The Pocket Oxford Russian Dictionary

The Pocket Oxford Russian Dictionary

Second Edition

Russian–English
Compiled by Jessie Coulson

English–Russian
Compiled by Nigel Rankin and Della Thompson

Revised and updated by **Colin Howlett**

Oxford New York
OXFORD UNIVERSITY PRESS
1994

Oxford University Press, Walton Street, Oxford OX2 6DP
Oxford New York
Athens Auckland Bangkok Bombay
Calcutta Cape Town Dar es Salaam Delhi
Florence Hong Kong Istanbul Karachi
Kuala Lumpur Madras Madrid Melbourne
Mexico City Nairobi Paris Singapore
Taipei Tokyo Toronto
and associated companies in
Berlin Ibadan

Oxford is a trade mark of Oxford University Press

British Library Cataloguing in Publication Data
Data available

Library of Congress Cataloging in Publication Data..
Data available

ISBN 0–19–864500–7

10 9 8 7 6 5 4 3 2 1

Typeset by AZbuka Ltd.
Printed in Great Britain by
Clays Ltd.,
Bungay, Suffolk.

Preface

The Pocket Oxford Russian Dictionary, the first edition of which was published in 1981, is designed primarily to meet the needs of English-speaking users who do not have an advanced knowledge of Russian. In addition to the linguistically inclined it caters for those whose interest in the language as such is minimal and whose requirements are confined to being able to find and translate a limited number of words encountered in their own particular field of interest or activity. It has therefore established its popularity with students, tourists, and business travellers alike.

This new edition offers a variety of enhancements over its predecessor: the text has been entirely reset to afford greater ease of consultation; to reflect change in both the English- and Russian-speaking worlds the word list of each section has been updated and expanded by a total of some 3,000 items; common geographical names are now included; and for the convenience of users who are non-native speakers of English the English headwords have been transcribed into the International Phonetic Alphabet.

COLIN HOWLETT

May 1994

Using this dictionary

Russian–English section

Stress

In Russian there are some classes of words—prepositions, conjunctions, particles—which are normally unstressed. Stress is indicated for all other words, except monosyllables, by the placing of a stress mark (´) over the vowel of the stressed syllable. Except in a few compound words, the vowel **ё** is always stressed and so has no stress mark. When two stress marks are found in the same word or form (as in **óбли́тый**) either of the two syllables may be stressed.

Treatment of entries

Articles consist of a word, prefix or other lexical element, or occasionally of two or more synonymous words or forms, or corresponding masculine and feminine forms, with basic grammatical information, translation(s), and sometimes usage examples. To save space related and alphabetically consecutive words may be grouped in paragraphs, as may consecutive but unrelated entries each consisting only of a cross-reference, and compound words of which the first element is a prefix or other combining form. All headwords, including those together in paragraphs, are printed in enlarged bold type. Conjugational and declensional information, as well as all usage examples, are printed in smaller bold type.

The swung dash (~) may be substituted in the body of an article for the whole of the headword or, in a list of compound words, for the prefix or other combining form which is common to all of them. In some headwords the ending may be separated from the stem by a thin vertical stroke; the swung dash will then represent the stem only, and the appropriate form of the ending will be appended to it, as in **са́харн|ый** sugar; sugary; **~ая голова́** sugar loaf; **~ый заво́д** sugar refinery.

The headword of an article is usually the nominative case of nouns or pronouns, the nominative singular masculine of adjectives, or the infinitive of verbs. The genitive ending of every noun is given and is followed by that of any case showing an irregularity of ending or a change of stress. In the singular any case is named, but in the plural the cases can be identified by their endings. The alternative genitive ending in **-у** is given in parentheses immediately after the genitive (see examples below); the term locative (abbreviated to *loc.*) is used for the prepositional form ending in **-у́** after **в** or **на**. In the case of those pronouns for which a list of case endings is given, the accusative is never included and the cases are shown in the order: genitive, dative, instrumental, and prepositional. Since the gender of Russian nouns can usually be deduced from the endings of the nominative and genitive it is indicated here only in exceptional instances, as in the case of masculine nouns ending in **-а** or **-я** and neuter nouns ending in **-мя**. Nouns ending in a soft sign (**-ь**) should be assumed to be feminine unless labelled *m*. All verbs are labelled *impf.* or *pf.* or, when bi-aspectual, *impf.* & *pf.* The form and stress of the first person singular of the present or future tense are indicated immediately after the infinitive and other forms of the present (or future) and past tenses are given if they show a change of stress or an irregularity of ending or contain the vowel **ё**. When a perfective verb is formed by the addition of a prefix to a simple imperfective, the prefix is divided from the rest of the infinitive by a thin vertical stroke. A single parenthesis, (, before the reflexive ending of an infinitive indicates, especially in cross-references, that the cross-reference etc. applies to both the active and the reflexive infinitive. When the construction of a verb demands the use of a case other than the accusative or genitive the case required is indicated, as in **махáть**... *impf.*, **махнýть**... *pf.+i.* wave; brandish.

Some adjectives have mobile stress in the short forms; in these the full nominative singular masculine form of the headword is followed immediately by a semicolon and then by the short forms.

The following examples illustrate many of the points made above:

адресовáть, -сýю *impf.* & *pf.* address, send; **~ся** address o.s.

нали́ть, -лью́, -льёшь; нáли́л, -а, -о *pf.* (*impf.* **наливáть**) pour (out).

плáмя, -мени *nt.* flame; fire, blaze.

пóвод[2], **-а (-у)**, *loc.* **-ý**; *pl.* **-óдья, -ьев** rein.

по|проси́ть(ся, -ошý(сь, -óсишь(ся *pf.*

прозвáть, -зовý, -зовёшь; -áл, -á, -о *pf.* (*impf.* **прозывáть**) nickname, name.

проси́ть, -ошý, -óсишь *impf.* (*pf.* **по~**) ask; beg; invite; **~ся** ask; apply.

про|слýшать, -аю *pf.*, **прослýшивать, -аю** *impf.* hear; listen to.

сестрá, -ы́; *pl.* **сёстры, сестёр, сёстрам** sister.

сок, -а (-у), *loc.* **-ý** juice; sap; **в (пóлном) ~ý** in the prime of life.

худóй; худ, -á, -о thin, lean.

English–Russian section

General

To save space several headwords are sometimes included in the same paragraph. They are printed in enlarged bold type and separated by full stops. Phrases and usage examples are printed in smaller bold type and separated by semicolons.

When a headword is used in a phrase or usage example it is replaced by a swung dash (~), e.g. **crash** ... **~ landing**. The swung dash is also used as a space-saving device in the Russian text, where it stands for the preceding Russian word, e.g. **Georgian** ... грузи́н, ~ка (where ~ка indicates грузи́нка) and **sing** ... петь *impf.*, про~, с~ *pf.* (where про~, с~ indicates пропéть, спеть).

In giving grammatical forms a hyphen is often used to stand for the whole or a part of the preceding or following Russian word, e.g. **grey** ... седóй (сед, -á, -о) = седóй (сед, седá, сéдо); **come** ... приходи́ть (-ожý, -óдишь) = приходи́ть (прихожý, прихóдишь); **prepare** ... при-, под-, готáвливаться = приготáвливаться, подготáвливаться. Superscript numerals are used to distinguish unrelated headwords spelt alike, and glosses may follow in parentheses, e.g. **bank**[1] *n.* (*of river*), **bank**[2] *n.* (*econ.*).

Stress

For guidance on the use of the stress indicator (ˈ) in the English text see *Pronunciation* below.

The stress of each Russian word is indicated above the vowel of the stressed syllable. It is not given for monosyllables, except those which bear the main stress in a phrase, e.g. **be** ... нé было; **year** ... год óт году; here, the stressed monosyllable and the next word are pronounced as one.

The vowel ё has no stress mark since it is almost always stressed; when the stress falls elsewhere this is shown, e.g. **quarterly** ... трёхмéсячный.

The presence of two stress marks indicates that either of the marked syllables may be stressed.

Changes of stress which take place in conjugation, or declension, or in the short forms of adjectives, are shown as follows:

(i) **suggest** ... предложи́ть (-жý, -жишь). Here, the absence of a stress mark on the second person singular indicates that the stress is on the preceding syllable: предлóжишь.

(ii) **begin** ... начáть (-чнý, -чнёшь; нáчал, -á, -о). When the stress of the two preceding forms is not identical as it is in (i) above, the final form takes the stress of the first of these: нáчало. Forms not shown at all, e.g. the rest of the conjugation of предложи́ть, and the rest of the future and the past plural of начáть, are stressed like the last form given: предлóжит etc., начнёт etc., нáчали.

(iii) **boring**[2] ... скýчный (-чен, -чнá, -чно) = (скýчен, скучнá, скýчно, скýчны); where the ending (e.g. -чны here) is not given, the stress is the same as for the previous form.

(iv) **rain** ... дождь (-дя́). The single form in parentheses is the genitive (see *Declension* below) and all other forms have the same stressed syllable. If only one case-labelled form is given in the singular it is an exception to the regular paradigm. For example, **leg** ... ногá (*a.* -гу; *pl.* -ги, -г, -гáм); the other singular forms have end-stress, while the unmentioned plural forms follow the stress of the last form given: ногáми, ногáх.

Pronunciation

For the convenience of users whose native language is not English all main headwords, i.e. those starting a paragraph, are transcribed into the International Phonetic Alphabet, a key to which is supplied below. To save space within the paragraph the transcription of a word is not given where its pronunciation can be deduced from that of a preceding word. It is also omitted in the case of compound words whose second element is listed elsewhere in the dictionary. Where the stress of an untranscribed word changes this is indicated by means of a stress indicator (ˈ) immediately before the stressed syllable.

In the case of abbreviations transcriptions are not supplied where the component letters are pronounced individually, e.g. **BBC**, or where the expanded form or key word therein is treated elsewhere as a separate entry.

Where the pronunciation of a word varies according to its part of speech both transcriptions are supplied, separated by a semicolon. The order of the transcriptions is the same as the order in which the parts of speech are treated (see **conduct**).

Nouns

Gender This can usually be deduced from the ending of the nominative singular: a final consonant or -й indicates a masculine noun, -а or -я or -ь feminine, -е or -о neuter. Gender is shown explicitly for masculine nouns ending in -а, -я or -ь, neuter nouns in -мя, and indeclinable nouns. If a noun is given only as a plural form either the gender or the genitive plural is indicated.

Declension When a single inflected form is added in parentheses with no indication of case or number it is the genitive singular, e.g. **Indian** ... индéец (-éйца), and all other inflected cases have the genitive stem. Apart from changes in stress (see *Stress* above), the following irregularities are among those indicated:

(i) The mobile vowel in masculine nouns, e.g. **stub** ... окýрок (-рка).

(ii) The alternative genitive singular in -у or -ю of masculine nouns, e.g. **cheese** ... сыр (-а(у)), i.e. сы́ра or сы́ру. For nouns denoting a substance, a number of objects, or a collective unit, the -у/-ю form has partitive value; with other nouns it is used only in certain set phrases.

(iii) The prepositional singular of masculine nouns, when ending in -ý (or -ю́) after в or на. Here the term *locative* is used, e.g. **shore** ... бéрег (*loc.* -ý).

(iv) Substantivized adjectives are followed by *sb.* to show that they retain the adjectival declension.

Adjectives

The short forms of adjectives are shown when they are irregular, when the stress moves (see *Stress* above), and for all adjectives ending in -нный or -нний, e.g. **sickly** ... болéзненный (-ен, -енна); **sincere** ... и́скренний (-нен, -нна, -нно & -нне).

Verbs

Persons and tenses treated as irregular, and changes of stress in conjugation, are shown in parentheses, e.g. **come** ... приходи́ть (-ожý, -óдишь) *impf.*, прийти́ (придý, -дёшь; пришёл, -шлá) *pf.* The first two forms in parentheses are the first and second persons singular of the present or future tense; other persons and the past tense follow where necessary. Each verb is labelled with its aspect. The case construction is indicated for transitive verbs *not* followed by the accusative.

The conjugation of быть is given only under **be**. Irregularities of imperative, participial and gerundial forms are not usually shown.

The following changes in the first person singular of the present or future tense of verbs in -ить are treated as regular (and therefore not provided):

(i) Insertion of л after a stem in -б, -в, -м, -п, or -ф, e.g. **add** ... добáвить: добáвлю, добáвишь.

(ii) Change of д or з to ж, к or т to ч, с or х to ш, ск or ст to щ, e.g. **annoy** ... досади́ть: досажý, досади́шь; **answer** ... отвéтить: отвéчу, отвéтишь; **paint** ... крáсить: крáшу, крáсишь; **clean** ... чи́стить: чи́щу, чи́стишь.

The reflexive suffix -ся or -сь is placed in parentheses when the verb may be used with or without it, usually as an intransitive or a transitive verb respectively, e.g. **open** *v.t. & i.* открывáть(ся) *impf.*, откры́ть(ся) (-рóю(сь), -рóешь(ся)) *pf.*

Phonetic symbols

Consonants

b	*b*ut	j	*y*es	p	*p*en	w	*w*e	ð	*th*is
d	*d*og	k	*c*at	r	*r*ed	z	*z*oo	ŋ	ri*ng*
f	*f*ew	l	*l*eg	s	*s*it	ʃ	*sh*e	x	lo*ch*
g	*g*et	m	*m*an	t	*t*op	ʒ	deci*s*ion	tʃ	*ch*ip
h	*h*e	n	*n*o	v	*v*oice	θ	*th*in	dʒ	*j*ar

Vowels

æ	c*a*t	iː	s*ee*	uː	t*oo*	əʊ	n*o*	aɪə	f*ire*
ɑː	*ar*m	ɒ	h*o*t	ə	*a*go	eə	h*air*	aʊə	s*our*
e	b*e*d	ɔː	s*aw*	aɪ	m*y*	ɪə	n*ear*		
ɜː	h*er*	ʌ	r*u*n	aʊ	h*ow*	ɔɪ	b*oy*		
ɪ	s*i*t	ʊ	p*u*t	eɪ	d*ay*	ʊə	p*oor*		

(ə) signifies the indeterminate sound as in gard*e*n, carn*a*l, and rhyth*m*.

(r) at the end of a word indicates an r that is sounded when a word beginning with a vowel follows, as in *clutter up* and *an acre of land.*

The mark ˜ indicates a nasalized sound, as in the following sounds that are not natural in English: æ̃ (t*im*bre) ɑ̃ (él*an*) ɔ̃ (garç*on*)

The main or primary stress of a word is shown by ˈ preceding the relevant syllable; any secondary stress in words of three or more syllables is shown by ˌ preceding the relevant syllable.

Proprietary terms

This dictionary includes some words which are, or are asserted to be, proprietary names or trade marks. These words are labelled (*prop.*). The presence or absence of this label should not be regarded as affecting the legal status of any proprietary name or trade mark.

Abbreviations

a.	accusative
abbr.	abbreviation (of)
abs.	absolute
adj., adjs.	adjective(s)
adv., advs.	adverb(s)
aeron.	aeronautics
agric.	agricultural
anat.	anatomy
approx.	approximate(ly)
archaeol.	archaeology
astron.	astronomy
attr.	attributive
aux.	auxiliary
bibl.	biblical
biol.	biology
bot.	botany
c.g.	common gender
chem.	chemistry
cin.	cinema(tography)
coll.	colloquial
collect.	collective(ly)
comb.	combination
comm.	commerce
comp.	comparative
comput.	computing
conj., conjs.	conjunction(s)
cul.	culinary
d.	dative
def.	definite
det.	determinate
dim.	diminutive
dipl.	diplomacy
eccl.	ecclesiastical
econ.	economics
elec.	electrical
emph.	emphatic
esp.	especially
etc.	etcetera
f.	feminine
fig.	figurative
fut.	future (tense)
g.	genitive
geog.	geography
geol.	geology
geom.	geometry
gram.	grammar
hist.	historical
hort.	horticulture
i.	instrumental; intransitive
imper.	imperative
impers.	impersonal
impf.	imperfective
indecl.	indeclinable
indef.	indefinite
indet.	indeterminate
inf.	infinitive
int.	interjection
interrog.	interrogative
journ.	journalism
leg.	legal
ling.	linguistics
liter.	literary
loc.	locative
m.	masculine
math.	mathematics
med.	medicine
meteor.	meteorology
mil.	military
min.	mineralogy
mus.	music
myth.	mythology
n.	noun
naut.	nautical
neg.	negative
nn.	nouns
nom.	nominative
nt.	neuter
o.s.	oneself
p.	prepositional
parl.	parliamentary
part.	particle
pej.	pejorative
pers.	person
pf.	perfective
phon.	phonetics
phot.	photography
phys.	physics
pl.	plural
poet.	poetical
pol.	political
poss.	possessive
pred.	predicate; predicative
pref.	prefix
prep.	preposition
pres.	present (tense)
print.	printing
pron., prons.	pronoun(s)
propr.	proprietary term
psych.	psychology
rail.	railway
refl.	reflexive
rel.	relative
relig.	religion; religious
Russ.	Russian
sb.	substantive
sg.	singular
sl.	slang
s.o.	someone
sth.	something
superl.	superlative
t.	transitive
tech.	technical
theatr.	theatre
theol.	theology
trig.	trigonometry
univ.	university
usu.	usually
v.	verb
var.	various
v.aux	auxiliary verb
vbl.	verbal
vet.	veterinary
v.i.	intransitive verb
voc.	vocative
v.t.	transitive verb
vv.	verbs
zool.	zoology

Russian–English dictionary

A

А *abbr.* (*of* **ампе́р**) amp, ampere.
а *nt.indecl.* the letter **а.**
а *conj.* and, but; **а (не) то́** or else, otherwise.
а *part.* eh?
а *int.* oh, ah.
абажу́р, -а lampshade.
абба́т, -а abbot; abbé. **аббати́са, -ы** abbess. **абба́тство, -а** abbey.
аббревиату́ра, -ы abbreviation; acronym.
абза́ц, -а indention; paragraph; **сде́лать ~** indent.
абонеме́нт, -а subscription, season ticket; **сверх ~а** extra. **абоне́нт, -а** subscriber; (*library*) borrower, reader; (*theatre etc.*) season-ticket holder. **абони́ровать, -рую** *impf.* & *pf.* subscribe for, subscribe to, take a (season-)ticket for; **~ся** subscribe, take out a subscription, be a subscriber.
абориге́н, -а aboriginal. **абориге́нный** aboriginal, native.
або́рт, -а abortion; abort, failure, cancellation; **подпо́льный ~** backstreet abortion; **сде́лать ~** have an abortion. **аборти́вный** abortive; causing abortion.
абрико́с, -а apricot.
а́брис, -а outline, contour.
абсолю́т, -а absolute. **абсолю́тно** *adv.* absolutely, utterly. **абсолю́тный** absolute; utter; **~ слух** perfect pitch.
абсу́рд, -а absurdity; the absurd. **абсу́рдный** absurd.
аванга́рд, -а advanced guard, van; vanguard; avant-garde. **авангарди́зм, -а** avant-gardism. **авангарди́ст, -а** avant-gardist. **авангарди́стский** avant-garde. **аванза́л, -а** anteroom. **аванпо́ст, -а** outpost; forward position.
ава́нс, -а advance, advance payment; *pl.* advances, overtures. **авանси́ровать, -рую** *impf.* & *pf.* advance. **ава́нсом** *adv.* in advance, on account.
авансце́на, -ы proscenium.
авантю́ра, -ы adventure; venture; escapade; shady, risky, or speculative enterprise. **авантюри́зм, -а** adventurism. **авантюри́ст, -а** adventurer. **авантюри́стка, -и** adventuress; (*sl.*) gold-digger. **авантю́рный** adventurous; adventure, of adventure.
авари́йно-спаса́тельный (emergency-)rescue, life-saving. **авари́йный** accident, breakdown, crash; emergency; spare; **~ сигна́л** distress signal. **ава́рия, -и** accident, crash, wreck; breakdown; damage; loss; **потерпе́ть ава́рию** have an accident.
а́вгуст, -а August.
а́виа *abbr.* (*of* **авиапо́чтой**) '(by) airmail'.
авиа... *abbr.* (*of* **авиацио́нный**) *in comb.* air-, aero-; aircraft; aviation. **авиабиле́т, -а** air-ticket. **~деса́нт, -а** airborne assault landing; airborne assault force. **~деса́нтник, -а** paratrooper. **~диспе́тчер, -а** air-traffic controller. **~каскадёр, -а** stunt flyer. **~катастро́фа, -ы** air crash. **~компа́ния, -и** airline. **~ли́ния, -и** air-route, airway. **~но́сец, -сца** aircraft carrier. **~пассажи́р, -а** airline passenger. **~письмо́, -а́**; *pl.* **-а, -сем** airmail letter; aerogram(me). **~по́чта, -ы** airmail. **~разве́дка, -и** air reconnaissance. **~спо́рт, -а** aerial sports. **~съёмка, -и** aerial survey.
авиацио́нно-косми́ческий aerospace. **авиацио́нный** aviation; flying; aircraft. **авиа́ция, -и** aviation; flying; aircraft; air-force.
авока́до *nt.indecl.* avocado (*tree*).
аво́сь *adv.* perhaps, maybe; **на ~** at random, on the off-chance. **аво́ська, -и** (*string*) shopping-bag.
авра́л, -а work involving all hands; emergency; rush job; *int.* all hands on deck! all hands to the pump! **авра́льный** rush, emergency.
австрали́ец, -и́йца, австрали́йка, -и Australian. **австрали́йский** Australian. **Австра́лия, -и** Australia.
австри́ец, -и́йца, австри́йка, -и Austrian. **австри́йский** Austrian. **А́встрия, -и** Austria.
авто... *in comb.* self-; auto-; automatic; motor-; bus. **автоава́рия, -и** road, traffic accident. **~а́тлас, -а** road atlas. **~ба́за, -ы** motor-transport depot. **~биогра́фия, -и** autobiography. **авто́бус, -а** bus; coach. **~вокза́л, -а** bus, coach station. **~во́р, -а** car thief. **~го́нщик, -а** racing-driver. **авто́граф, -а** autograph. **~да́ча, -и** mobile home, caravan, trailer. **~доро́га, -и** road; highway. **~запра́вочн|ый; ~ая ста́нция** petrol station. **~запра́вщик, -а** petrol tanker. **~ка́р, -а** motor trolley. **~каскадёр, -а** stunt driver. **~катастро́фа, -ы** road, traffic accident. **~кла́в, -а** autoclave. **~коло́нка, -и** petrol pump. **~коло́нна, -ы** motorcade; convoy. **~кори́дда, -ы** stock-car race; stock-car racing. **~кра́т, -а** autocrat. **~крати́ческий**

autocratic. **~лиха́ч, -а́** reckless driver, road-hog. **~магази́н, -а** car dealer's, motorcar showroom. **~магистра́ль, -и** (motor) highway; **скоростна́я ~** expressway. **~маши́на, -ы** motor vehicle. **~мотодро́м, -а** race-track. **~но́мия, -и** autonomy. **~но́мный** autonomous; self-contained. **~отве́тчик, -а** answerphone. **~павильо́н, -а** bus shelter. **~пило́т, -а** automatic pilot. **~портре́т, -а** self-portrait. **~прице́п, -а** trailer, caravan; **жило́й ~** camper, mobile home. **~ра́лли** *nt.indecl.* (car) rally. **~ралли́ст, -а** rallyist, rally driver. **~ру́чка, -и** fountain-pen. **~спо́рт, -а** motor sports. **~ста́нция, -и** bus, coach station. **~сто́п, -а** automatic brakes; hitch-hiking; hitch-hiking permit. **~стоя́нка, -и** car park. **~стра́да, -ы** motorway. **~суфлёр, -а** Autocue (*propr.*), teleprompter. **~трюка́ч, -а́** stunt driver. **~шко́ла, -ы** driving school.

автома́т, -а slot-machine; automatic device, weapon, etc.; sub-machine gun; robot; automaton; **де́нежный ~** cash dispenser; **игрово́й ~** slot machine; **парко́вочный ~** parking meter; **стира́льный ~** washing machine; **суши́льный ~** dryer; **(телефо́н-)~** dial telephone, automatic telephone; public call-box. **автоматиза́ция, -и** automation. **автоматизи́ровать, -рую** *impf.* & *pf.* automate; make automatic; **~ся** become automatic. **автомати́ческий, автомати́чный, автома́тный** automatic.

а́втор, -а author; composer, producer, inventor; (*fig.*) architect; **~ го́ла** scorer; **~ предложе́ния, ~ резолю́ции** mover of a resolution. **авториза́ция, -и** authorization. **авторизо́ванный** authorized. **авторизова́ть, -зу́ю** *pf.* & *impf.* authorize.

авторитари́зм, -а authoritarianism. **авторите́т, -а** authority; prestige. **авторите́тный** authoritative.

а́вторск|ий author's; **~ий гонора́р** royalty; **~ое пра́во** copyright; **«~ие права́ зая́влены»** 'all rights reserved'; **~ие** *sb., pl.* royalties. **а́вторско-правово́й** copyright. **а́вторство, -а** authorship.

ага́ *int.* ah; aha.

аге́нт, -а agent; attaché. **аге́нтство, -а** agency; **~ печа́ти** news agency; **бракопосре́дническое ~** marriage bureau. **аге́нту́ра, -ы** secret service; (network of) agents.

агит... *abbr.* (*of* **агитацио́нный**) *in comb.* agitation, campaign. **агитпро́п, -а** agitation and propaganda section. **~пу́нкт, -а** *abbr.* agitation centre; committee-rooms.

агита́тор, -а agitator, propagandist; canvasser, electioneer. **агитацио́нный** propaganda; campaign. **агита́ция, -и** propaganda, agitation; campaign; **предвы́борная ~** electioneering. **агити́ровать, -рую** *impf.* (*pf.* **с~**) agitate, campaign; electioneer; (try to) persuade, win over. **аги́тка, -и** piece of propaganda.

агонизи́ровать, -рую *impf.* & *pf.* be in the throes of death. **аго́ния, -и** agony of death, death-pangs.

агрега́т, -а aggregate; assembly, unit, outfit, set.

агресси́вность, -и aggression, aggressiveness. **агресси́вный** aggressive. **агре́ссия, -и** (*pol.*) aggression. **агре́ссор, -а** aggressor.

агроло́гия, -и agrology, soil science.

агроно́м, -а, -но́мша, -и agronomist. **агроно́мия, -и** agriculture. **агроте́хник, -а** agricultural technician. **агроте́хника, -и** agricultural technology.

ад, -а, *loc.* **-у́** hell.

адвока́т, -а lawyer, advocate. **адвокату́ра, -ы** legal profession; lawyers.

аде́пт, -а adherent, follower, disciple.

адида́ски, -сок *pl.* (*coll.*) trainers.

администрати́вный administrative. **администра́тор, -а** administrator, manager. **администра́торская** *sb.* (*hotel*) reception. **администра́ция, -и** administration; management. **администри́рование, -я** bureaucracy, red tape. **администри́ровать, -рую** *impf.* act as administrator or manager (of); send into exile.

адмира́л, -а admiral; (*zool.*) Red Admiral. **адмиралте́йский** Admiralty. **адмиралте́йство, -а** Admiralty; naval dockyard. **адмира́льский** admiral's; flag. **адмира́льша, -и** admiral's wife.

а́дов *adj.* infernal, diabolical.

а́дрес, -а; *pl.* **-а́, -о́в** address; **не по ~у** to the wrong address. **адреса́нт, -а** sender. **адреса́т, -а** addressee. **а́дресн|ый** address; **~ая кни́га** directory; **~ый стол** address bureau. **адресова́ть, -су́ю** *impf.* & *pf.* address, send; **~ся** address o.s.

а́дский infernal, hellish, fiendish, devilish.

адъю́нкт, -а service student.

адъюта́нт, -а aide-de-camp; **ста́рший ~** adjutant.

ажу́р, -а openwork; up-to-date; **в ~е** in order, (all) correct. **ажу́рн|ый** openwork; delicate, lacy; **~ая рабо́та** openwork; tracery.

аза́рт, -а heat; excitement; fervour, ardour, passion. **аза́ртн|ый** reckless, venturesome; heated; excitable; **~ая игра́** game of chance.

а́збука, -и alphabet; ABC; **дакти́льная ~** sign language; **~ Мо́рзе** Morse code. **а́збучный** alphabetical; elementary.

Азербайджа́н, -а Azerbaijan.

азиа́т, -а, азиа́тка, -и Asian. **азиа́тский** Asian. **А́зия, -и** Asia.

азо́т, -а nitrogen; **за́кись ~а** nitrous oxide.

а́ист, -а stork.

ай *int.* oh; oo; **ай да молоде́ц!** well done! good lad!

айва́, -ы́ quince, quinces.

айда́ *int.* come on! let's go!

акаде́мик, -а Academician; member or student of an academy. **академи́ческий,**

академи́чный academic. **акаде́мия, -и** academy.
аквала́нг, -а aqualung. **аквалангист, -а** skin-diver. **акварели́ст, -а** water-colour painter. **акваре́ль, -и** water-colour, water-colours. **аква́риум, -а** aquarium. **аквариуми́ст, -а** aquarist. **акведу́к, -а** aqueduct.
аккомпанеме́нт, -а accompaniment; **под** ~+*g.* to the accompaniment of. **аккомпаниа́тор, -а, -а́торша, -и** accompanist. **аккомпани́ровать, -рую** *impf.+d.* accompany.
акко́рд, -а chord; **взять** ~ strike a chord.
акко́рдн|ый agreed, by agreement; **~ая рабо́та** piece-work.
аккредити́в, -а letter of credit; credentials. **аккредитова́ть, -тую** *impf.* & *pf.* accredit.
аккумуля́ция, -и accumulation.
акку́ратный accurate, neat, careful; punctual; exact, thorough.
акри́л, -а acrylic. **акри́ловый** acrylic.
аксельба́нт, -а aiguillette.
аксессуа́р, -а accessory; (stage) property.
аксио́ма, -ы axiom; truism.
акт, -а act; deed, document; **обвини́тельный** ~ indictment.
актёр, -а actor. **актёрский** actor's. **актёрство, -а** acting; posing.
акти́в, -а activists; assets; advantages. **активиза́ция, -и** stirring up, making (more) active. **активизи́ровать, -рую** *impf.* & *pf.* make (more) active, stir up, arouse. **акти́вный** active; ~ **бала́нс** favourable balance.
акти́ровать, -рую *impf.* & *pf.* (*pf. also* **с~**) register, record, presence or absence of; (*sl.*) write off. **актиро́вка, -и** (*sl.*) writing off, write-off; cancellation.
а́ктов|ый; ~ая бума́га official document, stamped paper; **~ый зал** assembly hall.
актри́са, -ы actress.
актуа́льный actual; up-to-date, topical, urgent.
аку́ла, -ы shark.
акупункту́ра, -ы acupuncture.
аку́стика, -и acoustics. **акусти́ческий** acoustic.
акуше́р, -а obstetrician. **акуше́рка, -и** midwife. **акуше́рский** obstetric, obstetrical. **акуше́рство, -а** obstetrics; midwifery.
акце́нт, -а accent, stress. **акценти́ровать, -рую** *impf.* & *pf.* accent; accentuate.
акци́з, -а duty; Excise. **акци́зный** excise.
акционе́р, -а shareholder; stockholder. **акционе́рн|ый** joint-stock; **~ое о́бщество** joint-stock company. **а́кция[1], -и** share; *pl.* stock. **а́кция[2], -и** action.
але́ть, -е́ет *impf.* (*pf.* **за~**) redden, flush, blush; show red.
алка́ш, -а́ (*sl.*) boozer.
алкоголи́зм, -а alcoholism. **алкого́лик, -а** alcoholic; drunkard. **алкоголи́ческий** alcoholic. **алкого́ль, -я** *m.* alcohol. **алкого́льный** alcoholic.
аллерге́н, -а allergen. **алле́ргик, -а** allergy sufferer. **аллерги́я, -и** allergy.
алле́я, -и avenue; path, walk.
алло́ *int.* hello!
аллю́р, -а pace, gait.
алма́з, -а diamond. **алма́зный** diamond; of diamonds.
алта́рь, -я́ *m.* altar; chancel, sanctuary.
алфави́т, -а alphabet. **алфави́тный** alphabetical; ~ **указа́тель** index.
а́лчный greedy, grasping.
а́лый scarlet.
альбино́с, -а, альбино́ска, -и albino.
альбо́м, -а album; sketch-book.
альмана́х, -а literary miscellany; almanac.
альпи́йск|ий Alpine; **~ие луга́** alps, mountain meadows. **альпина́рий, -я** rock garden. **альпини́зм, -а** mountaineering. **альпини́ст, -а, альпини́стка, -и** (mountain) climber.
А́льпы, Альп *pl.* the Alps.
альт, -а́; *pl.* **-ы́** alto, contralto; viola. **альтера́ция, -и** change in pitch; **зна́ки альтера́ции** accidentals. **альти́ст, -а, -и́стка, -и** viola-player. **альто́вый** alto, contralto; viola.
альтруи́зм, -а altruism. **альтруи́ст, -а** altruist. **альтруисти́ческий** altruistic.
алья́нс, -а alliance.
алюми́ниевый aluminium. **алюми́ний, -я** aluminium.
Аля́ска, -и Alaska.
аляфурше́т, -а buffet.
Амазо́нка, -и the Amazon (*river*); **а~, -и** Amazon; horsewoman; riding-habit.
а́мба *f.indecl.* (*sl.*) finish, curtains, kibosh.
амба́р, -а barn; storehouse, warehouse. **амба́рный** barn.
амби́ция, -и pride; arrogance. **амбицио́зный** vainglorious, conceited; self-loving, egoistic.
а́мбра, -ы ambergris; scent, perfume, fragrance. **амбре́** *nt.indecl.* scent, perfume.
амбулато́рия, -и out-patients' department; surgery. **амбулато́рный; ~ больно́й** out-patient.
Аме́рика, -и America. **америка́нец, -нца, америка́нка, -и** American. **америка́нск|ий** American; US; **~ие го́ры** Big Dipper, switch-back; **~ий замо́к** Yale (*propr.*) lock; **~ий оре́х** Brazil nut.
амети́ст, -а amethyst.
ами́нь, -я *m.* amen; finis, finish, kibosh.
аммиа́к, -а ammonia. **аммиа́чный** ammonia, ammoniac, ammoniacal. **аммо́ний, -я** ammonium.
амнисти́ровать, -рую *impf.* & *pf.* amnesty. **амни́стия, -и** amnesty.
амора́льный amoral; immoral.
амортиза́тор, -а shock-absorber. **амортиза́ция, -и** depreciation, wear and tear; shock-absorption. **амортизи́ровать, -рую** *impf.* & *pf.* amortize; damp, make shock-proof.
ампе́р, -а; *g.pl.* **ампе́р** ampere.
ампи́р, -а Empire style. **ампи́рный** Empire.

амплуа́ *nt.indecl.* type; role; occupation, job.
ампута́ция, -и amputation. **ампути́ровать, -ую** *impf.* & *pf.* amputate.
аму́р, -а cupid; *pl.* amours, love-affairs. **аму́рный** love.
амфетами́н, -а amphetamine.
амфитеа́тр, -а amphitheatre; circle.
АН *abbr.* (*of* **Акаде́мия Нау́к**) Academy of Sciences.
ана́лиз, -а analysis; ~ **кро́ви** blood test. **анализи́ровать, -рую** *impf.* & *pf.* analyse. **анали́тик, -а** analyst. **аналити́ческий** analytic, analytical.
аналоги́чный analogous. **анало́ги|я, -и** analogy; **по ~и** (**с**+*i.*) by analogy (with).
анало́й, -я lectern.
анана́с, -а pineapple. **анана́сный, анана́совый** pineapple.
анархи́ст, -а, -и́стка, -и anarchist. **анархи́ческий** anarchic, anarchical. **ана́рхия, -и** anarchy.
анатоми́ческий anatomic(al). **анато́мия, -и** anatomy.
анаша́, -и́ (*sl.*) pot, hash. **анаши́ст, -а** (*sl.*) pot smoker; hash-head.
анга́р, -а hangar.
а́нгел, -а angel; **день ~а** name day. **а́нгельский** angels'; angelic.
анги́на, -ы quinsy, tonsillitis, ulcerated sore throat.
англизи́ровать, -рую *impf.* & *pf.* anglicize. **английск|ий** English; **~ая була́вка** safety-pin; **~ая соль** Epsom salts; **~ий рожо́к** cor anglais. **англика́нец, -нца, англика́нка, -нки** Anglican. **англици́зм, -а** Anglicism, English loan-word. **англича́нин, -а**; *pl.* **-ча́не, -чан** Englishman. **англича́нка, -и** Englishwoman. **А́нглия, -и** England, Britain. **англоязы́чный** English-speaking, anglophone.
андре́евский St. Andrew's.
А́нды, Анд *pl.* the Andes.
анекдо́т, -а anecdote, story; funny thing. **анекдоти́ческий** anecdotal; unlikely; funny, comical. **анекдоти́чный** improbable; odd; amusing, funny.
анеми́ческий, анеми́чный anaemic. **анеми́я, -и** anaemia.
анестезио́лог, -а anaesthetist. **анестези́ровать, -рую** *impf.* & *pf.* anaesthetize. **анестези́рующ|ий** anaesthetizing, anaesthetic; **~ее сре́дство** anaesthetic. **анестези́я, -и** anaesthesia.
ани́с, -а anise; variety of apple. **ани́сов|ый; ~ое се́мя** aniseed.
анке́та, -ы questionnaire, (application-)form; (opinion) poll, inquiry, survey.
аннота́ция, -и annotation; blurb.
аннули́ровать, -рую *impf.* & *pf.* annul, nullify; cancel, repeal, revoke, abolish. **аннуля́ция, -и** annulment, nullification; cancellation, revocation, repeal.
анони́м, -а anonymous author, work, letter. **анони́мка, -и** poison-pen letter. **анони́мный** anonymous. **анони́мщик, -а** poison-pen writer.
ано́нс, -а announcement, notice; advertisement. **анонси́ровать, -рую** *impf.* & *pf.* announce, make an announcement.
анорекси́я, -и anorexia.
анса́мбль, -я *m.* ensemble; company, troupe.
Антаркти́да, -ы Antarctica.
Анта́рктика, -и the Antarctic.
анте́нна, -ы antenna; aerial.
анти... *in comb.* anti-. **антиалкого́льный** temperance. **~веществó, -á** anti-matter. **~детона́тор, -а** anti-knock (compound). **~детонацио́нный** anti-knock. **~па́тия, -и** antipathy. **~прига́рный** non-stick. **~раке́та, -ы** anti-missile missile. **~раке́тчик, -а** ban-the-bomb campaigner. **~санита́рный** insanitary. **~се́птик, -а** antiseptic; preservative. **~септи́ческий** antiseptic. **~те́ло, -а**; *pl.* **-á** antibody. **~фри́з, -а** antifreeze. **~челове́ческий** inhuman.
антиква́р, -а, антиква́рий, -я antiquary, antiquarian; antique-dealer. **антиквариа́т, -а** antique-dealer's, antique-shop. **антиква́рный** antiquarian; antique. **анти́чность, -и** antiquity. **анти́чный** ancient, antique.
антоло́гия, -и anthology.
антра́кт, -а interval; entr'acte.
антреко́т, -а entrecôte, steak.
антрепренёр, -а impresario.
антресо́ли, -ей *pl.* mezzanine; attic floor; attics; gallery.
антропо́лог, -а anthropologist. **антропологи́ческий** anthropological. **антрополо́гия, -и** anthropology.
антропофа́г, -а cannibal. **антропофа́гия, -и** cannibalism.
антура́ж, -а surroundings, environment; entourage, associates.
анфа́с *adv.* full face.
анфила́да, -ы suite.
анчо́ус, -а anchovy.
аншла́г, -а 'house full' notice; **пройти́ с ~о́м** play to full houses.
апартейд, -а apartheid.
апати́чный apathetic. **апа́тия, -и** apathy.
апелли́ровать, -рую *impf.* & *pf.* appeal. **апелляцио́нный; ~ суд** Court of Appeal. **апелля́ция, -и** appeal.
апельси́н, -а orange; orange-tree. **апельси́нный, апельси́новый** orange; **апельси́нное варе́нье** (orange) marmalade.
аперити́в, -а apéritif.
аплике́ *indecl. adj.* plated; appliqué.
аплоди́ровать, -рую *impf.*+*d.* **аплодисме́нт, -а** clap; *pl.* applause; **под ~ы** to applause.
АПН *abbr.* (*of* **Аге́нтство печа́ти «Но́вости»**) APN, Novosti Press Agency.
аполити́зм, -а political apathy. **аполити́чный** politically apathetic.
апо́стол, -а apostle; Acts and Epistles. **апо́стольский** apostolic.

аппара́т, -а apparatus, apparat; machinery, organs; staff, establishment; camera; **ка́ссовый ~** cash register; **копирова́льный ~** photocopier; **ку́хонный ~** food processor; **слухово́й ~** hearing aid; **факсими́льный а.** fax (machine). **аппарату́ра, -ы** apparatus, gear; (*comput.*) hardware. **аппара́тчик, -а** operator; apparatchnik, functionary.

аппе́ндикс, -а appendix. **аппендици́т, -а** appendicitis.

аппликату́ра, -ы fingering. **апплика́ция, -и** appliqué, appliqué-work. **аппликацио́нный** appliqué.

апре́ль, -я *m.* April; **пе́рвое ~я** April Fool's Day; **с пе́рвым ~я!** April Fool! **апре́льский** April.

апроба́ция, -и approval. **апроби́ровать, -рую** *impf.* & *pf.* approve.

апси́да, -ы apse.

апте́ка, -и (dispensing) chemist's; medicine chest; first-aid kit. **апте́карский** chemist's; pharmaceutical. **апте́карь, -я** *m.* chemist, pharmacist. **апте́карша, -и** pharmacist; chemist's wife. **апте́чка, -и** medicine chest; first-aid kit. **апте́чный** medicine, drug.

апчхи́ *int.* atishoo!

ара́б, -а, ара́бка, -и Arab. **ара́бский** Arab, Arabian, Arabic; arabic. **арави́йский** Arabian.

Ара́вия, -и Arabia.

ара́п, -а Negro; trickster, swindler.

ара́пник, -а (*huntsman's*) whip.

ара́хис, -а peanut, groundnut. **ара́хисов|ый** peanut, groundnut; **~ая па́ста** peanut butter.

арба́, -ы́; *pl.* **-ы** (bullock-)cart.

арби́тр, -а arbitrator. **арбитра́ж, -а** arbitration.

арбу́з, -а water-melon.

арго́ *nt.indecl.* argot, slang. **арготи́зм, -а** slang expression. **арготи́ческий** slang.

аргуме́нт, -а argument. **аргумента́ция, -и** reasoning; arguments. **аргументи́ровать, -рую** *impf.* & *pf.* argue, (try to) prove.

аре́на, -ы arena; ring.

аре́нда, -ы lease; rent; **в аре́нду** on lease. **арендá́тор, -а** leaseholder, tenant. **арендова́ть, -ду́ю** *impf.* & *pf.* lease, take or hold on lease.

аре́ст, -а arrest; seizure, sequestration. **ареста́нт, -а, -а́нтка, -и** prisoner. **ареста́нтская** *sb.* lock-up, cells. **арестова́ть, -тую** *pf.*, **аресто́вывать, -аю** *impf.* arrest; seize, sequestrate.

арифме́тика, -и arithmetic. **арифмети́ческий** arithmetical. **арифмо́граф, -а, арифмо́метр, -а** calculating machine.

а́рка, -и arch. **арка́да, -ы** arcade.

арка́н, -а lasso. **арка́нить, -ню** *impf.* (*pf.* **за~**) lasso.

А́рктика, -и the Arctic.

армади́л, -а armadillo.

армату́ра, -ы fittings, accessories, equipment; reinforcement; armature; trophy (of arms). **армату́рщик, -а** fitter.

арме́ец, -е́йца soldier; *pl.* Soviet Army Sports-Club team. **арме́йский** army.

Арме́ния, -и Armenia.

а́рмия, -и army.

армя́к, -а́ peasant's heavy overcoat.

армяни́н, -а; *pl.* **-я́не, -я́н, армя́нка, -и** Armenian. **армя́нский** Armenian.

арома́т, -а scent, odour, aroma; fragrance; bouquet. **ароматиза́тор, -а** flavouring. **аромати́ческий, аромати́чный, арома́тный** aromatic, fragrant.

а́рочный arched, vaulted.

арсена́л, -а arsenal.

арта́читься, -чусь *impf.* jib, be restive; dig one's heels in; be pigheaded, be obstinate.

арте́ль, -и artel. **арте́льный** of an artel; common, collective. **арте́льщик, -а, арте́льщица, -ы** member, leader, of an artel.

артериа́льный arterial. **арте́рия, -и** artery.

артиллери́йский artillery, ordnance. **артилле́рия, -и** artillery.

арти́ст, -а, -и́стка, -и artiste, artist, performer; expert. **артисти́зм, -а** artistry. **артисти́ческая** *sb.* dressing-room, green-room, artists' room. **артисти́ческий** artistic.

а́рфа, -ы harp. **арфи́ст, -а, -и́стка, -и** harpist.

архео́лог, -а archaeologist. **археологи́ческий** archaeological. **археоло́гия, -и** archaeology.

архи́в, -а archives. **архива́риус, -а, архиви́ст, -а** archivist. **архи́вный** archive, archival.

архидья́кон, -а archdeacon. **архиепи́скоп, -а** archbishop. **архиере́й, -я** bishop.

архите́ктор, -а architect. **архитекту́ра, -ы** architecture. **архитекту́рный** architectural.

арши́н, -а; *g.pl.* **-ши́н(ов)** arshin (*old Russ. measurement, equivalent to approx. 71 cm.*); arshin-rule; **как бу́дто ~ проглоти́л** bolt upright, as stiff as a poker.

асе́ссор, -а; колле́жский ~ Collegiate Assessor (*8th grade*: *see* **чин**).

аске́т, -а ascetic. **аскети́зм, -а** asceticism. **аскети́ческий** ascetic.

а́спид[1], **-а** asp; viper.

а́спид[2], **-а** slate. **а́спидн|ый; ~ая доска́** slate.

аспира́нт, -а, -а́нтка, -и post-graduate student. **аспиранту́ра, -ы** post-graduate course; post-graduate students.

ассигна́ция, -и banknote.

ассамбле́я, -и assembly; ball.

ассисте́нт, -а assistant; junior lecturer, research assistant. **ассисти́ровать, -рую** *impf.+d.* assist.

ассоциа́ция, -и association. **ассоции́ровать, -рую** *impf.* & *pf.* associate.

АССР *abbr.* (*of* ***автоно́мная сове́тская социалисти́ческая респу́блика***) ASSR, Autonomous Soviet Socialist Republic.

астро... *in comb.* astro-. **астрона́вт, -а** astronaut. **~на́втика, -и** space-travel. **~но́м, -а** astronomer. **~номи́ческий** astronomical. **~но́мия, -и** astronomy.

ась *int.* eh?

атама́н, -а ataman; Cossack chieftain, commander; (gang-)leader, robber chieftain.

ателье́ *nt.indecl.* studio; atelier; **портно́вское ~** tailor's shop; **телевизио́нное ~** TV repair workshop.

Атланти́ческий; ~ океа́н the Atlantic (Ocean).

а́тлас[1], **-а** atlas.

атла́с[2], **-а** satin. **атла́систый, атла́сный** satin; like satin, satiny.

атле́т, -а athlete; acrobat; (*circus*) strongman. **атлети́зм, -а** athleticism; body-building. **атле́тика, -и** athletics; **лёгкая ~** track and field sports; **тяжёлая ~** weight-lifting, boxing, wrestling. **атлети́ческий** athletic.

атмосфе́ра, -ы atmosphere. **атмосфери́ческий, атмосфе́рный** atmospheric; **атмосфе́рные оса́дки** rainfall.

а́том, -а atom. **атоми́стика, -и** atomics; atomic theory. **атомисти́ческий** atomistic. **а́томник, -а** atomic scientist. **а́томный** atomic.

аттеста́т, -а testimonial, recommendation, reference; certificate; pedigree. **аттеста́ция, -и** attestation; testimonial; confidential report. **аттестова́ть, -ту́ю** *impf.* & *pf.* attest; recommend.

аттракцио́н, -а sideshow; **парк ~ов** amusement park.

ау́ *int.* halloo, cooee.

аудито́рия, -и auditorium, lecture-room; audience.

ау́кать(ся, -аю(сь *impf.* **ау́кнуть(ся, -ну(сь** *pf.* halloo, cooee.

аукцио́н, -а auction. **аукционе́р, -а** bidder (*at auction*). **аукциони́ст, -а** auctioneer. **аукцио́нный** auction; **~ зал** auction room.

ау́л, -а aul, Caucasian or Central Asian village.

а́утборт, -а outboard motor.

ауто́псия, -и autopsy, post-mortem.

афга́нец, -нца Afghan, Afghani; **«~»** (*Soviet*) Afghan war vet(eran).

афи́нский Athenian.

Афи́ны, Афи́н *pl.* Athens. **афи́нянин, -а**; *pl.* **-яне, афи́нянка, -и** Athenian.

афи́ша, -и placard, poster. **афиши́ровать, -рую** *impf.* & *pf.* parade, advertise; **~ся** be exhibitionist, seek the limelight.

афори́зм, -а aphorism. **афористи́ческий, афористи́чный** aphoristic.

А́фрика, -и Africa. **африка́анс, -а** Afrikaans. **африка́нер, -а** Afrikaner. **африка́нец, -нца, африка́нка, -и** African. **африка́нский** African.

аффе́кт, -а fit of passion, rage, nervous excitement; temporary insanity.

ах *int.* ah, oh. **а́хи, -ов**; *pl.* ahs, ohs. **а́ханье, -я** sighing; exclamations. **а́хать, -аю** *impf.* (*pf.* **а́хнуть**) sigh; exclaim; gasp.

ахине́я, -и nonsense, rubbish; **нести́ ахине́ю** talk nonsense.

а́хнуть, -ну *pf.* (*impf.* **а́хать**) gasp, exclaim; bang; strike.

аэро... *in comb.* aero-, air-, aerial. **аэро́бика, -и** aerobics. **~би́ст, -а, ~би́стка, -и** aerobicist. **аэро́бн|ый** aerobic; **~ая гимна́стика** aerobics, aerobic exercises. **аэровокза́л, -а** air terminal, airport building. **~дро́м, -а** aerodrome, air-field. **~зо́ль, -я** *m.* aerosol, spray. **~на́вт, -а** aeronaut; balloonist. **~по́рт, -а** airport. **~по́чта, -и** air-mail. **~сни́мок, -мка** aerial photograph. **~ста́т, -а** balloon. **~съёмка, -и** aerial photography.

аэрокосми́ческий aerospace.

АЭС *abbr.* (*of* **а́томная электроста́нция**) atomic power station.

аятолла́, -ы́ ayatollah.

а/я *abbr.* (*of* **абонеме́нтный я́щик**) PO, Post Office box.

Б

б *letter*: *see* **бэ**

б *part.*: *see* **бы**

б. *abbr.* (*of* **бы́вший**) former, ex-, one-time.

ба *int.* expressing surprise.

ба́ба, -ы (*married*) peasant woman; woman; **ка́менная ~** ancient stone image; **сне́жная ~** snowman. **ба́б|ий; ~ье ле́то** Indian summer; **~ьи ска́зки** old wives' tales. **ба́бка**[1], **-и** grandmother; **(повива́льная) ~** midwife.

ба́бка[2], **-и** knucklebone; pastern; **игра́ть в ба́бки** play at knucklebones.

ба́бочка, -и butterfly; **ночна́я ~** moth.

ба́бушка, -и grandmother; granny.

бага́ж, -а́ luggage. **бага́жник, -а** carrier; luggage-rack, compartment; boot. **бага́жничек, -чка** glove compartment. **бага́жный** luggage; **~ ваго́н** luggage-van.

багрове́ть, -ею *impf.* (*pf.* **по~**) crimson, flush, go red. **багро́вый, багря́ный** crimson, purple.

бадминто́н, -а badminton. **бадминтони́ст, -а** badminton-player.

бадья́, -и́; *g.pl.* **-де́й** tub, bucket, pail.

ба́за, -ы base; centre; stock, stores; basis; **~ да́нных** database; **плаву́чая ~** factory ship.

база́р, -а market, fair; bazaar; row, din. **база́рный** market.

бази́ровать, -рую *impf.* base; **~ся** be based, rest (on).
байда́рка, -и canoe; kayak. **байда́рочник, -а** canoeist. **байда́рочный** canoe.
ба́йка[1], **-и** flannelette, flannel. **ба́йковый** flannelette, flannel; ~ **плато́к** woollen shawl.
ба́йка[2], **-и** fairy story, cock-and-bull story.
ба́йт, -а (*comput.*) byte.
бак[1], **-а** tank, cistern; can, billy.
бак[2], **-а** forecastle, fo'c's'le.
бакале́йный grocer's, grocery. **бакале́йщик, -а** grocer. **бакале́я, -и** groceries.
ба́кан, -а, ба́кен, -а buoy.
бакенба́рды, -ба́рд *pl.*, **ба́кены, -ов** *pl.* whiskers; side-whiskers. **ба́ки, бак** *pl.* sideburns, (*short*) side-whiskers.
баклажа́н, -а; *g.pl.* **-ов** *or* **-жа́н** aubergine.
бактериа́льный, бактери́йный bacterial. **бактерио́лог, -а** bacteriologist. **бакте́рия, -и** bacterium.
бал, -а, *loc.* **-у́**; *pl.* **-ы́** dance, ball.
балага́н, -а booth; side-show; popular show; farce, buffoonery. **балага́нить, -ню** *impf.* play the fool. **балала́нщик, -а** showman; clown, buffoon.
балала́ечник, -а balalaika player. **балала́йка, -и** balalaika.
баламу́т, -а trouble-maker. **баламу́тить, -у́чу** *impf.* (*pf.* **вз~**) stir up, trouble; disturb; upset.
бала́нда, -ы (*sl.*) watery soup, skilly, swill.
балансёр, -а rope-walker.
баланси́р, -а balance, balance-wheel. **баланси́ровать, -рую** *impf.* (*pf.* **с~**) balance; keep one's balance.
балахо́н, -а loose overall; shapeless garment.
балбе́с, -а booby.
балдахи́н, -а canopy.
балери́на, -ы ballerina. **бале́т, -а** ballet.
ба́лка[1], **-и** beam, girder.
ба́лка[2], **-и** ravine, gully.
балл, -а mark, number, point, degree; force; **вы́сший** ~ top marks, an 'A'; **ве́тер в пять ~ов** wind force 5.
балла́да, -ы ballad.
балла́ст, -а ballast; lumber.
балло́н, -а container, carboy, cylinder; balloon tyre.
баллоти́ровать, -рую *impf.* ballot, vote; put to the vote; **~ся** stand, be a candidate (**в** *or* **на**+*a.* for). **баллотиро́вка, -и** vote, ballot, poll; polling, voting.
бало́ванный spoilt. **балова́ть, -лу́ю** *impf.* (*pf.* **из~**) spoil; indulge, pamper; play about, play up; +*i.* play with, play at, amuse o.s. with; **~ся** play about, get up to tricks; amuse o.s., play; +*i.* indulge in. **ба́ловень, -вня** *m.* spoilt child; pet, favourite. **баловство́, -а́** spoiling, over-indulgence; pampering; monkey tricks, mischief.
балти́йск|ий; Б~ое мо́ре the Baltic (Sea).
ба́льза, -ы balsa(wood).
бальза́м, -а balsam; balm; ~ **для воло́с** hair conditioner. **бальзами́ровать, -рую** *impf.* (*pf.* **на~**) embalm.
ба́льный ball, dance.
балюстра́да, -ы balustrade; banister. **баля́сина, -ы** baluster, banister. **баля́сы;** ~ **точи́ть** jest, joke.
БАМ *abbr.* (*of* ***Байка́ло-Аму́рская (железнодоро́жная) магистра́ль***) Baykal-Amur railway.
бамбу́к, -а bamboo. **бамбу́ков|ый** bamboo; **~ое положе́ние** awkward situation.
бан, -а, *loc.* **-у́** (*sl.*) railway station.
ба́нда, -ы band, gang.
банда́ж, -а́ truss; belt, bandage; tyre.
бандеро́ль, -и wrapper; printed matter, book-post.
банди́т, -а bandit, brigand; gangster; **вооружённый** ~ armed robber. **бандити́зм, -а** banditry, robbery; **возду́шный** ~ air piracy.
банк, -а bank; **Всеми́рный** ~ World Bank.
ба́нка[1], **-и** jar; tin.
ба́нка[2], **-и** (sand-)bank, shoal.
банке́т, -а banquet.
банки́р, -а banker. **банкро́т, -а** bankrupt.
бант, -а bow. **ба́нтик, -а** bow; **гу́бки ~ом** Cupid's bow. **бантов|о́й; ~а́я скла́дка** box-pleat.
ба́ня, -и bath, bath-house; **фи́нская** ~ sauna.
бар, -а bar; snack-bar; **пивно́й** ~ pub.
бараба́н, -а drum. **бараба́нить, -ню** *impf.* drum, thump. **бараба́нн|ый** drum; **~ая дробь** drum-roll; **~ая перепо́нка** ear-drum. **бараба́нщик, -а** drummer.
бара́к, -а barrack; *pl.* hutments.
бара́н, -а ram; sheep. **бара́ний** sheep's; sheepskin; mutton. **бара́нина, -ы** mutton.
бара́нка, -и baranka, ring-shaped roll; (steering-)wheel.
барахли́ть, -лю́ *impf.* pink, knock; talk rubbish.
барахло́, -а́ old clothes, jumble; odds and ends; trash, junk; rubbish. **барахо́лка, -и** second-hand market, junk-stall.
бара́хтаться, -аюсь *impf.* flounder, wallow, thrash about.
бара́шек, -шка young ram; lamb; lambskin; wing nut; catkin; *pl.* white horses; fleecy clouds. **бара́шковый** lambskin.
ба́ржа́, -и *or* **-и́**; *g.pl.* **барж(е́й)** barge.
ба́рин, -а; *pl.* **-ре** *or* **-ры, бар** barin; landowner; gentleman; master; sir.
ба́рка, -и barge.
баро́чный baroque.
барс, -а ounce, snow-leopard.
ба́рский gentleman's; lordly; grand. **ба́рственный** lordly, grand, arrogant.
барсу́к, -а́ badger. **барсу́чий** badger; badger-skin.
бархáн, -а sand-hill, dune.
ба́рхат, -а (-у) velvet. **бархати́стый** velvety. **ба́рхатка, -и** velvet ribbon **ба́рхатный** velvet; velvety.

барчо́нок, -нка; *pl.* **-ча́та, -ча́т, барчу́к, -а́** barin's son; young master, young gentleman.
ба́рыня, -и barin's wife; lady; mistress; madam.
бары́ш, -а́ profit. **бары́шник, -а** dealer; buyer for re-sale; jobber; (ticket) speculator. **бары́шничать, -аю** *impf.* deal, speculate, job (+*i.* in).
ба́рышня, -и; *g.pl.* **-шень** barin's daughter; young lady, young mistress; miss.
барье́р, -а barrier; obstacle; bar; fence, jump, hurdle. **барьери́ст, -а, -и́стка, -и** hurdler. **барье́рный** hurdle; ~ **бег** hurdle-race.
бас, -а; *pl.* **-ы́** bass. **баси́стый** bass.
баскетбо́л, -а basket-ball. **баскетболи́ст, -а, -и́стка, -и** basket-ball player **баскетбо́льный** basket-ball. **баске́тки, -ток** *pl.* basketball boots.
баснопи́сец, -сца fabulist, writer of fables. **баснослóвный** mythical, legendary; fabulous. **ба́сня, -и**; *g.pl.* **-сен** fable; legend; fabrication.
басо́вый bass.
бассе́йн, -а basin; pool, pond; reservoir; swimming-pool; **плеска́тельный** ~ paddling pool; **каменноуго́льный** ~, **у́гольный** ~ coal-field.
бастова́ть, -тую *impf.* be on strike.
батаре́ец, -е́йца gunner. **батаре́йка, -и, батаре́я, -и** battery; radiator.
бати́ст, -а (-у) batiste, cambric, lawn.
бато́н, -а long loaf; stick, bar. **бато́нчик, -а** stick, bar; **шокола́дный** ~ bar of chocolate.
батра́к, -а́, батра́чка, -и farm-hand, farm-worker, farm labourer. **батра́цкий** farm, farm labourer's.
бату́т, -а trampoline. **батути́ст, -а, батути́стка, -и** trampolinist.
ба́тька, -и *m.*, **ба́тюшка, -и** *m.*, **ба́тя, -и** *m.* father; my dear chap. **ба́тюшки** *int.* good gracious!
бах *int.* bang! **ба́хать(ся, -аю(сь** *impf. of* **ба́хнуть(ся**
бахва́л, -а boaster, braggart. **бахва́льство, -а** bragging, boasting.
ба́хнуть, -ну *pf.* (*impf.* **ба́хать**) bang; thump; **~ся** fall or bump heavily and noisily; let o.s. fall, plump down; **~ся голово́й** bang one's head.
бахрома́, -ы́ fringe. **бахро́мчатый** fringed.
бац *int.* bang! crack! **ба́цать, -аю** *impf.*, **ба́цнуть, -ну** *pf.* crack, bang, bash.
баци́лла, -ы bacillus. **бациллоноси́тель, -я** *m.* carrier.
ба́шенка, -и turret. **ба́шенный** tower, turret.
башка́, -и́ head. **башкови́тый** brainy.
ба́шли, -ей dosh, lolly.
башлы́к, -а́ hood.
башма́к, -а́ shoe; chock; **под** ~ **о́м у**+*g.* under the thumb of.
ба́шня, -и; *g.pl.* **-шен** tower, turret.
ба́ю-ба́й, ба́юшки-баю́ *int.* hushabye, lullaby. **баю́кать, -аю** *impf.* (*pf.* **у~**) lull, rock, sing to sleep.
бде́ние, -я vigil, wakefulness. **бди́тельность, -и** vigilance, watchfulness. **бди́тельный** vigilant, watchful.
бег, -а, *loc.* **-у́**; *pl.* **-а́** run, running; double; race; **оздорови́тельный** ~ jogging; *pl.* trotting-races. **бе́гать, -аю** *indet.* (*det.* **бежа́ть**) *impf.* run; move quickly.
бегемо́т, -а hippopotamus.
бегле́ц, -а́, бегля́нка, -и fugitive. **бе́глость, -и** speed, fluency, dexterity. **бе́глый** fugitive; quick, rapid, fluent; fleeting, cursory, passing; ~ **гла́сный** fugitive vowel, fill-vowel; *sb.* fugitive, runaway. **беговики́, -о́в** *pl.* running shoes. **бегово́й** running; race; ~ **круг** race-course, ring. **бего́м** *adv.* running, at a run, at the double. **беготня́, -и́** running about; bustle. **бе́гство, -а** flight, hasty retreat; escape. **бегу́н, -а́, бегу́нья, -и**; *g.pl.* **-ний** runner.
беда́, -ы́; *pl.* **-ы** misfortune; calamity, disaster; trouble; ~ **в том, что** the trouble is (that); ~ **как** terribly, awfully; **на беду́** unfortunately; **не** ~ it doesn't matter; **что за** ~! what does it matter? so what? **бедне́ть, -е́ю** *impf.* (*pf.* **о~**) grow poor. **бе́дность, -и** poverty, the poor; **у́ровень/поро́г бе́дности** poverty line. **бе́дный; -ден, -дна́, -дно** poor; poverty-stricken. **бедня́га, -и** *m.*, **бедня́жка, -и** *c.g.* poor thing, poor creature. **бедня́к, -а́, бедня́чка, -и** poor peasant; poor man, poor woman. **бедня́чество, -а** poor peasants.
бе́дренный femoral, thigh-. **бедро́, -а́**; *pl.* **бёдра, -дер** thigh; hip; leg.
бе́дственный disastrous, calamitous. **бе́дствие, -я** disaster, calamity; **райо́н бе́дствия** disaster area. **сигна́л бе́дствия** distress signal. **бе́дствовать, -твую** *impf.* be in want, live in poverty.
бежа́ть, бегу́ *det.* (*indet.* **бе́гать**) *impf.* (*pf.* **по~**) run; flow; fly; boil over; *impf.* & *pf.* escape. **бе́женец, -нца, бе́женка, -и** refugee.
без, безо *prep.*+*g.* without; in the absence of; minus, less, short of; ~ **вас** in your absence; ~ **ма́лого** almost, all but; ~ **пяти́ (мину́т)** five (minutes) to; ~ **ума́ (от**+*g.*) mad, crazy (about); ~ **че́тверти** a quarter to.
без..., безъ..., бес... *in comb.* in-, un-; non-; -less. **безавари́йный** accident-free; without breakdowns. **~ала́берный** disorderly, unsystematic; slovenly, careless. **~алкого́льный** non-alcoholic, soft. **~апелляцио́нный** without appeal; peremptory, categorical. **~биле́тник, -а, -ница, -ы** fare dodger; stowaway. **~бо́жие, -я** atheism, **~бо́жный** atheistic; irreligious, anti-religious; godless; shameless, scandalous, outrageous. **~боле́зненный** painless. **~бра́чность, -и** unmarried state, living in sin. **~бра́чный** celibate.

~бре́жный boundless. **~ве́рие, -я** unbelief. **~ве́стный** unknown; obscure. **~ве́тренный** calm, windless. **~ви́нный** guiltless, innocent. **~вку́сие, -я, ~вку́сица, -ы** lack of taste; bad taste. **~вку́сный** tasteless. **~вла́стие, -я** anarchy. **~во́дный** arid, waterless; anhydrous. **~возвра́тный** irrevocable; irretrievable; irrecoverable. **~возме́здный** free, gratis; unpaid. **~во́лие, -я** weakness of will, lack of will-power. **~во́льный** weak-willed, spineless. **~вре́дный** harmless, innocuous; **экологи́чески ~** eco-friendly. **~време́нный** untimely, premature. **~вы́ходный** hopeless, desperate; without going out; uninterrupted. **~гла́зый** one-eyed, eyeless. **~гла́сный** silent, dumb; powerless to protest. **~голо́сный** voiceless, unvoiced. **~гра́мотный** illiterate; ignorant. **~грани́чный** boundless, limitless, infinite. **~гре́шный** innocent, sinless, without sin. **~да́рник, -а** mediocrity, third-rater. **~да́рный** ungifted, untalented; third-rate; **~ актёр** ham; **~ певе́ц** third-rate singer. **~де́йственный** inactive; idle, passive. **~де́йствие, -я** inaction, inactivity, inertia, idleness; negligence. **~де́йствовать, -твую** *impf.* be idle, be inactive; stand idle, not work.

безде́лица, -ы, безде́лка, -и trifle, bagatelle. **безделу́шка, -и** trinket, knick-knack, toy. **безде́льник, -а** idler, loafer; ne'er-do-well. **безде́льничать, -аю** *impf.* idle, loaf. **безде́льный** idle; trifling.

бе́здна, -ы abyss, chasm; enormous numbers, a multitude, masses.

без... бездо́ждье, -я dry weather, drought. **~доказа́тельный** unsupported, unsubstantiated, unproved. **~до́мн|ый** homeless; **~ая ко́шка** stray cat. **~до́нный** bottomless, fathomless. **~доро́жный** without roads. **~доро́жье, -я** lack of (good) roads; season when roads are impassable. **~ду́шный** heartless, callous; soulless, lifeless. **~жа́лостный** pitiless, ruthless. **~жи́зненный** lifeless. **~забо́тный** carefree, untroubled, careless. **~заве́тный** selfless, wholehearted. **~зако́ние, -я** lawlessness; unlawful act. **~зако́нный** illegal, unlawful; lawless. **~засте́нчивый** shameless, unblushing, barefaced. **~защи́тный** defenceless, unprotected. **~земе́льный** landless. **~зло́бный** good-natured, kindly. **~ли́кий** featureless; faceless, impersonal. **~ли́чный** characterless, without personality, without individuality; impersonal. **~лу́нный** moonless. **~лю́дный** uninhabited; sparsely populated; lonely, solitary; empty, unfrequented.

безме́н, -а steelyard; spring balance.

без... безме́рный boundless, limitless. **~мо́зглый** brainless. **~мо́лвие, -я** silence. **~мо́лвный** silent, mute. **~мото́рный** engineless; **~мото́рный самолёт** glider. **~мяте́жный** serene, placid. **~надёжный** hopeless. **~надзо́рный** neglected. **~нака́занно** *adv.* with impunity, unpunished. **~нака́занный** unpunished. **~но́гий** legless; one-legged. **~нра́вственный** immoral.

безо *prep.*: *see* **без**

безобра́зие, -я ugliness; outrage; disgrace, scandal. **безобра́зить, -а́жу** *impf.* (*pf.* **о~**) disfigure, mutilate; create a disturbance, make a nuisance of o.s. **безобра́зничать, -аю** *impf.* behave outrageously; make a nuisance of o.s.

без... безогово́рочный unconditional. **~опа́сность, -и** safety, security; **по́яс/ реме́нь безопа́сности** seat belt. **~опа́сный** safe; secure; **~опа́сная бри́тва** safety razor. **~ору́жный** unarmed. **~оско́лочный** unsplinterable; splinter-proof, shatter-proof. **~основа́тельный** groundless. **~останово́чный** unceasing, continuous; without a break; sustained; non-stop. **~отве́тный** meek, unanswering; unanswered; dumb. **~отве́тственный** irresponsible. **~отка́зно** *adv.* without a hitch. **~отка́зный** trouble-free, smooth-(running). **~отлага́тельный, ~отло́жный** urgent. **~отлу́чный** uninterrupted; continual, continuous; ever-present. **~относи́тельно** *adv.*+**к**+*d.* irrespective of. **~относи́тельный** absolute, unconditional. **~отра́дный** cheerless, dreary. **~отчётный** uncontrolled; unaccountable; instinctive. **~оши́бочный** unerring; faultless; correct. **~рабо́тица, -ы** unemployment. **~рабо́тн|ый** unemployed; **постоя́нно ~ые** the long-term unemployed. **~разде́льный** undivided; whole-hearted; complete. **~разли́чие, -я** indifference. **~разли́чно** *adv.* indifferently; it is all the same. **~разли́чный** indifferent; neutral. **~разме́рный** one-size, stretch. **~рассу́дный** reckless, foolhardy, imprudent. **~ро́дный** alone in the world; without relatives; of unknown antecedents. **~ро́потный** uncomplaining, unmurmuring; meek, resigned. **~рука́вка, -и** sleeveless jacket, jerkin. **~ру́кий** armless; one-armed; awkward. **~уда́рный** unstressed, unaccented. **~у́держный** unrestrained, uncontrolled; uncontrollable. **~укори́зненный** irreproachable, impeccable.

безу́мец, -мца madman. **безу́мие, -я** madness, insanity; distraction. **безу́мный** mad, inane; crazy, senseless; terrible. **~у́мство, -а** madness.

без... безупре́чный irreproachable, faultless. **~уря́дица, -ы** disorder, confusion. **~уса́дочный** pre-shrunk, shrinkproof. **~усло́вно** *adv.* unconditionally, absolutely; of course, undoubtedly, certainly. **~усло́вный** unconditional, absolute; undoubted, indisputable, **~успе́шный** unsuccessful. **~уста́нный** tireless; ceaseless, unremitting. **~уте́шный** inconsolable. **~уча́стие, -я, ~уча́стность, -и** indifference, apathy. **~уча́стный** indifferent, apathetic, unconcerned. **~ъя́дерный** nuclear-free, non-nuclear. **~ыде́йный**

without ideas or ideals; unideological; unprincipled. **~ызве́стный** unknown, obscure. **~ымённый, ~ымя́нный** nameless, anonymous; **~ымя́нный па́лец** third finger, ring-finger. **~ынтере́сный** uninteresting. **~ыску́ственный, ~ыску́сный** artless, ingenuous, unsophisticated. **~ысхо́дный** hopeless, inconsolable; irreparable; interminable.

бейсбо́л, -а baseball. **бейсболи́ст, -а** baseball player.

Бе́йсик (*comput.*) Basic.

бека́р, -а, бека́р *indecl. adj.* natural.

бека́с, -а snipe. **бекаси́нник, -а** small shot.

беко́н, -а bacon.

Белару́сь, -и Belarus.

беле́ть, -е́ю *impf.* (*pf.* **по~**) grow white, turn white; show white; **~ся** show white.

белизна́, -ы́ whiteness. **бели́ла, -и́л** *pl.* whitewash, whiting; correction fluid, Tippex (*propr.*); ceruse. **бели́льный** bleaching. **бели́ть, -лю́, бе́лишь** *impf.* (*pf.* **вы́~, на~, по~**) whitewash; whiten; bleach; **~ся** put ceruse on.

бе́личий squirrel, squirrel's. **бе́лка, -и** squirrel.

белко́вый albuminous.

беллетри́ст, -а writer of fiction. **беллетри́стика, -и** fiction.

бело... *in comb.* white-, leuco-. **белогварде́ец, -е́йца** White Guard. **~дере́вец, -вца** joiner. **~кро́вие, -я** leukaemia. **~ку́рый** fair, blonde. **~ру́с, -а, ~ру́ска, -и, ~ру́сский** Belorussian. **~ры́бица** white salmon. **~сне́жный** snow-white.

белови́к, -а́ fair copy. **белово́й** clean, fair.

бело́к, -лка́ white; albumen, protein.

белошве́йка, -и seamstress. **белошве́йн|ый** linen; **~ая рабо́та** plain sewing.

белу́га, -и beluga, white sturgeon.

белу́ха, -и white whale.

бел|ый; бел, -а́, бе́ло́ white; clean, blank; **~ая берёза** silver birch; **~ый день** broad daylight; **~ое кале́ние** white heat; **~ый медве́дь** polar bear; **~ые но́чи** white nights, midnight sun; **~ые стихи́** blank verse.

Бе́льгия, -и Belgium.

бельё, -я́ linen; bedclothes, underclothes, underclothing; washing; **да́мское ~** lingerie.

бельмо́, -а́; *pl.* **-а** cataract; wall-eye.

бельэта́ж, -а first floor; dress circle.

бемо́ль, -я *m.*, **бемо́ль** *indecl. adj.* flat.

бенефи́с, -а benefit (performance).

бензи́н, -а petrol; benzine; **неэтили́рованный ~** unleaded. **бензи́нов|ый** petrol; **~ая коло́нка** petrol pump. **бензино́ме́р, -а** petrol-gauge **бензинопрово́д, -а** petrol pipe.

бензо... *in comb.* petrol. **бензоба́к, -а** petrol-tank. **~во́з, -а** petrol tanker. **~запра́вка, -и, ~запра́вочная** *sb.* filling-station, petrol-station. **~запра́вщик, -а** petrol bowser, **~коло́нка, -и** petrol pump. **~ме́р, -а** fuel gauge. **~очисти́тель, -я** *m.* petrol filter. **~прово́д, -а** petrol pipe, fuel line. **~хранили́ще, -а** petrol (storage) tank. **~цисте́рна, -ы** petrol tanker.

бензо́л, -а benzene; benzol.

берёг *etc.*: *see* **бере́чь**

бе́рег, -а, *loc.* **-у́**; *pl.* **-а́** bank, shore; coast; **на ~у́ мо́ря** at the seaside. **берегов|о́й** coast; coastal; **~о́е судохо́дство** coastal shipping.

бережёшь *etc.*: *see* **бере́чь. бережли́вый** thrifty, economical; careful. **бе́режный** careful; cautious; solicitous.

берёза, -ы birch. **берёзник, -а, березня́к, -а́** birch grove, birch wood. **берёзовый** birch.

берейтор, -а horse-breaker; riding-master.

бере́менеть, -ею *impf.* (*pf.* **за~**) become pregnant; be pregnant. **бере́менный** pregnant (+*i.* with). **бере́менность, -и** pregnancy; gestation.

бере́т, -а beret.

бере́чь, -регу́, -режёшь; -рёг, -ла́ *impf.* take care of, look after; keep; cherish; husband; be sparing of; **~ся** be careful, take care; beware; **береги́(те)сь!** look out!

Берли́н, -а Berlin. **берли́нск|ий** Berlin; **~ая лазу́рь** Prussian blue.

берло́га, -и den, lair.

берму́ды, -ов *pl.* Bermuda shorts.

беру́ *etc.*: *see* **брать**

бес, -а devil; the devil.

бес... *see* **без...**

бесе́да, -ы talk, conversation; discussion; **~ по душа́м** heart-to-heart (talk). **бесе́дка, -и** summer-house. **бесе́довать, -дую** *impf.* talk, converse.

беси́ть, бешу́, бе́сишь *impf.* (*pf.* **вз~**) enrage, madden, infuriate; **~ся** go mad; rage, be furious.

бес... бескла́ссовый classless. **~коне́чный** endless; infinite; interminable; **~коне́чная дробь** recurring decimal. **~коры́стие, -я** disinterestedness. **~коры́стный** disinterested. **~кофейновый** decaffeinated. **~кра́йний** boundless. **~кро́вный** bloodless.

бесновáтый like one possessed; raving, frenzied. **бесновáться, нýюсь** *impf.* rage, storm, rave; be possessed. **бесо́вский** devilish, devil's.

бес... беспа́мятный forgetful. **~па́мятство, -а** unconsciousness; forgetfulness; delirium **~пардо́нный** shameless, brazen. **~парти́йный** non-party. **~перспекти́вный** without prospects; hopeless. **~пе́чность, -и** carelessness, unconcern. **~пе́чный** carefree; careless, unconcerned. **~пило́тный** unmanned. **~пла́тно** *adv.* free. **~пла́тный** free; rent-free; complimentary. **~пло́дие, -я** sterility, barrenness. **~пло́дность, -и** fruitlessness, futility. **~пло́дный** sterile, barren; fruitless, futile. **~поворо́тный** irrevocable, final. **~подо́бный** incomparable, superb, magnificent. **~позвоно́чный** invertebrate.

беспоко́ить, -о́ю *impf.* (*pf.* **о~, по~**) disturb, make anxious, make uneasy; trouble; **~ся** worry, be anxious; trouble, put o.s. out. **беспоко́йный** restless; anxious; uneasy; troubled; disturbing; fidgety.

бес... бесполе́зный useless. **~по́лый** sexless, asexual. **~помо́щный** helpless, powerless; feeble. **~поро́дный** mongrel, not thoroughbred. **~поро́чный** blameless, irreproachable; immaculate. **~поря́док, -дка** disorder; untidy state; *pl.* disorders, disturbances, rioting. **~поря́дочный** disorderly; untidy. **~поса́дочный** non-stop. **~почве́нный** groundless; unsound. **~по́шлинный** duty-free; **~по́шлинная торго́вля** free trade. **~поща́дный** merciless, relentless. **~пра́вный** wihout rights, deprived of civil rights. **~преде́л, -а** chaos, mayhem. **~преде́льный** boundless, infinite. **~предме́тный** aimless, purposeless; abstract. **~прекосло́вный** unquestioning, absolute. **~препя́тственный** unhindered; free, clear, unimpeded. **~преры́вный** continuous, uninterrupted. **~преста́нный** continual, incessant. **~при́быльный** non-profit-making.

беспризо́рник, -а, -ница, -ы waif, homeless child. **беспризо́рный** neglected, stray; homeless; *sb.* waif, homeless child or young person.

бес... бесприме́рный unexampled, unparalleled **~пристра́стие, -я, ~пристра́стность, -и** impartiality. **~пристра́стный** impartial, unbiased. **~прию́тный** homeless; not affording shelter. **~про́волочный** wireless. **~просве́тный** pitch-dark, pitch-black; hopeless, gloomy; unrelieved. **~пу́тный** debauched, dissipated, dissolute. **~свя́зный** incoherent. **~семя́нный** seedless. **~серде́чие, -я, ~серде́чность, -и** heartlessness, callousness. **~серде́чный** heartless; callous, unfeeling, hard-hearted. **~си́лие, -я** impotence; debility, feebleness. **~си́льный** weak, feeble; impotent, powerless. **~сла́вие, -я** infamy. **~сла́вный** ignominious; infamous; inglorious. **~сле́дно** *adv.* without trace; utterly, completely. **~сле́дный** without leaving a trace, complete. **~слове́сный** dumb, speechless; silent, unmurmuring, meek, humble; walking-on. **~сме́нный** permanent, continuous. **~сме́ртие, -я** immortality. **~сме́ртный** immortal, undying. **~смы́сленный** senseless; foolish; meaningless, nonsensical. **~смы́слица, -ы** nonsense. **~со́вестный** unscrupulous; shameless. **~созна́тельный** unconscious; involuntary. **~со́нница, -ы** insomnia, sleeplessness. **~со́нный** sleepless. **~спо́рный** indisputable, undeniable, unquestionable; incontrovertible. **~сро́чный** indefinite; indeterminate; unlimited. **~стра́стный** impassive. **~стра́шный** intrepid, fearless. **~тала́нный** untalented, without talent.

бестолко́вщина, -ы muddle, confusion, disorder. **бестолко́вый** muddleheaded, slow, stupid; confused, incoherent. **бе́столочь, -и** confusion, muddle; stupid creature; blockheads.

бес... бестре́петный dauntless, undaunted, intrepid. **~фо́рменный** shapeless, formless. **~хара́ктерный** weak, spineless. **~хи́тростный** artless; ingenuous; unsophisticated. **~цве́тный** colourless. **~це́льный** aimless; pointless. **~це́нный** priceless. **~це́нок; за ~це́нок** very cheap, for a song. **~церемо́нный** unceremonious; cavalier; free and easy, familiar, off-hand. **~челове́чный** inhuman. **~че́стить, -е́щу** *impf.* (*pf.* **о~че́стить**) dishonour, disgrace. **~че́стный** dishonourable, disgraceful. **~чи́сленный** innumerable, countless.

бесчу́вственный insensible, unconscious; insensitive, unfeeling. **бесчу́вствие, -я** unconsciousness, insensibility; callousness, heartlessness; **пьян до бесчу́вствия** dead drunk.

бес... бесшо́вный seamless. **~шу́мный** noiseless.

бето́н, -а concrete. **бетони́ровать, -рую** *impf.* (*pf.* **за~**) concrete. **бето́нный** concrete. **бетономеша́лка, -и** concrete-mixer. **бето́нщик, -а** concrete-worker, concreter.

бечева́, -ы́ tow-rope; rope, cord, twine. **бечёвка, -и** twine, cord, string. **бечевни́к, -а́** tow-path, towing-path. **бечев|о́й** tow, towing; **~а́я** *sb.* tow-path, towing-path.

бе́шенство, -а hydrophobia, rabies; fury, rage. **бе́шеный** rabid, mad; furious, violent.

бешу́ *etc.*: *see* **беси́ть**

биатло́н, -а biathlon. **биатлони́ст, -а** biathlete, biathlon competitor.

бибабо́ *nt.indecl.* glove puppet.

библе́йский biblical. **библио́граф, -а** bibliographer. **библиографи́ческий** bibliographical. **библиоте́ка, -и** library; **~-чита́льня** reading-room. **библиоте́карь, -я** *m.*, **-те́карша, -и** librarian. **библиоте́чный** library. **би́блия, -и** bible.

бива́к, -а bivouac, camp.

би́вень, -вня *m.* tusk.

бигль, -я beagle (*dog*).

бигуди́ *indecl. pl.* curlers.

биде́ *nt.indecl.* bidet.

бидо́н, -а can; milk-churn.

бие́ние, -я beating; beat.

бижуте́рия, -и costume jewellery.

би́знес, -а business. **бизнесме́н, -а** businessman.

биле́т, -а ticket; card; pass, permit; **креди́тный ~** bank-note. **билетёр, -а, -тёрша, -и** ticket-collector; usherette. **биле́тный** ticket.

билья́рд, -а billiards. **бильярди́ст, -а** *m.* billiards-player. **билья́рдная** *sb.* billiard-hall.

бино́кль, -я *m.* binoculars; **полево́й ~** field-glasses; **театра́льный ~** opera-glasses. **бинокуля́рный** binocular.

бинт, -а́ bandage. **бинтова́ть, -ту́ю** *impf.* (*pf.* **за~**) bandage. **бинто́вка, -и** bandaging.

био́граф, -а biographer. **биографи́ческий**

biographical. **биогра́фия, -и** biography; curriculum vitae, CV.

био́лог, -а biologist. **биологи́ческий** biological. **биоло́гия, -и** biology. **биоресу́рсы, -ов** *pl.* bioresources. **биори́тмы, -ов** *pl.* biorhythms. **биохими́ческий** biochemical. **биохи́мия, -и** biochemistry.

би́ржа, -и exchange.

би́рка, -и tally; name-plate; label.

бирюза́, -ы́ turquoise

бис *int.* encore; **спеть на ~** repeat as encore. **биси́ровать, -рую** *impf.* & *pf.* repeat; give an encore.

би́сер, -а glass beads, bugles. **би́серина, -ы, би́серинка, -и** (*small*) glass bead.

бискви́т, -а sponge cake; biscuit. **бискви́тный** sponge; biscuit.

бит, -а (*comput.*) bit.

би́тва, -ы battle.

битко́м *adv.*; **~ наби́т** crowded, packed.

битло́вка, -и polo-neck (sweater).

бито́к, -тка́ rissole, hamburger.

би́т|ый beaten; broken, cracked; **~ые сли́вки** whipped cream; **~ый час** a full hour; hours, ages. **бить, бью, бьёшь** *impf.* (*pf.* **за~, по~, про~, уда́рить**) beat; hit; defeat; strike; whip; sound; thump, bang; kill, slaughter; smash, shatter; fight, struggle, wage war (**по**+*d.* on, against); spurt, gush; shoot, fire; **~ в бараба́н** beat a drum; **~ в ладо́ши** clap one's hands; **~ (в) наба́т** sound, raise the alarm; **~ в цель** hit the target; **~ ключо́м** gush out, well up; be in full swing; **~ на**+*a.* strive for, after; have a range of; **~ отбо́й** beat a retreat; **~ по**+*d.* damage, injure, wound; **~ трево́гу** sound, raise, the alarm; **~ хвосто́м** lash its tail; **~ся** fight; beat; writhe, struggle; break; +*i.* knock, hit, strike; +**над**+*i.* struggle with, rack one's brains over; **~ голово́й об сте́ну** be up against a blank wall; **~ об закла́д** bet, wager. **битьё, -я́** beating, thrashing, thumping, banging; smashing.

бифште́кс, -а (beef)steak. **бифште́ксная** *sb.* steakhouse.

би́ч, -а́ whip, lash; scourge. **бичева́ть, -чу́ю** *impf.* flog; lash, castigate.

бишь *part.* expressing effort to remember name, etc.: **как ~ его́?** what was the name again?; what's-his-name, thingamy; **то ~** that is to say.

бла́го, -а good; blessing; **всех благ!** all the best! **бла́го** *conj.* since.

бла́го... *in comb.* well-, good-. **Благове́щение, -я** Annunciation. **~ве́щенский** of the Annunciation. **~ви́дный** comely; plausible, specious. **~воле́ние, -я** goodwill; favour. **~воспи́танный** well-bred.

благодаре́ние, -я gratitude, thanks. **благодари́ть, -рю́** *impf.* (*pf.* **по~**) thank; **благодарю́ вас** thank you. **благода́рность, -и** gratitude; thanks; bribe; **не сто́ит благода́рности** don't mention it, not at all. **благода́рный** grateful; rewarding, promising. **благода́рственный** of gratitude, of thanks; thanksgiving. **благодаря́** *prep.+d.* thanks to, owing to; because of.

благо... благоде́тель, -я *m.*, **-ница, -ы** benefactor. **~де́тельный** beneficial; beneficent. **~ду́шный** placid, equable; good-humoured. **~жела́тель, -я** *m.* well-wisher. **~жела́тельный** well-disposed; benevolent. **~зву́чный** melodious, harmonious. **~мы́слящий** right-thinking, right-minded. **~надёжный** reliable, trustworthy, sure; loyal. **~наме́ренный** well-intentioned. **~нра́вие, -я** good behaviour. **~нравный** well-behaved; high-principled. **~полу́чие, -я** well-being; happiness. **~полу́чно** *adv.* all right, well; happily; safely. **~полу́чный** happy, successful; safe. **~присто́йный** decent, seemly, decorous. **~прия́тный** favourable. **~прия́тствовать** *impf.+d.* favour; **наибо́лее ~прия́тствуемая держа́ва** most-favoured nation. **~разу́мие, -я** sense; prudence. **~разу́мный** judicious; sensible, prudent. **~ро́дие, -я; ва́ше ~ро́дие** Your Honour. **~ро́дный** noble. **~ро́дство, -а** nobility. **~скло́нность, -и** favour, good graces. **~скло́нный** favourable; gracious. **~слови́ть, -влю́** *pf.*, **благословля́ть, -я́ю** *impf.* bless. **~состоя́ние, -я** prosperity. **~твори́тель, -я** *m.*, **-ница, -ы** philanthropist. **~твори́тельный** charitable, charity. **~тво́рный** salutary; beneficial; wholesome. **~устро́енный** well-equipped, well-arranged, well-planned; with all amenities.

блаже́нный blessed; blissful; simple-minded. **блаже́нство, -а** bliss, blessedness.

бланк, -а form; **анке́тный ~** questionnaire. **бла́нков|ый** form; **~ая на́дпись** endorsement.

блат, -а (*sl.*) thieves' cant, criminals' slang; pull, protection racket, fiddle; string-pulling, wangling. **блатн|о́й** criminal; soft, cushy; **~а́я му́зыка** thieves' cant; *sb.* criminal, thief.

бледне́ть, -е́ю *impf.* (*pf.* **по~**) grow pale; pale. **бледноли́цый** pale; *sb.* paleface. **бле́дность, -и** paleness, pallor. **бле́дный; -ден, -дна́, -о** pale; colourless; **~ как полотно́** as white as a sheet.

бле́йзер, -а blazer.

блёклый faded. **блёкнуть, -ну; блёк(нул)** *impf.* (*pf.* **по~**) fade, wither.

блеск, -а (-у) brightness, brilliance, lustre, shine; splendour, magnificence.

блесну́ть, -ну́, -нёшь *pf.* flash, gleam; shine. **блесте́ть, -ещу́, -сти́шь** *or* **бле́щешь** *impf.* shine; glitter; sparkle. **блёстка, -и** sparkle, flash; spangle, sequin. **блестя́щий** shining, bright; brilliant.

бле́яние, -я bleat, bleating. **бле́ять, -е́ет** *impf.* bleat.

ближа́йший nearest, closest; next; immediate; **~ ро́дственник** next of kin. **бли́же** *comp. of* **бли́зкий, бли́зко. ближневосто́чный**

Middle East; Middle Eastern. **бли́жний** near, close; neighbouring; *sb.* neighbour. **близ** *prep.+g.* near, close to, by. **бли́зиться, -зится** *impf.* approach, draw near. **бли́зкий; -зок, -и́зка́, -о** near, close; imminent; intimate; **~кие** *sb., pl.* one's nearest and dearest, near relatives. **бли́зко** *adv.* near, close (**от**+*g.* to); nearly, closely. **близне́ц, -а́** twin; *pl.* Gemini. **близору́кий** short-sighted. **бли́зость, -и** nearness, closeness, proximity; intimacy.

блик, -а spot or patch of light; light, highlight.

блин, -а́ pancake. **бли́нная** *sb.* pancake parlour.

блинда́ж, -а́ dug-out.

блиста́тельный brilliant, splendid. **блиста́ть, -а́ю** *impf.* shine; glitter; sparkle.

блиц, -а flash (attachment).

блиц(-)... *in comb.* lightning ...; whirlwind ... **блицвизи́т** flying visit. **бли́цкриг, -а** blitzkrieg.

блок[1], **-а** block, pulley, sheave.

блок[2], **-а** bloc; block; section, unit; slab; module; carton. **блока́дник, -а** victim of siege of Leningrad (1941–44). **блоки́ровать, -рую** *impf.* & *pf.* blockade; block; **~ся** form a bloc. **блокиро́вка, -и** block system.

блокно́т, -а writing-pad, note-pad, note-book.

блонди́н, -а, блонди́нка, -и blond(e).

блоха́, -и́; *pl.* **-и, -а́м** flea.

бло́чный modular.

блоши́ный flea. **бло́шки, -шек** *pl.* tiddlywinks.

блудни́ца, -ы whore.

блужда́ть, -а́ю *impf.* roam, wander, rove. **блужда́ющ|ий** wandering; **~ий огонёк** will-o'-the-wisp; **~ по́чка** floating kidney.

блу́за, -ы, блу́зка, -и blouse.

блю́дечко, -а saucer; small dish; **на блю́дечке** on a plate. **блю́до, -а** dish; course. **блюдоли́з, -а** lickspittle. **блю́дце, -а** saucer.

блюсти́, -юду́, -дёшь; блюл, -а́ *impf.* (*pf.* **со~**) guard, keep; watch over; observe. **блюсти́тель, -я** *m.* keeper, guardian.

боб, -а́ bean. **бобо́в|ый** bean; **~ые** *sb., pl.* **бобо́к, -бка́** leguminous plants.

бобр, -а́ beaver. **бо́брик, -а** beaver-cloth; **во́лосы ~ом** crew cut. **бобро́вый** beaver.

бо́бслей, -я bobsleigh; bobsleighing. **бобслеи́ст, -а** bobsleigher.

бобы́ль, -я́ *m.* poor landless peasant; solitary person.

Бог, бог, -а, *voc.* **Бо́же** God; god; **дай ~** God grant; **~ его́ зна́ет** who knows? **не дай ~** God forbid; **Бо́же (мой)!** my God! good God!; **ра́ди ~а** for God's sake; **с ~ом!** good luck!; **сла́ва ~у** thank God. **богаде́льня, -и** almshouse, workhouse.

богате́й, -я rich man. **богате́ть, -е́ю** *impf.* (*pf.* **раз~**) grow rich. **бога́тство, -а** riches, wealth; richness. **бога́тый** rich, wealthy; *sb.* rich man. **бога́ч, -а́** rich man.

боги́ня, -и goddess. **Богома́терь, -и** Mother of God. **богомо́лец, -льца́, богомо́лка, -и** devout person; pilgrim. **богомо́лье, -я** pilgrimage. **богомо́льный** religious, devout. **Богоро́дица, -ы** the Virgin Mary. **богосло́в, -а** theologian. **богосло́вие, -я** theology. **боготвори́ть, -рю́** *impf.* worship, idolize; deify. **Богоявле́ние, -я** Epiphany.

бода́ть(ся, -а́ю(сь *impf.*, **бодну́ть, -ну́, -нёшь** *pf.* (*pf. also* **забода́ть**) butt. **бодли́вый** inclined to butt.

бодри́ть, -рю́ *impf.* stimulate, invigorate, brace up; **~ся** try to keep up one's spirits. **бо́дрость, -и** cheerfulness, good spirits, courage. **бо́дрствовать, -твую** be awake; stay awake, keep awake; sit up. **бо́дрый; бодр, -а́, -о** cheerful, brisk, bright; hale and hearty. **бодря́щий** invigorating, bracing.

боеви́к, -а́ active revolutionary, militant; smash hit. **боеви́тость, -и** fighting spirit. **боев|о́й** fighting, battle, war; urgent; militant, determined, unyielding; **~ о́й клич** war-cry; **~о́е креще́ние** baptism of fire; **~о́й механи́зм** striking mechanism. **боеголо́вка, -и** warhead. **боеготóвность, -и** combat readiness. **боеприпа́сы, -ов** *pl.* ammunition. **боéц, бойца́** soldier; fighter, warrior; butcher, slaughterer; *pl.* men.

Бо́же *see* **Бог. бо́жеский** divine; fair, just. **божество́, -а́** deity; divinity. **бо́ж|ий** God's; **~ья коро́вка** ladybird; **ка́ждый ~ий день** every blessed day. **божи́ться, -жу́сь** *impf.* (*pf.* **по~**) swear. **божо́к, -жка́** idol.

бой, -я (-ю), *loc.* **-ю́**; *pl.* **-и́, -ёв** battle, action, fight; bout; fighting; killing, slaughtering; striking; breakage(s), broken glass, crockery, etc.; **бараба́нный ~** drumbeat; **~ быко́в** bullfight; **~ кито́в** whaling; **~ тюле́ней** sealing; **с бо́ю** by force; **часы́ с бо́ем** striking clock.

бо́й|кий; бо́ек, бойка́, -о bold, spry, smart, sharp; glib; lively, animated; busy.

бойни́ца, -ы loophole, embrasure.

бо́йня, -и; *g.pl.* **бо́ен** slaughter-house, abattoir, shambles; massacre, slaughter, butchery.

бо́йче *comp. of* **бо́йкий**

бок, -а (-у), *loc.* **-у́**; *pl.* **-а́** side; flank; **~ о́ ~** side by side; **в ~** sideways; **на́ ~** sideways, to the side; **на ~у́** on one side; **по́д ~ом** near by, close by; **с ~у** from the side, from the flank; **с ~у на́ бок** from side to side.

бока́л, -а glass; goblet.

боково́й side, flank; lateral; sidelong. **бо́ком** *adv.* sideways.

бокс, -а boxing. **боксёр, -а** boxer. **боксёрский** boxing. **бокси́ровать, -рую** *impf.* box.

болва́н, -а block; blockhead; twit; dummy; idol. **болва́нка, -и** block; pig; **желе́зо в ~х** pig-iron.

Болга́рия, -и Bulgaria.

болево́й of pain, painful.

бо́лее *adv.* more; **~ всего́** most of all; **тем ~**

especially as.

болéзнен|ный sickly; unhealthy; abnormal; morbid; painful. **болéзнь, -и** illness, disease, ailment; abnormality; ~ **рóста** growing pains.

болéльщик, -а, -щица, -ы fan, supporter. **болéть**[1], **-éю** *impf.* be ill, suffer; be worried; +**за**+*a.* support, be a fan of. **болéть**[2], **-лúт** *impf.* ache, hurt.

болóнья, -и (cape of) waterproof nylon.

болóтистый marshy, boggy, swampy. **болóто, -а** marsh, bog, swamp. **болóтный** marsh, bog.

болтáнка, -и air-pocket. **болтáть**[1], **-áю** *impf.* stir; shake; dangle; ~**ся** dangle, swing; hang loosely; hang about; fly bumpily, bump.

болтáть[2], **-áю** *impf.* chatter, jabber, natter. **болтлúвый** garrulous, talkative; indiscreet. **болтнýть, -нý, -нёшь** *pf.* blurt out. **болтовнЯ́, -ú** talk chatter; gossip. **болтýн**[1], **-á, болтýнья, -и** talker, chatterer; chatterbox; gossip.

болтýн[2], **-á** addled egg.

болтýшка, -и scrambled eggs; mixture; swill, mash; whisk.

боль, -и pain; ache; ~ **в бокý** stitch. **больнúца, -ы** hospital. **больнúчный** hospital; ~ **листóк** medical certificate. **бóльно**[1] *adv.* painfully, badly; *pred.*+*d.* it hurts. **бóльно**[2] *adv.* very, extremely, terribly. **больнóй; -лен, -льнá** ill, sick; diseased; sore; *sb.* patient, invalid.

большáк, -á high road. **бóльше** *comp. of* **большóй, велúкий, мнóго**; bigger, larger; greater; more; ~ **не** not any more, no more, no longer; ~ **тогó** and what is more; *adv.* for the most part. **бóльш|ий** greater, larger; ~**ей чáстью** for the most part; **сáмое** ~**ее** at most, at the utmost, at the outside. **большинствó, -á** majority; most people. **больш|óй** big, large; great; grown-up; ~**áя бýква** capital letter; ~**áя дорóга** high road; ~**óй пáлец** thumb; big toe; ~**óй свет** high society, the world; ~**úе** *sb., pl.* grown-ups. **большýщий** huge, enormous.

болЯ́чка, -и sore, scab; defect, weakness.

бóмба, -ы bomb; **зажигáтельная** ~ petrol bomb, Molotov cocktail. **бомбардировáть, -рýю** *impf.* bombard; bomb. **бомбардирóвка, -и** bombardment, bombing. **бомбардирóвщик, -а** bomber; bomber pilot. **бомбёжка, -и** bombing. **бомбúть, -блю́** bomb. **бомбовóз, -а** bomber. **бóмбовый** bomb. **бомбоубéжище, -а** bomb shelter.

бомж, -а *abbr.* (*of* ***без определённого мéста жúтельства***) homeless person, vagrant.

бóна, -ы bond, bill; money order; *pl.* paper money.

бор, -а, *loc.* **-ý**; *pl.* **-ы́** pine-wood, coniferous forest.

бордó *nt.indecl.* claret; red Bordeaux. **бордó** *indecl. adj.*, **бордóвый** wine-red, claret-coloured.

бордю́р, -а border.

борéц, -рцá fighter; wrestler; campaigner; activist; ~ **за мир** peace campaigner.

борзáя *sb.* borzoi; **англúйская** ~ greyhound. **бóрзый** swift.

бормотáние, -я muttering, mumbling; mutter, mumble. **бормотáть, -очý, -óчешь** *impf.* (*pf.* **про**~) mutter, mumble.

бóрный boric, boracic.

бóров, -а hog.

боровúк, -á (edible) boletus.

бородá, -ы́, *a.* **бóроду**; *pl.* **бóроды, -рóд, -áм** beard; wattles. **бородáвка, -и** wart. **бородáтый** bearded. **бородáч, -á** bearded man. **борóдка, -и** small beard, tuft; key-bit; barb.

бороздá, -ы́; *pl.* **бóрозды, -óзд, -áм** furrow; fissure. **бороздúть, -зжý** *impf.* (*pf.* **вз**~) furrow; plough; leave wake or track on; score. **борóздка, -и** furrow, groove. **борóздчатый** furrowed; grooved, scored.

боронá, -ы́, *a.* **бóрону**; *pl.* **бóроны, -рóн, -áм** harrow. **боронúть, -ню́** *impf.* (*pf.* **вз**~) harrow.

борóться, -рю́сь, бóрешься *impf.* wrestle, grapple; struggle, fight.

борт, -а, *loc.* **-ý**; *pl.* **-á, -óв** side, ship's side; front; cushion; **зá** ~, **за** ~**ом** overboard; **на** ~, **на** ~**ý** on board. **борт...** *in comb.* ship's; air, flight, flying.

бортов|óй ship's; side; onboard; flight, flying; ~**áя кáчка** rolling. **бортпроводнúк, -á** air steward. **бортпроводнúца, -ы** air hostess.

борщ, -á bor(t)sch.

борьбá, -ы́ wrestling; struggle, fight; conflict; **америкáнская** ~ all-in wrestling.

босикóм *adv.* barefoot. **босóй; бос, -á, -о, босонóгий** barefooted; **на бóсу нóгу** on one's bare feet. **босонóжка, -и** barefooted woman or girl; barefoot dancer; *pl.* sandals, mules. **босЯ́к, -á, босЯ́чка, -и** tramp; down-and-out.

бот, -а, бóтик[1], **-а** small boat.

ботáник, -а botanist. **ботáника, -и** botany. **ботанúческий** botanical; ~ **сад** botanical gardens.

бóтик[2], **-а** high overshoe. **ботúнок, -нка** boot.

бóцман, -а boatswain, boatswain's mate.

бочáг, -á pool; deep puddle.

бочкóм *adv.* sideways.

бóчка, -и barrel, cask. **бочóнок, -нка** keg, small barrel.

боязлúвый timid, timorous. **боЯ́знь, -и** fear, dread.

боЯ́рин, -а; *pl.* **-Я́ре, -Я́р** boyar. **боЯ́рск|ий** boyar's, boyars'; ~**ие дéти** small landowners.

боЯ́рышник, -а hawthorn.

боЯ́ться, бою́сь *impf.*+*g.* be afraid of, fear; dislike, be intolerant of.

бр. *abbr.* (*of* **брáтья**) bros., brothers.

бра *nt.indecl.* sconce, bracket.
бра́га, -и home-brewed beer.
бра́к[1], **-а** marriage.
бра́к[2], **-а** defective goods, defect, defective part; reject, waste. **бракёр, -а** inspector. **бракова́ть, -ку́ю** *impf.* (*pf.* **за~**) reject. **бракоде́л, -а** bad workman.
бракоразво́дный divorce.
брандахлы́ст, -а slops, swill.
брани́ть, -ню́ *impf.* (*pf.* **вы́~**) scold; abuse, curse; **~ся** (*pf.* **по~ся**) swear, curse; quarrel. **бра́нн|ый**[1] abusive, profane; **~ое сло́во** swear-word.
бра́нн|ый[2] martial, battle. **брань**[1], **-и** war; battle.
брань[2], **-и** swearing, bad language; abuse.
брасле́т, -а bracelet.
брасс, -а breast stroke. **брасси́ст, -а, -и́стка, -и** breast-stroke swimmer.
брат, -а; *pl.* **-тья, -тьев** brother; comrade; old man, my lad, mate; lay brother, monk, friar; *pl.* friends, boys; **на ~а** per head; **наш ~** we, the likes of us, our sort. **брата́ние, -я** fraternization. **брата́ться, -а́юсь** *impf.* (*pf.* **по~**) fraternize. **братва́, -ы́** comrades, friends. **бра́тия, -и**; *g.pl.* **-тий, бра́тья, -и** brotherhood, fraternity. **братоуби́йство, -а, братоуби́йца, -ы** *c.g.* fratricide. **бра́тский** brotherly, fraternal. **бра́тство, -а** brotherhood, fraternity.
брать, беру́, -рёшь; брал, -а́, -о *impf.* (*pf.* **взять**) take; get, obtain, book; hire; seize, grip; exact, demand, require; surmount, clear; work; be effective; take bribes; *+i.* succeed through, succeed by means of; *+adv.* bear; **~ верх** get the upper hand; **~ в ско́бки** put in brackets; **~ на**+*a.* have a range of; **~ на букси́р** take in tow; **~ на пору́ки** go bail for; **~ но́ту** sing (play) a note; **~ под аре́ст** put under arrest; **~ своё** get one's (own) way; take its toll, tell; **~ сло́во** take the floor; **~ся+за**+*a.* touch; take hold of, seize; take up; get down to; **+за**+*a. or inf.* undertake, take on o.s.; appear, come; **~ся за ум** come to one's senses; **~ся нарасхва́т** go (sell) like hot cakes.
бра́чный marriage; mating.
бреве́нчатый log. **бревно́, -а́**; *pl.* **-ёвна, -вен** log, beam.
бред, -а, *loc.* **-у́** delirium; raving(s); gibberish; **соба́чий ~** twaddle, poppycock. **бре́дить, -е́жу** *impf.* be delirious, rave; *+i.* rave about, be infatuated with. **бре́дни, -ей** *pl.* ravings; fantasies. **бредово́й, бредо́вый** delirious; fantastic, nonsensical.
бреду́ *etc.*: *see* **брести́. бре́жу** *etc.*: *see* **бре́дить**
бре́згать, -аю *impf.* (*pf.* **по~**) *+inf. or i.* be squeamish about, be fastidious about; be nauseated by, be sickened by; shrink from, scruple or hesitate to. **брезгли́вый** squeamish, fastidious.
брезе́нт, -а tarpaulin.
бре́зжить(ся, -ит(ся *impf.* dawn; gleam faintly, glimmer.
брейк, -а break dancing. **бре́йкер, -а** break dancer.
брёл *etc.*: *see* **бре́сти**
брело́к, -а charm, trinket; **~ для ключе́й** key ring, fob.
бремени́ть, -ню́ *impf.* (*pf.* **о~**) burden. **бре́мя, -мени** *nt.* burden; load.
бренча́ть, -чу́ *impf.* strum; jingle.
брести́, -еду́, -едёшь; брёл, -а́ *impf.* stroll, amble; struggle along, drag o.s. along.
брете́ль, -и, брете́лька, -и shoulder strap.
бре́ю *etc.*: *see* **брить**
брига́да, -ы brigade; squadron; crew, team, gang, squad. **бригади́р, -а** brigadier; brigade-leader; team-leader; foreman. **брига́дник, -а, -ница, -ы** member of brigade, crew, team.
бри́дер, -а breeder reactor.
бри́джи, -ей *pl.* breeches.
briза́нтный high-explosive.
бриллиа́нт, -а, брилья́нт, -а brilliant, diamond.
брита́нец, -нца, брита́нка, -и Briton, British subject; Englishman, Englishwoman. **брита́нск|ий** British; **Б~ие острова́** *pl.* the British Isles.
бри́тва, -ы razor. **бри́твенный** shaving. **бри́тый** shaved; clean-shaven. **брить, бре́ю** *impf.* (*pf.* **по~**) shave; **~ся** shave (o.s.). **бритьё, -я́** shave; shaving.
бри́чка, -и britzka, trap.
бро́вка, -и brow; edge. **бровь, -и**; *pl.* **-и, -е́й** eyebrow; brow.
брод, -а ford.
броди́ть, -ожу́, -о́дишь *impf.* wander, roam, stray; amble, stroll; ferment. **бродя́га, -и** *c.g.* **бродя́жка, -и** *c.g.* tramp, vagrant, down-and-out; wanderer. **бродя́жничать, -аю** *impf.* be on the road, be a tramp. **бродя́жничество, -а** vagrancy. **бродя́чий** vagrant; wandering, roving; strolling; stray; restless. **броже́ние, -я** ferment, fermentation.
бром, -а bromine; bromide. **бро́мистый** bromic, bromidic; **~ ка́лий** potassium bromide. **бро́мный, бро́мовый** bromine.
броне... *in comb.* armoured, armour. **бронебо́йный** armour-piercing. **~ви́к, -а́** armoured car. **~во́й** armoured, armour. **~жиле́т, -а** bulletproof vest. **~но́сец, -сца** battleship, ironclad; armadillo. **~но́сный, ~та́нковый** armoured.
бро́нза, -ы bronze; (collection of) bronzes. **бронзирова́ть, -ру́ю** *impf.* & *pf.* bronze. **бронзиро́вка, -и** bronzing. **бро́нзовый** bronze; bronzed.
брониро́ванный armoured. **бронирова́ть**[1], **-ру́ю** *impf.* & *pf.* (*pf. also* **за~**) armour.
брони́ровать[2], **-рую** *impf.* & *pf.* (*pf. also* **за~**) reserve, book.
бронхи́т, -а bronchitis.
броня́[1], **-и́** armour.

бро́ня[2], **-и** reservation; commandeering; warrant, permit; exemption.

броса́ть, -а́ю *impf.*, **бро́сить, -о́шу** *pf.* throw, cast, fling; drop, throw down; leave, abandon, desert; give up, leave off; **бро́сь(те)!** stop it! drop it!; **~ся** throw o.s., fling o.s., rush; *+inf.* begin, start; *+i.* throw away, squander; throw at one another, pelt one another with; **~ся в глаза́** be striking, arrest the attention; **~ся на коле́ни** fall on one's knees; **~ся на по́мощь**+*d.* rush to the assistance of. **бро́ский** arresting, striking; loud, garish, glaring. **бро́сов|ый** worthless, rubbishy; **~ая цена́** giveaway price; **~ый э́кспорт** dumping. **бросо́к, -ска́** throw; burst; bound, spurt; thrust.

бро́шка, -и, брошь, -и brooch.

брошю́ра, -ы pamphlet, booklet, brochure. **брошюрова́ть, -ру́ю** *impf.* (*pf.* **с~**) stitch. **брошюро́вка, -и** stitching. **брошюро́вщик, -а** stitcher.

брус, -а; *pl.* **-сья, -сьев** squared timber; beam, joist; bar; **(паралле́льные) ~ья** parallel bars. **бруско́вый** bar.

брусни́ка, -и cowberry, red whortleberry; cowberries, red whortleberries.

брусо́к, -ска́ bar; ingot; slug.

бру́ствер, -а breastwork, parapet.

бру́тто *indecl. adj.* gross.

бры́згалка, -и sprinkler; water-pistol.

бры́згать, -зжу *or* **-гаю** *impf.*, **бры́знуть, -ну** *pf.* splash, spatter; sprinkle; spurt, gush; **~ слюно́й** sputter, splutter; **~ся** splash o.s., splash one another; spray o.s. **бры́зги, брызг** *pl.* spray, splashes; fragments; sparks.

брыка́ть, -а́ю *impf.*, **брыкну́ть, -ну́, -нёшь** *pf.* kick; **~ся** kick, rebel.

брысь *int.* shoo!

брюзга́, -и́ *c.g.* grumbler. **брюзгли́вый** grumbling, peevish. **брюзжа́ть, -жу́** *impf.* grumble.

брю́ква, -ы swede.

брю́ки, брюк *pl.* trousers; **~-ю́бка** culottes.

брюне́т, -а dark man, dark-haired man. **брюне́тка, -и** brunette.

Брюссе́ль, -я Brussels.

брюха́стый, брюха́тый big-bellied. **брю́хо, -а**; *pl.* **-и** belly; paunch, corporation; stomach.

брю́чный trouser; **~ костю́м** trouser suit.

брюшко́, -а́; *pl.* **-и́, -о́в** abdomen; paunch. **брюшно́й** abdominal; **~ тиф** typhoid.

бря́канье, -я clatter. **бря́кать, -аю** *impf.*, **бря́кнуть, -ну** *pf.* crash down, drop with a crash; blurt out; (*+i.*) clatter, make a clatter; **~ся** crash, fall heavily. **бряца́ние, -я** rattling, rattle; clanking, clank; clang. **бряца́ть, -а́ю** *impf.* rattle; clank, clang.

бу́бен, -бна tambourine. **бубене́ц, -нца́, бубе́нчик, -а** small bell.

бу́бны, -бён, -бна́м *pl.* diamonds. **бубно́вый** diamond; **~ вале́т** knave of diamonds.

бугóр, -гра́ mound, hillock, knoll; bump, lump. **бугоро́к, -рка́** small mound or lump; protuberance; tubercle. **бугорча́тка, -и** tuberculosis, consumption. **бугри́стый** hilly, bumpy.

бу́дет that's enough, that will do; *+inf.* it's time to stop; **~ вам писа́ть** don't do any more writing.

буди́льник, -а alarm-clock. **буди́ть, бужу́, бу́дишь** *impf.* (*pf.* **про~, раз~**) wake, awaken; rouse, arouse.

бу́дка, -и box, booth; hut; stall; **соба́чья ~** dog-kennel.

бу́дни, -ней *pl.* weekdays; workdays, working days; humdrum existence. **бу́дний, бу́дничный** weekday; everyday; dull, humdrum.

бу́дто *conj.* as if, as though; **~ (бы), (как) ~** apparently, allegedly, ostensibly; *part.* really?

бу́ду *etc.*: *see* **быть. бу́дучи** being. **бу́дущ|ий** future; next, coming; to be, to come; **~ая мать** mother-to-be, expectant mother; **~ее** *sb.* future. **бу́дущность, -и** future. **бу́дь(те)** *see* **быть**

бу́ер, -а; *pl.* **-а́, -о́в** ice-boat, ice-yacht.

бужу́ *see* **буди́ть**

буза́, -ы́ home brew; (*sl.*) row, shindy; rubbish.

бузина́, -ы́ elder. **бузи́нник, -а** thicket of elders. **бузи́нный, бузи́новый** elder.

бузи́ть, -и́шь *impf.* (*sl.*) kick up a row.

бузотёр, -а (*sl.*) rowdy; trouble-maker.

буй, -я; *pl.* **-и́, -ёв** buoy.

бу́йвол, -а buffalo.

бу́йный; бу́ен, буйна́, -о violent, turbulent; tempestuous; ungovernable; wild; luxuriant, lush. **бу́йство, -а** tumult, uproar; unruly conduct, riotous behaviour. **бу́йствовать, -твую** *impf.* create uproar, behave violently.

бук, -а beech.

бука́шка, -и small insect.

бу́ква, -ы; *g.pl.* **бу́кв** letter; **~ в бу́кву** literally, word for word. **буква́льно** *adv.* literally. **буква́льный** literal. **буква́рь, -я́** ABC. **бу́квенно-цифрово́й** alphanumeric. **буквое́д, -а** pedant. **буквое́дство, -а** pedantry.

букети́ровать, -рую *impf.* thin out.

букини́ст, -а second-hand bookseller.

букле́т, -а (fold-out) leaflet.

буклиро́ванн|ый bouclé; **~ая ткань** bouclé fabric. **бу́кля, -и** curl, ringlet.

бу́ковый beech, beech-wood.

букс, -а box(-tree).

букси́р, -а tug, tug-boat; tow-rope, hawser. **букси́ровать, -рую** *impf.* tow, be towing, have in tow.

буксова́ние, -я wheel-spin. **буксова́ть, -су́ет** *impf.* spin, slip.

булава́, -ы́ mace. **була́вка, -и** pin; **англи́йская ~** safety-pin. **була́вочный** pin.

булими́я, -и bulimia.

бу́лка, -и roll; **сдо́бная ~** bun. **бу́лочная** *sb.* bakery; baker's shop. **бу́лочник, -а** baker.

булты́х *int.* splash, plump. **бултыха́ться, -а́юсь** *impf.*, **бултыхну́ться, -ну́сь, -нёшься** *pf.* fall with heavy splash, plunge, plump.

булы́жник, -а cobble-stone, cobbles. **булы́жный** cobbled.

бульва́р, -а avenue; boulevard. **бульва́рный** boulevard, avenue; trashy, rubbishy; vulgar.

бу́льканье, -я gurgling, gurgle. **бу́лькать, -аю** *impf.* gurgle.

бульо́н, -а broth, stock.

бум, -а beam.

бума́га, -и cotton; paper; document; **почто́вая ~** notepaper; *pl.* securities. **бумагодержа́тель, -я** *m.* security-holder, bond-holder; paper-clip. **бума́жка, -и** piece of paper; paper; note. **бума́жник, -а** wallet; paper-maker. **бума́жн|ый** cotton; paper; **~ая волоки́та** red tape; **~ змей** kite; **~ая фа́брика** paper-mill. **бумажо́нка, -и** scrap of paper.

бунт[1], -а bale; package; bundle.

бунт[2], -а; *pl.* **-ы́** rebellion, revolt, rising; riot; mutiny. **бунта́рский** seditious, mutinous; rebellious; turbulent. **бунта́рь, -я́** *m.* rebel; insurgent; mutineer; rioter; inciter to rebellion or mutiny. **бунтова́ть(ся, -ту́ю(сь** *impf.* (*pf.* **вз~**) revolt, rebel; mutiny, riot; incite to rebellion or mutiny. **бунтовско́й** rebellious, mutinous. **бунтовщи́к, -а́, -щи́ца, -ы** rebel, insurgent; mutineer; rioter.

бур, -а auger; bore; drill.

бура́, -ы́ borax.

бура́в, -а́; *pl.* **-а́** auger; gimlet. **бура́вить, -влю** *impf.* (*pf.* **про~**) bore, drill. **бура́вчик, -а** gimlet.

бура́н, -а snowstorm.

бурда́, -ы́ (*sl.*) slops, swill, hog-wash.

буреве́стник, -а stormy petrel. **бурево́й** storm; stormy. **бурело́м, -а** wind-fallen trees.

буре́ние, -я boring, drilling.

буржуа́ *m.indecl.* bourgeois. **буржуази́я, -и** bourgeoisie. **буржуа́зный** bourgeois. **буржу́й, -я** bourgeois. **буржу́йка, -и** bourgeois; small stove. **буржу́йский** bourgeois.

бури́льный boring, drilling. **бури́льщик, -а** borer, driller, drill-operator. **бури́ть, -рю́** *impf.* bore, drill.

бу́ркать, -аю *impf.*, **бу́ркнуть, -ну** *pf.* growl, grumble, mutter.

бурли́вый stormy; seething, turbulent. **бурли́ть, -лю́** *impf.* boil, seethe.

бу́рный; -рен, -рна́, -о stormy, rough; impetuous; rapid; energetic.

буров|о́й boring, bore, drilling; **~а́я вы́шка** derrick; **~а́я (сква́жина)** borehole; **~о́й стано́к, ~а́я устано́вка** drilling rig.

бурча́ть, -чу́ *impf.* (*pf.* **про~**) grumble; mumble, mutter; rumble; bubble.

бу́р|ый; бур, -а́, -о brown; (dark) chestnut; **~ая лиси́ца** red fox.

бурья́н, -а tall weeds.

бу́ря, -и storm; tempest; gale.

бу́сать, -аю *impf.* (*sl.*) drink, swallow.

бу́сина, -ы, бу́синка, -и bead. **бу́сы, бус** *pl.* beads.

бутафо́р, -а property-man, props. **бутафо́рия, -и** properties, props; window-dressing. **бутафо́рский** property.

бутербро́д, -а (open) sandwich; **зако́н ~а** Sod's Law, Murphy's Law. **бутербро́дная** *sb.* sandwich bar.

буто́н, -а bud. **бутонье́рка, -и** button-hole, spray of flowers.

бу́тсы, -ов *pl.* football boots.

буты́лка, -и bottle. **буты́лочный** bottle; **~ цвет** bottle green. **буты́ль, -и** large bottle; demijohn; carboy.

буфе́т, -а sideboard; buffet, refreshment room; bar, counter. **буфе́тная** *sb.* pantry. **буфе́тчик, -а** barman; steward. **буфе́тчица, -ы** barmaid; counter assistant.

бу́фы, буф *pl.* gathered fullness, close gathering, puffs.

бух *int.* thump, thud. **бу́хать, -аю** *impf.* (*pf.* **бу́хнуть**) thump, bang; drop noisily, bang down; thunder, thud; blurt out; **~ся** fall heavily; plump o.s. down.

бухга́лтер, -а book-keeper, accountant. **бухгалте́рия, -и** book-keeping, accountancy; counting-house; accounts office, department. **бухга́лтерский** book-keeping, account.

бу́хнуть[1], -ну; бух *impf.* swell.

бу́хнуть[2](ся, -ну(сь *pf. of* **бу́хать(ся**

бу́хта, -ы bay, bight. **бу́хточка, -и** cove, creek, inlet.

бушева́ть, -шу́ю *impf.* rage, storm.

бушла́т, -а pea-jacket; wadded jacket; (*sl.*) **деревя́нный ~** coffin.

буя́н, -а rowdy, brawler. **буя́нить, -ню** *impf.* make row, create uproar, brawl. **буя́нство, -а** rowdyism, brawling.

бы, б *part.* **I.** *+past tense or inf. indicates the conditional or subjunctive, expresses possibility, a wish, a polite suggestion or exhortation.* **II. (+ни)** *forms indef. prons. and conjs. see* **е́сли, как, когда́, кто,** *etc.*

быва́ло *part.* used to, would; **мать быва́ло ча́сто пе́ла э́ту пе́сню** my mother would often sing this song. **быва́лый** experienced; worldly-wise; past, former; not new; habitual, familiar. **быва́ть, -а́ю** *impf.* be, be present; happen; take place; be inclined to be, tend to be; **как не быва́ло**+*g.* have completely disappeared; **как ни в чём не быва́ло** as if nothing had happened, as though everything was all right. **бы́вший** former, formerly, ex-.

бык, -а́ bull, ox; stag; pier.

были́на, -ы bylina. **были́нный** of byliny; epic, heroic.

бы́ло *part.* nearly, on the point of; (only) just; **чуть ~ не** very nearly, all but. **был|о́й** former, past, bygone; **~о́е** *sb.* the past. **быль, -и** the past, what really happened; true story, true happening.

быстрина́, -ы́; *pl.* **-ы** rapids. **быстроно́гий** swift-footed, fleet-footed; fast. **быстрота́, -ы́** quickness, swiftness, rapidity; speed. **быстроте́чный** fleeting, transient. **быстро-хо́дный** fast, high-speed. **бы́стрый; быстр, -á, -o** rapid, fast, quick; prompt.

быт, -а, *loc.* **-у́** way of life, life; everyday life; **слу́жба ~а** consumer services. **быти́е, -я́** being, existence; objective reality; **книга́ Бытия́** Genesis. **бытова́ть, -ту́ет** *impf.* exist; occur; be current. **бытов|о́й** of everyday life; everyday; domestic; social; **~а́я жи́вопись** genre painting; **~о́е обслу́живание** consumer services; **~а́я ЭВМ** home computer; **~ы́е прибо́ры** domestic appliances.

бытописа́ние, -я annals, chronicles. **быто-писа́тель, -я** *m.* annalist, chronicler; writer on social themes.

быть *pres. 3rd sg.* **есть,** *pl.* **суть**; *fut.* **бу́ду**; *past* **был, -á, -o**; *imper.* **бу́дь(те)** *impf.* be; exist; be situated; happen, take place; *impers.+d.* be sure to happen, be inevitable; **будь, что бу́дет** come what may; **~ беде́** there's sure to be trouble; **должно́ ~** probably, very likely; **как ~?** what is to be done?; **не будь его́** but for him, if it weren't for him; **так и ~** so be it; all right, very well, have it your own way.

быча́чий, бы́чий bull, ox. **бычо́к**[1], **-чка́** young ox, steer.

бычо́к[2], **-чка́** (*sl.*) cigarette end, fag-end.

бью *etc.*: *see* **бить**

бэ *nt.indecl.* the letter **б.**

бюллете́нь, -я *m.* bulletin; voting-paper, ballot-paper; medical certificate; **информа-цио́нный ~** newsletter; **быть на бюллете́не** be on the sick-list, be on sick-leave.

бюро́ *nt.indecl.* bureau; office; writing-desk; **туристи́ческое ~** travel agency. **бюрокра́т, -а** bureaucrat. **бюрократи́зм, -а** bureaucracy. **бюрократи́ческий** bureaucratic. **бюрокра́тия, -и** bureaucracy; bureaucrats.

бюст, -а bust; bosom. **бюстга́льтер, -а** brassière, bra.

В

В *abbr.* (*of* **вольт**) volt; (*of* **восто́к**) E, East.

в *letter*: *see* **вэ**

в, во *prep.* **I.** *+a.* into, to; on; at; within; for; as; through; **быть в** take after, be like; **в два ра́за бо́льше** twice as big, twice the size; **в на́ши дни** in our day; **войти́ в дом** go into the house; **в понеде́льник** on Monday; **в тече́ние**+*g.* during, in the course of; **в четы́ре часа́** at four o'clock **высото́й в три ме́тра** three metres high; **игра́ть в ша́хматы** play chess; **моро́з в де́сять гра́дусов** ten degrees of frost; **пое́хать в Москву́** go to Moscow; **положи́ть в я́щик стола́** put in(to) a drawer; **преврати́ть во́ду в лёд** turn water into ice; **разби́ть в куски́** smash to pieces; **руба́шка в клётку** check(ed) shirt; **сесть в ваго́н** get into the carriage; **сказа́ть в шу́тку** say as a joke; **смотре́ть в окно́** look out of the window; **это мо́жно сде́лать в неде́лю** it can be done in a week. **II.** *+p.* in; on; at; of; at a distance of; **в двадца́том ве́ке** in the twentieth century; **в теа́тре** at the theatre; **в трёх киломе́трах от го́рода** three kilometres from the town; **в четвёртом часу́** between three (o'clock) and four; **в э́том году́** this year; **в январе́** in January; **лицо́ в весну́шках** freckled face; **пье́са в пяти́ а́ктах** a play in five acts, a five-act play; **роди́ться в Москве́** be born in Moscow; **саха́р в куска́х** lump sugar; **служи́ть в куха́рках** be a cook.

в. *abbr.* (*of* **век**) C, century.

в..., во..., въ... *vbl. pref. expressing direction of action or motion inwards or upwards; occurrence wholly within the agent.*

ваго́н, -а (railway-)carriage, coach; van; car; wagon-load; loads, stacks; **~-рестора́н** restaurant car, dining-car. **вагоне́тка, -и** truck, trolley. **вагоновожа́тый** *sb.* tram-driver.

ва́жничанье, -я airs. **ва́жничать, -аю** *impf.* give o.s. airs; *+i.* plume o.s., pride o.s., on. **ва́жность, -и** importance, consequence; significance; pomposity, pretentiousness. **ва́жный; -жен, -жна́, -o** important; weighty, consequential; pompous, pretentious.

ва́за, -ы vase, bowl.

ва́кса, -ы (shoe-)polish, blacking; **чи́стить ва́ксой** polish. **ва́ксить, -кшу** *impf.* (*pf.* **на~**) black, polish.

вал[1], **-а,** *loc.* **-у́**; *pl.* **-ы́** bank, earthen wall; rampart; billow, roller, wave; barrage.

вал[2], **-а,** *loc.* **-у́**; *pl.* **-ы́** shaft, spindle.

вал[3], **-а** gross output.

вала́ндаться, -аюсь *impf.* loiter, hang about; mess about.

валёк, -лька́ battledore; swingle-tree; roll; roller; flail; loom.

ва́ленок, -нка; *g.pl.* **-нок** felt boot. **ва́леный** felt.

вале́т, -а knave, Jack.

ва́лик, -а bolster; roller; cylinder; spindle, shaft; platen.

вали́ть[1], **-ли́т** *impf.* flock, throng; pour; **ва́лом ~** throng, flock; **вали́(те)!** go on! have a go!

вали́ть[2], **-лю́, -лишь** *impf.* (*pf.* **по~, с~**) throw down, bring down, knock down; overthrow; fell; lay low; heap, pile up; **~ся** fall, collapse; drop; topple; **у него́ всё из рук ва́лится** his fingers are all thumbs; he can't give his mind to anything.

ва́лка, -и felling. **ва́лкий; -лок, -лка́, -о** unsteady, shaky.
валово́й gross; wholesale.
валто́рна, -ы French-horn. **валторни́ст, -а** French-horn (player).
валу́н, -а́ boulder.
вальс, -а waltz. **вальси́ровать, -и́рую** *impf.* waltz.
вальцева́ть, -цу́ю *impf.* roll. **вальцо́вка, -и** rolling; rolling press. **вальцо́вый** rolling. **вальцы́**, *pl.* **-о́в** rolling press. **вальцо́вщик, -а** roller.
валю́та, -ы currency; foreign currency. **валю́тчик, -а, -чица, -ы** (foreign) currency speculator.
ва́ляный felt. **валя́ть, -я́ю** *impf.* (*pf.* **на~, с~**) drag; roll; shape; full, felt; botch, bungle; make a mess (of), mess about; **~ дурака́** play the fool; **валя́й(те)!** go ahead! carry on!; **~ся** lie, lie about, loll; roll, wallow; **~ся в нога́х у**+*g.* fall at the feet of.
вам, ва́ми *see* **вы**
вани́ль, -и vanilla, vanilla-pod.
ва́нна, -ы, ва́нночка, -и bath. **ва́нный** bath; **~ая** *sb.* bathroom.
ва́нька, -и *m.* cabby.
ва́рвар, -а barbarian. **варвари́зм, -а** loanword; barbarism. **ва́рварский** barbarian; barbarous; barbaric. **ва́рварство, -а** barbarity; vandalism.
ва́режка, -и mitten.
варёный boiled; limp. **варе́нье, -я** jam, marmalade.
вариа́нт, -а reading, variant; version; option; scenario; model.
вари́ть, -рю́, -ришь *impf.* (*pf.* **с~**) boil; cook; brew; make; digest; **~ся** boil; cook. **ва́рка, -и** boiling; cooking; making; brewing.
Варша́ва, -ы Warsaw.
вас *see* **вы**
василёк, -лька́ cornflower. **василько́вый** cornflower; cornflower blue.
ва́та, -ы cotton wool; wadding; **са́харная ~** candyfloss.
ват́ага, -и band, gang.
ватерли́ния, -и water-line. **ватерпа́с, -а** spirit-level.
Ватика́н, -а the Vatican.
вати́н, -а (sheet) wadding, quilting. **ва́тник, -а** quilted jacket. **ва́тный** quilted, wadded.
ватру́шка, -и open tart; curd tart, cheesecake.
ватт, -а; *g.pl.* **ватт** watt.
ва́учер, -а (privatization) voucher.
ва́фельный waffle. **ва́фля, -и**; *g.pl.* **-фель** waffle.
вахла́к, -а́ lout; sloven.
ва́хта, -ы watch. **ва́хтенный** watch; **~ журна́л** log, log-book; **~ команди́р** officer of the watch, duty officer.
ваш, -его *m.*, **ва́ша, -ей** *f.*, **ва́ше, -его** *nt.*, **ва́ши, -их** *pl.*, *pron.* your, yours.
Вашингто́н, -а Washington.
ваяние, -я sculpture. **вая́тель, -я** *m.* sculptor. **вая́ть, -я́ю** *impf.* (*pf.* **из~**) sculpture; carve, model.
вбега́ть, -а́ю *impf.*, **вбежа́ть, вбегу́** *pf.* run in, rush in.
вберу́ *etc.*: *see* **вобра́ть**
вбива́ть, -а́ю *impf.* *of* **вбить. вби́вка, -и** knocking in, driving in, hammering.
вбира́ть, -а́ю *impf.* *of* **вобра́ть**
вбить, вобью́, -бьёшь *pf.* (*impf.* **вбива́ть**) drive in, hammer in, knock in.
вблизи́ *adv.* (+**от**+*g.*) close (to), near (to), not far (from); closely.
вбок *adv.* sideways, to one side.
вбра́сывание, -я throw-in. **вбра́сывать, -аю** *impf.* *of* **вбро́сить**
вброд *adv.* by fording or wading; **переходи́ть ~** ford, wade.
вбро́сить, -о́шу *pf.* (*impf.*, **вбра́сывать**) throw in.
вв. *abbr.* (*of* **века́**) centuries.
вва́ливать, -аю *impf.*, **ввали́ть, -лю́, -лишь** *pf.* throw heavily, heave, fling, bundle, tumble; **~ся** fall heavily; sink, become hollow or sunken; burst in. **ввали́вшийся** sunken, hollow.
введе́ние, -я leading in; introduction. **введу́** *etc.*: *see* **ввести́**
ввезти́, -зу́, -зёшь; ввёз, -ла́ *pf.* (*impf.* **ввози́ть**) import; bring in, take in, carry in.
ввек *adv.* ever; for ever.
вве́рить, -рю *pf.* (*impf.* **вверя́ть)** entrust, confide; **~ся**+*d.* trust in, put one's faith in; put o.s. in the hands of.
вверну́ть, -ну́, -нёшь *pf.*, **ввёртывать, -аю** *impf.* screw in; insert; put in.
вверх *adv.* up, upward(s); **~дном, ~ нога́ми, ~ торма́шками** upside down, topsy-turvy; **~ (по ле́стнице)** upstairs; **~ (по тече́нию)** upstream. **вверху́** *adv.* above, overhead; upstairs; upstream; at the top.
вверя́ть(ся, -я́ю(сь *impf.* *of* **вве́рить(ся**
ввести́, -еду́, -едёшь; ввёл, -а́ *pf.* (*impf.* **вводи́ть**) bring in, lead in; introduce; insert, interpolate, incorporate; administer.
ввиду́ *prep.*+*g.* in view of.
ввинти́ть, -нчу́ *pf.*, **вви́нчивать, -аю** *impf.* screw in.
ввод, -а bringing in, leading in; lead-in, lead; input, intake. **вводи́ть, -ожу́, -о́дишь** *impf.* *of* **ввести́. вво́дн|ый** introductory; parenthetic; **~ое предложе́ние, ~ое сло́во** parenthesis; **~ый тон** leading note.
ввожу́ *see* **вводи́ть, ввози́ть**
ввоз, -а importation, importing; import, imports. **ввози́ть, -ожу́, -о́зишь** *impf.* *of* **ввезти́. вво́зный** imported; import.
вво́лю *adv.* to one's heart's content; enough and to spare; ad lib.
вво́сьмеро *adv.* eight times. **ввосьмеро́м** *adv.* eight together; **мы ~** eight of us.
ВВС *abbr.* (*of* **вое́нно-возду́шные си́лы**) air force.

ввысь *adv.* up, upward(s).
ввяза́ть, -яжу́, -я́жешь *pf.*, **ввя́зывать, -аю** *impf.* knit in; involve; **~ся** meddle, get involved, get or be mixed up (in).
вгиб, -а inward bend; concavity, dent, sag. **вгиба́ть(ся, -а́ю(сь** *impf. of* **вогну́ть(ся**
вглубь *adv.* deep, deep into, into the depths.
вгляде́ться, -яжу́сь *pf.*, **вгля́дываться, -аюсь** *impf.* peer, look closely or intently (**в**+*a.* at).
вгоня́ть, -я́ю *impf. of* **вогна́ть. вдава́ться, вдаю́сь, -ёшься** *impf. of* **вда́ться**
вдави́ть, -авлю́, -а́вишь *pf.*, **вда́вливать, -аю** *impf.* press in, crush in; **~ся** give , give way; be crushed or pressed in; press in.
вдалеке́, вдали́ *adv.* in the distance, far away; **~ от** a long way from. **вдаль** *adv.* into the distance.
вда́ться, -а́мся, -а́шься, -а́стся, -адимся; -а́лся, -ла́сь *pf.* (*impf.* **вдава́ться**) jut out; penetrate, go in; **~ в то́нкости** split hairs.
вдвига́ть(ся, -а́ю(сь *impf.*, **вдви́нуть(ся, -ну(сь** *pf.* push in, move in, thrust in.
вдво́е *adv.* twice; double; **~ бо́льше** twice as big, as much, as many. **вдвоём** *adv.* (the) two together, both. **вдвойне́** *adv.* twice as much, double; doubly.
вдева́ть, -а́ю *impf. of* **вдеть**
вдёжка, -и threading; thread, tape, cord, lace.
вде́лать, -аю *pf.*, **вде́лывать, -аю** *impf.* set in, fit in.
вдёржка, -и bodkin; threading. **вдёргивать, -аю** *impf.*, **вдёрнуть, -ну** *pf.* **в**+*a.* thread through, pull through.
вде́сятеро *adv.* ten times; **~ бо́льше** ten times as much, as many. **вдесятеро́м** *adv.* ten together; **мы ~** ten of us.
вдеть, -е́ну *pf.* (*impf.* **вдева́ть**) put in, thread.
ВДНХ *abbr.* (*of* ***Вы́ставка достиже́ний наро́дного хозя́йства***) Exhibition of National Economic Achievements.
вдоба́вок *adv.* in addition; besides, as well, into the bargain.
вдова́, -ы́; *pl.* **-ы** widow. **вдове́ц, -вца́** widower. **вдо́вий** widow's, widows'. **вдови́ца, -ы** widow.
вдо́воль *adv.* enough; in abundance; plenty (of).
вдо́вствующая *sb.* dowager. **вдо́вый** widowed.
вдого́нку *adv.* (**за**+*i.*) after, in pursuit (of).
вдоль *adv.* lengthways, lengthwise; **~ и поперёк** in all directions, far and wide; minutely, in detail; *prep.+g. or* **по**+*d.* along.
вдох, -а breath. **вдохнове́ние, -я** inspiration, **вдохнове́нный** inspired. **вдохнови́тель, -я** *m.*, **-тельница, -ы** inspirer, inspiration. **вдохнови́ть, -влю́** *pf.*, **вдохновля́ть, -я́ю** *impf.* inspire. **вдохну́ть, -ну́, -нёшь** *pf.* (*impf.* **вды́хать**) breathe in, inhale; +**в**+*a.* inspire with, breathe into.
вдре́безги *adv.* to pieces, to smithereens; **~ пьян** blotto, plastered.
вдруг *adv.* suddenly; all at once; what if? suppose; **все ~** all together.
вдува́ть, -а́ю *impf. of* **вду́нуть, вдуть**
вду́маться, -аюсь *pf.*, **вду́мываться, -аюсь** *impf.* ponder, meditate; +**в**+*a.* think over. **вду́мчивый** thoughtful.
вду́нуть, -ну *pf.*, **вдуть, -у́ю** *pf.* (*impf.* **вдува́ть**) blow in, pump in.
вдыха́ние, -я inhalation, inspiration. **вдыха́тельный** respiratory. **вдыха́ть, -а́ю** *impf. of* **вдохну́ть**
веда́ть, -аю *impf.* know; +*i.* manage, handle; be in charge of. **ве́дение[1], -я** authority, jurisdiction; **в ве́дении**+*g.* under the jurisdiction of; **вне моего́ ве́дения** outside my province.
веде́ние[2], -я conducting, conduct, management; **~ книг** book-keeping.
ве́домость, -и; *g.pl.* **-е́й** list, register; *pl.* gazette. **ве́домственный** departmental. **ве́домство, -а** department.
ведро́, -а́; *pl.* **вёдра, -дер** bucket, pail; vedro (*old Russ. liquid measure, equivalent to approx. 12 litres*).
веду́ *etc.*: *see* **вести́. веду́щ|ий** leading; **~ее колесо́** driving-wheel.
ведь *part. and conj.* you see, you know; but; why; isn't it? is it?
ве́дьма, -ы witch; old bag, hag.
ве́ер, -а; *pl.* **-а́** fan. **веерообра́зный** fan-shaped; **~ свод** fan vault(ing).
ве́жливость, -и politeness, courtesy, civility. **ве́жливый** polite, courteous, civil.
везде́ *adv.* everywhere. **вездехо́д, -а** cross-country vehicle. **вездехо́дный** cross-country.
везе́ние, -я luck. **везу́чий** fortunate, lucky. **везти́, -зу́, -зёшь; вёз, -ла́** *impf.* (*pf.* **по~**) cart, convey, carry; bring, take; *impers.+d.* be lucky, be in luck, have luck; **ему́ не везло́** he was unlucky.
Везу́вий, -я (Mt.) Vesuvius.
век, -а (-у), *loc.* **-у́**; *pl.* **-а́** century; age; life, lifetime; **испоко́н ~о́в** from time immemorial. **век** *adv.* for ages, for ever; always, constantly.
ве́ко, -а; *pl.* **-и, век** eyelid.
ве́кове́чный eternal, everlasting. **векову́й** ancient, age-old, secular.
ве́ксель, -я; *pl.* **-я́, -е́й** *m.* promissory note, bill (of exchange). **ве́ксельный; ~ курс** rate of exchange.
вёл *etc.*: *see* **вести́**
веле́ть, -лю́ *impf. & pf.* order, tell; **не ~** forbid, not allow.
велика́н, -а giant. **велика́нша, -и** giantess. **велика́нский** gigantic. **вели́к|ий; вели́к, -а** *or* **-а́** great; big, large; too big; **~ие держа́вы** Great Powers; **~ий князь** grand prince, grand duke; **~ий пост** Lent.
велико... *in comb.* great. **Великобрита́ния, -и** Great Britain. **~держа́вный** great-power.

~ду́шие, -я magnanimity, generosity. **~ду́шный** magnanimous; generous. **~ле́пие, -я** splendour, magnificence. **~ле́пный** splendid, magnificent; excellent. **~по́стный** Lenten. **~ру́с, -а, -ру́ска, -и** Great Russian. **~ру́сский** Great Russian.

велича́вый stately, majestic. **велича́йший** greatest, extreme, supreme. **вели́чественный** majestic, grand. **вели́чество, -а** Majesty. **вели́чие, -я** greatness, grandeur, sublimity. **величина́, -ы́**; *pl.* **-ы** size; quantity, magnitude; value; great figure.

велосипе́д, -а bicycle, bike; **трёхколёсный ~** tricycle. **велосипеди́ст, -а** cyclist. **велотренажёр, -а** exercise bicycle.

вельве́т, -а velveteen, cotton velvet; **~ в ру́бчик** corduroy. **вельве́товый** velveteen; corduroy.

вельмо́жа, -и *m.* grandee, dignitary, magnate.

Ве́на, -ы Vienna.

ве́на, -ы vein.

венге́рка, -и Hungarian; dolman; Hungarian ballroom dance. **венге́рский** Hungarian. **венгр, -а** Hungarian. **Ве́нгрия, -и** Hungary.

Вене́ра, -ы Venus. **вене́рин** *adj.* Venusian, of Venus; **~ волосо́к** maidenhair fern. **венери́ческий** venereal.

ве́нец[1]**, -нца** Viennese.

вене́ц[2]**, -нца́** crown; wreath, garland; corona; halo.

Вене́ция, -и Venice.

вене́чный coronal; coronary.

ве́нзель, -я; *pl.* **-я́, -е́й** *m.* monogram.

ве́ник, -а besom, (birch-)broom.

ве́нка, -и Viennese.

вено́зный venous.

вено́к, -нка́ wreath, garland.

ве́нский Viennese; **~ стул** ballroom chair.

ве́нтиль, -я *m.* valve.

вентиля́тор, -а ventilator; extractor (fan).

венча́льный wedding. **венча́ние, -я** wedding; coronation. **венча́ть, -а́ю** *impf.* (*pf.* **об~, по~, у~**) crown; marry; **~ся** be married, marry. **ве́нчик, -а** halo, nimbus; corolla; edge, rim; crown; ring, bolt.

ве́ра, -ы faith, belief; trust, confidence; **на ~у** on trust.

ве́рба, -ы willow, osier, pussy-willow; willow branch. **ве́рбн|ый; ~ое воскресе́нье** Palm Sunday.

верблю́д, -а, -ю́дица, -ы camel. **верблю́ж|ий** camel's; camelhair; **~ья шерсть** camel's hair.

ве́рбный *see* **ве́рба**

вербова́ть, -бу́ю *impf.* (*pf.* **за~**) recruit, enlist. **вербо́вка, -и** recruitment.

ве́рбовый willow; osier; wicker.

верёвка, -и rope; string; cord. **верёвочный** rope.

верени́ца, -ы row, file, line, string.

ве́реск, -а heather.

веретено́, -а́; *pl.* **-тёна** spindle, shank, axle.

вереща́ть, -щу́ *impf.* squeal; chirp.

ве́рить, -рю *impf.* believe, have faith; *+d. or* **в**+*a.* trust (in), believe in; **~ на́ сло́во** take on trust.

вермише́ль, -и vermicelli.

верне́е *adv.* rather. **верноподданный** loyal, faithful. **ве́рно** *part.* probably, I suppose; that's right! **ве́рность, -и** faithfulness, loyalty; truth, correctness.

верну́ть, -ну́, -нёшь *pf.* (*impf.* **возвраща́ть**) give back, return; get back, recover, retrieve; **~ся** return, revert.

ве́рный; -рен, -рна́, -о faithful, loyal; true; correct; sure; reliable; certain.

ве́рование, -я belief; creed. **ве́ровать, -рую** *impf.* believe. **вероисповеда́ние, -я** religion; denomination. **вероло́мный** treacherous, perfidious. **вероотсту́пник, -а** apostate. **веротерпи́мость, -и** (religious) toleration. **вероя́тно** *adv.* probably. **вероя́тность, -и** probability. **вероя́тный** probable, likely.

Верса́ль, -и Versailles.

ве́рсия, -и version.

верста́, -ы́, *a.* **-у́** *or* **вёрсту**; *pl.* **вёрсты** verst (*old Russ. measurement, equivalent to approx. 1.06 km.*); verst-post; **за́ ~у** miles away.

верста́к, -а́ bench.

верстово́й verst (*see* **верста́**); **~ столб** milestone.

ве́ртел, -а; *pl.* **-а́** spit, skewer. **верте́ть, -чу́, -тишь** *impf.* turn (round); twirl; spin; **~ся** rotate, turn (round), revolve, spin; move about, hang about, go round; fidget; turn and twist, dodge. **вёрткий; -ток, -тка** nimble, agile. **вертлю́г, -а́** swivel. **вертля́вый** restless, fidgety; flighty, frivolous.

вертодро́м, -а heliport. **вертолёт, -а** helicopter.

верту́н, -а́ fidget; tumbler-pigeon. **верту́шка, -и** revolving door, revolving stand; turntable; flibbertigibbet, coquette.

ве́рующий *sb.* believer.

верфь, -и dockyard, shipyard.

верх, -а (-у), *loc.* **-у́**; *pl.* **-и́** *or* **-а́** top, summit; height; upper part, upper side; upper reaches; bonnet, hood; upper hand; outside; right side; *pl.* upper ten, bosses, leadership, management, top brass; high notes. **ве́рхний** upper; outer; top. **верхо́вный** supreme. **верхово́й**[1] riding; *sb.* rider. **верхово́й**[2] upstream, up-river; upper. **верхо́вье, -я**; *g.pl.* **-вьев** upper reaches, head. **верхола́з, -а** steeple-jack. **ве́рхом**[1] *adv.* on high ground; quite full, brim-full. **верхо́м**[2] *adv.* on horseback; astride; **е́здить ~** ride. **верху́шка, -и** top, summit; apex; bosses, top brass, management.

верчу́ *etc.*: *see* **верте́ть**

верши́на, -ы top, summit; peak; height; apex, vertex. **верши́ть, -шу́** *impf.* top, top out; decide, settle; *+i.* manage, control, direct; control, sway.

вершо́к, -шка́ vershok (*old Russ. measurement, equivalent to approx. 4.4 cm.*); inch; smattering.

вес, -а (-у), *loc.* **-у́**; *pl.* **-а́** weight; authority, influence; **на ~** by weight; **на ~у́** suspended, balanced.

веселе́ть, -е́ю *impf.* (*pf.* **по~**) cheer up, be cheerful. **весели́ть, -лю́** *impf.* (*pf.* **раз~**) cheer up, gladden; amuse; **~ся** enjoy o.s.; amuse o.s. **ве́село** *adv.* gaily, merrily. **весёлость, -и** gaiety; cheerfulness. **весёлый; ве́сел, -а́, -о** gay, merry; cheerful, lively. **весе́лье, -я** gaiety, merriment.

весе́нн|ий spring; vernal; **~ее равноде́нствие** vernal equinox.

ве́сить, ве́шу *impf.* weigh. **ве́ский** weighty, solid.

весло́, -а́; *pl.* **вёсла, -сел** oar; scull; paddle.

весна́, -ы́; *pl.* **вёсны, -сен** spring; spring-time. **весно́й, -о́ю** *adv.* in (the) spring. **весну́шка, -и** freckle. **весну́шчатый** freckled. **весня́нка, -и** mayfly.

весово́й weight, of weight; sold by weight. **весо́мый** heavy, weighty; ponderable.

вест, -а west; west wind.

ве́стерн, а western.

вести́, веду́, -дёшь; вёл, -а́ *impf.* (*pf.* **по~**) lead, take; conduct, carry on; be engaged in, drive; conduct; direct, run; keep; *+i.* pass, run (**по**+*d.* over, across); **~ кора́бль** navigate a ship; **~ (своё) нача́ло** originate; **~ ого́нь** fire; **~ самолёт** pilot an aircraft; **~ свой род от** be descended from; **~ себя́** behave, conduct o.s.; **~сь** be observed, be the the custom.

ве́стник, -а messenger, herald; bulletin. **вестово́й** signal; *sb.* orderly. **весть, и**; *g.pl.* **-е́й** news; *pl.* tales, talk, gossip; **бе́з вести** without trace. **весть; Бог ~** God knows; **не ~** goodness knows, there's no knowing.

весы́, -о́в *pl.* scales, balance; Libra.

весь, всего́ *m.*, **вся, всей** *f.*, **всё, всего́** *nt.*, **все, всех** *pl.*, *pron.* all, the whole of; all gone; **бума́га вся** the paper has all gone, there's no paper left; **во ~ го́лос** at the top of one's voice; **во-всю́** like anything; **вот и всё** that's all; **при всём том** for all that; moreover; **всего́ хоро́шего!** goodbye; all the best!; **всё** everything; **без всего́** without anything, with nothing; **все** everybody.

весьма́ *adv.* very, highly; very much.

ветви́стый spreading, (many-) branched, branching. **ветви́ться, -влю́сь** *impf.* branch.

ветвра́ч, -а́ vet.

ветвь, -и; *g.pl.* **-е́й** branch; bough.

ве́тер, -тра (-у), *loc.* **-у́**; *g.pl.* **ветро́в** wind; *pl.* wind; **по ве́тру** before the wind; down wind; **подби́тый ве́тром** empty-headed; light, flimsy; **под ве́тром** (to) leeward; **про́тив ве́тра** close to the wind, against the wind. **ветеро́к, -рка́** breeze.

ве́тка, -и branch; twig.

ветла́, -ы́; *pl.* **вётлы** (white) willow.

ве́то *nt.indecl.* veto.

ве́точка, -и twig, sprig, shoot.

ветo̕шка, -и rag. **ветo̕шник, -а** old clothes dealer, rag-dealer. **ве́тошь, -и** old clothes, rags.

ветрене́ть, -е́ет *impf.* become windy, get windy. **ве́треный** windy; frivolous, inconstant, unstable. **ветров|о́й** wind, of wind; **~о́е окно́, ~о́е стекло́** windscreen. **ветроме́р, -а** anemometer. **ветроуказа́тель, -я** *m.* drogue, wind cone, wind sock. **ветря́к, -а́** wind motor; windmill. **ветряно́й, ве́тряный** wind; **ве́тряная о́спа** chicken-pox.

ве́тхий; ветх, -а́, -о old, ancient; dilapidated, ramshackle, tumbledown; decrepit; **В~ заве́т** Old Testament. **ветхозаве́тный** Old-Testament; antiquated, out-of-date. **ве́тхость, -и** decrepitude, dilapidation, decay.

ветчина́, -ы́ ham.

ветша́ть, -а́ю *impf.* (*pf.* **об~**) decay; become dilapidated.

ве́ха, -и landmark; marker post, stake.

ве́чер, -а; *pl.* **-а́** evening; party; soirée. **вече́рн|ий** evening; **~яя заря́** sunset; dusk. **вече́рник, -а** evening student, evening worker. **вече́рня, -и**; *g.pl.* **-рен** vespers. **ве́чером** *adv.* in the evening.

ве́чно *adv.* for ever, eternally; everlastingly. **вечнозелёный** evergreen. **ве́чность, -и** eternity; an age, ages. **ве́чн|ый** eternal, everlasting; endless; perpetual; **~ая мерзлота́** permafrost; **~ое перо́** fountain-pen.

ве́шалка, -и peg, rack, stand; hanger; cloakroom. **ве́шать, -аю** *impf.* (*pf.* **взве́сить, пове́сить, све́шать**) hang; weigh, weigh out; **~ся** be hung, be hanged; hang o.s.; weigh o.s.

ве́шний spring, vernal.

ве́шу *etc.*: *see* **ве́сить**

веща́ние, -я radio; prophecy. **веща́ть, -а́ю** *impf.* broadcast; prophesy; pontificate.

вещево́й clothing, kit; in kind; **~ мешо́к** knapsack; pack, hold-all, kit-bag; **~ склад** clothing store, stores. **веще́ственный** substantial, material, real. **вещество́, -а́** substance; matter. **вещмешо́к, -шка́** rucksack.

вещь, -и; *g.pl.* **-е́й** thing.

ве́ялка, -и winnowing-fan; winnowing-machine. **ве́яние, -я** winnowing; breathing, blowing; current, tendency, trend. **ве́ять, ве́ю** *impf.* (*pf.* **про~**) winnow, fan; blow, breathe; wave, flutter.

вз..., взо..., взъ..., вс... *vbl. pref. expressing direction of motion or action upwards or on to*; *rapidity or suddenness of occurrence*; *completion or finality of action.*

взад *adv.* backwards; **~ и вперёд** backwards and forwards, to and fro.

взаи́мность, -и reciprocity; requital, return. **взаи́мный** mutual, reciprocal.

взаимо... *in comb.* inter-. **взаимоде́йствие, -я** interaction; co-operation, coordination **~де́йствовать, -твую** *impf.* interact; cooperate. ~**отноше́ние, -я** interrelation; *pl.* relations. ~**по́мощь, -и** mutual aid. ~**свя́зь, -и** intercommunication; interdependence, correlation.

взаймы́ *adv.* as a loan; **взять** ~ borrow; **дать** ~ lend.

взаме́н *prep.+g.* instead of; in return for, in exchange for.

взаперти́ *adv.* under lock and key; in seclusion, in isolation.

взапра́вду *adv.* in truth, really and truly.

вз|баламу́тить, -у́чу *pf.*

взба́лмошный unbalanced, eccentric.

взба́лтывание, -я shaking (up). **взба́лтывать, -аю** *impf. of* **взболта́ть**

взбега́ть, -а́ю *impf.*, **взбежа́ть, -егу́** *pf.* run up.

взберу́сь *etc.*: *see* **взобра́ться. вз|беси́ть(ся, -ешу́(сь, -е́сишь(ся** *pf.* **взбива́ть, -а́ю** *impf. of* **взбить. взбира́ться, -а́юсь** *impf. of* **взобра́ться**

взби́тый whipped, beaten. **взбить, взобью́, -бьёшь** *pf.* (*impf.* **взбива́ть**) beat (up), whip; shake up, fluff up.

взболта́ть, -а́ю *pf.* (*impf.* **взба́лтывать**) shake (up).

вз|борозди́ть, -зжу́ *pf.* **вз|борони́ть, -ню́** *pf.* **взбра́сывать, -аю** *impf. of* **взбро́сить**

взбреда́ть, -а́ю *impf.*, **взбрести́, -еду́, -едёшь; -ёл, -ела́** *pf.* +**на**+*a.* climb (up), mount, with difficulty; struggle up; ~ **в го́лову, на ум** come into one's head.

взбро́сить, -о́шу *pf.* (*impf.* **взбра́сывать**) throw up, toss up.

вз|будора́жить, -жу *pf.* **вз|бунтова́ться, -ту́юсь** *pf.*

взбуха́ть, -а́ет *impf.*, **взбу́хнуть, -нет; -ух** *pf.* swell (out).

взва́ливать, -аю *impf.*, **взвали́ть, -лю́, -лишь** *pf.* hoist, heave (up); load; +**на**+*a.* saddle with.

взве́сить, -е́шу *pf.* (*impf.* **ве́шать, взве́шивать**) weigh.

взвести́, -еду́, -едёшь; -ёл, -а́ *pf.* (*impf.* **взводи́ть**) lead up, take up; lift up, raise; cock, arm; +**на**+*a.* impute to, bring against.

взвесь, -и suspension. **взве́шенный** weighed; suspended, of suspension. **взве́шивать, -аю** *impf. of* **взве́сить**

взвива́ть(ся, -а́ю(сь *impf. of* **взви́ть(ся**

взвизг, -а scream, squeal, screech; yelp. **взви́згивать, -аю** *impf.*, **взви́згнуть, -ну** *pf.* let out screams, a scream; scream, screech; yelp.

взвинти́ть, -нчу́ *pf.*, **взви́нчивать, -аю** *impf.* excite, work up; inflate; ~**ся** work o.s. up; spiral up. **взви́нченный** excited, worked up; nervy, on edge; highly strung; inflated.

взвить, взовью́, -ёшь; -ил, -а́, -о *pf.* (*impf.* **взвива́ть**) raise; ~**ся** rise, be hoisted; fly up, soar.

взвод[1]**, -а** platoon, troop.

взвод[2]**, -а** cocking; notch; **на боево́м** ~**е** cocked; **на пе́рвом** ~**е** at half cock. **взводи́ть, -ожу́, -о́дишь** *impf. of* **взвести́. взводно́й** cocking.

взво́дный platoon; *sb.* platoon commander.

вз|двои́ть, -ою́ *pf.*

взволно́ванный agitated, disturbed; ruffled; anxious, troubled, worried. **вз|волнова́ть(ся, -ну́ю(сь** *pf.*

взвыть, взво́ю *pf.* howl, set up a howl.

взгляд, -а look; glance; gaze, stare; view; opinion; **на** ~ to judge from appearances; **на пе́рвый** ~, **с пе́рвого** ~ at first sight. **взгля́дывать, -аю** *impf.*, **взгляну́ть, -яну́, -я́нешь** *pf.* look, glance.

взго́рок, -рка, взго́рье, -я hill, hillock.

взгроможда́ть, -а́ю *impf.*, **взгромозди́ть, -зжу́** *pf.* pile up; ~**ся** clamber up.

вздёргивать, -аю *impf.*, **вздёрнуть, -ну** *pf.* hitch up; jerk up; turn up; hang.

вздор, -а nonsense. **вздо́рный** cantankerous, quarrelsome; foolish, stupid.

вздорожа́ние, -я rise in price. **вз|дорожа́ть, -а́ет** *pf.*

вздох, -а sigh; deep breath. **вздохну́ть, -ну́, -нёшь** *pf.* (*impf.* **вздыха́ть**) sigh; heave a sigh; take a deep breath; take a breather, pause for breath.

вздра́гивать, -аю *impf.* (*pf.* **вздро́гнуть**) shudder, quiver.

вздремну́ть, -ну́, -нёшь *pf.* have a nap, doze.

вздро́гнуть, -ну *pf.* (*impf.* **вздра́гивать**) start, jump; wince, flinch.

вздува́ть(ся, -а́ю(сь *impf. of* **вздуть**[1]**(ся**

взду́мать, -аю *pf.* take it into one's head; **не взду́май(те)!** mind you don't, don't you dare! **взду́маться, -ается** *pf.*, *impers.* (+*d.*) come into one's head; **как взду́мается** as the fancy takes one, as one likes.

взду́тие, -я swelling; inflation. **взду́тый** swollen. **вздуть**[1]**, -у́ю** *pf.* (*impf.* **вздува́ть**) blow up, swell, inflate; ~**ся** swell.

вздуть[2]**, -у́ю** *pf.* thrash, lick, give a hiding.

вздыха́ние, -я sighing; sigh. **вздыха́тель, -я** *m.* admirer, suitor. **вздыха́ть, -а́ю** *impf.* (*pf.* **вздохну́ть**) breathe; sigh.

взима́ть, -а́ю *impf.* levy, collect.

взла́мывать, -аю *impf. of* **взлома́ть**

вз|леле́ять, -е́ю *pf.*

взлёт, -а flight; taking wing; take-off. **взлета́ть, -а́ю** *impf.*, **взлете́ть, -лечу́** *pf.* fly (up); take off. **взлётный** flying; take-off; **взлётно-поса́дочная полоса́** runway, landing strip.

взлом, -а breaking open, breaking in; break-in. **взлома́ть, -а́ю** *pf.* (*impf.* **взла́мывать**) break open, force; smash; break up, break through. **взло́мщик, -а** burglar, house-breaker.

взлохма́ченный dishevelled, tousled.

взмах, -а stroke, sweep, wave, flap. **взма́хивать, -аю** *impf.*, **взмахну́ть, -ну́, -нёшь** *pf.+i.* wave, flap.

взмо́рье, -я (sea-)shore, coast; seaside, beach;

coastal waters.

вз|мути́ть, -учу́, -у́ти́шь *pf.*

взнос, -а payment; fee, dues; subscription; instalment.

взнузда́ть, -а́ю *pf.*, **взну́здывать, -аю** *impf.* bridle.

взо... *see* **вз...**

взобра́ться, взберу́сь, -ёшься; -а́лся, -ла́сь, -а́ло́сь *pf.* (*impf.* **взбира́ться**) **на**+*a.* climb (up), clamber up.

взобью *etc.*: *see* **взбить. взовью** *etc.*: *see* **взвить**

взойти́, -йду́, -йдёшь; -ошёл, -шла́ *pf.* (*impf.* **вос-, всходи́ть**) rise, go up, come up; **на**+*a.* mount, ascend; enter.

взор, -а look, glance.

взорва́ть, -ву́, -вёшь; -а́л, -а́, -о *pf.* (*impf.* **взрыва́ть**) blow up; blast; fire, explode, detonate; exasperate, madden; **~ся** blow up, burst, explode.

взро́слый grown-up, adult.

взрыв, -а explosion; burst, outburst; plosion. **взрыва́тель, -я** *m.* fuse. **взрыва́ть, -а́ю** *impf.*, **взры́ть, -ро́ю** *pf.* (*pf. also* **взорва́ть**) blow up; **~ся** blow up, explode. **взрывн|о́й** explosive; explosion, blasting; plosive; **~а́я волна́** shock wave, blast. **взрывча́тка, -и** explosive. **взры́вчатый** explosive.

взъ... *see* **вз...**

взъеро́шенный tousled, dishevelled; ruffled. **взъеро́шивать, -аю** *impf.*, **взъ|еро́шить, -шу** *pf.* tousle, ruffle, rumple; **~ся** become dishevelled, bristle up, stand on end.

взыва́ть, -а́ю *impf. of* **воззва́ть**

взыска́ние, -я penalty, punishment; recovery, exaction; prosecution. **взыска́тельный** exacting; demanding. **взыска́ть, -ыщу́, -ы́щешь** *pf.*, **взы́скивать, -аю** *impf.* exact, recover; call to account, make answer.

взя́тие, -я taking, capture, seizure. **взя́тка, -и** bribe; trick. **взя́точничество, -а** bribery, corruption. **взять(ся, возьму(сь, -мёшь(ся; -ял(ся, -а́(сь, -о(сь** *pf. of* **брать(ся; ни дать ни ~** exactly, neither more nor less than; **отку́да ни возьми́сь** out of the blue, from nowhere.

вибра́ция, -и vibration. **вибри́ровать, -рует** *impf.* vibrate, oscillate.

вид[1], -а (-у), *loc.* **-у́** look; appearance; air; shape, form; condition; view; prospect; sight; **де́лать вид** pretend; **име́ть в ~у́** plan, intend; mean; bear in mind, not forget; **и́з ~у** out of sight; **на ~у́** in the public eye; **потеря́ть и́з ~у** lose sight of; **под ~ом** under the pretext; **при ~е** at the sight.

вид[2], -а kind, sort; species.

ви́данный seen; heard of. **вида́ть, -а́ю** *impf.* (*pf.* **по~, у~**) see; **~ся** meet; see one another. **ви́дение[1], -я** sight, vision. **виде́ние[2], -я** vision, apparition.

видео *in comb.* video. **видеоза́пись, -и** video recording. **~ка́мера, -ы** video camera. **~кассе́та, -ы** video cassette. **~ле́нта, -ы** videotape. **~магнитофо́н, -а** video recorder. **~те́ка, -и** video rental club. **~телефо́н, -а** videophone.

ви́деть, ви́жу *impf.* (*pf.* **у~**) see; **~ во сне** dream (of); **~ся** see one another, meet; appear. **ви́димо** *adv.* visibly; evidently; seemingly. **ви́димо-неви́димо** *adv.* immense numbers of. **ви́димость, -и** visibility, vision; appearance, semblance, show; appearances. **ви́димый** visible, in sight; apparent, evident, seeming. **видне́ться, -е́ется** be visible. **ви́дный; -ден, -дна́, -о, -ы** *or* **-ы́** visible; conspicuous; distinguished, prominent; stately, portly, dignified. **видово́й[1]** landscape; **~ фильм** travelogue, travel-film.

видово́й[2] specific; aspectual.

видоизмене́ние, -я modification; alteration; variety. **видоизмени́ть, -ню́** *pf.*, **видоизменя́ть, -я́ю** *impf.* modify, alter; **~ся** alter; be modified, be altered.

видоиска́тель, -я *m.* view-finder.

ви́жу *see* **ви́деть**

ви́за, -ы visa; official stamp.

визг, -а squeal; scream; yelp. **визгли́вый** shrill; screaming, squealing, squalling. **визжа́ть, -жу́** *impf.* squeal, scream, yelp, squeak.

визи́ровать, -рую *impf.* & *pf.* (*pf. also* **за~**) visa, visé.

визи́т, -а visit; call. **визита́ция, -и** call; round; search. **визи́тка, -и** morning coat.

виктори́на, -ы quiz.

ви́лка, -и fork; plug; bracket. **вилообра́зный** forked. **ви́лочный** fork-lift. **ви́лы, вил** *pl.* pitchfork.

вильну́ть, -ну́, -нёшь *pf.*, **виля́ть, -я́ю** *impf.* twist and turn; turn sharply; prevaricate, be evasive; +*i.* wag.

Ви́льнюс, -а Vilnius.

вина́, -ы́; *pl.* **ви́ны** fault, guilt; blame.

виндсёрфинг, -а windsurfing, sailboarding.

винегре́т, -а Russian salad; medley, farrago.

вини́тельный accusative. **вини́ть, -ню́** *impf.* accuse, blame; reproach; **~ся** (*pf.* **по~**) confess.

ви́нкель, -я; *pl.* **-я́** *m.* set-square.

виннока́менный tartaric. **ви́нн|ый** wine; winy; vinous; **~ый ка́мень** tartar; **~ая я́года** fig. **вино́, -а́**; *pl.* **-а** wine; vodka.

винова́тый guilty; to blame; **винова́т(а)!** (I'm) sorry. **вино́вник, -а** author, initiator; culprit; **~ торжества́** founder of the feast. **вино́вный** guilty.

виногра́д, -а (-у) vine; grapes. **виногра́дарь, -я** *m.* wine-grower. **виногра́дина, -ы** grape. **виногра́дник, -а** vineyard. **виногра́дный** vine; grape; wine, vintage. **виноку́р, -а** distiller. **винокуре́ние, -я** distillation. **виноку́ренный** distilling; **~ заво́д** distillery.

винт, -а́ screw; propeller; rotor; spiral; vint. **винти́ть, -нчу́** *impf.* screw in; unscrew; turn. **винто́вка, -и** rifle. **винтово́й** screw; spiral; helical. **винто́вочный** rifle-. **винто́м** *adv.* spirally.

вира́ж, -а́ turn; bend, curve.
вис, -а hang, hanging. **ви́селица, -ы** gallows. **висе́ть, вишу́** *impf.* hang; hover.
ви́ски *nt.indecl.* whisky; **шотла́ндское ~** Scotch (whisky).
вислоу́хий lop-eared. **ви́снуть, -ну; ви́с(нул)** *impf.* hang; droop.
висо́к, -ска́ temple.
високо́сный; ~ год leap-year.
висо́чный temporal.
вису́лька, -и pendant. **вися́чий** hanging; **~ замо́к** padlock; **~ мост** suspension bridge.
витами́н, -а vitamin. **витаминизи́ровать, -рую** *impf. & pf.* fortify, enrich with vitamins. **витами́нный** vitamin; vitamin-rich.
вито́й twisted, spiral. **вито́к, -тка́** turn, coil, loop; orbit.
витра́ж, -а́ stained-glass window, panel, etc. **витри́на, -ы** shop-window; showcase.
вить, вью, вьёшь; вил, -а́, -о *impf.* (*pf.* **с~**) twist, wind, weave; **~ гнездо́** build a nest; **~ верёвки из**+*g.* twist round one's little finger; **~ся** wind, twine; curl, wave; hover, circle; twist, turn; whirl, eddy; writhe.
вихо́р, -хра́ tuft. **вихра́стый** shaggy, wiry; shock-headed.
вихрево́й vortical. **вихрь, -я** *m.* whirlwind; whirl, eddy, vortex; **сне́жный ~** blizzard.
ви́це- *pref.* vice-. **вице-коро́ль, -я́** viceroy. **~президе́нт, -а** vice-president.
вицмунди́р, -а (*dress*) uniform.
ВИЧ *abbr.* (*of* **ви́рус иммунодефици́та челове́ка**) HIV (*human immunodeficiency virus*); **инфици́рованный ~** HIV-positive.
ви́шенник, -а, вишня́к, -а́ cherry-orchard, cherry-grove; wild cherry. **вишнёвый** cherry; cherry-coloured. **ви́шня, -и**; *g.pl.* **-шен** cherry, cherries; cherry-tree.
вишу́ *see* **висе́ть**
вишь *part.* look, just look; well!
вка́лывать, -аю *impf.* (*pf.* **вколо́ть**) (*sl.*) work hard, slave; get stuck in.
вка́пывать, -аю *impf. of* **вкопа́ть**
вкати́ть, -ачу́, -а́тишь *pf.*, **вка́тывать, -аю** *impf.* roll in, wheel in; roll up; put in, put on; administer; **~ся** roll in; run in.
вкл. (*abbr. of* **включи́тельно**) incl., including.
вклад, -а deposit; investment; endowment; contribution. **вкла́дка, -и, вкла́дыш, -а** supplementary sheet, inset. **вкладно́й** deposit; supplementary, inserted; **~ лист** loose leaf, insert. **вкла́дчик, -а** depositor; investor.
вкла́дывать, -аю *impf. of* **вложи́ть. вкла́дыш** *see* **вкла́дка**
вкле́ивать, -аю *impf.*, **вкле́ить, -е́ю** *pf.* stick in, glue in, paste in; put in. **вкле́йка, -и** sticking in; inset.
вкли́нивать, -аю *impf.*, **вкли́нить, -и́ню** *pf.* wedge in; put in; **~ся** edge one's way in; drive a wedge (into).
включа́тель, -я *m.* switch. **включа́ть, -а́ю** *impf.*, **включи́ть, -чу́** *pf.* include; insert; switch on, turn on, start; plug in, connect; engage, let in; **~ся в**+*a.* join in, enter into. **включа́я** including. **включе́ние, -я** inclusion, insertion; switching on, turning on. **включи́тельно** *adv.* inclusive.
вкола́чивать, -аю *impf.*, **вколоти́ть, -очу́, -о́тишь** *pf.* hammer in, knock in.
вколо́ть, -олю́, -о́лешь *pf.* (*impf.* **вка́лывать**) stick (in), pin (in).
вконе́ц *adv.* completely, absolutely.
вко́панный dug in; rooted to the ground. **вкопа́ть, -а́ю** *pf.* (*impf.* **вкапыва́ть**) dig in.
вкорени́ть, -ню́ *pf.*, **вкореня́ть, -я́ю** *impf.* inculcate; **~ся** take root.
вкось *adv.* obliquely, slantwise; **~ и вкривь, вкривь и ~** at random, all over the place; indiscriminately.
вкра́дчивый insinuating, ingratiating. **вкра́дываться, -аюсь** *impf.*, **вкра́сться, -аду́сь, -адёшься** *pf.* steal in, creep in; worm o.s., insinuate o.s., (into).
вкра́тце *adv.* briefly, succinctly.
вкривь *adv.* aslant; wrongly, perversely; **~ и вкось** *see* **вкось**
вкруг *see* **вокру́г**
вкруту́ю *adv.* hard(-boiled).
вку́пе *adv.* together.
вкус, -а taste; manner, style; **де́ло ~а** a matter of taste. **вкуси́ть, -ушу́, -у́сишь** *pf.*, **вкуша́ть, -а́ю** *impf.* taste; partake of; savour, experience. **вку́сный; -сен, -сна́, -о** tasty, nice, good; appetizing.
вла́га, -и moisture, damp, liquid.
влага́лище, -а vagina; sheath.
влага́ть, -а́ю *impf. of* **вложи́ть**
владе́лец, -льца, -лица, -ы owner; proprietor. **владе́ние, -я** ownership; possession; property; domain, estate. **владе́тель, -я** *m.*, **-ница, -ы** possessor; sovereign. **владе́тельный** sovereign. **владе́ть, -е́ю** *impf.*+*i.* own, possess; control; be in possession of; have (a) command of; have the use of.
влады́ка, -и *m.* master, sovereign; Orthodox prelate; my Lord. **влады́чество, -а** dominion, rule, sway.
влажне́ть, -е́ет *impf.* (*pf.* **по~**) become humid, grow damp. **вла́жный; -жен, -жна́, -о** damp, moist, humid.
вла́мываться, -аюсь *impf. of* **вломи́ться**
вла́ствовать, -твую *impf.*+(**над**+) *i.* rule, hold sway over. **власти́тель, -я** *m.* sovereign, ruler. **вла́стный** imperious, commanding; masterful; empowered, competent. **власть, -и**; *g.pl.* **-е́й** power; authority; control; *pl.* authorities; **ва́ша ~** as you like, please yourself, it's up to you.
вле́во *adv.* to the left.
влеза́ть, -а́ю *impf.*, **влезть, -зу; влез** *pf.* climb in, climb up; get in; fit in, go in, go on; **ско́лько вле́зет** as much as will go in, any amount.
влёк *etc.*: *see* **влечь**

влепи́ть, -плю́, -пишь *pf.*, **влепля́ть, -я́ю** *impf.* stick in, fasten in; ~ **пощёчину**+*d.* give a slap in the face.

влета́ть, -а́ю *impf.*, **влете́ть, -ечу́** *pf.* fly in; rush in.

влече́ние, -я attraction; bent, inclination. **влечь, -еку́, -ечёшь; влёк, -ла́** *impf.* draw, drag; attract; ~ **за собо́й** involve, entail; ~**ся** к+*d.* be drawn to, be attracted by.

влива́ть, -а́ю *impf.*, **влить, волью́, -ёшь; влил, -а́, -о** *pf.* pour in; infuse; instil; bring in; ~**ся** flow in.

влия́ние, -я influence. **влия́тельный** influential. **влия́ть, -я́ю** *impf.* (*pf.* **по**~) **на**+*a.* influence, have an influence on, affect.

вложе́ние, -я enclosure; investment. **вложи́ть, -ожу́, -о́жишь** *pf.* (*impf.* **вкла́дывать, влага́ть**) put in, insert; enclose; invest.

вломи́ться, -млю́сь, -мишься *pf.* (*impf.* **вла́мываться**) break in.

влюби́ть, -блю́, -бишь *pf.*, **влюбля́ть, -я́ю** *impf.* capture the heart of, make fall in love (**в**+*a.* with); ~**ся** fall in love, **влюблённый; -лён, -а́** in love; loving, tender; *sb.* lover. **влю́бчивый** amorous, susceptible.

вма́зать, -а́жу *pf.*, **вма́зывать, -аю** *impf.* cement in, putty in, mortar in.

вм. *abbr.* (*of* **вме́сто**) instead of, in place of.

вмени́ть, -ню́ *pf.*, **вменя́ть, -я́ю** *impf.* impute; ~ **в вину́** lay to the charge of; ~ **в обя́занность** impose as a duty. **вменя́емый** responsible, liable; of sound-mind.

вме́сте *adv.* together; at the same time; ~ **с тем** at the same time, also.

вмести́лище, -а receptacle. **вмести́мость, -и** capacity; tonnage. **вмести́тельный** capacious; spacious, roomy. **вмести́ть, -ещу́** *pf.* (*impf.* **вмеща́ть**) contain, hold, accommodate; find room for; put, place; ~**ся** go in.

вме́сто *prep.*+*g.* instead of, in place of.

вмеша́тельство, -а interference; intervention. **вмеша́ть, -а́ю** *pf.*, **вме́шивать, -аю** *impf.* mix in; mix up, implicate; ~**ся** interfere, meddle.

вмеща́ть(ся, -а́ю(сь *impf.* *of* **вмести́ться**

вмиг *adv.* in an instant, in a flash.

вмина́ть, -а́ю *impf.*, **вмять, вомну́, -нёшь** *pf.* crush in, press in, dent.

ВМФ *abbr.* (*of* **вое́нно-морско́й флот**) navy.

вмя́тина, -ы dent.

внаём, внаймы́ *adv.* to let; for hire; **брать** ~ hire, rent; **отдава́ться** ~ let, hire out, rent; **сдава́ться** ~ be to let.

внаки́дку *adv.* thrown over the shoulders.

внача́ле *adv.* at first, in the beginning.

вне *prep.*+*g.* outside; out of; without; ~ **себя́** beside o.s.; ~ **сомне́ния** without doubt, undoubtedly.

вне... *pref.* extra-; situated outside, lying outside the province or scope of; -less. **внебра́чный** extra-marital; illegitimate, born outside wedlock. ~**вре́менный** timeless. ~**кла́ссный** out-of-school, extracurricular. ~**ма́точный** extra-uterine. ~**очередно́й** out of turn, out of order; extraordinary; extra. ~**парти́йный** non-party. ~**пи́ковый** off-peak. ~**служе́бный** leisure-time, leisure. ~**студи́йный** outside. ~**шко́льный** adult; extra-scholastic; out-of-school. ~**шта́тник, а** freelancer; casual. ~**шта́тный** casual, part-time; untenured.

внедре́ние, -я introduction; inculcation, indoctrination; intrusion. **внедри́ть, -рю́** *pf.*, **внедря́ть, -я́ю** *impf.* inculcate, instil; introduce; ~**ся** take root.

внеза́пно *adv.* suddenly, all of a sudden, all at once. **внеза́пный** sudden, unexpected; surprise.

вне́млю *etc.*: *see* **внима́ть**

внесе́ние, -я bringing in, carrying in; paying in, deposit; entry, insertion; moving, submission. **внести́, -су́, -сёшь; внёс, -ла́** *pf.* (*impf.* **вноси́ть**) bring in, carry in; introduce, put in; pay in, deposit; move, table; insert, enter; bring about, cause.

вне́шне *adv.* outwardly. **вне́шний** outer, exterior; outward, external; outside; surface, superficial; foreign. **вне́шность, -и** exterior; surface; appearance.

вниз *adv.* down, downwards; downstream; ~ **по**+*d.* down; ~ **по тече́нию** downstream. **внизу́** *adv.* below; downstairs; *prep.*+*g.* at the foot of, in the lower part of.

вника́ть, -а́ю *impf.*, **вни́кнуть, -ну; вник** *pf.*+**в**+*a.* go carefully into, investigate thoroughly, get to the heart or root of.

внима́ние, -я attention; notice, note; heed; consideration; attentions, kindness; ~! look out!; ~ **на старт!** get set! **внима́тельный** attentive; thoughtful, considerate, kind. **внима́ть, -а́ю** *or* **вне́млю** *impf.* (*pf.* **внять**) listen to, hear; heed.

вничью́ *adv.*; **око́нчиться** ~ end in a draw, be drawn; **сыгра́ть** ~ draw.

вноси́ть, -ошу́, -о́сишь *impf.* *of* **внести́**

внук, -а grandson; *pl.* grandchildren, descendants.

вну́тренн|ий inner, interior; internal; intrinsic; home, inland; ~**ие дохо́ды** inland revenue. **вну́тренность, -и** interior; *pl.* entrails, intestines; internal organs; viscera. **внутри́** *adv.* & *prep.*+*g.* inside, within. **внутрь** *adv.* & *prep.*+*g.* inside, in; inwards.

внуча́та, -ча́т *pl.* grandchildren. **внуча́тный, внуча́тый** second, great-; ~ **брат** second cousin; ~ **племя́нник** great-nephew. **вну́чка, -и** grand-daughter; grandchild.

внуша́емость, -и suggestibility. **внуша́ть, -а́ю** *impf.*, **внуши́ть, -шу́** *pf.* instil; suggest; +*d.* inspire with, fill with. **внуше́ние, -я** suggestion; reproof, reprimand. **внуши́тельный** inspiring, impressive; imposing, striking.

вня́тный distinct; intelligible. **внять** *no fut.*; **-ял, -а́, -о** *pf.* *of* **внима́ть**

во *see* **в**²

во... *see* **в...**

вобра́ть, вберу́, -рёшь; -а́л, -а́, -о *pf.* (*impf.* **вбира́ть**) absorb, draw in, soak up, inhale.

вобью *etc.*: *see* **вбить**

вове́к, вовеки́ *adv.* for ever; ~ **не** never.

во́время *adv.* in time; on time; **не** ~ at the wrong time.

во́все *adv.* quite; ~ **не** not at all.

во-вторы́х *adv.* secondly, in the second place.

вогна́ть, вгоню́, -о́нишь; -гна́л, -а́, -о *pf.* (*impf.* **вгоня́ть**) drive in. **во́гнутый** concave; dented. **вогну́ть, -ну́, -нёшь** *pf.* (*impf.* **вгиба́ть**) bend or curve inwards; **~ся** bend inwards, curve inwards.

...вод *in comb.* -breeder, -grower, -raiser.

вода́, -ы́, *a.* **во́ду**; *pl.* **-ы** water; *pl.* the waters; watering-place, spa.

водворе́ние, -я settlement; establishment. **водвори́ть, -рю́** *pf.*, **водворя́ть, -я́ю** *impf.* settle, install, house; establish.

води́тель, -я *m.* driver; leader. **води́тельница, -ы** (*woman*) driver. **води́тельство, -а** leadership. **води́ть, вожу́, во́дишь** *impf.* lead; conduct; take; drive; *+i.* (**по**+*d.*) pass (over, across); ~ **автомоби́ль, маши́ну** drive a car; ~ **глаза́ми по**+*d.* cast one's eyes over; **~ся** be, be found; associate, play (with); be the custom, happen.

во́дка, -и vodka. **воднолы́жник, -а, -ница, -ы** water-skier. **во́дн|ый** water; watery; aquatic; aqueous; **~ые лы́жи** water-skiing; water-skis.

водо... *in comb.* water, water-; hydraulic; hydro-. **водобоя́знь, -и** hydrophobia. **~вмести́лище, -а** reservoir. **~во́з, -а** water-carrier. **~воро́т, -а** whirlpool, eddy; vortex, maelstrom, whirl. **~ём, -а** reservoir. **~измеще́ние, -я** displacement. **~ка́чка, -и** water-tower, pump-house, pumping station. **~ла́з, -а** diver; Newfoundland (*dog*). **~ла́зный** diving. **~ле́й, -я** Aquarius. **~непроница́емый** watertight; waterproof. **~но́сный** water-bearing. **~отво́д, -а** drain, overflow. **~отво́дный** drainage, overflow. **~отта́лкивающий** water-repellent. **~па́д, -а** waterfall; falls, cataract. **~по́й, -я** watering-place; water-supply; watering. **~прово́д, -а** water-pipe, water-main; water supply. **~прово́дный** water-main, mains; tap-. **~прово́дчик, -а** plumber. **~разде́л, -а** watershed. **~распыли́тель, -я** *m.* sprinkler. **~ро́д, -а** hydrogen. **во́доросль, -и** water-plant, water-weed; seaweed; alga. **~снабже́ние, -я** water supply **~сто́к, -а** drain, gutter. **~усто́йчивый** water-repellant.

во́дочный vodka.

водружа́ть, -а́ю *impf.*, **водрузи́ть, -ужу́** *pf.* hoist; set up, fix up.

водяни́стый watery. **водя́нка, -и** dropsy. **водяно́й** water; aquatic; ~ **знак** watermark; *sb.* water-sprite. **водя́ночный** dropsical.

воева́ть, вою́ю *impf.* wage war, make war, be at war; quarrel. **воево́да, -ы** *m.* voivode (*in ancient Russia, commander of army or governor of province*). **воево́дство, -а** office of voivode; voivode's province.

воеди́но *adv.* together, into one.

воен... *abbr.* (*of* **вое́нный**) *in comb.* military, war-. **военко́м, -а** military commissar. **~ко́р, -а** war correspondent.

военизá́ция, -и militarization. **военизи́рованный** militarized, armed; paramilitary.

военно... *in comb.* military; war-. **вое́нно-возду́шный** air-, air-force; **~-возду́шные си́лы** air force. **вое́нно-морско́й** naval; **~-морско́й флот** navy. **~пле́нный** *sb.* prisoner of war. **вое́нно-полево́й; ~-полево́й суд** (drumhead) court-martial. **~слу́жащий** *sb.* serviceman.

вое́нн|ый military; war; army; **~ое положе́ние** martial law; **~ый суд** court-martial; *sb.* soldier, serviceman; *pl.* the military.

вожа́к, -а́ guide; leader. **вожа́тый** *sb.* guide; leader; tram-driver. **вожде́ние, -я** leading; driving, steering, piloting. **вождь, -я́** *m.* leader, chief.

вожжа́, -и́; *pl.* **-и, -е́й** reins.

вожу́ *etc.*: *see* **води́ть, вози́ть**

воз, -а (-у), *loc.* **-у́**; *pl.* **-ы́** *or* **-а́** cart, wagon; cart-load; loads, heaps.

воз..., возо..., вос... *vbl. pref. expressing direction or movement upwards*; *renewed action*; *action in response*; *beginning of action*; *intensity*, *excitement*, *solemnity*.

возбуди́мый excitable, irritable. **возбуди́тель, -я** *m.* agent; stimulus; stimulant; exciter; instigator. **возбуди́ть, -ужу́** *pf.*, **возбужда́ть, -а́ю** *impf.* excite, rouse, arouse; stimulate, whet; stir up, incite; provoke; institute, bring, raise. **возбужда́ющ|ий; ~ее сре́дство** stimulant. **возбужде́ние, -я** excitement, agitation. **возбуждённый** excited, agitated.

возвести́, -еду́, -дёшь; -вёл, -ла́ *pf.* (*impf.* **возводи́ть**) elevate; raise; erect, put up; bring, advance, level; +**к**+*d.* trace to, derive from.

возвести́ть, -ещу́ *pf.*, **возвеща́ть, -а́ю** *impf.* proclaim, announce.

возводи́ть, -ожу́, -о́дишь *impf. of* **возвести́**

возвра́т, -а return; repayment, reimbursement; restitution; ~ **боле́зни** relapse; ~ **со́лнца** solstice. **возврати́ть, -ащу́** *pf.*, **возвраща́ть, -а́ю** *impf.* (*pf. also* **верну́ть**) return, give back, restore; pay back; recover, retrieve; send back, bring back; **~ся** return; go back, come back; revert. **возвра́тный** back, return; relapsing; recurrent; reflexive. **возвраще́ние, -я** return; recurrence; restoration, restitution.

возвы́сить, -ы́шу *pf.*, **возвыша́ть, -а́ю** *impf.* raise; ennoble; **~ся** rise, go up; tower. **возвыше́ние, -я** rise; raising; eminence; raised place. **возвы́шенность, -и** height; eminence; loftiness, sublimity. **возвы́шенный**

high, elevated; lofty, sublime.

возгла́вить, -влю *pf.*, **возглавля́ть, -я́ю** *impf.* head, be at the head of.

во́зглас, -а cry, exclamation. **возгласи́ть, -ашу́** *pf.*, **возглаша́ть, -а́ю** *impf.* proclaim. **возглаше́ние, -я** proclamation; exclamation.

возгора́емость, -и inflammability. **возгора́емый** inflammable. **возгора́ние, -я** ignition; **то́чка возгора́ния** flash-point. **возгора́ться, -а́юсь** *impf.*, **возгоре́ться, -рю́сь** *pf.* flare up; be seized (with); be smitten.

воздава́ть, -даю́, -даёшь *impf.*, **возда́ть, -а́м, -а́шь, -а́ст, -ади́м; -а́л, -а́, -о** *pf.* render; ~ **до́лжное**+*d.* do justice to.

воздвига́ть, -а́ю *impf.*, **воздви́гнуть, -ну; -дви́г** *pf.* raise, erect; ~**ся** rise, arise.

возде́йствие, -я influence; **физи́ческое** ~ coercion. **возде́йствовать, -твую** *impf.* & *pf.* influence, affect; act on, work on.

возде́лать, -аю *pf.*, **возде́лывать, -аю** *impf.* cultivate, till.

воздержа́вшийся *sb.* abstainer; abstention. **воздержа́ние, -я** abstinence; abstention. **возде́ржанный, возде́ржный** abstemious; temperate; abstinent. **воздержа́ться, -жу́сь, -жишься** *pf.*, **возде́рживаться, -аюсь** *impf.* refrain; abstain; withhold acceptance, decline.

во́здух, -а air; **в** ~**е** in the air; **на** ~, **на** ~**е** out of doors. **воздуходу́вка, -и** blower. **воздухонепронеца́емый** air-tight.

воздухоохлажда́емый air-cooled. **возду́шн|ый** air, aerial; overhead; air-raid; airy, light; flimsy; ~**ые за́мки** castles in the air; ~**ый змей** kite; ~**ая пе́тля** chain (stitch); ~**ый пиро́г** soufflé; ~**ый флот** air force; ~**ый шар** balloon.

воззва́ние, -я appeal. **воззва́ть, -зову́, -вёшь** *pf.* (*impf.* **взыва́ть**) appeal, call (**о**+*p.* for).

воззре́ние, -я view, opinion, outlook.

вози́ть, вожу́, во́зишь *impf.* cart, convey; carry; bring, take; drive; draw; beat, flog; ~**ся** romp, run about, play noisily; take trouble, spend time, busy o.s.; potter about; tinker, fiddle about, mess about. **во́зка, -и** carting, carriage.

возлага́ть, -а́ю *impf. of* **возложи́ть**

во́зле *adv.* & *prep.*+*g.* by, near; near by; past.

возложи́ть, -жу́, -жишь *pf.* (*impf.* **возлага́ть**) lay; place.

возлю́бленный beloved; *sb.* boy-friend, girl-friend; lover, mistress.

возме́здие, -я retribution; requital; punishment.

возмести́ть, -ещу́ *pf.*, **возмеща́ть, -а́ю** *impf.* compensate for, make up for; refund, reimburse. **возмеще́ние, -я** compensation, indemnity; damages; replacement; refund, reimbursement.

возмо́жно *adv.* possibly; +*comp.* as ... as possible. **возмо́жность, -и** possibility; opportunity; *pl.* means, resources; potentialities; **по (ме́ре) возмо́жности** as far as possible; **при пе́рвой возмо́жности** as soon as possible, at the first opportunity. **возмо́жный** possible; greatest possible.

возмужа́лость, -и maturity; manhood, womanhood. **возмужа́лый** mature; grown up. **возмужа́ть, -а́ю** *pf.* grow up, reach maturity; gain strength, become strong.

возмути́тельный disgraceful, scandalous; seditious, subversive. **возмути́ть, -ущу́** *pf.*, **возмуща́ть, -а́ю** *impf.* disturb, trouble; stir up, incite; anger, rouse to indignation; ~**ся** be indignant, be roused to indignation, be exasperated; rebel, rise in revolt. **возмуще́ние, -я** indignation; revolt, rebellion; perturbation; disturbance. **возмущённый; -щён, -щена́** indignant, troubled, disturbed.

вознагради́ть, -ажу́ *pf.*, **вознагражда́ть, -а́ю** *impf.* reward; recompense; make up to (**за**+*a.* for). **вознагражде́ние, -я** reward, recompense; compensation; fee, remuneration.

возненави́деть, -и́жу *pf.* conceive a hatred for, come to hate.

вознесе́ние, -я ascent; Ascension. **вознести́, -несу́, -несёшь; -нёс, -ла́** *pf.* (*impf.* **возноси́ть**) raise, lift up; ~**сь** rise; ascend.

возника́ть, -а́ет *impf.*, **возни́кнуть, -нет; -ни́к** *pf.* arise, spring up. **возникнове́ние, -я** rise, beginning, origin.

возни́ца, -ы *m.* coachman, driver. **возни́чий** *sb.* coachman, driver.

возноси́ть(ся, -ошу́(сь, -о́сишь(ся *impf. of* **вознести́(сь. возноше́ние, -я** raising, elevation.

возня́, -и́ row, noise; horse-play; bother, trouble.

возобнови́ть, -влю́ *pf.*, **возобновля́ть, -я́ю** *impf.* renew, resume; restore; ~**ся** begin again. **возобновле́ние, -я** renewal, resumption; revival.

возража́ть, -а́ю *impf.*, **возрази́ть, -ажу́** *pf.* object, have or raise an objection; take exception; retort; say. **возраже́ние, -я** objection; retort; answer.

во́зраст, -а age; **на** ~**е** grown up. **возраста́ние, -я** growth, increase; increment. **возраста́ть, -а́ет** *impf.*, **возрасти́, -тёт; -ро́с, -ла́** *pf.* grow, increase.

возроди́ть, -ожу́ *pf.*, **возрожда́ть, -а́ю** *impf.* regenerate; revive; ~**ся** revive. **возрожде́ние, -я** rebirth; revival; Renaissance.

возро́с *etc.*: *see* **возрасти́. возро́сший** increased.

во́зчик, -а carter, carrier; drayman.

возьму́ *etc.*: *see* **взять**

во́ин, -а warrior; soldier, serviceman. **во́инск|ий** military; soldierly; army, troop; ~**ая пови́нность** conscription. **вои́нственный** warlike; bellicose. **во́йнствующий** militant.

вои́стину *adv.* indeed; verily.

вой, -я howl, howling; wail, wailing.

войду́ *etc.*: *see* **войти́**

во́йлок, -а felt; strip of felt. **во́йлочный** felt.

войнá, -ы́; *pl.* **-ы** war.
вóйско, -а; *pl.* **-á** army; host; multitude; *pl.* troops, forces. **войсковóй** military; of the (Cossack) host.
войти́, -йду́, -йдёшь; вошёл, -шлá *pf.* (*impf.* **входи́ть**) go in, come in, enter; get in(to); ~ **в азáрт** grow heated; ~ **в летá** get on (in years); ~ **в мóду** become fashionable; ~ **во вкус** acquire a taste; ~ **в си́лу** come into force.
вокзáл, -а (railway-)station.
вокру́г *adv.* & *prep.+g.* round, around.
вол, -á ox, bullock.
волáн, -а flounce; shuttlecock.
Вóлга, -и the Volga.
волды́рь, -я́ *m.* blister; lump, bump.
волевóй volitional; strong-willed. **вóлей-невóлей** *adv.* willy-nilly.
вóлжский Volga, of the Volga.
волк, -а; *pl.* **-и, -óв** wolf. **волкодáв, -а** wolf-hound.
волнá, -ы́; *pl.* **-ы, вóлнáм** wave. **волнéние, -я** roughness, choppiness; agitation, disturbance; emotion, excitement; (*usu. pl.*) unrest. **волни́стый** wavy; undulating; corrugated; watered. **волновáть, -ну́ю** *impf.* (*pf.* **вз~**) disturb, agitate; excite; worry; **~ся** be disturbed or agitated; fret, worry, be nervous, be excited; be in a state of ferment or unrest; be rough or choppy; ripple, wave. **волнолóм, -а** breakwater. **волнообрáзный** wavelike; undulatory; wavy, undulating. **волнорéз, -а** breakwater. **волну́ющий** disturbing, worrying; exciting, thrilling, stirring.
вóлок, -а; *pl.* **-и** *or* **-á** portage.
волоки́та, -ы red tape.
волокни́стый fibrous, stringy. **волокнó, -á**; *pl.* **-а** fibre, filament.
волоку́ *etc.*: *see* **волóчь**
вóлос, -а; *pl.* **-ы** *or* **-á, -óс** hair; *pl.* hair. **волосáтый** hairy; hirsute; pilose. **волоси́стый** fibrous. **волоснóй** capillary. **волосóк, -скá** hair, fine hair; hair-spring; filament.
волостнóй of a volost (*see* **вóлость**). **вóлость, -и**; *pl.* **-и, -éй** volost (*smallest administrative division of tsarist Russia*).
волосянóй hair.
волочи́ть, -очу́, -óчишь *impf.* drag; draw; **~ся** drag, trail; **+за**+*i.* run after. **волóчь, -оку́, -очёшь; -óк, -лá** *impf.* drag; **~ся** drag, trail; drag o.s. along; shuffle.
волчáта *etc.*: *see* **волчóнок. вóлчий** wolf, wolf's; wolfish. **волчи́ха, -и, волчи́ца, -ы** she-wolf.
волчóк, -чкá top; gyroscope.
волчóнок, -нка; *pl.* **-чáта, -чáт** wolf cub.
волшéбник, -а magician; wizard. **волшéбница, -ы** enchantress. **волшéбн|ый** magic, magical; enchanted; bewitching, enchanting; **~ая пáлочка** magic wand; **~ое цáрство** fairyland, enchanted kingdom. **волшебствó, -á** magic, enchantment.
вóльно *adv.* freely; **~!** stand at ease! **вольнонаёмный** civilian. **вóльность, -и** freedom, liberty; license; familiarity **вóльный; -лен, -льнá, -о, -ы** *or* **-ы́** free; unrestricted; loose; free-style; familiar; private; at liberty; ~ **кáменщик** Freemason.
вольт[1], **-а** volt.
вольт[2], **-а**, *loc.* **-у́** vault; volte. **вольтижёр, -а** trick-rider. **вольтижи́ровать, -рую** *impf.* vault.
вóльтов *adj.* voltaic.
вольфрáм, -а tungsten; wolfram.
волью́ *etc.*: *see* **влить**
вóля, -и will; volition; wish(es); freedom, liberty; ~ **вáша** as you please, as you like; **дать вóлю**+*d.* give rein, vent to; **дать себé вóлю** let o.s. go; **на вóле** at liberty; **не по своéй вóле** against one's will; **по дóброй вóле** freely, of one's own free will.
вомну́ *etc.*: *see* **вмять**
вон *adv.* out; off, away.
вон *part.* there, over there.
вонзáть, -áю *impf.*, **вонзи́ть, -нжу́** *pf.* plunge, thrust; **~ся в**+*a.* pierce, penetrate.
вонь, -и stink, stench. **воню́чий** stinking, fetid. **воню́чка, -и** stinker; skunk. **воня́ть, -я́ю** stink, reek.
воображáемый imaginary; fictitious. **воображáть, -áю** *impf.*, **вообрази́ть, -ажу́** *pf.* imagine; fancy; **~ся** imagine o.s. **воображéние, -я** imagination; fancy. **вообрази́мый** imaginable.
вообщé *adv.* in general; generally (speaking); on the whole; always; altogether; at all; ~ **говоря́** generally speaking; as a matter of fact.
воодушеви́ть, -влю́ *pf.*, **воодушевля́ть, -я́ю** *impf.* inspire, rouse; in spirit, hearten. **воодушевлéние, -я** rousing; inspiration; inspiriting; animation; enthusiasm, fervour. **воодушевлённый** animated; enthusiastic, fervent.
вооружáть, -áю *impf.*, **вооружи́ть, -жу́** *pf.* arm, equip; fit out; set turn; ~ **прóтив себя́** antagonize; **~ся** arm o.s., provide o.s. **вооружéние, -я** arming; arms, armament; equipment. **вооружённый; -жён, -á** armed; equipped.
воóчию *adv.* with one's own eyes, for o.s.; clearly, plainly.
во-пéрвых *adv.* first, first of all, in the first place.
вопи́ть, -плю́ *impf.* yell, howl, wail. **вопию́щий** crying, glaring; flagrant, scandalous. **вопия́ть, -ию́, -иéшь** *impf.* cry out, clamour.
воплоти́ть, -ощу́ *pf.*, **воплощáть, -áю** *impf.* embody, incarnate; ~ **в себé** be the embodiment of. **воплощéние, -я** embodiment; incarnation. **воплощённый; -щён, -щенá** incarnate; personified.
вопль, -я *m.* cry, wail; wailing, howling.
вопреки́ *prep.+d.* despite, in spite of; against, contrary to.
вопрóс, -а question; problem; matter; ~ **по**

существу́ substance of the matter; **под ~ом** in question, undecided; **что за ~!** of course! **вопроси́тельный** interrogative; questioning; **~ знак** question-mark. **вопроша́ющий** questioning, inquiring.

вопью́ *etc.*: *see* **впить**

вор, -а; *pl.* **-ы, -о́в** thief; criminal.

ворва́ться, -ву́сь, -вёшься; -а́лся, -ла́сь, -а́ло́сь *pf.* (*impf.* **врыва́ться**) burst in.

воркова́ть, -ку́ю *impf.* coo; bill and coo.

воркотня́, -и́ grumbling.

воробе́й, -ья́ sparrow. **воробьи́ный** sparrow's; sparrow; passerine.

воро́ванный stolen. **ворова́тый** thievish; furtive. **ворова́ть, -ру́ю** *impf.* (*pf.* **с~**) steal; be a thief. **воро́вка, -и** (*woman*) thief. **воровски́** *adv.* furtively. **воровско́й** thieves'; illegal. **воровство́, -а́** stealing; theft.

во́рон, -а raven. **воро́на, -ы** crow. **воронёный** blued. **воро́ний** crow's; corvine. **ворони́ть, -ню́** *impf.* blue.

воро́нка, -и funnel; crater.

вороно́й black; *sb.* black horse.

вороньё, -я carrion crows.

во́рот[1], **-а** neckline; collar; neckband.

во́рот[2], **-а** winch; windlass.

воро́та, -ро́т *pl.* gate, gates; gateway; goal.

вороти́ть[1], **-очу́, -о́тишь** *impf.+i.* be in charge of; **~ нос** turn up one's nose; **меня́ воро́тит от э́того де́ла** this business makes me sick.

вороти́ть[2], **-очу́, -о́тишь** *pf.* bring back, get back; turn back, send back; **~ся** return, come back, go back.

воротни́к, -а́, воротничо́к, -чка́ collar.

воро́тн|ый gate; **~ая ве́на** portal vein.

во́рох, -а; *pl.* **-а́** heap, pile; masses, lots, heaps.

воро́чать, -аю *impf.* turn (over); move, shift; *+i.* control, have control of; boss; **~ глаза́ми** roll one's eyes; **~ миллио́нами** deal in millions; **~ся** move, turn; toss and turn.

ворочу́(сь *etc.*: *see* **вороти́ть(ся**

вороши́ть, -шу́ *impf.* stir up; turn (over); **~ся** move about, stir.

ворс, -а nap, pile. **ворси́нка, -и** hair, nap, lint; fibre. **ворси́стый** fleecy.

ворча́ть, -чу́ *impf.* grumble, growl. **ворчли́вый** querulous, peevish; grumpy.

вос... *see* **воз...**

восвоя́си *adv.* home; **отпра́виться ~** go back home.

восемна́дцатый eighteenth. **восемна́дцать, -и** eighteen. **во́семь, -сьми́,** *i.* **-сьмью́** *or* **-семью́** eight. **во́семьдесят, -сьми́десяти** eighty. **восемьсо́т, -сьмисо́т, -ста́ми** eight hundred. **во́семью** *adv.* eight times.

воск, -а (-у) wax, beeswax.

воскли́кнуть, -ну *pf.*, **восклица́ть, -а́ю** *impf.* exclaim. **восклица́ние, -я** exclamation. **восклица́тельный** exclamatory; **~ знак** exclamation mark.

воско́вка, -и waxed paper; stencil. **восков|о́й** wax, waxen; waxy; waxed; **~а́я бума́га** greaseproof paper.

воскреса́ть, -а́ю *impf.*, **воскре́снуть, -ну; -е́с** *pf.* rise again, rise from the dead; revive.

воскресе́ние, -я resurrection. **воскресе́нье, -я** Sunday. **воскреси́ть, -ешу́** *pf.*, **воскреша́ть, -а́ю** *impf.* raise from the dead, resurrect; revive. **воскре́сник, -а** voluntary Sunday work. **воскре́сный** Sunday. **воскреше́ние, -я** raising from the dead, resurrection; revival.

воспале́ние, -я inflammation. **воспалённый; -лён, -а́** inflamed; sore. **воспали́ть, -лю́** *pf.* **воспаля́ть, -я́ю** *impf.* inflame; **~ся** become inflamed.

воспита́ние, -я upbringing, education; training; (good) breeding. **воспи́танник, -а, -ница, -ы** pupil, schoolboy, schoolgirl; ward. **воспи́танность, -и** (good) breeding. **воспи́танный** well-brought-up. **воспита́тельный** educational; **~ дом** foundling hospital. **воспита́ть, -а́ю** *pf.*, **воспи́тывать, -аю** *impf.* bring up, rear; cultivate, foster; inculcate; educate; train.

воспламени́ть, -ню́ *pf.*, **воспламеня́ть, -я́ю** *impf.* kindle, set on fire, ignite; fire, inflame; **~ся** ignite, catch fire; blaze up; take fire, flare up. **воспламеня́емый** inflammable.

вос|по́льзоваться, -зуюсь *pf.*

воспомина́ние, -я recollection, memory; *pl.* memoirs; reminiscences.

вос|препя́тствовать, -твую *pf.*

воспрети́ть, -ещу́ *pf.*, **воспреща́ть, -а́ю** *impf.* forbid, prohibit. **воспреще́ние, -я** prohibition. **воспрещённый; -щён, -а́** forbidden, prohibited.

восприе́мник, -а godfather. **восприе́мница, -ы** godmother. **восприи́мчивый** receptive, impressionable; susceptible. **воспринима́емый** perceptible, apprehensible. **воспринима́ть, -а́ю** *impf.*, **восприня́ть, -иму́, -и́мешь; -и́нял, -а́, -о** *pf.* perceive, apprehend; grasp, take in; interpret, take (**как** for). **восприя́тие, -я** perception.

воспроизведе́ние, -я reproduction. **воспроизвести́, -еду́, -едёшь; -вёл, -а́** *pf.*, **воспроизводи́ть, -ожу́, -о́дишь** *impf.* reproduce; renew; recall. **воспроизводи́тельный** reproductive. **воспроизво́дство, -а** reproduction.

вос|проти́виться, -влюсь *pf.*

воссоедине́ние, -я reunion, reunification. **воссоедини́ть, -ню́** *pf.*, **воссоединя́ть, -я́ю** *impf.* reunite.

восстава́ть, -таю́, -таёшь *impf. of* **восста́ть.** **восстана́вливать, -аю** *impf. of* **восстанови́ть**

восста́ние, -я rising, insurrection.

восстанови́тельный of restoration of, reconstruction. **восстанови́ть, -влю́, -вишь** *pf.* (*impf.* **восстана́вливать**) restore, renew, re-establish, reinstate; recall, recollect; reduce; **~ про́тив**+*g.* set against; **~ про́тив себя́** antagonize. **восстановле́ние, -я** restoration, renewal, reinstatement; rehabilitation; reconstruction; reduction.

восста́ть, -а́ну *pf.* (*impf.* **восстава́ть**) rise (up), arise.

восто́к, -а east. **востокове́дение, -я** oriental studies.

восто́рг, -а delight, rapture; **в ~е от**+*g.* delighted with. **восторга́ть, -а́ю** *impf.* delight, enrapture; **~ся**+*i.* be delighted with, go into raptures over. **восто́рженный** enthusiastic. **восторжествова́ть, -тву́ю** *pf.* triumph.

восто́чник, -а orientalist. **восто́чный** east, eastern; oriental.

востре́бование, -я claiming, demand; **до востре́бования** to be called for, poste restante. **востре́бовать, -бую** *pf.* claim, call for.

восхвали́ть, -лю́, -лишь *pf.*, **восхваля́ть, -я́ю** *impf.* praise, extol.

восхити́тельный entrancing, ravishing; delightful; delicious. **восхити́ть, -хищу́** *pf.*, **восхища́ть, -а́ю** *impf.* carry away, delight, enrapture. **восхище́ние, -я** delight, rapture; admiration. **восхищённый; -щён, -а́** rapt, admiring.

восхо́д, -а rising; east. **восходи́ть, -ожу́, -о́дишь** *impf. of* **взойти́; ~ к**+*d.* go back to, date from. **восходи́тель, -я** mountaineer, climber. **восхожде́ние, -я** ascent. **восходя́щий** rising.

восше́ствие, -я accession.

восьма́я *sb.* eighth; octave. **восьмёрка, -и** eight; No.8; figure of eight. **во́сьмеро, -ры́х** eight; eight pairs.

восьми... *in comb.* eight-; octo-. **восьмигра́нник, -а** octahedron. **~деся́тый** eightieth. **~кла́ссник, -а, -ница, -ы** eighth-year pupil. **~кра́тный** eightfold, octuple. **~ле́тний** eight-year; eight-year-old. **~со́тый** eight-hundredth. **~уго́льник, -а** octagon. **~уго́льный** octagonal. **~часово́й** eight-hour.

восьмо́й eighth.

вот *part.* here (is), there (is); this (is); here's a ..! there's a ..!; well!; **~ ещё!** well, what next?; **~ и всё** and that's all; **~ как!** no! really! **~ та́к!** that's it! that's right! **~ тебе́!** take that!; **~ тебе́ и...** so much for ...; **~ что!** no! not really? **вот-во́т** *adv.* a moment more, and ...; this moment, just; *part.* that's it, that's right!

воткну́ть, -ну́, -нёшь *pf.* (*impf.* **втыка́ть**) stick in, drive in, thrust in.

вотру́ *etc.*: *see* **вотере́ть**

воцаре́ние, -я accesssion. **воцари́ться, -и́тся** *pf.*, **воцаря́ться, -я́ется** *impf.* come to the throne; fall, set in, reign; establish o.s.

вошёл *etc.*: *see* **войти́**

вошь, вши; *g.pl.* **вшей** louse.

вошью́ *etc.*: *see* **вшить**

воща́нка, -и wax paper, wax(ed) cloth; cobbler's wax. **вощано́й** wax. **вощи́ть, -щу́** *impf.* (*pf.* **на~**) wax, wax-polish.

во́ю *etc.*: *see* **выть**

вою́ю *etc.*: *see* **воева́ть. вою́ющий** warring; belligerent.

впада́ть, -а́ю *impf.*, **впасть, -аду́** *pf.* fall, flow; lapse, sink; fall in; **+в**+*a.* verge on, approximate to. **впаде́ние, -я** confluence, (river-)mouth. **впа́дина, -ы** cavity, hollow; socket. **впа́лый** hollow, sunken.

впервой, впервы́е *adv.* for the first time, first.

вперёд *adv.* forward(s), ahead; in future; in advance; **идти́ ~** be fast. **впереди́** *adv.* in front, ahead; in (the) future; *prep.*+*g.* in front of, ahead of, before.

вперемешку *adv.* pell-mell, higgledy-piggledy.

впери́ть, -рю́ *pf.*, **вперя́ть, -я́ю** *impf.* fix, fasten; direct; **~ся** be fixed; gaze fixedly, stare.

впечатле́ние, -я impression; effect. **впечатли́тельный** impressionable, sensitive.

впива́ть(ся, -а́ю(сь *impf. of* **впи́ть(ся**

вписа́ть, -ишу́, -и́шешь *pf.*, **впи́сывать, -аю** *impf.* enter, insert; inscribe; **~ся** be enrolled, join. **впи́ска, -и** entry; insertion.

впита́ть, -а́ю *pf.*, **впи́тывать, -аю** *impf.* absorb, take in; **~ся** soak.

впить, вопью́, -ьёшь; -и́л, -а́, -о *pf.* (*impf.* **впива́ть**) imbibe, absorb; **~ся** dig in, stick in; cling to; **~ся взо́ром, глаза́ми** fix one's gaze, one's eyes (on).

впи́хивать, -аю *impf.*, **впи́хнуть, -ну́, -нёшь** *pf.* stuff in, cram in; shove in.

вплавь *adv.* (by) swimming; **перепра́виться ~** swim across.

вплести́, -ету́, -етёшь; -ёл, -а́ *pf.*, **вплета́ть, -а́ю** *impf.* plait in, intertwine; involve.

вплотну́ю *adv.* close; closely; in earnest. **вплоть** *adv.*; **~ до**+*g.* (right) up to; **~ к**+*d.* right against, close to, right up to.

вполго́лоса *adv.* under one's breath, in an undertone.

вполза́ть, -а́ю *impf.*, **вползти́, -зу́, -зёшь; -з, -ла́** *pf.* creep in, creep up, crawl in.

вполне́ *adv.* fully, entirely; quite.

вполови́ну *adv.* (by) half.

впопа́д *adv.* to the point; opportunely.

впопыха́х *adv.* in a hurry, hastily; in one's haste.

впо́ру *adv.* at the right time, opportune(ly); just right, exactly; **быть ~** (+*d.*) fit.

впосле́дствии *adv.* subsequently, afterwards.

впотьма́х *adv.* in the dark.

впра́вду *adv.* really.

впра́ве *adv.*; **быть ~** have a right.

впра́вить, -влю *pf.*, **вправля́ть, -я́ю** *impf.* set, reduce; tuck in. **впра́вка, -и** setting, reduction.

впра́во *adv.* to the right (**от**+*g.* of).

впредь *adv.* in (the) future; **~ до**+*g.* until.

впро́чем *conj.* however, but; though; or rather.

впры́гивать, -аю *impf.*, **впры́гнуть, -ну** *pf.* jump in, jump up (on).

впры́скивание, -я injection. **впры́скивать,**

-аю *impf.*, **впры́снуть, -ну** *pf.* inject.
впряга́ть, -а́ю *impf.* **впрячь, -ягу́, -яжёшь; -яг, -ла́** *pf.* harness.
впуск, -а admission, admittance. **впуска́ть, -а́ю** *impf.*, **впусти́ть, -ущу́, -у́стишь** *pf.* admit, let in. **впускно́й** admittance; inlet.
впусту́ю *adv.* for nothing, to no purpose, in vain.
впу́тать, -аю *perf*,. **впу́тывать, -аю** *impf.* entangle, involve, implicate; **~ся** get mixed up in.
впущу́ *etc.*: *see* **впусти́ть**
впя́теро *adv.* five times. **впятеро́м** *adv.* five (together).
враг, -а́ enemy; the Devil. **вражда́, -ы́** enmity, hostility. **вражде́бный** hostile; enemy. **враждова́ть, -ду́ю** be at war, be at enmity, be hostile, quarrel. **вра́жеский** enemy. **вра́жий** enemy, hostile.
вразби́вку *adv.* at random.
вразбро́д *adv.* separately, not in concert, disunitedly.
вразре́з *adv.* contrary; **идти́ ~ с**+*i.* go against.
вразуми́тельный intelligible, clear; instructive; persuasive. **вразуми́ть, -млю** *pf.*, **вразумля́ть, -я́ю** *impf.* make understand, make listen to reason, make see sense.
враспло́х *adv.* unexpectedly, unawares, by surprise.
враста́ть, -а́ет *impf.*, **врасти́, -тёт; врос, -ла́** *pf.* grow in; take root. **враста́ющий** ingrowing.
врата́рь, -я́ *m.* gate-keeper; goalkeeper.
врать, вру, врёшь; -ал, -а́, -о *impf.* (*pf.* **на~, со~**) lie, tell lies; talk nonsense.
врач, -а́ doctor; medical officer; **де́тский ~** paediatrician; **зубно́й ~** dentist. **враче́бный** medical.
враща́тельный rotary. **враща́ть, -а́ю** *impf.* turn, rotate, revolve; **~ глаза́ми** roll one's eyes; **~ся** turn, revolve, rotate; **~ся в худо́жественных круга́х** move in artistic circles. **враще́ние, -я** rotation, revolution, gyration.
вред, -а́ harm, hurt, injury; damage. **вреди́тель, -я** *m.* pest; wrecker, saboteur; *pl.* vermin. **вреди́тельство, -а** wrecking, (act of) sabotage. **вреди́ть, -ежу́** *impf.* (*pf.* **по~**) +*d.* injure, harm, hurt; damage. **вре́дный; -ден, -дна́, -о** harmful, injurious; unhealthy.
врежу́ *see* **вреди́ть. вре́жу(сь** *etc.*: *see* **вреза́ть(ся**
вре́зать, -е́жу *pf.*, **вреза́ть, -а́ю** *impf.* cut in, engrave; set in, fit in, insert; (*sl.*) +*d.* hit, smash; slang, curse; **~ся** cut, force one's way, run (into); be engraved; fall in love; **~ся в зе́млю** plunge to the ground. **врезно́й** inset; mortise; notch.
времена́ми *adv.* at times, now and then, from time to time.
временни́к, -а́ chronicle, annals. **вре́менно** *adv.* temporarily; **~ исполня́ющий обя́занности** acting; **~ пове́ренный в дела́х** acting chargé d'affaires. **временно́й** temporal; time; of tense(s). **вре́менный** temporary; provisional; acting. **временщи́к, -а́** favourite. **вре́мя, -мени**; *pl.* **-мена́, -мён, -а́м** *nt.* time, times; tense; **~ го́да** season; **~ от вре́мени** at times, from time to time, now and then; **в своё ~** in one's time; once, at one time; in due course, in one's own time; **до того́ вре́мени** till then, till that time; **на ~** for a time; **са́мое ~** just the time, the (right) time; **ско́лько вре́мени?** what is the time? **тем вре́менем** meanwhile. **время́нка, -и** portable or makeshift stove; temporary structure.
врид, -а *abbr.* (*of* ***вре́менно исполня́ющий до́лжность***) temporary, acting (as).
вро́вень *adv.* level, on a level.
вро́де *prep.*+*g.* like; **не́что ~** a sort of, a kind of; *part.* such as, like; apparently, seemingly.
врождённый; -дён, -а́ innate; congenital; inherent.
врозь, врозь *adv.* separately, apart.
врос *etc.*: *see* **врасти́. вро́ю(сь**, *etc.*: *see* **вры́ть(ся. вру**, *etc.*: *see* **врать**
врун, -а́, вру́нья, -и liar.
вруча́ть, -а́ю *impf.*, **вручи́ть, -чу́** *pf.* hand, deliver; entrust; serve. **вручи́тель, -я** *m.* bearer.
вручну́ю *adv.* by hand.
врыва́ть(ся, -а́ю(сь *impf.* *of* **ворва́ться, вры́ть(ся**
вры́ть, вро́ю *pf.* (*impf.* **врыва́ть**) dig in, bury; **~ся** dig o.s. in.
вряд (ли) *adv.* it's not likely; hardly, scarcely; **~ ли сто́ит** it's hardly worth while.
вс... *see* **вз...**
всади́ть, -ажу́, -а́дишь *pf.*, **вса́живать, -аю** *impf.* thrust in, plunge in; set in; put in, sink in. **вса́дник, -а** rider, horseman; knight. **вса́дница, -ы** rider, horsewoman.
вса́сывание, -я suction; absorption. **вса́сывать(ся, -аю(сь** *impf.* *of* **всоса́ть(ся**
всё, все *pron.*: *see* **весь. всё** *adv.* always, all the time; only, all; **~ (ещё)** still; **~ из-за тебя́** all because of you; **~ лу́чше и лу́чше** better and better; *conj.* however, nevertheless; **~ же** all the same.
все... *in comb.* all-, omni-. **всевозмо́жный** of every kind; all possible. **~во́лновый** all-wave. **~ме́рно** *adv.* in every way, to the utmost. **~ме́рный** of every kind, every possible kind of. **~ми́рный** world, world-wide, universal. **~могу́щий** omnipotent, all-powerful. **~наро́дно** *adv.* publicly. **~наро́дный** national; nation-wide, **~ору́жие; во всеору́жии** completely ready; fully armed, equipped. **~плане́тный** global, worldwide. **~побежда́ющий** all-conquering. **~пого́дный** all-weather. **~росси́йский** All-Russian. **~сезо́нный** year-round. **~си́льный** omnipotent, all-powerful. **~славя́нский** pan-Slav. **~сою́зный** All-Union. **~сторо́нний** all-round; thorough, detailed; comprehensive.

всегда́ always, ever. **всегда́шний** usual, habitual, customary.
всего́ *adv.* in all, all told; only.
вселе́ние, -я installation, moving in.
вселе́нная *sb.* universe. **вселе́нский** universal; ecumenical.
всели́ть, -лю́ *pf.*, **вселя́ть, -я́ю** *impf.* install, settle, lodge; move; inspire, instill; **~ся** move in, install o.s., settle in; be implanted.
все́меро *adv.* seven times, **всемеро́м** *adv.* seven (together).
всео́буч, -а *abbr.* (*of* ***всео́бщее обуче́ние***) compulsory education. **всео́бщий** general, universal.
всерьёз *adv.* seriously, in earnest.
всё-таки *conj. and part.* all the same, for all that, still. **всеце́ло** *adv.* completely; exclusively.
вска́кивать, -аю *impf. of* **вскочи́ть**
вс|кара́бкаться, -аюсь *pf.*, **вскара́бкиваться, -аюсь** *impf.* scramble up, clamber up.
вскачь *adv.* at a gallop.
вски́дывать, -аю *impf.*, **вски́нуть, -ну** *pf.* throw up, toss; **~ся** leap up; +**на**+*a.* turn on, go for.
вскипа́ть, -а́ю *impf.*, **вс|кипе́ть, -плю́** *pf.* boil up; flare up.
вс|кипяти́ть(ся, -ячу́(сь *pf.*
всклоко́чивать, -аю *impf.*, **всклоко́чить, -чу** *pf.* dishevel, tousle.
всколыхну́ть, -ну́, -нёшь *pf.* stir; stir up, rouse.
вскользь *adv.* slightly; in passing.
вско́ре *adv.* soon, shortly after.
вскочи́ть, -очу́, -о́чишь *pf.* (*impf.* **вска́кивать**) jump up, spring up, leap up; come up.
вскри́кивать, -аю *impf.*, **вскри́кнуть, -ну** *pf.* cry out, shriek, scream. **вскрича́ть, -чу́** *pf.* exclaim.
вскрыва́ть, -а́ю *impf.*, **вскрыть, -ро́ю** *pf.* open; reveal, disclose; turn up; lance; cut open, dissect; **~ся** come to light, be revealed; become clear of ice, become open; burst. **вскры́тие, -я** opening; revelation, disclosure; lancing; dissection, post-mortem.
вслед *adv.* & *prep.*+*d.* after; **~ за**+*i.* after, following. **всле́дствие** *prep.*+*g.* in consequence of, because of, on account of.
вслепу́ю *adv.* blindly; blindfold; **печа́тать ~** to touch-type.
вслух *adv.* aloud.
вслу́шаться, -аюсь *pf.* **вслу́шиваться, -аюсь** *impf.* listen attentively, listen hard.
всма́триваться, -аюсь *impf.*, **всмотре́ться, -рю́сь, -ришься** *pf.* look closely, peer, look hard.
всмя́тку *adv.* soft(-boiled), lightly (boiled).
всо́вывать, -аю *impf. of* **всу́нуть**
всоса́ть, -су́, -сёшь *pf.* (*impf.* **вса́сывать**) suck in; absorb; imbibe; **~ся** be absorbed, soak in; sink in.
вспа́рхивать, -аю *impf. of* **вспорхну́ть**
вспа́рывать, -аю *impf. of* **вспоро́ть**
вс|паха́ть, -ашу́, -а́шешь *pf.*, **вспа́хивать, -аю** *impf.* plough up. **вспа́шка, -и** ploughing.
вс|пе́нить, -ню *pf.*
всплеск, -а splash; blip. **всплёскивать, -аю** *impf.*, **всплесну́ть, -ну́, -нёшь** *pf.* splash; **~ рука́ми** fling up, throw up, one's hands.
всплыва́ть, -а́ю *impf.*, **всплыть, -ыву́, -ывёшь; -ыл, -а́, -о** *pf.* rise to the surface, surface; arise, come up; come to light, be revealed.
вс|полоши́ть(ся, -шу́(сь *pf.*
вспомна́ть, -а́ю *impf.*, **вспо́мнить, -ню** *pf.* remember, recall, recollect; **~ся** *impers.*+*d.*: **мне вспо́мнилось** I remembered.
вспомога́тельный auxiliary; subsidiary, branch.
вспоро́ть, -орю́, -о́решь *pf.* (*impf.* **вспа́рывать**) rip open.
вспорхну́ть, -ну́, -нёшь *pf.* (*impf.* **вспа́рхивать**) take wing, start up, fly up.
вс|поте́ть, -е́ю *pf.*
вспры́гивать, -аю *impf.*, **вспры́гнуть, -ну** *pf.* jump up, spring up.
вспры́скивать, -аю *impf.*, **вспры́снуть, -ну** *pf.* sprinkle.
вспуха́ть, -а́ет *impf.*, **вс|пу́хнуть, -нет; -ух** *pf.* swell up.
вспыли́ть, -лю́ *pf.* flare up; fly into a rage (**на**+*a.* with) **вспы́льчивый** hot-tempered, irritable.
вспы́хивать, -аю *impf.*, **вспы́хнуть, -ну** *pf.* burst into flame, blaze up; flare up; break out; blush. **вспы́шка, -и** flash; flare, spurt; outburst, burst; outbreak.
встава́ние, -я rising, standing. **встава́ть, -таю, -таёшь** *impf. of* **встать**
вста́вить, -влю *pf.*, **вставля́ть, -я́ю** *impf.* put in, set in, insert. **вста́вка, -и** fixing, insertion; framing, mounting; inset; front; interpolation. **вставн|о́й** inserted; set in; **~ы́е зу́бы** false teeth; **~ы́е ра́мы** double window-frames.
встать, -а́ну *pf.* (*impf.* **встава́ть**) get up, rise; stand up; stand; arise, come up; stop; go, fit (**в**+*a.* into); **~ на коле́ни** kneel down; **~ с ле́вой ноги́** get out of bed on the wrong side.
встрево́женный *adj.* anxious, worried, alarmed. **вс|трево́жить, -жу** *pf.*
встрёпанный dishevelled.
встрепену́ться, -ну́сь, -нёшься *pf.* rouse o.s.; shake its wings; start, start up; beat faster, begin to thump.
встре́тить, -е́чу *pf.*, **встреча́ть, -а́ю** *impf.* meet, meet with, encounter; greet, welcome, receive; **~ся** meet; be found, be met with. **встре́ча, -и** meeting; reception; encounter; match. **встре́чный** coming to meet; contrary, head; counter; **~ ве́тер** head wind; **~ иск** counter-claim; *sb.* person met with; **ка́ждый ~ и попере́чный** anybody and everybody, every Tom, Dick and Harry; **пе́рвый**

~ the first person you meet, anybody.
встряска, -и shaking; shock. **встряхивать, -аю** *impf.*, **встряхнуть, -ну, -нёшь** *pf.* shake; shake up, rouse; **~ся** shake o.s.; rouse o.s., pull o.s. together; have a good time.
вступать, -аю *impf.*, **вступить, -плю, -пишь** *pf.*+**в**+*a.* enter, enter into, join, join in; come into; +**на**+*a.* go up, mount; ~ **в брак** marry; ~ **на престол** ascend the throne; **~ся** intervene; +**за**+*a.* stand up for. **вступительный** introductory; inaugural, opening; entrance. **вступление, -я** entry, joining; accession; prelude, opening, introduction, preamble.
всунуть, -ну *pf.* (*impf.* **всовывать**) put in, stick in, push in, slip in.
всхлипнуть, -ну *pf.*, **всхлипывать, -аю** *impf.* sob. **всхлипывание, -я** sobbing; sobs.
всходить, -ожу, -одишь *impf. of* **взойти. всходы, -ов** *pl.* new growth, shoots.
всхрапнуть, -ну, -нёшь *pf.*, **всхрапывать, -аю** *impf.* snore; snort; have a nap.
всю *see* **весь**
всюду *adv.* everywhere.
вся *see* **весь**
всяк|ий any; every, all kinds of; **~ом случае** in any case, anyhow, at any rate; **на ~ий случай** just in case, to be on the safe side; *pron.* anyone, everyone; anything. **всячески** *adv.* in every possible way, in all ways. **всяческий** all kinds of.
Вт *abbr.* (*of* **ватт**) W, watt.
втайне *adv.* secretly, in secret.
вталкивать, -аю *impf. of* **втолкнуть**
втаптывать, -аю *impf. of* **втоптать**
втаскивать, -аю *impf. of* **втащить**
втачать, -аю *pf.*, **втачивать, -аю** *impf.* sew in, sew on; set in. **втачка, -и** sewing in, sewing on; patch. **втачанный, втачной** sewn in, sewn on; set in.
втащить, -щу, -щишь *pf.* (*impf.* **втаскивать**) drag in, drag on, drag up; **~ся** drag o.s.
втекать, -ает *impf. of* **втечь**
втереть, вотру, вотрёшь; втёр *pf.* (*impf.* **втирать**) rub in; **~ся** insinuate o.s., worm o.s.
втечь, -чёт; втёк, -ла *pf.* (*impf.* **втекать**) flow in.
втирание, -я rubbing in; embrocation, liniment. **втирать(ся, -аю(сь** *impf. of* **втереть(ся**
втискивать, -аю *impf.*, **втиснуть, -ну** *pf.* squeeze in; **~ся** squeeze (o.s.) in.
втихомолку, втихую *advs.* surreptitiously; on the quiet.
втолкнуть, -ну, -нёшь *pf.* (*impf.* **вталкивать**) push in, shove in.
втоптать, -пчу, -пчешь *pf.* (*impf.* **втаптывать**) trample (in).
втора, -ы second voice, violin, etc. **вторить, -рю** *impf.* play or sing second; +*d.* repeat, echo. **вторичный** second, secondary. **вторник, -а** Tuesday. **втор|ой** second; **~ое** *sb.* second course. **второочередной** secondary.
второстепенный secondary, minor.
в-третьих *adv.* thirdly, in the third place. **втрое** *adv.* three times, treble. **втроём** *adv.* three (together). **втройне** *adv.* three times as much, treble.
втуз, -а *abbr.* (*of* ***высшее техническое учебное заведение***) technical college.
втулка, -и bush; plug; bung; liner, sleeve.
втыкать, -аю *impf. of* **воткнуть. втычка, -и** thrusting in, driving in, driving in; plug, bung.
втягивать, -аю *impf.*, **втянуть, -ну, -нешь** *pf.* draw in, up; pull in, up; absorb; take in; involve; **~ся** sink, fall in; +**в**+*a.* draw into enter; get used to; get keen on.
вуалетка, -и veil. **вуалировать, -рую** *impf.* (*pf.* **за~**) veil, draw a veil over; fog. **вуаль, -и** veil; fog.
вуз, -а *abbr.* (*of* ***высшее учебное заведение***) higher educational establishment; university, college, institute. **вузовец, -вца, -овка, -и** student.
вулкан, -а volcano. **вулканический** volcanic.
вульгарность, -и vulgarity. **вульгарный** vulgar.
вундеркинд, -а infant prodigy.
вход, -а entrance; entry. **входить, -ожу, -одишь** *impf. of* **войти. входн|ой** entrance, input; **~ое отверстие** inlet, inlet port. **входящий** incoming, entering; reentrant; male.
вхолостую *adv.* idle, free; **работать** ~ idle.
вцепиться, -плюсь, -пишься *pf.*, **вцепляться, -яюсь** *impf.* clutch, cling to; seize, catch hold of.
вчера *adv.* yesterday. **вчерашний** yesterday's.
вчерне in rough, roughly.
вчетверо *adv.* four times, by four, in four. **вчетвером** *adv.* four (together). **в-четвёртых** *adv.* fourthly, in the fourth place.
вши *etc.*: *see* **вошь**
вшестеро *adv.* six times, by six. **вшестером** *adv.* six (together).
вшивать, -аю *impf. of* **вшить. вшивка, -и** sewing in; patch. **вшивной** sewn in, set in.
вшивый lousy.
вширь *adv.* in breadth; widely.
вшить, вошью, -ьёшь *pf.* (*impf.* **вшивать**) sew in, set in.
въ... *see* **в...**
въедаться, -ается *impf. of* **въесться. въедливый, въедчивый** *adjs.* corrosive; caustic; acid.
въезд, -а entry; entrance. **въезжать, -аю** *impf. of* **въехать**
въесться, -естся, -едятся *pf.* (*impf.* **въедаться**) **в**+*a.* eat into, corrode.
въехать, -еду *pf.* (*impf.* **въезжать**) ride in, up; drive in, up; +**в**+*a.* move into; run into.
въявь *adv.* in reality; before one's eyes, with one's own eyes.
вы, вас, вам, вами, вас *pron.* you.
вы... *vbl. pref. expressing direction of mo-*

tion or action outwards; *achievement or attainment by means of action*; *completion of action or process.*

выбега́ть, -а́ю *impf.*, **вы́бежать, -егу** *pf.* run out.

вы́|белить, -лю *pf.* **вы́белка, -и** bleaching; whitening.

вы́беру *etc.*: *see* **вы́брать. выбива́ть(ся, -а́ю(сь** *impf. of* **вы́бить(ся. выбира́ть(ся, -а́ю(сь** *impf. of* **вы́брать(ся**

вы́бить, -бью *pf.* (*impf.* **выбива́ть**) knock out, kick out; dislodge; beat; beat down; beat out; stamp, strike; hammer out; **~ся** get out; break loose; come out, show; **~ся из сил** exhaust o.s., be exhausted.

вы́боина, -ы rut; pot-hole; dent; groove.

вы́бор, -а choice, option; selection, assortment; *pl.* election, elections, **вы́борка, -и** selection; excerpt. **вы́борн|ый** elective; electoral; elected; **~ бюллете́нь** ballot-paper; **~ый, ~ая** *sb.* delegate. **вы́борочный** selective.

вы́|бранить(ся, -ню(сь *pf.* **выбра́сывать(ся, -аю(сь** *impf. of* **вы́бросить(ся**

вы́брать, -беру *pf.* (*impf.* **выбира́ть**) choose, select, pick out; elect; take out; haul in; **~ся** get out; move, remove; manage to go out.

выбрива́ть, -а́ю *impf.*, **вы́брить, -рею** *pf.* shave; **~ся** shave (o.s.).

вы́брос, -а blip, pip. **вы́бросить, -ошу** *pf.* (*impf.* **выбра́сывать**) throw out; reject, discard, throw away; put out; **~ся** throw o.s. out, leap out; **~ся с парашю́том** bale out.

выбыва́ть, -а́ю *impf.*, **вы́быть, -буду** *pf.* **из**+*g.* leave, quit; be out of. **выбы́тие, -я** departure, removal, absence.

выва́ливать, -аю *impf.*, **вы́валить, -лю** *pf.* throw out; pour out; **~ся** fall out; pour out.

выва́ривать, -аю *impf.*, **вы́варить, -рю** *pf.* boil out; extract by boiling; boil thoroughly. **вы́варка, -и** decoction, extraction; residue, concentrate.

вы́везти, -зу; -ез *pf.* (*impf.* **вы́возить**) take out, remove; bring out; export; save, rescue.

вы́верить, -рю *pf.* (*impf.* **выверя́ть**) verify; regulate.

вы́вернуть, -ну *pf.*, **вывёртывать, -аю** *impf.* turn inside out; unscrew; pull out; twist, wrench; dislocate; **~ся** come unscrewed; slip out; get out, extricate o.s., wriggle out; be dislocated; emerge. **вы́верт, -а** caper; mannerism; affectation.

выверя́ть, -я́ю *impf. of* **вы́верить**

вы́весить, -ешу *pf.* (*impf.* **выве́шивать**) weigh; hang out; put up, post up. **вы́веска, -и** sign, signboard; screen, pretext; mug.

вы́вести, -еду; -ел *pf.* (*impf.* **выводи́ть**) lead out, bring out; drive out; turn out, force out; remove; exterminate; deduce, conclude; hatch; grow, breed, raise; put up, erect; depict, portray; write, draw, trace out; **~сь** go out of use; lapse; disappear; become extinct; come out; hatch out.

выве́тривание, -я airing; weathering. **выве́тривать, -аю** *impf.*, **вы́ветрить, -рю** *pf.* air; drive out, remove, efface; weather, erode; **~ся** weather; disappear, be driven out, be effaced.

выве́шивать, -аю *impf. of* **вы́весить**

вы́вих, -а dislocation; sprain; kink; oddity, quirk. **вы́вихнуть, -ну** *pf.* dislocate, put out; sprain.

вы́вод, -а deduction, conclusion; withdrawal, removal. **выводи́ть(ся, -ожу́(сь, -о́дишь(ся** *impf. of* **вы́вести(сь. вы́водка, -и** removal; exercising. **вы́водок, -дка** brood; hatch litter.

вывожу́ *see* **выводи́ть, вывози́ть**

вы́воз, -а export; removal. **вывози́ть, -ожу́, -о́зишь** *impf. of* **вы́везти. вы́возка, -и** carting out. **вывозно́й** export.

вы́гарки, -ов *pl.* slag, dross.

вы́гиб, -а curve, curvature. **выгиба́ть(ся, -а́ю(сь** *impf. of* **вы́гнуть(ся**

вы́|гладить, -ажу *pf.*

вы́глядеть, -яжу *impf.* look, look like. **выгля́дывать, -аю** *impf.*, **вы́глянуть, -ну** *pf.* look out; peep out, emerge, become visible.

вы́гнать, -гоню *pf.* (*impf.* **выгоня́ть**) drive out; expel; distil; force.

вы́гнутый curved, convex. **вы́гнуть, -ну** *pf.* (*impf.* **выгиба́ть**) bend, arch; **~ся** arch up.

выгова́ривать, -аю *impf.* **вы́говорить, -рю** *pf.* pronounce, utter, speak; reserve; stipulate for; +*d.* reprimand; **~ся** speak out, have one's say out. **вы́говор, -а** accent, pronunciation; reprimand, rebuke.

вы́года, -ы advantage, benefit; profit, gain; interest. **вы́годн|ый** advantageous, beneficial; profitable; **~о** it pays.

вы́гон, -а pasture, common. **вы́гонка, -и** distillation. **выгоня́ть, -я́ю** *impf. of* **вы́гнать**

выгора́живать, -аю *impf. of* **вы́городить**

выгора́ть, -а́ет *impf.*, **вы́гореть, -рит** *pf.* burn down; burn out; fade, bleach; turn out well, come off.

вы́городить, -ожу *pf.* (*impf.* **выгора́живать**) fence off; shield, screen.

вы́|гравировать, -рую *pf.*

выгружа́ть, -а́ю *impf.*, **вы́грузить, -ужу** *pf.* unload; discharge; disembark; **~ся** unload; disembark; detrain, debus. **вы́грузка, -и** unloading; disembarkation.

выдава́ть, -даю́, -даёшь *impf.*, **вы́дать, -ам, -ашь, -аст, -адим** *pf.* give out, issue, produce; give away, betray; deliver up, extradite; +**за**+*a.* pass off as, give out to be; **~ за́муж** give in marriage; **~ся** protrude, project, jut out; stand out; present itself, happen to be. **вы́дача, -и** issuing; issue; payment; extradition. **выдаю́щийся** prominent; salient; eminent, outstanding.

выдвига́ть, -а́ю *impf.*, **вы́двинуть, -ну** *pf.* move out; pull out, open; put forward, advance; promote; nominate, propose; **~ся** move forward, move out, come out; rise, get on. **выдвиже́нец, -нца, -же́нка, -и** worker promoted from rank and file. **выдвиже́ние, -я** nomination; promotion, advancement.

выделе́ние, -я secretion; excretion; isolation; apportionment. **вы́делить, -лю** *pf.*, **выделя́ть, -я́ю** *impf.* pick out, single out; detach, detail; assign, earmark; allot; secrete; excrete; isolate; ~ **курси́вом** italicize; **~ся** take one's share; ooze out, exude; stand out, be noted (+*i.* for).

вы́держанный consistent; self-possessed; firm; matured, seasoned. **вы́держать, -жу** *pf.* **выде́рживать, -аю** *impf.* bear, hold; stand, stand up to, endure; contain o.s.; pass; keep; lay up; mature; season; maintain, sustain. **вы́держка[1], -и** endurance; self-possession; exposure.

вы́держка[2], -и extract, excerpt, quotation.

вы́дох, -а expiration. **вы́дохнуть, -ну** *pf.* (*impf.* **выдыха́ть**) breathe out; **~ся** have lost fragrance or smell; be played out; be flat; be past one's best.

вы́дра, -ы otter.

вы́|драть, -деру *pf.* **вы́|дрессировать, -рую** *pf.* **вы́|дубить, -блю** *pf.*

выдува́льщик, -а glass-blower. **выдува́ть, -а́ю** *impf. of* **вы́дуть. вы́дувка, -и** glass-blowing. **выдувно́й** blown.

вы́думанный made-up, invented, fabricated. **вы́думать, -аю** *pf.*, **выду́мывать, -аю** *impf.* invent; make up, fabricate. **вы́думка, -и** invention; idea, gadget, device; inventiveness; fabrication, fiction.

вы́|дуть, -ую *pf.* (*impf. also* **выдува́ть**) blow; blow out; blow up.

выдыха́ние, -я expiration. **выдыха́ть(ся, -а́ю(сь** *impf. of* **вы́дохнуть(ся**

вы́езд, -а departure; exit; turn-out, equipage; going out.

выездн|о́й going-out; travelling, visiting; exit; away; **~о́й матч** away match; **~ая се́ссия суда́** assizes. **выезжа́ть, -а́ю** *impf. of* **вы́ехать**

вы́емка, -и taking out; seizure; collection; excavation; hollow, groove; fluting, flute; cutting, cut.

вы́ехать, -еду *pf.* (*impf.* **выезжа́ть**) go out, depart; drive out, ride out; move, remove, leave; +**на**+*p.* make use of, exploit, take advantage of.

вы́жать, -жму *pf.* (*impf.* **выжима́ть**) squeeze out; wring out, press out; lift, press-lift.

вы́ждать, -ду *pf.* (*impf.* **выжида́ть**) wait for, wait out.

вы́жечь, -жгу *pf.* (*impf.* **выжига́ть**) burn low, burn out; burn, scorch; cauterize. **вы́жженн|ый, ~ая земля́** scorched earth.

выжива́ние, -я survival. **выжива́ть, -а́ю** *impf. of* **вы́жить**

выжига́ние, -я burning out, scorching; cauterization; ~ **по де́реву** poker-work. **выжига́ть, -а́ю** *impf. of* **вы́жечь**

выжида́ние, -я waiting, temporizing. **выжида́тельный** waiting; expectant; temporizing. **выжида́ть, -а́ю** *impf. of* **вы́ждать**

вы́жим, -а press-up. **выжима́ние, -я** squeezing; wringing (out); (weight-)lifting. **выжима́ть, -а́ю** *impf. of* **вы́жать. вы́жимка, -и** squeezing, pressing, wringing; abstract, brief summary.

вы́жить, -иву *pf.* (*impf.* **выжива́ть**) survive; live through; stay alive, hold out, stick it out; drive out, hound out; get rid of; ~ **из ума́** become senile.

вы́звать, -зову *pf.* (*impf.* **вызыва́ть**) call, call out; send for; challenge; call forth, provoke; cause; stimulate, rouse; ~ **по телефо́ну** ring up; **~ся** volunteer, offer.

выздора́вливать, -аю *impf.*, **вы́здороветь, -ею** *pf.* recover, get better. **выздоровле́ние, -я** recovery; convalescence.

вы́зов, -а call; summons; challenge.

вы́|золотить, -лочу *pf.* **вы́золоченный** gilt.

вызу́бривать, -аю *impf.*, **вы́|зубрить, -рю** *pf.* learn by heart, cram.

вызыва́ть(ся, -а́ю(сь *impf. of* **вы́звать(ся. вызыва́ющий** defiant; challenging, provocative.

вы́играть, -аю *pf.*, **выи́грывать, -аю** *impf.* win; gain. **вы́игрыш, -а** win; winning; winnings; gain; prize. **вы́игрышный** winning; premium; lottery; advantageous; effective.

вы́йти, -йду; -шел, -шла *pf.* (*impf.* **выходи́ть**) go out; come out; get out; appear; turn out; come of; be used up; have expired; ~ **в свет** appear; ~ **в фина́л** reach the final; ~ **за́муж** (**за**+*a.*) marry; ~ **из грани́ц,** ~ **из преде́лов** exceed the bounds; ~ **из себя́** lose one's temper, be beside o.s.; ~ **на вы́зовы** take a call; ~ **на сце́ну** come onto the stage.

вы́казать, -ажу *pf.*, **выка́зывать, -аю** *impf.* show; display.

выка́лывать, -аю *impf. of* **вы́колоть**

выка́пчивать, -аю *impf. of* **вы́коптить**

выка́пывать, -аю *impf. of* **вы́копать**

вы́карабкаться, -аюсь *pf.*, **выкара́бкиваться, -аюсь** *impf.* scramble out; get out.

вы́|катать, -аю *pf.*

вы́качать, -аю *pf.*, **выка́чивать, -аю** *impf.* pump out.

выки́дывать, -аю *impf.*, **вы́кинуть, -ну** *pf.* throw out, reject; put out; miscarry, abort; ~ **флаг** hoist a flag. **вы́кидыш, -а** miscarriage, abortion.

вы́кладка, -и laying out; lay-out; facing; kit; computation, calculation. **выкла́дывать, -аю** *impf. of* **вы́ложить**

выклика́ть, -аю *impf.*, **вы́кликнуть, -ну** *pf.* call out.

выключа́тель, -я *m.* switch. **выключа́ть, -а́ю** *impf.*, **вы́ключить, -чу** *pf.* turn off, switch off; remove, exclude; justify.

вы́|клянчить, -чу *pf.*

выкола́чивать, -аю *impf.*, **вы́колотить, -лочу** *pf.* knock out, beat out; beat; extort, wring out.

вы́колоть, -лю *pf.* (*impf.* **выка́лывать**) put out; gouge out; tattoo.

вы́|копать, -аю *pf.* (*impf. also* **выка́пывать**) dig; dig up, dig out; exhume; unearth; **~ся** dig o.s. out.

вы́коптить, -пчу *pf.* (*impf.* **выка́пчивать**) smoke.

вы́корчевать, -чую *pf.*, **выкорчёвывать, -аю** *impf.* uproot, root out; extirpate, eradicate.

выкра́ивать, -аю *impf. of* **вы́кроить**

вы́|красить, -ашу *pf.*, **выкра́шивать, -аю** *impf.* paint; dye.

вы́крик, -а cry, shout; yell. **выкри́кивать, -аю** *impf.*, **вы́крикнуть, -ну** *pf.* cry out; yell.

вы́кроить, -ою *pf.* (*impf.* **выкра́ивать**) cut out; (manage to) find. **вы́кройка, -и** pattern.

вы́крутить, -учу *pf.*, **выкру́чивать, -аю** *impf.* unscrew; twist; **~ся** extricate o.s., get o.s. out.

вы́куп, -а ransom; redemption.

вы́|купать[1](ся, -аю(сь *pf.*

выкупа́ть[2], -а́ю *impf.*, **вы́купить, -плю** *pf.* ransom, redeem. **выкупно́й** ransom; redemption.

выку́ривать, -аю *impf.*, **вы́курить, -рю** *pf.* smoke; smoke out; distil.

выла́вливать, -аю *impf. of* **вы́ловить**

вы́лазка, -и sally, sortie; raid; ramble, excursion, outing.

вы́|лакать, -аю *pf.* **выла́мывать, -аю** *impf. of* **вы́ломать** **выла́щивать, -аю** *impf. of* **вы́лощить**

вылеза́ть, -а́ю *impf.*, **вы́лезти, вы́лезть, -зу; -лез** *pf.* crawl out; climb out; fall out, come out.

вы́|лепить, -плю *pf.*

вы́лет, -а flight; take-off, departure; emission, escape; overhang. **вылета́ть, -а́ю** *impf.*, **вы́лететь, -ечу** *pf.* fly out, off, away; take off; rush out, dash out; escape.

выле́чивать, -аю *impf.*, **вы́лечить, -чу** *pf.* cure, heal; **~ся** recover, be cured; **~ся от**+*g.* get over.

вылива́ть(ся, -а́ю(сь *pf. of* **вы́лить(ся**

вы́|линять, -яет *pf.*

вы́лить, -лью *pf.* (*impf.* **вылива́ть**) pour out; empty (out); cast, found; mould; **~ся** run out, flow (out); be expressed, express itself.

вы́ловить, -влю *pf.* (*impf.* **выла́вливать**) fish out, catch.

вы́ложить, -жу *pf.* (*impf.* **выкла́дывать**) lay out, spread out; cover, lay, face; tell, reveal.

вы́лом, -а breaking down, in, out, open; breach, break, gap. **вы́ломать, -аю** *pf.*, **вы́ломить, -млю** *pf.* (*impf.* **выла́мывать**) break down, break out, break open. **вы́ломка, -и** breaking off.

вы́лощенный glossy; polished, smooth. **вы́лощить, -щу** *pf.* (*impf.* **выла́щивать**) polish.

вы́|лудить, -ужу *pf.* **вы́лью** *etc.*: *see* **вы́лить**

вы́|мазать, -мажу *pf.*, **выма́зывать, -аю** *impf.* smear, daub, dirty; **~ся** get dirty, make o.s. dirty.

выма́ливать, -аю *impf. of* **вы́молить**

выма́нивать, -аю *impf.*, **вы́манить, -ню** *pf.* entice, lure; **+у**+*g.* swindle, cheat, out of; wheedle, coax out of.

вы́|марать, -аю *pf.* **вы́мени** *etc.*: *see* **вы́мя**

вы́мереть, -мрет; -мер *pf.* (*impf.* **вымира́ть**) die out; become extinct; be, become, deserted. **вы́мерший** extinct.

вымина́ть, -а́ю *impf. of* **вы́мять.** **вымира́ть, -а́ю** *impf. of* **вы́мереть.** **вы́мну** *etc.*: *see* **вы́мять**

вымога́тель, -я *m.*, **-ница, -ы** blackmailer, extortioner. **вымога́тельство, -а** blackmail, extortion. **вымога́ть, -а́ю** *impf.* extort, wring (out).

вымока́ть, -а́ю *impf.*, **вы́мокнуть, -ну; -ок** *pf.* be soaked, drenched, wet through; soak, steep; rot.

вымола́чивать, -аю *impf. of* **вы́молотить**

вы́молвить, -влю *pf.* say, utter.

вы́молить, -лю *pf.* (*impf.* **выма́ливать**) beg; obtain by prayer(s).

вы́молот, -а threshing; grain. **вы́молотить, -очу** *pf.* (*impf.* **вымола́чивать**) thresh. **вы́молотки, -ток** *or* **-тков** *pl.* chaff.

вы́|мостить, -ощу *pf.* **вы́мою** *etc.*: *see* **вы́мыть**

вы́мпел, -а pennant.

вы́мрет *see* **вы́мереть.** **вымыва́ть(ся** *impf. of* **вы́мыть(ся**

вы́мысел, -сла invention, fabrication; fantasy, flight of fancy. **вы́мыслить, -лю** *pf.* (*impf.* **вымышля́ть**) think up, make up, invent; imagine.

вы́|мыть, -мою *pf.* (*impf.* **вымыва́ть**) wash; wash out, off; wash away; **~ся** wash, wash o.s.

вы́мышленный fictitious, imaginary. **вымышля́ть, -я́ю** *impf. of* **вы́мыслить**

вы́мя, -мени *nt.* udder.

вы́мять, -мну *pf.* (*impf.* **вымина́ть**) knead, work; trample down.

вы́нести, -су; -нес *pf.* (*impf.* **выноси́ть**) carry out, take out; take away; carry away; bear, stand, endure; pass; **~ вопро́с** submit a question; **~ на бе́рег** wash up; **~сь** fly out, rush out.

вынима́ть(ся, -а́ю(сь *impf. of* **вы́нуть(ся**

вы́нос, -а carrying out; removal; drift; trace. **выноси́ть, -ошу́, -о́сишь** *impf. of* **вы́нести; не ~** be unable to bear, to stand; **~ся** *impf. of* **вы́нестись.** **вы́носка, -и** taking out, carrying out; removal; marginal note, footnote. **выно́сливость, -и** endurance, staying-power; hardiness.

вы́нудить, -ужу *pf.*, **вынужда́ть, -а́ю** *impf.* force, compel, oblige; extort. **вы́нужденный** forced, compulsory.

вы́нуть, -ну *pf.* (*impf.* **вынима́ть**) take out;

pull out; extract; draw out; **~ся** come out, pull out.

вы́пад, -а attack; lunge, thrust. **выпада́ть, -а́ю** *impf. of* **вы́пасть. выпаде́ние, -я** falling out; fall-out; precipitation; prolapsus.

выпа́лывать, -аю *impf. of* **вы́полоть**

выпа́ривать, -аю *impf.*, **вы́парить, -рю** evaporate.

выпа́рывать, -аю *impf. of* **вы́пороть**[2]

вы́пасть, -аду; -ал *pf.* (*impf.* **выпада́ть**) fall out; fall; occur, turn out; lunge, thrust.

выпека́ть, -а́ю *impf.*, **вы́печь, -еку; -ек** *pf.* bake. **вы́печка, -и** baking, batch.

выпива́ть, -а́ю *impf. of* **вы́пить**; enjoy a drink. **вы́пивка, -и** drinking; drinks.

выпи́ливать, -аю *impf.*, **вы́пилить, -лю** *pf.* saw, cut out, make with fretsaw.

вы́писать, -ишу *pf.*, **выпи́сывать, -аю** *impf.* copy out, excerpt; trace out; write out; order; subscribe to; send for, write for; strike off the list; **~ из больни́цы** discharge from hospital; **~ся** leave, be discharged. **вы́писка, -и** copying out, making extracts; writing out; extract, excerpt, cutting; ordering, subscription; discharge.

вы́|пить, -пью *pf.* (*impf. also* **выпива́ть**) drink; drink up, drink off.

вы́плавить, -влю *pf.*, **выплавля́ть, -я́ю** *impf.* smelt. **вы́плавка, -и** smelting; smelted metal.

вы́плата, -ы payment. **вы́платить, -ачу** *pf.*, **выпла́чивать, -аю** *impf.* pay out; pay off.

выплёвывать, -аю *impf. of* **вы́плюнуть**

вы́плести, -ету *pf.*, **выплета́ть, -а́ю** *impf.* undo, untie; unplait; weave.

выплыва́ть, -а́ю *impf.*, **вы́плыть, -ву** *pf.* swim out, sail out, come to surface, come up; emerge; appear, crop up.

вы́плюнуть, -ну *pf.* (*impf.* **выплёвывать**) spit out.

выполза́ть, -а́ю *impf.*, **вы́ползти, -зу; -олз** *pf.* crawl out, creep out.

выполне́ние, -я execution, carrying out; fulfilment. **выполни́мый** practical, feasible. **вы́полнить, -ню** *pf.*, **выполня́ть, -я́ю** *impf.* execute, carry out; fulfil; discharge.

вы́|полоскать, -ощу *pf.*

вы́|полоть, -лю *pf.* (*impf. also* **выпа́лывать**) weed out; weed.

вы́|пороть[1], **-рю** *pf.*

вы́пороть[2], **-рю** *pf.* (*impf.* **выпа́рывать**) rip out, rip up.

вы́|потрошить, -шу *pf.*

вы́править, -влю *pf.*, **выправля́ть, -я́ю** *impf.* straighten (out); correct; prove; get, obtain; **~ся** become straight; improve. **вы́правка, -и** bearing; correction.

выпра́шивать, -аю *impf. of* **вы́просить, -шу** solicit.

выпрова́живать, -аю *impf.*, **вы́проводить, -ожу** *pf.* send packing; show the door.

вы́просить, -ошу *pf.* (*impf.* **выпра́шивать**) (*ask for and*) obtain, get.

выпряга́ть, -а́ю *impf. of* **вы́прячь**

выпрями́тель, -я *m.* rectifier. **вы́прямить, -млю** *pf.*, **выпрямля́ть, -я́ю** *impf.* straighten (out); rectify; **~ся** come straight; straighten up, pull o.s. up.

вы́прячь, -ягу; -яг *pf.* (*impf.* **выпряга́ть**) unharness.

выпу́гивать, -аю *impf.*, **вы́пугнуть, -ну** *pf.* scare off; start.

вы́пукло *adv.* in relief. **вы́пукло-** convex-. **вы́пуклость, -и** protuberance; prominence, bulge; convexity; relief; clarity, distinctness. **вы́пуклый** protuberant; prominent, bulging; convex; in relief; clear, distinct.

вы́пуск, -а output; issue; discharge; part, number, instalment; final-year students, pupils; cut, omission; edging, piping. **выпуска́ть, -а́ю** *impf.*, **вы́пустить, -ущу** *pf.* let out, release; put out, issue; turn out, produce; cut, cut out, omit; let out, let down; show; see through the press. **выпускни́к, -а́** final-year student, pupil. **выпускн|о́й** output; discharge; exhaust; **~о́й экза́мен** finals, final examination; **~а́я цена́** market-price; **~о́й** *sb.* final-year student.

вы́путать, -аю *pf.*, **выпу́тывать, -аю** *impf.* disentangle; **~ся** disentangle o.s., extricate o.s.; **~ся из беды́** get out of a scrape.

вы́пушка, -и edging, braid, piping.

вы́пытать, -аю *pf.*, **выпы́тывать, -аю** *impf.* elicit, worm out.

выпь, -и bittern.

вы́пью *etc.*: *see* **вы́пить**

вы́пятить(ся, -ячу(сь *pf.*, **выпя́чивать(ся, -аю(сь** *impf.* stick out, protrude.

вырабатывать, -аю *impf.*, **вы́работать, -аю** *pf.* work out; work up; draw up; elaborate; manufacture; produce, make; earn. **вы́работка, -и** manufacture; production, making; working; working out, drawing up; output, yield; make.

выра́внивать(ся, -аю(сь *impf. of* **вы́ровнять(ся**

выража́ть, -а́ю *impf.*, **вы́разить, -ажу** *pf.* express; convey; voice; **~ся** express o.s.; manifest itself; amount, come (**в**+*p.* to). **выраже́ние, -я** expression. **вы́раженный** pronounced, marked. **вырази́тель, -я** *m.* spokesman, exponent; voice. **вырази́тельный** expressive; significant.

выраста́ть, -а́ю *impf.*, **вы́расти, -ту; -рос** *pf.* grow, grow up; develop; increase; appear, rise up; **~ из**+*g.* grow out of. **вы́растить, -ащу** *pf.*, **выра́щивать, -аю** *impf.* bring up; rear, breed; grow, cultivate.

вы́рвать[1], **-ву** *pf.* (*impf.* **вырыва́ть**) pull out, tear out; extort, wring out; **~ся** tear o.s. away; break out, break loose, break free; get away; come loose, come out; break, burst, escape; shoot up, shoot (out).

вы́|рвать[2], **-ву** *pf.*

вы́рез, -а cut; notch; décolletage. **вы́резать, -ежу** *pf.*, **выреза́ть, -а́ю** *impf.*, **выре́зы-**

вать, -аю *impf.* cut out; excise; cut, carve; engrave; slaughter, butcher. **вы́резка, -и** cutting out, excision; carving; engraving; cutting; fillet. **вырезно́й** cut; carved; low-necked, décolleté. **выре́зывание, -я** cutting out; excision; carving; engraving.

вы́рисовать, -сую *pf.*, **вырисо́вывать, -аю** *impf.* draw carefully, draw in detail; ~**ся** appear; stand out.

вы́ровнять, -яю *pf.* (*impf.* **выра́внивать**) smooth, level; straighten (out); draw up; ~**ся** become level, become even; form up; equalize; catch up, draw level; improve.

вы́родиться, -ится *pf.*, **вырожда́ться, -а́ется** *impf.* degenerate. **вы́родок, -дка** degenerate; black sheep. **вырожде́нец, -нца** degenerate. **вырожде́ние, -я** degeneration.

вы́ронить, -ню *pf.* drop.

вы́рос *etc.*: *see* **вы́расти. вы́рост, -а** growth, excrescence; offshoot. **вы́ростковый** calf.

вы́росток, -тка yearling; calf.

вы́рою *etc.*: *see* **вы́рыть**

выруба́ть, -а́ю *impf.*, **вы́рубить, -блю** *pf.* cut down, fell; hew out; cut (out); carve (out); ~**ся** cut one's way out. **вы́рубка, -и** cutting down, felling; hewing out; clearing.

вы́|ругать(ся, -аю(сь *pf.*

выру́ливать, -аю *impf.*, **вы́|рулить, -лю** *pf.* taxi.

выруча́ть, -а́ю *impf.*, **вы́ручить, -чу** *pf.* recue; help out; gain; make. **вы́ручка, -и** rescue, assistance; gain; proceeds, receipts; earnings.

вырыва́ние[1], -я pulling out, extraction; uprooting.

вырыва́ние[2], -я digging (up). **вырыва́ть[2], -а́ю** *impf.*, **вы́рыть, -рою** *pf.* dig up, dig out, unearth.

вырыва́ть[1](ся *impf. of* **вы́рвать(ся**

вы́садить, -ажу *pf.*, **выса́живать, -аю** *impf.* set down; help down; put off; detrain, debus; put ashore, land; plant out, transplant; smash; break in; ~**ся** alight, get off; land; disembark; detrain, debus. **вы́садка, -и** disembarkation; landing; transplanting, planting out.

выса́сывать, -аю *impf. of* **вы́сосать**

высве́рливать, -аю *impf.*, **вы́сверлить, -лю** *pf.* drill, bore.

вы́свободить, -божу *pf.*, **высвобожда́ть, -а́ю** *impf.* free; disengage, disentangle; release; help to escape.

высека́ть, -а́ю *impf. of* **вы́сечь[2]. вы́секу** *etc.*: *see* **вы́сечь**

выселе́нец, -нца evacuee. **выселе́ние, -я** eviction. **вы́селить, -лю** *pf.*, **выселя́ть, -я́ю** *impf.* evict; evacuate, move; ~**ся** move, remove. **вы́селок, -лка** settlement.

вы́сечка, -и carving; hewing. **вы́|сечь[1], -еку; -сек** *pf.* **вы́сечь[2], -еку; -сек** (*impf.* **высека́ть**) cut, cut out; carve; hew.

вы́сидеть, -ижу *pf.*, **выси́живать, -аю** *impf.* sit out; stay; hatch, hand out.

вы́ситься, -сится *impf.* rise, tower.

вы́сказать, -кажу *pf.*, **выска́зывать, -аю** *impf.* express; state; ~**ся** speak out; speak one's mind, have one's say; speak. **выска́зывание, -я** utterance; pronouncement, opinion.

выска́кивать, -аю *impf. of* **вы́скочить**

выска́льзывать, -аю *impf. of* **вы́скользнуть**

вы́скоблить, -лю *pf.* scrape out; erase; remove.

вы́скользнуть, -ну *pf.* (*impf.* **выска́льзывать**) slip out.

вы́скочить, -чу *pf.* (*impf.* **выска́кивать**) jump out; leap out, spring out, rush out; come up; drop out, fall out; ~ **с**+*i.* come out with. **вы́скочка, -и** upstart, parvenu.

вы́сланный *sb.* exile, deportee. **вы́слать, вы́шлю** *pf.* (*impf.* **высыла́ть**) send, send out, dispatch; exile; deport.

вы́следить, -ежу *pf.*, **высле́живать, -аю** *impf.* trace, track; stalk; shadow.

вы́слуга, -и; ~ **лет** long service. **выслу́живать, -аю** *impf.*, **вы́служить, -жу** *pf.* qualify for, earn; serve (out); ~**ся** gain promotion, be promoted; curry favour, get in (with).

вы́слушать, -аю *pf.*, **выслу́шивать, -аю** *impf.* hear out; sound; listen to. **выслу́шивание, -я** auscultation.

вы́|смолить, -лю *pf.* **вы́|сморкать(ся, -аю(сь** *pf.* **высо́вывать(ся, -аю(сь** *impf. of* **вы́сунуть(ся**

высо́кий; -о́к, -а́, -о́ко́ high; tall; lofty; elevated, sublime.

высоко... *in comb.* high-, highly. **высокоблагоро́дие, -я** (your) Honour, Worship. ~**во́льтный** high-tension. ~**го́рный** Alpine, mountain. ~**ка́чественный** high-quality. ~**ме́рие, -я** haughtiness, arrogance. ~**ме́рный** haughty, arrogant. ~**па́рный** high-flown, stilted; bombastic, turgid. ~**про́бный** sterling; standard; of high quality. ~**со́ртный** high-grade. ~**часто́тный** high-frequency.

вы́сосать, -осу *pf.* (*impf.* **выса́сывать**) suck out.

высота́, -ы́; *pl.* **-ы** height, altitude; pitch; eminence; high level; high quality. **высо́тник, -а** high-building worker; high-altitude flier. **высо́тн|ый** high; high-altitude; tall, multistorey, high-rise; ~**ое зда́ние** tower block. **высотоме́р, -а** altimeter, height-finder.

вы́|сохнуть, -ну; -ох *pf.* (*impf. also* **высыха́ть**) dry, dry out; dry up; wither, fade; waste away, fade away. **вы́сохший** dried up; shrivelled; wizened.

вы́ставить, -влю *pf.*, **выставля́ть, -я́ю** *impf.* bring out, bring forward; display, exhibit; post; put forward; adduce; put down, set down; take out, remove; send out, turn out, throw out; +*i.* represent as, make out to be; ~ **свою́ кандидату́ру** stand for election; ~**ся** lean out, thrust o.s. forward; show off. **вы́ставка, -и** exhibition, show; display;

showcase, (shop-)window. **выставно́й** removable.

вы́|стегать, -аю *pf.* **вы́стелю** *etc.*: *see* **вы́стлать. выстила́ть, -аю** *impf. of* **вы́стлать.**
вы́|стирать, -аю *pf.*

вы́стлать, -телю *pf.* (*impf.* **выстила́ть**) cover; line; pave.

вы́страдать, -аю *pf.* suffer, go through; gain through suffering.

выстра́ивать(ся, -аю(сь *impf. of* **вы́строиться. выстра́чивать, -аю** *impf. of* **вы́строчить**

вы́стрел, -а shot; report. **вы́стрелить, -лю** *pf.* shoot, fire.

вы́|строгать, -аю *pf.*

вы́строить, -ою *pf.* (*impf.* **выстра́ивать**) build; draw up, order, arrange; form up. **~ся** form up.

вы́строчить, -чу *pf.* (*impf.* **выстра́чивать**) hemstitch; stitch.

вы́стукать, -аю *pf.* **высту́кивать, -аю** *impf.* tap, percuss; tap out. **высту́кивание, -я** percussion; tapping.

вы́ступ, -а protuberance, projection, ledge; bulge, salient; lug. **выступа́ть, -а́ю** *impf.* **вы́ступить, -плю** *pf.* come forward, go forward; come out; appear; perform; speak; +**из**+*g.* go beyond, exceed; **~ из берего́в** overflow its banks; **~ с докла́дом** give a talk; **~ с ре́чью** make a speech. **высту́пление, -я** appearance, performance; speech; setting out.

вы́сунуть, -ну *pf.* (*impf.* **высо́вывать**) put out, thrust out; **~ся** show o.s., thrust o.s. forward; **~ ся в окно́** lean out of the window.

вы́|сушить(ся, -шу(сь *pf.*

вы́сш|ий highest; supreme; high; higher; **~ая то́чка** climax.

высыла́ть, -а́ю *impf. of* **вы́слать. вы́сылка, -и** sending, dispatching; expulsion, exile.

вы́сыпать, -плю *pf.*, **высыпа́ть, -а́ю** *impf.* pour out; empty (out); spill; **~ся** pour out, spill.

высыха́ть, -а́ю *impf. of* **вы́сохнуть**

высь, -и height; summit.

вытáлкивать, -аю *impf. of* **вы́толкать, вы́толкнуть. вы́|таращить, -щу** *pf.* **вытáскивать, -аю** *impf. of* **вы́тащить. вы́|тачать, -аю** *pf.* **вытáчивать, -аю** *impf. of* **вы́точить**

вы́тачка, -и tuck; dart.

вы́|тащить, -щу *pf.* (*impf. also* **вытáскивать**) drag out; pull out, extract; steal, pinch.

вы́|твердить, -ржу *pf.*

вытека́ть, -а́ю *impf.* (*pf.* **вы́течь**); **~ из**+*g.* flow from, out of; result from, follow from.

вы́|теребить, -блю *pf.*

вы́тереть, -тру; -тер *pf.* (*impf.* **вытира́ть**) wipe, wipe up; dry, rub dry; wear out.

вы́терпеть, -плю *pf.* bear, endure.

вы́тертый threadbare.

вытесне́ние, -я ousting; supplanting; displacement. **вы́теснить, -ню** *pf.*, **вытесня́ть, -я́ю** *impf.* crowd out; force out; oust; supplant; displace.

вы́течь, -чет; -ек *pf.* (*impf.* **вытека́ть**) flow out, run out.

вытира́ть, -а́ю *impf. of* **вы́тереть**

вы́тиснить, -ню *pf.*, **вытисня́ть, -я́ю** *impf.* stamp, imprint, impress.

вы́толкать, -аю *pf.*, **вы́толкнуть, -ну** *pf.* (*impf.* **вытáлкивать**) throw out, sling out; push out, force out.

вы́точенный turned; **сло́вно ~** chiselled; perfectly formed. **вы́|точить, -чу** *pf.* (*impf.*, *also* **вытáчивать**) turn; sharpen; gnaw through.

вы́|травить, -влю *pf.*, **вытра́вливать, -аю** *impf.*, **вытравля́ть, -я́ю** *impf.* exterminate, destroy, poison; remove, get out; etch; trample down, damage.

вы́требовать, -бую *pf.* summon, send for; get on demand.

вытрезви́тель, -я *m.* detoxification centre. **вы́трезвить(ся, -влю(сь** *pf.*, **вытрезвля́ть(ся, -я́ю(сь** *impf.* sober up.

вы́тру *etc.*: *see* **вы́тереть**

вытряса́ть, -а́ю *impf.*, **вы́|трясти, -су; -яс** *pf.* shake out.

вытря́хивать, -аю *impf.* **вы́тряхнуть, -ну** *pf.* shake out.

выть, во́ю *impf.* howl; wail. **вытьё, -я́** howling; wailing.

вытя́гивать, -аю *impf.*, **вы́тянуть, -ну** *pf.* stretch, stretch out; extend; draw out, extract; endure, stand, stick; weigh; **~ся** stretch, stretch out, stretch o.s.; grow, shoot up; draw o.s. up. **вы́тяжка, -и** drawing out, extraction; extract; stretching extension. **вытяжно́й** drawing; exhaust; ventilating; **~ шкаф** fume chamber.

вы́|утюжить, -жу *pf.*

выу́чивать, -аю *impf.*, **вы́|учить, -чу** *pf.* learn; teach; **~ся**+*d. or inf.* learn. **вы́учка, -и** teaching, training.

выха́живать, -аю *impf. of* **вы́ходить**

вы́хватить, -ачу *pf.*, **выхва́тывать, -аю** *impf.* snatch out, up; snatch away; pull out, draw; take out; take up.

вы́хлоп, -а exhaust.

выхлопа́тывать, -аю *impf. of* **вы́хлопотать**

выхлопно́й exhaust, discharge.

вы́хлопотать, -очу *pf.* (*impf.* **выхлопа́тывать**) obtain with much trouble.

вы́ход, -а going out; leaving, departure; way out, exit; outlet, vent; appearance; entrance; output, yield; outcrop; **все хо́ды и ~ы** all the ins and outs; **~ в отста́вку** retirement; **~ за́муж** marriage. **вы́ходец, -дца** emigrant; immigrant. **выходи́ть[1], -ожу́, -о́дишь** *impf. of* **вы́йти; +на**+*a.* look out on, give on, face.

вы́ходить[2], -ожу *pf.* (*impf.* **выха́живать**) tend, nurse; rear, bring up; grow.

вы́ходить[3], **-ожу** *pf.* (*impf.* **выха́живать**) pass through; go all over.
вы́ходка, -и trick; escapade, prank.
выходн|о́й exit, outlet; going-out, outgoing; leaving, departure, discharge; publication. issue; output; **~а́я дверь** street door; **~о́й день** day off, free day, rest-day; **~о́й лист** title-page; **~а́я роль** walking-on part; **~ы́е све́дения** imprint; **~о́й** *sb.* person off duty; day off; **~а́я** *sb.* person off duty. **вы́хожу** *etc.*: *see* **вы́ходить. выхожу́** *etc.*: *see* **выходи́ть**[1]
выхола́щивать, -аю *impf.*, **вы́холостить, -ощу** *pf.* castrate, geld; emasculate.
вы́хухоль, -я *m.* musk-rat; musquash. **вы́хухолевый** musquash.
вы́царапать, -аю *pf.*, **выцара́пывать, -аю** *impf.* scratch; scratch out; extract, get out.
вы́цвести, -ветет *pf.*, **выцвета́ть, -а́ет** *impf.* fade. **вы́цветший** faded.
вы́цедить, -ежу *pf.*, **выце́живать, -аю** *impf.* filter, rack off; strain; decant; drink off, drain.
вычека́нивать, -аю *impf.*, **вы́|чеканить, -ню** *pf.* mint; strike.
вычёркивать, -аю *impf.*, **вы́черкнуть, -ну** *pf.* cross out, strike out; expunge, erase.
вы́черпать, -аю *pf.*, **выче́рпывать, -аю** *impf.* bale out.
вы́честь, -чту; -чел, -чла *pf.* (*impf.* **вычита́ть**) subtract; deduct, keep back. **вы́чет, -а** deduction; **за ~ом** except; less, minus, allowing for.
вычисле́ние, -я calculation. **вычисли́тель, -я** *m.* calculator; plotter; computer **вычисли́тельн|ый** calculating, computing; **~ая маши́на** computer. **вы́числить, -лю** *pf.*, **вычисля́ть, -яю** *impf.* calculate, compute.
вы́|чистить, -ищу *pf.* (*impf. also* **вычища́ть**) clean, clean up, clean out; purge.
вычита́емое *sb.* subtrahend. **вычита́ние, -я** subtraction. **вычита́ть, -а́ю** *impf. of* **вы́честь**
вычища́ть, -а́ю *impf. of* **вы́чистить**
вы́чту *etc.*: *see* **вы́честь**
вы́швырнуть, -ну *pf.* **вышвы́ривать, -аю** *impf.* throw out, hurl out; chuck out.
вы́ше higher, taller; *prep.+g.* above, beyond; over; *adv.* above.
выше... *in comb.* above-, afore-. **вышеизло́женный** foregoing. **~на́званный** aforenamed. **~озна́ченный** aforesaid, above-mentioned. **~ска́занный, ~ука́занный** aforesaid. **~упомя́нутый** aforementioned.
вы́шел *etc.*: *see* **вы́йти**
вышиба́ла, -ы *m.* chucker-out, bouncer. **вышиба́ть, -а́ю** *impf.*, **вы́шибить, -бу; -иб** *pf.* knock out; chuck out.
вышива́льный embroidery. **вышива́льщица, -ы** embroideress, needlewoman. **вышива́ние, -я** embroidery, needlework. **вышива́ть, -а́ю** *impf. of* **вы́шить. вы́шивка, -и** embroidery.
вышина́, -ы́ height.
вы́шить, -шью *pf.* (*impf.* **вышива́ть**) embroider. **вы́шитый** embroidered.
вы́шка, -и turret; tower; **(бурова́я) ~** derrick.
вы́|школить, -лю *pf.* **вы́шлю** *etc.*: *see* **вы́слать. вы́шью** *etc.*: *see* **вы́шить**
вы́щипать, -плю *pf.* **вы́щипнуть, -ну** *pf.*, **выщи́пывать, -аю** *impf.* pluck out, pull out.
вы́явить, -влю *pf.*, **выявля́ть, -я́ю** *impf.* reveal; bring out; make known; display; show up, expose; **~ся** appear, come to light, be revealed. **выявле́ние, -я** revelation; showing up, exposure.
выясне́ние, -я elucidation; explanation. **вы́яснить, -ню** *pf.* **выясня́ть, -я́ю** *impf.* elucidate; clear up, explain; **~ся** become clear; turn out, prove.
Вьетна́м, -а Vietnam.
вью *etc.*: *see* **вить**
вью́га, -и snow-storm, blizzard.
вьюк, -а pack; load.
вьюно́к, -нка́ bindweed, convolvulus.
вью́чн|ый pack; **~ое живо́тное** pack animal, beast of burden; **~ая ло́шадь** pack-horse; **~ое седло́** pack-saddle.
вью́шка, -и damper.
вью́щийся creeping, climbing; curly, frizzy.
вэ *nt.indecl.* the letter **в.**
вяжу́ *etc.*: *see* **вяза́ть. вя́жущий** binding, cementing; astringent.
вяз, -а elm.
вяза́льный knitting, crochet. **вяза́ние, -я** knitting, crocheting; binding, tying. **вя́занка**[1], **-и** knitted garment. **вяза́нка**[2], **-и** bundle, truss. **вя́заный** knitted, crocheted. **вяза́нье, -я** knitting; crochet(-work). **вяза́ть, вяжу́, вя́жешь** (*impf. pf.* **с~**) tie, bind; clamp; knit, crochet; be astringent; **~ся** accord, agree; fit in, be in keeping, tally. **вя́зка, -и** tying, binding; knitting, crocheting; bunch, string.
вя́зкий; -зок, -зка́, -о viscous, glutinous, sticky; boggy; ductile, malleable; tough; astringent. **вя́знуть, -ну; вя́з(нул), -зла** *impf.* (*pf.* **за~, у~**) stick, get stuck; sink.
вя́зовый elm.
вя́зчик, -а binder. **вязь, -и** ligature; arabesque.
вял *etc.*: *see* **вя́нуть**
вя́ление, -я dry-curing; drying. **вя́леный** dried; sun-cured. **вя́лить, -лю** *impf.* (*pf.* **про~**) dry, dry-cure. **вя́лый** flabby, flaccid; limp; sluggish; inert; slack. **вя́нуть, -ну; вял** *impf.* (*pf.* **за~, у~**) fade, wither; droop, flag.

Г

г *letter*: *see* **гэ**

г *abbr.* (*of* **грамм**) g, gr, gram(me)(s).

г. *abbr.* (*of* **год**) year; (*of* **гора́**) Mt., mountain; (*of* **го́род**) city, town; (*of* **господи́н**) Mr.

га *abbr.* (*of* **гекта́р**) ha., hectare.

габари́т, -а clearance; clearance diagram; size, dimension. **габари́тн|ый** clearance; overall; **~ые воро́та** loading gauge; **~ая высота́** headroom.

га́вань, -и harbour.

га́врик, -а (*sl.*) petty crook; man, fellow, mate.

га́га, -и eider(-duck).

гага́ра, -ы loon, diver. **гага́рка, -и** razorbill.

гага́т, -а jet.

гага́чий eider-; **~ пух** eiderdown.

гад, -а reptile, amphibian; vile creature; *pl.* vermin.

гада́лка, -и fortune-teller. **гада́ние, -я** fortune-telling, divination; guess-work. **гада́тельный** fortune-telling; problematical, conjectural, hypothetical. **гада́ть, -а́ю** *impf.* (*pf.* **по~**) tell fortunes; guess, conjecture, surmise.

га́дина, -ы reptile; vile creature; *pl.* vermin. **га́дить, га́жу** *impf.* (*pf.* **на~**) +**в**+*p.*, **на**+*a.* foul, dirty, defile. **га́дкий; -док, -дка́, -о** nasty, vile, foul, loathsome; **~ утёнок** ugly duckling. **гадли́вость, -и** aversion, disgust. **гадли́вый** of disgust, disgusted. **га́дость, -и** filth, muck; dirty trick; *pl.* filthy expressions. **гадю́ка, -и** adder, viper; repulsive person.

га́ер, -а buffoon, clown. **га́ерничать, -аю** *impf.*, **га́ерствовать, -твую** *impf.* clown, play the fool.

га́ечный nut; **~ ключ** spanner, wrench.

га́же *comp. of* **га́дкий**

газ[1], -а gauze.

газ[2], -а (-у) gas; wind; **дать ~** step on the gas; **сба́вить ~** reduce speed; **на по́лном га́зе** at top speed. **газану́ть, -ну́, -нёшь** *pf.* (*impf.* **газова́ть**) accelerate; scram. **газа́ция, -и** aeration. **газго́льдер, -а** gasholder.

газе́ль, -и gazelle.

газе́та, -ы newspaper, paper. **газе́тный** newspaper, news. **газе́тчик, -а, -чица, -ы** journalist; newspaper-seller.

газиро́ванный aerated. **гази́ровать, -рую** *impf.* aerate. **газиро́вка, -и** aeration; aerated water. **газова́ть, -зу́ю** *impf.* (*pf.* **газану́ть**) accelerate, step on it; scram. **га́зовый[1]** gas; **~ счётчик** gas-meter.

га́зовый[2] gauze.

газокали́льный incandescent. **газоли́н, -а** gasolene. **газоме́р, -а** gas-meter.

газо́н, -а lawn, turf, grass. **газонокоси́лка, -и** lawn-mower.

газообра́зный gaseous. **газопрово́д, -а** gas pipeline; gas-main. **газопрово́дный** gas.

ГАИ *abbr.* (*of* ***Госуда́рственная автомоби́льная инспе́кция***) State Motor-vehicle Inspectorate.

га́йка, -и nut; female screw.

гала́ктика, -и galaxy.

галантере́йный haberdasher's, haberdashery. **галантере́я, -и** haberdashery, fancy goods.

галанти́р, -а galantine.

галдёж, -а́ din, racket, row. **галде́ть, -ди́шь** *impf.* make a din, make a row.

гале́ра, -ы galley.

галере́я, -и gallery. **галёрка, -и** gallery, gods.

га́лечник, -а shingle, pebbles.

галифе́ *indecl. pl.* riding-breeches; jodhpurs.

га́лка, -и jackdaw, daw.

галл, -а Gaul. **га́лльский** Gaulish; Gallic.

гало́п, -а gallop; galop. **галопи́ровать, -рую** *impf.* gallop.

га́лочий jackdaw's, daw's. **га́лочка, -и** tick.

гало́ша, -и galosh.

галс, -а tack.

га́лстук, -а tie; neckerchief.

галу́шка, -и dumpling.

га́лька, -и pebble; pebbles, shingle.

гам, -а (-у) din, uproar.

гама́к, -а́ hammock.

га́мбургер, -а (ham)burger. **га́мбургерная** *sb.* burger bar.

га́мма, -ы scale; gamut; range.

гангре́н, -а gangrene. **гангрено́зный** gangrenous.

гандбо́л, -а handball. **гандболи́ст, -а** handball-player.

ганте́ль, -и dumb-bell.

гара́ж, -а́ garage.

гаранти́ровать, -рую *impf.* & *pf.* guarantee, vouch for. **гара́нтия, -и** guarantee; safeguard.

гардеро́б, -а wardrobe; cloakroom. **гардеро́бная** *sb.* cloakroom. **гардеро́бщик, -а, -щица, -ы** cloakroom attendant.

гарди́на, -ы curtain.

гарев|о́й, га́рев|ый cinder; **~ая доро́жка** cinder track, cinder-path.

га́ркать, -аю *impf.*, **га́ркнуть, -ну** *pf.* shout, bark.

гармо́ника, -и accordion, concertina; pleats; **гармо́никой** (accordion-)pleated, in pleats. **гармони́ческий** harmonic; harmonious; rhythmic. **гармони́чный** harmonious. **гармо́ния, -и** harmony; concord; accordion,

concertina. **гармо́нь, -и, гармо́шка, -и** accordion, concertina.
гарнизо́н, -а garrison.
гарни́р, -а garnish; trimmings; vegetables.
гарниту́р, -а set; suite.
гарпу́н, -а́ harpoon.
гарт, -а type-metal.
гарь, -и burning; cinders, ashes.
гаси́льник, -а extinguisher, **гаси́тель, -я** *m.* extinguisher; damper; suppressor. **гаси́ть, гашу́, га́сишь** *impf.* (*pf.* **за~, по~**) put out, extinguish; slake; suppress, stifle; cancel; liquidate. **га́снуть, -ну; гас** *impf.* (*pf.* **за~, по~, у~**) be extinguished, go out; grow dim; sink.
гастролёр, -а, -ёрша, -и guest-artist; touring actor, actress; casual worker. **гастроли́ровать, -рую** *impf.* tour, be on tour. **гастро́ль, -и** tour; guest-appearance, performance; temporary engagement.
гастроно́м, -а gourmet; grocery, grocer's (shop). **гастрономи́ческий** gastronomic; provision. **гастроно́мия, -и** gastronomy; provisions; delicatessen.
га́убица, -ы howitzer.
гауптва́хта, -ы guardhouse, guardroom.
гаше́ние, -я extinguishing; slaking; cancellation, suppression. **гашёный** slaked.
гаше́тка, -и trigger; button.
гварде́ец, -е́йца guardsman. **гварде́йский** guards. **гва́рдия, -и** Guards.
гво́здик, -а tack; stiletto heel. **гвозди́ка, -и** pink(s), carnation(s); cloves. **гвоздь, -я́**; *pl.* **-и, -е́й** *m.* nail; tack; peg; crux; highlight, hit.
гг. *abbr.* (*of* **го́ды**) years.
где *adv.* where; somewhere; anywhere; how; **~ бы ни** wherever; **~ мне знать?** how should I know? **где́-либо** *adv.* anywhere. **где́-нибудь** *adv.* somewhere; anywhere. **где́-то** *adv.* somewhere.
ГДР *abbr.* **Герма́нская Демократи́ческая Респу́блика** German Democratic Republic.
гекта́р, -а hectare. **гекто...** *in comb.* hecto-.
ге́лий, -я helium.
геморро́й, -я haemorrhoids, piles.
гемофили́я, -и haemophilia.
ген, -а gene.
ген... *abbr.* (*of* **генера́льный**) *in comb.* general.
генеалоги́ческий genealogical. **генеало́гия, -и** genealogy.
генера́л, -а general; **~-губерна́тор** governor-general. **генералите́т, -а** generals; high command. **генера́льн|ый** general; radical, basic; **~ая репети́ция** dress rehearsal. **генера́льский** general's. **генера́льша, -и** general's wife.
генера́тор, -а generator. **генера́ция, -и** generation; oscillation.
гениа́льный of genius, great; brilliant. **ге́ний, -я** genius.
гео... *in comb.* geo-. **гео́граф, -а** geographer. **~графи́ческий** geographical. **~гра́фия, -и** geography. **гео́лог, -а** geologist. **~логи́ческий** geological. **~ло́гия, -и** geology. **гео́метр, -а** geometrician. **~метри́ческий** geometric, geometrical. **~ме́трия, -и** geometry.
георги́н, -а, георги́на, -ы dahlia.
гепа́рд, -а cheetah.
гера́нь, -и geranium.
герб, -а́ arms, coat of arms. **ге́рбов|ый** heraldic; bearing coat of arms; stamped; **~ая печа́ть** official stamp; **~ый сбор** stamp-duty.
геркуле́с, -а Hercules; rolled oats. **геркуле́совский** Herculean.
герма́нец, -нца Teuton, German. **Герма́ния, -и** Germany. **герма́нский** Germanic, Teutonic; German.
герметический, гермети́чный hermetic, secret; hermetically sealed, air-tight, water-tight, pressurized.
герои́зм, -а heroism. **геро́ика, -и** heroics; heroic spirit; heroic style. **герои́ня, -и** heroine. **герои́ческий** heroic. **геро́й, -я** hero. **геро́йский** heroic. **геро́йство, -а** heroism.
герц, -а; *g.pl.* **герц** hertz.
гетеросексуа́льный heterosexual.
ге́тман, -а hetman.
г-жа *abbr.* (*of* **госпожа́**) Mrs.; Miss; Ms.
гиаци́нт, -а hyacinth; jacinth.
ги́бель, -и death; destruction, ruin; loss; wreck; downfall. **ги́бельный** disastrous, fatal.
ги́бк|ий; -бок, -бка́, -бко flexible, pliant; floppy; lithe; adaptable, versatile, resourceful; tractable; **~ий диск** (*comput.*) floppy (disk). **ги́бкость, -и** flexibility, pliancy; suppleness.
ги́бнуть, -ну; ги́б(нул) *impf.* (*pf.* **по~**) perish.
Гибралта́р, -а Gibraltar.
гига́нт, -а giant. **гига́нтский** gigantic.
гигие́на, -ы hygiene. **гигиени́ческ|ий** hygienic, sanitary; **~ая повя́зка** sanitary towel; **~ая бума́га** toilet paper.
гид, -а guide.
гидро... *pf.* hydro-. **гидро́лиз, -а** hydrolysis. **~о́кись, -и** hydroxide. **~ста́нция, -и** hydro-electric power-station. **~те́хник, -а** hydraulic engineer. **~те́хника, -и** hydraulic engineering. **~фо́н, -а** hydrophone.
гие́на, -ы hyena.
гик, -а whoop, whooping. **ги́кать, -аю** *impf.*, **ги́кнуть, -ну** *pf.* whoop.
ги́льдия, -и guild.
ги́льза, -ы case; cartridge-case; sleeve; liner; (cigarette-)wrapper.
Гимала́и, -ев *pl.* the Himalayas.
гимн, -а hymn.
гимнази́ст, -а, -и́стка, -и grammar-school or high-school pupil. **гимна́зия, -и** grammar school, high school.
гимна́стика, -и gymnastics.
гипно́з, -а hypnosis. **гипнотизёр, -а** hypnotist. **гипнотизи́ровать, -рую** *impf.* (*pf.* **за~**) hypnotize. **гипноти́зм, -а** hypnotism.

гипноти́ческий hypnotic.
гипо́теза, -ы hypothesis. **гипотети́ческий, гипотети́чный** hypothetical.
гиппопота́м, -а hippopotamus.
гипс, -а gypsum, plaster of Paris; plaster; plaster cast. **ги́псовый** plaster.
гиреви́к, -а́ weight-lifter.
гирля́нда, -ы garland.
ги́ря, -и weight.
гита́ра, -ы guitar.
гл. *abbr.* (*of* **глава́**) chapter.
глав... (*abbr. of* **гла́вный**) *in comb.* head, chief, main; **гла́вное управле́ние** central administration, central board. **главбу́х, -а** chief accountant. **главк, -а** chief directorate; central committee, central administration. **~ре́ж, -а** head producer, chief director.
глава́, -ы́; *pl.* **-ы** head; chief; chapter; cupola. **глава́рь, -я́** *m.* leader, ring-leader. **главе́нство, -а** supremacy. **главе́нствовать, -твую** *impf.* be in command, lead, dominate. **главнокома́ндующий** *sb.* commander-in-chief. **гла́вн|ый** chief, main, principal; head, senior; **~ая кни́га** ledger; **~ый нерв** nerve-centre; **~ым о́бразом** chiefly, mainly, for the most part; **~ое** *sb.* the chief thing, the main thing; the essentials; **и са́мое ~ое** and above all.
глаго́л, -а verb; word. **глаго́льный** verbal.
глади́льный ironing. **гла́дить, -а́жу** *impf.* (*pf.* **вы́~, по~**) stroke; iron, press. **гла́дкий** smooth; sleek; plain; fluent, facile. **гла́дко** *adv.* smoothly; swimmingly; **~ вы́бритый** clean-shaven. **гладь, -и** smooth surface; satin-stitch. **гла́же** *comp. of* **гла́дкий, гла́дко. гла́женье, -я** ironing.
глаз, -а (-у), *loc.* **-у́**; *pl.* **-а́, глаз** eye; eyesight; **в ~а́** to one's face; **за ~а́**+*g.* in the absence of, behind the back of; **на ~а́, на ~а́х** before one's eyes; **с ~у на ~** without witnesses; **смотре́ть во все ~а́** be all eyes. **глаза́стый** big-eyed; quick-sighted.
глазиро́ванный glazed; glossy; iced, glacé. **глазирова́ть, -ру́ю** *impf. & pf.* glaze; candy; ice. **глазиро́вка, -и** glazing; icing.
глazни́к, -а́ oculist. **глазни́ца, -ы** eye-socket. **глазно́й** eye; optic; **~ врач** oculist, eye-specialist.
глазу́нья, -и fried eggs.
глазу́рь, -и glaze; syrup; icing.
гла́нда, -ы gland; tonsil.
глас, -а voice. **гласи́ть, -си́т** *impf.* announce; say, run. **гла́сность, -и** publicity; glasnost, openness. **гла́сный** open, public; vowel, vocalic; *sb.* vowel. **глаша́тай, -я** crier; herald.
гле́тчер, -а glacier.
гли́на, -ы clay. **гли́нистый** clay; clayey, argillaceous. **глинозём, -а** alumina. **гли́нян|ый** clay; earthenware, pottery; clayey; **~ая посу́да** earthenware.
гли́ссер, -а speed-boat; hydroplane.
глоба́льный global; (*fig.*) extensive.
гл. обр. *abbr.* (*of* **гла́вным о́бразом**) chiefly, mainly.
гло́бус, -а globe.
глода́ть, -ожу́, -о́жешь *impf.* gnaw.
глота́ть, -а́ю *impf.* swallow. **гло́тка, -и** gullet; throat. **глото́к, -тка́** gulp; mouthful.
гло́хнуть, -ну; глох *impf.* (*pf.* **за~, о~**) become deaf; die away, subside; decay; die; grow wild, become a wilderness, run to seed.
глу́бже *comp. of* **глубо́кий, глубоко́. глубина́, -ы́**; *pl.* **-ы** depth; depths, deep places; heart, interior; recesses; profundity; intensity. **глуби́нный** deep; deep-laid; deep-sea; depth; remote, out-of-the-way. **глубо́к|ий; -о́к, -а́, -о́ко́** deep; profound; intense; thorough, thorough-going; considerable, serious; late, advanced, extreme; **~ий вира́ж** steep turn; **~ой о́сенью** in the late autumn; **~ая ста́рость** extreme old age; **~ая таре́лка** soup-plate. **глубоко́** *adv.* deep; deeply, profoundly. **глубоково́дный** deep-water, deep-sea. **глубокомы́слие, -я** profundity; perspicacity. **глубоме́р, -а** depth gauge. **глубоча́йший** *superl. of* **глубо́кий. глубь, -и** depth; (the) depths.
глуми́ться, -млю́сь *impf.* mock, jeer (**над**+*i.* at). **глумле́ние, -я** mockery; gibe, jeer. **глумли́вый** mocking; gibing, jeering.
глупе́ть, -е́ю *impf.* (*pf.* **по~**) grow stupid. **глупе́ц, -пца́** fool, blockhead. **глупи́ть, -плю́** *impf.* (*pf.* **с~**) make a fool of o.s.; do something foolish. **глупова́тый** silly; rather stupid. **глу́пость, -и** foolishness, stupidity; nonsense; **глу́пости!** (stuff and) nonsense! **глу́пый; глуп, -а́, -о** foolish, stupid, silly.
глуха́рь, -я́ *m.* capercailzie; deaf person; coach screw. **глухова́тый** somewhat deaf, hard of hearing. **глухо́й; глух, -а́, -о** muffled, confused, indistinct; obscure, vague; voiceless; thick, dense; wild; remote, lonely, deserted; god-forsaken; sealed; blank, blind; buttoned up, done up; not open; late; **~а́я крапи́ва** dead-nettle; **~о́й, ~а́я** *sb.* deaf man, deaf woman. **глухонемо́й** deaf and dumb; *sb.* deaf mute. **глухота́, -ы́** deafness. **глу́ше** *comp. of* **глухо́й. глуши́лка, -и** jamming, jammer. **глуши́тель, -я** *m.* silencer, damper; suppressor; jammer. **глуши́ть, -шу́** *impf.* (*pf.* **за~, о~**) stun, stupefy; muffle; dull, deaden, damp; drown, jam; switch off; put out, extinguish; choke; stifle; suppress; soak up, swill. **глушь, -и** backwoods; solitary place.
глы́ба, -ы clod; lump, block.
гляде́ть, -яжу́ *impf.* (*pf.* **по~, гля́нуть**) look, gaze; heed, take notice; look for, seek; show, appear; **+за**+*i.* look after, see to; **+на**+*a.* look on (to), give on (to), face; take example from, imitate; +*i. or adv.* look, look like; **~ в о́ба** be on one's guard; **~ ко́со на** take a poor view of; **гляди́(те)** mind (out); **(того́ и) гляди́** it looks as if; I'm afraid; at any moment; **гля́дя по**+*d.* depending on; **не**

гля́дя на+*a.* unmindful of, heedless of; **~ся** look at o.s.
гля́нец, -нца gloss, lustre; polish.
гля́нуть, -ну *pf.* (*impf.* **гляде́ть**) glance.
глянцеви́тый glossy, lustrous.
гм *int.* hm!
г-н *abbr.* (*of* **господи́н**) Mr.
гнать, гоню́, го́нишь; гнал, -á, -o *impf.* drive; urge (on); whip up; drive hard; dash, tear; hunt, chase; persecute; turn out; distil; **~ся за**+*i.* pursue; strive for, strive after; keep up with.
гнев, -а anger, rage; wrath. **гне́ваться, -аюсь** *impf.* (*pf.* **раз~**) be angry. **гневи́ть, -влю** *impf.* (*pf.* **про~**) anger, enrage. **гневли́вый** irascible. **гне́вный** angry, irate.
гнедо́й bay.
гнезди́ться, -зжу́сь *impf.* nest, build a nest; roost; have its seat; be lodged. **гнездо́, -á**; *pl.* **гнёзда** nest; eyrie; den, lair; brood; cluster; socket; seat; housing. **гнездова́ние, -я** nesting.
гнести́, -ету́, -етёшь *impf.* oppress, weigh down; press. **гнёт, -а** press; weight; oppression. **гнету́щий** oppressive.
гни́да, -ы nit.
гние́ние, -я decay, putrefaction, rot. **гнило́й; -ил, -á, -o** rotten; decayed; putrid; corrupt; damp, muggy. **гнить, -ию́, -иёшь; -ил, -á, -o** *impf.* (*pf.* **с~**) rot, decay; decompose. **гное́ние, -я** suppuration. **гнои́ть, -ою́** *impf.* (*pf.* **с~**) let rot, leave to rot; allow to decay; **~ся** suppurate, discharge matter. **гной, -я (-ю)**, *loc.* **-ю́** pus, matter. **гнойни́к, -á** abscess; ulcer. **гно́йный** purulent.
гнуса́вить, -влю *impf.* talk, speak, through one's nose. **гнуса́вость, -и** nasal twang. **гнуса́вый, гнусли́вый** nasal.
гну́сный; -сен, -сна́, -o vile, foul.
гну́т|ый bent; **~ая ме́бель** bentwood furniture. **гнуть, гну, гнёшь** *impf.* (*pf.* **со~**) bend, bow; drive at, aim at; **~ся** bend; be bowed; stoop; be flexible. **гнутьё, -я́** bending.
гнуша́ться, -а́юсь *impf.* (*pf.* **по~**) disdain; +*g.* *or i.* shun; abhor, have an aversion to.
гобеле́н, -а tapestry.
гобои́ст, -а oboist. **гобо́й, -я** oboe.
гове́нье, -я fasting. **гове́ть, -е́ю** *impf.* fast.
говно́, -á shit.
го́вор, -а sound of voices; murmur, babble; talk, rumour; pronunciation, accent; dialect. **говори́льня, -и** talking-shop. **говори́ть, -рю́** *impf.* (*pf.* **сказа́ть**) speak, talk; say; tell; mean, convey, signify; point, testify; **говори́т Москва́** this is Moscow; **~ в по́льзу**+*g.* tell in favour of; support, back; **не говоря́ уже́ о**+*p.* not to mention; **не́чего (и) ~** it goes without saying, needless to say; **что и ~** it can't be denied; **~ся; как говори́тся** as they say, as the saying goes. **говорли́вый** garrulous, talkative. **говору́н, -á, -ру́нья, -и** talker, chatterer, chatterbox.
говя́дина, -ы beef. **говя́жий** beef.
го́гот, -а cackle; shouts of laughter. **гогота́нье, -я** cackling. **гогота́ть, -очу́, -о́чешь** *impf.* cackle; laugh aloud, shout with laughter.
год, -а (-у), *loc.* **-у́**; *pl.* **-ы** *or* **-á**, *g.* **-о́в** *or* **лет** year; *pl.* years, age, time; **бе́з ~у неде́ля** only a few days; **в ~ы** in the days (of), during; **в ~áх** advanced in years, getting on; **~ от ~у** every year; **из ~а в ~** year in, year out; **не по ~áм** beyond one's years, precocious(ly). **года́ми** *adv.* for years (on end). **годи́на, -ы** time; period; year.
годи́ться, -жу́сь *impf.* be fit, suitable, suited; do, serve; +**в**+*nom. or a.* be cut out for, be old enough to be; **не годи́тся** it's no good, it won't do; +*inf.* it does not do to, one should not.
годи́чный lasting a year, a year's; annual, yearly.
го́дный; -ден, -дна́, -о, -ы *or* **-ы́** fit, suitable, valid.
годова́лый a year-old; yearling. **годови́к, -á** yearling. **годово́й** annual, yearly. **годовщи́на, -ы** anniversary.
гожу́сь *etc.*: *see* **годи́ться**
гол, -а goal.
гола́вль, -я́ *m.* chub.
голена́ст|ый long-legged; **~ые** *sb., pl.* wading birds. **голени́ще, -а** (boot-)top. **го́лень, -и** shin.
голла́ндец, -дца Dutchman. **Голла́ндия, -и** Holland. **голла́ндка, -и** Dutchwoman; tiled stove; jumper. **голла́ндск|ий** Dutch; **~ая печь** tiled stove; **~ое полотно́** Holland.
голова́, -ы́, *a.* **го́лову**; *pl.* **го́ловы, -о́в, -а́м** head; brain, mind; wits; life; van; *c.g.* person in charge, head; **в пе́рвую го́лову** first of all; **городско́й ~** mayor; **~ сы́ру** a cheese; **на свою́ го́лову** to one's cost; **с головы́** per head. **голова́стик, -а** tadpole. **голо́вка, -и** head; cap, nose, tip; head-scarf; *pl.* vamp. **головн|о́й** head; brain, cerebral; leading, advance; **~а́я боль** headache; **~о́й го́лос** head-voice, falsetto; **~о́й мозг** brain, cerebrum; **~о́й убо́р** headgear, headdress. **головокруже́ние, -я** giddiness, dizziness; vertigo. **головокружи́тельный** dizzy, giddy. **головоло́мка, -и** puzzle, riddle, conundrum. **головоло́мный** puzzling. **головомо́йка, -и** reprimand, dressing-down, telling-off. **головоре́з, -а** cut-throat; bandit; blackguard, ruffian, rascal. **головотя́п, -а** bungler, muddler.
го́лод, -а (-у) hunger; starvation; famine; dearth, acute shortage. **голода́ние, -я** starvation; fasting. **голода́ть, -а́ю** *impf.* go hungry, hunger, starve; fast, go without food. **голо́дный; го́лоден, -дна́, -о, -ы** *or* **-ы́** hungry; hunger, starvation; meagre, scanty, poor. **голодо́вка, -и** starvation; hunger-strike.
голоно́гий bare-legged; bare-foot.
го́лос, -а (-у); *pl.* **-á, -о́в** voice; part; word,

opinion; say; vote; **во весь ~** at the top of one's voice; **пода́ть ~ за**+*a.* vote for; **пра́во ~а** vote, suffrage, franchise; **с ~а** by ear. **голоси́стый** loud-voiced; vociferous; loud. **голоси́ть, -ошу́** *impf.* sing loudly; cry; wail, keen.

голосло́вный unsubstantiated, unfounded; unsupported by evidence.

голосова́ние, -я voting; poll; hitching lifts, hitch-hiking; **всео́бщее ~** universal suffrage. **голосова́ть, -су́ю** *impf.* (*pf.* **про~**) vote; put to the vote, vote on; hitch lifts, hitch-hike. **голосово́й** vocal.

голошта́нник, -а ragamuffin.

голубе́ть, -е́ет *impf.* (*pf.* **по~**) turn blue, show blue. **голубизна́, -ы́** blueness. **голу́бка, -и** pigeon; (my) dear, darling. **голуб|о́й** blue; light blue, pale blue; gay, homosexual; **~о́е то́пливо** natural gas; **~о́й экра́н** television screen. **голу́бчик, -а** my dear, my dear fellow; darling. **го́лубь, -я**; *pl.* **-и, -е́й** *m.* pigeon, dove. **голубя́тник, -а** pigeon-fancier; dovecot. **голубя́тня, -и**; *g.pl.* **-тен** dovecot, pigeon-loft.

го́лый; гол, -ла́, -ло naked, bare; poor; unmixed, unadorned; pure, neat. **голытьба́, -ы́** the poor. **голы́ш, -а́** naked child, naked person; pauper; pebble, smooth round stone. **голышо́м** *adv.* stark naked. **голя́к, -а́** beggar, tramp.

гомеопа́т, -а homoeopath. **гомеопати́ческий** homoeopathic. **гомеопа́тия, -и** homoeopathy.

гомоге́нный homogeneous.

го́мон, -а (-у) hubbub. **гомони́ть, -ню́** *impf.* shout, talk noisily.

гомосексуали́ст, -а homosexual, gay. **гомосексуа́льный** homosexual, gay.

гондо́ла, -ы gondola; car; nacelle.

гоне́ние, -я persecution. **гони́тель, -я** *m.*, **~ница, -ы** persecutor. **го́нка, -и** race; dashing, rushing; haste, hurry. **го́нкий; -нок, -нка́, -нко** fast, swift; fast-growing.

Гонко́нг, -а Hong Kong.

гонора́р, -а fee.

го́ночный racing.

гонча́р, -а́ potter.

го́нщик, -а racer; drover. **гоню́** *etc.*: *see* **гнать. гоня́ть, -я́ю** *impf.* drive; send on errands; **~ся** race; +**за**+*i.* chase, pursue, hunt.

гор... *abbr.* (*of* **городско́й**) *in comb.* city, town. **горсове́т, -а** city soviet, town soviet.

гора́, -ы́, *a.* **го́ру**; *pl.* **го́ры, -а́м** mountain; hill; heap, pile, mass; **в го́ру** uphill; **по́д гору** downhill.

гора́здо *adv.* much, far, by far.

горб, -а́, *loc.* **-у́** hump; protuberance, bulge. **горба́тый** humpbacked, hunchbacked; **~ нос** hooked nose. **го́рбить, -блю** *impf.* (*pf.* **с~**) arch, hunch; **~ся** stoop, become bent. **горбоно́сый** hook-nosed. **горбу́н, -а́** *m.*, **горбу́нья, -и**; *g.pl.* **-ний** humpback, hunchback. **горбу́шка, -и**; *g.pl.* **-шек** crust, heel of loaf.

гордели́вый haughty, proud. **горди́ться, -ржу́сь** *impf.* put on airs, be haughty; +*i.* be proud of, pride o.s. on. **го́рдость, -и** pride. **го́рдый; горд, -а́, -о, го́рды́** proud. **горды́ня, -и** pride, arrogance.

го́ре, -я grief, sorrow; distress; woe; misfortune, trouble. **горева́ть, -рю́ю** *impf.* grieve, mourn.

горе́лка, -и burner. **горе́лый** burnt. **горе́ние, -я** burning, combustion; enthusiasm.

го́рестный sad, sorrowful; pitiful, mournful. **го́ресть, -и** sorrow, grief; *pl.* afflictions, misfortunes, troubles.

горе́ть, -рю́ *impf.* (*pf.* **с~**) burn; be on fire, be alight; glitter, shine.

го́рец, -рца mountain-dweller, highlander.

го́речь, -и bitterness; bitter taste; bitter stuff.

горизо́нт, -а horizon; skyline. **горизонта́ль, -и** horizontal; contour line.

го́ристый mountainous, hilly. **го́рка, -и** hill; hillock; steep climb.

горла́н, -а bawler. **горла́нить, -ню** *impf.* bawl, yell. **горла́стый** noisy, loud-mouthed. **го́рло, -а** throat; neck. **горлово́й** throat; of the throat; guttural; raucous. **го́рлышко, -а** neck.

горн[1], **-а** furnace, forge.

горн[2], **-а** bugle. **горни́ст, -а** bugler.

го́рничная *sb.* maid, chambermaid; stewardess.

горново́й furnace, forge; *sb.* furnaceman. **горнозаво́дский** mining and metallurgical. **горнопромы́шленность, -и** mining industry. **горнопромы́шленный** mining. **горнорабо́чий** *sb.* miner.

горноста́евый ermine. **горноста́й, -я** ermine.

го́рный mountain; mountainous; mineral; mining; **~ лён** asbestos; **~ хруста́ль** rock crystal.

го́род, -а; *pl.* **-а́** town; city; base, home. **городи́ть, -ожу́, -о́дишь** *impf.* fence, enclose; **~ глу́пости** talk nonsense; **огоро́д ~** make a fuss. **городово́й** *sb.* policeman. **городск|о́й** urban; city; municipal; **~а́я ла́сточка** (house-)martin. **го́род-спу́тник, -а** satellite town. **горожа́нин, -а**; *pl.* **-а́не, -а́н** *m.*, **-жа́нка, -и** town-dweller; townsman, townswoman.

горо́х, -а (-у) pea, peas. **горо́ховый** pea. **горо́шек, -шка** spotted design (*on material*), polka dots; **души́стый ~** sweet peas; **зелёный ~** green peas. **горо́шина, -ы** pea.

го́рсточка, -и, горсть, -и; *g.pl.* **-е́й** handful.

горта́нный guttural; laryngeal. **горта́нь, -и** larynx.

го́рче *comp. of* **го́рький. горчи́ть, -чи́т** *impf.* taste bitter. **горчи́ца, -ы** mustard. **горчи́чник, -а** mustard plaster. **горчи́чница, -ы** mustard-pot.

горшо́к, -шка́ pot; chamber-pot.

го́рький; -рек, -рька́, -о bitter; rancid; hapless, wretched.

горю́ч|ий combustible, inflammable; **~ее** *sb.* fuel. **горю́чка, -и** motor fuel.

горячело́мкий hot-short. **горя́чий; -ря́ч, -а́** hot; passionate; ardent, fervent; hot-tempered; mettlesome; heated; impassioned; busy; high-temperature.

горячи́ть, -чу́ *impf.* (*pf.* **раз~**) excite, irritate; **~ся** get excited, become impassioned. **горя́чка, -и** fever; feverish activity; feverish haste; *c.g.* hothead; firebrand; **поро́ть горя́чку** hurry, bustle; rush headlong. **горя́чность, -и** zeal, fervour, enthusiasm.

гос... *abbr.* (*of* **госуда́рственный**) *in comb.* state. **Госдепарта́мент, -а** State Department. **~пла́н, -а** State Planning Commission (*in former USSR*). **~стра́х** State Insurance.

го́спиталь, -я *m.* (military) hospital.

го́споди *int.* good Lord! good gracious! **господи́н, -а**; *pl.* **-ода́, -о́д, -а́м** master; gentleman; Mr.; Messrs. **госпо́дский** seigniorial, manorial; **~ дом** manor-house; the big house. **госпо́дство, -а** supremacy, dominion, mastery; predominance. **госпо́дствовать, -твую** *impf.* hold sway, exercise dominion; predominate, prevail; **~ над**+*i.* command, dominate; tower above. **госпо́дствующий** ruling; predominant, prevailing; commanding. **Госпо́дь, Го́спода,** *voc.* **Го́споди** *m.* God, the Lord. **госпожа́, -и́** mistress; lady; Mrs., Miss, Ms.

гостево́й guest, guests'. **гостеприи́мный** hospitable. **гостеприи́мство, -а** hospitality. **гости́ная** *sb.* drawing-room, sitting-room; drawing-room suite. **гости́ница, -ы** hotel; inn. **гости́ный; ~ двор** arcade, bazaar. **гости́ть, гощу́** *impf.* stay, be on a visit. **гость, -я**; *g.pl.* **-е́й** *m.*, **го́стья, -и**; *g.pl.* **-ий** guest, visitor.

госуда́рственный State, public. **госуда́рство, -а** State. **госуда́рыня, -и, госуда́рь, -я** *m.* sovereign; Your Majesty.

гот, -а Goth. **готи́ческий** Gothic; **~ шрифт** Gothic (type), black letter.

гото́вить, -влю *impf.* (*pf.* **с~**) prepare, get ready; train; cook; lay in, store; have in store; **~ся** get ready; prepare o.s., make preparations; be at hand, brewing, impending, imminent; loom ahead. **гото́вность, -и** readiness, preparedness, willingness. **гото́в|ый** ready, prepared; willing; on the point, on the verge; ready-made, finished; tight, plastered; **на всём ~ом** and all found.

гофриро́ванный corrugated; crimped, waved; pleated; goffered. **гофрирова́ть, -ру́ю** *impf.* & *pf.* corrugate; wave, crimp; goffer. **гофриро́вка, -и** corrugation; goffering; waving; waves.

гр. *abbr.* (*of* **граждани́н, гражда́нка**) citizen.

граб, -а hornbeam.

грабёж, -а́ robbery; pillage, plunder. **граби́тель, -я** *m.* robber. **граби́тельский** extortionate, exorbitant. **граби́тельство, -а** robbery. **гра́бить, -блю** *impf.* (*pf.* **о~**) rob, pillage. **гра́бленый** stolen.

гра́бли, -бель *or* **-блей** *pl.* rake.

гра́бовый hornbeam.

гравёр, -а, гравиро́вщик, -а engraver, etcher. **гравёрный** engraver's, etcher's; engraving, etching.

гра́вий, -я gravel. **грави́йный** gravel.

гравирова́льный engraving, etching. **гравирова́ть, -ру́ю** *impf.* (*pf.* **вы́~**) engrave; etch. **гравиро́вка, -и** engraving, print; etching. **гравю́ра, -ы** engraving, print; etching; **~ на де́реве** woodcut; **~ на лино́лиуме** linocut.

град[1], -а city, town.

град[2], -а hail; shower, torrent; volley; **~ом** thick and fast. **гра́дина, -ы** hailstone.

гради́рня, -и salt-pan; cooling-tower. **гради́ровать, -рую** *impf.* & *pf.* evaporate.

градово́й hail. **гра́дом** *see* **град**

градострои́тель, -я *m.* town-planner. **градострои́тельный, градострои́тельство, -а** town planning.

гра́дус, -а degree; pitch; stage. **гра́дусник, -а** thermometer. **гра́дусн|ый** degree; grade; **~ая се́тка** grid.

граждани́н, -а; *pl.* **гра́ждане, -дан, гражда́нка, -и** citizen. **гражда́нский** civil; citizens'; civic; secular; civilian. **гражда́нство, -а** citizenship, nationality.

грамза́пись, -и gramophone recording.

грамм, -а gram(me).

грамма́тик, -а grammarian. **грамма́тика, -и** grammar; grammar-book. **граммати́ческий** grammatical.

гра́мота, -ы ability to read and write, reading and writing; official document; deed. **гра́мотность, -и** literacy. **гра́мотный** literate; grammatically correct; competent.

грампласти́нка, -и disc, gramophone record.

гран, -а; *g.pl.* **гран** grain.

грана́т, -а pomegranate; garnet. **грана́та, -ы** shell, grenade. **грана́тник, -а** pomegranate. **грана́товый** pomegranate; garnet; rich red.

гране́ние, -я cutting. **гранёный** cut, faceted; cut-glass. **грани́льный** lapidary; diamond-cutting. **грани́льня, -и**; *g.pl.* **-лен** diamond-cutter's workshop. **грани́льщик, -а** lapidary, diamond-cutter.

грани́т, -а granite.

грани́ть, -ню́ *impf.* cut, facet.

грани́ца, -ы frontier, border; boundary, limit, bound; **за грани́цей, за грани́цу** abroad. **грани́чить, -чит** *impf.* border; verge.

гра́нка, -и galley proof, galley, slip (proof).

грань, -и border, verge; brink; side, facet; edge; period.

граф, -а count; earl.

графа́, -ы́ column. **гра́фик, -а** graph; chart; schedule; draughtsman, graphic artist. **гра́фика, -и** drawing, graphic art; script.

графи́н, -а carafe; decanter.

графи́ня, -и countess.

графи́т, -а graphite, black-lead; (pencil-)lead.
графи́ть, -флю́ *impf.* (*pf.* **раз~**) rule.
графи́ческий graphic.
графлёный ruled.
гра́фство, -а title of earl or count; county.
грацио́зный graceful. **гра́ция, -и** grace.
грач, -а́ rook.
гребёнка, -и comb; rack; hackle. **гре́бень, -бня** *m.* comb; hackle; crest; ridge. **гребе́ц, -бца́** rower, oarsman. **гребно́й** rowing. **гребо́к, -бка́** stroke; blade. **гребу́** *etc.*: *see* **грести́**
грёза, -ы day-dream, dream. **гре́зить, -е́жу** *impf.* dream.
гре́йдер, -а grader; unmetalled road.
грек, -а Greek.
гре́лка, -и heater; hot-water bottle, foot-warmer.
греме́ть, -млю́ *impf.* (*pf.* **про~**) thunder, roar; rumble; peal; rattle; resound, ring out. **грему́ч|ий** roaring, rattling; fulminating; **~ий газ** fire-damp; **~ая змея́** rattlesnake; **~ая ртуть** fulminate of mercury; **~ий сту́день** nitro-gelatine. **грему́шка, -и** rattle; sleigh-bell.
грести́, -ебу́, -ебёшь; грёб, -бла́ *impf.* row; scull, paddle; rake.
греть, -е́ю *impf.* warm, heat; give out heat; **~ся** warm o.s., bask.
грех, -а́ sin. **грехо́вный** sinful. **грехопаде́ние, -я** the Fall; fall.
Гре́ция, -и Greece. **гре́цкий** Greek, Grecian; **~ оре́х** walnut. **греча́нка, -и** Greek. **гре́ческий** Greek, Grecian.
гречи́ха, -и buckwheat. **гре́чневый** buckwheat.
греши́ть, -шу́ *impf.* (*pf.* **по~, со~**) sin. **гре́шник, -а, -ница, -ы** sinner. **гре́шный; -шен, -шна́, -о** sinful; culpable.
гриб, -а́ mushroom, toadstool, fungus. **грибно́й** mushroom.
гри́ва, -ы mane; wooded ridge; spit, shelf, sandbank.
гри́венник, -а ten-copeck piece.
грим, -а make-up; grease-paint.
грима́с|а, -ы grimace; **де́лать ~ы** make, pull faces.
гримёр, -а, -ёрша, -и make-up artist. **гримирова́ть, -ру́ю** *impf.* (*pf.* **за~, на~**) make up; *+i.* make up as; **~ся** make up. **гримиро́вка, -и** making up, make-up.
грипп, -а influenza.
гриф¹, -а gryphon; vulture.
гриф², -а finger-board.
гриф³, -а seal, stamp.
гри́фель, -я *m.* slate-pencil. **гри́фельн|ый** slate; **~ая доска́** slate.
гроб, -а, *loc.* **-у́**; *pl.* **-ы́** *or* **-а́** coffin; grave. **гробану́ть, -ну́, -нёшь** *pf.* damage, break; **~ся** have an accident, be killed in an accident. **гробово́й** coffin; deathly, sepulchral. **гробовщи́к, -а́** coffin-maker; undertaker.
гроза́, -ы́; *pl.* **-ы** (thunder-)storm; calamity, disaster; terror; threats.
гроздь, -и; *pl.* **-ди** *or* **-дья , -де́й** *or* **-дьев** cluster, bunch.
грози́ть(ся, -ожу́(сь *impf.* (*pf.* **по~, при~**) threaten; make a threatening gesture; **~ кулако́м** *+d.* shake one's fist at. **гро́зный; -зен, -зна́, -о** menacing, threatening; dread, terrible; formidable; stern, severe. **грозово́й** storm, thunder.
гром, -а; *pl.* **-ы, -о́в** thunder.
грома́да, -ы mass; bulk, pile; heaps, **грома́дина, -ы** vast object. **грома́дный** huge, vast, enormous, colossal.
громи́ть, -млю́ *impf.* destroy; smash, rout; thunder, fulminate, against.
гро́мкий; -мок, -мка́, -о loud; famous; notorious; fine-sounding, specious. **гро́мко** *adv.* loud(ly); aloud. **громкоговори́тель, -я** *m.* loud-speaker. **громово́й** thunder, of thunder; thunderous, deafening; crushing, smashing. **громогла́сный** loud; loud-voiced; public, open.
громозди́ть, -зжу́ *impf.* (*pf.* **на~**) pile up, heap up; **~ся** tower; clamber up. **громо́здкий** cumbersome, unwieldy.
гро́мче *comp. of* **гро́мкий, гро́мко**
громыха́ть, -а́ю *impf.* rumble, clatter.
гроссме́йстер, -а grand master.
грот, -а grotto.
гро́хать, -аю *impf.*, **гро́хнуть, -ну** *pf.* crash, bang; drop with a crash, bang down; **~ся** fall with a crash. **гро́хот¹, -а** crash, din.
гро́хот², -а screen, sieve, riddle.
грохота́ть, -очу́, -о́чешь *impf.* (*pf.* **про~**) crash; roll, rumble; thunder, roar; roar (with laughter).
грош, -а́ half-copeck piece; farthing, brass farthing, penny. **грошо́вый** dirt-cheap, shoddy; insignificant, trifling.
грубе́ть, -е́ю *impf.* (*pf.* **за~, о~, по~**) grow coarse, coarsen; become rough. **груби́ть, -блю́** *impf.* (*pf.* **на~**) be rude. **грубия́н, -а** boor. **грубия́нить, -ню** *impf.* (*pf.* **на~**) be rude; behave boorishly. **гру́бо** *adv.* coarsely, roughly; crudely; rudely. **гру́бость, -и** rudeness; coarseness; grossness; rude remark. **гру́бый; груб, -а́, -о** coarse; rough; crude, rude; gross, flagrant.
гру́да, -ы heap, pile.
груди́на, -ы breastbone. **груди́нка, -и** brisket; breast. **грудн|о́й** breast, chest; pectoral; **~а́я жа́ба** angina pectoris; **~о́й ребёнок** infant in arms. **грудобрю́шн|ый; ~ая прегра́да** diaphragm. **грудь, -и́** *or* **-и**, *i.* **-ю**, *loc.* **-и́**; *pl.* **-и, -е́й** breast; bosom, bust; chest; (shirt-)front.
груз, -а weight; load, cargo, freight; burden; bob. **грузи́ло, -а** sinker.
грузи́н, -а; *g.pl.* **-и́н, грузи́нка, -и** Georgian. **грузи́нский** Georgian.
грузи́ть, -ужу́, -у́зишь *impf.* (*pf.* **за~, на~, по~**) load, lade, freight; **~ся** load, take on cargo.

Гру́зия, -и Georgia.

гру́зка, -и lading. **гру́зный; -зен, -зна́, -о** weighty, bulky; unwieldy; corpulent. **грузови́к, -а́** lorry, truck. **грузово́й** goods, cargo, freight, load. **грузопото́к, -а** freight traffic, goods traffic. **грузотакси́** *nt.indecl.* taxi-lorry. **гру́зчик, -а** stevedore, docker; loader.

грунт, -а ground, soil, earth; subsoil; bottom; priming, primer. **грунтова́ть, -ту́ю** *impf.* (*pf.* **за~**) prime. **грунто́вка, -и** priming, ground coat, ground. **грунтово́й** soil, earth, ground; subsoil; bottom; priming; unpaved, unmetalled.

гру́ппа, -ы group. **группирова́ть, -ру́ю** *impf.* (*pf.* **с~**) group, classify; **~ся** group, form groups. **группиро́вка, -и** grouping; classification; group. **группово́й** group; team.

грусти́ть, -ущу́ *impf.* grieve, mourn; +**по**+*d.* pine for. **гру́стный; -тен, -тна́, -о** sad; melancholy; grievous, distressing. **грусть, -и** sadness, melancholy.

гру́ша, -и pear; pear-shaped thing. **гру́шевый** pear; **~ компо́т** stewed pears.

гры́жа, -и hernia, rupture. **гры́жевый** hernial; **~ банда́ж** truss.

грызня́, -и́ dog-fight, fight; squabble. **грызть, -зу́, -зёшь; грыз** *impf.* (*pf.* **раз~**) gnaw; nibble; nag; devour, consume; **~ся** fight; squabble, bicker. **грызу́н, -а́** rodent.

гряда́, -ы́; *pl.* **-ы, -а́м** ridge; bed; row, series; bank. **гря́дка, -и** (flower-)bed.

гряду́щий approaching; coming, future; to come; **на сон ~** at bedtime; last thing at night.

грязево́й mud. **грязни́ть, -ню́** *impf.* (*pf.* **за~, на~**) dirty, soil; sully, besmirch; make a mess, be untidy; **~ся** become dirty. **гря́зный; -зен, -зна́, -о** muddy, mud-stained; dirty; untidy, slovenly; filthy; refuse, garbage, slop. **грязь, -и,** *loc.* **-и́** mud; dirt, filth; *pl.* mud; mud-baths, mud-cure.

гря́нуть, -ну *pf.* burst out, crash out, ring out; strike up. **~ся** crash (down).

грясти́, -яду́, -ядёшь *impf.* approach.

губа́, -ы́; *pl.* **-ы, -а́м** lip; *pl.* pincers. **губа́стый** thick-lipped.

губерна́тор, -а governor. **губе́рния, -и** (*hist.*) guberniya, province. **губе́рнский** provincial; **~ секрета́рь** Provincial Secretary (*12th grade*: *see* **чин**).

губи́тельный destructive, ruinous; baneful, pernicious. **губи́ть, -блю́, -бишь** *impf.* (*pf.* **по~**) destroy; be the undoing of; ruin, spoil; **~ся** be destroyed; be wasted.

гу́бка, -и sponge.

губн|о́й lip; labial; **~а́я гармо́ника** harmonica, mouth organ.

гу́бчатый porous, spongy; **~ каучу́к** foam rubber.

гуверна́нтка, -и governess. **гувернёр, -а** tutor.

гугу́; ни ~! not a sound!; mum's the word!

гуде́ние, -я hum; drone; buzzing; hooting, hoot. **гуде́ть, гужу́** *impf.* (*pf.* **про~**) hum; drone; buzz; hoot. **гудо́к, -дка́** hooter, siren, horn, whistle; hoot, hooting.

гудро́н, -а tar. **гудрони́ровать, -рую** *impf.* & *pf.* (*pf. also* **за~**) tar. **гудро́нный** tar, tarred.

гул, -а rumble; hum; boom. **гу́лкий; -лок, -лка́, -о** resonant; booming, rumbling.

ГУЛАГ *abbr.* (*of* ***Гла́вное управле́ние исправи́тельно-трудовы́х лагере́й***) GULAG, Main Administration for Corrective Labour Camps.

гуля́нье, -я; *g.pl.* **-ний** walking, going for a walk, walk; fête; outdoor party. **гуля́ть, -я́ю** *impf.* (*pf.* **по~**) walk, stroll; go for a walk, take a walk; have time off, not be working; make merry, carouse, have a good time; +**с**+*i.* go with.

ГУМ, -а *abbr.* (*of* ***Госуда́рственный универса́льный магази́н***) GUM, State Department Store.

гумани́зм, -а humanism. **гумани́ст, -а** humanist. **гумани́тарный** of the humanities; humane. **гума́нный** humane.

гумно́, -а́; *pl.* **-а, -мен** *or* **-мён, -ам** threshing-floor; barn.

гурт, -а́ herd, drove; flock. **гуртовщи́к, -а́** herdsman; drover. **гурто́м** *adv.* wholesale; in bulk; together; in a body, en masse.

гуса́к, -а́ gander.

гу́сеница, -ы caterpillar; (caterpillar) track. **гу́сеничный** track, tracked.

гусёнок, -нка; *pl.* **-ся́та, -ся́т** gosling. **гуси́н|ый** goose; **~ая ко́жа** goose-flesh; **~ые ла́пки** crow's-feet.

густе́ть, -е́ет *impf.* (*pf.* **за~, по~**) thicken, get thicker. **густо́й; густ, -а́, -о** thick, dense; deep, rich. **густота́, -ы́** thickness, density; deepness, richness.

гусы́ня, -и goose. **гусь, -я**; *pl.* **-и, -е́й** *m.* goose. **гусько́м** *adv.* in single file. **гуся́тина, -ы** goose.

гутали́н, -а shoe-polish, boot-polish.

гу́ща, -и dregs, lees, grounds, sediment; thicket; thick, centre, heart. **гу́ще** *comp. of* **густо́й. гущина́, -ы́** thickness; thicket.

гэ *nt.indecl.* the letter **г**.

ГЭС *abbr.* (*of* ***гидроэлектроста́нция***) hydro-electric power station.

д *letter*: *see* **дэ**

д. *abbr.* (*of* **дере́вня**) village; (*of* **дом**) house.

да *conj.* and; but; **да (ещё)** and what is more;

да (и) and besides; **да и то́лько** and that's all.

да *part.* yes; yes? really? indeed; well; *+3rd pers. of v.*, may, let; **да здра́вствует...!** long live ..!

дава́ть, даю́, -ёшь *impf. of* **дать; дава́й(те)** let us, let's; come on; **~ся** yield; let o.s. be caught; come easy; **не ~ся**+*d.* dodge, evade; **ру́сский язы́к ему́ даётся легко́** Russian comes easy to him.

да́веча *adv.* lately, recently.

дави́ло, -а press. **дави́ть, -влю́, -вишь** *impf.* (*pf.* **за~, по~, раз~, у~**) press; squeeze; weigh, lie heavy; crush; oppress; trample; strangle; **~ся** choke; hang o.s. **да́вка, -и** crushing, squeezing; throng, crush. **давле́ние, -я** pressure.

да́вний ancient; of long standing. **давно́** *adv.* long ago; for a long time; long since. **давнопроше́дший** remote; long past; pluperfect. **да́вность, -и** antiquity; remoteness; long standing; prescription. **давны́м-давно́** *adv.* long long ago, ages ago.

дади́м *etc.*: *see* **дать. даю́** *etc.*: *see* **дава́ть**

да́же *adv.* even.

дакти́льн|ый; ~ая а́збука sign language.

да́лее *adv.* further; **и так ~** and so on, etc. **далёкий; -ёк, -а́, -ёко́** distant, remote; far (away). **далеко́, далёко** *adv.* far; far off; by a long way; **~ за** long after; **~ не** far from. **даль, -и**, *loc.* **-и́** distance. **да́льн|ий** distant, remote; long; **без ~их слов** without more ado; **~ Восто́к** the Far East. **дальнозо́ркий** long-sighted. **да́льность, -и** distance; range. **да́льше** *adv.* farther; further; then, next; longer.

дам *etc.*: *see* **дать**

да́ма, -ы lady; partner; queen.

да́мба, -ы dike, embankment; dam.

да́мка, -и king. **да́мский** ladies'.

Да́ния, -и Denmark.

да́нные *sb., pl.* data; facts, information; qualities, gifts; grounds; **необрабо́танные ~** raw data. **да́нный** given, present; in question, this. **дань, -и** tribute; debt.

дар, -а; *pl.* **-ы́** gift; donation; grant. **даре́ние, -я** donation. **дари́тель, -я** *m.* donor. **дари́ть, -рю́, -ришь** *impf.* (*pf.* **по~**) *+d.* give, make a present.

дармое́д, -а, -е́дка, -и parasite, sponger, scrounger. **дармое́дничать, -аю** *impf.* sponge, scrounge.

дарова́ние, -я gift, talent. **дарова́ть, -ру́ю** *impf. & pf.* grant, confer. **дарови́тый** gifted, talented. **дарово́й** free, gratuitous. **да́ром** *adv.* free, gratis; in vain, to no purpose.

да́та, -ы date.

да́тельный dative.

дати́ровать, -рую *impf. & pf.* date.

да́тский Danish. **датча́нин, -а**; *pl.* **-а́не, -а́н, датча́нка, -и** Dane.

дать, дам, дашь, даст, дади́м; дал, -а́, да́ло́ *pf.* (*impf.* **дава́ть**) give; administer; grant; let; **~ взаймы́** lend; **~ газ** step on the gas; **~ доро́гу** make way; **~ кля́тву** take an oath; **~ нача́ло**+*d.* give rise to; **~ сло́во** give one's word; *+d.* give the floor; **~ ход**+*d.* set in motion, get going; **~ся** *pf. of* **дава́ться**

да́ча, -и dacha; **на да́че** in the country; **на да́чу** (in)to the country. **да́чник, -а** (holiday) visitor.

два *m. & nt.*, **две** *f.*, **двух, -ум, -умя́, -ух** two; **~-три** two or three, a couple; **ка́ждые ~ дня** every other day. **двадцатиле́тний** twenty-year; twenty-year-old. **двадца́т|ый** twentieth; **~ые го́ды** the twenties. **два́дцать, -и́**, *i.* **-ью́** twenty. **два́дцатью** *adv.* twenty times. **два́жды** *adv.* twice; double. **двена́дцатый** twelfth. **двена́дцать, -и** twelve.

двер|о́й door; **~а́я коро́бка** door-frame. **две́рца, -ы**; *g.pl.* **-рец** door, hatch. **дверь, -и**, *loc.* **-и́**; *pl.* **-и, -е́й**, *i.* **-я́ми** *or* **-ьми́** door; *pl.* doors, door.

две́сти, двухсо́т, -умста́м, -умяста́ми, -ухста́х two hundred.

дви́гатель, -я *m.* engine, motor; (prime) mover, motive force. **дви́гательный** motive; motor. **дви́гать, -аю** *or* **-и́жу** *impf.*, **дви́нуть, -ну** *pf.* move; set in motion, get going; advance, further; **~ся** move; advance; start, get started. **движе́ние, -я** movement; motion; exercise; flow; traffic; promotion, advancement; impulse; **железнодоро́жное ~** train service. **дви́жимость, -и** movables, chattels; personal property. **дви́жимый** movable; moved, prompted, activated. **движко́в|ый** slide; **~ые регуля́торы** slide controls. **дви́жущий** motive; moving; driving.

дво́е, -и́х two; two pairs.

двое... *in comb.* two-; double(-). **двоебо́рец, -рца** competitor in double event. **~бо́рье, -я** double event. **~ду́шие, -я** duplicity, double-dealing. **~ду́шный** two-faced. **~же́нец, -нца, ~му́жница, -ы** bigamist. **~жёнство, -а, ~му́жие, -я** bigamy. **~то́чие, -я** colon.

двои́ть, -ою́ *impf.* (*pf.* **вз~**) double; divide into two; **~ся** divide in two; appear double. **двои́чный** binary. **дво́йка, -и** two; figure 2; No. 2; pair-oar. **двойни́к, -а́** double; twin. **двойно́й** double, twofold; binary. **дво́йня, -и**; *g.pl.* **-о́ен** twins. **дво́йственный** double-dealing, two-faced; dual; bipartite.

двор, -а́ yard; courtyard; homestead; court; **на ~е́** out of doors, outside; **при ~е́** at court. **дворе́ц, -рца́** palace. **дворе́цкий** *sb.* butler; majordomo. **дво́рник, -а** yardman; windscreen-wiper. **дво́рницк|ий** dvornik's. **~ая** *sb.* dvornik's lodge. **дво́рня, -и** servants, menials. **дворо́вый** yard, courtyard; *sb.* house-serf. **дворцо́вый** palace. **дворяни́н, -а**; *pl.* **-я́не, -я́н, дворя́нка, -и** member of the nobility or gentry. **дворя́нство, -а** nobility, gentry.

двою́родн|ый; ~ый брат, ~ая сестра́ (first)

cousin; ~**ый дя́дя,** ~**ая тётка** first cousin once removed. **двоя́кий** double; ambiguous; in two ways, of two kinds. **двояко...** double-, bi-, di-.

дву..., двух... *in comb.* two-; bi-, di-; double(-); diplo-. **двубо́ртный** double-breasted. ~**гла́вый** two-headed. ~**гла́сный** *sb.* diphthong. ~**гри́венный** *sb.* twenty-copeck piece. ~**жи́льный** strong; hardy; tough. ~**зна́чный** two-digit. ~**ли́кий** two-faced. ~**ли́чие, -я** double-dealing, duplicity. ~**ли́чный** two-faced; hypocritical. ~**пла́нный** two-dimensional. ~**по́лый** bisexual. ~**ру́чный** two-handed; two-handled. ~**ру́шник, -а** double-dealer. ~**сло́жный** disyllabic. ~**сме́нный** in two shifts, two-shift. ~**смы́сленный** ambiguous, equivocal. ~**(х)спа́льный** double. ~**сторо́нний** double-sided; two-way; bilateral. ~**ха́томный** diatomic. ~**хгоди́чный** two-year. ~**хкра́сочный** two-colour; two-tone. ~**хле́тний** two-year; two-year-old; biennial. ~**хме́стный** two-seater; two-berth. ~**хме́сячник, -а** bi-monthly. ~**хмото́рный** twin-engined, two-engined. ~**хпала́тный** bicameral. ~**хпарти́йный** bipartisan. ~**хсотле́тие, -я** bicentenary. ~**хсо́тый** two-hundredth. ~**хта́ктный** two-beat; two-stroke. ~**хъя́русный** two-layer, two-storey, two-tier, double-deck; two-lever. ~**хэта́жный** two-storey, double-deck; ~**чле́н, -а** binomial. ~**язы́чный** bilingual.

деба́ты, -ов *pl.* debate.

де́бет, -а debit. **дебетова́ть, -ту́ю** *impf.* & *pf.* debit.

де́бит, -а discharge, flow, yield, output.

де́бри, -ей *pl.* jungle; thickets; the wilds; maze, labyrinth.

дебю́т, -а début; opening.

де́ва, -ы maid, maiden; girl; spinster; Virgo; **ста́рая** ~ old maid.

девальва́ция, -и devaluation.

дева́ть(ся, -а́ю(сь *impf. of* **де́ть(ся**

деви́з, -а motto; device.

деви́ца, -ы spinster; girl. **деви́ческий, де́ви́ч|ий** girlish, maidenly; ~**ья фами́лия** maiden name. **де́вка, -и** girl, wench, lass; tart, whore. **де́вочка, -и** (little) girl. **де́вственник, -а, -ица, -ы** virgin. **де́вственный** virgin; virginal, innocent. **де́вушка, -и** girl; maid.

девяно́сто, -а ninety. **девяно́стый** ninetieth. **де́вятеро, -ы́х** nine; nine pairs. **девятисо́тый** nine-hundredth. **девя́тка, -и** nine; figure 9; No. 9; group of nine. **девятна́дцать, -и** nineteen. **девя́тый** ninth. **де́вять, -и́**, *i.* **-ью́** nine. **девятьсо́т, -тисо́т, -тиста́м, -тьюста́ми, -тиста́х** nine hundred. **де́вятью** *adv.* nine times.

дегенера́т, -а degenerate. **дегенерати́вный** degenerate. **дегенера́ция, -и** degeneration. **дегенери́ровать, -рую** *impf.* & *pf.* degenerate.

дёготь, -гтя tar, coal-tar, pitch. **дёгтебето́н, -а** tarmac, tar concrete. **дегтя́рный** tar, coal-tar, pich; tarry.

дед, -а grandfather; grandad, grandpa. **де́довский** grandfather's; old-world; old-fashioned. **де́душка, -и** grandfather; grandad.

дееприча́стие, -я gerund, adverbial participle.

дежу́рить, -рю *impf.* be on duty, be in (constant) attendance. **дежу́рный** duty; on duty. **дежу́рство, -а** (being on) duty.

дезерти́р, -а deserter. **дезерти́ровать, -рую** *impf.* & *pf.* desert. **дезерти́рство, -а** desertion.

дезинфе́кция, -и disinfection. **дезинфици́ровать, -рую** *impf.* & *pf.* disinfect.

дезодора́нт, -а deodorant; air freshener.

де́йственный efficacious; effective. **де́йствие, -я** action; operation; activity; functioning; effect; act; **под** ~**м** under the influence. **действи́тельно** *adv.* really; indeed. **действи́тельность, -и** reality; realities; conditions; validity; efficacy; **в действи́тельности** in reality, in fact. **действи́тельный** real, actual; true, authentic; valid, efficacious; effective; active. **де́йствовать, -твую** *impf.* (*pf.* **по**~) affect, have an effect; act; work, function; operate; +*i.* use; **не** ~ be out of order, not be working. **де́йствующ|ий** active; in force; working; ~**ее лицо́** character; active participant; ~**ие ли́ца** dramatis personae, cast.

де́ка, -и sounding-board.

декабри́ст, -а Decembrist. **дека́брь, -я́** *m.* December. **дека́брьский** December.

дека́да, -ы ten days; (ten-day) festival.

дека́н, -а dean. **декана́т, -а** office of dean.

деклама́тор, -а reciter, declaimer. **деклама́ция, -и** recitation, declamation. **деклами́ровать, -рую** *impf.* (*pf.* **про**~) recite, declaim. **деклара́ция, -и** declaration; **нало́говая** ~ tax return.

декорати́вный decorative, ornamental. **декора́тор, -а** decorator; scene-painter. **декора́ция, -и** scenery, décor; window-dressing.

декре́т, -а decree; maternity leave; **уйти́ в** ~ take maternity leave. **декрети́ровать, -ую** *impf.* & *pf.* decree. **декре́тный;** ~ **о́тпуск** maternity leave.

де́ланный artificial, forced, affected. **де́лать, -аю** *impf.* (*pf.* **с**~) make; do; give, produce; ~ **вид** pretend, feign; ~ **предложе́ние** propose; ~ **честь**+*d.* honour; do credit to; ~**ся** become, get, grow; happen; be going on; break out, appear.

делега́т, -а delegate. **делега́ция, -и** delegation; group. **делеги́ровать, -ую** *impf.* & *pf.* delegate.

делёж, -а́, делёжка, -и sharing, division; partition. **деле́ние, -я** division; point, degree, unit.

деле́ц, -льца́ business man, dealer; smart operator.

делика́тность, -и delicacy. **делика́тный** delicate.

дели́мое *sb.* dividend. **дели́мость, -и** divisibility. **дели́тель, -я** *m.* divisor. **дели́ть, -лю́, -лишь** *impf.* (*pf.* **по~, раз~**) divide; share; **~ шесть на́ три** divide six by three; **~ся** divide; be divisible; *+i.* share; communicate, impart.

де́ло, -а; *pl.* **-а́** business; affair, affairs; cause; occupation; matter; point; fact; deed; thing; case, action; file, dossier; battle, fighting; **в са́мом де́ле** really, indeed; **~ в том** the point is; **в то́м то и ~** that's just the point; **~ за ва́ми** it's up to you; **как (ва́ши) дела́?** how are things going? how are you getting on? **на са́мом де́ле** in actual fact, as a matter of fact; **по де́лу, по дела́м** on business; **то и ~** continually, time and again. **делови́тый** business-like, efficient. **делово́й** business, work; business-like. **де́льный** efficient, business-like; sensible, practical.

дельтапла́н, -а hang-glider (*craft*). **дельтапланери́ст, -а** hang-glider (*pers.*).

дельфи́н, -а dolphin.

демаго́г, -а demagogue. **демагоги́ческий** demagogic. **демаго́гия, -и** demagogy.

демокра́т, -а democrat; plebeian. **демократизи́ровать, -рую** *impf.* & *pf.* democratize. **демократи́ческий** democratic; plebeian. **демокра́тия, -и** democracy; common people, lower classes.

демонстра́ция, -и demonstration; (public) showing; display, show.

дендра́рий, -я arboretum.

де́нежн|ый monetary; money; moneyed; **~ый перево́д** money order, postal order; **~ая рефо́рма** currency reform; **~ый штраф** fine.

де́ну *etc.*: *see* **деть**

день, дня *m.* day; afternoon; **днём** in the afternoon; **на днях** the other day; one of these days; **че́рез ~** every other day.

де́ньги, -нег, -ьга́м *pl.* money.

департа́мент, -а department.

депо́ *nt.indecl.* depot.

депозита́рий, -я *m.* depository.

депорта́нт, -а deportee. **депорта́ция, -и** deportation. **депорти́ровать, -ую** *impf.* & *pf.* deport.

депута́т, -а deputy; delegate. **депута́ция, -и** deputation.

дёргать, -аю *impf.* (*pf.* **дёрнуть**) pull, tug; pull out; harass, pester; *+i.* move sharply, jerk, shrug; **~ся** twitch; jerk; move sharply.

дерга́ч, -а́ corncrake, landrail.

деревене́ть, -е́ю *impf.* (*pf.* **за~, о~**) grow stiff, grow numb. **дереве́нский** village; rural, country. **дере́вня, -и**; *pl.* **-и, -ве́нь, -вня́м** village; the country. **де́рево, -а**; *pl.* **-е́вья, -ьев** tree; wood. **дереву́шка, -и** hamlet. **деревя́нный** wood; wooden; expressionless, dead; dull.

держа́ва, -ы power; orb. **держа́вный** holding supreme power, sovereign; powerful.

держа́ть, -жу́, -жишь *impf.* hold; hold up, support; keep; **~ корректу́ру** read proofs; **~ пари́** bet; **~ себя́** behave; **~ экза́мен** take an examination; **~ся** hold; be held up, be supported; keep, stay, be; hold o.s.; behave; last; hold together; hold out, stand firm, hold one's ground; *+g.* keep to; adhere to, stick to; **~ся на ни́точке** hang by a thread.

дерза́ние, -я daring. **дерза́ть, -а́ю** *impf.*, **дерзну́ть, -ну́, -нёшь** *pf.* dare. **де́рзкий** impertinent, impudent, cheeky; insolent; daring, audacious. **дерзнове́нный** audacious, daring. **де́рзость, -и** impertinence; cheek; rudeness; insolence; daring, audacity.

дёрн, -а (-у) turf. **дерно́вый** turf. **дернова́ть, -ну́ю** *impf.* turf, edge with turf.

дёрнуть(ся, -ну(сь *pf. of* **дёргать(ся**

деру́ *etc.*: *see* **драть**

деса́нт, -а landing; landing force. **деса́нтник, -а** paratrooper. **деса́нтный** landing.

десна́, -ы́; *pl.* **дёсны, -сен** gum.

де́спот, -а despot.

десятерно́й tenfold. **де́сятеро, -ы́х** ten. **десятиле́тие, -я** decade; tenth anniversary. **десятиле́тка, -и** ten-year (*secondary*) school. **десятиле́тний** ten-year, decennial; ten-year-old. **десяти́чный** decimal. **деся́тка, -и** ten; No. 10; group of ten; tenner (*10-rouble note*). **деся́ток, -тка** ten; ten years, decade. **деся́тник, -а** foreman. **деся́тский** *sb.* peasant policeman. **деся́тый** tenth. **де́сять, -и́**, *i.* **-ью** ten. **де́сятью** *adv.* ten times.

дет... *abbr.* (*of* **де́тский**) *in comb.* children's. **детдо́м, -а** children's home. **~площа́дка, -и** playground. **~са́д, -а** kindergarten, nursery school.

дета́ль, -и detail; part, component. **дета́льный** detailed; minute.

детвора́, -ы children.

детекти́в, -а whodunit; detective story.

детёныш, -а young animal; cub, whelp, etc.; *pl.* young.

деterге́нт, -а detergent.

де́ти, -те́й, -тям, -тьми́, -тях *pl.* children. **де́тская** *sb.* nursery. **де́тский** child's, children's; childish. **де́тство, -а** childhood.

деть, де́ну *pf.* (*impf.* **дева́ть**) put; **куда́ ты дел моё перо́?** what have you done with my pen?; **~ся** get to, disappear to; **куда́ она́ де́лась?** what has become of her?

дефе́кт, -а defect. **дефекти́вный** defective; handicapped; **~ ребёнок** (*mentally or physically*) handicapped child. **дефе́ктный** imperfect, faulty.

дефи́с, -а hyphen; **писа́ть че́рез ~** hyphenate.

дефици́т, -а deficit; shortage, deficiency. **дефици́тный** showing a loss; in short supply; scarce.

децима́льный decimal.

дешеве́ть, -е́ет *impf.* (*pf.* **по~**) fall in price, get cheaper. **дешеви́зна, -ы** cheapness; low price. **дешéвле** *comp. of* **дёшево, дешёвый. дёшево** *adv.* cheap, cheaply; lightly. **дешёвый; дёшев, -á, -о** cheap; empty, worthless.

дешифри́ровать, -рую *impf.* & *pf.* decipher, decode. **дешифрóвка, -и** decipherment, decifering, decoding.

деяние, -я act, deed. **дéятель, -я** *m.*; **госудáрственный ~** statesman; **~ наýки** scientific worker, scientist; **общéственный ~** public figure. **дéятельность, -и** activity; activities; work; operation. **дéятельный** active, energetic.

джаз, -а jazz. **джаз-ансáмбль, -я** jazz-combo. **джази́ст, -а** jazz musician.

джéмпер, -а jumper, pullover, jersey.

джинсóвый denim. **джи́нсы, -ов** *pl.* jeans.

джип, -а jeep.

джóггинг, -а jogging, fun-running.

джóйстик, -а (*comput.*) joystick.

джýнгли, -ей *pl.* jungle.

ДЗУ *abbr.* (*of* ***долговрéменное запоминáющее устрóйство***) (*comput.*) ROM (*read-only memory*).

дзю(-)дó *nt. indecl.* judo. **дзюдои́ст, -а** judoist, judoka.

диáгноз, -а diagnosis. **диагности́ровать, -рую** *impf.* & *pf.* diagnose.

диагонáл|ь, -и diagonal; **по ~и** diagonally. **диагонáльный** diagonal.

диагрáмма, -ы diagram; **круговáя ~** pie chart.

диалéкт, -а dialect. **диалекти́ческий, диалéктный** dialectal.

диалóг, -а dialogue. **диалóговый** interactive.

диáметр, -а diameter.

диапазóн, -а diapason; range; compass; band.

диапозити́в, -а slide, transparency.

диафрáгма, -ы diaphragm; (*phot.*) aperture.

дивáн, -а sofa; divan.

диверсáнт, -а saboteur. **диверсиóнный** diversionary; sabotage, wrecking. **дивéрсия, -и** diversion; sabotage.

диви́зия, -и (*mil.*) division.

ди́вный amazing; marvellous, wonderful. **ди́во, -а** wonder, marvel.

диéз, -а sharp.

диéта, -ы diet. **диетéтика, -и** dietetics. **диетети́ческий** dietetic; **~ магази́н** health food shop. **диетóлог, -а** nutritionist.

ди́зель, -я *m.* diesel; diesel engine. **ди́зельный** diesel.

дизентери́я, -и dysentery.

дикáрь, -я́ *m.*, **дикáрка, -и** savage; barbarian; shy person. **ди́кий** wild; savage; shy, unsociable; queer, absurd; fantastic, preposterous, ridiculous. **дикобрáз, -а** porcupine. **дикóвина, -ы** marvel, wonder. **дикорастýщий** wild. **ди́кость, -и** wildness, savagery; shyness, unsociableness; absurdity, queerness.

диктáнт, -а dictation.

диктáтор, -а dictator. **диктáторский** dictatorial. **диктатýра, -ы** dictatorship.

диктовáть, -тýю *impf.* (*pf.* **про~**) dictate. **диктóвка, -и** dictation. **ди́ктор, -а** announcer.

дилетáнт, -а dilettante, dabbler. **дилетáнтство, -а** dilettantism.

дилижáнс, -а stage-coach.

ди́на, -ы dyne.

динáмик, -а loudspeaker. **динáмика, -и** dynamics; action, movement.

динозáвр, -а dinosaur.

диплóм, -а diploma; degree; degree work, research; pedigree.

дипломáт, -а diplomat; attaché case. **дипломати́ческий, дипломати́чный** diplomatic. **дипломáтия, -и** diplomacy; **~ канонéрок** gunboat diplomacy.

дипломи́рованный graduate; professionally qualified, certificated, diplomaed. **диплóмный** diploma, degree.

директи́ва, -ы instructions; directions, directives.

дирéктор, -а; *pl.* **~á** director, manager; **~ шкóлы** head (master, mistress); principal. **дирéкция, -и** management; board (of directors).

дирижáбль, -я *m.* airship.

дирижёр, -а conductor. **дирижи́ровать, -рую** *impf.+i.* conduct.

диск, -а disc, disk; discus; plate; dial; **компáктный ~** compact disk.

ди́скант, -а treble.

дискéт, -а (*comput.*) diskette; **пустóй ~** blank diskette. **диск-жокéй, -я** disc-jockey. **дисковóд, -а** (*comput.*) disk drive.

дискрéтность, -и discreteness, discontinuity. **дискрéтн|ый** discrete; digital; **~ая маши́на** digital computer.

дискриминациóнный discriminatory.

дискриминáция, -и discrimination; **~ жéнщин** sexism.

дискуссиóнный discussion, debating; debatable, open to question. **дискýссия, -и** discussion, debate. **дискути́ровать, -рую** *impf.* & *pf.* discuss, debate.

диспансéр, -а clinic, (health) centre.

диспéтчер, -а controller, dispatcher. **диспéтчерская** *sb.* controller's office; control tower.

диссертáция, -и dissertation, thesis.

дистанциóнн|ый distance, distant, remote; remote-control; **~ый взрывáтель** time fuse; **~ое управлéние** remote control. **дистáнция, -и** distance; range; division, region, sector.

дисципли́на, -ы discipline. **дисциплинáрный** disciplinary. **дисциплини́ровать, -рую** *impf.* & *pf.* discipline.

дитя́, -я́ти; *pl.* **дéти, -éй** *nt.* child; baby.

дифтери́т, -а, дифтери́я, -и diptheria.

дичáть, -áю *impf.* (*pf.* **о~**) grow wild; become unsociable; run wild. **дичи́на, -ы** game.

дичи́ться, -чу́сь *impf.* be shy; +*g.* shun, fight shy of. **дичь, -и,** *loc.* **-и́** game; wildfowl; wilderness, wilds.

длина́, -ы́ length; **длино́й** in length, long. **длинново́лновый** long-wave. **дли́нный; -нен, -нна́, -о** long; lengthy. **дли́тельность, -и** duration. **дли́тельный** long, protracted, long-drawn-out. **дли́ться, -и́тся** *impf.* (*pf.* **про~**) last, be protracted.

для *prep.*+*g.* for; for the sake of; to; of; **~ ви́ду** for the sake of appearances; **вре́дно ~ дете́й** bad for children; **высо́к ~ свои́х лет** tall for his age; **непроница́емый ~ воды́** waterproof, impervious to water; **~ того́, что́бы...** in order to ...; **э́то ~ вас** this is for you; **э́то типи́чно ~ них** it is typical of them.

днева́льный *sb.* orderly, man on duty. **дневни́к, -а́** diary, journal. **днев|но́й** day; daylight; day's, daily; **~а́я сме́на** day shift; **~о́й спекта́кль** matinée. **днём** *adv.* in the day time, by day; in the afternoon. **дни** *etc.*: *see* **день**

ДНК *abbr.* (*of* **дезоксирибонуклеи́новая кислота́**) DNA (*deoxyribonucleic acid*).

дно, дна; *pl.* **до́нья, -ьев** bottom.

до *nt.indecl.* C; doh.

до *prep.*+*g.* to, up to; as far as; until, till; before; to the point of; under; about, approximately; with regard to, concerning; **де́ти до пяти́ лет** children under five; **до бо́ли** until it hurt(s); **до войны́** before the war; **до на́шей э́ры** B.C. **до сих пор** up to now, till now, hitherto; **до тех пор** till then, before; **до того́, как** before; **до того́, что** to such an extent that, to the point where; **мне не до** I don't feel like, I'm not in the mood for; **от Санкт-Петербу́рга до Москвы́** from St. Petersburg to Moscow; **что до меня́** as far as I am concerned; **ю́бка до коле́н** knee-length skirt.

до... *pref.* up (to); pre-; sub- *in comb.* **I.** *with vv., etc. expresses completion of action, indicates that action is carried to a certain point, expresses supplementary action*; *with refl. vv. expresses eventual attainment of object, or continuation of action with injurious consequences.* **II.** *with adjs. indicates priority in time sequence.*

доба́вить, -влю *pf.*, **добавля́ть, -я́ю** *impf.* (+*a. or g.*) add. **доба́вка, -и** addition; second-helping. **добавле́ние, -я** addition; appendix, addendum, supplement; extra. **доба́вочный** additional, supplementary; extra; extension, booster.

добега́ть, -а́ю *impf.*, **добежа́ть, -егу́** *pf.*+**до**+*g.* run to, run as far as; reach.

добела́ *adv.* to white heat, white-hot; clean, white.

добива́ть, -а́ю *impf.*, **доби́ть, -бью, -бьёшь** *pf.* finish (off), kill off, deal the final blow to; **~ся**+*g.* get, obtain, secure; achieve; **~ся своего́** get one's way, gain one's end.

добира́ться, -а́юсь *impf. of* **добра́ться**

до́блестный valiant, valorous, brave. **до́блесть, -и** valour, prowess.

добра́ться, -беру́сь, -ёшься; -а́лся, -ла́сь, -а́ло́сь *pf.* (*impf.* **добира́ться**) +**до**+*g.* get to, reach.

добро́, -а́ good; good deed; goods, property; **э́то не к добру́** it is a bad sign, it augurs ill.

добро... *in comb.* good-, well-. **доброво́лец, -льца** volunteer. **~во́льно** *adv.* voluntarily, of one's own free will. **~во́льный** voluntary. **~де́тель, -и** virtue. **~де́тельный** virtuous. **~ду́шие, -я** good nature. **~ду́шный** good-natured; genial. **~жела́тельный** benevolent. **~ка́чественный** of good quality; benign. **~со́вестный** conscientious.

доброта́, -ы́ goodness, kindness. **до́бр|ый; добр, -а́, -о, до́бры́** good; kind; **бу́дьте добры́**+*imper.* please; would you be kind enough to; **в ~ый час!** good luck! **по ~ой во́ле** of one's own accord, of one's own free will.

добыва́ть, -а́ю *impf.*, **добы́ть, -бу́ду; до́был, -а́ , -о** *pf.* get, obtain, procure; extract, mine, quarry. **добы́ча, -и** output; extraction; mining, quarrying; booty, spoils, loot; bag, catch; mineral products.

добью *etc.*: *see* **доби́ть. доведу́** *etc.*: *see* **довести́**

довезти́, -езу́, -езёшь; -вёз, -ла́ *pf.* (*impf.* **довози́ть**) take (to), carry (to), drive (to).

дове́ренность, -и warrant; power of attorney; trust. **дове́ренн|ый** trusted; confidential; **~ое лицо́** confidential agent; **~ый** *sb.* agent, proxy. **дове́рие, -я** trust, confidence. **дове́рить, -рю** *pf.* (*impf.* **доверя́ть**) entrust; trust, confide; **~ся**+*d.* trust in; confide in. **дове́рчивый** trustful, credulous.

доверша́ть, -а́ю *impf.*, **доверши́ть, -шу́** *pf.* complete. **доверше́ние, -я** completion, accomplishment; **в ~ всего́** to crown all.

доверя́ть(ся, -я́ю(сь *impf. of* **дове́рить(ся**

дове́сок, -ска makeweight.

довести́, -еду́, -едёшь; -вёл, -а́ *pf.*, **доводи́ть, -ожу́, -о́дишь** *impf.* lead, take, accompany (to); bring, drive, reduce (to). **до́вод, -а** argument, reason.

довое́нный pre-war.

довози́ть, -ожу́, -о́зишь *impf. of* **довезти́**

дово́льно *adv.* enough; quite, fairly; rather; pretty. **дово́льный** contented, satisfied; content; pleased; considerable. **дово́льство, -а** content, contentment; ease, prosperity. **дово́льствоваться, -ствуюсь** *impf.* (*pf.* **у~**) be content, be satisfied.

дог, -а Great Dane; **далма́тский ~** Dalmation.

догада́ться, -а́юсь *pf.*, **дога́дываться, -аюсь** *impf.* guess; suspect. **дога́дка, -и** surmise, conjecture; shrewdness; imagination. **дога́дливый** quick witted, shrewd.

до́гма, -ы dogma, dogmatic assertion. **догмати́зм, -а** dogmatism. **догмати́ческий** dogmatic.

догна́ть, -гоню́, -го́нишь; -гна́л, -а́, -о *pf.* (*impf.* **догоня́ть**) catch up (with); drive; push up.

догова́риваться, -аюсь *impf.*, **договори́ться, -рю́сь** *pf.* come to an agreement or understanding; arrange; negotiate, treat; **догова́ривающиеся сто́роны** contracting parties. **до́гово́р, -а**; *pl.* **-ы** *or* **-а́, -о́в** agreement; contract; treaty, pact. **догово́рный** contractual; agreed; fixed by treaty.

догоня́ть, -я́ю *impf. of* **догна́ть**

догора́ть, -а́ет *impf.*, **догоре́ть, -ри́т** *pf.* burn out, burn down.

дое́ду *etc.*: *see* **дое́хать. доезжа́ть, -а́ю** *impf. of* **дое́хать**

дое́ние, -я milking.

дое́хать, -е́ду *pf.* (*impf.* **доезжа́ть**) +**до**+*g.* reach, arrive at.

дожда́ться, -ду́сь, -дёшься; -а́лся, -ла́сь, -а́ло́сь *pf.*+*g.* wait for, wait until.

дождеви́к, -а́ raincoat; puff-ball. **дождево́й** rain; rainy; ~ **червь** earthworm. **до́ждик, -а** shower. **дождли́вый** rainy. **дождь, -я́** *m.* rain; shower, hail; ~ **идёт** it is raining.

дожива́ть, -а́ю *impf.*, **дожи́ть, -иву́, -ивёшь; до́жи́л, -а́, -о** *pf.* live out; spend; +**до**+*g.* live until; reach; come to, be reduced to.

до́за, -ы dose.

доза́тор, -а metering device; hopper, feeder, dispenser.

дозволе́ние, -я permission. **дозво́ленный** permitted; legal. **дозво́лить, -лю** *pf.*, **дозволя́ть, -я́ю** *impf.* permit, allow.

дозвони́ться, -ню́сь *pf.* get through, reach by telephone; ring (*doorbell etc.*) until one gets an answer.

дозо́р, -а patrol; **ночно́й** ~ night watch. **дозо́рный** patrol, scout.

дозрева́ть, -а́ет *impf.*, **дозре́ть, -е́ет** *pf.* ripen. **дозре́лый** fully ripe.

доистори́ческий prehistoric. **доисто́рия, -и** prehistory.

дои́ть, дою́, до́ишь *impf.* (*pf.* **по~**) milk; **~ся** give milk. **до́йка, -и** milking. **до́йный** milch.

дойму́ *etc.*: *see* **доня́ть**

дойти́, дойду́, -дёшь; дошёл, -шла́ *pf.* (*impf.* **доходи́ть**) +**до**+*g.* reach; make an impression on, get through to, penetrate to, touch; come to, be a matter of.

док, -а dock.

доказа́тельный demonstrative, conclusive. **доказа́тельство, -а** proof, evidence; demonstration. **доказа́ть, -ажу́** *pf.*, **дока́зывать, -аю** *impf.* demonstrate, prove; argue, try to show. **доказу́емый** demonstrable.

докати́ться, -ачу́сь, -а́тишься *pf.*, **дока́тываться, -аюсь** *impf.* roll; thunder, boom; +**до**+*g.* sink into, come to.

докла́д, -а report; lecture; paper; talk, address; announcement. **докла́дчик, -а** speaker, lecturer; rapporteur. **докла́дывать(ся, -аю(сь** *impf. of* **доложи́ть(ся**

до́красна́ *adv.* to red heat, to redness; red-hot, red.

до́ктор, -а; *pl.* **-а́** doctor. **доктора́льный** didactic. **доктора́нт, -а** person working for doctorate. **до́кторский** doctor's; doctoral. **до́кторша, -и** woman doctor; doctor's wife.

доктри́на, -ы doctrine. **доктринёр, -а** doctrinaire. **доктринёрский** doctrinaire.

докуме́нт, -а document, paper; deed, instrument. **документа́льный** documentary. **документа́ция, -и** documentation; documents, papers.

долби́ть, -блю́ *impf.* hollow; chisel, gouge; repeat, say over and over again; swot up; learn by rote.

долг, -а (-у), *loc.* **-у́**; *pl.* **-и́** duty; debt; **в** ~ on credit; **в ~у́** indebted; **взять в** ~ borrow; **дать в** ~ lend.

до́лгий; до́лог, -лга́, -о long. **до́лго** *adv.* long, (for) a long time. **долгове́чный** lasting; durable.

долголе́тие, -я longevity. **долголе́тний** of many years; long-standing.

долгота́, -ы́; *pl.* **-ы** length; longitude.

долево́й lengthwise. **до́лее** *adv.* longer.

должа́ть, -а́ю *impf.* (*pf.* **за~**) borrow.

до́лжен, -жна́ *pred.*+*d.* in debt to; +*inf.* obliged, bound; likely; must, have to, ought to; **он ~ мне три рубля́** he owes me three roubles; **он ~ идти́** he must go; **он ~ был отказа́ться** he had to refuse; **он ~ ско́ро прийти́** he should be here soon; **должно́ быть** probably. **должни́к, -а́, -ни́ца, -ы** debtor. **должностн|о́й** official; **~о́е лицо́** official, functionary, public servant. **до́лжность, -и**; *g.pl.* **-е́й** post, appointment, office; duties. **до́лжный** due, fitting, proper.

доли́на, -ы valley.

до́ллар, -а dollar.

доложи́ть[1], -ожу́, -о́жишь *pf.* (*impf.* **докла́дывать**) add.

доложи́ть[2], -ожу́, -о́жишь *pf.* (*impf.* **докла́дывать**) +*a.* *or* **о**+*p.* report; give a report on; announce; **~ся** announce one's arrival.

доло́й *adv.* away, off; +*a.* down with!; **с глаз ~, из се́рдца вон** out of sight, out of mind; **с глаз мои́х ~!** get out of my sight!

долото́, -а́; *pl.* **-а** chisel.

до́лька, -и segment, section; clove.

до́льше *adv.* longer.

до́ля, -и; *g.pl.* **-е́й** part, portion; share; quota, allotment; lobe; lot, fate.

дом, -а (-у), *loc.* **-у́**; *pl.* **-а́** building, house; home; household; lineage; family; **на ~у́** at home. **до́ма** *adv.* at home; in(doors). **дома́шн|ий** house; home; domestic; home-made, homespun, home-brewed; tame; **~яя рабо́та** homework; housework; **~яя хозя́йка** housewife; **~ие** *sb.*, *pl.* family, people.

до́менн|ый blast-furnace, ironmaking; **~ая печь** blast-furnace.

доминúровать, -рует *impf.* dominate, predominate; +**над**+*i.* dominate, command.

домкра́т, -а jack.

до́мна, -ы blast-furnace.

домовладе́лец, -льца, -лица, -ы house-owner; landlord. **домово́дство, -а** household management; domestic science. **домо́в|ый** house; household; housing; **~ая кни́га** house-register, register of tenants; **~ая конто́ра** house-manager's office; **~ый трест** housing trust.

домога́тельство, -а solicitation, importunity; demand, bid. **домога́ться, -а́юсь** *impf.+g.* seek, solicit, covet, bid for.

домо́й *adv.* home, homewards. **домострое́ние, -я** housebuilding. **домострои́тельный** housebuilding. **домоуправле́ние, -я** house management (committee). **домохозя́йка, -и** housewife. **домрабо́тница, -ы** domestic servant, daily (maid).

дона́шиваться, -вается *impf. of* **доноси́ться**[2]

доне́льзя *adv.* in the extreme; to the utmost degree; **он ~ упря́м** he's as stubborn as a mule, he couldn't be more pigheaded.

донесе́ние, -я dispatch, report, message. **донести́, -су́, -сёшь; -нёс, -сла́** *pf.* (*impf.* **доноси́ть**) report, announce; *+d.* inform; **+на**+*a.* inform against, denounce; **~сь** be heard; **+до**+*g.* reach, reach the ears of; carry as far as.

до́низу *adv.* to the bottom; **све́рху ~** from top to bottom.

донима́ть, -а́ю *impf. of* **доня́ть**

до́нный bottom, base; **~ лёд** ground ice.

до́нор, -а blood-donor.

доно́с, -а denunciation, information. **доноси́ть(ся**[1]**, -ношу́(сь, -но́сишь(ся** *impf. of* **донести́(сь**

доноси́ться[2]**, -но́сится** *pf.* (*impf.* **дона́шиваться**) wear out, be worn out.

доно́счик, -а informer.

донско́й Don; **~ каза́к** Don Cossack.

до́нья *etc.*: *see* **дно**

до н.э. *abbr.* **до на́шей э́ры** B.C.

доня́ть, дойму́, -мёшь; до́нял, -а́, -о *pf.* (*impf.* **донима́ть**) weary to death, pester.

допла́та, -ы additional payment, extra charge, excess. **доплати́ть, -ачу́, -а́тишь** *pf.*, **допла́чивать, -аю** *impf.* pay in addition; pay the rest.

доплыва́ть, -а́ю *impf.*, **доплы́ть, -ыву́, -ывёшь; -ы́л, -а́, -о** *pf.* **до**+*g.* swim to, sail to; reach.

допо́длинно *adv.* for certain. **допо́длинный** authentic, genuine.

дополне́ние, -я supplement, addition; appendix; addendum; object. **дополни́тельно** *adv.* in addition. **дополни́тельн|ый** supplementary, additional, extra; complementary; **~ые вы́боры** by-election. **допо́лнить, -ню** *pf.*, **дополня́ть, -я́ю** *impf.* supplement, add to, amplify; complete; complement.

допото́пный antediluvian.

допра́шивать, -аю *impf.*, **допроси́ть, -ошу́, -о́сишь** *pf.* interrogate, question, examine. **допро́с, -а** interrogation, examination.

до́пуск, -а right of entry, admittance; tolerance. **допуска́ть, -а́ю** *impf.*, **допусти́ть, -ущу́, -у́стишь** *pf.* admit; allow, permit; tolerate; grant, assume, suppose. **допусти́мый** permissable, admissible, allowable, acceptable. **допуще́ние, -я** assumption.

доро́га, -и road; highway; way; journey; route; **в доро́ге** on the journey, on the way, en route; **по доро́ге** on the way; the same way; **туда́ ему́ и ~!** serves him right!

до́рого *adv.* dear, dearly. **дорогови́зна, -ы** expensiveness; high cost, high prices. **дорого́й; до́рог, -а́, -о** dear; expensive; costly.

доро́дный portly, corpulent, stout; healthy, strong.

дородово́й antenatal.

дорожа́ть, -а́ет *impf.* (*pf.* **вз~, по~**) rise in price, go up. **доро́же** *comp. of* **до́рого, дорого́й. дорожи́ть, -жу́** *impf.+i.* value; prize; care about.

доро́жка, -и path, walk; track; lane; runway; strip, runner, stair-carpet. **доро́жный** road; highway; travelling.

доса́да, -ы annoyance; disappointment; nuisance, pity. **досади́ть, -ажу́** *pf.*, **досажда́ть, -а́ю** *impf.+d.* annoy. **доса́дливый** annoyed, irritated, disappointed; of annoyance. **доса́дный** annoying; disappointing. **доса́довать, -дую** be annoyed (**на**+*a.* with).

досе́ле *adv.* up to now.

доска́, -и́, *a.* **до́ску**; *pl.* **-и, -со́к, -ска́м** board; plank; slab; plaque, plate.

досло́вный literal, verbatim; word-for-word.

досмо́тр, -а inspection, examination. **досмо́трщик, -а** inspector, examiner.

доспе́хи, -ов *pl.* armour.

досро́чный ahead of time, ahead of schedule, early.

достава́ть(ся, -таю́(сь, -ёшь(ся *impf. of* **доста́ть(ся**

доста́вить, -влю *pf.*, **доставля́ть, -я́ю** *impf.* deliver, convey; supply, furnish; cause, give. **доста́вка, -и** delivery; conveyance. **доста́вщик, -а** roundsman, delivery man.

доста́ну *etc.*: *see* **доста́ть**

доста́ток, -тка sufficiency; prosperity; *pl.* income. **доста́точно** *adv.* enough, sufficiently. **доста́точный** sufficient; adequate; prosperous, well-off.

доста́ть, -а́ну *pf.* (*impf.* **достава́ть**) fetch; get (out), take (out); obtain; *+g. or* **до**+*g.* touch; reach; *impers.* suffice, be sufficient; **~ся**+*d.* pass to, be inherited by; fall to the lot of; **ему́ доста́нется** he'll catch it.

достига́ть, -а́ю *impf.*, **дости́гнуть, дости́чь, -и́гну; -сти́г** *pf.+g.* attain, achieve; *+g. or* **до**+*g.* reach. **достиже́ние, -я** achievement, attainment. **достижи́мый** accessible; attainable.

досто... *in comb.* worthy (of). **достове́рный** reliable, trustworthy; authentic. **~па́мятный**

memorable. **~примеча́тельность, -и** notable place or object; *pl.* sights; **осма́тривать ~примеча́тельности** go sightseeing. **~примеча́тельный** noteworthy, remarkable, notable.

досто́инство, -а dignity; merit, virtue; value; rank, title. **досто́йно** *adv.* suitably, fittingly, adequately, properly; with dignity. **досто́йный** deserved; fitting, adequate; suitable, fit; worthy; +*g.* worthy of, deserving.

достоя́ние, -я property.

до́ступ, -а access; entrance; admission, admittance. **досту́пный** accessible; simple; easily understood; intelligible; approachable; moderate, reasonable; **~ для** open to; available to.

досу́г, -а leisure, (spare) time. **досу́жий** leisure, spare; idle.

до́суха *adv.* dry.

досяга́емый attainable, accessible.

дота́ция, -и grant, subsidy.

дотла́ utterly, completely, out; to the ground.

дото́шный meticulous.

дотра́гиваться, -аюсь *impf.*, **дотро́нуться, -нусь** *pf.* +**до**+*g.* touch.

дотя́гивать, -аю *impf.*, **дотяну́ть, -яну́, -я́нешь** *pf.* draw out; stretch out; hold out; live, last; put off; +**до**+*g.* draw, drag, haul as far as; reach, make; **~ся** stretch, reach; drag on; +**до**+*g.* reach, touch.

до́хлый dead; sickly, puny. **до́хнуть, -нет; дох** (*pf.* **из~, по~, с~**) die; croak, kick the bucket.

дохну́ть, -ну́, -нёшь *pf.* draw a breath.

дохо́д, -а income; receipts; revenue. **доходи́ть, -ожу́, -о́дишь** *impf. of* **дойти. дохо́дность, -и** profitability; income. **дохо́дный** profitable, lucrative, paying; income-producing, revenue-producing. **дохо́дчивый** intelligible, easy to understand.

до́чери *etc.*: *see* **дочь**

до́чиста *adv.* clean; completely.

до́чка, -и daughter. **дочь, -чери**, *i.* **-черью**; *pl.* **-чери, -чере́й**, *i.* **-черьми́** daughter.

дошёл *etc.*: *see* **дойти**

дошко́льник, -а, -ница, -ы preschooler. **дошко́льный** pre-school; nusery.

доща́тый plank, board, wooden. **доще́чка, -и** small plank, small board; door-plate, name-plate.

доя́рка, -и milkmaid.

др.: и ~ *abbr.* (*of* **други́е**) & co.; *et al.*

д-р *abbr.* (*of* **до́ктор**) Dr, Doctor; (*of* **дире́ктор**) Director.

драгоце́нность, -и jewel; gem; precious stone; treasure; *pl.* jewellery; valuables. **драгоце́нный** precious.

дразни́ть, -ню́, -нишь *impf.* tease.

дра́ка, -и fight; **доходи́ть до дра́ки** come to blows.

драко́н, -а dragon; wyvern.

дра́ма, -ы drama; tragedy, calamity. **драмати́зм, -а** dramatic effect; dramatic character, dramatic quality; tension. **драмати́ческий** dramatic; drama, theatre, of the theatre; theatrical; tense. **драмату́рг, -а** playwright, dramatist. **драматурги́я, -и** dramatic art; dramatic composition, play-writing; drama, plays.

драп, -а heavy woollen cloth.

драпиро́вка, -и draping; curtain; hangings. **драпиро́вщик, -а** upholsterer. **драпри́** *indecl. pl.* curtain(s), hangings.

дра́повый cloth.

драть, деру́, -рёшь; драл, -а́, -о *impf.* (*pf.* **вы́~, за~, со~**) tear, tear up; sting, irritate; run away, make off; tear off; kill; beat, flog, thrash; tear out; +**с**+*g.* fleece; sting; **~ го́рло** bawl; **~ у́ши** +*d.* jar on; **чёрт его́ (по)дери́!** damn him! **~ся** fight; use one's fists; struggle.

дре́безги *pl.*; **в ~** to smithereens. **дребезжа́ние, -я** rattle, clink, jingle, tinkle. **дребезжа́ть, -жи́т** *impf.* rattle, jingle, tinkle, clink.

древеси́на, -ы wood; wood-pulp; timber. **древе́сн|ый** wood; **~ая ма́сса** wood-pulp; **~ый пито́мник** arboretum; **~ый у́голь** charcoal.

дре́вко, -а; *pl.* **-и, -ов** pole, (flag-)staff; shaft.

древнеевре́йский Hebrew. **древнеру́сский** Old Russian. **дре́вний** ancient; very old, aged. **дре́вность, -и** antiquity.

дрези́на, -ы trolley.

дре́йф, -а drift; leeway. **дрейфова́ть, -фу́ет** *impf.* drift. **дрейфу́ющий** drifting; **~ лёд** drift-ice.

дрема́, -ы́, дрёма, -ы drowsiness, sleepiness. **дрема́ть, -млю́, -млешь** *impf.* doze; slumber; drowse; **не ~** be wakeful; be wide awake, on the alert. **дремо́та, -ы** drowsiness, somnolence.

дрему́чий thick, dense.

дрессиро́ванный trained; performing. **дрессирова́ть, -ру́ю** *impf.* (*pf.* **вы́~**) train, school. **дрессиро́вка, -и** training. **дрессиро́вщик, -а** trainer.

дроби́льный crushing, grinding. **дроби́на, -ы** pellet. **дроби́ть, -блю́** *impf.* (*pf.* **раз~**) break up, smash; crush, grind; divide, split up; **~ся** break to pieces, smash; crumble; divide, split up. **дроблёный** splintered, crushed, ground, fragmented. **дро́бный** separate; subdivided, split up; minute; staccato, abrupt; fractional; **~ дождь** fine rain. **дробови́к, -а́** shot-gun. **дробь, -и** (small) shot, pellets; drumming; tapping; trilling; fraction.

дрова́, дров *pl.* firewood. **дро́вни, дро́вне́й** *pl.* wood-sledge.

дро́ги, дрог *pl.* dray; hearse.

дро́гнуть, -ну *pf.*, **дрожа́ть, -жу́** *impf.* shake, move; tremble; shiver; quiver, quaver; flicker; waver, falter; +**над**+*i.* be concerned over, worry about; grudge.

дрожжево́й yeast. **дро́жжи, -е́й** *pl.* yeast.

дрóжки, -жек *pl.* droshky.
дрожь, -и shivering, trembling; tremor, quaver.
дрозд, -á thrush.
дрóссель, -я *m.* throttle, choke.
дрóтик, -а javelin, dart.
друг[1], **-а**; *pl.* **-узья́, -зéй** friend. **друг**[2]; **~ дрýга (дрýгу)** each other, one another; **~ за ~ом** one after another; in single file. **другóй** other, another; different; second; **на ~ день** (the) next day. **дрýжба, -ы** friendship. **дружелю́бный, дрýжеский, дрýжественный** friendly. **дружи́ть, -жý, -ýжишь** *impf.* be friends, be on friendly terms; **~ся** (*pf.* **по~ся**) make friends. **дрýжно** *adv.* harmoniously, in concord; simultaneously, in concert; rapidly, smoothly. **дрýжный; -жен, -жнá, -о** amicable; harmonious; simultaneous, concerted.
друммóндов свет limelight.
дря́блый; дрябл, -á, -о flabby; flaccid; sluggish.
дря́зги, -зг *pl.* squabbles; petty annoyances.
дряннóй worthless, rotten; good-for-nothing. **дрянь, -и** trash, rubbish.
дряхлéть, -éю *impf.* (*pf.* **о~**) become decrepit. **дря́хлый; -хл, -лá, -о** decrepit, senile.
дуб, -а; *pl.* **-ы́** oak; blockhead. **дуби́льный** tanning, tannic. **дуби́льня, -и**; *g.pl.* **-лен** tannery. **дуби́на, -ы** club, cudgel; blockhead. **дуби́нка, -и** truncheon, baton. **дуби́ть, -блю́** *impf.* (*pf.* **вы́~**) tan.
дублёр, -а understudy; actor dubbing a part. **дублéт, -а, дублика́т, -а** duplicate. **дубли́ровать, -рую** duplicate; understudy; dub.
дубовáтый coarse; stupid, thick. **дубóвый** oak; coarse; clumsy; thick.
Дувр, -а Dover.
дугá, -и́; *pl.* **-и** shaft-bow; arc; arch.
дýдка, -и pipe, fife. **дýжка, -и** small arch or bow; handle; (croquet-)hoop; wishbone.
дýло, -а muzzle; barrel. **дýльце, -а**; *g.pl.* **-лец** mouthpiece.
дýма, -ы thought; Duma; council. **дýмать, -аю** *impf.* (*pf.* **по~**) think; *+inf.* think of, intend.
Дунáй, -я the Danube.
дуновéние, -я puff, breath. **дýнуть, -ну** *pf. of* **дуть**
дупли́стый hollow. **дуплó, -á**; *pl.* **-а, -пел** hollow; hole; cavity.
дýра, -ы, дурáк, -á fool. **дурáчить, -чу** *impf.* (*pf.* **о~**) fool, dupe; **~ся** play the fool.
дурéть, -éю *impf.* (*pf.* **о~**) grow stupid.
дурмáн, -а datura; drug, narcotic; intoxicant. **дурмáнить, -ню** *impf.* (*pf.* **о~**) stupefy.
дурнóй; -рен, -рнá, -о bad, evil; nasty; ill, faint; ugly; **мне дýрно** I'm going to faint. **дурнотá, -ы́** faintness; nausea.
дýтый blown, blown up, hollow; inflated; pneumatic; exaggerated. **дуть, дýю** *impf.* (*pf.* **вы́~, по~, дýнуть**) blow; **дýет** there is a draught. **дутьё, -я́** blowing; draught; blast; glass-blowing. **дýться, дýюсь** *impf.* pout; sulk, be sulky.
дух, -а (-у) spirit; spirits; heart; mind; breath; air; ghost; smell; **в ~е** in high spirits, in a good mood; **во весь ~** at full speed, flat out; **не в моём ~е** not to my taste; **ни слýху ни ~у** no news, not a word, not a whisper; **одни́м ~ом** in one breath; at one go, at a stretch; **пáдать ~ом** lose heart, grow despondent. **духи́, -óв** *pl.* scent, perfume. **Дýхов день** Whit Monday. **духовéнство, -а** clergy, priesthood. **духови́дец, -дца** clairvoyant; medium. **духóвка, -и** oven. **духóвный** spiritual; inner, inward; ecclesiastical, church, religious. **духовóй** wind; air; steam; steamed. **духотá, -ы́** stuffiness, closeness; stuffy heat.
дýш, -а shower.
душá, -и́, *a.* **-у**; *pl.* **-и** soul; heart; feeling; spirit; moving spirit; inspiration; **в глубинé души́** in one's heart of hearts; **в душé** inwardly, secretly; at heart; **за душóй** to one's name; **на дýшу** per head; **от всéй души́** with all one's heart.
душевáя *sb.* shower-room.
душевнобольнóй mentally ill, insane; *sb.* mental patient; lunatic. **душéвный** mental; of the mind; sincere, cordial, heartfelt.
души́стый fragrant; sweet-scented; **~ горóшек** sweet pea(s). **души́ть**[1], **-шý, -шишь** *impf.* (*pf.* **на~**) scent, perfume; **~ся** use scent, put on scent.
души́ть[2], **-шý, -шишь** *impf.* (*pf.* **за~**) strangle; stifle, smother, suffocate; suppress; choke.
дýшный; -шен, -шнá, -о stuffy, close; sultry; stifling, suffocating.
дуэли́ст, -а duellist. **дуэ́ль, -и** duel.
ды́бом *adv.* on end; **у меня́ вóлосы встáли ~** my hair stood on end. **дыбы́: станови́ться на ~** rear; resist, jib, dig one's heels in.
дым, -а (-у), *loc.* **-ý**; *pl.* **-ы́** smoke. **дыми́ть, -млю́** *impf.* (*pf.* **на~**) smoke; **~ся** smoke, steam; billow. **ды́мка, -и** haze, mist. **ды́мный** smoky. **дымов|óй** smoke; **~áя трубá** flue, chimney; smoke-stack, funnel. **дымóк, -мкá** puff of smoke. **дымохóд, -а** flue. **ды́мчатый** smoky; smoked; smoke-coloured.
ды́ня, -и melon.
дырá, -ы́; *pl.* **-ы, ды́рка, -и**; *g.pl.* **-рок** hole; gap. **дыря́вый** full of holes; holed, perforated.
дыхáние, -я breathing, respiration; breath. **дыхáтельн|ый** respiratory; breathing, breather; **~ое гóрло** windpipe. **дышáть, -шý, -шишь** *impf.* breathe.
дья́вол, -а devil. **дья́вольский** devilish, diabolical; damnable.
дья́кон, -а; *pl.* **-á** deacon. **дьячóк, -чкá** sacristan, sexton; reader.
дю́жина, -ы dozen. **дю́жинный** ordinary, commonplace.

дэ *nt.indecl.* the letter **д.**
дюйм, -а inch.
дя́денька, -и *m.*, **дя́дюшка, -и** *m.* uncle. **дя́дя, -и**; *g.pl.* **-ей** uncle.
дя́тел, -тла woodpecker.

Е

е *nt.indecl.* the letter **е.**
ев... *pref.* eu-. **евге́ника, -и** eugenics. **е́внух, -а** eunuch. **еврази́йский** Eurasian. **евста́хиев** Eustachian.
ева́нгелие, -я gospel; the Gospels. **евангели́ческий** evangelical. **ева́нгельский** gospel.
евре́й, -я Jew; Hebrew; **ве́рующий ~** Orthodox Jew. **евре́йка, -и** Jewess. **евре́йский** Jewish.
Евро́па, -ы Europe. **Европарла́мент, -а** Europarliament. **европе́ец, -е́йца, европе́йка, -е́йки** European. **европе́йский** European; Western.
ЕВС *abbr.* (*of* ***Европе́йская валю́тная систе́ма***) EMS, European Monetary System.
Еги́пет, -а Egypt. **еги́петский** Egyptian. **египтя́нин, -а**; *pl.* **-я́не, -я́н, египтя́нка, -и** Egyptian.
его́ *see* **он, оно́**; *pron.* his; its, of it.
еда́, -ы́ food; meal; eating.
едва́ *adv.* & *conj.* hardly, barely; only just; scarcely; **~..., как** no sooner ... than; **~ ли** hardly, scarcely; **~ (ли) не** nearly, almost, all but.
еди́м *etc.*: *see* **есть**[1]
едине́ние, -я unity. **едини́ца, -ы** one; figure one; unity; unit; individual. **едини́чность, -и** singleness; single occurrence. **едини́чный** single, unitary; solitary, isolated; individual.
едино... *in comb.* mono-, uni-; one; co-. **единобо́жие, -я** monotheism. **~бо́рство, -а** single combat. **~бра́чие, -я** monogamy. **~бра́чный** monogamous. **~вла́стие, -я** autocracy, absolute rule. **~вла́стный** autocratic; dictatorial; absolute. **~вре́менно** *adv.* only once; simultaneously. **~вре́менный** extraordinary; unique; *+d. or* **с**+*i.* simultaneous with. **~гла́сие, -я, ~ду́шие, -я** unanimity. **~гла́сный, ~ду́шный** unanimous. **~кро́вный** consanguineous; **~кровный брат** half-brother. **~мы́слие, -я** like-mindedness; agreement in opinion. **~мы́шленник, -а** like-minded person; accomplice; **мы с ним ~мы́шленники** we are in agreement, we think the same way. **~нача́лие, -я** unified management command. **~обра́зие, -я** uniformity. **~обра́зный** uniform. **~ро́г, -а** unicorn; narwhal. **~утро́бный** uterine; **~утро́бный брат** half-brother.
еди́нственно *adv.* only, solely. **еди́нственный** only, sole; singular; unique, unequalled. **еди́нство, -а** unity. **еди́ный** one; single, sole; united, unified; common.
е́дкий; е́док, едка́, -о caustic, corrosive; acrid, pungent; sarcastic; **~ натр** caustic soda.
едо́к, -а́ mouth, head; eater.
е́ду *etc.*: *see* **е́хать. е́дче** *comp. of* **е́дкий**
её *see* **она́**; *pron.* her, hers; its.
ёж, ежа́ hedgehog.
еже... *in comb.* every; -ly. **ежего́дник, -а** annual, year-book. **~го́дный** annual, yearly. **~дне́вный** daily; everyday; quotidian. **~кварта́льный** quarterly. **~ме́сячник, -а, ~ме́сячный** monthly. **~неде́льник, -а, ~неде́льный** weekly. **~но́щный** nightly.
ежеви́ка, -и blackberries; blackberry bush, bramble. **ежеви́чный** blackberry.
ёжиться, ёжусь *impf.* (*pf.* **съ~**) huddle up; shrivel; shrink away; hesitate.
езда́, -ы́ ride, riding; drive, driving; going; journey; traffic. **е́здить, е́зжу** *impf.* go; ride, drive; slip; **~ верхо́м** ride. **ездо́к, -а́** rider; horseman.
ей *see* **она́**
ей-бо́гу *int.* really! I swear (to God).
ел *etc.*: *see* **есть**[1]
е́ле *adv.* hardly, barely, scarcely; only just.
ёлка, -и fir, fir-tree, spruce; Christmas tree, Christmas party; herring-bone pattern. **ело́вый** fir, spruce; deal, white-wood. **ёлочка, -и** herring-bone pattern, herring-boning. **ёлочный** Christmas-tree; herring-bone; dendritic. **ель, -и** fir, fir-tree; spruce; deal, white wood. **е́льник, -а** fir (spruce) plantation; fir-wood, fir-twigs.
ем *etc.*: *see* **есть**[1]
ёмкий capacious. **ёмкость, -и** capacity, cubic content; capacitance.
ему́ *see* **он, оно́**
ено́т, -а, ено́товый raccoon.
епи́скоп, -а bishop. **епи́скопский** episcopal.
е́ресь, -и heresy. **ерети́к, -а́** heretic. **ерети́ческий** heretical.
ёрзать, -аю *impf.* fidget.
еро́шить, -шу *impf.* (*pf.* **взъ~**) ruffle, rumple, tousle; dishevel; **~ся** bristle, stand on end, stick up.
ерунда́, -ы́ nonsense, rubbish; trifle, trifling matter.
е́сли if; **~ бы** if only; **~ бы не** but for, if it were not for; **~ не** unless; **~ то́лько** provided; if only; **что, ~ бы** what about, how about.
ест *see* **есть**[1]
есте́ственно *adv.* naturally. **есте́ственный** natural. **естество́, -а́** nature; essence. **естестве́дение, -я, естествозна́ние, -я** (natural) science; natural history; nature study.

есть[1], ем, ешь, ест, еди́м; ел *impf.* (*pf.* **съ~**) eat; corrode, eat away; sting, make smart; torment, nag (at).
есть[2] *see* **быть**; is, are; there is, there are; **и ~** yes, indeed; **как ~** entirely, completely; *int.* yes, sir; very good, sir; aye, aye sir.
ефре́йтор, -а lance-corporal.
е́хать, е́ду *impf.* (*pf.* **по~**) go; ride, drive; travel, journey, voyage; **~ верхо́м** ride.
ехи́дный malicious, spiteful; venomous.
ешь *see* **есть[1]**
ещё *adv.* still; yet; (some) more; any more; yet, further; again; *+comp.* still, yet even; **всё ~** still; **~ бы!** of course! oh yes! can you ask?; **~ не, нет ~** not yet; **~ раз** once more, again; encore!; **пока́ ~** for the present, for the time being.
ЕЭС *abbr.* (*of* ***Европе́йское экономи́ческое соо́бщество***) EEC, European Economic Community.
е́ю *see* **она́**

ж *letter*: *see* **жэ**
ж *conj.*: *see* **же**
жа́ба, -ы toad; quinsy.
жа́бра, -ы; *g.pl.* **-бр** gill, branchia.
жа́воронок, -нка lark.
жа́дничать, -аю *impf.* be greedy; be mean. **жа́дность, -и** greed; greediness; avidity; avarice, meanness. **жа́дный; -ден, -дна́, -о** greedy; avid; avaricious, mean.
жа́жда, -ы thirst; +*g.* thirst for, craving for. **жа́ждать, -ду** *impf.* thirst, long, yearn.
жаке́т, -а, жаке́тка, -и jacket.
жале́ть, -е́ю *impf.* (*pf.* **по~**) pity, feel sorry for; regret, be sorry; +*a. or g.* spare; grudge.
жа́лить, -лю *impf.* (*pf.* **у~**) sting, bite.
жа́лкий; -лок, -лка́, -о pitiful, pitiable, pathetic, wretched. **жа́лко** *pred.*: *see* **жаль**
жа́ло, -а sting.
жа́лоба, -ы complaint. **жа́лобный** plaintive; doleful; mournful.
жа́лованн|ый granted, conferred; **~ая гра́мота** charter, letters patent. **жа́лованье, -я** salary, pay, wage(s); reward; donation. **жа́ловать, -лую** *impf.* (*pf.* **по~**) +*a. or d.* of person, *i. or a.* of thing, grant, bestow on, confer on; +**к**+*d.* come to see, visit; **~ся** complain (**на**+*a.* of, about).
жа́лостливый compassionate, sympathetic; pitiful. **жа́лостный** piteous; compassionate, sympathetic. **жа́лость, -и** pity, compassion. **жаль, жа́лко** *pred.*, *impers.* (it is) a pity, a shame; +*d.* it grieves; +*d.* & *g.* regret; feel sorry for; +*g.* grudge; **ей ~ бы́ло себя́** she felt sorry for herself; **~, что вас там не́ было** it is a pity you were not there; **как ~** what a pity; **мне ~ его́** I'm sorry for him.
жанр, -а genre; genre-painting. **жанри́ст, -а** genre-painter.
жар, -а (-у), *loc.* **-у́** heat; heat of the day; hot place; embers; fever; (high) temperature; ardour. **жара́, -ы́** heat; hot weather.
жарго́н, -а jargon; slang, cant.
жа́рен|ый roast grilled; fried; **~ый карто́фель** chips; **~ое** *sb.* roast (meat). **жа́рить, -рю** *impf.* (*pf.* **за~, из~**) roast; grill; fry; scorch, burn; **~ся** roast, fry; **~ся на со́лнце** sunbathe. **жа́рк|ий; -рок, -рка́, -о** hot; torrid; tropical; heated; ardent; passionate; **-о́е** *sb.* roast (meat). **жаро́вня, -и**; *g.pl.* **-вен** brazier. **жаропро́чный** ovenproof. **жар-пти́ца, -ы.** Firebird. **жа́рче** *comp. of* **жа́ркий**
жа́тва, -ы harvest. **жа́твенн|ый** harvest; reaping; **~ая маши́на** harvester, reaper. **жа́тка, -и** harvester, reaper. **жа́ть[1], жну, жнёшь** *impf.* (*pf.* **с~**) reap, cut.
жать[2], жму, жмёшь *impf.* press, squeeze; pinch, be tight; oppress.
жва́чка, -и chewing, rumination; cud; chewing-gum. **жва́чн|ый** ruminant; **~ое** *sb.* ruminant.
жгу *etc.*: *see* **жечь**
жгут, -а́ plait; braid; tourniquet.
жгу́чий burning, smarting; scalding, baking; hot; caustic, corrosive. **жёг** *etc.*: *see* **жечь**
ж.д. *abbr.* (*of* ***желе́зная доро́га***) railway.
ждать, жду, ждёшь; -ал, -а́, -о *impf.*+*g.* wait for, await; expect.
же, ж *conj.* but; and; however; also; *part.* giving emphasis or expressing identity; **мне же ка́жется** it seems to me, however; **на пе́рвом же шагу́** at the very first step; **оди́н и тот же** one and the same; **он же ваш брат** he's your brother, after all; **сего́дня же** this very day; **так же** in the same way; **тако́й же, тот же** the same, idem; **там же** in the same place, ibid.; **что же ты де́лаешь?** what on earth are you doing?
жева́тельн|ый chewing; **~ая рези́нка** chewing-gum. **жева́ть, жую́, жуёшь** *impf.* chew; masticate; ruminate.
жезл, -а́ rod; staff; baton; crozier.
жела́ние, -я wish, desire. **жела́нный** wished-for, longed-for; desired; beloved. **жела́тельный** desirable; advisable, preferable; optative. **жела́ть, -а́ю** *impf.* (*pf.* **по~**) +*g.* wish for, desire; want; +**чтобы** *or inf.* wish, want. **жела́ющие** *sb.*, *pl.* those who wish.
желе́ *nt.indecl.* jelly.
железа́, -ы́; *pl.* **же́лезы, -лёз, -за́м** gland; *pl.* tonsils. **желе́зистый[1]** glandular.
желе́зистый[2] iron; ferrous; ferriferous; chalybeate. **железнодоро́жник, -а** railwayman. **железнодоро́жн|ый** railway; **~ая ве́тка** branch line; **~ое полотно́** permanent

way; **~ый у́зел** junction. **желе́зн|ый** iron; ferric; reliable, dependable; **~ая доро́га** railway; **~ый лом** scrap iron. **желе́зо, -а** iron.

железо... *in comb.* iron, ferro-, ferri-, ferric. **железобето́н, -а** reinforced concrete, ferroconcrete. **~бето́нный** reinforced-concrete. **~плави́льный** iron foundry. **~прока́тный** steel-rolling; **~прока́тный заво́д** rolling mill. **~ру́дный** iron-ore.

жёлоб, -а; *pl.* **-а́** gutter; trough; chute; channel; groove. **желобо́к, -бка́** groove, channel, flute; slot; furrow.

желте́ть, -е́ю *impf.* (*pf.* **по~**) turn yellow; show yellow. **желтова́тый** yellowish; sallow. **желто́к, -тка́** yolk. **желту́ха, -и** jaundice. **желту́шный** jaundiced. **жёлт|ый; жёлт, -а́, жёлто́** yellow; **~ая медь** brass.

желу́док, -дка stomach. **желу́дочный** stomach; gastric.

жёлудь, -я; *g.pl.* **-е́й** *m.* acorn.

жёлчный bilious; bile, gall; peevish, irritable. **жёлчь, -и** bile, gall.

жема́ниться, -нюсь *impf.* mince, be affected, put on airs. **жема́нный** mincing, affected.

же́мчуг, -а; *pl.* **-а́** pearl, pearls. **жемчу́жина, -ы** pearl. **жемчу́жный** pearl; pearly.

жена́, -ы́; *pl.* **жёны** wife. **жена́тик, -а** married man; *pl.* married couple. **жена́тый** married.

Жене́ва, -ы Geneva.

жени́ть, -ню́, -нишь *impf.* & *pf.* (*pf. also* **по~**) marry. **жени́тьба, -ы** marriage, wedding. **жени́ться, -ню́сь, -нишься** *impf.* & *pf.* (+**на**+*p.*) marry, get married (to). **жени́х, -а́** fiancé; bridegroom. **же́нский** woman's; feminine; female. **же́нственный** womanly, feminine. **же́нщина, -ы** woman.

жердь, -и; *g.pl.* **-е́й** pole; stake.

жеребёнок, -нка; *pl.* **-бя́та, -бя́т** foal. **жеребе́ц, -бца́** stallion.

жеребьёвка, -и casting of lots.

жерло́, -а́; *pl.* **-а** muzzle; vent, pipe, crater.

жёрнов, -а; *pl.* **-а́, -о́в** millstone.

же́ртва, -ы sacrifice; victim; **пасть же́ртвой**+*g.* fall victim to; **принести́ в же́ртву** sacrifice. **же́ртвенный** sacrificial. **же́ртвовать, -твую** *impf.* (*pf.* **по~**) present, donate, make a donation (of); +*i.* sacrifice, give up.

жест, -а gesture.

жёсткий; -ток, -тка́, -о hard, tough; rigid, strict.

жесто́кий; -то́к, -а́, -о cruel; brutal; severe, sharp. **жестокосе́рдный, -се́рдый** hard-hearted. **жесто́кость, -и** crulty, brutality.

жёстче *comp. of* **жёсткий**

жесть, -и tin(-plate). **жестя́нка, -и** tin, can; piece of tin. **жестян|о́й** tin; **~а́я посу́да** tinware.

жето́н, -а medal; counter; token; **проездно́й ~** travel token.

жечь, жгу, жжёшь; жёг, жгла *impf.* (*pf.* **с~**) burn; **~ся** burn, sting; burn o.s. **жжёный** burnt; scorched; **~ ко́фе** roasted coffee.

живи́тельный invigorating, revivifying; bracing. **жи́во** *adv.* vividly; with animation; keenly; strikingly; quickly; promptly. **жив|о́й; жив, -а́, -о** living, live, alive; lively; keen; brisk; animated; vivacious; poignant; bright, sparkling; **~а́я и́згородь** (quickset) hedge; **~о́й инвента́рь** livestock; **на ~у́ю ни́тку** hastily, anyhow; **шить на ~у́ю ни́тку** tack; **оста́ться в ~ы́х** survive, escape with one's life. **живопи́сец, -сца** painter. **живопи́сн|ый** pictorial; picturesque; **~ое ме́сто** beauty spot. **жи́вопись, -и** painting; paintings, art. **жи́вость, -и** liveliness, vivacity, animation.

живо́т, -а abdomen, belly; stomach. **живо́тик, -а** tummy. **животново́дство, -а** stock-breeding, animal husbandry. **живо́тное** *sb.* animal; beast; brute; **ко́мнатное ~** pet. **живо́тный** animal.

живу́ *etc.*: *see* **жить. живу́чий** tenacious of life; hardy; firm, stable. **живьём** *adv.* alive.

жи́дк|ий; -док, -дка́, -о liquid; fluid; watery; weak, thin; sparse, scanty; feeble; **~ий криста́лл** liquid crystal; **~ое те́ло** liquid. **жи́дкостный** liquid, fluid; liquid-fuel. **жи́дкость, -и** liquid, fluid; liquor; wateriness, weakness, thinness. **жи́жа, -и, жи́жица, -ы** sludge, slurry; slush; wash, swill; liquid, liquor. **жи́же** *comp. of* **жи́дкий**

жи́зненный life, of life; vital; living; close to life; lifelike; vitally important; **~ые си́лы** vitality, sap; **~ый у́ровень** standard of living. **жизнеописа́ние, -я** biography. **жизнера́достный** full of the joy of living; cheerful, buoyant. **жизнеспосо́бный** capable of living; viable; vigorous, flourishing. **жизнь, -и** life; existence.

жил... *abbr.* (*of* **жили́щный, жило́й**) *in comb.* living; housing. **жилмасси́в, -а** housing estate. **~отде́л, -а** housing department. **~пло́щадь, -и** floor-space; housing, accommodation. **~строи́тельство, -а** house building. **~фонд, -а** housing, accommodation.

жи́ла, -ы vein; tendon, sinew; lode, seam; core, strand; catgut.

жиле́т, -а, жиле́тка, -и waistcoat.

жиле́ц, -льца́, жили́ца, -ы lodger; tenant; inhabitant; **он не ~ (на бе́лом све́те)** he is not long for this world.

жи́листый sinewy; stringy; wiry.

жили́ца *see* **жиле́ц. жили́ще, -а** dwelling, abode; lodging; (living) quarters. **жили́щн|ый** housing; living; **~ые усло́вия** living conditions.

жи́лка, -и vein; fibre, rib; streak; bent.

жил|о́й dwelling; residential; inhabited; habitable, fit to live in; **~о́й дом** dwelling house; block of flats; **~а́я пло́щадь** floor-space; housing, accommodation. **жильё, -я́** habitation; dwelling; lodging; (living) accommodation.

жим, -а press.

жир, -а (-у), *loc.* **-у́**; *pl.* **-ы́** fat; grease. **жире́ть, -ре́ю** *impf.* (*pf.* **о~, раз~**) grow fat, stout, plump. **жи́рный; -рен, -рна́, -о** fatty; greasy; rich; plump; lush; bold, heavy. **жирова́ть, -ру́ю** *impf.* lubricate, oil, grease; fatten, grow fat. **жирово́й** fatty; adipose; fat.

жите́йский worldly; of life, of the world; everyday. **жи́тель, -я** *m.* inhabitant; dweller. **жи́тельство, -а** residence; **ме́сто жи́тельства** residence, domicile; **ме́сто постоя́нного жи́тельства** permanent address. **жи́тница, -ы** granary. **жи́тный** cereal. **жи́то, -а** corn, cereal. **жить, живу́, -вёшь; жил, -а́, -о** *impf.* live; +*i.* live for, live on, live in. **житьё, -я́** life; existence; habitation, residence.

жму *etc.*: *see* **жать**[2]

жму́риться, -рюсь *impf.* (*pf.* **за~**) screw up one's eyes, frown. **жму́рки, -рок** *pl.* blind-man's buff.

жмых, -а́, жмыхи́, -о́в *pl.* oil-cake.

жне́йка, -и reaper. **жнец, -а́, жни́ца, -ы** reaper. **жну** *etc.*: *see* **жать**[1]

жоке́й, -я jockey. **жоке́йка, -и** jockey cap.

жре́бий, -я lot; fate, destiny; **~ бро́шен** the die is cast.

жрец, -а́ priest. **жре́ческий** priestly. **жри́ца, -ы** priestess.

жужжа́ние, -я humming, buzzing; hum, buzz, drone. **жужжа́ть, -жжу́** hum, buzz, drone; whiz(z).

жук, -а́ beetle.

жу́лик, -а petty thief; cheat, swindler; card-sharper. **жу́льничать, -аю** *impf.* (*pf.* **с~**) cheat, swindle, defraud.

жура́вль, -я́ *m.* crane.

жури́ть, -рю́ *impf.* reprove, take to task.

журна́л, -а magazine, periodical; journal; diary; register; log; **~ заседа́ний** minute-book.

журнали́ст, -а journalist. **журнали́стика, -и** journalism. **журнали́стский** journalistic.

журча́ние, -я ripple, babble; murmur. **журча́ть, -чи́т** *impf.* babble, ripple, murmur.

жу́ткий; -ток, -тка́, -о awe-inspiring; uncanny; terrible, terrifying. **жу́тко** *adv.* terrifyingly; terribly, awfully.

жую́ *etc.*: *see* **жева́ть**

жэ *nt.indecl.* the letter **ж.**

жюри́ *nt.indecl.* jury, judges; umpire, referee; **член ~** judge.

З

з *letter*: *see* **зэ**

з. *abbr.* (*of* **за́пад**) W, West.

за *prep.* **I.** +*a.* (*indicating motion or action*) or *i.* (*indicating rest or state*) behind; beyond; across, the other side of; at; to; **вы́йти за́муж за**+*a.* marry, get married to; **за́мужем за**+*i.* married to; **за́ борт, за бо́ртом** overboard; **за́ городом** out of town; **за рубежо́м** abroad; **сесть за роя́ль** sit down at the piano; **сиде́ть за роя́лем** be at the piano; **за́ угол, за угло́м** round the corner. **II.** +*a.* after; over; during, in the space of; by; for; to; **боя́ться за** fear for; **за ва́ше здоро́вье!** your health!; **вести́ за́ руку** lead by the hand; **далеко́ за по́лночь** long after midnight; **за два дня до**+*g.* two days before; **ему́ уже́ за́ сорок** he is over forty already; **есть за трои́х** eat enough for three; **за́ три киломе́тра от дере́вни** three kilometres from the village; **за́ ночь** during the night, overnight; **плати́ть за биле́т** pay for a ticket; **за после́днее вре́мя** recently, lately, of late. **III.** +*i.* after; for; on account of, because of; at, during; **год за го́дом** year after year; **идти́ за молоко́м** go for milk; **за неиме́нием**+*g.* for want of; **за обе́дом** at dinner; **о́чередь за ва́ми** it is your turn; **посла́ть за до́ктором** send for a doctor; **следи́ть за** look after; **сле́довать за** follow.

за... *pref. in comb.* **I.** *with vv. forms the perfective aspect*; *indicates beginning of action, direction of action beyond a given point, continuation of action to excess.* **II.** *with nn. and adjs.*: trans-, beyond, on the far side.

за|але́ть, -е́ет *pf.* **за|арка́нить, -ню** *pf.*

заба́ва, -ы amusement; game; pastime; fun. **забавля́ть, -я́ю** *impf.* amuse, entertain, divert; **~ся** amuse o.s. **заба́вный** amusing, funny.

забаллоти́ровать, -рую *pf.* blackball, reject, fail to elect.

забастова́ть, -ту́ю *pf.* strike; go on strike, come out on strike. **забасто́вка, -и** strike; stoppage. **забасто́вщик, -а, -щица, -ы** striker.

забве́ние, -я oblivion; unconsciousness; drowsiness. **забве́нный** forgotten.

забе́г, -а heat, race; trial **забега́ть, -а́ю** *impf.* **забежа́ть, -егу́** *pf.* run up; run off; stray; +**к**+*d.* drop in on, look in to see; **~ вперёд** run ahead; anticipate.

забеле́ть(ся, -е́ет(ся *pf.* (begin to) turn white.

за|бере́менеть, -ею *pf.* become pregnant.

заберу́ *etc.*: *see* **забра́ть. за|бетони́ровать, -рую** *pf.*

забива́ние, -я jamming. **забива́ть(ся, -а́ю(сь** *impf.* *of* **заби́ть(ся**[1]. **заби́вка, -и** driving in; blocking up, stopping up.

за|бинтова́ть, -ту́ю *pf.*, **забинто́вывать** *impf.* bandage; **~ся** bandage o.s.

забира́ть(ся, -а́ю(сь *impf.* *of* **забра́ть(ся**

заби́тый cowed, downtrodden. **заби́ть**[1], **-бью́, -бьёшь** *pf.* (*impf.* **забива́ть**) drive in, hammer in, ram in; score; seal, stop up, block up; obstruct; choke; jam; cram, stuff; beat up, knock senseless; render defenceless;

beat; outdo, surpass; slaughter; ~ **себé в гóлову** get it firmly fixed in one's head; ~**ся** hide, take refuge; become cluttered, become clogged; +**в**+*a.* get into, penetrate. **за|би́ть(ся**[2] *pf.* begin to beat. **забия́ка, -и** *c.g.* quarrelsome person; squabbler; trouble-maker; bully.

заблаговре́менно *adv.* in good time; well in advance. **заблаговре́менный** timely, done in good time.

заблагорассу́диться, -ится *pf., impers.* (+*d.*) come into one's head; seem good (to); **он придёт, когда́ ему́ заблагорассу́дится** he will come when he thinks fit, feels so disposed.

заблесте́ть, -ещу́, -ести́шь *or* **-е́щешь** *pf.* begin to shine, glitter, glow.

заблуди́ться, -ужу́сь, -у́дишься *pf.* lose one's way, get lost. **заблу́дший** lost, stray. **заблужда́ться, -а́юсь** *impf.* be mistaken. **заблужде́ние, -я** error; delusion.

за|бода́ть, -а́ю *pf.*

забо́й, -я (pit-)face. **забо́йщик, -а** face-worker, cutter.

заболева́емость, -и sickness rate; number of cases. **заболева́ние, -я** sickness, illness, disease; falling ill. **заболева́ть**[1]**, -а́ю** *impf.*, **заболе́ть**[1]**, -е́ю** *pf.* fall ill, fall sick; be taken ill; +*i.* go down with. **заболева́ть**[2]**, -а́ет** *impf.*, **заболе́ть**[2]**, -ли́т** *pf.* (begin to) ache, (begin to) hurt; **у меня́ заболе́л зуб** I have tooth-ache.

забо́р[1]**, -а** fence. **забо́ристый** strong; pungent; risqué, racy. **забо́рный** fence; coarse, indecent; risqué.

забо́р[2]**, -а** taking away; obtaining on credit.

забо́ртный outboard.

забо́та, -ы concern; care, attention(s); cares, trouble(s). **забо́тить, -о́чу** *impf.* (*pf.* **о~**) trouble, worry, cause anxiety to; ~**ся** *impf.* (*pf.* **по~**) worry, be troubled; take care (**о**+*p.* of); take trouble; care. **забо́тливый** solicitous, thoughtful, caring.

забрако́ванный rejected; ~ **това́р** rejects. **за|бракова́ть, -ку́ю** *pf.*

забра́сывать, -аю *impf. of* **заброса́ть, забро́сить**

забра́ть, -беру́, -берёшь; -а́л, -а́, -о *pf.* (*impf.* **забира́ть**) take; take away; seize; appropriate; take in; turn off, turn aside; come over; catch; stop up, block up; ~**ся** climb; get to, get into; hide, go into hiding.

забреда́ть, -а́ю *impf.*, **забрести́, -еду́, -едёшь; -ёл, -а́** *pf.* stray, wander; drop in.

за|бронирова́ть[1]**, -ру́ю** *pf.* **за|брони́ровать**[2]**, -рую** *pf.*

заброса́ть, -а́ю *pf.* (*impf.* **забра́сывать**) fill up; shower, bespatter, deluge. **забро́сить, -о́шу** *pf.* (*impf.* **забра́сывать**) throw; fling; cast; throw up, give up, abandon; neglect, let go; take, bring; leave behind; mislay. **забро́шенный** neglected; deserted, desolate.

забры́згать, -аю *pf.*, **забры́згивать, -аю** *impf.* splash, spatter, bespatter.

забыва́ть, -а́ю *impf.*, **забы́ть, -бу́ду** *pf.* forget; ~**ся** doze off, drop off; lose consciousness; sink into a reverie; forget o.s. **забы́вчивый** forgetful; absent-minded. **забытьё, -я́** unconsciousness; drowsiness.

забью́ *etc.*: *see* **заби́ть**

зав, -а *abbr.* (*of* **заве́дующий**) manager; chief, head.

зав... *abbr.* (*of* **заве́дующий**) *in comb.* manager, director, superintendent; **заводско́й** factory, works. **завга́р, -а** garage manager. ~**ко́м, -а** factory committee. **за́вуч, -а** director of studies.

зава́ливать, -аю *impf.*, **завали́ть, -лю́, -лишь** *pf.* block up, obstruct; fill; pile; cram; overload; knock down, demolish; make a mess of; ~**ся** fall, tumble; collapse; overturn, tip up; come to grief.

зава́ривать, -аю *impf.*, **завари́ть, -арю́, -а́ришь** *pf.* make; brew; scald; weld. **зава́рка, -и** brewing; scalding; welding.

заведе́ние, -я establishment, institution; custom, habit. **заве́довать, -дую** *impf.*+*i.* manage, superintend; be in charge of.

заве́домо *adv.* wittingly. **заве́домый** notorious, undoubted; well-known.

заведу́ *etc.*: *see* **завести́**

заве́дующий *sb.* (+*i.*) manager; head; director, superintendent; person in charge.

завезти́, -зу́, -зёшь; -ёз, -ла́ *pf.* (*impf.* **завози́ть**) convey, deliver; supply; leave.

за|вербова́ть, -бу́ю *pf.*

заве́ренн|ый witnessed; certified; ~**ая ко́пия** certified true copy. **завери́тель, -я** *m.* witness. **заве́рить, -рю** *pf.* (*impf.* **заверя́ть**) assure; certify; witness.

заверну́ть, -ну́, -нёшь *pf.* (*impf.* **завёртывать, завора́чивать**) wrap, wrap up; tuck up, roll up; screw tight, screw up; turn off; drop in, call in; turn; come on, come down; ~**ся** wrap o.s. up, wrap up, muffle o.s.

заверте́ться, -рчу́сь, -ртишься *pf.* begin to turn, begin to spin; become flustered, lose one's head.

завёртка, -и wrapping up; package. **завёртывать(ся, -аю(сь** *impf. of* **заверну́ть(ся**

заверша́ть, -а́ю *impf.*, **заверши́ть, -шу́** *pf.* complete, conclude, crown. **заверше́ние, -я** completion; end, conclusion.

заверя́ть, -я́ю *impf. of* **заве́рить**

заве́са, -ы curtain; veil, screen. **заве́сить, -е́шу** *pf.* (*impf.* **заве́шивать**) cover; curtain, curtain off.

завести́, -еду́, -ёшь; -вёл, -а́ *pf.* (*impf.* **заводи́ть**) take, bring; leave, drop off; set up, start; acquire; institute, introduce; wind (up), crank; ~**сь** be; appear; be established, be set up; start.

заве́т, -а behest, bidding, ordinance; Testament. **заве́тный** cherished; intimate; secret.

заве́шивать, -аю *impf. of* **заве́сить**

завеща́ние, -я will, testament. **завеща́ть,**

-а́ю leave, bequeath; devise.
завя́тый inveterate, out-and-out, downright; incorrigible.
завива́ть(ся, -а́ю(сь *impf. of* **зави́ть(ся. зави́вка, -и** waving; curling; wave.
зави́дно *impers.+d.*: **мне** ~ I feel envious. **зави́дный** enviable. **зави́довать, -дую** *impf.* (*pf.* **по~**) *+d.* envy.
за|визи́ровать, -рую *pf.*
завинти́ть, -нчу́ *pf.*, **зави́нчивать, -аю** *impf.* screw up; **~ся** screw up.
зави́сеть, -и́шу *impf.* **+от+***g.* depend on; lie in the power of. **зави́симость, -и** dependence; **в зави́симости от** depending on, subject to. **зави́симый** dependent.
зави́стливый envious. **за́висть, -и** envy.
завито́й; за́вит, -а́, -о curled, waved. **завито́к, -тка́** curl, lock; flourish; volute, scroll; tendril; helix. **зави́ть, -вью́, -вьёшь; -и́л, -а́, -о** *pf.* (*impf.* **завива́ть**) curl, wave; twist, wind; **~ся** curl, wave, twine; curl, wave, one's hair; have one's hair waved.
завладева́ть, -а́ю *impf.*, **завладе́ть, -е́ю** *pf.+i.* take possession of; seize, capture.
завлека́тельный alluring; fascinating, captivating; attractive. **завлека́ть, -а́ю** *impf.*, **завле́чь, -еку́, -ечёшь; -лёк, -ла́** *pf.* lure, entice; fascinate; captivate.
заво́д¹, -а factory; mill; works; plant; stud(farm).
заво́д², -а winding up; winding mechanism. **заводи́ть(ся, -ожу́(сь, -о́дишь(ся** *impf. of* **завести́(сь. заво́дка, -и** winding up; starting, cranking. **заводно́й** clockwork, mechanical; winding, cranking, starting.
заво́дский, заводско́й factory, works, mill; prefabricated; stud; *sb.* factory worker. **заводча́не, -а́н** *pl.* factory workers. **заво́дчик, -а** manufacturer, mill-owner, factory owner.
за́водь, -и backwater.
завоева́ние, -я winning; conquest; achievement, gain. **завоева́тель, -я** *m.* conqueror. **завоева́тельный** aggressive; of aggression. **завоева́ть, -ою́ю** *pf.*, **завоёвывать, -аю** *impf.* conquer; win, gain; try to get.
завожу́ *etc.*: *see* **заводи́ть, завози́ть**
заво́з, -а delivery; carriage. **завози́ть, -ожу́, -о́зишь** *impf. of* **завезти́**
завора́чивать(ся, -аю(сь *impf. of* **заверну́ть(ся. заворо́т¹, -а** turn, turning; sharp bend. **за́ворот², -а; ~ кишо́к** twisted intestines, volvulus.
заво́ю *etc.*: *see* **завы́ть**
завсегда́ *adv.* always. **завсегда́тай, -я** habitué, frequenter.
за́втра tomorrow. **за́втрак, -а** breakfast; lunch; **второ́й** ~ elevenses, mid-morning snack. **за́втракать, -аю** *impf.* (*pf.* **по~**) have breakfast; have lunch. **за́втрашний** tomorrow's; ~ **день** tomorrow, the morrow; the (near) future.
за|вуали́ровать, -рую *pf.*
завыва́ть, -а́ю *impf.*, **завы́ть, -во́ю** *pf.* (begin to) howl.
завяза́ть, -яжу́, -я́жешь *pf.* (*impf.* **завя́зывать**) tie, tie up; knot; bind, bind up; start; **~ся** start; arise; (of fruit) set. **завя́зка, -и** string, lace, band; beginning, start; opening; plot.
за|вя́знуть, -ну; -я́з *pf.* **завя́зывать(ся, -аю(сь** *impf. of* **завяза́ть(ся**
завя́лый withered, faded; dead. **за|вя́нуть, -ну; -я́л** *pf.*
загада́ть, -а́ю *pf.*, **зага́дывать, -аю** *impf.* think of; plan ahead, look ahead; guess at the future; ~ **зага́дку** ask a riddle. **зага́дка, -и** riddle; enigma, mystery. **зага́дочный** enigmatic, mysterious.
зага́р, -а sunburn, tan.
за|гаси́ть, -ашу́, -а́сишь *pf.* **за|га́снуть, -ну** *pf.*
загво́здка, -и snag, obstacle; difficulty.
заги́б, -а fold; bend; exaggeration; deviation. **загиба́ть(ся, -а́ю(сь** *impf. of* **загну́ть(ся. заги́бщик, -а** deviationist.
за|гипнотизи́ровать, -рую *pf.*
загла́вие, -я title; heading. **загла́вн|ый** title; **~ая бу́ква** capital letter; **~ая роль** title-role, name-part.
загла́дить, -а́жу *pf.*, **загла́живать, -аю** *impf.* iron, iron out, press; make up for; expiate; **~ся** iron out, become smooth; fade.
за|гло́хнуть, -ну; -гло́х *pf.*
заглуша́ть, -а́ю *impf.*, **за|глуши́ть, -шу́** *pf.* drown, deaden, muffle; jam; choke; suppress, stifle; alleviate, soothe. **заглу́шка, -и** choke, plug, stopper.
загляде́нье, -я lovely sight. **загляде́ться, -яжу́сь** *pf.*, **загля́дываться, -аюсь** *impf.* **на+***a.* stare at; be lost in admiration of. **загля́дывать, -аю** *impf.*, **загляну́ть, -ну́, -нешь** *pf.* peep; glance; look in, drop in.
за́гнанный driven, at the end of one's tether; tired out, exhausted; downtrodden, cowed. **загна́ть, -гоню́, -го́нишь; -а́л, -а́, -о** *pf.* (*impf.* **загоня́ть**) drive in, drive home; drive; exhaust; sell, flog.
загнива́ние, -я rotting, putrescence; decay; suppuration. **загнива́ть, -а́ю** *impf.*, **загни́ть, -ию́, -иёшь; -и́л, -а́, -о** *pf.* rot; decay; fester.
загну́ть, -ну́, -нёшь *pf.* (*impf.* **загиба́ть**) turn up, turn down; bend, fold; crease; utter; **~ся** turn up, stick up; turn down; turn up one's toes.
загова́ривать, -аю *impf.*, **заговори́ть, -рю́** *pf.* begin to talk; begin to speak; talk to death, tire out with talk; cast a spell over; protect with a charm (**от+***g.* against); ~ **с+***i.* speak to. **за́говор, -а** plot, conspiracy; charm, spell. **загово́рщик, -а** conspirator.
заголо́вок, -вка title; heading; headline.
заго́н, -а enclosure, pen; driving in; rounding up. **заго́нщик, -а** beater. **загоня́ть¹, -я́ю** *impf. of* **загна́ть. загоня́ть², -я́ю** *pf.* tire out; work to death; grill.
загора́живать(ся, -аю(сь *impf. of* **загороди́ть**

загора́ть, -а́ю *impf.*, **загоре́ть, -рю́** *pf.* become sunburnt, brown, tan; **~ся** catch fire; blaze, break out, start; *impers.+d.* become eager, want very much.

за́город, -а suburbs; **~ом** in the suburbs.

загороди́ть, -рожу́, -ро́дишь *pf.* (*impf.* **загора́живать**) enclose, fence in; barricade; bar; obstruct, block. **загоро́дка, -и** fence, enclosure.

за́городный out-of-town; country; suburban.

загота́вливать, -аю *impf.*, **заготовля́ть, -я́ю** *impf.*, **загото́вить, -влю** *pf.* lay in; lay in a stock of, stockpile, store; prepare. **загото́вка, -и** (State) procurement, purchase; laying in; stocking up, stockpiling; semi-finished product.

загради́тельный defensive; barrage; minelaying. **загради́ть, -ажу́** *pf.*, **загражда́ть, -а́ю** *impf.* block, obstruct; bar. **загражде́ние, -я** blocking; obstruction; obstacle, barrier.

грани́ца

загрни́ца

заграни́ца, -ы abroad, foreign parts. **заграни́чный** foreign.

загреба́ть, -а́ю *impf.*, **загрести́, -ебу́, -ебёшь; -ёб, -ла́** *pf.* rake up, gather; rake in.

загри́вок, -вка withers; nape (of the neck).

за|гримирова́ть(ся, -ру́ю(сь *pf.*

загромозжда́ть, -а́ю *impf.*, **загромозди́ть, -зжу́** *pf.* block up, encumber; pack, cram; overload.

загрубе́лый coarsened, callous. **за|грубе́ть, -е́ю** *pf.*

загружа́ть, -а́ю *impf.*, **за|грузи́ть, -ужу́, -у́зи́шь** *pf.* load; overload; feed; keep fully occupied; **~ся**+*i.* load up with, take on. **загру́зка, -и** loading, feeding; charge, load, capacity.

за|грунтова́ть, -ту́ю *pf.*

загрусти́ть, -ущу́ *pf.* grow sad.

загрязне́ние, -я soiling; pollution; contamination. **за|грязни́ть, -ню́** *pf.*, **загрязня́ть, -я́ю** *impf.* soil, make dirty; contaminate, pollute; **~ся** make o.s. dirty, become dirty; be polluted.

загс, -а *abbr.* (*of* **(отде́л) за́писи а́ктов гражда́нского состоя́ния**) registry office.

загуби́ть, -блю́, -бишь *pf.* ruin; squander, waste.

за|гудрони́ровать, -рую *pf.*

загуля́ть, -я́ю *pf.*, **загу́ливать, -аю** *impf.* take to drink.

за|густе́ть, -е́ет *pf.* thicken, grow thick.

зад, -а (-у), *loc.* **-у́**; *pl.* **-ы́** back; hindquarters; buttocks, seat; croup, rump; *pl.* back-yard(s); **~ом напере́д** back to front; **е́хать ~ом** to reverse, back up.

зада́бривать, -аю *impf. of* **задо́брить**

задава́ть(ся, -даю́(сь *impf. of* **зада́ть(ся**

задави́ть, -влю́, -вишь *pf.* crush; run over, knock down.

зададим *etc.*, **за́дал** *etc.*, **зада́м** *etc.*: *see* **зада́ть**

зада́ние, -я task, job; commission, assignment.

зада́ривать, -аю *impf.*, **задари́ть, -рю́, -ришь** *pf.* load with presents; bribe.

зада́тки, -тков *pl.* instincts, inclinations.

зада́ток, -тка deposit, advance.

зада́ть, -а́м, -а́шь, -а́ст, -адим; за́дал, -а́, -о *pf.* (*impf.* **задава́ть**) set; give; put; **~ вопро́с** ask a question; **~ тя́гу** take to one's heels; **я ему́ зада́м!** I'll give him what-for!; **~ся** turn out well; work out, succeed; **~ся мы́слью, це́лью** set o.s., make up one's mind.

зада́ча, -и problem, sum; task; mission.

задвига́ть, -а́ю *impf.*, **задви́нуть, -ну** *pf.* bolt; bar; close; push, slide; **~ задви́жку** shoot a bolt; **~ за́навес** draw a curtain; **~ся** shut; slide. **задви́жка, -и** bolt; catch, fastening; slide-valve. **задвижно́й** sliding.

задво́рки, -рок *pl.* back-yard; back parts; out-of-the-way place, backwoods.

задева́ть, -а́ю *impf. of* **заде́ть**

заде́лать, -аю *pf.*, **заде́лывать, -аю** *impf.* do up; block up, close up; wall up; stop (up). **заде́лка, -и** doing up; blocking up, stopping up.

заде́ну *etc.*: *see* **заде́ть. задёргивать, -аю** *impf. of* **задёрнуть. за|деревене́ть, -е́ю** *pf.*

задержа́ние, -я detention, arrest; retention; suspension. **задержа́ть, -жу́, -жишь** *pf.*, **заде́рживать, -аю** *impf.* detain; delay; withhold, keep back; retard; arrest; **~ дыха́ние** hold one's breath; **~ся** stay too long; linger.

задёрнуть, -ну *pf.* (*impf.* **задёргивать**) pull; draw; cover; curtain off.

задеру́ *etc.*: *see* **задра́ть**

заде́ть, -е́ну *pf.* (*impf.* **задева́ть**) touch, brush (against), graze; offend, wound; catch (against), catch on; **~ за живо́е** touch on the raw.

зади́ра, -ы *c.g.* bully; trouble-maker. **задира́ть(ся, -а́ю(сь** *impf. of* **задра́ть(ся. зади́ристый** provocative, pugnacious; cocky, pert.

за́дн|ий back, rear; hind; **дать ~ий ход** back, reverse; **~яя мысль** ulterior motive; **~ий план** background; **~ий прохо́д** anus, back passage; **~ий фона́рь** tail-light. **за́дник, -а** back; back drop.

задо́брить, -рю *pf.* (*impf.* **зада́бривать**) cajole; coax; win over.

задо́к, -дка́ back.

задо́лго *adv.* long before.

за|должа́ть, -а́ю *pf.*; **~ся** run into debt. **задо́лженность, -и** debts; liabilities.

задо́р, -а fervour, ardour; enthusiasm; passion; temper. **задо́рный** provocative; fervent, ardent; impassioned; quick-tempered.

задохну́ться, -ну́сь, -нёшься; -о́хся *or* **-у́лся** *pf.* (*impf.* **задыха́ться**) suffocate; choke; pant; gasp for breath.

за|дра́ть, -деру́, -дерёшь; -а́л, -а́, -о *pf.* (*impf. also* **задира́ть**) tear to pieces, kill; lift up, stretch up; break, split; provoke, insult; **~ нос** put on airs; **~ся** break; split; ride up.

задрема́ть, -млю́, -млешь *pf.* doze off, begin to nod.

задува́ть, -а́ю *impf. of* **заду́ть**

заду́мать, -аю *pf.*, **заду́мывать, -аю** *impf.* plan; intend; think of; conceive the idea (of); **~ся** become thoughtful, pensive; meditate; ponder. **заду́мчивость, -и** thoughtfulness; reverie. **заду́мчивый** thoughtful, pensive.

заду́ть, -у́ю *pf.* (*impf.* **задува́ть**) blow out; blow in; begin to blow.

задуше́вный sincere; cordial; intimate; **~ разгово́р** heart-to-heart (talk).

за|души́ть, -ушу́, -у́шишь *pf.* **зады́** *etc.*: *see* **зад**

задыха́ться, -а́юсь *impf. of* **задохну́ться**

заеда́ние, -я jamming. **заеда́ть, -а́ю** *impf. of* **зае́сть. заеди́м** *etc.*: *see* **зае́сть**

зае́зд, -а calling in; lap, round, heat. **зае́здить, -зжу** *pf.* override; wear out; work too hard. **заезжа́ть, -а́ю** *impf. of* **зае́хать. зае́зженный** hackneyed, trite; worn out. **зае́зж|ий** visiting; **~ий двор** wayside inn; **~ая тру́ппа** touring company.

заём, за́йма loan. **заёмный** loan. **заёмщик, -а, -щица, -ы** borrower, debtor.

зае́сть, -е́м, -е́шь, -е́ст, -еди́м *pf.* (*impf.* **заеда́ть**) torment, oppress; jam; foul; *+i.* take with.

зае́хать, -е́ду *pf.* (*impf.* **заезжа́ть**) call in; enter, ride in, drive in; land o.s.; reach; +**за**+*a.* go beyond, go past; +**за**+*i.* call for, fetch.

за|жа́рить(ся, -рю(сь *pf.*

зажа́ть, -жму́, -жмёшь *pf.* (*impf.* **зажима́ть**) squeeze; press; clutch; grip; suppress.

зaже́чь, -жгу́, -жжёшь; -жёг, -жгла́ *pf.* (*impf.* **зажига́ть**) set fire to; kindle; light; strike; inflame; **~ся** catch fire; light up; flame up.

залива́ть(ся, -а́ю(сь *impf. of* **зажи́ть(ся. заживи́ть, -влю́** *pf.*, **заживля́ть, -я́ю** *impf.* heal. **за́живо** *adv.* alive. **заживу́** *etc.*: *see* **зажи́ть**

зажига́лка, -и lighter; incendiary. **зажига́ние, -я** ignition. **зажига́тельн|ый** inflammatory; incendiary; **~ая свеча́** sparking-plug. **зажига́ть(ся, -а́ю(сь** *impf. of* **заже́чь(ся**

зажи́м, -а clamp; clutch; clip; (screw) terminal; suppression, clamping down. **зажима́ть, -а́ю** *impf. of* **зажа́ть. зажи́мистый** strong, powerful; tight-fisted, stingy. **зажимно́й** tight-fisted. **зажи́мщик, -а** suppressor.

зажи́точность, -и prosperity. **зажи́точный** well-to-do; prosperous. **зажи́ть, -иву́, -ивёшь; -ил, -а́, -о** *pf.* (*impf.* **залива́ть**) heal; close up; begin to live; **~ся** live to a great age; live too long.

зажму́ *etc.*: *see* **зажа́ть. за|жму́риться, -рюсь** *pf.*

зазелене́ть, -е́ет *pf.* turn green.

заземле́ние, -я earthing; earth. **заземли́ть, -лю́** *pf.*, **заземля́ть, -я́ю** *impf.* earth.

зазнава́ться, -наю́сь, -наёшься *impf.*, **зазна́ться, -а́юсь** *pf.* give o.s. airs, become conceited.

зазу́бренный notched, jagged, serrated. **зазу́брина, -ы** notch, jag. **за|зубри́ть¹, -рю́** *pf.*

за|зубри́ть², -рю́, -у́бришь *pf.*

заи́грывать, -аю *impf.* make advances; flirt.

за́ика, -и *c.g.* stammerer, stutterer. **заика́ние, -я** stammer, stutter; stammering, stuttering. **заика́ться, -а́юсь** *impf.*, **заикну́ться, -ну́сь, -нёшься** *pf.* stammer, stutter; +**о**+*p.* hint at, mention, touch on.

заимообра́зно *adv.* on credit, on loan. **заи́мствование, -я** borrowing, adoption. **заи́мствованн|ый** borrowed, taken over; **~ое сло́во** loan-word. **заи́мствовать, -твую** *impf.* & *pf.* (*pf. also* **по~**) borrow, take over, adopt.

заинтересо́ванный interested, concerned. **заинтересова́ть, -су́ю** *pf.*, **заинтересо́вывать, -аю** *impf.* interest; excite the curiosity of; **~ся**+*i.* become interested in, take an interest in.

заи́скивать, -аю *impf.* make up (to), ingratiate o.s.

зайду́ *etc.*: *see* **зайти́. займу́** *etc.*: *see* **заня́ть**

зайти́, -йду́, -йдёшь; зашёл, -шла́ *pf.* (*impf.* **заходи́ть**) call; look in, drop in; go, go on; set; wane; +**в**+*a.* get to, reach; +**за**+*a.* go behind, turn; +**за**+*i.* call for, go for, fetch.

за́йца *etc.*: *see* **за́яц. за́йчик, -а** (dear) little hare; reflection of sunlight. **зайчи́ха, -и** doe (*of hare*). **зайчо́нок, -нка**; *pl.* **-ча́та, -ча́т** leveret.

закабали́ть, -лю́ *pf.*, **закабаля́ть, -я́ю** *impf.* enslave.

закавка́зский Transcaucasian. **Закавка́зье, -я** Transcaucasia.

закады́чный intimate, bosom.

зака́з, -а order; prohibition; **на ~** to order. **заказа́ть, -ажу́, -а́жешь** *pf.*, **зака́зывать, -аю** *impf.* order; reserve, book. **зака́зник, -а** reserve; preserve. **заказн|о́й** made to order, made to measure, bespoke; registered; **~о́е (письмо́)** registered letter. **зака́зчик, -а** customer, client.

зака́л, -а temper, tempering; stamp, cast; strength of character, backbone. **закалённый** tempered, hardened, hard; seasoned, tough; fully trained. **зака́ливать, -аю** *impf.*, **закали́ть, -лю́** *pf.* (*impf. also* **закаля́ть**) temper; harden, case-harden; harden off. **зака́лка, -и** tempering, hardening; temper, calibre.

зака́лывать, -аю *impf. of* **заколо́ть**

закаля́ть, -я́ю *impf. of* **закали́ть. зака́нчивать(ся, -аю(сь** *impf. of* **зако́нчить(ся**

зака́пать, -аю *pf.*, **зака́пывать¹, -аю** *impf.* begin to drip; rain, fall in drops; pour in drops; spot, spatter.

зака́пывать²(ся, -аю(сь *impf. of* **закопа́ть(ся**

зака́т, -а setting; sunset; decline; **на ~е** at sunset; **на ~е дней** in one's declining years. **заката́ть, -а́ю** *pf.*, **зака́тывать¹, -аю** *impf.* begin to roll; roll up; roll out; **~ в тюрьму́** throw into prison. **закати́ть, -ачу́, -а́тишь**

pf., **зака́тывать²**, **-аю** *impf.* roll; **~ся** roll; set; wane; vanish, disappear; go off; **~ся сме́хом** burst out laughing.

зака́тный sunset.

заква́сить, -а́шу *pf.*, **заква́шивать, -аю** *impf.* ferment; leaven. **заква́ска, -и** ferment; leaven.

закида́ть, -а́ю *pf.*, **заки́дывать¹, -аю** *impf.* shower; cover up; fill up; spatter, bespatter; **~ вопро́сами** ply with questions; **~ гря́зью** fling mud at.

заки́дывать², -аю *impf.*, **заки́нуть, -ну** *pf.* throw; throw out, away; fling, cast, toss.

закипа́ть, -а́ет *impf.*, **закипе́ть, -пи́т** *pf.* begin to boil, simmer; be in full swing.

закиса́ть, -а́ю *impf.*, **заки́снуть, -ну; -и́с, -ла** *pf.* turn sour; become apathetic. **за́кись, -и** oxide, protoxide; **~ азо́та** nitrous oxide.

закла́д, -а pawn; pledge; mortgage; bet, wager; **би́ться об ~** bet, wager; **в ~е** in pawn. **закла́дка, -и** laying, laying down; batch, charge; bookmark. **закладна́я** *sb.* mortgage. **закладно́й** mortgage; pawn. **закла́дывать, -аю** *impf. of* **заложи́ть**

закле́ивать, -аю *impf.*, **закле́ить, -е́ю** *pf.* glue up; stick up; seal; **~ся** stick.

за|клейми́ть, -млю́ *pf.*

заклепа́ть, -а́ю *pf.*, **заклёпывать, -аю** *impf.* rivet. **заклёпка, -и** rivet; riveting.

заклина́ние, -я incantation; spell, charm; exorcism. **заклина́тель, -я** *m.* exorcist; **~ змей** snake-charmer. **заклина́ть, -а́ю** *impf.* conjure; invoke; exorcize; adjure, entreat.

заключа́ть, -а́ю *impf.*, **заключи́ть, -чу́** *pf.* conclude; end; infer; enter into; contain; enclose; comprise; confine. **заключа́ться, -а́ется** consist; lie, be; be contained. **заключе́ние, -я** conclusion; end; inference; resolution, decision; confinement, detention. **заключённый** *sb.* prisoner, convict. **заключи́тельный** final, concluding.

закля́тие, -я oath, pledge. **закля́тый** sworn, inveterate; enchanted, bewitched.

закова́ть, -кую́, -куёшь *pf.*, **зако́вывать, -аю** *impf.* chain; shackle, put in irons.

закола́чивать, -аю *impf. of* **заколоти́ть**

заколдо́ванный bewitched, enchanted; spellbound; **~ круг** vicious circle. **заколдова́ть, -ду́ю** *pf.* bewitch, enchant; lay a spell on.

зако́лка, -и hairpin; hair-grip; hair-slide.

заколоти́ть, -лочу́, -ло́тишь *pf.* (*impf.* **закола́чивать**) board up; nail up; knock in, drive in; beat the life out of, knock insensible.

за|коло́ть, -олю́, -о́лешь *pf.* (*impf. also* **зака́лывать**) stab, spear, stick; kill; pin, pin up; fasten; (*impers.*) **у меня́ заколо́ло в боку́** I have a stitch in my side; **~ся** stab o.s.

зако́н, -а law; **~ бо́жий** scripture, divinity. **законнорождённый** legitimate. **зако́нный** lawful, legal; legitimate, rightful.

законо... *in comb.* law, legal. **законове́дение, -я** law, jurisprudence. **~да́тельный** legislative. **~ме́рность, -и** regularity, normality. **~ме́рный** regular, natural. **~положе́ние, -я** statute. **~прое́кт, -а** bill.

за|конопа́тить, -а́чу *pf.* **за|консерви́ровать, -рую** *pf.* **за|конспекти́ровать, -рую** *pf.* **за|контрактова́ть(ся, -ту́ю(сь** *pf.*

зако́нченность, -и finish; completeness. **зако́нченный** finished; complete; consummate. **зако́нчить, -чу** *pf.* (*impf.* **зака́нчивать**) end, finish; **~ся** end, finish; come to an end.

закопа́ть, -а́ю *pf.* (*impf.* **зака́пывать**) begin to dig; bury; **~ся** begin to rummage; bury o.s.; dig (o.s.) in.

закопте́лый sooty, grimy. **за|копте́ть, -ти́т** *pf.* **за|копти́ть, -пчу́** *pf.*

закорене́лый deep-rooted; ingrained; inveterate.

зако́рки, -рок *pl.* back, shoulders.

закосне́лый deep-rooted; incorrigible, inveterate. **за|косне́ть, -е́ю** *pf.*

закостене́лый ossified; stiff.

закоу́лок, -лка back street, alley, passage; secluded corner, nook; **знать все закоу́лки** know all the ins and outs.

закочене́лый numb with cold. **за|кочене́ть, -е́ю** *pf.*

закра́дываться, -аюсь *impf. of* **закра́сться.**

закра́ивать, -аю *impf. of* **закрои́ть**

закра́сить, -а́шу *pf.* (*impf.* **закра́шивать**) paint over, paint out.

закра́сться, -аду́сь, -адёшься *pf.* (*impf.* **закра́дываться**) steal in, creep in.

закра́шивать, -аю *impf. of* **закра́сить**

закре́па, -ы catch; fastener. **закрепи́тель, -я** *m.* fastener; fixative, fixing agent, fixer. **закрепи́ть, -плю́** *pf.*, **закрепля́ть, -я́ю** *impf.* fasten, secure; make fast; fix; consolidate; +**за**+*i.* allot to, assign to; appoint to, attach to; **~ за собо́й** secure; **~ ся, на**+*a.* consolidate one's hold on.

закрепости́ть, -ощу́ *pf.* **закрепоща́ть, -а́ю** *impf.* enslave; make a serf of. **закрепоще́ние, -я** enslavement; slavery, serfdom.

закрича́ть, -чу́ *pf.* cry out; begin to shout; give a shout.

закрои́ть, -ою́ *pf.* (*impf.* **закра́ивать**) cut out; groove. **закро́й, -я** cutting out; cut, style; groove. **закро́йный** cutting, cutting out. **закро́йщик, -а** cutter.

за́кром, -а; *pl.* **-а́** corn-bin.

закро́ю *etc.*: *see* **закры́ть. закрою́** *etc.*: *see* **закрои́ть**

закругле́ние, -я rounding, curving; curve; curvature; well-rounded period. **закруглённый; -ён, -а́** rounded; well-rounded. **закругли́ть, -лю́** *pf.*, **закругля́ть, -я́ю** *impf.* make round; round off; **~ся** become round.

закружи́ться, -ужу́сь, -у́жишься *pf.* begin to whirl, begin to go round; be in a whirl.

за|крути́ть, -учу́, -у́тишь *pf.*, **закру́чивать, -аю** *impf.* twist, twirl, whirl round; wind round; roll; turn; screw in; turn the head of;

~ся twist, twirl, whirl; wind round; begin to whirl.

закрыва́ть, -а́ю *impf.* **закры́ть, -ро́ю** *pf.* close, shut; shut off, turn off; close down, shut down; cover; **~ся** close, shut; end; close down; cover o.s., take cover; find shelter, shelter. **закры́тие, -я** closing; shutting; closing down; shelter, cover. **закры́т|ый** closed, shut; private; **~ое голосова́ние** secret ballot; **~ое заседа́ние** private meeting; closed session; **~ое мо́ре** inland sea; **~ое пла́тье** high-necked dress; **~ый просмо́тр** private view.

закули́сный behind the scenes; secret; underhand, under-cover.

закупа́ть, -а́ю *impf.*, **закупи́ть, -плю́, -пишь** *pf.* buy up; lay in; stock up with; bribe. **заку́пка, -и** purchase. **закупно́й** bought, purchased.

заку́поривать, -аю *impf.*, **заку́порить, -рю** *pf.* cork; stop up; plug, clog; shut up; coop up. **заку́порка, -и** corking; embolism, thrombosis.

заку́почный purchase. **заку́пщик, -а, -щица, -ы** purchaser; buyer.

заку́ривать, -аю *impf.*, **закури́ть, -рю́, -ришь** *pf.* light; light up; begin to smoke.

закуси́ть, -ушу́, -у́сишь *pf.*, **заку́сывать, -аю** *impf.* have a snack; have a bite; *+i.* have a bit of; ~ **удила́** take the bit between one's teeth. **заку́ска, -и** hors-d'oeuvre; appetizer, snack, titbit. **заку́сочная** *sb.* snack-bar.

за|ку́тать, -аю *pf.*, **заку́тывать, -аю** *impf.* wrap up; muffle; tuck up; **~ся** wrap o.s. up.

зал, -а hall, room; ~ **ожида́ния** waiting-room.

залёг *etc.*: *see* **зале́чь. залега́ние, -я** bedding; bed, seam. **залега́ть, -а́ю** *impf. of* **зале́чь**

за|ледене́ть, -е́ю *pf.*

залежа́лый stale, long unused. **залежа́ться, -жу́сь** *pf.*, **залёживаться, -аюсь** *impf.* lie too long; lie idle a long time; find no market; become stale. **за́лежь, -и** deposit, bed, seam; stale goods.

залеза́ть, -а́ю *impf.*, **зале́зть, -зу; -е́з** *pf.* climb, climb up; get in; creep in; ~ **в долги́** run into debt.

за|лепи́ть, -плю́, -пишь *pf.*, **залепля́ть, -я́ю** *impf.* paste up, paste over; glue up, stick up.

залета́ть, -а́ю *impf.*, **залете́ть, -ечу́** *pf.* fly; **+в**+*a.* fly into; land at; **+за**+*a.* fly over, fly beyond. **залётн|ый** flown in; **~ая пти́ца** bird of passage.

зале́чивать, -аю *impf.*, **залечи́ть, -чу́, -чишь** *pf.* heal, cure; **~ся** heal, heal up.

зале́чь, -ля́гу, -ля́жешь; залёг, -ла́ *pf.* (*impf.* **залега́ть**) lie down; lie low; lie in wait; lie, be deposited; take root, become ingrained; become blocked.

зали́в, -а bay; gulf; creek, cove. **залива́ть, -а́ю** *impf.*, **зали́ть, -лью́, -льёшь; за́лил, -а́, -о** *pf.* flood, inundate; quench, extinguish, put out; lay, spread; stop holes in; *+i.* pour over, spill on; ~ **ска́терть черни́лами** spill ink on the tablecloth; ~ **ту́шью** ink in; **~ся** be flooded; pour, spill; *+i.* break into, burst into; ~ **ся слеза́ми** burst into tears, dissolve in tears.

зало́г, -а deposit; pledge; security, mortgage; token; voice. **заложи́ть, -жу́, -жишь** *pf.* (*impf.* **закла́дывать**) lay; put; mislay; pile up, heap up; block up; pawn, mortgage; harness; lay in, store, put by. **зало́жник, -а** hostage.

залп, -а volley, salvo; **~ом** without pausing for breath, at one gulp.

залью́ *etc.*: *see* **зали́ть. заля́гу** *etc.*: *see* **зале́чь**

зам, -а *abbr.* (*of* **замести́тель**) assistant, deputy.

зам... *abbr.* (*of* **замести́тель**) *in comb.* assistant, deputy; vice-. **замдире́ктора** deputy director; vice-principal, assistant head. **~мини́стра** deputy minister. **~председа́теля** vice-chairman.

за|ма́зать, -а́жу *pf.*, **зама́зывать, -аю** *impf.* paint over; efface; slur over; putty; daub, smear; soil; **~ся** smear o.s.; get dirty. **зама́зка, -и** putty, paste, cement; puttying.

зама́лчивать, -аю *impf. of* **замолча́ть**

зама́нивать, -аю *impf.*, **замани́ть, -ню́, -нишь** *pf.* entice, lure; attract; decoy. **зама́нчивость, -и** allurements. **зама́нчивый** tempting, alluring.

за|мара́ть(ся, -а́ю(сь *pf.* **за|маринова́ть, -ну́ю** *pf.*

замаскиро́ванный masked; disguised; concealed. **за|маскирова́ть, -ру́ю** *pf.*, **замаскиро́вывать, -аю** *impf.* mask; disguise; camouflage; conceal; **~ся** disguise o.s.

зама́х, -а threatening gesture. **зама́хиваться, -аюсь** *impf.*, **замахну́ться, -ну́сь, -нёшься** *pf.* threaten; *+i.* raise threateningly; ~ **руко́й на**+*a.* lift one's hand against.

зама́чивать, -аю *impf. of* **замочи́ть**

зама́щивать, -аю *impf. of* **замости́ть**

замедле́ние, -я slowing down, deceleration; delay. **заме́дленный** retarded, delayed. **заме́длить, -лю** *pf.*, **замедля́ть, -я́ю** *impf.* slow down, retard; reduce, slacken; delay; hold back; be slow (to), be long (in); **~ся** slow down; slacken, grow slower.

замёл *etc.*: *see* **замести́**

заме́на, -ы substitution; replacement; commutation; substitute. **замени́мый** replaceable. **замени́тель, -я** *m.* (+*g.*) substitute (for). **замени́ть, -ню́, -нишь** *pf.*, **заменя́ть, -я́ю** *impf.* replace; take the place of; be a substitute for.

замере́ть, -мру́, -мрёшь; за́мер, -ла́, -о *pf.* (*impf.* **замира́ть**) stand still; freeze, be rooted to the spot; die down, die away; die.

замерза́ние, -я freezing. **замерза́ть, -а́ю** *impf.*, **за|мёрзнуть, -ну** *pf.* freeze, freeze up; freeze to death.

заме́рить, -рю *pf.* (*impf.* **замеря́ть**) measure, gauge. **заме́рн|ый** gauge, measuring;

~ая ре́йка dip-stick, gauge rod.

за́мертво *adv.* like one dead, in a dead faint.

замеря́ть, -я́ю *impf. of* **заме́рить**

замеси́ть, -ешу́, -е́сишь *pf.* (*impf.* **заме́шивать**) knead.

замести́, -ету́, -етёшь; -мёл, -а́ *pf.* (*impf.* **замета́ть**) sweep up; cover; ~ **следы́** cover one's traces.

замести́тель, -я *m.*, **~ница, -ы** substitute; assistant, deputy, vice-. **замести́ть, -ещу́** *pf.* (*impf.* **замеща́ть**) replace, be substitute for; deputize for, act for; serve in place of.

замета́ть[1], **-а́ю** *impf. of* **замести́**

замета́ть[2], **-а́ю** *pf.* (*impf.* **замётывать**) tack, baste.

заме́тить, -е́чу *pf.* (*impf.* **замеча́ть**) notice; take notice of, make a note of; remark, observe. **заме́тка, -и** paragraph; mark; note. **заме́тный** noticeable; appreciable; outstanding.

замётывать, -аю *impf. of* **замета́ть**[2]

замеча́ние, -я remark, observation; reprimand, reproof. **замеча́тельный** remarkable; splendid, wonderful. **замеча́ть, -а́ю** *impf. of* **заме́тить. заме́ченный** discovered; noticed; detected.

замеша́тельство, -а confusion; embarrassment. **замеша́ть, -а́ю** *pf.*, **заме́шивать, -аю** *impf.* mix up, entangle; **~ся** become mixed up, become entangled; mix, mingle. **заме́шивать, -аю** *impf. of* **замеси́ть, замеша́ть**

заме́шка, -и delay. **заме́шкаться, -аюсь** *pf.* linger, loiter.

замеща́ть, -а́ю *impf. of* **замести́ть. замеще́ние, -я** substitution; filling.

замина́ть, -а́ю *impf. of* **замя́ть. зами́нка, -и** hitch; hesitation.

замира́ние, -я dying out, dying down; sinking. **замира́ть, -а́ю** *impf. of* **замере́ть**

за́мкнутость, -и reserve, reticence. **за́мкнутый** reserved; closed, exclusive. **замкну́ть, -ну́, -нёшь** *pf.* (*impf.* **замыка́ть**) lock; close; **~ся** close; shut o.s. up; become reserved; **~ся в себя́** shrink into o.s.

замну́ *etc.*: *see* **замя́ть**

за́мок[1], **-мка** castle.

замо́к[2], **-мка́** lock; padlock; keystone; bolt; clasp, clip; **запере́ть на ~** lock; **под замко́м** under lock and key.

замо́лвить, -влю *pf.*; ~ **слове́чко** put in a word.

замолка́ть, -а́ю *impf.*, **замо́лкнуть, -ну; -мо́лк** *pf.* fall silent; stop, cease. **замолча́ть, -чу́** *pf.* (*impf.* **зама́лчивать**) fall silent; cease corresponding; keep silent about, hush up.

замора́живание, -я freezing; chilling, refrigeration; congealing; quenching. **замора́живать, -аю** *impf.*, **заморо́зить, -ро́жу** *pf.* freeze; refrigerate; ice, chill. **заморо́женный** frozen; iced. **за́морозки, -ов** *pl.* (slight) frosts.

замо́рский overseas.

замо́рыш, -а weakling, puny creature; runt.

за|мости́ть, -ощу́ *pf.* (*impf. also* **зама́щивать**) pave.

за|мочи́ть, -чу́, -чишь *pf.* (*impf. also* **зама́чивать**) wet; soak; ret.

замо́чн|ый lock; **~ая сква́жина** keyhole.

замру́ *etc.*: *see* **замере́ть**

за́муж *adv.*; **вы́йти ~** (**за**+*a.*) marry; **вы́дать ~ за**+*a.* marry (off) to. **за́мужем** *adv.* married (**за**+*i.* to). **заму́жество, -а** marriage.

замурова́ть, -ру́ю *pf.*, **замуро́вывать, -аю** *impf.* brick up; wall up; immure.

за|мути́ть(ся, -учу́(сь, -у́тишь(ся *pf.*

заму́чивать, -аю *impf.*, **за|му́чить, -чу** *pf.* torment; wear out; plague the life out of, bore to tears. **за|му́читься, -чусь** *pf.*

за́мша, -и suede; chamois leather, shammy. **замшеви́дный** suedette, suede-cloth.

замыка́ние, -я locking, closing; closure; short circuit, shorting. **замыка́ть(ся, -а́ю(сь** *impf. of* **замкну́ть(ся замыка́ющ|ий; идти́ ~им** bring up the rear.

за́мысел, -сла project, plan; design, scheme; idea. **замы́слить, -лю** *pf.*, **замышля́ть, -я́ю** *impf.* plan; contemplate, intend, think of. **замыслова́тый** intricate, complicated.

замя́ть, -мну́, -мнёшь *pf.* (*impf.* **замина́ть**) hush up, stifle, smother; suppress; put a stop to; distract attention from; **~ся** falter; stumble; stop short.

за́навес, -а, занаве́ска, -и curtain. **занаве́сить, -е́шу** *pf.*, **занаве́шивать, -аю** *impf.* curtain; hang; cover.

за|неме́ть, -е́ю *pf.*

занесённый сне́гом snowbound. **занести́, -су́, -сёшь; -ёс, -ла́** *pf.* (*impf.* **заноси́ть**) bring; leave, drop; raise, lift; note down, put down, enter; cover with snow, sand, etc.; ~ **в протоко́л** place on record, record in the minutes; **~сь** be carried away.

занима́тельный entertaining, diverting; absorbing. **занима́ть, -а́ю** *impf.* (*pf.* **заня́ть**) occupy; interest; engage, secure; take, take up; borrow; **~ся**+*i.* be occupied with, be engaged in; work at, work on; study; busy o.s. with; devote o.s. to.

зано́за, -ы splinter. **занози́ть, -ожу́** *pf.* get a splinter in.

зано́с, -а drift, accumulation; raising; lifting; skid, skidding. **заноси́ть(ся, -ошу́(сь, -о́сишь(ся** *impf. of* **занести́(сь зано́сный** alien, foreign, imported. **зано́счивый** arrogant, haughty.

за|нумерова́ть, -ру́ю *pf.*

заня́тие, -я occupation; pursuit; *pl.* studies, work. **заня́тный** entertaining, amusing; interesting. **за́нято** *adv.* engaged, number engaged. **занято́й** busy. **за́нятый; -нят, -а́, -о** occupied; taken; engaged; employed; busy. **заня́ть(ся, займу́(сь, -мёшь(ся; за́нял(ся, -а́(сь, -о(сь** *pf. of* **занима́ть(ся**

заодно́ *adv.* in concert; at one; at the same time.

заострённый pointed, sharp. **заостри́ть, -рю́**

pf., **заострять, -яю** *impf.* sharpen; stress, emphasize; **~ся** grow sharp; become pointed.

заочник, -а, -ница, -ы student taking correspondence course; external student. **заочно** *adv.* in one's absence; by correspondence course. **заочн|ый; ~ый курс** correspondence course; **~ое обучение** postal tuition; **~ый приговор** judgement by default.

запад, -а west; the West, the Occident. **западный** west, western; westerly.

западня, -и; *g.pl.* **-ней** trap; pitfall, snare.

запаздывать, -аю *impf. of* **запоздать**

запаивать, -аю *impf. of* **запаять. запайка, -и** soldering; sealing (off), seal.

за|паковать, -кую *pf.*, **запаковывать, -аю** *impf.* pack; wrap up, do up.

за|пакостить, -ощу *pf.*

запал, -а ignition; fuse; detonator. **запаливать, -аю** *impf.*, **запалить, -лю** light, ignite, kindle; set fire to. **запальн|ый** ignition; detonating; **~ая свеча** (sparking-)plug. **запальчивый** quick-tempered.

за|парковать(ся, -кую(сь *pf.*

запас, -а reserve; stock, supply; hem; *pl.* turnings; **выпустить ~** let out; **отложить про ~** put by; **про ~** for an emergency; **проверить ~** take stock; **~ слов** vocabulary. **запасать, -аю** *impf.*, **запасти, -су, -сёшь; -ас, -ла** *pf.* stock, store; lay in stock of; **~ся**+*i.* provide o.s. with; stock up with; arm o.s. with. **запасливый** thrifty; provident. **запасник, -а, запасной** *sb.* reservist. **запасной, запасный** spare; reserve; **~ выход** emergency exit; **~ путь** siding.

запах[1], **-а** smell.

запах[2], **-а** wrapover. **запахивать, -аю** *impf.*, **запахнуть**[2], **-ну, -нёшь** *pf.* wrap up; **~ся** wrap (o.s.) up.

запахнуть[1], **-ну; -ах** *pf.* begin to smell.

за|пачкать, -аю *pf.*

запашка, -и ploughing in, ploughing up; plough-land, arable land.

запаять, -яю *pf.* (*impf.* **запаивать**) solder; seal, seal off.

запев, -а solo part. **запевала, -ы** *c.g.* singer of solo part; leader of chorus; leader, instigator. **запевать, -аю** *impf.* (*pf.* **запеть**) lead the singing, set the tune.

запеканка, -и baked pudding, baked dish; spiced brandy. **запекать(ся, -аю** *impf. of* **запечь(ся. запеку** *etc.*: *see* **запечь**

за|пеленать, -аю *pf.*

запереть, -пру, -прёшь; запер, -ла, -ло *pf.* (*impf.* **запирать**) lock; lock in; shut up; bar; block up; **~ на засов** bolt; **~ся** lock o.s. in; shut (o.s.) up; +**в**+*p.* refuse to admit, refuse to speak about.

запеть, -пою, -поёшь *pf.* (*impf.* **запевать**) begin to sing; **~ другое** change one's tune; **~ песню** strike up a song; plug a song.

запечатать, -аю *pf.*, **запечатывать, -аю** *impf.* seal. **запечатлевать, -аю** *impf.* **запечатлеть, -ею** *pf.* imprint, impress, engrave; **~ся** imprint, stamp, impress, itself.

запечь, -еку, -ечёшь; -пёк, -ла *pf.* (*impf.* **запекать**) bake; **~ся** bake; become parched; clot, coagulate.

запивать, -аю *impf. of* **запить**

запинаться, -аюсь *impf. of* **запнуться. запинка, -и** hesitation; **без запинки** smoothly.

запирательство, -а denial, disavowal. **запирать(ся, -аю(сь** *impf. of* **запереть(ся**

записать, -ишу, -ишешь *pf.* **записывать, -аю** *impf.* note, make a note of, take notes; take down; record; enter, register, enrol; make over (to); begin to write, begin to correspond; **~ся** register, enter one's name, enrol; **~ся в клуб** join a club; **~ся к врачу** make an appointment with the doctor. **записка, -и** note; minute, memorandum; *pl.* notes; memoirs; transactions. **записн|ой** note, writing; regular; inveterate; **~ая книжка** notebook. **запись, -и** writing down; recording; registration; entry, record; deed.

запить, -пью, -пьёшь; запил, -а, -о *pf.* (*impf.* **запивать**) begin drinking, take to drink; wash down (with), take (with).

запихать, -аю *pf.*, **запихивать, -аю** *impf.*, **запихнуть, -ну, -нёшь** *pf.* push in, cram in.

запишу *etc.*: *see* **записать**

заплаканный tear-stained; in tears. **заплакать, -ачу** *pf.* begin to cry.

за|планировать, -рую *pf.*

заплата, -ы patch. **заплатанный** patched, mended.

за|платить, -ачу, -атишь *pf.* pay; +**за**+*a.* pay for; **~ по счёту** settle an account.

заплачу *etc.*: *see* **заплакать. заплачу** *see* **заплатить**

заплесневелый mouldy, mildewed. **за|плесневеть, -веет** *pf.*

заплести, -ету, -етёшь; -ёл, -а *pf.*, **заплетать, -аю** *impf.* plait, braid; **~сь** stumble; be unsteady in one's gait; falter.

за|пломбировать, -рую *pf.*

заплыв, -а heat, round. **заплывать, -аю** *impf.*, **заплыть, -ыву, -ывёшь; -ыл, -а, -о** *pf.* swim in, sail in; swim out, sail out; be swollen, be bloated.

запнуться, -нусь, -нёшься *pf.* (*impf.* **запинаться**) hesitate; stumble, halt; stammer; **~ ногой** trip (up).

заповедник, -а reserve; preserve; **государственный ~** national park. **заповедный** prohibited; **~ лес** forest reserve. **заповедь, -и** precept; commandment.

заподазривать, -аю *impf.*, **заподозрить, -рю** *pf.* suspect (**в**+*p.* of); be suspicious of.

запоем *see* **запой**

запоздалый belated; late; delayed. **запоздать, -аю** *pf.* (*impf.* **запаздывать**) be late.

запой, -я hard drinking; alcoholism; **курить запоем** smoke like a chimney; **пить запоем** have bouts of heavy drinking. **запойный** *adj.*; **~ пьяница** chronic drunk; old soak.

заполза́ть, -а́ю, заползти́, -зу́, -зёшь; -о́лз, -зла́ creep in, creep under; crawl in, crawl under.

запо́лнить, -ню *pf.*, **заполня́ть, -я́ю** *impf.* fill (in, up).

заполя́рный polar; trans-polar. **заполя́рье, -я** polar regions.

запомина́ть, -а́ю *impf.*, **запо́мнить, -ню** *pf.* remember, keep in mind; memorize; **~ся** be retained in memory, stay in one's mind. **запомина́ющ|ий; ~ее устро́йство** (*comput.*) storage device.

за́понка, -и cuff-link; (collar-)stud.

запо́р, -а bolt; lock; closing, locking, bolting; constipation; **на ~е** locked, bolted.

запороши́ть, -ши́т *pf.* powder, dust, scatter.

запоте́лый misted, dim. **за|поте́ть, -е́ет** *pf.* mist over.

запою́ *etc.*: *see* **запе́ть**

заправи́ла, -ы boss. **запра́вить, -влю** *pf.*, **заправля́ть, -я́ю** *impf.* insert, tuck in; prepare, set up; fuel, refuel, fill up; season, dress, flavour; mix in; **~ ла́мпу** trim a lamp; **заправля́ть дела́ми** boss the show; **~ся** refuel. **запра́вка, -и** refuelling, filling; servicing, setting up; seasoning, dressing, flavouring.

запра́шивать, -аю *impf. of* **запроси́ть**

запре́т, -а prohibition, ban; **под ~ом** banned, prohibited. **запрети́тельный** prohibitive. **запрети́ть, -ещу́** *pf.*, **запреща́ть, -а́ю** *impf.* prohibit, forbid, ban. **запре́тный** forbidden, prohibited. **запреще́ние, -я** prohibition; distraint. **запрещённый** forbidden, illicit.

за|прихо́довать, -ую *pf.* **за|программи́ровать, -ую** *pf.*

запроки́дывать, -аю *impf.*, **запроки́нуть, -ну** *pf.* throw back; **~ся** throw o.s. back; fall back, sink back.

запро́с, -а inquiry; overcharging; *pl.* requirements, needs. **запроси́ть, -ошу́, -о́сишь** *pf.* (*impf.* **запра́шивать**) inquire; inquire of, question; ask (*a high price*).

за́просто *adv.* without ceremony, without formality.

за|протоколи́ровать, -рую *pf.* **запрошу́** *etc.*: *see* **запроси́ть. запру́** *etc.*: *see* **запере́ть**

запру́да, -ы dam, weir; mill-pond. **за|пруди́ть, -ужу́, -у́ди́шь** *pf.*, **запру́живать, -аю** *impf.* block; dam; fill to overflowing, cram, jam.

запряга́ть, -а́ю *impf. of* **запря́чь. запрягу́** *etc.*: *see* **запря́чь. запря́жка, -и** harnessing; harness, team.

запря́тать(ся, -я́чу(сь *pf.*, **запря́тывать(ся, -аю(сь** *impf.* hide.

запря́чь, -ягу́, -яжёшь; -я́г, -ла́ *pf.* (*impf.* **запряга́ть**) harness; yoke.

запу́ганный cowed, intimidated, broken-spirited. **запуга́ть, -а́ю** *pf.*, **запу́гивать, -аю** *impf.* cow, intimidate.

запуска́ть, -а́ю *impf.*, **запусти́ть, -ущу́, -у́стишь** *pf.* thrust (in), push (in), dig (in); start, start up; launch; (*+a. or i.*) throw, fling; neglect, let go. **запусте́лый** neglected; desolate. **запусте́ние, -я** neglect; desolation.

запу́танный tangled; intricate, involved, knotty. **за|пу́тать, -аю** *pf.*, **запу́тывать, -аю** *impf.* tangle; confuse; complicate; muddle; involve; **~ся** get tangled, get entangled; be involved, get involved; become complicated.

запу́щенный neglected. **запущу́** *etc.*: *see* **запусти́ть**

запча́сть, -и; *g.pl.* **-е́й** *abbr.* (*of* ***запасна́я часть***) spare part, spare.

за|пыли́ть(ся, -лю́(сь *pf.*

запыха́ться, -а́юсь *pf.* be out of breath.

запью́ *etc.*: *see* **запи́ть**

запя́стье, -я wrist; bracelet.

запята́я *sb.* comma; difficulty, snag.

за|пятна́ть, -а́ю *pf.*

зараба́тывать, -аю *impf.*, **зарабо́тать, -аю** *pf.* earn; start (up), begin to work; **~ся** overwork. **за́работн|ый; ~ая пла́та** wages; pay, salary. **за́работок, -тка** earnings.

заража́ть, -а́ю *impf.*, **зарази́ть, -ажу́** *pf.* infect; **~ся**+*i.* be infected with, catch. **зара́за, -ы** infection, contagion; pest, plague. **зарази́тельный** infectious; catching. **зара́зный** infectious, contagious; *sb.* infectious case.

зара́нее *adv.* beforehand; in good time; in advance.

зараста́ть, -а́ю *impf.*, **зарасти́, -ту́, -тёшь; -ро́с, -ла́** *pf.* be overgrown; heal, skin over.

за́рево, -а glow.

за|регистри́ровать(ся, -и́рую(сь *pf.*

за|регули́ровать, -рую *pf.*

заре́з, -а (-у) disaster; **до ~у** desperately, badly, urgently. **за|ре́зать, -е́жу** *pf.* kill, knife; slaughter; **~ся** cut one's throat.

зарека́ться, -а́юсь *impf. of* **заре́чься**

зарекомендова́ть, -ду́ю *pf.*; **~ себя́** show o.s., present o.s.; +*i.* prove o.s., show o.s., to be.

заре́чься, -еку́сь, -ечёшься; -ёкся, -екла́сь *pf.* (*impf.* **зарека́ться**) +*inf.* renounce; swear off, promise to give up.

за|ржа́веть, -еет *pf.* **заржа́вленный** rusty.

зарисова́ть, -су́ю *pf.*, **зарисо́вывать, -аю** *impf.* sketch. **зарисо́вка, -и** sketching; sketch.

зарни́ца, -ы summer lightning.

зароди́ть, -ожу́ *pf.*, **зарожда́ть, -а́ю** *impf.* generate, engender; **~ся** be born; arise. **заро́дыш, -а** foetus; bud; embryo, germ. **заро́дышевый** embryonic. **зарожде́ние, -я** conception; origin.

заро́к, -а (solemn) promise, vow, pledge, undertaking.

заро́с *etc.*: *see* **зарасти́. за́росль, -и** thicket; brushwood.

заро́ю *etc.*: *see* **зары́ть**

зарпла́та, -ы *abbr.* (*of* ***за́работная пла́та***) wages; pay; salary.

заруба́ть, -а́ю *impf. of* **заруби́ть**

зарубе́жный foreign.

заруби́ть, -блю́, -бишь *pf.* (*impf.* **заруба́ть, -а́ю**) kill, cut down; notch, cut in. **зару́бка, -и** notch, incision.

за|румя́нить(ся, -ню(сь *pf.*

заруча́ться, -а́юсь *impf.*, **заручи́ться, -учу́сь** *pf.+i.* secure. **зару́чка, -и** pull, protection.

зарыва́ть, -а́ю *impf.*, **зары́ть, -ро́ю** *pf.* bury; **~ся** bury o.s.; dig in.

заря́, -и́; *pl.* **зо́ри, зорь** dawn, daybreak; sunset, nightfall; reveille, retreat.

заря́д, -а charge; cartridge; fund, supply. **заряди́ть, -яжу́, -я́ди́шь** *pf.*, **заряжа́ть, -а́ю** *impf.* load; charge; stoke; **~ся** be loaded; be charged. **заря́дка, -и** loading; charging; exercises, drill. **заряжа́ющий** *sb.* loader.

заса́да, -ы ambush. **засади́ть, -ажу́, -а́дишь** *pf.*, **заса́живать, -аю** *impf.* plant; plunge, drive; shut in, confine; keep in; set (**за**+*a.* to); **~ (в тюрьму́)** put in prison, lock up. **заса́дка, -и** planting. **заса́живаться, -аюсь** *impf. of* **засе́сть**

заса́ливать[1]**, -аю** *impf. of* **засоли́ть**

заса́ливать[2]**, -аю** *impf.*, **заса́лить, -лю** *pf.* soil, make greasy.

заса́сывать, -аю *impf. of* **засоса́ть**

заса́харенный candied, crystallized.

засвети́ть, -ечу́, -е́тишь *pf.* light; **~ся** light up. **за́светло** *adv.* before nightfall, before dark.

за|свиде́тельствовать, -твую *pf.*

засе́в, -а sowing; seed, seed-corn; sown area. **засева́ть, -а́ю** *impf. of* **засе́ять**

заседа́ние, -я meeting; session, sitting; conference. **заседа́тель, -я** *m.* assessor. **заседа́ть, -а́ю** *impf.* sit, meet, be in session.

засе́ивать, -аю *impf. of* **засе́ять. засе́к** *etc.*: *see* **засе́чь засека́ть, -а́ю** *impf. of* **засе́чь**

засекре́тить, -ре́чу *pf.*, **засекре́чивать, -аю** *impf.* classify; restrict; make secret; clear, give access to secret material. **засекре́ченный** classified; cleared; hush-hush, secret.

засеку́ *etc.*: *see* **засе́чь. засе́л** *etc.*: *see* **засе́сть**

заселе́ние, -я settlement; colonization. **заселённый; -ён, -ена́** populated, inhabited. **засели́ть, -лю́** *pf.*, **заселя́ть, -я́ю** *impf.* settle; colonize; populate; occupy.

засе́сть, -ся́ду; -се́л *pf.* (*impf.* **заса́живаться**) sit down (**за**+*a.* to); sit firm, sit tight; ensconce o.s.; lodge in, stick in.

засе́чка, -и notch, indentation, mark; intersection; fix; serif. **засе́чь, -еку́, -ечёшь; -е́к, -ла́** *pf.* (*impf.* **засека́ть**) flog to death; notch; intersect; locate; fix.

засе́ять, -е́ю *pf.* (*impf.* **засева́ть, засе́ивать**) sow.

засиде́ться, -ижу́сь *pf.*, **заси́живаться, -аюсь** *impf.* sit too long, stay too long; sit up late; stay late. **заси́женный** fly-specked, fly-blown.

за|силосова́ть, -су́ю *pf.*

заси́лье, -я dominance, sway.

засла́ть, зашлю́, -шлёшь *pf.* (*impf.* **засыла́ть**) send.

засло́н, -а screen; barrier, road-block; (*furnace, oven*) door. **заслони́ть, -оню́** *pf.*, **заслоня́ть, -я́ю** *impf.* cover; shield, screen; hide, push into the background. **засло́нка, -и** (stove-)lid; damper; slide; baffle-plate; (*furnace, oven*) door.

заслу́га, -и merit, desert; service. **заслу́женный, заслужённый** deserved, merited; meritorious, of merit, distinguished; Honoured; time-honoured, good old. **заслу́живать, -аю** *impf.*, **заслужи́ть, -ужу́, -у́жишь** *pf.* deserve, merit; win, earn; *+g.* be worthy or deserving of.

заслу́шать, -аю *pf.*, **заслу́шивать, -аю** *impf.* listen to, hear; **~ся** (*+g.*) listen spellbound (to).

засме́ивать, -аю *impf.*, **засмея́ть, -ею́, -ёешь** *pf.* ridicule; **~ся** begin to laugh; burst out laughing.

засмоли́ть, -лю́ *pf.* tar, pitch.

засну́ть, -ну́, -нёшь *pf.* (*impf.* **засыпа́ть**) go to sleep, fall asleep; die down.

засо́в, -а bolt, bar.

засо́вывать, -аю *impf. of* **засу́нуть**

засо́л, -а salting, pickling. **засоли́ть, -олю́, -о́ли́шь** *pf.* (*impf.* **заса́ливать**) salt, corn, pickle. **засо́лка, -и** salting, pickling; brine, pickle.

засоре́ние, -я littering; pollution, contamination; obstruction, clogging up. **засори́ть, -рю́** *pf.*, **засоря́ть, -я́ю** *impf.* litter; get dirt into; clog, block up, stop.

засоса́ть, -осу́, -осёшь *pf.* (*impf.* **заса́сывать**) suck in; engulf, swallow up.

за|со́хнуть, -ну; -со́х *pf.* (*impf. also* **засыха́ть**) dry, dry up; wither.

за́спанный sleepy.

заста́ва, -ы gate, gates; barrier; picket, picquet; outpost; **пограни́чная ~** frontier post.

застава́ть, -таю́, -таёшь *impf. of* **заста́ть**

заста́вить[1]**, -влю** *pf.*, **заставля́ть, -я́ю** *impf.* cram; fill; block up, obstruct.

заста́вить[2]**, -влю** *pf.*, **заставля́ть, -я́ю** *impf.* make; compel, force.

заста́иваться, -ается *impf. of* **застоя́ться. заста́ну** *etc.*: *see* **заста́ть**

застаре́лый chronic; rooted.

заста́ть, -а́ну *pf.* (*impf.* **застава́ть**) find; catch.

застёгивать, -аю *impf.*, **застегну́ть, -ну́, -нёшь** *pf.* fasten, do up; button up, hook up. **застёжка, -и** fastening; clasp, buckle; hasp; **~-мо́лния** zip fastener, zip.

застекли́ть, -лю́ *pf.*, **застекля́ть, -я́ю** *impf.* glaze, fit with glass.

застелю́ *etc.*: *see* **застла́ть**

засте́нчивый shy.

застига́ть, -а́ю *impf.*, **засти́гнуть, засти́чь, -и́гну; -сти́г** *pf.* catch; take unawares.

застила́ть, -а́ю *impf. of* **застла́ть. засти́лка, -и** covering; floor-covering.

засти́чь *see* **засти́гнуть**

застлáть, -телю́, -тéлешь *pf.* (*impf.* **застилáть**) cover; spread over; cloud; ~ **ковро́м** carpet.
застóй, -я stagnation; standstill; depression. **застóйный** stagnant; sluggish, immobile.
застóльн|ый table-; **~ая речь** after-dinner speech.
за|стóпорить, -рю *pf.*
застоя́ться, -и́тся *pf.* (*impf.* **застáиваться**) stagnate, stand too long, get stale.
застрáивать, -аю *impf.* *of* **застрóить**
застрахóванный insured. **за|страховáть, -хýю** *pf.*, **застрахóвывать, -аю** *impf.* insure (**от**+*g.* against).
застревáть, -áю *impf.* *of* **застря́ть**
застрели́ть, -елю́, -éлишь *pf.* shoot (dead); **~ся** shoot o.s.; blow one's brains out. **застрéльщик, -а** pioneer, leader.
застрóить, -óю *pf.* (*impf.* **застрáивать**) build over, build on, build up. **застрóйка, -и** building.
застря́ть, -я́ну *pf.* (*impf.* **застревáть**) stick; get stuck; be held up; be bogged down.
за|студенéть, -éет *pf.*
застуди́ть, -ужý, -ýдишь *pf.*, **застýживать, -аю** *impf.* expose to cold, chill; **~ся** catch cold.
зáступ, -а spade.
заступáться, -áюсь *impf.*, **заступи́ться, -плю́сь, -пишься** *pf.* +**за**+*a.* stand up for, take the part of; plead for. **застýпник, -а** defender; protector. **застýпничество, -а** protection; intercession, defence.
застывáть, -áю *impf.*, **засты́ть, -ы́ну** *pf.* congeal; thicken, harden, set; become stiff; freeze; be petrified, be paralysed. **засты́лый** congealed; stiff.
засýнуть, -ну *pf.* (*impf.* **засóвывать**) thrust in, push in, shove in; stuff in; tuck in.
зáсуха, -и drought.
засýчивать, -аю *impf.*, **засучи́ть, -чý, -чишь** *pf.* roll up.
засýшивать, -аю *impf.*, **засуши́ть, -шý, -шишь** *pf.* dry up, shrivel. **засýшливый** arid, dry, drought.
засылáть, -áю *impf.* *of* **заслáть**
засы́пать[1], -плю *pf.*, **засыпáть, -áю** *impf.* fill up, fill in; cover, strew; put in, add; ~ **вопрóсами** bombard with questions.
засыпáть[2](ся, -áю(сь *impf.* *of* **заснýть, засы́пать(ся**
засы́паться, -плюсь *pf.* (*impf.* **засыпáться**) be caught; come to grief, slip up; fail an examination.
засы́пка, -и filling; backfilling; filling up, charging; covering, strewing; putting in.
засыхáть, -áю *impf.* *of* **засóхнуть**
察сяду *etc.*: *see* **засéсть**
затаённый; -ён, -енá secret; repressed, suppressed. **затáивать, -аю** *impf.*, **затаи́ть, -аю́** *pf.* suppress, repress; conceal; harbour, cherish; ~ **дыхáние** hold one's breath; ~ **оби́ду** nurse a grievance, bear a grudge.
затáлкивать, -аю *impf.* *of* **затолкáть. затáпливать, -аю** *impf.* *of* **затопи́ть. затáптывать, -аю** *impf.* *of* **затоптáть**
затáсканный worn; threadbare; hackneyed, trite. **затаскáть, -áю** *pf.*, **затáскивать[1], -аю** *impf.* wear out; make hackneyed, make trite; drag about; ~ **по судáм** drag through the courts; **~ся** wear (out), get dirty or threadbare with use.
затáскивать[2], -аю *impf.*, **затащи́ть, -щý, -щишь** *pf.* drag in; drag off, drag away.
затвердевáть, -áет *impf.*, **за|твердéть, -éет** *pf.* harden, become hard; set; solidify; freeze. **затвердéвший, затвердéлый** hardened; solidified, set, congealed. **затвердéние, -я** hardening; induration, callosity; callus. **за|тверди́ть, -ржý** *pf.*
затвóр, -а bolt, bar; lock; breech-block; shutter; water-gate, flood-gate. **затвори́ть, -рю́, -ришь** *pf.*, **затворя́ть, -я́ю** *impf.* shut, close; **~ся** shut o.s. up, lock o.s. in. **затвóрник, -а** hermit, anchorite, recluse.
затевáть, -áю *impf.* *of* **затéять. затéйливый** ingenious; intricate, involved; original.
затёк *etc.*: *see* **затéчь. затекáть, -áет** *impf.* *of* **затéчь**
затéм *adv.* then, after that, next; for that reason; ~ **что** because, since, as.
затемнéние, -я darkening, obscuring; blacking out; black-out; fade-out. **затемни́ть, -ню́** *pf.*, **затемня́ть, -я́ю** *impf.* darken, obscure; black out. **зáтемно** *adv.* before dawn.
затерéть, -трý, -трёшь; -тёр *pf.* (*impf.* **затирáть**) rub out; block, jam; **сýдно затёрло льдáми** the ship was ice bound.
затéрянный lost; forgotten, forsaken. **затеря́ть, -я́ю** *pf.* lose, mislay; **~ся** be lost; be mislaid; be forgotten.
затéчь, -ечёт, -екýт; -тёк, -клá *pf.* (*impf.* **затекáть**) pour, flow; leak; swell up; become numb.
затéя, -и undertaking, enterprise, venture; escapade; joke. **затéять, -éю** *pf.* (*impf.* **затевáть**) undertake, venture; organize; ~ **дрáку** start a fight.
затирáть, -áю *impf.* *of* **затерéть**
затихáть, -áю *impf.*, **зати́хнуть, -ну; -ти́х** *pf.* die down, abate; die away, fade; become quiet. **зати́шье, -я** calm; lull; sheltered corner; backwater.
заткнýть, -нý, -нёшь *pf.* (*impf.* **затыкáть**) stop up; plug; stick, thrust; ~ **прóбкой** cork.
затмевáть, -áю *impf.*, **затми́ть, -ми́шь** *pf.* darken, obscure; eclipse; overshadow. **затмéние, -я** eclipse; darkening; black-out.
затó *conj.* but then, but on the other hand.
затовáренность, -и, затовáривание, -я overstocking; glut.
затолкáть, -áю *pf.* (*impf.* **затáлкивать**) jostle.
затóн, -а backwater; boat-yard. **затонýть, -óнет** *pf.* sink, be submerged.
затопи́ть[1], -плю́, -пишь *pf.* (*impf.* **затáп-**

ливать) light; turn on the heating.

затопи́ть[2], **-плю́, -пишь** *pf.*, **затопля́ть, -я́ю** *impf.* flood, submerge; sink, scuttle.

затопта́ть, -пчу́, -пчешь *pf.* (*impf.* **зата́птывать**) trample, trample down; trample underfoot.

зато́р, -а obstruction, block, jam; congestion.

за|тормози́ть, -ожу́ *pf.*

затoча́ть, -а́ю *impf.*, **заточи́ть, -чу́** *pf.* confine, shut up; incarcerate, imprison. **заточе́ние, -я** confinement; incarceration, captivity.

за|трави́ть, -влю́, -вишь *pf.*, **затра́вливать, -аю** *impf.* hunt down, bring to bay; persecute, harass, harry; badger.

затра́гивать, -аю *impf. of* **затро́нуть**

затра́та, -ы expense; outlay. **затра́тить, -а́чу** *pf.*, **затра́чивать, -аю** *impf.* expend, spend.

затре́бовать, -бую *pf.* request, require; ask for.

затро́нуть, -ну *pf.* (*impf.* **затра́гивать**) affect; touch, graze; touch on.

затрудне́ние, -я difficulty. **затрудни́тельный** difficult; embarrassing. **затрудни́ть, -ню́** *pf.*, **затрудня́ть, -я́ю** *impf.* trouble; cause trouble to; embarrass; make difficult; hamper; **~ся** be in difficulties; *+inf. or i.* find difficulty in.

затума́нивать, -ает *impf.*, **за|тума́нить, -ит** *pf.* befog; cloud, dim, obscure.

за|тупи́ть, -плю́, -пишь *pf.*

за|тушева́ть, -шу́ю *pf.*, **затушёвывать, -аю** *impf.* shade; conceal; draw a veil over.

за|туши́ть, -шу́, -шишь *pf.* put out, extinguish; suppress.

за́тхлый musty, mouldy; stuffy, close; stagnant.

затыка́ть, -а́ю *impf. of* **заткну́ть**

заты́лок, -лка back of the head; occiput; scrag, scrag-end. **заты́лочный** occipital.

затя́гивать, -аю *impf.*, **затяну́ть, -ну́, -нешь** *pf.* tighten; lace up; cover; close, heal; drag out, draw out, spin out; **~ся** lace o.s. up; be covered; close, skin over; be delayed; linger; be drawn out, drag on; inhale. **затя́жка, -и** inhaling; prolongation; dragging on; drawing out; delaying, putting off; lagging. **затяжно́й** long-drawn-out; lingering.

зауны́вный mournful, doleful.

зауря́дный ordinary, commonplace; mediocre.

заусе́нец, -нца, заусе́ница, -ы agnail, hangnail, wire-edge, burr.

за|фарширова́ть, -ру́ю *pf.* **за|фиксировать, -рую** *pf.* **за|фрахтова́ть, -ту́ю** *pf.*

захва́т, -а seizure, capture; usurpation; clamp, claw. **захвати́ть, -ачу́, -а́тишь** *pf.* **захва́тывать, -аю** *impf.* take; seize, capture; carry away; thrill, excite; catch; **у меня́ захвати́ло дух** it took my breath away. **захва́тнический** predatory; aggressive. **захва́тчик, -а** invader; aggressor. **захва́тывающий** gripping; **~ дух** breath-taking.

захвора́ть, -а́ю *pf.* fall ill, be taken ill.

за|хире́ть, -е́ю *pf.*

захлебну́ться, -ну́сь, -нёшься *pf.*, **захлёбываться, -аюсь** *impf.* choke (**от**+*g.* with).

захлестну́ть, -ну́, -нёшь *pf.* **захлёстывать, -аю** *impf.* flow over, swamp, overwhelm; overflow.

захло́пнуть, -ну *pf.*, **захло́пывать, -аю** *impf.* slam, bang; **~ся** slam (to), bang (to), shut with a bang.

захо́д, -а setting, sunset; stopping, calling, putting in. **заходи́ть, -ожу́, -о́дишь** *impf. of* **зайти́. захо́жий** newly-arrived.

захолу́стный remote, out-of-the-way, provincial. **захолу́стье, -я** backwoods; godforsaken hole.

за|хорони́ть, -ню́, -нишь *pf.* **за|хоте́ть(ся, -очу́(сь, -о́чешь(ся, -оти́м(ся** *pf.*

захуда́лый impoverished, poor, shabby; emaciated.

зацвести́, -етёт; -вёл, -а *pf.*, **зацвета́ть, -а́ет** *impf.* burst into flower, come into bloom.

зацепи́ть, -плю́, -пишь *pf.*, **зацепля́ть, -я́ю** *impf.* hook; engage; sting; catch (**за**+*a.* on); **~ся за**+*a.* catch on; catch hold of. **заце́пка, -и** catch, hook, peg; hooking; hitch, catch; pull, protection.

зачасту́ю *adv.* often, frequently.

зача́тие, -я conception. **зача́ток, -тка** embryo; rudiment; beginning, germ. **зача́точный** rudimentary. **зача́ть, -чну́, -чнёшь; -ча́л, -а́, -о** *pf.* (*impf.* **зачина́ть**) conceive; begin.

за|ча́хнуть, -ну; -ча́х *pf.* **зачёл** *etc.*: *see* **заче́сть**

заче́м *adv.* why; what for. **заче́м-то** *adv.* for some reason.

зачёркивать, -аю *impf.*, **зачеркну́ть, -ну́, -нёшь** *pf.* cross out, strike out; delete.

за|черни́ть, -ню́ *pf.*

зачерпну́ть, -ну́, -нёшь *pf.*, **заче́рпывать, -аю** *impf.* scoop up; ladle; draw up.

зачерстве́лый stale; hard-hearted. **за|черстве́ть, -е́ет** *pf.*

заче́сть, -чту́, -чтёшь; -чёл, -чла́ *pf.* (*impf.* **зачи́тывать**) take into account, reckon as credit. **зачёт, -а** reckoning; instalment; test; **в ~ пла́ты** in payment, on account; **получи́ть, сдать ~ по**+*d.* pass a test in; **поста́вить ~ по**+*d.* pass in. **зачётн|ый; ~ая квита́нция** receipt; **~ая кни́жка** (student's) record book.

за|чехли́ть, -лю́ *pf.*

зачина́тель, -я founder, author. **зачина́ть, -а́ю** *impf. of* **зача́ть. зачи́нщик, -а** instigator, ringleader.

зачи́слить, -лю *pf.*, **зачисля́ть, -я́ю** *impf.* include; enter; enrol, enlist; **~ся** join, enter.

зачи́тывать, -аю *impf. of* **заче́сть**

зачну́ *etc.*: *see* **зача́ть. зачту́** *etc.*: *see* **заче́сть. зашёл** *etc.*: *see* **зайти**

зашива́ть, -а́ю *impf.* **заши́ть, -шью́, -шьёшь** *pf.* sew up; suture; put stitches in.

зашифро́ванный encoded, in cipher **за|шифрова́ть, -ру́ю** *pf.* **зашифро́вывать, -аю**

impf. encipher, encode.

зашлю́ *etc.*: *see* **засла́ть**

за|шнурова́ть, -ру́ю *pf.*, **зашнуро́вывать, -аю** *impf.* lace up.

за|шпаклева́ть, -лю́ю *pf.* **за|штемпелева́ть, -лю́ю** *pf.* **за|што́пать, -аю** *pf.* **за|штрихова́ть, -ху́ю** *pf.*

зашью́ *etc.*: *see* **заши́ть**

защипну́ть, -ну́, -нёшь *pf.*, **защи́пывать, -аю** *impf.* pinch, nip, tweak; take; curl; punch.

защи́та, -ы defence; protection; the defence. **защити́ть, -ищу́** *pf.*, **защища́ть, -а́ю** *impf.* defend, protect; stand up for.

заяви́ть, -влю́, -вишь *pf.*, **завля́ть, -я́ю** *impf.* announce, declare; claim; show, attest; **~ся** appear, turn up. **зая́вка, -и** claim; demand, request. **заявле́ние, -я** statement, declaration; application.

зая́длый inveterate, confirmed.

за́яц, за́йца hare; stowaway; gate-crasher; **е́хать за́йцем** travel without a ticket. **за́ячий** hare, hare's; **~ щаве́ль** wood sorrel.

зва́ние, -я calling, profession; rank; title. **зва́ный** invited; **~ ве́чер** guest-night; **~ гость** guest; **~ обе́д** banquet, dinner, dinner-party. **зва́тельный** vocative. **звать, зову́, -вёшь; звал, -а́, -о** *impf.* (*pf.* **по~**) call; ask, invite; **как вас зову́т?** what is your name?; **~ся** be called.

звезда́, -ы́; *pl.* **звёзды** star. **звёздный** star; starry; starlit; stellar. **звездообра́зный** star-shaped; radial; stellate. **звездочёт, -а́** astrologer. **звёздочка, -и** little star; asterisk.

звене́ть, -ню́ *impf.* ring; *+i.* jingle, clink.

звено́, -а́; *pl.* **зве́нья, -ьев** link; bond; team, group, section, flight; unit; component, element; network. **звеньево́й** *sb.* team leader; section leader.

звери́нец, -нца menagerie. **звери́ный** wild-animal, wild-beast. **зверобо́й** hunter, sealer. **зверово́дство, -а** fur farming. **зверoло́в, -а** trapper. **зве́рски** *adv.* brutally, bestially; terribly, awfully. **зве́рский** brutal, bestial; terrific, tremendous. **зве́рство, -а** brutality; atrocity. **зве́рствовать, -твую** *impf.* commit atrocities. **зверь, -я**; *pl.* **-и, -е́й** *m.* wild animal, wild beast; brute. **зверьё, -я́** wild animals; wild beasts.

звон, -а ringing; ringing sound, chime, peal, chink, clink. **звони́ть, -ню́** *impf.* (*pf.* **по~**) ring; ring up; **~ в колокола́** ring the bells; **~ кому́-нибу́дь (по телефо́ну)** ring s.o. up, telephone s.o.; **вы не туда́ звони́те** you've got the wrong number; **звоня́т** the telephone's ringing; there's s.o. at the door; **~ся** ring the (door-)bell, ring. **зво́нк|ий; -нок, -нка́, -о** ringing, clear; voiced; **~ая моне́та** hard cash, coin. **звоно́к, -нка́** bell; **~ по телефо́ну** (telephone) call. **зво́нче, звонче́е** *comp. of* **зво́нкий, зво́нко**

звук, -а sound; **ни ~а** not a sound.

звуко... *in comb.* sound. **звукоза́пись, -и** sound recording. **~изоля́ция, -и** sound-proofing. **~непроница́емый** sound-proof. **~подража́тельный** onomatopoeic. **~прово́дный** sound conducting. **~снима́тель, -я** *m.* pick-up. **~ула́вливатель, -я** *m.* sound locator. **~часто́тный** audio, audio-frequency.

звуково́й sound; audio; acoustical, acoustic. **звуча́ние, -я** sound vibration; phonation. **звуча́ть, -чи́т** *impf.* be heard; sound; *+i.* express, convey; **~ и́скренно** ring true. **зву́чный; -чен, -чна́, -о** sonorous.

звя́канье, -я jingling; tinkling. **звя́кать, -аю** *impf.*, **звя́кнуть, -ну** *pf.* (*+i.*) jingle; tinkle.

зда́ние, -я building.

здесь *adv.* here; at this point; in this. **зде́шний** local; **не ~** a stranger here.

здоро́ваться, -аюсь *impf.* (*pf.* **по~**) exchange greetings; **~ за́ руку** shake hands. **здо́рово** *adv.* splendidly, magnificently; well done! fine! **здоро́вый** healthy, strong; well; health-giving, wholesome, sound. **здоро́вье, -я** health; **за ва́ше ~!** your health! **как ва́ше ~?** how are you? **здра́вица, -ы** toast. **здра́вница, -ы** sanatorium. **здра́во** *adv.* soundly; sensibly.

здраво... *in comb.* health; sound, sensible. **здравомы́слящий** sensible, judicious. **~охране́ние, -я** public health; health service. **~охрани́тельный** public-health.

здравпу́нкт, -а medical post, medical centre. **здра́вствовать, -твую** *impf.* be healthy; thrive, prosper; **здра́вствуй(те)!** how do you do?; good morning, afternoon, evening; **да здра́вствует!** long live! **здра́в|ый** sensible; healthy; **в ~ом уме́** in one's right mind; **~ый смысл** common sense.

зе́бра, -ы zebra; zebra crossing.

зев, -а pharynx; jaws. **зева́ка, -и** *c.g.* idler, gaper. **зева́ть, -а́ю** *impf.*, **зевну́ть, -ну́, -нёшь** *pf.* (*pf. also* **про~**) yawn; gape; miss, let slip, lose. **зево́к, -вка́, зево́та, -ы** yawn.

зелене́ть, -е́ет *impf.* (*pf.* **по~**) turn green, go green; show green. **зеленн|о́й; ~а́я ла́вка** greengrocer's. **зелено́ватый** greenish. **зелён|ый; зе́лен, -а́, -о** green; **~ый лук** spring onions; **~ая у́лица** go, green light. **зе́лень, -и** green; greenery, vegetation; greens; vegetables.

земле... *in comb.* land; earth. **землеве́дение, -я** physical geography. **~владе́лец, -льца** landowner. **~де́лец, -льца** farmer. **~де́лие, -я** farming, agriculture. **~де́льческий** agricultural. **~ко́п, -а** navvy. **~ме́р, -а** land-surveyor. **~ме́рный** surveying, surveyor's. **~ро́йный** earth-moving, excavating. **~трясе́ние, -я** earthquake. **~черпа́лка, -и** mechanical dredger, bucket dredger. **~черпа́ние, -я** dredging.

земли́стый earthy; sallow. **земля́, -и́**, *a.* **-ю**; *pl.* **-и, земе́ль, -ям** earth; land; soil. **земля́к, -а́** fellow-countryman. **земляни́ка, -и** strawberries; wild strawberries. **земля́нка, -и** dug-out; mud hut. **землян|о́й** earthen; earth;

earthy; **~ая гру́ша** Jerusalem artichoke. **земля́чка, -и** country-woman. **земно́й** earthly; terrestrial; ground; mundane; **~ шар** the globe.

зени́т, -а zenith. **зени́тный** zenith; anti-aircraft.

зе́ркало, -а; *pl.* **-а́** looking-glass; mirror; reflector. **зерка́льн|ый** mirror; looking-glass; reflecting; smooth; plate, plate-glass; **~ое изображе́ние** mirror image.

зерни́ст|ый granular, granulated; grainy; **~ая икра́** unpressed caviare. **зерно́, -а́**; *pl.* **зёрна, зёрен** grain; seed; kernel, core; corn; **ко́фе в зёрнах** coffee beans. **зернови́дный** granular. **зерново́й** grain, corn, seed. **зерновы́е** *sb., pl.* cereals; grain crop. **зернохрани́лище, -а** granary.

зерца́ло, -а looking-glass; *pl.* breast-plate.

зигза́г, -а zigzag.

зима́, -ы́, *a.* **-у**; *pl.* **-ы** winter. **зи́мний** winter, wintry. **зимова́ть, -му́ю** *impf.* (*pf.* **пере~, про~**) winter, spend the winter; hibernate. **зимо́вка, -и** wintering, winter stay; hibernation; polar station. **зимо́вщик, -а** winterer. **зимо́вье, -я** winter quarters. **зимо́й** *adv.* in winter. **зимосто́йкий** hardy.

зия́ние, -я gaping, yawning; gap; hiatus. **зия́ть, -я́ет** *impf.* gape, yawn.

злак, -а grass; cereal. **зла́ковый** grassy, herbaceous; cereal, grain.

зле́йший *superl. of* **злой; ~враг** worst enemy. **злить, злю** *impf.* (*pf.* **обо~, о~, разо~**) anger; irritate; **~ся** be angry, be in a bad temper; rage. **зло, -а**; *g.pl.* **зол** evil; harm; misfortune, disaster; malice, spite; vexation. **зло** *adv.* maliciously, spitefully.

зло... *in comb.* evil, harm, malice; wicked, malicious; bad-tempered. **злове́щий** ominous, ill-omened. **~во́ние, -я** stink, stench. **~во́нный** fetid, stinking. **~вре́дный** pernicious; noxious. **~ка́чественный** malignant; pernicious. **~наме́ренный** ill-intentioned. **~па́мятный** rancorous, unforgiving. **~полу́чный** unlucky, ill-starred. **~ра́дный** malevolent, gloating. **~сло́вие, -я** malicious gossip; backbiting. **~умы́шленник, -а** malefactor, criminal; plotter. **~умы́шленный** with criminal intent. **~язы́чие, -я** slander, backbiting. **~язы́чный** slanderous.

зло́ба, -ы malice; spite; anger; **~ дня** topic of the day, latest news. **зло́бный** malicious, spiteful; bad-tempered. **злободне́вн|ый** topical; **~ые вопро́сы** burning issues, topics of the day. **злоде́й, -я** villain; scoundrel. **злоде́йский** villainous. **злоде́йство, -а** villainy; crime, evil deed. **злодея́ние, -я** crime, evil deed. **злой; зол, зла** evil; bad; wicked; malicious; malevolent; vicious; bad-tempered; savage; dangerous; severe, cruel; bad, nasty; **«зла́я соба́ка»** 'beware of the dog'. **зло́стн|ый** malicious; conscious, intentional; persistent, hardened; **~ное банкро́тство** fraudulent bankruptcy. **злость, -и** malice, spite; fury. **злоупотреби́ть, -блю́** *pf.*, **злоупотребля́ть, -я́ю** *impf.+i.* abuse. **злоупотребле́ние, -я**+*i.* abuse of; **~ дове́рием** breach of confidence.

змеи́ный snake; snake's; cunning, crafty; wicked. **змеи́стый** serpentine; sinuous. **змей, -я** snake; dragon; kite. **змея́, -и́**; *pl.* **-и** snake. **змий, -я** serpent, dragon.

знак, -а sign; mark; token, symbol; omen; signal; **~и препина́ния** punctuation marks; **~и разли́чия** insignia, badges of rank.

знако́мить, -млю *impf.* (*pf.* **о~, по~**) acquaint; introduce; **~ся** become acquainted, acquaint o.s.; get to know; introduce o.s.; study, investigate; +**с**+*i.* meet, make the acquaintance of. **знако́мство, -а** acquaintance; (circle of) acquaintances; knowledge (**с**+*i.* of). **знако́м|ый** familiar; **быть ~ым с**+*i.* be acquainted with, know; **~ый, ~ая** *sb.* acquaintance, friend.

знамена́тель, -я *m.* denominator; **привести́ к одному́ знамена́телю** reduce to a common denominator. **знамена́тельный** significant, important; principal. **зна́мение, -я** sign. **знамени́тость, -и** celebrity. **знамени́тый** celebrated, famous, renowned; outstanding, superlative. **знаменова́ть, -ну́ю** *impf.* signify, mark. **знамено́сец, -сца** standard-bearer. **зна́мя, -мени**; *pl.* **-мёна** *nt.* banner; flag; standard.

зна́ние, -я knowledge; *pl.* learning; accomplishments; **со зна́нием де́ла** capably, competently.

зна́тный; -тен, -тна́, -о distinguished; outstanding, notable; noble, aristocratic; splendid.

знато́к, -а́ expert; connoisseur. **знать, -а́ю** *impf.* know; **дать ~** inform, let know; **да́йте мне ~ о вас** let me hear from you; **дать себе́ ~** make itself felt; **~ в лицо́** know by sight; **~ ме́ру** know where to stop; **~ себе́ це́ну** know one's own value; **~ толк в**+*p.* be knowledgeable about; **~ся** associate.

значе́ние, -я meaning; significance; importance; value. **зна́чит** so then; that means. **значи́тельный** considerable, sizeable; important; significant; meaningful. **зна́чить, -чу** *impf.* mean; signify; have significance, be of importance; **~ся** be; be mentioned, appear. **значо́к, -чка́** badge; mark.

зна́ющий expert; learned, erudite; knowledgeable; well-informed.

знobи́ть, -и́т *impf., impers.+a.*; **меня́**, *etc.*, **зноби́т** I feel shivery, feverish.

зной, -я intense heat. **зно́йный** hot, sultry; burning.

зов, -а (-у) call, summons; invitation. **зову́** *etc.*: *see* **звать**

зо́дческий architecture, architectural. **зо́дчество, -а** architecture. **зо́дчий** *sb.* architect.

зол *see* **зло, злой**

зола́, -ы́ ashes, cinders.

золо́вка, -и sister-in-law, husband's sister.
золоти́стый golden. **золоти́ть, -очу́** *impf.* (*pf.* **вы́~, по~**) gild. **зо́лото, -а** gold. **золот|о́й** gold; golden; **~о́е дно** gold-mine; **~о́й запа́с** gold reserves; **~о́й песо́к** gold-dust; **~ы́е про́мыслы** gold-fields. **золотоно́сный** auriferous; gold-bearing.
золоту́ха, -и scrofula. **золоту́шный** scrofulous.
золоче́ние, -я gilding. **золочёный** gilt, gilded.
зо́на, -ы zone; region; band, belt. **зона́льный** zonal, zone; regional.
зонд, -а probe; bore; sonde. **зонди́ровать, -рую** *impf.* sound, probe.
зонт, -а́ umbrella; awning. **зо́нтик, -а** umbrella; sunshade; umbrel. **зо́нтичный** umbellate, umbelliferous.
зоо́лог, -а zoologist. **зоологи́ческий** zoological. **зооло́гия, -и** zoology. **зоомагази́н, -а** pet-shop. **зоопа́рк, -а** zoo, zoological gardens. **зооферма, -ы** fur farm.
зо́ри *etc.*: *see* **заря́**
зо́ркий; -рок, -рка́, -о sharp-sighted; perspicacious, penetrating; vigilant.
зрачо́к, -чка́ pupil.
зре́лище, -а sight; spectacle; show; pageant.
зре́лость, -и ripeness; maturity; **аттеста́т зре́лости** school-leaving certificate. **зре́лый; зрел, -а́, -о** ripe, mature.
зре́ние, -я sight, eyesight, vision; **обма́н зре́ния** optical illusion; **по́ле зре́ния** field of vision, field of view; **то́чка зре́ния** point of view; **у́гол зре́ния** viewing angle, camera angle.
зреть, -е́ю *impf.* (*pf.* **со~**) ripen; mature.
зри́мый visible. **зри́тель, -я** *m.* spectator, observer; onlooker; *pl.* audience. **зри́тельный** visual; optic; **~ зал** hall, auditorium.
зря *adv.* to no purpose, for nothing, in vain.
зря́чий sighted, seeing.
зуб, -а; *pl.* **-ы** *or* **-бья, -о́в** *or* **-бьев** tooth; cog. **зуба́стый** large-toothed; sharp-tongued. **зубе́ц, -бца́** tooth, cog, tine; blip. **зуби́ло, -а** chisel. **зубно́й** dental; tooth; **~ врач** dentist. **зубовраче́бный** dentists', dental; **~ кабине́т** dental surgery. **зубоврачева́ние, -я** dentistry. **зубо́к, -бка́**; *pl.* **-бки́** tooth; cog; clove. **зубоска́л, -а** scoffer. **зубочи́стка, -и** toothpick.
зубр, -а (European) bison, aurochs; die-hard.
зубри́ть[1], -рю́ *impf.* (*pf.* **за~**) notch, serrate.
зубри́ть[2], -рю́, зу́бри́шь *impf.* (*pf.* **вы́~, за~**) cram, learn by rote.
зубча́тка, -и sprocket; gear-wheel, gear; rack-wheel. **зубча́тый** toothed, cogged; gear, gear-wheel; serrate, serrated, jagged, indented.
зуд, -а itch. **зуда́, -ы́** *c.g.* bore. **зуде́ть, -и́т** itch.
ЗУПВ *abbr.* (*of* **запомина́ющее устро́йство с произво́льной вы́боркой**) (*comput.*) RAM, (*random-access memory*).
зы́бкий; -бок, -бка́, -о unsteady, shaky; unstable, shifting; vacillating. **зыбу́ч|ий** unsteady, unstable, shifting; **~ие пески́** quicksands. **зыбь, -и**; *g.pl.* **-е́й** ripple, rippling.
зы́чный loud, stentorian.
зэ *nt.indecl.* the letter **з.**
зюйд, -а south; south wind.
зя́бкий chilly, sensitive to cold.
зя́блик, -а chaffinch.
зя́блый frozen; damaged by frost.
зя́бнуть, -ну; зяб *impf.* suffer from cold, feel the cold.
зять, -я; *pl.* **-тья́, -тьёв** son-in-law; brother-in-law, sister's husband.

И

и *nt.indecl.* the letter **и; и с кра́ткой, и кра́ткое** the letter **й.**
и *conj.* and; and so; even; just; too; as well; (*with neg.*) either; **в то́м-то и де́ло** that's just it, that's the whole point; **и... и** both ... and; **и он не знал** he didn't know either; **и про́чее, и так да́лее** etc., etcetera, and so on and so forth; **и тому́ подо́бное** and the like; **и тот и друго́й** both.
и́бо *conj.* for; because, since.
и́ва, -ы willow. **ивня́к, -а́** osier-bed; osiers, osier. **и́вовый** willow.
и́волга, -и oriole.
игла́, -ы́; *pl.* **-ы** needle; thorn; spine; quill. **иглотерапе́вт, -а** acupuncturist. **иглотерапи́я, -и** acupuncture.
и́го, -а yoke.
иго́лка, -и needle. **иго́лочка, -и** *dim.*: **с иго́лочки** brand-new, spick and span. **иго́льник, -а** needle-case. **иго́льный** needle, needle's. **иго́льчатый** needle-shaped; acicular; needle; **~ при́нтер** dot-matrix printer.
иго́рный gaming, gambling. **игра́, -ы́**; *pl.* **-ы** play, playing; game; hand; turn, lead; **~ приро́ды** sport, freak (of nature); **~ слов** pun. **игра́льн|ый** playing; **~ые ко́сти** dice. **игра́ть, -а́ю** *impf.* (*pf.* **сыгра́ть**) play; act; **~ в+*a.*** play (*game*); **~ на+*p.*** play (*an instrument*), play on; **+*i.*** *or* **с+*i.*** play with, toy with, trifle with; **~ в билья́рд, на билья́рде** play billiards; **э́то не игра́ет ро́ли** it is of no importance, of no significance. **игри́вый** playful. **игри́стый** sparkling. **игро́к, -а́** player; gambler. **игру́шечный** toy. **игру́шка, -и** toy; plaything.
идеа́л, -а ideal. **идеализи́ровать, -рую** *impf.* & *pf.* idealize. **идеали́зм, -а** idealism. **идеали́ст, -а** idealist. **идеалисти́ческий, идеалисти́чный** idealistic.

идеа́льн|ый ideal, perfect; **~ое состоя́ние** mint condition.

иде́йность, -и principle, integrity; ideological content. **иде́йный** high-principled; acting on principle; ideological.

идео́лог, -а ideologist. **идеологи́ческий** ideological. **идеоло́гия, -и** ideology.

идёт *etc.*: *see* **идти́**

иде́я, -и idea; notion, concept; **счастли́вая ~** happy thought.

идилли́ческий idyllic. **иди́ллия, -и** idyll.

идио́ма, -ы idiom. **идиомати́ческий** idiomatic.

идио́т, -а idiot, imbecile. **идиоти́зм, -а** idiocy, imbecility. **идиоти́ческий, идио́тский** idiotic, imbecile.

и́дол, -а idol. **идолопокло́нник, -а** idolater. **идолопокло́ннический** idolatrous.

идти́, иду́, идёшь; шёл, шла *impf.* (*pf.* **пойти́**) go; come; go round; run, work; pass; go on, be in progress; be on, be showing; fall; +**в**+*nom.-a.* become; +**в**+*a.* be used for, go for; +(**к**+)*d.* suit, become; +**на**+*a.* enter; go to make, go on; +**о**+*p.* be about; +*i. or* **с**+*g.* play, lead, move; **ей идёт тридца́тый год** she is in her thirtieth year; **~ в лётчики** become a flyer; **~ в лом** go for scrap; **~ на сме́ну**+*d.* take the place of, succeed; **~ ферзём** move the queen; **~ с черве́й** lead a heart; **хорошо́ ~** be selling well, be going well; **шли го́ды** years passed; **э́та шля́па е́й не идёт** that hat doesn't suit her.

иезуи́т, -а Jesuit. **иезуи́тский** Jesuit.

иере́й, -я priest. **иере́йство, -а** priesthood.

иеро́глиф, -а hieroglyph; ideogram, ideograph. **иероглифи́ческий** hieroglyphic.

иждиве́нец, -нца, -ве́нка, -и dependant. **иждиве́ние, -я** maintenance; means, funds; **на иждиве́нии** at the expense of; **жить на своём иждиве́нии** keep o.s.; **жить на иждиве́нии роди́телей** live on one's parents. **иждиве́нчество, -а** dependence.

из, изо *prep.*+*g.* from, out of, of; **вы́йти из до́ма** go out, leave the house; **изо всех сил** with all one's might; **из достове́рных исто́чников** from reliable sources, on good authority; **ло́жки из серебра́** silver spoons; **обе́д из трёх блюд** a three-course dinner; **оди́н из ста** one in a hundred.

из..., изо..., изъ..., ис... *vbl. pref. expressing motion outwards; action over entire surface of object, in all directions; expenditure of instrument or object in course of action; continuation or repetition of action to extreme point; exhaustiveness of action.*

изба́, -ы́; *pl.* **-ы** izba; **~-чита́льня** village reading-room.

избави́тель, -я *m.* deliverer. **изба́вить, -влю** *pf.*, **избавля́ть, -я́ю** *impf.* save, deliver; **изба́ви Бог!** God forbid; **~ся** be saved, escape; **~ся от** get rid of; get out of. **избавле́ние, -я** deliverance.

избало́ванный spoilt. **из|балова́ть, -лу́ю** *pf.*, **избало́вывать, -аю** *impf.* spoil.

изба́ч, -а́ village librarian.

избега́ть, -а́ю *impf.*, **избе́гнуть, -ну; -бе́г(нул)** *pf.*, **избежа́ть, -егу́** *pf.*+*g. or inf.* avoid; shun, escape, evade. **избежа́ние, -я; во ~**+*g.* (in order) to avoid.

изберу́ *etc.*: *see* **избра́ть**

избива́ть, -а́ю *impf. of* **изби́ть. избие́ние, -я** slaughter, massacre; beating, beating-up.

избира́тель, -я *m.*, **~ница, -ы** elector, voter. **избира́тельн|ый** electoral; election; selective; **~ый бюллете́нь** voting-paper; **~ая у́рна** ballot-box; **~ый уча́сток** polling station. **избира́ть, -а́ю** *impf. of* **избра́ть**

изби́тый beaten, beaten up; hackneyed, trite. **изби́ть, изобью́, -бьёшь** *pf.* (*impf.* **избива́ть**) beat unmercifully, beat up; slaughter, massacre; wear down, ruin.

избра́ние, -я election. **и́збранн|ый** selected; select; **~ые** *sb.*, *pl.* the elite. **избра́ть, -беру́, -берёшь; -а́л, -а́, -о** *pf.* (*impf.* **избира́ть**) elect; choose.

избу́шка, -и small hut.

избы́ток, -тка surplus, excess; abundance, plenty. **избы́точный** surplus; abundant, plentiful.

извая́ние, -я statue, sculpture. **извая́ть, -я́ю** *pf.*

изве́дать, -аю *pf.*, **изве́дывать, -аю** *impf.* come to know, learn the meaning of.

изведу́ *etc.*, **извёл** *etc.*: *see* **извести́**

и́зверг, -а monster. **изверга́ть, -а́ю** *impf.*, **изве́ргнуть, -ну; -е́рг** *pf.* disgorge; eject; throw out; excrete; expel; **~ся** erupt. **изверже́ние, -я** eruption; ejection, expulsion; excretion.

изверну́ться, -ну́сь, -нёшься *pf.*, **извёртываться, -аюсь** *impf.* (*impf. also* **извора́чиваться**) dodge, take evasive action; be evasive.

извести́, -еду́, -едёшь; -ёл, -ела́ *pf.* (*impf.* **изводи́ть**) use (up); waste; destroy, exterminate; exhaust; torment.

изве́стие, -я news; information; intelligence; *pl.* proceedings, transactions. **извести́ть, -ещу́** *pf.* (*impf.* **извеща́ть**) inform, notify.

извёстка, -и lime. **известкова́ть, -ку́ю** *impf.* & *pf.* lime. **известко́вый** lime; limestone; calcareous.

изве́стно it is (well) known; of course, certainly; **как ~** as everybody knows; **наско́лько мне ~** as far as I know. **изве́стность, -и** fame, reputation; repute; notoriety. **изве́стн|ый** known; well-known, famous; notorious; certain; **в ~ых слу́чаях** in certain cases.

известня́к, -а́ limestone. **и́звесть, -и** lime.

извеща́ть, -а́ю *impf. of* **извести́ть. извеще́ние, -я** notification, notice; advice.

изви́в, -а winding, bend. **извива́ть, -а́ю** *impf. of* **изви́ть; ~ся** coil; wriggle, writhe; twist, wind; meander. **изви́лина, -ы** bend, twist, winding; convolution. **изви́листый** winding;

tortuous; sinuous; meandering.

извинéние, -я excuse; apology, pardon. **извини́тельный** excusable, pardonable; apologetic. **извини́ть, -ню́** *pf.*, **извиня́ть, -я́ю** *impf.* excuse; **извини́те (меня́)** I beg your pardon, excuse me, (I'm) sorry; **извини́те, что я опозда́л** sorry I'm late; **~ся** apologize; make excuses, excuse o.s.; **извиня́юсь** I apologize, (I'm) sorry; **извини́тесь за меня́** present my apologies, make my excuses.

изви́ть, изовью́, -вьёшь; -и́л, -á, -о *pf.* (*impf.* **извива́ть**) coil, twist; wind; **~ся** coil; writhe, twist.

извлека́ть, -а́ю *impf.*, **извле́чь, -еку́, -ечёшь; -ёк, -ла́** *pf.* extract; derive, elicit; extricate; **~ уро́к из** learn a lesson from. **извлече́ние, -я** extraction; extract, excerpt.

извне́ *adv.* from outside.

изводи́ть, -ожу́, -о́дишь *impf. of* **извести́**

изво́зчик, -а cabman, cabby; carrier, carter, drayman; cab.

изво́лить, -лю *impf.+inf. or g.* wish, desire; *+inf.* deign, be pleased; **изво́льте** if you wish; all right; with pleasure.

извора́чиваться, -аюсь *impf. of* **изверну́ться. изворо́т, -а** bend, twist; *pl.* tricks, wiles. **изворо́тливый** resourceful, artful; wily, shrewd.

извратить, -ащу́ *pf.*, **извраща́ть, -а́ю** *impf.* distort; pervert; misinterpret, misconstrue. **извраще́ние, -я** perversion; misinterpretation, distortion. **извращённый** perverted, unnatural.

изга́дить, -а́жу *pf.* befoul, soil; spoil, make a mess of.

изги́б, -а bend, twist; winding; inflexion, nuance. **изгиба́ть(ся, -а́ю(сь** *impf. of* **изогну́ть(ся**

изгла́дить, -а́жу *pf.*, **изгла́живать, -аю** *impf.* efface, wipe out, blot out.

изгна́ние, -я banishment; expulsion; exile. **изгна́нник, -а** exile. **изгна́ть, -гоню́, -го́нишь; -а́л, -а́, -о** *pf.* (*impf.* **изгоня́ть**) banish, expel, exile; oust, do away with.

изголо́вье, -я bed-head; bedside; **служи́ть изголо́вьем** serve as a pillow.

изголода́ться, -а́юсь be famished, starve; *+***по***+d.* thirst for, yearn for.

изгоню́ *etc.*: *see* **изгна́ть. изгоня́ть, -я́ю** *impf. of* **изгна́ть**

и́згородь, -и fence, hedge.

изгота́вливать, -аю *impf.*, **изгото́вить, -влю** *pf.*, **изготовля́ть, -я́ю** *impf.* make, manufacture, produce; prepare; cook; **~ся** get ready, make ready. **изготови́тель, -я** manufacturer, producer. **изгото́вка, -и, изготовле́ние, -я** making, manufacture, production; preparation.

издава́ть, -даю́, -даёшь *impf. of* **изда́ть**

и́здавна *adv.* from time immemorial; for a very long time.

издади́м *etc.*: *see* **изда́ть**

издалека́, издалёка, и́здали *advs.* from afar, from far away, from a distance.

изда́ние, -я publication; edition; promulgation. **изда́тель, -я** *m.*, **~ница, -ы** publisher. **изда́тельство, -а** publishing house, press, publisher's. **изда́ть, -а́м, -а́шь, -а́ст, -ади́м; -а́л, -а́, -о** *pf.* (*impf.* **издава́ть**) publish; promulgate; issue; produce; emit; let out, utter; **~ся** be published.

издева́тельский mocking. **издева́тельство, -а** mocking, scoffing; mockery; taunt, insult. **издева́ться, -а́юсь** *impf.* (+**над**+*i.*) mock, scoff (at). **издёвка, -и** taunt, insult.

изде́лие, -я make, work; article; *pl.* wares.

издержа́ть, -жу́, -жишь *pf.* spend; **~ся** spend all one's money; be spent up. **изде́ржки, -жек** *pl.* expenses; costs; cost.

издеру́ *etc.*: *see* **изодра́ть. издира́ть, -а́ю** *impf. of* **изодра́ть**

из|до́хнуть, -ну; -до́х *pf.*, **издыха́ть, -а́ю** *impf.* die; peg out, kick the bucket. **издыха́ние, -я; после́днее ~** last breath, last gasp.

из|жа́рить(ся, -рю(сь *pf.*

изжива́ть, -а́ю *impf.*, **изжи́ть, -иву́, -вёшь; -и́л, -á, -о** *pf.* overcome, get over; eliminate, get rid of.

изжо́га, -и heartburn.

из-за *prep.+g.* from behind, from beyond; because of, through; **жени́ться ~ де́нег** marry for money.

излага́ть, -а́ю *impf. of* **изложи́ть**

изла́мывать, -аю *impf. of* **излома́ть**

излече́ние, -я treatment; recovery; cure. **изле́чивать, -аю** *impf.*, **излечи́ть, -чу́, -чишь** cure; **~ся** be cured, make a complete recovery; +**от**+*g.* rid o.s. of, shake off.

излива́ть, -а́ю *impf.*, **изли́ть, изолью́, -льёшь; -и́л, -á, -о** *pf.* pour out, give vent to; **~ ду́шу** unbosom o.s.; unburden one's heart.

изли́шек, -шка surplus; remainder; excess; **с изли́шком** enough and to spare. **изли́шество, -а** excess; over-indulgence. **изли́шний; -шен, -шня** superfluous; excessive; unnecessary.

излия́ние, -я outpouring, outflow, effusion, discharge.

изловчи́ться, -чу́сь *pf.* contrive, manage.

изложе́ние, -я exposition; account. **изложи́ть, -жу́, -жишь** *pf.* (*impf.* **излага́ть**) expound, state; set forth; word, draft; **~ на бума́ге** commit to paper.

изло́м, -а break, fracture; sharp bend; salient point. **изло́манный** broken, fractured; winding, tortuous; worn out. **излома́ть, -а́ю** *pf.* (*impf.* **изла́мывать**) break; smash; wear out; warp, corrupt.

излуча́ть, -а́ю *impf.* radiate, emit; **~ся** be emitted, be radiated; emanate. **излуче́ние, -я** radiation; emanation.

излу́чина, -ы bend, curve, meander. **излу́чистый** winding, meandering.

излю́бленный favourite.

из|мáзать, -áжу *pf.*, dirty, smear all over; use up; **~ся** get dirty, smear o.s. all over.

из|марáть, -áю *pf.* **из|мельчáть, -áю** *pf.* **из|мельчи́ть, -чу́** *pf.*

измéна, -ы betrayal; treachery, treason; infidelity.

изменéние, -я change, alteration; inflexion. **измени́ть**[1], **-ню́, -нишь** *pf.* (*impf.* **изменя́ть**) change, alter; **~ся** change, alter; vary; **~ся в лицé** change countenance.

измени́ть[2], **-ню́, -нишь** *pf.* (*impf.* **изменя́ть**) *+d.* betray; be unfaithful to; fail. **измéнник, -а** traitor **измéннический** treacherous, traitorous.

измéнчивый changeable; inconstant, fickle. **изменя́емый** variable. **изменя́ть(ся, -я́ю(сь** *impf. of* **измени́ть(ся**

измерéние, -я measurement, measuring; mensuration; sounding, fathoming; metering, gauging; taking; dimension. **измери́мый** measurable. **измери́тель, -я** *m.* gauge, meter; index. **измери́тельный** measuring; standard. **измéрить, -рю** *pf.*, **измеря́ть, -я́ю** *impf.* measure, gauge; sound; survey.

измождённый; -ён, -енá emaciated; worn out.

и́зморозь, -и hoar-frost; rime.

изму́чать, -аю *pf.*, **изму́чивать, -аю** *impf.*, **из|му́чить, -чу** *pf.* torment; tire out, exhaust; **~ся** be tired out, be exhausted. **изму́ченный** worn out, tired out.

измы́слить, -лю *pf.*, **измышля́ть, -я́ю** *impf.* fabricate, invent; contrive. **измышлéние, -я** fabrication, invention.

измя́тый crumpled, creased; haggard, jaded. **из|мя́ть(ся, изомну́(сь, -нёшь(ся** *pf.*

изнáнка, -и wrong side; under side; reverse; seamy side. **изнáночн|ый; ~ая петля́** purl (stitch).

из|наси́ловать, -лую *pf.* rape, assault, violate.

изнáшивание, -я wear (and tear). **изнáшивать(ся, -аю(сь** *impf. of* **износи́ть(ся**

изнéженный pampered; delicate; soft, effete; effeminate. **изнéживать, -аю** *impf.*, **изнéжить, -жу** *pf.* pamper, coddle; make effeminate; **~ся** go soft, grow effete; become effeminate.

изнемогáть, -áю *impf.*, **изнемóчь, -огу́, -óжешь; -óг, -лá** *pf.* be exhausted, be dead tired. **изнеможéние, -я** exhaustion. **изнеможённый; -ён, -á** exhausted.

изнóс, -а (-у) wear; wear and tear; deterioration; **не знать ~у** wear well, stand hard wear. **износи́ть, -ошу́, -óсишь** *pf.* (*impf.* **изнáшивать**) wear out; **~ся** wear out; be used up, be played out; age (*prematurely*). **износостóйкий** hard-wearing. **изнóшенный** worn out; threadbare; worn; aged.

изнóю *etc.*: *see* **изны́ть**

изнурéние, -я exhaustion; emaciation. **изнурённый; -ён, -енá** exhausted, worn out; jaded; **~ го́лодом** faint with hunger. **изнури́тельный** exhausting. **изнури́ть, -рю́** *pf.*, **изнуря́ть, -я́ю** *impf.* exhaust, wear out.

изнутри́ *adv.* from inside, from within.

изнывáть, -áю *impf.*, **изны́ть, -нóю** *pf.* languish, be exhausted; **~ от жáжды** be tormented by thirst; **~ по**+*d.* pine for.

изо *see* **из изо...**[1] *see* **из... . изо...**[2] iso-.

изоби́лие, -я abundance, plenty, profusion. **изоби́ловать, -лует** *impf.+i.* abound in, be rich in. **изоби́льный** abundant; *+i.* abounding in.

изобличáть, -áю *impf.*, **изобличи́ть, -чу́** *pf.* expose; unmask; reveal, show. **изобличéние, -я** exposure; conviction. **изобличи́тельн|ый** damning; **~ые докумéнты** documentary evidence.

изобрести́, -ету́, -етёшь; -ёл, -á *pf.*, **изобретáть, -áю** *impf.* invent; devise, contrive. **изобретáтель, -я** *m.* inventor. **изобретáтельный** inventive; resourceful. **изобретéние, -я** invention.

изображáть, -áю *impf.*, **изобрази́ть, -ажу́** *pf.* represent, depict, portray (*+i.* as); imitate, take off; **~ из себя́**+*a.* make o.s. out to be, represent o.s. as; **~ся** appear, show itself. **изображéние, -я** image; representation; portrayal; imprint. **изобрази́тельн|ый** graphic; decorative; **~ые искýсства** fine arts.

изобью́ *etc.*: *see* **изби́ть.** **изовью́** *etc.*: *see* **изви́ть**

изóгнутый bent, curved; winding. **изогну́ть(ся, -ну́(сь, -нёшь(ся** *pf.* (*impf.* **изгибáть(ся**) bend, curve.

изóдранный tattered. **изодрáть, издеру́, -дерёшь; -áл, -á, -о** *pf.* (*impf.* **издирáть**) tear to pieces; scratch all over.

изолгáться, -лгу́сь, -лжёшься; -áлся, -áсь, -óсь *pf.* become a hardened liar.

изоли́рованный isolated; separate; insulated. **изоли́ровать, -рую** *impf. & pf.* isolate; quarantine; insulate. **изолирóвка, -и** insulation; insulating tape.

изолью́ *etc.*: *see* **изли́ть**

изоля́тор, -а insulator; isolation ward; solitary confinement cell. **изоля́ция, -и** isolation; quarantine; insulation.

изомну́(сь *etc.*: *see* **измя́ть**

изóрванный tattered, torn. **изорвáть, -ву́, -вёшь; -áл, -á, -о** *pf.* tear, tear to pieces; **~ся** be in tatters.

изотру́ *etc.*: *see* **истерéть**

изощрённый; -рён, -á refined; keen. **изощри́ть, -рю́** *pf.*, **изощря́ть, -я́ю** *impf.* sharpen; cultivate, refine, develop; **~ся** acquire refinement; excel.

из-под *prep.+g.* from under; from near; from; **буты́лка ~ молокá** milk-bottle.

изразéц, -зцá tile. **изразцóвый** tile; tiled.

Изрáиль, -я Israel.

из|расхóдовать(ся, -дую(сь *pf.*

и́зредка *adv.* now and then; occasionally; from time to time.

изрéзанный cut up; indented, rugged.

изре́зать, -е́жу *pf.*, **изре́зывать, -аю** *impf.* cut up; cut to pieces; indent.
изрека́ть, -а́ю *impf.*, **изре́чь, -еку́, -ечёшь; -ёк, -ла́** *pf.* speak solemnly; utter. **изрече́ние, -я** dictum, saying.
изро́ю *etc.*: *see* **изры́ть**
изруба́ть, -а́ю *impf.*, **изруби́ть, -блю́, -бишь** *pf.* cut (up); chop, chop up, mince; cut down, cut to pieces.
изруга́ть, -а́ю *pf.* abuse, swear at, curse.
изрыва́ть, -а́ю *impf.*, **изры́ть, -ро́ю** *pf.* dig up, tear up, plough up. **изры́тый** pitted; cratered; torn up.
изря́дно *adv.* fairly, pretty; tolerably. **изря́дный** fair, handsome; fairly large.
изуве́чивать, -аю *impf.*, **изуве́чить, -чу** *pf.* maim, mutilate.
изуми́тельный amazing, astounding. **изуми́ть, -млю́** *pf.* **изумля́ть, -я́ю** *impf.* amaze, astonish; **~ся** be amazed. **изумле́ние, -я** amazement. **изумлённый; -лён, -а́** amazed, astonished; dumbfounded.
изумру́д, -а emerald.
изуро́дованный maimed, mutilated; disfigured. **из|уро́довать, -дую** *pf.*
изуча́ть, -а́ю *impf.*, **изучи́ть, -чу́, -чишь** *pf.* learn, study; master; come to know (very well). **изуче́ние, -я** study.
изъ... *see* **из...**
изъе́здить, -зжу *pf.* travel all over; wear out. **изъе́зженный** much-travelled, well-worn; rutted.
изъяви́тельн|ый; ~ое наклоне́ние indicative (mood). **изъяви́ть, -влю́, -вишь** *pf.*, **изъявля́ть, -я́ю** *impf.* express; **~ согла́сие** give consent. **изъявле́ние, -я** expression.
изъя́н, -а (-у) defect, flaw.
изъя́тие, -я withdrawal; removal; exception. **изъя́ть, изыму́, -мешь** *pf.* **изыма́ть, -а́ю** *impf.* withdraw; remove; confiscate.
изыска́ние, -я investigation, research; prospecting; survey. **изы́сканный** refined; recherché. **изыска́тель, -я** *m.* project surveyor; prospector. **изыска́ть, -ыщу́, -ы́щешь** *pf.*, **изы́скивать, -аю** *impf.* search (successfully) for, search out; (try to) find; prospect for.
изю́м, -а (-у) raisins; sultanas. **изю́мина, -ы** raisin. **изю́минка, -и** zest, go, spirit; sparkle; **с изю́минкой** spirited, piquant.
изя́щество, -а elegance, grace. **изя́щный** elegant, graceful.
ика́ние, -я hiccupping. **ика́ть, -а́ю** *impf.*, **икну́ть, -ну́, -нёшь** *pf.* hiccup.
ико́на, -ы icon. **иконогра́фия, -и** iconography; portraiture, portraits. **иконопи́сец, -сца** icon-painter. **и́конопись, -и** icon-painting.
ико́та, -ы hiccup, hiccups.
икра́[1], **-ы́** (hard) roe; spawn; caviare; pâté, paste.
икра́[2], **-ы́**; *pl.* **-ы** calf.
икс, -а (letter) x.
ил, -а silt, mud, ooze; sludge.
и́ли, иль *conj.* or; **~... ~** either ... or.
и́листый muddy, silty, oozy.
иллюзиони́ст, -а illusionist; conjurer, magician. **иллю́зия, -и** illusion. **иллюзо́рный** illusory.
иллюмина́тор, -а porthole.
иллюстри́рованный illustrated. **иллюстри́ровать, -рую** *impf.* & *pf.* illustrate.
иль *see* **и́ли. им** *see* **он, они́, оно́**
им. *abbr.* (*of* **и́мени**) named after.
и́мени *etc.*: *see* **и́мя**
име́ние, -я estate; property, possessions.
имени́ны, -и́н *pl.* name-day (party). **имени́тельный** nominative. **и́менно** *adv.* namely; to wit, viz.; just, exactly, precisely; to be exact; **вот ~!** exactly! precisely! **именно́й** named, nominal; bearing the owner's name; inscribed, autographed; name. **именова́ть, -ну́ю** *impf.* (*pf.* **на~**) name; **~ся**+*i.* be called; be termed. **имену́емый** called.
име́ть, -е́ю *impf.* have; **~ в виду́** bear in mind, think of, mean; **~ де́ло с**+*i.* have dealings with, have to do with; **~ значе́ние** be of importance, matter; **~ ме́сто** take place; **~ся** be; be present, be available.
и́ми *see* **они́**
иммигра́нт, -а immigrant. **иммиграцио́нный** immigration. **иммигра́ция, -и** immigration. **иммигри́ровать, -рую** *impf.* & *pf.* immigrate.
иммуниза́ция, -и immunization. **иммунизи́ровать, -рую** *impf.* & *pf.* immunize. **иммуните́т, -а** immunity. **иммунный (к**+*d.*) immune (to).
импера́тор, -а emperor. **импера́торский** imperial. **императри́ца, -ы** empress. **империали́зм, -а** imperialism. **импе́рия, -и** empire.
импони́ровать, -рую *impf.*+*d.* impress.
и́мпорт, -а import; foreign goods. **импортёр, -а** importer. **импорти́ровать, -ую** *impf.* & *pf.* import. **и́мпортный** imported, foreign.
импровиза́ция, -и improvisation. **импровизи́ровать, -рую** *impf.* (*pf.* **сымпровизи́ровать**) improvise; extemporize.
и́мпульс, -а impulse, impetus. **импульси́вный** impulsive.
иму́щественный property. **иму́щество, -а** property, belongings; stock; stores, equipment. **иму́щий** propertied; well off, wealthy.
и́мя, и́мени; *pl.* **имена́, -ён** *nt.* name; first name, christian name; reputation; noun; **во ~**+*g.* in the name of; **~ прилага́тельное** adjective; **~ существи́тельное** noun, substantive; **~ числи́тельное** numeral; **от и́мени**+*g.* on behalf of; **по и́мени** by name; in name, nominally; **Теа́тр и́мени Го́рького** the Gorky Theatre.
ин... *abbr.* (*of* **иностра́нный**) *in comb.* foreign. **инвалю́та, -ы** foreign currency. **инотде́л, -а** foreign department.
инакомы́слие, -я nonconformism, heterodoxy. **инакомы́слящий** nonconformist.

и́на́че *adv.* differently, otherwise; **так и́ли ~** in either case, in any event, at all events; *conj.* otherwise, or, or else.
инвали́д, -а disabled person; invalid. **инвали́дность, -и** disablement, disability.
инвента́рн|ый inventory, stock; **~ая о́пись** inventory. **инвента́рь, -я** *m.* stock; equipment, appliances; inventory.
инве́стор, -а investor.
инде́ец, -е́йца (*American*) Indian. **инде́йка, -и**; *g.pl.* **-е́ек** turkey(-hen). **инде́йский** (*American*) Indian; **~ пету́х** turkey-cock. **индиа́нка, -и** (*American*) Indian.
индивидуа́льность, -и individuality. **индивидуа́льный** individual. **индиви́дуум, -а** individual.
инди́ец, -и́йца Indian. **инди́йский** Indian. **И́ндия, -и** India.
Индоне́зия, -и Indonesia.
инду́с, -а, инду́ска, -и Hindu. **инду́сский** Hindu.
индустриализа́ция, -и industrialization. **индустриализи́ровать, -рую** *impf.* & *pf.* industrialize. **индустриа́льный** industrial. **инду́стрия, -и** industry.
индю́к, -а́, индю́шка, -и turkey.
и́ней, -я hoar-frost, rime.
ине́ртность, -и inertness, inertia; sluggishness, inaction, passivity. **ине́ртный** inert; passive; sluggish, inactive. **ине́рция, -и** inertia.
инжене́р, -а engineer; **~-меха́ник** mechanical engineer; **~-строи́тель** civil engineer. **инжене́рн|ый** engineering; **~ые войска́** Engineers; **~ое де́ло** engineering.
инициа́лы, -ов *pl.* initials.
инициати́в|а, -ы initiative; **по со́бственной ~е** on one's own initiative. **инициати́вный** enterprising, go-getting.
ин-ква́рто *nt.indecl.* quarto.
инкруста́ция, -и inlaid work, inlay. **инкрусти́ровать, -рую** *impf.* & *pf.* inlay.
ино... *in comb.* other, different; hetero-. **иногоро́дн|ый** of, from, for, another town. **~зе́мец, -мца** foreigner. **~зе́мный** foreign. **~планета́рный** alien, extraterrestrial. **~планетя́нин, -а,** *pl.* **-я́не, -я́н** alien, extraterrestrial. **~ро́дец, -дца** non-Russian. **~ро́дный** foreign. **~сказа́ние, -я** allegory. **~сказа́тельный** allegorical. **~стра́нец, -нца, ~стра́нка, -и**; *g.pl.* **-нок** foreigner. **~стра́нный** foreign. **~язы́чный** speaking, belonging to, another language; non-native, foreign.
иногда́ *adv.* sometimes.
ино́й different; other; some; **~ раз** sometimes; **ины́ми слова́ми** in other words.
и́нок, -а monk. **и́нокиня, -и** nun.
ин-окта́во *nt.indecl.* octavo.
инотде́л *see* **ин...**
и́ноходь, -и amble.
инспе́ктор, -а inspector; **~ мане́жа** ringmaster; **порто́вый ~** harbourmaster.
инспе́кция, -и inspection; inspectorate.
инсти́нкт, -а instinct. **инстинкти́вный** instinctive.
институ́т, -а institution; institute; young ladies' boarding school. **институ́тка, -и** boarding-school miss; innocent, unsophisticated girl.
инструкти́ровать, -рую *impf.* & *pf.* (*pf. also* **про~**) instruct, give instructions to; brief. **инстру́кция, -и** instructions; directions.
инструме́нт, -а instrument; tool, implement; tools, implements.
инсцени́ровать, -рую *impf.* & *pf.* dramatize, adapt; stage. **инсцениро́вка, -и** dramatization, adaptation; pretence, act.
интелле́кт, -а intellect; **иску́сственный ~** (*comput.*) artificial intelligence. **интеллектуа́льный** intellectual.
интеллиге́нт, -а intellectual, member of intelligentsia. **интеллиге́нтный** cultured, educated. **интеллиге́нтский** dilettante. **интеллиге́нция, -и** intelligentsia.
интенда́нт, -а commissary, quartermaster.
интенси́вный intensive. **интенсифици́ровать, -рую** *impf.* & *pf.* intensify.
интерва́л, -а interval.
интерве́нция, -и (*pol.*) intervention.
интервью́ *nt.indecl.* interview; **~ в прямо́м эфи́ре** live (*TV or radio*) interview. **интервьюе́р, -а** interviewer. **интервьюи́ровать, -рую** *impf.* & *pf.* interview.
интере́с, -а interest. **интере́сный** interesting; striking, attractive. **интересова́ть, -су́ю** *impf.* interest; **~ся** be interested (+*i.* in).
интерна́т, -а boarding-school.
интернационализа́ция, -и internationalization. **интернационализи́ровать, -рую** *impf.* & *pf.* internationalize. **интернационали́зм, -а** internationalism. **итнернационали́ст, -а** internationalist. **интернациона́льный** international.
интерни́ровать, -ую *impf.* & *pf.* intern.
интерфе́йс, -а (*comput.*) interface.
инти́мность, -и intimacy. **инти́мный** intimate.
интри́га, -и intrigue; plot.
интуити́вный intuitive. **интуи́ция, -и** intuition.
инфа́ркт, -а infarct; coronary (thrombosis), heart attack.
инфля́ция, -и inflation.
инфекцио́нн|ый infectious; **~ая больни́ца** isolation hospital. **инфе́кция, -и** infection.
инфля́ция, -и inflation.
ин-фо́лио *nt.indecl.* folio.
информа́тик, -а information scientist. **информа́тика, -и** information science. **информацио́нный** news. **информа́ция, -и** information; news item.
и.о. *abbr.* (*of* ***исполня́ющий обя́занности***) acting.
ио́д *etc.*: *see* **йод**
ипподро́м, -а hippodrome; racecourse.
Ира́к, -а Iraq.

Ира́н, -а Iran.
и́рис[1], **-а** (*bot.*) iris.
ири́с[2], **-а** toffee. **ири́ска, -и** (a) toffee.
ирла́ндец, -дца Irishman. **Ирла́ндия, -и** Ireland. **ирла́ндка, -и** Irishwoman. **ирла́ндский** Irish.
ирони́ческий, ирони́чный ironic(al). **иро́ния, -и** irony.
ис... *see* **из...**
иск, -а suit, action.
искажа́ть, -а́ю *impf.*, **искази́ть, -ажу́** *pf.* distort, pervert, twist; misrepresent. **искаже́ние, -я** distortion, perversion. **искажённый; -ён, -ена́** distorted, perverted.
искале́ченный crippled, maimed. **искале́чивать, -аю** *impf.*, **ис|кале́чить, -чу** *pf.* cripple, maim; break, damage; **~ся** become a cripple; be crippled.
иска́ние, -я search, quest; *pl.* strivings. **иска́тель, -я** seeker; searcher; view-finder; selector; scanner. **иска́ть, ищу́, и́щешь** *impf.* (+*a. or g.*) seek, look for, search for.
исключа́ть, -а́ю *impf.*, **исключи́ть, -чу́** *pf.* exclude; eliminate; expel; dismiss; rule out. **исключа́я** *prep.*+*g.* except, excepting, with the exception of; **~ прису́тствующих** present company excepted. **исключе́ние, -я** exception; exclusion; expulsion; elimination; **за исключе́нием**+*g.* with the exception of. **исключи́тельно** *adv.* exceptionally; exclusively, solely; exclusive. **исключи́тельный** exceptional; exclusive, sole; excellent.
искове́рканный corrupt, corrupted; broken; spoilt. **ис|кове́ркать, -аю** *pf.*
исколеси́ть, -ешу́ *pf.* travel all over.
ис|ко́мкать, -аю *pf.*
ископа́емое mineral; fossil. **ископа́емый** fossilized, fossil.
искорене́ние, -я eradication. **искорени́ть, -ню́** *pf.*, **искореня́ть, -я́ю** *impf.* eradicate.
и́скоса *adv.* sideways; sidelong; askance.
и́скра, -ы spark; flash; glimmer.
и́скренний sincere, candid. **и́скренно** *adv.* sincerely; candidly. **и́скренность, -и** sincerity; candour.
искриви́ть, -влю́ *pf.*, **искривля́ть, -я́ю** *impf.* bend; curve; distort, twist, warp. **искривле́ние, -я** bend; distortion, warping.
искри́стый sparkling. **искри́ть, -и́т** *impf.* spark; **~ся** sparkle; scintillate. **искрово́й** spark.
ис|кромса́ть, -а́ю *pf.* **ис|кроши́ть(ся, -шу́(сь, -шишь(ся** *pf.*
ис|купа́ть[1]**(ся, -а́ю(сь** *pf.*
искупа́ть[2], **-а́ю** *impf.*, **искупи́ть, -плю́, -пишь** *pf.* expiate, atone for; make up for, compensate for. **искупи́тель, -я** *m.* redeemer. **искупле́ние, -я** redemption, expiation, atonement.
искуси́ть, -ушу́ *pf. of* **искуша́ть**
иску́сный skilful; expert. **иску́сственный** artificial; synthetic; feigned, pretended. **иску́сство, -а** art; craftsmanship, skill.
искуша́ть, -а́ю *impf.* (*pf.* **искуси́ть**) tempt; seduce. **искуше́ние, -я** temptation, seduction. **искушённый; -ён, -ена́** experienced; tested.
исла́м, -а Islam.
ис|па́костить, -ощу *pf.*
испа́нец, -нца, испа́нка, -и Spaniard. **Испа́ния, -и** Spain. **испа́нский** Spanish.
испаре́ние, -я evaporation; *pl.* fumes. **испа́рина, -ы** perspiration. **испари́тель, -я** *m.* evaporator; vaporizer. **испари́ть, -рю́** *pf.*, **испаря́ть, -я́ю** *impf.* evaporate, volatilize; exhale; **~ся** evaporate, vaporize; be evaporated.
ис|па́чкать, -аю *pf.* **ис|пе́чь, -еку́, -ечёшь** *pf.*
испещрённый; -рён, -рена́ speckled. **испещри́ть, -рю́** *pf.*, **испещря́ть, -я́ю** *impf.* speckle, spot; mark all over, cover.
исписа́ть, -ишу́, -и́шешь *pf.*, **испи́сывать, -аю** *impf.* cover, fill with writing; use up.
испито́й haggard, gaunt; hollow-cheeked.
испове́довать, -дую *impf.* & *pf.* confess; profess; **~ся** confess; make one's confession; +**в**+*p.* unburden o.s. of, acknowledge. **и́споведь, -и** confession.
исподло́бья *adv.* sullenly, distrustfully.
исподтишка́ *adv.* in an underhand way; on the quiet, on the sly; **смея́ться ~** laugh in one's sleeve.
испоко́н веко́в, ве́ку *see* **ве́к**
исполи́н, -а giant. **исполи́нский** gigantic.
исполко́м, -а *abbr.* (*of* **исполни́тельный комите́т**) executive committee.
исполне́ние, -я fulfilment, execution, discharge; performance; **привести́ в ~** carry out, execute. **исполни́мый** feasible, practicable. **исполни́тель, -я** *m.*, **-тельница, -ы** executor; performer. **исполни́тельный** executive; assiduous, careful, attentive; **~ лист** writ, court order. **испо́лнить, -ню** *pf.*, **исполня́ть, -я́ю** *impf.* carry out, execute; fulfil; perform; **~ обеща́ние** keep a promise; **~ про́сьбу** grant a request; **~ся** be fulfilled; *impers.* (+*d.*); **испо́лнилось пять лет с тех пор, как** it is five years since; **ему́ испо́лнилось семь лет** he is seven years old. **исполня́ющий; ~ обя́занности**+*g.* acting.
испо́льзование, -я utilization; **повто́рное ~** recycling. **использова́ть, -зую** *impf.* & *pf.* make (good) use of, utilize; turn to account.
ис|по́ртить(ся, -рчу(сь *pf.* **испо́рченность, -и** depravity. **испо́рченный** depraved; corrupted; spoiled; bad, rotten.
исправи́тельный correctional; corrective; **~ дом** reformatory. **испра́вить, -влю** *pf.* **исправля́ть, -я́ю** *impf.* rectify, correct, emendate; repair, mend; reform, improve, amend; **~ся** improve, reform. **исправле́ние, -я** correcting; repairing; improvement; correction; emendation. **испра́вленный** improved, corrected; revised; reformed. **испра́вник, -а** district police superintendent. **испра́вность, -и** good repair, good condition; punctuality; preciseness; meticulous-

ness. **испра́вный** in good order; punctual; precise; meticulous.

ис|про́бовать, -бую *pf.*

испу́г, -а (-у) fright; alarm. **испу́ганный** frightened, scared, startled. **ис|пуга́ть(ся, -а́ю(сь** *pf.*

испуска́ть, -а́ю *impf.*, **испусти́ть, -ущу́, -у́стишь** *pf.* emit, let out; utter; **~ вздох** heave a sigh; **~ дух** breathe one's last.

испыта́ние, -я test, trial; ordeal; examination. **испы́танный** tried, well-tried; tested. **испыта́тельный** test, trial; examining; experimental; probationary. **испыта́ть, -а́ю** *pf.*, **испы́тывать, -аю** *impf.* test; try; feel, experience.

и́ссера- *in comb.* grey-, greyish; **~голубо́й** grey-blue.

и́ссиня- *in comb.* blue-, bluish.

иссле́дование, -я investigation; research; analysis; exploration; paper; study. **иссле́дователь, -я** *m.* researcher; investigator; explorer. **иссле́довательский** research. **иссле́довать, -дую** *impf.* & *pf.* investigate, examine; research into; explore, analyse.

и́сстари *adv.* from of old; **так ~ ведётся** it is an old custom.

исступле́ние, -я frenzy, transport. **исступлённый** frenzied; ecstatic.

иссуша́ть, -а́ю *impf.*, **иссуши́ть, -шу́, -шишь** *pf.* dry up; consume, waste.

иссяка́ть, -а́ет *impf.*, **исся́кнуть, -нет; -я́к** *pf.* run dry, dry up; run low, fail.

istáсканный worn out; threadbare; worn; haggard. **истаска́ть, -а́ю** *pf.*, **istáскивать, -аю** *impf.* wear out; **~ся** wear out; be worn out.

истека́ть, -а́ет *impf. of* **исте́чь. истёкший** past, last; preceding, previous.

истере́ть, изотру́, -трёшь; истёр *pf.* (*impf.* **истира́ть**) grate; wear away, wear down; **~ся** wear out; wear away, be worn away.

истёрзанный tattered, lacerated; tormented.

исте́рик, -а, истери́чка, -и hysterical subject. **исте́рика, -и** hysterics. **истери́чный** hysterical. **истери́я, -и** hysteria.

исте́ц, -тца́, исти́ца, -ы plaintiff; petitioner.

истече́ние, -я outflow; expiry, expiration; **~ кро́ви** haemorrhage. **исте́чь, -ечёт; -тёк, -ла́** *pf.* (*impf.* **истека́ть**) flow out; elapse; expire.

и́стина, -ы truth. **и́стинный** true.

истира́ние, -я abrasion. **истира́ть(ся, -а́ю(сь** *impf. of* **истере́ть(ся**

исти́ца *see* **исте́ц**

истлева́ть, -а́ю *impf.*, **истле́ть, -е́ю** *pf.* rot, decay; be reduced to ashes, smoulder away.

исто́к, -а source.

истолкова́ть, -ку́ю *pf.*, **истолко́вывать, -аю** *impf.* interpret, expound; comment on.

ис|толо́чь, -лку́, -лчёшь; -ло́к, -лкла́ *pf.*

исто́ма, -ы lassitude; languor. **ис|томи́ть, -млю́** *pf.*, **истомля́ть, -я́ю** *impf.* exhaust, weary; **~ся** be exhausted, be worn out; be weary. **истомлённый; -ён, -ена́** exhausted, tired out, worn out.

истопни́к, -а́ stoker, boilerman.

исторга́ть, -а́ю *impf.*, **исто́ргнуть, -ну; -о́рг** *pf.* throw out, expel; wrest, wrench; force, extort.

исто́рик, -а historian. **истори́ческий** historical; historic. **истори́чный** historical. **исто́рия, -и** history; story; incident, event; **заба́вная ~** a funny thing.

исто́чник, -а spring; source.

истоща́ть, -а́ю *impf.*, **истощи́ть, -щу́** *pf.* exhaust; drain, sap; deplete; emaciate. **истоще́ние, -я** emaciation; exhaustion; depletion. **истощённый; -ён, -ена́** emaciated; exhausted.

ис|тра́тить, -а́чу *pf.*

истреби́тель, -я *m.* destroyer; fighter. **истреби́тельный** destructive; fighter. **истреби́ть, -блю́** *pf.*, **истребля́ть, -я́ю** *impf.* destroy; exterminate, extirpate.

истрёпанный torn, frayed; worn. **ис|трепа́ть, -плю́, -плешь** *pf.*

истука́н, -а idol, image.

ис|тупи́ть, -плю́, -пишь *pf.*

и́стый true, genuine.

истяза́ние, -я torture. **истяза́ть, -а́ю** *impf.* torture.

исхо́д, -а outcome, issue; end; Exodus; **на ~е** nearing the end, coming to an end; **на ~е дня** towards evening. **исходи́ть, -ожу́, -о́дишь** *impf.* (+**из** *or* **от**+*g.*) issue (from), come (from); emanate (from); proceed (from), base o.s. (on). **исхо́дный** initial, original, starting; departure, of departure.

исхуда́лый emaciated, wasted. **исхуда́ть, -а́ю** *pf.* grow thin, become wasted.

исцеле́ние, -я healing, cure; recovery. **исцели́мый** curable. **исцели́ть, -лю́** *pf.*, **исцеля́ть, -я́ю** *impf.* heal, cure.

исчеза́ть, -а́ю *impf.*, **исче́знуть, -ну; -е́з** *pf.* disappear, vanish. **исчезнове́ние, -я** disappearance.

и́счерна- *in comb.* blackish-.

исче́рпать, -аю *pf.*, **исче́рпывать, -аю** *impf.* exhaust, drain; settle, conclude. **исче́рпывающий** exhaustive.

исчисле́ние, -я calculation; calculus. **исчи́слить, -лю** *pf.*, **исчисля́ть, -я́ю** *impf.* calculate, compute; estimate. **исчисля́ться, -я́ется** *impf.*+*i.* *or* **в**+*a.* amount to, come to; be calculated at.

ита́к *conj.* thus; so then; and so.

Ита́лия, -и Italy. **италья́нец, -нца, италья́нка, -и** Italian. **италья́нск|ий** Italian; **~ая забасто́вка** sit-down strike, work-to-rule, go-slow.

ито́г, -а sum; total; result, upshot. **итого́** *adv.* in all, altogether. **ито́говый** total, final.

иуде́й, -я, иуде́йка, -и Jew. **иуде́йский** Judaic.

их *see* **они́. их, и́хний** their, theirs.

ихтиоза́вр, -а ichthyosaurus. **ихтиоло́гия, -и** ichthyology.

иша́к, -а́ donkey, ass; hinny.
ище́йка, -и bloodhound; police dog; sleuth.
ищу́ *etc.*: *see* **иска́ть**
ию́ль, -я *m.* July. **ию́льский** July.
ию́нь, -я *m.* June. **ию́ньский** June.

й *letter*: *see* **и**
йе́ти *m. indecl.* yeti, abominable snowman.
йог, -а Yogi.
йо́га, -и yoga.
йогу́рт, -а yog(h)urt.
йод, -а iodine.
йо́та, -ы iota.

К

к *letter*: *see* **ка**
к, ко *prep.+d.* to, towards; by; for; on; on the occasion of; **к лу́чшему** for the better; **к (не)сча́стью** (un)fortunately, (un)luckily; **к пе́рвому января́** by the first of January; **к сро́ку** on time; **к тому́ вре́мени** by then, by that time; **к тому́ же** besides, moreover; **к чему́?** what for? **лицо́м к лицу́** face to face; **ни к чему́** no good, no use.
к. *abbr.* (*of* **ко́мната**) room; (*of* **копе́йка**) copeck.
ка *nt.indecl.* the letter **к.**
-ка *part. modifying force of imper. or expressing decision or intention*; **да́йте-ка пройти́** let me pass, please; **скажи́-ка мне** do tell me.
каба́к, -а tavern, drinking-shop; pub.
кабала́, -ы́ servitude, bondage. **кабали́ть, -лю́** *impf.* enslave.
каба́н, -а́ wild boar.
кабаре́ *nt.indecl.* cabaret.
кабачо́к[1], **-чка́** *dim. of* **каба́к**
кабачо́к[2], **-чка́** vegetable marrow.
ка́бель, -я *m.* cable. **ка́бельный** *adj.* **ка́бельтов, -а** cable, hawser; cable's length.
каби́на, -ы cabin; booth; cockpit; cab. **кабине́т, -а** study; consulting-room, surgery; room, classroom, laboratory, office; cabinet. **кабине́тский** cabinet.
каблу́к, -а heel. **каблучо́к, -чка́** heel; ogee; **~-шпи́лька** stiletto heel.
кабота́ж, -а cabotage; coastal shipping. **кабота́жник, -а** coaster. **кабота́жный** cabotage; coastal, coasting, coastwise. **кавале́р, -а** knight; partner, gentleman. **кавалерга́рд, -а** horse-guardsman. **кавалери́йский** cavalry. **кавалери́ст, -а** cavalryman. **кавале́рия, -и** cavalry.
ка́верза, -ы chicanery; mean trick, dirty trick. **ка́верзный** tricky, ticklish.
Кавка́з, -а Caucasus. **кавка́зец, -зца́, кавка́зка, -и** Caucasian. **кавка́зский** Caucasian.
кавы́чки, -чек *pl.* inverted commas, quotation marks; **откры́ть ~** quote; **закры́ть ~** unquote.
каде́т, -а cadet. **каде́тский** cadet; **~ корпу́с** military school.
ка́дка, -и tub, vat.
кадр, -а frame, still; close-up; cadre; *pl.* establishment; staff; personnel; specialists, skilled workers. **кадрови́к, -а́** member of permanent establishment, professional body, etc. **ка́дровый** regular; experienced, skilled; trained.
кады́к, -а́ Adam's apple.
каёмка, -и (narrow) border, (narrow) edging. **каёмчатый** with a border.
каждодне́вный daily, everyday. **ка́ждый** each, every; *sb.* everybody, everyone.
ка́жется *etc.*: *see* **каза́ться**
каза́к, -а́; *pl.* **-а́ки́, -а́ко́в, каза́чка, -и** Cossack. **Казахста́н, -а** Kazakhstan.
каза́рма, -ы barracks; barrack.
каза́ться, кажу́сь, ка́жешься *impf.* (*pf.* **по~**) seem, appear; *impers.* (*+d.*) **ка́жется, каза́лось** apparently; **каза́лось бы** it would seem, one would think; **мне ка́жется** it seems to me; I think.
каза́цкий, каза́чий Cossack. **каза́чка** *see* **каза́к. казачо́к, -чка́** page-boy.
казённый State; government; fiscal; public; bureaucratic, formal; banal, undistinguished, conventional; **~ язы́к** official jargon; **на ~ счёт** at the public expense. **казна́, -ы́** Exchequer, Treasury; public purse; the State; money, property. **казначе́й, -я** treasurer, bursar; paymaster; purser.
казни́ть, -ню́ *impf.* & *pf.* execute, put to death; punish, chastise; castigate. **казнь, -и** execution.
кайма́, -ы́; *g.pl.* **каём** border, edging; hem, selvage.
как *adv.* how; what; all of a sudden, all at once; **вот ~!** not really! you don't say!; **~ вы ду́маете?** what do you think?; **~ вы пожива́ете?** how are you? **~ дела́?** how are you getting on? **~ его зову́т?** what is his name? what is he called?; **~ есть** complete(ly), utter(ly); **~ же** naturally, of course; **~ же так?** how is that?; **~ ни** however; **~-ника́к** nevertheless, for all that; **~ есть**

дура́к he's a complete fool. **как** *conj.* as; like; when; since; *+neg.* but, except, than; **бу́дьте ~ до́ма** make yourself at home; **в то вре́мя ~** while, whereas; **~ вдруг** when suddenly; **~ мо́жно, ~ нельзя́**+*comp.* as ... as possible; **~ мо́жно скоре́е** as soon as possible; **~ нельзя́ лу́чше** as well as possible; **~ наро́чно** as luck would have it; **~..., так и** both ... and; **~ то́лько** as soon as, when; **ме́жду тем, ~** while, whereas; **я ви́дел, ~ она́ ушла́** I saw her go. **как бу́дто** *conj.* as if, as though; *part.* apparently, it would seem. **как бы** how; as if, as though; **как бы... не** what if, supposing; **бою́сь, как бы он не́ был в дурно́м настрое́нии** I am afraid he may be in a bad temper; **как бы не так!** not likely, certainly not; **как бы... ни** however. **ка́к-либо** *adv.* somehow. **ка́к-нибудь** *adv.* somehow; in some way or other; anyhow; some time. **как раз** *adv.* just, exactly. **как-то** *adv.* somehow; once, one day.

кака́о *nt.indecl.* cocoa. **кака́ов|ый; ~ые бобы́** cocoa-beans.

како́в *m.*, **какова́** *f.*, **каково́** *nt.*, **каковы́** *pl. pron.* what, what sort (of); **~ он?** what is he like?; **~ он собо́й?** what does he look like?; **пого́да-то какова́!** what weather! **каково́** *adv.* how. **како́й** *pron.* what; (such) as; which; **~... ни** whatever, whichever; **каки́м о́бразом?** how?; **~ тако́й?** which (exactly)?; **како́е там** nothing of the kind, quite the contrary. **како́й-либо, како́й-нибудь** *prons.* some; any; only. **како́й-то** *pron.* some; a; a kind of; something like.

как раз, ка́к-то *see* **как**

каламбу́р, -а pun. **каламбури́ст, -а** punster. **каламбу́рить, -ю** *impf.* (*pf.* **с~**) pun.

каланча́, -и́ watch-tower.

кале́ка, -и *c.g.* cripple.

календа́рь, -я́ *m.* calendar.

кале́ние, -я incandescence.

кале́чить, -чу *impf.* (*pf.* **ис~, по~**) cripple, maim, mutilate; twist, pervert; **~ся** become a cripple, be crippled.

кали́бр, -а calibre; bore; gauge.

ка́лий, -я potassium.

кали́тка, -и wicket, (wicket-)gate.

калори́йность, -и calorie content. **калори́йный** high-calorie; fattening. **кало́рия, -и** calorie.

кало́ша, -и galosh.

ка́лька, -и tracing-paper; tracing; calque.

калькуля́тор, -а calculator. **калькуля́ция, -и** calculation.

кальсо́ны, кальсо́н *pl.* (under)pants, drawers.

ка́льций, -я calcium.

ка́мбала, -ы flat-fish; plaice; flounder.

камени́стый stony, rocky. **каменноуго́льный** coal; **~ бассе́йн** coal-field. **ка́менн|ый** stone; rock; stony; hard, immovable; **~ый век** Stone Age; **~ая соль** rock-salt; **~ у́голь** coal. **каменоло́мня, -и**; *g.pl.* quarry. **ка́менщик, -а** (stone)mason; bricklayer. **ка́мень, -мня**; *pl.* **-мни, -мне́й** *m.* stone.

ка́мера, -ы chamber; compartment; cell, ward; camera; inner tube, (foot-ball) bladder; **~ хране́ния (багажа́)** cloak-room, left-luggage office. **ка́мерный** chamber. **камерто́н, -а** tuning-fork.

ками́н, -а fireplace; fire.

камко́рдер, -а camcorder.

камо́рка, -и closet, very small room.

кампа́ния, -и campaign; cruise.

камфара́, -ы́ camphor.

камы́ш, -а́ reed, rush; cane.

кана́ва, -ы ditch; gutter; drain; trench; inspection pit.

Кана́да, -ы Canada. **кана́дец, -дца, кана́дка, -и** Canadian. **кана́дский** Canadian.

кана́л, -а canal; channel; duct; bore. **канализа́ция, -и** sewerage, sewerage system; drainage; underground cable system.

канаре́ечный canary; canary-coloured. **канаре́йка, -и** canary.

кана́т, -а rope; cable, hawser. **канатохо́дец, -дца** rope-walker.

канва́, -ы canvas; groundwork; outline, design. **канво́вый** canvas.

кандалы́, -о́в *pl.* shackles, fetters, irons.

кандида́т, -а candidate; kandidat (*in former USSR, holder of first higher degree, awarded on dissertation*). **кандида́тская** *sb.* doctoral thesis. **кандидату́ра, -ы** candidature.

кани́кулы, -ул *pl.* vacation; holidays. **каникуля́рный** holiday.

кани́стра, -ы can, canister.

канифо́ль, -и rosin.

каннибáл, -а cannibal. **каннибали́зм, -а** cannibalism.

канои́ст, -а canoeist.

канона́да, -ы cannonade.

каноне́рка, -и gunboat. **каноне́рск|ий; ~ая ло́дка** gunboat. **канони́р, -а** gunner.

кано́э *nt.indecl.* canoe.

кант, -а edging, piping; welt; mount. **кантова́ть, -ту́ю** *impf.* (*pf.* **о~**) border, pipe; mount.

кану́н, -а eve; vigil, watch-night.

ка́нуть, -ну *pf.* drop, sink; **~ в ве́чность** sink into oblivion; **как в во́ду ~** vanish into thin air, disappear without trace.

канцеля́рия, -и office. **канцеля́рск|ий** office; clerical; **~ие принадле́жности** stationery. **канцеля́рщина, -ы** office-work; red-tape.

канцероге́н, -а carcinogen. **канцероге́нн|ый** carcinogenic; **~ое вещество́** carcinogen.

ка́нцлер, -а chancellor.

канцтова́р|ы, -ов *pl. abbr.* (*of* **канцеля́рские това́ры**) office supplies.

ка́пать, -аю *or* **-плю** *impf.* (*pf.* **ка́пнуть, на~**) drip, drop; trickle, dribble; fall in drops; pour out in drops; *+i.* spill. **ка́пелька, -и** small drop, droplet; a little; a bit, a grain,

a whit; ~ **росы** dew-drop.
капельмейстер, -а conductor; bandmaster.
капельный drip, drop, drip-feed, trickle; tiny.
капитал, -а capital. **капиталистический** capitalist, capitalistic. **капитальный** capital; main, fundamental; most important; ~ **ремонт** capital repairs, major overhaul.
капитан, -а captain; master, skipper.
капитель, -и capital; small caps.
капитуляция, -и capitulation.
капкан, -а trap. **капканный** trap; trapping.
капля, -и; *g.pl.* **-пель** drop; bit, scrap; **ни капли** not a bit, not a scrap, not a whit; **по капле** drop by drop. **капнуть, -ну** *pf. of* **капать**
капор, -а hood, bonnet.
капот, -а hood, cowl, cowling; bonnet; (*loose*) dressing-gown, house-coat.
каприз, -а caprice, whim; vagary; ~ **судьбы** twist of fate. **капризник, -а** capricious person, child. **капризничать, -аю** *impf.* behave capriciously; (*of a child*) play up, be naughty. **капризный** capricious; naughty; wilful.
капуста, -ы cabbage; **кормовая** ~ kale; **спаржевая** ~ broccoli.
капюшон, -а hood.
кара, -ы punishment, retribution.
карабин, -а carbine. **карабинер, -а** car(a)bineer.
карабкаться, -аюсь *impf.* (*pf.* **вс~**) clamber, scramble up.
каравай, -я round loaf, cob; pudding.
караван, -а caravan; convoy.
каракуль, -я *m.* Persian lamb.
каракуля, -и scrawl, scribble.
карамболь, -я *m.* cannon.
карамель, -и caramel; caramels. **карамелька, -и** caramel.
карандаш, -а pencil.
карапуз, -а chubby little fellow.
карась, -я *m.* crucian carp.
карательный punitive. **карать, -аю** *impf.* (*pf.* **по~**) punish, chastise.
караул, -а guard; watch; ~! help!; **нести** ~ be on guard. **караулить, -лю** *impf.* guard; watch for, lie in wait for. **караульный** guard; *sb.* sentry, sentinel, guard.
карболовый carbolic.
карбункул, -а carbuncle.
карбюратор, -а carburettor.
кардиолог, -а cardiologist. **кардиостимулятор, -а** pacemaker.
карета, -ы carriage, coach; ~ **скорой помощи** ambulance.
карий brown; hazel.
карикатура, -ы caricature; cartoon.
каркас, -а frame; framework.
каркать, -аю *impf.*, **каркнуть, -ну** *pf.* (*pf. also* **на~**) caw, croak.
карлик, -а, карлица, -ы dwarf; pygmy. **карликовый** dwarf, dwarfish; pygmy.
карман, -а pocket. **карманный** *adj.* pocket; ~ **вор** pickpocket.
карнавал, -а carnival.
карниз, -а cornice; ledge.
карта, -ы map; chart; (playing-)card.
картавить, -влю *impf.* burr. **картавость, -и** burr. **картавый** burring.
картер, -а gear casing, crank-case.
картечь, -и case-shot, grape-shot; buckshot.
картина, -ы picture; scene. **картинка, -и** picture; illustration; ~**-загадка** jig-saw puzzle. **картинный** picturesque; picture.
картон, -а cardboard, pasteboard; cartoon. **картонка, -и** cardboard box; hat-box, bandbox.
картотека, -и card-index.
картофелечистка, -и potato peeler. **картофелина, -ы** potato. **картофель, -я (-ю)** *m.* potatoes; potato(-plant). **картофельн|ый** potato; ~**ая запеканка** shepherd's pie; ~**ый крахмал** potato flour; ~**ое пюре** mashed potatoes.
карточка, -и card; season ticket; photograph; ~ **вин** wine-list; ~ **кушаний** menu, bill of fare. **карточный** card; ~ **домик** house of cards.
картошка, -и potatoes; potato.
картуз, -а (peaked) cap.
карусель, -и roundabout, merry-go-round.
карцер, -а cell, lock-up.
карьер[1], -а full gallop.
карьер[2], -а quarry; sand-pit.
карьера, -ы career. **карьеризм, -а** careerism. **карьерист, -а** careerist.
касание, -я contact. **касательная** *sb.* tangent. **касаться, -аюсь** *impf.* (*pf.* **коснуться**) +*g.* *or* **до**+*g.* touch; touch on; concern, relate to; **что касается** as to, as regards, with regard to.
каска, -и helmet.
Каспийск|ий: ~**ое море** the Caspian (Sea).
касса, -ы till; cash-box; booking-office; box-office; cash-desk; cash; case; ~**-автомат** slot-machine, ticket-machine; ~ **взаимопомощи** benefit fund, mutual aid fund, friendly society.
кассета, -ы cassette; plate-holder.
кассир, -а, кассирша, -и cashier. **кассовый** cash; box-office; ~ **аппарат** cash rgister. ~ **счёт** cash-account; ~ **успех** box-office success.
кастрат, -а eunuch. **кастрация, -и** castration. **кастрировать, -рую** *impf.* & *pf.* castrate, geld.
кастрюля, -и saucepan.
каталка, -и; детская ~ baby buggy, push-chair.
каталог, -а catalogue. **каталогизировать, -рую** *impf.* & *pf.* catalogue.
катание, -я rolling; driving; ~ **верхом** riding; ~ **на коньках** skating; ~ **на роликах** roller skating; ~ **с гор** tobogganing.
катать, -аю *impf.* (*pf.* **вы~, с~**) roll; wheel, trundle; drive, take for a drive, take out; roll out; mangle; ~**ся** roll, roll about; go for a drive; ~**ся верхом** ride, go riding; ~**ся на**

конькáх skate, go skating; **~ся сó смеху** split one's sides.

катастрóфа, -ы catastrophe, disaster; accident, crash.

катафáлк, -а catafalque; hearse.

категорúческий categorical.

кáтер, -а; *pl.* **-á** cutter; boat, motorboat, launch.

катúть, -ачý, -áтишь *impf.* bowl along, rip, tear; **~ся** rush, tear; flow, stream, roll; **~ся пóд гору** go downhill; **~ся с горы́** slide downhill; **катúсь, катúтесь** get out! clear off!

катóд, -а cathode. **катóдн|ый; ~ые лучú** cathode rays; **~ая трýбка** cathode-ray tube.

катóк, -ткá skating-rink; roller; mangle.

катóлик, -а (Roman) Catholic. **католúчка, -и** (Roman) Catholic. **католицúзм, -а** (Roman) Catholicism. **католúческий** (Roman) Catholic.

кáторга, -и penal servitude, hard labour. **каторжáнин, -а** convict, ex-convict. **кáторжник, -а** convict. **кáторжн|ый** penal, convict; **~ые рабóты** hard labour; drudgery.

катýшка, -и reel, bobbin; spool; coil.

каучýк, -а rubber.

кафé *nt.indecl.* café; **~-морóженое** ice-cream parlour.

кáфедра, -ы pulpit; rostrum, platform; chair; department.

качáлка, -и rocking-chair; **конь-~** rocking-horse. **качáние, -я** rocking, swinging, swing; pumping. **качáть, -áю** *impf.* (*pf.* **качнýть**) *+a. or i.* rock, swing; shake; lift up, chair; pump; **~ся** rock, swing; roll, pitch; reel, stagger. **качéли, -ей** *pl.* swing; see-saw.

кáчественный qualitative; high-quality. **кáчество, -а** quality; **в кáчестве**+*g.* as, in the capacity or character of; **вы́играть ~, потерять ~** gain, lose, by an exchange.

кáчка, -и rocking; tossing.

качнýть(ся, -нý(сь, -нёшь(ся *pf. of* **качáть(ся. качý** *etc.*: *see* **катúть**

кáша, -и kasha; gruel, porridge; **заварúть кáшу** stir up trouble. **кашевáр, -а** cook.

кáшель, -шля cough. **кáшлянуть, -ну** *pf.*, **кáшлять, -яю** *impf.* cough; have a cough.

кашнé *nt.indecl.* scarf, muffler.

каштáн, -а chestnut. **каштáновый** chestnut.

каю́та, -ы cabin, stateroom. **каю́т-компáния, -и** wardroom; passengers' lounge.

кáющийся repentant, contrite, penitent. **кáяться, кáюсь** *impf.* (*pf.* **по~, рас~**) repent; confess; **кáюсь** I am sorry to say, I (must) confess.

кв. *abbr.* (*of* **квадрáтный**) square; (*of* **квартúра**) flat, apartment.

квадрáт, -а square; quad; **в квадрáте** squared; **возвестú в ~** square. **квадрáтный** square; quadratic. **квадратýра, -ы** squaring; quadrature.

квáканье, -я croaking. **квáкать, -аю** *impf.*, **квáкнуть, -ну** *pf.* croak.

квалификáция, -и qualification. **квалифицúрованный** qualified, skilled, trained, specialized. **квалифицúровать, -рую** *impf.* & *pf.* check, test; qualify (as).

квант, -а, квáнта, -ы quantum.

квартáл, -а block; quarter. **квартáльный** quarterly; *sb.* police officer.

квартúра, -ы flat; lodging(s); apartment(s); quarters, billets. **квартирáнт, -а, -рáнтка, -и** lodger; tenant. **квартúрн|ый; ~ая плáта, квартплáта, -ы** rent.

кварц, -а quartz.

квас, -а (-у); *pl.* **~ы́** kvass (*sour Russ. beer*).

квáсить, -áшу *impf.* sour; ferment; pickle; leaven. **квасцóвый** alum. **квасцы́, -óв** *pl.* alum. **квáшен|ый** sour, fermented; **~ая капýста** sauerkraut.

квéрху *adv.* up, upwards.

квит, квúты quits.

квитáнция, -и receipt. **квитóк, -ткá** ticket, check.

кВт *abbr.* (*of* **киловáтт**) kW, kilowatt.

кг *abbr.* (*of* **килó, килогрáмм**) k, kg, kilo(s), kilogram(s).

КГБ *abbr.* (*of* ***Комитéт госудáрственной безопáсности***) KGB, State Security Committee.

кебáб, -а kebab. **кебáбная** *sb.* kebab house.

кегельбáн, -а bowling alley; skittle alley.

кегль, -я *m.* point size, body size.

кéгля, -и skittle.

кедр, -а cedar. **кедрóвый** cedar.

кéды, -ов *or* **кед** *pl.* sports shoes, plimsolls.

кекс, -а cake; fruit-cake.

Кёльн, -а Cologne.

кéлья, -и; *g.pl.* **-лий** cell.

кем *see* **кто**

кéмпинг, -а camp-site.

кенгурý *m.indecl.* kangaroo.

кенотáф, -а cenotaph.

кéпка, -и cap, cloth cap.

керáмика, -и ceramics. **керамúческий** ceramic.

керогáз, -а oil pressure stove. **керосúн, -а** paraffin, kerosene. **керосúнка, -и** oil-stove.

кéта, -ы Siberian salmon. **кéтов|ый; ~ая икрá** red caviare.

кефúр, -а kefir.

кибернéтика, -и cybernetics. **кибернетúческий** cybernetic.

кибúтка, -и covered wagon; nomad tent.

кивáть, -áю *impf.*, **кивнýть, -нý, -нёшь** *pf.* **(головóй)** nod, nod one's head; (**+на**+*a.*) motion (to). **кивóк, -вкá** nod.

кидáть, -áю *impf.* (*pf.* **кúнуть**) throw, fling, cast; **~ся** throw o.s., fling o.s.; rush; *+i.* throw, fling, shy.

Кúев, -а Kiev. **кúевский** Kiev; Kievan.

кий, -я́; *pl.* **-ú, -ёв** (*billiard*) cue.

килев|óй keel; **~áя кáчка** pitching.

килó *nt.indecl.* kilogram(me).

кило... *in comb.* kilo-. **килобáйт, -а** kilobyte. **~вáтт, -а** kilowatt. **~грáмм, -а** kilogram(me). **~мéтр, -а** kilometre.

киль, -я *m.* keel; fin. **кильвáтер, -а** wake.

кúлька, -и sprat.

кинжа́л, -а dagger.

кино́ *nt.indecl.* cinema.

кино... *in comb.* film-, cine-. **киноаппара́т, -а** cinecamera. **~арти́ст, -а, ~арти́стка, -и** film actor, actress. **~ателье́** *nt.indecl.* film studio. **~ве́дение, -я** film studies. **~журна́л, -а** news-reel. **~звезда́, -ы́** film-star. **~зри́тель, -я** *m.* film-goer. **~карти́на, -ы** film, picture. **~меха́ник, -а** projectionist. **~опера́тор, -а** cameraman. **~плёнка, -и** film. **~прока́тчик, -а** film distributor. **~режиссёр, -а** film director. **~съёмка, -и** filming, shooting. **~теа́тр, -а** cinema. **~хро́ника, -и** news-reel.

ки́нуть(ся, -ну(сь *pf. of* **кида́ть(ся**

кио́ск, -а kiosk, stall, stand.

ки́па, -ы pile, stack; pack, bale.

кипари́с, -а cypress.

кипе́ние, -я boiling. **кипе́ть, -плю́** *impf.* (*pf.* **вс~**) boil, seethe; **рабо́та кипе́ла** work was in full swing.

Кипр, -а Cyprus.

кипу́чий boiling, seething; ebullient, turbulent. **кипяти́льник, -а** kettle, boiler. **кипяти́льный** boiling, boiler. **кипяти́ть, -ячу́** *impf.* (*pf.* **вс~**) boil; **~ся** boil; get excited, be enraged, be in a rage. **кипято́к, -тка́** boiling water. **кипячёный** boiled.

Кирги́зия, -и Kirghizia.

кири́ллица, -ы Cyrillic alphabet.

кирка́, -и́ pickaxe, pick.

кирпи́ч, -а́ brick; bricks; 'no-entry' sign. **кирпи́чный** brick; brick-red; **~ заво́д** brick-works, brick-field, brick-yard.

кисе́йный muslin.

кисе́ль, -я́ *m.* kissel (*kind of blancmange*).

кисе́т, -а tobacco-pouch.

кисея́, -и́ muslin.

ки́ска, -и pussy.

кислоро́д, -а oxygen. **кислота́, -ы́**; *pl.* **-ы** acid; sourness, acidity. **кисло́тный** acid. **ки́сл|ый** sour; acid; **~ая капу́ста** sauerkraut. **ки́снуть, -ну; кис** *impf.* (*pf.* **про~**) turn sour, go sour; mope.

ки́сточка, -и brush; tassel. **кисть, -и**; *g.pl.* **-е́й** cluster, bunch; brush; tassel; hand.

кит, -а́ whale.

кита́ец, -а́йца; *pl.* **-цы, -цев, китая́нка, -и** Chinese. **Кита́й, -я** China. **кита́йка, -и** nankeen. **кита́йск|ий** Chinese; **~ая тушь** Indian ink.

китобо́й, -я whaler, whaling ship. **кито́вый** whale; **~ ус** whalebone. **китобо́йный** whaling. **китообра́зный** cetacean.

кичи́ться, -чу́сь *impf.* plume o.s.; strut. **кичли́вость, -и** conceit; arrogance. **кичли́вый** conceited, arrogant, haughty, strutting.

кише́ть, -ши́т *impf.* swarm, teem.

кише́чник, -а bowels, intestines. **кише́чный** intestinal. **кишка́, -и́** gut, intestine; hose.

кишмя́ *adv.*; **~ кише́ть** swarm.

к.-л. *abbr.* (*of* **како́й-ли́бо**) some.

клавеси́н, -а harpsichord. **клавиату́ра, -ы** keyboard. **кла́виш, -а, кла́виша, -ы** key. **кла́вишн|ый; ~ые инструме́нты** keyboard instruments.

клад, -а treasure.

кла́дбище, -а cemetery, graveyard, churchyard.

кла́дка, -и laying; masonry, walling. **кладова́я** *sb.* pantry, larder; store-room. **кладовщи́к, -а́** storeman; shopman. **кладу́** *etc.*: *see* **класть. кла́дчик, -а** bricklayer.

кла́няться, -яюсь *impf.* (*pf.* **поклони́ться**) *+d.* bow to; greet; send, convey greetings; humble o.s.; go cap in hand to.

кла́пан, -а valve; vent; flap.

кларне́т, -а clarinet.

класс, -а class; form; class-room; *pl.* hopscotch. **кла́ссн|ый** class; classroom; high-class; first-class; **~ый ваго́н** passenger coach; **~ая доска́** blackboard; **~ая каю́та** private cabin. **кла́ссовый** class.

класть, -аду́, -адёшь; -ал *impf.* (*pf.* **положи́ть, сложи́ть**) lay; put; place; construct, build.

клаустрофо́бия, -и claustrophobia.

клева́ть, клюю́, клюёшь *impf.* (*pf.* **клю́нуть**) peck; bite; **~ но́сом** nod.

кле́вер, -а; *pl.* **-а́** clover.

клевета́, -ы́ slander; calumny, aspersion; libel. **клевета́ть, -ещу́, -е́щешь** *impf.* (*pf.* **на~**) *+на+a.* slander, calumniate; libel. **клевetни́к, -а́, -ни́ца, -ы** slanderer. **клевetни́ческий** slanderous; libellous, defamatory.

клеево́й glue; adhesive; size. **клеёнка, -и** oilcloth; oilskin. **кле́ить, -е́ю** *impf.* (*pf.* **с~**) glue; gum; paste; stick; **~ся** stick; become sticky; get on, go well. **клей, -я (-ю)**, *loc.* **-ю́**; *pl.* **-и́** glue, adhesive, gum; size. **кле́йк|ий** sticky; **~ая ле́нта** adhesive tape.

клеймёный branded. **клейми́ть, -млю́** *impf.* (*pf.* **за~**) brand; stamp; stigmatize. **клеймо́, -а́**; *pl.* **-а** brand; stamp; mark.

кле́мма, -ы clamp, clip; terminal.

клён, -а maple.

клёпаный riveted. **клепа́ть, -а́ю** *impf.* rivet.

кле́тка, -и cage; coop; hutch; square; check; cell. **кле́точка, -и** cellule. **кле́точный** cage; cell, cellular. **клетча́тка, -и** cellulose. **кле́тчатый** checked; squared; cellular.

клёш, -а flare; **брю́ки ~** flares, bell-bottoms; **ю́бка ~** flared skirt.

клешня́, -и́; *g.pl.* **-е́й** claw.

кле́щи́, -е́й *pl.* pincers, tongs; pincer-movement.

клие́нт, -а client; customer. **клиенту́ра, -ы** clientèle.

кли́зма, -ы enema.

клик, -а cry, call. **кли́кать, -и́чу** *impf.*, **кли́кнуть, -ну** *pf.* call, hail; honk.

кли́макс, -а, климакте́рий, -я menopause.

клин, -а; *pl.* **-нья, -ньев** wedge; quoin; gore; gusset; field.

кли́ника, -и clinic. **клинаци́ст, -а** clinician. **клини́ческий** clinical.

клино́к, -нка́ blade. **кли́нопись, -и** cuneiform.
кли́рос, -а choir.
клич, -а call. **кли́чка, -и** name; alias; nickname. **кли́чу** *etc.*: *see* **кли́кать**
клише́ *nt.indecl.* cliché.
клок, -а́; *pl.* **-о́чья, -ьев** *or* **-и́, -о́в** rag, shred; tuft; ~ **се́на** wisp of hay.
кло́кот, -а bubbling; gurgling. **клокота́ть, -о́чет** *impf.* bubble; gurgle; boil up.
клони́ровать, -рую *impf.* & *pf.* clone.
клони́ть, -ню́, -нишь *impf.* bend; incline; +**к**+*d.* lead; drive at; **~ся** bow, bend; +**к**+*d.* near, approach, lead up to, head for; **день клони́лся к ве́черу** the day was declining.
клоп, -а́ bug.
кло́ун, -а clown.
клочо́к, -чка́ scrap, shred, wisp; plot. **кло́чья** *etc.*: *see* **клок**
клуб[1], -а club; ~ **здоро́вья** keep-fit club; **офице́рский** ~ officers' mess.
клуб[2], -а; *pl.* **-ы́** puff; **~ы́ пы́ли** clouds of dust.
клу́бень, -бня *m.* tuber.
клуби́ться, -и́тся *impf.* swirl; wreathe, curl.
клубни́ка, -и strawberry; strawberries. **клубни́чный** strawberry.
клубо́к, -бка́ ball; tangle, mass; ~ **в го́рле** lump in the throat.
клу́мба, -ы (flower-)bed.
клык, -а́ fang; tusk; canine (*tooth*).
клюв, -а beak.
клю́ква, -ы cranberry; cranberries; **разве́систая** ~ traveller's tale, tall story.
клю́нуть, -ну *pf. of* **клева́ть**
ключ[1], -а́ key; clue; keystone; clef; wrench, spanner; **запере́ть на** ~ lock.
ключ[2], -а́ spring; source; **бить ~о́м** spout, jet; be in full swing.
ключево́й key; ~ **знак** clef; ~ **ка́мень** keystone. **ключи́ца, -ы** collarbone, clavicle.
клю́шка, -и (hockey) stick; (golf-)club.
клюю́ *etc.*: *see* **клева́ть**
кля́кса, -ы blot, smudge.
кляну́ *etc.*: *see* **кля́сть**
кля́нчить, -чу *impf.* (*pf.* **вы́~**) beg.
клясть, -яну́, -янёшь; -ял, -а́, -о *impf.* curse; **~ся** (*pf.* **по~ся**) swear, vow. **кля́тва, -ы** oath, vow; **дать кля́тву** take an oath. **кля́твенный** sworn, on oath.
км *abbr.* (*of* **киломе́тр**) km, kilometre.
к.-н. *abbr.* (*of* **како́й-нибудь**) some, any.
кни́га, -и book.
книго... *in comb.* book, biblio-. **книгове́дение[1], -я** bibliography. **~веде́ние[2], -я** book-keeping. **~держа́тель, -я** *m.* book-end. **~е́д, -а** bookworm. **~изда́тель, -я** *m.* publisher. **~люб, -а** bibliophile, book-lover. **~храни́лище, -а** library; book-stack; book-storage, shelving.
кни́жечка, -и booklet. **кни́жка, -и** book; note-book; bank-book. **кни́жн|ый** book; **~ая по́лка** bookshelf; **~ый червь** bookworm; **~ый шкаф** bookcase.
кни́зу *adv.* downwards.
кно́пка, -и drawing-pin; press-stud; knob, (push-)button. **кно́почный;** ~ **телефо́н** push-button telephone.
кнут, -а́ whip; knout.
княги́ня, -и princess. **кня́жество, -а** principality. **княжна́, -ы́**; *g.pl.* **-жо́н** princess.
князь, -я; *pl.* **-зья́, -зе́й** *m.* prince.
К° *abbr.* (*of* **компа́ния**) Co., Company.
ко *see* **к** *prep.*
коали́ция, -и coalition.
кобура́, -ы́ holster.
кобы́ла, -ы mare; (vaulting-)horse. **кобы́лка, -и** filly; bridge.
ко́ваный forged; hammered; wrought; iron-bound, iron-tipped; terse.
кова́рный insidious, crafty; perfidious, treacherous. **кова́рство, -а** insidiousness, craftiness; perfidy, treachery.
кова́ть, кую́, -ёшь *impf.* (*pf.* **под~**) forge; hammer; shoe.
ковёр, -вра́ carpet; rug; **~-самолёт** magic carpet.
кове́ркать, -аю *impf.* (*pf.* **ис~**) distort, mangle, mispronounce; spoil, ruin.
ко́вка, -и forging; shoeing. **ко́вкий; -вок, -вка́, -вко** malleable, ductile.
коври́га, -и loaf. **коври́жка, -и** honeycake, gingerbread.
ко́врик, -а rug, mat. **ковроочисти́тель, -я** carpet cleaner. **коврочи́стка, -и** carpet sweeper.
ковш, -а́ scoop, ladle, dipper; bucket.
ковы́ль, -я *m.* feather-grass.
ковыля́ть, -я́ю *impf.* hobble; stump; toddle.
ковырну́ть, -ну́, -нёшь *pf.*, **ковыря́ть, -я́ю** *impf.* dig into; tinker, potter; +**в**+*p.* pick; pick at; ~ **в зуба́х** pick one's teeth; **~ся** rummage; tinker, potter.
когда́ *adv.* when; **~...**, ~ sometimes ..., sometimes; ~ **(бы) ни** whenever; ~ **как** it depends; *conj.* when; while, as; if; ~ **так** if so, if that is the case. **когда́-либо, когда́-нибудь** *advs.* some time, some day; ever. **когда́-то** *adv.* once, at one time; at some time; formerly; some day, some time.
кого́ *see* **кто**
ко́готь, -гтя; *pl.* **-гти, -гте́й** *m.* claw; talon; **показа́ть свой ко́гти** show one's teeth.
код, -а code; **персона́льный** ~ personal identification number; PIN.
ко́декс, -а code; codex.
кодоско́п, -а overhead projector.
ко́е-где́ *adv.* here and there, in places. **ко́е-ка́к** *adv.* anyhow; somehow (or other), just. **ко́е-како́й** *pron.* some. **ко́е-кто́, -кого́** *pron.* somebody; some people. **ко́е-что́, -чего́** *pron.* something; a little.
ко́жа, -и skin, hide; leather; peel, rind; epidermis. **кожа́н, -а́** leather coat. **ко́жанка, -и** leather jacket, leather coat. **ко́жаный** leather. **коже́венный** leather; tanning, leather-dress-

ing; ~ **завóд** tannery. **кожéвник, -а** tanner, leather-dresser, currier. **кóжица, -ы** thin skin; film, pellicle; peel, skin. **кóжный** skin; cutaneous. **кожурá, -ы́** rind, peel, skin.

козá, -ы́; *pl.* **-ы** she-goat, nanny-goat, **козёл, -злá** goat; he-goat, billy-goat. **козерóг, -а** ibex; Capricorn. **кóзий** goat; ~ **пух** angora. **козлёнок, -нка**; *pl.* **-лята, -лят** kid. **козлóвый** goatskin.

кóзлы, -зел *pl.* (coach-)box; trestle(s); saw-horse.

кóзни, -ей *pl.* machinations, intrigues.

козырёк, -рькá peak; eye-shade; **взять под** ~*+d.* salute.

козырнóй trump, of trumps. **козырнýть, -нý, -нёшь** *pf.*, **козырять, -яю** *impf.* lead trumps; trump; play one's trump card; salute. **кóзырь, -я**; *pl.* **-и, -éй** *m.* trump; **откры́ть свой кóзыри** put one's cards on the table.

кóйка, -и; *g.pl.* **кóек** berth, bunk; hammock; bed.

кокéтка, -и coquette. **кокéтливый** coquettish. **кокéтничать, -ю** *impf.* (**с**+*i.*) flirt (with); (+*i.*) show off, flaunt. **кокéтство, -а** coquetry.

коклю́ш, -а whooping-cough.

кóкон, -а cocoon.

кокóс, -а coco(-tree); coconut. **кокóсов|ый** coconut; ~**ый орéх** coconut; ~**ая пáльма** coconut tree.

кокс, -а coke.

коктéйль, -я *m.* cocktail; **молóчный** ~ milk shake.

кол, -á; *pl.* **-лья, -ьев** stake, picket; **ни** ~**á ни дворá** neither house nor home.

кóлба, -ы retort.

колбасá, -ы́; *pl.* **-ы** sausage; **кровянáя** ~ black pudding.

колгóтки, -ток *pl.* tights.

колдовствó, -á witchcraft, sorcery, magic. **колдýн, -á** sorcerer, magician, wizard. **колдýнья, -и**; *g.pl.* **-ний** witch, sorceress.

колебáние, -я oscillation, vibration; fluctuation, variation; hesitation; wavering, vacillation. **колебáтельный** oscillatory, vibratory. **колебáть, -éблю** *impf.* (*pf.* **по**~) shake; ~**ся** oscillate, vibrate, swing; shake; fluctuate, vary; hesitate; waver.

коленкóр, -а calico. **коленкóровый** calico.

колéно, -а; *pl.* **-и** *or* **-а** *or* **-нья, -ей** *or* **-лен** *or* **-ньев** knee, joint, node; bend; elbow, crank; **по** ~, **по колéни** knee deep, up to one's knees; **стать на колéни** kneel (down); **стоять на колéнях** be kneeling, be on one's knees. **колéнчатый** crank, cranked; bent, elbow; ~ **вал** crankshaft.

колéсник, -а wheelwright. **колесни́ца, -ы** chariot. **колёсный** wheel; wheeled. **колесó, -á**; *pl.* **-ёса** wheel.

колéчко, -а ringlet.

колея́, -и́ rut; track, gauge.

коли́бри *c.g. indecl.* humming-bird.

коли́чественн|ый quantitative; ~**ое числи́тельное** cardinal number. **коли́чество, -а** quantity, amount; number.

кóлкий; -лок, -лкá, -о prickly; sharp, biting, caustic.

коллáж, -а collage.

коллéга, -и colleague. **коллегиáльный** joint, collective; corporate. **коллéгия, -и** board; college. **коллéжский** collegiate; ~ **асéссор, регистрáтор, секретáрь, совéтник** (*8th, 14th, 10th, 6th grade*: *see* **чин**).

коллекти́в, -а group, body, team. **коллективизáция, -и** collectivization. **коллективизи́ровать, -рую** *impf.* & *pf.* collectivize. **коллективи́зм, -а** collectivism; team spirit. **коллекти́вн|ый** collective; joint; ~**ое владéние** joint ownership; ~**ое хозя́йство** collective farm; ~**ое руковóдство** collective leadership.

коллéктор, -а commutator; manifold.

коллекционéр, -а collector. **коллекциони́ровать, -рую** *impf.* collect. **коллéкция, -и** collection.

колли́зия, -и clash, conflict, collision.

колóда, -ы block; log; pack (*of cards*).

колóдезный well; well-deck. **колóдец, -дца** well; shaft.

колóдка, -и last; block, chock.

кóлокол, -а; *pl.* **-á, -óв** bell. **колокóльный** bell; ~ **звон** peal, chime. **колокóльня, -и** bell-tower. **колокóльчик, -а** small bell; handbell; campanula, harebell.

колониáльный colonial. **колонизáция, -и** colonization. **колонизовáть, -ýю** *impf.* & *pf.* colonize. **колони́ст, -а** colonist. **колóния, -и** colony; settlement.

колóнка, -и geyser; (street) fountain; stand-pipe; column; **бензи́новая** ~ petrol pump. **колóнна, -ы** column. **колóнный** columned. **колонти́тул, -а** running title, catchword. **колонци́фра, -ы** page number, folio.

колори́т, -а colouring, colour. **колори́тный** colourful, picturesque, graphic.

кóлос, -а; -óсья, -ьев ear, spike. **колоси́ться, -и́тся** *impf.* form ears.

колосники́, -óв *pl.* fire-bars; grate; flies.

колоти́ть, -очý, -óтишь *impf.* (*pf.* **по**~) beat; batter, pound; thrash, drub; break, smash; shake; ~**ся** pound, thump; shake; +**о**+*a.* beat; strike, against.

колóть[1], **-лю́, -лешь** *impf.* (*pf.* **рас**~) break, chop, split; ~ **орéхи** crack nuts.

колóть[2], **-лю́, -лешь** *impf.* (*pf.* **за**~, **кольнýть**) prick; stab; sting; taunt; slaughter; ~**ся** prick.

колпáк, -а cap; lamp-shade; hood, cover, cowl.

колýн, -á axe, chopper.

колхóз, -а *abbr.* (*of* **коллекти́вное хозя́йство**) collective farm.

колыбéль, -и cradle.

колыхáть, -ы́шу *impf.*, **колыхнýть, -нý, -нёшь** *pf.* sway, rock; ~**ся** sway, heave; flutter, flicker.

ко́лышек, -шка peg.

кольну́ть, -ну́, -нёшь *pf. of* **коло́ть**

кольцева́ть, -цу́ю *impf.* (*pf.* **о~**) ring. **кольцево́й** annular; circular. **кольцо́, -а́**; *pl.* **-а, -ле́ц, -льцам** ring; hoop.

колю́ч|ий prickly; thorny; sharp, biting; **~ая про́волока** barbed wire. **колю́чка, -и** prickle; thorn; quill; burr.

коля́ска, -и carriage; side-car; **де́тская ~** pram; pushchair; **инвали́дная ~** wheelchair; **~-су́мка** shopping trolley, shopper.

ком, -а; *pl.* **-мья, -мьев** lump; ball; clod.

ком *see* **кто**

ком... *abbr.* (*of* **коммунисти́ческий, команди́р, кома́ндный**) *in comb.* Communist; commander; command. **комба́т, -а** battalion commander. **~ди́в, -а** divisional commander. **~инте́рн, -а** Comintern. **~па́ртия, -и** Communist Party. **~сомо́л, -а** Komsomol, Young Communist League. **~сомо́лец, -льца, -о́лка, -и** member of Komsomol.

кома́нда, -ы command; order; party, detachment; crew; ship's company, team. **команди́р, -а** commander, commanding officer; captain. **командирова́ть, -ру́ю** *impf.* & *pf.* post, send, dispatch on mission, on official business. **командиро́вка, -и** posting, dispatching; mission, commission, business trip; warrant; authority. **командиро́вочн|ый** *adj.*; **~ые де́ньги** travelling allowance; **~ые** *sb., pl.* travelling allowance, expenses. **кома́ндн|ый** command; commanding; control; **~ая вы́шка** control tower; **~ый пункт** command post; **~ый соста́в** officers; executive (*body*). **кома́ндование, -я** commanding; command; headquarters. **кома́ндовать, -дую** *impf.* (*pf.* **с~**) give orders; be in command; *+i.* command; *+i. or* **над**+*i.* order about; +**над**+*i.* command. **кома́ндующий** *sb.* commander.

кома́р, -а́ mosquito.

комба́йн, -а combine, multi-purpose machine; **зерново́й ~** combine harvester; **ку́хонный ~** food processor.

комбина́т, -а industrial complex; combine; training centre. **комбина́ция, -и** combination; merger; scheme, system; manoeuvre; combinations, slip. **комбинезо́н, -а** overalls, boiler suit; dungarees. **комбини́ровать, -рую** *impf.* (*pf.* **с~**) combine.

коме́дия, -и comedy; play-acting; farce.

коменда́нт, -а commandant; manager; warden; superintendent. **комендату́ра, -ы** commandant's office.

коме́та, -ы comet.

коми́зм, -а humour; the funny side, the comic element; the comic. **ко́мик, -а** comic actor; comedian. **ко́микс, -а** comic, comic strip, comic book; *pl.* the funnies.

комисса́р, -а commissar. **комиссариа́т, -а** ministry department.

комиссионе́р, -а (commission-)agent, factor, broker. **комиссио́нн|ый** commission; committee, board; **~ый магази́н** second-hand shop; **~ые** *sb., pl.* commission. **коми́ссия, -и** commission; committee, board.

комите́т, -а committee.

коми́ческий comic; comical, funny. **коми́чный** comical, funny.

ко́мкать, -аю *impf.* (*pf.* **ис~, с~**) crumple; make a hash of, muff.

коммента́рий, -я commentary; *pl.* comment. **коммента́тор, -а** commentator. **комменти́ровать, -рую** *impf.* & *pf.* comment (upon).

коммерса́нт, -а merchant; businessman **комме́рция, -и** commerce, trade. **комме́рческий** commercial, mercantile.

комму́на, -ы commune. **коммуна́льн|ый** communal; municipal; **~ые услу́ги** public utilities. **коммуна́р, -а** Communard. **коммуни́зм, -а** communism.

коммуникацио́нн|ый; ~ая ли́ния line of communication. **коммуника́ция, -и** communication.

коммуни́ст, -а communist. **коммунисти́ческий** communist.

коммута́тор, -а commutator; switchboard.

ко́мната, -ы room. **ко́мнатный** room; indoor.

комо́д, -а chest of drawers.

комо́к, -мка́ lump; **~ не́рвов** bundle of nerves.

компа́кт-ди́ск, -а compact disk, CD; **прои́грыватель** *m.* **~ов** compact disk, CD player.

компа́ния, -и company. **компаньо́н, -а, -о́нка, -и** companion; partner.

ко́мпас, -а compass.

компенса́ция, -и compensation. **компенси́ровать, -рую** *impf.* & *pf.* compensate; indemnify; equilibrate.

компете́нтный competent. **компете́нция, -и** competence.

ко́мплексный complex, compound, composite; combined; over-all, all-in; **~ обед** table d'hote dinner. **компле́кт, -а** complete set; complement; specified number; **~ белья́** bedclothes. **компле́ктный** complete, **комплектова́ть, -ту́ю** *impf.* (*pf.* **с~, у~**) complete; replenish; bring up to strength, (re)man. **компле́кция, -и** build; constitution.

комплиме́нт, а compliment.

компози́тор, -а composer. **компози́ция, -и** composition.

компо́стер, -а punch. **компости́ровать, -рую** *impf.* (*pf.* **про~**) punch.

компре́сс, -а compress.

компромети́ровать, -рую *impf.* (*pf.* **с~**) compromise. **компроми́сс, -а** compromise.

компью́тер, -а computer; **ИБМ-совмести́мый ~** IBM(*propr.*)-compatible computer; **~-калькуля́тор** scientific calculator; **наколе́нный ~** laptop (computer). **компью́терный** computer; computerized.

кому́ *see* **кто**

комфо́рт, -а comfort. **комфорта́бельный** comfortable.

конве́йер, -а conveyor.

конвенциона́льный conventional. **конве́нция, -и** convention, agreement.

конве́рт, -а envelope; sleeve.

конвои́р, -а escort. **конвои́ровать, -рую** *impf.* escort, convoy. **конво́й, -я** escort, convoy.

конгре́сс, -а congress.

конденса́тор, -а capacitor; condenser.

конди́терская *sb.* confectioner's, sweet-shop, cake shop.

кондиционе́р, -а air-conditioner. **кондицио́нный** air-conditioning.

конду́ктор, -а; *pl.* **-а́, -торша, -и** conductor; guard.

конево́дство, -а horse-breeding. **конево́дческий** horse-breeding. **конёк, -нька́** *dim. of* **конь**; hobby-horse, hobby.

коне́ц, -нца́ end; distance, way; **в конце́ концо́в** in the end, after all; **в о́ба конца́** there and back; **в оди́н ~** one way; **и концы́ в во́ду** and nobody any the wiser **оди́н ~** it comes to the same thing in the end; **своди́ть концы́ с конца́ми** make (both) ends meet; **со всех концо́в** from all quarters. **коне́чно** *adv.* of course, certainly; no doubt. **коне́чность, -и** extremity. **коне́чн|ый** final, last; ultimate; terminal; finite; **~ая остано́вка, ~ая ста́нция** terminus.

кони́на, -ы horse-meat.

кони́ческий conic, conical.

конкре́тный concrete; specific.

конку́р, -а showjumping.

конкуре́нт, -а competitor. **конкуре́нция, -и** competition; **вне конкуре́нции** *hors concours.* **конкури́ровать, -рую** *impf.* compete. **ко́нкурс, -а** competition; **вне ~а** *hors concours.* **конкурса́нт, -а** competitor; contestant. **ко́нкурсный** competitive.

ко́нник, -а cavalryman; rider, equestrian. **ко́нница, -ы** cavalry; horse. **конногварде́ец, -е́йца** horse-guardsman; life-guard. **коннозаво́дство, -а** horse-breeding; stud, stud-farm. **ко́нный** horse; mounted; equestrian; **~ заво́д** stud.

конопа́тить, -а́чу *impf.* (*pf.* **за~**) caulk.

конопля́, -и́ hemp.

консе́нсус, -а consensus.

консерва́нт, -а preservative.

консервати́вный conservative. **консервати́зм, -а** conservatism. **консерва́тор, -а** conservative.

консервато́рия, -и conservatoire, academy of music.

консерва́ция, -и conservation; temporary closing down. **консерви́ровать, -рую** *impf.* & *pf.* (*pf. also* **за~**) preserve; can, bottle, pot; close down temporarily. **консе́рвн|ый** preserving; **~ая ба́нка** tin; can. **консервооткрыва́тель, -я** *m.* tin, can opener. **консе́рвы, -ов** *pl.* tinned goods; goggles.

конси́лиум, -а consultation.

консо́ль, -и console; cantilever; pedestal.

конспе́кт, -а synopsis, summary, abstract, précis. **конспекти́вный** concise, summary. **конспекти́ровать, -рую** *impf.* (*pf.* **за~, про~**) make an abstract of.

конспирати́вный secret, clandestine. **конспира́тор, -а** conspirator.

констата́ция, -и ascertaining; verification, establishment. **констати́ровать, -рую** *impf.* & *pf.* ascertain; verify, establish; certify.

конструи́ровать, -рую *impf.* & *pf.* (*pf. also* **с~**) construct; design; form (*government, etc.*).

конструкти́вный structural; constructional; constructive. **констру́ктор, -а** designer, constructor. **констру́кция, -и** construction; structure; design.

ко́нсул, -а consul. **ко́нсульский** consular. **ко́нсульство, -а** consulate.

консульта́ция, -и consultation; advice; advice bureau; clinic, surgery; tutorial; supervision. **консульти́ровать, -рую** *impf.* (*pf.* **про~**) advise; act as tutor (to); +**с**+*i.* consult; **~ся** have a consultation; obtain advice; +**с**+*i.* be a pupil of; consult.

конта́кт, -а contact; touch. **конта́ктный** contact; **~ рельс** live rail.

конте́йнер, -а container. **контейнерово́з, -а** container ship, carrier.

континге́нт, -а quota; contingent; batch; **~ войск** a military force.

контине́нт, -а continent. **континента́льный** continental.

конто́ра, -ы office. **конто́рск|ий** office; **~ая кни́га** account-book, ledger. **конто́рщик, -а** clerk.

контр... *in comb.* counter-.

контраба́нда, -ы contraband, smuggling. **контрабанди́ст, -а** smuggler. **контраба́ндный** contraband; bootleg.

контраба́с, -а double-bass.

контраге́нт, -а contracting party; subcontractor. **контра́кт, -а** contract. **контрактова́ть, -ту́ю** *impf.* (*pf.* **за~**) contract for; engage; **~ся** contract, undertake.

контрама́рка, -и complimentary ticket.

контрапу́нкт, -а counterpoint. **контрапункти́ческий, контрапу́нктный** contrapuntal.

контра́ст, -а, контра́стность, -и contrast.

контрата́ка, -и counter-attack. **контратакова́ть, -ву́ю** *impf.* & *pf.* counter-attack.

контрибу́ция, -и indemnity; contribution.

контрнаступле́ние, -я counter-offensive.

контролёр, -а inspector; ticket-collector. **контроли́ровать, -рую** *impf.* (*pf.* **про~**) check; inspect. **контро́ль, -я** *m.* control; check, checking; inspection; inspectors. **контро́льн|ый** control; check; monitoring; reference; **~ая вы́шка** conning-tower; **~ая рабо́та** test.

контрразве́дка, -и counter-intelligence; security service, secret service. **контрразве́дчик,**

-а counter-intelligence agent.

контршпиона́ж, -а counterespionage.

конту́женный contused, bruised; shell-shocked, **конту́зить, -у́жу** *pf.* contuse, bruise; shell-shock. **конту́зия, -и** contusion; shell-shock.

ко́нтур, -а contour, outline; circuit.

конура́, -ы́ kennel.

ко́нус, -а cone. **конусообра́зный** conical.

конферансье́ *m.indecl.* compère, master of ceremonies, MC.

конфере́нц-за́л, -а conference room. **конфере́нция, -и** conference.

конфе́т|а, -ы sweet, chocolate; **~ы-соса́лки** fruit drops. **конфе́тница, -ы** sweet bowl, dish.

конфиденциа́льный confidential.

конфли́кт, -а clash, conflict; dispute.

конфронта́ция, -и confrontation, showdown.

конфу́з, -а discomforture, embarrassment. **конфу́зить, -у́жу** *impf.* (*pf.* **с~**) confuse, embarrass; place in an awkward or embarrassing position; **~ся** feel awkward or embarrassed; be shy. **конфу́зливый** bashful; shy. **конфу́зный** awkward, embarrassing.

концентра́т, -а concentrate. **концентрацио́нный** concentration. **концентра́ция, -и** concentration. **концентри́ровать, -рую** *impf.* (*pf.* **с~**) concentrate; mass.

конце́рт, -а concert; recital; concerto. **концерта́нт, -а, -а́нтка, -и** performer. **концерти́на, -ы** concertina. **концертме́йстер, -а** first violin; leader; soloist; accompanist. **конце́ртный** concert.

концла́герь, -я *abbr.* (*of* **концентрацио́нный ла́герь**) concentration camp.

концо́вка, -и tail-piece; colophon; ending.

конча́ть, -а́ю *impf.*, **ко́нчить, -чу** *pf.* finish; end; *+inf.* stop; **~ся** end, finish; come to an end; be over; expire. **ко́нчен|ый** finished; decided, settled; **всё ~о** it's all over; it's all up. **ко́нчик, -а** tip; point. **кончи́на, -ы** decease, demise; end.

конь, -я́; *pl.* **-и, -е́й** horse; vaulting-horse; knight; **~-кача́лка** rocking-horse. **коньки́, -о́в** *pl.* skates; **~ на ро́ликах** roller skates. **конькобе́жец, -жца** skater. **конькобе́жный** skating. **ко́нюх, -а** groom, stable-boy. **коню́шня, -и**; *g.pl.* **-шен** stable.

кооперати́в, -а cooperative society. **кооперати́вный** cooperative. **коопера́тор, -а** co-operator, member of the co-operative society. **коопера́ция, -и** cooperation. **коопери́ровать, -рую** *impf.* & *pf.* organize on cooperative lines. **коопери́роваться, -руюсь** *impf.* & *pf.* cooperate.

координа́ция, -и co-ordination. **координи́ровать, -рую** *impf.* & *pf.* co-ordinate.

копа́ть, -а́ю *impf.* (*pf.* **копну́ть, вы́~**) dig; dig up; dig out; **~ся** rummage; root; dawdle.

копе́ечный worth, costing, a copeck; cheap; petty, trifling. **копе́йка, -и** copeck.

Копенга́ген, -а Copenhagen.

ко́пи, -ей *pl.* mines.

копи́лка, -и money-box.

копи́рка, -и carbon paper; copying paper. **копирова́льный** copying. **копи́ровать, -рую** *impf.* (*pf.* **с~**) copy; imitate, mimic. **копиро́вка, -и** copying. **копиро́вщик, -а, -щица, -ы** copyist.

копи́ть, -плю́, -пишь *impf.* (*pf.* **на~**) save (up); accumulate, amass; store up; **~ся** accumulate.

ко́пия, -и copy; duplicate; replica; **печа́тная ~** (*comput.*) hard copy; **резе́рвная ~** (*comput.*) backup.

копна́, -ы́; *pl.* **-ы, -пён** shock, stook; heap, pile; **~ се́на** hay-cock. **копни́ть, -ню́** *impf.* (*pf.* **с~**) shock, stook; cock.

копну́ть, -ну́, -нёшь *pf. of* **копа́ть**

ко́поть, -и soot; lamp-black.

копоши́ться, -шу́сь *impf.* swarm; potter (about).

копте́ть, -и́т *impf.* (*pf.* **за~**) be covered with soot; smoke. **копти́лка, -и** oil-lamp. **копти́ть, -пчу́** *impf.* (*pf.* **за~, на~**) smoke, (smoke-)cure; blacken with smoke; cover with soot. **копче́ние, -я** smoking, curing; smoked foods. **копчёный** smoked, cured.

копы́тный hoof; hoofed, ungulate. **копы́то, -а** hoof.

копьё, -я́; *pl.* **-я, -пий** spear, lance.

кора́, -ы́ bark, rind; cortex; crust.

корабе́льный ship's, ship; marine, naval. **корабе́льщик, -а** shipwright. **кораблевожде́ние, -я** navigation. **кораблекруше́ние, -я** shipwreck. **кораблестрое́ние, -я** shipbuilding. **кораблестрои́тель, -я** *m.* shipbuilder, naval architect. **кора́бль, -я́** *m.* ship, vessel; nave.

кора́лл, -а coral.

коревóй measles.

коре́ец, -е́йца, корея́нка, -и Korean. **коре́йский** Korean.

корена́стый thickset, stocky. **корени́ться, -и́тся** *impf.* be rooted. **коренн|о́й** radical, fundamental; **~о́й жи́тель** native; **~о́й зуб** molar; **~а́я ло́шадь** shaft-horse; **~о́е населе́ние** indigenous population. **ко́рень, -рня**; *pl.* **-и, -е́й** *m.* root; radical. **коре́нья, -ьев** *pl.* root vegetables. **корешо́к, -шка́** rootlet; root; back, spine; counterfoil; pal, mate.

Коре́я, -и Korea. **корея́нка** *see* **коре́ец**

корзи́на, -ы, корзи́нка, -и basket. **корзи́нный** basket.

коридо́р, -а corridor, passage.

кори́нка, -и currants.

кори́ца, -ы cinnamon.

кори́чневый brown.

ко́рка, -и crust; rind, peel; scab.

корм, -а (-у), *loc.* **-у́**; *pl.* **-а́** fodder, food, feed; forage.

корма́, -ы́ stern, poop.

корми́лец, -льца bread-winner; benefactor.

корми́лица, -ы wet-nurse; benefactress. **корми́ть, -млю́, -мишь** *impf.* (*pf.* **на~, по~, про~**) feed; keep, maintain; **~ся** eat, feed; +*i.* live on, make a living by. **кормле́ние, -я** feeding. **кормов|о́й**[1] fodder, forage; **~а́я свёкла** mangel-wurzel.

кормово́й[2] stern, poop; after.

корневи́ще, -а rhizome. **корнево́й** root; radical. **корнепло́ды, -ов** root-crops.

корнишо́н, -а gherkin.

коро́бить, -блю *impf.* (*pf.* **по~**) warp; jar upon, grate upon; **~ся** (*pf. also* **с~ся**) warp, buckle.

коро́бка, -и box, case; **~ скоросте́й** gear-box.

коро́ва, -ы cow. **коро́в|ий** cow, cow's; **~ье ма́сло** butter. **коро́вник, -а** cow-shed.

короле́ва, -ы queen. **короле́вич, -а** king's son. **короле́вна, -ы** king's daughter. **короле́вский** royal; king's; regal, kingly. **короле́вство, -а** kingdom. **королёк, -лька́** petty king, kinglet; gold-crest; blood-orange. **коро́ль, -я́** *m.* king.

коромы́сло, -а yoke; beam; rocking shaft, rocker (arm); balance arm.

коро́на, -ы crown; coronet; corona.

коронаротромбо́з, -а coronary thrombosis; coronary. **корона́рный** coronary.

коро́нка, -и crown. **коро́нный** crown, of state. **коронова́ть, -ну́ю** *impf.* & *pf.* crown.

коросте́ль, -я corncrake.

корота́ть, -а́ю *impf.* (*pf.* **с~**) while away, pass. **коро́тк|ий; ко́ро́ток, -тка́, ко́ро́тко́, ко́ро́тки́** short; brief; close, intimate; **~ая распра́ва** short shrift; **на ~ой ноге́** on intimate terms. **ко́ротко** *adv.* briefly; intimately; **~ говоря́** in short. **коротково́лновый** short-wave. **коро́че** *comp. of* **коро́ткий, ко́ротко**

корпе́ть, -плю́ *impf.* sweat, pore (**над**+*i.* over).

ко́рпус, -а; *pl.* **-ы, -ов** *or* **-а́, -о́в** corps; services high school; building; hull; housing, frame, case; long primer; body; trunk, torso; length.

корректи́в, -а amendment, correction. **корректи́ровать, -рую** *impf.* (*pf.* **про~, с~**) correct, read, edit. **корре́ктный** correct, proper. **корре́ктор, -а**; *pl.* **-а́** proof-reader, corrector. **корректу́ра, -ы** proof-reading; proof.

корреспонде́нт, -а correspondent. **корреспонде́нция, -и** correspondence; **заказна́я, проста́я ~** registered, non-registered mail. **корреспонди́ровать, -рую** *impf.* correspond.

корсе́т, -а corset.

корт, -а (tennis-)court.

ко́ртик, -а dirk.

ко́рточки, -чек *pl.*; **сесть на ~, сиде́ть на ко́рточках** squat.

корчева́ть, -чу́ю *impf.* grub up, root out. **корчёвка, -и** grubbing up, rooting out.

ко́рчить, -чу *impf.* (*pf.* **с~**) contort; **~ грима́сы, ро́жи** make faces, pull faces; **~ дурака́** play the fool; **~ из себя́** pose as; *impers.*+*a.* convulse; make writhe; **его́ ко́рчит от бо́ли** he is writhing in pain; **~ся** writhe.

ко́ршун, -а kite.

коры́стный mercenary. **корыстолюби́вый** self-interested, mercenary. **корыстолю́бие, -я** self-interest, cupidity. **коры́сть, -и** cupidity, avarice; profit, gain.

коры́то, -а trough; wash-tub.

корь, -и measles.

коря́вый rough, uneven; gnarled; clumsy, uncouth; pock-marked.

коса́[1], **-ы́**, *a.* **-у**; *pl.* **-ы** plait, tress, braid.

коса́[2], **-ы́**, *a.* **ко́су**; *pl.* **-ы** spit.

коса́[3], **-ы́**, *a.* **ко́су́**; *pl.* **-ы** scythe. **коса́рь, -я́** *m.* mower, hay-maker.

ко́свенн|ый indirect; oblique; **~ые ули́ки** circumstantial evidence.

коси́лка, -и mower, mowing-machine. **коси́ть**[1], **кошу́, ко́сишь** *impf.* (*pf.* **с~**) mow; cut; mow down.

коси́ть[2], **кошу́** *impf.* (*pf.* **по~, с~**) squint; be crooked; **~ся** slant; look sideways; look askance.

коси́ца, -ы lock; pigtail.

косма́тый shaggy.

косме́тика, -и cosmetics, make-up. **космети́ческ|ий** cosmetic; **~ий кабине́т** beauty parlour; **~ая ма́ска** face-pack; **~ая су́мочка** vanity bag, case; **~ий ремо́нт** redecoration; refurbishment.

косми́ческ|ий cosmic; space; **~ий кора́бль** spaceship, spacecraft; **~ое простра́нство** (outer) space; **~ое телеви́дение** satellite television broadcasting. **космодро́м, -а** cosmodrome, launching-site (*for spacecraft*). **космолёт, -а** (space) shuttle. **космона́втика, -и** astronautics, space exploration. **космоте́хника, -и** space technology. **космона́вт, -а, -на́втка, -и** spaceman, cosmonaut, astronaut. **ко́смос, -а** cosmos; (outer) space. **космоте́хника, -и** space technology.

косне́ть, -е́ю *impf.* (*pf.* **за~**) stagnate; stick. **косноязы́чный** tongue-tied.

косну́ться, -ну́сь, -нёшься *pf. of* **каса́ться**

ко́сный inert, sluggish; stagnant.

ко́со *adv.* slantwise, aslant, askew; sidelong, obliquely. **косогла́зие, -я** squint, cast. **косогла́зый** cross-eyed, squint-eyed. **косого́р, -а** slope, hillside. **косо́й; кос, -а́, -о** slanting; oblique; sloping; sidelong; squinting, cross-eyed; **скро́енный по ~** cut on the cross. **косола́пый** pigeon-toed; clumsy, awkward.

костёр, -тра́ bonfire; camp-fire.

кости́стый, костля́вый bony; **ко́стный** bone, bony, osseous. **ко́сточка, -и** *dim. of* **кость** bone; kernel, stone, pip.

косты́ль, -я́ *m.* crutch; tail-skid.

кость, -и, *loc.* **и́**; *pl.* **-и, -е́й** bone; die; **игра́ть в ко́сти** dice.

костю́м, -а dress, clothes; suit; costume;

англи́йский ~ tailor-made (coat and skirt); **вече́рний ~** dress suit; **купа́льный ~** swimsuit; **маскара́дный ~** fancy-dress. **костюме́р, -а** wardrobe master. **костюмиро́ванный** in costume; fancy-dress; **~ бал, ве́чер** fancy-dress ball. **костю́мн|ый** *adj.*; **~ая пье́са** period play, costume play.

костя́к, -а́ skeleton; backbone. **костяно́й** bone; ivory.

косы́нка, -и (*three-cornered*) head-scarf, shawl.

кот, -а́ tom-cat.

котёл, -тла́ boiler; copper, cauldron. **котело́к, -лка́** pot; mess-tin; bowler (hat); noddle, head. **коте́льная** *sb.* boiler-room, boiler-house.

котёнок, -нка; *pl.* **-тя́та, -тя́т** kitten. **ко́тик, -а** fur-seal; sealskin. **ко́тиковый** sealskin.

котле́та, -ы rissole, croquette; **отбивна́я ~** cutlet, chop.

котлова́н, -а foundation pit, excavation. **котлови́на, -ы** basin, hollow; trough.

кото́мка, -и knapsack.

кото́рый *pron.* which, what; who; that; **в кото́ром часу́** (at) what time; **кото́рые..., кото́рые** some ..., some; **~ раз** how many times; **~ час?** what time is it? **кото́рый-либо, кото́рый-нибудь** *prons.* some; one or other.

котя́та *etc.*: *see* **котёнок**

ко́фе *m.indecl.* coffee; **раствори́мый ~** instant coffee. **кофева́рка, -и** coffee-maker. **кофеи́н, -а** caffeine. **кофе́йник, -а** coffee-pot. **кофе́йный** coffee. **кофемо́лка, -и** coffee-mill, coffee-grinder.

ко́фта, -ы, ко́фточка, -и blouse.

коча́н, -а́ *or* **-чна́** (cabbage-)head.

кочева́ть, -чу́ю *impf.* lead a nomadic life; rove, wander; migrate. **кочёвка, -и** nomad camp; wandering, migration; nomadic existence. **коче́вник, -а** nomad. **кочево́й** nomadic; migratory. **коче́вье, -я**; *g.pl.* **-вий** nomad encampment; nomad territory.

кочега́р, -а stoker, fireman. **кочега́рка, -и** stokehold, stokehole.

кочене́ть, -е́ю *impf.* (*pf.* **за~, о~**) grow numb; stiffen.

кочерга́, -и́; *g.pl.* **-рёг** poker.

кочеры́жка, -и cabbage-stalk.

ко́чка, -и hummock; tussock. **кочкова́тый** hummocky, tussocky.

коша́чий cat, cat's; catlike; feline; **~ конце́рт** caterwauling; hooting, barracking.

кошелёк, -лька́ purse.

коше́рный kosher.

ко́шка, -и cat; grapnel, drag; *pl.* climbing-irons; cat(-o'-nine-tails).

кошма́р, -а nightmare. **кошма́рный** nightmarish; horrible, awful.

кошу́ *etc.*: *see* **коси́ть**

кощу́нственный blasphemous. **кощу́нство, -а** blasphemy.

коэффицие́нт, -а coefficient, factor; **~ у́мственных спосо́бностей** intelligence quotient, IQ.

КП *abbr.* (*of* **Коммунисти́ческая па́ртия**) Communist Party. **КПСС** *abbr.* (*of* **Коммунисти́ческая па́ртия Сове́тского Сою́за**) CPSU, Communist Party of the Soviet Union.

кра́деный stolen. **краду́** *etc.*: *see* **красть. кра́дучись** *adv.* stealthily, furtively.

краеве́дение, -я regional studies.

краеуго́льный; ~ ка́мень corner-stone.

кра́жа, -и theft; **магази́нная ~** shoplifting; **~ со взло́мом** burglary.

край, -я (-ю), *loc.* **-ю́**; *pl.* **-я́, -ёв** edge; brim; brink; land, country; territory, region; side (*of meat*); **в чужи́х края́х** in foreign parts; **на краю́ све́та** at the world's end; **че́рез ~** overmuch, beyond measure. **кра́йне** *adv.* extremely. **кра́йний** extreme; last; uttermost; outside, wing. **кра́йность, -и** extreme; extremity.

крал *etc.*: *see* **кра́сть**

кран, -а tap, cock, faucet; crane.

крапи́ва, -ы nettle. **крапи́вница, -ы** nettle-rash. **крапи́вный** nettle.

кра́пина, -ы, кра́пинка, -и speck, spot. **краплёный** marked.

краса́вец, -вца handsome man; Adonis. **краса́вица, -ы** beauty. **краси́вость, -и** (mere) prettiness. **краси́вый** beautiful; handsome; fine.

краси́льный dye; dyeing. **краси́льня, -и**; *g.pl.* **-лен** dye-house, dye-works. **краси́льщик, -а** dyer. **краси́тель, -я** *m.* dye, dyestuff. **кра́сить, -а́шу** *impf.* (*pf.* **вы́~, о~, по~**) paint; colour; dye; stain; **~ся** (*pf.* **на~**) make-up. **кра́ска, -и** paint, dye; colour; painting, colouring, dyeing; (*printer's*) ink; **~ для ресни́ц** mascara; **(водо-)эмульсио́нная ~** emulsion (paint). **краскораспыли́тель, -я** *m.* paint sprayer, spray-gun.

красне́ть, -е́ю *impf.* (*pf.* **по~**) blush; redden, grow red; show red; colour; **~ся** show red.

красно... *in comb.* red; beautiful. **красноарме́ец, -е́йца** Red Army man. **~арме́йский** Red Army. **~ва́тый** reddish. **~гварде́ец, -е́йца** Red Guard. **~дере́вец, -вца, ~дере́вщик, -а** cabinet-maker. **~знамённый** Red-Banner. **~ко́жий** red-skinned; *sb.* redskin. **~речи́вый** eloquent; expressive. **~ре́чие, -я** eloquence; oratory.

краснота́, -ы́ redness; red spot. **кра́сн|ый; -сен, -сна́, -о** red; beautiful; fine; of high quality or value; **~ое де́рево** mahogany; **~ый лес** coniferous forest; **~ая строка́** (first line of) new paragraph; **~ый у́гол** place of honour; **~ый уголо́к** Red Corner.

красова́ться, -су́юсь *impf.* (*pf.* **по~**) stand in beauty; show off; *+i.* flaunt. **красота́, -ы́**; *pl.* **-ы** beauty. **кра́сочный** paint; ink; colourful, (highly) coloured.

красть, -аду́, -адёшь; крал *impf.* (*pf.* **у~**) steal; **~ся** steal, creep, sneak.

кра́тк|ий; -ток, -тка́, -о short; brief; concise;

~ое содержа́ние summary. **кра́тко** *adv.* briefly. **кратковре́менный** short, brief; short-lived; transitory. **краткосро́чный** short-term.

кра́тное *sb.* multiple.

кратча́йший *superl. of* **кра́ткий. кра́тче** *comp. of* **кра́ткий, кра́тко**

крах, -а crash; failure.

крахма́л, -а starch. **крахма́лить, -лю** *impf.* (*pf.* **на~**) starch. **крахма́льный** starched.

кра́ше *comp. of* **краси́вый, краси́во**

кра́шеный painted; coloured; dyed; made up, wearing make-up. **кра́шу** *etc.*: *see* **кра́сить**

краю́ха, -и hunk, thick slice.

креве́тка, -и shrimp; prawn. **креветколо́вн|ый; ~ое су́дно** shrimper, shrimp boat.

креди́т, -а credit. **креди́тка, -и** credit card. **креди́тный** credit, on credit. **кредитова́ть, -ту́ю** *impf. & pf.* credit, give credit (to). **кредито́р, -а** creditor; **~ по закладно́й** mortgagee. **кредитоспосо́бность, -и** creditworthiness, credit rating.

кре́йсер, -а; *pl.* **-а́, -о́в** cruiser. **кре́йсерский** cruiser, cruising. **крейси́ровать, -рую** *impf.* cruise.

крем, -а cream.

креме́нь, -мня́ *m.*, **кремешо́к, -шка́** flint.

кремлеве́д, -а Kremlinologist. **кремлеве́дение, -я** Kremlinology. **кремлёвский** Kremlin. **кремль, -я́** *m.* citadel; Kremlin.

кремнёв|ый flint; silicon; siliceous; **~ое ружьё** flint-lock. **кремнезём, -а** silica. **кре́мний, -я** silicon. **кремни́стый** siliceous; stony.

кре́мовый cream; cream-coloured.

крен, -а list, heel; bank. **крени́ть, -ню́** *impf.* (*pf.* **на~**) heel; bank; **~ся** heel over, list; bank.

креп, -а crêpe; crape.

крепи́ть, -плю́ *impf.* strengthen; support, shore up timber; make fast, hitch, lash; furl; constipate, make costive; **~ся** hold out. **кре́пк|ий; -пок, -пка́, -о** strong; sound; sturdy, robust; firm; **~ий моро́з** hard frost; **~ие напи́тки** spirits; **~ое сло́во, словцо́** swear-word, curse. **кре́пко** *adv.* strongly; firmly; soundly. **крепле́ние, -я** strengthening; fastening; binding; timbering, shoring up; lashing, furling.

кре́пнуть, -ну; -еп *impf.* (*pf.* **о~**) get stronger.

крепостни́чество, -а serfdom. **крепостн|о́й** serf; **~о́е пра́во** serfdom; **~о́й** *sb.* serf.

кре́пость, -и fortress; strength. **крепча́ть, -а́ет** *impf.* (*pf.* **по~**) strengthen; get stronger, get harder, get up. **кре́пче** *comp. of* **кре́пкий, кре́пко**

кре́сло, -а; *g.pl.* **-сел** arm-chair, easy-chair; stall; **высо́кое ~** (*child's*) high chair; **инвали́дное ~** wheelchair; **~-кача́лка** rocking chair.

крест, -а́ cross; **постави́ть ~ на**+*p.* give up for lost. **крести́ны, -и́н** *pl.* christening. **крести́ть, крещу́, -е́стишь** *impf. & pf.* (*pf. also* **о~, пере~**) baptize, christen; nickname; make sign of the cross over; **~ся** cross o.s.; be baptized, be christened. **крестна́крест** *adv.* crosswise. **кре́стник, -а, кре́стница, -ы** god-child. **крёстн|ый; ~ая (мать)** godmother; **~ый оте́ц** godfather. **кресто́вый** of the cross; **~ похо́д** crusade. **крестоно́сец, -сца** crusader. **крестообра́зный** cruciform.

крестья́нин, -а; *pl.* **-я́не, -я́н, крестья́нка, -и** peasant. **крестья́нский** peasant. **крестья́нство, -а** peasants, peasantry.

креще́ние, -я baptism, christening; **К~** Epiphany. **крещён|ый; -ён, -ена́** baptized; *sb.* Christian. **крещу́** *etc.*: *see* **крести́ть**

крива́я *sb.* curve. **кривизна́, -ы́** crookedness; curvature. **криви́ть, -влю́** *impf.* (*pf.* **по~, с~**) bend, distort; **~ душо́й** go against one's conscience; **~ся** become crooked or bent; make a wry face. **кривля́ка, -и** *c.g.* poseur; affected person. **кривля́нье, -я** affectation. **кривля́ться, -я́юсь** *impf.* be affected, give o.s. airs.

криво... *in comb.* curved, crooked; one-sided. **кривобо́кий** lopsided. **~гла́зый** blind in one eye; one-eyed. **~лине́йный** curvilinear. **~но́гий** bandy-legged. **~то́лки, -ов** *pl.* false rumours. **~ши́п, -а** crank; crankshaft.

криво́й; крив, -а́, -о crooked; curved; one-eyed.

крик, -а cry, shout; *pl.* clamour, outcry. **крикли́вый** clamorous, shouting; bawling; loud; penetrating; blatant. **кри́кнуть, -ну** *pf. of* **крича́ть. крику́н, -а́** shouter, bawler; babbler.

криста́лл, -а crystal; **маги́ческий ~** crystal ball; (*comput.*) (silicon) chip.

кри́тик, -а critic. **кри́тика, -и** criticism; critique. **критикова́ть, -ку́ю** *impf.* criticize. **крити́ческий** critical.

крича́ть, -чу́ *impf.* (*pf.* **кри́кнуть**) cry, shout; yell, scream. **крича́щий** loud; blatant.

кров, -а roof; shelter; **лишённый ~а** homeless.

крова́вый bloody.

крова́ть, -и bed; bedstead.

кро́вельный roof, roofing.

кровено́сный blood-; circulatory. **крови́нка, -и** drop of blood.

кро́вля, -и; *g.pl.* **-вель** roof.

кро́вн|ый blood; thoroughbred; vital, deep, intimate; deadly; **~ая месть** blood-feud.

крово... *in comb.* blood, sangui-, haemo-. **кровожа́дный** bloodthirsty. **~излия́ние, -я** haemorrhage. **~обраще́ние, -я** circulation. **~подтёк, -а** bruise. **~проли́тие, -я** bloodshed. **~проли́тный** bloody; sanguinary. **~со́с, -а** vampire-bat; bloodsucker. **~тече́ние, -я** bleeding; haemorrhage. **~точи́вость, -и** haemophilia. **~точи́ть, -чи́т** *impf.* bleed. **~ха́ркание, -я** spitting of blood; haemoptysis.

кровь, -и, *loc.* **-й** blood. **кровянóй** blood.
кроúть, крою *impf.* (*pf.* **с~**) cut, cut out.
крóйка, -и cutting out.
крокодúл, -а crocodile.
крóкус, -а crocus.
крóлик, -а rabbit. **кроликовóдство, -а** rabbit-breeding. **крóликовый, крóличий** rabbit.
кроль, -я *m.* crawl(-stroke).
крольчáтник, -а rabbit-hutch; rabbit farm. **крольчúха, -и** doe, she-rabbit.
крóме *prep.+g.* except; besides, in addition to; ~ **тогó** besides, moreover, furthermore; ~ **шýток** joking apart.
крóмка, -и edge; selvage; rim; brim.
кромсáть, -áю *impf.* (*pf.* **ис~**) cut up carelessly, hack to pieces; shred.
крóна[1], **-ы** crown, top.
крóна[2], **-ы** (*coin*) crown.
кронштéйн, -а bracket; corbel.
кропотлúвый painstaking; minute; laborious; precise.
кросс, -а cross-country race.
кроссвóрд, -а crossword.
кроссмéн, -а cross-country runner.
крот, -á mole, moleskin.
крóткий; -ток, -ткá, -тко meek, gentle; mild. **крóтость, -и** gentleness; mildness, meekness.
крохá, -й, *a.* **-у**; *pl.* **-и, -ох, -áм** crumb. **крóхотный, крóшечный** tiny, minute. **крóшево, -а** hash; medley. **крошúть, -шý, -шишь** *impf.* (*pf.* **ис~, на~, рас~**) crumble; chop, hack; hack to pieces; *+i.* drop crumbs of; **~ся** crumble; break up small. **крóшка, -и** crumb; a bit.
круассáн, -а croissant.
круг, -а (-у), *loc.* **-ý**; *pl.* **-й** circle; ring; circuit, lap; sphere; range; compass; **на** ~ on average, taking it all round. **круглогодúчный** year-round. **круглосýточный** round-the-clock, 24-hour. **крýгл|ый; кругл, -á, -о** round; complete, utter, perfect; **~ый год** all the year round; **~ый, ~ая сиротá** (complete) orphan; **~ые сýтки** day and night. **кругов|óй** circular; all-round; cyclic; **~áя порýка** mutual responsibility guarantee; **~áя чáша** loving-cup. **кругозóр, -а** prospect; outlook, horizon, range of interests. **кругóм** *adv.* round, around; round about; completely; entirely; *prep.+g.* round, around. **кругооборóт, -а** circulation. **кругосвéтный** round-the-world.
кружевнóй lace; lacy. **крýжево, -а**; *pl.* **-á, -ев, -áм** lace.
крýжить, -ужý, -ýжúшь *impf.* whirl, spin round; circle; wander; **~ся** whirl, spin round, go round.
крýжка, -и mug; tankard; collecting-box.
крýжный roundabout, circuitous. **кружóк, -жкá** circle, society, group; disc; washer.
круúз, -а cruise.
крупá, -ы́; *pl.* **-ы** groats; sleet. **крупúнка, -и** grain. **крупúца, -ы** grain, fragment, atom.
крупно... *in comb.* large, coarse, macro-, megalo-; **крупномасштáбный** large-scale; ambitious. **крýпн|ый** large, big; large-scale; coarse; important; serious; prominent, outstanding; **~ый план** close-up; **~ый разговóр** high words; **~ый шаг** coarse pitch; **~ым шáгом** at a round pace.
крупчáтка, -и finest (white) flour. **крупчáтый** granular.
крутизнá, -ы́ steepness; steep slope.
крутúльный torsion, torsional; doubling. **крутúть, -учý, -ýтишь** *impf.* (*pf.* **за~, с~**) twist, twirl; roll; turn, wind; whirl; **~ся** turn, spin, revolve; whirl; be in a whirl.
крýто *adv.* steeply; suddenly; abruptly, sharply; sternly, severely; drastically; thoroughly. **крут|óй; крут, -á, -о** steep; sudden; abrupt, sharp; stern, severe; drastic; thick; well-done; **~óе яйцó** hard-boiled egg. **крýча, -и** steep slope, cliff. **крýче** *comp. of* **крутóй, крýто**
кручý *etc.*: *see* **крутúть**
крушéние, -я wreck; crash; ruin; collapse.
крыжóвенный gooseberry. **крыжóвник, -а** gooseberries; gooseberry bush.
крылáтый winged. **крылó, -á**; *pl.* **-лья, -льев** wing; sail, vane; splashboard, mudguard.
крыльцó, -á; *pl.* **-а, -лéц, -цáм** porch; (front, back) steps.
Крым, -а the Crimea. **кры́мский** Crimean.
кры́са, -ы rat. **крысолóв, -а** rat-catcher. **крысолóвка, -и** rat-trap.
кры́тый covered. **крыть, крóю** *impf.* cover; roof; coat; trump; **~ся** be, lie; be concealed. **кры́ша, -и** roof. **кры́шка, -и** lid; cover.
крюк, -á (-у); *pl.* **-кú, -кóв** *or* **-ючья, -чьев** hook; detour. **крючковáтый** hooked. **крючóк, -чкá** hook; hitch, catch.
кря́ду *adv.* in succession, running.
кряж, -а ridge.
кря́кать, -аю *impf.* **кря́кнуть, -ну** *pf.* quack; grunt.
кряхтéть, -хчý *impf.* groan.
ксерокóпия, -и xerox (copy). **ксéрокс, -а** Xerox(*propr.*)(-machine); xerox.
кстáти *adv.* to the point, to the purpose; opportunely; at the same time, incidentally; by the way.
кто, когó, комý, кем, ком *pron.* who; anyone, anybody; **комý как** tastes differ; ~ **(бы) ни** whoever; whosoever; ~ **идёт?** who goes there?; ~ **когó?** who will win, who will come out on top?; **~... ~** some ..., others; ~ **кудá** in all directions; ~ **что лю́бит** tastes differ. **ктó-либо, ктó-нибудь** *prons.* anyone, anybody; someone, somebody. **ктó-то** *pron.* someone, somebody.
куб, -а; *pl.* **-ы́** cube; cubic metre; boiler, water-heater, urn; still; vat; **в ~е** cubed.
куб. *abbr.* (*of* **кубúческий**) cubic.
кýбарем *adv.* head over heels; headlong.
кубатýра, -ы cubic content. **кýбик, -а** brick, block; cubic centimetre.

куби́нец, -нца, куби́нка, -и Cuban. **куби́нский** Cuban.
куби́ческий cubic, cubical; cube.
ку́бовый indigo.
ку́бок, -бка goblet, bowl, beaker; cup; **встре́ча на ~** cup-tie.
кубоме́тр, -а cubic metre.
кувши́н, -а jug; pitcher. **кувши́нка, -и** water-lily.
кувырка́ться, -а́юсь *impf.*, **кувыркну́ться, -ну́сь** *pf.* turn somersaults, go head over heels; **кувырко́м** *adv.* head over heels; topsy-turvy.
куда́ *adv.* where, where to; what for; *+comp.* much, far; **~ (бы) ни** wherever; **~ бы то ни́ было** anywhere; **~ лу́чше** much better; **хоть ~** fine, excellent. **куда́-либо, куда́-нибудь** *adv.* anywhere, somewhere. **куда́-то** *adv.* somewhere.
куда́хтанье, -я cackling, clucking. **куда́хтать, -хчу** *impf.* cackle, cluck.
ку́дри, -е́й *pl.* curls. **кудря́в|ый** curly; curly-headed; leafy, bushy; flowery, florid, ornate; **~ая капу́ста** curly kale. **кудря́шки, -шек** *pl.* ringlets.
кузне́ц, -а́ smith, blacksmith. **кузне́чик, -а** grasshopper. **кузне́чный** blacksmith's; **~ мех** bellows; **~ мо́лот** sledge-hammer. **ку́зница, -ы** forge, smithy.
ку́зов, -а; *pl.* **-а́** basket; body.
кукаре́кать, -ает *impf.*, **кукаре́кнуть, -нет** *pf.* (*pf. also* **про~**) crow. **кукареку́** cock-a-doodle-doo.
ку́киш, -а fico, fig.
ку́кла, -ы doll; puppet; **теа́тр ку́кол** puppet theatre.
кукова́ть, -ку́ю *impf.* (*pf.* **про~**) cuckoo.
ку́колка, -и dolly; chrysalis, pupa. **ку́кольник, -а** puppeteer. **ку́кольный** doll's; doll-like; puppet.
кукуру́за, -ы (Indian) corn, maize; **возду́шная ~** popcorn.
куку́шка, -и cuckoo.
кула́к, -а́ fist; striking force; kulak. **кула́цкий** kulak, kulak's. **кула́чный** fist.
кулёк, -лька́ bag.
кули́к, -а́ sandpiper.
кули́сы, -и́с wings; **за кули́сами** behind the scenes.
кули́ч, -а́ Easter cake.
кулуа́ры, -ов *pl.* lobby.
ку́льман, -а drawing-board.
культ... *abbr.* (*of* **культу́рно-, культу́рный**) *in comb.* cultural, educational, recreational. **культба́за, -ы** recreation centre. **~отде́л, -а** Cultural Section. **~похо́д, -а** cultural crusade; cultural outing. **~рабо́та, -ы** cultural and educational work.
культу́ра, -ы culture; standard, level; cultivation, growing.
культури́зм, -а body-building. **культури́ст, -а** body-builder.
культу́рно *adv.* in a civilized manner. **культу́рность, -и** (level of) culture. **культу́рный** cultured; cultivated; cultural.
культя́, -и́, культя́пка, -и stump.
кум, -а; *pl.* **-мовья́, -ьёв, кума́, -ы́** god-parent of one's child.
кума́ч, -а́ red calico.
куми́р, -а idol.
кумы́с, -а koumiss (*fermented mare's milk*).
ку́ний marten(-fur). **куни́ца, -ы** marten.
кун-фу́ *nt. indecl.* kung-fu.
купа́льный bathing, swimming. **купа́льня, -и** bathing-place. **купа́льщик, -а, -щица, -ы** bather. **купа́ть, -а́ю** *impf.* (*pf.* **вы́, ис~**) bathe; bath; **~ся** bathe; take a bath.
купе́ *nt.indecl.* compartment.
купе́ц, -пца́ merchant. **купе́ческий** merchant, mercantile. **купе́чество, -а** merchant class. **купи́ть, -плю́, -пишь** *pf.* (*impf.* **покупа́ть**) buy.
купле́т, -а stanza, strophe.
ку́пля, -и buying, purchase.
ку́пол, -а; *pl.* **-а́** cupola, dome.
купо́н, -а coupon.
купоро́с, -а vitriol.
купчи́ха, -и merchant's wife; woman of merchant class.
кура́нты, -ов *pl.* chiming clock; chimes.
курга́н, -а barrow; tumulus.
куре́ние, -я smoking; incense. **кури́льница, -ы** censer; incense-burner. **кури́льщик, -а, -щица, -ы** smoker.
кури́н|ый hen's; chicken's.
кури́тельн|ый smoking; **~ая бума́га** cigarette paper. **кури́ть, -рю́, -ришь** *impf.* (*pf.* **по~**) smoke; distil; *+a. or i.* burn; **~ся** burn; smoke; *+i.* produce, emit.
ку́рица, -ы; *pl.* **ку́ры, кур** hen, chicken.
курно́сый snub; snub-nosed.
куро́к, -рка́ cock, cocking-piece; **взвести́ ~** cock a gun; **спусти́ть ~** pull the trigger.
куропа́тка, -и partridge; ptarmigan.
куро́рт, -а health-resort; spa.
курс, -а course; policy; year; rate (of exchange). **курса́нт, -а** student.
курси́в, -а italics; **~ом** in italics. **курси́вный** italic.
курси́ровать, -рую *impf.* ply.
курси́стка, -и woman student.
ку́ртка, -и jacket.
курча́виться, -ится *impf.* curl. **курча́вый** curly; curly-headed.
ку́ры *etc.*: *see* **ку́рица**
курьёз, -а a funny thing; **для ~а, ра́ди ~а** for a joke, for amusement. **курьёзный** curious; funny.
курье́р, -а messenger; courier. **курье́рский** fast, express.
куря́тина, -ы chicken. **куря́тник, -а** hen-house, hen-coop.
куря́щий *sb.* smoker; **ваго́н для куря́щих** smoking-carriage, smoker.
куса́ть, -а́ю *impf.* bite; sting; **~ся** bite; bite one another.

кусковóй in lumps; lump. **кусóк, -скá** piece, bit; slice; lump; cake.

куст, -á bush, shrub. **кустáрник, -а** shrubbery; bush, shrub; bushes, shrubs.

кустáрн|ый hand-made, home-made; handicrafts; amateurish, primitive; **~ая промы́шленность** cottage industry. **кустáрь, -я́** *m.* handicraftsman.

кýтать, -аю *impf.* (*pf.* **за~**) wrap up, muffle up; **~ся** muffle o.s. up.

кутёж, -á drinking-bout; drunken revel, binge. **кутерьмá, -ы́** commotion, stir, bustle. **кути́ть, кучý, кýтишь** *impf.*, **кутнýть, -нý, -нёшь** *pf.* drink, carouse; go on a binge, the spree.

кухáрка, -и cook. **кýхня, -и**; *g.pl.* **-хонь** kitchen; cook-house; cooking, cuisine. **кýхонн|ый** kitchen; **~ая посýда** kitchen utensils.

кýцый tailless; bob-tailed; short; limited, abbreviated.

кýча, -и heap, pile; heaps, piles, lots. **кучевóй** cumulus.

кýчер, -а; *pl.* **-á** coachman, driver. **кучерскóй** coachman's.

кýчка, -и small heap; small group. **кýчный** closely-grouped.

кучý *see* **кути́ть**

кушáк, -á sash; (*plaited*) girdle; belt.

кýшанье, -я food; dish. **кýшать, -аю** *impf.* (*pf.* **по~, с~**) eat, take, have.

кушéтка, -и couch, chaise-longue.

кую́ *etc.*: *see* **ковáть**

кювéт, -а ditch, drain; tray, dish, bath.

Л

л *letter*: *see* **эль**

л *abbr.* (*of* **литр**) l., litre(s).

лабири́нт, -а labyrinth, maze.

лаборáнт, -а, -áнтка, -и laboratory assistant. **лаборатóрия, -и** laboratory. **лабораторный** laboratory.

лáва, -ы lava.

лави́на, -ы avalanche.

лáвка, -и bench; shop. **лáвочка, -и** small shop. **лáвочник, -а, -ница, -ы** shopkeeper, retailer.

лавр, -а bay-tree, laurel; *pl.* laurels.

лáвра, -ы monastery.

лáврóвый laurel, bay; **~ венóк** laurel wreath, laurels.

лáгерник, -а camp inmate. **лáгерн|ый** camp; **~ая жизнь** nomad existence; **~ый сбор** annual camp. **лáгерь, -я**; *pl.* **-я́** *or* **-и, -éй** *or* **-ей** *m.* camp.

лад, -а (-у), *loc.* **-ý**; *pl.* **-ы́, -óв** harmony, concord; manner, way; stop, fret key, stud; **в ~, не в ~** in, out of, tune; **идти́ на ~** go well, be successful; **на свой ~** in one's own way, after one's own fashion; **не в ~áх** at odds, at variance; **они́ не в ~áх** they don't get on.

лáдан, -а incense; **дышáть на ~** have one foot in the grave.

лáдить, лáжу *impf.* get on, be on good terms; **~ся** go well, succeed. **лáдно** *adv.* harmoniously; well; all right; very well! **лáдный** fine, excellent; harmonious.

ладóнный palmar. **ладóнь, -и** palm.

ладья́[1]**, -ьи́** rook, castle.

ладья́[2]**, -ьи́** boat, barge.

лáжу *etc.*: *see* **лáдить, лáзить**

лазарéт, -а (*mil.*) field hospital; sick quarters; sick-bay; infirmary.

лáзать *see* **лáзить. лазéйка, -и** hole, gap; loop-hole.

лáзер, -а laser. **лáзерный** laser; **~ при́нтер** laser printer.

лáзить, лáжу, лáзать, -аю *impf.* climb, clamber; +**в**+*a.* climb into, get into.

лазýрный sky-blue, azure. **лазýрь, -и** azure.

лазýтчик, -а scout; spy.

лай, -я bark, barking. **лáйка**[1]**, -и** husky.

лáйка[2]**, -и** kid. **лáйковый** kid; kidskin.

лáйнер, -а liner, airliner.

лак, -а (-у) varnish, lacquer; **~ для волóс** hair spray.

лакáть, -áю *impf.* (*pf.* **вы́~**) lap.

лакéй, -я footman, man-servant; lackey, flunkey. **лакéйский** man-servant's; servile.

лакирóванн|ый varnished, lacquered; **~ая кóжа** patent leather. **лакировáть, -рýю** *impf.* (*pf.* **от~**) varnish; lacquer. **лакирóвка, -и** varnishing, lacquering; varnish; gloss, polish.

лáкмус, -а litmus. **лáкмусов|ый** litmus; **~ая бумáга** litmus paper.

лáков|ый varnished, lacquered; **~ая кóжа** patent leather.

лáкомить, -млю *impf.* (*pf.* **по~**) regale, treat; **~ся**+*i.* treat o.s. to. **лáкомка, -и** *c.g.* gourmand; lover of sweet things. **лáкомство, -а** delicacy; *pl.* dainties, sweet things. **лáкомый** dainty, tasty; +**до** fond of, partial to.

лакони́ческий laconic.

Ла-Мáнш, -а the (English) Channel.

лáмпа, -ы lamp; valve, tube. **лáмпочка, -и** lamp; bulb; light.

ландшáфт, -а landscape.

лáндыш, -а lily of the valley.

лань, -и fallow deer; doe.

лáпа, -ы paw; tenon, dovetail; fluke; (*sl.*) bribe; **попáсть в лáпы к**+*d.* fall into the clutches of.

лáпоть, -птя; *pl.* **-и, -éй** *m.* bast shoe, bast sandal.

лáпочка, -и (my) darling, sweetheart (*form of direct address*).

лáпчатый palmate; web-footed.

лапшá, -и́ noodles; noodle soup.

ларёк, -рька́ stall. **ларёчник, -а** stall-keeper. **ларь, -я́** *m.* chest, coffer; bin; stall.

ла́ска, -и caress, endearment; kindness. **ласка́тельн|ый** caressing; affectionate; **~ое и́мя** pet name. **ласка́ть, -а́ю** *impf.* caress, fondle, pet; comfort, console; **~ся**+к+*d.* make up to; snuggle up to; coax; fawn upon. **ла́сковый** affectionate, tender.

ла́стик, -а (india-)rubber, eraser.

ла́сточка, -и swallow.

Ла́твия, -и Latvia.

ла́текс, -а latex.

лати́нский Latin.

лату́нный brass. **лату́нь, -и** brass.

ла́ты, лат *pl.* armour.

латы́нь, -и Latin.

латы́ш, -а́, латы́шка, -и Latvian, Lett. **латы́шский** Latvian, Lettish.

лауреа́т, -а prize-winner.

лафе́т, -а gun-carriage.

ла́цкан, -а lapel.

лачу́га, -и hovel, shack.

ла́ять, ла́ю *impf.* bark; bay.

лба *etc.*: *see* **лоб**

лгать, лгу, лжёшь; лгал, -а́, -о *impf.* (*pf.* **на~, со~**) lie; tell lies; +**на**+*a.* slander. **лгун, -а́, лгу́нья, -и** liar.

лебедёнок, -нка; *pl.* **-дя́та, -дя́т** cygnet. **лебеди́ный** swan, swan's. **лебёдка, -и** swan, pen; winch, windlass. **ле́бедь, -я**; *pl.* **-и, -е́й** *m.* swan, cob.

лебези́ть, -ежу́ *impf.* fawn, cringe.

лев, льва lion.

левко́й, -я stock.

лево... *in comb.* left, left-hand. **левобере́жный** left-bank. **левша́, -и́**; *g.pl.* **-е́й** *c.g.* left-handed person, left-hander, southpaw. **ле́в|ый** *adj.* left; left-hand; port; left-wing; unofficial, illegal; **~ая сторона́** left-hand side, near side, wrong side.

лёг *etc.*: *see* **лечь**

легализа́ция, -и legalization.

легализова́ть, -у́ю *impf.* & *pf.* legalize. **легализова́ться, -зу́юсь** *impf.* & *pf.* become legalized. **лега́льный** legal.

леге́нда, -ы legend. **легенда́рный** legendary.

легио́н, -а legion; **иностра́нный ~** the Foreign Legion; **о́рден почётного ~а** Legion of Honour. **легионе́р, -а** legionary, legionnaire.

лёгк|ий; -гок, -гка́, лёгки́ light; easy; slight, mild; **~ая атле́тика** field and track events; **лёгок на поми́не** talk of the devil! **у него́ ~ая рука́** he brings luck. **легко́** *adv.* easily, lightly, slightly.

легко... *in comb.* light, light-weight; easy, easily, readily. **легкове́рие, -я** credulity, gullibility. **~ве́рный** credulous, gullible. **~ве́с, -а, ~ве́сный** light-weight. **~ву́шка, -и** (private) car. **~мы́сленный** light-minded; thoughtless, careless, irresponsible; flippant, frivolous, superficial. **~мы́слие, -я** flippancy, frivolity, levity.

легков|о́й; ~о́й автомоби́ль, ~а́я маши́на (private) car. **лёгкое** *sb.* lung; lights. **лёгкость, -и** lightness; easiness. **лего́нько** *adv.* slightly; gently. **лёгочный** lung, pulmonary. **ле́гче** *comp. of* **лёгкий, легко́**

лёд, льда (-у), *loc.* **-у** ice. **ледене́ть, -е́ю** *impf.* (*pf.* **за~, о~**) freeze; grow numb with cold. **ледене́ц, -нца́** fruit-drop. **ледени́стый** frozen; icy. **ледени́ть, -и́т** *impf.* (*pf.* **о~**) freeze; chill. **леденя́щий** chilling, icy.

ле́дник[1]**, -а** ice-house; ice-box; **ваго́н-~** refrigerator van. **ледни́к**[2]**, -а́** glacier. **леднико́вый** glacial; glacier; ice; refrigerator; **~ пери́од** Ice Age. **ледоко́л, -а** ice-breaker. **ледору́б, -а** ice-axe. **ледян|о́й** ice; icy; ice-cold; **~а́я гора́** tobogganing run, ice slope; iceberg.

лежа́ть, -жу́ *impf.* lie; be, be situated. **лежа́чий** lying (down); **~ больно́й** bed-patient.

ле́звие, -я (cutting) edge; blade.

лезть, -зу; лез *impf.* (*pf.* **по~**) climb; clamber, crawl; make one's way; come on, keep on; creep, get, go; fall out; come to pieces; **~ в пе́тлю** stick one's neck out; **~ на́ стену** climb up the wall; **не ~ за сло́вом в карма́н** not be at a loss for words.

лейбори́ст, -а Labourite. **лейбори́стский** Labour.

ле́йка, -и watering-can; pourer; funnel.

лейтена́нт, -а lieutenant.

лека́рственный medicinal. **лека́рство, -а** medicine, drug.

ле́ксика, -и vocabulary. **лексико́н, -а** lexicon; vocabulary. **лекси́ческий** lexical.

ле́ктор, -а lecturer. **лекцио́нный** lecture. **ле́кция, -и** lecture; **чита́ть ле́кцию** lecture, deliver a lecture.

леле́ять, -е́ю *impf.* (*pf.* **вз~**) cherish, foster; coddle, pamper.

лён, льна flax.

лени́вый lazy, idle; sluggish.

Ленингра́д, -а Leningrad.

лени́ться, -ню́сь, -нишься *impf.* (*pf.* **по~**) be lazy, be idle; +*inf.* be too lazy to.

ле́нта, -ы ribbon; band; tape; film; belt; track.

лентя́й, -я, -я́йка, -и lazy-bones; sluggard. **лентя́йничать, -аю** *impf.* be lazy, be idle, loaf. **лень, -и** laziness, idleness; indolence; **ей ~ встать** she is too lazy to get up.

леопа́рд, -а leopard.

леота́рд, -а leotard.

лепесто́к, -тка́ petal.

ле́пет, -а babble; prattle. **лепета́ть, -ечу́, -е́чешь** *impf.* (*pf.* **про~**) babble, prattle.

лепёшка, -и scone; tablet, lozenge, pastille.

лепи́ть, -плю́, -пишь *impf.* (*pf.* **вы~, за~, на~, с~**) model, fashion; mould; stick; **~ся** cling; crawl. **ле́пка, -и** modelling. **лепн|о́й** modelled, moulded; **~о́е украше́ние** stucco moulding.

лес, -а (-у), *loc.* **-у́**; *pl.* **-а́** forest, wood, woods;

timber; **тропи́ческий** ~ rainforest; *pl.* scaffold, scaffolding.

ле́са́, -ы *or* **-ы́**; *pl.* **ле́сы** fishing-line.

лесби́йский lesbian. **лесбия́нка, -и** lesbian.

леси́стый wooded, forest, woodland. **лесни́к, -а́** forester; gamekeeper. **лесни́чество, -а** forestry area. **лесни́чий** *sb.* forestry officer; forest warden; gamekeeper. **лесно́й** forest, forestry; timber.

лесо... *in comb.* forest, forestry; timber wood. **лесово́дство, -а** forestry. **~загото́вка, -и** logging, lumbering. **~защи́тный** forest-protection. **~насажде́ние, -я** afforestration; (forest) plantation. **~пи́лка, -и, ~пи́льня, -и**; *g.pl.* **-лен** sawmill. **~ру́б, -а** woodcutter, logger. **~спла́в, -а** (timber) rafting. **~сте́пь, -и** partially wooded steppe. **~ту́ндра, -ы** forest-tundra.

ле́стница, -ы stairs, staircase; ladder; steps. **ле́стничн|ый; ~ая кле́тка** (stair-)well.

ле́стный flattering; complimentary. **лесть, -и** flattery; adulation.

лёт, -а, *loc.* **-у́** flight, flying; **на ~у́** in the air, on the wing; hurriedly, in passing.

лета́, лет *pl.* years; age; **в ~х** elderly, getting on (in years); **на ста́рости лет** in one's old age; **прошло́ мно́го лет** many years passed; **ско́лько вам лет?** how old are you? **сре́дних лет** middle-aged.

лета́тельный flying. **лета́ть, -а́ю** *impf.*, **лете́ть, лечу́** *impf.* (*pf.* **полете́ть**) fly; rush, tear; fall, drop.

ле́тний summer. **ле́тник, -а** annual.

лётный flying, flight; ~ **соста́в** air-crew.

ле́то, -а; *pl.* **-а́** summer; *pl.* years. **ле́том** *adv.* in summer.

летопи́сец, -сца chronicler, annalist. **ле́топись, -и** chronicle, annals.

летосчисле́ние, -я (system of) chronology; era.

лету́н, -а́, лету́нья, -и flyer; rolling stone, drifter. **лету́ч|ий** flying; passing, ephemeral; brief; volatile; **~ий листо́к** leaflet; **~ий ми́тинг** emergency meeting, extraordinary meeting, impromptu meeting; **~ая мышь** bat; hurricane lamp. **лету́чка, -и** leaflet; emergency meeting; mobile detachment, road patrol; mobile dressing station. **лётчик, -а, -чица, -ы** pilot; aviator, flyer; **~-испыта́тель** test pilot.

лече́бница, -ы clinic, hospital. **лече́бный** medical; medicinal. **лече́ние, -я** (medical) treatment; cure. **лечи́ть, -чу́, -чишь** *impf.* treat (**от** for); **~ся** be given, have treatment (**от** for); *+i.* take a course of.

лечу́ *etc.*: *see* **лете́ть, лечи́ть**

лечь, ля́гу, ля́жешь; лёг, -ла́ *pf.* (*impf.* **ложи́ться**) lie, lie down; go to bed, turn in; +**на**+*a.* fall on, rest on, lie on.

лещ, -а́ bream.

лже... *in comb.* false, pseudo-, mock-. **лженау́ка, -и** pseudo-science. **~свиде́тель, -я** *m.*, **~ница, -ы** perjuror, perjured witness. **~свиде́тельство, -а** false witness. **~уче́ние, -я** false doctrine.

лжец, -а́ liar. **лжи́вый** lying; mendacious; false, deceitful.

ли, ль *interrog. part.* & *conj.* whether, if; **ли,... ли** whether ... or; **ра́но ли, по́здно ли** sooner or later.

либера́л, -а liberal. **либерали́зм, -а** liberalism; tolerance. **либера́льный** liberal; tolerant.

ли́бо *conj.* or; **~... ~** either ... or.

ли́вень, -вня *m.* heavy shower, downpour, rainstorm; cloud-burst; hail.

ливре́йный livery, liveried. **ливре́я, -и** livery.

ли́га, -и league.

ли́дер, -а leader; flotilla leader. **ли́дерство, -а** leadership; first place, lead. **лиди́ровать, -рую** *impf.* & *pf.* be in the lead.

лиза́ть, лижу́, -ешь *impf.*, **лизну́ть, -ну́, -нёшь** *pf.* lick.

лик, -а face.

ликвида́тор, -а liquidator. **ликвида́ция, -и** liquidation; elimination, abolition; ~ **долго́в** settlement of debts. **ликвиди́ровать, -рую** *impf.* & *pf.* liquidate, wind up; eliminate, abolish.

ликёр, -а liqueur.

ликова́ние, -я rejoicing, exultation, triumph. **ликова́ть, -ку́ю** *impf.* rejoice, exult, triumph.

лиле́йный lily-white; liliaceous. **ли́лия, -и** lily.

лило́вый mauve, violet.

лима́н, -а estuary.

лими́т, -а quota; limit. **лимити́ровать, -рую** *impf.* & *pf.* establish a quota, maximum in respect of.

лимо́н, -а lemon. **лимона́д, -а** lemonade; fruit squash. **лимо́нн|ый** lemon; **~ая кислота́** citric acid.

ли́мфа, -ы lymph.

лингви́ст, -а linguist. **лингви́стика, -и** linguistics. **лингвисти́ческий** linguistic.

лине́йка, -и ruler; rule; line. **лине́йный** linear, line; of the line; ~ **кора́бль** battleship.

ли́нза, -ы lens.

ли́ния, -и line. **лино́ваный** lined, ruled. **линова́ть, -ну́ю** *impf.* (*pf.* **на~**) rule.

линогравю́ра, -ы linocut.

лино́леум, -а lino(leum).

Линч, -а; зако́н ~а, суд ~а lynch law.

линю́чий liable to fade, not fast. **линя́лый** faded, discoloured; moulted.

линя́ть, -я́ет *impf.* (*pf.* **вы́~, по~, с~**) fade, lose colour; run; cast the coat, skin; shed hair; moult; slough.

ли́па, -ы lime(-tree).

ли́пкий; -пок, -пка́, -о sticky, adhesive. **ли́пнуть, -ну; лип** *impf.* stick, adhere.

липня́к, -а́ lime-grove. **ли́повый** lime, linden.

ли́ра, -ы lyre. **ли́рик, -а** lyric poet. **ли́рика, -и** lyric poetry. **лири́ческий** lyric; lyrical.

лири́чный lyrical.
лиса́, -ы́; *pl.* **-ы** fox. **лисёнок, -нка**; *pl.* **-ся́та, -ся́т** fox-cub. **ли́сий** fox, fox's. **лиси́ца, -ы** fox.
лист, -а́; *pl.* **-ы́** *or* **-ья, -о́в** *or* **-ьев** leaf; sheet; quire; page; form; certificate; **в ~** in folio; **игра́ть с ~а́** play at sight; **корректу́ра в ~а́х** page proofs. **листа́ть, -а́ю** *impf.* leaf through, turn over the pages of. **листва́, -ы́** leaves, foliage. **ли́ственный** deciduous. **листо́вка, -и** leaflet. **листово́й** sheet, plate; leaf. **листо́к, -тка́** *dim. of* **лист**; leaflet; form, pro-forma. **листопа́д, -а** fall of the leaves.
лит... *abbr.* (*of* **литерату́ра, -ту́рный**) *in comb.* literature, literary.
Литва́, -ы Lithuania.
лите́йная *sb.* foundry, smelting house. **лите́йный** founding, casting. **лите́йщик, -а** founder.
ли́тера, -ы type, letter. **литера́тор, -а** literary man, man of letters. **литерату́ра, -ы** literature. **литерату́рн|ый** literary; **~ое воровство́** plagiarism.
ли́тий, -я lithium.
лито́вец, -вца, лито́вка, -и Lithuanian. **лито́вский** Lithuanian.
лито́й cast.
литр, -а litre. **литро́вый** litre.
лить, лью, льёшь; лил, -а́, -о *impf.* (*pf.* **с~**) pour; shed, spill; found, cast, mould. **литьё, -я́** founding, casting, moulding; castings, mouldings. **ли́ться, льётся; ли́лся, -а́сь, ли́ло́сь** *impf.* flow; stream, pour.
лиф, -а bodice.
лифт, -а lift, elevator. **лифтёр, -а** lift operator.
ли́фчик, -а bodice; bra.
лиха́ч, -а́ (driver of) smart cab; reckless driver, road-hog. **лихо́й**[1]; **лих, -а́, -о** dashing, spirited.
лихо́й[2]; **лих, -а́, -о, ли́хи́** evil.
лихора́дка, -и fever. **лихора́дочный** feverish.
лицева́ть, -цу́ю *impf.* (*pf.* **пере~**) turn. **лицев|о́й** facial; exterior; **~а́я ру́копись** illuminated manuscript; **~а́я пе́тля** plain (stitch); **~а́я сторона́** facade, front; right side; obverse.
лицеме́р, -а hypocrite, dissembler. **лицеме́рие, -я** hypocrisy, dissimulation. **лицеме́рный** hypocritical.
лице́нзия, -и licence.
лицо́, -а́; *pl.* **-а** face; exterior; right side; person; **быть к лицу́**+*d.* suit, become; befit; **в лице́**+*g.* in the person of; **знать в ~** know by sight; **~м к лицу́** face to face; **на нём лица́ нет** he looks awful; **невзира́я на ли́ца** without respect of persons; **от лица́**+*g.* in the name of, on behalf of; **сказа́ть в ~**+*d.* say to his, *etc.*, face; **черты́ лица́** features. **личи́на, -ы** mask; guise; escutcheon, keyplate. **личи́нка, -и** larva, grub; maggot. **ли́чно** *adv.* personally, in person. **лично́й** face; facial. **ли́чность, -и** personality; person, individual; *pl.* personalities, personal remarks. **ли́чный** personal; individual; private; **~ секрета́рь** private secretary; **~ соста́в** staff, personnel.
лиша́й, -я lichen; herpes; **опоя́сывающий ~** shingles. **лиша́йник, -а** lichen.
лиша́ть(ся, -а́ю(сь *impf. of* **лиши́ть(ся**
ли́шек, -шка (-у) surplus; **с ли́шком** odd, and more, just over.
лише́нец, -нца disfranchised person. **лише́ние, -я** deprivation; privation, hardship; **~ гражда́нских прав** disfranchisement. **лишённый; -ён, -ена́**+*g.* lacking in, devoid of. **лиши́ть, -шу́** *pf.* (*impf.* **лиша́ть**) +*g.* deprive of; **~ себя́ жи́зни** take one's own life; **~ся**+*g.* lose, be deprived of. **ли́шн|ий** superfluous; unnecessary; left over; spare, odd; **~ раз** once more; **с ~им** odd, and more.
лишь *adv.* only; *conj.* as soon as; **~ бы** if only, provided that; **~ (то́лько)** as soon as.
лоб, лба, *loc.* **лбу** forehead; brow.
ло́бби *nt. indecl.* lobby. **лобби́ст, -а** lobbyist.
ло́бзик, -а fret-saw.
ло́бн|ый frontal; front; **~ое ме́сто** place of execution. **лобово́й** frontal, front.
лове́ц, -ца́ fisherman; hunter. **лови́ть, -влю́, -вишь** *impf.* (*pf.* **пойма́ть**) catch, try to catch; **~ на сло́ве** take at his, *etc.*, word; **~ ста́нцию** try to pick up a (radio-)station.
ло́вкий; -вок, -вка́, -о adroit, dexterous, deft; cunning, smart; comfortable. **ло́вкость, -и** adroitness, dexterity, deftness; cunning, smartness.
ло́вля, -и; *g.pl.* **-вель** catching, hunting; fishing-ground. **лову́шка, -и** snare, trap.
ло́вче *comp. of* **ло́вкий**
логари́фм, -а logarithm. **логарифми́ческ|ий; ~ая лине́йка** slide-rule.
ло́гика, -и logic. **логи́ческий** logical. **логи́чность, -и** logicality.
ло́говище, -а, ло́гово, -а den, lair.
логопе́д, -а speech therapist. **логопе́дия, -и** speech therapy.
ло́дка, -и, ло́дочка, -и boat. **ло́дочник, -а** boatman. **ло́дочный** boat, boat-.
ло́дырничать, -аю *impf.* loaf, idle about. **ло́дырь, -я** *m.* loafer, idler.
ло́жа, -и box; (masonic) lodge.
ложби́на, -ы hollow.
ло́же, -а couch; bed; channel; gun-stock.
ложи́ться, -жу́сь *impf. of* **лечь**
ло́жка, -и spoon; spoonful.
ло́жн|ый false, erroneous; sham, dummy. **ложь, лжи** lie, falsehood.
лоза́, -ы́; *pl.* **-ы** vine. **лозня́к, -а́** willow-bush.
ло́зунг, -а slogan, catchword; watchword; pass-word.
локомоти́в, -а locomotive.
ло́кон, -а lock, curl, ringlet.
локотни́к, -а́ (chair-, sofa-)arm. **ло́коть, -ктя**; *pl.* **-и, -е́й** *m.* elbow.

лом, -а; *pl.* **-ы, -о́в** crowbar; scrap, waste. **ло́маный** broken. **лома́ть, -а́ю** *impf.* (*pf.* **по~, с~**) break; fracture; rack, cause to ache; **~ ка́мень** quarry stone; **~ ру́ки** wring one's hands; **~ себе́ го́лову** rack one's brains; **меня́ всего́ лома́ло** I was aching all over; **~ся** break; crack; pose, put on airs; make difficulties, be obstinate.

ломба́рд, -а pawnshop. **ломба́рдн|ый; ~ая квита́нция** pawn-ticket.

ло́мберный; ~ стол card-table.

ломи́ть, ло́мит *impf.* break; break through, rush; *impers.* cause to ache; **у меня́ ло́мит спи́ну** my back aches; **~ся** be (near to) breaking; +**в**+*a.* force; +**от**+*g.* be bursting, crammed, loaded, with. **ло́мка, -и** breaking; *pl.* quarry. **ло́мкий; -мок, -мка́, -о** fragile, brittle.

ломов|о́й dray, draught; **~о́й изво́зчик** drayman, carter; **~а́я ло́шадь** cart-horse, dray-horse, draught-horse.

ломо́та, -ы ache (in one's bones).

ломо́ть, -мтя́; *pl.* **-мти́** *m.* large slice, round; hunk; chunk. **ло́мтик, -а** slice.

Ло́ндон, -а London. **ло́ндонец, -ца, ло́ндонка, -ки** Londoner. **ло́ндонский** London.

ло́но, -а bosom, lap.

лопа́рь, -я́ *m.*, **лопа́рка, -и** Lapp, Lapplander. **лопа́рский** Lapp, Lappish.

ло́пасть, -и; *pl.* **-и, -е́й** blade; fan, vane; paddle; lamina; **~ оси́** axle-tree.

лопа́та, -ы spade; shovel. **лопа́тка, -и** shoulder-blade; shovel; trowel; blade.

ло́паться, -аюсь *impf.*, **ло́пнуть, -ну** *pf.* burst; split, crack; break; fail, be a failure; go bankrupt, crash.

лопоу́хий lop-eared.

лопу́х, -а́ burdock.

лоси́на, -ы elk-skin, chamois leather; elk-meat; *pl.* buckskins. **лоси́ный** elk, elk-.

лоск, -а (-у) lustre, gloss, shine.

лоску́т, -а́; *pl.* **-ы́** *or* **-ья, -о́в** *or* **-ьев** rag, shred, scrap. **лоску́тн|ый** scrappy; made of scraps, patchwork; **~ое одея́ло** patchwork quilt.

лосни́ться, -ню́сь *impf.* be glossy, shine.

лососи́на, -ы salmon. **ло́со́сь, -я** *m.* salmon.

лось, -я; *pl.* **-и, -е́й** *m.* elk.

лосьо́н, -а lotion; aftershave; make-up remover.

лот, -а lead, plummet.

лотере́йный lottery, raffle. **лотере́я, -и** lottery, raffle.

лото́ *nt. indecl.* lotto, bingo.

лото́к, -тка́ hawker's stand; hawker's tray; chute; gutter; trough. **лото́чник, -а, -ница, -ы** hawker.

поха́нка, -и, лоха́нь, -и (wash-)tub.

лохма́тить, -а́чу *impf.* (*pf.* **раз~**) tousle, ruffle; **~ся** become tousled, be dishevelled. **лохма́тый** shaggy(-haired); dishevelled, tousled.

лохмо́тья, -ьев *pl.* rags.

ло́цман, -а pilot; pilot-fish.

лошади́н|ый horse; equine; **~ая си́ла** horsepower. **лоша́дка, -и** (small) horse; hobby-horse; rocking-horse; **ло́шадь, -и**; *pl.* **-и, -е́й,** *i.* **-дьми́** *or* **-дя́ми** horse.

лощёный glossy, polished.

лощи́на, -ы hollow, depression.

лощи́ть, -щу́ *impf.* (*pf.* **на~**) polish; gloss, glaze.

лоя́льность, -и fairness; honesty; loyalty. **лоя́льный** fair; honest; loyal.

л.с. *abbr.* (*of* ***лошади́ная си́ла***) horsepower.

луб, -а bast. **лубо́к, -бка́** splint; wood-block; popular print. **лубо́чн|ый; ~ая карти́нка** popular print.

луг, -а, *loc.* **-у́**; *pl.* **-а́** meadow.

луди́ть, лужу́, лу́дишь *impf.* (*pf.* **вы́~, по~**) tin.

лу́жа, -и puddle, pool.

лужа́йка, -и grass-plot, lawn, (forest-)glade.

луже́ние, -я tinning. **лужёный** tinned, tin-plate. **лужу́** *etc.*: *see* **луди́ть**

лу́за, -ы pocket.

лук[1], -а (-у) onions; **зелёный лук** spring onions; **~-шнитт** chives.

лук[2], -а bow.

лука́вить, -влю *impf.* (*pf.* **с~**) be cunning. **лука́вство, -а** craftiness; slyness. **лука́вый** crafty, sly, cunning; arch.

лу́ковица, -ы onion; bulb; onion dome. **лу́ковичный** onion-shaped; bulbous.

лукомо́рье, -я cove, bay.

луна́, -ы́; *pl.* **-ы** moon. **луна́тик, -а** sleep-walker, somnambulist.

луко́шко, -а; *pl.* **-и** punnet, bast basket.

лу́нка, -и hole; socket, alveolus.

лу́нник, -а lunar probe. **лу́нн|ый** moon; lunar; **~ый ка́мень** moonstone; **~ая ночь** moonlit night; **~ый свет** moonlight. **луно-хо́д, -а** lunar rover, Moon buggy.

лу́па, -ы magnifying-glass.

лупи́ть, -плю́, -пишь *impf.* (*pf.* **об~, с~**) peel (off); bark; fleece; **~ся** peel (off), scale; come off, chip.

луч, -а́ ray; beam. **лучево́й** ray, beam; radial, radiating; radiation. **лучеза́рный** radiant, resplendent. **лучеиспуска́ние, -я** radiation. **лучепреломле́ние, -я** refraction.

лучи́на, -ы spill; chip; splinter.

лучи́стый radiant; radial.

лу́чше better; **~ всего́, ~ всех** best of all; **нам ~ верну́ться** we had better go back; **тем ~** so much the better. **лу́чш|ий** better; best; **в ~ем слу́чае** at best; **всего́ ~его!** all the (very) best! **к ~ему** for the better.

лущёный; -ён, -ена́ hulled, shelled, husked. **лущи́ть, -щу́** *impf.* (*pf.* **об~**) shell, husk, hull, pod.

лы́жа, -и ski; snow-shoe. **лы́жник, -а** skier. **лы́жный** ski, skiing; **~ спорт** skiing. **лыжня́, -и́** ski-track.

лы́ко, -а bast.

лысе́ть, -е́ю *impf.* (*pf.* **об~, по~**) grow bald.

лы́сина, -ы bald spot, bald patch; blaze, star, patch. **лы́сый; лыс, -á, -о** bald.
ль *see* **ли**
льва *etc.*: *see* **лев. львёнок, -нка**; *pl.* **львя́та, -я́т** lion-cub. **льви́ный** lion, lion's; ~ **зев** snapdragon. **льви́ца, -ы** lioness.
льго́та, -ы privilege; advantage. **льго́тн|ый** privileged; favourable; ~**ый биле́т** complimentary ticket, free ticket; **на** ~**ых усло́виях** on easy terms.
льда *etc.*: *see* **лёд. льди́на, -ы** block of ice; ice-floe. **льди́нка, -и** piece of ice. **льди́стый** icy; ice-covered.
льна *etc.*: *see* **лён. льново́дство, -а** flax-growing. **льнопряде́ние, -я** flax-spinning. **льнопряди́льный** flax-spinning. **льнопряди́льня, -и**; *g.pl.* **-лен** flax-mill.
льнуть, -ну, -нёшь *impf.* (*pf.* **при**~) +**к**+*d.* cling to, stick to; have a weakness for; make up to, try to get in with.
льняно́й flax, flaxen; linen; linseed.
льсте́ц, -á flatterer. **льсти́вый** flattering; smooth-tongued. **льстить, льщу** *impf.* (*pf.* **по**~) +*d.* flatter; gratify; +*a.* delude; ~**ся**+**на**+*a.* be tempted by.
лью *etc.*: *see* **лить**
любе́зность, -и courtesy; politeness, civility; kindness; compliment. **любе́зн|ый** courteous; polite; obliging; kind, amiable; **бу́дьте** ~**ы** be so kind (as to).
люби́мец, -мца, -мица, -ы pet, favourite. **люби́мый** beloved, loved; favourite. **люби́тель, -я** *m.*, **-ница, -ы** lover; amateur. **люби́тельский** amateur; amateurish; choice. **люби́ть, -блю́, -бишь** *impf.* love; like, fond of; need, require.
любова́ться, -бу́юсь *impf.* (*pf.* **по**~) admire; feast one's eyes (**на**+*a.* on).
любо́вник, -а lover. **любо́вница, -ы** mistress. **любо́вный** love-; loving. **любо́вь, -бви́**, *i.* **-бо́вью** love.
любозна́тельный inquisitive.
любо́й any; either; *sb.* anyone, anybody.
любопы́тн|ый curious; inquisitive; prying; interesting; ~**о знать** it would be interesting to know. **любопы́тство, -а** curiosity. **любопы́тствовать, -твую** *impf.* (*pf.* **по**~) be curious.
лю́бящий loving, affectionate; ~ **вас** yours affectionately.
лю́ди, -е́й, -ям, -дьми́, -ях *pl.* people; men; servants; **в** ~ away from home; **на лю́дях** in the presence of others, in company. **лю́дный** populous; crowded. **людое́д, -а** cannibal; ogre. **людско́й** human; servants'.
люк, -а hatch, hatchway; trap; manhole.
люкс, -а luxury (class).
Лю́ксембу́рг, -а Luxemburg.
лю́ксовый luxury(-class).
лю́лька, -и cradle.
лю́стра, -ы chandelier.
лю́тик, -а buttercup.
лю́тый; лют, -á, -о ferocious, fierce, cruel.
люце́рна, -ы lucerne.
ля *nt.indecl.* A; lah.
ляга́ть, -а́ю *impf.*, **лягну́ть, -ну́, -нёшь** *pf.* kick; ~**ся** kick.
ля́гу *etc.*: *see* **лечь**
лягуша́тник, -а paddling-pool. **лягу́шка, -и** frog.
ля́жка, -и thigh, haunch.
ля́згать, -аю *impf.* clank, clang; +*i.* rattle, clatter; **он ля́згал зуба́ми** his teeth were chattering.
ля́мка, -и strap; **тяну́ть ля́мку** toil, sweat, drudge.
ля́пис, -а silver nitrate, lunar caustic.
ля́псус, -а blunder; slip (*of the tongue*, *of the pen*).

М

м *letter*: *see* **эм**
м *abbr.* (*of* **метр**) m, metre(s).
м. *abbr.* (*of* **мину́та**) min., minute(s).
мавзоле́й, -я mausoleum.
мавр, -а, маврита́нка, -и Moor. **маврита́нский** Moorish; Moresque; Mauretanian.
магази́н, -а shop; store; depot; magazine. **магази́нный** *adj.*; ~ **вор** shoplifter.
магисте́рский master's. **маги́стр, -а** (holder of) master's degree; head of knightly or monastic order.
магистра́ль, -и main; main line, main road.
маги́ческий magic, magical. **ма́гия, -и** magic.
ма́гний, -я magnesium.
магни́т, -а magnet. **магни́тный** magnetic. **магнито́ла, -ы** radio cassette (recorder). **магнитоле́нта, -ы** magnetic tape. **магнитоте́ка, -и** tape library. **магнитофо́н, -а** tape-recorder; **видеокассе́тный** ~ video recorder. **магнитофо́нн|ый;** ~**ая за́пись** tape-recording.
мада́м *f.indecl.* madam, madame; governess; dressmaker.
мадемуазе́ль, -и mademoiselle; governess.
Мадри́д, -а Madrid.
мадья́р, -а; *pl.* **-ы, -я́р, мадья́рка, -и** Magyar, Hungarian. **мадья́рский** Magyar.
мажо́р, -а major (key); cheerful mood, good spirits. **мажо́рный** major; cheerful.
ма́заный dirty, soiled; cob, daub, clay, **ма́зать, ма́жу** *impf.* (*pf.* **вы**~, **за**~, **из**~, **на**~, **по**~, **про**~) oil, grease, lubricate; smear, spread; soil, dirty; daub; miss; ~**ся** get dirty; soil; make up. **мазо́к, -зка́** touch, dab; smear; miss. **мазу́т, -а** fuel oil. **мазь, -и** ointment; grease.

майс, -а maize. **майсов|ый; ~ая ка́ша** polenta.

май, -я May.

ма́йка, -и singlet, vest, T-shirt; **се́тчатая ~** string vest.

майоне́з, -а mayonnaise.

майо́р, -а major.

майора́н, -а marjoram.

ма́йский May; May-day; **~ жук** cockchafer.

мак, -а (-у) poppy, poppy-seeds.

мака́ть, -а́ю *impf.* (*pf.* **макну́ть**) dip.

маке́т, -а model; dummy.

макну́ть, -ну́, -нёшь *pf. of* **мака́ть**

ма́ковка, -и poppy-head; crown; cupola. **ма́ковый** poppy; poppy-seed.

макре́ль, -и mackerel.

максима́льный maximum. **ма́ксимум, -а** maximum; at most.

макулату́ра, -ы paper for recycling.

маку́шка, -и top, summit; crown.

мал *etc.*: *see* **ма́лый**

малева́ть, -лю́ю *impf.* (*pf.* **на~**) paint.

мале́йший least, slightest. **ма́ленький** little; small; slight; young.

мали́на, -ы raspberries; raspberry-bush, raspberry-cane; raspberry tea. **мали́нник, -а** raspberry-bushes. **мали́новый** raspberry; crimson.

ма́ло *adv.* little, few; not enough; **~ кто** few (people); **~ ли что!** what does it matter? **~ ли что мо́жет случи́ться** who knows what may happen; **~ того́** moreover; **~ того́ что...** not only ..., it is not enough that ...; **э́того ма́ло** this is not enough.

мало... *in comb.* (too) little, small-, low-, under-. **малова́жный** of little importance, insignificant. **~вероя́тный** unlikely, improbable. **~ве́сный** light, light-weight. **~во́дье, -я** shortage of water. **~во́льтный** low-voltage. **~гра́мотный** semi-literate; crude, ignorant. **~достове́рный** improbable; not well-founded. **~ду́шие, -я** faintheartedness, cowardice. **~ду́шный** fainthearted, cowardly. **~жи́рный** low-fat. **~заме́тный** barely visible, hardly noticeable; ordinary, undistinguished. **~земе́лье, -я** shortage of (arable) land. **~земе́льный** without enough (arable) land; land-hungry. **~изве́данный** little-known. **~иму́щий** needy, indigent, poor. **~калори́йный** low-calorie. **~кро́вие, -я** anaemia. **~кро́вный** anaemic. **~ле́тний** young; juvenile; minor, under-age. **~ле́тство, -а** infancy; nonage, minority. **~лю́дный** not crowded, unfrequented; poorly attended; thinly populated. **~обеспе́ченный** needy, poverty-stricken. **~опла́чиваемый** low-paid, badly-paid. **~ро́слый** undersized, stunted. **~содержа́тельный** empty, shallow. **~употреби́тельный** infrequent, rarely used. **~форма́тный** miniature. **~це́нный** of little value. **~чи́сленный** small (in number), few.

мало-ма́льски *adv.* in the slightest degree; at all. **малома́льский** slightest, most insignificant. **мало-пома́лу** *adv.* little by little, bit by bit.

ма́л|ый; мал, -а́ little, (too) small; **без ~ого** almost, all but; **са́мое ~ое** at the least; **с ~ых лет** from childhood; *sb.* fellow, chap; lad, boy. **малы́ш, -а́** child, kiddy; little boy. **ма́льчик, -а** boy, lad; child; apprentice. **мальчико́вый** boy's, boys'. **мальчи́шеский** boyish; childish, puerile. **мальчи́шка, -и** *m.* urchin, boy. **мальчуга́н, -а** little boy. **малю́тка, -и** *c.g.* baby, little one.

маля́р, -а́ (house-)painter, decorator.

маляри́я, -и malaria.

ма́ма, -ы mother, mummy, mamma. **мама́ша, -и, ма́менька, -и** mummy, mamma. **ма́менькин, ма́мин** mother's.

ма́монт, -а mammoth.

мандари́н, -а mandarin, tangerine.

манда́т, -а warrant; mandate, credentials. **манда́тн|ый** mandate, mandated; **~ая систе́ма голосова́ния** card-vote system.

манёвр, -а manoeuvre; shunting. **манёвренный** manoeuvre, manoeuvring, manoeuvrable; shunting, switching. **маневри́ровать, -рую** *impf.* (*pf.* **с~**) manoeuvre; shunt; *+i.* make good use of, use to advantage. **маневро́вый** shunting.

мане́ж, -а riding-school, manège; (*circus*) ring; **инспе́ктор ~а** ringmaster; **спорти́вный ~** sports hall; **(де́тский) ~** play-pen. **мане́жик, -а** play-pen.

манеке́н, -а lay figure; dummy; mannequin. **манеке́нщик, -а, -щица, -ы** model, mannequin.

мане́р, -а, мане́ра, -ы manner, way; style. **мане́рный** affected; precious.

манже́та, -ы cuff.

маникю́рша, -ы manicurist.

манипули́ровать, -рую *impf.* manipulate. **манипуля́ция, -и** manipulation; machination, intrigue.

мани́ть, -ню́, -нишь *impf.* (*pf.* **по~**) beckon; attract; lure, allure.

маните́ст, -а manifesto. **манифеста́нт, -а** demonstrator. **манифеста́ция, -и** demonstration. **манифести́ровать, -рую** *impf.* demonstrate.

мани́шка, -и false shirt-front, dickey.

ма́ния, -и mania; passion, craze; **~ вели́чия** megalomania.

манки́ровать, -рую *impf.* & *pf.* be absent; *+i.* neglect; *+d.* be impolite to.

ма́нн|ый; ~ая ка́ша, ~ая крупа semolina.

мано́метр, -а pressure-gauge, manometer.

ма́нтия, -и cloak; mantle; robe, gown.

мануфакту́ра, -ы manufacture; textiles; workshop; (textile) mill.

мара́тель, -я *m.* dauber; scribbler. **мара́ть, -а́ю** *impf.* (*pf.* **вы~, за~, из~, на~**) soil, stain; daub; scribble; cross out, strike out; **~ся** get dirty; soil one's hands.

марафо́нец, -ца marathon runner. **марафо́нский; ~ бег** marathon.
ма́рганец, -нца manganese.
маргари́тка, -и daisy.
марино́ванный pickled. **маринова́ть, -ну́ю** *impf.* (*pf.* **за~**) pickle, marinate; delay, hold up, shelve.
марионе́тка, -и puppet, marionette. **марионе́точный** puppet, marionette.
ма́рка, -и stamp; mark; counter; brand, make; trade-mark; grade, sort; name, reputation.
ма́ркетинг, -а marketing.
ма́ркий easily soiled. **маркирова́ть, -ру́ю** *impf.* & *pf.* mark; brand.
ма́рлевый gauze. **ма́рля, -и** gauze; butter muslin, cheesecloth.
мармела́д, -а fruit jellies. **мармела́дка, -и** fruit jelly.
мармори́ровать, -рую *impf.* & *pf.* marble.
Марс, -а Mars.
Марсе́ль, -я Marseilles.
марсиа́нин, -а; *pl.* **-а́не, -а́н, марсиа́нка, -и** Martian. **марсиа́нский** Martian.
март, -а March. **ма́ртовский** March.
марты́шка, -и marmoset; monkey.
марш, -а march; **~ проте́ста** protest march.
марширова́ть, -ру́ю *impf.* march; **~ на ме́сте** mark time. **марширо́вка, -и** marching.
маршру́т, -а route, itinerary. **маршру́тка, -и, маршру́тное та́кси** fixed-route taxi.
ма́ска, -и mask. **маскара́д, -а** masked ball; masquerade. **маскирова́ть, -ру́ю** *impf.* (*pf.* **за~**) mask, disguise; camouflage. **маскиро́вка, -и** masking, disguise; camouflage. **маскиро́вщик, -а** camouflage expert.
Ма́сленица, -ы Shrovetide; (Mardi Gras) carnival. **маслёнка, -и** butter-dish; oil-can. **ма́слен|ый** buttered; oiled; oily; unctuous; **~ая неде́ля** Shrovetide. **масли́на, -ы** olive. **ма́слить, -лю** *impf.* (*pf.* **на~, по~**) butter; oil, grease. **ма́сло, -а**; *pl.* **-а́, ма́сел, -сла́м** butter; oil; oil paints, oils; **как по ма́слу** swimmingly. **маслобо́йка, -и** churn; oil press. **маслобо́йный заво́д, маслобо́йня, -и**; *g.pl.* **-о́ен, маслозаво́д, -а** creamery; dairy; oil-mill. **масломе́р, -а** oil gauge; dipstick. **масляни́стый** oily. **ма́сляный** oil; butter.
ма́сса, -ы mass; paste, pulp; a lot, lots.
масса́ж, -а massage; **то́чечный ~** shiatsu, acupressure.
масси́в, -а massif; expanse, tract. **масси́вный** massive.
массо́вка, -и mass-meeting; outing; crowd scene. **ма́ссов|ый** mass; popular; bulk; **~ая поста́вка** bulk delivery; **~ые сце́ны** crowd scenes.
маста́к, -а́ expert, past master. **ма́стер, -а**; *pl.* **-а́, мастери́ца, -ы** foreman, forewoman; master craftsman, skilled worker; expert, master; (*sport*) vet(eran); **~ по ремо́нту** repairman; **телевизио́нный ~** TV repairman; **~ на все ру́ки** jack of all trades. **мастери́ть, -рю́** *impf.* (*pf.* **с~**) make, build, construct. **мастерска́я** *sb.* workshop; shop; studio. **мастерско́й** masterly. **мастерство́, -а́** trade, craft; skill, craftsmanship.
масти́ка, -и mastic; putty; floor-polish.
масти́тый venerable.
масть, -и; *pl.* **-и, -е́й** colour; suit; **ходи́ть в ~** follow suit.
масшта́б, -а scale. **масшта́бность, -и** (large) scale, range, dimensions. **масшта́бный** scale; large-scale.
мат, -а checkmate, mate; **объяви́ть ~** mate, checkmate.
матема́тик, -а mathematician. **матема́тика, -и** mathematics. **математи́ческ|ий** mathematical; **~ое обеспе́чение** (computer) software.
материа́л, -а material; stuff. **материа́льный** material; physical; financial, pecuniary, economic.
матери́к, -а́ continent; mainland; subsoil. **материко́вый** continental.
матери́нский maternal, motherly. **матери́нство, -а** maternity, motherhood.
мате́рия, -и material, cloth, stuff; matter; pus; subject, topic.
ма́тка, -и uterus, womb; female, queen; (submarine) tender, depot ship.
ма́тов|ый matt; dull; suffused; **~ое стекло́** frosted glass.
матра́с, -а, матра́ц, -а mattress; **надувно́й ~** air bed, inflatable mattress.
ма́трица, -ы matrix; die, mould.
матро́с, -а sailor, seaman. **матро́ска, -и** sailor's wife; sailor's blouse, sailor blouse. **матро́сский** sailor's, sailors', seaman's, seamens'; **~ воротни́к** sailor collar.
ма́тушка, -и mother; priest's wife.
матч, -а match; **междунаро́дный ~** test (match); **повто́рный ~** return match.
мать, ма́тери, *i.* **-рью**; *pl.* **-тери, -ре́й** mother; **бу́дущая ~** expectant mother; **~-одино́чка** single mother.
ма́фия, -и Mafia.
мах, -а (-у) swing, stroke; **дать ~у** let a chance slip, make a blunder; **одни́м ~ом** at one stroke, in a trice; **с ~у** rashly, without thinking. **маха́ть, машу́, ма́шешь** *impf.*, **махну́ть, -ну́, -нёшь** *pf.+i.* wave; brandish; wag; flap; go, travel; rush, leap; jump. **махови́к, -а́** fly-wheel. **махов|о́й; ~о́е колесо́** fly-wheel; **~ы́е пе́рья** wing-feathers.
ма́хонький very little, small, tiny.
махро́в|ый double; double-dyed, dyed-in-the-wool; terry; **~ая ткань** terry-towelling.
ма́чеха, -и stepmother.
ма́чта, -ы mast.
маши́на, -ы machine; mechanism; engine; (motor) vehicle; car; bicycle; train; **(посудо)мо́ечная ~** dishwasher; **~ «ско́рой по́мощи»** ambulance. **машина́льный** mechanical; automatic, absent-minded; machine-like. **машинизи́ровать, -рую** *impf.* & *pf.* mechanize.

машини́ст, -а operator, engineer; engine-driver; scene-shifter. **машини́стка, -и** typist; **~-стенографи́стка** shorthand-typist. **маши́нка, -и** machine; typewriter; sewing-machine; clippers. **маши́нно-тра́кторн|ый; ~ая ста́нция** machine and tractor station. **маши́нн|ый** machine, engine; mechanical, mechanized; power-driven; **~ое бюро́** typing bureau; **~ая гра́фика** computer graphics; **~ый зал** engine-room; machine-room; **~ое обуче́ние** computer-aided learning. **машинопи́сный** typewritten; **~ текст** typescript. **маши́нопись, -и** typewriting; typescript. **машинострое́ние, -я** mechanical engineering, machine-building.

мая́к, -а́ lighthouse; beacon.

ма́ятник, -а pendulum. **ма́ять, ма́ю** *impf.* wear out, exhaust, weary; **~ся** suffer, languish; loaf, loiter about.

мая́чить, -чу *impf.* loom, loom up; appear indistinctly.

мг *abbr.* (*of* **миллигра́мм**) mg, milligram(s).

мгла, -ы haze; mist; gloom, darkness. **мгли́стый** hazy.

мгнове́ние, -я instant, moment. **мгнове́нный** instantaneous, momentary.

МГУ *abbr.* (*of* ***Моско́вский госуда́рственный университе́т***) Moscow State University.

ме́бель, -и furniture. **ме́бельщик, -а** upholsterer; furniture-dealer. **меблиро́ванный** furnished. **меблирова́ть, -ру́ю** *impf.* & *pf.* furnish. **меблиро́вка, -и** furnishing; furniture.

мег..., мега... *in comb.* meg-, mega-. **мегава́тт, -а**; *g.pl.* **-а́тт** megawatt. **~ге́рц, -а** megacycle. **мего́м, -а** megohm. **~то́нна, -ы** megaton.

мёд, -а (-у), *loc.* **-у́**; *pl.* **-ы́** honey; mead.

мед... *abbr.* (*of* **медици́нский**) *in comb.* of medicine, medical. **медбра́т, -а** male nurse. **~ву́з, -а** medical school, school of medicine. **~институ́т, -а** medical school. **~осмо́тр, -а** medical (examination), check-up; **пройти́ ~** to have a checkup. **~пу́нкт, -а** first aid post, medical station; surgery. **~сестра́, -ы́** (*hospital*) nurse.

медали́ст, -а medallist; medal winner. **меда́ль, -и** medal. **медальо́н, -а** medallion, locket.

медве́дица, -ы she-bear; Bear, Ursa. **медве́дь, -я** *m.* bear; **бамбу́ковый ~** giant panda. **медве́жий** bear; bear's; bearskin; bear-like. **медвежо́нок, -нка**; *pl.* **-жа́та, -жа́т** bear cub; **плю́шевый ~** teddy bear.

медеплави́льный copper-smelting.

ме́дик, -а medical student; doctor. **медикаме́нт, -а** medicine; *pl.* medical supplies.

медита́ция, -и meditation. **медити́ровать, -рую** *impf.* to meditate.

медици́на, -ы medicine. **медици́нск|ий** medical; **~ое обслу́живание** medical attendance, medical care; **~ий пункт** dressing-station, first-aid post. **меди́чка, -и** medical student.

ме́дленно *adv.* slowly. **ме́дленный** slow. **медли́тельный** sluggish; slow, tardy. **ме́длить, -лю** *impf.* linger; tarry; be slow.

ме́дник, -а coppersmith; tinker. **ме́дный** copper; brass, brazen; cupric, cuprous.

медо́вый honey; honeyed; **~ ме́сяц** honeymoon.

меду́за, -ы jellyfish, medusa.

медь, -и copper.

меж *prep.+i.* between.

меж... *in comb.* inter-; between. **межгородско́й** intercity. **~континента́льный** intercontinental. **~ли́чностный** interpersonal. **~национа́льный** interethnic. **~плане́тный** interplanetary. **~ра́совый** interracial. **~сезо́нье, -я** off season.

межа́, -и́; *pl.* **-и, меж, -а́м** boundary; boundary-strip.

междоме́тие, -я interjection.

ме́жду *prep.+i.* between; among, amongst; **~ на́ми (говоря́)** between ourselves, between you and me; **~ про́чим** incidentally, by the way; **~ тем** meanwhile; all the same; **~ тем как** while, whereas.

между... *in comb.* inter-, between. **междугоро́дный** inter-urban, inter-city; **~городный телефо́н** trunk-line. **~наро́дный** international.

мезони́н, -а attic (storey); mezzanine (floor).

Ме́ксика, -и Mexico.

мел, -а, *loc.* **-у́** chalk; whiting; whitewash.

мёл *etc.*: *see* **мести́**

меланхо́лик, -а melancholic person. **меланхоли́ческий** melancholy. **меланхо́лия, -и** melancholy.

меле́ть, -е́ет *impf.* (*pf.* **об~**) grow shallow.

мели́ть, -лю́ *impf.* (*pf.* **на~**) chalk.

ме́лк|ий; -лок, -лка́, -о small; shallow; shallow-draught; fine; petty, small-minded; **~ая таре́лка** flat plate. **ме́лко** *adv.* fine, small.

мелко... *in comb.* small; fine, finely; petty; shallow. **мелкобуржуа́зный** petty-bourgeois. **~во́дный** shallow. **~во́дье, -я** shallow water; shallow. **~зерни́стый** fine-grained, small-grained **~со́бственнический** relating to small property holders.

мело́к, -лка́ chalk.

ме́лочность, -и pettiness, small-mindedness, meanness. **ме́лочный** petty, trifling; paltry; small-minded. **ме́лочь, -и**; *pl.* **-и, -е́й** small items; small fry; small coin; (small) change; *pl.* minutiae; trifles, trivialities.

мель, -и, *loc.* **-и́** shoal; bank; **на мели́** aground; on the rocks in low water; **сесть на ~** run aground.

мелька́ть, -а́ю *impf.*, **мелькну́ть, -ну́, -нёшь** *pf.* be glimpsed fleetingly; flash, gleam (for a moment). **ме́льком** *adv.* in passing; for a moment.

ме́льник, -а miller. **ме́льница, -ы** mill. **ме́льничный** mill; **~ лото́к** mill-race.

мельча́йший *superl. of* **ме́лкий. мельча́ть, -а́ю** *impf.* (*pf.* **из~**) grow shallow; become small(er); become petty. **ме́льче** *comp. of* **ме́лкий, ме́лко. мельчи́ть, -чу́** *impf.* (*pf.* **из~, раз~**) crush, crumble; pulverize; grind; mill; reduce size or significance of. **мелюзга́, -и́** small fry.

мелю́ *etc.*: *see* **моло́ть**

мембра́на, -ы membrane; diaphragm.

мемуа́ры, -ов *pl.* memoirs.

ме́на, -ы exchange, barter.

ме́неджер, -а manager; **~ по сбы́ту** sales manager.

ме́нее *adv.* less; **~ всего́** least of all; **тем не ~** none the less, all the same.

мензу́рка, -и measuring-glass; graduated measure.

меново́й exchange; barter.

ме́ньше smaller; less. **ме́ньш|ий** lesser, smaller; younger; **по ~ей ме́ре** at least; **са́мое ~ее** at the least. **меньшинство́, -а́** minority.

меню́ *nt.indecl.* menu, bill of fare.

меня́ *see* **я** *pron.*

меня́ть, -я́ю *impf.* (*pf.* **об~, по~**) change; exchange; **~ся** change; +*i.* exchange.

ме́ра, -ы measure; **в ме́ру** fairly, moderately; **в ме́ру**+*g.* to the extent of; **по ме́ре возмо́жности** as far as possible; **по ме́ре того, как** (in proportion) as; **не в ме́ру, сверх ме́ры, чрез ме́ру** excessively, immoderately.

мере́жка, -и hem-stitching, open-work.

мере́щиться, -щусь *impf.* (*pf.* **по~**) seem, appear; appear dimly, glimmer.

мерза́вец, -вца blackguard, scoundrel. **ме́рзкий; -зок, -зка́, -о** disgusting, loathsome; abominable, foul.

мерзлота́, -ы́; ве́чная ~ permafrost. **мёрзлый** frozen, congealed. **мёрзнуть, -ну; мёрз** *impf.* (*pf.* **за~**) freeze.

ме́рзость, -и vileness, loathsomeness; loathsome thing, nasty thing; abomination.

мери́ло, -а standard, criterion. **мери́льный** measuring.

ме́рить, -рю *impf.* (*pf.* **по~, с~**) measure; try on; **~ся**+*i.* measure. **ме́рка, -и** measure.

ме́ркнуть, -нет; ме́рк(нул) *impf.* (*pf.* **по~**) grow dark, grow dim; fade.

ме́рный measured; rhythmical; measuring. **мероприя́тие, -я** measure.

ме́ртвенный deathly, ghastly. **мертве́ть, -е́ю** *impf.* (*pf.* **о~, по~**) grow numb; mortify; be benumbed. **мертве́ц, -а́** corpse, dead man. **мертве́цкая** *sb.* mortuary, morgue. **мёртв|ый; мёртв, -а́, мёртво́** dead; **~ая зыбь** swell; **~ая петля́** loop; noose; **спать ~ым сном** sleep like the dead.

мерца́ть, -а́ет *impf.* twinkle; shimmer, glimmer; flicker.

ме́сиво, -а mash; medley; jumble. **меси́ть, мешу́, ме́сишь** *impf.* (*pf.* **с~**) knead.

места́ми *adv.* here and there, in places. **месте́чко, -а;** *pl.* **-и, -чек** small town.

мести́, мету́, -тёшь; мёл, -а́ *impf.* sweep; whirl; **метёт** there is a snow-storm.

местко́м, -а *abbr.* (*of* **ме́стный комите́т**) local (trade-union) committee. **ме́стность, -и** locality, district; area; ground, country, terrain. **ме́стный** local; localized; locative. **...ме́стный** *in comb.* -berth, -seater, -place.

ме́сто, -а; *pl.* **-а́** place; site; seat; berth; space, room; post, situation, job; passage; piece of luggage; *pl.* the provinces, the country; **без ме́ста** out of work; **име́ть ~** take place; **~ де́йствия** scene (of action); **на ме́сте преступле́ния** in the act, red-handed; **не к ме́сту** out of place; **ни с ме́ста!** don't move! stay where you are! **местожи́тельство, -а** (place of) residence; **без определённого местожи́тельства** of no fixed abode. **местоиме́ние, -я** pronoun. **местоиме́нный** pronominal. **местонахожде́ние, -я** location, whereabouts. **местопребыва́ние, -я** abode, residence. **месторожде́ние, -я** birthplace; deposit, bed; layer; **~ у́гля** coal-field.

месть, -и vengeance, revenge.

ме́сяц, -а month; moon. **ме́сячный** monthly.

метаболи́зм, -а metabolism.

мета́лл, -а metal. **металли́ст, -а** metalworker. **металли́ческий** metal, metallic. **металлоиска́тель, -я** *m.* metal-detector. **металлоло́м, -а** scrap(-metal).

мета́ние, -я throwing, casting, flinging; **~ копья́** throwing the javelin. **мета́тель, -я** *m.* thrower. **мета́ть**[1]**, мечу́, ме́чешь** *impf.* (*pf.* **метну́ть**) throw, cast, fling; **~ банк** keep the bank; **~ икру́** spawn; **~ся** rush about; toss (and turn).

мета́ть[2]**, -а́ю** *impf.* (*pf.* **на~, с~**) tack, baste.

метёлка, -и whisk; panicle.

мете́ль, -и snow-storm; blizzard.

метео... *abbr.* (*of* **метеорологи́ческий**) *in comb.* meteorological; weather-. **метеосво́дка, -и** weather report. **~слу́жба, -ы** weather service. **~ста́нция** weather-station. **~усло́вия** weather conditions.

метео́р, -а meteor; hydrofoil.

метеоро́лог, -а meteorologist; weatherman. **метеорологи́ческ|ий** meteorological; **~ая сво́дка** weather report **метеороло́гия, -и** meteorology.

ме́тить[1]**, ме́чу** *impf.* (*pf.* **на~, по~**) mark.

ме́тить[2]**, ме́чу** *impf.* (*pf.* **на~**) aim; **+в**+*a. pl.* aim at, aspire to; **+в** *or* **на**+*a.* drive at, mean.

ме́тка, -и marking, mark.

ме́ткий; -ток, -тка́, -о well-aimed, accurate. **ме́ткость, -и** marksmanship; accuracy; neatness, pointedness.

метла́, -ы́; *pl.* **мётлы, -тел** broom.

метну́ть, -ну́, -нёшь *pf. of* **мета́ть**[1]

ме́тод, -а method. **мето́дика, -и** method(s), system; principles; methodology. **методи́ческий** methodical, systematic. **методи́чный** methodical, orderly.

метр, -а metre. **метра́ж, -а́** metric area; length in metres.

ме́трика, -и birth-certificate. **метри́ческ|ий**[1]**; ~ая кни́га** register of births deaths and

marriages; **~ое свиде́тельство** birth-certificate.
метри́ческий[2] metric; metrical.
метро́ *nt.indecl.* metro; underground; **на ~** by metro, by underground.
мету́ *etc.*: *see* **мести́**
ме́тче *comp. of* **ме́ткий**
мех[1], **-а**, *loc.* **-у́**; *pl.* **-а́** fur; **на ~у́** fur lined.
мех[2], **-а**; *pl.* **-и́** wine-skin, water-skin; *pl.* bellows.
механиза́ция, -и mechanization. **механизи́рованный** mechanized. **механизи́ровать, -рую** *impf.* & *pf.* mechanize. **механи́зм, -а** mechanism; gear, gearing; *pl.* machinery. **меха́ник, -а** mechanic. **меха́ника, -и** mechanics; trick; knack. **механи́ческий** mechanical; power-driven; of mechanics; mechanistic; **~ моме́нт** momentum; **~ цех** machine shop. **механи́чный** mechanical, automatic.
мехово́й fur. **меховщи́к, -а́** furrier.
меч, -а́ sword.
ме́ченый marked; labelled, tagged; **~ а́том** tracer, tracer element.
мече́ть, -и mosque.
мечта́, -ы́ dream, day-dream. **мечта́тельный** dreamy. **мечта́ть, -а́ю** *impf.* dream.
ме́чу *etc.*: *see* **ме́тить. мечу́** *etc.*: *see* **мета́ть**
меша́лка, -и mixer, stirrer.
меша́ть[1], **-а́ю** *impf.* (*pf.* **по~**) *+d.* hinder, impede, hamper; prevent; disturb; **не меша́ло бы**+*inf.* it would do no harm to, it would not be a bad thing to.
меша́ть[2], **-а́ю** *impf.* (*pf.* **по~, с~**) stir; agitate; mix, blend, confuse, mix up; **~ся** (**в**+*a.*) interfere (in), meddle (with).
ме́шкать, -аю *impf.* linger, delay; loiter.
мешкова́тый baggy; awkward, clumsy. **мешкови́на, -ы** sacking, hessian. **мешо́к, -шка́** bag; sack; clumsy fellow.
мещани́н, -а; *pl.* **-а́не, -а́н** petty bourgeois; Philistine. **меща́нский** lower middle-class; bourgeois, vulgar, narrow-minded; Philistine. **меща́нство, -а** petty bourgeoisie, lower middle-class; philistinism, vulgarity, narrow-mindedness.
ми *nt.indecl.* E; me.
миг, -а moment, instant.
мига́ть, -а́ю *impf.*, **мигну́ть, -ну́, -нёшь** *pf.* blink; wink, twinkle; *+d.* wink at.
ми́гом *adv.* in a flash; in a jiffy.
мигре́нь, -и migraine.
ми́дия, -и mussel.
мизе́рный scanty, wretched.
мизи́нец, -нца little finger; little toe.
микро... *in comb.* micro-; small. **микроавто́бус, -а** minibus. **~ампе́р, -а** microampere. **~во́лнов|ый; ~ая пе́чка** microwave (oven). **~ди́ск, -а** (*comput.*) floppy (disk), diskette. **~компью́тер, -а** microcomputer. **~органи́зм, -а** micro-organism. **~ско́п, -а** microscope. **~скопи́ческий, ~скопи́чный** microscopic. **~фо́н, -а** microphone.
микро́н, -а micron.
ми́ксер, -а (*cul.*) blender, liquidizer.
миксту́ра, -ы medicine, mixture.
ми́ленький pretty; nice; sweet; dear, darling.
милитари́зм, -а militarism. **милитари́ст, -а** militarist. **милитаристи́ческий** militaristic.
милицио́не́р, -а militiaman, policeman. **мили́ция, -и** militia, police force.
милли... *in comb.* milli-. **миллигра́мм, -а** milligram(me). **~ли́тр, -а** millilitre. **~ме́тр, -а** millimetre.
миллиа́рд, -а billion, a thousand millions. **миллиарде́р, -а** multi-millionaire. **миллио́н, -а** million. **миллионе́р, -а** millionaire. **миллио́нный** millionth; worth, numbered in, millions.
милосе́рдие, -я mercy, charity; **сестра́ милосе́рдия** (*hospital*) nurse. **милосе́рдный** merciful, charitable.
ми́лостив|ый gracious, kind; **~ый госуда́рь** sir; (Dear) Sir; **~ая госуда́рыня** madam; (Dear) Madam. **ми́лостыня, -и** alms. **ми́лость, -и** favour, grace; mercy; charity; **ва́ша ~** your worship; **ми́лости про́сим!** welcome!; you are always welcome; come and see us. **ми́лочка, -и** dear, darling. **ми́лый; мил, -а́, -о** nice; kind; sweet, lovable; dear, darling.
ми́ля, -и mile.
ми́мика, -и (facial) expression; miming.
ми́мо *adv.* & *prep.+g.* by, past. **мимое́здом** *adv.* in passing. **мимолётный** fleeting, transient. **мимохо́дом** *adv.* in passing.
мин. *abbr.* (*of* **мину́та**) min., minute(s).
ми́на[1], **-ы** mine; bomb; rocket.
ми́на[2], **-ы** expression; face, countenance.
миндалеви́дн|ый almond-shaped. **минда́лина, -ы** almond; tonsil. **минда́ль, -я́** *m.* almond(-tree); almonds. **минда́льн|ый** almond; **~ое пече́нье** macaroon.
минера́л, -а mineral. **минерало́гия, -и** mineralogy. **минера́льный** mineral.
мини- *in comb.* mini-.**мини-трусы́, -о́в** *pl.* briefs, panties. **~футбо́л, -а** five-a-side (football). **~ю́бка, -и** miniskirt.
миниатю́рный diminutive, tiny, dainty.
минима́льный minimum. **ми́нимум, -а** minimum; at the least.
министе́рский ministerial. **министе́рство, -а** ministry. **мини́стр, -а** minister.
минова́ть, -ну́ю *impf.* & *pf.* pass, pass by, pass over; be over, be past; *impers.+d.* escape, avoid; **тебе́ э́того не ~** you can't escape it.
миномёт, -а mortar. **миноно́сец, -сца** torpedo-boat.
мино́р, -а minor (key); blues.
мину́вш|ий past; **~ее** *sb.* the past.
ми́нус, -а minus; defect, shortcoming. **ми́нусовый** negative.
мину́та minute. **мину́тный** minute; momentary; transient, ephemeral, brief.
мину́ть, -нешь; ми́нул *pf.* pass; pass by; be over, be past; **ему́ ми́нуло два́дцать лет** he is turned twenty.

мир[1], **-а**; *pl.* **-ы́** world; universe; mir (*Russ. village community*); **живо́тный ~** fauna; **расти́тельный ~** flora; **престу́пный ~** the underworld.

мир[2], **-а** peace. **мири́ть, -рю́** *impf.* (*pf.* **по~, при~**) reconcile; **~ся** be reconciled, make it up; reconcile o.s. (**с**+*i.* to). **ми́рный** peace; peaceful; peaceable.

мировоззре́ние, -я (world-)outlook; philosophy. **миров|о́й** world; **~а́я держа́ва** world power.

миролюби́вость, -и peaceable disposition. **миролюби́вый** peace-loving, peaceful.

ми́ска, -и basin, bowl, tureen.

миссионе́р, -а missionary.

ми́ссия, -и mission; legation.

мисте́рия, -и mystery(-play).

ми́стика, -и mysticism.

мистифика́тор, -а hoaxer. **мистифика́ция, -и** hoax, leg-pull.

мисти́ческий mystic, mystical.

ми́тинг, -а mass meeting. **митингова́ть, -гу́ю** *impf.* hold a mass meeting; discuss endlessly.

миф, -а myth. **мифи́ческий** mythical. **мифологи́ческий** mythological. **мифоло́гия, -и** mythology.

мише́нь, -и target.

ми́шка, -и bear; Teddy bear.

мишура́, -ы́ tinsel; tawdriness, show. **мишу́рный** tinsel; trumpery, tawdry.

мл *abbr.* (*of* **миллили́тр**) ml, millilitre(s).

младе́нец, -нца baby; infant. **младе́нческий** infantile. **младе́нчество, -а** infancy, babyhood. **мла́дший** younger; youngest; junior; **~ кома́ндный соста́в** non-commissioned officers; **~ офице́рский соста́в** junior officers.

млекопита́ющие *sb.*, *pl.* mammals. **мле́чный** milk; lactic; **~ Путь** Milky Way, Galaxy.

млн. *abbr.* (*of* **миллио́н**) m, million(s).

млрд. *abbr.* (*of* **миллиа́рд**) b., billion(s) (= *thousand million*).

мм *abbr.* (*of* **миллиме́тр**) mm., millimetre(s).

мне *see* **я** *pron.*

мне́ние, -я opinion; **по моему́ мне́нию** in my opinion.

мни́мый imaginary; sham, pretended. **мни́тельный** hypochondriac; mistrustful, suspicious. **мнить, мню** *impf.* think, imagine; **мно́го мнить о себе́** think a lot of o.s.

мно́г|ий much; many; **~ие** *sb.*, *pl.* many (people); **~ое** *sb.* much, a great deal, many things; **во мно́гом** in many respects. **мно́го** *adv.*+*g.* much; many; a great deal; a lot of; **~ лу́чше** much better; **на ~** by far; **ни ~ ни ма́ло** neither more nor less (than), no less (than).

много... *in comb.* many-, poly-, multi-, multiple-. **многобо́жие, -я** polytheism. **~бо́рец, -рца** multi-eventer; all-rounder. **~бо́рье, -я** multi-discipline event. **~бра́чие, -я** polygamy. **~веково́й** centuries-old. **~во́дный** full, in spate; well-watered, abounding in water. **~гра́нник, -а** polyhedron. **~гра́нный** polyhedral; many-sided. **~де́тный** having many children. **~же́нец, -нца** polygamist. **~жёнство, -а** polygamy. **~значи́тельный** significant. **~зна́чный** multi-digit; polysemantic. **~каска́дный** multi-stage. **~кра́тный** repeated, re-iterated; multiple; frequentative, iterative. **~ле́тний** lasting, living, many years; of many years' standing; perennial. **~ле́тник, -а** perennial. **~лю́дный** populous; crowded. **~му́жие, -я** polyandry. **~национа́льный** multinational. **~обеща́ющий** promising, hopeful; significant. **~обра́зие, -я** variety, diversity. **~обра́зный** varied, diverse. **~ра́совый** multiracial. **~семе́йный** having a large family. **~сло́вный** verbose, prolix. **~сло́жный** complex, complicated; polysyllabic. **~сло́йный** multi-layer; multi-ply; **~сло́йная фане́ра** plywood. **~сторо́нний** polygonal; multi-lateral; many-sided, versatile. **~ступе́нчатый** multistage. **~тира́жка, -и** factory newspaper; house organ. **~то́мный** multi-volume. **~то́чие, -я** ellipsis, suspension points. **~уважа́емый** respected; Dear. **~уго́льник, -а** polygon. **~уго́льный** polygonal. **~цве́тный** many-coloured, multicoloured; polychromatic; multiflorous, floribunda. **~целево́й** multipurpose. **~чи́сленный** numerous. **~чле́н, -а** polynomial. **~эта́жный** multi-storey. **~язы́чный** polyglot; multilingual.

мно́жественный plural. **мно́жество, -а** great number; value; set; aggregate; great quantities; multitude. **мно́жимое** *sb.* multiplicand. **мно́житель, -я** *m.* multiplier; factor. **мно́жить, -жу** *impf.* (*pf.* **по~, у~**) multiply; increase, augment; **~ся** multiply, increase.

мной *etc.*: *see* **я** *pron.* **мог** *etc.*: *see* **мочь.**

мну *etc.*: *see* **мять**

мобилиза́ция, -и mobilization. **мобилизова́ть, -зу́ю** *impf.* & *pf.* (**на**+*a.*) mobilize (for). **моби́льный** mobile.

моги́ла, -ы grave. **моги́льник, -а** burial ground, cemetery. **моги́льн|ый** grave; of the grave; sepulchral; **~ая плита́** tombstone, gravestone, headstone. **моги́льщик, -а** grave-digger.

могу́ *etc.*: *see* **мочь. могу́чий** mighty, powerful. **могу́щественный** powerful. **могу́щество, -а** power, might.

мо́да, -ы fashion, vogue.

модели́ровать, -рую *impf.* & *pf.* design. **моде́ль, -и** model; pattern. **моделье́р, -а** dress-designer. **моде́льный** model; fashionable.

мо́дем, -а modem.

модерниза́ция, -и modernization; updating. **модернизи́ровать, -рую** *impf.* & *pf.* modernize; update.

моди́стка, -и milliner; modiste.

модифика́ция, -и modification. **модифици́ровать, -рую** *impf.* & *pf.* modify.
мо́дный; -ден, -дна́, -о fashionable, stylish; fashion.
мо́жет *see* **мочь**
можжеве́льник, -а juniper.
мо́жно one may, one can; it is permissible; it is possible; **как** ~+*comp.* as ... as possible; **как** ~ **лу́чше** as well as possible, to the best of one's abilities; **как** ~ **скоре́е** as soon as possible.
моза́ика, -и mosaic; inlay. **моза́ичный** inlaid, mosaic.
мозг, -а (-у), *loc.* **-у́**; *pl.* **-и́** brain; marrow; **шевели́ть** ~**а́ми** use one's head. **мозгови́тый** brainy. **мозгово́й** cerebral; brain.
мозо́листый calloused; horny. **мозо́ль, -и** corn; callus, callosity.
мой, моего́ *m.*, **моя́, мое́й** *f.*, **моё, моего́** *nt.*, **мои́, -и́х** *pl. pron.* my; mine; **по-мо́ему** in my opinion, I think; in my way; as I wish, as I think right.
мо́йщик, -а washer; cleaner; ~ **о́кон** window-cleaner.
мо́кнуть, -ну; мок *impf.* get wet, get soaked; soak. **мокрова́тый** moist, damp. **мокро́та**[1], **-ы** phlegm. **мокрота́**[2], **-ы́** humidity, damp. **мо́крый** wet, damp; soggy.
мол, -а, *loc.* **-у́** mole, pier.
молва́, -ы́ rumour, talk. **мо́лвить, -влю** *impf.* & *pf.* utter; say.
Молда́вия, -и Moldavia.
моле́кула, -ы molecule. **молекуля́рный** molecular.
моле́ние, -я prayer; entreaty, supplication. **моли́тва, -ы** prayer. **моли́ть, -лю́, -лишь** *impf.* pray; entreat, supplicate, beg (**о**+*p.* for); ~**ся** (*pf.* **по**~**ся**) pray, offer prayers; say one's prayers; +**на**+*a.* idolize.
мо́лкнуть, -ну; молк *impf.* fall silent.
молниено́сн|ый lightning; ~**ая война́** blitzkrieg. **молниеотво́д, -а** lighning-conductor. **мо́лния, -и** lightning; zip(-fastener); **(телегра́мма-)**~ express telegram.
молодёжь, -и youth, young people; the younger generation. **молоде́ть, -е́ю** *impf.* (*pf.* **по**~) get younger, look younger. **молоде́ц, -дца́** fine fellow; brick; ~! well done! good man!; **вести́ себя́ молодцо́м** put up a good show. **молоде́цкий** dashing, spirited. **молодня́к, -а́** saplings; young animals; youth, young people. **молод|о́й; мо́лод, -а́, -о** young, youthful; ~**о́й карто́фель** new potatoes; ~**о́й ме́сяц** new moon; ~**о́й** *sb.* bridegroom; ~**а́я** *sb.* bride; ~**ы́е** *sb.*, *pl.* young couple, newly-weds. **мо́лодость, -и** youth; youthfulness. **моложа́вый** young-looking; **име́ть** ~ **вид** look young for one's age. **моло́же** *comp. of* **молодо́й**
молоко́, -а́ milk. **молокосо́с, -а** greenhorn, raw youth.
мо́лот, -а hammer. **молоти́лка, -и** threshing-machine. **молоти́ть, -очу́, -о́тишь** *impf.* (*pf.* **с**~) thresh; hammer. **молото́к, -тка́** hammer; **отбо́йный** ~ pneumatic drill.
мо́лотый ground. **моло́ть, мелю́, ме́лешь** *impf.* (*pf.* **с**~) grind, mill; ~ **вздор** talk nonsense, talk rot.
молотьба́, -ы́ threshing.
моло́чник, -а milk-jug, milk-can; milkman. **моло́чница, -ы** milkwoman, milk-seller. **моло́чн|ый** milk; dairy; milky; lactic; ~**ый брат** foster-brother; ~**ое стекло́** frosted-glass, opal glass; ~**ое хозя́йство** dairy farm(ing); ~**ая** *sb.* dairy; creamery.
мо́лча *adv.* silently, in silence. **молчали́вый** silent, taciturn; tacit; unspoken. **молча́ние, -я** silence. **молча́ть, -чу́** *impf.* be silent, keep silence.
моль, -и (clothes-)moth.
мольба́, -ы́ entreaty, supplication.
мольбе́рт, -а easel.
моме́нт, -а moment; instant; feature, element, factor. **момента́льно** *adv.* in a moment, instantly. **момента́льный** instantaneous; ~ **сни́мок** snap(shot). **моме́нтами** *adv.* now and then.
мона́рх, -а monarch. **монархи́зм, -а** monarchism. **монархи́ст, -а** monarchist. **монархи́ческий** monarchic(al). **мона́рхия, -и** monarchy.
монасты́рь, -я́ *m.* monastery; convent. **мона́х, -а** monk; friar. **мона́хиня, -и** nun. **мона́шеский** monastic; monkish.
Монбла́н, -а Mont Blanc.
Монго́лия, -и Mongolia.
моне́та, -ы coin; **приня́ть за чи́стую моне́ту** take at face value, take in good faith. **монетари́ст, -а** (*econ.*) monetarist. **монетари́стский** monetarist. **моне́тный** monetary; ~ **двор** mint.
монито́ринг, -а monitoring.
монога́мия, -и monogamy. **монога́мный** monogamous.
моноли́т, -а monilith. **моноли́тность, -и** monolithic character; solidity. **моноли́тный** monolithic; massive, united.
моноло́г, -а monologue, soliloquy.
монополиза́ция, -и monopolization. **монополизи́ровать, -рую** *impf.* & *pf.* monopolize. **монополи́ст, -а** monopolist. **монополисти́ческий** monopolistic. **монопо́лия, -и** monopoly.
моното́нный monotonous. **монохро́мный** monochrome. **моноци́кл, -а** unicycle.
монта́ж, -а́ assembling, mounting, installation; montage; editing, cutting; arrangement. **монта́жник, -а** rigger, erector, fitter. **монтёр, -а** fitter, maintenance man, mechanic. **монти́ровать, -рую** *impf.* (*pf.* **с**~) mount; install, fit; erect; edit, cut.
мор, -а pestilence, plague.
мора́ль, -и moral; morals, ethics. **мора́льн|ый** moral; ethical; ~**ое состоя́ние** morale.
морга́ть, -а́ю *impf.*, **моргну́ть, -ну́, -нёшь** *pf.* blink; wink.

мо́рда, -ы snout, muzzle; face, (ugly) mug.

мо́ре, -я; *pl.* **-я́, -е́й** sea; **в откры́том мо́ре** on the open sea; **за́ морем** oversea(s).

море́на, -ы moraine.

морепла́вание, -я navigation; voyaging. **морепла́ватель, -я** *m.* navigator, seafarer. **морепла́вательный** nautical, navigational. **морехо́д, -а** seafarer.

морж, -а́, моржи́ха, -и walrus; (*open-air*) winter bather. **моржо́вый** walrus, walrus-hide.

Мо́рзе Morse; **а́збука ~** Morse code. **морзя́нка, -и** Morse code.

мори́ть, -рю́ *impf.* (*pf.* **по~, у~**) exterminate; exhaust, wear out; **~ го́лодом** starve.

морко́вка, -и carrot. **морко́вный** carrot; carroty. **морко́вь, -и** carrots.

моро́женое *sb.* ice-cream, ice. **моро́женый** frozen, chilled. **моро́з, -а** frost; *pl.* intensely cold weather. **морози́лка, -и** freezer compartment; freezer. **моро́зить, -о́жу** freeze. **моро́зный** frost, frosty. **морозоусто́йчивый** frost-resistant, hardy.

мороси́ть, -и́т *impf.* drizzle.

морс, -а fruit-juice, fruit syrup; fruit drink.

морск|о́й sea; maritime; marine, nautical; shipping; naval; **~о́й волк** old salt; **~а́я звезда́** starfish; **~о́й конёк** sea-horse; **~а́я пе́нка** meerschaum; **~а́я пехо́та** marines; **~о́й разбо́йник** pirate; **~а́я свинья́** porpoise; **~о́й флот** navy, fleet.

мо́рфий, -я morphia, morphine.

морфоло́гия, -и morphology; accidence.

морщи́на, -ы wrinkle; crease. **морщи́нистый** wrinkled, lined; creased. **мо́рщить**[1], **-щу** *impf.* (*pf.* **на~, по~, с~**) wrinkle; pucker; **~ лоб** knit one's brow; **~ся** make a wry face; knit one's brow; wince; crease, wrinkle. **морщи́ть**[2], **-и́т** *impf.* crease; ruck up.

моря́к, -а́ sailor, seaman.

Москва́, -ы́ Moscow; the Moskva (*river*). **москви́ч, -а́, москви́чка, -и** Muscovite.

моски́т, -а mosquito.

моско́вский Moscow, of Moscow.

мост, мо́ста (-у), *loc.* **-у́**; *pl.* **-ы́** bridge. **мо́стик, -а** bridge. **мости́ть, -ощу́** *impf.* (*pf.* **вы́~, за~, на~**) pave; lay. **мостки́, -о́в** *pl.* planked footway, board-walk; wooden platform. **мостова́я** *sb.* roadway; pavement. **мостово́й** bridge.

мота́льный winding. **мота́ть**[1], **-а́ю** *impf.* (*pf.* **мотну́ть, на~**) wind, reel; shake.

мота́ть[2], **-а́ю** *impf.* (*pf.* **про~**) squander.

мота́ться, -а́юсь *impf.* dangle; wander; rush about; **~ по́ свету** knock about the world.

моти́в, -а motive; reason; tune; motif. **мотиви́ровать, -рую** *impf.* & *pf.* give reasons for, justify. **мотивиро́вка, -и** reason(s); motivation; justification.

мотну́ть, -ну́, -нёшь *pf. of* **мота́ть**

мото... *in comb.* motor-, engine-; motor cycle; motorized; power. **мотого́нки, -нок** *pl.* motor-cycle races. **~дро́м, -а** motor cycle race-track. **~кро́сс, -а** motocross. **~пе́д, -а** moped. **~пехо́та, -ы** motorized infantry. **~пила́, -ы́** power saw. **~планёр, -а** powered glider. **~ро́ллер, -а** (motor-)scooter. **~спо́рт, -а** motorcycle racing. **~цикл, -а, ~цикле́т, -а** motor cycle. **~цикли́ст, -а** motorcyclist, biker; **~ свя́зи** despatch-rider.

мотовско́й wasteful, extravagant. **мотовство́, -а́** wastefulness, extravagance, prodigality.

мото́к, -тка́ skein, hank.

мото́р, -а motor, engine. **мотори́ст, -а** motor-mechanic. **мото́рка, -и** motorboat. **мото́рный** motor; engine.

моты́га, -и hoe, mattock. **моты́жить, -жу** *impf.* hoe.

мотылёк, -лька́ butterfly, moth.

мох, мха *or* **мо́ха**, *loc.* **мху**; *pl.* **мхи, мхов** moss. **мохна́т|ый** hairy, shaggy; **~ое полоте́нце** Turkish towel.

моцио́н, -а exercise.

моча́, -и́ urine; water.

моча́лка, -и loofah. **моча́ло, -а** bast.

мочеви́на, -ы urea. **мочево́й** urinary; uric; **~ пузы́рь** bladder. **мо́ченный** wetted; steeped; soused. **мочёный** soaked, steeped. **мочи́ть, -чу́, -чишь** *impf.* (*pf.* **за~, на~**) wet, moisten; soak; steep, macerate; **~ся** (*pf.* **по~ся**) urinate, make water.

мочь, могу́, мо́жешь; мог, -ла́ *impf.* (*pf.* **с~**) be able; **мо́жет (быть)** perhaps, maybe; **не могу́ знать** I don't know. **мочь, -и** power, might; **во всю ~, изо всей мо́чи, что есть мо́чи** with all one's might and main.

моше́нник, -а rogue, scoundrel; swindler. **моше́нничать, -аю** *impf.* (*pf.* **с~**) play the rogue, cheat, swindle. **моше́ннический** rascally, swindling.

мо́шка, -и midge. **мошкара́, -ы́** (swarm of) midges.

мощёный paved.

мо́щность, -и power; capacity, rating; output. **мо́щный; -щен, -щна́, -о** powerful; vigorous.

мощу́ *etc.*: *see* **мости́ть**

мощь, -и power, might.

мо́ю *etc.*: *see* **мыть. мо́ющий** washing; detergent.

мрак, -а darkness, gloom. **мракобе́с, -а** obscurantist. **мракобе́сие, -я** obscurantism.

мра́мор, -а marble. **мра́морный** marble; marbled; marmoreal.

мрачне́ть, -е́ю *impf.* (*pf.* **по~**) grow dark; grow gloomy. **мра́чный** dark, sombre; gloomy, dismal.

мсти́тель, -я *m.* avenger. **мсти́тельный** vindictive. **мстить, мщу** *impf.* (*pf.* **ото~**) take vengeance on, revenge o.s.; +**за**+*a.* avenge.

мудрёный; -рён, -а́ strange, queer, odd; difficult, abstruse, complicated; **не мудрено́, что** no wonder (that). **мудре́ц, -а́** sage, wise man. **мудри́ть, -рю́** *impf.* (*pf.* **на~, с~**) subtilize, complicate matters unnecessarily.

му́дрость, -и wisdom. **му́дрый; -др, -á, -о** wise, sage.

муж, -а; *pl.* **-жья́** *or* **-и́** husband; man. **мужа́ть, -а́ю** *impf.* grow up; mature, ripen; grow strong; **~ся** take heart, take courage. **мужеподо́бный** mannish; masculine. **му́жеский** male; masculine. **му́жественный** manly, steadfast. **му́жество, -а** courage, fortitude.

мужи́к, -á muzhik, moujik (*Russ. peasant*); peasant; man, fellow.

мужск|о́й masculine; male; **~о́й род** masculine gender; **~а́я шко́ла** boys' school. **мужчи́на, -ы** *m.* man.

музе́й, -я museum.

му́зыка, -и music; instrumental music; band; business, affair. **музыка́льность, -и** melodiousness; musical talent. **музыка́льный** musical. **музыка́нт, -а** musician; **у́личный ~** busker.

му́ка[1], **-и** torment; torture; suffering; pangs, throes.

мука́[2], **-и́** meal; flour. **мукомо́л, -а** miller.

мул, -а mule.

мультиплика́тор, -а multiplier; multiplying camera; animator, animated-cartoon artist. **мультипликацио́нный** cartoon, animated-cartoon **мультиплика́ция, -и, мультфи́льм, -а** cartoon (*film*).

му́мия, -и mummy (*embalmed corpse*).

мунди́р, -а (full-dress) uniform; **карто́фель в ~е** baked potatoes, jacket-potatoes.

мундшту́к, -á mouthpiece; cigarette-holder, cigar-holder; curb.

мураве́й, -вья́ ant. **мураве́йник, -а** ant-hill; ant-bear. **мура́шка, -и** small ant; **мура́шки по спине́ бе́гают** it sends a shiver down one's spine.

мурлы́кать, -ы́чу *or* **-каю** *impf.* purr; hum.

муска́т, -а nutmeg; muscat, muscatel. **муска́тный; ~ оре́х** nutmeg; **~ цвет** mace.

му́скул, -а muscle. **му́скулистый** muscular, sinewy, brawny. **му́скульный** muscular.

му́сор, -а refuse; sweepings, dust; rubbish; garbage; debris. **му́сорн|ый; ~ая пово́зка** dust-cart; **~ая сва́лка** rubbish heap; **~ый я́щик** dustbin. **мусородроби́лка, -и** waste-disposal unit. **мусоропрово́д, -а** refuse chute. **мусоросжига́тель, -я** incinerator.

муссо́н, -а monsoon.

мусульма́нин, -ина; *pl.* **-а́не, -а́н** Muslim, Moslem. **мусульма́нский** Muslim, Moslem. **мусульма́нство, -а** Islam, Mohammedanism.

мута́нт, -а mutant.

мути́ть, мучу́, му́тишь *impf.* (*pf.* **вз~, за~, по~**) trouble, make muddy; stir up, upset; dull, make dull; **~ся** grow turbid, muddy, dull; dim. **мутне́ть, -е́ет** *impf.* (*pf.* **по~**) grow or become turbid, muddy, dull. **му́тность, -и** turbidity; dullness. **му́тный; -тен, -тна́, -о** turbid, troubled; dull, dulled, lack-lustre; confused.

му́фта, -ы muff; sleeve, coupling, clutch; **~ сцепле́ния** clutch.

му́ха, -и fly. **мухомо́р, -а** fly-agaric, toadstool.

муче́ние, -я torment, torture. **му́ченик, -а, му́ченица, -ы** martyr. **мучи́тель, -я** *m.* torturer; tormentor. **му́чить, -чу** *impf.* (*pf.* **за~, из~**) torment; worry, harass; **~ся** torment o.s.; worry, feel unhappy; suffer agonies; **~ся от бо́ли** be racked with pain.

мучни́стый farinaceous, starchy; mealy, floury. **мучно́й** flour, meal; farinaceous, starchy; **~о́е** *sb.* starchy foods.

мха *etc.*: *see* **мох**

МХАТ, -а, *abbr.* (*of* ***Моско́вский худо́жественный (академи́ческий) теа́тр***) Moscow Arts Theatre.

мчать, мчу *impf.* rush along, whirl along; **~ся** rush, race, tear along.

мши́стый mossy.

мще́ние, -я vengeance.

мщу *etc.*: *see* **мстить**

мы, нас, нам, на́ми, нас *pron.* we; **мы с ва́ми, мы с тобо́й** you and I.

мы́лить, -лю *impf.* (*pf.* **на~**) soap, lather; **~ся** soap o.s.; lather, make a lather. **мы́лкий** lathering easily; soapy. **мы́ло, -а**; *pl.* **-á** soap; foam, lather. **мыловаре́ние, -я** soap-boiling, soap-making. **мылова́ренный** soap-making; **~ заво́д** soap works. **мы́льница, -ы** soap-dish; soap-box. **мы́льн|ый** soap, soapy; **~ый ка́мень** soapstone; **~ые хло́пья** soap-flakes.

мыс, -а cape, promontory.

мы́сленный mental. **мы́слимый** conceivable, thinkable. **мысли́тель, -я** *m.* thinker. **мысли́тельный** intellectual; thought, of thought. **мы́слить, -лю** *impf.* think; reason; conceive. **мысль, -и** thought; idea. **мы́слящий** thinking.

мыть, мо́ю *impf.* (*pf.* **вы~, по~**) wash; **~ся** wash (o.s.); **~ся в ва́нне** have a bath; **~ся под ду́шем** take a shower.

мыча́ть, -чу́ *impf.* (*pf.* **про~**) low, moo; bellow; mumble.

мышело́вка, -и mousetrap.

мы́шечный muscular.

мышле́ние, -я thinking, thought.

мы́шца, -ы muscle.

мышь, -и; *g.pl.* **-е́й** mouse. **мышья́к, -á (-у́)** arsenic.

мэр, -а mayor. **мэ́рия, -и** town council; town hall.

Мю́нхен, -а Munich.

мя́гк|ий; -гок, -гка́, -о soft; mild; gentle; **~ий ваго́н** 'soft-class' carriage, sleeping-car, sleeper; **~ий знак** soft sign, the letter **ь**; **~ое кре́сло** easy-chair; **~ий хлеб** new bread. **мя́гко** *adv.* softly; mildly; gently. **мя́гче** *comp. of* **мя́гкий, мя́гко. мя́киш, -а** soft part (of loaf), crumb. **мя́кнуть, -нет; мяк** *impf.* (*pf.* **раз~**) soften, become soft. **мя́коть, -и** fleshy part, flesh; pulp.

мя́млить, -лю *impf.* (*pf.* **про~**) mumble; vacillate; procrastinate.

мяси́стый fleshy; meaty; pulpy. **мясни́к, -а́** butcher. **мясн|о́й** meat; **~ы́е консе́рвы** tinned meat; **~а́я** *sb.* butcher's (shop). **мя́со, -а** flesh; meat; beef. **мясору́бка, -и** mincer.

мя́та, -ы mint; peppermint.

мяте́ж, -а́ mutiny, revolt. **мяте́жник, -а** mutineer, rebel. **мяте́жный** rebellious, mutinous; restless; stormy.

мя́тный mint, peppermint.

мя́тый crushed; rumpled, crumpled; **~ пар** exhaust steam. **мять, мну, мнёшь** *impf.* (*pf.* **из~, раз~, с~**) work up; knead; crumple, rumple; **~ся** become crumpled; get creased, get crushed; crush (easily); hesitate, vacillate, hum and haw.

мяу́кать, -аю *impf.* mew, miaow.

мяч, -а́, мя́чик, -а ball.

н *letter*: *see* **эн**

на *prep.* **I.** +*a.* on; on to, to, into; at; till, until; for; by; **ко́мната на двои́х** a room for two; **коро́че на дюйм** shorter by an inch, an inch shorter; **на беду́** unfortunately; **на вес** by weight; **на друго́й день** (the) next day; **на́ зиму** for the winter; **на Но́вый год** on New Year's Day; **на рубль ма́рок** a rouble's worth of stamps; **на се́вер от** (to the) north of; **на со́лнце** in the sun; **на чёрный день** for a rainy day; **на что э́то вам ну́жно?** what do you want it for? **на э́тот раз** this time, for this once; **отложи́ть на за́втра** put off till tomorrow; **перевести́ на** translate into; **сесть на** get on, get in, go on board. **II.** +*p.* on, upon; in; at; **жа́рить на ма́сле** fry (in butter); **игра́ть на роя́ле** play the piano; **на ва́те** padded; **на дворе́, на у́лице** out of doors; **на его́ па́мяти** within his recollection; **на кани́кулах** during the holidays, in the holidays; **на конце́рте** at a concert; **на лету́** in flight; **на лю́дях** in public; **на мои́х глаза́х** in my presence; **на́ море** at sea; **на рабо́те** at work; **на э́тих днях** one of these days; **на э́той неде́ле** this week; **рабо́тать на не́фти** run on oil.

на *part.* here; here you are; here, take it.

на... *pref.* **I.** *of vv., forms the perfective aspect; indicates direction on to, action applied to a surface, or to a certain quantity or number, or continued to sufficiency, excess, or the point of satisfaction or exhaustion.* **II.** *of nn. and adjs.*: on. **III.** *of advs.*: extremely, very.

наб. *abbr.* (*of* **на́бережная**) embankment, quay.

наба́вить, -влю *pf.*, **набавля́ть, -я́ю** *impf.* add; add to, increase, raise. **наба́вка, -и** adding, addition, increase, rise. **наба́вочный** extra, additional.

набалда́шник, -а knob.

на|бальзами́ровать, -рую *pf.*

наба́т, -а alarm, alarm-bell; **бить в ~** sound the alarm, raise an alarm.

набе́г, -а raid, foray. **набега́ть, -а́ю** *impf.*, **набежа́ть, -егу́** *pf.* run against, run into; come running, pour in; spring up; *impers.* pucker, wrinkle.

набекре́нь *adv.* on one side, over one ear.

на|бели́ть(ся, -елю́(сь, -е́ли́шь(ся *pf.* **на́бело** *adv.*; **переписа́ть ~** make a fair copy of.

на́бережная *sb.* embankment, quay.

наберу́ *etc.*: *see* **набра́ть**

набива́ть(ся, -а́ю(сь *impf.* *of* **наби́ть(ся. наби́вка, -и** stuffing, padding, packing; (textile) printing. **набивно́й** printed.

набира́ть(ся, -а́ю(сь *impf.* *of* **набра́ть(ся**

наби́т|ый packed, stuffed, filled; crowded; **битко́м ~** crammed, packed out; **~ый дура́к** utter fool. **наби́ть, -бью́, -бьёшь** *pf.* (*impf.* **набива́ть**) stuff, pack in, fill; break to pieces, smash; kill, bag; print; beat, hammer, drive, knock; **~ оско́мину** set the teeth on edge; **~ ру́ку** get one's hand in, become skilled; **~ це́ну** put up the price; bid up; **~ся** crowd in; be crowded; +*d.* impose or force o.s. on.

наблюда́тель, -я *m.* observer; spectator. **наблюда́тельность, -и** (power of) observation. **наблюда́тельный** observant; observation. **наблюда́ть, -а́ю** *impf.* observe,watch; +**за**+*i.* take care of, look after; supervise, superintend, control. **наблюде́ние, -я** observation; supervision, superintendence, control.

на́божный devout, pious.

набо́йка, -и print; printed fabric; printed pattern; (*rubber etc.*) heel.

на́бок *adv.* on one side, crooked.

наболе́вший sore, painful; **~ вопро́с** burning question, pressing problem. **наболе́ть, -е́ет** *pf.* ache, be painful.

набо́р, -а recruiting, enlisting, engaging; collection, set; setting up, composing; matter set up; metal plaques, (horse-)brasses; **~ слов** mere verbiage. **набо́рная** *sb.* composing room. **набо́рщик, -а** compositor.

набра́сывать(ся, -аю(сь *impf.* *of* **наброса́ть, набро́сить(ся**

набра́ть, -беру́, -берёшь; -а́л, -а́, -о *pf.* (*impf.* **набира́ть**) gather, collect, assemble; enlist, engage; compose, set up; **~ высоту́** gain height; **~ но́мер** dial a number; **~ ско́рость** pick up speed, gather speed; **~ся** assemble, collect; +*g.* find, acquire, pick up; **~ся сме́лости** pluck up courage.

набрести́, -еду́, -дёшь; -ёл, -ела́ *pf.* +**на**+*a.* come across, hit upon.

набросáть, -áю *pf.* (*impf.* **набрáсывать**) throw, throw down; sketch, outline; jot down. **набрóсить, -óшу** *pf.* (*impf.* **набрáсывать**) throw; **~ся** throw o.s., fling o.s.; **~ся на** attack, assail. **набрóсок, -ска** sketch, outline, (rough) draft.

набухáть, -áет *impf.*, **набýхнуть, -нет; -ýх** *pf.* swell.

набью *etc.*: *see* **набúть**

наваждéние, -я delusion, hallucination.

на|вáксить, -кшу *pf.*

навáливать, -аю *impf.*, **навалúть, -лю́, -лишь** *pf.* heap, pile up; put on top; load, overload; **~ся** lean, bring one's weight to bear; +**на**+*a.* fall (up)on. **навáлка, -и** loading; list, listing; **в навáлку** in bulk, loose. **навáлом** *adv.* in bulk, loose.

на|валя́ть, -я́ю *pf.*

навáр, -а fat; goodness. **навáристый, навáрный** rich and nourishing. **навáривать, -аю** *impf.*, **наварúть, -рю́, -ришь** *pf.* weld (on); boil, cook. **наварнóй** welded.

навевáть, -áю *impf. of* **навéять**

навéдаться, -аюсь *pf.*, **навéдываться, -аюсь** *impf.* call, look in.

наведéние, -я laying, laying on; placing; induction; **~ спрáвок** making inquiries; **~ поря́дка** putting in order.

наведý *etc.*: *see* **навестú**

навезтú, -зý, -зёшь; -вёз, -лá *pf.* (*impf.* **навозúть**) cart, bring in; +**на**+*a.* drive against, drive into.

навéивать, -аю *impf. of* **навéять**

навéк, навéки *adv.* for ever, for good.

навёл *etc.*: *see* **навестú**

навéрно, навéрное *adv.* probably, most likely; certainly, for sure. **наверня́кá** *adv.* certainly, for sure; safely; **держáть парú ~** bet on a certainty.

наверстáть, -áю *pf.*, **навёрстывать, -аю** *impf.* make up for, compensate for.

навéрх *adv.* up, upwards; upstairs; to the top. **наверхý** *adv.* above; upstairs.

навéс, -а awning, roof, canopy; penthouse; (*open*) shed; car-port.

навеселé *adv.* merry, a bit tight.

навéсистый overhanging, jutting. **навéсить, -éшу** *pf.* (*impf.* **навéшивать**) hang, hang up. **навéска, -и** hanging; hinge. **навесн|óй** hanging; **~áя дверь** hinged door.

навестú, -едý, -едёшь; -вёл, -á *pf.* (*impf.* **наводúть**) direct, lead; aim; cover, coat; cover with, spread; introduce, bring, produce; make; cause; **~ красотý** make up; **~ спрáвку** make inquiries.

навестúть, -ещý *pf.* (*impf.* **навещáть**) visit, call on.

навéтренный windward, exposed to the wind.

навéчно *adv.* for ever; in perpetuity.

навéшать, -аю *pf.* **навéшивать**[1], **-аю** *impf.* hang, hang out; weigh out.

навéшивать[2], **-аю** *impf. of* **навéсить**

навещáть, -áю *impf. of* **навестúть**

навéять, -éю *pf.* (*impf.* **навевáть, навéивать**) blow; cast, bring, bring about; winnow.

нáвзничь *adv.* backwards, on one's back.

навзры́д *adv.*; **плáкать ~** sob.

нависáть, -áет *impf.*, **навúснуть, -нет; -вúс** *pf.* hang, overhang, hang over; threaten, impend. **навúслый, навúсшый** beetling, overhanging.

навлекáть, -áю *impf.*, **навлéчь, -екý, -ечёшь; -ёк, -лá** *pf.* bring, draw, call down; incur.

наводúть, -ожý, -óдишь *impf. of* **навестú; наводя́щий вопрóс** leading question. **навóдка, -и** aiming, directing; applying.

наводнéние, -я flood. **наводнúть, -ню́** *pf.*, **наводня́ть, -я́ю** *impf.* flood; inundate.

навóжу *see* **навóзить. навожý** *see* **навозúть**

навóз, -а (-у) dung, manure, muck. **навóзить**[1], **-óжу** *impf.* (*pf.* **у~**) manure. **навóзн|ый** dung-, muck-; **~ая кýча** dunghill.

навозúть[2], **-ожý, -óзишь** *impf. of* **навезтú**

нáволока, -и, нáволочка, -и pillowcase.

навострúть, -рю́ *pf.* sharpen; prick up; **~ лы́жи** clear off, clear out; **~ся** train o.s., grow skilful, become good.

на|вощúть, -щý *pf.*

на|врáть, -рý, -рёшь; -áл, -á, -о *pf.* tell lies, romance; talk nonsense; +**в**+*p.* make a mistake (mistakes) in; get wrong.

навредúть, -ежý *pf.*+*d.* harm.

навсегдá *adv.* for ever, for good; **раз ~** once and for all.

навстрéчу *adv.* to meet; **идтú ~** go to meet; meet halfway; compromise with; consider sympathetically.

навы́ворот *adv.* inside out; back to front.

нáвык, -а habit; knack; experience, skill.

навы́кат(е) *adv.* protuberant, bulging.

навы́лет *adv.* right through.

навы́нос *adv.* to take away; for consumption off the premises, off-licence.

навы́пуск *adv.* worn outside.

навы́тяжку *adv.*; **стоя́ть ~** stand at attention.

навью́чивать, -аю *impf.*, **на|вью́чить, -чу** *pf.* load.

навязáть[1], **-áет** *impf.*, **навя́знуть, -нет; -я́з** *pf.* stick; **э́то навя́зло у меня́ в зубáх** I'm sick and tired of it.

навязáть[2], **-яжý, -я́жешь** *pf.*, **навя́зывать, -аю** *impf.* tie, fasten; knit; thrust, force, foist, press; **~ся** thrust o.s., intrude; be importunate. **навя́зчив|ый** importunate, intrusive; persistent; **~ая идéя** fixed idea, obsession.

нагадáть, -áю *pf.* predict, foretell.

на|гáдить, -áжу *pf.*

нагáйка, -и whip; riding-crop.

нагáн, -а revolver.

нагáр, -а snuff, scale.

нагибáть(ся, -áю(сь *impf. of* **нагнýть(ся**

нагишóм *adv.* stark naked.

наглáзник, -а blinker; eye-shade, patch.

наглéц, -á impudent fellow. **нáглость, -и**

impudence, insolence, effrontery.

на́глухо *adv.* tightly, hermetically.

нагля́дн|ый clear, graphic; visual; **~ые посо́бия** visual aids; **~ый уро́к** object-lesson.

нагна́ть, -гоню́, -го́нишь; -а́л, -а́, -о *pf.* (*impf.* **нагоня́ть**) overtake, catch up (with); drive; inspire, arouse, cause.

нагнести́, -ету́, -етёшь *pf.*, **нагнета́ть, -а́ю** *impf.* compress; supercharge. **нагнета́тель, -я** *m.* supercharger.

на́глый; -гл, -а́, -о impudent, insolent, impertinent; bold-faced, brazen.

нагное́ние, -я suppuration. **нагнои́ться, -и́тся** *pf.* fester, suppurate.

нагну́ть, -ну́, -нёшь *pf.* (*impf.* **нагиба́ть**) bend; **~ся** bend, stoop.

нагова́ривать, -аю *impf.*, **наговори́ть, -рю́** *pf.* slander, calumniate; talk a lot (of); record; **~ пласти́нку** make a record; **~ся** talk o.s. out.

наго́й; наг, -а́, -о naked, bare.

на́голо́ *adv.* naked, bare; **остри́женный на́голо** close-cropped; **с ша́шками наголо́** with drawn swords.

нагоня́й, -я scolding, telling-off. **нагоня́ть, -я́ю** *impf. of* **нагна́ть**

нагора́живать, -аю *impf. of* **нагороди́ть**

нагора́ть, -а́ет *impf.*, **нагоре́ть, -ри́т** *pf.* gutter; be consumed; *impers.+d.* catch it, be told off; **ему́ за э́то нагоре́ло** he was told off for it.

наго́рн|ый upland, mountain; mountainous; **~ая про́поведь** Sermon on the Mount.

нагороди́ть, -ожу́, -о́ди́шь *pf.* (*impf.* **нагора́живать**) pile up; erect, build; **~ вздо́р(а)** talk a lot of nonsense.

нагота́, -ы́ nakedness, nudity, bareness.

нагота́вливать, -аю *impf.*, **наготó́вить, -влю** *pf.* get in, lay in; prepare. **наготó́ве** *adv.* in readiness, ready.

награ́бить, -блю *pf.* amass by dishonest means; acquire as loot.

награ́да, -ы reward; award; decoration; prize. **награди́ть, -ажу́** *pf.*, **награжда́ть, -а́ю** *impf.* reward; decorate; award prize to. **наградны́е** *sb.*, *pl.* bonus. **награжде́ние, -я** rewarding; award, decoration.

нагрева́тельный heating. **нагрева́ть, -а́ю** *impf.*, **нагре́ть, -е́ю** *pf.* warm, heat; **~ся** get hot, warm up.

на|гримирова́ть, -ру́ю *pf.*

нагроможда́ть, -а́ю *impf.*, **на|громозди́ть, -зжу́** *pf.* heap up, pile up.

на|груби́ть, -блю́ *pf.* **на|грубия́нить, -ню** *pf.*

нагру́дник, -а bib; breastplate. **нагру́дный** breast; pectoral; **~ крест** pectoral cross.

нагружа́ть, -а́ю *impf.*, **на|грузи́ть, -ужу́, -у́зишь** *pf.* load, burden; **~ся** load o.s., burden; o.s. **нагру́зка, -и** loading; load; work; commitments, obligation(s).

на|грязни́ть, -ню́ *pf.*

нагря́нуть, -ну *pf.* appear unexpectedly; +**на**+*a.* descend on, take unawares.

над, надо *prep.+i.* over, above; on, at; **~ голово́й** overhead; **рабо́тать ~ диссерта́цией** be working on a dissertation; **смея́ться над** laugh at.

над..., надо... *pref. in comb.* **I.** *with vv. indicates increase, addition; incomplete or partial action, superficiality, slightness.* **II.** *with nn. and adjs.*: over-, super-, above-. **надво́дный** above-water, surface-. **~гро́бие, -я** epitaph. **~гро́бный** on or over a grave. **~ду́в, -а** supercharge, boost; pressurization. **~зе́мный** overground; surface-. **~по́чечник, -а** adrenal (gland). **~по́чечный** adrenal.

надави́ть, -влю́, -вишь *pf.*, **нада́вливать, -аю** *impf.* press; squeeze out; crush.

надба́вить, -влю *pf.*, **надбавля́ть, -я́ю** *impf.* add; add to, increase, raise. **надба́вка, -и** addition, increase; rise.

надвига́ть, -а́ю *impf.*, **надви́нуть, -ну** *pf.* move, pull, push; **~ся** approach, advance, draw near.

на́двое *adv.* in two; ambiguously.

надво́рный; ~ сове́тник Court Councillor (*7th grade: see* **чин**).

надёванный worn, used. **надева́ть, -а́ю** *impf. of* **наде́ть**

наде́жда, -ы hope; **в наде́жде**+*inf. or* **на**+*a.* in the hope of. **надёжный** reliable, trustworthy, safe.

наде́л, -а allotment.

наде́лать, -аю *pf.* make; cause; do.

надели́ть, -лю́, -лишь *pf.*, **наделя́ть, -я́ю** *impf.* endow, provide; allot to, give to.

наде́ть, -е́ну *pf.* (*impf.* **надева́ть**) put on.

наде́яться, -е́юсь *impf.* (*pf.* **по~**) hope, expect; rely.

надзира́тель, -я *m.* overseer, supervisor, superintendent; (police) inspector. **надзира́ть, -а́ю** *impf.*+**за**+*i.* supervise, superintend, oversee. **надзо́р, -а** supervision; surveillance; inspectorate.

надла́мывать(ся, -аю(сь *impf. of* **надломи́ть(ся**

надлежа́щ|ий fitting, proper, appropriate; **~им о́бразом** properly. **надлежи́т; -жа́ло** *impers.* (+*d.*) it is necessary, required; **вам ~ яви́ться в де́сять часо́в** you are (required) to present yourself at ten o'clock; **~ э́то сде́лать** it must be done.

надло́м, -а break; fracture; crack; breakdown, crack-up. **надломи́ть, -млю́, -мишь** *pf.* (*impf.* **надла́мывать**) break; fracture; crack; breakdown; **~ся** break, crack, breakdown. **надло́мленный** broken, cracked.

надме́нный haughty, arrogant, supercilious.

на днях *adv.* one of these days; the other day, recently, lately.

на́до[1], **на́добно** (+*d.*) it is necessary; I, *etc.*, must, ought to; I, *etc.*, need; **так ему́ и ~** serve him right!; **~ быть** probably. **на́добность, -и** necessity, need; **в слу́чае на́добности** in case of need.

надо[2] *see* **над. надо...** *see* **над...**

надоеда́ть, -а́ю *impf.*, **надое́сть, -е́м, -е́шь,**

-ест, -едим *pf.+d.* bore, bother, pester, plague; annoy. **надоедливый** boring, tiresome.
надолго *adv.* for a long time, for long.
надорвать, -ву, -вёшь; -ал, -а, -о *pf.* (*impf.* **надрывать**) tear; strain, overtax; **~ся** tear; overstrain o.s., rupture o.s.
надоумить, -млю *pf.*, **надоумливать, -аю** *impf.* advise, suggest an idea to.
надошью *etc.*: *see* **надшить**
надписать, -ишу, -ишешь *pf.*, **надписывать, -аю** *impf.* inscribe, write. **надпись, -и** inscription; notice; writing, legend; superscription, address.
надрез, -а cut, incision; notch. **надрезать, -ежу** *pf.*, **надрезать, -аю** *impf.*, **надрезывать, -аю** *impf.* make an incision in.
надругательство, -а outrage. **надругаться, -аюсь** *pf.*+**над**+*i.* outrage, insult, abuse.
надрыв, -а tear; strain; breakdown; outburst. **надрывать(ся, -аю(сь** *impf.* *of* **надорвать(ся. надрывный** violent, hysterical; heartrending.
надсмотр, -а supervision; surveillance. **надсмотрщик, -а, -щица, -ы** overseer; supervisor.
надставить, -влю *pf.*, **надставлять, -яю** *impf.* lengthen. **надставка, -и** lengthening; piece put on.
надстраивать, -аю *impf.*, **надстроить, -ою** *pf.* build on top; extend upwards. **надстройка, -и** building upwards; superstructure.
надувала, -ы *c.g.* swindler, cheat. **надувательство, -а** swindle, cheating, trickery. **надувать(ся, -аю(сь** *impf.* *of* **надуть(ся надувной** pneumatic, inflatable.
надуманный far-fetched, artificial, invented.
надумать, -аю *pf.*, **надумывать, -аю** *impf.* make up one's mind; think up, make up.
надутый swollen, inflated; haughty; sulky. **надуть, -ую** *pf.* (*impf.* **надувать**) inflate, blow up; puff out; dupe, swindle; **~ губы** pout; **~ся** fill out, swell out; be puffed up; pout, sulk.
надушенный scented, perfumed. **на|душить(ся, -ушу(сь, -ушишь(ся** *pf.*
надшивать, -аю *impf.*, **надшить, -дошью, -дошьёшь** *pf.* lengthen; sew on.
на|дымить, -млю *pf.* **наедаться, -аюсь** *impf.* *of* **наесться**
наедине *adv.* privately, alone.
наезд, -а flying visit; raid. **наездить, -зжу** *pf.*, **наезживать, -аю** *impf.* travel, cover; travel over; make by driving; break in. **наездник, -а** horseman, rider; jockey. **наездница, -ы** horsewoman, rider. **наезжать, -аю** *impf.* *of* **наездить, наехать** pay occasional visits. **наезженный** well-travelled. **наезжий** newly-arrived.
наём, найма hire, hiring; renting; **взять в ~** rent; **сдать в ~** let. **наёмник, -а** hireling; mercenary. **наёмный** hired, rented. **наёмщик, -а** tenant, lessee.
наесться, -емся, -ешься, -естся, -едимся *pf.* (*impf.* **наедаться**) eat one's fill; stuff o.s.
наехать, -еду *pf.* (*impf.* **наезжать**) come down, arrive unexpectedly; +**на**+*a.* run into, collide with.
нажать[1], **-жму, -жмёшь** *pf.* (*impf.* **нажимать**) press; squeeze; press on; put pressure (on).
нажать[2], **-жну, -жнёшь** *pf.* (*impf.* **нажинать**) reap harvest.
наждак, -а emery. **наждачн|ый; ~ая бумага** emery paper.
нажива, -ы profit, gain.
наживать(ся, -аю(сь *impf.* *of* **нажить(ся**
нажим, -а pressure; clamp. **нажимать, -аю** *impf.* *of* **нажать**[1] **нажимистый** exacting. **нажимной, нажимный** pressure.
нажинать, -аю *impf.* *of* **нажать**[2]
нажить, -иву, -ивёшь; нажил, -а, -о *pf.* (*impf.* **наживать**) acquire, gain; contract, incur; **~ врагов** make enemies; **~ся; -жился, -ась** get rich, make a fortune.
нажму *etc.*: *see* **нажать**[1]. **нажну** *etc.*: *see* **нажать**[2]
назавтра *adv.* (the) next day.
назад *adv.* back, backwards; **(тому) ~** ago.
назади *adv.* behind.
название, -я name; title. **названый** adopted; sworn. **назвать, -зову, -зовёшь; -ал, -а, -о** *pf.* (*impf.* **называть**) call, name; invite; **~ся** be called; call o.s.; give one's name.
наземный ground, surface. **наземь** *adv.* to the ground.
назидание, -я edification. **назидательный** edifying.
назло *adv.* out of spite; to spite.
назначать, -аю *impf.*, **назначить, -чу** *pf.* appoint; nominate; fix, set; prescribe.
назову *etc.*: *see* **назвать**
назойливый importunate, persistent; tiresome.
назревать, -ает *impf.*, **назреть, -еет** *pf.* ripen, mature; become urgent, imminent, inevitable.
назубок *adv.*; **знать ~** know by heart.
называемый; так ~ so-called. **называть(ся, -аю(сь** *impf.* *of* **назвать(ся; что называется** as they say.
наи... *pref. used with comparatives and superlatives to signify the very highest degree.* **наиболее** *adv.* (the) most. **~больший** greatest, biggest; **~больший общий делитель** highest common factor. **~высший** highest. **~лучший** best. **~менее** *adv.* (the) least. **~меньший** least, smallest; **~меньшее общее кратное** lowest common multiple. **~худший** worst.
наигранный put on, assumed; forced. **наиграть, -аю** *pf.*, **наигрывать, -аю** *impf.* win; play, strum, pick out; **~ пластинку** make a recording. **наигрыш, -а** folk-tune; artificiality, staginess.
наизнанку *adv.* inside out.

наизу́сть *adv.* by heart.
наименова́ние, -я name; title. **на|именова́ть, -ну́ю** *pf.*
наискосо́к, на́искось *adv.* obliquely, diagonally, aslant.
нали́тие, -я inspiration; influence; **по найтию** instinctively, by intuition.
найдёныш, -а foundling.
наймит, -а hireling.
найму́ *etc.*: *see* **наня́ть**
найти́, -йду́, -йдёшь; нашёл, -шла́, -шло́ *pf.* (*impf.* **находи́ть**) find; find out, discover; gather, collect; +**на**+*a.* come across, come over, come upon; **~сь** be found; be, be situated; turn up; rise to the occasion, find the right thing (*to do, say, etc.*); **не ~сь** be at a loss.
нака́з, -а order, instructions; mandate. **наказа́ние, -я** punishment. **наказа́ть, -ажу́, -а́жешь** *pf.*, **нака́зывать, -аю** *impf.* punish; order, tell. **наказу́емый** punishable.
нака́л, -а heating; incandescence, (white-)heat. **накалённый** heated; red-hot, white-hot, incandescent; strained, tense. **нака́ливать, -аю** *impf.*, **накали́ть, -лю́** *pf.*, **накаля́ть, -я́ю** *impf.* heat; make red-hot, white-hot; strain, make tense; **~ся** glow, become incandescent; heat up; become strained, become tense.
нака́лывать(ся, -аю(сь *impf. of* **наколо́ть(ся**
накану́не *adv.* the day before; *prep.*+*g.* on the eve of the day before.
на|ка́пать, -аю *pf.* (*impf.* **нака́пывать**) pour out (*drop by drop*), measure out; +*i.* spill.
нака́пливать(ся, -аю(сь *impf. of* **накопи́ть(ся нака́пывать, -аю** *impf. of* **нака́пать. на|ка́ркать, -аю** *pf.*
накача́ть, -а́ю *pf.*, **нака́чивать, -аю** *impf.* pump; pump up; **~ся** get tight.
наки́д, -а loop; made stitch. **накида́ть, -а́ю** *pf.*, **наки́дывать, -аю** *impf.* throw, throw down. **наки́дка, -и** cloak, cape; wrap; pillow-cover; increase, extra charge. **наки́нуть, -ну** *pf.*, **наки́дывать, -аю** *impf.* throw; throw on, slip on; **~ся** throw o.s., fling o.s.; **~ся на** attack, assail.
накипа́ть, -а́ет *impf.*, **накипе́ть, -пи́т** *pf.* form a scum, form a scale; boil up. **на́кипь, -и** scum; scale, fur, deposit.
накла́дка, -и bracket; hair piece, wig; appliqué. **накладна́я** *sb.* invoice, way-bill. **накладн|о́й** laid on; false; **~о́е зо́лото** rolled gold; **~о́й карма́н** patch pocket; **~о́е серебро́** plated silver, (silver) plate; **~ы́е расхо́ды** overheads. **накла́дывать, -аю** *impf. of* **наложи́ть**
на|клеветать, -ещу́, -е́щешь *pf.* **наклёвываться, -а́ется** *impf. of* **наклю́нуться**
накле́ивать, -аю *impf.*, **накле́ить, -е́ю** *pf.* stick on, paste on. **накле́йка, -и** sticking (on, up); sticker; label; patch.
наклепа́ть, -а́ю *pf.*, **наклёпывать, -аю** *impf.* rivet; make roughly, knock together.
накло́н, -а slope, inclination, incline; bend. **наклоне́ние, -я** inclination; mood. **наклони́ть, -ню́, -нишь** *pf.* **наклоня́ть, -я́ю** *impf.* incline, bend; **~ся** stoop, bend; bow. **накло́нность, -и** learning, inclination, propensity. **накло́нный** inclined, sloping.
наклю́нуться, -нется *pf.* (*impf.* **наклёвываться**) peck its way out of the shell; turn up.
накова́льня, -и anvil.
нако́жный cutaneous, skin.
нако́лка, -и pinning, sticking; head-dress; tattooing, tattoo. **наколо́ть**[1]**, -лю́, -лешь** *pf.* (*impf.* **нака́лывать**) prick; pin; stick; **~ся** prick o.s.
наколо́ть[2]**, -лю́, -лешь** *pf.* (*impf.* **нака́лывать**) chop, split.
наконе́ц *adv.* at last; in the end; finally. **наконе́чник, -а** tip, point. **наконе́чный** final; on the end.
на|копи́ть, -плю́, -пишь *pf.*, **накопля́ть, -я́ю** *impf.* (*impf. also* **нака́пливать**) accumulate, amass, pile up, store; **~ся** accumulate. **накопле́ние, -я** accumulation; storage; build-up; **~ да́нных** data storage.
на|копти́ть, -пчу́ *pf.* **на|корми́ть, -млю́, -мишь** *pf.*
накра́пывать, -ает *impf.* spit, drizzle.
накра́сить, -а́шу *pf.* (*impf.* **накра́шивать**) paint; make up. **на|кра́ситься, -а́шусь** *pf.*
на|крахма́лить, -лю *pf.* **накра́шивать, -аю** *impf. of* **накра́сить**
на|крени́ть, -ню́ *pf.* **накрени́ться, -ни́тся** *pf.*, **накреня́ться, -я́ется** *impf.* tilt; list, take a list, heel.
на́крепко *adv.* fast, tight; strictly.
на́крест *adv.* crosswise.
накрича́ть, -чу́ *pf.* (+**на**+*a.*) shout (at).
на|кроши́ть, -шу́, -шишь *pf.* **накро́ю** *etc.*: *see* **накры́ть**
накрути́ть, -учу́, -у́тишь *pf.*, **накру́чивать, -аю** *impf.* wind, twist.
накрыва́ть, -а́ю *impf.*, **накры́ть, -ро́ю** *pf.* cover; catch; **~ (на) стол** lay the table; **~ на ме́сте** catch red-handed; **~ся** cover o.s.
накупа́ть, -а́ю *impf.*, **накупи́ть, -плю́, -пишь** *pf.* buy up.
наку́ренный smoky, smoke-filled. **накури́ть, -рю́, -ришь** *pf.* fill with smoke; distil.
налага́ть, -а́ю *impf. of* **наложи́ть**
нала́дить, -а́жу *pf.* **нала́живать, -аю** *impf.* regulate, adjust; tune; repair; organize; **~ся** come right; get going.
на|лга́ть, -лгу́, -лжёшь; -а́л, -а́, -о *pf.*
нале́во *adv.* to the left; on the side.
налёг *etc.*: *see* **нале́чь. налега́ть, -а́ю** *impf. of* **нале́чь**
налегке́ *adv.* lightly dressed; without luggage.
на|лепи́ть, -плю́, -пишь *pf.*
налёт, -а raid, swoop; flight; thin coating, bloom, patina; touch, shade; **с ~а** suddenly, without warning or preparation, just like that.

налета́ть[1], **-а́ю** *pf.* have flown. **налета́ть**[2], **-а́ю** *impf.*, **налете́ть, -лечу́** *pf.* swoop down; come flying; spring up; +**на**+*a.* fly or drive into, run into. **налётчик, -а** raider, robber.

нале́чь, -ля́гу, -ля́жешь; -лёг, -ла́ *pf.* (*impf.* **налега́ть**) lean, apply one's weight, lie; apply o.s.; +**на**+*a.* put one's weight behind.

налжёшь *etc.*: *see* **налга́ть**

нали́в, -а pouring in; ripening, swelling. **налива́ть(ся, -а́ю(сь** *impf. of* **нали́ть(ся. нали́вка, -и** (*fruit-flavoured*) liqueur. **наливн|о́й** ripe, juicy; for carriage of liquids; overshot; **~о́й док** wet dock; **~о́е су́дно** tanker.

на|линова́ть, -ну́ю *pf.*

налипа́ть, -а́ет *impf.*, **нали́пнуть, -нет; -и́п** *pf.* stick.

налито́й plump, juicy; **~ кро́вью** bloodshot. **нали́ть, -лью́, -льёшь; на́лил, -а́, -о** *pf.* (*impf.* **налива́ть**) pour (out), fill; pour on; **~ся; -и́лся́, -а́сь, -и́ло́сь** pour in, run in; ripen, swell.

налицо́ *adv.* present, manifest; available, on hand.

нали́чие, -я presence. **нали́чность, -и** presence; amount on hand; cash, ready money. **нали́чн|ый** on hand, in hand, available; cash; **~ые (де́ньги)** cash, ready money.

наловчи́ться, -чу́сь *pf.* become skilful.

нало́г, -а tax. **нало́говый** tax. **налогоплате́льщик, -а** taxpayer. **нало́женн|ый; ~ым платежо́м** C.O.D. **наложи́ть, -жу́, -жишь** *pf.* (*impf.* **накла́дывать, налага́ть**) lay (in, on), put (in, on); apply; impose; **~ отпеча́ток** leave traces; **~ штра́ф** impose a fine; **~ на себя́ ру́ки** lay hands on o.s., commit suicide.

на|лощи́ть, -щу́ *pf.* **налью́** *etc.*: *see* **нали́ть**

налюбова́ться, -бу́юсь *pf.*+*i. or* **на**+*a.* gaze one's fill at, admire (sufficiently).

наля́гу *etc.*: *see* **нале́чь**

нам *etc.*: *see* **мы**

на|ма́зать, -а́жу *pf.*, **нама́зывать, -аю** *impf.* oil, grease; smear, spread; daub; **~ся** make up.

на|малева́ть, -лю́ю *pf.* **на|мара́ть, -а́ю** *pf.* **на|ма́слить, -лю** *pf.* **нама́тывать, -аю** *impf. of* **намота́ть. нама́чивать, -аю** *impf. of* **намочи́ть**

наме́дни *adv.* the other day, recently.

намёк, -а hint. **намека́ть, -а́ю** *impf.*, **намекну́ть, -ну́, -нёшь** *pf.* hint, allude.

на|мели́ть, -лю́ *pf.*

намерева́ться, -а́юсь *impf.*+*inf.* intend to, mean to, be about to. **наме́рен** *pred.*; **я ~**+*inf.* I intend to, I mean to; **что она́ ~а сде́лать?** what is she going to do? **наме́рение, -я** intention, purpose. **наме́ренный** intentional, deliberate.

на|мета́ть, -а́ю *pf.* **на|ме́тить**[1], **-е́чу** *pf.*

наме́тить[2], **-е́чу** *pf.* (*impf.* **намеча́ть**) plan, project; outline; nominate, select; **~ся** be outlined, take shape. **намётка**[1], **-и** draft, preliminary outline.

намётка[2], **-и** tacking, basting; tacking thread.

намеча́ть(ся, -а́ю(сь *impf. of* **наме́тить(ся**

намно́го *adv.* much, far.

намока́ть, -а́ю *impf.*, **намо́кнуть, -ну** *pf.* get wet.

намо́рдник, -а muzzle.

на|мо́рщить(ся, -щу(сь *pf.* **на|мости́ть, -ощу́** *pf.*

на|мота́ть, -а́ю *pf.* (*impf. also* **нама́тывать**) wind, reel.

на|мочи́ть, -очу́, -о́чишь *pf.* (*impf. also* **нама́чивать**) wet; soak, steep; splash, spill.

намы́в, -а alluvium. **намывно́й** alluvial.

намы́ливать, -аю *impf.*, **на|мы́лить, -лю** *pf.* soap. **намы́ть, -мо́ю** *pf.* wash; wash down, wash up.

нанести́, -су́, -сёшь; -ёс, -ла́ *pf.* (*impf.* **наноси́ть**) carry, bring; draw, plot; cause, inflict; **~ оскорбле́ние** insult; **~ уда́р**+*d.* deal a blow; hit, punch, strike; **~ ущёрб** damage.

на|низа́ть, -ижу́, -и́жешь *pf.*, **нани́зывать, -аю** *impf.* string, thread.

нанима́тель, -я *m.* tenant; employer. **нанима́ть(ся, -а́ю(сь** *impf. of* **наня́ть(ся**

нано́с, -а alluvial deposit; drift. **наноси́ть, -ошу́, -о́сишь** *impf. of* **нанести́. нано́сный** alluvial; alien, borrowed.

наня́ть, найму́, -мёшь; на́нял, -а́, -о *pf.* (*impf.* **нанима́ть**) hire, engage; rent; **~ся** get a job, get work.

наоборо́т *adv.* on the contrary; back to front; the other, the wrong, way (round); **и ~** and vice versa.

наобу́м *adv.* without thinking, at random.

нао́тмашь *adv.* with a wild swing (of the hand), violently, full.

наотре́з *adv.* flatly, point-blank.

напада́ть, -а́ю *impf. of* **напа́сть. напада́ющий** *sb.* forward. **нападе́ние, -я** attack; forwards. **напа́дки, -док** *pl.* attacks, accusations.

на|па́костить, -ощу *pf.*

напа́рник, -а co-driver, fellow-worker; team-mate; mate.

напа́сть, -аду́, -адёшь; -а́л *pf.* (*impf.* **напада́ть**) **на**+*a.* attack; descend on; grip, seize, come over; come upon, come across. **напа́сть, -и** misfortune, disaster.

на|па́чкать, -аю *pf.*

напе́в, -а melody, tune. **напева́ть, -а́ю** *impf. of* **напе́ть напе́вный** melodious.

напербо́й, наперебы́в *adv.* interrupting, vying with, one another.

напере́д *adv.* in advance, beforehand.

наперекóр *adv.*+*d.* in defiance of, counter to.

наперебы́в *see* **напербо́й**

напёрсток, -тка thimble.

на|пе́рчить, -чу *pf.*

напе́ть, -пою́, -поёшь *pf.* (*impf.* **напева́ть**) sing; hum, croon; **~ пласти́нку** make a record.

на|печа́тать(ся, -аю(сь *pf.* **напива́ться, -а́юсь** *impf. of* **напи́ться**

напи́лок, -лка, напи́льник, -а file.
на|писа́ть, -ишу́, -и́шешь *pf.*
напи́ток, -тка drink, bevarage. **напи́ться, -пью́сь, -пьёшься; -и́лся, -а́сь, -и́ло́сь** *pf.* (*impf.* **напива́ться**) quench one's thirst, drink; get drunk.
напиха́ть, -а́ю *pf.*, **напи́хивать, -аю** *impf.* cram, stuff.
на|плева́ть, -плюю́, -плюёшь *pf.*; ~! to hell with it! who cares?
напле́чник, -а shoulder strap. **напле́чный** shoulder-.
наплы́в, -а flow, influx; accumulation; dissolve; canker.
наплюю́ *etc.*: *see* **наплева́ть**
напова́л outright, on the spot.
наподо́бие *prep.+g.* like, not unlike.
на|пои́ть, -ою́, -о́ишь *pf.*
напока́з *adv.* for show; **выставля́ть** ~ display; show off.
наполне́ние, -я filling; inflation. **наполни́тель, -я** *m.* filler. **напо́лнить(ся, -ню(сь** *pf.*, **наполня́ть(ся, -я́ю(сь** *impf.* fill.
наполови́ну *adv.* half.
напомина́ние, -я reminder. **напомина́ть, -а́ю** *impf.*, **напо́мнить, -мню** *pf.* remind.
напо́р, -а pressure. **напо́ристость, -и** energy; push, go. **напо́ристый** energetic, pushing. **напо́рный** pressure.
напо́ртить, -рчу *pf.* spoil; damage; +*d.* injure, harm.
напосле́док *adv.* in the end; after all.
напою́ *etc.*: *see* **напе́ть, напои́ть**
напр. *abbr.* (*of* **наприме́р**) e.g., for example.
напра́вить, -влю *pf.*, **направля́ть, -я́ю** *impf.* direct; aim; send; refer; sharpen, whet; organize; **~ся** make (for), go (towards); get going, get underway. **напра́вка, -и** setting, whetting. **направле́ние, -я** direction; trend, tendency, turn; order, warrant, directive; action, effect; sector. **напра́вленный** purposeful, unswerving; directional. **направля́ющая** *sb.* guide. **направля́ющий** guiding, guide; leading.
напра́во *adv.* to the right, on the right.
напра́сно *adv.* vainly, in vain, to no purpose, for nothing; wrong, unjustly, mistakenly. **напра́сный** vain, idle; unfounded, unjust.
напра́шиваться, -аюсь *impf. of* **напроси́ться**
наприме́р for example, for instance.
на|прока́зить, -а́жу *pf.* **на|прока́зничать, -аю** *pf.*
напрока́т *adv.* for hire, on hire; **взять** ~ hire.
напролёт *adv.* through, without a break; **всю ночь** ~ all night long.
напроло́м *adv.* straight, regardless of obstacles; **идти́** ~ push one's way through.
на|проро́чить, -чу *pf.*
напроси́ться, -ошу́сь, -о́сишься *pf.* (*impf.* **напра́шиваться**) thrust o.s., force o.s.; suggest itself; ~ **на** ask for, invite; ~ **на комплиме́нты** fish for compliments.
напро́тив *adv.* opposite; on the contrary; +*d.* against, to spite. **напро́тив** *prep.+g.* opposite.
напру́живать, -аю *impf.*, **напру́жить, -жу** *pf.* strain; tense; **~ся** become tense, become taut.
напряга́ть(ся, -а́ю(сь *impf. of* **напря́чь(ся. напряже́ние, -я** tension; effort, exertion, strain; stress; voltage; ~ **смеще́ния** grid bias. **напряжённый** tense, strained; intense; intensive.
напрями́к *adv.* straight, straight out.
напря́чь, -ягу́, -яжёшь; -я́г, -ла́ *pf.* (*impf.* **напряга́ть**) tense, strain; **~ся** exert o.s., strain o.s.; become tense.
на|пуга́ть(ся, -а́ю(сь *pf.* **на|пу́дрить(ся, -рю(сь** *pf.*
на́пуск, -а letting in; slipping, letting loose; bloused or loosely hanging part. **напуска́ть, -а́ю** *impf.*, **напусти́ть, -ущу́, -у́стишь** *pf.* let in, admit; let loose, slip; ~ **на себя́** affect, put on, assume; **~ся**+**на**+*a.* fly at, go for. **напускно́й** assumed, put on, artificial.
напу́тать, -аю *pf.* +**в**+*p.* make a mess of, make a hash of; confuse; get wrong.
напу́тственный parting, farewell. **напу́тствие, -я** parting words, farewell speech.
напуха́ть, -а́ет *impf.*, **напу́хнуть, -нет** *pf.* swell (up).
на|пыли́ть, -лю́ *pf.*
напы́щенный pompous, bombastic, high-flown.
напью́сь *etc.*: *see* **напи́ться**
наравне́ *adv.* level, keeping pace; equally; on an equal footing.
нараспа́шку *adv.* unbuttoned; **у него́ душа́** ~ he wears his heart on his sleeve.
нараспе́в *adv.* in a sing-song (way).
нараста́ние, -я growth, accumulation; build-up. **нараста́ть, -а́ет** *impf.*, **нарасти́, -тёт; -ро́с, -ла́** *pf.* grow, form; increase, swell; accumulate.
нарасхва́т *adv.* very quickly, like hot cakes; **раскупа́ться** ~ be in great demand.
нарва́ть[1], **-рву́, -рвёшь; -а́л, -а́, -о** *pf.* (*impf.* **нарыва́ть**) pick; tear up.
нарва́ть[2], **-вёт; -а́л, -а́, -о** *pf.* (*impf.* **нарыва́ть**) gather, come to a head.
нарва́ться, -ву́сь, -вёшься; -а́лся, -ала́сь, -а́ло́сь *pf.* (*impf.* **нарыва́ться**) +**на**+*a.* run into, run up against.
наре́з, -а thread, groove; rifling; plot. **наре́зать, -е́жу** *pf.*, **нареза́ть, -а́ю** *impf.* cut, cut up, slice, carve; thread, rifle; allot, parcel out. **наре́зка, -и** cutting, slicing; thread, rifling. **нарезно́й** rifled.
нарека́ние, -я censure.
наре́чие[1], **-я** dialect.
наре́чие[2], **-я** adverb. **наре́чный** adverbial.
на|рисова́ть, -су́ю *pf.*
нарица́тельн|ый nominal; **и́мя ~ое** common noun; **~ая сто́имость** face value, nominal value.

наркоделе́ц, -ьца́ drug trafficker, pusher. **нарко́з, -а** anaesthesia; narcosis; anaesthetic. **наркома́н, -а, -ма́нка, -и** drug addict. **наркома́ния, -и** drug addiction. **наркосиндика́т, -а** drug ring. **нарко́тик, -а** narcotic, drug.

наро́д, -а (-у) people.

народи́ться, -ожу́сь *pf.* (*impf.* **нарожда́ться**) be born; come into being, arise.

наро́дник, -а narodnik, populist. **наро́днический** populist. **наро́дность, -и** nationality; people; national character. **наро́дный** national; folk; popular; people's. **народонаселе́ние, -я** population.

нарожда́ться, -а́юсь *impf. of* **народи́ться. нарожде́ние, -я** birth, springing up.

наро́с *etc.*: *see* **нарасти́. наро́ст, -а** outgrowth, excrescence; burr, tumour; incrustation, scale.

нарочи́тый deliberate, intentional. **наро́чно** *adv.* on purpose, purposely, deliberately; for fun, jokingly. **на́рочный** *sb.* courier; express messenger, special messenger; **с ~м** express delivery.

на́рты, нарт *pl.*, **на́рта, -ы** sledge.

нару́жно *adv.* outwardly, on the surface. **нару́жность, -и** exterior, (outward) appearance. **нару́жный** external, exterior, outward; for external use only, not to be taken. **нару́жу** *adv.* outside, out.

на|румя́нить(ся, -ню(сь *pf.*

нару́чник, -а handcuff, manacle. **нару́чн|ый; ~ые часы́** wrist-watch.

наруше́ние, -я breach; infringement, violation; offence. **наруши́тель, -я** *m.* transgressor, infringer, violator; **~ грани́цы** illegal entrant. **нару́шить, -шу** *pf.*, **наруша́ть, -а́ю** *impf.* break; disturb, infringe, violate, transgress.

на́ры, нар *pl.* plank-bed.

навы́в, -а abscess, boil. **нарыва́ть(ся, -а́ю(сь** *impf. of* **нарва́ть(ся**

наря́д[1]**, -а** order, warrant; duty; detail.

наря́д[2]**, -а** attire; apparel; dress. **наряди́ть, -яжу́** *pf.* (*impf.* **наряжа́ть**) dress array; dress up; **~ся** dress up, array o.s. **наря́дный** well-dressed, elegant, smart.

наряду́ *adv.* alike, equally; side by side; **~ с э́тим** at the same time.

наряжа́ть(ся, -а́ю(сь *impf. of* **наряди́ть(ся**

нас *see* **мы**

НАСА NASA *abbr.* (*of* National Aeronautics and Space Administration).

насади́ть, -ажу́, -а́дишь *pf.*, **насажда́ть, -а́ю** *impf.* (*impf. also* **наса́живать**) plant; seat; propagate; implant, inculcate; set; fix, stick, pin. **наса́дка, -и** setting, fixing, putting on; hafting; bait; nozzle, mouthpiece. **насажа́ть, -а́ю** *pf.* (*impf.* **наса́живать**) plant, seat. **насажде́ние, -я** planting; plantation stand, wood; spreading, dissemination, propagation. **наса́живать, -аю** *impf. of* **насади́ть, насажа́ть**

наса́ливать, -аю *impf. of* **насоли́ть**

наса́сывать, -аю *impf. of* **насоса́ть**

насви́стывать, -аю *impf.* whistle.

наседа́ть, -а́ю *impf.* (*pf.* **насе́сть**) press; settle, collect. **насе́дка, -и** sitting hen.

насека́ть, -а́ю *impf. of* **насе́чь. насеко́мое** *sb.* insect. **насеку́** *etc.*: *see* **насе́чь**

населе́ние, -я population, inhabitants; settling, peopling. **населённость, -и** density of population. **населённый** populated, settled, inhabited; thickly populated, populous; **~ пункт** settlement; inhabited place; built-up area. **насели́ть, -лю́** *pf.*, **населя́ть, -я́ю** *impf.* settle, people, inhabit. **насе́льник, -а** inhabitant.

насе́ст, -а roost, perch. **насе́сть, -ся́ду, -се́л** *pf. of* **наседа́ть**

насе́чка, -и incision, cut; notch; inlay. **насе́чь, -еку́, -ечёшь; -ёк, -ла́** *pf.* (*impf.* **насека́ть**) cut; cut up; incise; damascene.

насиде́ть, -ижу́ *pf.*, **наси́живать, -аю** *impf.* hatch; warm. **наси́женн|ый** long occupied; **~ое ме́сто** old haunt, old home.

наси́лие, -я violence, force, aggression. **наси́ловать, -лую** *impf.* (*pf.* **из~**) coerce, constrain; rape. **наси́лу** *adv.* with difficulty, hardly. **наси́льник, -а** aggressor, user of violence, violator. **наси́льно** *adv.* by force, forcibly. **наси́льственный** violent, forcible.

наска́кивать, -аю *impf. of* **наскочи́ть**

на|сканда́лить, -лю *pf.*

наскво́зь *adv.* through, throughout.

наско́лько *adv.* how much? how far?; as far as, so far as.

на́скоро *adv.* hastily, hurriedly.

наскочи́ть, -очу́, -о́чишь *pf.* (*impf.* **наска́кивать**) +**на**+*a.* run into, collide with; fly at.

наскреба́ть, -а́ю *impf.*, **наскрести́, -ебу́, -ебёшь; -ёб, -ла́** *pf.* scrape up, scrape together.

наску́чить, -чу *pf.* bore.

наслади́ть, -ажу́ *pf.*, **наслажда́ть, -а́ю** *impf.* delight, please; **~ся** enjoy, take pleasure, delight. **наслажде́ние, -я** delight, pleasure, enjoyment.

насла́иваться, -ается *impf. of* **наслои́ться**

насле́дие, -я legacy; heritage. **на|следи́ть, -ежу́** *pf.* **насле́дник, -а** heir, legatee; successor. **насле́дница, -ы** heiress. **насле́дный** next in succession; **~ принц** crown prince. **насле́дование, -я** inheritance, succession. **насле́довать, -дую** *impf.* & *pf.* (*pf. also* **у~**) inherit, succeed to. **насле́дственный** hereditary, inherited. **насле́дство, -а** inheritance, legacy; heritage.

наслое́ние, -я stratification; stratum, layer, deposit. **наслои́ться, наслои́тся** *pf.* (*impf.* **насла́иваться**) form a layer or stratum, be deposited.

наслы́шаться, -шусь *pf.* have heard a lot. **наслы́шка, -и; по наслы́шке** by hearsay.

на́смерть *adv.* to death; to the death.

насмеха́ться, -а́юсь *impf.* jeer, gibe; +**над**+*i.* ridicule. **на|смеши́ть, -шу́** *pf.* **насме́шка, -и** mockery, ridicule; gibe. **насме́шливый** mocking, derisive; sarcastic.

на́сморк, -а cold in the head.

насмотре́ться, -рю́сь, -ришься *pf.* see a lot; ~ **на** see enough of, have looked enough at.

насоли́ть, -олю́, -о́ли́шь *pf.* (*impf.* **наса́ливать**) salt, pickle; oversalt; annoy, spite, injure.

на|сори́ть, -рю́ *pf.*

насо́с, -а pump. **насоса́ть, -осу́, -осёшь** *pf.* (*impf.* **наса́сывать**) pump; suck; ~**ся** suck one's fill; drink o.s. drunk. **насо́сный** pumping.

на́спех *adv.* hastily.

на|спле́тничать, -аю *pf.* **наства́ть, -таёт** *impf. of* **наста́ть**

настави́тельный edifying, instructive. **наста́вить**[1], **-влю** *pf.* (*impf.* **наставля́ть**) edify; exhort, admonish.

наста́вить[2], **-влю** *pf.* (*impf.* **наставля́ть**) lengthen; add, add on; aim, point; set up, place. **наста́вка, -и** addition. **наставле́ние, -я** exhortation, admonition; directions, instructions, manual.

наставля́ть, -я́ю *impf. of* **наста́вить**

наста́вник, -а tutor, teacher, mentor; **кла́ссный** ~ form-master. **наста́вничество, -а** tutorship, tutelage.

наставно́й lengthened; added.

наста́ивать(ся, -аю(сь *impf. of* **настоя́ть(ся**

наста́ть, -а́нет *pf.* (*impf.* **настава́ть**) come, begin, set in.

на́стежь *adv.* wide, wide open.

настелю́ *etc.*: *see* **настла́ть**

насте́нн|ый hanging; ~**ые часы́** wall-clock.

настига́ть, -а́ю *impf.*, **насти́гнуть, насти́чь, -и́гну; -и́г** *pf.* catch up with, overtake.

насти́л, -а flooring, planking. **настила́ть, -а́ю** *impf. of* **настла́ть**

насти́чь *see* **настига́ть**

настла́ть, -телю́, -те́лешь *pf.* (*impf.* **настила́ть**) lay, spread.

насто́й, -я infusion; (*fruit-flavoured*) liqueur, cordial. **насто́йка, -и** (*fruit-flavoured*) liqueur, cordial.

насто́йчивый persistent; urgent, insistent.

насто́лько *adv.* so, so much; ~, **наско́лько** as much as.

насто́льник, -а table-lamp, desk-lamp. **насто́льный** table, desk; for constant reference, in constant use.

настора́живать, -аю *impf.*, **насторожи́ть, -жу́** *pf.* set; prick up, strain; ~**ся** prick up one's ears. **настороже́** *adv.* on the alert, on one's guard. **насторо́женный; -ен, -енна, насторожённый; -ён, -ена́** *or* **-ённа** guarded; alert.

настоя́ние, -я insistence. **настоя́тельный** persistent, insistent; urgent, pressing. **настоя́ть**[1], **-ою́** *pf.* (*impf.* **наста́ивать**) insist.

настоя́ть[2], **-ою́** *pf.* (*impf.* **наста́ивать**) brew, draw, infuse; ~**ся** draw, stand; stand a long time.

настоя́щее *sb.* the present. **настоя́щий** (the) present, this; real, genuine.

настра́ивать(ся, -аю(сь *impf. of* **настро́ить(ся**

настри́г, -а shearing, clipping; clip. **настри́чь, -игу́, -ижёшь; -и́г** *pf.* shear, clip.

на́строго *adv.* strictly.

настрое́ние, -я mood, temper, humour; ~ **умо́в** public feeling, general mood.

настро́ить, -о́ю *pf.* (*impf.* **настра́ивать**) tune, tune in; dispose, incline; incite; ~**ся** dispose o.s., incline, settle; make up one's mind. **настро́йка, -и** tuning; tuning in; tuning signal. **настро́йщик, -а** tuner.

на|строчи́ть, -чу́ *pf.*

настря́пать, -аю *pf.* cook; cook up.

наступа́тельный offensive; aggressive. **наступа́ть**[1], **-а́ю** *impf. of* **наступи́ть**[1]

наступа́ть[2], **-а́ет** *impf. of* **наступи́ть**[2]. **наступа́ющий** coming, beginning.

наступа́ющий *sb.* attacker.

наступи́ть[1], **-плю́, -пишь** *pf.* (*impf.* **наступа́ть**) tread, step; attack; advance.

наступи́ть[2], **-у́пит** *pf.* (*impf.* **наступа́ть**) come, set in; fall; **наступи́ла ночь** night had fallen; **наступи́ла тишина́** silence fell. **наступле́ние**[1], **-я** coming, approach; **с** ~**м но́чи** at nightfall.

наступле́ние[2], **-я** offensive, attack.

насу́питься, -плюсь *pf.*, **насу́пливаться, -аюсь** *impf.* frown, knit one's brows.

на́сухо *adv.* dry. **насуши́ть, -шу́, -шишь** *pf.* dry.

насу́щность, -и urgency. **насу́щный** urgent, vital, essential; **хлеб** ~ daily bread.

насчёт *prep.*+*g.* about, concerning; as regards.

насчита́ть, -а́ю *pf.*, **насчи́тывать, -аю** *impf.* count; hold, contain; ~**ся**+*g.* number.

насы́пать, -плю *pf.*, **насыпа́ть, -а́ю** *impf.* pour in, pour on; fill; spread, scatter; raise, heap up. **насы́пка, -и** pouring; filling. **насыпно́й** bulk; piled up; ~ **холм** artificial mound. **на́сыпь, -и** embankment.

насы́тить, -ы́щу *pf.*, **насыща́ть, -а́ю** *impf.* sate, satiate; saturate, impregnate; ~**ся** be full, be sated; be saturated. **насы́щенный** saturated; rich, concentrated.

нася́ду *etc.*: **насе́сть**

ната́лкивать(ся, -аю(сь *impf. of* **натолкну́ть(ся** **ната́пливать, -аю** *impf. of* **натопи́ть**

натаска́ть, -а́ю *pf.*, **ната́скивать, -аю** *impf.* train; coach, cram; bring in, lay in; fish out, drag out, fetch out.

натвори́ть, -рю́ *pf.* do, get up to.

натере́ть, -тру́, -трёшь; -тёр *pf.* (*impf.* **натира́ть**) rub on, rub in; polish; chafe, rub; grate; ~**ся** rub o.s.

натерпе́ться, -плю́сь, -пишься *pf.* have suffered much, have gone through a great deal.

натира́ть(ся, -а́ю(сь *impf. of* **натере́ть(ся**

на́тиск, -а onslaught, charge, onset; pressure; impress, impression. **нати́скать, -аю** *pf.* impress; cram in; shove, push about.

наткну́ться, -ну́сь, -нёшься *pf.* (*impf.* **натыка́ться**) +**на**+*a.* run against, run into; strike, stumble on, come across.

НАТО NATO *abbr.* (*of* North Atlantic Treaty Organization).

натолкну́ть, -ну́, -нёшь *pf.* (*impf.* **ната́лкивать**) push, lead; ~ **на** suggest; **~ся** run against, run across.

натопи́ть, -плю́, -пишь *pf.* (*impf.* **ната́пливать**) heat, heat up; stoke up; melt.

на|точи́ть, -чу́, -чишь *pf.*

натоща́к *adv.* on an empty stomach.

натр, -а natron, soda; **е́дкий** ~ caustic soda.

натрави́ть, -влю́, -вишь *pf.*, **натра́вливать, -аю** *impf.*, **натравля́ть, -я́ю** *impf.* set (on); stir up; etch; exterminate (*by poison*).

натрениро́ванный trained. **на|тренирова́ть(ся, -ру́ю(сь** *pf.*

на́трий, -я sodium.

нату́га, -и effort, strain. **на́туго** *adv.* tight, tightly. **нату́жный** strained, forced.

нату́ра, -ы nature; kind; model; **на нату́ре** on location; **плати́ть нату́рой** pay in kind; **с нату́ры** from life. **натура́льно** *adv.* naturally, of course. **натура́льный** natural; real, genuine; in kind; ~ **обме́н** barter. **нату́рный** life, from life; on location.

натуропа́т, -а naturopath. **натуропа́тия, -и** naturopathy.

нату́рщик, -а, -щица, -ы artist's model.

натыка́ть(ся, -а́ю(сь *impf. of* **наткну́ть(ся**

натюрмо́рт, -а still life.

натя́гивать, -аю *impf.*, **натяну́ть, -ну́, -нешь** *pf.* stretch; draw; pull tight, tauten; pull on; **~ся** stretch. **натя́жка, -и** stretching, straining; tension; stretch; **допусти́ть натя́жку** stretch a point; **с натя́жкой** be stretching a point, at a pinch. **натяжно́й** tension. **натя́нутость, -и** tension. **натя́нутый** tight; strained, forced.

науга́д *adv.* at random; by guesswork.

нау́ка, -и science; learning, scholarship; study; lesson. **наукообра́зный** scientific; pseudo-scientific.

наутёк *adv.*: **пусти́ться** ~ take to one's heels, take to flight.

нау́тро *adv.* (the) next morning.

на|учи́ть, -чу́, -чишь *pf.*

нау́чн|ый scientific; **~ая фанта́стика** science fiction.

нау́шник, -а ear-flap, ear-muff; ear-phone, head-phone; informer, tale-bearer. **нау́шничать, -аю** *impf.* tell tales, inform.

нафтали́н, -а (-у) naphthalene. **нафтали́новый** naphthalene; ~ **ша́рик** moth-ball.

наха́л, -а, -ха́лка, -и impudent creature, brazen creature; lout, hussy. **наха́льный** impudent, impertinent, cheeky; brazen, bold-faced. **наха́льство, -а** impudence, effrontery.

нахвата́ть, -а́ю *pf.*, **нахва́тывать, -аю** *impf.* pick up, get hold of, come by; **~ся**+*g.* pick up, get a smattering of.

нахле́бник, -а parasite, hanger-on; boarder, paying guest.

нахлобу́чивать, -аю *impf.*, **нахлобу́чить, -чу** *pf.* pull down; +*d.* tell off, dress down. **нахлобу́чка, -и** telling-off, dressing-down.

нахлы́нуть, -нет *pf.* well up; surge; flow, gush; crowd.

нахму́ренный frowning, scowling. **на|хму́рить(ся, -рю(сь** *pf.*

находи́ть(ся, -ожу́(сь, -о́дишь(ся *impf. of* **найти́(сь. нахо́дка, -и** find; godsend. **нахо́дчивый** resourceful, ready, quick-witted.

на|холоди́ть, -ожу́ *pf.*

нацеди́ть, -ежу́, -е́дишь *pf.*, **наце́живать, -аю** *impf.* strain.

наце́ливать, -аю *impf.*, **на|це́лить, -лю** *pf.* aim, level, direct; **~ся** aim, take aim.

наце́нка, -и extra, addition; additional charge.

национализи́ровать, -рую *impf.* & *pf.* nationalize. **националисти́ческий** nationalist, nationalistic. **национа́льность, -и** nationality; ethnic group; national character. **национа́льный** national. **на́ция, -и** nation.

нацме́н, -а, -ме́нка, -и *abbr.* member of national minority. **нацменьши́нство, -а** *abbr.* national minority.

на|чади́ть, -ажу́ *pf.*

нача́ло, -а beginning, start; origin, source; principle, basis; command, authority; **для нача́ла** to start with; **с нача́ла** at, from, the beginning. **нача́льник, -а** head, chief; superior, boss. **нача́льный** initial, first; primary. **нача́льственный** overbearing, domineering. **нача́льство, -а** the authorities; command, direction; head, boss. **нача́льствование, -я** command. **нача́льствовать, -твую** *impf.* be in command; +**над**+*i.* command. **нача́тки, -ков** *pl.* rudiments, elements. **нача́ть, -чну́, -чнёшь; на́чал, -а́, -о** *pf.* (*impf.* **начина́ть**) begin, start; **~ся** begin, start.

начеку́ *adv.* on the alert, ready.

на|черни́ть, -ню́ *pf.* **на́черно** *adv.* roughly, in rough.

начерта́ние, -я tracing; outline. **начерта́тельн|ый; ~ая геоме́трия** descriptive geometry. **начерта́ть, -а́ю** *pf.* trace, inscribe.

на|черти́ть, -рчу́, -ртишь *pf.*

начина́ние, -я undertaking; project; initiative. **начина́тель, -я** *m.*, **-тельница, -ы** originator, initiator. **начина́тельный** inchoative, inceptive. **начина́ть(ся, -а́ю(сь** *impf. of* **нача́ть(ся. начина́ющий** *sb.* beginner. **начина́я с** *prep.*+*g.* as from, starting with.

начи́нивать, -аю *impf.*, **начини́ть**[1]**, -ню́, -нишь** *pf.* mend; sharpen.

начини́ть[2]**, -ню́** *pf.*, **начиня́ть, -я́ю** *impf.* stuff, fill. **начи́нка, -и** stuffing, filling.

начисле́ние, -я extra charge, supplement, addition. **начи́слить, -лю** *pf.*, **начисля́ть, -я́ю** *impf.* add.

начи́стить, -и́щу *pf.* (*impf.* **начища́ть**) clean;

polish, shine; peel. **на́чисто** *adv.* flatly, decidedly; openly, frankly; **переписа́ть ~** make a clean copy (of). **начистоту́, начисту́ю** *adv.* openly, frankly.

начи́танность, -и learning, erudition; wide reading. **начи́танный** well-read; **начита́ть, -а́ю** *pf.* have read; **~ся** have read (too) much, have read enough.

начища́ть, -а́ю *impf. of* **начи́стить**

наш, -его *m.*, **на́ша, -ей** *f.*, **на́ше, -его** *nt.*, **на́ши, -их** *pl.*, *pron.* our, ours; **~а взяла́** we've won; **~его** (*after comp.*) than we (*have etc.*); **~и** our (own) people; **оди́н из ~их** one of us; **служи́ть, угожда́ть, и ~им и ва́шим** run with the hare and hunt with the hounds.

нашаты́рный; ~ спирт ammonia. **нашаты́рь, -я́** *m.* sal-ammoniac; ammonia.

нашёл *etc.*: *see* **найти́**

нашепта́ть, -пчу́, -пчешь *pf.*, **нашёптывать, -аю** *impf.* whisper; cast a spell.

наше́ствие, -я invasion.

нашива́ть, -а́ю *impf.*, **наши́ть, -шью́, -шьёшь** *pf.* sew on. **наши́вка, -и** stripe, chevron; tab. **нашивно́й** sewn on; **~ карма́н** patch pocket.

нашинкова́ть, -ку́ю *pf.*, **нашинко́вывать, -аю** *impf.* shred, chop.

нашпи́ливать, -аю *impf.*, **нашпи́лить, -лю** *pf.* pin on.

нашлёпать, -аю *impf.* slap.

нашуме́ть, -млю́ *pf.* make a din; cause a sensation.

нашью́ *etc.*: *see* **наши́ть**

нащу́пать, -аю *pf.*, **нащу́пывать, -аю** *impf.* grope for, fumble for, feel (about) for; grope one's way to, find by groping.

на|электризова́ть, -зу́ю *pf.*

на|я́бедничать, -аю *pf.*

наяву́ *adv.* awake; in reality; **сон ~** waking dream.

не *part.* not; **не раз** more than once.

не... *pref.* un-, in-, non-, mis-, dis-; -less; not. **неаккура́тный** careless, inaccurate; unpunctual; untidy.

Неа́поль, -я Naples.

небезопа́сный unsafe. **небезразли́чный** not indifferent. **небезызве́стн|ый** not unknown; notorious; well-known; **~о, что** it is no secret that; **нам ~о** we are not unaware. **небезынтере́сный** not without interest.

небеса́ *etc.*: *see* **не́бо²**. **небе́сный** heavenly, of heaven; celestial.

не... небесполе́зный of some use, useful. **неблагода́рный** ungrateful, thankless. **неблагожела́тельный** malevolent, ill-disposed. **неблагозву́чие, -я** disharmony, dissonance. **неблагозву́чный** inharmonious, discordant. **неблагонадёжный** unreliable. **неблагополу́чие, -я** trouble. **неблагополу́чный** unsuccessful, bad, unfavourable. **неблагопристо́йный** obscene, indecent, improper. **неблагоразу́мный** imprudent, ill-advised, unwise. **неблагоро́дный** ignoble, base.

нёбный palatal, palatine. **нёбо¹, -а** palate.

не́бо², -а; *pl.* **-беса́, -бе́с** sky; heaven.

не... небога́тый of modest means, modest. **небольшо́й** small, not great; **с небольши́м** a little over.

небосво́д, -а firmament, vault of heaven. **небоскло́н, -а** horizon. **небоскрёб, -а** skyscraper.

небо́сь *adv.* I dare say; probably, very likely; I suppose.

не... небре́жничать, -аю *impf.* be careless. **небре́жный** careless, negligent; slipshod; offhand. **небыва́лый** unprecedented; fantastic, imaginary; inexperienced. **небыли́ца, -ы** fable, cock-and-bull story. **небытие́, -я́** non-existence. **небьющийся** unbreakable.

Нева́, -ы́ the Neva.

нева́жно *adv.* not too well, indifferently. **нева́жный** unimportant, insignificant; poor, indifferent. **невдалеке́** *adv.* not far away. **неве́дение, -я** ignorance. **неве́домо** *adv.* God (only) knows. **неве́домый** unknown; mysterious. **неве́жа, -и** *c.g.* boor, lout. **неве́жда, -ы** *c.g.* ignoramus. **неве́жественный** ignorant. **неве́жество, -а** ignorance; rudeness, bad manners, discourtesy. **неве́жливый** rude, impolite, ill-mannered. **неве́ликий; -и́к, -а́, -ико́** small, short; slight, insignificant. **неве́рие, -я** unbelief, atheism; lack of faith, scepticism. **неве́рный; -рен, -рна́, -о** incorrect, wrong; inaccurate, uncertain, unsteady; false; faithless, disloyal; unfaithful; **Фома́ ~** doubting Thomas. **невероя́тный** improbable, unlikely; incredible, unbelievable. **неве́рующий** unbelieving; *sb.* unbeliever, atheist. **невесёлый** joyless, sad. **невесо́мость, -и** weightlessness. **невесо́мый** weightless; imponderable, insignificant.

неве́ста, -ы fiancée; bride. **неве́стка, -и** daughter-in-law; brother's wife, sister-in-law.

не... невзго́да, -ы adversity, misfortune. **невзирая на** *prep.+a.* in spite of; regardless of. **невзнача́й** *adv.* by chance, unexpectedly. **невзра́чный** unattractive, plain. **невзыска́тельный** unexacting, undemanding. **не́видаль, -и** wonder, prodigy. **неви́данный** unprecedented, unheard-of; mysterious. **неви́димый** invisible. **неви́дящий** unseeing. **неви́нность, -и** innocence. **неви́нный** innocent. **невино́вный** innocent, not guilty. **невку́сный** tasteless, unappetizing, not nice. **невменя́емый** irresponsible, not responsible; beside o.s. **невмеша́тельство, -а** non-intervention; non-interference. **невмоготу́, невмо́чь** *advs.* unbearable, unendurable, too much (for). **невнима́ние, -я** inattention; carelessness; lack of consideration. **невнима́тельный** inattentive, thoughtless. **невня́тный** indistinct, incomprehensible.

не́вод, -а seine, seine-net.

не... невозврати́мый, невозвра́тный irrevocable, irrecoverable. **невозвращéнец, -нца** defector. **невозде́ланный** untilled, waste. **невозде́ржанный, невозде́ржный** intemperate; incontinent; uncontrolled, unrestrained. **невозмо́жный** impossible; insufferable. **невозмути́мый** imperturbable; calm, unruffled. **невозобновля́емый** non-renewable.

нево́лить, -лю *impf.* (*pf.* **при~**) force, compel. **нево́льник, -а, -ница, -ы** slave. **нево́льно** *adv.* involuntarily; unintentionally. **нево́льный** involuntary; unintentional; forced; **~ная поса́дка** forced landing. **нево́ля, -и** bondage, captivity; necessity.

не... невообрази́мый unimaginable, inconceivable. **невооружённ|ый** unarmed; **~ным гла́зом** with the naked eye. **невоспи́танность, -и** ill breeding, bad manners. **невоспи́танный** ill-bred. **невоспламеня́емый** non-inflammable. **невосприи́мчивый** unreceptive; immune. **невпопа́д** *adv.* out of place; irrelevant, inopportune.

невралги́ческий neuralgic. **невралги́я, -и** neuralgia.

невреди́мый safe, unharmed, uninjured.

неври́т, -а neuritis. **невро́з, -а** neurosis. **неврологи́ческий** neurological. **невроло́гия, -и** neurology. **невро́тик, -а** neurotic. **невроти́ческий** neurotic.

не... невручéние, -я non-delivery. **невы́года, -ы** disadvantage, loss. **невы́годный** disadvantageous, unfavourable; unprofitable, unremunerative. **невы́держанный** lacking self-control; unmatured. **невыноси́мый** unbearable, insufferable, intolerable. **невыполнéние, -я** non-fulfilment, non-compliance. **невыполни́мый** impracticable. **невырази́мый** inexpressible, unmentionable. **невысо́кий; -со́к, -á, -о́ко́** not high, low; not tall, short. **невы́ясненный** obscure, uncertain. **неувя́зка, -и** discrepancy.

нéга, -и luxury; bliss, delight; voluptuousness.

негашён|ый unslaked; **~ая и́звесть** quicklime.

нéгде *adv.* there is nowhere.

не... неги́бкий; -бок, -бкá, -о inflexible, stiff. **негла́сный** secret. **неглубо́кий; -о́к, -á, -о** rather shallow; superficial. **неглу́п|ый; -у́п, -á, -о** sensible, quite intelligent; **он ~** he is no fool. **него́дник, -а** reprobate, scoundrel, good-for-nothing. **него́дный; -ден, -днá, -о** unfit, unsuitable; worthless. **негодова́ние, -я** indignation. **негодова́ть, -ду́ю** *impf.* be indignant. **негоду́ющий** indignant. **негодя́й, -я** scoundrel, rascal. **негостеприи́мный** inhospitable.

негр, -а Negro.

негра́мотность, -и illiteracy. **негра́мотный** illiterate.

негритёнок, -нка; *pl.* **-тя́та, -тя́т** Negro child. **негритя́нка, -и** Negress. **негритя́нский, нéгрский** Negro.

не... неда́вний recent. **неда́вно** *adv.* recently. **недалёкий; -ёк, -á, -ёко́** not far away, near; short; not bright, dull-witted. **недалёко́** *adv.* not far, near. **неда́ром** *adv.* not for nothing, not without reason, not without purpose. **недви́жимость, -и** real property, real estate. **недви́жимый** immovable; motionless. **недвусмы́сленный** unequivocal. **недействи́тельный** ineffective, ineffectual; invalid, null and void. **недели́мый** indivisible.

недéльный of a week, week's. **недéля, -и** week.

не... недёшево *adv.* not cheap(ly), dear(ly). **недоброжела́тель, -я** *m.* ill-wisher **недоброжела́тельность, -и, недоброжела́тельство, -а** hostility, ill-will, malevolence. **недоброжела́тельный** ill-disposed, hostile, malevolent. **недоброка́чественный** of poor quality, low-grade; bad. **недобросо́вестный** unscrupulous; not conscientious, careless. **недо́брый; -о́бр, -брá, -о** unkind, unfriendly; bad; evil, wicked. **недовéрие, -я** distrust; mistrust; lack of confidence. **недовéрчивый** distrustful, not confident, mistrustful. **недовéс, -а** short weight. **недово́льный** dissatisfied, discontented, displeased; *sb.* malcontent.**недово́льство, -а** dissatisfaction, discontent, displeasure. **недога́дливый** slow-witted. **недоглядéть, -яжу́** *pf.* overlook; take insufficient care of. **недоеда́ние, -я** malnutrition. **недоеда́ть, -а́ю** *impf.* be undernourished, be underfed, not eat enough. **недозво́ленный** unlawful; illicit.

недои́мка, -и arrears. **недои́мочность, -и** non-payment. **недои́мщик, -а** defaulter, person in arrears.

не... недо́лг|ий; -лог, -лгá, -о short, brief; **вот и вся ~á** that's all there is to it. **недо́лго** *adv.* not long. **недолговéчный** short-lived, ephemeral. **недомéр, -а** short measure. **недомéрок, -рка** undersized object; small size. **недомога́ние, -я** indisposition. **недомога́ть, -а́ю** *impf.* be unwell, be indisposed. **недомо́лвка, -и** reservation, omission. **недомы́слие, -я** thoughtlessness. **недоно́сок, -ска** premature child. **недоно́шенный** premature. **недооцéнивать, -аю** *impf.*, **недооцени́ть, -ню́, -нишь** *pf.* underestimate, underrate. **недооцéнка, -и** underestimation. **недопроизво́дство, -а** underproduction. **недопусти́мый** inadmissible, intolerable. **недоразумéние, -я** misunderstanding. **недорого́й, -до́рог, -á, -о** not dear, inexpensive; reasonable, modest. **недоро́д, -а** crop failure, bad harvest. **недосмо́тр, -а** oversight. **недосмотрéть, -рю́, -ришь** *pf.* overlook, miss; take insufficient care. **недоспа́ть, -плю́; -а́л, -á, -о** *pf.* (*impf.* **недосыпа́ть**) not have enough sleep.

недостава́ть, -таёт *impf.*, **недоста́ть, -а́нет** *pf. impers.* be missing, be lacking, be wanting. **недоста́ток, -тка** shortage, lack, deficiency, want; shortcoming, defect. **недоста́точно** *adv.* insufficiently, not enough. **недоста́точный** insufficient, inadequate; ~ **глаго́л** defective verb. **недоста́ча, -и** lack, shortage, deficit.

не... недостижи́мый unattainable. **недостове́рный** not authentic, doubtful, apocryphal. **недосто́йный** unworthy, **недосту́пный** inaccessible. **недосу́г, -а** lack of time, being too busy; **за ~ом** for lack of time. **недосчита́ться, -а́юсь** *pf.* **недосчи́тываться, -аюсь** *impf.* miss, find missing, be short (of). **недосыпа́ть, -а́ю** *impf. of* **недоспа́ть. недосяга́емый** unattainable. **недотро́га, -и** *c.g.* touchy person; *f.* mimosa.

недоумева́ть, -а́ю *impf.* be puzzled, be at a loss, be bewildered. **недоуме́ние, -я** perplexity, bewilderment. **недоуме́нный** puzzled, perplexed.

не... недоу́чка, -и *c.g.* half-educated person. **недохва́тка, -и** shortage, lack. **недочёт, -а** deficit, shortage; shortcoming, defect.

не́дра, недр *pl.* depths, heart, bowels; **бога́тство недр** mineral wealth.

не... недре́млющий unsleeping, watchful, vigilant. **не́друг, -а** enemy. **недружелю́бный** unfriendly.

неду́г, -а illness, disease.

недурно́й not bad; not bad looking.

недю́жинный out of the ordinary, outstanding, exceptional.

не... неесте́ственный unnatural. **нежда́нно** *adv.* unexpectedly; **~-нега́данно** quite unexpectedly. **нежда́нный** unexpected, unlooked-for. **нежела́ние, -я** unwillingness, disinclination. **нежела́тельный** undesirable, unwanted. **нежена́тый** unmarried.

не́женка, -и *c.g.* mollycoddle.

нежило́й uninhabited; not habitable.

не́жить, -жу *impf.* pamper; indulge; caress; **~ся** luxuriate, bask. **не́жничать, -аю** *impf.* bill and coo; be soft, be over-indulgent. **не́жность, -и** tenderness; delicacy; *pl.* endearments, display of affection, compliments, flattery. **не́жный** tender; delicate; affectionate.

не... незабве́нный unforgettable. **незабу́дка, -и** forget-me-not. **незабыва́емый** unforgettable. **незаве́ренный** uncertified. **незави́симо** *adv.* independently; ~ **от** irrespective of. **незави́симый** independent; sovereign. **незави́сящ|ий; по ~им от нас обстоя́тельствам** owing to circumstances beyond our control. **незада́ча, -и** ill luck, bad luck. **незада́чливый** unlucky; luckless. **незадо́лго** *adv.* not long. **незако́нн|ый** illegal, illicit, unlawful; illegitimate; **~ая жена́** common-law wife. **незако́нченный** unfinished, incomplete. **незамени́мый** irreplaceable, indispensable. **незамерза́ющ|ий** ice-free; anti-freeze; **~ая смесь** antifreeze. **незаме́тно** *adv.* imperceptibly, insensibly. **незаме́тный** imperceptible; inconspicuous, insignificant. **незаму́жняя** unmarried, single. **незамыслова́тый** simple, uncomplicated. **незапа́мятный** immemorial. **незапя́тнанный** unstained, unsullied. **незара́зный** non-contagious. **незаслу́женный** unmerited, undeserved. **незастро́енный** not built on, undeveloped; vacant. **незате́йливый** simple, plain; modest. **незауря́дный** uncommon, outstanding, out of the ordinary.

не́зачем *adv.* there is no need; it is useless, pointless, no use.

не... незащищённый unprotected. **незва́ный** uninvited. **нездоро́виться, -ится** *impf., impers.+d.*; **мне нездоро́вится** I don't feel well, I am not well. **нездоро́вый** unhealthy, sickly; morbid; unwholesome; unwell. **нездоро́вье, -я** indisposition; ill health. **неземно́й** not of the earth; unearthly. **незло́бивый** gentle, mild, forgiving. **незнако́мец, -мца, незнако́мка, -и** stranger. **незнако́мый** unknown, unfamiliar; unacquainted. **незна́ние, -я** ignorance. **незна́чащий, незначи́тельный** insignificant, unimportant, of no consequence. **незре́лый** unripe, immature. **незри́мый** invisible. **незы́блемый** unshakable, stable, firm. **неизбе́жный** inevitable, unavoidable, inescapable. **неизве́данный** unknown, unexplored; not experienced before.

неизве́стное *sb.* unknown quantity. **неизве́стность, -и** uncertainty; ignorance; obscurity. **неизве́стный** unknown; *sb.* stranger, unknown.

не... неизглади́мый indelible, uneffaceable. **неи́зданный** unpublished. **неизлечи́мый** incurable. **неизме́нный** unchanged, unchanging; devoted, true. **неизменя́емый** invariable, unalterable. **неизмери́мый** immeasurable, immense. **неизу́ченный** unstudied; obscure, unknown; unexplored. **неиме́ние, -я** lack, want; absence; **за ~м**+*g.* for want of. **неимове́рный** incredible, unbelievable. **неиму́щий** indigent, needy, poor. **неи́скренний** insincere; false. **неиску́сный** unskilful, inexpert. **неискушённый** inexperienced, innocent, unsophisticated. **неисполне́ние, -я** non-performance, non-observance, non-execution. **неисполни́мый** impracticable, unrealizable. **неисправи́мый** incorrigible; irremediable, irreparable. **неиспра́вность, -и** disrepair, fault, defect; carelessness. **неиспра́вный** out of order, faulty, defective; careless. **неиссле́дованный** unexplored, uninvestigated. **неиссяка́емый** inexhaustible. **неи́стовство, -а** fury, frenzy; violence; savagery, atrocity. **неи́стовый** furious, frenzied, uncontrolled. **неистощи́мый, неисчерпа́емый** inexhaustible. **неисчисли́мый** innumerable, incalculable.

нейло́н, -а, нейло́новый nylon.

нейро́н, -а neuron.

нейтрализа́ция, -и neutralization. **нейтрализова́ть, -зу́ю** *impf.* & *pf.* neutralize. **нейтралите́т, -а, нейтра́льность, -и** neutrality. **нейтра́льный** neutral. **нейтри́но, -а** neutrino. **нейтро́н, -а** neutron.

неквалифици́рованный unskilled; unqualified.

не́кий *pron.* a certain, some.

не́когда[1] *adv.* once, long ago, in the old days.

не́когда[2] *adv.* there is no time; **мне** ~ I have no time.

не́кого, не́кому, не́кем, не́ о ком *pron.* (*with separable pref.*) there is nobody.

неколеби́мый unshakeable.

некомпете́нтный not competent, unqualified.

не́котор|ый *pron.* some; **~ым о́бразом** somehow, in a way; **~ые** *sb.*, *pl.* some, some people.

некраси́вый plain, ugly, unsightly, unpleasant.

некро́з, -а necrosis. **некроло́г, -а** obituary (notice). **некрома́нтия, -и** necromancy; telling fortunes.

некры́тый roofless.

некста́ти *adv.* malapropos, unseasonably, at the wrong time, out of place.

не́кто *pron.* somebody; one, a certain.

не́куда *adv.* there is nowhere.

не... некульту́рный uncivilized, uncultured; uncultivated; barbarous, ill-mannered, uncouth, boorish. **некуря́щий** *sb.* non-smoker. **нела́дн|ый** wrong; **здесь что́-то ~о** something is wrong here; **будь он ~ен!** blast him! **нелады́, -о́в** *pl.* discord, disagreement; trouble, something wrong. **нелега́льный** illegal. **нелега́льщина, -ы** illegal literature, illegal activity. **нелёгкая** *sb.* the devil, the deuce. **нелёгкий** difficult, not easy; heavy, not light. **неле́пость, -и** absurdity, nonsense. **неле́пый** absurd, ridiculous. **нело́вк|ий** awkward, clumsy, gauche; uncomfortable, embarrassing; **мне ~о** I'm uncomfortable. **нело́вко** *adv.* awkwardly, uncomfortably. **нело́вкость, -и** awkwardness, gaucherie, clumsiness; blunder. **нельзя́** *adv.* it is impossible, it is not allowed; one ought not, one should not, one can't; **здесь кури́ть** ~ smoking is not allowed here; **как ~ лу́чше** in the best possible way.

не... нелюбе́зный ungracious; discourteous. **нелюби́мый** unloved. **нелюди́м, -а, нелюди́мка, -и** unsociable person. **нелюди́мый** unsociable; unpeopled, lonely. **нема́ло** *adv.* not a little, not a few; a considerable amount or number. **немалова́жный** of no small importance. **нема́лый** no small, considerable. **неме́дленно** *adv.* immediately, at once, without delay. **неме́дленный** immediate.

неме́ть, -е́ю *impf.* (*pf.* **за~, о~**) become dumb; grow numb. **не́мец, -мца** German. **неме́цк|ий** German; **~ая овча́рка** Alsation (*dog*).

неми́лость, -и disgrace, disfavour.

немину́емый inevitable, unavoidable.

не́мка, -и German.

немно́г|ий a little; not much; (a) few; **~ие** *sb.*, *pl.* few, a few. **немно́го** *adv.* a little; some, not much; a few; somewhat, slightly. **немногосло́вный** laconic, brief, terse. **немно́жко** *adv.* a little, a bit, a trifle.

немну́щийся uncrushable, crease-resistant.

нем|о́й; нем, -а́, -о dumb, mute, (utterly) silent; **~а́я а́збука** deaf-and-dumb alphabet; **~о́й согла́сный** voiceless consonant; **~о́й фильм** silent film. **немота́, -ы́** dumbness.

не́мощный feeble, ill, sick. **не́мощь, -и** sickness; feebleness, infirmity.

немудрёный simple, easy; **немудрено́** no wonder.

ненави́деть, -и́жу *impf.* hate, detest, loathe. **ненави́стник, -а** hater. **ненави́стный** hated, hateful. **не́нависть, -и** hatred.

не... ненагля́дный dear, beloved. **ненадёжный** insecure; unreliable, untrustworthy. **нена́добность, -и** uselessness. **ненадо́лго** *adv.* for a short time, not for long. **ненападе́ние, -я** non-aggression. **ненаруши́мый** inviolable. **ненаси́лие, -я** non-violence. **ненаси́льственный** non-violent. **нена́стный** bad, foul, rainy. **нена́стье, -я** bad weather, wet weather. **ненастоя́щий** artificial, imitation, counterfeit. **ненасы́тный** insatiable. **ненорма́льность, -и** abnormality. **ненорма́льный** abnormal; deranged. **нену́жный** unnecessary, superfluous.

нео... *pref.* neo-. **неозо́йский** neozoic. **~классици́зм, -а** neo-classicism. **~колониали́зм, -а** neo-colonialism. **~фаши́стский** neo-fascist. **~фи́т, -а** neophyte.

не... необду́манный thoughtless, hasty, precipitate. **необеспе́ченный** without means, unprovided for, not provided (with). **необита́емый** uninhabited; ~ **о́стров** desert island. **необозна́ченный** not indicated, not marked. **необозри́мый** boundless, immense, **необосно́ванный** unfounded, groundless. **необрабо́танный** uncultivated, untilled; raw, crude; unpolished, untrained. **необразо́ванный** uneducated. **необу́зданный** unbridled, ungovernable. **необу́ченный** untrained.

необходи́мость, -и necessity; **по необходи́мости** of necessity, perforce. **необходи́мый** necessary, essential.

не... необъясни́мый inexplicable, unaccountable. **необъя́тный** immense, unbounded. **необыкнове́нный** unusual, uncommon. **необыча́йный** extraordinary, exceptional, unaccustomed. **необы́чный** unusual, singular. **необяза́тельный** optional. **неограни́ченный** unlimited, absolute. **неоднокра́тно** *adv.* repeatedly, more than once. **неоднокра́тный** repeated. **неодобре́ние, -я** disapproval. **неодобри́тельный** disapproving. **неодушевлённый** inanimate.

неожи́данность, -и unexpectedness, suddenness; surprise. **неожи́данный** unexpected, sudden.

не... неоконча́тельный inconclusive. **неоко́нченный** unfinished. **неопису́емый** indescribable. **неопла́тный** that cannot be repaid; insolvent. **неопла́ченный** unpaid. **неопра́вданный** unjustified, unwarranted. **неопределённый** indefinite, indeterminate; infinitive; vague, uncertain. **неопредели́мый** indefinable. **неопроверживый** irrefutable; incontestable. **неопря́тный** slovenly, untidy, sloppy. **неопублико́ванный** unpublished. **нео́пытность, -и** inexperience. **нео́пытный** inexperienced. **неосведомлённый** ill-informed. **неосе́длый** nomadic. **неосла́бный** unremitting, unabated, untiring. **неосмотри́тельный** imprudent, incautious; indiscreet. **неоснова́тельный** unfounded, unwarranted; frivolous. **неоспори́мый** unquestionable, incontestable, indisputable. **неосторо́жный** careless, imprudent, indiscreet, incautious. **неосуществи́мый** impracticable, unrealizable. **неосяза́емый** intangible. **неотврати́мый** inevitable. **неотвя́зный, неотвя́зчивый** importunate; obsessive. **неотёсанный** rough, undressed; unpolished, uncouth.

не́откуда *adv.* there is nowhere; there is no reason; **мне ~ э́то получи́ть** there is nowhere I can get it from.

не... неотло́жн|ый urgent, pressing; **~ая по́мощь** first aid. **неотлу́чно** *adv.* constantly, continually, unremittingly; permanent. **неотлу́чный** continual, constant, permanent. **неотрази́мый** irresistible; incontrovertible, irrefutable. **неотсту́пный** persistent, importunate. **неотъе́млемый** inalienable; inseparable, integral. **неохо́та, -ы** reluctance. **неохо́тно** *adv.* reluctantly; unwillingly. **неоцени́мый** inestimable, invaluable. **неощути́мый** imperceptible. **непа́рный** odd. **непарти́йный** non-party; unbefitting a member of the (Communist) Party. **непереводи́мый** untranslatable. **непередава́емый** incommunicable, inexpressible. **неперехо́дный** intransitive. **непеча́тный** unprintable.

неплатёж, -ежа́ non-payment. **неплатёжеспосо́бный** insolvent. **неплате́льщик, -а** defaulter; person in arrears.

не... неплодоро́дный infertile. **непло́хо** *adv.* not badly, quite well. **неплохо́й** not bad, quite good. **непобеди́мый** invincible; unbeatable. **неповинове́ние, -я** insubordination, disobedience. **неповоро́тливый** clumsy, awkward; sluggish, slow. **неповтори́мый** inimitable, unique. **непого́да, -ы** bad weather. **непогреши́мый** infallible. **неподалёку** *adv.* not far(away). **неподა́тливый** stubborn, intractable, unyielding. **неподви́жный** motionless, immobile, immovable; fixed, stationary. **неподде́льный** genuine; sincere, unfeigned. **неподку́пный** incorruptible, unbribable. **неподража́емый** inimitable. **неподходя́щий** unsuitable, inappropriate. **непоко́йный** troubled, disturbed, restless. **непоколеби́мый** unshakable, steadfast. **непоко́рный** recalcitrant, unruly, insubordinate. **непокры́тый** uncovered, bare.

не... непола́дки, -док *pl.* defects. **неполноце́нность, -и; ко́мплекс неполноце́нности** inferiority complex. **неполноце́нный** defective, imperfect; inadequate. **непо́лный** incomplete; defective; not quite, not (a) full. **непоме́рный** excessive, inordinate. **непонима́ние, -я** incomprehension, lack of understanding. **непоня́тливый** slow-witted, stupid, dull. **непоня́тный** unintelligible, incomprehensible. **непоправи́мый** irreparable, irremediable. **непоря́док, -дка** disorder. **непоря́дочный** dishonourable. **непосвящённый** uninitiated. **непосе́да, -ы** *c.g.* fidget, restless person. **непоси́льный** beyond one's strength, excessive. **непосле́довательный** inconsistent; inconsequent. **непослуша́ние, -я** disobedience. **непослу́шный** disobedient, naughty. **непосре́дственный** immediate, direct; spontaneous; ingenuous. **непостижи́мый** incomprehensible. **непостоя́нный** inconstant, changeable. **непостоя́нство, -а** inconstancy. **непотопля́емый** unsinkable. **непотре́бный** obscene, indecent; useless; bad. **непоча́тый** untouched, not begun; **~ край, у́гол** a lot, a wealth, no end. **непочте́ние, -я** disrespect. **непочти́тельный** disrespectful.

не... непра́вда, -ы untruth, falsehood, lie. **неправдоподо́бие, -я** improbability, unlikelihood. **неправдоподо́бный** improbable, unlikely, implausible. **непра́вильно** *adv.* wrong; irregularly; incorrectly; erroneously. **непра́вильность, -и** irregularity; anomaly; incorrectness. **непра́вильн|ый** irregular; anomalous; incorrect, erroneous, wrong, mistaken; **~ая дробь** improper fraction. **неправомо́чный** incompetent; not entitled. **неправоспосо́бный** disqualified. **неправота́, -ы́** error; injustice. **непра́вый** wrong, mistaken; unjust. **непракти́чный** unpractical. **непревзойдённый** unsurpassed, matchless. **непредви́денный** unforeseen. **непредубеждённый** unprejudiced. **непредусмо́тренный** unforeseen; unprovided for. **непредусмотри́тельный** improvident, short-sighted. **непреклóнный** inflexible, unbending; inexorable, adamant. **непрело́жный** immutable, unalterable; indisputable.

не... непреме́нно *adv.* without fail; certainly; absolutely. **непреме́нный** indispensable, necessary; **~ секрета́рь** permanent secretary. **непреодоли́мый** insuperable, insurmountable; irresistible. **непреры́вно** *adv.* uninterruptedly, continuously. **непреры́вный** uninterrupted, unbroken; continuous. **непреста́нный** incessant, continual. **неприве́тливый** unfriendly, ungracious; bleak. **непривлека́тельный** unattractive. **непривы́чный** unaccustomed, unwonted, unusual. **непригля́дный** unattractive, unsightly. **неприго́дный** unfit, unserviceable, useless; ineligible. **неприе́млемый** unacceptable. **неприкоснове́нность, -и** inviolability, immunity. **неприкоснове́нный** inviolable; to be kept intact; reserve, emergency. **неприкра́шенный** plain, unadorned, unvarnished. **неприли́чный** indecent, improper; unseemly, unbecoming. **неприме́ни́мый** inapplicable. **непримири́мый** irreconcilable. **непринуждённый** unconstrained; natural, relaxed, easy; spontaneous. **неприспосо́бленный** unadapted; maladjusted. **непристо́йный** obscene, indecent. **непристу́пный** inaccessible, impregnable; unapproachable, haughty. **непритво́рный** unfeigned. **непритяза́тельный, неприхотли́вый** modest, unpretentious, simple, plain. **неприя́зненный** hostile, inimical. **неприя́знь, -и** hostility, enmity. **неприя́тель, -я** *m.* enemy. **неприя́тельский** hostile, enemy. **неприя́тный** unpleasant, disagreeable; annoying, troublesome; obnoxious.

не... непрове́ренный unverified, unchecked. **непроводни́к, -а́** non-conductor. **непроводя́щий** non-conducting. **непрогля́дный** impenetrable; pitch-dark. **непродолжи́тельный** short, short-lived. **непроду́манный** rash, unconsidered. **непрое́зжий** impassable. **непрозра́чный** opaque. **непроизводи́тельный** unproductive; wasteful. **непроизво́льный** involuntary. **непроля́зный** impassable, impenetrable. **непромока́емый** waterproof. **непроница́емый** impenetrable, impervious; inscrutable; +**для**+*g.* proof against. **непрости́тельный** unforgivable, unpardonable, inexcusable. **непроходи́мый** impassable; complete, utter, hopeless. **непро́чный; -чен, -чна́, -о** fragile, flimsy; precarious, unstable; not durable.

не прочь *pred.* not averse; **я ~ пойти́ туда́** I wouldn't mind going there.

не... непро́шеный uninvited, unasked(-for). **неработоспосо́бный** incapacitated, disabled. **нерабо́чий; ~ день** day off, free day. **нера́венство, -а** inequality, disparity. **неравноме́рный** uneven, irregular. **нера́вный** unequal. **ненади́вый** negligent, indolent, careless, remiss. **неразбери́ха, -и** muddle, confusion. **неразбо́рчивый** not fastidious; unscrupulous; illegible. **неразвито́й; -ра́звит, -а́, -о** undeveloped; backward. **неразгово́рчивый** taciturn, not talkative. **неразделимый, неразде́льный** indivisible, inseparable. **неразличи́мый** indistinguishable. **неразлу́чный** inseparable. **неразрешённый** unsolved; forbidden, prohibited. **неразреши́мый** insoluble. **неразры́вный** indissoluble, inseparable. **неразу́мный** unwise, unreasonable. **нерасположе́ние, -я** dislike; disinclination. **нерасполо́женный** ill-disposed; unwilling, disinclined. **нерастворимый** insoluble. **нерасчётливый** extravagant, wasteful; improvident.

нерв, -а nerve; **гла́вный ~** nerve-centre. **нерви́ровать, -рую** *impf.* get on s.o.'s nerves, irritate. **не́рвничать, -аю** *impf.* be fidgety, fret; be irritable. **нерви́ческий** nervous. **нервнобольно́й** *sb.* neurotic, nervous case. **не́рвный; -вен, -вна́, -о** nervous; neural; irritable, highly strung; **~ у́зел** ganglion. **нерво́зный** nervy, irritable, excitable. **нервю́ра, -ы** rib.

не... нереа́льный unreal; unrealistic. **нере́дкий; -док, -дка́, -о** not infrequent, not uncommon. **нере́дко** not infrequently. **нереши́мость, -и, нереши́тельность, -и** indecision; irresolution. **нереши́тельный** indecisive, irresolute, undecided. **нержаве́ющ|ий** rustless; **~ая сталь** stainless steel. **неро́вный; -вен, -вна́, -о** uneven, rough; unequal, irregular. **нерукотво́рный** not made with hands. **неруши́мый** inviolable, indestructible, indissoluble.

неря́ха, -и *c.g.* sloven; slattern, slut. **неря́шливый** slovenly, untidy, slatternly; careless, slipshod.

не... несбы́точн|ый unrealizable; **~ые мечты́** castles in the air; **~ые наде́жды** vain hopes. **несваре́ние, -я; ~ желу́дка** indigestion. **несве́жий; -е́ж, -а́** not fresh; stale; tainted; weary, washed-out. **несвоевре́менный** ill-timed, inopportune; overdue, not at the right time. **несво́йственный** not characteristic, unusual, unlike. **несвя́зный** disconnected, incoherent. **несгиба́емый** unbending, inflexible. **несгово́рчивый** intractable. **несгора́емый** fireproof; **~ шкаф** safe.

несессе́р, -а dressing-case.

нескла́дный incoherent; ungainly, awkward; absurd.

несклоня́емый indeclinable.

не́сколько, -их *pron.* some, several; a number, a few; *adv.* somewhat, a little, rather.

не... несконча́емый interminable, never-ending. **нескро́мный; -мен, -мна́, -о** immodest; vain; indelicate, tactless, indiscreet. **несло́жный** simple. **неслы́ханный** unheard-of, unprecedented. **неслы́шный** inaudible; noiseless. **несме́тный** countless, incalculable, innumerable. **несмина́емый** uncrushable, crease-resistant. **несмолка́емый** ceaseless, unremitting.

несмотря́ на *prep.+a.* in spite of, despite, notwithstanding.

не... несно́сный intolerable, insupportable, unbearable. **несоблюде́ние, -я** non-observance. **несовершенноле́тие, -я** minority.

несовершеннолéтний under-age; *sb.* minor. **несовершéнный** imperfect, incomplete; imperfective. **несовмести́мость, -и** incompatibility. **несовмести́мый** incompatible. **несоглáсие, -я** disagreement, difference; discord, variance; refusal. **несоглáсный** not agreeing; inconsistent, incompatible; discordant; not consenting. **несогласовáние, -я** non-agreement. **несоглáсованный** uncoordinated. **несознáтельный** irresponsible. **несоизмери́мый** incommensurable. **несокруши́мый** indestructible; unconquerable. **несóлоно; уйти́ ~ хлебáвши** get nothing for one's pains, go away empty-handed. **несомнéнно** *adv.* undoubtedly, doubtless, beyond question. **несомнéнный** undoubted, indubitable, unquestionable. **несообрáзный** incongruous, incompatible; absurd. **несоотвéтствие, -я** disparity, incongruity. **несоразмéрный** disproportionate. **несостоя́тельный** insolvent, bankrupt; not wealthy, of modest means; groundless, unsupported. **неспéлый** unripe. **неспокóйный** restless; uneasy. **неспосóбный** dull, not able; incapable, not competent. **несправедли́вый** unjust, unfair; incorrect, unfounded. **неспростá** *adv.* not without purpose; with an ulterior motive. **несравнéнно** *adv.* incomparably, matchlessly; far, by far. **несравнéнный; -éнен, -éнна** incomparable, matchless. **несравни́мый** not comparable; incomparable, unmatched. **нестерпи́мый** unbearable, unendurable.

нести́, -сý, -сёшь; нёс, -лá *impf.* (*pf.* **по~, с~**) carry; bear; bring, take; support; suffer; incur; perform; talk; lay; *impers.+i.* stink of, reek of; **~сь** rush, tear, fly; float, drift, be carried; skim; spread, be diffused; lay, lay eggs.

не... нестóйкий unstable. **нестроеви́к, -á** non-combatant. **нестроевóй** non-combatant. **нестрóйный; -óен, -ойнá, -о** discordant, dissonant; disorderly; clumsily built. **несудохóдный** unnavigable. **несущéственный** immaterial, inessential.

несý *etc.*: *see* **нести́. несýщий** supporting, carrying, bearing, lifting.

несхóдный unlike, dissimilar; unreasonable.

несчастли́вец, -вца, -вица, -ы unlucky person; unfortunate. **несчастли́вый** unfortunate, unlucky; unhappy. **несчáстный** unhappy, unfortunate, unlucky; *sb.* wretch, unfortunate. **несчáстье, -я** misfortune; accident; **к несчáстью** unfortunately.

несчётный innumerable, countless.

нет *part.* no, not; nothing; **~ да ~, ~ как ~** absolutely not; **свести́ на ~** bring to naught; **~-~ да и** from time to time, every now and then. **нет, нéту** there is not, there are not.

не... нетакти́чный tactless. **нетвёрдый; -ёрд, -á, -о** unsteady, shaky; not firm. **нетерпели́вый** impatient. **нетерпéние, -я** impatience. **нетерпи́мый** intolerable, intolerant. **нетóчный; -чен, -чнá, -о** inaccurate, inexact. **нетрадициóнный** unconventional. **нетрéбовательный** not exacting, undemanding; unpretentious. **нетрéзвый** drunk, intoxicated. **нетрóнутый** untouched; chaste, virginal. **нетрудовóй; ~ дохóд** unearned income. **нетрудоспосóбность, -и** disablement, disability.

нéтто *indecl. adj. & adv.* net, nett.

нéту *see* **нет**

не... неубеди́тельный unconvincing. **неуважéние, -я** disrespect. **неуважи́тельный** inadequate; disrespectful. **неувéренный** uncertain; hesitant; **~ в себé** diffident. **неувядáемый, неувядáющий** unfading, eternal, immortal. **неувя́зка, -и** lack of coordination; misunderstanding. **неугаси́мый** inextinguishable, unquenchable; never extinguished. **неугомóнный** restless; unsleeping, indefatigable. **неудáча, -и** failure. **неудáчливый** unlucky. **неудáчник, -а, -ница, -ы** unlucky person, failure. **неудáчный** unsuccessful, unfortunate. **неудержи́мый** irrepressible. **неудóбный** uncomfortable; inconvenient, awkward, embarrassing. **неудóбство, -а** discomfort, inconvenience, embarrassment. **неудовлетворéние, -я** dissatisfaction. **неудовлетворённый** dissatisfied, discontented. **неудовлетвори́тельный** unsatisfactory. **неудовóльствие, -я** displeasure.

неужéли? *part.* indeed? really? surely not? **~ он так дýмает?** does he really think that?

не... неузнавáемый unrecognizable. **неуклóнный** steady, steadfast; undeviating, unswerving, strict. **неуклю́жий** clumsy, awkward. **неукроти́мый** ungovernable, untameable. **неукрощённый; -ён, -á** untamed. **неулови́мый** elusive, difficult to catch; imperceptible, subtle. **неумéлый** unskilful; clumsy. **неумéренный** immoderate; excessive. **неумéстный** inappropriate; out of place, misplaced; irrelevant. **неумоли́мый** implacable, inexorable. **неумы́шленный** unintentional.

не... неуплáта, -ы non-payment. **неупотреби́тельный** not in use, not current. **неуравновéшенный** unbalanced. **неурожáй, -я** bad harvest, crop failure. **неурóчный** untimely, unseasonable, inopportune. **неуря́дица, -ы** disorder, mess; squabbling, squabble. **неуспевáемость, -и** poor progress; underachievement. **неуспевáющий** backward; underachieving. **неуспéх, -а** failure. **неустóйка, -и** forfeit, penalty; failure. **неустóйчивый** unstable; unsteady. **неустраши́мый** fearless, intrepid. **неуступчивый** unyielding, uncompromising. **неусы́пный** vigilant, unremitting. **неутéшный** inconsolable, disconsolate. **неутоли́мый** unquenchable; unappeasable; insatiable. **неутоми́мый** tireless, indefatigable. **нéуч, -а** ignoramus.

неучти́вый discourteous, impolite. **неуязви́мый** invulnerable; unassailable.

неф, -а nave.

нефри́т, -а jade.

нефте... *in comb.* oil, petroleum. **нефтево́з, -а** tanker. **~но́сный** oil-bearing. **~перего́нный заво́д** oil refinery. **~прово́д, -а** (oil) pipeline. **~проду́кты, -ов** *pl.* petroleum products. **~та́нкер, -а** oil-tanker (*ship*). **~хими́ческий** petrochemical.

нефть, -и oil, petroleum; **~-сыре́ц** crude oil. **нефтян|о́й** oil, petroleum; oil-fired; **~о́е покрыва́ло, -а́я плёнка** oil-slick.

не... нехва́тка, -и shortage, deficiency. **нехорошо́** *adv.* badly. **нехоро́ш|ий; -о́ш, -а́** bad; **~о́** it is bad, it is wrong; **как ~о́!** what a shame!; **чу́вствовать себя́ ~о́** feel unwell. **не́хотя** *adv.* reluctantly, unwillingly; unintentionally. **нецелесообра́зн|ый** inexpedient; purposeless, pointless; **~ая тра́та** waste. **нецензу́рный** unprintable. **нечая́нный** unexpected; accidental; unintentional.

не́чего, не́чему, -чем, не́ о чем *pron.* (*with separate pref.*) (there is) nothing; it's no good, it's no use; there is no need; **~ де́лать** there is nothing to be done; it can't be helped; **~ сказа́ть!** well, really! well, I must say!; **от ~ де́лать** for want of something better to do, idly.

нечелове́ческий inhuman, superhuman.

нечести́вый impious, profane. **нече́стно** *adv.* dishonestly, unfairly. **нече́стный** dishonest, unfair.

не́чет, -а odd number. **нечётный** odd.

нечистопло́тный dirty; slovenly; unscrupulous. **нечистота́, -ы́**; *pl.* **-о́ты, -о́т** dirtiness, dirt, filth; *pl.* sewage. **нечи́стый; -и́ст, -а́, -о** dirty, unclean; impure; adulterated; careless, inaccurate; dishonourable, dishonest; *sb.* the evil one, the devil. **не́чисть, -и** evil spirits; scum, vermin.

нечленоразде́льный inarticulate.

не́что *pron.* something.

не... *pref.* **нешу́точн|ый** grave, serious; **~ое де́ло** no joke, no laughing matter. **неща́дный** merciless, pitiless. **нея́вка, -и** non-appearance, absence. **неядови́тый** non-poisonous, non-toxic. **нея́сный; -сен, -сна́, -о** unclear; vague, obscure.

ни *part.* not a; **ни оди́н (одна́, одно́)** not one, not a single; (*with prons. and pronominal advs.*) -ever; **как... ни** however; **кто... ни** whoever; **что... ни** whatever; **како́й ни на есть** any whatsoever. **ни** *conj.*; **ни... ни** neither ... nor; **ни за что ни про что** for no reason, without rhyme or reason; **ни ры́ба ни мя́со** neither fish, flesh, nor good red herring; **ни с того́, ни с сего́** all of a sudden, for no apparent reason; **ни то ни сё** neither one thing nor the other.

ни́ва, -ы cornfield, field.

нивели́р, -а level. **нивели́ровать, -рую** *impf.* & *pf.* level; survey, contour. **нивелиро́вщик, -а** surveyor.

нигде́ *adv.* nowhere.

нидерла́ндец, -дца; *g.pl.* **-дцев** Dutchman. **нидерла́ндка, -и** Dutchwoman. **нидерла́ндский** Dutch.

Нидерла́нды, -ов *pl.* the Netherlands.

нижа́йший lowest, humblest; very low, very humble. **ни́же** *adj.* lower, humbler; *adv.* below; *prep.+g.* below, beneath. **нижеподписа́вшийся** (the) undersigned. **нижесле́дующий** following. **нижестоя́щий** subordinate. **нижеупомя́нутый** (the) undermentioned. **ни́жн|ий** lower, under-; **~ее бельё** underclothes; **~ий эта́ж** ground floor.

низ, -а (-у), *loc.* **-у́**; *pl.* **-ы́** bottom; ground floor; *pl.* lower classes; low notes.

низ..., нис... *vbl. pref.* down, downward(s).

низа́ть, нижу́, ни́жешь *impf.* (*pf.* **на~**) string, thread.

низверга́ть, -а́ю *impf.*, **низве́ргнуть, -ну; -е́рг** *pf.* precipitate; throw down, overthrow; **~ся** crash down; be overthrown. **низверже́ние, -я** overthrow.

низи́на, -ы depression, hollow. **ни́зкий; -зок, -зка́, -о** low; humble; base, mean. **ни́зко** *adv.* low; basely, meanly, despicably. **низкопокло́нник, -а** toady, crawler. **низкопокло́нничать, -аю** *impf.* crawl, cringe, grovel. **низкопокло́нство, -а** obsequiousness, cringing, servility. **низкопро́бный** base; low-grade; inferior. **низкоро́слый** undersized, stunted, dwarfish. **низкосо́ртный** low-grade, of inferior quality.

ни́зменность, -и lowland; baseness. **ни́зменный** low-lying; low, base, vile.

низово́й lower; down-stream, from lower down the Volga; local. **низо́вье, -я**; *g.pl.* **-ьев** the lower reaches; **низо́вья Во́лги** the lower Volga. **ни́зость, -и** lowness; baseness, meanness. **ни́зш|ий** lower, lowest; **~ее образова́ние** primary education; **~ий сорт** inferior quality.

ника́к *adv.* by no means, in no way. **никако́й** *pron.* no; no ... whatever

ни́кель, -я *m.* nickel.

нике́м *see* **никто́**. **никогда́** *adv.* never. **ник|о́й** no; **~о́им о́бразом** by no means, in no way. **никто́, -кого́, -кому́, -ке́м, ни о ко́м** *pron.* (*with separable pref.*) nobody, no one. **никуда́** nowhere; **~ не годи́тся** (it) is worthless, (it) is no good at all, (it) won't do. **никуды́шный** useless, worthless, good-for-nothing. **никчёмный** pointless, useless; no good. **нима́ло** *adv.* not at all, not in the least.

нимб, -а halo, nimbus.

ни́мфа, -ы nymph; pupa. **нимфома́нка, -и** nymphomaniac.

ниотку́да *adv.* from nowhere; not from anywhere.

нипочём *adv.* it is nothing; for nothing, dirt cheap; never, in no circumstances.

ни́ппель, -я; *pl.* **-я́** nipple.

нис... *see* **низ...**
ниско́лько *adv.* not at all, not in the least.
ниспроверга́ть, -а́ю *impf.*, **ниспрове́ргнуть, -ну; -е́рг** *pf.* overthrow, overturn. **ниспроверже́ние, -я** overthrow.
нисходя́щий descending, of descent; falling.
ни́тка, -и thread; string; **до ни́тки** to the skin; **на живу́ю ни́тку** hastily, carelessly, anyhow. **ни́точка, -и** thread. **ни́точный** thread; spinning.
нитро... *in comb.* nitro-. **нитробензо́л, -а** nitrobenzene. **~глицери́н, -а** nitroglycerine. **~клетча́тка, -и** nitrocellulose.
ни́тчатый filiform. **нить, -и** thread; filament; suture; **(путево́дная) ~** clue. **нитяно́й, ни́тяный** cotton, thread.
Ни́цца, -ы Nice.
ничего́ *etc.*: *see* **ничто. ничего́** *adv.* all right; so-so, passably, not too badly; *as indecl. adj.* not bad, passable. **ниче́й, -чья́, -чьё** *pron.* nobody's, no-one's; **ничья́ земля́** no man's land. **ничья́** *sb.* draw, drawn game; tie; dead heat.
ничко́м *adv.* face downwards, prone.
ничто́, -чего́, -чему́, -че́м, ни о чём *pron.* (*with separable pref.*) nothing; naught; nil; **ничего!** that's all right! it doesn't matter! never mind! **ничто́жество, -а** nonentity, nobody; nothingness. **ничто́жный** insignificant; paltry, worthless.
ничу́ть *adv.* not at all, not in the least, not a bit.
ничьё *etc.*: *see* **ниче́й**
ни́ша, -и niche, recess; bay.
ни́щенка, -и beggar-woman. **ни́щенский** beggarly. **ни́щенствовать, -твую** *impf.* beg, be a beggar; be destitute. **нищета́, -ы́** destitution, indigence, poverty; beggars, the poor. **ни́щий; нищ, -а́, -е** destitute, indigent, poverty-stricken, poor; *sb.* beggar, mendicant, pauper.
НЛО *abbr.* (*of* **неопо́знанный лета́ющий объе́кт**) UFO, unidentified flying object.
но *conj.* but; still, nevertheless; *sb.* snag, difficulty.
но *int.* gee up!
нова́тор, -а innovator. **нова́торство, -а** innovation.
Но́вая Зела́ндия, -ой -и New Zealand.
нове́йший newest, latest.
нове́лла, -ы short story. **новелли́ст, -а** short-story writer.
но́веньк|ий brand-new; **~ий, ~ая** *sb.* new boy, new girl.
новизна́, -ы́ novelty; newness. **нови́нка, -и** novelty. **новичо́к, -чка́** novice, beginner, tyro; new recruit; new boy, new girl.
ново... *in comb.* new, newly; recent, recently; modern. **новобра́нец, -нца** new recruit. **~бра́чный** *sb.* bridegroom; **~бра́чная** *sb.* bride; **~бра́чные** *sb.*, *pl.* newly-weds. **~введе́ние, -я** innovation. **~го́дний** new year's, new-year. **~зела́ндец, -дца**; *g.pl.* **-дцев**, **~зела́ндка, -и** New-Zealander. **~зела́ндский** New Zealand. **~лу́ние, -я** new moon. **~мо́дный** up-to-date, fashionable; newfangled. **~прибы́вший** newly-arrived; *sb.* newcomer. **~рождённый** newborn; *sb.* neonate. **~сёл, -а, ~сёлка, -и** new settler. **~се́лье, -я** new home; house-warming.
но́вость, -и news; novelty. **но́вшество, -а** innovation, novelty. **но́вый; нов, -а́, -о** new, novel, fresh; modern, recent; **~ год** New Year's Day. **новь, -и** virgin soil.
нога́, -и́, *a.* **но́гу**; *pl.* **но́ги, нога́м** foot, leg; **без (за́дних) ног** dead beat; **встать с ле́вой ноги́** get out of bed on the wrong side; **дать но́гу** get in step; **идти́ в но́гу с**+*i.* keep in step with; **на коро́ткой ноге́ с**+*i.* intimate with, on good terms with; **на широ́кую (большу́ю, ба́рскую) но́гу** in style, like a lord; **протяну́ть но́ги** turn up one's toes; **сбить с ног** knock down; **сби́ться с ноги́** get out of step; **со всех ног** as fast as one's legs will carry one; **стать на́ ноги, стоя́ть на нога́х** stand on one's own feet.
ногото́к, -тка́ nail; *pl.* marigold. **но́готь, -гтя**; *pl.* **-и** *m.* finger-nail, toe-nail.
нож, -а́ knife; **на ~а́х** at daggers drawn. **ножев|о́й** knife; **~ы́е изде́лия, ~о́й това́р** cutlery; **~о́й ма́стер** cutler.
но́жка, -и small foot or leg; leg; stem, stalk.
но́жницы, -иц *pl.* scissors, shears.
ножно́й foot, pedal, treadle.
но́жны, -жен *pl.* sheath, scabbard.
ножо́вка, -и saw, hacksaw.
ножо́вщик, -а cutler.
ноздрева́тый porous, spongy. **ноздря́, -и́**; *pl.* **-и, -е́й** nostril.
нока́ут, -а knock-out. **нокаути́ровать, -рую** *impf.* & *pf.* knock out.
нолево́й, нулево́й zero. **ноль, -я́, нуль, -я́** *m.* nought, zero, nil, love; cipher; **абсолю́тный ~** absolute zero; **в семна́дцать ~-~** at seventeen hundred hours, at five p.m.
но́мер, -а; *pl.* **-а́** number; size; (hotel-)room; item, turn; trick. **номера́тор** *etc.*: *see* **нумера́тор** *etc.* **номерно́й** *sb.* floor waiter, hotel servant. **номеро́к, -рка́** tag; label, ticket; small room.
номина́л, -а face value. **номина́льный** nominal; rated, indicated.
нора́, -ы́; *pl.* **-ы** burrow, hole; lair, form.
Норве́гия, -и Norway. **норве́жец, -жца, норве́жка, -и** Norwegian. **норве́жский** Norwegian.
норд, -а north; north wind. **норд-ве́ст, -а** north-west, north-wester. **норд-о́ст, -а** north-east, north-easter.
но́рка, -и mink.
но́рма, -ы standard, norm; rate; **~ вре́мени** time limit. **нормализа́ция, -и** standardization. **нормализова́ть, -зу́ю** *impf.* & *pf.* standardize. **норма́льный** normal; standard.
Норма́ндск|ий: ~ие острова́ *pl.* the Channel Islands.

норматив, -а norm, standard **нормирова́ние, -я, нормиро́вка, -и** regulation, normalization; rate-fixing. **нормирова́ть, -ру́ю** *impf. & pf.* regulate, standardize, normalize. **нормиро́вщик, -а, -щица, -ы** rate-fixer, rate-setter.

нос, -а (-у), *loc.* **-у́;** *pl.* **-ы́** nose; beak; bow, prow; **на ~у́** near (at hand), imminent; **оста́вить с ~ом** dupe, make a fool of; **пове́сить ~** be crestfallen, be discouraged. **но́сик, -а** (small) nose; toe; spout.

носи́лки, -лок *pl.* stretcher; litter; hand-barrow. **носи́льщик, -а** porter. **носи́тель, -я** *m.*, **-тельница, -ы** bearer; carrier; vehicle. **носи́ть, -ошу́, -о́сишь** *impf.* carry, bear; wear; **~ на рука́х** make much of, make a fuss of, spoil; **~ся** rush, tear along, fly; float, drift, be carried; wear; +**с**+*i.* make much of, make a fuss of. **но́ска, -и** carrying, bearing, wearing; laying. **но́ский** hard-wearing, durable; laying, that lays well.

носово́й of or for the nose; nasal; bow, fore; **~ плато́к** (pocket) handkerchief. **носо́к, -ска́** little nose; toe; sock. **носоро́г, -а** rhinoceros.

но́та, -ы note; *pl.* music.

нота́риус, -а notary.

нота́ция, -и notation; lecture, reprimand.

ночева́ть, -чу́ю *impf.* (*pf.* **пере~**) spend the night. **ночёвка, -и** spending the night. **ночле́г, -а** shelter for the night, a night's lodging; passing the night. **ночле́жка, -и, ночле́жный дом** doss-house, common lodging-house. **ночни́к, -а́** night-light. **ночн|о́й** night, nocturnal; **~а́я ба́бочка** moth; **~а́я руба́шка** nightdress, nightgown, nightshirt; **~о́й сто́лик** bedside table; **~ы́е ту́фли** bedroom slippers. **ночь, -и,** *loc.* **-и́;** *g.pl.* **-е́й** night; **глуха́я ~** dead of night. **но́чью** *adv.* at night, by night.

но́ша, -и burden. **но́шеный** in use, worn; part-worn, second-hand.

но́ю *etc.*: *see* **ныть**

ноя́брь, -я́ *m.* November. **ноя́брьский** November.

нрав, -а disposition, temper; *pl.* manners, customs, ways; **по ~у** to one's taste, pleasing. **нра́виться, -влюсь** *impf.* (*pf.* **по~**) +*d.* please; **мне нра́вится** I like. **нравоуче́ние, -я** moralizing, moral lecture; moral. **нравоучи́тельный** edifying. **нра́вственность, -и** morality, morals. **нра́вственный** moral.

н. ст. *abbr.* (*of* **но́вый стиль**) NS, New Style (*of calendar*).

ну *int. & part.* well, well then; what?; really; what a ..!; there's a ..!; **а ну́**+*g.* to hell with; **(да) ну́?** not really?; **ну́ как**+*fut.* suppose, what if?

ну́дный tedious, boring.

нужда́, -ы́; *pl.* **-ы** want, straits; need; indigence; necessity; call of nature; **нужды́ нет** never mind, it doesn't matter. **нужда́ться, -а́юсь** *impf.* be in want, be poor, be hard up; +**в**+*p.* need, require, want. **ну́жник, -а** lavatory, public convenience, latrine. **ну́жн|ый; -жен, -жна́, -о, ну́жны́** necessary, requisite; **~о** it is necessary; +*d.* I, *etc.*, must, ought to, should, need.

нуклейновый nucleic.

нулево́й, нуль *see* **нолево́й, ноль**

нумера́тор, ном-, -а numberer, numbering machine; annunciation. **нумера́ция, ном-, -и** numeration; numbering. **нумерова́ть, ном-, -ру́ю** *impf.* (*pf.* **за~, про~**) number.

нутро́, -а́ inside, interior; core, kernel; instinct(s), intuition; **всем ~м** with one's whole being, completely; **по нутру́**+*d.* to the liking of. **нутряно́й** internal.

ны́не *adv.* now; today. **ны́нешний** the present, this; today's. **ны́нче** *adv.* today; now.

нырну́ть, -ну́, -нёшь *pf.*, **ныря́ть, -я́ю** *impf.* dive, plunge; duck. **ныро́к, -рка́** dive, plunge; duck, ducking; diver. **ныря́ло, -а** plunger.

ны́тик, -а whiner, moaner. **ныть, но́ю** *impf.* ache; whine, moan. **нытьё, -я́** whining, moaning.

Нью-Йо́рк, -а New York.

н.э. *abbr.* (*of* **на́шей э́ры**) AD; **до н. э.** BC.

нюх, -а scent; nose, flair. **ню́хательный таба́к** snuff. **ню́хать, -аю** *impf.* (*pf.* **по~**) smell, sniff; **~ таба́к** take snuff.

ня́нчить, -чу *impf.* nurse, look after; dandle; **~ся с**+*i.* be nurse to, act as nurse to; fuss over, make a fuss of. **ня́нька, -и** nanny. **ня́ня, -и** (*children's*) nurse, nanny; hospital nurse; **приходя́щая ~** babysitter; childminder.

о *nt.indecl.* the letter **о**.

о, об, обо *prep.* **I.** +*p.* of, about, concerning; on; with, having; **стол о трёх но́жках** a three-legged table. **II.** +*a.* against; on, upon; **бок о́ бок** side by side; **опере́ться о сте́ну** lean against the wall; **рука́ о́б руку** hand in hand; **споткну́ться о ка́мень** stumble against a stone. **III.** +*a. or p.* on, at, about; **об э́ту по́ру** about this time; **о заре́** about dawn.

о *int.* oh!

о. *abbr.* (*of* **о́стров**) Is., Island, Isle.

о..., об..., обо..., объ... *vbl. pref. indicates transformation, process of becoming, action applied to entire surface of object or to series of objects.*

об *see* **о** *prep.*

об..., обо..., объ... *vbl. pref.* = **о...** *or indicates action or motion about an object.*

о́ба, обо́их *m.* & *nt.*, **о́бе, обе́их** *f.* both; **обе́ими рука́ми** with both hands; very willingly, readily; **смотре́ть в о́ба** keep one's eyes open, be on one's guard.

обагри́ть, -рю́ *pf.*, **обагря́ть, -я́ю** *impf.* crimson, incarnadine; ~ **кро́вью** stain with blood; ~ **ру́ки в крови́** steep one's hands in blood; ~**ся** be crimsoned; ~**ся (кро́вью)** be stained with blood.

обалдева́ть, -а́ю *impf.*, **обалде́ть, -е́ю** *pf.* go crazy; become dulled; be stunned.

обанкро́титься, -о́чусь *pf.* go bankrupt.

обая́ние, -я fascination, charm. **обая́тельный** fascinating, charming.

обва́л, -а fall, falling, crumbling; collapse; caving-in; landslide; **(сне́жный)** ~ avalanche. **обва́ливать(ся, -аю(сь** *impf.* *of* **обвали́ть(ся, обваля́ть. обва́листый** liable to fall, liable to cave in. **обвали́ть, -лю́, -лишь** *pf.* (*impf.* **обва́ливать**) cause to fall, cause to collapse; crumble; heap round; ~**ся** fall, collapse, cave in; crumble.

обваля́ть, -я́ю *pf.* (*impf.* **обва́ливать**) roll; ~ **в сухаря́х** roll in bread-crumbs.

обва́ривать, -аю *impf.*, **обвари́ть, -рю́, -ришь** *pf.* pour boiling water over; scald; ~**ся** scald o.s.

обведу́ *etc.*: *see* **обвести́. обвёл** *etc.*: *see* **обвести́ об|венча́ть(ся, -а́ю(сь** *pf.*

обверну́ть, -ну́, -нёшь *pf.*, **обвёртывать, -аю** *impf.* wrap, wrap up.

обве́с, -а short weight. **обве́сить, -е́шу** *pf.* (*impf.* **обве́шивать**) give short weight (to); cheat in weighing.

обвести́, -еду́, -едёшь; -ёл, -ела́ *pf.* (*impf.* **обводи́ть**) lead round, take round; encircle; surround; outline; dodge, get past; deceive, fool, cheat; ~ **взо́ром, глаза́ми** look round (at), take in; ~ **вокру́г па́льца** twist round one's little finger.

обве́тренный weather-beaten; chapped.

обветша́лый decrepit, decayed; dilapidated. **об|ветша́ть, -а́ю** *pf.*

обве́шивать, -аю *impf.* *of* **обве́сить**

обвива́ть(ся, -а́ю(сь *impf.* *of* **обви́ть(ся**

обвине́ние, -я charge, accusation; prosecution; **вы́нести** ~ **в**+*p.* find guilty of. **обвини́тель, -я** *m.* accuser; prosecutor. **обвини́тельн|ый** accusatory; ~**ый акт** indictment; ~**ый пригово́р** verdict of guilty; ~**ая речь** speech for the prosecution. **обвини́ть, -ню́** *pf.*, **обвиня́ть, -я́ю** *impf.* prosecute, indict; +**в**+*p.* accuse of, charge with. **обвиня́емый** *sb.* the accused; defendant.

обвиса́ть, -а́ет *impf.*, **обви́снуть, -нет; -ви́с** *pf.* sag; droop; grow flabby. **обви́слый** flabby; hanging, drooping.

обви́ть, обовью́, обовьёшь; обви́л, -а́, -о *pf.* (*impf.* **обвива́ть**) wind round, entwine; ~**ся** wind round, twine o.s. round.

обво́д, -а enclosing, surrounding; outlining. **обводи́ть, -ожу́, -о́дишь** *impf.* *of* **обвести́**

обводне́ние, -я irrigation; filling up. **обводни́тельный** irrigation. **обводни́ть, -ню́** *pf.*, **обводня́ть, -я́ю** *impf.* irrigate; fill with water.

обво́дный bypass, leading round.

обвора́живать, -аю *impf.*, **обворожи́ть, -жу́** *pf.* charm, fascinate, enchant. **обворожи́тельный** charming, fascinating, enchanting.

обвяза́ть, -яжу́, -я́жешь *pf.*, **обвя́зывать, -аю** *impf.* tie round; edge; ~**ся**+*i.* tie round o.s.

обгла́дывать, -аю *impf.*, **обглода́ть, -ожу́, -о́жешь** *pf.* pick, gnaw (round). **обгло́док, -дка** bare bone.

обго́н, -а passing. **обгоня́ть, -я́ю** *impf.* *of* **обогна́ть**

обгора́ть, -а́ю *impf.*, **обгоре́ть, -рю́** *pf.* be burnt, be scorched. **обгоре́лый** burnt, charred, scorched.

обдава́ть, -даю́, -даёшь *impf.*, **обда́ть, -а́м, -а́шь, -а́ст, -ади́м; о́бдал, -а́, -о** *pf.*+*i.* pour over, cover with; overcome, overwhelm with; ~**ся**+*i.* pour over o.s.

обде́лать, -аю *pf.* (*impf.* **обде́лывать**) finish; cut, polish, set; manage, arrange; cheat.

обдели́ть, -лю́, -лишь *pf.* (*impf.* **обделя́ть**) +*i.* do out of one's (fair) share of.

обде́лывать, -аю *impf.* *of* **обде́лать**

обделя́ть, -я́ю *impf.* *of* **обдели́ть**

обдеру́ *etc.*: *see* **ободра́ть. обдира́ть, -а́ю** *impf.* *of* **ободра́ть. обди́рка, -и** peeling; hulling, shelling; skinning, flaying; groats. **обди́рный** peeled, hulled.

обдува́ла, -ы *c.g.* cheat, trickster. **обдува́ть, -а́ю** *impf.* *of* **обду́ть**

обду́манно *adv.* after careful consideration, deliberately. **обду́манный** deliberate, well-considered, well-weighed, carefully-thought-out. **обду́мать, -аю** *pf.*, **обду́мывать, -аю** *impf.* consider, think over, weigh.

обду́ть, -у́ю *pf.* (*impf.* **обдува́ть**) blow on, blow round; cheat, fool, dupe.

о́бе *see* **о́ба. обега́ть, -а́ю** *impf.* *of* **обежа́ть. обегу́** *etc.*: *see* **обежа́ть**

обе́д, -а dinner; **пе́ред** ~**ом** in the morning; **по́сле** ~**а** in the afternoon. **обе́дать, -аю** *impf.* (*pf.* **по**~) have dinner, dine. **обе́денный** dinner; ~ **переры́в** dinner hour.

обедне́вший, обедне́лый impoverished. **обедне́ние, -я** impoverishment. **о|бедне́ть, -е́ю** *pf.*, **обедни́ть, -ню́** *pf.*, **обедня́ть, -я́ю** *impf.* impoverish.

обе́дня, -и; *g.pl.* **-ден** mass.

обежа́ть, -егу́ *pf.* (*impf.* **обега́ть**) run round; run past; outrun, pass.

обезбо́ливание, -я anaesthetization. **обезбо́ливать, -аю** *impf.*, **обезбо́лить, -лю** *pf.* anaesthetize.

обезвре́дить, -е́жу *pf.*, **обезвре́живать, -аю** *impf.* render harmless; neutralize.

обездо́ленный deprived; unfortunate, hapless. **обездо́ливать, -аю** *impf.*, **обездо́лить, -лю** *pf.* deprive of one's share.

обеззара́живать, -аю *impf.*, **обеззара́зить,**

-а́жу *pf.* disinfect. **обеззара́живающий** disinfectant.

обезле́сение, -я deforestation.

обезли́ченный depersonalized; generalized, reduced to a standard; mechanical. **обезли́чивать, -аю** *impf.*, **обезли́чить, -чу** *pf.* deprive of individuality, depersonalize; do away with personal responsibility for. **обезли́чка, -и** lack of personal responsibility.

обезобра́живать, -аю *impf.*, **о|безобра́зить, -а́жу** *pf.* disfigure, mutilate.

обезопа́сить, -а́шу *pf.* secure, make safe; **~ся** secure o.s.

обезору́живание, -я disarmament. **обезору́живать, -аю** *impf.*, **обезору́жить, -жу** *pf.* disarm.

обезу́меть, -ею *pf.* lose one's senses, lose one's head; **~ от испу́га** become panic-stricken.

обезья́на, -ы monkey; ape. **обезья́ний** monkey; simian; ape-like. **обезья́нник, -а** monkey-house. **обезья́нничать, -аю** *impf.* (*pf.* **с~**) ape.

обели́ть, -лю́ *pf.*, **обеля́ть, -я́ю** *impf.* vindicate, prove the innocence of; clear of blame; whitewash; **~ся** vindicate o.s., prove one's innocence.

оберега́ть, -а́ю *impf.*, **обере́чь, -егу́, -ежёшь; -рёг, -ла́** *pf.* guard; protect; **~ся** guard o.s., protect o.s.

оберну́ть, -ну́, -нёшь *pf.*, **обёртывать, -аю** *impf.* (*impf. also* **обора́чивать**) wind, twist; wrap up; turn; turn over; **~ кни́гу** jacket a book; cover a book; **~ся** turn, turn around; turn out; come back; manage, get by; +*i. or* **в**+*a.* turn into; **~ся лицо́м к** turn towards. **обёртка, -и** wrapper; envelope; (dust-)jacket, cover. **обёрточн|ый** wrapping; **~ая бума́га** brown paper, wrapping paper.

оберу́ *etc.*: *see* **обобра́ть**

обескура́живать, -аю *impf.*, **обескура́жить, -жу** *pf.* discourage; dismay.

обескро́вить, -влю *pf.*, **обескро́вливать, -аю** *impf.* drain of blood, bleed white; render lifeless. **обескро́вленный** bloodless; pallid, anaemic, lifeless.

обеспече́ние, -я securing, guaranteeing; ensuring; providing, provision; guarantee; security; safeguard(s); protection. **обеспе́ченность, -и** security; +*i.* being provided with, provision of. **обеспе́ченный** well-to-do; well provided for. **обеспе́чивать, -аю** *impf.*, **обеспе́чить, -чу** *pf.* provide for; secure, guarantee; ensure, assure; safeguard, protect; +*i.* provide with, guarantee supply of.

о|беспоко́ить(ся, -о́ю(сь *pf.*

обесси́леть, -ею *pf.* grow weak, lose one's strength; collapse, break down. **обесси́ливать, -аю** *impf.*, **обесси́лить, -лю** *pf.* weaken.

о|бесcла́вить, -влю *pf.*

обессме́ртить, -рчу *pf.* immortalize.

обесцве́тить, -е́чу *pf.*, **обесцве́чивать, -аю** *impf.* fade, deprive of colour; make colourless, tone down; **~ся** fade; become colourless.

обесцене́ние, -я depreciation; loss of value. **обесце́нивать, -аю** *impf.*, **обесце́нить, -ню** *pf.* depreciate; cheapen; **~ся** depreciate, lose value.

о|бесче́стить, -е́щу *pf.*

обе́т, -а vow, promise. **обетова́нный** promised. **обеща́ние, -я** promise; **дать ~** give a promise, give one's word; **сдержа́ть ~** keep a promise, keep one's word. **обеща́ть, -а́ю** *impf. & pf.* (*pf. also* **по~**) promise.

обжа́лование, -я appeal. **обжа́ловать, -лую** *pf.* appeal against, lodge a complaint against.

обже́чь, обожгу́, обожжёшь; обжёг, обожгла́ *pf.*, **обжига́ть, -а́ю** *impf.* burn; scorch; bake; fire, calcine; sting; **~ся** burn o.s.; scald o.s.; burn one's fingers; **~ся крапи́вой** be stung by a nettle. **обжига́тельн|ый** glazing; baking; roasting; **~ая печь** kiln.

обжо́ра, -ы *c.g.* glutton, gormandizer. **обжо́рливый** gluttonous. **обжо́рство, -а** gluttony.

обзаведе́ние, -я providing, fitting out; establishment; fittings, appointments; bits and pieces. **обзавести́сь, -еду́сь, -едёшься; -вёлся, -ла́сь** *pf.*, **обзаводи́ться, -ожу́сь, -о́дишься** *impf.* +*i.* provide o.s. with; set up.

обзову́ *etc.*: *see* **обозва́ть**

обзо́р, -а survey, review.

обзыва́ть, -а́ю *impf. of* **обозва́ть**

обива́ть, -а́ю *impf. of* **оби́ть. оби́вка, -и** upholstering; upholstery.

оби́да, -ы offence, injury, insult; annoying thing, nuisance; **не в оби́ду будь ска́зано** no offence meant; **не дать себя́ в оби́ду** stand up for o.s. **оби́деть, -и́жу** *pf.*, **обижа́ть, -а́ю** *impf.* offend; hurt, wound; **му́хи не оби́дит** he would not harm a fly; **~ся** take offence, take umbrage; feel hurt; **~ся на**+*a.* resent; **не обижа́йтесь** don't be offended. **оби́дный** offensive; annoying, tiresome; **мне оби́дно** I feel hurt, it pains me; **оби́дно** it is a pity, it is a nuisance. **оби́дчивый** touchy, sensitive. **оби́женный** offended, hurt, aggrieved.

оби́лие, -я abundance, plenty. **оби́льный** abundant, plentiful; +*i.* rich in.

обиня́к, -а́ circumlocution; hint, evasion; **без ~о́в** plainly, in plain terms; **говори́ть ~а́ми** beat about the bush.

обира́ть, -а́ю *impf. of* **обобра́ть**

обита́емый inhabited. **обита́тель, -я** *m.* inhabitant; resident; inmate. **обита́ть, -а́ю** *impf.* live, dwell, reside.

оби́ть, обобью́, -ьёшь *pf.* (*impf.* **обива́ть**) upholster, cover; knock off, knock down; **~ гвоздя́ми** stud; **~ желе́зом** bind with iron.

обихо́д, -а custom, (general) use, practice; **в дома́шнем ~е** in domestic use, in the household. **обихо́дный** everyday.

обката́ть, -а́ю *pf.*, **обка́тывать, -аю** *impf.*

roll; roll smooth; run in. **обка́тка, -и** running in.

обкла́дка, -и facing; ~ **дёрном** turfing. **обкла́дывать(ся, -аю(сь** *impf. of* **обложи́ть(ся**

обко́м, -а *abbr.* (*of* ***областно́й комите́т***) regional committee.

обкра́дывать, -аю *impf. of* **обокра́сть**

обл. *abbr.* (*of* **о́бласть**) oblast, region.

обла́ва, -ы raid, swoop; round-up; cordon, cordoning off; battue.

облага́емый taxable. **облага́ть(ся, -а́ю(сь** *impf. of* **обложи́ть(ся;** ~**ся нало́гом** be liable to tax, be taxable.

облагора́живать, -аю *impf.*, **облагоро́дить, -о́жу** *pf.* ennoble.

облада́ние, -я possession. **облада́тель, -я** *m.* possessor. **облада́ть, -а́ю** *impf.+i.* possess, be possessed of; ~ **пра́вом** have the right; ~ **хоро́шим здоро́вьем** enjoy good health.

о́блако, -а; *pl.* **-а́, -о́в** cloud.

обла́мывать(ся, -аю(сь *impf. of* **облома́ть(ся, обломи́ться**

обласка́ть, -а́ю *pf.* treat with affection, show much kindness or consideration to.

областно́й oblast; provincial; regional; dialectal. **о́бласть, -и;** *g.pl.* **-е́й** oblast, province; region; district; belt; tract; field, sphere, realm, domain.

обла́тка, -и wafer; capsule; paper seal.

о́блачко, -а; *pl.* **-а́, -о́в** *dim. of* **о́блако. о́блачность, -и** cloudiness; cloud. **о́блачный** cloudy.

облёг *etc.*: *see* **обле́чь. облега́ть, -а́ет** *impf. of* **обле́чь облега́ющий** tight-fitting.

облегча́ть, -а́ю *impf.*, **облегчи́ть, -чу́** *pf.* lighten; relieve; alleviate, mitigate; commute; facilitate. **облегче́ние, -я** relief.

обледене́лый ice-covered. **обледене́ние, -я** icing over; **пери́од обледене́ния** Ice Age. **обледене́ть, -е́ет** *pf.* ice over, become covered with ice.

облеза́ть, -а́ет *impf.*, **облé́зть, -зет; -лéз** *pf.* come out, fall out, come off; grow bare, grow mangy; peel off. **облéзлый** shabby, bare; mangy.

облека́ть(ся, -а́ю(сь *impf. of* **обле́чь**[2]**(ся. облеку́** *etc.*: *see* **обле́чь**[2]

обле́ниваться, -аюсь *impf.*, **облени́ться, -ню́сь, -нишься** *pf.* grow lazy, get lazy.

облепи́ть, -плю́, -пишь *pf.*, **облепля́ть, -я́ю** *impf.* stick to, cling to; surround, throng round; paste all over, plaster.

облета́ть, -а́ю *impf.*, **облете́ть, -лечу́** fly (round); spread (round, all over); fall.

обле́чь[1]**, -ля́жет; -лёг, -ла́** *pf.* (*impf.* **облега́ть**) cover, surround, envelop; fit tightly.

обле́чь[2]**, -еку́, -ечёшь; -ёк, -кла́** *pf.* (*impf.* **облека́ть**) clothe, invest; wrap, shroud; ~**ся** clothe o.s., dress o.s.; *+g.* take the form of, assume the shape of.

облива́ние, -я spilling over, pouring over; shower-bath; sponge down. **облива́ть(ся, -а́ю(сь** *impf. of* **обли́ть(ся; се́рдце у меня́ кро́вью облива́ется** my heart bleeds. **обли́вка, -и** glazing; glaze. **обливно́й** glazed.

облига́ция, -и bond, debenture.

обли́занный smooth. **облиза́ть, -ижу́, -и́жешь** *pf.*, **обли́зывать, -аю** *impf.* lick (all over); lick clean; ~**ся** smack one's lips; lick itself.

о́блик, -а look, aspect, appearance; cast of mind, temper.

облисполко́м, -а *abbr.* (*of* ***областно́й исполни́тельный комите́т***) regional executive committee.

о́бли́тый; о́бли́т, -á, -о covered, enveloped; ~ **све́том луны́** bathed in moonlight. **обли́ть, оболью́, -льёшь; о́бли́л, -ила́, -о** *pf.* (*impf.* **облива́ть**) pour, sluice, spill; glaze; ~**ся** sponge down, take a shower; pour over o.s., spill over o.s.; ~**ся по́том** be bathed in sweat; ~**ся слеза́ми** melt into tears.

облицева́ть, -цу́ю *pf.*, **облицо́вывать, -аю** *impf.* face, revet. **облицо́вка, -и** facing, revetment; lining, coating.

облича́ть, -а́ю *impf.*, **обличи́ть, -чу́** *pf.* expose, unmask, denounce; reveal, display, manifest; point to. **обличе́ние, -я** exposure, unmasking, denunciation. **обличи́тельн|ый** denunciatory; ~**ая речь,** ~**ая статья́** diatribe, tirade.

обложе́ние, -я taxation; assessment, rating. **обложи́ть, -жу́, -жишь** *pf.* (*impf.* **обкла́дывать, облага́ть**) put round; edge; surface; face; cover; surround; close round, corner; assess; **круго́м обложи́ло (не́бо)** the sky is completely overcast; ~ **ме́стным нало́гом** rate; ~ **нало́гом** tax; **обложи́ло язы́к** the tongue is furred; ~**ся***+i.* put round o.s., surround o.s. with. **обло́жка, -и** (dust-)cover; folder.

облока́чиваться, -аюсь *impf.*, **облокоти́ться, -очу́сь, -о́ти́шься** *pf.* **на***+a.* lean one's elbows on.

обло́м, -а breaking off; break; profile. **облома́ть, -а́ю** *pf.* (*impf.* **обла́мывать**) break off; make yield; ~**ся** break off, snap. **обломи́ться, -ло́мится** *pf.* (*impf.* **обла́мываться**) break off. **обло́мок, -мка** fragment; debris, wreckage.

об|лупи́ть, -плю́, -пишь *pf.*, **облу́пливать, -аю** *impf.* peel; shell; fleece; ~**ся** peel, peel off, scale; come off, chip. **облу́пленный** chipped.

облучи́ть, -чу́ *pf.*, **облуча́ть, -а́ю** *impf.* irradiate. **облуче́ние, -я** irradiation.

об|лущи́ть, -щу́ *pf.* **об|лысе́ть, -е́ю** *pf.*

облюбова́ть, -бу́ю *pf.*, **облюбо́вывать, -аю** *impf.* pick, choose, select.

обля́жет *etc.*: *see* **обле́чь**[1]

обма́зать, -а́жу *pf.*, **обма́зывать, -аю** *impf.* coat; putty; soil, besmear. ~**ся***+i.* besmear o.s. with, get covered with. **обма́зка, -и** coating, puttying.

обма́кивать, -аю *impf.*, **обмакну́ть, -ну́, -нёшь** *pf.* dip.

обма́н, -а fraud, deception; illusion; ~ **зре́ния** optical illusion. **обма́нный** fraudulent, deceitful. **обману́ть, -ну́, -нешь** *pf.*, **обма́нывать, -аю** *impf.* deceive; cheat, swindle; betray, disappoint; ~**ся** be deceived, be disappointed. **обма́нчивый** deceptive, delusive. **обма́нщик, -а** deceiver; cheat, fraud.

обма́тывать(ся, -аю(сь *impf. of* **обмота́ть(ся**

обма́хивать, -аю *impf.*, **обмахну́ть, -ну́, -нёшь** *pf.* brush off, dust (off); fan; ~**ся** fan o.s.

обмёл *etc.*: *see* **обмести́**

обмеле́ние, -я shallowing, shoaling. **об|меле́ть, -е́ет** *pf.* become shallow, shoal; run aground.

обме́н, -а exchange, interchange; barter; **в** ~ **за**+*a.* in exchange for; ~ **веще́ств** metabolism; ~ **мне́ниями** exchange of opinions. **обме́нивать, -аю** *impf.*, **обмени́ть, -ню́, -нишь** *pf.*, **об|меня́ть, -я́ю** *pf.* exchange; barter; swap; ~**ся**+*i.* exchange; **обменя́ться впечатле́ниями** compare notes. **обме́нный** exchange; metabolic.

обме́р, -а measurement; false measure.

обмере́ть, обомру́, -рёшь; о́бмер, -ла́, -ло *pf.* (*impf.* **обмира́ть**) faint; ~ **от у́жаса** be horror-struck; **я о́бмер** my heart stood still.

обме́ривать, -аю *impf.*, **обме́рить, -рю** *pf.* measure; cheat in measuring, give short measure (to); ~**ся** make a mistake in measuring.

обмести́, -ету́, -етёшь; -мёл, -а́ *pf.*, **обмета́ть**[1]**, -а́ю** *impf.* sweep off, dust.

обмета́ть[2]**, -ечу́** *or* **-а́ю, -е́чешь** *or* **-а́ешь** *pf.* (*impf.* **обмётывать**) oversew, overcast, whip; blanket-stitch.

обмету́ *etc.*: *see* **обмести́. обмётывать, -аю** *impf. of* **обмета́ть. обмира́ть, -а́ю** *impf. of* **обмере́ть**

обмозгова́ть, -гу́ю *pf.*, **обмозго́вывать, -аю** *impf.* think over, turn over (in one's mind).

обмола́чивать, -аю *impf. of* **обмолоти́ть**

обмо́лвиться, -влюсь *pf.* make a slip of the tongue; +*i.* say, utter. **обмо́лвка, -и** slip of the tongue.

обмоло́т, -а threshing. **обмолоти́ть, -лочу́, -ло́тишь** *pf.* (*impf.* **обмола́чивать**) thresh.

обмора́живать, -аю *impf.*, **обморо́зить, -ро́жу** *pf.* expose to frost, subject to frostbite, get frost-bitten; **я обморо́зил себе́ ру́ки** I have got my hands frost-bitten; ~**ся** suffer frost-bite, be frost-bitten. **обморо́женный** frost-bitten.

о́бморок, -а fainting-fit, swoon; syncope.

обмота́ть, -а́ю *pf.* (*impf.* **обма́тывать**) wind round; ~**ся**+*i.* wrap o.s. in. **обмо́тка, -и** winding; lagging; taping; *pl.* puttees, leg-wrappings.

обмо́ю *etc.*: *see* **обмы́ть**

обмундирова́ние, -я, обмундиро́вка, -и fitting out (with uniform), issuing of uniform; uniform. **обмундирова́ть, -ру́ю** *pf.*, **обмундиро́вывать, -аю** *impf.* fit out (with uniform), issue with clothing; ~**ся** fit o.s. out; draw uniform. **обмундиро́вочный;** ~**ые де́ньги** uniform allowance.

обмыва́ние, -я bathing, washing. **обмыва́ть, -а́ю** *impf.*, **обмы́ть, -мо́ю** *pf.* bathe, wash; sponge down. ~**ся** wash, bathe; sponge down.

обмяка́ть, -а́ю *impf.*, **обмя́кнуть, -ну; -мя́к** *pf.* become soft; go limp, become flabby.

обнадёживать, -аю *impf.*, **обнадёжить, -жу** *pf.* give hope to, reassure.

обнажа́ть, -а́ю *impf.*, **обнажи́ть, -жу́** *pf.* bare, uncover; unsheathe; lay bare, reveal. **обнажённый; -ён, -ена́** naked, bare; nude.

обнаро́дование, -я publication, promulgation. **обнаро́довать, -дую** *impf.* & *pf.* publish, promulgate.

обнару́же́ние, -я disclosure; displaying, revealing; discovery; detection. **обнару́живать, -аю** *impf.*, **обнару́жить, -жу** *pf.* disclose; display; reveal, betray; discover, bring to light; detect; ~**ся** be revealed, come to light.

обнести́, -су́, -сёшь; -нёс, -ла́ *pf.* (*impf.* **обноси́ть**) enclose; +*i.* serve round, pass round; pass over, leave out; **меня́ обнесли́ вино́м** I have not been offered wine; ~ **и́згородью** fence (in); ~ **пери́лами** rail in, rail off.

обнима́ть(ся, -а́ю(сь *impf. of* **обня́ть(ся.**

обниму́ *etc.*: *see* **обня́ть**

обнища́лый impoverished; beggarly. **обнища́ние, -я** impoverishment.

обнови́ть, -влю́ *pf.*, **обновля́ть, -я́ю** *impf.* renovate; renew; re-form; repair, restore; use or wear for the first time; ~**ся** revive, be restored. **обно́вка, -и** new acquisition, new toy; new dress. **обновле́ние, -я** renovation, renewal; **вне́шнее** ~ face-lift.

обноси́ть, -ошу́, -о́сишь *impf. of* **обнести́;** ~**ся** have worn out one's clothes; be out at the elbow. **обно́ски, -ов** *pl.* old clothes, cast-offs.

обню́хать, -аю *pf.*, **обню́хивать, -аю** *impf.* smell, sniff at.

обня́ть, -ниму́, -ни́мешь; о́бнял, -а́, -о *pf.* (*impf.* **обнима́ть**) embrace; clasp in one's arms; take in; ~ **взгля́дом** survey; ~ **умо́м** comprehend, take in; ~**ся** embrace; hug one another.

обо *see* **о** *prep.* **обо...** *see* **о...**

обобра́ть, оберу́, -рёшь; обобра́л, -а́, -о *pf.* (*impf.* **обира́ть**) rob; clean out; pick; gather all of.

обобща́ть, -а́ю *impf.*, **обобщи́ть, -щу́** *pf.* generalize. **обобще́ние, -я** generalization. **обобществи́ть, -влю́** *pf.*, **обобществля́ть, -я́ю** *impf.* socialize; collectivize. **обобществле́ние, -я** socialization; collectivization.

обобью *etc.*: *see* **оби́ть. обовью** *etc.*: *see* **обви́ть**

обогати́ть, -ащу́ *pf.*, **обогаща́ть, -а́ю** *impf.*

enrich; concentrate; **~ся** become rich; enrich o.s. **обогаще́ние, -я** enrichment; concentration.

обогна́ть, обгоню́, -о́нишь; обогна́л, -а́, -о *pf.* (*impf.* **обгоня́ть**) pass, leave behind; outstrip, outdistance. **обогну́ть, -ну́, -нёшь** *pf.* (*impf.* **огиба́ть**) round, skirt; double; bend round.

обогре́в, -а heating. **обогрева́ние, -я** heating, warming. **обогрева́тель, -я** *m.* heater. **обогрева́ть, -а́ю** *impf.*, **обогре́ть, -е́ю** *pf.* heat, warm; **~ся** warm o.s.; warm up.

о́бод, -а; *pl.* **-о́дья, -ьев** rim; felloe. **ободо́к, -дка́** thin rim, narrow border; fillet.

ободра́нец, -нца ragamuffin, ragged fellow. **обо́дранный** ragged. **ободра́ть, обдеру́, -рёшь; -а́л, -а́, -о** *pf.* (*impf.* **обдира́ть**) strip; skin, flay; peel; fleece.

ободре́ние, -я encouragement, reassurance. **ободри́тельный** encouraging, reassuring. **ободри́ть, -рю́** *pf.*, **ободря́ть, -я́ю** *impf.* cheer up; encourage, reassure; **~ся** cheer up, take heart.

обожа́ние, -я adoration. **обожа́тель, -я** *m.* adorer; admirer. **обожа́ть, -а́ю** *impf.* adore, worship.

обожгу́ *etc.*: *see* **обже́чь**

обожестви́ть, -влю́ *pf.*, **обожествля́ть, -я́ю** *impf.* deify; worship, idolize. **обожествле́ние, -я** deification, worship.

обожжённый; -ён, -ена́ burnt, scorched; scalded; stung.

обо́з, -а string of carts, string of sledges; transport; collection of vehicles.

обозва́ть, обзову́, -вёшь; -а́л, -а́, -о *pf.* (*impf.* **обзыва́ть**) call; call names; **~ дурако́м** call a fool.

обозлённый; -ён, -а́ angered; embittered. **обо|зли́ть, -лю́** *pf.*, **о|зли́ть, -лю́** *pf.* enrage, anger; embitter; **~ся** get angry, grow angry.

обознача́ть, -а́ю *impf.*, **обозна́чить, -чу** *pf.* mean; mark; reveal; emphasize; **~ся** appear, reveal o.s. **обозначе́ние, -я** marking; sign, symbol.

обо́зник, -а driver.

обозрева́тель, -я *m.* reviewer, observer; columnist; **полити́ческий ~** political correspondent. **обозрева́ть, -а́ю** *impf.*, **обозре́ть, -рю́** *pf.* survey; view; look round; (pass in) review. **обозре́ние, -я** surveying, viewing; looking round; survey; review; revue. **обозри́мый** visible.

обо́и, -ев *pl.* wallpaper.

обо́йма, -ы; *g.pl.* **-о́йм** cartridge clip.

обойти́, -йду́, -йдёшь; -ошёл, -ошла́ *pf.* (*impf.* **обходи́ть**) go round, pass; make the round of, go (all) round; avoid; leave out; pass over; **~ молча́нием** pass over in silence; **~сь** cost, come to; manage, make do; turn out, end; +**с**+*i.* treat.

обо́йщик, -а upholsterer.

обокра́сть, обкраду́, -дёшь *pf.* (*impf.* **обкра́дывать**) rob.

оболо́чка, -и casing; membrane; cover, envelope, jacket; shell; coat.

обо́лтус, -а blockhead, booby.

обольсти́тель, -я *m.* seducer. **обольсти́тельный** seductive, captivating. **обольсти́ть, -льщу́** *pf.*, **обольща́ть, -а́ю** *impf.* captivate; seduce. **обольще́ние, -я** seduction; delusion.

оболью́ *etc.*: *see* **обли́ть**

обомле́ть, -е́ю *pf.* be stupefied, be stunned.

обомру́ *etc.*: *see* **обмере́ть**

обомшёлый moss-grown.

обоня́ние, -я (sense of) smell. **обоня́тельный** olfactory. **обоня́ть, -я́ю** *impf.* smell.

обопру́ *etc.*: *see* **опере́ть**

обора́чиваемость, -и turnover. **обора́чивать(ся, -а́ю(сь** *impf. of* **оберну́ть(ся, обороти́ть(ся**

обо́рванец, -нца ragamuffin, ragged fellow. **обо́рванный** torn, ragged. **оборва́ть, -ву́, -вёшь; -а́л, -а́, -о** *pf.* (*impf.* **обрыва́ть**) tear off, pluck; strip; break; snap; cut short, interrupt; **~ся** break; snap; fall; come away; stop suddenly, stop short.

обо́рка, -и frill, flounce.

оборо́на, -ы defence; defences. **оборони́тельный** defensive. **оборони́ть, -ню́** *pf.*, **обороня́ть, -я́ю** *impf.* defend; **~ся** defend o.s. **оборо́нный** defence, defensive. **обороноспосо́бность, -и** defensive capability.

оборо́т, -а turn; revolution, rotation; circulation; turnover; back; **~ ре́чи** (turn of) phrase; locution; **смотри́ на ~е** P.T.O., please turn over; see other side. **оборо́тистый** resourceful. **обороти́ть, -рочу́, -ро́тишь** *pf.* (*impf.* **обора́чивать**) turn; **~ся** turn (round); +*i. or* **в**+*a.* turn into. **оборо́тливый** resourceful. **оборо́тн|ый** circulating, working; turn-round; reverse; **~ый капита́л** working capital; **~ая сторона́** reverse side; verso; **э ~ое** the letter **э.**

обору́дование, -я equipping; equipment; **вспомога́тельное ~** (*comput.*) peripherals. **обору́довать, -дую** *impf.* & *pf.* equip, fit out; manage, arrange.

обоснова́ние, -я basing; basis, ground. **обосно́ванный** well-founded, well-grounded. **обоснова́ть, -ную́, -нуёшь** *or* **-ну́ю, -ну́ешь** *pf.*, **обосно́вывать, -аю** *impf.* ground, base; substantiate; **~ся** settle down.

обосо́бить, -блю *pf.*, **обособля́ть, -я́ю** *impf.* isolate; **~ся** stand apart; keep aloof. **обособле́ние, -я** isolation. **обосо́бленный** isolated, solitary.

обостре́ние, -я aggravation, exacerbation. **обострённый** keen; strained, tense; sharp, pointed. **обостри́ть, -рю́** *pf.*, **обостря́ть, -я́ю** *impf.* sharpen, intensify; strain; aggravate, exacerbate; **~ся** become sharp, become pointed; become keener, become more sensitive; become strained; be aggravated; become acute.

оботру́ *etc.*: *see* **обтере́ть**
обо́чина, -ы verge; shoulder, edge, side.
обошёл *etc.*: *see* **обойти́. обошью́** *etc.*: *see* **обши́ть**
обою́дность, -и mutuality, reciprocity. **обою́дный** mutual, reciprocal. **обоюдоо́стрый** double-edged, two-edged.
обраба́тывать, -аю *impf.*, **обрабо́тать, -аю** *pf.* till, cultivate; work, work up; treat, process; machine; polish, perfect; work upon, win round. **обраба́тывающ|ий; ~ая промы́шленность** manufacturing industry. **обрабо́тка, -и** working (up); treatment, processing; cultivation.
обра́довать(ся, -дую(сь *pf.*
о́браз, -а shape, form; appearance; image; type; figure; mode, manner; way; icon; **гла́вным ~ом** mainly, chiefly, largely; **каки́м ~ом?** how?; **~ де́йствий** line of action, policy; **~ жи́зни** way of life; **~ мы́слей** way of thinking; **~ правле́ния** form of government; **таки́м ~ом** thus. **образе́ц, -зца́** model; pattern; example; specimen, sample. **о́бразный** picturesque, graphic; figurative; employing images. **образова́ние, -я** formation; education. **образо́ванный** educated. **образова́тельный** educational. **образова́ть, -зу́ю** *impf.* & *pf.*, **образо́вывать, -аю** *impf.* form; make (up); organize; educate; **~ся** form; arise; turn out well.
образу́мить, -млю *pf.* bring to reason; make listen to reason; **~ся** come to one's senses, see reason.
образцо́вый model; exemplary. **обра́зчик, -а** specimen, sample; pattern.
обра́мить, -млю *pf.*, **обрамля́ть, -я́ю** *impf.* frame. **обрамле́ние, -я** framing; frame; setting.
обраста́ть, -а́ю *impf.*, **обрасти́, -ту́, -тёшь; -ро́с, -ла́** *pf.* be overgrown; be covered, surrounded, cluttered; +*i.* acquire, accumulate.
обрати́м|ый reversible, convertible; **~ая валю́та** convertible currency. **обрати́ть, -ащу́** *pf.*, **обраща́ть, -а́ю** *impf.* turn; convert; **~ в бе́гство** put to flight; **~ внима́ние на**+*a.* pay attention to, take notice of, notice; call, draw, attention to; **~ на себя́ внима́ние** attract attention (to o.s.); **~ в шу́тку** turn into a joke; **~ся** turn; revert; appeal; apply; accost, address; circulate; +**в**+*a.* turn into, become; +**с**+*i.* treat; handle, manage; **~ся в бе́гство** take to flight; **~ся в слух** be all ears; prick up one's ears. **обра́тно** *adv.* back; backwards; conversely; inversely; **~ пропорциона́льный** inversely proportional; **туда́ и ~** there and back. **обра́тн|ый** reverse; return; opposite; inverse; **в ~ую сто́рону** in the opposite direction; **~ый а́дрес** sender's address, return address; **~ая вспы́шка** backfiring; **~ой по́чтой** by return (of post); **~ый уда́р** backfire; **~ый ход** reverse motion, back stroke. **обраще́ние, -я** appeal, address; conversion; circulation; manner; (+**с**+*i.*) treatment (of); handling (of); use (of).
об|ревизова́ть, -зу́ю *pf.*
обре́з, -а edge, side; sawn-off gun; **в ~**+*g.* only just enough; **де́нег у меня́ в ~** I haven't a penny to spare. **обре́зать, -е́жу** *pf.*, **обреза́ть, -а́ю** *impf.* cut; cut off; clip, trim; pare; prune; bevel; circumcise; cut short, snub; **~ся** cut o.s. **обре́зок, -зка** scrap; remnant; *pl.* ends; clippings.
обрека́ть, -а́ю *impf. of* **обре́чь. обреку́** *etc.*: *see* **обре́чь обрёл** *etc.*: *see* **обрести́**
обремени́тельный burdensome, onerous. **о|бремени́ть, -ню́** *pf.*, **обременя́ть, -я́ю** *impf.* burden.
обрести́, -ету́, -етёшь; -рёл, -а́ *pf.*, **обрета́ть, -а́ю** *impf.* find. **обрета́ться, -а́юсь** *impf.* be; live.
обрече́ние, -я doom. **обречённый** doomed. **обре́чь, -еку́, -ечёшь; -ёк, -ла́** *pf.* (*impf.* **обрека́ть**) condemn, doom.
обрисова́ть, -су́ю *pf.*, **обрисо́вывать, -аю** *impf.* outline, delineate, depict; **~ся** appear (in outline), take shape.
обро́к, -а quit-rent.
оброни́ть, -ню́, -нишь *pf.* drop; let drop, let fall.
обро́с *etc.*: *see* **обрасти́. обро́сший** overgrown.
обруба́ть, -а́ю *impf.*, **обруби́ть, -блю́, -бишь** *pf.* chop off; lop off, cut off; dock; hem seam. **обру́бок, -бка** stump.
об|руга́ть, -а́ю *pf.*
о́бруч, -а; *pl.* **-и, -е́й** hoop. **обруча́льн|ый** engagement, betrothal; **~ое кольцо́** betrothal ring, wedding ring. **обруча́ть, -а́ю** *impf.*, **обручи́ть, -чу́** betroth; **~ся**+**с**+*i.* become engaged to. **обруче́ние, -я** betrothal.
обру́шивать, -аю *impf.*, **об|ру́шить, -шу** *pf.* bring down, rain down; **~ся** come down, collapse, cave in; +**на**+*a.* beat down on; come down on, fall on, pounce on.
обры́в, -а precipice; break, rupture. **обрыва́ть(ся, -а́ю(сь** *impf. of* **оборва́ть(ся. обры́вистый** steep, precipitous; abrupt. **обры́вок, -вка** scrap; snatch.
обры́згать, -аю *pf.*, **обры́згивать, -аю** *impf.*, **обры́знуть, -ну** *pf.* splash, spatter; sprinkle.
обрю́зглый, обрю́згший flabby.
обря́д, -а rite, ceremony. **обря́дный, обря́довый** ritual, ceremonial.
обслу́живание, -я service; servicing, maintenance; **бытово́е ~** consumer service(s); **медици́нское ~** medical attendance, medical care. **обслу́живать, -аю** *impf.*, **обслужи́ть, -жу́, -жишь** *pf.* serve, attend to; service; mind, operate; **обслу́живающий персона́л** staff; assistants, attendants.
обсле́дование, -я inspection; inquiry; investigation. **обсле́дователь, -я** *m.* inspector, investigator. **обсле́довать, -дую** *impf.* & *pf.* inspect; investigate; examine.
обсо́хнуть, -ну; -о́х *pf.* (*impf.* **обсыха́ть**) dry, dry up.

обстáвить, -влю *pf.*, **обставля́ть, -я́ю** *impf.* surround, encircle; furnish; arrange; organize; **~ся** establish o.s., furnish one's home. **обстанóвка, -и** furniture; décor; situation, conditions; environment; set-up.

обстоя́тельный thorough, reliable; detailed, circumstantial. **обстоя́тельственный** adverbial. **обстоя́тельство, -а** circumstance; adverbial modifier, adverb, adverbial phrase. **обстоя́ть, -ои́т** *impf.* be; get on go; **как обстои́т дéло?** how is it going? how are things going?

обстрáгивать, -аю *impf. of* **обстрогáть**

обстрáивать(ся, -аю(сь *impf. of* **обстрóить(ся**

обстрéл, -а firing, fire; **под ~ом** under fire. **обстрéливать, -аю** *impf.*, **обстреля́ть, -я́ю** *pf.* fire at, fire on; bombard; **~ся** become seasoned (in battle), receive one's baptism of fire. **обстрéлянный** seasoned, experienced.

обстрогáть, -áю, обстругáть, -áю *pf.* (*impf.* **обстрáгивать**) plane; whittle.

обстрóить, -óю *pf.* (*impf.* **обстрáивать**) build up, build round; **~ся** be built; spring up; build for o.s.

обстругáть *see* **обстрогáть**

обступáть, -áет *impf.*, **обступи́ть, -ýпит** *pf.* surround; cluster round.

обсуди́ть, -ужý, -ýдишь *pf.*, **обсуждáть, -áю** *impf.* discuss; consider. **обсуждéние, -я** discussion.

обсчитáть, -áю *pf.*, **обсчи́тывать, -аю** *impf.* cheat (*in reckoning*); **~ся** make a mistake (*in counting*), miscalculate; **вы обсчитáлись на шесть копéек** you were six copecks out.

обсы́пать, -плю *pf.* **обсыпáть, -áю** *impf.* strew; sprinkle.

обсыхáть, -áю *impf. of* **обсóхнуть. обтáчивать, -аю** *impf. of* **обточи́ть**

обтекáемый streamlined, streamline. **обтекáтель, -я** *m.* fairing, cowling.

обтерéть, оботрý, -трёшь; обтёр *pf.* (*impf.* **обтирáть**) wipe; wipe dry; rub; **~ся** wipe o.s. dry, dry o.s.; sponge down.

обтерпéться, -плю́сь, -пишься *pf.* become acclimatized, get used.

о(б)тесáть, -ешý, -éшешь *pf.*, **о(б)тёсывать, -аю** *impf.* square; rough-hew; dress, trim; lick into shape.

обтирáние, -я sponge-down; lotion. **обтирáть(ся, -áю(сь** *pf. of* **обтерéть(ся**

обточи́ть, -чý, -чишь *pf.* (*impf.* **обтáчивать**) grind; turn, machine, round off. **обтóчка, -и** turning, machining, rounding off.

обтрёпанный frayed; shabby. **обтрепáть, -плю́, -плешь** *pf.* fray; **~ся** fray; become frayed; get shabby.

обтя́гивать, -аю *impf.*, **обтянýть, -нý, -нешь** *pf.* cover; fit close, fit tight. **обтя́жка, -и** cover; skin; **в обтя́жку** close-fitting.

обувáть(ся, -áю(сь *impf. of* **обýть(ся. обýвка, -и** boots, shoes. **обувнóй** shoe. **óбувь, -и** footwear; boots, shoes.

обýгливание, -я carbonization. **обýгливать, -аю** *impf.*, **обýглить, -лю** *pf.* char; carbonize; **~ся** char, become charred.

обýживать, -аю *impf. of* **обýзить**

обýза, -ы burden, encumbrance.

обуздáть, -áю *pf.*, **обýздывать, -аю** *impf.* bridle, curb; restrain, control.

обýзить, -ýжу *pf.* (*impf.* **обýживать**) make too tight, too narrow.

обуревáемый possessed; *+i.* a prey to. **обуревáть, -áет** *impf.* shake; grip; possess.

обуслóвить, -влю *pf.*, **обуслóвливать, -аю** *impf.* cause, bring about; *+i.* make conditional on, limit by; **~ся***+i.* be conditioned by, be conditional on; depend on.

обýтый shod. **обýть, -ýю** *pf.* (*impf.* **обувáть**) put boots, shoes on; provide with boots, shoes; **~ся** put on one's boots, shoes.

óбух, -а *or* **-á** butt, back.

обучáть, -áю *impf.*, **об|учи́ть, -чý, -чишь** *pf.* teach; train, instruct; **~ся***+d. or inf.* learn. **обучéние, -я** teaching; instruction, training.

обхвáт, -а girth; **в ~е** in circumference. **обхвати́ть, -ачý, -áтишь** *pf.*, **обхвáтывать, -аю** *impf.* embrace; clasp.

обхóд, -а round; beat; roundabout way; bypass; evasion, circumvention. **обходи́тельный** amiable; courteous; pleasant. **обходи́ть(ся, -ожý(сь, -óдишь(ся** *impf. of* **обойти́(сь. обхóдный** roundabout, circuitous; **~ путь** detour. **обхождéние, -я** manners; treatment; behaviour.

обшáривать, -аю *impf.*, **обшáрить, -рю** *pf.* rummage through, ransack.

обшивáть, -áю *impf. of* **обши́ть. обши́вка, -и** edging, bordering; trimming, facing; boarding, panelling; sheathing; plating; **~ фанéрой** veneering.

обши́рный extensive; spacious; vast.

обши́ть, обошью́, -шьёшь *pf.* (*impf.* **обшивáть**) edge, border; sew round; trim, face; fit out, make outfit(s) for; plank; panel; sheathe, plate.

обшлáг, -á; *pl.* **-á, -óв** cuff.

общáться, -áюсь *impf.* associate, mix.

обще... *in comb.* common(ly), general(ly). **общедостýпный** moderate in price; popular. **~жи́тие, -я** hostel; community; communal life. **~извéстный** well-known, generally known; notorious. **~нарóдный** general, national, public; **~нарóдный прáздник** public holiday. **~образовáтельный** general, of general education. **~при́нятый** generally accepted. **~сою́зный** All-Union. **~употреби́тельный** in general use. **~человéческий** common to all mankind; human; universal, general, ordinary.

общéние, -я intercourse; relations, links; **ли́чное ~** personal contact.

общéственник, -а, -ица, -ы social activist, public-spirited person. **общéственность, -и** (the) public; public opinion; community;

communal organizations; **дух общественности** public spirit. **обще́ственн|ый** social, public; voluntary, unpaid, amateur; **на ~ых нача́лах** voluntary, unpaid; **~ые нау́ки** social sciences; **~ое пита́ние** public catering. **о́бщество, -а** society; association; company; **нау́чное ~** learned body.

о́бщ|ий general; common; **в ~ем** on the whole, in general, in sum; **~ий ито́г, ~ая су́мма** sum total. **о́бщи́на, -ы** community; commune. **о́бщи́нный** communal; common.

об|щипа́ть, -плю́, -плешь *pf.*

общи́тельный sociable. **о́бщность, -и** community.

объ... *see* **о..., об...**

объеда́ть(ся, -а́ю(сь *impf. of* **объе́сть(ся**

объедине́ние, -я unification; merger; union, association. **объединённый; -ён, -á** united. **объедини́тельный** unifying, uniting. **объедини́ть, -ню́** *pf.*, **объединя́ть, -я́ю** *impf.* unite; join; pool, combine; **~ся** unite.

объе́дки, -ов *pl.* leavings, leftovers, scraps.

объе́здить, -зжу, -здишь *pf.* (*impf.* **объезжа́ть**) travel over; break in.

объезжа́ть, -а́ю *impf. of* **объе́здить, объе́хать. объе́зжий** roundabout, circuitous.

объе́кт, -а object; objective; establishment, works. **объекти́в, -а** objective, lens. **объекти́вный** objective; unbiased.

объём, -а volume; bulk, size, capacity. **объёмистый** voluminous, bulky. **объёмный** by volume, volumetric.

объе́сть, -е́м, -е́шь, -е́ст, -еди́м *pf.* (*impf.* **объеда́ть**) gnaw (round), nibble; **~ся** overeat.

объе́хать, -е́ду *pf.* (*impf.* **объезжа́ть**) drive round; go round; go past, skirt; visit, make the round of; travel over.

объяви́ть, -влю́, -вишь *pf.*, **объявля́ть, -я́ю** *impf.* declare, announce; publish, proclaim; advertise; **~ся** turn up, appear; *+i.* announce o.s., declare o.s. **объявле́ние, -я** declaration, announcement; notice; avertisement.

объясне́ние, -я explanation; **~ в любви́** declaration of love. **объясни́мый** explicable, explainable. **объясни́тельный** explanatory. **объясни́ть, -ню́** *pf.*, **объясня́ть, -я́ю** *impf.* explain; **~ся** explain o.s.; become clear, be explained; speak, make o.s. understood; **+с**+*i.* have a talk with; have it out with; *+i.* be explained, accounted for, by.

объя́тие, -я embrace.

обыва́тель, -я *m.* man in the street; inhabitant, resident. **обыва́тельский** commonplace; of the local inhabitants; narrow-minded.

обыгра́ть, -а́ю *pf.*, **обы́грывать, -аю** *impf.* beat; win; use with effect, play up; turn to advantage, turn to account.

обы́денный ordinary, usual; commonplace, everyday.

обыкнове́ние, -я habit, wont; **име́ть ~**+*inf.* be in the habit of; **по обыкнове́нию** as usual. **обыкнове́нно** *adv.* usually; as a rule. **обыкнове́нный** usual; ordinary; commonplace; everyday.

о́быск, -а search. **обыска́ть, -ыщу́, -ы́щешь** *pf.* **обы́скивать, -аю** *impf.* search.

обы́чай, -я custom; usage. **обы́чно** *adv.* usually, as a rule. **обы́чный** usual, ordinary.

обя́занность, -и duty; responsibility; **исполня́ющий обя́занности** acting. **обя́занный** (*+inf.*) obliged, bound; *+d.* obliged to, indebted to (*+i.* for). **обяза́тельно** *adv.* without fail; **он ~ там бу́дет** he is sure to be there, he is bound to be there. **обяза́тельный** obligatory; compulsory; binding; obliging, kind. **обяза́тельство, -а** obligation; engagement; *pl.* liabilities; **взять на себя́ ~** pledge o.s., undertake. **обяза́ть, -яжу́, -я́жешь** *pf.*, **обя́зывать, -аю** *impf.* bind; commit; oblige; **~ся** bind o.s., pledge o.s., undertake; **не хочу́ ни пе́ред кем обя́зываться** I do not want to be beholden to anybody.

овдове́вший widowed. **овдове́ть, -е́ю** *pf.* become a widow, widower.

ове́н, овна́ Aries, the Ram.

овёс, овса́ oats.

ове́чий sheep, sheep's. **ове́чка, -и** *dim. of* **овца́**; lamb, harmless person, gentle creature.

ови́н, -а barn.

овладева́ть, -а́ю *impf.*, **овладе́ть, -е́ю** *pf.*+*i.* take possession of; master; seize; **~ собо́й** get control of o.s., regain self-control. **овладе́ние, -я** mastery; mastering.

о-во *abbr.* (*of* **общество**) Soc., Society.

о́вод, -а; *pl.* **-ы** *or* **-á, оводо́в** gadfly.

о́вощ, -а; *pl.* **-и, -е́й** vegetable, vegetables. **овощно́й** vegetable; **~ магази́н** greengrocer's, greengrocery.

овра́г, -а ravine, gully.

овся́нка, -и oatmeal; porridge. **овсяно́й** oat, of oats. **овся́н|ый** oat, oatmeal; **~ая крупа́** (coarse) oatmeal.

овца́, -ы́; *pl.* **-ы, ове́ц, о́вцам** sheep; ewe. **овцево́дство, -а** sheep-breeding. **овча́р, -а** shepherd. **овча́рка, -и** sheep-dog. **овчи́на, -ы** sheepskin. **овчи́нный** sheepskin.

ога́рок, -рка candle-end.

огиба́ть, -а́ю *impf. of* **обогну́ть**

оглавле́ние, -я table of contents.

огласи́ть, -ашу́ *pf.*, **оглаша́ть, -а́ю** *impf.* proclaim; announce; divulge, make public; fill (with sound); **~ся** resound, ring. **огла́ска, -и** publicity; **получи́ть огла́ску** be given publicity. **оглаше́ние, -я** proclaiming, publication; **не подлежи́т оглаше́нию** confidential, not for publication.

огло́бля, -и; *g.pl.* **-бель** shaft.

о|гло́хнуть, -ну; -óх *pf.*

оглуша́ть, -а́ю *impf.*, **о|глуши́ть, -шу́** *pf.* deafen; stun. **оглуши́тельный** deafening.

огляде́ть, -яжу́ *pf.*, **огля́дывать, -аю** *impf.*, **огляну́ть, -ну́, -нешь** *pf.* look round; look over, examine, inspect; **~ся** look round, look about; look back; turn to look; adapt o.s., become acclimatized. **огля́дка, -и** looking round, looking back; care, caution; **бежа́ть без огля́дки** run for one's life.

огнево́й fire; fiery; igneous. **огнебезопа́сный** non-inflammable. **огнемёт, -а** flame-thrower. **о́гненный** fiery. **огнеопа́сный** inflammable. **огнеприпа́сы, -ов** *pl.* ammunition. **огнесто́йкий** fire-proof, fire-resistant. **огнестре́льн|ый; ~ое ору́жие** fire-arm(s). **огнетуши́тель, -я** fire-extinguisher. **огнеупо́рн|ый** fire-resistant, fire-proof; refractory; **~ая гли́на** fire-clay; **~ый кирпи́ч** fire brick.

ого́ *int.* oho!

огова́ривать, -аю *impf.*, **оговори́ть, -рю́** *pf.* slander; stipulate (for); fix, agree on; **~ся** make a reservation, make a proviso; make a slip (of the tongue); **я оговори́лся** it was a slip of the tongue. **огово́р, -а** slander. **огово́рка, -и** reservation, proviso; slip of the tongue; **без огово́рок** without reserve.

оголённый bare, nude; uncovered, exposed. **оголи́ть, -лю́** *pf.* (*impf.* **оголя́ть**) bare; strip, uncover; **~ся** strip, strip o.s.; become exposed.

оголте́лый wild, frantic; frenzied; unbridled.

оголя́ть(ся, -я́ю(сь *impf. of* **оголи́ть(ся**

огонёк, -нька́ (*small*) light; zest, spirit. **ого́нь, огня́** *m.* fire; firing; light.

огора́живать, -аю *impf.*, **огороди́ть, -рожу́, -ро́дишь** *pf.* fence in, enclose; **~ся** fence o.s. in. **огоро́д, -а** kitchen-garden; market-garden. **огоро́дник, -а** market-gardener. **огоро́дничество, -а** market-gardening. **огоро́дный** kitchen-garden, market-garden.

огоро́шить, -шу *pf.* take aback, dumbfound; startle.

огорча́ть, -а́ю *impf.*, **огорчи́ть, -чу́** *pf.* grieve, distress, pain; **~ся** grieve, distress o.s., be distressed, be pained. **огорче́ние, -я** grief, affliction; chagrin. **огорчи́тельный** distressing.

о|гра́бить, -блю *pf.* **ограбле́ние, -я** robbery; burglary; **у́личное ~** mugging.

огра́да, -ы fence. **огради́ть, -ажу́** *pf.*, **огражда́ть, -а́ю** *impf.* guard, protect; enclose, fence in; **~ся** defend o.s., protect o.s., guard o.s.

ограниче́ние, -я limitation, restriction. **ограни́ченный** limited, narrow. **ограни́чивать, -аю** *impf.*, **ограни́чить, -чу** *pf.* limit, restrict, cut down; **~ся**+*i.* limit o.s. to, confine o.s. to; be limited, be confined to.

огро́мный huge; vast; enormous.

огрубе́лый coarse, hardened, rough. **о|грубе́ть, -е́ю** *pf.*

огрыза́ться, -а́юсь *impf.*, **огрызну́ться, -ну́сь, -нёшься** *pf.* snap (**на**+*a.* at).

огры́зок, -зка bit, end; stub, stump.

огу́зок, -зка rump.

огу́лом *adv.* all together; wholesale, indiscriminately. **огу́льно** *adv.* without grounds. **огу́льный** wholesale, indiscriminate; unfounded, groundless.

огуре́ц, -рца́ cucumber.

одарённый gifted, talented. **ода́ривать, -аю** *impf.*, **одари́ть, -рю́** *pf.*, **одаря́ть, -я́ю** *impf.* give presents (to); +*i.* endow with.

одева́ть(ся, -а́ю(сь *impf. of* **оде́ть(ся**

оде́жда, -ы clothes; garments; clothing; revetment; surfacing.

одеколо́н, -а eau-de-Cologne.

одели́ть, -лю́ *pf.*, **оделя́ть, -я́ю** *impf.* (+*i.*) present (with); endow (with).

оде́ну *etc.*: *see* **оде́ть. одёргивать, -аю** *impf. of* **одёрнуть**

одеревене́лый numb; lifeless. **о|деревене́ть, -е́ю** *pf.*

одержа́ть, -жу́, -жишь *pf.*, **оде́рживать, -аю** *impf.* gain, win; **~ верх** gain the upper hand, prevail. **одержи́мый** possessed.

одёрнуть, -ну *pf.* (*impf.* **одёргивать**) pull down, straighten; call to order; silence.

оде́тый dressed; clothed. **оде́ть, -е́ну** *pf.* (*impf.* **одева́ть**) dress; clothe; **~ся** dress (o.s.); +**в**+*a.* put on. **одея́ло, -а** blanket; coverlet; **~-гре́лка** electric blanket. **одея́ние, -я** garb, attire.

оди́н, одного́, одна́, одно́й, одно́, одного́; *pl.* **одни́, одни́х** *num.* one; a, an; a certain; alone; only; by o.s.; nothing but; same; **в оди́н го́лос** with one voice, with one accord; **все до одного́** (all) to a man; **мне это всё одно́** it is all one to me; **одни́..., други́е** some ..., others; **оди́н за други́м** one after the other; **оди́н и тот же** one and the same; **одно́ и то же** the same thing; **оди́н на оди́н** in private, tete-á-tete; face to face; **одни́ но́жницы** one pair of scissors; **оди́н раз** once; **одни́м сло́вом** in a word, in short; **по одному́** one by one, one at a time; in single file.

одина́ково *adv.* equally. **одина́ковый** identical, the same, equal. **одина́рный** single.

оди́ннадцатый eleventh. **оди́ннадцать, -и** eleven.

одино́кий solitary; lonely; single. **одино́чество, -а** solitude; loneliness, **одино́чка, -и** *c.g.* (one) person alone; **в одино́чку** alone, on one's own; **мать-~** unmarried mother; **по одино́чке** one by one. **одино́чкой** *adv.* alone, by o.s., by itself. **одино́чн|ый** individual; one-man; single; **~ое заключе́ние** solitary confinement. **одино́чник, -а** individual competitor; skiff.

одио́зный odious.

одича́лый wild, gone wild. **одича́ние, -я** running wild. **о|дича́ть, -а́ю** *pf.*

одна́жды *adv.* once; one day; once upon a time; **~ у́тром, ~ ве́чером, ~ но́чью** one morning, evening, night.

одна́ко *conj.* however; but; though; *int.* you don't say so! not really!

одно... *in comb.* single, one; uni-, mono-, homo-. **однобо́кий** one-sided. **~бо́ртный**

single-breasted. **~вре́ме́нно** *adv.* simultaneously, at the same time. **~го́док, -дка, ~го́дка, -и** person of the same age (**с**+*i.* as). **~дне́вный** one-day. **~зву́чный** monotonous. **~зна́чащий** synonymous; monosemantic. **~зна́чный** synonymous; monosemantic; simple; one-digit. **~имённый** of the same name; eponymous. **~кла́ссник** classmate. **~кле́точный** unicellular. **~коле́йный** single-track. **~кра́тный** single; **~кра́тный вид** momentary aspect. **~ле́тний** one-year; annual. **~ле́тник, -а** annual. **~ле́ток, -тка, ~ле́тка, -и** (person) of the same age (**с**+*i.* as). **~ме́стный** for one (person); single-seater. **~мото́рный** single-engined. **~обра́зие, -я, ~обра́зность, -и** monotony. **~обра́зный** monotonous. **~по́люсный** unipolar. **~пу́тка, -и** single-track railway. **~пу́тный** one-way. **~ро́дность, -и** homogeneity, uniformity. **~ро́дный** homogeneous, uniform; similar. **~сло́жный** monosyllabic; terse, abrupt. **~сло́йный** single-layer; one-ply, single-ply. **~сторо́нний** one-sided; unilateral; one-way; one-track. **~та́ктный** one-stroke; single-cycle. **~ти́пный** of the same type; of the same kind. **~то́мник, -а** one-volume edition. **~то́мный** one-volume. **~фами́лец, -льца** person bearing the same surname; namesake. **~цве́тный** one-colour; monochrome. **~эта́жный** single-stage; one-storeyed. **~язы́чный** monolingual. **~я́русный** single-tier, single-deck; single-layer.

одобре́ние, -я approval. **одобри́тельный** approving. **одо́брить, -рю** *pf.*, **одобря́ть, -я́ю** *impf.* approve of, approve.

одолева́ть, -а́ю *impf.*, **одоле́ть, -е́ю** *pf.* overcome, conquer; master, cope with.

одолжа́ть, -а́ю *impf.*, **одолжи́ть, -жу́** *pf.* lend; +**у**+*g.* borrow from; **~ся** be obliged, be beholden; borrow, get into debt. **одолже́ние, -я** favour, service.

одома́шненный domesticated. **одома́шнивать, -аю** *impf.*, **одома́шнить, -ню** *pf.* domesticate, tame.

о|дряхле́ть, -е́ю *pf.*

одува́нчик, -а dandelion.

оду́маться, -аюсь *pf.*, **оду́мываться, -аюсь** *impf.* change one's mind; think better of it; have time to think. **одура́чивать, -аю** *impf.*, **о|дура́чить, -чу** *pf.* fool, make a fool of.

одуре́лый stupid. **одуре́ние, -я** stupefaction, torpor. **о|дуре́ть, -е́ю** *pf.*

одурма́нивать, -аю *impf.*, **о|дурма́нить, -ню** *pf.* stupefy. **о́дурь, -и** stupefaction, torpor. **одуря́ть, -я́ю** *impf.* stupefy; **одуря́ющий за́пах** overpowering scent.

одухотворённый inspired; spiritual. **одухотвори́ть, -рю́** *pf.*, **одухотворя́ть, -я́ю** *impf.* inspire.

одушеви́ть, -влю́ *pf.*, **одушевля́ть, -я́ю** *impf.* animate; **~ся** be animated. **одушевле́ние, -я** animation. **одушевлённый** animated; animate.

одышка, -и shortness of breath; **страда́ть оды́шкой** be short-winded.

ожере́лье, -я necklace.

ожесточа́ть, -а́ю *impf.*, **ожесточи́ть, -чу́** *pf.* embitter, harden; **~ся** become embittered, become hard. **ожесточе́ние, -я, ожесточённость, -и** bitterness; hardness. **ожесточённый** bitter, embittered; hard.

ожива́ть, -а́ю *impf. of* **ожи́ть**

оживи́ть, -влю́ *pf.*, **оживля́ть, -я́ю** *impf.* revive; enliven, vivify, animate; **~ся** become animated, liven up. **оживле́ние, -я** animation, gusto; reviving; enlivening. **оживлённый** animated, lively.

ожида́ние, -я expectation; waiting; **в ожида́нии** expecting; +*g.* pending; **про́тив ожида́ния** unexpectedly; **сверх ожида́ния** beyond expectation. **ожида́ть, -а́ю** *impf.*+*g.* wait for; expect, anticipate.

ожире́ние, -я obesity. **о|жиреть, -е́ю** *pf.*

ожи́ть, -иву́, -ивёшь; о́жил, -а́, -о *pf.* (*impf.* **ожива́ть**) come to life, revive.

ожо́г, -а burn, scald.

оз. *abbr.* (*of* **о́зеро**) L., Lake.

о|забо́тить, -о́чу *pf.*, **озабо́чивать, -аю** *impf.* trouble, worry; cause anxiety to; **~ся**+*i.* attend to, see to. **озабо́ченность, -и** preoccupation; anxiety. **озабо́ченный** preoccupied; anxious, worried.

озагла́вить, -лю *pf.*, **озагла́вливать, -аю** *impf.* entitle, call; head. **озада́ченный** perplexed, puzzled. **озада́чивать, -аю** *impf.*, **озада́чить, -чу** *pf.* perplex, puzzle; take aback.

озари́ть, -рю́ *pf.*, **озаря́ть, -я́ю** *impf.* light up, illuminate; **их озари́ло** it dawned on them; **~ся** light up. **озвере́лый** brutal; brutalized. **о|звере́ть, -е́ю** *pf.*

озву́ченный фильм sound film.

оздорови́тельный sanitary; fitness, keep-fit; **~ бег** jogging; **~ ла́герь** health camp. **оздорови́ть, -влю́** *pf.*, **оздоровля́ть, -я́ю** *impf.* render (more) healthy; improve sanitary conditions of.

озелени́ть, -ню́ *pf.*, **озеленя́ть, -я́ю** *impf.* plant (*with trees, grass, etc.*).

озёрный lake; **~ райо́н** lake district. **о́зеро, -а**; *pl.* **озёра** lake.

ози́мые *sb., pl.* winter crops. **ози́мый** winter. **о́зимь, -и** winter crop.

озира́ться, -а́юсь *impf.* look round; look back.

о|зли́ть(ся *see* **обозли́ть(ся**

озло́бить, -блю *pf.*, **озлобля́ть, -я́ю** *impf.* embitter; **~ся** grow bitter, be embittered. **озлобле́ние, -я** bitterness, animosity. **озло́бленный** embittered, bitter; angry.

о|знако́мить, -млю *pf.*, **ознакомля́ть, -я́ю** *impf.* **с**+*i.* acquaint with; **~ся с**+*i.* familiarize o.s. with.

ознаменова́ние, -я marking, commemoration; **в ~**+*g.* to mark, to commemorate, in commemoration of. **ознаменова́ть, -ну́ю**

pf., **ознамено́вывать, -аю** *impf.* mark, commemorate; celebrate.
означа́ть, -а́ет *impf.* mean, signify, stand for. **озна́ченный** aforesaid.
озно́б, -а shivering, chill.
озо́н, -а ozone. **озо́нный; ~ слой** ozone layer. **озонобезвре́дный** ozone-friendly.
озорни́к, -а́ naughty child, mischievous child; rowdy. **озорнича́ть, -а́ю** *impf.* (*pf.* **с~**) be naughty, get up to mischief. **озорно́й** naughty, mischievous; rowdy. **озорство́, -а́** naughtiness, mischief.
озя́бнуть, -ну; озя́б *pf.* be cold, be freezing.
ой *int.* oh; ow!; ouch!; oops!
ок. *abbr.* (*of* **о́коло**) approx., c., circa.
оказа́ть, -ажу́, -а́жешь *pf.* (*impf.* **ока́зывать**) render, show; **~ влия́ние на**+*a.* influence, exert influence on; **~ де́йствие** have an effect, take effect; **~ предпочте́ние** show preference; **~ услу́гу** do a service, do a good turn; **~ честь** do honour; **~ся** turn out, prove; find o.s., be found.
ока́зия, -и opportunity; unexpected happening, funny thing.
ока́зывать(ся, -аю(сь *impf. of* **оказа́ть(ся**
окайми́ть, -млю́ *pf.*, **окаймля́ть, -я́ю** *impf.* border, edge.
окамене́лость, -и fossil. **окамене́лый** fossil; fossilized; petrified. **о|камене́ть, -е́ю** *pf.*
о|кантова́ть, -ту́ю *pf.* **оканто́вка, -и** mount; edge.
ока́нчивать(ся, -аю(сь *impf. of* **око́нчить(ся** **ока́пывать(ся, -аю(сь** *impf. of* **окопа́ть(ся**
окая́нный damned, cursed.
океа́н, -а ocean. **океа́нский** ocean; oceanic; ocean-going; **~ парохо́д** ocean liner.
оки́дывать, -аю *impf.*, **оки́нуть, -ну** *pf.* cast round; **~ взгля́дом** take in at a glance, glance over.
о́кисел, -сла oxide. **окисле́ние, -я** oxidation. **окисли́ть, -лю́** *pf.* **окисля́ть, -я́ю** *impf.* oxidize; **~ся** oxidize. **о́кись, -и** oxide.
оккупа́нт, -а invader; *pl.* occupying forces, occupiers. **оккупа́ция, -и** occupation. **оккупи́ровать, -рую** *impf.* & *pf.* occupy.
окла́д, -а salary scale; (basic) pay; tax(-rate); metal overlay, setting.
оклевета́ть, -ещу́, -е́щешь *pf.* slander, calumniate, defame.
окле́ивать, -аю *impf.*, **окле́ить, -е́ю** *pf.* cover; glue over, paste over; **~ обо́ями** paper.
окно́, -а́; *pl.* **о́кна** window; port; gap; aperture; interval, free period.
о́ко, -а; *pl.* **о́чи, оче́й** eye; **в мгнове́ние о́ка** in the twinkling of an eye.
окова́ть, окую́, -ёшь *pf.*, **око́вывать, -аю** *impf.* bind; fetter, shackle. **око́вы, око́в** *pl.* fetters.
окола́чиваться, -аюсь *impf.* lounge about, kick one's heels.
околдова́ть, -ду́ю *pf.*, **околдо́вывать, -аю** *impf.* bewitch, entrance, enchant.
околева́ть, -а́ю *impf.*, **околе́ть, -е́ю** *pf.* die. **околе́лый** dead.
о́коло *adv.* & *prep.*+*g.* by; close (to), near; around; about; **где́-нибудь ~** hereabouts, somewhere here; **~ э́того, ~ того́** thereabouts.
око́лыш, -а cap-band.
око́льн|ый roundabout; **~ым путём** in a roundabout way.
о|кольцева́ть, -цу́ю *pf.*
око́нный window; **~ переплёт** sash.
оконча́ние, -я end; conclusion, termination; ending; **~ сле́дует** to be concluded. **оконча́тельно** *adv.* finally, definitively; completely. **оконча́тельный** final; definitive, decisive. **око́нчить, -чу** *pf.* (*impf.* **ока́нчивать**) finish, end; **~ся** finish, end, terminate; be over.
око́п, -а trench; entrenchment. **окопа́ть, -а́ю** *pf.* (*impf.* **ока́пывать**) dig up, dig round; **~ся** entrench o.s., dig in. **око́пн|ый** trench; **~ая война́** trench warfare.
о́корок, -а; *pl.* **-а́, -о́в** ham, gammon; leg.
окостенева́ть, -а́ю *impf.*, **окостене́ть, -е́ю** *pf.* ossify; stiffen. **окостене́лый** ossified; stiff.
окочене́лый stiff with cold. **о|кочене́ть, -е́ю** *pf.*
око́шечко, -а, око́шко, -а (small) window; opening.
окра́ина, -ы outskirts, outlying districts; borders, marches.
о|кра́сить, -а́шу *pf.*, **окра́шивать, -аю** *impf.* paint, colour; dye; stain. **окра́ска, -и** painting; colouring; dyeing, staining; colouration; tinge, tint, touch, slant.
о|кре́пнуть, -ну *pf.* **о|крести́ть(ся, -ещу́(сь, -е́стишь(ся** *pf.*
окре́стность, -и environs; neighbourhood, vicinity. **окре́стный** neighbouring, surrounding.
о́крик, -а hail, call; cry, shout. **окри́кивать, -аю** *impf.*, **окри́кнуть, -ну** *pf.* hail, call, shout to.
окрова́вленный blood-stained, bloody.
окро́шка, -и okroshka (*a cold soup*); hotchpotch, jumble.
о́круг, -а okrug; region, district; circuit. **окру́га, -и** neighbourhood. **округлённый; -лён, -а́** rounded. **округли́ть, -лю́** *pf.*, **округля́ть, -я́ю** *impf.* round; round off; express in round numbers; **~ся** become rounded; be expressed in round numbers. **окру́глый** rounded, roundish. **окружа́ть, -а́ю** *impf.*, **окружи́ть, -жу́** *pf.* surround; encircle. **окружа́ющ|ий** surrounding; **~ая среда́** environment; **~ее** *sb.* environment; **~ие** *sb.*, *pl.* associates; entourage. **окруже́ние, -я** encirclement; surroundings; environment; milieu; **в окруже́нии**+*g.* accompanied by; surrounded by, in the midst of. **окружн|о́й** okrug, district, circuit; circle;

~ая желе́зная доро́га circle line. **окру́жность, -и** circumference; circle; neighbourhood; **на три ми́ли в окру́жности** within a radius of three miles, for three miles round. **окру́жный** neighbouring.

окрыли́ть, -лю́ *pf.*, **окрыля́ть, -я́ю** *impf.* inspire, encourage.

окта́н, -а octane. **окта́нов|ый** octane; **~ое число́** octane rating.

октя́брь, -я́ *m.* October. **октя́брьский** October.

окуна́ть, -а́ю *impf.*, **окуну́ть, -ну́, -нёшь** *pf.* dip; **~ся** dip; plunge; become absorbed, become engrossed.

о́кунь, -я; *pl.* **-и, -е́й** *m.* perch.

окупа́ть, -а́ю *impf.*, **окупи́ть, -плю́, -пишь** *pf.* compensate, repay, make up for; **~ся** be compensated, be repaid, pay for itself; pay; be justified, be requited, be rewarded.

оку́ривание, -я fumigation. **оку́ривать, -аю** *impf.*, **окури́ть, -рю́, -ришь** *pf.* fumigate.

оку́рок, -рка cigarette-end; (cigar-)stub.

оку́тать, -аю *pf.*, **оку́тывать, -аю** *impf.* wrap up; shroud, cloak; **~ся** wrap up; be shrouded, be cloaked.

оку́чивать, -аю *impf.*, **оку́чить, -чу** earth up.

ола́дья, -и; *g.pl.* **-ий** fritter; girdle scone, drop-scone.

оледене́лый frozen. **о|ледене́ть, -е́ю** *pf.* **о|ледени́ть, -и́т** *pf.*

оле́н|ий deer, deer's; reindeer; hart, hart's; **~ий мох** reindeer moss; **~ьи рога́** antlers. **оле́нина, -ы** venison. **оле́нь, -я** *m.* deer; reindeer.

оли́ва, -ы olive. **оли́вковый** olive; olive(-coloured).

олимпиа́да, -ы olympiad; competition. **олимпи́йск|ий** Olympic; Olympian; **~ие и́гры** Olympic games, Olympics. **олимпи́ец, -и́йца, олимпи́йка, -и** Olympian, Olympic contender.

оли́фа, -ы drying oil.

олицетворе́ние, -я personification; embodiment. **олицетворённый; -рён, -а́** personified. **олицетвори́ть, -рю́** *pf.*, **олицетворя́ть, -я́ю** *impf.* personify, embody.

о́лово, -а tin. **оловя́нн|ый** tin; stannic; **~ая посу́да** tinware; pewter; **~ая фольга́** tinfoil.

ом, -а ohm.

омерзе́ние, -я loathing. **омерзе́ть, -е́ю** *pf.* become loathsome. **омерзи́тельн|ый** loathsome, sickening; **~ое настрое́ние** foul mood.

омертве́лость, -и stiffness, numbness; necrosis, mortification. **омертве́л|ый** stiff, numb; necrotic; **~ая ткань** dead tissue. **омертве́ние, -я** necrosis. **о|мертве́ть, -е́ю** *pf.*

омле́т, -а omelette.

омоложе́ние, -я rejuvenation.

омо́ним, -а homonym.

омо́ю *etc.*: *see* **омы́ть**

омрача́ть, -а́ю *impf.*, **омрачи́ть, -чу́** *pf.* darken, cloud, overcloud; **~ся** become darkened, become clouded.

о́мут, -а pool; whirlpool; whirl, maelstrom.

омыва́ть, -а́ю *impf.*, **омы́ть, омо́ю** *pf.* wash; wash away, wash out; wash down; **~ся** be washed.

он, его́, ему́, им, о нём *pron.* he. **она́, её, ей, ей (е́ю), о ней** *pron.* she.

онда́тра, -ы musk-rat, musquash. **онда́тровый** musquash.

онеме́лый dumb; numb. **о|неме́ть, -е́ю** *pf.*

они́, их, им, и́ми, о них *pron.* they. **оно́, его́, ему́, им, о нём** *pron.* it; this, that.

ООН *abbr.* (*of* ***Организа́ция объединённых на́ций***) UN(O), United Nations (Organization). **оо́новский** United Nations.

опада́ть, -а́ет *impf. of* **опа́сть. опада́ющий** deciduous.

опа́здывать, -аю *impf. of* **опозда́ть**

опа́ла, -ы disgrace, disfavour.

о|пали́ть, -лю́ *pf.*

опа́ловый opal; opaline.

опа́лубка, -и shuttering, casing.

опаса́ться, -а́юсь *impf.+g.* fear, be afraid of; *+g. or inf.* beware (of); avoid, keep off. **опасе́ние, -я** fear; apprehension; misgiving(s). **опа́сливый** cautious; wary.

опа́сность, -и danger; peril. **опа́сный** dangerous, perilous.

опа́сть, -адёт *pf.* (*impf.* **опада́ть**) fall, fall off; subside, go down.

опе́ка, -и guardianship, tutelage; trusteeship; guardians, trustees; care; surveillance. **опека́емый** *sb.* ward. **опека́ть, -а́ю** *impf.* be guardian of; take care of, watch over. **опеку́н, -а́, -у́нша, -и** guardian; tutor; trustee.

операти́вность, -и drive, energy. **операти́вный** energetic; efficient; executive; operative, surgical; operation(s); operational; strategical. **опера́тор, -а** operator; cameraman. **опера́торная** *sb.* management and control centre. **операцио́нн|ый** operating; surgical; **~ая** *sb.* operating theatre. **опера́ция, -и** operation.

опереди́ть, -режу́ *pf.*, **опережа́ть, -а́ю** *impf.* outstrip, leave behind; forestall.

опере́ние, -я plumage. **оперённый; -ён, -а́** feathered.

опере́тта, -ы, -е́тка, -и musical comedy, operetta.

опере́ть, обопру́, -прёшь; опёр, -ла́ *pf.* (*impf.* **опира́ть**) +**о**+*a.* lean against; **~ся, на** *or* **о**+*a.* lean on, lean against.

опери́ровать, -рую *impf.* & *pf.* operate on; operate, act; +*i.* operate with; use, handle.

опери́ть, -рю́ *pf.* (*impf.* **оперя́ть**) feather; adorn with feathers; **~ся** be fledged; stand on one's own feet.

о́перный opera; operatic; **~ теа́тр** opera-house.

оперуполномо́ченный *sb.* C.I.D. officer; security officer.

опершись на+*a.* leaning on.

оперя́ть(ся, -я́ю(сь *impf. of* **опери́ть(ся**

опеча́лить(ся, -лю(сь *pf.*

опеча́тать, -аю *pf.* (*impf.* **опеча́тывать**) seal up.

опеча́тка, -и misprint; **спи́сок опеча́ток** errata.

опеча́тывать, -аю *impf. of* **опеча́тать**

опе́шить, -шу *pf.* be taken aback.

опи́вки, -вок *pl.* dregs.

опи́лки, -лок *pl.* sawdust; (metal) filings.

опира́ть(ся, -а́ю(сь *impf. of* **опере́ть(ся**

описа́ние, -я description; account. **опи́санный** circumscribed. **описа́тельный** descriptive. **описа́ть, -ишу́, -и́шешь** *pf.*, **опи́сывать, -аю** *impf.* describe; list, inventory; circumscribe; distrain; **~ся** make a slip of the pen. **о́пись, -и** list, schedule; inventory.

опла́кать, -а́чу *pf.*, **опла́кивать, -аю** *impf.* mourn for; bewail, deplore.

опла́та, -ы pay, payment; remuneration. **оплати́ть, -ачу́, -а́тишь** *pf.*, **опла́чивать, -аю** *impf.* pay for, pay; **~ расхо́ды** meet the expenses, foot the bill; **~ счёт** settle the account, pay the bill. **опла́ченн|ый** paid; **с ~ым отве́том** reply-paid.

опла́чу *etc.*: *see* **опла́кать. оплачу́** *etc.*: *see* **оплати́ть**

оплева́ть, -люю́, -люёшь *pf.*, **оплёвывать, -аю** *impf.* spit on; humiliate.

оплеу́ха, -и slap in the face.

о|плеши́веть, -ею *pf.*

оплодотворе́ние, -я impregnation, fecundation; fertilization. **оплодотвори́тель, -я** *m.* fertilizer. **оплодотвори́ть, -рю́** *pf.*, **оплодотворя́ть, -я́ю** *impf.* impregnate, fecundate; fertilize.

о|пломбирова́ть, -ру́ю *pf.*

опло́т, -а stronghold, bulwark.

опло́шность, -и blunder, oversight. **опло́шный** mistaken, blundering.

оплюю́ *etc.*: *see* **оплева́ть**

оповести́ть, -ещу́ *pf.*, **оповеща́ть, -а́ю** *impf.* notify, inform. **оповеще́ние, -я** notification; warning.

о|пога́нить, -ню *pf.*

опозда́вший *sb.* late-comer. **опозда́ние, -я** being late, lateness; delay; **без опозда́ния** on time; **с ~м на де́сять мину́т** ten minutes late. **опозда́ть, -а́ю** *pf.* (*impf.* **опа́здывать**) be late; be overdue; be slow.

опознава́тельный distinguishing; **~ знак** landmark, beacon; marking. **опознава́ть, -наю́, -наёшь** *impf.*, **опозна́ть, -а́ю** *pf.* identify. **опозна́ние, -я** identification.

опозо́рение, -я defamation. **о|позо́рить(ся, -рю(сь** *pf.*

ополا́скиватель, -я *m.*: **~ (для воло́с)** hair conditioner.

оползáть, -а́ет *impf.*, **оползти́, -зёт; -о́лз, -ла́** *pf.* slip, slide. **о́ползень, -зня** *m.* landslide, landslip.

ополча́ться, -а́юсь *impf.*, **ополчи́ться, -чу́сь** *pf.* take up arms; be up in arms; **+на**+*a.* fall on, attack. **ополче́нец, -нца** militiaman. **ополче́ние, -я** militia; irregulars, levies.

опо́мниться, -нюсь *pf.* come to one's senses, collect o.s.

опо́р, -а; во весь ~ at full speed, at top speed, full tilt.

опо́ра, -ы support; bearing; pier; buttress; **то́чка опо́ры** fulcrum, bearing.

опора́жнивать, -аю *impf. of* **опорожни́ть**

опо́рн|ый support, supporting, supported; bearing; **~ый прыжо́к** vault; **~ый пункт** strong point; **~ая то́чка** fulcrum.

опоро́жни́ть, -ню́ *or* **-ню** *pf.*, **опорожня́ть, -я́ю** *impf.* (*impf. also* **опора́жнивать**) empty; drain.

о|пороси́ться, -и́тся *pf.* **о|поро́чить, -чу** *pf.*

опохмели́ться, -лю́сь *pf.*, **опохмеля́ться, -я́юсь** *impf.* take a hair of the dog that bit you.

опо́шлить, -лю *pf.*, **опошля́ть, -я́ю** *impf.* vulgarize, debase.

опоя́сать, -я́шу *pf.*, **опоя́сывать, -аю** *impf.* gird on; girdle.

оппозицио́нный opposition, in opposition; antagonistic, of opposition. **оппози́ция, -и** opposition.

оппони́ровать, -рую *impf.* (+*d.*) oppose.

опра́ва, -ы setting, mounting; case; rim.

оправда́ние, -я justification; excuse; acquital, discharge. **оправда́тельный пригово́р** verdict of not guilty. **оправда́ть, -а́ю** *pf.*, **опра́вдывать, -аю** *impf.* justify, warrant; vindicate; authorize; excuse; acquit, discharge; **~ся** justify o.s.; vindicate o.s.; be justified.

опра́вить, -влю *pf.*, **оправля́ть, -я́ю** *impf.* put in order, set right; adjust; set, mount; **~ся** put one's dress in order; recover; **+от**+*g.* get over.

опра́шивать, -аю *impf. of* **опроси́ть**

определе́ние, -я definition; determination; decision; attribute. **определённый** definite; determinate; fixed; certain. **определи́мый** definable. **определи́ть, -лю́** *pf.*, **определя́ть, -я́ю** *impf.* define; determine; fix, appoint; allot, assign; **~ на слу́жбу** appoint; **~ся** be formed; take shape; be determined; obtain a fix, find one's position.

опроверга́ть, -а́ю *impf.*, **опрове́ргнуть, -ну; -ве́рг** *pf.* refute, disprove. **опроверже́ние, -я** refutation; disproof; denial.

опрокидн|о́й tipping, tip-up. **опроки́дывать, -аю** *impf.*, **опроки́нуть, -ну** *pf.* overturn; upset; topple; overthrow; overrun; refute; knock back; **~ся** overturn; topple over, tip over, tip up; capsize.

опроме́тчивый precipitate, rash, hasty, unconsidered. **о́прометью** *adv.* headlong.

опро́с, -а interrogation; (cross-)examination; referendum; (opinion) poll. **опроси́ть, -ошу́, -о́сишь** *pf.* (*impf.* **опра́шивать**) interrogate, question; (cross-)examine. **опро́сный** interrogatory; **~ лист** questionnaire.

опроти́веть, -ею *pf.* become loathsome, become repulsive.

опры́скать, -аю *pf.*, **опры́скивать, -аю** *impf.* sprinkle; spray. **опры́скиватель, -я** *m.* sprinkler, spray(er).

опря́тный neat, tidy.

о́птик, -а optician. **о́птика, -и** optics; optical instruments. **опти́ческий** optic, optical; ~ **обма́н** optical illusion.

опто́вый wholesale. **о́птом** *adv.* wholesale; ~ **и в ро́зницу** wholesale and retail.

опубликова́ние, -я publication; promulgation. **о|публикова́ть, -ку́ю** *pf.*, **опублико́вывать, -аю** *impf.* publish; promulgate.

опуска́ть(ся, -а́ю(сь *impf. of* **опусти́ть(ся**

опускн|о́й movable; **~а́я дверь** trap-door.

опусте́лый deserted. **о|пусте́ть, -е́ет** *pf.*

опусти́ть, -ущу́, -у́стишь *pf.* (*impf.* **опуска́ть**) lower; let down; turn down; omit; ~ **глаза́** look down; ~ **го́лову** hang one's head; ~ **ру́ки** lose heart; ~ **што́ры** draw the blinds; **~ся** lower o.s.; sink; fall; go down; let o.s. go, go to pieces.

опустоша́ть, -а́ю *impf.*, **опустоши́ть, -шу́** *pf.* devastate, lay waste, ravage. **опустоше́ние, -я** devastation, ruin. **опустоши́тельный** devastating.

опу́тать, -аю *pf.*, **опу́тывать, -аю** *impf.* enmesh, entangle; ensnare.

опуха́ть, -а́ю *impf.*, **о|пу́хнуть, -ну; опу́х** *pf.* swell, swell up. **опу́хлый** swollen. **о́пухоль, -и** swelling; tumour.

опущу́ *etc.*: *see* **опусти́ть**

опыле́ние, -я pollination. **опыли́ть, -лю́** *pf.*, **опыля́ть, -я́ю** *impf.* pollinate.

о́пыт, -а experience; experiment; test, trial; attempt. **о́пытный** experienced; experimental.

опьяне́лый intoxicated. **опьяне́ние, -я** intoxication. **о|пьяне́ть, -е́ю** *pf.*, **о|пьяни́ть, -и́т** *pf.*, **опьяня́ть, -я́ет** *impf.* intoxicate, make drunk. **опьяня́ющий** intoxicating.

опя́ть *adv.* again.

ора́ва, -ы crowd, horde.

ора́кул, -а oracle.

ора́нжевый orange. **оранжере́йный** hothouse, greenhouse. **оранжере́я, -и** hothouse, greenhouse, conservatory.

ора́тор, -а orator, (public) speaker. **ора́торский** orator's, speaker's; oratorical. **ора́торствовать, -твую** *impf.* orate, harangue, speechify.

ора́ть, ору́, орёшь *impf.* bawl, yell.

орби́та, -ы orbit; (eye-)socket; **вы́вести на орби́ту** put into orbit; ~ **влия́ния** sphere of influence.

орг... *abbr. in comb.* organization, organizational.

о́рган¹, -а organ; organization; unit, element; department, body; **исполни́тельный о́рган** executive; agency. **орга́н², -а** (*mus.*) organ. **организа́тор, -а** organizer. **организацио́нный** organization, organizational. **организа́ция, -и** organization; ~ **Объединённых на́ций** United Nations Organization.

органи́зм, -а organism.

организо́ванный organized; orderly, disciplined. **организова́ть, -зу́ю** *impf.* & *pf.* (*pf. also* **с~**) organize; **~ся** be organized; organize. **органи́ческий, органи́чный** organic.

о́ргия, -и orgy.

оргте́хника, -и office equipment.

орда́, -ы́; *pl.* **-ы** horde.

о́рден, -а; *pl.* **-а́** order. **орденоно́сец, -сца** holder of an order or decoration. **орденоно́сный** decorated with an order.

о́рдер, -а; *pl.* **-а́** order; warrant; writ.

ордина́рец, -рца orderly; batman.

ордина́тор, -а house-surgeon. **ординату́ра, -ы** house-surgeon's appointment; clinical studies.

орды́нский of the (Tartar) horde(s).

орёл, орла́ eagle; ~ **или ре́шка?** heads or tails?

орео́л, -а halo, aureole.

оре́х, -а nut, nuts; nut-tree; walnut. **оре́ховый** nut; walnut. **орехоко́лка, -и** nutcrackers. **оре́шник, -а** hazel; hazel-thicket.

оригина́л, -а original; eccentric, oddity. **оригина́льный** original.

ориента́ция, -и orientation (**на**+*a.* towards); understanding, grasp (**в**+*p.* of). **ориенти́р, -а** landmark; reference point, guiding line. **ориенти́рование, -я** orienteering. **ориенти́роваться, -руюсь** *impf.* & *pf.* orient o.s.; find, get, one's bearings; +**на**+*a.* head for, make for; aim at. **ориентиро́вка, -и** orientation. **ориентиро́вочный** serving for orientation, position-finding; tentative; provisional; rough; approximate.

орке́стр, -а orchestra; band.

орли́ный eagle's, eagle; aquiline. **орли́ца, -ы** female eagle.

орна́мент, -а ornament; ornamental design; plaster cast.

орнито́лог, -а ornithologist; **~-люби́тель** bird-watcher. **орнитоло́гия, -и** ornithology.

оробе́лый timid; frightened. **о|робе́ть, -е́ю** *pf.*

ороси́тельный irrigation. **ороси́ть, -ошу́** *pf.*, **ороша́ть, -а́ю** *impf.* irrigate. **ороше́ние, -я** irrigation; **поля́ ороше́ния** sewage farm.

ору́ *etc.*: *see* **ора́ть**

ору́дие, -я instrument; implement; tool; gun. **оруди́йный** gun. **ору́довать, -дую** *impf.*+*i.* handle; be active in; run; **он там всем ору́дует** he runs the whole show there. **оруже́йн|ый** arms; gun; **~ый заво́д** arms factory; **~ая пала́та** armoury. **ору́жие, -я** arm, arms; weapons.

орфографи́ческ|ий orthographic, orthographical; **~ая оши́бка** spelling mistake. **орфогра́фия, -и** orthography, spelling.

орхиде́я, -и orchid.

оса́, -ы́; *pl.* **-ы** wasp.

оса́да, -ы siege. **осади́ть¹, -ажу́** *pf.* (*impf.* **осажда́ть**) besiege, lay siege to; beleaguer; ~ **вопро́сами** ply with questions; ~ **про́сьбами** bombard with requests.

осади́ть[2], **-ажу́, -а́дишь** *pf.* (*impf.* **осажда́ть**) precipitate.

осади́ть[3], **-ажу́, -а́дишь** *pf.* (*impf.* **оса́живать**) check, halt; force back; rein in; put in his (her) place; take down a peg.

оса́дн|ый siege; **~ое положе́ние** state of siege.

оса́док, -дка sediment; precipitate; fall-out; after-taste; *pl.* precipitation, fall-out. **оса́дочный** precipitation; sedimentary.

осажда́ть, -а́ю *impf. of* **осади́ть. осажда́ться, -а́ется** *impf.* fall; be precipitated, fall out.

оса́живать, -аю *impf. of* **осади́ть. осажу́** *see* **осади́ть**

оса́нистый portly. **оса́нка, -и** carriage, bearing.

осва́ивать(ся, -аю(сь *impf. of* **осво́ить(ся**

осведоми́тель, -я *m.* informer. **осведоми́тельный** informative; information. **осве́домить, -млю** *pf.*, **осведомля́ть, -я́ю** *impf.* inform; **~ся о**+*p.* inquire about, ask after. **осведомле́ние, -я** informing, notification. **осведомлённость, -и** knowledge, information. **осведомлённый** well-informed, knowledgeable; conversant, versed.

освежа́ть, -а́ю *impf.*, **освежи́ть, -жу́** *pf.* refresh; freshen; air; revive. **освежи́тельный** refreshing.

освети́тельный lighting, illuminating. **освети́ть, -ещу́** *pf.*, **освеща́ть, -а́ю** *pf.* light; light up; illuminate, illumine; throw light on; **~ся** light up, brighten; be lighted. **освеще́ние, -я** light, lighting, illumination. **освещённый; -ён, -а́** lit; **~ луно́й** moonlit.

о|свиде́тельствовать, -твую *pf.*

освиста́ть, -ищу́, -и́щешь *pf.*, **осви́стывать, -аю** *impf.* hiss (off); boo, hoot; greet with catcalls.

освободи́тель, -я *m.* liberator. **освободи́тельный** liberation, emancipation. **освободи́ть, -ожу́** *pf.*, **освобожда́ть, -а́ю** *impf.* free, liberate; release, set free; emancipate; dismiss; vacate; clear, empty; **~ся** free o.s.; become free. **освобожде́ние, -я** liberation; release; emancipation; discharge; dismissal; vacation. **освобождённый; -ён, -а́** freed, free; exempt; **~ от нало́га** tax-free.

освое́ние, -я assimilation, mastery, familiarization; reclamation, opening up. **осво́ить, -о́ю** *pf.* (*impf.* **осва́ивать**) assimilate, master; cope with; become familiar with; acclimatize; **~ся** familiarize o.s.; feel at home.

о|святи́ть, -ящу́ *pf.* **освящённый; -ён, -ена́** consecrated; sanctified, hallowed; **обы́чай, ~ века́ми** time-honoured custom.

осево́й axle; axis; axial.

оседа́ние, -я settling, subsidence; settlement. **оседа́ть, -а́ю** *impf. of* **осе́сть**

осёдланный saddled. **о|седла́ть, -а́ю** *pf.*, **осёдлывать, -аю** *impf.* saddle.

осе́длый settled.

осека́ться, -а́юсь *impf. of* **осе́чься**

осёл, -сла́ donkey; ass.

осело́к, -лка́ touchstone; hone, whetstone, oil-stone.

осени́ть, -ню́ *pf.* (*impf.* **осеня́ть**) cover; overshadow; shield; dawn upon, strike; **~ся кресто́м** cross o.s.

осе́нний autumn, autumnal. **о́сень, -и** autumn. **о́сенью** *adv.* in autumn.

осеня́ть(ся, -я́ю(сь *impf. of* **осени́ть(ся**

осерди́ться, -ржу́сь, -рдишься *pf.* (+**на**+*a.*) become angry (with).

осеребри́ть, -ри́т *pf.* silver (over).

осе́сть, ося́ду; осе́л *pf.* (*impf.* **оседа́ть**) settle; subside; sink; form a sediment.

осётр, -а́ sturgeon. **осетри́на, -ы** sturgeon. **осетро́вый** sturgeon, sturgeon's.

осе́чка, -и misfire. **осе́чься, -еку́сь, -ечёшься** *pf.* (*impf.* **осека́ться**) misfire; stop short, break (off).

оси́ливать, -аю *impf.*, **оси́лить, -лю** *pf.* overpower; master; manage.

оси́на, -ы aspen. **оси́новый** aspen.

оси́ный wasp, wasp's; hornets'.

оси́плый hoarse, husky. **о|си́пнуть, -ну; оси́п** get hoarse, grow hoarse.

осироте́лый orphaned. **осироте́ть, -е́ю** *pf.* be orphaned.

оска́ливать, -аю *impf.*, **о|ска́лить, -лю** *pf.*; **~ зу́бы, ~ся** show one's teeth, bare one's teeth.

о|сканда́лить(ся, -лю(сь *pf.*

оскверне́ние, -я defilement; profanation. **оскверни́ть, -ню́** *pf.*, **оскверня́ть, -я́ю** *impf.* profane; defile.

оскла́биться, -блюсь *pf.* grin.

оско́лок, -лка splinter; fragment. **оско́лочный** *adj.* splinter; fragmentation.

оско́мина, -ы bitter taste (in the mouth); **наби́ть оско́мину** set the teeth on edge. **оско́мистый** sour, bitter.

оскорби́тельный insulting, abusive. **оскорби́ть, -блю́** *pf.*, **оскорбля́ть, -я́ю** *impf.* insult; offend; **~ся** take offence; be offended, be hurt. **оскорбле́ние, -я** insult; **~ де́йствием** assault and battery. **оскорблённ|ый; -ён, -а́** offended, insulted; **~ая неви́нность** outraged innocence.

ослабева́ть, -а́ю *impf.*, **о|слабе́ть, -е́ю** *pf.* weaken, become weak; slacken; abate. **ослабе́лый** weakened, enfeebled. **осла́бить, -блю** *pf.*, **ослабля́ть, -я́ю** *impf.* weaken; slacken, relax; loosen. **ослабле́ние, -я** weakening; slackening, relaxation.

ослепи́тельный blinding, dazzling. **ослепи́ть, -плю́** *pf.*, **ослепля́ть, -я́ю** *impf.* blind, dazzle. **ослепле́ние, -я** blinding, dazzling; blindness. **о|сле́пнуть, -ну; -е́п** *pf.*

осли́ный donkey; ass's, asses'; asinine. **осли́ца, -ы** she-ass.

осложне́ние, -я complication. **осложни́ть, -ню́** *pf.*, **осложня́ть, -я́ю** *impf.* complicate; **~ся** become complicated.

ослуша́ние, -я disobedience. **ослу́шаться,**

-аюсь *pf.*, **ослу́шиваться, -аюсь** *impf.* disobey.

ослы́шаться, -шусь *pf.* mishear. **ослы́шка, -и** mishearing, mistake of hearing.

осма́тривать(ся, -аю(сь *impf. of* **осмотре́ть(ся. осме́ивать, -аю** *impf. of* **осмея́ть**

о|смеле́ть, -е́ю *pf.* **осме́ливаться, -аюсь** *impf.*, **осме́литься, -люсь** *pf.* dare; beg to, take the liberty of.

осмея́ть, -ею́, -еёшь *pf.* (*impf.* **осме́ивать**) mock, ridicule.

о|смоли́ть, -лю́ *pf.*

осмо́тр, -а examination, inspection. **осмотре́ть, -рю́, -ришь** *pf.* (*impf.* **осма́тривать**) examine, inspect; look round, look over; **~ся** look round; take one's bearings, see how the land lies. **осмотри́тельный** circumspect. **осмо́трщик, -а** inspector.

осмы́сленный sensible, intelligent. **осмы́сливать, -аю** *impf.*, **осмы́слить, -лю** *pf.*, **осмысля́ть, -я́ю** *impf.* interpret, give a meaning to; comprehend.

оснасти́ть, -ащу́ *pf.*, **оснаща́ть, -а́ю** *impf.* rig; fit out, equip. **осна́стка, -и** rigging. **оснаще́ние, -я** rigging; fitting out; equipment.

осно́ва, -ы base, basis, foundation; *pl.* principles, fundamentals; stem (*of a word*); warp (*of cloth*); **на осно́ве**+*g.* on the basis of; **положи́ть в осно́ву** take as a principle. **основа́ние, -я** founding, foundation; base; basis; ground, reason; **на како́м основа́нии?** on what grounds?; **разру́шить до основа́ния** raze to the ground. **основа́тель, -я** *m.* founder. **основа́тельный** well-founded; just; solid, sound; thorough; bulky. **основа́ть, -ную́, -нуёшь** *pf.*, **осно́вывать, -аю** *impf.* found; base; **~ся** settle; base o.s.; be founded, be based. **основно́й** fundamental, basic; principal, main; primary; **в основно́м** in the main, on the whole. **основополо́жник, -а** founder, initiator.

осо́ба, -ы person, individual, personage. **осо́бенно** *adv.* especially; particularly; unusually; **не ~** not very, not particularly; not very much. **осо́бенность, -и** peculiarity; **в осо́бенности** especially, in particular; (more) particularly. **осо́бенный** special, particular, peculiar; **ничего́ осо́бенного** nothing in particular; nothing (very) much. **особня́к, -а́** private residence; detached house. **особняко́м** *adv.* by o.s. **осо́бо** *adv.* apart, separately; particularly, especially. **осо́бый** special; particular; peculiar.

осовреме́нивать, -аю *impf.*, **осовреме́нить, -ню, -нишь** *pf.* modernize.

осознава́ть, -наю́, -наёшь *impf.*, **осозна́ть, -а́ю** *pf.* realize.

осо́ка, -и sedge.

о́спа, -ы smallpox; pock-marks; vaccination marks.

оспа́ривать, -аю *impf.*, **оспо́рить, -рю** *pf.* dispute, question; challenge, contest; contend for.

о|срами́ть(ся, -млю́(сь *pf.*

ост, -а east; east wind.

остава́ться, -таю́сь, -таёшься *impf. of* **оста́ться**

оста́вить, -влю *pf.*, **оставля́ть, -я́ю** *impf.* leave; abandon, give up; reserve, keep; **~ в поко́е** leave alone, let alone; **~ за собо́й пра́во** reserve the right; **~ь(те)!** stop it! stop that! lay off!

остальн|о́й the rest of; **в ~о́м** in other respects; **~о́е** *sb.* the rest; **~ы́е** *sb.*, *pl.* the others.

остана́вливать(ся, -аю(сь *impf. of* **останови́ть(ся**

оста́нки, -ов *pl.* remains.

остано́в, -а stop, stopper, ratchet-gear. **останови́ть, -влю́, -вишь** *pf.* (*impf.* **остана́вливать**) stop; interrupt; pull up, restrain; check; direct, concentrate; **~ся** stop, come to a stop, come to a halt; stay, put up; +**на**+*p.* dwell on; settle on, rest on. **остано́вка, -и** stop; stoppage; hold-up; **~ за ва́ми** you are holding us up.

оста́ток, -тка remainder; rest; residue; remnant; residuum; balance; *pl.* remains; leavings; leftovers. **оста́точный** residual. remaining. **оста́ться, -а́нусь** *pf.* (*impf.* **остава́ться**) remain; stay; be left, be left over; **за ним оста́лось пять рубле́й** he owes five roubles; **~ в живы́х** survive, come through; **~ на́ ночь** stay the night; *impers.* (+*d.*) it is necessary; **нам не остаётся ничего́ друго́го, как согласи́ться** we have no choice but to agree.

о|стеклене́ть, -е́ет *pf.* **остекли́ть, -лю́** *pf.*, **остекля́ть, -я́ю** *impf.* glaze.

остепени́ться, -ню́сь *pf.*, **остепеня́ться, -я́юсь** *impf.* settle down; become staid, become respectable; mellow.

остерега́ть, -а́ю *impf.*, **остере́чь, -регу́, -режёшь; -рёг, -ла́** *pf.* warn, caution; **~ся** (+*g.*) beware (of); be careful (of), be on one's guard (against).

о́стов, -а frame, framework; shell; hull; skeleton.

остолбене́лый dumbfounded. **о|столбене́ть, -е́ю** *pf.*

осторо́жно *adv.* carefully; cautiously; guardedly; **~!** look out! 'with care'. **осторо́жность, -и** care, caution; prudence. **осторо́жный** careful, cautious; prudent.

остригá́ть(ся, -а́ю(сь *impf. of* **остри́чь(ся**

остриё, -я́ point; spike; (cutting) edge. **остри́ть**[1]**, -рю́** *impf.* sharpen, whet. **остри́ть**[2]**, -рю́** *impf.* (*pf.* **с~**) be witty.

о|стри́чь, -игу́, -ижёшь; -и́г *pf.* (*impf. also* **острига́ть**) cut, clip; **~ся** cut one's hair; have one's hair cut.

остро... *in comb.* sharp, pointed. **остроглá́зый** sharp-sighted, keen-eyed. **~коне́чный** pointed. **~ли́ст, -а** holly. **~но́сый** sharp-nosed; pointed, tapered. **~сло́в, -а** wit. **~уго́льный** acute-angled. **~у́мие, -я**

wit. **~у́мный** witty.

о́стров, -а; *pl.* **-а́** island; isle. **островно́й** island; insular. **острово́к, -вка́** islet; **~ безопа́сности** (traffic) island.

остро́та[1], **-ы** witticism, joke. **острота́**[2], **-ы́** sharpness; keenness; acuteness; pungency, poignancy.

о́стр|ый; остр, -а́, -о sharp; pointed; acute; keen; **~ое положе́ние** critical situation; **~ый сыр** strong cheese; **~ый у́гол** acute angle. **остря́к, -а́** wit.

о|студи́ть, -ужу́, -у́дишь *pf.*, **остужа́ть, -а́ю** *impf.* cool.

оступа́ться, -а́юсь *impf.*, **оступи́ться, -плю́сь, -пишься** *pf.* stumble.

остыва́ть, -а́ю *impf.*, **осты́ть, -ы́ну** *pf.* get cold; cool, cool down.

осуди́ть, -ужу́, -у́дишь *pf.*, **осужда́ть, -а́ю** *impf.* condemn, sentence; convict; censure, blame. **осужде́ние, -я** censure, condemnation; conviction. **осуждённый; -ён, -а́** condemned, convicted; *sb.* convict, convicted person.

осу́нуться, -нусь *pf.* grow thin, get pinched-looking.

осуша́ть, -а́ю *impf.*, **осуши́ть, -шу́, -шишь** *pf.* drain; dry. **осуше́ние, -я** drainage. **осуши́тельный** drainage.

осуществи́мый practicable, realizable, feasible. **осуществи́ть, -влю́** *pf.*, **осуществля́ть, -я́ю** *impf.* realize, bring about; accomplish, carry out; implement; **~ся** be fulfilled, come true. **осуществле́ние, -я** realization; accomplishment; implementation.

осчастли́вить, -влю *pf.*, **осчастли́вливать, -аю** *impf.* make happy.

осы́пать, -плю *pf.*, **осыпа́ть, -а́ю** *impf.* strew; shower; heap; pull down, knock down; **~ уда́рами** rain blows on; **~ся** crumble; fall. **о́сыпь, -и** scree.

ось, -и; *g.pl.* **-е́й** axis; axle; spindle; pin.

ося́ду *etc.*: *see* **осе́сть**

осяза́емый tangible; palpable. **осяза́ние, -я** touch. **осяза́тельный** tactile, tactual; tangible, palpable, sensible. **осяза́ть, -а́ю** *impf.* feel.

от, ото *prep.+g.* from; of; for; against; **бли́зко от го́рода** near the town; **вре́мя от вре́мени** from time to time; **день ото дня** from day to day; **дрожа́ть от стра́ха** tremble with fear; **застрахова́ть от огня́** insure against fire; **ключ от две́ри** door-key; **на се́вер от Москвы́** north of Moscow; **от всей души́** with all one's heart; **от и́мени**+*g.* on behalf of; **от нача́ла до конца́** from beginning to end; **от ра́дости** for joy; **письмо́ от пе́рвого а́вгуста** letter of the first of August; **рабо́чий от станка́** machine operative; **сре́дство от** a remedy for; **сын от пре́жнего бра́ка** a son by a previous marriage; **умере́ть от го́лода** die of hunger; **це́ны от рубля́ и вы́ше** prices from a rouble upwards.

от..., ото..., отъ... *vbl. pref. indicating completion of action or task, fulfilment of duty or obligation; action or motion away from a point; action continued through a certain time; (with vv. reflexive in form) action of negative character, cancelling or undoing of a state, omission, etc.*

ота́пливать, -аю *impf. of* **отопи́ть**

отба́вить, -влю *pf.*, **отбавля́ть, -я́ю** *impf.* take away; pour off; **хоть отбавля́й** more than enough.

отбега́ть, -а́ю *impf.*, **отбежа́ть, -егу́** *pf.* run off.

отберу́ *etc.*: *see* **отобра́ть**

отбива́ть(ся, -а́ю(сь *impf. of* **отби́ть(ся.** **отби́вка, -и** marking out, delineation; whetting, sharpening.

отбивн|о́й; ~а́я котле́та cutlet, chop.

отбира́ть, -а́ю *impf. of* **отобра́ть**

отби́тие, -я repulse; repelling. **отби́ть, отобью́, -ёшь** *pf.* (*impf.* **отбива́ть**) beat off, repulse, repel; parry; take; win over; break off, knock off; knock up; damage by knocks or blows; whet, sharpen; **~ся** break off; drop behind, straggle; +**от**+*g.* defend o.s. against; repulse, beat off; **~ся от рук** get out of hand.

от|бла́говестить, -ещу *pf.*

о́тблеск, -а reflection.

отбо́й, -я (-ю) repulse, repelling; retreat; ringing off; **бить ~** beat a retreat; **дать ~** ring off; **~ возду́шной трево́ги** the all-clear; **~ мяча́** return; **отбо́ю нет от** there is no getting rid of.

отбо́р, -а selection. **отбо́рный** choice, select(ed); picked. **отбо́рочн|ый** selection; **~ая коми́ссия** selection board; **~ое соревнова́ние** knock-out competition.

отбра́сывать, -аю *impf.*, **отбро́сить, -о́шу** *pf.* throw off; cast away; throw back, thrust back, hurl back, hurl back; give up, reject, discard; **~ тень** cast a shadow. **отбро́с, -а** garbage, refuse; offal.

отбыва́ть, -а́ю *impf.*, **отбы́ть, -бу́ду; о́тбыл, -а́, -о** *pf.* depart, leave; serve, do; **~ наказа́ние** serve one's sentence, do time.

отва́га, -и courage, bravery.

отва́дить, -а́жу *pf.*, **отва́живать, -аю** *impf.* scare away; +**от**+*g.* break of, cure of.

отва́живаться, -аюсь *impf.*, **отва́житься, -жусь** *pf.* dare, venture; have the courage. **отва́жный** courageous, brave.

отва́л, -а mould-board; dump, slag-heap; putting off, pushing off, casting off; **до ~а** to satiety; **нае́сться до ~а** eat one's fill, stuff o.s. **отва́ливать, -аю** *impf.*, **отвали́ть, -лю́, -лишь** *pf.* heave off; push aside; put off, push off, cast off; fork out, stump up.

отва́р, -а broth; decoction. **отва́ривать, -аю** *impf.*, **отвари́ть, -рю́, -ришь** *pf.* boil. **отварно́й** boiled.

отве́дать, -аю *pf.* (*impf.* **отве́дывать**) taste, try.

отведённый allotted. **отведу́** *etc.*: *see* **отвести́**

отве́дывать, -аю *impf. of* **отве́дать**

отвезти́, -зу́, -зёшь; -вёз, -ла́ *pf.* (*impf.* **отвози́ть**) take, take away; cart away.

отвёл *etc.*: *see* **отвести́**

отверга́ть, -а́ю *impf.*, **отве́ргнуть, -ну; -ве́рг** *pf.* reject, turn down; repudiate; spurn.

отвердева́ть, -а́ет *impf.*, **отверде́ть, -е́ет** *pf.* harden. **отверде́лость, -и** hardening; callus. **отверде́лый** hardened.

отве́рженец, -нца outcast. **отве́рженный** outcast.

отверну́ть, -ну́, -нёшь *pf.* (*impf.* **отвёртывать, отвора́чивать**) turn away, turn aside; turn down; turn on; unscrew; screw off, twist off; **~ся** turn away, turn aside; come on; come unscrewed.

отве́рстие, -я opening, aperture, orifice; hole; slot.

отверте́ть, -рчу́, -ртишь *pf.* (*impf.* **отвёртывать**) unscrew; screw off, twist off; **~ся** come unscrewed; get off; get out, wriggle out. **отвёртка, -и** screwdriver.

отвёртывать(ся, -аю(сь *impf. of* **отверну́ть(ся, отверте́ть(ся**

отве́с, -а plumb, plummet; slope. **отве́сить, -е́шу** *pf.* (*impf.* **отве́шивать**) weigh out. **отве́сно** *adv.* plumb; sheer. **отве́сный** perpendicular, sheer.

отвести́, -еду́, -едёшь; -вёл, -а́ *pf.* (*impf.* **отводи́ть**) lead, take, conduct; draw aside, take aside; deflect; draw off; reject; challenge; allot, assign; **~ глаза́** look aside, look away; **~ глаза́ от** take one's eyes off; **~ ду́шу** unburden one's heart; **~ обвине́ние** justify o.s.

отве́т, -а answer, reply, response; responsibility; **быть в отве́те (за)** be answerable (for).

ответви́ться, -и́тся *pf.*, **ответвля́ться, -я́ется** *impf.* branch off. **ответвле́ние, -я** branch, offshoot; branch pipe; tap, shunt.

отве́тить, -е́чу *pf.*, **отвеча́ть, -а́ю** *impf.* answer, reply; +**на**+*a.* return; +**за**+*a.* answer for, pay for. **отве́тный** given in answer, answering. **отве́тственность, -и** responsibility; **привле́чь к отве́тственности** call to account, bring to book. **отве́тственный** responsible; crucial; **~ реда́ктор** editor-in-chief. **отве́тчик, -а** defendant, respondent; bearer of responsibility; **телефо́нный ~** answerphone, telephone answering machine.

отве́шивать, -аю *impf. of* **отве́сить. отве́шу** *etc.*: *see* **отве́сить**

отви́ливать, -аю *impf.*, **отвильну́ть, -ну́, -нёшь** *pf.* dodge.

отвинти́ть, -нчу́ *pf.*, **отви́нчивать, -аю** *impf.* unscrew; **~ся** unscrew, come unscrewed.

отвиса́ть, -а́ет *impf.*, **отви́снуть, -нет; -и́с** *pf.* hang down, sag. **отви́сл|ый** hanging, baggy; **с ~ыми уша́ми** lop-eared.

отвлека́ть, -а́ю *impf.*, **отвле́чь, -еку́, -ечёшь; -влёк, -ла́** *pf.* distract, divert; draw away attention of; **~ся** be distracted; become abstracted. **отвлече́ние, -я** abstraction; distraction. **отвлечённый** abstract.

отво́д, -а taking aside; deflection; diversion; leading, taking, conducting; withdrawal; rejection; challenge; allotment, allocation; tap, tapping. **отводи́ть, -ожу́, -о́дишь** *impf. of* **отвести́. отво́дка, -и** branch; diversion; shifting device, shifter. **отво́док, -дка** cutting, layer.

отвоева́ть, -ою́ю *pf.*, **отвоёвывать, -аю** *impf.* win back, reconquer; fight, spend in fighting; finish fighting, finish the war.

отвози́ть, -ожу́, -о́зишь *impf. of* **отвезти́.**

отвора́чивать(ся, -аю(сь *impf. of* **отверну́ть(ся**

отвори́ть, -рю́, -ришь *pf.* (*impf.* **отворя́ть**) open; **~ся** open.

отворо́т, -а lapel flap; top.

отворя́ть(ся, -я́ю(сь *impf. of* **отвори́ть(ся.**

отвою́ю *etc.*: *see* **отвоева́ть**

отврати́тельный, отвра́тный repulsive, disgusting, loathsome; abominable. **отврати́ть, -ащу́** *pf.*, **отвраща́ть, -а́ю** *impf.* avert, stave off; deter, stay the hand of. **отвраще́ние, -я** aversion, disgust, repugnance; loathing.

отвяза́ть, -яжу́, -я́жешь *pf.*, **отвя́зывать, -аю** *impf.* untie, unfasten; untether; **~ся** come untied, come loose; +**от**+*g.* get rid of, shake off, get shut of; leave alone, leave in peace; stop nagging at; **отвяжи́сь от меня́!** leave me alone!

отвыка́ть, -а́ю *impf.*, **отвы́кнуть, -ну; -вы́к** *pf.* +**от** *or inf.* break o.s. of, give up; lose the habit of; grow out of.

отгада́ть, -а́ю *pf.*, **отга́дывать, -аю** *impf.* guess. **отга́дка, -и** answer. **отга́дчик, -а** guesser, solver, diviner.

отгиба́ть(ся, -а́ю(сь *impf. of* **отогну́ть(ся**

отглаго́льный verbal.

отгла́дить, -а́жу *pf.*, **отгла́живать, -аю** *impf.* iron (out).

отгова́ривать, -аю *impf.* **отговори́ть, -рю́** *pf.* dissuade; talk out of; **~ся**+*i.* plead, excuse o.s. on the ground of. **отгово́рка, -и** excuse, pretext.

отголо́сок, -ска echo.

отго́н, -а driving off; distillation; distillate. **отго́нка, -и** driving off; distillation. **отго́нн|ый; ~ые па́стбища** distant pastures.

отгоня́ть, -я́ю *impf. of* **отогна́ть**

отгора́живать, -аю *impf.*, **отгороди́ть, -ожу́, -о́дишь** *pf.* fence off; partition off, screen off; **~ся** fence o.s. off; shut o.s. off, cut o.s. off.

отгрыза́ть, -а́ю *impf.*, **отгры́зть, -зу́, -зёшь** *pf.* gnaw off, bite off.

отдава́ть[1]**(ся, -даю́(сь** *impf. of* **отда́ть(ся.**

отдава́ть[2]**, -аёт** *impf.*, *impers.*+*i.* taste of; smell of; smack of; **от него́ отдаёт во́дкой** he reeks of vodka.

отдави́ть, -влю́, -вишь *pf.* crush; **~ но́гу**+*d.* tread on the foot of.

отдале́ние, -я removal; estrangement; distance; **держа́ть в отдале́нии** keep at a distance. **отдалённость, -и** remoteness. **отдалённый** distant, remote. **отдали́ть, -лю́** *pf.*, **отдаля́ть, -я́ю** *impf.* remove; estrange, alienate; postpone, put off; **~ся** move away; digress.

отда́ние, -я giving back, returning. **отда́ть, -а́м, -а́шь, -а́ст, -адим; о́тдал, -а́, -о** *pf.* (*impf.* **отдава́ть**) give back, return; give; give up, devote; give in marriage, give away; put, place; make; sell, let have; recoil, kick; let go; cast off; **~ в шко́лу** send to school; **~ до́лжное**+*d.* render his due to; **~ под суд** prosecute; **~ прика́з** issue an order, give orders; **~ честь**+*d.* salute; **~ся** give o.s. (up); devote o.s.; resound; reverberate; ring. **отда́ча, -и** return; payment, reimbursement; letting go, casting off; efficiency, performance; output; recoil, kick.

отде́л, -а department; section, part.

отде́лать, -аю *pf.* (*impf.* **отде́лывать**) finish, put the finishing touches to; trim; decorate. **~ся**+**от**+*g.* get rid of, finish with; +*i.* escape with, get off with.

отделе́ние, -я separation; department, branch; compartment; section; part; **~ шка́фа** pigeon-hole. **отделённый** section; *sb.* section commander. **отделе́нский, отделе́нческий** department(al), branch. **отдели́мый** separable. **отдели́ть, -елю́, -е́лишь** *pf.* (*impf.* **отделя́ть**) separate, part; detach; separate off; cut off; **~ся** separate, part; detach o.s., itself; get detached; come apart; come off.

отде́лка, -и finishing; trimming; finish, decoration; décor. **отде́лочник, -а** (interior) decorator. **отде́лывать(ся, -аю(сь** *impf. of* **отде́лать(ся**

отде́льно separately; apart. **отде́льность, -и; в отде́льности** taken separately, individually. **отде́льный** separate, individual; independent. **отделя́ть(ся, -я́ю(сь** *impf. of* **отдели́ть(ся**

отдёргивать, -аю *impf.*, **отдёрнуть, -ну** *pf.* draw aside, pull aside; draw back, pull back; jerk back.

отдеру́ *etc.*: *see* **отодра́ть. отдира́ть, -а́ю** *impf. of* **отодра́ть**

отдохну́ть, -ну́, -нёшь *pf.* (*impf.* **отдыха́ть**) rest; have a rest, take a rest.

отду́шина, -ы air-hole, vent; safety-valve. **отду́шник, -а** air-hole, vent.

о́тдых, -а rest; relaxation; holiday. **отдыха́ть, -а́ю** *impf.* (*pf.* **отдохну́ть**) be resting; be on holiday. **отдыха́ющий** *sb.* holiday-maker.

отдыша́ться, -шу́сь, -шишься *pf.* recover one's breath.

отека́ть, -а́ю *impf. of* **оте́чь. о|тели́ться, -е́лится** *pf.* **отеса́ть** *etc.*: *see* **обтеса́ть**

оте́ц, отца́ father; **~-одино́чка** single father. **оте́ческий** fatherly, paternal. **оте́чествен|ный** home, native; **~ая промы́шленность** home industry; **Вели́кая О~ая война́** Great Patriotic War. **оте́чество, -а** native land, fatherland, home country.

оте́чь, -еку́, -ечёшь; отёк, -ла́ *pf.* (*impf.* **отека́ть**) swell, become swollen; gutter.

отжива́ть, -а́ю *impf.* **отжи́ть, -иву́, -ивёшь; о́тжил, -а́, -о** *pf.* become obsolete; become outmoded; **~ свой век** have had one's day; go out of fashion. **отжи́вший** obsolete; outmoded.

о́тзвук, -а echo.

о́тзыв[1]**, -а** opinion, judgement; reference; testimonial; review; reply, response; **похва́льный ~** honourable mention. **отзы́в**[2]**, -а** recall. **отзыва́ть(ся, -а́ю(сь** *impf. of* **отозва́ть(ся. отзывн|о́й; ~ы́е гра́моты** letters of recall. **отзы́вчивый** responsive.

отка́з, -а refusal; denial; repudiation; rejection; renunciation; giving up; failure; natural; **де́йствовать без ~а** run smoothly; **получи́ть ~** be refused, be turned down; **по́лный до ~а** full to capacity, cram-full. **отказа́ть, -ажу́, -а́жешь** *pf.*, **отка́зывать, -аю** *impf.* fail, break down; (+*d.* **в**+*p.*) refuse, deny; +*d.* **от**+*g.* dismiss, discharge; **~ от до́ма** forbid the house; **~ся** (+**от**+*g.* *or* +*inf.*) refuse, decline; turn down; retract; renounce, give up; relinquish, abdicate; **~ся от свое́й по́дписи** repudiate one's signature; **~ся служи́ть** be out of order. **отка́зник, -а, отка́зница, -цы** refusenik.

отка́лывать(ся, -аю(сь *impf. of* **отколо́ть(ся. отка́пывать, -аю** *impf. of* **откопа́ть. отка́рмливать, -аю** *impf. of* **откорми́ть**

откати́ть, -ачу́, -а́тишь *pf.*, **отка́тывать, -аю** *impf.* roll away; **~ся** roll away; roll back, be forced back.

откача́ть, -а́ю *pf.*, **отка́чивать, -аю** *impf.* pump out; resuscitate, give artificial respiration to.

отка́шливаться, -аюсь *impf.*, **отка́шляться, -яюсь** *pf.* clear one's throat.

откидно́й folding, collapsible. **отки́дывать, -аю** *impf.*, **отки́нуть, -ну** *pf.* turn back, fold back; throw aside, cast away.

откла́дывать, -аю *impf. of* **отложи́ть**

откла́няться, -яюсь *pf.* take one's leave.

откле́ивать, -аю *impf.*, **откле́ить, -е́ю** *pf.* unstick; **~ся** come unstuck.

о́тклик, -а response; comment; echo; repercussion. **отклика́ться, -а́юсь** *impf.*, **откли́кнуться, -нусь** *pf.* answer, respond.

отклоне́ние, -я deviation; divergence; declining, refusal; deflection, declination; error; diffraction; **~ в сто́рону** deviation; **~ от те́мы** digression. **отклони́ть, -ню́, -нишь** *pf.*, **отклоня́ть, -я́ю** *impf.* deflect; decline; **~ся** deviate; diverge; swerve.

отключа́ть, -а́ю *impf.*, **отключи́ть, -чу́** *pf.* cut off, disconnect.

отколоти́ть, -очу́, -о́тишь *pf.* knock off; beat up, thrash, give a good hiding.

отколо́ть, -лю́, -лешь *pf.* (*impf.* **отка́лы-**

вать) break off; chop off; unpin; **~ся** break off; come unpinned; come undone; break away, cut o.s. off.

откопа́ть, -а́ю *pf.* (*impf.* **отка́пывать**) dig out; exhume, disinter; dig up, unearth.

откорми́ть, -млю́, -мишь *pf.* (*impf.* **отка́рмливать**) fatten, fatten up. **отко́рмленный** fat, fatted, fattened.

отко́с, -а slope; **пусти́ть под ~** derail.

открепи́ть, -плю́ *pf.*, **открепля́ть, -я́ю** *impf.* unfasten, untie; **~ся** become unfastened.

открове́ние, -я revelation. **открове́нничать, -аю** *impf.* be candid, be frank; open one's heart. **открове́нный** candid, frank; blunt, outspoken; open, unconcealed; revealing. **откро́ю** *etc.*: *see* **откры́ть**

открути́ть, -учу́, -у́тишь *pf.*, **откру́чивать, -аю** *impf.* untwist, unscrew; **~ся** come untwisted; +**от**+*g.* get out of.

открыва́лка, -и tin-, can-opener; corkscrew. **открыва́ть, -а́ю** *impf.*, **откры́ть, -ро́ю** *pf.* open; uncover, reveal, bare; discover; turn on; **~ па́мятник** unveil a monument; **~ся** open; come to light, be revealed; confide. **откры́тие, -я** discovery; revelation; opening; inauguration; unveiling. **откры́тка, -и** postcard. **откры́то** openly. **откры́т|ый** open; **на ~ом во́здухе, под ~ым не́бом** out of doors, in the open air; **~ое заседа́ние** public sitting; **~ое письмо́** postcard; open letter.

отку́да *adv.* whence; where from; from which; **~ вы об э́том зна́ете?** how do you come to know about that?; **~ ни возьми́сь** quite unexpectedly, suddenly. **отку́да-либо, -нибу́дь** from somewhere or other. **отку́да-то** from somewhere.

отку́поривать, -аю *impf.*, **отку́порить, -рю** *pf.* uncork; open. **отку́порка, -и** opening, uncorking.

откуси́ть, -ушу́, -у́сишь *pf.*, **отку́сывать, -аю** *impf.* bite off; snap off, nip off.

отлага́тельство, -а delay; procrastination; **де́ло не те́рпит отлага́тельства** the matter is urgent. **отлага́ть(ся, -а́ю(сь** *impf.* *of* **отложи́ть(ся**

от|лакирова́ть, -ру́ю *pf.* **отла́мывать, -аю** *impf.* *of* **отлома́ть, отломи́ть**

отлежа́ть, -жу́ *pf.*, **отлёживать, -аю** *impf.*; **я отлежа́л но́гу** my foot has gone to sleep.

отлепи́ть, -плю́, -пишь *pf.*, **отлепля́ть, -я́ю** *impf.* unstick, take off; **~ся** come unstuck, come off.

отлёт, -а flying away; departure; **на ~е** on the point of departure, about to leave; in one's outstretched hand; (standing) by itself. **отлета́ть, -а́ю** *impf.*, **отлете́ть, -лечу́** *pf.*, fly, fly away, fly off; vanish; rebound, bounce back; come off, burst off.

отли́в, -а ebb, ebb-tide; tint; play of colours; **с золоты́м ~ом** shot with gold. **отлива́ть, -а́ю** *impf.*, **отли́ть, отолью́; о́тлил, -а́, -о** *pf.* pour off; pump out; cast, found; (*no pf.*) +*i.* to be shot with. **отли́вка, -и** casting, founding; cast, ingot, moulding. **отливно́й** cast, casting; founded, moulded.

отлича́ть, -а́ю *impf.*, **отличи́ть, -чу́** *pf.* distinguish; single out; **~ одно́ от друго́го** tell one (thing) from another; **~ся** distinguish o.s., excel; differ; +*i.* be notable for. **отли́чие, -я** difference; distinction; **в ~ от** unlike, as distinguished from, in contradistinction to; **знак отли́чия** order, decoration; **с отли́чием** with honours. **отли́чник, -а** outstanding student, worker, etc. **отличи́тельный** distinctive; distinguishing. **отли́чно** *adv.* excellently; perfectly; extremely well. **отли́чный** different; excellent; perfect; extremely good.

отло́гий sloping. **отло́гость, -и** slope. **отло́же** *comp. of* **отло́гий**

отложе́ние, -я sediment, precipitation; deposit. **отложи́ть, -ожу́, -о́жишь** *pf.* (*impf.* **откла́дывать, отлага́ть**) put aside; put away, put by; put off, postpone; adjourn; turn back, turn down; unharness; deposit; **~ся** detach o.s., separate; deposit, be deposited. **отложно́й воротни́к** turn-down collar.

отлома́ть, -а́ю, отломи́ть, -млю́, -мишь *pf.* (*impf.* **отла́мывать**) break off.

отлуча́ть, -а́ю *impf.*, **отлучи́ть, -чу́** *pf.* separate, remove; **~ (от це́ркви)** excommunicate; **~ся** absent o.s. **отлу́чка, -и** absence; **быть в отлу́чке** be absent, be away.

отлы́нивать, -аю *impf.*+**от**+*g.* shirk.

отма́лчиваться, -аюсь *impf.* *of* **отмолча́ться**

отма́хивать, -аю *impf.*, **отмахну́ть, -ну́, -нёшь** *pf.* brush off; wave away; **~ся от**+*g.* brush off; brush aside.

отмежева́ться, -жу́юсь *pf.*, **отмежёвываться, -аюсь** *impf.* **от**+*g.* dissociate o.s. from; refuse to acknowledge.

о́тмель, -и bar, (sand-)bank; shallow.

отме́на, -ы abolition; abrogation, repeal, revocation; cancellation, countermand. **отмени́ть, -ню́, -нишь** *pf.*, **отменя́ть, -я́ю** *impf.* abrogate, repeal, revoke, rescind; abolish; cancel, countermand; disaffirm.

отмере́ть, отомрёт; о́тмер, -ла́, -ло *pf.* (*impf.* **отмира́ть**) die off; die out, die away.

отме́ривать, -аю *impf.*, **отме́рить, -рю** *pf.*, **отмеря́ть, -я́ю** *impf.* measure off.

отмести́, -ету́, -етёшь; -ёл, -а́ *pf.* (*impf.* **отмета́ть**) sweep aside.

отме́стка, -и revenge.

отмета́ть, -а́ю *impf. of* **отмести́**

отме́тина, -ы mark, notch; star, blaze. **отме́тить, -е́чу** *pf.*, **отмеча́ть, -а́ю** *impf.* mark, note; make a note of; point to, mention, record; celebrate, mark by celebration; **~ся** sign one's name; sign out. **отме́тка, -и** note; mark; blip. **отме́тчик, -а** marker.

отмира́ние, -я dying off; dying away, fading away, withering away. **отмира́ть, -а́ет** *impf.* *of* **отмере́ть**

отмолча́ться, -чу́сь *pf.* (*impf.* **отма́лчиваться**) keep silent, say nothing.

отмора́живать, -аю *impf.*, **отморо́зить, -о́жу** *pf.* injure by frost-bite. **отморо́жение, -я** frost-bite. **отморо́женный** frost-bitten.

отмо́ю *etc.*: *see* **отмы́ть**

отмыва́ть, -а́ю *impf.*, **отмы́ть, -мо́ю** *pf.* wash clean; wash off, wash away; **~ся** wash o.s. clean; come out, come off.

отмы́чка, -и picklock; master key.

отне́киваться, -аюсь *impf.* refuse.

отнести́, -су́, -сёшь; -нёс, -ла́ *pf.* (*impf.* **относи́ть**) take; carry away, carry off; ascribe, attribute, refer; **~сь к**+*d.* treat; regard; apply to; concern, have to do with; date from; **э́то к де́лу не отно́сится** that's beside the point, that is not relevant.

отнима́ть(ся, -а́ю(сь *impf. of* **отня́ть(ся**

относи́тельно *adv.* relatively; *prep.*+*g.* concerning, about, with regard to. **относи́тельность, -и** relativity. **относи́тельн|ый** relative; **~ое местоиме́ние** relative pronoun.

относи́ть[1]**(ся, -ошу́(сь, -о́сишь(ся** *impf. of* **отнести́(сь. относи́ть**[2]**, -ошу́, -о́сишь** *pf.* stop wearing. **отноше́ние, -я** attitude; treatment; relation; respect; ratio; letter, memorandum; *pl.* relations; terms; **в не́которых отноше́ниях** in some respects; **в отноше́нии**+*g.*, **по отноше́нию к**+*d.* with respect to, with regard to; **в прямо́м (обра́тном) отноше́нии** in direct (inverse) ratio; **не име́ть отноше́ния к**+*d.* bear no relation to, have nothing to do with.

отны́не *adv.* henceforth, henceforward.

отня́тие, -я taking away; amputation. **отня́ть, -ниму́, -ни́мешь; о́тнял, -а́, -о** *pf.* (*impf.* **отнима́ть**) take (away); amputate; **~ от груди́** wean; **~ три от шести́** take three away from six; **э́то о́тняло у меня́ три часа́** it took me three hours; **~ся** be paralysed; **у него́ отняла́сь пра́вая рука́** he has lost the use of his right arm.

ото *see* **от. ото...** *see* **от...**

отобража́ть, -а́ю *impf.*, **отобрази́ть, -ажу́** *pf.* reflect; represent. **отображе́ние, -я** reflection; representation.

отобра́ть, отберу́, -рёшь; отобра́л, -а́, -о *pf.* (*impf.* **отбира́ть**) take (away); seize; select, pick out.

отобью́ *etc.*: *see* **отби́ть**

отовсю́ду *adv.* from everywhere.

отогна́ть, отгоню́, -о́нишь; отогна́л, -а́, -о *pf.* (*impf.* **отгоня́ть**) drive away, off; keep off; distil (off).

отогну́ть, -ну́, -нёшь *pf.* (*impf.* **отгиба́ть**) bend back; flange; **~ся** bend back.

отогрева́ть, -а́ю *impf.*, **отогре́ть, -е́ю** *pf.* warm; **~ся** warm o.s.

отодвига́ть, -а́ю *impf.*, **отодви́нуть, -ну** *pf.* move aside; put off, put back; **~ся** move aside.

отодра́ть, отдеру́, -рёшь; отодра́л, -а́, -о *pf.* (*impf.* **отдира́ть**) tear off, rip off; flog.

отож(д)естви́ть, -влю́ *pf.*, **отож(д)ествля́ть, -я́ю** *impf.* identify.

отожжённый; -ён, -а́ annealed.

отозва́ть, отзову́, -вёшь; отозва́л, -а́, -о *pf.* (*impf.* **отзыва́ть**) take aside; recall; **~ся на**+*a.* answer; respond to; **о**+*a.* speak of; **на**+*a. or p.* tell on; have an affect on.

отойти́, -йду́, -йдёшь; отошёл, -шла́ *pf.* (*impf.* **отходи́ть**) move away; move off; leave, depart; withdraw; recede; fall back; digress, diverge; come out, come away, come off; recover; come to o.s., come round; pass, go; be lost.

отолью́ *etc.*: *see* **отли́ть. отомрёт** *etc.*: *see* **отмере́ть**

ото|мсти́ть, -мщу́ *pf.*

отопи́тельный heating. **отопи́ть, -плю́, -пишь** *pf.* (*impf.* **ота́пливать**) heat. **отопле́ние, -я** heating.

отопру́ *etc.*: *see* **отпере́ть. отопью́** *etc.*: *see* **отпи́ть**

ото́рванность, -и detachment, isolation; loneliness. **ото́рванный** cut off, isolated, out of touch. **оторва́ть, -ву́, -вёшь** *pf.* (*impf.* **отрыва́ть**) tear off; tear away; **~ся** come off, be torn off; be cut off, lose touch, lose contact; break away; tear o.s. away; **~ся от земли́** take off.

оторопе́лый dumbfounded. **оторопе́ть, -е́ю** *pf.* be struck dumb.

отосла́ть, -ошлю́, -ошлёшь *pf.* (*impf.* **отсыла́ть**) send (off), dispatch; send back; +**к**+*d.* refer to.

отошёл *etc.*: *see* **отойти́. отошлю́** *etc.*: *see* **отосла́ть**

отоща́лый emaciated. **о|тоща́ть, -а́ю** *pf.*

отпада́ть, -а́ет *impf. of* **отпа́сть. отпаде́ние, -я** falling away; defection.

от|пари́ровать, -рую *pf.* **отпа́рывать, -аю** *impf. of* **отпоро́ть**

отпа́сть, -адёт *pf.* (*impf.* **отпада́ть**) fall off, drop off; fall away; defect, drop away; pass, fade.

отпере́ть, отопру́, -прёшь; о́тпер, -ла́, -ло *pf.* (*impf.* **отпира́ть**) unlock; open; **~ся** open; +**от**+*g.* deny; disown.

отпе́тый arrant, inveterate.

от|печа́тать, -аю *pf.*, **отпеча́тывать, -аю** *impf.* print (off); type (out); imprint; unseal, open (up); **~ся** leave an imprint; be printed. **отпеча́ток, -тка** imprint, print; impress.

отпива́ть, -а́ю *impf. of* **отпи́ть**

отпи́ливать, -аю *impf.*, **отпили́ть, -лю́, -лишь** *pf.* saw off.

отпира́тельство, -а denial, disavowal. **отпира́ть(ся, -а́ю(сь** *impf. of* **отпере́ть(ся**

отпи́ть, отопью́, -пьёшь; о́тпил, -а́, -о *pf.* (*impf.* **отпива́ть**) sip, take a sip of.

отпи́хивать, -аю *impf.*, **отпихну́ть, -ну́, -нёшь** *pf.* push off; shove aside.

отпла́та, -ы repayment. **отплати́ть, -ачу́, -а́тишь** *pf.*, **отпла́чивать, -аю** *impf.*+*d.* pay back, repay, requite; **~ той же моне́той** pay back in his own coin.

отплыва́ть, -а́ю *impf.*, **отплы́ть, -ыву́, -ывёшь; -ы́л, -а́, -о** *pf.* sail, set sail; swim off.

отплы́тие, -я sailing, departure.

о́тповедь, -и reproof, rebuke.

отполза́ть, -а́ю *impf.* **отползти́, -зу́, -зёшь; -о́лз, -ла́** *pf.* crawl away.

от|полирова́ть, -ру́ю *pf.* **от|полоска́ть, -ощу́** *pf.*

отпо́р, -а repulse; rebuff; **встре́тить ~** meet with a rebuff; **дать ~** repulse.

отporо́ть[1], **-рю́, -решь** *pf.* (*impf.* **отпа́рывать**) rip off, rip out.

отпоро́ть[2], **-рю́, -решь** *pf.* flog, thrash, give a thrashing.

отправи́тель, -я *m.* sender. **отпра́вить, -влю** *pf.*, **отправля́ть, -я́ю** *impf.* send, forward, dispatch; **~ся** set out, set off, start; leave, depart. **отпра́вка, -и** sending off, forwarding, dispatch. **отправле́ние, -я** sending; departure; exercise, performance; **~ обя́занностей** performance of one's duties. **отправн|о́й; ~о́й пункт, ~а́я то́чка** starting-point.

от|пра́здновать, -ную *pf.*

отпра́шиваться, -аюсь *impf.*, **отпроси́ться, -ошу́сь, -о́сишься** *pf.* ask for leave, get leave.

отпры́гивать, -аю *impf.*, **отпры́гнуть, -ну** *pf.* jump back, spring back; jump aside, spring aside; bounce back.

о́тпрыск, -а offshoot, scion.

отпряга́ть, -а́ю *impf. of* **отпря́чь**

отпря́дывать, -аю *impf.*, **отпря́нуть, -ну** *pf.* recoil, start back.

отпря́чь, -ягу́, -яжёшь; -я́г, -ла́ *pf.* (*impf.* **отпряга́ть**) unharness.

отпу́гивать, -аю *impf.*, **отпугну́ть, -ну́, -нёшь** *pf.* frighten off, scare away.

о́тпуск, -а, *loc.* **-у́**; *pl.* **-а́** leave, holiday(s); furlough; issue, delivery, distribution; tempering, drawing; **в ~е, в ~у́** on leave; **~ по боле́зни** sick-leave. **отпуска́ть, -а́ю** *impf.*, **отпусти́ть, -ущу́, -у́стишь** *pf.* let go, let off; let out; set free; release; give leave (of absence); relax, slacken; (let) grow; issue, give out; serve; assign, allot; remit; forgive; temper, draw; **~ шу́тку** crack a joke. **отпускни́к, -а́** person on leave, holiday-maker; soldier on leave. **отпускн|о́й** holiday; leave; on leave; **~ы́е де́ньги** holiday pay; **~а́я цена́** (wholesale) selling price. **отпуще́ние, -я** remission; **козёл отпуще́ния** scapegoat. **отпу́щенник, -а** freedman.

отраба́тывать, -аю *impf.*, **отрабо́тать, -аю** *pf.* work off; work (for); finish work; finish working on; master. **отрабо́танный** worked out; waste, spent, exhaust.

отра́ва, -ы poison; bane. **отрави́тель, -я** *m.* poisoner. **отрави́ть, -влю́, -вишь** *pf.*, **отравля́ть, -я́ю** *impf.* poison; **~ся** poison o.s.

отра́да, -ы joy, delight; comfort. **отра́дный** gratifying, pleasing; comforting.

отража́тель, -я *m.* reflector; scanner; ejector. **отража́тельный** reflecting, deflecting; reverberatory. **отража́ть, -а́ю** *impf.*, **отрази́ть, -ажу́** *pf.* reflect; repulse, repel, parry; ward off; **~ся** be reflected; reverberate; +**на**+*p.* affect, tell on.

отраслево́й branch. **о́трасль, -и** branch.

отраста́ть, -а́ет *impf.*, **отрасти́, -тёт; отро́с, -ла́** *pf.* grow. **отрасти́ть, -ащу́** *pf.*, **отра́щивать, -аю** *impf.* (let) grow.

от|реаги́ровать, -рую *pf.* **от|регули́ровать, -рую** *pf.* **от|редакти́ровать, -рую** *pf.*

отре́з, -а cut; length; **~ на пла́тье** dress-length. **отре́зать, -е́жу** *pf.*, **отреза́ть, -а́ю** *impf.* cut off; divide, apportion; snap.

о|трезве́ть, -е́ю *pf.* **отрезви́тельный** sobering. **отрезви́ть, -влю́, -ви́шь** *pf.*, **отрезвля́ть, -я́ю** *impf.* sober; **~ся** become sober, sober up. **отрезвле́ние, -я** sobering (up).

отрезно́й cutting; tear-off, cut-off. **отре́зок, -зка** piece, cut; section; portion; segment; **~ вре́мени** period, space of time.

отрека́ться, -а́юсь *impf. of* **отре́чься**

от|рекомендова́ть(ся, -ду́ю(сь *pf.* **отрёкся** *etc.*: *see* **отре́чься. от|ремонти́ровать, -рую** *pf.* **от|репети́ровать, -рую** *pf.*

отре́пье, -я, отре́пья, -ьев *pl.* rags.

от|реставри́ровать, -и́рую *pf.*

отрече́ние, -я renunciation; **~ от престо́ла** abdication. **отре́чься, -еку́сь, -ечёшься** *pf.* (*impf.* **отрека́ться**) renounce, disavow, give up.

отреша́ть, -а́ю *impf.*, **отреши́ть, -шу́** *pf.* release; dismiss, suspend; **~ся** renounce, give up; get rid of. **отрешённость, -и** estrangement, aloofness.

отрица́ние, -я denial; negation. **отрица́тельный** negative; bad, unfavourable. **отрица́ть, -а́ю** *impf.* deny; disclaim.

отро́г, -а spur.

отро́дье, -я race, breed, spawn.

отро́с *etc.*: *see* **отрасти́. отро́сток, -тка** shoot, sprout; branch, extension; appendix.

о́троческий adolescent. **о́трочество, -а** adolescence.

отруба́ть, -а́ю *impf. of* **отруби́ть**

о́труби, -ей *pl.* bran.

отруби́ть, -блю́, -бишь *pf.* (*impf.* **отруба́ть**) chop off; snap back.

от|руга́ть, -а́ю *pf.*

отры́в, -а tearing off; alienation, isolation; loss of contract, estrangement; **без ~а от произво́дства** while remaining at work; **в ~е от**+*g.* out of touch with; **~ (от земли́)** take-off. **отрыва́ть(ся, -а́ю(сь** *impf. of* **оторва́ть(ся. отры́вистый** jerky, abrupt; curt. **отрывно́й** detachable, tear-off. **отры́вок, -вка** fragment, except; passage. **отры́вочный** fragmentary, scrappy.

отры́жка, -и belch; belching, eructation; survival, throw-back.

от|ры́ть, -ро́ю *pf.*

отря́д, -а detachment; order. **отряди́ть, -яжу́** *pf.*, **отряжа́ть, -а́ю** *impf.* detach, detail, tell off.

отря́хивать, -аю *impf.*, **отряхну́ть, -ну́, -нёшь** *pf.* shake down, shake off; **~ся** shake o.s. down.

от|салютова́ть, -ту́ю *pf.*

отса́сывание, -я suction. **отса́сыватель, -я** *m.* suction pump. **отса́сывать, -аю** *impf. of* **отсоса́ть**

о́тсве́т, -а reflection; reflected light. **отсве́чивать, -аю** *impf.* be reflected; +*i.* shine with, reflect.

отсебя́тина, -ы words of one's own; ad-libbing.

отсе́в, -а sifting, selection; siftings, residue. **отсева́ть(ся, -а́ю(сь, отсе́ивать(ся, -аю(сь** *impf. of* **отсе́ять(ся. отсе́вки, -ов** *pl.* siftings, residue.

отсе́к, -а compartment. **отсека́ть, -а́ю** *impf.*, **отсе́чь, -еку́, -ечёшь; -сёк, -ла́** *pf.* sever, chop off, cut off. **отсече́ние, -я** cutting off, severance; **дать го́лову на ~** stake one's life. **отсе́чка, -и** cut-off.

отсе́ять, -е́ю *pf.* (*impf.* **отсева́ть, отсе́ивать**) sift, screen; eliminate; **~ся** fall out, fall off; fall away, drop out.

отска́кивать, -аю *impf.*, **отскочи́ть, -чу́, -чишь** *pf.* jump aside, jump away; rebound, bounce back; come off, break off.

отслу́живать, -аю *impf.*, **отслужи́ть, -жу́, -жишь** *pf.* serve; serve one's time; have served its turn, be worn out.

отсове́товать, -тую *pf.*+*d.* dissuade.

отсоса́ть, -осу́, -осёшь *pf.* (*impf.* **отса́сывать**) suck off, draw off; filter by suction.

отсро́чивать, -аю *impf.*, **отсро́чить, -чу** *pf.* postpone, delay, defer; adjourn; extend (date of). **отсро́чка, -и** postponement, delay, deferment; adjournment; respite; extension.

отстава́ние, -я lag; lagging behind. **отстава́ть, -таю́, -аёшь** *impf. of* **отста́ть**

отста́вить, -влю *pf.*, **отставля́ть, -я́ю** *impf.* set aside, put aside; dismiss, discharge; rescind; **~!** as you were! **отста́вка, -и** dismissal, discharge; resignation; retirement; **в отста́вке** retired, in retirement; **вы́йти в отста́вку** resign, retire. **отставно́й** retired.

отста́ивать(ся, -аю(сь *impf. of* **отстоя́ть(ся**

отста́лость, -и backwardness. **отста́лый** backward; **у́мственно ~** mentally retarded; **физи́чески ~** physically handicapped. **отста́ть, -а́ну** *pf.* (*impf.* **отстава́ть**) fall behind, drop behind; lag behind; be backward, be retarded; be behind(hand); be left behind, become detached; lose touch; break (off); break o.s.; be slow; come off; **~ на полчаса́** be half an hour late; **~ от** break o.s. of, give up; leave alone.

от|стега́ть, -а́ю *pf.*

отстёгивать, -аю *impf.*, **отстегну́ть, -ну́, -нёшь** *pf.* unfasten, undo; unbutton; **~ся** come unfastened, come undone.

отсто́й, -я sediment, deposit. **отсто́йник, -а** settling tank; sedimentation tank; cesspool.

отстоя́ть¹, -ою́ *pf.* (*impf.* **отста́ивать**) defend, save; stand up for; **~ свои́ права́** assert one's rights. **отстоя́ть², -ои́т** *impf.* be ... away; **ста́нция отстои́т от це́нтра го́рода на два киломе́тра** the station is two kilometres from the town centre. **отстоя́ться, -ои́тся** *pf.* (*impf.* **отста́иваться**) settle; precipitate; become stabilized, become fixed.

отстра́ивать(ся, -аю(сь *impf. of* **отстро́ить(ся**

отстране́ние, -я pushing aside; dismissal, discharge. **отстрани́ть, -ню́** *pf.*, **отстраня́ть, -я́ю** *impf.* push aside, lay aside; dismiss, discharge, remove; suspend; **~ся** move away; keep out of the way, keep aloof; **~ся от** dodge; relinquish.

отстре́ливаться, -аюсь *impf.*, **отстреля́ться, -я́юсь** *pf.* fire back.

отстрига́ть, -а́ю *impf.*, **отстри́чь, -игу́, -ижёшь; -ри́г** *pf.* cut off, clip.

отстро́ить, -о́ю *pf.* (*impf.* **отстра́ивать**) complete the construction of, finish building; build up; **~ся** finish building; be built up.

отступа́ть, -а́ю *impf.*, **отступи́ть, -плю́, -пишь** *pf.* step back; recede; retreat, fall back; back down; **~ от**+*g.* go back on; give up; swerve from, deviate from; **~ся от**+*g.* give up, renounce; go back on. **отступле́ние, -я** retreat; deviation; digression. **отсту́пник, -а** apostate; recreant. **отступн|о́й; ~ы́е де́ньги, ~о́е** *sb.* indemnity, compensation. **отступя́** *adv.* (farther) off, away (**от**+*g.* from).

отсу́тствие, -я absence; lack, want; **за ~м**+*g.* in the absence of; for lack of, for want of; **находи́ться в отсу́тствии** be absent. **отсу́тствовать, -твую** *impf.* be absent; default. **отсу́тствующий** absent; *sb.* absentee.

отсчита́ть, -а́ю *pf.*, **отсчи́тывать, -аю** *impf.* count off, count out; read off.

отсыла́ть, -а́ю *impf. of* **отосла́ть. отсы́лка, -и** dispatch; reference; **~ де́нег** remittance.

отсы́пать, -плю *pf.*, **отсыпа́ть, -а́ю** *impf.* pour off; measure off; **~ся** pour out.

отсыре́лый damp. **от|сыре́ть, -е́ет** *pf.*

отсю́да *adv.* from here; hence; from this.

отта́ивать, -аю *impf. of* **отта́ять**

отта́лкивание, -я repulsion. **отта́лкивать, -аю** *impf. of* **оттолкну́ть. отта́лкивающий** repulsive, repellent.

отта́чивать, -аю *impf. of* **отточи́ть**

отта́ять, -а́ю *pf.* (*impf.* **отта́ивать**) thaw out.

оттени́ть, -ню́ *pf.*, **оттеня́ть, -я́ю** *impf.* shade, shade in; set off, make more prominent. **отте́нок, -нка** shade, nuance; tint, hue.

о́ттепель, -и thaw.

оттесни́ть, -ню́ *pf.*, **оттесня́ть, -я́ю** *impf.* drive back, press back; push aside, shove aside.

оттого́ *adv.* that is why; **~, что** because.

о́ттиск, -а impression; off-print, reprint.

оттолкну́ть, -ну́, -нёшь *pf.* (*impf.* **отта́лкивать**) push away, push aside; antagonize, alienate; **~ся** push off.

оттопы́ренный protruding, sticking out. **оттопы́ривать, -аю** *impf.*, **оттопы́рить, -рю** *pf.* stick out; ~ **гу́бы** pout; **~ся** protrude, stick out; bulge.

отточи́ть, -чу́, -чишь *pf.* (*impf.* **отта́чивать**) sharpen, whet.

отту́да *adv.* from there.

оття́гивать, -аю *impf.*, **оттяну́ть, -ну́, -нешь** *pf.* draw out, pull away; draw off; delay. **оття́жка, -и** delay, procrastination; guy-rope; strut, brace, stay.

отупе́лый stupefied, dulled. **отупе́ние, -я** stupefaction, dullness, torpor. **о|тупе́ть, -е́ю** *pf.* grow dull, sink into torpor.

от|утю́жить, -жу *pf.*

отуча́ть, -а́ю *impf.*, **отучи́ть, -чу́, -чишь** *pf.* break (of); **~ся** break o.s. (of).

от|футбо́лить, -лю *pf.*, **отфутбо́ливать, -аю** *impf.* pass on; send on; send from pillar to post.

отха́ркать, -аю *pf.*, **отха́ркивать, -аю** expectorate. **отха́ркивающ|ий** *adv.*; **~ее (сре́дство)** expectorant.

отхлебну́ть, -ну́, -нёшь *pf.*, **отхлёбывать, -аю** *impf.* sip, take a sip of; take a mouthful of.

отхлы́нуть, -нет *pf.* flood back, rush back, rush away.

отхо́д, -а departure, sailing; withdrawal, retirement, falling back; ~ **от** deviation from; break with. **отходи́ть, -ожу́, -о́дишь** *impf. of* **отойти́. отхо́дчивый** not bearing grudges. **отхо́ды, -ов** *pl.* waste; siftings, screenings; tailings.

отцвести́, -ету́, -етёшь; -ёл, -а́ *pf.*, **отцвета́ть, -а́ю** *impf.* finish blossoming, fade.

отцепи́ть, -плю́, -пишь *pf.*, **отцепля́ть, -я́ю** *impf.* unhook; uncouple; **~ся** come unhooked, come uncoupled; +**от**+*g.* leave alone. **отце́пка, -и** uncoupling.

отцо́вский father's; paternal. **отцо́вство, -а** paternity.

отча́иваться, -аюсь *impf. of* **отча́яться**

отча́ливать, -аю *impf.*, **отча́лить, -лю** *pf.* cast off; push off.

отча́сти *adv.* partly.

отча́яние, -я despair. **отча́янный** despairing; desperate; daredevil. **отча́яться, -а́юсь** *pf.* (*impf.* **отча́иваться**) despair.

отчего́ *adv.* why. **отчего́-либо, -нибу́дь** *adv.* for some reason or other. **отчего́-то** *adv.* for some reason.

от|чека́нить, -ню *pf.*

о́тчество, -а patronymic; **как его́ по о́тчеству?** what is his patronymic?

отчёт, -а account; **дать** ~ **в**+*p.* give an account of; report on; **отда́ть себе́** ~ **в**+*p.* be aware of, realize. **отчётливый** distinct; precise; intelligible, clear. **отчётность, -и** book-keeping; accounts. **отчётный** *adj.*; ~ **год** financial year, current year; ~ **докла́д** report.

отчи́зна, -ы country, native land; fatherland.

о́тчий paternal. **о́тчим, -а** step-father.

отчисле́ние, -я deduction; assignment; dismissal. **отчи́слить, -лю** *pf.*, **отчисля́ть, -я́ю** *impf.* deduct; assign; dismiss.

отчита́ть, -а́ю *pf.*, **отчи́тывать, -аю** *impf.* scold, read a lecture, tell off; **~ся** report back; +**в**+*p.* give an account of, report on.

отчуди́ть, -ужу́ *pf.*, **отчужда́ть, -а́ю** *impf.* alienate; estrange. **отчужде́ние, -я** alienation; estrangement.

отшатну́ться, -ну́сь, -нёшься *pf.*, **отша́тываться, -аюсь** *impf.* start back, recoil; +**от**+*g.* give up, forsake, break with.

отшвы́ривать, -аю *impf.*, **отшвырну́ть, -ну́, -нёшь** *pf.* fling away; throw off.

отше́льник, -а hermit, anchorite; recluse.

от|шлифова́ть, -фу́ю *pf.* **от|штукату́рить, -рю** *pf.*

отшути́ться, -учу́сь, -у́тишься *pf.*, **отшу́чиваться, -аюсь** *impf.* reply with a joke; laugh it off.

отщепе́нец, -нца renegade.

отъ... *see* **от...**

отъе́зд, -а departure. **отъезжа́ть, -а́ю** *impf.*, **отъе́хать, -е́ду** *pf.* drive off, go off. **отъе́зжий** distant.

отъя́вленный thorough; inveterate.

отыгра́ть, -а́ю *pf.*, **оты́грывать, -аю** *impf.* win back; **~ся** win, get, back what one has lost; get one's own back, get one's revenge.

отыска́ть, -ыщу́, -ы́щешь *pf.*, **оты́скивать, -аю** *impf.* find; track down, run to earth; look for, try to find; **~ся** turn up, appear.

офице́р, -а officer. **офице́рский** officer's, officers'. **офице́рство, -а** officers; commissioned rank.

официа́льный official.

официа́нт, -а waiter. **официа́нтка, -и** waitress.

официо́з, -а semi-official organ (*of the press*). **официо́зный** semi-official.

оформи́тель, -я *m.* decorator, stage-painter. **офо́рмить, -млю** *pf.*, **оформля́ть, -я́ю** *impf.* get up, mount, put into shape; register officially, legalize; ~ **пье́су** stage a play; **~ся** take shape; be registered; legalize one's position; be taken on the staff, join the staff. **оформле́ние, -я** get-up; mounting, staging; registration, legalization.

офса́йд, -а (*sport*) offside.

ох *int.* oh! ah!

оха́пка, -и armful; **взять в оха́пку** take in one's arms.

о|характеризова́ть, -зу́ю *pf.*

о́хать, -аю *impf.* (*pf.* **о́хнуть**) moan, groan; sigh.

охва́т, -а scope, range; inclusion; outflanking, envelopment. **охвати́ть, -ачу́, -а́тишь** *pf.*, **охва́тывать, -аю** *impf.* envelop; enclose; grip, seize; comprehend, take in; outflank; +*i.* draw into, involve in. **охва́ченный** seized, gripped; ~ **у́жасом** terror-stricken.

охладева́ть, -а́ю *impf.*, **охладе́ть, -е́ю** *pf.* grow cold. **охладе́лый** cold; grown cold.

охлади́тельный cooling, cool. **охлади́ть, -ажу́** *pf.*, **охлажда́ть, -а́ю** *impf.* cool, chill; refrigerate, freeze; **~ся** become cool, cool down. **охлажда́ющ|ий** cooling, refrigerating; **~ая жи́дкость** coolant. **охлажде́ние, -я** cooling, chilling; refrigerating, freezing; coolness; **с возду́шным ~м** air-cooled.

о|хмеле́ть, -е́ю *pf.* **о́хнуть, -ну** *pf. of* **о́хать**

охо́та[1], -ы hunt, hunting; chase.

охо́та[2], -ы desire, wish; inclination.

охо́титься, -о́чусь *impf.* hunt. **охо́тник[1], -а** hunter; sportsman.

охо́тник[2], -а volunteer; +**до**+*g. or inf.* lover of, enthusiast for.

охо́тничий hunting; sporting, shooting.

охо́тно *adv.* willingly, gladly, readily.

о́хра, -ы ochre.

охра́на, -ы guarding; protection; conservation, preservation; guard. **охрани́ть, -ню́** *pf.*, **охраня́ть, -я́ю** *impf.* guard, protect; preserve. **охра́нка, -и** secret police. **охра́нн|ый** guard, protection; **~ая гра́мота, ~ый лист** safe-conduct, pass.

охри́плый, охри́пший hoarse, husky. **о|хри́пнуть, -ну; охри́п** *pf.* become hoarse.

о|хроме́ть, -е́ю *pf.*

о|цара́пать(ся, -аю(сь *pf.*

оце́нивать, -аю *impf.*, **оцени́ть, -ню́, -нишь** *pf.* estimate, evaluate; appraise; appreciate. **оце́нка, -и** estimation, evaluation; appraisal; estimate; appreciation. **оце́нщик, -а** valuer.

оцепене́лый torpid, benumbed. **о|цепене́ть, -е́ю** *pf.*

оцепи́ть, -плю́, -пишь *pf.*, **оцепля́ть, -я́ю** *impf.* surround; cordon off. **оцепле́ние, -я** surrounding; cordoning off; cordon.

оцинко́ванный galvanized.

оча́г, -а́ hearth; centre, seat; focus; nidus; **дома́шний ~** hearth, home; **~ зара́зы** nidus of affection; **~ землетрясе́ния** focus of earthquake; **~ сопротивле́ния** pocket of resistance.

очарова́ние, -я charm, fascination. **очарова́тельный** charming, fascinating. **очарова́ть, -ру́ю** *pf.*, **очаро́вывать, -аю** charm, fascinate.

очеви́дец, -дца eye-witness. **очеви́дно** *adv.* obviously, evidently. **очеви́дный** obvious, evident, manifest, patent.

о́чень *adv.* very; very much.

очередн|о́й next; next in turn; periodic, periodical; recurrent; usual, regular; routine; **~а́я зада́ча** immediate task; **~о́й о́тпуск** usual holiday. **о́чередь, -и**; *g.pl.* **-е́й** turn; queue, line; burst, salvo; **на о́череди** next (in turn); **по о́череди** in turn, in order, in rotation; **в пе́рвую ~** in the first place, in the first instance; **~ за ва́ми** it is your turn; **стоя́ть в о́череди (за+*i*)** queue (for), stand in line (for).

о́черк, -а essay, sketch, study; outline.

о|черни́ть, -ню́ *pf.*

очерстве́лый hardened, callous. **о|черстве́ть, -е́ю** *pf.*

очерта́ние, -я outline(s), contour(s). **очерти́ть, -рчу́, -ртишь** *pf.*, **оче́рчивать, -аю** *impf.* outline, trace.

очёски, -ов *pl.* combings; flocks.

очёчник, -а spectacle case.

о́чи *etc.*: *see* **о́ко**

очи́нивать, -аю *impf.* **о|чини́ть, -ню́, -нишь** *pf.* sharpen, point.

очисти́тельный purifying, cleansing. **о|чи́стить, -и́щу** *pf.*, **очища́ть, -а́ю** *impf.* clean; cleanse, purify; refine; rectify; clear; free; peel; **~ся** clear o.s.; become clear (**от**+*g.* of). **очи́стка, -и** cleaning; cleansing, purification; refinement, rectification; clearance; freeing; mopping up; **для очи́стки со́вести** for conscience sake. **очи́стки, -ов** *pl.* peelings. **очище́ние, -я** cleansing; purification.

очки́, -о́в *pl.* glasses, spectacles; goggles; **защи́тные ~** protective goggles. **очко́, -а́**; *g.pl.* **-о́в** pip; point; hole. **очко́в|ый[1]; ~ая систе́ма** points system. **очко́в|ый[2]; ~ая змея́** cobra.

очну́ться, -ну́сь, -нёшься *pf.* wake, wake up; come to (o.s.), regain consciousness.

о́чн|ый; ~ое обуче́ние internal courses; **~ая ста́вка** confrontation.

очути́ться, -у́тишься *pf.* find o.s.; come to be.

о|швартова́ть, -ту́ю *pf.*

оше́йник, -а collar.

ошеломи́тельный stunning. **ошеломи́ть, -млю́** *pf.*, **ошеломля́ть, -я́ю** *impf.* stun. **ошеломле́ние, -я** stupefaction.

ошиба́ться, -а́юсь *impf.*, **ошиби́ться, -бу́сь, -бёшься; -и́бся** *pf.* be mistaken, make a mistake, make mistakes; be wrong; err, be at fault. **оши́бка, -и** mistake; error; blunder; **по оши́бке** by mistake. **оши́бочный** erroneous, mistaken.

ошпа́ривать, -аю *impf.*, **о|шпа́рить, -рю** *pf.* scald.

о|штрафова́ть, -фу́ю *pf.* **о|штукату́рить, -рю** *pf.* **о|щени́ться, -и́тся** *pf.*

ощети́ниваться, -ается *impf.*, **о|щети́ниться, -нится** *pf.* bristle (up).

о|щипа́ть, -плю́, -плешь *pf.*, **ощи́пывать, -аю** *impf.* pluck.

ощу́пать, -аю *pf.*, **ощу́пывать, -аю** *impf.* feel, touch; grope about. **о́щупь, -и; на ~** to the touch; by touch; **идти́ на ~** grope one's way; feel one's way. **о́щупью** *adv.* gropingly, fumblingly; by touch; blindly; **идти́ ~** grope one's way, feel one's way; **иска́ть ~** grope for.

ощути́мый, ощути́тельный perceptible, tangible, palpable; appreciable. **ощути́ть, -ущу́** *pf.*, **ощуща́ть, -а́ю** *impf.* feel, sense, experience. **ощуще́ние, -я** sensation; feeling, sense.

П

п *letter*: *see* **пэ**
па *nt.indecl.* step, *pas.*
па́ва, -ы peahen.
павиа́н, -а baboon.
павильо́н, -а pavilion; film studio.
павли́н, -а peacock.
па́водок, -дка (sudden) flood, freshet.
па́вш|ий fallen; **~ие в бою́** (those) who fell in action.
па́губа, -ы ruin, destruction; bane. **па́губный** pernicious, ruinous; baneful; fatal.
па́даль, -и carrion.
па́дать, -аю *impf.* (*pf.* **пасть, упа́сть**) fall; sink; drop; decline; fall out, drop out; die; **~ ду́хом** lose heart, lose courage; **~ от уста́лости** be ready to drop. **па́дающ|ий** falling; incident; incoming; **~ие звёзды** shooting stars. **паде́ж, -а́** case. **паде́ние, -я** fall; drop, sinking; degradation; slump; incidence; dip. **па́дкий на**+*a.* or **до**+*g.* having a weakness for; susceptible to; greedy for. **паду́ч|ий** falling; **~ая (боле́знь)** falling sickness, epilepsy.
па́дчерица, -ы step-daughter.
па́дш|ий fallen; **~ие** *sb., pl.* the fallen.
паёк, пайка́ ration.
па́зуха, -и bosom; sinus; axil; **за па́зухой** in one's bosom.
пай, -я; *pl.* **-и́, -ёв** share. **па́йщик, -а** shareholder.
пак, -а pack-ice.
Пакиста́н, -а Pakistan.
паке́т, -а parcel, package; packet; (*official*) letter; paper bag.
па́кля, -и tow; oakum.
пакова́ть, -ку́ю *impf.* (*pf.* **за~, у~**) pack.
па́костить, -ощу *impf.* (*pf.* **за~, ис~, на~**) soil, dirty; spoil, mess up; +*d.* play dirty tricks on. **па́костный** dirty, mean, foul; nasty. **па́кость, -и** filth; dirty trick; obscenity, dirty word.
пакт, -а pact; **~ догово́ра** covenant; **~ о ненападе́нии** non-agression pact.
паланти́н, -а (fur) stole, cape.
пала́та, -ы ward; chamber, house; hall; *pl.* palace; **Оруже́йная ~** Armoury; **~ мер и весо́в** Board of Weights and Measures; **~ о́бщин** House of Commons; **торго́вая ~** Chamber of Commerce. **пала́тка, -и** tent; marquee; stall, booth; **в ~х** under canvas. **пала́тн|ый** ward; **~ая сестра́** (ward) sister. **пала́точный** tent; tented, of tents.
пала́ч, -а́ hangman; executioner; butcher.
па́лец, -льца finger; toe; pin, peg; cam, cog, tooth; **знать как свой пять па́льцев** have at one's finger-tips; **он па́льцем никого́ не тро́нет** he wouldn't harm a fly; **~ о ~ не уда́рить** not lift a finger; **смотре́ть скво́зь па́льцы на**+*a.* close one's eyes to.
палиса́д, -а paling; palisade, stockade. **палиса́дник, -а** (*small*) front garden.
палиса́ндр, -а rosewood.
пали́тра, -ы palette.
пали́ть[1]**, -лю́** *impf.* (*pf.* **о~, с~**) burn; scorch.
пали́ть[2]**, -лю́** *impf.* (*pf.* **вы́~, пальну́ть**) fire, shoot.
па́лка, -и stick; walking-stick, cane; staff; **из-под па́лки** under the lash, under duress; **~ о двух конца́х** double-edged weapon.
пало́мник, -а pilgrim. **пало́мничество, -а** pilgrimage.
па́лочка, -и stick; bacillus; **дирижёрская ~** (conductor's) baton. **па́лочковый** bacillary. **па́лочный** stick, cane.
па́луба, -ы deck. **па́лубный; ~ груз** deck cargo.
пальба́, -ы́ fire, cannonade.
па́льма, -ы palm(-tree). **па́льмов|ый** palm; **~ая ветвь** olive-branch; **~ое де́рево** boxwood.
пальну́ть, -ну́, -нёшь *pf.* of **пали́ть**
пальто́ *nt.indecl.* (over)coat; topcoat.
паля́щий burning, scorching.
па́мятник, -а monument; memorial; tombstone. **па́мятн|ый** memorable; memorial; **~ая кни́жка** notebook, memorandum book. **па́мять, -и** memory; recollection, remembrance; mind, consciousness; **без па́мяти** unconscious; **на ~** by heart; **по па́мяти** from memory; **подари́ть на ~** give as a keepsake.
пана́ма, -ы, пана́мка, -и panama (hat).
пане́ль, -и pavement, footpath; panel(ling), wainscot(ing). **пане́льн|ый** panelling; **~ая обши́вка** panelling, wainscot.
па́ника, -и panic. **паникёр, -а** panicmonger, scaremonger, alarmist.
панихи́да, -ы office for the dead; requiem; **гражда́нская ~** (civil) funeral. **панихи́дный** requiem; funereal.
пани́ческий panic; panicky.
панк, -а punk. **па́нковый** punk.
панно́ *nt.indecl.* panel.
пансио́н, -а boarding-school; boarding-house; board and lodging; **ко́мната с ~ом** room and board. **пансиона́т, -а** living in; holiday hotel. **пансионе́р, -а** boarder; guest.
пантало́ны, -о́н *pl.* trousers; knickers, panties.
панте́ра, -ы panther.
па́па[1]**, -ы** *m.* (the) Pope.
па́па[2]**, -ы** *m.*, **папа́ша, -и** *m.* daddy; papa.
папиро́са, -ы (*Russian*) cigarette. **папиро́сн|ый** *adj.*; **~ая бума́га** rice-paper.
па́пка, -и file; document case, folder; cardboard, pasteboard.

па́поротник, -а fern.
па́пский papal. **па́пство, -а** papacy.
пар[1], **-а (-у)**, *loc.* **-у́**; *pl.* **-ы́** steam; exhalation; **на всех пара́х** full steam ahead, at full speed.
пар[2], **-а**, *loc.* **-у́**; *pl.* **-ы́** fallow.
па́ра, -ы pair, couple; (two-piece) suit.
пара́граф, -а paragraph.
пара́д, -а parade; review; **возду́шный ~** air-display, fly-past. **пара́дность, -и** magnificence; ostentation. **пара́дн|ый** parade; gala; main, front; **~ая дверь** front door; **~ые ко́мнаты** state rooms, (suite of) reception rooms; **~ый подъе́зд** main entrance; **~ая фо́рма** full dress (uniform).
парализо́ванный paralysed. **парализова́ть, -зу́ю** *impf.* & *pf.* paralyse. **парали́ч, -а́** paralysis, palsy. **паралі́чный** paralytic.
паралле́ль, -и parallel. **паралле́льн|ый** parallel; **~ые бру́сья** parallel bars; **~ая медици́на** alternative, complementary medicine.
пара́ф, -а flourish; initials. **парафи́ровать, -рую** *impf.* & *pf.* initial.
парашю́т, -а parachute; **на ~е** by parachute; **прыжо́к с ~ом** parachute jump. **парашюти́ст, -а** parachute jumper; paratrooper.
паре́ние, -я soaring.
па́рень, -рня; *g.pl.* **-рне́й** *m.* boy, lad; chap, fellow.
пари́ *nt.indecl.* bet; **держа́ть ~** bet, lay a bet.
Пари́ж, -а Paris. **парижа́нин, -а**; *pl.* **-а́не, -а́н, парижа́нка, -и** Parisian. **пари́жский** Parisian.
пари́к, -а́ wig. **парикма́хер, -а** barber; hairdresser. **парикма́херская** *sb.* barber's, hairdresser's.
пари́ровать, -и́рую *impf.* & *pf.* (*pf. also* **от~**) parry, counter.
парите́т, -а parity. **парите́тн|ый; на ~ых нача́лах** on a par, on an equal footing.
пари́ть[1], **-рю́** *impf.* soar, swoop, hover.
па́рить[2], **-рю** *impf.* steam, induce sweating in; stew; *impers.* **па́рит** it is sultry; **~ся** (*pf.* **по~ся**) steam, sweat; stew.
парк, -а park; yard, depot; fleet; stock; pool; **ваго́нный ~** rolling-stock.
па́рка, -и steaming; stewing.
парке́т, -а parquet.
па́ркий steamy.
па́ркинг, -а car park. **паркова́ть, -ку́ю** *impf.* (*pf.* **за~**) park; **~ся** park. **парко́вочный; ~ автома́т, ~ счётчик** parking meter.
парла́мент, -а parliament. **парламента́рный** parliamentarian. **парламентёр, -а** envoy; bearer of flag of truce. **парламентёрский; ~ флаг** flag of truce. **парла́ментский** parliamentary; **~ зако́н** Act of Parliament.
парни́к, -а́ hot bed, seed-bed; frame. **парнико́в|ый** *adj.*; **~ые расте́ния** hothouse plants.
парни́шка, -и boy, lad.
парн|о́й fresh; steamy; **~о́е молоко́** milk fresh from the cow. **па́рный**[1] steamy.
па́рный[2] pair; forming a pair; twin; pair-horse.
паро... *in comb.* steam-. **парово́з, -а** locomotive, (steam-)engine. **~во́зник, -а** engine-driver, engineer. **~во́зный** engine. **~выпускно́й** exhaust. **~непроница́емый** steam-tight, steam-proof. **~обра́зный** vaporous. **~прово́д, -а** steam-pipe. **~силово́й** steam-power. **~хо́д, -а** steamer; steamship; **колёсный ~** paddle-boat. **~хо́дный** steam; steamship; **~хо́дное о́бщество** steamship company. **~хо́дство, -а** steam-navigation; steamship-line.
паров|о́й steam; steamed; **~а́я маши́на** steam-engine; **~о́е отопле́ние** steam heating; central heating.
пароди́ст, -а mimic, impressionist.
паро́ль, -я *m.* password, countersign.
паро́м, -а ferry(-boat). **паро́мщик, -а** ferryman.
паро́сский Parian.
парт... *abbr. in comb.* Party. **партакти́в, -а** Party activists. **~биле́т, -а** Party (membership) card. **~кабине́т, -а** Party educational centre. **~ко́м, -а** Party committee. **~о́рг, -а** Party organizer. **~организа́ция, -и** Party organization. **~съезд, -а** Party congress.
па́рта, -ы (*school*) desk.
парте́р, -а stalls; pit.
парти́ец, -и́йца Party member.
партиза́н, -а; *g.pl.* **-а́н** partisan; guerilla. **партиза́нск|ий** partisan, guerilla; unplanned, haphazard; **~ая война́** guerilla warfare; **~ое движе́ние** Resistance (movement).
парти́йка, -и Party member. **парти́йность, -и** Party membership; Party spirit, Party principles. **парти́йный** party; Party; *sb.* Party member.
партиту́ра, -ы score.
па́ртия, -и party; group; batch; lot; consignment; game, set; part.
партнёр, -а partner. **партнёрство, -а** partnership.
па́рус, -а; *pl.* **-а́, -о́в** sail; **идти́ под ~а́ми** sail, be under sail; **на всех ~а́х** in full sail; **подня́ть ~а́** set sail. **паруси́на, -ы** canvas, sail-cloth; duck. **па́русник, -а** sailing vessel. **па́русный** sail; **~ спорт** sailing.
парфюме́рия, -и perfumery.
парча́, -и́; *g.pl.* **-е́й** brocade. **парчо́вый** brocade.
паря́щ|ий soaring, hovering; **~ая маши́на** hovercraft.
пас[1], **-а** (*cards*) pass; **в э́том де́ле я ~** (*coll.*) I'm no good at this.
пас[2], **-а** (*sport*) pass; **~ сюда́!** pass!
па́сека, -и apiary, beehive. **па́сечный** *adj.* beekeeper's, beekeeping.
пасётся *see* **пасти́сь**
па́сквиль, -я *m.* libel, lampoon. **па́сквильный** libellous.
па́смурный dull, cloudy; overcast; gloomy, sullen. **пасова́ть, -су́ю** *impf.* (*pf.* **с~**) pass;

be unable to cope (with), give up, give in.
па́спорт, -а; *pl.* **-а́** passport; registration certificate.
пасса́ж, -а passage; arcade.
пассажи́р, -а passenger. **пассажи́рск|ий** passenger; **~ое движе́ние** passenger services.
пасси́в, -а (*gram.*) passive voice. **пасси́вность, -и** passiveness, passivity. **пасси́вный** passive.
па́ста, -ы paste; purée.
па́стбище, -а pasture.
пастерна́к, -а parsnip.
пасти́, -су́, -сёшь; пас, -ла́ *impf.* graze, pasture; shepherd, tend.
пасти́сь, -сётся; па́сся, -ла́сь *impf.* graze; browse. **пасту́х, -а́** shepherd; herdsman. **пасту́шеский** shepherd's, herdsman's; pastoral. **пастушо́к, -шка́** shepherd. **пасту́шка, -и** shepherdess.
пасть, -и mouth; jaws.
пасть, паду́, -дёшь; пал *pf. of* **па́дать**
Па́сха, -и Easter; Passover. **пасха́льный** Easter, paschal.
па́сынок, -нка stepson, stepchild; outcast.
пат, -а stalemate.
пате́нт, -а (**на**+*a.*) patent (for); licence (for); **владе́лец ~а** patentee. **патентова́ть, -ту́ю** *impf.* patent, take out a patent (for).
патети́ческий, патети́чный pathetic.
патефо́н, -а (*portable*) gramophone.
па́тока, -и treacle; syrup. **па́точный** treacle; treacly.
патрио́т, -а patriot. **патриоти́зм, -а** patriotism. **патриоти́ческий** patriotic.
патро́н, -а cartridge; chuck, holder; lamp-socket; lamp-holder; pattern.
патрона́ж, -а patronage; home health service. **патрона́жн|ый; ~ая сестра́** health visitor, district nurse.
патро́нка, -и pattern.
патро́нный cartridge.
патрули́ровать, -рую *impf.* patrol. **патру́ль, -я́** *m.* patrol.
па́уза, -ы pause; interval; rest.
пау́к, -а́ spider. **паути́на, -ы** cobweb, spider's web; gossamer; web. **пау́чий** spider, spider's.
па́фос, -а (excessive) feeling; zeal, enthusiasm; spirit.
пах, -а, *loc.* **-у́** groin.
па́ханый ploughed. **па́харь, -я** *m.* ploughman. **паха́ть, пашу́, па́шешь** *impf.* (*pf.* **вс~**) plough, till.
па́хнуть[1]**, -ну; пах** *impf.*+*i.* smell of; reek of; savour of, smack of.
пахну́ть[2]**, -нёт** *pf.* puff, blow.
па́хота, -ы ploughing, tillage. **па́хотный** arable.
паху́чий odorous, strong-smelling.
пацие́нт, -а patient.
па́чка, -и bundle; batch; packet, pack; tutu.
па́чкать, -аю *impf.* (*pf.* **за~, ис~, на~**) dirty, soil, stain, sully; daub. **пачкотня́, -и́** daub. **пачку́н, -а́** sloven; dauber.
пашу́ *etc.*: *see* **паха́ть. па́шня, -и**; *g.pl.* **-шен** ploughed field.
пашо́т, -а; яйцо́-~ poached egg.
паште́т, -а pie; pâté.
пае́лья, -и paella.
па́юсн|ый; ~ая икра́ pressed caviare.
пая́льник, -а soldering iron. **пая́льн|ый** soldering; **~ая ла́мпа** blow-lamp. **пая́льщик, -а** tinman, tinsmith. **па́яный** soldered. **пая́ть, -я́ю** *impf.* solder.
пая́ц, -а clown.
пе́вец, -вца́, певи́ца, -ы singer. **певу́чий** melodious. **пе́вч|ий** singing; **~ая пти́ца** song-bird; *sb.* chorister.
пе́гий skewbald, piebald.
пед... *abbr.* (*of* **педагоги́ческий**) *in comb.* pedagogic(al); teachers'; education, educational. **педву́з, -а, ~институ́т, -а** (teachers') training college. **~ку́рсы, -ов** *pl.* teachers' training courses. **~сове́т, -а** staff-meeting. **~фа́к, -а** education department.
педаго́г, -а teacher; pedagogue, educationist. **педаго́гика, -и** pedagogy, pedagogics. **педагоги́ческий** pedagogical; educational; **~ институ́т** (teachers') training college; **~ факульте́т** education department.
педа́ль, -и pedal; treadle. **педа́льный** pedal.
педа́нт, -а pedant. **педанти́ческий** pedantic. **педанти́чность, -и** pedantry.
пединститу́т, -а teacher training college.
педофи́л, -а paedophile.
пейза́ж, -а landscape; scenery. **пейзажи́ст, -а** landscape painting.
пёк *see* **печь. пека́рный** baking, bakery. **пека́рня, -и**; *g.pl.* **-рен** bakery, bakehouse. **пе́карь, -я**; *pl.* **-я́, -е́й** *m.* baker.
Пеки́н, -а Peking; Beijing.
пе́кло, -а scorching heat; hell-fire. **пеку́** *etc.*: *see* **печь**
пелена́, -ы́; *g.pl.* **-лён** shroud. **пелена́ть, -а́ю** *impf.* (*pf.* **за~, с~**) swaddle; put nappy on, change.
пе́ленг, -а bearing. **пеленга́тор, -а** direction finder. **пеленгова́ть, -гу́ю** *impf.* & *pf.* take the bearings of.
пелёнка, -и napkin, nappy; *pl.* swaddling-clothes; **с пелёнок** from the cradle.
пельме́ни, -ей *pl.* pelmeni (*kind of ravioli*).
пе́мза, -ы pumice(-stone). **пе́мзовый** pumice.
пе́на, -ы foam, spume; scum; froth, head; lather; **(мы́льная) ~** soapsuds.
пена́л, -а pencil-box, pencil-case.
пе́ние, -я singing; **~ петуха́** crowing.
пе́нист|ый foamy; frothy; **~ое вино́** sparkling wine. **пе́нить, -ню** *impf.* (*pf.* **вс~**) froth; **~ся** foam, froth.
пеницилли́н, -а penicillin.
пе́нка, -и skin; **(морска́я) ~** meerschaum. **пе́нковый** meerschaum. **пенопла́ст, -а** foam plastic.
пенсионе́р, -а pensioner. **пенсио́нный** pen-

sion; ~ во́зраст retirement age. **пе́нсия, -и** pension; ~ **по инвали́дности** disability pension; ~ **по ста́рости** old-age pension.
пенсне́ *nt.indecl.* pince-nez.
пень, пня *m.* stump, stub.
пенька́, -и́ hemp. **пеньќо́вый** hempen.
пе́ня, -и fine. **пеня́ть, -я́ю** *impf.* (*pf.* **по~**) +*d.* reproach; +**на**+*a.* blame.
пе́пел, -пла ash, ashes. **пепели́ще, -а** site of fire; (hearth and) home; **родно́е** ~ old home. **пе́пельница, -ы** ashtray. **пе́пельный** ashy.
пер. *abbr.* (*of* **переу́лок**) Street, Lane.
перве́йший the first, the most important; first-class. **пе́рвенец, -нца** first-born; first of its kind. **пе́рвенство, -а** first place; championship; ~ **по футбо́лу** football championship. **пе́рвенствова́ть, -твую** *or* **-тву́ю** *impf.* take first place; take precedence, take priority. **перви́чный** primary; initial.
перво... *in comb.* first, primary; prime, top; newly, just; arch-, archaeo-, proto-; prim(o)-. **первобы́тный** primitive; primordial; primeval; pristine. **~зда́нный** primordial; primitive, primary. **~исто́чник, -а** primary source; origin. **~катего́рник, -а** first-ranker. **~кла́ссный** first-class, first-rate. **~ку́рсник, -а** first-year student, freshman. **~ма́йский** Mayday. **~нача́льно** *adv.* originally. **~нача́льный** original; primary; initial; prime; elementary. **~о́браз, -а** prototype, original; protoplast. **~очередно́й, ~очерёдный** first and foremost, immediate. **~печа́тный** early printed, incunabular; first printed, first edition; **~печа́тные кни́ги** incunabula. **~причи́на, -ы** first cause. **~разря́дный** first-class, first-rank. **~ро́дный** first-born; primal original. **~рождённый** first-born. **~со́ртный** best-quality; first-class, first-rate. **~степе́нный** paramount, of the first order.
пе́рвое *sb.* first course. **пе́рво-на́перво** *adv.* first of all. **пе́рв|ый** first; former; earliest; **быть ~ым, идти́ ~ым** come first; lead; **~ое де́ло, ~ым де́лом** first of all, first thing; **с ~ого ра́за** from the first.
перга́мент, -а parchment; greaseproof paper. **перга́ментный** parchment; parchment-like; greaseproof.
пере... *vbl. pref. indicating action across or through something*; *repetition of action*; *superiority*, *excess*, *etc.*; *extension of action to encompass many or all objects or cases of a given kind*; *division into two or more parts*; *reciprocity of action*: trans-, re-, over-, out-.
переадресова́ть, -су́ю *pf.*, **переадресо́вывать, -аю** *impf.* re-address.
перебега́ть, -а́ю *impf.*, **перебежа́ть, -бегу́** *pf.* run across; desert, go over. **перебе́жка, -и** bound, rush; re-run. **перебе́жчик, -а** deserter; turncoat.
перебе́ливать, -аю *impf.*, **перебели́ть, -елю́, -е́ли́шь** *pf.* re-whitewash; make a fair copy of.
переберу́ *etc.*: *see* **перебра́ть**
перебива́ть(ся, -а́ю(сь *impf. of* **переби́ть(ся. переби́вка, -и** re-upholstering.
перебира́ть(ся, -а́ю(сь *impf. of* **перебра́ть(ся**
переби́ть, -бью́, -бьёшь *pf.* (*impf.* **перебива́ть**) interrupt; intercept; kill, slay, slaughter; beat; beat up again; break; re-upholster; **~ся** break; make ends meet; get by. **перебо́й** interruption, intermission; stoppage, hold-up; irregularity; misfire. **перебо́йный** interrupted, intermittent.
перебо́рка, -и sorting out; re-assembly; partition; bulkhead.
переборо́ть, -рю́, -решь *pf.* overcome; master.
переборщи́ть, -щу́ *pf.* go too far; overdo it.
перебра́нка, -и wrangle, squabble.
перебра́сывать(ся, -аю(сь *impf. of* **перебро́сить(ся**
перебра́ть, -беру́, -берёшь; -а́л, -а́, -о *pf.* (*impf.* **перебира́ть**) sort out, pick over; look through, look over; turn over; turn over in one's mind; finger; dismantle and re-assemble; reset; take in excess; score more than enough; **~ся** get over, cross; move.
перебро́сить, -о́шу *pf.* (*impf.* **перебра́сывать**) throw over; transfer; **~ся** fling o.s.; spread; +*i.* throw to one another; **~ся не́сколькими слова́ми** exchange a few words. **перебро́ска, -и** transfer.
перебью́ *etc.*: *see* **переби́ть**
перева́л, -а passing, crossing; pass. **перева́ливать, -аю** *impf.*, **перевали́ть, -лю́, -лишь** *pf.* transfer, shift; cross, pass; *impers.* (+*d.*) **перевали́ло за́ полночь** it is past midnight; **ей перевали́ло за́ сорок** she's turned forty; **~ся** waddle.
перева́ривать, -аю *impf.*, **перевари́ть, -рю́, -ришь** *pf.* boil again; reheat; overdo, overcook; digest; swallow, bear, stand.
переведу́ *etc.*: *see* **перевести́**
перевезти́, -зу́, -зёшь; -вёз, -ла́ *pf.* (*impf.* **перевози́ть**) take across, put across; transport, convey; (re)move.
переверну́ть, -ну́, -нёшь *pf.*, **перевёртывать, -аю** *impf.* (*impf. also* **перевора́чивать**) turn (over); overturn, upset; turn inside out; ~ **вверх дном** turn upside-down; **~ся** turn (over).
переве́с, -а preponderance; predominance; advantage, superiority; **с ~ом в пять голосо́в** with a majority of five votes. **переве́сить, -е́шу** *pf.* (*impf.* **переве́шивать**) reweigh, weigh again; outweigh, outbalance; tip the scales; hang somewhere else.
перевести́, -веду́, -ведёшь; -вёл, -а́ *pf.* (*impf.* **переводи́ть**) take across; transfer, move, switch, shift; translate; convert, express; copy; ~ **дух** take breath; ~ **часы́ вперёд (наза́д)** put a clock forward (back); **~сь**

be transferred; come to an end, run out; become extinct; **у меня́ перевели́сь де́ньги** my money ran out.

переве́шивать, -аю *impf. of* **переве́сить**

перевира́ть, -а́ю *impf. of* **перевра́ть**

перево́д, -а (-у) transfer, move, switch, shift; translation; version; conversion; spending, using up, waste; **нет ~у**+*d.* there is no shortage of, there is an inexhaustible supply of. **переводи́ть(ся, -ожу́(сь, -о́дишь(ся** *impf. of* **перевести́(сь. переводн|о́й** transfer; **~а́я бума́га** carbon paper, transfer paper; **~а́я карти́нка** transfer. **перево́дный** transfer; translated. **перево́дчик, -а** translator; interpreter.

перево́з, -а transporting, conveyance; crossing; ferry. **перевози́ть, -ожу́, -о́зишь** *impf. of* **перевезти́. перево́зка, -и** conveyance, carriage. **перево́зчик, -а** ferryman; boatman; carrier, carter, removal man.

перевооружа́ть, -а́ю *impf.*, **перевооружи́ть, -жу́** *pf.* rearm; **~ся** rearm. **перевооруже́ние, -я** rearmament.

перевоплоти́ть, -лощу́ *pf.*, **перевоплоща́ть, -а́ю** *impf.* reincarnate; transform; **~ся** be reincarnated; transform o.s., be transformed. **перевоплоще́ние, -я** reincarnation; transformation.

перевора́чивать(ся, -аю(сь *impf. of* **перевернуть(ся. переворо́т, -а** revolution; overturn; cataclysm; **госуда́рственный ~** coup d'état.

перевоспита́ние, -я re-education; rehabilitation. **перевоспита́ть, -а́ю** *pf.*, **перевоспи́тывать, -аю** *impf.* re-educate; rehabilitate.

перевра́ть, -ру́, -рёшь; -а́л, -а́, -о *pf.* (*impf.* **перевира́ть**) garble, confuse; misinterpret; misquote.

перевыполне́ние, -я over-fulfilment. **перевы́полнить, -ню** *pf.*, **перевыполня́ть, -я́ю** *impf.* over-fulfil.

перевяза́ть, -яжу́, -я́жешь *pf.*, **перевя́зывать, -аю** *impf.* dress, bandage; tie up, cord; tie again, re-tie; knit again. **перевя́зка, -и** dressing, bandage. **перевя́зочный; ~ материа́л** dressing; **~ пункт** dressing station. **пе́ревязь, -и** cross-belt, shoulder-belt; sling.

переги́б, -а bend, twist; fold; exaggeration; **допусти́ть ~ в**+*p.* carry too far. **перегиба́ть(ся, -а́ю(сь** *impf. of* **перегну́ть(ся**

перегля́дываться, -аюсь *impf.*, **перегляну́ться, -ну́сь, -нешься** *pf.* exchange glances.

перегна́ть, -гоню́, -го́нишь; -а́л, -а́, -о *pf.* (*impf.* **перегоня́ть**) outdistance, leave behind; overtake, surpass; drive; ferry; distil, sublimate.

перегно́й, -я humus.

перегну́ть, -ну́, -нёшь *pf.* (*impf.* **перегиба́ть**) bend; **~ па́лку** go too far; **~ся** bend; lean over.

перегова́ривать, -аю *impf.* **переговори́ть, -рю́** *pf.* talk, speak; silence, out-talk; **+о**+*p.* talk over, discuss; **~ся (с**+*i.*) exchange remarks (with). **перегово́р, -а** (telephone) call, conversation; *pl.* negotiations, parley; **вести́ ~ы** negotiate, conduct negotiations, parley. **перегово́рн|ый** *adj.*; **~ая бу́дка** call-box, telephone booth; **~ый пункт** public call-boxes; trunk-call office.

перего́н, -а driving; stage. **перего́нка, -и** distillation. **перего́нный** distilling, distillation; **~ заво́д** distillery; **~ куб** still. **перегоню́** *etc.*: *see* **перегна́ть. перегоня́ть, -я́ю** *impf. of* **перегна́ть**

перегора́живать, -аю *impf. of* **перегороди́ть**

перегора́ть, -а́ет *impf.*, **перегоре́ть, -ри́т** *pf.* burn out, fuse; burn through; rot through.

перегороди́ть, -рожу́, -ро́ди́шь *pf.* (*impf.* **перегора́живать**) partition off; block. **перегоро́дка, -и** partition; baffle (plate). **перегоро́женный** partitioned off; blocked.

перегре́в, -а overheating; superheating. **перегрева́ть, -а́ю** *impf.*, **перегре́ть, -е́ю** *pf.* overheat; **~ся** overheat; burn, burn out, get burned.

перегружа́ть, -а́ю *impf.*, **перегрузи́ть, -ужу́, -у́зишь** *pf.* overload; transfer, trans-ship; overwork. **перегру́зка, -и** overload; overwork; transfer; reloading.

перегрыза́ть, -а́ю *impf.*, **перегры́зть, -зу́, -зёшь; -гры́з** *pf.* gnaw through, bite through; **~ся** fight; quarrel, wrangle.

пе́ред, пе́редо, пред, пре́до *prep.*+*i.* before; in front of; in the face of; to; compared to, in comparison with; **извини́ться ~** apologize to. **перёд, пе́реда**; *pl.* **-а́** front, forepart.

передава́ть, -даю́, -даёшь *impf.*, **переда́ть, -а́м, -а́шь, -а́ст, -ади́м; пе́редал, -а́, -о** *pf.* pass, hand, hand over; hand down; make over; tell; communicate; transmit, convey; pay too much, give too much; **вы пе́редали три рубля́** you have paid three roubles too much; **~ де́ло в суд** take a matter to court, sue; **~ приве́т** convey one's greetings, send one's regards; **переда́й(те) им приве́т** remember me to them; **~ся** pass; be transmitted; be communicated; be inherited; +*d.* go over to. **переда́точн|ый; ~ый механи́зм** drive, driving mechanism, transmission; **~ое число́** gear ratio. **переда́тчик, -а** transmitter, sender; conductor. **переда́ча, -и** passing; transmission; communication; broadcast; drive; gear, gearing; transfer; **пряма́я ~** live broadcast; **рекла́мная ~** commercial, advert.

передвига́ть, -а́ю *impf.*, **передви́нуть, -ну** *pf.* move, shift; **~ часы́ вперёд (наза́д)** put the clock forward (back); **~ сро́ки экза́менов** change the date of examinations; **~ся** move, shift; travel. **передвиже́ние, -я** movement, moving; conveyance; travel; **сре́дства передвиже́ния** means of transport. **передви́жка, -и** movement; moving;

travel; *in comb.* travelling; itinerant; **библиоте́ка-**~ travelling library, mobile library; **теа́тр-**~ strolling players. **передвижно́й** movable, mobile; travelling, itinerant.

переде́л, -а re-partition; re-division, redistribution; re-allotment.

переде́лать, -аю *pf.*, **переде́лывать, -аю** *impf.* alter; change; refashion, recast; do. **переде́лка, -и** alteration; adaptation; **отда́ть в переде́лку** have altered; **попа́сть в переде́лку** get into a pretty mess.

передёргивать(ся, -аю(сь *impf. of* **передёрнуть(ся**

передержа́ть, -жу́, -жишь *pf.*, **переде́рживать, -аю** *impf.* keep too long; overdo; overcook; overexpose. **переде́ржка, -и** overexposure.

передёрнуть, -ну *pf.* (*impf.* **передёргивать**) pull aside, pull across; cheat; distort, misrepresent; ~ **фа́кты** juggle with facts; ~**ся** flinch, wince.

пере́дний front, fore; anterior; first, leading; ~ **план** foreground. **пере́дник, -а** apron; pinafore. **пере́дняя** *sb.* ante-room; (entrance) hall, lobby. **пе́редо** *see* **пе́ред.** **передови́к, -а́** outstanding worker. **передови́ца, -ы** leading article, leader; editorial. **передов|о́й** forward; advanced; foremost; ~**ы́е взгля́ды** advanced views; ~**о́й отря́д** advanced detachment; vanguard; ~**а́я (статья́)** leading article, leader; editorial.

передозиро́вка, -и overdose.

передохну́ть, -ну́, -нёшь *pf.* pause for breath, take a breather.

передра́знивать, -аю *impf.*, **передразни́ть, -ню́, -нишь** *pf.* take off, mimic.

передря́га, -и scrape, tight corner; unpleasantness.

переду́мать, -аю *pf.*, **переду́мывать, -аю** *impf.* change one's mind, think better of it; do a lot of thinking.

переды́шка, -и respite, breathing-space.

перее́зд, -а crossing; removal. **переезжа́ть, -а́ю** *impf.*, **перее́хать, -е́ду** *pf.* cross; run over, knock down; move, remove.

пережа́ренный overdone; burnt. **пережа́ривать, -аю** *impf.*, **пережа́рить, -рю** *pf.* overdo, overcook.

пережда́ть, -жду́, -ждёшь; -а́л, -а́, -о *pf.* (*impf.* **пережида́ть**) wait; wait through, wait for the end of.

пережёвывать, -аю *impf.* masticate, chew; repeat over and over again.

пережива́ние, -я experience. **пережива́ть, -а́ю** *impf. of* **пережи́ть**

пережида́ть, -а́ю *impf. of* **пережда́ть**

пережито́е *sb.* the past. **пережи́ток, -тка** survival; vestige. **пережи́ть, -иву́, -ивёшь; пе́режил, -а́, -о** *pf.* (*impf.* **пережива́ть**) live through; experience; go through; endure; suffer; outlive, outlast, survive.

перезаряди́ть, -яжу́, -я́дишь *pf.*, **перезаряжа́ть, -а́ю** *impf.* recharge, reload. **перезаря́дка, -и** recharging, reloading.

перезво́н, -а ringing, chime.

пере|зимова́ть, -му́ю *pf.*

перезрева́ть, -а́ю *impf.*, **перезре́ть, -е́ю** *pf.* become overripe; be past one's prime. **перезре́лый** overripe; past one's first youth, past one's prime.

переизбира́ть, -а́ю *impf.*, **переизбра́ть, -беру́, -берёшь; -бра́л, -а́, -о** *pf.* re-elect. **переизбра́ние, -я** re-election.

переиздава́ть, -даю́, -даёшь *impf.*, **переизда́ть, -а́м, -а́шь, -а́ст, -адим; -а́л, -а́, -о** *pf.* republish, reprint. **переизда́ние, -я** republication; new edition, reprint.

переименова́ть, -ну́ю *pf.*, **переимено́вывать, -аю** *impf.* rename.

переиму́ *etc.*: *see* **переня́ть**

перейти́, -йду́, -йдёшь; перешёл, -шла́ *pf.* (*impf.* **переходи́ть**) cross; get across, get over, go over; pass; turn (**в**+*a.* to, into); ~ **в наступле́ние** go over to the offensive; ~ **грани́цу** cross the frontier; ~ **из рук в ру́ки** change hands; ~ **на другу́ю рабо́ту** change one's job; ~ **че́рез мост** cross a bridge.

перека́рмливать, -аю *impf. of* **перекорми́ть**

переквалифика́ция, -и training for a new profession; retraining. **переквалифици́роваться, -руюсь** *impf. & pf.* change one's profession; retrain.

перекидно́й; ~ **мо́стик** footbridge, gangway; ~ **календа́рь** loose-leaf calendar. **переки́дывать, -аю** *impf.*, **переки́нуть, -ну** *pf.* throw over; ~**ся** leap; spread; go over, defect; ~**ся слова́ми** exchange a few remarks.

перекиса́ть, -а́ет *impf.*, **переки́снуть, -нет** *pf.* turn sour, go sour. **пе́рекись, -и** peroxide.

перекла́дина, -ы cross-beam, cross-piece, transom; joist; horizontal bar.

перекла́дывать, -аю *impf. of* **переложи́ть**

перeклика́ться, -а́юсь *impf.*, **перекли́кнуться, -нусь** *pf.* call to one another. **перекли́чка, -и** roll-call, call-over; hook-up.

переключа́тель, -я *m.* switch. **переключа́ть, -а́ю** *impf.*, **переключи́ть, -чу́** *pf.* switch, switch over; ~**ся** switch (over).

перекова́ть, -кую́, -куёшь *pf.*, **переко́вывать, -аю** *impf.* re-shoe; re-forge; hammer out, beat out.

переколоти́ть, -лочу́, -ло́тишь *pf.* break, smash.

перекорми́ть, -млю́, -мишь *pf.* (*impf.* **перека́рмливать**) overfeed, surfeit; feed.

перекоси́ть, -ошу́, -о́сишь *pf.* warp; distort; ~**ся** warp, be warped; become distorted.

перекочева́ть, -чу́ю *pf.*, **перекочёвывать, -аю** *impf.* migrate, move on.

переко́шенный distorted, twisted.

перекра́ивать, -аю *impf. of* **перекрои́ть**

перекра́сить, -а́шу *pf.*, **перекра́шивать, -аю** *impf.* (re-)colour, (re-)paint; (re-)dye; ~**ся** change colour; turn one's coat.

пере|крести́ть, -ещу́, -е́стишь *pf.*, **перекре́щивать, -аю** *impf.* cross; **~ся** cross, intersect; cross o.s. **перекрёстн|ый** cross; **~ый допро́с** cross-examination; **~ый ого́нь** cross-fire; **~ая ссы́лка** cross-reference. **перекрёсток, -тка** cross-roads, crossing.

перекри́кивать, -аю *impf.*, **перекрича́ть, -чу́** *pf.* out-shout, outroar; shout down.

перекрои́ть, -ою́ *pf.* (*impf.* **перекра́ивать**) cut out again; rehash; reshape.

перекрыва́ть, -а́ю *impf.*, **перекры́ть, -ро́ю** *pf.* re-cover; exceed; **~ реко́рд** break a record.

перекую́ *etc.*: *see* **перекова́ть**

перекупа́ть, -а́ю *impf.*, **перекупи́ть, -плю́, -пишь** *pf.* buy; buy up; buy secondhand. **переку́пщик, -а** second-hand dealer.

перекуси́ть, -ушу́, -у́сишь *pf.*, **переку́сывать, -аю** *impf.* bite through; have a bite, have a snack.

перелага́ть, -а́ю *impf. of* **переложи́ть**

перела́мывать, -аю *impf. of* **переломи́ть**

перелеза́ть, -а́ю *impf.* **переле́зть, -зу; -е́з** *pf.* climb over, get over.

перелёт, -а migration; flight. **перелета́ть, -а́ю** *impf.*, **перелете́ть, -лечу́** *pf.* fly over, fly across; overshoot the mark. **перелётн|ый** migratory; **~ая пти́ца** bird of passage.

перелива́ние, -я decanting; transfusion; **~ кро́ви** blood transfusion. **перелива́ть, -а́ю** *impf. of* **перели́ть. перелива́ться, -а́ется** *impf. of* **перели́ться** play; modulate. **перели́вчатый** iridescent; shot; modulating.

перелиста́ть, -а́ю *pf.*, **перели́стывать, -аю** *impf.* turn over, leaf through; look through, glance at.

перели́ть, -лью́, -льёшь; -и́л, -а́, -о *pf.* (*impf.* **перелива́ть**) pour; decant; let overflow; transfuse. **перели́ться, -льётся; -ли́лся, -лила́сь, -ли́ло́сь** *pf.* (*impf.* **перелива́ться**) flow; overflow, run over.

пере|лицева́ть, -цу́ю *pf.*, **перелицо́вывать, -аю** *impf.* turn; have turned.

переложе́ние, -я arrangement. **переложи́ть, -жу́, -жишь** *pf.* (*impf.* **перекла́дывать, перелага́ть**) put somewhere else; shift, move; transfer; interlay; re-set, re-lay; put in too much; put, set, arrange; transpose; **~ в стихи́** put into verse; **~ на му́зыку** set to music.

перело́м, -а break, breaking; fracture; turning-point, crisis; sudden change; **на ~е**+*g.* on the eve of. **перелома́ть, -а́ю** *pf.* break; **~ся** break, be broken. **переломи́ть, -млю́, -мишь** *pf.* (*impf.* **перела́мывать**) break in two; break; fracture; master; **~ себя́** master o.s., restrain one's feelings. **перело́мный; ~ моме́нт** critical moment, crucial moment.

перелью́ *etc.*: *see* **перели́ть. перема́лывать, -аю** *impf. of* **перемоло́ть**

перема́нивать, -аю *impf.*, **перемани́ть, -ню́, -нишь** *pf.* win over; entice.

перемежа́ться, -а́ется *impf.* alternate; **перемежа́ющаяся лихора́дка** intermittent fever.

перемелю́ *etc.*: *see* **перемоло́ть**

переме́на, -ы change, alteration; change (of clothes); interval, break. **перемени́ть, -ню́, -нишь** *pf.*, **переменя́ть, -я́ю** *impf.* change; **~ся** change. **переме́нный** variable, changeable; **~ ток** alternating current. **переме́нчивый** changeable.

перемести́ть, -мещу́ *pf.* (*impf.* **перемеща́ть**) move; transfer; **~ся** move.

перемеша́ть, -а́ю *pf.*, **переме́шивать, -аю** *impf.* mix, intermingle; mix up; confuse; **~ся** get mixed; get mixed up.

перемеща́ть(ся, -а́ю(сь *impf. of* **перемести́ть(ся. перемеще́ние, -я** transference, shift; displacement; dislocation; travel. **перемещённ|ый** displaced; **~ые ли́ца** displaced persons.

переми́гиваться, -аюсь *impf.*, **перемигну́ться, -ну́сь, -нёшься** *pf.* wink at each other; +**с**+*i.* wink at.

переми́рие, -я armistice, truce.

перемога́ть, -а́ю *impf.* (try to) overcome; **~ся** struggle (*against illness, tears, etc.*).

перемоло́ть, -мелю́, -ме́лешь *pf.* (*impf.* **перема́лывать**) grind, mill; pulverize.

перемыва́ть, -а́ю *impf.*, **перемы́ть, -мо́ю** *pf.* wash (up) again.

перенапряга́ть, -а́ю *impf.*, **перенапря́чь, -ягу́, -яжёшь: -я́г, -ла́** *pf.* overstrain; **~ся** overstrain o.s.

перенаселе́ние, -я overpopulation. **перенаселённый; -лён, -а́** overpopulated; overcrowded. **перенасели́ть, -лю́** *pf.*, **перенаселя́ть, -я́ю** *impf.* overpopulate; overcrowd.

перенести́, -су́, -сёшь; -нёс, -ла́ *pf.* (*impf.* **переноси́ть**) carry, move, take; transport; transfer; carry over; take over; put off, postpone; endure, bear, stand; **~сь** be carried; be borne; be carried away.

перенима́ть, -а́ю *impf. of* **переня́ть**

перено́с, -а transfer; transportation; division of words; **знак ~а** hyphen. **переноси́мый** bearable, endurable. **переноси́ть(ся, -ошу́(сь, -о́сишь(ся** *impf. of* **перенести́(сь**

перено́сица, -ы bridge (*of the nose*).

перено́ска, -и carrying over; transporting; carriage. **перено́сный** portable; figurative, metaphorical.

пере|ночева́ть, -чу́ю *pf.* **переношу́** *etc.*: *see* **переноси́ть**

переня́ть, -ейму́, -еймёшь; пе́реня́л, -а́, -о *pf.* (*impf.* **перенима́ть**) imitate, copy; adopt.

переобору́довать, -дую *impf.* & *pf.* re-equip.

переодева́лка, -и changing-room.

переосвиде́тельствовать, -твую *impf.* & *pf.* re-examine.

переоце́нивать, -аю *impf.*, **переоцени́ть, -ню́, -нишь** *pf.* overestimate, overrate; revalue, reappraise. **переоце́нка, -и** overestimation; revaluation, reappraisal.

перепа́чкать, -аю *pf.* dirty, make dirty; **~ся** get dirty.

пе́репел, -а; *pl.* **-а́, перепёлка, -и** quail.

перепеча́тать, -аю *pf.*, **перепеча́тывать, -аю** *impf.* reprint; type (out). **перепеча́тка, -и** reprinting; reprint.

перепи́ливать, -аю *impf.*, **перепили́ть, -лю́, -лишь** *pf.* saw in two.

переписа́ть, -ишу́, -и́шешь *pf.*, **перепи́сывать, -аю** *impf.* copy; type; re-write; list, make a list of. **перепи́ска, -и** copying; typing; correspondence; letters; **быть в перепи́ске с**+*i.* be in correspondence with. **перепи́счик, -а, -чица, -ы** copyist; typist. **перепи́сываться, -аюсь** *impf.* correspond. **пе́репись, -и** census; inventory.

перепла́вить, -влю *pf.*, **переплавля́ть, -я́ю** *impf.* smelt.

перепла́та, -ы overpayment; surplus. **переплати́ть, -ачу́, -а́тишь** *pf.*, **перепла́чивать, -аю** *impf.* overpay, pay too much.

переплести́, -лету́, -летёшь; -лёл, -а́ *pf.*, **переплета́ть, -а́ю** *impf.* bind; interlace, interknit; re-plait; **~ся** interlace, interweave; get mixed up. **переплёт, -а** binding; cover; transom; caning; mess, scrape. **переплётная** *sb.* bindery; bookbinder's. **переплётчик, -а** bookbinder.

переплыва́ть, -а́ю *impf.*, **переплы́ть, -ыву́, -ывёшь; -ы́л, -а́, -о** *pf.* swim (across); sail across, row across, cross.

переподгота́вливать, -аю *impf.*, **переподгото́вить, -влю** *pf.* retrain; give further training. **переподгото́вка, -и** further training; retraining; **ку́рсы по переподгото́вке** refresher courses.

переполза́ть, -а́ю *impf.*, **переползти́, -зу́, -зёшь; -о́лз, -ла́** *pf.* crawl across; creep across.

переполне́ние, -я overfilling; overcrowding. **перепо́лненный** overcrowded; overfull. **перепо́лнить, -ню** *pf.*, **переполня́ть, -я́ю** *impf.* overfill; overcrowd; **~ся** be overflowing; be overcrowded.

переполо́х, -а alarm; commotion, rumpus. **переполоши́ть, -шу́** *pf.* alarm; arouse, alert; **~ся** take alarm, become alarmed.

перепо́нка, -и membrane; web. **перепо́нчатый** membranous; webbed; web-footed.

перепра́вить, -влю *pf.*, **переправля́ть, -я́ю** *impf.* convey, transport; take across; forward; correct; **~ся** cross, get across.

перепродава́ть, -даю́, -даёшь *impf.*, **перепрода́ть, -а́м, -а́шь, -а́ст, -ади́м; -про́дал, -а́, -о** *pf.* re-sell. **перепрода́жа, -и** re-sale.

перепроизво́дство, -а overproduction.

перепры́гивать, -аю *impf.*, **перепры́гнуть, -ну** *pf.* jump, jump over.

перепу́г, -а (-у) fright. **перепуга́ть, -а́ю** *pf.* frighten, give a fright, give a turn; **~ся** get a fright.

пере|пу́тать, -аю *pf.*, **перепу́тывать, -аю** *impf.* entangle; confuse, mix up, muddle up.

перепу́тье, -я cross-roads.

перераба́тывать, -аю *impf.*, **перерабо́тать, -аю** *pf.* work up, make; convert; treat; remake; recast, re-shape; process; work overtime; overwork; **~ся** overwork.

перераспределе́ние, -я redistribution. **перераспредели́ть, -лю́** *pf.*, **перераспределя́ть, -я́ю** *impf.* redistribute.

перераста́ние, -я outgrowing; escalation; growing (into), development (into). **перераста́ть, -а́ю** *impf.*, **перерасти́, -ту́, -тёшь; -ро́с, -ла́** *pf.* outgrow, overtop; outstrip; be too old (for); **+в**+*a.* grow into, develop into, turn into.

перерасхо́д, -а over-expenditure; overdraft. **перерасхо́довать, -дую** *impf.* & *pf.* overspend, expend too much of; overdraw.

перерасчёт, -а recalculation, recomputation.

перерва́ть, -ву́, -вёшь; -а́л, -а́, -о *pf.* (*impf.* **перерыва́ть**) break, tear asunder; **~ся** break, come apart.

перерегистра́ция, -и re-registration. **перерегистри́ровать, -рую** *impf.* & *pf.* re-register.

перере́зать, -е́жу *pf.*, **перереза́ть, -а́ю** *impf.*, **перере́зывать, -аю** *impf.* cut; cut off; cut across; break; kill, slaughter.

перереша́ть, -а́ю *impf.*, **перереши́ть, -шу́** *pf.* re-solve; decide differently; change one's mind, reconsider one's decision.

перероди́ть, -ожу́ *pf.*, **перерожда́ть, -а́ю** *impf.* regenerate; **~ся** be reborn; be regenerated; degenerate. **перерожде́ние, -я** regeneration; degeneration.

переро́с *etc.*: *see* **перерасти́. переро́ю** *etc.*: *see* **переры́ть**

перепруба́ть, -а́ю *impf.*, **перерруби́ть, -блю́, -бишь** *pf.* chop in two; cut up, chop up.

переры́в, -а interruption; interval, break, intermission; **с ~ами** off and on.

перерыва́ть[1](ся, -а́ю(сь *impf.* *of* **перерва́ть(ся**

перерыва́ть[2], -а́ю *impf.*, **переры́ть, -ро́ю** *pf.* dig up; rummage through, search thoroughly.

пересади́ть, -ажу́, -а́дишь *pf.*, **переса́живать, -аю** *impf.* transplant; graft; seat somewhere else; make change, help change; **~ че́рез**+*a.* help across. **переса́дка, -и** transplantation; grafting; change, changing.

переса́живаться, -аюсь *impf.* *of* **пересе́сть. переса́ливать, -аю** *impf.* *of* **пересоли́ть. пересека́ть(ся, -а́ю(сь** *impf.* *of* **пересе́чь(ся**

переселе́нец, -нца settler; migrant, emigrant; immigrant. **переселе́ние, -я** migration, emigration; immigration, resettlement; move, removal. **пересели́ть, -лю́** *pf.*, **переселя́ть, -я́ю** *impf.* move; transplant; resettle; **~ся** move; migrate.

пересе́сть, -ся́ду *pf.* (*impf.* **переса́живаться**) change one's seat; change (*trains etc.*).

пересече́ние, -я crossing, intersection. **пересе́чь, -секу́, -сечёшь; -сёк, -ла́** *pf.* (*impf.*

пересекать) cross; traverse; intersect; cut, cut up; **~ся** cross, intersect.

пересиливать, -аю *impf.*, **пересилить, -лю** *pf.* overpower; overcome, master.

пересказ, -а (re)telling; exposition. **пересказать, -ажу, -ажешь** *pf.*, **пересказывать, -аю** *impf.* tell, retell; expound; retail, relate.

перескакивать, -аю *impf.*, **перескочить, -чу, -чишь** *pf.* jump (over), vault (over); skip (over).

переслать, -ешлю, -шлёшь *pf.* (*impf.* **пересылать**) send; remit; send on, forward.

пересматривать, -аю *impf.*, **пересмотреть, -трю, -тришь** *pf.* revise; reconsider; review. **пересмотр, -а** revision; reconsideration; review; re-trial.

пересолить, -олю, -олишь *pf.* (*impf.* **пересаливать**) put too much salt in, over-salt; exaggerate, overdo it.

пересохнуть, -нет; -ох *pf.* (*impf.* **пересыхать**) dry up, become parched; dry out.

переспать, -плю; -ал, -а, -о *pf.* oversleep; spend the night; **~ с**+*i.* sleep with.

переспелый overripe.

переспорить, -рю *pf.* out-argue, defeat in argument.

переспрашивать, -аю *impf.*, **переспросить, -ошу, -осишь** *pf.* ask again; ask to repeat.

пересориться, -рюсь *pf.* quarrel, fall out.

переставать, -таю, -таёшь *impf.* *of* **перестать**

переставить, -влю *pf.*, **переставлять, -яю** *impf.* move, shift; re-arrange; transpose; **~ часы вперёд (назад)** put the clock forward (back).

перестараться, -аюсь *pf.* overdo it, try too hard.

перестать, -ану *pf.* (*impf.* **переставать**) stop, cease.

перестрадать, -аю *pf.* have suffered, have gone through.

перестраивать(ся, -аю(сь *impf.* *of* **перестроить(ся**

перестрелка, -и exchange of fire; firing; skirmish. **перестрелять, -яю** *pf.* shoot (down).

перестроить, -ою *pf.* (*impf.* **перестраивать**) rebuild, reconstruct; re-design, refashion, reshape; reorganize; retune; **~ся** reform; reorganize o.s.; switch over, retune (**на**+*a.* to). **перестройка, -и** rebuilding, reconstruction; reorganization; retuning; (*pol.*) perestroika.

переступать, -аю *impf.*, **переступить, -плю, -пишь** *pf.* step over; cross; overstep; **~ с ноги на ногу** shuffle one's feet.

пересуды, -ов *pl.* gossip.

пересчитать, -аю *pf.*, **пересчитывать, -аю** *impf.* (*pf.* **перечесть**) re-count; count; **+на**+*a.* convert to, express in terms of.

пересылать, -аю *impf.* *of* **переслать. пересылка, -и** sending, forwarding; **~ бесплатно** post free; carriage paid; **стоимость пересылки** postage. **пересыльный** transit.

пересыхать, -ает *impf.* *of* **пересохнуть**

пересяду *etc.*: *see* **пересесть. перетапливать, -аю** *impf.* *of* **перетопить**

перетаскивать, -аю *impf.*, **перетащить, -щу, -щишь** *pf.* drag (over, through); move, remove.

перетереть, -тру, -трёшь; -тёр *pf.*, **перетирать, -аю** *impf.* wear out, wear down; grind; wipe, dry; **~ся** wear out, wear through.

перетопить, -плю, -пишь *pf.* (*impf.* **перетапливать**) melt.

перетру *etc.*: *see* **перетереть**

перетягивание, -я; ~ каната tug-of-war. **перетягивать, -аю** *impf.*, **перетянуть, -ну, -нешь** *pf.* pull, draw; attract, win over; outbalance, outweigh; **~ на свою сторону** win over.

переулок, -лка narrow street; cross-street; lane, passage.

переустройство, -а reconstruction, reorganization.

переутомить, -млю *pf.*, **переутомлять, -яю** *impf.* overtire, overstrain; overwork; **~ся** overtire o.s., overstrain o.s.; overwork; be run down. **переутомление, -я** overstrain; overwork.

переформировать, -рую *pf.*, **переформировывать, -аю** *impf.* re-form.

перехватить, -ачу, -атишь *pf.*, **перехватывать, -аю** *impf.* intercept, catch; snatch a bite (of); borrow; go too far, overdo it. **перехватчик, -а** interceptor.

перехитрить, -рю *pf.* outwit.

переход, -а passage, transition; crossing; day's march; going over, conversion; **подземный ~** underpass, subway. **переходить, -ожу, -одишь** *impf.* *of* **перейти. переходный** transitional; transitive; transient. **переходящий** transient, transitory; intermittent; brought forward, carried over; **~ кубок** challenge cup.

перец, -рца pepper.

перечёл *etc.*: *see* **перечесть**

перечень, -чня *m.* list, enumeration.

перечёркивать, -аю *impf.*, **перечеркнуть, -ну, -нёшь** *pf.* cross out, cancel.

перечесть, -чту, -чтёшь; -чёл, -чла *pf.*: *see* **пересчитать, перечитать**

перечисление, -я enumeration; list; transfer, transferring. **перечислить, -лю** *pf.*, **перечислять, -яю** *impf.* enumerate, list; transfer.

перечитать, -аю *pf.*, **перечитывать, -аю** *impf.* (*pf.* **перечесть**) re-read.

перечить, -чу *impf.* contradict; cross, go against.

перечница, -ы pepper-pot. **перечн|ый** pepper; **~ая мята** peppermint.

перечту *etc.*: *see* **перечесть. перечу** *etc.*: *see* **перечить**

перешагивать, -аю *impf.*, **перешагнуть, -ну,**

-нёшь *pf.* step over; ~ **порóг** cross the threshold.
перешéек, -éйка isthmus, neck.
перешёл *etc.*: *see* **перейтú**
перешёптываться, -аюсь *impf.* whisper (together), exchange whispers.
перешивáть, -áю *impf.*, **перешúть, -шью́, -шьёшь** *pf.* alter; have altered. **перешúвка, -и** altering, alteration.
перешлю́ *etc.*: *see* **переслáть**
перещеголя́ть, -я́ю *pf.* outdo, surpass.
переэкзаменовáть, -нýю *pf.*, **переэкзаменóвывать, -аю** re-examine; ~**ся** take an examination again.
перúла, -úл *pl.* rail, railing(s); handrail; banisters.
перúна, -ы feather-bed.
перúод, -а period. **периóдика, -и** periodicals, journals. **периодúческ|ий** periodic; periodical; recurring, recurrent; ~**ая дробь** recurring decimal.
пéристо-кучевóй cirro-cumulus. **пéрист|ый** feathery; plumose; pinnate; ~**ые облакá** fleecy clouds; cirrus.
периферúя, -и periphery; the provinces; outlying districts.
перл, -а pearl. **перламýтр, -а** mother-of-pearl, nacre. **перламýтров|ый;** ~**ая пýговица** pearl button. **перлóв|ый;** ~**ая крупá** pearl barley.
перманéнт, -а permanent wave, perm. **перманéнтный** permanent.
пернáтый feathered. **пернáтые** *sb.*, *pl.* birds. **перó, -á**; *pl.* **пéрья, -ьев** feather; pen; fin; blade, paddle. **перочúнный нож, нóжик** penknife.
перрóн, -а platform.
перс, -а Persian. **персúдский** Persian.
пéрсик, -а peach.
персия́нин, -а; *pl.* **-я́не, -я́н, персия́нка, -и** Persian.
персóна, -ы person; **сóбственной персóной** in person. **персонáж, -а** character; personage. **персонáл, -а** personnel, staff. **персонáльный** personal; individual; ~ **состáв** staff, personnel.
перспектúва, -ы perspective; vista; prospect; outlook. **перспектúвный** perspective; prospective, forward-looking; long-term; promising.
перст, -á finger. **пéрстень, -тня** *m.* ring; signet-ring.
перфокáрта, -ы punched card.
пéрхоть, -и dandruff, scurf.
перцóвый pepper.
перчáтка, -и glove; gauntlet.
перчúнка, -и peppercorn. **пéрчить, -чу** *impf.* (*pf.* **на**~, **по**~) pepper.
першúть, -úт *impf.*, *impers.*; **у меня́ першúт в гóрле** I have a tickle in my throat.
пёс, пса dog.
пéсенник, -а song-book; (choral) singer; song-writer. **пéсенный** song; of songs.
песéц, -сцá (polar) fox.
пёсий dog; dog's, dogs'; **пéсья звездá** dog-star, Sirius.
песнь, -и; *g.pl.* **-ей** song; canto, book; **П**~ **Пéсней** Song of Songs. **пéсня, -и**; *g.pl.* **-сен** song; air.
песóк, -скá (-ý) sand; *pl.* sands, stretches of sand. **песóчница, -ы** sand-box; sand-pit. **песóчн|ый** sand; sandy; short; ~**ое печéнье**, ~**ое тéсто** shortbread; ~**ые часы́** sand-glass, hourglass.
пест, -á pestle. **пéстик, -а** pistil; pestle.
пестротá, -ы́ variegation, diversity of colours; mixed character. **пёстрый** motley, variegated, many-coloured, particoloured; colourful.
песчáник, -а sandstone. **песчáный** sand, sandy. **песчúнка, -и** grain of sand.
петáрда, -ы petard; squib, cracker.
петлúца, -ы buttonhole; tab. **петля́, -и**; *g.pl.* **-тель** loop; noose; button-hole; stitch; hinge.
петрýшка[1]**, -и** parsley.
петрýшка[2]**, -и** *m.* Punch; *f.* Punch-and-Judy show; foolishness, absurdity.
петýх, -á cock; **встать с** ~**áми** be up with the lark; ~**-боéц** fighting-cock. **петýший, петушúный** cock, cock's. **петушóк, -шкá** cockerel.
петь, пою́, поёшь *impf.* (*pf.* **про**~, **с**~) sing; chant, intone; crow; ~ **вполгóлоса** hum.
пехóта, -ы infantry, foot. **пехотúнец, -нца** infantryman. **пехóтный** infantry.
печáлить, -лю *impf.* (*pf.* **о**~) grieve, sadden; ~**ся** grieve, be sad. **печáль, -и** grief, sorrow. **печáльный** sad, mournful, sorrowful; sorry, bad.
печáтание, -я printing. **печáтать, -аю** *impf.* (*pf.* **на**~, **от**~) print; type; ~**ся** write, be published; be at the printer's. **печáтка, -и** signet, seal, stamp. **печáтн|ый** printing; printer's; printed; ~**ые бýквы** block letters, block capitals; ~**ая крáска** printer's ink; ~**ый лист** quire, sheet; ~**ый станóк** printing-press. **печáть, -и** seal, stamp; print; printing; type; press.
печéние, -я baking.
печёнка, -и liver.
печёный baked.
пéчень, -и liver.
печéнье, -я pastry; biscuit; cake. **пéчка, -и** stove. **печнóй** stove; oven; furnace; kiln. **печь, -и**, *loc.* **-ú**; *g.pl.* **-éй** stove; oven; furnace, kiln; ~ **сверхвысóкой частоты́** microwave oven. **печь, пекý, -чёшь; пёк, -лá** *impf.* (*pf.* **ис**~) bake; scorch, parch; ~**ся** bake; broil.
пешехóд, -а pedestrian. **пешехóдн|ый** pedestrian; foot-; ~**ая дорóжка**, ~**ая тропá** footpath; ~**ый мост** foot-bridge. **пéшечный** pawn, pawn's. **пéший** pedestrian; unmounted, foot. **пéшка, -и** pawn. **пешкóм** *adv.* on foot.

пещéра, -ы cave, cavern; grotto. **пещéристый** cavernous. **пещéрник, -а** caver, pot-holer. **пещéрный** cave; ~ **человéк** caveman, cave-dweller.

ПЗУ *abbr.* (*of* **постоя́нное запоминáющее устрóйство**) (*comput.*) ROM, (*read-only memory*).

пианúно *nt.indecl.* (*upright*) piano.

пивнáя *sb.* pub; alehouse. **пивн|óй** beer; **~ы́е дрóжжи** brewer's yeast. **пи́во, -а** beer, ale. **пивовáр, -а** brewer.

пиджáк, -á jacket, coat. **пиджáчн|ый; ~ый костю́м, ~ая пáра** (lounge-)suit.

пижáма, -ы pyjamas.

пик, -а peak; **часы́ пик** rush-hour.

пи́ка, -и pike, lance.

пикáнтный piquant; spicy; savoury.

пикáп, -а pick-up (*van*).

пикé *nt.indecl.* dive.

пикéт, -а picket; piquet. **пикéтчик, -а** picket.

пи́ки, пик *pl.* spades.

пики́рование, -я dive, diving. **пики́ровать, -рую** *impf.* & *pf.* (*pf. also* **с~**) dive.

пики́роваться, -руюсь *impf.* exchange caustic remarks, cross swords. **пикирóвка, -и** altercation, slanging match.

пикирóвщик, -а dive-bomber. **пики́рующий** diving; ~ **бомбардирóвщик** dive-bomber.

пи́кнуть, -ну *pf.* squeak, let out a squeak; make a sound.

пи́ковый of spades; awkward, unfavourable.

пилá, -ы́; *pl.* **-ы** saw; nagger. **пилёный** sawed, sawn; ~ **сáхар** lump sugar. **пили́ть, -лю́, -лишь** *impf.* saw; nag (at). **пи́лка, -и** sawing; fret-saw; nail-file. **пилообрáзный** serrated, notched.

пилóтка, -и forage-cap.

пилоти́ровать, -рую *impf.* pilot. **пилоти́руемый** manned.

пилю́ля, -и pill.

пинáть, -áю *impf.* (*pf.* **пнуть**) kick.

пингви́н, -а penguin.

пинóк, -нкá kick.

пинцéт, -а pincers, tweezers.

пиóн, -а peony.

пионéр, -а pioneer. **пионéрский** pioneer.

пир, -а, *loc.* **-ý**; *pl.* **-ы́** feast, banquet.

пирами́да, -ы pyramid.

пирáт, -а pirate; **воздýшный** ~ air pirate, sky-jacker.

Пиренéи, -ев *pl.* the Pyrenees.

пировáть, -рýю *impf.* feast; celebrate.

пирóг, -á pie; tart. **пирóжное** *sb.* pastries; cake, pastry. **пирожóк, -жкá** patty, pastry, pie.

пирýшка, -и party, celebration. **пи́ршество, -а** feast, banquet; celebration.

писáка, -и *c.g.* scribbler, quill-driver, pen-pusher. **пи́сан|ый** written, manuscript; **~ая красáвица** as pretty as a picture. **пи́сарь, -я**; *pl.* **-я́** *m.* clerk. **писáтель, -я** *m.*, **писáтельница, -ы** writer, author. **писáть, пишý, пи́шешь** *impf.* (*pf.* **на~**) write; paint; ~ **мáслом** paint in oils; **~ся** be written, be spelt. **писéц, -сцá** clerk; scribe.

писк, -а squeak, cheep, chirp, peep. **пискли́вый, пискля́вый** squeaky. **пи́скнуть, -ну** *pf. of* **пищáть**

пистолéт, -а pistol; gun; **~-пулемёт** sub-machine gun.

пистóн, -а (percussion-)cap; piston; hollow rivet.

писчебумáжный writing-paper; stationery; ~ **магази́н** stationer's (shop). **пи́сч|ий** writing; **~ая бумáга** writing paper. **пи́сьменно** *adv.* in writing. **пи́сьменн|ый** writing, written; **в ~ом ви́де, в ~ой фóрме** in writing; **~ый знак** letter; **~ый стол** writing-table, desk. **письмó, -á**; *pl.* **-а, -сем** letter; writing; script; hand(-writing). **письмонóсец, -сца** postman.

питáние, -я nourishment, nutrition; feeding; feed. **питáтельн|ый** nourishing, nutritious; alimentary; feed, feeding; **~ая средá** culture medium; breeding-ground. **питáть, -áю** *impf.* (*pf.* **на~**) feed; nourish; sustain; supply; **~ся** be fed, eat; *+i.* feed on, live on.

пи́терский of St. Petersburg.

питóмец, -мца foster-child, nursling; charge; pupil; alumnus. **питóмник, -а** nursery.

пить, пью, пьёшь; пил, -á, -о *impf.* (*pf.* **вы́~**) drink; have, take; **мне хóчется ~, я хочý ~** I am thirsty. **питьё, -я́** drinking; drink, beverage. **питьев|óй** drinkable; **~áя водá** drinking-water.

пи́хта, -ы (silver) fir.

пи́цца, -ы pizza. **пиццери́я, -и** pizza parlour, pizzeria.

пи́чкать, -аю *impf.* (*pf.* **на~**) stuff, cram.

пи́шущ|ий writing; **~ая маши́нка** typewriter.

пи́ща, -и food.

пищáть, -щý *impf.* (*pf.* **пи́скнуть**) squeak; cheep, peep; whine; sing.

пищеварéние, -я digestion; **расстрóйство пищеварéния** indigestion. **пищевóд, -а** oesophagus, gullet. **пищев|óй** food; **~ы́е продýкты** foodstuffs; foods; eatables. **пищекомбинáт, -а** catering combine.

пия́вка, -и leech.

пл. *abbr.* (*of* **плóщадь**) Sq., Square.

плáвание, -я swimming; sailing; navigation; voyage; **сýдно дáльнего плáвания** ocean-going ship. **плáвательный** swimming, bathing; ~ **бассéйн** swimming-bath, pool. **плáвать, -аю** *impf.* swim; float; sail. **плавбáза, -ы** factory ship.

плави́льник, -а crucible. **плави́льный** melting, smelting; fusion. **плави́льня, -и** foundry. **плави́льщик, -а** founder, smelter. **плáвить, -влю** *impf.* (*pf.* **рас~**) melt, smelt; fuse; **~ся** melt; fuse. **плáвка, -и** fusing; fusion.

плáвки, -вок *pl.* bathing trunks.

плáвк|ий fusible; fuse; **~ая встáвка, ~ий предохрани́тель, ~ая прóбка** fuse. **плавлéние, -я** melting, fusion. **плáвленый; ~**

сыр processed cheese.
плавни́к, -а́ fin; flipper. **пла́вный** smooth, flowing; liquid. **плаву́ч|ий** floating; buoyant; **~ая льди́на** ice-floe; **~ий мая́к** lightship, floating light; **~ий рыбозаво́д** factory ship.
плагиа́т, -а plagiarism. **плагиа́тор, -а** plagiarist.
плака́т, -а poster, bill; placard. **плакати́ст, -а** poster artist.
пла́кать, -а́чу *impf.* cry, weep; cry for, weep for; mourn; **~ навзры́д** sob; **~ся** complain, lament; +**на**+*a.* complain of; lament, bewail, bemoan.
плакирова́ть, -ру́ю *impf.* & *pf.* plate. **плакиро́вка, -и** plating.
пла́кса, -ы cry-baby. **плакси́вый** whining; piteous, pathetic. **плаку́чий** weeping.
пла́менность, -и ardour. **пла́менный** flaming, fiery; ardent, burning. **пла́мя, -мени** *nt.* flame; fire, blaze.
план, -а plan; scheme; plane.
планёр, -а glider. **планери́зм, -а** gliding. **планери́ст, -а** glider-pilot. **планёрный** gliding; **~ спорт** gliding.
плане́та, -ы planet. **плане́тный** planetary.
плани́рование[1], -я planning.
плани́рование[2], -я gliding; glide.
плани́ровать[1], -рую *impf.* (*pf.* **за~**) plan.
плани́ровать[2], -рую *impf.* (*pf.* **с~**) glide, glide down.
пла́нка, -и lath, slat.
пла́новый planned, systematic; planning. **планоме́рный** systematic, planned, balanced, regular.
планта́тор, -а planter. **планта́ция, -и** plantation.
планше́т, -а plane-table; map-case.
пласт, -а́ layer; sheet; course; stratum, bed. **пласти́на, -ы** plate. **пласти́нка, -и** plate; (*gramophone*) record, disc.
пласти́ческий plastic. **пласти́чность, -и** plasticity. **пласти́чный** plastic; supple, pliant; rhythmical; fluent, flowing. **пластма́сса, -ы** plastic. **пластма́ссовый** plastic.
пла́та, -ы pay; salary; payment, charge; fee; fare. **платёж, -а́** payment. **платёжеспосо́бный** solvent. **платёжный** payment; pay. **плате́льщик, -а** payer.
пла́тина, -ы platinum. **пла́тиновый** platinum.
плати́ть, -ачу́, -а́тишь *impf.* (*pf.* **за~, у~**) pay; +*i.* pay back, return; **~ся** (*pf.* **по~ся**) **за**+*a.* pay for. **пла́тн|ый** paid; requiring payment, chargeable; paying; **~ая доро́га** toll road.
плато́к, -тка́ shawl; head-scarf; handkerchief.
платфо́рма, -ы platform; truck.
пла́тье, -я; *g.pl.* **-ьев** clothes, clothing; dress; gown, frock. **платяно́й** clothes; **~ шкаф** wardrobe.
плафо́н, -а ceiling; lamp shade, ceiling light; bowl.
плац, -а, *loc.* **-у́** parade-ground. **плацда́рм, -а** bridgehead, beach-head; base; springboard.
плацка́рта, -ы reserved-seat ticket.
плач, -а weeping, crying; wailing; keening; lament. **плаче́вный** mournful, sad; sorry; lamentable, deplorable. **пла́чу** *etc.*: *see* **пла́кать**
плачу́ *etc.*: *see* **плати́ть**
плашмя́ *adv.* flat, prone.
плащ, -а́ cloak; raincoat; waterproof cape.
плебисци́т, -а plebiscite.
плева́тельница, -ы spittoon. **плева́ть, плюю́, плюёшь** *impf.* (*pf.* **на~, плю́нуть**) spit; **~ в потоло́к** idle, fritter away the time; *impers.*+*d.*: **мне ~** I don't give a damn, a toss (**на**+*a.* about); **~ся** spit. **плево́к, -вка́** spit, spittle.
плеври́т, -а pleurisy.
плед, -а rug; plaid.
пле́ер, -а personal stereo, Walkman (*propr.*).
плёл *etc.*: *see* **плести́**
племенно́й tribal; pedigree. **пле́мя, -мени**; *pl.* **-мена́, -мён** *nt.*, tribe; breed; stock. **племя́нник, -а** nephew. **племя́нница, -ы** niece.
плен, -а, *loc.* **-у́** captivity.
плена́рный plenary.
плени́тельный captivating, fascinating, charming. **плени́ть, -ню́** *pf.* (*impf.* **пленя́ть**) take prisoner, take captive; captivate, fascinate, charm; **~ся** be captivated, be fascinated.
плёнка, -и film; pellicle.
пле́нник, -а prisoner, captive. **пле́нный** captive.
плёночный film; filmy.
пле́нум, -а plenum, plenary session.
пленя́ть(ся, -я́ю(сь *impf. of* **плени́ть(ся**
пле́сенный mouldy, musty. **пле́сень, -и** mould.
плеск, -а splash, plash. lapping. **плеска́тельный бассе́йн** paddling pool. **плеска́ть, -ещу́, -е́щешь** *impf.* (*pf.* **плесну́ть**) splash, plash; lap; **~ся** splash; lap.
пле́сневеть, -еет *impf.* (*pf.* **за~**) go mouldy, grow musty.
плесну́ть, -ну́, -нёшь *pf. of* **плеска́ть**
плести́, -ету́, -етёшь; плёл, -а́ *impf.* (*pf.* **с~**) plait, braid; weave; tat; spin; net; **~ вздор, ~ чепуху́** talk rubbish; **~сь** drag o.s. along; trudge; **~сь в хвосте́** lag behind. **плете́ние, -я** plaiting, braiding; wickerwork. **плетёнка, -и** (wicker) mat, basket; hurdle. **плетён|ый** woven; wattled; wicker. **плете́нь, -тня́** *m.* hurdle; wattle fencing. **плётка, -и, плеть, -и**; *g.pl.* **-е́й** lash.
пле́чико, -а; *pl.* **-и, -ов** shoulder-strap; *pl.* coat-hanger; padded shoulders. **плечи́стый** broad-shouldered. **плечо́, -а́**; *pl.* **-и, -а́м** shoulder; arm.
плеши́веть, -ею *impf.* (*pf.* **о~**) grow bald. **плеши́вый** bald. **плеши́на, -ы, плешь, -и** bald patch; bare patch.
плещу́ *etc.*: *see* **плеска́ть**
пли́нтус, -а plinth; skirting-board.

плис, -а velveteen. **пли́совый** velveteen.

плиссиро́ванный pleated. **плиссирова́ть, -ру́ю** *impf.* pleat.

плита́, -ы́; *pl.* **-ы** plate, slab; flag-(stone); stove, cooker; **моги́льная ~** gravestone, tombstone. **пли́тка, -и** tile; (thin) slab; stove, cooker; **~ шокола́да** bar, block, of chocolate. **пли́точный** tile, of tiles; **~ пол** tiled floor.

плове́ц, -вца́, пловчи́ха, -и swimmer; **~ на доске́** surfer. **плову́чий** floating; buoyant.

плод, -а́ fruit; **приноси́ть ~ы́** bear fruit. **плоди́ть, -ожу́** *impf.* (*pf.* **рас~**) produce, procreate; engender; **~ся** multiply; propagate. **пло́дный** fertile; fertilized.

плодо... *in comb.* fruit-. **плодови́тый** fruitful, prolific; fertile. **~во́дство, -а** fruit-growing. **~но́сный** fruit-bearing, fruitful. **~овощно́й** fruit and vegetable. **~ро́дный** fertile. **~сме́нн|ый; ~сме́нная систе́ма** rotation of crops. **~тво́рный** fruitful. **~я́дный** frugivorous.

пло́мба, -ы stamp, seal; stopping; filling. **пломбирова́ть, -ру́ю** *impf.* (*pf.* **за~, о~**) seal; stop, fill.

пло́ский; -сок, -ска́, -о flat; plane; trivial, tame.

плоско... *in comb.* flat. **плоского́рье, -я** plateau; tableland. **~гру́дый** flat-chested. **~гу́бцы, -ев** *pl.* pliers. **~до́нный** flat-bottomed. **~сто́пие, -я** flat feet.

пло́скость, -и; *g.pl.* **-е́й** flatness; plane; platitude, triviality.

плот, -а́ raft.

плоти́на, -ы dam; weir; dike, dyke.

пло́тник, -а carpenter, joiner.

пло́тно *adv.* close(ly), tight(ly). **пло́тность, -и** thickness; compactness; solidity, strength; density. **пло́тный; -тен, -тна́, -о** thick; compact; dense; solid, strong; thickset, solidly built; tightly-filled; square, hearty.

плотоя́дный carnivorous; lustful. **плоть, -и** flesh.

пло́хо *adv.* badly; ill; bad; **~ ко́нчить** come to a bad end; **чу́вствовать себя́ ~** feel unwell, feel bad; *sb.* bad mark. **плохова́тый** rather bad, not too good. **плохо́й** bad; poor.

площа́дка, -и area, (sports) ground, playground; site; landing; platform; **киносъёмочная ~** (*film*) set. **пло́щадь, -и**; *g.pl.* **-е́й** area; space; square.

пло́ще *comp. of* **пло́ский**

плуг, -а; *pl.* **-и́** plough.

плут, -а́ cheat, swindler, knave; rogue. **плутова́тый** cunning. **плутова́ть, -ту́ю** *impf.* (*pf.* **с~**) cheat, swindle. **плутовско́й** knavish; roguish, mischievous; picaresque.

плыть, -ыву́, -ывёшь; плыл, -а́, -о *impf.* swim; float; drift; sail; **~ сто́я** tread water.

плю́нуть, -ну *pf. of* **плева́ть**

плюс, -а plus; advantage.

плюш, -а plush. **плю́шевый** plush; plush-covered.

плющ, -а́ ivy.

плюю́ *etc.*: *see* **плева́ть**

пляж, -а beach.

плясა́ть, -яшу́, -я́шешь *impf.* (*pf.* **с~**) dance. **пля́ска, -и** dance; dancing. **плясов|о́й** dancing; **~а́я** *sb.* dance tune, dancing song. **плясу́н, -а́, плясу́нья, -и**; *g.pl.* **-ий** dancer.

пневма́тик, -а pneumatic tyre. **пневмати́ческий** pneumatic.

пнуть, пну, пнёшь *pf. of* **пина́ть**

пня *etc.*: *see* **пень**

по *prep.* **I.** *+d.* on; along; round, about; by; over; according to; in accordance with; for; in; at; by (reason of); on account of; from; **жить по сре́дствам** live within one's means; **идти́ по следа́м**+*g.* follow in the track(s) of; **идти́ по траве́** walk on the grass; **лу́чший по ка́честву** better in quality; **переда́ть по ра́дио** broadcast; **по а́дресу**+*g.* to the address of; **по во́здуху** by air; **по де́лу** on business; **по и́мени** by name; **по любви́** for love; **по ма́тери** on the mother's side; **по оши́бке** by mistake; **по положе́нию** by one's position; ex officio; **по понеде́льникам** on Mondays; **по по́чте** by post; **по пра́ву** by right, by rights; **по происхожде́нию** by descent, by origin; **по профе́ссии** by profession; **по ра́дио** over the radio; **по рассе́янности** from absent mindedness; **по утра́м** in the mornings; **това́рищ по шко́ле** school fellow; **тоска́ по до́му, по ро́дине** homesickness; **чемпио́н по ша́хматам** chess champion. **II.** *+d. or a. of cardinal number, forms distributive number*; **по́ два, по́ двое** in twos, two by two; **по пять рубле́й шту́ка** at five roubles each; **по рублю́ шту́ка** one rouble each; **по ча́су в день** an hour a day. **III.** *+a.* to, up to; for, to get; **идти́ по грибы́** go to get mushrooms; **по пе́рвое сентября́** up to (and including) the first of September; **по по́яс** up to the waist; **по ту сто́рону** on that side. **IV.** *+p.* on, (immediately) after; for; **носи́ть тра́ур по** be in mourning for; **по нём** to his liking; **по прибы́тии** on arrival.

по- *pref. in comb. with d. case of adjs., or with advs. ending in* **-и**, *indicates manner of action, conduct, etc., use of a named language, or accordance with the opinion or wish of*; **говори́ть по-ру́сски** speak Russian; **жить по-ста́рому** live in the old style; **по-мо́ему** in my opinion.

по...[1] *vbl. pref. forms the perfective aspect*; *indicates action of short duration or incomplete or indefinite character, and action repeated at intervals or of indeterminate duration.*

по...[2] *pref.* **I.** *in comb. with adjs. and nn., indicates situation along or near something.* **пово́лжский** situated on the Volga. **пово́лжье, -я** the Volga region. **помо́ры, -ов** *pl.* native Russian inhabitants of White-sea coasts. **помо́рье, -я** seaboard, coastal region. **II.** *in comb. with comp. of adjs., indicates a* *smaller degree of comparison*, *slightly more* (*or less*) ...; **помéньше** a little less; **помолóже** rather younger.

по|багровéть, -éю *pf.*

побáиваться, -аюсь *impf.* be rather afraid.

побéг[1], -а flight; escape.

побéг[2], -а sprout, shoot; sucker; set; graft.

побегýшки; быть на побегýшках у+*g.* run errands for; be at the beck and call of.

побéда, -ы victory. **победúтель, -я** *m.* victor, conqueror; winner. **победúть, -úшь** *pf.* (*impf.* **побеждáть**) conquer, vanquish; defeat; master, overcome. **побéдный, победонóсный** victorious, triumphant.

побеждáть, -áю *impf. of* **победúть**

по|белéть, -éю *pf.* **по|белúть, -лю́, -éлишь** *pf.*

поберéжный coastal. **поберéжье, -я** seaboard, (sea-)coast, littoral.

по|беспокóить(ся, -óю(сь *pf.*

побирáться, -áюсь *impf.* beg; live by begging.

по|бúть(ся, -бью́(сь, -бьёшь(ся *pf.*

по|благодарúть, -рю́ *pf.*

поблáжка, -и indulgence.

по|побледнéть, -éю *pf.* **по|блёкнуть, -ну; -блёк** *pf.*

поблúзости *adv.* near at hand, hereabouts.

по|божúться, -жýсь, -жúшься *pf.*

побóи, -ев *pl.* beating, blows. **побóище, -а** slaughter, carnage; bloody battle.

побóрник, -а champion, upholder, advocate. **поборóть, -рю́, -решь** *pf.* overcome; fight down; beat.

побóчн|ый secondary, accessory; collateral; **~ый продýкт** by-product; **~ая рабóта** sideline; **~ый сын** natural son.

по|бранúться, -ню́сь *pf.*

по|братáться, -áюсь *pf.* **по-брáтски** *adv.* like a brother; fraternally. **побратúмы, -ов** *pl.* twin cities.

по|брéзгать, -аю *pf.* **по|брúть(ся, -брéю(сь** *pf.*

побудúтельный stimulating. **побудúть, -ужý** *pf.*, **побуждáть, -áю** *impf.* induce, impel, prompt, spur. **побуждéние, -я** motive; inducement; incentive.

побывáть, -áю *pf.* have been, have visited; look in, visit. **побы́вка, -и** leave, furlough; **приéхать на побы́вку** come on leave. **побы́ть, -бýду, -дешь; пóбыл, -á, -о** *pf.* stay (for a short time).

побью́(сь *etc.*: *see* **побúть(ся**

повáдить, -áжу *pf.*, **повáживать, -аю** *impf.* accustom; train; **~ся** get into the habit (of). **повáдка, -и** habit.

по|валúть(ся, -лю́(сь, -лишь(ся *pf.*

повáльно *adv.* without exception. **повáльный** general, mass; epidemic.

пóвар, -а; *pl.* **-á** cook, chef. **повáренный** culinary; cookery, cooking.

по-вáшему *adv.* in your opinion; as you wish.

поведéние, -я conduct, behaviour.

поведý *etc.*: *see* **повестú. по|везтú, -зý, -зёшь; -вёз, -лá** *pf.* **повёл** *etc.*: *see* **повестú**

повелевáть, -áю *impf.*+*i.* command, rule; +*d.* enjoin. **повелéние, -я** command, injunction. **повелúтельный** imperious, peremptory; authoritative; imperative.

по|венчáть(ся, -áю(сь *pf.*

повергáть, -áю *impf.*, **повéргнуть, -ну; -вéрг** *pf.* throw down; lay low; plunge.

повéренная *sb.* confidante. **повéренный** *sb.* attorney; confidant; **~ в делáх** chargé d'affaires. **повéрить, -рю** *pf.* (*impf.* **поверя́ть**) believe; check, verify; confide, entrust. **повéрка, -и** check-up, check; verification; proof; roll-call; **~ врéмени** time-signal.

повернýть, -нý, -нёшь *pf.*, **повёртывать, -аю** *impf.* (*impf. also* **поворáчивать**) turn; change; **~ся** turn; **~ся спинóй к**+*d.* turn one's back on.

повéрх *prep.*+*g.* over, above. **повéрхностн|ый** surface, superficial; shallow; perfunctory; **~ое унавóживание** top dressing. **повéрхность, -и** surface.

повéрье, -я; *g.pl.* **-ий** popular belief, superstition. **поверя́ть, -я́ю** *impf. of* **повéрить**

по|веселéть, -éю *pf.* **повéсить(ся, -вéшу(сь** *pf. of* **вéшать(ся**

повествовáние, -я narrative, narration. **повествовáтельный** narrative. **повествовáть, -твýю** *impf.* +**о**+*p.* narrate, recount, relate, tell about.

по|вестú, -едý, -едёшь; -вёл, -á *pf.* (*impf.* **поводúть**) +*i.* move; **~ бровя́ми** raise one's eyebrows.

повéстка, -и notice, notification; summons; writ; signal; last post; **~ (дня)** agenda.

пóвесть, -и; *g.pl.* **-éй** story, tale.

повéтрие, -я epidemic; infection.

повéшу *etc.*: *see* **повéсить. по|вздóрить, -рю** *pf.*

повивáльн|ый obstetric; **~ая бáбка** midwife.

по|видáть(ся, -áю(сь *pf.* **по|винúться, -ню́сь** *pf.*

повúнность, -и duty, obligation; **вóинская ~** conscription. **повúнный** guilty; obliged, bound.

повиновáться, -нýюсь *impf.* & *pf.* obey. **повиновéние, -я** obedience.

повисáть, -áю *impf.*, **по|вúснуть, -ну; -вúс** *pf.* hang on; hang down, droop; hang; **~ в вóздухе** hang in mid-air.

по|влажнéть, -éет *pf.*

повлéчь, -екý, -ечёшь; -ёк, -лá *pf.* drag; pull behind one; **~ (за собóй)** entail, bring in its train.

по|влия́ть, -я́ю *pf.*

пóвод[1], -а occasion, cause, ground; **по ~у**+*g.* apropos of, as regards, concerning.

пóвод[2], -а, *loc.* **-ý;** *pl.* **-óдья, -ьев** rein; **быть на ~ý у**+*g.* be under the thumb of. **поводúть, -ожý, -óдишь** *impf. of* **повестú. поводóк, -дкá** rein; lead.

пово́зка, -и cart; vehicle, conveyance; (*unsprung*) carriage.

пово́лжский, пово́лжье *see* **по...**[2] **I.**

повора́чивать(ся, -аю(сь *impf. of* **поверну́ть(ся, повороти́ть(ся; повора́чивайся, -айтесь!** get a move on! look sharp! look lively!

по|ворожи́ть, -жу́ *pf.*

поворо́т, -а turn, turning; bend; turning-point. **повороти́ть(ся, -рочу́(сь, -ро́тишь(ся** *pf.* (*impf.* **повора́чивать(ся)** turn. **поворо́тливый** nimble, agile, quick; manoeuvrable. **поворо́тный** turning; rotary, rotating; revolving; ~ **круг** turntable; ~ **мост** swing bridge; ~ **пункт** turning point.

по|вреди́ть, -ежу́ *pf.*, **поврежда́ть, -а́ю** *impf.* damage; injure, hurt; ~**ся** be damaged; be injured, be hurt. **поврежде́ние, -я** damage, injury.

повремени́ть, -ню́ *pf.* wait a little; +**с**+*i.* linger over, delay. **повреме́нный** periodic, periodical; by time.

повседне́вно *adv.* daily, every day. **повседне́вный** daily; everyday.

повсеме́стно *adv.* everywhere, in all parts. **повсеме́стный** universal, general.

повста́нец, -нца rebel, insurgent, insurrectionist. **повста́нческий** rebel; insurgent.

повсю́ду *adv.* everywhere.

повто́р, -а replay. **повторе́ние, -я** repetition; reiteration. **повтори́тельный** repeated; revision. **повтори́ть, -рю́** *pf.*, **повторя́ть, -я́ю** *impf.* repeat; ~**ся** repeat o.s.; be repeated; recur. **повто́рный** repeated; recurring.

повы́сить, -ы́шу *pf.*, **повыша́ть, -а́ю** *impf.* raise, heighten; promote, prefer, advance; ~ **вдво́е, втро́е** double, treble; ~ **го́лос,** ~ **тон** raise one's voice; ~**ся** rise; improve; be promoted, receive advancement. **повыше́ние, -я** rise, increase; advancement. **повы́шенн|ый** heightened, increased; ~**ое настрое́ние** state of excitement; ~**ая температу́ра** high temperature.

повяза́ть, -яжу́, -я́жешь *pf.*, **повя́зывать, -аю** *impf.* tie. **повя́зка, -и** bandeau, fillet; bandage.

по|гада́ть, -а́ю *pf.*

пога́нец, -нца swine; scoundrel. **пога́нить, -ню** *impf.* (*pf.* **о**~) pollute, defile. **пога́нка, -и** toadstool. **пога́ный** foul; unclean; filthy, vile; ~ **гриб** toadstool, poisonous mushroom.

погаса́ть, -а́ю *impf.*, **по|га́снуть, -ну** *pf.* go out, be extinguished. **по|гаси́ть, -ашу́, -а́сишь** *pf.* **погаша́ть, -а́ю** *impf.* liquidate, cancel. **пога́шенный** used, cancelled, cashed.

погиба́ть, -а́ю *impf.*, **по|ги́бнуть, -ну; -ги́б** *pf.* perish; be lost. **поги́бель, -и** ruin, perdition. **поги́бельный** ruinous, fatal. **поги́бший** lost; ruined; killed; **число́ поги́бших** death-roll.

по|гла́дить, -а́жу *pf.*

поглоти́ть, -ощу́, -о́тишь *pf.*, **поглоща́ть, -а́ю** *impf.* swallow up; take up; absorb.

по|глупе́ть, -е́ю *pf.*

по|гляде́ть(ся, -яжу́(сь *pf.* **погля́дывать, -аю** *impf.* glance; look from time to time; +**за**+*i.* keep an eye on.

погна́ть, -гоню́, -го́нишь; -гна́л, -а́, -о *pf.* drive; begin to drive; ~**ся за**+*i.* run after; start in pursuit of, give chase to; strive for, strive after.

по|гну́ть(ся, -ну́(сь, -нёшь(ся *pf.* **по|гнуша́ться, -а́юсь** *pf.*

погово́рка, -и saying, proverb; byword.

пого́да, -ы weather.

погоди́ть, -ожу́ *pf.* wait a little, wait a bit; **немно́го погодя́** a little later.

поголо́вно *adv.* one and all; to a man. **поголо́вный** general, universal, across-the-board; capitation, poll. **поголо́вье, -я** head, number.

по|голубе́ть, -е́ет *pf.*

пого́н, -а; *g.pl.* **-о́н** shoulder-strap; (rifle-)sling.

пого́нщик, -а driver. **погоню́** *etc.*: *see* **погна́ть. пого́ня, -и** pursuit, chase. **погоня́ть, -я́ю** *impf.* urge on, drive.

погоре́ть, -рю́ *pf.* burn down; be burnt out; lose everything in a fire. **погоре́лец, -льца** one who has lost all his possessions in a fire.

пограни́чник, -а frontier guard. **пограни́чн|ый** frontier; boundary; ~**ая полоса́** border; ~**ая стра́жа** frontier guards.

по́греб, -а; *pl.* **-а́** cellar. **погреба́льн|ый** funeral; ~**ая колесни́ца** hearse. **погреба́ть, -а́ю** *impf. of* **погрести́. погребе́ние, -я** burial.

погрему́шка, -и rattle.

погрести́[1]**, -ебу́, -ебёшь; -рёб, -ла́** *pf.* (*impf.* **погреба́ть**) bury.

погрести́[2]**, -ебу́, -ебёшь; -рёб, -ла́** *pf.* row for a while.

погре́ть, -е́ю *pf.* warm; ~**ся** warm o.s.

по|греши́ть, -шу́ *pf.* sin; err. **погре́шность, -и** error, mistake, inaccuracy.

по|грози́ть(ся, -ожу́(сь *pf.* **по|грубе́ть, -е́ю** *pf.*

погружа́ть, -а́ю *impf.*, **по|грузи́ть, -ужу́, -у́зишь** *pf.* load; ship; dip, plunge, immerse; submerge; duck; ~**ся** sink, plunge; submerge, dive; be plunged, absorbed, buried, lost. **погруже́ние, -я** sinking, submergence; immersion; dive, diving. **погру́зка, -и** loading; shipment.

погряза́ть, -а́ю *impf.*, **по|гря́знуть, -ну; -я́з** *pf.* be bogged down, be stuck.

по|губи́ть, -блю́, -бишь *pf.* **по|гуля́ть, -я́ю** *pf.* **по|густе́ть, -е́ет** *pf.*

под, подо *prep.* **I.** +*a. or i.* under; near, close to; **быть** ~ **ружьём** be under arms; **взять по́д руку**+*a.* take the arm of; ~ **ви́дом**+*g.* under the guise of; **по́д гору** downhill; ~ **замко́м** under lock and key; ~ **землёй** underground; ~ **Москво́й** in the neighbourhood of Moscow; ~ **руко́й** (close) at hand, to hand. **II.** +*i.* occupied by, used as; (meant, implied) by; in, with; **говя́дина** ~ **хре́ном**

beef with horse-radish; **пóле ~ картóфелем** potato-field. **III.** *+a.* towards; on the eve of; to (the accompaniment of); in imitation of; on; for, to serve as; **емý ~ пятьдесят (лет)** he is getting on for fifty; **~ аплодисмéнты** to applause; **~ вéчер** towards evening; **поддéлка ~ жéмчуг** fake pearls; **~ диктóвку** from dictation; **~ звýки мýзыки** to the sound of music; **~ конéц** towards the end; **~ Нóвый год** on New Year's Eve; **шýба ~ кóтик** imitation sealskin coat.

под..., подо..., подъ... *pref. in comb.* **I.** *with vv. indicates action from beneath or affecting lower part of something, motion upwards or towards a point, slight or insufficient action or effect, supplementary action, underhand action.* **II.** *with nn. and adjs.*: under-, sub-.

подавáльщик, -а waiter; supplier. **подавáльщица, -ы** waitress. **подавáть(ся, -даю(сь, -даёшь(ся** *impf. of* **подáть(ся**

подави́ть, -влю́, -вишь *pf.*, **подавля́ть, -я́ю** *impf.* suppress, put down; repress; depress; crush, overwhelm. **по|дави́ться, -влю́сь, -вишься** *pf.* **подавлéние, -я** suppression; repression. **подáвленность, -и** depression; blues. **подáвленный** suppressed; depressed, dispirited. **подавля́ющ|ий** overwhelming; overpowering; **~ее большинствó** overwhelming majority.

подáвно *adv.* much less, all the more.

подáгра, -ы gout. **подагри́ческий** gouty.

подáльше *adv.* a little further.

по|дари́ть, -рю́, -ришь *pf.* **подáрок, -рка** present; gift.

подáтель, -я *m.* bearer; **~ прошéния** petitioner. **подáтливый** pliant, pliable; complaisant. **пóдать, -и**; *g.pl.* **-éй** tax, duty, assessment. **подáть, -áм, -áшь, -áст, -ади́м; пóдал, -á, -о** *pf.* (*impf.* **подавáть**) serve; give; put, move, turn; put forward, present, hand in; display; **обéд пóдан** dinner is served; **~ в отстáвку** send in one's resignation; **~ в суд на**+*a.* bring an action against; **~ гóлос** vote; **~ жáлобу** lodge a complaint; **~ заявлéние** hand in an application; **~ мяч** serve; **~ рýку** hold out one's hand; **~ телегрáмму** send a telegram; **~ся** move; give way; yield; cave in, collapse; **+на**+*a.* make for, set out for; **~ся в стóрону** move aside; **~ся назáд** draw back. **подáча, -и** giving, presenting; service, serve; feed, supply; introduction; **~ голосóв** voting. **подáчка, -и** (charitable) gift; pittance. **подаю** *etc.*: *see* **подавáть. подая́ние, -я** charity, alms; dole.

подбегáть, -áю *impf.*, **подбежáть, -егý** *pf.* run up, come running up.

подбивáть, -áю *impf. of* **подби́ть. подби́вка, -и** lining; re-soling.

подберý *etc.*: *see* **подобрáться. подбирáть(ся, -áю(сь** *impf. of* **подобрáть(ся**

подби́тый bruised; lined; padded; **~ глаз** black eye. **подби́ть, -добью́, -добьёшь** *pf.* (*impf.* **подбивáть**) line; pad, wad; re-sole; injure, bruise; put out of action, knock out, shoot down; incite, instigate.

подбодри́ть, -рю́ *pf.*, **подбодря́ть, -я́ю** *impf.*, cheer up, encourage; **~ся** cheer up, take heart.

подбóйка, -и lining; re-soling.

подбóр, -а selection, assortment; **в ~** run on; **(как) на ~** choice, well-matched.

подбородóк, -дка chin.

подбочéниваться, -аюсь *impf.*, **подбочéниться, -нюсь** *pf.* place one's arms akimbo. **подбочéнившись** *adv.* with arms akimbo, with hands on hips.

подбрáсывать, -аю *impf.*, **подбрóсить, -рóшу** *pf.* throw up, toss up; throw in, throw on; abandon, leave surreptitiously.

подвáл, -а cellar; basement; (article appearing at) foot of page. **подвáльный** basement, cellar.

подведý *etc.*: *see* **подвести́**

подвезти́, -зý, -зёшь; -вёз, -лá *pf.* (*impf.* **подвози́ть**) bring, take; give a lift.

подвенéчн|ый wedding; **~ое плáтье** wedding-dress.

подвергáть, -áю *impf.*, **подвéргнуть, -ну; -вéрг** *pf.* subject; expose; **~ опáсности** expose to danger; **~ сомнéнию** call in question. **подвéрженный** subject, liable; susceptible.

подвéсить, -éшу *pf.* (*impf.* **подвéшивать**) hang up, suspend; **~ся** hang, be suspended. **подвеснóй** hanging, suspended, pendant; overhead; suspension; **~ дви́гатель, motóр** outboard motor, engine.

подвести́, -едý, -едёшь; -вёл, -á *pf.* (*impf.* **подводи́ть**) lead up, bring up; place (under); bring under, subsume; put together; let down; **~ итóги** reckon up; sum up; **~ фундáмент** underpin.

подвéшивать(ся, -аю(сь *impf. of* **подвéсить(ся**

пóдвиг, -а exploit, feat; heroic deed.

подвигáть(ся, -áю(сь *impf. of* **подви́нуть(ся**

подвижнóй mobile; movable; travelling; lively; agile; **~ состáв** rolling-stock. **подви́жный** mobile; lively; agile.

подвизáться, -áюсь *impf.* (**в** *or* **на**+*p.*) work (in), make a career (in).

подви́нуть, -ну *pf.* (*impf.* **подвигáть**) move; push; advance, push forward; **~ся** move; advance, progress.

подвлáстный+*d.* subject to; under the jurisdiction of.

подвóда, -ы cart. **подводи́ть, -ожý, -óдишь** *impf. of* **подвести́**

подвóдник, -а submariner. **подвóдн|ый** submarine; underwater; **~ая скалá** reef.

подвóз, -а transport; supply. **подвози́ть, -ожý, -óзишь** *impf. of* **подвезти́**

подворóтня, -и; *g.pl.* **-тен** gateway.

подвóх, -а trick.

подвы́пивший tipsy, tiddly.

подвяза́ть, -яжу́, -я́жешь *pf.*, **подвя́зывать, -аю** *impf.* tie up; keep up. **подвя́зка, -и** garter; suspender.

подгиба́ть(ся, -а́ю(сь *impf. of* **подогну́ть(ся**

подгляде́ть, -яжу́ *pf.*, **подгля́дывать, -аю** *impf.* peep; spy, watch furtively.

подгова́ривать, -аю *impf.*, **подговори́ть, -рю́** *pf.* put up, incite, instigate.

подголо́сок, -ска second part, supporting voice; yes-man.

подгоню́ *etc.*: *see* **подогна́ть. подгоня́ть, -я́ю** *impf. of* **подогна́ть**

подгора́ть, -а́ет *impf.*, **подгоре́ть, -ри́т** *pf.* get a bit burnt. **подгоре́лый** slightly burnt.

подготови́тельный preparatory. **подгото́вить, -влю** *pf.*, **подготовля́ть, -я́ю** *impf.* prepare; ~ **по́чву** pave the way; ~**ся** prepare, get ready. **подгото́вка, -и** preparation, training; grounding, schooling. **подгото́вленность, -и** preparedness.

поддава́ться, -даю́сь, -даёшься *impf. of* **подда́ться**

подда́кивать, -аю *impf.* agree, assent.

по́дданный *sb.* subject; national. **по́дданство, -а** citizenship, nationality. **подда́ться, -а́мся, -а́шься, -а́стся, -ади́мся; -а́лся, -ла́сь** *pf.* (*impf.* **поддава́ться**) yield, give way, give in; **не ~ описа́нию** beggar description.

подде́лать, -аю *pf.*, **подде́лывать, -аю** *impf.* counterfeit, falsify, fake; forge; fabricate. **подде́лка, -и** falsification; forgery; counterfeit; imitation, fake; ~ **под же́мчуг** artificial pearls. **подде́льный** false, counterfeit; forged; sham, spurious.

поддержа́ние, -я maintenance, support. **поддержа́ть, -жу́, -жишь** *pf.* **подде́рживать, -аю** *impf.* support; back up, second; keep up, maintain; bear; ~ **поря́док** maintain order. **подде́ржка, -и** support; encouragement, backing; seconding; prop, stay; **при подде́ржке**+*g.* with the support of.

поддра́знивать, -аю *impf.*, **поддразни́ть, -ню́, -нишь** *pf.* tease (slightly).

поддува́ло, -а ash-pit.

по|де́йствовать, -твую *pf.*

поде́лать, -аю *pf.* do; **ничего́ не поде́лаешь** it can't be helped, there's nothing to be done about it.

по|дели́ть(ся, -лю́(сь, -лишь(ся *pf.*

поде́лка, -и *pl.* small (hand-made) articles.

подело́м *adv.*; ~ **ему́**, *etc.* it serves him, *etc.*, right.

подённо *adv.*, **подённый** by the day; **подённая опла́та** payment by the day. **подёнщик, -а** day-labourer, workman hired by the day. **подёнщица, -ы** daily, char.

подёргивание, -я twitch, twitching; jerk. **подёргиваться, -аюсь** *impf.* twitch.

поде́ржанный second-hand.

подёрнуть, -нет *pf.* cover, coat; ~**ся** be covered.

подеру́ *etc.*: *see* **подра́ть. по|дешеве́ть, -е́ет** *pf.*

поджа́ривать(ся, -аю(сь *impf.*, **поджа́рить(ся, -рю(сь** *pf.* fry, roast, grill; brown, toast. **поджа́ристый** brown, browned; crisp.

поджа́рый lean, wiry, sinewy.

поджа́ть, -дожму́, -дожмёшь *pf.* (*impf.* **поджима́ть**) draw in, draw under; ~ **гу́бы** purse one's lips; ~ **хвост** have one's tail between one's legs.

подже́чь, -дожгу́, -ожжёшь; -жёг, -дожгла́ *pf.*, **поджига́ть, -а́ю** *impf.* set fire to, set on fire; burn. **поджига́тель, -я** *m.* incendiary; instigator; ~ **войны́** warmonger. **поджига́тельский** inflammatory.

поджида́ть, -а́ю *impf.* (+*g.*) wait (for); lie in wait (for).

поджима́ть, -а́ю *impf. of* **поджа́ть**

поджо́г, -а arson.

подзаголо́вок, -вка subtitle, sub-heading.

подзадо́ривать, -аю *impf.*, **подзадо́рить, -рю** *pf.* egg on, set on.

подзащи́тный *sb.* client.

подземе́лье, -я; *g.pl.* **-лий** cave; dungeon. **подзе́мка, -и** underground, tube. **подзе́мный** underground, subterranean.

подзо́рн|ый; ~ая труба́ telescope.

подзову́ *etc.*: *see* **подозва́ть. подзыва́ть, -а́ю** *impf. of* **подозва́ть**

подиви́ть, -влю́ *pf.* astonish, amaze. **по|диви́ться, -влю́сь** *pf.*

подка́пывать(ся, -аю(сь *impf. of* **подкопа́ть(ся**

подкарау́ливать, -аю *impf.*, **подкарау́лить, -лю** *pf.* be on the watch (for), lie in wait (for); catch.

подка́рмливать, -аю *impf. of* **подкорми́ть**

подкати́ть, -ачу́, -а́тишь *pf.*, **подка́тывать, -аю** *impf.* roll up, drive up; roll.

подка́шивать(ся, -аю(сь *impf. of* **подкоси́ть(ся**

подки́дывать, -аю *impf.*, **подки́нуть, -ну** *pf.* throw up, toss up; throw in, throw on; abandon. **подки́дыш, -а** foundling.

подкла́дка, -и lining; **на шёлковой подкла́дке** silk-lined. **подкла́дочный** lining. **подкла́дывать, -аю** *impf. of* **подложи́ть**

подкле́ивать, -аю *impf.*, **подкле́ить, -е́ю** *pf.* glue, paste; glue up, paste up; stick together, mend. **подкле́йка, -и** glueing, pasting; sticking.

подко́ва, -ы (horse-)shoe. **под|кова́ть, -кую́, -ёшь** *pf.*, **подко́вывать, -аю** *impf.* shoe.

подко́жный subcutaneous, hypodermic.

подкоми́ссия, -и, подкомите́т, -а subcommittee.

подко́п, -а undermining; underground passage; intrigue, underhand plotting. **подкопа́ть, -а́ю** *pf.* (*impf.* **подка́пывать**) undermine, sap; ~**ся под**+*a.* undermine, sap; burrow under; intrigue against.

подкорми́ть, -млю́, -мишь *pf.* (*impf.* **подка́рмливать**) top-dress, give a top-dressing;

feed up. **подко́рмка, -и** top-dressing.

подкоси́ть, -ошу́, -о́сишь *pf.* (*impf.* **подка́шивать**) cut down; fell, lay low; **~ся** give way, fail one.

подкра́дываться, -аюсь *impf. of* **подкра́сться**

подкра́сить, -а́шу *pf.* (*impf.* **подкра́шивать**) touch up; tint, colour; **~ся** make up lightly.

подкра́сться, -аду́сь, -адёшься *pf.* (*imp* **подкра́дываться**) steal up, sneak up.

подкра́шивать(ся, -аю(сь *impf. of* **подкра́сить(ся. подкра́шу** *etc.*: *see* **подкра́сить**

подкрепи́ть, -плю́ *pf.*,**подкрепля́ть, -я́ю** *impf.* reinforce; support; back; confirm, corroborate; fortify, recruit the strength of; **~ся** fortify o.s. **подкрепле́ние, -я** confirmation, corroboration; sustenance; reinforcement.

по́дкуп, -а bribery. **подкупа́ть, -а́ю** *impf.*, **подкупи́ть, -плю́, -пишь** *pf.* bribe; suborn; win over.

подла́диться, -а́жусь *pf.*, **подла́живаться, -аюсь** *impf.* **+к**+*d.* adapt o.s. to, fit in with; humour; make up to.

подла́мываться, -ается *impf. of* **подломи́ться**

по́дле *prep.*+*g.* by the side of, beside.

подлежа́ть, -жу́ *impf.*+*d.* be liable to, be subject to; **не подлежи́т сомне́нию** it is beyond doubt; unquestionably. **подлежа́щее** *sb.* subject. **подлежа́щий**+*d.* liable to, subject to; **не ~ оглаше́нию** confidential, private; off the record.

подлеза́ть, -а́ю *impf.*, **подле́зть, -зу; -е́з** *pf.* crawl (under), creep (under).

подле́ц, -а́ scoundrel, villain.

подлива́ть, -а́ю *impf. of* **подли́ть. подли́вка, -и** sauce, dressing; gravy. **подливн|о́й; ~о́е колесо́** undershot wheel.

подли́за, -ы *c.g.* lickspittle, toady. **подлиза́ться, -ижу́сь, -и́жешься** *pf.*, **подли́зываться, -аюсь** *impf.* **+к**+*d.* make up to, suck up to; wheedle.

по́длинник, -а original. **по́длинно** *adv.* really; genuinely. **по́длинн|ый** genuine; authentic; original; true, real; **с ~ым ве́рно** certified true copy.

подли́ть, -долью́, -дольёшь; по́длил, -а́, -о *pf.* (*impf.* **подлива́ть**) pour; add; **~ ма́сла в ого́нь** add fuel to the flames.

подло́г, -а forgery.

подло́дка, -и submarine; sub.

подложи́ть, -жу́, -жишь *pf.* (*impf.* **подкла́дывать**) add; **+под**+*a.* lay under; line.

подло́жный false, spurious; counterfeit, forged.

подломи́ться, -о́мится *pf.* (*impf.* **подла́мываться**) break; give way under one.

по́длость, -и meanness, baseness; mean trick, low trick.

подлу́нный sublunar.

по́длый; подл, -а́, -о mean, base, ignoble.

подма́зать, -а́жу *pf.*, **подма́зывать, -аю** *impf.* grease, oil; paint; give bribes, grease palms.

подманда́тный mandated.

подмасте́рье, -я; *g.pl.* **-ьев** *m.* apprentice.

подме́н, -а, подме́на, -ы replacement. **подме́нивать, -аю** *impf.*, **подмени́ть, -ню́, -нишь** *pf.*, **подменя́ть, -я́ю** *impf.* replace.

подмести́, -ету́, -етёшь; -мёл, -а́ *pf.*, **подмета́ть**[1], **-а́ю** *impf.* sweep.

подмета́ть[2], **-а́ю** *pf.* (*impf.* **подмётывать**) baste, tack.

подме́тить, -е́чу *pf.* (*impf.* **подмеча́ть**) notice.

подмётка, -и sole.

подмётывать, -аю *impf. of* **подмета́ть**[2]

подмеча́ть, -а́ю *impf. of* **подме́тить**

подмеша́ть, -а́ю *pf.*, **подме́шивать, -аю** *impf.* mix in, stir in.

подми́гивать, -аю *impf.*, **подмигну́ть, -ну́, -нёшь** *pf.*+*d.* wink at.

подмо́га, -и help, assistance; **идти́ на подмо́гу** lend a hand.

подмока́ть, -а́ет *impf.*, **подмо́кнуть, -нет; -мо́к** *pf.* get damp, get wet.

подмора́живать, -ает *impf.*, **подморо́зить, -зит** *pf.* freeze. **подморо́женный** frost-bitten, frozen.

подмо́стки, -ов *pl.* scaffolding, staging; stage.

подмо́ченный damp; tarnished, tainted, blemished.

подмы́в, -а washing away, undermining. **подмыва́ть, -а́ю** *impf.*, **подмы́ть, -о́ю** *pf.* wash; wash away, undermine; **его́ так и подмыва́ет** he feels an urge (to), he can hardly help (doing).

подмы́шка, -и armpit. **подмы́шник, -а** dress-preserver.

поднево́льный dependent; subordinate; forced.

поднести́, -су́, -сёшь; -ёс, -ла́ *pf.* (*impf.* **подноси́ть**) present; take, bring.

поднима́ть(ся, -а́ю(сь *impf. of* **подня́ть(ся**

поднови́ть, -влю́ *pf.*, **подновля́ть, -я́ю** *impf.* renew, renovate.

подно́жие, -я foot; pedestal. **подно́жка, -и** step; running-board. **подно́жный; ~ корм** pasture.

подно́с, -а tray; salver. **подноси́ть, -ошу́, -о́сишь** *impf. of* **поднести́. подноше́ние, -я** giving; present, gift.

подня́тие, -я raising; rise; rising. **подня́ть, -ниму́, -ни́мешь; по́днял, -а́, -о** *pf.* (*impf.* **поднима́ть, подыма́ть**) raise; lift (up); hoist; pick up; rouse, stir up; open up; improve, enhance; **~ на́ смех** hold up to ridicule; **~ пе́тли** pick up stitches; **~ ору́жие** take up arms; **~ целину́** break fresh ground; open up virgin lands; **~ся** rise; go up; get up; climb, ascend; arise; break out, develop; improve; recover.

подо *see* **под. подо...** *see* **под...**

подоба́ть, -а́ет *impf.* be becoming, be fitting. **подоба́ющий** proper, fitting.

подо́бие, -я likeness; similarity. **подо́бн|ый** like, similar; **и тому́ ~ое** and the like, and so on, and such like; **ничего́ ~ого!** nothing of the sort!

подобостра́стие, -я servility. **подобостра́стный** servile.

подобра́ть, -дберу́, -дберёшь; -бра́л, -а́, -о *pf.* (*impf.* **подбира́ть**) pick up; tuck up, put up; select, pick; **~ся** steal up, approach stealthily; make o.s. tidy.

подобью́ *etc.*: *see* **подби́ть**

подогна́ть, -дгоню́, -дго́нишь; -а́л, -а́, -о *pf.* (*impf.* **подгоня́ть**) drive; drive on, urge on, hurry; adjust, fit.

подогну́ть, -ну́, -нёшь *pf.* (*impf.* **подгиба́ть**) tuck in; bend under; **~ся** bend.

подогрева́ть, -а́ю *impf.*, **подогре́ть, -е́ю** *pf.* warm up, heat up; arouse.

пододвига́ть, -а́ю *impf.*, **пододви́нуть, -ну** *pf.* move up, push up.

пододея́льник, -а quilt cover, blanket cover; top sheet.

подожгу́ *etc.*: *see* **подже́чь**

подожда́ть, -ду́, -дёшь; -а́л, -а́, -о *pf.* wait (+*g. or a.* for).

подожму́ *etc.*: *see* **поджа́ть**

подозва́ть, -дзову́, -дзовёшь; -а́л, -а́, -о *pf.* (*impf.* **подзыва́ть**) call up; beckon.

подозрева́емый suspected; suspect. **подозрева́ть, -а́ю** *impf.* suspect. **подозре́ние, -я** suspicion. **подозри́тельный** suspicious; suspect; shady, fishy.

по|дои́ть, -ою́, -о́ишь *pf.* **подо́йник, -а** milk-pail.

подойти́, -йду́, -йдёшь; -ошёл, -шла́ *pf.* (*impf.* **подходи́ть**) approach; come up, go up; +*d.* do for; suit, fit.

подоко́нник, -а window-sill.

подо́л, -а hem; lower part, lower slopes, foot.

подо́лгу *adv.* for a long time; for ages; for hours, *etc.*, together.

подолью́ *etc.*: *see* **подли́ть**

подо́нки, -ов *pl.* dregs; scum.

подоплёка, -и underlying cause, hidden motive.

подопру́ *etc.*: *see* **подпере́ть**

подо́пытный experimental; **~ кро́лик** guinea-pig.

подорва́ть, -рву́, -рвёшь; -а́л, -а́, -о *pf.* (*impf.* **подрыва́ть**) undermine, sap; damage severely; blow up; blast.

по|дорожа́ть, -а́ет *pf.*

подоро́жник, -а plantain; provisions for a journey. **подоро́жный** on the road; along the road; **~ столб** milestone.

подосла́ть, -ошлю́, -ошлёшь *pf.* (*impf.* **подсыла́ть**) send (secretly).

подоспева́ть, -а́ю *impf.* **подоспе́ть, -е́ю** *pf.* arrive, appear (at the right moment).

подостла́ть, -дстелю́, -дсте́лешь *pf.* (*impf.* **подстила́ть**) lay underneath.

подотде́л, -а section, subdivision.

подотру́ *etc.*: *see* **подтере́ть**

подотчётный accountable; on account.

по|до́хнуть, -ну *pf.* (*impf. also* **подыха́ть**) die; peg out, kick the bucket.

подохо́дный; ~ нало́г income-tax.

подо́шва, -ы sole; foot; base.

подошёл *etc.*: *see* **подойти́. подошлю́** *etc.*: *see* **подосла́ть. подошью́** *etc.*: *see* **подши́ть. подпада́ть, -а́ю** *impf. of* **подпа́сть. подпа́ивать, -аю** *impf. of* **подпои́ть**

подпа́сть, -аду́, -адёшь; -а́л *pf.* (*impf.* **подпада́ть**) **под**+*a.* fall under; **~ под влия́ние**+*g.* fall under the influence of.

подпева́ла, -ы *c.g.* yes-man.

подпере́ть, -допру́; -пёр *pf.* (*impf.* **подпира́ть**) prop up.

подпи́ливать, -аю *impf.*, **подпили́ть, -лю́, -лишь** *pf.* saw a little off; file, file down. **подпи́лок, -лка** file.

подпира́ть, -а́ю *impf. of* **подпере́ть**

подписа́вший *sb.* signatory. **подписа́ние, -я** signing, signature. **подписа́ть, -ишу́, -и́шешь** *pf.*, **подпи́сывать, -аю** *impf.* sign; write underneath, add; **~ся** sign; subscribe. **подпи́ска, -и** subscription; engagement, written undertaking; signed statement. **подписно́й** subscription; **~ лист** subscription list. **подпи́счик, -а** subscriber. **по́дпись, -и** signature; caption; inscription; **за ~ю**+*g.* signed by; **за ~ю и печа́тью** signed and sealed.

подпои́ть, -ою́, -о́ишь *pf.* (*impf.* **подпа́ивать**) make tipsy.

подполко́вник, -а lieutenant-colonel.

подпо́лье, -я cellar; underground. **подпо́льный** under-floor; underground.

подпо́ра, -ы, подпо́рка, -и prop, support; brace, strut.

подпры́гивать, -аю *impf.*, **подпры́гнуть, -ну** *pf.* leap up, jump up.

подпуска́ть, -а́ю *impf.*, **подпусти́ть, -ущу́, -у́стишь** *pf.* allow to approach; add in; get in, put in; **~ шпи́льку** sting.

подража́ние, -я imitation. **подража́ть, -а́ю** *impf.* imitate.

подразде́л, -а subsection. **подразделе́ние, -я** subdivision; sub-unit. **подраздели́ть, -лю́** *pf.*, **подразделя́ть, -я́ю** subdivide.

подразумева́ть, -а́ю *impf.* imply, mean; **~ся** be implied, be meant, be understood.

подраста́ть, -а́ю *impf.*, **подрасти́, -ту́, -тёшь; -ро́с, -ла́** *pf.* grow.

по|дра́ть(ся, -деру́(сь, -дерёшь(ся, -а́л(ся, -ла́(сь, -о́(сь *or* **-о(сь** *pf.*

подреза́ть, -е́жу *pf.*, **подреза́ть, -а́ю** *impf.* cut; clip, trim; prune, lop; +*g.* cut (off) more of.

подро́бно *adv.* minutely, in detail; at (great) length. **подро́бность, -и** detail; minuteness. **подро́бный** detailed, minute.

подровня́ть, -я́ю *pf.* level, even; trim.

подро́с *etc.*: *see* **подрасти́. подро́сток, -тка** adolescent; teenager; youth, young girl.

подро́ю *etc.*: *see* **подры́ть**

подруба́ть[1], -а́ю *impf.*, **подруби́ть, -блю́,**

-бишь *pf.* chop down; cut short(er); hew.

подрубáть[2], **-áю** *impf.*, **подрубúть, -блю́, -бишь** *pf.* hem.

подру́га, -и friend. **по-дру́жески** *adv.* in a friendly way; as a friend. **по|дружи́ться, -жу́сь** *pf.*

подру́ливать, -аю *impf.*, **подрули́ть, -лю́** *pf.* taxi up.

подру́чный at hand, to hand; improvised, makeshift; *sb.* assistant, mate.

подры́в, -а undermining; injury, blow, detriment.

подрывáть[1], **-áю** *impf. of* **подорвáть**

подрывáть[2], **-áю** *impf.*, **подры́ть, -ро́ю** undermine, sap. **подрывно́й** blasting, demolition; undermining, subversive.

подря́д *adv.* in succession; running; on end.

подря́д, -а contract. **подря́дный** (done by) contract. **подря́дчик, -а** contractor.

подсáживаться, -аюсь *impf. of* **подсéсть**

подсвéчник, -а candlestick.

подсéсть, -ся́ду; -сéл *pf.* (*impf.* **подсáживаться**) sit down, take a seat (**к**+*d.* by, near, next to).

под|сини́ть, -ню́ *pf.*

подсказáть, -ажу́, -áжешь *pf.*, **подскáзывать, -аю** *impf.* prompt; suggest. **подскáзка, -и** prompting.

подскáкивать, -аю *impf.*, **подскочи́ть, -чу́, -чишь** *pf.* jump (up), leap up, soar; run up, come running.

подслеповáтый weak-sighted.

подслу́шать, -аю *pf.*, **подслу́шивать, -аю** *impf.* overhear; eavesdrop, listen.

подсмáтривать, -аю *impf. of* **подсмотрéть**

подсмéиваться, -аюсь *impf.* **над**+*i.* laugh at, make fun of.

подсмотрéть, -рю́, -ришь *pf.* (*impf.* **подсмáтривать**) spy (on).

подснéжник, -а snowdrop.

подсо́бный subsidiary, supplementary; secondary; auxiliary; accessory.

подсо́вывать, -аю *impf. of* **подсу́нуть**

подсознáние, -я subconscious (mind). **подсознáтельный** subconscious.

подсо́лнечник, -а sunflower. **подсо́лнечн|ый** sunflower; **~ое мáсло** sunflower(-seed) oil. **подсо́лнух, -а** sunflower; sunflower seed.

подсо́хнуть, -ну *pf.* (*impf.* **подсыхáть**) get dry, dry out a little.

подспо́рье, -я help, support.

подстáвить, -влю *pf.*, **подставля́ть, -я́ю** *impf.* put (under); bring up, put up; hold up; expose, lay bare; substitute; **~ но́жку**+*d.* trip up. **подстáвка, -и** stand; support, rest, prop. **подставн|о́й** false; substitute; **~о́е лицо́** dummy, figure-head.

подстакáнник, -а glass-holder.

подстелю́ *etc.*: *see* **подостлáть**

подстерегáть, -áю *impf.*, **подстерéчь, -егу́, -ежёшь; -рёг, -лá** *pf.* be on the watch for, lie in wait for.

подстилáть, -áю *impf. of* **подостлáть. подсти́лка, -и** bedding; litter.

подстрáивать, -аю *impf. of* **подстро́ить**

подстрекáтель, -я *m.* instigator. **подстрекáтельский** inflammatory. **подстрекáтельство, -а** instigation, incitement, setting-on. **подстрекáть, -áю** *impf.*, **подстрекну́ть, -ну́, -нёшь** *pf.* instigate, incite, set on; excite.

подстрéливать, -аю *impf.*, **подстрели́ть, -лю́, -лишь** *pf.* wound; wing.

подстригáть, -áю *impf.*, **подстри́чь, -игу́, -ижёшь; -и́г** *pf.* cut; clip, trim; prune; **~ся** trim one's hair; have a hair-cut, a trim.

подстро́ить, -о́ю *pf.* (*impf.* **подстрáивать**) build on; tune (up); arrange, contrive.

подстро́чн|ый interlinear; literal, word-for-word; **~ое примечáние** footnote.

по́дступ, -а approach. **подступáть, -áю** *impf.* **подступи́ть, -плю́, -пишь** *pf.* approach, come up, come near; **~ся к**+*d.* approach.

подсуди́мый *sb.* defendant; the accused. **подсу́дн|ый**+*d.* under the jurisdiction of, within the competence of; **~ое дéло** punishable offence.

подсу́нуть, -ну *pf.* (*impf.* **подсо́вывать**) put, thrust, shove; slip, palm off.

подсчёт, -а calculation; count. **подсчитáть, -áю** *pf.*, **подсчи́тывать, -аю** count (up); calculate.

подсылáть, -áю *impf. of* **подослáть**

подсыхáть, -áю *impf. of* **подсо́хнуть**

подся́ду *etc.*: *see* **подсéсть. подтáлкивать, -аю** *impf. of* **подтолкну́ть**

подтасовáть, -су́ю *pf.*, **подтасо́вывать, -аю** *impf.* shuffle unfairly; garble, juggle with.

подтáчивать, -аю *impf. of* **подточи́ть**

подтверди́тельный confirmatory; of acknowledgement. **подтверди́ть, -ржу́** *pf.*, **подтверждáть, -áю** *impf.* confirm; corroborate, bear out; **~ получéние**+*g.* acknowledge receipt of. **подтверждéние, -я** confirmation, corroboration; acknowledgement.

подтёк, -а bruise. **подтекáть, -áет** *impf. of* **подтéчь** leak, be leaking.

подтерéть, -дотру́, -дотрёшь; подтёр *pf.* (*impf.* **подтирáть**) wipe, wipe up.

подтéчь, -ечёт; -тёк, -лá *pf.* (*impf.* **подтекáть**) **под**+*a.* flow under, run under.

подтирáть, -áю *impf. of* **подтерéть**

подтолкну́ть, -ну́, -нёшь *pf.* (*impf.* **подтáлкивать**) push, nudge; urge on.

подточи́ть, -чу́, -чишь *pf.* (*impf.* **подтáчивать**) sharpen slightly, give an edge (to); eat away, gnaw; undermine.

подтру́нивать, -аю *impf.*, **подтруни́ть, -ню́** *pf.* **над**+*i.* chaff, tease.

подтя́гивать, -аю *impf.*, **подтяну́ть, -ну́, -нешь** *pf.* tighten; pull up, haul up; bring up; move up; take in hand, chase up; **~ся** tighten one's belt, etc.; pull o.s. up; move up, move in; pull o.s. together, take o.s. in hand.

подтя́жки, -жек *pl.* braces, suspenders. **подтя́нутый** smart.

по|ду́мать, -аю *pf.* think; think a little, think for a while. **поду́мывать, -аю**+*inf. or* **о**+*p.* think of, think about.

по|ду́ть, -у́ю *pf.*

поду́чивать, -аю *impf.*, **подучи́ть, -чу́, -чишь** *pf.*+*a.* study, learn; +*a.* and *d.* instruct in; **~ся** (+*d.*) learn.

поду́шка, -и pillow; cushion.

подхали́м, -а *m.* toady, lickspittle. **подхали́мничать, -аю** *impf.* toady. **подхали́мство, -а** toadying, grovelling.

подхвати́ть, -ачу́, -а́тишь *pf.*, **подхва́тывать, -аю** *impf.* catch (up), pick up, take up; **~ пе́сню** take up, join in a song.

подхо́д, -а approach. **подходи́ть, -ожу́, -о́дишь** *impf. of* **подойти́. подходя́щий** suitable, proper, appropriate.

подцепи́ть, -плю́, -пишь *pf.*, **подцепля́ть, -я́ю** *impf.* hook on, couple on; pick up.

подча́с *adv.* sometimes, at times.

подчёркивать, -аю *impf.*, **подчеркну́ть, -ну́, -нёшь** *pf.* underline; emphasize.

подчине́ние, -я subordination; submission, subjection. **подчинённый** subordinate; tributary; *sb.* subordinate. **подчини́ть, -ню́** *pf.*, **подчиня́ть, -я́ю** subordinate, subject; place (under); **~ся**+*d.* submit to, obey.

подше́фный aided, assisted; +*d.* under the patronage of, sponsored by.

подшива́ть, -а́ю *impf. of* **подши́ть. подши́вка, -и** hemming; lining; soling; hem, facing; filing, file.

подши́пник, -а bearing.

подши́ть, -дошью́, -дошьёшь *pf.* (*impf.* **подшива́ть**) hem, line, face; sole; sew underneath; file.

подшути́ть, -учу́, -у́тишь *pf.*, **подшу́чивать, -аю** *impf.* **над**+*i.* chaff, mock; play a trick on.

подъ... *see* **под... . подъе́ду** *etc.*: *see* **подъе́хать**

подъе́зд, -а porch, entrance, doorway; approach, approaches. **подъездн|о́й** approach; **~а́я алле́я** drive; **~а́я доро́га** access road; **~о́й путь** spur (track). **подъе́здный** entrance. **подъезжа́ть, -а́ю** *impf. of* **подъе́хать**

подъём, -а lifting; raising; hoisting; ascent; climb; rise; upward slope; development; élan; enthusiasm, animation; instep; reveille; **тяжёл (лёгок) на ~** slow (quick) off the mark, (not) easily persuaded to go somewhere. **подъёмник, -а** lift, elevator, hoist; jack. **подъёмн|ый** lifting; **~ые де́ньги** removal allowance; travelling expenses; **~ кран** crane, jenny, derrick; **~ маши́на** lift; **~ мост** drawbridge; **~ые** *sb., pl.* removal allowance, travelling expenses.

подъе́хать, -е́ду *pf.* (*impf.* **подъезжа́ть**) drive up, draw up; call; get round.

подыма́ть(ся, -а́ю(сь *impf. of* **подня́ть(ся**

подыска́ть, -ыщу́, -ы́щешь *pf.*, **поды́скивать, -аю** *impf.* seek (out), (try to) find.

подыто́живать, -аю *impf.*, **подыто́жить, -жу** *pf.* sum up.

подыха́ть, -а́ю *impf. of* **подо́хнуть**

подыша́ть, -шу́, -шишь *pf.* breathe; **~ све́жим во́здухом** have, get, a breath of fresh air.

поеда́ть, -а́ю *impf. of* **пое́сть**

поеди́нок, -нка duel; single combat.

по́езд, -а; *pl.* **-а́** train; convoy, procession; **~ом** by train. **пое́здка, -и** journey; trip, excursion, outing, tour. **поездн|о́й** train; **~а́я брига́да** train crew.

пое́сть, -е́м, -е́шь, -е́ст, -еди́м; -е́л *pf.* (*impf.* **поеда́ть**) eat, eat up; have a bite to eat.

по|е́хать, -е́ду *pf.* go; set off, depart.

по|жале́ть, -е́ю *pf.*

по|жа́ловать(ся, -лую(сь *pf.* **пожа́луй** *adv.* perhaps; very likely; it may be. **пожа́луйста** *part.* please; certainly! by all means! with pleasure!; not at all, don't mention it.

пожа́р, -а fire; conflagration. **пожа́рник, -а, пожа́рный** *sb.* fireman. **пожа́рн|ый** fire; **~ая кома́нда** fire-brigade; **~ая ле́стница** fire-escape; **~ая маши́на** fire-engine.

пожа́тие, -я; ~ руки́ handshake. **пожа́ть**[1], **-жму́, -жмёшь** *pf.* (*impf.* **пожима́ть**) press, squeeze; **~ ру́ку**+*d.* shake hands with; **~ плеча́ми** shrug one's shoulders; **~ся** shrink; huddle up, hug o.s.

пожа́ть[2], **-жну́, -жнёшь** *pf.* (*impf.* **пожина́ть**) reap.

пожела́ние, -я wish, desire. **по|жела́ть, -а́ю** *pf.*

пожелте́лый yellowed; gone yellow. **по|желте́ть, -е́ю** *pf.*

по|жени́ть, -ню́, -нишь *pf.* **пожени́ться, -же́нимся** *pf.* get married.

поже́ртвование, -я donation; sacrifice. **по|же́ртвовать, -твую** *pf.*

пожива́ть, -а́ю *impf.* live; **как (вы) пожива́ете?** how are you (getting on)?; **ста́ли они́ жить-~ да добра́ нажива́ть** they lived happily ever after. **поживи́ться, -влю́сь** *pf.* (+*i.*) profit (by), live (off). **пожи́вший** experienced. **пожило́й** middle-aged; elderly.

пожима́ть(ся, -а́ю(сь *impf. of* **пожа́ть**[1]**(ся. пожина́ть, -а́ю** *impf. of* **пожа́ть**[2]

пожира́ть, -а́ю *impf. of* **пожра́ть**

пожи́тки, -ов *pl.* belongings, things; goods and chattels; **со всеми пожи́тками** bag and baggage.

пожму́ *etc.*: *see* **пожа́ть**[1]. **пожну́** *etc.*: **пожа́ть**[2]

пожра́ть, -ру́, -рёшь; -а́л, -а́, -о *pf.* (*impf.* **пожира́ть**) devour.

по́за, -ы pose; attitude, posture.

по|забо́титься, -о́чусь *pf.* **по|зави́довать, -дую** *pf.* **по|за́втракать, -аю** *pf.*

позавчера́ *adv.* the day before yesterday.

позади́ *adv. & prep.*+*g.* behind.

по|заи́мствовать, -твую *pf.* **по|зва́ть, -зову́,**

-зовёшь; -áл, -á, -о *pf.*

позволéние, -я permission, leave; **с вáшего позволéния** with your permission, by your leave; **с позволéния сказáть** if one may say so. **позволи́тельный** permissible. **позвóлить, -лю** *pf.*, **позволя́ть, -я́ю** *impf.+d. or a.* allow, permit; ~ **себé поéздку в Пáриж** be able to afford a trip to Paris; **позвóль(те)** allow me; excuse me.

по|звони́ться, -ню́(сь) *pf.*

позвонóк, -нкá vertebra. **позвонóчник, -а** spine, backbone; spinal column. **позвонóчн|ый** spinal, vertebral; vertebrate; **~ые** *sb., pl.* vertebrates.

позднéе *adv.* later. **позднéйший** latest. **пóздний** late; **пóздно** it is late. **пóздно** *adv.* late.

по|здорóваться, -аюсь *pf.* **поздрáвить, -влю** *pf.*, **поздравля́ть, -я́ю** *impf.* **с**+*i.* congratulate on; ~ **с днём рождéния** wish many happy returns. **поздрави́тельн|ый** congratulatory; **~ая кáрточка** greetings card. **позравлéние, -я** congratulation.

по|зеленéть, -éет *pf.*

珍

поземéльный land; ~ **налóг** land-tax.

пóзже *adv.* later (on.).

позициóнн|ый positional, position; static; **~ая войнá** trench warfare. **пози́ция, -и** position; stand; **заня́ть пози́цию** take one's stand.

познавáемый cognizable, knowable. **познавáтельный** cognitive. **познавáть, -наю́, -наёшь** *impf. of* **познáть. познавáться, -наю́сь, -наёшься** *impf.* become known, be recognized.

по|знакóмить(ся, -млю(сь *pf.*

познáние, -я cognition; *pl.* knowledge. **познáть, -áю** *pf.* (*impf.* **познавáть**) get to know, become acquainted with.

позолóта, -ы gilding, gilt. **по|золоти́ть, -лочу́** *pf.*

позóр, -а shame, disgrace; infamy, ignominy. **позóрить, -рю** *impf.* (*pf.* **о~**) disgrace; **~ся** disgrace o.s. **позóрный** shameful, disgraceful; infamous, ignominious.

позы́в, -а urge, call; inclination. **позывн|óй** call; **~óй сигнáл, ~ы́е** *sb., pl.* call sign.

поимённо *adv.* by name; **вызывáть** ~ call over, call the roll of. **поимённый** nominal; ~ **спи́сок** list of names.

пóиски, -ов *pl.* search; **в пóисках**+*g.* in search of, in quest of.

пои́стине *adv.* indeed, in truth.

пои́ть, пою́, пóишь *impf.* (*pf.* **на~**) give something to drink; water.

пойду́ *etc.*: *see* **пойти́**

пóйло, -а swill, mash.

поймáть, -áю *pf. of* **лови́ть. пойму́** *etc.*: *see* **поня́ть**

пойти́, -йду́, -йдёшь; пошёл, -шлá *pf. of* **идти́, ходи́ть**; go, walk; begin to walk; +*inf.* begin; +**в**+*a.* take after; **пошёл!** off you go! I'm off; **пошёл вон!** be off! get out!; **(так) не пойдёт** that won't work, that won't wash; **э́то ей не пойдёт** it won't suit her.

покá *adv.* for the present, for the time being; ~ **что** in the meanwhile. **покá** *conj.* while; ~ **не** until, till.

покáз, -а showing, demonstration. **показáние, -я** testimony, evidence; deposition; affidavit; reading. **показáтель, -я** *m.* index, exponent; showing. **показáтельный** significant; instructive, revealing; model; demonstration; exponential; ~ **суд** show-trial. **показáть, -ажу́, -áжешь** *pf.*, **покáзывать, -аю** *impf.* show; display, reveal; register, read; testify, give evidence; +**на**+*a.* point at, point to; ~ **вид** pretend; ~ **лу́чшее врéмя** clock (make) the best time; ~ **на дверь**+*d.* show the door (to). **по|казáться, -ажу́сь, -áжешься** *pf.*, **покáзываться, -аюсь** *impf.* show o.s. (itself); come in sight; appear; seem. **показнóй** for show; ostentatious.

по-какóвски *adv.* in what language?

по|калéчить(ся, -чу(сь *pf.*

покáмест *adv. & conj.* for the present; while; meanwhile.

по|карáть, -áю *pf.*

покáтость, -и slope, incline. **покáтый** sloping; slanting.

покачáть, -áю *pf.* rock, swing; ~ **головóй** shake one's head. **покáчивать, -аю** rock slightly; **~ся** rock; swing; stagger, totter. **покачну́ть, -ну́, -нёшь** shake; rock; **~ся** sway, totter, lurch.

покаяние, -я confession; penitence, repentance. **покая́нный** penitential. **по|кáяться, -áюсь** *pf.*

поквитáться, -áюсь *pf.* be quits; get even.

покидáть, -áю *impf.*, **поки́нуть, -ну** *pf.* leave; desert, abandon, forsake. **поки́нутый** deserted; abandoned.

поклáдистый complaisant, obliging; easy to get on with.

поклáжа, -и load; baggage, luggage.

поклёп, -а slander, calumny.

поклóн, -а bow; greeting; **передáть мой** ~+*d.* remember me to, give my regards to; **послáть** ~ send one's compliments, one's kind regards. **поклонéние, -я** worship. **поклони́ться, -ню́сь, -нишься** *pf. of* **клáняться. поклóнник, -а** admirer; worshipper. **поклоня́ться, -я́юсь** *impf.+d.* worship.

по|кля́сться, -яну́сь, -нёшься; -я́лся, -лáсь *pf.*

покóиться, -óюсь *impf.* rest, repose, be based; lie. **покóй, -я** rest, peace; room, chamber. **покóйник, -а** the deceased. **покóйн|ый** calm, quiet; comfortable; restful; **~ой нóчи!** good night!

по|колебáть(ся, -éблю(сь *pf.*

поколéние, -я generation.

по|колоти́ть(ся, -очу́(сь, -óтишь(ся *pf.*

покóнчить, -чу *pf.* **с**+*i.* finish; finish with, have done with; put an end to, do away with; ~ **с собóй** commit suicide; **с э́тим покóнчено** that's done with.

покоре́ние, -я subjugation, subdual; conquest. **покори́ть, -рю́** *pf.* (*impf.* **покоря́ть**) subjugate, subdue; conquer; **~ся** submit, resign o.s.

по|корми́ть(ся, -млю́(сь, -мишь(ся *pf.*

поко́рно *adv.* humbly; submissively, obediently.

по|коро́бить(ся, -блю(сь *pf.* **покоро́бленный** warped.

покоря́ть(ся, -я́ю(сь *impf. of* **покори́ть(ся**

поко́с, -а mowing, haymaking; meadow(-land); **второ́й ~** aftermath.

покоси́вшийся rickety, crazy, ramshackle; leaning. **по|коси́ть(ся, -ошу́(сь** *pf.*

покра́жа, -и theft; stolen goods.

по|кра́сить, -а́шу *pf.* **покра́ска, -и** painting, colouring.

по|красне́ть, -е́ю *pf.* **по|красова́ться, -су́юсь** *pf.* **по|крепча́ть, -а́ет** *pf.* **по|криви́ть(ся, -влю́(сь** *pf.*

покри́кивать, -аю *impf.* shout (**на**+*a.* at).

покро́в, -а cover; covering; pall; cloak, shroud; protection. **покрови́тель, -я** *m.*, **покрови́тельница, -ы** patron; sponsor. **покрови́тельственный** protective; condescending, patronizing. **покрови́тельство, -а** protection, patronage. **покрови́тельствовать, -твую** *impf.+d.* protect, patronize.

покро́й, -я cut.

покроши́ть, -шу́, -шишь *pf.* crumble; mince, chop.

покрыва́ло, -а cover; bedspread, counterpane; shawl; veil. **покрыва́ть, -а́ю** *impf.*, **по|кры́ть, -ро́ю** *pf.* cover; coat; roof; drown; shield, cover up for; hush up; discharge, pay off; **~ся** cover o.s.; get covered. **покры́тие, -я** covering; surfacing; discharge, payment. **покры́шка, -и** cover, covering; outer cover.

покупа́тель, -я *m.* buyer, purchaser; customer, client. **покупа́тельный** purchasing. **покупа́ть, -а́ю** *impf. of* **купи́ть. поку́пка, -и** buying; purchasing; purchase. **покупн|о́й** bought, purchased; purchase, purchasing; **~а́я цена́** purchase price.

по|кури́ть, -рю́, -ришь *pf.*, **поку́ривать, -аю** *impf.* smoke a little; have a smoke.

по|ку́шать, -аю *pf.*

пол[1]**, -а (-у)**, *loc.* **-у́**; *pl.* **-ы́** floor

пол[2]**, -а** sex.

пол... *in comb. with n. in g.*, *in oblique cases usu.* **полу...** half. **полве́ка** half a century. **~го́да** half a year, six months. **~доро́ги** half-way. **~дю́жины** half a dozen. **~милли́она** half a million. **~мину́ты** half a minute. **~цены́** half price. **~часа́** half an hour.

пола́, -ы́; *pl.* **-ы** skirt, flap; **из-под полы́** on the sly, under cover.

полага́ть, -а́ю *impf.* suppose, think, believe; lay, place. **полага́ться, -а́юсь** *impf. of* **положи́ться;** *impers.* **полага́ется** one is supposed to; **не полага́ется** it is not done; **так полага́ется** it is the custom, done thing; *+d.* it is due to; **нам э́то полага́ется** it is our due; we have a right to it.

пола́дить, -а́жу *pf.* come to an understanding; get on good terms.

по|ла́комить(ся, -млю(сь *pf.*

по́лдень, -дня *or* **-лу́дня** *m.* noon, midday; south. **полдне́вный** *adj.*

по́ле, -я; *pl.* **-я́** field; ground; margin; brim; **~ де́ятельности** sphere of action. **полев|о́й** field; **~ы́е цветы́** wild flowers; **~о́й шпат** feldspar.

поле́зн|ый useful; helpful; good, wholesome; effective; **~ая нагру́зка** payload.

по|ле́зть, -зу; -ле́з *pf.*

поле́мика, -и controversy, dispute; polemics. **полемизи́ровать, -рую** *impf.* argue, debate, engage in controversy. **полеми́ческий** controversial; polemical.

по|лени́ться, -ню́сь, -нишься *pf.*

поле́но, -а; *pl.* **-е́нья, -ьев** log.

поле́сье, -я woodlands, wooded region.

полёт, -а flight; flying; **вид с пти́чьего ~а** bird's eye view. **по|лете́ть, -лечу́** *pf.*

по́лзать, -аю *indet. impf.*, **ползти́, -зу́, -зёшь; полз, -ла́** *det. impf.* crawl, creep; ooze; spread; fray, ravel; slip, slide, collapse. **ползу́ч|ий** creeping; **~ие расте́ния** creepers.

поли... *in comb.* poly-.

поли́ва, -ы glaze. **полива́ть(ся, -а́ю(сь** *impf. of* **поли́ть(ся.**

поливитами́ны, -ов *pl.* multivitamins.

поли́вка, -и watering.

полиграфи́ст, -а printing trades worker. **полиграфи́ческ|ий** printing-trades; **~ая промы́шленность** printing industry. **полиграфи́я, -и** printing.

полиго́н, -а range; **уче́бный ~** training ground.

поликли́ника, -и polyclinic; outpatients' (department).

полиненасы́щенный; ~ые жиры́ polyunsaturated fats.

полиня́лый faded, discoloured. **по|линя́ть, -я́ет** *pf.*

полирова́льн|ый polishing; **~ая бума́га** sandpaper. **полирова́ть, -ру́ю** *impf.* (*pf.* **от~**) polish. **полиро́вка, -и** polishing; polish. **полиро́вочный** polishing; buffing. **полиро́вщик, -а** polisher.

по́лис, -а policy; **страхово́й ~** insurance policy.

полит... *abbr.* (*of* **полити́ческий**) *in comb.* political. **политбюро́** *nt.indecl.* Politburo (*executive organ of Central Committee of CPSU*). **~гра́мота, -ы** elementary political education. **~заключённый** *sb.* political prisoner. **~кружо́к, -жка́** political study circle. **~просве́т, -а** political education. **~рабо́тник, -а** political worker.

полите́хник, -а polytechnic student. **полите́хникум, -а** polytechnic. **политехни́ческий** polytechnic, polytechnical.

поли́тика, -и policy; politics. **полити́ческий** political.

поли́ть, -лью́, -льёшь; по́ли́л, -а́, -о *pf.* (*impf.* **полива́ть**) pour on, pour over; ~ **(водо́й)** water; ~**ся**+*i.* pour over o.s.

полихлорвини́л, -а PVC (*polyvinyl chloride*).

полице́йский police; *sb.* policeman. **поли́ция, -и** police.

поли́чн|ое *sb.*: **с** ~**ым** red-handed.

полк, -а́, *loc.* **-у́** regiment.

по́лка[1], **-и** shelf; berth.

по́лка[2], **-и** weeding.

полко́вник, -а colonel. **полково́дец, -дца** commander; general. **полково́й** regimental.

поллюта́нт, -а pollutant.

полне́ть, -е́ю *impf.* (*pf.* **по**~) put on weight, fill out.

по́лно *adv.* that's enough! that will do! stop it! ~ **ворча́ть!** stop grumbling.

полно... *in comb.* full; completely. **полновла́стный** sovereign. ~**кро́вный** full-blooded. ~**лу́ние, -я** full moon. ~**метра́жный** full-length. ~**пра́вный** enjoying full rights; competent; ~**пра́вный член** full member. ~**сбо́рный** prefabricated. ~**це́нный** of full value.

полномо́чие, -я authority, power; plenary powers; commission; proxy; *pl.* terms of reference; credentials; **дать полномо́чия**+*d.* empower, commission; **превы́сить полномо́чия** exceed one's commission. **полномо́чный** plenipotentiary.

по́лностью *adv.* fully, in full; completely, utterly. **полнота́, -ы́** fullness, completeness; plenitude; stoutness, corpulence, plumpness.

по́лночь, -л(у́)ночи midnight; north; **за** ~ after midnight.

по́лн|ый; -лон, -лна́, по́лно́ full; complete; entire, total; absolute; stout, portly; plump; **в** ~**ом соста́ве** in full force; in a body; ~**ым го́лосом** at the top of one's voice; ~**ы́м-полно́** chock-full, cram-full; ~**ый сбор** full house; ~**ое собра́ние сочине́ний** complete works; ~**ый стенографи́ческий отчёт** verbatim record.

полови́к, -а́ mat, matting; door-mat.

полови́на, -ы half; middle; **два с полови́ной** two and a half; ~ **(две́ри)** leaf; ~ **шесто́го** half past five. **полови́нка, -и** half; leaf. **полови́нчатый** halved; half-and-half; half-hearted; undecided; indeterminate.

полово́й[1] floor.

полово́й[2] sexual.

по́лог, -а curtains; cover, blanket.

поло́гий gently sloping.

положе́ние, -я position; whereabouts; posture; attitude; condition, state; situation; status, standing; circumstances; regulations, statute; thesis; tenet; clause, provisions; **быть на высоте́ положе́ния** rise to the situation; **по положе́нию** according to the regulations.

поло́женный agreed; determined. **поло́жим** let us assume; suppose; though, even if. **положи́тельный** positive; affirmative; favourable; complete, absolute; practical.

положи́ть, -жу́, -жишь *pf.* (*impf.* **класть**) put, place; lay (down); decide; agree; propose, offer; fix; ~**ся** (*impf.* **полага́ться**) rely, count; pin one's hopes.

по́лоз, -а; *pl.* **-о́зья, -ьев** runner.

по|лома́ть(ся, -а́ю(сь *pf.* **поло́мка, -и** breakage.

полоса́, -ы́, *a.* **по́лосу́**; *pl.* **по́лосы, -ло́с, -а́м** stripe, streak; strip; band; region; zone, belt; period; phase; spell, run. **полоса́тый** striped, stripy.

полоска́ние, -я rinse, rinsing; gargle, gargling. **полоска́тельница, -ы** slop-basin. **полоска́ть, -ощу́, -о́щешь** *impf.* (*pf.* **вы́**~, **от**~, **про**~) rinse; ~ **го́рло** gargle; ~**ся** paddle; flap.

по́лость[1], **-и**; *g.pl.* **-е́й** cavity.

по́лость[2], **-и**; *g.pl.* **-е́й** carriage-rug.

полоте́нце, -а; *g.pl.* **-нец** towel.

полотёр, -а floor-polisher.

поло́тнище, -а width; panel. **полотно́, -а́**; *pl.* **-а, -тен** linen; canvas. **полотня́ный** linen.

поло́ть, -лю́, -лешь *impf.* (*pf.* **вы́**~) weed.

полоши́ть, -шу́ *impf.* (*pf.* **вс**~) agitate, alarm; ~**ся** take alarm, take fright.

полощу́ *etc.*: *see* **полоска́ть**

полтерге́йст, -а poltergeist.

полти́на, -ы, полти́нник, -а fifty copecks; fifty-copeck piece.

полтора́, -лу́тора *m.* & *nt.*, **полторы́, -лу́тора** *f.* one and a half. **полтора́ста, полу́т-** a hundred and fifty.

полу...[1] *see* **пол...**[1]

полу...[2] *in comb.* half-, semi-, demi-. **полуботи́нок, -нка**; *g.pl.* **-нок** shoe. ~**вое́нный** paramilitary. ~**го́дие, -я** six months, half a year. ~**годи́чный** six months', lasting six months. ~**годова́лый** six-month-old. ~**годово́й** half-yearly, six-monthly. ~**гра́мотный** semi-literate. ~**гра́ция, -и** pantie-girdle. ~**гу́сеничный** half-track. ~**защи́та, -ы** half backs; **центр** ~**защи́ты** centre half. ~**защи́тник, -а** half-back. ~**комбина́ция, -и** half-slip, waist petticoat. ~**кру́г, -а** semicircle. ~**кру́глый** semicircular. ~**ме́ра, -ы** half-measure. ~**ме́сяц, -а** crescent (moon). ~**носки́, -о́в** *pl.* ankle socks. ~**оборо́т, -а** half-turn. ~**о́стров, -а** peninsula. ~**откры́тый** half-open; ajar. ~**официа́льный** semi-official. ~**подва́льный** semi-basement. ~**проводни́к, -а́** semi-conductor, transistor. ~**проводнико́вый** transistor, transistorized. ~**со́нный** half-asleep; dozing. ~**ста́нок, -нка** halt. ~**то́нка, -и** half-ton lorry. ~**тьма́, -ы́** semi-darkness; twilight, dusk. ~**фабрика́т, -а** semi-finished product, convenience food. ~**фина́л, -а** semi-final. ~**ша́рие, -я** hemisphere. ~**шу́бок, -бка** sheepskin coat.

полу́да, -ы tinning. **по|луди́ть, -ужу́, -у́дишь** *pf.*
полу́денный midday.
полу́торка, -и thirty-hundredweight lorry.
получа́тель, -я *m.* recipient. **получа́ть, -а́ю** *impf.*, **получи́ть, -чу́, -чишь** *pf.* get, receive, obtain; **~ся** come, arrive, turn up; turn out, prove, be; **из э́того ничего́ не получи́лось** nothing came of it; **результа́ты получи́лись нева́жные** the results are poor. **получе́ние, -я** receipt. **полу́чка, -и** receipt; pay(-packet).
полу́чше *adv.* rather better, a little better.
по́лчище, -а horde; mass, flock.
полы́нн|ый wormwood; **~ая во́дка** absinthe. **полы́нь, -и** wormwood.
по|лысе́ть, -е́ю *pf.*
по́льза, -ы use; advantage, benefit, profit; **в по́льзу**+*g.* in favour of, on behalf of. **по́льзовани|е, -я** use; **многокра́тного ~я** re-usable. **по́льзователь, -я** *m.* user. **по́льзоваться, -зуюсь** *impf.* (*pf.* **вос~**) +*i.* make use of, utilize; profit by; enjoy; take advantage of; **~ дове́рием**+*g.* enjoy the confidence of; **~ креди́том** be credit-worthy; **~ слу́чаем** take the opportunity; **~ уваже́нием** be held in respect.
по́лька, -и Pole; polka. **по́льский** Polish; *sb.* polonaise.
по|льсти́ть(ся, -льщу́(сь *pf.*
По́льша, -и Poland.
полью́ *etc.*: *see* **поли́ть**
полюби́ть, -блю́, -бишь *pf.* come to like, take to; fall in love with.
по|любова́ться, -бу́юсь *pf.*
полюбо́вный amicable.
по|любопы́тствовать, -твую *pf.*
по́люс, -а pole.
поля́к, -а Pole.
поля́на, -ы glade, clearing.
поля́рник, -а polar explorer, member of polar expedition. **поля́рн|ый** polar, arctic; diametrically opposed; **~ая звезда́** pole-star; **(се́верное) ~ое сия́ние** aurora borealis, Northern Lights.
пом... *abbr.* (*of* **помо́щник**) *in comb.* assistant. **помбу́х, -а** assistant accountant. **~дире́ктор, -а** assistant manager. **~на́ч, -а** assistant chief, assistant head.
пома́да, -ы pomade; lipstick.
по|ма́зать(ся, -а́жу(сь *pf.* **помазо́к, -зка́** small brush.
помале́ньку *adv.* gradually, little by little; gently; in a small way, modestly; tolerably, so-so.
пома́лкивать, -аю *impf.* hold one's tongue, keep mum.
по|мани́ть, -ню́, -нишь *pf.*
пома́рка, -и blot; pencil mark; correction.
по|ма́слить, -лю *pf.*
помаха́ть, -машу́, -ма́шешь *pf.*, **пома́хивать, -аю** *impf.*+*i.* wave; brandish, swing; wag.
поме́ньше somewhat smaller, rather smaller, a little smaller; somewhat less, a little less, rather less.
по|меня́ть(ся, -я́ю(сь *pf.* **по|мере́щиться, -щусь** *pf.* **по|ме́рить(ся, -рю(сь** *pf.* **по|ме́ркнуть, -нет; -ме́рк(нул)** *pf.*
помертве́лый deathly pale. **по|мертве́ть, -е́ю** *pf.*
помести́тельный roomy; capacious; spacious. **помести́ть, -ещу́** *pf.* (*impf.* **помеща́ть**) lodge, accommodate; put up; place, locate; invest; **~ статью́** publish an article; **~ся** lodge; find room; put up; go in. **поме́стье, -я**; *g.pl.* **-тий, -тьям** estate.
по́месь, -и cross-breed, hybrid; cross; mongrel; mixture, hotch-potch.
поме́сячный monthly.
помёт, -а dung, excrement; droppings; litter, brood, farrow.
поме́та, -ы mark, note. **по|ме́тить, -е́чу** *pf.* (*impf. also* **помеча́ть**) mark; date; **~ га́лочкой** tick.
поме́ха, -и hindrance; obstacle; encumbrance; *pl.* interference; **быть (служи́ть) поме́хой**+*d.* hinder, impede, stand in the way of. **помехоусто́йчивый** anti-static, anti-interference.
помеча́ть, -а́ю *impf. of* **поме́тить**
поме́шанный mad, crazy; insane; *sb.* madman, madwoman. **помеша́телство, -а** madness, craziness; lunacy, insanity; craze. **по|меша́ть, -а́ю** *pf.* **помеша́ться, -а́юсь** *pf.* go made, go crazy.
поме́шивать, -аю *impf.* stir slowly.
помеща́ть, -а́ю *impf. of* **помести́ть. помеща́ться, -а́юсь** *impf. of* **помести́ться** be; be located, be situated; be housed; be accommodated, find room; **в э́тот стадио́н помеща́ются се́мьдесят ты́сяч челове́к** this stadium holds seventy thousand people. **помеще́ние, -я** premises; apartment, room, lodging; placing, location; investment; **жило́е ~** housing, living accommodation. **поме́щик, -а** landowner, landlord. **поме́щичий** landowner's; **~ дом** manor-house, gentleman's residence.
помидо́р, -а tomato.
поми́лование, -я forgiveness, pardon. **поми́ловать, -лую** *pf.* forgive, pardon.
поми́мо *prep.*+*g.* apart from; besides; without the knowledge of, unbeknown to.
поми́н, -а (-у) mention; **лёгок на ~е** talk of the devil. **помина́ть, -а́ю** *impf. of* **помяну́ть; не ~ ли́хом** remember kindly; not bear a grudge against; **помина́й как зва́ли** he, *etc.*, has vanished into thin air; **~ добро́м** speak well of. **поми́нки, -нок** *pl.* funeral repast.
по|мири́ть(ся, -рю́(сь *pf.*
по́мнить, -ню *impf.* remember.
помножа́ть, -а́ю *impf.*, **по|мно́жить, -жу** *pf.* multiply; **~ два на́ три** multiply two by three.
помога́ть, -а́ю *impf. of* **помо́чь**
по-мо́ему *adv.* I think; in my opinion; to my

mind, to my way of thinking; as I (would) wish, as I would have it.

помо́и, -ев *pl.* slops. **помо́йка, -и**; *g.pl.* **-óек** dustbin; rubbish heap, rubbish dump; cesspit. **помо́йн|ый** slop; **~ое ведро́** slop-pail.

помо́л, -а grinding, milling; grist.

помо́лвка, -и betrothal, engagement.

по|моли́ться, -лю́сь, -лишься *pf.*

по|молоде́ть, -е́ю *pf.*

помолча́ть, -чу́ *pf.* be silent for a time. pause.

помо́р, помо́рский *etc.*: *see* **по...[2] I.**

по|мори́ть, -рю́ *pf.* **по|мо́рщиться, -щу́сь** *pf.*

помо́ст, -а dais; platform, stage, rostrum; scaffold.

по|мочи́ться, -чу́сь, -чишься *pf.*

помо́чь, -огу́, -о́жешь; -о́г, -ла́ *pf.* (*impf.* **помога́ть**) help, aid, assist; relieve, bring relief. **помо́щник, -а, помо́щница, -ы** assistant, mate; help, helper, helpmeet. **по́мощь, -и** help, aid, assistance; relief; **без посторо́нней по́мощи** unaided, single-handed; **на ~!** help!; **пода́ть ру́ку по́мощи** lend a hand, give a helping hand; **при по́мощи, с по́мощью**+*g.* with the help of, by means of.

помо́ю *etc.*: *see* **помы́ть**

по́мпа, -ы pump.

по|мрачне́ть, -е́ю *pf.*

по|мути́ть(ся, -учу́(сь, -у́тишь(ся *pf.* **помутне́ние, -я** dimness, dullness, clouding. **по|мутне́ть, -е́ет** *pf.*

помча́ться, -чу́сь *pf.* dash, rush, tear; dart off.

помыка́ть, -а́ю *impf.*+*i.* order about.

по́мысел, -сла intention, design; thought.

по|мы́ть(ся, -мо́ю(сь *pf.*

помяну́ть, -ну́, -нешь *pf.* (*impf.* **помина́ть**) mention; remember in one's prayers; **помяни́ моё сло́во** mark my words.

помя́тый crushed; flabby, baggy. **по|мя́ться, -мнётся** *pf.*

по|наде́яться, -е́юсь *pf.* count, rely.

пона́добиться, -блюсь *pf.* become necessary, be needed; **е́сли пона́добится** if necessary.

понапра́сну *adv.* in vain.

понаслы́шке *adv.* by hearsay.

по-настоя́щему *adv.* in the right way, properly, truly.

понево́ле *adv.* willynilly; against one's will.

понеде́льник, -а Monday. **понеде́льный** weekly.

понемно́гу, понемно́жку *adv.* little by little; a little.

по|нести́(сь, -су́(сь, -сёшь(ся; -нёс(ся, -ла́(сь *pf.*

понижа́ть, -а́ю *impf.*, **пони́зить, -ни́жу** *pf.* lower; reduce; **~ся** fall, drop, go down, fall off. **пониже́ние, -я** fall, drop; lowering; reduction.

поника́ть, -а́ю *impf.*, **по|ни́кнуть, -ну; -ни́к** *pf.* droop, flag, wilt; **~ голово́й** hang one's head.

понима́ние, -я understanding; comprehension; interpretation, conception. **понима́ть, -а́ю** *impf. of* **поня́ть**

по-но́вому *adv.* in a new fashion; **нача́ть жить ~** begin a new life, turn over a new leaf.

поно́с, -а diarrhoea.

поноси́ть[1], -ошу́, -о́сишь *pf.* carry; wear.

поноси́ть[2], -ошу́, -о́сишь *impf.* abuse, revile. **поно́сный** abusive, defamatory.

поно́шенный worn; shabby, threadbare.

по|нра́виться, -влюсь *pf.*

понто́н, -а pontoon; pontoon bridge. **понто́нный** pontoon.

понуди́тельный compelling, pressing; coercive. **пону́дить, -у́жу** *pf.* **понужда́ть, -а́ю** *impf.* force, compel, coerce; impel.

понука́ть, -а́ю *impf.* urge on.

пону́рить, -рю *pf.*; **~ го́лову** hang one's head. **пону́рый** downcast, depressed.

по|ню́хать, -аю *pf.* **понюшка, -и; ~ табаку́** pinch of snuff.

поня́тие, -я concept, conception; notion, idea. **поня́тливость, -и** comprehension, understanding. **поня́тливый** bright, quick. **поня́тн|ый** understandable; clear, intelligible; perspicuous; **~о** of course, naturally; **~о?** (do you) see? is that clear?; **~о!** I see; I understand; quite! **поня́ть, пойму́, -мёшь; по́нял, -а́, -о** *pf.* (*impf.* **понима́ть**) understand, comprehend; realize.

по|обе́дать, -аю *pf.* **по|обеща́ть, -а́ю** *pf.*

поо́даль *adv.* at some distance, a little way away.

поодино́чке *adv.* one by one, one at a time.

поочерёдно *adv.* in turn, by turns.

поощре́ние, -я encouragement; incentive, spur. **поощри́ть, -рю́** *pf.*, **поощря́ть, -я́ю** *impf.* encourage.

поп, -а́ priest.

поп- *in comb.* pop-. **поп-анса́мбль, -я** *m.* pop group. **~-му́зыка, -и** pop (music). **~-певе́ц, -ца́, ~-певи́ца, -ы** pop singer.

попада́ние, -я hit. **попада́ть(ся, -а́ю(сь** *impf. of* **попа́сть(ся**

попадья́, -и́ priest's wife.

попа́ло *see* **попа́сть. по|па́риться, -рюсь** *pf.*

попа́рно *adv.* in pairs, two by two.

попа́сть, -аду́, -адёшь; -а́л *pf.* (*impf.* **попада́ть**) **+в**+*a.* hit; get to, get into, find o.s. in; **+на**+*a.* hit upon, come on; **не туда́ ~** get the wrong number; **~ в плен** be taken prisoner; **~ в цель** hit the target; **~ на по́езд** catch a train; **~ на рабо́ту** land a job; **~ся** be caught; find o.s.; turn up; **пе́рвый попа́вшийся** the first person one happens to meet; **~ся на у́дочку** swallow the bait; **что попадётся** anything. **попа́ло** *with prons. and advs.*; **где ~** anywhere; **как ~** anyhow; helter-skelter; **что ~** the first thing to hand.

по|пеня́ть, -я́ю *pf.*

попере́к *adv.* & *prep.*+*g.* across; **вдоль и ~** far and wide; **знать вдоль и ~** know inside out, know the ins and outs of; **стать ~**

го́рла+*d.* stick in the throat of; **стоя́ть ~ доро́ги**+*d.* be in the way of.

попереме́нно *adv.* in turns, by turn.

попере́чник, -а diameter. **попере́чн|ый** transverse, diametrical, cross; dihedral; **~ый разре́з, ~ое сече́ние** cross-section.

по|перчи́ть, -чу́ *pf.*

попече́ние, -я care; charge; **быть на попече́нии**+*g.* be under the charge of, be left to the care of. **попечи́тель, -я** *m.* guardian, trustee.

попира́ть, -а́ю *impf.* (*pf.* **попра́ть**) trample on; flout.

поплавко́в|ый float; **~ая ка́мера** float chamber. **поплаво́к, -вка́** float; floating restaurant.

popла́кать — **popла́кать, -а́чу** *pf.* cry a little; shed a few tears.

по|плати́ться, -чу́сь, -тишься *pf.*

попо́йка, -и drinking-bout.

попола́м *adv.* in two, in half; half-and-half; fifty-fifty.

поползнове́ние, -я feeble impulse; half-formed intention, half a mind; pretension(s).

пополне́ние, -я replenishment; re-stocking; re-fuelling; reinforcement. **по|полне́ть, -е́ю** *pf.* **попо́лнить, -ню** *pf.*, **пополня́ть, -я́ю** *impf.* replenish, supplement, fill up; re-stock; re-fuel; reinforce.

пополу́дни *adv.* in the afternoon, p.m.

пополу́ночи *adv.* after midnight, a.m.

попо́на, -ы horse-cloth.

поправи́мый reparable, remediable. **попра́вить, -влю** *pf.*, **поправля́ть, -я́ю** *impf.* mend, repair; correct, set right, put right; adjust, set straight, tidy; improve, better; **~ причёску** tidy one's hair; **~ся** correct o.s.; get better, recover; put on weight; look better; improve. **попра́вка, -и** correction, amendment; mending, repairing; adjustment; recovery.

попра́ть; -а́л *pf. of* **попира́ть**

по-пре́жнему *adv.* as before; as usual.

попрёк, -а reproach. **попрека́ть, -а́ю** *impf.*, **попрекну́ть, -ну́, -нёшь** *pf.* reproach.

по́прище, -а field; walk of life, profession, career.

по|про́бовать, -бую *pf.* **по|проси́ть(ся, -ошу́(сь, -о́сишь(ся** *pf.*

по́просту *adv.* simply; without ceremony.

попроша́йка, -и *c.g.* cadger; beggar. **попроша́йничать, -аю** *impf.* beg; cadge.

попуга́й, -я parrot.

популя́рность, -и popularity. **популя́рный** popular.

попусти́тельство, -а connivance; toleration; tolerance.

по-пусто́му, по́пусту *adv.* in vain, to no purpose.

попу́тно *adv.* at the same time; in passing; incidentally. **попу́тный** accompanying; following; passing; incidental; **~ ве́тер** fair wind. **попу́тчик, -а** fellow-traveller.

попыта́ть, -а́ю *pf.* try; **~ сча́стья** try one's luck. **по|пыта́ться, -а́юсь** *pf.* **попы́тка, -и** attempt, endeavour.

по|пя́титься, -я́чусь *pf.* **попя́тный** backward; **идти́ на ~** go back on one's word.

пора́, -ы́, *a.* **-у**; *pl.* **-ы, пор, -а́м** time, season; it is time; **в (са́мую) по́ру** opportunely, at the right time; **давно́ ~** it is high time; **до поры́ до вре́мени** for the time being; **до каки́х пор?** till when? till what time? how long? **до сих пор** till now, up to now, so far; hitherto; **на пе́рвых ~х** at first; **с каки́х пор? с кото́рых пор?** since when?

поработи́ть, -ощу́ *pf.*, **порабоща́ть, -а́ю** *impf.* enslave. **порабоще́ние, -я** enslavement.

по|ра́довать(ся, -дую(сь *pf.*

поража́ть, -а́ю *impf.*, **по|рази́ть, -ажу́** *pf.* rout; hit; strike; defeat; affect; stagger, startle; **~ся** be astounded, be startled; be staggered. **пораже́нец, -нца** defeatist. **пораже́ние, -я** defeat; hitting; striking; affection; lesion; **~ в права́х** disfranchisement. **пораже́нчество, -а** defeatism. **порази́тельный** striking; staggering, startling.

пора́нить, -ню *pf.* wound; injure; hurt.

порва́ть, -ву́, -вёшь; -ва́л, -а́, -о *pf.* (*impf.* **порыва́ть**) tear (up); break, break off; **~ся** tear; break (off); snap; be broken off.

по|реде́ть, -е́ет *pf.*

поре́з, -а cut. **поре́зать, -е́жу** *pf.* cut; kill, slaughter; **~ся** cut o.s.

поре́й, -я leek.

по|рекомендова́ть, -ду́ю *pf.* **по|ржа́веть, -еет** *pf.*

по́ристый porous.

порица́ние, -я censure; reproof, reprimand; blame; **обще́ственное ~** public censure. **порица́тельный** disapproving; reproving. **порица́ть, -а́ю** *impf.* blame; censure.

по́ровну *adv.* equally, in equal parts.

поро́г, -а threshold; rapids.

поро́да, -ы breed, race, strain, species, stock; kind, sort, type; breeding; rock; layer, bed, stratum; matrix. **поро́дистый** thoroughbred, pedigree. **породи́ть, -ожу́** *pf.* (*impf.* **порожда́ть**) give birth to, beget; raise, generate, engender, give rise to.

породнённ|ый; ~ые города́ twin cities, **по|родни́ть(ся, -ню́(сь** *pf.* **поро́дность, -и** race, breed; stock, strain, **поро́дный** pedigree.

порожда́ть, -а́ю *impf. of* **породи́ть**

поро́жний empty.

по́рознь *adv.* separately, apart.

поро́й, поро́ю *adv.* at times, now and then.

поро́к, -а vice; defect; flaw, blemish; **~ се́рдца** heart-disease.

пороло́н, -а foam rubber. **поропла́ст, -а** foam plastic.

поросёнок, -нка; *pl.* **-ся́та, -ся́т** piglet; sucking-pig. **порос́иться, -и́тся** *impf.* (*pf.* **о~**) farrow.

по́росль, -и suckers, shoots; young wood.

поро́ть[1], **-рю́, -решь** *impf.* (*pf.* **вы́~**) flog, thrash; whip, lash.

поро́ть[2], **-рю́, -решь** *impf.* (*pf.* **рас~**) undo, unpick; rip (out); **~ вздор, ерунду́, чушь** talk rot, talk nonsense; **~ горя́чку** be in a frantic hurry; **~ся** come unstitched, come undone.

по́рох, -а (-у); *pl.* **~а́** gunpowder, powder; **он ~а не вы́думает** he'll never set the Thames on fire. **порохово́й** powder; **~ по́греб, ~ склад** powder-magazine.

поро́чить, -чу *impf.* (*pf.* **о~**) discredit; bring into disrepute; defame, denigrate, blacken, smear. **поро́чный** vicious, depraved; wanton; faulty, defective, fallacious.

порошо́к, -шка́ powder.

порт, -а, *loc.* **-у́**; *pl.* **-ы, -о́в** port; harbour; dockyard.

по́ртить, -чу *impf.* (*pf.* **ис~**) spoil, mar; damage; corrupt; **~ся** deteriorate; go bad; decay, rot; get out of order; be corrupted, become corrupt.

портни́ха, -и dressmaker, tailor. **портно́вский** tailor's, tailoring. **портно́й** *sb.* tailor.

портови́к, -а́ docker. **порто́вый** port, harbour; **~ рабо́чий** docker.

портре́т, -а portrait; likeness.

портсига́р, -а cigarette-case; cigar-case.

Португа́лия, -и Portugal.

портфе́ль, -я *m.* brief-case; portfolio.

портье́ра, -ы curtain(s), portière.

портя́нка, -и foot-binding, puttee.

пору́ганный profaned, desecrated; outraged. **поруга́ть, -а́ю** *pf.* scold, swear at; **~ся** curse, swear; fall out, quarrel.

пору́ка, -и bail; guarantee; surety; **на пору́ки** on bail.

по-ру́сски *adv.* (in) Russian; **говори́ть ~** speak Russian.

поруча́ть, -а́ю *impf.* *of* **поручи́ть. пору́ченец, -нца** special messenger. **поруче́ние, -я** commission, errand; message; mission.

по́ручень, -чня *m.* handrail.

пору́чик, -а lieutenant.

поручи́ть, -чу́, -чишь *pf.* (*impf.* **поруча́ть**) charge, commission; entrust; instruct.

поручи́ться, -чу́сь, -чишься *pf.* *of* **руча́ться**

порха́ть, -а́ю *impf.*, **порхну́ть, -ну́, -нёшь** *pf.* flutter, flit; fly about.

порцио́н, -а ration. **порцио́нный** à la carte. **по́рция, -и** portion; helping.

по́рча, -и spoiling; damage; wear and tear.

по́ршень, -шня *m.* piston; plunger. **поршнев|о́й** piston, plunger; reciprocating; **~о́е кольцо́** piston ring.

поры́в[1], **-а** gust; rush; fit; uprush, upsurge; impulse.

поры́в[2], **-а** breaking, snapping. **порыва́ть(ся**[1], **-а́ю(сь)** *impf.* *of* **порва́ть(ся**

порыва́ться[2], **-а́юсь** *impf.* make jerky movements; try, endeavour, strive. **поры́висто** *adv.* fitfully, by fits and starts. **поры́вистый** gusty; jerky; impetuous, violent; fitful.

поря́дковый ordinal. **поря́дком** *adv.* pretty, rather; properly, thoroughly. **поря́док, -дка (-у)** order; sequence; manner, way; procedure; *pl.* customs, usages, observances; **в обяза́тельном поря́дке** without fail; **всё в поря́дке** everything is alright, it's all in order; **в спе́шном поря́дке** quickly, in haste; **не в поря́дке** out of order; **по поря́дку** in order, in succession; **~ дня** agenda, order of business, order of the day. **поря́дочно** *adv.* decently; honestly; respectably; fairly, pretty; a fair amount; fairly well, quite decently. **поря́дочный** decent; honest; respectable; fair, considerable.

пос. *abbr.* (*of* **посёлок**) settlement, housing estate.

посади́ть, -ажу́, -а́дишь *pf.* *of* **сади́ть, сажа́ть. поса́дка, -и** planting; embarkation; boarding; landing; seat. **поса́дочн|ый** planting; landing; **~ые огни́** flare-path; **~ фа́ры** landing lights.

посажу́ *etc.*: *see* **посади́ть. по|са́харить, -рю** *pf.* **по|сва́тать(ся, -аю(сь** *pf.* **по|свеже́ть, -е́ет** *pf.* **по|свети́ть, -ечу́, -е́тишь** *pf.* **по|светле́ть, -е́ет** *pf.*

по́свист, -а whistle; whistling. **посви́стывать, -аю** *impf.* whistle.

по-сво́ему *adv.* (in) one's own way.

посвяти́ть, -ящу́ *pf.*, **посвяща́ть, -а́ю** *impf.* devote, give up; dedicate; initiate, let in; ordain, consecrate. **посвяще́ние, -я** dedication; initiation; consecration, ordination.

посе́в, -а sowing; crops. **посевн|о́й** sowing; **~а́я пло́щадь** sown area, area under crops.

по|седе́ть, -е́ю *pf.* **посёкся** *etc.*: *see* **посе́чься**

поселе́нец, -нца settler; deportee, exile. **поселе́ние, -я** settling, settlement; deportation, exile. **по|сели́ть, -лю́** *pf.*, **поселя́ть, -я́ю** *impf.* settle; lodge; inspire, arouse, engender; **~ся** settle, take up residence, make one's home. **посёлок, -лка** settlement; housing estate.

посеребрённый; -рён, -а́ silver-plated; silvered. **по|серебри́ть, -рю́** *pf.*

по|сере́ть, -е́ю *pf.*

посети́тель, -я *m.* visitor; caller; guest. **посети́ть, -ещу́** *pf.* (*impf.* **посеща́ть**) visit; call on; attend.

по|се́товать, -тую *pf.* **по|се́чься, -ечётся, -еку́тся; -сёкся, -ла́сь** *pf.*

посеща́емость, -и attendance, (number of) visitors. **посеща́ть, -а́ю** *impf.* *of* **посети́ть. посеще́ние, -я** visiting; visit.

по|се́ять, -е́ю *pf.*

поси́льн|ый within one's powers.

посине́лый gone blue. **по|сине́ть, -е́ю** *pf.*

по|скака́ть, -ачу́, -а́чешь *pf.*

поскользну́ться, -ну́сь, -нёшься *pf.* slip.

поско́льку *conj.* as far as, as much as, (in) so far as; since.

по|скро́мничать, -аю *pf.* **по|скупи́ться, -плю́сь** *pf.*

посла́нец, -нца messenger, envoy. **посла́ние, -я** message; epistle. **посла́нник, -а** envoy, minister. **посла́ть, -шлю́, -шлёшь** *pf.* (*impf.* **посыла́ть**) send, dispatch; move, thrust; ~ **за до́ктором** send for the doctor; ~ **по по́чте** post.

по́сле *adv.* & *prep.+g.* after; afterwards, later (on); since; ~ **всего́** after all, when all is said and done; ~ **всех** last (of all).

после... *in comb.* post-; after-. **послевое́нный** post-war. **~за́втра** *adv.* the day after tomorrow. **~обе́денный** after-dinner. **~родово́й** post-natal. **~сло́вие, -я** epilogue; concluding remarks. **~уда́рный** post-tonic.

после́дн|ий last; final; recent; latest; latter; **(в) ~ее вре́мя, за ~ее вре́мя** lately, recently; **(в) ~ий раз** for the last time; **до ~его вре́мени** until very recently; **~яя ка́пля** the last straw; **~яя мо́да** the latest fashion. **после́дователь, -я** *m.* follower. **после́довательный** successive, consecutive; consistent, logical. **по|сле́довать, -дую** *pf.* **после́дствие, -я** consequence, sequel; after-effect. **после́дующий** subsequent, succeeding, following, ensuing; consequent.

посло́вица, -ы proverb, saying. **посло́вичный** proverbial.

по|служи́ть, -жу́, -жишь *pf.* **послужно́й** service; ~ **спи́сок** service record.

послуша́ние, -я obedience. **по|слу́шать(ся, -аю(сь** *pf.* **послу́шный** obedient, dutiful.

по|слы́шаться, -шится *pf.*

посма́тривать, -аю *impf.* look from time to time (at), glance occasionally.

посме́иваться, -аюсь *impf.* chuckle, laugh softly.

посме́ртный posthumous.

по|сме́ть, -е́ю *pf.*

посме́шище, -а laughing-stock, butt. **посмея́ние, -я** mockery, ridicule. **посмея́ться, -ею́сь, -еёшься** *pf.* laugh; +**над**+*i.* laugh at, ridicule, make fun of.

по|смотре́ть(ся, -рю́(сь, -ришь(ся *pf.*

посо́бие, -я aid, help, relief, assistance; allowance, benefit; textbook; (*educational*) aid; *pl.* teaching equipment; **уче́бные посо́бия** educational supplies. **посо́бник, -а** accomplice; abettor.

по|сове́товать(ся, -тую(сь *pf.* **по|соде́йствовать, -твую** *pf.*

посо́л, -сла́ ambassador.

по|соли́ть, -олю́, -о́ли́шь *pf.*

посо́льский ambassadorial, ambassador's; embassy. **посо́льство, -а** embassy.

поспа́ть, -сплю́; -а́л, -а́, -о *pf.* sleep; have a nap.

поспева́ть¹, -а́ет *impf.*, **по|спе́ть¹, -е́ет** *pf.* ripen; be done, be ready.

поспева́ть², -а́ю *impf.*, **поспе́ть², -е́ю** *pf.* have time; be in time; (**к**+*d.*, **на**+*a.* for); +**за**+*i.* keep up with, keep pace with; **не ~ к по́езду** miss the train; ~ **на по́езд** catch the train.

по|спеши́ть, -шу́ *pf.* **поспе́шно** *adv.* in a hurry, hurriedly, hastily. **поспе́шный** hasty, hurried.

по|спо́рить, -рю *pf.* **по|спосо́бствовать, -твую** *pf.*

посреди́ *adv.* & *prep.+g.* in the middle (of), in the midst (of). **посреди́не** *adv.* in the middle. **посре́дник, -а** mediator, intermediary; go-between; middleman; umpire. **посре́дничество, -а** mediation. **посре́дственно** *adv.* so-so, (only) fairly well; satisfactory. **посре́дственность, -и** mediocrity. **посре́дственный** mediocre, middling; fair, satisfactory. **посре́дством** *prep.+g.* by means of; by dint of; with the aid of.

по|ссо́рить(ся, -рю(сь *pf.*

пост¹, -а́, *loc.* **-у́** post; **занима́ть ~** occupy a post; **на ~у́** at one's post; on one's beat; on point duty.

пост², -а́, *loc.* **-у́** fasting; abstinence; fast.

по|ста́вить¹, -влю *pf.*

поста́вить², -влю *pf.*, **поставля́ть, -я́ю** *impf.* supply, purvey. **поста́вка, -и** supply; delivery. **поставщи́к, -а́** supplier, purveyor, provider; caterer; outfitter.

постанови́ть, -влю́, -вишь *pf.* (*impf.* **постановля́ть**) decree, enact, ordain; decide, resolve.

постано́вка, -и staging, production; arrangement, organization; putting, placing, setting; erection, raising; ~ **го́лоса** voice training; ~ **па́льцев** fingering.

постановле́ние, -я decree, enactment; decision, resolution. **постановля́ть, -я́ю** *impf. of* **постанови́ть**

постано́вочный stage, staging, production. **постано́вщик, -а** producer, stage-manager; (film) director.

по|стара́ться, -а́юсь *pf.*

по|старе́ть, -е́ю *pf.* **по-ста́рому** *adv.* as before; as of old.

посте́ль, -и bed; bottom. **посте́льн|ый** bed; **~ое бельё** bed-clothes; ~ **режи́м** confinement to bed. **постелю́** *etc.*: *see* **постла́ть**

постепе́нно *adv.* gradually, little by little. **постепе́нный** gradual.

по|стесня́ться, -я́юсь *pf.*

постига́ть, -а́ю *impf. of* **пости́чь. пости́гнуть** *see* **пости́чь постиже́ние, -я** comprehension, grasp. **постижи́мый** comprehensible.

постила́ть, -а́ю *impf. of* **постла́ть. пости́лка, -и** spreading, laying; bedding; litter.

пости́чь, пости́гнуть, -и́гну; -и́г(нул) *pf.* (*impf.* **постига́ть**) comprehend, grasp; befall.

по|стла́ть, -стелю́, -сте́лешь *pf.* (*impf. also* **постила́ть**) spread, lay; ~ **посте́ль** make a bed.

по́стн|ый lenten; lean; glum; **~ое ма́сло** vegetable oil.

посто́й, -я billeting, quartering.

посто́льку *conj.* to the same extent, to the same degree; (so).

по|сторони́ться, -ню́сь, -ни́шься *pf.* **посторо́нн|ий** strange; foreign; extraneous, outside; *sb.* stranger, outsider; **~им вход запрещён** no admission; private.

постоя́нно *adv.* constantly, continually, perpetually, always. **постоя́нн|ый** permanent; constant; continual; invariable; steadfast, unchanging; **~ый а́дрес** permanent address; **~ая (величина́)** constant; **~ый ток** direct current. **постоя́нство, -а** constancy; permanency.

по|стоя́ть, -ою́ *pf.* stand, stop; +**за**+*a.* stand up for.

пострада́вший *sb.* victim. **по|страда́ть, -а́ю** *pf.*

построе́ние, -я construction; building; formation. **по|стро́ить(ся, -ро́ю(сь** *pf.* **постро́йка, -и** building; erection, construction; building-site.

постро́мка, -и trace; strap.

поступа́тельный progressive, forward, advancing. **поступа́ть, -а́ю** *impf.*, **поступи́ть, -плю́, -пишь** *pf.* act; do; come through, come in, be received; +**в** *or* **на**+*a.* enter, join, go to, go into; +**с**+*i.* treat, deal with; **~ в прода́жу** be on sale, come on the market; **~ в шко́лу** go to school, start school; **поступи́ла жа́лоба** a complaint has been received; **~ся**+*i.* waive, forgo; give up. **поступле́ние, -я** entering, joining; receipt; entry. **посту́пок, -пка** action; act, deed; *pl.* conduct, behaviour. **по́ступь, -и** gait; step, tread.

по|стуча́ть(ся, -чу́(сь *pf.*

по|стыди́ться, -ыжу́сь *pf.* **посты́дный** shameful.

посу́да, -ы crockery; plates and dishes; service; ware; utensils; vessel, crock. **посу́дн|ый** china; dish; **~ое полоте́нце** tea-towel; **~ый шкаф** dresser, china-cupboard.

по|сули́ть, -лю́ *pf.*

посу́точный 24-hour, round-the-clock; by the day.

посчастли́виться, -ится *pf. impers.* (+*d.*) turn out well, go well (for); **ей посчастли́вилось**+*inf.* she had the luck to, she was lucky enough to.

посчита́ть, -а́ю *pf.* count (up). **по|счита́ться, -а́юсь** *pf.*

посыла́ть, -а́ю *impf. of* **посла́ть. посы́лка, -и** sending; parcel, package; errand; premise. **посы́лочн|ый** parcel; **~ая фи́рма** mail-order firm. **посы́льный** *sb.* messenger.

посы́пать, -плю, -плешь *pf.*, **посыпа́ть, -а́ю** *impf.* strew; sprinkle; powder.

посяга́тельство, -а encroachment; infringement. **посяга́ть, -а́ю** *impf.*, **посягну́ть, -ну́, -нёшь** *pf.* encroach, infringe; make an attempt (**на**+*a.* on).

пот, -а (-у), *loc.* **-у́**; *pl.* **-ы́** sweat, perspiration.

потаённый, потайно́й secret.

по-тво́ему *adv.* in your opinion; as you wish; as you advise; **пусть бу́дет ~** have it your own way; just as you think.

потака́ть, -а́ю *impf.*+*d.* indulge, pander to.

потасо́вка, -и brawl, fight; hiding, beating.

потво́рствовать, -твую *impf.* (+*d.*) be indulgent (towards), connive (at), pander (to).

потёмки, -мок *pl.* darkness. **по|темне́ть, -е́ет** *pf.*

по|тепле́ть, -е́ет *pf.*

потерпе́вший *sb.* victim; survivor. **по|терпе́ть, -плю́, -пишь** *pf.*

поте́ря, -и loss; waste; *pl.* losses, casualties. **по|теря́ть(ся, -я́ю(сь** *pf.*

по|тесни́ть, -ню́ *pf.* **по|тесни́ться, -ню́сь** *pf.*; make room; sit closer, stand closer, squeeze up, move up.

поте́ть, -е́ю *impf.* (*pf.* **вс~, за~**) sweat, perspire; mist over, steam up; (+**над**+*i.*) sweat, toil (over).

поте́ха, -и fun, amusement. **по|те́шить(ся, -шу(сь** *pf.* **поте́шный** funny, amusing.

потира́ть, -а́ю *impf.* rub.

потихо́ньку *adv.* noiselessly, softly; secretly, by stealth, on the sly; slowly.

по́тн|ый; -тен, -тна́, -тно sweaty, damp with perspiration; misty, steamed up; **~ые ру́ки** clammy hands.

пото́к, -а stream; flow; torrent; flood; production line; group; **пото́к маши́н** traffic flow.

потоло́к, -лка́ ceiling.

по|толсте́ть, -е́ю *pf.*

пото́м *adv.* afterwards; later (on); then, after that. **пото́мок, -мка** descendant; scion; offspring, progeny. **пото́мство, -а** posterity, descendants.

потому́ *adv.* that is why; **~ что** *conj.* because, as.

по|тону́ть, -ну́, -нешь *pf.* **пото́п, -а** flood, deluge. **по|топи́ть, -плю́, -пишь** *pf.*, **потопля́ть, -я́ю** *impf.* sink. **потопле́ние, -я** sinking.

по|топта́ть, -пчу́, -пчешь *pf.* **по|торопи́ть(ся, -плю́(сь, -пишь(ся** *pf.*

пото́чн|ый continuous; production-line; **~ая ли́ния** production line; **~ое произво́дство** mass production.

по|тра́тить, -а́чу *pf.*

потреби́тель, -я *m.* consumer, user. **потреби́тельск|ий** consumer; consumer's, consumers'; **~ие това́ры** consumer goods. **потреби́ть, -блю́** *pf.*, **потребля́ть, -я́ю** *impf.* consume, use. **потребле́ние, -я** consumption, use. **потре́бность, -и** need, want, necessity, requirement. **потре́бный** necessary, required, requisite. **по|тре́бовать(ся, -бую(сь** *pf.*

по|трево́жить(ся, -жу(сь *pf.*

потрёпанный shabby; ragged, tattered; battered; worn, seedy. **по|трепа́ть(ся, -плю́(сь, -плешь(ся** *pf.*

по|тре́скаться, -ается *pf.* **потре́скивать, -ает** *impf.* crackle.

потроха́, -о́в *pl.* giblets; pluck. **потроши́ть, -шу́** *impf.* (*pf.* **вы́~**) disembowel, clean; draw.

потруди́ться, -ужу́сь, -у́дишься *pf.* take some pains, do some work; take the trouble.

потряса́ть, -а́ю *impf.*, **потрясти́, -су́, -сёшь; -я́с, -ла́** *pf.* shake; rock; stagger, stun; *+a. or i.* brandish, shake; ~ **кулако́м** shake one's fist. **потряса́ющий** staggering, stupendous, tremendous.

поту́га, -и muscular contraction; *pl.* labours, vain attempts; **родовы́е поту́ги** labour.

поту́пить, -плю *pf.*, **потупля́ть, -я́ю** *impf.* lower, cast down; **~ся** look down, cast down one's eyes.

потускне́лый tarnished; lack-lustre. **по|тускне́ть, -е́ет** *pf.*

потуха́ть, -а́ет *impf.*, **по|ту́хнуть, -нет, -у́х** *pf.* go out; die out. **поту́хший** extinct; lifeless, lack-lustre.

по|туши́ть, -шу́, -шишь *pf.* **по|тяга́ться, -а́юсь** *pf.*

потя́гиваться, -аюсь *impf.*, **по|тяну́ться, -ну́сь, -нешься** *pf.* stretch o.s. **по|тяну́ть, -ну́, -нешь** *pf.*

по|у́жинать, -аю *pf.* **по|умне́ть, -е́ю** *pf.*

поучи́тельный instructive.

похвала́, -ы́ praise. **по|хвали́ть(ся, -лю́(сь, -лишь(ся** *pf.* **похвальба́, -ы́** bragging, boasting. **похва́льный** praiseworthy, laudable, commendable; laudatory.

по|хва́стать(ся, -аю(сь *pf.*

похити́тель, -я *m.* kidnapper; abductor; thief. **похи́тить, -хи́щу** *pf.*, **похища́ть, -а́ю** *impf.* kidnap; abduct, carry off; steal. **похище́ние, -я** theft; kidnapping; abduction.

похлёбка, -и broth, soup.

по|хлопота́ть, -очу́, -о́чешь *pf.*

похме́лье, -я hangover.

похо́д, -а campaign; march; cruise; (long) walk, hike; outing, excursion; **вы́ступить в ~** take the field; set out; **на ~е** on the march.

по|ходáтайствовать, -твую *pf.*

походи́ть, -ожу́, -о́дишь *impf.* **на**+*a.* be like, look like, resemble.

похо́дка, -и gait, walk, step. **похо́дн|ый** mobile, field; marching, cruising; **~ая крова́ть** camp-bed; **~ая ку́хня** mobile kitchen, field kitchen; **~ый мешо́к** kit-bag; **~ый поря́док** marching order; **~ая ра́ция** walkie-talkie. **похожде́ние, -я** adventure, escapade.

похо́жий similar, alike; ~ **на** like.

по|хорони́ть, -ню́, -нишь *pf.* **похоро́нный** funeral. **по́хороны, -ро́н** *pl.* funeral; burial.

по|хороше́ть, -е́ю *pf.*

по́хоть, -и lust.

по|худе́ть, -е́ю *pf.*

по|целова́ть(ся, -лу́ю(сь *pf.* **поцелу́й, -я** kiss.

по|церемо́ниться, -нюсь *pf.*

по́чва, -ы soil, earth; ground; basis, footing. **по́чвенный** soil, ground; ~ **покро́в** top-soil.

почём *adv.* how much; how; ~ **знать?** who can tell? how is one to know?; ~ **сего́дня я́блоки** how much are apples today?; ~ **я зна́ю?** how should I know?

почему́ *adv.* why; (and) so, that's why. **почему́-либо, -нибу́дь** *advs.* for some reason or other. **почему́-то** *adv.* for some reason.

по́черк, -а hand(writing).

почерне́лый blackened, darkened. **по|черне́ть, -е́ю** *pf.*

почерпа́ть, -а́ю *impf.*, **почерпну́ть, -ну́, -нёшь** *pf.* get, draw, scoop up; pick up.

по|черстве́ть, -е́ю *pf.* **по|чеса́ть(ся, -ешу́(сь, -е́шешь(ся** *pf.*

по́честь, -и honour. **почёт, -а** honour; respect, esteem. **почётный** honoured, respected, esteemed; of honour; honourable; honorary; ~ **карау́л** guard of honour.

по́чечный renal; kidney.

почива́ть, -а́ю *impf. of* **почи́ть**

почи́н, -а initiative; beginning, start.

по|чини́ть, -ню́, -нишь *pf.*, **починя́ть, -я́ю** *impf.* repair, mend. **почи́нка, -и** repairing, mending.

по|чи́стить(ся, -ищу(сь *pf.*

почита́ние, -я honouring; respect, esteem. **почита́ть[1], -а́ю** *impf.* honour, respect, esteem; revere; worship.

почита́ть[2], -а́ю *pf.* read for a while, look at.

почи́ть, -и́ю *pf.* (*impf.* **почива́ть**) rest, take one's rest; pass away; ~ **на ла́врах** rest on one's laurels.

по́чка[1], -и bud.

по́чка[2], -и kidney; **иску́сственная ~** kidney machine.

по́чта, -ы post, mail; post-office; **электро́нная ~** e-mail. **почтальо́н, -а** postman. **почтальо́нша, -и** postwoman. **почта́мт, -а** (head) post-office.

почте́ние, -я respect; esteem; deference. **почте́нный** honourable; respectable, estimable; venerable; considerable.

почти́ *adv.* almost, nearly.

почти́тельный respectful, deferential; considerable. **почти́ть, -чту́** *pf.* honour.

почто́в|ый post, mail; postal; **~ая каре́та** stage coach, mail; **~ая ка́рточка** postcard; **~ый перево́д** postal order; **~ый по́езд** mail (train); **~ый я́щик** letter-box.

по|чу́диться, -ишься *pf.* **по|шаба́шить, -шу** *pf.*

пошатну́ть, -ну́, -нёшь *pf.* shake; **~ся** shake; totter, reel, stagger; be shaken.

по|шевели́ть(ся, -елю́(сь, -е́ли́шь(ся *pf.* **пошёл** *etc.*: *see* **пойти́**

поши́вка, -и sewing. **поши́вочный** sewing.

по́шлина, -ы duty; customs.

по́шлость, -и vulgarity, commonness; triviality; triteness, banality. **по́шлый** vulgar, common; commonplace, trivial; trite, banal. **пошля́к, -а́** vulgarian, Philistine.

поштýчно *adv.* by the piece. **поштýчный** by the piece; piece-work.

по|шути́ть, -учу́, -у́тишь *pf.*

пощáда, -ы mercy. **по|щадúть, -ажý** *pf.*
по|щекотáть, -очý, -óчешь *pf.*
пощёчина, -ы box on the ear; slap in the face.
по|щýпать, -аю *pf.*
поэ́зия, -и poetry. **поэ́ма, -ы** poem. **поэ́т, -а** poet.
поэтáпный phased.
поэтúческий poetic, poetical.
поэ́тому *adv.* therefore, and so.
пою́ *etc.*: *see* **петь, поúть**
появúться, -влю́сь, -вишься *pf.*, **появля́ться, -я́юсь** *impf.* appear; show up; emerge. **появлéние, -я** appearance.
пóяс, -а; *pl.* **-á** belt; girdle; waist-band; waist; zone; **по ~** up to the waist, waist-deep, waist-high.
пояснéние, -я explanation, elucidation. **пояснúтельный** explanatory. **пояснúть, -ню́** *pf.* (*impf.* **поясня́ть**) explain, elucidate.
пояснúца, -ы small of the back. **поясн|óй** waist; to the waist, waist-high; zone, zonal; **~áя вáнна** hip-bath.
поясня́ть, -я́ю *impf. of* **пояснúть**
пр. *abbr.* (*of* **проéзд**) passage, thoroughfare; (*of* **проспéкт**) Prospect, Avenue; **и ~** (*of* **и прóчее**) etc. etcetera; and so on; (*of* **и прóчие**) *et al.*, and Co.
пра... *pref.* original, first, oldest; great-. **прабáбушка, -и** great-grandmother. **прáвнук, -а** great-grandson. **прáвнучка, -и** great-granddaughter. **прáдед, -а** great-grandfather; *pl.* ancestors, forefathers. **~дéдовский** great-grandfather's; ancestral; ancient. **~дéдушка, -и** *m.* great-grandfather. **прáотец, -тца** forefather. **~прáдед, -а** great-great-grandfather. **~родúтель, -я** *m.* primogenitor; forefather.
прáвда, -ы (the) truth; true; justice; **всéми ~ми и непрáвдами** by fair means or foul, by hook or by crook; **э́то ~** that's true. **правдúвый** true; truthful; honest, upright. **правдоподóбный** probable, likely; plausible.
прáвило, -а rule; regulation; principle; **взять за ~, положúть за ~** make it a rule; **взять себé за ~** make a point of; **как ~** as a rule; **прáвила ýличного движéния** traffic regulations.
прáвильно *adv.* rightly; correctly; regularly. **прáвильн|ый** right, correct; regular; rectilinear, rectilineal; **~о!** that's right! exactly!
правúтельственный government, governmental. **правúтельство, -а** government. **прáвить**[1], **-влю**+*i.* rule, govern; drive.
прáвить[2], **-влю** *impf.* correct; **~ корректýру** read proofs, correct proofs. **прáвка, -и** correcting; (proof-)reading.
правлéние, -я board, governing body; administration, management; governing, government.
прáвленый corrected.
прá|внук, ~внучка *see* **пра...**
прáво, -а; *pl.* **-á** law; right; **(водúтельские) правá** driving licence; **на правáх**+*g.* in the capacity, character, or position of; **на правáх рýкописи** all rights reserved; **~ гóлоса** the vote, suffrage.
прáво *adv.* really, truly, indeed.
право...[1] *in comb.* law; right. **правовéд, -а** jurist; law-student. **~вéдение, -я** jurisprudence. **~вéрный** orthodox; *sb.* true believer (*esp. of Moslems*). **~мéрный** lawful, rightful. **~мóчие, -я** competence. **~мóчный** competent, authorized. **~нарушéние, -я** infringement of the law, offence. **~нарушúтель, -я** *m.* offender, delinquent. **~писáние, -я** spelling, orthography. **~слáвный** orthodox; *sb.* member of Orthodox Church. **~сýдие, -я** justice.
право...[2] *in comb.* right, right-hand. **правобережный** on the right bank, right-bank. **~охранúтельн|ый** law-enforcement; **~ые óрганы** law-enforcement agencies. **~сторóнний** right; right-hand. **~флангóвый** right-flank, right-wing.
правовóй legal, of the law; lawful, rightful.
правотá, -ы́ rightness; innocence.
прáвый[1] right; right-hand; right-wing.
прáв|ый[2]**; прав, -á, -о** right, correct; righteous, just; innocent, not guilty; **~ое дéло** a just cause.
прáвящий ruling.
Прáга, -и Prague.
прáдед *etc.*: *see* **пра...**
прáздник, -а (public) holiday; feast; festival; festive occasion. **прáзднование, -я** celebration. **прáздновать, -ную** *impf.* (*pf.* **от~**) celebrate. **прáздность, -и** idleness, inactivity; emptiness. **прáздный** idle; inactive; empty; vain, useless.
прáктика, -и practice; practical work; **на прáктике** in practice. **практиковáть, -кýю** *impf.* practise; apply in practice; **~ся** (*pf.* **на~ся**) practice; be used, be practised; +**в**+*p.* have practice in. **прáктикум, -а** practical work. **практúческий, практúчный** practical.
прáотец *see* **пра...**
прáпорщик, -а ensign.
прапрáдед *etc.*: *see* **пра...**
прах, -а dust; ashes, remains; **пойтú ~ом** go to rack and ruin.
прáчечная *sb.* laundry; wash-house; **~-автомáт** launderette. **прáчка, -и** laundress.
пре... *pref. in comb.* **I.** *with vv. indicates action in extreme degree or superior measure*: sur-, over-, out-. **II.** *with adjs. and advs. indicates superlative degree*: very, most, exceedingly.
пребывáние, -я stay; residence; tenure, period; **~ в дóлжности, ~ на постý** tenure of office, period in office. **пребывáть, -áю** *impf.* be; reside; **~ в невéдении** be in the dark; **~ у влáсти** be in power.
превзойтú, -йдý, -йдёшь; -ошёл, -шлá *pf.* (*impf.* **превосходúть**) surpass; excel; ~

самого́ себя́ surpass o.s.; ~ **чи́сленностью** outnumber.

превозмога́ть, -а́ю *impf.*, **превозмо́чь, -огу́, -о́жешь; -о́г, -ла́** *pf.* overcome, surmount.

превознести́, -су́, -сёшь; -ёс, -ла́ *pf.*, **превозноси́ть, -ошу́, -о́сишь** *impf.* extol, praise.

превосходи́тельство, -а Excellency. **превосходи́ть, -ожу́, -о́дишь** *impf. of* **превзойти́. превосхо́дн|ый** superlative; superb, outstanding, excellent; superior; **~ая сте́пень** superlative (degree). **превосходя́щий** superior.

преврати́ть, -ащу́ *pf.*, **превраща́ть, -а́ю** *impf.* convert, turn, reduce; transmute; **~ся** turn, change. **превра́тно** *adv.* wrongly; ~ **истолкова́ть** misinterpret; ~ **поня́ть** misunderstand. **превра́тный** wrong, false; changeful, inconstant, perverse. **превраще́ние, -я** transformation, conversion; transmutation; metamorphosis.

превы́сить, -ы́шу *pf.*, **превыша́ть, -а́ю** *impf.* exceed. **превыше́ние, -я** exceeding, excess.

прегра́да, -ы obstacle; bar, barrier. **прегради́ть, -ажу́** *pf.*, **прегражда́ть, -а́ю** *impf.* bar, obstruct, block.

пред *see* **пе́ред**

пред...[1], **предъ...** *pref.* pre-, fore-, ante-.

пред...[2] *abbr.* (*of* **председа́тель**) *in comb.* chairman.

...пре́д, -а *abbr.* (*of* **председа́тель**) *in comb.* representative, spokesman.

предава́ть(ся, -даю́(сь, -даёшь(ся *impf. of* **преда́ть(ся**

преда́ние, -я legend; tradition; handing over, committal. **пре́данность, -и** devotion; faithfulness; loyalty. **пре́данный** devoted, faithful. **преда́тель, -я** *m.* traitor; betrayer. **преда́тельский** traitorous; perfidious; treacherous. **преда́тельство, -а** treachery, betrayal, perfidy. **преда́ть, -а́м, -а́шь, -а́ст, -ади́м; пре́дал, -а́, -о** *pf.* (*impf.* **предава́ть**) hand over, commit; betray; ~ **забве́нию** bury in oblivion; ~ **земле́** commit to the earth; ~ **суду́** bring to trial; **~ся** give o.s. up, abandon o.s.; give way, indulge; *+d.* go over to, put o.s. in the hands of.

преда́ю *etc.*: *see* **предава́ть**

предвари́тельн|ый preliminary; prior; **по ~ому соглаше́нию** by prior arrangement; **~ое заключе́ние** detention before trial; **~ая прода́жа биле́тов** advance sale of tickets, advance booking. **предвари́ть, -рю́** *pf.*, **предваря́ть, -я́ю** *impf.* forestall, anticipate; forewarn, inform beforehand.

предве́стник, -а forerunner, precursor; herald, harbinger; presage, portent. **предвеща́ть, -а́ю** *impf.* foretell; herald, presage, portend; **э́то предвеща́ет хоро́шее** this augurs well.

предвзя́тый preconceived; prejudiced, biased.

предви́деть, -и́жу *impf.* foresee; **~ся** be foreseen; be expected.

предвкуси́ть, -ушу́, -у́сишь *pf.*, **предвкуша́ть, -а́ю** *impf.* look forward to, anticipate (with pleasure).

предводи́тель, -я *m.* leader. **предводи́тельствовать, -твую** *impf.+i.* lead.

предвое́нный pre-war.

предвосхи́тить, -и́щу *pf.*, **предвосхища́ть, -а́ю** *impf.* anticipate.

предвы́борный (pre-)election.

предго́рье, -я foothills.

преде́л, -а limit; bound, boundary; end; *pl.* range; **положи́ть ~***+d.* put an end to, terminate. **преде́льн|ый** boundary; limiting; maximum; utmost; critical; saturated; **~ый во́зраст** age-limit; **~ое напряже́ние** breaking load, maximum stress; **~ая ско́рость** maximum speed; **~ый срок** time-limit, deadline.

предзнаменова́ние, -я omen, augury. **предзнаменова́ть, -ну́ю** *impf.* bode, augur, portend.

предисло́вие, -я preface, foreword.

предлага́ть, -а́ю *impf. of* **предложи́ть.**

предло́г[1], **-а** pretext; **под ~ом***+g.* on the pretext of.

предло́г[2], **-а** preposition.

предложе́ние[1], **-я** sentence; clause; proposition.

предложе́ние[2], **-я** offer; proposition; proposal; motion; suggestion; supply; **внести́ ~** move, introduce, put down, a motion; **сде́лать ~***+d.* make an offer to; propose to; **спрос и ~** supply and demand. **предложи́ть, -жу́, -жишь** *pf.* (*impf.* **предлага́ть**) offer; propose; suggest; put, set, propound; order, require; ~ **резолю́цию** move a resolution.

предло́жный prepositional.

предме́т, -а object; article, item; subject; topic, theme; *pl.* goods; **на сей ~** to this end, with this object; ~ **спо́ра** point at issue; **~ы пе́рвой необходи́мости** necessities. **предме́тный** object; ~ **катало́г** subject catalogue; ~ **сто́лик** stage; ~ **уро́к** object-lesson.

предназнача́ть, -а́ю *impf.*, **предназна́чить, -чу** destine, intend, mean; earmark, set aside. **предназначе́ние, -я** earmarking; destiny.

преднаме́ренный premeditated; aforethought; deliberate.

пре́до *see* **пе́ред**

пре́док, -дка forefather, ancestor; *pl.* forebears.

предоста́вить, -влю *pf.*, **предоставля́ть, -я́ю** *impf.* grant; leave; give; ~ **в его́ распоряже́ние** put at his disposal; ~ **пра́во** concede a right; ~ **сло́во***+d.* give the floor to, call on to speak.

предостерега́ть, -а́ю *impf.*, **предостере́чь, -егу́, -ежёшь; -ёг, -ла́** *pf.* warn, caution. **предостереже́ние, -я** warning, caution. **предосторо́жность, -и** caution; precaution; **ме́ры предосторо́жности** precautionary measures.

предосуди́тельный wrong, reprehensible, blameworthy.

предотврати́ть, -ащу́ *pf.*, **предотвраща́ть, -а́ю** *impf.* avert, prevent; ward off, stave off.

предохране́ние, -я protection; preservation. **предохрани́тель, -я** *m.* guard; safety device, safety-catch; fuse. **предохрани́тельн|ый** preservative; preventive; safety; protective; **~ый кла́пан** safety-valve; **~ая коро́бка** fuse-box. **предохрани́ть, -ню́** *pf.*, **предохраня́ть, -я́ю** *impf.* preserve, protect.

предписа́ние, -я order, injunction; *pl.* directions, instructions; prescription; **согла́сно предписа́нию** by order. **предписа́ть, -ишу́, -и́шешь** *pf.*, **предпи́сывать, -аю** *impf.* order, direct, instruct; prescribe.

предполага́емый supposed, conjectural. **предполага́ть, -а́ю** *impf.*, **предположи́ть, -жу́, -о́жишь** *pf.* suppose, assume; conjecture, surmise; intend, propose; contemplate; presuppose; **предполага́ется** *impers.* it is proposed, it is intended. **предположе́ние, -я** supposition, assumption; intention. **предположи́тельно** *adv.* supposedly, presumably; probably. **предположи́тельный** conjectural; hypothetical.

предпосле́дний penultimate, last-but-one, next-to-last.

предпосы́лка, -и prerequisite, precondition; premise.

предпоче́сть, -чту́, -чтёшь; -чёл, -чла́ *pf.*, **предпочита́ть, -а́ю** *impf.* prefer; **я предпочёл бы** I would rather. **предпочте́ние, -я** preference. **предпочти́тельный** preferable.

предприи́мчивость, -и enterprise. **предприи́мчивый** enterprising.

предпринима́тель, -я *m.* owner; employer; entrepreneur; contractor. **предпринима́тельство, -а** business undertakings; **свобо́дное ~** free enterprise. **предпринима́ть, -а́ю** *impf.*, **предприня́ть, -иму́, -и́мешь; -и́нял, -а́, -о** *pf.* undertake; **~ ата́ку** launch an attack; **~ шаги́** take steps. **предприя́тие, -я** undertaking, enterprise; business; concern; works; **риско́ванное ~** venture, risky undertaking.

предрасположе́ние, -я predisposition. **предрасполо́женный** predisposed.

предрассу́док, -дка prejudice.

предреша́ть, -а́ю *impf.* **предреши́ть, -шу́** *pf.* decide beforehand; predetermine.

председа́тель, -я *m.*, **председа́тельница, -ы** chairman. **председа́тельск|ий** chairman's; **~ое кре́сло** the chair. **председа́тельствовать, -твую** *impf.* preside, be in the chair.

предсказа́ние, -я prediction, forecast, prophecy; prognostication. **предсказа́тель, -я** *m.* foreteller, forecaster; soothsayer. **предсказа́ть, -ажу́, -а́жешь** *pf.*, **предска́зывать, -аю** *impf.* foretell, predict; forecast, prophesy.

предсме́ртный dying; **~ час** one's last hour.

представа́ть, -таю́, -таёшь *impf. of* **предста́ть**

представи́тель, -я *m.* representative; spokesman; specimen. **представи́тельный** representative; imposing. **представи́тельство, -а** representation; representatives; delegation.

предста́вить, -влю *pf.*, **представля́ть, -я́ю** *impf.* present; produce, submit; introduce; recommend, put forward; display; perform; play; represent; **~ себе́** imagine, fancy, picture, conceive; **представля́ть собо́й** represent, be; constitute; **~ся** present itself, occur, arise; seem; introduce o.s.; *+i.* pretend to be, pass o.s. off as. **представле́ние, -я** presentation, introduction; declaration; statement; representation; performance; idea, notion, conception.

предста́ть, -а́ну *pf.* (*impf.* **представа́ть**) appear; **~ пе́ред судо́м** appear in court.

предстоя́ть, -ои́т *impf.* be in prospect, lie ahead, be at hand; **мне предстои́т пойти́ туда́** I shall have to go there. **предстоя́щий** coming, forthcoming; impending, imminent.

предте́ча, -и *c.g.* forerunner, precursor; **Иоа́нн ~** John the Baptist.

предубежде́ние, -я prejudice, bias.

предугада́ть, -а́ю *pf.*, **предуга́дывать, -аю** *impf.* guess; foresee.

предупреди́тельность, -и courtesy; attentiveness. **предупреди́тельный** preventive, precautionary; courteous, attentive; obliging. **предупреди́ть, -ежу́** *pf.*, **предупрежда́ть, -а́ю** *impf.* notify in advance, let know beforehand; warn; give notice; prevent, avert; anticipate, forestall. **предупрежде́ние, -я** notice; notification; warning, caution; prevention; anticipation; forestalling.

предусма́тривать, -аю *impf.*, **предусмотре́ть, -рю́, -ришь** *pf.* envisage, foresee; provide for, make provision for. **предусмотри́тельный** prudent; provident; far-sighted.

предчу́вствие, -я presentiment; foreboding, misgiving, premonition. **предчу́вствовать, -твую** *impf.* have a presentiment (about), have a premonition of.

предше́ственник, -а predecessor; forerunner, precursor. **предше́ствовать, -твую** *impf.+d.* go in front of; precede.

предъ... *see* **пред...**[1]

предъяви́тель, -я *m.* bearer; **а́кция на предъяви́теля** ordinary share. **предъяви́ть, -влю́, -вишь** *pf.*, **предъявля́ть, -я́ю** *impf.* show, produce, present; bring, bring forward; **~ иск к**+*d.* bring suit against; **~ обвине́ние**+*d.* charge; **~ пра́во на**+*a.* lay claim to.

предыду́щ|ий previous, preceding; **~ее** *sb.* the foregoing.

пре́емник, -а successor. **пре́емственность, -и** succession; continuity.

пре́жде *adv.* before; first; formerly, in former times; **~ чем** before; *prep.+g.* before; **~**

всего́ first of all, to begin with; first and foremost. **преждевре́менный** premature, untimely. **пре́жний** previous, former.

презента́ция, -и presentation; launch.

презервати́в, -а condom.

президе́нт, -а president, **президе́нтский** presidential. **прези́диум, -а** presidium.

презира́ть, -а́ю *impf.* despise; hold in contempt; disdain; scorn. **презре́ние, -я** contempt; scorn. **презре́нный** contemptible, despicable. **презри́тельный** contemptuous, scornful.

преиму́щественно *adv.* mainly, chiefly, principally. **преиму́щественный** main, principal, primary, prime; preferential; priority. **преиму́щество, -а** advantage; preference; **по преиму́ществу** for the most part, chiefly.

прейскура́нт, -а price-list.

преклоне́ние, -я admiration, worship. **преклони́ть, -ню́** *pf.*, **преклоня́ть, -я́ю** *impf.* bow, bend; ~ **го́лову** bow; ~ **коле́на** genuflect, kneel; **~ся** bow down; *+d. or* **перед***+i.* admire, worship. **прекло́нный;** ~ **во́зраст** old age; declining years.

прекра́сно *adv.* excellently; perfectly well. **прекра́сный** beautiful; fine; excellent, capital, first-rate; **в оди́н ~ день** one fine day; ~ **пол** the fair sex.

прекрати́ть, -ащу́ *pf.*, **прекраща́ть, -а́ю** *impf.* stop, cease, discontinue; put a stop to, end; break off, sever, cut off; ~ **войну́** end the war; ~ **подпи́ску** discontinue a subscription, stop subscribing; **~ся** cease, end.

преле́стный charming, delightful, lovely. **пре́лесть, -и** charm; fascination.

преломи́ть, -млю́, -мишь *pf.*, **преломля́ть, -я́ю** *impf.* refract; **~ся** be refracted. **преломле́ние, -я** refraction.

пре́лый fusty, musty; rotten. **прель, -и** mouldiness, mould, rot.

прельсти́ть, -льщу́ *pf.*, **прельща́ть, -а́ю** *impf.* attract; lure, entice; **~ся** be attracted; be tempted; fall (*+i.* for).

прелю́дия, -и prelude.

премиа́льн|ый bonus; prize; **~ые** *sb., pl.* bonus.

преми́нуть, -ну *pf. with neg.* (not) fail.

премирова́ть, -ру́ю *impf. & pf.* award a prize to; give a bonus. **пре́мия, -и** prize; bonus; bounty, gratuity; premium.

премье́р, -а prime minister; leading actor, lead. **премье́ра, -ы** première, first performance. **премье́рша, -и** leading lady, lead.

пренебрега́ть, -а́ю *impf.*, **пренебре́чь, -егу́, -ежёшь; -ёг, -ла́** *pf.+i.* scorn, despise; neglect, disregard. **пренебреже́ние, -я** scorn, contempt, disdain; neglect, disregard. **пренебрежи́тельный** scornful; slighting; disdainful.

пре́ния, -ий *pl.* debate; discussion; pleadings; **вы́ступить в ~х** take part in a discussion.

преоблада́ние, -я predominance. **преоблада́ть, -а́ет** *impf.* predominate; prevail.

преобража́ть, -а́ю *impf.*, **преобрази́ть, -ажу́** *pf.* transform. **преображе́ние, -я** transformation; Transfiguration. **преобразова́ние, -я** transformation; reform; reorganization. **преобразова́ть, -зу́ю** *pf.*, **преобразо́вывать, -аю** *impf.* transform; reform, reorganize.

преодолева́ть, -а́ю *impf.*, **преодоле́ть, -е́ю** *pf.* overcome, get over, surmount.

препара́т, -а preparation.

препина́ние, -я; зна́ки препина́ния punctuation marks.

препира́тельство, -а altercation, wrangling, squabbling. **препира́ться, -а́юсь** *impf.* wrangle, squabble.

преподава́ние, -я teaching, tuition, instruction. **преподава́тель, -я** *m.*, **-ница, -ы** teacher; lecturer, instructor. **преподава́тельский** teaching; teacher's, teachers'; ~ **соста́в** (teaching) staff. **преподава́ть, -даю́, -даёшь** *impf.* teach.

преподнести́, -су́, -сёшь; -ёс, -ла́ *pf.*, **преподноси́ть, -ошу́, -о́сишь** present with, make a present of.

препроводи́тельный accompanying. **препроводи́ть, -вожу́, -во́дишь** *pf.*, **препровожда́ть, -а́ю** *impf.* send, forward, dispatch.

препя́тствие, -я obstacle, impediment, hindrance; hurdle; **ска́чки (бег) с препя́тствиями** steeplechase; hurdle-race, obstacle-race. **препя́тствовать, -твую** *impf.* (*pf.* **вос~**) *+d.* hinder, impede, hamper; stand in the way of.

прерва́ть, -ву́, -вёшь; -а́л, -а́, -о *pf.* (*impf.* **прерыва́ть**) interrupt; break off; cut off, sever; cut short; **нас прерва́ли** we've been cut off; **~ся** be interrupted; be broken off; break down; break.

пререка́ние, -я altercation, argument, wrangle. **пререка́ться, -а́юсь** *impf.* argue, wrangle, dispute.

прерыва́ть(ся, -а́ю(сь *impf. of* **прерва́ть(ся**

пресека́ть, -а́ю *impf.*, **пресе́чь, -еку́, -ечёшь; -ёк, -екла́** *pf.* stop, cut short; put an end to; ~ **в ко́рне** nip in the bud; **~ся** stop; break.

пресле́дование, -я pursuit, chase; persecution, victimization; prosecution. **пресле́довать, -дую** *impf.* pursue, chase, be after; haunt; persecute, torment; victimize; prosecute.

преслову́тый notorious.

пресмыка́ться, -а́юсь *impf.* grovel, cringe; creep, crawl. **пресмыка́ющееся** *sb.* reptile.

пре́сный fresh; unsalted; unleavened; flavourless, tasteless; insipid, vapid, flat.

пре́сса, -ы the press. **пресс-атташе́** *m.indecl.* press attaché. **пресс-бюро́** *nt.indecl.* press department. **пресс-конфере́нция, -и** press conference.

престаре́лый aged; advanced in years.

престо́л, -а throne; altar.

преступле́ние, -я crime, offence; felony; transgression. **престу́пник, -а** criminal, offender, delinquent; felon; **вое́нный ~** war criminal. **престу́пность, -и** criminality; crime, delinquency. **престу́пный** criminal; felonious.

пресы́титься, -ы́щусь *pf.*, **пресыща́ться, -а́юсь** *impf.* be satiated, be surfeited. **пресыще́ние, -я** surfeit, satiety.

претвори́ть, -рю́ *pf.*, **претворя́ть, -я́ю** *impf.* (**в**+*a.*) turn, change, convert; **~ в жизнь** put into practice, realize, carry out; **~ся в**+*a.* turn into, become; **~ в жизнь** be realized, come true.

претенде́нт, -а claimant; aspirant; candidate; contestant; pretender. **претендова́ть, -ду́ю** *impf.* **на**+*a.* claim, lay claim to; have pretensions to; aspire to. **прете́нзия, -и** claim; pretension; **быть в прете́нзии на**+*a.* have a grudge, a grievance against; bear a grudge.

претерпева́ть, -а́ю *impf.*, **претерпе́ть, -плю́, -пишь** *pf.* undergo; suffer, endure.

преувеличе́ние, -я exaggeration; overstatement. **преувели́чивать, -аю** *impf.*, **преувели́чить, -чу** *pf.* exaggerate; overstate.

преуменьша́ть, -а́ю *impf.*, **преуме́ньшить, -е́ньшу́** *pf.* underestimate; minimize; belittle; understate.

преуспева́ть, -а́ю *impf.*, **преуспе́ть, -е́ю** *pf.* succeed, be successful; thrive, prosper, flourish.

преходя́щий transient.

при *prep.* +*p.* by, at; in the presence of; attached to, affiliated to, under the auspices of; with; about; on; for, notwithstanding; in the time of, in the days of; under; during; when, in case of; **би́тва ~ Бородине́** the battle of Borodino; **~ всём том** with it all, moreover; for all that; **~ де́тях** in front of the children; **~ дневно́м све́те** by daylight; **~ доро́ге** by the road(-side); **~ Ива́не Гро́зном** in the reign of Ivan the Terrible; under Ivan the Terrible; **при мне** in my presence; **~ перехо́де че́рез у́лицу** when crossing the street; **~ Пу́шкине** in Pushkin's day; **~ слу́чае** when the occasion arises; **~ све́те ла́мпы** by lamplight; **у него́ не́ было ~ себе́ де́нег** he had no money on him.

при... *pref.* **I.** *with vv. indicates action or motion continued to a given terminal point*; *action of attaching or adding*; *direction of action towards speaker or from above downward*; *incomplete or tentative action*; *exhaustive action*; *action to an accompaniment*. **II.** *with nn. and adjs. indicates juxtaposition or proximity.*

приба́вить, -влю *pf.*, **прибавля́ть, -я́ю** add, put on; increase, augment; exaggerate, lay it on (thick); **~ (в ве́се)** put on weight; **~ хо́ду** put on speed; **~ ша́гу** mend one's pace; **~ся** increase; rise; wax; **день приба́вился** the days are getting longer, are drawing out. **приба́вка, -и** addition, augmentation; increase, supplement, rise. **прибавле́ние, -я** addition, augmentation; supplement, appendix. **приба́вочный** additional; surplus.

прибалти́йский Baltic. **Приба́лтика, -и** the Baltic States.

прибега́ть[1], **-а́ю** *impf.* *of* **прибежа́ть**

прибега́ть[2], **-а́ю** *impf.*, **прибе́гнуть, -ну; -бе́г** *pf.* +**к**+*d.* resort to, fall back on.

прибежа́ть, -егу́ *pf.* (*impf.* **прибега́ть**) come running, run up.

прибе́жище, -а refuge; **после́днее ~** last resort.

приберега́ть, -а́ю *impf.*, **прибере́чь, -егу́, -ежёшь; -ёг, -ла́** *pf.* save (up), reserve.

приберу́ *etc.*: *see* **прибра́ть. прибива́ть, -а́ю** *impf.* *of* **приби́ть прибира́ть, -а́ю** *impf.* *of* **прибра́ть**

приби́ть, -бью́, -бьёшь *pf.* (*impf.* **прибива́ть**) nail, fix with nails; lay, flatten; drive, carry; beat up.

прибл. *abbr.* (*of* **приблизи́тельно**) approx., approximately.

приближа́ть, -а́ю *impf.*, **прибли́зить, -и́жу** *pf.* bring nearer, move nearer; hasten, advance; **~ся** approach, draw near; draw (come) nearer. **приблизи́тельно** *adv.* approximately, roughly. **приблизи́тельный** approximate, rough.

прибо́й, -я surf, breakers.

прибо́р, -а instrument, device, apparatus, appliance, gadget; set, service, things; fittings; **бри́твенный ~** shaving things; **ча́йный ~** tea service, tea things. **прибо́рн|ый** instrument; **~ая доска́** dash-board, instrument panel.

прибра́ть, -беру́, -берёшь; -а́л, -а́, -о *pf.* (*impf.* **прибира́ть**) tidy (up), clear up, clean up; put away; **~ ко́мнату** do (out) a room; **~ посте́ль** make a bed.

прибре́жн|ый coastal; littoral, riverside; riparian; **~ые острова́** off-shore islands.

прибыва́ть, -а́ю *impf.*, **прибы́ть, -бу́ду; при́был, -а́, -о** *pf.* arrive; get in; increase, grow; rise, swell; wax. **при́быль, -и** profit, gain; return; increase, rise. **при́быльный** profitable, lucrative. **прибы́тие, -я** arrival.

прибью́ *etc.*: *see* **приби́ть**

прива́л, -а halt, stop; stopping-place.

приватиза́ция, -и privatization. **приватизи́ровать, -ую** *impf.* & *pf.* privatize.

приведу́ *etc.*: *see* **привести́**

привезти́, -зу́, -зёшь; -ёз, -ла́ (*impf.* **привози́ть**) bring.

привере́дливый fastidious, squeamish, hard to please. **привере́дничать, -аю** *impf.* be hard to please, be fastidious, be squeamish.

приве́рженец, -нца adherent; follower. **приве́рженный** attached, devoted.

приве́сить, -е́шу *pf.* (*impf.* **приве́шивать**) hang up, suspend.

привести́, -еду́, -едёшь; -ёл, -а́ *pf.* (*impf.* **приводи́ть**) bring; lead; take; reduce; adduce, cite; +**к**+*d.* lead to, bring to, conduce to, result in; +**в**+*a.* put in(to), set; **~ в движе́ние, в де́йствие** set in motion, set going; ~ **в изумле́ние** astonish, astound; ~ **в исполне́ние** execute, carry out; ~ **в отча́яние** drive to despair; ~ **в поря́док** put in order, tidy (up); arrange, fix; ~ **в у́жас** horrify.

приве́т, -а greeting(s); regards; **переда́йте** ~+*d.* remember me to, my regards to; **с серде́чным ~ом** yours sincerely. **приве́тливость, -и** affability; cordiality. **приве́тливый** cordial, friendly; affable. **приве́тствие, -я** greeting, salutation; speech of welcome. **приве́тствовать, -твую** *impf.* & *pf.* greet, salute, hail; welcome; ~ **сто́я** give a standing ovation (to).

приве́шивать, -аю *impf. of* **приве́сить**

прививать(ся, -а́ю(сь, -а́ешь(ся *impf. of* **приви́ть(ся. приви́вка, -и** inoculation; vaccination; grafting, graft.

привиде́ние, -я ghost, spectre; apparition.

при|ви́деться, -дится *pf.*

привилегиро́ванн|ый privileged; **~ая а́кция** preference share. **привиле́гия, -и** privilege.

привинти́ть, -нчу́ *pf.*, **приви́нчивать, -аю** *impf.* screw on.

приви́ть, -вью́, -вьёшь; -и́л, -а́, -о *pf.* (*impf.* **привива́ть**) inoculate, vaccinate; graft; implant; inculcate; cultivate, foster; ~ **о́спу**+*d.* vaccinate; **~ся** take; become established, find acceptance, catch on.

при́вкус, -а after-taste; smack.

привлека́тельный attractive. **привлека́ть, -а́ю** *impf.*, **привле́чь, -еку́, -ечёшь; -ёк, -ла́** *pf.* attract; draw; draw in, win over; have up; ~ **внима́ние** attract attention; ~ **к суду́** sue, take to court; prosecute; put on trial.

при́вод, -а drive, driving-gear. **приводи́ть, -ожу́, -о́дишь** *impf. of* **привести́. приводно́й** driving.

привожу́ *etc.*: *see* **приводи́ть, привози́ть**

приво́з, -а bringing, supply; importation; import. **привози́ть, -ожу́, -о́зишь** *impf. of* **привезти́. привозно́й, приво́зный** imported.

приво́льный free.

привстава́ть, -таю́, -таёшь *impf.*, **привста́ть, -а́ну** *pf.* half-rise; rise, stand up.

привыка́ть, -а́ю *impf.*, **привы́кнуть, -ну; -ы́к** *pf.* get used, get accustomed; get into the habit, get into the way. **привы́чка, -и** habit. **привы́чный** habitual, usual, customary; accustomed, used; of habit.

привью́ *etc.*: *see* **приви́ть**

привя́занность, -и attachment; affection. **привя́занный** attached. **привяза́ть, -яжу́, -я́жешь** *pf.*, **привя́зывать, -аю** *impf.* attach; tie, bind, fasten, secure, tether; **~ся** become attached; attach o.s.; +**к**+*d.* pester, bother. **привязно́й** fastened, secured, tethered. **привя́зчивый** importunate, insistent, annoying; affectionate; susceptible. **при́вязь, -и** tie; lead, leash; tether.

пригласи́ть, -ашу́ *pf.*, **приглаша́ть, -а́ю** *impf.* invite, ask; call (in); ~ **на обе́д** ask to dinner. **приглаше́ние, -я** invitation; offer.

пригляде́ться, -яжу́сь *pf.*, **пригля́дываться, -аюсь** *impf.* look closely; +**к**+*d.* scutinize, examine; get used to, get accustomed to.

пригна́ть, -гоню́, -го́нишь; -а́л, -а́, -о *pf.* (*impf.* **пригоня́ть**) drive in, bring in; fit, adjust.

пригова́ривать[1], -аю *impf.* keep saying, keep (on) repeating.

пригова́ривать[2], -аю *impf.*, **приговори́ть, -рю́** *pf.* sentence, condemn.

пригоди́ться, -ожу́сь *pf.* prove useful; be of use; come in useful, come in handy. **приго́дный** fit, suitable, good; useful. **приго́жий** fine.

пригоня́ть, -я́ю *impf. of* **пригна́ть**

пригора́ть, -а́ет *impf.*, **пригоре́ть, -ри́т** *pf.* be burnt. **пригоре́лый** burnt.

при́город, -а suburb. **при́городный** suburban.

приго́рок, -рка hillock, knoll.

при́горшня, -и; *g.pl.* **-ей** handful.

приготови́тельный preparatory. **пригото́вить, -влю** *pf.*, **приготовля́ть, -я́ю** *impf.* prepare, cook, ~ **роль** learn a part; **~ся** prepare; prepare o.s. **приготовле́ние, -я** preparation.

пригрева́ть, -а́ю *impf. of* **пригре́ть**

при|гре́зиться, -е́жусь *pf.*

пригре́ть, -е́ю *pf.* (*impf.* **пригрева́ть**) warm; cherish.

при|грози́ть, -ожу́ *pf.*

придава́ть, -даю́, -даёшь *impf.*, **прида́ть, -а́м, -а́шь, -а́ст, -ади́м; при́дал, -а́, -о** *pf.* add; increase, strengthen; give, impart; attach; ~ **значе́ние**+*d.* attach importance to. **прида́ча, -и** adding; addition, supplement; **в прида́чу** into the bargain, in addition.

придвига́ть, -а́ю *impf.* **придви́нуть, -ну** *pf.* move up, draw up; **~ся** move up, draw near.

придво́рный court; *sb.* courtier.

приде́лать, -аю *pf.*, **приде́лывать, -аю** *impf.* fix, attach.

приде́рживаться, -аюсь *impf.* hold on, hold; +*g.* hold to, keep to; stick to, adhere to; ~ **пра́вой стороны́** keep to the right; ~ **мне́ния** be of the opinion.

придеру́сь *etc.*: *see* **придра́ться. придира́ться, -а́юсь** *impf. of* **придра́ться. приди́рка, -и** cavil, captious objection; fault-finding; carping. **приди́рчивый** niggling; captious.

придоро́жный roadside, wayside.

придра́ться, -деру́сь, -дерёшься; -а́лся, -а́сь, -а́ло́сь *pf.* (*impf.* **придира́ться**) find fault, cavil, carp; seize; ~ **к слу́чаю** seize an opportunity.

приду́ *etc.*: *see* **прийти́**

приду́мать, -аю *pf.*, **приду́мывать, -аю** *impf.* think up, devise, invent; think of.

придыха́тельное *sb.* aspirate.

приеду *etc.*: *see* **приехать. приезд, -а** arrival, coming. **приезжать, -аю** *impf. of* **приехать. приезжий** newly arrived; *sb.* newcomer; visitor.

приём, -а receiving; reception; surgery; welcome; admittance; dose; go; motion, movement; method, way, mode; device, trick; hold, grip; **в один ~** at one go. **приемлемый** acceptable; admissible. **приёмная** *sb.* waiting-room; reception room. **приёмник, -а** radio, wireless, receiver. **приёмн|ый** receiving; reception; entrance; foster, adoptive, adopted; **~ый день** visiting day; **~ая комиссия** selection board; **~ая мать** foster-mother; **~ые часы** (business) hours; surgery (hours); **~ый экзамен** entrance examination. **приёмо-передающий** two-way. **приёмщик, -а** inspector, examiner. **приёмочный** inspection, examining.

приехать, -еду *pf.* (*impf.* **приезжать**) arrive, come.

прижать, -жму, -жмёшь *pf.* (*impf.* **прижимать**) press; clasp; **~ся** press o.s.; cuddle up, snuggle up, nestle up.

прижечь, -жгу, -жжёшь; -жёг, -жгла *pf.* (*impf.* **прижигать**) cauterize, sear.

приживалка, -и, приживальщик, -а dependant; hanger-on, sponger, parasite.

прижигание, -я cauterization. **прижигать, -аю** *impf. of* **прижечь**

прижимать(ся, -аю(сь *impf. of* **прижать(ся. прижимистый** tight-fisted, stingy. **прижму** *etc.*: *see* **прижать**

приз, -а; *pl.* **-ы** prize.

призадуматься, -аюсь *pf.*, **призадумываться, -аюсь** *impf.* become thoughtful, become pensive.

призвание, -я vocation, calling; **по призванию** by vocation. **призвать, -зову, -зовёшь; -ал, -а, -о** *pf.* (*impf.* **призывать**) call, summon; call upon, appeal to; call up; **~ся** be called up.

приземистый stocky, squat; thickset.

приземление, -я landing, touchdown. **приземлиться, -люсь** *pf.*, **приземляться, -яюсь** *impf.* land, touch down.

призёр, -а, призёрша, -и prizewinner.

призма, -ы prism. **призматический** prismatic.

признавать, -наю, -наёшь *impf.*, **признать, -аю** *pf.* recognize; spot, identify; admit, own, acknowledge; deem, vote; **(не) ~ себя виновным** plead (not) guilty; **~ся** confess, own; **~ся (сказать)** to tell the truth. **признак, -а** sign, symptom; indication. **признание, -я** confession, declaration; admission, acknowledgement; recognition. **признанный** acknowledged, recognized. **признательный** grateful.

призову *etc.*: *see* **призвать**

призрак, -а spectre, ghost, phantom, apparition. **призрачный** spectral, ghostly, phantasmal; illusory, imagined.

призыв, -а call, appeal; slogan; call-up, conscription. **призывать(ся, -аю(сь** *impf. of* **призвать(ся. призывной** conscription; **~ возраст** military age; *sb.* conscript.

прииск, -а mine; **золотые ~и** gold-field(s).

прийти, приду, -дёшь; пришёл, -шла *pf.* (*impf.* **приходить**) come; arrive; **~ в себя** come round, regain consciousness; **~ в ужас** be horrified; **~ к концу** come to an end; **~ к заключению** come to the conclusion, arrive at a conclusion; **~сь+по**+*d.* fit; suit; +**на**+*a.* fall on; *impers.* (+*d.*) have to; happen (to), fall to the lot (of); +**на**+*a. or* **с**+*g.* be owing to, from; **нам пришлось вернуться в Москву** we had to return to Moscow; **как придётся** anyhow, at haphazard.

приказ, -а order, command; order of the day; office, department. **приказание, -я** order, command, injunction. **приказать, -ажу, -ажешь** *pf.*, **приказывать, -аю** *impf.* order, command; give orders, direct.

прикалывать, -аю *impf. of* **приколоть**

прикасаться, -аюсь *impf. of* **прикоснуться**

прикидывать, -аю *impf.*, **прикинуть, -ну** *pf.* throw in, add; weigh; estimate; calculate, reckon; **~ся**+*i.* pretend (to be), feign; **~ся больным** pretend to be ill, feign illness.

приклад[1], -а butt.

приклад[2], -а trimmings, findings. **прикладной** applied. **прикладывать(ся, -аю(сь** *impf. of* **приложить(ся**

приклеивать, -аю *impf.*, **приклеить, -ею** *pf.* stick; glue; paste; affix; **~ся** stick, adhere.

приключаться, -ается *impf.*, **приключиться, -ится** *pf.* happen, occur. **приключение, -я** adventure. **приключенческий** adventure.

приковать, -кую, -куёшь *pf.*, **приковывать, -аю** *impf.* chain; rivet.

прикол, -а stake; **на ~е** laid up, idle.

приколачивать, -аю *impf.*, **приколотить, -очу, -отишь** *pf.* nail, fasten with nails; beat up.

приколоть, -лю, -лешь *pf.* (*impf.* **прикалывать**) pin, fasten with a pin; stab, transfix.

прикомандировать, -рую *pf.*, **прикомандировывать, -аю** *impf.* attach, second.

прикосновение, -я touch, contact; concern. **прикосновенный** concerned, involved, implicated (**к**+*d.* in). **прикоснуться, -нусь, -нёшься** *pf.* (*impf.* **прикасаться**) **к**+*d.* touch.

прикрасить, -ашу *pf.*, **прикрашивать, -аю** *impf.* embellish, embroider.

прикрепить, -плю *pf.*, **прикреплять, -яю** *impf.* fasten, attach. **прикрепление, -я** fastening; attachment; registration.

прикрывать, -аю *impf.*, **прикрыть, -рою** *pf.* cover; screen; protect, shelter, shield; cover up, conceal; close down, wind up; **~ся** cover o.s.; close down, go out of business; +*i.* use as cover, take refuge in, shelter behind.

прику́ривать, -аю *impf.*, **прикури́ть, -рю́, -ришь** *pf.* get a light; light a cigarette from another.

прику́с, -а bite. **прикуси́ть, -ушу́, -у́сишь** *pf.*, **прику́сывать, -аю** *impf.* bite; ~ **язы́к** hold one's tongue, keep one's mouth shut.

прила́вок, -вка counter; **рабо́тник прила́вка** counter-hand; (shop) assistant.

прилага́тельн|ый adjective; **~ое** *sb.* adjective. **прилага́ть, -а́ю** *impf. of* **приложи́ть**

прила́дить, -а́жу *pf.*, **прила́живать, -аю** *impf.* fit, adjust.

приласка́ть, -а́ю *pf.* caress, fondle, pet; **~ся** snuggle up, nestle up.

прилега́ть, -а́ет *impf.* (*pf.* **приле́чь**) **к**+*d.* fit; adjoin, be adjacent to, border (on). **прилега́ющий** close-fitting, tight-fitting; adjoining, adjacent, contiguous.

прилежа́ние, -я diligence, industry; application. **приле́жный** diligent, industrious, assiduous.

прилепи́ть(ся, -плю́(сь, -пишь(ся *pf.*, **прилепля́ть(ся, -я́ю(сь** *impf.* stick.

прилёт, -а arrival. **прилета́ть, -а́ю** *impf.*, **прилете́ть, -ечу́** *pf.* arrive, fly in; fly, come flying.

приле́чь, -ля́гу, -ля́жешь; -ёг, -гла́ *pf.* (*impf.* **прилега́ть**) lie down; be laid flat; +**к**+*d.* fit.

прили́в, -а flow, flood; rising tide; surge, influx; congestion; ~ **кро́ви** rush of blood; ~ **эне́ргии** burst of energy. **прилива́ть, -а́ет** *impf. of* **прили́ть. прили́вный** tidal.

прилипа́ть, -а́ет *impf.*, **прили́пнуть, -нет; -ли́п** *pf.* stick, adhere. **прили́пчивый** sticking, adhesive; clinging; not to be shaken off; tiresome; catching.

прили́ть, -льёт; -и́л, -а́, -о *pf.* (*impf.* **прилива́ть**) flow; rush.

прили́чие, -я decency, propriety; decorum. **прили́чный** decent; proper, decorous, seemly; tolerable, fair.

приложе́ние, -я application; affixing; enclosure; supplement; appendix; schedule, exhibit; apposition. **приложи́ть, -жу́, -жишь** *pf.* (*impf.* **прикла́дывать, прилага́ть**) put; apply; affix; add, join; enclose; ~ **все стара́ния** do one's best, try one's hardest; **~ся** take aim; +*i.* put, apply; +**к**+*d.* kiss.

прилуни́ться, -ню́сь *pf.* land on the Moon.

прильёт *etc.*: *see* **прили́ть. при|льну́ть, -ну́, -нёшь** *pf.* **приля́гу** *etc.*: *see* **приле́чь**

прима́нивать, -аю *impf.*, **примани́ть, -ню́, -нишь** *pf.* lure; entice, allure. **прима́нка, -и** bait, lure; enticement, allurement.

примене́ние, -я application; employment, use. **примени́ть, -ню́, -нишь** *pf.*, **применя́ть, -я́ю** *impf.* apply; employ, use; ~ **на пра́ктике** put into practice; **~ся** adapt o.s., conform.

приме́р, -а example; instance; model; **не в** ~+*d.* unlike; +*comp.* far more, by far; **подава́ть** ~ set an example; **привести́ в** ~ cite as an example.

при|ме́рить, -рю *pf.* (*impf. also* **примеря́ть**) try on; fit. **приме́рка, -и** trying on; fitting.

приме́рно *adv.* in exemplary fashion; approximately, roughly. **приме́рный** exemplary, model; approximate, rough.

приме́рочная *sb.* fitting-room.

примеря́ть, -я́ю *impf. of* **приме́рить**

при́месь, -и admixture; dash; **без при́месей** unadulterated.

приме́та, -ы sign, token; mark. **приме́тный** perceptible, visible, noticeable; conspicuous, prominent.

примеча́ние, -я note, footnote; *pl.* comments.

примеша́ть, -а́ю *pf.*, **приме́шивать, -аю** *impf.* add, mix in.

примина́ть, -а́ю *impf. of* **примя́ть**

примире́ние, -я reconciliation. **примире́нчество, -а** appeasement, compromise. **примири́мый** reconcilable. **примири́тель, -я** *m.* reconciler, conciliator, peace-maker. **примири́тельный** conciliatory. **при|мири́ть, -рю́** *pf.*, **примиря́ть, -я́ю** *impf.* reconcile; conciliate; **~ся** be reconciled, make it up; +**с**+*i.* reconcile o.s. to, put up with.

примити́вный primitive; crude.

примкну́ть, -ну́, -нёшь *pf.* (*impf.* **примыка́ть**) join; fix, attach.

примну́ *etc.*: *see* **примя́ть**

примо́рский seaside; maritime. **примо́рье, -я** seaside; littoral.

примо́чка, -и wash, lotion.

приму́ *etc.*: *see* **приня́ть**

примча́ться, -чу́сь *pf.* come tearing along.

примыка́ние, -я contiguity; agglutination. **примыка́ть, -а́ю** *impf. of* **примкну́ть;** +**к**+*d.* adjoin, abut on, border on. **примыка́ющий** affiliated.

примя́ть, -мну́, -мнёшь *pf.* (*impf.* **примина́ть**) crush, flatten; trample down.

принадлежа́ть, -жу́ *impf.* belong. **принадле́жност|ь, -и** belonging; membership; *pl.* accessories, appurtenances; equipment; outfit, tackle; **туале́тные ~и** toiletries.

при|неволи́ть, -лю *pf.*

принести́, -су́, -сёшь *pf.* (*impf.* **приноси́ть**) bring; fetch; bear, yield; bring in; ~ **в же́ртву** sacrifice; ~ **по́льзу** be of use, be of benefit.

принима́ть(ся, -а́ю(сь *impf. of* **приня́ть(ся; принима́ющая сторона́** host country.

принора́вливать, -аю *impf.*, **приноровить, -влю́** *pf.* fit, adapt, adjust; **~ся** adapt o.s., accommodate o.s.

приноси́ть, -ошу́, -о́сишь *impf. of* **принести́. приноше́ние, -я** gift, offering.

при́нтер, -а printer; **ла́зерный** ~ laser printer.

принуди́тельн|ый compulsory; forced, coercive; **~ые рабо́ты** forced labour, hard labour. **принуди́ть, -у́жу** *pf.*, **принужда́ть, -а́ю** *impf.* force, compel, coerce, constrain. **принужде́ние, -я** compulsion, constraint; duress. **принуждённый** constrained, forced.

при́нцип, -а principle. **принципиа́льно** *adv.* on principle; in principle. **принципиа́льный**

of principle; in principle; general.

приня́тие, -я taking; taking up; assumption; acceptance, adoption; admission, admittance. **при́нято** it is accepted, it is usual; **не** ~ it is not done. **приня́ть, -иму́, -и́мешь; при́нял, -а́, -о** *pf.* (*impf.* **принима́ть**) take; accept; take up; take over; pass, approve; admit; receive; +**за**+*a.* take for; ~ **ва́нну** take (have) a bath; ~ **в шко́лу** admit to, accept for, a school; ~ **зако́н** pass a law; ~ **лека́рство** take medicine; ~ **ме́ры** take measures; ~ **резолю́цию** pass, adopt, carry a resolution; ~ **уча́стье** take part; ~**ся** begin; start; take; take root, strike root; +**за**+*a.* take in hand; set to, get down to; ~ **за рабо́ту** set to work.

приободри́ть, -рю́ *pf.*, **приободря́ть, -я́ю** *impf.* cheer up, encourage, hearten; ~**ся** cheer up.

приобрести́, -ету́, -етёшь; -рёл, -а́ *pf.*, **приобрета́ть, -а́ю** *impf.* acquire, gain. **приобрете́ние, -я** acquisition; gain; bargain, find.

приобща́ть, -а́ю *impf.*, **приобщи́ть, -щу́** *pf.* join, attach, unite; ~ **к де́лу** file; ~**ся к**+*d.* join in.

приозёрный lakeside, lakeland.

приостана́вливать, -аю *impf.* **приостанови́ть, -влю́, -вишь** *pf.* stop, suspend, check; ~**ся** halt, stop, pause. **приостано́вка, -и** halt, check, stoppage, suspension.

приотвори́ть, -рю́, -ришь *pf.*, **приотворя́ть, -я́ю** *impf.* open slightly, half-open, set ajar.

припа́док, -дка fit; attack; paroxysm.

припаса́ть, -а́ю *impf.*, **припасти́, -су́, -сёшь; -а́с, -ла́** *pf.* store, lay in, lay up. **припа́сы, -ов** *pl.* stores, supplies; provisions; munitions.

припе́в, -а refrain, burden.

приписа́ть, -ишу́, -и́шешь *pf.*, **припи́сывать, -аю** *impf.* add; attribute, ascribe; put down, impute. **припи́ска, -и** addition; postscript; codicil.

припла́та, -ы extra pay; additional payment. **приплати́ть, -ачу́, -а́тишь** *pf.* **припла́чивать, -аю** *impf.* pay in addition.

припло́д, -а issue, increase.

приплыва́ть, -а́ю *impf.*, **приплы́ть, -ыву́, -ывёшь; -ы́л, -а́, -о** *pf.* swim up, sail up.

приплю́снуть, -ну *pf.*, **приплю́щивать, -аю** *impf.* flatten.

приподнима́ть, -а́ю *impf.*, **приподня́ть, -ниму́, -ни́мешь; -о́днял, -а́, -о** *pf.* raise (a little); ~**ся** raise o.s. (a little), rise.

припо́й, -я solder.

припомина́ть, -а́ю *impf.*, **припо́мнить, -ню** *pf.* remember, recollect, recall; +*d.* remind.

припра́ва, -ы seasoning, flavouring; relish, condiment, dressing. **припра́вить, -влю** *pf.*, **приправля́ть, -я́ю** *impf.* season, flavour, dress.

припря́тать, -я́чу *pf.*, **припря́тывать, -аю** *impf.* secrete, put by.

припу́гивать, -аю *impf.*, **припугну́ть, -ну́, -нёшь** *pf.* intimidate, scare.

при́пуск, -а allowance, margin.

прираба́тывать, -аю *impf.*, **прирабо́тать, -аю** *pf.* earn ... extra, earn in addition. **при́работок, -тка** supplementary earnings, additional earnings.

прира́внивать, -аю *impf.*, **приравня́ть, -я́ю** *pf.* equate, place on the same footing; compare (**к**+*d.* to).

прираста́ть, -а́ю *impf.*, **прирасти́, -тёт; -ро́с, -ла́** *pf.* adhere; take; increase; accrue; ~ **к ме́сту** be rooted to the spot.

прире́чный riverside.

приро́да, -ы nature; character. **приро́дный** natural; native; born, by birth; inborn, innate. **природосберега́ющий** environment-friendly. **прирождённый** inborn, innate; born.

приро́с *etc.*: *see* **прирасти́. приро́ст, -а** increase, growth.

прируча́ть, -а́ю *impf.*, **приручи́ть, -чу́** *pf.* tame; domesticate. **прируче́ние, -я** taming, domestication.

приса́живаться, -аюсь *impf. of* **присе́сть**

присва́ивать, -аю *impf.*, **присво́ить, -о́ю** *pf.* appropriate; give, award, confer; ~ **и́мя**+*d.* & *g.* name after.

приседа́ть, -а́ю *impf.*, **присе́сть, -ся́ду** *pf.* (*impf. also* **приса́живаться**) sit down, take a seat; squat; cower.

прискака́ть, -ачу́, -а́чешь *pf.* come galloping, arrive at a gallop; rush, tear.

приско́рбный sorrowful, regrettable, lamentable.

присла́ть, -ишлю́, -ишлёшь *pf.* (*impf.* **присыла́ть**) send, dispatch.

прислони́ть(ся, -оню́(сь, -о́ни́шь(ся *pf.*, **прислоня́ть(ся, -я́ю(сь** *impf.* lean, rest (**к**+*d.* against).

прислу́га, -и maid, servant; servants, domestics; crew. **прислу́живать, -аю** *impf.* (**к**+*d.*) wait (upon);~**ся к**+*d.* fawn upon, cringe to.

прислу́шаться, -аюсь *pf.*, **прислу́шиваться, -аюсь** *impf.* listen; +**к**+*d.* listen to; heed, pay attention to; get used to (the sound of), cease to notice.

присма́тривать, -аю *impf.*, **присмотре́ть, -рю́, -ришь** *pf.* look for, find; +**за**+*i.* look after, keep an eye on; supervise, superintend; ~ **за ребёнком** mind the baby; ~**ся** (**к**+*d.*) look closely (at); get accustomed, get used (to).

присни́ться, -ню́сь *pf.*

присовокупи́ть, -плю́ *pf.*, **присовокупля́ть, -я́ю** *impf.* add; attach.

присоедине́ние, -я joining; addition; annexation; connection. **присоедини́ть, -ню́** *pf.* **присоединя́ть, -я́ю** *impf.* join; add; annex; connect; ~**ся к**+*d.* join; associate o.s. with; ~ **к мне́нию** subscribe to an opinion.

приспосо́бить, -блю *pf.*, **приспособля́ть, -я́ю** *impf.* fit, adjust, adapt, accommodate; ~**ся** adapt o.s., accommodate o.s. **приспособле́ние, -я** adaptation, accommodation; device, contrivance; appliance, gadget. **приспосо́бленность, -и** fitness, suitability. **приспособля́емость, -и** adaptability.

при́став, -а; *pl.* **-а́** *or* **-ы** police officer, police sergeant.

придтава́ть, -таю́, -таёшь *impf. of* **приста́ть**

приста́вить, -влю *pf.* (*impf.* **приставля́ть**) **к**+*d.* put, place, set to, against; lean against; add to; appoint to look after.

приста́вка, -и prefix.

приставля́ть, -я́ю *impf. of* **приста́вить. приставн|о́й** added, attached; **~а́я ле́стница** step-ladder.

при́стальный fixed, intent.

при́стань, -и; *g.pl.* **-е́й** landing-stage, jetty; pier; wharf; refuge; haven.

приста́ть, -а́ну *pf.* (*impf.* **пристава́ть**) stick, adhere; attach o.s.; pester, bother, badger; put in, come alongside.

пристёгивать, -аю *impf.*, **пристегну́ть, -ну́, -нёшь** *pf.* fasten. **пристежно́й; ~ воротничо́к** separate collar.

пристра́ивать(ся, -аю(сь *impf. of* **пристро́ить(ся**

пристра́стие, -я weakness, predilection, passion; partiality, bias. **пристра́стный** partial, biased.

пристро́ить, -о́ю *pf.* (*impf.* **пристра́ивать**) add, build on; place, settle, fix up; **~ся** be placed, be settled, be fixed up, get a place; join up, form up. **пристро́йка, -и** annexe, extension; outhouse; lean-to.

при́ступ, -а assault, storm; fit, attack; bout, touch; access, approach. **приступа́ть, -а́ю** *impf.* **приступи́ть, -плю́, -пишь** *pf.* **к**+*d.* set about, start; get down to; approach; importune, pester. **присту́пок, -пка** step.

при|стыди́ть, -ыжу́ *pf.* **пристыжённый; -жён, -а́** ashamed.

при|стыкова́ться, -ку́ется *pf.*

пристя́жка, -и, пристяжна́я *sb.* trace-horse, outrunner.

присуди́ть, -ужу́, -у́дишь *pf.*, **присужда́ть, -а́ю** *impf.* sentence, condemn; award; confer; **~ к штра́фу** fine, impose a fine on. **присужде́ние, -я** awarding, adjudication; conferment.

прису́тственн|ый; ~ое ме́сто government office. **прису́тствие, -я** presence; attendance; government office; **~ ду́ха** presence of mind. **прису́тствовать, -твую** be present, attend. **прису́тствующ|ий** present; **~ие** *sb.*, *pl.* those present, present company.

прису́щий inherent; characteristic; distinctive.

присыла́ть, -а́ю *impf. of* **присла́ть**

прися́га, -и oath; **привести́ к прися́ге** swear in, administer the oath to. **присяга́ть, -а́ю** *impf.*, **присягну́ть, -ну́, -нёшь** *pf.* take one's oath, swear; **~ в ве́рности** swear allegiance.

прися́ду *etc.*: *see* **присе́сть**

прися́жный sworn; born, inveterate; **~ заседа́тель** juror, juryman; **~ пове́ренный** barrister.

прита́йться, -а́юсь *pf.* hide, conceal o.s.

прита́скивать, -аю *impf.*, **притащи́ть, -ащу́, -а́щишь** *pf.* bring, drag, haul; **~ся** drag o.s.

притвори́ться, -рю́сь *pf.*, **притворя́ться -я́юсь** *impf.*+*i.* pretend to be; feign; sham; **~ больны́м** pretend to be ill, feign illness. **притво́рный** pretended, feigned, sham. **притво́рство, -а** pretence, sham. **притво́рщик, -а** sham; dissembler, hypocrite.

притека́ть, -а́ю *impf. of* **прите́чь**

притесне́ние, -я oppression. **притесни́ть, -ню́** *pf.*, **притесня́ть, -я́ю** *impf.* oppress.

прите́чь, -ечёт, -еку́т; -ёк, -ла́ *pf.* (*impf.* **притека́ть**) flow in, pour in.

притиха́ть, -а́ю *impf.*, **прити́хнуть, -ну; -и́х** *pf.* quiet down, grow quiet, hush.

прито́к, -а tributary; flow, influx; intake.

прито́м *conj.* (and) besides.

прито́н, -а den, haunt.

при́торный sickly-sweet, luscious, cloying.

притра́гиваться, -аюсь *impf.*, **притро́нуться, -нусь** *pf.* touch.

притупи́ть, -плю́, -пишь *pf.*, **притупля́ть, -я́ю** *impf.* blunt, dull; deaden; **~ся** become blunt, lose its edge; become dull.

при́тча, -и parable.

притяга́тельный attractive, magnetic. **притя́гивать, -аю** *impf. of* **притяну́ть**

притяжа́тельный possessive.

притяже́ние, -я attraction; **земно́е ~** gravity.

притяза́ние, -я claim, pretension. **притяза́ть, -а́ю** *impf.* **на**+*a.* lay claim to, have pretensions to.

притя́нутый; ~ за́ уши, за́ волосы far fetched. **притяну́ть, -ну́, -нешь** *pf.* (*impf.* **притя́гивать**) draw, attract; drag (up), pull (up).

приуро́чивать, -аю *impf.*, **приуро́чить, -чу** *pf.* **к**+*d.* time for, time to coincide with.

приуса́дебный; ~ уча́сток personal plot individual holding.

приуча́ть, -а́ю *impf.*, **приучи́ть, -чу́, -чишь** *pf.* accustom; train, school.

прихва́рывать, -аю *impf.*, **прихворну́ть -ну́, -нёшь** *pf.* be unwell, be indisposed.

при́хвостень, -тня *m.* hanger-on.

прихлеба́тель, -я *m.* sponger, parasite.

прихо́д, -а coming, arrival; advent; receipts parish; **~ и расхо́д** credit and debit. **приходи́ть(ся, -ожу́(сь, -о́дишь(ся** *impf. of* **прийти́(сь. прихо́дный** receipt. **прихо́довать -дую** *impf.* (*pf.* **за~**) credit. **приходя́щ|ий** non-resident; **~ий больно́й** outpatient; **~ая домрабо́тница** daily (maid), char(woman).

прихотли́вый capricious, whimsical; fanciful intricate. **при́хоть, -и** whim, caprice, fancy.

прихра́мывать, -аю limp (slightly).

прице́л, -а sight; aiming. **прице́ливаться -аюсь** *impf.*, **прице́литься, -люсь** *pf.* aim take aim.

прицéниваться, -аюсь *impf.*, **прицени́ться, -ню́сь, -ни́шься** (**к**+*d.*) ask the price (of).

прицéп, -а trailer. **прицепи́ть, -плю́, -пишь** *pf.*, **прицепля́ть, -я́ю** *impf.* hitch, hook on; couple; **~ся к**+*d.* stick to, cling to; pester; nag at. **прицéпка, -и** hitching, hooking on; coupling; trailer; pestering; nagging. **прицепнóй; ~ вагóн** trailer.

причáл, -а mooring, making fast; mooring line; berth, moorings. **причáливать, -аю** *impf.*, **причáлить, -лю** *pf.* moor.

причáстие[1], **-я** participle. **причáстие**[2], **-я** communion.

причáстный[1] participial. **причáстный**[2] participating, concerned; involved; accessary, privy.

причём *conj.* moreover, and; while. **причём** *adv.* why? what for? **а ~ же я тут?** what has it to do with me?

причесáть, -ешу́, -éшешь *pf.*, **причёсывать, -аю** *impf.* brush, comb; do the hair (of); **~ся** do one's hair, have one's hair done. **причёска, -и** hair-do, hair-style; haircut.

причи́на, -ы cause; reason. **причини́ть, -ню́** *pf.*, **причиня́ть, -я́ю** *impf.* cause; occasion.

причи́слить, -лю *pf.*, **причисля́ть, -я́ю** *impf.* reckon, number, rank (**к**+*d.* among); add on; attach.

причитáние, -я lamentation.

причитáться, -áется *impf.* be due; **вам причитáется два рубля́** you have two roubles to come; **с вас причитáется два рубля́** you have two roubles to pay.

причу́да, -ы caprice, whim, fancy; oddity, vagary.

при|чу́диться, -ится *pf.*

причу́дливый odd, queer; fantastic; capricious, whimsical.

при|швартовáть, -ту́ю *pf.* **пришёл** *etc.*: *see* **прийти́**

приши́бленный crest-fallen, dejected.

пришивáть, -áю *impf.*, **приши́ть, -шью́, -шьёшь** *pf.* sew on, attach; nail (on).

пришлю́ *etc.*: *see* **прислáть**

пришпóривать, -аю *impf.*, **пришпóрить, -рю** *pf.* spur (on).

прищеми́ть, -млю́ *pf.* **прищемля́ть, -я́ю** *impf.* pinch, squeeze.

прищéпка, -и, прищéпок, -пка clothes-peg.

прищу́риваться, -аюсь *impf.*, **прищу́риться, -рюсь** *pf.* screw up one's eyes.

прию́т, -а asylum, orphanage; shelter, refuge. **приюти́ть, -ючу́** *pf.* shelter, give refuge; **~ся** take shelter.

прия́тель, -я *m.*, **прия́тельница, -ы** friend. **прия́тельский** friendly, amicable. **прия́тный** nice, pleasant, agreeable, pleasing; **~ на вкус** nice, palatable, tasty.

про *prep.*+*a.* about; for; **~ себя́** to o.s.

про... *pref. in comb.* **I.** *with vv. indicates action through, across, or past object*; *action continued throughout given period of time*; *overall or exhaustive action or effect*; *loss or failure.* **II.** *with nn. and adjs.*: pro-.

прóба, -ы trial, test; try-out; assay; hallmark; sample; standard, measure of fineness of gold; **зóлото 96-óй прóбы** 24-carat gold, pure gold.

пробéг, -а run; race; mileage, distance. **пробегáть, -áю** *impf.*, **пробежáть, -егу́** *pf.* run; cover; pass, run past, run by; run through; run along, run over.

пробéл, -а blank, gap; hiatus; lacuna; deficiency, flaw.

проберу́ *etc.*: *see* **пробрáть. пробивáть(ся, -áю(сь** *impf. of* **проби́ть(ся. пробирáть(ся, -áю(сь** *impf. of* **пробрáть(ся**

проби́рка, -и test-tube. **проби́рный** test, assay; **~ое клеймó** hallmark. **проби́ровать, -рую** *impf.* test, assay.

про|би́ть, -бью́, -бьёшь *pf.* (*impf. also* **пробивáть**) make a hole in; hole, pierce; punch; strike; **~ся** fight, force, make, one's way through; break through, strike through.

прóбка, -и cork; stopper; plug; fuse; (traffic) jam, blockage, congestion. **прóбковый** cork; **~ пóяс** life-belt, life-jacket.

проблéма, -ы problem. **проблемати́ческий** problematic(al).

прóблеск, -а flash; gleam, ray.

прóбный trial, test, experimental; hallmarked; **~ кáмень** touchstone. **прóбовать, -бую** *impf.* (*pf.* **ис~, по~**) try; attempt, endeavour; test; taste, feel.

пробóина, -ы hole.

проболтáться, -áюсь *pf.* blab, let out a secret; hang about.

пробóр, -а parting; **дéлать (себé) ~** part one's hair.

про|бормотáть, -очу́, -óчешь *pf.*

пробрáть, -беру́, -берёшь; -áл, -á, -о *pf.* (*impf.* **пробирáть**) go through; scold, rate; clear, weed; **~ся** make one's way; force one's way; steal (through); **~ óщупью** feel one's way.

пробу́ду *etc.*: *see* **пробы́ть**

про|буди́ть, -ужу́, -у́дишь *pf.*, **пробуждáть, -áю** *impf.* wake (up); awaken, rouse, arouse; **~ся** wake, wake up. **пробуждéние, -я** waking (up), awakening.

про|бурáвить, -влю *pf.*, **пробурáвливать, -аю** *impf.* bore (through), drill.

про|бурчáть, -чу́ *pf.*

пробы́ть, -бу́ду; прóбыл, -á, -о *pf.* remain, stay; be.

пробью́ *etc.*: *see* **проби́ть**

провáл, -а failure; flop; downfall; gap; funnel. **провáливать, -аю** *impf.*, **провали́ть, -лю́, -лишь** *pf.* cause to fall in, bring down; ruin, make a mess of; reject, fail; **~ся** collapse; fall in, come down; fall through; fail; disappear, vanish.

прованск|ий Provençal; **~ое мáсло** olive oil.

провéдать, -аю *pf.*, **провéдывать, -аю** *impf.* come to see, call on; find out, learn.

провезти́, -зу́, -зёшь; -ёз, -лá *pf.* (*impf.*

провози́ть) convey, transport; smuggle (through, in, out); bring.

прове́рить, -рю *pf.* **проверя́ть, -я́ю** *impf.* check, check up on; verify; audit; control; test; ~ **биле́ты** examine tickets; ~ **тетра́ди** correct exercise-books; ~ **на алкого́ль** breathalyse. **прове́рка, -и** checking, check; examination; verification; control; testing.

про|вести́, -еду́, -едёшь; -ёл, -а́ *pf.* (*impf. also* **проводи́ть**) lead, take; pilot; build; install; carry out, carry on; conduct, hold; carry through; carry; pass; advance, put forward; draw; spend; +*i.* pass over, run over; ~ **в жизнь** put into effect, put into practice; ~ **водопрово́д** lay on water; ~ **вре́мя** pass the time; ~ **черту́** draw a line; **хорошо́** ~ **вре́мя** have a good time.

прове́тривать, -аю *impf.*, **прове́трить, -рю** *pf.* air; ventilate.

про|ве́ять, -е́ю *pf.*

провиде́ние, -я Providence. **прови́деть, -и́жу** *impf.* foresee.

прови́зия, -и provisions.

провизо́рный preliminary, provisional; temporary.

провини́ться, -ню́сь *pf.* be guilty; do wrong; ~ **пе́ред**+*i.* wrong.

провинциа́льный provincial. **прови́нция, -и** province; the provinces.

про́вод, -а; *pl.* **-а́** wire, lead, conductor. **проводи́мость, -и** conductivity; conductance. **проводи́ть**[1], **-ожу́, -о́дишь** *impf. of* **провести́** conduct, be a conductor.

проводи́ть[2], **-ожу́, -о́дишь** *pf.* (*impf.* **провожа́ть**) accompany; see off; ~ **глаза́ми** follow with one's eyes; ~ **домо́й** see home.

прово́дка, -и leading, taking; building; installation; wiring, wires.

проводни́к[1], **-а́** guide; conductor, guard.

проводни́к[2], **-а́** conductor; bearer; transmitter. **проводно́й** wire, line.

про́воды, -ов *pl.* seeing off, send-off. **провожа́тый** *sb.* guide, escort. **провожа́ть, -а́ю** *impf. of* **проводи́ть**

прово́з, -а carriage, conveyance, transport.

провозгласи́ть, -ашу́ *pf.*, **провозглаша́ть, -а́ю** *impf.* proclaim, declare; announce; +*i.* proclaim, hail as; ~ **тост** propose a toast. **провозглаше́ние, -я** proclamation; declaration.

провози́ть, -ожу́, -о́зишь *impf. of* **провезти́**

провока́тор, -а agent provocateur; instigator, provoker. **провокацио́нный** provocative. **провока́ция, -и** provocation. **про́волока, -и** wire. **про́волочн|ый** wire; ~**ая сеть** wire netting.

прово́рный quick, swift, prompt; agile, nimble, adroit, dexterous. **прово́рство, -а** quickness, swiftness; agility, nimbleness, adroitness, dexterity.

провоци́ровать, -рую *impf.* & *pf.* (*pf.* **с**~) provoke.

про|вя́лить, -лю *pf.*

прогада́ть, -а́ю *pf.*, **прога́дывать, -аю** *impf.* miscalculate.

прога́лина, -ы glade; (clear) space.

прогла́тывать, -аю *impf.*, **проглоти́ть, -очу́, -о́тишь** *pf.* swallow.

прогляде́ть, -яжу́ *pf.*, **прогля́дывать**[1], **-аю** *impf.* overlook, miss; look through, glance through. **проглянуть, -я́нет** *pf.*, **прогля́дывать**[2], **-ает** *impf.* show, show through, peep out, peep through, appear.

прогна́ть, -гоню́, -го́нишь; -а́л, -а́, -о *pf.* (*impf.* **прогоня́ть**) drive away; banish; drive; sack, fire.

про|гневи́ть, -влю́ *pf.*

прогнива́ть, -а́ет *impf.*, **прогни́ть, -ниёт; -и́л, -а́, -о** *pf.* rot through, be rotten.

прогно́з, -а prognosis; (weather) forecast. **прогнози́рование, -я** forecasting. **прогнози́ст, -а** forecaster.

проголода́ться, -а́юсь *pf.* get hungry, grow hungry.

про|голосова́ть, -су́ю *pf.* **прогоня́ть, -я́ю** *impf. of* **прогна́ть**

прогора́ть, -а́ю *impf.*, **прогоре́ть, -рю́** *pf.* burn; burn out; get burnt; go bankrupt, go bust.

прого́рклый rancid, rank.

програ́мма, -ы programme; schedule; syllabus, curriculum. **программи́ровать, -рую** *impf.* (*pf.* **за**~) programme.

прогре́в, -а warming up. **прогрева́ть, -а́ю** *impf.*, **прогре́ть, -е́ю** *pf.* heat, warm thoroughly; warm up; ~**ся** get warmed through, get thoroughly warmed; warm up.

про|греме́ть, -млю́ *pf.*

прогре́сс, -а progress. **прогресси́вный** progressive. **прогресси́ровать, -рую** *impf.* progress, make progress.

про|грохота́ть, -очу́, -о́чешь *pf.*

прогрыза́ть, -а́ю *impf.*, **прогры́зть, -зу́, -зёшь; -ы́з** *pf.* gnaw through.

про|гуде́ть, -гужу́ *pf.*

прогу́л, -а absence (from work); absenteeism. **прогу́ливать, -аю** *impf.*, **прогуля́ть, -я́ю** *pf.* be absent from work; miss; take for a walk, walk; ~ **уро́ки** (play) truant; ~**ся** stroll, saunter; take a walk. **прогу́лка, -и** walk, stroll; ramble; outing. **прогу́льщик, -а** absentee, truant.

прод... *abbr.* (*of* **продово́льственный**) *in comb.* food-, provision-. **продма́г, -а** grocery; provision-shop. ~**пу́нкт, -а** food centre. ~**това́ры, -ов** *pl.* food products.

продава́ть, -даю́, -даёшь *impf.*, **прода́ть, -а́м, -а́шь, -а́ст, -ади́м; про́дал, -а́, -о** *pf.* sell. **продава́ться, -даётся** *impf.* be for sale; sell. **продаве́ц, -вца́** seller, vender; salesman; shop-assistant. **продавщи́ца, -ы** seller, vendor; saleswoman; shop-assistant, shop-girl. **прода́жа, -и** sale, selling. **прода́жный** for sale, to be sold; mercenary, venal.

продвига́ть, -а́ю *impf.*, **продви́нуть, -ну** *pf.* move forward, push forward; promote, further, advance; **~ся** advance; move on, move forward; push on, push forward, forge ahead; be promoted.

про|декламировать, -рую *pf.*

проделать, -аю *pf.*, **проделывать, -аю** *impf.* do, perform, accomplish. **проделка, -и** trick; prank, escapade.

продёргивать, -аю *impf. of* **продёрнуть**

продержать, -жу, -жишь *pf.* hold; keep; **~ся** hold out.

продёрнуть, -ну, -нешь *pf.* (*impf.* **продёргивать**) pass, run; put through; criticize, pull to pieces; **~ нитку в иголку** thread a needle.

продешевить, -влю *pf.* sell too cheap.

про|диктовать, -тую *pf.*

продлевать, -аю *impf.*, **продлить, -лю** *pf.* extend, prolong. **продление, -я** extension, prolongation. **про|длиться, -ится** *pf.*

продмаг, -а grocer's (shop).

продовольственн|ый food, provision; **~ая карточка** ration book, ration card; **~ый магазин** grocery, provision shop. **продовольствие, -я** food, food-stuffs; provisions.

продолговатый oblong.

продолжатель, -я *m.* continuer, successor. **продолжать, -аю** *impf.*, **продолжить, -жу** *pf.* continue, go on (with), proceed (with); extend, prolong; **~ся** continue, last, go on, be in progress. **продолжение, -я** continuation; sequel; extension, prolongation; **в ~**+*g.* in the course of, during, for, throughout; **~ следует** to be continued. **продолжительность, -и** duration, length. **продолжительный** long; prolonged, protracted.

продольный longitudinal, lengthwise, linear.

продрогнуть, -ну; -ог *pf.* be chilled to the marrow, be half-frozen.

продукт, -а product; produce; provisions, food-stuffs; **натуральные ~ы** wholefoods. **продуктивно** *adv.* productively; to good effect, with a good result. **продуктивность, -и** productivity. **продуктивный** productive; fruitful. **продуктовый** food, provision; **~ магазин** grocery, food-shop.

продукция, -и production, output.

продумать, -аю *pf.*, **продумывать, -аю** *impf.* think over; think out.

продырявить, -влю *pf.* make a hole in, pierce.

продюсер, -а (film-)producer.

проедать, -аю *impf. of* **проесть. проеду** *etc.*: *see* **проехать**

проезд, -а passage, thoroughfare; journey; «**~а нет**» 'no thoroughfare'. **проездить, -зжу** *pf.* (*impf.* **проезжать**) spend on a journey, spend in travelling; spend travelling (driving, riding). **проездн|ой** travelling; **~ой билет** ticket; **~ая плата** fare; **~ые** *sb.*, *pl.* travelling expenses. **проездом** *adv.* en route, in transit, while passing through. **проезжать, -аю** *impf. of* **проездить, проехать. проезж|ий** passing (by); **~ая дорога** highway, thoroughfare; **~ий** *sb.* passer-by.

проект, -а project, scheme, design; draft; **~ договора** draft treaty; **~ резолюции** draft resolution. **проектировать, -рую** *impf.* (*pf.* **с~**) project; plan, design. **проектный** planning, designing; planned. **проектор, -а** projector.

проекционный; ~ фонарь projector. **проекция, -и** projection.

проесть, -ем, -ешь, -ест, -едим; -ел *pf.* (*impf.* **проедать**) eat through, corrode; spend on food.

проехать, -еду *pf.* (*impf.* **проезжать**) pass by, through; drive by, through; ride by, through; go past, pass; go, do, make, cover.

прожаренный well-done.

прожектор, -а; *pl.* **-ы** *or* **-а** searchlight; floodlight.

прожечь, -жгу, -жжёшь; -жёг, -жгла *pf.* (*impf.* **прожигать**) burn; burn through.

проживать, -аю *impf. of* **прожить**

прожигать, -аю *impf. of* **прожечь**

прожиточный enough to live on; **~ минимум** living wage. **прожить, -иву, -ивёшь; -ожил, -а, -о** *pf.* (*impf.* **проживать**) live; spend; run through.

прожорливый voracious, gluttonous.

проза, -ы prose. **прозаический** prose; prosaic; prosy.

прозвание, -я, прозвище, -а nickname. **прозвать, -зову, -зовёшь; -ал, -а, -о** *pf.* (*impf.* **прозывать**) nickname, name.

про|зевать, -аю *pf.* **про|зимовать, -мую** *pf.*

прозову *etc.*: *see* **прозвать**

прозодежда, -ы *abr.* working clothes; overalls.

прозорливый sagacious; perspicacious.

прозрачный transparent; limpid, pellucid.

прозывать, -аю *impf. of* **прозвать**

прозябание, -я vegetation. **прозябать, -аю** *impf.* vegetate.

проиграть, -аю *pf.*, **проигрывать, -аю** *impf.* lose; play; **~ся** lose everything, gamble away all one's money. **проигрыватель, -я** *m.* record-player; **~ компакт-дисков** CD player. **проигрыш, -а** loss.

произведение, -я work; production; product. **произвести, -еду, -едёшь; -ёл, -а** *pf.*, **производить, -ожу, -одишь** *impf.* make; carry out; execute; produce; cause; effect; give birth to; +**в**+*a./nom. pl.* promote to (the rank of); **~ впечатление** make an impression, create an impression; **~ на свет** bring into the world. **производительность, -и** productivity, output; productiveness. **производительный** productive; efficient. **производн|ый** derivative, derived; **~ое слово** derivative. **производственный** industrial; production; commercial; **~ стаж** industrial experience, industrial work record. **производство, -а** production, manufacture; factory, works; carrying out, execution.

произвол, -а arbitrariness; arbitrary rule; **оставить на ~ судьбы** leave to the mercy of fate; **чини́ть ~** impose arbitrary rule. **произво́льный** arbitrary.

произнести́, -су́, -сёшь; -ёс, -ла́ *pf.*, **произноси́ть, -ошу́, -о́сишь** *impf.* pronounce; articulate; say, utter; **~ речь** deliver a speech. **произноше́ние, -я** pronunciation; articulation.

произойти́, -ойдёт; -ошёл, -шла́ *pf.* (*impf.* **происходи́ть**) happen, occur, take place; spring, arise, result; come, descend, be descended.

про|инструкти́ровать, -рую *pf.*

про́иски, -ов *pl.* intrigues; machinations, schemes, underhand plotting.

проистека́ть, -а́ет *impf.*, **происте́чь, -ечёт; -ёк, -ла́** *pf.* spring, result; stem.

происходи́ть, -ожу́, -о́дишь *impf. of* **произойти́**; go on, be going on. **происхожде́ние, -я** origin; provenance; parentage, descent, extraction, birth; **по происхожде́нию** by birth.

происше́ствие, -я event, incident, happening, occurrence; accident.

пройти́, -йду́, -йдёшь; -ошёл, -шла́ *pf.* (*impf.* **проходи́ть**) pass; go; go past, go by, elapse; do, cover; be over; pass off, abate, let up; go off; take, study, learn; go through, get through; fall; **~ в**+*a./nom. pl.*, become, be made; be taken on; **ему́ э́то да́ром не пройдёт** he will have to pay for it; **~ ми́мо** pass by, go by, go past; overlook, disregard; **~ че́рез** pass, get through; **э́то не пройдёт** it won't work; **~сь** walk up and down; take a stroll, a walk; dance.

прок, -а (-у) use benefit.

прокажённый *sb.* leper. **прока́за¹, -ы** leprosy.

прока́за², -ы mischief, prank, trick. **прока́зить, -а́жу** *impf.*, **прока́зничать, -аю** *impf.* (*pf.* **на~**) be up to mischief, play pranks. **прока́зник, -а** mischievous child.

прока́лывать, -аю *impf. of* **проколо́ть**

прока́т, -а hire.

прокати́ться, -ачу́сь, -а́тишься *pf.* roll; go for a drive, go for a run.

прока́тный rolling; rolled; **~ стан** rolling-mill.

прокипяти́ть, -ячу́ *pf.* boil; boil thoroughly.

прокиса́ть, -а́ет *impf.*, **про|ки́снуть, -нет** *pf.* turn (sour).

прокла́дка, -и laying; building, construction; washer, gasket; packing. **прокла́дывать, -аю** *impf. of* **проложи́ть**

проклама́ция, -и proclamation, leaflet.

проклина́ть, -а́ю *impf.*, **прокля́сть, -яну́, -янёшь; -о́клял, -а́, -о** *pf.* curse, damn; swear at. **прокля́тие, -я** curse; damnation, perdition; imprecation. **прокля́тый; -я́т, -а́, -о** accursed, damned; damnable, confounded.

проколо́ть, -лю́, -лешь *pf.* (*impf.* **прока́лывать**) prick, pierce; perforate; run through.

про|компости́ровать, -рую *pf.* **про|конспекти́ровать, -рую** *pf.* **про|консульти́ровать(ся, -рую(сь** *pf.* **про|контроли́ровать, -рую** *pf.*

проко́рм, -а nourishment, sustenance.

про|корми́ть(ся, -млю́(сь, -мишь(ся *pf.*

про|корректи́ровать, -рую *pf.*

прокра́дываться, -аюсь *impf.*, **прокра́сться, -аду́сь, -адёшься** *pf.* steal in.

про|кукаре́кать, -ает *pf.* **про|кукова́ть, -ку́ю** *pf.*

прокуро́р, -а public prosecutor; procurator; investigating magistrate.

прокути́ть, -учу́, -у́тишь *pf.*, **проку́чивать, -аю** *impf.* squander, dissipate; go on the spree, go on the binge.

пролага́ть, -а́ю *impf. of* **проложи́ть**

пролега́ть, -а́ет *impf.* lie, run.

про́лежень, -жня *m.* bedsore.

пролеза́ть, -а́ю *impf.*, **проле́зть, -зу; -ле́з** *pf.* get through, climb through; get in, worm o.s. in.

про|лепета́ть, -ечу́, -е́чешь *pf.*

пролёт, -а span; stair-well; bay.

пролетариа́т, -а proletariat. **пролета́рий, -я** proletarian; **пролета́рии всех стран, соединя́йтесь!** workers of the world, unite! **пролета́рский** proletarian.

пролета́ть, -а́ю *impf.*, **пролете́ть, -ечу́** *pf.* fly; cover; fly by, fly past, fly through; flash, flit.

проли́в, -а strait, sound. **пролива́ть, -а́ю** *impf.*, **проли́ть, -лью́, -льёшь; -о́ли́л, -а́, -о** *pf.* spill, shed; **~ свет на**+*a.* throw light on; shed light on.

проложи́ть, -жу́, -жишь *pf.* (*impf.* **прокла́дывать, пролага́ть**) lay; build, construct; interlay; insert; interleave; **~ доро́гу** build a road; pave the way, blaze a trail; **~ себе́ доро́гу** carve one's way.

проло́м, -а breach, break; gap; fracture. **пролома́ть, -а́ю** *pf.* break, break through.

пролью́ *etc.*: *see* **проли́ть**

пром... *abbr.* (*of* **промы́шленный**) *in comb.* industrial. **промтова́ры, -ов** *pl.* manufactured goods. **~финпла́н, -а** industrial and financial plan.

про|ма́зать, -а́жу *pf.* **прома́тывать(ся, -аю(сь** *impf. of* **промота́ть(ся**

про́мах, -а miss; slip, blunder. **прома́хиваться, -аюсь** *impf.*, **промахну́ться, -ну́сь, -нёшься** *pf.* miss; miss the mark; miscue; be wide of the mark, make a mistake, miss an opportunity.

прома́чивать, -аю *impf. of* **промочи́ть**

промедле́ние, -я delay; procrastination. **проме́длить, -лю** *pf.* delay, dally; procrastinate.

промежу́ток, -тка interval; space. **промежу́точный** intermediate; intervening; interim.

промелькну́ть, -ну́, -нёшь *pf.* flash; flash past, fly by; be perceptible, be discernible.

проме́нивать, -аю *impf.*, **променя́ть, -я́ю** *pf.* exchange, trade, barter; change.

промерза́ть, -а́ю *impf.*, **промёрзнуть, -ну; -ёрз** *pf.* freeze through. **промёрзлый** frozen.

промока́тельн|ый; ~ая бума́га blotting-paper. **промока́ть, -а́ю** *impf.*, **промо́кнуть, -ну; -мо́к** *pf.* get soaked, get drenched.

промо́лвить, -влю *pf.* say, utter.

про|мота́ть, -а́ю *pf.* (*impf. also* **прома́тывать**) squander; **~ся** run through one's money.

промочи́ть, -чу́, -чишь *pf.* (*impf.* **прома́чивать**) get wet (through); soak, drench; **~ но́ги** get one's feet wet.

промо́ю *etc.*: *see* **промы́ть**

промча́ться, -чу́сь *pf.* tear, dart, rush (by, past, through); fly.

промыва́ние, -я washing (out, down); bathing; irrigation. **промыва́ть, -а́ю** *impf. of* **промы́ть**

про́мысел, -сла trade, business; *pl.* works; **го́рный ~** mining; **охо́тничий ~** hunting, trapping; **ры́бный ~** fishing, fishery. **промысло́в|ый** producers'; business; hunters', trappers'; game; **~ая коопера́ция** producers' cooperative.

промы́ть, -мо́ю *pf.* (*impf.* **промыва́ть**) wash well, wash thoroughly; bathe, irrigate; wash; scrub; **~ мозги́**+*d.* brain-wash.

про|мыча́ть, -чу́ *pf.*

промы́шленник, -а manufacturer, industrialist. **промы́шленность, -и** industry. **промы́шленный** industrial.

про|мя́млить, -лю *pf.*

пронести́, -су́, -сёшь; -ёс, -ла́ *pf.* (*impf.* **проноси́ть**) carry; carry by, past, through; pass (over), be over, be past; **~сь** rush by, past, through; scud (past); fly; be carried, spread; **пронёсся слух** there was a rumour.

пронза́ть, -а́ю *impf.*, **пронзи́ть, -нжу́** *pf.* pierce, run through, transfix. **пронзи́тельный** penetrating; piercing; shrill, strident.

пронiза́ть, -ижу́, -и́жешь *pf.*, **прони́зывать, -аю** *impf.* pierce; permeate, penetrate; run through. **прони́зывающий** piercing, penetrating.

проника́ть, -а́ю *impf.*, **прони́кнуть, -ну; -и́к** *pf.* penetrate; percolate; run through; **~ся** be imbued, be filled. **проникнове́ние, -я** penetration; feeling; heartfelt conviction. **проникнове́нный** full of feeling; heartfelt. **прони́кнутый**+*i.* imbued with, full of.

проница́емый permeable, pervious. **проница́тельный** penetrating; perspicacious; acute, shrewd.

проноси́ть(ся, -ошу́(сь, -о́сишь(ся *impf. of* **пронести́(сь** **про|нумерова́ть, -ру́ю** *pf.*

проны́рливый pushful, pushing.

проню́хать, -аю *pf.*, **проню́хивать, -аю** *impf.* smell out, nose out, get wind of.

прообраз, -а prototype.

пропага́нда, -ы propaganda. **пропаганди́ровать, -рую** *impf.* engage in propaganda (for); propagandize. **пропаганди́ст, -а** propagandist.

пропада́ть, -а́ю *impf. of* **пропа́сть. пропа́жа, -и** loss; lost object, missing thing.

пропа́лывать, -аю *impf. of* **пропо́лоть**

пропа́н, -а propane.

про́пасть, -и precipice; abyss; a mass, masses.

пропа́сть, -аду́, -адёшь *pf.* (*impf.* **пропада́ть**) be missing; be lost; disappear, vanish; be done for, die; be wasted; **мы пропа́ли** we're lost, we're done for; **~ бе́з вести** be missing.

пропека́ть(ся, -а́ю(сь *impf. of* **пропе́чь(ся.**

про|пе́ть, -пою́, -поёшь *pf.*

пропе́чь, -еку́, -ечёшь; -ёк, -ла́ *pf.* (*impf.* **пропека́ть**) bake well, bake thoroughly; **~ся** bake well; get baked through.

пропива́ть, -а́ю *impf. of* **пропи́ть**

прописа́ть, -ишу́, -и́шешь *pf.*, **пропи́сывать, -аю** *impf.* prescribe; register; **~ся** register. **пропи́ска, -и** registration; residence permit. **прописн|о́й** capital; commonplace, trivial; **~а́я бу́ква** capital letter; **~а́я и́стина** truism. **про́пись, -и** copy; copy-book maxim. **про́писью** *adv.* in words, in full; **писа́ть ци́фры ~** write out figures in words.

пропита́ние, -я subsistence, sustenance, food; **зарабо́тать себе́ на ~** earn one's living. **пропита́ть, -а́ю** *pf.*, **пропи́тывать, -аю** *impf.* impregnate, saturate; soak, steep; keep, provide for; **~ся** be saturated, be steeped; keep o.s.

пропи́ть, -пью́, -пьёшь; -о́пи́л, -а́, -о *pf.* (*impf.* **пропива́ть**) spend on drink, squander on drink.

пропл́ыв, -а (swimming) race, heat. **проплыва́ть, -а́ю** *impf.*, **проплы́ть, -ыву́, -ывёшь; -ы́л, -а́, -о** *pf.* swim, swim by, past, through; sail by, past, through; float; drift by, past, through; **~ стометро́вку** swim the hundred metres.

пропове́довать, -дую *impf.* preach; advocate. **про́поведь, -и** sermon; homily; preaching, advocacy; **наго́рная ~** Sermon on the Mount.

пропо́лка, -и weeding. **пропо́лоть, -лю́, -лешь** *pf.* (*impf.* **пропа́лывать**) weed.

про|полоска́ть, -ощу́, -о́щешь *pf.*

пропорциона́льный proportional, proportionate. **пропо́рция, -и** proportion; ratio.

про́пуск, -а; *pl.* **-а́** *or* **-и, -о́в** *or* **-ов** pass, permit; password; admission; omission, lapse; absence, non-attendance; blank, gap. **пропуска́ть, -а́ю** *impf.*, **пропусти́ть, -ущу́, -у́стишь** *pf.* let pass, let through; let in, admit; absorb; pass; omit, leave out; skip; miss; let slip; **~ ми́мо уше́й** pay no heed to, turn a deaf ear to; **не пропуска́ть воды́** be waterproof; **пропуска́ть во́ду** leak. **пропускн|о́й; ~а́я бума́га** blotting-paper; **~о́й свет** transmitted light; **~а́я спосо́бность** capacity.

пропью́ *etc.*: *see* **пропи́ть**

прораба́тывать, -аю *impf.*, **прорабо́тать, -аю** *pf.* work, work through; work at, study; get up; slate, pick holes in. **прорабо́тка, -и**

study, studying, getting up; slating.

прораста́ть, -а́ет *impf.*, **прорасти́, -тёт; -ро́с, -ла́** *pf.* germinate, sprout, shoot.

прорва́ть, -ву́, -вёшь; -а́л, -а́, -о *pf.* (*impf.* **прорыва́ть**) break through; tear, make a hole in; burst; ~ **блока́ду** run the blockade; ~**ся** burst open, break; tear; break out, break through.

про|реаги́ровать, -рую *pf.*

проре́з, -а cut; slit, notch, nick. **про|ре́зать, -е́жу** *pf.*, **прореза́ть, -а́ю** *impf.* (*impf. also* **проре́зывать**) cut through; ~**ся** be cut, come through.

прорези́нивать, -аю *impf.*, **прорези́нить, -ню** *pf.* rubberize. **проре́зывать(ся, -аю(сь** *impf. of* **проре́зать(ся. про|репети́ровать, -рую** *pf.*

проре́ха, -и rent, tear, slit; fly, flies; gap, deficiency.

про|рецензи́ровать, -рую *pf.*

проро́к, -а prophet.

проро́с *etc.*: *see* **прорасти́**

產рони́ть, -ню́, -нишь *pf.* utter, breathe, drop.

проро́ческий prophetic, oracular. **проро́чество, -а** prophecy **проро́чить, -чу** *impf.* (*pf.* **на**~) prophesy; predict.

проро́ю *etc.*: *see* **проры́ть**

проруба́ть, -а́ю *impf.*, **прорруби́ть, -блю́, -бишь** *pf.* cut through, hack through; break. **про́рубь, -и** ice-hole.

проры́в, -а break; break-through, breach; hitch, hold-up. **ликвиди́ровать** ~ put things right; **по́лный** ~ breakdown. **прорыва́ть**[1]**(ся, -а́ю(сь** *impf. of* **прорва́ть(ся**

прорыва́ть[2]**, -а́ю** *impf.*, **проры́ть, -ро́ю** *pf.* dig through; ~**ся** dig one's way through, tunnel through.

проса́чиваться, -ается *impf. of* **просочи́ться**

просве́рливать, -аю *impf.*, **про|сверли́ть, -лю́** *pf.* drill, bore; perforate, pierce.

просве́т, -а (clear) space; shaft of light; ray of hope; aperture, opening. **просвети́тельный** educational; cultural. **просвети́тельство, -а** educational activities, cultural activities. **просвети́ть**[1]**, -ещу́** *pf.* (*impf.* **просвеща́ть**) educate; enlighten.

просвети́ть[2]**, -ечу́, -е́тишь** *pf.* (*impf.* **просве́чивать**) X-ray.

просветле́ние, -я clearing-up; brightening (up); clarity, lucidity. **просветлённый** clear, lucid. **про|светле́ть, -е́ет** *pf.*

просве́чивание, -я fluoroscopy; radioscopy. **просве́чивать, -аю** *impf. of* **просвети́ть**; be translucent; be visible; show, appear, shine.

просвеща́ть, -а́ю *impf. of* **просвети́ть. просвеще́ние, -я** enlightenment; education, instruction; **наро́дное** ~ public education. **просвещённый** enlightened; educated, cultured.

про́седь, -и streak(s) of grey; **во́лосы с** ~**ю** greying hair.

просе́ивать, -аю *impf. of* **просе́ять**

про́сека, -и cutting, ride.

просёлок, -лка country road, cart-track.

просе́ять, -е́ю *pf.* (*impf.* **просе́ивать**) sift, riddle, screen.

про|сигнализи́ровать, -рую *pf.*

просиде́ть, -ижу́ *pf.*, **проси́живать, -аю** *impf.* sit; ~ **всю ночь** sit up all night.

проси́тель, -я *m.* applicant; supplicant; petitioner. **проси́тельный** pleading. **проси́ть, -ошу́, -о́сишь** *impf.* (*pf.* **по**~) ask; beg; plead, intercede; invite; **«про́сят не кури́ть»** 'No smoking, please'; ~**ся** ask; apply.

просия́ть, -я́ю *pf.* brighten; begin to shine; beam, light up.

проска́кивать, -аю *impf. of* **проскочи́ть**

проска́льзывать, -аю *impf.*, **проскользну́ть, -ну́, -нёшь** *pf.* slip in, creep in; ~ **ми́мо** slip past.

проскочи́ть, -чу́, -о́чишь *pf.* (*impf.* **проска́кивать**) rush, tear; slip through; slip in, creep in.

про|сла́бить, -бит *pf.*

просла́вить, -влю *pf.*, **прославля́ть, -я́ю** *impf.* glorify; bring fame to; make famous; ~**ся** become famous, be renowned. **просла́вленный** famous, renowned, celebrated, illustrious.

проследи́ть, -ежу́ *pf.* track (down); trace.

прослези́ться, -ежу́сь *pf.* shed a tear, a few tears.

прослои́ть, -ою́ *pf.* layer; sandwich. **просло́йка, -и** layer, stratum; seam, streak.

про|слу́шать, -аю *pf.*, **прослу́шивать, -аю** *impf.* hear; listen to; miss, not catch.

про|слы́ть, -ыву́, -ывёшь; -ы́л, -а́, -о *pf.*

просма́тривать, -аю *impf.*, **просмотре́ть, -рю́, -ришь** *pf.* look over, look through; glance over, glance through; survey; view; run over; overlook, miss. **просмо́тр, -а** survey; view, viewing; examination; **закры́тый** ~ private view; **предвари́тельный** ~ preview.

просну́ться, -ну́сь, -нёшься *pf.* (*impf.* **просыпа́ться**) wake up, awake.

про́со, -а millet.

просо́вывать(ся, -аю(сь *impf. of* **просу́нуть(ся**

про|со́хнуть, -ну; -о́х *pf.* (*impf. also* **просыха́ть**) get dry, dry out. **просо́хший** dried.

просочи́ться, -и́тся *pf.* (*impf.* **проса́чиваться**) percolate; filter; leak, ooze; seep out; filter through, leak out.

проспа́ть, -плю́; -а́л, -а́, -о *pf.* (*impf.* **просыпа́ть**) sleep (for, through); oversleep; miss.

проспе́кт, -а avenue; prospectus; summary.

проспо́рить, -рю *pf.* lose, lose a bet; argue.

про|спряга́ть, -а́ю *pf.*

просро́чен|ный overdue; out-of-date, expired; **па́спорт** ~ the passport is out of date. **просро́чивать, -аю** *impf.*, **просро́чить, -чу** *pf.* allow to run out; be behind with; overstay; ~ **о́тпуск** overstay one's leave. **просро́чка, -и** delay; expiration of time limit.

проста́к, -а́ simpleton. **просте́йший** *superl. of* **просто́й**

просте́нок, -нка pier; partition.

простере́ться, -трётся; -тёрся *pf.*, **простира́ться, -а́ется** *impf.* stretch, extend.

прости́тельный pardonable, excusable, justifiable.

проститу́тка, -и prostitute. **проститу́ция, -и** prostitution.

прости́ть, -ощу́ *pf.* (*impf.* **проща́ть**) forgive, pardon; excuse; **~ся** (**с**+*i.*) say goodbye (to), take (one's) leave (of), bid farewell.

про́сто *adv.* simply; **~ так** for no particular reason.

просто... *in comb.* simple; open; mere. **простоволо́сый** bare-headed, with head uncovered. **~ду́шный** open-hearted; simple-hearted, simple-minded; ingenuous, artless. **~ква́ша, -и** (thick) sour milk, yoghurt. **~люди́н, -а** man of the common people. **~наро́дный** of the common people. **~ре́чие, -я** popular speech; **в ~ре́чии** colloquially. **~ре́чный** popular, of popular speech. **~серде́чный** simple-hearted; frank; open.

просто́й, -я standing idle, enforced idleness; stoppage.

прост|о́й simple; easy; ordinary; plain; unaffected, unpretentious; mere; **~ы́м гла́зом** with the naked eye; **~ы́е лю́ди** ordinary people; **~о́й наро́д** the common people; **~о́е предложе́ние** simple sentence; **~о́е число́** prime number. **про́сто-на́просто** *adv.* simply.

просто́р, -а spaciousness; space, expanse; freedom, scope; elbow-room; **дать ~** give scope, free range, full play. **просто́рн|ый** spacious, roomy; ample; **здесь ~о** there is plenty of room here.

простота́, -ы́ simplicity.

простра́нный extensive, vast; diffuse; verbose. **простра́нственный** spatial. **простра́нство, -а** space; expanse; area.

простре́л, -а lumbago. **простре́ливать, -аю** *impf.*, **прострели́ть, -лю́, -лишь** *pf.* shoot through.

прострётся *etc.*: *see* **простере́ться**

про|строчи́ть, -очу́, -о́чишь *pf.*

просту́да, -ы cold; chill. **простуди́ть, -ужу́, -у́дишь** *pf.*, **простужа́ть, -а́ю** *impf.* let catch cold; **~ся** catch (a) cold, a chill.

просту́пок, -пка fault; misdemeanour.

просты́нн|ый sheet; **~ое полотно́** sheeting. **простыня́, -и́**; *pl.* **про́стыни, -ы́нь, -ня́м** sheet.

просты́ть, -ы́ну *pf.* get cold; cool; catch cold.

просу́нуть, -ну *pf.* (*impf.* **просо́вывать**) push, shove, thrust; **~ся** push through, force one's way through.

просу́шивать, -аю *impf.*, **просуши́ть, -шу́, -шишь** *pf.* dry (*thoroughly, properly*); **~ся** dry, get dry. **просу́шка, -и** drying.

просуществова́ть, -тву́ю *pf.* exist; last, endure.

просчита́ться, -а́юсь *pf.*, **просчи́тываться, -аюсь** *impf.* miscalculate.

про́сы́п, -а (-у); без ~у without waking, without stirring.

просыпа́ть, -плю́ *pf.*, **просыпа́ть**[1], **-а́ю** *impf.* spill; **~ся** spill, get spilt.

просыпа́ть[2], **-а́ю** *impf.* of **проспа́ть. просыпа́ться, -а́юсь** *impf. of* **просну́ться. просыха́ть, -а́ю** *impf. of* **просо́хнуть**

про́сьба, -ы request; application, petition; **«~ не кури́ть»** 'No smoking, please'; **у меня́ к вам ~** I have a favour to ask you.

прота́лкивать, -аю *impf. of* **протолкну́ть. прота́пливать, -аю** *impf. of* **протопи́ть**

прота́скивать, -аю *impf.*, **протащи́ть, -щу́, -щишь** *pf.* pull, drag, trail.

проте́з, -а artificial limb; (*artificial*) aid; prosthesis, prosthetic appliance; **зубно́й ~** false teeth, denture; **слухово́й ~** hearing aid. **проте́зный** prosthetic.

протека́ть, -а́ет *impf. of* **проте́чь. протёкший** past, last.

проте́кция, -и patronage, influence.

протере́ть, -тру́, -трёшь; -тёр *pf.* (*impf.* **протира́ть**) wipe (over); wipe dry; rub (through).

проте́ст, -а protest; objection.

протеста́нт, -а Protestant. **протеста́нтский** Protestant. **протеста́нтство, -а** Protestantism.

протестова́ть, -ту́ю *impf.* & *pf.* (**про́тив**+*g.*) protest (against), object (to).

проте́чь, -ечёт; -тёк, -ла́ *pf.* (*impf.* **протека́ть**) flow, run; leak; ooze, seep; elapse, pass; take its course.

про́тив *prep.*+*g.* against; opposite; facing; contrary to, as against; in proportion to, according to; **име́ть что́-нибудь ~** have something against, mind, object; **ничего́ не име́ть ~** not mind, not object.

про́тивень, -вня *m.* dripping-pan; meat-tin; girdle, griddle.

проти́виться, -влюсь *impf.* (*pf.* **вос~**) +*d.* oppose; resist, stand up against. **проти́вник, -а** opponent, adversary, antagonist; the enemy. **проти́вно** *prep.*+*d.* against; contrary to. **проти́вн|ый**[1] opposite; contrary; opposing, opposed; **в ~ом слу́чае** otherwise; **~ый ве́тер** contrary wind, head wind. **проти́вный**[2] nasty, offensive, disgusting; unpleasant, disagreeable; **мне проти́вно** I am disgusted.

противо... *in comb.* anti-, contra-, counter-. **противове́с, -а** counterbalance, counterpoise. **~возду́шный** anti-aircraft. **~га́з, -а** gas-mask, respirator. **~га́зовый** anti-gas. **~де́йствие, -я** opposition, counteraction. **~де́йствовать, -твую** *impf.*+*d.* oppose, counteract. **~есте́ственный** unnatural. **~зако́нный** unlawful; illegal. **~зача́точ-**

ный contraceptive. **~лежа́щий** opposite. **~обще́ственный** anti-social. **~пожа́рный** fire-fighting, fire-prevention. **~поло́жность, -и** opposition; contrast; opposite, antithesis; **пряма́я ~поло́жность** exact opposite. **~поло́жный** opposite; opposed, contrary. **~поста́вить, -влю** *pf.*, **~поставля́ть, -я́ю** *impf.* oppose; contrast, set off. **~пига́рный** non-stick. **~раке́та, -ы** anti-missile. **~раке́тный** anti-missile. **~речи́вый** contradictory; discrepant, conflicting. **~ре́чие, -я** contradiction; inconsistency; conflict, clash. **~ре́чить, -чу** *impf.+d.* contradict; be at variance with, conflict with, be contrary to, run counter to. **~стоя́ть, -ою́** *impf.+d.* resist, withstand. **~та́нковый** anti-tank. **~уго́нный** anti-theft. **~хими́ческий** anti-gas. **~шу́мы, -ов** *pl.* earplugs. **~я́дие, -я** antidote.

протира́ть, -а́ю *impf. of* **протере́ть. проти́рка, -и** cleaning rag.

проткну́ть, -ну́, -нёшь *pf.* (*impf.* **протыка́ть**) pierce; transfix; spit, skewer.

протоко́л, -а minutes, record of proceedings; report; statement; charge-sheet; protocol; **вести́ ~** take, record, the minutes; **занести́ в ~** enter in the minutes. **протоколи́ровать, -рую** *impf.* & *pf.* (*pf. also* **за~**) minute, record. **протоко́льный** of protocol; exact, factual.

протолкну́ть, -ну́, -нёшь *pf.* (*impf.* **прота́лкивать**) push through.

протопи́ть, -плю́, -пишь *pf.* (*impf.* **прота́пливать**) heat (*thoroughly*).

проторённ|ый beaten, well-trodden; **~ая доро́жка** beaten track.

прото́чный flowing, running.

про|тра́лить, -лю *pf.* **протру́** *etc.*: *see* **протере́ть. про|труби́ть, -блю́** *pf.*

протуха́ть, -а́ет *impf.*, **проту́хнуть, -нет; -у́х** *pf.* become foul, become rotten; go bad. **проту́хший** foul, rotten; bad, tainted.

протыка́ть, -а́ю *impf. of* **проткну́ть**

протя́гивать, -аю *impf.*, **протяну́ть, -ну́, -нешь** *pf.* stretch; extend; stretch out, hold out; reach out; protract; drawl out; last; **~ся** stretch out; reach out; extend, stretch, reach; last, go on. **протяже́ние, -я** extent, stretch; distance, expanse, area; space; **на всём протяже́нии**+*g.* along the whole length of, all along; **на протяже́нии** during, for the space of. **протяжённость, -и** extent, length. **протя́жность, -и** slowness; **~ ре́чи** drawl. **протя́жный** long-drawn-out; drawling.

проу́чивать, -аю *impf.*, **проучи́ть, -чу́, -чишь** *pf.* study, learn (up); teach a lesson, punish.

проф. *abbr.* (*of* **профе́ссор**) professor.

проф... *abbr.* (*of* **профессиона́льный, профсою́зный**) *in comb.* professional, occupational; trade-union. **профбиле́т, -а** trade-union card. **~боле́знь, -и** occupational disease. **~ко́м, -а** trade-union committee. **~о́рг, -а** trade-union organizer. **~ориента́ция, -и** vocational guidance. **~рабо́тник, -а** trade-union official. **~сою́з, -а** trade-union. **~сою́зный** trade-union. **~техучи́лище, -а** technical college. **~техшко́ла, -ы** trade school. **~шко́ла, -ы** trade-union school.

профа́н, -а layman; ignoramus.

профессиона́льн|ый professional; occupational; **~ая ориента́ция** career guidance; **~ый риск** occupational hazard; **~ый сою́з** trade-union. **профе́ссия, -и** profession, occupation, trade.

профе́ссор, -а; *pl.* **~а́** professor. **профе́ссорский** professorial.

профила́ктика, -и prophylaxis; preventive measures, precautions. **профилакти́ческий** prophylactic; preventive, precautionary.

про́филь, -я *m.* profile; side-view; outline; section; type.

профо́рма, -ы form, formality.

прохла́да, -ы coolness, cool. **прохлади́тельный** refreshing, cooling. **прохла́дный** cool, fresh.

прохо́д, -а (-у) passage; passageway; gangway, aisle; duct; **пра́во ~а** right of way; **«~а нет»** 'no thoroughfare'. **проходи́мец, -мца** rogue, rascal. **проходи́мый** passable. **проходи́ть, -ожу́, -о́дишь** *impf. of* **пройти́. прохо́дка, -и** going through, getting through; tunnelling, driving. **проходно́й** of passage; through, communciating. **прохо́жий** passing, in transit; *sb.* passer-by.

процвета́ние, -я prosperity, well-being; flourishing, thriving. **процвета́ть, -а́ю** *impf.* prosper, flourish, thrive.

процеди́ть, -ежу́, -е́дишь *pf.* (*impf.* **проце́живать**) filter, strain; **~ сквозь зу́бы** mutter, mumble.

процеду́ра, -ы procedure; treatment; **лече́бные процеду́ры** medical treatment.

проце́живать, -аю *pf. of* **процеди́ть**

проце́нт, -а percentage; per cent; interest; **сто ~ов** a hundred per cent.

проце́сс, -а process; trial; legal action, legal proceedings; lawsuit; cause, case. **проце́ссия, -и** procession.

проце́ссор, -а (*comput.*) processor.

процессуа́льный trial; legal.

про|цити́ровать, -рую *pf.*

прочёска, -и screening; combing.

проче́сть, -чту́, -чтёшь; -чёл, -чла́ *pf. of* **чита́ть**

про́ч|ий other; **и ~ее** etc., etcetera, and so on; **ме́жду ~им** incidentally, by the way; **~ие** *sb.*, *pl.* (the) others.

прочи́стить, -и́щу *pf.* (*impf.* **прочища́ть**) clean; cleanse thoroughly.

про|чита́ть, -а́ю *pf.*, **прочи́тывать, -аю** *impf.* read (through).

прочища́ть, -а́ю *impf. of* **прочи́стить**

про́чно *adv.* firmly, soundly, solidly, well. **про́чн|ый; -чен, -чна́, -о** firm, sound, stable, solid; durable, lasting; enduring. **~ая**

крáска fast colour.

прочтéние, -я reading; reciting; giving, delivering. **прочтý** *etc.*: *see* **прочéсть**

прочýвствовать, -твую *pf.* feel; feel deeply, acutely, keenly; experience, go through; get the feel of.

прочь *adv.* away, off; averse to; **(подú) ~!** go away! be off!; **(пошёл) ~ отсю́да!** get out of here!; **~ с дорóги!** get out of the way!; **рýки ~!** hands off!; **я не прочь** I have no objection, I am not averse to, I am quite willing.

прошéдш|ий past; last; **~ее** *sb.* the past. **прошёл** *etc.*: *see* **пройтú**

прошéние, -я application, petition.

прошептáть, -пчý, -пчешь *pf.* whisper.

прошéствие, -я; по прошéствии+*g.* after the lapse of, after the expiration of.

прошивáть, -áю *impf.*, **прошúть, -шью́, -шьёшь** *pf.* sew, stitch. **прошúвка, -и** insertion.

прошлогóдний last year's. **прóшл|ый** past; of the past; bygone, former; last; **в ~ом годý** last year; **~ое** *sb.* the past.

про|шнуровáть, -рýю *pf.* **про|штудúровать, -рую** *pf.* **прошью́** *etc.*: *see* **прошúть**

прощáй(те) goodbye; farewell. **прощáльный** parting; farewell. **прощáние, -я** farewell; parting, leave-taking. **прощáть(ся, -áю(сь** *impf. of* **простúть(ся**

прóще simpler, plainer, easier.

прощéние, -я forgiveness, pardon; **прошý прощéния** I beg your pardon; (I'm) sorry.

прощýпать, -аю *pf.*, **прощýпывать, -аю** *impf.* feel; detect; sound (out).

про|экзаменовáть, -нýю *pf.*

проявúтель, -я *m.* developer. **проявúть, -влю́, -вишь** *pf.*, **проявля́ть, -я́ю** *impf.* show, display, manifest, reveal; develop.

проя́снеть[1], **-еет** *pf.* clear; **прояснéло** it cleared up. **прояснéть**[2], **-éет** *pf.* brighten (up). **прояснúться, -úтся** *pf.*, **проясня́ться, -я́ется** *impf.* clear, clear up.

пруд, -á, *loc.* **-ý** pond. **прудúть, -ужý, -ýдúшь** *impf.* (*pf.* **за~**) dam. **прудовóй** pond.

пружúна, -ы spring. **пружúнистый** springy, elastic. **пружúнка, -и** mainspring; hairspring. **пружúнный** spring.

прусáк, -á cockroach.

пруссáк, -á, пруссáчка, -и Prussian. **прýсский** Prussian.

прут, -а *or* **-á**; *pl.* **-тья** twig; switch; rod.

пры́галка, -и skipping-rope. **пры́гать, -аю** *impf.*, **пры́гнуть, -ну** *pf.* jump, leap, spring; bound; hop; bounce; **~ со скакáлкой** skip; **~ с упóром** vault; **~ с шестóм** pole-vault. **прыгýн, -á, прыгýнья, -и**; *g.pl.* **-ний** jumper. **прыжкóв|ый; ~ая вы́шка** diving board. **прыжóк, -жкá** jump; leap, spring; caper; **прыжкú** jumping; **прыжкú на батýте** trampolining; **прыжкú в вóду** diving; **~ в высотý** high jump; **~ в длинý** long jump; **~ с мéста** standing jump; **прыжкú с парашю́том** parachute-jumping, sky-diving; **~ с разбéга** running jump; **~ с упóром** vault, vaulting; **~ с шестóм** pole-vault.

пры́скать, -аю *impf.*, **пры́снуть, -ну** *pf.* spurt, gush; **~ на** *or* **в**+*a.* spray, sprinkle; **~ (сó смеху)** burst out laughing.

пры́ткий quick, lively, sharp. **прыть, -и** speed; quickness, liveliness, go.

прыщ, -á, пры́щик, -а pimple; postule, **прыщáвый** pimply, pimpled.

прядéние, -я spinning. **пря́деный** spun. **прядúльный** spinning. **прядúльня, -и**; *g.pl.* **-лен** (spinning-)mill. **прядúльщик, -а** spinner. **прядý** *etc.*: *see* **прясть. прядь, -и** lock; strand. **пря́жа, -и** yarn, thread.

пря́жка, -и buckle, clasp.

пря́лка, -и distaff; spinning-wheel.

прямáя *sb.* straight line; **по прямóй** on the straight. **пря́мо** *adv.* straight; straight on; directly; frankly, openly, bluntly; really.

прямо... *in comb.* straight-; direct; ortho-, rect(i)-, right. **прямодýшие, -я** directness, frankness, straightforwardness. **~дýшный** direct, frank, straightforward. **~кры́лый** orthopterous. **~линéйный** rectilinear; straightforward, forthright. **~слóйный** straight-grained. **~угóльник, -а** rectangle. **~угóльный** right-angled, rectangular.

прямóй; -ям, -á, -о straight; upright, erect; through; direct; straightforward; real.

пря́ник, -а spice cake; gingerbread; honey-cake. **пря́ничный** gingerbread. **пря́ность, -и** spice; spiciness. **пря́ный** spicy; heady.

прясть, -ядý, -ядёшь; -ял, -я́лá, -о *impf.* (*pf.* **с~**) spin.

пря́тать, -я́чу *impf.* (*pf.* **с~**) hide, conceal; **~ся** hide, conceal o.s. **пря́тки, -ток** *pl.* hide-and-seek.

пря́ха, -и spinner.

пса *etc.*: *see* **пёс**

псалóм, -лмá psalm. **псалóмщик, -а** (psalm-)reader; sexton.

псевдонúм, -а pseudonym; pen-name.

псих, -а madman, lunatic, crank. **психбольнúца, -ы** mental hospital. **психиáтр, -а** psychiatrist. **психиатрúческ|ий** psychiatric(al); **~ая лечéбница** mental hospital. **психиатрúя, -и** psychiatry. **псúхика, -и** state of mind; psyche; psychology. **психúческий** mental, psychical.

психоанáлиз, -а psychoanalysis. **психоаналúтик, -а** psychoanalyst. **психоаналитúческий** psychoanalytic(al). **психóз, -а** psychosis. **психóлог, -а** psychologist. **психологúческий** psychological. **психолóгия, -и** psychology. **психопáт, -а** psychopath; lunatic. **психотерапéвт, -а** psychotherapist. **психотерапúя, -и** psychotherapy.

псориáз, -а psoriasis.

птенéц, -нцá nestling; fledgeling. **птúца, -ы** bird; **вáжная ~** big noise; **домáшняя ~** poultry. **птицевóд, -а** poultry-farmer, poultry-breeder. **птúч|ий** bird, bird's, poultry; **вид с ~ьего полёта** bird's-eye view; **~ий**

двор poultry-yard. **пти́чка, -и** bird.

пу́блика, -и public; audience. **публика́ция, -и** publication; notice, advertisement. **публикова́ть, -ку́ю** *impf.* (*pf.* **о~**) publish. **публици́ст, -а** publicist; commentator on current affairs. **публици́стика, -и** social and political journalism; writing on current affairs. **публицисти́ческий** publicistic. **публи́чно** *adv.* publicly; in public; openly. **публи́чность, -и** publicity. **публи́чн|ый** public; **~ый дом** brothel; **~ая же́нщина** prostitute.

пу́гало, -а scarecrow. **пу́ганый** scared, frightened. **пуга́ть, -а́ю** *impf.* (*pf.* **ис~, на~**) frighten, scare; intimidate; *+i.* threaten with; **~ся** (*+g.*) be frightened (of), be scared (of); take fright (at); shy (at). **пуга́ч, -а́** toy pistol; screech owl. **пугли́вый** fearful, timorous; timid. **пугну́ть, -ну́, -нёшь** *pf.* scare, frighten; give a fright.

пу́говица, -ы, пу́говка, -и button.

пуд, -а; *pl.* **-ы́** pood (*old Russ. measurement, equivalent to approx. 16.38 kg*). **пудово́й, пудо́вый** one pood in weight.

пу́дра, -ы powder. **пу́дреный** powdered. **пу́дрить, -рю** *impf.* (*pf.* **на~**) powder; **~ся** powder one's face, use powder.

пуза́тый big-bellied, pot-bellied.

пузырёк, -рька́ phial, vial; bubble; bleb. **пузы́рь, -я́** *m.* bubble; blister; bladder.

пук, -а; *pl.* **-и́** bunch, bundle; tuft; wisp.

пулево́й bullet. **пулемёт, -а** machine-gun. **пулемётный** machine-gun. **пулемётчик, -а** machine-gunner. **пулесто́йкий** bullet-proof.

пульс, -а pulse. **пульса́р, -а** pulsar. **пульси́ровать, -рует** *impf.* pulse; pulsate; beat, throb.

пульт, -а desk, stand; control panel.

пу́ля, -и bullet.

пункт, -а point; spot; post; centre; item; plank; **по всем ~ам** at all points. **пункти́р, -а** dotted line. **пункти́рный** dotted, broken.

пунктуа́льность, -и punctuality. **пунктуа́льный** punctual.

пунктуа́ция, -и punctuation.

пунцо́вый crimson.

пунш, -а punch (*drink*).

пуп, -а́ navel; umbilicus; **~ земли́** hub of the universe. **пупови́на, -ы** umbilical cord. **пупо́к, -пка́** navel; gizzard. **пупо́чный** umbilical.

пурга́, -и́ snow-storm, blizzard.

пу́рпур, -а purple, crimson. **пурпу́рный, пурпу́ровый** purple, crimson.

пуск, -а starting (up); setting in motion. **пуска́й** *see* **пусть. пуска́ть(ся, -а́ю(сь** *impf. of* **пусти́ть(ся. пусков|о́й** starting; initial; **~а́я площа́дка** (rocket-)launching platform.

пусте́ть, -е́ет *impf.* (*pf.* **о~**) empty; become deserted.

пусти́ть, пущу́, пу́стишь *pf.* (*impf.* **пуска́ть**) let go; set free; let in, allow to enter; let, allow, permit; start; set, put; send; set in motion, set going, set working; throw, shy; put forth, put out; **не ~** keep out; **~ во́ду** turn on the water; **~ в ход** start, launch, set going, set in train; **~ ко́рни** take root; **~ ростки́** shoot, sprout; **~ слух** start, spread, a rumour; **~ фейерве́рк** let off fireworks; **~ся** set out; start; begin; **~ся в путь** set out, get on one's way.

пустобрёх, -а chatterbox, windbag.

пустова́ть, -ту́ет *impf.* be empty, stand empty; lie fallow. **пуст|о́й; -ст, -а́, -о** empty; void; tenantless, vacant, uninhabited; deserted; idle; shallow; futile, frivolous; vain, ungrounded; **~о́е ме́сто** blank space; **~а́я отгово́рка** lame excuse, hollow pretence; **~ы́е слова́** mere words; **~о́й чай** just tea. **пустота́, -ы́**; *pl.* **-ы** emptiness; void; vacuum; shallowness; futility, frivolousness. **пустоте́лый** hollow.

пусты́нник, -а hermit, anchorite. **пусты́нный** uninhabited; deserted; **~ о́стров** desert island. **пу́стынь, -и** hermitage, monastery. **пусты́ня, -и** desert, wilderness. **пусты́рь, -я́** *m.* waste land; vacant plot; desolate area.

пусты́шка, -и blank; hollow object; *(baby's)* dummy; empty-headed person.

пусть, пуска́й *part.* let; all right, very well; though, even if; **~ бу́дет так** so be it; **~ х ра́вен 3** let x = 3.

пустя́к, -а́ trifle; bagatelle. **пустяко́вый** trifling, trivial.

пу́таница, -ы muddle, confusion; mess, tangle. **пу́таный** muddled, confused; tangled; confusing; muddle-headed. **пу́тать, -аю** *impf.* (*pf.* **за~, пере~, с~**) tangle; confuse; muddle; mix up; **~ся** get tangled; get confused; get muddled; get mixed up.

путёвка, -и pass, authorization; permit; **проси́ть путёвку в санато́рий** apply for a place in a sanatorium. **путеводи́тель, -я** *m.* guide, guide-book. **путево́дн|ый** guiding; **~ая звезда́** guiding star; lodestar. **путев|о́й** travelling, itinerary; **~а́я ка́рта** road-map; **~а́я ско́рость** ground-speed. **путём** *prep.+g.* by means of, by dint of. **путепрово́д, -а** overpass; underpass; bridge. **путеше́ственник, -а** traveller. **путеше́ствие, -я** journey; trip; voyage; cruise; *pl.* travels. **путеше́ствовать, -твую** *impf.* travel; voyage. **путь, -и́**, *i.* **-ём**, *p.* **-и́** way; track; path; road; course; journey; voyage; passage, duct; means; use, benefit; **во́дный ~** water-way; **в пути́** en route, on one's way; **в четырёх днях пути́ от** four day's journey from; **ми́рным путём** amicably, peaceably; **морски́е пути́** shipping-routes, sea-lanes; **нам с ва́ми по пути́** we are going the same way; **на обра́тном пути́** on the way back; **пойти́ по пути́***+g.* take, follow, the path of; **по пути́** on the way; **пути́ сообще́ния** communications; **стоя́ть на пути́** be in the way.

путч, -а coup, putsch. **путчи́ст, -а** coup-leader, putschist.

пух, -а (-у), *loc.* **-у́** down; fluff; **разби́ть в ~ и прах** put to complete rout.

пу́хл|ый; -хл, -а́, -о chubby, plump. **пу́хнуть, -ну; пух** *impf.* (*pf.* **вс~, о~**) swell.

пухови́к, -а́ feather-bed; down quilt; eiderdown. **пухо́вка, -и** powder-puff. **пухо́вый** downy.

пучегла́зый goggle-eyed.

пучи́на, -ы gulf, abyss; the deep.

пучо́к, -чка́ bunch, bundle; tuft, fascicle; wisp.

пу́шечн|ый gun, cannon; **~ое мя́со** cannon-fodder.

пуши́нка, -и bit of fluff; **~ сне́га** snowflake. **пуши́стый** fluffy, downy.

пу́шка, -и gun, cannon.

пушни́на, -ы furs, fur-skins, pelts. **пушно́й** fur; fur-bearing; **~ зверь** fur-bearing animals.

пу́ще *adv.* more; **~ всего́** most of all.

пущу́ *etc.*: *see* **пусти́ть**

пчела́, -ы́; *pl.* **-ёлы** bee. **пчели́ный** bee, bee's, of bees; **~ воск** beeswax. **пчелово́д, -а** bee-keeper, apiarist. **пче́льник, -а** apiary.

пшени́ца, -ы wheat. **пшени́чный** wheat, wheaten.

пшённый millet. **пшено́, -а́** millet.

пыл, -а (-у), *loc.* **-у́** heat, ardour, passion. **пыла́ть, -а́ю** *impf.* blaze, flame; burn; glow.

пылеви́дный powdered, pulverized. **пылесо́с, -а** vacuum cleaner. **пылесо́сить, -сю** *impf.* vacuum(-clean), hoover. **пыли́нка, -и** speck of dust. **пыли́ть, -лю́** *impf.* (*pf.* **за~, на~**) raise a dust, raise the dust; cover with dust, make dusty; **~ся** get dusty, get covered with dust.

пы́лкий ardent, passionate; fervent; fervid. **пы́лкость, -и** ardour, passion; fervency.

пыль, -и, *loc.* **-и́** dust. **пы́льн|ый; -лен, -льна́, -о** dusty; **~ый котёл** dust-bowl; **~ая тря́пка** duster. **пыльца́, -ы́** pollen.

пыта́ть, -а́ю *impf.* torture, torment. **пыта́ться, -та́юсь** *impf.* (*pf.* **по~**) try. **пы́тка, -и** torture, torment. **пытли́вый** inquisitive, searching.

пы́хать, пы́шет *impf.* blaze.

пыхте́ть, -хчу́ *impf.* puff, pant.

пы́шет *see* **пы́хать**

пы́шка, -и bun; doughnut; chubby child; plump woman.

пы́шность, -и splendour, magnificence. **пы́шный; -шен, -шна́, -шно** splendid, magnificent; fluffy, light; luxuriant.

пьедеста́л, -а pedestal.

пье́ксы, -с *pl.* ski-boots.

пье́са, -ы play; piece.

пью *etc.*: *see* **пить**

пьяне́ть, -е́ю *impf.* (*pf.* **о~**) get drunk. **пьяни́ть, -ни́т** *impf.* (*pf.* **о~**) intoxicate, make drunk; go to one's head. **пья́ница, -ы** *c.g.* drunkard; tippler, toper. **пья́нство, -а** drunkenness; hard drinking. **пья́нствовать, -твую** *impf.* drink hard, drink heavily. **пья́ный** drunk; drunken; tipsy, tight; intoxicated; heady, intoxicating.

пэ *nt.indecl.* the letter **п.**

пюпи́тр, -а desk; reading-desk; music-stand.

пюре́ *nt.indecl.* purée.

пядь, -и; *g.pl.* **-е́й** span; **ни пя́ди** not an inch.

пя́льцы, -лец *pl.* tambour; embroidery frame.

пята́, -ы́; *pl.* **-ы, -а́м** heel.

пята́к, -а́, пятачо́к, -чка́ five-copeck piece. **пятёрка, -и** five; figure 5; No.5; group of five; fiver, five-rouble note. **пя́теро, -ы́х** five.

пяти... *in comb.* five; penta-. **пятибо́рье, -я** pentathlon. **~гла́вый** five-headed; five-domed. **~две́рн|ый; ~ая маши́на** hatchback. **~десятиле́тие, -я** fifty years; fiftieth anniversary; fiftieth birthday. **П~деся́тница, -ы** Pentecost. **~деся́тый** fiftieth; **~деся́тые го́ды** the fifties. **~кла́ссник, -а, -ница, -ы, ~кла́шка, -и** *c.g.* class-five pupil. **~кни́жие, -я** Pentateuch. **~коне́чный** five-pointed. **~кра́тный** fivefold, quintuple. **~ле́тие, -я** five years; fifth anniversary. **~ле́тка, -и** five years; five-year plan; five-year-old. **~со́тенный** five-hundred-rouble. **~сотле́тие, -я** five centuries; quincentenary. **~со́тый** five-hundredth. **~сто́пный** pentameter. **~то́нка, -и** five-ton lorry. **~ты́сячный** five-thousandth. **~уго́льник, -а** pentagon. **~уго́льный** pentagonal.

пя́тка, -и heel.

пятна́дцатый fifteenth. **пятна́дцать, -и** fifteen.

пятна́ть, -а́ю *impf.* (*pf.* **за~**) spot, stain, smirch; tig, catch. **пятна́шки, -шек** *pl.* tag, tig. **пятни́стый** spotted, dappled.

пя́тница, -ы Friday.

пятно́, -а́; *pl.* **-а, -тен** stain; spot; patch; blot; stigma, blemish; **роди́мое ~** birth-mark.

пято́к, -тка́ five. **пя́тый** fifth. **пять, -и́,** *i.* **-ью** five. **пятьдеся́т, -и́десяти,** *i.* **-ью́десятью** fifty. **пятьсо́т, -тисо́т, -тиста́м** five hundred. **пя́тью** *adv.* five times.

Р

р *letter*: *see* **эр**

р. *abbr.* (*of* **река́**) R., River.; (*of* **рубль**) r., rouble(s).

раб, -а́ slave, bondsman.

раб... *abbr.* (*of* **рабо́чий**) *in comb.* worker. **рабко́р, -а** worker correspondent. **~селько́р, -а** worker-peasant correspondent. **~си́ла, -ы** manpower, labour force.

раба́, -ы́ slave; bondswoman. **рабовладе́лец, -льца** slave-owner. **рабовладе́ль-**

ческий slave-owning. **раболе́пие, -я** servility. **раболе́пный** servile. **раболе́пствовать, -твую** cringe, fawn.

рабо́та, -ы work; labour; job, employment; working; functioning; running; workmanship. **рабо́тать, -аю** *impf.* work; run, function; be open; *+i.* work, operate; **не ~** not work, be out of order; **~ над**+*i.* work at, work on. **рабо́тник, -а, рабо́тница, -ы** worker; workman; hand, labourer. **рабо́тный** working; **~ дом** workhouse. **работома́н, -а, работома́нка, -ки** workaholic. **работоспосо́бность, -и** capacity for work, efficiency. **работоспосо́бный** able-bodied, efficient. **работя́щий** hardworking, industrious. **рабо́чий** *sb.* worker; working man; workman; hand, labourer. **рабо́ч|ий** worker's; work; working; working-class; driving; **~ее движе́ние** working-class movement, labour movement; **~ий день** working day; **~ее колесо́** driving wheel; **~ая ло́шадь** draught-horse; **~ие ру́ки** hands; **~ая си́ла** man-power, labour force; labour.

ра́бский slave; servile. **ра́бство, -а** slavery, servitude.

равви́н, -а rabbi.

ра́венство, -а equality; **знак ра́венства** equals sign.

равио́ли *nt.* & *pl. indecl.* ravioli.

равне́ние, -я dressing, alignment; **~ напра́во!** eyes right! **равни́на, -ы** plain. **равни́нный** plain; level, flat.

равно́ *adv.* alike; equally; **~ как** as well as; and also, as also. **равно́** *pred.*: *see* **ра́вный**

равно... *in comb.* equi-, iso-. **равнобе́дренный** isosceles. **~ве́сие, -я** equilibrium; balance, equipoise; **привести́ в ~ве́сие** balance. **~де́йствующая** *sb.* resultant force. **~де́нствие, -я** equinox. **~ду́шие, -я** indifference. **~ду́шный** indifferent. **~зна́чащий, ~зна́чный** equivalent, equipollent. **~ме́рный** even; uniform. **~отстоя́щий** equidistant. **~пра́вие, -я** equality of rights. **~пра́вный** equal in rights, having equal rights. **~си́льный** of equal strength; equal, equivalent, tantamount. **~сторо́нний** equilateral. **~уго́льный** equiangular. **~це́нный** of equal value, of equal worth; equivalent.

ра́вн|ый; -вен, -вна́ equal; **на ~ых** as equals, on an equal footing; **при про́чих ~ых усло́виях** other things being equal; **~ым о́бразом** equally, likewise; **равно́** *pred.* make(s), equals; **всё ~о́** it is all the same, it makes no difference; all the same; **мне всё ~о́** I don't mind, it's all the same to me; **не всё ли ~о́?** what difference does it make? what does it matter? **равня́ть, -я́ю** *impf.* (*pf.* **с~**) make even; treat equally; +**с**+*i.* compare with, treat as equal to; **~ счёт** equalize; **~ся** compete, compare; be equal; be equivalent, be tantamount; dress; *+d.* equal, amount to; +**с**+*i.* compete with, match.

рагу́ *nt. indecl.* ragout; **кита́йское ~** chop suey.

рад, -а, -о *pred.* glad.

ра́ди *prep.* *+g.* for the sake of; **чего́ ~?** what for?

радиа́тор, -а radiator.

радиацио́нный radiation. **радиа́ция, -и** radiation.

ра́диевый radium. **ра́дий, -я** radium.

радика́л, -а radical. **радикали́зм, -а** radicalism. **радика́льность, -и** radicalism. **радика́льн|ый** radical, drastic; **~ые измене́ния** sweeping changes.

ра́дио *nt.indecl.* radio, wireless; radio set; **переда́ть по ~** broadcast; **слу́шать ~** listen in.

радио... *in comb.* radio-; radioactive. **радиоакти́вность, -и** radioactivity. **~акти́вный** radioactive. **~аппара́т, -а** radio set. **~бесе́да, -ы** phone-in. **~веща́ние, -я** broadcasting. **~веща́тельный** broadcasting. **~гра́мма, -ы** radiogram; wireless message. **~журнали́ст, -а** broadcaster. **~зо́нд, -а** radiosonde. **радио́лог, -а** radiologist. **~логи́ческий** radiological. **~ло́гия, -и** radiology. **~лока́тор, -а** radar (set). **~люби́тель, -я** *m.* radio amateur, ham. **~мая́к, -а́** radio beacon. **~мо́ст, -а** satellite (radio) link-up. **~переда́тчик, -а** transmitter. **~переда́ча, -и** transmission, broadcast. **~перекли́чка, -и** radio link-up. **~приёмник, -а** receiver radio (set). **~свя́зь, -и** radio communication, radio link. **~слу́шатель, -я** *m.* listener. **~ста́нция, -и** radio station, set. **~те́хника, -и** radio-engineering. **~управля́емый** remote-controlled. **~фици́ровать, -рую** *impf.* & *pf.* instal radio in, equip with radio. **~хими́ческий** radiochemical. **~хи́мия, -и** radiochemistry. **~электро́ника, -и** radioelectronics.

радио́ла, -ы radiogram.

ради́ровать, -рую *impf.* & *pf.* radio. **ради́ст, -а** radio operator; telegraphist.

ра́диус, -а radius.

ра́довать, -дую *impf.* (*pf.* **об~, по~**) gladden, make glad, make happy; **~ся** be glad, be happy, rejoice. **ра́достный** glad, joyous, joyful. **ра́дость, -и** gladness, joy; **от ра́дости** for joy, with joy; **с ~ю** with pleasure, gladly.

ра́дуга, -и rainbow. **ра́дужн|ый** iridescent, opalescent, rainbow-coloured; cheerful; optimistic; **~ая оболо́чка** iris.

раду́шие, -я cordiality. **раду́шный** cordial; **~ приём** hearty welcome.

раёк, райка́ gallery; gods.

ражу́ *etc.*: *see* **рази́ть**

раз, -а; *pl.* **-ы́, раз** time, occasion; one; **в друго́й ~** another time, some other time; **в са́мый ~** at the right moment, just right; **ещё ~** (once) again, once more; **как ~** just, exactly; **как ~ то** the very thing; **на э́тот ~** this time, on this occasion, (for) this once; **не ~** more than once; time and again; **ни ~у** not once, never; **оди́н ~** once; **~ (и) навсегда́** once (and) for all. **раз** *adv.* once,

one day. **раз** *conj.* if, since; ~ **так** in that case.
раз..., разо..., разъ..., рас... *vbl. pref. indicating division into parts; distribution; action in different directions; action in reverse; termination of action or state; intensification of action*: dis-, un-.
разба́вить, -влю *pf.*, **разбавля́ть, -я́ю** *impf.* dilute.
разбаза́ривание, -я squandering; sell-out. **разбаза́ривать, -аю** *impf.*, **разбаза́рить, -рю** *pf.* squander, waste.
разба́лтывать(ся, -аю(сь *impf. of* **разболта́ть(ся**
разбе́г, -а (-у) run, running start; **прыжо́к с разбе́га (-е́гу)** running jump. **разбега́ться, -а́юсь** *impf.*, **разбежа́ться, -е́гусь** *pf.* take a run, run up; scatter, disperse; be scattered; **у меня́ разбежа́лись глаза́** I was dazzled.
разберу́ *etc.*: *see* **разобра́ть**
разбива́ть(ся, -а́ю(сь *impf. of* **разби́ть(ся. разби́вка, -и** laying out; spacing (out).
разбинтова́ть, -ту́ю *pf.*, **разбинто́вывать, -аю** *impf.* unbandage, remove a bandage from; **~ся** remove one's bandage(s); come off, come undone; come unbandaged, lose its bandage.
разбира́тельство, -а examination, investigation. **разбира́ть, -а́ю** *impf. of* **разобра́ть**; be particular; **не разбира́я** indiscriminately; **~ся** *impf. of* **разобра́ться**
разби́ть, -зобью́, -зобьёшь *pf.* (*impf.* **разбива́ть**) break; smash; break up, break down; divide (up), split; damage; fracture; beat, defeat; lay out, mark out; space (out); **~ся** break, get broken, get smashed; hurt o.s. badly; smash o.s. up. **разби́тый** broken; jaded.
раз|бла́говестить, -ещу *pf.* **раз|богате́ть, -е́ю** *pf.*
разбо́й, -я robbery, brigandage. **разбо́йник, -а** robber, brigand, bandit. **разбо́йнич|ий** robber; thieves'; **~ья ша́йка** gang of robbers.
разболе́ться[1], **-ли́тся** *pf.* ache; **у меня́ разболе́лась голова́** I've got a (bad) headache.
разболе́ться[2], **-е́юсь** *pf.* become ill, lose one's health.
разболта́ть[1], **-а́ю** *pf.* (*impf.* **разба́лтывать**) divulge, let out, give away.
разболта́ть[2], **-а́ю** *pf.* (*impf.* **разба́лтывать**) shake up, stir up; loosen; **~ся** mix; come loose, work loose; get slack, get out of hand.
разбомби́ть, -блю́ *pf.* bomb, destroy by bombing.
разбо́р, -а (-у) analysis; parsing; criticism, critique; selectiveness, discrimination; investigation; stripping, dismantling; buying up; sorting out; sort, quality; **без ~у (-а)** indiscriminately. **разбо́рный** collapsible. **разбо́рчивость, -и** legibility; scrupulousness; fastidiousness. **разбо́рчивый** legible; scrupulous; fastidious, exacting; discriminating.
разбра́сывать, -аю *impf. of* **разброса́ть**
разбреда́ться, -а́ется *impf.*, **разбрести́сь, -едётся; -ёлся, -ла́сь** *pf.* disperse; straggle. **разбро́д, -а** disorder.
разбро́санный sparse, scattered; straggling; disconnected, incoherent. **разброса́ть, -а́ю** *pf.* (*impf.* **разбра́сывать**) throw about; scatter, spread, strew.
раз|буди́ть, -ужу́, -у́дишь *pf.*
разбуха́ние, -я swelling; ~ **шта́та** over-staffing. **разбуха́ть, -а́ет** *impf.*, **разбу́хнуть, -нет; -бу́х** *pf.* swell.
разбушева́ться, -шу́юсь *pf.* fly into a rage; blow up; run high.
разва́л, -а breakdown, disintegration, disruption; disorganization. **разва́ливать, -аю** *impf.*, **развали́ть, -лю́, -лишь** *pf.* pull down; break up; mess up; **~ся** collapse; go to pieces, fall to pieces; fall down, tumble down; break down; sprawl, lounge. **разва́лина, -ы** ruin; wreck; **гру́да разва́лин** a heap of ruins.
разварно́й boiled soft.
ра́зве *part.* really?; ~ **вы не зна́ете?** don't you know?; ~ **(то́лько),** ~ **(что)** only; perhaps; except that, only. **ра́зве** *conj.* unless.
развева́ться, -а́ется *impf.* fly, flutter.
развед... *abbr.* (*of* **разве́дывательный**) *in comb.* reconnaissance; intelligence. **развед-гру́ппа, -ы** reconnaissance party. **~о́рган, -а** intelligence agency; reconnaissance unit. **~сво́дка, -и** intelligence summary. **~слу́жба, -ы** intelligence service.
разве́дать, -аю *pf.* (*impf.* **разве́дывать**) find out; investigate; reconnoitre; prospect.
разведе́ние, -я breeding, rearing; cultivation.
разведённ|ый divorced; **~ый, ~ая** *sb.* divorcee.
разве́дка, -и intelligence; secret service, intelligence service; reconnaissance; prospecting; **идти́ в разве́дку** reconnoitre. **разве́дочный** prospecting, exploratory.
разведу́ *etc.*: *see* **развести́**
разве́дчик, -а intelligence officer; scout; prospector. **разве́дывать, -аю** *impf. of* **разве́дать**
развезти́, -зу́, -зёшь; -ёз, -ла́ *pf.* (*impf.* **развози́ть**) convey, transport; deliver; exhaust, wear out; make impassable, make unfit for traffic.
разве́ивать(ся, -аю(сь *impf. of* **разве́ять(ся. развёл** *etc.*: *see* **развести́**
развенча́ть, -а́ю *pf.*, **разве́нчивать, -аю** *impf.* dethrone; debunk.
развёрнутый extensive, large-scale, all-out; detailed; deployed, extended. **разверну́ть, -ну́, -нёшь** *pf.* (*impf.* **развёртывать, развора́чивать**) unfold, unwrap, open; unroll; unfurl; deploy; expand; develop; turn, swing; scan; show, display; **~ся** unfold, unroll, come unwrapped; deploy; develop; spread; expand; turn, swing.
разверста́ть, -а́ю *pf.*, **развёрстывать, -аю** *impf.* distribute, allot, apportion. **развёрстка, -и** allotment, apportionment; distribution.

развёртывать(ся, -аю(сь *impf. of* **разверну́ть(ся**
разве́с, -а weighing out.
раз|весели́ть, -лю́ *pf.* cheer up, amuse; **~ся** cheer up.
разве́систый branchy, spreading. **разве́сить[1], -е́шу** *pf.* (*impf.* **разве́шивать**) spread; hang (out).
разве́сить[2], -е́шу *pf.* (*impf.* **разве́шивать**) weigh out. **развесно́й** sold by weight.
развести́, -еду́, -едёшь; -ёл, -а́ *pf.* (*impf.* **разводи́ть**) take, conduct; part, separate; divorce; dilute; dissolve; start; breed, rear; cultivate; **~ мост** raise a bridge, swing a bridge open; **~ ого́нь** light a fire; **~сь** be divorced; breed, multiply.
разветви́ться, -ви́тся *pf.* **разветвля́ться, -я́ется** *impf.* branch; fork; ramify. **разветвле́ние, -я** branching, ramification, forking; branch; fork.
разве́шать, -аю *pf.*, **разве́шивать, -аю** *impf.* hang.
разве́шивать, -аю *impf. of* **разве́сить, разве́шать. разве́шу** *etc.*: *see* **разве́сить**
разве́ять, -е́ю *pf.* (*impf.* **разве́ивать**) scatter, disperse; dispel; destroy; **~ся** disperse; be dispelled.
развива́ть(ся, -а́ю(сь *impf. of* **разви́ть(ся**
развинти́ть, -нчу́ *pf.*, **разви́нчивать, -аю** *impf.* unscrew. **разви́нченный** unstrung; unsteady; lurching.
разви́тие, -я development; evolution; progress; maturity. **развито́й; ра́звит, -а́, -о** developed; mature, adult. **разви́ть, -зовью́; -зовьёшь; -и́л, -а́, -о** *pf.* (*impf.* **развива́ть**) develop; unwind, untwist; **~ся** develop.
развлека́ть, -а́ю *impf.*, **развле́чь, -еку́, -ечёшь; -ёк, -ла́** *pf.* entertain, amuse; divert; **~ся** have a good time; amuse o.s.; be diverted, be distracted.
разво́д, -а divorce. **разводи́ть(ся, -ожу́(сь, -о́дишь(ся** *impf. of* **развести́(сь. разво́дка, -и** separation. **разводно́й; ~ ключ** adjustable spanner, monkey-wrench; **~ мост** drawbridge, swing bridge.
развози́ть, -ожу́, -о́зишь *impf. of* **развезти́**
разволнова́ть(ся, -ну́ю(сь *pf.* get excited, be agitated.
развора́чивать(ся, -аю(сь *impf. of* **разверну́ть(ся**
раз|вороши́ть, -шу́ *pf.*
развра́т, -а debauchery, depravity, dissipation. **разврати́ть, -ащу́** *pf.* **развраща́ть, -а́ю** *impf.* debauch, corrupt; deprave. **развра́тничать, -аю** *impf.* indulge in debauchery, lead a depraved life. **развра́тный** debauched, depraved, profligate; corrupt. **развращённый; -ён, -а́** corrupt.
развяза́ть, -яжу́, -я́жешь *pf.*, **развя́зывать, -аю** *impf.* untie, unbind, undo; unleash; **~ся** come untied, come undone; **~ся с**+*i.* rid o.s. of, have done with. **развя́зка, -и** dénouement; outcome, issue, upshot; (*motorway*) junction; **де́ло идёт к развя́зке** things are coming to a head. **развя́зный** familiar; free-and-easy.
разгада́ть, -а́ю *pf.*, **разга́дывать, -аю** *impf.* solve, guess, puzzle out, make out; **~ сны** interpret dreams; **~ шифр** break a cipher. **разга́дка, -и** solution.
разга́р, -а height, peak, climax; **в по́лном ~е** in full swing; **в ~е ле́та** in the height of summer.
разгиба́ть(ся, -а́ю(сь *impf. of* **разогну́ть(ся**
разглаго́льствовать, -твую *impf.* hold forth, expatiate.
разгла́дить, -а́жу *pf.*, **разгла́живать, -аю** *impf.* smooth out; iron out, press.
разгласи́ть, -ашу́ *pf.*, **разглаша́ть, -а́ю** *impf.* divulge, give away, let out; +**о**+*p.* spread, broadcast; herald, trumpet. **разглаше́ние, -я** divulging, disclosure.
разгляде́ть, -яжу́ *pf.*, **разгля́дывать, -аю** *impf.* make out, discern, descry; examine closely, scrutinize.
разгне́ванный angry. **разгне́вать, -аю** *pf.* anger, incense. **раз|гне́ваться, -аюсь** *pf.*
разгова́ривать, -аю *impf.* talk, speak, converse. **разгово́р, -а (-у)** talk, conversation. **разгово́рник, -а** phrase-book. **разгово́рный** colloquial; conversational. **разгово́рчивый** talkative, loquacious.
разго́н, -а dispersal; breaking up; run, running start; distance; space. **разго́нистый** widely-spaced. **разгоня́ть(ся, -я́ю(сь** *impf. of* **разогна́ть(ся**
разгора́живать, -аю *impf. of* **разгороди́ть**
разгора́ться, -а́юсь *impf.*, **разгоре́ться, -рю́сь** *pf.* flame up, flare up; flush; **стра́сти разгоре́лись** feelings ran high, passions rose.
разгороди́ть, -ожу́, -о́ди́шь *pf.* (*impf.* **разгора́живать**) partition off.
раз|горячи́ть(ся, -чу́(сь *pf.*; **~ся от вина́** be flushed with wine.
разгра́бить, -блю *pf.* plunder, pillage, loot. **разграбле́ние, -я** plunder, pillage; looting.
разграниче́ние, -я demarcation, delimitation; differentiation. **разграни́чивать, -аю** *impf.*, **разграни́чить, -чу** *pf.* delimit, demarcate; differentiate, distinguish.
раз|графи́ть, -флю́ *pf.*, **разграфля́ть, -я́ю** *impf.* rule, square. **разграфле́ние, -я** ruling.
разгреба́ть, -а́ю *impf.*, **разгрести́, -ебу́, -ебёшь; -ёб, -ла́** *pf.* rake (away), shovel (away).
разгро́м, -а rout, crushing defeat; knock-out blow; havoc, devastation. **разгроми́ть, -млю́** *pf.* rout, defeat.
разгружа́ть, -а́ю *impf.*, **разгрузи́ть, -ужу́, -у́зи́шь** *pf.* unload; relieve; **~ся** unload; be relieved. **разгру́зка, -и** unloading; relief, relieving.
разгрыза́ть, -а́ю *impf.*, **раз|гры́зть, -зу́, -зёшь; -ы́з** *pf.* crack; bite through.
разгу́л, -а revelry, debauch; raging; (wild)

outburst. **разгу́ливать, -аю** *impf.* stroll about, walk about. **разгу́ливаться, -аюсь** *impf.*, **разгуля́ться, -я́юсь** *pf.* spread o.s.; have free scope; wake up, be wide awake; clear up; improve. **разгу́льный** loose, wild, rakish.

раздава́ть(ся, -даю́(сь, -даёшь(ся *impf. of* **разда́ть(ся**

раз|дави́ть, -влю́, -вишь *pf.* **разда́вливать, -аю** *impf.* crush; squash; run down, run over; overwhelm.

разда́ть, -а́м, -а́шь, -а́ст, -ади́м; ро́з- *or* **раз-да́л, -а́, -о** *pf.* (*impf.* **раздава́ть**) distribute, give out, serve out, dispense; **~ся** be heard; resound; ring out; make way; stretch, expand; put on weight. **разда́ча, -и** distribution. **раз-даю́** *etc.*: *see* **раздава́ть**

раздва́ивать(ся, -аю(сь *impf. of* **раз-двои́ть(ся**

раздвига́ть, -а́ю *impf.*, **раздви́нуть, -ну** *pf.* move apart, slide apart; draw back; **~ стол** extend a table; **~ся** move apart, slide apart; be drawn back; **за́навес раздви́нулся** the curtain rose. **раздвижно́й** expanding; sliding; extensible.

раздвое́ние, -я division into two; bifurcation; **~ ли́чности** split personality. **раздво́ен-ный, раздвоённый** forked; bifurcated; cloven; split. **раздвои́ть, -ою́** *pf.* (*impf.* **раз-два́ивать**) divide into two; bisect; **~ся** bifurcate, fork; split, become double.

раздева́лка, -и, раздева́льня, -и; *g.pl.* **-лен** cloakroom. **раздева́ть(ся, -а́ю(сь** *impf. of* **разде́ть(ся**

разде́л, -а division; partition; allotment; section, part.

разде́латься, -аюсь *pf.* +**с**+*i.* finish with, be through with; settle accounts with; pay off; get even with.

разделе́ние, -я division; **~ труда́** division of labour. **раздели́мый** divisible. **раз|дели́ть, -лю́, -лишь** *pf.*, **разделя́ть, -я́ю** *impf.* divide; separate, part; share; **~ся** divide; be divided; be divisible; separate, part. **раз-де́льный** separate; clear, distinct.

разде́ну *etc.*: *see* **разде́ть. раздеру́** *etc.*: *see* **разодра́ть**

разде́ть, -де́ну *pf.* (*impf.* **раздева́ть**) undress; **~ся** undress (o.s.), strip; take off one's coat, one's things.

раздира́ть, -а́ю *impf. of* **разодра́ть. раз-дира́ющий (ду́шу)** heart-rending, harrowing.

раздобыва́ть, -а́ю *impf.*, **раздобы́ть, -бу́ду** *pf.* get, procure, come by, get hold of.

раздо́лье, -я expanse; freedom, liberty. **раз-до́льный** free.

раздо́р, -а discord, dissension; **се́ять ~** breed strife, sow discord.

раздоса́довать, -дую *pf.* vex.

раздража́ть, -а́ю *impf.*, **раздражи́ть, -жу́** *pf.* irritate; annoy, exasperate, put out; **~ся** lose one's temper, get annoyed; get irritated; become inflamed. **раздраже́ние, -я** irritation; **в раздраже́нии** in a temper. **раздра-жи́тельный** irritable; short-tempered.

раздразни́ть, -ню́, -нишь *pf.* tease; arouse, stimulate.

раз|дроби́ть, -блю́ *pf.*, **раздробля́ть, -я́ю** *impf.* break; smash to pieces, splinter; turn, convert, reduce. **раздро́бленный, раз-дроблённый** shattered; small-scale; fragmented.

раздува́ть(ся, -а́ю(сь *impf. of* **разду́ть(ся**

разду́мать, -аю *pf.*, **разду́мывать, -аю** *impf.* change one's mind; +*inf.* decide not to; ponder, consider; hesitate; **не разду́мывая** without a moment's thought. **разду́мье, -я** meditation; thought, thoughtful mood; hesitation; **в глубо́ком ~** deep in thought.

разду́ть, -у́ю *pf.* (*impf.* **раздува́ть**) blow; fan; blow out; exaggerate; whip up; inflate, swell; blow about; **~ся** swell.

разева́ть, -а́ю *impf. of* **рази́нуть**

разжа́лобить, -блю *pf.* move (to pity).

разжа́ловать, -лую *pf.* degrade, demote.

разжа́ть, -зожму́, -мёшь *pf.* (*impf.* **разжи-ма́ть**) unclasp, open; release, unfasten, undo.

разжева́ть, -жую́, -жуёшь *pf.*, **разжёвы-вать, -аю** *impf.* chew, masticate; chew over.

разже́чь, -зожгу́, -зожжёшь; -жёг, -зожгла́ *pf.*, **разжига́ть, -а́ю** *impf.* kindle; rouse, stir up.

разжима́ть, -а́ю *impf. of* **разжа́ть. раз|жи-ре́ть, -е́ю** *pf.*

рази́нуть, -ну *pf.* (*impf.* **разева́ть**) open; **~ рот** gape; **рази́нув рот** open-mouthed. **рази́-ня, -и** *c.g.* scatter-brain.

рази́тельный striking. **рази́ть, ражу́** *impf.* (*pf.* **по~**) strike.

разлага́ть(ся, -а́ю(сь *impf. of* **разложи́ть(ся**

разла́д, -а discord, dissension; disorder.

разла́мывать(ся, -аю(сь *impf. of* **разло-ма́ть(ся, разломи́ть(ся. разлёгся** *etc.*: *see* **разле́чься**

разлеза́ться, -а́ется *impf.*, **разле́зться, -зется; -ле́зся** *pf.* come to pieces; come apart, fall apart.

разлени́ться, -ню́сь, -нишься *pf.* get very lazy, sink into sloth.

разлета́ться, -а́юсь *impf.*, **разлете́ться, -лечу́сь** *pf.* fly away; fly about, scatter; shatter; vanish, be shattered; fly, rush; rush up.

разле́чься, -ля́гусь; -лёгся, -гла́сь *pf.* stretch out; sprawl.

разли́в, -а bottling; flood; overflow. **разли-ва́ть, -а́ю** *impf.*, **разли́ть, -золью́, -зольёшь; -и́л, -а́, -о** *pf.* pour out; spill; flood (with), drench (with); **~ся** spill; overflow, flood; spread. **разли́вка, -и** bottling. **разливн|о́й** on tap, on draught; **~о́е вино́** wine from the wood. **разли́тие, -я** flooding.

различа́ть, -а́ю *impf.*, **различи́ть, -чу́** *pf.* distinguish; tell the difference; discern, make out; **~ся** differ. **разли́чие, -я** distinction; difference; **зна́ки разли́чия** badges of rank.

различи́тельный distinctive, distinguishing. **разли́чный** different; various, diverse.

разложе́ние, -я breaking down; decomposition; decay; putrefaction; demoralization, corruption; disintegration; expansion; resolution. **разложи́ть, -жу́, -жишь** *pf.* (*impf.* **разлага́ть, раскла́дывать**) put away; lay out; spread (out); distribute, apportion; break down; decompose; expand; resolve; demoralize, corrupt; ~ **костёр** make a fire; ~**ся** decompose; rot, decay; become demoralized; be corrupted; disintegrate, crack up, go to pieces.

разло́м, -а breaking; break. **разлома́ть, -а́ю, разломи́ть, -млю́, -мишь** *pf.* (*impf.* **разла́мывать**) break, break to pieces; pull down; ~**ся** break to pieces.

раз|лохма́тить, -а́чу *pf.*

разлу́ка, -и separation; parting. **разлуча́ть, -а́ю** *impf.*, **разлучи́ть, -чу́** *pf.* separate, part, sever; ~**ся** separate, part.

разлюби́ть, -блю́, -бишь *pf.* cease to love, stop loving; stop liking, no longer like.

разля́гусь *etc.*: *see* **разле́чься**

разма́зать, -а́жу *pf.*, **разма́зывать, -аю** *impf.* spread, smear.

разма́лывать, -аю *impf.* *of* **размоло́ть**

разма́тывать, -аю *impf.* *of* **размота́ть**

разма́х, -а (-у) sweep; swing; span; amplitude; scope, range, scale. **разма́хивать, -аю** *impf.*+*i.* swing; brandish; ~ **рука́ми** gesticulate. **разма́хиваться, -аюсь** *impf.*, **размахну́ться, -ну́сь, -нёшься** *pf.* swing one's arm. **разма́шистый** sweeping.

размежева́ние, -я demarcation, delimitation. **размежева́ть, -жу́ю** *pf.*, **размежёвывать, -аю** *impf.* divide out, delimit; ~**ся** fix one's boundaries; delimit functions or spheres of action.

размёл *etc.*: *see* **размести́**

размельча́ть, -а́ю *impf.*, **раз|мельчи́ть, -чу́** *pf.* crumble, crush, pulverize.

размелю́ *etc.*: *see* **размоло́ть**

разме́н, -а exchange; changing. **разме́нивать, -аю** *impf.*, **разменя́ть, -я́ю** *pf.* change; ~**ся**+*i.* exchange; dissipate. **разме́нн|ый** exchange; ~**ая моне́та** (small) change.

разме́р, -а dimension(s); size; measurement; rate, amount; scale, extent; metre; measure; *pl.* proportions. **разме́ренный** measured. **разме́рить, -рю** *pf.*, **размеря́ть, -я́ю** *impf.* measure off; measure.

размести́, -ету́, -етёшь; -мёл, -а́ *pf.* (*impf.* **размета́ть**) sweep clear; clear; sweep away.

размести́ть, -ещу́ *pf.* (*impf.* **размеща́ть**) place, accommodate; quarter; stow; distribute; ~**ся** take one's seat.

размета́ть, -а́ю *impf.* *of* **размести́**

разме́тить, -е́чу *pf.*, **размеча́ть, -а́ю** *impf.* mark.

размеша́ть, -а́ю *pf.*, **разме́шивать, -аю** *impf.* stir (in).

размеща́ть(ся, -а́ю(сь *impf.* *of* **размести́ть(ся. размеще́ние, -я** placing; accommodation; distribution, disposal, allocation; investment. **размещу́** *etc.*: *see* **размести́ть**

размина́ть(ся, -а́ю(сь *impf.* *of* **размя́ть(ся**

размину́ться, -ну́сь, -нёшься *pf.* pass (one another); cross; +**с**+*i.* pass; miss.

размножа́ть, -а́ю *impf.*, **размно́жить, -жу** *pf.* multiply, manifold, duplicate; breed, rear; ~**ся** propagate itself; breed; spawn.

размозжи́ть, -жу́ *pf.* smash.

размо́лвка, -и tiff, disagreement.

размоло́ть, -мелю́, -ме́лешь *pf.* (*impf.* **разма́лывать**) grind.

размора́живать, -аю *impf.*, **разморо́зить, -о́жу** *pf.* unfreeze, defreeze, defrost; ~**ся** unfreeze; become defrozen, defrosted.

размота́ть, -а́ю *pf.* (*impf.* **разма́тывать**) unwind, unreel; squander.

размыва́ть, -а́ет *impf.*, **размы́ть, -о́ет** *pf.* wash away; erode.

размышле́ние, -я reflection; meditation, thought. **размышля́ть, -я́ю** *impf.* reflect, ponder; think (things) over.

размягча́ть, -а́ю *impf.*, **размягчи́ть, -чу́** *pf.* soften; ~**ся** soften, grow soft. **размягче́ние, -я** softening.

размяка́ть, -а́ю *impf.*, **раз|мя́кнуть, -ну; -мя́к** *pf.* soften, become soft.

раз|мя́ть, -зомну́, -зомнёшь *pf.* (*impf.* *also* **размина́ть**) knead; mash; ~**ся** soften, grow soft; stretch one's legs; limber up, loosen up.

разна́шивать, -аю *impf.* *of* **разноси́ть**

разнести́, -су́, -сёшь; -ёс, -ла́ *pf.* (*impf.* **разноси́ть**) carry, convey; take round, deliver; spread; enter, note down; smash, break up, destroy; blow up; scatter, disperse; *impers.*+*a.* swell (up); **у меня́ щёку разнесло́** my cheek is swollen.

разнима́ть, -а́ю *impf.* *of* **разня́ть**

ра́зниться, -нюсь *impf.* differ. **ра́зница, -ы** difference; disparity; **кака́я** ~? what difference does it make?

разно... *in comb.* different, vari-, hetero-. **разнобо́й, -я** lack of co-ordination; difference, disagreement. ~**ве́с, -а** (set of) weights. ~**ви́дность, -и** variety. ~**гла́сие, -я** difference, disagreement; discrepancy. ~**голо́сый** discordant. ~**кали́берный** of different calibres; mixed, heterogeneous. ~**мы́слие, -я** difference of opinions. ~**обра́зие, -я** variety, diversity; **для** ~**обра́зия** for a change. ~**обра́зить, -а́жу** *impf.* vary, diversify. ~**обра́зный** various, varied, diverse. ~**рабо́чий** *sb.* unskilled labourer. ~**речи́вый** contradictory, conflicting. ~**ро́дный** heterogeneous. ~**склоня́емый** irregularly declined. ~**сторо́нний** many-sided; versatile; all-round; scalene. ~**хара́ктерный** diverse, varied. ~**цве́тный** of different colours; many-coloured, variegated, motley. ~**чте́ние, -я** variant reading. ~**ше́рстный**, ~**шёрстый** with coats of different colours; mixed, ill-assorted. **~язычный** polyglot.

разносить[1], -ошу, -осишь *pf.* (*impf.* **разнашивать**) break in, wear in; **~ся** become comfortable with wear.

разносить[2], -ошу, -осишь *impf. of* **разнести. разноска, -и** delivery. **разносн|ый** delivery; abusive; **~ые слова** swear-words.

разность, -и difference; diversity. **разносчик, -а** pedlar, hawker.

разношу *etc.*: *see* **разносить**

разнузданный unbridled, unruly.

разн|ый different, differing; various, diverse; **~ое** *sb.* different things; various matters, any other business.

разнять, -ниму, -нимешь; роз- *or* **разнял, -а, -о** *pf.* (*impf.* **разнимать**) take to pieces, dismantle, disjoint; part, separate.

разо... *see* **раз...**

разоблачать, -аю *impf.*, **разоблачить, -чу** *pf.* expose, unmask. **разоблачение, -я** exposure, unmasking.

разобрать, -зберу, -рёшь; -ал, -а, -о *pf.* (*impf.* **разбирать**) take; take to pieces, strip, dismantle; buy up; sort out; investigate, look into; analyse, parse; make out, understand; **ничего нельзя ~** one can't make head or tail of it; **~ся** sort things out; +**в**+*p.* investigate, look into; understand.

разобщать, -аю *impf.*, **разобщить, -щу** *pf.* separate; estrange, alienate; disconnect, uncouple, disengage. **разобщение, -я** disconnection, uncoupling. **разобщённо** *adv.* apart, separately.

разобью *etc.*: *see* **разбить. разовью** *etc.*: *see* **развить**

разогнать, -згоню, -онишь; -гнал, -а, -о *pf.* (*impf.* **разгонять**) scatter, drive away; disperse; dispel; drive fast, race; space. **~ся** gather speed, gather momentum.

разогнуть, -ну, -нёшь *pf.* (*impf.* **разгибать**) unbend, straighten; **~ся** straighten (o.s.) up.

разогревать, -аю *impf.*, **разогреть, -ею** *pf.* warm up; **~ся** warm up, grow warm.

разодеть(ся, -ену(сь *pf.* dress up.

разодрать, -здеру, -рёшь; -ал, -а, -о *pf.* (*impf.* **раздирать**) tear (up); lacerate, harrow.

разожгу *etc.*: *see* **разжечь. разожму** *etc.*: *see* **разжать**

разо|злить, -лю *pf.* anger, enrage; **~ся** get angry, fly into a rage.

разойтись, -йдусь, -йдёшься; -ошёлся, -ошлась *pf.* (*impf.* **расходиться**) go away; break up, disperse; branch off, diverge; radiate; differ, be at variance, conflict; part, separate, be divorced; dissolve, melt; be spent; be sold out; be out of print; gather speed; be carried away.

разолью *etc.*: *see* **разлить**

разом *adv.* all at once, all at one go.

разомну *etc.*: *see* **размять**

разорвать, -ву, -вёшь; -ал, -а, -о *pf.* (*impf.* **разрывать**) tear; break (off), sever; blow up, burst; **~ся** tear, become torn; break, snap; blow up, burst; explode, go off.

разорение, -я ruin; destruction, havoc. **разорительный** ruinous; wasteful. **разорить, -рю** *pf.* (*impf.* **разорять**) ruin, bring to ruin; destroy, ravage; **~ся** ruin o.s., be ruined.

разоружать, -аю *impf.*, **разоружить, -жу** *pf.* disarm; **~ся** disarm. **разоружение, -я** disarmament.

разорять(ся, -яю(сь *impf. of* **разорить(ся**

разослать, -ошлю, -ошлёшь *pf.* (*impf.* **рассылать**) send round, distribute, circulate; send out, dispatch.

разостлать, расстелить, -стелю, -телешь *pf.* (*impf.* **расстилать**) spread (out); lay; **~ся** spread.

разотру *etc.*: *see* **растереть**

разочарование, -я disappointment. **разочарованный** disappointed, disillusioned.

разочаровать, -рую *pf.*, **разочаровывать, -аю** *impf.* disappoint, disillusion, disenchant; **~ся** be disappointed, be disillusioned.

разочту *etc.*: *see* **расчесть. разошёлся** *etc.*: *see* **разойтись разошлю** *etc.*: *see* **разослать. разошью** *etc.*: *see* **расшить**

разрабатывать, -аю *impf.*, **разработать, -аю** *pf.* cultivate; work, exploit; work out, work up; develop; elaborate. **разработка, -и** cultivation; working, exploitation; working out, working up; elaboration; field; pit, working, quarry.

разражаться, -аюсь *impf.*, **разразиться, -ажусь** *pf.* break out; burst out; **~ смехом** burst out laughing.

разрастаться, -ается *impf.*, **разрастись, -тётся; -росся, -лась** *pf.* grow, grow up; grow thickly; spread.

разрежённ|ый; -ён, -а rarefied, rare; **~ое пространство** vacuum.

разрез, -а cut; slit, slash; section; point of view; **в ~е**+*g.* from the point of view of, in the context of; **в этом ~е** in this connection. **разрезать, -ежу** *pf.*, **разрезать, -аю** *impf.* cut; slit. **разрезной** cutting; slit, with slits; **~ нож** paper-knife.

разрешать, -аю *impf.*, **разрешить, -шу** *pf.* (+*d.*) allow, permit; authorize; (+*a.*) release, absolve; solve; settle; **разрешите пройти** let me pass; do you mind letting me pass?; **~ся** be allowed; be solved; be settled; **~ся от бремени** be delivered of; **«курить не разрешается»** 'No smoking'. **разрешение, -я** permission; authorization, permit; solution; settlement. **разрешимый** solvable.

разрозненный uncoordinated; odd; incomplete, broken.

разросся *etc.*: *see* **разрастись. разрою** *etc.*: *see* **разрыть**

разрубать, -аю *impf.*, **разрубить, -блю, -бишь** *pf.* cut, cleave; hack; chop.

разруха, -и ruin, collapse. **разрушать, -аю** *impf.*, **разрушить, -шу** *pf.* destroy; demolish, wreck; ruin; frustrate, blast, blight; **~ся**

go to ruin, collapse. **разрушéние, -я** destruction. **разрушúтельный** destructive.

разрыв, -а breach; break; gap; rupture, severance; burst, explosion. **разрывáть[1](ся, -áю(сь** *impf. of* **разорвáть(ся**

разрывáть[2], -áю *impf. of* **разрыть**

разрывнóй explosive, bursting.

разрыть, -рóю *pf.* (*impf.* **разрывáть**) dig (up); turn upside down, rummage through.

раз|рыхлúть, -лю́ *pf.*, **разрыхля́ть, -я́ю** *impf.* loosen; hoe.

разря́д[1], -а category, rank; sort; class, rating.

разря́д[2], -а discharge. **разрядúть, -яжу́, -я́дишь** *pf.* (*impf.* **разряжáть**) unload; discharge; space out; **~ся** run down; clear, ease. **разря́дка, -и** spacing (out); discharging; unloading; **~ напряжённости** lessening of tension, détente.

разря́дник, -а, -ница, -ы ranking player or competitor.

разряжáть(ся, -áю(сь *impf. of* **разрядúть(ся**

разубедúть, -ежу́ *pf.*, **разубеждáть, -áю** *impf.* dissuade; **~ся** change one's mind, change one's opinion.

разувáться, -áюсь *impf. of* **разу́ться**

разувéрить, -рю *pf.*, **разуверя́ть, -я́ю** *impf.* dissuade, undeceive; +**в**+*p.* argue out of; **~ся** (**в**+*p.*) lose faith (in), cease to believe.

разузнавáть, -наю́, -наёшь *impf.*, **разузнáть, -áю** *pf.* (try to) find out; make inquiries.

разукрáсить, -áшу *pf.*, **разукрáшивать, -аю** *impf.* adorn, decorate, embellish.

разукрупнúть(ся, -ню́(сь *pf.*, **разукрупня́ть(ся, -я́ю(сь** *impf.* break up into smaller units.

рáзум, -а reason; mind, intellect; **у негó ум за ~ зашёл** he is (was) at his wit's end. **разумéться, -éется** *impf.* be understood, be meant; **(самó собóй) разумéется** of course; it stands to reason, it goes without saying. **разу́мный** possessing reason; judicious, intelligent; sensible; reasonable; wise.

разу́ться, -у́юсь *pf.* (*impf.* **разувáться**) take off one's shoes.

разу́чивать, -аю *impf.*, **разучúть, -чу́, -чишь** *pf.* study; learn (up). **разу́чиваться, -аюсь** *impf.*, **разучúться, -чу́сь, -чишься** *pf.* forget (how to).

разъ... *see* **раз...**

разъедáть, -áет *impf. of* **разъéсть**

разъединúть, -ню́ *pf.*, **разъединя́ть, -я́ю** *impf.* separate, disunite; disconnect; **нас разъединúли** we were cut off.

разъéдусь *etc.*: *see* **разъéхаться**

разъéзд, -а departure; dispersal; passing loop, siding (track); mounted patrol; travelling (about), journeys. **разъезднóй** travelling. **разъезжáть, -áю** *impf.* drive about, ride about; travel, wander; **~ся** *impf. of* **разъéхаться**

разъéсть, -éст, -едя́т; -éл *pf.* (*impf.* **разъедáть**) eat away; corrode.

разъéхаться, -éдусь *pf.* (*impf.* **разъезжáться**) depart; disperse; separate; (be able to) pass; pass one another, miss one another; slide apart.

разъярённый; -ён, -á furious, in a furious temper, frantic with rage. **разъярúть, -рю́** *pf.*, **разъяря́ть, -я́ю** *impf.* infuriate, rouse to fury; **~ся** get furious, become frantic with rage.

разъяснéние, -я explanation, elucidation; interpretation. **разъяснúтельный** explanatory, elucidatory. **разъя́сниваться, -ается** *impf.*, **разъя́сниться, -ится** *pf.* clear (up).

разъяснúть, -ню́ *pf.*, **разъясня́ть, -я́ю** *impf.* explain, elucidate; interpret; **~ся** become clear, be cleared up.

разыгрáть, -áю *pf.*, **разы́грывать, -аю** *impf.* play (through); perform; draw; raffle; play a trick on; **~ся** rise, get up; run high.

разыскáть, -ыщу́, -ы́щешь *pf.* find. **разы́скивать, -аю** *impf.* look for, search for; **~ся** be wanted.

рай, -я, *loc.* **-ю́** paradise; garden of Eden.

рай... *abbr.* (*of* **райóнный**) *in comb.* district. **райкóм, -а** district committee. **~совéт, -а** district soviet.

райóн, -а region; area; zone; (*administrative*) district. **райóнный** district.

рáйский heavenly.

рак, -а crawfish, crayfish; cancer, canker; Crab; Cancer.

ракéта[1], -ы, ракéтка, -и racket.

ракéта[2], -ы rocket; (*ballistic*) missile; flare; **~-носúтель, -я** carrier rocket, launch vehicle. **ракéтный** rocket; jet.

рáковина, -ы shell; sink.

рáковый cancer; cancerous.

рáлли *nt. indecl.* rally. **раллúст, -а** rallier.

рáма, -ы frame; chassis, carriage; **встáвить в рáму** frame.

рамазáн, -а (*relig.*) Ramadan.

рáмка, -и frame; *pl.* framework, limits; **в рáмке** framed.

рáмпа, -ы footlights.

рáна, -ы wound. **ранéние, -я** wounding; wound, injury. **рáненый** wounded; injured.

рáнец, -нца knapsack, haversack; satchel.

рáнить, -ню *impf.* & *pf.* wound; injure.

рáнний early. **рáно** *pred.* it is (too) early. **рáно** *adv.* early; **~ или пóздно** sooner or later. **рáньше** *adv.* earlier; before; formerly; first (of all).

рапúра, -ы foil. **рапирúст, -а, рапирúстка, -и** fencer.

рáпорт, -а report. **рапортовáть, -ту́ю** *impf.* & *pf.* report.

рапсóдия, -и rhapsody.

рас... *see* **раз...** .

рáса, -ы race. **расúзм, -а** rac(ial)ism. **расúст, -а** rac(ial)ist.

раскáиваться, -аюсь *impf. of* **раскáяться**

раскалённый; -ён, -á scorching, burning hot;

incandescent. **раскали́ть, -лю́** *pf.* (*impf.* **раскаля́ть**) make very hot, make red-hot, white-hot; **~ся** heat up, glow, become red-hot, white-hot. **раска́лывать(ся, -аю(сь** *impf. of* **расколо́ть(ся раскаля́ть(ся, -я́ю(сь** *impf. of* **раскали́ть(ся. раска́пывать, -аю** *impf. of* **раскопа́ть**

раска́т, -а roll, peal. **раската́ть, -а́ю** *pf.*, **раска́тывать, -аю** *impf.* roll, roll out, smooth out, level; drive, ride, (about). **раска́тистый** rolling, booming. **раскати́ться, -ачу́сь, -а́тишься** *pf.*, **раска́тываться, -аюсь** *impf.* gather speed; roll away; peal, boom.

раскача́ть, -а́ю *pf.*, **раска́чивать, -аю** *impf.* swing; rock; loosen, shake loose; shake up, stir up; **~ся** swing, rock; shake loose; bestir o.s.

раска́яние, -я repentance, remorse. **рас|ка́яться, -а́юсь** *pf.* (*impf. also* **раска́иваться**) repent.

расквита́ться, -а́юсь *pf.* settle accounts; get even, be quits.

раски́дывать, -аю *impf.*, **раски́нуть, -ну** *pf.* stretch (out); spread; scatter; set up, pitch; **~ умо́м** ponder, think things over, consider; **~ся** spread out, lie, sprawl.

раскла́дка, -и laying; putting up; allotment. **раскладн|о́й** folding; **~а́я крова́ть** camp-bed. **раскладу́шка, -и** camp-bed. **раскла́дывать, -аю** *impf. of* **разложи́ть**

раскла́няться, -яюсь *pf.* bow; exchange bows; take leave.

раскле́ивать, -аю *impf.*, **раскле́ить, -е́ю** *pf.* unstick; stick (up), paste (up); **~ся** come unstuck; fall through, fail to come off; feel seedy, be off colour.

раскле́шенный flared.

раско́л, -а split, division; schism; dissent. **рас|коло́ть, -лю́, -лешь** *pf.* (*impf. also* **раска́лывать**) split; chop; break; disrupt, break up; **~ся** split; crack, break. **раско́льник, -а** dissenter, schismatic. **раско́льнический** dissenting, schismatic.

раскопа́ть, -а́ю *pf.* (*impf.* **раска́пывать**) dig up, unearth, excavate. **раско́пка, -и** digging up; *pl.* excavation, excavations.

раско́сый slanting, slant.

раскраду́ *etc.*: *see* **раскра́сть. раскра́дывать, -аю** *impf. of* **раскра́сть. раскра́ивать, -аю** *impf. of* **раскрои́ть**

раскра́сить, -а́шу *pf.* (*impf.* **раскра́шивать**) paint, colour. **раскра́ска, -и** painting, colouring; colours, colour scheme.

раскрасне́ться, -е́юсь *pf.* flush, go red.

раскра́сть, -аду́, -адёшь *pf.* (*impf.* **раскра́дывать**) loot, clean out.

раскра́шивать, -аю *impf. of* **раскра́сить**

раскрепости́ть, -ощу́ *pf.*, **раскрепоща́ть, -а́ю** *impf.* set free, liberate, emancipate. **раскрепоще́ние, -я** liberation, emancipation.

раскритикова́ть, -ку́ю *pf.* criticize harshly, slate.

раскрои́ть, -ою́ *pf.* (*impf.* **раскра́ивать**) cut out; cut open.

рас|кроши́ть(ся, -шу́(сь, -шишь(ся *pf.* **раскро́ю** *etc.*: *see* **раскры́ть**

раскрути́ть, -учу́, -у́тишь *pf.*, **раскру́чивать, -аю** *impf.* untwist, undo; **~ся** come untwisted, come undone.

раскрыва́ть, -а́ю *impf.*, **раскры́ть, -о́ю** *pf.* open; expose, bare; reveal, disclose, lay bare; discover; **~ся** open; uncover o.s.; come out, come to light, be discovered.

раскупа́ть, -а́ет *impf.*, **раскупи́ть, -у́пит** *pf.* buy up.

раску́поривать, -аю *impf.*, **раску́порить, -рю** *pf.* uncork, open.

раскуси́ть, -ушу́, -у́сишь *pf.*, **раску́сывать, -аю** *impf.* bite through; get to the core of; see through.

раску́тать, -аю *pf.* unwrap.

ра́совый racial.

распа́д, -а disintegration, break-up; collapse; decomposition. **распада́ться, -а́ется** *impf. of* **распа́сться**

распа́ивать, -аю *impf. of* **распая́ть**

распакова́ть, -ку́ю *pf.*, **распако́вывать, -аю** *impf.* unpack; **~ся** unpack; come undone.

распа́рывать(ся, -аю(сь *impf. of* **распоро́ть(ся**

распа́сться, -адётся *pf.* (*impf.* **распада́ться**) disintegrate, fall to pieces; break up; collapse; decompose, dissociate.

распаха́ть, -ашу́, -а́шешь *pf.*, **распа́хивать[1], -аю** *impf.* plough up.

распа́хивать[2], -аю *impf.*, **распахну́ть, -ну́, -нёшь** *pf.* open (wide); fling open, throw open; **~ся** open; fly open, swing open; throw open one's coat.

распая́ть, -я́ю *pf.* (*impf.* **распа́ивать**) unsolder; **~ся** come unsoldered.

распева́ть, -а́ю *impf.* sing.

распеча́тать, -аю *pf.*, **распеча́тывать, -аю** *impf.* open; unseal; print out. **распеча́тка, -и** printout.

распи́вочн|ый for consumption on the premises; **~ая** *sb.* tavern, bar.

распи́ливать, -аю *impf.*, **распили́ть, -лю́, -лишь** *pf.* saw up.

распина́ть, -аю *impf. of* **распя́ть**

расписа́ние, -я time-time, schedule. **расписа́ть, -ишу́, -и́шешь** *pf.*, **распи́сывать, -аю** *impf.* enter; assign, allot; paint; decorate; **~ся** sign; register one's marriage; **+в**+*p.* sign for; acknowledge; testify to. **распи́ска, -и** receipt. **расписно́й** painted, decorated.

рас|пла́вить, -влю *pf.*, **расплавля́ть, -я́ю** *impf.* melt, fuse. **расплавле́ние, -я** melting, fusion.

распла́каться, -а́чусь *pf.* burst into tears.

распласта́ть, -а́ю *pf.* spread; flatten; split, divide into layers; **~ся** sprawl.

распла́та, -ы payment; retribution; **час распла́ты** day of reckoning. **расплати́ться, -ачу́сь, -а́тишься** *pf.*, **распла́чиваться,**

-аюсь *impf.* (+**с**+*i.*) pay off; settle accounts, get even; +**за**+*a.* pay for.
расплеска́ть(ся, -ещу́(сь, -е́щешь(ся *pf.*, **расплёскивать(ся, -аю(сь** *impf.* spill.
расплести́, -ету́, -етёшь; -ёл, -а́ *pf.*, **расплета́ть, -а́ю** *impf.* unplait; untwine, untwist, undo; **~сь** come unplaited, come undone; untwine, untwist.
рас|плоди́ть(ся, -ожу́(сь *pf.*
расплыва́ться, -а́ется *impf.*, **расплы́ться, -ывётся; -ы́лся, -а́сь** *pf.* run; spread. **расплы́вчатый** dim, indistinct; diffuse, vague.
расплю́щивать, -аю *impf.*, **расплю́щить, -щу** *pf.* flatten out, hammer out.
распну́ *etc.*: *see* **распя́ть**
распознава́емый recognizable, identifiable. **распознава́ть, -наю́, -наёшь** *impf.*, **распозна́ть, -а́ю** *pf.* recognize, identify; distinguish; diagnose.
располага́ть, -а́ю *impf.* (*pf.* **расположи́ть**) +*i.* dispose of, have at one's disposal, have available; **не ~ вре́менем** have no time to spare. **располага́ться, -а́юсь** *impf. of* **расположи́ться располага́ющий** prepossessing.
располза́ться, -а́ется *impf.*, **расползти́сь, -зётся; -о́лзся, -зла́сь** *pf.* crawl, crawl away; ravel out; give (at the seams).
расположе́ние, -я disposition; arrangement; situation, location; inclination; tendency, propensity; bias, penchant; favour, liking; sympathies; mood, humour. **располо́женный** well-disposed; disposed, inclined, in the mood; **я не о́чень располо́жен сего́дня рабо́тать** I don't feel much like working today. **расположи́ть, -жу́, -жишь** *pf.* (*impf.* **располага́ть**) dispose; arrange, set out; win over, gain; **~ся** settle down; compose o.s., make o.s. comfortable.
рас|поро́ть, -рю́, -решь *pf.* (*impf. also* **распа́рывать**) unpick, undo, rip; **~ся** rip, come undone.
распоряди́тель, -я *m.* manager. **распоряди́тельность, -и** good management; efficiency; **отсу́тствие распоряди́тельности** mismanagement. **распоряди́тельный** capable; efficient; active. **распоряди́ться, -яжу́сь** *pf.*, **распоряжа́ться, -а́юсь** *impf.* order, give orders; see; +*i.* manage, deal with, dispose of. **распоря́док, -дка** order; routine; **пра́вила вну́треннего распоря́дка на фа́брике** factory regulations. **распоряже́ние, -я** order; instruction, direction; disposal, command; **быть в распоряже́нии**+*g.* be at the disposal of; **до осо́бого распоряже́ния** until further notice.
распра́ва, -ы punishment, execution; violence; reprisal; **крова́вая ~** massacre, butchery.
распра́вить, -влю *pf.*, **расправля́ть, -я́ю** *impf.* straighten; smooth out; spread, stretch; **~ кры́лья** spread one's wings.
распра́виться, -влюсь *pf.*, **расправля́ться, -я́юсь** *impf.* **с**+*i.* deal with, make short work of; give short shrift to.
распределе́ние, -я distribution; allocation, assignment. **распредели́тель, -я** *m.* distributor; retailer. **распредели́тельный** distributive, distributing; **~ щит** switchboard. **распредели́ть, -лю́** *pf.*, **распределя́ть, -я́ю** *impf.* distribute; allocate, allot, assign; **~ своё вре́мя** allocate one's time.
распродава́ть, -даю́, -даёшь *impf.*, **распрода́ть, -а́м, -а́шь, -а́ст, -ади́м; -о́дал, -а́, -о** *pf.* sell off; sell out. **распрода́жа, -и** sale; clearance sale.
распростёрт|ый outstretched; prostrate, prone; **с ~ыми объя́тиями** with open arms.
распрости́ться, -ощу́сь *pf.*, **распроща́ться, -а́юсь** *pf.* take leave, bid farewell.
распростране́ние, -я spreading, diffusion; dissemination; circulation. **распространённый; -ён, -а́** widespread, prevalent. **распространи́ть, -ню́** *pf.*, **распространя́ть, -я́ю** *impf.* spread; give currency to; diffuse; disseminate, propagate; popularize; extend; give off, give out; **~ся** spread; extend; apply; enlarge, expatiate, dilate (**о**+*p.* on).
распроща́ться *etc.*: *see* **распрости́ться**
ра́спря, -и; *g.pl.* **-ей** quarrel, feud.
распряга́ть, -а́ю *impf.*, **распря́чь, -ягу́, -яжёшь; -я́г, -ла́** *pf.* unharness.
распуска́ть, -а́ю *impf.*, **распусти́ть, -ущу́, -у́стишь** *pf.* dismiss; dissolve; disband; let out; relax; let get out of hand; spoil; dissolve; melt; spread; **~ во́лосы** loosen one's hair; **~ на кани́кулы** dismiss for the holidays; **~ся** open, come out; come loose; dissolve; melt; get out of hand; let o.s. go.
распу́тать, -аю *pf.* (*impf.* **распу́тывать**) disentangle, untangle; unravel; untie, loose; puzzle out.
распу́тица, -ы season of bad roads; slush.
распу́тный dissolute, dissipated, debauched.
распу́тывать, -аю *impf. of* **распу́тать**
распу́тье, -я crossroads; parting of the ways.
распуха́ть, -а́ю *impf.*, **распу́хнуть, -ну; -у́х** *pf.* swell (up).
распу́щенный undisciplined; spoilt; dissolute, dissipated.
распыле́ние, -я dispersion, scattering; spraying; atomization. **распыли́тель, -я** *m.* spray, atomizer. **распыли́ть, -лю́** *pf.*, **распыля́ть, -я́ю** *impf.* spray; atomize; pulverize; disperse, scatter; **~ся** disperse, get scattered.
распя́тие, -я crucifixion; crucifix, cross. **распя́ть, -пну́, -пнёшь** *pf.* (*impf.* **распина́ть**) crucify.
расса́да, -ы seedlings. **рассади́ть, -ажу́, -а́дишь** *pf.*, **расса́живать, -аю** *impf.* plant out, transplant; seat, offer seats; separate, seat separately.
расса́живаться, -ается *impf. of* **рассе́сться. расса́сываться, -ается** *impf. of* **рассоса́ться**
рассвести́, -етёт; -ело́ *pf.*, **рассвета́ть, -а́ет**

impf. dawn; **рассветáет** day is breaking; **совершéнно рассвелó** it is (was) broad daylight. **рассвéт, -а** dawn, daybreak.

рас|свирипéть, -éю *pf.*

расседлáть, -áю *pf.* unsaddle.

рассéивание, -я dispersion; dispersal, scattering, dissipation. **рассéивать(ся, -аю(сь** *impf. of* **рассéять(ся**

рассекáть, -áю *impf. of* **рассéчь**

расселéние, -я settling, resettlement; separation.

рассéлина, -ы cleft, fissure; crevasse.

расселúть, -лю́ *pf.*, **расселя́ть, -я́ю** *impf.* settle, resettle; separate, settle apart.

рас|сердúть(ся, -жу́(сь, -рдишь(ся *pf.* **рассéрженный** angry.

рассéсться, -ся́дусь *pf.* (*impf.* **рассáживаться**) take seats; sprawl.

рассéчь, -еку́, -ечёшь; -ёк, -лá *pf.* (*impf.* **рассекáть**) cut, cut through; cleave.

рассéянность, -и absent-mindedness, distraction; diffusion; dispersion; dissipation. **рассéянный** absent-minded; diffused; scattered, dispersed; dissipated; ~ **свет** diffused light. **рассéять, -éю** *pf.* (*impf.* **рассéивать**) sow, broadcast; place at intervals, dot about; disperse, scatter; dispel; ~**ся** disperse, scatter; clear, lift; divert o.s., have some distraction.

расскáз, -а story, tale; account, narrative. **рассказáть, -ажу́, -áжешь** *pf.*, **расскáзывать, -аю** *impf.* tell, narrate, recount. **расскáзчик, -а** story-teller, narrator.

расслáбить, -блю *pf.*, **расслабля́ть, -я́ю** *impf.* weaken, enfeeble; enervate. **расслаблéние, -я** weakening, enfeeblement; relaxation.

расслáивать(ся, -аю(сь *impf. of* **расслоúть(ся**

расслéдование, -я investigation, examination; inquiry; **произвестú** ~+*g.* hold an inquiry into. **расслéдовать, -дую** *impf.* & *pf.* investigate, look into, hold an inquiry into.

расслоéние, -я stratification; exfoliation. **расслоúть, -ою́** *pf.* (*impf.* **расслáивать**) divide into layers, stratify; ~**ся** become stratified; exfoliate, flake off.

расслы́шать, -шу *pf.* catch.

рассмáтривать, -аю *impf. of* **рассмотрéть**; examine, scrutinize; regard as, consider.

рас|смешúть, -шу́ *pf.*

рассмея́ться, -ею́сь, -еёшься *pf.* burst out laughing.

рассмотрéние, -я examination, scrutiny; consideration; **представить на** ~ submit for consideration. **рассмотрéть, -рю́, -ришь** *pf.* (*impf.* **рассмáтривать**) examine, consider; descry, discern, make out.

рассовáть, -сую́, -суёшь *pf.*, **рассóвывать, -аю** *impf.* **по**+*d.* shove into, stuff into.

рассóл, -а (-у) brine; pickle.

рассóриться, -рюсь *pf.* **с**+*i.* fall out with, quarrel with.

рас|сортировáть, -ру́ю *pf.*, **рассортирóвывать, -аю** *impf.* sort out.

рассосáться, -сётся *pf.* (*impf.* **рассáсываться**) resolve.

рассóхнуться, -нется; -óхся *pf.* (*impf.* **рассыхáться**) warp, crack, shrink.

расспрáшивать, -аю *impf.*, **расспросúть, -ошу́, -óсишь** *pf.* question; make inquiries of.

рассрóчить, -чу *pf.* spread (over), divide into instalments. **рассрóчка, -и** instalment; **в рассрóчку** in instalments, by instalments.

расставáние, -я parting. **расставáться, -таю́сь, -таёшься** *impf. of* **расстáться**

расстáвить, -влю *pf.*, **расставля́ть, -я́ю** *impf.*, **расстанáвливать, -аю** *impf.* place, arrange, post; move apart, set apart; let out; ~ **часовы́х** post sentries. **расстанóвка, -и** placing; arrangement; pause; spacing; **говорúть с расстанóвкой** speak slowly and deliberately.

расстáться, -áнусь *pf.* (*impf.* **расставáться**) part, separate; +**с**+*i.* leave; give up.

расстёгивать, -аю *impf.*, **расстегну́ть, -ну́, -нёшь** *pf.* undo, unfasten; unbutton; unhook, unclasp, unbuckle; ~**ся** come undone; undo one's coat.

расстелúть(ся, *etc.*: *see* **разостлáть(ся. расстилáть(ся, -áю(сь** *impf. of* **разостлáть(ся**

расстоя́ние, -я distance, space, interval; **на далёком расстоя́нии** a long way off, in the far distance.

расстрáивать(ся, -аю(сь *impf. of* **расстрóить(ся**

расстрéл, -а execution, shooting. **расстрéливать, -аю** *impf.*, **расстреля́ть, -я́ю** *pf.* shoot.

расстрóенный disordered, deranged; upset; out of tune. **расстрóить, -óю** *pf.* (*impf.* **расстрáивать**) upset; thwart; frustrate; put out; disorder, derange; disturb; throw into confusion; unsettle; put out of tune; ~ **ряды́ протúвника** break the enemy's ranks; ~**ся** be frustrated; be shattered; be upset, be put out; get out of tune; fall into confusion, fall apart; fall through. **расстрóйство, -а** disorder, disarray; derangement; confusion; frustration; discomposure; ~ **желу́дка** indigestion; diarrhoea.

расступáться, -áется *impf.*, **расступúться, -у́пится** *pf.* part, make way.

расстыковáться, -ку́ется *pf.* disengage, cast off. **расстыкóвка, -и** disengagement, casting off.

рассудúтельность, -и reasonableness; good sense. **рассудúтельный** reasonable; sober-minded; sensible. **рассудúть, -ужу́, -у́дишь** *pf.* judge, arbitrate; think, consider; decide. **рассу́док, -дка** reason; intellect, mind; good sense. **рассуждáть, -áю** *impf.* reason; deliberate; debate; argue; +**о**+*p.* discuss. **рассуждéние, -я** reasoning; discussion; debate; argument; **без рассуждéний** without arguing.

рассую́ *etc.*: *see* **рассова́ть**

рассчи́танный calculated, deliberate; meant, intended, designed. **рассчита́ть, -а́ю** *pf.*, **рассчи́тывать, -аю** *impf.*, **расче́сть, разочту́, -тёшь; расчёл, разочла́** *pf.* calculate; compute; rate; count, reckon; expect, hope; rely, depend; **~ся** settle accounts, reckon.

рассыла́ть, -а́ю *impf. of* **разосла́ть. рассы́лка, -и** delivery, distribution. **рассы́льный** *sb.* messenger; delivery man.

рассы́пать, -плю *pf.*, **рассыпа́ть, -а́ю** *impf.* spill; strew, scatter; **~ся** spill, scatter; spread out, deploy; crumble; go to pieces, disintegrate; be profuse; **~ся в похвала́х**+*d.* shower praises on. **рассыпно́й** (sold) loose. **рассы́пчатый** friable; short, crumbly; floury.

рассыха́ться, -а́ется *impf. of* **рассо́хнуться. расся́дусь** *etc.*: *see* **рассе́сться.**

раста́лкивать, -аю *impf. of* **растолка́ть**

раста́пливать(ся, -аю(сь *impf. of* **растопи́ть(ся раста́птывать, -аю** *impf. of* **растопта́ть**

растаска́ть, -а́ю *pf.*, **раста́скивать, -аю** *impf.*, **растащи́ть, -щу́, -щишь** *pf.* pilfer, filch.

раста́чивать, -аю *impf. of* **расточи́ть. растащи́ть** *see* **растаска́ть. рас|та́ять, -а́ю** *pf.*

раство́р², **-а** (extent of) opening, span. **раство́р¹**, **-а** solution; mortar. **раствори́мый** soluble; ~ **ко́фе** instant coffee. **раствори́тель, -я** *m.* solvent. **раствори́ть¹**, **-рю́** *pf.* (*impf.* **растворя́ть**) dissolve; mix; **~ся** dissolve.

раствори́ть², **-рю́, -ришь** *pf.* (*impf.* **растворя́ть**) open; **~ся** open.

растворя́ть(ся, -я́ю(сь *impf. of* **раствори́ть(ся. растека́ться, -а́ется** *impf. of* **расте́чься**

расте́ние, -я plant.

растере́ть, разотру́, -трёшь; растёр *pf.* (*impf.* **растира́ть**) grind; pound; triturate; spread; rub; massage; **~ся** rub o.s. briskly.

растерза́ть, -а́ю *pf.*, **расте́рзывать, -аю** *impf.* tear to pieces; lacerate, harrow.

расте́рянность, -и confusion, perplexity, dismay. **расте́рянный** confused, perplexed, dismayed. **растеря́ть, -я́ю** *pf.* lose; **~ся** get lost; lose one's head, get confused.

расте́чься, -ечётся, -еку́тся; -тёкся, -ла́сь *pf.* (*impf.* **растека́ться**) spill; run; spread.

расти́, -ту́, -тёшь; рос, -ла́ *impf.* grow; increase; grow up; advance, develop.

растира́ние, -я grinding; rubbing, massage. **растира́ть(ся, -а́ю(сь** *impf. of* **растере́ть(ся**

расти́тельность, -и vegetation; hair. **расти́тельный** vegetable. **расти́ть, ращу́** *impf.* raise, bring up; train; grow, cultivate.

растолка́ть, -а́ю *pf.* (*impf.* **раста́лкивать**) push apart; shake. **растолкну́ть, -ну́, -нёшь** *pf.* part forcibly, push apart.

растолкова́ть, -ку́ю *pf.*, **растолко́вывать, -аю** *impf.* explain, make clear.

рас|толо́чь, -лку́, -лчёшь; -ло́к, -лкла́ *pf.*

растолсте́ть, -е́ю *pf.* put on weight, grow stout.

растопи́ть¹, **-плю́, -пишь** *pf.* (*impf.* **раста́пливать**) melt; thaw; **~ся** melt.

растопи́ть², **-плю́, -пишь** *pf.* (*impf.* **раста́пливать**) light, kindle; **~ся** begin to burn. **расто́пка, -и** lighting; kindling, firewood.

растопта́ть, -пчу́, -пчешь *pf.* (*impf.* **раста́птывать**) trample, stamp on, crush.

расторга́ть, -а́ю *impf.*, **расто́ргнуть, -ну; -о́рг** *pf.* cancel, dissolve, annul, abrogate. **расторже́ние, -я** cancellation, dissolution, annulment, abrogation.

расторо́пный quick, prompt, smart; efficient.

расточа́ть, -а́ю *impf.*, **расточи́ть¹**, **-чу́** *pf.* waste, squander, dissipate; lavish, shower. **расточи́тельный** extravagant, wasteful.

расточи́ть², **-чу́, -чишь** *pf.* (*impf.* **раста́чивать**) bore, bore out.

растрави́ть, -влю́, -вишь *pf.*, **растравля́ть, -я́ю** *impf.* irritate.

растра́та, -ы spending; waste; squandering; embezzlement. **растра́тить, -а́чу** *pf.*, **растра́чивать, -аю** *impf.* spend; waste, squander, dissipate; fritter away; embezzle. **растра́тчик, -а** embezzler.

растрёпанный tousled, dishevelled; tattered. **рас|трепа́ть, -плю́, -плешь** *pf.* disarrange; tousle, dishevel; tatter, tear; **~ся** get tousled; be dishevelled; get tattered.

растре́скаться, -ается *pf.*, **растре́скиваться, -ается** *impf.* crack, chap.

растро́гать, -аю *pf.* move, touch; **~ся** be moved.

растя́гивать, -аю *impf.*, **растяну́ть, -ну́, -нешь** *pf.* stretch (out); strain, sprain; prolong, drag out; ~ **себе́ мы́шцу** pull a muscle; **~ся** stretch; lengthen; be prolonged, drag out; stretch o.s. out, sprawl; measure one's length, fall flat. **растяже́ние, -я** tension; stretch, stretching; strain, sprain. **растяжи́мость, -и** stretchability; tensility; extensibility. **растяжи́мый** tensile; extensible; stretchable. **растя́нутый** stretched; long-winded, prolix.

рас|фасова́ть, -су́ю *pf.*

расформирова́ние, -я breaking up; disbandment. **расформирова́ть, -ру́ю** *pf.*, **расформиро́вывать, -аю** *impf.* break up; disband.

расха́живать, -аю *impf.* walk about; pace up and down; ~ **по ко́мнате** pace the floor.

расха́ливать, -аю *impf.*, **расхвали́ть, -лю́, -лишь** *pf.* lavish, shower, praises on.

расхва́рываться, -аюсь *impf. of* **расхвора́ться**

расхвата́ть, -а́ю *pf.*, **расхва́тывать, -аю** *impf.* seize on, buy up.

расхвора́ться, -а́юсь *pf.* (*impf.* **расхва́рываться**) fall (seriously) ill.

расхити́тель, -я *m.* plunderer. **расхи́тить, -и́щу** *pf.*, **расхища́ть, -а́ю** *impf.* plunder, misappropriate. **расхище́ние, -я** plundering, misappropriation.

расхля́банный loose; unstable; lax, undisciplined.

расхо́д, -а expenditure; consumption; outlay; expenses; *pl.* expenses, outlay, cost; **списа́ть в ~** write off. **расходи́ться, -ожу́сь, -о́дишься** *impf. of* **разойти́сь. расхо́дование, -я** expense, expenditure. **расхо́довать, -дую** *impf.* (*pf.* **из~**) spend, expend; use up, consume; **~ся** spend money; be spent, be consumed. **расхожде́ние, -я** divergence; **~ во мне́ниях** difference of opinion.

расхола́живать, -аю *impf.*, **расхолоди́ть, -ожу́** *pf.* damp the ardour of.

расхоте́ть, -очу́, -о́чешь, -оти́м *pf.* cease to want, no longer want.

расхохота́ться, -очу́сь, -о́чешься *pf.* burst out laughing.

расцара́пать, -аю *pf.* scratch (all over).

расцвести́, -ету́, -етёшь; -ёл, -а́ *pf.*, **расцвета́ть, -а́ю** *impf.* blossom, come into bloom; flourish. **расцве́т, -а** bloom, blossoming (out); flourishing; flowering, heyday; **в ~е сил** in the prime of life, in one's prime.

расцве́тка, -и colours; colouring.

расце́нивать, -аю *impf.*, **расцени́ть, -ню́, -нишь** *pf.* estimate, assess, value; rate; consider, think. **расце́нка, -и** valuation; price; (wage-)rate.

расцепи́ть, -плю́, -пишь *pf.*, **расцепля́ть, -я́ю** *impf.* uncouple, unhook; disengage, release. **расцепле́ние, -я** uncoupling, unhooking; disengaging, release.

расчеса́ть, -ешу́, -е́шешь *pf.* (*impf.* **расчёсывать**) comb; scratch. **расчёска, -и** comb.

расче́сть *etc.*: *see* **рассчита́ть. расчёсывать, -аю** *impf. of* **расчеса́ть**

расчёт[1], -а calculation; computation; estimate, reckoning; gain, advantage; settling, settlement; dismissal, discharge; **быть в ~е** be quits, be even; **дать ~**+*d.* dismiss, sack; **не принима́ть в ~** leave out of account; **приня́ть в ~** take into consideration. **расчётливый** economical, thrifty; careful. **расчётный** calculation, computation, reckoning; pay; accounts; rated, calculated, designed; **~ день** pay-day; **~ отде́л** accounts department.

расчи́стить, -и́щу *pf.*, **расчища́ть, -а́ю** *impf.* clear; **~ся** clear. **расчи́стка, -и** clearing.

расчлене́ние, -я dismemberment; partition. **рас|члени́ть, -ню́** *pf.*, **расчленя́ть, -я́ю** *impf.* dismember; partition; break up, divide.

расшата́ть, -а́ю *pf.*, **расша́тывать, -аю** *impf.* shake loose, make rickety; shatter, impair; **~ся** get loose, get rickety; go to pieces, crack up.

расшеве́ливать, -аю *impf.*, **расшевели́ть, -лю́, -е́ли́шь** *pf.* stir, shake; rouse.

расшиба́ть, -а́ю *impf.*, **расшиби́ть, -бу́, -бёшь; -и́б** *pf.* break up, smash to pieces; hurt; knock, stub; **~ся** hurt o.s., knock o.s.; **~ся в лепёшку** go flat out.

расшива́ть, -а́ю *impf. of* **расши́ть. расшивно́й** embroidered.

расшире́ние, -я broadening, widening; expansion; extension; dilation, dilatation; distension. **расши́рить, -рю** *pf.*, **расширя́ть, -я́ю** *impf.* broaden, widen; enlarge; expand; extend; **~ся** broaden, widen, gain in breadth; extend; expand, dilate.

расши́ть, разошью́, -шьёшь *pf.* (*impf.* **расшива́ть**) embroider; undo, unpick.

расшифрова́ть, -ру́ю *pf.*, **расшифро́вывать, -аю** *impf.* decipher, decode; interpret.

расшнурова́ть, -ру́ю *pf.*, **расшнуро́вывать, -аю** *impf.* unlace, undo.

расще́дриться, -рюсь be generous, turn generous.

расще́лина, -ы cleft, crevice, crack.

расще́п, -а split. **расщепи́ть, -плю́** *pf.*, **расщепля́ть, -я́ю** *impf.* split; splinter; break up; **~ся** split, splinter. **расщепле́ние, -я** splitting; splintering; fission; break-up, disintegration; **~ ядра́** nuclear fission. **расщепля́емый, расщепля́ющийся** fissile, fissionable.

ратифика́ция, -и ratification. **ратифици́ровать, -рую** *impf.* & *pf.* ratify.

рафина́д, -а lump sugar.

рахи́т, -а rickets.

рационализа́тор, -а efficiency expert. **рационализа́торский** rationalization. **рационализа́ция, -и** rationalization, improvement. **рационализи́ровать, -рую** *impf.* & *pf.* rationalize, improve. **рациона́льный** rational; efficient.

ра́ция, -и portable radio transmitter; walkie-talkie.

рвану́ться, -ну́сь, -нёшься *pf.* dart, rush, dash.

рва́ный torn; lacerated. **рвать[1], рву, рвёшь; рвал, -а́, -о** *impf.* tear; rend; rip; pull out, tear out; pick, pluck; blow up; break off, sever; **~ и мета́ть** rant and rave; **~ся** break; tear; burst, explode; strive; be eager, be bursting; **~ с при́вязи** strain at the leash.

рвать[2], рвёт; рва́ло́ *impf.* (*pf.* **вы~**), *impers.*+*a.* vomit, be sick, throw up; **его́ рвёт** he's vomiting.

рве́ние, -я zeal, fervour, ardour.

рво́та, -ы vomiting; retching; vomit. **рво́тн|ый** emetic; **~ое** *sb.* emetic.

ре *nt.indecl.* (*mus.*) D; ray.

реабилита́ция, -и rehabilitation. **реабилити́ровать, -рую** *impf.* & *pf.* rehabilitate.

реаги́ровать, -рую *impf.* (*pf.* **от~, про~**) react; respond.

реакти́вный reactive; jet, jet-propelled; rocket; **~ самолёт** jet (plane). **реа́ктор, -а** reactor, pile.

реакционе́р, -а reactionary. **реакцио́нный** reactionary. **реа́кция, -и** reaction.

реали́зм, -а realism. **реализова́ть, -зу́ю** *impf.* & *pf.* realize (*assets*). **реали́ст, -а** realist. **реалисти́ческий** realistic. **реа́льность, -и** reality; practicability. **реа́льный** real; realizable, practicable, workable; realistic; practical.

ребёнок, -нка; *pl.* **ребя́та, -я́т** *and* **де́ти, -е́й** child; infant.

ребро́, -а́; *pl.* **рёбра, -бер** rib; fin; edge, verge; **поста́вить вопро́с ~м** put a question point-blank.

ребя́та, -я́т *pl.* children; boys, lads. **ребя́ческий** child's; childish; infantile, puerile. **ребя́чество, -а** childishness, puerility. **ребя́чий** childish. **ребя́читься, -чусь** *impf.* behave like a child.

рёв, -а roar; bellow, howl.

рев... *abbr.* (*of* **революцио́нный, ревизио́нный**) *in comb.* revolutionary; inspection. **ревко́м, -а** revolutionary committee. **~коми́ссия, -и** Inspection Board.

рева́нш, -а revenge; return match.

реве́ть, -ву́, -вёшь *impf.* roar; bellow; howl.

ревизио́нный inspection; auditing. **реви́зия, -и** inspection; audit; revision. **ревизова́ть, -зу́ю** *impf.* & *pf.* (*pf. also* **об~**) inspect; revise. **ревизо́р, -а** inspector.

ревмати́зм, -а rheumatism; rheumatics; **суставно́й ~** rheumatic fever. **ревмати́ческий** rheumatic; **~ артри́т** rheumatoid arthritis.

ревни́вый jealous. **ревнова́ть, -ну́ю** *impf.* (*pf.* **при~**) be jealous. **ре́вностный** zealous, earnest, fervent. **ре́вность, -и** jealousy; zeal, earnestness, fervour.

револьве́р, -а revolver, pistol.

революционе́р, -а revolutionary. **революцио́нный** revolutionary. **револю́ция, -и** revolution.

ре́гби *nt. indecl.* rugby (football); **люби́тельское ~** rugby union; **профессиона́льное ~** rugby league.

реги́стр, -а register. **регистра́тор, -а** registrar. **регистрату́ра, -ы** registry. **регистра́ция, -и** registration. **регистри́ровать, -рую** *impf.* & *pf.* (*pf. also* **за~**) register, record; **~ся** register; register one's marriage.

регла́мент, -а regulations; standing orders; time-limit; **установи́ть ~** agree on procedure. **регламента́ция, -и** regulation. **регламенти́ровать, -рую** *impf.* & *pf.* regulate.

регресси́вный regressive. **регресси́ровать, -рую** *impf.* regress.

регули́рование, -я regulation, control; adjustment. **регули́ровать, -рую** *impf.* (*pf.* **за~, от~, у~**) regulate; control; adjust, tune. **регулиро́вщик, -а** traffic controller; man on point duty.

регуля́рность, -и regularity. **регуля́рный** regular. **регуля́тор, -а** regulator; control.

ред... *abbr.* (*of* **редакцио́нный**) *in comb.* editorial. **редколле́гия, -и** editorial board. **~отде́л, -а** editorial department. **~сове́т, -а** editorial committee.

...ред *abbr.* (*of* **реда́ктор**) *in comb.* editor.

редакти́рование, -я editing. **редакти́ровать, -рую** *impf.* (*pf.* **от~**) edit, be editor of; word. **реда́ктор, -а** editor; **гла́вный ~** editor-in-chief; **~ отде́ла** sub-editor. **реда́кторский** editorial. **редакцио́нн|ый** editorial, editing; **~ая коми́ссия** drafting committee. **реда́кция, -и** editorial staff; editorial office; editing; wording; **под реда́кцией**+*g.* edited by.

реде́ть, -е́ет *impf.* (*pf.* **по~**) thin, thin out.

реди́с, -а radishes. **реди́ска, -и** radish.

ре́дкий; -док, -дка́, -о thin; sparse; rare; uncommon. **ре́дко** *adv.* sparsely; far apart; rarely, seldom. **ре́дкость, -и** rarity; curiosity, curio.

ре́дька, -и black radish.

рее́стр, -а list, roll, register.

режи́м, -а régime; routine; procedure; regimen; mode of operation; conditions; rate; **~ пита́ния** diet.

режиссёр, -а producer; director. **режисси́ровать, -рую** *impf.* produce; direct.

ре́жущий cutting, sharp. **ре́зать, ре́жу** *impf.* (*pf.* **за~, про~, с~**) cut; slice; carve; engrave; pass close to, shave; cut into; kill, slaughter, knife; speak bluntly; **~ся** be cut, come through; gamble.

резви́ться, -влю́сь *impf.* sport, gambol, play. **ре́звый** frisky, playful, sportive.

резе́рв, -а reserve(s); **име́ть в ~е** have in reserve. **резерва́ция, -и** reservation. **резерви́ровать, -рую** *impf.* & *pf.* reserve. **резерви́ст, -а** reservist. **резе́рвн|ый** reserve; back-up; **~ая ко́пия** back-up copy. **резервуа́р, -а** reservoir, vessel, tank.

резе́ц, -зца́ cutter; cutting tool; chisel; incisor.

рези́на, -ы rubber. **рези́нка, -и** rubber; (piece of) elastic. **рези́нов|ый** rubber; elastic; **~ые сапоги́** wellingtons, gum-boots.

ре́зкий sharp; harsh; abrupt; shrill. **резно́й** carved, fretted. **резня́, -и́** slaughter, butchery, carnage.

резолю́ция, -и resolution.

резо́н, -а reason, basis; **в э́том есть свой ~** there is a reason for this. **резона́нс, -а** resonance; echo, response; **име́ть ~** have repercussions. **резо́нный** reasonable.

результа́т, -а result, outcome. **результати́вный** successful.

резьба́, -ы́ carving, fretwork.

резюме́ *nt.indecl.* summary, résumé. **резюми́ровать, -рую** *impf.* & *pf.* sum up, summarize.

рейд[1], **-а** roads, roadstead.

рейд[2], **-а** raid.

Рейн, -а the Rhine. **рейнве́йн, -а (-у)** hock. **ре́йнский** Rhine.

рейс, -а trip, run; voyage, passage; flight.

река́, -и́, *а.* ре́ку; *pl.* **-и, ре́ка́м** river.

реквизи́т, -а properties, props.

рекла́ма, -ы advertising, advertisement; publicity. **рекламировать, -рую** *impf.* & *pf.* advertise, publicize, push. **рекламный** publicity.

рекомендательн|ый of recommendation; **~ое письмо** letter of introduction. **рекомендация, -и** recommendation; reference. **рекомендовать, -дую** *impf.* & *pf.* (*pf. also* **от~, по~**) recommend; speak well for; advise; **~ся** introduce o.s.; be advisable.

реконструировать, -рую *impf.* & *pf.* reconstruct.

рекорд, -а record; **побить ~** break, beat, a record. **рекордный** record, record-breaking. **рекордсмен, -а, -енка, -и** record-holder.

ректор, -а rector, vice-chancellor, principal (*head of a university*).

религиоведение, -я religious studies. **религиозный** religious; of religion; pious. **религия, -и** religion.

реликвия, -и relic.

рельеф, -а relief. **рельефно** *adv.* boldly. **рельефный** relief; raised, embossed, bold.

рельс, -а rail; **сойти с ~ов** be derailed, go off the rails. **рельсовый** rail, railway.

ремарка, -и stage direction.

ремень, -мня *m.* strap; belt; thong; **~ безопасности** seat belt.

ремесленник, -а artisan, craftsman; hack. **ремесленничество, -а** workmanship, craftsmanship; hack-work. **ремесленн|ый** handicraft; trade; mechanical; stereotyped; **~ое училище** trade school. **ремесло, -а**; *pl.* **-ёсла, -ёсел** handicraft; trade; profession.

ремонт, -а repair, repairs; maintenance; **косметический ~** face-lift. **ремонтировать, -рую** *impf.* & *pf.* (*pf. also* **от~**) repair; refit, recondition, overhaul. **ремонтный** repair, repairing.

рента, -ы rent; income. **рентабельный** paying, profitable.

рентген, -а X-rays; roentgen. **рентгенизировать, -рую** *impf.* & *pf.* X-ray. **рентгеновский** X-ray. **рентгенолог, -а** radiologist. **рентгенология, -и** radiology.

реорганизация, -и reorganization. **реорганизовать, -зую** *impf.* & *pf.* reorganize.

репа, -ы turnip.

репарация, -и reparation.

репатриант, -а repatriate. **репатриация, -и** repatriation. **репатриировать, -рую** *impf.* & *pf.* repatriate.

репеллент, -а insect repellant.

репертуар, -а repertoire.

репетировать, -рую *impf.* (*pf.* **от~, про~, с~**) rehearse; coach. **репетитор, -а** coach. **репетиция, -и** rehearsal; repeater mechanism; **часы с репетицией** repeater.

реплика, -и rejoinder, retort; cue.

репортаж, -а reporting; account. **репортёр, -а** reporter.

репрессалии, -ий *pl.* reprisals.

репрессивный repressive. **репрессировать, -рую** *impf.* & *pf.* subject to repression. **репрессия, -и** punitive measure.

репродуктор, -а loud-speaker.

республика, -и republic. **республиканец, -нца** republican. **республиканский** republican.

рессора, -ы spring. **рессорный** spring; sprung.

реставрация, -и restoration. **реставрировать, -рую** *impf.* & *pf.* (*pf. also* **от~**) restore.

ресторан, -а restaurant.

ресурс, -а resource; **последний ~** the last resort.

ретивый zealous, ardent.

ретироваться, -руюсь *impf.* & *pf.* retire, withdraw; make off.

ретранслятор, -а (radio-)relay. **ретрансляция, -и** relaying, retransmission.

ретроракета, -ы retro-rocket.

ретушировать, -рую *impf.* & *pf.* (*pf. also* **от~**) retouch. **ретушь, -и** retouching.

реферат, -а synopsis, abstract; paper, essay.

реформа, -ы reform. **реформатор, -а** reformer. **Реформация, -и** (*hist.*) Reformation. **реформизм, -а** reformism. **реформировать, -рую** *impf.* & *pf.* reform. **реформист, -а** reformist.

рецензент, -а reviewer. **рецензировать, -рую** *impf.* (*pf.* **про~**) review, criticize. **рецензия, -и** review; notice.

рецепт, -а prescription; recipe; method, way, practice.

рецидив, -а recurrence; relapse; repetition. **рецидивист, -а** recidivist.

рециркуляция, -и recycling.

речевой speech; vocal.

речка, -и river. **речной** river; riverine; fluvial; **~ вокзал** river-steamer and water-bus station; **~ трамвай** water-bus.

речь, -и; *g.pl.* **-ей** speech; enunciation, way of speaking; language; discourse; oration; address; **выступить с ~ю** make a speech; **не об этом ~** that's not the point; **об этом не может быть и речи** it is (quite) out of the question; **о чём ~?** what are you talking about? what is it all about?; **~ идёт о том...** the question is ... .

решать(ся, -аю(сь *impf. of* **решить(ся. решающий** decisive, deciding; key, conclusive. **решение, -я** decision; decree, judgement; verdict; solution, answer; **вынести ~** pass a resolution.

решётка, -и grating; grille, railing; lattice; trellis; fender, (fire)guard; (fire)-grate; tail. **решето, -а**; *pl.* **-ёта** sieve. **решётчатый** lattice, latticed; trellised.

решимость, -и resolution, resoluteness; resolve. **решительно** *adv.* resolutely; decidedly, definitely; absolutely; **~ всё равно** it makes no difference whatever. **решительность, -и** resolution, determination, firmness. **решительный** resolute, determined; decided; firm; definite; decisive; crucial; absolute. **решить, -шу** *pf.* (*impf.* **решать**) de-

cide, determine; make up one's mind; solve, settle; **~ся** make up one's mind, resolve; bring o.s.; +*g.* lose, be deprived of.
ре́шка; орёл или ~? heads or tails?
ржа́веть, -еет *impf.* (*pf.* **за~, по~**) rust. **ржа́вчина, -ы** rust; mildew. **ржа́вый** rusty.
ржано́й rye.
ржать, ржу, ржёшь *impf.* neigh.
Ри́га, -и Riga.
ри́га, -и (threshing-)barn.
Рим, -а Rome. **ри́млянин, -а**; *pl.* **-яне, -ян, ри́млянка, -и** Roman. **ри́мск|ий** Roman; **па́па ~ий** the Pope; **~ие ци́фры** Roman numerals.
ри́нуться, -нусь *pf.* rush, dash, dart.
рис, -а (-у) rice.
рис. *abbr.* (*of* **рису́нок**) fig., figure.
риск, -а risk; hazard; **пойти́ на ~** run risks, take chances. **риско́ванный** risky; risqué. **рискова́ть, -ку́ю** *impf.* run risks, take chances; *+i. or inf.* risk, take the risk of.
рисова́ние, -я drawing. **рисова́ть, -су́ю** *impf.* (*pf.* **на~**) draw; paint, depict, portray; **~ся** be silhouetted; appear, present o.s.; pose, act.
ри́сов|ый rice; **~ая ка́ша** rice pudding; boiled rice.
рису́нок, -нка drawing; illustration; figure; pattern, design; outline; draughtsmanship.
ритм, -а rhythm. **ритми́ческий, ритми́чный** rhythmic(al).
риф, -а reef.
ри́фма, -ы rhyme. **рифмова́ть, -му́ю** *impf.* (*pf.* **с~**) rhyme; **~ся** rhyme. **рифмо́вка, -и** rhyming (system).
р-н *abbr.* (*of* **райо́н**) district.
robе́ть — **робе́ть, -е́ю** *impf.* (*pf.* **о~**) be timid; be afraid, quail. **ро́бкий; -бок, -бка́, -о** timid, shy. **ро́бость, -и** timidity, shyness.
роботе́хника, -и robotics.
ро́бче *comp. of* **ро́бкий**
ров, рва, *loc.* **-у** ditch.
рове́сник, -а person of the same age, coeval. **ро́вно** *adv.* regularly, evenly; exactly; sharp; absolutely; just as, exactly like; **~ в час** at one sharp, on the stroke of one; **~ ничего́** absolutely nothing, nothing at all. **ро́вный** flat; even; level; regular; equable; exact; equal. **ро́вня́, ро́вни́** *c.g.* equal; match. **ровня́ть, -я́ю** *impf.* (*pf.* **с~**) even, level; **~ с землёй** raze to the ground.
рог, -а; *pl.* **-а́, -о́в** horn; antler; bugle. **рога́тый** horned. **рогови́ца, -ы** cornea. **рогово́й** horn; horny; horn-rimmed.
рого́жа, -ы bast mat(ting).
род, -а (-у), *loc.* **-у́**; *pl.* **-ы́** family, kin, clan; birth, origin, stock; generation; genus; sort, kind; **без ~у, без пле́мени** without kith or kin; **в э́том ~е** of this sort, of the kind; **ей де́сять лет о́т ~у** she is ten years old; **он своего́ ~а ге́ний** he is a genius in his (own) way; **~ом** by birth; **своего́ ~а** a kind of, a sort of; **челове́ческий ~** mankind, the human race. **роди́льный** maternity; puerperal.
ро́дина, -ы native land, mother country; home, homeland. **ро́динка, -и** birth-mark.
роди́тель, -я *m.* father; **~ница, -ы** mother; **роди́тели, -ей** *pl.* parents. **роди́тельный** genitive. **роди́тельский** parental, parents'; paternal. **роди́ть, рожу́, -и́л, -ила́, -о** *impf.* & *pf.* (*impf. also* **рожа́ть, рожда́ть**) bear; give birth to; give rise to; **~ся** be born; arise, come into being; spring up, thrive.
родни́к, -а́ spring. **роднико́вый** spring.
родни́ть, -ни́т (*pf.* **по~**) make related, link; make similar, make alike; **~ся** become related, be linked. **родн|о́й** own; native; home; **~о́й брат** brother; **~о́й язы́к** mother tongue; **~ы́е** *sb.*, *pl.* relations, relatives, family. **родня́, -и́** relation(s), relative(s); kinsfolk. **родово́й** clan, tribal; ancestral; generic; gender. **родонача́льник, -а** ancestor, forefather; father. **родосло́вн|ый** genealogical; **~ая** *sb.* genealogy, pedigree. **ро́дственник, -а** relation, relative. **ро́дственный** kindred, related; allied; cognate; familiar, intimate. **родство́, -а́** relationship, kinship; relations, relatives. **ро́ды, -ов** *pl.* birth; childbirth, delivery; labour.
ро́жа, -и (ugly) mug; **стро́ить ро́жы** pull faces.
рожа́ть, -а́ю, рожда́ть(ся, -а́ю(сь *impf. of* **роди́ть(ся. рожда́емость, -и** birth-rate. **рожде́ние, -я** birth; birthday. **рождённый; -ён, -а́** born. **Рождество́, -а́** Christmas.
рожь, ржи rye.
ро́за, -ы rose; rose-bush, rose-tree; rose window.
ро́зга, -и; *g.pl.* **-зог** birch.
ро́здал *etc.*: *see* **разда́ть**
розе́тка, -и rosette; socket; wall-plug.
розмари́н, -а rosemary.
ро́зница, -ы retail; **в ~у** retail. **ро́зничный** retail. **ро́зно** *adv.* apart, separately. **рознь, -и** difference; dissension.
ро́знял *etc.*: *see* **разня́ть**
ро́зовый pink; rose-coloured; rosy; rose.
ро́зыгрыш, -а draw; drawing; drawn game; playing off; tournament, competition, championship.
ро́зыск, -а search; inquiry; investigation.
ройться, -йтся swarm. **рой, -я**, *loc.* **-ю́**; *pl.* **-и́, -ёв** swarm.
рок, -а fate.
рокирова́ть(ся, -ру́ю(сь *impf.* & *pf.* castle. **рокиро́вка, -и** castling.
рок-му́зыка, -и rock music. **рок-н-ро́лл, -а** rock 'n' roll.
роково́й fateful; fated; fatal.
ро́кот, -а roar, rumble. **рокота́ть, -о́чет** *impf.* roar, rumble.
ро́лик, -а roller; castor; *pl.* roller skates. **ро́ликов|ый; ~ая доска́** skateboard. **ролидро́м, -а** roller-skating rink. **ро́ллер, -а** scooter. **ро́ллинг, -а** skateboard; skateboarding.

роль, -и; *g.pl.* **-е́й** role, part.
ром, -а (-у) rum.
рома́н, -а novel; romance; love affair. **рома-ни́ст, -а** novelist.
рома́нс, -а song; romance.
рома́шка, -и, рома́шковый camomile.
роня́ть, -я́ю *impf.* (*pf.* **урони́ть**) drop, let fall; shed; lower, injure, discredit.
ро́пот, -а murmur, grumble. **ропта́ть, -пщу́, -пщешь** *impf.* murmur, grumble.
рос *etc.*: *see* **расти́**
роса́, -ы́; *pl.* **-ы** dew. **роси́стый** dewy.
роско́шный luxurious, sumptuous; luxuriant; splendid. **ро́скошь, -и** luxury; luxuriance; splendour.
ро́слый tall, strapping.
ро́спись, -и list, inventory; painting(s), mural(s).
ро́спуск, -а dismissal; disbandment; breaking up.
росси́йский Russian. **Росси́я, -и** Russia.
россия́нин, -а; *pl.* **-я́не, -я́н, россия́нка, -и** Russian.
ро́ссказни, -ей *pl.* old wives' tales, cock-and-bull stories.
ро́ссыпь, -и scattering; *pl.* deposit; **~ю** in bulk, loose.
рост, -а (-у) growth; increase, rise; height, stature; **во весь ~** upright, straight; **~ом** in height.
ростовщи́к, -а́ usurer, money-lender.
росто́к, -тка́ sprout, shoot; **пусти́ть ростки́** put out shoots.
ро́счерк, -а flourish, **одни́м ~ом пера́** with a stroke of the pen.
рот, рта (рту), *loc.* **рту** mouth.
ро́та, -ы company.
рота́тор, -а duplicator. **ротацио́нн|ый** rotary; **~ая маши́на** rotary press. **рота́ция, -и** rotary press.
ро́тный company; *sb.* company commander.
ротозе́й, -я, -зе́йка, -и gaper, rubberneck; scatter-brain. **ротозе́йство, -а** carelessness, absent-mindedness.
ро́ща, -и, ро́щица, -ы grove.
ро́ю *etc.*: *see* **рыть**
роя́ль, -я *m.* (grand) piano; **игра́ть на роя́ле** play the piano.
РСФСР *abbr.* (*of* ***Росси́йская Сове́тская Федерати́вная Социалисти́ческая Респу́блика***) Russian Soviet Federal Socialist Republic.
рту́тный mercury, mercurial. **ртуть, -и** mercury; quicksilver.
руба́нок, -нка plane.
руба́шка, -и shirt; **ночна́я ~** night-shirt, nightgown, nightdress.
рубе́ж, -а́ boundary, border(line), frontier; line; **за ~о́м** abroad.
рубе́ц, -бца́ scar, cicatrice; weal; hem; seam; tripe.
руби́н, -а ruby. **руби́новый** ruby; ruby-coloured.
руби́ть, -блю́, -бишь *impf.* (*pf.* **с~**) fell; hew, chop, hack; mince, chop up; build (of logs), put up, erect.
ру́бище, -а rags, tatters.
ру́бка[1]**, -и** felling; hewing, hacking; chopping; mincing.
ру́бка[2]**, -и** deck house, deck cabin; **боева́я ~** conning-tower; **рулева́я ~** wheelhouse.
рублёвка, -и one-rouble note. **рублёвый** (one-)rouble.
ру́блен|ый minced, chopped; log, of logs; **~ые котле́ты** rissoles; **~ое мя́со** mince, minced meat, hash.
рубль, -я́ *m.* rouble.
ру́брика, -и rubric, heading; column.
ру́бчатый ribbed. **ру́бчик, -а** scar, seam, rib.
ру́гань, -и abuse, bad language, swearing. **руга́тельн|ый** abusive; **~ые слова́** bad language, swear-words. **руга́тельство, -а** oath, swear-word. **руга́ть, -а́ю** *impf.* (*pf.* **вы́~, об~, от~**) curse, swear at; abuse; tear to pieces; criticize severely; **~ся** curse, swear, use bad language; swear at, abuse, one another.
руда́, -ы́; *pl.* **-ы** ore. **рудни́к, -а́** mine, pit. **рудни́чный** mine, pit; mining; **~ газ** firedamp. **рудоко́п, -а** miner.
руже́йный rifle, gun; **~ вы́стрел** rifle-shot. **ружьё, -ья́**; *pl.* **-ья, -жей, -ьям** gun, rifle.
рука́, -и́, *a.* **-у**; *pl.* **-и, рук, -а́м** hand; arm; **в со́бственные ру́ки** personal; **игра́ть в четы́ре руки́** play duets; **идти́ по́д руку с**+*i.*, walk arm in arm with; **маха́ть руко́й** wave one's hand; **махну́ть руко́й на**+*a.* give up as lost; **на ско́рую ру́ку** hastily; extempore; **не поднима́ется ~**+*inf.* one cannot bring o.s. to; **под руко́й** at hand; **по рука́м!** done! it's a bargain!; **приложи́ть ру́ку** append one's signature; **рука́ми не тро́гать!** (please) don't touch!; **ру́ки вверх!** hands up; **ру́ки прочь!** hands off!; **руко́й пода́ть** a stone's throw away; **у вас на ~х** on you; **чёткая ~** a clear hand; **э́то мне на́ руку** that suits me.
рука́в, -а́; *pl.* **-а́, -о́в** sleeve; branch, arm; hose; **пожа́рный ~** fire-hose. **рукави́ца, -ы** mitten; gauntlet.
руководи́тель, -я *m.* leader; manager; instructor; guide. **руководи́ть, -ожу́** *impf.*+*i.* lead; guide; direct, manage. **руково́дство, -а** leadership; guidance; direction; guide; handbook, manual; instructions; leaders; governing body. **руково́дствоваться, -твуюсь**+*i.* follow; be guided by, be influenced by. **руководя́щ|ий** leading; guiding; **~ая статья́** leader; **~ий комите́т** steering committee.
рукоде́лие, -я needlework; *pl.* hand-made goods.
рукомо́йник, -а wash-stand.
рукопа́шн|ый hand-to-hand; **~ая** *sb.* hand-to-hand fighting.
рукопи́сный manuscript. **ру́копись, -и** manuscript.
рукоплеска́ние, -я applause. **рукоплеска́ть, -ещу́, -е́щешь** *impf.*+*d.* applaud, clap.

рукопожа́тие, -я handshake; **обменя́ться рукопожа́тиями** shake hands.
рукоя́тка, -и handle; hilt; haft, helve; shaft; grip.
рулев|о́й steering; **~о́е колесо́** steering wheel; *sb.* helmsman, man at the wheel.
руле́тка, -и tape-measure; roulette.
рули́ть, -лю́ *impf.* (*pf.* **вы́~**) taxi.
руль, -я́ *m.* rudder; helm; (steering-)wheel; handlebar.
румы́н, -а; *g.pl.* **-ы́н, румы́нка, -и** Romanian, Rumanian. **Румы́ния, -и** Romania, Rumania. **румы́нский** Romanian, Rumanian.
румя́на, -я́н *pl.* rouge. **румя́нец, -нца** (high) colour; flush; blush. **румя́нить, -ню** *impf.* (*pf.* **за~, на~**) redden, bring colour to; rouge; brown; **~ся** redden; glow; flush; use rouge, put on rouge. **румя́ный** rosy, ruddy; brown.
ру́пор, -а megaphone, speaking-trumpet; loud-hailer; mouthpiece.
руса́лка, -и mermaid. **руса́лочий** mermaid, mermaid's.
ру́сский Russian; *sb.* Russian.
ру́сый light brown.
рути́на, -ы routine; rut, groove. **рути́нный** routine.
ру́хлядь, -и junk, lumber.
ру́хнуть, -ну *pf.* crash down; fall heavily; crash (*to the ground*).
руча́тельство, -а guarantee; **с ~м** warranted, guaranteed. **руча́ться, -а́юсь** *impf.* (*pf.* **поручи́ться**) answer, vouch; +**за**+*a.* warrant, guarantee, certify.
руче́й, -чья́ stream, brook.
ру́чка, -и handle; (door-)knob; (chair-)arm; pen; penholder. **ручн|о́й** hand; arm; manual; hand-made; tame; **~ы́е часы́** wrist-watch.
ру́шить, -у *impf.* (*pf.* **об~**) pull down; **~ся** fall, fall in; collapse.
ры́ба, -ы fish; *pl.* Pisces. **рыба́к, -а́** fisherman. **рыба́лка, -и** fishing. **рыба́цкий, рыба́чий** fishing. **ры́бий** fish; fishlike, fishy; **~ жир** cod-liver oil. **ры́бн|ый** fish; **~ые консе́рвы** tinned fish. **рыбово́дческ|ий; ~ая фе́рма** fish farm. **рыболо́в, -а** fisherman; angler. **рыболо́вный** fishing. **рыбопито́мник, -а** fish hatchery.
рыво́к, -вка́ jerk; dash, burst, spurt.
рыда́ние, -я sobbing, sobs. **рыда́ть, -а́ю** *impf.* sob.
ры́жий; рыж, -а́, -е red, red-haired; ginger; chestnut; reddish-brown, brown with age; gold.
ры́ло, -а snout; (ugly) mug.
ры́нок, -нка market; market-place. **ры́ночный** market.
рыса́к, -а́ trotter.
ры́сий lynx.
рыси́стый trotting. **рыси́ть, -и́шь** *impf.* trot.
рысь[1]**, -и,** *loc.* **-и́** trot; **~ю, на рыся́х** at a trot.
рысь[2]**, -и** lynx.
ры́твина, -ы rut, groove. **рыть, ро́ю** *impf.* (*pf.* **вы́~, от~**) dig; rummage about (in), ransack, burrow in; **~ся** dig; rummage.
рыхли́ть, -лю́ *impf.* (*pf.* **вз~, раз~**) loosen, make friable. **ры́хлый; -л, -а́, -о** friable; loose; porous; pudgy, podgy.
ры́царский knightly; chivalrous. **ры́царь, -я** *m.* knight.
рыча́г, -а́ lever.
рыча́ть, -чу́ *impf.* growl, snarl.
рья́ный zealous, ardent.
рэ́ггей *m. indecl.* reggae.
рюкза́к, -а rucksack, backpack. **рюкза́чник, -а** backpacker.
рю́мка, -и wineglass.
ряби́на[1]**, -ы** rowan (tree), mountain ash; rowan-berry.
ряби́на[2]**, -ы** pit, pock. **ряби́ть, -и́т** *impf.* ripple; *impers.* **у меня́ ряби́т в глаза́х** I am dazzled. **рябо́й** pitted, pock-marked; speckled. **ря́бчик, -а** hazel-hen, hazel grouse. **рябь, -и** ripple, ripples; dazzle.
ря́вкать, -аю *impf.*, **ря́вкнуть, -ну** *pf.* bellow, roar.
ряд, -а (-у), *loc.* **-у́**; *pl.* **-ы́** row; line; file, rank; series; numbers; **из ~а вон выходя́щий** outstanding, exceptional, out of the common run; **пе́рвый ~** front row; **после́дний ~** back row; **стоя́ть в одно́м ~у́ с**+*i.* rank with. **рядово́й** ordinary; common; **~ соста́в** rank and file; men, other ranks; *sb.* private. **ря́дом** *adv.* alongside; near, close by, next door; +**с**+*i.* next to.
ря́са, -ы cassock.

С

С *abbr.* (*of* **се́вер**) N, North.
с *letter*: *see* **эс**
с, со *prep.* **I.** +*g.* from; since; off; for, with; on; by; **дово́льно с тебя́!** that's enough from you!; **перево́д с ру́сского** translation from Russian; **с большо́й бу́квы** with a capital letter; **сда́ча с рубля́** change for a rouble; **с ле́вой стороны́** on the left-hand side; **с одно́й стороны́, с друго́й стороны́** on the one hand, on the other hand; **со сна** just up, half awake; **со стыда́** for shame, with shame; **с пе́рвого взгля́да** at first sight; **с ра́дости** for joy; **с утра́** since morning. **II.** +*a.* about; the size of; **ма́льчик с па́льчик** Tom Thumb; **на́ша до́чка ро́стом с ва́шу** our daughter is about the same height as yours; **с неде́лю** for about a week. **III.** +*i.* with; and; **мы с ва́ми** you and I; **получи́ть с пе́рвой по́чтой** receive by the first post; **что с ва́ми?** what is the matter with you? what's up?

с. *abbr.* (*of* **село́**) village; (*of* **страни́ца**) p., page.

с..., со..., съ... *vbl. pref. indicating perfective aspect; unification, joining, fastening; accompaniment, participation; comparison; copying; removal; movement away (from), to one side, downwards, down (from), off, there and back, directed to a point or centre; action in concert.*

СА *abbr.* (*of* **Сове́тская А́рмия**) Soviet Army.

са́бельный sabre.

сабза́, -ы́ sultanas.

са́бля, -и; *g.pl.* **-бель** sabre; (cavalry) sword.

сабота́ж, -а sabotage. **сабота́жник, -а** saboteur. **саботи́ровать, -рую** *impf.* & *pf.* sabotage.

са́ван, -а shroud; blanket.

с|агити́ровать, -рую *pf.*

сад, -а, *loc.* **-у́**; *pl.* **-ы́** garden, gardens. **сади́ть, сажу́, са́дишь** *impf.* (*pf.* **по~**) plant; **~ на дие́ту** put on a diet. **сади́ться, сажу́сь** *impf. of* **сесть. садо́вник, -а, -ница, -ы** gardener. **садово́дство, -а** gardening; horticulture; nursery; garden(s). **садо́вый** garden; cultivated.

садо-мазохи́зм, -а sado-masochism.

са́жа, -и soot.

сажа́ть, -а́ю *impf.* (*pf.* **посади́ть**) plant; seat; set put; **~ в тюрьму́** put in prison, imprison, jail; **~ под аре́ст** put under arrest. **са́женец, -нца** seedling; sapling.

са́же́нь, -и; *pl.* **-и, -жен** *or* **-же́не́й** sazhen (*old Russ. measure of length, equivalent to 2.13 metres*).

сажу́ *etc.*: *see* **сади́ть**

са́йка, -и roll.

саквоя́ж, -а travelling-bag, grip.

с|акти́ровать, -рую *pf.*

сала́зки, -зок *pl.* sled, toboggan.

сала́т, -а (-у) salad; **~-лату́к** lettuce. **сала́тник, -а, сала́тница, -ы** salad-dish, salad-bowl.

са́ло, -а fat, lard; suet; tallow.

сало́н, -а salon; saloon; **да́мский ~** beauty parlour.

салфе́тка, -и napkin, serviette.

са́льный greasy; fat; tallow; obscene, bawdy.

салю́т, -а salute. **салютова́ть, -ту́ю** *impf.* & *pf.* (*pf.* **от~**) *+d.* salute.

сам, -ого́ *m.*, **сама́, -о́й,** *a.* **-оё** *f.*, **само́, -ого́** *nt.*, **са́ми, -и́х** *pl.*, *pron.* -self, -selves; myself, *etc.*, ourselves, *etc.*; **она́ — ~а́ доброта́** she is kindness itself; **~ по себе́** in itself; by o.s., unassisted; **~ собо́й** of itself, of its own accord; **~о́ собо́й (разуме́ется)** of course; it goes without saying.

са́мбо *nt.indecl. abbr.* (*of* **самозащи́та без ору́жия**) unarmed combat.

саме́ц, -мца́ male. **са́мка, -и** female.

само... *in comb.* self-, auto-. **самобы́тный** original, distinctive. **~внуше́ние, -я** auto-suggestion. **~возгора́ние, -я** spontaneous combustion. **~во́льный** wilful, self-willed; unauthorized; unwarranted. **~дви́жущийся** self-propelled. **~де́лка, -и** home-made product. **~де́льный** home-made; self-made. **~держа́вие, -я** autocracy. **~держа́вный** autocratic. **~де́ятельность, -и** amateur work, amateur performance; initiative. **~дово́льный** self-satisfied, smug, complacent. **~ду́р, -а** petty tyrant; wilful person. **~ду́рство, -а** petty tyranny, obstinate wilfulness. **~забве́ние, -я** selflessness. **~забве́нный** selfless. **~защи́та, -ы** self-defence. **~зва́нец, -нца** imposter, pretender. **~зва́нство, -а** imposture. **~ка́т, -а** scooter; bicycle. **~кри́тика, -и** self-criticism. **~люби́вый** proud; touchy. **~лю́бие, -я** pride, self-esteem. **~мне́ние, -я** conceit, self-importance. **~наде́янный** presumptuous. **~облада́ние, -я** self-control, self-possession; composure. **~обма́н, -а** self-deception. **~оборо́на, -ы** self-defence. **~образова́ние, -я** self-education. **~обслу́живание, -я** self-service. **~определе́ние, -я** self-determination. **~опроки́дывающийся** self-tipping; **~опроки́дывающийся грузови́к** tip-up lorry. **~отверже́ние, -я, ~отве́рженность, -и** selflessness. **~отве́рженный** selfless, self-sacrificing. **~пи́шущий** recording, registering; **~пи́шущее перо́** fountain-pen. **~поже́ртвование, -я** self-sacrifice. **~пу́ск, -а** self-starter. **~рекла́ма, -ы** self-advertisement. **~ро́дный** native. **~ро́док, -дка** nugget; rough diamond. **~сва́л, -а** tip-up lorry. **~созна́ние, -я** self-consciousness. **~сохране́ние, -я** self-preservation. **~стоя́тельно** *adv.* independently; on one's own. **~стоя́тельность, -и** independence. **~стоя́тельный** independent. **~су́д, -а** lynch law, mob law. **~тёк, -а** drift. **~тёком** *adv.* by gravity; haphazard of its own accord; **идти́ ~тёком** drift. **~уби́йственный** suicidal. **~уби́йство, -а** suicide (*act*). **~уби́йца, -ы** *c.g.* suicide (*person*). **~уве́ренность, -и** self-confidence, self-assurance. **~уве́ренный** self-confident, self-assured; cocksure. **~униже́ние, -я** self-abasement, self-disparagement. **~управле́ние, -я** self-government; local authority. **~управля́ющийся** self-governing. **~упра́вный** arbitrary. **~упра́вство, -а** arbitrariness. **~учи́тель, -я** *m.* (self-tuition) manual, self-instructor. **~у́чка, -и** *c.g.* self-taught person. **~хо́дный** self-propelled. **~чу́вствие, -я** general state; **как ва́ше ~чу́вствие?** how do you feel?

самова́р, -а samovar.

самолёт, -а aeroplane, aircraft, plane.

самоцве́т, -а semi-precious stone.

са́м|ый *pron.* (the) very (the) right; (the) same; (the) most; **в ~ое вре́мя** at the right time; **в ~ом де́ле** indeed; **в ~ом де́ле?** indeed? really? **в ~ый раз** just right; **на ~ом де́ле** actually, in fact; **~ый глу́пый** the stupidest, the most stupid; **~ые пустяки́** the merest trifles; **с ~ого нача́ла** from the very beginning, right from the start; **с ~ого утра́** since first thing.

сан, -а dignity, office.

сан... *abbr.* (*of* **санита́рный**) *in comb.* medical, hospital; sanitary. **санвра́ч, -а́** medical officer of health; sanitary inspector. **~по́езд, -а** hospital train, ambulance train. **~пу́нкт, -а** medical centre; dressing-station, aid-post. **~у́зел, -зла́** sanitary unit; lavatory. **~ча́сть, -и** medical unit.

са́ни, -е́й *pl.* sledge, sleigh.

санита́р, -а medical orderly, hospital orderly, male nurse; stretcher-bearer. **санитари́я, -и** hygiene, public health. **санита́рка, -и** nurse. **санита́рн|ый** medical; hospital; (public) health; sanitary; **~ый автомоби́ль, ~ая каре́та, ~ая маши́на** ambulance; **~ый у́зел** sanitary unit; lavatory.

са́нки, -нок *pl.* sledge; toboggan.

Санкт-Петербу́рг, -а St. Petersburg. **санкт-петербу́ргский** St. Petersburg. **санкт-петербуржа́нка, -и, санкт-петербу́ржец, -ца** St. Petersburger.

санкциони́ровать, -рую *impf.* & *pf.* sanction. **са́нкция, -и** sanction, approval.

са́нный sledge, sleigh; **~ путь** sleigh-road.

сано́вник, -а dignitary, high official. **сано́вный** of exalted rank.

са́ночник, -а tobogganist.

сантиме́тр, -а centimetre; tape-measure, ruler.

сапёр, -а sapper; pioneer. **сапёрный** sapper, pioneer; engineer.

сапо́г, -а́; *g.pl.* **-о́г** boot; top-boot, jackboot. **сапо́жник, -а** shoemaker, bootmaker; cobbler. **сапо́жный** boot, shoe.

сапфи́р, -а sapphire.

сара́й, -я shed; barn, barrack.

саранча́, -и́ locust; locusts.

сарафа́н, -а sarafan (*Russ. peasant womens' dress, without sleeves and buttoning in front*); pinafore (dress).

сарде́лька, -и (*small, fat*) sausage.

сарди́н|а, -ы sardine, pilchard; **~ы в ма́сле** (tinned) sardines.

сатана́, -ы́ *m.* Satan. **сатани́нский** satanic.

сати́н, -а sateen. **сати́новый** sateen.

сати́ра, -ы satire. **сати́рик, -а** satirist. **сатири́ческий** satirical.

Сау́довская Ара́вия, -ой -и Saudi Arabia.

са́уна, -ы sauna.

сафа́ри *nt. indecl.* safari; **«~» зоопа́рк** safari park.

сафья́н, -а morocco. **сафья́новый** morocco.

са́хар, -а (-у) sugar.

Саха́ра, -ы the Sahara.

сахари́н, -а saccharine. **са́харистый** sugary; saccharine. **са́харить, -рю** *impf.* (*pf.* **по~**) sugar, sweeten. **са́харница, -ы** sugar-basin. **са́харн|ый** sugar; sugary; **~ая голова́** sugar-loaf; **~ый заво́д** sugar-refinery; **~ый песо́к** granulated sugar; **~ая пу́дра** castor sugar; **~ая свёкла** sugar-beet.

сачо́к, -чка́ net; landing net; butterfly-net.

сб. *abbr.* (*of* **сбо́рник**) collection.

сба́вить, -влю *pf.* **сбавля́ть, -я́ю** *impf.* take off, deduct; reduce; **~ в ве́се** lose weight; **~ газ** throttle down; **~ с цены́** reduce the price

с|баланси́ровать, -рую *pf.*

сбе́гать[1], -аю *pf.* run; +**за**+*i.* run for. **сбега́ть[2], -а́ю** *impf.*, **сбежа́ть, -егу́** *pf.* run down (from); run away; disappear, vanish; **~ся** come running; gather, collect.

сберега́тельн|ый; ~ая ка́сса savings bank. **сберега́ть, -а́ю** *impf.*, **сбере́чь, -егу́, -ежёшь; -ёг, -ла́** *pf.* save; save up, put aside; preserve, protect. **сбереже́ние, -я** economy; saving, preservation; savings. **сберка́сса, -ы** *abbr.* savings bank. **сберкни́жка, -и** savings book.

сбива́ть, -а́ю *impf.*, **с|бить, собью́, -бьёшь** *pf.* bring down, knock down, throw down; knock off, dislodge; put out; distract; deflect; wear down, tread down; knock together; churn; beat up, whip, whisk; **~ с доро́ги** misdirect; **~ с ног** knock down; **~ с то́лку** muddle, confuse; **~ це́ну** beat down the price; **~ся** be dislodged; slip; be deflected; go wrong; be confused; be inconsistent; **~ся в ку́чу, ~ся толпо́й** bunch, huddle; **~ся с доро́ги, ~ся с пути́** lose one's way, go astray; **~ся с ног** be run off one's feet; **~ся со счёта** lose count. **сби́вчивый** confused, indistinct; inconsistent, contradictory. **сби́т|ый; ~ые сли́вки** whipped cream.

сближа́ть, -а́ю *impf.*, **сбли́зить, -и́жу** *pf.* bring (closer) together, draw together; **~ся** draw together, converge; become good friends. **сближе́ние, -я** rapprochement; intimacy; approach, closing in.

сбо́ку *adv.* from one side; on one side; at the side.

сбор, -а collection; dues; duty; charge(s), fee, toll; takings, returns; salvage; assemblage, gathering; course of instruction; **быть в ~е** be assembled, be in session; **~ урожа́я** harvest. **сбо́рище, -а** crowd, mob. **сбо́рка, -и** assembling, assembly, erection; gather. **сбо́рник, -а** collection; **~ пра́вил** code of rules. **сбо́рн|ый** assembly; mixed, combined; that can be taken to pieces; prefabricated, sectional; detachable; **~ая кома́нда** combined team, representative team; picked team; scratch team; **~ый пункт** assembly point, rallying point. **сбо́рочный** assembly; **~ цех** assembly shop. **сбо́рчатый** gathered. **сбо́рщик, -а** collector; assembler, fitter, mounter.

сбра́сывать(ся, -аю(сь *impf.* *of* **сбро́сить(ся**

сбрива́ть, -а́ю *impf.*, **сбрить, сбре́ю** *pf.* shave off.

сброд, -а riff-raff, rabble.

сброс, -а fault, break. **сбро́сить, -о́шу** *pf* (*impf.* **сбра́сывать**) throw down, drop throw off; cast off; shed; throw away, discard; **~ся** throw o.s. down, leap (+*g.* off from).

с|брошюрова́ть, -ру́ю *pf.*
сбру́я, -и harness.
сбыва́ть, -а́ю *impf.*, **сбыть, сбу́ду; сбыл, -а́, -о** *pf.* sell, market; get rid of; dump; ~ **с рук** get off one's hands; ~**ся** come true, be realized; happen; **что сбу́дется с ней?** what will become of her? **сбыт, -а** sale; market. **сбытово́й** selling, marketing.
св. *abbr.* (*of* **свято́й**) St., Saint.
сва́дебный wedding; nuptial. **сва́дьба, -ы;** *g.pl.* **-деб** wedding.
сва́ливать, -аю *impf.*, **с|вали́ть, -лю́, -лишь** *pf.* throw down, bring down; overthrow; lay low; heap up, pile up; abate; ~**ся** fall, fall down, collapse. **сва́лка, -и** dump; scrap-heap, rubbish-heap; scuffle; **вы́бросить на сва́лку** dump.
с|валя́ть, -я́ю *pf.* **сваля́ться, -я́ется** *pf.* get tangled, get matted.
сва́ривать, -аю *impf.*, **с|вари́ть, -рю́, -ришь** *pf.* boil; cook; weld; ~**ся** boil, cook; weld (together), unite. **сва́рка, -и** welding.
сварли́вый peevish; shrewish.
сварно́й welded. **сва́рочный** welding. **сва́рщик, -а** welder.
сва́тать, -аю *impf.* (*pf.* **по~, со~**) propose as a husband or wife; ask in marriage; ~**ся** **к**+*d.* *or* **за**+*a.* ask, seek in marriage.
сва́я, -и pile.
све́дение, -я piece of information; knowledge; attention, notice; report, minute; *pl.* information, intelligence; knowledge. **све́дущ|ий** knowledgeable; versed, experienced; ~**ие ли́ца** experts, informed persons.
сведу́ *etc.*: *see* **свести́**
свежезаморо́женный fresh-frozen; chilled. **све́жесть, -и** freshness; coolness. **свеже́ть, -е́ет** *impf.* (*pf.* **по~**) become cooler; freshen. **све́ж|ий; -еж, -а́** fresh; ~**ее бельё** clean underclothes; ~**ие проду́кты** fresh food; ~**ий хлеб** new bread.
свезти́, -зу́, -зёшь; свёз, -ла́ *pf.* (*impf.* **свози́ть**) take, convey; bring down, take down; take away, clear away.
свёкла, -ы beet, beetroot.
свёкор, -кра father-in-law. **свекро́вь, -и** mother-in-law.
свёл *etc.*: *see* **свести́**
сверга́ть, -а́ю *impf.*, **све́ргнуть, -ну; сверг** *pf.* throw down, overthrow. **сверже́ние, -я** overthrow; ~ **с престо́ла** dethronement.
све́рить, -рю *pf.* (*impf.* **сверя́ть**) collate; check.
сверка́ние, -я sparkling, sparkle; twinkling, twinkle; glitter; glare. **сверка́ть, -а́ю** *impf.* sparkle, twinkle; glitter; gleam. **сверкну́ть, -ну́, -нёшь** *pf.* flash.
сверли́льный drill, drilling; boring. **сверли́ть, -лю́** *impf.* (*pf.* **про~**) drill; bore through; nag, gnaw. **сверло́, -а́** drill. **сверля́щий** nagging, gnawing, piercing.
сверну́ть, -ну́, -нёшь *pf.* (*impf.* **свёртывать, свора́чивать**) roll, roll up; turn; reduce, contract, curtail, cut down; wind up; ~ **ла́герь** break camp; ~ **ше́ю**+*d.* wring the neck of; ~**ся** roll up, curl up; coil up; fold; curdle, coagulate, turn; contract.
све́рстник, -а person of the same age, coeval; **мы с ним ~и** he and I are the same age
свёрток, -тка package, parcel, bundle. **свёртывание, -я** rolling, rolling up; curdling, turning; coagulation; reduction, curtailment, cutting down, cuts. **свёртывать(ся, -аю(сь** *impf. of* **сверну́ть(ся**
сверх *prep.*+*g.* over, above, on top of; beyond; over and above; in addition to; in excess of; ~ **того́** moreover, besides.
сверх... *in comb.* super-, supra-, extra-, over-, preter-, hyper-. **сверхзвезда́, -ы́** quasar. ~**звуково́й** supersonic. ~**пла́новый** over and above the plan. ~**при́быль, -и** excess profit. ~**проводни́к, -а́** superconductor. ~**секре́тный** top-secret. ~**совреме́нный** ultra-modern. ~**уро́чный** overtime. ~**уро́чные** *sb.*, *pl.* overtime. ~**челове́к, -а** superman. ~**челове́ческий** superhuman. ~**шпио́н, -а** super-spy. ~**шта́тный** supernumerary. ~**ъесте́ственный** supernatural, preternatural.
све́рху *adv.* from above; from the top; on the surface; ~ **до́низу** from top to bottom.
сверчо́к, -чка́ cricket.
сверя́ть, -я́ю *impf. of* **све́рить**
свес, -а overhang. **све́сить, -е́шу** *pf.* (*impf.* **све́шивать**) let down, lower; dangle; weigh; ~**ся** hang over, overhang; lean over.
свести́, -еду́, -едёшь; -ёл, -а́ *pf.* (*impf.* **своди́ть**) take; take down; take away, lead off; remove, take out; bring together, put together; unite; reduce, bring; cramp, convulse; ~ **дру́жбу**, ~ **знако́мство** make friends; ~ **концы́ с конца́ми** make (both) ends meet; ~ **на нет** bring to naught; ~ **с ума́** drive mad; ~ **счёты** settle accounts, get even; **у меня́ свело́ но́гу** I've got cramp in the leg.
свет[1]**, -а (-у)** light; daybreak; **при ~е**+*g.* by the light of.
свет[2]**, -а (-у)** world; society, beau monde.
света́ть, -а́ет *impf.*, *impers.* dawn; ~**а́ет** day is breaking, it is getting light. **светёлка, -и** attic. **свети́ло, -а** luminary. **свети́льный** illuminating; ~ **газ** coal-gas. **свети́ть, -ечу́, -е́тишь** *impf.* (*pf.* **по~**) shine; +*d.* light; hold a light for, light the way for; ~**ся** shine, gleam. **светле́ть, -е́ет** *impf.* (*pf.* **по~, про~**) brighten; grow lighter; clear up, brighten up. **све́тлый** light; light-coloured; radiant; joyous; pure, unclouded; lucid, clear. **светля́к, -а́, светлячо́к, -чка́** glow-worm; fire-fly.
свето... *in comb.* light, photo-. **светобоя́знь, -и** photophobia. ~**ко́пия, -и** photocopy, Photostat (*propr.*); blueprint. ~**маскиро́вка, -и** black-out. ~**непроница́емый** light-proof, light-tight, opaque. ~**си́ла, -ы** candlepower; rapidity, speed, focal ratio.

~фильтр, -а light filter; (colour) filter. **~фо́р, -а** traffic light(s). **~чувстви́тельный** photosensitive, light-sensitive, photographic, sensitized.

светов|о́й light, lighting; luminous; **~о́й год** light-year; **~а́я рекла́ма** illuminated sign(s).

све́тский society, fashionable; genteel, refined; temporal, lay, secular; **~ челове́к** man of the world, man of fashion.

светя́щийся luminous, luminescent, fluorescent, phosphorescent. **свеча́, -и́**; *pl.* **-и, -е́й** candle; taper; (sparking-)plug. **свече́ние, -я** luminescence, fluorescence; phosphorescence. **све́чка, -и** candle. **свечно́й** candle; **~ огáрок** candle-end. **свечу́** *etc.*: *see* **свети́ть**

с|ве́шать, -аю *pf.* **све́шивать(ся, -аю(сь** *impf. of* **све́сить(ся. свива́ть, -а́ю** *impf. of* **свить**

свида́ние, -я meeting; appointment; rendezvous; date; **до свида́ния!** goodbye!; **назна́чить ~** make an appointment; make a date.

свиде́тель, -я *m.*, **-ница, -ы** witness. **свиде́тельство, -а** evidence; testimony; certificate; **~ о бра́ке** marriage certificate; **~ о прода́же** bill of sale. **свиде́тельствовать, -твую** *impf.* (*pf.* **за~, о~**) give evidence, testify; be evidence (of), show; witness; attest, certify; examine, inspect.

свина́рник, -а, свина́рня, -и pigsty.

свине́ц, -нца́ lead.

свини́на, -ы pork. **свин|о́й** pig; pork; **~а́я ко́жа** pigskin; **~о́е са́ло** lard.

свинцо́в|ый lead; leaden; lead-coloured; **~ые бели́ла** white lead.

свинья́, -и́; *pl.* **-и, -е́й, -ям** pig, swine; hog; sow.

свире́ль, -и (reed-)pipe.

свирепе́ть, -е́ю *impf.* (*pf.* **рас~**) grow fierce, grow savage. **свире́пствовать, -твую** *impf.* rage; be rife. **свире́пый** fierce, ferocious, savage; violent.

свиса́ть, -а́ю *impf.*, **сви́снуть, -ну; -ис** *pf.* hang down, droop, dangle; trail.

свист, -а whistle; whistling; singing, piping, warbling. **свиста́ть, -ищу́, -и́щешь** *impf.* whistle; sing, pipe, warble. **свисте́ть, -ищу́** *impf.*, **сви́стнуть, -ну** *pf.* whistle; hiss. **свисто́к, -тка́** whistle.

сви́та, -ы suite; retinue; series, formation.

сви́тер, -а sweater; **спорти́вный ~** sweatshirt.

сви́ток, -тка roll, scroll. **с|вить, совью́, совьёшь; -ил, -а́, -о** *pf.* (*impf. also* **свива́ть**) twist, wind; **~ся** roll up, curl up, coil.

свищ, -а́ flaw; (knot-)hole; fistula.

свищу́ *etc.*: *see* **свиста́ть, свисте́ть**

свобо́да, -ы freedom, liberty; **на свобо́де** at leisure; at large, at liberty; **~ рук** a free hand; **~ сло́ва** freedom of speech. **свобо́дно** *adv.* freely; easily, with ease; fluently; loose, loosely. **свобо́дн|ый** free; easy; vacant; spare; free-and-easy; loose, loose-fitting; flowing. **~ое вре́мя** free time, time off; spare time; **~ый до́ступ** easy access; **~ый уда́р** free kick. **свободолюби́вый** freedom-loving. **свободомы́слие, -я** free-thinking. **свободомы́слящий** free-thinking; *sb.* free-thinker.

свод, -а code; collection; arch, vault; **~ зако́нов** code of laws.

своди́ть, -ожу́, -о́дишь *impf. of* **свести́**

сво́дка, -и summary, résumé; report; communiqué; revise. **сво́дный** composite, combined; collated; step-; **~ брат** step-brother.

сво́дчатый arched, vaulted.

своево́лие, -я self-will, wilfulness. **своево́льный** self-willed, wilful.

своевре́менно *adv.* in good time; opportunely. **своевре́менный** timely, opportune; well-timed.

своенра́вие, -я wilfulness, waywardness, capriciousness. **своенра́вный** wilful, wayward, capricious.

своеобра́зие, -я originality; peculiarity. **своеобра́зный** original; peculiar, distinctive.

свожу́ *etc.*: *see* **своди́ть, свози́ть. свози́ть, -ожу́, -о́зишь** *impf. of* **свезти́**

свой, своего́ *m.*, **своя́, свое́й** *f.*, **своё, своего́** *nt.*, **свои́, свои́х** *pl.*, *pron.* one's (own); my, his, her, its; our, your, their; **доби́ться своего́** get one's own way; **она́ сама́ не своя́** she is not herself; **он не в своём уме́** he is not in his right mind. **сво́йственный** peculiar, characteristic. **сво́йство, -а** property, quality, attribute, characteristic.

сво́ра, -ы leash, pair; pack; gang.

свора́чивать, -аю *impf. of* **сверну́ть, своротить. с|ворова́ть, -ру́ю** *pf.*

своротить, -очу́, -о́тишь *pf.* (*impf.* **свора́чивать**) dislodge, displace, shift; turn, swing; twist, dislocate.

свыка́ться, -а́юсь *impf.*, **сво́кнуться, -нусь; -ы́кся** *pf.* get used, accustom o.s.

свысока́ *adv.* haughtily; condescendingly. **свы́ше** *adv.* from above; from on high. **свы́ше** *prep.+g.* over, more than; beyond.

свя́занный constrained; combined, fixed; bound; coupled. **с|вяза́ть, -яжу́, -я́жешь** *pf.*, **свя́зывать, -аю** *impf.* tie together; tie, bind; connect, link; associate; **~ся** get in touch, communicate; get involved, get mixed up. **связи́ст, -а, -и́стка, -и** signaller; worker in communication services. **свя́зка, -и** sheaf, bunch, bundle; chord; ligament; copula. **связно́й** liaison, communication. **свя́зный** connected, coherent. **связу́ющий** connecting, linking; liaison. **связь, -и**, *loc.* **-и́** connection; causation; link, tie, bond; liaison, association; communication(s); signals; tie, stay, brace, strut; coupling; *pl.* connections, contacts.

святи́лище, -а sanctuary. **святи́тель, -я** *m.* prelate. **святи́ть, -ячу́** *impf.* (*pf.* **о~**) consecrate; bless, sanctify. **свя́тки, -ток** *pl.* Christmas-tide. **свя́то** *adv.* piously; religiously; ~ **бере́чь** treasure; ~ **чти́ть** hold sacred. **свят|о́й; -ят, -á, -о** holy; sacred; saintly; pious; **~о́й, ~áя** *sb.* saint. **свяще́нник, -а** priest. **свяще́нный** holy; sacred. **свяще́нство, -а** priesthood; priests.

сгиб, -а bend. **сгибáемый** flexible, pliable. **сгибáть, -áю** *impf. of* **согну́ть**

сглáдить, -áжу *pf.*, **сглáживать, -аю** *impf.* smooth out; smooth over, soften; **~ся** smooth out, become smooth; be smoothed over, be softened; diminish, abate.

с|глупи́ть, -плю́ *pf.*

сгнивáть, -áю *impf.*, **с|гнить, -ию́, -иёшь; -ил, -á, -о** *pf.* rot, decay.

с|гнои́ть, -ою́ *pf.*

сговáриваться, -аюсь *impf.*, **сговори́ться, -рю́сь** *pf.* come to an arrangement, reach an understanding; arrange; make an appointment. **сго́вор, -а** agreement, compact, deal; betrothal. **сгово́рчивый** compliant, complaisant, tractable.

сгон, -а driving; herding, rounding-up. **сго́нка, -и** rafting, floating. **сго́нщик, -а** herdsman, drover; rafter. **сгоня́ть, -я́ю** *impf. of* **согнáть**

сгорáние, -я combustion; **двигатель вну́треннего сгорáния** internal-combustion engine. **сгорáть, -áю** *impf. of* **сгоре́ть**

с|го́рбить(ся, -блю(сь *pf.* **сго́рбленный** crooked, bent; hunchbacked.

с|горе́ть, -рю́ *pf.* (*impf. also* **сгорáть**) burn down; be burnt out, be burnt down; be burned; be used up; burn; burn o.s. out; ~ **от стыдá** burn with shame. **сгорячá** *adv.* in the heat of the moment; in a fit of temper.

с|гото́вить, -влю *pf.*

сгребáть, -áю *impf.*, **сгрести́, -ебу́, -ебёшь; -ёб, -лá** *pf.* rake up, rake together; shovel away, off.

сгружáть, -áю *impf.*, **сгрузи́ть, -ужу́, -у́зи́шь** *pf.* unload.

с|группировáть(ся, -ру́ю(сь *pf.*

сгусти́ть, -ущу́ *pf.*, **сгущáть, -áю** *impf.* thicken; condense; **~ся** thicken; condense; clot. **сгу́сток, -тка** clot. **сгуще́ние, -я** thickening, condensation; clotting. **сгущённ|ый; -ён, -á** condensed; **~ое молоко́** condensed milk; evaporated milk.

сдáбривать, -аю *impf. of* **сдо́брить**

сдавáть, сдаю́, сдаёшь *impf. of* **сдать;** ~ **экзáмен** take, sit for, an examination; **~ся** *impf. of* **сдáться**

сдави́ть, -влю́, -вишь *pf.*, **сдáвливать, -аю** *impf.* squeeze. **сдáвленный** squeezed; constrained.

сдáточн|ый delivery; **~ая квитáнция** receipt. **сдать, -ам, -ашь, -аст, -ади́м; -ал, -á, -о** *pf.* (*impf.* **сдавáть**) hand over; pass; let, let out, hire out; give in change; surrender, yield, give up; deal; ~ **багáж на хранéние** deposit, leave, one's luggage; ~ **экзáмен** pass an examination; **~ся** surrender, yield. **сдáча, -и** handing over; letting out, hiring out; surrender; change; deal; **дать сдáчи** give change; give as good as one gets.

сдви́г, -а displacement; fault, dislocation; change, improvement. **сдвигáть, -áю** *impf.*, **сдви́нуть, -ну** *pf.* shift, move, displace; move together, bring together; **~ся** move, budge; come together. **сдвижно́й** movable.

с|дéлать(ся, -аю(сь *pf.* **сдéлка, -и** transaction; deal, bargain; agreement. **сдéльн|ый** piece-work; **~ая рабо́та** piece-work. **сдéльщик, -а** piece-worker. **сдéльщина, -ы** piece-work.

сдёргивать, -аю *impf. of* **сдёрнуть**

сдéржанно *adv.* with restraint, with reserve. **сдéржанный** restrained, reserved. **сдержáть, -жу́, -жишь** *pf.*, **сдéрживать, -аю** *impf.* hold, hold back; hold in check, contain; keep back, restrain; keep; ~ **сло́во** keep one's word.

сдёрнуть, -ну *pf.* (*impf.* **сдёргивать**) pull off.

сдеру́ *etc.*: *see* **содрáть. сдирáть, -áю** *impf. of* **содрáть**

сдо́ба, -ы shortening; fancy bread, bun(s). **сдо́бн|ый; -бен, -бнá, -о** rich, short; **~ая бу́лка** bun. **сдо́брить, -рю** *pf.* (*impf.* **сдáбривать**) flavour; spice; enrich.

с|до́хнуть, -нет; сдох *pf.* (*impf. also* **сдыхáть**) die, croak, kick the bucket.

сдружи́ться, -жу́сь *pf.* become friends.

сдубли́рованный bonded.

сдувáть, -áю *impf.*, **сду́нуть, -ну** *pf.*, **сдуть, -у́ю** *pf.* blow away, blow off; crib.

сдыхáть, -áет *impf. of* **сдо́хнуть**

сеáнс, -а performance; showing, house; sitting.

себесто́имость, -и prime cost; cost (price).

себя́, *d. & p.* **себé**, *i.* **собо́й** *or* **собо́ю** *refl. pron.* oneself; myself, yourself, himself, *etc.*; **собо́й** -looking, in appearance; **хоро́ш собо́й** good-looking, nice-looking; **ничего́ себé** not bad; **так себé** so-so.

сев, -а sowing.

сéвер, -а north. **сéвернее** *adv.+g.* northwards of, to the north of. **сéверн|ый** north, northern; northerly; **С~ый Ледови́тый океáн** the Arctic Ocean; **~ый олéнь** reindeer; **~ое сия́ние** northern lights, aurora borealis. **сéверо-восто́к, -а** north-east **сéверо-восто́чный** north-east, north-eastern. **сéверо-зáпад, -а** north-west. **сéверо-зáпадный** north-west, north-western. **северя́нин, -а**; *pl.* **-я́не, -я́н** northerner.

севооборо́т, -а rotation of crops.

сего́ *see* **сей. сего́дня** *adv.* today; ~ **вéчером** this evening, tonight. **сего́дняшний** of today, today's.

седéльник, -а saddler. **седéльный** saddle.

седéть, -éю *impf.* (*pf.* **по~**) go grey, turn grey. **седéющий** grizzled, greying. **сединá, -ы́**; *pl.* **-ы** grey hairs; grey streak.

седла́ть, -а́ю *impf.* (*pf.* **о~**) saddle. **седло́, -а́**; *pl.* **сёдла, -дел** saddle. **седлови́на, -ы** arch; saddle; col.

седоборо́дый grey-bearded. **седовла́сый, седоволо́сый** grey-haired. **седо́й; сед, -а́, -о** grey; hoary; grey-haired; flecked with white.

седо́к, -а́ fare, passenger; rider, horseman.

седьмо́й seventh.

сезо́н, -а season. **сезо́нник, -а** seasonal worker. **сезо́нный** seasonal.

сей, сего́ *m.*, **сия́, сей** *f.*, **сие́, сего́** *nt.*, **сии́, сих** *pl.*, *pron.* this; these; **на сей раз** this time, for this once; **сего́ ме́сяца** this month's; **сию́ мину́ту** this (very) minute; at once, instantly.

сейча́с *adv.* now, at present, at the (present) moment; just, just now; presently, soon; straight away, immediately.

сёк *etc.*: *see* **сечь**

сек. *abbr.* (*of* **секу́нда**) sec., second(s).

секре́т, -а secret; hidden mechanism; listening post; **по ~у** secretly; confidentially, in confidence.

секретариа́т, -а secretariat. **секрета́рский** secretarial; secretary's. **секрета́рша, -и, секрета́рь, -я́** *m.* secretary.

секре́тно *adv.* secretly, in secret; secret, confidential; **соверше́нно ~** top secret. **секре́тный** secret; confidential; **~ сотру́дник** secret agent, under-cover agent.

секс, -а sex; **~ вне бра́ка** extramarital sex. **сексапи́льность, -и** sex appeal. **сексапи́льный** sexy. **сексуа́льность, -и** sexuality. **сексуа́льный** sexual.

се́кта, -ы sect. **секта́нт, -а** sectarian, sectary. **секта́нство, -а** sectarianism.

се́ктор, -а sector, section, part, sphere.

секу́ *etc.*: *see* **сечь**

секу́нда, -ы second; **сию́ секу́нду!** (in) just a moment! **секунда́нт, -а** second; second string. **секу́ндн|ый** second; **~ая стре́лка** second hand. **секундоме́р, -а** stop-watch.

секцио́нный sectional. **се́кция, -и** section.

селёдка, -и herring. **селёдочный** herring, of herring(s).

се́лезень, -зня *m.* drake.

селе́ктор, -а intercom.

селе́ние, -я settlement, village.

сели́тра, -ы saltpetre, nitre. **сели́трян|ый** saltpetre; **~ая кислота́** nitric acid.

сели́ть, -лю́ *impf.* (*pf.* **по~**) settle; **~ся** settle. **сели́тебный** built-up; building, development. **сели́тьба, -ы**; *g.pl.* **-и́тьб** developed land; built-up area; settlement. **село́, -а́**; *pl.* **сёла** village.

сель... *abbr.* (*of* **се́льский**) *in comb.* village; country, rural. **селько́р, -а** rural correspondent. **~ма́г, -а, ~по́** *nt.indecl.* village shop. **~сове́т, -а** village soviet.

сельдере́й, -я celery.

сельдь, -и; *pl.* **-и, -е́й** herring. **сельдяно́й** herring.

се́льск|ий country, rural; village; **~ое хозя́йство** agriculture, farming. **сельскохозя́йственный** agricultural, farming.

семафо́р, -а semaphore; signal.

сёмга, -и salmon; smoked salmon.

семе́йный family; domestic; **~ челове́к** married man, family man. **семе́йство, -а** family.

се́мени *etc.*: *see* **се́мя**

семени́ть, -ню́ *impf.* mince.

семени́ться, -и́тся *impf.* seed. **семенни́к, -а** testicle; pericarp, seed-vessel; seed-plant. **семенно́й** seed; seminal, spermatic.

семери́чный septenary. **семёрка, -и** seven; figure 7; No. 7; group of seven. **семерно́й** sevenfold, septuple. **се́меро, -ы́х** seven.

семе́стр, -а term, semester. **семестро́вый** terminal.

се́мечко, -а; *pl.* **-и** seed; *pl.* sunflower seeds.

семидесятиле́тие, -я seventy years; seventieth anniversary, birthday. **семидесятиле́тний** seventy-year, seventy years'; seventy-year-old. **семидеся́т|ый** seventieth; **~ые го́ды** the seventies. **семикра́тный** sevenfold, septuple. **семиле́тка, -и** seven-year school; seven-year plan; seven-year-old. **семиле́тний** seven-year; septennial; seven-year-old; **~ ребёнок** child of seven, seven-year-old.

семина́р, -а seminar.

семинари́ст, -а seminarist. **семина́рия, -и** seminary; training college.

семисо́тый seven-hundredth. **семиты́сячный** seven-thousandth. **семиуго́льник, -а** heptagon. **семиуго́льный** heptagonal. **семна́дцатый** seventeenth. **семна́дцать, -и** seventeen. **семь, -ми́, -мью́** seven. **се́мьдесят, -ми́десяти, -мью́десятью** seventy. **семьсо́т, -мисо́т,** *i.* **-мьюста́ми** seven hundred. **се́мью** *adv.* seven times.

семья́, -и́; *pl.* **-и, -е́й, -ям** family. **семьяни́н, -а** family man.

се́мя, -мени; *pl.* **-мена́, -мя́н, -мена́м** seed; semen, sperm.

Се́на, -ы the Seine.

сена́т, -а senate. **сена́тор, -а** senator. **сена́торский** senatorial.

се́ни, -е́й *pl.* (entrance-)hall; (*enclosed*) porch.

сенно́й hay. **се́но, -а** hay. **сенова́л, -а** hayloft, hay-mow. **сеноко́с, -а** mowing, haymaking; hayfield. **сенокоси́лка, -и** mowing machine. **сеноко́сный** haymaking.

сенсацио́нный sensational. **сенса́ция, -и** sensation.

сентимента́льность, -и sentimentality. **сентимента́льный** sentimental.

сентя́брь, -я́ *m.*, **сентя́брьский** September.

сепарати́вный separatist. **сепарати́зм, -а** separatism. **сепарати́ст, -а** separatist. **сепара́тный** separate.

се́псис, -а sepsis, septicaemia. **септи́ческий** septic.

се́ра, -ы sulphur; brimstone; ear-wax.

сервáнт, -а sideboard.

сервúз, -а service, set. **сервировáть, -рýю** *impf.* & *pf.* serve; ~ **стол** lay a table. **сервирóвка, -и** laying; serving, service.

сердéчник, -а core. **сердéчность, -и** cordiality; warmth. **сердéчный** heart; of the heart; cardiac; cordial, hearty; heartfelt, sincere; warm, warm-hearted. **сердúтый** angry, cross; irate; strong. **сердúть, -ржý, -рдишь** *impf.* (*pf.* **рас**~) anger, make angry; ~**ся** be angry, be cross. **сéрдце, -а**; *pl.* **-á, -дéц** heart; **в сердцáх** in anger, in a fit of temper; **от всегó сéрдца** from the bottom of one's heart, wholeheartedly. **сердцебиéние, -я** palpitation. **сердцевúдный** heart-shaped; cordate. **сердцевúна, -ы** core, pith, heart.

серебрёный silver-plated. **серебрúстый** silvery. **серебрúть, -рю** *impf.* (*pf.* **по**~) silver, silver-plate; ~**ся** silver, become silvery. **серебрó, -á** silver. **серéбряник, -а** silversmith. **серéбрян|ый** silver; ~**ая свáдьба** silver wedding.

середúна, -ы middle, midst; **золотáя** ~ golden mean. **середúнный** middle, mean, intermediate. **серёдка, -и** middle, centre.

серёжка, -и earring; catkin.

сéренький grey; dull, drab. **серéть, -éю** *impf.* (*pf.* **по**~) turn grey, go grey; show grey.

сержáнт, -а sergeant.

серúйн|ый serial; ~**ое произвóдство** mass production. **сéрия, -и** series; range; part.

сéрн|ый sulphur; sulphuric; ~**ая кислотá** sulphuric acid.

серовáтый greyish. **сероглáзый** grey-eyed.

серп, -á sickle, reaping-hook; ~ **луны́** crescent moon.

серпантúн, -а paper streamer; serpentine road.

серповúдный crescent(-shaped).

серсó *nt.indecl.* hoop.

сéрфинг, -а surfing. **серфингúст, -а** surfer.

сéрый; сер, -á, -о grey; dull; drab; dim; ignorant, uncouth, uneducated.

серьгá, -ú; *pl.* **-и, -рёг** earring.

серьёзно *adv.* seriously; earnestly; in earnest. **серьёзный** serious; earnest; grave.

сéссия, -и session, sitting; conference, congress; term.

сестрá, -ы́; *pl.* **сёстры, сестёр, сёстрам** sister.

сесть, сяду *pf.* (*impf.* **садúться**) sit down; alight; settle, perch; land; set; shrink; +**на**+*a.* board, take, get on; ~ **за рабóту** set to work; ~ **на корáбль** go on board, go aboard; ~ **на лóшадь** mount a horse; ~ **на пóезд** board a train.

сетевóй net, netting, mesh. **сéтка, -и** net, netting; (luggage-)rack; string bag; grid; coordinates; scale.

сéтовать, -тую *impf.* (*pf.* **по**~) complain; lament, mourn.

сéточный net; grid. **сетчáтка, -и** retina. **сéтчатый** netted, network; reticular. **сеть, -и**, *loc.* **-ú**; *pl.* **-и, -éй** net; network; circuit, system.

сечéние, -я cutting; section. **сечь, секý, сечёшь; сек** *impf.* (*pf.* **вы́**~) cut to pieces; beat, flog; ~**ся** (*pf.* **по**~**ся**) split; cut.

сéялка, -и sowing-machine, seed drill. **сéяльщик, -а, сéятель, -я** *m.* sower. **сéять, сéю** *impf.* (*pf.* **по**~) sow; throw about.

сжáлиться, -люсь *pf.* take pity (**над**+*i.*) on.

сжáтие, -я pressing, pressure; grasp, grip; compression; condensation. **сжáтость, -и** compression; conciseness, concision. **сжáтый** compressed; condensed, compact; concise, brief.

с|жать[1], **сожнý, -нёшь** *pf.*

сжать[2], **сожмý, -мёшь** *pf.* (*impf.* **сжимáть**) squeeze; compress; grip; clench; ~ **зýбы** grit one's teeth; ~**ся** tighten, clench; shrink, contract.

с|жечь, сожгý, сожжёшь; сжёг, сожглá *pf.* (*impf.* **сжигáть**) burn; burn up, burn down; cremate.

сживáться, -áюсь *impf. of* **сжúться**

сжигáть, -áю *impf. of* **сжечь**

сжим, -а clip, grip, clamp. **сжимáемость, -и** compressibility, condensability. **сжимáть(ся** *impf. of* **сжáть**[2]**(ся**

сжúться, -ивýсь, -ивёшься; -úлся, -áсь *pf.* (*impf.* **сживáться**) **с**+*i.* get used to, get accustomed to.

с|жýльничать, -аю *pf.*

сзáди *adv.* from behind; behind; from the end; from the rear. **сзáди** *prep.*+*g.* behind.

сзывáть, -áю *impf. of* **созвáть**

си *nt.indecl.* B; te.

сибúрский Siberian; ~ **кедр** Siberian pine. **Сибúрь, -и** Siberia. **сибиря́к, -á, сибиря́чка, -и** Siberian.

сигáра, -ы cigar. **сигарéта, -ы** cigarette; small cigar. **сигáрка, -и** (*home-made*) cigarette. **сигáрный** cigar.

сигнáл, -а signal. **сигнализáция, -и** signalling. **сигнализúровать, -рую** *impf.* & *pf.* (*pf. also* **про**~) signal; give warning. **сигнáльный** signal. **сигнáльщик, -а** signaller, signal-man.

сидéлка, -и (*untrained*) nurse, sick-nurse. **сидéние, -я** sitting. **сидéнье, -я** seat. **сидéть, -ижý** *impf.* sit; be; fit; **плáтье хорошó сидúт на ней** the dress fits her; ~ **без дéла** have nothing to do; ~ **верхóм** be on horseback; ~ **(в тюрьмé)** be in prison; ~ **на насéсте** roost, perch.

Сúдней, -я Sydney.

сидр, -а cider.

сидя́чий sitting; sedentary; sessile.

сиé *etc.*: *see* **сей**

сúзый; сиз, -á, -о dove-coloured, (blue-)grey; bluish, blue.

сий *see* **сей**

сикх, -а Sikh. **сúкхский** Sikh.

сúла, -ы strength; force; power; energy; quantity, multitude; point, essence; *pl.* force(s); **в**

си́ле in force, valid; **в си́лу**+*g.* on the strength of, by virtue of, because of; **имéющий си́лу** valid; **не по ~ам** beyond one's powers, beyond one's strength; **свои́ми ~ами** unaided; **си́лой** by force. **силáч, -á** strong man. **си́литься, -люсь** *impf.* try, make efforts. **силов|óй** power; of force; **~óе пóле** field of force; **~áя стáнция** power-station, power-house; **~áя устанóвка** power-plant.

силóк, -лкá noose, snare.

си́лос, -а silo, silage. **силосовáть, -сýю** *impf.* & *pf.* (*pf. also* **за~**) silo, ensile.

си́льно *adv.* strongly, violently; very much, greatly; badly. **си́льный; -лен** *or* **-лён, -льнá, -о** strong; powerful; intense, keen, hard; **он не силён в языкáх** he is not good at languages; **~морóз** hard frost.

си́мвол, -а symbol; emblem; **~ вéры** creed. **символизи́ровать, -рую** *impf.* symbolize. **символи́зм, -а** symbolism. **символи́ческий** symbolic.

симметри́ческий symmetrical. **симметри́я, -и** symmetry.

симпатизи́ровать, -рую *impf.+d.* be in sympathy with, sympathize with. **симпати́ческий** sympathetic. **симпати́чный** likeable, attractive, nice. **симпáтия, -и** liking; sympathy.

симули́ровать, -рую *impf.* & *pf.* simulate, feign, sham. **симуля́нт, -а** malingerer, sham. **симуля́ция, -и** simulation, pretence.

симфони́ческий symphonic. **симфóния, -и** symphony; concordance.

синагóга, -и synagogue.

синдикáт, -а syndicate. **синдици́ровать, -рую** *impf.* & *pf.* syndicate.

синевá, -ы́ blue; **~ под глазáми** dark rings under the eyes. **синевáтый** bluish. **синеглáзый** blue-eyed. **сине́ть, -éю** *impf.* (*pf.* **по~**) turn blue, become blue; show blue. **си́ний; синь, -ня́, -не** (dark) blue. **сини́льная кислотá** prussic acid. **сини́ть, -ню́** *impf.* (*pf.* **под~**) paint blue; blue.

синóд, -а synod. **синодáльный** synodal.

синóним, -а synonym. **синони́мика, -и** synonymy; synonyms.

синóптик, -а weather-forecaster. **синóптика, -и** weather-forecasting.

си́нтаксис, -а syntax. **синтакси́ческий** syntactical.

си́нтез, -а synthesis. **синтезáтор, -а** synthesizer. **синтези́ровать, -рую** *impf.* & *pf.* synthesize. **синтети́ческий** synthetic.

си́нус, -а sine; sinus.

синхрони́зм, -а synchronism. **синхронизáция, -и** synchronization. **синхронизи́ровать, -рую** *impf.* & *pf.* synchronize. **синхрони́ст, -а** simultaneous interpreter.

синь[1]**, -и** blue. **синь**[2] *see* **си́ний. си́нька, -и** blue, blueing; blue-print. **синя́к, -á** bruise; **~ (под глáзом)** black eye.

си́плый hoarse, husky. **си́пнуть, -ну; сип** *impf.* (*pf.* **о~**) become hoarse, become husky.

сирéна, -ы siren; hooter.

сирéневый lilac(-coloured). **сирéнь, -и** lilac.

Си́рия, -и Syria.

сирóп, -а syrup.

сиротá, -ы́ *pl.* **-ы** *c.g.* orphan. **сиротли́вый** lonely. **сирóтский** orphan's, orphans'; **~ дом** orphanage.

систéма, -ы system; type. **систематизи́ровать, -рую** *impf.* & *pf.* systematize. **системáтика, -и** systematics; classification; taxonomy. **системати́ческий, системати́чный** systematic; methodical.

си́тец, -тца (-тцу) (cotton) print, (printed) cotton; chintz.

си́то, -а sieve; screen; riddle.

си́тцевый print, chintz; chintz-covered.

сия́ *see* **сей**

сия́ние, -я radiance; halo. **сия́ть, -я́ю** *impf.* shine, beam; be radiant.

сказ, -а tale, lay; skaz. **сказáние, -я** story, tale, legend, lay. **сказáть, -ажý, -áжешь** *pf.* (*impf.* **говори́ть**) say; speak; tell; **как ~** how shall I put it?; **скáзано — сдéлано** no sooner said than done; **так сказáть** so to say. **сказáться, -ажýсь, -áжешься** *pf.*, **скáзываться, -аюсь** *impf.* give notice, give warning; tell (on); declare o.s.; **~ больны́м** report sick. **сказúтель, -я** *m.* narrator, storyteller. **скáзка, -и** tale; story; fairy-tale; fib. **скáзочник, -а** story-teller. **скáзочный** fairy-tale; fabulous, fantastic; **~ ая странá** fairyland. **сказýемое** *sb.* predicate.

скакáлка, -и skipping-rope. **скакáть, -ачý, -áчешь** *impf.* (*pf.* **по~**) skip, jump; hop; gallop. **скаковóй** race, racing. **скакýн, -á** fast horse, race-horse.

скалá, -ы́; *pl.* **-ы** rock face, crag; cliff; **подвóдная ~** reef. **скали́стый** rocky; precipitous.

скáлить, -лю *impf.* (*pf.* **о~**); **~ зýбы** bare one's teeth; grin.

скáлка, -и rolling-pin.

скалолáз, -а rock-climber. **скалолáзание, -я** rock-climbing.

скáлывать, -аю *impf. of* **сколóть**

скамéечка, -и footstool; small bench. **скамéйка, -и** bench. **скамья́, и́**; *pl.* **скáмьи́, -éй** bench; **~ подсуди́мых** dock; **со шкóльной скамьи́** straight from school.

скандáл, -а scandal; disgrace; brawl, rowdy scene. **скандали́ст, -а** brawler; trouble-maker; rowdy. **скандáлить, -лю** *impf.* (*pf.* **на~, о~**) brawl; kick up a row; shame; **~ся** disgrace o.s.; cut a poor figure **скандáльный** scandalous; rowdy; scandal.

Скандинáвия, -и Scandinavia.

сканди́рование, -я scansion.

скáнер, -а scanner.

скáпливать(ся, -аю(сь *impf. of* **скопи́ть(ся**

скарб, -а goods and chattels, bits and pieces.

скáред, -а, скáреда, -ы *c.g.* miser. **скáредничать, -аю** *impf.* be stingy. **скáредный** stingy, miserly, niggardly.

скарлатúна, -ы scarlet fever, scarlatina.

скат, -а slope, incline; pitch.

с|катáть, -áю *pf.* (*impf.* **скáтывать**) roll (up); furl.

скáтерть, -и; *pl.* **-и, -éй** table-cloth; **~ью дорóга!** good riddance!

скатúть, -ачý, -áтишь *pf.*, **скáтывать**[1], **-аю** *impf.* roll down; **~ся** roll down; slip, slide. **скáтывать**[2], **-аю** *impf. of* **скатáть**

скафáндр, -а diving-suit; space-suit.

скáчка, -и gallop, galloping. **скáчки, -чек** *pl.* horse-race; races, race-meeting; **~ с препятствиями** steeple-chase, obstacle-race. **скачкообрáзный** spasmodic; uneven. **скачóк, -чкá** jump, leap, bound.

скáшивать, -аю *impf. of* **скосúть**

СКВ *abbr.* (*of* ***свобóдно конвертúруемая валюта***) freely convertible currency, hard currency.

сквáжина, -ы slit, chink; bore-hole; well **сквáжистый, сквáжный** porous.

сквер, -а public garden; square.

сквéрно badly; bad, poorly. **сквернослóвить, -влю** *impf.* use foul language. **сквéрный** nasty, foul; bad.

сквозúть, -úт *impf.* be transparent, show light through; show through; **сквозúт** *impers.* there is a draught. **сквознóй** through; all-round; transparent; **~ вéтер** draught. **сквозняк, -á** draught. **сквозь** *prep.+g.* through.

скворéц, -рцá starling.

скелéт, -а skeleton.

скéптик, -а sceptic. **скептицúзм, -а** scepticism. **скептúческий** sceptical.

скетч, -а (*theatr.*) sketch.

скúдка, -и rebate, reduction, discount; allowance(s); **со скúдкой в**+*a.* with a reduction of, at a discount of. **скúдывать, -аю** *impf.*, **скúнуть, -ну** *pf.* throw off, throw down; knock off.

скúпетр, -а sceptre.

скипидáр, -а (-у) turpentine.

скирд, -á; *pl.* **-ы́, скирдá, -ы́**; *pl.* **-ы, -áм** stack, rick.

скисáть, -áю *impf.*, **скúснуть, -ну; скис** *pf.* go sour, turn (sour).

скитáлец, -льца wanderer. **скитáльческий** wandering. **скитáться, -áюсь** *impf.* wander.

скиф, -а Scythian. **скúфский** Scythian.

склад[1], **-а** storehouse; depot; store.

склад[2], **-а (-у)** stamp, mould; turn; logical connection; **~ умá** turn of mind, mentality.

склáдка, -и fold; pleat, tuck; crease; wrinkle.

склáдно *adv.* smoothly, coherently.

складн|óй folding, collapsible; **~áя кровáть** camp-bed; **~áя лéстница** steps, step-ladder.

склáдный; -ден, -дна, -о well-knit, well-built; well-made; rounded, smooth, coherent.

склáдочный, складскóй storage, warehousing; **склáдочное мéсто** store-room, lumber-room, box-room.

склáдчатый plicated, folded.

склáдчина, -ы clubbing; pooling; **в склáдчину** by clubbing together. **склáдывать(ся, -аю(сь** *impf. of* **сложúть(ся**

склéивать, -аю *impf.*, **с|клéить, -éю** *pf.* stick together; glue together, paste together; **~ся** stick together. **склéйка, -и** glueing, pasting, together.

склеп, -а (burial) vault, crypt.

склепáть, -áю *pf.* **склёпывать, -аю** *impf.* rivet. **склёпка, -и** riveting.

склерóз, -а sclerosis; **рассéянный, мнóжественный ~** multiple sclerosis.

склóка, -и squabble; row.

склон, -а slope; **на ~е лет** in one's declining years. **склонéние, -я** inclination; declination; declension. **склонúть, -ню́, -нишь** *pf.*, **склонять, -яю** *impf.* incline; bend, bow; win over, gain over; decline; **~ся** bend, bow; give in, yield; decline, be declined. **склóнность, -и** inclination; disposition; susceptibility; bent, penchant. **склóнный; -нен, -ннá, -нно** inclined, disposed, susceptible, given, prone. **склоняемый** declinable.

склóчник, -а squabbler, trouble-maker. **склóчный** troublesome, trouble-making.

склянка, -и phial; bottle; hour-glass; bell; **шесть склянок** six bells.

скобá, -ы́; *pl.* **-ы, -áм** cramp, clamp; staple; catch, fastening; shackle.

скóбель, -я *m.* spoke-shave, draw(ing)-knife.

скóбка, -и *dim. of* **скобá**; bracket; *pl.* parenthesis, parentheses; **в ~х** in brackets; in parenthesis, by the way, incidentally.

скоблúть, -облю́, -óблишь *impf.* scrape, plane.

скóбочн|ый cramp, clamp, staple, shackle; bracket; **~ая машúна** stapler, stapling machine.

скóванность, -и constraint. **скóванный** constrained; locked, bound; **~ льдáми** ice-bound. **сковáть, скую́, скуёшь** *pf.* (*impf.* **скóвывать**) forge; hammer out; chain; fetter, bind; pin down, hold, contain; lock; **лёд сковáл рéку** the river is ice-bound.

сковородá, -ы́; *pl.* **скóвороды, -рóд, -áм, сковорóдка, -и** frying-pan.

скóвывать, -аю *impf. of* **сковáть**

сколáчивать, -аю *impf.*, **сколотúть, -очý, -óтишь** *pf.* knock together; knock up; put together.

сколóть, -лю́, -лешь *pf.* (*impf.* **скáлывать**) split off, chop off; pin together.

скольжéние, -я sliding, slipping; glide; **~ на крылó** side-slip. **скользúть, -льжý** *impf.*, **скользнýть, -нý, -нёшь** *pf.* slide; slip; glide. **скóльзкий; -зок, -зкá, -о** slippery. **скользящий** sliding; **~ ýзел** slip-knot.

скóлько *adv.* how much; how many; as far as, so far as; **~ вам лет?** how old are you?; **~ врéмени?** what time is it? how long?; ~

раз? how many times? **ско́лько-нибудь** *adv.* any.

с|кома́ндовать, -дую *pf.* **с|комбини́ровать, -рую** *pf.* **с|ко́мкать, -аю** *pf.* **с|комплектова́ть, -ту́ю** *pf.* **с|компромети́ровать, -рую** *pf.*

сконфу́женный embarrassed, confused, abashed, disconcerted. **с|конфу́зить(ся, -у́жу(сь** *pf.*

с|концентри́ровать, -рую *pf.*

сконча́ние, -я end; passing, death. **сконча́ться, -а́юсь** *pf.* pass away, die.

с|копи́ровать, -рую *pf.*

скопи́ть, -плю́, -пишь *pf.* (*impf.* **ска́пливать**) save, save up; amass, pile up; **~ся** accumulate, pile up; gather, collect. **скопле́ние, -я** accumulation; crowd; concentration, conglomeration.

с|копни́ть, -ню́ *pf.* **ско́пом** *adv.* in a crowd, in a bunch, en masse.

скорбе́ть, -блю́ *impf.* grieve, mourn, lament. **ско́рбный** sorrowful, mournful, doleful. **скорбь, -и**; *pl.* **-и, -е́й** sorrow, grief.

скоре́е, скоре́й *comp. of* **ско́ро, ско́рый**; *adv.* rather, sooner; **как мо́жно ~** as soon as possible; **~ всего́** most likely, most probably.

скорлупа́, -ы́; *pl.* **-ы** shell.

скорня́жн|ый fur, fur-dressing; **~ое де́ло** furriery; **~ый това́р** furs. **скорня́к, -а́** furrier, fur-dresser.

ско́ро *adv.* quickly, fast; soon.

скоро... *in comb.* quick-, fast-. **скорова́рка, -и** pressure-cooker. **~гово́рка, -и** patter; tongue-twister. **~ду́м, -а** quick-witted person. **~пи́сный** cursive. **ско́ропись, -и** cursive; shorthand. **~подъёмность, -и** rate of climb. **~по́ртящийся** perishable. **~пости́жный** sudden. **~спе́лый** early; fast-ripening; premature; hasty. **~стре́льный** rapid-firing, quick-firing. **~сшива́тель, -я** *m.* loose-leaf binder; folder, file. **~те́чный** transient, short-lived; **~те́чная чахо́тка** galloping consumption. **~хо́д, -а** runner, messenger; fast runner; high-speed skater.

с|коро́биться, -ится *pf.*

скоростни́к, -а́ high-speed worker, performer. **скоростно́й** high-speed; **~ авто́бус** express bus. **ско́рость, -и**; *g.pl.* **-е́й** speed; velocity; rate; **в ско́рости** soon, in the near future; **коро́бка скоросте́й** gear-box.

с|корота́ть, -а́ю *pf.*

скорпио́н, -а scorpion; Scorpio.

с|корректи́ровать, -рую *pf.* **с|ко́рчить(ся, -чу(сь** *pf.*

ско́р|ый; скор, -а́, -о quick, fast; rapid; near; short; forthcoming; **в ~ом бу́дущем** in the near future; **в ~ом вре́мени** shortly, before long; **на ~ую ру́ку** off-hand, in a rough-and-ready way; **~ый по́езд** fast train, express; **~ая по́мощь** first-aid; ambulance service.

скос, -а mowing. **с|коси́ть**[1]**, -ошу́, -о́сишь** *pf.* (*impf. also* **ска́шивать**) mow.

с|коси́ть[2]**, -ошу́** *pf.* (*impf. also* **ска́шивать**) squint; be drawn to one side; cut on the cross.

скот, -а́, ското́ина, -ы cattle; livestock; beast, swine. **ско́тник, -а** herdsman; cowman. **ско́тный** cattle, livestock; **~ двор** cattle-yard, farmyard.

ското... *in comb.* cattle. **скотобо́йня, -и**; *g.pl.* **-о́ен** slaughter-house. **~во́д, -а** cattle-breeder, stock-breeder. **~во́дство, -а** cattle-raising, stock-breeding. **~кра́дство, -а** cattle-stealing. **~приго́нный двор** stock-yard. **~промы́шленник, -а** cattle-dealer. **~сбра́сыватель, -я** *m.* cow-catcher.

ско́тский cattle; brutal, brutish, bestial. **ско́тство, -а** brutish condition; brutality, bestiality.

скра́сить, -а́шу *pf.*, **скра́шивать, -аю** *impf.* smooth over; relieve, take the edge off; improve.

скребо́к, -бка́ scraper. **скребу́** *etc.*: *see* **скрести́**

скре́жет, -а grating; gnashing, grinding. **скрежета́ть, -ещу́, -е́щешь** *impf.* grate, grit; *+i.* scrape, grind, gnash.

скре́па, -ы tie, clamp, brace; counter-signature, authentication.

скре́пер, -а scraper.

скрепи́ть, -плю́ *pf.*, **скрепля́ть, -я́ю** *impf.* fasten (together), make fast; pin (together); clamp, brace; countersign, authenticate, ratify; **скрепя́ се́рдце** reluctantly, grudgingly. **скре́пка, -и** paper-clip. **скрепле́ние, -я** fastening; clamping; tie, clamp.

скрести́, -ебу́, -ебёшь; -ёб, -ла́ *impf.* scrape; scratch, claw; **~сь** scratch.

скрести́сь, -ещу́ *pf.*, **скре́щивать, -аю** *impf.* cross; interbreed; **~ся** cross; clash; interbreed. **скреще́ние, -я** crossing; intersection. **скре́щивание, -я** crossing; interbreeding.

с|криви́ть(ся, -влю́(сь *pf.*

скрип, -а squeak, creak. **скрипа́ч, -а́** violinist; fiddler. **скрипе́ть, -плю́** *impf.*, **скри́пнуть, -ну** *pf.* squeak, creak; scratch. **скрипи́чный** violin; **~ ключ** treble clef. **скри́пка, -и** violin, fiddle. **скрипу́чий** squeaking, creaking; rasping, scratching.

с|кро́ить, -ою́ *pf.*

скро́мник, -а modest man. **скро́мничать, -аю** *impf.* (*pf.* **по~**) be (too) modest. **скро́мность, -и** modesty. **скро́мный; -мен, -мна́, -о** modest.

скро́ю *etc.*: *see* **скрыть. скрою́** *etc.*: *see* **скро́ить**

скру́пул, -а scruple. **скрупулёзный** scrupulous.

с|крути́ть, -учу́, -у́тишь *pf.*, **скру́чивать, -аю** *impf.* twist; roll; bind, tie up.

скрыва́ть, -а́ю *impf.*, **скры́ть, -о́ю** *pf.* hide, conceal; **~ся** hide, go into hiding, be hidden; steal away, escape; disappear, vanish. **скры́тничать, -аю** *impf.* be secretive, be reticent. **скры́тный** reticent, secretive. **скры́тый** secret, concealed, hidden; latent.

скря́га, -и *c.g.* miser. **скря́жничать, -аю** *impf.* pinch, scrape; be miserly.

ску́дный; -ден, -дна́, -о scanty, poor; slender, meagre; scant; +*i.* poor in, short of. **ску́дость, -и** scarcity, poverty.

ску́ка, -и boredom, tedium.

скула́, -ы́; *pl.* **-ы** cheek-bone. **скула́стый** with high cheek-bones.

скули́ть, -лю́ *impf.* whine, whimper.

ску́льптор, -а sculptor. **скульпту́ра, -ы** sculpture. **скульпту́рный** sculptural; statuesque.

ску́мбрия, -и mackerel.

скунс, -а skunk.

скупа́ть, -а́ю *impf. of* **скупи́ть**

скупе́ц, -пца́ miser.

скупи́ть, -плю́, -пишь *pf.* (*impf.* **скупа́ть**) buy (up); corner.

скупи́ться, -плю́сь *impf.* (*pf.* **по~**) pinch, scrape, be stingy, be miserly; be sparing; +**на**+*a.* stint, grudge; **~ на де́ньги** be close-fisted.

ску́пка, -и buying (up); cornering.

ску́по *adv.* sparingly. **скупо́й; -п, -а́, -о** stingy, miserly, niggardly; inadequate. **ску́пость, -и** stinginess, miserliness, niggardliness.

ску́пщик, -а buyer (up); **~ кра́деного** fence.

ску́тер, -а; *pl.* **-а́** outboard speed-boat.

скуча́ть, -а́ю *impf.* be bored; +**по**+*d. or p.* miss, yearn for.

ску́ченность, -и density, congestion; **~ населе́ния** overcrowding. **ску́ченный** dense, congested. **ску́чивать, -аю** *impf.*, **ску́чить, -чу** *pf.* crowd (together); **~ся** flock, cluster; crowd together, huddle together.

ску́чный; -чен, -чна́, -о boring, tedious, dull; bored; **мне ску́чно** I'm bored.

с|ку́шать, -аю *pf.* **скую́** *etc.*: *see* **скова́ть**

слабе́ть, -е́ю *impf.* (*pf.* **о~**) weaken, grow weak; slacken, droop. **слабина́, -ы́** slack; weak spot, weak point. **слаби́тельн|ый** laxative, purgative; **~ое** *sb.* purge. **сла́бить, -ит** *impf.* (*pf.* **про~**) purge, act as a laxative; *impers.*+*a.* **его́ сла́бит** he has diarrhoea.

слабо... *in comb.* weak, feeble, slight. **слабоалкого́льный** low-alcohol. **~во́лие, -я** weakness of will. **~во́льный** weak-willed. **~ду́шный** faint-hearted. **~не́рвный** nervy, nervous; neurasthenic. **~ра́звитый** underdeveloped. **~си́льный** weak, feeble; low-powered. **~то́чный** low-current, weak-current, low-power. **~у́мие, -я** feeble-mindedness, imbecility; dementia. **~у́мный** feeble-minded, imbecile. **~хара́ктерный** characterless, of weak character.

сла́бый; -б, -а́, -о weak; feeble; slack, loose; poor.

сла́ва, -ы glory; fame; name, repute, reputation; rumour; **на сла́ву** wonderfully well, excellently, famously. **сла́вить, -влю** *impf.* celebrate, hymn, sing the praises of; **~ся** (+*i.*) be famous, famed, renowned, (for); have a reputation (for). **сла́вный** glorious, famous, renowned; nice, splendid.

славяни́н, -а; *pl.* **-я́не, -я́н, славя́нка, -и** Slav. **славянофи́л, -а** Slavophil(e). **славя́нский** Slav, Slavonic.

слага́емое *sb.* component, term, member. **слага́ть, -а́ю** *impf. of* **сложи́ть**

сла́дить, -а́жу *pf.* **с**+*i.* cope with, manage, handle; make, construct.

сла́дк|ий; -док, -дка́, -о sweet; sugary, sugared, honeyed; **~кое мя́со** sweetbread; **~ое** *sb.* sweet course. **сладостра́стник, -а** voluptuary. **сладостра́стный** voluptuous. **сла́дость, -и** joy; sweetness; sweetening; *pl.* sweets.

сла́женность, -и co-ordination, harmony, order. **сла́женный** co-ordinated, harmonious, orderly.

сла́нец, -нца shale, slate; schist. **сланцева́тый, сла́нцевый** shale; shaly, slaty, schistose.

сластёна *c.g.* person with a sweet tooth. **сласть, -и**; *pl.* **-и, -е́й** delight, pleasure; *pl.* sweets, sweet things.

слать, шлю, шлёшь *impf.* send.

слаща́вый sugary, sickly-sweet. **сла́ще** *comp. of* **сла́дкий**

сле́ва *adv.* from (the) left; on, to, the left; **~ напра́во** from left to right.

слёг *etc.*: *see* **слечь**

слегка́ *adv.* slightly; lightly, gently; somewhat.

след, следа́ (-у), *d.* **-у**, *loc.* **-у́**; *pl.* **-ы́** track; trail, footprint, footstep; trace, sign, vestige. **следи́ть**[1]**, -ежу́** *impf.* +**за**+*i.* watch; track; shadow; follow; keep up with; look after; keep an eye on. **следи́ть**[2]**, -ежу́** *impf.* (*pf.* **на~**) leave traces, marks, footmarks, footprints. **сле́дование, -я** movement, proceeding. **сле́дователь, -я** *m.* investigator. **сле́довательно** *adv.* consequently, therefore, hence. **сле́довать, -дую** *impf.* (*pf.* **по~**) **I.** +*d. or* **за**+*i.* follow; go after; comply with; result; go, be bound; **по́езд сле́дует до Москвы́** the train goes to Moscow; **II.** *impers.* (+*d.*) ought, should; be owing, be owed; **вам сле́дует**+*inf.* you should, you ought to; **как и сле́довало ожида́ть** as was to be expected; **как сле́дует** properly, well; as it should be; **куда́ сле́дует** to the proper quarter; **ско́лько с меня́ сле́дует?** how much do I owe (you)? **сле́дом** *adv.* (**за**+*i.*) immediately after, behind, close behind. **следопы́т, -а** pathfinder, tracker. **сле́дственн|ый** investigation, inquiry; **~ая коми́ссия** commission (committee) of inquiry. **сле́дствие**[1]**, -я** consequence, result. **сле́дствие**[2]**, -я** investigation. **сле́дующ|ий** following, next; **в ~ий раз** next time; **на ~ей неде́ле** next week; **~им о́бразом** in the following way. **сле́жка, -и** shadowing.

слеза́, -ы́; *pl.* **-ёзы, -а́м** tear.

слеза́ть, -а́ю *impf. of* **слезть**

слези́ться, -и́тся *impf.* water. **слезли́вый** tearful, lachrymose. **слёзный** tear; lachrymal; tearful, plaintive. **слезоточи́вый** watering, running; lachrymatory; ~ **газ** tear-gas.

слезть, -зу; слез *pf.* (*impf.* **слеза́ть**) climb down, get down; dismount; alight, get off; come off, peel.

сленг, -а slang. **сле́нговый** slang.

слепе́нь, -пня́ *m.* gadfly, horse-fly.

слепе́ц, -пца́ blind man. **слепи́ть**[1], **-пи́т** *impf.* blind; dazzle.

с|лепи́ть[2], **-плю́, -пишь** *pf.*, **слепля́ть, -я́ю** *impf.* stick together; mould, model.

сле́пнуть, -ну; слеп *impf.* (*pf.* **о~**) go blind, become blind. **сле́по** *adv.* blindly; indistinctly. **слеп|о́й; -п, -а́, -о** blind; indistinct; **~ы́е** *sb., pl.* the blind.

сле́пок, -пка cast.

слепота́, -ы́ blindness.

сле́сарь, -я; *pl.* **-я́** *or* **-и** *m.* metal worker; locksmith.

слёт, -а gathering, meeting; rally. **слета́ть, -а́ю** *impf.*, **слете́ть, -ечу́** *pf.* fly down; fall down, fall off; fly away; **~ся** fly together; congregate.

слечь, сля́гу, -я́жешь; слёг, -ла́ *pf.* take to one's bed.

сли́ва, -ы plum; plum-tree.

слива́ть(ся, -а́ю(сь *impf. of* **сли́ть(ся.**

сли́вки, -вок *pl.* cream. **сли́вочник, -а** cream-jug. **сли́вочн|ый** cream; creamy; **~ое ма́сло** butter; **~ое моро́женое** ice-cream.

сли́зистый mucous; slimy. **слизня́к, -а́** slug.

слизь, -и mucus; slime.

с|линя́ть, -я́ет *pf.*

слипа́ться, -а́ется *impf.*, **сли́пнуться, -нётся; -и́пся** *pf.* stick together.

сли́тно together, as one word. **сли́ток, -тка** ingot, bar. **с|лить, солью́, -ьёшь; -ил, -а́, -о** *pf.* (*impf. also* **слива́ть**) pour, pour out, pour off; fuse, merge, amalgamate; **~ся** flow together; blend, mingle; merge, amalgamate.

слича́ть, -а́ю *impf.*, **сличи́ть, -чу́** *pf.* collate; check. **сличе́ние, -я** collation, checking. **сличи́тельный** checking, check.

сли́шком *adv.* too; too much.

слия́ние, -я confluence; blending, merging, amalgamation; merger.

слова́рный lexical; lexicographic(al), dictionary. **слова́рь, -я́** *m.* dictionary; glossary; vocabulary. **слове́сник, -а, -ница, -ы** philologist; student of philology; (*Russian*) language and literature teacher. **слове́сность, -и** literature; philology. **слове́сный** verbal, oral; literary; philological. **сло́вник, -а** glossary; word-list, vocabulary. **сло́вно** *conj.* as if; like, as. **сло́во, -а**; *pl.* **-а́** word; speech; speaking; address; lay, tale; **к сло́ву** by the way, by the by; **одни́м ~м** in a word. **сло́вом** *adv.* in a word, in short. **словообразова́ние, -я** word-formation. **словоохо́тливый** talkative, loquacious. **словосочета́ние, -я** word combination, word-group, phrase. **словоупотребле́ние, -я** use of words, usage. **словцо́, -а́** word; apt word, the right word; **для кра́сного словца́** for effect, to display one's wit.

слог[1], **-а** style.

слог[2], **-а**; *pl.* **-и, -о́в** syllable. **слогово́й** syllabic.

слое́ние, -я stratification. **слоён|ый** flaky; **~ое те́сто** puff pastry, flaky pastry.

сложе́ние, -я adding; composition; addition; build, constitution. **сложи́ть, -жу́, -жишь** *pf.* (*impf.* **класть, скла́дывать, слага́ть**) put (together), lay (together); pile, heap, stack; add, add up; fold (up); make up, compose; take off, put down, set down; lay down; **сложа́ ру́ки** with arms folded; idle; ~ **ве́щи** pack, pack up; ~ **наказа́ние** remit a punishment; **~ся** form, turn out; take shape; arise; club together, pool one's resources. **сложносокращённ|ый: ~ое сло́во** acronym. **сло́жность, -и** complication; complexity; **в о́бщей сло́жности** all in all, in sum. **сло́жный; -жен, -жна́, -о** compound; complex; multiple; complicated, intricate; **~ое сло́во** compound (word).

слои́стый stratified; lamellar; flaky, foliated; schistose. **слои́ть, -ою́** *impf.* stratify; layer; make flaky. **слой, -я**; *pl.* **-и́, -ёв** layer; stratum; coat, coating, film.

слом, -а demolition, pulling down, breaking up; **пойти́ на ~** be scrapped. **с|лома́ть(ся, -а́ю(сь** *pf.* **сломи́ть, -млю́, -мишь** *pf.* break, smash; overcome; **сломя́ го́лову** like mad, at breakneck speed; **~ся** break.

слон, -а́ elephant; bishop. **слони́ха, -и** she-elephant. **слоно́в|ый** elephant; elephantine; **~ая кость** ivory.

слою́ *etc.*: *see* **слои́ть**

слоня́ться, -я́юсь *impf.* loiter (about), mooch about.

слуга́, -и́; *pl.* **-и** *m.* man, (man)servant. **служа́нка, -и** servant, maid. **слу́жащий** *sb.* employee; *pl.* staff. **слу́жба, -ы** service; work; employment. **служе́бн|ый** service; office; official; work; auxiliary; secondary; **~ый вход** staff entrance; **~ое вре́мя** office hours; **~ое де́ло** official business. **служе́ние, -я** service, serving. **служи́ть, -жу́, -жишь** *impf.* (*pf.* **по~**) serve; work, be employed, be; be used, do; be in use, do duty; *+d.* devote o.s. to; ~ **доказа́тельством***+g.* serve as evidence of; ~ **при́знаком** indicate, be a sign of.

с|лука́вить, -влю *pf.* **с|лупи́ть, -плю́, -пишь** *pf.*

слух, -а hearing; ear; rumour, hearsay; **по ~у** be ear. **слуха́ч, -а́** monitor. **слухов|о́й** acoustic, auditory, aural; **~о́й аппара́т** hearing aid; **~о́е окно́** dormer (window).

слу́чай, -я incident, occurrence, event; case; accident; opportunity, occasion; chance; **ни в ко́ем слу́чае** in no circumstances; **по слу́чаю** secondhand; *+g.* by reason of, on account of; on the occasion of. **случа́йно** *adv.* by chance, by accident, accidentally; by any chance. **случа́йность, -и** chance; **по счастли́вой случа́йности** by a lucky chance, by sheer luck. **случа́йн|ый** accidental, fortuitous; chance; casual, incidental; **~ая встре́ча** chance meeting. **случа́ться, -а́ется** *impf.*, **случи́ться, -и́тся** *pf.* happen; come about, come to pass, befall; turn up show up; **что случи́лось?** what has happened? what's up?

слу́шатель, -я *m.* hearer, listener; student; *pl.* audience. **слу́шать, -аю** *impf.* (*pf.* **по~, про~**) listen to; hear; attend lectures on; **(я) слу́шаю!** hello!; very well, very good; yes, sir; **~ся**+*g.* obey, listen to.

слыть, -ыву́, -ывёшь; -ыл, -а́, -о *impf.* (*pf.* **про~**) have the reputation, be known, be said; pass (+*i.* *or* **за**+*a.* for).

слыха́ть *impf.*, **слы́шать, -шу** *impf.* (*pf.* **у~**) hear; notice; feel, sense. **слы́шаться, -шится** *impf.* (*pf.* **по~**) be heard, be audible. **слы́шимость, -и** audibility. **слы́шимый** audible. **слы́шно** *adv.* audibly. **слы́шн|ый** audible; **~о** *pred.*, *impers.* (+*d.*) one can hear; it is said, they say; **нам никого́ не́ было ~о** we could not hear anyone; **что ~о?** what's new?

слюда́, -ы́ mica. **слюдяно́й** mica.

слюна́, -ы́; *pl.* **-и, -е́й** saliva; spit; *pl.* slobber, spittle. **слюня́вый** dribbling, drivelling, slavering.

сля́гу *etc.*: *see* **слечь**

сля́котный slushy. **сля́коть, -и** slush.

см *abbr.* (*of* **сантиме́тр**) cm, centimetre(s).

см. *abbr.* (*of* **смотри́**) see, *vide.*

сма́зать, -а́жу *pf.*, **сма́зывать, -аю** *impf.* oil, lubricate; grease; smudge; rub over; slur over. **сма́зка, -и** oiling, lubrication; oil, lubricant; greasing; grease. **сма́зочн|ый** oil; lubricating; **~ое ма́сло** lubricating oil. **сма́зчик, -а** greaser. **сма́зывание, -я** oiling, lubrication; greasing; slurring over.

смак, -а (-у) relish, savour. **смакова́ть, -ку́ю** *impf.* relish, enjoy; savour.

с|маневри́ровать, -рую *pf.*

сма́нивать, -аю *impf.*, **смани́ть, -ню́, -нишь** *pf.* entice, lure.

с|мастери́ть, -рю́ *pf.* **сма́тывать, -аю** *impf.* *of* **смота́ть**

сма́хивать, -аю *impf.*, **смахну́ть, -ну́, -нёшь** *pf.* brush away, off; flick away, off.

сма́чивать, -аю *impf.* *of* **смочи́ть**

сме́жный adjacent, contiguous, adjoining, neighbouring.

смека́лка, -и native wit, mother wit; sharpness.

смёл *etc.*: *see* **смести́**

смеле́ть, -е́ю *impf.* (*pf.* **о~**) grow bold, grow bolder. **сме́ло** *adv.* boldly; easily, with ease. **сме́лость, -и** boldness, audacity, courage. **сме́лый** bold, audacious, courageous, daring. **смельча́к, -а́** bold spirit; daredevil.

смелю́ *etc.*: *see* **смоло́ть**

сме́на, -ы changing, change; replacement(s); relief; shift; change; **идти́ на сме́ну**+*d.* take the place of, relieve; **~ карау́ла** changing of the guard. **смени́ть, -ню́, -нишь** *pf.*, **сменя́ть**[1], **-я́ю** *impf.* change; replace; relieve; succeed; **~ся** hand over; be relieved; take turns; +*i.* give place to. **сме́нность, -и** shift system; shiftwork. **сме́нн|ый** shift; changeable; **~ое колесо́** spare wheel. **сме́нщик, -а** relief; *pl.* new shift. **сменя́емый** removable, interchangeable. **сменя́ть**[2], **-я́ю** *pf.* exchange.

с|ме́рить, -рю *pf.*

смерка́ться, -а́ется *impf.*, **сме́ркнуться, -нется** *pf.* get dark.

смерте́льно *adv.* mortally; extremely, terribly; **~ уста́ть** be dead tired. **смерте́льный** mortal, fatal, death; extreme, terrible. **сме́ртность, -и** mortality, death-rate. **сме́ртн|ый** mortal; death; deadly, extreme; **~ая казнь** death penalty; capital punishment; **~ый пригово́р** death sentence. **смерть, -и**; *g.pl.* **-е́й** death; decease; **до́ сме́рти** to death; **умере́ть свое́й сме́ртью** die a natural death; **~ как** *adv.* awfully, terribly.

смерч, -а whirlwind, tornado; waterspout; sandstorm.

смеси́тельный mixing. **с|меси́ть, -ешу́, -е́сишь** *pf.*

смести́, -ету́, -етёшь; -ёл, -а́ *per.* (*impf.* **смета́ть**) sweep off, sweep (away).

смести́ть, -ещу́ *pf.* (*impf.* **смеща́ть**) displace; remove; move; dismiss; **~ся** change position, become displaced.

смесь, -и mixture; blend, miscellany, medley.

сме́та, -ы estimate.

смета́на, -ы smetana, sour cream.

с|мета́ть[1], **-а́ю** *pf.* (*impf.* *also* **смётывать**) tack (together).

смета́ть[2], **-а́ю** *impf.* *of* **смести́**

сме́тливый quick, sharp; resourceful.

сме́тный estimated,budget, planned.

смету́ *etc.*: *see* **смести́. смётывать, -аю** *impf.* *of* **смета́ть**

сметь, -е́ю *impf.* (*pf.* **по~**) dare; have the right.

смех, -а (-у) laughter; laugh; **~а ра́ди** for a joke, for fun. **смехотво́рный** laughable, ludicrous, ridiculous.

сме́шанн|ый mixed; combined; **~ое акционе́рное о́бщество** joint-stock company. **с|меша́ть, -а́ю** *pf.*, **сме́шивать, -аю** *impf.* mix, blend; lump together; confuse, mix up; **~ся** mix, (inter)blend, blend in; mingle; become confused, get mixed up. **смеше́ние, -я** mixture, blending, merging; confusion, mixing up.

смеши́ть, -шу́ *impf.* (*pf.* **на~, рас~**) amuse, make laugh. **смешли́вость, -и** risibility. **смешли́вый** inclined to laugh, easily amused, given to laughing. **смешн|о́й** funny; amusing; absurd, ridiculous, ludicrous; **здесь нет ничего́ ~о́го** there's nothing to laugh at, it is no laughing matter; **~о́** *pred.* it is funny; it makes one laugh.

смешу́ *etc.*: *see* **смеси́ть, смеши́ть**

смеща́ть(ся, -а́ю(сь *impf. of* **смести́ть(ся.** **смеще́ние, -я** displacement, removal; shifting, shift; drift; bias. **смещу́** *etc.*: *see* **смести́ть**

смея́ться, -ею́сь, -еёшься *impf.* laugh; +**над**+*i.* laugh at, make fun of.

смире́ние, -я humility, meekness. **смире́нный** humble, meek. **смири́тельн|ый; ~ая руба́шка** straitjacket. **смири́ть, -рю́** *pf.*, **смиря́ть, -я́ю** *impf.* restrain, subdue; humble; **~ся** submit; resign o.s. **сми́рно** *adv.* quietly; **~!** attention! **сми́рный** quiet; submissive.

см. на об. *abbr.* (*of* ***смотри́ на оборо́те***) PTO (= *please turn over*), see over.

смогу́ *etc.*: *see* **смочь**

смо́кинг, -а dinner-jacket.

смола́, -ы́; *pl.* **-ы** resin; pitch, tar; rosin. **смолёный** resined; tarred, pitched. **смоли́стый** resinous. **смоли́ть, -лю́** *impf.* (*pf.* **вы́~, о~**) resin; tar, pitch.

смолка́ть, -а́ю *impf.*, **смо́лкнуть, -ну; -олк** *pf.* fall silent, be silent; cease.

смо́лоду *adv.* from one's youth.

с|молоти́ть, -очу́, -о́тишь *pf.* **с|моло́ть, смелю́, сме́лешь** *pf.*

смоляно́й pitch, tar, resin.

с|монти́ровать, -рую *pf.*

сморка́ть, -а́ю *impf.* (*pf.* **вы́~**) blow; **~ся** blow one's nose.

сморо́дина, -ы currants; currant(-bush). **сморо́динный** currant.

смо́рщенный wrinkled. **с|мо́рщить(ся, -щу(сь** *pf.*

смота́ть, -а́ю *pf.* (*impf.* **сма́тывать**) wind, reel; **~ся** hurry (away); go, drop in.

смотр, -а, *loc.* **-у́**; *pl.* **-о́тры́** review, inspection; public showing; **произвести́ ~**+*d.* inspect, review; **~ худо́жественной самоде́ятельности** amateur arts festival. **смотре́ть, -рю́, -ришь** *impf.* (*pf.* **по~**) look; see; watch; look through; examine; review, inspect; +**за**+*i.* look after; be in charge of, supervise; +**в**+*a.*, **на**+*a.* look on to, look over; +*i.* look (like); **смотри́(те)!** mind! take care!; **~ за поря́дком** keep order; **смотря́** it depends; **смотря́ по** depending on, in accordance with; **~ся** look at o.s. **смотри́тель, -я** *m.* supervisor; custodian keeper. **смотрово́й** review; observation, inspection, sight.

смочи́ть, -чу́, -чишь *pf.* (*impf.* **сма́чивать**) damp, wet, moisten.

с|мочь, -огу́, -о́жешь; смог, -ла́ *pf.*

с|моше́нничать, -аю *pf.* **смо́ю** *etc.*: *see* **смы́ть**

смрад, -а stink stench. **смра́дный** stinking.

смуглоли́цый, сму́глый; -гл, -а́, -о dark-complexioned; swarthy.

с|мудри́ть, -рю́ *pf.*

сму́та, -ы disturbance, sedition. **смути́ть, -ущу́** *pf.*, **смуща́ть, -а́ю** *impf.* embarrass, confuse; disturb, trouble; **~ся** be embarrassed, be confused. **сму́тн|ый** vague; confused; dim; disturbed, troubled; **~ое вре́мя** Time of Troubles. **смутья́н, -а** trouble-maker. **смуще́ние, -я** embarrassment, confusion. **смущённый; -ён, -а́** embarrassed, confused.

смыва́ть(ся, -а́ю(сь *impf. of* **смыть(ся**

смыка́ть(ся, -а́ю(сь *impf. of* **сомкну́ть(ся**

смысл, -а sense; meaning; purport; point; **в по́лном ~е сло́ва** in the full sense of the word; **нет ~а** there is no sense, there is no point. **смы́слить, -лю** *impf.* understand. **смыслово́й** sense, semantic; of meaning.

смыть, смо́ю *pf.* (*impf.* **смыва́ть**) wash off; wash away; **~ся** wash off, come off; slip away, run away, disappear.

смы́чка, -и union; linking. **смычо́к, -чка́** bow.

смышлёный clever, bright.

смягча́ть, -а́ю *impf.*, **смягчи́ть, -чу́** *pf.* soften; mollify; ease, alleviate; assuage; palatalize; **~ся** soften, become soft, grow softer; be mollified; relent, relax; grow mild; ease (off).

смяте́ние, -я confusion, disarray; commotion; **приводи́ть в ~** confuse, perturb. **с|мять(ся, сомну́(сь, -нёшь(ся** *pf.*

снабди́ть, -бжу́ *pf.*, **снабжа́ть, -а́ю** *impf.*+*i.* supply with, furnish with, provide with. **снабже́ние, -я** supply, supplying, provision.

сна́добье, -я; *g.pl.* **-ий** drug; concoction.

сна́йпер, -а sniper; sharp-shooter.

снару́жи *adv.* on the outside; from (the) outside. **снаря́д, -а** projectile, missile; shell; contrivance, machine, gadget; tackle, gear. **снаряди́ть, -яжу́** *pf.*, **снаряжа́ть, -а́ю** *impf.* equip, fit out; **~ся** equip o.s., get ready. **снаря́дн|ый** shell, projectile; ammunition; apparatus. **снаряже́ние, -я** equipment, outfit.

снасть, -и; *g.pl.* **-е́й** tackle, gear; *pl.* rigging.

снача́ла *adv.* at first, at the beginning; all over again.

сна́шивать, -аю *impf. of* **сноси́ть**

СНГ *abbr.* (*of* ***Соо́бщество незави́симых госуда́рств***) CIS, Commonwealth of Independent States.

снег, -а (-у); *pl.* **-а́** snow; **мо́крый ~** sleet.

снеги́рь, -я́ bullfinch.

снегово́й snow. **снегоочисти́тель, -я** *m.* snow-plough. **снегопа́д, -а** snowfall, fall of snow. **снегосту́пы, -ов** *pl.* snow-shoes. **снегохо́д, -а** snow-tractor. **Снегу́рочка, -и** Snow Maiden. **снежи́нка, -и** snow-flake. **сне́жн|ый** snow; snowy; **~ая ба́ба** snowman. **снежо́к, -жка́** light snow; snowball.

снести́[1]**, -су́, -сёшь; -ёс, -ла́** *pf.* (*impf.* **сноси́ть**) take; bring together, pile up; bring down, fetch down; carry away; blow off; take off; demolish, take down, pull down; bear, endure, stand, put up with; **~сь** communicate (**с**+*i.* with).

с|нести́²(сь, -су́(сь, -сёшь(ся; снёс(ся, -сла́(сь *pf.*

снижа́ть, -а́ю *impf.*, **сни́зить, -и́жу** *pf.* lower; bring down; reduce; **~ся** descend; come down; lose height; fall, sink. **сниже́ние, -я** lowering; reduction; loss of height.

снизойти́, -йду́, -йдёшь; -ошёл, -шла́ *pf.* (*impf.* **снисходи́ть**) condescend, deign.

сни́зу *adv.* from below; from the bottom; **~ до́верху** from top to bottom.

снима́ть(ся, -а́ю(сь *impf. of* **снять(ся. сни́мок, -мка** photograph; print. **сниму́** *etc.*: *see* **снять**

сниска́ть, -ищу́, -и́щешь *pf.*, **сни́скивать, -аю** *impf.* gain, get, win.

снисходи́тельность, -и condescension; indulgence, tolerance, leniency. **снисходи́тельный** condescending; indulgent, tolerant, lenient. **снисходи́ть, -ожу́, -о́дишь** *impf. of* **снизойти́. снисхожде́ние, -я** indulgence, leniency.

сни́ться, снюсь *impf.* (*pf.* **при~**), *impers.+d.* dream; **ей сни́лось** she dreamed; **мне сни́лся сон** I had a dream.

сно́ва *adv.* again, anew, afresh.

сновиде́ние, -я dream.

сноп, -а́ sheaf; **~ лучей** shaft of light. **сноповяза́лка, -и** binder.

сноро́вистый quick, smart, nimble, clever. **сноро́вка, -и** knack, skill.

снос, -а demolition, pulling down; drift; wear. **сноси́ть¹, -ошу́, -о́сишь** *pf.* (*impf.* **сна́шивать**) wear out. **сноси́ть²(ся, -ошу́(сь, -о́сишь(ся** *impf. of* **снести́(сь. сно́ска, -и** footnote. **сно́сно** *adv.* tolerably, so-so. **сно́сный** tolerable; fair, reasonable.

снотво́рн|ый soporific; **~ые** *sb.*, *pl.* sleeping-pills.

снoха́, -и́; *pl.* **-и** daughter-in-law.

snоше́ние, -я intercourse; relations, dealings.

сношу́ *etc.*: *see* **сноси́ть**

сня́тие, -я taking down; removal, lifting; raising; taking, making; **~ ко́пии** copying. **снят|о́й; ~о́е молоко́** skim milk. **снять, сниму́, -и́мешь; -ял, -а́, -о** *pf.* (*impf.* **снима́ть**) take off; take down; gather in; remove; withdraw, cancel; take; make; photograph; **~ запре́т** lift a ban; **~ с рабо́ты** discharge, sack; **~ с учёта** strike off the register; **~ фильм** shoot, make, a film; **~ся** come off; move off; have one's photograph taken; **~ с я́коря** weigh anchor; get under way.

со *see* **с** *prep.*

со...¹ *vbl.pref. used instead of* **с...** *before* **и, й, о**, *before two or more consonants, and before single consonants followed by* **ь**.

со...² *pref. in comb. with nn. and adjs.*: co-, joint. **соа́втор, -а** co-author, joint author. **~а́вторство, -а** co-authorship, joint authorship. **~бра́т, -а**; *pl.* **-ья, -ьев** colleague. **~владе́лец, -льца** joint owner, joint proprietor. **~владе́ние, -я** joint ownership. **~вме́стно** *adv.* in common, jointly. **~вме́стный** joint, combined; **~вме́стное обуче́ние** co-education; **~вме́стная рабо́та** team-work. **~вою́ющий** co-belligerent. **~граждани́н, -а**; *pl.* **-а́ждане, -ан** fellow-citizen. **~докла́д, -а** supplementary report, paper. **~жи́тель, -я** *m.* room-mate, flat-mate; cohabitee, lover. **~жи́тельница, -ы** room-mate, flat-mate; cohabitee, mistress. **~жи́тельство, -а** living together, lodging together; cohabitation. **~квартира́нт, -а** co-tenant, sharer of flat or lodgings. **~насле́дник, -а** co-heir. **~о́бщник, -а** accomplice, confederate. **~оте́чественник, -а** compatriot, fellow-countryman. **~племе́нник, -а** fellow-tribesman. **~подчине́ние, -я** co-ordination. **~преде́льный** contiguous. **~прича́стность, -и** complicity, participation. **~ра́тник, -а** comrade-in-arms. **~служи́вец, -вца** colleague, fellow-employee. **~существова́ние, -я** co-existence. **~умы́шленник, -а** accomplice. **~учени́к, -а́** schoolfellow. **~чле́н, -а** fellow-member.

соба́ка, -и dog; hound; **~-поводы́рь** guide-dog. **соба́чий** dog, dog's; canine. **соба́чка, -и** little dog, doggie; trigger. **соба́чник, -а** dog-lover.

с|обезья́нничать, -аю *pf.*

соберу́ *etc.*: *see* **собра́ть**

СОБЕС, а *or* **собе́с, а** *abbr.* (*of* **(отде́л) социа́льного обеспе́чения**) social security department (*of local authority*).

собесе́дник, -а interlocutor, party to conversation, companion; **он — заба́вный ~** he is amusing to talk to, amusing company.

собира́ние, -я collecting, collection. **собира́тель, -я** *m.* collector. **собира́тельный** collective. **собира́ть(ся, -а́ю(сь** *impf. of* **собра́ть(ся**

собла́зн, -а temptation. **соблазни́тель, -я** *m.* tempter; seducer. **соблазни́тельница, -ы** temptress. **соблазни́тельный** tempting; alluring; seductive; suggestive, corrupting. **соблазни́ть, -ню́** *pf.*, **соблазня́ть, -я́ю** *impf.* tempt; seduce, entice.

соблюда́ть, -а́ю *impf.*, **со|блюсти́, -юду́, -дёшь; -ю́л, -а́** *pf.* observe; keep (to), stick to. **соблюде́ние, -я** observance; maintenance.

собо́й, собо́ю *see* **себя́**

соболе́знование, -я sympathy, condolence(s). **соболе́зновать, -ную** *impf.+d.* sympathize with, condole with.

собо́лий, соболи́ный sable. **со́боль, -я**; *pl.* **-и** *or* **-я́** *m.* sable.

собо́р, -а cathedral; council, synod, assembly. **собо́рный** cathedral; synod, council.

собра́ние, -я meeting; gathering; assembly; collection; **~ сочине́ний** collected works. **со́бранный** collected; concentrated. **собра́ть, -беру́, -берёшь; -а́л, -а́, -о** *pf.* (*impf.* **собира́ть**) gather; collect; pick; assemble, muster; convoke, convene; mount; obtain, poll; prepare, make ready, equip; make gathers in, take in; **~ся** gather, assemble, muster; be amassed; prepare, make ready, get ready; intend, be about, be going; +**с**+*i*. collect; **~ся с ду́хом** take a deep breath; pluck up one's courage; pull o.s. together; **~ся с мы́слями** collect one's thoughts.

со́бственник, -а owner, proprietor. **со́бственнический** proprietary; proprietorial, possessive. **со́бственно** *adv*. strictly; **~ (говоря́)** strictly speaking, properly speaking, as a matter of fact. **собственнору́чно** *adv*. personally, with one's own hand. **собственнору́чн|ый** done, made, written, with one's own hand(s); **~ая по́дпись** autograph. **со́бственность, -и** property; possession, ownership. **со́бственн|ый** (one's) own; proper; true; natural; internal; **в ~ые ру́ки** personal; **и́мя ~ое** proper name; **~ой персо́ной** in person.

собы́тие, -я event; **теку́щие собы́тия** current affairs.

собью́ *etc*.: *see* **сбить**

сов... *abbr*. (*of* **сове́т**) *in comb*. soviet, Soviet, council; **сове́тский** Soviet. **совми́н, -а** Council of Ministers. **~нарко́м, -а** Council of People's Commissars. **~нархо́з, -а** (Regional) Economic Council. **~хо́з, -а** sovkhoz, State farm.

сова́, -ы́; *pl*. **-ы** owl.

сова́ть, сую́, -ёшь *impf*. (*pf*. **су́нуть**) thrust, shove, poke; **~ся** push, push in; poke one's nose in, butt in.

соверша́ть, -а́ю *impf*. **соверши́ть, -шу́** *pf*. accomplish; carry out; perform; commit, perpetuate; complete, conclude; **~ся** happen; be accomplished, be completed. **соверше́ние, -я** accomplishment, fulfilment; perpetration, commission. **соверше́нно** *adv*. perfectly; absolutely, utterly, completely, totally. **совершенноле́тие, -я** majority. **совершенноле́тний** of age. **соверше́нный**[1] perfect; absolute, utter, complete, total. **соверше́нный**[2] perfective. **соверше́нство, -а** perfection. **соверше́нствовать, -твую** *impf*. (*pf*. **у~**) perfect; improve; **~ся в**+*i*. perfect o.s. in; pursue advanced studies in.

со́вестливый conscientious. **со́вестно** *impers*.+*d*. be ashamed; **ему́ бы́ло ~** he was ashamed. **со́весть, -и** conscience; **по со́вести (говоря́)** to be honest.

сове́т, -а advice, counsel; opinion; council; conference; soviet, Soviet; **~ Безопа́сности** Security Council. **сове́тник, -а** adviser; counsellor. **сове́товать, -тую** *impf*. (*pf*. **по~**) advise; **~ся с**+*i*. consult, ask advice of, seek advice from. **советове́д, -а** Sovietologist. **советолог, -а** Kremlinologist, Kremlin-watcher. **сове́тск|ий** Soviet; of soviets; of the Soviet Union; **~ая власть** the Soviet regime; **~ий Сою́з** the Soviet Union. **сове́тчик, -а** adviser, counsellor.

совеща́ние, -я conference, meeting. **совеща́тельный** consultative, deliberative. **совеща́ться, -а́юсь** *impf*. deliberate; consult; confer.

совлада́ть, -а́ю *pf*. **с**+*i*. control, cope with.

совмести́мый compatible. **совмести́тель, -я** *m*. person holding more than one office, combining jobs; pluralist. **совмести́ть, -ещу́** *pf*., **совмеща́ть, -а́ю** *impf*. combine; **~ся** coincide; be combined, combine. **совме́стн|ый** joint, combined; **~ое обуче́ние** co-education; **~ое предприя́тие** joint venture.

сово́к, -вка́ shovel; scoop; dust-pan; **садо́вый ~** trowel.

совокупи́ть, -плю́ *pf*., **совокупля́ть, -я́ю** *impf*. combine, unite; **~ся** copulate. **совокупле́ние, -я** copulation. **совоку́пно** *adv*. in common, jointly. **совоку́пность, -и** aggregate, sum total; totality. **совоку́пный** joint, combined, aggregate.

совпада́ть, -а́ет *impf*., **совпа́сть, -адёт** *pf*. coincide; agree, concur, tally.

соврати́ть, -ащу́ *pf*. (*impf*. **совраща́ть**) pervert, seduce; **~ся** go astray.

со|вра́ть, -вру́, -врёшь; -а́л, -а́, -о *pf*.

совраща́ть(ся, -а́ю(сь *impf*. *of* **соврати́ть(ся. совраще́ние, -я** perverting, seducing, seduction.

совреме́нник, -а contemporary. **совреме́нность, -и** the present (time); contemporaneity. **совреме́нный** contemporary, present-day; modern; up-to-date; +*d*. contemporaneous with, of the time of.

совру́ *etc*.: *see* **совра́ть**

совсе́м *adv*. quite; entirely, completely, altogether; **~ не** not at all, not in the least.

совью́ *etc*.: *see* **свить**

согла́сие, -я consent; assent; agreement; accordance; accord; concord, harmony. **согласи́ть, -ашу́** *pf*. (*impf*. **соглаша́ть**) reconcile; **~ся** consent; agree; concur. **согла́сно** *adv*. in accord, in harmony, in concord; *prep*.+*d*. in accordance with; according to. **согла́сность, -и** harmony, harmoniousness. **согла́сн|ый**[1] agreeable (to); in agreement; concordant; harmonious; **быть ~ым** agree (with). **согла́сный**[2] consonant, consonantal; *sb*. consonant.

согласова́ние, -я co-ordination; concordance; agreement; concord. **согласо́ванность, -и** co-ordination; **~ во вре́мени** synchronization. **согласова́ть, -су́ю** *pf*., **согласо́вывать, -аю** *impf*. co-ordinate; agree; make agree; **~ся** accord; conform; agree.

соглаша́тель, -я *m*. appeaser; compromiser. **соглаша́тельский** conciliatory. **соглаша́тельство, -а** appeasement; compromise. **соглаша́ть(ся, -а́ю(сь** *impf*. *of* **согласи́ть(ся. соглаше́ние, -я** agreement; understanding; covenant. **соглашу́** *etc*.: *see* **согласи́ть**

согна́ть, сгоню́, сго́нишь; -а́л, -а́, -о *pf*. (*impf*. **сгоня́ть**) drive away; drive together, round up.

со|гну́ть, -ну́, -нёшь *pf.* (*impf. also* **сгиба́ть**) bend, curve, crook; **~ся** bend (down), bow (down); stoop.

согрева́ть, -а́ю *impf.*, **согре́ть, -е́ю** *pf.* warm, heat; **~ся** get warm; warm o.s.

согреше́ние, -я sin, trespass. **со|греши́ть, -шу́** *pf.*

соде́йствие, -я assistance, help; good offices. **соде́йствовать, -твую** *impf.* & *pf.* (*pf. also* **по~**) +*d.* assist, help; further, promote; make for, contribute to.

содержа́ние, -я maintenance, upkeep; keeping; allowance; pay; content; matter, substance; contents; plot; table of contents; **быть на содержа́нии у**+*g.* be kept, supported, by. **содержа́нка, -и** kept woman. **содержа́тельный** rich in content; pithy. **содержа́ть, -жу́, -жишь** *impf.* keep; maintain; support; have, contain; **~ся** be kept; be maintained; be contained. **содержи́мое** *sb.* contents.

со|дра́ть, сдеру́, -рёшь; -а́л, -а́, -о *pf.* (*impf. also* **сдира́ть**) tear off, strip off; fleece.

содрога́ние, -я shudder. **содрога́ться, -а́юсь** *impf.*, **содрогну́ться, -ну́сь, -нёшься** *pf.* shudder, shake, quake.

содру́жество, -а concord; community, commonwealth.

со́евый soya.

соедине́ние, -я joining, conjunction, combination; joint, join, junction; compound; formation. **соединённ|ый; -ён, -а́** united, joint. **С~ое Короле́вство** United Kingdom. **С~ые Шта́ты (Аме́рики)** United States (of America).

соедини́тельный connective, connecting; copulative. **соедини́ть, -ню́** *pf.*, **соединя́ть, -я́ю** *impf.* join, unite; connect, link; combine; **~ (по телефо́ну)** put through; **~ся** join, unite; combine.

сожале́ние, -я regret; pity; **к сожале́нию** unfortunately. **сожале́ть, -е́ю** *impf.* regret, deplore.

сожгу́ *etc.*: *see* **сжечь. сожже́ние, -я** burning; cremation.

сожму́ *etc.*: *see* **сжать**[2]. **сожну́** *etc.*: *see* **сжать**[1] **созва́ниваться, -аюсь** *impf. of* **созвони́ться**

созва́ть, -зову́, -зовёшь; -а́л, -а́, -о *pf.* (*impf.* **сзыва́ть, созыва́ть**) call together; call; invite; summon; convoke, convene.

созве́здие, -я constellation.

созвони́ться, -ню́сь *pf.* (*impf.* **созва́ниваться**) ring up; speak on the telephone.

созву́чие, -я accord, consonance; assonance. **созву́чный** harmonious; +*d.* consonant with, in keeping with.

создава́ть, -даю́, -даёшь *impf.*, **созда́ть, -а́м, -а́шь, -а́ст, -ади́м; со́зда́л, -а́, -о** *pf.* create; found, originate; set up, establish; **~ся** be created; arise, spring up. **созда́ние, -я** creation; making; work; creature. **созда́тель, -я** *m.* creator; founder, originator.

созерца́ние, -я contemplation. **созерца́тельный** contemplative, meditative. **созерца́ть, -а́ю** *impf.* contemplate.

сознава́ть, -наю́, -наёшь *impf.*, **созна́ть, -а́ю** *pf.* be conscious of, realize; recognize, acknowledge; **~ся** confess; plead guilty. **созна́ние, -я** consciousness; recognition, acknowledgement; admission, confession; **прийти́ в ~** recover consciousness; **~ до́лга** sense of duty. **созна́тельность, -и** awareness, consciousness; intelligence, acumen; deliberation, deliberateness. **созна́тельный** conscious; politically conscious; intelligent; deliberate.

созову́ *etc.*: *see* **созва́ть. с|озорнича́ть, -а́ю** *pf.*

созрева́ть, -а́ю *impf.*, **со|зре́ть, -е́ю** *pf.* ripen, mature; come to a head.

созы́в, -а convocation; summoning, calling. **созыва́ть, -а́ю** *impf. of* **созва́ть**

соизво́лить, -лю *pf.*, **соизволя́ть, -я́ю** *impf.* deign, condescend, be pleased.

соизмери́мый commensurable.

соиска́ние, -я competition, candidacy. **соиска́тель, -я** *m.*, **-ница, -ы** competitor, candidate.

сойти́, -йду́, -йдёшь; сошёл, -шла́ *pf.* (*impf.* **сходи́ть**) go down, come down; descend, get off, alight; leave; come off; pass, go off; +**за**+*a.* pass for, be taken for; **снег сошёл** the snow has melted; **сойдёт и так** it will do (as it is); **~ с доро́ги** get out of the way, step aside; **~ с ума́** go mad, go out of one's mind; **сошло́ благополу́чно** it went off all right; **~сь** meet; come together, gather; become friends; become intimate; agree; tally; **~сь хара́ктером** get on, hit it off.

сок, -а (-у), *loc.* **-у́** juice; sap; **в (по́лном) ~у́** in the prime of life. **соковыжима́лка, -и** juicer, juice-extractor.

со́кол, -а falcon.

сократи́ть, -ащу́ *pf.*, **сокраща́ть, -а́ю** *impf.* shorten; curtail; abbreviate; abridge; reduce, cut down; dismiss, discharge, lay off; cancel; **~ся** grow shorter, get shorter; decrease, decline; cut down; be cancelled; contract. **сокраще́ние, -я** shortening; abridgement; abbreviation; reduction, cutting down; curtailment; cancellation; contraction; **~ шта́тов** staff reduction; **уво́лить по сокраще́нию шта́тов** dismiss as redundant. **сокращённ|ый** brief; abbreviated; **~ое сло́во** abbreviation.

сокрове́нный secret, concealed; innermost. **сокро́вище, -а** treasure. **сокро́вищница, -ы** treasure-house, treasury.

сокруша́ть, -а́ю *impf.*, **сокруши́ть, -шу́** *pf.* shatter; smash; crush; distress, grieve; **~ся** grieve, be distressed. **сокруше́ние, -я** smashing, shattering; grief, distress. **сокрушённый; -ён, -а́** grief-stricken. **сокруши́тельный** shattering; crippling, withering, destructive.

сокры́тие, -я concealment. **сокры́ть, -ро́ю** *pf.* conceal, hide, cover up; **~ся** hide, conceal o.s.

со|лга́ть, -лгу́, -лжёшь; -а́л, -а́, -о *pf.*
солда́т, -а; *g.pl.* **-а́т** soldier. **солда́тский** soldier's; army.
соле́ние, -я salting; pickling. **солёный; со́лон, -а́, -о** salt; salty; salted; pickled; corned; spicy; hot. **соле́нье, -я** salted food(s); pickles.
солида́рность, -и solidarity; collective (joint) responsibility. **солида́рный** at one, in sympathy; collective, joint, solidary. **соли́дность, -и** solidity; reliability. **соли́дн|ый** solid; strong, sound; reliable; respectable; sizeable; **~ый во́зраст** middle age; **челове́к ~ых лет** a middle-aged man.
соли́ст, -а, соли́стка, -и soloist.
солите́р, -а solitaire (diamond).
соли́ть, -лю́, со́лишь *impf.* (*pf.* **по~**) salt; pickle, corn.
со́лнечн|ый sun; solar; sunny; **~ый свет** sunlight; sunshine; **~ый уда́р** sunstroke; **~ые часы́** sundial. **со́лнце, -а** sun. **солнцепёк, -а; на ~е** right in the sun, in the full blaze of the sun. **солнцестоя́ние, -я** solstice.
солове́й, -вья́ nightingale. **соловьи́ный** nightingale's.
со́лод, -а (-у) malt.
соло́дка, -и liquorice. **солодко́вый** liquorice.
соло́ма, -ы straw; thatch. **соло́менн|ый** straw; straw-coloured; **~ая вдова́** grass widow; **~ая кры́ша** thatch, thatched roof. **соло́минка, -и** straw.
со́лон *etc.*: *see* **солёный. солони́на, -ы** salted beef, corned beef. **соло́нка, -и** salt-cellar. **солонча́к, -а́** saline soil; *pl.* salt marshes. **соль**[1], **-и**; *pl.* **-и, -е́й** salt.
соль[2] *nt.indecl.* G; sol. soh.
со́льный solo.
солью́ *etc.*: *see* **слить**
соляно́й, соля́ный salt, saline; **соля́ная кислота́** hydrochloric acid.
со́мкнутый close; **~ строй** close order. **сомкну́ть, -ну́, -нёшь** *pf.* (*impf.* **смыка́ть**) close; **~ся** close, close up.
сомнева́ться, -а́юсь *impf.* doubt, have doubts; question; worry; **не ~ в**+*p.* have no doubts of. **сомне́ние, -я** doubt; uncertainty; **без сомне́ния** without doubt, undoubtedly. **сомни́тельн|ый** doubtful, questionable; dubious; equivocal; **~о** it is doubtful, it is open to question.
сомну́ *etc.*: *see* **смять**
сон, сна sleep; dream; **ви́деть во сне** dream, dream about. **сонли́вость, -и** sleepiness, drowsiness; somnolence. **сонли́вый** sleepy, drowsy; somnolent. **со́нный** sleepy, drowsy; somnolent; slumberous; sleeping, soporific.
сообража́ть, -а́ю *impf.*, **сообрази́ть, -ажу́** *pf.* consider, ponder, think out; weigh; understand, grasp; think up, arrange; have a quick one, have a round of drinks. **сообрази́тельный** quick-witted, quick, sharp, bright.
сообра́зный с+*i.* conformable to, in conformity with, consistent with. **сообразова́ть, -зу́ю** *impf.* & *pf.* conform, make conformable; adapt; **~ся** conform, adapt o.s.
сообща́ *adv.* together, jointly. **сообща́ть, -а́ю** *impf.*, **сообщи́ть, -щу́** *pf.* communicate, report, announce; impart; +*d.* inform of, tell that. **сообще́ние, -я** communication, report; information; announcement; connection.
сооруди́ть, -ужу́ *pf.*, **сооружа́ть, -а́ю** *impf.* build, erect. **сооруже́ние, -я** building; erection; construction; structure.
соотве́тственно *adv.* accordingly, correspondingly; *prep.*+*d.* according to, in accordance with, in conformity with, in compliance with. **соотве́тственный** corresponding. **соотве́тствие, -я** accordance, conformity, correspondence. **соотве́тствовать, -твую** *impf.* correspond, conform, be in keeping. **соотве́тствующий** corresponding; proper, appropriate, suitable.
сопе́рник, -а rival. **сопе́рничать, -аю** *impf.* be rivals; compete, vie. **сопе́рничество, -а** rivalry.
сопе́ть, -плю́ *impf.* breathe heavily; sniff; snuffle; huff and puff.
со́пка, -и knoll, hill, mound.
сопли́вый snotty.
сопостави́мый comparable. **сопоста́вить, -влю** *pf.*, **сопоставля́ть, -я́ю** *impf.* compare. **сопоставле́ние, -я** comparison.
соприкаса́ться, -а́юсь *impf.*, **соприкосну́ться, -ну́сь, -нёшься** *pf.* adjoin, be contiguous (to); come into contact. **соприкоснове́ние, -я** contiguity; contact.
сопроводи́тель, -я *m.* escort. **сопроводи́тельный** accompanying. **сопроводи́ть, -ожу́** *pf.*, **сопровожда́ть, -а́ю** *impf.* accompany; escort. **сопровожде́ние, -я** accompaniment; escort; **звуково́е ~** soundtrack.
сопротивле́ние, -я resistance; opposition. **сопротивля́ться, -я́юсь** *impf.*+*d.* resist, oppose.
сопу́тствовать, -твую *impf.*+*d.* accompany.
сопью́сь *etc.*: *see* **спи́ться**
сор, -а (-у) litter, dust, rubbish.
соразме́рить, -рю *pf.*, **соразмеря́ть, -я́ю** *impf.* proportion, balance, match. **соразме́рный** proportionate, commensurate.
сорва́ть, -ву́, -вёшь; -а́л, -а́, -о *pf.* (*impf.* **срыва́ть**) tear off, away, down; break off; pick, pluck; get, extract; break; smash, wreck, ruin, spoil; vent; **~ся** break away, break loose; fall, come down; fall through, fall to the ground, miscarry; **~ с ме́ста** dart off; **~ с пете́ль** come off its hinges.
с|организова́ть, -зу́ю *pf.*
соревнова́ние, -я competition; contest; tournament; event; emulation. **соревнова́ться, -ну́юсь** *impf.* compete, contend. **соревну́ющийся** *sb.* competitor, contestant, contender. **сори́ть, -рю́** *impf.* (*pf.* **на~**) +*a. or i.* litter; throw about. **со́рн|ый** dust, rubbish, refuse; **~ая трава́** weed, weeds. **сорня́к, -а́** weed.

со́рок, -а́ forty.
соро́ка, -и magpie.
сороков|о́й fortieth; **~ы́е го́ды** the forties.
соро́чка, -и shirt; blouse; shift.
сорт, -а; *pl.* **-а́** grade, quality; brand; sort, kind, variety. **сортирова́ть, -ру́ю** *impf.* (*pf.* **рас~**) sort, assort, grade, size. **сортиро́вка, -и** sorting, grading, sizing. **сортиро́вочный** sorting; **~ая** *sb.* marshalling-yard. **сортиро́вщик, -а** sorter. **со́ртность, -и** grade, quality. **со́ртный** of high quality. **сортово́й** high-grade, of high quality.
соса́ть, -су́, -сёшь *impf.* suck.
со|сва́тать, -аю *pf.*
сосе́д, -а; *pl.* **-и, сосе́дка, -и** neighbour; **~ по кварти́ре** flatmate. **сосе́дний** neighbouring; adjacent, next; **~ дом** the house next door. **сосе́дский** neighbours', neighbouring, next-door. **сосе́дство, -а** neighbourhood, vicinity. **соси́ска, -и** sausage; frankfurter.
со́ска, -и (*baby's*) dummy.
соска́кивать, -аю *impf. of* **соскочи́ть**
соска́льзывать, -аю *impf.*, **соскользну́ть, -ну́, -нёшь** *pf.* slide down, glide down; slip off, slide off.
соскочи́ть, -чу́, -чишь *pf.* (*impf.* **соска́кивать**) jump off, leap off; jump down, leap down; come off; vanish suddenly.
соску́читься, -чусь *pf.* get bored, be bored; **~ по** miss.
сослага́тельный subjunctive.
сосла́ть, сошлю́, -лёшь *pf.* (*impf.* **ссыла́ть**) exile, banish, deport; **~ся на**+*a.* refer to, allude to; cite, quote; plead, allege.
сосло́вие, -я estate; corporation, professional association.
сосна́, -ы́; *pl.* **-ы, -сен** pine(-tree). **сосно́вый** pine; deal.
сосну́ть, -ну́, -нёшь *pf.* have a nap.
сосо́к, -ска́ nipple, teat.
сосредото́ченность, -и concentration. **сосредото́ченный** concentrated. **сосредото́чивать, -аю** *impf.*, **сосредото́чить, -чу** *pf.* concentrate; focus; **~ся** concentrate.
соста́в, -а composition, make-up; structure; compound; staff; personnel; membership; strength; train; **в ~е**+*g.* numbering, consisting of, amounting to; **в по́лном ~е** with its full complement; in, at, full strength; in a body. **составит́ель, -я** *m.* compiler, author. **соста́вить, -влю** *pf.*, **составля́ть, -я́ю** *impf.* put together; make (up); compose; draw up; compile; work out; construct; be, constitute; amount to, total; **~ в сре́днем** average; **~ся** form, be formed, come into being. **составно́й** compound, composite; sectional; component, constituent.
со|ста́рить(ся, -рю(сь *pf.*
состоя́ние, -я state, condition; position; status; fortune; **в состоя́нии**+*inf.* able to, in a position to. **состоя́тельный** solvent; well-off, well-to-do; well-grounded. **состоя́ть, -ою́** *impf.* be; +**из**+*g.* consist of, comprise, be made up of; +**в**+*p.* consist in, lie in, be; **~ в до́лжности**+*g.* occupy the post of. **состоя́ться, -ои́тся** *pf.* take place.
сострада́ние, -я compassion, sympathy. **сострада́тельный** compassionate, sympathetic.
с|остри́ть, -рю́ *pf.* **со|стря́пать, -аю** *pf.*
со|стыкова́ть, -у́ю *pf.*, **состыко́вывать, -аю** *impf.* dock; **~ся** dock.
состяза́ние, -я competition, contest; match; **уча́стник состяза́ния** competitor. **состяза́ться, -а́юсь** *impf.* compete, contend.
сосу́д, -а vessel.
сосу́лька, -и icicle.
со|счита́ть, -а́ю *pf.* **сот** *see* **сто. со|твори́ть, -рю́** *pf.*
со́тенная *sb.* hundred-rouble note.
со|тка́ть, -ку́, -кёшь; -а́л, -ала́, -о *pf.*
со́тня, -и; *g.pl.* **-тен** a hundred.
сотови́дный honeycomb. **со́товый** honeycomb; **~ мёд** honey in the comb.
сотру́ *etc.*: *see* **стере́ть**
сотру́дник, -а collaborator; employee, assistant, official; contributor. **сотру́дничать, -аю** *impf.* collaborate; +**в**+*p.* contribute to. **сотру́дничество, -а** collaboration; cooperation.
сотряса́ть, -а́ю *impf.*, **сотрясти́, -су́, -сёшь; -я́с, -ла́** *pf.* shake; **~ся** shake, tremble. **сотрясе́ние, -я** shaking; concussion.
со́ты, -ов *pl.* honeycomb; **мёд в со́тах** honey in the comb.
со́тый hundredth.
со́ул, -а; (му́зыка) ~ soul music.
со́ус, -а (-у) sauce; gravy; dressing.
соуча́стие, -я participation; taking part; complicity. **соуча́стник, -а** partner; participant; accessory, accomplice.
соха́, -и́; *pl.* **-и** (*wooden*) plough.
со́хнуть, -ну; сох *impf.* (*pf.* **вы́~, за~, про~**) dry, get dry; become parched; wither.
сохране́ние, -я preservation; conservation; care, custody, charge, keeping; retention. **сохрани́ть, -ню́** *pf.*, **сохраня́ть, -я́ю** *impf.* preserve, keep; keep safe; retain, reserve; **~ся** remain (intact); last out, hold out; be well preserved. **сохра́нность, -и** safety, undamaged state; safe-keeping. **сохра́нный** safe.
соц... *abbr.* (*of* **социа́льный, социалисти́ческий**) *in comb.* social; socialist. **соцреали́зм, -а** socialist realism. **~соревнова́ние, -я** socialist emulation. **~стра́х, -а** social insurance.
социа́л-демокра́т, -а Social Democrat. **социа́л-демократи́ческий** Social Democratic. **социализа́ция, -и** socialization. **социализи́ровать, -рую** *impf.* & *pf.* socialize. **социали́зм, -а** socialism. **социали́ст, -а** socialist. **социалисти́ческий** socialist. **социа́льн|ый** social; **~ое обеспече́ние** social security; **~ое положе́ние** social status; **~ое страхова́ние** social insurance.
социо́лог, -а sociologist. **социологи́ческий** sociological. **социоло́гия, -и** sociology.

соч. *abbr.* (*of* **сочине́ния**) works.
сочета́ние, -я combination. **сочета́ть, -а́ю** *impf.* & *pf.* combine; +**с**+*i.* go with, harmonize with; match; ~ **бра́ком** marry; ~**ся** combine; harmonize; match; ~**ся бра́ком** be married.
сочине́ние, -я composition; work; essay; co-ordination. **сочини́ть, -ню́** *pf.*, **сочиня́ть, -я́ю** *impf.* compose; write; make up, fabricate.
сочи́ться, -и́тся *impf.* ooze (out), trickle; ~ **кро́вью** bleed.
сочлени́ть, -ню́ *pf.*, **сочленя́ть, -я́ю** *impf.* join, couple.
со́чный; -чен, -чна́, -о juicy; succulent; rich; lush.
сочту́ *etc.*: *see* **счесть**
сочу́вственный sympathetic. **сочу́вствие, -я** sympathy. **сочу́вствовать, -твую** *impf.*+*d.* sympathize with, feel for.
сошёл *etc.*: *see* **сойти́. сошлю́** *etc.*: *see* **сосла́ть. сошью́** *etc.*: *see* **сшить**
сощу́ривать, -аю *impf.*, **со|щу́рить, -рю** *pf.* screw up, narrow; ~**ся** screw up one's eyes; narrow.
сою́з[1], **-а** union; alliance; agreement; league. **сою́з**[2], **-а** conjunction. **сою́зник, -а** ally. **сою́зный** allied; of the (Soviet) Union.
со́я, -и soya bean.
спаге́тти *nt.* & *pl. indecl.* spaghetti.
спад, -а slump, recession; abatement. **спада́ть, -а́ет** *impf. of* **спасть**
спа́ивать, -аю *impf. of* **спая́ть, спои́ть**
спа́йка, -и soldered joint; solidarity, unity.
с|пали́ть, -лю́ *pf.*
спа́льник, -а sleeping-bag. **спа́льн|ый** sleeping; ~**ый ваго́н** sleeper, sleeping car; ~**ое ме́сто** berth, bunk. **спа́льня, -и**; *g.pl.* **-лен** bedroom; bedroom suite; ~**-гости́ная** bedsitting room.
спа́ржа, -и asparagus.
спартакиа́да, -ы sports meeting.
спа́рывать, -аю *impf. of* **споро́ть**
спаса́ние, -я rescuing, life-saving. **спаса́тель, -я** *m.* (*at sea*) lifeguard; rescuer; (*pl.*) rescue party; lifeboat. **спаса́тельн|ый** rescue, life-saving; ~**ый круг** lifebuoy; ~**ый по́яс** lifebelt; ~**ая экспеди́ция** rescue party. **спаса́ть(ся, -а́ю(сь** *impf. of* **спасти́(сь. спасе́ние, -я** rescuing, saving; rescue, escape; salvation.
спаси́бо thanks; thank you.
спаси́тель, -я *m.* rescuer, saver; saviour. **спаси́тельный** saving; of rescue, of escape; salutary.
с|пасова́ть, -су́ю *pf.*
спасти́, -су́, -сёшь; спас, -ла́ *pf.* (*impf.* **спаса́ть**) save; rescue; ~**сь** save o.s., escape; be saved.
спасть, -адёт *pf.* (*impf.* **спада́ть**) fall (down); abate.
спать, сплю; -ал, -а́, -о *impf.* sleep, be asleep; **лечь** ~ go to bed; **пора́** ~ it is bedtime.
спа́янность, -и cohesion, unity; solidarity. **спа́янный** united. **спая́ть, -я́ю** *pf.* (*impf.* **спа́ивать**) solder together, weld; unite, knit together.
спекта́кль, -я *m.* performance.
спектр, -а spectrum.
спекули́ровать, -рую *impf.* speculate; profiteer; gamble; +**на**+*p.* gamble on, reckon on; profit by. **спекуля́нт, -а** speculator, profiteer. **спекуля́ция, -и** speculation; profiteering; gamble.
с|пелена́ть, -а́ю *pf.*
спелео́лог, -а caver, pot-holer.
спе́лый ripe.
сперва́ *adv.* at first; first.
спе́реди *adv.* in front, at the front, from the front; *prep.*+*g.* (from) in front of.
спёртый close, stuffy.
спеси́вый arrogant, haughty, lofty. **спесь, -и** arrogance, haughtiness, loftiness.
спеть[1], **-е́ет** *impf.* (*pf.* **по**~) ripen.
с|петь[2], **спою́, споёшь** *pf.*
спец, -е́ца́; *pl.* **-е́цы́, -ев** *or* **-о́в** *abbr.* (*of* **специали́ст**) specialist, expert, authority.
спец... *abbr.* (*of* **специа́льный**) *in comb.* special. **спецко́р, -а** special correspondent. ~**ку́рс, -а** special course (of lectures). ~**оде́жда, -ы** working clothes, protective clothing; overalls.
специализи́роваться, -руюсь *impf.* & *pf.* specialize. **специали́ст, -а** specialist, expert, authority. **специа́льность, -и** speciality, special interest; profession; trade. **специа́льный** special; specialist; ~ **те́рмин** technical term.
специ́фика, -и specific character. **специфи́ческий** specific.
спецо́вка, -и protective clothing, working clothes; overall(s).
спеши́ть, -шу́ *impf.* (*pf.* **по**~) hurry, be in a hurry; make haste, hasten; hurry up; be fast.
спе́шка, -и hurry, haste, rush. **спе́шн|ый** urgent, pressing; ~**ый зака́з** rush order; ~**ая по́чта** express delivery.
спива́ться, -а́юсь *impf. of* **спи́ться**
СПИД, а *abbr.* (*of* ***синдро́м приобретённого имму́нного дефици́та***) AIDS (*acquired immune deficiency syndrome*).
с|пики́ровать, -рую *pf.*
спи́ливать, -аю *impf.*, **спили́ть, -лю́, -лишь** *pf.* saw down; saw off.
спина́, -ы́, *a.* **-у**; *pl.* **-ы** back. **спи́нка, -и** back. **спинно́й** spinal; ~ **мозг** spinal cord; ~ **хребе́т** spinal column.
спирт, -а (-у) alcohol, spirit(s). **спиртн|о́й** spirituous; ~**ы́е напи́тки** spirits; ~**о́е** *sb.* spirits. **спирто́вка, -и** spirit-stove. **спиртово́й** spirit, spirituous.
списа́ть, -ишу́, -и́шешь *pf.*, **спи́сывать, -аю** *impf.* copy; crib; write off; ~**ся** exchange letters. **спи́сок, -ска** list; roll; record; manuscript copy; ~ **избира́телей** voters' list, electoral roll; ~ **уби́тых и ра́неных** casualty list.

спи́ться, сопью́сь, -ьёшься; -и́лся, -а́сь *pf.* (*impf.* **спива́ться**) take to drink, become a drunkard.

спи́хивать, -аю *impf.*, **спихну́ть, -ну́, -нёшь** *pf.* push aside; push down.

спи́ца, -ы knitting-needle; spoke.

спи́чечн|ый match; **~ая коро́бка** match-box. **спи́чка, -и** match.

спишу́ *etc.*: *see* **списа́ть**

сплав[1], **-а** floating, rafting. **сплав**[2], **-а** alloy. **спла́вить**[1], **-влю** *pf.*, **сплавля́ть**[1], **-я́ю** *impf.* float; raft; get rid of. **спла́вить**[2], **-влю** *pf.*, **сплавля́ть**[2], **-я́ю** *impf.* alloy; **~ся** fuse, coalesce.

с|плани́ровать, -рую *pf.* **спла́чивать(ся, -аю(сь** *impf. of* **сплоти́ть(ся**

сплёвывать, -аю *impf. of* **сплю́нуть**

с|плести́, -ету́, -етёшь; -ёл, -а́ *pf.*, **сплета́ть, -а́ю** *impf.* weave; plait; interlace. **сплете́ние, -я** interlacing; plexus.

спле́тник, -а, -ница, -ы gossip, scandal-monger. **спле́тничать, -аю** *impf.* (*pf.* **на~**) gossip, tittle-tattle; talk scandal. **спле́тня, -и**; *gen pl.* **-тен** gossip, scandal.

сплоти́ть, -очу́ *pf.* (*impf.* **спла́чивать**) join; unite, rally; **~ ряды́** close the ranks; **~ся** unite, rally; close the ranks. **сплочённость, -и** cohesion, unity. **сплочённый; -ён, -а́** united, firm; unbroken.

сплошно́й solid; all-round, complete; unbroken, continuous; sheer, utter, unreserved. **сплошь** *adv.* all over; throughout; without a break; completely, utterly; without exception; **~ да ря́дом** nearly always; pretty often.

с|плутова́ть, -ту́ю *pf.*

сплыва́ть, -а́ет *impf.*, **сплыть, -ывёт; -ыл, -а́, -о** *pf.* sail down, float down; be carried away; overflow, run over; **бы́ло да сплы́ло** those were the days; it's all over. **~ся** run (together), merge, blend.

сплю *see* **спать**

сплю́нуть, -ну *pf.* (*impf.* **сплёвывать**) spit; spit out.

сплю́щенный flattened out. **сплю́щивать, -аю** *impf.*, **сплю́щить, -щу** *pf.* flatten; **~ся** become flat.

с|пляса́ть, -яшу́, -я́шешь *pf.*

сподви́жник, -а comrade-in-arms.

спои́ть, -ою́, -о́ишь *pf.* (*impf.* **спа́ивать**) accustom to drinking, make a drunkard of.

споко́йн|ый quiet; calm, tranquil; placid, serene; composed; comfortable; **~ой но́чи** good night! **споко́йствие, -я** quiet; tranquillity; calm, calmness; order; composure, serenity.

спола́скивать, -аю *impf. of* **сполосну́ть**

сполза́ть, -а́ю *impf.*, **сползти́, -зу́, -зёшь; -олз, -ла́** *pf.* climb down; slip (down); fall away.

сполна́ *adv.* completely, in full.

сполосну́ть, -ну́, -нёшь *pf.* (*impf.* **спола́скивать**) rinse.

спо́нсор, -а sponsor, backer.

спор, -а (-у) argument; controversy; debate; dispute. **спо́рить, -рю** *impf.* (*pf.* **по~**) argue; dispute; debate; bet, have a bet. **спо́рный** disputable, debatable, questionable; disputed, at issue; **~ вопро́с** moot point, vexed question; **~ мяч** jump ball; held ball.

споро́ть, -рю́, -решь *pf.* (*impf.* **спа́рывать**) rip off.

спорт, -а sport, sports; **бату́тный ~** trampolining; **ко́нный ~** equestrianism; **лы́жный ~** skiing; **парашю́тный ~** parachute-jumping. **спорти́вн|ый** sports; **~ый зал** gymnasium; **~ая площа́дка** sports-ground, playing-field; **~ые состяза́ния** sports. **спортсме́н, -а, спортсме́нка, -и** athlete, player.

спо́рый; -ор, -а́, -о successful, profitable; skilful, efficient.

спо́соб, -а way, manner, method; mode; means; **~ употребле́ния** directions for use; **таки́м ~ом** in this way. **спосо́бность, -и** ability, talent, aptitude, flair; capacity. **спосо́бный** able; talented, gifted, clever; capable. **спосо́бствовать, -твую** *impf.* (*pf.* **по~**) *+d.* assist; be conducive to, further, promote, make for.

споткну́ться, -ну́сь, -нёшься *pf.*, **спотыка́ться, -а́юсь** *impf.* stumble; get stuck, come to a stop.

спохвати́ться, -ачу́сь, -а́тишься *pf.*, **спохва́тываться, -аюсь** *impf.* remember suddenly.

спою́ *etc.*: *see* **спеть, спои́ть**

спра́ва *adv.* to the right.

справедли́вость, -и justice; equity; fairness; truth, correctness. **справедли́вый** just; equitable, fair; justified.

спра́вить, -влю *pf.*, **справля́ть, -я́ю** *impf.* celebrate. **спра́виться**[1], **-влюсь** *pf.* **справля́ться, -я́юсь** *impf.* **с**+*i.* cope with, manage; deal with. **спра́виться**[2], **-влюсь** *pf.*, **справля́ться, -я́юсь** *impf.* ask, inquire; inform o.s.; **~ в словаре́** consult a dictionary. **спра́вка, -и** information; reference; certificate; **навести́ спра́вку** inquire; **наводи́ть спра́вку** make inquiries. **спра́вочник, -а** reference-book, handbook, guide, directory. **спра́вочн|ый** inquiry, information; **~ая кни́га** reference-book, handbook.

спра́шивать(ся, -аю(сь *impf. of* **спроси́ть(ся.** **с|провоци́ровать, -рую** *pf.*

с|проекти́ровать, -рую *pf.*

спрос, -а (-у) demand; asking; **без ~у** without asking leave, without permission; **по́льзоваться (бо́льшим) ~ом** be in (great) demand; **~ на**+*a.* demand for, run on. **спроси́ть, -ошу́, -о́сишь** *pf.* (*impf.* **спра́шивать**) ask (for); inquire; ask to see; +**с**+*g.* make answer for, make responsible for; **~ся** ask permission.

спросо́нок *adv.* (being) only half-awake.

спры́гивать, -аю *impf.*, **спры́гнуть, -ну** *pf.*

jump off, jump down.

спры́скивать, -аю *impf.*, **спры́снуть, -ну** *pf.* sprinkle.

спряга́ть, -а́ю *impf.* (*pf.* **про~**) conjugate; **~ся** be conjugated. **спряже́ние, -я** conjugation.

с|прясть, -яду́, -ядёшь; -ял, -я́ла́, -о *pf.*

с|пря́тать(ся, -я́чу(сь *pf.*

спу́гивать, -аю *impf.*, **спугну́ть, -ну́, -нёшь** *pf.* frighten off, scare off.

спуртова́ть, -ту́ю *impf.* & *pf.* spurt.

спуск, -а lowering, hauling down; descent; descending; landing; release; draining; slope. **спуска́ть, -а́ю** *impf.*, **спусти́ть, -ущу́, -у́стишь** *pf.* let down, lower; haul down; let go, let loose, release; let out, drain; send out; go down; forgive, let off, let go, let pass; lose; throw away, squander; **~ кора́бль** launch a ship; **~ куро́к** pull the trigger; **~ пе́тлю** drop a stitch; **~ с це́пи** unchain; **спустя́ рукава́** carelessly. **спускн|о́й** drain; **~а́я труба́** drain-pipe. **спусково́й** trigger. **спустя́** *prep.+a.* after; later; **немно́го ~** not long after.

с|пу́тать(ся, -аю(сь *pf.*

спу́тник, -а satellite, sputnik; (travelling) companion; fellow-traveller; concomitant.

спущу́ *etc.*: *see* **спусти́ть**

спя́чка, -и hibernation; sleepiness, lethargy.

ср. *abbr.* (*of* ***сравни́***) cf., compare; (*of* **сре́дний**) mean.

сравне́ние, -я comparison; simile; **по сравне́нию с**+*i.* as compared with, as against.

сра́внивать, -аю *impf.* *of* **сравни́ть, сравня́ть**

сравни́тельно *adv.* comparatively; **~ с**+*i.* compared with. **сравни́тельный** comparative. **сравни́ть, -ню́** *pf.* (*impf.* **сра́внивать**) compare; **~ся с**+*i.* compare with, come up to, touch.

с|равня́ть, -я́ю *pf.* (*impf. also* **сра́внивать**) make even, make equal; level.

сража́ть, -а́ю *impf.*, **срази́ть, -ажу́** *pf.* slay, strike down, fell; overwhelm, crush; **~ся** fight, join battle. **сраже́ние, -я** battle, engagement.

сра́зу *adv.* at once; straight away, right away.

срам, -а (-у) shame. **срами́ть, -млю́** *impf.* (*pf.* **о~**) shame, put to shame; **~ся** cover o.s. with shame. **срамни́к, -а́** shameless person. **срамно́й** shameless. **срамота́, -ы́** shame.

сраста́ние, -я growing together; knitting. **сраста́ться, -а́ется** *impf.*, **срасти́сь, -тётся; сро́сся, -ла́сь** *pf.* grow together; knit.

сребролюби́вый money-grubbing. **сребро-но́сный** argentiferous.

среда́[1], **-ы́**; *pl.* **-ы** environment, surroundings; milieu; habitat; medium; **в на́шей среде́** in our midst, among us. **среда́**[2], **-ы́**, *a.* **-у**; *pl.* **-ы, -а́м** *or* **-ам** Wednesday. **среди́** *prep.+g.* among, amongst; amidst; in the middle of; **~ бе́ла дня** in broad daylight.

Средизе́мное мо́ре, -ого -я the Mediterranean (Sea). **средиземномо́рский** Mediterranean.

среди́на, -ы middle. **сре́дне** *adv.* middling, so-so. **средневеко́вый** medieval. **средневеко́вье, -я** the Middle Ages. **средневи́к, -а́** middle-distance runner. **сре́дн|ий** middle; medium; mean; average; middling; secondary; neuter; **~ие века́** the Middle Ages; **~яя величина́** mean value; **~ий па́лец** middle finger, second finger; **~ее** *sb.* mean, average; **вы́ше ~его** above (the) average.

сре́дство, -а means; remedy; *pl.* means; resources; credits; **жить не по сре́дствам** live beyond one's means.

срез, -а cut; section; shear, shearing; slice, slicing. **с|ре́зать, -е́жу** *pf.* **среза́ть, -а́ю** *impf.* cut off; slice, cut, chop; fail, plough; **~ся** fail, be ploughed.

с|репети́ровать, -рую *pf.*

срисова́ть, -су́ю *pf.*, **срисо́вывать, -аю** *impf.* copy.

с|рифмова́ть(ся, -му́ю(сь *pf.* **с|ровня́ть, -я́ю** *pf.*

сродство́, -а́ affinity.

срок, -а (-у) date; term; time, period; **в ~, к ~у** in time, to time; **~ хране́ния** shelf life.

сро́сся *etc.*: *see* **срасти́сь**

сро́чно *adv.* urgently; quickly. **сро́чность, -и** urgency; hurry; **что за ~?** what's the hurry? **сро́чный** urgent, pressing; at a fixed date; for a fixed period; periodic, routine; **~ зака́з** rush order.

сро́ю *etc.*: *see* **срыть**

сруб, -а felling; framework. **сруба́ть, -а́ю** *impf.*, **с|руби́ть, -блю́, -бишь** *pf.* fell, cut down; build (*of logs*).

срыв, -а disruption; derangement, frustration; foiling, spoiling, ruining, wrecking; **~ перегово́ров** breaking-off of talks, breakdown in negotiations. **срыва́ть**[1]**(ся, -а́ю(сь** *impf. of* **сорва́ть(ся**

срыва́ть[2], **-а́ю** *impf.*, **срыть, сро́ю** *pf.* raze, level to the ground.

сря́ду *adv.* running.

ссади́на, -ы scratch, abrasion. **ссади́ть, -ажу́, -а́дишь** *pf.*, **сса́живать, -аю** *impf.* set down; help down, help to alight; put off, turn off.

ссо́ра, -ы quarrel; falling-out; slanging-match; **быть в ссо́ре** be on bad terms, have fallen out. **ссо́рить, -рю** *impf.* (*pf.* **по~**) cause to quarrel, embroil; **~ся** quarrel, fall out.

СССР *abbr.* (*of* ***Сою́з Сове́тских Социалисти́ческих Респу́блик***) USSR, Union of Soviet Socialist Republics.

ссу́да, -ы loan. **ссуди́ть, -ужу́, -у́дишь** *pf.*, **ссужа́ть, -а́ю** *impf.* lend, loan.

с|сучи́ть, -чу́, -у́чи́шь *pf.*

ссыла́ть(ся, -а́ю(сь *impf. of* **сосла́ть(ся. ссы́лка**[1], **-и** exile, banishment; deportation. **ссы́лка**[2], **-и** reference. **ссы́льный, ссы́льная** *sb.* exile.

ссы́пать, -плю *pf.*, **ссыпа́ть, -а́ю** *impf.* pour. **ссыпно́й; ~ пункт** grain-collecting station.

ст. *abbr.* (*of* **статья́**) Art., Article (*of law, etc.*); (*of* **столéтие**) c., century.

стабилизáтор, -а stabilizer; tail-plane. **стабилизи́ровать, -рую** *impf.* & *pf.*, **стабилизовáть, -зу́ю** *impf.* & *pf.* stabilize; **~ся** become stable. **стаби́льный** stable, firm; **~ учéбник** standard textbook.

стáвень, -вня; *g.pl.* **-вней** *m.*, **стáвня, -и**; *g.pl.* **-вен** shutter.

стáвить, -влю *impf.* (*pf.* **по~**) put, place, set; stand; station; put up, erect; install; put in; put on; apply; present, stage, stake. **стáвка**[1], **-и** rate; stake; **~ зарплáты** rate of pay. **стáвка**[2], **-и** headquarters.

стáвня *see* **стáвень**

стадио́н, -а stadium.

стáдия, -и stage.

стáдность, -и herd instinct. **стáдный** gregarious. **стáдо, -а**; *pl.* **-á** herd, flock.

стаж, -а length of service; record; probation. **стажёр, -а** probationer, houseman; trainee. **стажировáть(ся, -ру́ю(сь** *impf.* go through period of training.

стáивать, -ает *impf. of* **стáять**

стáйер, -а long-distance runner.

стакáн, -а glass, tumbler, beaker.

сталелитéйный steel-founding, steel-casting; **~ завóд** steel foundry. **сталеплави́льный** steel-making; **~ завóд** steel works. **сталепрокáтный** (steel-)rolling; **~ стан** rolling-mill.

стáлкивать(ся, -аю(сь *impf. of* **столкну́ть(ся**

стáло быть *conj.* consequently, therefore, so.

сталь, -и steel. **стальнóй** steel.

стамéска, -и chisel.

стан[1], **-а** figure, torso.

стан[2], **-а** camp.

стан[3], **-а** mill.

стандáрт, -а standard. **стандартизáция, -и** standardization. **стандáртный** standard.

станкóвый machine; mounted; (free-)standing. **станкостроéние, -я** machine-tool engineering.

станови́ться, -влю́сь, -вишься *impf. of* **стать**

станóк, -нкá machine tool, machine; bench; mount, mounting.

стáну *etc.*: *see* **стать**

станцио́нный station. **стáнция, -и** station.

стáпель, -я; *pl.* **-я́** *m.* stocks.

стáптывать(ся, -аю(сь *impf. of* **стоптáть(ся**

старáние, -я effort, endeavour, pains, diligence. **старáтель, -я** *m.* prospector (*for gold*), (gold-)digger. **старáтельность, -и** application, diligence. **старáтельный** diligent, painstaking, assiduous. **старáться, -áюсь** *impf.* (*pf.* **по~**) try, endeavour; take pains; make an effort.

старéть, -éю *impf.* (*pf.* **по~, у~**) grow old, age. **стáрец, -рца** elder, (*venerable*) old man; hermit. **стари́к, -á** old man. **старинá, -ы́** antiquity, olden times; antique(s); old man, old fellow. **стари́нный** ancient; old; antique. **стáрить, -рю** *impf.* (*pf.* **со~**) age, make old; **~ся** age, grow old.

старо... *in comb.* old. **старовéр, -а** Old Believer. **~дáвний** ancient. **~жи́л, -а** old inhabitant; old resident. **~завéтный** old-fashioned, conservative; antiquated. **~мóдный** old-fashioned, out-moded; out-of-date. **~печáтный; ~печáтные кни́ги** early printed books. **~свéтский** old-world; old-fashioned. **~славя́нский** Old Slavonic.

стáроста, -ы head; senior; monitor; churchwarden. **стáрость, -и** old age.

старт, -а start; **на ~!** on your marks! **стáртёр, -а** starter. **стартовáть, -ту́ю** *impf.* & *pf.* start. **стáртовый** starting.

стару́ха, -и old woman. **стáрческ|ий** old man's; senile; **~ое слабоу́мие** senility, senile decay. **стáрше** *comp. of* **стáрый.** **стáрш|ий** oldest, eldest; senior; superior; chief, head; upper, higher; **~ий адъютáнт** adjutant; **~ие** *sb.*, *pl.* (one's) elders; **~ий** *sb.* chief; man in charge; **кто здесь ~ий?** who is in charge here? **старшинá, -ы́** *m.* sergeant-major; petty officer; leader, senior representative, doyen, foreman. **старшинствó, -á** seniority; **по старшинству́** by right of, in order of, seniority. **стáрый; -ар, -á, -о** old. **старьё, -я́** old things, old clothes, old junk.

стáскивать, -аю *impf. of* **стащи́ть**

с|тасовáть, -су́ю *pf.*

стати́ст, -а super, extra.

стати́стика, -и statistics. **статисти́ческий** statistical.

стáтный stately.

стáтский civil, civilian; State; **~ совéтник** State Councillor (*5th grade*: *see* **чин**).

стáтуя, -и statue.

стать, -áну *pf.* (*impf.* **станови́ться**) stand; take up position; stop, come to a halt; cost; suffice, do; begin, start; +*i.* become, get, grow; +**с**+*i.* become of, happen to; **не ~** *impers.*+*g.* cease to be; disappear, be gone; **егó не стáло** he is no more; **её отцá давнó не стáло** her father has been dead a long time; **~ в óчередь** queue up; **~ в пóзу** strike an attitude; **~ на колéни** kneel; **~ на рабóту** begin work; **часы́ стáли** the clock (has) stopped.

стать, -и; *g.pl.* **-éй** need, necessity; physique, build; points; **быть под ~** be well-matched; +*d.* be like; **с какóй стáти?** why? what for?

стáться, -áнется *pf.* happen; become; **вполнé мóжет ~** it is quite possible.

статья́, -и́; *g.pl.* **-éй** article; clause; item; matter, job; class, rating; **э́то осóбая ~** that is another matter.

стационáр, -а permanent establishment; hospital. **стационáрный** stationary; permanent, fixed; **~ больнóй** in-patient.

с|тачáть, -áю *pf.*

ста́чечник, -а striker. **ста́чка, -и** strike.

с|тащи́ть, -щу́, -щишь *pf.* (*impf. also* **ста́скивать**) drag off, pull off; drag down; pinch, swipe, whip.

ста́я, -и flock, flight; school, shoal; pack.

ста́ять, -ает *pf.* (*impf.* **ста́ивать**) melt.

ствол, -а́ trunk; stem; bole, barrel; tube, pipe; shaft.

ство́рка, -и leaf, fold; door, gate, shutter. **ство́рчатый** folding; valved.

сте́бель, -бля; *g.pl.* **-бле́й** *m.* stem, stalk. **стебе́льчатый** stalky, stalk-like; ~ **шов** feather-stitch.

стёганка, -и quilted jacket. **стёган|ый** quilted; **~ое одея́ло** quilt. **стега́ть**[1], **-а́ю** *impf.* (*pf.* **вы́~**) quilt.

стега́ть[2], **-а́ю** *impf.*, **стегну́ть, -ну́** *pf.* (*pf. also* **от~**) whip, lash.

стежо́к, -жка́ stitch.

стёк *etc.*: *see* **стечь. стека́ть(ся, -а́ет(ся** *impf. of* **сте́чь(ся**

стеклене́ть, -е́ет *impf.* (*pf.* **о~**) become glassy. **стекло́, -а́**; *pl.* **-ёкла, -кол** glass; lens; (window-)pane.

стекло... *in comb.* glass. **стекловолокно́, -а́** glass fibre. **~ду́в, -а** glass-blower. **~ма́сса, -ы** molten glass. **~очисти́тель, -я** *m.* windscreen-wiper.

стекля́нн|ый glass; glassy; **~ый колпа́к** bell-glass, glass case; **~ая посу́да** glassware. **стеко́льный** glass; vitreous. **стеко́льщик, -а** glazier.

стели́ть *see* **стлать**

стелла́ж, -а́ shelves, shelving; rack, stand.

сте́лька, -и insole, sock.

сте́льная коро́ва cow in calf.

стелю́ *etc.*: *see* **стлать**

с|темне́ть, -е́ет *pf.*

стена́, -ы́, *a.* **-у**; *pl.* **-ы, -а́м** wall. **стенгазе́та, -ы** wall newspaper. **стенно́й** wall; mural.

стеногра́мма, -ы shorthand record. **стено́граф, -а, стенографи́ст, -а, стенографи́стка, -и** stenographer, shorthand-writer. **стенографи́ровать, -рую** *impf.* & *pf.* take down in shorthand. **стенографи́ческий** shorthand. **стеногра́фия, -и** shorthand, stenography.

сте́нопись, -и mural.

степе́нный staid, steady; middle-aged.

сте́пень, -и; *g.pl.* **-е́й** degree; extent; power.

степно́й steppe. **степня́к, -а́** steppe-dweller; steppe horse. **степь, -и**, *loc.* **-и́**; *g.pl.* **-е́й** steppe.

стерегу́ *etc.*: *see* **стере́чь**

стереоти́п, -а stereotype. **стереоти́пн|ый** stereotype; **-ая фра́за** stock phrase.

стереофони́ческий stereophonic.

стере́ть, сотру́, сотрёшь; стёр *pf.* (*impf.* **стира́ть**) wipe off; rub out, erase; rub sore; grind down; **~ся** rub off; fade; wear down; be effaced, be obliterated.

стере́чь, -регу́, -режёшь; -ёг, -ла́ *impf.* guard; watch (over); watch for.

сте́ржень, -жня *m.* pivot; shank, rod; core. **стержнево́й** pivoted; ~ **вопро́с** key question.

стерилиза́тор, -а sterilizer. **стерилиза́ция, -и** sterilization. **стерилизова́ть, -зу́ю** *impf.* & *pf.* sterilize. **стери́льность, -и** sterility. **стери́льный** sterile; germ-free.

сте́рлинг, -а sterling; **фунт ~ов** pound sterling.

сте́рлядь, -и; *g.pl.* **-е́й** sterlet.

стеро́ид, -а steroid.

стерпе́ть, -плю́, -пишь *pf.* bear, suffer, endure.

стёртый worn, effaced.

стесне́ние, -я constraint. **стесни́тельный** shy; inhibited; difficult, inconvenient. **с|тесни́ть, -ню́** *pf.*, **стесня́ть, -я́ю** *impf.* constrain; hamper; inhibit. **с|тесни́ться, -ню́сь** *pf.*, **стесня́ться, -я́юсь** *impf.* (*pf. also* **по~**) +*inf.* feel too shy to, be ashamed to; (+*g.*) feel shy (of).

стече́ние, -я confluence; ~ **наро́да** concourse; ~ **обстоя́тельств** coincidence. **стечь, -чёт; -ёк, -ла́** *pf.* (*impf.* **стека́ть**) flow down; **~ся** flow together; gather, throng.

стиль, -я *m.* style. **сти́льный** stylish; period.

сти́мул, -а stimulus, incentive. **стимули́ровать, -рую** *impf.* & *pf.* stimulate.

стипендиа́т, -а grant-aided student. **стипе́ндия, -и** grant.

стира́льный washing.

стира́ть[1]**(ся, -а́ю(сь** *impf. of* **стере́ть(ся**

стира́ть[2], **-а́ю** *impf.* (*pf.* **вы́~**) wash, launder; **~ся** wash. **сти́рка, -и** washing, wash, laundering, laundry.

сти́скивать, -аю *impf.*, **сти́снуть, -ну** *pf.* squeeze; clench; hug.

стих, -а́ verse; line; *pl.* verses, poetry.

стиха́ть, -а́ю *impf. of* **сти́хнуть**

стихи́йн|ый elemental; spontaneous, uncontrolled; **~ое бе́дствие** disaster. **стихи́я, -и** element.

сти́хнуть, -ну; стих *pf.* (*impf.* **стиха́ть**) abate, subside; die down; calm down.

стихове́дение, -я prosody. **стихосложе́ние, -я** versification; prosody. **стихотворе́ние, -я** poem. **стихотво́рный** in verse form; of verse; poetic; ~ **разме́р** metre.

стлать, стели́ть, стелю́, сте́лешь *impf.* (*pf.* **по~**) spread; ~ **посте́ль** make a bed; ~ **ска́терть** lay the cloth; **~ся** spread; drift, creep.

сто, ста; *g.pl.* **сот** a hundred.

стог, -а, *loc.* **-е** & **-у́**; *pl.* **-а́** stack, rick.

стогра́дусный centigrade.

сто́имость, -и cost; value. **сто́ить, -о́ю** *impf.* cost; be worth; be worthy of, deserve; **не сто́ит** don't mention it; **сто́ит** it is worth while; ~ **то́лько**+*inf.* one has only to.

стой *see* **стоя́ть**

сто́йка, -и counter, bar; support, prop; stanchion, upright; strut; set; stand, stance.

сто́йкий firm; stable; persistent; steadfast, staunch, steady. **сто́йкость, -и** firmness, stability; steadfastness, staunchness; determination. **сто́йло, -а** stall. **стоймя́** *adv.* upright.

сток, -а flow; drainage, outflow; drain, gutter; sewer.

Стокго́льм, -а Stockholm.

стол, -а́ table; desk; board; cooking, cuisine; department, section; office, bureau.

столб, -а́ post, pole, pillar, column. **столбене́ть, -е́ю** *impf.* (*pf.* **о~**) be rooted to the ground, be transfixed. **столбе́ц, -бца́** column. **сто́лбик, -а** column; style; double crochet, treble. **столбня́к, -а́** stupor; tetanus. **столбово́й** main, chief.

столе́тие, -я century; centenary. **столе́тний** of a hundred years; a hundred years old; **~ стари́к** centenarian.

столи́ца, -ы capital; metropolis. **столи́чный** capital; of the capital.

столкнове́ние, -я collision; clash. **столкну́ть, -ну́, -нёшь** *pf.* (*impf.* **ста́лкивать**) push off, push away; cause to collide, bring into collision; bring together; **~ся** collide, come into collision; clash, conflict; +**с**+*i.* run into, bump into.

столова́ться, -лу́юсь *impf.* have meals, board, mess. **столо́вая** *sb.* dining-room; mess; canteen; dining-room suite. **столо́вый** table; dinner; feeding, catering, messing.

столп, -а́ pillar, column.

столпи́ться, -и́тся *pf.* crowd.

столь *adv.* so. **сто́лько** *adv.* so much, so many.

столя́р, -а́ joiner, carpenter. **столя́рный** joiner's, carpenter's.

стометро́вка, -и (the) hundred metres; hundred-metre event.

стон, -а groan, moan. **стона́ть, -ну́, -нешь** *impf.* groan, moan.

стоп! *int.* stop!; *indecl. adj.* stop.

стопа́[1], **-ы́**; *pl.* **-ы** foot.

стопа́[2], **-ы́**; *pl.* **-ы** goblet.

стопа́[3], **-ы́**; *pl.* **-ы** ream; pile, heap.

сто́пка[1], **-и** pile, heap.

сто́пка[2], **-и** small glass.

сто́пор, -а stop, catch, pawl. **сто́порить, -рю** *impf.* (*pf.* **за~**) stop, lock; slow down, bring to a stop; **~ся** slow down, come to a stop.

стопроце́нтный hundred-per-cent.

стоп-сигна́л, -а brake-light.

стопта́ть, -пчу́, -пчешь *pf.* (*impf.* **ста́птывать**) wear down; trample; **~ся** wear down, be worn down.

с|торгова́ть(ся, -гу́ю(сь *pf.*

сто́рож, -а; *pl.* **-а́** watchman, guard. **сторожев|о́й** watch; **~а́я бу́дка** sentry-box; **~о́й кора́бль** escort vessel; **~о́е су́дно** patrol-boat. **сторожи́ть, -жу́** *impf.* guard, watch, keep watch over.

сторона́, -ы́, *a.* **сто́рону**; *pl.* **сто́роны, -ро́н, -а́м** side; quarter; hand; feature, aspect; part; party; land, place; parts; **в стороне́** aside, aloof; **в сто́рону** aside; **на чужо́й стороне́** in foreign parts; **по ту сто́рону**+*g.* across; on the other, the far, side of; **с моéй стороны́** for my part; **с одно́й стороны́** on the one hand; **шу́тки в сто́рону** joking apart. **сторони́ться, -ню́сь, -ни́шься** *impf.* (*pf.* **по~**) stand aside, make way; +*g.* shun, avoid. **сторо́нний** strange, foreign; detached; indirect. **сторо́нник, -а** supporter, adherent, advocate; **~ ми́ра** peace campaigner.

сто́чн|ый sewage, drainage; **~ые во́ды** sewage; **~ая труба́** drainpipe, sewer.

стоя́к, -а́ post, stanchion, upright; stand-pipe; chimney. **стоя́нка, -и** stop; parking; stopping place, parking space; stand; rank; moorage; site; **«~ запрещена́!»** 'No parking'; **~ такси́** taxi-rank. **стоя́ть, -ою́** *impf.* (*pf.* **по~**) stand; be; be situated, lie; continue; stay; be stationed; stop; have stopped, have come to a stop; +**за**+*a.* stand up for; **мой часы́ стоя́т** my watch has stopped; **рабо́та стои́т** work has come to a standstill; **сто́й(те)!** stop! halt!; **~ во главе́**+*g.* head, be at the head of; **~ ла́герем** be encamped, be under canvas; **~ на коле́нях** kneel, be kneeling; **~ у вла́сти** be in power, be in office; **стоя́ла хоро́шая пого́да** the weather kept fine. **стоя́чий** standing; upright, vertical; stagnant.

сто́ящий deserving; worthwhile.

стр. *abbr.* (*of* **страни́ца**) p., page.

страда́лец, -льца sufferer. **страда́ние, -я** suffering. **страда́тельный** passive. **страда́ть, -а́ю** *or* **-ра́жду** *impf.* (*pf.* **по~**) suffer; be subject; be in pain; be weak, be poor; **~ за**+*g.* feel for; **~ по**+*d. or p.* miss, long for, pine for; **~ от зубно́й бо́ли** have toothache.

стра́жа, -и guard, watch; **взять под стра́жу** take into custody; **под стра́жей** under arrest, in custody; **стоя́ть на стра́же**+*g.* guard.

страна́, -ы́; *pl.* **-ы** country; land; **~ све́та** cardinal point.

страни́ца, -ы page.

стра́нник, -а, стра́нница, -ы wanderer; pilgrim.

стра́нно *adv.* strangely, oddly. **стра́нность, -и** strangeness; oddity, eccentricity, singularity. **стра́нн|ый; -а́нен, -анна́, -о** strange; funny, odd, queer.

стра́нствие, -я wandering, journeying, travelling. **стра́нствовать, -твую** *impf.* wander, journey, travel.

Страсбу́рг, -а Strasbourg.

Страстн|о́й of Holy Week; **~а́я пя́тница** Good Friday.

стра́стный; -тен, -тна́, -о passionate; impassioned; ardent. **стра́сть, -и**; *g.pl.* **-е́й** passion; +**к**+*d.* passion for; **до стра́сти** passionately. **страсть** *adv.* awfully, frightfully; an awful lot, a terrific number.

страте́г, -а strategist. **стратеги́ческий** strategic. **страте́гия, -и** strategy.

стратоста́т, -а stratosphere balloon. **страто-**

сфéра, -ы stratosphere. **стратосфéрный** stratospheric.
стрáус, -а ostrich. **стрáусовый** ostrich.
страх, -а (-у) fear; terror; risk, responsibility; **на свой ~** at one's own risk; **под ~ом смéрти** on pain of death. **страх** *adv.* terribly.
страхкáсса, -ы insurance office. **страховáние, -я** insurance; **~ жи́зни** life insurance; **~ от огня́** fire insurance. **страховáть, -хýю** *impf.* (*pf.* **за~**) insure (**от**+*g.* against); **~ся** insure o.s. **страхóвка, -и** insurance; guarantee.
стрáшно *adv.* terribly, awfully. **стрáшн|ый; -шен, -шнá, -о** terrible, awful, dreadful, frightful, fearful; terrifying, frightening; **~ый сон** bad dream.
стрекозá, -ы́; *pl.* **-ы** dragonfly.
стрéкот, -а, стрекотня́, -и́ chirr; rattle, chatter, clatter. **стрекотáть, -очý, -óчешь** *impf.* chirr; rattle, chatter, clatter.
стрелá, -ы́; *pl.* **-ы** arrow; shaft; dart; arm, boom, jib; derrick. **стрелéц, -льцá** Sagittarius. **стрéлка, -и** pointer, indicator; needle; arrow; spit; points. **стрелкóвый** rifle; shooting, fire; small-arms; infantry. **стрелови́дность, -и** angle, sweep. **стрелови́дн|ый** arrow-shaped; **~ое крылó** swept-back wing. **стрелóк, -лкá** shot; rifleman, gunner. **стрéлочник, -а** pointsman. **стрельбá, -ы́**; *pl.* **-ы** shooting, firing; shoot, fire. **стрельнýть, -нý, -нёшь** *pf.* fire, fire a shot; rush away. **стрéльчатый** lancet; arched, pointed. **стрéляный** shot; used, fired, spent; that has been under fire. **стреля́ть, -я́ю** *impf.* shoot; fire; **~ глазáми** dart glances; make eyes; **~ кнутóм** crack a whip.
стремглáв *adv.* headlong.
стременнóй stirrup.
стреми́тельный swift, headlong; impetuous. **стреми́ться, -млю́сь** *impf.* strive; seek, aspire; try; rush, speed, charge. **стремлéние, -я** striving, aspiration. **стремни́на, -ы** rapid, rapids; precipice.
стрéмя, -мени; *pl.* **-менá, -мя́н, -áм** *nt.* stirrup. **стремя́нка, -и** step-ladder, steps. **стремя́нный** stirrup.
стрехá, -и́; *pl.* **-и** eaves.
стригáльщик, -а shearer. **стри́женый** short; short-haired, cropped; shorn, sheared; clipped. **стри́жка, -и** hair-cut; cut; shearing; clipping. **стричь, -игý, -ижёшь; -иг** *impf.* (*pf.* **о~**) cut, clip; cut the hair of; shear; cut into pieces; **~ся** cut one's hair, have one's hair cut; wear one's hair short.
строгáль, -я́ *m.*, **строгáльщик, -а** plane operator, planer. **строгáльный** planing; **~ резéц** planer, cutter. **строгáть, -áю** *impf.* (*pf.* **вы́~**) plane, shave.
стрóгий strict; severe; stern. **стрóгость, -и** strictness; severity; *pl.* strong measures.
строев|óй combatant; line; drill; **~áя слýжба** combatant service. **строéние, -я** building; structure; composition; texture.
строжáйший, стрóже *superl.* & *comp.* of **стрóгий**
строи́тель, -я *m.* builder. **строи́тельн|ый** building, construction; **~ое искýсство** civil engineering; **~ая площáдка** building site. **строи́тельство, -а** building, construction; building site, construction site. **стрóить, -óю** *impf.* (*pf.* **по~**) build; construct; make; formulate, express; base; draw up, form up; **~ся** be built, be under construction; draw up, form up; **стрóйся!** fall in! **строй, -я,** *loc.* **-ю́**; *pl.* **-и** *or* **-и́, -ев** *or* **-ёв** system; order; régime; structure; pitch; formation; service, commission. **стрóйка, -и** building, construction; building-site. **стрóйность, -и** proportion; harmony; balance, order. **стрóйный; -óен, -ойнá, -о** harmonious, well-balanced, orderly, well put together, well-proportioned, shapely.
строкá, -и́, *a.* **-óкý**; *pl.* **-и, -áм** line; **крáсная ~** break-line, new paragraph.
строп, -а, стрóпа, -ы sling; shroud line.
стропи́ло, -а rafter, truss, beam.
стропти́в|ый obstinate, refractory; **~ая** *sb.* shrew.
строфá, -ы́; *pl.* **-ы, -áм** stanza, strophe.
строчёный stitched; hem-stitched. **строчи́ть, -чý, -óчи́шь** *impf.* (*pf.* **на~, про~**) sew, stitch; back-stitch; scribble, dash off. **стрóчка, -и** stitch; back-stitching; hem-stitching; line.
строчнóй lower-case, small.
стрóю *etc.*: *see* **стрóить**
струг, -а plane. **стругáть, -áю** *impf.* (*pf.* **вы́~**) plane, shave. **стрýжка, -и** shaving, filing.
струи́ться, -и́тся *impf.* stream, flow.
структýра, -ы structure. **структýрный** structural; structured.
струнá, -ы́; *pl.* **-ы** string. **стрýнный** stringed.
с|трýсить, -ýшу *pf.*
стручкóвый leguminous, podded; **~ пéрец** capsicum; **~ горóшек** peas in the pod. **стручóк, -чкá** pod.
струя́, -и́; *pl.* **-и, -уй** jet, spurt, stream; current; spirit; impetus.
стря́пать, -аю *impf.* (*pf.* **со~**) cook; cook up; concoct. **стряпня́, -и́** cooking. **стряпýха, -и** cook.
стря́хивать, -аю *impf.*, **стряхнýть, -нý, -нёшь** *pf.* shake off.
ст. ст. *abbr.* (*of* **стáрый стиль**) OS, Old Style (*of calendar*).
студенéть, -éет *impf.* (*pf.* **за~**) thicken, set. **студени́стый** jelly-like.
студéнт, -а, студéнтка, -и student. **студéнческий** student.
стýдень, -дня *m.* jelly; galantine; aspic.
студи́ец, -и́йца, студи́йка, -и student. **студи́йный** studio.
студи́ть, -ужý, -ýдишь *impf.* (*pf.* **о~**) cool.
стýдия, -и studio, workshop; school.
стук, -а knock; tap; thump; rumble; clatter.

сту́кать, -аю *impf.*, **сту́кнуть, -ну** *pf.* knock; bang; tap; rap; hit, strike; **~ся** knock (o.s.), bang, bump.

стул, -а; *pl.* **-лья, -льев** chair. **стульча́к, -а́** (*lavatory*) seat. **сту́льчик, -а** stool.

сту́па, -ы mortar.

ступа́ть, -а́ю *impf.*, **ступи́ть, -плю́, -пишь** *pf.* step; tread; **ступа́й(те)!** be off! clear out! **ступе́нчатый** stepped, graduated, graded; multi-stage. **ступе́нь, -и**; *g.pl.* **-е́не́й** step, rung; stage, grade, level, phase. **ступня́, -и́** foot; sole.

стуча́ть, -чу́ *impf.* (*pf.* **по~**) knock; bang; tap; rap; chatter; hammer, pulse, thump, pound; **~ся в**+*a.* knock at.

стушева́ться, -шу́юсь *pf.* **стушёвываться, -аюсь** *impf.* efface o.s., retire to the background; be covered with confusion; shade off, fade out.

с|туши́ть, -шу́, -шишь *pf.*

стыд, -а́ shame. **стыди́ть, -ыжу́** *impf.* (*pf.* **при~**) shame, put to shame; **~ся** (*pf.* **по~ся**) be ashamed. **стыдли́вый** bashful. **сты́дн|ый** shameful; **~о!** (for) shame! **~о** *impers.+d.* **ему́ ~о** he is ashamed; **как тебе́ не ~о!** you ought to be ashamed of yourself!

стык, -а joint; junction; meeting-point. **стыкова́ть, -ку́ю** *impf.* (*pf.* **со~**) join end to end; dock; **~ся** (*pf.* **при~ся**) dock. **стыко́вка, -и** docking. **стыко́вочный** docking.

сты́нуть, стыть, -ы́ну; стыл *impf.* cool; get cold; run cold; freeze.

сты́чка, -и skirmish, clash; squabble.

стюарде́сса, -ы stewardess; air hostess.

стя́гивать, -аю *impf.*, **стяну́ть, -ну́, -нешь** *pf.* tighten; pull together; gather, assemble; pull off; pinch, steal; **~ся** tighten; gird o.s. tightly; gather, assemble.

суббо́та, -ы Saturday.

субсиди́ровать, -рую *impf.* & *pf.* subsidize. **субси́дия, -и** subsidy, grant.

субти́тр, -а subtitle.

субтропи́ческий subtropical.

субъе́кт, -а subject; self, ego; person, individual; character, type. **субъекти́вный** subjective.

сувере́н, -а sovereign. **суверените́т, -а** sovereignty. **сувере́нный** sovereign.

сугли́нок, -нка loam.

сугро́б, -а snowdrift.

сугу́бо *adv.* especially, particularly; exclusively.

суд, -а́ court; law-court; legal proceedings; the judges; the bench; judgement, verdict; **пода́ть в ~ на**+*a.* bring an action against; **~ че́сти** court of honour.

суда́ *etc.*: *see* **суд, су́дно**[1]

суда́к, -а́ pike-perch.

суде́бный judicial; legal; forensic. **суде́йский** judge's; referee's, umpire's. **суде́йство, -а** refereeing, umpiring; judging. **суди́мость, -и** previous convictions, record.

суди́ть, сужу́, су́дишь *impf.* judge; form an opinion; try; pass judgement; referee, umpire; foreordain; **~ся** go to law.

су́дно[1]**, -а**; *pl.* **-да́, -о́в** vessel, craft.

су́дно[2]**, -а**; *g.pl.* **-ден** bed-pan.

судоводи́тель, -я *m.* navigator. **судовожде́ние, -я** navigation. **судово́й** ship's; marine.

судомо́йка, -и kitchen-maid, scullery maid, washer-up; scullery.

судопроизво́дство, -а legal proceedings.

су́дорога, -и cramp, convulsion, spasm. **су́дорожный** convulsive, spasmodic.

судострое́ние, -я shipbuilding. **судострои́тельный** shipbuilding. **судохо́дный** navigable; shipping; **~ кана́л** ship canal.

судьба́, -ы́; *pl.* **-ы, -деб** fate, fortune, destiny, lot; **каки́ми судьба́ми?** how do you come to be here?

судья́, -и́; *pl.* **-и, -е́й, -ям** *m.* judge; referee; umpire.

суеве́р, -а superstitious person. **суеве́рие, -я** superstition. **суеве́рный** superstitious.

суета́, -ы́ bustle, fuss. **суети́ться, -ечу́сь** *impf.* bustle, fuss. **суетли́вый** fussy, bustling.

сужде́ние, -я opinion; judgement.

су́женая *sb.* fiancée; intended (*wife*). **су́женый** *sb.* fiancé; intended (*husband*).

суже́ние, -я narrowing; constriction. **су́живать, -аю** *impf.*, **су́зить, -у́жу** *pf.* narrow, contract; make too narrow; **~ся** narrow; taper.

сук, -а́, *loc.* **-у́**; *pl.* **су́чья, -ьев** *or* **-и́, -о́в** bough; knot.

су́ка, -и bitch. **су́кин** *adj.*; **~ сын** son of a bitch.

сукно́, -а́; *pl.* **-а, -кон** cloth; **положи́ть под ~** shelve. **суко́нный** cloth; rough, clumsy, crude.

сули́ть, -лю́ *impf.* (*pf.* **по~**) promise.

султа́н[1]**, -а** sultan.

султа́н[2]**, -а** plume.

сума́, -ы́ bag; pouch.

сумасбро́д, -а, сумасбро́дка, -и madcap. **сумасбро́дный** wild, extravagant. **сумасбро́дство, -а** extravagance, wild behaviour. **сумасше́дш|ий** mad; lunatic; **~ий** *sb.* madman, lunatic; **~ая** *sb.* madwoman, lunatic. **сумасше́ствие, -я** madness, lunacy.

сумато́ха, -и hurly-burly, turmoil; bustle; confusion, chaos.

сумбу́р, -а confusion, chaos. **сумбу́рный** confused, chaotic.

су́меречный twilight; crepuscular. **су́мерки, -рек** *pl.* twilight, dusk; half-light.

суме́ть, -е́ю *pf.+inf.* be able to, manage to.

су́мка, -и bag; handbag; shopping-bag; case; satchel; pouch.

су́мма, -ы sum. **сумма́рный** summary; total. **сумми́ровать, -рую** *impf.* & *pf.* sum up, total up; summarize.

су́мрак, -а dusk, twilight; murk. **су́мрачный** gloomy; murky; dusky.

су́мчатый marsupial.
сунду́к, -а́ trunk, box, chest.
су́нуть(ся, -ну(сь *pf. of* **сова́ть(ся**
суп, -а (-у); *pl.* **-ы́** soup.
суперобло́жка, -и dust-jacket.
супов|о́й soup; **~а́я ло́жка** soup-spoon; **~а́я ми́ска** soup-tureen.
супру́г, -а husband, spouse; *pl.* husband and wife, (*married*) couple. **супру́га, -и** wife, spouse. **супру́жеск|ий** conjugal, matrimonial; **~ая изме́на** infidelity. **супру́жество, -а** matrimony, wedlock.
сургу́ч, -а́ sealing-wax.
surди́нка —

сурди́нка, -и mute; **под сурди́нку** on the quiet, on the sly. **сурдока́мера, -ы** soundproof room.
суро́вость, -и severity, sternness. **суро́в|ый** severe, stern; rigorous; bleak; unbleached, brown; **~ое полотно́** crash; brown holland.
суро́к, -рка́ marmot.
суррога́т, -а substitute.
су́слик, -а ground-squirrel.
су́сло, -а must; wort; grape-juice.
суста́в, -а joint, articulation.
су́тки, -ток *pl.* twenty-four hours; a day (and a night); **дво́е с полови́ной су́ток** sixty hours.
су́толока, -и commotion, hubbub, hurly-burly.
су́точн|ый twenty-four hour; daily; per diem; round-the-clock; **~ые де́ньги, ~ые** *sb., pl.* per diem allowance.
суту́литься, -люсь *impf.* stoop. **суту́лый** round-shouldered, stooping.
суть, -и essence, main point; **по су́ти де́ла** as a matter of fact, in point of fact; **~ де́ла** the heart of the matter.
суфлёр, -а prompter. **суфлёрск|ий** prompt; **~ая бу́дка** prompt-box. **суфли́ровать, -рую** *impf.+d.* prompt.
суха́рь, -я́ *m.* rusk; *pl.* bread-crumbs. **су́хо** *adv.* drily; coldly.
сухожи́лие, -я tendon, sinew.
сухо́й; сух, -а́, -о dry; dried-up; arid; dried; withered; chilly, cold. **сухопу́тный** land. **су́хость, -и** dryness, aridity; chilliness, coldness. **сухоща́вый** lean, skinny.
сучи́ть, -чу́, су́чишь *impf.* (*pf.* **с~**) twist, spin; throw; roll out.
сучкова́тый knotty; gnarled. **сучо́к, -чка́** twig; knot.
су́ша, -и (dry) land. **су́ше** *comp. of* **сухо́й.** **сушёный** dried. **суши́лка, -и** dryer; drying-room. **суши́льня, -и**; *g.pl.* **-лен** drying-room. **суши́ть, -шу́, -шишь** *impf.* (*pf.* **вы́~**) dry, dry out, dry up; **~ся** dry, get dry.
суще́ственный essential, vital; material; important. **существи́тельное** *sb.* noun, substantive. **существо́, -а́** being, creature; essence. **существова́ние, -я** existence. **существова́ть, -тву́ю** *impf.* exist. **су́щий** existing; real; absolute, utter, downright. **су́щность, -и** essence; **~ де́ла** the point; **в су́щности** in essence, at bottom; as a matter of fact.
сую́ *etc.*: *see* **сова́ть.** **с|фабрикова́ть, -ку́ю** *pf.* **с|фальши́вить, -влю** *pf.*
с|фантази́ровать, -рую *pf.*
сфе́ра, -ы sphere; realm; zone, area; **~ влия́ния** sphere of influence. **сфери́ческий** spherical
с|формирова́ть(ся, -ру́ю(сь *pf.* **с|формова́ть, -му́ю** *pf.* **с|формули́ровать, -рую** *pf.*
с|фотографи́ровать(ся, -рую(сь *pf.*
с.-х. *abbr.* (*of* **се́льское хозя́йство**) agriculture.
схвати́ть, -ачу́, -а́тишь *pf.* **схва́тывать, -аю** *impf.* (*impf. also* **хвата́ть**) seize; catch; grasp, comprehend; clamp together; **~ся** snatch, catch; grapple, come to grips. **схва́тка, -и** skirmish, fight, encounter; squabble; *pl.* contractions; fit, spasm; **родовы́е схва́тки** labour.
схе́ма, -ы diagram, chart; sketch; outline, plan; circuit. **схемати́ческий** diagrammatic, schematic; sketchy, over-simplified. **схемати́чный** sketchy, over-simplified.
с|хитри́ть, -рю́ *pf.*
схлы́нуть, -нет *pf.* (break and) flow back; break up, rush away; subside, vanish.
сход, -а coming off, alighting; descent; gathering, assembly. **сходи́ть[1](ся, -ожу́(сь, -о́дишь(ся** *impf. of* **сойти́(сь.** **с|ходи́ть[2], -ожу́, -о́дишь** *pf.* go; +**за**+*i.* go for, go to fetch. **схо́дка, -и** gathering, assembly, meeting. **схо́дный; -ден, -дна́, -о** similar; reasonable, fair. **схо́дня, -и**; *g.pl.* **-ей** (*usu. pl.*) gangway, gang-plank. **схо́дство, -а** likeness, similarity, resemblance.
схола́стика, -и scholasticism. **схоласти́ческий** scholastic.
с|хорони́ть(ся, -ню́(сь, -нишь(ся *pf.*
сцеди́ть, -ежу́, -е́дишь *pf.*, **сце́живать, -аю** *impf.* strain off, pour off, decant.
сце́на, -ы stage; scene. **сцена́рий, -я** scenario; script; stage directions. **сценари́ст, -а** script-writer. **сцени́ческ|ий** stage; **~ая рема́рка** stage direction. **сцени́чный** good theatre.
сцеп, -а coupling; drawbar. **сцепи́ть, -плю́, -пишь** *pf.*, **сцепля́ть, -я́ю** *impf.* couple; **~ся** be coupled; grapple, come to grips. **сце́пка, -и** coupling. **сцепле́ние, -я** coupling; adhesion; cohesion; accumulation, chain; clutch.
счастли́вец, -вца, счастли́вчик, -а lucky man. **счастли́вица, -ы** lucky woman. **счастли́в|ый; сча́стли́в** happy; lucky, fortunate; successful; **~ая иде́я** happy thought; **~ого пути́, ~ого пла́вания** bon voyage, pleasant journey. **сча́стье, -я** happiness; luck, good fortune.
сче́сть(ся, сочту́(сь, -тёшь(ся; счёл(ся, сочла́(сь *pf. of* **счита́ть(ся.** **счёт, -а (-у)**, *loc.* **-у́**; *pl.* **-а́** bill; account; counting, calculation, reckoning; score; expense; **быть на хоро́шем ~у́** be in good repute, stand well; **в два ~а**

in two ticks, in two shakes; **за ~**+*g.* at the expense of; **на ~** on account; +*g.* on the account, to the account, of; **потеря́ть ~**+*d.* lose count of. **счётн|ый** counting, calculating, computing; accounts, accounting; **~ая лине́йка** slide-rule; **~ая маши́на** calculating machine. **счетово́д, -а** accountant, book-keeper. **счетово́дчество, -а** accounting, book-keeping. **счётчик, -а, счётчица, -ы** teller; counter; meter. **счёты, -ов** *pl.* abacus.

счи́стить, -и́щу *pf.* (*impf.* **счища́ть**) clean off; clear away; **~ся** come off, clean off.

счита́ть, -а́ю *impf.* (*pf.* **со~, счесть**) count; compute, reckon; consider, think; regard (as); **~ся** (*pf. also* **по~ся**) settle accounts; be considered, be thought, be reputed; be regarded (as); **+с**+*i.* take into consideration; take into account, reckon with.

счища́ть(ся, -а́ю(сь *impf. of* **счи́стить(ся**

США *abbr.* (*of* ***Соединённые Шта́ты Аме́рики***) USA, United States of America.

сшиба́ть, -а́ю *impf.*, **сшиби́ть, -бу́, -бёшь; сшиб** *pf.* strike, hit, knock (off); **~ с ног** knock down; **~ся** collide; come to blows.

сшива́ть, -а́ю *impf.*, **с|шить, сошью́, -ьёшь** *pf.* sew; sew together, sew up. **сши́вка, -и** sewing together.

съ... *vbl. pref.*: *see* **с...**

съеда́ть, -а́ю *impf. of* **съесть. съедо́бный** edible; eatable, nice.

съе́ду *etc.*: *see* **съе́хать**

съёживаться, -аюсь *impf.*, **съ|ёжиться, -жусь** *pf.* huddle up; shrivel, shrink.

съезд, -а congress; conference, convention; arrival, gathering. **съе́здить, -зжу** *pf.* go, drive, travel.

съезжа́ть(ся, -а́ю(сь *impf. of* **съе́хать(ся**

съел *etc.*: *see* **съесть**

съём, -а removal. **съёмка, -и** removal; survey, surveying; plotting; exposure; shooting. **съёмный** detachable, removable. **съёмщик, -а, съёмщица, -ы** tenant, lessee; surveyor.

съестн|о́й food; **~ы́е припа́сы, ~о́е** *sb.* food supplies, provisions, eatables, food-stuffs. **съ|есть, -ем, -ешь, -ест, -еди́м; съел** *pf.* (*impf. also* **съеда́ть**)

съе́хать, -е́ду *pf.* (*impf.* **съезжа́ть**) go down; come down; move, remove; slip; **~ся** meet; arrive, gather, assemble.

съ|язви́ть, -влю́ *pf.*

сы́воротка, -и whey; serum. **сы́вороточный** serum; serous.

сы́гранность, -и team-work. **сыгра́ть, -а́ю** *pf. of* **игра́ть; ~ся** play (well) together, play as a team.

сымпровизи́ровать, -рую *pf.* of **импровизи́ровать**

сын, -а; *pl.* **сыновья́, -е́й** *or* **-ы́, -о́в** son. **сыно́вий, сыно́вний** filial. **сыно́к, -нка́** little son, little boy; sonny.

сы́пать, -плю *impf.* pour; strew; pour forth; **~ся** fall; pour out, run out; scatter; fly; rain down; fray. **сыпно́й тиф** typhus. **сыпу́ч|ий** friable; free-flowing; shifting; **ме́ры ~их тел** dry measures; **~ий песо́к** quicksand; shifting sand. **сыпь, -и** rash, eruption.

сыр, -а (-у), *loc.* **-у́**; *pl.* **-ы́** cheese.

сыре́ть, -е́ю *impf.* (*pf.* **от~**) become damp.

сыре́ц, -рца́ unfinished product, raw product; **шёлк-~** raw silk.

сы́рник, -а curd fritter. **сы́рный** cheese; cheesy. **сырова́р, -а** cheese-maker. **сырова́рение, -я, сыроде́лие, -я** cheese-making.

сыр|о́й; сыр, -а́, -о damp; raw; uncooked; unfinished; green, unripe; **~а́я вода́** unboiled water; **~ы́е материа́лы** raw materials. **сы́рость, -и** dampness, humidity. **сырьё, -я́** raw material(s).

сыск, -а investigation, detection. **сыска́ть, сыщу́, сы́щешь** *pf.* find; **~ся** be found, come to light. **сыскно́й** investigation.

сы́тный; -тен, -тна́, -о satisfying, substantial, copious. **сы́тость, -и** satiety, repletion. **сы́тый; сыт, -а́, -о** satisfied, replete, full; fat; **~ по го́рло** full up; **~ скот** fat stock.

сыч, -а́ little owl.

сы́щик, -а, сы́щица, -ы detective.

с|эконо́мить, -млю *pf.*

сюда́ *adv.* here, hither.

сюже́т, -а subject; plot; topic. **сюже́тный** subject; based on, having, a theme.

сюи́та, -ы (*mus.*) suite.

сюрпри́з, -а surprise.

сюрреали́зм, -а surrealism. **сюрреали́ст, -а** surrealist.

сюрту́к, -а́ frock-coat.

сюсю́кать, -аю *impf.* lisp.

сяк *adv.*: *see* **так сям** *adv.*: *see* **там**

Т

т *letter*: *see* **тэ**

т *abbr.* (*of* **то́нна**) t., ton(s), tonne(s).

т. *abbr.* (*of* **това́рищ**) Comrade; (*of* **том**) vol., volume.

та *see* **тот**

таба́к, -а́ (-у́) tobacco; snuff. **табаке́рка, -и** snuff-box. **таба́чн|ый** tobacco; **~ого цве́та** snuff-coloured.

та́бель, -я; *pl.* **-и, -ей** *or* **-я́, -е́й** *m.* table, list, scale. **та́бельн|ый** table; time; **~ые часы́** time-clock. **та́бельщик, -а, -щица, -ы** time-keeper.

табле́тка, -и tablet.

табли́ца, -ы table; list; plate; **~ вы́игрышей** prize-list; **табли́цы логари́фмов** logarithm tables; ~ **Менделе́ева** periodic table; ~ **умноже́ния** multiplication table. **табли́чный** tabular; standard.

та́бор, -а camp; gipsy encampment. **та́борный** camp; gypsy.

табуля́тор, -а tabulator.

табу́н, -а́ herd.

табуре́т, -а, табуре́тка, -и stool.

таврёный branded. **тавро́, -а́**; *pl.* **-а, -а́м** brand.

Таджикиста́н, -а Tadzhikistan.

таёжник, -а, -ница, -ы taiga dweller. **таёжный** taiga.

таз, -а, *loc.* **-у́**; *pl.* **-ы́** basin; wash-basin; pelvis. **тазобе́дренный** hip; ~ **суста́в** hip-joint. **та́зовый** pelvic.

таи́нственный mysterious; enigmatic; secret; secretive. **таи́ть, таю́** *impf.* hide, conceal; harbour; **~ся** hide, be in hiding; lurk.

Тайва́нь, -я Taiwan.

тайга́, -и́ taiga.

тайко́м *adv.* in secret, surreptitiously, by stealth; ~ **от**+*g.* behind the back of.

тайм, -а half; period of play.

та́йна, -ы mystery; secret. **тайни́к, -а́** hiding-place; *pl.* secret places, recesses. **тайнопи́сный** cryptographic. **та́йнопись, -и** cryptography, cryptogram. **та́йный** secret; clandestine; privy; ~ **сове́тник** Privy Councillor (*3rd grade*: *see* **чин**).

так *adv.* so; thus, in this way, like this; in such a way; as it should be; just like that; **и** ~ even so; as it is, as it stands; **и** ~ **да́лее** and so on, and so forth; **и** ~ **и сяк** this way and that; **мы сде́лали** ~ this is what we did, we did it this way; **не** ~ amiss, wrong; **про́сто** ~, ~ **(то́лько)** for no special reason, just for fun; ~ **же** in the same way; ~ **же... как** as ... as; ~ **и** simply, just; ~ **и быть** all right, right you are; ~ **и есть** I thought so!; ~ **ему́ и на́до** serves him right; ~ **и́ли ина́че** in any event, whatever happens; one way or another; ~ **себе́** so-so, middling, not too good; **что́-то бы́ло не совсе́м** ~ something was amiss, something was not quite right; **я** ~ **и забы́л** I clean forgot. **так** *conj.* then; so; **не сего́дня,** ~ **за́втра** if not today, then tomorrow; ~ **как** as, since. **так** *part.* yes.

такела́ж, -а rigging; tackle, gear. **такела́жник, -а** rigger, scaffolder. **такела́жный** rigging; scaffolding.

та́кже *adv.* also, too, as well.

-таки *part.* after all; **всё~** nevertheless; **опя́ть~** again; **та́к~** after all, really.

тако́в *m.*, **-а́** *f.*, **-о́** *nt.*, **-ы́** *pl.*, *pron.* such; **все они́ ~ы́** they are all the same.

так|о́й *pron.* such; so; a kind of; **в ~о́м слу́чае** in that case; **кто он ~о́й?** who is he?; **~о́й же** the same; **~и́м о́бразом** thus, in this way; **что ~о́е?** what's that? what did you say?; **что э́то ~о́е?** what is this? **тако́й-то** *pron.* so-and-so; such-and-such.

та́кса, -ы fixed price, statutory price; tariff. **takса́тор, -а** price-fixer; valuer. **такса́ция, -и** price-fixing; valuation.

такси́ *nt.indecl.* taxi.

такси́ровать, -рую *impf.* & *pf.* fix the price of, value.

такси́ст, -а taxi-driver. **таксомото́рный** taxi. **таксомото́рщик, -а** taxi-driver. **таксопа́рк, -а** taxi-depot, fleet of taxis.

такт, -а time; measure; bar; stroke; tact.

та́к-таки *see* **-таки**

та́ктик, -а tactician. **та́ктика, -и** tactics. **такти́ческий** tactical. **такти́чность, -и** tact. **такти́чный** tactful.

та́ктов|ый time, timing; **~ая черта́** bar-line.

тала́нт, -а talent, gift; talented man. **тала́нтливый** talented, gifted.

та́лия, -и waist.

Та́ллин, -а Tallin(n).

тало́н, -а, тало́нчик, -а coupon; stub; ~ **на обе́д** luncheon voucher; **поса́дочный** ~ boarding pass; landing card.

та́л|ый thawed, melted; **~ая вода́** melted snow; **~ый снег** slush.

там *adv.* there; **и** ~ **и сям** here, there, and everywhere; ~ **же** in the same place; ibid, *ibidem.*

тамада́, -ы́ *m.* master of ceremonies; toast-master.

та́мбур¹, -а tambour; lobby; platform. **та́мбур², -а** tambour-stitch, chain-stitch. **та́мбурный** tambour; ~ **шов** tambour-stitch; chain-stitch.

тамо́женный customs. **тамо́жня, -и** custom-house.

тампо́н, -а (*med.*) tampon, plug; **гигиени́ческий** ~ sanitary towel, pad.

та́нгенс, -а tangent. **тангенциа́льный** tangential.

та́нец, -нца dance; dancing.

та́нковый tank, armoured.

танцева́льный dancing; ~ **ве́чер** dance. **танцева́ть, -цу́ю** *impf.* dance. **танцо́вщик, -а, танцо́вщица, -ы** (ballet) dancer. **танцо́р, -а, танцо́рка, -и** dancer.

та́пка, -и, та́почка, -и (*heelless*) slipper; sports shoe, gym shoe.

та́ра, -ы packing, packaging; tare.

align="left"тарака́н, -а cockroach; black-beetle.

тара́щить, -щу *impf.* (*pf.* **вы́~**); ~ **глаза́** goggle.

таре́лка, -и plate; disc; **быть не в свое́й таре́лке** feel uneasy, feel unsettled, be not quite o.s. **таре́льчатый** plate; disc.

тари́ф, -а tariff, rate. **тарифици́ровать, -рую** *impf.* & *pf.* tariff.

таска́ть, -а́ю *impf.* drag, lug; carry; pull; take; drag off; pull out; pinch, swipe; wear; **~ся** drag, trail; roam about, hang about.

тасова́ть, -су́ю *impf.* (*pf.* **с~**) shuffle. **тасо́вка, -и** shuffle, shuffling.

ТАСС *abbr.* (*of* ***Телегра́фное аге́нство Сове́тского Сою́за***) TASS, Telegraph Agency of the Soviet Union.

тафта́, -ы́ taffeta.
тахта́, -ы́ divan, ottoman.
тача́ть, -а́ю *impf.* (*pf.* **вы́~, с~**) stitch.
та́чка, -и wheelbarrow.
тащи́ть, -щу́, -щишь *impf.* (*pf.* **вы́~, с~**) pull; drag, lug; carry; take; drag off; pull out; pinch, swipe; **~ся** drag o.s. along; drag, trail.
та́яние, -я thaw, thawing. **та́ять, та́ю** *impf.* (*pf.* **рас~**) melt; thaw; melt away, dwindle, wane; waste away.
Тбили́си *m.indecl.* Tbilisi.
тварь, -и creature; creatures; wretch.
тверде́ть, -е́ет *impf.* (*pf.* **за~**) harden, become hard. **тверди́ть, -ржу́** *impf.* (*pf.* **вы́~, за~**) repeat, say again and again; memorize, learn by heart. **твёрдо** *adv.* hard; firmly, firm. **твердоло́бый** thick-skulled; diehard. **твёрд|ый** hard; firm; solid; stable; steadfast; **~ый знак** hard sign, ъ; **~ое те́ло** solid; **~ые це́ны** fixed prices. **тверды́ня, -и** stronghold.
твой, -его́ *m.*, **твоя́, -е́й** *f.*, **твоё, -его́** *nt.*, **твои́, -и́х** *pl.* your, yours; **твои́** *sb.*, *pl.* your people.
творе́ние, -я creation, work; creature; being. **творе́ц, -рца́** creator. **твори́тельный** instrumental. **твори́ть, -рю́** *impf.* (*pf.* **со~**) create; do; make; **~ чудеса́** work wonders; **~ся** happen, go on; **что тут твори́тся?** what is going on here?
тво́ро́г, -а́ (-у́) *or* **-а (-у)** curds; cottage cheese. **творо́жный** curd.
тво́рческий creative. **тво́рчество, -а** creation; creative work; works.
т.д.: и ~ (*of* **так да́лее**) etc., and so on.
те *see* **тот**
т.е. *abbr.* (*of* **то есть**) that is, i.e.
теа́тр, -а theatre; stage; plays, dramatic works. **театра́л, -а** theatre-goer, playgoer. **театра́льн|ый** theatre; theatrical; stagy; **~ая ка́сса** box-office. **театрове́дение, -я** drama studies.
тебя́ *etc.*: *see* **ты**
те́зис, -а thesis; proposition, point.
тёзка, -и namesake.
тёк *see* **течь**
текст, -а text; words, libretto, lyrics.
тексти́ль, -я *m.* textiles. **тексти́льный** textile. **тексти́льщик, -а, -щица, -ы** textile worker.
тексту́альный verbatim, word-for-word; textual.
теку́честь, -и fluidity; fluctuation; instability. **теку́чий** fluid; fluctuating, unstable. **теку́щ|ий** current, of the present moment; instant; routine, ordinary; **~ий ремо́нт** running repair(s), routine maintenance; **~ие собы́тия** current affairs; **~ий счёт** current account; **6-го числа́ ~его ме́сяца** the 6th inst.
тел. *abbr.* (*of* **телефо́н**) tel., telephone.
теле... *in comb.* tele-; television. **телеателье́** *nt.indecl.* TV repair workshop. **~ви́дение, -я** television. **~визио́нный** television, T.V. **~ви́зор, -а** television (set). **~гра́мма, -ы** telegram, wire. **~гра́ф, -а** telegraph (office). **~графи́ровать, -рую** *impf.* & *pf.* telegraph, wire. **~гра́фный** telegraph; telegraphic; **~гра́фный столб** telegraph-pole. **~журна́л, -а** current affairs programme (*on TV*). **~зри́тель, -я** *m.* (television) viewer. **~ма́н, -а** TV addict. **~мо́ст, -а** satellite (TV) link-up. **~объекти́в, -а** telephoto lens. **~пати́ческий** telepathic. **~па́тия, -и** telepathy. **~ско́п, -а** telescope. **~скопи́ческий** telescopic. **~ста́нция, -и** television station. **~сту́дия, -и** television studio. **~суфлёр, -а** teleprompter, Autocue (*propr.*). **~управле́ние, -я** remote control. **~фа́кс, -а** fax (machine). **~фо́н, -а** telephone; (telephone) number; **(по)звони́ть по ~фо́ну**+*d.* telephone, ring up; **~фон-автома́т, -а** public telephone, call-box. **~фони́ровать, -рую** *impf.* & *pf.* telephone. **~фони́ст, -а, -и́стка, -и** telephonist, (switchboard) operator. **~фони́я, -и** telephony. **~фо́нный** telephone; **~фо́нная кни́га** telephone directory; **~фо́нная ста́нция** telephone exchange; **~фо́нная тру́бка** handset, receiver. **~фотогра́фия, -и** telephotography. **~це́нтр, -а** television centre.
теле́га, -и cart, waggon. **теле́жка, -и** small cart; handcart; bogie, trolley. **теле́жный** cart.
телёнок, -нка; *pl.* **-я́та, -я́т** calf.
теле́сн|ый bodily; corporal; somatic; physical; corporeal; **~ое наказа́ние** corporal punishment; **~ого цве́та** flesh-coloured.
тели́ться, -ится *impf.* (*pf.* **о~**) calve. **тёлка, -и** heifer.
те́ло, -а; *pl.* **-а́** body; **держа́ть в чёрном те́ле** ill-treat, maltreat. **телогре́йка, -и** quilted jacket, padded jacket. **телодвиже́ние, -я** movement, motion; gesture. **телосложе́ние, -я** build, frame. **телохрани́тель, -я** *m.* bodyguard. **тельня́шка, -и** vest.
теля́та *etc.*: *see* **телёнок. теля́тина, -ы** veal. **теля́чий** calf; veal.
тем *conj.* (so much) the; **~ лу́чше** so much the better; **~ не ме́нее** none the less, nevertheless.
тем *see* **тот, тьма**[2]
те́ма, -ы subject; topic; theme. **тема́тика, -и** subject-matter; themes, subjects. **темати́ческий** subject; thematic.
тембр, -а timbre.
Те́мза, -ы the Thames.
темне́ть, -е́ет *impf.* (*pf.* **по~, с~**) grow dark, become dark; darken; show dark; **темне́ет** it gets dark, it is getting dark. **темни́ца, -ы** dungeon. **темно́** *pred.* it is dark. **темноко́жий** dark-skinned, dusky, swarthy. **тёмно-си́ний** dark blue. **темнота́, -ы́** dark, darkness; ignorance; backwardness. **тёмный** dark; obscure; vague; sombre; shady, fishy, suspicious; ignorant, benighted.
темп, -а tempo; rate, speed, pace.

те́мпера, -ы distemper; tempera.

темпера́мент, -а temperament. **темпера́ментный** temperamental; spirited.

температу́ра, -ы temperature; ~ **кипе́ния** boiling-point; ~ **замерза́ния** freezing-point.

те́мя, -мени *nt.* crown, top of the head.

тенденцио́зный tendentious, biased. **тенде́нция, -и** tendency; bias.

те́ндер, -а tender.

тенево́й, тени́стый shady.

те́ннис, -а tennis. **теннеси́ст, -а, -и́стка, -и** tennis-player. **те́ннисн|ый** tennis; **~ая площа́дка** tennis-court.

те́нор, -а; *pl.* **-а́, -о́в** (*mus.*) tenor.

тент, -а awning, canopy.

тень, -и, *loc.* **-и́**; *pl.* **-и, -е́й** shade; shadow; phantom; ghost; particle, vestige, atom; suspicion.

теологи́ческий theological. **теоло́гия, -и** theology.

теоре́ма, -ы theorem. **теоретизи́ровать, -рую** *impf.* theorize. **теоре́тик, -а** theorist. **теорети́ческий** theoretical. **тео́рия, -и** theory.

теософи́ческий theosophical. **теосо́фия, -и** theosophy.

тепе́решн|ий present; **в ~ее вре́мя** at the present time, nowadays. **тепе́рь** *adv.* now; nowadays, today.

тепле́ть, -е́ет *impf.* (*pf.* **по~**) get warm. **те́плиться, -ится** *impf.* flicker; glimmer. **тепли́ца, -ы** greenhouse, hothouse, conservatory. **тепли́чный** hothouse. **тепло́, -а́** heat; warmth. **тепло́** *adv.* warmly; *pred.* it is warm.

тепло... *in comb.* heat; thermal; thermo-. **теплово́з, -а** diesel locomotive. **~во́зный** diesel. **~ёмкость, -и** heat capacity, thermal capacity; heat. **~кро́вный** warm-blooded. **~обме́н, -а** heat exchange. **~прово́д, -а** hot-water system. **~прово́дный** heat-conducting. **~сто́йкий** heat-proof, heat-resistant. **~те́хник, -а** heating engineer. **~те́хника, -и** heat engineering. **~хо́д, -а** motor ship. **~центра́ль, -и** (district) heating plant.

теплово́й heat; thermal; ~ **дви́гатель** heat-engine; ~ **уда́р** heat-stroke; thermal shock. **теплота́, -ы́** heat; warmth. **теплу́шка, -и** heated railway van. **тёплый; -пел, -пла́, тёпло́** warm; warmed, heated; cordial; kindly, affectionate; heartfelt.

терапе́вт, -а therapeutist. **терапи́я, -и** therapy; **интенси́вная** ~ intensive care.

тереби́ть, -блю́ *impf.* (*pf.* **вы́~**) pull, pick; pull at, pull about; pester, bother.

тере́ть, тру, трёшь; тёр *impf.* rub; grate, grind; chafe; **~ся** rub o.s.; **~ся о**+*a.* rub against; **~ся о́коло**+*g.* hang about, hang around; **~ся среди́**+*g.* mix with, hobnob with.

терза́ть, -а́ю *impf.* tear to pieces; pull about; torment, torture; **~ся**+*i.* suffer; be a prey to.

тёрка, -и grater.

те́рмин, -а term. **терминоло́гия, -и** terminology.

терми́ческий thermic, thermal. **термодина́мика, -и** thermodynamics. **термодинами́ческий** thermodynamic. **термо́метр, -а** thermometer. **термоста́т, -а** thermostat. **те́рмос, -а** thermos (flask). **термоя́дерный** thermonuclear.

тёрн, -а, терно́вник, -а sloe, blackthorn. **терни́стый, терно́вый** thorny, prickly.

терпели́вый patient. **терпе́ние, -я** patience; endurance, perseverance; **запасти́сь ~м** be patient. **терпе́ть, -плю́, -пишь** *impf.* (*pf.* **по~**) suffer; undergo; bear, endure, stand; have patience; tolerate, put up with; **вре́мя не те́рпит** there is no time to be lost, time is getting short; **вре́мя те́рпит** there is plenty of time; ~ **не могу́** I can't stand, I hate. **терпе́ться, -пится** *impf.*, *impers.*+*d.* **ему́ не те́рпится**+*inf.* he is impatient to. **терпи́мость, -и** tolerance; indulgence. **терпи́мый** tolerant; indulgent, forbearing; tolerable, bearable, supportable.

те́рпкий; -пок, -пка́, -о astringent; tart, sharp. **те́рпкость, -и** astringency; tartness, sharpness, acerbity.

терра́са, -ы terrace.

территориа́льный territorial. **террито́рия, -и** territory, confines, grounds; area.

терро́р, -а terror. **терроризи́ровать, -рую** *impf.* & *pf.* terrorize. **террори́зм, -а** terrorism; **возду́шный** ~ air piracy. **террори́ст, -а** terrorist; **возду́шный** ~ air pirate. **террористи́ческий** terrorist.

тёртый ground; grated; hardened, experienced.

теря́ть, -я́ю *impf.* (*pf.* **по~, у~**) lose; shed; ~ **в ве́се** lose weight; ~ **из виду** lose sight of; ~ **си́лу** become invalid; **~ся** get lost; disappear, vanish; fail, decline, decrease, weaken; become flustered; be at a loss; **~ся в дога́дках** be at a loss.

тёс, -а (-у) boards, planks. **теса́ть, тешу́, те́шешь** *impf.* cut, hew; trim, square.

тесёмка, -и tape, ribbon, lace, braid. **тесёмчатый** ribbon, braid; ~ **глист** tapeworm.

тесни́ть, -ню́ *impf.* (*pf.* **по~, с~**) press; crowd; squeeze, constrict; be too tight; **~ся** press through, push a way through; move up, make room; crowd, cluster, jostle. **те́сно** *adv.* closely; tightly; narrowly. **теснота́, -ы́** crowded state; narrowness; crush, squash. **те́сн|ый** crowded, cramped; narrow; (too) tight; close; compact; hard, difficult; **~о** it is crowded, there is not enough room.

тесо́вый board, plank.

те́сто, -а dough; pastry; paste.

тесть, -я *m.* father-in-law.

тесьма́, -ы́ tape, ribbon, lace, braid.

те́терев, -а; *pl.* **-а́** black grouse, blackcock. **тетёрка, -и** grey hen.

тётка, -и aunt.

тетра́дка, -и, тетра́дь, -и exercise book; copy-book; part, fascicule.

тётя, -и; *g.pl.* **-ей** aunt.

тех... *abbr.* (*of* **техни́ческий**) *in comb.* technical. **техми́нимум, -а** minimum (technical) qualifications. **~персона́л, -а** technical personnel. **~ре́д, -а** technical editor.

те́хник, -а technician. **те́хника, -и** machinery, technical equipment; technical devices; engineering; technology; technique, art. **те́хникум, -а** technical college, technical school. **техни́ческий** technical; engineering; maintenance; industrial; commercial(-grade); assistant, subordinate; **~ие усло́вия** specifications.

техно́лог, -а technologist. **технологи́ческий** technological. **техноло́гия, -и** technology; **высокосло́жная ~** high technology.

тече́ние, -я flow; course; current, stream; trend, tendency; **вверх по тече́нию** upstream.

течь, -чёт; тёк, -ла́ *impf.* flow; stream; pass; leak, be leaky.

те́шить, -шу *impf.* (*pf.* **по~**) amuse, entertain; gratify, please; **~ся** (+*i.*) amuse o.s. (with), play (with).

тешу́ *etc.*: *see* **теса́ть**

тёща, -и mother-in-law.

тигр, -а tiger. **тигри́ца, -ы** tigress. **тигро́вый** tiger.

ти́на, -ы slime, mud; mire. **ти́нистый** slimy, muddy.

тип, -а type. **типи́чный** typical. **типово́й** standard; model; type. **типогра́фия, -и** printing-house, press. **типогра́фск|ий** typographical; printing, printer's; **~ая кра́ска** printer's ink.

тир, -а shooting-range; shooting-gallery. **тира́да, -ы** tirade; sally.

тира́ж, -а́ draw; circulation; edition; **вы́йти в тира́ж** be drawn; have served one's turn, become redundant, be superannuated.

тира́н, -а tyrant **тирани́ческий** tyrannical. **тирани́я, -и** tyranny. **тира́нствовать, -вую** *impf.* (**над**+*i.*) tyrannize (over).

тире́ *nt.indecl.* dash.

ти́скать, -аю *impf.*, **ти́снуть, -ну** *pf.* press, squeeze; pull. **тиски́, -о́в** *pl.* vice; **в тиска́х**+*g.* in the grip of, in the clutches of. **тисне́ние, -я** stamping, printing; imprint; design. **тиснёный** stamped, printed.

ти́тул, -а title; title-page. **ти́тульный** title; **~ лист** title-page; **~ спи́сок** itemized list. **титуля́рный** titular; **~ сове́тник** Titular Councillor (*9th grade*: *see* **чин**).

тиф, -а, *loc.* **-у́** typhus; typhoid.

ти́хий; тих, -а́, -о quiet; low, soft, faint; silent, noiseless; still; calm; gentle; slow, slow-moving; **Т~ океа́н** the Pacific (Ocean); **~ ход** slow-speed, slow pace. **ти́хо** *adv.* quietly; softly; gently; silently, noiselessly; calmly; still; slowly. **тихоокеа́нский** Pacific. **ти́ше** *comp.* *of* **ти́хий, ти́хо; ти́ше!** quiet! silence! hush! gently! careful! **тишина́, -ы́** quiet, silence; stillness; **нару́шить тишину́** break the silence; **соблюда́ть тишину́** keep quiet.

т. к. *abbr.* (*of* **так как**) as, since.

тка́невый tissue. **тка́ный** woven. **ткань, -и** fabric, cloth; tissue; substance, essence. **ткать, тку, ткёшь; -ал, -ала́, -о** *impf.* (*pf.* **со~**) weave. **тка́цкий** weaver's, weaving; **~ стано́к** loom. **ткач, -а́, ткачи́ха, -и** weaver.

ткну́ть(ся, -у(сь, -ёшь(ся *pf.* *of* **ты́кать(ся**

тле́ние, -я decay, decomposition, putrefaction; smouldering. **тлеть, -е́ет** *impf.* rot, decay, decompose, putrefy; moulder; smoulder; **~ся** smoulder.

тмин, -а (-у) caraway-seeds.

то *pron.* that; **а не то́** or else, otherwise; **(да) и то́** and even then, and that; **то́ есть** that is (to say); **то и де́ло** every now and then. **то** *conj.* then; **не то..., не то** either ... or; whether ... or; half ..., half; **не то, что́бы..., но** it is (was) not that ..., (but); **то..., то** now ..., now; **то ли..., то ли** whether ... or; **то тут, то там** now here, now there.

-то *part.* just, precisely, exactly; **в то́м-то и де́ло** that's just it.

тобо́й *see* **ты**

тов. *abbr.* (*of* **това́рищ**) Comrade.

това́р, -а goods; wares; article; commodity.

това́рищ, -а comrade; friend; companion; colleague; person; assistant, deputy, vice-; **~ по рабо́те** colleague; mate; **~ по шко́ле** schoolfriend; **~ председа́теля** vice-president. **това́рищеск|ий** comradely; friendly; communal; unofficial; **с ~им приве́том** with fraternal greetings.

това́рищество, -а comradeship, fellowship; company; association, society.

това́рность, -и marketability. **това́рный** goods; freight; commodity; marketable; **~ ваго́н** goods truck; **~ склад** warehouse; **~ соста́в** goods train.

това́ро... *in comb.* commodity; goods. **товарообме́н, -а** barter, commodity exchange. **~оборо́т, -а** (sales) turnover; commodity circulation. **~отправи́тель, -я** *m.* consignor, forwarder (*of goods*). **~получа́тель, -я** *m.* consignee.

тогда́ *adv.* then; **~ как** whereas, while. **тогда́шний** of that time, of those days; the then.

того́ *see* **тот**

тожде́ственный identical, one and the same. **то́ждество, -а** identity.

то́же *adv.* also, as well, too.

ток, -а (-у); *pl.* **-и** current.

тока́рный turning; **~ стано́к** lathe. **то́карь, -я**; *pl.* **-я́, -е́й** *or* **-и, -ей** *m.* turner, lathe operator.

То́кио *m.indecl.* Tokyo.

толк, -а (-у) sense; understanding; use, profit; **бе́з ~у** senselessly, wildly; to no purpose;

знать ~ в+*p.* know what's what in; be a good judge of; **сбить с ~у** confuse, muddle; **с ~ом** sensibly, intelligently.

толкáть, -áю *impf.* (*pf.* **толкнýть**) push, shove; jog; **~ лóктем** nudge; **~ ядрó** put the shot; **~ся** jostle.

тóлки, -ов *pl.* talk; rumours, gossip.

толкнýть(ся, -нý(сь, -нёшь(ся *pf. of* **толкáть(ся**

толковáние, -я interpretation; *pl.* commentary. **толковáть, -кýю** *impf.* interpret; explain; talk; say; **лóжно ~** misinterpret, misconstrue. **толкóвый** intelligent, sensible; intelligible, clear; **~ словáрь** defining dictionary. **тóлком** *adv.* plainly, clearly.

толкотня́, -и́ crush, scrum, squash; crowding.

толкý *etc.*: *see* **толóчь**

толкýчий ры́нок flea market. **толкýчка, -и** crush, scrum, squash; crowded place; flea market.

толокнó, -á oatmeal.

толóчь, -лкý, -лчёшь; -лóк, -лклá *impf.* (*pf.* **ис~, рас~**) pound, crush.

толпá, -ы́; *pl.* **-ы** crowd; throng; multitude. **толпи́ться, -и́тся** *impf.* crowd; throng; cluster.

толстéть, -éю *impf.* (*pf.* **по~**) grow fat, get stout; put on weight. **толсти́ть, -и́т** *impf.* fatten; make look fat. **толстокóжий** thick-skinned; pachydermatous. **толстомóрдый** fat-faced. **тóлстый; -á, -о** fat; stout; thick; heavy. **толстя́к, -á** fat man; fat boy.

толчёный pounded, crushed; ground. **толчёт** *etc.*: *see* **толóчь**

толчея́, -и́ crush, scrum, squash.

толчóк, -чкá push, shove; put; jolt, bump; shock, tremor; incitement, stimulus.

тóлща, -и thickness; thick. **тóлще** *comp. of* **тóлстый. толщинá, -ы́** thickness; fatness, stoutness.

тóлько *adv.* only, merely; solely; just; **~ что** just, only just; **~-~** barely; *conj.* only, but; **(как) ~, (лишь) ~** as soon as; **~ бы** if only.

том, -а; *pl.* **~á** volume. **тóмик, -а** small volume, slim volume.

томи́тельный wearisome, tedious, wearing; tiresome, trying; agonizing. **томи́ть, -млю́** *impf.* (*pf.* **ис~**) tire, wear, weary; torment; wear down; stew, steam, braise; **~ся** pine; languish; be tormented. **томлéние, -я** languor. **томлёный** stewed, steamed, braised. **тóмность, -и** languor. **тóмный; -мен, -мнá, -о** languid, languorous.

тон, -а; *pl.* **-á** *or* **-ы, -óв** tone; note; shade; tint; **дурнóй ~** bad form; **хорóший ~** good form. **тонáльность, -и** key; tonality.

тóненький thin; slender, slim. **тóнкий; -нок, -нкá, -о** thin; slender, slim; fine; delicate; refined; dainty; subtle; nice; keen; crafty, sly; **~ вкус** refined taste; **~зáпах** delicate perfume; **~ знатóк** connoisseur; **~ слух** good ear; **~ сон** light sleep. **тóнкость, -и** thinness; slenderness, slimness; fineness; subtlety; nice point; nicety.

тóнна, -ы (*metric*) ton, tonne. **тоннáж, -а** tonnage.

тоннéль *see* **туннéль**

тонýть, -нý, -нешь *impf.* (*pf.* **по~, у~**) sink; drown; go down; be lost, be hidden, be covered.

тонфи́льм, -а sound film; (sound) recording.

тóньше *comp. of* **тóнкий**

тóпать, -аю *impf.* (*pf.* **тóпнуть**) stamp; **~ ногóй** stamp one's foot.

топи́ть[1]**, -плю́, -пишь** *impf.* (*pf.* **по~, у~**) sink; drown; wreck, ruin; **~ся** drown o.s.

топи́ть[2]**, -плю́, -пишь** *impf.* stoke; heat; melt (down); render; **~ся** burn, be alight; melt. **тóпка, -и** stoking; heating; melting (down); furnace, fire-box.

тóпкий boggy, marshy, swampy.

тóпливн|ый fuel; **~ая нефть** fuel oil. **тóпливо, -а** fuel.

тóпнуть, -ну *pf. of* **тóпать**

топóграф, -а topographer. **топографи́ческий** topographical. **топогрáфия, -и** topography.

тóполевый poplar. **тóполь, -я**; *pl.* **-я́** *or* **-и** *m.* poplar.

топóр, -á axe. **топóрик, -а** hatchet. **топори́ще, -а** axe-handle. **топóрный** axe; clumsy, crude; uncouth.

тóпот, -а tread; tramp; **кóнский ~** clatter of hooves. **топтáть, -пчý, -пчешь** *impf.* (*pf.* **по~**) trample (down); **~ся** stamp; **~ся на мéсте** mark time.

торг, -а, *loc.* **-ý**; *pl.* **-и́** trading; bargaining, haggling; market; *pl.* auction. **торговáть, -гýю** *impf.* (*pf.* **с~**) trade, deal; bargain for; be open; +*i.* sell; **~ся** bargain, haggle. **торгóвец, -вца** merchant; trader, dealer; tradesman. **торгóвка, -и** market-woman; stall-holder; street-trader. **торгóвля, -и** trade, commerce. **торгóв|ый** trade, commercial; mercantile; **~ое сýдно** merchant ship; **~ый флот** merchant navy. **торгпрéд, -а** *abbr.* trade representative. **торгпрéдство, -а** *abbr.* trade delegation. **торгфлóт, -а** merchant navy.

торжéственный solemn; ceremonial; festive; gala. **торжествó, -á** celebration; triumph; exultation; *pl.* festivities, rejoicings. **торжествовáть, -твýю** *impf.* celebrate; triumph, exult. **торжествýющий** triumphant, exultant.

торможéние, -я braking; deceleration; inhibition. **тóрмоз, -а**; *pl.* **-á** *or* **-ы** brake; drag, hindrance, obstacle. **тормози́ть, -ожý** *impf.* (*pf.* **за~**) brake, apply the brake(s); hamper, impede, be a drag on; retard, damp; inhibit. **тормознóй** brake, braking.

тормоши́ть, -шý *impf.* pester, plague, worry, torment; bother.

торопи́ть, -плю́, -пишь *impf.* (*pf.* **по~**) hurry; hasten; press; **~ся** hurry, be in a hurry; make haste. **торопли́вый** hurried, hasty.

торпе́да, -ы torpedo. **торпеди́ровать, -рую** *impf. & pf.* torpedo.

торт, -а cake.

торф, -а peat. **торфоболо́тный** peat-moss. **торфяни́стый** peaty. **торфян|о́й** peat; **~о́е боло́то** peat-moss, peat-bog.

торча́ть, -чу́ *impf.* stick up, stick out; protrude, jut out; hang about. **торчко́м** *adv.* on end, sticking up.

торше́р, -а standard lamp.

тоска́, -и́ melancholy; anguish; pangs; depression; boredom; nostalgia; **~ по** longing for, yearning for; **~ по ро́дине** homesickness. **тоскли́вый** melancholy; depressed, miserable; dull, dreary, depressing. **тоскова́ть, -ку́ю** *impf.* be melancholy, depressed, miserable; long, yearn, pine; **~ по** miss.

тост, -а toast; toasted sandwich; **~ с сы́ром** Welsh rarebit. **то́стер, -а** toaster.

тот *m.*, **та** *f.*, **то** *nt.*, **те** *pl. pron.* that; the former; he, she, it; the other; the opposite; the one; the same; the right; *pl.* those; **в том слу́чае** in that case; **и тому́ подо́бное** and so on, and so forth; **и ~ и друго́й** both; **к тому́ же** moreover; **на той стороне́** on the other side; **не ~** the wrong; **не ~, так друго́й** if not one, then the other; **ни с того́ ни с сего́** for no reason at all; without rhyme or reason; **ни ~ ни друго́й** neither; **одно́ и то же** one and the same thing, the same thing over again; **по ту сто́рону**+*g.* beyond, on the other side of; **с тем, что́бы** in order to, with a view to; on condition that, provided that; **с того́ бе́рега** from the other shore; **тем вре́менем** in the meantime; **того́ и гляди́** any minute now; before you know where you are; **тот, кто** the one who, the person who; **э́то не та дверь** that's the wrong door. **то́тчас** *adv.* at once; immediately.

точи́лка, -и steel, knife-sharpener; pencil-sharpener. **точи́ло, -а** whetstone, grindstone. **точи́льный** grinding, sharpening; **~ ка́мень** whetstone, grindstone. **точи́льщик, -а** (knife-)grinder. **точи́ть, -чу́, -чишь** *impf.* (*pf.* **вы́~, на~**) sharpen; grind; whet, hone; turn; eat away, gnaw away; corrode; gnaw at, prey upon.

то́чка, -и spot; dot; full stop; point; **попа́сть в то́чку** hit the nail on the head; **~ в то́чку** exactly; to the letter, word for word; **~ зре́ния** point of view; **~ с запято́й** semicolon. **то́чно[1]** *adv.* exactly, precisely; punctually; **~ в час** at one o'clock sharp. **то́чно[2]** *conj.* as though, as if; like. **то́чность, -и** punctuality; exactness; precision; accuracy; **в то́чности** exactly, precisely; accurately; to the letter. **то́чн|ый; -чен, -чна́, -о** exact, precise; accurate; punctual; **~ые нау́ки** exact sciences; **~ый прибо́р** precision instrument. **то́чь-в-то́чь** *adv.* exactly; to the letter; word for word.

тошни́ть, -и́т *impf.*, *impers.+a.*; **меня́ тошни́т** I feel sick; **меня́ от э́того тошни́т** it makes me sick, it sickens me. **тошнота́, -ы́** sickness, nausea. **тошнотво́рный** sickening, nauseating.

тоща́ть, -а́ю *impf.* (*pf.* **о~**) become thin, get thin. **то́щ|ий; тощ, -а́, -е** gaunt, emaciated; scraggy, skinny, scrawny; lean; empty; poor; **~ая по́чва** poor soil.

т.п.: и ~ *abbr.*: (*of* ***тому́ подо́бное***) etc., and so on.

тпру *int.* whoa!

трава́, -ы́; *pl.* **-ы** grass; herb. **трави́нка, -и** blade of grass.

трави́ть, -влю́, -вишь *impf.* (*pf.* **вы́~, за~**) poison; exterminate, destroy; etch; hunt; persecute, torment; badger; bait; worry the life out of. **травле́ние, -я** extermination, destruction; etching. **тра́вленый** etched. **тра́вля, -и** hunting; persecution, tormenting; badgering.

тра́вма, -ы trauma, injury; shock. **травмати́зм, -а** traumatism; injuries. **травматологи́ческий; ~ пункт** casualty (department).

травокоси́лка, -и lawn mower. **траволече́ние, -я** herbal medicine. **травоя́дный** herbivorous. **травяни́стый** grass; herbaceous; grassy; tasteless, insipid. **травяно́й** grass; herbaceous; herb; grassy.

траге́дия, -и tragedy. **тра́гик, -а** tragic actor; tragedian. **траги́ческий, траги́чный** tragic.

традицио́нный traditional. **тради́ция, -и** tradition.

тракт, -а high road, highway; route; channel.

тракта́т, -а treatise; treaty.

тракти́р, -а inn, tavern. **тракти́рный** inn. **тракти́рщик, -а, тракти́рщица, -ы** innkeeper.

трактова́ть, -ту́ю *impf.* interpret; treat, discuss. **тракто́вка, -и** treatment; interpretation.

тра́ктор, -а tractor; **гу́сеничный ~** caterpillar tractor. **трактори́ст, -а, ~ка, -ки** tractor driver.

трал, -а trawl. **тра́лить, -лю** *impf.* (*pf.* **про~**) trawl; sweep. **тра́льщик, -а** trawler; minesweeper.

трамбова́ть, -бу́ю *impf.* (*pf.* **у~**) ram, tamp. **трамбо́вка, -и** ramming; rammer; beetle.

трамва́й, -я tram-line; tram. **трамва́йный** tram.

трампли́н, -а spring-board; ski-jump; trampoline; jumping-off place.

транзи́стор, -а transistor; transistor radio, transistor set. **транзи́сторный** transistor; transistorized.

транзи́т, -а transit.

транквилиза́тор, -а tranquillizer.

транс, -а trance.

трансаге́нтство, -а removal company.

транскриби́ровать, -рую *impf. & pf.* transcribe. **транскри́пция, -и** transcription.

транслúровать, -рую *impf. & pf.* broadcast, transmit; relay. **транслятор, -а** repeater. **трансляциóнный** transmission; broadcasting; relaying. **трансляция, -и** broadcast, transmission; relay.

трáнспорт, -а transport; transportation, conveyance, consignment; train; supply ship; troopship. **транспортáбельный** transportable, mobile. **транспортёр, -а** conveyor; carrier. **транспортúр, -а** protractor. **транспортúровать, -рую** *impf. & pf.* transport. **трáнспортник, -а** transport worker; transport plane.

трансформáтор, -а transformer; quick-change artist; conjurer, illusionist.

траншéйный trench. **траншéя, -и** trench.

трап, -а ladder; steps.

трáпеза, -ы (*monastery*) dining-table; meal; refectory. **трáпезная** *sb.* refectory.

трапéция, -и trapezium; trapeze.

трáсса, -ы line, course, direction; route, road. **трассúровать, -рую** *impf. & pf.* mark out, trace. **трассúрующий** tracer.

трáта, -ы expenditure; expense; waste. **трáтить, -áчу** *impf.* (*pf.* **ис~, по~**) spend, expend; waste.

трáулер, -а trawler.

трáур, -а mourning. **трáурный** mourning; funeral; mournful, sorrowful.

трафарéт, -а stencil; conventional pattern; cliché. **трафарéтный** stencilled; conventional, stereotyped; trite, hackneyed.

трáчу *etc.*: *see* **трáтить**

трéбование, -я demand; request; claim; requirement, condition; requisition, order; *pl.* aspirations; needs. **трéбовательный** demanding, exacting; particular; requisition, order. **трéбовать, -бую** *impf.* (*pf.* **по~**) send for, call, summon; *+g.* demand, request, require; expect, ask; need, call for; **~ся** be needed, be required; **на э́то трéбуется мнóго врéмени** it takes a lot of time; **что и трéбовалось доказáть** (*math.*) Q.E.D.

тревóга, -и alarm; anxiety; uneasiness, disquiet; alert. **тревóжить, -жу** *impf.* (*pf.* **вс~, по~**) alarm; disturb; worry, trouble; interrupt; **~ся** worry, be anxious, be alarmed, be uneasy; worry o.s., trouble o.s., put o.s. out. **тревóжный** worried, anxious, uneasy, troubled; alarming, disturbing, disquieting; alarm.

трéзвенник, -а teetotaller, abstainer. **трéзвеннический** temperance. **трезвéть, -éю** *impf.* (*pf.* **о~**) sober up, become sober.

трезвóн, -а peal (*of bells*); rumours, gossip; row, shindy.

трéзвый; -зв, -á, -о sober; teetotal, abstinent.

трéйлер, -а trailer.

трель, -и trill, shake; warble.

тренажёр, -а training apparatus; **гребнóй ~** rowing machine; **лётный ~** flight simulator. **трéнер, -а** trainer, coach. **трéнерский** trainer's, training.

трéние, -я friction; rubbing; *pl.* friction.

тренировáть, -рýю *impf.* (*pf.* **на~**) train, coach; **~ся** train o.s.; be in training. **тренирóвка, -и** training, coaching. **тренирóвочный** training; practice.

трепáть, -плю́, -плешь *impf.* (*pf.* **ис~, по~, рас~**) scutch, swingle; pull about; blow about; dishevel, tousle; tear; wear out; pat; **его́ трéплет лихорáдка** he is feverish; **~ся** tear, fray; wear out; flutter, blow about; go round; hang out; blather, talk rubbish; play the fool. **трéпет, -а** trembling, quivering; trepidation. **трепетáть, -ещý, -éщешь** *impf.* tremble; quiver; flicker; palpitate. **трéпетный** trembling; flickering; anxious; timid.

треск, -а crack, crash; crackle, crackling; noise, fuss.

трескá, -ú cod.

трéскаться[1], -ается *impf.* (*pf.* **по~**) crack; chap.

трéскаться[2], -аюсь *impf. of* **трéснуться**

трескóвый cod.

трескотня́, -ú crackle, crackling; chirring; chatter, blather. **трескýчий** crackling; highfalutin(g), high-flown; **~ морóз** hard frost. **трéснуть, -нет** *pf.* snap, crackle; crack; chap; **~ся** (*impf.* **трéскаться**) *+i.* bang.

трест, -а trust.

третéйский arbitration; **~ суд** arbitration tribunal.

трéт|ий, -ья, -ье third; **в ~ьем часý** between two and three; **половúна ~ьего** half past two; **~ьего дня́** the day before yesterday; **~ье** *sb.* sweet (course).

третúровать, -рую *impf.* slight.

третúчный tertiary, ternary. **треть, -и**; *g.pl.* **-éй** third. **трéтье** *etc.*: *see* **трéтий. треугóльник, -а** triangle. **треугóльный** three-cornered, triangular.

трефóвый of clubs. **трéфы, треф** *pl.* clubs.

трёх... *in comb.* three-, tri-. **трёхгодúчный** three-year. **~годовáлый** three-year-old. **~голóсный** three-part. **~грáнный** three-edged; trihedral. **~днéвный** three-day; tertian. **~знáчный** three-digit, three-figure. **~колёсный** three-wheeled. **~лéтний** three-year; three-year old. **~мéрный** three-dimensional. **~мéстный** three-seater. **~мéсячный** three-month; quarterly; three-month-old. **~слóжный** trisyllabic. **~слóйный** three-layered; three-ply. **~сóтый** three-hundredth. **~сторóнний** three-sided; trilateral; tripartite. **~тóнка, -и** three-ton lorry. **~ходовóй** three-way, three-pass; three-move. **~цвéтный** three-coloured; tricolour; trichromatic. **~этáжный** three-storey(ed).

трещáть, -щý *impf.* crack; crackle; creak; chirr; crack up; jabber, chatter. **трéщина, -ы** crack, split; cleft, fissure; chap.

три, трёх, -ём, -емя́, -ёх three.

трибýна, -ы platform, rostrum; tribune; stand.

тригономéтрия, -и trigonometry.

тридцатилéтний thirty-year; thirty-year old.

тридца́тый thirtieth. **три́дцать, -и́**, *i.* **-ью** thirty. **три́дцатью** *adv.* thirty times. **три́жды** *adv.* three times; thrice.

трико́ *nt.indecl.* jersey, tricot, stockinet; knitted fabric; tights; pants, knickers. **трико́вый** jersey, tricot. **трикота́ж, -а** jersey, tricot, stockinet; knitted fabric; knitted wear, knitted garments. **трикота́жный** jersey, tricot; knitted.

трило́гия, -и trilogy. **тримара́н, -а** trimaran. **триме́стр, -а** term (*at educational establishment*).

трина́дцатый thirteenth. **трина́дцать, -и** thirteen. **трино́м, -а** trinomial.

трио́ль, -и triplet.

три́ста, трёхсо́т, -ёмста́м, -емяста́ми, -ёхста́х three hundred.

триу́мф, -а triumph; **с ~ом** triumphantly, in triumph. **триумфа́льный** triumphal.

тро́гательный touching, moving, affecting. **тро́гать(ся, -аю(сь** *impf. of* **тро́нуть(ся**

тро́е, -и́х *pl.* three. **троебо́рье, -я** triathlon. **троекра́тный** thrice-repeated. **трои́ть, -ою́** *impf.* treble; divide into three; **~ся** be trebled; appear treble. **Тро́ица, -ы** Trinity; Whit Sunday. **Тро́ицын день** Whit Sunday. **тро́йка, -и** (*figure*) three; troika; No. 3; three-piece suite; three-man commission. **тройно́й** triple, threefold, treble; three-ply. **тро́йственный** triple; tripartite.

тролле́й, -я trolley. **тролле́йбус, -а** trolley-bus. **тролле́йбусный** trolley-bus.

трон, -а throne. **тро́нный** throne.

тро́нуть, -ну *pf.* (*impf.* **тро́гать**) touch; disturb, trouble; move, affect; start; **~ся** start, set out; go bad; be touched; be moved, be affected; be cracked.

тропа́, -ы́ path.

тро́пик, -а tropic.

тропи́нка, -и path.

тропи́ческий tropical; **~ по́яс** torrid zone.

трос, -а rope, cable, hawser.

тростни́к, -а́ reed, rush. **тростнико́вый** reed.

тро́сточка, -и, трость, -и; *g.pl.* **~е́й** cane, walking-stick.

тротуа́р, -а pavement.

трофе́й, -я trophy; spoils (*of war*), booty; captured material. **трофе́йный** captured.

трою́родн|ый; ~ый брат, ~ая сестра́ second cousin.

тру *etc.*: *see* **тере́ть**

труба́, -ы́; *pl.* **-ы** pipe; conduit; chimney, flue; funnel, smoke-stack; trumpet; tube; duct. **труба́ч, -а́** trumpeter; trumpet-player. **труби́ть, -блю́** *impf.* (*pf.* **про~**) blow, sound; blare; **~ в**+*a.* blow. **тру́бка, -и** tube; pipe; fuse; (*telephone*) receiver, handset. **тру́бный** trumpet. **трубопрово́д, -а** pipe-line; piping, tubing; manifold. **трубочи́ст, -а** chimney-sweep. **тру́бочный** pipe; **~ таба́к** pipe tobacco. **тру́бчатый** tubular.

труд, -а́ labour; work; effort; *pl.* works; transactions; **не сто́ит ~а́** it is not worth the trouble; **с ~о́м** with difficulty, hardly. **труди́ться, -ужу́сь, -у́дишься** *impf.* toil, labour, work; trouble. **тру́дно** *pred.* it is hard, it is difficult. **тру́дность, -и** difficulty; obstacle. **тру́дный; -ден, -дна́, -о** difficult; hard; arduous; awkward; serious, grave.

трудо... *in comb.* labour, work. **трудоде́нь, -дня́** *m.* work-day (*unit of payment*). **~люби́вый** hard-working, industrious. **~лю́бие, -я** industry, diligence. **~сберега́ющий** labour-saving. **~спосо́бность, -и** ability to work, capacity for work. **~спосо́бный** able-bodied; capable of working.

трудово́й labour, work; working; earned; hard-earned; **~ стаж** working life. **трудя́щ|ийся** working; **~иеся** *sb.*, *pl.* the workers. **тру́женик, -а, тру́женица, -ы** toiler. **тру́женический** toiling; of toil.

труп, -а dead body, corpse; carcass. **тру́пный** corpse; post-mortem; ptomaine.

тру́ппа, -ы troupe, company.

трус, -а coward.

тру́сики, -ов *pl.* shorts; (*swimming*) trunks.

труси́ть[1], **-ушу́** *impf.* trot along, jog along.

тру́сить[2], **-у́шу** *impf.* (*pf.* **с~**) be a coward; lose one's nerve; quail; be afraid, be frightened. **труси́ха, -и** coward. **трусли́вый** cowardly; faint-hearted, timorous; apprehensive. **тру́сость, -и** cowardice.

трусы́, -о́в *pl.* shorts; trunks; pants.

трушу́ *etc.*: *see* **труси́ть, тру́сить**

трущо́ба, -ы slum; godforsaken hole.

трюк, -а feat, stunt; trick. **трю́ковый** trick.

трюм, -а hold.

трюмо́ *nt.indecl.* pier-glass.

тряпи́чный rag; soft, spineless. **тря́пка, -и** rag; duster; spineless creature; *pl.* finery, clothes. **тряпьё, -я́** rags; clothes, things.

тряси́на, -ы bog, swampy ground; quagmire. **тря́ска, -и** shaking, jolting. **тря́ский** shaky, jolty; bumpy. **трясти́, -су́, -сёшь; -яс, -ла́** *impf.*, **тряхну́ть, -ну́, -нёшь** *pf.* (*pf. also* **вы~**) shake; shake out; jolt; +*i.* shake, swing, toss; **~сь** shake; tremble, shiver; quake; bump along, jolt.

тсс *int.* sh! hush!

тт. *abbr.* (*of* **това́рищи**) Comrades; (*of* **тома́**) vols, volumes.

туале́т, -а dress; toilet; dressing; dressing-table; lavatory, cloak-room; **обще́ственный ~** public convenience. **туале́тный** toilet; **~ сто́лик** dressing-table. **туале́тчик, -а, туале́тчица, -ы** lavatory attendant, cloak-room attendant.

туберкулёз, -а tuberculosis, consumption. **туберкулёзник, -а, -ница, -ы** consumptive. **туберкулёзный** tubercular, consumptive; tuberculosis.

ту́го *adv.* tight(ly), taut; with difficulty; **~ наби́ть** pack tight, cram; *pred.*, *impers.* **с деньга́ми у нас ~** money is tight with us, we're strapped for cash; **ему́ ~ прихо́дится**

he is in a (tight) spot. **тугóй; туг, -á, -о** tight; taut; tightly filled, tightly stuffed; blown up hard; close-fisted; difficult; ~ **нá ухо** hard of hearing, **тугоплáвкий** refractory.

тудá *adv.* there, thither; that way; to the right place; **не** ~! not that way!; **ни** ~ **ни сюдá** neither one way nor the other; ~ **и обрáтно** there and back.

тýже *comp. of* **тýго, тугóй**

тужýрка, -и (*man's*) double-breasted jacket.

туз, -á, *a.* **-á** ace; dignitary; big name.

тузéмец, -мца, тузéмка, -и native. **тузéмный** native, indigenous.

тýловище, -а trunk; torso.

тулýп, -а sheepskin coat.

тумáн, -а (-у) fog; mist; haze. **тумáнить, -ит** *impf.* (*pf.* **за**~) dim, cloud, obscure; ~**ся** grow misty, grow hazy; be enveloped in mist; be befogged; grow gloomy, be depressed. **тумáнность, -и** fog, mist; nebula; haziness, obscurity. **тумáнный** foggy; misty; hazy; dull, lacklustre; obscure, vague.

тýмба, -ы post; bollard; pedestal. **тýмбочка, -и** bedside table.

тунея́дец, -дца parasite, sponger. **тунея́дствовать, -твую** *impf.* be a parasite, sponge.

тунúка, -и tunic.

туннéль, -я *m.*, **тоннéль, -я** *m.* tunnel; subway. **туннéльный, тоннéльный** tunnel; subway.

тупéть, -éю *impf.* (*pf.* **о**~) become blunt; grow dull. **тупúк, -á** blind alley, cul-de-sac, dead end; siding; impasse, deadlock; **зайтú в** ~ reach a deadlock; **постáвить в** ~ stump, nonplus. **тупúть, -плю́, -пишь** *impf.* (*pf.* **за**~, **ис**~) blunt; ~**ся** become blunt. **тупúца, -ы** *c.g.* dimwit, blockhead, dolt. **тупóй; туп, -á, -о** blunt; obtuse; dull; vacant, stupid, meaningless; slow; dim; blind, unquestioning. **тýпость, -и** bluntness; vacancy; dullness, slowness. **тупоýмный** dull, obtuse.

тур, -а turn; round.

турбáза, -ы tourist centre.

турбúна, -ы turbine.

турéцкий Turkish; ~ **барабáн** big drum, bass drum.

турúзм, -а tourism; outdoor pursuits; **вóдный** ~ boating; **гóрный** ~ mountaineering.

турúст, -а, -úстка, -и tourist; hiker. **турúстский** tourist; ~ **похóд** *see* **турпохóд**

Туркменистáн, -а Turkmenistan.

турнé *nt.indecl.* tour.

турнúк, -á horizontal bar.

турникéт, -а turnstile; tourniquet.

турнúр, -а tournament.

тýрок, -рка Turk. **турчáнка, -и** Turkish woman.

турпохóд, -а *abbr.* (*of* ***турúстский похóд***) walking-tour; tourist excursion; outing.

Тýрция, -и Turkey.

тýсклый dim, dull; matt; tarnished; wan; lacklustre; colourless, tame. **тускнéть, -éет** *impf.* (*pf.* **по**~) dim; grow dim, grow dull; tarnish; pale.

тут *adv.* here; now; ~ **же** there and then. **тýт-то** *adv.* just here; there and then.

тýфля, -и shoe; slipper.

тýхлый; -хл, -á, -о rotten, bad. **тýхнуть**[1], **-нет; тух** go bad.

тýхнуть[2], **-нет; тух** *impf.* (*pf.* **по**~) go out.

тýча, -и cloud; storm-cloud; swarm, host. **тучевóй** cloud.

тýчный; -чен, -чнá, -чно fat, obese; rich, fertile; succulent.

туш, -а flourish.

тýша, -и carcass.

тушевáть, -шýю *impf.* (*pf.* **за**~) shade. **тушёвка, -и** shading.

тушёный braised, stewed. **тушúть**[1], **-шý, -шишь** *impf.* (*pf.* **с**~) braise, stew.

тушúть[2], **-шý, -шишь** *impf.* (*pf.* **за**~, **по**~) extinguish, put out; suppress, stifle, quell.

тушýю *etc.*: *see* **тушевáть. тушь, -и** Indian ink; ~ **(для реснúц)** mascara.

тчк *abbr.* (*of* **тóчка**) stop (*in telegram*).

тщáтельность, -и thoroughness, carefulness; care. **тщáтельный** thorough, careful; painstaking.

тщедýшный feeble, frail, weak; puny.

тщеслáвие, -я vanity, vainglory. **тщеслáвный** vain, vainglorious. **тщетá, -ы́** vanity. **тщéтно** *adv.* vainly, in vain. **тщéтный** vain, futile; unavailing.

ты, тебя́, -бé, тобóй, тебé you; thou; **быть на ты с**+*i.* be on familiar terms with.

ты́кать, ты́чу *impf.* (*pf.* **ткнуть**) poke; prod; jab; stick; ~ **пáльцем** point; ~**ся** knock (**в**+*a.* against, into); rush about, fuss about.

ты́ква, -ы pumpkin; gourd.

тыл, -а (-у), *loc.* **-ý**; *pl.* **-ы́** back; rear; the interior. **тыловóй** rear; ~ **гóспиталь** base hospital. **ты́льный** back; rear.

тын, -а paling; palisade, stockade.

ты́сяча, -и, *i.* **-ей** *or* **-ью** thousand. **тысячелéтие, -я** a thousand years; millennium; thousandth anniversary. **тысячелéтний** thousand-year; millennial. **ты́сячный** thousandth; of (many) thousands.

тычúнка, -и stamen.

тьма[1], **-ы** dark, darkness.

тьма[2], **-ы**; *g.pl.* **тем** ten thousand; host, swarm, multitude.

тэ *nt.indecl.* the letter **т**.

тю́бик, -а tube.

тюк, -á bale, package.

тюлéневый sealskin. **тюлéний** seal. **тюлéнь, -я** *m.* seal.

тюль, -я *m.* tulle.

тюльпáн, -а tulip.

тюрéмн|ый prison; ~**ое заключéние** imprisonment. **тюрéмщик, -а** gaoler, warder; enslaver. **тюрéмщица, -ы** wardress. **тюрьмá, -ы́**; *pl.* **-ы, -рем** prison; jail, gaol; imprisonment.

тюфя́к, -á mattress. **тюфя́чный** mattress.

тя́га, -и traction; locomotion; locomotives;

thrust; draught; pull, attraction; thirst, craving; taste; **дать тя́гу** take to one's heels. **тяга́ться, -а́юсь** *impf.* (*pf.* **по~**) measure one's strength (against); vie, contend; have a tug-of-war. **тяга́ч, -а́** tractor.

тя́гостный burdensome, onerous; painful, distressing. **тя́гость, -и** weight, burden; fatigue. **тяготе́ние, -я** gravity, gravitation; attraction, taste; bent, inclination. **тяготе́ть, -е́ю** *impf.* gravitate; be drawn, be attracted; **~ над** hang over, threaten. **тяготи́ть, -ощу́** *impf.* burden, be a burden on; lie heavy on, oppress.

тягу́чий malleable, ductile; viscous; slow, leisurely, unhurried.

тя́жба, -ы lawsuit; litigation; competition, rivalry.

тяжело́ *adv.* heavily; seriously, gravely; with difficulty. **тяжело́** *pred.* it is hard; it is painful; it is distressing; **ему́ ~** he feels miserable, he feels wretched. **тяжелоатле́т, -а** weight-lifter. **тяжелове́с, -а** heavy-weight. **тяжелове́сный** heavy; ponderous, clumsy. **тяжелово́з, -а** heavy (draught-)horse; heavy lorry. **тяжёлый; -ёл, -а́** heavy; difficult; slow; severe; serious, grave, bad; seriously ill; painful; ponderous, unwieldy. **тя́жесть, -и** gravity; weight; heavy object; heaviness; difficulty; severity. **тя́жкий** heavy, hard; severe; serious, grave.

тяну́ть, -ну́, -нешь *impf.* (*pf.* **по~**) pull; draw; haul; drag; tug; drawl; drag out, protract, delay; weigh, weigh down; draw up; take in; extract; extort; *impers.* (+*a.*) draw, attract; be tight; **его́ тя́нет домо́й** he wants to go home; **тя́нет в плеча́х** it feels tight across the shoulders; **~ жре́бий** draw lots; **~ на букси́ре** tow; **~ся** stretch; extend; stretch out; stretch o.s.; drag on; crawl; drift; move along one after another; last out, hold out; reach (out), strive (**к**+*d.* after); +**за**+*i.* try to keep up with, try to equal.

тяну́чка, -и toffee, caramel.

у *nt.indecl.* the letter **у**.

у *int.* oh.

у *prep.*+*g.* by; at; from, of; belonging to; **спроси́те у него́ о́ттиск** ask him to let you have an offprint; **у вла́сти** in power; **у воро́т** at the gate; **у меня́ (есть)** I have; **у меня́ к вам ма́ленькая про́сьба** I have a small favour to ask of you; **у нас** at our place, with us; here, in our country; **у неё нет вре́мени** she has no time; **у окна́** by the window; **я за́нял де́сять рубле́й у сосе́да** I borrowed ten roubles from a neighbour.

у... *vbl. pref. indicating movement away from a place, insertion in something, covering all over, reduction or curtailment, achievement of aim; and, with adjectival roots, forming vv. expressing comp. degree.*

уба́вить, -влю *pf.*, **убавля́ть, -я́ю** *impf.* reduce, lessen, diminish; **~ в ве́се** lose weight.

у|ба́юкать, -аю *pf.*, **убаю́кивать, -аю** *impf.* lull (to sleep); rock to sleep, sing to sleep.

убега́ть, -а́ю *impf. of* **убежа́ть**

убеди́тельн|ый convincing, persuasive, cogent; pressing; earnest; **быть ~ым** carry conviction. **убеди́ть, -и́шь** *pf.* (*impf.* **убежда́ть**) convince; persuade; prevail on; **~ся** be convinced; make certain, satisfy o.s.

убежа́ть, -егу́ *pf.* (*impf.* **убега́ть**) run away, run off, make off; escape; boil over.

убежда́ть(ся, -а́ю(сь *impf. of* **убеди́ть(ся. убежде́ние, -я** persuasion; conviction, belief. **убеждённость, -и** conviction. **убеждённый; -ён, -а́** convinced; persuaded; confirmed; staunch, stalwart.

убе́жище, -а refuge, asylum; sanctuary; shelter; dug-out; **иска́ть убе́жища** seek refuge; seek sanctuary; **пра́во убе́жища** right of asylum.

убелённый; -ён, -а́ whitened, white; **~ седи́нами** white-haired; **~ седино́й** white. **убели́ть, -и́т** *pf.* whiten.

уберега́ть, -а́ю *impf.*, **убере́чь, -регу́, -режёшь; -рёг, -гла́** *pf.* protect, guard, keep safe, preserve; **~ся от**+*g.* protect o.s. against, guard against.

уберу́ *etc.*: *see* **убра́ть**

убива́ть(ся, -а́ю(сь *impf. of* **уби́ть(ся. уби́йственный** deadly; murderous; killing. **уби́йство, -а** murder, assassination. **уби́йца, -ы** *c.g.* murderer; killer; assassin.

убира́ть(ся, -а́ю(сь *impf. of* **убра́ть(ся; убира́йся!** clear off! hop it! **убира́ющийся** retractable.

уби́тый killed; crushed, broken; *sb.* dead man. **уби́ть, убью́, -ьёшь** *pf.* (*impf.* **убива́ть**) kill; murder; assassinate; finish; break, smash; expend; waste; **~ся** hurt o.s., bruise o.s.; grieve.

убо́гий wretched; poverty-stricken, beggardly; squalid; *sb.* pauper, beggar. **убо́жество, -а** poverty; squalor; mediocrity; physical disability; infirmity.

убо́й, -я slaughter; **корми́ть на ~** fatten; feed up, stuff. **убо́йность, -и** effectiveness, destructive power. **убо́йный** killing, destructive, lethal; for slaughter.

убо́р, -а dress, attire; **головно́й ~** headgear, head-dress.

убо́ристый close, small.

убо́рка, -и harvesting, reaping, gathering in; picking; collection, removal; clearing up, tidying up. **уборная** *sb.* lavatory; public convenience; dressing-room. **уборочн|ый** harvest, harvesting; **~ая машина** harvester. **уборщик, -а, уборщица, -ы** cleaner. **убранство, -а** furniture; appointments; decoration; attire. **убрать, уберу, -рёшь; -ал, -а, -о** *pf.* (*impf.* **убирать**) remove; take away; kick out; sack; put away, store; harvest, reap, gather in; clear up, tidy up; decorate, adorn; **~ комнату** do a room; **~ постель** make a bed; **~ с дороги** put out of the way; **~ со стола** clear the table; **~ся** clear up, tidy up, clean up; clear off, clear out; attire o.s.

убывать, -аю *impf.*, **убыть, убуду; убыл, -а, -о** *pf.* decrease, diminish; subside,fall, go down; wane; go away, leave. **убыль, -и** diminution, decrease; subsidence; losses, casualties. **убыток, -тка (-тку)** loss; *pl.* damages. **убыточно** *adv.* at a loss. **убыточн|ый** unprofitable; **~ая продажа** sale at a loss.

убью *etc.*: *see* **убить**

уважаемый respected, esteemed, honoured; dear. **уважать, -аю** *impf.* respect, esteem. **уважение, -я** respect, esteem; **с ~м** yours sincerely. **уважительный** valid, good; respectful, deferential.

увариваться, -ается *impf.*, **увариться, -арится** *pf.* be thoroughly cooked; boil down, boil away.

уведомительн|ый notifying, informing; **~ое письмо** letter of advice; notice. **уведомить, -млю** *pf.*, **уведомлять, -яю** *impf.* inform, notify. **уведомление, -я** information, notification.

уведу *etc.*: *see* **увести**

увезти, -зу, -зёшь; увёз, -ла *pf.* (*impf.* **увозить**) take (away); take with one; steal; abduct, kidnap.

увековечивать, -аю *impf.*, **увековечить, -чу** *pf.* immortalize; perpetuate.

увёл *etc.*: *see* **увести**

увеличение, -я increase; augmentation; extension; magnification; enlargement. **увеличивать, -аю** *impf.*, **увеличить, -чу** *pf.* increase; augment; extend; enhance; magnify; enlarge; **~ся** increase, grow, rise. **увеличитель, -я** *m.* enlarger. **увеличительн|ый** magnifying; enlarging; augmentative; **~ое стекло** magnifying glass.

у|венчать, -аю *pf.*, **увенчивать, -аю** *impf.* crown; **~ся** be crowned.

уверение, -я assurance; protestation. **уверенность, -и** confidence; certitude, certainty; **в полной уверенности** in the firm belief, quite certain. **уверенный** confident; sure; certain; **будь(те) уверен(ы)!** you may be sure, you may rely on it. **уверить, -рю** *pf.* (*impf.* **уверять**) assure; convince, persuade; **~ся** assure o.s., satisfy o.s.; be convinced.

увернуться, -нусь, -нёшься *pf.*, **увёртываться, -аюсь** *impf.* **от**+*g.* dodge; evade. **увёртка, -и** dodge, evasion; subterfuge; *pl.* wiles. **увёртливый** evasive, shifty.

увертюра, -ы overture.

уверять(ся, -яю(сь *impf. of* **уверить(ся**

увеселение, -я amusement, entertainment. **увеселительн|ый** amusement, entertainment; pleasure; **~ая поездка** pleasure trip. **увеселять, -яю** *impf.* amuse, entertain.

увесистый weighty; heavy.

увести, -еду, -едёшь; -ёл, -а *pf.* (*impf.* **уводить**) take (away); take with one; carry off, walk off with.

увечить, -чу *impf.* maim, mutilate, cripple. **увечный** maimed, mutilated, crippled; *sb.* cripple. **увечье, -я** maiming, mutilation; injury.

увешать, -аю *pf.*, **увешивать, -аю** *impf.* hang, cover (+*i.* with).

увещание, -я exhortation, admonition. **увещать, -аю** *impf.*, **увещевать, -аю** *impf.* exhort, admonish.

у|видать(ся, -аю(сь *pf.* **у|видеть(ся, -ижу(сь** *pf.*

увиливать, -аю *impf.*, **увильнуть, -ну, -нёшь** *pf.* **от**+*g.* dodge; evade, shirk; (try to) wriggle out of.

увлажнить, -ню *pf.*, **увлажнять, -яю** *impf.* moisten, damp, wet.

увлекательный fascinating; absorbing. **увлекать, -аю** *impf.*, **увлечь, -еку, -ечёшь; -ёк, -ла** *pf.* carry along; carry away, distract; captivate, fascinate; entice, allure; **~ся** be carried away; become keen; become mad (+*i.* about); become enamoured, fall (+*i.* for).

увод, -а taking away, withdrawal; carrying off; stealing. **уводить, -ожу, -одишь** *impf. of* **увести**

увожу *etc.*: *see* **уводить, увозить**

увоз, -а abduction; carrying off; **свадьба ~ом** elopement. **увозить, -ожу, -одишь** *impf. of* **увезти**

уволить, -лю *pf.*, **увольнять, -яю** *impf.* discharge, dismiss; retire; sack, fire; **~ся** retire; resign, leave the service. **увольнение, -я** discharge, dismissal; retiring, pensioning off. **увольнительный** discharge, dismissal; leave.

увы *int.* alas!

увядание, -я fading, withering **увядать, -аю** *impf. of* **увянуть. увядший** withered.

увязать[1], -аю *impf. of* **увязнуть**

увязать[2], -яжу, -яжешь *pf.* (*impf.* **увязывать**) tie up; pack up; co-ordinate; **~ся** pack; tag along. **увязка, -и** tying up, roping, strapping; co-ordination.

у|вязнуть, -ну; -яз *pf.* (*impf. also* **увязать**) get bogged down, get stuck.

увязывать(ся, -аю(сь *impf. of* **увязать(ся**

у|вянуть, -ну *pf.* (*impf. also* **увядать**) fade, wither, wilt, droop.

угадать, -аю *pf.*, **угадывать, -аю** *impf.* guess (right).

угар, -а charcoal fumes; carbon monoxide (poisoning); ecstasy, intoxication.

уга́рный full of (monoxide) fumes; ~ **газ** carbon monoxide.

угаса́ть, -а́ет *impf.*, **у|га́снуть, -нет; -а́с** *pf.* go out; die down.

угле... *in comb.* coal; charcoal; carbon. **углево́д, -а** carbohydrate. **~водоро́д, -а** hydrocarbon. **~добы́ча, -и** coal extraction. **~жже́ние, -я** charcoal burning. **~жо́г, -а** charcoal-burner. **~кислота́, -ы́** carbonic acid; carbon dioxide. **~ки́слый** carbonate (of); **~ки́слый аммо́ний** ammonium carbonate. **~ро́д, -а** carbon.

углова́тый angular; awkward. **углово́й** corner; angle; angular.

углуби́ть, -блю́ *pf.*, **углубля́ть, -я́ю** *impf.* deepen; make deeper; sink deeper; extend; **~ся** deepen; become deeper; become intensified; go deep; delve deeply; become absorbed. **углубле́ние, -я** hollow, depression, dip; draught; deepening; extending; intensification. **углублённый** deepened; deep; profound; absorbed.

угна́ть, угоню́, -о́нишь; -а́л, -а́, -о *pf.* (*impf.* **угоня́ть**) drive away; send off, despatch; steal; **~ся за**+*i.* keep pace with, keep up with.

угнета́тель, -я *m.* oppressor. **угнета́тельский** oppressive. **угнета́ть, -а́ю** *impf.* oppress; depress, dispirit. **угнете́ние, -я** oppression; depression. **угнетённ|ый** oppressed; depressed; **~ое состоя́ние** low spirits, depression.

угова́ривать, -аю *impf.*, **уговори́ть, -рю́** *pf.* persuade, induce; urge; talk into; **~ся** arrange, agree. **угово́р, -а (-у)** persuasion; agreement; compact.

уго́да, -ы; в уго́ду+*d.* to please. **угоди́ть, -ожу́** *pf.*, **угожда́ть, -а́ю** *impf.* fall, get; bang; (+*d.*) hit; +*d.* *or* **на**+*a.* please, oblige. **уго́дливый** obsequious. **уго́дно** *pred.*+*d.*: **как вам** ~ as you wish, as you please; please yourself; **что вам ~?** what would you like? what can I do for you?; *part.* **кто** ~ anyone (you like), whoever you like; **что** ~ anything (you like), whatever you like. **уго́дный** pleasing, welcome.

у́гол, угла́, *loc.* **-у́** corner; angle; part of a room; place; **из-за угла́** (from) round the corner; on the sly; **име́ть свой у́гол** have a place of one's own; ~ **зре́ния** visual angle; point of view.

уголо́вник, -а, -ница, -ы criminal. **уголо́вный** criminal.

уголо́к, -лка́, *loc.* **-у́** corner.

у́голь, у́гля́; *pl.* **у́гли, -ей** *or* **-е́й** *m.* coal; charcoal.

уго́льник, -а set square; angle iron, angle bracket. **уго́льный**[1] corner.

у́гольный[2] coal; carbon; carbonic. **у́гольщик, -а** collier; coal-miner; coal-man; charcoal-burner.

угомони́ть, -ню́ *pf.* calm down, pacify; **~ся** calm down.

уго́н, -а driving away; stealing. **уго́нщик, -а** thief; hijacker; ~ **маши́ны** car thief.

угоня́ть, -я́ю *impf.* *of* **угна́ть**

угора́ть, -а́ю *impf.*, **угоре́ть, -рю́** *pf.* get carbon monoxide poisoning; be mad, be crazy. **угоре́лый; как** ~ like a madman, like one possessed.

у́горь[1]**, угря́** *m.* eel.

у́горь[2]**, угря́** *m.* blackhead.

угости́ть, -ощу́ *pf.*, **угоща́ть, -а́ю** *impf.* entertain; treat. **угоще́ние, -я** entertaining, treating; refreshments; fare.

угро́бить, -блю *pf.* (*sl.*) do in; ruin, wreck.

угрожа́ть, -а́ю *impf.* threaten. **угрожа́ющий** threatening, menacing. **угро́за, -ы** threat, menace.

угрызе́ние, -я pangs; **угрызе́ния со́вести** remorse.

угрю́мый sullen, morose, gloomy.

уда́в, -а boa, boa-constrictor.

удава́ться, удаётся *impf.* *of* **уда́ться**

у|дави́ть(ся, -влю́(сь, -вишь(ся *pf.* **уда́вка, -и** running-knot, half hitch. **удавле́ние, -я** strangling, strangulation.

удале́ние, -я removal; extraction; sending away, sending off; moving off. **удали́ть, -лю́** *pf.* (*impf.* **удаля́ть**) remove; extract; send away; move away; **~ся** move off, move away; leave, withdraw, retire.

удало́й, уда́лый; -а́л, -а́, -о daring, bold. **у́даль, -и, удальство́, -а́** daring, boldness.

удаля́ть(ся, -я́ю(сь *impf.* *of* **удали́ть(ся**

уда́р, -а blow; stroke; shock; attack; thrust; seizure; **быть в ~е** be in good form; **нанести́** ~ strike a blow; ~ **гро́ма** thunder-clap. **ударе́ние, -я** accent; stress; stress-mark; emphasis. **уда́ренный** stressed, accented. **уда́рить, -рю** *pf.*, **ударя́ть, -я́ю** *impf.* (*impf.* *also* **бить**) strike; hit; sound; beat; attack; set in; **~ся** strike, hit; **~ся в бе́гство** break into a run; **~ся в слёзы** burst into tears. **уда́рник, -а, -ница, -ы** shock-worker. **уда́рный** percussive; percussion; shock; of shock-workers; urgent, rush. **ударопро́чный, ударосто́йкий** shockproof, shock-resistant.

уда́ться, -а́стся, -аду́тся; -а́лся, -ла́сь *pf.* (*impf.* **удава́ться**) succeed, be a success, turn out well, work. **уда́ча, -и** good luck, good fortune; success. **уда́чный** successful; felicitous, apt, good.

удва́ивать, -аю *impf.*, **удво́ить, -о́ю** *pf.* double, redouble; reduplicate. **удвое́ние, -я** doubling; reduplication. **удво́енный** doubled, redoubled; reduplicated.

уде́л, -а lot, destiny; apanage; crown lands.

удели́ть, -лю́ *pf.* (*impf.* **уделя́ть**) spare, devote, give.

уде́льный[1] specific; ~ **вес** specific gravity.

уде́льный[2] apanage, crown.

уделя́ть, -я́ю *impf.* *of* **удели́ть**

у́держ, -у; без ~у unrestrainedly, without restraint, uncontrollably. **удержа́ние, -я** deduction; retention, keeping, holding. **удер-**

жа́ть, -жу́, -жишь *pf.*, **уде́рживать, -аю** *impf.* hold, hold on to, not let go; keep, retain; hold back, keep back; restrain; keep down, suppress; deduct; ~ **в па́мяти** bear in mind, retain in one's memory; **~ся** hold one's ground, hold on, hold out; stand firm; keep one's feet; keep (from), refrain (from); **мы не могли́ ~ся от сме́ха** we couldn't help laughing; **~ся от собла́зна** resist a temptation.

удеру́ *etc.*: *see* **удра́ть**

удешеви́ть, -влю́ *pf.*, **удешевля́ть, -я́ю** *impf.* reduce the price of; **~ся** become cheaper. **удешевле́ние, -я** price-reduction.

удиви́тельный astonishing, surprising, amazing; wonderful, marvellous; **не удиви́тельно, что** no wonder (that). **удиви́ть, -влю́** *pf.*, **удивля́ть, -я́ю** *impf.* astonish, surprise, amaze; **~ся** be astonished, be surprised, be amazed; marvel. **удивле́ние, -я** astonishment, surprise, amazement; **к моему́ удивле́нию** to my surprise; **на** ~ excellently, splendidly, marvellously.

удила́, -и́л *pl.* bit.

уди́лище, -а fishing-rod. **уди́льщик, -а, -щица, -ы** angler.

удира́ть, -а́ю *impf. of* **удра́ть**

уди́ть, ужу́, у́дишь *impf.* fish for; ~ **ры́бу** fish; **~ся** bite.

удлине́ние, -я lengthening; extension. **удлини́ть, -ню́** *pf.*, **удлиня́ть, -я́ю** *impf.* lengthen; extend, prolong; **~ся** become longer, lengthen; be extended, be prolonged.

удо́бно *adv.* comfortably; conveniently. **удо́бн|ый** comfortable; cosy; convenient, suitable, opportune; proper, in order; **~ый слу́чай** opportunity; **~о**+*d.* it is convenient for, it suits.

удобо... *in comb.* conveniently, easily, well. **удобовари́мый** digestible. **~исполни́мый** easy to carry out. **~обтека́емый** streamlined. **~переноси́мый** portable, easily carried. **~поня́тный** comprehensible, intelligible. **~произноси́мый** easy to pronounce. **~управля́емый** easily controlled. **~усвоя́емый** easily assimilated. **~чита́емый** legible, easy to read.

удобре́ние, -я fertilization, manuring; fertilizer. **удо́брить, -рю** *pf.*, **удобря́ть, -я́ю** *impf.* fertilize.

удо́бство, -а comfort; convenience; amenity; **кварти́ра со все́ми удо́бствами** flat with all conveniences.

удовлетворе́ние, -я satisfaction; gratification. **удовлетворённый; -рён, -а́** satisfied, contented. **удовлетвори́тельно** *adv.* satisfactorily; fair, satisfactory. **удовлетвори́тельный** satisfactory. **удовлетвори́ть, -рю́** *pf.*, **удовлетворя́ть, -я́ю** *impf.* satisfy; gratify; give satisfaction to; comply with; +*d.* answer, meet; +*i.* supply with, furnish with; ~ **жела́ние** gratify a wish; ~ **потре́бности** satisfy the requirements; ~ **про́сьбу** comply with a request; **~ся** content o.s.; be satisfied.

удово́льствие, -я pleasure; amusement. **у|дово́льствоваться, -твуюсь** *pf.*

удо́й, -я milk-yield; milking. **удо́йлив|ый** yielding much milk; **~ая коро́ва** good milker.

удоста́ивать(ся, -аю(сь *impf. of* **удосто́ить(ся**

удостовере́ние, -я certification, attestation; certificate; ~ **ли́чности** identity card. **удостове́рить, -рю** *pf.*, **удостоверя́ть, -я́ю** *impf.* certify, attest, witness; ~ **ли́чность**+*g.* prove the identity of, identify; **~ся** make sure (**в**+*p.* of), assure o.s.

удосто́ить, -о́ю *pf.* (*impf.* **удоста́ивать**) make an award to; +*g.* award to, confer on; +*i.* favour with, vouchsafe to; **~ся**+*g.* receive, be awarded; be favoured with, be vouchsafed; be found worthy.

удосу́живаться, -аюсь *impf.*, **удосу́житься, -жусь** *pf.* find time.

у́дочка, -и (fishing-)rod.

удра́ть, удеру́, -ёшь; удра́л, -а́, -о *pf.* (*impf.* **удира́ть**) make off, clear out, run away.

удружи́ть, -жу́ *pf.*+*d.* do a good turn.

удруча́ть, -а́ю *impf.*, **удручи́ть, -чу́** *pf.* depress, dispirit. **удручённый; -чён, -а́** depressed, despondent.

удуша́ть, -а́ю *impf.*, **удуши́ть, -шу́, -шишь** *pf.* smother, stifle, suffocate; asphyxiate. **удуше́ние, -я** suffocation; asphyxiation. **уду́шливый** stifling, suffocating; asphyxiating. **уду́шье, -я** asthma; suffocation, asphyxia.

уедине́ние, -я solitude; seclusion. **уединённый** solitary, secluded; lonely. **уедини́ться, -ню́сь** *pf.*, **уединя́ться, -я́юсь** *impf.* retire, withdraw; seclude o.s.

уе́зд, -а uyezd (*administrative unit*).

уезжа́ть, -а́ю *impf.*, **уе́хать, уе́ду** *pf.* go away, leave, depart.

уж, -а́ grass-snake.

уж *adv. see* **уже́. уж, уже́** *part.* to be sure, indeed, certainly; really.

у|жа́лить, -лю *pf.*

у́жас, -а horror, terror; *pred.* it is awful, it is terrible; ~ **(как)** awfully, terribly; ~ **ско́лько** an awful lot of. **ужаса́ть, -а́ю** *imp.*, **ужасну́ть, -ну́, -нёшь** *pf.* horrify, terrify; **~ся** be horrified, be terrified. **ужа́сно** *adv.* horribly, terribly; awfully; frightfully. **ужа́сный** awful, terrible, ghastly, frightful.

у́же *comp. of* **у́зкий**

уже́, уж *adv.* already; now; by now; ~ **давно́** it's a long time ago; ~ **не** no longer. **уже́** *part.*: *see* **уж** *part.*

уже́ние, -я fishing, angling.

ужесточа́ться, -а́ется *impf.* become, be made, stricter, tighter, more rigorous. **ужесточе́ние, -я** tightening up, intensification; making stricter, more rigorous. **ужесточи́ть, -чу́** *pf.* make stricter, make more rigorous;

intensify, tighten (up).

уживáться, -áюсь *impf. of* **ужи́ться. ужи́вчивый** easy to get on with.

ужи́мка, -и grimace.

у́жин, -а supper. **у́жинать, -аю** *impf.* (*pf.* **по~**) have supper.

ужи́ться, -иву́сь, -ивёшься; -и́лся, -лáсь *pf.* (*impf.* **уживáться**) get on.

ужу́ *see* **уди́ть**

узаконéние, -я legalization; legitimization; statute. **узакóнивать, -аю** *impf.*, **узакóнить, -ню** *pf.*, **узаконя́ть, -я́ю** *impf.* legalize, legitimize.

Узбекистáн, -а Uzbekistan.

уздá, -ы́; *pl.* **-ы** bridle.

у́зел, узлá knot; bend, hitch; junction; centre; node; bundle, pack; **нéрвный ~** nerve-centre, ganglion.

у́зк|ий; у́зок, узкá, -о narrow; tight; limited; narrow-minded; **~ое мéсто** bottleneck. **узкоколéйка, -и** narrow-gauge railway. **узкоколéйный** narrow-gauge.

узловáтый knotty; nodose; gnarled. **узлов|óй** junction; main, principal, central, key; **~áя стáнция** junction.

узнавáть, -наю́, -наёшь *impf.*, **узнáть, -áю** *pf.* recognize; get to know, become familiar with; learn, find out.

у́зник, -а, у́зница, -ы prisoner.

узóр, -а pattern, design. **узóрный** pattern; patterned. **узóрчатый** patterned.

у́зость, -и narrowness; tightness.

у́зы *pl.* bonds, ties.

уйду́ *etc.*: *see* **уйти́. уйму́** *etc.*: *see* **уня́ть**

уйти́, уйду́, -дёшь; ушёл, ушлá *pf.* (*impf.* **уходи́ть**) go away, leave, depart; escape; get away; evade; retire; sink; bury o.s.; be used up, be spent; pass away, slip away; boil over; spill; **~ (вперёд)** gain, be fast; **на э́то уйдёт мнóго врéмени** it will take a lot of time; **так вы далекó не уйдёте** you won't get very far like that; **~ на пéнсию** retire on a pension; **~ со сцéны** quit the stage; **~ с рабóты** leave work, give up work.

укáз, -а decree; edict, ukase. **указáние, -я** indication, pointing out; instruction, direction. **укáзанный** fixed, appointed, stated. **указáтель, -я** *m.* indicator; marker; gauge; index; guide, directory; **~ направлéния** road-sign. **указáтельн|ый** indicating; demonstrative; **~ый пáлец** index finger, forefinger; **~ая стрéлка** pointer. **указáть, -ажу́, -áжешь** *pf.*, **укáзывать, -аю** *impf.* show; indicate; point; point out; explain; give directions; give orders. **укáзка, -и** pointer; orders; **по чужóй укáзке** at s.o. else's bidding.

укáлывать, -аю *impf. of* **уколóть**

укатáть, -áю *pf.*, **укáтывать[1], -аю** *impf.* roll, roll out; flatten; wear out, tire out; **~ся** become smooth. **укати́ть, -ачу́, -áтишь** *pf.*, **укáтывать[2], -аю** *impf.* roll away; drive off; **~ся** roll away.

укачáть, -áю *pf.*, **укáчивать, -аю** *impf.* rock to sleep; make sick.

уклáд, -а structure; form; organization, set-up; **~ жи́зни** style of life, mode of life; **óбщественно-экономи́ческий ~** social and economic structure. **уклáдка, -и** packing; stacking, piling; stowing; laying; setting, set. **уклáдчик, -а** packer; layer. **уклáдывать(ся[1], -аю(сь** *impf. of* **уложи́ть(ся**

уклáдываться[2], -аюсь *impf. of* **улéчься**

уклóн, -а slope, declivity; inclination; incline; gradient; bias, tendency; deviation. **уклонéние, -я** deviation; evasion; digression. **уклони́ст, -а** deviationist. **уклони́ться, -ню́сь, -ни́шься** *pf.*, **уклоня́ться, -я́юсь** *impf.* deviate; +**от**+*g.* turn, turn off, turn aside; avoid; evade. **уклóнчивый** evasive.

уклю́чина, -ы rowlock.

укóл, -а prick; jab; injection; thrust. **уколóть, -лю́, -лешь** *pf.* (*impf.* **укáлывать**) prick; sting, wound.

укомплектовáние, -я bringing up to strength. **укомплектóванный** complete, at full strength. **у|комплектовáть, -ту́ю** *pf.*, **укомплектóвывать, -аю** *impf.* complete; bring up to (full) strength; man; +*i.* equip with, furnish with.

укóр, -а reproach.

укорáчивать, -аю *impf. of* **укороти́ть**

укорени́ть, -ню́ *pf.*, **укореня́ть, -я́ю** *impf.* implant, inculcate; **~ся** take root, strike root.

укори́зна, -ы reproach. **укори́зненный** reproachful. **укори́ть, -рю́** *pf.* (*impf.* **укоря́ть**) reproach (**в**+*p.* with).

укороти́ть, -очу́ *pf.* (*impf.* **укорáчивать**) shorten.

укоря́ть, -я́ю *impf. of* **укори́ть**

укóс, -а (hay-)crop.

укрáдкой *adv.* stealthily, by stealth, furtively. **украду́** *etc.*: *see* **укрáсть**

Укрáина, -ы (the) Ukraine. **украи́нец, -нца, украи́нка, -и** Ukrainian. **украи́нский** Ukrainian.

укрáсить, -áшу *pf.* (*impf.* **украшáть**) adorn, decorate, ornament; **~ся** be decorated; adorn o.s.

у|крáсть, -аду́, -дёшь *pf.*

украшáть(ся, -áю(сь *impf. of* **укрáсить(ся. украшéние, -я** adorning; decoration; adornment; ornament.

укрепи́ть, -плю́ *pf.*, **укрепля́ть, -я́ю** *impf.* strengthen; reinforce; fix, make fast; fortify; consolidate; brace; enhance; **~ся** become stronger; fortify one's position. **укреплéние, -я** strengthening; reinforcement; consolidation; fortification; work. **укрепля́ющее** *sb.* tonic, restorative.

укрóмный secluded, sheltered, cosy.

укрóп, -а (-у) dill.

укроти́тель, -я *m.* (animal-)tamer. **укроти́ть, -ощу́** *pf.*, **укрощáть, -áю** *impf.* tame; curb, subdue, check; **~ся** become tame, be tamed; calm down, die down. **укрощéние, -я** taming.

укрóю *etc.*: *see* **укрыть**
укрупнéние, -я enlargement, extension; amalgamation. **укрупнúть, -ню́** *pf.*, **укрупня́ть, -я́ю** *impf.* enlarge, extend; amalgamate.
укрывáтель, -я *m.* concealer, harbourer; ~ **крáденого** receiver (of stolen goods). **укрывáтельство, -а** concealment, harbouring; receiving. **укрывáть, -áю** *impf.*, **укры́ть, -рóю** *pf.* cover, cover up; conceal, harbour; give shelter (to); receive, act as receiver of; **~ся** cover o.s.; take cover; find shelter; escape notice. **укры́тие, -я** cover; concealment; shelter.
ýксус, -а (-у) vinegar.
укýс, -а bite; sting. **укусúть, -ушý, -ýсишь** *pf.* bite; sting.
укýтать, -аю *pf.*, **укýтывать, -аю** *impf.* wrap up; **~ся** wrap o.s. up.
укушý *etc.*: *see* **укусúть**
ул. *abbr.* (*of* **ýлица**) St., Street; Rd., Road.
улáвливать, -аю *impf. of* **уловúть**
улáдить, -áжу *pf.*, **улáживать, -аю** *impf.* settle, arrange; reconcile.
улáмывать, -аю *impf. of* **уломáть**
ýлей, ýлья (bee)hive.
улетáть, -áю *impf.*, **улетéть, улечý** *pf.* fly, fly away; vanish. **улетýчиваться, -аюсь** *impf.*, **улетýчиться, -чусь** *pf.* evaporate, volatilize; vanish, disappear.
улéчься, уля́гусь, -я́жешься; улёгся, -глáсь *pf.* (*impf.* **уклáдываться**) lie down; find room; settle; subside; calm down.
улизнýть, -нý, -нёшь *pf.* slip away, steal away.
улúка, -и clue; evidence.
улúтка, -и snail.
ýлица, -ы street; **на ýлице** in the street; out of doors, outside.
уличáть, -áю *impf.*, **уличúть, -чý** *pf.* establish the guilt of; ~ **в**+*p.* catch out in.
ýличный street.
улóв, -а catch, take, haul. **уловúмый** perceptible; audible. **уловúть, -влю́, -вишь** *pf.* (*impf.* **улáвливать**) catch, pick up, locate; detect, perceive; seize. **улóвка, -и** trick, ruse, subterfuge.
уложéние, -я code. **уложúть, -жý, -жишь** *pf.* (*impf.* **уклáдывать**) lay; pack; stow; pile, stack; cover; set; ~ **спать** put to bed; **~ся** pack, pack up; go in; fit in; sink in; +**в**+*a.* keep within, confine o.s. to.
уломáть, -áю (*impf.* **улáмывать**) talk round, prevail on.
улучáть, -áю *impf.*, **улучúть, -чý** *pf.* find, seize, catch.
улучшáть, -áю *impf.*, **улýчшить, -шу** *pf.* improve; ameliorate; better; **~ся** improve; get better. **улучшéние, -я** improvement; amelioration.
улыбáться, -áюсь *impf.*, **улыбнýться, -нýсь, -нёшься** *pf.* smile; +*d.* appeal to. **улы́бка, -и** smile.
ультра... *in comb.* ultra-. **ультравысóкий** ultra-high. **~звуковóй** supersonic, ultrasonic. **~корóткий** ultra-short. **~фиолéтовый** ultra-violet.
уля́гусь *etc.*: *see* **улéчься**
ум, -á mind, intellect; wits; head; **свестú с ~á** drive mad; **склад ~á** mentality; turn of mind; **сойтú с ~á** go mad; go crazy.
умалéние, -я belittling, disparagement. **умалúть, -лю́** *pf.* (*impf.* **умаля́ть**) belittle, disparage; decrease, lessen.
умалишённый mad, lunatic; *sb.* lunatic, madman, madwoman.
умáлчивать, -аю *impf. of* **умолчáть**
умаля́ть, -я́ю *impf. of* **умалúть**
умéлец, -льца skilled workman, craftsman. **умéлый** able, skilful; capable; skilled. **умéние, -я** ability, skill; know-how.
уменьшáть, -áю *impf.*, **умéньшúть, -шу** *or* **-шý** *pf.* reduce, diminish, decrease, lessen; ~ **расхóды** cut down expenditure; ~ **скóрость** slow down; **~ся** diminish, decrease, drop, dwindle; abate. **уменьшéние, -я** decrease, reduction, diminution, lessening, abatement. **уменьшúтельный** diminutive.
умéренность, -и moderation. **умéренный** moderate; temperate.
умерéть, умрý, -рёшь; ýмер, -лá, -о *pf.* (*impf.* **умирáть**) die.
умéрить, -рю *pf.* (*impf.* **умеря́ть**) moderate; restrain.
умертвúть, -рщвлю́ *pf.*, **умерщвля́ть, -я́ю** *impf.* kill, destroy; mortify. **ýмерший** dead; *sb.* the deceased. **умерщвлéние, -я** killing, destruction; mortification.
умеря́ть, -я́ю *impf. of* **умéрить**
уместúть, -ещý *pf.* (*impf.* **умещáть**) get in, fit in, find room for; **~ся** go in, fit in, find room. **умéстно** *adv.* appropriately; opportunely; to the point. **умéстный** appropriate; pertinent, to the point; opportune, timely.
умéть, -éю *impf.* be able, know how.
умещáть(ся, -áю(сь *impf. of* **уместúть(ся**
умилéние, -я tenderness; emotion. **умилúтельный** moving, touching, affecting. **умилúть, -лю́** *pf.*, **умиля́ть, -я́ю** *impf.* move, touch; **~ся** be moved, be touched.
умирáние, -я dying. **умирáть, -áю** *impf. of* **умерéть. умирáющий** dying; *sb.* dying person.
умнéть, -éю *impf.* (*pf.* **по~**) grow wiser.
ýмник, -а good boy; clever person. **ýмница, -ы** good girl; *c.g.* clever person. **ýмнó** *adv.* cleverly, wisely; sensibly.
умножáть, -áю *impf.*, **у|мнóжить, -жу** *pf.* multiply; increase; augment; **~ся** increase, multiply. **умножéние, -я** multiplication; increase, rise. **умножúтель, -я** *m.* multiplier.
ýмный; умён, умнá, ýмнó clever, wise, intelligent; sensible. **умозаключáть, -áю** *impf.*, **умозаключúть, -чý** *pf.* deduce; infer, conclude. **умозаключéние, -я** deduction; conclusion, inference.
умолúть, -лю́ *pf.* (*impf.* **умоля́ть**) move by entreaties.

ýмолк, -у; без ~у without stopping, incessantly. **умолка́ть, -а́ю** *impf.*, **умо́лкнуть, -ну; -о́лк** *pf.* fall silent; stop; cease. **умолча́ть, -чý** *pf.* (*impf.* **ума́лчивать**) pass over in silence, fail to mention, suppress.

умоля́ть, -я́ю *impf. of* **умоли́ть**; beg, entreat, implore, beseech. **умоля́ющий** imploring, pleading.

умопомеша́тельство, -а derangement, madness, insanity.

умори́тельный incredibly funny, killing. **у|мори́ть, -рю́** *pf.* kill; tire out, exhaust.

умо́ю *etc.*: *see* **умы́ть.** **умрý** *etc.*: *see* **умере́ть**

ýмственный mental, intellectual; **~ труд** brainwork.

умудри́ть, -рю́ *pf.*, **умудря́ть, -я́ю** *impf.* make wise, make wiser; **~ся** contrive, manage.

умча́ть, -чý *pf.* whirl away, dash away; **~ся** whirl away, dash away.

умыва́льная *sb.* lavatory, cloak-room. **умыва́льник, -а** wash-stand, wash-basin. **умыва́льный** wash, washing. **умыва́ть(ся, -а́ю(сь** *impf. of* **умы́ть(ся**

ýмысел, -сла design, intention; **злой ~** evil intent; **с ýмыслом** of set purpose.

умы́ть, умо́ю *pf.* (*impf.* **умыва́ть**) wash; **~ся** wash (o.s.).

умы́шленный intentional, deliberate.

унаво́живать, -аю *impf.*, **у|наво́зить, -о́жу** *pf.* manure.

у|насле́довать, -дую *pf.*

унести́, -сý, -сёшь; -ёс, -ла́ *pf.* (*impf.* **уноси́ть**) take away; carry off, make off with; carry away, remove; **~сь** whirl away; fly away, fly by; be carried (away).

универма́г, -а *abbr.* department store. **универса́льн|ый** universal; all-round; many-sided; versatile; multi-purpose, all-purpose; **~ магази́н** department store; **~ое сре́дство** panacea. **универса́м, -а** *abbr.* supermarket.

университе́т, -а university. **университе́тский** university.

унижа́ть, -а́ю *impf.*, **уни́зить, -и́жу** *pf.* humble; humiliate; lower, degrade; **~ся** debase o.s., lower o.s., stoop. **униже́ние, -я** humiliation, degradation, abasement. **уни́женный** humble. **унижённый** oppressed, degraded. **унизи́тельный** humiliating, degrading.

унима́ть(ся, -а́ю(сь *impf. of* **уня́ть(ся**

унита́з, -а lavatory pan.

уничтожа́ть, -а́ю *impf.*, **уничто́жить, -жу** *pf.* destroy, annihilate; wipe out; exterminate, obliterate; abolish; do away with, eliminate; put an end to; crush. **уничтожа́ющий** destructive, annihilating. **уничтоже́ние, -я** destruction, annihilation; extermination, obliteration; abolition, elimination.

уноси́ть(ся, -ошý(сь, -о́сишь(ся *impf. of* **унести́(сь**

ýнтер, -а, ýнтер-офице́р, -а non-commissioned officer, NCO.

унывáть, -а́ю *impf.* be depressed, be dejected. **уны́лый** depressed, dejected, despondent, downcast; melancholy, doleful, cheerless. **уны́ние, -я** depression, dejection, despondency.

уня́ть, уймý, -мёшь; -я́л, -а́, -о *pf.* (*impf.* **унима́ть**) calm, soothe, pacify; stop, check; suppress; **~ся** calm down; stop, abate, die down.

упа́док, -дка decline; decay, collapse; decadence; depression; **~ дýха** depression. **упа́дочнический** decadent. **упа́дочный** depressive; decadent. **упадý** *etc.*: *see* **упа́сть**

у|пакова́ть, -кýю *pf.*, **упако́вывать, -аю** *impf.* pack (up); wrap (up), bale. **упако́вка, -и** packing; wrapping, baling; package. **упако́вочный** packing. **упако́вщик, -а** packer.

упа́сть, -адý, -адёшь *pf. of* **па́дать**

упере́ть, упрý, -рёшь; -ёр *pf.*, **упира́ть, -а́ю** *impf.* rest, prop, lean (heavily); (*sl.*) pinch, steal; **~ глаза́ в**+*a.* fix one's eyes on; **~ на**+*a.* stress, insist on; **~ся** rest, lean, prop o.s.; resist; jib; dig one's heels in; +**в**+*a.* come up against; run into

упи́танный well-fed; fattened; plump.

упла́та, -ы payment, paying. **у|плати́ть, -ачý, -а́тишь** *pf.*, **упла́чивать, -аю** *impf.* pay.

уплотне́ние, -я compression; condensation; consolidation; sealing. **уплотни́ть, -ню́** *pf.*, **уплотня́ть, -я́ю** *impf.* condense; consolidate, concentrate, compress; pack (in).

уплыва́ть, -а́ю *impf.*, **уплы́ть, -ывý, -ывёшь; -ы́л, -а́, -о** *pf.* swim away; sail away, steam away; pass, elapse; be lost to sight; vanish, ebb.

уподо́биться, -блюсь *pf.*, **уподобля́ться, -я́юсь** *impf.*+*d.* become like; be assimilated to. **уподобле́ние, -я** likening, comparison; assimilation.

упое́ние, -я ecstasy, rapture, thrill. **упоённый** intoxicated, thrilled, in raptures. **упои́тельный** intoxicating, ravishing.

уполза́ть, -а́ю *impf.*, **уползти́, -зý, -зёшь; -о́лз, -зла́** *pf.* creep away, crawl away.

уполномо́ченный *sb.* (authorized) agent, delegate, representative; proxy; commissioner. **уполнома́чивать, уполномо́чивать, -аю** *impf.*, **уполномо́чить, -чу** *pf.* authorize, empower. **уполномо́чие, -я** authorization; authority; credentials.

упомина́ние, -я mention; reference; reminder. **упомина́ть, -а́ю** *impf.*, **упомянýть, -нý, -нешь** *pf.* mention, refer to.

упо́р, -а rest, prop, support; stay, brace; **в ~** point-blank; **сде́лать ~ на**+*a. or p.* lay stress on; **смотре́ть в ~ на**+*a.* stare straight at. **упо́рный** stubborn, unyielding, obstinate; dogged, persistent; sustained. **...упо́рный** *in comb.* -resistant. **упо́рство, -а** stubbornness, obstinacy; doggedness, persistence. **упо́рствовать, -твую** *impf.* be stubborn; persist (**в**+*p.* in).

упоря́дочивать, -аю *impf.*, **упоря́дочить, -чу** *pf.* regulate, put in (good) order, set to rights.

употреби́тельный (widely-)used; common, generally accepted, usual. **употреби́ть, -блю́** *pf.*, **употребля́ть, -я́ю** *impf.* use; make use of; take. **употребле́ние, -я** use; usage; application; **вы́йти из употребле́ния** go out of use, fall into disuse; **спо́соб употребле́ния** directions for use.

управде́л, -а *abbr.* office manager, business manager. **управдо́м, -а** *abbr.* manager (*of block of flats*), house manager. **управи́тель, -я** *m.* manager; bailiff, steward. **упра́виться, -влюсь** *pf.*, **управля́ться, -я́юсь** *impf.* cope, manage; +**с**+*i.* deal with. **управле́ние, -я** management; administration; direction; control; driving, piloting, steering; government; authority, directorate, board; controls; **под управле́нием**+*g.* conducted by; ~ **автомоби́лем** driving; ~ **на расстоя́нии** remote control; ~ **по ра́дио** radio control. **управля́емый снаря́д** guided missile. **управля́ть, -я́ю** *impf.*+*i.* manage, administer, direct, run; govern; be in charge of; control, operate; drive, pilot, steer, navigate; ~ **весло́м** paddle. **управля́ющий** control, controlling; *sb.* manager; bailiff, steward; ~ **по́ртом** harbour-master.

упражне́ние, -я exercise. **упражня́ть, -я́ю** *impf.* exercise, train; ~**ся** practise, train.

упраздне́ние, -я abolition; cancellation, annulment. **упраздни́ть, -ню́** *pf.*, **упраздня́ть, -я́ю** *impf.* abolish; cancel, annul.

упра́шивать, -аю *impf. of* **упроси́ть**

упрева́ть, -а́ет *impf. of* **упре́ть**

упрёк, -а reproach, reproof. **упрека́ть, -а́ю** *impf.*, **упрекну́ть, -ну́, -нёшь** *pf.* reproach, reprove; accuse, charge.

у|пре́ть, -е́ет *pf.* (*impf. also* **упрева́ть**) stew.

упроси́ть, -ошу́, -о́сишь *pf.* (*impf.* **упра́шивать**) beg, entreat; prevail upon.

упрости́ть, -ощу́ *pf.* (*impf.* **упроща́ть**) simplify; over-simplify; ~**ся** be simplified, get simpler.

упро́чивать, -аю *impf.*, **упро́чить, -чу** *pf.* strengthen, consolidate; fix; secure; establish firmly; +**за**+*i.* leave to; establish for, ensure for; ~**ся** be strengthened, be consolidated; become firmer; be firmly established; establish o.s.; settle o.s.; +**за**+*i.* become attached to, stick to.

упрошу́ *etc.*: *see* **упроси́ть**

упроща́ть(ся, -а́ю(сь *impf. of* **упрости́ть(ся. упроще́ние, -я** simplification. **упрощённый; -щён, -а́** simplified; over-simplified.

упру́ *etc.*: *see* **упере́ть**

упру́гий elastic; resilient, flexible; springy. **упру́гость, -и** elasticity; pressure, tension; spring, bound. **упру́же** *comp. of* **упру́гий**

упря́жка, -и harness, gear; team, relay. **упряжн|о́й** draught; ~**а́я ло́шадь** draught-horse, carriage-horse. **у́пряжь, -и** harness, gear.

упря́миться, -млюсь *impf.* be obstinate; persist. **упря́мство, -а** obstinacy, stubbornness. **упря́мый** obstinate, stubborn; persistent.

упря́тать, -я́чу *pf.*, **упря́тывать, -аю** *impf.* hide, conceal; put away, banish ~**ся** hide.

упуска́ть, -а́ю *impf.*, **упусти́ть, -ущу́, -у́стишь** *pf.* let go, let slip, let fall; miss; lose; neglect; ~ **из виду** lose sight of, overlook, fail to take account of. **упуще́ние, -я** omission; slip; negligence.

ура́ *int.* hurray!, hurrah!

уравне́ние, -я equalization; equation. **ура́внивать, -аю** *impf.*, **уравня́ть, -я́ю** *pf.* equalize, make equal, make level; equate. **уравни́тельный** equalizing, levelling. **уравнове́сить, -е́шу** *pf.*, **уравнове́шивать, -аю** *impf.* balance; equilibrate; counterbalance; neutralize. **уравнове́шенность, -и** balance, steadiness, composure. **уравнове́шенный** balanced, steady, composed.

урага́н, -а hurricane; storm.

Ура́л, -а the Urals.

ура́н, -а uranium; Uranus. **ура́новый** uranium; uranic.

урва́ть, -ву́, -вёшь; -а́л, -а́, -о *pf.* (*impf.* **урыва́ть**) snatch, grab.

урегули́рование, -я regulation; settlement, adjustment. **у|регули́ровать, -рую** *pf.*

уре́з, -а reduction, cut. **уре́зать, -е́жу** *pf.*, **уреза́ть, -а́ю, уре́зывать, -аю** *impf.* cut off; shorten; cut down, reduce; axe.

у́рна, -ы urn; ballot-box; refuse-bin, litter-bin.

у́ровень, -вня *m.* level; plane; standard; grade; gauge.

уро́д, -а freak, monster; deformed person; ugly person; depraved person.

уроди́ться, -ожу́сь *pf.* ripen; grow; be born; +**в**+*a.* take after.

уро́дливость, -и deformity; ugliness. **уро́дливый** deformed, misshapen; ugly; bad; abnormal; faulty; distorting, distorted. **уро́довать, -дую** *impf.* (*pf.* **из**~) deform, disfigure, mutilate; make ugly; distort. **уро́дство, -а** deformity; disfigurement; ugliness; abnormality.

урожа́й, -я harvest; crop, yield; abundance. **урожа́йность, -и** yield; productivity. **урожа́йный** harvest; productive, high-yield; ~ **год** good year.

урождённый née; inborn, born. **уроже́нец, -нца, уроже́нка, -и** native. **урожу́сь** *see* **уроди́ться**

уро́к, -а lesson; homework; task.

уро́н, -а losses, casualties; damage. **урони́ть, -ню́, -нишь** *pf. of* **роня́ть**

уро́чный fixed, agreed; usual, established.

урыва́ть, -а́ю *impf. of* **урва́ть. уры́вками** *adv.* in snatches, by fits and starts; at odd moments. **уры́вочный** fitful; occasional.

ус, -а; *pl.* **-ы́** whisker; antenna; tendril; awn; *pl.* moustache.

усади́ть, -ажу́, -а́дишь *pf.*, **уса́живать, -аю** *impf.* seat, offer a seat; make sit down; set; plant; cover; ~ **в тюрьму́** clap in prison. **уса́дьба, -ы**; *g.pl.* **-деб** *or* **-дьб** country estate, country seat; farmstead; farm centre. **уса́живаться, -аюсь** *impf. of* **усе́сться**

уса́тый moustached; whiskery; whiskered.

усва́ивать, -аю *impf.*, **усво́ить, -о́ю** *pf.* master; assimilate; adopt, acquire; imitate; pick up. **усвое́ние, -я** mastering; assimilation; adoption.

усе́ивать, -аю *impf. of* **усе́ять**

усе́рдие, -я zeal; diligence. **усе́рдный** zealous; diligent, painstaking.

усе́сться, уся́дусь; -е́лся *pf.* (*impf.* **уса́живаться**) take a seat; settle; set (to), settle down (to).

усе́ять, -е́ю *pf.* (*impf.* **усе́ивать**) sow; cover, dot, stud; litter, strew.

усиде́ть, -ижу́ *pf.* keep one's place, remain seated, sit still; hold down a job. **уси́дчивость, -и** assiduity. **уси́дчивый** assiduous; painstaking.

у́сик, -а tendril; awn; runner; antenna; *pl.* small moustache.

усиле́ние, -я strengthening; reinforcement; intensification; aggravation; amplification. **уси́ленный** reinforced; intensified, increased; earnest, urgent, importunate; copious. **уси́ливать, -аю** *impf.*, **уси́лить, -лю** *pf.* intensify, increase, heighten; aggravate; amplify; strengthen, reinforce; **~ся** increase, intensify; become stronger; become aggravated; swell, grow louder; make efforts, try. **уси́лие, -я** effort; exertion. **усили́тель, -я** *m.* amplifier; booster. **усили́тельный** amplifying; booster.

ускака́ть, -ачу́, -а́чешь *pf.* bound away; skip off; gallop off.

ускольза́ть, -а́ю *impf.*, **ускользну́ть, -ну́, -нёшь** *pf.* slip off; steal away; get away; disappear; escape; +**от**+*g.* evade, avoid.

ускоре́ние, -я acceleration; speeding-up. **ускори́тель, -я** *m.* accelerator. **уско́рить, -рю** *pf.*, **ускоря́ть, -я́ю** *impf.* quicken; speed up, accelerate; hasten; precipitate; **~ся** accelerate, be accelerated; quicken.

усла́вливаться *see* **усло́виться**

услади́ть, -ажу́ *pf.*, **услажда́ть, -а́ю** *impf.* delight, charm; soften, mitigate.

уследи́ть, -ежу́ *pf.* +**за**+*i.* keep an eye on, mind; follow.

усло́вие, -я condition; clause, term; stipulation, proviso; agreement; *pl.* conditions; **усло́вия приёма** reception. **усло́виться, -влюсь** *pf.*, **усло́вливаться, усла́вливаться, -аюсь** *impf.* agree, settle; arrange, make arrangements. **усло́вленный** agreed, fixed, stipulated. **усло́вность, -и** convention, conventionality; conditional character. **усло́вный** conditional; conditioned; conventional; agreed, prearranged; relative; theoretical; **~ знак** conventional sign.

усложне́ние, -я complication. **усложни́ть, -ню́** *pf.*, **усложня́ть, -я́ю** *impf.* complicate; **~ся** become complicated.

услу́га, -и service; good turn; *pl.* service(s), public utilities; **оказа́ть услу́гу** do a service. **услу́живать, -аю** *impf.* **услужи́ть, -жу́, -жишь** *pf.* serve, act as a servant; +*d.* do a service, do a good turn. **услу́жливый** obliging.

услыха́ть, -ы́шу *pf.*, **у|слы́шать, -ы́шу** *pf.* hear; sense; scent.

усма́тривать, -аю *impf. of* **усмотре́ть**

усмеха́ться, -а́юсь *impf.*, **усмехну́ться, -ну́сь, -нёшься** *pf.* smile; grin; sneer; smirk. **усме́шка, -и** smile; grin; sneer.

усмире́ние, -я pacification; suppression, putting down. **усмири́ть, -рю́** *pf.*, **усмиря́ть, -я́ю** *impf.* pacify; calm, quieten; tame; suppress, put down.

усмотре́ние, -я discretion, judgement; **по усмотре́нию** at one's discretion, as one thinks best. **усмотре́ть, -рю́, -ришь** *pf.* (*impf.* **усма́тривать**) perceive, observe; see; regard, interpret.

усну́ть, -ну́, -нёшь *pf.* go to sleep, fall asleep.

усоверше́нствование, -я perfecting; finishing, qualifying; advanced studies; improvement, refinement. **усоверше́нствованный** improved; finished, complete. **у|соверше́нствовать(ся, -твую(сь** *pf.*

усомни́ться, -ню́сь *pf.* doubt.

усо́пший *sb.* (the) deceased.

успева́емость, -и progress. **успева́ть, -а́ю** *impf.*, **успе́ть, -е́ю** *pf.* have time; manage; succeed, be successful. **успе́ется** *impers.* there is still time, there is no hurry. **успе́х, -а** success; progress. **успе́шный** successful.

успока́ивать, -аю *impf.*, **успоко́ить, -о́ю** *pf.* calm, quiet, soothe, tranquillize; reassure, set one's mind at rest; assuage, deaden; reduce to order, control; **~ся** calm down; compose o.s.; rest content; abate; become still; drop. **успока́ивающ|ий** calming, soothing, sedative; **~ее сре́дство** sedative, tranquillizer. **успокое́ние, -я** calming, quieting, soothing; calm; peace, tranquillity. **успокои́тельн|ый** calming, soothing; reassuring; **~ое** *sb.* sedative, tranquillizer.

уста́в, -а regulations, rules, statutes; service regulations; rule; charter.

устава́ть, -таю́, -ёшь *impf. of* **уста́ть; не устава́я** incessantly, uninterruptedly.

уста́вить, -влю *pf.*, **уставля́ть, -я́ю** *impf.* set, arrange, dispose; cover, fill, pile; direct, fix; **~ся** find room, go in; fix one's gaze, stare; become fixed, become steady. **уста́вный** regulation, statutory, prescribed.

уста́лость, -и fatigue, tiredness, weariness. **уста́лый** tired, weary, fatigued.

устана́вливать, -аю *impf.*, **установи́ть, -влю́, -вишь** *pf.* place, put, set up; install, mount, rig up; adjust, regulate, set; establish; institute; fix, prescribe; secure; obtain; determine; ascertain; **~ся** take position, dispose o.s.; be settled, be established; set in; be formed; be fixed. **устано́вка, -и** placing, putting, setting up, arrangement; installation;

mounting, rigging; adjustment, regulation, setting; plant, unit; directions, directive. **установлéние, -я** establishment; statute; institution. **установленный** established, fixed, prescribed, regulation.

устáну *etc.*: *see* **устáть**

устаревáть, -áю *impf.*, **у|старéть, -éю** *pf.* grow old; become obsolete; become antiquated, go out of date. **устарéлый** obsolete; antiquated, out-of-date.

устáть, -áну *pf.* (*impf.* **уставáть**) become tired, tire; **я устáла** I am tired.

ýстно *adv.* orally, by word of mouth. **ýстн|ый** oral, verbal; **~ая речь** spoken language.

устóй, -я abutment, buttress, pier; foundation, support; *pl.* foundations, bases. **устóйчивость, -и** stability, steadiness, firmness; resistance. **устóйчивый** stable, steady, firm; settled; resistant (**к**+*d.* to). **устоять, -ою** *pf.* keep one's balance, keep one's feet; stand firm, stand one's ground; resist, hold out.

устрáивать(ся, -аю(сь *impf. of* **устрóить(ся**

устранéние, -я removal, elimination, clearing. **утсранúть, -ню** *pf.*, **устранять, -яю** *impf.* remove; eliminate, clear; dismiss; **~ся** resign, retire, withdraw.

устрашáть, -áю *impf.*, **устрашúть, -шý** *pf.* frighten; scare; **~ся** be afraid; be frightened, be terrified. **устрашáющий** frightening; deterrent. **устрашéние, -я** frightening; fright, fear; **срéдство устрашéния** deterrent.

устремúть, -млю *pf.*, **устремлять, -яю** *impf.* direct, fix; **~ся** rush; head; be directed, be fixed, be concentrated; concentrate. **устремлéние, -я** rush; striving, aspiration. **устремлённость, -и** tendency.

ýстрица, -ы oyster. **ýстричный** oyster.

устроéние, -я arranging, organization. **устрóитель, -я** *m.*, **тельница, -ы** organizer. **устрóить, -óю** *pf.* (*impf.* **устрáивать**) arrange, organize; establish; make; construct; cause, create; settle, order, put in order; place, fix up; get, secure; suit, be convenient; **~ на рабóту** find, fix up with, a job; **~ скандáл** make a scene; **~ся** work out; come right; manage, make arrangements; settle down, get settled; be found, get fixed up. **устрóйство, -а** arrangement, organization; (mode of) construction; layout; apparatus, mechanism, device; structure, system; **запоминáющее ~** (*comput.*) storage (device), memory; **постоянное запоминáющее ~** (*comput.*) ROM (*read-only memory*).

устýп, -а shelf, ledge; terrace; bench. **уступáть, -áю** *impf.*, **уступúть, -плю, -пишь** *pf.* yield; give in; cede; concede; let have, give up; be inferior; take off, knock off; **~ дорóгу** make way; **~ мéсто** give up one's place, seat. **устýпка, -и** concession, compromise; reduction. **устýпчатый** ledged, stepped, terraced. **устýпчивый** pliant, pliable; compliant, tractable.

устыдúться, -ыжýсь *pf.* (+*g.*) be ashamed (of).

ýстье, -я; *g.pl.* **-ьев** mouth; estuary.

усугýбить, -ýблю *pf.*, **усугублять, -яю** *impf.* increase; intensify; aggravate, make worse.

усы́ *see* **ус**

усыновúть, -влю *pf.*, **усыновлять, -яю** *impf.* adopt. **усыновлéние, -я** adoption.

усы́пать, -плю *pf.*, **усыпáть, -áю** *impf.* strew, scatter; cover.

усыпúтельный soporific. **усыпúть, -плю** *pf.*, **усыплять, -яю** *impf.* put to sleep; lull; weaken, undermine, neutralize; **~ боль** deaden pain.

усядусь *etc.*: *see* **усéсться**

утáивать, -аю *impf.*, **утаúть, -аю** *pf.* conceal; keep to o.s., keep secret; appropriate.

утáптывать, -аю *impf. of* **утоптáть**

утáскивать, -аю *impf.*, **утащúть, -щý, -щишь** *pf.* drag away, drag off; make off with.

ýтварь, -и utensils, equipment.

утвердúтельный affirmative. **утвердúть, -ржý** *pf.*, **утверждáть, -áю** *impf.* confirm; approve; sanction, ratify; establish; assert, maintain, hold, claim, allege. **утверждéние, -я** approval; confirmation; ratification; assertion, affirmation, claim, allegation; establishment.

утекáть, -áю *impf. of* **утéчь**

утёнок, -нка; *pl.* **утята, -ят** duckling.

утерéть, утрý, -рёшь; утёр *pf.* (*impf.* **утирáть**) wipe; wipe off; wipe dry; **~ нос**+*d.* score off.

утерпéть, -плю, -пишь *pf.* restrain o.s.

утéря, -и loss. **у|терять, -яю** *pf.*

утёс, -а cliff, crag. **утёсистый** steep, precipitous.

утéчка, -и leak, leakage; escape; loss, wastage, dissipation; **~ гáза** escape of gas. **утéчь, -екý, -ечёшь; утёк, -лá** *pf.* (*impf.* **утекáть**) flow away; leak, escape; run away; pass, elapse, go by.

утешáть, -áю *impf.*, **утéшить, -шу** *pf.* comfort, console; **~ся** console o.s. **утешéние, -я** comfort, consolation. **утешúтельный** comforting, consoling.

утúль, -я *m.*, **утильсырьё, -я** salvage; scrap; rubbish, refuse. **утúльный** scrap.

утúный duck, duck's.

утирáть(ся, -áю(сь *impf. of* **утерéть(ся**

утихáть, -áю *impf.*, **утúхнуть, -ну; -úх** *pf.* abate, subside; cease, die away; slacken; drop; become calm, calm down.

ýтка, -и duck; canard.

уткнýть, -нý, -нёшь *pf.* bury; fix; **~ся** bury o.s.; **~ся головóй в подýшку** bury one's head in the pillow.

утолúть, -лю *pf.* (*impf.* **утолять**) quench, slake; satisfy; relieve, alleviate, soothe.

утолстúть, -лщý *pf.*, **утолщáть, -áю** *impf.* thicken, make thicker; **~ся** thicken, become thicker. **утолщéние, -я** thickening; thickened part, bulge; reinforcement, rib, boss.

утолять, -яю *impf. of* **утолúть**

утомúтельный tiresome; tedious; wearisome,

tiring, fatiguing. **утоми́ть, -млю́** *pf.*, **утомля́ть, -я́ю** *impf.* tire, weary, fatigue; **~ся** get tired. **утомле́ние, -я** tiredness, weariness, fatigue. **утомлённый** tired, weary, fatigued.

у|тону́ть, -ну́, -нешь *pf.* (*impf. also* **утопа́ть**) drown, be drowned; sink, go down.

утончённость, -и refinement. **утончённый** refined; exquisite, subtle.

утопа́ть, -а́ю *impf. of* **утону́ть** roll, wallow.

у|топи́ть(ся, -плю́(сь, -пишь(ся *pf.* **уто́пленник, -а** drowned man.

утопта́ть, -пчу́, -пчешь *pf.* (*impf.* **ута́птывать**) trample down, pound.

уточне́ние, -я more precise definition; amplification, elaboration. **уточни́ть, -ню́** *pf.*, **уточня́ть, -я́ю** *impf.* define more precisely; amplify, elaborate.

утра́ивать, -аю *impf. of* **утро́ить**

у|трамбова́ть, -бу́ю *pf.*, **утрамбо́вывать, -аю** *impf.* ram, tamp; **~ся** become flat, become level.

утра́та, -ы loss. **утра́тить, -а́чу** *pf.*, **утра́чивать, -аю** *impf.* lose.

у́тренний morning, early. **у́тренник, -а** morning performance, matinée; early-morning frost.

утри́ровать, -рую *impf.* & *pf.* exaggerate; overplay. **утриро́вка, -и** exaggeration.

у́тро, -а *or* **-а́, -у** *or* **-у́**; *pl.* **-а, -ам** *or* **-а́м** morning.

утро́ба, -ы womb; belly.

утро́ить, -о́ю *pf.* (*impf.* **утра́ивать**) triple, treble.

у́тром *adv.* in the morning; **сего́дня ~** this morning.

утру́ *etc.*: *see* **утере́ть, у́тро**

утруди́ть, -ужу́ *pf.*, **утружда́ть, -а́ю** *impf.* trouble, tire.

утю́г, -а́ iron. **утю́жить, -жу** *impf.* (*pf.* **вы́~, от~**) iron, press; smooth. **утю́жка, -и** ironing, pressing.

ух *int.* oh, ooh, ah.

уха́, -и́ fish soup.

уха́б, -а pot-hole. **уха́бистый** full of pot-holes; bumpy.

уха́живать, -аю *impf.* **за**+*i.* nurse, tend; look after; court; pay court to, make advances to.

у́хать, -аю *impf. of* **у́хнуть**

ухвати́ть, -ачу́, -а́тишь *pf.*, **ухва́тывать, -аю** *impf.* catch, lay hold of; seize; grasp; **~ся за**+*a.* grasp, lay hold of; set to, set about; seize; jump at; take up. **ухва́тка, -и** grip; grasp; skill; trick; manner.

ухитри́ться, -рю́сь *pf.*, **ухитря́ться, -я́юсь** *impf.* manage, contrive.

ухло́пать, -аю *pf.*, **ухло́пывать, -аю** *impf.* squander, waste; (*sl.*) kill.

ухмы́лка, -и smirk, grin. **ухмыльну́ться, -ну́сь, -нёшься** *pf.*, **ухмыля́ться, -я́юсь** *impf.* smirk, grin.

у́хнуть, -ну *pf.* (*impf.* **у́хать**) cry out; hoot; crash; bang; rumble; slip, fall; come a cropper; come to grief; drop; lose, squander, spend up.

у́хо, -а; *pl.* **у́ши, уше́й** ear; ear-flap, ear-piece; lug, hanger; **заткну́ть у́ши** stop one's ears; **кра́ем ~а** with half an ear; **по́ уши** up to one's eyes; **слу́шать во все у́ши** be all ears; **туго́й на́ ~** hard of hearing.

ухо́д[1], **-а** +**за**+*i.* care of; maintenance of; nursing, tending, looking after.

ухо́д[2], **-а** going away, leaving, departure; withdrawal. **уходи́ть, -ожу́, -о́дишь** *impf. of* **уйти́**; stretch, extend.

ухудша́ть, -а́ю *impf.*, **уху́дшить, -шу** *pf.* make worse, aggravate; **~ся** get worse.

уцеле́ть, -е́ю *pf.* remain intact, escape destruction; survive; escape.

уцепи́ть, -плю́, -пишь *pf.*, **уцепля́ть, -я́ю** *impf.* catch hold of, grasp, seize; **~ся за**+*a.* catch hold of, grasp, seize; jump at.

уча́ствовать, -твую *impf.* take part, participate; have a share, hold shares. **уча́ствующий** *sb.* participant. **уча́стие, -я** participation, taking part; share, sharing; sympathy, concern.

участи́ть, -ащу́ *pf.* (*impf.* **учаща́ть**) make more frequent, quicken; **~ся** become more frequent, become more rapid.

уча́стливый sympathetic. **уча́стник, -а** participant, member; **~ состяза́ния** competitor. **уча́сток, -тка** plot, strip; allotment; lot, parcel; part, section, portion; length; division; sector, area, zone, district; police district, police-station; field, sphere. **у́часть, -и** lot, fate, portion.

учаща́ть(ся, -а́ю(сь *impf. of* **участи́ть(ся. учащённый; -ён, -ена́** quickened; faster.

уча́щийся *sb.* student; pupil. **учёба, -ы** studies; course; studying, learning; drill, training. **уче́бник, -а** text-book; manual, primer. **уче́бн|ый** educational; school; training, practice; **~ый год** academic year, school year; **~ые посо́бия** teaching aids; **~ое су́дно** training-ship. **уче́ние, -я** learning; studies; apprenticeship; teaching, instruction; doctrine; exercise; *pl.* training. **учени́к, -а́, учени́ца, -ы** pupil; student; learner; apprentice; disciple, follower. **учени́ческий** pupil'(s); apprentice('s); unskilled; raw, crude, immature. **учени́чество, -а** time spent as pupil or student; apprenticeship; rawness, immaturity. **учёность, -и** learning, erudition. **учён|ый** learned, erudite; educated; scholarly; academic; scientific; trained, performing; **~ая сте́пень** (*university*) degree; **~ый** *sb.* scholar; scientist.

уче́сть, учту́, -тёшь; учёл, учла́ *pf.* (*impf.* **учи́тывать**) take stock of, make an inventory of; take into account, take into consideration; allow for; bear in mind; discount.

учёт, -а stock-taking; reckoning, calculation; taking into account; registration; discount, discounting; **без ~а**+*g.* disregarding; **взять на ~** register. **учётн|ый** registration; discount; ~**ое отделе́ние** records section.

учи́лище, -а school; (training) college.

у|чини́ть, -ню́ *pf.*, **учиня́ть, -я́ю** *impf.* make; carry out, execute; commit.

учи́тель, -я; *pl.* **-я́** *m.*, **учи́тельница, -ы** teacher. **учи́тельск|ий** teacher's, teachers'; ~**ая** *sb.* staff-room.

учи́тывать, -аю *impf. of* **уче́сть**

учи́ть, учу́, у́чишь *impf.* (*pf.* **вы́~, на~, об~**) teach; be a teacher; learn, memorize; ~**ся** be a student; *+d. or inf.* learn, study.

учреди́тель, -я *m.* founder. **учреди́тельница, -ы** foundress. **учреди́тельн|ый** constituent; ~**ый акт** constituent act; ~**ое собра́ние** constituent assembly. **учреди́ть, -ежу́** *pf.*, **учрежда́ть, -а́ю** *impf.* found, establish, set up; introduce, institute. **учрежде́ние, -я** founding, setting up; establishment; institution.

учти́вый civil, courteous, polite.

учту́ *etc.*: *see* **уче́сть**

ушёл *etc.*: *see* **уйти́. у́ши** *etc.*: *see* **у́хо**

уши́б, -а injury; knock; bruise, contusion. **ушиба́ть, -а́ю** *impf.*, **ушиби́ть, -бу́, -бёшь; уши́б** *pf.* injure; bruise; hurt, shock; ~**ся** hurt o.s., give o.s. a knock; bruise o.s.

ушко́, -а́; *pl.* **-и́, -о́в** eye; lug; tab, tag.

ушно́й ear, aural.

уще́лье, -я ravine, gorge, canyon.

ущеми́ть, -млю́ *pf.*, **ущемля́ть, -я́ю** *impf.* pinch, jam, nip; limit; encroach on; wound, hurt. **ущемле́ние, -я** pinching, jamming, nipping; limitation; wounding, hurting. **уще́рб, -а** detriment; loss; damage, injury; prejudice; **на ~е** waning. **уще́рбный** waning.

ущипну́ть, -ну́, -нёшь *pf. of* **щипа́ть**

Уэ́льс, -а Wales.

ую́т, -а cosiness, comfort. **ую́тный** cosy, comfortable.

уязви́мый vulnerable. **уязви́ть, -влю́** *pf.*, **уязвля́ть, -я́ю** *impf.* wound, hurt.

уясне́ние, -я explanation, elucidation. **уясни́ть, -ню́** *pf.* **уясня́ть, -я́ю** *impf.* understand, make out; explain.

Ф

ф *letter*: *see* **эф**

фа *nt.indecl.* F; fah.

фаб... *abbr.* (*of* **фабри́чный**) *in comb.* factory, works. **фабко́м, -а** works committee.

фа́брика, -и factory, mill, works. **фабрика́нт, -а** manufacturer. **фабрика́т, -а** finished product, manufactured product. **фабрикова́ть, -ку́ю** *impf.* (*pf.* **с~**) manufacture, make, fabricate, forge. **фабри́чн|ый** factory; industrial, manufacturing; factory-made; ~**ая ма́рка**, ~**ое клеймо́** trade-mark.

фа́була, -ы plot, story.

фаго́т, -а bassoon. **фаготи́ст, -а** bassoon-player.

фа́за, -ы phase; stage.

фаза́н, -а, фазани́ха, -и pheasant. **фаза́ний** pheasant, pheasants'.

фа́зис, -а phase. **фа́зный, фа́зовый** phase.

фа́кел, -а torch, flare, flame. **факе́льный** torch(-light). **фа́кельщик, -а** torch-bearer; incendiary.

фа́кс, -а fax; **посла́ть по ~у** to fax. **факси́мильный; ~ аппара́т** fax (machine).

факт, -а fact; **соверши́вшийся ~** fait accompli. **факти́чески** *adv.* in fact, actually; practically, virtually, to all intents and purposes. **факти́ческий** actual; real; virtual.

факту́ра, -ы invoice, bill; style, execution, texture; structure.

факультати́вный optional. **факульте́т, -а** faculty, department. **факульте́тский** faculty.

фа́лда, -ы tail, skirt.

фальсифика́тор, -а falsifier, forger. **фальсифика́ция, -и** falsification; forging; adulteration; forgery, fake, counterfeit. **фальсифици́ровать, -рую** *impf.* & *pf.* falsify; forge; adulterate. **фальши́вить, -влю** *impf.* (*pf.* **с~**) be a hypocrite, act insincerely; sing or play out of tune. **фальши́вка, -и** forged document. **фальши́вый** false; spurious; forged, fake; artificial, imitation; off-key, out-of-tune; hypocritical, insincere. **фальшь, -и** deception, trickery; falsity; falseness; hypocrisy, insincerity.

фами́лия, -и surname; family, kin. **фами́льный** family. **фамилья́рничать, -аю** be over familiar, take liberties. **фамилья́рность, -и** familiarity; liberty, liberties. **фамилья́рный** (over-)familiar; unceremonious; offhand, casual.

фанати́зм, -а fanaticism. **фана́тик, -а** fanatic. **фанати́ческий** fanatical.

фане́ра, -ы veneer; plywood. **фане́рный** veneer, of veneer; plywood.

фантазёр, -а dreamer, visionary. **фантази́ровать, -рую** *impf.* (*pf.* **с~**) dream, indulge in fantasies; make up, dream up; improvise. **фанта́зия, -и** fantasy; fancy; imagination; whim; fabrication. **фанта́стика, -и** fiction, fantasy; the fantastic; works of fantasy; **нау́чная ~** science fiction. **фантасти́ческий, фантасти́чный** fantastic; fabulous; imaginary.

фа́ра, -ы headlight; **поса́дочные фа́ры** landing-lights.

фарао́н, -а pharaoh; faro. **фарао́нов** pharaoh's.

фарва́тер, -а fairway, channel.

фармазо́н, -а freemason.

фармаце́вт, -а pharmaceutical chemist. **фармацевти́ческий** pharmaceutical.

фарт, -а (*sl.*) luck, success.
фартук, -а apron; carriage-rug.
фарфор, -а china; porcelain. **фарфоров|ый** china; **~ая посуда** china.
фарцовщик, -а spiv, black marketeer.
фарш, -а stuffing, force-meat; minced meat, sausage-meat. **фаршированный** stuffed. **фаршировать, -рую** *impf.* (*pf.* **за~**) stuff.
фасовать, -сую *impf.* (*pf.* **рас~**) package, pre-pack. **фасовка, -и** packaging, pre-packing.
фасоль, -и kidney bean(s), French bean(s); haricot beans.
фасон, -а cut; fashion; style; manner, way; **держать ~** show off, put on airs. **фасонистый** fashionable, stylish. **фасонный** fashioned, shaped; form, forming, shape, shaping.
фаталист, -а fatalist. **фаталистический** fatalistic. **фатальность, -и** fatality, fate. **фатальный** fatal, fated; **~ вид** resigned appearance.
фашизм, -а Fascism. **фашист, -а** Fascist. **фашистский** Fascist.
фаянс, -а faience, pottery. **фаянсовый** pottery.
ФБР *abbr.* (*of* ***Федеральное бюро расследований***) FBI, Federal Bureau of Investigation.
февраль, -я *m.* February. **февральский** February.
федеративный federative, federal. **федерация, -и** federation.
феерический fairy-tale, magical.
фейерверк, -а firework, fireworks.
фельдмаршал, -а Field Marshal. **фельдшер, -а**; *pl.* **-а, -шерица, -ы** doctor's assistant; (*partly-qualified*) medical attendant; hospital attendant; trained nurse.
фельетон, -а feuilleton, feature.
фен, -а (hair-)dryer.
феномен, -а phenomenon; phenomenal occurrence, person. **феноменальный** phenomenal.
феодализм, -а feudalism. **феодальный** feudal.
ферзевый queen's. **ферзь, -я** *m.* (*chess*) queen.
ферма[1], **-ы** farm.
ферма[2], **-ы** girder, truss. **ферменный** lattice.
фермер, -а farmer.
фестиваль, -я *m.* festival.
фетр, -а felt. **фетровый** felt.
фехтовальный fencing, of fencing. **фехтовальщик, -а, -щица, -ы** fencer. **фехтование, -я** fencing. **фехтовать, -тую** *impf.* fence.
фея, -и fairy.
фиалка, -и violet.
фибергласс, -а fibreglass. **фиберглассовый** fibreglass.
фибра, -ы fibre. **фиброзный** fibrous.
фибролит, -а chipboard.
фига, -и fig(-tree).
фигаро *nt.indecl.* bolero.
фигляр, -а (*circus*) acrobat; clown; mountebank; buffoon. **фиглярить, -рю, фиглярничать, -аю, фиглярствовать, -твую** *impf.* put on an act.
фигура, -ы figure; court-card; (chess-)piece. **фигуральный** figurative, metaphorical; ornate, involved. **фигурант, -а** figurant; super, extra. **фигурировать, -ирую** *impf.* figure, appear. **фигурист, -а, -истка, -и** figure-skater. **фигурка, -и** figurine, statuette; figure. **фигурн|ый** figured; ornamented, patterned; figure; **~ое катание** figure-skating.
физик, -а physicist. **физика, -и** physics. **физиолог, -а** physiologist. **физиологический** physiological. **физиология, -и** physiology. **физиономия, -и** physiognomy. **физиотерапевт, -а** physiotherapist. **физиотерапия, -и** physiotherapy. **физическ|ий** physical; physics; **~ая культура** physical culture; gymnastics. **физкультура, -ы** *abbr.* P.E., gymnastics. **физкультурник, -а, -урница, -ы** *abbr.* gymnast, athlete. **физкультурный** *abbr.* gymnastics; athletic; sports; **~ зал** gymnasium.
фиксаж, -а fixing; fixer, fixing, solution. **фиксировать, -рую** *impf.* & *pf.* (*pf. also* **за~**) fix; record, register.
фиктивный fictitious. **фикция, -и** fiction.
филантроп, -а philanthropist. **филантропический** philanthropic. **филантропия, -и** philanthropy.
филателист, -а philatelist, stamp collector. **филателия, -и** philately.
филе *nt.indecl.* sirloin; fillet; drawn-thread work, filet (lace). **филей, -я** sirloin. **филейн|ый** sirloin; filet-lace, drawn-thread; **~ая работа** drawn-thread work, filet.
филиал, -а branch. **филиальный** branch.
филин, -а eagle-owl.
филистер, -а philistine. **филистерский** philistine. **филистерство, -а** philistinism.
филолог, -а philologist; student of language and literature. **филологический** philological. **филология, -и** philology, study of language and literature.
филон, -а (*sl.*) skiver, slacker. **филонить, -ню** *impf.* (*sl.*) slack, skive (off).
философ, -а philosopher. **философия, -и** philosophy. **философский** philosophic(al). **философствовать, -вую** *impf.* philosophize.
фильм, -а film.
фильтр, -а filter. **фильтровать, -рую** *impf.* (*pf.* **про~**) filter; screen, check.
фин... *abbr.* of **финансовый** financial, finance. **фининспектор, -а** financial officer. **~отдел, -а** finance department.
финал, -а finale; final. **финальный** final.
финансировать, -рую *impf.* & *pf.* finance. **финансист, -а** financier; financial expert. **финансовый** financial. **финансы, -ов** *pl.*

finance, fianances; money.

фи́ник, -а date. **фи́никовый** date.

фи́ниш, -а finish; finishing post. **фи́нишный** finishing.

фи́нка, -и Finn; Finnish knife; Finnish cap; Finnish pony. **Финля́ндия, -и** Finland. **финля́ндский** Finnish. **финн, -а** Finn. **фи́нно-уго́рский** Finno-Ugrian. **фи́нский** Finnish.

финт, -а feint.

фиоле́товый violet.

фи́рма, -ы firm; company; combine; large enterprise; trade name; appearance, guise.

фисгармо́ния, -и harmonium.

фити́ль, -я́ *m.* wick; fuse.

флаг, -а flag; **под ~ом** *+g.* flying under the flag of; under the guise of; **приспу́щенные ~и** flags at half-mast; **спусти́ть ~** lower a flag.

флако́н, -а (scent-)bottle, flask.

флама́ндец, -дца, флама́ндка, -и Fleming. **флама́ндский** Flemish.

флане́левый flannel. **флане́ль, -и** flannel.

флегмати́ческий phlegmatic.

фле́йта, -ы flute. **флейти́ст, -а, -и́стка, -и** flautist. **фле́йтовый** flute.

фле́ксия, -и inflexion. **флекти́вный** inflexional; inflected.

фли́гель, -я; *pl.* **-я́** *m.* wing; pavilion, extension, annexe.

флирт, -а flirtation. **флиртова́ть, -ту́ю** *impf.* (**с**+*i.*) flirt (with).

флома́стер, -а felt-tip (pen); marker (pen).

Флоре́нция, -и Florence.

Флори́да, -ы Florida.

флот, -а fleet; **возду́шный ~** air force; aviation. **фло́тский** naval; *sb.* sailor.

флю́гер, -а; *pl.* **-а́** weather-vane, weathercock; pennant.

флюс[1], **-а** gumboil, abscess.

флюс[2], **-а**; *pl.* **-ы́** flux.

фля́га, -и flask; water-bottle; (milk-)churn, milk-can. **фля́жка, -и** flask.

фойе́ *nt.indecl.* foyer.

фо́кус[1], **-а** trick; conjuring trick.

фо́кус[2], **-а** focus. **фокуси́ровать, -рую** *impf.* focus. **фокусиро́вка, -и** focusing.

фо́кусник, -а conjurer, juggler.

фо́кусный focal.

фольга́, -и́ foil.

фолькло́р, -а folklore.

фо́мка, -и (*sl.*) jemmy.

фон, -а background.

фона́рик, -а small lamp; torch, flashlight. **фона́рный** lamp; **~ столб** lamp-post. **фона́рщик, -а** lamplighter. **фона́рь, -я́** *m.* lantern; lamp; light; skylight; black-eye, shiner.

фонд, -а fund; stock; reserves, resources; stocks; foundation.

фоне́тика, -и phonetics. **фонети́ческий** phonetic.

фонта́н, -а fountain; stream; gusher.

форе́ль, -и trout.

фо́рзац, -а fly-leaf.

фо́рма, -ы form; shape; mould, cast; uniform; *pl.* contours; **в пи́сьменной фо́рме** in writing; **в фо́рме** in form; **отли́ть в фо́рму** mould, cast. **форма́льный** formal. **форма́ция, -и** structure; stage; formation; stamp, mentality. **фо́рменный** uniform; regulation; formal; proper, regular, positive. **формирова́ние, -я** forming; organization; unit, formation. **формирова́ть, -ру́ю** *impf.* (*pf.* **с~**) form; organize; shape; **~ся** form, shape, develop. **формова́ть, -му́ю** *impf.* (*pf.* **с~**) form, shape; model; mould, cast. **формо́вщик, -а** moulder.

фо́рмула, -ы formula; formulation. **формули́ровать, -рую** *impf.* & *pf.* (*pf. also* **с~**) formulate. **формулиро́вка, -и** formulation; wording; formula. **формуля́р, -а** record of service; log-book; library card; (*sl.*) dossier.

форпо́ст, -а (*mil.*) advanced post; outpost.

форси́рованный forced; accelerated. **форси́ровать, -рую** *impf.* & *pf.* force; speed up.

фо́рточка, -и fortochka; small hinged window-pane; air vent.

фосфа́т, -а phosphate.

фо́сфор, -а phosphorus. **фо́сфористый** phosphorous.

фо́то *nt.indecl.* photo(graph).

фото... *in comb.* photo-, photo-electric. **фотоаппара́т, -а** camera. **~бума́га, -и** photographic paper. **~гени́чный** photogenic. **фото́граф, -а** photographer. **~графи́ровать, -рую** *impf.* (*pf.* **с~**) photograph; **~графи́роваться** be photographed, have one's photograph taken. **~графи́ческий** photographic. **~гра́фия, -и** photography; photograph; photographer's studio. **~копирова́льный; ~ аппара́т** photocopier. **~ко́пия** photocopy. **~ла́мпа, -ы** dark-room lamp; photoelectric cell. **~люби́тель, -я** *m.* amateur photographer. **~набо́р, -а** film-setting; photo typesetting. **~объекти́в, -а** (camera) lens. **~панно́** *nt.indecl.* photo-mural; blow-up. **~репортёр, -а** press photographer. **~хро́ника, -и** news in pictures. **~элеме́нт, -а** photoelectric cell.

фрагме́нт, -а fragment, detail; **~ фи́льма** film clip.

фра́за, -ы sentence; phrase. **фразёр, -а** phrase-monger.

фрак, -а tail-coat, dress coat, tails; evening dress.

фракцио́нный fractional; factional. **фра́кция, -и** fraction; faction.

франки́ровать, -рую *impf.* & *pf.* prepay, pay the postage (of). **франкиро́вка, -и** prepayment.

франкоязы́чный Francophone.

франкомасо́н, -а Freemason.

франт, -а dandy. **франтовско́й** dandyish, dandified. **франтовство́, -а́** dandyism.

Фра́нция, -и France. **францу́женка, -и** Frenchwoman. **францу́з, -а** Frenchman. **францу́зский** French; **~ ключ** monkey-wrench.

фрахт, -а freight. **фрахтовáть, -тýю** *impf.* (*pf.* **за~**) charter.
фрейли́на, -ы maid of honour.
френч, -а service jacket.
фрéска, -и fresco.
фронт, -а; *pl.* **-ы, -óв** front; **стать во ~** stand to attention. **фронтови́к, -á** front-line soldier. **фронтовóй** front(-line).
фронтóн, -а pediment.
фрукт, -а fruit. **фруктóвый** fruit; **~ сад** orchard.
фтор, -а fluorine. **фтóристый** fluorine; fluoride. **~ кáльций** calcium fluoride.
фу *int.* ugh! oh!
фугáс, -а landmine. **фугáсный** high-explosive.
фундáмент, -а foundation, base; substructure; seating. **фундаментáльный** fundamental; solid, sound; thorough(-going); main; basic.
фунди́рованный funded, consolidated.
функциони́ровать, -рую *impf.* function. **фýнкция, -и** function.
фунт, -а pound. **фýнтик, -а** paper bag, paper cone, screw of paper.
фурáж, -á forage, fodder. **фурáжка, -и** peaked cap, service cap, forage-cap.
фургóн, -а van; estate car, station wagon; caravan; pantechnicon.
фýрия, -и termagant, virago.
фурнитýра, -ы accessories; parts, components; fittings.
фурýнкул, -а furuncle.
фут, -а foot; foot-rule. **футбóл, -а** football, soccer. **футболи́ст, -а** footballer. **футбóлить, -лю** *impf.* & *pf.* (*pf. also* **от~**) give, be given, the run-around. **футбóлка, -и** football jersey, sports shirt. **футбóльный** football; **~ мяч** football.
футля́р, -а case, container; sheath; cabinet; casing, housing.
фýтовый one-foot.
футуролóгия, -и futurology.
фуфáйка, -и jersey; sweater.
фы́ркать, -аю *impf.*, **фы́ркнуть, -ну** *pf.* snort; chuckle; grouse, grumble.

Х

ха *nt.indecl.* the letter **х**.
хаврóнья, -и sow.
хáки *nt.indecl.* & *adj.* khaki.
халáт, -а robe; dressing-gown; overall. **халáтность, -и** carelessness, negligence. **халáтный** careless, negligent.
халтýра, -ы pot-boiler; hackwork; money made on the side, extra earnings. **халтýрить, -рю** *impf.* do hackwork; earn a little extra. **халтýрщик, -а** hack.
хам, -а boor, lout. **хáмский** boorish, loutish. **хáмство, -а** boorishness, loutishness.
хан, -а khan.
хандрá, -ы́ depression, dejection. **хандри́ть, -рю́** *impf.* suffer from melancholy; be dejected, be depressed.
ханжá, -и́ canting hypocrite, sanctimonious person. **хáнжеский, ханжескóй** sanctimonious, hypocritical.
хáнство, -а khanate.
хаóс, -а chaos.
харáктер, -а character; personality; nature; disposition; type. **характеризовáть, -зýю** *impf.* & *pf.* (*pf. also* **о~**) describe; characterize, be characteristic of; **~ся** be characterized. **характери́стика, -и** reference; description. **характéрный**[1] characteristic; typical; distinctive; character. **харáктерный**[2] of strong character, strong-willed; temperamental; quick-tempered.
хáркать, -аю *impf.*, **хáркнуть, -ну** *pf.* spit, hawk; **~ крóвью** spit blood.
хáртия, -и charter.
хáря, -и mug, face.
хáта, -ы peasant hut.
хáять, хáю *impf.* run down; abuse; slate, slang, swear at, curse.
хвалá, -ы́ praise. **хвалéбный** laudatory, eulogistic, complimentary. **хвалёный** highly-praised, much-vaunted. **хвали́ть, -лю́, -лишь** *impf.* (*pf.* **по~**) praise, compliment; **~ся** boast.
хвáстать(ся, -аю(сь *impf.* (*pf.* **по~**) boast, brag. **хвастли́вый** boastful. **хвастовствó, -á** boasting, bragging. **хвастýн, -á** boaster, braggart.
хватáть[1], **-áю** *impf.*, **хвати́ть, -ачý, -áтишь** *pf.* (*pf. also* **схвати́ть**) snatch, seize, catch hold of; grab, grasp; bite; hit, strike, knock; **~ся** wake up (to), remember; +*g.* realize the absence of; +**за**+*a.* snatch at, clutch at; catch at; take up, try out; **пóздно хвати́лись** you thought of it too late; **~ся за ум** come to one's senses.
хватáть[2], **-áет** *impf.*, **хвати́ть, -áтит** *pf.*, *impers.* (+*g.*) suffice, be sufficient, be enough; last out; **врéмени не хватáло** there was not enough time; **мне егó не хватáет** I miss him; **на сегóдня хвáтит** that will do for today, let's call it a day; **у нас не хватáет дéнег** we haven't enough money; **хвáтит!** that will do!; that's enough!; **э́того ещё не хватáло!** that's all we needed!; that's the last straw!; **э́того мне хвáтит на мéсяц** this will last me a month. **хвáтка, -и** grasp, grip, clutch; method, technique; skill. **хвáткий** strong; tenacious; skilful, crafty.
хвóйн|ый coniferous; **~ые** *sb.*, *pl.* conifers.
хворáть, -áю *impf.* be ill.

хво́рост, -а (-у) brushwood; straws. **хворости́на, -ы** stick, switch. **хворостяно́й** brushwood.

хвост, -á tail; end, tail-end; train; queue. **хво́стик, -а** tail; **с ~ом** and a bit; **сто с ~ом** a hundred odd. **хвостово́й** tail.

хво́я, -и needle, needles; (*coniferous*) branch(es).

Хе́льсинки *m.indecl.* Helsinki.

хи́жина, -ы shack, hut, cabin.

хим... *abbr.* (*of* **хими́ческий**) *in comb.* chemical. **химкомбина́т, -а** chemical plant. **~проду́кты, -ов** chemical products. **~чи́стка, -и** dry-cleaning; dry-cleaner's.

химе́ра, -ы chimera. **химери́ческий** chimerical.

хи́мик, -а chemist. **хими́ческ|ий** chemical; **~ая война́** chemical warfare. **хи́мия, -и** chemistry.

химотерапи́я, -и chemotherapy.

хи́на, -ы, хини́н, -а quinine.

хире́ть, -е́ю *impf.* (*pf.* **за~**) grow sickly; wither; decay.

хиропра́ктик, -а chiropractor.

хиру́рг, -а surgeon. **хирурги́ческ|ий** surgical; **~ая сестра́** theatre nurse, theatre sister. **хирурги́я, -и** surgery.

хитре́ц, -á sly, cunning person. **хитри́ть, -рю́** *impf.* (*pf.* **с~**) use cunning, be cunning, be crafty; dissemble. **хи́трость, -и** cunning, craftiness; ruse, stratagem; skill, resource; intricacy, subtlety. **хи́трый** cunning, sly, crafty, wily; skilful, resourceful; intricate, subtle; complicated.

хихи́кать, -аю *impf.*, **хихи́кнуть, -ну** *pf.* giggle, titter, snigger.

хище́ние, -я theft; embezzlement, misappropriation. **хи́щник, -а** predator, bird of prey, beast of prey; plunderer, despoiler. **хи́щнический** predatory, rapacious; destructive; injurious. **хи́щн|ый** predatory; rapacious, grasping, greedy; **~ые пти́цы** birds of prey.

хладнокро́вие, -я coolness, composure, presence of mind, sang-froid; **сохраня́ть ~** keep one's head. **хладнокро́вный** cool, composed, self-possessed. **хладосто́йкий** cold-resistant; anti-freeze.

хлам, -а rubbish, trash, lumber.

хлеб, -а; *pl.* **-ы, -ов** *or* **-á, -о́в** bread; loaf; grain, corn, cereal; **~-соль** bread and salt, hospitality. **хлеба́ть, -а́ю** *impf.*, **хлебну́ть, -ну́, -нёшь** *pf.* gulp down, drink down; eat; go through, experience. **хле́бный** bread; baker's; grain, corn, cereal; rich, abundant; grain-producing.

хлебо... *in comb.* bread; baking; grain. **хлебobу́лочный** bread. **~загото́вка, -и** grain-procurement. **~заво́д, -а** (*mechanized*) bakery. **~пека́рня, -и**; *g.pl.* **-рен** bakery; bakehouse. **~поста́вка, -и** grain delivery. **~ре́з, -а, ~ре́зка, -и** bread-cutter. **~ро́дный** grain-growing; rich; **~ро́дный год** good year (for cereals).

хлев, -а, *loc.* **-ý**; *pl.* **-á** cow-house, cattle-shed, byre.

хлеста́ть, -ещу́, -е́щешь *impf.*, **хлестну́ть, -ну́, -нёшь** *pf.* lash; whip; beat (down), teem, pour; gush, spout.

хлоп *int.* bang! **хлоп, -а** bang, clatter. **хло́пать, -аю** *impf.* (*pf.* **хло́пнуть**) bang; slap; **~ (в ладо́ши)** clap, applaud.

хлопково́дство, -а cotton-growing. **хло́пковый** cotton.

хло́пнуть, -ну *pf. of* **хло́пать**

хлопо́к[1], -пкá clap.

хло́пок[2], -пка cotton.

хлопота́ть, -очу́, -о́чешь *impf.* (*pf.* **по~**) busy o.s.; bustle about; take trouble, make efforts; +**о**+*p. or* **за**+*a.* petition for, plead for, solicit for. **хлопотли́вый** troublesome, bothersome; exacting; busy, bustling, restless. **хло́поты, -о́т** *pl.* trouble; efforts; pains.

хлопча́тка, -и cotton. **хлопчатобума́жный** cotton.

хло́пья, -ьев *pl.* flakes.

хлор, -а chlorine. **хлорвини́ловый** vinyl chloride. **хло́ристый, хло́рный** chlorine; chloride; **хло́рная и́звесть** chloride of lime. **хло́рка, -и** bleaching powder, bleach liquor.

хлорофи́лл, -а chlorophyll.

хлорофо́рм, -а chloroform. **хлороформи́ровать, -рую** *impf.* & *pf.* (*pf. also* **за~**) chloroform.

хлы́нуть, -нет *pf.* gush, pour; rush, surge.

хлыст, -á whip, switch.

хмелево́д, -а hop-grower. **хмелево́й** hop. **хмеле́ть, -е́ю** *impf.* (*pf.* **за~, о~**) get tipsy, get tight. **хмель, -я** *loc.* **-ю́** *m.* hop, hops; drunkenness, tipsiness; **во хмелю́** tipsy, tight. **хмельн|о́й; -лён, -льнá** drunken, drunk; tipsy; intoxicating.

хму́рить, -рю *impf.* (*pf.* **на~**); **~ бро́ви** knit one's brows; **~ся** frown; become gloomy; be overcast, be cloudy. **хму́рый** gloomy, sullen; overcast, dull, cloudy; lowering.

хны́кать, -ы́чу *or* **-аю** *impf.* whimper, snivel; whine.

хо́бот, -а trunk, proboscis. **хобото́к, -ткá** proboscis.

ход, -а (-у), *loc.* **-ý**; *pl.* **-ы, -ов** *or* **-ы́** *or* **-á, -о́в** motion, movement; travel, going; speed, pace; procession; course, progress; work, operation, running; stroke; move; lead; gambit, manoeuvre; entrance; passage, thoroughfare, covered way; wheel-base; runners; **быть в ~ý** be in demand, be in vogue; **дать за́дний ~** back, reverse; **дать ~** set in motion, set going; **знать все ~ы и вы́ходы** know all the ins and outs; **на ~ý** in transit, on the move, without halting; in motion; in operation; **по́лным ~ом** at full speed, in full swing; **пусти́ть в ~** start, set in motion, set going; put into operation, put into service; **три часá ~у** three hours' journey.

хода́тай, -я intercessor, mediator. **хода́тайство, -а** petitioning; entreaty, pleading; petition, application. **ходáтайствовать, -твую** *impf.* (*pf.* **по~**) petition, apply.

хóдики, -ов *pl.* wall-clock.

ходи́ть, хожý, хóдишь *impf.* (*pf.* **с~**) walk; go; run; pass, go round; lead, play; move; sway, shake; +**в**+*p.* be; wear; +**за**+*i.* look after, take care of, tend; **~ с пик** lead a spade; **~ ферзём** move one's queen. **хóдкий; -док, -дкá, -о** fast; saleable, marketable; popular, in demand, sought after; current. **ходýли, -ей** *pl.* stilts. **ходýльный** stilted. **ходьбá, -ы́** walking; walk; **полчасá ходьбы́** half an hour's walk. **ходя́ч|ий** walking; able to walk; popular; current; **~ая добродéтель** virtue personified; **~ая монéта** currency.

хозрасчёт, -а *abbr.* (*of* **хозя́йственный расчёт**) self-financing system.

хозя́ин, -а; *pl.* **-я́ева, -я́ев** owner, proprietor; master; boss; landlord; host; **хозя́ева пóля** home team. **хозя́йка, -и** owner; mistress; hostess; landlady; wife, missus. **хозя́йничать, -аю** *impf.* keep house; be in charge; play the master, take charge. **хозя́йственник, -а** financial manager, economic manager. **хозя́йственный** economic, of the economy; management; household; economical, thrifty. **хозя́йство, -а** economy; management; housekeeping; equipment; farm, holding; **домáшнее ~** housekeeping; **сéльское ~** agriculture.

хоккеи́ст, -а (ice-)hockey-player. **хоккéй, -я** hockey, ice-hockey; **кóнный ~** polo. **хоккéйный** (ice-)hockey.

холéра, -ы cholera.

холестери́н, -а cholesterol. **холестери́новый** cholesteric.

холм, -á hill. **холми́стый** hilly.

хóлод, -а (-у); *pl.* **-á, -óв** cold; coldness; cold spell, cold weather. **холоди́льник, -а** refrigerator; cooler, condenser; **двухсекциóнный ~** fridge-freezer. **холоди́льный** cooling; refrigerating, freezing, freezing. **холоди́ть, -ожý** *impf.* (*pf.* **на~**) cool; chill; produce feeling of cold. **хóлодно** *adv.* coldly. **хóлодность, -и** coldness. **холóдн|ый; хóлоден, -днá, -о** cold; inadequate, thin; **~ое орýжие** side-arms, cold steel; **~ая** *sb.* cooler, lock-up.

холóп, -а serf. **холóпий** serf's, of serfdom, servile.

холостóй; хóлост, -á unmarried, single; bachelor; idle, free; blank, dummy. **холостя́к, -á** bachelor. **холостя́цкий** bachelor.

холст, -á canvas; sackcloth. **холщóвый** canvas; sackcloth.

хомýт, -á (horse-)collar; burden; clamp, clip.

хор, -а; *pl.* **хóры́** choir; chorus.

хорвáт, -а, хорвáтка, -и Croat. **хорвáтский** Croatian.

хорёк, -рькá polecat.

хори́ст, -а member of choir or chorus. **хоровóд, -а** round dance.

хорони́ть, -ню́, -нишь *impf.* (*pf.* **за~, по~, с~**) bury; hide conceal; **~ся** hide, conceal o.s.

хорóшенький pretty; nice. **хорошéнько** *adv.* properly, thoroughly, well and truly. **хорошéть, -éю** *impf.* (*pf.* **по~**) grow prettier. **хорóший; -óш, -á, -ó** good; nice; pretty, nice-looking; **хорошó** *pred.* it is good; it is nice, it is pleasant. **хорошó** *adv.* well; nicely; all right! very well!; good.

хóры, хор *or* **-ов** *pl.* gallery.

хотéние, -я desire, wish. **хотéть, хочý, хóчешь, хоти́м** *impf.* (*pf.* **за~**) wish; +*g.* want; **éсли хоти́те** perhaps; **~ пить** be thirsty; **~ сказáть** mean; **~ся** *impers.* +*d.* want; **мне хотéлось бы** I should like; **ей хóчется** she wants; **емý хóчется спать** he is sleepy.

хоть *conj.* although; even if; *part.* at least, if only; for example, even; **~ бы** if only. **хотя́** *conj.* although, though; **~ бы** even if; if only.

хохлáтый crested, tufted.

хóхот, -а guffaw, loud laugh. **хохотáть, -очý, -óчешь** *impf.* guffaw, laugh loudly.

хочý *etc.*: *see* **хотéть**

храбрéц, -á brave man. **храбри́ться, -рю́сь** make a show of bravery; pluck up one's courage. **хрáбрость, -и** bravery, courage. **хрáбрый** brave, courageous, valiant.

храм, -а temple, church.

хранéние, -я keeping, custody; storage; conservation; **кáмера хранéния** cloakroom, left-luggage office; **сдать на ~** store, deposit, leave in a cloakroom. **храни́лище, -а** storehouse, depository. **храни́тель, -я** *m.* keeper, custodian; repository; curator. **храни́ть, -ню́** *impf.* keep; preserve, maintain; store; **~ся** be, be kept; be preserved.

храпéть, -плю́ *impf.* snore; snort.

хребéт, -бтá spine; back; (mountain) range; ridge; crest, peak. **хребтóвый** spinal; range, ridge, crest.

хрен, -а (-у) horseradish. **хренóвый** horseradish.

хрестомáтия, -и reader.

хрип, -а wheeze; hoarse sound. **хрипéть, -плю́** *impf.* wheeze. **хри́плый; -пл, -á , -о** hoarse,wheezing. **хри́пнуть, -ну; хрип** *impf.* (*pf.* **о~**) become hoarse, lose one's voice. **хрипотá, -ы́** hoarseness.

христиани́н, -а; *pl.* **-áне, -áн, христиáнка, -и** Christian. **христиáнский** Christian. **христиáнство, -а** Christianity; Christendom. **Христóс, -истá** Christ.

хром, -а box-calf.

хромáть, -áю *impf.* limp, be lame; be poor, be shaky. **хромéть, -éю** *impf.* (*pf.* **о~**) go lame. **хромóй; хром, -á, -о** lame, limping; game, gammy; shaky, rickety; *sb.* lame man, woman. **хромотá, -ы́** lameness.

хрóник, -а chronic invalid.

хрóника, -и chronicle; news items; newsreel; historical film. **хроникáльный** news; documentary.

хрони́ческий chronic.

хронологи́ческий chronological. **хроно-**

ло́гия, -и chronology. **хроно́метр, -а** chronometer. **хронометра́ж, -а** time-study.

хру́пкий; -пок, -пка́, -о fragile; brittle; frail; delicate. **хру́пкость, -и** fragility; brittleness; frailness.

хруст, -а crunch; crackle.

хруста́лик, -а crystalline lens. **хруста́ль, -я́** *m.* cut glass; crystal. **хруста́льный** cut-glass; crystal; crystal-clear.

хрусте́ть, -ущу́ *impf.*, **хру́стнуть, -ну** *pf.* crunch; crackle. **хрустя́щий** crackling; crisp, crunchy; ~ **карто́фель** potato crisps.

хрю́кать, -аю *impf.*, **хрю́кнуть, -ну** *pf.* grunt.

хрящ[1], **-а́** cartilage, gristle.

хрящ[2], **-а́** gravel, shingle. **хрящева́тый**[2], **хрящево́й**[2] gravelly, shingly.

хрящева́тый[1], **хрящево́й**[1] cartilaginous, gristly.

худе́ть, -е́ю *impf.* (*pf.* **по~**) grow thin.

ху́до, -а harm, ill; evil. **ху́до** *adv.* ill, badly.

худо́жественный art, arts; artistic; aesthetic; ~ **фильм** feature film. **худо́жество, -а** art; artistry; *pl.* the arts. **худо́жник, -а** artist.

худо́й[1]**; худ, -а́, -о** thin, lean.

худо́й[2]**; худ, -а́, -о** bad; full of holes; worn; tumbledown; **ему́ ху́до** he feels bad; **на ~ коне́ц** if the worst comes to the worst, at (the) worst.

худоща́вый thin, lean.

ху́дший *superl. of* **худо́й, плохо́й** (the) worst. **ху́же** *comp. of* **худо́й, ху́до, плохо́й, пло́хо** worse.

хула́, -ы́ abuse, criticism.

хулига́н, -а hooligan. **хулига́нить, -ню** *impf.* behave like a hooligan. **хулига́нство, -а** hooliganism.

ху́нта, -а junta. **хунти́ст, -а** member of a junta.

ху́тор, -а; *pl.* **-а́** farm; farmstead; small village.

Ц

ц *letter*: *see* **цэ**

ца́пля, -и; *g.pl.* **-пель** heron.

цара́пать, -аю *impf.*, **цара́пнуть, -ну** *pf.* (*pf. also* **на~, о~**) scratch; scribble; **~ся** scratch; scratch one another; scramble, scrabble. **цара́пина, -ы** scratch; abrasion.

царе́вич, -а tsarevich (*son of a tsar*). **царе́вна, -ы**; *g.pl.* **-ен** tsarevna (*daughter of a tsar*). **цари́зм, -а** tsarism. **цари́стский** tsarist. **цари́ть, -рю́** *impf.* be tsar; hold sway; reign, prevail. **цари́ца, -ы** tsarina; queen. **ца́рский** of the tsar, tsar's; royal; tsarist; regal, kingly. **ца́рство, -а** kingdom, realm; reign; domain. **ца́рствование, -я** reign. **ца́рствовать, -твую** *impf.* reign. **царь, -я́** *m.* tsar; king, ruler.

цвести́, -ету́, -етёшь; -ёл, -а́ *impf.* flower, bloom, blossom; prosper, flourish; grow mouldy.

цвет[1], **-а**; *pl.* **-а́** colour; ~ **лица́** complexion.

цвет[2], **-а (-у)**, *loc.* **-у́**; *pl.* **-ы́** flower; cream, pick; blossom-time; prime; blossom; **во ~е лет** in the prime of life; **во ~е сил** at the height of one's powers; **в цвету́** in blossom. **цветни́к, -а́** flower-bed, flower-garden.

цветн|о́й coloured; colour; non-ferrous; **~а́я капу́ста** cauliflower; **~ы́е мета́ллы** non-ferrous metals; **~о́е стекло́** stained glass; **~о́й фильм** colour-film.

цветово́дство, -а flower-growing, floriculture.

цветов|о́й colour; **~а́я слепота́** colour-blindness.

цвето́к, -тка́; *pl.* **цветы́** *or* **цветки́, -о́в** flower. **цвето́чный** flower; ~ **магази́н** flower-shop. **цвету́щий** flowering, blossoming, blooming; prosperous, flourishing.

цеди́лка, -и strainer, filter. **цеди́ть, цежу́, це́дишь** *impf.* strain, filter; percolate; say (through clenched teeth).

целе́бный curative, healing.

целево́й special; targeted, earmarked for a specific purpose. **целенапра́вленный** purposeful. **целесообра́зный** expedient. **целеустремлённый; -ён, -ённа** *or* **-ена́** purposeful.

целико́м *adv.* whole; wholly, entirely.

целина́, -ы́ virgin lands, virgin soil. **цели́нн|ый** virgin; **~ые зе́мли** virgin lands.

цели́тельный curative, healing, medicinal.

це́лить(ся, -лю(сь *impf.* (*pf.* **на~**) aim, take aim.

целко́вый *sb.* one rouble.

целлофа́н, -а cellophane. **целлуло́ид, -а** celluloid. **целлюло́за, -ы** cellulose.

целова́ть, -лу́ю *impf.* (*pf.* **по~**) kiss; **~ся** kiss.

це́лое *sb.* whole; integer. **целому́дренный** chaste. **целому́дрие, -я** chastity. **це́лостность, -и** integrity. **це́лостный** integral; entire, complete. **це́лый; цел, -а́, -о** whole, entire; safe, intact.

цель, -и target; aim, object, goal, end, purpose; **с це́лью** with the object (of), in order to.

цельнометалли́ческий all-metal. **це́льный; -лен, -льна́, -о** one-piece, solid; entire; whole; integral; single; undiluted. **це́льность, -и** wholeness, entirety, integrity.

цеме́нт, -а cement. **цементи́ровать, -рую** *impf. & pf.* cement; case-harden.

цена́, -ы́, *a.* **-у**; *pl.* **-ы** price, cost; worth, value; **цено́й**+*g.* at the price of, at the cost of; **любо́й цено́й** at any price.

ценз, -а qualification. **це́нзовый** qualifying.

це́нзор, -а censor. **цензу́ра, -ы** censorship.

цени́тель, -я *m.* judge, connoisseur, expert. **цени́ть, -ню́, -нишь** *impf.* value; assess; estimate; appreciate. **це́нник, -а** price-list. **це́нность, -и** value; price; importance; *pl.* valuables; values. **це́нный** valuable; costly; precious; important.

центр, -а centre. **централиза́ция, -и** centralization. **централизова́ть, -зу́ю** *impf.* & *pf.* centralize. **центра́ль, -и** main. **центра́льный** central. **центробе́жный** centrifugal.

цеп, -а́ flail.

цепене́ть, -е́ю *impf.* (*pf.* **о~**) freeze; be numbed; be rooted to the spot. **це́пкий** tenacious, strong; prehensile; sticky, tacky, loamy; obstinate, persistent, strong-willed. **це́пкость, -и** tenacity, strength; obstinacy, persistence. **цепля́ться, -я́юсь** *impf.* **за**+*a.* clutch at, try to grasp; cling to; stick to.

цепн|о́й chain; **~а́я реа́кция** chain reaction. **цепо́чка, -и** chain; file, series. **цепь, -и**, *loc.* **-и́**; *g.pl.* **-е́й** chain; row; series; range; line, file; succession; circuit; *pl.* chains, bonds.

церемо́ниться, -нюсь *impf.* (*pf.* **по~**) stand on ceremony; be (over-)considerate. **церемо́ния, -и** ceremony; **без церемо́ний** informally. **церемо́нный** ceremonious.

церковнославя́нский Church Slavonic. **церко́вный** church; ecclesiastical. **це́рковь, -кви**; *g.pl.* **-е́й** church.

цех, -а, *loc.* **-у́**; *pl.* **-и** *or* **-а́** shop; section; guild, corporation.

цивилиза́ция, -и civilization. **цивилизо́ванный** civilized. **цивилизова́ть, -зу́ю** *impf.* & *pf.*

цигейка, -и beaver lamb. **цигейковый** beaver-lamb.

цика́да, -ы cicada.

цикл, -а cycle. **цикли́ческий** cyclic(al).

цикло́н, -а cyclone.

циклотро́н, -а cyclotron.

цико́рий, -я chicory. **цико́рный** chicory.

цили́ндр, -а cylinder; drum; top hat. **цилиндри́ческий** cylindrical.

цимба́лы, -а́л *pl.* cymbals.

цинга́, -и́ scurvy. **цинго́тный** scurvy; scorbutic.

цини́зм, -а cynicism. **ци́ник, -а** cynic. **цини́ческий** cynical.

цинк, -а zinc. **ци́нковый** zinc.

цино́вка, -и mat. **цино́вочный** mat, of mats.

цирк, -а circus. **цирково́й** circus.

циркули́ровать, -рует *impf.* circulate. **ци́ркуль, -я** *m.* (pair of) compasses; dividers. **циркуля́р, -а** circular.

цирю́льник, -а barber.

цисте́рна, -ы cistern, tank.

цитаде́ль, -и citadel; bulwark, stronghold.

цита́та, -ы quotation. **цити́ровать, -рую** *impf.* (*pf.* **про~**) quote.

ци́тра, -ы zither.

ци́трус, -а citrus. **ци́трусов|ый** citrous; **~ые** *sb.*, *pl.* citrus plants.

цифербла́т, -а dial, face.

ци́фра, -ы figure; number, numeral. **цифров|о́й** numerical, in figures; **~а́я за́пись** digital recording; **~ы́е да́нные** figures.

ЦК *abbr.* (*of* ***Центра́льный Комите́т***) Central Committee.

цо́кать, -аю *impf.*, **цо́кнуть, -ну** *pf.* clatter, clang; click.

цо́коль, -я *m.* socle, plinth, pedestal. **цо́кольный** plinth; **~ эта́ж** ground floor.

ЦРУ *abbr.* (*of* ***Центра́льное разве́довательное управле́ние***) CIA, Central Intelligence Agency.

цука́т, -а candied fruit, candied peel.

цыга́н, -а; *pl.* **-е, -а́н** or **-ы, -ов, цыга́нка, -и** gipsy. **цыга́нский** gipsy.

цыплёнок, -нка *pl.* **-ля́та, -ля́т** chicken; chick.

цы́почки; на ~, на цы́почках on tip-toe.

цэ *nt.indecl.* the letter **ц**.

Цю́рих, -а Zurich.

Ч

ч *letter: see* **чэ**

ч. *abbr.* (*of* **час**) hour, (*after numerals*) o'clock; (*of* **часть**) part.

чад, -а (-у) *loc.* **-у́** fumes, smoke. **чади́ть, чажу́** *impf.* (*pf.* **на~**) smoke. **ча́дный** smoky, smoke-laden; stupefied, stupefying.

чай, -я (-ю); *pl.* **-и́, -ёв** tea.

чай *part.* probably, perhaps; no doubt; I suppose; after all.

ча́йка, -и; *g.pl.* **ча́ек** gull, sea-gull.

ча́йник, -а teapot; kettle. **ча́йн|ый** tea; **~ая посу́да** tea-service; **~ая ро́за** tea-rose. **чайхана́, -ы́** tea-house.

чалма́, -ы turban.

ча́лый roan.

чан, -а, *loc.* **-у́**; *pl.* **-ы́** vat, tub, tank.

ча́рка, -и cup, goblet, small glass.

чарова́ть, -ру́ю *impf.* bewitch; charm, captivate, enchant.

ча́ртерный chartered.

час, -а (-у), with numerals **-а́**, *loc.* **-у́**; *pl.* **-ы** hours, time, period; *pl.* guard-duty; **~** one o'clock; **в два ~а́** at two o'clock; **стоя́ть на ~а́х** stand guard; **~ы́ пик** rush-hour. **часо́вня, -и**; *g.pl.* **-вен** chapel. **часово́й** *sb.* sentry, sentinel, guard. **часов|о́й** clock, watch; of one hour, an hour's; by the hour; one o'clock; **~о́й переры́в** an hour's interval; **~а́я пла́та** payment by the hour; **~о́й по́яс** time zone; **~а́я стре́лка** (hour-)hand.

часовщи́к, -а́ watchmaker. **ча́сом** *adv.* sometimes, at times; by the way.

части́ца, -ы small part, element; particle. **части́чно** *adv.* partly, partially. **части́чный** partial.

ча́стность, -и detail; **в ча́стности** in particular. **ча́стн|ый** private; personal; particular, individual; local; district; **~ая со́бственность** private property.

ча́сто *adv.* often, frequently; close, thickly. **частоко́л, -а** paling, palisade. **частота́, -ы́**; *pl.* **-ы** frequency. **часто́тный** frequency. **часту́шка, -и** ditty, folk-song. **ча́стый; част, -а́, -о** frequent; close, close together; dense, thick; close-woven; quick, rapid; **~ гре́бень** fine-tooth comb.

часть, -и; *g.pl.* **-е́й** part; portion; section, department, side; sphere, field; share; unit; **ча́сти ре́чи** parts of speech.

часы́, -о́в *pl.* clock, watch; **нару́чные ~, ручны́е ~** wrist-watch.

ча́хлый stunted; poor, sorry; weakly, sickly, puny. **ча́хнуть, -ну; чах** *impf.* (*pf.* **за~**) wither away; become weak, go into a decline. **чахо́тка, -и** consumption. **чахо́точный** consumptive; poor, sorry, feeble.

ча́ша, -и cup, bowl; chalice; **~ весо́в** scale, pan. **ча́шка, -и** cup; bowl; scale, pan.

ча́ща, -и thicket.

ча́ще *comp. of* **ча́сто, ча́стый; ~ всего́** most often, mostly.

ча́яние, -я expectation; hope. **ча́ять, ча́ю** *impf.* hope, expect; think, suppose.

чва́ниться, -нюсь *impf.* (+*i.*) boast (of). **чва́нство, -а** conceit, arrogance, pride.

чего́ *see* **что**

чей *m.*, **чья** *f.*, **чьё** *nt.*, **чьи** *pl.*, *pron.* whose. **че́й-либо, че́й-нибудь** anyone's. **че́й-то** someone's.

чек, -а cheque; check, bill; receipt.

чека́н, -а stamp, die. **чека́нить, -ню** *impf.* (*pf.* **вы́~, от~**) mint, coin; stamp, engrave, emboss, chase; **~ слова́** enunciate words clearly; rap out; **~ шаг** step out. **чека́нный** stamping, engraving, embossing; stamped, engraved, embossed, chased; precise, expressive, chiselled; **~ шаг** measured tread.

чёлка, -и fringe; forelock.

чёлн, -а́; *pl.* **чёлны́** dug-out canoe; boat. **челно́к, -а́** dug-out canoe; shuttle.

челове́к, -а; *pl.* **лю́ди**; with numerals, *g.* **-ве́к, -ам** man, person, human being; (man-)servant, waiter.

человеко... *in comb.* man-, anthropo-. **челове́ко-де́нь, -дня́** *m.* man-day. **~любѝвый** philanthropic. **~лю́бие, -я** philanthropy; humanity; humaneness. **~ненави́стнический** misanthropic. **~обра́зный** anthropomorphous; anthropoid. **челове́ко-ча́с, -а**; *pl.* **-ы́** man-hour.

челове́чек, -чка little man. **челове́ческий** human; humane. **челове́чество, -а** humanity, mankind. **челове́чий** human. **челове́чный** humane.

че́люсть, -и jaw, jaw-bone; denture, dental plate, false teeth.

чем, чём *see* **что. чем** *conj.* than; +*inf.* rather than, instead of; **~..., тем...**+*comp.* the more ..., the more.

чемода́н, -а suitcase.

чемпио́н, -а, чемпио́нка, -и champion(s), title-holder(s). **чемпиона́т, -а** championship.

чему́ *see* **что**

чепе́ *nt. indecl.* incident, emergency.

чепуха́, -и́ nonsense, rubbish; trifle, triviality.

че́пчик, -а cap; bonnet.

че́рви, -е́й, че́рвы, черв *pl.* hearts. **черво́нн|ый** of hearts; red; **~ое зо́лото** pure gold; **~ый туз** ace of hearts.

червь, -я́; *pl.* **-и́, -е́й** *m.* worm; maggot; bug, virus, germ. **червя́к, -а́** worm; screw.

черда́к, -а́ attic, loft.

черёд, -а́ *loc.* **-у́** turn; queue; **идти́ свои́м ~о́м** take its course. **чередова́ние, -я** alternation, interchange, rotation; (vowel) gradation, ablaut. **чередова́ть, -ду́ю** *impf.* alternate; **~ся** alternate, take turns.

че́рез, чрез *prep.*+*a.* across; over; through; via; in; after; (further) on; every (other); **~ день** every other day, on alternate days; **~ полчаса́** in half an hour; **~ три киломе́тра** three kilometres further on; **~ ка́ждые три страни́цы** every three pages.

черёмуха, -и bird cherry.

че́реп, -а; *pl.* **-а́** skull, cranium.

черепа́ха, -и tortoise; turtle; tortoiseshell. **черепа́ховый** tortoise; turtle; tortoiseshell. **черепа́ший** tortoise, turtle; very slow.

черепи́ца, -ы tile. **черепи́чный** tile; tiled.

черепо́к, -пка́ crock, potsherd, broken piece of pottery.

чересчу́р *adv.* too; too much.

чере́шневый cherry; cherry-wood. **чере́шня, -и**; *g.pl.* **-шен** cherry; cherry-tree.

черке́с, -а, черке́шенка, -и Circassian. **черке́сский** Circassian.

черкну́ть, -ну́, -нёшь *pf.* scrape; leave a mark on; scribble, dash off.

черне́ть, -е́ю *impf.* (*pf.* **по~**) turn black, go black; show black. **черни́ка, -и** bilberry, whortleberry. **черни́ла, -и́л** *pl.* ink. **черни́льница, -ы** ink-pot, ink-well. **черни́льный** ink; **~ каранда́ш** indelible pencil. **черни́ть, -ню́** *impf.* (*pf.* **за~, на~, о~**) blacken; paint black; slander. **черни́чный** bilberry.

черно... *in comb.* black; unskilled; rough. **чёрно-бе́лый** black-and-white. **черноб́у́рка, -и** silver fox (fur). **~бу́рый** dark-brown; **~бу́рая лиса́** silver fox, **~воло́сый** black-haired. **~гла́зый** black-eyed. **~зём, -а** chernozem, black earth. **~зёмный** black-earth. **~ко́жий** black, coloured; *sb.* Negro, black. **~мо́рский** Black-Sea. **~рабо́чий** *sb.* unskilled worker, labourer. **~сли́в, -а (-у)** prunes. **~сморо́динный** blackcurrant.

черновик, -а́ rough copy, draft. **черново́й** rough; draft, preparatory; heavy, dirty; crude.

чернота́, -ы́ blackness; darkness. **чёрн|ый; -рен, -рна́** black; back; heavy, unskilled; ferrous; gloomy, melancholy; **на ~ый день** for a rainy day; **~ые мета́ллы** ferrous metals; **~ый хлеб** black bread, rye-bread; **~ый ход** back way, back door; **~ый** *sb.* Negro, black.

черпа́к, -а́ scoop; bucket; grab. **черпа́лка, -и** scoop; ladle. **че́рпать, -аю** *impf.*, **черпну́ть, -ну́, -нёшь** *pf.* draw; scoop; ladle; extract, derive.

черстве́ть, -е́ю *impf.* (*pf.* **за~, о~, по~**) grow stale, get stale; become hardened, grow callous. **чёрствый; чёрств, -а́, -о** stale; hard, callous.

чёрт, -а; *pl.* **че́рти, -е́й** devil; the devil.

черта́, -ы́ line; boundary; trait, characteristic; **в о́бщих ~х** in general outline; **в черте́ го́рода** within the town boundary. **чертёж, -а́** drawing; blueprint, plan, scheme. **чертёжная** *sb.* drawing-office. **чертёжник, -а** draughtsman. **чертёжный** drawing. **черти́ть, -рчу́, -ртишь** *impf.* (*pf.* **на~**) draw; draw up.

чёртов *adj.* devil's; devilish, hellish. **черто́вский** devilish, damnable.

чёрточка, -и line; hyphen. **черче́ние, -я** drawing. **черчу́** *etc.*: *see* **черти́ть**

чеса́ть, чешу́, -шешь *impf.* (*pf.* **по~**) scratch; comb; card; **~ся** scratch o.s.; comb one's hair; **у него́ ру́ки че́шутся**+*inf.* he is itching to.

чесно́к, -а́ (-у́) garlic. **чесно́чный** garlic.

чесо́тка, -и scab; rash; mange; itch.

че́ствование, -я celebration. **че́ствовать, -твую** *impf.* celebrate; honour. **че́стность, -и** honesty, integrity. **че́стный; -тен, -тна́, -о** honest, upright. **честолюби́вый** ambitious. **честолю́бие, -я** ambition. **честь, -и** *loc.* **-и́** honour; regard, respect; **отда́ть ~**+*d.* salute.

четве́рг, -а́ Thursday. **четвере́ньки; на ~, на четвере́ньках** on all fours, on hands and knees. **четвёрка, -и** figure 4; No. 4; four; (*mark*) good. **че́тверо, -ы́х** four. **четверо-но́г|ий** four-legged; **~ое** *sb.* quadruped. **четверости́шие, -я** quatrain. **четвёртый** fourth. **че́тверть, -и**; *g.pl.* **-е́й** quarter; quarter of an hour; term; **без че́тверти час** a quarter to one. **четверть-фина́л, -а** quarter-final.

чёткий; -ток, -тка́, -о precise; clear-cut; clear, well-defined; legible; plain, distinct; articulate. **чёткость, -и** precision; clarity, clearness, definition; legibility; distinctness.

чётный even.

четы́ре, -рёх, -рьмя́, -рёх four. **четы́реста, -рёхсо́т, -ьмяста́ми, -ёхста́х** four hundred.

четырёх... *in comb.* four-, tetra-. **четырёх-голо́сный** four-part. **~гра́нник, -а** tetrahedron. **~кра́тный** fourfold. **~ле́тие, -я** four-year period; fourth anniversary. **~ме́стный** four-seater. **~мото́рный** four-engined. **~со́тый** four-hundredth. **~сто́пный** tetrameter. **~та́ктный** four-stroke. **~уго́льник, -а** square, quadrangle. **~уго́льный** square, quadrangular. **~часово́й** four hours', four-hour; four-o'clock.

четы́рнадцатый fourteenth. **четы́рнадцать, -и** fourteen.

чех, -а Czech.

чехарда́, -ы leap-frog.

чехли́ть, -лю́ *impf.* (*pf.* **за~**) cover. **чехо́л, -хла́** cover, case; loose cover.

Чехослова́кия, -и Czechoslovakia.

чечеви́ца, -ы lentil; lens. **чечеви́чн|ый** lentil; **~ая похлёбка** mess of pottage.

че́шка, -и Czech. **че́шский** Czech.

чешу́ *etc.*: *see* **чеса́ть**

чешу́йка, -и scale. **чешуя́, -и́** scales.

чиж, -а́, чи́жик, -а siskin.

чин, -а; *pl.* **-ы́** rank; *any of fourteen grades* (*numbered from the top*) *of tsarist Civil Service*; official; rite, ceremony, order; **быть в ~а́х** hold high rank, be of high rank.

чини́ть[1], **-ню́, -нишь** *impf.* (*pf.* **по~**) repair, mend.

чини́ть[2], **-ню́, -нишь** *impf.* (*pf.* **о~**) sharpen.

чини́ть[3], **-ню́** *impf.* (*pf.* **у~**) carry out, execute; cause; **~ препя́тствия**+*d.* put obstacles in the way of.

чино́вник, -а civil servant; official, functionary; bureaucrat. **чино́внический, чино́вничий** civil-service; bureaucratic.

чи́псы, -ов *pl.* (potato) crisps.

чири́кать, -аю *impf.*, **чири́кнуть, -ну** *pf.* chirp.

чи́ркать, -аю *impf.*, **чи́ркнуть, -ну** *pf.*+*i.* strike; **~ спи́чкой** strike a match.

чи́сленность, -и numbers; strength. **чи́сленный** numerical. **числи́тель, -я** *m.* numerator. **числи́тельное** *sb.* numeral. **чи́слить, -лю** *impf.* count, reckon; **~ся** be; +*i.* be reckoned, be on paper; be attributed; **за ним чи́слится мно́го недоста́тков** he has many failings; **~ся больны́м** be on the sick-list; **~ся в спи́ске** be on the list. **число́, -а́**; *pl.* **-а, -сел** number; date, day; **в числе́**+*g.* among; **в том числе́** including; **еди́нственное ~** singular; **мно́жественное ~** plural; **сего́дня восемна́дцатое ~** today is the eighteenth. **числово́й** numerical.

чи́стильщик, -а cleaner; **~ сапо́г** bootblack, shoeblack. **чи́стить, чи́щу** *impf.* (*pf.* **вы~, о~, по~**) clean; brush, scour, sweep; peel, shell; purge; clear; dredge. **чи́стка, -и** cleaning; purge; **этни́ческая ~** ethnic cleansing; **отда́ть в чи́стку** have cleaned, send to the cleaner's. **чи́сто** *adv.* cleanly, clean; purely, merely; completely. **чистов|о́й** fair, clean; **~а́я ко́пия, ~о́й экземпля́р** fair copy, clean copy. **чистокро́вный** thoroughbred, pure-blooded. **чистописа́ние, -я** calligraphy, (hand)writing. **чистопло́тный** clean; neat, tidy; decent. **чистосерде́чный** frank, sincere, candid. **чистота́, -ы́** cleanness, cleanliness; neatness, tidiness; purity, innocence. **чи́ст|ый** clean; neat; tidy; pure; unsullied; undiluted; clear; net; utter; mere, sheer; complete, absolute; **на ~ом во́здухе** in the open air; **~ый вес** net weight; **~ые де́ньги** cash; **~ый лист** blank sheet; **~ая при́быль** clear profit; **~ая случа́йность** pure chance.

чита́емый widely-read, popular. **чита́льный** reading. **чита́льня, -и**; *g.pl.* **-лен** reading-room. **чита́тель, -я** *m.* reader. **чита́ть, -а́ю** *impf.* (*pf.* **про~, проче́сть**) read; recite, say; **~ ле́кции** lecture, give lectures; **~ с губ** lip-read; **~ся** be legible; be visible, be discernible. **чи́тка, -и** reading; reading through.

чих, -а sneeze. **чиха́ть, -а́ю** *impf.*, **чихну́ть, -ну́, -нёшь** *pf.* sneeze, cough, splutter.

чи́ще *comp. of* **чи́сто, чи́стый**

чи́щу *etc.*: *see* **чи́стить**

член, -а member; limb; term; part; article. **члене́ние, -я** articulation. **члени́ть, -ню́** *impf.* (*pf.* **рас~**) divide; articulate. **членко́р, -а** *abbr.*, (*of* **член-корреспонде́нт**) *abbr.* corresponding member, associate. **членоразде́льный** articulate. **чле́нск|ий** membership; **~ие взно́сы** membership fee, dues. **чле́нство, -а** membership.

чмо́кать, -аю *impf.*, **чмо́кнуть, -ну** *pf.* make smacking or sucking sound; kiss noisily; **~ губа́ми** smack one's lips.

чо́канье, -я clinking of glasses. **чо́каться, -аюсь** *impf.*, **чо́кнуться, -нусь** *pf.* clink glasses.

чо́порный prim, stiff; stuck-up, stand-offish.

чрева́тый+*i.* fraught with, pregnant with. **чре́во, -а** belly, womb. **чревовеща́ние, -я** ventriloquism. **чревовеща́тель, -я** *m.* ventriloquist.

чрез *see* **че́рез. чрезвыча́йн|ый** extraordinary; special, extreme; **~ое положе́ние** state of emergency. **чрезме́рный** excessive, inordinate, extreme.

чте́ние, -я reading; reading-matter; **~ с губ** lip-reading. **чтец, -а́, чти́ца, -ы** reader; reciter. **чти́во, -а** (*trashy*) reading-matter.

чтить, чту *impf.* honour.

чти́ца *see* **чтец**

что, чего́, чему́, чем, о чём *pron.* what?; how?; why?; how much?; which, what, who; anything; **в чём де́ло?** what is the matter? **для чего́?** what ... for? why?; **е́сли ~ случи́тся** if anything happens; **к чему́?** why?; **~ ему́ до э́того?** what does it matter to him?; **~ каса́ется меня́** as for me, as far as I am concerned; **~ с тобо́й?** what's the matter (with you)?; **я зна́ю, ~ вы име́ете в виду́** I know what you mean; **~ ж** yes; all right, right you are; **~ за** what? what sort of?; what (a) ..!; **(а) ...!; ~ за ерунда́!** what (utter) nonsense! **что** *conj.* that. **что (бы) ни** *pron.* whatever, no matter what; **во что бы то ни ста́ло** at whatever cost.

чтоб, что́бы *conj.* in order (to), so as; that; to; **он сказа́л, что́бы вы к нему́ зашли** he said you were to go and see him; **он хо́чет, что́бы я сде́лал э́то сейча́с же** he wants me to do it at once. **что-ли́бо, что-нибу́дь** *prons.* anything. **что́-то** *pron.* something. **что́-то** *adv.* somewhat, slightly; somehow, for some reason.

чу́вственность, -и sensuality. **чу́вственный** sensual; perceptible, sensible. **чувстви́тельность, -и** sensitivity, sensitiveness, sensibility; perceptibility; sentimentality; tenderness, feeling; (*film*) speed. **чувстви́тельный** sensitive, susceptible; sensible, perceptible; sentimental; tender. **чу́вство, -а** feeling; sense; senses; **прийти́ в ~** come round, regain consciousness. **чу́вствовать, -твую** *impf.* feel; realize; appreciate, have a feeling for; **~ся** be perceptible; make itself felt.

чугу́н, -а́ cast iron. **чугу́нка, -и** (*cast-iron*) pot; (*cast-iron*) stove; railway. **чугу́нный** cast-iron.

чуда́к, -а́, чуда́чка, -и eccentric, crank. **чуда́ческий** eccentric, extravagant. **чуда́чество, -а** eccentricity, extravagance.

чудеса́ *etc.*: *see* **чу́до. чуде́сный** miraculous; marvellous, wonderful.

чу́диться, -ишься *impf.* (*pf.* **по~, при~**) seem.

чу́дно *adv.* wonderfully, beautifully. **чудно́й; -дён, -дна́** odd, strange. **чу́дный** wonderful, marvellous; beautiful, lovely; magical. **чу́до, -а**; *pl.* **-деса́** miracle; wonder, marvel. **чудо́вище, -а** monster. **чудо́вищный** monstrous; enormous. **чудоде́й, -я, -де́йка, -и** miracle-worker. **чудоде́йственный** miracle-working; miraculous. **чу́дом** *adv.* miraculously. **чудотво́рный** miraculous, miracle-working.

чужби́на, -ы foreign land, foreign country. **чужда́ться, -а́юсь** *impf.*+*g.* shun, avoid; stand aloof from, be untouched by. **чу́ждый; -жд, -а́, -о** alien (to); +*g.* free from, devoid of, a stranger to. **чужезе́мец, -мца, -зе́мка, -и** foreigner, stranger. **чужезе́мный** foreign. **чуж|о́й** someone else's, another's, others'; strange, alien; foreign; **на ~о́й счёт** at s.o. else's expense; **~и́е края́** foreign lands; *sb.* stranger.

чула́н, -а store-room, lumber-room; larder; built-in-cupboard.

чуло́к, -лка́; *g.pl.* **-ло́к** stocking. **чуло́чн|ый** stocking; **~ая вя́зка** stocking-stitch.

чум, -а tent.

чума́, -ы́ plague.

чурба́н, -а block, chock; blockhead. **чу́рка, -и** block, lump.

чу́ткий; -ток, -тка́, -о keen, sharp, quick; sensitive; sympathetic; tactful, delicate, considerate; **~ сон** light sleep. **чу́ткость, -и** keeness, sharpness, quickness; delicacy, tact, consideration.

чу́точка, -и; ни чу́точки not in the least; **чу́точку** a little (bit), a wee bit.

чу́тче *comp. of* **чу́ткий**

чуть *adv.* hardly, scarcely; just; a little, very slightly; ~ **не** almost, nearly, all but; ~ **свет** at daybreak, at first light; **~-чуть** a tiny bit.

чухо́нец, -нца, чухо́нка, -и Finn. **чухо́нск|ий** Finnish; **~ое ма́сло** butter.

чу́чело, -а stuffed animal, stuffed bird; scarecrow.

чушь, -и nonsense, rubbish.

чу́ять, чу́ю *impf.* scent, smell; sense, feel.

чьё *etc.*: *see* **чей**

чэ *nt.indecl.* the letter **ч.**

ша *nt.indecl.* the letter **ш.**

ша́баш[1], **-а** sabbath. **шаба́ш**[2], **-а́** end of work, break; finish; **~!** that's all! that's enough! that'll do! **шаба́шить, -шу** *impf.* (*pf.* **по~**) (*sl.*) knock off, stop work; take a break. **шаба́шник, -а** moonlighter. **шаба́шничать, -аю** *impf.* moonlight.

шабло́н, -а template, pattern; mould, form; stencil; cliché; routine. **шабло́нный** stencil, pattern; trite, banal; stereotyped; routine.

шаг, -а (-у), with numerals **-а́**, *loc.* **-у́**; *pl.* **-и́** step; footstep; pace; stride.

шага́ть, -а́ю *impf.*, **шагну́ть, -ну́, -нёшь** *pf.* step; walk, stride; pace; go, come; make progress. **ша́гом** *adv.* at walking pace, at a walk; slowly.

ша́йба, -ы washer; puck.

ша́йка[1], **-и** tub.

ша́йка[2], **-и** gang, band.

шака́л, -а jackal.

шала́нда, -ы barge, lighter.

шала́ш, -а́ cabin, hut.

шали́ть, -лю́ *impf.* be naughty; play up, play tricks. **шаловли́вый** naughty, mischievous, playful. **ша́лость, -и** prank, game; *pl.* mischief, naughtiness. **шалу́н, -а́, шалу́нья, -и**; *g.pl.* **-ний** naughty child.

шаль, -и shawl.

шальн|о́й mad, crazy; wild; **~а́я пу́ля** stray bullet.

ша́мкать, -аю *impf.* mumble, lisp.

шампа́нское *sb.* champagne.

шампиньо́н, -а (*cultivated*) mushroom.

шампу́нь, -я *m.* shampoo.

шанс, -а chance.

шансо́н, -а ballad. **шансонье́** *m. indecl.* balladeer; singer-songwriter.

шанта́ж, -а́ blackmail. **шантажи́ровать, -рую** *impf.* blackmail.

ша́пка, -и cap; banner, headline. **ша́почка, -и** cap.

шар, -а, with numerals **-а́**; *pl.* **-ы́** sphere; ball; balloon; ballot; *pl.* (*sl.*) peepers, eyes.

шара́хать, -аю *impf.*, **шара́хнуть, -ну** hit; **~ся** rush, dash; shy.

шарж, -а caricature, cartoon. **шаржи́ровать, -рую** *impf.* caricature.

ша́рик, -а ball; corpuscle. **ша́риков|ый; ~ая (авто)ру́чка** ball-point pen; **~ый подши́пник** ball-bearing. **шарикоподши́пник, -а** ball-bearing.

ша́рить, -рю *impf.* grope, feel, fumble; sweep.

ша́ркать, -аю *impf.*, **ша́ркнуть, -ну** *pf.* shuffle; scrape; ~ **ного́й** click one's heels.

шарма́нка, -и barrel-organ, street organ. **шарма́нщик, -а** organ-grinder.

шарни́р, -а hinge, joint.

шарова́ры, -а́р *pl.* (*wide*) trousers; bloomers.

шарови́дный spherical, globular. **шарово́й** ball; globular. **шарообра́зный** spherical, globular.

шарф, -а scarf.

шасси́ *nt.indecl.* chassis; undercarriage.

шата́ть, -а́ю *impf.* rock, shake; *impers.+a.* **его́ шата́ет** he is reeling, staggering; **~ся** rock, sway; reel, stagger, totter; come loose, be loose; be unsteady; wander; loaf, lounge about. **шата́ющийся** loose.

шатёр, -тра́ tent; marquee; tent-shaped roof or steeple.

ша́ткий unsteady; shaky; loose; unstable, insecure; unreliable; vacillating.

шатро́вый tent-shaped.

шату́н, -а́ connecting-rod.

ша́фер, -а; *pl.* **-а́** best man.

шафра́н, -а saffron. **шафра́нный, шафра́новый** saffron.

шах[1], **-а** Shah.

шах[2], **-а** check; ~ **и мат** checkmate. **шахмати́ст, -а** chess-player. **ша́хматн|ый** chess; chess-board, chequered, check; **~ая па́ртия** game of chess. **ша́хматы, -ат** *pl.* chess; chessmen.

ша́хта, -ы mine, pit; shaft. **шахтёр, -а** miner. **шахтёрский** miner's, miners'; mining. **ша́хтный** pit, mine.

ша́шечница, -ы draught-board, chess-board. **ша́шка**[1], **-и** draught; *pl.* draughts.

ша́шка[2], **-и** sabre, cavalry sword.

шашлы́к, -а́ shashlik, kebab.

шва *etc.*: *see* **шов**

шва́бра, -ы mop, swab.

шваль, -и rubbish; trash; riff-raff.

шварто́в, -а hawser; mooring-line; *pl.* moorings. **швартова́ть, -ту́ю** *impf.* (*pf.* **о~, при~**) moor; **~ся** moor, make fast.

швах *indecl.* weak, poor; bad; in a bad way.

швед, -а, шве́дка, -и Swede. **шве́дский** Swedish.

шве́йн|ый sewing; **~ая маши́на** sewing-machine. **~ая мастерска́я** dress-maker's.

швейца́р, -а (hall-)porter, door-keeper, commissionaire.

швейца́рец, -рца, -ца́рка, -и Swiss. **Швейца́рия, -и** Switzerland. **швейца́рский** Swiss.

Шве́ция, -и Sweden.

швея́, -и́ seamstress, machinist.

швырну́ть, -ну́, -нёшь *pf.* **швыря́ть, -я́ю** *impf.* throw, fling, chuck, hurl; **~ся**+*i.* throw; throw about, treat carelessly, muck about.

шевели́ть, -елю́, -е́ли́шь *impf.*, **шевельну́ть, -ну́, -нёшь** *pf.* (*pf. also* **по~**) turn (over); (+*i.*) move, stir, budge; **~ся** move, stir, budge.

шевро́ *nt.indecl.* kid.

шеде́вр, -а masterpiece, chef d'oeuvre.

шезло́нг, -а deck-chair; lounger.

шёл *see* **идти́**

ше́лест, -а rustle, rustling. **шелесте́ть, -сти́шь** *impf.* rustle.

шёлк, -а (-у), *loc.* **-у́**; *pl.* **-а́** silk. **шелкови́стый** silk, silky. **шелко́вица, -ы** mulberry(-tree). **шелкови́чный** mulberry; **~ червь** silkworm. **шёлковый** silk. **шёлкогра́фия, -и** silk-screen printing.

шелохну́ть, -ну́, -нёшь *pf.* stir, agitate; **~ся** stir, move.

шелуха́, -и́ skin; peel, peelings; pod; scale. **шелуши́ть, -шу́** peel; shell; **~ся** peel; peel off, flake off.

шепеля́вить, -влю *impf.* lisp. **шепеля́вый** lisping; hissing.

шепну́ть, -ну́, -нёшь *pf.*, **шепта́ть, -пчу́, -пчешь** *impf.* whisper; **~ся** whisper (together). **шёпот, -а** whisper. **шёпотом** *adv.* in a whisper.

шере́нга, -и rank; file, column.

шерохова́тый rough; uneven; rugged.

шерсть, -и wool, woollen; fleece; hair, coat. **шерстяно́й** wool, woollen.

шерша́веть, -еет *impf.* become rough, get rough. **шерша́вый** rough.

шест, -а́ pole; staff.

ше́ствие, -я procession. **ше́ствовать, -твую** walk in procession, process; march, pace, proceed.

шестёрка, -и six; figure 6; No. 6; group of six.

шестерня́, -и́; *g.pl.* **-рён** gear-wheel, cogwheel, pinion.

ше́стеро, -ы́х six.

шести... *in comb.* six-, hexa-, sex(i)-. **шестигра́нник, -а** hexahedron. **~дне́вка, -и** six-day (*working*) week. **~деся́тый** sixtieth. **~кла́ссник, -а, ~кла́ссница, -ы** sixth-year pupil. **~ле́тний** six-year; six-year-old. **~ме́сячный** six-month; six-month-old. **~сотле́тие, -я** six hundred years; sexcentenary, six-hundredth anniversary. **~со́тый** six-hundredth. **~уго́льник, -а** hexagon. **~уго́льный** hexagonal. **~часово́й** six-hour; six-o'clock.

шестнадцатиле́тний sixteen-year; sixteen-year old. **шестна́дцатый** sixteenth. **шестна́дцать, -и** sixteen. **шестови́к, -а́** pole-vaulter.

шест|о́й sixth; **одна́ ~а́я** one-sixth. **шесть, -и́**, *i.* **-ью** six. **шестьдеся́т, -и́десяти**, *i.* **-ью́десятью** sixty. **шестьсо́т, -исо́т, -иста́м, -ьюста́ми, -иста́х** six hundred. **ше́стью** *adv.* six times.

шеф, -а boss, chief; patron, sponsor, **ше́фский** patronage, sponsorship, adoption; sponsored. **ше́фство, -а** patronage, adoption. **ше́фствовать, -твую** *impf.* **+над**+*i.* adopt; sponsor.

ше́я, -и neck; **сиде́ть на ше́е у** be a burden to.

ши́ворот, -а collar.

шизофрени́я, -и schizophrenia.

шика́рный chic, smart, stylish; splendid, magnificent; done for effect.

ши́кать, -аю *impf.*, **ши́кнуть, -ну** *pf.*+*d.* hiss, boo; **+на**+*a.* hush, call 'sh' to.

ши́ло, -а; *pl.* **-ья, -ьев** awl.

ши́на, -ы tyre; splint.

шине́ль, -и greatcoat, overcoat.

шинко́ванный shredded, chopped. **шинкова́ть, -ку́ю** *impf.* shred, chop.

ши́нный tyre. **шиноремо́нтный** tyre-repairing, tyre-maintenance.

шип, -а́ thorn, spike, crampon, nail; pin; tenon.

шипе́ние, -я hissing; sizzling; sputtering. **шипе́ть, -плю́** *impf.* hiss; sizzle; fizz; sputter.

шипо́вник, -а wild rose, dog-rose.

шипу́чий sparkling; fizzy. **шипу́чка, -и** fizzy drink. **шипя́щий** sibilant.

ши́ре *comp. of* **широ́кий, широ́ко́. ширина́, -ы́** width, breadth; gauge. **ши́рить, -рю** *impf.* extend, expand; **~ся** spread, extend.

ши́рма, -ы screen.

широ́к|ий; -о́к, -а́, -о́ко́ wide, broad; **това́ры ~ого потребле́ния** consumer goods; **~ие ма́ссы** the broad masses; **~ое пла́тье** loose dress; **~ая пу́блика** the general public; **~ий экра́н** wide screen. **широ́ко́** *adv.* wide, widely, broadly; extensively, on a large scale; **~ смотре́ть на ве́щи** be broad-minded.

широко... *in comb.* wide-, broad-. **широковеща́ние, -я** broadcasting. **~веща́тельный** broadcasting. **~коле́йный** broad-gauge. **~ко́стный** big-boned. **~пле́чий** broad-shouldered. **~по́лый** wide-brimmed; full-skirted. **~форма́тный, ~экра́нный** wide-screen.

широта́, -ы́; *pl.* **-ы** width, breadth; latitude. **широ́тный** of latitude; latitudinal. **широча́йший** *superl. of* **широ́кий. ширпотре́б, -а** *abbr.* consumption; consumer goods.

ширь, -и (wide) expanse; **во всю ~** to full width; to the full extent.

ши́тый embroidered. **шить, шью, шьёшь** *impf.* (*pf.* **с~**) sew; make; embroider. **шитьё, -я́** sewing, needlework; embroidery.

шифр, -а cipher, code; press-mark; monogram. **шифро́ванный** in cipher, coded. **шифрова́ть, -ру́ю** *impf.* (*pf.* **за~**) encipher, code. **шифро́вка, -и** enciphering, coding; coded communication, communication in cipher.

шиш, -а́ fico, fig; nothing; ruffian, brigand; **ни ~а́** damn all. **ши́шка, -и** cone; bump; lump, knob; core; (*sl.*) big shot, big noise. **шишкова́тый** knobby, knobbly; bumpy. **шишкови́дный** cone-shaped. **шишконо́сый** coniferous.

шкала́, -ы́; *pl.* **-ы** scale; dial.

шкату́лка, -и box, casket, case.

шкаф, -а, *loc.* **-у́**; *pl.* **-ы́** cupboard; wardrobe; dresser; **кни́жный ~** bookcase; **несгора́емый ~** safe. **шка́фчик, -а** cupboard, locker.

шквал, -а squall. **шква́листый** squally.

шкет, -а (*sl.*) boy, lad.

шкив, -а; *pl.* **-ы́** pulley; sheave.

шко́ла, -ы school; **~-интерна́т** boarding-school. **шко́лить, -лю** *impf.* (*pf.* **вы́~**) train, discipline. **шко́льник, -а** schoolboy. **шко́льница, -ы** schoolgirl. **шко́льный** school; **~ учи́тель** school-teacher, school-master.

шку́ра, -ы skin, hide, pelt. **шку́рка, -и** skin; rind; emery paper, sandpaper. **шку́рник, -а, -ница, -ы** self-seeker. **шку́рный** self-centred, selfish.

шла *see* **идти́**

шлагба́ум, -а barrier; arm.

шлак, -а slag; dross; cinder; clinker. **шлакобло́к, -а** breeze-block. **шла́ковый** slag.

шланг, -а hose.

шлейф, -а train.

шлем, -а helmet; **вя́заный ~** balaclava.

шлёпать, -аю *impf.*, **шлёпнуть, -ну** *pf.* smack, spank; shuffle; tramp; (*sl.*) shoot, execute by shooting; **~ся** fall flat, plop down, plump down.

шли *see* **идти́**

шлифова́льный polishing; grinding; abrasive. **шлифова́ть, -фу́ю** *impf.* (*pf.* **от~**) polish; grind; abrade. **шлифо́вка, -и** polishing; grinding; polish.

шло *see* **идти́. шлю** *etc.*: *see* **слать**

шлюз, -а lock, sluice, floodgate. **шлю́зный, шлюзово́й** lock, sluice.

шлю́пка, -и launch, boat.

шля́па, -ы hat; helpless, feeble creature; **де́ло в шля́пе** it's in the bag. **шля́пка, -и** hat, bonnet; head; cap. **шля́пник, -а, шля́пница, -ы** milliner, hatter. **шля́пный** hat.

шмель, -я́ bumble-bee.

шмы́гать, -аю *impf.*, **шмыгну́ть, -ы́гну́, -ы́гнёшь** *pf.* dart, rush, slip, sneak; *+i.* rub, brush; **~ но́сом** sniff.

шнур, -а́ cord; lace; flex, cable. **шнурова́ть, -ру́ю** *impf.* (*pf.* **за~, про~**) lace up; tie. **шнуро́к, -рка́** lace.

шныря́ть, -я́ю *impf.* dart about, run in and out.

шов, шва seam; stitch; suture; joint; weld.

шок, -а shock. **шоки́ровать, -рую** *impf.* shock. **шо́ков|ый; ~ая терапи́я** shock therapy.

шокола́д, -а chocolate. **шокола́дка, -и** chocolate, bar of chocolate. **шокола́дный** chocolate; chocolate-coloured.

шо́рох, -а rustle.

шо́рты, шорт *pl.* shorts.

шо́ры, шор *pl.* blinkers.

шоссе́ *nt.indecl.* highway, main road; (*surfaced*) road.

шотла́ндец, -дца Scotsman, Scot. **Шотла́ндия, -и** Scotland. **шотла́ндка**[1], **-и** Scot(swoman). **шотла́ндка**[2], **-и** tartan, plaid. **шотла́ндский** Scottish, Scots.

шофёр, -а, driver; chauffeur. **шофёрский** driver's; driving.

шпа́га, -и sword.

шпага́т, -а cord; twine; string; splits.

шпаклева́ть, -лю́ю *impf.* (*pf.* **за~**) caulk; fill, stop, putty. **шпаклёвка, -и** filling, puttying, stopping; putty.

шпа́ла, -ы sleeper.

шпана́, -ы́ (*sl.*) hooligan(s), rowdy, rowdies; riff-raff, rabble; petty criminals.

шпарга́лка, -и crib.

шпа́рить, -рю *impf.* (*pf.* **о~**) scald.

шпат, -а spar.

шпиль, -я *m.* spire, steeple; capstan, windlass. **шпи́лька, -и** hairpin; hat-pin; tack, brad; stiletto heel.

шпина́т, -а spinach.

шпингале́т, -а bolt; catch, latch.

шпио́н, -а spy. **шпиона́ж, -а** espionage. **шпио́нить, -ню** *impf.* be a spy; spy (**за**+*i.* on). **шпио́нский** spy's; espionage.

шпо́ра, -ы spur.

шприц, -а syringe.

шпро́та, -ы sprat; *pl.* smoked sprats in oil.

шпу́лька, -и spool, bobbin.

шрам, -а scar.

шрифт, -а; *pl.* **-ы́** type, print; script; **курси́вный ~** italic(s). **шрифтово́й** type.

шт. *abbr.* (*of* **шту́ка**) item, piece.

штаб, -а; *pl.* **-ы́** staff; headquarters.

шта́бель, -я; *pl.* **-я́** *m.* stack, pile.

штаби́ст, -а, штабни́к, -а́ staff-officer. **штабно́й** staff headquarters.

штамп, -а die, punch; stamp; impress; letter-head; cliché, stock phrase. **штампо́ванный** punched, stamped, pressed; trite, hackneyed; stock, standard.

шта́нга, -и bar, rod, beam; weight; crossbar. **штанги́ст, -а** weight-lifter.

штани́шки, -шек *pl.* (*child's*) shorts. **штаны́, -о́в** trousers.

штат[1], **-а** State.

штат[2], **-а, шта́ты, -ов** *pl.* staff, establishment.

штати́в, -а tripod, base, support, stand.

шта́тный staff; established, permanent.

шта́тск|ий civilian; **~ое (пла́тье)** civilian clothes, mufti, civvies; **~ий** *sb.* civilian.

штемпелева́ть, -лю́ю *impf.* (*pf.* **за~**) stamp; frank, postmark. **штемпе́ль, -я**; *pl.* **-я́** *m.* stamp; **почто́вый ~** postmark.

ште́псель, -я; *pl.* **-я́** *m.* plug, socket. **ште́псельный** plug, socket.

штиль, -я *m.* calm.

што́льня, -и; *g.pl.* **-лен** gallery.

што́пальный darning. **што́паный** darned.

што́пать, -аю *impf.* (*pf.* **за~**) darn. **што́пка, -и** darning; darn; darning wool, darning thread.
што́пор, -а corkscrew; spin.
што́ра, -ы blind.
шторм, -а gale, storm.
штормо́вка, -и anorak; parka.
штраф, -а fine. **штрафно́й** penal; penalty; **~ батальо́н** penal battalion; **~ уда́р** penalty kick. **штрафова́ть, -фу́ю** *impf.* (*pf.* **о~**) fine.
штрих, -а́ stroke; hatching; feature, trait. **штрихова́ть, -ху́ю** *impf.* (*pf.* **за~**) shade, hatch.
штуди́ровать, -рую *impf.* (*pf.* **про~**) study.
шту́ка, -и item, one; piece; trick; thing; **вот так ~!** well, I'll be damned! **в том-то и ~!** that's just the point; **пять штук яиц** five eggs.
штукату́р, -а plasterer. **штукату́рить, -рю** *impf.* (*pf.* **от~, о~**) plaster, parget. **штукату́рка, -и** plastering; plaster; facing, rendering; stucco. **штукату́рный** plaster, stucco.
штурва́л, -а (steering-)wheel, helm; controls. **штурва́льный** steering, control; *sb.* helmsman, pilot.
штурм, -а storm, assault.
шту́рман, -а; *pl.* **-ы** *or* **-а́** navigator.
штурмова́ть, -му́ю *impf.* storm, assault. **штурмов|о́й** assault; storming; **~а́я авиа́ция** ground-attack aircraft; **~а́я ле́стница** scaling-ladder; **~а́я полоса́** assault course. **штурмовщи́на, -ы** rushed work, production spurt, sporadic effort.
шту́чн|ый piece, by the piece; **~ый пол** parquet floor; **~ая рабо́та** piece-work; **~ый това́р** piece-goods.
штык, -а́ bayonet. **штыково́й** bayonet.
штырь, -я́ *m.* pintle, pin.
шу́ба, -ы winter coat, fur coat.
шу́лер, -а; *pl.* **-а́** card-sharper, cheat. **шу́лерство, -а** card-sharping, sharp practice.
шум, -а (-у) noise; din, uproar, racket; sensation, stir; **мно́го ~у из-за ничего́** much ado about nothing; **наде́лать ~у** cause a sensation. **шуме́ть, -млю́** *impf.* make a noise; row, wrangle; make a stir; make a fuss; cause a sensation. **шу́мный; -мен, -мна́, -о** noisy; loud; sensational. **шумови́к, -а́** sound effects man.
шумо́вка, -и perforated spoon; skimmer.
шумов|о́й sound, noise; **~ы́е эффе́кты** sound effects. **шумо́к, -мка́** noise; **под ~** under cover, on the quiet.
шу́рин, -а brother-in-law.
шурша́ть, -шу́ *impf.* rustle, crackle.
шу́стрый; -тёр, -тра́, -о smart, bright, sharp.
шут, -а́ fool; jester; buffoon, clown. **шути́ть, -чу́, -тишь** *impf.* (*pf.* **по~**) joke, jest; play, trifle; **+над**+*i.* laugh at, make fun of. **шу́тка, -и** joke, jest; trick; farce; **без шу́ток, кро́ме шу́ток** joking apart; **в шу́тку** as a joke, in jest; **не на шу́тку** in earnest; **сыгра́ть шу́тку с**+*i.* play a trick on. **шутли́вый** humorous; joking, light-hearted. **шу́точн|ый** comic; joking; **де́ло не ~ое** it's no joke, no laughing matter. **шутя́** *adv.* for fun, in jest; easily, lightly.
шушу́каться, -аюсь *impf.* whisper together.
шху́на, -ы schooner.
шью *etc.*: *see* **шить**

ща *nt.indecl.* the letter **щ.**
щаве́ль, -я́ *m.* sorrel.
щади́ть, щажу́ *impf.* (*pf.* **по~**) spare; have mercy on.
щебёнка, -и, щё́бень, -бня *m.* gravel, crushed stone, ballast; road-metal.
щё́бет, -а twitter, chirp. **щебета́ть, -ечу́, -е́чешь** *impf.* twitter, chirp.
щего́л, -гла́ goldfinch.
щёголь, -я *m.* dandy, fop. **щегольну́ть, -ну́, -нёшь** *pf.*, **щеголя́ть, -я́ю** *impf.* dress fashionably; strut about; *+i.* show off, parade, flaunt. **щегольско́й** foppish, dandified.
ще́дрость, -и generosity. **ще́дрый; -др, -а́, -о** generous; lavish, liberal.
щека́, -и́, *a.* **щёку**; *pl.* **щёки, -а́м** cheek.
щеко́лда, -ы latch, catch.
щекота́ть, -очу́, -о́чешь *impf.* (*pf.* **по~**) tickle. **щеко́тка, -и** tickling, tickle. **щекотли́вый** ticklish, delicate.
щёлкать, -аю *impf.*, **щёлкнуть, -ну** *pf.* crack; flick, fillip, flip; trill; *+i.* click, snap, pop; **он щёлкает зуба́ми** his teeth are chattering; **~ па́льцами** snap one's fingers.
щёлок, -а lye, liquor. **щелочно́й** alkaline. **щёлочь, -и**; *g.pl.* **-е́й** alkali.
щелчо́к, -чка́ flick, fillip; slight; blow.
щель, -и; *g.pl.* **-е́й** crack; chink; slit; fissure, crevice; slit trench; **голосова́я ~** glottis.
щени́ться, -и́тся *impf.* (*pf.* **о~**) pup, whelp, cub. **щено́к, -нка́**; *pl.* **-нки́, -о́в** *or* **-ня́та, -я́т** puppy, pup; whelp, cub.
щепа́, -ы́; *pl.* **-ы, -а́м, ще́пка, -и** splinter, chip; kindling; **худо́й как ще́пка** as thin as a rake. **щепа́ть, -плю́, -плёшь** *impf.* chip, chop.
щепети́льный punctilious, correct; pernickety, fussy, finicky.
ще́пка *see* **щепа́**
щепо́тка, -и, ще́по́ть, -и pinch.
щети́на, -ы bristle; stubble. **щети́нистый** bristly, bristling. **щети́ниться, -ится** *impf.* (*pf.* **о~**) bristle. **щётка, -и** brush; fetlock. **щёточный** brush.

щёчный cheek.
щи, щей *or* **щец, щам, щами** *pl.* shchi, cabbage soup.
щиколотка, -и ankle.
шипать, -плю, -плешь *impf.*, **щипнуть, -ну, -нёшь** *pf.* (*pf. also* **об~, о~, ущипнуть**) pinch, nip, tweak; sting, bite; burn; pluck; nibble; **~ся** pinch. **щипком** *adv.* pizzicato. **щипок, -пка** pinch, nip, tweak. **щипцы, -ов** *pl.* tongs, pincers, pliers; forceps. **щипчики, -ов** *pl.* tweezers.
щит, -а shield; screen; sluice-gate; (*tortoise*) shell; hoarding; board; panel; **распределительный ~** switchboard; **~ управления** control panel. **щитовидный** thyroid. **щиток, -тка** dashboard.
щука, -и pike.
щуп, -а probe. **щупальце, -а**; *g.pl.* **-лец** tentacle; antenna. **щупать, -аю** (*pf.* **по~**) feel, touch; feel for; probe.
щуплый; -пл, -а, -о weak, puny, frail.
щурить, -рю *impf.* (*pf.* **со~**) screw up, narrow; **~ся** screw up one's eyes; narrow.
щуч|ий pike's; **(как) по ~ьему веленью** of its own accord, as if by magic.

Э

э *nt.indecl.*, **э оборотное** the letter **э**.
эвакуационный evacuation. **эвакуация, -и** evacuation. **эвакуированный** *sb.* evacuee. **эвакуировать, -рую** *impf.* & *pf.* evacuate.
Эверест, -а (Mt.) Everest.
ЭВМ *abbr.* (*of* ***электронная вычислительная машина***) (electronic) computer.
эволюционировать, -рую *impf.* & *pf.* evolve. **эволюционный** evolutionary. **эволюция, -и** evolution; manoeuvre.
эгоизм, -а egoism, selfishness. **эгоист, -а** egoist. **эгоистический** egoistic, selfish. **эготизм, -а** egotism.
Эдинбург, -а Edinburgh.
эй *int.* hi! hey!
Эйре *nt.indecl.* Eire.
эйтаназия, -и euthanasia.
Эйфелева башня, -ой -и the Eiffel Tower.
экватор, -а equator. **экваториальный** equatorial.
эквивалент, -а equivalent. **эквивалентный** equivalent.
экз. *abbr.* (*of* **экземпляр**) copy, specimen.
экзамен, -а examination, exam; **~ на вождение** driving test; **выдержать, сдать ~** pass an examination. **экзаменатор, -а** examiner. **экзаменовать, -ную** *impf.* (*pf.* **про~**) examine; **~ся** take an examination.
экзема, -ы eczema.
экземпляр, -а specimen, example; copy.
экипаж[1], -а carriage.
экипаж[2], -а crew; ship's company. **экипировать, -рую** *impf.* & *pf.* equip. **экипировка, -и** equipping; equipment.
экологический ecological. **экология, -и** ecology.
эконом, -а steward, housekeeper; economist. **экономика, -и** economics; economy. **экономить, -млю** *impf.* (*pf.* **с~**) use sparingly, husband; save; economize. **экономический** economic; economical. **экономичный** economical. **экономия, -и** economy; saving. **экономка, -и** housekeeper. **экономный** economical; careful, thrifty.
экосистема, -ы ecosystem.
экран, -а screen; **голубой ~** television (screen). **экранизация, -и** filming, screening; film version. **экранный** on-screen.
экскаватор, -а excavator, earth-moving machine.
экскурсант, -а tourist. **экскурсионный** excursion. **экскурсия, -и** (conducted) tour; excursion, trip; outing; group, party (*of tourists*). **экскурсовод, -а** guide.
экспансивный effusive, expansive, talkative.
экспедировать, -рую *impf.* & *pf.* dispatch. **экспедиция, -и** expedition; dispatch, forwarding; forwarding office.
эксперт, -а expert. **экспертиза, -ы** (expert) examination, expert opinion; commission of experts.
эксплуататор, -а exploiter. **эксплуатационн|ый** exploitational, operating; **~ые расходы** running costs; **~ые условия** working conditions. **эксплуатация, -и** exploitation; utilization; operation, running. **эксплуатировать, -рую** *impf.* exploit; operate, run, work.
экспо *f.indecl.* Expo. **экспозиция, -и** layout; exposition; exposure. **экспонат, -а** exhibit. **экспонент, -а** exhibitor. **экспонировать, -рую** *impf.* & *pf.* exhibit; expose. **экспонометр, -а** exposure meter.
экспорт, -а export. **экспортёр, -а** exporter. **экспортировать, -рую** *impf.* & *pf.* export.
экспресс, -а express (*train, coach, etc.*).
экспромт, -а impromptu. **экспромтом** *adv.* impromptu; suddenly, without warning; **играть ~** improvise.
экстерн, -а external student. **экстернат, -а** extramural course(s).
экстравагантный extravagant, eccentric, bizarre, preposterous.
экстракт, -а (*cul.*) extract; résumé, précis.
экстрасенс, -а psychic.
экстренн|ый urgent; emergency; extra, special; **~ое заседание** extraordinary session; **~ое издание, ~ый выпуск** special edition; **~ые расходы** unforeseen expenses.
эксцентричный eccentric.

экю́ *m.* & *nt. indecl.* écu.

эласти́чн|ый elastic; springy, resilient; **~ые брю́ки** stretch pants.

элега́нтность, -и elegance. **элега́нтный** elegant, smart.

электризова́ть, -зу́ю *impf.* (*pf.* **на~**) electrify. **эле́ктрик, -а** electrician. **электрифици́ровать, -рую** *impf.* & *pf.* electrify. **электри́ческий** electric; **~ фона́рик** torch, flashlight. **электри́чество, -а** electricity; electric light. **электри́чка, -и** electric train.

электро... *in comb.* electro-, electric, electrical. **электробытово́й** electrical. **~во́з, -а** electric locomotive. **~дви́гатель, -я** *m.* electric motor. **~дина́мика, -и** electrodynamics. **~дугово́й** electric-arc. **~изгородь, -и** electric fence. **электро́лиз, -а** electrolysis. **~маши́нка, -и** electric typewriter. **~монтёр, -а** electrician. **~одея́ло, -а** electric blanket. **~подогрева́тель, -я** *m.* electric heater. **~по́езд, -а** electric train. **~полоте́нце, -а** hand-drier. **~полотёр, -а** electric floor-polisher. **~прибо́р, -а** electrical appliance. **~про́вод, -а**; *pl.* **-а́** electric cable. **~прово́дка, -и** electric wiring. **~прои́грыватель, -я** *m.* record-player. **~сва́рка, -и** electric welding. **~ста́нция, -и** power-station. **~те́хник, -а** electrical engineer. **~те́хника, -и** electrical engineering. **~тя́га, -и** electric traction. **~шо́к, -а** electric-shock treatment. **~энцефалогра́мма, -ы** (electro-)encephalogram. **~энцефало́граф, -а** (electro-)encephalograph.

электро́н, -а electron. **электро́ника, -и** electronics.

электронно- *in comb.* electron, electronic. **электро́нно-лучево́й** electron-beam, cathode-ray. **~микроскопи́ческий** electron-microscope.

электро́нный electron; electronic.

элеме́нт, -а element; cell; type, character. **элемента́рный** elementary; simple.

эль *nt.indecl.* the letter **л**.

эм *nt.indecl.* the letter **м**.

эма́левый enamel. **эмалиро́ванный** enamelled. **эмалирова́ть, -ру́ю** *impf.* enamel. **эма́ль, -и** enamel.

эмансипа́ци|я, -и emancipation; **боре́ц за ~ю же́нщин** women's liberationist. **эмансипи́ровать, -рую** *impf.* & *pf.* emancipate.

эмба́рго *nt.indecl.* embargo.

эмбле́ма, -ы emblem; insignia.

эмбрио́н, -а embryo.

эмигра́нт, -а emigrant, émigré. **эмигра́ция, -и** emigration. **эмигри́ровать, -рую** *impf.* & *pf.* emigrate.

эмоциона́льный emotional. **эмо́ция, -и** emotion.

эмпири́зм, -а empiricism. **эмпи́рик, -а** empiricist. **эмпири́ческий** empiricist; empirical.

э́му *indecl.* emu.

эму́льсия, -и emulsion.

эн *nt.indecl.* the letter **н**.

э́ндшпиль, -я *m.* end-game.

энерге́тика, -и power engineering. **энерги́чный** energetic, vigorous, forceful. **эне́ргия, -и** energy; vigour, effort.

энерго... *in comb.* power, energy. **энерговооружённость, -и** power capacity, power supply. **~ёмкий** power-consuming. **~затра́та, -ы** energy expenditure. **~систе́ма, -ы** electric power system.

энтомо́лог, -а entomologist. **энтомологи́ческий** entomological. **энтомоло́гия, -и** entomology.

энтузиа́зм, -а enthusiasm. **энтузиа́ст, -а** (+*g.*) enthusiast (about, for), devotee (of).

энциклопеди́ческий encyclopaedic; **~ слова́рь** encyclopaedia. **энциклопе́дия, -и** encyclopaedia.

эпигра́мма, -ы epigram. **эпи́граф, -а** epigraph.

эпиде́мия, -и epidemic.

эпизо́д, -а episode. **эпизоди́ческий** episodic; occasional, sporadic.

эпикуре́ец, -йца epicurean. **эпикуре́йский** epicurean.

эпиле́псия, -и epilepsy. **эпиле́птик, -а** epileptic. **эпилепти́ческий** epileptic.

эпило́г, -а epilogue. **эпита́фия, -и** epitaph. **эпи́тет, -а** epithet. **эпице́нтр, -а** epicentre.

эпи́ческий epic. **эпопе́я, -и** epic.

эполе́ты, эполе́т *pl.* epaulettes.

эпо́ха, -и epoch, age, era. **эпоха́льный** epoch-making.

эр *nt.indecl.* the letter **р**.

э́ра, -ы era; **до на́шей э́ры** B.C.; **на́шей э́ры** A.D.

эроге́нн|ый erogenous; **~ые зо́ны** erogenous zones.

эро́тика, -и sensuality. **эроти́ческий, эроти́чный** erotic, sensual.

эруди́ция, -и erudition.

эрцге́рцог, -а archduke. **эрцгерцоги́ня, -и** archduchess. **эрцге́рцогство, -а** archduchy.

эс *nt.indecl.* the letter **с**.

эска́дра, -ы squadron. **эска́дренный** squadron; **~ миноно́сец** destroyer. **эскадри́льный** squadron. **эскадри́лья, -и**; *g.pl.* **-лий** squadron. **эскадро́н, -а** squadron, troop. **эскадро́нный** squadron, troop.

эскала́тор, -а escalator.

эскало́п, -а cutlet(s).

эски́з, -а sketch, study; draft, outline. **эски́зный** sketch; sketchy; draft.

эскимо́ *nt.indecl.* choc-ice.

эскимо́с, -а, эскимо́ска, -и Eskimo. **эскимо́сский** Eskimo.

эско́рт, -а (*mil.*) escort. **эскорти́ровать, -рую** *impf.* & *pf.* (*mil.*) escort.

эсми́нец, -нца *abbr.* (*of* **эска́дренный миноно́сец**) destroyer.

эссе́нция, -и essence.

эстака́да, -ы trestle, platform; trestle bridge; gantry; overpass; pier, boom.

эста́мп, -а print, engraving, plate.

эстафе́та, -ы relay race; baton.
эсте́тика, -и aesthetics; design. **эстети́ческий** aesthetic.
Эсто́ния, -и Estonia.
эстра́да, -ы stage, platform; variety, music hall; **арти́ст эстра́ды** variety performer, artiste; entertainer. **эстра́дный** stage; variety; ~ **конце́рт** variety show; entertainment.
эта́ж, -а́ storey, floor. **этаже́рка, -и** shelves; whatnot; stand. **эта́жность, -и** number of storeys.
э́так *adv.* so, thus; about, approximately. **э́такий** such (a), what (a).
эталóн, -а standard.
эта́п, -а stage, phase; lap; halting-place; transport, shipment, of prisoners. **этапи́ровать, -рую** *impf.* ship, transport.
э́тика, -и ethics.
этике́т, -а etiquette.
этике́тка, -и label.
этимóлог, -а etymologist. **этимологи́ческий** etymological. **этимолóгия, -и** etymology.
эти́ческий, эти́чный ethical.
этни́ческий ethnic.
этногра́фия, -и ethnography.
э́то *part.* this (is), that (is), it (is). **э́тот** *m.*, **э́та** *f.*, **э́то** *nt.*, **э́ти** *pl. pron.* this, these.
этю́д, -а study, sketch; étude; exercise; problem.
эф *nt.indecl.* the letter **ф.**
эфе́с, -а hilt, handle.
эфиóп, -а, эфиóпка, -и Ethiopian. **эфиóпский** Ethiopian.
эфи́р, -а ether; air. **эфи́рн|ый** ethereal; ether, ester; **~ое ма́сло** essential oil; volatile oil.
эффе́кт, -а effect, impact; result, consequences; *pl.* effects; **тепли́чный** ~ greenhouse effect. **эффекти́вный** effective; efficient. **эффе́ктный** effective; striking; done for effect.
эх *int.* eh! oh!
э́хо, -а echo. **эхолóт, -а** echo-sounder. **эхолока́ция, -и** echo location.
эшафóт, -а scaffold.
эшелóн, -а echelon; special train, troop-train.

Ю

ю *nt.indecl.* the letter **ю.**
ю. *abbr.* (*of* **юг**) S., south.
ЮАР *abbr.* (*of* ***Ю́жно-Африка́нская Респу́блика***) Republic of South Africa.
юбиле́й, -я anniversary; jubilee. **юбиле́йный** jubilee.
ю́бка, -и skirt; **~-брю́ки** split skirt, culottes.
ю́бочка, -и short skirt.
ювели́р, -а jeweller. **ювели́рный** jeweller's, jewellery; fine, intricate; ~ **магази́н** jeweller's.
юг, -а south; **на ~е** in the south. **ю́го-востóк, -а** south-east. **ю́го-за́пад, -а** south-west. **югосла́в, -а, югосла́вка, -и** Yugoslav. **Югосла́вия, -и** Yugoslavia. **югосла́вский** Yugoslav. **южа́нин, -а**; *pl.* **-а́не, -а́н, южа́нка, -и** southerner. **ю́жный** southern; **Ю́~ океа́н** the Antarctic Ocean.
ю́мор, -а humour. **юморе́ска, -и** humoresque. **юмори́ст, -а** humourist. **юмори́стика, -и** humour. **юмористи́ческий** humorous, comic, funny.
юниóр, -а, юниóрка, -и junior; junior competitor, player, etc. **юнкóр, -а** *abbr.* youth correspondent.
ю́ность, -и youth. **ю́ноша, -и** *m.* youth. **ю́ношеский** youthful. **ю́ношество, -а** youth; young people. **ю́ный; юн, -а́, -о** young; youthful.
юпи́тер, -а floodlight.
юриди́ческ|ий legal, juridical; **~ие нау́ки** jurisprudence, law; **~ий факульте́т** faculty of law. **юрискóнсульт, -а** legal adviser. **юри́ст, -а** legal expert, lawyer.
ю́ркий; -рок, -рка́, -рко quick-moving, brisk; sharp, smart.
ю́рта, -ы yurt (*nomad's tent in Central Asia*).
юсти́ция, -и justice.
юти́ться, ючу́сь *impf.* huddle (together); take shelter.

Я

я *nt.indecl.* the letter **я.**
я, меня́, мне, мной (-óю), (обо) мне *pron.* I.
я́беда, -ы *c.g.*, **я́бедник, -а** sneak, tell-tale; informer. **я́бедничать, -аю** *impf.* (*pf.* **на~**) inform, tell tales, sneak.
я́блоко, -а; *pl.* **-и, -ок** apple; **в я́блоках** dappled, dapple; **глазнóе** ~ eyeball. **я́блоневый, я́блонный, я́блочный** apple. **я́блоня, -и** apple-tree.
яви́ться, явлю́сь, я́вишься *pf.*, **явля́ться, -я́юсь** *impf.* appear; present o.s., report; turn up, arrive, show up; arise, occur; *+i.* be, serve as. **я́вка, -и** appearance, attendance, presence; secret rendez-vous; ~ **обяза́тельна** attendance obligatory. **явле́ние, -я** phenomenon; appearance; occurrence, happening; scene. **я́вный** obvious, manifest, patent; overt, explicit. **я́вственный** clear, distinct. **я́вствовать, -твует** appear; be clear, be obvious; follow.

ягнёнок, -нка; *pl.* **-ня́та, -я́т** lamb.
я́года, -ы berry; berries.
я́годица, -ы buttock, buttocks.
яд, -а (-у) poison; venom.
я́дерщик, -а nuclear physicist. **я́дерный** nuclear.
ядови́тый poisonous; venomous; toxic.
ядрёный vigorous, healthy; bracing; sound, crisp, juicy. **ядро́, -а́**; *pl.* **-а, я́дер** kernel, core; nucleus; main body; (cannon-)ball; shot. **ядротолка́тель, -я** *m.* shot-putter.
я́зва, -ы ulcer, sore. **я́звенн|ый** ulcerous; **~ая боле́знь** ulcers. **я́звина, -ы** large ulcer; indentation, pit. **язви́тельный** caustic, biting, sarcastic. **язви́ть, -влю́** *impf.* (*pf.* **съ~**) wound, sting; be sarcastic.
язы́к, -а́ tongue; clapper; language; **англи́йский ~** English. **языка́стый** sharp-tongued. **языкове́д, -а** linguist(ician). **языкове́дение, -я, языкозна́ние, -я** linguistics. **языково́й** linguistic. **языко́вый** tongue; lingual. **язычко́вый** uvular; reed. **язы́чник, -а** heathen, pagan. **язы́чный** lingual. **язычо́к, -чка́** tongue; uvula; reed; catch.
яи́чко, -а; *pl.* **-и, -чек** egg; testicle. **яи́чник, -а** ovary. **яи́чница, -ы** fried eggs. **яйцеви́дный** oval; oviform, ovoid, egg-shaped. **яйцо́, -а́**; *pl.* **я́йца, яи́ц** egg; ovum.
як, -а yak.
я́кобы *conj.* as if, as though; *part.* supposedly, ostensibly, allegedly.
я́корн|ый anchor; mooring; **~ая стоя́нка** anchorage. **я́корь, -я**; *pl.* **-я́** *m.* anchor; armature.
ял, -а whaleboat, whaler; yawl. **я́лик, -а** skiff, dinghy; yawl. **я́личник, -а** ferryman.
Я́лта, -ы Yalta.
я́ма, -ы pit, hole; depression, hollow.
ямщи́к, -а́ coachman.
янва́рский January. **янва́рь, -я́** *m.* January.
янта́рный amber. **янта́рь, -я́** *m.* amber.
япо́нец, -нца, япо́нка, -и Japanese. **Япо́ния, -и** Japan. **япо́нский** Japanese; **~ лак** Japan.
ярд, -а yard (*measure*).
я́ркий; я́рок, ярка́, -о bright; colourful, striking; vivid, graphic; **~ приме́р** striking example, glaring example.
ярлы́к, -а́ label; tag.
я́рмарка, -и fair. **я́рмарочный** fair, market.
ярмо́, -а́; *pl.* **-а** yoke.
ярово́й spring, spring-sown.
я́ростный furious, fierce, savage, frenzied. **я́рость, -и** fury, rage, frenzy.
я́рус, -а circle; tier; layer.
я́рче *comp. of* **я́ркий**
я́рый vehement, fervent; furious, raging; violent.
я́сельный crèche, day-nursery.
я́сеневый ash. **я́сень, -я** *m.* ash(-tree).
я́сли, -ей *pl.* manger, crib; crèche, day nursery.
ясне́ть, -е́ет *impf.* become clear, clear. **я́сно** *adv.* clearly. **яснови́дение, -я** clairvoyance. **яснови́дец, -дца, яснови́дица, -ы** clairvoyant. **я́сный; я́сен, ясна́, -о** clear; bright; fine; distinct; serene; plain; lucid; precise, logical.
я́ства, яств *pl.* viands, victuals.
я́стреб, -а; *pl.* **-а́** hawk. **ястреби́н|ый** hawk; **с ~ым взгля́дом** hawk-eyed. **ястребо́к, -бка́** hawk; fighter (*plane*).
я́хта, -ы yacht.
яче́истый cellular, porous. **яче́йка, -и, ячея́, -и́** cell.
ячме́нный barley. **ячме́нь[1], -я́** *m.* barley.
ячме́нь[2], -я́ *m.* stye.
я́щерица, -ы lizard.
я́щик, -а box, chest, case; cabinet; drawer; **му́сорный ~** dustbin; **откла́дывать в до́лгий ~** shelve, put off.
я́щур, -а foot-and-mouth disease.

English–Russian dictionary

A [eɪ] *n.* (*mus.*) ля *nt.indecl.*; **from A to Z** с нача́ла до конца́.

a [ə, eɪ], **an** [æn, ən] *indef. article, not usu. translated*; *adj.* оди́н, не́кий, како́й-то; **fifty miles an hour** пятьдеся́т миль в час; **twice a week** два ра́за в неде́лю.

AA *abbr.* (*of* ***Automobile Association***) Ассоциа́ция автомобили́стов.

aback [ə'bæk] *adv.*: **take ~** поража́ть *impf.*, порази́ть *pf.*; засти́гнуть *pf.* враспло́х.

abacus ['æbəkəs] *n.* счёты *m.pl.*

abandon [ə'bænd(ə)n] *v.t.* (*leave*) оставля́ть *impf.*, оста́вить *pf.*; (*desert*) покида́ть *impf.*, поки́нуть *pf.*; (*give up*) броса́ть *impf.*, бро́сить *pf.*; **~ o.s. to** предава́ться (-даю́сь, -даёшься) *impf.*, преда́ться (-а́мся, -а́шься, -а́стся, -ади́мся; -а́лся, -ала́сь) *pf.+d.* **abandoned** *adj.* забро́шенный, поки́нутый; (*profligate*) распу́тный. **abandonment** *n.* (*action*) оставле́ние; (*state*) забро́шенность.

abase [ə'beɪs] *v.t.* унижа́ть *impf.*, уни́зить *pf.* **abasement** *n.* униже́ние.

abate [ə'beɪt] *v.i.* (*lessen*) уменьша́ться *impf.*, уме́ньшиться *pf.*; (*weaken*) слабе́ть *impf.*, о~ *pf.*; (*calm*) успока́иваться *impf.*, успоко́иться *pf.*; (*die down*) затиха́ть *impf.*, зати́хнуть (-х) *pf.* **abatement** *n.* уменьше́ние.

abattoir ['æbəˌtwɑː(r)] *n.* скотобо́йня (*g.pl.* -бен).

abbess ['æbɪs] *n.* аббати́са. **abbey** ['æbɪ] *n.* абба́тство. **abbot** ['æbət] *n.* абба́т.

abbreviate [ə'briːvɪˌeɪt] *v.t.* сокраща́ть *impf.*, сократи́ть (-ащу́, -ати́шь) *pf.* **abbrevi'ation** *n.* сокраще́ние.

ABC [ˌeɪbiː'siː] *n.* а́збука, алфави́т.

abdicate ['æbdɪˌkeɪt] *v.i.* отрека́ться *impf.*, отре́чься (-еку́сь, -ечёшься; -ёкся, -екла́сь) *pf.* от престо́ла. **abdi'cation** *n.* отрече́ние (от престо́ла).

abdomen ['æbdəmən] *n.* брюшна́я по́лость (*pl.* -ти, -те́й); (*entom.*) брюшко́ (*pl.* -ки́, -ко́в). **abdominal** [æb'dɒmɪn(ə)l] *adj.* брюшно́й.

abduct [əb'dʌkt] *v.t.* наси́льно увози́ть (-ожу́, -о́зишь) *impf.*, увезти́ (увезу́, -зёшь; увёз, -ла́) *pf.* **abduction** *n.* наси́льственный уво́з.

aberration [ˌæbə'reɪʃ(ə)n] *n.* аберра́ция; (*mental*) помраче́ние ума́.

abet [ə'bet] *v.t.* подстрека́ть *impf.*, подстрекну́ть *pf.* (к соверше́нию преступле́ния *etc.*); соде́йствовать *impf.* & *pf.* соверше́нию (преступле́ния *etc.*).

abhor [əb'hɔː(r)] *v.t.* пита́ть *impf.* отвраще́ние к+*d.*; (*hate*) ненави́деть (-и́жу, -и́дишь) *impf.* **abhorrence** [əb'hɒrəns] *n.* отвраще́ние. **abhorrent** *adj.* отврати́тельный.

abide [ə'baɪd] *v.t.* (*tolerate*) выноси́ть (-ошу́, -о́сишь) *impf.*, вы́нести (-су́, -сешь; -с) *pf.*; *v.i.* (*remain*) остава́ться (-таю́сь, -таёшься) *impf.*, оста́ться (-а́нусь, -а́нешься) *pf.*; **~ by** (*promise etc.*) выполня́ть *impf.*, вы́полнить *pf.*

ability [ə'bɪlɪtɪ] *n.* спосо́бность; уме́ние.

abject ['æbdʒekt] *adj.* (*miserable*) жа́лкий (-лок, -лка́, -лко); (*low*) ни́зкий (-зок, -зка́, -зко); (*craven*) малоду́шный.

abjure [əb'dʒʊə(r)] *v.t.* отрека́ться *impf.*, отре́чься (-еку́сь, -ечёшься; -ёкся, -екла́сь) *pf.* от+*g.*

ablative ['æblətɪv] *n.* абляти́в.

ablaze [ə'bleɪz] *pred.*: **be ~** горе́ть (-ри́т) *impf.*; сверка́ть *impf.*

able ['eɪb(ə)l] *adj.* спосо́бный, уме́лый; (*talented*) тала́нтливый; **be ~ to** мочь (могу́, мо́жешь; мог, -ла́) *impf.*, с~ *pf.*; быть в состоя́нии; (*know how to*) уме́ть *impf.*, с~ *pf.*

abnormal [æb'nɔːm(ə)l] *adj.* ненорма́льный. **abnormality** [ˌæbnɔː'mælɪtɪ] *n.* ненорма́льность.

aboard [ə'bɔːd] *adv.* на борт(у́); (*train*) на по́езд(е).

abolish [ə'bɒlɪʃ] *v.t.* отменя́ть *impf.*, отмени́ть (-ню́, -нишь) *pf.*; уничтожа́ть *impf.*, уничто́жить *pf.* **abolition** [ˌæbə'lɪʃ(ə)n] *n.* отме́на; уничтоже́ние.

abominable [ə'bɒmɪnəb(ə)l] *adj.* отврати́тельный; (*bad*) ужа́сный; **the A~ Snowman** «сне́жный челове́к», йе́ти *m.indecl.* **abomi'nation** *n.* отвраще́ние; (*also object of ~*) ме́рзость.

aboriginal [ˌæbə'rɪdʒɪn(ə)l] *adj.* иско́нный, коренно́й; *n.* абориге́н, коренно́й жи́тель *m.* **aborigines** *n.* абориге́ны *m.pl.*, коренны́е жи́тели *m.pl.*

abort [ə'bɔːt] *v.i.* (*med.*) выки́дывать *impf.*, вы́кинуть *pf.*; *v.t.* (*terminate*) прекраща́ть *impf.*, прекрати́ть (-ащу́, -ати́шь) *pf.*; обрыва́ть *impf.*, оборва́ть (-ву́, -вёшь; оборва́л, -а́, -о) *pf.* **abortion** *n.* або́рт, вы́кидыш; **backstreet ~** подпо́льный або́рт. **abortive** *adj.* неуда́вшийся, безуспе́шный.

abound [ə'baʊnd] *v.i.* быть в большо́м коли́честве; **~ in** изоби́ловать *impf.+i.*; **~ with**

кише́ть (-ши́т) *impf.+i.*
about [ə'baʊt] *adv. & prep.* о́коло+*g.*; (*concerning*) о+*p.*, насчёт+*g.*; (*up and down*) по+*d.*; **be ~ to** собира́ться *impf.*, собра́ться (соберу́сь, -рёшся; собра́лся, -ала́сь, -а́ло́сь) *pf.+inf.*
above [ə'bʌv] *adv.* наверху́; (*higher up*) вы́ше; **from ~** све́рху; свы́ше; *prep.* над+*i.*; (*more than*) свы́ше+*g.* **above-board** *adj.* че́стный (-ен, -тна́, -тно), прямо́й (прям, -а́, -о). **above-mentioned** *adj.* вышеупомя́нутый.
abrasion [ə'breɪʒ(ə)n] *n.* стира́ние, истира́ние; (*wound*) сса́дина. **abrasive** [ə'breɪsɪv] *adj.* абрази́вный; *n.* абрази́в, шлифова́льный материа́л.
abreast [ə'brest] *adv.* (*in line*) в ряд, ря́дом; (*on a level*) в у́ровень.
abridge [ə'brɪdʒ] *v.t.* сокраща́ть *impf.*, сократи́ть (-ащу́, -ати́шь) *pf.* **abridgement** *n.* сокраще́ние.
abroad [ə'brɔːd] *adv.* за грани́цей, за грани́цу; **from ~** из-за грани́цы.
abrupt [ə'brʌpt] *adj.* (*steep*) обры́вистый, круто́й (крут, -а́, -о, кру́ты́); (*sudden*) внеза́пный; (*manner*) ре́зкий (-зок, -зка́, -зко).
abscess ['æbsɪs] *n.* абсце́сс, нары́в, гнойни́к (-а́).
abscond [əb'skɒnd] *v.i.* скрыва́ться *impf.*, скры́ться (-ро́юсь, -ро́ешься) *pf.*; бежа́ть (бегу́, бежи́шь) *impf. & pf.*
absence ['æbs(ə)ns] *n.* отсу́тствие; (*temporary*) отлу́чка; (*from work*) нея́вка, невы́ход, на рабо́ту; **~ of mind** рассе́янность. **absent** ['æbs(ə)nt; əb'sent] *adj.* отсу́тствующий; в отлу́чке; **be ~** отсу́тствовать *impf.*; *v.t.*: **~ o.s.** отлуча́ться *impf.*, отлучи́ться *pf.* **absentee** [,æbsən'tiː] *n.* отсу́тствующий *sb.*; (*habitual*) прогу́льщик, -ица. **absenteeism** *n.* прогу́л, абсентеи́зм. **absent-minded** *adj.* рассе́янный (-ян, -янна).
absolute ['æbsə,luːt, -,ljuːt] *adj.* абсолю́тный; (*complete*) по́лный (-лон, -лна́, по́лно́), соверше́нный (-нен, -нна); (*unrestricted*) безусло́вный, неограни́ченный (-ен, -енна); (*pure*) чи́стый (чист, -а́, -о, чи́сты́); **~ alcohol** чи́стый спирт (-а(у), *loc.* -е & -у́); **~ pitch** (*of sound*) абсолю́тная высота́; (*in person*) абсолю́тный слух; **~ proof** несомне́нное доказа́тельство; **~ zero** абсолю́тный нуль (-ля́) *m.*
absolution [,æbsə'luːʃ(ə)n, -'ljuːʃ(ə)n] *n.* отпуще́ние грехо́в. **absolve** [əb'zɒlv] *v.t.* проща́ть *impf.*, прости́ть *pf.*
absorb [əb'sɔːb, -'zɔːb] *v.t.* (*take in*) впи́тывать *impf.*, впита́ть *pf.*; (*swallow, also fig.*) поглоща́ть *impf.*, поглоти́ть (-ощу́, -о́тишь); *pf.*; (*suck in*) вса́сывать *impf.*, всоса́ть (-су́, -сёшь); *pf.*; (*tech.*) абсорби́ровать *impf. & pf.*; (*engross*) захва́тывать *impf.*, захвати́ть (-ачу́, -а́тишь) *pf.* **absorbed** *adj.* поглощённый (-ён, -ена́), захва́ченный (-ен). **absorbent** *adj.* вса́сывающий; поглоща́ющий. **absorption** *n.* впи́тывание; вса́сывание; поглоще́ние; абсо́рбция; (*mental*) погружённость.
abstain [əb'steɪn] *v.i.* возде́рживаться *impf.*, воздержа́ться (-жу́сь, -жишься) *pf.* (**from** от+*g.*). **abstemious** [æb'stiːmɪəs] *adj.* возде́ржанный (-ан, -анна) **abstention** [əb'stenʃ(ə)n] *n.* воздержа́ние; (*from vote*) уклоне́ние, отка́з, от голосова́ния; (*person*) воздержа́вшийся *sb.* **abstinence** ['æbstɪnəns] *n.* воздержа́ние; (*total ~*) тре́звость. **abstinent** *adj.* возде́ржанный (-ан, -анна).
abstract ['æbstrækt; əb'strækt] *adj.* абстра́ктный, отвлечённый (-ён, -ённа); *n.* конспе́кт, рефера́т; **in the ~** абстра́ктно, отвлечённо; (*journal of*) **~(s)** реферати́вный журна́л; *v.t.* (*steal*) похища́ть *impf.*, похити́ть (-и́щу, -и́тишь) *pf.*; красть (-аду́, -адёшь; -ал) *impf.*, у- *pf.*; (*make ~ of*) рефери́ровать *impf. & pf.*, конспекти́ровать *impf.*, за~, про~ *pf.* **ab'stracted** *adj.* погружённый (-ён, -ена́) в мы́сли, рассе́янный (-ян, -янна). **ab'straction** *n.* абстра́кция, отвлечённость; (*abstractedness*) погружённость в мы́сли, рассе́янность; (*theft*) похище́ние, кра́жа.
absurd [əb'sɜːd] *adj.* неле́пый, абсу́рдный. **absurdity** *n.* неле́пость, абсу́рд(ность).
abundance [ə'bʌnd(ə)ns] *n.* (из)оби́лие. **abundant** *adj.* (из)оби́льный.
abuse [ə'bjuːz; ə'bjuːs] *v.t.* (*revile*) руга́ть *impf.*, вы́~, об~, от~ *pf.*; брани́ть *impf.*, вы́~ *pf.*; (*misuse*) злоупотребля́ть *impf.*, злоупотреби́ть *pf.*; *n.* (*curses*) брань, ру́гань, руга́тельства *nt.pl.*; (*misuse*) злоупотребле́ние. **abusive** [ə'bjuːsɪv] *adj.* оскорби́тельный, бра́нный.
abut [ə'bʌt] *v.i.* примыка́ть *impf.* (**on** к+*d.*). **abutment** *n.* (берегово́й) усто́й.
abysmal [ə'bɪzm(ə)l] *adj.* бездо́нный (-нен, -нна); (*bad*) ужа́сный. **abyss** [ə'bɪs] *n.* бе́здна, про́пасть. **abyssal** *adj.* абисса́льный.
AC *abbr.* (*of* ***alternating current***) переме́нный ток.
a/c [ə'kaʊnt] *n. abbr.* (*of* **account**) теку́щий счёт.
acacia [ə'keɪʃə] *n.* ака́ция.
academia [,ækə'diːmɪə] *n.* академи́ческий мир; учёные круги́. **academic** [,ækə'demɪk] *adj.* академи́ческий, университе́тский; (*abstract*) академи́чный. **acade'mician** *n.* акаде́мик. **academy** [ə'kædəmɪ] *n.* акаде́мия; учё́бное заведе́ние.
accede [æk'siːd] *v.i.* вступа́ть *impf.*, вступи́ть (-плю́, -пишь) *pf.* (**to** в, на+*a.*); (*assent*) соглаша́ться *impf.*, согласи́ться *pf.*
accelerate [ək'selə,reɪt] *v.t. & i.* ускоря́ть(ся) *impf.*, уско́рить(ся) *pf.*; *v.i.* ускоря́ть *impf.*, уско́рить *pf.* ход. **accele'ration** *n.* ускоре́ние. **accelerator** *n.* ускори́тель *m.*; (*pedal*) акселера́тор.

accent ['æks(ə)nt, -sent; æk'sent] *n.* акце́нт; (*stress*) ударе́ние, знак ударе́ния; *v.t.* де́лать *impf.*, с~ *pf.* ударе́ние на+*a.*; ста́вить *impf.*, по~ *pf.* зна́ки ударе́ния над+*i.* **accentuate** [æk'sentjʊ,eɪt] *v.t.* подчёркивать *impf.*, подчеркну́ть *pf.* **accentu'ation** *n.* подчёркивание.

accept [ək'sept] *v.t.* принима́ть *impf.*, приня́ть (приму́, -мешь; при́нял, -а́, -о) *pf.*; (*agree*) соглаша́ться *impf.*, согласи́ться *pf.* **acceptable** *adj.* прие́млемый; (*pleasing*) уго́дный. **acceptance** *n.* приня́тие. **accep't-ation** *n.* при́нятое значе́ние. **accepted** *adj.* (обще)при́нятый.

access ['ækses] *n.* до́ступ; (*attack*) при́ступ. **ac'cessary** *n.* (*after the fact*) соуча́стник, -ица (преступле́ния по́сле собы́тия). **ac'cessible** *adj.* досту́пный. **ac'cession** *n.* вступле́ние, восше́ствие (на престо́л); (*acquisition*) приобрете́ние. **ac'cessories** *n.* принадле́жности *f.pl.* **ac'cessory** *adj.* доба́вочный, вспомога́тельный.

accidence ['æksɪd(ə)ns] *n.* морфоло́гия.

accident ['æksɪd(ə)nt] *n.* (*chance*) слу́чай, случа́йность; (*mishap*) несча́стный слу́чай; (*crash*) ава́рия, катастро́фа; **by** ~ случа́йно. **acci'dental** *adj.* случа́йный; *n.* (*mus.*) знак альтера́ции.

acclaim [ə'kleɪm] *v.t.* приве́тствовать *impf.* (*in past also pf.*); *n.* приве́тствие.

acclimatization [ə,klaɪmətaɪ'zeɪʃ(ə)n] *n.* акклиматиза́ция. **a'cclimatize** *v.t.* акклиматизи́ровать *impf.* & *pf.*

accommodate [ə'kɒmə,deɪt] *v.t.* помеща́ть *impf.*, помести́ть *pf.*; размеща́ть *impf.*, размести́ть *pf.* **accommodating** *adj.* услу́жливый. **accommo'dation** *n.* помеще́ние; (*lodging*) жильё; ~ **ladder** нару́жный трап.

accompaniment [ə'kʌmpənɪmənt] *n.* сопровожде́ние; (*mus.*) аккомпанеме́нт. **accompanist** *n.* аккомпаниа́тор. **accompany** *v.t.* сопровожда́ть *impf.*, сопроводи́ть *pf.*; (*mus.*) аккомпани́ровать *impf.+d.*

accomplice [ə'kʌmplɪs, -'kɒm-] *n.* соо́бщник, -ица, соуча́стник, -ица.

accomplish [ə'kʌmplɪʃ, ə'kɒm-] *v.t.* соверша́ть *impf.*, соверши́ть *pf.* **accomplished** *adj.* завершённый (-ён, -ена́); (*skilled*) превосхо́дный. **accomplishment** *n.* выполне́ние, заверше́ние; *pl.* досто́инства *nt.pl.*, соверше́нства *nt.pl.*

accord [ə'kɔːd] *n.* согла́сие; **of one's own** ~ доброво́льно; **of its own** ~ сам собо́й, сам по себе́; **with one** ~ единогла́сно, единоду́шно. **accordance** *n.*: **in** ~ **with** в соотве́тствии с+*i.*, согла́сно+*d.*, с+*i.* **according** *adv.*: ~ **to** по+*d.*, соотве́тственно+*d.*, с+*i.*; ~ **to him** по его́ слова́м. **accordingly** *adv.* соотве́тственно.

accordion [ə'kɔːdɪən] *n.* гармо́ника, аккордео́н.

account [ə'kaʊnt] *n.* счёт (-а(у); *pl.* -а́); расчёт; отчёт; (*description, narrative*) описа́ние, расска́з; **call to** ~ призыва́ть *impf.*, призва́ть (-зову́, -зовёшь; призва́л, -а́, -о) *pf.* к отве́ту; **keep** ~ **of** вести́ (веду́, -дёшь; вёл, -а́) *impf.* счёт+*d.*; **not on any** ~, **on no** ~ ни в ко́ем слу́чае; **on** ~ в счёт причита́ющейся су́ммы; **on** ~ **of** из-за+*g.*, по причи́не+*g.*; **settle** ~**s with** своди́ть (-ожу́, -о́дишь) *impf.*, свести́ (сведу́, -дёшь; свёл, -а́) *pf.* счёты с+*i.*; **take into** ~ принима́ть *impf.*, приня́ть (приму́, -мешь; при́нял, -а́) *pf.* во внима́ние, в расчёт; **turn to (good)** ~ обраща́ть *impf.*, обрати́ть (-ащу́, -ати́шь) *pf.* в свою́ по́льзу; *v.i.*: ~ **for** объясня́ть *impf.*, объясни́ть *pf.* **accountable** *adj.* отве́тственный (-ен, -енна), подотчётный. **accountancy** *n.* бухгалте́рия. **accountant** *n.* бухга́лтер.

accredited [ə'kredɪtɪd] *adj.* аккредито́ванный (-ан).

accretion [ə'kriːʃ(ə)n] *n.* прираще́ние, приро́ст.

accrue [ə'kruː] *v.i.* нараста́ть *impf.*, нарасти́ (-тёт; наро́с, -ла́) *pf.*; ~**d interest** наро́сшие проце́нты *m.pl.*

accumulate [ə'kjuːmjʊ,leɪt] *v.t.* & *i.* нака́пливать(ся) *impf.*, копи́ть(ся) (-плю́, -пит(ся)) *impf.*, на~ *pf.*; *v.i.* ска́пливаться *impf.*, скопи́ться (-ится) *pf.* **accumu'lation** *n.* накопле́ние, скопле́ние. **accumulator** *n.* аккумуля́тор.

accuracy ['ækjʊrəsɪ] *n.* то́чность, ме́ткость. **accurate** *adj.* то́чный (-чен, -чна́, -чно), ме́ткий (-ток, -тка́, -тко).

accursed [ə'kɜːsɪd, ə'kɜːst] *adj.* прокля́тый.

accusation [,ækjuː'zeɪʃ(ə)n] *n.* обвине́ние. **accusative** [ə'kjuːzətɪv] *adj.* (*n.*) вини́тельный (паде́ж (-а́)). **accuse** [ə'kjuːz] *v.t.* обвиня́ть *impf.*, обвини́ть *pf.* (**of** в+*p.*); **the** ~**d** обвиня́емый *sb.*, подсуди́мый *sb.*

accustom [ə'kʌstəm] *v.t.* приуча́ть *impf.*, приучи́ть (-учу́, -чишь) *pf.* (**to** к+*d.*). **accustomed** *adj.* привы́чный, обы́чный; **be, get** ~ привыка́ть *impf.*, привы́кнуть (-к) *pf.* (**to** к+*d.*).

ace [eɪs] *n.* (*cards*) туз (-а́); (*expert*) ас.

acetic [ə'siːtɪk] *adj.* у́ксусный. **acetylene** [ə'setɪ,liːn] *n.* ацетиле́н; *adj.* ацетиле́новый.

ache [eɪk] *n.* боль; *v.i.* боле́ть (-ли́т) *impf.*

achieve [ə'tʃiːv] *v.t.* достига́ть *impf.*, дости́чь & дости́гнуть (-и́гну, -и́гнешь; -и́г) *pf.+g.*; добива́ться *impf.*, доби́ться (-бью́сь, -бьёшся) *pf.+g.* **achievement** *n.* достиже́ние.

acid ['æsɪd] *n.* кислота́; *adj.* ки́слый (-сел, -сла́, -сло); ~ **rain** кисло́тные дожди́ (*m.pl.*). **a'cidity** *n.* кислота́, кисло́тность.

acknowledge [ək'nɒlɪdʒ] *v.t.* (*admit*) признава́ть (-наю́, -наёшь) *impf.*, призна́ть *pf.*; сознава́ть (-наю́, -наёшь) *impf.*, созна́ть *pf.*; (*express gratitude*) благодари́ть *impf.*, по~ *pf.* за+*a.*; (~ *receipt of*) подтвержда́ть *impf.*, подтверди́ть *pf.* получе́ние+*g.* **acknowledgement** *n.* призна́ние; благода́рность;

подтверждéние; **in ~ of** в знак благодáрности за+*a*.

acme ['ækmɪ] *n.* вершѝна, верх (*pl.* -ѝ), вы́сшая тóчка.

acne ['æknɪ] *n.* прыщѝ *m.pl.*

acorn ['eɪkɔːn] *n.* жёлудь (*pl.* -ди, -дéй) *m.*

acoustic [ə'kuːstɪk] *adj.* (*of sound*) акустѝческий, звуковóй; (*of hearing*) слуховóй; (*sound-absorbing*) звукопоглощáющий. **acoustics** *n.* акýстика.

acquaint [ə'kweɪnt] *v.t.* знакóмить *impf.*, по~ *pf.*; ознакомля́ть *impf.*, ознакóмить *pf.* **acquaintance** *n.* знакóмство; (*person*) знакóмый *sb.* **acquainted** *adj.* знакóмый.

acquiesce [,ækwɪ'es] *v.i.* соглашáться *impf.*, согласѝться *pf.* **acquiescence** *n.* (молчалѝвое, неохóтное) соглáсие. **acquiescent** *adj.* (молчалѝво) согласáющийся.

acquire [ə'kwaɪə(r)] *v.t.* приобретáть *impf.*, приобрестѝ (-етý, -етёшь; -ёл, -елá) *pf.*; (*habit etc.*) усвáивать *impf.*, усвóить *pf.* **acquired** *adj.* приобретённый (-ён, -енá); **~ taste** благоприобретённый вкус. **acquisition** [,ækwɪ'zɪʃ(ə)n] *n.* приобретéние. **acquisitive** [ə'kwɪzɪtɪv] *adj.* жáдный (-ден, -днá, -дно).

acquit [ə'kwɪt] *v.t.* oпрáвдывать *impf.*, оправдáть *pf.*; **~ o.s.** вестѝ (ведý, -дёшь; вёл, -á) *impf.* себя́. **acquittal** *n.* оправдáние.

acre ['eɪkə(r)] *n.* акр; *pl.* зéмли (-мéль, -млям) *f.pl.*, помéстье. **acreage** ['eɪkərɪdʒ] *n.* плóщадь в áкрах.

acrid ['ækrɪd] *adj.* óстрый (остр & остёр, острá, óстрó), éдкий (éдок, едкá, éдко).

acrimonious [,ækrɪ'məʊnɪəs] *adj.* язвѝтельный, жёлчный.

acrobat ['ækrə,bæt] *n.* акробáт. **acro'batic** *adj.* акробатѝческий. **acro'batics** *n.* акробáтика.

acronym ['ækrənɪm] *n.* акрóним, аббревиатýра.

across [ə'krɒs] *adv.* & *prep.* чéрез+*a.*; поперёк (+*g.*); (*to, on, other side*) на, по, ту стóрону (+*g.*), на той сторонé (+*g.*); (*crosswise*) крест-нáкрест. **across-the-board** *adj.* всеóбщий, всеобъéмлющий, поголóвный.

acrylic [ə'krɪlɪk] *n.* акрѝл; *adj.* акрѝловый.

act [ækt] *n.* (*deed*) акт, постýпок (-пка); (*law*) закóн; (*of play*) дéйствие; **A~s (of the Apostles)** Дея́ния *nt.pl.* апóстолов; *v.i.* поступáть *impf.*, поступѝть (-плю́, -пишь) *pf.*; дéйствовать *impf.*, по~ *pf.*; *v.t.* игрáть *impf.*, сыгрáть *pf.* **acting** *n.* игрá на сцéне; *adj.* исполня́ющий обя́занности+*g.* **action** ['ækʃ(ə)n] *n.* дéйствие, постýпок (-пка); (*leg.*) иск, (судéбный) процéсс; (*battle*) бой (*loc.* бою́). **active** *adj.* актѝвный, дéятельный, энергѝчный; **~ service** действѝтельная слýжба; **~ voice** действѝтельный залóг. **ac'tivity** *n.* дéятельность; актѝвность; *pl.* дéятельность. **actor** ['æktə(r)] *n.* актëр. **actress** *n.* актрѝса.

actual ['æktʃʊəl, 'æktjʊəl] *adj.* действѝтельный, фактѝческий. **actuality** [,æktʃʊ'ælɪtɪ, ,æktjʊ-] *n.* действѝтельность. **actually** *adv.* на сáмом дéле, фактѝчески.

actuate ['æktʃʊ,eɪt] *v.t.* приводѝть (-ожý, -óдишь) *impf.*, привестѝ (приведý, -дёшь; привёл, -á) *pf.* в движéние.

acuity [ə'kjuːɪtɪ] *n.* остротá.

acupuncture ['ækjuː,pʌŋktʃə(r)] *n.* акупунктýра, иглоукáлывание.

acute [ə'kjuːt] *adj.* óстрый (остр & остёр, острá, óстрó); (*penetrating*) проницáтельный; **~ accent** акýт.

AD *abbr.* (*of* ***Anno Domini***) н.э., (нáшей э́ры).

adamant ['ædəmənt] *adj.* непреклóнный (-нен, -нна).

adapt [ə'dæpt] *v.t.* приспособля́ть *impf.*, приспосóбить *pf.*; (*for stage etc.*) инсценѝровать *impf.* & *pf.*; **~ o.s.** приспособля́ться *impf.*, приспосóбиться *pf.*; применя́ться *impf.*, применѝться (-ню́сь, -нишься) *pf.* **adaptable** *adj.* приспособля́ющийся. **adap'tation** *n.* приспособлéние, адаптáция, передéлка; инсценирóвка.

add [æd] *v.t.* прибавля́ть *impf.*, прибáвить *pf.*; добавля́ть *impf.*, добáвить *pf.*; **~ together** склáдывать *impf.*, сложѝть (-жý, -жишь) *pf.*; **~ up to** сводѝться (-ится) *impf.*, свестѝсь (сведётся; свёлся, -лáсь) *pf.* к+*d.* **addenda** [ə'dendə] *n.* дополнéния *nt.pl.*, приложéния *nt.pl.*

adder ['ædə(r)] *n.* гадю́ка.

addict ['ædɪkt] *n.* (*drug* ~) наркомáн, ~ка. **a'ddicted** *adj.*: **be ~ to** быть рабóм+*g.*; **~ to drink** предаю́щийся пья́нству. **a'ddiction** *n.* пáгубная привы́чка; (*to drugs*) наркомáния.

addition [ə'dɪʃ(ə)n] *n.* прибавлéние, добавлéние; дополнéние; (*math.*) сложéние; **in ~** вдобáвок, крóме тогó, к томý же. **additional** *adj.* добáвочный, дополнѝтельный. **'additive** *n.* добáвка.

address [ə'dres] *n.* áдрес (*pl.* -á); (*speech*) обращéние, речь; *v.t.* адресовáть *impf.* & *pf.*; (*apply*) обращáться *impf.*, обратѝться (-ащýсь, -атѝшься) *pf.* к+*d.*; **~ a meeting** выступáть *impf.*, вы́ступить *pf.* с рéчью на собрáнии. **addre'ssee** *n.* адресáт.

adept ['ædept; ə'dept] *n.* знатóк (-á), экспéрт; *adj.* свéдущий.

adequacy ['ædɪkwəsɪ] *n.* адеквáтность, достáточность. **adequate** *adj.* адеквáтный, достáточный.

adhere [əd'hɪə(r)] *v.i.* прилипáть *impf.*, прилѝпнуть (-нет; прилѝп) *pf.* (**to** к+*d.*); (*fig.*) придéрживаться *impf.*+*g.* **adherence** *n.* привéрженность, вéрность. **adherent** *n.* привéрженец (-нца); послéдователь *m.*, ~ница. **adhesion** [əd'hiːʒ(ə)n] *n.* прилипáние, склéивание. **adhesive** [əd'hiːsɪv] *adj.* лѝпкий (-пок, -пкá, -пко), клéйкий; **~ tape** скотч; *n.* клей (-éя(ю), *loc.* -ею́; *pl.* -éи).

adjacent [ə'dʒeɪs(ə)nt] *adj.* смéжный, сосéдний.

adjectival [ˌædʒɪk'taɪv(ə)l] *adj.* адъекти́вный. **'adjective** *n.* (и́мя *nt.*) прилага́тельное *sb.*
adjoin [ə'dʒɔɪn] *v.t.* прилега́ть *impf.* к+*d.*
adjourn [ə'dʒɜːn] *v.t.* откла́дывать *impf.*, отложи́ть (-жу́, -жишь) *pf.*; *v.i.* объявля́ть *impf.*, объяви́ть (-влю́, -вишь) *pf.* переры́в; (*to another place*) переходи́ть (-ожу́, -о́дишь) *impf.*, перейти́ (перейду́, -дёшь; перешёл, -шла́) *pf.*
adjudicate [ə'dʒuːdɪˌkeɪt] *v.i.* выноси́ть (-ошу́, -о́сишь) *impf.*, вы́нести (-су, -сешь; -с) *pf.* (суде́бное, арбитра́жное) реше́ние; разреша́ть *impf.*, разреши́ть *pf.* спор; рассма́тривать *impf.*, рассмотре́ть (-рю́, -ришь) *pf.* де́ло.
adjust [ə'dʒʌst] *v.t.* & *i.* приспособля́ть(ся) *impf.*, приспосо́бить(ся) *pf.*; *v.t.* пригоня́ть *impf.*, пригна́ть (-гоню́, -го́нишь; пригна́л, -а́, -о) *pf.*; (*regulate*) регули́ровать *impf.*, от~ *pf.* **adjustable** *adj.* регули́руемый; ~ **spanner** разводно́й ключ (-а́). **adjustment** *n.* регули́рование, регулиро́вка, подго́нка.
adjutant ['ædʒʊt(ə)nt] *n.* адъюта́нт.
administer [əd'mɪnɪstə(r)] *v.t.* (*manage*) управля́ть *impf.*+*i.*; (*dispense*) отправля́ть *impf.*; (*give*) дава́ть (даю́, даёшь) *impf.*, дать (дам, дашь, даст, дади́м; дал, -а́, да́ло́, -и) *pf.* **admini'stration** *n.* администра́ция, управле́ние; (*government*) прави́тельство. **ad'ministrative** *adj.* администрати́вный, управле́нческий. **ad'ministrator** *n.* администра́тор.
admirable ['ædmərəb(ə)l] *adj.* похва́льный; (*excellent*) замеча́тельный.
admiral ['ædmər(ə)l] *n.* адмира́л. **Admiralty** *n.* адмиралте́йство.
admiration [ˌædmɪ'reɪʃ(ə)n] *n.* любова́ние, восхище́ние. **admire** [əd'maɪə(r)] *v.t.* любова́ться *impf.*, по~ *pf.*+*i.*, на+*a.*; восхища́ться *impf.*, восхити́ться (-ищу́сь, -ити́шься) *pf.*+*i.* **admirer** *n.* покло́нник.
admissible [əd'mɪsɪb(ə)l] *adj.* допусти́мый, прие́млемый. **admission** *n.* до́ступ, впуск, вход; (*confession*) призна́ние. **admit** *v.t.* впуска́ть *impf.*, впусти́ть (-ущу́, -у́стишь) *pf.*; (*allow*) допуска́ть *impf.*, допусти́ть (-ущу́, -у́стишь) *pf.*; (*accept*) принима́ть *impf.*, приня́ть (приму́, -мешь; при́нял, -а́, -о) *pf.*; (*confess*) признава́ть (-наю́, -наёшь) *impf.*, призна́ть *pf.* **admittance** *n.* до́ступ. **admittedly** *adv.* призна́ться.
admixture [æd'mɪkstʃə(r)] *n.* при́месь.
adolescence [ˌædə'lesəns] *n.* ю́ность. **adolescent** *adj.* подро́стковый; *n.* подро́сток (-тка).
adopt [ə'dɒpt] *v.t.* (*child*) усыновля́ть *impf.*, усынови́ть *pf.*; (*thing*) усва́ивать *impf.*, усво́ить *pf.*; (*approve*) принима́ть *impf.*, приня́ть (приму́, -мешь; при́нял, -а́, -о) *pf.* **adopted, adoptive** *adj.* приёмный. **adoption** *n.* усыновле́ние; приня́тие.
adorable [ə'dɔːrəb(ə)l] *adj.* восхити́тельный, преле́стный. **ado'ration** *n.* обожа́ние. **adore** *v.t.* обожа́ть *impf.* **adorer** *n.* обожа́тель *m.*
adorn [ə'dɔːn] *v.t.* украша́ть *impf.*, укра́сить *pf.* **adornment** *n.* украше́ние.
adroit [ə'drɔɪt] *adj.* ло́вкий (-вок, -вка́, -вко, ло́вки́).
adult [ə'dʌlt, 'ædʌlt] *adj.* & *n.* взро́слый (*sb.*).
adulterate [ə'dʌltəˌreɪt] *v.t.* фальсифици́ровать *impf.* & *pf.* **adulte'ration** *n.* фальсифика́ция.
adultery [ə'dʌltərɪ] *n.* адъюлте́р, внебра́чная связь.
advance [əd'vɑːns] *n.* (*going forward*) продвиже́ние (вперёд); (*progress*) прогре́сс; (*mil.*) наступле́ние; (*rise*) повыше́ние; (*of pay etc.*) ава́нс; (*loan*) ссу́да; **in** ~ зара́нее, вперёд; ава́нсом; **make ~s to** уха́живать *impf.* за+*i.*; ~ **information** предвари́тельные све́дения *nt.pl.*; ~ **copy** сигна́льный экземпля́р; *v.i.* (*go forward*) продвига́ться *impf.*, продви́нуться *pf.* вперёд; идти́ (иду́, идёшь; шёл, шла) *impf.* вперёд; (*mil.*) наступа́ть *impf.*; *v.t.* продвига́ть *impf.*, продви́нуть *pf.*; (*put forward*) выдвига́ть *impf.*, вы́двинуть *pf.*; (*promote*) повыша́ть *impf.*, повы́сить *pf.* (*pay in* ~) выпла́чивать *impf.*, вы́платить *pf.* ава́нсом. **advanced** *adj.* передово́й, продви́нутый; ~ **in years** престаре́лый; ~ **studies** вы́сший курс. **advancement** *n.* продвиже́ние, повыше́ние.
advantage [əd'vɑːntɪdʒ] *n.* преиму́щество; (*profit*) вы́года, по́льза; **take ~ of** по́льзоваться *impf.*, вос~ *pf.*+*i.*; **to** ~ вы́годно, хорошо́; в вы́годном све́те; **to the best** ~ в са́мом вы́годном све́те. **advan'tageous** *adj.* вы́годный.
adventure [əd'ventʃə(r)] *n.* приключе́ние; ~ **story** приключе́нческий рома́н. **adventurer** *n.* авантюри́ст. **adventuress** *n.* авантюри́стка. **adventurism**. *n.* авантюри́зм. **adventurist** *n.* авантюри́ст. **adventurous** *adj.* (*rash*) риско́ванный (-ан, -анна); (*enterprising*) предприи́мчивый.
adverb ['ædvɜːb] *n.* наре́чие. **adverbial** *adj.* наре́чный, обстоя́тельственный.
adversary ['ædvəsərɪ] *n.* проти́вник. **adverse** *adj.* неблагоприя́тный; ~ **winds** проти́вные ве́тры *m.pl.* **ad'versity** *n.* несча́стье.
advert ['ædvɜːt] *abbr.* объявле́ние, рекла́ма. **advertise** *v.t.* реклами́ровать *impf.* & *pf.*; афиши́ровать *impf.* & *pf.*; *v.i.* помеща́ть *impf.*, помести́ть *pf.*, дава́ть (даю́, даёшь) *impf.*, дать (дам, дашь, даст, дади́м; дал, -а́, да́ло́, -и) *pf.* объявле́ние (**for** о+*p.*). **ad'vertisement** *n.* объявле́ние, рекла́ма.
advice [əd'vaɪs] *n.* сове́т; (*specialist*) консульта́ция; (*notice*) ави́зо *nt.indecl.*; **a piece, word of** ~ сове́т. **advisability** [ədˌvaɪzə'bɪlɪtɪ] *n.* жела́тельность. **advisable** *adj.* рекоменду́емый, жела́тельный. **advise** [əd'vaɪz] *v.t.* сове́товать *impf.*, по~ *pf.*+*d.* & *inf.*; рекомендова́ть *impf.* & *pf.*, по~ *pf.*+*a.* & *inf.*; (*notify*) уведомля́ть *impf.*, уве́домить *pf.* **~dly** *adv.* обду́манно, наме́ренно. **adviser** *n.* сове́тник, -ица; консульта́нт; **legal** ~

юриско́нсульт; **medical** ~ врач (-а́). **advisory** *adj.* совеща́тельный; консультати́вный.

advocacy ['ædvəkəsɪ] *n.* (*profession*) адвокату́ра; (*support*) пропага́нда. **advocate** *n.* адвока́т; сторо́нник; *v.t.* пропаганди́ровать *impf.*; выступа́ть *impf.*, вы́ступить *pf.* в защи́ту+*g.*

aerial ['eərɪəl] *n.* анте́нна; *adj.* возду́шный.

aero- ['eərəʊ] *in comb.* авиа..., аэро... . **aerobicist** [eə'rəʊbɪsɪst] *n.* аэроби́ст, ~ка. **ae'robics** *n.* аэро́бика, аэро́бная гимна́стика. **aerodrome** ['eərəˌdrəʊm] *n.* аэродро́м. **aero-dy'namics** *n.* аэродина́мика. **aero-engine** *n.* авиацио́нный дви́гатель *m.* **aero'nautical** *adj.* авиацио́нный. **aeroplane** *n.* самолёт. **aerosol** ['eərəˌsɒl] *n.* аэрозо́ль *m.* **aerospace** *adj.* авиацио́нно-косми́ческий.

aesthetic [iːs'θetɪk] *adj.* эстети́ческий.

affable ['æfəb(ə)l] *adj.* приве́тливый. **affa'bility** *n.* приве́тливость.

affair [ə'feə(r)] *n.* (*business*) де́ло (*pl.* -ла́); (*love*) рома́н.

affect [ə'fekt] *v.t.* де́йствовать *impf.*, по~ *pf.* на+*a.*; влия́ть *impf.*, по~ *pf.* на+*a.*; (*touch*) тро́гать *impf.*, тро́нуть *pf.*; затра́гивать *impf.*, затро́нуть *pf.*; (*concern*) каса́ться *impf.*+*g.*; **it doesn't ~ me** э́то меня́ не каса́ется. **affec'tation** *n.* притво́рство, жема́нство. **affected** *adj.* притво́рный, жема́нный (-нен, -нна). **affecting** *adj.* тро́гательный. **affection** *n.* привя́занность, любо́вь (-бви́, *i.* -бо́вью); (*malady*) боле́знь. **affectionate** *adj.* лю́бящий, не́жный (-жен, -жна́, -жно, не́жны́), ла́сковый.

affiliate [ə'fɪlɪˌeɪt] *v.t.* &*i.* присоединя́ть(ся) *impf.*, присоедини́ть(ся) *pf.* как филиа́л, отделе́ние. **affiliated** *adj.* филиа́льный. **affili'ation** *n.* присоедине́ние как филиа́л; (*of child*) установле́ние отцо́вства+*g.*

affinity [ə'fɪnɪtɪ] *n.* (*relationship*) родство́; (*resemblance*) схо́дство, бли́зость; (*attraction*) увлече́ние.

affirm [ə'fɜːm] *v.t.* утвержда́ть *impf.*; *v.i.* торже́ственно заявля́ть *impf.*, заяви́ть (-влю́, -вишь) *pf.* **affir'mation** *n.* заявле́ние. **affirmative** *adj.* утверди́тельный.

affix [ə'fɪks; 'æfɪks] *v.t.* прикрепля́ть *impf.*, прикрепи́ть *pf.*; *n.* а́ффикс.

afflict [ə'flɪkt] *v.t.* огорча́ть *impf.*, огорчи́ть *pf.*; причиня́ть *impf.*, причини́ть *pf.* страда́ния+*d.* **affliction** *n.* огорче́ние.

affluence ['æflʊəns] *n.* бога́тство. **affluent** *adj.* бога́тый; ~ **society** богате́ющее о́бщество.

afford [ə'fɔːd] *v.t.* позволя́ть *impf.*, позво́лить *pf.* себе́; быть в состоя́нии+*inf.*; (*supply*) предоставля́ть *impf.*, предоста́вить *pf.*; доставля́ть *impf.*, доста́вить *pf.*; **I can't ~ it** мне э́то не по сре́дствам, не по карма́ну.

afforest [ə'fɒrɪst, æ-] *v.t.* заса́живать *impf.*, засади́ть (-ажу́, -а́дишь) *pf.* ле́сом; облеси́ть *pf.* **affore'station** *n.* лесонасажде́ние, облесе́ние.

affront [ə'frʌnt] *n.* (публи́чное) оскорбле́ние, оби́да; *v.t.* оскорбля́ть *impf.*, оскорби́ть *pf.*

Afghan (hound) ['æfgæn] *n.* афга́нская борза́я.

afoot [ə'fʊt] *adv.*: **set** ~ пуска́ть *impf.*, пусти́ть (пущу́, пу́стишь) *pf.* в ход.

aforesaid [ə'fɔːsed] *adj.* вышеупомя́нутый. **aforethought** [ə'fɔːθɔːt] *adj.* преднаме́ренный (-ен, -енна).

afraid [ə'freɪd] *pred.*: **be** ~ боя́ться (бою́сь, бои́шься) *impf.*

afresh [ə'freʃ] *adv.* сно́ва.

Africa ['æfrɪkə] *n.* А́фрика. **African** *adj.* африка́нский; *n.* африка́нец (-нца), -нка.

Afro-American [ˌæfrəʊ-] *adj.* афроамерика́нский.

after ['ɑːftə(r)] *adv.* впосле́дствии; по́сле, пото́м; *prep.* по́сле+*g.*, спустя́+*a.*; за+*a.*, *i.*; ~ **all** в конце́ концо́в; **day ~ day** день за днём; **long ~ midnight** далеко́ за по́лночь.

after- ['ɑːftə(r)] *in comb.* после... . **afterbirth** *n.* после́д. **after-dinner** *adj.* послеобе́денный. **afterlife** *n.* загро́бная жизнь. **aftermath** ['ɑːftəˌmæθ, -ˌmɑːθ] *n.* после́дствия *nt.pl.* **afternoon** *n.* втора́я полови́на дня; **in the** ~ днём, пополу́дни. **aftershock** *n.* повто́рные толчки́ *m.pl.* **afterthought** *n.* запозда́лая мысль.

afterwards ['ɑːftəwədz] *adv.* впосле́дствии; пото́м, по́зже.

again [ə'geɪn, ə'gen] *adv.* опя́ть; (*once more*) ещё раз; (*anew*) сно́ва.

against [ə'geɪnst, ə'genst] *prep.* (*opposed to*) про́тив+*g.*; (~ *background of*) на фо́не+*g.*

agate ['ægət] *n.* ага́т.

age [eɪdʒ] *n.* во́зраст; (*period*) век (на веку́; *pl.* -а́), эпо́ха; *v.t.* ста́рить *impf.*, со~ *pf.*; *v.i.* старе́ть *impf.*, по~ *pf.*; ста́риться *impf.*, со~ *pf.* **aged** ['eɪdʒɪd] *adj.* ста́рый (стар, -а́, ста́ро́), престаре́лый; **the** ~ пожилы́е лю́ди *m.pl.*, престаре́лые *m.pl.* **ageism** *n.* дискримина́ция по во́зрасту. **ageist** *n.* сторо́нник дискримина́ции по во́зрасту.

agency ['eɪdʒənsɪ] *n.* аге́нтство; (*mediation*) посре́дничество; **by, through the ~ of** посре́дством, при по́мощи, при соде́йствии, +*g.* **agenda** [ə'dʒendə] *n.* пове́стка дня. **agent** *n.* аге́нт.

agglomerate [ə'glɒmərət] *n.* агломера́т. **agglome'ration** *n.* скопле́ние, агломера́ция.

agglutination [əˌgluːtɪ'neɪʃ(ə)n] *n.* агглютина́ция. **a'gglutinative** *adj.* агглютинати́вный.

aggravate ['ægrəˌveɪt] *v.t.* ухудша́ть *impf.*, уху́дшить *pf.*; (*annoy*) раздража́ть *impf.*, раздражи́ть *pf.* **aggra'vation** *n.* ухудше́ние; раздраже́ние.

aggregate ['ægrɪgət] *adj.* совоку́пный; *n.* совоку́пность, агрега́т; **in the** ~ в совоку́пности, в це́лом.

aggression [ə'greʃ(ə)n] *n.* агре́ссия; агресси́вность. **aggressive** *adj.* агресси́вный.

aggressor *n.* агрéссор.
aggrieved [ə'gri:vd] *adj.* оби́женный (-ен).
aghast [ə'gɑ:st] *pred.* поражён (-á) у́жасом; в у́жасе (**at** от+*g.*).
agile ['ædʒaɪl] *adj.* прово́рный. **agility** [ə'dʒɪlɪtɪ] *n.* прово́рство.
agitate ['ædʒɪˌteɪt] *v.t.* волнова́ть *impf.*, вз~ *pf.*; *v.i.* агити́ровать *impf.* **agi'tation** *n.* волне́ние; агита́ция.
agnostic [æg'nɒstɪk] *n.* агно́стик; *adj.* агности́ческий. **agnosticism** *n.* агностици́зм.
ago [ə'gəʊ] *adv.* (тому́) наза́д; **long** ~ давно́.
agonizing ['ægəˌnaɪzɪŋ] *adj.* мучи́тельный. **agony** *n.* мучи́тельная боль; (*of death*) аго́ния.
agrarian [ə'greərɪən] *adj.* агра́рный, земе́льный.
agree [ə'gri:] *v.i.* соглаша́ться *impf.*, согласи́ться *pf.*; усла́вливаться *impf.*, усло́виться *pf.* (**on** о+*p.*); (*reach agreement*) догова́риваться *impf.*, договори́ться *pf.*; (*gram.*) согласова́ться *impf.* & *pf.* **agreeable** *adj.* согла́сный; (*pleasing*) прия́тный. **agreed** *adj.* согласо́ванный (-ан), усло́вленный (-ен). **agreement** *n.* согла́сие, соглаше́ние, догово́р; (*gram.*) согласова́ние; **in** ~ согла́сен (-сна).
agricultural [ˌægrɪ'kʌltʃər(ə)l] *adj.* сельскохозя́йственный, земледе́льческий. **'agriculture** *n.* се́льское хозя́йство, земледе́лие; (*science*) агроно́мия.
aground [ə'graʊnd] *pred.* на мели́; *adv.*: **run** ~ сади́ться *impf.*, сесть (ся́ду, -дешь; сел) *pf.* на мель.
ahead [ə'hed] *adv.* (*forward*) вперёд; (*in front*) впереди́; ~ **of time** досро́чно.
aid [eɪd] *v.t.* помога́ть *impf.*, помо́чь (-огу́, -о́жешь; -о́г, -огла́) *pf.*+*d.*; *n.* по́мощь; (*teaching*) посо́бие; ~ **agency** организа́ция по оказа́нию по́мощи; **in** ~ **of** в по́льзу+*g.*; **come to the** ~ **of** прийти́ (приду́, -дёшь; пришёл, -шла́) *pf.* на по́мощь+*d.*
aide-de-camp [ˌeɪd də 'kɑ̃] *n.* адъюта́нт (генера́ла).
AIDS [eɪdz] *n. abbr.* (*of* ***acquired immune deficiency syndrome***) СПИД, (синдро́м приобретённого иммýнного дефици́та).
aileron ['eɪləˌrɒn] *n.* элеро́н.
ailing ['eɪlɪŋ] *adj.* (*ill*) больно́й (-лен, -льна́); (*sickly*) хи́лый (хил, -á, -о).
ailment ['eɪlmənt] *n.* неду́г.
aim [eɪm] *n.* (*aiming*) прице́л; (*purpose*) цель, намере́ние; *v.i.* це́литься *impf.*, на~ *pf.* (**at** в+*a.*); прице́ливаться *impf.*, прице́литься *pf.* (**at** в+*a.*); (*also fig.*) ме́тить *impf.*, на~ *pf.* (**at** в+*a.*); *v.t.* наце́ливать *impf.*, наце́лить *pf.*; (*also fig.*) наводи́ть (-ожу́, -о́дишь) *impf.*, навести́ (наведу́, наведёшь; навёл, -á) *pf.* **aimless** *adj.* бесце́льный.
air [eə(r)] *n.* во́здух; (*look*) вид; (*mus.*) пе́сня (*g.pl.* -сен), мело́дия; ~ **crash** авиакатастро́фа; ~ **force** ВВС (вое́нно-возду́шные си́лы) *f.pl.*; ~ **hostess** стюарде́сса; ~ **piracy** возду́шный бандити́зм; **by** ~ самолётом; **change of** ~ переме́на обстано́вки; **on the** ~ по ра́дио; *attr.* возду́шный; *v.t.* (*ventilate*) прове́тривать *impf.*, прове́трить *pf.*; (*make known*) выставля́ть *impf.*, вы́ставить *pf.* напока́з; заявля́ть *impf.*, заяви́ть (-влю́, -вишь) *pf.* во всеуслы́шание.
air- [eə(r)] *in comb.* **airborne** ['eəbɔ:n] *adj.* (*mil.*) возду́шно-деса́нтный; *pred.* в во́здухе. **air-conditioner** *n.* кондиционе́р (во́здуха). **air-conditioning** *n.* кондициони́рование во́здуха. **air-cooled** *adj.* с возду́шным охлажде́нием. **aircraft** *n.* самолёт; (*collect.*) самолёты *m.pl.*, авиа́ция. **aircraft-carrier** *n.* авиано́сец (-сца).
airer ['eərə(r)] *n.* (напо́льная) суши́лка.
airless ['eəlɪs] *adj.* (*stuffy*) ду́шный (-шен, -шна́, -шно); безвозду́шный. **airlift** *n.* возду́шные перево́зки *f.pl.*; *v.t.* перевози́ть (-ожу́, -о́зишь) *impf.*, перевезти́ (перевезу́, -зёшь; перевёз, -ла́) *pf.* по во́здуху. **airline** *n.* авиали́ния. **airlock** *n.* возду́шная про́бка. **airmail** *n.* а́виа(по́чта). **airman** *n.* лётчик. **airport** *n.* аэропо́рт (*loc.* -у́). **airship** *n.* дирижа́бль *m.* **airspeed** *n.* возду́шная ско́рость. **airstrip** *n.* лётная полоса́ (*a.* полосу́; *pl.* -осы, -о́с, -оса́м). **airtight** *adj.* непроница́емый для во́здуха. **airworthy** *adj.* приго́дный к полёту.
aisle [aɪl] *n.* боково́й неф; (*passage*) прохо́д.
alabaster ['æləˌbɑ:stə(r), -ˌbæstə(r), ˌælə'b-] *n.* алеба́стр.
alacrity [ə'lækrɪtɪ] *n.* жи́вость; (*readiness*) гото́вность.
alarm [ə'lɑ:m] *n.* трево́га; *v.t.* трево́жить *impf.*, вс~ *pf.*; ~ **clock** буди́льник. **alarming** *adj.* трево́жный. **alarmist** *n.* паникёр; *adj.* паникёрский.
alas [ə'læs, ə'lɑ:s] *int.* увы́!
Alaska [ə'læskə] *n.* Аля́ска.
albatross ['ælbəˌtrɒs] *n.* альбатро́с.
albino [æl'bi:nəʊ] *n.* альбино́с.
album ['ælbəm] *n.* альбо́м.
alchemist ['ælkəmɪst] *n.* алхи́мик. **alchemy** *n.* алхи́мия.
alcohol ['ælkəˌhɒl] *n.* алкого́ль *m.*, спирт (-а(у), *loc.* -е & -у́); спиртны́е напи́тки *m.pl.* **alco'holic** *adj.* алкаго́льный, спиртно́й; *n.* алкаго́лик, -и́чка.
alcove ['ælkəʊv] *n.* альќо́в, ни́ша.
alder ['ɔ:ldə(r)] *n.* ольха́.
alderman ['ɔ:ldəmən] *n.* о́лдермен.
ale [eɪl] *n.* пи́во, эль *m.*
alert [ə'lɜ:t] *adj.* бди́тельный, живо́й (жив, -á, -о); *pred.* на стороже́; *n.* трево́га; *v.t.* предупрежда́ть *impf.*, предупреди́ть *pf.*
algebra ['ældʒɪbrə] *n.* а́лгебра. **algebraic** [ˌældʒɪ'breɪɪk] *adj.* алгебраи́ческий. **algorithm** ['ælgəˌrɪð(ə)m] *n.* алгори́тм.
alias ['eɪlɪəs] *adv.* ина́че (называ́емый); *n.* кли́чка, вы́мышленное и́мя *nt.*
alibi ['ælɪˌbaɪ] *n.* а́либи *nt.indecl.*
alien ['eɪlɪən] *n.* иностра́нец (-нца), -нка;

(*extraterrestrial*) инопланетя́нин (*pl.* -я́не, -я́н); *adj.* иностра́нный, чужо́й, чу́ждый (чужд, -а́, -о); (*extraterrestrial*) внеземно́й. **alienate** *v.t.* отчужда́ть *impf.*; отдаля́ть *impf.*, отдали́ть *pf.* **alie'nation** *n.* отчужде́ние, охлажде́ние; (*insanity*) умопомеша́тельство.

alight¹ [ə'laɪt] *v.i.* сходи́ть (-ожу́, -о́дишь) *impf.*, сойти́ (сойду́, -дёшь; сошёл, -шла́) *pf.*; (*come down*) сади́ться *impf.*, сесть (ся́ду, -дешь; сел) *pf.*; (*dismount*) спе́шиваться *impf.*, спе́шиться *pf.*

alight² [ə'laɪt] *pred.* зажжён (-а́); **be ~** горе́ть (-ри́т) *impf.*; (*shine*) сия́ть *impf.*

align [ə'laɪn] *v.t.* располага́ть *impf.*, расположи́ть (-жу́, -жишь) *pf.* по одно́й ли́нии; ста́вить *impf.*, по~ *pf.* в ряд. **alignment** *n.* выра́внивание, равне́ние.

alike [ə'laɪk] *pred.* похо́ж, одина́ков; *adv.* одина́ково, то́чно так же.

alimentary [ˌælɪ'mentərɪ] *adj.* пищево́й; **~ canal** пищевари́тельный кана́л.

alimony ['ælɪmənɪ] *n.* алиме́нты *m.pl.*

alive [ə'laɪv] *pred.* жив (-а́, -о), в живы́х; (*brisk*) бодр (-а́, -о); **~ with** киша́щий+*i.*

alkali ['ælkəˌlaɪ] *n.* щёлочь (*pl.* -чи, -че́й). **alkaline** *adj.* щелочно́й.

all [ɔ:l] *adj.* весь (вся, всё; все); вся́кий; *n.* всё, все *pl.*; *adv.* всеце́ло, целико́м, по́лностью; совсе́м, соверше́нно; **~ along** всё вре́мя; **~ but** почти́, едва́ не; **~ in** кра́йне утомлён (-а́); **~ over** повсю́ду; **~ right** хорошо́, ла́дно; (*satisfactory*) так себе́; непло́х (-а́, -о); **~ the same** всё равно́; **in ~** всего́; **love ~** по нулю́; **two, etc., ~** по́ два и т.д.; **not at ~** ниско́лько; **on ~ fours** на четвере́ньках. **all-in** *adj.*: **~ wrestling** кетч. **all-round** *adj.* разносторо́нний (-нен, -ння).

allay [ə'leɪ] *v.t.* облегча́ть *impf.*, облегчи́ть *pf.*; успока́ивать *impf.*, успоко́ить *pf.*; утоля́ть *impf.*, утоли́ть *pf.*

allegation [ˌælɪ'geɪʃ(ə)n] *n.* заявле́ние, утвержде́ние. **allege** [ə'ledʒ] *v.t.* заявля́ть *impf.*, заяви́ть (-влю́, -вишь) *pf.*; утвержда́ть *impf.* **allegedly** *adv.* я́кобы.

allegiance [ə'li:dʒ(ə)ns] *adv.* ве́рность.

allegorical [ˌælɪ'gɒrɪk(ə)l] *adj.* аллегори́ческий, иносказа́тельный. **allegory** ['ælɪgərɪ] *n.* аллего́рия, иносказа́ние.

allegretto [ˌælɪ'gretəʊ] *adv.* (*n.*) аллегре́тто (*nt.indecl.*). **allegro** [ə'leɪgrəʊ, ə'leg-] *adv.* (*n.*) алле́гро (*nt.indecl.*).

allergen ['ælədʒ(ə)n] *n.* аллерге́н. **allergic** [ə'lɜ:dʒɪk] *adj.* аллерги́ческий. **allergy** *n.* аллерги́я.

alleviate [ə'li:vɪˌeɪt] *v.t.* облегча́ть *impf.*, облегчи́ть *pf.*; смягча́ть *impf.*, смягчи́ть *pf.* **allevi'ation** *n.* облегче́ние, смягче́ние.

alley ['ælɪ] *n.* переу́лок (-лка), прохо́д.

alliance [ə'laɪəns] *n.* сою́з. **allied** ['ælaɪd] *adj.* сою́зный.

alligator ['ælɪˌgeɪtə(r)] *n.* аллига́тор.

alliterate [ə'lɪtəˌreɪt] *v.i.* аллитери́ровать *impf.* **allite'ration** *n.* аллитера́ция.

allocate ['æləˌkeɪt] *v.t.* распределя́ть *impf.*, распредели́ть *pf.*; ассигнова́ть *impf.* & *pf.* **allo'cation** *n.* распределе́ние; ассигнова́ние.

allot [ə'lɒt] *v.t.* предназнача́ть *impf.*, предназна́чить *pf.*; распределя́ть *impf.*, распредели́ть *pf.*; отводи́ть (-ожу́, -о́дишь) *impf.*, отвести́ (отведу́, -дёшь; отвёл, -ла́) *pf.*; выделя́ть *impf.*, вы́делить *pf.* **allotment** *n.* выделе́ние; (*plot of land*) уча́сток (-тка).

allow [ə'laʊ] *v.t.* позволя́ть *impf.*, позво́лить *pf.*; разреша́ть *impf.*, разреши́ть *pf.*; допуска́ть *impf.*, допусти́ть (-ущу́, -у́стишь) *pf.*; **~ for** принима́ть *impf.*, приня́ть (приму́, -мешь; при́нял, -ла́, -о) *pf.* во внима́ние, в расчёт; учи́тывать *impf.*, уче́сть (учту́, -тёшь; учёл, учла́) *pf.* **allowance** *n.* (*financial*) содержа́ние, посо́бие; (*expenses*) де́ньги (-нег, -ньга́м) *pl.* на расхо́ды; (*deduction, also fig.*) ски́дка; **make ~(s) for** принима́ть *impf.*, приня́ть (приму́, -мешь; при́нял, -ла́, -о) *pf.* во внима́ние, в расчёт; де́лать *impf.*, с~ *pf.* ски́дку на+*a.*

alloy ['ælɔɪ; ə'lɔɪ] *n.* сплав; *v.t.* сплавля́ть *impf.*, спла́вить *pf.*

allude [ə'lu:d, ə'lju:d] *v.i.* ссыла́ться *impf.*, сосла́ться (сошлю́сь, -лёшься) *pf.* (**to** на+*a.*); намека́ть *impf.*, намекну́ть *pf.* (**to** на+*a.*).

allure [ə'ljʊə(r)] *v.t.* зама́нивать *impf.*, замани́ть (-ню́, -нишь) *pf.*; завлека́ть *impf.*, завле́чь (-еку́, -ечёшь; -ёк, -екла́) *pf.* **allurement** *n.* прима́нка. **alluring** *adj.* зама́нчивый, завлека́тельный, соблазни́тельный.

allusion [ə'lu:ʒ(ə)n, ə'lju:-] *n.* ссы́лка, намёк.

alluvial [ə'lu:vɪəl] *adj.* аллювиа́льный, нано́сный.

all-weather *adj.* всепого́дный.

ally ['ælaɪ] *n.* сою́зник; *v.t.* соединя́ть *impf.*, соедини́ть *pf.*

almanac ['ɔ:lməˌnæk, 'ɒl-] *n.* календа́рь (-ря́) *m.*

almighty [ɔ:l'maɪtɪ] *adj.* всемогу́щий.

almond ['ɑ:mənd] *n.* (*tree*; *pl. collect.*) минда́ль (-ля́) *m.*; (*nut*) минда́льный оре́х; *attr.* минда́льный.

almost ['ɔ:lməʊst] *adv.* почти́, едва́ (ли) не, чуть (бы́ло) не.

alms [ɑ:mz] *n.* ми́лостыня. **almshouse** *n.* богаде́льня (*g.pl.* -лен).

aloe(s) ['æləʊ] *n.* ало́э *nt.indecl.*

aloft [ə'lɒft] *adv.* наве́рх (-у́).

alone [ə'ləʊn] *pred.* оди́н (одна́, одно́; одни́); одино́к; *adv.* то́лько; сам по себе́; **~ with** наедине́ с+*i.*; **leave ~** оставля́ть *impf.*, оста́вить *pf.* в поко́е; **let ~** не говоря́ уже́ о+*p.*

along [ə'lɒŋ] *prep.* по+*d.*, вдоль+*g.*, вдоль по+*d.*; *adv.* (*onward*) да́льше, вперёд; (*with o.s.*) с собо́й; **all ~** всё вре́мя; **~ with** вме́сте с+*i*. **along'side** *adv.*, *prep.* ря́дом (с+*i*.), бок о́ бок (с+*i*.).

aloof [ə'lu:f] *pred.*, *adv.* (*apart*) в стороне́, вдали́; (*distant*) хо́лоден (-дна́, -дно, хо́лодны́), равноду́шен (-шна).

aloud [ə'laʊd] *adv.* вслух, гро́мко.

alphabet ['ælfə,bet] *n.* алфави́т, а́збука. **alpha'betical** *adj.* алфави́тный. **alphanumeric** [,ælfənju:'merɪk] *adj.* алфави́тно-цифрово́й.

alpine ['ælpaɪn] *adj.* альпи́йский.

Alps [ælpz] *n.*: **the ~** А́льпы (-п) *pl.*

already [ɔ:l'redɪ] *adv.* уже́.

also ['ɔ:lsəʊ] *adv.* та́кже, то́же.

altar ['ɔ:ltə(r), 'ɒl-] *n.* алта́рь (-ря́) *m.* **altarpiece** *n.* запресто́льный о́браз (*pl.* -а́).

alter ['ɔ:ltə(r), 'ɒl-] *v.t.* переде́лывать *impf.*, переде́лать *pf.*; *v.t.* & *i.* изменя́ть(ся) *impf.*, измени́ть(ся) (-ню́(сь), -нишь(ся)) *pf.* **alte'ration** *n.* переде́лка; переме́на; измене́ние.

altercation [,ɔ:ltə'keɪʃ(ə)n, ,ɒl-] *n.* препира́тельство.

alternate [ɔ:l'tɜ:nət, ɒl-; 'ɔ:ltə,neɪt, 'ɒl-] *adj.* череду́ющийся, перемежа́ющийся; *v.t.* & *i.* чередова́ть(ся) *impf.*; **alternating current** переме́нный ток; **on ~ days** че́рез день. **alternation** [,ɔ:ltə'neɪʃ(ə)n, ,ɒl-] *n.* чередова́ние. **al'ternative** *n.* альтернати́ва; *adj.* альтернати́вный; **~ medicine** паралле́льная медици́на; **~ technology** алтернати́вная техноло́гия.

although [ɔ:l'ðəʊ] *conj.* хотя́.

altimeter ['æltɪ,mi:tə(r)] *n.* альтиме́тр, высотоме́р. **altitude** ['æltɪ,tju:d] *n.* высота́ (*pl.* -о́ты). **alto** *n.* альт (-а́); контра́льто *f.* & *nt.indecl.*; *attr.* альто́вый; контра́льтовый.

altogether [,ɔ:ltə'geðə(r)] *adv.* (*fully*) совсе́м; (*in total*) всего́; (*wholly*) всеце́ло.

alum ['æləm] *n.* квасцы́ *m.pl.* **aluminium** [,ælju'mɪnɪəm] *n.* алюми́ний; *attr.* алюми́ниевый.

always ['ɔ:lweɪz] *adv.* всегда́; (*constantly*) постоя́нно.

Alzheimer's disease ['ælts,haɪməz] *n.* боле́знь Альцге́ймера.

a.m. *abbr.* (*of* **ante meridiem**) утра́; **6 ~** шесть часо́в утра́.

amalgamate [ə'mælgə,meɪt] *v.t.* & *i.* амальгами́ровать(ся) *impf.* & *pf.*; объединя́ть(ся) *impf.*, объедини́ть(ся) *pf.* **amalga'mation** *n.* амальгами́рование; объедине́ние.

amanuensis [ə,mænju:'ensɪs] *n.* перепи́счик, -ица.

amass [ə'mæs] *v.t.* копи́ть (-плю́, -пишь) *impf.*, на~ *pf.*

amateur ['æmətə(r)] *n.* люби́тель *m.*, ~ница; *adj.* самоде́ятельный, люби́тельский. **amateurish** *adj.* люби́тельский.

amatory ['æmətərɪ] *adj.* любо́вный.

amaze [ə'meɪz] *v.t.* удивля́ть *impf.*, удиви́ть *pf.*; изумля́ть *impf.*, изуми́ть *pf.* **amazement** *n.* удивле́ние, изумле́ние. **amazing** *adj.* удиви́тельный, изуми́тельный.

Amazon ['æməz(ə)n] *n.* Амазо́нка.

ambassador [æm'bæsədə(r)] *n.* посо́л (-сла́). **ambassadorial** [,æmbæsə'dɔ:rɪəl] *adj.* посо́льский.

amber ['æmbə(r)] *n.* янта́рь (-ря́) *m.*; *adj.* янта́рный; (*coloured*) жёлтый (жёлт, -а́, жёлто́). **ambergris** ['æmbəgrɪs, -,gri:s] *n.* а́мбра.

ambidextrous [,æmbɪ'dekstrəs] *adj.* одина́ково свобо́дно владе́ющий обе́ими рука́ми.

ambiguity [,æmbɪ'gju:ɪtɪ] *n.* двусмы́сленность. **am'biguous** *adj.* двусмы́сленный (-ен, -енна).

ambition [æm'bɪʃ(ə)n] *n.* честолю́бие. **ambitious** *adj.* честолюби́вый.

amble ['æmb(ə)l] *v.i.* (*horse*) бе́гать *indet.*, бежа́ть (-жи́т) *det.* и́ноходью; (*ride*) е́здить *indet.*, е́хать (е́ду, е́дешь) *det.* верхо́м на инохо́дце; (*on foot*) ходи́ть (хожу́, хо́дишь) *indet.*, идти́ (иду́, идёшь; шел, шла) *det.* нетороплйвым ша́гом; *n.* и́ноходь.

ambrosia [æm'brəʊzɪə, -ʒjə] *n.* амбро́зия.

ambulance ['æmbjʊləns] *n.* маши́на ско́рой по́мощи; ско́рая по́мощь; **air ~** санита́рный самолёт.

ambush ['æmbʊʃ] *n.* заса́да; *v.t.* напада́ть *impf.*, напа́сть (-аду́, -адёшь; -а́л) *pf.* из заса́ды на+*a.*; устра́ивать *impf.*, устро́ить *pf.* заса́ду на+*a.*

ameliorate [ə'mi:lɪə,reɪt] *v.t.* & *i.* улучша́ть(ся) *impf.*, улу́чшить(ся) *pf.* **amelio'ration** *n.* улучше́ние.

amen [ɑ:'men, eɪ-] *int.* ами́нь!

amenable [ə'mi:nəb(ə)l] *adj.* усту́пчивый, сгово́рчивый (**to** +*d.*).

amend [ə'mend] *v.t.* исправля́ть *impf.*, испра́вить *pf.*; вноси́ть (-ошу́, -о́сишь) *impf.*, внести́ (внесу́, -сёшь; внёс, -ла́) *pf.* измене́ния, попра́вки, в+*a.* **amendment** *n.* попра́вка, исправле́ние, поправле́ние. **amends** [ə'mendz] *n.*: **make ~ for** загла́живать *impf.*, загла́дить *pf.*

amenities [ə'mi:nɪtɪz, ə'menɪtɪz] *n.* пре́лести *f.pl.*, удо́бства *nt.pl.*

America [ə'merɪkə] *n.* Аме́рика. **American** *adj.* америка́нский; *n.* америка́нец (-нца), -нка. **Americanism** *n.* американи́зм. **Americanization** [ə,merɪkənaɪ'zeɪʃ(ə)n] *n.* американиза́ция. **A'mericanize** *v.t.* американизи́ровать *impf.* & *pf.*

amethyst ['æmɪθɪst] *n.* амети́ст.

amiability [,eɪmɪə'bɪlɪtɪ] *n.* любе́зность. **'amiable** *adj.* любе́зный. **amicability** [,æmɪkə'bɪlɪtɪ] *n.* дружелю́бие. **'amicable** *adj.* дружелю́бный.

amid(st) [ə'mɪdst] *prep.* среди́+*g.*

amiss [ə'mɪs] *adv.* ду́рно, пло́хо; **take it ~** обижа́ться *impf.*, оби́деться (-и́жусь, -и́дишься) *pf.*

amity ['æmɪtɪ] *n.* дру́жественные отноше́ния *nt.pl.*

ammonia [ə'məʊnɪə] *n.* аммиа́к; (*liquid ~*) нашаты́рный спирт (-а(у), *loc.* -е & -у́). **ammoniac(al)** *adj.* аммиа́чный.

ammunition [,æmjʊ'nɪʃ(ə)n] *n.* боеприпа́сы

m.pl., снаря́ды *m.pl.*, патро́ны *m.pl.*, дробь.

amnesty ['æmnɪstɪ] *n.* амни́стия; '**A~ International**' «Междунаро́дная амни́стия»; *v.t.* амнисти́ровать *impf.* & *pf.*

among(st) [ə'mʌŋst] *prep.* среди́+*g.*, ме́жду+*i.*

amoral [eɪ'mɒr(ə)l] *adj.* амора́льный.

amorous ['æmərəs] *adj.* влю́бчивый; (*in love*) влюблённый (-ён, -ена́).

amorphous [ə'mɔːfəs] *adj.* امо́рфный, бесфо́рменный (-ен, -енна).

amortization [əˌmɔːtaɪ'zeɪʃ(ə)n] *n.* амортиза́ция. **amortize** [ə'mɔːtaɪz] *v.t.* амортизи́ровать *impf.* & *pf.*

amount [ə'maʊnt] *n.* коли́чество; *v.i.*: ~ **to** составля́ть *impf.*, соста́вить *pf.*; равня́ться *impf.*+*d.*; быть равноси́льным+*d.*

amp [æmp] *n. abbr.* (*of* **ampere**) A, (ампе́р).

ampere ['æmpeə(r)] *n.* ампе́р (*g.pl.* -р).

amphibian [æm'fɪbɪən] *n.* амфи́бия. **amphibious** *adj.* земново́дный.

amphitheatre ['æmfɪˌθɪətə(r)] *n.* амфитеа́тр.

ample ['æmp(ə)l] *adj.* (*enough*) (вполне́) доста́точно; (*abundant*) оби́льный; (*spacious*) обши́рный. **amplification** [ˌæmplɪfɪ'keɪʃ(ə)n] *n.* усиле́ние. **amplifier** ['æmplɪˌfaɪə(r)] *n.* усили́тель *m.* **amplify** *v.t.* (*strengthen*) уси́ливать *impf.*, уси́лить *pf.*; (*enlarge*) расширя́ть *impf.*, расши́рить *pf.* **amplitude** ['æmplɪˌtjuːd] *n.* обши́рность, просто́р. **amply** *adv.* доста́точно.

ampoule ['æmpuːl] *n.* а́мпула.

amputate ['æmpjʊˌteɪt] *v.t.* ампути́ровать *impf.* & *pf.* **ampu'tation** *n.* ампута́ция.

amuse [ə'mjuːz] *v.t.* забавля́ть *impf.*; развлека́ть *impf.*, развле́чь (-еку́, -ечёшь; -ёк, -екла́) *pf.*; увеселя́ть *impf.* **amusement** *n.* заба́ва, развлече́ние, увеселе́ние; *pl.* аттракцио́ны *m.pl.* **amusing** *adj.* заба́вный; (*funny*) смешно́й (-шо́н, -шна́).

anachronism [ə'nækrəˌnɪz(ə)m] *n.* анахрони́зм. **anachro'nistic** *adj.* анахрони́чный, -ческий.

anaemia [ə'niːmɪə] *n.* малокро́вие, анеми́я. **anaemic** *adj.* малокро́вный, анеми́чный, -ческий.

anaesthesia [ˌænɪs'θiːzɪə] *n.* анестези́я, обезбо́ливание. **anaesthetic** [ˌænɪs'θetɪk] *n.* анестези́рующее, обезбо́ливающее, сре́дство; *adj.* анестези́рующий, обезбо́ливающий. **anaesthetist** [ə'niːsθətɪst] *n.* наркотиза́тор. **anaesthetize** [ə'niːsθəˌtaɪz] *v.t.* анестези́ровать *impf.* & *pf.*; обезбо́ливать *impf.*, обезбо́лить *pf.*

anagram ['ænəˌgræm] *n.* анагра́мма.

anal ['eɪn(ə)l] *adj.* ана́льный.

analogical [ˌænə'lɒdʒɪk(ə)l] *adj.* аналоги́ческий. **analogous** [ə'næləgəs] *adj.* аналоги́чный. **analogue** ['ænəˌlɒg] *n.* ана́лог; ~ **computer** анало́говая вычисли́тельная маши́на, АВМ. **a'nalogy** *n.* анало́гия.

analyse ['ænəˌlaɪz] *v.t.* анализи́ровать *impf.* & *pf.*; (*gram.*) разбира́ть *impf.*, разобра́ть (разберу́, -рёшь; разобра́л, -á, -o) *pf.* **analysis** [ə'nælɪsɪs] *n.* ана́лиз. **analyst** ['ænəlɪst] *n.* анали́тик; психоанали́тик. **analytical** [ˌænə'lɪtɪk(ə)l] *adj.* аналити́ческий.

anarchic [ə'nɑːkɪk] *adj.* анархи́чный. '**anarchism** *n.* анархи́зм. '**anarchist** *n.* анархи́ст, ~ка; *adj.* анархи́стский. '**anarchy** *n.* ана́рхия.

anatomical [ˌænə'tɒmɪk(ə)l] *adj.* анатоми́ческий. **a'natomist** *n.* ана́том. **a'natomy** *n.* анато́мия.

ancestor ['ænsestə(r)] *n.* пре́док (-дка), прароди́тель *m.* **an'cestral** *adj.* родово́й, насле́дственный. **ancestress** *n.* прароди́тельница. **ancestry** *n.* происхожде́ние; пре́дки *m.pl.*, прароди́тели *m.pl.*

anchor ['æŋkə(r)] *n.* я́корь (*pl.* -ря́) *m.*; *v.t.* ста́вить *impf.*, по~ *pf.* на я́корь; *v.i.* станови́ться (-влю́сь, -вишься) *impf.*, стать (ста́ну, -нешь) *pf.* на я́корь. **anchorage** *n.* я́корная стоя́нка. **anchorman** *n.* (*TV*, *radio*) веду́щий.

anchovy ['æntʃəvɪ, æn'tʃəʊvɪ] *n.* анчо́ус.

ancient ['eɪnʃ(ə)nt] *adj.* анти́чный, дре́вний (-вен, -вня), стари́нный.

and [ænd, ənd] *conj.* и, а; с+*i.*; **you ~ I** мы с ва́ми; **my wife ~ I** мы с жено́й.

andante [æn'dæntɪ] *adv.* (*n.*) анда́нте (*nt.indecl.*).

Andes ['ændiːz] *n.*: **the ~** А́нды (-д) *pl.*

anecdotal [ˌænɪk'dəʊt(ə)l] *adj.* анекдоти́ческий. '**anecdote** *n.* анекдо́т.

anemometer [ˌænɪ'mɒmɪtə(r)] *n.* анемо́метр, ветроме́р.

anemone [ə'nemənɪ] *n.* анемо́н, ве́треница.

aneroid (barometer) ['ænəˌrɔɪd] *n.* анеро́ид, баро́метр-анеро́ид.

anew [ə'njuː] *adv.* сно́ва.

angel ['eɪndʒ(ə)l] *n.* а́нгел. **angelic** [æn'dʒelɪk] *adj.* а́нгельский.

anger ['æŋgə(r)] *n.* гнев; *v.t.* серди́ть (-ржу́, -рдишь) *impf.*, рас~ *pf.*

angle[1] ['æŋg(ə)l] *n.* у́гол (угла́); (*fig.*) то́чка зре́ния.

angle[2] ['æŋg(ə)l] *v.i.* уди́ть (ужу́, у́дишь) *impf.* ры́бу. **angler** ['æŋglə(r)] *n.* рыболо́в. **angling** *n.* уже́ние.

Anglican ['æŋglɪkən] *n.* англика́нец (-нца), -нка; *adj.* англика́нский.

anglophile ['æŋgləʊˌfaɪl] *n.* англофи́л; *adj.* англофи́льский.

angrily ['æŋgrɪlɪ] *adv.* серди́то, гне́вно. **angry** *adj.* серди́тый, гне́вный (-вен, -вна́, -вно); (*inflamed*) воспалённый (-ён, -ена́).

anguish ['æŋgwɪʃ] *n.* страда́ние, боль. **anguished** *adj.* страда́ющий.

angular ['æŋgjʊlə(r)] *adj.* углово́й; (*sharp*) углова́тый.

aniline ['ænɪˌliːn, -lɪn, -ˌlaɪn] *adj.* анили́новый.

animal ['ænɪm(ə)l] *n.* живо́тное *sb.*; зверь (*pl.* -ри, -ре́й) *m.*; *adj.* живо́тный. **animate** *adj.* живо́й (жив, -á, -o). **animated** ['ænɪˌmeɪtɪd] *adj.* оживлённый (-ён, -ена́), живо́й (жив, -á, -o); воодушевлённый (-ён, -ена́); (*film*) мультипликацио́нный; ~ **cartoon** мультфи́льм. **ani'mation** *n.* оживле́ние, жи́вость, воодушевле́ние.

animosity [ˌænɪ'mɒsɪtɪ], **animus** ['ænɪməs] *n.* вражде́бность, неприя́знь.

aniseed ['ænɪˌsiːd] *n.* ани́совое се́мя *nt.*

ankle ['æŋk(ə)l] *n.* лоды́жка, щи́колотка; ~ **socks** коро́ткие носки́ *m.pl.* **anklet** *n.* ножно́й брасле́т.

annals ['æn(ə)lz] *n.* ле́топись, анна́лы *m.pl.* **'annalist** *n.* летопи́сец (-сца).

annex [æ'neks, ə'n-] *v.t.* аннекси́ровать *impf.* & *pf.*; присоединя́ть *impf.*, присоедини́ть *pf.*; прилага́ть *impf.*, приложи́ть (-жу́, -жишь) *pf.* **anne'xation** *n.* анне́ксия; присоедине́ние. **'annexe** *n.* (*building*) пристро́йка; дополне́ние.

annihilate [ə'naɪəˌleɪt, ə'naɪl-] *v.t.* уничтожа́ть *impf.*, уничто́жить *pf.* **annihi'lation** *n.* уничтоже́ние.

anniversary [ˌænɪ'vɜːsərɪ] *n.* годовщи́на.

annotate ['ænəʊˌteɪt, 'ænəˌteɪt] *v.t.* анноти́ровать *impf.* & *pf.* **annotated** *adj.* снабжённый (-ён, -ена́) примеча́ниями, коммента́риями. **anno'tation** *n.* примеча́ние, коммента́рий, аннота́ция.

announce [ə'naʊns] *v.t.* объявля́ть *impf.*, объяви́ть (-влю́, -вишь) *pf.*; (*declare*) заявля́ть *impf.*, заяви́ть (-влю́, -вишь) *pf.*; (*radio*) сообща́ть *impf.*, сообщи́ть *pf.*; (*guest*) докла́дывать *impf.*, доложи́ть (-жу́, -жишь) *pf.* о+*p.* **announcement** *n.* объявле́ние; сообще́ние. **announcer** *n.* ди́ктор.

annoy [ə'nɔɪ] *v.t.* досажда́ть *impf.*, досади́ть *pf.*; раздража́ть *impf.*, раздражи́ть *pf.*; **I was ~ed** мне бы́ло доса́дно; **annoyance** *n.* доса́да, раздраже́ние; (*nuisance*) неприя́тность. **annoying** *adj.* доса́дный.

annual ['ænjʊəl] *adj.* ежего́дный, годово́й, годи́чный; (*bot.*) одноле́тний; *n.* ежего́дник; одноле́тник. **annually** *adv.* ежего́дно. **annuity** [ə'njuːɪtɪ] *n.* (ежего́дная) ре́нта.

annul [ə'nʌl] *v.t.* аннули́ровать *impf.* & *pf.* **annulment** *n.* аннули́рование.

annunciation [əˌnʌnsɪ'eɪʃ(ə)n] *n.* Благове́щение.

anode ['ænəʊd] *n.* ано́д.

anodyne ['ænəˌdaɪn] *n.* болеутоля́ющее сре́дство.

anoint [ə'nɔɪnt] *v.t.* пома́зывать *impf.*, пома́зать (-а́жу, -а́жешь) *pf.*

anomalous [ə'nɒmələs] *adj.* анома́льный. **anomaly** *n.* анома́лия.

anon [ə'nɒn] *abbr.*, **anonymous** [ə'nɒnɪməs] *adj.* анони́мный. **anonymity** [ˌænə'nɪmɪtɪ] *n.* анони́мность.

anorak ['ænəˌræk] *n.* ку́ртка с капюшо́ном; штормо́вка.

anorexia [ˌænə'reksɪə] *n.* анорекси́я. **anorexic** *n.* больно́й анорекси́ей; *adj.* страда́ющий анорекси́ей.

another [ə'nʌðə(r)] *adj.*, *pron.* друго́й; ~ **one** ещё (оди́н); **ask me ~** почём я зна́ю?; **in ~ ten years** ещё че́рез де́сять лет; **many ~** мно́гие други́е.

answer ['ɑːnsə(r)] *n.* отве́т; *v.t.* отвеча́ть *impf.*, отве́тить *pf.*+*d.*, на+*a.*; ~ **back** дерзи́ть *impf.*, на~ *pf.*+*d.*; ~ **for** руча́ться *impf.*, поручи́ться (-чу́сь, -чишься) *pf.* за+*a.*; ~ **the door** отворя́ть *impf.*, отвори́ть (-рю́, -ришь) *pf.* дверь на звоно́к, на стук. **answerable** *adj.* отве́тственный (-ен, -енна). **answerphone** *n.* автоотве́тчик, телефо́н-отве́тчик.

ant [ænt] *n.* мураве́й (-вья́).

antagonism [æn'tægəˌnɪz(ə)m] *n.* антагони́зм, вражда́. **antagonist** *n.* антагони́ст, проти́вник. **antago'nistic** *adj.* антагонисти́ческий, вражде́бный. **antagonize** *v.t.* порожда́ть *impf.*, породи́ть *pf.* антагони́зм, вражду́, у+*g.*

Antarctic [ænt'ɑːktɪk] *n.*: **the ~** Анта́рктика; *adj.* антаркти́ческий; ~ **Ocean** Ю́жный океа́н. **Antarctica** *n.* Антаркти́да.

anteater ['æntˌiːtə(r)] *n.* муравье́д.

antecedent [ˌæntɪ'siːd(ə)nt] *n.* антецеде́нт; *pl.* про́шлое *sb.*; *adj.* антецеде́нтный; предше́ствующий, предыду́щий.

antechamber ['æntɪˌtʃeɪmbə(r)] *n.* пере́дняя *sb.*, прихо́жая *sb.*

antedate [ˌæntɪ'deɪt] *v.t.* дати́ровать *impf.* & *pf.* за́дним число́м; (*precede*) предше́ствовать *impf.*+*d.*

antediluvian [ˌæntɪdɪ'luːvɪən, -'ljuːvɪən] *adj.* допото́пный.

antelope ['æntɪˌləʊp] *n.* антило́па.

antenatal [ˌæntɪ'neɪt(ə)l] *adj.* дородово́й.

antenna [æn'tenə] *n.* (*zool.*) у́сик, щу́пальце (*g.pl.* -лец & -льцев); (*also radio*) анте́нна.

anterior [æn'tɪərɪə(r)] *adj.* пере́дний; ~ **to** предше́ствующий+*d.*

anteroom ['æntɪˌruːm, -ˌrʊm] *n.* пере́дняя.

anthem ['ænθəm] *n.* гимн.

anthill ['ænthɪl] *n.* мураве́йник.

anthology [æn'θɒlədʒɪ] *n.* антоло́гия.

anthracite ['ænθrəˌsaɪt] *n.* антраци́т; *adj.* антраци́товый.

anthropoid ['ænθrəˌpɔɪd] *adj.* человекообра́зный; *n.* антрапо́ид. **anthropological** [ˌænθrəpə'lɒdʒɪk(ə)l] *adj.* антропологи́ческий. **anthro'pologist** *n.* антропо́лог. **anthro'pology** антрополо́гия.

anti- ['æntɪ] *in comb.* анти..., противо... . **anti-aircraft** *adj.* противовозду́шный, зени́тный. **antibiotic** [ˌæntɪbaɪ'ɒtɪk] *n.* антибио́тик. **antibody** *n.* антите́ло (*pl.* -ла́). **Antichrist** *n.* анти́христ.

anticipate [æn'tɪsɪˌpeɪt] *v.t.* ожида́ть *impf.*+*g.*; (*with pleasure*) предвкуша́ть *impf.*, предвкуси́ть (-ушу́, -у́сишь) *pf.*; (*forestall*) предупрежда́ть *impf.*, предупреди́ть *pf.* **antici'pation** *n.* ожида́ние; предвкуше́ние; предупрежде́ние.

anticlimax [ˌæntɪ'klaɪmæks] *n.* неосуществлённые ожида́ния *nt.pl.*, антикли́макс.

antics ['æntɪks] *n.* вы́ходки *f.pl.*, ша́лости *f.pl.*

anticyclone [ˌæntɪ'saɪkləʊn] *n.* антицикло́н.

antide'pressant *n.* антидепрессáнт. **antidote** ['æntɪˌdəʊt] *n.* противоя́дие. **antifascist** *n.* антифаши́ст, ~ка; *adj.* антифаши́стский. **'antifreeze** *n.* антифри́з, хладностóйкий состáв. **'antihero** *n.* антигерóй. **'antimatter** *n.* антивеществó. **anti-missile missile** *n.* антиракéта.

antimony ['æntɪmənɪ] *n.* сурьмá.

antipathetic [ˌæntɪpə'θetɪk] *adj.* антипати́чный. **antipathy** [æn'tɪpəθɪ] *n.* антипáтия. **anti'perspirant** *n.* антиперспирáнт, срéдство от потéния. **antipodes** [æn'tɪpəˌdiːz] *n.* антипóд.

antiquarian [ˌæntɪ'kweərɪən] *adj.* антиквáрный; *n.*, **'antiquary** *n.* антиквáр. **antiquated** ['æntɪˌkweɪtɪd] *adj.* устарéлый. **antique** [æn'tiːk] *adj.* стари́нный; *n.* анти́к; *pl.* старинá. **an'tiquity** *n.* дрéвность, старинá; *pl.* дрéвности *f.pl.*

anti-Semite [ˌæntɪ'siːmaɪt, -semaɪt] *n.* антисеми́т. **anti-Se'mitic** *adj.* антисеми́тский. **anti-Semitism** [-'semɪtɪz(ə)m] *n.* антисемити́зм. **antiseptic** *adj.* антисепти́ческий; *n.* антисéптик. **anti-Soviet** *adj.* антисовéтский; ~ **propaganda** антисовéтчина; ~ **propagandist** антисовéтчик. **anti-submarine** *adj.* противолóдочный. **anti-tank** *adj.* противотáнковый. **antithesis** [æn'tɪθɪsɪs] *n.* антитéза; (*opposition*) противоположность. **antithetical** [ˌæntɪ'θetɪk(ə)l] *adj.* антитети́ческий; противоположный.

antler ['æntlə(r)] *n.* олéний рог (*pl.* -á).

anus ['eɪnəs] *n.* зáдний прохóд.

anvil ['ænvɪl] *n.* наковáльня (*g.pl.* -лен).

anxiety [æŋ'zaɪətɪ] *n.* беспокóйство, тревóга, озабóченность. **anxious** ['æŋkʃəs] *adj.* беспокóйный, тревóжный, озабóченный (-ен, -енна); **be** ~ беспокóиться *impf.*; тревóжиться *impf.*

any ['enɪ] *adj., pron.* какóй-нибудь; скóлько-нибудь; вся́кий, любóй; ктó-нибудь, чтó-нибудь; (*with neg.*) никакóй, ни оди́н; нискóлько; никтó, ничтó; *adv.* скóлько-нибудь; (*with neg.*) нискóлько, ничу́ть. **anybody, anyone** *pron.* ктó-нибудь; вся́кий, любóй; (*with neg.*) никтó. **anyhow** *adv.* кáк-нибудь; кóе-как; (*with neg.*) никáк; *conj.* во вся́ком слу́чае; всё же, всё равнó. **anyone** *see* **anybody. anything** *pron.* чтó-нибудь; всё (что угóдно); (*with neg.*) ничегó. **anyway** *adv.* во вся́ком слу́чае; как бы то ни́ было. **anywhere** *adv.* где, кудá, откýда, угóдно; (*with neg., interrog.*) где-, кудá-, откýда-нибудь.

a.o.b. *abbr.* (*of* ***any other business***) рáзное.

aorta [eɪ'ɔːtə] *n.* аóрта.

apart [ə'pɑːt] *adv.* (*aside*) в сторонé, в стóрону; (*separately*) раздéльно, врозь; (*into pieces*) на чáсти; ~ **from** крóме+*g.*, не считáя+*g.*; **take** ~ разбирáть *impf.*, разобрáть (разберý, -рёшь; разобрáл, -лá, -о) *pf.* (на чáсти); **tell** ~ различáть *impf.*, различи́ть *pf.*; отличáть *impf.*, отличи́ть *pf.* друг от дрýга.

apartheid [ə'pɑːteɪt] *n.* апартеи́д.

apartment [ə'pɑːtmənt] *n.* кварти́ра; *pl.* меблирóванные кóмнаты *f.pl.*

apathetic [ˌæpə'θetɪk] *adj.* апати́чный. **'apathy** *n.* апáтия, безразли́чие.

ape [eɪp] *n.* обезья́на; *v.t.* обезья́ничать *impf.*, с~ *pf.* с+*g.*

aperient [ə'pɪərɪənt] *adj.* слаби́тельный; *n.* слаби́тельное *sb.*

aperture ['æpəˌtjʊə(r)] *n.* отвéрстие.

apex ['eɪpeks] *n.* верши́на.

aphorism ['æfəˌrɪz(ə)m] *n.* афори́зм. **apho'ristic** *adj.* афористи́чный, -ческий.

apiarist ['eɪpɪərɪst] *n.* пчеловóд. **apiary** *n.* пáсека, пчéльник.

apiece [ə'piːs] *adv.* (*persons*) на кáждого; (*things*) за штýку; (*amount*) по+*d. or a. with 2, 3, 4, 90, 100, etc.*

Apocalypse [ə'pɒkəlɪps] *n.* Апокáлипсис. **apoca'lyptic** *adj.* апокалипти́ческий.

Apocrypha [ə'pɒkrɪfə] *n.* апóкрифы *m.pl.* **apocryphal** *adj.* апокрифи́чный, -ческий.

apogee ['æpəˌdʒiː] *n.* апогéй.

apolitical [ˌeːpə'lɪtɪk(ə)l] *adj.* аполити́чный.

apologetic [əˌpɒlə'dʒetɪk] *adv.* извиня́ющийся; **be** ~ извиня́ться *impf.*; **feel** ~ чýвствовать *impf.* свою́ винý. **apologetics** *n.* апологéтика. **apologia** [ˌæpə'ləʊdʒɪə] *n.* аполóгия. **a'pologize** *v.i.* извиня́ться *impf.*, извини́ться *pf.* (**to** пéред+*i.*; **for** за+*a.*). **a'pology** *n.* извинéние; ~ **for** жáлкое подóбие+*g.*

apoplectic [ˌæpə'plektɪk] *adj.* апоплекси́ческий. **'apoplexy** *n.* апоплéкси́я.

apostasy [ə'pɒstəsɪ] *n.* (веро)отстýпничество. **apostate** *n.* (веро)отстýпник, -ица; *adj.* (веро)отстýпнический.

apostle [ə'pɒs(ə)l] *n.* апóстол. **apo'stolic** *adj.* апóстольский.

apostrophe [ə'pɒstrəfɪ] *n.* апострóф.

apotheosis [əˌpɒθɪ'əʊsɪs] *n.* апофеóз, прославлéние.

appal [ə'pɔːl] *v.i.* ужасáть *impf.*, ужаснýть *pf.* **appalling** *adj.* ужасáющий, ужáсный.

apparatus [ˌæpə'reɪtəs, 'æp-] аппарáт; прибóр; (*gymnastic*) гимнасти́ческие снаря́ды *m.pl.*

apparel [ə'pær(ə)l] *n.* одея́ние.

apparent [ə'pærənt] *adj.* (*seeming*) ви́димый; (*manifest*) очеви́дный, я́вный; **heir** ~ прямóй наслéдник. **apparently** *adv.* кáжется, по-ви́димому; очеви́дно.

apparition [ˌæpə'rɪʃ(ə)n] *n.* видéние, при́зрак.

appeal [ə'piːl] *n.* (*request*) при́зыв, воззвáние, обращéние; (*leg.*) апелля́ция, обжáлование; (*attraction*) привлекáтельность; ~ **court** апелляциóнный суд (-á); *v.i.* (*request*) взывáть *impf.*, воззвáть (-зовý, -зовёшь) *pf.* (**to** к+*d.*; **for** о+*p.*); обращáться *impf.*, обрати́ться (-ащýсь, -ати́шься) *pf.* (с при́зывом); (*leg.*) апелли́ровать *impf.* & *pf.*; ~ **against** обжáловать *pf.*; ~ **to** (*attract*) привлекáть *impf.*, привлéчь (-екý,

-ечёшь; -ёк, -еклá) *pf.*

appear [ə'pɪə(r)] *v.i.* появля́ться *impf.*, появи́ться (-влю́сь, -вишься) *pf.*; выступа́ть *impf.*, вы́ступить *pf.*; (*seem*) каза́ться (кажу́сь, -жешься) *impf.*, по~ *pf.* **appearance** *n.* появле́ние, выступле́ние; (*aspect*) вид, нару́жность; (*pl.*) ви́димость.

appease [ə'pi:z] *v.t.* умиротворя́ть *impf.*, умиротвори́ть *pf.* **appeasement** *n.* умиротворе́ние.

appellant [ə'pelənt] *n.* апелля́нт. **appellate** *adj.* апелляцио́нный.

append [ə'pend] *v.t.* прилага́ть *impf.*, приложи́ть (-жу́, -жишь) *pf.*; прибавля́ть *impf.*, приба́вить *pf.* **appendicitis** [ə,pendɪ'saɪtɪs] *n.* аппендици́т. **appendix** *n.* приложе́ние, прибавле́ние; (*anat.*) аппе́ндикс.

appertain [,æpə'teɪn] *v.i.*: ~ **to** принадлежа́ть (-жи́т) *impf.*+*d.*; относи́ться (-ится) *impf.*+*d.*

appetite ['æpɪ,taɪt] *n.* аппети́т. **'appetizing** *adj.* аппети́тный.

applaud [ə'plɔ:d] *v.t.* аплоди́ровать *impf.*+*d.*; рукоплеска́ть (-ещу́, -е́щешь) *impf.*+*d.* **applause** *n.* аплодисме́нты *m.pl.*, рукоплеска́ние.

apple ['æp(ə)l] *n.* я́блоко (*pl.* -ки); *adj.* я́блочный; ~ **charlotte** шарло́тка; ~**-tree** я́блоня.

appliance [ə'plaɪəns] *n.* приспособле́ние, прибо́р. **applicable** ['æplɪkəb(ə)l, ə'plɪkəb(ə)l] *adj.* примени́мый. **'applicant** *n.* пода́тель *m.*, ~ница, заявле́ния; проси́тель *m.*, ~ница; кандида́т. **appli'cation** *n.* (*use*) примене́ние, приложе́ние; (*putting on*) накла́дывание; (*request*) заявле́ние. **applied** *adj.* прикладно́й. **appliqué** [æ'pli:keɪ] *n.* аппплика́ция. **apply** *v.t.* (*use*) применя́ть *impf.*, примени́ть (-ню́, -нишь) *pf.*; прилага́ть *impf.*, приложи́ть (-жу́, -жишь) *pf.*; (*put on*) накла́дывать *impf.*, наложи́ть (-жу́, -жишь) *pf.*; *v.i.* (*request*) обраща́ться *impf.*, обрати́ться (-ащу́сь, -ати́шься) *pf.* с про́сьбой (**for** о+*p.*); подава́ть (-даю́, -даёшь) *impf.*, пода́ть (-а́м, -а́шь, -а́ст, -ади́м; по́дал, -ла́, -о) *pf.* заявле́ние.

appoint [ə'pɔɪnt] *v.t.* назнача́ть *impf.*, назна́чить *pf.* **appointment** *n.* назначе́ние; (*office*) до́лжность, пост (-а́, *loc.* -у́); (*meeting*) свида́ние.

apposite ['æpəzɪt] *adj.* уме́стный. **appo'sition** *n.* приложе́ние; **in** ~ прило́женный (-ен).

appraisal [ə'preɪz(ə)l] *n.* оце́нка. **appraise** *v.t.* оце́нивать *impf.*, оцени́ть (-ню́, -нишь) *pf.*

appreciable [ə'pri:ʃəb(ə)l] *adj.* ощути́мый, ощути́тельный. **appreciate** *v.t.* цени́ть (-ню́, -нишь) *impf.*; (пра́вильно) оце́нивать *impf.*, оцени́ть (-ню́, -нишь) *pf.*; *v.i.* повыша́ться *impf.*, повы́ситься *pf.* **appreciation** [ə,pri:ʃɪ'eɪʃ(ə)n, ə,pri:s-] *n.* (*estimation*) оце́нка; (*recognition*) призна́тельность; (*rise in value*) повыше́ние це́нности, цены́. **appreciative** *adj.* призна́тельный (**of** за+*a.*).

apprehend [,æprɪ'hend] *v.t.* (*arrest*) аресто́вывать *impf.*, арестова́ть *pf.*; (*understand*) понима́ть *impf.*, поня́ть (пойму́, -мёшь; по́нял, -ла́, -о) *pf.*; (*anticipate*) опаса́ться *impf.*+*g.*, *inf.* **apprehension** *n.* аре́ст; опасе́ние. **apprehensive** *adj.* опаса́ющийся.

apprentice [ə'prentɪs] *n.* учени́к (-а́), подмасте́рье (*g.pl.* -в) *m.*; *v.t.* отдава́ть (-даю́, -даёшь) *impf.*, отда́ть (-а́м, -а́шь, -а́ст, -ади́м; о́тдал, -а́, -о) *pf.* в уче́ние. **apprenticeship** *n.* учени́чество; обуче́ние.

appro *abbr.* (*of* **approval**): **on** ~ на про́бу.

approach [ə'prəʊtʃ] *v.t.* подходи́ть (-ожу́, -о́дишь) *impf.*, подойти́ (подойду́, -дёшь; подошёл, -шла́) *pf.* к+*d.*; приближа́ться *impf.*, прибли́зиться *pf.* к+*d.*; (*apply to*) обраща́ться *impf.*, обрати́ться (-ащу́сь, -ати́шься) *pf.* к+*d.*; *n.* приближе́ние; подхо́д; подъе́зд, по́дступ.

approbation [,æprə'beɪʃ(ə)n] *n.* одобре́ние.

appropriate [ə'prəʊprɪət; ə'prəʊprɪ,eɪt] *adj.* подходя́щий, соотве́тствующий; *v.t.* присва́ивать *impf.*, присво́ить *pf.*; (*assign money*) ассигнова́ть *impf.* & *pf.* **appropri'ation** *n.* присвое́ние, присво́енное *sb.*; ассигнова́ние.

approval [ə'pru:v(ə)l] *n.* одобре́ние; утвержде́ние. **approve** *v.t.* утвержда́ть *impf.*, утверди́ть *pf.*; *v.t.* & *i.* ~ **of** одобря́ть *impf.*, одо́брить *pf.*

approximate [ə'prɒksɪmət] *adj.* приблизи́тельный; *v.i.* приближа́ться *impf.* (**to** к+*d.*). **approxi'mation** *n.* приближе́ние.

apricot ['eɪprɪ,kɒt] *n.* абрико́с.

April ['eɪprɪl, 'eɪpr(ə)l] *n.* апре́ль *m.*; ~ **Fool!** с пе́рвым апре́ля!; *attr.* апре́льский.

apron ['eɪprən] *n.* пере́дник; (*theatre*) авансце́на; (*airfield*) площа́дка.

apropos ['æprə,pəʊ, -'pəʊ] *adv.* кста́ти; ~ **of** по по́воду+*g.*; относи́тельно+*g.*; что каса́ется+*g.*

apse [æps] *n.* апси́да.

apt [æpt] *adj.* (*suitable*) уда́чный; (*quick*) спосо́бный; (*inclined*) скло́нный (-о́нен, -о́нна́, -о́нно). **aptitude** ['æptɪ,tju:d] *n.* спосо́бность.

aqualung ['ækwə,lʌŋ] *n.* аквала́нг. **aquamarine** [,ækwəmə'ri:n] *n.* аквамари́н. **aquarist** ['ækwərɪst] *n.* аквариуми́ст. **aquarium** [ə'kweərɪəm] *n.* аква́риум. **Aquarius** [ə'kweərɪəs] *n.* Водоле́й. **aquatic** [ə'kwætɪk] *adj.* водяно́й, во́дный. **aqueduct** ['ækwɪ,dʌkt] *n.* акведу́к. **aqueous** ['eɪkwɪəs] *adj.* во́дный; (*watery*) водяни́стый.

aquiline ['ækwɪ,laɪn] *adj.* орли́ный.

Arab ['ærəb] *n.* (*person*) ара́б, ~ка; (*horse*) ара́бская ло́шадь (*pl.* -ди, -де́й, *i.* -дьми́); *adj.* ара́бский. **arabesque** [,ærə'besk] *n.* арабе́ска. **Arabia** [ə'reɪbɪə] *n.* Ара́вия. **Arabic** *adj.* ара́бский.

arable ['ærəb(ə)l] *adj.* па́хотный.

arbitrary ['ɑ:bɪtrərɪ] *adj.* произво́льный.

arbitrate *v.i.* де́йствовать *impf.* в ка́честве трете́йского судьи́. **arbi'tration** *n.* арбитра́ж, трете́йское реше́ние. **arbitrator** *n.* арби́тр, трете́йский судья́ (*pl.* -дьи, -де́й, -дья́м) *m.*
arboreal [ɑː'bɔːrɪəl] *adj.* древе́сный; (*living in trees*) обита́ющий на дере́вьях. **arbour** ['ɑːbə(r)] *n.* бесе́дка.
arc [ɑːk] *n.* дуга́ (*pl.* -ги); ~ **lamp** дугова́я ла́мпа. **ar'cade** *n.* арка́да, пасса́ж.
arch[1] [ɑːtʃ] *n.* а́рка, свод, дуга́ (*pl.* -ги); *v.t.* & *i.* выгиба́ть(ся) *impf.*, вы́гнуть(ся) *pf.*; изгиба́ть(ся) *impf.*, изогну́ть(ся) *pf.*
arch[2] [ɑːtʃ] *adj.* игри́вый.
arch- [ɑːtʃ] *in comb.* архи...; эрц... . **archangel** ['ɑːk-] *n.* арха́нгел. **archbishop** *n.* архиепи́скоп. **archdeacon** *n.* архидиа́кон. **archduchess** *n.* эрцгерцоги́ня. **archduchy** *n.* эрцге́рцогство. **archduke** *n.* эрцге́рцог.
archaeological [ˌɑːkɪə'lɒdʒɪk(ə)l] *adj.* археологи́ческий. **archae'ologist** *n.* архео́лог. **archae'ology** *n.* археоло́гия.
archaic [ɑː'keɪɪk] *adj.* архаи́чный. **archaism** *n.* архаи́зм.
archer ['ɑːtʃə(r)] *n.* стрело́к (-лка́) из лу́ка. **archery** *n.* стрельба́ из лу́ка.
archipelago [ˌɑːkɪ'peləˌgəʊ] *n.* архипела́г.
architect ['ɑːkɪˌtekt] *n.* архите́ктор, зо́дчий *sb.* **archi'tectural** *adj.* архитекту́рный. **architecture** *n.* архитекту́ра.
archives ['ɑːkaɪvz] *n.* архи́в. **archivist** ['ɑːkɪvɪst] *n.* архива́риус, архиви́ст.
archway ['ɑːtʃweɪ] *n.* прохо́д под а́ркой, сво́дчатый прохо́д.
arctic ['ɑːktɪk] *n.*: **the A~** А́рктика; *adj.* аркти́ческий; **A~ Ocean** Се́верный Ледови́тый океа́н.
ardent ['ɑːd(ə)nt] *adj.* горя́чий (-ч, -ча́), пы́лкий (-лок, -лка́, -лко) **ardour** *n.* пыл (-а(у), *loc.* -у́), пы́лкость, рве́ние.
arduous ['ɑːdjuːəs] *adj.* тру́дный (-ден, -дна́, -дно).
area ['eərɪə] *n.* (*extent*) пло́щадь (*pl.* -ди, -де́й); (*region*) райо́н, зо́на.
arena [ə'riːnə] *n.* аре́на.
argon ['ɑːgɒn] *n.* арго́н.
arguable ['ɑːgjʊəb(ə)l] *adj.* утвержда́емый, доказу́емый; (*disputed*) спо́рный. **argue** *v.t.* (*try to prove*) аргументи́ровать *impf.* & *pf.*; (*maintain*) утвержда́ть *impf.*; (*prove*) дока́зывать *impf.*; *v.i.* (*dispute*) спо́рить *impf.*, по~ *pf.* **argument** *n.* аргуме́нт, до́вод; (*dispute*) спор. **argu'mentative** *adj.* лю́бящий спо́рить.
argy-bargy [ˌɑːdʒɪ'bɑːdʒɪ] *n.* (*coll.*) перебра́нка, перепа́лка.
arid ['ærɪd] *adj.* сухо́й (сух, -а́, -о), безво́дный. **a'ridity** *n.* су́хость.
Aries ['eəriːz] *n.* Ове́н (Овна́).
arise [ə'raɪz] *v.i.* возника́ть *impf.*, возни́кнуть (-к) *pf.*; происходи́ть (-ит) *impf.*, произойти́ (-ойдёт; -ошёл, -ошла́) *pf.*
aristocracy [ˌærɪ'stɒkrəsɪ] *n.* аристокра́тия. **'aristocrat** *n.* аристокра́т, ~ка. **aristo'cratic** *adj.* аристократи́ческий, -и́чный.
arithmetic [ə'rɪθmətɪk] *n.* арифме́тика. **arith'metical** *adj.* арифмети́ческий. **arithme'tician** *n.* арифме́тик.
ark [ɑːk] *n.* (Но́ев) ковче́г.
arm[1] [ɑːm] *n.* (*of body*) рука́ (*a.* -ку; *pl.* -ки, -к, -ка́м); (*of sea*) морско́й зали́в; (*of chair*) ру́чка; (*of river*) рука́в (-а́; *pl.* -а́); (*of tree*) больша́я ветвь (*pl.* -ви); ~ **in** ~ по́д руку; **at ~'s length** (*fig.*) на почти́тельном расстоя́нии; **with open ~s** с распростёртыми объя́тиями.
arm[2] [ɑːm] *n.* (*mil.*) род войск; *pl.* (*weapons*) ору́жие; *pl.* (*coat of ~s*) герб (-а́); *v.t.* вооружа́ть *impf.*, вооружи́ть *pf.* **armaments** ['ɑːməmənts] *n.* вооруже́ния *nt.pl.*
armature ['ɑːməˌtjʊə(r)] *n.* армату́ра.
armchair *n.* кре́сло (*g.pl.* -сел).
Armenia [ɑː'miːnɪə] *n.* Арме́ния.
armful *n.* оха́пка. **armhole** *n.* про́йма.
armistice ['ɑːmɪstɪs] *n.* переми́рие.
armorial [ɑː'mɔːrɪəl] *adj.* ге́рбовый, геральди́ческий. **armour** ['ɑːmə(r)] *n.* (*hist.*) доспе́хи *m.pl.*; броня́; (*vehicles, collect.*) бронеси́лы *f.pl.* **armoured** *adj.* брониро́ванный (-ан), броново́й; (*vehicles etc.*) бронета́нковый, броне...; ~ **car** броневи́к (-а́), бронеавтомоби́ль *m.*; ~ **forces** бронета́нковые войска́ *nt.pl.*, бронеси́лы *f.pl.* **armourer** *n.* оруже́йник. **armoury** *n.* арсена́л, склад ору́жия.
armpit *n.* подмы́шка.
army ['ɑːmɪ] *n.* а́рмия; *adj.* арме́йский.
aroma [ə'rəʊmə] *n.* арома́т. **aro'matic** *adj.* аромати́чный.
around [ə'raʊnd] *adv.* круго́м, вокру́г; *prep.* вокру́г+*g.*; **all** ~ повсю́ду.
arouse [ə'raʊz] *v.t.* пробужда́ть, буди́ть (бужу́, бу́дишь) *impf.*, про~ *pf.*; возбужда́ть *impf.*, возбуди́ть *pf.*
arraign [ə'reɪn] *v.t.* привлека́ть *impf.*, привле́чь (-еку́, -ечёшь; -ёк, -екла́) *pf.* к суду́. **arraignment** *n.* привлече́ние к суду́.
arrange [ə'reɪndʒ] *v.t.* (*put in order*) приводи́ть (-ожу́, -о́дишь) *impf.*, привести́ (приведу́, -дёшь; привёл, -а́) *pf.* в поря́док; расставля́ть *impf.*, расста́вить *pf.*; (*plan*) устра́ивать *impf.*, устро́ить *pf.*; (*mus.*) аранжи́ровать *impf.* & *pf.*; *v.i.*: ~ **for** усла́вливаться *impf.*, усло́виться *pf.* о+*p.*; ~ **to** угова́риваться *impf.*, уговори́ться *pf.*+*inf.* **arrangement** *n.* расположе́ние; устро́йство; (*agreement*) соглаше́ние; (*mus.*) аранжиро́вка; *pl.* приготовле́ния *nt.pl.*
array [ə'reɪ] *v.t.* наряжа́ть *impf.*, наряди́ть (-яжу́, -я́дишь) *pf.*; (*marshal*) стро́ить *impf.*, вы́~ *pf.*; *n.* наря́д; (*series*) совоку́пность.
arrears [ə'rɪəz] *n.* задо́лженность, недои́мка.
arrest [ə'rest] *v.t.* аресто́вывать *impf.*, арестова́ть *pf.*; заде́рживать *impf.*, задержа́ть (-жу́, -жишь) *pf.*; (*attention*) прико́вывать *impf.*, прикова́ть (-кую́, -куёшь) *pf.*;

n. аре́ст, задержа́ние.

arrival [ə'raɪv(ə)l] *n.* прибы́тие, прие́зд; (*new* ~) вновь прибы́вший *sb.*; (*child*) новорождённый *sb.* **arrive** *v.i.* прибыва́ть *impf.*, прибы́ть (прибу́ду, -дешь; при́был, -а́, -о) *pf.*; приезжа́ть *impf.*, прие́хать (-е́ду, -е́дешь) *pf.*; (*succeed*) доби́ться (-бью́сь, -бьёшься) *pf.* успе́ха.

arrogance ['ærəgəns] *n.* высокоме́рие, кичли́вость. **arrogant** *adj.* высокоме́рный, кичли́вый.

arrow ['ærəʊ] *n.* стрела́ (*pl.* -лы); (*pointer etc.*) стре́лка. **arrowhead** *n.* наконе́чник стрелы́.

arsenal ['ɑ:sən(ə)l] *n.* арсена́л.

arsenic ['ɑ:sənɪk] *n.* мышья́к (-а́); *adj.* мышьяко́вый.

arson ['ɑ:s(ə)n] *n.* поджо́г.

art [ɑ:t] *n.* иску́сство; ~ **nouveau** стиль *m.* «ар нуво́»; *pl.* гумани́тарные нау́ки *f.pl.*; *adj.* худо́жественный.

arterial [ɑ:'tɪərɪəl] *adj.* (*anat.*) артериа́льный; магистра́льный; ~ **road** магистра́ль. '**artery** *n.* (*anat.*) арте́рия; магистра́ль.

artesian [ɑ:'ti:zɪən, -ʒ(ə)n] *adj.* артезиа́нский.

artful ['ɑ:tfʊl] *adj.* хи́трый (-тёр, -тра́, хи́тро́), ло́вкий (-вок, -вка́, -вко, ло́вки́).

arthritic [ɑ:'θrɪtɪk] *adj.* артрити́ческий. **arthritis** [ɑ:'θraɪtɪs] *n.* артри́т.

artichoke ['ɑ:tɪ,tʃəʊk] *n.* артишо́к; (*Jerusalem* ~) землянáя гру́ша.

article ['ɑ:tɪk(ə)l] *n.* (*literary*) статья́ (*g.pl.* -е́й); (*clause*) пункт; (*thing*) предме́т; (*gram.*) арти́кль *m.*, член; *v.t.* отдава́ть (-даю́, -даёшь) *impf.*, отда́ть (-а́м, -а́шь, -а́ст, -ади́м; о́тдал, -а́, -о) *pf.* в уче́ние.

articulate [ɑ:'tɪkjʊlət] *adj.* членоразде́льный, я́сный (я́сен, ясна́, я́сно, ясны́); *v.t.* произноси́ть (-ошу́, -о́сишь) *impf.*, произнести́ (-есу́, -есёшь; -ёс, -есла́) *pf.*; артикули́ровать *impf.* **articulated** *adj.* сочленённый (-ён, -ена́). **articu'lation** *n.* артикуля́ция; сочлене́ние.

artifice ['ɑ:tɪfɪs] *n.* хи́трость, (иску́сная) вы́думка. **artificer** [ɑ:'tɪfɪsə(r)] *n.* (вое́нный) те́хник. **artificial** [,ɑ:tɪ'fɪʃ(ə)l] *adj.* иску́сственный (-ен(ен), -енна).

artillery [ɑ:'tɪlərɪ] *n.* артилле́рия; *adj.* артиллери́йский. **artilleryman** *n.* артиллери́ст.

artisan [,ɑ:tɪ'zæn, 'ɑ:-] *n.* реме́сленник.

artist ['ɑ:tɪst] *n.* худо́жник; арти́ст. **artiste** [ɑ:'ti:st] *n.* арти́ст, ~ка. **ar'tistic** *adj.* худо́жественный (-ен, -енна); артисти́ческий.

artless ['ɑ:tlɪs] *adj.* бесхи́тростный, простоду́шный.

Aryan ['eərɪən] *n.* ари́ец (-и́йца), ари́йка; *adj.* ари́йский.

as [æz, əz] *adv.* как; *conj.* (*time*) когда́; в то вре́мя как; (*cause*) так как; (*manner*) как; (*concession*) как ни; *rel. pron.* како́й; кото́рый; что; **as ... as** так (же)... как; **as for, to** относи́тельно+*g.*; что каса́ется+*g.*; **as if** как бу́дто; **as it were** ка́к бы; так сказа́ть; **as soon as** как то́лько; **as well** также; то́же.

a.s.a.p. *abbr.* (*of* **as soon as possible**) как мо́жно скоре́е.

asbestos [æz'bestɒs, æs-] *n.* асбе́ст; *adj.* асбе́стовый.

ascend [ə'send] *v.t.* поднима́ться *impf.*, подня́ться (-ниму́сь, -ни́мешься; -я́лся́, -яла́сь) *pf.* на+*a.*; всходи́ть (-ожу́, -о́дишь) *impf.*, взойти́ (взойду́, -дёшь; взошёл, -шла́) *pf.* на+*a.*; *v.i.* возноси́ться (-ошу́сь, -о́сишься) *impf.*, вознести́сь (-есу́сь, -есёшься; -ёсся, -есла́сь) *pf.* **ascendancy** *n.* доминиру́ющее влия́ние (**over** на+*a.*). **ascendant** *adj.* восходя́щий. **Ascension** *n.* (*eccl.*) Вознесе́ние. **ascent** *n.* восхожде́ние (**of** на+*a.*).

ascertain [,æsə'teɪn] *v.t.* устана́вливать *impf.*, установи́ть (-влю́, -вишь) *pf.*

ascetic [ə'setɪk] *adj.* аскети́ческий; *n.* аске́т. **asceticism** *n.* аскети́зм.

ascribe [ə'skraɪb] *v.t.* припи́сывать *impf.*, приписа́ть (-ишу́, -и́шешь) *pf.* (**to** +*d.*). **ascription** [ə'skrɪpʃ(ə)n] *n.* припи́сывание.

asepsis [eɪ'sepsɪs, ə-] *n.* асе́птика. **aseptic** *adj.* асепти́ческий.

asexual [eɪ'seksjʊəl, æ-] *adj.* беспо́лый.

ash[1] [æʃ] *n.* (*tree*) я́сень *m.*

ash[2] [æʃ], **ashes** [æʃɪz] *n.* зола́, пе́пел (-пла); (*human remains*) прах.

ashamed [ə'ʃeɪmd] *pred.*: **he is** ~ ему́ сты́дно; **be, feel,** ~ **of** стыди́ться *impf.*, по~ *pf.*+*g.*

ashen ['æʃ(ə)n] *adj.* (*of* **ash**[2]) пе́пельный; (*pale*) ме́ртвенно-бле́дный.

ashore [ə'ʃɔ:(r)] *adv.* на бе́рег(у́).

ashtray ['æʃtreɪ] *n.* пе́пельница.

Asia ['eɪʃə, -ʒə] *n.* А́зия. **Asian, Asiatic** [,eɪʃɪ'ætɪk, ,eɪz-] *adj.* азиа́тский; *n.* азиа́т, ~ка.

aside [ə'saɪd] *adv.* в сто́рону, в стороне́; *n.* слова́ *nt.pl.*, произноси́мые в сто́рону.

asinine ['æsɪ,naɪn] *adj.* осли́ный; (*stupid*) глу́пый (глуп, -а́, -о).

ask [ɑ:sk] *v.t.* (*inquire of*) спра́шивать *impf.*, спроси́ть (-ошу́, -о́сишь) *pf.*; (*request*) проси́ть (-ошу́, -о́сишь) *impf.*, по~ *pf.* (**for** *a.*, *g.*, о+*p.*); (*invite*) приглаша́ть *impf.*, пригласи́ть *pf.*; (*demand*) тре́бовать *impf.*+*g.* (**of** от+*g.*); ~ **after** осведомля́ться *impf.*, осве́домиться *pf.* о+*p.*; ~ **a question** задава́ть (-даю́, -даёшь) *impf.*, зада́ть (-а́м, -а́шь, -а́ст, -ади́м; за́дал, -а́, -о) *pf.* вопро́с; **it's yours for the ~ing** сто́ит то́лько попроси́ть.

askance [ə'skæns, -'skɑ:ns] *adv.* ко́со, с подозре́нием.

askew [ə'skju:] *adv.* кри́во.

asleep [ə'sli:p] *pred., adv.*: **be** ~ спать (сплю, спишь; спал, -а́, -о) *impf.*; **fall** ~ засыпа́ть *impf.*, засну́ть *pf.*; **my foot's** ~ нога́ затекла́.

asp [æsp] *n.* а́спид.

asparagus [ə'spærəgəs] *n.* спа́ржа.

aspect ['æspekt] *n.* аспе́кт, вид (-а(у), на виду́), сторона́ (*a.* -ону; *pl.* -оны, -о́н, -она́м).

aspen ['æspən] *n.* оси́на.

asperity [ə'sperɪtɪ] *n.* ре́зкость.
aspersion [ə'spɜːʃ(ə)n] *n.* клевета́.
asphalt ['æsfælt] *n.* асфа́льт; *adj.* асфа́льтовый; *v.t.* асфальти́ровать *impf.* & *pf.*
asphyxia [æs'fɪksɪə] *n.* асфи́ксия, уду́шье. **asphyxiate** *v.t.* удуша́ть *impf.*, удуши́ть (-шу́, -шишь) *pf.*
aspic ['æspɪk] *n.* заливно́е *sb.*; **in** ~ заливно́й.
aspirant ['æspɪrənt] *n.* претенде́нт. **aspirate** *n.* придыха́тельный *sb.* **aspi'ration** *n.* (*ling.*) придыха́ние; (*desire*) стремле́ние. **aspire** [ə'spaɪə(r)] *v.i.* стреми́ться *impf.* (**to** к+*d.*).
aspirin ['æsprɪn] *n.* аспири́н; (*tablet*) табле́тка аспири́на.
ass [æs] *n.* осёл (осла́).
assail [ə'seɪl] *v.t.* напада́ть *impf.*, напа́сть (-аду́, -адёшь; -а́л) *pf.* на+*a.*; (*with questions*) забра́сывать *impf.*, заброса́ть *pf.* вопро́сами. **assailant** *n.* напада́ющий *sb.*
assassin [ə'sæsɪn] *n.* (наёмный, -ная) уби́йца *c.g.* **assassinate** *v.t.* (вероло́мно) убива́ть *impf.*, уби́ть (убью́, убьёшь) *pf.* **assassi'nation** *n.* (преда́тельское) уби́йство.
assault [ə'sɔːlt, ə'sɒlt] *n.* нападе́ние; (*mil.*) штурм; (*rape*) изнаси́лование; ~ **and battery** оскорбле́ние де́йствием; *v.t.* напада́ть *impf.*, напа́сть (-аду́, -адёшь; -а́л) *pf.* на+*a.*; штурмова́ть *impf.*; наси́ловать *impf.*, из~ *pf.*
assay [ə'seɪ, 'æseɪ] *n.* про́ба; *v.t.* производи́ть (-ожу́, -о́дишь) *impf.*, произвести́ (-еду́, -едёшь; -ёл, -ела́) *pf.* ана́лиз+*g.*; про́бовать *impf.*, по~ *pf.*
assemblage [ə'semblɪdʒ] *n.* сбор, собира́ние. **assemble** *v.t.* собира́ть *impf.*, собра́ть (соберу́, -рёшь; собра́л, -а́, -о) *pf.*; (*machine*) монти́ровать *impf.*, с~ *pf.*; *v.i.* собира́ться *impf.*, собра́ться (-берётся; собра́лся, -ала́сь, -а́ло́сь) *pf.* **assembly** *n.* собра́ние, ассамбле́я; (*of machine*) сбо́рка.
assent [ə'sent] *v.i.* соглаша́ться *impf.*, согласи́ться *pf.* (**to** на+*a.*, *inf.*); *n.* согла́сие; (*royal*) са́нкция.
assert [ə'sɜːt] *v.t.* утвержда́ть *impf.*; ~ **o.s.** отста́ивать *impf.*, отстоя́ть (-ою́, -ои́шь) *pf.* свои́ права́. **assertion** *n.* утвержде́ние. **assertive** *adj.* насто́йчивый, самонаде́янный (-ян, -янна).
assess [ə'ses] *v.t.* (*amount*) определя́ть *impf.*, определи́ть *pf.*; (*tax*) облага́ть *impf.*, обложи́ть (-жу́, -жишь) *pf.* нало́гом; (*value*) оце́нивать *impf.*, оцени́ть (-ню́, -нишь) *pf.* **assessment** *n.* определе́ние; обложе́ние; оце́нка.
asset ['æset] *n.* це́нное ка́чество; бла́го; *pl.* иму́щество; ~**s and liabilities** акти́в и пасси́в.
assiduity [ˌæsɪ'djuːɪtɪ] *n.* прилежа́ние, усе́рдие. **assiduous** [ə'sɪdjʊəs] *adj.* приле́жный, усе́рдный.
assign [ə'saɪn] *v.t.* назнача́ть *impf.*, назна́чить *pf.*; ассигнова́ть *impf.* & *pf.* **assignation** [ˌæsɪg'neɪʃ(ə)n] *n.* (*meeting*) усло́вленная встре́ча, свида́ние. **assignment** *n.* (*task*) зада́ние; (*mission*) командиро́вка.
assimilate [ə'sɪmɪˌleɪt] *v.t.* ассимили́ровать *impf.* & *pf.*; усва́ивать *impf.*, усво́ить *pf.* **assimi'lation** *n.* ассимиля́ция; усвое́ние.
assist [ə'sɪst] *v.t.* помога́ть *impf.*, помо́чь (-огу́, -о́жешь; -о́г, -огла́) *pf.*+*d.*; соде́йствовать *impf.* & *pf.*+*d.* **assistance** *n.* по́мощь, соде́йствие. **assistant** *n.* помо́щник, ассисте́нт.
assizes [ə'saɪzɪz] *n.* выездна́я се́ссия суда́.
associate [ə'səʊʃɪˌeɪt, -sɪˌeɪt; ə'səʊʃɪət, -sɪət] *v.t.* ассоции́ровать *impf.* & *pf.*; *v.i.* присоединя́ться *impf.*, присоедини́ться *pf.* (**with** к+*d.*); обща́ться *impf.* (**with** с+*i.*); *n.* (*colleague*) колле́га *c.g.*; (*subordinate member*) мла́дший член, член-корреспонде́нт. **associ'ation** *n.* о́бщество, ассоциа́ция; присоедине́ние; **A~ football** футбо́л.
assonance ['æsənəns] *n.* ассона́нс.
assorted [ə'sɔːtɪd] *adj.* подо́бранный (-ан). **assortment** *n.* ассортиме́нт.
assuage [ə'sweɪdʒ] *v.t.* успока́ивать *impf.*, успоко́ить *pf.*; смягча́ть *impf.*, смягчи́ть *pf.*
assume [ə'sjuːm] *v.t.* (*accept*) принима́ть *impf.*, приня́ть (приму́, -мешь; при́нял, -а́, -о) *pf.*; (*pretend*) напуска́ть *impf.*, напусти́ть (-ущу́, -у́стишь) *pf.* на себя́; (*suppose*) предполога́ть *impf.*, предположи́ть (-ожу́, -о́жишь) *pf.*; ~**d name** вы́мышленное и́мя *nt.* **assumption** [ə'sʌmpʃ(ə)n] *n.* приня́тие на себя́; (*pretence*) притво́рство; (*supposition*) предположе́ние, допуще́ние; (*eccl.*, **the A~**) Успе́ние.
assurance [ə'ʃʊərəns] *n.* увере́ние; (*self* ~) самоуве́ренность; (*insurance*) страхова́ние. **assure** *v.t.* уверя́ть *impf.*, уве́рить *pf.*; гаранти́ровать *impf.* & *pf.*; (*insure*) страхова́ть *impf.*, за~ *pf.* (**against** от+*g.*). **assuredly** *adv.* несомне́нно.
aster ['æstə(r)] *n.* а́стра.
asterisk ['æstərɪsk] *n.* звёздочка.
astern [ə'stɜːn] *adv.* позади́, наза́д.
asteroid ['æstəˌrɔɪd] *n.* астеро́ид.
asthma ['æsmə] *n.* а́стма. **asth'matic** *adj.* астмати́ческий.
astigmatic [ˌæstɪg'mætɪk] *adj.* астигмати́ческий. **a'stigmatism** *n.* астигмати́зм.
astir [ə'stɜː(r)] *pred.*, *adv.* (*in motion*) в движе́нии; (*out of bed*) на нога́х; (*excited*) в возбужде́нии.
astonish [ə'stɒnɪʃ] *v.t.* удивля́ть *impf.*, удиви́ть *pf.* **astonishing** *adj.* удиви́тельный. **astonishment** *n.* удивле́ние.
astound [ə'staʊnd] *v.t.* изумля́ть *impf.*, изуми́ть *pf.* **astounding** *adj.* изуми́тельный.
astrakhan [ˌæstrə'kæn] *n.* кара́куль *m.*
astral ['æstr(ə)l] *adj.* астра́льный, звёздный.
astray [ə'streɪ] *adv.*: **go** ~ сбива́ться *impf.*, сби́ться (собью́сь, собьёшься) *pf.* с пути́; **lead** ~ сбива́ть *impf.*, сбить (собью́, собьёшь) *pf.* с пути́.
astride [ə'straɪd] *adv.* расста́вив но́ги; верхо́м (**of** на+*p.*); *prep.* верхо́м на+*p.*

astringent [ə'strɪndʒ(ə)nt] *adj.* вя́жущий; *n.* вя́жущее сре́дство.

astro- [æstrəʊ] *in comb.* астро..., звездо... . **astrologer** [ə'strɒlədʒə(r)] *n.* астро́лог. **astrological** [ˌæstrə'lɒdʒɪk(ə)l] *adj.* астрологи́ческий. **astrology** [ə'strɒlədʒɪ] *n.* астроло́гия. **astronaut** ['æstrəˌnɔ:t] *n.* астрона́вт. **astronomer** [ə'strɒnəmə(r)] *n.* астроно́м. **astronomical** [ˌæstrə'nɒmɪk(ə)l] *adj.* астрономи́ческий. **a'stronomy** *n.* астроно́мия. **astrophysical** *adj.* астрофизи́ческий. **astrophysics** *n.* астрофи́зика.

astute [ə'stju:t] *adj.* проница́тельный; (*crafty*) хи́трый (хитр, -а́, хи́тро́).

asunder [ə'sʌndə(r)] *adv.* (*apart*) врозь; (*in pieces*) на ча́сти.

asylum [ə'saɪləm] *n.* психиатри́ческая больни́ца; (*refuge*) убе́жище.

asymmetrical [ˌeɪsɪ'metrɪk(ə)l, ˌæsɪ'metrɪk(ə)l] *adj.* асимметри́ческий. **a'symmetry** *n.* асимметри́я.

at [æt, *unstressed* ət] *prep.* (*position, condition*) на+*p.*, в+*p.*, у+*g.*; (*time, direction*) на+*a.*, в+*a.*; *with* vv. *etc.*: *see* vv. *etc.*, *e.g.* **look** смотре́ть (**at** на+*a.*); ~ **all** вообще́; **not** ~ **all** совсе́м не; ~ **first** снача́ла, сперва́; ~ **home** до́ма; ~ **last** наконе́ц; ~ **least** по кра́йней ме́ре; ~ **most** са́мое бо́льшее; ~ **night** но́чью; ~ **once** (*immediately*) сра́зу; (*simultaneously*) одновре́ме́нно; ~ **present** в настоя́щее вре́мя; ~ **that** на том; (*moreover*) к тому́ же; ~ **work** (*working*) за рабо́той; (~ *place of work*) на рабо́те.

atheism ['eɪθɪˌɪz(ə)m] *n.* атеи́зм. **atheist** *n.* атеи́ст. **athe'istic** *adj.* атеисти́ческий.

Athens ['æθɪnz] *n.* Афи́ны (-н) *pl.*

athlete ['æθli:t] *n.* атле́т; легкоатле́т, ~ка; спортсме́н, ~ка. **athletic** [æθ'letɪk] *adj.* атлети́ческий. **athletics** *n.* (лёгкая) атле́тика.

Atlantic [ət'læntɪk]: ~ **Ocean** Атланти́ческий океа́н.

atlas ['ætləs] *n.* а́тлас.

atmosphere ['ætməsˌfɪə(r)] *n.* атмосфе́ра. **atmospheric** [ˌætməs'ferɪk] *adj.* атмосфе́рный. **atmospherics** *n.* атмосфе́рные поме́хи *f.pl.*

atom ['ætəm] *n.* а́том; ~ **bomb** а́томная бо́мба. **a'tomic** *adj.* а́томный.

atone [ə'təʊn] *v.i.* искупа́ть *impf.*, искупи́ть (-плю́, -пишь) *pf.* (**for** +*a.*). **atonement** *n.* искупле́ние.

atrocious [ə'trəʊʃəs] *adj.* отврати́тельный, ужа́сный. **atrocity** [ə'trɒsɪtɪ] *n.* зве́рство, у́жас.

atrophy ['ætrəfɪ] *n.* атрофи́я, притупле́ние; *v.i.* атрофи́роваться *impf.* & *pf.*

attach [ə'tætʃ] *v.t.* (*fasten*) прикрепля́ть *impf.*, прикрепи́ть *pf.*; (*fig.*) привя́зывать *impf.*, привяза́ть (-яжу́, -я́жешь) *pf.*; (*second*) прикомандиро́вывать *impf.*, прикомандирова́ть *pf.*; (*attribute*) придава́ть (придаю́, -даёшь) *impf.*, прида́ть (-а́м, -а́шь, -а́ст, -ади́м; при́дал, -а́, -о) *pf.* **attaché** [ə'tæʃeɪ] *n.* атташе́ *m.indecl.* **attachment** *n.* прикрепле́ние; привя́занность; *pl.* принадле́жности *f.pl.*

attack [ə'tæk] *v.t.* напада́ть *impf.*, напа́сть (-аду́, -адёшь; -а́л) *pf.* на+*a.*; *n.* нападе́ние; (*mil. also*) ата́ка; (*of illness*) припа́док (-дка).

attain [ə'teɪn] *v.t.* достига́ть *impf.*, дости́чь & дости́гнуть (-и́гну, -и́гнешь; -и́г) *pf.*+*g.*, до+*g.*; ~ **the age of** дожива́ть *impf.*, дожи́ть (-иву́, -ивёшь; до́жил, -а́, -о) *pf.* до+*g.* **attainment** *n.* достиже́ние.

attempt [ə'tempt] *v.t.* пыта́ться *impf.*, по~ *pf.*+*inf.*; про́бовать *impf.*, по~ *pf.*+*inf.*; *n.* попы́тка; (*on the life of*) покуше́ние (на жизнь+*g.*); **make an** ~ **on the life of** покуша́ться *impf.*, покуси́ться *pf.* на жизнь+*g.*

attend [ə'tend] *v.i.* занима́ться *impf.*, заня́ться (займу́сь, -мёшься; -я́лся́, -яла́сь) *pf.* (**to** +*i.*); (*be present*) прису́тствовать *impf.* (**at** на+*p.*); *v.t.* (*accompany*) сопровожда́ть *impf.*, сопроводи́ть *pf.*; (*serve*) обслу́живать *impf.*, обслужи́ть (-жу́, -жишь) *pf.*; (*visit*) посеща́ть *impf.*, посети́ть (-ещу́, -ети́шь) *pf.* **attendance** *n.* (*presence*) прису́тствие; посеща́емость; обслу́живание. **attendant** *adj.* сопровожда́ющий; *n.* (*escort*) провожа́тый *sb.*

attention [ə'tenʃ(ə)n] *n.* внима́ние; **pay** ~ **to** обраща́ть *impf.*, обрати́ть (-ащу́, -ати́шь) *pf.* внима́ние на+*a.*; *int.* (*mil.*) сми́рно! **attentive** *adj.* внима́тельный; (*polite*) ве́жливый.

attenuated [ə'tenjʊˌeɪtɪd] *adj.* утончённый (-ён, -ена́). **attenu'ation** *n.* утонче́ние.

attest [ə'test] *v.t.* заверя́ть *impf.*, заве́рить *pf.*; свиде́тельствовать *impf.*, за~ *pf.*

attic ['ætɪk] *n.* манса́рда, черда́к (-а́); (*storey*) мезони́н.

attire [ə'taɪə(r)] *v.t.* наряжа́ть *impf.*, наряди́ть (-яжу́, -я́дишь) *pf.*; *n.* наря́д.

attitude ['ætɪˌtju:d] *n.* (*posture*) по́за; (*opinion*) отноше́ние (**towards** к+*d.*); (~ *of mind*) склад ума́.

attn. [ə'tenʃ(ə)n] *n. abbr.* (*of* **for the attention of**) вним., (внима́нию)+*g.*

attorney [ə'tɜ:nɪ] *n.* пове́ренный *sb.*; **by** ~ че́рез пове́ренного; **power of** ~ дове́ренность; **A~ General** генера́льный атто́рней.

attract [ə'trækt] *v.t.* притя́гивать *impf.*, притяну́ть (-ну́, -нешь) *pf.*; прельща́ть *impf.*, прельсти́ть *pf.*; привлека́ть *impf.*, привле́чь (-еку́, -ечёшь; -ёк, -екла́) *pf.* **attraction** [ə'trækʃ(ə)n] *n.* притяже́ние; привлека́тельность; (*entertainment*) аттракцио́н. **attractive** *adj.* привлека́тельный, притяга́тельный.

attribute [ə'trɪbju:t; 'ætrɪˌbju:t] *v.t.* припи́сывать *impf.*, приписа́ть (-ишу́, -и́шешь) *pf.*; *n.* (*object*) атрибу́т; (*quality*) сво́йство; (*gram.*) определе́ние. **attri'bution** [ˌætrɪ'bju:ʃ(ə)n] *n.* припи́сывание. **a'ttributive** *adj.* атрибути́вный, определи́тельный.

attrition [ə'trɪʃ(ə)n] *n.* истира́ние; **war of** ~

война на истощение.
aubergine ['əʊbəˌʒi:n] *n.* баклажан.
auburn ['ɔ:bən] *adj.* каштанового цвета, рыжеватый.
auction ['ɔ:kʃ(ə)n] *n.* аукцион; *v.t.* продавать (-даю, -даёшь) *impf.*, продать (-ам, -ашь, -аст, -адим; продал, -а, -о) *pf.* с аукциона. **auctio'neer** *n.* аукционист.
audacious [ɔ:'deɪʃəs] *adj.* (*bold*) смелый (смел, -а, -о); (*imprudent*) дерзкий (-зок, -зка, -зко) **audacity** [ɔ:'dæsɪtɪ] *n.* смелость; дерзость.
audibility [ˌɔ:dɪ'bɪlɪtɪ] *n.* слышимость. **'audible** *adj.* слышный (-шен, -шна, -шно). **'audience** *n.* публика, аудитория; (радио)слушатели *m.pl.*, (теле)зрители *m.pl.*; (*interview*) аудиенция.
audio-lingual [ˌɔ:dɪəʊ 'lɪŋgw(ə)l] *adj.* аудиоречевой. **audiotape** *n.* плёнка звукозаписи. **audiotypist** *n.* фономашинистка. **audiovisual** *adj.* аудио-визуальный.
audit ['ɔ:dɪt] *n.* проверка счетов, ревизия; *v.t.* проверять *impf.*, проверить *pf.* (счета+*g.*). **au'dition** *n.* проба; *v.t.* & *i.* устраивать *impf.*, устроить *pf.* пробу+*g.* **'auditor** *n.* ревизор. **auditorium** [ˌɔ:dɪ'tɔ:rɪəm] *n.* зрительный зал, аудитория. **'auditory** *adj.* слуховой.
auger ['ɔ:gə(r)] *n.* бурав (-а), сверло (*pl.* свёрла).
augment [ɔ:g'ment] *n.* увеличивать *impf.*, увеличить *pf.*; прибавлять *impf.*, прибавить *pf.*+*g.* **augmen'tation** *n.* увеличение, прибавка. **augmentative** *adj.* увеличительный.
augur ['ɔ:gə(r)] *v.t.* & *i.* предвещать *impf.*
August ['ɔ:gəst] *n.* август; *attr.* августовский. **august** [ɔ:'gʌst] *adj.* величественный (-ен, -енна).
aunt [ɑ:nt] *n.* тётя (*g.pl.* -тей), тётка. **auntie** *n.* тётушка.
aureole ['ɔ:rɪˌəʊl] *n.* ореол.
auriferous [ɔ:'rɪfərəs] *adj.* золотоносный.
aurochs ['ɔ:rɒks, 'aʊrɒks] *n.* тур.
aurora [ɔ:'rɔ:rə] *n.* аврора; ~ **borealis** северное сияние.
auspices ['ɔ:spɪsɪz] *n.* покровительство. **auspicious** [ɔ:'spɪʃəs] *adj.* благоприятный.
austere [ɒ'stɪə(r), ɔ:'stɪə(r)] *adj.* строгий (строг, -а, -о), суровый. **austerity** [ɒ'sterɪtɪ, ɔ:'sterɪtɪ] *n.* строгость, суровость.
austral ['ɔ:str(ə)l, 'ɒstr(ə)l] *adj.* южный.
Australia [ɒ'streɪlɪə] *n.* Австралия. **Australian** *n.* австралиец (-ийца), -ийка; *adj.* австралийский.
Austria ['ɒstrɪə] *n.* Австрия. **Austrian** *n.* австриец (-ийца), -ийка; *adj.* австрийский.
authentic [ɔ:'θentɪk] *adj.* (*genuine*) подлинный (-нен, -нна), аутентичный; (*reliable*) достоверный. **authenticate** *v.t.* удостоверять *impf.*, удостоверить *pf.*; устанавливать *impf.*, установить (-влю, -вишь) *pf.* подлинность+*g.* **authen'ticity** *n.* подлинность, аутентичность; достоверность.
author ['ɔ:θə(r)] *n.* автор, писатель *m.* ~ница; *v.t.* писать (пишу, -шешь) *impf.* на~ *pf.* **authoress** ['ɔ:θrɪs, ˌɔ:θə'res] *n.* писательница.
authoritarian [ɔ:ˌθɒrɪ'teərɪən] *adj.* авторитарный; *n.* сторонник авторитарной власти **au'thoritative** *adj.* авторитетный. **au'thority** *n.* (*power*) власть (*pl.* -ти, -тей), полномочие; (*evidence*) авторитет; (*source*) авторитетный источник. **'authorize** *v.t.* (*action*) разрешать *impf.*, разрешить *pf.* (*person*) уполномочивать *impf.*, уполномочить *pf.*
authorship ['ɔ:θəʃɪp] *n.* авторство.
auto- [ɔ:təʊ] *in comb.* авто... . **autobio'grapher** *n.* автобиограф. **autobio'graphical** автобиографический. **autobi'ography** *n* автобиография. **autoclave** ['ɔ:təˌkleɪv] *n* автоклав. **autocracy** [ɔ:'tɒkrəsɪ] *n.* автократия. **autocrat** ['ɔ:təˌkræt] *n.* автократ **auto'cratic** *adj.* автократический. **autocross** *n.* автокросс. **Autocue** *n.* (*propr.*) автосуфлёр. **autograph** *n.* автограф; *adj* написанный рукой автора; *v.t.* писать (пишу, -шешь) *impf.*, на~ *pf.* автограф в+*p.*, на+*p.* **automatic** [ˌɔ:tə'mætɪk] *adj.* автоматический; *n.* автоматический пистолет **auto'mation** *n.* автоматизация. **automaton** [ɔ:'tɒmət(ə)n] *n.* автомат. **autonomous** [ɔ:'tɒnəməs] *adj.* автономный. **au'tonomy** *n* автономия. **autopilot** *n.* автопилот. **autopsy** ['ɔ:tɒpsɪ, ɔ:'tɒpsɪ] *n.* вскрытие трупа аутопсия. **autosuggestion** *n.* самовнушение.
autumn ['ɔ:təm] *n.* осень. **autumn(al)** [ɔ:'tʌmn(ə)l] *adj.* осенний.
auxiliary [ɔ:g'zɪljərɪ] *adj.* вспомогательный *n.* помощник, -ица; (*gram.*) вспомогательный глагол; *pl.* вспомогательные войска *nt.pl.*
avail [ə'veɪl] *n.*: **of no** ~ бесполезен (-зна) **to no** ~ напрасно; *v.t.*: ~ **o.s. of** пользоваться *impf.*, вос~ *pf.*+*i.* **available** [ə'veɪləb(ə)l] *adj.* доступный, наличный; *pred* налицо, в наличии.
avalanche ['ævəˌlɑ:nʃ] *n.* лавина.
avarice ['ævərɪs] *n.* жадность. **avaricious** [ˌævə'rɪʃəs] *adj.* жадный (-ден, -дна, -дно).
Av(e). ['ævəˌnju:] *n. abbr.* (*of* **avenue**) пр. (проспект); авеню.
avenge [ə'vendʒ] *v.t.* мстить *impf.*, ото~ *pf* за+*a.* **avenger** *n.* мститель *m.*
avenue ['ævəˌnju:] *n.* (*of trees*) аллея; (*wide street*) проспект; (*approach*) путь (-ти, -тём) *m.*
aver [ə'vɜ:(r)] *v.t.* утверждать *impf.*; заявлять *impf.*, заявить (-влю, -вишь) *pf.*
average ['ævərɪdʒ] *n.* среднее число (*pl.* -ла -сел, -слам), среднее *sb.*; **on** ~ в среднем *adj.* средний; *v.t.* составлять *impf.* в среднем; делать *impf.* в среднем.
averse [ə'vɜ:s] *adj.* нерасположенный (-ен)

несклóнный (-нен, -ннá, -нно); **not ~ to** не прочь+*inf.*, не прóтив+*g.* **aversion** *n.* отвращéние. **avert** *v.t.* (*ward off*) предотвращáть *impf.*, предотвратúть (-ащý, -атúшь) *pf.*; (*turn away*) отводúть (-ожý, -óдишь) *impf.*, отвестú (отведý, -дёшь; отвёл, -á) *pf.*
aviary [ˈeɪvɪərɪ] *n.* птúчник.
aviation [ˌeɪvɪˈeɪʃ(ə)n] *n.* авиáция. **ˈaviator** *n.* лётчик.
avid [ˈævɪd] *adj.* áлчный, жáдный (-ден, -днá, -дно). **aˈvidity** *n.* áлчность, жáдность.
avionics [ˌeɪvɪˈɒnɪks] *n.* авиациóнная электрóника.
avoid [əˈvɔɪd] *v.t.* избегáть *impf.*, избежáть (-егý, -жúшь) *pf.*+*g.*; уклоня́ться *impf.*, уклонúться (-ню́сь, -нишься) *pf.* от+*g.* **avoidance** *n.* избежáние, уклонéние.
avoirdupois [ˌævədəˈpɔɪz; ˌævwɑːdjuːˈpwɑː] *n.* эвердьюпóйс.
avowal [əˈvaʊ(ə)l] *n.* признáние.
await [əˈweɪt] *v.t.* ждать (жду, ждёшь; ждал, -á, -о) *impf.*+*g.*; **'to ~ arrival'** «до востребования».
awake [əˈweɪk] *pred.*: **be ~** не спать (сплю, спишь) *impf.*; **be ~ to** понимáть *impf.*; **stay ~** бóдрствовать *impf.* **awake(n)** *v.t.* пробуждáть *impf.*, пробудúть (-ужý, -ýдишь) *pf.*; *v.i.* просыпáться *impf.*, проснýться *pf.*
award [əˈwɔːd] *v.t.* присуждáть *impf.*, присудúть (-ужý, -ýдишь) *pf.*; награждáть *impf.*, наградúть *pf.*; *n.* (*prize*) нагрáда, прéмия; (*decision*) присуждéние.
aware [əˈweə(r)] *pred.*: **be ~ of** сознавáть (-аю́, -аёшь) *impf.*+*a.*; знать *impf.*+*a.*
away [əˈweɪ] *adv.* прочь; **far ~** (*from*) далекó (от+*g.*); **~ game** игрá (*pl.* -ры) на чужóм пóле; **~ team** комáнда гостéй.
awe [ɔː] *n.* благоговéйный страх; **stand in ~ of** испы́тывать *impf.* благоговéйный трéпет пéред+*i.*; *v.t.* внушáть *impf.*, внушúть *pf.* (благоговéйный) страх+*d.* **awe-struck** *adj.* преиспóлненный (-ен) благоговéйного стрáха, благоговéния. **awful** *adj.* ужáсный, стрáшный (-áшен, -нá, -но, стрáшны́) **awfully** *adv.* ужáсно, óчень, стрáшно.
awkward [ˈɔːkwəd] *adj.* нелóвкий (-вок, -вкá, -вко). **awkwardness** *n.* нелóвкость.
awl [ɔːl] *n.* шúло (*pl.* -лья, -льев)
awning [ˈɔːnɪŋ] *n.* навéс, тент.
AWOL [ˈeɪwɒl] *pred. adj. abbr.* (*of* ***absent without leave***) в самовóльной отлýчке.
awry [əˈraɪ] *adv.* крúво, нáбок; **go ~** провалúться (-ится) *pf.*
axe [æks] *n.* топóр (-á); *v.t.* урéзывать, урезáть *impf.*, урéзать (-éжу, -éжешь) *pf.*
axial [ˈæksɪəl] *adj.* осевóй.
axiom [ˈæksɪəm] *n.* аксиóма. **axioˈmatic** *adj.* аксиоматúческий.
axis [ˈæksɪs], **axle** *n.* ось (*pl.* óси, осéй).
ay [aɪ] *int.* да!; *n.* положúтельный отвéт; (*in vote*) гóлос (*pl.* -á) „за“; **the ~es have it** большинствó „за“.
ayatollah [ˌaɪəˈtɒlə] *n.* аятоллá *m.*
Azerbaijan [ˌæzəbaɪˈdʒɑːn] *n.* Азербайджáн.
azure [ˈæʒə(r), -zjə(r)] *n.* лазýрь; *adj.* лазýрный.

B

B [biː] *n.* (*mus.*) си *nt.indecl.* **BA** *abbr.* (*of* ***Bachelor of Arts***) бакалáвр гуманитáрных наýк.
babble [ˈbæb(ə)l] *n.* (*voices*) болтовня́; (*water*) журчáние; *v.i.* болтáть *impf.*; журчáть (-чúт) *impf.*
babel [ˈbeɪb(ə)l] *n.* галдёж (-á); **tower of B~** столпотворéние вавилóнское.
baboon [bəˈbuːn] *n.* павиáн.
baby [ˈbeɪbɪ] *n.* младéнец (-нца); *adj.* мáлый (мал, -á, мáлó, -ы́), дéтский. **babyish** *adj.* ребя́ческий. **babysitter** *n.* приходя́щая ня́ня.
Bacchanalia [ˌbækəˈneɪlɪə] *n.* вакханáлия. **Bacchanalian** *adj.* вакхúческий.
bachelor [ˈbætʃələ(r)] *n.* холостя́к (-á); (*degree-holder*) бакалáвр; *adj.* холостóй (-ост).
bacillus [bəˈsɪləs] *n.* бацúлла.
back [bæk] *n.* (*of body*) спинá (*a.* -ну; *pl.* -ны); (*rear*) зáдняя часть (*pl.* -ти, -тéй); (*reverse*) оборóт; (*of book*) корешóк (-шкá); (*of seat*) спúнка; (*sport*) защúтник; *adj.* зáдний; (*overdue*) просрóченный (-ен); *v.t.* поддéрживать *impf.*, поддержáть (-жý, -жишь) *pf.*; *v.i.* пя́титься *impf.*, по~ *pf.*; отступáть *impf.*, отступúть (-плю́, -пишь) *pf.*; **~ down** уступáть *impf.*, уступúть (-плю́, -пишь) *pf.*; **~ out** уклоня́ться *impf.*, уклонúться (-ню́сь, -нишься) *pf.* (**of** от+*g.*). **backbiter** *n.* клеветнúк (-á). **backbiting** *n.* клеветá. **backbone** *n.* позвонóчник; (*support*) глáвная опóра; (*firmness*) твёрдость харáктера. **backer** *n.* лицó (*pl.* -ца), субсидúрующее úли поддéрживающее предприя́тие; сторóнник. **background** *n.* фон, зáдний план; (*person's*) воспитáние, происхождéние, окружéние. **backpack** *n.* рюкзáк. **backpacker** *n.* рюкзáчник. **backside** *n.* зад (*loc.* -ý; *pl.* -ы́). **backslider** *n.* ренегáт, рецидивúст. **back-up** *adj.* запаснóй; (*comput.*) резéрвный. **backward** *adj.* отстáлый; *adv.* назáд. **backwash** *n.* откáт (воды́). **backwater** *n.* зáводь, затóн.
bacon [ˈbeɪkən] *n.* бекóн, грудúнка.
bacterium [bækˈtɪərɪəm] *n.* бактéрия.
bad [bæd] *adj.* плохóй (плох, -á, -о, плóхú); (*food etc.*) испóрченный (-ен); (*language*) грýбый (груб, -á, -о); **~ taste** безвкýсица.

badge [bædʒ] *n.* значóк (-чкá), эмблéма.
badger ['bædʒə(r)] *n.* барсýк (-á); *v.t.* приставáть (-таю́, -таёшь) *impf.*, пристáть (-áну, -áнешь) *pf.* к+*d.*; трави́ть (-влю́, -вишь) *impf.*, за~ *pf.*
badly ['bædlɪ] *adv.* плóхо; (*very much*) óчень, си́льно.
baffle ['bæf(ə)l] *v.t.* стáвить *impf.*, по~ *pf.* в тупи́к; приводи́ть (-ожу́, -óдишь) *impf.*, привести́ (-еду́, -едёшь; привёл, -á) *pf.* в недоумéние; *n.* экрáн.
bag [bæg] *n.* мешóк (-шкá), сýмка; *v.t.* (*game*) убивáть *impf.*, уби́ть (убью́, убьёшь) *pf.*; *v.i.* (*clothes*) сидéть (сиди́т) *impf.*, сесть (ся́дет; сел) *pf.* мешкóм.
baggage ['bægɪdʒ] *n.* багáж (-á(ý)); *adj.* багáжный.
baggy ['bægɪ] *adj.* мешковáтый.
bagpipe ['bægpaɪp] *n.* волы́нка. **bagpiper** *n.* волы́нщик.
bail¹ [beɪl] *n.* (*security*) поручи́тельство, залóг; (*surety*) поручи́тель *m.*, -ница; *v.t.* (~ *out*) брать (берý, -рёшь; брал, -á, -о) *impf.*, взять (возьмý, -мёшь; взял, -á, -о) *pf.* на порýки.
bail² [beɪl] *n.* (*cricket*) переклáдина ворóт.
bail³, bale² [beɪl] *v.t.* вычéрпывать *impf.*, вы́черпнуть *pf.* (вóду из+*g.*); ~ **out** *v.i.* выбрáсываться *impf.*, вы́броситься *pf.* с парашю́том. **bailer** *n.* черпáк (-á).
bait [beɪt] *n.* нажи́вка; примáнка (*also fig.*); (*fig.*) соблáзн; *v.t.* (*torment*) трави́ть (-влю́, -вишь) *impf.*, за~ *pf.*
baize [beɪz] *n.* бáйка.
bake [beɪk] *v.t.* печь (пекý, печёшь; пёк, -лá) *impf.*, ис~ *pf.*; (*bricks*) обжигáть *impf.*, обжéчь (обожгý, -жжёшь; обжёг, обожглá) *pf.* **baker** *n.* пéкарь *m.*, бýлочник. **bakery** *n.* пекáрня (*g.pl.* -рен), бýлочная *sb.* **baking** *n.* печéние, вы́печка.
Balaclava [ˌbælə'klɑːvə] *n.*: ~ **(helmet)** вя́заный шлем.
balance ['bæləns] *n.* (*scales*) весы́ *m.pl.*; (*equilibrium*) равновéсие; (*econ.*) бaлáнс; (*remainder*) остáток (-тка); ~ **sheet** балáнс; *v.t.* уравновéшивать *impf.*, уравновéсить *pf.*; (*econ.*) баланси́ровать *impf.*, с~ *pf.*
balcony ['bælkənɪ] *n.* балкóн.
bald [bɔːld] *adj.* лы́сый (лыс, -á, -о), плеши́вый; ~ **patch** лы́сина.
baldness *n.* плеши́вость.
bale¹ [beɪl] *n.* (*bundle*) тюк (-á), ки́па; *v.t.* уклáдывать *impf.*, уложи́ть (-жý, -жишь) *pf.* в тюки́, ки́пы.
bale² [beɪl] *see* **bail³**
baleful ['beɪlfʊl] *adj.* пáгубный, мрáчный (-чен, -чнá, -чно).
balk [bɔːk] *n.* бáлка; (*hindrance*) препя́тствие; *v.t.* препя́тствовать *impf.*, вос~ *pf.*+*d.*
ball¹ [bɔːl] *n.* (*sphere*) мяч (-á), шар (-á *with 2, 3, 4*; *pl.* -ы́); клубóк (-бкá); ~ **and socket** шаровóй шарни́р.
ball² [bɔːl] *n.* (*dancing*) бал (*loc.* -ý; *pl.* -ы́)
ballad ['bæləd] *n.* баллáда; шансóн.
ballast ['bæləst] *n.* баллáст; *v.t.* грузи́ть (-ужý, -ýзи́шь) *impf.*, за~, на~ *pf.* баллáстом.
ball-bearing [ˌbɔːl'beərɪŋ] *n.* шарикоподши́пник.
ballerina [ˌbælə'riːnə] *n.* балери́на.
ballet ['bæleɪ] *n.* балéт. **ballet-dancer** *n.* арти́ст, ~ка, балéта, танцóвщик, -ица.
balloon [bə'luːn] *n.* воздýшный шар (-á *with 2, 3, 4*; *pl.* -ы́); *v.t.* раздувáться *impf.*, раздýться (-ýется) *pf.*
ballot ['bælət] *n.* голосовáние, баллотирóвка. **ballot-paper** *n.* избирáтельный бюллетéнь *m.*; *v.i.* голосовáть *impf.*, про~ *pf.*
ball-point ['bɔːlpɔːnt] *n.* (*pen*) шáриковая рýчка, шáрик.
ballyhoo [ˌbælɪ'huː] *n.* шуми́ха.
balm [bɑːm] *n.* бальзáм. **balmy** *adj.* души́стый.
Baltic ['bɔːltɪk, 'bɒl-] *n.*: **the ~ (Sea)** Балти́йское мóре; ~ **States** прибалти́йские госудáрства, Прибáлтика.
baluster ['bæləstə(r)] *n.* баля́сина. **balu'strade** *n.* балюстрáда.
bamboo [bæm'buː] *n.* бамбýк.
bamboozle [bæm'buːz(ə)l] *v.t.* одурáчивать *impf.*, одурáчить *pf.*
ban [bæn] *n.* запрéт, запрещéние; *v.t.* запрещáть *impf.*, запрети́ть (-ещý, -ети́шь) *pf.*
banal [bə'nɑːl] *adj.* банáльный.
banana [bə'nɑːnə] *n.* банáн.
band [bænd] *n.* (*strip*) óбод (*pl.* ободья, -ьев)), тесьмá, полóска, каймá (*g.pl.* каём); (*of people*) грýппа; (*mus.*) оркéстр; (*radio*) полосá (*a.* пóлосу; *pl.* -осы, -óс, -осáм)) частóт; *v.i.*: ~ **together** объединя́ться *impf.*, объедини́ться *pf.*
bandage ['bændɪdʒ] *n.* бинт (-á), повя́зка; *v.t.* бинтовáть *impf.*, за~ *pf.*
bandit ['bændɪt] *n.* банди́т.
bandoleer [ˌbændə'lɪə(r)] *n.* патронтáш.
bandy ['bændɪ] *v.t.* (*throw about*) перебрáсываться *impf.*, перебрóситься *pf.*+*i.*
bandy-legged ['bændɪˌlegɪd] *adj.* кривонóгий.
bane [beɪn] *n.* (*ruin*) ги́бель; (*poison*; *fig.*) отрáва. **baneful** *adj.* ги́бельный, ядови́тый.
bang [bæŋ] *n.* (*blow*) (си́льный) удáр; (*noise*) (грóмкий) слух; (*of gun*) вы́стрел; *v.t.* ударя́ть *impf.*, удáрить *pf.*; хлóпать *impf.*, хлóпнуть *pf.*; стучáть (-чý, -чи́шь) *impf.*, стýкнуть *pf.*
bangle ['bæŋg(ə)l] *n.* браслéт.
banish ['bænɪʃ] *v.t.* изгоня́ть *impf.*, изгнáть (-гоню́, -гóнишь; изгнáл, -á, -о) *pf.*; высылáть *impf.*, вы́слать (вы́шлю, -шлешь) *pf.* **banishment** *n.* изгнáние, вы́сылка, ссы́лка.
banisters ['bænɪstəz] *n.* пери́ла *nt.pl.*
banjo ['bændʒəʊ] *n.* бáнджо *nt.indecl.*
bank¹ [bæŋk] *n.* (*of river*) бéрег (*loc.* -ý; *pl.* -á); (*in sea*) óтмель; (*of earth*) вал (*loc.* -ý; *pl.* -ы́); (*aeron.*) крен; *v.t.* сгребáть *impf.*, сгрести́ (-ебý, -ебёшь; сгрёб, -лá) *pf.* в кýчу.

bank² [bæŋk] *n.* (*econ.*) банк, фонд; ~ **holiday** устано́вленный пра́здник; *v.i.* (*keep money*) держа́ть (-жу́, -жишь) *impf.* де́ньги (в ба́нке); *v.t.* (*put in* ~) класть (кладу́, -дёшь; клал) *impf.*, положи́ть (-жу́, -жишь) *pf.* в банк; ~ **on** полага́ться *impf.*, положи́ться (-жу́сь, -жишься) *pf.* на+*a.*

bankrupt [ˈbæŋkrʌpt] *n.* банкро́т; *adj.* обанкро́тившийся; *v.t.* доводи́ть (-ожу́, -о́дишь) *impf.*, довести́ (-еду́, -едёшь; -ёл, -ела́) *pf.* до банкро́тства. **bankruptcy** *n.* банкро́тство.

banner [ˈbænə(r)] *n.* зна́мя (*pl.* -ёна) *nt.*, флаг; ~ **headline** ша́пка.

banquet [ˈbæŋkwɪt] *n.* банке́т, пир (*loc.* -у́; *pl.* -ы́).

bantam [ˈbæntəm] *n.* бента́мка. **bantamweight** *n.* легча́йший вес.

banter [ˈbæntə(r)] *n.* подшу́чивание; *v.i.* шути́ть (шучу́, шу́тишь) *impf.*

baptism [ˈbæptɪz(ə)m] *n.* креще́ние. **baptize** [bæpˈtaɪz] *v.t.* крести́ть (-ещу́, -е́стишь) *impf.*, о~ *pf.*

bar [bɑː(r)] *n.* (*beam*) брус (*pl.* -ья, -ьев), полоса́ (*a.* по́лосу́; *pl.* -осы, -о́с, -оса́м); (*of chocolate*) пли́тка; (*of soap*) кусо́к (-ска́); (*barrier*) прегра́да, барье́р; (*leg.*) колле́гия юри́стов; (*counter*) сто́йка; (*room*) бар; (*mus.*) такт; *v.t.* (*obstruct*) прегражда́ть *impf.*, прегради́ть *pf.*; (*prohibit*) запреща́ть *impf.*, запрети́ть (-ещу́, -ети́шь) *pf.*

barb [bɑːb] *n.* зубе́ц (-бца́); ~**ed wire** колю́чая про́волока.

barbarian [bɑːˈbeərɪən] *n.* ва́рвар; *adj.* ва́рварский. **barbaric** [bɑːˈbærɪk], **barbarous** [ˈbɑːbərəs] *adj.* ва́рварский, гру́бый (груб, -а́, -о).

barber [ˈbɑːbə(r)] *n.* парикма́хер; ~**'s shop** парикма́херская *sb.*

bar-code [ˈbɑːkəʊd] *n.* бар-ко́д.

bard [bɑːd] *n.* бард, певе́ц (-вца́).

bare [beə(r)] *adj.* (*naked*) го́лый (гол, -а́, -о); (*barefoot*) босо́й (бос, -а́, -о); (*exposed*) обнажённый (-ён, -ена́); (*unadorned*) неприкра́шенный (-ен); (*scanty*) минима́льный; *v.t.* обнажа́ть *impf.*, обнажи́ть *pf.*; ~ **one's head** снима́ть *impf.*, снять (сниму́, -мешь; снял, -а́, -о) *pf.* шля́пу, ша́пку. **barefaced** *adj.* на́глый (нагл, -а́, -о). **barely** *adv.* едва́, чуть не, е́ле-е́ле, лишь (с трудо́м).

bargain [ˈbɑːgɪn] *n.* вы́годная сле́лка, дешёвая поку́пка; *v.i.* торгова́ться *impf.*, с~ *pf.*

barge [bɑːdʒ] *n.* ба́ржа, ба́рка; *v.i.*: ~ **into** ната́лкиваться *impf.*, натолкну́ться *pf.* на+*a.* **barˈgee** *n.* ло́дочник.

baritone [ˈbærɪˌtəʊn] *n.* барито́н.

barium [ˈbeərɪəm] *n.* ба́рий.

bark¹ [bɑːk] *n.* (*sound*) лай; *v.i.* ла́ять (ла́ю, ла́ешь) *impf.*

bark² [bɑːk] *n.* (*of tree*) кора́.

barley [ˈbɑːlɪ] *n.* ячме́нь (-ня́) *m.*

barm [bɑːm] *n.* заква́ска.

barmaid *n.* буфе́тчица. **barman** *n.* ба́рмен, буфе́тчик.

barn [bɑːn] *n.* амба́р.

barometer [bəˈrɒmɪtə(r)] *n.* баро́метр. **barometric(al)** [ˌbærəʊˈmetrɪk] *adj.* барометри́ческий.

baron [ˈbærən] *n.* баро́н. **baroness** *n.* бароне́сса. **baronet** *n.* бароне́т. **baronial** [bəˈrəʊnɪəl] *adj.* баро́нский.

baroque [bəˈrɒk] *n.* баро́кко *nt.indecl.*

barrack¹ [ˈbærək] *n.* каза́рма.

barrack² [ˈbærək] *v.t.* осви́стывать *impf.*, освиста́ть (-ищу́, -и́щешь) *pf.*

barrage [ˈbærɑːʒ] *n.* загражде́ние, барра́ж.

barrel [ˈbær(ə)l] *n.* (*vessel*) бо́чка; (*of gun*) ду́ло; ~ **organ** шарма́нка.

barren [ˈbærən] *adj.* беспло́дный.

barricade [ˌbærɪˈkeɪd] *n.* баррика́да, прегра́да; *v.t.* баррикади́ровать *impf.*, за~ *pf.*

barrier [ˈbærɪə(r)] *n.* барье́р, прегра́да, шлагба́ум.

barring [ˈbɑːrɪŋ] *prep.* за исключе́нием+*g.*

barrister [ˈbærɪstə(r)] *n.* адвока́т.

barrow¹ [ˈbærəʊ] *n.* (*tumulus*) курга́н.

barrow² [ˈbærəʊ] *n.* (*cart*) та́чка.

barter [ˈbɑːtə(r)] *n.* менова́я торго́вля; *v.i.* обме́ниваться *impf.*, обменя́ться *pf.* това́рами.

base¹ [beɪs] *n.* осно́ва, основа́ние; (*also mil.*) ба́за; *v.t.* осно́вывать *impf.*, основа́ть (-ную́, -нуёшь) *pf.* **baseless** *adj.* необосно́ванный. **baseline** *n.* (*sport*) за́дняя ли́ния площа́дки. **basement** *n.* цо́кольный эта́ж (-а́), подва́л.

base² [beɪs] *adj.* (*low*) ни́зкий (-зок, -зка́, -зко), по́длый (подл, -а́, -о); (*metal*, *also fig.*) низкопро́бный.

bash [bæʃ] *v.t.* колоти́ть (-очу́, -о́тишь) *impf.*, по~ *pf.*

bashful [ˈbæʃfʊl] *adj.* засте́нчивый. **bashfulness** *n.* засте́нчивость.

basic [ˈbeɪsɪk] *adj.* основно́й.

basil [ˈbæz(ə)l] *n.* базили́к.

basin [ˈbeɪs(ə)n] *n.* (*vessel*) ми́ска, таз (*loc.* -у́; *pl.* -ы́); (*geog.*, *geol.*) бассе́йн; (*pool*) водоём.

basis [ˈbeɪsɪs] *n.* ба́зис, осно́ва.

bask [bɑːsk] *v.i.* гре́ться *impf.*; (*fig*) наслажда́ться *impf.*, наслади́ться *pf.* (**in** +*i.*).

basket [ˈbɑːskɪt] *n.* корзи́на, корзи́нка. **basketball** *n.* баскетбо́л; *adj.* баскетбо́льный.

bas-relief [ˌbɑː rɪˈliːf] *n.* барелье́ф.

bass¹ [beɪs] *n.* (*mus.*) бас (*pl.* -ы́); *adj.* басо́вый; ~ **drum** большо́й бараба́н.

bass² [bæs] *n.* (*fish*) о́кунь (*pl.* -ни, -не́й) *m.*

bassoon [bəˈsuːn] *n.* фаго́т.

bastard [ˈbɑːstəd, ˈbæ-] *n.* внебра́чный, побо́чный, ребёнок (-нка; *pl.* де́ти, дете́й); *adj.* незаконнорождённый.

baste¹ [beɪst] *v.t.* (*tack*) мета́ть *impf.*, на~, с~ *pf.*

baste² [beɪst] *v.t.* (*cul.*) полива́ть *impf.*, поли́ть (-лью́, -льёшь) *pf.* жи́ром.

bastion [ˈbæstɪən] *n.* бастио́н.

bat¹ [bæt] *n.* (*zool.*) летýчая мышь (*pl.* -ши, -шéй).
bat² [bæt] *n.* (*sport*) битá; *v.i.* бить (бью, бьёшь) *impf.*, по~ *pf.* по мячý.
bat³ [bæt] *v.t.* (*wink*) моргáть *impf.*, моргнýть *pf.+i.*, *abs.*
batch [bætʃ] *n.* пáчка; (*of loaves*) вы́печка.
bated ['beɪtɪd] *adj.* умéренный (-ен); **with ~ breath** затаи́в дыхáние.
bath [bɑːθ] *n.* (*vessel*) вáнна; *pl.* плáвательный бассéйн; **~ robe** купáльный халáт; *v.t.* купáть *impf.*, вы́~, ис~ *pf.* **bathe** [beɪð] *v.i.* купáться *impf.*, вы́~, ис~ *pf.*; *v.t.* омывáть *impf.*, омы́ть (омóю, омóешь) *pf.* **bather** *n.* купáльщик, -ица. **bathhouse** *n.* бáня. **bathing** *n.* купáние; **~ costume** купáльный костю́м. **bathroom** *n.* вáнная *sb.*
batiste [bæ'tiːst] *n.* бати́ст.
batman ['bætmən] *n.* (*mil.*) денщи́к (-á).
baton ['bæt(ə)n] *n.* (*mil.*) жезл (-á); (*police*) дуби́нка; (*sport*) эстафéта; (*mus.*) дирижёрская пáлочка.
battalion [bə'tælɪən] *n.* батальóн.
batten ['bæt(ə)n] *n.* рéйка; *v.t.* заколáчивать *impf.*, заколоти́ть (-очý, -óтишь) *pf.* доскáми.
batter ['bætə(r)] *n.* жи́дкое тéсто; *v.t.* разбивáть *impf.*, разби́ть (разобью́, -ьёшь) *pf.*; размозжи́ть *pf.*; **~ing ram** тарáн.
battery ['bætərɪ] *n.* (*mil.*, *tech.*) батарéя; (*leg.*) оскорблéние дéйствием.
battle ['bæt(ə)l] *n.* би́тва, сражéние, бой (*loc.* бою́; *pl.* бои́); *adj.* боевóй. **battlefield** *n.* пóле (*pl.* -ля́) бóя. **battlement** *n.* зубчáтая стенá (*a.* -ну; *pl.* -ны, -н, -нáм). **battleship** *n.* линéйный корáбль (-ля́) *m.*, линкóр.
bauble ['bɔːb(ə)l] *n.* безделýшка.
bawdy ['bɔːdɪ] *adj.* непристóйный.
bawl [bɔːl] *v.i.* орáть (орý, орёшь) *impf.*
bay¹ [beɪ] *n.* (*bot.*) лáвр(овое дéрево); *pl.* лаврóвый венóк (-нкá), лáвры *m.pl.*; *adj.* лаврóвый.
bay² [beɪ] *n.* (*geog.*) зали́в, бýхта.
bay³ [beɪ] *n.* (*recess*) пролёт; **~ window** фонáрь (-ря́) *m.*; **sick ~** лазарéт.
bay⁴ [beɪ] *v.i.* (*bark*) лáять (лáю, лáешь) *impf.*; (*howl*) выть (вóю, вóешь) *impf.*; *n.* лай; вой.
bay⁵ [beɪ] *adj.* (*colour*) гнедóй.
bayonet ['beɪəˌnet] *n.* штык (-á); *v.t.* колóть (-лю́, -лешь) *impf.*, за~ *pf.* штыкóм.
bazaar [bə'zɑː(r)] *n.* базáр.
BBC *abbr.* (*of* ***British Broadcasting Corporation***) Би-Би-Си́ *nt. indecl.*.
BC *abbr.* (*of* ***before Christ***) до н.э., до нáшей э́ры.
be¹ [biː, bɪ] *v.* **1.** быть (*fut.* бýду, -дешь; был, -á, -о; нé был, -á, -о): *usually omitted in pres.*: **he is a teacher** он учи́тель; *+i. or nom. in past and fut.*: **he was, will ~, a teacher** он был, бýдет учи́телем. **2.** (*exist*) существовáть *impf.* **3.** (*frequentative*) бывать *impf.* **4.** (*~ situated*) находи́ться (-ожýсь, -óдишься) *impf.*: **where is the information office?** где нахóдится спрáвочное бюрó?; (*upright*) стоя́ть (стою́, -ои́шь) *impf.*: **the piano is against the wall** роя́ль стои́т у стены́; (*laid flat*) лежáть (-жý, -жи́шь) *impf.*: **the letter is on the table** письмó лежи́т на столé. **5.** (*in general definitions*) явля́ться *impf.+i.*: **Moscow is the capital of Russia** столи́цей Росси́и явля́ется гóрод Москвá. **6.: there is, are** имéется, имéются; (*emph.*) есть.
be² [biː, bɪ] *v.aux.* **1.** *be+inf.*, *expressing duty, plan*: дóлжен (-жнá)+*inf.*: **he is to leave on Monday** он дóлжен отпрáвиться в понедéльник. **2.** *be+past part. pass.*, *expressing passive*: быть+*past part.pass. in short form*: **this was made by my son** э́то бы́ло сдéлано мои́м сы́ном; *impers. construction of 3 pl.+a.*: **I was beaten** меня́ би́ли; *reflexive construction*: **music was heard** слы́шалась мýзыка. **3.** *be+pres.part. act.*, *expressing continuous tenses*: *imperfect aspect*: **I am reading** я читáю.
beach [biːtʃ] *n.* пляж, бéрег (*loc.* -ý; *pl.* -á). **beachhead** *n.* плацдáрм; *v.t.* вытáскивать *impf.*, вы́тащить *pf.* на бéрег.
beacon ['biːkən] *n.* мая́к (-á), сигнáльный огóнь (огня́) *m.*
bead [biːd] *n.* бýсина; (*of liquid*) кáпля (*g.pl.* -пель); *pl.* бýсы *f.pl.*
beadle ['biːd(ə)l] *n.* церкóвный стóрож (*pl.* -á).
beagle ['biːg(ə)l] *n.* бигль*m.*, англи́йская гóнчая *sb.*
beak [biːk] *n.* клюв.
beaker ['biːk(ə)r] *n.* стакáн.
beam [biːm] *n.* (*timber etc.*) бáлка; (*ray*) луч (-á); (*naut.*) бимс; (*breadth*) ширинá; *v.t.* испускáть *impf.*, испусти́ть (-ущý, -ýстишь) *pf.*; *v.i.* (*shine*) сия́ть *impf.*
bean [biːn] *n.* фасóль, боб (-á).
bear¹ [beə(r)] *n.* медвéдь *m.*, -дица; **Great, Little, B~** Большáя, Мáлая, Медвéдица; **~ cub** медвежóнок (-жóнка; *pl.* -жáта, -жáт).
bear² [beə(r)] *v.t.* (*carry*) носи́ть (ношý, нóсишь) *indet.*, нести́ (несý, -сёшь; нёс, -лá) *det.*, по~ *pf.*; (*support*) поддéрживать *impf.*, поддержáть (-жý, -жишь) *pf.*; (*endure*) терпéть (-плю́, -пишь) *impf.*; выноси́ть (-ошý, -óсишь) *impf.*, вы́нести (-су, -сешь; -с) *pf.*; (*give birth to*) рождáть *impf.*, роди́ть *impf.* & *pf.* (*pf.* роди́л, -á, -о). **bearable** *adj.* снóсный, терпи́мый.
beard ['bɪəd] *n.* бородá (*a.* -оду; *pl.* -оды, -óд, -одáм). **bearded** *adj.* бородáтый.
bearer ['beərə(r)] *n.* носи́тель *m.*; (*of cheque*) предъяви́тель *m.*; (*of letter*) подáтель *m.*
bearing ['beərɪŋ] *n.* ношéние; (*behaviour*) поведéние; (*relation*) отношéние; (*position*) пéленг; (*tech.*) подши́пник, опóра.
beast [biːst] *n.* живóтное *sb.*, зверь (*pl.* -ри, -рéй) *m.*; (*fig.*) скоти́на *c.g.* **beastly** *adj.* (*coll.*) проти́вный, отврати́тельный.
beat [biːt] *n.* бой; (*round*) обхóд; (*mus.*) такт; *v.t.* бить (бью, бьёшь) *impf.*, по~ *pf.*; (*cul.*)

взбива́ть *impf.*, взбить (взобью́, -ьёшь) *pf.*; ~ **a carpet** выбива́ть *impf.*, вы́бить (-бью, -бьешь) *pf.* ковёр; ~ **off** отбива́ть *impf.*, отби́ть (отобью́, -ьёшь) *pf.*; ~ **time** отбива́ть *impf.*, отби́ть (отобью́, -ьёшь) *pf.* такт; ~ **up** избива́ть *impf.*, изби́ть (изобью́, -ьёшь) *pf.* **beating** *n.* битьё; (*defeat*) пораже́ние; бие́ние.

beatific [ˌbiːəˈtɪfɪk] *adj.* блаже́нный (-е́н, -е́нна). **beatify** [biːˈætɪˌfaɪ] *v.t.* канонизи́ровать *impf.* & *pf.* **be'atitude** *n.* блаже́нство.

beau [bəʊ] *n.* (*fop*) франт; (*ladies' man*) ухажёр.

beautiful [ˈbjuːtɪˌfʊl] *adj.* краси́вый, прекра́сный. **beautify** *v.t.* украша́ть *impf.* укра́сить *pf.* **beauty** *n.* (*quality*) красота́; (*person*) краса́вица.

beaver [ˈbiːvə(r)] *n.* (*animal*) бобр (-а́); (*fur*) бобёр (-бра́), бобро́вый мех (-а(у), *loc.* -е & -у́; *pl.* -а́).

becalmed [bɪˈkɑːmd] *adj.*: **be** ~ штилева́ть (-лю́ю, -лю́ешь) *impf.*

because [bɪˈkɒz] *conj.* потому́, что; так как; *adv.*: ~ **of** из-за́+*g.*

beckon [ˈbekən] *v.t.* мани́ть (-ню́, -нишь) *impf.*, по~ *pf.* к себе́.

become [bɪˈkʌm] *v.i.* станови́ться (-влю́сь, -вишься) *impf.*, стать (-а́ну, -а́нешь) *pf.*+*i.*; ~ **of** ста́ться (-а́нется) *pf.* с+*i.* **becoming** *adj.* подоба́ющий, иду́щий к лицу́+*d.*

bed [bed] *n.* крова́ть, посте́ль; (*garden*) гря́дка; (*sea*) дно, *pl.* до́нья, -ьев; (*river*) ру́сло; (*geol.*) пласт (-а́, *loc.* -у́). **bedclothes, bedding** *n.* посте́льное бельё. **bedridden** *adj.* прико́ванный (-на) к посте́ли боле́знью. **bedrock** *n.* материко́вая поро́да. **bedroom** *n.* спа́льня (*g.pl.* -лен). **bedtime** *nt.* вре́мя *nt.* ложи́ться спать.

bedeck [bɪˈdek] *v.t.* украша́ть *impf.*, укра́сить *pf.*

bedevil [bɪˈdev(ə)l] *v.t.* терза́ть *impf.*; му́чить *impf.*, за~ *pf.*

bedlam [ˈbedləm] *n.* бедла́м, сумасше́дший дом.

bedraggled [bɪˈdræg(ə)ld] *adj.* заво́женный (-ен).

bee [biː] *n.* пчела́ (*pl.* -ёлы). **beehive** *n.* у́лей (у́лья).

beech [biːtʃ] *n.* бук.

beef [biːf] *n.* говя́дина. **beefburger** *n.* ру́бленый бифште́кс.

beer [bɪə(r)] *n.* пи́во. **beer(y)** *adj.* пивно́й.

beep [biːp] *n.* гудо́к; *v.i.* гуде́ть (-ди́т) *impf.*

beet [biːt] *n.* свёкла.

beetle [ˈbiːt(ə)l] *n.* жук (-а́).

beetroot [ˈbiːtruːt] *n.* свёкла.

befall [bɪˈfɔːl] *v.t.* & *i.* случа́ться *impf.*, случи́ться *pf.* (+*d.*).

befit [bɪˈfɪt] *v.t.* подходи́ть (-ит) *impf.*, подойти́ (-ойдёт; -ошёл, -ошла́) *pf.*+*d.*

before [bɪˈfɔː(r)] *adv.* пре́жде, ра́ньше; *prep.* пе́ред+*i.*, до+*g.*; *conj.* до того́ как; пре́жде чем; (*rather than*) скоре́е чем; **the day** ~ **yesterday** позавчера́. **beforehand** *adv.* зара́нее, вперёд.

befriend [bɪˈfrend] *v.t.* ока́зывать *impf.*, оказа́ть (-ажу́, -а́жешь) *pf.* дру́жескую по́мощь+*d.*

beg [beg] *v.i.* ни́щенствовать *impf.*; *v.t.* (*ask*) проси́ть (-ошу́, -о́сишь) *impf.*, по~ *pf.*; (*of dog*) служи́ть (-ит) *impf.*; ~ **pardon** проси́ть (-ошу́, -о́сишь) *impf.* проще́ние.

beget [bɪˈget] *v.t.* порожда́ть *impf.*, породи́ть *pf.*

beggar [ˈbegə(r)] *n.* ни́щий *sb.*; *v.t.* разоря́ть *impf.*, разори́ть *pf.* **beggarliness** *n.* нищета́. **beggarly** *adj.* (*poor*) бе́дный (-ден, -дна́, -дно); (*mean*) жа́лкий (-лок, -лка́, -лко).

begin [bɪˈgɪn] *v.t.* начина́ть *impf.*, нача́ть (-чну́, -чнёшь; на́чал, -а́, -о) *pf.*; *v.i.* начина́ться *impf.*, нача́ться (-чну́сь, -чнёшься; -алcя́, -ала́сь) *pf.* **beginner** *n.* начина́ющий *sb.*, новичо́к (-чка́). **beginning** *n.* нача́ло.

begonia [bɪˈgəʊnjə] *n.* бего́ния.

begrudge [bɪˈgrʌdʒ] *v.t.* (*spare*) скупи́ться *impf.*, по~ *pf.* на+*a.*, +*inf.*

beguile [bɪˈgaɪl] *v.t.* (*amuse*) развлека́ть *impf.*, развле́чь (-еку́, -ечёшь; -ёк, -екла́) *pf.*

behalf [bɪˈhɑːf] *n.*: **on** ~ **of** от и́мени+*g.*; (*in interest of*) в по́льзу+*g.*

behave [bɪˈheɪv] *v.i.* вести́ (веду́, -дёшь; вёл, -а́) *impf.* себя́. **behaviour** *n.* поведе́ние.

behead [bɪˈhed] *v.t.* обезгла́вливать *impf.*, обезгла́вить *pf.*

behest [bɪˈhest] *n.* заве́т.

behind [bɪˈhaɪnd] *adv.*, *prep.* сза́ди (+*g.*), позади́ (+*g.*), за (+*a.*, *i.*); *n.* зад (*loc.* -у́; *pl.* -ы́).

behold [bɪˈhəʊld] *int.* се! **beholden** *pred.*: ~ **to** обя́зан+*d.*

beige [beɪʒ] *adj.* беж *indecl.*, бе́жевый.

Beijing [beɪˈdʒɪŋ] *n.* Пеки́н.

being [ˈbiːɪŋ] *n.* (*existence*) бытие́ (*i.* -ие́м, *p.* -ии́); (*creature*) существо́; **for the time** ~ на не́которое вре́мя; вре́менно.

belabour [bɪˈleɪbə(r)] *v.t.* бить (бью, бьёшь) *impf.*, по~ *pf.*

Belarus [beləˈrʌs] *n.* Белару́сь.

belated [bɪˈleɪtɪd] *adj.* запозда́лый.

belch [beltʃ] *n.* отры́жка; *v.i.* рыга́ть *impf.*, рыгну́ть *pf.*; *v.t.* изверга́ть *impf.*, изве́ргнуть (-г(нул), -гла) *pf.*

beleaguer [bɪˈliːgə(r)] *v.t.* осажда́ть *impf.*, осади́ть *pf.*

belfry [ˈbelfrɪ] *n.* колоко́льня (*g.pl.* -лен).

Belgium [ˈbeldʒəm] *n.* Бе́льгия.

belie [bɪˈlaɪ] *v.t.* противоре́чить *impf.*+*d.*

belief [bɪˈliːf] *n.* (*faith*) ве́ра; (*confidence*) убежде́ние. **believable** *adj.* вероя́тный, правдоподо́бный. **believe** *v.t.* ве́рить *impf.*, по~ *pf.*+*d.*; **I** ~ **so** ка́жется так; **I** ~ **not** ду́маю, что нет; едва́ ли.

belittle [bɪˈlɪt(ə)l] *v.t.* умаля́ть *impf.*, умали́ть *pf.*

bell [bel] *n.* ко́локол (*pl.* -а́); (*small*) колоко́льчик, бубе́нчик; ~ **tower** колоко́льня

(*g.pl.* -лен). **bell-bottomed** *adj.*: ~ **trousers** брю́ки (-к) *pl.* с растру́бами.
belle [bel] *n.* краса́вица.
belles-lettres [bel 'letr] *n.* худо́жественная литерату́ра.
bellicose ['belɪ,kəʊz] *adj.* вои́нственный (-ен, -енна), агресси́вный. **belligerency** [bɪ'lɪdʒərənsɪ] *n.* вои́нственность. **belligerent** *n.* вою́ющая сторона́ (*a.* -ону; *pl.* -оны, -о́н, -она́м); *adj.* вою́ющий.
bellow ['beləʊ] *n.* мыча́ние, рев; *v.t. & i.* мыча́ть (-чу́, -чи́шь *impf.*; реве́ть (-ву́, -вёшь) *impf.*
bellows ['beləʊz] *n.* мехи́ *m.pl.*
bell-ringer ['belrɪŋə(r)] *n.* звона́рь (-ря́) *m.*
belly ['belɪ] *n.* живо́т (-а́), брю́хо (*pl.* -хи).
belong [bɪ'lɒŋ] *v.i.* принадлежа́ть (-жу́, -жи́шь) *impf.* (**to** (к)+*d.*). **belongings** [bɪ'lɒŋɪŋz] *n.* пожи́тки (-ков) *pl.*, ве́щи (-ще́й) *f.pl.*
beloved [bɪ'lʌvɪd, *pred. also* -lʌvd] *adj.* люби́мый, возлю́бленный (-ен, -енна).
below [bɪ'ləʊ] *adv.* вниз, внизу́, ни́же; *prep.* ни́же+*g.*
belt [belt] *n.* (*strap*) по́яс (*pl.* -а́), реме́нь (-мня́); (*zone*) зо́на, полоса́ (*a.* -осу; *pl.* -осы, -о́с, -оса́м); *v.t.* подпоя́сывать *impf.*, подпоя́сать (-я́шу, -я́шешь) *pf.*
bench [bentʃ] *n.* (*seat*) скамья́ (*pl.* ска́мьи́, -ме́й), скаме́йка; (*for work*) стано́к (-нка́); (*court*) полице́йские су́дьи (*g.* -де́й) *pl.*; (*parl.*) ме́сто (*pl.* -та́); **back ~es** ска́мьи́ рядовы́х чле́нов парла́мента.
bend [bend] *n.* сгиб, изги́б, накло́н; *v.t.* сгиба́ть *impf.*, согну́ть *pf.*
beneath [bɪ'ni:θ] *prep.* под+*i.*
benediction [,benɪ'dɪkʃ(ə)n] *n.* благослове́ние.
benefaction [,benɪ'fækʃ(ə)n] *n.* ми́лость, дар (*pl.* -ы́). **benefactor** *n.* благоде́тель *m.*
benefice ['benɪfɪs] *n.* бенефи́ция. **be'neficence** *n.* благодея́ние, милосе́рдие. **be'neficent** *adj.* благотво́рный, поле́зный.
bene'ficial *adj.* поле́зный, вы́годный. **bene'ficiary** *n.* лицо́ (*pl.* -ца), получа́ющее дохо́ды; (*in will*) насле́дник. **benefit** *n.* по́льза, вы́года; (*allowance*) посо́бие; (*theatr.*) бенефи́с; *v.t.* приноси́ть (-ошу́, -о́сишь) *impf.*, принести́ (-есу́, -есёшь; -ёс, -есла́) *pf.* по́льзу+*d.*; *v.i.* извлека́ть *impf.*, извле́чь (-еку́, -ечёшь; -ёк, -екла́) *pf.* вы́году.
be'nevolence *n.* благожела́тельность, благодея́ние. **be'nevolent** *adj.* благоскло́нный (-нен, -нна), благотвори́тельный.
benign [bɪ'naɪn] *adj.* до́брый (добр, -а́, -о, -ы́), мя́гкий (мя́гок, мягка́, мя́гко, мя́гки́); (*of tumour*) доброка́чественный (-нен, -нна).
bent [bent] *n.* скло́нность, накло́нность.
benumbed [bɪ'nʌmd] *adj.* окочене́вший, оцепене́лый.
benzene ['benzi:n] *n.* бензо́л.
bequeath [bɪ'kwi:ð] *v.t.* завеща́ть *impf. & pf.* (+*a.* & *d.*). **bequest** *n.* насле́дство, посме́ртный дар (*pl.* -ы́).
berate [bɪ'reɪt] *v.t.* руга́ть *impf.*, вы́~ *pf.*
bereave [bɪ'ri:v] *v.t.* лиша́ть *impf.*, лиши́ть *pf.* (**of** +*g.*). **bereavement** *n.* поте́ря (бли́зкого).
Berlin [bɜ:'lɪn] *n.* Берли́н.
berry ['berɪ] *n.* я́года.
berserk [bə'sɜ:k, -'zɜ:k] *adj.* неи́стовый; **go ~** неи́стовствовать *impf.*
berth [bɜ:θ] *n.* (*bunk*) ко́йка; (*naut.*) стоя́нка; **give a wide ~ to** обходи́ть (-ожу́, -о́дишь) *impf.*; избега́ть *impf.*, избе́гнуть (избе́г(нул), -гла) *pf.*+*g.*; *v.t.* ста́вить *impf.*, по~ *pf.* на я́корь, на прича́л.
beryl ['berɪl] *n.* бери́лл.
beseech [bɪ'si:tʃ] *v.t.* умоля́ть *impf.*, умоли́ть *pf.* **beseeching** *adj.* умоля́ющий.
beset [bɪ'set] *v.t.* осажда́ть *impf.*, осади́ть *pf.*
beside [bɪ'saɪd] *prep.* о́коло+*g.*, во́зле+*g.*, ря́дом с+*i.*; **~ the point** некста́ти; **~ o.s.** вне себя́. **besides** *adv.* кро́ме того́, поми́мо; *prep.* кро́ме+*g.*
besiege [bɪ'si:dʒ] *v.t.* осажда́ть *impf.*, осади́ть *pf.*
besom ['bi:z(ə)m] *n.* садо́вая метла́ (*pl.* мётлы, -тел, -тлам), ве́ник.
besotted [bɪ'sɒtɪd] *adj.* одуре́лый.
bespoke [bɪ'spəʊk] *adj.* зака́занный (-ан); **~ tailor** портно́й *sb.*, рабо́тающий на зака́з.
best [best] *adj.* лу́чший, са́мый лу́чший; *adv.* лу́чше всего́, бо́льше всего́; **do one's ~** де́лать *impf.*, с~ *pf.* всё возмо́жное; **~ man** ша́фер (*pl.* -а́). **bestseller** *n.* бестсе́ллер, хо́дкая кни́га.
bestial ['bestɪəl] *adj.* ско́тский, зве́рский. **bestiality** [,bestɪ'ælɪtɪ] *n.* ско́тство, зве́рство.
bestow [bɪ'stəʊ] *v.t.* дарова́ть *impf. & pf.*
bestride [bɪ'straɪd] *v.t.* (*sit*) сиде́ть (сижу́, сиди́шь) *impf.* верхо́м на+*p.*; (*stand*) стоя́ть (-ою́, -ои́шь) *impf.*, расста́вив но́ги над+*i.*
bet [bet] *n.* пари́ *nt.indecl.*; (*stake*) ста́вка; *v.t.* держа́ть (-жу́, -жишь) *impf.* пари́ (на+*a.*). **betting** *n.* заключе́ние пари́.
betide [bɪ'taɪd] *v.t. & i.* случа́ться *impf.*, случи́ться *pf.* (+*d.*); **whate'er ~** что бы ни случи́лось; **woe ~ you** го́ре тебе́.
betray [bɪ'treɪ] *v.t.* изменя́ть *impf.*, измени́ть (-ню́, -нишь) *pf.*+*d.*; предава́ть (-даю́, -даёшь) *impf.*, преда́ть (-а́м, -а́шь, -а́ст, -ади́м; пре́дал, -а́, -о) *pf.* **betrayal** *n.* изме́на, преда́тельство.
betroth [bɪ'trəʊð] *v.t.* обруча́ть *impf.*, обручи́ть *pf.* **betrothal** *n.* обруче́ние.
better ['betə(r)] *adj.* лу́чший; *adv.* лу́чше; (*more*) бо́льше; *v.t.* улучша́ть *impf.*, улу́чшить *pf.*; **get the ~ of** брать (беру́, -рёшь; брал, -а́, -о)) *impf.*, взять (возьму́, -мёшь; взял, -а́, -о) *pf.* верх над+*i.*; **had ~: you had ~ go** вам (*d.*) лу́чше бы пойти́; **think ~ of** переду́мывать *impf.*, переду́мать *pf.* **betterment** *n.* улучше́ние.
between [bɪ'twi:n] *prep.* ме́жду+*i.*

bevel ['bev(ə)l] *n.* (*tool*) ма́ска.
beverage ['bevərɪdʒ] *n.* напи́ток (-тка).
bevy ['bevɪ] *n.* собра́ние, компа́ния.
bewail [bɪ'weɪl] *v.t.* сокруша́ться *impf.*, сокруши́ться *pf.* о+*p.*
beware [bɪ'weə(r)] *v.i.* остерега́ться *impf.*, остере́чься (-егу́сь, -ежёшься; -ёгся, -егла́сь) *pf.* (**of** +*g.*).
bewilder [bɪ'wɪldə(r)] *v.t.* сбива́ть *impf.*, сбить (собью́, -ьёшь) *pf.* с то́лку. **bewildered** *adj.* смущённый (-ён, -ена́), озада́ченный (-ен). **bewilderment** *n.* смуще́ние, замеша́тельство.
bewitch [bɪ'wɪtʃ] *v.t.* заколдо́вывать *impf.*, заколдова́ть *pf.*; очаро́вывать *impf.*, очарова́ть *pf.* **bewitching** *adj.* очарова́тельный.
beyond [bɪ'jɒnd] *prep.* за+*a.* & *i.*; по ту сто́рону+*g.*; (*above*) сверх+*g.*; (*outside*) вне+*g.*; **the back of ~** глушь (-ши́), край (*loc.* -аю́) све́та.
bias ['baɪəs] *n.* (*inclination*) укло́н; (*prejudice*) предупрежде́ние; **to cut on the ~** крои́ть *impf.*, с~ *pf.* по косо́й. **biased** *adj.* предупреждённый (-ён, -ена́).
bib [bɪb] *n.* нагру́дник.
Bible ['baɪb(ə)l] *n.* Би́блия. **biblical** ['bɪblɪk(ə)l] *adj.* библе́йский.
bibliography [ˌbɪblɪ'ɒgrəfɪ] *n.* библиогра́фия.
bibliophile ['bɪblɪəʊˌfaɪl] *n.* библиофи́л.
bibulous ['bɪbjʊləs] *adj.* пья́нствующий.
bicarbonate (of soda) [baɪ'kɑːbənɪt] *n.* со́да.
bicentenary [ˌbaɪsen'tiːnərɪ] *n.* двухсотле́тие; *adj.* двухсотле́тний.
biceps ['baɪseps] *n.* би́цепс, двугла́вая мы́шца.
bicker ['bɪkə(r)] *v.i.* пререка́ться *impf.*; препира́ться *impf.* **bickering** *n.* пререка́ния *nt.pl.*, ссо́ры *f.pl.* из-за мелоче́й.
bicycle ['baɪsɪk(ə)l] *n.* велосипе́д.
bid [bɪd] *n.* предложе́ние цены́, зая́вка; *v.t.* & *i.* предлага́ть *impf.*, предложи́ть (-жу́, -жишь) *pf.* (це́ну) (**for** за+*a.*); *v.t.* (*command*) прика́зывать *impf.*, приказа́ть (-ажу́, -а́жешь) *pf.*+*d.* **bidding** *n.* предложе́ние цены́, торги́ *m.pl.*; (*command*) прика́зание.
bide [baɪd] *v.t.*: **~ one's time** ожида́ть *impf.* подходя́щего моме́нта.
biennial [baɪ'enɪəl] *adj.* двухле́тний; *n.* двухле́тник.
bier [bɪə(r)] *n.* (похоро́нные) дро́ги (-г) *pl.*
bifocal [baɪ'fəʊk(ə)l] *adj.* двухфо́кусный.
big [bɪg] *adj.* большо́й, кру́пный (-пен, -пна́, -пно, кру́пны́); (*important*) ва́жный (-жен, -жна́, -жно, ва́жны́); **~ business** де́ло большо́го масшта́ба; **~ end** больша́я, ни́жняя, кривоши́пная голо́вка; **~ name** знамени́тость; **~ noise** ши́шка; **~ top** цирк; **talk ~** хва́статься *impf.*
bigamist ['bɪgəmɪst] *n.* (*man*) двоеже́нец (-нца); (*woman*) двуму́жница. **bigamous** *adj.* двубра́чный. **bigamy** *n.* двубра́чие.
bike [baɪk] *n.* велосипе́д; (*motorcycle*) мотоци́кл; *v.i.* е́здить *indet.*, е́хать (е́ду, е́дешь) *det.*, по~ на мотоци́кле. **biker** *n.* мотоцикли́ст, ~ка. **bikeway** *n.* велосипе́дная доро́жка.
bikini [bɪ'kiːnɪ] *n.* бики́ни *nt.indecl.*
bilateral [baɪ'lætər(ə)l] *adj.* двусторо́нний.
bilberry ['bɪlbərɪ] *n.* черни́ка.
bile [baɪl] *n.* жёлчь. **bilious** ['bɪljəs] *adj.* жёлчный.
bilge [bɪldʒ] *n.* (*sl.*) ерунда́.
bilingual [baɪ'lɪŋgw(ə)l] *adj.* двуязы́чный. **bilingualism** *n.* двуязы́чие.
bill [bɪl] *n.* (*account*) счёт (*pl.* -а́); (*draft of law*) законопрое́кт; (**~** *of exchange*) ве́сель (*pl.* -ля́); (*theatr.*) програ́мма; (*poster*) афи́ша; *v.t.* (*announce*) объявля́ть *impf.*, объяви́ть (-влю́, -вишь) *pf.* в афи́шах; раскле́ивать *impf.*, раскле́ить *pf.* афи́ши+*g.*; **~ of fare** меню́ *nt.indecl.*; **~ of health** санита́рное удостовере́ние; **~ of lading** накладна́я *sb.*; **B~ of Rights** билль *m.* о права́х.
billet ['bɪlɪt] *n.* помеще́ние для посто́я, кварти́ры *f.pl.*; *v.t.* расквартиро́вывать *impf.*, расквартирова́ть *pf.*; **~ing officer** квартирье́р.
billhead ['bɪlhed] *n.* бланк.
billiard-ball ['bɪljəd] *n.* билья́рдный шар (-а́ with *2,3,4*; *pl.* -ы́). **billiard-cue** *n.* кий (кия́; *pl.* кии́). **billiard-room** *n.* бильярдная *sb.* **billiard-table, billiards** *n.* билья́рд.
billion ['bɪljən] *n.* биллио́н.
billow ['bɪləʊ] *n.* больша́я волна́ (*pl.* -ны, -н, -на́м), вал (*loc.* -у́; *pl.* -ы́); *v.i.* вздыма́ться *impf.* **billowy** *adj.* вздыма́ющийся, волни́стый.
billposter ['bɪlˌpəʊstə(r)] *n.* раскле́йщик афи́ш.
bimonthly [baɪ'mʌnθlɪ] *adj.* (*twice a month*) выходя́щий два ра́за в ме́сяц; (*every two months*) выходя́щий раз в два ме́сяца.
bin [bɪn] *n.* (*refuse*) му́сорное ведро́ (*pl.* вёдра, -дер, -дра́м); (*corn*) за́кром (*pl.* -а́), ларь (-ря́) *m.*
bind [baɪnd] *v.t.* (*tie*) свя́зывать *impf.*, связа́ть (-яжу́, -я́жешь) *pf.*; (*oblige*) обя́зывать *impf.*, обяза́ть (-яжу́, -я́жешь) *pf.*; (*book*) переплета́ть *impf.*, переплести́ (-ету́, -етёшь; -ёл, -ела́) *pf.* **binder** *n.* (*person*) переплётчик, -ица; (*agric.*) вяза́льщик; (*for papers*) па́пка. **binding** *n.* (*book*) переплёт; (*braid*) оторо́чка. **bindweed** *n.* вьюно́к (-нка́).
binge [bɪndʒ] *n.* кутёж (-а́).
bingo ['bɪŋgəʊ] *n.* би́нго *nt.indecl.*
binoculars [bɪ'nɒkjʊləz] *n.* бино́кль *m.*
binomial [baɪ'nəʊmɪəl] *adj.* двучле́нный.
biochemical [ˌbaɪəʊ'kemɪk(ə)l] *adj.* биохими́ческий. **biochemist** *n.* биохи́мик. **biochemistry** *n.* биохи́мия. **biographer** [baɪ'ɒgrəfə(r)] *n.* био́граф. **bio'graphical** *adj.* биографи́ческий. **biography** *n.* биогра́фия, жизнеописа́ние. **biological** [ˌbaɪə'lɒdʒɪk(ə)l] *adj.* биологи́ческий. **bi'ologist** *n.* био́лог.

bi'ology *n.* биоло́гия.

bipartisan [baɪ'pɑːtɪz(ə)n] *adj.* двухпарти́йный. **bipartite** [baɪ'pɑːtaɪt] *adj.* двусторо́нний. **biped** ['baɪped] *n.* двуно́гое живо́тное *sb.* **biplane** *n.* бипла́н.

birch [bɜːtʃ] *n.* (*tree*) берёза; (*rod*) ро́зга (*g.pl.* -зог); *v.t.* сечь (секу́, сечёшь; сек, -ла́) *impf.*, вы́~ *pf.* ро́згой.

bird [bɜːd] *n.* пти́ца; ~ **of passage** перелётная пти́ца; ~ **of prey** хи́щная пти́ца; ~**'s-eye view** вид с пти́чьего полёта.

Biro ['baɪərəʊ] *n.* (*propr.*) ша́риковая ру́чка, ша́рик.

birth [bɜːθ] *n.* рожде́ние; (*origin*) происхожде́ние; ~ **certificate** ме́трика; ~ **control** противозача́точные ме́ры *f.pl.* **birthday** *n.* день (дня) *m.* рожде́ния. **birthplace** *n.* ме́сто (*pl.* -а́) рожде́ния. **birthright** *n.* пра́во по рожде́нию.

biscuit ['bɪskɪt] *n.* сухо́е пече́нье.

bisect [baɪ'sekt] *v.t.* разреза́ть *impf.*, разре́зать (-е́жу, -е́жешь) *pf.* попола́м.

bishop ['bɪʃəp] *n.* епи́скоп; (*chess*) слон (-а́). **bishopric** *n.* епа́рхия.

bismuth ['bɪzməθ] *n.* ви́смут.

bison ['baɪs(ə)n] *n.* бизо́н.

bit[1] [bɪt] *n.* (*piece*) кусо́чек (-чка), до́ля (*pl.* -ли, -ле́й); **a** ~ немно́го; **not a** ~ ничу́ть.

bit[2] [bɪt] *n.* (*tech.*) сверло́ (*pl.* -ёрла), бура́в (-а́); (*bridle*) удила́ (-л) *pl.*

bitch [bɪtʃ] *n.* су́ка.

bite [baɪt] *n.* уку́с; (*fishing*) клёв; *v.t.* куса́ть *impf.*, укуси́ть (-ушу́, -у́сишь) *pf.*; (*fish*) клева́ть (клюёт) *impf.*, клю́нуть *pf.* **biting** *adj.* е́дкий (е́док, -едка́, е́дко), ре́зкий (-зок, -зка́, -зко).

bitter ['bɪtə(r)] *adj.* го́рький (-рек, -рька́, -рько). **bitterness** *n.* го́речь.

bittern ['bɪt(ə)n] *n.* выпь.

bitumen ['bɪtjʊmɪn] *n.* биту́м. **bituminous** [bɪ'tjuːmɪnəs] *adj.* биту́м(ино́з)ный.

bivouac ['bɪvʊ,æk] *n.* бива́к.

bi-weekly [baɪ'wiːklɪ] *adj.* (*twice a week*) выходя́щий два ра́за в неде́лю; (*fortnightly*) выходя́щий раз в две неде́ли, двухнеде́льный.

bizarre [bɪ'zɑː(r)] *adj.* стра́нный (-нен, -нна́, -нно), причу́дливый.

blab [blæb] *v.t.* выба́лтывать *impf.*, вы́болтать *pf.*

black [blæk] *adj.* чёрный (-рен, -рна́); (*dark-skinned*) чернoко́жий; ~ **eye** подби́тый глаз (*pl.* -а́, глаз, -а́м), фона́рь (-ря́) *m.*; *n.* (*negro*) чёрный *sb.*; (*mourning*) тра́ур. **blackberry** *n.* ежеви́ка (*collect.*). **blackbird** *n.* чёрный дрозд (-а́). **blackboard** *n.* кла́ссная доска́ (*a.* -ску; *pl.* -ски, -со́к, -ска́м). **black'currant** *n.* чёрная сморо́дина. **blacken** *v.t.* черни́ть *impf.*, за~, на~, (*fig.*) о~ *pf.* **blackguard** [blægɑːd, -gəd] *n.* подле́ц (-ца́), мерза́вец (-вца). **blackleg** *n.* штрейкбре́хер. **blackmail** *n.* шанта́ж (-а́); *v.t.* шантажи́ровать *impf.*

bladder ['blædə(r)] *n.* пузы́рь (-ря́) *m.*

blade [bleɪd] *n.* (*knife etc.*) ле́звие, клино́к (-нка́); (*oar etc.*) ло́пасть (*pl.* -ти, -те́й); (*grass*) были́нка.

blame [bleɪm] *n.* вина́, порица́ние; *v.t.* вини́ть *impf.* (**for** в+*p.*); **be to** ~ быть винова́тым. **blameless** *adj.* безупре́чный, неви́нный (-нен, -нна).

blanch [blɑːntʃ] *v.t.* бели́ть *impf.*, вы́~ *pf.*; (*food*) обва́ривать *impf.*, обвари́ть (-рю́, -ришь) *pf.*; *v.i.* бледне́ть *impf.*, по~ *pf.*

bland [blænd] *adj.* мя́гкий (-гок, -гка́, -гко, мя́гки́); (*in manner*) ве́жливый.

blandishment ['blændɪʃmənt] *n.*: *pl.* льсти́вые ре́чи (-че́й) *pl.*

blank [blæŋk] *n.* (*space*) пробе́л; (*form*) бланк; (*ticket*) пусто́й биле́т; *adj.* пусто́й (пуст, -а́, -о, -ы́); незапо́лненный (-ен); чи́стый (чист, -а́, -о, чи́сты́); ~ **cartridge** холосто́й патро́н; ~ **wall** глуха́я стена́ (*a.* -ну; *pl.* -ны, -н, -на́м); ~ **verse** бе́лый стих (-а́).

blanket ['blæŋkɪt] *n.* одея́ло.

blare [bleə(r)] *n.* звук трубы́; *v.i.* труби́ть *impf.*, про~ *pf.*; (*shout*) ора́ть (ору́, орёшь) *impf.*

blasphemous ['blæsfiməs] *adj.* богоху́льный. **blasphemy** *n.* богоху́льство.

blast [blɑːst] *n.* (*wind*) поры́в ве́тра; (*air*) струя́ (*pl.* -у́и); (*sound*) гудо́к (-дка́); (*of explosion*) взрывна́я волна́ (*pl.* -ны, -н, -на́м); *v.t.* взрыва́ть *impf.*, взорва́ть (-ву́, -вёшь; взорва́л, -а́, -о) *pf.*; ~ **off** стартова́ть *impf.* & *pf.*; взлета́ть *impf.*, взлете́ть (-ечу́, -ети́шь) *pf.* **blast-furnace** *n.* до́менная печь (*pl.* -чи, -че́й).

blatant ['bleɪt(ə)nt] *adj.* (*clear*) я́вный; (*flagrant*) вопию́щий.

blaze[1] [bleɪz] *n.* (*flame*) я́ркое пла́мя *nt.*; (*light*) я́ркий цвет; *v.i.* (*flame*) пыла́ть *impf.*; (*with light*) сверка́ть *impf.*

blaze[2] [bleɪz] *v.t.* (*mark*) ме́тить *impf.*, на~ *pf.*; ~ **the trail** прокла́дывать *impf.* путь.

blazer ['bleɪzə(r)] *n.* спорти́вная ку́ртка.

bleach [bliːtʃ] *n.* хло́рная и́звесть; *v.t.* бели́ть *impf.*, вы́~ *pf.* **bleaching** *n.* отбе́ливание, беле́ние.

bleak [bliːk] *adj.* (*bare*) оголённый (-ён, -ена́); (*dreary*) уны́лый.

bleary ['blɪərɪ] *adj.* му́тный (-тен, -тна́, -тно, му́тны́), затума́ненный (-ен). **bleary-eyed** *adj.* с затума́ненными глаза́ми.

bleat [bliːt] *v.i.* бле́ять (-е́ю, -е́ешь) *impf.*; *n.* бле́яние.

bleed [bliːd] *v.i.* кровоточи́ть *impf.*; *v.t.* пуска́ть *impf.*, пусти́ть (пущу́, пу́стишь) *pf.* кровь+*d.*; *n.* кровотече́ние; кровопуска́ние; **my heart** ~**s** се́рдце облива́ется кро́вью.

bleep [bliːp] *n.* бип.

blemish ['blemɪʃ] *n.* недоста́ток (-тка), пятно́ (*pl.* -тна, -тен, -тнам), поро́к; **without** ~ непоро́чный, незапя́танный (-ан).

blench [blentʃ] *v.i.* вздро́гнуть *pf.*

blend [blend] *n.* смесь; *v.t.* сме́шивать *impf.*, смеша́ть *pf.*; *v.i.* гармони́ровать *impf.* **blender** *n.* смеси́тель *m.*; (*cul.*) ми́ксер.

bless [bles] *v.t.* благословля́ть *impf.*, благослови́ть *pf.* **blessed** *adj.* благослове́нный (-е́н, -е́нна), счастли́вый (сча́стлив). **blessing** *n.* (*action*) благослове́ние; (*object*) бла́го.

blind [blaɪnd] *adj.* слепо́й (слеп, -а́, -о); ~ **alley** тупи́к (-а́); ~ **flying** слепо́й полёт; *n.* што́ра; *v.t.* ослепля́ть *impf.*, ослепи́ть *pf.*

blink [blɪŋk] *v.i.* мига́ть *impf.*, мигну́ть *pf.*; морга́ть *impf.*, моргну́ть *pf.*; *n.* мига́ние. **blinkers** *n.* шо́ры (-р) *pl.*

blip [blɪp] *n.* сигна́л на экра́не.

bliss [blɪs] *n.* блаже́нство. **blissful** *adj.* блаже́нный (-е́н, -е́нна).

blister ['blɪstə(r)] *n.* пузы́рь (-ря́) *m.*, волды́рь (-ря́) *m.*; *v.i.* покрыва́ться *impf.*, покры́ться (-ро́юсь, -ро́ешься) *pf.* пузыря́ми, волдыря́ми; *v.t.* вызыва́ть *impf.*, вы́звать (-зовет) *pf.* пузы́рь, волды́рь на+*p.*, на ко́же+*g.*

blithe [blaɪð] *adj.* весёлый (ве́сел, -а́, -о, ве́селы́); (*carefree*) беспе́чный.

blitz [blɪts] *n.* стреми́тельное нападе́ние; (*aerial*) стреми́тельный налёт. **blitzkrieg** ['blɪtskri:g] *n.* молниено́сная война́.

blizzard ['blɪzəd] *n.* мете́ль, вью́га.

bloated ['bləʊtɪd] *adj.* наду́тый, разду́тый.

bloater ['bləʊtə(r)] *n.* копчёная селёдка.

blob [blɒb] *n.* (*liquid*) ка́пля (*g.pl.* -пель); (*spot*) пя́тнышко (*pl.* -шки, -шек, -шкам).

bloc [blɒk] *n.* блок.

block [blɒk] *n.* (*of wood*) чурба́н, коло́да; (*of stone*) глы́ба; (*obstruction*) зато́р; (*traffic*) про́бка; (*tech.*) блок; (~ *of flats*) жило́й дом (*pl.* -а́); ~ **and tackle** та́ли (-лей) *pl.*; ~ **letters** печа́тные бу́квы *f.pl.*; *v.t.* прегражда́ть *impf.*, прегради́ть *pf.*; ~ **out** набра́сывать *impf.*, наброса́ть *pf.* вчерне́.

blockade [blɒ'keɪd] *n.* блока́да; *v.t.* блоки́ровать *impf.* & *pf.*

blockage ['blɒkɪdʒ] *n.* зато́р.

blond [blɒnd] *n.* блонди́н, ~ка; *adj.* белоку́рый.

blood [blʌd] *n.* кровь (*loc.* -ви́; *pl.* -ви, -ве́й); (*descent*) происхожде́ние; ~ **bank** храни́лище кро́ви и пла́змы; ~ **donor** до́нор; ~ **orange** королёк (-лька́); ~ **pressure** кровяно́е давле́ние; ~ **relation** бли́зкий ро́дственник, -ая ро́дственница; ~ **transfusion** перелива́ние кро́ви. **bloodhound** *n.* ище́йка. **bloodless** *adj.* бескро́вный. **blood-poisoning** *n.* зараже́ние кро́ви. **blood-vessel** *n.* кровено́сный сосу́д. **bloody** *adj.* крова́вый, окрова́вленный (-ен, -енна).

bloom [blu:m] *n.* расцве́т; *v.i.* расцвета́ть *impf.*, расцвести́ (-ету́, -етёшь; -ёл, -ела́) *pf.*

blossom ['blɒsəm] *n.* цвето́к (-тка́; *pl.* цветы́); *collect.* цвет; **in** ~ в цвету́.

blot [blɒt] *n.* кля́кса; пятно́ (*pl.* -тна, -тен, -тнам); *v.t.* промока́ть *impf.*, промокну́ть *pf.*; па́чкать *impf.*, за~ *pf.*

blotch [blɒtʃ] *n.* пятно́ (*pl.* -тна, -тен, -тнам). **blotchy** *adj.* запя́танный (-ан).

blotter ['blɒtə(r)], **blotting-paper** *n.* промока́тельная бума́га.

blouse [blaʊz] *n.* ко́фточка, блу́зка.

blow[1] [bləʊ] *n.* уда́р.

blow[2] [bləʊ] *v.t.* & *i.* дуть (ду́ю, ду́ешь) *impf.*; ве́ять (ве́ет) *impf.*; выдува́ть *impf.*, вы́дуть (-ую, -уешь) *pf.*; ~ **away** сноси́ть (-ошу́, -о́сишь) *impf.*, снести́ (-есу́, -есёшь; снёс, -ла́) *pf.*; ~ **down** сва́ливать *impf.*, свали́ть (-лю́, -лишь) *pf.*; ~ **up** взрыва́ть *impf.*, взорва́ть (-ву́, -вёшь; взорва́л, -а́, -о) *pf.* **blow-lamp** *n.* пая́льная ла́мпа. **blow-up** *n.* фотопанно́ *nt.indecl.*

blubber[1] ['blʌbə(r)] *n.* во́рвань.

blubber[2] ['blʌbə(r)] *v.i.* реве́ть (-ву́, -вёшь) *impf.*

bludgeon ['blʌdʒ(ə)n] *n.* дуби́нка.

blue [blu:] *adj.* (*dark*) си́ний (-нь, -ня́, -не); (*light*) голубо́й; *n.* си́ний, голубо́й цвет; (*sky*) не́бо. **bluebell** *n.* колоко́льчик. **bluebottle** *n.* си́няя му́ха. **blueprint** *n.* си́нька, светоко́пия; (*fig.*) прое́кт.

bluff[1] [blʌf] *n.* (*deceit*) обма́н, блеф; *v.i.* притворя́ться *impf.*, притвори́ться *pf.*

bluff[2] [blʌf] *n.* (*cliff*) отве́сный бе́рег (*loc.* -у́; *pl.* -а́); *adj.* (*person*) грубова́то-доброду́шный.

blunder ['blʌndə(r)] *n.* гру́бая оши́бка, опло́шность; *v.i.* ошиба́ться *impf.*, ошиби́ться (-бу́сь, -бёшься; -бся) *pf.*; (*stumble*) спотыка́ться *impf.*, споткну́ться *pf.*

blunt [blʌnt] *adj.* (*knife*) тупо́й (туп, -а́, -о, ту́пы́); (*person*) прямо́й (прям, -а́, -о, пря́мы́); (*words*) ре́зкий (-зок, -зка́, -зко) *v.t.* тупи́ть (-плю́, -пишь) *impf.*, за~, ис~ *pf.*; притупля́ть *impf.*, притупи́ть (-плю́, -пишь) *pf.*

blur [blɜ:(r)] *n.* расплы́вчатая фо́рма; *v.t.* тума́нить *impf.*, за~ *pf.*; изгла́живать *impf.*, изгла́дить *pf.*

blurb [blɜ:b] *n.* (изда́тельская) аннота́ция.

blurred ['blɜ:d] *adj.* расплы́вчатый, нея́сный (-сен, -сна́, -сно, нея́сны́).

blurt [blɜ:t] *v.t.*: ~ **out** выба́лтывать *impf.*, вы́болтать *pf.*

blush [blʌʃ] *v.i.* красне́ть *impf.*, по~ *pf.*; зарде́ться *pf.*; *n.* румя́нец (-нца).

bluster ['blʌstə(r)] *v.i.* бушева́ть (-шу́ю, -шу́ешь) *impf.*; *n.* пусты́е угро́зы *f.pl.*

boa ['bəʊə] *n.* боа́ *m.indecl.* (*snake*), *nt.indecl.* (*wrap*); ~ **constrictor** уда́в.

boar [bɔ:(r)] *n.* бо́ров (*pl.* -ы, -о́в); (*wild*) вепрь *m.*

board [bɔ:d] *n.* доска́ (*a.* -ску; *pl.* -ски, -со́к, -ска́м); (*table*) стол (-а́); (*food*) пита́ние; (*committee*) правле́ние, сове́т; *pl.* сце́на, подмо́стки (-ков) *pl.*; (*naut.*) борт (*loc.* -у́; *pl.* -а́); **on** ~ на борт(у́); *v.i.* столова́ться *impf.*; *v.t.* сади́ться *impf.*, сесть (ся́ду, -дешь; сел) *pf.* (на кора́бль, в по́езд и т.д.); **~ing**

pass поса́дочный тало́н; (*naut.*) брать (беру́, -рёшь; брал, -а́, -о) *impf.*, взять (возьму́, -мёшь; взял, -а́, -о) *pf.* на аборда́ж. **boarder** *n.* пансионе́р. **boarding-house** *n.* пансио́н. **boarding-school** *n.* интерна́т.

boast [bəʊst] *v.i.* хва́статься *impf.*, по~ *pf.*; *v.t.* горди́ться *impf.*+*i.*; *n.* хвастовство́. **boaster** *n.* хвасту́н (-а́). **boastful** *adj.* хвастли́вый.

boat [bəʊt] *n.* ло́дка, су́дно (*pl.* -да́, -до́в), кора́бль (-ля́) *m.*; ~ **building** судострое́ние. **boat-hook** *n.* баго́р (-гра́). **boatswain** ['bəʊs(ə)n] *n.* бо́цман.

bob[1] [bɒb] *n.* (*weight*) баланси́р; (*hair*) коро́ткая стри́жка.

bob[2] [bɒb] *v.i.* подпры́гивать *impf.*, подпры́гнуть *pf.*

bobbin ['bɒbɪn] *n.* кату́шка, шпу́лька.

bobby ['bɒbɪ] *n.* полисме́н, бо́бби *m.indecl.*

bobsleigh ['bɒbsleɪ] *n.* бо́бсле́й.

bobtail ['bɒbteɪl] *n.* обре́занный хвост (-а́).

bode [bəʊd] *v.t.* предвеща́ть *impf.*

bodice ['bɒdɪs] *n.* лиф, корса́ж.

bodily ['bɒdɪlɪ] *adv.* целико́м; *adj.* теле́сный, физи́ческий.

bodkin ['bɒdkɪn] *n.* тупа́я игла́ (*pl.* -лы).

body ['bɒdɪ] *n.* те́ло (*pl.* -ла́), ту́ловище; (*corpse*) труп; (*frame*) о́стов; (*troops etc.*) ко́рпус (*pl.* -а́); (*carriage*) ку́зов (*pl.* -а́); (*main part*) основна́я часть. **body-builder** *n.* культури́ст. **body-building** *n.* культури́зм. **bodyguard** *n.* телохрани́тель *m.*; *collect.* ко́рпус телохрани́телей.

bog [bɒg] *n.* боло́та, трясина; **get ~ged down** увяза́ть *impf.*, увя́знуть (-з) *pf.* **boggy** *adj.* боло́тистый.

bogus ['bəʊgəs] *adj.* подде́льный, фальши́вый.

bogy ['bəʊgɪ] *n.* бу́ка, пу́гало.

boil[1] [bɔɪl] *n.* (*med.*) фуру́нкул, нары́в.

boil[2] [bɔɪl] *v.i.* кипе́ть (-пи́т) *impf.*, вс~ *pf.*; *v.t.* кипяти́ть *impf.*, с~ *pf.*; (*cook*) вари́ть (-рю́, -ришь) *impf.*, с~ *pf.*; *n.* кипе́ние; **bring to the ~** доводи́ть (-ожу́, -о́дишь) *impf.*, довести́ (-еду́, -дёшь; -ёл, -ела́) *pf.* до кипе́ния. **boiled** *adj.* варёный, кипячёный. **boiler** *n.* (*vessel*) котёл (-тла́); (*fowl*) ку́рица го́дная для ва́рки; ~ **suit** комбинезо́н. **boilerhouse** *n.* коте́льная *sb.* **boiling** *n.* кипе́ние; *adj.* кипя́щий; ~ **water** кипято́к (-тка́).

boisterous ['bɔɪstərəs] *adj.* бу́рный (-рен, бу́рна́, -рно), шумли́вый.

bold [bəʊld] *adj.* сме́лый (смел, -а́, -о), хра́брый (храбр, -а́, -о, хра́бры́), де́рзкий (-зок, -зка́, -зко); (*clear*) чёткий (-ток, -тка́, -тко); (*type*) жи́рный.

bole [bəʊl] *n.* ствол (-а́).

bolster ['bəʊlstə(r)] *n.* ва́лик; *v.t.*: ~ **up** подпира́ть *impf.*, подпере́ть (подопру́, -рёшь; подпёр) *pf.*

bolt [bəʊlt] *n.* засо́в, задви́жка; (*tech.*) болт (-а́); (*flight*) бе́гство; *v.t.* запира́ть *impf.*, запере́ть (-пру́, -прёшь; за́пер, -ла́, -ло) *pf.* на засо́в; скрепля́ть *impf.*, скрепи́ть *pf.* болта́ми; *v.i.* (*flee*) удира́ть *impf.*, удра́ть (удеру́, -рёшь; удра́л, -ла́, -ло) *pf.*; (*horse*) понести́ (-есёт; -ёс, -есла́) *pf.*

bomb [bɒm] *n.* бо́мба; *v.t.* бомби́ть *impf.*; бомбарди́ровать *impf.* **bombard** [bɒm'bɑːd] *v.t.* бомбарди́ровать *impf.* **bombardment** *n.* бомбардиро́вка. **bomber** *n.* бомбардиро́вщик.

bombastic [bɒm'bæstɪk] *adj.* напы́щенный (-ен, -енна).

bonanza [bə'nænzə] *n.* золото́е дно.

bond [bɒnd] *n.* (*econ.*) облига́ция; связь; *pl.* око́вы (-в) *pl.*, (*fig.*) у́зы (уз) *pl.*

bone [bəʊn] *n.* кость (*pl.* -ти, -те́й); *pl.* прах; ~ **of contention** я́блоко раздо́ра.

bonfire ['bɒn,faɪə(r)] *n.* костёр (-тра́).

bonnet ['bɒnɪt] *n.* ка́пор, че́пчик; (*car*) капо́т.

bonny ['bɒnɪ] *adj.* здоро́вый, хоро́шенький.

bony ['bəʊnɪ] *adj.* кости́стый.

booby ['buːbɪ] *n.* болва́н, о́лух; ~ **trap** лову́шка.

book [bʊk] *n.* кни́га; *v.t.* (*order*) зака́зывать *impf.*, заказа́ть (-ажу́, -а́жешь) *pf.*; (*reserve*) брони́ровать *impf.*, за~ *pf.* **bookbinder** *n.* переплётчик, -ица. **bookkeeper** *n.* бухга́лтер. **bookmaker, bookie** *n.* букме́кер. **booking** *n.* (*order*) зака́з; (*sale*) прода́жа биле́тов; ~ **clerk** касси́р; ~ **office** ка́сса.

boom[1] [buːm] *n.* (*barrier*) бон.

boom[2] [buːm] *n.* (*sound*) гул; (*econ.*) бум, экономи́ческий подъём; *v.i.* гуде́ть (гужу́, гуди́шь) *impf.*; (*flourish*) процвета́ть *impf.*

boon[1] [buːn] *n.* бла́го.

boon[2] [buːn] *adj.*: ~ **companion** весёлый друг (*pl.* друзья́, -зе́й).

boor ['bʊə(r)] *n.* гру́бый, мужикова́тый челове́к. **boorish** *adj.* мужикова́тый.

boost [buːst] *v.t.* (*raise*) поднима́ть *impf.*, подня́ть (-ниму́, -ни́мешь; по́днял, -а́, -о) *pf.*; (*increase*) увели́чивать *impf.*, увели́чить *pf.*

boot [buːt] *n.* боти́нок (-нка; *g.pl.* -нок), сапо́г (-а́; *g.pl.* -г); (*football*) бу́тса; *v.t.*: ~ **out** выгоня́ть *impf.*, вы́гнать (вы́гоню, вы́гнишь) *pf.* **boo'tee** *n.* де́тский вя́заный башмачо́к (-чка́). **boots** *n.* коридо́рный *sb.*

booth [buːð, buːθ] *n.* кио́ск, бу́дка; (*polling*) каби́на (для голосова́ния).

bootlegger ['buːtlegə(r)] *n.* торго́вец (-вца) контрабанд́ными спиртны́ми напи́тками.

booty ['buːtɪ] *n.* добы́ча; (*mil.*) трофе́и *m.pl.*

booze [buːz] *n.* вы́пивка; *v.i.* выпива́ть *impf.*

boracic [bə'ræsɪk] *adj.* бо́рный. **borax** ['bɔːræks] *n.* бура́.

border ['bɔːdə(r)] *n.* (*boundary*) грани́ца; (*edge*) край (*loc.* -аю́; *pl.* -ая́); (*edging*) кайма́, бордю́р; *v.i.* грани́чить *impf.* (**on** с+*i.*); *v.t.* окаймля́ть *impf.*, окайми́ть *pf.* **borderline** *n.* грани́ца.

bore[1] [bɔː(r)] *n.* (*tedium*) ску́ка; (*person*) ну́дный челове́к; *v.t.* надоеда́ть *impf.*, надое́сть (-е́м, -е́шь, -е́ст, -еди́м; -е́л) *pf.* **boredom** *n.* ску́ка. **boring**[1] *adj.* ску́чный (-чен, -чна́, -чно).

bore[2] [bɔ:(r)] *n.* (*calibre*) кана́л (ствола́), кали́бр (ору́жия); (*borehole*) бурова́я сква́жина; *v.t.* сверли́ть *impf.*, про~ *pf.* **boring**[2] *adj.* сверля́щий, буро́вой.

born [bɔ:n] *adj.* прирождённый; **be ~** роди́ться *impf.*, (-и́лся́, -ила́сь) *pf.*

borough ['bʌrə] *n.* го́род (*pl.* -а́).

borrow ['bɒrəʊ] *v.t.* занима́ть *impf.*, заня́ть (займу́, -мёшь; за́нял, -а́, -о) *pf.* (**from** у+*g.*); заи́мствовать *impf.* & *pf.*

bosh [bɒʃ] *n.* чепуха́.

bosom ['bʊz(ə)m] *n.* (*breast*) грудь (-ди́, *i.* -дью́; *pl.* -ди, -де́й); (*heart*) се́рдце; (*depths*) не́дра (-р) *pl.*; **~ friend** закады́чный друг (*pl.* друзья́, -зе́й).

boss [bɒs] *n.* хозя́ин (*pl.* -я́ева, -я́ев), шеф; *v.t.* кома́ндовать *impf.*, с~ *pf.*+*i.* **bossy** *adj.* вла́стный.

botanical [bə'tænɪk(ə)l] *adj.* ботани́ческий. **botanist** ['bɒtənɪst] *n.* бота́ник. **botany** ['bɒtənɪ] *n.* бота́ника.

botch [bɒtʃ] *v.t.* по́ртить *impf.*, ис~ *pf.*

both [bəʊθ] *adj.*, *pron.* о́ба (обо́их, -им, -ими) *m.* & *nt.*, о́бе (обе́их, -им, -ими) *f.*; *adv.* то́же; **~ ... and** и... и; не то́лько... но и; как... так и.

bother ['bɒðə(r)] *n.* беспоко́йство, хло́поты (*g.* -о́т) *pl.*; *v.t.* беспоко́ить *impf.*; надоеда́ть *impf.*, надое́сть (-е́м, -е́шь, -е́ст, -еди́м; -е́л) *pf.*

bottle ['bɒt(ə)l] *n.* буты́лка; *v.t.* разлива́ть *impf.*, разли́ть (разолью́, -ьёшь; разли́л, -а́, -о) *pf.* по буты́лкам; **~ up** (*conceal*) зата́ивать *impf.*, затаи́ть *pf.*; (*restrain*) подавля́ть *impf.*, подави́ть (-влю́, -вишь) *pf.* **bottleneck** *n.* у́зкое ме́сто (*pl.* -та́), зато́р.

bottom ['bɒtəm] *n.* ни́жняя часть (*pl.* -ти, -те́й); (*of river etc.*) дно (*pl.* до́нья, -ьев); (*buttocks*) зад (*loc.* -у́; *pl.* -ы́); *adj.* са́мый ни́жний. **bottomless** *adj.* бездо́нный (-нен, -нна); **~ pit** ад (*loc.* -у́).

bough [baʊ] *n.* сук (-а́, *loc.* -у́; *pl.* -и́, -о́в & су́чья, -ьев), ветвь (*pl.* -ви, -ве́й).

boulder ['bəʊldə(r)] *n.* валу́н (-а́), глы́ба.

bounce [baʊns] *n.* прыжо́к (-жка́), скачо́к (-чка́); *v.i.* подпры́гивать *impf.*, подпры́гнуть *pf.* **bouncing** *adj.* ро́слый, здоро́вый.

bound[1] [baʊnd] *n.* (*limit*) преде́л; *v.t.* ограни́чивать *impf.*, ограни́чить *pf.*

bound[2] [baʊnd] *n.* (*spring*) прыжо́к (-жка́), скачо́к (-чка́); *v.i.* пры́гать *impf.*, пры́гнуть *pf.*; скака́ть (-ачу́, -а́чешь) *impf.*

bound[3] [baʊnd] *adj.* (*tied*) свя́занный (-ан); **he is ~ to be there** он обяза́тельно там бу́дет.

bound[4] [baʊnd] *adj.*: **to be ~ for** направля́ться *impf.*, напра́виться *pf.* на+*a.*

boundary ['baʊndərɪ, -drɪ] *n.* грани́ца, межа́ (*pl.* -жи, -ж, -жа́м).

bounder ['baʊndə(r)] *n.* хам.

boundless ['baʊndlɪs] *adj.* беспреде́льный, безграни́чный.

bounteous ['baʊntɪəs], **bountiful** *adj.* (*generous*) ще́дрый (ще́др, -а́, -о); (*ample*) оби́льный. **bounty** *n.* ще́дрость; (*gratuity*) пре́мия.

bouquet [bu:'keɪ, bəʊ-] *n.* буке́т.

bourgeois ['bʊəʒwɑ:] *n.* буржуа́ *m.indecl.*; *adj.* буржуа́зный. **bourgeoisie** [,bʊəʒwɑ:'zi:] *n.* буржуази́я.

bout [baʊt] *n.* (*of illness*) при́ступ; (*sport*) схва́тка, встре́ча.

boutique [bu:'ti:k] *n.* (небольшо́й) мо́дный магази́н.

bovine ['bəʊvaɪn] *adj.* быча́чий (-чья, -чье); (*fig.*) тупо́й (туп, -а́, -о, ту́пы́).

bow[1] [bəʊ] *n.* (*weapon*) лук; (*knot*) бант; (*mus.*) смычо́к (-чка́).

bow[2] [baʊ] *n.* (*obeisance*) покло́н; *v.i.* кла́няться *impf.*, поклони́ться (-ню́сь, -нишься) *pf.*

bow[3] [baʊ] *n.* (*naut.*) нос (*loc.* -у́; *pl.* -ы́); (*rowing*) пе́рвый но́мер (*pl.* -а́).

bowdlerize ['baʊdlə,raɪz] *v.t.* очища́ть *impf.*, очи́стить *pf.*

bowels ['baʊəlz] *n.* кише́чник; (*depths*) не́дра (-р) *pl.*

bower ['baʊə(r)] *n.* бесе́дка.

bowl[1] [bəʊl] *n.* (*vessel*) ми́ска, таз (*loc.* -у́; *pl.* -ы́), ча́ша.

bowl[2] [bəʊl] *n.* (*ball*) шар (-а́ *with* 2,3,4; *pl.* -ы́); *v.i.* мета́ть (мечу́, -чешь) *impf.*, метну́ть *pf.* мяч; подава́ть (-даю́, -даёшь) *impf.*, пода́ть (-а́м, -а́шь, -а́ст, -ади́м; по́дал, -а́, -о) *pf.* мяч. **bowler (hat)** *n.* котело́к (-лка́). **bowling-alley** *n.* кегельба́н. **bowls** *n.* игра́ в шары́; **play ~** игра́ть *impf.*, сыгра́ть *pf.* в шары́.

box[1] [bɒks] *n.* (*container*) коро́бка, я́щик, сунду́к (-а́); (*theatr.*) ло́жа; (*coach*) ко́злы (-зел) *pl.*; (*horse*) сто́йло; **~ office** ка́сса; **~ pleat** бантова́я скла́дка.

box[2] [bɒks], **boxwood** *n.* (*bot.*) самши́т.

box[3] [bɒks] *v.i.* бокси́ровать *impf.* **boxer** *n.* боксёр. **boxing** *n.* бокс.

boy [bɔɪ] *n.* ма́льчик, ю́ноша *m.*; **~ scout** бойска́ут. **boyfriend** *n.* друг (*pl.* друзья́, -зе́й). **boyhood** *n.* о́трочество. **boyish** *adj.* мальчи́шеский.

boycott ['bɔɪkɒt] *n.* бойко́т; *v.t.* бойкоти́ровать *impf.* & *pf.*

bra [brɑ:] *n.* бюстга́лтер.

brace [breɪs] *n.* (*clamp*) скре́па; *pl.* подтя́жки *f.pl.*; (*pair*) па́ра; *v.t.* скрепля́ть *impf.*, скрепи́ть *pf.*; **~ o.s.** напряга́ть *impf.*, напря́чь (-ягу́, -я́жешь; -я́г, -ягла́) *pf.* си́лы.

bracelet ['breɪslɪt] *n.* брасле́т.

bracing ['breɪsɪŋ] *adj.* бодря́щий.

bracket ['brækɪt] *n.* (*support*) кроншт́ейн; *pl.* ско́бки *f.pl.*; (*category*) катего́рия, ру́брика.

brad [bræd] *n.* шти́фчик. **bradawl** ['brædɔ:l] *n.* ши́ло (*pl.* ши́лья, -ьев).

brag [bræg] *v.i.* хва́статься *impf.*, по~ *pf.*

braggart ['brægət] *n.* хвасту́н (-а́).
braid [breɪd] *n.* тесьма́.
Braille [breɪl] *n.* шрифт Бра́йля.
brain [breɪn] *n.* мозг (-а(у), *loc.* -е & -у́; *pl.* -и́); (*intellect*) ум (-а́); ~ **drain** уте́чка умо́в; *v.t.* размозжи́ть *pf.* го́лову+*d.* **brainstorm** *n.* припа́док (-дка) безу́мия. **brainwashing** *n.* идеологи́ческая обрабо́тка. **brainwave** *n.* блестя́щая иде́я.
braise [breɪz] *v.t.* туши́ть (-шу́, -шишь) *impf.*, с~ *pf.*
brake [breɪk] *n.* то́рмоз (*pl.* -а́, *fig.* -ы); *v.t.* тормози́ть *impf.*, за~ *pf.*
bramble ['bræmb(ə)l] *n.* ежеви́ка.
brambling ['bræmblɪŋ] *n.* вьюро́к (-рка́).
bran [bræn] *n.* о́труби (-бе́й) *pl.*
branch [brɑːntʃ] *n.* ве́тка; (*subject*) о́трасль; (*department*) отделе́ние, филиа́л; *v.i.* разветвля́ться *impf.*, разветви́ться *pf.*
brand [brænd] *n.* (*mark*) клеймо́ (*pl.* -ма); (*make*) ма́рка; (*sort*) сорт (*pl.* -а́); *v.t.* клейми́ть *impf.*, за~ *pf.*
brandish ['brændɪʃ] *v.t.* разма́хивать *impf.*+*i.*
brandy ['brændɪ] *n.* конья́к (-а́(у́)).
brass [brɑːs] *n.* лату́нь, жёлтая медь; (*mus.*) ме́дные инструме́нты *m.pl.*; *adj.* лату́нный, ме́дный; ~ **band** ме́дный духово́й орке́стр; **bold as** ~ на́глый (нагл, -а́, -о); ~ **hats** нача́льство, ста́ршие офице́ры *m.pl.*; **top** ~ вы́сшее нача́льство.
brassière ['bræzɪə(r), -sɪˌeə(r)] *n.* бюстга́лтер.
brat [bræt] *n.* ребёнок (-нка; *pl.* де́ти, -те́й); (*pej.*) постре́л.
bravado [brə'vɑːdəʊ] *n.* брава́да.
brave [breɪv] *adj.* хра́брый (храбр, -а́, -о, хра́бры́), сме́лый (смел, -а́, -о); *v.t.* хра́бро встреча́ть *impf.*, встре́тить *pf.* **bravery** *n.* хра́брость, сме́лость.
brawl [brɔːl] *n.* у́личная дра́ка, сканда́л; *v.i.* дра́ться (деру́сь, -рёшься; дра́лся, -ала́сь, -а́ло́сь) *impf.*, по~ *pf.*; сканда́лить *impf.*, на~ *pf.*
brawn [brɔːn] *n.* му́скульная си́ла; (*cul.*) свино́й сту́день (-дня) *m.* **brawny** дю́жий (дюж, -а́, -е), си́льный (си́лён, -льна́, -льно, си́льны́).
bray [breɪ] *n.* крик осла́; *v.i.* крича́ть (-чи́т) *impf.*; издава́ть (-даю́, -даёшь) *impf.*, изда́ть (-а́м, -а́шь, -а́ст, -ади́м; изда́л, -а́, -о) *pf.* ре́зкий звук.
brazen ['breɪz(ə)n] *adj.* ме́дный, бро́нзовый; (~*-faced*) бессты́дный.
brazier ['breɪzɪə(r), -ʒə(r)] *n.* жаро́вня (*g.pl.* -вен).
breach [briːtʃ] *n.* наруше́ние; (*break*) проло́м; (*mil.*) брешь; *v.t.* прола́мывать *impf.*, пролома́ть, проломи́ть (-млю́, -мишь) *pf.*
bread [bred] *n.* хлеб; (*white*) бу́лка. **breadwinner** *n.* корми́лец (-льца).
breadth [bredθ] *n.* ширина́, широта́.
break [breɪk] *n.* проло́м, разры́в; (*pause*) переры́в, па́уза; ~ **of day** рассве́т; *v.t.* лома́ть *impf.*, с~ *pf.*; разбива́ть *impf.*, разби́ть (разобью́, -ьёшь) *pf.*; (*violate*) наруша́ть *impf.*, нару́шить *pf.*; ~ **in(to)** вла́мываться *impf.*, вломи́ться (-млю́сь, -мишься) *pf.* в+*a.*; ~ **off** отла́мывать *impf.*, отломи́ть (-млю́, -мишь) *pf.*; (*interrupt*) прерыва́ть *impf.*, прерва́ть (-ву́, -вёшь; -ва́л, -вала́, -ва́ло) *pf.*; ~ **out** вырыва́ться *impf.*, вы́рваться (-вусь, -вешься) *pf.*; ~ **through** пробива́ться *impf.*, проби́ться (-бью́сь, -бьёшься) *pf.*; ~ **up** разбива́ть(ся) *impf.*, разби́ть(ся) (разобью́, -бьёт(ся) *pf.*; ~ **with** порыва́ть *impf.*, порва́ть (-ву́, -вёшь; порва́л, -а́, -о) *pf.* с+*i.* **breakage** *n.* поло́мка. **breakdown** *n.* ава́рия; **nervous** ~ не́рвное расстро́йство. **breaker** *n.* буру́н (-а́). **breakfast** ['brekfəst] *n.* у́тренний за́втрак; *v.i.* за́втракать *impf.*, по~ *pf.* **breakneck** *adj.*: **at** ~ **speed** сломя́ го́лову. **breakwater** *n.* мол (*loc.* -у́).
breast [brest] *n.* грудь (-ди́, *i.* -дью; *pl.* -ди, -де́й). **breast-feeding** *n.* кормле́ние гру́дью. **breaststroke** *n.* брасс.
breath [breθ] *n.* дыха́ние, дунове́ние. **breathalyse** ['breθəlaɪz] *v.t.* проверя́ть*impf.*, прове́рить *pf.* на алкого́ль *m.* **Breathalyser** *n.* (*propr.*) алкоме́тр. **breathe** [briːð] *v.i.* дыша́ть (-шу́, -шишь) *impf.*; ~ **in** вдыха́ть *impf.*, вдохну́ть *pf.*; ~ **out** выдыха́ть *impf.*, вы́дохнуть *pf.* **breather, breathing-space** *n.* переды́шка. **breathless** *adj.* запыха́вшийся.
breeches [brɪtʃɪz] *n.* бри́джи (-же́й) *pl.*, брю́ки (-к) *pl.*
breed [briːd] *n.* поро́да; *v.i.* размножа́ться *impf.*, размно́житься *pf.*; *v.t.* разводи́ть (-ожу́, -о́дишь) *impf.*, развести́ (-еду́, -едёшь; -ёл, -ела́) *pf.* **breeder** *n.* ...во́д: **cattle** ~ скотово́д; **poultry** ~ птицево́д. **breeding** *n.* разведе́ние, ...во́дство; (*upbringing*) воспи́танность.
breeze [briːz] *n.* ветеро́к (-рка́); (*naut.*) бриз. **breezy** *adj.* све́жий (свеж, -а́, -о́, све́жи́); (*lively*) живо́й (жив, -а́, -о).
breviary ['briːvɪərɪ] *n.* тре́бник.
brevity ['brevɪtɪ] *n.* кра́ткость.
brew [bruː] *v.t.* (*beer*) вари́ть (-рю́, -ришь) *impf.*, с~ *pf.*; (*tea*) зава́ривать *impf.*, завари́ть (-рю́, -ришь) *pf.* **brewer** *n.* пивова́р. **brewery** *n.* пивова́ренный заво́д.
bribe [braɪb] *n.* взя́тка; *v.t.* дава́ть (даю́, даёшь) *impf.*, дать (дам, дашь, даст, дади́м; дал, -а́, да́ло́, -и) *pf.* взя́тку+*d.*; подкупа́ть *impf.*, подкупи́ть (-плю́, -пишь) *pf.* **bribery** *n.* по́дкуп.
brick [brɪk] *n.* кирпи́ч (-а́) (*also collect.*); (*toy*) (де́тский) ку́бик; *adj.* кирпи́чный. **brickbat** *n.* обло́мок (-мка) кирпича́. **bricklayer** *n.* ка́менщик.
bridal ['braɪd(ə)l] *adj.* сва́дебный. **bride** *n.* неве́ста; (*after wedding*) новобра́чная *sb.* **bridegroom** *n.* жени́х (-а́); новобра́чный *sb.* **bridesmaid** *n.* подру́жка неве́сты.
bridge[1] [brɪdʒ] *n.* мост (мо́ста́, *loc.* -у́; *pl.* -ы́),

мо́стик; (*of nose*) перено́сица; *v.t.* наводи́ть (-ожу́, -о́дишь) *impf.*, навести́ (-еду́, -едёшь; -ёл, -ела́) *pf.* мост че́рез+*a.*; стро́ить *impf.*, по~ *pf.* мост че́рез+*a.* **bridgehead** *n.* плацда́рм.

bridge² [brɪdʒ] *n.* (*cards*) бридж.

bridle ['braɪd(ə)l] *n.* узда́ (*pl.* -ды), у́здечка; *v.t.* обу́здывать *impf.*, обузда́ть *pf.*; *v.i.* возмуща́ться *impf.*, возмути́ться (-ущу́сь, -ути́шься) *pf.*

brief [bri:f] *adj.* недо́лгий (-лог, -лга́, -лго), кра́ткий (-ток, -тка́, -тко); *n.* инструкта́ж; *v.t.* инструкти́ровать *impf.* & *pf.* **brief-case** *n.* портфе́ль *m.* **briefing** *n.* инструкти́рование. **briefly** *adv.* кра́тко, сжа́то. **briefs** *n.* трусы́ (-о́в), тру́сики (-ов) *pl.*

brier ['braɪə(r)] *n.* шипо́вник.

brig [brɪg] *n.* бриг.

brigade [brɪ'geɪd] *n.* брига́да. **brigadier** [ˌbrɪgə'dɪə(r)] *n.* бригади́р.

bright [braɪt] *adj.* я́ркий (я́рок, ярка́, я́рко), блестя́щий; (*clever*) смышлёный (-ён). **brighten** *v.i.* проясня́ться *impf.*, проясни́тся *pf.*; *v.t.* придава́ть (-даю́, -даёшь) *impf.*, прида́ть (-а́м, -а́шь, -а́ст, -ади́м; при́дал, -а́, -о) *pf.* блеск, красоту́. **brightness** *n.* я́ркость.

brilliant ['brɪlɪənt] *adj.* блестя́щий.

brim [brɪm] *n.* край (*pl.* -ая́); (*hat*) поля́ (-ле́й) *pl.* **brimful** *adj.* по́лный (-лон, -лна́, по́лно́) до краёв.

brimstone ['brɪmstəʊn] *n.* саморо́дная се́ра.

brine [braɪn] *n.* рассо́л.

bring [brɪŋ] *v.t.* (*carry*) приноси́ть (-ошу́, -о́сишь) *impf.*, принести́ (-есу́, -есёшь; -ёс, -есла́) *pf.*; (*lead*) приводи́ть (-ожу́, -о́дишь) *impf.*, привести́ (-еду́, -едёщь; -ёл, -ела́) *pf.*; (*transport*) привози́ть (-ожу́, -о́зишь) *impf.*, привезти́ (-езу́, -езёшь; -ёз, -езла́) *pf.*; ~ **about** быть причи́ной+*g.*; ~ **back** возвраща́ть *impf.*, возврати́ть (-ащу́, -ати́шь) *pf.*; ~ **down** сва́ливать *impf.*, свали́ть (-лю́, -лишь) *pf.*; ~ **forward** переноси́ть (-ошу́, -о́сишь) *impf.*, перенести́ (-есу́, -есёшь; -ёс, -есла́) *pf.* на сле́дующую страни́цу; ~ **up** (*educate*) воспи́тывать *impf.*, воспита́ть *pf.*; (*question*) поднима́ть *impf.*, подня́ть (-ниму́, -ни́мешь; по́днял, -а́, -о) *pf.*

brink [brɪŋk] *n.* край (*pl.* -ая́), грань.

brisk [brɪsk] *adj.* (*lively*) живо́й (жив, -а́, -о), оживлённый (-ён, -ённа); (*air etc.*) све́жий (свеж, -а́, -о́, све́жи́), бодря́щий.

brisket ['brɪskɪt] *n.* груди́нка.

brisling ['brɪzlɪŋ, 'brɪs-] *n.* бри́слинг, шпро́та.

bristle ['brɪs(ə)l] *n.* щети́на; *v.i.* ощети́ниваться *impf.*, ощети́ниться *pf.*; ~ **with** изоби́ловать *impf.*+*i.*

Britain ['brɪt(ə)n] Великобрита́ния, А́нглия. **British** *adj.* брита́нский, англи́йский; ~ **Isles** Брита́нские острова́. **Britisher, Briton** *n.* брита́нец (-нца), -нка; англича́нин (*pl.* -а́не), -а́нка.

brittle ['brɪt(ə)l] *adj.* хру́пкий (-пок, -пка́, -пко). **brittleness** *n.* хру́пкость.

broach [brəʊtʃ] *v.t.* начина́ть *impf.*, нача́ть (-чну́, -чнёшь; на́чал, -а́, -о) *pf.* обсужда́ть; затра́гивать *impf.*, затро́нуть *pf.*

broad [brɔ:d] *adj.* (*wide*) широ́кий (-о́к, -ока́, -о́ко́); (*general*) о́бщий (общ, -а́); (*clear*) я́сный (я́сен, ясна́, я́сно, я́сны́); **in ~ daylight** средь бе́ла дня; **in ~ outline** в о́бщих черта́х. **broad-minded** *adj.* с широ́кими взгля́дами. **broadly** *adv.*: ~ **speaking** вообще́ говоря́.

broadcast ['brɔ:dkɑ:st] *n.* радио-, теле-, переда́ча; радио-, теле-, програ́мма; *adj.* радио..., теле...; *v.t.* передава́ть (-даю́, -даёшь) *impf.*, переда́ть (-а́м, -а́шь, -а́ст, -ади́м; пе́редал, -а́, -о) *pf.* по ра́дио, по телеви́дению; (*seed*) се́ять (се́ю, се́ешь) *impf.*, по~ *pf.* вразбро́с. **broadcaster** *n.* ди́ктор. **broadcasting** *n.* радио-, теле-, веща́ние.

brocade [brə'keɪd, brəʊ-] *n.* парча́; *adj.* парчо́вый.

broccoli ['brɒkəlɪ] *n.* спа́ржевая капу́ста.

brochure ['brəʊʃə(r), brəʊ'ʃjʊə(r)] *n.* брошю́ра.

brogue [brəʊg] *n.* (*shoe*) спорти́вный боти́нок (-нка; *g.pl.* -нок); (*accent*) ирла́ндский акце́нт.

broiler ['brɔɪlə(r)] *n.* бро́йлер.

broke [brəʊk] *pred.* разорён (-а́); **be ~ to the world** не име́ть *impf.* ни гроша́. **broken** *adj.* сло́манный (-ан), разби́тый, нару́шенный (-ен). **broken-hearted** *adj.* уби́тый го́рем.

broker ['brəʊkə(r)] *n.* бро́кер, ма́клер. **brokerage** *n.* комиссио́нное вознагражде́ние.

bromide ['brəʊmaɪd] *n.* броми́д. **bromine** ['brəʊmi:n] *n.* бром (-а(у)).

bronchitis [brɒŋ'kaɪtɪs] *n.* бронхи́т.

bronze [brɒnz] *n.* бро́нза; *adj.* бро́нзовый; *v.t.* бронзирова́ть *impf.* & *pf.*

brooch [brəʊtʃ] *n.* брошь, бро́шка.

brood [bru:d] *n.* вы́водок (-дка); *v.i.* мра́чно размышля́ть *impf.* **broody** *adj.* сидя́щий на я́йцах; ~ **hen** насе́дка.

brook¹ [brʊk] *n.* руче́й (-чья́).

brook² [brʊk] *v.t.* терпе́ть (-плю́, -пишь) *impf.*

broom [bru:m] *n.* метла́ (*pl.* мётлы, -тел, -тлам); (*plant*) раки́тник, дрок. **broomstick** *n.* (*witches'*) помело́ (*pl.* -лья, -льев).

Bros. *abbr.* (*of* **Brother(s)**) Бра́тья (в назва́нии фи́рмы).

broth [brɒθ] *n.* бульо́н.

brothel ['brɒθ(ə)l] *n.* публи́чный дом (*pl.* -а́).

brother ['brʌðə(r)] *n.* брат (*pl.* -ья, -ьев); ~ **in arms** собра́т (*pl.* -ья, -ьев) по ору́жию. **brother-in-law** *n.* (*sister's husband*) зять (*pl.* -я́, -ёв); (*husband's brother*) де́верь (*pl.* -рья́, -ре́й); (*wife's brother*) шу́рин *pl.* (шурья́, -ьёв); (*wife's sister's husband*) своя́к (-а́). **brotherhood** *n.* бра́тство. **brotherly** *adj.* бра́тский.

brow [braʊ] *n.* (*eyebrow*) бровь (*pl.* -ви, -вéй); (*forehead*) лоб (лба, *loc.* лбу); (*of cliff*) вы́ступ. **browbeaten** *adj.* запу́ганный (-ан).
brown [braʊn] *adj.* кори́чневый; (*eyes*) ка́рий; ~ **paper** обёрточная бума́га; *v.t.* (*cul.*) подрумя́нивать *impf.*, подрумя́нить *pf.*
browse [braʊz] *v.i.* (*feed*) пасти́сь (пасётся; па́сся, пасла́сь) *impf.*; (*read*) чита́ть *impf.* бессисте́мно.
bruise [bru:z] *n.* синя́к (-а́), уши́б; *v.t.* ушиба́ть *impf.*, ушиби́ть (-бу́, -бёшь; -б) *pf.* **bruised** *adj.* (*fruit*) повреждённый (-ён, -ена́).
brunette [bru:'net] *n.* брюне́тка.
brush [brʌʃ] *n.* щётка; (*paint*) кисть (*pl.* -ти, -те́й); *v.t.* (*clean*) чи́стить *impf.*, вы́~ *pf.* щёткой; (*touch*) легко́ каса́ться *impf.*, косну́ться *pf.+g.*; ~ **one's hair** причёсываться *impf.*, причеса́ться (-ешу́сь, -е́шешься) *pf.* щёткой; ~ **aside** отстраня́ть *impf.*, отстрани́ть *pf.*; ~ **up** собира́ть *impf.*, собра́ть (соберу́, -рёшь; собра́л, -а́, -о) *pf.* щёткой; (*renew*) возобновля́ть *impf.*, возобнови́ть *pf.* знако́мство с+*i.* **brush-off** *n.*: **give the** ~ отма́хиваться *impf.*, отмахну́ться *pf.+g.*
brushwood ['brʌʃwʊd] *n.* хво́рост (-а(у)).
Brussels ['brʌs(ə)lz] *n.* Брюссе́ль *m.* **Brussels sprouts** *n.* брюссе́льская капу́ста.
brutal ['bru:t(ə)l] *adj.* жесто́кий (-о́к, -о́ка́, -о́ко), зве́рский, гру́бый (груб, -а́, -о). **bru'tality** *n.* жесто́кость, зве́рство. **brutalize** *v.t.* (*treat brutally*) гру́бо обраща́ться *impf.*, с+*i.*; (*make brutal*) доводи́ть (-ожу́, -о́дишь) *impf.*, довести́ (-еду́, -едёшь; -ёл, -ела́) *pf.* до озвере́ния. **brute** *n.* живо́тное *sb.*; (*person*) скоти́на. **brutish** *adj.* гру́бый (груб, -а́, -о), жесто́кий (-о́к, -о́ка́, -о́ко).
B.Sc. *abbr.* (*of* ***Bachelor of Science***) бакала́вр (есте́ственных).
BST *abbr.* (*of* ***British Summer Time***) Брита́нское ле́тнее вре́мя.
bubble ['bʌb(ə)l] *n.* пузы́рь (-ря́) *m.*, пузырёк (-рька́); *v.i.* пузы́риться *impf.*; кипе́ть (-пи́т) *impf.*, вс~ *pf.* **bubbly** *n.* шампа́нское *sb.*
buccaneer [ˌbʌkə'nɪə(r)] *n.* пира́т.
buck [bʌk] *n.* (*male animal*) саме́ц (-мца́); *v.i.* брыка́ться *impf.*
bucket ['bʌkɪt] *n.* ведро́ (*pl.* вёдра, -дер, -драм), ведёрко (*pl.* -рки, -рок, -ркам).
buckle ['bʌk(ə)l] *n.* пря́жка; *v.t.* застёгивать *impf.*, застегну́ть *pf.* пря́жкой; *v.i.* (*crumple*) коро́биться *impf.*, по~, с~ *pf.*
buckshot ['bʌkʃɒt] *n.* карте́чь.
buckskins ['bʌkskɪnz] *n.* лоси́ны (-н) *pl.*
buckthorn ['bʌkθɔ:n] *n.* круши́на.
buckwheat ['bʌkwi:t] *n.* гречи́ха.
bucolic [bju:'kɒlɪk] *adj.* буколи́ческий, дереве́нский.
bud [bʌd] *n.* по́чка, буто́н; *v.i.* развива́ться *impf.* **budding** *n.* окулиро́вка, почкова́ние.
Buddha ['bʊdə] *n.* Бу́дда. **Buddhism** *n.* будди́зм. **Buddhist** *n.* будди́ст; *adj.* будди́йский.
budge [bʌdʒ] *v.t.* & *i.* шевели́ть(ся) (-елю́(сь), -е́ли́шь(ся)) *impf.*, по~ *pf.*
budgerigar ['bʌdʒərɪˌgɑ:(r)] *n.* попуга́йчик.
budget ['bʌdʒɪt] *n.* бюдже́т; *v.i.*: ~ **for** предусма́тривать *impf.*, предусмотре́ть (-рю́, -ришь) *pf.* в бюдже́те.
buff [bʌf] *n.* (*leather*) ко́жа; **in, to, the** ~ нагишо́м; *adj.* желтова́то-бе́жевый.
buffalo ['bʌfəˌləʊ] *n.* бу́йвол.
buffoon [bə'fu:n] *n.* шут (-а́); **act the** ~ пая́сничать *impf.*
bug [bʌg] *n.* (*bedbug*) клоп (-а́); (*virus*) ви́рус; (*microphone*) потайно́й микрофо́н; *v.t.* (*install* ~) устана́вливать *impf.*, установи́ть (-влю́, -вишь) *pf.* аппарату́ру для подслу́шивания в+*p.*; (*listen*) подслу́шивать *impf.*
bugle ['bju:g(ə)l] *n.* рог (*pl.* -а́), горн. **bugler** *n.* горни́ст.
build [bɪld] *n.* (*person*) телосложе́ние; *v.t.* стро́ить *impf.*, вы́~, по~ *pf.* **builder** *n.* строи́тель *m.* **building** *n.* (*edifice*) зда́ние; (*action*) строи́тельство; ~ **society** о́бщество, предоставля́ющее сре́дства для поку́пки жилы́х помеще́ний.
bulb [bʌlb] *n.* лу́ковица; (*electric*) ла́мпочка. **bulbous** *adj.* лу́ковичный.
Bulgaria [bʌl'geərɪə] *n.* Болга́рия.
bulge [bʌldʒ] *n.* вы́пуклость, вы́ступ; *v.i.* выпя́чиваться *impf.*; выпира́ть *impf.* **bulging** *adj.* разбу́хший, оттопы́ривающийся; ~ **eyes** глаза́ (-з) *pl.* на вы́кате.
bulk [bʌlk] *n.* (*size*) объём; (*greater part*) бо́льшая часть; (*mass*) основна́я ма́сса; (*large object*) грома́да; ~ **buying** заку́пки *f.pl.* гурто́м; ~ **cargo** груз нава́лом.
bull [bʊl] *n.* (*ox*) бык (-а́); (*male animal*) саме́ц (-мца́); *adj.* быча́чий (-чья, -чье). **bulldog** *n.* бульдо́г. **bulldoze** *v.t.* расчища́ть *impf.*, расчи́стить *pf.* бульдо́зером. **bulldozer** *n.* бульдо́зер. **bullfinch** *n.* снеги́рь (-ря́) *m.* **bullock** ['bʊlək] *n.* вол (-а́). **bull's-eye** *n.* (*target*) я́блоко.
bullet ['bʊlɪt] *n.* пу́ля. **bullet-proof** *adj.* пулесто́йкий.
bulletin ['bʊlɪtɪn] *n.* бюллете́нь *m.*
bullion ['bʊlɪən] *n.* сли́ток (-тка).
bully ['bʊlɪ] *n.* зади́ра *c.g.*, забия́ка *c.g.*; *v.t.* запу́гивать *impf.*, запуга́ть *pf.*; задира́ть *impf.*
bulrush ['bʊlrʌʃ] *n.* камы́ш (-а́)
bulwark ['bʊlwək] *n.* бастио́н, опло́т.
bum [bʌm] *n.* зад (*loc.* -у́; *pl.* -ы́).
bumble-bee ['bʌmb(ə)lˌbi:] *n.* шмель (-ля́) *m.*
bump [bʌmp] *n.* (*blow*) уда́р, толчо́к (-чка́); (*swelling*) ши́шка; *v.i.* ударя́ться *impf.*, уда́риться *pf.*; ~ **into, against** налета́ть *impf.*, налете́ть (-ечу́, -ети́шь) *pf.* на+*a.*; ната́лкиваться *impf.*, натолкну́ться *pf.* на+*a.* **bumper** *n.* ба́мпер; *adj.* о́чень кру́пный, оби́льный.

bumpkin ['bʌmpkɪn] *n.* неотёсанный па́рень (-рня; *pl.* -рни, -рне́й) *m.*; **country** ~ деревéнщина *c.g.*

bumptious ['bʌmpʃəs] *adj.* наха́льный, самоуве́ренный (-ен, -енна).

bun [bʌn] *n.* сдо́бная бу́лка.

bunch [bʌntʃ] *n.* пучо́к (-чка́), свя́зка, гроздь (*pl.* -ди, -де́й & -дья, -дьев); *v.t.* собира́ть *impf.*, собра́ть (соберу́, -рёшь; собра́л, -а́, -о) *pf.* в пучки́.

bundle ['bʌnd(ə)l] *n.* у́зел (узла́), узело́к (-лка́); *v.t.* свя́зывать *impf.*, связа́ть (-яжу́, -я́жешь) *pf.* в у́зел; ~ **away, off** спрова́живать *impf.*, спрова́дить *pf.*

bung [bʌŋ] *n.* вту́лка.

bungalow ['bʌŋgə,ləʊ] *n.* бу́нгало *nt.indecl.*

bungle ['bʌŋg(ə)l] *v.t.* по́ртить *impf.*, ис~ *pf.*; *n.* пу́таница. **bungler** *n.* пу́таник.

bunk [bʌŋk] *n.* (*berth*) ко́йка.

bunker ['bʌŋkə(r)] *n.* бу́нкер (*pl.* -а́ & -ы).

bunkum ['bʌŋkəm] *n.* чепуха́.

buoy [bɔɪ] *n.* бу́й (*pl.* буи́), ба́кен. **buoyancy** *n.* плаву́честь; (*fig.*) бо́дрость, оживле́ние. **buoyant** *adj.* плаву́чий; бо́дрый (бодр, -а́, -о), жизнера́достный.

bur, burr [bɜ:(r)] *n.* колю́чка.

burden ['bɜ:d(ə)n] *n.* бре́мя *nt.*; *v.t.* обременя́ть *impf.*, обремени́ть *pf.*

bureau ['bjʊərəʊ, -'rəʊ] *n.* бюро́ *nt.indecl.* **bureaucracy** [bjʊə'rɒkrəsɪ] *n.* бюрокра́тия (*also collect.*), бюрократи́зм. **'bureaucrat** *n.* бюрокра́т. **bureau'cratic** *adj.* бюрократи́ческий.

burger ['bɜ:gə(r)] *n.* га́мбургер, котле́та; ~ **bar** га́мбургерная *sb.*

burglar ['bɜ:glə(r)] *n.* взло́мщик. **burglary** *n.* кра́жа со взло́мом. **burgle** *v.i.* соверша́ть *impf.*, соверши́ть *pf.* кра́жу со взло́мом; *v.t.* гра́бить *impf.*, о~ *pf.*

burial ['berɪəl] *n.* погребе́ние; ~ **service** заупоко́йная слу́жба.

burlesque [bɜ:'lesk] *n.* паро́дия; *v.t.* пароди́ровать *impf.* & *pf.*; *adj.* пароди́ческий, пароди́йный.

burly ['bɜ:lɪ] *adj.* здорове́нный.

burn [bɜ:n] *v.t.* жечь (жгу, жжёшь, жгут; жёг, жгла) *impf.*, с~ (сожгу́, сожжёшь, сожгу́т; сжёг, сожгла́) *pf.*; *v.t.* & *i.* (*injure*) обжига́ть(ся) *impf.*, обже́чь(ся) (обожгу́(сь), обожжёшь(ся), обожгу́т(ся); обжёг(ся), обожгла́(сь)) *pf.*; *v.i.* горе́ть (-рю́, -ришь) *impf.*, с~ *pf.*; (*by sun*) загора́ть *impf.*, загоре́ть (-рю́, -ри́шь) *pf.*; *n.* ожо́г. **burner** *n.* горе́лка. **burning** *adj.* горя́чий (-ч, -ча́).

burnish ['bɜ:nɪʃ] *v.t.* полирова́ть *impf.*, на~, от~ *pf.* **burnishing** *n.* полиро́вка; *adj.* полирова́льный.

burr *see* **bur**

burrow ['bʌrəʊ] *n.* нора́ (*pl.* -ры), но́рка; *v.i.* рыть (ро́ю, ро́ешь) *impf.*, вы́~ *pf.* нору́; (*fig.*) ры́ться (ро́юсь, ро́ешься) *impf.*

bursar ['bɜ:sə] *n.* казначе́й. **bursary** *n.* стипе́ндия.

burst [bɜ:st] *n.* разры́в, вспы́шка; *v.i.* разрыва́ться *impf.*, разорва́ться (-вётся; -ва́лся, -вала́сь, -вало́сь) *pf.*; ло́паться *impf.*, ло́пнуть *pf.*; *v.t.* разрыва́ть *impf.*, разорва́ть (-ву́, -вёшь; разорва́л, -а́, -о) *pf.*

bury ['berɪ] *v.t.* (*dead*) хорони́ть (-ню́, -нишь) *impf.*, по~ *pf.*; (*hide*) зарыва́ть *impf.*, зары́ть (-ро́ю, -ро́ешь) *pf.*

bus [bʌs] *n.* авто́бус; ~ **conductor** конду́ктор (*pl.* -а́).

bush [bʊʃ] *n.* куст (-а́); (*collect.*) куста́рник. **bushy** *adj.* густо́й (густ, -а́, -о, гу́сты́).

business ['bɪznɪs] *n.* (*matter*) де́ло; (*occupation*) заня́тие; (*firm*) комме́рческое предприя́тие; (*buying and selling*) би́знес; **big** ~ кру́пный капита́л; **mind your own** ~ не ва́ше де́ло; **no monkey** ~ без фо́кусов; **on** ~ по де́лу. **businessman** *n.* бизнесме́н.

busker [bʌskə(r)] *n.* у́личный музыка́нт.

bust [bʌst] *n.* (*sculpture*) бюст; (*bosom*) грудь (-ди́, *i.* -дью; *pl.* -ди, -де́й).

bustle[1] ['bʌs(ə)l] *n.* (*fuss*) сумато́ха, суета́; *v.i.* суети́ться *impf.*

bustle[2] ['bʌs(ə)l] *n.* (*garment*) турню́р.

busy ['bɪzɪ] *adj.* занято́й (за́нят, -а́, -о); *v.t.*: ~ **o.s.** занима́ться *impf.*, заня́ться (займу́сь, -мёшься; заня́лся́, -ла́сь) *pf.* (**with** +*i.*). **busybody** ['bɪzɪ,bɒdɪ] *n.* челове́к, сую́щий нос в чужи́е дела́.

but [bʌt] *conj.* но, а, кро́ме; ~ **then** но зато́; *prep.* кро́ме+*g.*

butcher ['bʊtʃə(r)] *n.* мясни́к (-а́); *v.t.* ре́зать (ре́жу, -жешь) *impf.*, за~ *pf.*; **~'s shop** мясна́я *sb.* **butchery** *n.* резня́.

butler ['bʌtlə(r)] *n.* дворе́цкий *sb.*

butt[1] [bʌt] *n.* (*cask*) бо́чка.

butt[2] [bʌt] *n.* (*of gun*) прикла́д; (*end*) то́лстый коне́ц (-нца́).

butt[3] [bʌt] *n.* (*target*) мише́нь.

butt[4] [bʌt] *v.t.* бода́ть *impf.*, за~ *pf.*; *v.i.* бода́ться *impf.*

butter ['bʌtə(r)] *n.* (сли́вочное) ма́сло; *v.t.* нама́зывать *impf.*, намаза́ть (-ажу́, -а́жешь) *pf.* ма́слом. **buttercup** *n.* лю́тик. **butterfly** *n.* ба́бочка.

buttock ['bʌtək] *n.* я́годица.

button ['bʌt(ə)n] *n.* пу́говица; (*knob*) кно́пка; *v.t.* застёгивать *impf.*, застегну́ть *pf.*

buttress ['bʌtrɪs] *n.* контрфо́рс; *v.t.* подпира́ть *impf.*, подпере́ть (подопру́, -рёшь; подпёр) *pf.*

buy [baɪ] *n.* поку́пка; *v.t.* покупа́ть *impf.*, купи́ть (-плю́, -пишь) *pf.* **buyer** *n.* покупа́тель *m.*

buzz [bʌz] *n.* жужжа́ние; *v.i.* жужжа́ть (-жи́т) *impf.*; гуде́ть (гужу́, гуди́шь) *impf.*

buzzard ['bʌzəd] *n.* каню́к (-а́)

buzzer ['bʌzə(r)] *n.* зу́ммер.

by [baɪ] *adv.* ми́мо; ~ **and** ~ вско́ре; *prep.* (*near*) о́коло+*g.*, у+*g.*; (*beside*) ря́дом с+*i.*; (*via*) че́рез+*a.*; (*past*) ми́мо+*g.* (*time*) к+*d.*; (*means*) *i. without prep.*; ~ **means of** посре́дством+*g.*

bye-bye ['baɪbaɪ, bə'baɪ] *int.* пока́!; всего́!
by-election ['baɪɪ,lekʃ(ə)n] *n.* дополни́тельные вы́боры *m.pl.* **bygone** *adj.* пережи́тый, про́шлый; *n.*: *pl.* про́шлое *sb.*; (*objects*) предме́ты *m.pl.*, вы́шедшие из употребле́ния; **let ~s be ~s** что пропа́ло, то быльём поросло́. **by-law** *n.* пастановле́ние ме́стной вла́сти. **bypass** *n.* (*road*) обхо́д, обхо́дный путь (-ти́, -тём) *m.*; (*pipe*) обво́дный кана́л; *v.t.* обходи́ть (-ожу́, -о́дишь) *impf.*, обойти́ (обойду́, -дёшь; обошёл, -шла́) *pf.*; объезжа́ть *impf.*, объе́хать (-е́ду, -е́дешь) *pf.* **by-product** *n.* побо́чный проду́кт. **bystander** *n.* наблюда́тель *m.*
byte [baɪt] *n.* (*comput.*) байт.
byway *n.* просёлочная доро́га. **byword** *n.* (*proverb*) погово́рка; (*example*) приме́р.

C

C[1] [siː] *n.* (*mus.*) до *nt.indecl.*
C[2] *abbr.* (*of* **Celsius** *or* **centigrade**) (шкала́) Це́льсия; **20°C** 20°Ц (гра́дусов Це́льсия (*or* по Це́льсию)).
c. *abbr.* (*of* **century**) в., век; ст., столе́тие; (*of* **circa**) ок., о́коло; (*of* **cent(s)**) це́нт.
cab [kæb] *n.* (*taxi*) такси́ *nt.indecl.*; (*of lorry*) каби́на.
cabaret ['kæbə,reɪ] *n.* кабаре́, эстра́дное представле́ние.
cabbage ['kæbɪdʒ] *n.* капу́ста; **~ white** капу́стница.
cabin ['kæbɪn] *n.* (*hut*) хи́жина; (*bathing etc.*) каби́на; (*ship's*) каю́та. **cabin-boy** *n.* ю́нга *m.*
cabinet ['kæbɪnɪt](*pol.*) кабине́т; (*cupboard*) (застеклённый) шкаф (*loc.* -у́; *pl.* -ы́); **C~ Minister** мини́стр-член кабине́та. **cabinet-maker** *n.* краснодере́вец (-вца).
cable ['keɪb(ə)l] *n.* (*rope*) кана́т, трос; (*electric*) ка́бель *m.*; (*cablegram*) каблогра́мма; **~ stitch** жгут (-а́); *v.t.* & *i.* телеграфи́ровать *impf.* & *pf.* (по подво́дному ка́белью).
cabotage ['kæbə,tɑːʒ, -tɪdʒ] *n.* кабота́ж.
cacao [kə'kɑːəʊ, -'keɪəʊ] *n.* кака́о *nt.indecl.*
cache [kæʃ] *n.* укры́тый, та́йный, запа́с.
cackle ['kæk(ə)l] *n.* (*geese*) го́гот, гогота́нье; (*hens*) куда́хтанье; *v.i.* гогота́ть (-очу́, -о́чешь) *impf.*; куда́хтать (-хчу, -хчешь) *impf.*
cactus ['kæktəs] *n.* ка́ктус; *adj.* ка́ктусовый.
cad [kæd] *n.* хам.
cadaverous [kə'dævərəs] *adj.* мёртвенно-бле́дный (-ден, -дна́, -дно, -бле́дны́).
caddie ['kædɪ] *n.* челове́к, прислу́живающий при игре́ в гольф.
caddish ['kædɪʃ] *adj.* ха́мский.
caddy ['kædɪ] *n.* (*box*) ча́йница.
cadence ['keɪd(ə)ns] *n.* (*rhythm*) ритм, такт; (*mus.*) каде́нция. **cadenced** *adj.* ме́рный, ритми́чный. **cadenza** [kə'denzə] *n.* каде́нция.
cadet [kə'det] *n.* каде́т (*g.pl.* -т & -тов); *adj.* каде́тский.
cadge [kædʒ] *v.t.* выпра́шивать *impf.*, вы́просить *pf.*
cadre ['kɑːdə(r), 'kɑːdrə] *n.* ка́дры *m.pl.*
Caesarean (section) [sɪ'zeərɪən] *n.* ке́сарево сече́ние.
caesura [sɪ'zjʊərə] *n.* цезу́ра.
cafe ['kæfeɪ, 'kæfɪ] *n.* кафе́ *nt.indecl.* **cafeteria** [,kæfɪ'tɪərɪə] *n.* кафете́рий.
caffeine ['kæfiːn] *n.* кофеи́н.
cage [keɪdʒ] *n.* кле́тка; (*in mine*) клеть (*loc.* -ети́; *pl.* -ти, -те́й); *v.t.* сажа́ть *impf.*, посади́ть (-ажу́, -а́дишь) *pf.* в кле́тку; **a ~d lion** лев в кле́тке.
cairn [keən] *n.* гру́да камне́й.
caisson ['keɪs(ə)n, kə'suːn] *n.* кессо́н.
cajole [kə'dʒəʊl] *v.t.* ума́сливать *impf.*, ума́слить *pf.* **cajolery** *n.* лесть, ума́сливание.
cake [keɪk] *n.* торт, пиро́жное *sb.*; (*fruit-~*) кекс; (*soap*) кусо́к (-ска́); *v.i.* тверде́ть *impf.*, за~ *pf.*; отвердева́ть *impf.*, отверде́ть *pf.*
calabrese [,kælə'briːz] *n.* спа́ржевая капу́ста.
calamitous [kə'læmɪtəs] *adj.* па́губный, бе́дственный (-ен, -енна). **calamity** *n.* бе́дствие.
calcareous [kæl'keərɪəs] *adj.* известко́вый. **calcium** ['kælsɪəm] *n.* ка́льций; *adj.* ка́льциевый.
calculate ['kælkjʊ,leɪt] *v.t.* вычисля́ть *impf.*, вы́числить *pf.*; *v.i.* рассчи́тывать *impf.*, рассчита́ть *pf.* (**on** на+*a.*); **~ing-machine** вычисли́тельная маши́на. **calculated** *adj.* преднаме́ренный (-ен, -енна). **calcu'lation** *n.* вычисле́ние, расчёт. **calculator** *n.* калькуля́тор. **calculus** *n.* (*math.*) исчисле́ние; (*stone*) ка́мень (-мня; *pl.* -мни, -мне́й) *m.*
calendar ['kælɪndə(r)] *n.* календа́рь (-ря́) *m.*; (*register*) спи́сок (-ска).
calf[1] [kɑːf] *n.* (*cow*) телёнок (-нка; *pl.* теля́та, -т); (*other animal*) детёныш; (*leather*) теля́чья ко́жа; **~ love** ребя́ческая любо́вь (-бви́, -бо́вью)
calf[2] [kɑːf] *n.* (*leg*) икра́ (*pl.* -ры).
calibrate ['kælɪ,breɪt] *v.t.* калибри́ровать *impf.* & *pf.*; калиброва́ть *impf.* **cali'bration** *n.* калибро́вка. **calibre** *n.* кали́бр.
calico ['kælɪ,kəʊ] *n.* коленко́р (-а(у)), митка́ль (-ля́) *m.*
call [kɔːl] *v.* звать (зову́, -вёшь; звал, -а́, -о) *impf.*, по~ *pf.*; (*name*) называ́ть *impf.*, назва́ть (назову́, -вёшь; назва́л, -а́, -о) *pf.*;

(*cry*) кричáть (-чý, -чи́шь) *impf.*, кри́кнуть *pf.*; (*wake*) буди́ть (бужý, бýдишь) *impf.*, раз~ *pf.*; (*visit*) заходи́ть (-ожý, -óдишь) *impf.*, зайти́ (зайдý, -дёшь; зашёл, -шлá) *pf.* (**on** к+*d.*; **at** в+*a.*); (*stop at*) останáвливаться *impf.*, останови́ться (-вится) *pf.* (**at** в, на, +*p.*); (*summon*) вызывáть *impf.*, вы́звать (вы́зову, -вешь; *pf.*; (*ring up*) звони́ть *impf.*, по~ *pf.*+*d.*; ~ **for** (*require*) трéбовать *impf.*, по~ *pf.*+*g.*; (*fetch*) заходи́ть (-ожý, -óдишь) *impf.*, зайти́ (зайдý, -дёшь; зашёл, -шлá) *pf.* за+*i.*; ~ **off** отменя́ть *impf.*, отмени́ть (-ню́, -нишь) *pf.*; ~ **out** вскри́кивать *impf.*, вскри́кнуть *pf.*; ~ **up** призывáть *impf.*, призвáть (призовý, -вёшь; призвáл, -á, -о) *pf.*; *n.* (*cry*) крик; (*summons*) зов, призы́в; (*telephone*) (телефóнный) вы́зов, разговóр; (*visit*) визи́т; (*signal*) сигнáл. **call-box** *n.* телефóн-автомáт. **call-boy** *n.* мáльчик, вызывáющий актёров на сцéну.

caller *n.* посети́тель *m.*, ~ница; гость (*pl.* -ти, -тéй) *m.*, гóстья (*g.pl.* -тий). **calling** *n.* (*summons*) призвáние; (*profession*) профéссия; (*occupation*) заня́тие; (*trade*) ремеслó. **call-over** *n.* перекли́чка. **call-sign** *n.* позывнóй сигнáл, позывны́е *sb.* **call-up** призы́в.

callous ['kæləs] *adj.* (*person*) бессердéчный, бесчýвственный (-ен(ен), -енна).

callow ['kæləʊ] *adj.* (*unfledged*) неопери́вшийся; (*raw*) неóпытный.

callus ['kæləs] *n.* мозóль.

calm [kɑːm] *adj.* (*tranquil*) спокóйный, хладнокрóвный; (*quiet*) ти́хий (тих, -á, -о); (*windless*) безвéтренный (-ен, -енна); *n.* спокóйствие; безвéтрие; *v.t.* & *i.* (~ *down*) успокáивать(ся) *impf.*, успокóить(ся) *pf.*

calorie ['kælərɪ] *n.* калóрия.

calumniate [kə'lʌmnɪˌeɪt] *v.t.* клеветáть (-ещý, -éщешь) *impf.*, на~ *pf.* на+*a.* **calumniation, 'calumny** *n.* клеветá.

calve [kɑːv] *v.i.* тели́ться (-ится) *impf.*, о~ *pf.*

calypso [kə'lɪpsəʊ] *n.* кали́псо *nt.indecl.*

calyx ['keɪlɪks, 'kæl-] *n.* чáшечка.

cam [kæm] *n.* кулачóк (-чкá), кулáк (-á).

camber ['kæmbə(r)] *n.* вы́пуклость. **cambered** *adj.* вы́пуклый.

camcorder ['kæmˌkɔːdə(r)] *n.* камкóрдер.

camel ['kæm(ə)l] *n.* верблю́д.

cameo ['kæmɪˌəʊ] *n.* камéя.

camera ['kæmrə, -ərə] *n.* фотоаппарáт; кино-, теле-, кáмера. **cameraman** *n.* кинооперáтор.

camomile ['kæməˌmaɪl] *n.* ромáшка.

camouflage ['kæməˌflɑːʒ] *n.* маскирóвка; камуфля́ж; *adj.* маскирóвочный; *v.t.* маскировáть *impf.*, за~ *pf.*

camp [kæmp] *n.* лáгерь (*pl.* -я́, -éй) *m.*; *v.i.* располагáться *impf.*, расположи́ться (-жýсь, -жишься) *pf.* лáгерем. **camp-bed** *n.* раскладнáя кровáть, раскладýшка. **camp-chair** *n.* складнóй стул (*pl.* -ья, -ьев). **camp-fire** *n.* бивáчный костёр (-трá).

campaign [kæm'peɪn] *n.* кампáния; похóд; *v.i.* (*conduct* ~) проводи́ть (-ожý, -óдишь) *impf.*, провести́ (-едý, -едёшь; -ёл, -елá) *pf.* кампáнию; (*serve in* ~) учáствовать *impf.* в похóде, в кампáнии.

campanula [kæm'pænjʊlə] *n.* колокóльчик.

camphor ['kæmfə(r)] *n.* камфарá. **camphorated oil** *n.* камфóрное мáсло.

campus ['kæmpəs] *n.* акеми́ческий городóк (-дкá), академгородóк (-дкá).

camshaft ['kæmʃɑːft] *n.* распредели́тельный, кулачкóвый, вал (*loc.* -ý; *pl.* -ы́).

can[1] [kæn] *n.* жестя́нка, (консéрвная) корóбка, бáнка; *v.t.* консерви́ровать *impf.*, за~ *pf.*

can[2] [kæn] *v.aux.* (*be able*) мочь (могý, мóжешь; мог, -лá) *impf.*, с~ *pf.*+*inf.*; (*know how*) умéть *impf.*, с~ *pf.*+*inf.*

Canada ['kænədə] *n.* Канáда. **Canadian** [kə'neɪdɪən] *n.* канáдец (-дца), -дка; *adj.* канáдский.

canal [kə'næl] *n.* канáл.

canary [kə'neərɪ] *n.* канарéйка.

cancel ['kæns(ə)l] *v.t.* аннули́ровать *impf.* & *pf.*; отменя́ть *impf.*, отмени́ть (-ню́, -нишь) *pf.*; (*math.*) сокращáть *impf.*, сократи́ть (-ащý, -ати́шь) *pf.*; (*print.*) вычёркивать *impf.*, вы́черкнуть *pf.*; (*stamp*) гаси́ть (гашý, гáсишь) *impf.*, по~ *pf.*; *n.* (*print.*) перепечáтанный лист (-á). **cance'llation** *n.* аннули́рование, отмéна; (*math.*) сокращéние; (*print.*) перепечáтка.

cancer ['kænsə(r)] *n.* рак; (**C**~) Рак; *adj.* рáковый; ~ **patient** больнóй рáком. **cancerous** *adj.* рáковый.

candelabrum [ˌkændɪ'lɑːbrəm] *n.* канделя́бр.

candid ['kændɪd] *adj.* откровéнный (-нен, -нна), и́скренний (-нен, -нна, -нне & -нно); ~ **camera** скры́тый фотоаппарáт.

candidacy ['kændɪdəsɪ] *n.* кандидатýра. **candidate** *n.* кандидáт. **candidature** *n.* кандидатýра.

candied ['kændɪd] *adj.* засáхаренный; ~ **peel** цукáт(ы).

candle ['kænd(ə)l] *n.* свечá (*pl.* -чи, -чéй); ~ **end** огáрок (-рка). **candlestick** *n.* подсвéчник. **candlewick** *n.* фити́ль (-ля́) *m.*, вы́шивка фитилькáми.

candour ['kændə(r)] *n.* откровéнность, и́скренность.

candy ['kændɪ] *n.* слáдости *f.pl.*; *v.t.* засáхаривать *impf.*, засáхарить *pf.* **candyfloss** *n.* сáхарная вáта.

cane [keɪn] *n.* (*plant*) тростни́к (-á); (*stick*) трость (*pl.* -ти, -тéй), пáлка; ~ **sugar** тростникóвый сáхар (-а(у)); *v.t.* бить (бью, бьёшь) *impf.*, по~ *pf.* трóстью, пáлкой.

canine ['keɪnaɪn, 'kæn-] *adj.* собáчий (-чья, -чье); *n.* (*tooth*) клык (-á).

canister ['kænɪstə(r)] *n.* жерстянáя корóбка.

canker ['kæŋkə(r)] *n.* рак.

cannibal [ˈkænɪb(ə)l] *n.* каннибáл, людоéд; *adj.* каннибáльский, людоéдский. **cannibalism** *n.* каннибали́зм, людоéдство. **canniba'listic** *adj.* каннибáльский, людоéдский. **cannibalize** *v.t.* снимáть *impf.*, снять (сниму́, -мешь; снял, -á, -о) *pf.* чáсти с+*g.*

cannon [ˈkænən] *n.* (*gun*) пу́шка; (*billiards*) карамбóль *m.*; *adj.* пу́шечный; *v.i.*: ~ **into** налетáть *impf.*, налетéть (-лечу́, -лети́шь) *pf.* на+*a.*; ~ **off** отскáкивать *impf.*, отскочи́ть (-очу́, -óчишь) *pf.* от+*g.* **cannon-ball** *n.* пу́шечное ядрó (*pl.* я́дра, я́дер, я́драм); ~ **service** пу́шечная подáча. **cannon-fodder** *n.* пу́шечное мя́со. **canno'nade** *n.* канонáда.

canoe [kəˈnu:] *n.* канóэ *nt.indecl.*; челнóк (-á); *v.i.* плáвать *indet.*, плыть (плыву́, -вёшь; плыл, -á, -о) *det.* в челнокé, на канóэ.

canon [ˈkænən] *n.* канóн; (*person*) канóник; ~ **law** канони́ческое прáво. **ca'nonical** *adj.* канони́ческий; ~ **hours** устáвные часы́ *m.pl.* моли́тв. **ca'nonicals** *n.* церкóвное облачéние. **canoni'zation** *n.* канонизáция. **canonize** *v.t.* канонизовáть *impf.* & *pf.*

canopy [ˈkænəpɪ] *n.* балдахи́н.

cant[1] [kænt] *n.* (*slant*) наклóн, наклóнное положéние; *v.t.* наклоня́ть *impf.*, наклони́ть (-ню́, -ишь) *pf.*; придавáть (-даю́, -даёшь) *impf.*, придáть (-áм, -áшь, -áст, -ади́м; при́дал, -á, -о) *pf.*+*d.* наклóнное положéние.

cant[2] [kænt] *n.* (*hypocrisy*) хáнжество; (*jargon*) жаргóн, аргó *nt.indecl.*

cantaloup [ˈkæntə,lu:p] *n.* канталу́па.

cantankerous [kænˈtæŋkərəs] *adj.* ворчли́вый.

cantata [kænˈtɑ:tə] *n.* кантáта.

canteen [kænˈti:n] *n.* столóвая *sb.*, буфéт; (*case*) я́щик; (*flask*) фля́га.

canter *n.* кéнтер, лёгкий галóп; *v.i.* (*rider*) éздить *indet.*, éхать (éду, éдешь) *det.* лёгким галóпом; (*horse*) ходи́ть (-дит) *indet.*, идти́ (идёт; шёл, шла) *det.* лёгким галóпом; *v.t.* пускáть *impf.*, пусти́ть (пущу́, пу́стишь) *pf.* лёгким галóпом.

cantilever [ˈkæntɪ,li:və(r)] *n.* консóль, укóсина; ~ **bridge** консóльный мост (мóстá, *loc.* -у́; *pl.* -ы́).

canto [ˈkæntəʊ] *n.* песнь.

canton [ˈkæntɒn] *n.* кантóн.

canvas [ˈkænvəs] *n.* холст (-á), канвá, пару- си́на; (*painting*) карти́на; (*sails*) парусá *m.pl.*; **under** ~ (*on ship*) под парусáми; (*in tent*) в палáтках.

canvass [ˈkænvəs] *v.i.* собирáть *impf.*, собрáть (соберу́, -рёшь; собрáл, -á, -о) *pf.* голосá; ~ **for** агити́ровать *impf.*, с~ *pf.* за+*a.*; *n.* собирáние голосóв; агитáция. **canvasser** *n.* собирáтель *m.* голосóв.

canyon [ˈkænjən] *n.* каньóн.

cap [kæp] *n.* шáпка, фурáжка; (*cloth*) кéпка; (*woman's*) чепéц (-пцá); (*percussion*) кáпсюль *m.*, пистóн; (*lid*) кры́шка; *v.t.* (*surpass*) перещеголя́ть *pf.*; превосходи́ть (-ожу́, -óдишь) *impf.*, превзойти́ (-ойду́, -ойдёшь; -ошёл, -ошлá) *pf.*

capability [,keɪpəˈbɪlɪtɪ] *n.* спосóбность. **'capable** *adj.* спосóбный; (*skilful*) умéлый; ~ **of** (*admitting*) поддающийся+*d.*; (*able*) спосóбный на+*a.*

capacious [kəˈpeɪʃəs] *adj.* простóрный, вмести́тельный, ёмкий (ёмок, ёмка). **capacitance** [kəˈpæsɪt(ə)ns] *n.* ёмкость. **capacity** [kəˈpæsɪtɪ] *n.* ёмкость, вмести́мость; (*ability*) спосóбность; (*power*) мóщность; **in the** ~ **of** в кáчестве+*g.*

cape[1] [keɪp] *n.* (*geog.*) мыс (*loc.* -е & -у́; *pl.* мысы́).

cape[2] [keɪp] *n.* (*cloak*) пелери́на, плащ (-á). **caped** *adj.* с пелери́ной.

caper[1] [ˈkeɪpə(r)] *n.* (*plant*) кáперс; *pl.* кáперсы *m.pl.*

caper[2] [ˈkeɪpə(r)] *n.* (*leap*) прыжóк (-жкá); **cut** ~**s** выдéлывать *impf.* антрашá; *v.i.* дéлать *impf.* прыжки́.

capillary [kəˈpɪlərɪ] *n.* капилля́р; *adj.* капилля́рный.

capital [ˈkæpɪt(ə)l] *adj.* (*city*) столи́чный; (*letter*) прописнóй; (*main*) капитáльный; (*excellent*) отли́чный; ~ **goods** срéдства *nt.pl.* произвóдства; ~ **punishment** смéртная казнь; ~ **ship** кру́пный боевóй корáбль (-ля́) *m.*; *n.* (*town*) столи́ца; (*letter*) прописнáя бу́ква; (*econ.*) капитáл; (*arch.*) капитéль. **capitalism** *n.* капитали́зм. **capitalist** *n.* капитали́ст; *adj.* капиталисти́ческий. **capita'listic** *adj.* капиталисти́ческий. **capitali'zation** *n.* капитализáция. **capitalize** *v.t.* капитализи́ровать *impf.* & *pf.*

capitation [,kæpɪˈteɪʃ(ə)n] *attr.* поголóвный.

capitulate [kəˈpɪtjʊ,leɪt] *v.i.* капитули́ровать *impf.* & *pf.* **capitu'lation** *n.* капитуля́ция.

capon [ˈkeɪpən] *n.* каплу́н (-á).

caprice [kəˈpri:s] *n.* капри́з. **capricious** *adj.* капри́зный.

Capricorn [ˈkæprɪ,kɔ:n] *n.* Козерóг.

capsize [kæpˈsaɪz] *v.t.* & *i.* опроки́дывать(ся) *impf.*, опроки́нуть(ся) *pf.*

capstan [ˈkæpst(ə)n] *n.* кабестáн.

capsule [ˈkæpsju:l] *n.* кáпсула, облáтка.

captain [ˈkæptɪn] *n.* капитáн; *v.t.* быть капитáном+*g.* **captaincy** *n.* звáние, чин, дóлжность, капитáна.

caption [ˈkæpʃ(ə)n] *n.* нáдпись, пóдпись; (*cin.*) титр.

captious [ˈkæpʃəs] *adj.* приди́рчивый.

captivate [ˈkæptɪ,veɪt] *v.t.* пленя́ть *impf.*, плени́ть *pf.* **captivating** *adj.* плени́тельный. **captive** *adj.* & *n.* плéнный. **cap'tivity** *n.* невóля; (*esp. mil.*) плен (*loc.* -у́). **capture** *n.* взя́тие, захвáт, пóимка; *v.t.* брать (беру́, -рёшь; брал, -á, -о) *impf.*, взять (возьму́, -мёшь; взял, -á, -о) *pf.* в плен; захвáтывать *impf.*, захвати́ть (-ачу́, -áтишь) *pf.*

car [kɑ:(r)] *n.* маши́на, автомоби́ль *m.*; ~ **park** пáркинг; *attr.* автомоби́льный.

carafe [kəˈræf, -rɑ:f] *n.* графи́н.

caramel(s) ['kærəˌmel] *n.* караме́ль.
carat ['kærət] *n.* кара́т (*g.pl.* -т &-тов).
caravan ['kærəˌvæn] *n.* (*convoy*) карава́н; (*cart*) фурго́н; (*house*) дом-автоприце́п.
caraway (seeds) ['kærəˌweɪ] *n.* тмин (-а(у)).
carbide ['kɑːbaɪd] *n.* карби́д.
carbine ['kɑːbaɪn] *n.* карби́на.
carbohydrate [ˌkɑːbə'haɪdreɪt] *n.* углево́д. **carbolic (acid)** [kɑː'bɒlɪk] *n.* карбо́ловая кислота́. **carbon** *n.* углеро́д; ко́пия; ~ **copy** ко́пия (че́рез копи́рку); ~ **dioxide** углекислота́; ~ **paper** копирова́льная бума́га. **carbonaceous** *adj.* (*carbon*) углеро́дистый; (*coal*) у́глистый. **'carbonate** *n.* углеки́слая соль. **carboniferous** [ˌkɑːbə'nɪfərəs] *adj.* углено́сный. **carborundum** [ˌkɑːbə'rʌndəm] *n.* карбору́нд.
carboy ['kɑːbɔɪ] *n.* буты́ль.
carbuncle ['kɑːbʌŋk(ə)l] *n.* карбу́нкул.
carburettor [ˌkɑːbjʊ'retə(r), ˌkɑːbə-] *n.* карбюра́тор.
carcase, carcass ['kɑːkəs] *n.* ту́ша, труп.
carcinogen [kɑː'sɪnədʒ(ə)n] *n.* канцероге́н. **carcino'genic** *n.* канцероге́нный.
card [kɑːd] *n.* ка́рта, ка́рточка; (*ticket*) биле́т; **a house of ~s** ка́рточный до́мик; ~ **index** картоте́ка. **cardboard** *n.* карто́н; *adj.* карто́нный. **card-sharp(er)** *n.* шу́лер (*pl.* -а́). **card-table** *n.* ло́мберный, ка́рточный, стол (-а́).
cardiac ['kɑːdɪˌæk] *adj.* серде́чный.
cardigan ['kɑːdɪgən] *n.* вя́заная ко́фта, кардига́н.
cardinal ['kɑːdɪn(ə)l] *adj.* (*important*) кардина́льный; ~ **number** коли́чественное числи́тельное *sb.*; *n.* кардина́л.
care [keə(r)] *n.* (*trouble*) забо́та, попече́ние; (*attention*) внима́тельность; (*tending*) ухо́д; **take ~** осторо́жно!; береги́(те)сь!; смотри́(те)!; **take ~ of** забо́титься *impf.*, по~ *pf.* о+*p.*; **I don't ~** мне всё равно́; **what do I ~?; who ~s?** а мне всё равно́!; а мне-то что?
career [kə'rɪə(r)] *n.* (*movement*) карье́р; (*profession*) карье́ра; ~ **guidance** профессиона́льная ориента́ция.
carefree ['keəfriː] *adj.* беззабо́тный. **careful** *adj.* (*cautious*) осторо́жный; (*thorough*) тща́тельный. **careless** *adj.* (*negligent*) небре́жный; (*incautious*) неосторо́жный; (*carefree*) беззабо́тный.
caress [kə'res] *n.* ла́ска (*g.pl.* -ск); *v.t.* ласка́ть *impf.*
caretaker ['keəˌteɪkə(r)] *n.* смотри́тель *m.*, ~ница; сто́рож (*pl.* -а́); *attr.* вре́менный.
careworn ['keəwɔːn] *adj.* изму́ченный (-ен) забо́тами.
cargo ['kɑːgəʊ] *n.* груз.
caricature ['kærɪkətjʊə(r)] *n.* карикату́ра; *v.t.* изобража́ть *impf.*, изобрази́ть *pf.* в карикату́рном ви́де.
caries ['keəriːz, -rɪˌiːz] *n.* карио́з.
carmine ['kɑːmaɪn] *n.* карми́н, карми́нный цвет; *adj.* карми́нный.
carnage ['kɑːnɪdʒ] *n.* резня́.
carnal ['kɑːn(ə)l] *adj.* пло́тский.
carnation [kɑː'neɪʃ(ə)n] *n.* (садо́вая) гвозди́ка.
carnival ['kɑːnɪv(ə)l] *n.* карнава́л; (*Shrovetide*) ма́сленица.
carnivore ['kɑːnɪˌvɔː(r)] *n.* плотоя́дное живо́тное *sb.* **car'nivorous** *adj.* плотоя́дный.
carol ['kær(ə)l] *n.* (рожде́ственский) гимн.
carotid artery [kə'rɒtɪd] *n.* со́нная арте́рия.
carousal [kə'raʊzəl] *n.* попо́йка.
carp¹ [kɑːp] *n.* (*wild*) саза́н; (*domesticated*) карп.
carp² [kɑːp] *v.i.* придира́ться *impf.*, придра́ться (-деру́сь, -дерёшься; -дра́лся, -драла́сь, -дра́ло́сь) *pf.* (**at** к+*d.*)
carpenter ['kɑːpɪntə(r)] *n.* пло́тник. **carpentry** *n.* пло́тничество.
carpet ['kɑːpɪt] *n.* ковёр (-вра́); *v.t.* устила́ть *impf.*, устла́ть (-телю́, -те́лешь) *pf.* ковра́ми.
carping ['kɑːpɪŋ] *adj.* приди́рчивый; *n.* приди́рки (-рок) *pl.*
carriage ['kærɪdʒ] *n.* (*vehicle*) каре́та, экипа́ж; (*rail.*) ваго́н; (*of machine*) каре́тка; (*conveyance*) прово́з, перево́зка; (*bearing*) оса́нка; ~ **forward** с опла́той доста́вки получа́телем; ~ **free** беспла́тная пересы́лка; ~ **paid** за пересы́лку упла́чено. **carriageway** *n.* прое́зжая часть доро́ги, у́лицы. **carrier** *n.* (*person*) во́зчик; (*object*) бага́жник; ~ **pigeon** почто́вый го́лубь (*pl.* -би, -бе́й) *m.*; ~ **wave** несу́щая волна́ (*pl.* -ны, -н, -на́м).
carrion ['kærɪən] *n.* па́даль; *pl.* чёрная воро́на.
carrot ['kærət] *n.* морко́вка; *pl.* морко́вь (*collect.*).
carry ['kærɪ] *v.t.* (*by hand*) носи́ть (ношу́, но́сишь) *indet.*, нести́ (несу́, -сёшь; нёс, -ла́) *det.*; переноси́ть (-ошу́, -о́сишь) *impf.*, перенести́ (-есу́, -есёшь; -ёс, -есла́) *pf.*; (*in vehicle*) вози́ть (вожу́, во́зишь) *indet.*, везти́ (везу́, -зёшь; вёз, -ла́) *det.*; *v.i.* нести́сь (несётся; нёсся, несла́сь); (*sound*) быть слы́шен (-шна́, -шно); ~ **forward** переноси́ть (-ошу́, -о́сишь) *impf.*, перенести́ (-есу́, -есёшь; -ёс, -есла́) *pf.*; ~ **on** (*continue*) продолжа́ть *impf.*; (*behaviour*) вести́ (веду́, ведёшь; вёл, -а́) *impf.* себя́ несде́ржанно; ~ **out** выполня́ть *impf.*, вы́полнить *pf.*; доводи́ть (-ожу́, -о́дишь) *impf.*, довести́ (-еду́, -едёшь; -ёл, -ела́) *pf.* до конца́; ~ **over** переноси́ть (-ошу́, -о́сишь) *impf.*, перенести́ (-есу́, -есёшь; -ёс, -есла́) *pf.*
cart [kɑːt] *n.* теле́га, пово́зка; *v.t.* вози́ть (вожу́, во́зишь) *indet.*, везти́ (везу́, -зёшь; вёз, -ла́) *det.* в теле́ге. **cartage** *n.* сто́имость перево́зки. **cart-horse** *n.* ломова́я ло́шадь (*pl.* -ди, -де́й, *i.* -дьми́). **cart-load** *n.* воз. **cart-track** *n.* гужева́я доро́га, просёлок (-лка). **cartwheel** колесо́ (*pl.* -ёса) теле́ги;

(*somersault*) переворо́т бо́ком в сто́рону.
cartel [kɑːˈtel] *n.* карте́ль *m.*
cartilage [ˈkɑːtɪlɪdʒ] *n.* хрящ (-а́). **cartilaginous** [ˌkɑːtɪˈlædʒɪnəs] *adj.* хрящево́й.
cartographer [kɑːˈtɒgrəfə(r)] *n.* карто́граф. **cartoˈgraphic** *adj.* картографи́ческий. **cartography** *n.* картогра́фия.
carton [ˈkɑːt(ə)n] *n.* (карто́нная) коро́бка; блок.
cartoon [kɑːˈtuːn] *n.* карикату́ра; (*design*) карто́н; (*cin.*) мультфи́льм. **cartoonist** *n.* карикатури́ст, ~ка.
cartridge [ˈkɑːtrɪdʒ] *n.* патро́н. **cartridge-belt** *n.* патронта́ш.
carve [kɑːv] *v.t.* ре́зать (ре́жу, -жешь) *impf.* по+*d.*; (*wood*) выреза́ть *impf.*, вы́резать (-ежу, -ежешь) *pf.*; (*stone*) высека́ть *impf.*, вы́сечь (-еку, -ечешь; -ек); (*meat etc.*) нареза́ть *impf.*, наре́зать (-е́жу, -е́жешь) *pf.* **carver** *n.* (*person*) ре́зчик; *pl.* (*cutlery*) большо́й нож (-а́) и ви́лка. **carving** *n.* резьба́; резно́й орна́мент; ~ **knife** нож (-а́) для нареза́ния мя́са.
cascade [kæsˈkeɪd] *n.* каска́д.
case¹ [keɪs] *n.* (*instance*) слу́чай; (*leg.*) де́ло (*pl.* -ла́); (*med.*) больно́й *sb.*; (*gram.*) паде́ж (-а́); **as the ~ may be** в зави́симости от обстоя́тельств; **in ~** (в слу́чае) е́сли; **in any ~** во вся́ком слу́чае; **in no ~** не в ко́ем слу́чае; **just in ~** на вся́кий слу́чай, на аво́сь.
case² [keɪs] *n.* (*box*) я́щик, коро́бка; (*suitcase*) чемода́н; (*casing*) футля́р, чехо́л; (*print.*) ка́сса; *v.t.* покрыва́ть *impf.*, покры́ть (-ро́ю, -ро́ешь) *pf.* **case-harden** *v.t.* цементи́ровать *impf.* & *pf.*
casement window [ˈkeɪsmənt] *n.* ство́рное окно́ (*pl.* о́кна, о́кон, о́кнам).
cash [kæʃ] *n.* нали́чные *sb.*; де́ньги (-нег, -ньга́м) *pl.*; ка́сса; ~ **and carry** прода́жа за нали́чный расчёт без доста́вки на́ дом; ~ **down** де́ньги на бо́чку; ~ **on delivery** нало́женным платежо́м; ~ **register** ка́сса; *v.t.* превраща́ть *impf.*, преврати́ть (-щу́, -ти́шь) *pf.* в нали́чные *sb.*; ~ **a cheque** получа́ть *impf.*, получи́ть (-чу́, -чишь) *pf.* де́ньги по че́ку. **cashcard** *n.* ка́рточка для де́нежного автома́та. **cashier¹** [kæˈʃɪə(r)] *n.* касси́р. **cashier²** *v.t.* увольня́ть *impf.*, уво́лить *pf.* со слу́жбы.
cashmere [ˈkæʃmɪə(r)] *n.* кашеми́р.
casing [ˈkeɪsɪŋ] *n.* (*tech.*) кожу́х (-а́).
casino [kəˈsiːnəʊ] *n.* казино́ *nt.indecl.*
cask [kɑːsk] *n.* бо́чка.
casket [ˈkɑːskɪt] *n.* шкату́лка, ларе́ц (-рца́).
Caspian [ˈkæspɪən]: ~ **Sea** Каспи́йское мо́ре.
casserole [ˈkæsəˌrəʊl] *n.* тяжёлая кастрю́ля; блю́до, приготовля́емое в ней.
cassette [kæˈset, kə-] *n.* кассе́та.
cassock [ˈkæsək] *n.* ря́са.
cast [kɑːst] *v.t.* (*throw*) броса́ть *impf.*, бро́сить *pf.*; (*shed*) сбра́сывать *impf.*, сбро́сить *pf.*; (*theatr.*) распределя́ть *impf.*, распредели́ть *pf.* ро́ли+*d.*; (*found*) лить (лью, льёшь; лил, -а́, -о) *impf.*, с~ (солью́, -льёшь; слил, -а́, -о) *pf.*; (*horoscope*) составля́ть *impf.*, соста́вить *pf.*; ~ **ashore** выбра́сывать *impf.*, вы́бросить *pf.* на бе́рег; ~ **off** (*knitting*) спуска́ть *impf.*, спусти́ть (-ущу́, -у́стишь) *pf.* пе́тли; (*naut.*) отплыва́ть *impf.*, отплы́ть (-ыву́, -ывёшь; отплы́л, -а́, -о) *pf.*; ~ **on** (*knitting*) набира́ть *impf.*, набра́ть (наберу́, -рёшь; набра́л, -а́, -о) *pf.* пе́тли; *n.* (*throw*) бросо́к (-ска́), броса́ние; (*of mind etc.*) склад; (*mould*) фо́рма; (*med.*) ги́псовая повя́зка; (*theatr.*) де́йствующие ли́ца (-ц) *pl.*; (*in eye*) лёгкое косогла́зие. **castaway** *n.* потерпе́вший *sb.* кораблекруше́ние. **cast iron** *n.* чугу́н (-а́). **cast-iron** *adj.* чугу́нный. **cast-offs** *n.* (*clothes*) но́шеное пла́тье.
castanet [ˌkæstəˈnet] *n.* кастанье́та.
caste [kɑːst] *n.* ка́ста; ка́стовая систе́ма.
castigate [ˈkæstɪˌgeɪt] *v.t.* бичева́ть *impf.*
castle [ˈkɑːs(ə)l] *n.* за́мок (-мка); (*chess*) ладья́.
castor [ˈkɑːstə(r)] *n.* (*wheel*) ро́лик, колёсико (*pl.* -ки, -ков); ~ **sugar** са́харная пу́дра.
castor oil [ˈkɑːstə(r)] *n.* касто́ровое ма́сло.
castrate [kæˈstreɪt] *v.t.* кастри́ровать *impf.* & *pf.* **castration** *n.* кастра́ция.
casual [ˈkæʒʊəl, -zjʊəl] *adj.* случа́йный; (*careless*) несерьёзный. **casualty** *n.* (*wounded*) ра́неный *sb.*; (*killed*) уби́тый *sb.*; *pl.* поте́ри (-рь) *pl.*; ~ **ward** пала́та ско́рой по́мощи.
casuist [ˈkæzjuːɪst, ˈkæʒʊɪst] *n.* казуи́ст. **casuˈistic(al)** *adj.* казуисти́ческий. **casuistry** *n.* казуи́стика.
cat [kæt] *n.* ко́шка; (*tom*) кот (-а́). **catcall** *n.* свист, осви́стывание; *v.t.* & *i.* осви́стывать *impf.*, освиста́ть (-ищу́, -и́щешь) *pf.* **cat-o'-nine-tails** *n.* ко́шки *f.pl.* **cat's-eye** *n.* (*min.*) коша́чий глаз (*loc.* -у́; *pl.* -за́, -з); (**C~**, *propr.*) (*on road*) (доро́жный) рефле́ктор. **catwalk** *n.* у́зкий мо́стик; рабо́чий помо́ст.
cataclysm [ˈkætəˌklɪz(ə)m] *n.* катакли́зм.
catalogue [ˈkætəˌlɒg] *n.* катало́г; (*price list*) прейскура́нт; *v.t.* каталогизи́ровать *impf.* & *pf.*
catalysis [kəˈtælɪsɪs] *n.* ката́лиз. **catalyst** [ˈkætəlɪst] *n.* катализа́тор. **cataˈlytic** *adj.* каталити́ческий.
catamaran [ˌkætəməˈræn] *n.* катамара́н.
catapult [ˈkætəˌpʌlt] *n.* (*child's*) рога́тка; (*hist.*, *aeron.*) катапу́льта; *v.t.* катапульти́ровать *impf.* & *pf.*
cataract [ˈkætəˌrækt] *n.* (*waterfall*) водопа́д; (*med.*) катара́кта.
catarrh [kəˈtɑː(r)] *n.* ката́р.
catastrophe [kəˈtæstrəfɪ] *n.* катастро́фа. **catastrophic** [ˌkætəˈstrɒfɪk] *adj.* катастрофи́ческий.
catch [kætʃ] *v.t.* (*captive*) лови́ть (-влю́, -вишь) *impf.*, пойма́ть *pf.*; (*seize*) захва́тывать *impf.*, захвати́ть (-ачу́, -а́тишь) *pf.*; (*surprise*)

застава́ть (-таю́, -таёшь) *impf.*, заста́ть (-а́ну, -а́нешь) *pf.*; (*disease*) заража́ться *impf.*, зарази́ться *pf.*+*i.*; (*be in time for*) успева́ть *impf.*, успе́ть *pf.* на+*a.*; ~ **on** зацепля́ть(ся) *impf.*, зацепи́ть(ся) (-плю́(сь), -пишь(ся)) *pf.* за+*a.*; (*v.i.*) (*become popular*) привива́ться *impf.*, приви́ться (-вьётся; -ви́лся, -вила́сь) *pf.*; ~ **up with** догоня́ть *impf.*, догна́ть (догоню́, -нишь; догна́л, -а́, -о) *pf.*; *n.* (*action*) пои́мка; (*of fish*) уло́в; (*trick*) уло́вка; (*on door etc.*) защёлка, задви́жка; ~ **crops** междупосевны́е культу́ры *f.pl.* **catching** *adj.* зара́зный; зарази́тельный. **catchment area** *n.* водосбо́рная пло́щадь (*pl.* -ди, -де́й). **catchword** *n.* (*slogan*) ло́зунг; (*running title*) колонти́тул; (*headword*) загла́вное сло́во (*pl.* -ва́). **catchy** *adj.* привлека́тельный, легко́ запомина́ющийся.

catechism ['kætɪ,kɪz(ə)m] *n.* (*eccl.*) катехи́зис; допро́с. **catechize** ['kætɪ,kaɪz] *v.t.* допра́шивать *impf.*, допроси́ть (-ошу́, -о́сишь) *pf.*

categorical [,kætɪ'gɒrɪk(ə)l] *adj.* категори́ческий. '**category** *n.* катего́рия.

cater ['keɪtə(r)] *v.i.* поставля́ть *impf.* прови́зию; ~ **for** снабжа́ть *impf.*, снабди́ть *pf.*; обслу́живать *impf.*, обслужи́ть (-жу́, -жишь) *pf.* **caterer** *n.* поставщи́к (-а́) (прови́зии).

caterpillar ['kætə,pɪlə(r)] *n.* гу́сеница; *adj.* гу́сеничный; **C~ track** (*propr.*) гу́сеничная ле́нта.

caterwaul ['kætə,wɔːl] *v.i.* крича́ть (-чу́, -чи́шь) кото́м; задава́ть (-даёт) *impf.*, зада́ть (-а́ст; за́дал, -а́, -о) *pf.* коша́чий конце́рт. **caterwauling** *n.* коша́чий конце́рт.

catgut ['kætgʌt] *n.* кетгу́т.

catharsis [kə'θɑːsɪs] *n.* ка́тарсис.

cathedral [kə'θiːdr(ə)l] *n.* (кафедра́льный) собо́р.

catheter ['kæθɪtə(r)] *n.* кате́тер.

cathode ['kæθəʊd] *n.* като́д; ~ **rays** като́дные лучи́ *m.pl.*

Catholic ['kæθəlɪk, 'kæθlɪk] *adj.* католи́ческий; *n.* като́лик, -ичка. **Ca'tholicism** *n.* католи́чество, католици́зм.

catkin ['kætkɪn] *n.* серёжка.

cattle ['kæt(ə)l] *n.* скот (-а́).

Caucasus ['kɔːkəsəs] *n.* Кавка́з.

cauldron ['kɔːldrən] *n.* котёл (-тла́).

cauliflower ['kɒlɪ,flaʊə(r)] *n.* цветна́я капу́ста.

caulk [kɔːk] *v.t.* конопа́тить *impf.*, за~ *pf.*

causal ['kɔːz(ə)l] *adj.* причи́нный (-нен, -нна). **cau'sality** *n.* причи́нность. **cau'sation** *n.* причине́ние; причи́нность. **cause** *n.* причи́на, по́вод; (*leg. etc.*) де́ло (*pl.* -ла́); *v.t.* причиня́ть *impf.*, причини́ть *pf.*; вызыва́ть *impf.*, вы́звать (-зову, -зовешь) *pf.*; (*induce*) заставля́ть *impf.*, заста́вить *pf.* **causeless** *adj.* беспричи́нный (-нен, -нна).

caustic ['kɔːstɪk] *adj.* каусти́ческий, е́дкий (е́док, едка́, е́дко) ~ **soda** е́дкий натр; *n.* е́дкое вещество́.

cauterization [,kɔːtəraɪ'zeɪʃ(ə)n] *n.* прижига́ние. '**cauterize** *v.t.* прижига́ть *impf.*, приже́чь (-жгу́, -жжёшь; -жёг, -жгла́) *pf.* '**cautery** *n.* термока́утер.

caution ['kɔːʃ(ə)n] *n.* осторо́жность; (*warning*) предупрежде́ние; *v.t.* предостерега́ть *impf.*, предостере́чь (-егу́, -жёшь; -ёг, -егла́) *pf.* **cautious** *adj.* осторо́жный. **cautionary** *adj.* предостерега́ющий.

cavalcade [,kævəl'keɪd] *n.* кавалька́да. **cavalier** [,kævə'lɪə(r)] *adj.* бесцеремо́нный (-нен, -нна); (**C~**, *hist.*) рояли́стский; рояли́ст. **cavalry** ['kævəlrɪ] *n.* кавале́рия. **cavalryman** *n.* кавалери́ст.

cave [keɪv] *n.* пеще́ра; *v.i.*: ~ **in** обва́ливаться *impf.*, обвали́ться (-ится) *pf.*; (*yield*) уступа́ть *impf.*, уступи́ть (-плю́, -пишь) *pf.* **caveman** *n.* пеще́рный челове́к. **cavern** ['kæv(ə)n] *n.* пеще́ра. **cavernous** *adj.* пеще́ристый.

caviare ['kævɪ,ɑː(r)] *n.* икра́.

cavil ['kævɪl] *v.i.* придира́ться *impf.*, придра́ться (-деру́сь, -дерёшься; -а́лся, -ала́сь, -а́ло́сь) *pf.* (**at** к+*d.*).

cavity ['kævɪtɪ] *n.* впа́дина, по́лость (*pl.* -ти, -те́й).

caw ['kɔː] *v.i.* ка́ркать *impf.*, ка́ркнуть *pf.*; *n.* ка́рканье.

cayman ['keɪmən] *n.* кайма́н.

CD *abbr.* (*of* ***compact disk***) компа́кт-ди́ск; **CD player** прои́грыватель (*m.*) компа́кт-ди́сков.

CD-ROM *abbr.* (*of* ***compact disk — read-only memory***) компа́кт-ди́ск ПЗУ; ~ **player** прои́грыватель *m.* компа́кт-ди́сков ПЗУ.

cease [siːs] *v.t.* & *i.* прекраща́ть(ся) *impf.*, прекрати́ть(ся) (-ащу́, -ати́т(ся)) *pf.*; *v.i.* перестава́ть (-таю́, -таёшь) *impf.*, переста́ть (-а́ну, -а́нешь) *pf.* (+*inf.*). **cease-fire** *n.* прекраще́ние огня́. **ceaseless** *adj.* непреста́нный (-а́нен, -а́нна).

cedar ['siːdə(r)] *n.* кедр.

ceiling ['siːlɪŋ] *n.* потоло́к (-лка́); (*prices etc.*) максима́льная цена́ (*a.* -ну), максима́льный у́ровень (-вня) *m.*

celandine ['selən,daɪn] *n.* чистоте́л.

celebrate ['selɪ,breɪt] *v.t.* пра́здновать *impf.*, от~ *pf.*; **be ~d** сла́виться *impf.* (**for** +*i.*). **celebrated** *adj.* знамени́тый. **cele'bration** *n.* пра́зднование. **ce'lebrity** *n.* знамени́тость.

celery ['selərɪ] *n.* сельдере́й.

celestial [sɪ'lestɪəl] *adj.* небе́сный.

celibacy ['selɪbəsɪ] *n.* безбра́чие. **celibate** *adj.* безбра́чный; (*person*) холосто́й (-ост), незаму́жняя.

cell [sel] *n.* (*room*) ке́лья; (*prison*) (тюре́мная) ка́мера; (*biol.*) кле́тка, клё́точка; (*pol.*) яче́йка.

cellar ['selə(r)] *n.* подва́л, по́греб (*pl.* -а́); *adj.* подва́льный.

cellist ['tʃelɪst] *n.* виолончели́ст. **cello** ['tʃeləʊ] *n.* виолонче́ль.

cellophane ['selə,feɪn] *n.* целлофа́н; *adj.*

целлофа́новый. **cellular** ['seljʊlə(r)] *adj.* кле́точный. **cellule** *n.* кле́точка. **celluloid** *n.* целлуло́ид; (кино)фи́льм. **cellulose** *n.* целлюло́за; клетча́тка.

Celsius ['selsɪəs]: ~ **scale** шкала́ термоме́тра Це́льсия; ~ **thermometer** тероме́тр Це́льсия; **10°** ~ 10° по Це́льсию.

Celt [kelt, selt] *n.* кельт. **Celtic** *adj.* ке́льтский.

cement [sɪ'ment] *n.* цеме́нт; *v.t.* цементи́ровать *impf.*, за~ *pf.*

cemetery ['semɪtərɪ] *n.* кла́дбище.

cenotaph ['senəˌtɑ:f] *n.* кенота́ф.

censer ['sensə(r)] *n.* кади́ло.

censor ['sensə(r)] *n.* це́нзор; *v.t.* подверга́ть *impf.*, подве́ргнуть (-г) *pf.* цензу́ре. **censorious** [sen'sɔ:rɪəs] *adj.* стро́гий (строг, -а́, -о); скло́нный (-о́нен, -о́нна́, -о́нно) осужда́ть. **censorship** *n.* цензу́ра. **censure** *n.* осужде́ние; порица́ние; *v.t.* осужда́ть *impf.*, осуди́ть (-ужу́, -у́дишь) *pf.*; порица́ть *impf.*

census *n.* пе́репись (населе́ния).

cent [sent] *n.* цент; **per** ~ проце́нт.

centaur ['sentɔ:(r)] *n.* кента́вр.

centenarian [ˌsentɪ'neərɪən] *adj.* столе́тний; *n.* столе́тний челове́к, челове́к в во́зрасте ста лет. **centenary** [sen'ti:nərɪ] *n.* столе́тие. **cen'tennial** *adj.* столе́тний; *n.* столе́тняя годовщи́на. **'centigrade** *adj.* стогра́дусный; **10°** ~ 10° по Це́льсию. **'centigram** *n.* сантигра́мм. **'centilitre** *n.* центили́тр. **'centimetre** *n.* сантиме́тр. **'centipede** *n.* сороконо́жка.

central ['sentr(ə)l] *adj.* центра́льный; ~ **heating** центра́льное отопле́ние. **centralism** *n.* централи́зм. **centrali'zation** *n.* централиза́ция. **centralize** *v.t.* централизова́ть *impf.* & *pf.* **centre** *n.* центр; середи́на; ~ **back** центр защи́ты; ~ **forward** центр нападе́ния; ~ **half** центр полузащи́ты; *v.i.* сосредото́чиваться *impf.*, сосредото́читься *pf.* **centri'fugal** *adj.* центробе́жный. **centrifuge** ['sentrɪˌfju:dʒ] *n.* центрифу́га. **cen'tripetal** *adj.* центростреми́тельный.

centurion [sen'tjʊərɪən] *n.* центурио́н. **'century** *n.* столе́тие, век (*loc.* в -е, на -у́; *pl.* -а́); (*sport*) сто очко́в.

ceramic [sɪ'ræmɪk, kɪ-] *adj.* керами́ческий. **ceramics** *n.* кера́мика.

cereal ['sɪərɪəl] *adj.* хле́бный; *n.*: *pl.* хлеба́ *m.pl.*, хле́бные, зерновы́е, зла́ки *m.pl.*; **breakfast** ~**s** зерновы́е хло́пья (-ьев) *pl.*

cerebral ['serɪbr(ə)l] *adj.* мозгово́й.

ceremonial [ˌserɪ'məʊnɪəl] *adj.* форма́льный; торже́ственный (-ен, -нна), пара́дный; *n.* церемониа́л. **ceremonious** *adj.* церемо́нный (-нен, -нна). **'ceremony** *n.* церемо́ния.

cerise [sə'ri:z, -'ri:s] *adj.* (*n.*) све́тло-вишнёвый (цвет).

cert [sɜ:t] *n.* (*sl.*) ве́рное де́ло. **certain** ['sɜ:t(ə)n, -tɪn] *adj.* (*definite*) определённый (-ёнен, -ённа); (*reliable*) ве́рный (-рен, -рна́, -рно, ве́рны́); (*doubtless*) несомне́нный (-нен, -нна); *pred.* уве́рен (-нна); **for** ~ наверняка́. **certainly** *adv.* (*of course*) коне́чно, безусло́вно; (*without fail*) непреме́нно; (*beyond question*) несомне́нно. **certainty** *n.* (*conviction*) уве́ренность; (*undoubted fact*) несомне́нный факт; безусло́вность; **bet on a** ~ держа́ть (-жу́, -жишь) *impf.* пари́ наверняка́.

cer'tificate *n.* удостовере́ние, свиде́тельство; сертифика́т; аттеста́т; **birth** ~ ме́трика. **certify** *v.t.* удостоверя́ть *impf.*, удостове́рить *pf.*; свиде́тельствовать *impf.*, за~ *pf.*; (*as insane*) признава́ть (-наю́, -наёшь) *impf.*, призна́ть *pf.* сумасше́дшим.

certitude *n.* уве́ренность.

cessation [se'seɪʃ(ə)n] *n.* прекраще́ние.

cesspit ['sespɪt] *n.* помо́йная я́ма. **cesspool** *n.* выгребна́я я́ма; (*fig.*) клоа́ка.

cf. *abbr.* ср., сравни́.

CFCs *abbr.* (*of* ***chloro-fluorocarbons***) хлори́рованные фторуглеро́ды.

chafe [tʃeɪf] *v.t.* (*rub*) тере́ть (тру, трёшь; тёр) *impf.*; (*rub sore*) натира́ть *impf.*, натере́ть (-тру́, -трёшь; -тёр) *pf.*; *v.i.* (*fret*) раздража́ться *impf.*, раздражи́ться *pf.*

chaff [tʃɑ:f] *n.* (*husks*) мяки́на; (*chopped straw*) се́чка; (*banter*) подшу́чивание; *v.t.* поддра́знивать *impf.*, поддразни́ть (-ню́, -нишь) *pf.*; подшу́чивать *impf.*, подшути́ть (-учу́, -у́тишь) *pf.* над+*i.*

chaffinch ['tʃæfɪntʃ] *n.* зя́блик.

chagrin ['ʃægrɪn, ʃə'gri:n] *n.* огорче́ние.

chain [tʃeɪn] *n.* цепь (*loc.* -пи́; *pl.* -пи, -пе́й); (*crochet*) коси́чка; ~ **reaction** цепна́я реа́кция. **chain-stitch** *n.* тамбу́рный шов (шва), тамбу́рная стро́чка.

chair [tʃeə(r)] *n.* стул (*pl.* -ья, -ьев), кре́сло (*g.pl.* -сел); (*chairmanship*) председа́тельство; (*chairman*) председа́тель *m.*, ~ница; (*univ.*) ка́федра; *v.t.* (*preside*) председа́тельствовать *impf.* на+*p.*; (*carry aloft*) поднима́ть *impf.*, подня́ть (-ниму́, -ни́мешь; по́днял, -а́, -о) *pf.* и нести́ (несу́, -сёшь; нёс, -ла́) *impf.* **chairman, -woman** *n.* председа́тель *m.*, ~ница.

chalice ['tʃælɪs] *n.* ча́ша.

chalk [tʃɔ:k] *n.* мел (-а(у), *loc.* -у́ & -е); (*piece of* ~) мело́к (-лка́); **not by a long** ~ отню́дь нет, далеко́ не; *v.t.* писа́ть (пишу́, пи́шешь) *impf.*, на~ *pf.* ме́лом; черти́ть (-рчу́, -ртишь) *impf.*, на~ *pf.* ме́лом. **chalky** *adj.* мелово́й, известко́вый.

challenge ['tʃælɪndʒ] *n.* (*summons*) вы́зов; (*sentry's call*) о́клик (часово́го); (*leg.*) отво́д; *v.t.* вызыва́ть *impf.*, вы́звать (вы́зову, -вешь) *pf.*; оклика́ть *impf.*, окли́кнуть *pf.*; отводи́ть (-ожу́, -о́дишь) *impf.*, отвести́ (-еду́, -едёшь; -ёл, -ела́) *pf.*

chamber ['tʃeɪmbə(r)] *n.* ко́мната; (*pol.*) пала́та; *pl.* меблиро́ванные ко́мнаты *f.pl.*; *pl.* (*judge's*) кабине́т (судьи́); ~ **music** ка́мерная му́зыка. **chamberlain** ['tʃeɪmbəlɪn] *n.* камерге́р; (**C**~) гофме́йстер.

chambermaid *n.* го́рничная *sb.* **chamber-pot** *n.* ночно́й горшо́к (-шка́).
chameleon [kə'mi:lɪən] *n.* хамелео́н.
chamois ['ʃæmwɑ:; 'ʃæmɪ] *n.* (*animal*) се́рна; (*~-leather*) за́мша; *adj.* за́мшевый.
champ [tʃæmp] *v.i.* ча́вкать *impf.*, ча́вкнуть *pf.*; ~ **the bit** грызть (-зёт; -з) *impf.* удила́ (*pl.*).
champagne [ʃæm'peɪn] *n.* шампа́нское *sb.*
champion ['tʃæmpɪən] *n.* (*athletic etc.*) чемпио́н, ~ка; (*animal, plant etc*) пе́рвый призёр; (*upholder*) побо́рник, -ица; *adj.* получи́вший пе́рвый приз; *v.t.* защища́ть *impf.*, защити́ть (-ищу́, -ити́шь) *pf.* **championship** *n.* пе́рвенство, чемпиона́т; побо́рничество.
chance [tʃɑ:ns] *n.* случа́йность; (*opportunity*) слу́чай; (*possibility*) шанс; *adj.* случа́йный; *v.i.* (*happen*) случа́ться *impf.*, случи́ться *pf.*; ~ **it** рискну́ть *pf.*
chancel ['tʃɑ:ns(ə)l] *n.* алта́рь (-ря́) *m.*
chancellery ['tʃɑ:nsələrɪ] *n.* канцеля́рия. **chancellor** *n.* ка́нцлер; (*univ.*) ре́ктор университе́та; **Lord C~** лорд-ка́нцлер; **C~ of the Exchequer** ка́нцлер казначе́йства. **Chancery** *n.* суд (-а́) лорда-ка́нцлера; **c~** канцеля́рия.
chancy ['tʃɑ:nsɪ] *adj.* риско́ванный (-ан, -анна).
chandelier [ˌʃændɪ'lɪə(r)] *n.* лю́стра.
change [tʃeɪndʒ] *n.* переме́на; измене́ние; (*of clothes etc.*) сме́на; (*money*) сда́ча; (*of trains etc.*) переса́дка; ~ **for the better** переме́на к лу́чшему; ~ **of air** переме́на обстано́вки; ~ **of life** климакте́рий; ~ **of scene** переме́на обстано́вки; **for a** ~ для разнообра́зия; *v.t.* & *i.* меня́ть(ся) *impf.*; изменя́ть(ся) *impf.*, измени́ть(ся) (-ню́(сь), -нишь(ся)) *pf.*; *v.i.* (*one's clothes*) переодева́ться *impf.*, переоде́ться (-е́нусь, -е́нешься) *pf.*; (*trains etc.*) переса́живаться *impf.*, пересе́сть (-ся́ду, -ся́дешь; -се́л) *pf.*; *v.t.* (*a baby*) перепелёнывать *impf.*, перепелена́ть *pf.*; (*give ~ for*) разме́нивать *impf.*, разменя́ть *pf.*; ~ **into** превраща́ться *impf.*, преврати́ться (-ащу́сь, -ати́шься) *pf.* в+*a.* **changeable** *adj.* непостоя́нный (-нен, -нна), неусто́йчивый, изме́нчивый. **changeless** *adj.* неизме́нный (-нен, -нна), постоя́нный (-нен, -нна). **changing-room** *n.* раздева́лка; приме́рочная *sb.*
channel ['tʃæn(ə)l] *n.* кана́л, проли́в, прото́к; (*fig.*) ру́сло (*g.pl.* -сл & -сел), путь (-ти́, -тём) *m.*; **the (English) C~** Ла-Ма́нш; **the C~ Islands** Норма́ндские острова́; **C~ tunnel** тонне́ль под Ла-Ма́ншем; *v.t.* пуска́ть *impf.*, пусти́ть (пущу́, пу́стишь) *pf.* по кана́лу; (*fig., direct*) направля́ть *impf.*
chaos ['keɪɒs] *n.* ха́ос. **cha'otic** *adj.* хаоти́чный.
chap¹ [tʃæp] *n.* (*person*) ма́лый *sb.*, па́рень (-рня; *pl.* -рни, -рне́й) *m.*
chap² [tʃæp] *n.* (*crack*) тре́щина; *v.i.* тре́скаться *impf.*, по~ *pf.*
chapel ['tʃæp(ə)l] *n.* часо́вня (*g.pl.* -вен), капе́лла; моле́льня (*g.pl.* -лен).
chaplain ['tʃæplɪn] *n.* капелла́н.
chapter ['tʃæptə(r)] *n.* глава́ (*pl.* -вы); (*eccl.*) капи́тул; ~ **house** зда́ние капи́тула.
char¹ [tʃɑ:(r)] *n.* приходя́щая домрабо́тница.
char² [tʃɑ:(r)] *v.t.* & *i.* обу́гливать(ся) *impf.*, обу́глить(ся) *pf.*
character ['kærɪktə(r)] *n.* хара́ктер; (*testimonial*) рекоменда́ция; (*personage*) персона́ж; (*theatr.*) де́йствующее лицо́ (*pl.* -ца); (*letter*) бу́ква; (*numeral*) ци́фра; (*mark*) знак. **characte'ristic** *adj.* характе́рный; *n.* характе́рная черта́. **characterize** *v.t.* характеризова́ть *impf.* & *pf.*
charade [ʃə'rɑ:d] *n.* шара́да.
charcoal ['tʃɑ:kəʊl] *n.* древе́сный у́голь (у́гля́) *m.*
charge [tʃɑ:dʒ] *n.* (*load*) нагру́зка; (*for gun; elec.*) заря́д; (*fee*) пла́та; (*care*) попече́ние; (*person*) пито́мец (-мца), -мица; (*accusation*) обвине́ние; (*mil.*) ата́ка; **be in ~ of** заве́довать *impf.*+*i.*; име́ть *impf.* на попече́нии; **in the ~ of** на попече́нии+*g.*; *v.t.* (*gun; elec.*) заряжа́ть *impf.*, заряди́ть (-яжу́, -я́ди́шь) *pf.*; (*accuse*) обвиня́ть *impf.*, обвини́ть *pf.* (**with** в+*p.*); (*mil.*) атакова́ть *impf.* & *pf.*; *v.i.* броса́ться *impf.*, бро́ситься *pf.* в ата́ку; ~ **(for)** брать (беру́, -ерёшь; брал, -а́, -о) *impf.*, взять (возьму́, -мёшь; взял, -а́, -о) *pf.* (за+*a.*); назнача́ть *impf.*, назна́чить *pf.* пла́ту (за+*a.*); ~ **to (the account of)** запи́сывать *impf.*, записа́ть (-ишу́, -и́шешь) *pf.* на счёт+*g.*
chargé d'affaires [ˌʃɑ:ʒeɪ dæ'feə(r)] *n.* пове́ренный *sb.* в дела́х.
chariot ['tʃærɪət] *n.* колесни́ца.
charisma [kə'rɪzmə] *n.* (*divine gift*) бо́жий дар; (*charm*) обая́ние. **charis'matic** *adj.* боговдохнове́нный; вдохнове́нный; с бо́жьей и́скрой; обая́тельный.
charitable ['tʃærɪtəb(ə)l] *adj.* благотвори́тельный; (*merciful*) милосе́рдный; (*lenient*) снисходи́тельный. **charity** *n.* (*kindness*) милосе́рдие; (*leniency*) снисходи́тельность; благотвори́тельность; (*organization*) благотвори́тельное о́бщество; *pl.* благотвори́тельная де́ятельность.
charlatan ['ʃɑ:lət(ə)n] *n.* шарлата́н.
charlotte ['ʃɑ:lɒt] *n.*: **apple ~** шарло́тка.
charm [tʃɑ:m] *n.* очарова́ние; пре́лесть; (*spell*) за́говор; *pl.* ча́ры (чар) *pl.*; (*amulet*) талисма́н; (*trinket*) брело́к; **act, work, like a ~** твори́ть *impf.*, со~ *pf.* чудеса́; *v.t.* очаро́вывать *impf.*, очарова́ть *pf.*; ~ **away** отгоня́ть *impf.*, отогна́ть (отгоню́, -нишь; отогна́л, -а́, -о) *pf.* (как бы) колдовство́м; **bear a ~ed life** быть неуязви́мым. **charming** *adj.* очарова́тельный, преле́стный.
charring ['tʃɑ:rɪŋ] *n.* рабо́та по до́му; **do, go out, ~** служи́ть (-жу́, -жишь) *impf.* приходя́щей домрабо́тницей.
chart [tʃɑ:t] *n.* (*naut.*) морска́я ка́рта; (*table*) гра́фик; *v.t.* наноси́ть (-ошу́, -о́сишь) *impf.*,

нанести́ (-су́, -сёшь; нанёс, -ла́) *pf.* на ка́рту; составля́ть *impf.*, соста́вить *pf.* гра́фик+*g.* **charter** *n.* (*document*) ха́ртия; (*statutes*) уста́в; (~-*party*) ча́ртер; *v.t.* (*ship*) фрахтова́ть *impf.*, за~ *pf.*; (*vehicle etc.*) нанима́ть *impf.*, наня́ть (найму́, -мёшь; на́нял, -а́, -о) *pf.*

charwoman ['tʃɑ:ˌwʊmən] *n.* приходя́щая домрабо́тница.

chase [tʃeɪs] *v.t.* гоня́ться *indet.*, гна́ться (гоню́сь, го́нишься; гна́лся, -ла́сь, гна́ло́сь) *det.* за+*i.*; *n.* (*pursuit*) пого́ня, пресле́дование; (*hunting*) охо́та.

chased [tʃeɪsd] *adj.* укра́шенный (-н) гравиро́ванием, релье́фом.

chasm ['kæz(ə)m] *n.* (*abyss*) бе́здна; (*fissure*) глубо́кая рассе́лина.

chassis ['ʃæsɪ] *n.* шасси́ *nt.indecl.*

chaste [tʃeɪst] *adj.* целому́дренный (-ен, -енна).

chastise [tʃæs'taɪz] *v.t.* подверга́ть *impf.*, подве́ргнуть (-г) *pf.* наказа́нию.

chastity ['tʃæstɪtɪ] *n.* целому́дрие.

chat [tʃæt] *n.* бесе́да, разгово́р; *v.i.* бесе́довать *impf.*; разгова́ривать *impf.*

chattels ['tʃæt(ə)lz] *n.* дви́жимость.

chatter ['tʃætə(r)] *n.* болтовня́; трескотня́; *v.i.* болта́ть *impf.*; треща́ть (-щу́, -щи́шь) *impf.*; (*of teeth*) стуча́ть (-ча́т) *impf.* **chatterbox** *n.* болту́н (-а́). **chatty** *adj.* разгово́рчивый.

chauffeur ['ʃəʊfə(r), -'fɜ:(r)] *n.* шофёр.

chauvinism ['ʃəʊvɪˌnɪz(ə)m] *n.* шовини́зм. **chauvinist** *n.* шовини́ст, ~ка; *adj.* шовини́стский.

cheap [tʃi:p] *adj.* дешёвый (дёшев, -а́, -о). **cheapen** *v.t.* & *i.* обесце́нивать(ся) *impf.*, обесце́нить(ся) *pf.*; удешевля́ть(ся) *impf.*, удешеви́ть(ся) *pf.* **cheaply** *adv.* дёшево. **cheapness** *n.* дешеви́зна.

cheat [tʃi:t] *v.t.* обма́нывать *impf.*, обману́ть (-ну́, -нешь) *pf.*; *v.i.* плутова́ть *impf.*, на~, с~ *pf.*; моше́нничать *impf.*, с~ *pf.*; *n.* (*person*) обма́нщик, -ица; (*act*) обма́н. **cheating** *n.* моше́нничество, плутовство́.

check¹ [tʃek] *n.* контро́ль *m.*, прове́рка; (*stoppage*) заде́ржка; (*chess*) шах; *adj.* контро́льный; *v.t.* (*examine*) проверя́ть *impf.*, прове́рить *pf.*; контроли́ровать *impf.*, про~ *pf.*; (*restrain*) сде́рживать *impf.*, сдержа́ть (-жу́, -жишь) *pf.*

check² [tʃek] *n.* (*pattern*) кле́тка. **check(ed)** *adj.* кле́тчатый.

check-list ['tʃeklɪst] *n.* контро́льный спи́сок (-ска́). **checkmate** *n.* шах и мат; *v.t.* наноси́ть (-ошу́, -о́сишь) *impf.*, нанести́ (-су́, -сёшь; нанёс, -ла́) *pf.*+*d.* пораже́ние. **checkout** *n.* ка́сса. **checkpoint** *n.* контро́льно-пропускно́й пункт. **check-up** *n.* (*med.*) медосмо́тр; (*tech.*) техосмо́тр.

cheek [tʃi:k] *n.* щека́ (*a.* щёку; *pl.* щёки, щёк, -а́м); (*impertinence*) наха́льство, де́рзость; *v.t.* дерзи́ть (-и́шь) *impf.*, на~ *pf.*+*d.* **cheekbone** *n.* скула́ (*pl.* -лы). **cheeky** *adj.* де́рзкий (-зок, -зка́, -зко), наха́льный.

cheep [tʃi:p] *n.* писк; *v.i.* пища́ть (-щу́, -щи́шь) *impf.*, пи́скнуть *pf.*

cheer ['tʃɪə(r)] *n.* одобри́тельное восклица́ние; *pl.* (*applause*) аплодисме́нты (-тов); *pl.*; ~**s!** за (ва́ше) здоро́вье!; **three ~s for ...** да здра́вствует (-уют)+*nom.*; *v.t.* (*applaud*) аплоди́ровать *impf.*+*d.*; ~ **up** ободря́ть(ся) *impf.*, ободри́ть(ся) *pf.* **cheerful** *adj.* весёлый (ве́сел, -а́, -о, ве́селы́), бо́дрый (бодр, -а́, -о). **cheerless** *adj.* уны́лый. **cheery** *adj.* бо́дрый (бодр, -а́, -о).

cheese [tʃi:z] *n.* сыр (-а(у); *pl.* -ы́); ~ **straw** сы́рная па́лочка. **cheesecake** *n.* ватру́шка. **cheesecloth** *n.* ма́рля. **cheese-paring** *n.* ску́пость, грошо́вая эконо́мия; *adj.* скупо́й (скуп, -а́, -о).

cheetah ['tʃi:tə] *n.* гепа́рд.

chef [ʃef] *n.* (шеф-)по́вар (*pl.* -а́)

chef-d'oeuvre [ʃeɪ'dɜ:vr] *n.* шеде́вр.

chemical ['kemɪk(ə)l] *adj.* хими́ческий; ~ **warfare** хими́ческая война́; *n.* химика́т; *pl.* химика́лии (-ий) *pl.* **chemically** *adv.* хими́чески. **chemist** *n.* хи́мик; (*druggist*) апте́карь *m.*; **~'s (shop)** апте́ка. **chemistry** *n.* хи́мия. **chemotherapy** [ˌki:mə'θerəpɪ] *n.* химотерапи́я.

chenille [ʃə'ni:l] *n.* сине́ль; *adj.* сине́льный.

cheque [tʃek] *n.* чек. **cheque-book** *n.* че́ковая кни́жка.

chequered ['tʃekə(r)d] *adj.* (*varied*) разнообра́зный; (*changing*) изме́нчивый.

cherish ['tʃerɪʃ] *v.t.* (*foster*) леле́ять (-е́ю, -е́ешь) *impf.*; (*hold dear*) дорожи́ть *impf.*+*i.*; (*preserve in memory*) храни́ть *impf.* (в па́мяти); (*love*) не́жно люби́ть (-блю́, -бишь) *impf.* **cherished** *adj.* заве́тный.

cheroot [ʃə'ru:t] *n.* мани́льская сига́ра.

cherry ['tʃerɪ] *n.* ви́шня (*g.pl.* -шен); чере́шня (*g.pl.* -шен); (*tree*) вишнёвое де́рево (*pl.* -е́вья, -е́вьев); (*colour*) вишнёвый цвет; *adj.* вишнёвый, вишнёвого цве́та; (*cherry-wood*) древеси́на вишнёвого де́рева.

cherub ['tʃerəb] *n.* херуви́м, херуви́мчик. **cherubic** *adj.* пу́хлый и розовощёкий.

chervil ['tʃɜ:vɪl] *n.* ке́рвель *m.*

chess [tʃes] *n.* ша́хматы (-т) *pl.*; *adj.* ша́хматный; ~ **champion** чемпио́н по ша́хматам; ~ **player** шахмати́ст, ~ка. **chessboard** *n.* ша́хматная доска́ (*a.* -ску; *pl.* -ски, -со́к, -скам). **chessman** *n.* ша́хматная фигу́ра.

chest [tʃest] *n.* я́щик, сунду́к (-а́); (*anat.*) грудь (-ди́, *i.* -дью; *pl.* -ди, -де́й); ~ **of drawers** комо́д.

chestnut ['tʃesnʌt] *n.* (*tree*, *fruit*) кашта́н; (*colour*) кашта́новый цвет; (*horse*) гнеда́я *sb.*; *adj.* кашта́новый; (*horse*) гнедо́й.

chevron ['ʃevrən] *n.* наши́вка.

chew [tʃu:] *v.t.* жева́ть (жую́, жуёшь) *impf.*; ~ **over** пережёвывать *impf.*, пережева́ть (-жую́, -жуёшь) *pf.*; ~ **the cud** жева́ть (жую́, жуёшь) *impf.* жва́чку. **chewing** *n.*

жева́ние. **chewing-gum** *n.* жева́тельная рези́нка, жва́чка.
chicane [ʃɪ'keɪn] *n.* вре́менное и́ли передвижно́е препя́тствие на доро́ге, го́ночном тре́ке. **chicanery** *n.* крючкотво́рство; махина́ция.
chick [tʃɪk] *n.* цыплёнок (-нка; *pl.* цепля́та, -т). **chicken** ['tʃɪkɪn] *n.* ку́рица (*pl.* ку́ры, кур); цыплёнок (-нка; *pl.* цепля́та, -т); (*meat*) куря́тина; *adj.* трусли́вый. **chicken-hearted, -livered** *adj.* трусли́вый. **chicken-pox** *n.* ве́тряная о́спа, ветря́нка.
chicory ['tʃɪkərɪ] *n.* цико́рий.
chief [tʃi:f] *n.* глава́ (*pl.* -вы) *c.g.*; (*mil. etc.*) нача́льник; (*of tribe*) вождь (-дя́) *m.*; (*robber*) атама́н; *adj.* гла́вный; ста́рший. **chiefly** *adv.* гла́вным о́бразом. **chieftain** *n.* вождь (-дя́) *m.*; (*robber*) атама́н.
chiffon ['ʃɪfɒn] *n.* шифо́н; *adj.* шифо́новый.
child [tʃaɪld] *n.* ребёнок (-нка; *pl.* де́ти, -те́й); ~ **prodigy** вундерки́нд; ~**'s play** де́тские игру́шки *f.pl.* **childbirth** *n.* ро́ды (-дов) *pl.* **childhood** *n.* де́тство. **childish** *adj.* де́тский; ребя́ческий. **childless** *adj.* безде́тный. **childlike** *adj.* де́тский. **child-minder** *n.* приходя́щая ня́ня. **childrens'** ['tʃɪldrənz] *adj.* де́тский.
chili ['tʃɪlɪ] *n.* стручко́вый пе́рец (-рца(у)).
chill [tʃɪl] *n.* хо́лод (-а(у); *pl.* -а́), охлажде́ние; (*ailment*) просту́да, озно́б; (*fig.*) холодо́к (-дка́); *v.t.* охлажда́ть *impf.*, охлади́ть *pf.*; студи́ть (-ужу́, -у́дишь) *impf.*, о~ *pf.* **chilled** *adj.* охлаждённый (-ён, -ена́), моро́женый. **chilly** *adj.* холо́дный (хо́лоден, -дна́, -дно, хо́лодны́), прохла́дный.
chime [tʃaɪm] *n.* (*set of bells*) набо́р колоколо́в; *pl.* (*sound*) колоко́льный перезво́н; (*of clock*) бой; *v.t.* звони́ть *impf.*, по~ *pf.* в+*a.*; *v.i.* звене́ть (-ни́т) *impf.*, про~ *pf.*; (*correspond*) соотве́тствовать *impf.* (**to** +*d.*); ~ **in** вме́шиваться *impf.*, вмеша́ться *pf.*
chimera [kaɪ'mɪərə, kɪ-] *n.* химе́ра. **chimerical** [tʃɪ'merɪk(ə)l] *adj.* химери́ческий.
chimney ['tʃɪmnɪ] *n.* (дымова́я) труба́ (*pl.* -бы). **chimney-pot** *n.* дефле́ктор. **chimney-sweep** *n.* трубочи́ст.
chimpanzee [,tʃɪmpən'zi:] *n.* шимпанзе́ *m.indecl.*
chin [tʃɪn] *n.* подборо́док (-дка); *v.t.*: ~ **the bar, o.s.** подтя́гиваться *impf.*, подтяну́ться (-ну́сь, -нешься) *pf.* до у́ровня подборо́дка.
China ['tʃaɪnə] *n.* Кита́й; *adj.* кита́йский.
china ['tʃaɪnə] *n.* (*material*) фарфо́р; (*objects*) посу́да; *adj.* фарфо́ровый.
chinchilla [tʃɪn'tʃɪlə] *n.* (*animal, fur*) шинши́лла.
Chinese [tʃaɪ'ni:z] *n.* (*person*) кита́ец (-а́йца), -aя́нка; *adj.* кита́йский; ~ **lantern** кита́йский фона́рик; ~ **white** кита́йские бели́ла (-л) *pl.*
chink[1] [tʃɪŋk] *n.* (*sound*) звон; *v.i.* звене́ть (-и́т) *impf.*, про~ *pf.*
chink[2] [tʃɪŋk] *n.* (*opening, crack*) щель (*pl.* -ли, -ле́й), сква́жина.
chintz [tʃɪnts] *n.* глазиро́ванный, ме́бельный си́тец (-тца(у)).
chip [tʃɪp] *v.t.* отбива́ть *impf.*, отби́ть (отобью́, -ьёшь) края́+*g.*; *n.* (*of wood*) щепа́ (*pl.* -пы, -п, -па́м), ще́пка, лучи́на; щерби́на, щерби́нка; (*in games*) фи́шка; (*microelectronics*) криста́лл; *pl.* жа́реная карто́шка (*collect.*).
chiropody [kɪ'rɒpədɪ] *n.* педикю́р.
chiropractor ['kaɪərəʊ,præktə(r)] *n.* хиропра́ктик.
chirp [tʃɜ:p] *v.i.* чири́кать *impf.*
chisel ['tʃɪz(ə)l] *n.* долото́ (*pl.* -та); стаме́ска; дуби́ло; резе́ц (-зца́); *v.t.* высека́ть *impf.*, вы́сечь (-еку, -ечешь; -ек) *pf.*; выреза́ть *impf.*, вы́резать (-ежу, -ежешь) *pf.* **chiseller** *n.* моше́нник.
chit [tʃɪt] *n.* (*note*) запи́ска.
chit-chat ['tʃɪttʃæt] *n.* болтовня́.
chivalrous ['ʃɪvəlrəs] *adj.* ры́царский. **chivalry** *n.* ры́царство.
chive [tʃaɪv] *n.* лук(-а)-ре́занец (-нца).
chloral ['klɔ:r(ə)l] *n.* хлоралгидра́т. **chloride** *n.* хлори́д. **chlorinate** *v.t.* хлори́ровать *impf.* & *pf.* **chlorine** *n.* хлор. **chloroform** *n.* хлорофо́рм; *v.t.* хлороформи́ровать *impf.* & *pf.* **chlorophyll** *n.* хлорофи́лл.
chock [tʃɒk] *n.* клин (*pl.* -ья, -ьев); (тормозна́я) коло́дка. **chock-a-block, chock-full** *adj.* битко́м наби́тый, перепо́лненный (-ен, -енна) (**of** +*i.*).
chocolate ['tʃɒkələt, 'tʃɒklət] *n.* шокола́д (-а(у)); (*sweet*) шокола́дка; (*colour*) шокола́дный цвет; *adj.* шокола́дный; шокола́дного цве́та.
choice [tʃɔɪs] *n.* вы́бор; *adj.* отбо́рный.
choir ['kwaɪə(r)] *n.* хор (*pl.* хо́ры́); хорово́й анса́мбль *m.* **choirboy** *n.* пе́вчий *sb.*, ма́льчик-хори́ст.
choke [tʃəʊk] *n.* (*valve*) дро́ссель *m.*; (*artichoke*) сердцеви́на артишо́ка; *v.i.* дави́ться (-влю́сь, -вишься) *impf.*, по~ *pf.*; задыха́ться *impf.*, задохну́ться (-о́х(нул)ся, -о́х(ну́)лась) *pf.*; *v.t.* (*suffocate*) души́ть (-шу́, -шишь) *impf.*, за~ *pf.*; (*of plants*) заглуша́ть, глуши́ть *impf.*, за~ *pf.* **choker** *n.* (*collar*) высо́кий крахма́льный воротничо́к (-чка́); (*necklace*) коро́ткое ожере́лье.
cholera ['kɒlərə] *n.* холе́ра.
choleric ['kɒlərɪk] *adj.* вспы́льчивый.
cholesterol [kə'lestə,rɒl] *n.* холестери́н.
choose [tʃu:z] *v.t.* (*select*) выбира́ть *impf.*, вы́брать (-беру, -берешь) *pf.*; (*decide*) реша́ть *impf.*, реши́ть *pf.* **choosy** *adj.* разбо́рчивый.
chop[1] [tʃɒp] *v.t.* руби́ть (-блю́, -бишь) *impf.*, рубну́ть, рубану́ть *pf.*; (*chop up*) кроши́ть (-шу́, -шишь) *impf.*, ис~, на~, рас~ *pf.*; коло́ть (-лю́, -лешь) *impf.*, рас~ *pf.*; ~ **off** отруба́ть *impf.*, отруби́ть (-блю́, -бишь) *pf.*;

n. (*blow*) рубя́щий уда́р; (*cul.*) отбивна́я котле́та.

chop[2] [tʃɒp] *v.i.*: ~ **and change** постоя́нно меня́ться *impf.*; колеба́ться (-блюсь, -блешься) *impf.*

chopper ['tʃɒpə(r)] *n.* (*knife*) се́чка, коса́рь (-ря́) *m.*; (*axe*) колу́н (-а́). **choppy** *adj.* неспоко́йный; ~ **sea** зыбь на́ море.

chops [tʃɒpz] *n.* (*jaws*) че́люсти (-тей) *pl.*; **lick one's** ~ обли́зываться *impf.*, облиза́ться (-жу́сь, -жешься) *pf.*

chop-sticks ['tʃɒpstɪkz] *n.* па́лочки *f.pl.* для еды́. **chop-suey** [tʃɒp'su:ɪ] *n.* кита́йское рагу́ *nt.indecl.*

choral ['kɔ:r(ə)l] *adj.* хорово́й. **chorale** [kɔ:'rɑ:l] *n.* хора́л.

chord[1] [kɔ:d] *n.* (*math.*) хо́рда; (*anat.*) свя́зка.

chord[2] [kɔ:d] *n.* (*mus.*) акко́рд.

choreographer [ˌkɒrɪ'ɒgrəfə(r)] *n.* хорео́граф. **choreo'graphic** *adj.* хореографи́ческий. **choreography** *n.* хореогра́фия.

chorister ['kɒrɪstə(r)] *n.* пе́вчий *sb.*, хори́ст, ~ка.

chortle ['tʃɔ:t(ə)l] *v.i.* фы́ркать *impf.*, фы́ркнуть *pf.* от сме́ха.

chorus ['kɔ:rəs] *n.* хор (*pl.* хо́ры́); (*refrain*) припе́в; ~ **girl** хори́стка; *v.i.* (*sing*) петь (поёт) *impf.*, про~ *pf.* хо́ром; (*speak*) говори́ть *impf.*, сказа́ть (-а́жет) *pf.* хо́ром.

christen ['krɪs(ə)n] *v.t.* (*baptise*) крести́ть (-ещу́, -е́стишь) *impf.* & *pf.*; (*give name*) дава́ть (даю́, даёшь) *impf.*, дать (дам, дашь, даст, дади́м; дал, -а́, да́ло́, -и) *pf.*+*d.* и́мя при креще́нии. **Christian** ['krɪstɪən, 'krɪstʃ(ə)n] *n.* христиани́н (*pl.* -а́не, -а́н), -а́нка; *adj.* христиа́нский; ~ **name** и́мя *nt.* **Christi'anity** *n.* христиа́нство. **Christmas** *n.* Рождество́; ~ **Eve** соче́льник; ~ **tree** ёлка. **Christmastide** *n.* свя́тки (-ток) *pl.*

chromatic [krə'mætɪk] *adj.* хромати́ческий. **chrome** [krəʊm] *n.* крон; ~ **leather** хроми́рованная ко́жа; ~ **steel** хро́мистая сталь; ~ **yellow** (жёлтый) крон. **chromium** *n.* хром. **chromium-plated** *adj.* хромиро́ванный. **chromoli'thograph(y)** *n.* хромолитогра́фия. **chromosome** ['krəʊməˌsəʊm] *n.* хромосо́ма.

chronic ['krɒnɪk] *adj.* хрони́ческий.

chronicle ['krɒnɪk(ə)l] *n.* хро́ника, ле́топись; **(Book of) C~s** Паралипомено́н; *v.t.* заноси́ть (-ошу́, -о́сишь) *impf.*, занести́ (-есу́, -есёшь; -ёс, -есла́) *pf.* (в дневни́к, в ле́топись); отмеча́ть *impf.*, отме́тить *pf.* **chronicler** *n.* летопи́сец (-сца).

chronological [ˌkrɒnə'lɒdʒɪk(ə)l] *adj.* хронологи́ческий. **chronology** [krə'nɒlədʒɪ] *n.* хроноло́гия. **chronometer** *n.* хроно́метр.

chrysalis ['krɪsəlɪs] *n.* ку́колка.

chrysanthemum [krɪ'sænθəməm] *n.* хризанте́ма.

chub [tʃʌb] *n.* гола́вль (-ля́) *m.*

chubby ['tʃʌbɪ] *adj.* пу́хлый (пухл, -а́, -о).

chuck [tʃʌk] *v.t.* броса́ть *impf.*, бро́сить *pf.*; ~ **it!** брось!; ~ **out** вышиба́ть *impf.*, вы́шибить (-бу, -бешь; -б) *pf.*; ~ **under the chin** трепа́ть (-плю́, -плешь) *impf.*, по~ *pf.* по подборо́дку; ~ **up** броса́ть *impf.*, бро́сить *pf.* **chucker-out** *n.* вышиба́ла *m.*

chuckle ['tʃʌk(ə)l] *v.i.* посме́иваться *impf.*

chug [tʃʌg] *v.i.* идти́ (идёт) *impf.* с пыхте́нием; ~ **along** пропыхте́ть (-ти́т) *pf.*

chum [tʃʌm] *n.* това́рищ.

chump [tʃʌmp] *n.* чурба́н; то́лстый коне́ц (-нца́); **off one's** ~ спя́тивший с ума́.

chunk [tʃʌŋk] *n.* ломо́ть (-мтя́) *m.*, кусо́к (-ска́). **chunky** *adj.* коро́ткий (ко́роток, -тка́, -тко, ко́ротки́) и то́лстый (толст, -а́, -о, то́лсты́); корена́стый.

church [tʃɜ:tʃ] *n.* це́рковь (-кви, -ковью; *pl.* -кви, -кве́й, -ква́м); **C~ of England** англика́нская це́рковь. **churchyard** *n.* (церко́вное) кла́дбище.

churlish ['tʃɜ:lɪʃ] *adj.* гру́бый (груб, -а́, -о), нелюбе́зный.

churn [tʃɜ:n] *n.* маслобо́йка; *v.t.* сбива́ть *impf.*, сбить (собью́, -ьёшь) *pf.*; *v.i.* (*foam*) пе́ниться *impf.*, вс~ *pf.*; (*seethe*) кипе́ть (-пи́т) *impf.*, вс~ *pf.*

chute [ʃu:t] *n.* скат, жёлоб (*pl.* -а́); (*parachute*) парашю́т.

CIA *abbr.* (*of* ***Central Intelligence Agency***) ЦРУ, Центра́льное разве́дывательное управле́ние.

cicada [sɪ'kɑ:də, -'keɪdə] *n.* цика́да.

CID *abbr.* (*of* ***Criminal Investigation Department***) отде́л/департа́мент уголо́вного ро́зыска.

cider ['saɪdə(r)] *n.* сидр.

cigar [sɪ'gɑ:(r)] *n.* сига́ра. **ciga'rette** *n.* сигаре́та; папиро́са; ~ **lighter** зажига́лка.

cinder ['sɪndə(r)] *n.* шлак; *pl.* зола́; ~ **track** гарева́я доро́жка.

cine-camera ['sɪnɪ-] *n.* киноаппара́т. **cinema** ['sɪnɪˌmɑ:, -mə] *n.* кино́ *nt.indecl.*, кинематогра́фия. **cine'matic** *adj.* кинематографи́ческий.

cinnamon ['sɪnəmən] *n.* кори́ца; (*colour*) све́тло-кори́чневый цвет.

cipher ['saɪfə(r)] *n.* (*math.*) ноль (-ля́) *m.*, нуль (-ля́) *m.*; шифр.

circle ['sɜ:k(ə)l] *n.* круг (*loc.* -е & -у́; *pl.* -и́); (*theatre*) я́рус; *v.t.* & *i.* кружи́ть(ся) (-ужу́(сь), -у́жи́шь(ся)) *impf.*; *v.i.* дви́гаться (-аюсь, -аешься & дви́жусь, -жешься) *impf.*, дви́нуться *pf.* по кру́гу. **circlet** *n.* кружо́к (-жка́); вено́к (-нка́). **circuit** ['sɜ:kɪt] *n.* кругооборо́т; объе́зд, обхо́д; (*tour*) турне́ *nt.indecl.*; (*leg.*) выездна́я се́ссия суда́; (*elec.*) цепь, ко́нтур; **short** ~ коро́ткое замыка́ние. **circuitous** [sɜ:'kju:ɪtəs] *adj.* кру́жный, око́льный. **circular** *adj.* кру́глый (кругл, -а́, -о, кру́глы́), кругово́й; (*circulating*) циркуля́рный; *n.* циркуля́р. **circularize** *v.t.* рассыла́ть *impf.*, разосла́ть (-ошлю́, -ошлёшь) *pf.* +*d.* циркуля́ры. **circulate** *v.i.* циркули́ровать *impf.*; *v.t.* рассыла́ть *impf.*, разосла́ть (-ошлю́, -ошлёшь) *pf.*; (*spread*) распространя́ть *impf.*, распространи́ть *pf.* **circu'lation** *n.* (*movement*) циркуля́ция; (*distribution*) распростране́ние; (*of newspaper*) тира́ж (-а́); (*econ.*) обраще́ние; (*med.*) кровообраще́ние.

circumcise ['sɜːkəm,saɪz] *v.t.* обреза́ть *impf.*, обре́зать (-е́жу, -е́жешь) *pf.* **circum'cision** *n.* обреза́ние.

circumference [sɜː'kʌmfərəns] *n.* окру́жность.

circumscribe ['sɜːkəm,skraɪb] *v.t.* оче́рчивать *impf.*, очерти́ть (-рчу́, -ртишь) *pf.*; (*restrict*) ограни́чивать *impf.*, ограни́чить *pf.*

circumspect ['sɜːkəm,spekt] *adj.* осмотри́тельный. **circum'spection** *n.* осмотри́тельность.

circumstance ['sɜːkəmst(ə)ns] *n.* обстоя́тельство; *pl.* (*material situation*) материа́льное положе́ние; **in, under the ~s** при да́нных обстоя́тельствах, в тако́м слу́чае; **in, under, no ~s** ни при каки́х обстоя́тельствах, ни в ко́ем слу́чае. **circumstantial** [,sɜːkəm'stænʃ(ə)l] *adj.* (*detailed*) подро́бный; **~ evidence** ко́свенные доказа́тельства *nt.pl.*

circumvent [,sɜːkəm'vent] *v.t.* (*outwit*) перехитри́ть *pf.*; (*evade*) обходи́ть (-ожу́, -о́дишь) *impf.*, обойти́ (обойду́, -дёшь; обошёл, -шла́) *pf.*

circus ['sɜːkəs] *n.* (*show*) цирк; (*arena*) кру́глая пло́щадь (*pl.* -ди, -де́й).

cirrhosis [sɪ'rəʊsɪs] *n.* цирро́з.

CIS *abbr.* (*of* ***Commonwealth of Independent States***) СНГ, Содру́жество незави́симых госуда́рств.

cistern ['sɪst(ə)n] *n.* бак; резервуа́р.

citadel ['sɪtəd(ə)l, -,del] *n.* цитаде́ль.

citation [saɪ'teɪʃ(ə)n] *n.* (*quotation*) ссы́лка, цита́та. **cite** *v.t.* цити́ровать *impf.*, про~ *pf.*; ссыла́ться *impf.*, сосла́ться (сошлю́сь, -льёшься) *pf.* на+*a.*

citizen ['sɪtɪz(ə)n] *n.* граждани́н (*pl.* -ане, -ан), -а́нка. **citizenship** *n.* гражда́нство.

citric ['sɪtrɪk] *adj.* лимо́нный. **citron** *n.* цитро́н. **citro'nella** *n.* цитроне́лла. **citrous** *adj.* ци́трусовый. **citrus** *n.* ци́трус; *adj.* ци́трусовый.

city ['sɪtɪ] *n.* го́род (*pl.* -а́).

civet ['sɪvɪt] *n.* (*perfume*) цибети́н; (~ *cat*) виве́рра.

civic ['sɪvɪk] *adj.* гражда́нский. **civil** *adj.* гражда́нский; (*polite*) ве́жливый; **~ engineer** гражда́нский инжене́р; **~ engineering** гражда́нское стро́ительство; **~ servant** госуда́рственный гражда́нский слу́жащий *sb.*; чино́вник; **~ service** госуда́рственная слу́жба; **~ war** гражда́нская война́. **ci'vilian** *n.* шта́тский *sb.*; *adj.* шта́тский; гражда́нский. **ci'vility** *n.* ве́жливость. **civili'zation** *n.* цивилиза́ция, культу́ра. **civilize** *v.t.* цивилизова́ть *impf.* & *pf.*; де́лать *impf.*, с~ *pf.* культу́рным. **civilized** *adj.* цивилизо́ванный; культу́рный.

claim [kleɪm] *n.* (*demand*) тре́бование, притяза́ние, прете́нзия; (*piece of land*) отведённый уча́сток (-тка); *v.t.* заявля́ть *impf.*, заяви́ть (-влю́, -вишь) *pf.* права́ *pl.* на+*a.*; претендова́ть *impf.* на+*a.*

clairvoyance [kleə'vɔɪəns] *n.* яснови́дение. **clairvoyant** *n.* яснови́дец (-дца), -дица; *adj.* яснови́дящий.

clam [klæm] *n.* вене́рка, рази́нька.

clamber ['klæmbə(r)] *v.i.* кара́бкаться *impf.*, вс~ *pf.*

clammy ['klæmɪ] *adj.* холо́дный и вла́жный на о́щупь.

clamorous ['klæmərəs] *adj.* крикли́вый. **clamour** *n.* кри́ки *m.pl.*, шум (-а(у)); *v.i.* крича́ть (-чу́, -чи́шь) *impf.*; **~ for** шу́мно тре́бовать *impf.*, по~ *pf.+g.*

clamp[1] [klæmp] *n.* (*clasp*) зажи́м, скоба́ (*pl.* -бы, -б, -ба́м), ско́бка; *v.t.* скрепля́ть *impf.*, скрепи́ть *pf.*

clamp[2] [klæmp] *n.* (*of potatoes*) бурт (бу́рта́; *pl.* -ы́).

clan [klæn] *n.* клан.

clandestine [klæn'destɪn] *adj.* та́йный.

clang [klæŋ], **clank** [klæŋk] *n.* лязг, бряца́ние; *v.t.* & *i.* ля́згать *impf.*, ля́згнуть *pf.* (+*i.*); бряца́ть *impf.*, про~ *pf.* (+*i.*, на+*p.*).

clap [klæp] *v.t.* хло́пать *impf.*, хло́пнуть *pf.+d.*; аплоди́ровать *impf.+d.*; *n.* хлопо́к (-пка́); рукоплеска́ния *nt. pl.*; (*thunder*) уда́р. **clapper** *n.* язы́к (-а́). **claptrap** ['klæptræp] *n.* треску́чая фра́за; (*nonsense*) вздор.

claret ['klærət] *n.* бордо́ *nt.indecl.*

clarification [,klærɪfɪ'keɪʃ(ə)n] *n.* (*explanation*) разъясне́ние; (*of liquid, chem.*) осветле́ние; (*purification*) очище́ние. **'clarify** *v.t.* разъясня́ть *impf.*, разъясни́ть *pf.*; осветля́ть *impf.*, осветли́ть *pf.*; очища́ть *impf.*, очи́стить *pf.*

clarinet [,klærɪ'net] *n.* кларне́т.

clarity ['klærɪtɪ] *n.* я́сность.

clash [klæʃ] *n.* (*conflict*) столкнове́ние; (*disharmony*) дисгармо́ния; (*sound*) гро́хот, лязг; *v.i.* ста́лкиваться *impf.*, столкну́ться *pf.*; (*coincide*) совпада́ть *impf.*, совпа́сть (-адёт; -а́л) *pf.*; не гармони́ровать *impf.*; (*sound*) ля́згать *impf.*, ля́згнуть *pf.*

clasp [klɑːsp] *n.* (*buckle etc.*) пря́жка, застёжка; (*handshake*) пожа́тие руки́; (*embrace*) объя́тие; *v.t.* обнима́ть *impf.*, обня́ть (обниму́, -мешь; о́бнял, -а́, -о) *pf.*; сжима́ть *impf.*, сжать (сожму́, -мёшь) *pf.* в объя́тиях. **clasp-knife** *n.* складно́й нож (-а́).

class [klɑːs] *n.* класс; (*category*) разря́д; **~ war** кла́ссовая борьба́; *v.t.* причисля́ть *impf.*, причи́слить *pf.* (**as** к+*d.*); классифици́ровать *impf.* & *pf.* **class-conscious** *adj.* (кла́ссово) созна́тельный. **class-consciousness** *n.* кла́ссовое созна́ние.

classic ['klæsɪk] *adj.* класси́ческий; (*renowned*) знамени́тый; *n.* кла́ссик; класси́ческое произведе́ние; *pl.* кла́ссика; класси́-

ческие языки́ *m.pl.* **classical** *adj.* класси́ческий.

classification [ˌklæsɪfɪˈkeɪʃ(ə)n] *n.* классифика́ция. ˈ**classify** *v.t.* классифици́ровать *impf.* & *pf.*; (~ *as secret*) засекре́чивать *impf.*, засекре́тить *pf.*

classroom [ˈklɑːsruːm, -rʊm] *n.* класс.

classy [ˈklɑːsɪ] *adj.* кла́ссный, первокла́ссный.

clatter [ˈklætə(r)] *n.* стук, лязг; *v.i.* стуча́ть (-чу́, -чи́шь) *impf.*, по~ *pf.*; ля́згать *impf.*, ля́згнуть *pf.*

clause [klɔːz] *n.* статья́; (*leg.*) кла́узула; (*gram.*) предложе́ние.

claw [klɔː] *n.* ко́готь (-гтя; *pl.* -гти, -гте́й); (*of crustacean*) клешня́; *v.t.* скрести́ (-ебу́, -ебёшь; ёб, -ебла́) *impf.*

clay [kleɪ] *n.* гли́на; (*pipe*) гли́няная тру́бка; *adj.* гли́няный. **clayey** *adj.* гли́нистый.

clean [kliːn] *adj.* чи́стый (чист, -а́, -о, чи́сты́); *adv.* (*fully*) соверше́нно, по́лностью; *v.t.* чи́стить *impf.*, вы́~, по~ *pf.*; очища́ть *impf.*, очи́стить *pf.* **cleaner** *n.* чи́стильщик, -ица; убо́рщик, -ица. **cleaner's** *n.* химчи́стка. **cleaning** *n.* чи́стка, убо́рка; очи́стка. **clean(li)ness** [ˈklenlɪnɪs] *n.* чистота́.

cleanse [klenz] *v.t.* очища́ть *impf.*, очи́стить *pf.*

clear [klɪə(r)] *adj.* я́сный (я́сен, ясна́, я́сно, я́сны́); (*transparent*) прозра́чный; (*distinct*) отчётливый; (*free*) свобо́дный (**of** от+*g.*); *v.t.* & *i.* очища́ть(ся) *impf.*, очи́стить(ся) *pf.*; *v.t.* (*jump over*) перепры́гивать *impf.*, перепры́гнуть *pf.*; (*acquit*) опра́вдывать *impf.*, оправда́ть *pf.*; ~ **away** убира́ть *impf.*, убра́ть (уберу́, -рёшь; убра́л, -а́, -о) *pf.* со стола́; ~ **off** (*go away*) убира́ться *impf.*, убра́ться (уберу́сь, -рёшься; убра́лся, -ала́сь, -а́ло́сь) *pf.*; ~ **out** (*v.t.*) вычища́ть *impf.*, вы́чистить *pf.*; (*v.i.*) (*make off*) удира́ть *impf.*, удра́ть (удеру́, -рёшь; удра́л, -а́, -о) *pf.*; ~ **up** (*make tidy*) приводи́ть (-ожу́, -о́дишь) *impf.*, привести́ (-еду́, -едёшь; -ёл, -ела́) *pf.* в поря́док; (*explain*) выясня́ть *impf.*, вы́яснить *pf.* **clearance** *n.* расчи́стка; (*permission*) разреше́ние. **clearing** *n.* расчи́стка; (*in forest*) поля́на. **clearly** *adv.* я́сно; отчётливо.

cleavage [ˈkliːvɪdʒ] *n.* разделе́ние. **cleaver** [ˈkliːvə(r)] *n.* нож (-а́) мясника́.

clef [klef] *n.* (*mus.*) ключ (-а́).

cleft [kleft] *n.* тре́щина, расще́лина; *adj.*: **in a ~ stick** в тупике́.

clematis [ˈklemətɪs, kləˈmeɪtɪs] *n.* ломоно́с.

clemency [ˈklemənsɪ] *n.* милосе́рдие.

clench [klentʃ] *v.t.* (*fist*) сжима́ть *impf.*, сжа́ть (сожму́, -мёшь) *pf.*; (*teeth*) сти́скивать *impf.*, сти́снуть *pf.*

clergy [ˈklɜːdʒɪ] *n.* духове́нство. **clergyman** *n.* свяще́нник. **clerical** [ˈklerɪk(ə)l] *adj.* (*of clergy*) духо́вный; (*of clerk*) канцеля́рский.

clerk [klɑːk] *n.* конто́рский слу́жащий *sb.*

clever [ˈklevə(r)] *adj.* у́мный (умён, -умна́, у́мно́), спосо́бный. **cleverness** *n.* уме́ние.

cliche [ˈkliːʃeɪ] *n.* клише́ *nt.indecl.*, изби́тая фра́за.

click [klɪk] *v.t.* щёлкать *impf.*, щёлкнуть *pf.*+*i.*; *n.* щёлк.

client [ˈklaɪənt] *n.* клие́нт. **clientele** [ˌkliːɒnˈtel] *n.* клиенту́ра.

cliff [klɪf] *n.* утёс, отве́сная скала́ (*pl.* -лы)

climacteric [klaɪˈmæktərɪk, ˌklaɪmækˈterɪk] *n.* климакте́рий; *adj.* климактери́ческий.

climate [ˈklaɪmɪt] *n.* кли́мат. **climatic** [ˌklaɪˈmætɪk] *adj.* климати́ческий.

climax [ˈklaɪmæks] *n.* кульминацио́нный пункт.

climb [klaɪm] *v.t.* & *i.* ла́зить *indet.*, лезть (ле́зу, -зешь; лез) *det.* на+*a.*; влеза́ть *impf.*, влезть (вле́зу, -зешь, влез) *pf.* на+*a.*; поднима́ться *impf.*, подня́ться (-ниму́сь, -ни́мешься; -ня́лся́, -няла́сь) *pf.* на+*a.*; (*aeron.*) набира́ть *impf.*, набра́ть (наберу́, -рёшь; набра́л, -а́, -о) *pf.* высоту́; ~ **down** спуска́ться *impf.*, спусти́ться (-ущу́сь, -у́стишься) *pf.* с+*g.*; (*give in*) уступа́ть *impf.*, уступи́ть (-плю́, -пишь) *pf.* **climber** *n.* (*mountain-~*) альпини́ст, ~ка; (*social ~*) карьери́ст, ~ка; (*plant*) выю́щееся расте́ние. **climbing** *n.* (*sport*) альпини́зм; (*ascent*) восхожде́ние; *adj.* (*plant*) выю́щийся.

clinch [klɪntʃ] *n.* (*boxing*) клинч, захва́т.

cling [klɪŋ] *v.i.* прилипа́ть *impf.*, прили́пнуть (-п) *pf.* (**to** к+*d.*); ~ **to** (*clothes*) облега́ть (-а́ет) *impf.*

clinic [ˈklɪnɪk] *n.* (*consultation*) консульта́ция; (*place*) кли́ника. **clinical** *adj.* клини́ческий.

clink [klɪŋk] *v.t.* & *i.* звене́ть (-ню́, -ни́шь) *impf.*, про~ *pf.* (+*i.*); ~ **glasses** чо́каться *impf.*, чо́кнуться *pf.*; *n.* звон.

clinker [ˈklɪŋkə(r)] *n.* (*brick*) кли́нкер; (*slag*) шлак.

clip[1] [klɪp] *n.* зажи́м; (*mil.*) обо́йма; *v.t.* скрепля́ть *impf.*, скрепи́ть *pf.*

clip[2] [klɪp] *v.t.* стричь (стригу́, -ижёшь, -иг) *impf.*, об~, о~ *pf.*; подреза́ть *impf.*, подре́зать (-е́жу, -е́жешь) *pf.* **clipped** *adj.* подре́занный, подстри́женный; ~ **tones** отры́вочная речь. **clipper** *n.* (*naut.*) кли́пер; *pl.* но́жницы *f.pl.* **clipping** *n.* стри́жка; (*newspaper ~*) газе́тная вы́резка; *pl.* настри́г, обре́зки *f.pl.*

clique [kliːk] *n.* кли́ка. **cliquish** *adj.* за́мкнутый.

cloak [kləʊk] *n.* плащ (-а́); *v.t.* покрыва́ть *impf.*, покры́ть (-ро́ю, -ро́ешь) *pf.* **cloakroom** *n.* (*for clothing*) гардеро́б; (*for luggage*) ка́мера хране́ния; (*lavatory*) убо́рная *sb.*, туале́т.

clock [klɒk] *n.* часы́ *m.pl.*; ~ **face** цифербла́т; *v.i.*: ~ **in** регистри́ровать *impf.*, за~ *pf.* прихо́д на рабо́ту. **clockmaker** *n.* часовщи́к (-а́). **clockwise** *adv.* по часово́й стре́лке. **clockwork** *n.* часово́й механи́зм.

clod [klɒd] *n.* ком (*pl.* -ья, -ьев), глы́ба. **clodhopper** *n.* у́вален (-льня) *m.*, дереве́нщина *c.g.*

clog [klɒg] *n.* башма́к (-а́) на деревя́нной подо́шве; *v.t.*: ~ **up** засоря́ть *impf.*, засори́ть *pf.*

cloister ['klɔɪstə(r)] *n.* (*monastery*) монасты́рь (-ря́) *m.*; (*arcade*) кры́тая арка́да.

clone [kləʊn] *n.* клон; *v.t.* клони́ровать *impf.* & *pf.*

close [kləʊs; kləʊz] *adj.* (*near*) бли́зкий (-зок, -зка́, -зко, бли́зки́); (*stuffy*) ду́шный (-шен, -шна́, -шно); (*secret*) скры́тый; *v.t.* (*shut*) закрыва́ть *impf.*, закры́ть *pf.*; (*conclude*) зака́нчивать *impf.*, зако́нчить *pf.*; *adv.* бли́зко (**to** от+*g.*). **closed** *adj.* закры́тый. **closeted** ['klɒzɪtɪd] *adj.*: **be** ~ **together** совеща́ться *impf.* наедине́. **close-up** *n.* съёмка, сня́тая на кру́пном пла́не; **in** ~ кру́пным пла́ном. **closing** *n.* закры́тие; *adj.* заключи́тельный. **closure** *n.* закры́тие.

clot [klɒt] *n.* сгу́сток (-тка́); *v.i.* сгуща́ться *impf.*, сгусти́ться *pf.* **clotted** *adj.* сгущённый; ~ **cream** густы́е топлёные сли́вки (-вок) *pl.*

cloth [klɒθ] *n.* ткань, сукно́ (*pl.* -кна, -кон, -кнам); (*duster*) тря́пка; (*table-*~) ска́терть (*pl.* -ти, -те́й)

clothe [kləʊð] *v.t.* одева́ть *impf.*, оде́ть (-е́ну, -оде́нешь) (**in** +*i.*, в+*a.*) *pf.* **clothes** *n.* оде́жда, пла́тье.

cloud [klaʊd] *n.* о́блако (*pl.* -ка́, -ко́в); (*rain, storm* ~) ту́ча; *v.t.* затемня́ть *impf.*, затемни́ть *pf.*; омрача́ть *impf.*, омрачи́ть *pf.*; ~ **over** покрыва́ться *impf.*, покры́ться (-ро́ется) *pf.* облака́ми, ту́чами.

clout [klaʊt] *v.t.* ударя́ть *impf.*, уда́рить *pf.*; *n.* затре́щина.

clove [kləʊv] *n.* гвозди́ка; (*garlic*) зубо́к (-бка́).

cloven ['kləʊv(ə)n] *adj.* раздво́енный (-ен, -енна).

clover ['kləʊvə(r)] *n.* кле́вер (*pl.* -а́).

clown [klaʊn] *n.* кло́ун.

club [klʌb] *n.* (*stick*) дуби́нка; *pl.* (*cards*) тре́фы *f.pl.*; (*association*) клуб; *v.t.* (*beat*) бить (бью, бьёшь) *impf.*, по~ *pf.* дуби́нкой; *v.i.*: ~ **together** устра́ивать *impf.*, устро́ить *pf.* скла́дчину.

cluck [klʌk] *v.i.* куда́хтать (-а́хчет) *impf.*

clue [klu:] *n.* (*evidence*) ули́ка; (*to puzzle*) ключ (-а́) (к разга́дке).

clump [klʌmp] *n.* гру́ппа дере́вьев; *v.i.* тяжело́ ступа́ть *impf.*, ступи́ть (-плю́, -пишь) *pf.*

clumsiness ['klʌmzɪnɪs] *n.* неуклю́жесть; беста́ктность. **clumsy** *adj.* неуклю́жий.

cluster ['klʌstə(r)] *n.* (*bunch*) пучо́к (-чка́); (*group*) гру́ппа; *v.i.* собира́ться *impf.*, собра́ться (-берётся; собра́лся, -ала́сь, -а́ло́сь) *pf.* гру́ппами.

clutch[1] [klʌtʃ] *n.* (*grasp*) хва́тка; ко́гти (-те́й) *m.pl.*; (*tech.*) сцепле́ние, му́фта; *v.t.* зажима́ть *impf.*, зажа́ть (зажму́, -мёшь) *pf.*; *v.i.*: ~ **at** хвата́ться *impf.*, хвати́ться (-ачу́сь, -а́тишься) *pf.* за+*a.*

clutch[2] [klʌtʃ] *n.* (*of eggs*) я́йца *pl.* (яи́ц, я́йцам).

clutter ['klʌtə(r)] *n.* беспоря́док (-дка); *v.t.* приводи́ть (-ожу́, -о́дишь) *impf.*, привести́ (-еду́, -едёшь; -ёл, -ела́) *pf.* в беспоря́док.

cm *abbr.* (*of* **centimetre(s)**) см, сантиме́тр.

Co. [kəʊ] *abbr.* (*of* **company**) К°, компа́ния.

c/o *abbr.* (*of* **care of**) по а́дресу+*g.*; че́рез+*a.*

coach [kəʊtʃ] *n.* (*carriage*) каре́та; (*rail.*) ваго́н; (*bus*) авто́бус; (*tutor*) репети́тор; (*sport*) тре́нер; *v.t.* репети́ровать *impf.*; тренирова́ть *impf.*, на~ *pf.*

coagulate [kəʊ'ægjʊˌleɪt] *v.i.* сгуща́ться *impf.*, сгусти́ться *pf.*

coal [kəʊl] *n.* у́голь (угля́; *pl.* у́гли, угле́й) *m.* **coal-bearing** *adj.* углено́сный.

coalesce [ˌkəʊə'les] *v.i.* соединя́ться *impf.*, соедини́ться *pf.*

coalface *n.* у́гольный забо́й. **coalfield** *n.* каменноуго́льный бассе́йн.

coalition [ˌkəʊə'lɪʃ(ə)n] *n.* коали́ция.

coalmine *n.* у́гольная ша́хта. **coalminer** *n.* шахтёр. **coal-scuttle** *n.* ведёрко (*pl.* -рки, -рок, -ркам) для угля́. **coal-seam** *n.* у́гольный пласт (-а́).

coarse [kɔ:s] *adj.* гру́бый (груб, -а́, -о); (*vulgar*) вульга́рный.

coast [kəʊst] *n.* побере́жье, бе́рег (*loc.* -у́; *pl.* -а́); *v.i.* (*trade*) кабота́жничать *impf.*; (*move without power*) дви́гаться (-и́гается & -и́жется) *impf.*, дви́нуться *pf.* по ине́рции. **coastal** *adj.* берегово́й, прибре́жный. **coaster** *n.* кабота́жное су́дно (*pl.* -да́, -до́в). **coastguard** *n.* берегова́я охра́на.

coat [kəʊt] *n.* (*overcoat*) пальто́ *nt.indecl.*; (*jacket*) пиджа́к (-а́), ку́ртка; (*layer*) слой (*pl.* слои́); (*animal*) шерсть (*pl.* -ти, -те́й), мех (*loc.* -у́; *pl.* -а́); ~ **of arms** герб (-а́); *v.t.* покрыва́ть *impf.*, покры́ть (-ро́ю, -ро́ешь) *pf.* (**with** сло́ем+*g.*).

coax [kəʊks] *v.t.* зада́бривать *impf.*, задо́брить *pf.*

cob [kɒb] *n.* (*corn-*~) поча́ток (-тка) кукуру́зы; (*swan*) ле́бедь(*pl.* -ди, -де́й)-саме́ц (-мца́); (*horse*) ни́зкая верхова́я ло́шадь (*pl.* -ди, -де́й, *i.* -дьми́).

cobalt ['kəʊbɔ:lt, -bɒlt] *n.* ко́бальт.

cobble ['kɒb(ə)l] *n.* булы́жник (*also collect.*); *v.t.* мости́ть *impf.*, вы́, за~ *pf.* булы́жником.

cobbler ['kɒblə(r)] *n.* сапо́жник.

cobra ['kəʊbrə, 'kɒbrə] *n.* очко́вая змея́ (*pl.* зме́и).

cobweb ['kɒbweb] *n.* паути́на.

cocaine [kə'keɪn, kəʊ-] *n.* кокаи́н.

cochineal ['kɒtʃɪˌni:l, -'ni:l] *n.* кошени́ль.

cock [kɒk] *n.* (*bird*) пету́х (-а́); (*tap*) кран; (*of gun*) куро́к (-рка́); *v.t.* (*gun*) взводи́ть (-ожу́, -о́дишь) *impf.*, взвести́ (-еду́, -едёшь; -ёл, -ела́) *pf.* куро́к+*g.*; ~ **a snook** пока́зывать *impf.*, показа́ть (-ажу́, -а́жешь) *pf.* дли́нный нос. **cocked hat** *n.* треуго́лка.

cockade [kɒ'keɪd] *n.* кока́рда.

cockatoo [ˌkɒkə'tu:] *n.* какаду́ *m.indecl.*

cockchafer ['kɒkˌtʃeɪfə(r)] *n.* ма́йский жук (-а́).

cockerel ['kɒkər(ə)l] *n.* петушо́к (-шка́).
cockle ['kɒk(ə)l] *n.* съедо́бная сердцеви́дка.
cockney ['kɒknɪ] *n.* уроже́нец (-нца), -нка, Ло́ндона.
cockpit ['kɒkpɪt] *n.* (*arena*) аре́на; (*aeron.*) каби́на.
cockroach ['kɒkrəʊʃ] *n.* тарака́н.
cocktail ['kɒkteɪl] *n.* кокте́йль *m.*
cocky ['kɒkɪ] *adj.* (*cheeky*) де́рзкий (-зок, -зка́, -зко); (*conceited*) чва́нный.
cocoa ['kəʊkəʊ] *n.* кака́о *nt.indecl.*
coco(nut) ['kəʊkəʊ] *n.* коко́с; *adj.* коко́совый.
cocoon [kə'ku:n] *n.* ко́кон.
cod [kɒd] *n.* треска́.
coda ['kəʊdə] *n.* (*mus.*) ко́да.
coddle ['kɒd(ə)l] *v.t.* изне́живать *impf.*, изне́жить *pf.*
code [kəʊd] *n.* (*collection of laws*) ко́декс, зако́ны *m.pl.*; (*cipher*) код, шифр; **civil** ~ гражда́нский ко́декс; ~ **of honour** зако́ны *m.pl.* че́сти; **penal** ~ уголо́вный ко́декс; **Morse** ~ а́збука Мо́рзе; *v.t.* шифрова́ть *impf.*, за~ *pf.* **codicil** *n.* припи́ска. **codify** *v.t.* кодифици́ровать *impf.* & *pf.*
cod-liver ['kɒdlɪvə(r)] *adj.*: ~ **oil** ры́бий жир (-а(у)).
co-education [ˌkəʊedju:'keɪʃ(ə)n] *n.* совме́стное обуче́ние.
coefficient [ˌkəʊɪ'fɪʃ(ə)nt] *n.* коэффицие́нт.
coerce [kəʊ'ɜ:s] *v.t.* принужда́ть *impf.*, прину́дить *pf.* **coercion** *n.* принужде́ние; **under** ~ по принужде́нию.
coexist [ˌkəʊɪg'zɪst] *v.i.* сосуществова́ть *impf.* **coexistence** *n.* сосуществова́ние.
C. of E. *abbr.* (*of* ***Church of England***) Англика́нская це́рковь.
coffee ['kɒfɪ] *n.* ко́фе *m.* (*nt.* (*coll.*)) *indecl.* **coffee-maker** *n.* кофева́рка. **coffee-mill** *n.* кофе́йница. **coffee-pot** *n.* кофе́йник.
coffer ['kɒfə(r)] *n.* сунду́к(-а́); *pl.* казна́.
coffin ['kɒfɪn] *n.* гроб (*loc.* -у́; *pl.* -ы́).
cog [kɒg] *n.* зубе́ц (-бца́); ~ **in the machine** ви́нтик маши́ны. **cogwheel** *n.* зубча́тое колесо́ (*pl.* -ёса), шестерня́ (*g.pl.* -рён).
cogent ['kəʊdʒ(ə)nt] *adj.* убеди́тельный.
cogitate ['kɒdʒɪˌteɪt] *v.i.* размышля́ть *impf.*, размы́слить *pf.* **cogi'tation** *n.*: *pl.* мы́сли (-лей) *f.pl.*, размышле́ния *nt.pl.*
cognate ['kɒgneɪt] *n. adj.* ро́дственный (-ен, -енна); *n.* ро́дственное сло́во.
cohabit [kəʊ'hæbɪt] *v.i.* сожи́тельствовать *impf.* **cohabi'tation** *n.* сожи́тельство.
coherence [kəʊ'hɪərəns] *n.* свя́зность. **coherent** *adj.* свя́зный. **cohesion** [kəʊ'hi:ʒ(ə)n] *n.* сплочённость; сцепле́ние. **cohesive** *adj.* спосо́бный к сцепле́нию.
cohort ['kəʊhɔ:t] *n.* кого́рта.
coil [kɔɪl] *v.t.* свёртывать *impf.*, сверну́ть *pf.* кольцо́м, спира́лью; укла́дывать *impf.*, уложи́ть (-жу́, -ожишь) *pf.* в бу́хту; *n.* кольцо́ (*pl.* -льца, -лец, -льцам), бу́хта; (*elec.*) кату́шка.
coin [kɔɪn] *n.* моне́та; *v.t.* чека́нить *impf.*, от~ *pf.* **coinage** *n.* (*coining*) чека́нка; (*system*) моне́та; моне́тная систе́ма.
coincide [ˌkəʊɪn'saɪd] *v.i.* совпада́ть *impf.*, совпа́сть (-аду́, -ёшь; -а́л) *pf.* **coincidence** [kəʊ'ɪnsɪd(ə)ns] *n.* совпаде́ние. **coinci'dental** *adj.* случа́йный.
Coke[1] [kəʊk] *n.* (*propr.*) «Ко́ка-ко́ла».
coke[2] [kəʊk] *n.* кокс; *adj.* ко́ксовый; *v.t.* коксова́ть *impf.*; ~ **oven** коксова́льная печь (*pl.* -чи, -че́й).
colander ['kʌləndə(r)] *n.* дуршла́г.
cold [kəʊld] *n.* хо́лод (-а(у); *pl.* -а́); (*illness*) просту́да, на́сморк; *adj.* холо́дный (хо́лоден, -дна́, -дно, хо́лодны́); ~ **steel** холо́дное ору́жие; ~ **war** холо́дная война́. **cold-blooded** *adj.* жесто́кий (-о́к, -о́ка́, -о́ко); (*zool.*) холоднокро́вный.
colic ['kɒlɪk] *n.* ко́лики *f.pl.*
collaborate [kə'læbəˌreɪt] *v.i.* сотру́дничать *impf.* **collabo'ration** *n.* сотру́дничество. **collaborator** *n.* сотру́дник, -ица.
collapse [kə'læps] *v.i.* ру́шиться *impf.*, об~ *pf.*; вали́ться (-лю́сь, -лишься) *impf.*, по~, с~ *pf.*; *n.* паде́ние; крах; прова́л. **collapsible** *adj.* разбо́рный, складно́й, откидно́й.
collar ['kɒlə(r)] *n.* воротни́к (-а́), воротничо́к (-чка́); (*dog-*~) оше́йник; (*horse-*~) хому́т (-а́); *v.t.* (*seize*) хвата́ть *impf.*, схвати́ть (-ачу́, -а́тишь) *pf.* **collar-bone** *n.* ключи́ца.
collate [kə'leɪt] *v.t.* слича́ть *impf.*, сличи́ть *pf.*
collateral [kə'lætər(ə)l] *adj.* побо́чный, дополни́тельный; *n.* (~ *security*) дополни́тельное обеспе́чение.
collation [kə'leɪʃ(ə)n] *n.* лёгкая заку́ска.
colleague ['kɒli:g] *n.* колле́га *c.g.*
collect [kə'lekt] *v.t.* собира́ть *impf.*, собра́ть (соберу́, -рёшь; собра́л, -а́, -о) *pf.*; (*as hobby*) коллекциони́ровать *impf.* **collected** *adj.* со́бранный; ~ **works** собра́ние сочине́ний. **collection** *n.* сбор, собира́ние; колле́кция. **collective** *n.* коллекти́в; *adj.* коллекти́вный; ~ **farm** колхо́з; ~ **farmer** колхо́зник, -ица; ~ **noun** собира́тельное существи́тельное *sb.* **collectivization** [kəˌlektɪvaɪ'zeɪʃ(ə)n] *n.* коллективиза́ция. **collector** *n.* сбо́рщик; коллекционе́р.
college ['kɒlɪdʒ] *n.* колле́дж. **collegiate** [kə'li:dʒət] *adj.* университе́тский.
collide [kə'laɪd] *v.i.* ста́лкиваться *impf.*, столкну́ться *pf.* **collision** [kə'lɪʒ(ə)n] *n.* столкнове́ние.
collie ['kɒlɪ] *n.* шотла́ндская овча́рка.
collier ['kɒlɪə(r)] *n.* (*miner*) шахтёр; (*ship*) у́гольщик. **colliery** *n.* каменноуго́льная ша́хта.
colloquial [kə'ləʊkwɪəl] *adj.* разгово́рный. **colloquialism** *n.* разгово́рное выраже́ние.
collusion [kə'lu:ʒ(ə)n, -'lju:ʒ(ə)n] *n.* та́йный сго́вор.
Cologne [kə'ləʊn] *n.* Кёльн.

colon¹ ['kəʊlən, -lɒn] *n.* (*anat.*) то́лстая кишка́ (*g.pl.* -шо́к).

colon² ['kəʊlən, -lɒn] *n.* (*punctuation mark*) двоето́чие.

colonel ['kɜːn(ə)l] *n.* полко́вник.

colonial [kə'ləʊnɪəl] *adj.* колониа́льный. **colonialism** *n.* колониали́зм. **colonist** ['kɒlənɪst] *n.* колони́ст, ~ка. **coloni'zation** *n.* колониза́ция. **colonize** *v.t.* колонизова́ть *impf.* & *pf.* **colony** *n.* коло́ния.

colonnade [ˌkɒlə'neɪd] *n.* колонна́да.

coloration [ˌkʌlə'reɪʃ(ə)n] *n.* окра́ска, расцве́тка.

coloratura [ˌkɒlərə'tʊərə] *n.* (*mus.*) колорату́ра.

colossal [kə'lɒs(ə)l] *adj.* колосса́льный, грома́дный.

colour ['kʌlə(r)] *n.* цвет (*pl.* -á), кра́ска; (*pl.*) (*flag*) зна́мя (*pl.* -мена́) *nt.*; ~ **film** цветна́я плёнка; ~ **prejudice** ра́совая дискримина́ция; *v.t.* кра́сить *impf.*, вы́~, о~, по~ *pf.*; раскра́шивать *impf.*, раскра́сить *pf.*; *v.i.* красне́ть *impf.*, по~ *pf.* **colou'ration** *see* **coloration. colour-blind** *adj.* страда́ющий дальтони́змом. **coloured** *adj.* цветно́й, раскра́шенный, окра́шенный. **colouring** *n.* кра́сящее вещество́; окра́ска.

colt [kəʊlt] *n.* жеребёнок (-бёнка; *pl.* -бя́та, -бя́т).

column ['kɒləm] *n.* (*archit.*, *mil.*) коло́нна; столб (-á); (*of print*) столбе́ц (-бца́). **columnist** *n.* обозрева́тель *m.*

coma ['kəʊmə] *n.* ко́ма. **comatose** *adj.* комато́зный.

comb [kəʊm] *n.* гребёнка; гре́бень (-бня) *m.*; *v.t.* чеса́ть (чешу́, -шешь) *impf.*; причёсывать *impf.*, причеса́ть (-ешу́, -е́шешь) *pf.*

combat ['kɒmbæt, 'kʌm-] *n.* бой (*loc.* бою́), сраже́ние; *v.t.* боро́ться (-рю́сь, -решься) *impf.* с+*i.*, про́тив+*g.* **'combatant** *n.* комбата́нт; *adj.* строево́й.

combination [ˌkɒmbɪ'neɪʃ(ə)n] *n.* сочета́ние; соедине́ние; комбина́ция. **combine** ['kɒmbaɪn; kəm'baɪn] *n.* комбина́т; (~-*harvester*) комба́йн; *v.t.* & *i.* совмеща́ть(ся) *impf.*, совмести́ть(ся) *pf.* **combined** *adj.* совме́стный.

combustible [kəm'bʌstɪb(ə)l] *adj.* горю́чий. **combustion** *n.* горе́ние; **internal ~ engine** дви́гатель *m.* вну́треннего сгора́ния.

come [kʌm] *v.i.* (*on foot*) приходи́ть (-ожу́, -о́дишь) *impf.*, прийти́ (приду́, -дёшь; пришёл, -шла́) *pf.*; (*by transport*) приезжа́ть *impf.*, прие́хать (-е́ду, -е́дешь) *pf.*; ~ **about** случа́ться *impf.*, случи́ться *pf.*; ~ **across** случа́йно ната́лкиваться *impf.*, натолкну́ться *pf.* на+*a.*; ~ **back** возвраща́ться *impf.*, возврати́ться (-ащу́сь, -ати́шься) *pf.*; ~ **from** происходи́ть (-ожу́, -о́дишь) *impf.*, произойти́ (-ойду́, -ойдёшь; -ошёл, -ошла́) *pf.* из, от+*g.*; ~ **in** входи́ть (-ожу́, -о́дишь) *impf.*, войти́ (войду́, -дёшь; вошёл, -шла́) *pf.*; ~ **in handy** пригоди́ться *pf.*; ~ **through** проника́ть *impf.*, прони́кнуть (-к) *pf.*; ~ **up to** доходи́ть (-ожу́, -о́дишь) *impf.*, дойти́ (дойду́, -дёшь; дошёл, -шла́) *pf.* до+*g.* **come-back** *n.* возвра́т. **come-down** *n.* паде́ние, ухудше́ние.

comedian [kə'miːdɪən] *n.* комеди́йный актёр, ко́мик. **comedi'enne** *n.* комеди́йная актри́са. **comedy** ['kɒmɪdɪ] *n.* коме́дия.

comet ['kɒmɪt] *n.* коме́та.

comfort ['kʌmfət] *n.* комфо́рт, удо́бство; (*consolation*) утеше́ние; *v.t.* утеша́ть *impf.*, уте́шить *pf.* **comfortable** *adj.* удо́бный. **comforter** *n.* (*person*) утеши́тель *m.*; (*dummy*) со́ска.

comic ['kɒmɪk] *adj.* коми́ческий, юмористи́ческий; ~ **opera** опере́тта; *n.* ко́мик; (*magazine*) ко́микс. **comical** *adj.* смешно́й, коми́чный.

coming ['kʌmɪŋ] *adj.* наступа́ющий.

comma ['kɒmə] *n.* запята́я *sb.*; **inverted ~** кавы́чка.

command [kə'mɑːnd] *n.* (*order*) прика́з; (*order*, *authority*) кома́нда; *v.t.* прика́зывать *impf.*, приказа́ть (-ажу́, -а́жешь) *pf.*+*d.*; кома́ндовать *impf.*, с~ *pf.*+*i.*, над (*terrain*) +*i.*; (*have ~ of*, *master*) владе́ть *impf.*+*i.* **'commandant** *n.* коменда́нт. **comman'deer** *v.t.* (*men*) набира́ть *impf.*, набра́ть (наберу́, -рёшь; набра́л, -á, -о) *pf.* в а́рмию; (*goods*) реквизи́ровать *impf.* & *pf.* **commander** *n.* команди́р; кома́ндующий *sb.* (**of** +*i.*). **commander-in-chief** *n.* главнокома́ндующий *sb.* **commanding** *adj.* кома́ндующий. **commandment** *n.* за́поведь. **commando** *n.* солда́т деса́нтно-диверсио́нного отря́да.

commemorate [kə'meməˌreɪt] *v.t.* ознамено́вывать *impf.*, ознаменова́ть *pf.* **commemo'ration** *n.* ознаменова́ние. **commemorative** *adj.* па́мятный, мемориа́льный.

commence [kə'mens] *v.t.* начина́ть *impf.*, нача́ть (-чну́, -чнёшь; на́чал, -á, -о) *pf.* **commencement** *n.* нача́ло.

commend [kə'mend] *v.t.* (*praise*) хвали́ть (-лю́, -лишь) *impf.*, по~ *pf.* **commendable** *adj.* похва́льный. **commen'dation** *n.* похвала́.

commensurable [kə'menʃərəb(ə)l, -sjərəb(ə)l] *adj.* соизмери́мый. **commensurate** *adj.* соразме́рный.

comment ['kɒment] *n.* замеча́ние; *v.i.* де́лать *impf.*, с~ *pf.* замеча́ния; ~ **on** комменти́ровать *impf.* & *pf.*, про~ *pf.* **commentary** *n.* коммента́рий. **commentator** *n.* коммента́тор.

commerce ['kɒmɜːs] *n.* торго́вля, комме́рция. **co'mmercial** *adj.* торго́вый, комме́рческий; *n.* рекла́мная переда́ча. **commercialize** *v.t.* превраща́ть *impf.*, преврати́ть (-ащу́, -ати́шь) *pf.* в исто́чник дохо́дов.

commiserate [kə'mɪzəˌreɪt] *v.i.*: ~ **with** соболе́зновать *impf.*+*d.* **commise'ration** *n.* соболе́знование.

commissar ['kɒmɪˌsɑː(r)] *n.* комисса́р.

commi'ssariat *n.* (*pol.*) комиссариа́т; (*mil. etc.*) интенда́нтство.
commission [kə'mɪʃ(ə)n] *n.* (*command*) поруче́ние; (*agent's fee*) комиссио́нные *sb.*; (~ *of inquiry etc.*) коми́ссия; (*mil.*) офице́рское зва́ние; **put into** ~ вводи́ть (-ожу́, -о́дишь) *impf.*, ввести́ (введу́, -дёшь; ввёл, -а́) *pf.* в строй; *v.t.* поруча́ть *impf.*, поручи́ть (-чу́, -чишь) *pf.+d.* **commissio'naire** *n.* швейца́р. **commissioner** *n.* уполномо́ченный представи́тель *m.*; комисса́р.
commit [kə'mɪt] *v.t.* соверша́ть *impf.*, соверши́ть *pf.*; ~ **o.s.** обя́зываться *impf.*, обяза́ться (-яжу́сь, -я́жешься) *pf.*; ~ **to** предава́ть (-даю́, -даёшь) *impf.*, преда́ть (-да́м, -да́шь, -а́ст, -ади́м; пре́дал, -а́, -о) *pf.+d.*; ~ **to prison** помеща́ть *impf.*, помести́ть *pf.* в тюрьму́. **commitment** *n.* обяза́тельство.
committee [ˌkɒmɪ'tiː] *n.* комите́т, коми́ссия.
commodity [kə'mɒdɪtɪ] *n.* това́р; **scarce** ~ дефици́тный това́р.
commodore ['kɒməˌdɔː(r)] *n.* (*officer*) коммодо́р.
common ['kɒmən] *adj.* о́бщий, просто́й; обыкнове́нный; *n.* общи́нная земля́ (*a.* -млю; *pl.* -мли, -ме́ль, -млям); ~ **sense** здра́вый смысл. **commonly** *adv.* обы́чно, обыкнове́нно. **commonplace** *adj.* изби́тый, бана́льный. **common-room** *n.* о́бщая ко́мната, учи́тельская *sb.* **commonwealth** *n.* содру́жество.
commotion [kə'məʊʃ(ə)n] *n.* сумато́ха, волне́ние.
communal ['kɒmjʊn(ə)l] *adj.* общи́нный, комму́нальный. **commune** *n.* комму́на; *v.i.* обща́ться *impf.*
communicate [kə'mjuːnɪˌkeɪt] *v.t.* передава́ть (-даю́, -даёшь) *impf.*, переда́ть (-да́м, -а́шь, -а́ст, -ади́м; пе́редал, -а́, -о) *pf.*; сообща́ть *impf.*, сообщи́ть *pf.* **communi'cation** *n.* сообще́ние; связь; коммуника́ция. **communicative** *adj.* разгово́рчивый.
communion [kə'mjuːnɪən] *n.* (*eccl.*) прича́стие.
communiqué [kə'mjuːnɪˌkeɪ] *n.* коммюнике́ *nt.indecl.*
Communism ['kɒmjʊˌnɪz(ə)m] *n.* коммуни́зм. **Communist** *n.* коммуни́ст, ~ка; *adj.* коммунисти́ческий.
community [kə'mjuːnɪtɪ] *n.* о́бщи́на; содру́жество; о́бщность.
commute [kə'mjuːt] *v.t.* заменя́ть *impf.*, замени́ть (-ню́, -нишь) *pf.* **commuter** *n.* пассажи́р, име́ющий сезо́нный биле́т.
compact[1] ['kɒmpækt] *n.* (*agreement*) соглаше́ние.
compact[2] [kəm'pækt] *adj.* компа́ктный; пло́тный (-тен, -на́, -тно, пло́тны́); ~ **disk** компа́кт-ди́ск; ~ **disk player** прои́грыватель *m.* компа́кт-ди́сков; *n.* пу́дреница.
companion [kəm'pænjən] *n.* това́рищ; компаньо́н, ~ка; (*fellow traveller*) спу́тник; (*lady's* ~) компаньо́нка; (*handbook*) спра́вочник. **companionable** *adj.* общи́тельный, компане́йский. **companionship** *n.* дру́жеское обще́ние. **company** ['kʌmpənɪ] *n.* о́бщество, компа́ния; (*theatr.*) тру́ппа; (*mil.*) ро́та; **ship's** ~ экипа́ж.
comparable ['kɒmpərəb(ə)l] *adj.* сравни́мый. **comparative** [kəm'pærətɪv] *adj.* сравни́тельный; *n.* сравни́тельная сте́пень (*pl.* -ни, -не́й). **compare** [kəm'peə(r)] *v.t.* & *i.* сра́внивать(ся) *impf.*, сравни́ть(ся) *pf.* (**to, with** с+*i.*). **comparison** [kəm'pærɪs(ə)n] *n.* сравне́ние.
compartment [kəm'pɑːtmənt] *n.* отделе́ние; (*rail.*) купе́ *nt.indecl.*
compass ['kʌmpəs] *n.* ко́мпас; *pl.* ци́ркуль *m.*; (*extent*) преде́лы *m.pl.*
compassion [kəm'pæʃ(ə)n] *n.* сострада́ние, жа́лость. **compassionate** *adj.* сострада́тельный.
compatibility [kəmˌpætə'bɪlɪtɪ] *n.* совмести́мость. **com'patible** *adj.* совмести́мый.
compatriot [kəm'pætrɪət] *n.* соотéчественник, -ица.
compel [kəm'pel] *v.t.* заставля́ть *impf.*, заста́вить *pf.*; принужда́ть *impf.*, прину́дить *pf.* **compelling** *adj.* неотрази́мый.
compendium [kəm'pendɪəm] *n.* кра́ткое руково́дство; конспе́кт.
compensate ['kɒmpenˌseɪt] *v.t.*: ~ **for** вознагражда́ть *impf.*, вознагради́ть *pf.* за+*a.*; возмеща́ть *impf.*, возмести́ть *pf.+d.*; компенси́ровать *impf.* & *pf.* **compen'sation** *n.* возмеще́ние, вознагражде́ние, компенса́ция.
compère ['kɒmpeə(r)] *n.* конферансье́ *m.indecl.*
compete [kəm'piːt] *v.i.* конкури́ровать *impf.*; соревнова́ться *impf.*; состяза́ться *impf.*
competence ['kɒmpɪt(ə)ns] *n.* компете́нция; компете́нтность; правомо́чие. **competent** *adj.* компете́нтный; правомо́чный.
competition [ˌkɒmpə'tɪʃ(ə)n] *n.* соревнова́ние, состяза́ние; конкуре́нция; ко́нкурс. **competitive** [kəm'petɪtɪv] *adj.* соревну́ющийся, конкури́рующий; ~ **examination** ко́нкурсный экза́мен. **competitor** *n.* соревну́ющийся *sb.*; конкуре́нт, ~ка.
compilation [ˌkɒmpɪ'leɪʃ(ə)n] *n.* компиля́ция; составле́ние. **compile** [kəm'paɪl] *v.t.* составля́ть *impf.*, соста́вить *pf.*; компили́ровать *impf.*, с~ *pf.* **compiler** *n.* состави́тель *m.*, ~ница; компиля́тор.
complacency [kəm'pleɪsənsɪ] *n.* самодово́льство. **complacent** *adj.* самодово́льный.
complain [kəm'pleɪn] *v.i.* жа́ловаться *impf.*, по~ *pf.* **complaint** *n.* жа́лоба; (*ailment*) боле́знь, неду́г.
complement ['kɒmplɪmənt] *n.* дополне́ние; (*full number*) (ли́чный) соста́в. **comple'mentary** *adj.* дополни́тельный; ~ **medicine** паралле́льная медици́на.
complete [kəm'pliːt] *v.t.* заверша́ть *impf.*, заверши́ть *pf.*; *adj.* по́лный (-лон, -лна́,

по́лно́); зако́нченный (-ен). **completion** *n.* заверше́ние, оконча́ние.

complex ['kɒmpleks] *adj.* сло́жный (-жен, -жна́, -жно); *n.* ко́мплекс. **com'plexity** *n.* сло́жность.

complexion [kəm'plekʃ(ə)n] *n.* цвет лица́.

compliance [kəm'plaɪəns] *n.* усту́пчивость. **compliant** *adj.* усту́пчивый.

complicate ['kɒmplɪˌkeɪt] *v.t.* осложня́ть *impf.*, осложни́ть *pf.* **complicated** *adj.* сло́жный (-жен, -жна́, -жно). **compli'cation** *n.* осложне́ние.

complicity [kəm'plɪsɪtɪ] *n.* соуча́стие.

compliment ['kɒmplɪmənt] *n.* комплиме́нт; *pl.* приве́т; *v.t.* говори́ть *impf.* комплиме́нт(ы)+*d.*; хвали́ть (-лю́, -лишь) *impf.*, по~ *pf.* **complimentary** [ˌkɒmplɪ'mentərɪ] *adj.* ле́стный, хвале́бный; (*ticket*) беспла́тный.

comply [kəm'plaɪ] *v.i.*: ~ **with** (*fulfil*) исполня́ть *impf.*, испо́лнить *pf.*; (*submit to*) подчиня́ться *impf.*, подчини́ться *pf.*+*d.*

component [kəm'pəʊnənt] *n.* компоне́нт, составна́я часть (*pl.* -ти, -те́й); *adj.* составно́й.

comport [kəm'pɔːt] *v.t.*: ~ **o.s.** вести́ (веду́, -дёшь; вёл, -а́) *impf.* себя́. **comportment** *n.* поведе́ние.

compose [kəm'pəʊz] *v.t.* (*liter.*, *mus.*) сочиня́ть *impf.*, сочини́ть *pf.*; (*institute*) составля́ть *impf.*, соста́вить *pf.*; (*print.*) набира́ть *impf.*, набра́ть (наберу́, -рёшь; набра́л, -а́, -о) *pf.* **composed** *adj.* споко́йный; **be ~ of** состоя́ть (-ои́т) *impf.* из+*g.* **composer** *n.* компози́тор. **composite** ['kɒmpəzɪt, -ˌzaɪt] *adj.* составно́й. **composition** [ˌkɒmpə'zɪʃ(ə)n] *n.* построе́ние; сочине́ние; соста́в. **compositor** [kəm'pɒzɪtə(r)] *n.* набо́рщик.

compost ['kɒmpɒst] *n.* компо́ст.

composure [kəm'pəʊʒə(r)] *n.* самооблада́ние.

compound¹ ['kɒmpaʊnd] *n.* (*mixture*) соедине́ние, соста́в; *adj.* составно́й; сло́жный.

compound² ['kɒmpaʊnd] *n.* (*enclosure*) огоро́женное ме́сто (*pl.* -та́).

comprehend [ˌkɒmprɪ'hend] *v.t.* понима́ть *impf.*, поня́ть (пойму́, -мёшь; по́нял, -а́, -о) *pf.* **comprehensible** *adj.* поня́тный. **comprehensive** *adj.* всесторо́нний (-нен, -ння); всеобъе́млющий; ~ **school** общеобразова́тельная шко́ла.

compress [kəm'pres] *v.t.* сжима́ть *impf.*, сжать (сожму́, -мёшь) *pf.*; сда́вливать *impf.*, сдави́ть (-влю́, -вишь) *pf.*; *n.* компре́сс. **compressed** *adj.* сжа́тый. **compression** *n.* сжа́тие. **compressor** *n.* компре́ссор.

comprise [kəm'praɪz] *v.t.* заключа́ть *impf.* в себе́; состоя́ть (-ою́, -ои́шь) *impf.* из+*g.*

compromise ['kɒmprəˌmaɪz] *n.* компроми́сс; *v.t.* компромети́ровать *impf.*, с~ *pf.*; *v.i.* идти́ (иду́, идёшь; шёл, шла) *impf.*, пойти́ (пойду́, -дёшь; пошёл, -шла́) *pf.* на компроми́сс.

compulsion [kəm'pʌlʃ(ə)n] *n.* принужде́ние. **compulsory** *adj.* обяза́тельный.

compunction [kəm'pʌŋkʃ(ə)n] *n.* угрызе́ние со́вести.

computation [ˌkɒmpjuː'teɪʃ(ə)n] *n.* вычисле́ние. **compute** [kəm'pjuːt] *v.t.* вычисля́ть *impf.*, вы́числить *pf.* **computer** *n.* вычисли́тельная маши́на; (*electronic*) ЭВМ; компью́тер. **computer-assisted** *adj.* автоматизи́рованный.

comrade ['kɒmreɪd, -rɪd] *n.* това́рищ. **comrade-in-arms** *n.* сора́тник. **comradeship** *n.* това́рищество.

concave ['kɒnkeɪv] *adj.* во́гнутый. **concavity** [kɒn'kævɪtɪ] *n.* во́гнутая пове́рхность.

conceal [kən'siːl] *v.t.* скрыва́ть *impf.*, скрыть (-ро́ю, -ро́ешь) *pf.* **concealment** [kən'siːlmənt] *n.* сокры́тие, ута́ивание.

concede [kən'siːd] *v.t.* уступа́ть *impf.*, уступи́ть (-плю́, -пишь) *pf.*

conceit [kən'siːt] *n.* самомне́ние; чва́нство. **conceited** *adj.* чва́нный (-нен, -нна).

conceivable [kən'siːvəb(ə)l] *adj.* постижи́мый; мы́слимый. **conceive** *v.t.* (*plan*, *contemplate*) замышля́ть *impf.*, замы́слить *pf.*; (*become pregnant*) зачина́ть *impf.* зача́ть (зачну́, -чнёшь; зача́л, -а́, -о) *pf.*

concentrate ['kɒnsənˌtreɪt] *n.* концентра́т; *v.t.* & *i.* сосредото́чивать(ся) *impf.*, сосредото́чить(ся) *pf.* (**on** на+*p.*); *v.t.* концентри́ровать *impf.*, с~ *pf.* **concentrated** *adj.* концентри́рованный, сосредото́ченный (-ен, -енна) **concen'tration** *n.* сосредото́ченность, концентра́ция.

concentric [kən'sentrɪk] *adj.* концентри́ческий.

concept ['kɒnsept] *n.* поня́тие; конце́пция. **con'ception** *n.* понима́ние; представле́ние; (*physiol.*) зача́тие.

concern [kən'sɜːn] *n.* (*worry*) забо́та; (*business*) предприя́тие; *v.t.* каса́ться *impf.*+*g.*; ~ **o.s. with** занима́ться *impf.*, заня́ться (займу́сь, -мёшься; заня́лся́, -яла́сь) *pf.*+*i.* **concerned** *adj.* озабо́ченный (-ен, -енна); ~ **with** свя́занный (-ан) с+*i.*; за́нятый (-т, -та́, -то)+*i.* **concerning** *prep.* относи́тельно+*g.*

concert ['kɒnsət] *n.* конце́рт; *v.t.* согласо́вывать *impf.*, согласова́ть *pf.* **con'certed** *adj.* согласо́ванный.

concertina [ˌkɒnsə'tiːnə] *n.* гармо́ника.

concession [kən'seʃ(ə)n] *n.* усту́пка; (*econ.*) конце́ссия. **concessio'naire** *n.* концессионе́р.

conch [kɒŋk, kɒntʃ] *n.* ра́ковина.

conciliate [kən'sɪlɪˌeɪt] *v.t.* умиротворя́ть *impf.*, умиротвори́ть *pf.* **concili'ation** *n.* умиротворе́ние. **conciliatory** *adj.* примири́тельный.

concise [kən'saɪs] *adj.* сжа́тый, кра́ткий (-ток, -тка́, -тко). **conciseness** *n.* сжа́тость, кра́ткость.

conclave ['kɒnkleɪv] *n.* конкла́в.

conclude [kən'kluːd] *v.t.* (*complete*) зака́нчивать *impf.*, закóнчить *pf.*; (*infer, arrange, complete*) заключáть *impf.*, заключи́ть *pf.* **concluding** *adj.* заключи́тельный; заверша́ющий. **conclusion** *n.* заключéние, окончáние; (*deduction*) вы́вод. **conclusive** *adj.* заключи́тельный; (*decisive*) решáющий.

concoct [kən'kɒkt] *v.t.* стря́пать *impf.*, со~ *pf.* **concoction** *n.* стряпня́.

concomitant [kən'kɒmɪt(ə)nt] *adj.* сопу́тствующий.

concord ['kɒnkɔːd, 'kɒŋ-] *n.* соглáсие; согласовáние. **con'cordance** *n.* соглáсие; соответствие; (*to Bible etc.*) словáрь (-ря́) *m.* **con'cordat** *n.* конкордáт.

concourse ['kɒnkɔːs, 'kɒŋ-] *n.* скоплéние; (*area*) откры́тое мéсто.

concrete ['kɒnkriːt, 'kɒŋ-] *n.* бетóн; *adj.* (*made of* ~) бетóнный; (*not abstract*) конкрéтный. **concrete-mixer** *n.* бетономешáлка.

concubine ['kɒŋkjʊˌbaɪn] *n.* налóжница; млáдшая женá.

concur [kən'kɜː(r)] *v.i.* соглашáться *impf.*, согласи́ться *pf.*

concussion [kən'kʌʃ(ə)n] *n.* сотрясéние.

condemn [kən'dem] *v.t.* осуждáть *impf.*, осуди́ть (-ужу́, -у́дишь) *pf.*; (*as unfit for use*) браковáть *impf.*, за~ *pf.* **condem'nation** *n.* осуждéние.

condensation [ˌkɒnden'seɪʃ(ə)n] *n.* конденсáция. **con'dense** *v.t.* (*liquid etc.*) конденси́ровать *impf.* & *pf.*; (*text etc.*) сжáто излагáть *impf.*, изложи́ть (-жу́, -жишь) *pf.* **con'densed** *adj.* сжáтый, крáткий (-ток, -ткá, -тко); сгущённый (-ён, -енá); конденси́рованный. **con'denser** *n.* конденсáтор.

condescend [ˌkɒndɪ'send] *v.i.* снисходи́ть (-ожу́, -óдишь) *impf.*, снизойти́ (-ойду́, -ойдёшь; -ошёл, -ошлá) *pf.* **condescending** *adj.* снисходи́тельный. **condescension** *n.* снисхождéние.

condiment ['kɒndɪmənt] *n.* припрáва.

condition [kən'dɪʃ(ə)n] *n.* услóвие; (*state of being*) состоя́ние; положéние; *v.t.* обуслóвливать *impf.*, обуслóвить *pf.* **conditional** *adj.* услóвный. **conditioned** *adj.* обуслóвленный (-ен); ~ **reflex** услóвный рефлéкс.

condole [kən'dəʊl] *v.i.*: ~ **with** соболéзновать *impf.*+*d.* **condolence** *n.*: *pl.* соболéзнование.

condom ['kɒndɒm] *n.* презервати́в.

condone [kən'dəʊn] *v.t.* закрывáть *impf.*, закры́ть (-рóю, -рóешь) *pf.* глазá на+*a.*

conduce [kən'djuːs] *v.i.*: ~ **to** спосóбствовать *impf.*+*d.* **conducive** *adj.* спосóбствующий (**to** +*d.*).

conduct ['kɒndʌkt; kən'dʌkt] *n.* ведéние; (*behaviour*) поведéние; *v.t.* вести́ (веду́, -дёшь; вёл, -á) *impf.*, по~, про~ *pf.*; (*mus.*) дирижи́ровать *impf.*+*i.*; (*phys.*) проводи́ть (-ит) *impf.* **con'duction** *n.* проводи́мость. **con'ductor** *n.* (*bus, tram*) кондýктор (*pl.* -á); (*phys.*) проводни́к (-á); (*mus.*) дирижёр.

conduit ['kɒndɪt, -djʊɪt] *n.* трубопровóд; (*for wires*) кабелепровóд.

cone [kəʊn] *n.* кóнус; (*of pine, fir*) ши́шка.

confection [kən'fekʃ(ə)n] *n.* изготовлéние; конди́терское издéлие. **confectioner** *n.* конди́тер; ~**'s** (*shop*) конди́терская *sb.* **confectionery** *n.* конди́терские издéлия *nt.pl.*

confederacy [kən'fedərəsɪ] *n.* конфедерáция. **confederate** *adj.* конфедерати́вный; *n.* сообщник. **confede'ration** *n.* конфедерáция.

confer [kən'fɜː(r)] *v.t.* жáловать *impf.*, по~ *pf.* (+*a.* & *i.*, +*d.* & *a.*); присуждáть *impf.*, присуди́ть (-ужу́, -у́дишь) (**on** +*d.*) *pf.*; *v.i.* совещáться *impf.* **conference** ['kɒnfərəns] *n.* совещáние; конферéнция; ~ **hall** конферéнц-зáл. **conferment** [kən'fɜːmənt] *n.* присвоéние; присуждéние.

confess [kən'fes] *v.t.* (*acknowledge*) признавáть (-наю́, -наёшь) *impf.*, признáть *pf.*; (*eccl., of sinner & priest*) исповéдовать *impf.* & *pf.* **confession** *n.* признáние; и́споведь. **confessor** *n.* духовни́к (-á).

confidant(e) [ˌkɒnfɪ'dænt, 'kɒn-] *n.* довéренное лицó (*pl.* -ца). **confide** [kən'faɪd] *v.t.* поверя́ть *impf.*, повéрить *pf.* **confidence** ['kɒnfɪd(ə)ns] *n.* (*trust*) довéрие; (*certainty*) увéренность; ~ **trick** мошéнничество; **'confident** *adj.* увéренный (-ен, -енна). **confi'dential** *adj.* секрéтный; конфиденциáльный.

configuration [kənˌfɪgjʊ'reɪʃ(ə)n, -gə'reɪʃ(ə)n] *n.* конфигурáция.

confine [kən'faɪn] *v.t.* ограни́чивать *impf.*, ограни́чить *pf.*; (*in prison*) заключáть *impf.*, заключи́ть *pf.* **confinement** *n.* (*for birth*) рóды (-дов) *pl.*; заключéние. **confines** ['kɒnfaɪnz] *n.* предéлы *m.pl.*

confirm [kən'fɜːm] *v.t.* подтверждáть *impf.*, подтверди́ть *pf.* **confir'mation** *n.* подтверждéние; (*eccl.*) конфирмáция. **confirmed** *adj.* закоренéлый.

confiscate ['kɒnfɪˌskeɪt] *v.t.* конфисковáть *impf.* & *pf.* **confis'cation** *n.* конфискáция.

conflagration [ˌkɒnflə'greɪʃ(ə)n] *n.* пожáрище.

conflict ['kɒnflɪkt; kən'flɪkt] *n.* конфли́кт; противорéчие; *v.i.*: ~ **with** (*contradict*) противорéчить *impf.*+*d.* **conflicting** *adj.* противоречи́вый.

confluence ['kɒnflʊəns] *n.* слия́ние.

conform [kən'fɔːm] *v.i.*: ~ **to** подчиня́ться *impf.*, подчини́ться *pf.*+*d.* **conformity** *n.* соответствие; (*compliance*) подчинéние.

confound [kən'faʊnd] *v.t.* сбивáть *impf.*, сбить (собью́, -ьёшь) *pf.* с тóлку; ~ **it!** к чёрту! **confounded** *adj.* прокля́тый.

confront [kən'frʌnt] *v.t.* стоя́ть (-ою́, -ои́шь) *impf.* лицóм к лицу́ с+*i.*; **be confronted with** быть постáвленным пéред+*i.*

confuse [kən'fjuːz] *v.t.* приводи́ть (-ожу́, -óдишь) *impf.*, привести́ (-еду́, -едёшь; -ёл,

-ела́) *pf.* в замеша́тельство; пу́тать *impf.*, за~, с~ *pf.* **confusion** *n.* замеша́тельство, пу́таница.

congeal [kən'dʒiːl] *v.t.* застыва́ть *impf.*, засты́(ну)ть (-ы́ну, -ы́нешь; -ы́(ну)л, -ы́ла) *pf.*

congenial [kən'dʒiːnɪəl] *adj.* бли́зкий (-зок, -зка́, -зко, бли́зки́) по ду́ху.

congenital [kən'dʒenɪt(ə)l] *adj.* врождённый (-ён, -ена́).

conger (eel) ['kɒŋgə(r)] *n.* морско́й у́горь (угря́) *m.*

congested [kən'dʒestɪd] *adj.* перепо́лненный (-ен); (*med.*) засто́йный. **congestion** [kən'dʒestʃ(ə)n] *n.* (*population*) перенаселённость; (*traffic*) зато́р; (*med.*) засто́й кро́ви.

congratulate [kən'grætjʊ,leɪt] *v.t.* поздравля́ть *impf.*, поздра́вить *pf.* (**on** с+*i.*). **congratu'lation** *n.* поздравле́ние. **congratu'latory** *adj.* поздрави́тельный.

congregate ['kɒŋgrɪ,geɪt] *v.i.* собира́ться *impf.*, собра́ться (-берётся; -бра́лся, -брала́сь, -бра́ло́сь) *pf.* **congre'gation** *n.* собра́ние; (*eccl.*) прихожа́не (-н) *pl.*

congress ['kɒŋgres] *n.* конгре́сс, съезд. **con'gressional** *adj.* относя́щийся к конгре́ссу. **Congressman** *n.* конгрессме́н.

congruent ['kɒŋgrʊənt] *adj.* конгруэ́нтный.

conic(al) ['kɒnɪk(ə)l] *adj.* кони́ческий.

conifer ['kɒnɪfə(r), 'kəʊn-] *n.* хво́йное *sb.* **co'niferous** *adj.* хво́йный, шишконо́сный.

conjectural [kən'dʒektʃər(ə)l] *adj.* предположи́тельный. **conjecture** *n.* предположе́ние; *v.t.* предполага́ть *impf.*, предположи́ть (-жу́, -жишь) *pf.*

conjugal ['kɒndʒʊg(ə)l] *adj.* супру́жеский.

conjugate ['kɒndʒʊ,geɪt] *v.t.* (*gram.*) спряга́ть *impf.*, про~ *pf.* **conju'gation** *n.* (*gram.*) спряже́ние.

conjunction [kən'dʒʌŋkʃ(ə)n] *n.* (*gram.*) сою́з.

conjure ['kʌndʒə(r)] *v.i.*: ~ **up** (*in mind*) вызыва́ть *impf.*, вы́звать (-зову, -зовешь) *pf.* в воображе́нии. **conjurer** *n.* фо́кусник. **conjuring** *n.* пока́зывание фо́кусов; ~ **trick** фо́кус.

conker ['kɒŋkə(r)] *n.* ко́нский кашта́н; *pl.* де́тская игра́ в кашта́ны.

connect [kə'nekt] *v.t.* свя́зывать *impf.*, связа́ть (-яжу́, -я́жешь) *pf.*; соединя́ть *impf.*, соедини́ть *pf.* **connected** *adj.* свя́занный (-ан). **connecting** *adj.* соедини́тельный, связу́ющий. **connecting-rod** *n.* шату́н (-а́). **connection, -exion** *n.* связь (*loc.* связи́).

conning-tower ['kɒnɪŋ] *n.* боева́я ру́бка.

connivance [kə'naɪv(ə)ns] *n.* попусти́тельство. **connive** *v.i.*: ~ **at** попусти́тельствовать *impf.+d.*

connoisseur [,kɒnə'sɜː(r)] *n.* знато́к (-а́).

conquer ['kɒŋkə(r)] *v.t.* (*country*) завоёвывать *impf.*, завоева́ть (-ою́ю, -ою́ешь) *pf.*; (*enemy*) побежда́ть *impf.*, победи́ть (-еди́шь, -еди́т) *pf.*; (*habit*) преодолева́ть *impf.*, преодоле́ть *pf.* **conqueror** *n.* завоева́тель *m.*; победи́тель *m.* **conquest** ['kɒŋkwest] *n.* завоева́ние; покоре́ние.

consanguinity [,kɒnsæŋ'gwɪnɪtɪ] *n.* кро́вное родство́.

conscience ['kɒnʃ(ə)ns] *n.* со́весть; **pangs of** ~ угрызе́ние со́вести. **consci'entious** *adj.* добросо́вестный. **conscious** *adj.* сознáтельный; *pred.* в созна́нии; **be ~ of** сознава́ть (-аю́, -аёшь) *impf.+a.* **consciousness** *n.* созна́ние.

conscript [kən'skrɪpt; 'kɒnskrɪpt] *v.t.* призыва́ть *impf.*, призва́ть (призову́, -вёшь; призва́л, -а́, -о) *pf.* на вое́нную слу́жбу; *n.* новобра́нец (-нца), призывни́к (-а́). **conscription** *n.* во́инская пови́нность.

consecrate ['kɒnsɪ,kreɪt] *v.t.* (*church etc.*) освяща́ть *impf.*, освяти́ть (-ящу́, -яти́шь) *pf.*; (*bishop etc.*) посвяща́ть *impf.*, посвяти́ть (-ящу́, -яти́шь) *pf.* (в епи́скопы и т.д.) **conse'cration** *n.* освяще́ние; посвяще́ние.

consecutive [kən'sekjʊtɪv] *adj.* после́довательный.

consensus [kən'sensəs] *n.* согла́сие.

consent [kən'sent] *v.i.* дава́ть (даю́, даёшь) *impf.*, дать (дам, дашь, даст, дади́м; дал, -а́, да́ло́, -и) *pf.* согла́сие; соглаша́ться *impf.*, согласи́ться *pf.* (**to** +*inf.*, на+*a.*); *n.* согла́сие.

consequence ['kɒnsɪkwəns] *n.* после́дствие; **of great** ~ большо́го значе́ния; **of some** ~ дово́льно ва́жный. **consequent** *adj.* после́довательный; ~ **on** вытека́ющий из+*g.* **consequently** *adv.* сле́довательно. **conse'quential** *adj.* ва́жный (-жен, -жна́, -жно, -жны́).

conservancy [kən'sɜːvənsɪ] *n.* охра́на (рек и лесо́в). **conser'vation** *n.* сохране́ние; охра́на приро́ды. **conservative** *adj.* консервати́вный; *n.* консерва́тор. **conservatory** *n.* оранжере́я. **conserve** *v.t.* сохраня́ть *impf.*, сохрани́ть *pf.*

consider [kən'sɪdə(r)] *v.t.* обду́мывать *impf.*, обду́мать *pf.*; рассма́тривать *impf.*, рассмотре́ть (-рю́, -ришь) *pf.*; (*regard as, be of opinion that*) счита́ть *impf.*, счесть (сочту́, -тёшь; счёл, сочла́) *pf.+i.*, за+*a.*, что. **considerable** *adj.* значи́тельный. **considerate** *adj.* внима́тельный. **conside'ration** *n.* рассмотре́ние; внима́ние; **take into** ~ принима́ть *impf.*, приня́ть (приму́, -мешь; при́нял, -а́, -о) *pf.* во внима́ние. **considered** *adj.* проду́манный (-ан). **considering** *prep.* принима́я+*a.* во внима́ние.

consign [kən'saɪn] *v.t.* отправля́ть *impf.*, отпра́вить *pf.* **consi'gnee** *n.* грузополуча́тель *m.* **consignment** *n.* (*goods consigned*) па́ртия; (*consigning*) отпра́вка това́ров; ~ **note** накладна́я *sb.* **consignor** *n.* грузоотправи́тель *m.*

consist [kən'sɪst] *v.i.*: ~ **of** состоя́ть *impf.* из+*g.* **consistency, -ce** *n.* после́довательность; консисте́нция. **consistent** *adj.*

послéдовательный; ~ **with** совмести́мый с+*i*. **consistently** *adv*. послéдовательно; соглáсно с+*i*.

consolation [ˌkɒnsəˈleɪʃ(ə)n] *n*. утешéние. **consolatory** [kənˈsɒlətərɪ] *adj*. утеши́тельный. **console**[1] [kənˈsəʊl] *v.t*. утешáть *impf*., утéшить *pf*. **consoling** *adj*. утеши́тельный.

console[2] [ˈkɒnsəʊl] *n*. пульт управлéния.

consolidate [kənˈsɒlɪˌdeɪt] *v.t*. укрепля́ть *impf*., укрепи́ть *pf*. **consolidated** *adj*. (*econ*.) консолиди́рованный (-ан, -анна). **consoliˈdation** *n*. укреплéние; (*econ*.) консолидáция.

consonance [ˈkɒnsənəns] *n*. созву́чие. **consonant** *n*. соглáсный *sb*.; *adj*. созву́чный; соглáсный; совмести́мый.

consort [kənˈsɔːt; ˈkɒnsɔːt] *v.i*. общáться *impf*.; *n*. супру́г, ~а; **Prince C~** супру́г цáрствующей королéвы.

consortium [kənˈsɔːtɪəm] *n*. консóрциум.

conspicuous [kənˈspɪkjʊəs] *adj*. замéтный; ви́дный (-ден, -нá, -дно, ви́дны́). **conspicuously** *adv*. я́сно, замéтно.

conspiracy [kənˈspɪrəsɪ] *n*. зáговор. **conspirator** *n*. заговóрщик, -ица. **conspiraˈtorial** *adj*. заговóрщицкий. **conspire** [kənˈspaɪə(r)] *v.i*. устрáивать *impf*., устрóить *pf*. зáговор.

constable [ˈkʌnstəb(ə)l] *n*. полицéйский *sb*. **constabulary** [kənˈstæbjʊlərɪ] *n*. поли́ция.

constancy [ˈkɒnstənsɪ] *n*. постоя́нство. **constant** *adj*. постоя́нный (-нен, -нна); (*faithful*) вéрный (-рен, -рнá, -рно, вéрны́). **constantly** *adv*. постоя́нно.

constellation [ˌkɒnstəˈleɪʃ(ə)n] *n*. созвéздие.

consternation [ˌkɒnstəˈneɪʃ(ə)n] *n*. тревóга.

constipation [ˌkɒnstɪˈpeɪʃ(ə)n] *n*. запóр.

constituency [kənˈstɪtjʊənsɪ] *n*. (*area*) избирáтельный óкруг (*pl*. -á); (*voters*) избирáтели *m.pl*. **constituent** *n*. (*component*) составнáя часть (*pl*. -ти, -тéй); (*voter*) избирáтель *m*.; *adj*. составнóй; ~ **assembly** учреди́тельное собрáние. **ˈconstitute** *v.t*. составля́ть *impf*., состáвить *pf*. **constiˈtution** *n*. (*pol*., *med*.) конститу́ция; (*composition*) составлéние. **constiˈtutional** *adj*. (*med*.) конституционáльный; (*pol*.) конституциóнный (-нен, -нна). **constiˈtutionally** *adv*. закóнно; в соотвéтствии с конститу́цией.

constrain [kənˈstreɪn] *v.t*. принуждáть *impf*., прину́дить *pf*. **constrained** *adj*. принуждённый (-ён, -енá). **constraint** *n*. принуждéние; **without** ~ свобóдно, непринуждённо.

constrict [kənˈstrɪkt] *v.t*. (*compress*) сжимáть *impf*., сжать (сожму́, -мёшь) *pf*.; (*narrow*) су́живать *impf*., су́зить *pf*. **constriction** *n*. сжáтие, сужéние.

construct [kənˈstrʌkt] *v.t*. стрóить *impf*., по~ *pf*. **construction** *n*. строи́тельство; (*also gram*.) констру́кция; (*interpretation*) истолковáние; ~ **site** стрóйка. **constructional** *adj*. строи́тельный; (*structural*) структу́рный. **constructive** *adj*. конструкти́вный. **constructor** *n*. строи́тель *m*., констру́ктор.

construe [kənˈstruː] *v.t*. истолкóвывать *impf*., истолковáть *pf*.

consul [ˈkɒns(ə)l] *n*. кóнсул; **honorary** ~ почётный кóнсул; ~ **general** генерáльный кóнсул. **consular** *adj*. кóнсульский. **consulate** *n*. кóнсульство.

consult [kənˈsʌlt] *v.t*. консульти́ровать *impf*., про~ *pf*. с+*i*.; совéтоваться *impf*., по~ *pf*. с+*i*. **consulˈtation** *n*. консультáция, совещáние. **consultative** *adj*. консультати́вный, совещáтельный. **consulting** *adj*. консульти́рующий; ~ **room** врачéбный кабинéт.

consume [kənˈsjuːm] *v.t*. потребля́ть *impf*., потреби́ть *pf*.; расхóдовать *impf*., из~ *pf*. **consumer** *n*. потреби́тель *m*.; ~ **goods** товáры *m.pl*. ширóкого потреблéния, ширпотрéб; ~ **society** óбщество потреблéния.

consummate [kənˈsʌmɪt, ˈkɒnsəmɪt; ˈkɒnsəˌmeɪt] *adj*. закóнченный (-ен, -енна); совершéнный (-нен, -нна); *v.t*. завершáть *impf*., заверши́ть *pf*.; доводи́ть (-ожу́, -óдишь) *impf*., довести́ (-еду́, -едёшь; довёл, -á) *pf*. до концá. **consuˈmmation** *n*. завершéние.

consumption [kənˈsʌmpʃ(ə)n] *n*. потреблéние, расхóд; (*disease*) чахóтка. **consumptive** [kənˈsʌmptɪv] *adj*. чахóточный, туберкулёзный; *n*. больнóй *sb*. чахóткой, туберкулёзом.

contact [ˈkɒntækt] *n*. контáкт, соприкосновéние; *v.t*. соприкасáться *impf*., соприкосну́ться *pf*. с+*i*.; входи́ть (-ожу́, -óдишь) *impf*., войти́ (войду́, -дёшь; вошёл, -шлá) *pf*. в контáкт с+*i*.

contagion [kənˈteɪdʒ(ə)n] *n*. зарáза, инфéкция. **contagious** *adj*. зарáзный, инфекциóнный; ~ **laughter** зарази́тельный смех.

contain [kənˈteɪn] *v.t*. содержáть (-жу́, -жишь) *impf*.; вмещáть *impf*., вмести́ть *pf*.; (*restrain*) сдéрживать *impf*., сдержáть (-жу́, -жишь) *pf*. **container** *n*. (*vessel*) сосу́д; (*transport*) контéйнер. **containment** *n*. сдéрживание.

contaminate [kənˈtæmɪˌneɪt] *v.t*. заражáть *impf*., зарази́ть *pf*.; загрязня́ть *impf*., загрязни́ть *pf*. **contamiˈnation** *n*. заражéние, загрязнéние.

contemplate [ˈkɒntəmˌpleɪt] *v.t*. созерцáть *impf*.; размышля́ть *impf*.; (*intend*) предполагáть *impf*., предположи́ть (-жу́, -жишь) *pf*. **contemˈplation** *n*. созерцáние; размышлéние. **conˈtemplative** *adj*. созерцáтельный.

contemporary [kənˈtempərərɪ] *n*. совремéнник; *adj*. совремéнный.

contempt [kənˈtempt] *n*. презрéние; ~ **of court** неуважéние к суду́; **hold in** ~ презирáть *impf*. **contemptible** *adj*. презрéнный (-ен, -енна). **contemptuous** *adj*. презри́тельный.

contend [kənˈtend] *v.i*. (*compete*) состязáться *impf*.; ~ **for** оспáривать *impf*.; *v.t*. утверждáть *impf*. **contender** *n*. соревну́ющийся *sb*.

content[1] ['kɒntent] *n.* содержа́ние; *pl.* содержи́мое *sb.*; **(table of) contents** содержа́ние.
content[2] [kən'tent] *n.* дово́льство; *pred.* дово́лен (-льна); *v.t.*: ~ **o.s. with** дово́льствоваться *impf.*, у~ *pf.*+*i.* **contented** *adj.* дово́льный; удовлетворённый (-ён, -ена́).
contention [kən'tenʃ(ə)n] *n.* (*dispute*) спор, разногла́сие; (*claim*) утвержде́ние. **contentious** *adj.* (*disputed*) спо́рный; (*quarrelsome*) вздо́рный.
contest ['kɒntest; kən'test] *n.* соревнова́ние, состяза́ние; *v.t.* оспа́ривать *impf.*, оспо́рить *pf.* **con'testant** *n.* уча́стник, -ица, соревнова́ния; конкуре́нт, ~ка.
context ['kɒntekst] *n.* конте́кст.
contiguity [ˌkɒntɪ'gju:ɪtɪ] *n.* соприкоснове́ние; бли́зость. **con'tiguous** *adj.* (*adjoining*) прилега́ющий (**to** к+*d.*); (*touching*) соприкаса́ющийся (**to** с+*i.*); (*near*) бли́зкий (-зок, -зка́, -зко, бли́зки́) (**to** от+*g.*).
continence ['kɒntɪnəns] *n.* воздержа́ние. **continent**[1] *adj.* возде́ржанный (-ан, -анна).
continent[2] ['kɒntɪnənt] *n.* матери́к (-а́), контине́нт. **conti'nental** *adj.* материко́вый, континента́льный.
contingency [kən'tɪndʒənsɪ] *n.* случа́йность. **contingent** *adj.* случа́йный, непредви́денный (-ен, -енна); ~ **on** в зави́симости от+*g.*; *n.* континге́нт.
continual [kən'tɪnjʊəl] *adj.* непреста́нный (-нен, -нна). **continuance, continu'ation** *n.* продолже́ние. **continue** *v.t.* & *i.* продолжа́ть(ся) *impf.*, продо́лжить(ся) *pf.* **continuous** *adj.* непреры́вный.
contort [kən'tɔ:t] *v.t.* искажа́ть *impf.*, искази́ть *pf.* **contortion** *n.* искаже́ние; искривле́ние. **contortionist** *n.* «челове́к-змея́».
contour ['kɒntʊə(r)] *n.* ко́нтур, очерта́ние; ~ **line** горизонта́ль.
contraband ['kɒntrəˌbænd] *n.* контраба́нда; *adj.* контраба́ндный.
contraception [ˌkɒntrə'sepʃ(ə)n] *n.* предупрежде́ние бере́менности. **contraceptive** *n.* противозача́точное сре́дство; *adj.* противозача́точный.
contract ['kɒntrækt; kən'trækt] *n.* контра́кт, догово́р; *v.i.* (*make a* ~) заключа́ть *impf.*, заключи́ть *pf.* контра́кт, догово́р; *v.t.* & *i.* сокраща́ть(ся) *impf.*, сократи́ть(ся) (-ащу́(сь), -ати́шь(ся)) *pf.* **contracting** *adj.* догова́ривающийся; ~ **parties** догова́ривающиеся сто́роны (-о́н, -она́м) *f.pl.* **contraction** *n.* сокраще́ние, сжа́тие. **contractor** *n.* подря́дчик.
contradict [ˌkɒntrə'dɪkt] *v.t.* противоре́чить *impf.*+*d.* **contradiction** *n.* противоре́чие. **contradictory** *adj.* противоречи́вый.
contralto [kən'træltəʊ] *n.* контра́льто (*voice*) *nt.* & (*person*) *f.indecl.*
contraption [kən'træpʃ(ə)n] *n.* штуко́вина; устро́йство.
contrariness ['kɒntrərɪnɪs] *n.* своенра́вие, упря́мство. **contrary** *adj.* (*opposite*) противополо́жный; (*perverse*) упря́мый; ~ **to** вопреки́+*d.*; **on the** ~ наоборо́т.
contrast ['kɒntrɑ:st] *n.* контра́ст, противополо́жность; *v.t.* противопоставля́ть *impf.*, противопоста́вить *pf.* (**with** +*d.*).
contravene [ˌkɒntrə'vi:n] *v.t.* наруша́ть *impf.*, нару́шить *pf.* **contravention** *n.* наруше́ние.
contribute [kən'trɪbju:t] *v.t.* (*to fund etc.*) же́ртвовать *impf.*, по~ *pf.* (**to** в+*a.*); ~ **to** (*further*) соде́йствовать *impf.* & *pf.* по~ *pf.*+*d.*; (*to publication etc.*) сотру́дничать *impf.* в+*p.* **contri'bution** *n.* поже́ртвование; вклад. **contributor** *n.* же́ртвователь *m.*; сотру́дник; соуча́стник.
contrite ['kɒntraɪt, kən'traɪt] *adj.* сокруша́ющийся, ка́ющийся. **con'trition** *n.* раска́яние.
contrivance [kən'traɪv(ə)ns] *n.* приспособле́ние; вы́думка. **contrive** *v.t.* умудря́ться *impf.*, умудри́ться *pf.*+*inf.*
control [kən'trəʊl] *n.* (*check*) контро́ль *m.*, прове́рка; (*direction*) управле́ние; (*restraint*) сде́ржанность; (*remote* ~) телеуправле́ние; ~ **point** контро́льный пункт; ~ **tower** диспе́тчерская вы́шка; *v.t.* (*check*) контроли́ровать *impf.*, про~ *pf.*; управля́ть *impf.*+*i.*; ~ **o.s.** сде́рживаться *impf.*, сдержа́ться (-жу́сь, -жишься) *pf.* **control-gear** *n.* механи́зм управле́ния. **controllable, controlled** *adj.* управля́емый, регули́руемый. **controller** *n.* контролёр; (*elec.*) контро́ллер.
controversial [ˌkɒntrə'vɜ:ʃ(ə)l] *adj.* спо́рный. **controversy** ['kɒntrəˌvɜ:sɪ] *n.* спор, диску́ссия.
contuse [kən'tju:z] *v.t.* конту́зить *pf.* **contusion** *n.* конту́зия.
conundrum [kə'nʌndrəm] *n.* головоло́мка.
convalesce [ˌkɒnvə'les] *v.i.* поправля́ться *impf.* **convalescence** *n.* попра́вка, выздора́вливание. **convalescent** *n.* & *adj.* выздора́вливающий.
convection [kən'vekʃ(ə)n] *n.* конве́кция.
convene [kən'vi:n] *v.t.* созыва́ть *impf.*, созва́ть (созову́, -вёшь; созва́л, -а́, -о) *pf.*
convenience [kən'vi:nɪəns] *n.* удо́бство; (*public* ~) убо́рная *sb.*; ~ **foods** полуфабрика́ты *m.pl.* **convenient** *adj.* удо́бный.
convent ['kɒnv(ə)nt, -vent] *n.* же́нский монасты́рь (-ря́) *m.*
convention [kən'venʃ(ə)n] *n.* (*assembly*) съезд, собра́ние; (*agreement*) конве́нция; (*practice, use, custom*) обы́чай; (*conventionality*) усло́вность. **conventional** *adj.* общепри́нятый, обы́чный; усло́вный; ~ **weapons** обы́чные ви́ды *m.pl.* ору́жия.
converge [kən'vɜ:dʒ] *v.i.* сходи́ться (-дятся) *impf.*, сойти́сь (-йду́тся; сошли́сь) *pf.* в одну́ то́чку. **convergence** *n.* сходи́мость, конверге́нция. **converging** *adj.* сходя́щийся в одно́й то́чке.
conversant [kən'vɜ:s(ə)nt] *pred.*: ~ **with** осведомлён (-а́) в+*p.*; знако́м с+*i.*
conversation [ˌkɒnvə'seɪʃ(ə)n] *n.* разгово́р,

бесе́да. **conversational** *adj.* разгово́рный. **con'verse**[1] *v.i.* разгова́ривать *impf.*; бесе́довать *impf.*

converse[2] ['kɒnvɜːs] *adj.* обра́тный, противополо́жный. **conversely** *adv.* наоборо́т. **conversion** [kən'vɜːʃ(ə)n] *n.* (*change*) превраще́ние; (*of faith*) обраще́ние; (*of building*) перестро́йка. **con'vert** *v.t.* (*change*) превраща́ть *impf.*, преврати́ть (-ащу́, -ати́шь) *pf.* (**into** в+*a.*); (*to faith*) обраща́ть *impf.*, обрати́ть (-ащу́, -ати́шь) *pf.* (**to** в+*a.*); (*a building*) перестра́ивать *impf.*, перестро́ить *pf.* **con'vertible** *adj.* обрати́мый; *n.* кабриоле́т, фаэто́н.

convex ['kɒnveks] *adj.* вы́пуклый.

convey [kən'veɪ] *v.t.* (*transport*) перевози́ть (-ожу́, -о́зишь) *impf.*, перевезти́ (-езу́, -езёшь; -ёз, -езла́) *pf.*; (*communicate*) сообща́ть *impf.*, сообщи́ть *pf.*; (*transmit*) передава́ть (-даю́, -даёшь) *impf.*, переда́ть (-а́м, -а́шь, -а́ст, -ади́м; пе́редал, -а́, -о) *pf.* **conveyance** *n.* перево́зка, переда́ча. **conveyancing** *n.* оформле́ние перехо́да пра́ва на недви́жимость. **conveyer** *n.* конве́йер, транспортёр.

convict ['kɒnvɪkt; kən'vɪkt] *n.* осуждённый *sb.*, ка́торжник; *v.t.* осужда́ть *impf.*, осуди́ть (-ужу́, -у́дишь) *pf.* **con'viction** *n.* (*leg.*) осужде́ние; (*belief*) убежде́ние. **con'vince** *v.t.* убежда́ть *impf.*, убеди́ть (-и́шь, -и́т) *pf.* **con'vincing** *adj.* убеди́тельный.

convivial [kən'vɪvɪəl] *adj.* компане́йский; весёлый.

convocation [,kɒnvə'keɪʃ(ə)n] *n.* созы́в; собра́ние; (*eccl.*) собо́р, сино́д. **convoke** [kən'vəʊk] *v.t.* созыва́ть *impf.*, созва́ть (созову́, -вёшь; созва́л, -а́, -о) *pf.*

convoluted ['kɒnvə,luːtɪd] *adj.* свёрнутый спира́лью, изви́листый.

convolvulus [kən'vɒlvjʊləs] *n.* вьюно́к (-нка́).

convoy ['kɒnvɔɪ] *n.* конво́й; коло́нна под конво́ем; *v.t.* конвои́ровать *impf.*

convulse [kən'vʌls] *v.t.*: **be convulsed with** содрога́ться *impf.*, содрогну́ться *pf.* от+*g.* **convulsion** *n.* (*med.*) конву́льсия; су́дороги *f.pl.*

coo [kuː] *n.* воркова́ние; *v.i.* воркова́ть *impf.*

cooee ['kuːiː] *int.* ау́!

cook [kʊk] *n.* куха́рка, по́вар (*pl.* -а́), ~и́ха; *v.t.* стря́пать *impf.*, со~ *pf.*; (*roast*) жа́рить *impf.*, за~, из~ *pf.*; (*boil*) вари́ть (-рю́, -ришь) *impf.*, с~ *pf.* **cooker** *n.* плита́ (*pl.* -ы), печь (*loc.* -чи́; *pl.* -чи, -че́й). **cookery** *n.* кулина́рия, стряпня́. **cooking** *adj.* ку́хонный; ~ **salt** пова́ренная соль.

cool [kuːl] *adj.* прохла́дный; (*of persons*) хладнокро́вный; *v.t.* студи́ть (-ужу́, -у́дишь) *impf.*, о~ *pf.*; охлажда́ть *impf.*, охлади́ть *pf.*; ~ **down, off** остыва́ть *impf.*, осты́(ну)ть (-ы́ну, -ы́нешь; -ы́(ну)л, -ы́ла) *pf.* **coolant** *n.* сма́зочно-охлажда́ющая жи́дкость. **cooler** *n.* охлади́тель *m.* **cooling** *adj.* охлажда́ющий.

coop [kuːp] *n.* куря́тник; *v.t.*: ~ **up** держа́ть (-жу́, -жишь) *impf.* взаперти́.

cooper ['kuːpə(r)] *n.* бо́нда́рь (бо́ндаря́) *m.*, боча́р (-а́).

cooperate [kəʊ'ɒpə,reɪt] *v.i.* сотру́дничать *impf.*; коопери́роваться *impf.* & *pf.* **coope'ration** *n.* сотру́дничество; коопера́ция. **cooperative, co-op** *n.* кооперати́в; *adj.* совме́стный, кооперати́вный. **co-operator** *n.* коопера́тор.

co-opt [kəʊ'ɒpt] *v.t.* коопти́ровать *impf.* & *pf.*

coordinate [kəʊ'ɔːdɪnət] *v.t.* координи́ровать *impf.* & *pf.*; согласо́вывать *impf.*, согласова́ть *pf.*; *n.* координа́та; *adj.* согласо́ванный (-ан), координи́рованный (-ан, -анна). **coordi'nation** *n.* координа́ция.

coot [kuːt] *n.* лысу́ха.

co-owner [kəʊ'əʊnə(r)] *n.* совладе́лец (-льца).

cop [kɒp] *n.* полице́йский *sb.*; *v.t.* пойма́ть *pf.*

cope[1] [kəʊp] *n.* ри́за.

cope[2] [kəʊp] *v.i.*: ~ **with** справля́ться *impf.*, спра́виться *pf.* с+*i.*

Copenhagen [,kəʊpən'heɪgən] *n.* Копенга́ген.

copious ['kəʊpɪəs] *adj.* оби́льный. **copiousness** *n.* изоби́лие.

copper ['kɒpə(r)] *n.* (*metal*) медь; (*vessel*) ме́дный котёл (-тла́); (*coin*) медя́к (-а́); (*policeman*) полице́йский *sb.* **copperplate** *n.* (*handwriting*) каллиграфи́ческий по́черк.

coppice ['kɒpɪs], **copse** [kɒps] *n.* ро́щица.

Copt [kɒpt] *n.* копт. **Coptic** ['kɒptɪk] *adj.* ко́птский.

copulate ['kɒpjʊ,leɪt] *v.i.* спа́риваться *impf.*, спа́риться *pf.* **copu'lation** *n.* копуля́ция.

copy ['kɒpɪ] *n.* ко́пия; (*specimen of book etc.*) экземпля́р; **fair** ~ чистови́к (-а́); **rough** ~ чернови́к (-а́); *v.t.* копи́ровать *impf.*, с~ *pf.*; (*transcribe*) перепи́сывать *impf.*, переписа́ть (-ишу́, -и́шешь) *pf.*. **copybook** *n.* тетра́дь. **copyright** *n.* а́вторское пра́во.

coquetry ['kɒkɪtrɪ, 'kəʊk-] *n.* коке́тство. **coquette** [kɒ'ket, kə'ket] *n.* коке́тка. **coquettish** *adj.* коке́тливый.

coracle ['kɒrək(ə)l] *n.* ло́дка из ивняка́, обтя́нутая ко́жей и́ли паруси́ной.

coral ['kɒr(ə)l] *n.* кора́лл; *adj.* кора́лловый.

corbel ['kɔːb(ə)l] *n.* вы́ступ; консо́ль; кронште́йн.

cord [kɔːd] *n.* шнур (-а́), верёвка; **umbilical** ~ пупови́на; **vocal cords** голосовы́е свя́зки *f.pl.*; *v.t.* свя́зывать *impf.*, связа́ть (-яжу́, -я́жешь) *pf.* верёвкой. **cordage** *n.* сна́сти (-те́й) *pl.*, такела́ж.

cordial ['kɔːdɪəl] *adj.* серде́чный, раду́шный; *n.* (*drink*) фрукто́вый напи́ток (-тка). **cordi'ality** *n.* серде́чность, раду́шие.

cordless ['kɔːdlɪs] *adj.* беспроводно́й, бесшнурово́й.

corduroy ['kɔːdə,rɔɪ] *n.* вельве́т (-а(у)) в ру́бчик; плис; *pl.* вельве́товые штаны́ (-но́в) *pl.*

core [kɔː(r)] *n.* сердцеви́на; (*fig.*) суть; *v.t.* удаля́ть *impf.*, удали́ть *pf.* сердцеви́ну из+*g.*

cork [kɔ:k] *n.* (*stopper*) про́бка; (*float*) поплаво́к (-вка́); *attr.* пробко́вый; *v.t.* заку́поривать *impf.*, заку́порить *pf.* **corkscrew** *n.* што́пор; *v.i.* дви́гаться (-и́гается & -и́жется) *impf.*, дви́нуться *pf.* по спира́ли.

corm [kɔ:m] *n.* клубнелу́ковица.

cormorant ['kɔ:mərənt] *n.* бакла́н.

corn[1] [kɔ:n] *n.* зерно́, зерновы́е хлеба́ *m.pl.*; (*wheat*) пшени́ца; (*oats*) овёс (овса́); (*maize*) кукуру́за. **corn-cob** *n.* поча́ток (-тка). **cornflakes** *n.* кукуру́зные хло́пья (-ьев) *pl.* **cornflour** *n.* кукуру́зная мука́. **cornflower** *n.* василёк (-лька́). **corny** *adj.* зерново́й; (*coll.*) бана́льный.

corn[2] [kɔ:n] *n.* (*on foot*) мозо́ль.

corn[3] [kɔ:n] *v.t.* заса́ливать *impf.*, засоли́ть (-олью́, -о́ли́шь) *pf.*; **~ed beef** солони́на.

cornea ['kɔ:nɪə] *n.* рогова́я оболо́чка.

cornelian [kɔ:'ni:lɪən] *n.* сердоли́к.

corner ['kɔ:nə(r)] *n.* у́гол (угла́, *loc.* углу́); *v.t.* загоня́ть *impf.*, загна́ть (-гоню́, -го́нишь; загна́л, -а́, -о) *pf.* в у́гол. **cornerstone** *n.* краеуго́льный ка́мень (-мня; *pl.* -мни, -мне́й) *m.*

cornet ['kɔ:nɪt] *n.* (*mus.*, *mil.*) корне́т; (*paper*) фу́нтик; (*ice-cream*) рожо́к (-жка́).

cornice ['kɔ:nɪs] *n.* карни́з.

cornucopia [ˌkɔ:njʊ'kəʊpɪə] *n.* рог изоби́лия.

corolla [kə'rɒlə] *n.* ве́нчик.

corollary [kə'rɒlərɪ] *n.* сле́дствие; вы́вод.

corona [kə'rəʊnə] *n.* коро́на, вене́ц (-нца́). **coronary (thrombosis)** ['kɒrənərɪ] *n.* вене́чный тромбо́з. **coro'nation** *n.* корона́ция. **coroner** ['kɒrənə(r)] *n.* сле́дователь *m.* **coronet** ['kɒrənɪt, -ˌnet] *n.* небольша́я коро́на; (*garland*) вено́к (-нка́).

Corp. *abbr.* (*of* **Corporation**) корпора́ция.

corporal[1] ['kɔ:pr(ə)l] *n.* капра́л.

corporal[2] ['kɔ:pr(ə)l] *adj.* теле́сный; ~ **punishment** теле́сное наказа́ние.

corporate ['kɔ:pərət] *adj.* корпорати́вный. **corpo'ration** *n.* корпора́ция.

corps [kɔ:(r)] *n.* ко́рпус (*pl.* -а́).

corpse [kɔ:ps] *n.* труп.

corpulence ['kɔ:pjʊləns] *n.* ту́чность. **corpulent** *adj.* ту́чный (-чен, -чна́, -чно).

corpuscle ['kɔ:pʌs(ə)l] *n.* части́ца, те́льце (*pl.* -льца́, -ле́ц, -льца́м); **red, white,** ~ кра́сные, бе́лые, ша́рики *m.pl.* **corpuscular** [kɔ:'pʌskjʊlə(r)] *adj.* корпускуля́рный.

corral [kɒ'rɑ:l] *n.* заго́н; *v.t.* загоня́ть *impf.*, загна́ть (-гоню́, -го́нишь; загна́л, -а́, -о) *pf.* в заго́н.

correct [kə'rekt] *adj.* пра́вильный, ве́рный (-рен, -рна́, -рно, ве́рны́); (*conduct*) корре́ктный; *v.t.* исправля́ть *impf.*, испра́вить *pf.* **correction** *n.* исправле́ние; попра́вка. **corrective** *adj.* исправи́тельный. **corrector** *n.* корре́ктор (*pl.* -ы & -а́).

correlate ['kɒrəˌleɪt, 'kɒrɪ-] *v.t.* соотноси́ть (-ошу́, -о́сишь) *impf.*, соотнести́ (-есу́, -есёшь; -ёс, -есла́) *pf.* **corre'lation** *n.* соотноше́ние, корреля́ция.

correspond [ˌkɒrɪ'spɒnd] *v.i.* соотве́тствовать *impf.* (**to, with** +*d.*); (*by letter*) перепи́сываться *impf.* **correspondence** *n.* соотве́тствие; корреспонде́нция. **correspondent** *n.* корреспонде́нт. **corresponding** *adj.* соотве́тствующий (**to** +*d.*).

corridor ['kɒrɪˌdɔ:(r)] *n.* коридо́р.

corroborate [kə'rɒbəˌreɪt] *v.t.* подтвержда́ть *impf.*, подтверди́ть *pf.* **corrobo'ration** *n.* подтвержде́ние.

corrode [kə'rəʊd] *v.t.* разъеда́ть *impf.*, разъе́сть (-е́ст, -едя́т; -е́л) *pf.* **corrosion** *n.* разъеда́ние, корро́зия. **corrosive** *adj.* е́дкий (е́док, едка́, е́дко); *n.* е́дкое, разъеда́ющее, вещество́.

corrugate ['kɒrʊˌgeɪt] *v.t.* гофрирова́ть *impf.* & *pf.*; **~d iron** рифлёное желе́зо.

corrupt [kə'rʌpt] *adj.* испо́рченный (-ен, -енна); развра́тный; *v.t.* развраща́ть *impf.*, разврати́ть (-ащу́, -ати́шь) *pf.*; по́ртить *impf.*, ис~ *pf.* **corruption** *n.* по́рча; развращённость; корру́пция.

corsage [kɔ:'sɑ:ʒ] *n.* корса́ж.

corsair ['kɔ:seə(r)] *n.* корса́р; пира́т.

corset ['kɔ:sɪt] *n.* корсе́т.

cortège [kɔ:'teɪʒ] *n.* торже́ственное ше́ствие, корте́ж.

cortex ['kɔ:teks] *n.* кора́.

corundum [kə'rʌndəm] *n.* кору́нд.

corvette [kɔ:'vet] *n.* корве́т.

cos [kɒs] *n.* сала́т ромэ́н.

cosh [kɒʃ] *n.* дуби́нка; *v.t.* ударя́ть *impf.*, уда́рить *pf.* дуби́нкой.

cosine ['kəʊsaɪn] *n.* ко́синус.

cosmetic [kɒz'metɪk] *adj.* космети́ческий; *n.* космети́ческое сре́дство; *pl.* косме́тика.

cosmic ['kɒzmɪk] *adj.* косми́ческий. **cosmonaut** ['kɒzməˌnɔ:t] *n.* космона́вт.

cosmopolitan [ˌkɒzmə'pɒlɪt(ə)n] *adj.* космополити́ческий; *n.* космополи́т.

Cossack ['kɒsæk] *n.* каза́к (-а́; *pl.* -аки́), -а́чка; *adj.* каза́чий (-чья, -чье), каза́цкий.

cosset ['kɒsɪt] *v.t.* не́жить *impf.*

cost [kɒst] *n.* сто́имость, цена́ (*a.* -ну; *pl.* -ы); *pl.* (*leg.*) суде́бные изде́ржки *f.pl.*; ~ **price** себесто́имость; *v.t.* сто́ить *impf.*

costermonger ['kɒstəˌmʌŋgə(r)] *n.* у́личный торго́вец.

costly ['kɒstlɪ] *adj.* дорого́й (до́рог, -а́, -о), це́нный (-нен, -нна).

costume ['kɒstju:m] *n.* костю́м, оде́жда; ~ **jewellery** ювели́рное украше́ние без драгоце́нных камне́й; ~ **play** истори́ческая пье́са.

cosy ['kəʊzɪ] *adj.* ую́тный; *n.* тёплая покры́шка.

cot [kɒt] *n.* (*child's*) де́тская крова́тка; (*hospital bed*) ко́йка.

cottage ['kɒtɪdʒ] *n.* котте́дж.

cotton ['kɒt(ə)n] *n.* хло́пок (-пка); (*cloth*) хлопчатобума́жная ткань; (*thread*) (бума́жная) ни́тка; ~ **plant** хлопча́тник; ~ **wool** ва́та; *adj.* хло́пковый, хлопчатобума́жный.

couch [kaʊtʃ] *n.* куше́тка, ло́же.
couch-grass [ku:tʃ] *n.* пыре́й.
cough [kɒf] *n.* ка́шель (-шля) *m.*; *v.i.* ка́шлять *impf.*
council ['kaʊns(ə)l] *n.* сове́т; (*eccl.*) собо́р. **councillor** *n.* сове́тник; член сове́та.
counsel ['kaʊns(ə)l] *n.* (*consultation*) обсужде́ние; (*advice*) сове́т; (*lawyer*) адвока́т; ~ **for the defence** защи́тник; ~ **for the prosecution** обвини́тель *m.*; *v.t.* сове́товать *impf.*, по~ *pf.*+*d.*
count[1] [kaʊnt] *n.* (*title*) граф.
count[2] [kaʊnt] *v.t.* счита́ть *impf.*, со~, счесть (сочту́, -тёшь; счёл, сочла́) *pf.*; *n.* счёт (-а(у)), подсчёт. **countdown** *n.* отсчёт вре́мени.
countenance ['kaʊntɪnəns] *n.* лицо́ (*pl.* -ца); *v.t.* одобря́ть *impf.*, одо́брить *pf.*
counter ['kaʊntə(r)] *n.* прила́вок (-вка), сто́йка; (*token*) фи́шка, жето́н; *adj.* обра́тный; *adv.*: **run** ~ **to** де́йствовать *impf.* про́тив+*g.*; *v.t.* пари́ровать *impf.*, от~ *pf.* **counte'ract** *v.t.* противоде́йствовать *impf.* **counte'raction** *n.* противоде́йствие. **counterbalance** *n.* противове́с; *v.t.* уравнове́шивать *impf.*, уравнове́сить *pf.* **counterfeit** *adj.* подло́жный, фальши́вый. **counterin'telligence** *n.* контрразве́дка. **counter'mand** *v.t.* отменя́ть *impf.*, отмени́ть (-ню́, -нишь) *pf.* **counterpane** *n.* покрыва́ло. **counterpart** *n.* соотве́тственная часть (*pl.* -ти, -те́й). **counterpoint** *n.* контрапу́нкт. **counter-revo'lutionary** *n.* контрреволюционе́р; *adj.* контрреволюцио́нный. **countersign** *n.* паро́ль *m.*
countess ['kaʊntɪs] *n.* графи́ня.
counting-house ['kaʊntɪŋ] *n.* бухгалте́рия.
countless ['kaʊntlɪs] *adj.* несчётный, бесчи́сленный (-ен, -енна).
countrified ['kʌntrɪˌfaɪd] *adj.* дереве́нский. **country** *n.* (*nation*) страна́; (*land of birth*) ро́дина; (*rural areas*) дере́вня; *adj.* дереве́нский, се́льский. **countryman, -woman** *n.* земля́к, -я́чка; се́льский жи́тель *m.*, -ая жи́тельница.
county ['kaʊntɪ] *n.* гра́фство.
coup (d'état) [ˌku: deɪ'tɑ:] *n.* госуда́рственный переворо́т; путч.
couple ['kʌp(ə)l] *n.* па́ра; два *m.* & *nt.*, две *f.* (двух, двум, двумя́); **married** ~ супру́ги *m.pl.*; *v.t.* сцепля́ть *impf.*, сцепи́ть (-плю́, -пишь) *pf.* **couplet** *n.* двусти́шье. **coupling** *n.* соедине́ние, сцепле́ние.
coupon ['ku:pɒn] *n.* купо́н; тало́н.
courage ['kʌrɪdʒ] *n.* му́жество, хра́брость. **courageous** [kə'reɪdʒəs] *adj.* хра́брый (храбр, -а́, -о, хра́бры).
courier ['kʊrɪə(r)] *n.* (*messenger*) курье́р; (*guide*) гид.
course [kɔ:s] *n.* курс, ход, путь (-ти́, -тём) *m.*; (*of meal*) блю́до; **of** ~ коне́чно; *v.t.* гна́ться (гоню́сь, го́нишься; гна́лся, гнала́сь, гна́ло́сь) *impf.* за+*i.* **coursing** *n.* охо́та с го́нчими.
court [kɔ:t] *n.* двор (-а́); (*sport*) корт, площа́дка; (*law*) суд (-а́); ~ **martial** вое́нный трибуна́л; *v.t.* уха́живать *impf.* за+*i.* **courteous** ['kɜ:tɪəs] *adj.* ве́жливый, любе́зный. **courtesy** ['kɜ:tɪsɪ] *n.* ве́жливость. **courtier** *n.* придво́рный *sb.*
cousin ['kʌz(ə)n] *n.* двою́родный брат (*pl.* -ья, -ьев)), -ная сестра́ (*pl.* сёстры, -тёр, -трам); **second** ~ троюро́дный брат (*pl.* -ья, -ьев), -ая сестра́ (*pl.* сёстры, -тёр, -трам).
cove [kəʊv] *n.* небольша́я бу́хта.
covenant ['kʌvənənt] *n.* догово́р; *v.i.* заключа́ть *impf.*, заключи́ть *pf.* догово́р.
cover ['kʌvə(r)] *n.* покры́шка; покро́в; укры́тие; чехо́л (-хла́); (*bed*) покрыва́ло; (*book*) переплёт, обло́жка; **under separate** ~ в отде́льном конве́рте; *v.t.* покрыва́ть *impf.*, покры́ть (-ро́ю, -ро́ешь) *pf.*; скрыва́ть *impf.*, скрыть (-ро́ю, -ро́ешь) *pf.* **coverage** *n.* репорта́ж, информа́ция. **covering** *n.* покры́шка, оболо́чка; *adj.* покрыва́ющий; ~ **letter** сопроводи́тельное письмо́ (*pl.* -сьма, -сем, -сьмам). **covert** *adj.* скры́тый, та́йный.
covet ['kʌvɪt] *v.t.* домога́ться *imp.*+*g.*; пожела́ть *pf.*+*g.* **covetous** *adj.* зави́стливый, а́лчный.
covey ['kʌvɪ] *n.* вы́водок (-дка).
cow[1] [kaʊ] *n.* коро́ва. **cowboy** *n.* ковбо́й. **cowshed** *n.* хлев (*loc.* -е & -у́; *pl.* -а́).
cow[2] [kaʊ] *v.t.* запу́гивать *impf.*, запуга́ть *pf.*
coward ['kaʊəd] *n.* трус. **cowardice** *n.* трусли́вость. **cowardly** *adj.* трусли́вый.
cower ['kaʊə(r)] *v.i.* съёживаться *impf.*, съёжиться *pf.*
cowl [kaʊl] *n.* (*hood*) капюшо́н; (*of chimney*) колпа́к (-а́) дымово́й трубы́.
cowslip ['kaʊslɪp] *n.* первоцве́т.
cox(swain) ['kɒkswein, -s(ə)n] *n.* рулево́й *m.*
coxcomb ['kɒkskəʊm] *n.* фат.
coy [kɔɪ] *adj.* скро́мный (-мен, -мна́, -мно).
CPSU *abbr.* (*of* ***Communist Party of the Soviet Union***) КПСС, Коммунисти́ческая па́ртия Сове́тского Сою́за.
crab [kræb] *n.* краб; **catch a** ~ пойма́ть *pf.* леща́.
crab-apple [kræb] *n.* (*fruit*) ди́кое я́блоко (*pl.* -ки, -к); (*tree*) ди́кая я́блоня.
crack [kræk] *n.* тре́щина; треск; уда́р; *adj.* первокла́ссный, великоле́пный; *v.t.* (*break*) коло́ть (-лю́, -лешь) *impf.*, рас~ *pf.*; *v.i.* (*sound*) тре́снуть *pf.*
cracker ['krækə(r)] *n.* (*Christmas* ~) хлопу́шка; (*firework*) фе́йерверк. **crackle** *v.i.* потре́скивать *impf.*; хрусте́ть (-щу́, -сти́шь) *impf.*; *n.* потре́скивание, хруст (-а(у)). **crackpot** *n.* поме́шанный *sb.*
cradle ['kreɪd(ə)l] *n.* колыбе́ль, лю́лька; *v.t.* убаю́кивать *impf.*
craft [krɑ:ft] *n.* (*trade*) ремесло́ (*pl.* -ёсла, -ёсел, -ёслам); (*boat*) су́дно (*pl.* суда́, -до́в).

craftiness *n.* хи́трость, лука́вство. **craftsman** *n.* реме́сленник.

crafty *adj.* хи́трый (-тёр, -тра́, хи́тро́), кова́рный.

crag [kræg] *n.* утёс. **craggy** *adj.* скали́стый.

cram [kræm] *v.t.* набива́ть *impf.*, наби́ть (набью́, -ьёшь) *pf.*; впи́хивать *impf.*, впихну́ть *pf.*; пи́чкать *impf.*, на~ *pf.*; (*coach*)ната́скивать *impf.*, натаска́ть *pf.* **crammed** *adj.* битко́м наби́тый.

cramp[1] [kræmp] *n.* (*med.*) су́дорога.

cramp[2] [kræmp] *n.* зажи́м, скоба́ (*pl.* -бы, -б, -ба́м); *v.t.* стесня́ть *impf.*, стесни́ть *pf.*; ограни́чивать *impf.*, ограни́чить *pf.* **cramped** *adj.* сти́снутый; ограни́ченный (-ен, -енна).

cranberry ['krænbərɪ] *n.* клю́ква.

crane [kreɪn] *n.* (*bird*) жура́вль (-ля́) *m.*; (*machine*) кран; *v.t.* (& *i.*) вытя́гивать *impf.*, вы́тянуть *pf.* (ше́ю).

cranium ['kreɪnɪəm] *n.* че́реп (*pl.* -а́).

crank[1] [kræŋk] *n.* кривоши́п, заводна́я ру́чка; *v.t.* заводи́ть (-ожу́, -о́дишь) *impf.*, завести́ (-еду́, -едёшь; -ёл, -ела́) *pf.*

crank[2] [kræŋk] *n.* (*eccentric*) чуда́к (-а́).

crankshaft ['kræŋkʃɑːft] *n.* коле́нчатый вал (*loc.* -у́; *pl.* -ы́).

cranky *adj.* чуда́ческий; эксцентри́чный.

cranny ['krænɪ] *n.* щель (*loc.* ще́ли́; *pl.* ще́ли, щеле́й).

crape [kreɪp] *n.* креп; (*mourning*) тра́ур.

crash [kræʃ] *n.* (*noise*) гро́хот, треск; (*accident*) круше́ние, ава́рия; (*financial*) крах, банкро́тство; ~ **helmet** защи́тный шлем; ~ **landing** вы́нужденная поса́дка; *v.i.* ру́шиться *impf.* с тре́ском; разбива́ться *impf.*, разби́ться (разобью́сь, -ьёшься) *pf.*

crass [kræs] *adj.* по́лный (-лон, -лна́, по́лно́), соверше́нный (-нен, -нна).

crate [kreɪt] *n.* упако́вочный я́щик.

crater ['kreɪtə(r)] *n.* кра́тер, жерло́ (*pl.* -ла).

crave [kreɪv] *v.t.* стра́стно жела́ть *impf.*+*g.*; ~ **for** жа́ждать (-ду, -дешь) *impf.*+*g.* **craving** *n.* стра́стное жела́ние.

craven ['kreɪv(ə)n] *adj.* трусли́вый, малоду́шный.

crawl [krɔːl] *v.i.* по́лзать *indet.*, ползти́ (-зу́, -зёшь; -з, -зла́) *det.*; тащи́ться (-щу́сь, -щишься) *impf.*; *n.* полза́ние; ме́дленный ход (-а(у)); (*sport*) кроль *m.*

crayfish ['kreɪfɪʃ] *n.* речно́й рак.

crayon ['kreɪən, -ɒn] *n.* цветно́й мело́к (-лка́), цветно́й каранда́ш (-а́); (*drawing*) пасте́ль; *v.t.* рисова́ть *impf.*, на~ *pf.* цветны́м мелко́м, карандашо́м.

craze [kreɪz] *n.* ма́ния. **crazy** *adj.* поме́шанный (-ан).

creak [kriːk] *n.* скрип; *v.i.* скрипе́ть (-плю́, -пи́шь) *impf.* **creaking, creaky** *adj.* скрипу́чий.

cream [kriːm] *n.* сли́вки (-вок) *pl.*, крем; ~ **cheese** сли́вочный сыр (-а(у)); **sour** ~ смета́на; *v.t.* сбива́ть *impf.*, сбить (собью́, -ьёшь) *pf.* **creamed** *adj.* взби́тый, стёртый. **creamy** *adj.* сли́вочный, кре́мовый, густо́й.

crease [kriːs] *n.* мя́тая скла́дка; *v.t.* мять (мну, мнёшь) *impf.*, из~ (изомну́, -нёшь), с~ (сомну́, -нёшь) *pf.* **creased** *adj.* мя́тый.

create [kriː'eɪt] *v.t.* создава́ть (-даю́, -даёшь) *impf.*, созда́ть (-а́м, -а́шь, -а́ст, -ади́м; со́здал, -а́, -о) *pf.*; твори́ть *impf.*, со~ *pf.* **creation** *n.* творе́ние; созда́ние. **creative** *adj.* тво́рческий, созда́тельный; *n.* творе́ц (-рца́), созда́тель *m.* **creature** ['kriːtʃə(r)] *n.* существо́; созда́ние; тварь.

crêche [kreʃ, kreɪʃ] *n.* (де́тские) я́сли (-лей) *pl.*

credence ['kriːd(ə)ns] *n.* дове́рие; **letter of** ~ рекоменда́тельное письмо́ (*pl.* -сьма, -сем, -сьмам); **give** ~ ве́рить *impf.* (**to** +*d.*). **credentials** [krɪ'denʃ(ə)lz] *n.* манда́т; удостовере́ние ли́чности; вери́тельные гра́моты *f.pl.* **credibility** [ˌkredɪ'bɪlɪtɪ] *n.* правдоподо́бие. '**credible** *adj.* заслу́живающий дове́рия. '**credibly** *adv.* достове́рно.

credit ['kredɪt] *n.* дове́рие; креди́т; прихо́д; ~ **card** креди́тная ка́рточка, креди́тка; *v.t.*: ~ **with** припи́сывать *impf.*, приписа́ть (-ишу́, -и́шешь) *pf.*+*d.*; **give** ~ кредитова́ть *impf.* & *pf.*+*a.*; отдава́ть (-даю́, -даёшь) *impf.*, отда́ть (-а́м, -а́шь, -а́ст, -ади́м; о́тдал, -а́, -о) *pf.* до́лжное+*d.*; **it is to your** ~ э́то вам де́лает честь. **creditable** *adj.* де́лающий честь. **creditor** *n.* кредито́р. **creditworthy** *adj.* кредитоспосо́бный.

credulity [krɪ'djuːlɪtɪ] *n.* легкове́рие. '**credulous** *adj.* легкове́рный.

creed [kriːd] *n.* убежде́ние; (*eccl.*) вероиспове́дание.

creep [kriːp] *v.i.* по́лзать *indet.*, ползти́ (-зу́, -зёшь; -з, -зла́) *det.*; кра́сться (-аду́сь, -адёшься; -а́лся) *impf.* **creeper** *n.* (*plant*) ползу́чее расте́ние. **creeping** *adj.* ползу́чий; ~ **paralysis** прогресси́вный парали́ч (-а́).

cremate [krɪ'meɪt] *v.t.* креми́ровать *impf.* & *pf.* **cremation** *n.* крема́ция. **crematorium** [ˌkremə'tɔːrɪəm] *n.* кремато́рий.

Creole ['kriːəʊl] *n.* крео́л, ~ка.

crêpe [kreɪp] *n.* креп; ~ **de Chine** крепдеши́н.

crescendo [krɪ'ʃendəʊ] *adv.*, *adj.* & *n.* креще́ндо *indecl.*

crescent ['krez(ə)nt, 'kres-] *n.* полуме́сяц; *adj.* серпови́дный.

cress [kres] *n.* кресс(-сала́т).

crest [krest] *n.* гре́бень (-бня) *m.*; верши́на. **crestfallen** *adj.* удручённый (-ён, -ённа).

cretin ['kretɪn] *n.* крети́н.

cretonne [kre'tɒn, 'kre-] *n.* крето́н.

crevasse [krə'væs], **crevice** ['krevɪs] *n.* расще́лина, рассе́лина.

crew [kruː] *n.* брига́да; (*of ship*) экипа́ж, кома́нда.

crib [krɪb] *n.* (*bed*) де́тская крова́тка; (*in school*) шпарга́лка; *v.i.* спи́сывать *impf.*, списа́ть (-ишу́, -и́шешь) *pf.* (**from** с+*g.*).

crick [krɪk] *n.* растяже́ние мышц.

cricket[1] ['krɪkɪt] *n.* (*sport*) кри́кет; ~ **bat** бита́.

cricket² ['krɪkɪt] *n.* (*insect*) сверчо́к (-чка́).
crier ['kraɪə(r)] *n.* глаша́тай.
crime [kraɪm] *n.* преступле́ние.
Crimea [kraɪ'mɪə] *n.* Крым.
criminal ['krɪmɪn(ə)l] *n.* престу́пник; *adj.* престу́пный, уголо́вный.
crimp [krɪmp] *v.t.* ме́лко завива́ть *impf.*, зави́ть (-вью́, -вьёшь; зави́л, -а́, -о) *pf.*
crimson ['krɪmz(ə)n] *adj.* мали́новый, кармази́нный.
cringe [krɪndʒ] *v.i.* (*cower*) съёживаться *impf.*, съёжиться *pf.*; (*of behaviour*) раболе́пствовать *impf.* **cringing** *adj.* подобостра́стный.
crinkle ['krɪŋk(ə)l] *n.* морщи́на.
crinoline ['krɪnəlɪn] *n.* кринoли́н.
cripple ['krɪp(ə)l] *n.* кале́ка *c.g.*; *v.t.* кале́чить *impf.*, ис~ *pf.*; (*fig.*) наноси́ть (-ошу́, -о́сишь) *impf.*, нанести́ (нанесу́, -сёшь; нанёс, -ла́) вред, поврежде́ние, +*d.*
crisis ['kraɪsɪs] *n.* кри́зис.
crisp [krɪsp] *adj.* (*brittle*) хрустя́щий; (*fresh*) све́жий (свеж, -а́, -о́, све́жи́); (*abrupt*) ре́зкий (-зок, -зка́, -зко); *n.*: *pl.* чи́псы (-сов) *pl.*
criss-cross ['krɪskrɒs] *adv.* крест-на́крест.
criterion [kraɪ'tɪərɪən] *n.* крите́рий.
critic ['krɪtɪk] *n.* кри́тик. **critical** *adj.* крити́ческий; (*dangerous*) опа́сный. **criticism** *n.* кри́тика. **criticize** *v.t.* критикова́ть *impf.* **critique** [krɪ'ti:k] *n.* кри́тика.
croak [krəʊk] *n.* ква́канье; *v.i.* ква́кать *impf.*, ква́кнуть *pf.*; хрипе́ть (-плю́, -пи́шь) *impf.*
Croat ['krəʊæt], **Croatian** [krəʊ'eɪʃ(ə)n] *n.* хорва́т, ~ка; *adj.* хорва́тский.
crochet ['krəʊʃeɪ, -ʃɪ] *n.* вяза́ние крючко́м; *v.t.* вяза́ть (вяжу́, вя́жешь) *impf.*, с~ *pf.* (крючко́м).
crock [krɒk] *n.* (*broken pottery*) гли́няный черепо́к (-пка́). **crockery** *n.* гли́няная, фая́нсовая, посу́да.
crocodile ['krɒkə,daɪl] *n.* крокоди́л.
crocus ['krəʊkəs] *n.* кро́кус.
croft [krɒft] *n.* ме́лкое хозя́йство. **crofter** *n.* ме́лкий аренда́тор.
croissant ['krwʌsɑ̃] *n.* круасса́н.
crone [krəʊn] *n.* сго́рбленная стару́ха.
crony ['krəʊnɪ] *n.* закады́чный друг (*pl.* друзья́, -зе́й, -зья́м).
crook [krʊk] *n.* (*staff*) по́сох; (*bend*) изги́б; (*swindler*) жу́лик, моше́нник; *v.t.* сгиба́ть *impf.*, согну́ть *pf.* **crooked** *adj.* криво́й (крив, -а́, -о); (*dishonest*) нече́стный. **crookedness** *n.* кривизна́; (*dishonesty*) жу́льничество.
croon [kru:n] *v.t.* & *i.* напева́ть *impf.*; мурлы́кать (-ы́чу, -ы́чешь) *impf.* **crooner** *n.* эстра́дный певе́ц (-вца́).
crop [krɒp] *n.* (*yield*) урожа́й; *pl.* культу́ры *f.pl.*; (*bird's*) зоб (*pl.* -ы́); (*haircut*) коро́ткая стри́жка; *v.t.* (*cut*) подстрига́ть *impf.*, подстри́чь (-игу́, -ижёшь; -и́г) *pf.*; ~ **up** неожи́данно возника́ть *impf.*, возни́кнуть (-к) *pf.*
croquet ['krəʊkeɪ, -kɪ] *n.* кроке́т.
cross [krɒs] *n.* крест (-а́); (*biol.*) (*action*) скре́щивание, (*result*) по́месь; *adj.* (*transverse*) попере́чный; (*angry*) серди́тый; *v.t.* пересека́ть *impf.*, пересе́чь (-еку́, -ечёшь; -е́к, -екла́) *pf.*; (*biol.*) скре́щивать *impf.*, скрести́ть *pf.*; ~ **off, out** вычёркивать *impf.*, вы́черкнуть *pf.*; ~ **o.s.** крести́ться (-ещу́сь, -е́стишься) *impf.*, пере~ *pf.*; ~ **over** переходи́ть (-ожу́, -о́дишь) *impf.*, перейти́ (-ейду́, -ейдёшь; -ешёл, -ешла́) *pf.* (че́рез)+*a.*. **crossbar** *n.* попере́чина. **crossbow** *n.* самостре́л. **cross-breed** *n.* по́месь; *v.t.* скре́щивать *impf.*, скрести́ть *pf.* **cross-country** *adj.*: ~ **race** кросс. **cross-examination** *n.* перекрёстный допро́с. **cross-examine, cross-question** *v.t.* подверга́ть *impf.*, подве́ргнуть (-г) *pf.* перекрёстному допро́су. **cross-eyed** *adj.* косогла́зый. **cross-legged** *adj.*: **sit** ~ сиде́ть (сижу́, сиди́шь) *impf.* по-туре́цки. **cross-reference** *n.* перекрёстная ссы́лка. **crossroad(s)** *n.* перекрёсток (-тка); (*fig.*) распу́тье. **cross-section** *n.* перекрёстное сече́ние. **crossways, crosswise** *adv.* крест-на́крест. **crossword (puzzle)** *n.* кроссво́рд. **crossing** *n.* (*intersection*) перекрёсток (-тка); (*foot*) перехо́д; (*transport*; *rail.*) перее́зд.
crotch [krɒtʃ] *n.* (*anat.*) проме́жность.
crotchet ['krɒtʃɪt] *n.* (*mus.*) четвертна́я но́та.
crotchety ['krɒtʃɪtɪ] *adj.* сварли́вый, приди́рчивый.
crouch [kraʊtʃ] *v.i.* пригиба́ться *impf.*, пригну́ться *pf.*
croup [kru:p] *n.* круп.
crow [krəʊ] *n.* воро́на; **as the ~ flies** по прямо́й ли́нии; *v.i.* кукаре́кать *impf.*; (*exult*) ликова́ть *impf.* **crowbar** *n.* лом (*pl.* ло́мы́, ломо́в).
crowd [kraʊd] *n.* толпа́ (*pl.* -пы); *v.i.* тесни́ться *impf.*, с~ *pf.*; ~ **into** вти́скиваться *impf.*, вти́снуться *pf.*; ~ **out** вытесня́ть *impf.*, вы́теснить *pf.* **crowded** *adj.* перепо́лненный (-ен).
crown [kraʊn] *n.* коро́на, вене́ц (-нца́); (*tooth*) коро́нка; (*head*) маку́шка; (*hat*) тулья́; (*coin*) кро́на; *v.t.* коронова́ть *impf.* & *pf.*; (*fig.*) венча́ть *impf.*, у~ *pf.*; **C~ prince** кронпри́нц.
crucial ['kru:ʃ(ə)l] *adj.* (*decisive*) реша́ющий; (*critical*) крити́ческий.
crucible ['kru:sɪb(ə)l] *n.* пла́вильный ти́гель (-гля) *m.*
crucifix ['kru:sɪfɪks], **cruci'fixion** *n.* распя́тие. **crucify** *v.t.* распина́ть *impf.*, распя́ть (-пну́, -пнёшь) *pf.*
crude [kru:d] *adj.* (*rude*) гру́бый (груб, -а́, -о); (*raw*) сыро́й (сыр, -а́, -о). **crudeness, crudity** *n.* гру́бость.
cruel ['kru:əl] *adj.* жесто́кий (-о́к, -о́ка́, -о́ко). **cruelty** *n.* жесто́кость.
cruet ['kru:ɪt] *n.* судо́к (-дка́).
cruise [kru:z] *n.* круи́з; морско́е путеше́ст-

вие; *v.i.* крейси́ровать *impf.*; **cruising speed** сре́дняя, экономи́ческая, ско́рость; **cruising taxi** свобо́дное такси́ *nt.indecl.* **cruiser** *n.* кре́йсер (*pl.* -а́ & -ы).

crumb [krʌm] *n.* кро́шка; *v.t.* обсыпа́ть *impf.*, обсы́пать (-плю, -плешь) *pf.* кро́шками.

crumble ['krʌmb(ə)l] *v.t.* кроши́ть (-ошу́, -о́шишь) *impf.*, ис~, на~, рас~ *pf.*; *v.i.* обва́ливаться *impf.*, обвали́ться (-ится) *pf.* **crumbling** *adj.* осыпа́ющийся, обва́ливающийся. **crumbly** *adj.* рассы́пчатый, кроша́щийся.

crumpet ['krʌmpɪt] *n.* сдо́бная лепёшка.

crumple ['krʌmp(ə)l] *v.t.* мять (мну, мнёшь) *impf.*, с~ (сомну́, -нёшь) *pf.*; ко́мкать *impf.*, с~ *pf.*

crunch [krʌntʃ] *n.* хруст; треск; *v.t.* грызть (-зу́, -зёшь; -з) *impf.*, раз~ *pf.*; *v.i.* хрусте́ть (-ущу́, -усти́шь) *impf.*, хру́стнуть *pf.*

crusade [kruː'seɪd] *n.* кресто́вый похо́д; (*fig.*) кампа́ния (в защи́ту+*g.*); *v.i.* боро́ться (-рю́сь, -решься) *impf.* (**for** за+*a.*). **crusader** *n.* крестоно́сец (-сца); (*fig.*) боре́ц (-рца́) (за+*a.*).

crush [krʌʃ] *n.* да́вка, толкотня́; (*infatuation*) си́льное увлече́ние; *v.t.* дави́ть (-влю́, -вишь) *impf.*, за~, раз~ *pf.*; мять (мну, мнёшь) *impf.*, с~ *pf.*; (*fig.*) подавля́ть *impf.*, подави́ть (-влю́, -вишь) *pf.* **crusher** *n.* дроби́лка. **crushing** *adj.* сокруши́тельный, уничтожа́ющий.

crust [krʌst] *n.* (*of earth*) кора́; (*bread etc.*) ко́рка.

crustacean [krʌ'steɪʃ(ə)n] *n.* ракообра́зное *sb.*

crusty ['krʌstɪ] *adj.* с твёрдой ко́ркой; (*irritable*) сварли́вый, раздражи́тельный.

crutch [krʌtʃ] *n.* косты́ль *m.*

crux [krʌks] *n.* затрудни́тельный вопро́с; ~ **of the matter** суть де́ла.

cry [kraɪ] *n.* плач; крик; **a far ~ to** далеко́ от+*g.*; *v.i.* (*weep*) пла́кать (-а́чу, -а́чешь) *impf.*; (*shout*) крича́ть (-чу́, -чи́шь) *impf.*; ~ **off** отка́зываться *impf.*, отказа́ться (-ажу́сь, -а́жешься) *pf.* (от+*g.*). **crying** *adj.* пла́чущий; вопию́щий; **it's a ~ shame** позо́рно!; жа́лко!

crypt [krɪpt] *n.* склеп. **cryptic** *adj.* зага́дочный. **cryptogram** *n.* та́йнопись.

crystal ['krɪst(ə)l] *n.* криста́лл; (*mineral*) хруста́ль (-ля́) *m.* **crystallize** *v.t.* & *i.* кристаллизова́ть(ся) *impf.* & *pf.*; *v.t.* (*fruit*) заса́харивать *impf.*, заса́харить *pf.*

cub [kʌb] *n.* детёныш (ди́кого зве́ря); **bear ~** медвежо́нок (-жо́нка; *pl.* -жа́та, -жа́т); **fox ~** лисёнок (-нка; *pl.* лися́та, -т); **lion ~** львёнок (-нка; *pl.* львя́та, -т); **wolf ~** волчёнок (-нка; *pl.* волча́та, -т).

cubby-hole ['kʌbɪ-] *n.* чула́н.

cube [kjuːb] *n.* куб. **cubic** *adj.* куби́ческий.

cubicle ['kjuːbɪk(ə)l] *n.* каби́на; бокс.

cuckoo ['kʊkuː] *n.* (*bird*) куку́шка; (*fool*) глупе́ц (-пца́); *v.i.* кукова́ть *impf.*, про~ *pf.*

cucumber ['kjuːkʌmbə(r)] *n.* огуре́ц (-рца́).

cud [kʌd] *n.* жва́чка.

cuddle ['kʌd(ə)l] *v.t.* обнима́ть *impf.*, обня́ть (обниму́, -мешь; о́бнял, -а́, -о) *pf.*; *v.i.* обнима́ться *impf.*, обня́ться (обниму́сь, -мешься; обня́лся́, -ла́сь) *pf.*

cudgel ['kʌdʒ(ə)l] *n.* дуби́на, дуби́нка.

cue[1] [kjuː] *n.* (*theatr.*) ре́плика.

cue[2] [kjuː] *n.* (*billiards*) кий (кия́; *pl.* кии́).

cuff[1] [kʌf] *n.* манже́та, обшла́г (-а́; *pl.* -а́); **off the ~** экспро́мтом.

cuff[2] [kʌf] *v.t.* (*hit*) дава́ть (даю́, даёшь) *impf.*, дать (дам, дашь, даст, дади́м; дал, -а́, да́ло́, -и) *pf.* пощёчину+*d.*

cuff-link ['kʌflɪnk] *n.* за́понка.

cul-de-sac ['kʌldəˌsæk, 'kʊl-] *n.* тупи́к (-а́).

culinary ['kʌlɪnərɪ] *adj.* кулина́рный.

cull [kʌl] *v.t.* отбира́ть *impf.*, отобра́ть (отберу́, -рёшь; отобра́л, -а́, -о) *pf.*

culminate ['kʌlmɪˌneɪt] *v.i.* достига́ть *impf.*, дости́чь & дости́гнуть (-и́гну, -и́гнешь; -и́г) *pf.* вы́сшей то́чки. **culmi'nation** *n.* кульминацио́нный пункт.

culottes [kjuː'lɒts] *n.* ю́бка-брю́ки.

culpability [ˌkʌlpə'bɪlɪtɪ] *n.* вино́вность. **'culpable** *adj.* вино́вный. **'culprit** *n.* вино́вный *sb.*

cult [kʌlt] *n.* культ; ~ **of personality** культ ли́чности.

cultivate ['kʌltɪˌveɪt] *v.t.* (*land*) обраба́тывать *impf.*, обрабо́тать *pf.*; (*crops*; *fig.*) культиви́ровать *impf.*; (*develop*) развива́ть *impf.*, разви́ть (разовью́, -ьёшь; разви́л, -а́, -о) *pf.* **cultivated** *adj.* (*land*) обрабо́танный (-ан); (*plants*) вы́ращенный (-ен); (*person*) культу́рный; ~ **crop** пропашна́я культу́ра. **culti'vation** *n.* обрабо́тка, возде́лывание; культива́ция; выра́щивание; **area under ~** посевна́я пло́щадь. **cultivator** *n.* культива́тор.

cultural ['kʌltʃər(ə)l] *adj.* культу́рный. **culture** *n.* культу́ра; (*of land*) возде́лывание; (*of animals*) разведе́ние; (*of bacteria*) выра́щивание. **cultured** *adj.* культу́рный; развито́й (ра́звит, -а́, -о); ~ **pearls** культиви́рованный же́мчуг (-а(у); *pl.* -а́).

culvert ['kʌlvət] *n.* водопропускна́я труба́ (*pl.* -бы).

cumbersome ['kʌmbəsəm] *adj.* обремени́тельный; громо́здкий.

cumulative ['kjuːmjʊlətɪv] *adj.* постепе́нно увели́чивающийся. **cumulus** ['kjuːmjʊləs] *n.* кучевы́е облака́ (-ко́в) *pl.*

cuneiform ['kjuːnɪˌfɔːm] *adj.* клинообра́зный; *n.* кли́нопись.

cunning ['kʌnɪŋ] *n.* хи́трость, лука́вство; *adj.* хи́трый (-тёр, -тра́, хи́тро́), лука́вый.

cup [kʌp] *n.* ча́шка, ча́ша; (*prize*) ку́бок (-бка).

cupboard ['kʌbəd] *n.* шкаф (*loc.* -у́; *pl.* -ы́).

Cupid ['kjuːpɪd] *n.* Купидо́н.

cupidity [kjuː'pɪdɪtɪ] *n.* а́лчность.

cupola ['kjuːpələ] *n.* ку́пол (*pl.* -а́).

cur [kɜ:(r)] *n.* (*dog*) дворня́жка; (*person*) гру́бый, ни́зкий, челове́к.
curable ['kjʊərəb(ə)l] *adj.* излечи́мый.
curate ['kjʊərət] *n.* свяще́нник (мла́дшего са́на).
curative ['kjʊərətɪv] *adj.* целе́бный.
curator [kjʊə'reɪtə(r)] храни́тель *m.* музе́я.
curb [kɜ:b] *v.t.* обу́здывать *impf.*, обузда́ть *pf.*; *n.* (*check*) обузда́ние, узда́ (*pl.* -ды); (*kerb*) край (*loc.* краю́; *pl.* края́) тротуа́ра.
curd [kɜ:d] (*cheese*) *n.* тво́ро́г (тво́рога́(у́)) **curdle** *v.t.* & *i.* свёртывать(ся) *impf.*, сверну́ть(ся) *pf.*; *v.t.* (*blood*) леденить *impf.*, о~ *pf.*
cure ['kjʊə(r)] *n.* (*treatment*) лече́ние; (*means*) сре́дство (**for** про́тив+*g.*); *v.t.* (*person*) выле́чивать *impf.*, вы́лечить *pf.*; (*smoke*) копти́ть *impf.*, за~ *pf.*; (*salt*) соли́ть (солю́, со́ли́шь) *impf.*, по~ *pf.*
curfew ['kɜ:fju:] *n.* коменда́нтский час.
curing ['kjʊərɪŋ] *n.* лече́ние; (*cul.*) копче́ние, соле́ние.
curio ['kjʊərɪəʊ] *n.* ре́дкая антиква́рная вещь (*pl.* -щи, -ще́й).
curiosity [ˌkjʊərɪ'ɒsɪtɪ] *n.* любопы́тство. '**curious** *adj.* любопы́тный.
curl [kɜ:l] *n.* (*hair*) ло́кон; (*spiral*; *hair*) завито́к (-тка́); *v.t.* завива́ть *impf.*, зави́ть (-вью́, -вьёшь; зави́л, -а́, -о) *pf.*; крути́ть (-учу́, -у́тишь) *impf.*, за~ *pf.*
curlew ['kɜ:lju:] *n.* кро́ншнеп.
curling ['kɜ:lɪŋ] *n.* кэ́рлинг.
curly ['kɜ:lɪ] *adj.* вью́щийся; кудря́вый. **curly-haired, curly-headed** *adj.* курча́вый.
curmudgeon [kə'mʌdʒ(ə)n] *n.* скря́га *c.g.*
currants ['kʌrəntz] *n.* (*collect.*) кори́нка.
currency ['kʌrənsɪ] *n.* валю́та; (*prevalence*) распространённость. **current** *adj.* теку́щий; *n.* тече́ние; (*air*) струя́ (*pl.* -у́и); (*water*; *elec.*) ток (-а(у)).
curriculum [kə'rɪkjʊləm] *n.* курс обуче́ния. **curriculum vitae** *n.* кра́ткое жизнеописа́ние, биогра́фия.
curry[1] ['kʌrɪ] *n.* кэ́рри *nt.indecl.*
curry[2] ['kʌrɪ] *v.t.*: ~ **favour with** заи́скивать *impf.* пе́ред+*i.*, у+*g.*
curse [kɜ:s] *n.* прокля́тие, руга́тельство; *v.t.* проклина́ть *impf.*, прокля́сть (-яну́, -янёшь; про́клял, -а́, -о) *pf.*; *v.i.* руга́ться *impf.*, по~ *pf.* **cursed** *adj.* прокля́тый, окая́нный.
cursive ['kɜ:sɪv] *n.* ско́ропись; *adj.* скоропи́сный.
cursory ['kɜ:sərɪ] *adj.* бе́глый; пове́рхностный.
curt [kɜ:t] *adj.* кра́ткий (-ток, -тка́, -тко); ре́зкий (-зок, -зка́, -зко).
curtail [kɜ:'teɪl] *v.t.* сокраща́ть *impf.*, сократи́ть (-ащу́, -ати́шь) *pf.* **curtailment** *n.* сокраще́ние.
curtain ['kɜ:t(ə)n] *n.* за́навес; занаве́ска. **curtain-call** *n.* вы́зов актёра; *v.t.* занаве́шивать *impf.*, занаве́сить *pf.*
curts(e)y ['kɜ:tsɪ] *n.*ревера́нс.
curvature ['kɜ:vətʃə(r)] *n.* кривизна́; искривле́ние. **curve** [kɜ:v] *n.* изги́б; (*math. etc.*) крива́я *sb.*; *v.t.* гнуть *impf.*, со~ *pf.*; *v.i.* изгиба́ться *impf.*, изогну́ться *pf.* **curvilinear** [ˌkɜ:vɪ'lɪnɪə(r)] *adj.* криволине́йный.
cushion ['kʊʃ(ə)n] *n.* поду́шка; *v.t.* смягча́ть *impf.*, смягчи́ть *pf.*
cusp [kʌsp] *n.* о́стрый вы́ступ; (*geom.*) то́чка пересе́чения двух кривы́х.
custard ['kʌstəd] *n.* сла́дкий заварно́й крем, со́ус.
custodian [kʌ'stəʊdɪən] *n.* храни́тель *m.*; сто́рож (*pl.* -а́). **custody** ['kʌstədɪ] *n.* опе́ка; хране́ние; (*of police*) аре́ст; **to be in** ~ находи́ться (нахожу́сь, -о́дишься) *impf.* под стра́жей, аре́стом; **to take into** ~ аресто-ва́ть *pf.*
custom ['kʌstəm] *n.* обы́чай; привы́чка; (*customers*) клиенту́ра; *pl.* (*duty*) тамо́женные по́шлины *f.pl.*; **to go through the** ~ проходи́ть (-ожу́, -о́дишь) *impf.*, пройти́ (пройду́, пройдёшь; прошёл, -шла́) *pf.* тамо́женный осмо́тр. **customary** *adj.* обы́чный, привы́чный. **customer** *n.* клие́нт; покупа́тель *m.*; зака́зчик. **custom-house** *n.* тамо́жня.
cut [kʌt] *v.t.* ре́зать (ре́жу, -жешь) *impf.*, по~ *pf.*; (*hair*) стричь (-игу́, -ижёшь; -и́г) *impf.*, о~ *pf.*; (*hay*) коси́ть (кошу́, ко́сишь) *impf.*, с~ *pf.*; (*price*) снижа́ть *impf.*, сни́зить *pf.*; (*cards*) снима́ть *impf.*, снять (сниму́, -мешь; снял, -а́, -о) *pf.* коло́ду; ~ **down** сруба́ть *impf.*, сруби́ть (-блю́, -бишь) *pf.* ~ **off** отреза́ть *impf.*, отре́зать (-е́жу, -е́жешь) *pf.*; (*interrupt*) прерыва́ть *impf.*, прерва́ть (-ву́, -вёшь; -ва́л, -вала́, -ва́ло) *pf.*; ~ **out** выре́зывать *impf.*, вы́резать (-ежу, -ежешь) *pf.*; крои́ть *impf.*, вы́~, с~ *pf.*; ~ **up** разреза́ть *impf.*, разре́зать (-е́жу, -е́жешь) *pf.*; *n.* поре́з, разре́з; покро́й; сниже́ние; *adj.* разре́занный (-ан); (*glass etc.*) гранёный; ~ **out** скро́енный (-ен); ~ **rate** сни́женная цена́ (*a.* -ну); ~ **up** огорчённый (-ён, -ена́)
cute [kju:t] *adj.* симпати́чный.
cuticle ['kju:tɪk(ə)l] *n.* ко́жица.
cutlass ['kʌtləs] *n.* абορда́жная са́бля (*g.pl.* -бель).
cutler ['kʌtlə(r)] *n.* ножо́вщик. **cutlery** *n.* ножевы́е изде́лия *nt.pl.*; ножи́, ви́лки и ло́жки *pl.*
cutlet ['kʌtlɪt] *n.* отбивна́я котле́та.
cut-out ['kʌtaʊt] *n.* (*switch*) предохрани́тель *m.*, выключа́тель *m.*; (*figure*) вы́резанная фигу́ра.
cutter ['kʌtə(r)] *n.* (*tailor*) закро́йщик, -ица; (*naut.*) ка́тер (*pl.* -а́).
cutthroat ['kʌtθrəʊt] *n.* головоре́з; *adj.* ожесточённый (-ён, -ённа).
cutting ['kʌtɪŋ] *n.* ре́зание; разреза́ние; (*press*) вы́резка; (*from plant*) черено́к (-нка́); (*rail.*) вы́емка; *adj.* ре́жущий; прони́зывающий; ре́зкий (-зок, -зка́, -зко).
cuttlefish ['kʌt(ə)lfɪʃ] *n.* карака́тица.

c.v. *abbr.* (*of* **curriculum vitae**) кра́ткое жизнеописа́ние, биогра́фия.
cwt ['hʌndrəd,weɪt] *abbr.* (*of* ***hundredweight***) (*Imperial — approx. 50.8 kg*) англи́йский це́нтнер; (*US — approx. 45.4 kg*) америка́нский це́нтнер.
cyanide ['saɪə,naɪd] *n.* циани́д.
cybernetics [,saɪbə'netɪks] *n.* киберне́тика.
cyclamen ['sɪkləmən] *n.* цикламе́н.
cycle ['saɪk(ə)l] *n.* цикл; (*elec.*) герц (*g.pl.* -ц); (*bicycle*) велосипе́д; *v.i.* е́здить *impf.* на велосипе́де. **cyclic(al)** ['saɪklɪk(ə)l, 'sɪk-] *adj.* цикли́ческий. **cycling** *n.* езда́ на велосипе́де; велоспо́рт. **cyclist** *n.* велосипеди́ст.
cyclone ['saɪkləʊn] *n.* цикло́н.
cyclotron ['saɪklə,trɒn] *n.* циклотро́н.
cygnet ['sɪgnɪt] *n.* лебедёнок (-нка; *pl.* лебедя́та, -т).
cylinder ['sɪlɪndə(r)] *n.* цили́ндр. **cy'lindrical** *adj.* цилиндри́ческий.
cymbals ['sɪmb(ə)lz] *n.* таре́лки *f.pl.*
cynic ['sɪnɪk] *n.* ци́ник. **cynical** *adj.* цини́чный. **cynicism** *n.* цини́зм.
cynosure ['saɪnə,zjʊə(r), 'sɪn-] *n.* центр внима́ния.
cypress ['saɪprəs] *n.* кипари́с.
Cypriot ['sɪprɪət] *n.* киприо́т, ~ка; **Greek (Turkish)** ~ киприо́т, ~ка, гре́ческого (туре́цкого) происхожде́ния.
Cyprus ['saɪprəs] *n.* Кипр.
Cyrillic [sɪ'rɪlɪk] *n.* кири́ллица.
cyst [sɪst] *n.* киста́.
czar, czarina *see* **tsar, tsarina**
Czech [tʃek] *n.* чех, че́шка; *adj.* че́шкий; ~ **Republic** Че́шская Респу́блика.

D

D [di:] *n.* (*mus.*) ре *nt.indecl.*
dab¹ [dæb] *n.* лёгкое каса́ние; мазо́к (-зка́); *v.t.* легко́ прикаса́ться *impf.*, прикосну́ться *pf.* к+*d.*; ~ **on** накла́дывать *impf.*, наложи́ть (-жу́, -жишь) *pf.* мазка́ми.
dab² [dæb] *adj.*: **be a ~ hand at** соба́ку съесть (-ем, -ешь, -ест, -еди́м; -ел) *pf.* на+*p.*
dabble ['dæb(ə)l] *v.i.* плеска́ться (-ещу́сь, -е́щешься) *impf.*; ~ **in** пове́рхностно, полюби́тельски, занима́ться *impf.*, заня́ться (займу́сь, -мёшься; -я́лся, -яла́сь) *pf.+i.* **dabbler** *n.* дилета́нт.
dachshund ['dækshʊnd] *n.* та́кса.
dad [dæd], **daddy** *n.* па́па. **daddy-long-legs** *n.* долгоно́жка.
dado ['deɪdəʊ] *n.* вну́тренняя пане́ль.
daffodil ['dæfədɪl] *n.* жёлтый нарци́сс.
daft [dɑ:ft] *adj.* глу́пый (глуп, -а́, -о); бессмы́сленный (-ен, -енна).
dagger ['dægə(r)] *n.* кинжа́л.
dahlia ['deɪlɪə] *n.* георги́н.
daily ['deɪlɪ] *adv.* ежедне́вно; *adj.* ежедне́вный, повседне́вный; ~ **bread** хлеб насу́щный; ~ **dozen** заря́дка; *n.* (*charwoman*) приходя́щая домрабо́тница; (*newspaper*) ежедне́вная газе́та.
daintiness ['deɪntɪnɪs] *n.* изя́щество. **dainty** *adj.* изя́щный; изы́сканный (-ан, -анна).
dairy ['deərɪ] *n.* маслобо́йня; (*shop*) моло́чная *sb.*; ~ **farm** моло́чное хозя́йство. **dairymaid** *n.* доя́рка.
dais ['deɪɪs] *n.* помо́ст.
daisy ['deɪzɪ] *n.* маргари́тка.
dale [deɪl] *n.* доли́на.
dalliance ['dælɪəns] *n.* пра́здное времяпрепровожде́ние. **dally** *v.i.* развлека́ться *impf.*, развле́чься (-еку́сь, -ечёшься; -ёкся, -екла́сь) *pf.*
Dalmation [dæl'meɪʃ(ə)n] *n.* далма́тский дог.
dam¹ [dæm] *n.* (*barrier*) плоти́на; перемы́чка; *v.t.* прегражда́ть *impf.*, прегради́ть *pf.* плоти́ной; пруди́ть (-ужу́, -у́ди́шь) *impf.*, за~ *pf.*
dam² [dæm] *n.* (*animal*) ма́тка.
damage ['dæmɪdʒ] *n.* поврежде́ние; уще́рб; *pl.* убы́тки *m.pl.*; *v.t.* поврежда́ть *impf.*, повреди́ть *pf.*; по́ртить *impf.*, ис~ *pf.*
damascene ['dæmə,si:n, ,dæmə'si:n] *v.t.* насека́ть *impf.*, насе́чь (-еку́, -ечёшь; -ёк, -екла́) *pf.* зо́лотом, серебро́м.
damask ['dæməsk] *n.* камча́тная ткань; *adj.* дама́сский; камча́тный.
damn [dæm] *v.t.* проклина́ть *impf.*, прокля́сть (-яну́, -янёшь; про́клял, -а́, -о) *pf.*; (*censure*) осужда́ть *impf.*, осуди́ть (-ужу́, -у́дишь) *pf.* **damnable** *adj.* отврати́тельный, прокля́тый. **dam'nation** *n.* прокля́тие. **damned** *adj.* прокля́тый.
damp [dæmp] *n.* сы́рость, вла́жность; *adj.* сыро́й (сыр, -а́, -о); вла́жный (-а́жен, -ажна́, -а́жно, -а́жны́); *v.t.* сма́чивать *impf.*, смочи́ть (-чу́, -чишь) *pf.*; увлажня́ть *impf.*, увлажни́ть *pf.* **dampcourse** *n.* гидроизоля́ция. **damp-proof** *adj.* влагонепроница́емый.
damson ['dæmz(ə)n] *n.* тернosли́ва.
dance [dɑ:ns] *v.i.* танцева́ть *impf.*; пляса́ть (-яшу́, -я́шешь) *impf.*, с~ *pf.*; *n.* та́нец (-нца), пля́ска; (*party*) танцева́льный ве́чер (*pl.* -а́). **dancer** *n.* танцо́р, ~ка; (*ballet*) танцо́вщик, -ица; балери́на.
dandelion ['dændɪ,laɪən] *n.* одува́нчик.
dandruff ['dændrʌf] *n.* пе́рхоть.
dandy ['dændɪ] *n.* де́нди *m.indecl.*, франт.
Dane [deɪn] *n.* датча́нин (*pl.* -а́не, -а́н), -а́нка; **Great** ~ дог. **Danish** *adj.* да́тский.
danger ['deɪndʒə(r)] *n.* опа́сность. **dangerous** *adj.* опа́сный.
dangle ['dæŋg(ə)l] *v.t.* болта́ть *impf.+i.*; *v.i.* болта́ться *impf.*; свиса́ть *impf.*

Danish ['deɪnɪʃ] *adj.* да́тский.
dank [dæŋk] *adj.* вла́жный, сыро́й.
Danube ['dænju:b] *n.* Дуна́й.
dapper ['dæpə(r)] *adj.* аккура́тный; франтова́тый.
dappled ['dæp(ə)ld] *adj.* пятни́стый. **dapple-grey** *adj.* се́рый (сер, -а́, -о) в я́блоках.
dare [deə(r)] *v.i.* сметь *impf.*, по *pf.*; отва́живаться *impf.*, отва́житься *pf.*; **I ~ say** полага́ю; *n.* вы́зов. **daredevil** *n.* сорвиголова́ *c.g.* (*pl.* -овы, -о́в, -ова́м). **daring** *n.* сме́лость; *adj.* сме́лый (смел, -а́, -о); де́рзкий (-зок, -зка́, -зко).
dark [dɑ:k] *adj.* тёмный (-мен, -мна́); **D~ Ages** ра́ннее средневеко́вье; **~ secret** вели́кая та́йна; *n.* темнота́, тьма, мрак. **darken** *v.t.* затемня́ть *impf.*, затемни́ть *pf.* **darkly** *adv.* мра́чно. **darkness** *n.* темнота́, тьма, мрак. **dark-room** *n.* тёмная ко́мната.
darling ['dɑ:klɪŋ] *n.* дорого́й *sb.*, ми́лый *sb.*; люби́мец (-мца); *adj.* дорого́й (до́рог, -а́, -о), люби́мый.
darn [dɑ:n] *v.t.* што́пать *impf.*, за~ *pf.*; *n.* зашто́панное ме́сто (*pl.* -та́). **darning** *n.* што́пка; *adj.* што́пальный; **~ thread, wool** што́пка.
dart [dɑ:t] *n.* стрела́ (*pl.* -лы); стре́лка; (*tuck*) вы́тачка; *v.t.* мета́ть (мечу́, ме́чешь) *impf.*; броса́ть *impf.*, бро́сить *pf.*; *v.i.* носи́ться (ношу́сь, но́сишься) *indet.*, нести́сь (несу́сь, -сёшься; нёсся, несла́сь) *det.*, по~ *pf.*
dash [dæʃ] *n.* (*hyphen*) тире́ *nt.indecl.*; (*admixture*) при́месь; (*rush*) рыво́к (-вка́); *v.t.* швыря́ть *impf.*, швырну́ть *pf.*; *v.i.* броса́ться *impf.*, бро́ситься *pf.*; носи́ться (ношу́сь, но́сишься) *indet.*, нести́сь (несу́сь, -сёшься; нёсся, несла́сь) *det.*, по~ *pf.*; мча́ться (мчусь, мчи́шься) *impf.* **dashboard** *n.* прибо́рная доска́ (*a.* -ску; *pl.* -ски, -со́к, -ска́м). **dashing** *adj.* лихо́й (лих, -а́, -о, ли́хи́), удало́й (уда́л, -а́, -о).
data *n.* да́нные *sb.*; фа́кты *m.pl.* **database** *n.* ба́за да́нных.
date[1] [deɪt] *n.* число́ (*pl.* -сла, -сел, -слам), да́та; (*engagement*) свида́ние; **out of ~** устаре́лый; (*overdue*) просро́ченный (-ен); **up to ~** совреме́нный (-нен, -нна); в ку́рсе де́ла; *v.t. & i.* дати́ровать(ся) *impf. & pf.*; (*make engagement*) назнача́ть *impf.*, назна́чить *pf.* свида́ние с+*i.*
date[2] [deɪt] *n.* (*fruit*) фи́ник(овая па́льма).
dative ['deɪtɪv] *adj.* (*n.*) да́тельный (паде́ж (-а́)).
daub [dɔ:b] *v.t.* ма́зать (ма́жу, -жешь) *impf.*, на~ *pf.*; малева́ть (-лю́ю, -лю́ешь) *impf.*, на~ *pf.*; *n.* плоха́я карти́на.
daughter ['dɔ:tə(r)] *n.* дочь (до́чери, *i.* -рью; *pl.* -ри, -ре́й, *i.* -рьми́). **daughter-in-law** *n.* неве́стка (*in relation to mother*), сноха́ (*pl.* -хи) (*in relation to father*).
dauntless ['dɔ:ntlɪs] *adj.* неустраши́мый.
davit ['dævɪt, 'deɪvɪt] *n.* шлюпба́лка.
dawdle ['dɔ:d(ə)l] *v.i.* безде́льничать *impf.*
dawn [dɔ:n] *n.* рассве́т; заря́ (*pl.* зо́ри, зорь, зо́рям); *v.i.* (*day*) рассвета́ть *impf.*, рассвести́ (-етёт, -ело́) *pf. impers.*; **~ (up)on** осеня́ть *impf.*, осени́ть *pf.*; **it ~ed on me** меня́ осени́ло.
day [deɪ] *n.* день (дня) *m.*; (*working ~*) рабо́чий день (дня) *m.*; (*24 hours*) су́тки (-ток) *pl.*; *pl.* (*period*) пери́од, вре́мя *nt.*; **~ after ~** изо дня́ в де́нь; **the ~ after tomorrow** послеза́втра; **all ~ long** день-денско́й; **the ~ before** накану́не; **the ~ before yesterday** позавчера́; **by ~** днём; **every other ~** че́рез день; **~ off** выходно́й день (дня) *m.*; **one ~** одна́жды; **this ~ week** че́рез неде́лю; **carry, win, the ~** оде́рживать *impf.*, одержа́ть (-жу́, -жишь) *pf.* побе́ду; **lose the ~** потерпе́ть (-плю́, -пишь) *pf.* пораже́ние. **daybreak** *n.* рассве́т. **day-dreams** *n.* мечты́ (*g.* мечта́ний) *f.pl.*, грёзы *f.pl.* **day-labourer** *n.* подёнщик, -ица. **daylight** *n.* дневно́й свет; **in broad ~** средь бе́ла дня́.
daze [deɪz] *v.t.* ошеломля́ть *impf.*, ошеломи́ть *pf.*; *n.* изумле́ние. **dazed** *adj.* изумлённый (-ён, -ена́), потрясённый (-ён, -ена́).
dazzle ['dæz(ə)l] *v.t.* ослепля́ть *impf.*, ослепи́ть *pf.* **dazzling** *adj.* блестя́щий, ослепи́тельный.
DC *abbr.* (*of* ***direct current***) постоя́нный ток.
deacon ['di:kən] *n.* дья́кон (*pl.* -а́).
dead [ded] *adj.* мёртвый (мёртв, -а, -о & (*fig.*) -о́), уме́рший; (*animals*) до́хлый; (*plants*) увя́дший; (*numb*) онеме́вший; (*lifeless*) безжи́зненный (-ен, -енна); (*sound*) глухо́й (глух, -а́, -о); (*complete*) соверше́нный (-нен, -нна); **~ to** глухо́й (глух, -а́, -о) к+*d.*; *n.*: **the ~** мёртвые *sb.*, уме́ршие *sb.*; **~ of night** глубо́кая ночь (*loc.* -чи́); *adv.* соверше́нно; **~ beat** смерте́льно уста́лый; **~ calm** (*naut.*) мёртвый штиль *m.*; **~ drunk** мертве́цки пья́ный (пьян, -а́, -о); **~ end** тупи́к (-а́); **~ heat** одновре́ме́нный фи́ниш; **~ march** похоро́нный марш; **~ reckoning** счисле́ние пути́; **~ set** мёртвая сто́йка; **~ weight** мёртвый груз.
deaden ['ded(ə)n] *v.t. & i.* притупля́ть(ся) *impf.*, притупи́ть(ся) (-плю́(сь), -пишь(ся)) *pf.*
dead-end ['dedend] *adj.* безвы́ходный. **deadline** (*time*) преде́льный срок (-а(у)). **deadlock** ['dedlɒk] *n.* тупи́к (-а́); **reach ~** зайти́ (зайду́, -дёшь; зашёл, -шла́) *pf.* в тупи́к. **deadly** ['dedlɪ] *adj.* смерте́льный, смертоно́сный; **~ nightshade** беллад́онна; **~ sin** сме́ртный грех (-а́). **dead-nettle** ['dednet(ə)l] *n.* глуха́я крапи́ва.
deaf [def] *adj.* глухо́й (глух, -а́, -о); **~ and dumb, ~ mute** глухонемо́й (*sb.*). **deafen** *v.t.* оглуша́ть *impf.*, оглуши́ть *pf.* **deafness** *n.* глухота́.
deal[1] [di:l] *n.*: **a great, good, ~** мно́го (+*g.*); (*with comp.*) гора́здо.
deal[2] [di:l] *n.* (*bargain*) сде́лка; (*cards*) сда́ча; *v.t.* (*cards*) сдава́ть (сдаю́, -аёшь) *impf.*,

сдать (-ам, -ашь, -аст, -ади́м; сдал, -а́, -о) *pf.*; (*blow*) наноси́ть (-ошу́, -о́сишь) *impf.*, нанести́ (-есу́, -есёшь; -ёс, -есла́) *pf.*; **~ in** торгова́ть *impf.+i.*; **~ out** распределя́ть *impf.*, распредели́ть *pf.*; **~ with** (*engage in*) занима́ться *impf.*, заня́ться (займу́сь, -мёшься; заня́лся́, -ла́сь) *pf.+i.*; (*behave towards*) обходи́ться (-ожу́сь, -о́дишься) *impf.*, обойти́сь (обойду́сь, -дёшься; обошёлся, -шла́сь) *pf.* с+*i.* **dealer** *n.* (*trader*) торго́вец (-вца) (**in** +*i.*).

deal³ [di:l] *n.* (*wood*) ело́вая, сосно́вая, древеси́на; *adj.* ело́вый, (*pine*) сосно́вый.

dean [di:n] *n.* (*univ.*) дека́н; (*church*) настоя́тель *m.* собо́ра. **deanery** *n.* декана́т.

dear [dɪə(r)] *adj.* дорого́й (до́рог, -а́, -о); (*also n.*) ми́лый (мил, -а́, -о, ми́лы́) (*sb.*).

dearth [dɜ:θ] *n.* недоста́ток (-тка); нехва́тка.

death [deθ] *n.* смерть (*pl.* -ти, -те́й); *adj.* сме́ртный, смерте́льный; **at ~'s door** при́ смерти; **put to ~** казни́ть *impf.* & *pf.*; **~ certificate** свиде́тельство о сме́рти; **~ duty** нало́г на насле́дство; **~ penalty** сме́ртная казнь; **~ rate** сме́ртность. **deathbed** *n.* сме́ртное ло́же. **deathblow** *n.* смерте́льный уда́р. **deathless** *adj.* бессме́ртный. **deathly** *adj.* смерте́льный. **death-roll** *n.* спи́сок (-ска́) уби́тых. **death-warrant** *n.* сме́ртный пригово́р (*also fig.*).

debar [dɪ'bɑ:(r)] *v.t.* **~ from** не допуска́ть *impf.* до+*g.*

debase [dɪ'beɪs] *v.t.* понижа́ть *impf.*, пони́зить *pf.* ка́чество+*g.*

debatable [dɪ'beɪtəb(ə)l] *adj.* спо́рный. **debate** *n.* пре́ния (-ий) *pl.*, деба́ты (-тов) *pl.*; *v.t.* обсужда́ть *impf.*, обсуди́ть (-ужу́, -у́дишь) *pf.*; дебати́ровать *impf.*

debauch [dɪ'bɔ:tʃ] *v.t.* развраща́ть *impf.*, разврати́ть (-ащу́, -ати́шь) *pf.*; *n.* о́ргия. **debauched** *adj.* развращённый (-ён, -ённа), развра́тный. **debauchery** *n.* развра́т.

debenture [dɪ'bentʃə(r)] *n.* долгово́е обяза́тельство.

debilitate [dɪ'bɪlɪˌteɪt] *v.t.* рас-, о-, слабля́ть; *impf.*, рас-, о-, сла́бить *pf.* **debility** *n.* бесси́лие, тщеду́шие.

debit ['debɪt] *n.* де́бет; **~s and credits** прихо́д и расхо́д; *v.t.* дебетова́ть *impf.* & *pf.*; запи́сывать *impf.*, записа́ть (-ишу́, -и́шешь) *pf.* в де́бет+*d.*

debouch [dɪ'baʊtʃ, -'bu:ʃ] *v.i.* (*mil.*) дебуши́ровать *impf.* & *pf.*; (*river*) впада́ть *impf.*, впасть (впадёт; впал) *pf.*

debris ['debri:, 'deɪ-] *n.* оско́лки *m.pl.*, обло́мки *m.pl.*

debt [det] *n.* долг (-а(у), *loc.* -у́; *pl.* -и́). **debtor** *n.* должни́к (-а́)

debunk [di:'bʌŋk] *v.t.* разве́нчивать *impf.*, развенча́ть *pf.*

début ['deɪbju:, -bu:] *n.* дебю́т; **make one's ~** дебюти́ровать *impf.* & *pf.* **debutante** *n.* дебюта́нтка.

deca- *in comb.* дека..., десяти... .

decade ['dekeɪd] *n.* десятиле́тие.

decadence ['dekəd(ə)ns] *n.* декаде́нтство; упа́дочничество. **decadent** *adj.* декаде́нтский; упа́дочный.

decaffeinated [di:'kæfɪˌneɪtɪd] *adj.*: **~ coffee** бескофеи́новый ко́фе.

decamp [dɪ'kæmp] *v.i.* удира́ть *impf.*, удра́ть (удеру́, -рёшь; удра́л, -а́, -о) *pf.*

decant [dɪ'kænt] *v.t.* сце́живать *impf.*, сцеди́ть (-ежу́, -е́дишь) *pf.*; (*wine*) перелива́ть *impf.*, перели́ть (-лью́, -льёшь; перели́л, -а́, -о) *pf.* (в графи́н). **decanter** *n.* графи́н.

decapitate [dɪ'kæpɪˌteɪt] *v.t.* обезгла́вливать *impf.*, обезгла́вить *pf.*

decarbonize [di:'kɑ:bəˌnaɪz] *v.t.* очища́ть *impf.*, очи́стить *pf.* от нага́ра.

decathlon [dɪ'kæθlən] *n.* десятибо́рье.

decay [dɪ'keɪ] *v.i.* гнить (-ию́, -иёшь; гнил, -а́, -о) *impf.*, с~ *pf.*; *n.* гние́ние; распа́д (*also physical*). **decayed** *adj.* прогни́вший, гнило́й (гнил, -а́, -о). **decaying** *adj.* гнию́щий.

decease [dɪ'si:s] *n.* кончи́на. **deceased** *adj.* поко́йный; *n.* поко́йный *sb.*, поко́йник, -ица.

deceit [dɪ'si:t] *n.* обма́н. **deceitful** *adj.* лжи́вый. **deceive** *v.t.* обма́нывать *impf.*, обману́ть (-ну́, -нешь) *pf.*

deceleration [di:ˌselə'reɪʃ(ə)n] *n.* замедле́ние.

December [dɪ'sembə(r)] *n.* дека́брь (-ря́) *m.*; *attr.* дека́брьский.

decency ['di:sənsɪ] *n.* прили́чие, поря́дочность. **decent** *adj.* прили́чный, поря́дочный.

decentralization [di:ˌsentrəlaɪ'zeɪʃ(ə)n] *n.* децентрализа́ция. **de'centralize** *v.t.* децентрализова́ть *impf.* & *pf.*

deception [dɪ'sepʃ(ə)n] *n.* обма́н. **deceptive** *adj.* обма́нчивый.

deci- [desɪ-] *in comb.* деци... .

decibel ['desɪˌbel] *n.* децибе́л.

decide [dɪ'saɪd] *v.t.* реша́ть *impf.*, реши́ть *pf.* **decided** *adj.* (*resolute*) реши́тельный; (*definite*) несомне́нный (-нен, -нна). **decidedly** *adv.* реши́тельно, бесспо́рно, я́вно.

deciduous [dɪ'sɪdjʊəs] *adj.* листопа́дный.

decimal ['desɪm(ə)l] *n.* десяти́чная дробь (*pl.* -би, -бе́й); *adj.* десяти́чный; **~ point** запята́я *sb.*

decimate ['desɪˌmeɪt] *v.t.* (*fig.*) коси́ть (-ит) *impf.*, с~ *pf.*

decipher [dɪ'saɪfə(r)] *v.t.* расшифро́вывать *impf.*, расшифрова́ть *pf.*

decision [dɪ'sɪʒ(ə)n] *n.* реше́ние. **decisive** [dɪ'saɪsɪv] *adj.* реша́ющий, реши́тельный.

deck [dek] *n.* па́луба; (*bus etc.*) эта́ж (-а́); *v.t.*: **~ out** украша́ть *impf.*, укра́сить *pf.* **deck-chair** *n.* шезло́нг. **deck-hand** *n.* па́лубный матро́с. **deckhouse** *n.* ру́бка.

declaim [dɪ'kleɪm] *v.t.* деклами́ровать *impf.*, про~ *pf.*

declaration [ˌdeklə'reɪʃ(ə)n] *n.* объявле́ние; (*document*) деклара́ция. **de'clare** *v.t.* за~, объ-, явля́ть *impf.*, за~, объ-, яви́ть (-влю́, -вишь) *pf.*

declassify [diːˈklæsɪˌfaɪ] *v.t.* рассекре́чивать *impf.*, рассекре́тить *pf.*

declension [dɪˈklenʃ(ə)n] *n.* склоне́ние. **decline** [dɪˈklaɪn] *n.* упа́док (-дка); (*price*) пониже́ние; *v.i.* приходи́ть (-ит) *impf.*, прийти́ (придёт; пришёл, -шла́) *pf.* в упа́док; *v.t.* (*refuse*) отклоня́ть *impf.*, отклони́ть (-ню́, -нишь) *pf.*; (*gram.*) склоня́ть *impf.*, про~ *pf.* **declining** *adj.*: ~ **years** преклóнный во́зраст.

declivity [dɪˈklɪvɪtɪ] *n.* укло́н.

decoction [dɪˈkɒkʃ(ə)n] *n.* отва́р (-а(у)).

decode [diːˈkəʊd] *v.t.* расшифро́вывать *impf.*, расшифрова́ть *pf.*

decompose [ˌdiːkəmˈpəʊz] *v.t.* разлага́ть *impf.*, разложи́ть (-жу́, -жишь) *pf.*; *v.i.* распада́ться *impf.*, распа́сться (-адётся; -а́лся) *pf.*; (*rot*) гнить (гнию́, -иёшь; гнил, -а́, -о) *impf.*, с~ *pf.*

decompress [ˌdiːkəmˈpres] *v.t.* снижа́ть *impf.*, сни́зить *pf.* давле́ние на+*a.* **decompression** [ˌdiːkəmˈpreʃ(ə)n] *n.* декомпре́ссия.

decontaminate [ˌdiːkənˈtæmɪˌneɪt] *v.t.* (*gas*) дегази́ровать *impf.* & *pf.*; (*radioactivity*) дезактиви́ровать *impf.* & *pf.*

decontrol [ˌdiːkənˈtrəʊl] *v.t.* снима́ть *impf.*, снять (сниму́, -мешь; снял, -а́, -о) *pf.* контро́ль *m.* с+*g.*

decorate [ˈdekəˌreɪt] *v.t.* украша́ть *impf.*, укра́сить *pf.*; (*with medal etc.*) награжда́ть *impf.*, награди́ть *pf.* о́рденом (-на́ми). **decoˈration** *n.* украше́ние, отде́лка; о́рден (*pl.* -а́). **decorative** *adj.* декорати́вный. **decorator** *n.* маля́р (-а́).

decorous [ˈdekərəs] *adj.* прили́чный; чи́нный (-нен, -нна́, -нно). **decorum** [dɪˈkɔːrəm] *n.* прили́чие, деко́рум; (*etiquette*) этике́т.

decoy [ˈdiːkɔɪ, dɪˈkɔɪ] *n.* (*trap*) западня́; (*bait*) прима́нка; *v.t.* за~, при~, ма́нивать *impf.*, за~, при~, мани́ть (-ню́, -нишь) *pf.*

decrease [ˈdiːkriːs] *v.t.* & *i.* уменьша́ть(ся) *impf.*, уме́ньши́ть(ся) *pf.*; *n.* уменьше́ние, пониже́ние.

decree [dɪˈkriː] *n.* ука́з, декре́т, постановле́ние; *v.t.* постановля́ть *impf.*, постанови́ть (-влю́, -вишь) *pf.*

decrepit [dɪˈkrepɪt] *adj.* дря́хлый (дряхл, -а́, -о); (*dilapidated*) ве́тхий (ветх, -а́, -о). **decrepitude** *n.* дря́хлость; ве́тхость.

dedicate [ˈdedɪˌkeɪt] *v.t.* посвяща́ть *impf.*, посвяти́ть (-ящу́, -яти́шь) *pf.* **dediˈcation** *n.* посвяще́ние.

deduce [dɪˈdjuːs] *v.t.* заключа́ть *impf.*, заключи́ть *pf.*; де́лать *impf.*, с~ *pf.* вы́вод.

deduct [dɪˈdʌkt] *v.t.* вычита́ть *impf.*, вы́честь (-чту, -чтешь; -чел, -чла) *pf.* **deduction** *n.* (*amount*) вы́чет; (*deducting*) вычита́ние; (*inference*) вы́вод.

deed [diːd] *n.* посту́пок (-пка); (*heroic*) по́двиг; (*leg.*) акт.

deem [diːm] *v.t.* счита́ть *impf.*, счесть (сочту́, -тёшь; счёл, сочла́) *pf.*+*a.* & *i.*

deep [diːp]*adj.* глубо́кий (-о́к, -ока́, -о́ко́); (*colour*) тёмный (-мен, -мна́); (*sound*) ни́зкий (-зок, -зка́, -зко, ни́зки́); *n.* мо́ре. **deepen** *v.t.* углубля́ть *impf.*, углуби́ть *pf.*; сгуща́ть *impf.*, сгусти́ть *pf.* **deep-rooted** *adj.* закорене́лый. **deep-seated** *adj.* укорени́вшийся.

deer [dɪə(r)] *n.* оле́нь *m.* **deerskin** *n.* лоси́на. **deer-stalker** *n.* охо́тничья ша́пка.

deface [dɪˈfeɪs] *v.t.* по́ртить *impf.*, ис~ *pf.*; (*erase*) стира́ть *impf.*, стере́ть (сотру́, -рёшь; стёр) *pf.* **defacement** *n.* по́рча; стира́ние.

defamation [ˌdefəˈmeɪʃ(ə)n, ˌdiːf-] *n.* диффама́ция, клевета́. **deˈfamatory** *adj.* дискредити́рующий, позо́рящий. **defame** [dɪˈfeɪm] *v.t.* поро́чить *impf.*, о~ *pf.*; позо́рить *impf.*, о~ *pf.*

default [dɪˈfɔːlt, -ˈfɒlt] *n.* невыполне́ние обяза́тельств; (*leg.*) нея́вка в суд; *v.i.* не выполня́ть *impf.* обяза́тельств.

defeat [dɪˈfiːt] *n.* пораже́ние; *v.t.* побежда́ть *impf.*, победи́ть (-и́шь) *pf.* **defeatism** *n.* пораже́нчество. **defeatist** *n.* пораже́нец (-нца).

defecate [ˈdefɪˌkeɪt] *v.i.* испражня́ться *impf.*, испражни́ться *pf.* **defeˈcation** *n.* испражне́ние.

defect [ˈdiːfekt; dɪˈfekt] *n.* дефе́кт, недоста́ток (-тка), изъя́н; *v.i.* дезерти́ровать *impf.* & *pf.* **defection** *n.* дезерти́рство. **defective** *adj.* неиспра́вный, повреждённый (-ён, -ена́); дефе́ктный, с изъя́ном. **defector** *n.* дезерти́р, невозвраще́нец (-нца).

defence [dɪˈfens] *n.* защи́та (*also leg.*, *sport*), оборо́на (*also mil.*); *pl.* (*mil.*) закрепле́ния *nt.pl.* **defenceless** *adj.* беззащи́тный. **defend** *v.t.* защища́ть *impf.*, защити́ть (-ищу́, -ити́шь) *pf.*; обороня́ть *impf.*, оборони́ть *pf.*; (*uphold*) подде́рживать *impf.*, поддержа́ть (-жу́, -жишь) *pf.* **defendant** *n.* подсуди́мый *sb.* **defender** *n.* защи́тник. **defensive** *adj.* оборони́тельный.

defer[1] [dɪˈfɜː(r)] *v.t.* (*postpone*) отсро́чивать *impf.*, отсро́чить *pf.*

defer[2] [dɪˈfɜː(r)] *v.i.*: ~ **to** подчиня́ться *impf.*+*d.* **deference** [ˈdefərəns] *n.* уваже́ние, почте́ние. **defeˈrential** *adj.* почти́тельный.

defiance [dɪˈfaɪəns] *n.* откры́тое неповинове́ние; **in ~ of** вопреки́+*d.*, напеке́р+*d.* **defiant** *adj.* вызыва́ющий, непоко́рный.

deficiency [dɪˈfɪʃənsɪ] *n.* нехва́тка, дефици́т. **deficient** *adj.* недоста́точный; (*mentally* ~) слабоу́мный. **deficit** [ˈdefɪsɪt] *n.* дефици́т, недочёт.

defile [dɪˈfaɪl] *v.t.* оскверня́ть *impf.*, оскверни́ть *pf.* **defilement** *n.* оскверне́ние, профана́ция.

define [dɪˈfaɪn] *v.t.* определя́ть *impf.*, определи́ть *pf.* **definite** [ˈdefɪnɪt] *adj.* определённый (-нен, -нна) **definitely** *adv.* несомне́нно. **defiˈnition** *n.* определе́ние. **deˈfinitive** *adj.* оконча́тельный.

deflate [dɪˈfleɪt] *v.t.* & *i.* спуска́ть *impf.*, спусти́ть (-ущу́, -у́стишь) *pf.*; *v.t.* (*person*) сбива́ть *impf.*, сбить (собью́, -ьёшь) *pf.* спесь c+*g.*; *v.i.* (*econ.*) проводи́ть (-ожу́, -о́дишь) *impf.*, провести́ (-еду́, -едёшь; -ёл, -ела́) *pf.* поли́тику дефля́ции. **deflation** *n.* дефля́ция.

deflect [dɪ'flekt] *v.t.* отклоня́ть *impf.*, отклони́ть (-ню́, -нишь) *pf.* **deflection** *n.* отклоне́ние.

defoliate [di:'fəʊlɪˌeɪt] *v.t.* уничтожа́ть *impf.*, уничто́жить *pf.* расти́тельность+*g.* **defoli'ation** *n.* дефолиа́ция.

deforest [di:'fɒrɪst] *v.t.* обезле́сивать *impf.*, обезле́сить *pf.* **deforest'ation** *n.* обезле́сение.

deform [dɪ'fɔ:m] *v.t.* уро́довать *impf.*, из~ *pf.*; деформи́ровать *impf.* & *pf.* **deformity** *n.* уро́дство.

defraud [dɪ'frɔ:d] *v.t.* обма́нывать *impf.*, обману́ть (-ну́, -нешь) *pf.*; ~ **of** выма́нивать *impf.*, вы́манить *pf.*+*a.* & у+*g.* (*of person*).

defray [dɪ'freɪ] *v.t.* опла́чивать *impf.*, оплати́ть (-ачу́, -а́тишь) *pf.*

defrost [di:'frɒst] *v.t.* размора́живать *impf.*, разморо́зить *pf.*

deft [deft] *adj.* ло́вкий (-вок, -вка́, -вко, ло́вки́).

defunct [dɪ'fʌŋkt] *adj.* усо́пший.

defy [dɪ'faɪ] *v.t.* (*challenge*) вызыва́ть *impf.*, вы́звать (вы́зову, -вешь) *pf.*; (*resist*) откры́то не повинова́ться *impf.*+*d.*

degeneracy [dɪ'dʒenərəsɪ] *n.* вырожде́ние, дегенера́ция. **degenerate** *n.* дегенера́т, вы́родок (-дка); *adj.* дегенерати́вный; *v.i.* вырожда́ться *impf.*, вы́родиться *pf.* **degenerative** *adj.* дегенерати́вный.

degradation [ˌdegrə'deɪʃ(ə)n] *n.* деграда́ция; униже́ние. **degrade** [dɪ'greɪd] *v.t.* унижа́ть *impf.*, уни́зить *pf.* **degrading** *adj.* унизи́тельный.

degree [dɪ'gri:] *n.* сте́пень (*pl.* -ни, -не́й); (*math.etc.*) гра́дус; (*univ.*) учёная сте́пень (*pl.* -ни, -не́й).

dehydrate [di:'haɪdreɪt, ˌdi:haɪ'dreɪt] *v.t.* обезво́живать *impf.*, обезво́дить *pf.* **dehy'dration** *n.* дегидрата́ция.

deify ['di:ɪˌfaɪ, 'deɪɪ-] *v.t.* обожествля́ть *impf.*, обожестви́ть *pf.*

deign [deɪn] *v.i.* соизволя́ть *impf.*, соизво́лить *pf.*

deity ['di:ɪtɪ, 'deɪɪ-] *n.* божество́.

dejected [dɪ'dʒektɪd] *adj.* удручённый (-ён, -ённа & -ена́), уны́лый. **dejection** *n.* уны́ние.

delay [dɪ'leɪ] *n.* заде́ржка; замедле́ние; **without** ~ неме́дленно; *v.t.* заде́рживать *impf.*, задержа́ть (-жу́, -жишь) *pf.*; замедля́ть *impf.*, заме́длить *pf.*

delegate ['delɪgət] *n.* делега́т; *v.t.* делеги́ровать *impf.* & *pf.* **dele'gation** *n.* делега́ция.

delete [dɪ'li:t] *v.t.* вычёркивать *impf.*, вы́черкнуть *pf.*

deliberate [dɪ'lɪbərət; dɪ'lɪbəˌreɪt] *adj.* (*intentional*) преднаме́ренный (-ен, -енна); (*unhurried*) неторопли́вый; *v.t.* & *i.* размышля́ть *impf.*, размы́слить *pf.* (о+*p.*). **delibe'ration** *n.* размышле́ние; (*discussion*) обсужде́ние, совеща́ние.

delicacy ['delɪkəsɪ] *n.* (*tact*) делика́тность; (*dainty*) ла́комство. **delicate** *adj.* то́нкий (-нок, -нка́, -нко, то́нки́); лёгкий (лёгок, -гка́, -гко́, лёгки́); (*health*) боле́зненный (-ен, -енна).

delicious [dɪ'lɪʃəs] *adj.* восхити́тельный; (*tasty*) о́чень вку́сный (-сен, -сна́, -сно).

delight [dɪ'laɪt] *n.* наслажде́ние, пре́лесть. **delightful** *adj.* преле́стный.

delimit [dɪ'lɪmɪt] *v.t.* размежёвывать *impf.*, размежева́ть (-жу́ю, -жу́ешь) *pf.* **delimi'tation** *n.* размежева́ние.

delinquency [dɪ'lɪŋkwənsɪ] *n.* правонаруше́ние, престу́пность. **delinquent** *n.* правонаруши́тель *m.*, ~ница.

delirious [dɪ'lɪrɪəs] *adj.* бредово́й; **be** ~ бре́дить *impf.* **delirium** *n.* бред (-а(у), *loc.* -у́); ~ **tremens** бе́лая горя́чка.

deliver [dɪ'lɪvə(r)] *v.t.* доставля́ть *impf.*, доста́вить *pf.*; (*rescue*) избавля́ть *impf.*, изба́вить *pf.* (**from** от+*g.*); (*lecture*) прочита́ть *impf.*, проче́сть (-чту́, -чтёшь; -чёл, -чла́) *pf.*; (*letters*) разноси́ть (-ошу́, -о́сишь) *impf.*, разнести́ (-есу́, -есёшь; -ёс, -есла́) *pf.*; (*speech*) произноси́ть (-ошу́, -о́сишь) *impf.*, произнести́ (-есу́, -есёшь; -ёс, -есла́) *pf.* **deliverance** *n.* избавле́ние, освобожде́ние. **delivery** *n.* доста́вка.

dell [del] *n.* лощи́на.

delphinium [del'fɪnɪəm] *n.* дельфи́ниум.

delta ['deltə] *n.* де́льта.

delude [dɪ'lu:d, -'lju:d] *v.t.* вводи́ть (-ожу́, -о́дишь) *impf.*, ввести́ (-еду́, -едёшь; ввёл, -а́) *pf.* в заблужде́ние.

deluge ['delju:dʒ] *n.* (*flood*) пото́п; (*rain*) ли́вень (-вня) *m.*

delusion [dɪ'lu:ʒ(ə)n, -'lju:ʒ(ə)n] *n.* заблужде́ние; ~**s of grandeur** ма́ния вели́чия.

demagogue ['deməˌgɒg] *n.* демаго́г. **dema'gogic** *adj.* демагоги́ческий. **demagogy** *n.* демаго́гия.

demand [dɪ'mɑ:nd] *n.* тре́бование; (*econ.*) спрос (**for** на+*a.*); *v.t.* тре́бовать *impf.*, по~ *pf.*+*g.*

demarcate ['di:mɑ:ˌkeɪt] *v.t.* разграни́чивать *impf.*, разграни́чить *pf.* **demar'cation** *n.* демарка́ция; **line of** ~ демаркацио́нная ли́ния.

demented [dɪ'mentɪd] *adj.* умалишённый (-ён, -ённа). **dementia** *n.* слабоу́мие.

demi- [demɪ-] *in comb.* полу... .

demigod ['demɪˌgɒd] *n.* полубо́г (*pl.* -и, -о́в).

demilitarization [di:ˌmɪlɪtəraɪ'zeɪʃ(ə)n] *n.* демилитариза́ция. **de'militarize** *v.t.* демилитаризова́ть *impf.* & *pf.*

demise [dɪ'maɪz] *n.* конч́ина.

demobbed [di:'mɒbd] *adj.* демобилизо́ванный (-ан). **demobilization** [di:ˌməʊbɪlaɪ'zeɪʃ(ə)n] *n.* демобилиза́ция. **de'mobilize** *v.t.* демобилизова́ть *impf.* & *pf.*

democracy [dɪ'mɒkrəsɪ] *n.* демокра́тия. **democrat** ['deməˌkræt] *n.* демокра́т. **democratic** *adj.* демократи́ческий, демократи́чный.

demolish [dɪ'mɒlɪʃ] *v.t.* разруша́ть *impf.*, разру́шить *pf.*; (*building*) сноси́ть (-ошу́, -о́сишь) *impf.*, снести́ (-су́, -сёшь; снёс, -ла́) *pf.*; (*refute*) опроверга́ть *impf.*, опрове́ргнуть (-ве́рг(нул), -ве́ргла) *pf.* **demo'lition** *n.* разруше́ние, снос.

demon ['diːmən] *n.* де́мон. **de'monic** *adj.* дья́вольский, демони́ческий.

demonstrable ['demɒnstrəb(ə)l, dɪ'mɒnstrəb(ə)l] *adj.* доказу́емый. **demonstrably** *adv.* очеви́дно, нагля́дно. **demonstrate** *v.t.* демонстри́ровать *impf.* & *pf.*; *v.i.* уча́ствовать *impf.* в демонстра́ции. **demon'stration** *n.* демонстра́ция, пока́з. **de'monstrative** *adj.* (*behaviour etc.*) экспанси́вный, несде́ржанный (-ан, -анна); (*gram.*) указа́тельный. **demonstrator** *n.* (*laboratory*) демонстра́тор; (*pol.*) демонстра́нт.

demoralization [dɪˌmɒrəlaɪ'zeɪʃ(ə)n] *n.* деморализа́ция. **de'moralize** *v.t.* деморализова́ть *impf.* & *pf.*

demote [dɪ'məʊt, diː-] *v.t.* понижа́ть *impf.*, пони́зить *pf.* в до́лжности; (*mil.*) разжа́ловать *pf.* **demotion** *n.* пониже́ние.

demur [dɪ'mɜː(r)] *v.i.* возража́ть *impf.*, возрази́ть *pf.* (**at, to** про́тив+*g.*); *n.*: **without** ~ без возраже́ний.

demure [dɪ'mjʊə(r)] *adj.* (притво́рно) скро́мный (-мен, -мна́, -мно).

den [den] *n.* (*animal's*) ло́гово, берло́га; (*thieves' etc.*) прито́н.

denial [dɪ'naɪəl] *n.* отрица́ние, опроверже́ние; (*refusal*) отка́з.

denigrate ['denɪˌgreɪt] *v.t.* черни́ть *impf.*, о~ *pf.*

denim ['denɪm] *adj.* джинсо́вый.

Denmark ['denmɑːk] *n.* Да́ния.

denomination [dɪˌnɒmɪ'neɪʃ(ə)n] *n.* (*name*) назва́ние; (*category*) катего́рия; (*relig.*) вероисповеда́ние. **de'nominator** *n.* знамена́тель *m.*

denote [dɪ'nəʊt] *v.t.* означа́ть *impf.*, озна́чить *pf.*

dénouement [deɪ'nuːmɑ̃] *n.* развя́зка.

denounce [dɪ'naʊns] *v.t.* (*accuse*) облича́ть *impf.*, обличи́ть *pf.*; (*inform on*) доноси́ть (-ошу́, -о́сишь) *impf.*, донести́ (-есу́, -есёшь; -ёс, -есла́) *pf.* на+*a.*; (*treaty*) денонси́ровать *impf.* & *pf.*

dense [dens] *adj.* (*thick*) густо́й (густ, -а́, -о, гу́сты́); (*stupid*) тупо́й (туп, -а́, -о, ту́пы́). **density** *n.* (*phys. etc.*) пло́тность.

dent [dent] *n.* вы́боина, вмя́тина; *v.t.* вмина́ть *impf.*, вмять (вомну́, -нёшь) *pf.*

dental ['dent(ə)l] *adj.* зубно́й. **dentifrice** ['dentɪfrɪs] *n.* (*paste*) зубна́я па́ста; (*powder*) зубно́й порошо́к (-шка́). **dentist** *n.* зубно́й врач (-а́). **dentistry** *n.* зубоврачева́ние. **denture** *n.* зубно́й проте́з.

denunciation [dɪˌnʌnsɪ'eɪʃ(ə)n] *n.* (*accusation*) обличе́ние; (*informing*) доно́с; (*treaty*) денонса́ция.

deny [dɪ'naɪ] *v.t.* отрица́ть *impf.*; ~ **o.s.** отка́зывать *impf.*, отказа́ть (-ажу́, -а́жешь) *pf.* себе́ в+*p.*

deodorant [diː'əʊdərənt] *n.* дезодора́тор.

depart [dɪ'pɑːt] *v.i.* отбыва́ть *impf.*, отбы́ть (отбу́ду, -дешь; о́тбы́л, -а́, -о) *pf.*; ~ **from** отклоня́ться *impf.*, отклони́ться (-ню́сь, -нишься) *pf.* от+*g.*

department [dɪ'pɑːtmənt] *n.* отде́л; (*government*) департа́мент, ве́домство; (*univ.*) факульте́т, ка́федра; ~ **store** универма́г. **depart'mental** *adj.* ве́домственный.

departure [dɪ'pɑːtʃə(r)] *n.* отбы́тие; отклоне́ние.

depend [dɪ'pend] *v.i.* зави́сеть (-и́шу, -и́сишь) *impf.* (**on** от+*g.*); (*rely*) полага́ться *impf.*, положи́ться (-жу́сь, -жишься) *pf.* (**on** на+*a.*). **dependable** *adj.* надёжный. **dependant** *n.* иждиве́нец (-нца); *pl.* семья́ и дома́шние *sb.* **dependence** *n.* зави́симость. **dependent** *adj.* зави́симый, зави́сящий.

depict [dɪ'pɪkt] *v.t.* изобража́ть *impf.*, изобрази́ть *pf.*; (*in words*) опи́сывать *impf.*, описа́ть (-ишу́, -и́шешь) *pf.*

deplete [dɪ'pliːt] *v.t.* истоща́ть *impf.*, истощи́ть *pf.* **depleted** *adj.* истощённый (-ён, -ённа). **depletion** *n.* истоще́ние.

deplorable [dɪ'plɔːrəb(ə)l] *adj.* приско́рбный, плаче́вный. **deplore** *v.t.* сожале́ть *impf.* о+*p.*

deploy [dɪ'plɔɪ] *v.t.* & *i.* развёртывать(ся) *impf.*, разверну́ть(ся) *pf.* **deployment** *n.* развёртывание.

depopulate [diː'pɒpjʊˌleɪt] *v.t.* истребля́ть *impf.*, истреби́ть *pf.* населе́ние+*g.*

deport [dɪ'pɔːt] *v.t.* высыла́ть *impf.*, вы́слать (вы́шлю, вы́шлешь) *pf.*; (*internal exile*) ссыла́ть *impf.*, сосла́ть (сошлю́, -лёшь) *pf.* **depor'tation** *n.* вы́сылка; ссы́лка. **depor'tee** *n.* высыла́емый *sb.*; ссы́льный *sb.*

deportment [dɪ'pɔːtmənt] *n.* поведе́ние, оса́нка.

depose [dɪ'pəʊz] *v.t.* сверга́ть *impf.*, све́ргнуть (-г(нул), -гла) *pf.* (с престо́ла); *v.i.* (*leg.*) пока́зывать *impf.*, показа́ть (-ажу́, -а́жешь) *pf.* **deposit** [dɪ'pɒzɪt] *n.* (*econ.*) вклад; (*pledge*) взнос; (*sediment*) оса́док (-дка); (*coal etc.*) месторожде́ние; *v.t.* (*econ.*) вноси́ть (-ошу́, -о́сишь) *impf.*, внести́ (-есу́, -есёшь; -ёс, -есла́) *pf.*; (*geol.*) отлага́ть *impf.*, отложи́ть (-жу́, -жишь) *pf.* **deposition** [ˌdiːpə'zɪʃ(ə)n, ˌdep-] *n.* сверже́ние (с престо́ла); (*leg.*) показа́ние; (*geol.*) отложе́ние. **depositor** *n.* вкла́дчик. **depository** *n.* храни́лище.

depot ['depəʊ] *n.* склад; депо́ *nt.indecl.*; ~ **ship** су́дно-ба́за (*pl.* суда́-ба́зы, судо́в-баз).

deprave [dɪ'preɪv] *v.t.* развраща́ть *impf.*, разврати́ть (-ащу́, -ати́шь) *pf.* **depraved** *adj.* развращённый (-ён, -ённа). **depravity** [dɪ'prævɪtɪ] *n.* развра́т.

deprecate ['deprɪ,keɪt] *v.t.* возражáть *impf.*, возразúть *pf.* прóтив+*g.* **depre'cation** *n.* неодобрéние.

depreciate [dɪ'priːʃɪ,eɪt, -sɪ,eɪt] *v.t.* & *i.* обесцéнивать(ся) *impf.*, обесцéнить(ся) *pf.* **depreci'ation** *n.* обесцéнение. **de'preciatory** *adj.* обесцéнивающий.

depress [dɪ'pres] *v.t.* (*lower*) понижáть *impf.*, понúзить *pf.*; (*dispirit*) удручáть *impf.*, удручúть *pf.* **depressed** *adj.* удручённый (-ён, -ённа & -енá) **depressing** *adj.* нагоня́ющий тоскý. **depression** *n.* (*hollow*) впáдина; (*econ.*, *med.*, *meteor.*, *etc.*) депрéссия.

deprivation [,deprɪ'veɪʃ(ə)n, ,diːpraɪ-] *n.* лишéние. **deprive** [dɪ'praɪv] *v.t.* лишáть *impf.*, лишúть *pf.* (**of** +*g.*)

depth [depθ] *n.* глубинá (*pl.* -ны); ~ **of feeling** сúла переживáния; ~**s of the country** глушь (-шú); **in the** ~ **of winter** в разгáре зимы́. **depth-bomb, depth-charge** *n.* глуби́нная бóмба.

deputation [,depjʊ'teɪʃ(ə)n] *n.* делегáция, депутáция. **depute** [dɪ'pjuːt] *v.t.* делегúровать *impf.* & *pf.* **'deputize** *v.i.* замещáть *impf.*, заместúть *pf.* (**for** +*a.*). **'deputy** *n.* заместúтель *m.*; помóщник, -ица; (*parl.*) депутáт.

derail [dɪ'reɪl, diː-] *v.t.* спускáть *impf.*, спустúть (-ущý, -ýстишь) *pf.* под откóс; **be derailed** сходúть (-ожý, -óдишь) *impf.*, сойтú (сойдý, -дёшь; сошёл, -шлá) *pf.* с рéльсов. **derailment** *n.* крушéние, сход с рéльсов.

derange [dɪ'reɪndʒ] *v.t.* расстрáивать *impf.*, расстрóить *pf.* **deranged** *adj.* (*mentally*) душевнобольнóй, ненормáльный. **derangement** *n.* (психúческое) расстрóйство.

derelict ['derəlɪkt, 'derɪ-] *adj.* брóшенный (-шен). **dere'liction** *n.* упущéние; (*of duty*) нарушéние дóлга.

deride [dɪ'raɪd] *v.t.* высмéивать *impf.*, вы́смеять (-ею, -еешь) *pf.* **derision** [dɪ'rɪʒ(ə)n] *n.* высмéивание; **object of** ~ посмéшище. **derisive** *adj.* (*mocking*) насмéшливый. **derisory** *adj.* (*ridiculous*) смехотвóрный.

derivation [,derɪ'veɪʃ(ə)n] *n.* происхождéние. **de'rivative** *n.* производное *sb.*; *adj.* произвóдный. **derive** [dɪ'raɪv] *v.t.* извлекáть *impf.*, извлéчь (-екý, -ечёшь; -ёк, -еклá) *pf.*; *v.i.*: ~ **from** происходúть (-ожý, -óдишь) *impf.*, произойтú (-ойдý, -ойдёшь; -ошёл, -ошлá) *pf.* от+*g.*

dermatitis [,dɜːmə'taɪtɪs] *n.* дерматúт.

derogatory [dɪ'rɒgətərɪ] *adj.* умаля́ющий, унижáющий.

derrick ['derɪk] *n.* дéррик; (*oil-well etc.*) буровáя вы́шка.

dervish ['dɜːvɪʃ] *n.* дéрвúш.

descend [dɪ'send] *v.t.* спускáться *impf.*, спустúться (-ущýсь, -ýстишься) *pf.* с+*g.*; сходúть (-ожý, -óдишь) *impf.*, сойтú (сойдý, -дёшь; сошёл, -шлá) *pf.* с+*g.*; *v.i.* (*go down*) спускáться *impf.*, спустúться (-ущýсь, -ýстишься) *pf.*; (*sink*) понижáться *impf.*, понúзиться *pf.*; ~ **on** (*attack*) обрýшиваться *impf.*, обрýшиться *pf.* на+*a.*; ~ **to** (*property*; *to details etc.*) переходúть (-ожý, -óдишь) *impf.*, перейтú (-йдý, -йдёшь; перешёл, -шлá) *pf.* к+*d.*; **be descended from** происходúть (-ожý, -óдишь) *impf.*, произойтú (-ойдý, -ойдёшь; -ошёл, -ошлá) *pf.* из, от, +*g.* **descendant** *n.* потóмок (-мка). **descent** *n.* спуск; (*sinking*) понижéние; (*lineage*) происхождéние; (*property*) наслéдование.

describe [dɪ'skraɪb] *v.t.* опúсывать *impf.*, описáть (-ишý, -úшешь) *pf.* **description** [dɪ'skrɪpʃ(ə)n] *n.* описáние. **descriptive** *adj.* описáтельный.

descry [dɪ'skraɪ] *v.t.* различáть *impf.*, различúть *pf.*

desecrate ['desɪ,kreɪt] *v.t.* оскверня́ть *impf.*, осквернúть *pf.* **dese'cration** *n.* осквернéние, профанáция.

desert[1] ['dezet] *n.* (*wilderness*) пусты́ня; *adj.* пусты́нный (-нен, -нна).

desert[2] [dɪ'zɜːt] *v.t.* покидáть *impf.*, покúнуть *pf.*; (*mil.*) дезертúровать *impf.* & *pf.* **deserter** *n.* дезертúр. **desertion** *n.* дезертúрство.

desert[3] [dɪ'zɜːt] *n.*: *pl.* заслýги *f.pl.* **deserve** *v.t.* заслýживать *impf.*, заслужúть (-жý, -жишь) *pf.* **deserving** *adj.* заслýживающий (**of** +*g.*). достóйный (-óин, -óйна) (**of** +*g.*).

desiccated ['desɪ,keɪtɪd] *adj.* сушёный.

design [dɪ'zaɪn] *n.* (*scheme*) зáмысел (-сла); (*sketch*) рисýнок (-нка); (*model*) конструкция, проéкт; **school of** ~ шкóла изобразúтельных искýсств; *v.t.* конструúровать *impf.*, с~ *pf.*; создавáть (-даю́, -даёшь) *impf.*, создáть (-áм, -áшь, -áст, -адúм; сóздáл, -á, -о) *pf.*

designate ['dezɪgnət; 'dezɪg,neɪt] *adj.* назнáченный (-чен); *v.t.* обозначáть *impf.*, обознáчить *pf.*; (*appoint*) назначáть *impf.*, назнáчить *pf.* **desig'nation** *n.* обозначéние, назвáние.

designer [dɪ'zaɪnə(r)] *n.* констрýктор, проектирóвщик, дизáйнер; (*of clothes*) модельéр.

desirable [dɪ'zaɪərəb(ə)l] *adj.* желáтельный. **desire** *n.* желáние; *v.t.* желáть *impf.*, по~ *pf.*+*g.* **desirous** *adj.* желáющий.

desist [dɪ'zɪst] *v.i.* переставáть (-таю́, -таёшь) *impf.*, перестáть (-áну, -áнешь) *pf.*

desk [desk] *n.* пúсьменный стол (-á); контóрка; (*school*) пáрта.

desolate ['desələt] *adj.* (*deserted*) покúнутый; (*dreary*) уны́лый. **desolation** [,desə'leɪʃ(ə)n] *n.* запустéние.

despair [dɪ'speə(r)] *n.* отчáяние; *v.i.* отчáиваться *impf.*, отчáяться (-áюсь, -áешься) *pf.* **despairing** *adj.* отчáянный (-ян, -янна). **desperado** [,despə'rɑːdəʊ] *n.* сорвиголовá (*pl.* -овы, -óв, -овáм). **desperate** ['despərət] *adj.* отчáянный (-ян, -янна). **despe'ration** *n.* отчáяние.

despatch *see* **dispatch**

despicable [ˈdespɪkəb(ə)l, dɪˈspɪk-] *adj.* презре́нный (-е́н, -е́нна), жа́лкий (-лок, -лка́, -лко). **despise** [dɪˈspaɪz] *v.t.* презира́ть *impf.*, презре́ть (-рю́, -ри́шь) *pf.*

despite [dɪˈspaɪt] *prep.* вопреки́+*d.*, несмотря́ на+*a.*

despondency [dɪˈspɒndənsɪ] *n.* уны́ние, пода́вленность. **despondent** *adj.* уны́лый.

despot [ˈdespɒt] *n.* де́спот. **deˈspotic** *adj.* деспоти́ческий, деспоти́чный. **despotism** *n.* деспоти́зм, деспоти́чность.

dessert [dɪˈzɜːt] *n.* десе́рт; сла́дкое *sb.*

destination [ˌdestɪˈneɪʃ(ə)n] *n.* ме́сто (*pl.* -та́) назначе́ния, цель. **ˈdestiny** *n.* судьба́, у́часть.

destitute [ˈdestɪˌtjuːt] *adj.* си́льно нужда́ющийся; без вся́ких средств. **destiˈtution** *n.* нищета́, нужда́.

destroy [dɪˈstrɔɪ] *v.t.* уничтожа́ть *impf.*, уничто́жить *pf.*; губи́ть (-блю́, -бишь) *impf.*, по~ *pf.* **destroyer** *n.* (*naut.*) эсми́нец (-нца). **destruction** [dɪˈstrʌkʃ(ə)n] *n.* разруше́ние, уничтоже́ние. **destructive** *adj.* разруши́тельный, уничтожа́ющий.

desultory [ˈdezəltərɪ] *adj.* беспоря́дочный.

detach [dɪˈtætʃ] *v.t.* отделя́ть *impf.*, отдели́ть *pf.* **detachable** *adj.* съёмный, отделя́емый. **detached** *adj.* отде́льный; ~ **house** особня́к (-а́). **detachment** *n.* отделе́ние, разъедине́ние; (*mil.*) отря́д.

detail [ˈdiːteɪl] *n.* дета́ль, подро́бность; (*mil.*) наря́д; **in detail** подро́бно; *v.t.* подро́бно расска́зывать *impf.*, рассказа́ть (-ажу́, -а́жешь) *pf.*; выделя́ть *impf.*, вы́делить *pf.*; назнача́ть *impf.*, назна́чить *pf.* в наря́д; ~ **for guard duty** назна́чить *pf.* в карау́л. **detailed** *adj.* дета́льный, подро́бный.

detain [dɪˈteɪn] *v.t.* заде́рживать *impf.*, задержа́ть (-жу́, -жишь) *pf.*; аресто́вывать *impf.*, арестова́ть *pf.* **detaiˈnee** *n.* аресто́ванный *sb.*, (челове́к) под стра́жей.

detect [dɪˈtekt] *v.t.* обнару́живать *impf.*, обнару́жить *pf.* **detection** *n.* обнаруже́ние; рассле́дование. **detective** *n.* сы́щик, детекти́в; *adj.* сыскно́й, детекти́вный; ~ **film, story,** *etc.* детекти́в. **detector** *n.* дете́ктор, обнаружи́тель *m.*

détente [deɪˈtɑ̃t] *n.* разря́дка.

detention [dɪˈtenʃ(ə)n] *n.* задержа́ние, аре́ст.

deter [dɪˈtɜː(r)] *v.t.* уде́рживать *impf.*, удержа́ть (-жу́, -жишь) *pf.* (**from** от+*g.*).

detergent [dɪˈtɜːdʒ(ə)nt] *n.* мо́ющее сре́дство; *adj.* мо́ющий, очища́ющий.

deteriorate [dɪˈtɪərɪəˌreɪt] *v.i.* ухудша́ться *impf.*, уху́дшиться *pf.* **deterioˈration** *n.* ухудше́ние.

determination [dɪˌtɜːmɪˈneɪʃ(ə)n] *n.* (*resoluteness*) реши́тельность, реши́мость. **deˈtermine** *v.t.* устана́вливать *impf.*, установи́ть (-влю́, -вишь) *pf.*; определя́ть *impf.*, определи́ть *pf.* **deˈtermined** *adj.* (*resolute*) реши́тельный.

deterrent [dɪˈterənt] *n.* уде́рживающее сре́дство, сре́дство устраше́ния; *adj.* сде́рживающий, уде́рживающий.

detest [dɪˈtest] *v.t.* ненави́деть (-и́жу, -и́дишь) *impf.* **detestable** *adj.* отврати́тельный. **deteˈstation** *n.* отвраще́ние, не́нависть.

dethrone [diːˈθrəʊn] *v.t.* сверга́ть *impf.*, све́ргнуть (-г(нул), -гла) *pf.* с престо́ла; развс́нчивать *impf.*, развенча́ть *pf.* **dethronement** *n.* сверже́ние с престо́ла; развенча́ние.

detonate [ˈdetəˌneɪt] *v.t.* & *i.* взрыва́ть(ся) *impf.*, взорва́ть(ся) (-ву́, -вёт(ся); взорва́л(ся), -а́(сь), -о/-а́ло́сь) *pf.* **detoˈnation** *n.* детона́ция, взрыв. **detonator** *n.* детона́тор.

detour [ˈdiːtʊə(r)] *n.* обхо́д, объе́зд.

detract [dɪˈtrækt] *v.i.*: ~ **from** умаля́ть *impf.*, умали́ть *pf.*+*a.*

detriment [ˈdetrɪmənt] *n.* уще́рб, вред (-а́). **detriˈmental** *adj.* вре́дный (-ден, -дна́, -дно), па́губный.

detritus [dɪˈtraɪtəs] *n.* детри́т.

deuce [djuːs] *n.* (*tennis*) ра́вный счёт.

devaluation [diːˌvæljuːˈeɪʃ(ə)n] *n.* девальва́ция. **deˈvalue** *v.t.* проводи́ть (-ожу́, -о́дишь) *impf.*, провести́ (-еду́, -едёшь; -ёл, -ела́) *pf.* девальва́цию+*g.*

devastate [ˈdevəˌsteɪt] *v.t.* опустоша́ть *impf.*, опустоши́ть *pf.* **devaˈstation** опустоше́ние.

develop [dɪˈveləp] *v.t.* & *i.* развива́ть(ся) *impf.*, разви́ть(ся) (разовью́(сь), -вьёшь(ся); разви́л(ся), -а́(сь), -о/-и́ло́сь) *pf.*; *v.t.* (*phot.*) проявля́ть *impf.*, прояви́ть (-влю́, -вишь) *pf.*; (*natural resources*) разраба́тывать *impf.*, разрабо́тать *pf.* **developer** *n.* (*of land etc.*) застро́йщик но́вого райо́на; (*phot.*) прояви́тель *m.* **development** *n.* разви́тие; (*phot.*) проявле́ние.

deviate [ˈdiːvɪˌeɪt] *v.i.* отклоня́ться *impf.*, отклони́ться (-ню́сь, -нишься) *pf.* (**from** от+*g.*). **deviˈation** *n.* отклоне́ние; (*pol.*) укло́н.

device [dɪˈvaɪs] *n.* устро́йство, прибо́р.

devil [ˈdev(ə)l] *n.* дья́вол, чёрт (*pl.* че́рти, -те́й), бес. **devilish** *adj.* дья́вольский, черто́вский. **devil-may-care** *adj.* бесшаба́шный.

devious [ˈdiːvɪəs] *adj.* (*indirect*) непрямо́й (-м, -ма́, -мо); (*person*) хи́трый (-тёр, -тра́, хи́тро́).

devise [dɪˈvaɪz] *v.t.* приду́мывать *impf.*, приду́мать *pf.*

devoid [dɪˈvɔɪd] *adj.* лишённый (-ён, -ена́) (**of** +*g.*).

devolution [ˌdiːvəˈluːʃ(ə)n, -ˈljuːʃ(ə)n] *n.* переда́ча; перехо́д. **devolve** [dɪˈvɒlv] *v.t.* передава́ть (-даю́, -даёшь) *impf.*, переда́ть (-а́м, -а́шь, -а́ст, -ади́м; пе́редал, -а́, -о) *pf.*; *v.i.* переходи́ть (-ожу́, -о́дишь) *impf.*, перейти́ (-йду́, -йдёшь; перешёл, -шла́) *pf.*

devote [dɪˈvəʊt] *v.t.* посвяща́ть *impf.*, посвяти́ть (-ящу́, -яти́шь) *pf.* **devoted** *adj.* пре́данный (-ан). **devotion** *n.* пре́данность, приве́рженность; *pl.* религио́зные обязан-

ности *f.pl.* **devotional** *adj.* религио́зный.
devour [dɪ'vaʊə(r)] *v.t.* пожира́ть *impf.*, пожра́ть (-ру́, -рёшь; пожра́л, -а́, -о) *pf.*
devout [dɪ'vaʊt] *adj.* на́божный, благочести́вый. **devoutness** *n.* на́божность, благоче́стие.
dew [dju:] *n.* роса́. **dewdrop** *n.* роси́нка. **dewy** *adj.* вла́жный (-жен, -жна́, -жно), роси́стый.
dexterity [dek'sterɪtɪ] *n.* прово́рство, ло́вкость; сноро́вка. **'dext(e)rous** *adj.* прово́рный; ло́вкий (-вок, -вка́, -вко, ло́вки́).
diabetes [ˌdaɪə'bi:ti:z] *n.* са́харная боле́знь, диабе́т. **diabetic** [ˌdaɪə'betɪk] *n.* диабе́тик; *adj.* диабети́ческий.
diabolic(al) [ˌdaɪə'bɒlɪk(l)] *adj.* дья́вольский; зве́рский.
diagnose ['daɪəgˌnəʊz] *v.t.* ста́вить *impf.*, по~ *pf.* диа́гноз+*g.* **diag'nosis** *n.* диа́гноз.
diagonal [daɪ'ægən(ə)l] *n.* диагона́ль; *adj.* диагона́льный. **diagonally** *adv.* по диагона́ли.
diagram ['daɪəˌgræm] *n.* диагра́мма; чертёж (-а́); схе́ма.
dial ['daɪ(ə)l] *n.* цифербла́т; шкала́ (*pl.* -лы); (*telephone*) диск набо́ра; *v.t.* набира́ть *impf.*, набра́ть (наберу́, -рёшь; набра́л, -а́, -о) *pf.*
dialect ['daɪəˌlekt] *n.* диале́кт, наре́чие; *adj.* диале́ктный. **dia'lectical** *adj.* диалекти́ческий.
dialogue ['daɪəˌlɒg] *n.* диало́г.
diameter [daɪ'æmɪtə(r)] *n.* диа́метр. **dia'metrical** *adj.* диаметра́льный; **~ly opposed** диаметра́льно противополо́жный.
diamond ['daɪəmənd] *n.* алма́з, бриллиа́нт; (*rhomb*) ромб; (*cards*) бу́бна (*pl.* бу́бны, бу́бён, бубна́м); **play a ~** ходи́ть (хожу́, хо́дишь) *impf.*, пойти́ (пойду́, -дёшь; пошёл, -шла́) *pf.* с бубён; *adj.* алма́зный, бриллиа́нтовый; бубно́вый.
diaper ['daɪəpə(r)] *n.* пелёнка.
diaphanous [daɪ'æfənəs] *adj.* прозра́чный.
diaphragm ['daɪəˌfræm] *n.* диафра́гма; мембра́на.
diarrhoea [ˌdaɪə'rɪə] *n.* поно́с.
diary ['daɪərɪ] *n.* дневни́к (-а́).
diatribe ['daɪəˌtraɪb] *n.* обличи́тельная речь (*pl.* -чи, -че́й).
dice *see* **die**[1]
dicey ['daɪsɪ] *adj.* риско́ванный (-ан, -анна).
dictaphone ['dɪktəˌfəʊn] *n.* диктафо́н. **dictate** ['dɪkteɪt; dɪk'teɪt] *n.* веле́ние; *v.t.* диктова́ть *impf.*, про~ *pf.* **dictation** *n.* дикто́вка, дикта́нт. **dictator** *n.* дикта́тор. **dicta'torial** *adj.* дикта́торский, повели́тельный. **dictatorship** *n.* диктату́ра.
diction ['dɪkʃ(ə)n] *n.* ди́кция.
dictionary ['dɪkʃənrɪ, -nərɪ] *n.* слова́рь (-ря́) *m.*
dictum ['dɪktəm] *n.* авторите́тное заявле́ние; (*maxim*) изрече́ние.
didactic [daɪ'dæktɪk, dɪ-] *adj.* дидакти́ческий.
diddle ['dɪd(ə)l] *v.t.* надува́ть *impf.*, наду́ть (-у́ю, -у́ешь) *pf.*
die[1] [daɪ] *n.* (*pl.* **dice**) игра́льная кость (*pl.* -ти, -те́й); (*pl.* **dies**) (*stamp*) штамп, ште́мпель (*pl.* -ля́) *m.*; (*mould*) ма́трица.
die[2] [daɪ] *v.i.* (*person*) умира́ть *impf.*, умере́ть (умру́, умрёшь; у́мер, -ла́, -ло) *pf.*; (*animal*) до́хнуть (до́х(нул), до́хла) *impf.*, из~, по~ *pf.*; (*plant*) вя́нуть (вя́(ну)л, вя́ла) *impf.*, за~ *pf.*; сконча́ться *pf.* **die-hard** *adj.* твердоло́бый *sb.*
diesel ['di:z(ə)l] *n.* (*engine*) ди́зель *m.*; *attr.* ди́зельный.
diet ['daɪət] *n.* дие́та; (*habitual food*) пита́ние, стол (-а́); *v.i.* соблюда́ть *impf.*, соблюсти́ (-юду́, -юдёшь; -ю́л, -юла́) *pf.* дие́ту. **dietary** *adj.* диети́ческий. **diet'etics** *n.* диете́тика.
differ ['dɪfə(r)] *v.i.* отлича́ться *impf.*; различа́ться *impf.*; (*disagree*) не соглаша́ться *impf.* **difference** *n.* ра́зница; (*disagreement*) разногла́сие. **different** *adj.* разли́чный, ра́зный. **diffe'rential** *n.* (*math.*) дифференциа́л; ра́зница; *adj.* дифференциа́льный. **diffe'rentiate** *v.t.* различа́ть *impf.*, различи́ть *pf.* **differenti'ation** *n.* различе́ние; дифференциа́ция.
difficult ['dɪfɪkəlt] *adj.* тру́дный (-ден, -дна́, -дно, тру́дны́), затрудни́тельный. **difficulty** *n.* тру́дность; затрудне́ние; **without ~** без труда́.
diffidence ['dɪfɪdəns] *n.* неуве́ренность в себе́. **diffident** *adj.* ро́бкий (-бок, -бка́, -бко), неуве́ренный (-ен) в себе́.
diffused [dɪ'fju:zd] *adj.* рассе́янный (-ян, -янна).
dig [dɪg] *n.* (*archaeol.*) раско́пки *f.pl.*; (*poke*) тычо́к (-чка́); *pl.* (*lodgings*) кварти́ра; **give a ~ in the ribs** ткнуть *pf.* ло́ктем под ребро́; *v.t.* копа́ть *impf.*, вы́~ *pf.*; рыть (ро́ю, ро́ешь) *impf.*, вы́~ *pf.*; (*prod*) ты́кать (ты́чу, -чешь) *impf.*, ткнуть *pf.*
digest ['daɪdʒest; daɪ'dʒest, dɪ-] *n.* (*synopsis*) кра́ткое изложе́ние, резюме́ *nt.indecl.*; (*collection*) сбо́рник резюме́; *v.t.* перева́ривать *impf.*, перевари́ть (-рю́, -ришь) *pf.* **digestible** *adj.* удобовари́мый. **digestion** *n.* пищеваре́ние. **digestive** *adj.* пищевари́тельный.
digger ['dɪgə(r)] *n.* копа́тель *m.*, землеко́п. **digging** *n.* копа́нье, рытьё; *pl.* земляны́е рабо́ты *f.pl.*
digit ['dɪdʒɪt] *n.* (*math.*) ци́фра, однозна́чное число́ (*pl.* -сла, -сел, -слам); (*anat.*) па́лец (-льца). **digital** ['dɪdʒɪt(ə)l] *adj.* цифрово́й; **~ recording** цифрова́я за́пись.
dignified ['dɪgnɪˌfaɪd] *adj.* с чу́вством со́бственного досто́инства. **dignify** *v.t.* облагора́живать *impf.*, облагоро́дить *pf.* **dignitary** *n.* сано́вник. **dignity** *n.* досто́инство.
digress [daɪ'gres] *v.i.* отклоня́ться *impf.*, отклони́ться (-ню́сь, -нишься) *pf.* (**from** от+*g.*). **digression** *n.* отступле́ние, отклоне́ние.

dike [daɪk] *n.* на́сыпь; (*ditch*) ров (рва, *loc.* во рву́).

dilapidated [dɪ'læpɪˌdeɪtɪd] *adj.* обветша́лый. **dilapi'dation** *n.* (*eccl.*) поврежде́ние.

dilate [daɪ'leɪt] *v.t. & i.* расширя́ть(ся) *impf.*, расши́рить(ся) *pf.*

dilatory ['dɪlətərɪ] *adj.* оття́гивающий.

dilemma [daɪ'lemə, dɪ-] *n.* диле́мма.

dilettante [ˌdɪlɪ'tæntɪ] *n.* дилета́нт; *adj.* дилета́нтский, люби́тельский.

diligence ['dɪlɪdʒ(ə)ns] *n.* прилежа́ние, усе́рдие. **diligent** *adj.* приле́жный, усе́рдный.

dill [dɪl] *n.* укро́п (-а(у)).

dilly-dally [ˌdɪlɪ'dælɪ] *v.i.* ме́шкать *impf.*

dilute [daɪ'lju:t] *v.t.* разбавля́ть *impf.*, разба́вить *pf.*; *adj.* разба́вленный (-ен). **dilution** *n.* разбавле́ние.

dim [dɪm] *adj.* ту́склый (тускл, -а́, -о), сму́тный (-тен, -тна́, -тно).

dimension [daɪ'menʃ(ə)n, dɪ-] *n.* величина́; *pl.* разме́ры *m.pl.*; (*math.*) измере́ние.

diminish [dɪ'mɪnɪʃ] *v.t. & i.* уменьша́ть(ся) *impf.*, уме́ньши́ть(ся) *pf.* **diminished** *adj.* уме́ньшенный (-ен). **dimi'nution** *n.* уменьше́ние. **diminutive** *adj.* ма́ленький; (*gram.*) уменьши́тельный; *n.* уменьши́тельное *sb.*

dimity ['dɪmɪtɪ] *n.* канифа́с.

dimness ['dɪmnɪs] *n.* ту́склость, полусве́т.

dimple ['dɪmp(ə)l] *n.* я́мочка.

dim-sighted *adj.* недальнови́дный. **dim-witted** *adj.* тупо́й (туп, -а́, -о, ту́пы́).

din [dɪn] *n.* шум и гам; *v.t.*: ~ **into one's ears** прожужжа́ть (-жу́, -жи́шь) у́ши+*d.*

dine [daɪn] *v.i.* обе́дать *impf.*, по~ *pf.*; *v.t.* угоща́ть *impf.*, угости́ть *pf.* обе́дом. **diner** *n.* обе́дающий *sb.*; (*rail.*) ваго́н(-а)-рестора́н(-а).

ding-dong ['dɪŋdɒŋ] *adj.* чреду́ющийся.

dinghy ['dɪŋɪ, 'dɪŋgɪ] *n.* шлю́пка, я́лик.

dingy ['dɪndʒɪ] *adj.* (*drab*) ту́склый (тускл, -а́, -о); (*dirty*) гря́зный (-зен, -зна́, -зно).

dining-car ['daɪnɪŋ] *n.* ваго́н(-а)-рестора́н(-а). **dining-room** *n.* столо́вая *sb.* **dinner** ['dɪnə(r)] *n.* обе́д. **dinner-hour** *n.* обе́денный переры́в. **dinner-jacket** *n.* смо́кинг. **dinner-time** *n.* обе́денное вре́мя *nt.*

dinosaur ['daɪnəˌsɔ:(r)] *n.* диноза́вр.

dint [dɪnt] *n.*: **by** ~ **of** посре́дством+*g.*; с по́мощью+*g.*

diocesan [daɪ'ɒsɪs(ə)n] *adj.* епархиа́льный. **diocese** ['daɪəsɪs] *n.* епа́рхия.

diode ['daɪəʊd] *n.* дио́д.

dioxide [daɪ'ɒksaɪd] *n.* двуо́кись.

dip [dɪp] *v.t. & i.* окуна́ть(ся) *impf.*, окуну́ть(ся) *pf.*; *v.t.* (*flag*) припуска́ть *impf.*, припусти́ть (-ущу́, -у́стишь) *pf.*; ~ **into** (*book*) перели́стывать *impf.*, перелиста́ть *pf.*; *n.* окуна́ние; (*depression*) впа́дина; (*slope*) укло́н; (*phys.*; *astr.*) наклоне́ние; **have a** ~ (*bathe*) купа́ться *impf.*, вы́~ *pf.*

diphtheria [dɪf'θɪərɪə] *n.* дифтери́я.

diphthong ['dɪfθɒŋ] *n.* дифто́нг.

diploma [dɪ'pləʊmə] *n.* дипло́м. **diplomacy** *n.* диплома́тия. **'diplomat** *n.* диплома́т. **diplo'matic** *adj.* дипломати́ческий, дипломати́чный; ~ **bag** дипломати́ческая по́чта.

dipper ['dɪpə(r)] *n.* (*ladle*) ковш (-а́); (*bird*) оля́пка.

dipsomania [ˌdɪpsə'meɪnɪə] *n.* алкоголи́зм.

dire ['daɪə(r)] *adj.* стра́шный (-шен, -шна́, -шно, стра́шны́); (*ominous*) злове́щий.

direct [daɪ'rekt, dɪ-] *adj.* прямо́й (прям, -а́, -о, пря́мы́); непосре́дственный (-ен, -енна); ~ **current** постоя́нный ток (-а(у)); *v.t.* направля́ть *impf.*, напра́вить *pf.*; (*guide, manage*) руководи́ть *impf.*+*i.*; (*film*) режисси́ровать *impf.* **direction** *n.* направле́ние; (*guidance*) руково́дство; (*instruction*) указа́ние; (*film*) режиссу́ра; **stage** ~ рема́рка. **directive** *n.* директи́ва, указа́ние. **directly** *adv.* пря́мо; (*at once*) сра́зу. **director** *n.* дире́ктор (*pl.* -а́), член правле́ния; (*film*) режиссёр; **board of directors** правле́ние. **directory** *n.* спра́вочник, указа́тель *m.*; **telephone** ~ телефо́нная кни́га.

dirge [dɜ:dʒ] *n.* погреба́льная песнь.

dirt [dɜ:t] *n.* грязь (*loc.* -зи́); ~ **cheap** деше́вле па́реной ре́пы; ~ **floor** земляно́й пол (*loc.* -у́; *pl.* -ы́). **dirty** *adj.* гря́зный (-зен, -зна́, -зно); (*mean*) по́длый (подл, -а́, -о); (*obscene*) непристо́йный; *v.t. & i.* па́чкать(ся) *impf.*, за~ *pf.*

disability [ˌdɪsə'bɪlɪtɪ] *n.* (*physical*) нетрудоспосо́бность. **disable** [dɪs'eɪb(ə)l] *v.t.* де́лать *impf.*, с~ *pf.* неспосо́бным; (*cripple*) кале́чить *impf.*, ис~ *pf.* **disabled** *adj.* искале́ченный (-ен); ~ **serviceman** инвали́д войны́. **disablement** *n.* инвали́дность.

disabuse [ˌdɪsə'bju:z] *v.t.* выводи́ть (-ожу́, -о́дишь) *impf.*, вы́вести (-еду, -едешь; -ел) *pf.* из заблужде́ния; ~ **of** освобожда́ть *impf.*, освободи́ть *pf.* от+*g.*

disadvantage [ˌdɪsəd'vɑ:ntɪdʒ] *n.* невы́годное положе́ние; (*defect*) недоста́ток (-тка). **disadvan'tageous** *adj.* невы́годный.

disaffected [ˌdɪsə'fektɪd] *adj.* недово́льный, нелоя́льный. **disaffection** *n.* недово́льство, нелоя́льность.

disagree [ˌdɪsə'gri:] *v.i.* не соглаша́ться *impf.*, согласи́ться *pf.*; расходи́ться (-ожу́сь, -о́дишься) *impf.*, разойти́сь (-ойду́сь, -ойдёшься; -ошёлся, -ошла́сь) *pf.* **disagreeable** *adj.* неприя́тный. **disagreement** *n.* расхожде́ние, несогла́сие; (*quarrel*) ссо́ра.

disallow [ˌdɪsə'laʊ] *v.t.* отка́зывать *impf.*, отказа́ть (-ажу́, -а́жешь) *pf.* в+*p.*

disappear [ˌdɪsə'pɪə(r)] *v.i.* исчеза́ть *impf.*, исче́знуть (-е́з) *pf.*; пропада́ть *impf.*, пропа́сть (-аду́, -адёшь; -а́л) *pf.*; скрыва́ться *impf.*, скры́ться (-ро́юсь, -ро́ешься) *pf.* **disappearance** *n.* исчезнова́ние, пропа́жа.

disappoint [ˌdɪsə'pɔɪnt] *v.t.* разочаро́вывать *impf.*, разочарова́ть *pf.* **disappointed** *adj.* разочаро́ванный (-ан, -ан(н)а). **disappointing** *adj.* вызыва́ющий разочарова́ние. **disappointment** *n.* разочарова́ние; доса́да.

disapproval [ˌdɪsəˈpruːvəl] *n.* неодобре́ние. **disapprove** *v.t.* не одобря́ть *impf.*
disarm [dɪsˈɑːm] *v.t.* разоружа́ть *impf.*, разоружи́ть *pf.*; обезору́живать *impf.*, обезору́жить *pf.* **disarmament** *n.* разоруже́ние.
disarray [ˌdɪsəˈreɪ] *n.* беспоря́док (-дка), смяте́ние.
disaster [dɪˈzɑːstə(r)] *n.* бе́дствие, несча́стье. **disastrous** *adj.* бе́дственный (-ен, -енна); ги́бельный, губи́тельный.
disavow [ˌdɪsəˈvaʊ] *v.t.* отрека́ться *impf.*, отре́чься (-еку́сь, -ечёшься; -ёкся, -екла́сь) *pf.* от+*g.*; отрица́ть *impf.*
disband [dɪsˈbænd] *v.t.* распуска́ть *impf.*, распусти́ть (-ущу́, -у́стишь) *pf.*; (*mil.*) расформиро́вывать *impf.*, расформирова́ть *pf.*; *v.i.* расходи́ться (-ожу́сь, -о́дишься) *impf.*, разойти́сь (-ойду́сь, -ойдёшься; -ошёлся, -ошла́сь) *pf.*
disbelief [ˌdɪsbɪˈliːf] *n.* неве́рие. **disbelieve** *v.t.* не ве́рить *impf.+d.*
disburse [dɪsˈbɜːs] *v.t.* выпла́чивать *impf.*, вы́платить *pf.* **disbursement** *n.* вы́плата.
disc, disk [dɪsk] *n.* диск, круг (*pl.* -и́); (*gramophone record*) грампласти́нка; (*comput.*) диск, диске́т; ~ **brake** ди́сковый то́рмоз (*pl.* -а́); ~ **drive** дисково́д, накопи́тель *m.* на ди́сках; ~ **jockey** диск-жоке́й.
discard [ˈdɪskɑːd] *v.t.* отбра́сывать *impf.*, отбро́сить *pf.*; (*cards*) сбра́сывать *impf.*, сбро́сить *pf.*; *n.* (*card*) сбро́шенная ка́рта.
discern [dɪˈsɜːn] *v.t.* различа́ть *impf.*, различи́ть *pf.*; разгляде́ть (-яжу́, -яди́шь) *pf.* **discernible** *adj.* различи́мый. **discerning** *adj.* проница́тельный. **discernment** *n.* распозна́ние; уме́ние различа́ть.
discharge [dɪsˈtʃɑːdʒ; ˈdɪstʃɑːdʒ,] *v.t.* (*ship etc.*) разгружа́ть *impf.*, разгрузи́ть (-ужу́, -у́зи́шь) *pf.* (*gun*; *elec.*) разряжа́ть *impf.*, разряди́ть *pf.*; (*dismiss*) увольня́ть *impf.*, уво́лить *pf.*; (*prisoner*) освобожда́ть *impf.*, освободи́ть *pf.*; (*debt*; *duty*) выполня́ть *impf.*, вы́полнить *pf.*; (*med.*) выделя́ть *impf.*, вы́делить *pf.*; *n.* разгру́зка; (*gun*) вы́стрел; (*elec.*) разря́д; увольне́ние; освобожде́ние; выполне́ние; (*med.*) (*action*) выделе́ние; (*matter*) выделе́ния *nt.pl.*
disciple [dɪˈsaɪp(ə)l] *n.* учени́к (-а́).
disciplinarian [ˌdɪsɪplɪˈneərɪən] *n.* сторо́нник стро́гой дисципли́ны. **disciˈplinary** *adj.* дисциплина́рный. **ˈdiscipline** *n.* дисципли́на; *v.t.* дисциплини́ровать *impf.* & *pf.*
disclaim [dɪsˈkleɪm] *v.t.* отрека́ться *impf.*, отре́чься (-еку́сь, -ечёшься; -ёкся, -екла́сь) *pf.* от+*g.* **disclaimer** *n.* отрече́ние.
disclose [dɪsˈkləʊz] *v.t.* обнару́живать *impf.*, обнару́жить *pf.* **disclosure** *n.* обноруже́ние.
discoloured [dɪsˈkʌlə(r)d] *adj.* измени́вший цвет, обесцве́ченный (-ен, -енна), вы́цветший.
discomfit [dɪsˈkʌmfɪt] *v.t.* приводи́ть (-ожу́, -о́дишь) *impf.*, привести́ (-еду́, -едёшь; -ёл, -ела́) *pf.* в замеша́тельство. **discomfiture** *n.* замеша́тельство.
discomfort [dɪsˈkʌmfət] *n.* неудо́бство, нело́вкость.
disconcert [ˌdɪskənˈsɜːt] *v.t.* (*plans*) расстра́ивать *impf.*, расстро́ить *pf.*; (*person*) смуща́ть *impf.*, смути́ть (-ущу́, -ути́шь) *pf.*
disconnect [ˌdɪskəˈnekt] *v.t.* разъединя́ть *impf.*, разъедини́ть *pf.*; (*elec.*) выключа́ть *impf.*, вы́ключить *pf.* **disconnected** *adj.* (*incoherent*) бессвя́зный.
disconsolate [dɪsˈkɒnsələt] *adj.* неуте́шный.
discontent [ˌdɪskənˈtent] *n.* недово́льство. **discontented** *adj.* недово́льный.
discontinue [ˌdɪskənˈtɪnjuː] *v.t.* & *i.* прекраща́ть(ся) *impf.*, прекрати́ть(ся) (-ащу́, -ати́т(ся)) *pf.*
discord [ˈdɪskɔːd] *n.* (*disagreement*) разногла́сие, разла́д; (*mus.*) диссона́нс. **disˈcordant** *adj.* несогласу́ющийся; диссони́рующий.
discount [ˈdɪskaʊnt] *n.* ски́дка; *v.t.* (*econ.*) учи́тывать *impf.*, уче́сть (учту́, -ёшь; учёл, -чла́) *pf.*; (*disregard*) не принима́ть *impf.*, приня́ть (-иму́, -и́мешь; при́нял, -а́, -о) *pf.* в расчёт, во внима́ние.
discourage [dɪˈskʌrɪdʒ] *v.t.* обескура́живать *impf.*, обескура́жить *pf.* **discouragement** *n.* обескура́живание.
discourteous [dɪsˈkɜːtɪəs] *adj.* нелюбе́зный, невоспи́танный (-ан, -анна). **discourtesy** *n.* нелюбе́зность, невоспи́танность.
discover [dɪˈskʌvə(r)] *v.t.* открыва́ть *impf.*, откры́ть (-ро́ю, -ро́ешь) *pf.*; обнару́живать *impf.*, обнару́жить *pf.* **discoverer** *n.* иссле́дователь *m.* **discovery** *n.* откры́тие.
discredit [dɪsˈkredɪt] *n.* позо́р; *v.t.* дискредити́ровать *impf.* & *pf.*
discreet [dɪˈskriːt] *adj.* осмотри́тельный, благоразу́мный. **discretion** [dɪˈskreʃ(ə)n] *n.* усмотре́ние; (*prudence*) благоразу́мие; **at one's** ~ по своему́ усмотре́нию.
discrepancy [dɪsˈkrepənsɪ] *n.* ра́зница, несоотве́тствие.
discriminate [dɪˈskrɪmɪˌneɪt] *v.t.* различа́ть *impf.*, различи́ть *pf.*; ~ **against** дискримини́ровать *impf.* & *pf.* **discrimiˈnation** *n.* дискримина́ция.
discus [ˈdɪskəs] *n.* диск; ~ **throwing** мета́ние ди́ска.
discuss [dɪˈskʌs] *v.t.* обсужда́ть *impf.*, обсуди́ть (-ужу́, -у́дишь) *pf.* **discussion** *n.* обсужде́ние, диску́ссия.
disdain [dɪsˈdeɪn] *n.* презре́ние. **disdainful** *adj.* презри́тельный, надме́нный (-е́нен, -е́нна).
disease [dɪˈziːz] *n.* боле́знь. **diseased** *adj.* больно́й (-лен, -льна́).
disembark [ˌdɪsɪmˈbɑːk] *v.t.* & *i.* выса́живать(ся) *impf.*, вы́садить(ся) *pf.* **disembarˈkation** *n.* вы́садка.
disembodied [ˌdɪsɪmˈbɒdɪd] *adj.* беспло́тный.
disembowel [ˌdɪsɪmˈbaʊəl] *v.t.* потроши́ть *impf.*, вы́~ *pf.*

disenchantment [ˌdɪsɪn'tʃɑːntmənt] *n.* разочарова́ние.

disenfranchise [ˌdɪsɪn'fræntʃaɪz] *v.t.* лиша́ть *impf.*, лиши́ть *pf.* (гражда́нских, избира́тельных) прав, привиле́гий. **disenfranchisement** *n.* лише́ние гражда́нских, избира́тельных, прав.

disengage [ˌdɪsɪn'geɪdʒ] *v.t.* высвобожда́ть *impf.*, вы́свободить *pf.*; (*tech.*) разобща́ть *impf.*, разобщи́ть *pf.*; выключа́ть *impf.*, вы́ключить *pf.* **disengaged** *adj.* свобо́дный. **disengagement** *n.* освобожде́ние; разобще́ние, выключе́ние.

disentangle [ˌdɪsɪn'tæŋg(ə)l] *v.t.* распу́тывать *impf.*, распу́тать *pf.*

disestablishment [ˌdɪsɪ'stæblɪʃmənt] *n.* отделе́ние це́ркви от госуда́рства.

disfavour [dɪs'feɪvə(r)] *n.* неми́лость, неприя́знь.

disfigure [dɪs'fɪgə(r)] *v.t.* уро́довать *impf.*, из~ *pf.*

disgorge [dɪs'gɔːdʒ] *v.t.* изверга́ть *impf.*, изве́ргнуть (-г(нул), -гла) *pf.*

disgrace [dɪs'greɪs] *n.* позо́р; (*disfavour*) неми́лость, опа́ла; *v.t.* позо́рить *impf.*, о~ *pf.* **disgraceful** *adj.* позо́рный.

disgruntled [dɪs'grʌnt(ə)ld] *adj.* недово́льный.

disguise [dɪs'gaɪz] *n.* маскиро́вка; измене́ние вне́шности; *v.t.* маскирова́ть *impf.*, за~ *pf.*; изменя́ть *impf.*, измени́ть (-ню́, -нишь) *pf.* вне́шность+*g.*; (*conceal*) скрыва́ть *impf.*, скрыть (-ро́ю, -ро́ешь) *pf.* **disguised** *adj.* замаскиро́ванный (-ан, -анна); ~ **as** переоде́тый в+*a.*

disgust [dɪs'gʌst] *n.* отвраще́ние; *v.t.* внуша́ть *impf.*, внуши́ть *pf.* отвраще́ние+*d.* **disgusting** *adj.* отврати́тельный, проти́вный.

dish [dɪʃ] *n.* блю́до; *pl.* посу́да *collect.*; *v.t.*: ~ **up** класть (-аду́, -адёшь; -ал) *impf.*, положи́ть (-ожу́, -о́жишь) *pf.* на блю́до.

disharmony [dɪs'hɑːmənɪ] *n.* дисгармо́ния; (*disagreement*) разногла́сие.

dishearten [dɪs'hɑːt(ə)n] *v.t.* обескура́живать *impf.*, обескура́жить *pf.*

dishevelled [dɪ'ʃev(ə)ld] *adj.* растрёпанный (-ан, -анна).

dishonest [dɪs'ɒnɪst] *adj.* нече́стный, недобросо́вестный. **dishonesty** *n.* нече́стность. **dishonour** *n.* бесче́стье; *v.t.* бесче́стить *impf.*, о~ *pf.* **dishonourable** *adj.* бесче́стный, по́длый (подл, -а́, -о).

dish-towel ['dɪʃtaʊəl] *n.* ку́хонное полоте́нце (*g.pl.* -нец). **dish-washer** *n.* (посу́до)мо́ечная маши́на. **dish-water** *n.* помо́и (-о́ев) *pl.*

disillusion [ˌdɪsɪ'luːʒ(ə)n, -'ljuːʒ(ə)n] *v.t.* разочаро́вывать *impf.*, разочарова́ть *pf.* **disillusionment** *n.* разочаро́ванность.

disinclination [ˌdɪsɪnklɪ'neɪʃ(ə)n] *n.* несклонность, неохо́та. **disinclined** [ˌdɪsɪn'klaɪnd] *adj.* **be** ~ не хоте́ться (хо́чется) *impers.+d.*

disinfect [ˌdɪsɪn'fekt] *v.t.* дезинфици́ровать *impf.* & *pf.* **disinfectant** *n.* дезинфици́рующее сре́дство; *adj.* дезинфици́рующий. **disinfection** *n.* дезинфе́кция, обеззара́живание.

disingenuous [ˌdɪsɪn'dʒenjʊəs] *adj.* нейскренный (-нен, -нна, -нне & -нно).

disinherit [ˌdɪsɪn'herɪt] *v.t.* лиша́ть *impf.*, лиши́ть *pf.* насле́дства.

disintegrate [dɪs'ɪntɪˌgreɪt] *v.t.* дезинтегри́ровать *impf.* & *pf.*; *v.i.* разлага́ться *impf.*, разложи́ться (-жу́сь, -жишься); *pf.* **disinte'gration** *n.* разложе́ние, дезинтегра́ция, распа́д.

disinterested [dɪs'ɪntrɪstɪd] *adj.* бескоры́стный.

disjointed [dɪs'dʒɔɪntɪd] *adj.* бессвя́зный.

disk *see* **disc**

diskette *n.* диске́т.

dislike [dɪs'laɪk] *n.* нелюбо́вь (-бви́, *i.* -бо́вью) (**for** к+*d.*); нерасположе́ние (**for** к+*d.*); *v.t.* не люби́ть (-блю́, -бишь) *impf.*

dislocate ['dɪsləˌkeɪt] *v.t.* (*med.*) выви́хивать *impf.*, вы́вихнуть *pf.*; расстра́ивать *impf.*, расстро́ить *pf.* **dislo'cation** *n.* вы́вих; беспоря́док (-дка).

dislodge [dɪs'lɒdʒ] *v.t.* смеща́ть *impf.*, смести́ть *pf.*

disloyal [dɪs'lɔɪəl] *adj.* нелоя́льный, неве́рный (-рен, -рна́, -рно, неве́рны́). **disloyalty** *n.* нелоя́льность, неве́рность.

dismal ['dɪzm(ə)l] *adj.* мра́чный (-чен, -чна́, -чно); уны́лый.

dismantle [dɪs'mænt(ə)l] *v.t.* разбира́ть *impf.*, разобра́ть (разберу́, -рёшь; разобра́л, -а́, -о) *pf.*; демонти́ровать *impf.* & *pf.*

dismay [dɪs'meɪ] *v.t.* приводи́ть (-ожу́, -о́дишь) *impf.*, привести́ (-еду́, -едёшь; -ёл, -ела́) *pf.* в у́жас, уны́ние; *n.* (*alarm*) испу́г (-а(у)); (*despair*) уны́ние.

dismember [dɪs'membə(r)] *v.t.* расчленя́ть *impf.*, расчлени́ть *pf.* **dismemberment** *n.* расчлене́ние.

dismiss [dɪs'mɪs] *v.t.* (*discharge*) увольня́ть *impf.*, уво́лить *pf.*; (*disband*) распуска́ть *impf.*, распусти́ть (-ущу́, -у́стишь) *pf.*; ~! *int.* (*mil.*) разойди́сь! **dismissal** *n.* увольне́ние; ро́спуск.

dismount [dɪs'maʊnt] *v.i.* (*from horse*) спе́шиваться *impf.*, спе́шиться *pf.*

disobedience [ˌdɪsə'biːdɪəns] *n.* непослуша́ние. **disobedient** *adj.* непослу́шный. **disobey** [ˌdɪsə'beɪ] *v.t.* не слу́шаться *impf.+g.*

disorder [dɪs'ɔːdə(r)] *n.* беспоря́док (-дка). **disordered** *adj.* расстро́енный (-ен). **disorderly** *adj.* (*untidy*) беспоря́дочный; (*unruly*) бу́йный (бу́ен, буйна́, -но).

disorganization [dɪsˌɔːgənaɪ'zeɪʃ(ə)n] *n.* дезорганиза́ция. **dis'organize** *v.t.* дезорганизова́ть *impf.* & *pf.*

disorientation [dɪsˌɔːrɪən'teɪʃ(ə)n] *n.* дезориента́ция.

disown [dɪs'əʊn] *v.t.* не признава́ть (-наю́, -наёшь) *impf.*, призна́ть *pf.*; отрица́ть *impf.*

disparage [dɪ'spærɪdʒ] *v.t.* умаля́ть *impf.*,

умали́ть *pf.* **disparagement** *n.* умале́ние.
disparity [dɪ'spærɪtɪ] *n.* нера́венство.
dispassionate [dɪ'spæʃənət] *adj.* беспристра́стный.
dispatch, des- [dɪ'spætʃ] *v.t.* (*send*) отправля́ть *impf.*, отпра́вить *pf.*; (*deal with*) расправля́ться *impf.*, распра́виться *pf.* с+*i.*; *n.* отпра́вка; (*message*) донесе́ние; (*rapidity*) быстрота́. **dispatch-box** *n.* вали́за. **dispatch-rider** *n.* мотоцикли́ст свя́зи.
dispel [dɪ'spel] *v.t.* рассе́ивать *impf.*, рассе́ять (-е́ю, -е́ешь) *pf.*
dispensary [dɪ'spensərɪ] *n.* апте́ка.
dispensation [ˌdɪspen'seɪʃ(ə)n] *n.* (*exemption*) освобожде́ние (от обяза́тельства, обе́та). **di'spense** *v.t.* (*distribute*) раздава́ть (-даю́, -даёшь) *impf.*, разда́ть (-а́м, -а́шь, -а́ст, -ади́м; ро́здал & разда́л, раздала́, ро́здало & разда́ло) *pf.*; (*justice, medicine*) отпуска́ть *impf.*, отпусти́ть (-ущу́, -у́стишь) *pf.*; ~ **with** (*do without*) обходи́ться (-ожу́сь, -о́дишься) *impf.*, обойти́сь (обойду́сь, -дёшься; обошёлся, -шла́сь) *pf.* без+*g.* **di'spenser** *n.* (*person*) фармаце́вт; (*device*) торго́вый автома́т.
dispersal [dɪ'spɜːsəl] *n.* распростране́ние. **disperse** *v.t.* разгоня́ть *impf.*, разогна́ть (разгоню́, -нишь; разогна́л, -а́, -о) *pf.*; рассе́ивать *impf.*, рассе́ять (-е́ю, -е́ешь) *pf.*; *v.t.* расходи́ться (-дится) *impf.*, разойти́сь (-ойдётся; -ошёлся, -ошла́сь) *pf.*
dispirited [dɪ'spɪrɪtɪd] *adj.* удручённый (-ён, -ена́).
displaced [dɪs'pleɪsd] *adj.*: ~ **persons** перемещённые ли́ца *nt.pl.* **displacement** [dɪs'pleɪsmənt] *n.* (*of fluid*) водоизмеще́ние.
display [dɪ'spleɪ] *n.* пока́з; проявле́ние; демонстра́ция; *v.t.* пока́зывать *impf.*, показа́ть (-ажу́, -а́жешь) *pf.*; проявля́ть *impf.*, прояви́ть (-влю́, -вишь) *pf.*; демонстри́ровать *impf.* &*pf.*
displease [dɪs'pliːz] *v.t.* раздража́ть *impf.*, раздражи́ть *pf.* **displeased** *pred.* недово́лен (-льна).
disposable [dɪ'spəʊzəb(ə)l] *adj.* име́ющийся в распоряже́нии; однора́зового по́льзования. **disposal** *n.* удале́ние, избавле́ние (**of** от+*g.*); **at your** ~ (*service*) к ва́шим услу́гам; (*use*) в ва́шем распоряже́нии. **dispose** *v.i.*: ~ **of** избавля́ться *impf.*, изба́виться *pf.* от+*g.* **disposed** *pred.*: ~ **to** скло́нен (-о́нна́, -о́нно) к+*d.*, располо́жен+*inf.* *or* к+*d.* **dispo'sition** *n.* расположе́ние, скло́нность; (*temperament*) нрав.
disproof [dɪs'pruːf] *n.* опроверже́ние.
disproportionate [ˌdɪsprə'pɔːʃənət] *adj.* непропорциона́льный.
disprove [dɪs'pruːv] *v.t.* опроверга́ть *impf.*, опрове́ргнуть (-г(нул), -гла) *pf.*
dispute [dɪ'spjuːt, 'dɪspjuːt; dɪ'spjuːt] *n.* (*debate*) спор; (*quarrel*) ссо́ра; *v.t.* оспа́ривать *impf.*, оспо́рить *pf.*
disqualification [dɪsˌkwɒlɪfɪ'keɪʃ(ə)n] *n.* дисквалифика́ция. **dis'qualify** *v.t.* лиша́ть *impf.*, лиши́ть *pf.* права́+*inf.*; дисквалифици́ровать *impf.* & *pf.*
disquiet [dɪs'kwaɪət] *n.* беспоко́йство, трево́га. **disquieting** *adj.* трево́жный.
disregard [ˌdɪsrɪ'gɑːd] *n.* невнима́ние к+*d.*; пренебреже́ние+*i.*; *v.t.* игнори́ровать *impf.* & *pf.*; пренебрега́ть *impf.*, пренебре́чь (-егу́, -ежёшь; -ёг, -егла́) *pf.*+*i.*
disrepair [ˌdɪsrɪ'peə(r)] *n.* неиспра́вность.
disreputable [dɪs'repjʊtəb(ə)l] *adj.* по́льзующийся дурно́й сла́вой, дурно́й репута́цией. **disre'pute** *n.* дурна́я сла́ва.
disrespect [ˌdɪsrɪ'spekt] *n.* неуваже́ние, непочте́ние. **disrespectful** *adj.* непочти́тельный.
disrupt [dɪs'rʌpt] *v.t.* срыва́ть *impf.*, сорва́ть (-ву́, -вёшь; сорва́л, -а́, -о) *pf.* **disruptive** *adj.* подрывно́й, разруши́тельный.
dissatisfaction [ˌdɪsætɪs'fækʃ(ə)n] *n.* неудовлетворённость; недово́льство. **di'ssatisfied** *adj.* неудовлетворённый (-ён, -ена́ & -ённа), недово́льный.
dissect [dɪ'sekt] *v.t.* разреза́ть *impf.*, разре́зать (-е́жу, -е́жешь) *pf.*; (*med. etc.*) вскрыва́ть *impf.*, вскрыть (-ро́ю, -ро́ешь) *pf.*
dissemble [dɪ'semb(ə)l] *v.t.* скрыва́ть *impf.*, скры́ть (-ро́ю, -ро́ешь) *pf.*; *v.i.* притворя́ться *impf.*, притвори́ться *pf.*
dissemination [dɪˌsemɪ'neɪʃ(ə)n] *n.* рассе́ивание; распростране́ние.
dissension [dɪ'senʃ(ə)n] *n.* разногла́сие, раздо́р. **dissent** *n.* расхожде́ние, несогла́сие; (*eccl.*) раско́л. **dissenter** *n.* (*eccl.*) раско́льник, секта́нт.
dissertation [ˌdɪsə'teɪʃ(ə)n] *n.* диссерта́ция.
disservice [dɪs'sɜːvɪs] *n.* плоха́я услу́га.
dissident ['dɪsɪd(ə)nt] *n.* диссиде́нт, инакомы́слящий *sb.*
dissimilar [dɪ'sɪmɪlə(r)] *adj.* несхо́дный, непохо́жий, разли́чный. **dissimilation** ['dɪsɪmɪ'leɪʃ(ə)n] *n.* диссимиля́ция.
dissipate ['dɪsɪˌpeɪt] *v.t.* (*dispel*) рассе́ивать *impf.*, рассе́ять (-е́ю, -е́ешь) *pf.*; (*squander*) прома́тывать *impf.*, промота́ть *pf.* **dissipated** *adj.* распу́тный, беспу́тный.
dissociate [dɪ'səʊʃɪˌeɪt, -sɪˌeɪt] *v.t.*: ~ **o.s.** отмежёвываться *impf.*, отмежева́ться (-жу́юсь, -жу́ешься) *pf.* (**from** от+*g.*). **dissoci'ation** *n.* разобще́ние, отмежева́ние.
dissolute ['dɪsəˌluːt, -ˌljuːt] *adj.* распу́щенный (-ен, -енна), развра́тный. **dissolution** *n.* (*treaty etc.*) расторже́ние; (*parl.*) ро́спуск; (*solution*) растворе́ние. **dissolve** [dɪ'zɒlv] *v.t.* & *i.* (*in liquid*) растворя́ть(ся) *impf.*, раствори́ть(ся) *pf.*; *v.t.* (*annul*) расторга́ть *impf.*, расто́ргнуть (-г(нул), -гла) *pf.*; (*parl.*) распуска́ть *impf.*, распусти́ть (-ущу́, -у́стишь) *pf.*
dissonance ['dɪsənəns] *n.* диссона́нс. **dissonant** *adj.* диссони́рующий.
dissuade [dɪ'sweɪd] *v.t.* отгова́ривать *impf.*, отговори́ть *pf.* **dissuasion** *n.* отгова́ривание.

distaff ['dɪstɑːf] *n.* пря́лка; **on the ~ side** по же́нской ли́нии.

distance ['dɪst(ə)ns] *n.* расстоя́ние; (*distant point*) даль (*loc.* -ли́); (*sport*) диста́нция; **at a great ~** вдали́. **distant** *adj.* да́льний, далёкий (-ёк, -ека́, -ёко́); (*reserved*) сде́ржанный (-ан, -анна).

distaste [dɪs'teɪst] *n.* неприя́знь. **distasteful** *adj.* проти́вный, неприя́тный.

distemper[1] [dɪ'stempə(r)] *n.* (*vet.*) чума́.

distemper[2] [dɪ'stempə(r)] *n.* (*paint*) те́мпера; *v.t.* кра́сить *impf.*, по~ *pf.* те́мперой.

distend [dɪ'stend] *v.t.* расширя́ть *impf.*, расши́рить *pf.*; надува́ть *impf.*, наду́ть (-у́ю, -у́ешь) *pf.* **distension** *n.* расшире́ние, надува́ние.

distil [dɪ'stɪl] *v.t.* перегоня́ть *impf.*, перегна́ть (-гоню́, -го́нишь; перегна́л, -а́, -о) *pf.*; дистилли́ровать *impf.* & *pf.* **disti'llation** *n.* перего́нка, дистилля́ция. **distillery** *n.* виноку́ренный, перего́нный, заво́д.

distinct [dɪ'stɪŋkt] *adj.* (*separate*) отде́льный; (*clear*) отчётливый; (*definite*) определённый (-ёнен, -ённа); **~ from** отлича́ющийся от+*g.* **distinction** *n.* отли́чие, разли́чие. **distinctive** *adj.* осо́бенный, отличи́тельный. **distinctly** *adj.* я́сно, определённо.

distinguish [dɪ'stɪŋgwɪʃ] *v.t.* различа́ть *impf.*, различи́ть *pf.*; **~ o.s.** отлича́ться *impf.*, отличи́ться *pf.* **distinguished** *adj.* выдаю́щийся.

distort [dɪ'stɔːt] *v.t.* искажа́ть *impf.*, искази́ть *pf.*; (*misrepresent*) извраща́ть *impf.*, изврати́ть (-ащу́, -ати́шь) *pf.* **distortion** *n.* искаже́ние, искривле́ние.

distract [dɪ'strækt] *v.t.* отвлека́ть *impf.*, отвле́чь (-еку́, -ечёшь; -ёк, -екла́) *pf.* **distracted** *adj.* (*maddened*) обезу́мевший. **distraction** *n.* (*amusement*) развлече́ние; (*madness*) безу́мие.

distrain [dɪ'streɪn] *v.i.*: **~ upon** накла́дывать *impf.*, наложи́ть (-жу́, -жишь) *pf.* аре́ст на+*a.* **distraint** *n.* наложе́ние аре́ста.

distraught [dɪ'strɔːt] *adj.* обезу́мевший.

distress [dɪ'stres] *n.* (*calamity*) беда́; (*ship etc.*) бе́дствие; (*poverty*) нужда́; (*physical*) недомога́ние; *v.t.* огорча́ть *impf.*, огорчи́ть *pf.*; му́чить *impf.*, из~ *pf.*

distribute [dɪ'strɪbjuːt, 'dɪ-] *v.t.* распределя́ть *impf.*, распредели́ть *pf.* **distri'bution** *n.* распределе́ние, разда́ча. **distributive** *adj.* распредели́тельный. **distributor** *n.* распредели́тель *m.*; (*cin.*) кинопрока́тчик.

district ['dɪstrɪkt] *n.* о́круг (*pl.* -а́), райо́н.

distrust [dɪs'trʌst] *n.* недове́рие; *v.t.* не доверя́ть *impf.* **distrustful** *adj.* недове́рчивый.

disturb [dɪ'stɜːb] *v.t.* беспоко́ить *impf.*, о~ *pf.* **disturbance** *n.* наруше́ние поко́я; *pl.* (*pol. etc.*) беспоря́дки *m.pl.*

disuse [dɪs'juːs] *n.* неупотребле́ние; **fall into ~** выходи́ть (-ит) *impf.*, вы́йти (-йдёт; вы́шел, -шла) *pf.* из употребле́ния. **disused** *adj.* вы́шедший из употребле́ния.

ditch [dɪtʃ] *n.* кана́ва, ров (рва, *loc.* во рву́).

dither ['dɪðə(r)] *v.i.* колеба́ться (-блюсь, -блешься) *impf.*; *n.*: **all of a ~** в си́льном возбужде́нии.

ditto ['dɪtəʊ] *n.* то же са́мое; *adv.* так же.

ditty ['dɪtɪ] *n.* пе́сенка.

diuretic [ˌdaɪjʊ'retɪk] *n.* мочего́нное сре́дство; *adj.* мочего́нный.

diurnal [daɪ'ɜːn(ə)l] *adj.* дневно́й.

divan [dɪ'væn, daɪ-, 'daɪ-] *n.* тахта́, дива́н.

dive [daɪv] *v.i.* ныря́ть *impf.*, нырну́ть *pf.*; пры́гать *impf.*, пры́гнуть *pf.* в во́ду; (*aeron.*) пики́ровать *impf.* & *pf.*; (*submarine*) погружа́ться *impf.*, погрузи́ться *pf.*; *n.* ныро́к (-рка́), прыжо́к (-жка́) в во́ду. **dive-bomber** *n.* пики́рующий бомбардиро́вщик. **diver** *n.* водола́з; (*bird*) гага́ра.

diverge [daɪ'vɜːdʒ] *v.i.* расходи́ться (-ится) *impf.*, разойти́сь (-ойдётся; -ошёлся, -ошла́сь) *pf.*; (*deviate*) отклоня́ться *impf.*, отклони́ться (-ню́сь, -нишься) *pf.* (**from** от+*g.*). **divergence** *n.* расхожде́ние; отклоне́ние. **divergent** *adj.* расходя́щийся.

diverse [daɪ'vɜːs, 'daɪ-, dɪ-] *adj.* различный, разнообра́зный. **diversifi'cation** *n.* расшире́ние ассортиме́нта. **diversified** *adj.* многообра́зный. **diversify** *v.t.* разнообра́зить *impf.* **diversion** *n.* (*deviation*) отклоне́ние; (*detour*) объе́зд; (*amusement*) развлече́ние; (*mil.*) диве́рсия. **diversionist** *n.* диверса́нт. **diversity** *n.* разнообра́зие; разли́чие. **divert** *v.t.* отклоня́ть *impf.*, отклони́ть (-ню́, -нишь) *pf.*; отводи́ть (-ожу́, -о́дишь) *impf.*, отвести́ (-еду́, -едёшь; -ёл, -ела́) *pf.*; (*amuse*) развлека́ть *impf.*, развле́чь (-еку́, -ечёшь; -ёк, -екла́) *pf.* **diverting** *adj.* заба́вный.

divest [daɪ'vest] *v.t.* (*unclothe*) разоблача́ть *impf.*, разоблачи́ть *pf.*; (*deprive*) лиша́ть *impf.*, лиши́ть *pf.* (**of** +*g.*).

divide [dɪ'vaɪd] *v.t.* дели́ть (-лю́, -лишь) *impf.*, по~ *pf.*; разделя́ть *impf.*, раздели́ть (-лю́, -лишь) *pf.* **dividend** ['dɪvɪˌdend] *n.* дивиде́нд. **dividers** *n.* ци́ркуль *m.*

divination [ˌdɪvɪ'neɪʃ(ə)n] *n.* гада́ние; предсказа́ние. **divine** [dɪ'vaɪn] *adj.* боже́ственный (-ен, -енна); *n.* богосло́в; *v.t.* предска́зывать *impf.*, предсказа́ть (-ажу́, -а́жешь) *pf.* **diviner** [dɪ'vaɪnə(r)] *n.* предсказа́тель *m.*

diving ['daɪvɪŋ] *n.* ныря́ние; (*profession*) водола́зное де́ло; (*aeron.*) пики́рование; (*naut.*) погруже́ние. **diving-board** *n.* трампли́н.

divining-rod [dɪ'vaɪnɪŋ] *n.* волше́бная лоза́ (*pl.* -зы).

divinity [dɪ'vɪnɪtɪ] *n.* божество́; (*theology*) богосло́вие; теоло́гия.

divisible [dɪ'vɪzɪb(ə)l] *adj.* дели́мый. **division** *n.* (*dividing*) деле́ние, разделе́ние; (*section*) отде́л, подразделе́ние; (*mil.*) диви́зия. **divisional** *adj.* дивизио́нный. **divisive** [dɪ'vaɪsɪv] *adj.* разделя́ющий, вызыва́ющий разногла́сия. **divisor** [dɪ'vaɪzə(r)] *n.* дели́тель *m.*

divorce [dɪ'vɔːs] *n.* разво́д; *v.i.* разводи́ться (-ожу́сь, -о́дишься) *impf.*, развести́сь (-еду́сь, -едёшься; -ёлся, -ела́сь) *pf.* **divorced** *adj.* разведённый (-ён, -ена́). **divor'cee** *n.* разведённая жена́ (*pl.* жёны).

divulge [daɪ'vʌldʒ, dɪ-] *v.t.* разглаша́ть *impf.*, разгласи́ть *pf.*

DIY *abbr.* (*of* ***do it yourself***): ~ **store** магази́н «уме́лые ру́ки».

dizziness ['dɪzɪnɪs] *n.* головокруже́ние. **dizzy** *adj.* головокружи́тельный; **I am** ~ у меня́ кру́жится голова́.

DJ *abbr.* (*of* ***disc jockey***) диск-жоке́й.

DNA *abbr.* (*of* ***deoxyribonucleic acid***) ДНК, (*дезоксирибонуклеи́новая кислота́*).

do [du:, də] *v.t.* де́лать *impf.*, с~ *pf.*; выполня́ть *impf.*, вы́полнить *pf.*; (*coll.*) (*cheat*) надува́ть *impf.*, наду́ть (-у́ю, -у́ешь) *pf.*; *v.i.* (*be suitable*) годи́ться *impf.*; (*suffice*) быть доста́точным; **that will** ~ хва́тит!; **how** ~ **you** ~**?** здра́вствуйте!; как вы пожива́ете?; ~ **away with** (*abolish*) уничтожа́ть *impf.*, уничто́жить *pf.*; ~ **in** (*kill*) убива́ть *impf.*, уби́ть (убью́, -ьёшь) *pf.*; ~ **up** (*restore*) ремонти́ровать *impf.*, от~ *pf.*; (*wrap up*) завёртывать *impf.*, заверну́ть *pf.*; (*fasten*) застёгивать *impf.*, застегну́ть *pf.*; ~ **without** обходи́ться (-ожу́сь, -о́дишься) *impf.*, обойти́сь (обойду́сь, -дёшься; обошёлся, -шла́сь) *pf.* без+*g.*

docile ['dəʊsaɪl] *adj.* поко́рный. **docility** [dəʊ'sɪlɪtɪ] *n.* поко́рность.

dock[1] [dɒk] *n.* (*bot.*) щаве́ль (-ля́) *m.*

dock[2] [dɒk] *v.t.* (*tail*) отруба́ть *impf.*, отруби́ть (-блю́, -бишь) *pf.*; (*money*) уре́зывать, уреза́ть *impf.*, уре́зать (-е́жу, -е́жешь) *pf.*

dock[3] [dɒk] *n.* (*naut.*) док; *v.t.* ста́вить *impf.*, по~ *pf.* в док; *v.i.* входи́ть (-ожу́, -о́дишь) *impf.*, войти́ (войду́, -дёшь; вошёл, -шла́) *pf.* в док; *v.t.* & *i.* (*spacecraft*) стыкова́ть(ся) *impf.*, со~ *pf.* **docker** *n.* до́кер, порто́вый рабо́чий *sb.* **docking** *n.* (*ship*) постано́вка в док; (*spacecraft*) стыко́вка. **dockyard** *n.* верфь.

dock[4] [dɒk] *n.* (*leg.*) скамья́ (*pl.* ска́мьи, -ме́й) подсуди́мых.

docket ['dɒkɪt] *n.* квита́нция; (*label*) ярлы́к (-а́), этике́тка.

doctor ['dɒktə(r)] *n.* врач (-а́); (*also univ. etc.*) до́ктор (*pl.* -а́); *v.t.* (*med.*) лечи́ть (-чу́, -чишь) *impf.*; (*falsify*) фальсифици́ровать *impf.* & *pf.* **doctor(i)al** ['dɒktər(ə)l, ˌdɒk'tɔ:rɪəl] *adj.* до́кторский. **doctorate** *n.* сте́пень (*pl.* -ни, -не́й) до́ктора.

doctrinaire [ˌdɒktrɪ'neə(r)] *n.* доктринёр; *adj.* доктринёрский. **'doctrine** *n.* доктри́на.

document ['dɒkjʊmənt] *n.* докуме́нт; *v.t.* документи́ровать *impf.* & *pf.* **docu'mentary** *adj.* документа́льный; *n.* документа́льный фильм. **documen'tation** *n.* документа́ция.

dodder ['dɒdə(r)] *v.i.* дрожа́ть (-жу́, -жи́шь) *impf.* **dodderer** *n.* дря́хлый стари́к.

dodge [dɒdʒ] *n.* (*trick*) ло́вкий приём, увёртка; *v.t.* уклоня́ться *impf.*, уклони́ться (-ню́сь, -нишься) *pf.* от+*g.*; уви́ливать *impf.*, увильну́ть *pf.* от+*g.*

doe [dəʊ] *n.* са́мка. **doeskin** *n.* за́мша.

dog [dɒg] *n.* соба́ка, пёс (пса); (*male dog*) кобе́ль (-ля́) *m.*; (*male animal*) саме́ц (-мца́); *v.t.* сле́довать *impf.*, по~ *pf.* по пята́м за+*i.*; (*fig.*) пресле́довать *impf.* **dog-collar** *n.* оше́йник. **dog-fight** *n.* возду́шный бой (*loc.* бою́; *pl.* бои́).

doggerel ['dɒgər(ə)l] *n.* ви́рши (-шей) *pl.*

dogma ['dɒgmə] *n.* до́гма. **dog'matic** *adj.* догмати́ческий.

doing ['du:ɪŋ] *n.*: *pl.* дела́ *nt.pl.*; (*events*) собы́тия *nt.pl.*

doldrums ['dɒldrəmz] *n.*: **be in the** ~ хандри́ть *impf.*

dole [dəʊl] *n.* посо́бие по безрабо́тице.

doleful ['dəʊlfʊl] *adj.* ско́рбный.

doll ['dɒl] *n.* ку́кла (*g.pl.* -кол).

dollar ['dɒlə(r)] *n.* до́ллар.

dollop ['dɒləp] *n.* здоро́вый кусо́к (-ска́).

dolly ['dɒlɪ] *n.* ку́колка; (*stick*) валёк (-лька́); (*cin.*) опера́торская теле́жка.

dolphin ['dɒlfɪn] *n.* дельфи́н, белобо́чка.

dolt [dəʊlt] *n.* болва́н. **doltish** *adj.* тупо́й (туп, -а́, -о, ту́пы́).

domain [də'meɪn] *n.* (*estate*) владе́ние; (*field*) о́бласть, сфе́ра.

dome [dəʊm] *n.* ку́пол (*pl.* -а́). **domed** *adj.* с ку́полом.

domestic [də'mestɪk] *adj.* (*of household*; *animals*) дома́шний; (*of family*) семе́йный; (*pol.*) вну́тренний; *n.* прислу́га. **domesticate** *v.t.* прируча́ть *impf.*, приручи́ть *pf.* **domesticity** [ˌdɒmə'stɪsɪtɪ, ˌdəʊ-] *n.* дома́шняя, семе́йная, жизнь.

domicile ['dɒmɪˌsaɪl, -sɪl] *n.* постоя́нное местожи́тельство; *v.t.* сели́ть *impf.*, по~ *pf.* на постоя́нное жи́тельство. **domiciliary** [ˌdɒmɪ'sɪlɪərɪ] *adj.* дома́шний.

dominance ['dɒmɪnəns] *n.* госпо́дство. **dominant** *adj.* преоблада́ющий; госпо́дствующий; *n.* домина́нта. **dominate** *v.t.* госпо́дствовать *impf.* над+*i.* **domi'neering** *adj.* вла́стный, деспоти́ческий.

dominion [də'mɪnɪən] *n.* доминио́н; влады́чество.

domino ['dɒmɪˌnəʊ] *n.* кость (*pl.* -ти, -те́й) домино́; *pl.* (*game*) домино́ *nt.indecl.*

don[1] [dɒn] *n.* (**D**~, *title*) дон; (*univ.*) преподава́тель *m.*

don[2] [dɒn] *v.t.* надева́ть *impf.*, наде́ть (-е́ну, -е́нешь) *pf.*

donate [dəʊ'neɪt] *v.t.* же́ртвовать *impf.*, по~ *pf.* **donation** *n.* дар (*pl.* -ы́), поже́ртвование.

donkey ['dɒŋkɪ] *n.* осёл (-сла́); ~ **engine** вспомога́тельный дви́гатель *m.*

donnish ['dɒnɪʃ] *adj.* педанти́чный.

donor ['dəʊnə(r)] *n.* же́ртвователь *m.*; (*med.*) до́нор.

doom [du:m] *n.* рок, судьба́; (*ruin*) ги́бель; *v.t.* обрека́ть *impf.*, обре́чь (-еку́, -ечёшь;

-ёк, -еклá) *pf.* **doomsday** *n.* стрáшный суд (-á); конéц (-нцá) свéта.

door [dɔː(r)] *n.* (*house*) дверь (*loc.* -ри́; *pl.* -ри, -рéй, *i.* -рьми́ & -ря́ми); (*smaller*) двéрца (*g.pl.* -рец). **doorbell** *n.* (дверно́й) звоно́к (-нкá). **doorknob** *n.* (дверна́я) ру́чка. **doorman** *n.* швейцáр. **doormat** *n.* полови́к (-á). **doorpost** *n.* (дверно́й) кося́к (-á). **doorstep** *n.* поро́г. **doorway** *n.* дверно́й проём.

dope [dəʊp] *n.* (*drug*) нарко́тик; информáция; ~ **fiend** наркомáн, ~ка; *v.t.* давáть (даю́, даёшь) *impf.*, дать (дам, дашь, даст, дади́м; дал, -á, дáло́, -и) *pf.* нарко́тик+*d.*

dormant ['dɔːmənt] *adj.* (*sleeping*) спя́щий; (*inactive*) бездéйствующий.

dormer window ['dɔːmə(r)] *n.* мансáрдное окно́ (*pl.* о́кна, о́кон, о́кнам).

dormitory ['dɔːmɪtərɪ] *n.* дортуáр.

dormouse ['dɔːmaʊs] *n.* со́ня.

dorsal ['dɔːs(ə)l] *adj.* спинно́й.

dose [dəʊs] *n.* до́за; *v.t.* давáть (даю́, даёшь) *impf.*, дать (дам, дашь, даст, дади́м; дал, -á, дáло́, -и) *pf.* лекáрство+*d.*

dosh [dɒʃ] *n.* (*sl.*) бáшли (-ей) *pl.*

doss-house [dɒs] *n.* ночлéжный дом (*pl.* -á).

dossier ['dɒsɪə(r), -ɪˌeɪ] *n.* досьé *nt.indecl.*

dot [dɒt] *n.* то́чка; *v.t.* стáвить *impf.*, по~ *pf.* то́чки на+*a.*; (*scatter*) усéивать *impf.*, усéять (-éю, -éешь) *pf.* (**with** +*i.*); ~**ted line** пункти́р.

dotage ['dəʊtɪdʒ] *n.* (стáрческое) слабоу́мие. **dotard** ['dəʊtəd] *n.* вы́живший из умá стари́к (-á). **dote** *v.i.*: ~ **on** обожáть *impf.*

dotty ['dɒtɪ] *adj.* рехну́вшийся.

double ['dʌb(ə)l] *adj.* двойно́й, пáрный; ~ **bed** двуспáльная кровáть; (*doubled*) удво́енный (-ен); *adv.* вдво́е; (*two together*) вдвоём; *n.* двойно́е коли́чество; (*person's*) двойни́к (-á); (*understudy*) дублёр; *pl.* (*sport*) пáрная игрá; **at the** ~ бéглым шáгом; *v.t.* удвáивать *impf.*, удво́ить *pf.*; (*fold*) склáдывать *impf.*, сложи́ть (-жу́, -жишь) *pf.* вдво́е; ~ **the parts of** (*theatr.*) игрáть *impf.*, сыгрáть *pf.* ро́ли+*g.* **double-barrelled** *adj.* двуство́льный. **double-bass** *n.* контрабáс. **double-breasted** *adj.* двубо́ртный. **double-cross** *v.t.* обмáнывать *impf.*, обману́ть (-ну́, -нешь) *pf.* **double-dealer** *n.* двуру́шник. **double-dealing** *n.* двуру́шничество; *adj.* двуру́шнический. **double-decker** *n.* двухэтáжный авто́бус. **double-edged** *adj.* обоюдоо́стрый. **double-faced** *adj.* двули́чный.

doubt [daʊt] *n.* сомнéние; *v.t.* сомневáться *impf.* в+*p.* **doubtful** *adj.* сомни́тельный. **doubting** *adj.* сомневáющийся. **doubtless** *adv.* несомнéнно.

douche [duːʃ] *n.* душ; *v.t.* обливáть *impf.*, обли́ть (оболью́, -ьёшь; о́бли́л, -á, -о) *pf.* водо́й.

dough [dəʊ] *n.* тéсто. **doughnut** *n.* по́нчик, пы́шка.

dour [dʊə(r)] *adj.* угрю́мый, мрáчный (-чен, -чнá, -чно).

douse [daʊs] *v.t.* (*light*) туши́ть (-шу́, -шишь) *impf.*, за~, по~ *pf.*

dove [dʌv] *n.* го́лубь (*pl.* -би, -бéй) *m.*, го́рлица. **dove-coloured** *adj.* си́зый (сиз, -á, -о). **dovecot(e)** *n.* голубя́тня (*g.pl.* -тен). **dovetail** *n.* лáсточкин хвост (-á); *v.i.*: ~ **(into one another)** соотвéтствовать *impf.* друг дру́гу.

Dover ['dəʊvə(r)] *n.* Дувр.

dowager ['daʊədʒə(r)] *n.* вдовá (*pl.* -вы); ~ **empress** вдо́вствующая императри́ца.

dowdy ['daʊdɪ] *adj.* безвку́сный, неэлегáнтный.

down[1] [daʊn] *n.* (*geog.*) безлéсная возвы́шенность; *pl.* Дáунс.

down[2] [daʊn] *n.* (*fluff*) пух (-а(у), *loc.* -у́), пушо́к (-шкá).

down[3] [daʊn] *adv.* (*motion*) вниз; (*position*) внизу́; **be** ~ **with** (*ill*) болéть *impf.*+*i.*; ~ **with** (*int.*) доло́й+*a.*; *prep.* вниз с+*g.*, по+*d.*; (*along*) (вдоль) по+*d.*; *v.t.*: ~ **tools** (*strike*) бастовáть *impf.*, за~ *pf.* **down-and-out** *n.* бедня́к (-á), оборвáнец (-нца). **downcast, down-hearted** *adj.* уны́лый. **downfall** *n.* (*ruin*) ги́бель. **downpour** *n.* ли́вень (-вня) *m.* **downright** *adj.* прямо́й (прям, -á, -о, пря́мы́); (*out-and-out*) я́вный; *adv.* совершéнно. **downstream** *adv.* вниз по течéнию.

dowry ['daʊərɪ] *n.* придáное *sb.*

doyen ['dɔɪən, 'dwɑːjæ̃] *n.* старшинá (*pl.* -ны) *m.*

doze [dəʊz] *v.i.* дремáть (-млю́, -млешь) *impf.*

dozen ['dʌz(ə)n] *n.* дю́жина; **baker's** ~ чёртова дю́жина.

Dr. *abbr.* (*of* **Doctor**) д-р, до́ктор.

drab [dræb] *adj.* бесцвéтный; (*boring*) скучный (-чен, -чнá, -чно).

draft [drɑːft] *n.* (*sketch*) чернови́к (-á); (*of document*) проéкт; (*econ.*) трáтта; *see also* **draught**; *v.t.* составля́ть *impf.*, состáвить *pf.* план, проéкт, +*g.*

drag [dræg] *v.t.* & *i.* тащи́ть(ся) (-щу́(сь), -щишь(ся)) *impf.*; волочи́ться (-чу́(сь), -чишь(ся)) *impf.*; *v.t.* (*river etc.*) драги́ровать *impf.* & *pf.*; *n.* (*grapnel*) ко́шка; (*lure*) примáнка; (*burden*) обу́за; (*brake*) тормозно́й башмáк (-á); (*aeron.*) лобово́е сопротивлéние. **dragnet** *n.* брéдень (-дня) *m.*

dragon ['drægən] *n.* драко́н. **dragonfly** *n.* стрекозá (*pl.* -зы).

dragoon [drə'guːn] *n.* драгу́н (*g.pl.* -н (*collect.*) & -нов).

drain [dreɪn] *n.* водосто́к; (*leakage*, *also fig.*) утéчка; *v.t.* осушáть *impf.*, осуши́ть (-шу́, -шишь) *pf.* **drainage** *n.* сток; канализáция; дренáж. **drain-pipe** *n.* водосто́чная трубá (*pl.* -бы).

drake [dreɪk] *n.* сéлезень (-зня) *m.*

dram [dræm] *n.* глото́к (-ткá).

drama ['drɑːmə] *n.* дрáма. **dramatic** [drə'mætɪk] *adj.* драмати́ческий. **dramatis personae** [ˌdræmətɪs pɜːˈsəʊnaɪ, -niː] *n.* де́йствующие ли́ца *nt.pl.* **dramatist** [ˈdræmətɪst] *n.* драмату́рг. **dramatize** *v.t.* инсцени́ровать *impf.* & *pf.*; (*fig.*) преувели́чивать *impf.*, преувели́чить *pf.*

drape [dreɪp] *v.t.* драпирова́ть *impf.*, за~ *pf.*; *n.* драпиро́вка. **draper** *n.* торго́вец (-вца) тка́нями. **drapery** *n.* драпиро́вка; (*cloth*; *collect.*) тка́ни *f.pl.*

drastic [ˈdræstɪk, ˈdrɑː-] *adj.* круто́й (крут, -á, -о), радика́льный.

drat [dræt] *int.* чёрт возьми́! **dratted** *adj.* проклятый.

draught [drɑːft] *n.* (*drink*) глото́к (-тка́); (*air*) тя́га, сквозня́к (-а́); (*naut.*) оса́дка; *pl.* (*game*) ша́шки *f.pl.*; *see* **draft; be in a ~** быть на сквозняке́; **~ animals** тя́гло *collect.*; **~ beer** пи́во из бо́чки; **~ horse** ломова́я ло́шадь (*pl.* -ди, -де́й, *i.* -дьми́) **draughtsman** *n.* (*person*) чертёжник; (*counter*) ша́шка. **draughty** *adj.*: **it is ~ here** здесь ду́ет.

draw [drɔː] *n.* (*action*) вытя́гивание; (*lottery*) лотере́я; (*attraction*) прима́нка; (*drawn game*) ничья́; *v.t.* (*pull*) тяну́ть (тя́ну, -нешь) *impf.*, по~ *pf.*; таска́ть *indet.*, тащи́ть (-щу́, -щишь) *det.*; (*curtains*) задёргивать *impf.*, задёрнуть *pf.* (занаве́ски); (*attract*) привлека́ть *impf.*, привле́чь (-еку́, -ечёшь; -ёк, -екла́) *pf.*; (*pull out*) вытаскивать *impf.*, вы́тащить *pf.*; (*sword*) обнажа́ть *impf.*, обнажи́ть *pf.*; (*lots*) броса́ть *impf.*, бро́сить *pf.* (жре́бий); (*water*; *inspiration*) че́рпать *impf.*, черпну́ть *pf.*; (*game*) конча́ть *impf.*, ко́нчить *pf.* (игру́) вничью́; (*evoke*) вызыва́ть *impf.*, вы́звать (вы́зову, -вешь) *pf.*; (*conclusion*) выводи́ть (-ожу́, -о́дишь) *impf.*, вы́вести (-еду́, -едешь; -ел) *pf.* (заключе́ние); (*fowl*) потроши́ть *impf.*, вы́~ *pf.*; (*diagram*) черти́ть (-рчу́, -ртишь) *impf.*, на~ *pf.*; (*picture*) рисова́ть *impf.*, на~ *pf.*; **~ aside** отводи́ть (-ожу́, -о́дишь) *impf.*, отвести́ (-еду́, -едёшь; -ёл, -ела́) *pf.* в сто́рону; **~ back** (*withdraw*) отступа́ть *impf.*, отступи́ть (-плю́, -пишь) *pf.*; **~ in** (*involve*) вовлека́ть *impf.*, вовле́чь (-еку́, -ечёшь; -ёк, -екла́) *pf.*; **~ up** (*document*) составля́ть *impf.*, соста́вить *pf.* **drawback** *n.* недоста́ток (-тка), поме́ха. **drawbridge** *n.* подъёмный мост (мо́ста́, *loc.* -у́; *pl.* -ы́). **drawer** *n.* (*person*) чертёжник, рисова́льщик; (*of table etc.*) выдвижно́й я́щик; *pl.* кальсо́ны (-н) *pl.* **drawing** *n.* (*action*) рисова́ние, черче́ние; (*object*) рису́нок (-нка), чертёж(-а́). **drawing-board** *n.* чертёжная доска́ (*a.* -ску; *pl.* -ски, -со́к, -ска́м). **drawing-pen** *n.* рейсфе́дер. **drawing-pin** *n.* кно́пка. **drawing-room** *n.* гости́ная *sb.*

drawl [drɔːl] *n.* протя́жное, медли́тельное, произноше́ние; *v.i.* растя́гивать *impf.*, растяну́ть (-ну́, -нешь) *pf.* слова́.

dray [dreɪ] *n.* подво́да. **dray-horse** *n.* ломова́я ло́шадь (*pl.* -ди, -де́й, *i.* -дьми́). **drayman** *n.* ломово́й изво́зчик.

dread [dred] *n.* страх; *v.t.* боя́ться (бою́сь, бои́шься) *impf.*+*g.* **dreadful** *adj.* стра́шный (-шен, -шна́, -шно, стра́шны́). **dreadnought** *n.* дредно́ут.

dream [driːm] *n.* сон (сна); мечта́ (*g.pl.* -а́ний); *v.i.* ви́деть (ви́жу, -дишь) *impf.*, у~ *pf.* сон; **~ of** ви́деть (ви́жу, -дишь) *impf.*, у~ *pf.* во сне́; (*fig.*) мечта́ть *impf.* о+*p.* **dreamer** *n.* мечта́тель *m.*, фантазёр.

dreariness [ˈdrɪərɪnɪs] *n.* тоскли́вость. **dreary** *adj.* тоскли́вый; ску́чный (-чен, -чна́, -чно).

dredge[1] [dredʒ] *v.t.* (*river etc.*) драги́ровать *impf.* & *pf.* **dredger**[1] *n.* землечерпа́лка; дра́га.

dredge[2] [dredʒ] *v.t.* (*sprinkle*) посыпа́ть *impf.*, посы́пать (-плю, -плешь) *pf.* **dredger**[2] *n.* си́течко (*pl.* -чки, -чек, -чка́м).

dreg [dreg] *n.*:*pl.* оса́дки (-ков) *pl.*, отбро́сы (-сов) *pl.*; **~ of society** подо́нки (-ков) *pl.* о́бщества.

drench [drentʃ] *v.t.* (*wet*) прома́чивать *impf.*, промочи́ть (-чу́, -чишь) *pf.*; **get ~ed** промока́ть *impf.*, промо́кнуть (-к) *pf.*

dress [dres] *n.* пла́тье (*g.pl.* -в), оде́жда; **~ circle** бельэта́ж; **~ coat** фрак; **~ rehearsal** генера́льная репети́ция; *v.t.* & *i.* одева́ть(ся) *impf.*, оде́ть(ся) (-е́ну(сь), -е́нешь(ся)) *pf.*; *v.t.* (*cul.*) приправля́ть *impf.*, припра́вить *pf.*; (*med.*) перевя́зывать *impf.*, перевяза́ть (-яжу́, -я́жешь) *pf.*; *v.i.* (*mil.*) равня́ться *impf.* **dresser**[1] *n.* (*theatr.*) костюме́р, ~ша.

dresser[2] [ˈdresə(r)] *n.* ку́хонный шкаф (*loc.* -у́; *pl.* -ы́).

dressing [ˈdresɪŋ] *n.* (*cul.*) припра́ва; (*med.*) перевя́зка. **dressing-case** *n.* несессе́р. **dressing-down** *n.* вы́говор. **dressing-gown** *n.* хала́т. **dressing-room** *n.* убо́рная *sb.* **dressing-station** *n.* перевя́зочный пункт. **dressing-table** *n.* туале́тный стол (-а́).

dressmaker [ˈdresˌmeɪkə(r)] *n.* портни́ха.

dribble [ˈdrɪb(ə)l] *v.i.* (*water*) ка́пать *impf.*; (*child*) пуска́ть *impf.*, пусти́ть (пущу́, пу́стишь) *pf.* слю́ни; (*sport*) вести́ (веду́, -дёшь; вёл, -а́) *impf.* мяч. **driblet** [ˈdrɪblɪt] *n.* ка́пелька.

dried [draɪd] *adj.* сушёный. **drier** [ˈdraɪə(r)] *n.* суши́лка.

drift [drɪft] *n.* тече́ние; (*naut.*) дрейф; (*aeron.*) снос; (*inaction*) безде́йствие; (*purpose*) тенде́нция; (*meaning*) смысл; (*snow*) сугро́б; (*sand*) нано́с; *v.i.* плыть (плыву́, -вёшь; плыл, -а́, -о) *impf.* по тече́нию; (*naut.*) дрейфова́ть *impf.*; (*snow etc.*) скопля́ться *impf.*, скопи́ться (-ится) *pf.*; *v.t.* (*snow*) наноси́ть (-ит) *impf.*, нанести́ (-есёт; -ёс, -есла́) *pf.*; заноси́ть (-ит) *impf.*, занести́ (-сёт; -сло́) *pf.* (сне́гом, песко́м) *impers.*+*a.*

drill[1] [drɪl] *n.* сверло́ (*pl.* -ёрла), дрель, бур; *v.t.* сверли́ть *impf.*, про~ *pf.*

drill[2] [drɪl] *n.* (*agric. machine*) се́ялка.

drill[3] [drɪl] *v.t.* (*mil.*) обуча́ть *impf.*, обучи́ть (-чу́, -чишь) *pf.* стро́ю; муштрова́ть *impf.*, вы́~ *pf.*; *v.i.* проходи́ть (-ожу́, -о́дишь) *impf.*, пройти́ (-ойду́, -ойдёшь; -ошёл, -ошла́) *pf.* строеву́ю подгото́вку; *n.* строева́я подгото́вка.

drink [drɪŋk] *n.* питьё, напи́ток (-тка); (*mouthful*) глото́к (-тка́); (*alcoholic*) спиртно́й напи́ток (-тка); **soft** ~ безалкого́льный напи́ток (-тка); *v.t.* пить (пью, пьёшь; пил, -а́, -о) *impf.*, вы́~ *pf.* (**to excess** си́льно); (*plants*; *fig.*) впи́тывать *impf.*, впита́ть *pf.* **drinking-bout** *n.* запо́й. **drinking-song** *n.* засто́льная пе́сня (*g.pl.* -сен). **drinking-water** *n.* питьева́я вода́ (*a.* -ду).

drip [drɪp] *n.* (*action*) ка́панье; (*object*) ка́пля (*g.pl.* -пель); *v.i.* ка́пать *impf.*, ка́пнуть *pf.* **drip-dry** *adj.* быстросо́хнущий. **dripping** *n.* (*fat*) жир (-а(у), *loc.* -е & -у́); ~ **wet** промо́кший насквозь.

drive [draɪv] *n.* (*journey*) езда́; (*excursion*) ката́нье, прогу́лка; (*campaign*) похо́д, кампа́ния; (*energy*) эне́ргия; (*tech.*) приво́д; (*driveway*) подъездна́я доро́га; *v.t.* (*urge*; *chase*) гоня́ть *indet.*, гнать (гоню́, -нишь; гнал, -а́, -о) *det.*; (*vehicle*) води́ть (вожу́, во́дишь) *indet.*, везти́ (веду́, -дёшь; вёл, -а́) *det.*; управля́ть *impf.*+*i.*; (*convey*) вози́ть (вожу́, во́зишь) *indet.*, везти́ (везу́, -зёшь; вёз, -ла́) *det.*, по~ *pf.*; *v.i.* (*travel*) е́здить *indet.*, е́хать (е́ду, -е́дешь) *det.*, по~ *pf.*; *v.t.* (*compel*) заставля́ть *impf.*, заста́вить *pf.*; (*nail etc.*) вбива́ть *impf.*, вбить (вобью́, -ьёшь) *pf.* (**into** в+*a.*); (*machine*) приводи́ть (-ожу́, -о́дишь) *impf.*, привести́ (-еду́, -едёшь; -ёл, -ела́) *pf.* в движе́ние (*by steam etc.*, +*i.*); ~ **away** *v.t.* прогоня́ть *impf.*, прогна́ть (прогоню́, -нишь; прогна́л, -а́, -о) *pf.*; *v.i.* уезжа́ть *impf.*, уе́хать (-е́ду, -е́дешь) *pf.*; ~ **out** *v.t.* (*knock out*) выбива́ть *impf.*, вы́бить (вы́бью, -ьешь); *pf.*; (*expel*) выгоня́ть *impf.*, вы́гнать (вы́гоню, -нишь) *pf.*; ~ **up** подъезжа́ть *impf.*, подъе́хать (-е́ду, -е́дешь) *pf.* (**to** к+*d.*).

drivel ['drɪv(ə)l] *n.* чепуха́; *v.i.* поро́ть (-рю́, -решь) *impf.* чепуху́.

driver ['draɪvə(r)] *n.* (*of vehicle*) води́тель *m.*, шофёр. **driving** *n.* вожде́ние; ката́ние; *adj.* дви́жущий; ~ **force** дви́жущая си́ла; ~ **school** автошко́ла; ~ **test** экза́мен на вожде́ние. **driving-belt** *n.* приводно́й реме́нь (-мня́) *m.* **driving-licence** *n.* води́тельские права́ *nt.pl.* **driving-wheel** *n.* веду́щее колесо́ (*pl.* -ёса).

drizzle ['drɪz(ə)l] *n.* ме́лкий до́ждь (-дя́) *m.*; *v.i.* мороси́ть *impf.*

droll [drəʊl] *adj.* смешно́й (-шо́н, -шна́), заба́вный. **drollery** *n.* шу́тка.

dromedary ['drɒmɪdərɪ, 'drʌm-] *n.* дромаде́р.

drone [drəʊn] *n.* (*bee*; *idler*) тру́тень (-тня) *m.*; (*buzz*) жужжа́ние; *v.i.* (*buzz*) жужжа́ть (-жжу́, -жжи́шь) *impf.*; (*mutter*) бубни́ть *impf.*

drool [dru:l] *v.i.* пуска́ть *impf.*, пусти́ть (пущу́, пу́стишь) *pf.* слюни.

droop [dru:p] *v.i.* ни́кнуть (ник) *impf.*, по~, с~ *pf.*

drop [drɒp] *n.* (*of liquid*) ка́пля (*g.pl.* -пель); (*pendant*) висю́лька; (*sweet*) ледене́ц (-нца́); (*fall*) паде́ние, пониже́ние; *v.t.* & *i.* ка́пать *impf.*, ка́пнуть *pf.*; (*price*) снижа́ть(ся) *impf.*, сни́зить(ся) *pf.*; *v.i.* (*fall*) па́дать *impf.*, упа́сть (-аду́, -адёшь; -а́л) *pf.*; *v.t.* роня́ть *impf.*, урони́ть (-ню́, -нишь) *pf.*; (*abandon*) броса́ть *impf.*, бро́сить *pf.*; (*eyes*) опуска́ть *impf.*, опусти́ть (-ущу́, -у́стишь) *pf.*; ~ **behind** отстава́ть (-таю́, -таёшь) *impf.*, отста́ть (-а́ну, -а́нешь) *pf.*; ~ **in** заходи́ть (-ожу́, -о́дишь) *impf.*, зайти́ (зайду́, -дёшь; зашёл, -шла́) *pf.* (**on** к+*d.*); ~ **off** (*fall asleep*) засыпа́ть *impf.*, засну́ть *pf.*; ~ **out** выбыва́ть *impf.*, вы́быть (-буду, -будешь) *pf.* (**of** из+*g.*). **droplet** *n.* ка́пелька. **drop-out** *n.* вы́бывший *sb.* **dropper** *n.* пипе́тка. **droppings** *n.* помёт, наво́з (-а(у)).

dropsy ['drɒpsɪ] *n.* водя́нка.

dross [drɒs] *n.* шлак; (*refuse*) отбро́сы (-сов) *pl.*

drought [draʊt] *n.* за́суха. **drought-resistant** *adj.* засухоусто́йчивый.

drove [drəʊv] *n.* ста́до (*pl.* -да́), гурт (-а́). **drover** *n.* гуртовщи́к (-а́).

drown [draʊn] *v.t.* топи́ть (-плю́, -пишь) *impf.*, у~ *pf.*; (*sound*) заглуша́ть *impf.*, заглуши́ть *pf.*; *v.i.* тону́ть (-ну́, -нешь) *impf.*, у~ *pf.*

drowse [draʊz] *v.i.* дрема́ть (-млю́, -млешь) *impf.* **drowsiness** *n.* сонли́вость, дремо́та. **drowsy** *adj.* сонли́вый, дре́млющий.

drub [drʌb] *v.t.* поро́ть (-рю́, -решь) *impf.*, вы́~ *pf.*

drudge [drʌdʒ] *n.* работя́га. **drudgery** *n.* тяжёлая, ну́дная, рабо́та.

drug [drʌg] *n.* медикаме́нт; нарко́тик; ~ **addict** наркома́н, ~ка; ~ **trafficker** наркоделе́ц (-льца́); *v.t.* дава́ть (даю́, даёшь) *impf.*, дать (дам, дашь, даст, дади́м; дал, -а́, да́ло́, -и) *pf.* нарко́тик+*d.*

druid ['dru:ɪd] *n.* друи́д.

drum [drʌm] *n.* бараба́н; *v.i.* бить (бью, бьёшь) *impf.* в бараба́н; бараба́нить *impf.* **drummer** *n.* бараба́нщик.

drunk [drʌŋk] *adj.* пья́ный (пьян, -а́, -о). **drunkard** *n.* пья́ница *c.g.* **drunken** *adj.* пья́ный. **drunkenness** *n.* пья́нство.

dry [draɪ] *adj.* сухо́й (сух, -а́, -о); ~ **land** су́ша; *v.t.* суши́ть (-шу́, -шишь) *impf.*, вы́~ *pf.*; (*wipe dry*) вытира́ть *impf.*, вы́тереть (-тру, -трешь; -тер) *pf.*; *v.i.* со́хнуть (сох) *impf.*, вы́~, про~ *pf.* **dry-cleaning** *n.* химчи́стка. **drying** *n.* су́шка; *adj.* суши́льный. **dryness** *n.* су́хость.

DSS *abbr.* (*of* ***Department of Social Security***) Министе́рство социа́льного обеспе́чения.

dual ['dju:əl] *adj.* двойно́й, двойственный (-ен, -енна). **duality** [ˌdju:'ælɪtɪ] *n.* двойственность, раздвóенность. **dual-purpose** *adj.* двойнóго назначéния.

dub¹ [dʌb] *v.t.* (*nickname*) давáть (даю́, даёшь) *impf.*, дать (дам, дашь, даст, дади́м; дал, -á, дáлó, -и) *pf.* прóзвище+*d.*

dub² [dʌb] *v.t.* (*cin.*) дубли́ровать *impf.* & *pf.* **dubbing** *n.* дубля́ж.

dubious ['dju:bɪəs] *adj.* сомни́тельный.

ducal ['dju:k(ə)l] *adj.* гéрцогский. **duchess** ['dʌtʃɪs] *n.* герцоги́ня. **duchy** ['dʌtʃɪ] *n.* гéрцогство.

duck¹ [dʌk] *n.* (*bird*) у́тка.

duck² [dʌk] *v.t.* окунáть *impf.*, окуну́ть *pf.*; *v.i.* увёртываться *impf.*, уверну́ться *pf.* от удáра.

duck³ [dʌk] *n.* (*cloth*) паруси́на.

duckling ['dʌklɪŋ] *n.* утёнок (-нка; *pl.* утя́та, -т).

duct ['dʌkt] *n.* прохóд, трубопровóд; (*anat.*) протóк.

ductile ['dʌktaɪl] *adj.* (*metal*) кóвкий (-вок, -вкá, -вко); (*clay*) пласти́чный. **ductility** [,dʌk'tɪlɪtɪ] *n.* кóвкость; пласти́чность.

dud [dʌd] *n.* (*forgery*) поддéлка; (*shell*) неразорвáвшийся заря́д; *adj.* поддéльный; (*worthless*) негóдный (-ден, -днá, -дно).

dudgeon ['dʌdʒ(ə)n] *n.* оби́да, возмущéние; **in high** ~ в глубóком возмущéнии.

due [dju:] *n.* дóлжное *sb.*; *pl.* сбóры *m.pl.*, взнóсы *m.pl.*; *adj.* дóлжный, надлежáщий; *pred.* дóлжен (-жнá); **in** ~ **course** со врéменем; *adv.* тóчно, пря́мо; ~ **to** благодаря́+*d.*, вслéдствие+*g.*

duel ['dju:əl] *n.* дуэ́ль, поеди́нок (-нка).

duet [dju:'et] *n.* дуэ́т.

duffer ['dʌfə(r)] *n.* дурáк (-á), недотёпа *c.g.*

dug-out ['dʌgaʊt] *n.* (*boat*) челнóк (-á); (*mil.*) блиндáж (-á).

duke [dju:k] *n.* гéрцог; **Grand D~** вели́кий князь (*pl.* -зья́, -зéй) *m.*

dulcet ['dʌlsɪt] *adj.* слáдкий (-док, -дкá, -дко), нéжный (-жен, -жнá, -жно, нéжны́).

dulcimer ['dʌlsɪmə(r)] *n.* цимбáлы (-л) *pl.*

dull [dʌl] *adj.* тупóй (туп, -á, -о, ту́пы́); (*tedious*) скучный (-чен, -чнá, -чно); (*colour*) ту́склый (-л, -лá, -ло), мáтовый; (*weather*) пáсмурный; *v.t.* притупля́ть *impf.*, притупи́ть (-плю́, -пишь) *pf.* **dullard** ['dʌləd] *n.* тупи́ца *c.g.* **dullness** *n.* ту́пость; ску́чность.

duly ['dju:lɪ] *adv.* надлежáщим óбразом; (*punctually*) в дóлжное врéмя, своеврéменно.

dumb [dʌm] *adj.* немóй (нем, -á, -о); (*taciturn*) молчали́вый; **deaf and** ~ глухонемóй. **dumb-bell** *n.* гантéль. **dumb'found** *v.t.* ошеломля́ть *impf.*, ошеломи́ть *pf.*

dummy ['dʌmɪ] *n.* макéт; (*tailor's*) манекéн; (*cards*) болвáн; (*baby's*) сóска(-пусты́шка); *adj.* ненастоя́щий, фальши́вый.

dump [dʌmp] *n.* свáлка; *v.t.* свáливать *impf.*, свали́ть (-лю́, -лишь) *pf.* **dumping** *n.* (*econ.*) дéмпинг, брóсовый э́кспорт.

dumpling ['dʌmplɪŋ] *n.* клёцка.

dumpy ['dʌmpɪ] *adj.* призéмистый, корéнáстый.

dun [dʌn] *adj.* серовáто-кори́чневый.

dunce [dʌns] *n.* болвáн, тупи́ца *c.g.*

dune [dju:n] *n.* дю́на.

dung [dʌŋ] *n.* помёт, навóз (-а(у)).

dungarees [,dʌŋgə'ri:z] *n.* (рабóчий) комбинезóн.

dungeon ['dʌndʒ(ə)n] *n.* темни́ца.

dunk [dʌŋk] *v.t.* макáть *impf.*, макну́ть *pf.*

dupe [dju:p] *v.t.* обмáнывать *impf.*, обману́ть (-ну́, -нешь) *pf.*; *n.* жéртва обмáна; простофи́ля *c.g.*

duplicate ['dju:plɪkət] *n.* дубликáт, кóпия; **in** ~ в двух экземпля́рах; *adj.* (*double*) двойнóй; (*identical*) иденти́чный; *v.t.* дубли́ровать *impf.*; снимáть *impf.*, снять (сниму́, -мешь; снял, -á, -о) *pf.* кóпию с+*g.* **duplicator** *n.* копировáльный аппарáт.

duplicity [dju:'plɪsɪtɪ] *n.* двули́чность.

durability [,djʊərə'bɪlɪtɪ] *n.* прóчность. '**durable** *adj.* прóчный (-чен, -чнá, -чно, прóчны́). **du'ration** *n.* продолжи́тельность; срок (-а(у)).

duress [djʊə'res, 'djʊə-] *n.* принуждéние; **under** ~ под давлéнием.

during ['djʊərɪŋ] *prep.* в течéние+*g.*, во врéмя+*g.*

dusk [dʌsk] *n.* су́мерки (-рек) *pl.*, су́мрак. **dusky** *adj.* су́меречный; тёмный (-мен, -мнá); (*complexion*) смуглый (смугл, -á, -о).

dust [dʌst] *n.* пыль (*loc.* -ли́); *v.t.* (*clean*) стирáть *impf.*, стерéть (сотру́, -рёшь; стёр) *pf.* пыль с+*g.*; (*sprinkle*) посыпáть *impf.*, посы́пать (-плю, -плешь) *pf.*+*i.* **dustbin** *n.* му́сорный я́щик. **duster** *n.* пы́льная тря́пка. **dusting** *n.* вытирáние, смáхивание, пы́ли. **dust-jacket** *n.* суперобложка. **dustman** *n.* му́сорщик. **dustpan** *n.* совóк (-вкá). **dusty** *adj.* пы́льный (-лен, -льнá, -льно), запылённый (-ён, -енá).

Dutch [dʌtʃ] *adj.* голлáндский; ~ **courage** хрáбрость во хмелю́; ~ **treat** склáдчина; *n.*: **the** ~ голлáндцы *m.pl.* **Dutchman** *n.* голлáндец (-дца).

dutiable ['dju:tɪəb(ə)l] *adj.* подлежáщий обложéнию пóшлиной. **dutiful** *adj.* послу́шный. **duty** *n.* (*obligation*) долг (-а(у), *loc.* -у́; *pl.* -и́), обя́занность; (*office*) дежу́рство; (*tax*) пóшлина; **on** ~ дежу́рный; **be on** ~ дежу́рить *impf.*; **do one's** ~ исполня́ть *impf.*, испóлнить *pf.* свой долг. **duty-free** *adj.* беспóшлинный. **duty-paid** *adj.* оплáченный пóшлиной.

dwarf [dwɔ:f] *n.* кáрлик, -ица; *adj.* кáрликовый; *v.t.* (*stunt*) останáвливать *impf.*, остановить (-влю́, -вишь) *pf.* рост, разви́тие+*g.*; (*tower above*) возвышáться *impf.*, возвы́ситься *pf.* над+*i.*

dwell [dwel] *v.i.* обитáть *impf.*; ~ **upon** останáвливаться *impf.* на+*p.* **dweller** *n.* жи́тель *m.*, ~ница. **dwelling** *n.* (~-*place*)

местожи́тельство. **dwelling-house** *n.* жило́й дом (-а(у); *pl.* -á).
dwindle ['dwɪnd(ə)l] *v.i.* убыва́ть *impf.*, убы́ть (убу́ду, -дешь; у́был, -á, -о) *pf.*
dye [daɪ] *n.* краси́тель *m.*, кра́ска; *v.t.* окра́шивать *impf.*, окра́сить *pf.* **dyed-in-the-wool** *adj.* (*fig.*) закорене́лый. **dyeing** *n.* кра́шение. **dyer** *n.* краси́льщик. **dye-works** *n.* краси́льня (*g.pl.* -лен).
dying ['daɪɪŋ] *adj.* умира́ющий; (*at time of death*) предсме́ртный; *n.* умира́ние, угаса́ние.
dynamic [daɪ'næmɪk] *adj.* динами́ческий. **dynamics** *n.* дина́мика.
dynamite ['daɪnə,maɪt] *n.* динами́т; *v.t.* взрыва́ть *impf.*, взорва́ть (-ву́, -вёшь; взорва́л, -á, -о) *pf.* динами́том.
dynamo ['daɪnə,məʊ] *n.* дина́мо-маши́на.
dynastic [dɪ'næstɪk] *adj.* династи́ческий. **dynasty** *n.* дина́стия.
dysentery ['dɪsəntərɪ, -trɪ] *n.* дизентери́я.
dyspepsia [dɪs'pepsɪə] диспепси́я. **dyspeptic** *n.* & *adj.* страда́ющий (*sb.*) диспепси́ей.

E [iː] *n.* (*mus.*) ми *nt.indecl.*
each [iːtʃ] *adj.* & *pron.* ка́ждый; ~ **other** друг дру́га (*d.* -гу, *etc.*).
eager ['iːgə(r)] *adj.* стремя́щийся (**for** к+*d.*); (*impatient*) нетерпели́вый. **eagerness** *n.* пыл (-а(у), *loc.* -у́), рве́ние.
eagle ['iːg(ə)l] *n.* орёл (орла́), орли́ца; ~ **owl** фи́лин. **eagle-eyed** *adj.* зо́ркий (-рок, -рка́, -рко). **eaglet** *n.* орлёнок (-нка; *pl.* орля́та, -т).
ear[1] [ɪə(r)] *n.* (*corn*) ко́лос (*pl.* -о́сья, -о́сьев); *v.i.* колоси́ться *impf.*, вы́~ *pf.*
ear[2] [ɪə(r)] *n.* (*organ*) у́хо (*pl.* у́ши, уше́й); (*sense*) слух; ~ **lobe** мо́чка; **by** ~ по слу́ху; **to be all ~s** слу́шать *impf.* во все у́ши. **earache** *n.* боль в у́хе. **eardrum** *n.* бараба́нная перепо́нка.
earl [ɜːl] *n.* граф. **earldom** *n.* гра́фство, ти́тул гра́фа.
earless ['ɪələs] *adj.* безу́хий.
early ['ɜːlɪ] *adj.* ра́нний; (*initial*) нача́льный; *adv.* ра́но.
earmark ['ɪəmɑːk] *n.* клеймо́ (*pl.* -ма); *v.t.* клейми́ть *impf.*, за~ *pf.*; (*assign*) предназнача́ть *impf.*, предназна́чить *pf.*
earn [ɜːn] *v.t.* зараба́тывать *impf.*, зарабо́тать *pf.*; (*deserve*) заслу́живать *impf.*, заслужи́ть (-жу́, -жишь) *pf.* **earnings** *n.* за́работок (-тка).
earnest ['ɜːnɪst] *adj.* серьёзный; *n.*: **in** ~ всерьёз.
earphone ['ɪəfəʊn] *n.* нау́шник. **earplugs** *n.* противошу́мы (-ов) *pl.* **earring** *n.* серьга́ (*pl.* -рьги, -рёг, -рьга́м). **earshot** *n.*: **within** ~ в преде́лах слы́шимости; **out of** ~ вне преде́лов слы́шимости. **ear-splitting** *adj.* оглуши́тельный.
earth [ɜːθ] *n.* земля́ (*a.* -лю); (*soil*) по́чва; (*fox's*) нора́ (*pl.* -ры); (*elec.*) заземле́ние; *v.t.* заземля́ть *impf.*, заземли́ть *pf.*; ~ **up** оку́чивать *impf.*, оку́чить *pf.* **earthen** *adj.* земляно́й. **earthenware** *n.* гли́няная посу́да (*collect.*); *adj.* гли́няный. **earthly** *adj.* земно́й, жите́йский. **earth-moving** *adj.* землеро́йный. **earthquake** *n.* землетрясе́ние. **earthwork** *n.* земляно́е укрепле́ние. **earthworm** *n.* земляно́й червь (-вя́; *pl.* -ви, -ве́й) *m.* **earthy** *adj.* земляно́й, земли́стый; (*coarse*) гру́бый (груб, -á, -о).
earwig ['ɪəwɪg] *n.* уховёртка.
ease [iːz] *n.* (*facility*) лёгкость; (*unconstraint*) непринуждённость; **at** ~ *int.* во́льно!; **with** ~ легко́, без труда́; *v.t.* облегча́ть *impf.*, облегчи́ть *pf.*
easel ['iːz(ə)l] *n.* мольбе́рт.
east [iːst] *n.* восто́к; (*naut.*) ост; *adj.* восто́чный; о́стовый. **eastern** *adj.* восто́чный. **eastwards** *adv.* на восто́к, к восто́ку.
Easter ['iːstə(r)] *n.* Па́сха.
easy ['iːzɪ] *adj.* лёгкий (-гок, -гка́, -гко́, лёгки́); (*unconstrained*) непринуждённый (-ён, -ённа). **easy-going** *adj.* доброду́шный.
eat [iːt] *v.t.* есть (ем, ешь, ест, еди́м; ел) *impf.*, с~ *pf.*; ку́шать *impf.*, по~, с~ *pf.*; ~ **away** разъеда́ть *impf.*, разъе́сть (-е́ст; -е́л) *pf.*; ~ **into** въеда́ться *impf.*, въе́сться (-е́стся; -е́лся) *pf.* в+*a.*; ~ **up** доеда́ть *impf.*, дое́сть (-е́м, -е́шь, -е́ст, -еди́м; -е́л) *pf.* **eatable** *adj.* съедо́бный.
eau-de-Cologne [,əʊdəkə'ləʊn] *n.* одеколо́н.
eaves [iːvz] *n.* стреха́ (*pl.* -и). **eavesdrop** *v.t.* подслу́шивать *impf.*, подслу́шать *pf.*
ebb [eb] *n.* (*tide*) отли́в; (*fig.*) упа́док (-дка).
ebony ['ebənɪ] *n.* чёрное де́рево.
ebullience [ɪ'bʌlɪəns] *n.* кипу́честь. **ebullient** *adj.* кипу́чий.
eccentric [ɪk'sentrɪk, ek-] *n.* чуда́к (-á), -а́чка; (*tech.*) эксце́нтрик; *adj.* эксцентри́чный. **eccen'tricity** *n.* эксцентри́чность, чуда́чество.
ecclesiastic [ɪ,kliːzɪ'æstɪk] *n.* духо́вное лицо́ (*pl.* -ца). **ecclesiastical** *adj.* духо́вный, церко́вный.
echelon ['eʃə,lɒn, 'eɪʃə,lɔ̃] *n.* эшело́н; *v.t.* эшелони́ровать *impf.* & *pf.*
echo ['ekəʊ] *n.* э́хо; (*imitation*) о́тклик; *v.i.* (*resound*) оглаша́ться *impf.*, огласи́ться *pf.* э́хом; *v.t.* & *i.* (*repeat*) повторя́ть(ся) *impf.*, повтори́ть(ся) *pf.* **echo-sounder** *n.* эхоло́т.
eclipse [ɪ'klɪps] *n.* затме́ние; (*fig.*) упа́док (-дка); *v.t.* затмева́ть *impf.*, затми́ть *pf.*
economic [,iːkə'nɒmɪk, ,ek-] *adj.* экономи́ческий, хозя́йственный; (*profitable*) рента́-

бельный. **economical** *adj.* эконóмный, бережли́вый. **e'conomist** *n.* экономи́ст. **e'conomize** *v.t.* & *i.* эконóмить *impf.*, с~ *pf.* **e'conomy** *n.* хозя́йство, эконóмика; (*saving*) эконóмия, сбереже́ние.

ecosystem ['iːkəʊˌsɪstəm] *n.* экосисте́ма.

ecstasy ['ekstəsɪ] *n.* экстáз, восхище́ние. **ecstatic** [ɪk'stætɪk] *adj.* исступлённый (-ён, -ённа).

écu ['ekjuː] *n.* экю́ *m.* & *nt.indecl.*

eddy ['edɪ] *n.* (*water*) водоворóт; (*wind*) вихрь *m.*; *v.i.* (*water*) крути́ться (-ится) *impf.*; (*wind*) клуби́ться *impf.*

edelweiss ['eɪd(ə)lˌvaɪs] *n.* эдельвéйс.

edge [edʒ] *n.* край (*loc.* -áе & аю́; *pl.* -ая́), крóмка; (*blade*) ле́звие; **on** ~ (*excited*) взволнóванный (-ан); (*irritable*) раздражённый (-ён, -енá); *v.t.* (*sharpen*) точи́ть (-чу́, -чишь) *impf.*, на~ *pf.*; (*border*) окаймля́ть *impf.*, окайми́ть *pf.*; *v.i.* пробирáться *impf.*, пробрáться (-беру́сь, -берёшься; -áлся, -алáсь, -áлóсь) *pf.* **edging** *n.* каймá. **edgy** *adj.* раздражи́тельный.

edible ['edɪb(ə)l] *adj.* съедóбный.

edict ['iːdɪkt] *n.* укáз.

edification [ˌedɪfɪ'keɪʃ(ə)n] *n.* назидáние. **edifice** ['edɪfɪs] *n.* здáние, сооруже́ние. **'edify** *v.t.* наставля́ть *impf.*, настáвить *pf.* **'edifying** *adj.* назидáтельный.

Edinburgh ['edɪnbərə, -brə] *n.* Э́динбург.

edit ['edɪt] *v.t.* редакти́ровать *impf.*, от~ *pf.*; (*cin.*) монти́ровать *impf.*, с~ *pf.* **edition** [ɪ'dɪʃ(ə)n] *n.* издáние; (*number of copies*) тирáж (-á). **editor** *n.* редáктор. **edi'torial** *n.* передовáя статья́; *adj.* редáкторский, редакциóнный.

educate ['edjʊˌkeɪt] *v.t.* воспи́тывать *impf.*, воспитáть *pf.* **educated** *adj.* образóванный (-ан, -анна). **edu'cation** *n.* образовáние, воспитáние; (*instruction*) обуче́ние. **edu'cational** *adj.* образовáтельный, воспитáтельный; учéбный.

EEC *abbr.* (*of* ***European Economic Community***) ЕЭС, Европéйское экономи́ческое сообщество.

eel [iːl] *n.* у́горь (угря́) *m.*

eerie ['ɪərɪ] *adj.* (*gloomy*) мрáчный (-чен, -чнá, -чно); (*strange*) стрáнный (-нен, -ннá, -нно).

efface [ɪ'feɪs] *v.t.* изглáживать *impf.*, изглáдить *pf.*; ~ **o.s.** стушёвываться *impf.*, стушевáться (-шу́юсь, -шу́ешься) *pf.*

effect [ɪ'fekt] *n.* (*result*) слéдствие; (*efficacy*) дéйствие; (*impression*; *theatr.*, *cin.*) эффéкт; *pl.* иму́щество; (*personal*) ли́чные вéщи (-щéй) *f.pl.*; **in** ~ факти́чески; **bring into** ~ осуществля́ть *impf.*, осуществи́ть *pf.*; **take** ~ вступáть *impf.*, вступи́ть (-ит) *pf.* в си́лу; *v.t.* производи́ть (-ожу́, -óдишь) *impf.*, произвести́ (-еду́, -едёшь; -ёл, -елá) *pf.* **effective** *adj.* дéйственный (-ен, -енна), эффекти́вный; (*striking*) эффéктный; (*actual*) факти́ческий. **effectiveness** *n.* дéйственность, эффекти́вность. **effectual** *adj.* дéйственный (-ен, -енна).

effeminate [ɪ'femɪnət] *adj.* изнéженный (-ен, -енна).

effervesce [ˌefə'ves] *v.i.* пéниться *impf.* **effervescent** *adj.* шипу́чий.

efficacious [ˌefɪ'keɪʃəs] *adj.* дéйственный (-ен, -енна), эффекти́вный. **efficacy** ['efɪkəsɪ] *n.* дéйственность, эффекти́вность. **efficiency** [ɪ'fɪʃənsɪ] *n.* дéйственность, эффекти́вность; (*of person*) умéние; (*mech.*) коэффициéнт полéзного дéйствия. **efficient** *adj.* дéйственный (-ен, -ена), эффекти́вный; (*person*) умéлый.

effigy ['efɪdʒɪ] *n.* изображéние.

effort ['efət] *n.* (*exertion*) уси́лие; (*attempt*) попы́тка.

effrontery [ɪ'frʌntərɪ] *n.* нáглость.

e.g. *abbr.* (*of* ***exempli gratia***) напр., напримéр.

egg[1] [eg] *n.* яйцó (*pl.* я́йца, яи́ц, я́йцам); *attr.* яи́чный.

egg[2] [eg] *v.t.*: ~ **on** подстрекáть *impf.*, подстрекну́ть *pf.*

egg-beater ['egbiːtə(r)] *n.* взбивáлка. **eggcup** *n.* рю́мка для яйцá. **eggplant** *n.* баклажáн. **eggshell** *n.* яи́чная скорлупá (*pl.* -пы).

ego ['iːgəʊ] *n.* э́го *indecl.*; я *nt.indecl.* **egoism** *n.* эгои́зм. **egoist** *n.* эгои́ст. **ego'istic** *adj.* эгоисти́ческий. **egotism** *n.* эготи́зм.

egret ['iːgrɪt] *n.* бéлая цáпля (*g.pl.* -пель).

Egypt ['iːdʒɪpt] *n.* Еги́пет. **Egyptian** [ɪ'dʒɪpʃ(ə)n] *n.* египтя́нин (*pl.* -я́не, -я́н), -я́нка; *adj.* еги́петский.

eider ['aɪdə(r)] *n.* (*duck*) гáга; (~*-down*) гагáчий пух (*loc.* -у́). **eiderdown** *n.* (*quilt*) пухóвое одея́ло.

Eiffel Tower ['aɪf(ə)l] *n.* Э́йфелева бáшня.

eight [eɪt] *adj.* & *n.* вóсемь (-сьми́, -семью́ & -сьмю́); (*collect.*; *8 pairs*) вóсьмеро (-ры́х); (*cards*; *boat*; *number 8*) восьмёрка; (*time*) вóсемь (часóв); (*age*) вóсемь лет. **eigh'teen** *adj.* & *n.* восемнáдцать (-ти, -тью); (*age*) восемнáдцать лет. **eigh'teenth** *adj.* & *n.* восемнáдцатый; (*fraction*) восемнáдцатая (часть (*pl.* -ти, -тéй)); (*date*) восемнáдцатое (числó). **eighth** *adj.* & *n.* восьмóй; (*fraction*) восьмáя (часть (*pl.* -ти, -тéй)); (*date*) восьмóе (числó). **eightieth** *adj.* & *n.* восьмидеся́тый; (*fraction*) восьмидеся́тая (часть (*pl.* -ти, -тéй)). **eighty** *adj.* & *n.* вóсемьдесят (-сьми́десяти, -сьмью́десятью); (*age*) вóсемьдесят лет; *pl.* (*decade*) восьмидеся́тые гóды (-дóв) *m.pl.*

Eire ['eərə] *n.* Э́йре *nt.indecl.*

either ['aɪðə(r), 'iːðə(r)] *adj.* & *pron.* (*one of two*) оди́н из двух, тот и́ли другóй; (*each of two*) и тот, и другóй; óба; любóй; *adv.* & *conj.*: ~ **... or** и́ли… и́ли, ли́бо… ли́бо.

eject [ɪ'dʒekt] *v.t.* извергáть *impf.*, изве́ргнуть (-г(ну)л, -гла) *pf.* **ejection** *n.* изверже́ние; ~ **seat** катапульти́руемое крéсло (*g.pl.* -сел).

eke [iːk] *v.t.*: ~ **out a living** перебивáться

impf., переби́ться (-бью́сь, -бьёшься) *pf.* ко́е-как.

elaborate [ɪ'læbərət; ɪ'læbə,reɪt] *adj.* (*complicated*) сло́жный (-жен, -жна́, -жно); (*detailed*) подро́бный; *v.t.* разраба́тывать *impf.*, разрабо́тать *pf.*; уточня́ть *impf.*, уточни́ть *pf.* **elabo'ration** *n.* разрабо́тка; уточне́ние.

elapse [ɪ'læps] *v.i.* проходи́ть (-о́дит) *impf.*, пройти́ (пройдёт; прошёл, -шла́) *pf.*; истека́ть *impf.*, исте́чь (-ечёт; -ёк, -екла́) *pf.*

elastic [ɪ'læstɪk, ɪ'lɑːstɪk] *n.* рези́нка; *adj.* эласти́чный, упру́гий. **elas'ticity** *n.* эласти́чность, упру́гость.

elate [ɪ'leɪt] *v.t.* возбужда́ть *impf.*, возбуди́ть *pf.* **elation** *n.* восто́рг.

elbow ['elbəʊ] *n.* ло́коть (-ктя; *pl.* -кти, -кте́й) *m.*; *v.t.* толка́ть *impf.*, толкну́ть *pf.* ло́ктем, -тя́ми; ~ **(one's way) through** прота́лкиваться *impf.*, протолкну́ться *pf.* че́рез+*a.*

elder¹ ['eldə(r)] *n.* (*tree*) бузина́.

elder² ['eldə(r)] *n.* (*person*) ста́рец (-рца); *pl.* ста́ршие *sb.*; *adj.* ста́рший. **elderberry** ['eldəbərɪ] *n.* я́года бузины́.

elderly *adj.* пожило́й. **eldest** *adj.* ста́рший.

elect [ɪ'lekt] *adj.* и́збранный; *v.t.* выбира́ть *impf.*, вы́брать (вы́беру, -решь) *pf.*; избира́ть *impf.*, избра́ть (изберу́, -рёшь; избра́л, -а́, -о) *pf.* **election** *n.* вы́боры *m.pl.*, избра́ние; *adj.* избира́тельный. **elective** *adj.* вы́борный. **elector** *n.* избира́тель *m.* **electoral** *adj.* избира́тельный, вы́борный. **electorate** *n.* избира́тели *m.pl.*

electric(al) [ɪ'lektrɪk(ə)l] *adj.* электри́ческий; ~ **blanket** одея́ло-гре́лка; ~ **shock** уда́р электри́ческим то́ком. **elec'trician** *n.* эле́ктрик, электромонтёр. **elec'tricity** *n.* электри́чество. **electrify** *v.t.* (*convert to electricity*) электрифици́ровать *impf.* & *pf.*; (*charge with electricity*; *fig.*) электризова́ть *impf.*, на~ *pf.* **electrode** *n.* электро́д. **electron** *n.* электро́н. **elec'tronic** *adj.* электро́нный. **elec'tronics** *n.* электро́ника.

electro- [ɪ'lektrəʊ] *in comb.* электро... . **electrocute** [ɪ'lektrə,kjuːt] *v.t.* убива́ть *impf.*, уби́ть (убью́, -ьёшь) *pf.* электри́ческим то́ком; (*execute*) казни́ть *impf.* & *pf.* на электри́ческом сту́ле. **electrolysis** [,ɪlek'trɒlɪsɪs, ,el-] *n.* электро́лиз. **electrolyte** [ɪ'lektrə,laɪt] *n.* электроли́т. **electromagnetic** *adj.* электромагни́тный. **electrotype** *n.* (*print.*) гальва́но *nt.indecl.*

elegance ['elɪgəns] *n.* элега́нтность, изя́щество. **elegant** *adj.* элега́нтный, изя́щный.

elegiac [,elɪ'dʒaɪək] *adj.* элеги́ческий. **'elegy** *n.* эле́гия.

element ['elɪmənt] *n.* элеме́нт; (*4 ~s*) стихи́я; *pl.* (*rudiments*) нача́тки (-ков) *pl.*; **be in one's ~** быть в свое́й стихи́и. **ele'mental** *adj.* стихи́йный. **ele'mentary** *adj.* (*rudimentary*) элемента́рный; (*school etc.*) нача́льный.

elephant ['elɪfənt] *n.* слон (-а́), ~и́ха. **ele'phantine** *adj.* слоно́вый; (*clumsy*) тяжелове́сный, неуклю́жий.

elevate ['elɪ,veɪt] *v.t.* поднима́ть *impf.*, подня́ть (подниму́, -мешь; по́дня́л, -а́, -о) *pf.*; (*in rank*) возводи́ть (-ожу́, -о́дишь) *impf.*, возвести́ (-еду́, -едёшь; -ёл, -ела́) *pf.* **ele'vation** *n.* подня́тие; возведе́ние; (*height*) высота́; (*angle*) у́гол (угла́) возвыше́ния; (*drawing*) вертика́льная прое́кция. **elevator** *n.* подъёмник; (*for grain*) элева́тор.

eleven [ɪ'lev(ə)n] *adj.* & *n.* оди́ннадцать (-ти, -тью); (*time*) оди́ннадцать (часо́в); (*age*) оди́ннадцать лет; (*team*) кома́нда (из оди́ннадцати челове́к). **elevenses** [ɪ'levənzɪz] *n.* второ́й за́втрак. **eleventh** *adj.* & *n.* оди́ннадцатый; (*fraction*) оди́ннадцатая (часть (*pl.* -ти, -те́й)); (*date*) оди́ннадцатое (число́); **at the ~ hour** в после́днюю мину́ту.

elf [elf] *n.* эльф.

elicit [ɪ'lɪsɪt, e'lɪsɪt] *v.t.* извлека́ть *impf.*, извле́чь (-еку́, -ечёшь; -ёк, -екла́) *pf.* (**from** из+*g.*); (*evoke*) вызыва́ть *impf.*, вы́звать (вы́зову, -вешь) *pf.*

eligibility [,elɪdʒɪ'bɪlɪtɪ] *n.* пра́во на избра́ние. **'eligible** *adj.* могу́щий, име́ющий пра́во, быть и́збранным.

eliminate [ɪ'lɪmɪ,neɪt] *v.t.* (*exclude*) устраня́ть *impf.*, устрани́ть *pf.*; (*remove*) уничтожа́ть *impf.*, уничто́жить *pf.* **elimi'nation** *n.* устране́ние; уничтоже́ние.

élite [eɪ'liːt, ɪ-] *n.* эли́та; *adj.* эли́тный.

elk [elk] *n.* лось (*pl.* -си, -се́й) *m.*

ellipse [ɪ'lɪps] *n.* э́ллипс. **ellipsis** *n.* э́ллипсис. **elliptic(al)** *adj.* эллипти́ческий.

elm [elm] *n.* вяз.

elocution [,elə'kjuːʃ(ə)n] *n.* ора́торское иску́сство.

elongate ['iːlɒŋ,geɪt] *v.t.* удлиня́ть *impf.*, удлини́ть *pf.*

elope [ɪ'ləʊp] *v.i.* сбега́ть *impf.*, сбежа́ть (-егу́, -ежи́шь) *pf.* **elopement** *n.* (та́йный) побе́г.

eloquence ['eləkwəns] *n.* красноре́чие. **eloquent** *adj.* красноречи́вый, вырази́тельный.

else [els] *adv.* (*besides*) ещё; (*instead*) друго́й; (*with neg.*) бо́льше; **nobody ~** никто́ бо́льше; **or ~** ина́че; а (не) то; и́ли же; **s.o. ~** кто-нибу́дь друго́й; **something ~?** ещё что́-нибудь? **elsewhere** *adv.* (*place*) в друго́м ме́сте; (*direction*) в друго́е ме́сто.

elucidate [ɪ'luːsɪ,deɪt, ɪ'ljuːs-] *v.t.* по-, разъ-, ясня́ть *impf.*, по-, разъ-, ясни́ть *pf.* **eluci'dation** *n.* по-, разъ-, ясне́ние.

elude [ɪ'luːd, ɪ'ljuːd] *v.t.* избега́ть *impf.*+*g.*; уклоня́ться *impf.*, уклони́ться (-ню́сь, -нишься) *pf.* от+*g.* **elusive** [ɪ'luːsɪv, ɪ'ljuːsɪv] *adj.* неуловимый.

emaciate [ɪ'meɪsɪ,eɪt, ɪ'meɪʃɪ,eɪt] *v.t.* истоща́ть *impf.*, истощи́ть *pf.* **emaci'ation** *n.* истоще́ние.

e-mail ['iːmeɪl] *n.* электро́нная по́чта.

emanate ['emə,neɪt] *v.i.* исходи́ть (-ит) *impf.*

(**from** из, от, +*g*.); (*light*) излуча́ться *impf.*, излучи́ться *pf.* **ema'nation** *n.* излуче́ние, эмана́ция.

emancipate [ɪ'mænsɪˌpeɪt] *v.t.* освобожда́ть *impf.*, освободи́ть *pf.*; эмансипи́ровать *impf.* & *pf.* **emanci'pation** *n.* освобожде́ние, эмансипа́ция.

emasculate [ɪ'mæskjʊˌleɪt] *v.t.* кастри́ровать *impf.* & *pf.*; (*fig.*) выхола́щивать *impf.*, вы́холостить *pf.* **emascu'lation** *n.* выхола́щивание.

embalm [ɪm'bɑːm] *v.t.* бальзами́ровать *impf.*, на~ *pf.* **embalmer** *n.* бальзамиро́вщик. **embalmment** *n.* бальзамиро́вка.

embankment [ɪm'bæŋkmənt] *n.* (*river*) да́мба, на́бережная *sb.*; (*rail.*) на́сыпь.

embargo [em'bɑːgəʊ, ɪm-] *n.* эмба́рго *nt.indecl.*; *v.t.* накла́дывать *impf.*, наложи́ть (-жу́, -жишь) *pf.* эмба́рго на+*a*.

embark [ɪm'bɑːk] *v.t.* грузи́ть (-ужу́, -у́зи́шь) *impf.*, по~ *pf.* на кора́бль; *v.i.* сади́ться *impf.*, сесть (ся́ду, -дешь; сел) *pf.* на кора́бль; ~ **upon** предпринима́ть *impf.*, предприня́ть (-иму́, -и́мешь; предпри́нял, -а́, -о) *pf.* **embar'kation** *n.* поса́дка (на кора́бль).

embarrass [ɪm'bærəs] *v.t.* смуща́ть *impf.*, смути́ть (-ущу́, -ути́шь) *pf.*; (*impede*) затрудня́ть *impf.*, затрудни́ть *pf.*; стесня́ть *impf.*, стесни́ть *pf.* **embarrassing** *adj.* неудо́бный. **embarrassment** *n.* смуще́ние, замеша́тельство.

embassy ['embəsɪ] *n.* посо́льство.

embed [ɪm'bed] *v.t.* вставля́ть *impf.*, вста́вить *pf.*; вде́лывать *impf.*, вде́лать *pf.*

embellish [ɪm'belɪʃ] *v.t.* (*adorn*) украша́ть *impf.*, укра́сить *pf.*; (*story*) прикра́шивать *impf.*, прикра́сить *pf.* **embellishment** *n.* украше́ние; преувеличе́ние.

embers ['embəz] *n.* горя́чая зола́, тле́ющие угольки́ *m.pl.*

embezzle [ɪm'bez(ə)l] *v.t.* растра́чивать *impf.*, растра́тить *pf.* **embezzlement** *n.* растра́та. **embezzler** *n.* растра́тчик.

embitter [ɪm'bɪtə(r)] *v.t.* ожесточа́ть *impf.*, ожесточи́ть *pf.*

emblem ['embləm] *n.* эмбле́ма, си́мвол.

embodiment [ɪm'bɒdɪmənt] *n.* воплоще́ние, олицетворе́ние. **embody** *v.t.* воплоща́ть *impf.*, воплоти́ть (-ощу́, -оти́шь) *pf.*; олицетворя́ть *impf.*, олицетвори́ть *pf.*

emboss [ɪm'bɒs] *v.t.* чека́нить *impf.*, вы́~, от~ *pf.* **embossed** *adj.* чека́ный (-нен, -нна).

embrace [ɪm'breɪs] *n.* объя́тие; *v.i.* обнима́ться *impf.*, обня́ться (обни́мемся, -етесь; -ня́лся́, -няла́сь) *pf.*; *v.t.* обнима́ть *impf.*, обня́ть (обниму́, -мешь; о́бнял, -а́, -о) *pf.*; (*accept*) принима́ть *impf.*, приня́ть (приму́, -мешь; при́нял, -а́, -о) *pf.*; (*comprise*) охва́тывать *impf.*, охвати́ть (-ачу́, -а́тишь) *pf.*

embrasure [ɪm'breɪʒə(r)] *n.* амбразу́ра.

embrocation [ˌembrəʊ'keɪʃ(ə)n] *n.* жи́дкая мазь.

embroider [ɪm'brɔɪdə(r)] *v.t.* (*cloth*) вышива́ть *impf.*, вы́шить (вы́шью, -ьешь) *pf.*; (*story*) прикра́шивать *impf.*, прикра́сить *pf.* **embroidery** *n.* вышива́ние, вы́шивка; преувеличе́ние; ~ **frame** пя́льцы (-лец) *pl.*

embryo ['embrɪəʊ] *n.* заро́дыш, эмбрио́н. **embryonic** *adj.* заро́дышевый, эмбриона́льный; (*fig.*) элемента́рный.

emend [ɪ'mend] *v.t.* исправля́ть *impf.*, испра́вить *pf.* **emen'dation** *n.* исправле́ние.

emerald ['emər(ə)ld] *n.* изумру́д; *adj.* изумру́дный.

emerge [ɪ'mɜːdʒ] *v.i.* появля́ться *impf.*, появи́ться (-влю́сь, -вишься) *pf.* **emergence** *n.* появле́ние. **emergency** *n.* непредви́денный слу́чай; **in case of** ~ в слу́чае кра́йней необходи́мости; **state of** ~ чрезвыча́йное положе́ние; ~ **brake** э́кстренный то́рмоз (*pl.* -а́); ~ **exit** запа́сный вы́ход; ~ **landing** вы́нужденная поса́дка; ~ **powers** чрезвыча́йные полномо́чия *nt.pl.* **emergent** *adj.* появля́ющийся; (*nation*) неда́вно получи́вший незави́симость.

emeritus [ɪ'merɪtəs] *adj.*: ~ **professor** заслу́женный профе́ссор (*pl.* -а́) в отста́вке.

emery ['emərɪ] *n.* нажда́к (-а́); ~ **paper** нажда́чная бума́га.

emetic [ɪ'metɪk] *adj.* рво́тный; *n.* рво́тное *sb.*

emigrant ['emɪgrənt] *n.* эмигра́нт, ~ка. **emigrate** *v.i.* эмигри́ровать *impf.* & *pf.* **emi'gration** *n.* эмигра́ция. **émigré** ['emɪˌgreɪ] *n.* эмигра́нт; *adj.* эмигра́нтский.

eminence ['emɪnəns] *n.* высота́, возвы́шенность; (*title*) высокопреосвяще́нство. **eminent** *adj.* выдаю́щийся. **eminently** *adv.* чрезвыча́йно.

emission [ɪ'mɪʃ(ə)n] *n.* испуска́ние, излуче́ние. **emit** *v.t.* испуска́ть *impf.*, испусти́ть (-ущу́, -у́стишь) *pf.*; (*light*) излуча́ть *impf.*, излучи́ть *pf.*; (*sound*) издава́ть (-даю́, -даёшь) *impf.*, изда́ть (-а́м, -а́шь, -а́ст, -ади́м; изда́л, -а́, -о) *pf.*

emotion [ɪ'məʊʃ(ə)n] *n.* (*state*) волне́ние; (*feeling*) эмо́ция, чу́вство. **emotional** *adj.* эмоциона́льный, волну́ющий.

emperor ['empərə(r)] *n.* императо́р.

emphasis ['emfəsɪs] *n.* ударе́ние; (*expressiveness*) вырази́тельность. **emphasize** *v.t.* подчёркивать *impf.*, подчеркну́ть *pf.*; выделя́ть *impf.*, вы́делить *pf.* **em'phatic** *adj.* вырази́тельный, подчёркнутый; (*person*) насто́йчивый.

empire ['empaɪə(r)] *n.* импе́рия.

empirical [ɪm'pɪrɪk(ə)l] *adj.* эмпири́ческий, -чный. **empiricism** *n.* эмпири́зм. **empiricist** *n.* эмпи́рик.

employ [ɪm'plɔɪ] *v.t.* (*thing*) по́льзоваться *impf.*+*i.*; (*person*) нанима́ть *impf.*, наня́ть (найму́, -мёшь; на́нял, -а́, -о) *pf.*; (*busy*) занима́ть *impf.*, заня́ть (займу́, -мёшь; заня́л, -ла́, -о) *pf.*; ~ **o.s.** занима́ться *impf.*, заня́ться (займу́сь, -мёшься; заня́лся́, -ла́сь) *pf.* **em'ploy'ee** *n.* сотру́дник, слу́жащий *sb.*

employer *n.* работода́тель *m.* **employment** *n.* рабо́та, слу́жба; испо́льзование; ~ **exchange** би́ржа труда́; **full** ~ по́лная за́нятость.

empower [ɪm'paʊə(r)] *v.t.* уполномо́чивать *impf.*, уполномо́чить *pf.* (**to** на+*a.*).

empress ['emprɪs] *n.* императри́ца.

emptiness ['emptɪnɪs] *n.* пустота́. **empty** *adj.* пусто́й (пуст, -а́, -о, пу́сты́); *v.t.* опорожня́ть *impf.*, опоро́жни́ть *pf.*; (*solid*) высыпа́ть *impf.*, вы́сыпать (-плю, -плешь) *pf.*; (*liquid*) вылива́ть *impf.*, вы́лить (-лью, -льешь) *pf.*; *v.i.* пусте́ть *impf.*, о~ *pf.*; (*river*) впада́ть *impf.*, впасть (-адёт, -ал) *pf.* **empty-headed** *adj.* пустоголо́вый.

EMS *abbr.* (*of* ***European Monetary System***) ЕВС, Европе́йская валю́тная систе́ма.

emu ['i:mju:] *n.* э́му *m.indecl.*

emulate ['emjʊˌleɪt] *v.t.* соревнова́ться *impf.* c+*i.*; подража́ть *impf.*+*d.* **emu'lation** *n.* соревнова́ние; подража́ние.

emulsion [ɪ'mʌlʃ(ə)n] *n.* эму́льсия.

enable [ɪ'neɪb(ə)l] *v.t.* дава́ть (даю́, даёшь) *impf.*, дать (дам, дашь, даст, дади́м; дал, -а́, да́ло́, -и) *pf.* возмо́жность+*d.* & *inf.*

enact [ɪ'nækt] *v.t.* (*ordain*) постановля́ть *impf.*, постанови́ть (-влю́, -вишь) *pf.*; (*law etc.*) вводи́ть (-ожу́, -о́дишь) *impf.*, ввести́ (введу́, -дёшь; ввёл, -а́) *pf.* в де́йствие; (*part, scene*) игра́ть *impf.*, сыгра́ть *pf.*

enamel [ɪ'næm(ə)l] *n.* эма́ль; *adj.* эма́левый; *v.t.* эмалирова́ть *impf.* & *pf.*

enamoured [ɪ'næmə(r)d] *pred.*: **be** ~ **of** быть влюблённым (-ён, -ена́) в+*a.*; увлека́ться *impf.*, увле́чься (-еку́сь, -ечёшься; -ёкся, -екла́сь) *pf.*+*i.*

encamp [ɪn'kæmp] *v.i.* располага́ться *impf.*, расположи́ться (-жу́сь, -жишься) *pf.* ла́герем. **encampment** *n.* ла́герь (*pl.* -ря́) *m.*

enchant [ɪn'tʃɑ:nt] *v.t.* (*bewitch*) заколдо́вывать *impf.*, заколдова́ть *pf.*; (*charm*) очаро́вывать *impf.*, очарова́ть *pf.* **enchanting** *adj.* очарова́тельный, волше́бный. **enchantment** *n.* очарова́ние, волшебство́. **enchantress** *n.* волше́бница.

encircle [ɪn'sɜ:k(ə)l] *v.t.* окружа́ть *impf.*, окружи́ть *pf.* **encirclement** *n.* окруже́ние.

enclave ['enkleɪv] *n.* анкла́в.

enclose [ɪn'kləʊz] *v.t.* огора́живать *impf.*, огороди́ть (-ожу́, -о́ди́шь) *pf.*; обноси́ть (-ошу́, -о́сишь) *impf.*, обнести́ (-есу́, -есёшь; -ёс, -есла́) *pf.*; (*in letter*) вкла́дывать *impf.*, вложи́ть (-жу́, -жишь) *pf.*; **please find** ~**d** прилага́ется (-а́ются)+*nom.* **enclosure** *n.* огоро́женное ме́сто (*pl.* -та́); в-, при-, ложе́ние.

encode [ɪn'kəʊd] *v.t.* шифрова́ть *impf.*, за~ *pf.*

encompass [ɪn'kʌmpəs] *v.t.* (*encircle*) окружа́ть *impf.*, окружи́ть *pf.*; (*contain*) заключа́ть *impf.*, заключи́ть *pf.*

encore ['ɒŋkɔ:(r)] *int.* бис!; *n.* вы́зов на бис; **give an** ~ биси́ровать *impf.* & *pf.*; *v.t.* вызыва́ть *impf.*, вы́звать (вы́зову, -вешь) *pf.* на бис.

encounter [ɪn'kaʊntə(r)] *n.* встре́ча; (*in combat*) столкнове́ние; *v.t.* встреча́ть *impf.*, встре́тить *pf.*; ста́лкиваться *impf.*, столкну́ться *pf.* c+*i.*

encourage [ɪn'kʌrɪdʒ] *v.t.* ободря́ть *impf.*, ободри́ть *pf.*; поощря́ть *impf.*, поощри́ть *pf.* **encouragement** *n.* ободре́ние, поощре́ние, подде́ржка. **encouraging** *adj.* ободри́тельный.

encroach [ɪn'krəʊtʃ] *v.t.* вторга́ться *impf.*, вто́ргнуться (-г(нул)ся, -глась) *pf.* (**on** в+*a.*); (*fig.*) посяга́ть *impf.*, посягну́ть *pf.* (**on** на+*a.*). **encroachment** *n.* вторже́ние; посяга́тельство.

encumber [ɪn'kʌmbə(r)] *v.t.* загроможда́ть *impf.*, загромозди́ть *pf.*; обременя́ть *impf.*, обремени́ть *pf.* **encumbrance** *n.* обу́за, препя́тствие.

encyclopaedia [enˌsaɪklə'pi:dɪə, ɪn-] *n.* энциклопе́дия. **encyclopaedic** *adj.* энциклопеди́ческий.

end [end] *n.* коне́ц (-нца́), край (*loc.* -аю́; *pl.* -ая́); (*conclusion*) оконча́ние; (*death*) смерть; (*purpose*) цель; **an** ~ **in itself** самоце́ль; **in the** ~ в конце́ концо́в; **no** ~ без конца́; **no** ~ **of** ма́сса+*g.*; **on** ~ (*upright*) стоймя́, ды́бом; (*continuously*) подря́д; **at a loose** ~ не у дел; **to the bitter** ~ до после́дней ка́пли кро́ви; **come to the** ~ **of one's tether** дойти́ (дойду́, -дёшь; дошёл, -шла́) *pf.* до то́чки; **make** ~**s meet** своди́ть (-ожу́, -о́дишь) *impf.*, свести́ (сведу́, -дёшь; свёл, -а́) *pf.* концы́ с конца́ми; *v.t.* конча́ть *impf.*, ко́нчить *pf.*; зака́нчивать *impf.*, зако́нчить *pf.*; прекраща́ть *impf.*, прекрати́ть (-ащу́, -ати́шь) *pf.*; *v.i.* конча́ться *impf.*, ко́нчиться *pf.*

endanger [ɪn'deɪndʒə(r)] *v.t.* подверга́ть *impf.*, подве́ргнуть (-г) *pf.* опа́сности.

endear [ɪn'dɪə(r)] *v.t.* внуша́ть *impf.*, внуши́ть *pf.* любо́вь к+*d.* (**to** +*d.*). **endearing** *adj.* привлека́тельный. **endearment** *n.* ла́ска (*g.pl.* -ск).

endeavour [ɪn'devə(r)] *n.* попы́тка, стара́ние; *v.i.* стара́ться *impf.*, по~ *pf.*

endemic [en'demɪk] *adj.* эндеми́ческий.

end-game ['endgeɪm] *n.* (*chess*) э́ндшпиль *m.*

ending ['endɪŋ] *n.* оконча́ние (*also gram.*), заключе́ние. **endless** *adj.* бесконе́чный, беспреде́льный.

endorse [ɪn'dɔ:s] *v.t.* (*document*) подпи́сывать *impf.*, подписа́ть (-ишу́, -и́шешь) *pf.*; (*bill*) индосси́ровать *impf.* & *pf.* (**to** в по́льзу+*g.*); (*approve*) одобря́ть *impf.*, одо́брить *pf.* **endorsement** *n.* по́дпись (на оборо́те+*g.*); индоссаме́нт; одобре́ние.

endow [ɪn'daʊ] *v.t.* обеспе́чивать *impf.*, обеспе́чить *pf.* постоя́нным дохо́дом; (*fig.*) одаря́ть *impf.*, одари́ть *pf.* **endowment** *n.* вклад, поже́ртвование; (*talent*) дарова́ние.

end-product ['endˌprɒdʌkt] *n.* гото́вое изде́лие.

endurance [ɪn'djʊərəns] *n.* (*of person*) выно́сливость, терпе́ние; (*of object*) про́чность. **endure** *v.t.* выноси́ть (-ошу́, -о́сишь) *impf.*, вы́нести (-есу, -есешь; -ес) *pf.*; терпе́ть (-плю́, -пишь) *impf.*, по~ *pf.*; *v.i.* продолжа́ться *impf.*, продо́лжиться *pf.*

enema ['enɪmə] *n.* кли́зма.

enemy ['enəmɪ] *n.* враг (-а́), проти́вник, неприя́тель *m.*; *adj.* вра́жеский.

energetic [ˌenə'dʒetɪk] *adj.* энерги́чный, си́льный (си́лён, -льна́, -льно, си́льны́). **'energy** *n.* эне́ргия, си́ла; *pl.* уси́лия *nt.pl.*

enervate ['enəˌveɪt] *v.t.* расслабля́ть *impf.*, рассла́бить *pf.*

enfeeble [ɪn'fi:b(ə)l] *v.t.* ослабля́ть *impf.*, осла́бить *pf.*

enfilade [ˌenfɪ'leɪd] *n.* продо́льный ого́нь (огня́) *m.*; *v.t.* обстре́ливать *impf.*, обстреля́ть *pf.* продо́льным огнём.

enforce [ɪn'fɔ:s] *v.t.* принужда́ть *impf.*, прину́дить *pf.* к+*d.* (**upon** +*a.*); (*law*) проводи́ть (-ожу́, -о́дишь) *impf.*, провести́ (-еду́, -едёшь; -ёл, -ела́) *pf.* в жизнь. **enforcement** *n.* принужде́ние; (*law etc.*) осуществле́ние, наблюде́ние за+*i.*, за соблюде́нием+*g.*

enfranchise [ɪn'fræntʃaɪz] *v.t.* предоставля́ть *impf.*, предоста́вить *pf.* избира́тельные права́ (*nt.pl.*)+*d.*; (*set free*) освобожда́ть *impf.*, освободи́ть *pf.*

engage [ɪn'geɪdʒ] *v.t.* (*hire*) нанима́ть *impf.*, наня́ть (найму́, -мёшь; на́нял, -а́, -о) *pf.*; (*tech.*) зацепля́ть *impf.*, зацепи́ть (-ит) *pf.*; ~ **the enemy in battle** завя́зывать *impf.*, завяза́ть (-яжу́, -я́жешь) *pf.* бой с проти́вником. **engaged** *adj.* (*occupied*) за́нятый (-т, -та́, -то); **be ~ in** занима́ться *impf.*, заня́ться (займу́сь, -мёшься; заня́лся́, -ла́сь) *pf.*+*i.*; **become ~** обруча́ться *impf.*, обручи́ться *pf.* (**to** с+*i.*). **engagement** *n.* (*appointment*) свида́ние; (*obligation*) обяза́тельство; (*betrothal*) обруче́ние; (*battle*) бой (*loc.* бою́; *pl.* бои́); ~ **ring** обруча́льное кольцо́ (*pl.* -льца, -ле́ц, -льцам). **engaging** *adj.* привлека́тельный.

engender [ɪn'dʒendə(r)] *v.t.* порожда́ть *impf.*, породи́ть *pf.*

engine ['endʒɪn] *n.* мото́р, маши́на, дви́гатель *m.*; (*rail.*) парово́з. **engine-driver** *n.* (*rail.*) машини́ст. **engi'neer** *n.* инжене́р; *pl.* (*mil.*) инжене́рные войска́ (-к) *pl.*; *v.t.* (*construct*) сооружа́ть *impf.*, сооруди́ть *pf.*; (*arrange*) устра́ивать *impf.*, устро́ить *pf.* **engi'neering** *n.* инжене́рное де́ло, те́хника, машинострое́ние; *adj.* инжене́рный, техни́ческий. **engine-room** *n.* маши́нное отделе́ние.

England ['ɪŋglənd] *n.* А́нглия. **English** *adj.* англи́йский; *n.*: **the ~** *pl.* англича́не (-н) *pl.*; ~ **Channel** Ла-Ма́нш. **Englishman, woman** *n.* англича́нин (*pl.* -а́не, -а́н), -а́нка.

engrave [ɪn'greɪv] *v.t.* гравирова́ть *impf.*, вы́~ *pf.*; (*fig.*) запечатлева́ть *impf.*, запечатле́ть *pf.* **engraver** *n.* гравёр. **engraving** *n.* (*picture*) гравю́ра; (*action*) гравиро́вка; *adj.* гравирова́льный, гравёрный.

engross [ɪn'grəʊs] *v.t.* завладева́ть *impf.*, завладе́ть *pf.*+*i.*; поглоща́ть *impf.*, поглоти́ть (-ощу́, -о́тишь) *pf.*; **be ~ed in** быть поглощённым+*i.* **engrossing** *adj.* увлека́тельный.

engulf [ɪn'gʌlf] *v.t.* заса́сывать *impf.*, засоса́ть (-су́, -сёшь) *pf.*

enhance [ɪn'hɑ:ns] *v.t.* увели́чивать *impf.*, увели́чить *pf.*

enigma [ɪ'nɪgmə] *n.* зага́дка. **enigmatic** [ˌenɪg'mætɪk] *adj.* зага́дочный.

enjoin [ɪn'dʒɔɪn] *v.t.* предпи́сывать *impf.*, предписа́ть (-ишу́, -и́шешь) *pf.*+*d.*; прика́зывать *impf.*, приказа́ть (-ажу́, -а́жешь) *pf.*+*d.*; (*leg.*) запреща́ть *impf.*, запрети́ть (-ещу́, -ети́шь) *pf.*+*d.* (**from** +*inf.*).

enjoy [ɪn'dʒɔɪ] *v.t.* получа́ть *impf.*, получи́ть (-чу́, -чишь) *pf.* удово́льствие от+*g.*; наслажда́ться *impf.*, наслади́ться *pf.*+*i.*; (*have use of*) по́льзоваться *impf.*+*i.*; облада́ть *impf.*+*i.* **enjoyable** *adj.* прия́тный. **enjoyment** *n.* удово́льствие, наслажде́ние; облада́ние (**of** +*i.*).

enlarge [ɪn'lɑ:dʒ] *v.t.* & *i.* увели́чивать(ся) *impf.*, увели́чить(ся) *pf.*; (*widen*) расширя́ть(ся) *impf.*, расши́рить(ся) *pf.*; ~ **upon** распространя́ться *impf.*, распространи́ться *pf.* о+*p.* **enlargement** *n.* увеличе́ние; расшире́ние. **enlarger** *n.* (*phot.*) увеличи́тель *m.*

enlighten [ɪn'laɪt(ə)n] *v.t.* просвеща́ть *impf.*, просвети́ть (-ещу́, -ети́шь) *pf.*; (*inform*) осведомля́ть *impf.*, осве́домить *pf.* **enlightenment** *n.* просвеще́ние.

enlist [ɪn'lɪst] *v.i.* поступа́ть *impf.*, поступи́ть (-плю́, -пишь) *pf.* на вое́нную слу́жбу; *v.t.* (*mil.*) вербова́ть *impf.*, за~ *pf.*; (*support etc.*) заруча́ться *impf.*, заручи́ться *pf.*+*i.*

enliven [ɪn'laɪv(ə)n] *v.t.* оживля́ть *impf.*, оживи́ть *pf.*

enmesh [ɪn'meʃ] *v.t.* опу́тывать *impf.*, опу́тать *pf.*

enmity ['enmɪtɪ] *n.* вражда́, неприя́знь.

ennoble [ɪ'nəʊb(ə)l] *v.t.* облагора́живать *impf.*, облагоро́дить *pf.*

ennui [ɒ'nwi:] *n.* тоска́.

enormity [ɪ'nɔ:mɪtɪ] *n.* чудо́вищность. **enormous** *adj.* грома́дный, огро́мный. **enormously** *adv.* кра́йне, чрезвыча́йно.

enough [ɪ'nʌf] *adj.* доста́точный; *adv.* доста́точно, дово́льно; ~ **money** доста́точно де́нег (*g.*); **be ~** хвата́ть *impf.*, хвати́ть (-ит) *pf. impers.*+*g.*; **I've had ~ of him** он мне надое́л.

enquire, enquiry *see* **inquire, inquiry**

enrage [ɪn'reɪdʒ] *v.t.* беси́ть (бешу́, бе́сишь) *impf.*, вз~ *pf.*

enrapture [ɪn'ræptʃə(r)] *v.t.* восхища́ть *impf.*, восхити́ть (-ищу́, -ити́шь) *pf.*

enrich [ɪn'rɪtʃ] *v.t.* обогаща́ть *impf.*, обогати́ть (-ащу́, -ати́шь) *pf.*

enrol [ɪn'rəʊl] *v.t.* & *i.* запи́сывать(ся) *impf.*, записа́ть(ся) (-ишу́(сь), -и́шешь(ся)) *pf.*; *v.t.* (*mil.*) вербова́ть *impf.*, за~ *pf.*; *v.i.* (*mil.*) поступа́ть *impf.*, поступи́ть (-плю́, -пишь) *pf.* на вое́нную слу́жбу. **enrolment** *n.* регистра́ция, за́пись.

en route [ɑ̃ 'ruːt] *adv.* по пути́ (**to, for** в+*a.*).

ensconce [ɪn'skɒns] *v.t.*: ~ **o.s.** заса́живаться *impf.*, засе́сть (converted зася́ду, -дешь; засе́л) *pf.* (**with** за+*a.*).

ensemble [ɒn'sɒmb(ə)l] *n.* (*mus.*) анса́мбль *m.*

enshrine [ɪn'ʃraɪn] *v.t.* (*relic*) класть (кладу́, -дёшь; клал) *impf.*, положи́ть (-жу́, -жишь) *pf.* в ра́ку; (*fig.*) храни́ть *impf.*

ensign ['ensaɪn, -s(ə)n] *n.* (*flag*) флаг; (*rank*) пра́порщик.

enslave [ɪn'sleɪv] *v.t.* порабоща́ть *impf.*, поработи́ть (-ощу́, -оти́шь) *pf.* **enslavement** *n.* порабоще́ние.

ensnare [ɪn'sneə(r)] *v.t.* опу́тывать *impf.*, опу́тать *pf.*

ensue [ɪn'sjuː] *v.i.* сле́довать *impf.*; вытека́ть *impf.* **ensuing** *adj.* после́дующий.

ensure [ɪn'ʃʊə(r)] *v.t.* обеспе́чивать *impf.*, обеспе́чить *pf.*

entail [ɪn'teɪl, en-] *n.* майора́т(ное насле́дование); *v.t.* (*leg.*) определя́ть *impf.*, определи́ть *pf.* насле́дование+*g.*; (*necessitate*) влечь (влечёт; влёк, -ла́) *impf.* за собо́й.

entangle [ɪn'tæŋg(ə)l] *v.t.* запу́тывать *impf.*, запу́тать *pf.*

enter ['entə(r)] *v.t.* & *i.* входи́ть (-ожу́, -о́дишь) *impf.*, войти́ (войду́, -дёшь; вошёл, -шла́) *pf.* в+*a.*; (*by transport*) въезжа́ть *impf.*, въе́хать (въе́ду, -дешь) *pf.* в+*a.*; *v.t.* (*join*) поступа́ть *impf.*, поступи́ть (-плю́, -пишь) *pf.* в, на, +*a.*; (*competition*) вступа́ть *impf.*, вступи́ть (-плю́, -пишь) *pf.* в+*a.*; (*in list*) вноси́ть (-ошу́, -о́сишь) *impf.*, внести́ (внесу́, -сёшь; внёс, -ла́) *pf.* в+*a.*

enteric [en'terɪk] *adj.* кише́чный. **enteritis** [ˌentə'raɪtɪs] *n.* энтери́т.

enterprise ['entəˌpraɪz] *n.* (*undertaking*) предприя́тие; (*initiative*) предприи́мчивость; **free, private,** ~ ча́стное предпринима́тельство. **enterprising** *adj.* предприи́мчивый.

entertain [ˌentə'teɪn] *v.t.* (*amuse*) развлека́ть *impf.*, развле́чь (-еку́, -ечёшь; -ёк, -екла́) *pf.*; (*guests*) принима́ть *impf.*, приня́ть (приму́, -мешь; при́нял, -а́, -о) *pf.*; угоща́ть *impf.*, угости́ть *pf.* (**to** +*i.*); (*hopes*) пита́ть *impf.* **entertaining** *adj.* занима́тельный, развлека́тельный. **entertainment** *n.* развлече́ние; приём; угоще́ние; (*show*) дивертисме́нт.

enthral [ɪn'θrɔːl] *v.t.* порабоща́ть *impf.*, поработи́ть (-ощу́, -оти́шь) *pf.*

enthrone [ɪn'θrəʊn] *v.t.* возводи́ть (-ожу́, -о́дишь) *impf.*, возвести́ (-еду́, -едёшь; -ёл, -ела́) *pf.* на престо́л. **enthronement** *n.* возведе́ние на престо́л. **enthusiasm** [ɪn'θjuːzɪˌæz(ə)m, -'θuːzɪˌæz(ə)m] *n.* энтузиа́зм, воодушевле́ние. **enthusiast** *n.* энтузиа́ст, ~ка. **enthusi'astic** *adj.* восто́рженный (-ен, -енна), воодушевлённый (-ён, -ённа).

entice [ɪn'taɪs] *v.t.* зама́нивать *impf.*, замани́ть (-ню́, -нишь) *pf.*; соблазня́ть *impf.*, соблазни́ть *pf.* **enticement** *n.* собла́зн, прима́нка, зама́нивание. **enticing** *adj.* соблазни́тельный, зама́нчивый.

entire [ɪn'taɪə(r)] *adj.* по́лный, це́лый, весь (вся, всё; все). **entirely** *adv.* вполне́, соверше́нно; (*solely*) исключи́тельно. **entirety** *n.* це́льность, полнота́; **in its** ~ по́лностью, в це́лом.

entitle [ɪn'taɪt(ə)l] *v.t.* (*book*) озагла́вливать *impf.*, озагла́вить *pf.*; (*give right to*) дава́ть (даю́, даёшь) *impf.*, дать (дам, дашь, даст, дади́м; дал, -а́, да́ло́, -и) *pf.* пра́во+*d.* (**to** на+*a.*); **be** ~**d to** име́ть пра́во на+*a.*

entity ['entɪtɪ] *n.* существо́; (*existence*) бытие́ (*i.* -ие́м, *p.* -ии́).

entomb [ɪn'tuːm] *v.t.* погреба́ть *impf.*, погрести́ (-ебу́, -ебёшь; -ёб, -ебла́) *pf.* **entombment** *n.* погребе́ние.

entomological [ˌentəmə'lɒdʒɪk(ə)l] *adj.* энтомологи́ческий. **ento'mologist** *n.* энтомо́лог. **ento'mology** *n.* энтомоло́гия.

entrails ['entreɪlz] *n.* вну́тренности (-тей) *pl.*, кишки́ (-шо́к) *pl.*; (*fig.*) не́дра (-р) *pl.*

entrance[1] ['entrəns] *n.* вход, въезд; (*theatr.*) вы́ход; (*into office etc.*) вступле́ние, поступле́ние; ~ **examinations** вступи́тельные экза́мены *m.pl.*; ~ **hall** вестибю́ль *m.*; **back** ~ чёрный вход; **front** ~ пара́дный вход. **entrant** *n.* (*sport*) уча́стник (**for** +*g.*).

entrance[2] [ɪn'trɑːns] *v.t.* приводи́ть (-ожу́, -о́дишь) *impf.*, привести́ (-еду́, -дёшь; -ёл, -ела́) *pf.* в состоя́ние тра́нса; (*charm*) очаро́вывать *impf.*, очарова́ть *pf.* **entrancing** *adj.* очарова́тельный.

entrap [ɪn'træp] *v.t.* пойма́ть *pf.* в лову́шку; (*fig.*) запу́тывать *impf.*, запу́тать *pf.*

entreat [ɪn'triːt] *v.t.* умоля́ть *impf.*, умоли́ть *pf.* **entreaty** *n.* мольба́, про́сьба.

entrench [ɪn'trentʃ] *v.t.* ока́пывать *impf.*, окопа́ть *pf.*; **be, become** ~**ed** (*fig.*) укореня́ться *impf.*, укорени́ться *pf.*

entropy ['entrəpɪ] *n.* энтропи́я.

entrust [ɪn'trʌst] *v.t.* (*secret*) вверя́ть *impf.*, вве́рить *pf.* (**to** +*d.*); (*object*; *person*) поруча́ть *impf.*, поручи́ть (-чу́, -чишь) *pf.* (**to** +*d.*).

entry ['entrɪ] *n.* вход, въезд; вступле́ние; (*theatr.*) вы́ход; (*in book etc.*) за́пись, статья́; (*sport*) записа́вшийся.

entwine [ɪn'twaɪn] *v.t.* (*interweave*) сплета́ть *impf.*, сплести́ (-ету́, -етёшь; -ёл, -ела́) *pf.*; (*wreathe*) обвива́ть *impf.*, обви́ть (обовью́, -ьёшь; обви́л, -а́, -о) *pf.*

enumerate [ɪ'njuːməˌreɪt] *v.t.* перечисля́ть *impf.*, перечи́слить *pf.* **enume'ration** *n.* перечисле́ние, пе́речень (-чня) *m.*

enunciate [ɪ'nʌnsɪˌeɪt] *v.t.* (*proclaim*) объявля́ть *impf.*, объяви́ть (-влю́, -вишь) *pf.*; (*express*) излага́ть *impf.*, изложи́ть (-жу́,

-жишь) *pf.*; (*pronounce*) произноси́ть (-ошу́, -о́сишь) *impf.*, произнести́ (-есу́, -есёшь; -ёс, -есла́) *pf.* **enunci'ation** *n.* объявле́ние; изложе́ние; произноше́ние.

envelop [ɪn'veləp] *v.t.* оку́тывать *impf.*, оку́тать *pf.*; завёртывать *impf.*, заверну́ть *pf.* **envelope** ['envə,ləʊp, 'ɒn-] *n.* (*letter*) конве́рт; (*other senses*) обёртка, оболо́чка

enviable ['envɪəb(ə)l] *adj.* зави́дный. **envious** *adj.* зави́стливый.

environment [ɪn'vaɪərənmənt] *n.* окружа́ющая среда́ (*pl.* -ды). **environs** [ɪn'vaɪərənz, 'envɪrənz] *n.* окре́стности *f.pl.*

envisage [ɪn'vɪzɪdʒ] *v.t.* предусма́тривать *impf.*, предусмотре́ть (-рю́, -ришь) *pf.*

envoy ['envɔɪ] *n.* посла́нник, аге́нт.

envy ['envɪ] *n.* за́висть; *v.t.* зави́довать *impf.*, по~ *pf.+d.*

enzyme ['enzaɪm] *n.* энзи́м.

epaulette [,epə'let] *n.* эполе́т(а).

ephemeral [ɪ'femər(ə)l, ɪ'fi:m-] *adj.* эфеме́рный, недолгове́чный.

epic ['epɪk] *n.* эпи́ческая поэ́ма, эпопе́я; *adj.* эпи́ческий.

epicentre ['epɪ,sentə(r)] *n.* эпице́нтр.

epicure ['epɪ,kjʊə(r)] *n.* эпикуре́ец (-е́йца). **epicu'rean** *adj.* эпикуре́йский.

epidemic [,epɪ'demɪk] *n.* эпиде́мия; *adj.* эпидеми́ческий.

epigram ['epɪ,græm] *n.* эпигра́мма. **epigra'mmatic(al)** *adj.* эпиграммати́ческий.

epigraph ['epɪ,grɑ:f] *n.* эпигра́ф.

epilepsy ['epɪ,lepsɪ] *n.* эпиле́псия. **epi'leptic** *n.* эпиле́птик; *adj.* эпилепти́ческий.

epilogue ['epɪ,lɒg] *n.* эпило́г.

Epiphany [e'pɪfənɪ, ɪ'pɪf-] *n.* (*eccl.*) Богоявле́ние.

episcopal [ɪ'pɪskəp(ə)l] *adj.* епи́скопский. **episcopate** *n.* епи́скопство.

episode ['epɪ,səʊd] *n.* эпизо́д. **epi'sodic** *adj.* эпизоди́ческий.

epistle [ɪ'pɪs(ə)l] *n.* посла́ние. **epistolary** *adj.* эпистоля́рный.

epitaph ['epɪ,tɑ:f] *n.* эпита́фия, надгро́бная на́дпись.

epithet ['epɪ,θet] *n.* эпи́тет.

epitome [ɪ'pɪtəmɪ] *n.* (*summary*) конспе́кт; (*embodiment*) воплоще́ние. **epitomize** *v.t.* конспекти́ровать *impf.*, за~, про~ *pf.*; воплоща́ть *impf.*, воплоти́ть (-ощу́, -оти́шь) *pf.*

epoch ['i:pɒk] *n.* эпо́ха, век (*pl.* -а́), пери́од.

equable ['ekwəb(ə)l] *adj.* равноме́рный, ро́вный (-вен, -вна́, -вно).

equal ['i:kw(ə)l] *adj.* ра́вный (-вен, -вна́), одина́ковый; (*capable of*) спосо́бный (**to** на+*a.*, +*inf.*); *n.* ра́вный *sb.*, ро́вня́ *c.g.*; *v.t.* равня́ться *impf.+d.* **equality** [ɪ'kwɒlɪtɪ] *n.* ра́венство, равнопра́вие. **equali'zation** *n.* уравне́ние. **equalize** *v.t.* ура́внивать *impf.*, уравня́ть *pf.*; *v.i.* (*sport*) равня́ть *impf.*, с~ *pf.* счёт. **equally** *adv.* равно́, ра́вным о́бразом.

equanimity [,ekwə'nɪmɪtɪ, ,i:k-] *n.* хладнокро́вие, невозмути́мость.

equate [ɪ'kweɪt] *v.t.* прира́внивать *impf.*, приравня́ть *pf.* (**with** к+*d.*).

equation [ɪ'kweɪʒ(ə)n] *n.* (*math.*) уравне́ние.

equator [ɪ'kweɪtə(r)] *n.* эква́тор. **equatorial** [,ekwə'tɔ:rɪəl, ,i:k-] *adj.* экваториа́льный.

equestrian [ɪ'kwestrɪən] *n.* вса́дник; *adj.* ко́нный. **equestrianism** *n.* ко́нный спорт. **equestri'enne** *n.* вса́дница.

equidistant [,i:kwɪ'dɪst(ə)nt] *adj.* равностоя́щий. **equilateral** [,i:kwɪ'lætər(ə)l] *adj.* равносторо́нний (-нен, -ння). **equilibrium** [,i:kwɪ'lɪbrɪəm] *n.* равнове́сие.

equine ['i:kwaɪn, 'ek-] *adj.* лошади́ный.

equinox ['i:kwɪ,nɒks, 'ek-] *n.* равноде́нствие.

equip [ɪ'kwɪp] *v.t.* обору́довать *impf.* & *pf.*; снаряжа́ть *impf.*, снаряди́ть *pf.* **equipment** *n.* обору́дование, снаряже́ние.

equitable ['ekwɪtəb(ə)l] *adj.* справедли́вый, беспристра́стный. **equity** *n.* справедли́вость, беспристра́стность; (*econ.*) ма́ржа; *pl.* (*econ.*) обыкнове́нные а́кции *f.pl.*

equivalence [ɪ'kwɪvələns] *n.* эквивале́нтность, равноце́нность. **equivalent** *adj.* эквивале́нтный, равноце́нный (-нен, -нна), равноси́льный; *n.* эквивале́нт.

equivocal [ɪ'kwɪvək(ə)l] *adj.* (*ambiguous*) двусмы́сленный (-ен, -енна); (*suspicious*) сомни́тельный. **equivocate** *v.i.* говори́ть *impf.* двусмы́сленно.

era ['ɪərə] *n.* э́ра, эпо́ха.

eradicate [ɪ'rædɪ,keɪt] *v.t.* искореня́ть *impf.*, искорени́ть *pf.* **eradi'cation** *n.* искорене́ние.

erase [ɪ'reɪz] *v.t.* стира́ть *impf.*, стере́ть (сотру́, -рёшь; стёр) *pf.*; подчища́ть *impf.*, подчи́стить *pf.* **eraser** *n.* ла́стик. **erasure** *n.* стира́ние, подчи́стка.

erect [ɪ'rekt] *adj.* прямо́й (прям, -а́, -о, пря́мы́); *v.t.* (*building*) сооружа́ть *impf.*, сооруди́ть *pf.*; воздвига́ть *impf.*, воздви́гнуть (-г) *pf.*; (*straighten*) выпрямля́ть *impf.*, вы́прямить *pf.* **erection** *n.* постро́йка, сооруже́ние; выпрямле́ние.

ermine ['ɜ:mɪn] *n.* горноста́й.

erode [ɪ'rəʊd] *v.t.* разъеда́ть *impf.*, разъе́сть (-е́ст, -едя́т; -е́л) *pf.*; (*geol.*) эроди́ровать *impf.* & *pf.*

erogenous [ɪ'rɒdʒɪnəs] *adj.* эроге́нный; ~ **zones** эроге́нные зо́ны.

erosion *n.* разъеда́ние; эро́зия.

erotic [ɪ'rɒtɪk] *adj.* эроти́ческий, любо́вный.

err [ɜ:(r)] *v.i.* ошиба́ться *impf.*, ошиби́ться (-бу́сь, -бьёшься; -бся) *pf.*; заблужда́ться *impf.*; (*sin*) греши́ть *impf.*, со~ *pf.*

errand ['erənd] *n.* поруче́ние; **run ~s** быть на посы́лках (**for** у+*g.*).

errant ['erənt] *adj.* (*knight*) стра́нствующий; (*thoughts*) блужда́ющий.

erratic [ɪ'rætɪk] *adj.* непостоя́нный (-нен, -нна), изме́нчивый.

erratum [ɪ'rɑ:təm] *n.* (*print*) опеча́тка; (*in writing*) опи́ска. **erroneous** [ɪ'rəʊnɪəs] *adj.* оши́бочный, ло́жный. **error** ['erə(r)] *n.* оши́бка, заблужде́ние.

erudite [ˈeruːˌdaɪt] *adj.* учёный. **erudition** [ˌeruːˈdɪʃ(ə)n] *n.* эруди́ция, учёность.

erupt [ɪˈrʌpt] *v.i.* прорыва́ться *impf.*, прорва́ться (-ву́сь, -вёшься; -ва́лся, -вала́сь, -ва́ло́сь) *pf.*; (*volcano*) изверга́ться *impf.*, изве́ргнуться (-гся) *pf.* **eruption** *n.* (*volcano*) изверже́ние; (*mirth*) взрыв; (*med.*) сыпь.

escalator [ˈeskəˌleɪtə(r)] *n.* эскала́тор.

escapade [ˈeskəˌpeɪd, ˌeskəˈpeɪd] *n.* вы́ходка, проде́лка. **escape** [ɪˈskeɪp] *n.* (*from prison*) бе́гство, побе́г; (*from danger*) спасе́ние; (*from reality*) ухо́д; (*of gas*) уте́чка; **have a narrow** ~ быть на волосо́к (**from** от+*g.*); *v.i.* (*flee*) бежа́ть (бегу́, бежи́шь) *impf.* & *pf.*; убега́ть *impf.*, убежа́ть (-егу́, -ежи́шь) *pf.*; (*save o.s.*) спаса́ться *impf.*, спасти́сь (-су́сь, -сёшься; -сся, -сла́сь) *pf.*; (*leak*) утека́ть *impf.*, уте́чь (-ечёт; -ёк, -екла́) *pf.*; *v.t.* избега́ть *impf.*, избежа́ть (-егу́, -ежи́шь) *pf.*+*g.*; (*groan*) вырыва́ться *impf.*, вы́рваться (-вется) *pf.* из, у, +*g.* **escaˈpee** *n.* бегле́ц (-а́).

escort [ˈeskɔːt; ɪˈskɔːt] *n.* конво́й, эско́рт; *v.t.* сопровожда́ть *impf.*, сопроводи́ть *pf.*; (*mil.*) конвои́ровать *impf.*, от~ *pf.*; эскорти́ровать *impf.* & *pf.*

escutcheon [ɪˈskʌtʃ(ə)n] *n.* щит (-а́) герба́.

Eskimo [ˈeskɪˌməʊ] *n.* эскимо́с, ~ка; *adj.* эскимо́сский.

especial [ɪˈspeʃ(ə)l] *adj.* осо́бенный, осо́бый; (*particular*) ча́стный. **especially** *adv.* осо́бенно; в ча́стности.

espionage [ˈespɪəˌnɑːʒ] *n.* шпиона́ж.

espousal [ɪˈspaʊz(ə)l] *n.* (*fig.*) подде́ржка. **espouse** *v.t.* (*fig.*) подде́рживать *impf.*, поддержа́ть (-жу́, -жишь) *pf.*

espy [ɪˈspaɪ] *v.t.* уви́деть (-и́жу, -и́дишь) *pf.*; (*detect*) замеча́ть *impf.*, заме́тить *pf.*

essay [ˈeseɪ] *n.* о́черк, эссе́ *nt.indecl.*; (*attempt*) попы́тка, про́ба; *v.t.* пыта́ться *impf.*, по~ *pf.*+*inf.* **essayist** *n.* очерки́ст, ~ка; эссеи́ст.

essence [ˈes(ə)ns] *n.* су́щность, существо́; (*extract*) эссе́нция. **essential** [ɪˈsenʃ(ə)l] *adj.* суще́ственный, необходи́мый, неотъе́млемый; *n.* основно́е *sb.*; *pl.* предме́ты *m.pl.* пе́рвой необходи́мости. **essentially** *adv.* по существу́, в основно́м.

establish [ɪˈstæblɪʃ] *v.t.* (*set up*) учрежда́ть *impf.*, учреди́ть *pf.*; (*fact etc.*) устана́вливать *impf.*, установи́ть (-влю́, -вишь) *pf.*; (*appoint*) устра́ивать *impf.*, устро́ить *pf.*; (*secure*) упро́чивать *impf.*, упро́чить *pf.* **establishment** *n.* (*action*) учрежде́ние, установле́ние; (*institution*) учрежде́ние, заведе́ние; (*staff*) штат.

estate [ɪˈsteɪt] *n.* (*property*) поме́стье (*g.pl.* -тий), име́ние; (*class*) сосло́вие; **real** ~ недви́жимость; ~ **agent** аге́нт по прода́же недви́жимости; ~ **duty** нало́г на насле́дство.

esteem [ɪˈstiːm] *n.* уваже́ние, почте́ние; *v.t.* уважа́ть *impf.*; почита́ть *impf.* **estimable** [ˈestɪməb(ə)l] *adj.* досто́йный (-о́ин, -о́йна) уваже́ния. **estimate** *n.* (*of quality*) оце́нка; (*of cost*) сме́та; *v.t.* оце́нивать *impf.*, оцени́ть (-ню́, -нишь) *pf.* **estimated** *adj.* предполага́емый, приме́рный. **estiˈmation** *n.* оце́нка, мне́ние.

Estonia [ɪˈstəʊnɪə] *n.* Эсто́ния.

estrange [ɪˈstreɪndʒ] *v.t.* отдаля́ть *impf.*, отдали́ть *pf.* **estrangement** *n.* отчужде́ние, отчуждённость.

estuary [ˈestjʊərɪ] *n.* у́стье (*g.pl.* -в).

et al [etˈæl] *abbr.* (*of* ***et alii***) и др., и други́е.

etc. [et ˈsetərə, ˈsetrə] *adv. abbr.* (*of* **et cetera**) и т.д., и так да́лее; и т.п., и тому́ подо́бное. **et cetera** и так да́лее, и тому́ подо́бие.

etch [etʃ] *v.t.* трави́ть (-влю́, -вишь) *impf.*, вы́~ *pf.* **etching** *n.* (*action*) травле́ние; (*object*) офо́рт.

eternal [ɪˈtɜːn(ə)l] *adj.* ве́чный. **eternity** *n.* ве́чность.

ether [ˈiːθə(r)] *n.* эфи́р. **ethereal** [ɪˈθɪərɪəl] *adj.* эфи́рный.

ethical [ˈeθɪk(ə)l] *adj.* эти́ческий, эти́чный. **ethics** *n.* э́тика.

ethnic [ˈeθnɪk] *adj.* этни́ческий; ~ **cleansing** этни́ческая чи́стка. **ethˈnography** *n.* этногра́фия.

etiquette [ˈetɪˌket, -ˈket] *n.* этике́т.

étude [ˈeɪtjuːd, -ˈtjuːd] *n.* этю́д.

etymological [ˌetɪməˈlɒdʒɪk(ə)l] *adj.* этимологи́ческий. **etymologist** [ˌetɪˈmɒlədʒɪst] *n.* этимо́лог. **etyˈmology** *n.* этимоло́гия.

eucalyptus [ˌjuːkəˈlɪptəs] *n.* эвкали́пт.

Eucharist [ˈjuːkərɪst] *n.* евхари́стия, прича́стие.

eulogize [ˈjuːləˌdʒaɪz] *v.t.* превозноси́ть (-ошу́, -о́сишь) *impf.*, превознести́ (-есу́, -есёшь; -ёс, -есла́) *pf.* **eulogy** *n.* похвала́.

eunuch [ˈjuːnək] *n.* е́внух.

euphemism [ˈjuːfɪˌmɪz(ə)m] *n.* эвфеми́зм. **eupheˈmistic** *adj.* эвфемисти́ческий.

euphonious [juːˈfəʊnɪəs] *adj.* благозву́чный. **euphony** [ˈjuːfənɪ] *n.* благозву́чие.

Eurasian [jʊəˈreɪʒ(ə)n] *adj.* еврази́йский.

Europe [ˈjʊərəp] *n.* Евро́па.

European [ˌjʊərəˈpɪən] *n.* европе́ец (-е́йца), -е́йка; *adj.* европе́йский.

euthanasia [ˌjuːθəˈneɪzɪə] *n.* эйтана́зия.

evacuate [ɪˈvækjʊˌeɪt] *v.t.* (*person*) эваку́ировать *impf.* & *pf.*; (*med.*) опорожня́ть *impf.*, опорожни́ть *pf.* **evacuˈation** *n.* эвакуа́ция; опорожне́ние. **evacuˈee** *n.* эваку́ированный *sb.*

evade [ɪˈveɪd] *v.t.* уклоня́ться *impf.*, уклони́ться (-ню́сь, -нишься) *pf.* от+*g.*; (*law*) обходи́ть (-ожу́, -о́дишь) *impf.*, обойти́ (обойду́, -дёшь; обошёл, -шла́) *pf.*

evaluate [ɪˈvæljʊˌeɪt] *v.t.* оце́нивать *impf.*, оцени́ть (-ню́, -нишь) *pf.* **evaluˈation** *n.* оце́нка.

evangelical [ˌiːvænˈdʒelɪk(ə)l] *adj.* ева́нгельский. **eˈvangelist** *n.* евангели́ст.

evaporate [ɪˈvæpəˌreɪt] *v.t.* & *i.* испаря́ть(ся)

impf., испари́ть(ся) *pf.*; *v.i.* (*lose moisture*) улету́чиваться *impf.*, улету́читься *pf.* **evapo'ration** *n.* испаре́ние.

evasion [ɪ'veɪʒ(ə)n] *n.* уклоне́ние (**of** от+*g.*); (*of law*) обхо́д; (*subterfuge*) увёртка. **evasive** *adj.* укло́нчивый.

eve [iːv] *n.* кану́н; **on the** ~ накану́не.

even ['iːv(ə)n] *adj.* ро́вный (-вен, -вна́, -вно) (*uniform*) равноме́рный; (*balanced*) уравнове́шенный; (*number*) чётный; **get** ~ расквита́ться *pf.* (**with** с+*i.*); *adv.* да́же; (*just*) как раз; (*with comp.*) ещё; ~ **if** да́же е́сли, хотя́ бы и; ~ **though** хотя́ бы; ~ **so** всё-таки; **not** ~ да́же не; *v.t.* выра́внивать *impf.*, вы́ровнять *pf.*

evening ['iːvnɪŋ] *n.* ве́чер (*pl.* -а́); *adj.* вече́рний.

evenly ['iːvənlɪ] *adv.* по́ровну, ро́вно, одина́ково. **evenness** *n.* ро́вность; равноме́рность.

evensong ['iːvənˌsɒŋ] *n.* вече́рня.

event [ɪ'vent] *n.* собы́тие, происше́ствие; **in the** ~ **of** в слу́чае+*g.*; **at all** ~**s** во вся́ком слу́чае. **eventual** [ɪ'ventjʊəl] *adj.* (*possible*) возмо́жный; (*final*) коне́чный. **eventu'ality** *n.* возмо́жность. **eventually** *adv.* в конце́ концо́в.

ever ['evə(r)] *adv.* (*at any time*) когда́-либо, когда́-нибудь; (*always*) всегда́; (*emph.*) же; ~ **since** с тех пор (как); ~ **so** о́чень; **for** ~ навсегда́; **hardly** ~ почти́ никогда́.

Everest ['evərɪst]: **Mt** ~ гора́ Эвере́ст.

evergreen ['evəˌgriːn] *adj.* вечнозелёный; *n.* вечнозелёное расте́ние. **ever'lasting** *adj.* ве́чный, постоя́нный. **ever'more** *adv.*: **for** ~ навсегда́, наве́ки.

every ['evrɪ] *adj.* ка́ждый, вся́кий, все (*pl.*); ~ **now and then** вре́мя от вре́мени; ~ **other** ка́ждый второ́й; ~ **other day** че́рез день. **everybody, everyone** *pron.* ка́ждый, все (*pl.*). **everyday** *adj.* (*daily*) ежедне́вный; (*commonplace*) повседне́вный. **everything** *pron.* всё. **everywhere** *adv.* всю́ду, везде́.

evict [ɪ'vɪkt] *v.t.* выселя́ть *impf.*, вы́селить *pf.* **eviction** *n.* выселе́ние.

evidence ['evɪd(ə)ns] *n.* свиде́тельство, доказа́тельство, ули́ка; **in** ~ (*pred.*) заме́тен (-тна, -тно); **give** ~ свиде́тельствовать *impf.* (о+*p.*; +*a.*; +что). **evident** *adj.* очеви́дный, я́сный (я́сен, ясна́, я́сно, ясны́).

evil ['iːv(ə)l, -ɪl] *n.* зло (*g.pl.* зол), поро́к; *adj.* злой (зол, зла), дурно́й (ду́рён, -рна́, -рно, ду́рны́). **evil-doer** *n.* злоде́й.

evince [ɪ'vɪns] *v.t.* проявля́ть *impf.*, прояви́ть (-влю́, -вишь) *pf.*

evoke [ɪ'vəʊk] *v.t.* вызыва́ть *impf.*, вы́звать (вы́зову, -вешь) *pf.*

evolution [ˌiːvə'luːʃ(ə)n, -'ljuːʃ(ə)n] *n.* разви́тие, эволю́ция. **evolutionary** *adj.* эволюцио́нный. **evolve** [ɪ'vɒlv] *v.t.* & *i.* развива́ть(ся) *impf.*, разви́ть(ся) (разовью́(сь), -ьёшь(ся); разви́л(ся), -ила́(сь), -и́ло/-и́ло́(сь) *pf.*; *v.i.* эволюциони́ровать *impf.* &*pf.*

ewe [juː] *n.* овца́ (*pl.* о́вцы, ове́ц, о́вцам).

ex- [eks] *in comb.* бы́вший.

exacerbate [ek'sæsəˌbeɪt, ɪg-] *v.t.* обостря́ть *impf.*, обостри́ть *pf.* **exacer'bation** *n.* обостре́ние.

exact [ɪg'zækt] *adj.* то́чный (-чен, -чна́, -чно), аккура́тный; *v.t.* взы́скивать *impf.*, взыска́ть (взыщу́, -щешь) *pf.* (**from, of** с+*g.*). **exacting** *adj.* (*person*) взыска́тельный, требова́тельный; (*circumstance*) суро́вый. **exactitude, exactness** *n.* то́чность. **exactly** *adv.* то́чно, как раз, и́менно.

exaggerate [ɪg'zædʒəˌreɪt] *v.t.* преувели́чивать *impf.*, преувели́чить *pf.* **exagge'ration** *n.* преувеличе́ние.

exalt [ɪg'zɔːlt] *v.t.* возвыша́ть *impf.*, возвы́сить *pf.*; (*extol*) превозноси́ть (-ошу́, -о́сишь) *impf.*, превознести́ (-есу́, -есёшь; -ёс, -есла́) *pf.* **exaltation** [ˌegzɔːl'teɪʃ(ə)n] *n.* возвыше́ние; (*elation*) восто́рг.

examination [ɪgˌzæmɪ'neɪʃ(ə)n] *n.* осмо́тр, иссле́дование; (*of knowledge*) экза́мен; (*leg.*) допро́с. **ex'amine** *v.t.* осма́тривать *impf.*, осмотре́ть (-рю́. -ришь) *pf.*; иссле́довать *impf.* & *pf.*; экзаменова́ть *impf.*, про~ *pf.*; допра́шивать *impf.*, допроси́ть (-ошу́, -о́сишь) *pf.* **examiner** *n.* экзамена́тор.

example [ɪg'zɑːmp(ə)l] *n.* приме́р, образе́ц (-зца́); **for** ~ наприме́р.

exasperate [ɪg'zɑːspəˌreɪt] *v.t.* раздража́ть *impf.*, раздражи́ть *pf.* **exasperation** *n.* раздраже́ние.

excavate ['ekskəˌveɪt] *v.t.* выка́пывать *impf.*, вы́копать *pf.*; (*archaeol.*) раска́пывать *impf.*, раскопа́ть *pf.* **exca'vation** *n.* выка́пывание; раско́пки *f.pl.* **excavator** *n.* экскава́тор.

exceed [ɪk'siːd] *v.t.* превыша́ть *impf.*, превы́сить *pf.* **exceedingly** *adv.* чрезвыча́йно.

excel [ɪk'sel] *v.t.* превосходи́ть (-ожу́, -о́дишь) *impf.*, превзойти́ (-ойду́, -ойдёшь; -ошёл, -ошла́) *pf.* (**in** в+*p.*, +*i.*); *v.i.* отлича́ться *impf.*, отличи́ться *pf.* (**at, in** в+*p.*). **excellence** ['eksələns] *n.* превосхо́дство. **'excellency** *n.* превосходи́тельство. **'excellent** *adj.* превосхо́дный, отли́чный.

except [ɪk'sept] *v.t.* исключа́ть *impf.*, исключи́ть *pf.*; *prep.* исключа́я+*a.*, за исключе́нием+*g.*, кро́ме+*g.* **exception** *n.* исключе́ние; **take** ~ **to** возража́ть *impf.*, возрази́ть *pf.* про́тив+*g.* **exceptional** *adj.* исключи́тельный.

excerpt ['eksɜːpt] *n.* отры́вок (-вка), вы́держка.

excess [ɪk'ses, 'ekses] *n.* избы́ток (-тка), изли́шек (-шка), изли́шество; ~ **fare** допла́та. **excessive** *adj.* чрезме́рный, изли́шний (-шен, -шня).

exchange [ɪks'tʃeɪndʒ] *n.* обме́н (**of** +*i.*); (*of currency*) разме́н; (*rate of* ~) курс; (*building*) би́ржа; (*telephone*) центра́льная телефо́нная ста́нция; *v.t.* обме́нивать *impf.*, обменя́ть *pf.* (**for** на+*a.*); обме́ниваться *impf.*, обменя́ться *pf.*+*i.*

Exchequer [ɪks'tʃekə(r)] *n.* казначе́йство, казна́.

excise[1] ['eksaɪz] *n.* (*duty*) акци́з(ный сбор); *v.t.* облага́ть *impf.*, обложи́ть (-жу́, -жишь) *pf.* акци́зным сбо́ром.

excise[2] ['eksaɪz] *v.t.* (*cut out*) выреза́ть *impf.*, вы́резать (-ежу, -ежешь) *pf.* **excision** [ɪk'sɪʒ(ə)n] *n.* вы́резка.

excitable [ɪk'saɪtəb(ə)l] *adj.* возбуди́мый. **excite** *v.t.* возбужда́ть *impf.*, возбуди́ть *pf.*; волнова́ть *impf.*, вз~ *pf.* **excitement** *n.* возбужде́ние, волне́ние.

exclaim [ɪk'skleɪm] *v.i.* восклица́ть *impf.*, воскли́кнуть *pf.* **exclamation** [,ekskləˈmeɪʃ(ə)n] *n.* восклица́ние; ~ **mark** восклица́тельный знак.

exclude [ɪk'sklu:d] *v.t.* исключа́ть *impf.*, исключи́ть *pf.* **exclusion** *n.* исключе́ние. **exclusive** *adj.* исключи́тельный; ~ **of** за исключе́нием+*g.*, не счита́я+*g.*

excommunicate [,ekskə'mju:nɪ,keɪt] *v.t.* отлуча́ть *impf.*, отлучи́ть *pf.* (от це́ркви). **excommuni'cation** *n.* отлуче́ние.

excrement ['ekskrɪmənt] *n.* экскреме́нты (-тов) *pl.*

excrescence [ɪk'skres(ə)ns] *n.* наро́ст.

excrete [ɪk'skri:t] *v.t.* выделя́ть *impf.*, вы́делить *pf.* **excretion** *n.* выделе́ние.

excruciating [ɪk'skru:ʃɪ,eɪtɪŋ] *adj.* мучи́тельный.

exculpate ['ekskʌl,peɪt] *v.t.* опра́вдывать *impf.*, оправда́ть *pf.* **excul'pation** *n.* оправда́ние.

excursion [ɪk'skɜ:ʃ(ə)n] *n.* экску́рсия.

excusable [ɪk'skju:zəb(ə)l] *adj.* извини́тельный, прости́тельный. **excuse** [ɪk'skju:s, ek-] *n.* извине́ние, оправда́ние, отгово́рка; *v.t.* извиня́ть *impf.*, извини́ть *pf.*; проща́ть *impf.*, прости́ть *pf.*; (*release*) освобожда́ть *impf.*, освободи́ть *pf.* (**from** от+*g.*); ~ **me!** извини́те (меня́)!; прости́те (меня́)!; прошу́ проще́ния!

execrable ['eksɪkrəb(ə)l] *adj.* отврати́тельный, ме́рзкий (-ок, -зка́, -зко).

execute ['eksɪ,kju:t] *v.t.* исполня́ть *impf.*, испо́лнить *pf.*; выполня́ть *impf.*, вы́полнить *pf.*; (*criminal*) казни́ть *impf.* & *pf.* **exe'cution** *n.* выполне́ние, исполне́ние; казнь. **exe'cutioner** *n.* пала́ч (-а́). **e'xecutive** *n.* исполни́тельный о́рган; (*person*) руководи́тель *m.*; *adj.* исполни́тельный; ~ **committee** исполни́тельный комите́т, исполко́м.

exegesis [,eksɪ'dʒi:sɪs] *n.* толкова́ние.

exemplary [ɪg'zemplərɪ] *adj.* приме́рный, образцо́вый. **exemplify** *v.t.* (*illustrate by example*) поясня́ть *impf.*, поясни́ть *pf.* приме́ром, на приме́ре; (*serve as example*) служи́ть (-жу́, -жишь) *impf.*, по~ *pf.* приме́ром+*g.*

exempt [ɪg'zempt] *adj.* освобождённый (-ён, -ена́) (**from** от+*g.*), свобо́дный (**from** от+*g.*); *v.t.* освобожда́ть *impf.*, освободи́ть *pf.* (**from** от+*g.*).

exemption *n.* освобожде́ние (**from** от+*g.*).

exercise ['eksə,saɪz] *n.* (*application*) примене́ние, осуществле́ние; (*physical* ~; *task*) упражне́ние; **take** ~ упражня́ться *impf.*; ~ **bicycle** *n.* велотренажёр; ~ **book** тетра́дь; *v.t.* (*apply*) применя́ть *impf.*, примени́ть (-ню́, -нишь) *pf.*; (*employ*) испо́льзовать *impf.* & *pf.*; (*train*) упражня́ть *impf.*

exert [ɪg'zɜ:t] *v.t.* ока́зывать *impf.*, оказа́ть (-ажу́, -а́жешь) *pf.*; ~ **o.s.** стара́ться *impf.*, по~ *pf.* **exertion** *n.* напряже́ние, уси́лие.

exhalation [,ekshə'leɪʃ(ə)n] *n.* выдыха́ние, вы́дох; (*vapour*) испаре́ние. **exhale** [eks'heɪl, ɪgz-] *v.t.* (*breathe out*) выдыха́ть *impf.*, вы́дохнуть *pf.*; (*as vapour*) испаря́ть *impf.*, испари́ть *pf.*

exhaust [ɪg'zɔ:st] *n.* вы́хлоп; ~ **pipe** выхлопна́я труба́ (*pl.* -бы); *v.t.* (*use up*) истоща́ть *impf.*, истощи́ть *pf.*; (*person*) изнуря́ть *impf.*, изнури́ть *pf.*; (*subject*) исче́рпывать *impf.*, исче́рпать *pf.* **exhausted** *adj.*: **be** ~ (*person*) изнемога́ть *impf.*, изнемо́чь (-огу́, -о́жешь; -о́г, -огла́) *pf.* **exhausting** *adj.* изнури́тельный. **exhaustion** *n.* изнуре́ние, истоще́ние, изнеможе́ние. **exhaustive** *adj.* исче́рпывающий.

exhibit [ɪg'zɪbɪt] *n.* экспона́т; (*leg.*) веще́ственное доказа́тельство; *v.t.* (*show*) пока́зывать *impf.*, показа́ть (-ажу́, -а́жешь) *pf.*; (*manifest quality*) проявля́ть *impf.*, прояви́ть (-влю́, -вишь) *pf.*; (*publicly*) выставля́ть *impf.*, вы́ставить *pf.* **exhi'bition** *n.* пока́з, проявле́ние; (*public* ~) вы́ставка. **exhibitor** *n.* экспоне́нт.

exhilarate [ɪg'zɪlə,reɪt] *v.t.* (*gladden*) весели́ть *impf.*, раз~ *pf.*; (*enliven*) оживля́ть *impf.*, оживи́ть *pf.* **exhila'ration** *n.* весе́лье, оживле́ние.

exhort [,egzɔ:t, ,eks-] *v.t.* увещева́ть *impf.* **exhor'tation** *n.* увещева́ние.

exhume [eks'hju:m, ɪg'zju:m] *v.t.* выка́пывать *impf.*, вы́копать *pf.*

exile ['eksaɪl, 'egz-] *n.* изгна́ние, ссы́лка; (*person*) изгна́нник, ссы́льный *sb.*; *v.t.* изгоня́ть *impf.*, изгна́ть (изгоню́, -нишь; изгна́л, -а́, -о) *pf.*; ссыла́ть *impf.*, сосла́ть (сошлю́, -лёшь) *pf.*

exist [ɪg'zɪst] *v.i.* существова́ть *impf.*; (*live*) жить (живу́, -вёшь; жил, -а́, -о) *impf.* **existence** *n.* существова́ние, нали́чие. **existent, existing** *adj.* существу́ющий, нали́чный.

exit ['eksɪt, 'egzɪt] *n.* вы́ход; (*theatr.*) ухо́д (со сце́ны); (*death*) смерть; ~ **visa** выездна́я ви́за; *v.i.* уходи́ть (-ожу́, -о́дишь) *impf.*, уйти́ (уйду́, -дёшь; ушёл, ушла́) *pf.*

exonerate [ɪg'zɒnə,reɪt] *v.t.* освобожда́ть *impf.*, освободи́ть *pf.* (**from** от+*g.*); (*from blame*) снима́ть *impf.*, снять (сниму́, -мешь; снял, -а́, -о) *pf.* обвине́ние с+*g.*

exorbitant [ɪg'zɔ:bɪt(ə)nt] *adj.* непоме́рный, чрезме́рный.

exorcism ['eksɔːˌsɪz(ə)m] *n.* изгна́ние ду́хов. **exorcize** *v.t.* (*spirits*) изгоня́ть *impf.*, изгна́ть (изгоню́, -нишь; изгна́л, -á, -о) *pf.*
exotic [ɪg'zɒtɪk] *adj.* экзоти́ческий.
expand [ɪk'spænd] *v.t.* & *i.* (*broaden*) расширя́ть(ся) *impf.*, расши́рить(ся) *pf.*; (*develop*) развива́ть(ся) *impf.*, разви́ть(ся) (разовью́(сь), -ьёшь(ся); разви́л(ся), -ила́(сь), -и́ло/-и́ло́(сь) *pf.*; (*increase*) увели́чивать(ся) *impf.*, увели́чить(ся) *pf.* **expanse** *n.* простра́нство. **expansion** *n.* расшире́ние; разви́тие; увеличе́ние; (*of territory*) экспа́нсия. **expansive** *adj.* (*extensive*) обши́рный; (*effusive*) экспанси́вный.
expatiate [ɪk'speɪʃɪˌeɪt] *v.i.* распространя́ться *impf.*, распространи́ться *pf.* (**on** о+*p.*).
expatriate [eks'pætrɪət, -'peɪtrɪət] *n.* экспатриа́нт.
expect [ɪk'spekt] *v.t.* (*await*) ожида́ть *impf.*+*g.*; ждать (жду, ждёшь; ждал, -á, -о) *impf.*+*g.*, что; (*anticipate*) наде́яться (-е́юсь, -е́ешься) *impf.*, по~ *pf.*; (*require*) тре́бовать *impf.*+*g.*, что́бы. **expectant** *adj.* ожида́ющий (**of** +*g.*); ~ **mother** бере́менная же́нщина, бу́дущая мать. **expec'tation** *n.* ожида́ние, наде́жда.
expectorant [ek'spektərənt] *n.* отха́ркивающее (сре́дство) *sb.* **expectorate** *v.t.* отха́ркивать *impf.*, отха́ркать *pf.*
expediency [ɪk'spiːdɪənsɪ] *n.* целесообра́зность. **expedient** *n.* сре́дство, приём; *adj.* целесообра́зный. **expedite** ['ekspɪˌdaɪt] *v.t.* ускоря́ть *impf.*, ускóрить *pf.*; бы́стро выполня́ть *impf.*, вы́полнить *pf.* **expedition** [ˌekspɪ'dɪʃ(ə)n] *n.* экспеди́ция. **expeditionary** *adj.* экспедицио́нный. **expeditious** *adj.* бы́стрый (быстр, -á, -о, бы́стры́).
expel [ɪk'spel] *v.t.* выгоня́ть *impf.*, вы́гнать (вы́гоню, -нишь) *pf.*; (*from school etc.*) исключа́ть *impf.*, исключи́ть *pf.*
expend [ɪk'spend] *v.t.* тра́тить *impf.*, ис~, по~ *pf.*; расхо́довать *impf.*, из~ *pf.* **expenditure** *n.* расхо́дование, расхо́д, тра́та. **expense** *n.* расхо́д; *pl.* расхо́ды *m.pl.*, изде́ржки *f.pl.*; **at the** ~ **of** ценóю+*g.*, за счёт+*g.* **expensive** *adj.* дорого́й (до́рог, -á, -о).
experience [ɪk'spɪərɪəns] *n.* óпыт, óпытность; (*incident*) пережива́ние; *v.t.* испы́тывать *impf.*, испыта́ть *pf.*; (*undergo*) пережива́ть *impf.*, пережи́ть (-иву́, -ивёшь; пе́режи́л, -á, -о) *pf.* **experienced** *adj.* óпытный.
experiment [ɪk'sperɪmənt, -ˌment] *n.* óпыт, экспериме́нт; *v.i.* производи́ть (-ожу́, -óдишь) *impf.*, произвести́ (-еду́, -едёшь; -ёл, -ела́) *pf.* óпыты (**on** на+*a.*); эксперименти́ровать *impf.* (**on, with** над, с+*i.*). **experi'mental** эксперимента́льный, óпытный. **experimen'tation** *n.* эксперименти́рование.
expert ['ekspɜːt] *n.* специали́ст (**at, in** в+*p.*, по+*d.*), знато́к (-á) (+*g.*); *adj.* óпытный. **expertise** [ˌekspɜː'tiːz] *n.* (*opinion*) эксперти́за; (*knowledge*) специа́льные зна́ния *nt.pl.*
expiate ['ekspɪˌeɪt] *v.t.* искупа́ть *impf.*, искупи́ть (-плю́, -пишь) *pf.* **expi'ation** *n.* искупле́ние.
expiration [ˌekspɪ'reɪʃ(ə)n] *n.* (*breathing out*) выдыха́ние; (*termination*) истече́ние. **expire** [ɪk'spaɪə(r)] *v.t.* (*exhale*) выдыха́ть *impf.*, вы́дохнуть *pf.*; *v.i.* (*period*) истека́ть *impf.*, исте́чь (-ечёт; -ёк, -екла́) *pf.*; (*die*) умира́ть *impf.*, умере́ть (умру́, -рёшь; у́мер, -ла́, -ло) *pf.* **ex'piry** *n.* истече́ние.
explain [ɪk'spleɪn] *v.t.* объясня́ть *impf.*, объясни́ть *pf.*; (*justify*) опра́вдывать *impf.*, оправда́ть *pf.* **expla'nation** *n.* объясне́ние. **ex'planatory** *adj.* объясни́тельный.
expletive [ɪk'spliːtɪv] *adj.* вставно́й; *n.* вставно́е сло́во (*pl.* -ва́); (*oath*) бра́нное сло́во (*pl.* -ва́).
explicit [ɪk'splɪsɪt] *adj.* я́вный, определённый (-ёнен, -ённа).
explode [ɪk'spləʊd] *v.t.* & *i.* взрыва́ть(ся) *impf.*, взорва́ть(ся) (-ву́, -вётся; взорва́л(ся), -ала́(сь), -а́ло/-áло́(сь) *pf.*; *v.t.* (*discredit*) разоблача́ть *impf.*, разоблачи́ть *pf.*; *v.i.* (*with anger etc.*) разража́ться *impf.*, разрази́ться *pf.*
exploit ['eksplɔɪt; ɪk'splɔɪt] *n.* по́двиг; *v.t.* эксплуати́ровать *impf.*; (*mine etc.*) разраба́тывать *impf.*, разрабо́тать *pf.* **exploi'tation** *n.* эксплуата́ция; разрабо́тка. **ex'ploiter** *n.* эксплуата́тор.
exploration [ˌeksplə'reɪʃ(ə)n] *n.* иссле́дование. **exploratory** [ɪk'splɒrətərɪ] *adj.* иссле́довательский. **explore** [ɪk'splɔː(r)] *v.t.* иссле́довать *impf.* & *pf.* **ex'plorer** *n.* иссле́дователь *m.*
explosion [ɪk'spləʊʒ(ə)n] *n.* взрыв; (*anger etc.*) вспы́шка. **explosive** *n.* взры́вчатое вещество́; *adj.* взры́вчатый, взрывно́й.
exponent [ɪk'spəʊnənt] *n.* (*interpreter*) истолкова́тель *m.*; (*representative*) представи́тель *m.*; (*math.*) показа́тель *m.* сте́пени. **exponential** [ˌekspə'nenʃ(ə)l] *adj.* (*math.*) показа́тельный.
export ['ekspɔːt; ek'spɔːt] *n.* вы́воз, э́кспорт; *v.t.* вывози́ть (-ожу́, -óзишь) *impf.*, вы́везти (-езу, -езешь; -ез) *pf.*; экспорти́ровать *impf.* & *pf.* **ex'porter** *n.* экспортёр.
expose [ɪk'spəʊz] *v.t.* (*to risk etc.*) подверга́ть *impf.*, подве́ргнуть (-г) *pf.* (**to** +*d.*); (*phot.*) экспони́ровать *impf.* & *pf.*; (*display*) выставля́ть *impf.*, вы́ставить *pf.*; (*discredit*) разоблача́ть *impf.*, разоблачи́ть *pf.*
exposition [ˌekspə'zɪʃ(ə)n] *n.* изложе́ние, толкова́ние.
exposure [ɪk'spəʊʒə(r)] *n.* подверга́ние (**to** +*d.*); (*phot.*) вы́держка; выставле́ние; разоблаче́ние.
expound [ɪk'spaʊnd] *v.t.* толкова́ть *impf.*; излага́ть *impf.*, изложи́ть (-жу́, -жишь) *pf.*
express [ɪk'spres] *n.* (*train*) экспре́сс; (*messenger*) на́рочный *sb.*, курье́р; *adj.* (*definite*) определённый (-ёнен, -ённа), то́чный (-чен, -чна́, -чно); *v.t.* выража́ть *impf.*, вы́разить

pf. **expression** *n.* выраже́ние; (*expressiveness*) вырази́тельность. **expressive** *adj.* вырази́тельный. **expressly** *adv.* наро́чно, наме́ренно.

expropriate [eks'prəʊprɪˌeɪt] *v.t.* экспроприи́ровать *impf.* & *pf.* **expropri'ation** *n.* экспроприа́ция.

expulsion [ɪk'spʌlʃ(ə)n] *n.* изгна́ние; (*from school etc.*) исключе́ние.

expunge [ɪk'spʌndʒ] *v.t.* вычёркивать *impf.*, вы́черкнуть *pf.*

exquisite [ek'skwɪzɪt] *adj.* утончённый (-ён, -ённа).

extant [ek'stænt] *adj.* сохрани́вшийся, существу́ющий.

extemporaneous [ɪkˌstempə'reɪnɪəs] *adj.* неподгото́вленный (-ен), импровизи́рованный (-ан). **ex'tempore** *adv.* без подгото́вки, экспро́мптом. **ex'temporize** *v.t.* & *i.* импровизи́ровать *impf.*, сымпровизи́ровать *pf.*

extend [ɪk'stend] *v.t.* простира́ть *impf.*, простере́ть (-тру́, -трёшь; -тёр) *pf.*; протя́гивать *impf.*, протяну́ть (-ну́, -нешь) *pf.*; (*enlarge*) расширя́ть *impf.*, расши́рить *pf.*; (*prolong*) продлева́ть *impf.*, продли́ть *pf.*; *v.i.* простира́ться *impf.*, простере́ться (-трётся; -тёрся) *pf.*; тяну́ться (-нется) *impf.*, по~ *pf.* **extension** *n.* расшире́ние; продле́ние. **extensive** *adj.* обши́рный, простра́нный (-нен, -нна), протяжённый (-ён, -ённа). **extent** *n.* протяже́ние; (*degree*) сте́пень (*pl.* -ни, -не́й); (*large space*) простра́нство.

extenuate [ɪk'stenjʊˌeɪt] *v.t.* уменьша́ть *impf.*, уме́ньшить *pf.*; **extenuating circumstances** смягча́ющие вину́ обстоя́тельства *nt.pl.*

exterior [ɪk'stɪərɪə(r)] *n.* вне́шность, нару́жность; *adj.* вне́шний, нару́жный.

exterminate [ɪk'stɜːmɪˌneɪt] *v.t.* уничтожа́ть *impf.*, уничто́жить *pf.*; истребля́ть *impf.*, истреби́ть *pf.* **extermi'nation** *n.* уничтоже́ние, истребле́ние.

external [ɪk'stɜːn(ə)l] *adj.* вне́шний, нару́жный.

extinct [ɪk'stɪŋkt] *adj.* (*volcano*) поту́хший; (*species*) вы́мерший; **become ~** ту́хнуть (-х) *impf.*, по~ *pf.*; вымира́ть *impf.*, вы́мереть (-мрет; -мер) *pf.* **extinction** *n.* потуха́ние, вымира́ние.

extinguish [ɪk'stɪŋgwɪʃ] *v.t.* гаси́ть (гашу́, га́сишь) *impf.*, по~ *pf.*; туши́ть (-шу́, -шишь) *impf.*, по~ *pf.*; (*debt.*) погаша́ть *impf.*, погаси́ть (-ашу́, -а́сишь) *pf.* **extinguisher** *n.* гаси́тель *m.*; (*fire ~*) огнетуши́тель *m.*

extirpate ['ekstəˌpeɪt] *v.t.* истребля́ть *impf.*, истреби́ть *pf.*; искореня́ть *impf.*, искорени́ть *pf.* **extir'pation** *n.* истребле́ние, искорене́ние.

extol [ɪk'stəʊl, ɪk'stɒl] *v.t.* превозноси́ть *impf.*, превознести́ (-есу́, -есёшь; -ёс, -есла́) *pf.*

extort [ɪk'stɔːt] *v.t.* вымога́ть *impf.* (**from** у+*g.*); (*information etc.*) выпы́тывать *impf.*, вы́пытать *pf.* (**from** у+*g.*). **extortion** *n.* вымога́тельство. **extortionate** *adj.* вымога́тельский, граби́тельский.

extra ['ekstrə] *n.* (*theatr.*) стати́ст, ~ка; (*payment*) припла́та, добавле́ние; *adj.* доба́вочный, дополни́тельный, э́кстренный; осо́бый; *adv.* осо́бо, осо́бенно, дополни́тельно.

extra- ['ekstrə] *in comb.* вне... .

extract ['ekstrækt; ɪk'strækt] *n.* экстра́кт; (*from book etc.*) вы́держка; *v.t.* извлека́ть *impf.*, извле́чь (-еку́, -ечёшь; -ёк, -екла́) *pf.*; (*pull out*) выта́скивать *impf.*, вы́тащить *pf.*; (*tooth*) удаля́ть *impf.*, удали́ть *pf.* **ex'traction** *n.* извлече́ние; выта́скивание; удале́ние; (*descent*) происхожде́ние. **extractor (fan)** *n.* вентиля́тор.

extradite ['ekstrəˌdaɪt] *v.t.* выдава́ть (-даю́, -даёшь) *impf.*, вы́дать (-ам, -ашь, -аст, -адим) *pf.* **extradition** [ˌekstrə'dɪʃ(ə)n] *n.* вы́дача.

extraneous [ɪk'streɪnɪəs] *adj.* чу́ждый (чужд, -а́, -о) (**to** +*d.*), посторо́нний.

extraordinary [ɪk'strɔːdɪnərɪ, ˌekstrə'ɔːdɪnərɪ] *adj.* необыча́йный, чрезвыча́йный; (*surprising*) удиви́тельный.

extraterrestrial [ˌekstrətɪ'restrɪəl] *n.* инопланетя́нин (*pl.* -я́не, -я́н); *adj.* инопланета́рный.

extravagance [ɪk'strævəgəns] *adj.* (*wild spending*) расточи́тельность; (*wildness*) сумасбро́дство. **extravagant** *adj.* расточи́тельный; сумасбро́дный.

extreme [ɪk'striːm] *n.* кра́йность; *adj.* кра́йний, чрезвыча́йный. **extremity** [ɪk'stremɪtɪ] *n.* (*end*) край (*loc.* -а́е & -аю́; *pl.* -ая́), коне́ц (-нца́); (*adversity*) кра́йность; *pl.* (*hands & feet*) коне́чности *f.pl.*

extricate ['ekstrɪˌkeɪt] *v.t.* (*disentangle*) распу́тывать *impf.*, распу́тать *pf.*; ~ **o.s.** выпу́тываться *impf.*, вы́путаться *pf.*

exuberance [ɪg'zjuːbərəns] *n.* изоби́лие, ро́скошь; (*of person*) жизнера́достность. **exuberant** *adj.* оби́льный, роско́шный; жизнера́достный.

exude [ɪg'zjuːd] *v.t.* & *i.* выделя́ть(ся) *impf.*, вы́делить(ся) *pf.*

exult [ɪg'zʌlt] *v.i.* ликова́ть *impf.* **exultant** *adj.* лику́ющий. **exul'tation** *n.* ликова́ние.

eye [aɪ] *n.* глаз (*loc.* -зу́; *pl.* -за́, -з, -за́м); (*poet.*) о́ко (*pl.* о́чи, оче́й); (*needle etc.*) ушко́ (*pl.* -ки́, -ко́в); **an eye for an eye** о́ко за о́ко; **up to the eyes in** по́ уши, по го́рло, в+*p.*; *v.t.* всма́триваться *impf.*, всмотре́ться (-рю́сь, -ришься) *pf.* в+*a.* **eyeball** *n.* глазно́е я́блоко (*pl.* -ки, -к). **eyebrow** *n.* бровь (*pl.* -ви, -ве́й). **eye-catching** *adj.* эффе́ктный. **eyelash** *n.* ресни́ца. **eyelid** *n.* ве́ко (*pl.* -ки, -к). **eyepiece** *n.* окуля́р. **eyesight** *n.* зре́ние. **eyewitness** *n.* очеви́дец (-дца).

eyrie ['ɪərɪ] *n.* (орли́ное) гнездо́ (*pl.* -ёзда).

F

F¹ [ef] *n.* (*mus.*) фа *nt.indecl.*

F² ['færən,haɪt] *abbr.* (*of* **Fahrenheit**) °Ф, (шкала́ термо́метра Фаренге́йта); **30°F** 30°Ф (гра́дусов по Фаренге́йту).

fable ['feɪb(ə)l] *n.* ба́сня (*g.pl.* -сен), небыли́ца.

fabric ['fæbrɪk] *n.* (*structure*) структу́ра, устро́йство; (*cloth*) ткань. **fabricate** *v.t.* (*invent*) выду́мывать *impf.*, вы́думать *pf.*; (*forge*) подде́лывать *impf.*, подде́лать *pf.* **fabri'cation** *n.* вы́думка; подде́лка.

fabulous ['fæbjʊləs] *adj.* ска́зочный.

facade [fə'sɑːd] *n.* фаса́д.

face [feɪs] *n.* лицо́ (*pl.* -ца); (*expression*) выраже́ние; (*grimace*) грима́са; (*outward aspect*) вне́шний вид; (*surface*) пове́рхность; (*clock etc.*) цифербла́т; **have the ~** име́ть *impf.* наха́льство; **make faces** ко́рчить *impf.* ро́жи; **~ down** (*cards*) руба́шкой вверх; **~ to ~** лицо́м к лицу́; **in the ~ of** пе́ред лицо́м+*g.*, вопреки́+*d.*; **on the ~ of it** на пе́рвый взгляд; **~ value** номина́льная сто́имость; **take at ~ value** принима́ть *impf.*, приня́ть (приму́, -мешь; при́нял, -а́, -о) *pf.* за чи́стую моне́ту; *v.t.* (*be turned towards*) быть обращённым к+*d.*; (*meet firmly*) смотре́ть (-рю́, -ришь) *impf.* в лицо́+*d.*; (*cover*) облицо́вывать *impf.*, облицева́ть (-цу́ю, -цу́ешь) *pf.*; **~ the music** расхлёбывать *impf.*, расхлеба́ть *pf.* ка́шу. **faceless** *adj.* безли́чный. **face-lift** *n.* космети́ческий ремо́нт; (*fig.*) вне́шнее обновле́ние.

facet ['fæsɪt] *n.* грань; (*aspect*) аспе́кт.

facetious [fə'siːʃəs] *adj.* шутли́вый.

facial ['feɪʃ(ə)l] *adj.* лицево́й.

facile ['fæsaɪl] *adj.* лёгкий (-гок, -гка́, -гко́, лёгки́), свобо́дный; (*pej.*) пове́рхностный. **facilitate** [fə'sɪlɪ,teɪt] *v.t.* облегча́ть *impf.*, облегчи́ть *pf.* **fa'cility** *n.* (*ease*) лёгкость; (*ability*) спосо́бность; (*opportunity*) возмо́жность.

facing ['feɪsɪŋ] *n.* облицо́вка; (*of garment*) отде́лка, обши́вка.

facsimile [fæk'sɪmɪlɪ] *n.* факси́миле *nt.indecl.*

fact [fækt] *n.* факт; (*reality*) действи́тельность; *pl.* (*information*) да́нные *sb.*; **the ~ is that ...** де́ло в том, что...; **as a matter of ~** со́бственно говоря́; **in ~** действи́тельно, на са́мом де́ле.

faction ['fækʃ(ə)n] *n.* фра́кция. **factional** *adj.* фракцио́нный.

factor ['fæktə(r)] *n.* (*circumstance*) фа́ктор; (*merchant*) комиссионе́р; (*math.*) мно́житель *m.*; (*of safety etc.*) коэффицие́нт.

factory ['fæktərɪ] *n.* фа́брика, заво́д. **factory-ship** *n.* плаву́чий рыбозаво́д.

factual ['fæktjʊəl] *adj.* факти́ческий, действи́тельный.

faculty ['fækəltɪ] *n.* сросо́бность, дар (*pl.* -ы́); (*univ.*) факульте́т.

fade [feɪd] *v.i.* вя́нуть (вял) *impf.*, за~ *pf.*; увяда́ть *impf.*, увя́нуть (-я́л) *pf.*; (*colour*) выцвета́ть *impf.*, вы́цвести (-етет; -ел) *pf.*; (*sound*) замира́ть *impf.*, замере́ть (-мрёт; за́мер, -ла́, -ло) *pf.*

faeces ['fiːsiːz] *n.* кал.

fag [fæg] *v.i.* корпе́ть (-плю́, -пишь) (**over** над+*i.*); *v.t.* утомля́ть *impf.*, утоми́ть *pf.*; *n.* (*drudgery*) тяжёлая рабо́та; (*cigarette*) сигаре́тка. **fag-end** *n.* оку́рок (-рка).

faggot ['fægət] *n.* (*wood*) вяза́нка хво́роста, -ту.

faience ['faɪɑ̃s] *n.* фая́нс.

fail [feɪl] *n.*: **without ~** обяза́тельно, непреме́нно; *v.t.* & *i.* (*be insufficient*) не хвата́ть *impf.*, не хвати́ть (-ит) *pf. impers.*+*g.* (*subject*) & у+*g.* (*object*); *v.i.* (*weaken*) ослабева́ть *impf.*, ослабе́ть *pf.*; *v.i.* (*not succeed*) терпе́ть (-плю́, -пишь) *impf.*, по~ *pf.* неуда́чу; не удава́ться (удаётся) *impf.*, уда́ться (-а́стся; -ало́сь) *pf. impers.*+*d.* (**in** +*inf.*); *v.t.* & *i.* (*examination*) прова́ливать(ся) *impf.*, провали́ть(ся) (-лю́(сь), -лишь(ся)) *pf.* **failing** *n.* недоста́ток (-тка), сла́бость; *prep.* за неиме́нием+*g.*, в слу́чае отсу́тствия+*g.* **failure** *n.* неуда́ча, прова́л; (*person*) неуда́чник, -ица.

faint [feɪnt] *n.* о́бморок; *adj.* (*weak*) сла́бый (слаб, -а́, -о); (*pale*) бле́дный (-ден, -дна́, -дно, бле́дны́); *v.i.* па́дать *impf.*, упа́сть (упаду́, -дёшь; упа́л) *pf.* в о́бморок. **faint-hearted** *adj.* малоду́шный.

fair¹ [feə(r)] *n.* я́рмарка.

fair² [feə(r)] *adj.* (*beautiful*) краси́вый; (*just*) че́стный (-тен, -тна́, -тно), справедли́вый; (*considerable*) поря́дочный; (*blond*) белоку́рый; **~ copy** чистови́к (-а́). **fairly** *adv.* (*tolerably*) дово́льно; (*completely*) соверше́нно. **fairway** *n.* фарва́тер.

fairy ['feərɪ] *n.* фе́я; **~ tale** ска́зка.

faith [feɪθ] *n.* (*belief*) ве́ра; (*trust*) дове́рие; (*loyalty*) ве́рность. **faithful** *adj.* ве́рный (-рен, -рна́, -рно, ве́рны́). **faithless** *adj.* вероло́мный, неве́рный (-е́рен, -ерна́, -е́рно, -е́рны́).

fake [feɪk] *n.* подде́лка; *v.t.* подде́лывать *impf.*, подде́лать *pf.*

falcon ['fɔːlkən, 'fɒlkən] *n.* со́кол. **falconry** *n.* соколи́ная охо́та.

fall [fɔːl] *n.* паде́ние; *pl.* водопа́д; *v.i.* па́дать *impf.*, (у)па́сть ((у)паду́, -дёшь; (у)па́л) *pf.*; понижа́ться *impf.*, пони́зиться *pf.*; **~ apart** распада́ться *impf.*, распа́сться (-адётся; -а́лся) *pf.*; **~ asleep** засыпа́ть *impf.*, засну́ть *pf.*; ~ **back on** прибега́ть *impf.*, прибе́гнуть (-г(нул), -гла) *pf.* к+*d.*; ~ **off** отпада́ть *impf.*, отпа́сть (-аду́, -адёшь; -а́л) *pf.*; ~ **over** опроки́дываться *impf.*, опроки́нуться *pf.*; ~ **through** прова́ливаться *impf.*, провали́ться (-ится) *pf.*

fallacious [fəˈleɪʃəs] *adj.* оши́бочный, ло́жный. **fallacy** [ˈfæləsɪ] *n.* оши́бка, заблужде́ние.

fallibility [ˌfælɪˈbɪlɪtɪ] *n.* оши́бочность. ˈ**fallible** *adj.* подве́рженный (-ен) оши́бкам.

fall-out [ˈfɔːlaʊt] *n.* радиоакти́вные оса́дки (-ков) *pl.*

fallow [ˈfæləʊ] *n.* пар (*pl.* -ы́), земля́ (*a.* -лю) под па́ром; *adj.* под па́ром; **lie** ~ лежа́ть (-жи́т) *impf.* под па́ром.

fallow deer [ˈfæləʊ] *n.* лань.

false [fɒls, fɔːls] *adj.* ло́жный, фальши́вый. **falsehood** *n.* ложь (лжи, *i.* ло́жью). **falsetto** [fɒlˈsetəʊ, fɔːl-] *n.* фальце́т. **falsifiˈcation** *n.* фальсифика́ция, подде́лка. **falsify** *v.t.* фальцифици́ровать *impf.* & *pf.*; подде́лывать *impf.*, подде́лать *pf.* **falsity** *n.* ло́жность.

falter [ˈfɒltə(r), ˈfɔːl-] *v.i.* (*stumble*) спотыка́ться *impf.*, споткну́ться *pf.*; (*stammer*) запина́ться *impf.*, запну́ться *pf.*; (*waver*) колеба́ться (-блюсь, -блешься) *impf.*

fame [feɪm] *n.* сла́ва, репута́ция. **famed** *adj.* изве́стный.

familiar [fəˈmɪlɪə(r)] *adj.* (*close*) бли́зкий (-зок, -зка́, -зко, бли́зки́); (*well known*) знако́мый; (*usual*) обы́чный; (*informal*) фамилья́рный. **famili'arity** *n.* бли́зость; знако́мство; фамилья́рность. **fa'miliarize** *v.t.* ознакомля́ть *impf.*, ознако́мить *pf.* (**with** с+*i.*).

family [ˈfæmɪlɪ, ˈfæmlɪ] *n.* семья́ (*pl.* -мьи, -ме́й, -мьям); (*lineage etc.*) род (-а(у), *loc.* -у́; *pl.* -ы́); (*generic group*) семе́йство; *attr.* семе́йный, фами́льный; ~ **tree** родосло́вная *sb.*

famine [ˈfæmɪn] *n.* (*scarcity of food*) го́лод (-а(у)); (*dearth*) недоста́ток (-тка). **famish** [ˈfæmɪʃ] *v.t.* мори́ть *impf.*, у~ *pf.* го́лодом; *v.i.* **be** ~**ed** голода́ть *impf.*

famous [ˈfeɪməs] *adj.* знамени́тый, изве́стный, просла́вленный.

fan[1] [fæn] *n.* (*device etc.*) ве́ер (*pl.* -а́); (*ventilator*) вентиля́тор; *v.t.* обма́хивать *impf.*, обмахну́ть *pf.*; (*flame*) раздува́ть *impf.*, разду́ть (-у́ю, -у́ешь) *pf.*

fan[2] [fæn] *n.* (*devotee*) боле́льщик, -ица. **fanatic** *n.* фана́тик, -и́чка. **fanatical** [fəˈnætɪk(ə)l] *adj.* фанати́ческий.

fanciful [ˈfænsɪˌfʊl] *adj.* (*capricious*) прихотли́вый; (*imaginary*) вообража́емый. **fancy** [ˈfænsɪ] *n.* фанта́зия, воображе́ние; (*whim*) прихо́да; *adj.* орнамента́льный; *v.t.* (*imagine*) представля́ть *impf.*, предста́вить *pf.* себе́; (*suppose*) каза́ться (ка́жется; каза́лось) *impf.*, по~ *pf. impers.*+*d.*; (*like*) нра́виться *impf.*, по~ *pf. impers.*+*d.*; ~ **dress** маскара́дный костю́м. **fancy-dress** *adj.* костюми́рованный; ~ **ball** (бал-)маскара́д.

fanfare [ˈfænfeə(r)] *n.* фанфа́ра.

fang [fæŋ] *n.* клык (-а́); (*serpent's*) ядови́тый зуб (*pl.* -ы, -о́в).

fantastic [fænˈtæstɪk] *adj.* фантасти́ческий, причу́дливый. ˈ**fantasy** *n.* фанта́зия, воображе́ние.

f.a.o. *abbr.* (*of* ***for the attention of***) вним.+*g.*, внима́нию+*g.*

far [fɑː(r)] *adj.* да́льний, далёкий (-ёк, -ека́, -ёко́); (*remote*) отдалённый; *adv.* далёко́; (*fig.*) намно́го; **as** ~ **as** (*prep.*) до+*g.*; (*conj.*) поско́льку; **by** ~ намно́го; **(in) so** ~ **as** поско́льку; **so** ~ до сих пор.

farce [fɑːs] *n.* фарс. **farcical** *adj.* фа́рсовый, смехотво́рный.

fare [feə(r)] *n.* (*price*) проездна́я пла́та; (*passenger*) пассажи́р; (*food*) пи́ща; *v.i.* пожива́ть *impf.* **farewell** *int.* проща́й(те)!; *n.* проща́ние; *attr.* проща́льный; **bid** ~ проща́ться *impf.*, прости́ться *pf.* (**to** с+*i.*).

far-fetched [fɑːˈfetʃd] *adj.* натя́нутый; притя́нутый за́ волосы, за́ уши.

farinaceous [ˌfærɪˈneɪʃəs] *adj.* мучни́стый, мучно́й.

farm [fɑːm] *n.* фе́рма, хозя́йство. **farmer** *n.* фе́рмер. **farming** *n.* се́льское хозя́йство.

far-reaching [fɑːˈriːtʃɪŋ] *adj.* далеко́ иду́щий.

farrier [ˈfærɪə(r)] *n.* (*smith*) кузне́ц (-а́); (*horse-doctor*) корова́л.

far-seeing [fɑːˈsiːɪŋ] *adj.* дальнови́дный. **far-sighted** *adj.* дальнови́дный; (*physically*) дальнозо́ркий.

farther [ˈfɑːðə(r)] *comp. adj.* бо́лее отдалённый (-ён, -ённа); дальне́йший; (*additional*) дополни́тельный; *adv.* да́льше. **farthermost** *adj.* са́мый да́льний. **farthest** *superl. adj.* са́мый да́льний, са́мый отдалённый; *adv.* да́льше всего́.

fascicle [ˈfæsɪk(ə)l] *n.* (*bot.*) пучо́к (-чка́); (*book*) вы́пуск.

fascinate [ˈfæsɪˌneɪt] *v.t.* очаро́вывать *impf.*, очарова́ть *pf.* **fascinating** *adj.* очарова́тельный. **fasciˈnation** *n.* очарова́ние.

Fascism [ˈfæʃɪz(ə)m] *n.* фаши́зм. **Fascist** *n.* фаши́ст, ~ка; *adj.* фаши́стский.

fashion [ˈfæʃ(ə)n] *n.* (*manner*) мане́ра; (*pattern*) фасо́н; (*style*) стиль *m.*; (*style of dress etc.*) мо́да; **after a** ~ не́которым о́бразом; **after the** ~ **of** по образцу́+*g.*; *v.t.* придава́ть (-даю́, -даёшь) *impf.*, прида́ть (-а́м, -а́шь, -а́ст, -ади́м; при́дал, -а́, -о) *pf.* фо́рму+*d.*; формирова́ть *impf.*, с~ *pf.* **fashionable** *adj.* мо́дный (-ден, -дна, -дно), фешене́бельный.

fast[1] [fɑːst] *n.* пост (-а́, *loc.* -у́); *v.i.* пости́ться *impf.*; **break (one's)** ~ разговля́ться *impf.*, разгове́ться *pf.*

fast[2] [fɑːst] *adj.* (*firm*) про́чный (-чен, -чна́, -чно, про́чны́), кре́пкий (-пок, -пка́, -пко), твёрдый (-д, -да́, -до), сто́йкий (-о́ек, -ойка́, -о́йко); (*rapid*) ско́рый (скор, -а́, -о), бы́стрый (быстр, -а́, -о, бы́стры́); (*immoral*) беспу́тный; **be** ~ (*timepiece*) спеши́ть *impf.*

fasten *v.t.* (*attach*) прикрепля́ть *impf.*, прикрепи́ть *pf.* (**to** к+*d.*); (*tie*) привя́зывать *impf.*, привяза́ть (-яжу́, -я́жешь) *pf.* (**to** к+*d.*); (*garment*) застёгивать *impf.*, застегну́ть *pf.* **fastener, fastening** *n.* запо́р, задви́жка; (*on garment*) застёжка.

fastidious [fæ'stɪdɪəs] *adj.* брезгли́вый.

fat [fæt] *n.* жир (-а(у), *loc.* -у́; *pl.* -ы́), са́ло; *adj.* (*greasy*) жи́рный (-рен, -рна́, -рно); (*plump*) то́лстый (-т, -та́, -то, то́лсты́), ту́чный (-чен, -чна́, -чно); **get, grow ~** толсте́ть *impf.*, по~ *pf.*

fatal ['feɪt(ə)l] *adj.* фата́льный, роково́й; (*deadly*) па́губный, смерте́льный. **fatality** [fə'tælətɪ] *n.* па́губность, фата́льность; (*calamity*) несча́стье; (*death*) смерть. **fate** *n.* судьба́ (*pl.* -дьбы, -деб, -дьбам), рок, жре́бий. **fated** *pred.* обречён (-а́). **fateful** *adj.* роково́й.

father ['fɑːðə(r)] *n.* оте́ц (-тца́). **father-in-law** *n.* (*husband's ~*) свёкор (-кра); (*wife's ~*) тесть *m.* **fatherland** *n.* оте́чество. **fatherly** *adj.* оте́ческий.

fathom ['fæð(ə)m] *n.* шесть (-ти́, -тью́) фу́тов (глубины́ воды́); *v.t.* измеря́ть *impf.*, изме́рить *pf.* глубину́ (воды́); (*understand*) понима́ть *impf.*, поня́ть (пойму́, -мёшь; по́нял, -а́, -о) *pf.*

fatigue [fə'tiːg] *n.* уста́лость, утомле́ние; *v.t.* утомля́ть *impf.*, утоми́ть *pf.*

fatness ['fætnɪs] *n.* ту́чность. **fatten** *v.t.* отка́рмливать *impf.*, откорми́ть (-млю́, -мишь) *pf.*; *v.i.* толсте́ть *impf.*, по~ *pf.* **fattening** *adj.* калори́йный. **fatty** *adj.* жи́рный (-рен, -рна́, -рно), жирово́й.

fatuous ['fætjʊəs] *adj.* тупо́й (туп, -а́, -о, ту́пы́).

fault [fɒlt, fɔːlt] *n.* недоста́ток (-тка), дефе́кт; (*blame*) вина́; (*geol.*) сброс. **faultless** *adj.* безупре́чный, безоши́бочный. **faulty** *adj.* дефе́ктный.

fauna ['fɔːnə] *n.* фа́уна.

favour ['feɪvə(r)] *n.* (*goodwill*) благоскло́нность; (*aid*) одолже́ние; **in (s.o.'s) ~** в по́льзу+*g.*; **be in ~ of** стоя́ть (-ою́, -ои́шь) *impf.* за+*a.*; *v.t.* благоволи́ть *impf.* к+*d.*; благоприя́тствовать *impf.*+*d.* **favourable** *adj.* (*propitious*) благоприя́тный; (*approving*) благоскло́нный (-нен, -нна). **favourite** *n.* люби́мец (-мца), -мица; фаври́т, ~ка; *adj.* люби́мый.

fawn[1] [fɔːn] *n.* оленёнок (-нка; *pl.* оленя́та, -т); *adj.* (*~-coloured*) желтова́то-кори́чневый.

fawn[2] [fɔːn] *v.i.* (*animal*) ласка́ться *impf.* (**upon** к+*d.*); (*person*) подли́зываться *impf.*, подлиза́ться (-ижу́сь, -и́жешься) *pf.* (**upon** к+*d.*).

fax [fæks] *n.* факс; **~ machine** факсими́льный аппара́т; *v.t.* передава́ть (-даю́, -даёшь) *impf.*, переда́ть (-а́м, -а́шь, -а́ст, -ади́м; пе́редал, -а́, -о) *pf.* по фа́ксу.

FBI *abbr.* (*of* **Federal Bureau of Investigation**) ФБР, Федера́льное бюро́ рассле́дований.

fealty ['fiːəltɪ] *n.* (прися́га на) ве́рность.

fear [fɪə(r)] *n.* страх, боя́знь, опасе́ние; *v.t.* & *i.* боя́ться (бою́сь, бои́шься) *impf.*+*g.*; опаса́ться *impf.*+*g.* **fearful** *adj.* (*terrible*) стра́шный (-шен, -шна́, -шно, стра́шны́); (*timid*) пугли́вый. **fearless** *adj.* бесстра́шный. **fearsome** *adj.* гро́зный (-зен, -зна́, -зно).

feasibility [ˌfiːzɪ'bɪlɪtɪ] *n.* осуществи́мость. **'feasible** *adj.* осуществи́мый, возмо́жный.

feast [fiːst] *n.* (*meal*) пир (*loc.* -е & -у́; *pl.* -ы́); (*festival*) пра́здник; *v.i.* пирова́ть *impf.*; *v.t.* угоща́ть *impf.*, угости́ть *pf.*; **~ one's eyes on** любова́ться *impf.*, по~ *pf.*+*i.*, на+*a.*

feat [fiːt] *n.* по́двиг.

feather ['feðə(r)] *n.* перо́ (*pl.* пе́рья, -ьев); *pl.* (*plumage*) опере́ние; *v.t.* оперя́ть *impf.*, опери́ть *pf.*; **~ bed** пери́на. **feather-brained** *adj.* ве́треный. **feathery** *adj.* перна́тый.

feature ['fiːtʃə(r)] *n.* осо́бенность, черта́; (*newspaper*) (темати́ческая) статья́; *pl.* (*of face*) черты́ *f.pl.* лица́; **~ film** худо́жественный фильм; *v.t.* (*in film*) пока́зывать *impf.*, показа́ть (-ажу́, -а́жешь) *pf.* (на экра́не); *v.i.* (*take part*) уча́ствовать *impf.* (**in** в+*p.*).

febrile ['fiːbraɪl] *adj.* лихора́дочный.

February ['febrʊərɪ] *n.* февра́ль (-ля́) *m.*; *attr.* февра́льский.

fecund ['fiːkənd, 'fek-] *adj.* плодоро́дный. **fe'cundity** *n.* плодоро́дие.

federal ['fedər(ə)l] *adj.* федера́льный. **fede'ration** *n.* федера́ция.

fee [fiː] *n.* гонора́р; (*entrance ~ etc.*) взнос; *pl.* (*regular payment, school, etc.*) пла́та.

feeble ['fiːb(ə)l] *adj.* сла́бый (слаб, -а́, -о), не́мощный. **feeble-minded** *adj.* слабоу́мный. **feebleness** *n.* сла́бость.

feed [fiːd] *n.* корм (-а(у), *loc.* -е & -у́; *pl.* -а́); *v.t.* корми́ть (-млю́, -мишь) *impf.*, на~, по~ *pf.*; пита́ть *impf.*, на~ *pf.*; *v.i.* корми́ться (-млю́сь, -мишься) *impf.*, по~ *pf.*; пита́ться *impf.* (**on** +*i.*); **~ up** (*fatten*) отка́рмливать *impf.*, откорми́ть (-млю́, -мишь) *pf.*; **I am fed up with** мне надое́л (-а, -о, -и)+*nom.* **feedback** *n.* обра́тная связь; (*fig.*) о́тклик, реа́кция.

feel [fiːl] *v.t.* осяза́ть *impf.*; ощуща́ть *impf.*, ощути́ть (-ущу́, -ути́шь) *pf.*; чу́вствовать *impf.*, по~ *pf.*; (*undergo*) испы́тывать *impf.*, испыта́ть *pf.*; *v.i.* (*~ bad etc.*) чу́вствовать *impf.*, по~ *pf.* себя́+*adv.*, +*i.*; **~ like** хоте́ться (хо́чется) *impf.* *impers.*+*d.* **feeling** *n.* (*sense*) ощуще́ние; (*emotion*) чу́вство; (*impression*) впечатле́ние; (*mood*) настрое́ние.

feign [feɪn] *v.t.* притворя́ться *impf.*, притвори́ться *pf.*+*i.* **feigned** *adj.* притво́рный.

feint [feɪnt] *n.* ло́жный уда́р; (*pretence*) притво́рство.

felicitate [fə'lɪsɪˌteɪt] *v.t.* поздравля́ть *impf.*, поздра́вить *pf.* (**on** с+*i.*). **felici'tation** *n.*

поздравлéние.
felicitous [fə'lɪsɪtəs] *adj.* удáчный, счастли́вый (счáстли́в). **felicity** *n.* счáстье, блажéнство.
feline ['fi:laɪn] *adj.* кошáчий (-чья, -чье).
fell [fel] *v.t.* (*tree*) срубáть *impf.*, сруби́ть (-блю́, -бишь) *pf.*; (*person*) сбивáть *impf.*, сбить (собью́, -ьёшь) *pf.* с ног.
fellow ['feləʊ] *n.* человéк, пáрень (-рня; *pl.* -рни, -рнéй) *m.*, товáрищ; член (коллéджа, наýчного óбщества и т.п.). **fellowship** *n.* товáрищество, сооóбщество, содрýжество.
felon ['felən] *n.* уголóвный престýпник, -ая престýпница. **felonious** [fɪ'ləʊnɪəs] *adj.* престýпный. **felony** *n.* углолóвное преступлéние.
fel(d)spar ['felspɑ:(r)] *n.* полевóй шпат.
felt [felt] *n.* фетр, вóйлок; *adj.* фéтровый, вóйлочный; ~ **boots** вáленки (-нок) *pl.* **felt-tip (pen)** *n.* фломáстер.
female ['fi:meɪl] *n.* (*animal*) сáмка; (*person*) жéнщина; *adj.* жéнский. **feminine** ['femɪnɪn] *adj.* жéнский, жéнственный (-ен, -енна); (*gram.*) жéнского рóда.
femoral ['femər(ə)l] *adj.* бéдренный. **femur** ['fi:mə(r)] *n.* бедрó (*pl.* бёдра, -дер, -драм).
fen [fen] *n.* болóто, болоти́стая мéстность.
fence [fens] *n.* ограда, забóр, и́згородь; *v.t.*: ~ **in** огорáживать *impf.*, огороди́ть (-ожý, -óди́шь) *pf.*; ~ **off** отгорáживать *impf.*, отгороди́ть (-ожý, -óди́шь) *pf.*; *v.i.* (*sport*) фехтовáть *impf.* **fencer** *n.* фехтовáльщик, -ица. **fencing** *n.* огорáживание; (*enclosure*) забóр, и́згородь; (*sport*) фехтовáние; *adj.* фехтовáльный.
fend [fend] *v.t.*: ~ **off** отражáть *impf.*, отрази́ть *pf.*; (*blow*) пари́ровать *impf.*, от~ *pf.*; ~ **for o.s.** забóтиться *impf.*, по~ *pf.* о себé. **fender** *n.* (*guard*) решётка; (*naut.*) крáнец (-нца).
fennel ['fen(ə)l] *n.* фéнхель *m.*
ferment ['fɜ:ment; fə'ment] *n.* (*substance*) заквáска; (*action, also fig.*) брожéние; *v.i.* броди́ть (-дит) *impf.*; *v.t.* квáсить (-áшу, -áсишь) *impf.*, за~ *pf.*; (*excite*) возбуждáть *impf.*, возбуди́ть *pf.* **fermen'tation** *n.* брожéние; (*excitement*) возбуждéние.
fern [fɜ:n] *n.* пáпоротник.
ferocious [fə'rəʊʃəs] *adj.* свирéпый, лю́тый (лют, -á, -о). **ferocity** [fə'rɒsɪtɪ] *n.* свирéпость, лю́тость.
ferret ['ferɪt] *n.* хорёк (-рькá); *v.t.*: ~ **out** выгоня́ть *impf.*, вы́гнать (вы́гоню, -нишь) *pf.*; (*search out*) разню́хивать *impf.*, разню́хать *pf.*; *v.i.*: ~ **about** (*rummage*) ры́ться (рóюсь, рóешься) *impf.*
ferro- ['ferəʊ] *in comb.* ферро..., железо... . **ferroconcrete** *n.* железобетóн. **ferrous** ['ferəs] *adj.* желéзный; ~ **metals** чёрные метáллы *m.pl.*
ferry ['ferɪ] *n.* парóм, перевóз; *v.t.* перевози́ть (-ожý, -óзишь) *impf.*, перевезти́ (-езý, -езёшь; -ёз, -езлá) *pf.* **ferryman** *n.* парóмщик, перевóзчик.
fertile ['fɜ:taɪl] *adj.* плодорóдный, плодови́тый. **fertility** [ˌfɜ:'tɪlɪtɪ] *n.* плодорóдие, плодови́тость. **fertilize** *v.t.* (*soil*) удобря́ть *impf.*, удобри́ть *pf.*; (*egg*) оплодотворя́ть *impf.*, оплодотвори́ть *pf.* **fertilizer** *n.* удобрéние.
fervent ['fɜ:v(ə)nt], **fervid** ['fɜ:vɪd] *adj.* горя́чий, пы́лкий (-лок, -лкá, -лко). **fervour** ['fɜ:və(r)] *n.* пыл (-а(у), *loc.* -ý), горя́чность, рвéние.
festal ['fest(ə)l] *adj.* (*of feast*) прáздничный; (*gay*) весёлый (вéсел, -á, -о, вéселы́).
fester ['festə(r)] *v.i.* гнои́ться *impf.*
festival ['festɪv(ə)l] *n.* прáздник, фестивáль *m.* **festive** *adj.* прáздничный; (*jovial*) весёлый (вéсел, -á, -о, вéселы́). **fe'stivity** *n.* весéлье; *pl.* торжествá *nt.pl.*
festoon [fe'stu:n] *n.* гирля́нда; (*archit.*) фестóн; *v.t.* украшáть *impf.*, укрáсить *pf.* гирля́ндами, фестóнами.
fetch [fetʃ] *v.t.* (*carrying*) приноси́ть (-ошý, -óсишь) *impf.*, принести́ (-есý, -есёшь; -ёс, -еслá) *pf.*; (*leading*) приводи́ть (-ожý, -óдишь) *impf.*, привести́ (-едý, -едёшь; -ёл, -елá) *pf.*; (*go and come back with*) (*on foot*) сходи́ть (-ожý, -óдишь) *pf.* за+*i.*; заходи́ть (-ожý, -óдишь) *impf.*, зайти́ (зайдý, -дёшь; зашёл, -шлá) *pf.* за+*i.*; (*by vehicle*) заезжáть *impf.*, заéхать (-éду, -éдешь) *pf.* за+*i.*; (*cause*) вызывáть *impf.*, вы́звать (вы́зову, -вешь) *pf.*; (*price*) выручáть *impf.*, вы́ручить *pf.* **fetching** *adj.* привлекáтельный.
fetid ['fetɪd, 'fi:tɪd] *adj.* зловóнный (-нен, -нна).
fetish ['fetɪʃ] *n.* фети́ш.
fetlock ['fetlɒk] *n.* щётка.
fetter ['fetə(r)] *v.t.* скóвывать *impf.*, сковáть (скую́, скуёшь) *pf.*; *n.*: *pl.* кандалы́ (-лóв) *pl.*, окóвы (-в) *pl.*
fettle ['fet(ə)l] *n.* состоя́ние.
feud [fju:d] *n.* крóвная месть.
feudal ['fju:d(ə)l] *adj.* феодáльный. **feudalism** *n.* феодоли́зм.
fever ['fi:və(r)] *n.* (*med.*) жар (-а(у), *loc.* -ý), лихорáдка; (*agitation*) возбуждéние. **feverish** *adj.* лихорáдочный; возбуждённый (-ён, -енá).
few, a ~ [fju:] *adj.* & *pron.* немнóгие (-их) *pl.*; немнóго+*g.*, мáло+*g.*, нéсколько+*g.*; **quite a** ~ немáло+*g.*
fez [fez] *n.* фéска.
fiancé [fɪ'ɒnseɪ, fɪ'ɑ̃seɪ] *n.* жени́х (-á). **fiancée** *n.* невéста.
fiasco [fɪ'æskəʊ] *n.* провáл.
fiat ['faɪæt, 'faɪət] *n.* (*sanction*) сáнкция; (*decree*) декрéт.
fib [fɪb] *n.* враньё; *v.i.* привирáть *impf.*, приврáть (-рý, -рёшь; приврáл, -á, -о) *pf.* **fibber** *n.* враль (-ля́) *m.*
fibre ['faɪbə(r)] *n.* фи́бра, волокнó (*pl.* -óкна, -óкон, -óкнам); (*character*) харáктер. **fibreglass** *n.* стекловолокнó. **fibrous** *adj.* фибрóзный, волокни́стый.

fickle [ˈfɪk(ə)l] *adj.* непостоя́нный (-нен, -нна), изме́нчивый. **fickleness** *n.* непостоя́нство, изме́нчивость.

fiction [ˈfɪkʃ(ə)n] *n.* (*literature*) беллетри́стика, худо́жественная литерату́ра; (*invention*) вы́думка. **fictional** *adj.* беллетристи́ческий; вы́мышленный. **ficˈtitious** *adj.* вы́мышленный, фикти́вный.

fiddle [ˈfɪd(ə)l] *n.* (*violin*) скри́пка; (*swindle*) обма́н; *v.i.* игра́ть *impf.* (**with** c+*i.*); ~ **about** безде́льничать *impf.*; *v.t.* (*cheat*) надува́ть *impf.*, наду́ть (-у́ю, -у́ешь) *pf.*

fidelity [fɪˈdelɪtɪ] *n.* ве́рность.

fidget [ˈfɪdʒɪt] *n.* непосе́да *c.g.*; *v.i.* ёрзать *impf.*; не́рвничать *impf.* **fidgety** *adj.* непосе́дливый.

field [fi:ld] *n.* по́ле (*pl.* -ля́, -ле́й); (*sport*) площа́дка; (*sphere*) о́бласть, сфе́ра; *attr.* полево́й; **F~ Marshal** фельдмарша́л. **field-glasses** *n.* полево́й бино́кль *m.* **field-mouse** *n.* полева́я мышь (*pl.* -ши, -ше́й).

fiend [fi:nd] *n.* (*demon*) дья́вол, де́мон; (*cruel person*) и́зверг. **fiendish** *adj.* дья́вольский.

fierce [ˈfɪəs] *adj.* свире́пый, лю́тый (лют, -а́, -о); (*strong*) си́льный (силён, -льна́, -льно, си́льны́).

fiery [ˈfaɪərɪ] *adj.* о́гненный.

fife [faɪf] *n.* ду́дка.

fifteen [fɪfˈti:n, ˈfɪf-] *adj.* & *n.* пятна́дцать (-ти, -тью); (*age*) пятна́дцать лет. **fifteenth** *adj.* & *n.* пятна́дцатый; (*fraction*) пятна́дцатая (часть (*pl.* -ти, -те́й)); (*date*) пятна́дцатое (число́). **fifth** *adj.* & *n.* пя́тый; (*fraction*) пя́тая (часть (*pl.* -ти, -те́й)); (*date*) пя́тое (число́); (*mus.*) кви́нта. **fiftieth** *adj.* & *n.* пятидеся́тый; (*fraction*) пятидеся́тая (часть (*pl.* -ти, -те́й)). **fifty** *adj.* & *n.* пятьдеся́т (-тидесяти́, -тью́десятью); (*age*) пятьдеся́т лет; *pl.* (*decade*) пятидеся́тые го́ды (-до́в) *m.pl.* **fifty-fifty** *adj.* ра́вный (-вен, -вна́); *adv.* по́ровну.

fig [fɪg] *n.* фи́га, ви́нная я́года, инжи́р.

fig. *abbr.* (*of* **figure**) рис., рису́нок.

fight [faɪt] *n.* дра́ка; (*battle*) бой (*loc.* бою́; *pl.* бои́); (*fig.*) борьба́; *v.t.* боро́ться (-рю́сь, -решься) *impf.* c+*i.*; сража́ться *impf.*, срази́ться *pf.* c+*i.*; *v.i.* дра́ться (деру́сь, -рёшься; дра́лся, -ла́сь, дра́ло́сь) *impf.* **fighter** *n.* боéц (бойца́); (*aeron.*) истреби́тель *m.* **fighting** *n.* бой *m.pl.*, сраже́ние, дра́ка; *adj.* боево́й.

figment [ˈfɪgmənt] *n.* вы́мысел (-сла), плод (-а́) воображе́ния.

figuration [fɪgjʊˈreɪʃ(ə)n] *n.* оформле́ние; (*ornamentation*) орнамента́ция. **ˈfigurative** *adj.* о́бразный, перено́сный. **ˈfigure** *n.* (*form, body, person*) фигу́ра; (*number*) ци́фра; (*diagram*) рису́нок (-нка); (*image*) изображе́ние; (*person*) ли́чность; (*of speech*) оборо́т ре́чи; *v.t.* (*represent*) изобража́ть *impf.*, изобрази́ть *pf.*; (*imagine*) представля́ть *impf.*, предста́вить *pf.* себе́; ~ **out** вычисля́ть *impf.*, вы́числить *pf.* **figure-head** *n.* (*naut.*) носово́е украше́ние; (*person*) подставно́е лицо́ (*pl.* -ца). **figurine** [ˌfɪgjʊˈri:n] *n.* статуэ́тка.

filament [ˈfɪləmənt] *n.* волокно́ (*pl.* -о́кна, -о́кон, -о́кнам), нить.

filch [fɪltʃ] *v.t.* стяну́ть (-ну́, -нешь) *pf.*

file[1] [faɪl] *n.* (*tool*) напи́льник; *v.t.* подпи́ливать *impf.*, подпили́ть (-лю́, -лишь) *pf.*

file[2] [faɪl] *n.* (*folder*) подши́вка, па́пка; (*set of papers*) де́ло (*pl.* -ла́); *v.t.* подшива́ть *impf.*, подши́ть (подошью́, -ьёшь) *pf.*; влага́ть *impf.*, вложи́ть (-жу́, -жишь) *pf.* в па́пки.

file[3] [faɪl] *n.* (*row*) ряд (-а́ *with* 2,3,4, *loc.* -у́; *pl.* -ы́), шере́нга; **in (single)** ~ гусько́м.

filial [ˈfɪlɪəl] *adj.* (*of son*) сыно́вний; (*of daughter*) доче́рний.

filigree [ˈfɪlɪˌgri:] *n.* филигра́нь; *adj.* филигра́нный.

fill [fɪl] *v.t.* & *i.* наполня́ть(ся) *impf.*, напо́лнить(ся) *pf.*; *v.t.* заполня́ть *impf.*, запо́лнить *pf.*; (*tooth*) пломбирова́ть *impf.*, за~ *pf.*; (*occupy*) занима́ть *impf.*, заня́ть (займу́, -мёшь; за́нял, -а́, -о) *pf.*; (*satiate*) насыща́ть *impf.*, насы́тить (-ы́щу, -ы́тишь) *pf.*; ~ **in** (*v.t.*) заполня́ть *impf.*, запо́лнить *pf.*; (*words*) впи́сывать *impf.*, вписа́ть (-ишу́, -и́шешь) *pf.*; (*v.i.*) замеща́ть *impf.*, замести́ть *pf.*

fillet [ˈfɪlɪt] *n.* (*ribbon*) повя́зка; (*cul.*) филе́ *nt.indecl.*

filling [ˈfɪlɪŋ] *n.* наполне́ние; (*tooth*) пло́мба; (*cul.*) начи́нка.

fillip [ˈfɪlɪp] *n.* щелчо́к (-чка́); толчо́к (-чка́).

filly [ˈfɪlɪ] *n.* кобы́лка.

film [fɪlm] *n.* (*haze*) ды́мка; (*layer*; *phot.*) плёнка; (*cin.*) фильм; ~ **star** кинозвезда́ (*pl.* -ёзды); ~ **studies** *n.* кинове́дение; *v.t.* экранизи́ровать *impf.* & *pf.*; *v.i.* производи́ть (-ожу́, -о́дишь) *impf.*, произвести́ (-еду́, -едёшь; -ёл, -ела́) *pf.* киносъёмку; снима́ть *impf.*, снять (сниму́, -мешь; снял, -а́, -о) *pf.* фильм. **filmy** *adj.* тума́нный (-нен, -нна).

filter [ˈfɪltə(r)] *n.* фильтр; *v.t.* фильтрова́ть *impf.*, про~ *pf.*; проце́живать *impf.*, процеди́ть *pf.*; ~ **through, out** проса́чиваться *impf.*, просочи́ться *pf.*

filth [fɪlθ] *n.* грязь (*loc.* -зи́); (*obscenity*) непристо́йность. **filthy** *adj.* гря́зный (-зен, -зна́, -зно); непристо́йный.

fin [fɪn] *n.* плавни́к (-а́); (*aeron.*) киль *m.*

final [ˈfaɪn(ə)l] *n.* фина́л; *pl.* выпускны́е экза́мены *m.pl.*; *adj.* после́дний, оконча́тельный. **finale** [fɪˈnɑ:lɪ, -leɪ] *n.* фина́л, развя́зка. **fiˈnality** *n.* зако́нченность. **finally** *adv.* в конце́ концо́в, оконча́тельно.

finance [ˈfaɪnæns, faɪˈnæns] *n.* фина́нсы (-сов) *pl.*; *pl.* дохо́ды *m.pl.*; *v.t.* финанси́ровать *impf.* & *pf.* **fiˈnancial** *adj.* фина́нсовый. **fiˈnancier** *n.* финанси́ст.

finch *n. see comb., e.g.* **bullfinch**

find [faɪnd] *n.* нахо́дка; *v.t.* находи́ть (-ожу́, -о́дишь) *impf.*, найти́ (найду́, -дёшь; нашёл,

-шла́) *pf.*; (*person*) застава́ть (-таю́, -таёшь) *impf.*, заста́ть (-а́ну, -а́нешь) *pf.*; ~ **out** узнава́ть (-наю́, -наёшь) *impf.*, узна́ть *pf.*; ~ **fault with** придира́ться *impf.*, придра́ться (придеру́сь, -рёшься; придра́лся, -ала́сь, -а́ло́сь) *pf.* к+*d.* **finding** *n.* (*leg.*) пригово́р; *pl.* (*of inquiry*) вы́воды *m.pl.*

fine[1] [fi:n] *n.* (*penalty*) штраф; *v.t.* штрафова́ть *impf.*, о~ *pf.*

fine[2] [fi:n] *adj.* (*excellent*) прекра́сный, превосхо́дный; (*delicate*) то́нкий (-нок, -нка́, -нко, то́нки́); (*of sand etc.*) ме́лкий (-лок, -лка́, -лко); ~ **arts** изобрази́тельные иску́сства *nt.pl.* **fineness** *n.* то́нкость, изя́щество, острота́. **finery** ['faɪnərɪ] *n.* наря́д, украше́ние. **finesse** [fɪ'nes] *n.* хи́трость.

finger ['fɪŋgə(r)] *n.* па́лец (-льца) (**index** указа́тельный; **middle** сре́дний; **ring** безымя́нный; **little** мизи́нец (-нца)); *v.t.* тро́гать *impf.*, тро́нуть *pf.* **fingerprint** *n.* отпеча́ток (-тка) па́льца. **fingertip** *n.*: **have at (one's)** ~**s** знать *impf.* как свои́ пять па́льцев.

finish ['fɪnɪʃ] *n.* коне́ц (-нца́), оконча́ние; (*of furniture etc.*) отде́лка; (*sport*) фи́ниш; *v.t.* & *i.* конча́ть(ся) *impf.*, ко́нчить(ся) *pf.*; *v.t.* ока́нчивать *impf.*, око́нчить *pf.*; ~**ing touches** после́дние штрихи́ *m.pl.*

finite ['faɪnaɪt] *adj.* определённый (-нен, -нна); (*gram.*) ли́чный.

Finland ['fɪnlənd] *n.* Финля́ндия.

Finn [fɪn] *n.* финн, фи́нка. **Finnish** *adj.* фи́нский.

fir [fɜ:(r)] *n.* ель, пи́хта. **fir-cone** *n.* ело́вая ши́шка.

fire ['faɪə(r)] *n.* ого́нь (огня́) *m.*; (*grate*) ками́н; (*conflagration*) пожа́р; (*bonfire*) костёр (-тра́); (*fervour*) пыл (-а(у), *loc.* -у́); **be on** ~ горе́ть (-рю́, -ри́шь) *impf.*; **catch** ~ загора́ться *impf.*, загоре́ться (-рю́сь, -ри́шься) *pf.*; **set** ~ **to, set on** ~ поджига́ть *impf.*, подже́чь (подожгу́, -жжёшь; поджёг, подожгла́) *pf.*; *v.t.* зажига́ть *impf.*, заже́чь (-жгу́, -жжёшь; -жёг, -жгла́) *pf.*; воспламеня́ть *impf.*, воспламени́ть *pf.*; (*gun*) стреля́ть *impf.* из+*g.* (**at** в+*a.*, по+*d.*); (*dismiss*) увольня́ть *impf.*, уво́лить *pf.*; ~ **brigade** пожа́рная кома́нда; ~ **extinguisher** огнетуши́тель *m.*; ~ **station** пожа́рное депо́ *nt.indecl.* **fire-alarm** *n.* пожа́рная трево́га. **firearm(s)** *n.* огнестре́льное ору́жие. **fire-engine** *n.* пожа́рная маши́на. **fire-escape** *n.* пожа́рная ле́стница. **firefly** *n.* светля́к (-а́). **fire-guard** *n.* ками́нная решётка. **fireman** *n.* пожа́рный *sb.*; (*tending furnace*) кочега́р. **fireplace** *n.* ками́н. **fireproof, fire-resistant** *adj.* огнеупо́рный. **fireside** *n.* ме́сто у ками́на. **firewood** *n.* дрова́ (-в) *pl.* **firework** *n.* фейерве́рк. **firing** *n.* (*of gun*) стрельба́.

firm[1] [fɜ:m] *n.* (*business*) фи́рма.

firm[2] [fɜ:m] *adj.* твёрдый (твёрд, -а́, -о), кре́пкий (-пок, -пка́, -пко), сто́йкий (-о́ек, -о́йка́, -о́йко). **firmament** *n.* небе́сный свод. **firmness** *n.* твёрдость.

first [fɜ:st] *adj.* пе́рвый; (*foremost*) выдаю́щийся; *n.* (*date*) пе́рвое (число́); пе́рвый *sb.*; *adv.* сперва́, снача́ла, в пе́рвый раз; **in the** ~ **place** во-пе́рвых; ~ **of all** пре́жде всего́; **at** ~ **sight** на пе́рвый взгляд, с пе́рвого взгля́да; ~ **aid** пе́рвая по́мощь; **give** ~ **aid** ока́зывать *impf.*, оказа́ть (-ажу́, -а́жешь) *pf.* пе́рвую по́мощь (**to** +*d.*); ~ **cousin** двою́родный брат (*pl.* -ья, -ьев), двою́родная сестра́ (*pl.* сёстры, сестёр, сёстрам). **first-born** *n.* пе́рвенец (-нца). **first-class** *adj.* первокла́ссный, превосхо́дный. **firsthand** *adv.* из пе́рвых рук. **first-rate** *adj.* первокла́ссный, превосхо́дный.

fiscal ['fɪsk(ə)l] *adj.* фина́нсовый, фиска́льный.

fish [fɪʃ] *n.* ры́ба; *adj.* ры́бный, ры́бий (-бья, -бье); *v.i.* лови́ть (-влю́, -вишь) *impf.* ры́бу; уди́ть (ужу́, у́дишь) *impf.* ры́бу; ~ **for** (*compliments etc.*) напра́шиваться *impf.*, напроси́ться (-ошу́сь, -о́сишься) *pf.* на+*a.*; ~ **out** вытаскивать *impf.*, вы́таскать *pf.* **fisherman** *n.* рыба́к (-а́), рыболо́в. **fishery** *n.* ры́бный про́мысел (-сла). **fishing** *n.* ры́бная ло́вля; ~ **boat** рыболо́вное су́дно (*pl.* суда́, -до́в); ~ **line** ле́са́ (*pl.* лёсы); ~ **rod** уди́лище, у́дочка. **fishmonger** *n.* торго́вец (-вца) ры́бой. **fishy** *adj.* ры́бний, ры́бий (-бья, -бье); (*dubious*) подозри́тельный.

fission ['fɪʃ(ə)n] *n.* расщепле́ние; **nuclear** ~ деле́ние ядра́; **cell** ~ деле́ние кле́ток. **fissure** *n.* трещи́на.

fist [fɪst] *n.* кула́к (-а́). **fisticuffs** ['fɪstɪ,kʌfs] *n.* кула́чный бой (*loc.* бою́; *pl.* бои́).

fit[1] [fɪt] *n.*: **be a good** ~ (*clothes*) хорошо́ сиде́ть (-ди́т, -дя́т) *impf.*; *adj.* подходя́щий, го́дный (-ден, -дна́, -дно); (*healthy*) здоро́вый; *v.t.* (*be suitable*) годи́ться *impf.*+*d.*, на+*a.*, для+*g.*; подходи́ть (-ожу́, -о́дишь) *impf.*, подойти́ (подойду́, -дёшь; подошёл, -шла́) *pf.*+*d.*; (*adjust*) прила́живать *impf.*, прила́дить *pf.* (**to** к+*d.*); *v.t.* & *i.* приспоса́бливать(ся) *impf.*, приспосо́бить(ся) *pf.*; ~ **out** снабжа́ть *impf.*, снабди́ть *pf.*

fit[2] [fɪt] *n.* (*attack*) припа́док (-дка), при́ступ; (*fig.*) поры́в. **fitful** *adj.* поры́вистый.

fitter ['fɪtə(r)] *n.* монтёр, устано́вщик. **fitting** *n.* (*of clothes*) приме́рка; прила́живание, монта́ж; *pl.* армату́ра; *adj.* подходя́щий, го́дный (-ден, -дна́, -дно). **fitting-room** *n.* приме́рочная *sb.*

five [faɪv] *adj.* & *n.* пять (-ти́, -тью́); (*collect.*; *5 pairs*) пя́теро (-ры́х); (*cards*; *number 5*) пятёрка; (*time*) пять (часо́в); (*age*) пять лет. **five-year** *adj.*: ~ **plan** пятиле́тка.

fix [fɪks] *n.* (*dilemma*) диле́мма; (*radio etc.*) засе́чка; *v.t.* устана́вливать *impf.*, установи́ть (-влю́, -вишь) *pf.*; (*arrange*) устра́ивать *impf.*, устро́ить *pf.*; (*repair*) поправля́ть *impf.*, попра́вить *pf.*; *v.t.* & *i.* остана́вливать(ся) *impf.*, останови́ть(ся) (-влю́(сь), -вишь(ся)) *pf.* (**on** на+*a.*). **fi'xation** *n.* фикса́ция. **fixed** *adj.* неподви́жный, постоя́нный (-нен, -нна).

fizz [fɪz] *v.i.* шипе́ть (-плю́, -пи́шь) *impf.*, *n.* (*coll.*) шипу́чка. **fizzy** *adj.* шипу́чий.

flabbergast ['flæbəˌgɑːst] *v.t.* ошеломля́ть *impf.*, ошеломи́ть *pf.*

flabby ['flæbɪ], **flaccid** ['flæksɪd, 'flæsɪd] *adj.* дря́блый (-л, -ла́, -ло), вя́лый.

flag¹ [flæg] *n.* (*standard*) флаг, зна́мя (*pl.* -мёна) *nt.*; *v.t.* (*signal*) сигнализи́ровать *impf.* & *pf.*, про~ *pf.* фла́гами.

flag² [flæg] *n.* (*stone*) плита́ (*pl.* -ты); *v.t.* мости́ть *impf.*, вы́~, за~ *pf.* пли́тами.

flag³ [flæg] *v.i.* (*droop*) поника́ть *impf.*, пони́кнуть (-к) *pf.*

flagellate ['flædʒɪlɪt] *v.t.* бичева́ть (-чу́ю, -чу́ешь) *impf.*

flagon ['flægən] *n.* кувши́н.

flagrant ['fleɪgrənt] *adj.* вопию́щий, очеви́дный, сканда́льный.

flagship ['flægʃɪp] *n.* флагма́н. **flagstaff** *n.* флагшто́к.

flail [fleɪl] *n.* цеп (-а́).

flair ['fleə(r)] *n.* чутьё.

flake [fleɪk] *n.* слой (*pl.* -ои́); *pl.* хло́пья (-ьев) *pl.*; *v.i.* слои́ться *impf.*; лупи́ться (-пится) *impf.*, об~ *pf.* **flaky** *adj.* слои́стый.

flamboyant [flæm'bɔɪənt] *adj.* цвети́стый.

flame [fleɪm] *n.* пла́мя *nt.*, ого́нь (огня́) *m.*; (*passion*) пыл (-а(у), *loc.* -у́); *v.i.* пыла́ть *impf.*; ~ **up** разгора́ться *impf.*, разгоре́ться (-ри́тся) *pf.* **flame-thrower** *n.* огнемёт.

flamingo [flə'mɪŋgəʊ] *n.* flами́нго *m.indecl.*

flange [flændʒ] *n.* фла́нец (-нца).

flank [flæŋk] *n.* бок (*loc.* -у́; *pl.* -а́), фланг; *v.t.* быть располо́женным сбо́ку, на фла́нге, +*g.*; (*mil.*) фланки́ровать *impf.* & *pf.*

flannel ['flæn(ə)l] *n.* флане́ль; *attr.* флане́левый.

flap [flæp] *n.* мах; (*wings*) взмах; (*board*) откидна́я доска́ (*a.* -ску; *pl.* -ски, -со́к, -ска́м); *v.t.* маха́ть (машу́, -шешь) *impf.*, махну́ть *pf.*+*i.*; взма́хивать *impf.*, взмахну́ть *pf.*+*i.*; *v.i.* развева́ться *impf.*

flare [fleə(r)] *n.* вспы́шка; (*signal*) светово́й сигна́л; *v.i.* вспы́хивать *impf.*, вспы́хнуть *pf.*; ~ **up** вспыли́ть *pf.*

flash [flæʃ] *n.* вспы́шка, пробле́ск; **in a** ~ ми́гом; *v.i.* сверка́ть *impf.*, сверкну́ть *pf.* **flashy** *adj.* показно́й.

flask [flɑːsk] *n.* фля́жка.

flat¹ [flæt] *n.* (*dwelling*) кварти́ра.

flat² [flæt] *n.* (~ *region*) равни́на; (*mus.*) бемо́ль *m.*; (*tyre*) спу́щенная ши́на; *adj.* пло́ский (-сок, -ска́, -ско), ро́вный (-вен, -вна́, -вно); (*dull*) ску́чный (-чен, -чна́, -чно); ~ **foot** плоскосто́пие. **flat-fish** *n.* ка́мбала. **flat-iron** *n.* утю́г (-а́).

flatmate ['flætmeɪt] *n.* сосе́д по кварти́ре.

flatten *v.t.* де́лать *impf.*, с~ *pf.* пло́ским; *v.i.* станови́ться (-ится) *impf.*, стать (ста́нет) *pf.* пло́ским; *v.t.* & *i.* выра́внивать(ся) *impf.*, вы́ровнять(ся) *pf.*

flatter *v.t.* льстить *impf.*, по~ *pf.*+*d.* **flatterer** *n.* льсте́ц (-а́). **flattering** *adj.* льсти́вый, ле́стный. **flattery** *n.* лесть.

flaunt [flɔːnt] *v.t.* щеголя́ть *impf.*, щегольну́ть *pf.*+*i.*; ~ **o.s.** выставля́ться *impf.*, вы́ставиться *pf.*

flautist ['flɔːtɪst] *n.* флейти́ст.

flavour ['fleɪvə(r)] *n.* арома́т, вкус; (*fig.*) при́вкус, отте́нок (-нка); *v.t.* приправля́ть *impf.*, припра́вить *pf.* **flavourless** *adj.* безвку́сный.

flaw [flɔː] *n.* (*crack*) трещи́на; (*defect*) изъя́н.

flax [flæks] *n.* лён (льна). **flaxen** *adj.* льняно́й; (*colour*) соло́менный.

flay [fleɪ] *v.t.* сдира́ть *impf.*, содра́ть (сдеру́, -рёшь; содра́л, -а́, -о) *pf.* ко́жу с+*g.*

flea [fliː] *n.* блоха́ (*pl.* -хи, -х, -ха́м). **flea-bite** *n.* блоши́ный уку́с.

fleck [flek] *n.* пятно́ (*pl.* -тна, -тен, -тнам), кра́пина.

fledge [fledʒ] *v.t.* оперя́ть *impf.*, опери́ть *pf.*; **be(come) fledged** оперя́ться *impf.*, опери́ться *pf.* **fledg(e)ling** *n.* птене́ц (-нца́).

flee [fliː] *v.i.* бежа́ть (бегу́, бежи́шь) *impf.* & *pf.* (**from** от+*g.*); (*vanish*) исчеза́ть *impf.*, исче́знуть (-з) *pf.*

fleece [fliːs] *n.* ове́чья шерсть, руно́ (*pl.* -на); *v.t.* обдира́ть *impf.*, ободра́ть (обдеру́, -рёшь; ободра́л, -а́, -о) *pf.* **fleecy** *adj.* шерсти́стый.

fleet [fliːt] *n.* флот (*pl.* -о́ты, -о́то́в); (*vehicles*) парк.

fleeting *adj.* мимолётный.

flesh [fleʃ] *n.* (*as opposed to mind*) плоть; (*meat*) мя́со; (*of fruit*) мя́коть; **in the** ~ во плоти́. **fleshly** *adj.* пло́тский. **fleshy** *adj.* мяси́стый.

flex [fleks] *n.* электрошну́р (-а́); *v.t.* сгиба́ть *impf.*, согну́ть *pf.* **flexibility** *adj.* ги́бкость, пода́тливость. **flexible** *adj.* ги́бкий (-бок, -бка́, -бко), пода́тливый. **flexion** *n.* сгиб(а́ние); (*gram.*) фле́ксия.

flick [flɪk] *n.* щелчо́к (-чка́); *v.t.* & *i.* щёлкать *impf.*, щёлкнуть *pf.* (+*i.*); ~ **off** сма́хивать *impf.*, смахну́ть *pf.*

flicker ['flɪkə(r)] *n.* мерца́ние; *v.i.* мерца́ть *impf.*

flick-knife ['flɪknaɪf] *n.* пружи́нный нож (-а́).

flier *see* **flyer**

flight¹ [flaɪt] *n.* (*fleeing*) бе́гство; **put to** ~ обраща́ть *impf.*, обрати́ть (-ащу́, -ати́шь) *pf.* в бе́гство.

flight² [flaɪt] *n.* (*flying*) полёт, перелёт; (*trip*) рейс; (*flock*) ста́я; (*aeron. unit*) звено́ (*pl.* -нья, -ньев); ~ **of stairs** ле́стничный марш. **flighty** *adj.* ве́треный.

flimsy ['flɪmzɪ] *adj.* непро́чный (-чен, -чна́, -чно).

flinch [flɪntʃ] *v.i.* уклоня́ться *impf.*, уклони́ться (-ню́сь, -нишься) *pf.* (**from** от+*g.*); (*wince*) вздра́гивать *impf.*, вздро́гнуть *pf.*

fling [flɪŋ] *v.t.* швыря́ть *impf.*, швырну́ть *pf.*;

v.i. (*also* ~ *o.s.*) броса́ться *impf.*, бро́ситься *pf.*
flint [flɪnt] *n.* кре́мень (-мня́) *m.*; *attr.* кремнёвый.
flip [flɪp] *n.* щелчо́к (-чка́); *v.t.* щёлкать *impf.*, щёлкнуть *pf.*+*i.*
flippancy ['flɪpənsɪ] *n.* легкомы́слие. **flippant** *adj.* легкомы́сленный (-ен, -енна).
flipper ['flɪpə(r)] *n.* плавни́к (-а́), ласт.
flirt [flɜːt] *n.* коке́тка; *v.i.* флиртова́ть *impf.* (**with** с+*i.*); (*fig.*) заи́грывать *impf.* (**with** с+*i.*). **flir'tation** *n.* флирт.
flit [flɪt] *v.i.* (*migrate*) переезжа́ть *impf.*, перее́хать (-е́ду, -е́дешь) *pf.*; (*fly*) порха́ть *impf.*, порхну́ть *pf.*
float [fləʊt] *n.* поплаво́к (-вка́), плот (-а́); *v.i.* пла́вать *indet.*, плыть (плыву́, -вёшь; плыл, -а́, -о) *det.*; *v.t.* (*loan*) выпуска́ть *impf.*, вы́пустить *pf.*; (*company*) пуска́ть *impf.*, пусти́ть (пущу́, пу́стишь) *pf.* в ход.
flock [flɒk] *n.* (*animals*) ста́до (*pl.* -да́); (*birds*) ста́я; (*people*) толпа́ (*pl.* -пы); *v.i.* стека́ться *impf.*, стечься (стечётся; стёкся, -кла́сь) *pf.*; толпи́ться *impf.*
floe [fləʊ] *n.* плаву́чая льди́на.
flog [flɒg] *v.t.* сечь (секу́, сечёшь; сек, -ла́) *impf.*, вы́~ *pf.*
flood [flʌd] *n.* наводне́ние, разли́в, пото́п; *v.i.* (*river etc.*) выступа́ть *impf.*, вы́ступить *pf.* из берего́в; *v.t.* наводня́ть *impf.*, наводни́ть *pf.*; затопля́ть *impf.*, затопи́ть (-плю́, -пишь) *pf.* **floodgate** *n.* шлюз. **floodlight** *n.* проже́ктор (*pl.* -ы & -а́). **flood-tide** *n.* прили́в;
floor [flɔː(r)] *n.* пол (*loc.* -у́; *pl.* -ы́); (*of sea*) дно (*no pl.*); (*storey*) эта́ж (-а́); **ground, first** (*etc.*) ~ пе́рвый, второ́й, (и т.д.) эта́ж (-а́); **take the** ~ брать (беру́, -рёшь; брал, -а́, -о) *impf.*, взять (возьму́, -мёшь; взял, -а́, -о) *pf.* сло́во; *v.t.* настила́ть *impf.*, настла́ть (-телю́, -те́лешь) *pf.* пол+*g.*; (*knock down*) вали́ть (-лю́, -лишь) *impf.*, по~ *pf.* на́ пол; (*confound*) ста́вить *impf.*, по~ *pf.* в тупи́к. **floorboard** *n.* полови́ца. **floorcloth** *n.* полова́я тря́пка. **flooring** *n.* насти́л(ка).
flop [flɒp] *v.i.* шлёпаться *impf.*, шлёпнуться *pf.*; (*fail*) прова́ливаться *impf.*, провали́ться (-ится) *pf.* **floppy** *adj.* вися́щий, болта́ющийся; *n.* (*comput.*) ~ **(disk)** ги́бкий диск.
flora ['flɔːrə] *n.* фло́ра. **floral** *adj.* цвето́чный.
Florence ['flɒrəns] *n.* Флоре́нция.
florescence [flɔː'res(ə)ns, flɒ-] *n.* цвете́ние. **florid** ['flɒrɪd] *adj.* цвети́стый; (*ruddy*) румя́ный. **'florist** *n.* торго́вец (-вца) цвета́ми.
flotilla [flə'tɪlə] *n.* флоти́лия.
flotsam ['flɒtsəm] *n.* пла́вающие обло́мки *m.pl.*
flounce¹ [flaʊns] *n.* (*of skirt*) обо́рка.
flounce² [flaʊns] *v.i.* броса́ться *impf.*, бро́ситься *pf.*
flounder¹ ['flaʊndə(r)] *n.* (*fish*) ка́мбала.
flounder² ['flaʊndə(r)] *v.i.* бара́хтаться *impf.*; пу́таться *impf.*, с~ *pf.*
flour ['flaʊə(r)] *n.* мука́. **flour-mill** *n.* ме́льница.
flourish ['flʌrɪʃ] *n.* (*movement*) разма́хивание (+*i.*); (*of pen*) ро́счерк; (*mus.*) туш; *v.i.* (*thrive*) процвета́ть *impf.*; *v.t.* (*wave*) разма́хивать *impf.*, размахну́ть *pf.*+*i.*
floury ['flaʊərɪ] *adj.* мучни́стый.
flout [flaʊt] *v.t.* пренебрега́ть *impf.*, пренебре́чь (-егу́, -ежёшь; -ёг, -егла́) *pf.*+*i.*
flow [fləʊ] *v.i.* течь (течёт; тёк, -ла́) *impf.*; ли́ться (льётся; ли́лся, лила́сь, ли́ло́сь) *impf.*; *n.* тече́ние, пото́к; (*tide*) прили́в.
flower ['flaʊə(r)] *n.* цвето́к (-тка́; *pl.* -ты́); (*pick*; *prime*) цвет; *v.i.* цвести́ (цветёт; цвёл, -а́) *impf.* **flower-bed** *n.* клу́мба. **flowerpot** *n.* цвето́чный горшо́к (-шка́). **flowery** *adj.* покры́тый цвета́ми; (*florid*) цвети́стый.
flu [fluː] *n.* грипп.
fluctuate ['flʌktjʊˌeɪt] *v.i.* колеба́ться (-блюсь, -блешься) *impf.*, по~ *pf.* **fluctu'ation** *n.* колеба́ние.
flue [fluː] *n.* дымохо́д.
fluency ['fluːənsɪ] *n.* пла́вность, бе́глость. **fluent** *adj.* пла́вный, бе́глый. **fluently** *adv.* бе́гло, свобо́дно.
fluff [flʌf] *n.* пух (-а(у), *loc.* -у́), пушо́к (-шка́). **fluffy** *adj.* пуши́стый.
fluid ['fluːɪd] *n.* жи́дкость; *adj.* жи́дкий (-док, -дка́, -дко), теку́чий.
flunkey ['flʌŋkɪ] *n.* лаке́й.
fluorescence [flʊə'res(ə)ns] *n.* флюоресце́нция. **fluorescent** *adj.* флюоресци́рующий.
fluoride ['flʊəraɪd] *n.* фтори́д. **fluorine** ['flʊəriːn] *n.* фтор.
flurry ['flʌrɪ] *n.* (*squall*) поры́в ве́тра; (*commotion*) сумато́ха; *v.t.* (*agitate*) волнова́ть *impf.*, вз~ *pf.*
flush [flʌʃ] *n.* прили́в; (*redness*) румя́нец (-нца); *v.i.* (*redden*) красне́ть *impf.*, по~ *pf.*; *v.t.* спуска́ть *impf.*, спусти́ть (-ущу́, -у́стишь) *pf.* во́ду в+*a.*
fluster ['flʌstə(r)] *n.* волне́ние; *v.t.* волнова́ть *impf.*, вз~ *pf.*
flute [fluːt] *n.* (*mus.*) фле́йта; (*groove*) желобо́к (-бка́).
flutter ['flʌtə(r)] *v.i.* порха́ть *impf.*, порхну́ть *pf.*; развева́ться *impf.*; (*with excitement*) трепета́ть (-ещу́, -е́щешь) *impf.*; *n.* порха́ние; тре́пет.
fluvial ['fluːvɪəl] *adj.* речно́й.
flux [flʌks] *n.* тече́ние; **in a state of** ~ в состоя́нии измене́ния.
fly¹ [flaɪ] *n.* (*insect*) му́ха.
fly² [flaɪ] *v.i.* лета́ть *indet.*, лете́ть (лечу́, лети́шь) *det.*, по~ *pf.*; (*flag*) развева́ться *impf.*; (*hasten*) нести́сь (несу́сь, -сёшься; нёсся, несла́сь) *impf.*, по~ *pf.*; (*flee*) бежа́ть (бегу́, бежи́шь) *impf.* & *pf.*; *v.t.* (*aircraft*) управля́ть *impf.*+*i.*; (*transport*) перевози́ть (-ожу́, -о́зишь) *impf.*, перевезти́ (-езу́, -езёшь; -ёз, -езла́) *pf.* (самолётом); (*flag*) поднима́ть *impf.*, подня́ть (-ниму́, -ни́мешь; под-

ня́л, -á, -о) *pf.* **flyer, flier** *n.* лётчик. **flying** *n.* полёт(ы).
flywheel *n.* махови́к (-á).
foal [fəʊl] *n.* (*horse*) жеребёнок (-нка; *pl.* жеребя́та, -т); (*ass*) ослёнок (-нка; *pl.* осля́та, -т); **in ~** жерёбая; *v.i.* жереби́ться *impf.*, о~ *pf.*
foam [fəʊm] *n.* пе́на; **~ plastic** пенопла́ст; **~ rubber** пенорези́на; *v.i.* пе́ниться *impf.*, вс~ *pf.* **foamy** *adj.* пени́стый.
focal ['fəʊk(ə)l] *adj.* фо́кусный.
fo'c's'le *see* **forecastle**
focus ['fəʊkəs] *n.* фо́кус, центр; *v.t.* фокуси́ровать *impf.*, с~ *pf.*; (*concentrate*) сосредото́чивать *impf.*, сосредото́чить *pf.*
fodder ['fɒdə(r)] *n.* корм (*loc.* -е & -ý; *pl.* -á), фура́ж (-á).
foe [fəʊ] *n.* враг (-á).
fog [fɒg] *n.* тума́н, мгла. **foggy** *adj.* тума́нный (-нен, -нна), нея́сный (-сен, -сна́, -сно).
foible ['fɔɪb(ə)l] *n.* сла́бость.
foil[1] [fɔɪl] *n.* (*metal*) фо́льга.
foil[2] [fɔɪl] *v.t.* (*frustrate*) расстра́ивать *impf.*, расстро́ить *pf.* (пла́ны+*g.*).
foil[3] [fɔɪl] *n.* (*sword*) рапи́ра.
foist [fɔɪst] *v.t.* навя́зывать *impf.*, навяза́ть (-яжу́, -я́жешь) *pf.* (**on** +*d*).
fold[1] [fəʊld] *n.* скла́дка, сгиб; *v.t.* скла́дывать *impf.*, сложи́ть (-жу́, -жишь) *pf.*; сгиба́ть *impf.*, согну́ть *pf.* **folder** *n.* па́пка. **folding** *adj.* складно́й, откидно́й, ство́рчатый.
fold[2] [fəʊld] *n.* (*sheep*-~) овча́рня (*g.pl.* -рен).
foliage ['fəʊlɪɪdʒ] *n.* листва́.
folk [fəʊk] *n.* наро́д (-а(у)), лю́ди (-де́й, -дям, -дьми́) *pl.*; *pl.* (*relatives*) родня́; *collect.*; *attr.* наро́дный. **folklore** *n.* фолькло́р.
follow ['fɒləʊ] *v.t.* сле́довать *impf.*, по~ *pf.*+*d.*, за+*i.*; идти́ (иду́, идёшь; шёл, шла) *det.* за+*i.*; следи́ть *impf.* за+*i.* **follower** *n.* после́дователь *m.*, ~ница. **following** *adj.* сле́дующий.
folly ['fɒlɪ] *n.* глу́пость, безу́мие.
fond [fɒnd] *adj.* лю́бящий, не́жный; **be ~ of** люби́ть (-блю́, -бишь) *impf.*+*a.*
fondle ['fɒnd(ə)l] *v.t.* ласка́ть *impf.*
fondness ['fɒndnɪs] *n.* не́жность, любо́вь (-бви́, *i.* -бо́вью).
font [fɒnt] *n.* (*eccl.*) купе́ль.
food [fu:d] *n.* пи́ща, еда́; **~ processor** *n.* ку́хонный комба́йн; **~ value** пита́тельность. **foodstuff** *n.* пищево́й проду́кт.
fool [fu:l] *n.* дура́к (-á), глупе́ц (-пца́); *v.t.* дура́чить *impf.*, о~ *pf.*; *v.i.*: **~ about, play the ~** дура́читься *impf.* **foolery** *n.* дура́чество. **foolhardy** *adj.* безрассу́дно хра́брый (храбр, -á, -о). **foolish** *adj.* глу́пый (глуп, -á, -о). **foolishness** *n.* глу́пость.
foot [fʊt] *n.* нога́ (*a.* -гу; *pl.* -ги, -г, -га́м), ступня́; (*measure*) фут; (*of hill etc.*) подно́жие; (*mil.*) пехо́та; **on ~** пешко́м; **put one's ~ in it** сесть (ся́ду, -дешь; сел) *pf.* в лу́жу. **football** *n.* футбо́л; *attr.* футбо́льный. **footballer** *n.* футболи́ст. **footfall** *n.* по́ступь. **footlights** *n.* ра́мпа. **footman** *n.* лаке́й. **footnote** *n.* сно́ска, примеча́ние. **footpath** *n.* тропи́нка; (*pavement*) тротуа́р. **footprint** *n.* след (*pl.* -ы́) (ноги́). **footstep** *n.* (*tread*) шаг (-а(у) & (*with 2,3,4*) -á, *loc.* -ý; *pl.* -и́); (*footprint*) след (*pl.* -ы́) (ноги́). **footwear** *n.* о́бувь.
fop [fɒp] *n.* щёголь *m.*, фат. **foppish** *adj.* щеголско́й, фатова́тый.
for [fə(r), fɔ:(r)] *prep.* (*of time*) в тече́ние+*g.*, на+*a.*; (*of purpose*) для+*g.*, за+*a.*, +*i.*; (*of destination*) в+*a.*; (*on account of*) из-за+*g.*; (*in place of*) вме́сто+*g.*; **~ the sake of** ра́ди+*g.*; **as ~** что каса́ется+*g.*; *conj.* так как, и́бо.
forage ['fɒrɪdʒ] *n.* фура́ж (-á), корм (*loc.* -е & -ý; *pl.* -á); *v.i.* фуражи́ровать *impf.*
foray ['fɒreɪ] *n.* набе́г.
forbear [fɔ:'beə(r)] *v.i.* (*refrain*) возде́рживаться *impf.*, воздержа́ться (-жу́сь, -жишься) *pf.* (**from** от+*g.*) **forbearance** *n.* возде́ржанность.
forbid [fə'bɪd] *v.t.* запреща́ть *impf.*, запрети́ть (-ещу́, -ети́шь) *pf.* (+*d.* (*person*) & *a.* (*thing*)); воспреща́ть *impf.*, воспрети́ть (-ещу́, -ети́шь) *pf.*+*a.*, +*inf.*
force [fɔ:s] *n.* (*strength*) си́ла; (*violence*) наси́лие; (*meaning*) смысл; *pl.* (*armed ~*) вооружёные си́лы *f.pl.*; **by ~** си́лой; **by ~ of** в си́лу+*g.*; **in ~** в си́ле; (*in large numbers*) толпа́ми; *v.t.* (*compel*) заставля́ть *impf.*, заста́вить *pf.*; принужда́ть *impf.*, прину́дить *pf.*; (*lock etc.*) взла́мывать *impf.*, взлома́ть *pf.*; (*hasten*) форси́ровать *impf.* & *pf.* **forceful** *adj.* си́льный (си́лён, -льна́, -льно, си́льны́); (*speech*) убеди́тельный. **forcible** *adj.* наси́льственный.
forceps ['fɔ:seps] *n.* щипцы́ (-цо́в) *pl.*
ford [fɔ:d] *n.* брод; *v.t.* переходи́ть (-ожу́, -о́дишь) *impf.*, перейти́ (-ейду́, -ейдёшь; -ешёл, -ешла́) *pf.* вброд+*a.*, че́рез+*a.*
fore [fɔ:(r)] *n.*: **to the ~** на пере́днем пла́не.
forearm ['fɔ:rɑ:m] *n.* предпле́чье (*g.pl.* -чий). **forebear** ['fɔ:beə(r)] *n.* (*ancestor*) пре́док (-дка). **forebode** [fɔ:'bəʊd] *v.t.* (*betoken*) предвеща́ть *impf.*; (*have presentiment*) предчу́вствовать *impf.* **foreboding** *n.* предчу́вствие. **forecast** *n.* предсказа́ние; (*of weather*) прогно́з; *v.t.* предска́зывать *impf.*, предсказа́ть (-ажу́, -а́жешь) *pf.* **forecastle, fo'c's'le** ['fəʊks(ə)l] *n.* (*naut.*) бак. **forefather** *n.* пре́док (-дка). **forefinger** *n.* указа́тельный па́лец (-льца). **foreground** *n.* пере́дний план. **forehead** ['fɒrɪd, 'fɔ:hed] *n.* лоб (лба, *loc.* лбу).
foreign ['fɒrɪn, 'fɒrən] *adj.* (*from abroad*) иностра́нный (-нен, -нна); (*alien*) чужо́й; (*external*) вне́шний; **~ body** иноро́дное те́ло (*pl.* -ла́). **foreigner** *n.* иностра́нец (-нца).
forelock ['fɔ:lɒk] *n.* чёлка. **foreman** *n.* (*jury*) старшина́ (*pl.* -ны) *m.* прися́жных; (*factory*) ма́стер (*pl.* -á).
foremost ['fɔ:məʊst] *adj.* передово́й, пере́д-

ний; (*notable*) выдающийся.

forensic [fə'rensɪk] *adj.* судебный.

forerunner ['fɔ:ˌrʌnə(r)] *n.* предвестник. **fore'see** *v.t.* предвидеть (-ижу, -идишь) *impf.* **fore'shadow** *v.t.* предвещать *impf.* **foresight** *n.* предвидение; (*caution*) предусмотрительность.

forest ['fɒrɪst] *n.* лес (-а(у), *loc.* -у́; *pl.* -а́).

forestall [fɔ:'stɔ:l] *v.t.* предупреждать *impf.*, предупредить *pf.*

forester ['fɒrɪstə(r)] *n.* лесник (-а́), лесничий *sb.* **forestry** *n.* лесоводство.

foretaste ['fɔ:teɪst] *n.* предвкушение; *v.t.* предвкушать *impf.*, предвкусить (-ушу́, -у́сишь) *pf.* **fore'tell** *v.t.* предсказывать *impf.*, предсказать (-ажу́, -а́жешь) *pf.* **forethought** *n.* (*intention*) преднамеренность; (*caution*) предусмотрительность. **fore'warn** *v.t.* предостерегать *impf.*, предостеречь (-егу́, -ежёшь; -ёг, -егла́) *pf.* **foreword** *n.* предисловие.

forfeit ['fɔ:fɪt] *n.* (*fine*) штраф; (*deprivation*) лишение, конфискация; (*in game*) фант; *pl.* (*game*) игра в фанты; *v.t.* лишаться *impf.*, лишиться *pf.*+*g.*; (*pay with*) платиться (-ачу́сь, -а́тишься) *impf.*, по~ *pf.*+*i.* **forfeiture** *n.* лишение, конфискация, потеря.

forge[1] [fɔ:dʒ] *n.* (*smithy*) кузница; (*furnace*) горн; *v.t.* ковать (кую́, куёшь) *impf.*, вы́~ *pf.*; (*fabricate*) подделывать *impf.*, подделать *pf.*

forge[2] [fɔ:dʒ] *v.i.*: ~ **ahead** продвигаться *impf.*, продвинуться *pf.* вперёд.

forger ['fɔ:dʒə(r)] *n.* подделыватель *m.*; (*of money*) фальшивомонетчик. **forgery** *n.* подделка, подлог.

forget [fə'get] *v.t.* забывать *impf.*, забыть (забу́ду, -дешь) *pf.* **forgetful** *adj.* забывчивый. **forget-me-not** *n.* незабудка.

forgive [fə'gɪv] *v.t.* прощать *impf.*, простить *pf.* **forgiveness** *n.* прощение.

forgo [fɔ:'gəʊ] *v.t.* воздерживаться *impf.*, воздержаться (-жу́сь, -жишься) *pf.* от+*g.*

fork [fɔ:k] *n.* (*eating*) вилка; (*digging*) вилы (-л) *pl.*; разветвление; *v.i.* работать *impf.* вилами; (*form* ~) разветвляться *impf.*, разветвиться *pf.*

forlorn [fɔ:'lɔ:n] *adj.* унылый.

form [fɔ:m] *n.* форма, вид, фигура; (*formality*) формальность; (*class*) класс; (*document*) бланк, анкета; (*bench*) скамейка; *v.t.* (*shape*) придавать (-даю́, -даёшь) *impf.*, придать (-да́м, -да́шь, -да́ст, -дади́м; при́дал, -а́, -о) *pf.* форму+*d.*; (*make up*) составлять *impf.*, составить *pf.*; образовывать *impf.*, образовать *pf.*; формировать *impf.*, с~ *pf.*; *v.i.* принимать *impf.*, принять (-и́мет; при́нял, -а́, -о) *pf.* форму; образовываться *impf.*, образоваться *pf.* **formal** *adj.* официальный, формальный. **for'mality** *n.* формальность. **for'mation** *n.* образование, формирование, формация.

former ['fɔ:mə(r)] *adj.* бывший, прежный; **the** ~ (*of two*) первый. **formerly** *adv.* прежде.

formidable ['fɔ:mɪdəb(ə)l] *adj.* (*dread*) грозный (-зен, -зна́, -зно); (*arduous*) трудный (-ден, -дна́, -дно, тру́дны́).

formless ['fɔ:mlɪs] *adj.* бесформенный (-ен, -енна).

formula ['fɔ:mjʊlə] *n.* формула. **formulate** *v.t.* формулировать *impf.*, с~ *pf.* **formu'lation** *n.* формулировка.

forsake [fə'seɪk, fɔ:-] *v.t.* (*desert*) покидать *impf.*, покинуть *pf.*; (*renounce*) отказываться *impf.*, отказаться (-ажу́сь, -а́жешься) *pf.* от+*g.*

forswear [fɔ:'sweə(r)] *v.t.* отрекаться *impf.*, отречься *pf.* (-еку́сь, -ечёшься; -ёкся, -екла́сь) от+*g.*

fort [fɔ:t] *n.* форт (*loc.* -у́; *pl.* -ы́).

forth [fɔ:θ] *adv.* вперёд, дальше; **back and** ~ взад и вперёд; **and so** ~ и так далее. **forthcoming** *adj.* предстоящий. **forth'with** *adv.* немедленно.

fortieth ['fɔ:tɪɪθ] *adj.* & *n.* сороковой; (*fraction*) сороковая (часть (*pl.* -ти, -те́й)).

fortification [ˌfɔ:tɪfɪ'keɪʃ(ə)n] *n.* фортификация, укрепление. **fortify** ['fɔ:tɪˌfaɪ] *v.t.* укреплять *impf.*, укрепить *pf.*; подкреплять *impf.*, подкрепить *pf.*; (*food*) витаминизировать *impf.* & *pf.* **'fortitude** *n.* мужество.

fortnight ['fɔ:tnaɪt] *n.* две недели. **fortnightly** *adj.* двухнедельный; *adv.* раз в две недели.

fortress ['fɔ:trɪs] *n.* крепость.

fortuitous [fɔ:'tju:ɪtəs] *adj.* случайный.

fortunate ['fɔ:tjʊnət, -tʃənət] *adj.* счастливый (сча́стлив). **fortunately** *adv.* к счастью. **fortune** *n.* (*destiny*) судьба (*pl.* -дьбы, -деб, -дьбам); (*good* ~) счастье; (*wealth*) состояние. **fortune-teller** *n.* гадальщик, -ица; гадалка. **fortune-telling** *n.* гадание.

forty ['fɔ:tɪ] *adj.* & *n.* сорок (*oblique cases* -а́); (*age*) сорок лет; *pl.* (*decade*) сороковые годы (-до́в) *m.pl.*

forward ['fɔ:wəd] *adj.* передний, передовой; (*early*) ранний; *n.* (*sport*) нападающий *sb.*; *adv.* вперёд, дальше; *v.t.* (*promote*) способствовать *impf.*, по~ *pf.*+*d.*; (*letter etc.*) пересылать *impf.*, переслать (перешлю́, -лёшь) *pf.*

fossil ['fɒs(ə)l] *n.* окаменелость, ископаемое *sb.*; *adj.* окаменелый, ископаемый. **fossilize** *v.t.* & *i.* превращать(ся) *impf.*, превратить(ся) *pf.* (-ащу́(сь), -ати́шь(ся)) в окаменелость.

foster ['fɒstə(r)] *v.t.* воспитывать *impf.*, воспитать *pf.*; (*feeling*) лелеять (-е́ю, -е́ешь) *impf.*; *adj.* приёмный. **foster-child** *n.* приёмыш.

foul [faʊl] *adj.* (*dirty*) грязный (-зен, -зна́, -зно); (*repulsive*) отвратительный; (*obscene*) непристойный; *n.* (*collision*) столкновение; (*sport*) нарушение правил; *v.t.* & *i.* (*dirty*) пачкать(ся) *impf.*, за~, ис~ *pf.*; (*entangle*) запутывать(ся) *impf.*, запутать(ся) *pf.*

found¹ [faʊnd] *v.t.* (*establish*) осно́вывать *impf.*, основа́ть (-ную́, -нуёшь) *pf.*; (*building*) закла́дывать *impf.*, заложи́ть (-жу́, -жишь) *pf.*
found² [faʊnd] *v.t.* (*metal*) отлива́ть *impf.*, отли́ть (отолью́, -ьёшь; о́тли́л, -а́, -о) *pf.*
foundation [faʊn'deɪʃ(ə)n] *n.* (*of building*) фунда́мент; (*basis*) осно́ва, основа́ние; (*institution*) учрежде́ние; (*funds*) фонд. '**founder¹** *n.* основа́тель *m.*, -ница.
founder² ['faʊndə(r)] *n.* (*of metal*) лите́йщик, плави́льщик.
founder³ ['faʊndə(r)] *v.i.* (*naut.*) идти́ (идёт; шёл, шла) *impf.*, пойти́ (пойдёт; пошёл, -шла́) *pf.* ко дну́.
foundling ['faʊndlɪŋ] *n.* подки́дыш.
foundry ['faʊndrɪ] *n.* лите́йная *sb.*
fount¹ [faʊnt] *n.* (*print.*) компле́кт шри́фта.
fount² [faʊnt] *n.* исто́чник. **fountain** *n.* фонта́н, исто́чник. **fountain-pen** *n.* автору́чка.
four [fɔː(r)] *adj.* & *n.* четы́ре (-рёх, -рём, -рьмя́); (*collect.*; *4 pairs*) че́тверо (-ры́х); (*cards*; *boat*; *number 4*) четвёрка; (*time*) четы́ре (часа́); (*age*) четы́ре го́да; **on all ~s** на четвере́ньках. **four'teen** *adj.* & *n.* четы́рнадцать (-ти, -тью); (*age*) четы́рнадцать лет. **four'teenth** *adj.* & *n.* четы́рнадцатый; (*fraction*) четы́рнадцатая (часть (*pl.* -ти, -те́й)); (*date*) четы́рнадцатое (число́). **fourth** *adj.* & *n.* четвёртый; (*quarter*) че́тверть (*pl.* -ти, -те́й); (*date*) четвёртое (число́); (*mus.*) ква́рта.
fowl [faʊl] *n.* (*bird*) пти́ца; (*domestic*) дома́шняя пти́ца; (*wild*) дичь *collect.*
fox [fɒks] *n.* лиса́ (*pl.* -сы), лиси́ца; *attr.* ли́сий (-сья, -сье); *v.t.* обма́нывать *impf.*, обману́ть (-ну́, -нешь) *pf.* **foxglove** *n.* наперстя́нка. **foxhole** *n.* (*mil.*) яче́йка. **foxy** *adj.* ли́сий (-сья, -сье); (*crafty*) хи́трый (-тёр, -тра́, хитро́).
foyer ['fɔɪeɪ] *n.* фойе́ *nt.indecl.*
fraction ['frækʃ(ə)n] *n.* (*math.*) дробь (*pl.* -би, -бе́й); (*portion*) части́ца. **fractional** *adj.* дро́бный.
fractious ['frækʃəs] *adj.* раздражи́тельный.
fracture ['fræktʃə(r)] *n.* перело́м; *v.t.* & *i.* лома́ть(ся) *impf.*, с~ *pf.*
fragile ['frædʒaɪl, -dʒɪl] *adj.* ло́мкий (-мок, -мка́, -мко), хру́пкий (-пок, -пка́, -пко). **fragility** [frə'dʒɪlɪtɪ] *n.* ло́мкость, хру́пкость.
fragment ['frægmənt] *n.* обло́мок (-мка), оско́лок (-лка); (*of writing etc.*) отры́вок (-вка), фрагме́нт. **fragmentary** *adj.* отры́вочный.
fragrance ['freɪgrəns] *n.* арома́т. **fragrant** *adj.* арома́тный, души́стый.
frail [freɪl] *adj.* хру́пкий (-пок, -пка́, -пко).
frame [freɪm] *n.* о́стов; (*body*) те́ло (*pl.* -ла́); (*build*) телосложе́ние; (*picture*) ра́ма, ра́мка; (*cin.*) кадр; **~ of mind** настрое́ние; *v.t.* (*devise*) создава́ть (-даю́, -даёшь) *impf.*, созда́ть (-а́м, -а́шь, -а́ст, -ади́м; со́зда́л, -а́, -о) *pf.*; (*adapt*) приспоса́бливать *impf.*, приспособля́ть *pf.*; (*picture*) вставля́ть *impf.*, вста́вить *pf.* в ра́му; (*surround*) обрамля́ть *impf.*, обрами́ть *pf.* **framework** *n.* о́стов, структу́ра; (*fig.*) ра́мки *f.pl.*
franc [fræŋk] *n.* франк.
France [frɑːns] *n.* Фра́нция.
franchise ['fræntʃaɪz] *n.* (*privilege*) привиле́гия; (*right to vote*) пра́во го́лоса.
frank¹ [fræŋk] *adj.* (*open*) открове́нный (-нен, -нна).
frank² [fræŋk] *v.t.* (*letter*) франки́ровать *impf.* & *pf.*
frantic ['fræntɪk] *adj.* неи́стовый, бе́шеный.
fraternal [frə'tɜːn(ə)l] *adj.* бра́тский. **fraternity** *n.* бра́тство, общи́на. **fraternize** ['frætə,naɪz] *v.t.* брата́ться *impf.*, по~ *pf.* (**with** с+*i.*).
fraud [frɔːd] *n.* (*deception*) обма́н; (*person*) обма́нщик. **fraudulent** *adj.* обма́нный (-нен, -нна).
fraught [frɔːt] *adj.*: **~ with** чрева́тый+*i.*, по́лный (-лон, -лна́, по́лно́)+*g.* & *i.*
fray¹ [freɪ] *n.* (*brawl*) дра́ка.
fray² [freɪ] *v.t.* & *i.* обтрёпывать(ся) *impf.*, обтрепа́ть(ся) (-плю́(сь), -плешь(ся)) *pf.*
freak [friːk] *n.* (*caprice*) причу́да; (*monstrosity*) уро́д.
freckle ['frek(ə)l] *n.* весну́шка. **freckled** *adj.* весну́шчатый.
free [friː] *adj.* свобо́дный, во́льный; (*gratis*) беспла́тный; **of one's own ~ will** по до́брой во́ле; **~ speech** свобо́да сло́ва; **~ thinker** вольноду́мец (-мца); *v.t.* освобожда́ть *impf.*, освободи́ть *pf.* **freedom** *n.* свобо́да. **freelance** *attr.* внешта́тный. **freelancer** *n.* внешта́тник (*coll.*). **Freemason** *n.* франкмасо́н.
freeze [friːz] *v.i.* замерза́ть *impf.*, мёрзнуть (-з) *impf.*, за~ *pf.*; *v.t.* замора́живать *impf.*, заморо́зить *pf.* **freezer** *n.* морози́лка.
freight [freɪt] *n.* фрахт, груз. **freighter** *n.* (*ship*) грузово́е су́дно (*pl.* -да́, -до́в).
French [frentʃ] *adj.* францу́зский; **~ bean** фасо́ль; **~ leave** ухо́д без проща́ния, без разреше́ния. **Frenchman** *n.* францу́з. **Frenchwoman** *n.* францу́женка.
frenetic [frə'netɪk] *adj.* неи́стовый.
frenzied ['frenzɪd] *adj.* неи́стовый. **frenzy** *n.* неи́стовство.
frequency ['friːkwənsɪ] *n.* частота́ (*pl.* -ты). **frequent** *adj.* ча́стый (част, -а́, -о); *v.t.* ча́сто посеща́ть *impf.*
fresco ['freskəʊ] *n.* фре́ска.
fresh [freʃ] *adj.* све́жий (свеж, -а́, -о́, све́жи́); (*new*) но́вый (нов, -а́, -о); (*vigorous*) бо́дрый (бодр, -а́, -о, бо́дры́); **~ water** пре́сная вода́ (*a.* -ду). **freshen** *v.t.* освежа́ть *impf.*, освежи́ть *pf.*; *v.i.* свеже́ть *impf.*, по~ *pf.* **freshly** *adv.* свежо́; (*recently*) неда́вно. **freshness** *n.* све́жесть; бо́дрость. **freshwater** *adj.* пресново́дный.
fret¹ [fret] *n.* (*irritation*) раздраже́ние; *v.t.* (*eat away*) разъеда́ть *impf.*, разъе́сть (-е́м, -е́шь, -е́ст, -еди́м; -е́л) *pf.*; *v.t.* & *i.* (*distress*) беспоко́ить(ся) *impf.*, о~ *pf.* **fretful** *adj.*

беспоко́йный.
fret[2] [fret] *n.* (*mus.*) лад (*loc.* -у́; *pl.* -ы́).
fretsaw ['fretsɔ:] *n.* ло́бзик.
friar ['fraɪə(r)] *n.* мона́х. **friary** *n.* мужско́й монасты́рь (-ря́) *m.*
friction ['frɪkʃ(ə)n] *n.* тре́ние; (*fig.*) тре́ния *nt.pl.*
Friday ['fraɪdeɪ, -dɪ] *n.* пя́тница; **Good ~** Вели́кая пя́тница.
fridge [frɪdʒ] *n.* холоди́льник. **fridge-freezer** *n.* двухсекцио́нный холоди́льник.
friend [frend] *n.* друг (*pl.* друзья́, -зе́й), подру́га; прия́тель *m.*, ~ница; (*acquaintance*) знако́мый *sb.* **friendly** *adj.* дру́жеский, дру́жественный. **friendship** *n.* дру́жба.
frigate ['frɪgɪt] *n.* фрега́т.
fright [fraɪt] *n.* испу́г (-а(у)). **frighten** *v.t.* пуга́ть *impf.*, ис~, на~ *pf.* **frightful** *adj.* стра́шный (-шен, -шна́, -шно, стра́шны́), ужа́сный.
frigid ['frɪdʒɪd] *adj.* холо́дный (хо́лоден, -дна́, -дно, хо́лодны́). **fri'gidity** *n.* хо́лодность.
frill [frɪl] *n.* обо́рка.
fringe [frɪndʒ] *n.* бахрома́.
frisk [frɪsk] *n.* (*leap*) прыжо́к (-жка́); *v.i.* (*frolic*) резви́ться *impf.* **frisky** *adj.* игри́вый, ре́звый (резв, -а́, -о).
fritter[1] ['frɪtə(r)] *n.* ола́дья (*g.pl.* -дий).
fritter[2] ['frɪtə(r)] *v.t.*: **~ away** растра́чивать *impf.*, растра́тить *pf.* (по мелоча́м и т.п.).
frivolity [ˌfrɪ'vɒlɪtɪ] *n.* легкомы́сленность. **'frivolous** *adj.* легкомы́сленный (-ен, -енна).
fro [frəʊ] *adv.*: **to and ~** взад и вперёд.
frock [frɒk] *n.* пла́тье (*g.pl.* -в). **frock-coat** *n.* сюрту́к (-а́).
frog [frɒg] *n.* лягу́шка.
frolic ['frɒlɪk] *v.i.* резви́ться *impf.*; (*play pranks*) прока́зничать *impf.*, на~ *pf.*; *n.* весе́лье; (*prank*) прока́за.
from [frəm, frɒm] *prep. expressing*: **1.** *starting-point*: (*away ~*; *~ person*) от+*g.*; (*~ off*, *down ~*; *in time*) с+*g.*; (*out of*) из+*g.*; **2.** *change of state*; *distinction*: от+*g.*, из+*g.*; **3.** *escape*, *avoidance*: от+*g.*; **4.** *source*: из+*g.*; **5.** *giving*, *sending*: от+*g.*; (*stressing sense of possession*) у+*g.*; **6.** *model*: по+*d.*; **7.** *reason*, *cause*: от+*g.*; **8.** *motive*: из-за+*g.*; **9.**: *in phrasal vv. see vv.*; **10. ~ ... to** (*time*) с+*g.*... до+*g.*; (*with strictly defined starting point*) от+*g.*... по+*g.*; (*up to and including*) с+*g.*... по+*a.*; (*space*) (*emphasizing distance*) от+*g.*... до+*g.*; (*emphasizing journey*) из+*g.*... в+*a.*; **11. ~ above** све́рху; **~ abroad** из-за грани́цы; **~ afar** и́здали; **~ among** из числа́+*g.*; **~ behind** из-за+*g.*; **~ day to day** изо дня́ в день; **~ everywhere** отовсю́ду; **~ here** отсю́да; **~ long ago** и́здавна; **~ memory** по па́мяти; **~ nature** с нату́ры; **~ now on** отны́не; **~ off** с+*g.*; **~ there** отту́да; **~ time to time** вре́мя от вре́мени; **~ under** из-под+*g.*
front [frʌnt] *n.* фаса́д, пере́дняя сторона́ (*a.* -ону; *pl.* -оны, -о́н, -она́м); (*mil.*) фронт (*pl.* -ы, -о́в); **in ~ of** впереди́+*g.*, пе́ред+*i.*; *adj.* пере́дний, пара́дный. **frontal** *adj.* (*anat.*) ло́бный; (*mil.*) лобово́й, фронта́льный.
frontier ['frʌntɪə(r), -'tɪə(r)] *n.* грани́ца; *adj.* пограни́чный.
frost [frɒst] *n.* моро́з. **frost-bite** *n.* отмороже́ние. **frost-bitten** *adj.* отморо́женный (-ен). **frosted** *adj.*: **~ glass** ма́товое стекло́. **frosty** *adj.* моро́зный; (*fig.*) ледяно́й.
froth [frɒθ] *n.* пе́на; *v.t.* & *i.* пе́нить(ся) *impf.*, вс~ *pf.* **frothy** *adj.* пе́нистый.
frown [fraʊn] *n.* хму́рый взгляд; *v.i.* хму́риться *impf.*, на~ *pf.*
frugal ['fru:g(ə)l] *adj.* (*careful*) бережли́вый; (*scanty*) ску́дный (-ден, -дна́, -дно).
fruit [fru:t] *n.* плод (-а́); *collect.* фру́кты *m.pl.* **fruitful** *adj.* плодови́тый, плодотво́рный. **fruition** [fru:'ɪʃ(ə)n] *n.* осуществле́ние; **come to ~** осуществи́ться *pf.* **fruitless** *adj.* беспдо́дный, бесполе́зный.
frustrate [frʌ'streɪt, 'frʌs-] *v.t.* расстра́ивать *impf.*, расстро́ить *pf.* **fru'stration** *n.* расстро́йство.
fry[1] [fraɪ] *n.* (*collect.*, *fishes*) мальки́ *m.pl.*
fry[2] [fraɪ] *v.t.* & *i.* жа́рить(ся) *impf.*, за~, из~ *pf.* **frying-pan** *n.* сковорода́ (*pl.* ско́вороды, -о́д, -ода́м).
fuel ['fju:əl] *n.* то́пливо, горю́чее *sb.*
fugitive ['fju:dʒɪtɪv] *n.* бегле́ц (-а́); *adj.* (*transient*) мимолётный.
fugue [fju:g] *n.* фу́га.
fulcrum ['fʊlkrəm, 'fʌl-] *n.* то́чка опо́ры, враще́ния.
fulfil [fʊl'fɪl] *v.t.* (*perform*) вы́-, ис-, полня́ть *impf.*, вы́-, ис-, по́лнить *pf.*; (*bring about*) осуществля́ть *impf.*, осуществи́ть *pf.* **fulfilment** *n.* вы́-, ис-, полне́ние; осуществле́ние.
full [fʊl] *adj.* по́лный (-лон, -лна́, по́лно́) (**of** +*g.*, *i.*); (*complete*) це́лый; (*abundant*) изоби́лующий, бога́тый; (*replete*) сы́тый (сыт, -а́, -о); **~ back** защи́тник; **~ stop** то́чка; *n.*: **in ~** по́лностью; **to the ~** в по́лной ме́ре; *adv.* (*very*) о́чень; (*exactly*) пря́мо, как раз. **full-blooded** *adj.* полнокро́вный. **fullness** *n.* полнота́. **fully** *adv.* по́лностью.
fulsome ['fʊlsəm] *adj.* чрезме́рный.
fumble ['fʌmb(ə)l] *v.i.*: **~ for** нащу́пывать *impf.*+*a.*; **~ with** нело́вко обраща́ться *impf.* с+*i.*
fume [fju:m] *n.* испаре́ние; *v.i.* испаря́ться *impf.*, испари́ться *pf.*; (*with anger*) кипе́ть (-плю́, -пи́шь) *impf.*, вс~ *pf.* от зло́сти. **fumigate** *v.t.* оку́ривать *impf.*, окури́ть (-рю́, -ришь) *pf.* **fumi'gation** *n.* оку́ривание.
fun [fʌn] *n.* заба́ва, весе́лье; **make ~ of** смея́ться (-ею́сь, -еёшься) *impf.*, по~ *pf.* над+*i.*
function ['fʌŋkʃ(ə)n] *n.* фу́нкция, назначе́ние; *pl.* (*duties*) обя́занности *f.pl.*; *v.i.* функциони́ровать *impf.*; де́йствовать *impf.* **functional** *adj.* функциона́льный. **functionary** *n.* должностно́е лицо́ (*pl.* -ца).
fund [fʌnd] *n.* запа́с; (*of money*) фонд, капита́л.

fundamental [ˌfʌndəˈment(ə)l] *n.* осно́ва; *adj.* основно́й.

funeral [ˈfjuːnər(ə)l] *n.* по́хороны (-о́н, -она́м) *pl.*; *adj.* похоро́нный, тра́урный. **funereal** [fjuːˈnɪərɪəl] *adj.* (*gloomy*) мра́чный (-чен, -чна́, -чно).

fungoid [ˈfʌŋgɔɪd] *adj.* грибно́й. **fungus** *n.* гриб (-а́).

funnel [ˈfʌn(ə)l] *n.* воро́нка; (*chimney*) дымова́я труба́ (*pl.* -бы).

funny [ˈfʌnɪ] *adj.* смешно́й (-шо́н, -шна́), заба́вный; (*odd*) стра́нный (-нен, -нна́, -нно).

fur [fɜː(r)] *n.* мех (*loc.* -у́; *pl.* -а́); *pl.* (*collect.*) пушни́на, меха́ *m.pl.*; *attr.* мехово́й; ~ **coat** шу́ба; ~ **farm** зверофе́рма; ~ **farming** зверово́дство.

furious [ˈfjʊərɪəs] *adj.* бе́шеный, я́ростный.

furl [fɜːl] *v.t.* свёртывать *impf.*, сверну́ть *pf.*

furnace [ˈfɜːnɪs] *n.* то́пка, горн.

furnish [ˈfɜːnɪʃ] *v.t.* (*provide*) снабжа́ть *impf.*, снабди́ть *pf.* (**with** с+*i.*); доставля́ть *impf.*, доста́вить *pf.*; (*house*) меблирова́ть *impf.* & *pf.*; обставля́ть *impf.*, обста́вить *pf.* **furniture** *n.* ме́бель, обстано́вка.

furrier [ˈfʌrɪə(r)] *n.* меховщи́к (-а́), скорня́к (-а́).

furrow [ˈfʌrəʊ] *n.* борозда́ (*a.* бо́розду; *pl.* бо́розды, -о́зд, -озда́м); (*wrinkle*) морщи́на; *v.t.* борозди́ть *impf.*, вз~, из~ *pf.*

furry [ˈfɜːrɪ] *adj.* мехово́й, пуши́стый.

further [ˈfɜːðə(r)] *comp. adj.* дальне́йший; (*additional*) доба́вочный; *adv.* да́льше, да́лее; *v.t.* продвига́ть *impf.*, продви́нуть *pf.*; соде́йствовать *impf.* & *pf.*+*d.*; спосо́бствовать *impf.*, по~ *pf.*+*d.* **further'more** *adv.* к тому́ же. **furthest** *superl. adj.* са́мый да́льний.

furtive [ˈfɜːtɪv] *adj.* скры́тый, та́йный. **furtively** *adv.* укра́дкой, кра́дучись.

fury [ˈfjʊərɪ] *n.* я́рость, неистовство, бе́шенство.

fuse[1] [fjuːz] *v.t.* & *i.* (*of metal*) сплавля́ть(ся) *impf.*, спла́вить(ся) *pf.*

fuse[2] [fjuːz] *n.* (*in bomb*) запа́л, фити́ль (-ля́) *m.*, взрыва́тель *m.*

fuse[3] [fjuːz] *n.* (*elec.*) пла́вкая про́бка, пла́вкий предохрани́тель *m.*; ~ **wire** пла́вкая про́волока.

fuselage [ˈfjuːzəˌlɑːʒ, -lɪdʒ] *n.* фюзеля́ж.

fusillade [ˌfjuːzɪˈleɪd] *n.* расстре́л.

fusion [ˈfjuːʒ(ə)n] *n.* пла́вка, слия́ние; (*nuclear* ~) си́нтез (я́дер).

fuss [fʌs] *n.* суета́; *v.i.* суети́ться *impf.* **fussy** *adj.* суетли́вый.

fusty [ˈfʌstɪ] *adj.* за́тхлый.

futile [ˈfjuːtaɪl] *adj.* бесполе́зный, тще́тный. **futility** [ˌfjuːˈtɪlɪtɪ] *n.* бесполе́зность, тще́тность.

future [ˈfjuːtʃə(r)] *n.* бу́дущее *sb.*, бу́дущность; (*gram.*) бу́дущее вре́мя *nt.*; *adj.* бу́дущий.

G

G [dʒiː] *n.* (*mus.*) соль *nt.indecl.*

g. *abbr.* (*of* **gram(me)(s)**) гм, (грамм).

gab [gæb] *n.* болтовня́.

gabble [ˈgæb(ə)l] *v.i.* тарато́рить *impf.*

gable [ˈgeɪb(ə)l] *n.* щипе́ц (-пца́).

gad [gæd] *v.i.*: ~ **about** шата́ться *impf.*

gadfly [ˈgædflaɪ] *n.* о́вод (*pl.* -ы & -а́), слепе́нь (-пня́) *m.*

gadget [ˈgædʒɪt] *n.* приспособле́ние.

gag [gæg] *n.* кляп; *v.t.* засо́вывать *impf.*, засу́нуть *pf.* кляп в рот+*d.*

gaggle [ˈgæg(ə)l] *n.* (*flock*) ста́я.

gaiety [ˈgeɪətɪ] *n.* весе́лье, весёлость. **gaily** *adv.* ве́село.

gain [geɪn] *n.* при́быль; *pl.* дохо́ды *m.pl.*; (*increase*) приро́ст; *v.t.* получа́ть *impf.*, получи́ть (-чу́, -чишь) *pf.*; приобрета́ть *impf.*, приобрести́ (-ету́, -етёшь; -ёл, -ела́) *pf.*; ~ **on** нагоня́ть *impf.*, нагна́ть (нагоню́, -нишь; нагна́л, -а́, -о) *pf.*

gainsay [geɪnˈseɪ] *v.t.* (*deny*) отрица́ть *impf.*; (*contradict*) противоре́чить *impf.*+*d.*

gait [geɪt] *n.* похо́дка.

gala [ˈgɑːlə] *n.* пра́зднество.

galaxy [ˈgæləksɪ] *n.* гала́ктика; (**G**~) (*Milky Way*) Мле́чный путь (-ти́, -тём) *m.*; (*fig.*) плея́да.

gale [geɪl] *n.* си́льный ве́тер (-тра; *loc.* на -тру́); (*naut.*) шторм.

gall[1] [gɔːl] *n.* (*bile*) жёлчь; (*bitterness*) жёлчность.

gall[2] [gɔːl] *n.* (*sore*) сса́дина; (*irritation*) раздраже́ние; *v.t.* (*vex*) раздража́ть *impf.*, раздражи́ть *pf.*

gallant [ˈgælənt; gəˈlænt] *adj.* (*brave*) хра́брый (храбр, -а́, -о); (*courtly*) гала́нтный. **ˈgallantry** *n.* хра́брость; гала́нтность.

gall-bladder [ˈgɔːlblædə(r)] *n.* жёлчный пузы́рь (-ря́) *m.*

gallery [ˈgælərɪ] *n.* галере́я; (*theatr.*) галёрка.

galley [ˈgælɪ] *n.* (*ship*) гале́ра; (*kitchen*) ка́мбуз.

gallon [ˈgælən] *n.* галло́н.

gallop [ˈgæləp] *n.* гало́п; *v.i.* скака́ть (-ачу́, -а́чешь) *impf.* (гало́пом).

gallows [ˈgæləʊz] *n.* ви́селица.

gallstone [ˈgɔːlstəʊn] *n.* жёлчный ка́мень (-мня; *pl.* -мни, -мне́й) *m.*

galore [gəˈlɔː(r)] *adv.* в изоби́лии.

galosh [gəˈlɒʃ] *n.* гало́ша.

galvanic [gælˈvænɪk] *adv.* гальвани́ческий.

galvanize [ˈgælvəˌnaɪz] *v.t.* гальванизи́ровать *impf.* & *pf.*; (*coat with zinc*) оцинко́вывать *impf.*, оцинкова́ть *pf.*
gambit [ˈgæmbɪt] *n.* гамби́т.
gamble [ˈgæmb(ə)l] *n.* аза́ртная игра́ (*pl.* -ры); (*undertaking*) риско́ванное предприя́тие; *v.i.* игра́ть *impf.* в аза́ртные и́гры; рискова́ть *impf.* (**with** +*i.*); ~ **away** прои́грывать *impf.*, проигра́ть *pf.* **gambler** *n.* игро́к (-а́). **gambling** *n.* аза́ртные и́гры *f.pl.*
gambol [ˈgæmb(ə)l] *v.i.* резви́ться *impf.*
game [geɪm] *n.* игра́ (*pl.* -ры); (*single* ~) па́ртия; (*collect.*, *animals*) дичь; *adj.* (*ready*) гото́вый. **gamekeeper** *n.* лесни́к (-а́). **gaming-house** *n.* иго́рный дом (*pl.* -а́). **gaming-table** *n.* иго́рный стол (-а́).
gammon [ˈgæmən] *n.* о́корок.
gamut [ˈgæmət] *n.* га́мма, диапазо́н.
gander [ˈgændə(r)] *n.* гуса́к (-а́).
gang [gæŋ] *n.* брига́да, ба́нда, ша́йка.
gangrene [ˈgæŋgriːn] *n.* гангре́на.
gangster [ˈgæŋstə(r)] *n.* га́нгстер, банди́т.
gangway [ˈgæŋweɪ] *n.* (*passage*) прохо́д; (*naut.*) схо́дни (-ней) *pl.*
gaol *see* **jail. gaoler** *see* **jailer**
gap [gæp] *n.* (*breach*) брешь, проло́м; (*crack*) щель (*pl.* -ли, -ле́й); (*blank space*) пробе́л.
gape [geɪp] *v.i.* (*person*) разева́ть *impf.*, рази́нуть *pf.* рот; (*chasm*) зия́ть; *impf.*; ~ **at** глазе́ть *impf.*, по~ *pf.* на+*a.*
garage [ˈgærɑːdʒ, -rɪdʒ] *n.* гара́ж (-а́).
garb [gɑːb] *n.* одея́ние.
garbage [ˈgɑːbɪdʒ] *n.* му́сор; (*fig.*) вздор.
garble [ˈgɑːb(ə)l] *v.t.* подтасо́вывать *impf.*, подтасова́ть *pf.*
garden [ˈgɑːd(ə)n] *n.* сад (*loc.* -у́; *pl.* -ы́); (*kitchen* ~) огоро́д; *pl.* парк; *attr.* садо́вый. **gardener** *n.* садо́вник, садово́д. **gardening** *n.* садово́дство.
gargle [ˈgɑːg(ə)l] *n.* полоска́ние; *v.i.* полоска́ть (-ощу́, -о́щешь) *impf.*, про~ *pf.* го́рло.
gargoyle [ˈgɑːgɔɪl] *n.* горгу́лья.
garish [ˈgeərɪʃ] *adj.* я́ркий (я́рок, ярка́, я́рко), крича́щий.
garland [ˈgɑːlənd] *n.* гирля́нда, вено́к (-нка́); *v.t.* украша́ть *impf.*, укра́сить *pf.* гирля́ндами.
garlic [ˈgɑːlɪk] *n.* чесно́к (-а́).
garment [ˈgɑːmənt] *n.* предме́т оде́жды; *pl.* оде́жда *collect.*
garnish [ˈgɑːnɪʃ] *n.* (*dish*) гарни́р; (*embellishment*) украше́ние; *v.t.* гарни́ровать *impf.* & *pf.*; украша́ть *impf.*, укра́сить *pf.*
garret [ˈgærɪt] *n.* манса́рда.
garrison [ˈgærɪs(ə)n] *n.* гарнизо́н.
garrulous [ˈgærʊləs] *adj.* болтли́вый.
garter [ˈgɑːtə(r)] *n.* подвя́зка.
gas [gæs] *n.* газ (-а(у)); *attr.* га́зовый; ~ **cooker** га́зовая плита́ (*pl.* -ты); ~ **main** газопрово́д; ~ **mask** противога́з; *v.i.* отравля́ть *impf.*, отрави́ть (-влю́, -вишь) *pf.* га́зом. **gaseous** [ˈgæsɪəs] *adj.* газообра́зный.
gash [gæʃ] *n.* глубо́кая ра́на, разре́з.
gasket [ˈgæskɪt] *n.* прокла́дка.
gasp [gɑːsp] *v.i.* задыха́ться *impf.*, задохну́ться (-х(ну́л)ся, -х(ну́)лась) *pf.*; (*exclaim*) а́хнуть *pf.*
gastric [ˈgæstrɪk] *adj.* желу́дочный.
gasworks [ˈgæswɜːks] *n.* га́зовый заво́д.
gate [geɪt] *n.* (*large*) воро́та (-т) *pl.*; (*small*) кали́тка. **gatekeeper** *n.* привра́тник. **gateway** *n.* (*gate*) воро́та (-т) *pl.*; (*entrance*) вход.
gather [ˈgæðə(r)] *v.t.* на-, со-, бира́ть *impf.*, на-, со-, бра́ть (-беру́, -берёшь; -бра́л, -брала́, -бра́ло) *pf.*; (*infer*) заключа́ть *impf.*, заключи́ть *pf.*; *v.i.* собира́ться *impf.*, собра́ться (-берётся; -бра́лся, -брала́сь, -бра́ло́сь) *pf.* **gathering** *n.* (*action*) собира́ние; (*assembly*) собра́ние.
gaudy [ˈgɔːdɪ] *adj.* я́ркий (я́рок, ярка́, -я́рко), крича́щий.
gauge [geɪdʒ] *n.* (*measure*) ме́ра; (*instrument*) кали́бр, измери́тельный прибо́р; (*rail.*) коле́я; (*criterion*) крите́рий; *v.t.* измеря́ть *impf.*, изме́рить *pf.*; (*estimate*) оце́нивать *impf.*, оцени́ть (-ню́, -нишь) *pf.*
gaunt [gɔːnt] *adj.* то́щий (тощ, -а́, -е).
gauntlet [ˈgɔːntlɪt] *n.* рукави́ца.
gauze [gɔːz] *n.* ма́рля, газ.
gay [geɪ] *adj.* весёлый (ве́сел, -а́, -о, ве́селы́); (*bright*) пёстрый (пёстр, -а́, пёстро́); (*homosexual*) гомосексуа́льный; *n.* гомосексуали́ст.
gaze [geɪz] *n.* при́стальный взгляд; *v.t.* при́стально гляде́ть (-яжу́, -яди́шь) *impf.* (**at** на+*a.*).
gazelle [gəˈzel] *n.* газе́ль.
gazetteer [ˌgæzɪˈtɪə(r)] *n.* географи́ческий спра́вочник.
GB *abbr.* (*of* ***Great Britain***) Великобрита́ния.
GCSE *abbr.* (*of* ***General Certificate of Secondary Education***) аттеста́т о сре́днем образова́нии.
gear [gɪə(r)] *n.* (*appliance*) приспособле́ние, механи́зм, устро́йство; (*in motor*) переда́ча; (*high*, *low*, ~ *etc.*) ско́рость (*pl.* -ти, -те́й); **in** ~ включённый (-ён, -ена́) **gearbox** *n.* коро́бка скоросте́й. **gearwheel** *n.* зубча́тое колесо́ (*pl.* -ёса), шестерня́ (*g.pl.* -рён).
geld [geld] *v.t.* кастри́ровать *impf.* & *pf.* **gelding** *n.* ме́рин.
gelignite [ˈdʒelɪgˌnaɪt] *n.* гелигни́т.
gem [dʒem] *n.* драгоце́нный ка́мень (-мня; *pl.* -мни, -мне́й) *m.*; (*fig.*) драгоце́нность.
Gemini [ˈdʒemɪˌnaɪ, -ˌniː] *n.* Близнецы́ *m.pl.*
gender [ˈdʒendə(r)] *n.* род (*pl.* -ы́).
gene [dʒiːn] *n.* ген.
genealogical [ˌdʒiːnɪəˈlɒdʒɪk(ə)l] *adj.* генеалоги́ческий. **geneˈalogy** *n.* генеало́гия, родосло́вная *sb.*
general [ˈdʒenər(ə)l] *n.* генера́л; *adj.* о́бщий (общ, -а́, -о), всео́бщий; (*chief*) генера́льный, гла́вный; **in** ~ вообще́. **geneˈrality** *n.* всео́бщность; (*majority*) большинство́. **generaliˈzation** *n.* обобще́ние. **generalize** *v.t.* обобща́ть *impf.*, обобщи́ть *pf.*; *v.i.*

говори́ть *impf.* неопределённо. **generally** *adv.* обы́чно, вообще́.
generate ['dʒenə,reɪt] *v.t.* порожда́ть *impf.*, породи́ть *pf.*; производи́ть (-ожу́, -о́дишь) *impf.*, произвести́ (-еду́, -едёшь; -ёл, -ела́) *pf.* **gene'ration** *n.* порожде́ние, произво́дство; (*in descent*) поколе́ние. **generator** *n.* генера́тор.
generic [dʒɪ'nerɪk] *adj.* родово́й; (*general*) о́бщий (общ, -а́, -о).
generosity [,dʒenə'rɒsɪtɪ] *n.* (*magnanimity*) великоду́шие; (*munificence*) ще́дрость. **'generous** *adj.* великоду́шный; ще́дрый (щедр, -а́, -о); (*abundant*) оби́льный.
genesis ['dʒenɪsɪs] *n.* происхожде́ние; (**G~**) Кни́га Бытия́.
genetic [dʒɪ'netɪk] *adj.* генети́ческий. **genetics** *n.* гене́тика.
Geneva [dʒɪ'ni:və] *n.* Жене́ва.
genial ['dʒi:nɪəl] *adj.* (*of person*) доброду́шный. **geni'ality** *n.* доброду́шие.
genital ['dʒenɪt(ə)l] *adj.* полово́й. **genitals** *n.* половы́е о́рганы *m.pl.*
genitive ['dʒenɪtɪv] *adj.* (*n.*) роди́тельный (паде́ж (-а́)).
genius ['dʒi:nɪəs] *n.* (*person*) ге́ний; (*ability*) гениа́льность; (*spirit*) дух.
genocide ['dʒenə,saɪd] *n.* геноци́д.
genre ['ʒɑ̃rə] *n.* жанр.
genteel [dʒen'ti:l] *adj.* благовоспи́танный (-ан, -анна).
gentian ['dʒenʃ(ə)n, -ʃɪən] *n.* гореча́вка.
gentile ['dʒentaɪl] *adj.* неевре́йский; *n.* нееврей.
gentility [dʒen'tɪlɪtɪ] *n.* благовоспи́танность.
gentle ['dʒent(ə)l] *adj.* (*mild*) мя́гкий (-гок, -гка́, -гко); (*meek*) кро́ткий (-ток, -тка́, -тко); (*quiet*) ти́хий (тих, -а́, -о); (*light*) лёгкий (-гок, -гка́, -гко́, лёгки́). **gentleman** *n.* джентльме́н; господи́н (*pl.* -ода́, -о́д, -ода́м). **gentleness** *n.* мя́гкость.
genuine ['dʒenjʊɪn] *adj.* (*authentic*) по́длинный (-нен, -нна), настоя́щий; (*sincere*) и́скренний (-нен, -нна, -нно & -нне). **genuineness** *n.* по́длинность; и́скренность.
genus ['dʒi:nəs, 'dʒenəs] *n.* род (*pl.* -ы́).
geo- ['dʒi:əʊ] *in comb.* гео... . **geographer** [dʒɪ'ɒgrəfə(r)] *n.* гео́граф. **geo'graphical** *adj.* географи́ческий. **ge'ography** *n.* геогра́фия. **geo'logical** *adj.* геологи́ческий. **ge'ologist** *n.* гео́лог. **ge'ology** *n.* геоло́гия. **geo'metric(al)** *adj.* геометри́ческий. **geome'trician** *n.* гео́метр. **ge'ometry** *n.* геоме́трия.
Georgia ['dʒɔ:dʒɪə] *n.* Гру́зия. **Georgian** *n.* (*Caucasian*) грузи́н (*g.pl.* -н), **~ка**; *adj.* грузи́нский.
geranium [dʒə'reɪnɪəm] *n.* гера́нь.
germ [dʒɜ:m] *n.* микро́б; (*fig.*) заро́дыш.
German ['dʒɜ:mən] *n.* не́мец (-мца), не́мка; *adj.* неме́цкий; **~ measles** красну́ха.
germane [dʒɜ:'meɪn] *adj.* уме́стный.
Germanic [dʒɜ:'mænɪk] *adj.* герма́нский. **Germany** ['dʒɜ:mənɪ] *n.* Герма́ния.
germinate ['dʒɜ:mɪ,neɪt] *v.i.* прораста́ть *impf.*, прорасти́ (-тёт; проро́с, -ла́) *pf.*
gesticulate [dʒe'stɪkjʊ,leɪt] *v.i.* жестикули́ровать *impf.* **gesticu'lation** *n.* жестикуля́ция. **'gesture** *n.* жест.
get [get] *v.t.* (*obtain*) достава́ть (-таю́, -таёшь) *impf.*, доста́ть (-а́ну, -а́нешь) *pf.*; добива́ться *impf.*, доби́ться (добью́сь, -ьёшься) *pf.+g.*; (*receive*) получа́ть *impf.*, получи́ть (-чу́, -чишь) *pf.*; (*understand*) понима́ть *impf.*, поня́ть (пойму́, -мёшь; по́нял, -а́, -о) *pf.*; (*disease*) схва́тывать *impf.*, схвати́ть (-ачу́, -а́тишь) *pf.*; (*induce*) угова́ривать *impf.*, уговори́ть *pf.* (**to do** *+inf.*); *v.i.* (*become*) станови́ться (-влю́сь, -вишься) *impf.*, стать (ста́ну, -нешь) *pf.+i.*; **have got** (*have*) име́ть *impf.*; **have got to** быть до́лжен (-жна́)*+inf.*; **~ about** (*spread*) распространя́ться *impf.*, распространи́ться *pf.*; **~ away** ускольза́ть *impf.*, ускользну́ть *pf.*; **~ back** (*recover*) получа́ть *impf.*, получи́ть (-чу́, -чишь) *pf.* обра́тно; (*return*) возвраща́ться *impf.*, верну́ться *pf.*; **~ down to** принима́ться *impf.*, приня́ться (приму́сь, -мешься; приня́лся́, -ла́сь) *pf.* за*+a.*; **~ off** слеза́ть *impf.*, слезть (-зу, -зешь) *pf.* с*+g.*; **~ on** сади́ться *impf.*, сесть (ся́ду, -дешь; сел) *pf.* в, на, *+a.*; (*prosper*) преуспева́ть *impf.*, преуспе́ть *pf.*; **~ on with** (*person*) ужива́ться *impf.*, ужи́ться (уживу́сь, -вёшься; ужи́лся, -ла́сь) *pf.* с*+i.*; **~ out of** (*avoid*) избавля́ться *impf.*, изба́виться *pf.* от*+g.*; **~ to** (*reach*) достига́ть *impf.*, дости́гнуть & дости́чь (-и́гну, -и́гнешь; -и́г) *pf.+g.*; **~ up** (*from bed*) встава́ть (-таю́, -таёшь) *impf.*, встать (-а́ну, -а́нешь) *pf.*
geyser ['gaɪzə(r), 'gi:-] *n.* (*spring*) ге́йзер; (*water-heater*) (га́зовая) коло́нка.
ghastly ['gɑ:stlɪ] *adj.* стра́шный (-шен, -шна́, -шно, стра́шны́), ужа́сный.
gherkin ['gɜ:kɪn] *n.* огуре́ц (-рца́).
ghetto ['getəʊ] *n.* ге́тто *nt.indecl.*
ghost [gəʊst] *n.* привиде́ние, при́зрак, дух, тень (*pl.* -ни, -не́й). **ghostly** *adj.* при́зрачный.
giant ['dʒaɪənt] *n.* велика́н, гига́нт; *adj.* грома́дный.
gibberish *n.* тараба́рщина.
gibbet ['dʒɪbɪt] *n.* ви́селица.
gibe [dʒaɪb] *n.* насме́шка; *v.i.* насмеха́ться *impf.* (**at** над*+i.*).
giblets ['dʒɪblɪts] *n.* потроха́ (-хо́в) *pl.*
Gibraltar [gɪ'brɔ:ltə] *n.* Гибралта́р; **Strait of ~** Гибралта́рский проли́в.
giddiness ['gɪdɪnɪs] *n.* головокруже́ние; (*frivolity*) легкомы́слие. **giddy** *adj.* (*frivolous*) легкомы́сленный (-ен, -енна); *pred.*: **I am, feel, ~** у меня́ кру́жится голова́.
gift [gɪft] *n.* (*present*) пода́рок (-рка); (*donation; ability*) дар (*pl.* -ы́); (*talent*) тала́нт (к*+d.*); (*ability*) спосо́бность (к*+d.*). **gifted** *adj.* одарённый (-ён, -ённа), тала́нтливый.
gig [gɪg] *n.* (*carriage*) кабриоле́т; (*boat*) ги́чка.

gigantic [dʒaɪˈgæntɪk] *adj.* гига́нтский, грома́дный.

giggle [ˈgɪg(ə)l] *n.* хихи́канье; *v.i.* хихи́кать *impf.*, хихи́кнуть *pf.*

gild [gɪld] *v.t.* золоти́ть *impf.*, вы́~, по~ *pf.*

gill [gɪl] *n.* (*of fish*) жа́бра.

gilt [gɪlt] *n.* позоло́та; *adj.* золочённый, позоло́ченный.

gimlet [ˈgɪmlɪt] *n.* бура́вчик.

gin[1] [dʒɪn] *n.* (*snare*) западня́; (*winch*) лебёдка; (*cotton-*~) джин.

gin[2] [dʒɪn] *n.* (*spirit*) джин.

ginger [ˈdʒɪndʒə(r)] *n.* имби́рь (-ря) *m.*; *attr.* имби́рный; (*in colour*) ры́жий (рыж, -а́, -е). **gingerbread** *n.* имби́рный пря́ник.

gingerly [ˈdʒɪndʒəlɪ] *adv.* осторо́жно.

gipsy [ˈdʒɪpsɪ] *n.* цыга́н (*pl.* -не, -н), ~ка; *attr.* цыга́нский.

giraffe [dʒɪˈrɑːf, -ˈræf] *n.* жира́ф.

gird [gɜːd] *v.t.* опоя́сывать *impf.*, опоя́сать (-я́шу, -я́шешь) *pf.*; (*encircle*) окружа́ть *impf.*, окружи́ть *pf.* **girder** *n.* ба́лка, фе́рма. **girdle** *n.* по́яс (*pl.* -а́); *v.t.* подпоя́сывать *impf.*, подпоя́сать (-я́шу, -я́шешь) *pf.*

girl [gɜːl] *n.* де́вочка, де́вушка. **girlfriend** *n.* подру́га. **girlish** *adj.* де́вичий (-чья, -чье).

girth [gɜːθ] *n.* (*band*) подпру́га; (*measurement*) обхва́т.

gist [dʒɪst] *n.* суть, су́щность.

give [gɪv] *v.t.* дава́ть (даю́, даёшь) *impf.*, дать (дам, дашь, даст, дади́м; дал, -а́, -да́ло́, -и) *pf.*; дари́ть (-рю́, -ришь) *impf.*, по~ *pf.*; ~ **away** выдава́ть (-даю́, -даёшь) *impf.*, вы́дать (-ам, -ашь, -аст, -адим) *pf.*; ~ **back** возвраща́ть *impf.*, возврати́ть (-ащу́, -ати́шь) *pf.*; ~ **in** (*yield, v.i.*) уступа́ть *impf.*, уступи́ть (-плю́, -пишь) *pf.* (**to** +*d.*); (*hand in, v.t.*) вруча́ть *impf.*, вручи́ть *pf.*; ~ **out** (*emit*) издава́ть (-даю́, -даёшь) *impf.*, изда́ть (-а́м, -а́шь, -а́ст, -ади́м; изда́л, -а́, -о) *pf.*; (*distribute*) раздава́ть (-даю́, -даёшь) *impf.*, разда́ть (-а́м, -а́шь, -а́ст, -ади́м; ро́здал & разда́л, раздала́, ро́здало & разда́ло) *pf.*; (*cease*) конча́ться *impf.*, ко́нчиться *pf.*; ~ **up** отка́зываться *impf.*, отказа́ться (-ажу́сь, -а́жешься) *pf.* от+*g.*; (*habit etc.*) броса́ть *impf.*, бро́сить *pf.*; ~ **o.s. up** сдава́ться (сдаю́сь, сдаёшься) *impf.*, сда́ться (-а́мся, -а́шься, -а́стся, -ади́мся; сда́лся, -ла́сь, сда́ло́сь) *pf.* **given** *pred.* (*inclined*) скло́нен (-о́нна́, -о́нно) (**to** к+*d.*); (*devoted*) пре́дан (-а) (**to** +*d.*).

gizzard [ˈgɪzəd] *n.* (*of bird*) му́скульный желу́док (-дка).

glacial [ˈgleɪʃ(ə)l, -sɪəl] *adj.* леднико́вый; (*fig.*) ледяно́й. **glacier** [ˈglæsɪə(r)] *n.* ледни́к (-а́), гле́тчер.

glad [glæd] *adj.* ра́достный, весёлый; *pred.* рад. **gladden** *v.t.* ра́довать *impf.*, об~ *pf.* **gladness** *n.* ра́дость.

glade [gleɪd] *n.* прога́лина, поля́на.

gladiolus [ˌglædɪˈəʊləs] *n.* шпа́жник.

glamorous [ˈglæmərəs] *adj.* (*charming*) обая́тельный; (*attractive*) привлека́тельный.

glamour [ˈglæmə(r)] *n.* обая́ние; привлека́тельность.

glance [glɑːns] *n.* (*look*) бе́глый взгляд; *v.i.*: ~ **at** взгля́дывать *impf.*, взгляну́ть (-ну́, -нешь) *pf.* на+*a.*; ~ **off** скользи́ть *impf.*, скользну́ть *pf.* по пове́рхности+*g.*

gland [glænd] *n.* железа́ (*pl.* же́лезы, -ёз, -еза́м). **glandular** *adj.* желе́зистый.

glare [gleə(r)] *n.* (*light*) ослепи́тельный блеск; (*look*) при́стальный, свире́пый, взгляд; *v.i.* ослепи́тельно сверка́ть *impf.*; при́стально, свире́по, смотре́ть (-рю́, -ришь) *impf.* (**at** на+*a.*). **glaring** *adj.* (*bright*) я́ркий; (*dazzling*) ослепи́тельный; (*mistake*) гру́бый.

glasnost [ˈglæznɒst, ˈglɑːs-] *n.* гла́сность.

glass [glɑːs] *n.* (*substance*) стекло́; (*drinking vessel*) стака́н, рю́мка; (*glassware*) стекля́нная посу́да; (*mirror*) зе́ркало (*pl.* -ла́); *pl.* (*spectacles*) очки́ (-ко́в) *pl.*; *attr.* стекля́нный; ~ **fibre** стекловолокно́. **glass-blower** *n.* стеклоду́в. **glasshouse** *n.* тепли́ца. **glassy** *adj.* (*of glass*) стекля́нный; (*water*) зерка́льный, гла́дкий (-док, -дка́, -дко); (*look*) ту́склый (тускл, -а́, -о).

glaze [gleɪz] *n.* глазу́рь; *v.t.* (*picture*) застекля́ть *impf.*, застекли́ть *pf.*; (*cover with* ~) покрыва́ть *impf.*, покры́ть (-ро́ю, -ро́ешь) *pf.* глазу́рью. **glazier** *n.* стеко́льщик.

gleam [gliːm] *n.* сла́бый свет; (*also of hope etc.*) про́блеск; *v.i.* свети́ться (-ится) *impf.*

glean [gliːn] *v.t.* тща́тельно собира́ть *impf.*, собра́ть (соберу́, -рёшь; собра́л, -а́, -о) *pf.*; *v.i.* подбира́ть *impf.*, подобра́ть (подберу́, -рёшь; подобра́л, -а́, -о) *pf.* коло́сья.

glee [gliː] *n.* весе́лье. **gleeful** *adj.* весёлый (ве́сел, -а́, -о, ве́селы́).

glib [glɪb] *adj.* бо́йкий (бо́ек, бойка́, бо́йко).

glide [glaɪd] *v.i.* скользи́ть *impf.*; (*aeron.*) плани́ровать *impf.*, с~ *pf.* **glider** *n.* (*aircraft*) планёр; (*person*) планери́ст.

glimmer [ˈglɪmə(r)] *n.* мерца́ние; *v.i.* мерца́ть *impf.*

glimpse [glɪmps] *n.* (*appearance*) про́блеск; (*view*) мимолётный взгляд; *v.t.* мелько́м ви́деть (ви́жу, ви́дишь) *impf.*, у~ *pf.*

glint [glɪnt], **glitter** [ˈglɪtə(r)] *n.* блеск; *v.i.* блесте́ть (-ещу́, -ести́шь & -е́щешь) *impf.*; сверка́ть *impf.*

gloat [gləʊt] *v.i.* пожира́ть *impf.*, пожра́ть (-ру́, -рёшь; пожра́л, -а́, -о) *pf.* глаза́ми (**over** +*a.*); (*maliciously*) злора́дствовать *impf.*

global [ˈgləʊb(ə)l] *adj.* (*world-wide*) мирово́й; (*total*) всео́бщий. **globe** *n.* (*sphere*) шар (-а́ *with 2,3,4*; *pl.* -ы́); (*the earth*) земно́й шар; (*chart*) гло́бус.

globular [ˈglɒbjʊlə(r)] *adj.* шарови́дный, сфери́ческий. **globule** *n.* ша́рик.

gloom [gluːm] *n.* мрак. **gloomy** *adj.* мра́чный (-чен, -чна́, -чно).

glorification [ˌglɔːrɪfɪˈkeɪʃ(ə)n] *n.* прославле́ние. ˈ**glorify** *v.t.* прославля́ть *impf.*, просла́-

вить *pf.* '**glorious** *adj.* сла́вный (-вен, -вна́, -вно); (*splendid*) великоле́пный. '**glory** *n.* сла́ва; *v.i.* торжествова́ть *impf.*

gloss [glɒs] *n.* (*lustre*) лоск, гля́нец (-нца); (*appearance*) ви́димость; *v.t.* наводи́ть (-ожу́, -о́дишь) *impf.*, навести́ (-еду́, -едёшь; навёл, -а́) *pf.* лоск, гля́нец, на+*a.*; ~ **over** зама́зывать *impf.*, зама́зать (-а́жу, -а́жешь) *pf.*

glossary ['glɒsərɪ] *n.* глосса́рий, слова́рь (-ря́) *m.*

glove [glʌv] *n.* перча́тка. **glover** *n.* перча́точник, -ица.

glow [gləʊ] *n.* нака́л, за́рево; (*of cheeks*) румя́нец (-нца); (*ardour*) пыл (-а(у), *loc.* -у́); *v.i.* (*incandescence*) накаля́ться *impf.*, накали́ться *pf.*; (*shine*) сия́ть *impf.* **glow-worm** *n.* светля́к (-а́).

glucose ['glu:kəʊs, -kəʊz] *n.* глюко́за.

glue [glu:] *n.* клей (-е́я (-е́ю), *loc.* -е́е & -ею́; *pl.* -еи́); *v.t.* кле́ить *impf.*, с~ *pf.*; (*attach*) прикле́ивать *impf.*, прикле́ить *pf.* (**to** к+*d.*).

glum [glʌm] *adj.* угрю́мый.

glut [glʌt] *n.* (*surfeit*) пресыще́ние; (*excess*) избы́ток (-тка); (*in market*) затова́ривание (рынка́); *v.t.* пресыща́ть *impf.*, пресы́тить (-ы́щу, -ы́тишь) *pf.*; (*overstock*) затова́ривать *impf.*, затова́рить *pf.*

glutton ['glʌt(ə)n] *n.* обжо́ра *c.g.* **gluttonous** *adj.* обжо́рливый. **gluttony** *n.* обжо́рство.

GMT *abbr.* (*of* ***Greenwich Mean Time***) вре́мя по Гри́нвичу.

gnarled [nɑ:ld] *adj.* (*hands*) шишкова́тый; (*tree*) сучкова́тый.

gnash [næʃ] *v.t.* скрежета́ть (-ещу́, -е́щешь) *impf.*+*i.* **gnashing** *n.* скре́жет.

gnat [næt] *n.* кома́р (-а́).

gnaw [nɔ:] *v.t.* глода́ть (-ожу́, -о́жешь) *impf.*; грызть (-зу́, -зёшь; -з) *impf.*

gnome [nəʊm] *n.* гном.

go [gəʊ] *n.* (*movement*) движе́ние; (*energy*) эне́ргия; (*attempt*) попы́тка; **be on the** ~ быть в движе́нии; **have a** ~ пыта́ться *impf.*, по~ *pf.*; *v.i.* (*on foot*) ходи́ть (хожу́, хо́дишь) *indet.*, идти́ (иду́, идёшь; шёл, шла) *det.*, пойти́ (пойду́, -дёшь; пошёл, -шла́ *pf.*; (*by transport*) е́здить *indet.*, е́хать (е́ду, е́дешь) *det.*, по~ *pf.*; (*work*) рабо́тать *impf.*; (*become*) станови́ться (-влю́сь, -вишься) *impf.*, стать (ста́ну, -нешь) *pf.*+*i.*; **be** ~**ing** (*to do*) собира́ться *impf.*, собра́ться (соберу́сь, -рёшься; собра́лся, -ала́сь, -а́ло́сь) *pf.* (+*inf.*); ~ **about** (*set to work at*) бра́ться (беру́сь, -рёшься; бра́лся, -ла́сь) *impf.*, взя́ться (возьму́сь, -мёшься; взя́лся, -ла́сь) *pf.* за+*a.*; (*wander*) броди́ть (-ожу́, -о́дишь) *indet.*; ~ **at** (*attack*) набра́сываться *impf.*, набро́ситься *pf.* на+*a.*; ~ **away** (*on foot*) уходи́ть (-ожу́, -о́дишь) *impf.*, уйти́ (уйду́, -дёшь; ушёл, ушла́) *pf.*; (*by transport*) уезжа́ть *impf.*, уе́хать (уе́ду, -дешь) *pf.*; ~ **down** спуска́ться *impf.*, спусти́ться (-ущу́сь, -у́стишься) *pf.*; ~ **into** (*enter*) входи́ть (-ожу́, -о́дишь) *impf.*, войти́ (войду́, -дёшь; вошёл, -шла́) *pf.* в+*a.*; (*investigate*) рассле́довать *impf.* & *pf.*; ~ **off** (*go away*) уходи́ть (-ожу́, -о́дишь) *impf.*, уйти́ (уйду́, -дёшь; ушёл, ушла́) *pf.*; (*deteriorate*) по́ртиться *impf.*, ис~ *pf.*; ~ **on** (*continue*) продолжа́ть(ся) *impf.*, продо́лжить(ся) *pf.*; ~ **out** выходи́ть (-ожу́, -о́дишь) *impf.*, вы́йти (вы́йду, -дешь; вы́шел, -шла) *pf.*; (*flame etc.*) га́снуть (-с) *impf.*, по~ *pf.*; ~ **over** (*inspect*) пересма́тривать *impf.*, пересмотре́ть (-рю́, -ришь) *pf.*; (*rehearse*) повторя́ть *impf.*, повтори́ть *pf.*; (*change allegiance etc.*) переходи́ть (-ожу́, -хо́дишь) *impf.*, перейти́ (перейду́, -дёшь; перешёл, -шла́) *pf.* (**to** в, на, +*a.*, к+*d.*); ~ **through** (*scrutinize*) разбира́ть *impf.*, разобра́ть (разберу́, -рёшь; разобра́л, -а́, -о) *pf.*; ~ **through with** доводи́ть (-ожу́, -о́дишь) *impf.*, довести́ (-еду́, -едёшь; -ёл, -ела́) *pf.* до конца́; ~ **without** обходи́ться (-ожу́сь, -о́дишься) *impf.*, обойти́сь (обойду́сь, -дёшься; обошёлся, -шла́сь) *pf.* без+*g.*

goad [gəʊd] *v.t.* подгоня́ть *impf.*, подогна́ть (подгоню́, -о́нишь; подогна́л, -а́, -о) *pf.*; ~ **on** (*instigate*) подстрека́ть *impf.*, подстрекну́ть *pf.* (**to** к+*d.*).

go-ahead ['gəʊəhed] *n.* разреше́ние, добро́; *adj.* предприи́мчивый.

goal [gəʊl] *n.* (*aim*) цель; (*sport*) воро́та (-т) *pl.*, (*also point(s) won*) гол (*pl.* -ы́); **score a** ~ забива́ть *impf.*, заби́ть (-бью́, -бьёшь) *pf.* гол. **goalkeeper** *n.* врата́рь (-ря́) *m.*

goat [gəʊt] *n.* коза́ (*pl.* -зы), козёл (-зла́); *attr.* ко́зий (-зья, -зье). **goatherd** *n.* ко́зий пасту́х (-а́).

gobble[1] ['gɒb(ə)l] *v.t.* (*eat*) жрать (жру, жрёшь; жрал, -а́, -о) *impf.*; ~ **up** пожира́ть *impf.*, пожра́ть (-ру́, -рёшь; пожра́л, -а́, -о) *pf.*

gobble[2] ['gɒb(ə)l] *v.i.* (*of turkeys*) кулды́кать *impf.*

go-between ['gəʊbɪˌtwi:n] *n.* посре́дник.

goblet ['gɒblɪt] *n.* бока́л, ку́бок (-бка).

god [gɒd] *n.* бог (*pl.* -и, -о́в); (*idol*) куми́р; (**G**~) Бог (*voc.* Бо́же); *pl.* (*theatr.*) галёрка. **godchild** *n.* кре́стник, -ица. **god-daughter** *n.* кре́стница. **goddess** *n.* боги́ня. **godfather** *n.* крёстный *sb.* **God-fearing** *adj.* богобоя́зненный (-ен, -енна). **godless** *adj.* безбо́жный. **godlike** *adj.* богоподо́бный. **godly** *adj.* на́божный. **godmother** *n.* крёстная *sb.* **godparent** *n.* крёстный *sb.* **godson** кре́стник.

goggle ['gɒg(ə)l] *v.i.* тара́щить *impf.* глаза́ (**at** на+*a.*). **goggle-eyed** *adj.* пучегла́зый. **goggles** *n.* защи́тные очки́ (-ко́в) *pl.*

going ['gəʊɪŋ] *adj.* де́йствующий. **goings-on** *n.* поведе́ние; дела́ *nt.pl.*

goitre ['gɔɪtə(r)] *n.* зоб (*loc.* -е & -у́; *pl.* -ы́).

gold [gəʊld] *n.* зо́лото; *adj.* золото́й; ~ **leaf** золота́я фо́льга; ~ **plate** золота́я посу́да *collect.* **gold-bearing** *adj.* золотоно́сный. **gold-beater** *n.* золотобо́й. **gold-digger** *n.* золотоиска́тель *m.*; (*sl.*) авантюри́стка.

gold-dust *n.* золотоно́сный песо́к (-ска́ (-ску́)). **golden** *adj.* золото́й, золоти́стый; ~ **eagle** бе́ркут. **gold-field** *n.* золото́й при́иск. **goldfinch** *n.* щего́л (-гла́). **goldfish** *n.* золота́я ры́бка. **gold-mine** *n.* золото́й рудни́к (-а́); (*fig.*) золото́е дно. **gold-plate** *v.t.* золоти́ть *impf.*, по~ *pf.* **goldsmith** *n.* золоты́х дел ма́стер (*pl.* -а́).

golf [gɒlf] *n.* гольф. **golfer** *n.* игро́к (-а́) в гольф.

gondola ['gɒndələ] *n.* гондо́ла. **gondo'lier** *n.* гондолье́р.

gong [gɒŋ] *n.* гонг.

good [gʊd] *n.* добро́, бла́го; *pl.* (*wares*) това́р(ы); **do** ~ (*benefit*) идти́ (идёт; шёл, шла) *impf.*, пойти́ (пойдёт; пошёл, -шла́) *pf.* на по́льзу+*d.*; *adj.* хоро́ший (-ш, -ша́), до́брый (добр, -а́, -о, до́бры́); ~ **morning** до́брое у́тро!; ~ **night** споко́йной но́чи! **good'bye** *int.* проща́й(те)!; до свида́ния! **good-humoured** *adj.* доброду́шный. **good-looking** *adj.* краси́вый. **goodness** *n.* доброта́.

goose [gu:s] *n.* гусь (*pl.* -си, -се́й) *m.*, гусы́ня; (*cul.*) гуся́тина. **goose-flesh** *n.* гуси́ная ко́жа.

gooseberry ['gʊzbərɪ] *n.* крыжо́вник (*plant or* (*collect.*) *berries*).

gore¹ [gɔ:(r)] *n.* (*blood*) запёкшаяся кровь (*loc.* -ви́).

gore² [gɔ:(r)] *v.t.* (*pierce*) бода́ть *impf.*, за~ *pf.*

gorge [gɔ:dʒ] *n.* гло́тка; (*narrow opening*) уще́лье (*g.pl.* -лий); *v.t.* жрать (жру, жрёшь; жрал, -а́, -о) *impf.*, со~ *pf.*; *v.i.* объеда́ться *impf.*, объе́сться (-е́мся, -е́шься, -е́стся, -еди́мся; -е́лся) *pf.* (**on** +*i.*).

gorgeous ['gɔ:dʒəs] *adj.* пы́шный (-шен, -шна́, -шно), великоле́пный.

gorilla [gə'rɪlə] *n.* гори́лла.

gormless ['gɔ:mlɪs] *adj.* непоня́тливый, бестолко́вый.

gorse [gɔ:s] *n.* утёсник.

gory ['gɔ:rɪ] *adj.* окрова́вленный.

gosh [gɒʃ] *int.* бо́же мой!

goshawk ['gɒshɔ:k] *n.* большо́й я́стреб (*pl.* -ы & -а́).

gosling ['gɒzlɪŋ] *n.* гусёнок (-нка; *pl.* гуся́та, -т).

Gospel ['gɒsp(ə)l] *n.* Ева́нгелие.

gossamer ['gɒsəmə(r)] *n.* (*web*) паути́на; (*gauze*) то́нкая ткань.

gossip ['gɒsɪp] *n.* (*talk*) болтовня́, спле́тня (*g. pl.* -тен); (*person*) болту́н (-а́), ~ья (*g.pl.* -ний), спле́тник, -ица; *v.i.* болта́ть *impf.*; спле́тничать *impf.*, на~ *pf.*

Goth [gɒθ] *n.* гот. **Gothic** го́тский; (*archit.*; *print.*) готи́ческий.

gouache [gʊ'ɑ:ʃ, gwɑ:ʃ] *n.* гуа́шь.

gouge [gaʊdʒ] *v.t.*: ~ **out** выда́лбливать *impf.*, вы́долбить *pf.*; (*eyes*) выка́лывать *impf.*, вы́колоть (-лю, -лешь) *pf.*

goulash ['gu:læʃ] *n.* гуля́ш (-я́ша́).

gourd [gʊəd] *n.* ты́ква.

gourmand ['gʊəmænd] *n.* лако́мка *c.g.*

gourmet ['gʊəmeɪ] *n.* гурма́н.

gout [gaʊt] *n.* пода́гра. **gouty** *adj.* подагри́ческий.

govern ['gʌv(ə)n] *v.t.* пра́вить *impf.*+*i.*; управля́ть *impf.*+*i.* **governess** *n.* гуверна́нтка. **government** *n.* (*of state*) прави́тельство; управле́ние (**of** +*i.*). **govern'mental** *adj.* прави́тельственный. **governor** *n.* прави́тель *m.*, губерна́тор; (*head of institution*) заве́дующий *sb.* (**of** +*i.*).

gown [gaʊn] *n.* (*woman's*) пла́тье (*g.pl.* -в); (*official's*) ма́нтия.

grab [græb] *n.* (*grasp*) захва́т; (*device*) черпа́к (-а́); *v.t.* хвата́ть *impf.*, (с)хвати́ть (-ачу́, -а́тишь) *pf.*; захва́тывать *impf.*, захвати́ть (-ачу́, -а́тишь) *pf.*

grace [greɪs] *n.* (~*fulness*) гра́ция; (*refinement*) изя́щество; (*kindness*) любе́зность; (*favour*) ми́лость; (*theol.*) благода́ть; *v.t.* (*adorn*) украша́ть *impf.*, укра́сить *pf.*; (*confer*) удоста́ивать *impf.*, удосто́ить *pf.* (**with** +*g.*). **graceful** *adj.* грацио́зный, изя́щный.

gracious ['greɪʃəs] *adj.* ми́лостивый, снисходи́тельный.

gradation [grə'deɪʃ(ə)n] *n.* града́ция.

grade [greɪd] *n.* (*level*) сте́пень (*pl.* -ни, -не́й); (*quality*) ка́чество; (*sort*) сорт (*pl.* -а́); (*slope*) укло́н; *v.t.* распределя́ть *impf.*, распредели́ть *pf.* по степеня́м, гру́ппам и т.п.; сортирова́ть *impf.*, рас~ *pf.*; (*road etc.*) нивели́ровать *impf.* & *pf.*

gradient ['greɪdɪənt] *n.* укло́н.

gradual ['grædjʊəl] *adj.* постепе́нный (-нен, -нна).

graduate ['grædjʊət; 'grædjʊ,eɪt] *n.* око́нчивший *sb.* университе́т, вуз; *v.i.* конча́ть *impf.*, око́нчить *pf.* (университе́т, вуз); *v.t.* градуи́ровать *impf.* & *pf.*

graffiti [grə'fi:ti:] *n.* (стенны́е) на́дписи (*f.pl.*).

graft¹ [grɑ:ft] *n.* (*agric.*) приво́й, приви́вка; (*med.*) переса́дка (живо́й тка́ни); *v.t.* (*agric.*) привива́ть *impf.*, приви́ть (-вью́, -вьёшь; приви́л, -а́, -о) *pf.* (**to** +*d.*); (*med.*) переса́живать *impf.*, пересади́ть (-ажу́, -а́дишь) *pf.*

graft² [grɑ:ft] *n.* (*bribe*) взя́тка, по́дкуп; *v.i.* (*give*) дава́ть (даю́, -аёшь) *impf.*, дать (дам, дашь, даст, дади́м; дал, -а́, да́ло́, -и) *pf.* взя́тки; (*take*) брать (беру́, -рёшь; брал, -а́, -о) *impf.*, взять (возьму́, -мёшь; взял, -а́, о) *pf.* взя́тки.

grain [greɪn] *n.* (*seed*; *collect.*) зерно́ (*pl.* зёрна, -рен, -рнам); (*particle*) крупи́нка; (*of sand*) песчи́нка; (*measure*) гран (*g.pl.* -н); (*smallest amount*) крупи́ца; (*of wood*) (древе́сное) волокно́; **against the** ~ не по нутру́; **not a** ~ **of** ни гра́на+*g.*

gram(me) [græm] *n.* грамм (*g.pl.* -м & -мов).

grammar ['græmə(r)] *n.* грамма́тика; ~ **school** гимна́зия. **grammarian** [grə'meərɪən] *n.* грамма́тик. **gra'mmatical** *adj.* граммати́ческий.

gramophone ['græmə,fəʊn] *n.* граммофо́н, прои́грыватель *m.*; ~ **record** грампласти́нка.
grampus ['græmpəs] *n.* се́рый дельфи́н.
granary ['grænərɪ] *n.* амба́р.
grand [grænd] *adj.* (*in titles*) вели́кий; (*main*) гла́вный; (*majestic*) вели́чественный (-ен, -енна); (*splendid*) великоле́пный; ~ **duke** вели́кий ге́рцог; (*in Russia*) вели́кий князь (*pl.* -зья́, -зе́й); ~ **master** гроссме́йстер; ~ **piano** роя́ль *m.* **grandchild** *n.* внук, вну́чка; *pl.* внуча́та (-т) *pl.* **granddaughter** *n.* вну́чка. **grandfather** *n.* де́душка *m.* **grandmother** *n.* ба́бушка. **grandparents** *n.* ба́бушка и де́душка. **grandson** *n.* внук. **grandstand** *n.* трибу́на.
grandee [græn'di:] *n.* (*Spanish, Portuguese*) гранд; вельмо́жа *m.*
grandeur ['grændjə(r), -ndʒə(r)] *n.* вели́чие.
grandiloquence [,græn'dɪləkwəns] *n.* напы́щенность. **grandiloquent** *adj.* напы́щенный (-ен, -енна).
grandiose ['grændɪ,əʊs] *adj.* грандио́зный.
grange [greɪndʒ] *n.* фе́рма.
granite ['grænɪt] *n.* грани́т; *attr.* грани́тный.
grannie, granny ['grænɪ] *n.* ба́бушка.
grant [grɑ:nt] *n.* дар (*pl.* -ы́); (*financial*) дота́ция, субси́дия; *v.t.* дарова́ть *impf.* & *pf.*; предоставля́ть *impf.*, предоста́вить *pf.*; (*concede*) допуска́ть *impf.*, допусти́ть (-ущу́, -у́стишь) *pf.*; **take for ~ed** счита́ть *impf.*, счесть (сочту́, -тёшь; счёл, сочла́) *pf.* само́ собо́й разуме́ющимся.
granular ['grænjʊlə(r)] *adj.* зерни́стый.
granulate ['grænjʊ,leɪt] *v.t.* гранули́ровать *impf.* & *pf.*; **~d sugar** са́харный песо́к (-ска́(у́)).
granule ['grænju:l] *n.* зёрнышко (*pl.* -шки, -шек, -шкам).
grape [greɪp] *n.* виногра́д (-а(у)) (*collect.*). **grapefruit** *n.* гре́йпфрут. **grapeshot** *n.* карте́чь. **grapevine** *n.* виногра́дная лоза́ (*pl.* -зы).
graph [grɑ:f, græf] *n.* гра́фик.
graphic ['græfɪk] *adj.* графи́ческий; (*vivid*) я́ркий (я́рок, ярка́, я́рко).
graphite ['græfaɪt] *n.* графи́т.
grapnel ['græpn(ə)l] *n.* дрек, ко́шка.
grapple ['græp(ə)l] *n.* (*grapnel*) дрек, ко́шка; (*grip*) захва́т; *v.i.* сцепля́ться *impf.*, сцепи́ться (-плю́сь, -пишься) *pf.* (**with** с+*i.*); боро́ться (-рю́сь, -решься) *impf.* (**with** с+*i.*); **grappling hook, iron** дрек, ко́шка.
grasp [grɑ:sp] *n.* (*grip*) хва́тка; (*control*) власть; (*mental hold*) схва́тывание; *v.t.* (*clutch*) хвата́ть *impf.*, схвати́ть (-ачу́, -а́тишь) *pf.*; (*comprehend*) понима́ть *impf.*, поня́ть (пойму́, -мёшь; по́нял, -а́, -о) *pf.* **grasping** *adj.* жа́дный (-ден, дна́, -дно).
grass [grɑ:s] *n.* трава́ (*pl.* -вы), злак; (*pasture*) па́стбище; ~ **snake** уж (-а́); ~ **widow** соло́менная вдова́ (*pl.* -вы). **grasshopper** *n.* кузне́чник. **grassy** *adj.* травяни́стый, травяно́й.
grate[1] [greɪt] *n.* (*in fireplace*) (ками́нная) решётка.
grate[2] [greɪt] *v.t.* (*rub*) тере́ть (тру, трёшь; тёр) *impf.*, на~ *pf.*; *v.i.* (*sound*) скрипе́ть (-пи́т) *impf.*; ~ **(up)on** (*irritate*) раздража́ть *impf.*, раздражи́ть *pf.*
grateful ['greɪtfʊl] *n.* благода́рный.
grater ['greɪtə(r)] *n.* тёрка.
gratify ['grætɪ,faɪ] *v.t.* удовлетворя́ть *impf.*, удовлетвори́ть *pf.*
grating ['greɪtɪŋ] *n.* решётка.
gratis ['grɑ:tɪs] *adv.* беспла́тно, да́ром.
gratitude ['grætɪ,tju:d] *n.* благода́рность.
gratuitous [grə'tju:ɪtəs] *adj.* (*free*) дарово́й; (*motiveless*) беспричи́нный (-нен, -нна).
gratuity [grə'tju:ɪtɪ] *n.* де́нежный пода́рок (-рка); (*tip*) чаевы́е *sb.*; (*mil.*) наградны́е *sb.*
grave[1] [greɪv] *n.* моги́ла. **gravedigger** *n.* моги́льщик. **gravestone** *n.* надгро́бный ка́мень (-мня; *pl.* -мни, -мне́й) *m.* **graveyard** *n.* кла́дбище.
grave[2] [greɪv] *adj.* (*serious*) серьёзный, ва́жный (-жен, -жна́, -жно, -жны́).
gravel ['græv(ə)l] *n.* гра́вий; ~ **pit** грави́йный карье́р.
gravitate ['grævɪ,teɪt] *v.i.* тяготе́ть *impf.* (**towards** к+*d.*). **gravi'tation** *n.* тяготе́ние.
gravity ['grævɪtɪ] *n.* (*seriousness*) серьёзность; (*force*) тя́жесть; **specific** ~ уде́льный вес.
gravy ['greɪvɪ] *n.* (мясна́я) подли́вка. **gravy-boat** *n.* со́усник.
graze[1] [greɪz] *v.t.* & *i.* (*feed*) пасти́ (пасу́(сь), пасёшь(ся); па́с(ся), пасла́(сь)) *impf.*
graze[2] [greɪz] *n.* (*abrasion*) цара́пина; *v.t.* (*touch lightly*) задева́ть *impf.*, заде́ть (-е́ну, -е́нешь) *pf.*; (*abrade*) цара́пать *impf.*, о~ *pf.*
grease [gri:s] *n.* жир (-а(у), *loc.* -е & -у́), топлёное са́ло; (*lubricant*) сма́зка; *v.t.* сма́зывать *impf.*, сма́зать (-а́жу, -а́жешь) *pf.* **grease-gun** *n.* таво́тный шприц. **grease-paint** *n.* грим. **greasy** *adj.* жи́рный (-рен, -рна́, -рно), са́льный.
great [greɪt] *adj.* (*large*) большо́й; (*eminent*) вели́кий; (*long*) до́лгий (-лог, -лга́, -лго); (*strong*) си́льный (си́лён, -льна́, -льно, си́льны́); **G~ Britain** Великобрита́ния; **to a ~ extent** в большо́й сте́пени; **a ~ deal** мно́го (+*g.*); **a ~ many** мно́гие; мно́жество (+*g.*). **great-aunt** *n.* двою́родная ба́бушка. **great-granddaughter** *n.* пра́внучка. **great-grandfather** *n.* пра́дед. **great-grandmother** *n.* праба́бка. **great-grandson** *n.* пра́внук.
greatly ['greɪtlɪ] *adv.* о́чень.
great-uncle [greɪt'ʌŋk(ə)l] *n.* двою́родный де́душка *m.*
Grecian ['gri:ʃ(ə)n] *adj.* гре́ческий. **Greece** *n.* Гре́ция.
greed [gri:d] *n.* жа́дность (**for** к+*d.*), а́лчность. **greedy** *adj.* жа́дный (-ден, -дна́, -дно) (**for** к+*d.*), а́лчный; (*for food*) прожо́рливый.
Greek [gri:k] *n.* грек, греча́нка; *adj.* гре́ческий.

green [griːn] *n.* (*colour*) зелёный цвет; (*piece of land*) лужо́к (-жка́); *pl.* зе́лень *collect.*; *adj.* зелёный (зе́лен, -а́, -о); (*inexperienced*) нео́пытный. **greenery** *n.* зе́лень. **greenfly** *n.* тля (*g.pl.* тлей). **greengage** *n.* ренкло́д. **greengrocer** *n.* зеленщи́к (-а́). **greenhorn** *n.* новичо́к (-чка́). **greenhouse** *n.* тепли́ца, оранжере́я; ~ **effect** тепли́чный эффе́кт.

greet [griːt] *v.t.* кла́няться *impf.*, поклони́ться (-ню́сь, -ни́шься) *pf.*+*d.*; приве́тствовать *impf.* (& *pf. in past tense*). **greeting** *n.* приве́т(ствие).

gregarious [grɪˈgeərɪəs] *adj.* ста́дный; (*person*) общи́тельный.

grenade [grɪˈneɪd] *n.* грана́та.

grey [greɪ] *adj.* се́рый (сер, -а́, -о); (*hair*) седо́й (сед, -а́, -о); ~ **hair** седина́ (*pl.* -ы).

greyhound [ˈgreɪhaʊnd] *n.* борза́я *sb.*

grid [grɪd] *n.* (*grating*) решётка; (*network*) сеть (*pl.* -ти, -те́й); (*map*) координа́тная се́тка.

grief [griːf] *n.* го́ре, печа́ль; **come to** ~ попада́ть *impf.*, попа́сть (попаду́, -дёшь; попа́л) *pf.* в беду́.

grievance [ˈgriːv(ə)ns] *n.* жа́лоба, оби́да.

grieve [griːv] *v.t.* огорча́ть *impf.*, огорчи́ть *pf.*; *v.i.* горева́ть (-рю́ю, -рю́ешь) *impf.* (**for** о+*p.*).

grievous [ˈgriːvəs] *adj.* тя́жкий (-жек, -жка́, -жко); (*flagrant*) вопию́щий.

grill¹ [grɪl] *n.* ра́шпер; *v.t.* (*cook*) жа́рить *impf.*, за~, из~ *pf.* (на ра́шпере); (*question*) допра́шивать *impf.*, допроси́ть (-ошу́, -о́сишь) *pf.*

grille, grill² [grɪl] *n.* (*grating*) решётка.

grim [grɪm] *adj.* (*stern*) суро́вый; (*sinister*) мра́чный (-чен, -чна́, -чно); (*unpleasant*) неприя́тный.

grimace [ˈgrɪməs, grɪˈmeɪs] *n.* грима́са; *v.i.* грима́сничать *impf.*

grime [graɪm] *n.* (*soot*) са́жа; (*dirt*) грязь (*loc.* -зи́). **grimy** *adj.* гря́зный (-зен, -зна́, -зно).

grin [grɪn] *n.* усме́шка; *v.i.* усмеха́ться *impf.*, усмехну́ться *pf.*

grind [graɪnd] *v.t.* (*flour etc.*) моло́ть (мелю́, -лешь) *impf.*, с~ *pf.*; (*axe*) точи́ть (-очу́, -чишь) *impf.*, на~ *pf.*; (*oppress*) му́чить *impf.*, за~, из~ *pf.*; ~ **one's teeth** скрежета́ть (-ещу́, -е́щешь) *impf.* зуба́ми.

grip [grɪp] *n.* схва́тывание; (*control*) власть; *v.t.* схва́тывать *impf.*, схвати́ть (-ачу́, -а́тишь) *pf.*

grisly [ˈgrɪzlɪ] *adj.* ужа́сный.

gristle [ˈgrɪs(ə)l] *n.* хрящ (-а́). **gristly** *adj.* хрящева́тый.

grit [grɪt] *n.* кру́пный песо́к (-ска́(у́)); (*firmness*) сто́йкость. **gritty** *adj.* песча́ный.

grizzly [ˈgrɪzlɪ] *adj.* се́рый (сер, -а́, -о); ~ **bear** гри́зли *m.indecl.*

groan [grəʊn] *n.* стон; *v.i.* стона́ть (-ну́, -нешь) *impf.*

grocer [ˈgrəʊsə(r)] *n.* бакале́йщик; **~'s (shop)** бакале́йная ла́вка, гастроно́м(и́ческий магази́н). **groceries** *n.* бакале́я *collect.*

groin [grɔɪn] *n.* (*anat.*) пах (*loc.* -у́).

groom [gruːm] *n.* грум, ко́нюх; (*bridegroom*) жени́х (-а́); *v.t.* (*horse*) чи́стить *impf.*, по~ *pf.*; (*person*) хо́лить *impf.*, вы́~ *pf.*; (*prepare*) гото́вить *impf.*, под~ *pf.* (**for** к+*d.*).

groove [gruːv] *n.* желобо́к (-бка́), паз (*loc.* -у́; *pl.* -ы́); (*routine*) колея́.

grope [grəʊp] *v.i.* нащу́пывать *impf.* (**for, after** +*a.*); ~ **one's way** идти́ (иду́, идёшь; шёл, шла) *impf.*, пойти́ (пойду́, -дёшь; пошёл, -шла́) *pf.* о́щупью.

gross¹ [grəʊs] *n.* (*12 dozen*) гросс; **by the** ~ о́птом.

gross² [grəʊs] *adj.* (*luxuriant*) пы́шный (-шен, -шна́, -шно); (*fat*) ту́чный (-чен, -чна́, -чно); (*coarse*) гру́бый (груб, -а́, -о); (*total*) валово́й; ~ **weight** вес бру́тто.

grotesque [grəʊˈtesk] *adj.* гроте́скный; (*absurd*) нele̓пый.

grotto [ˈgrɒtəʊ] *n.* грот, пеще́ра.

ground [graʊnd] *n.* земля́ (*a.* -лю), по́чва, грунт; *pl.* (*dregs*) гу́ща; (*sport*) площа́дка; *pl.* (*of house*) парк; (*background*) фон; (*reason*) основа́ние, причи́на; **break fresh** ~ прокла́дывать *impf.*, проложи́ть (-жу́, -жишь) *pf.* но́вые пути́; **gain** ~ де́лать *impf.*, с~ *pf.* успе́хи; **give, lose,** ~ уступа́ть *impf.*, уступи́ть (-плю́, -пишь) *pf.* (**to** +*d.*); **stand one's** ~ стоя́ть (-ою́, -ои́шь) *impf.* на своём; ~ **floor** цо́кольный, пе́рвый, эта́ж (-а́); *v.t.* (*base*) обосно́вывать *impf.*, обоснова́ть (-ну́ю, -нуёшь) *pf.*; (*instruct*) обуча́ть *impf.*, обучи́ть (-чу́, -чишь) *pf.* осно́вам (**in** +*g.*); *v.i.* (*naut.*) сади́ться *impf.*, сесть (ся́дет; сел) *pf.* на мель. **groundless** *adj.* беспричи́нный (-нен, -нна), необосно́ванный (-ан, -анна). **groundnut** *n.* земляно́й оре́х. **groundsheet** *n.* поло́тнище пала́тки. **groundwork** *n.* фунда́мент, осно́ва, основа́ние.

group [gruːp] *n.* гру́ппа; ~ **captain** полко́вник авиа́ции; *v.t. & i.*, группирова́ть(ся) *impf.*, с~ *pf.*

grouse¹ [graʊs] *n.* (*bird*) те́терев (*pl.* -а́); **(red)** ~ шотла́ндская куропа́тка.

grouse² [graʊs] *v.i.* (*grumble*) ворча́ть (-чу́, -чи́шь) *impf.*

grove [grəʊv] *n.* ро́ща.

grovel [ˈgrɒv(ə)l] *v.i.* пресмыка́ться *impf.* (**before** пе́ред+*i.*).

grow [grəʊ] *v.i.* расти́ (-ту́, -тёшь; рос, -ла́) *impf.*; (*become*) станови́ться (-влю́сь, -вишься) *impf.*, стать (ста́ну, -нешь) *pf.*+*i.*; *v.t.* (*cultivate*) выра́щивать *impf.*, вы́растить *pf.*; ~ **up** (*person*) выраста́ть *impf.*, вы́расти (-ту, -тешь; вы́рос, -ла) *pf.*; (*custom*) возника́ть *impf.*, возни́кнуть (-к) *pf.*

growl [graʊl] *n.* ворча́ние; *v.i.* ворча́ть (-чу́, -чи́шь) *impf.* (**at** на+*a.*).

grown-up [grəʊˈnʌp] *adj.* взро́слый *sb.*

growth [grəʊθ] *n.* рост (-а(у)); (*tumour*) о́пухоль.

grub [grʌb] *n.* (*larva*) личи́нка; (*sl.*) (*food*) жратва́; *v.i.*: ~ **about** ры́ться (ро́юсь, ро́ешься) *impf.* **grubby** *adj.* гря́зный, чума́зый.

grudge [grʌdʒ] *n.* недово́льство, за́висть; **have a ~ against** име́ть *impf.* зуб про́тив+*g.*; *v.t.* жале́ть *impf.*, по~ *pf.*+*a.*, +*g.*; неохо́тно дава́ть (даю́, даёшь) *impf.*, дать (дам, дашь, даст, дади́м; дал, -а́, да́ло́, -и) *pf.*; неохо́тно де́лать *impf.*, с~ *pf.* **grudgingly** *adv.* неохо́тно.

gruel ['gru:əl] *n.* жи́дкая ка́ша; *v.t.* утомля́ть *impf.*, утоми́ть *pf.* **gruelling** *adj.* изнури́тельный, суро́вый.

gruesome ['gru:səm] *adj.* отврати́тельный.

gruff [grʌf] *adj.* (*surly*) грубова́тый; (*voice*) хри́плый (-л, -ла́, -ло).

grumble ['grʌmb(ə)l] *n.* ворча́ние, ро́пот; *v.i.* ворча́ть (-чу́, -чи́шь) *impf.* (**at** на+*a.*).

grumpy ['grʌmpɪ] *adj.* брюзгли́вый.

grunt [grʌnt] *n.* хрю́канье; *v.i.* хрю́кать *impf.*, хрю́кнуть *pf.*

guarantee [ˌgærən'ti:] *n.* (*person*) поручи́тель *m.*, ~ница; (*security*) гара́нтия, зало́г; *v.t.* гаранти́ровать *impf.* & *pf.* (**against** от+*g.*); руча́ться *impf.*, поручи́ться (-чу́сь, -чишься) *pf.* за+*a.* **guarantor** *n.* поручи́тель *m.*, ~ница.

guard [gɑ:d] *n.* (*protection*) охра́на; (*watch, body of soldiers*) карау́л; (*sentry*) часово́й *sb.*; (*watchman*) сто́рож (*pl.* -а́); (*rail.*) конду́ктор (*pl.* -а́); *pl.* (**G~**) гва́рдия; ~ **of honour** почётный карау́л; *v.t.* охраня́ть *impf.*, охрани́ть *pf.*; *v.i.*: ~ **against** остерега́ться *impf.*, остере́чься (-егу́сь, -ежёшься; -ёгся, -егла́сь) *pf.*+*g.*, *inf.* **guard-house, -room** *n.* гауптва́хта. **guardsman** *n.* гварде́ец (-е́йца).

guardian ['gɑ:dɪən] *n.* храни́тель *m.*, ~ница; (*leg.*) опеку́н (-а́).

guer(r)illa [gə'rɪlə] *n.* партиза́н; ~ **warfare** партиза́нская война́.

guess [ges] *n.* дога́дка; *v.t.* & *i.* дога́дываться *impf.*, догада́ться *pf.* (о+*p.*); *v.t.* (~ *correctly*) уга́дывать *impf.*, угада́ть *pf.*

guest [gest] *n.* гость (*pl.* -ти, -те́й) *m.*, ~я (*g.pl.* -тий).

guffaw [gʌ'fɔ:] *n.* хо́хот; *v.i.* хохота́ть (-очу́, -о́чешь) *impf.*

guidance ['gaɪd(ə)ns] *n.* руково́дство. **guide** *n.* проводни́к (-а́), -и́ца; гид; (*adviser*) сове́тчик; (*manual*) руково́дство; (*guidebook*) путеводи́тель *m.*; *v.t.* води́ть (вожу́, во́дишь) *indet.*, вести́ (веду́, -дёшь; вёл, -а́) *det.*; (*direct*) руководи́ть *impf.*+*i.*; (*control*) управля́ть *impf.*+*i.*; **~ed missile** управля́емая раке́та. **guide-dog** *n.* соба́ка-поводы́рь (-ря́). **guide-post** *n.* указа́тельный столб(-а́).

guild [gɪld] *n.* ги́льдия, цех.

guile [gaɪl] *n.* кова́рство, хи́трость. **guileful** *adj.* кова́рный. **guileless** *adj.* простоду́шный.

guillotine ['gɪləˌti:n] *n.* гильоти́на; (*for paper etc.*) бумагоре́зальная маши́на; *v.t.* гильоти́ровать *impf.* & *pf.*

guilt [gɪlt] *n.* вина́, вино́вность. **guiltless** *adj.* неви́нный (-нен, -нна), невино́вный. **guilty** *adj.* вино́вный (**of** в+*p.*), винова́тый.

guinea ['gɪnɪ] *n.* гине́я. **guinea-fowl** *n.* цеса́рка. **guinea-pig** *n.* морска́я сви́нка; (*fig.*) подо́пытный кро́лик.

guise [gaɪz] *n.* вид, о́блик; **under the ~ of** под ви́дом+*g.*

guitar [gɪ'tɑ:(r)] *n.* гита́ра.

gulf [gʌlf] *n.* зали́в; (*chasm*) про́пасть; **G~ Stream** гольфстри́м.

gull [gʌl] *n.* ча́йка.

gullet ['gʌlɪt] *n.* пищево́д; (*throat*) го́рло.

gullible ['gʌlɪb(ə)l] *adj.* легкове́рный.

gully ['gʌlɪ] *n.* (*ravine*) овра́г; (*channel*) кана́ва.

gulp [gʌlp] *n.* глото́к (-тка́); *v.t.* жа́дно глота́ть *impf.*

gum[1] [gʌm] *n.* (*anat.*) десна́ (*pl.* дёсны, -сен, -снам).

gum[2] [gʌm] *n.* (*glue*) каме́дь, клей (-е́я(ю), *loc.* -е́е & ею́; *pl.* -е́й); *v.t.* скле́ивать *impf.*, скле́ить *pf.* **gumboot** *n.* рези́новый сапо́г (-а́; *g.pl.* -г). **gum-tree** *n.* эвкали́пт.

gumption ['gʌmpʃ(ə)n] *n.* нахо́дчивость.

gun [gʌn] *n.* (*piece of ordnance*) ору́дие, пу́шка; (*rifle etc.*) ружьё (*pl.* -жья, -жей); (*pistol*) пистоле́т; **starting ~** ста́ртовый пистоле́т; *v.t.*: ~ **down** расстре́ливать *impf.*, расстреля́ть *pf.* **gunboat** *n.* каноне́рская ло́дка. **gun-carriage** *n.* лафе́т. **gunner** *n.* артиллери́ст; (*aeron.*) стрело́к (-лка́). **gunpowder** *n.* по́рох (-а(у)). **gunsmith** *n.* оруже́йный ма́стер (*pl.* -а́).

gunwale ['gʌn(ə)l] *n.* планши́рь *m.*

gurgle ['gɜ:g(ə)l] *v.i.* бу́лькать *impf.*, бу́лькнуть *pf.*

gush [gʌʃ] *n.* си́льный пото́к; излия́ние; *v.i.* хлы́нуть *pf.*; излива́ться *impf.*, изли́ться (изолью́сь, -ьёшься; изли́лся, -ила́сь, -и́ло́сь) *pf.*

gusset ['gʌsɪt] *n.* клин (*pl.* -ья, -ьев), ла́стовица.

gust [gʌst] *n.* поры́в. **gusty** *adj.* поры́вистый.

gusto ['gʌstəʊ] *n.* удово́льствие, смак.

gut [gʌt] *n.* кишка́ (*g.pl.* -шо́к); *pl.* (*entrails*) вну́тренности *f.pl.*; *pl.* (*coll., bravery*) мужество́; *v.t.* потроши́ть *impf.*, вы~ *pf.*; (*devastate*) опустоша́ть *impf.*, опустоши́ть *pf.*

gutta-percha [ˌgʌtə'pɜ:tʃə] *n.* гуттапе́рча.

gutter ['gʌtə(r)] *n.* (водосто́чный) жёлоб (*pl.* -а́), сто́чная кана́ва; ~ **press** бульва́рная пре́сса.

guttural ['gʌtər(ə)l] *adj.* горта́нный, горлово́й.

guy[1] [gaɪ] *n.* (*rope*) оття́жка.

guy[2] [gaɪ] *n.* (*fellow*) па́рень (-рня; *pl.* -рни, -рне́й) *m.*

guzzle ['gʌz(ə)l] *v.t.* (*food*) пожира́ть *impf.*, пожра́ть (-ру́, -рёшь; пожра́л, -а́, -о) *pf.*; (*liquid*) хлеба́ть *impf.*, хлебну́ть *pf.*

gym [dʒɪm] *n.* (*gymnasium*) гимнасти́ческий зал; (*gymnastics*) гимна́стика. **gymnasium** [dʒɪm'neɪzɪəm] *n.* гимнасти́ческий зал; (*school*) гимна́зия. **'gymnast** *n.* гимна́ст, ~ка. **gym'nastic** *adj.* гимнасти́ческий. **gym'nastics** *n.* гимна́стика.

gynaecology [ˌgaɪnɪ'kɒlədʒɪ] *n.* гинеколо́гия.

gypsum ['dʒɪpsəm] *n.* гипс.

gyrate [ˌdʒaɪə'reɪt] *v.i.* враща́ться *impf.* по кру́гу; дви́гаться (дви́гается & дви́жется) *impf.* по спира́ли.

gyro(scope) ['dʒaɪərəˌskəʊp] *n.* гироско́п. **gyro-compass** *n.* гироко́мпас.

H

ha. *abbr.* (*of* **hectare(s)**) га, гекта́р.

haberdasher ['hæbəˌdæʃə(r)] *n.* торго́вец (-вца) галантере́ей. **haberdashery** *n.* (*articles*) галантере́я; (*shop*) галантере́йный магази́н.

habit ['hæbɪt] *n.* привы́чка; (*dress*) одея́ние.

habitable ['hæbɪtəb(ə)l] *adj.* го́дный (-ден, -дна́, -дно) для жилья́. **habi'tation** *n.* жили́ще.

habitual [hə'bɪtjʊəl] *adj.* обы́чный, привы́чный. **habitué** *n.* завсегда́тай.

hack[1] [hæk] *v.t.* руби́ть (-блю́, -бишь) *impf.*; дроби́ть *impf.*, раз~ *pf.*

hack[2] [hæk] *n.* писа́ка *c.g.* **hackneyed** ['hæknɪd] *adj.* изби́тый, бана́льный.

hacksaw ['hæksɔ:] *n.* ножо́вка.

haddock ['hædək] *n.* пи́кша.

haemophilia [ˌhi:mə'fɪlɪə] *n.* гемафили́я. **haemorrhage** ['hemərɪdʒ] *n.* кровоизлия́ние, кровотече́ние. **haemorrhoids** ['heməˌrɔɪdz] *n.* геморро́й *collect.*

hag [hæg] *n.* ве́дьма, карга́.

haggard ['hægəd] *adj.* измождённый (-ён, -ена́).

haggle ['hæg(ə)l] *v.i.* торгова́ться *impf.*, с~ *pf.*

hail[1] [heɪl] *n.* град; *v.i.* **it is ~ing** идёт (*past* пошёл) град; *v.t.* осыпа́ть *impf.*, осы́пать (-плю, -плешь) *pf.*+*a.* & *i.*; *v.i.* сы́паться (-плется) *impf.* гра́дом. **hailstone** *n.* гра́дина.

hail[2] [heɪl] *v.t.* (*greet*) приве́тствовать *impf.* (& *pf. in past*); (*call*) оклика́ть *impf.*, окли́кнуть *pf.*; *v.i.*: **~ from** (*of persons only*) быть ро́дом из+*g.*; происходи́ть (-ожу́, -о́дишь) *impf.*, произойти́ (произойду́, -дёшь; произошёл, -шла́) *pf.* из+*g.*

hair [heə(r)] *n.* (*single* ~) во́лос (*pl.* -осы, -о́с, -оса́м); *collect.* (*human*) во́лосы (-о́с, -оса́м) *pl.*; (*animal*) шерсть; **do one's ~** причёсываться *impf.*, причеса́ться (-ешу́сь, -е́шешься) *pf.* **haircut** *n.* стри́жка. **hairdo** *n.* причёска. **hairdresser** *n.* парикма́хер. **hairspray** *n.* лак для воло́с. **hairy** *adj.* волоса́тый.

hake [heɪk] *n.* хек.

halberd ['hælbəd] *n.* алеба́рда.

hale [heɪl] *adj.* здоро́вый.

half [hɑ:f] *n.* полови́на; (*sport*) тайм; *in comb.* пол(у)...; *adj.* полови́нный; **in ~** попола́м; **one and a ~** полтора́ *m.* & *nt.*, -ры́ *f.* +*g.sg.* (*oblique cases*: полу́тора+*pl.*); **~ moon** полуме́сяц; **~ past** (*one etc.*) полови́на (второ́го и т.д.). **half-back** *n.* полузащи́тник. **half-hearted** *adj.* равноду́шный. **half-hour** *n.* полчаса́ (*oblique cases* полу́часа). **half-mast** *adv.*: **flag at ~** приспущённый флаг. **half-time** *n.* переры́в ме́жду та́ймами. **halfway** *adv.* на полпути́. **halfwitted** *adj.* слабоу́мный.

halibut ['hælɪbət] *n.* па́лтус.

hall [hɔ:l] *n.* (*large room*) зал; (*entrance ~*) холл, вестибю́ль *m.*; (*dining ~*) столо́вая (колле́джа); (*~ of residence*) общежи́тие. **hallmark** *n.* проби́рное клеймо́ (*pl.* -ма); (*fig.*) при́знак.

hallo *see* **hello**

hallow ['hæləʊ] *v.t.* освяща́ть *impf.*, освяти́ть (-ящу́, -яти́шь) *pf.*

hallucination [həˌlu:sɪ'neɪʃ(ə)n] *n.* галлюцина́ция.

halo ['heɪləʊ] *n.* гало́ *nt.indecl.*; (*around Saint*) ве́нчик, нимб; (*fig.*) орео́л.

halogen ['hælədʒ(ə)n] *n.* галоге́н.

‹[1] [hɒlt, hɔ:lt] *n.* (*stoppage*) остано́вка; (*rail.*) полуста́нок (-нка) *v.t.* & *i.* остана́вливать(ся) *impf.*, останови́ть(ся) (-влю́(сь), -вишь(ся)) *pf.*; *int.* (*mil.*) стой(те)!

halt[2] [hɒlt, hɔ:lt] *v.i.* (*hesitate*) колеба́ться (-блюсь, -блешься) *impf.*

halter ['hɒltə(r), 'hɔ:l-] *n.* недоу́здок (-дка).

halve [hɑ:v] *v.t.* дели́ть (-лю́, -лишь) *impf.*, раз~ *pf.* попола́м.

ham [hæm] *n.* (*cul.*) ветчина́, о́корок; (*theatr.*) плохо́й актёр; (*radio ~*) радиолюби́тель *m.*; *v.i.* (*theatr.*) переи́грывать *impf.*, переигра́ть *pf.*

hamlet ['hæmlɪt] *n.* дереву́шка.

hammer ['hæmə(r)] *n.* мо́лот, молото́к (-тка́); **come under the ~** продава́ться (-даётся) *impf.*, прода́ться (-да́стся; -да́лся, -дала́сь) *pf.* с молотка́; *v.t.* бить (бью, бьёшь) *impf.* мо́лотом, молотко́м.

hammock ['hæmək] *n.* гама́к (-а́); (*naut.*) ко́йка.

hamper[1] ['hæmpə(r)] *n.* (*basket*) корзи́на с кры́шкой.

hamper[2] ['hæmpə(r)] *v.t.* (*hinder*) меша́ть *impf.*, по~ *pf.*+*d.*

hamster ['hæmstə(r)] *n.* хомя́к (-а́).

hand [hænd] *n.* рука́ (*a.* -ку; *pl.* -ки, -к, -ка́м); (*worker*) рабо́чий *sb.*; (*~writing*) по́черк;

(*clock* ~) стре́лка; **at** ~ под руко́й; **on** ~**s and knees** на четвере́ньках; *v.t.* передава́ть (-даю́, -даёшь) *impf.*, переда́ть (-а́м, -а́шь, -а́ст, -ади́м; -пе́редал, -а́, -о) *pf.*; вруча́ть *impf.*, вручи́ть *pf.* **handbag** *n.* су́мка, су́мочка. **handball** *n.* гандбо́л. **handbook** *n.* спра́вочник, руково́дство. **handcuffs** *n.* нару́чники *m.pl.* **hand-drier, -dryer** *n.* электрополоте́нце. **handful** *n.* горсть (*pl.* -ти, -те́й).

handicap ['hændɪˌkæp] *n.* (*sport*) гандика́п; (*hindrance*) поме́ха. **handicapped** *adj.*: ~ **person** инвали́д.

handicraft ['hændɪˌkrɑːft] *n.* ремесло́ (*pl.* -ёсла, -ёсел, -ёслам).

handiwork ['hændɪˌwɜːk] *n.* ручна́я рабо́та.

handkerchief ['hæŋkətʃɪf, -ˌtʃiːf] *n.* носово́й плато́к (-тка́).

handle ['hænd(ə)l] *n.* ру́чка, рукоя́тка; *v.t.* (*treat*) обраща́ться *impf.* с+*i.*; (*manage*) управля́ть *impf.*+*i.*; (*touch*) тро́гать *impf.*, тро́нуть *pf.* руко́й, рука́ми. **handlebar(s)** *n.* руль (-ля́) *m.*

handsome ['hænsəm] *adj.* краси́вый; (*generous*) ще́дрый (щедр, -а́, -о).

handwriting ['hændˌraɪtɪŋ] *n.* по́черк.

handy ['hændɪ] *adj.* (*convenient*) удо́бный; (*skilful*) ло́вкий (-вок, -вка́, -вко, ло́вки́); **come in** ~ пригоди́ться *pf.*

hang [hæŋ] *v.t.* ве́шать *impf.*, пове́сить *pf.*; подве́шивать *impf.*, подве́сить *pf.*; *v.i.* висе́ть (вишу́, виси́шь) *impf.*; ~ **about** слоня́ться *impf.*; ~ **back** колеба́ться (-блюсь, -блешься) *impf.*; ~ **on** (*remain*) держа́ться (-жу́сь, -жишься) *impf.* **hanger-on** *n.* прижива́льщик. **hang-glider** *n.* (*craft*) дельтапла́н; (*operator*) дельтапланери́ст. **hangman** *n.* пала́ч (-а́).

hangar ['hæŋə(r)] *n.* анга́р.

hangover ['hæŋˌəʊvə(r)] *n.* похме́лье.

hanker ['hæŋkə(r)] *v.i.*: ~ **after** стра́стно жела́ть *impf.*, по~ *pf.*+*g.*

haphazard [hæp'hæzəd] *adj.* случа́йный; *adv.* случа́йно, науда́чу.

hapless ['hæplɪs] *adj.* злополу́чный.

happen ['hæpən] *v.i.* (*occur*) случа́ться *impf.*, случи́ться *pf.*; происходи́ть (-и́т) *impf.*, произойти́ (-ойдёт; -ошёл, -шла́) *pf.*; (~ *to be somewhere*) ока́зываться *impf.*, оказа́ться (-ажу́сь, -а́жешься) *pf.*; ~ **upon** ната́лкиваться *impf.*, натолкну́ться *pf.* на+*a.*

happiness ['hæpɪnɪs] *n.* сча́стье. **happy** *adj.* счастли́вый (сча́стли́в); (*apt*) уда́чный; **H~ Birthday!** (поздравля́ю вас) с днём рожде́ния!; **H~ New Year!** с Но́вым го́дом!

harass ['hærəs] *v.t.* беспоко́ить *impf.*, о~ *pf.*

harbinger ['hɑːbɪndʒə(r)] *n.* предве́стник.

harbour ['hɑːbə(r)] *n.* га́вань, порт (*loc.* -у́; *pl.* -ы, -о́в); (*shelter*) убе́жище; *v.t.* (*person*) укрыва́ть *impf.*, укры́ть (-ро́ю, -ро́ешь) *pf.*; (*thoughts*) зата́ивать *impf.*, затаи́ть *pf.*

hard [hɑːd] *adj.* твёрдый (твёрд, -а́, -о), жёсткий (-ток, -тка́, -тко); (*difficult*) тру́дный (-ден, -дна́, -дно, тру́дны́); (*difficult to bear*) тяжёлый (-л, -ла́); (*severe*) суро́вый; ~ **copy** (*comput.*) печа́тная ко́пия; ~ **hat** защи́тный шлем. **hard-boiled** *adj.*: ~ **egg** яйцо́ (*pl.* я́йца, яи́ц, я́йцам) вкруту́ю.

harden ['hɑːd(ə)n] *v.t.* де́лать *impf.*, с~ *pf.* твёрдым; закаля́ть *impf.*, закали́ть *pf.*; *v.i.* затвердева́ть *impf.*, затверде́ть *pf.*; (*become callous*) ожесточа́ться *impf.*, ожесточи́ться *pf.*

hard-headed [hɑːd'hedɪd] *adj.* практи́чный. **hard-hearted** *adj.* жестокосе́рдный.

hardly ['hɑːdlɪ] *adv.* (*scarcely*) едва́ (ли); (*with difficulty*) с трудо́м.

hardship ['hɑːdʃɪp] *n.* (*privation*) нужда́.

hardware ['hɑːdweə(r)] *n.* скобяны́е изде́лия *nt.pl.*; (*comput.*) аппарату́ра, аппара́тное обору́дование.

hard-working [hɑːd'wɜːkɪŋ] *adj.* приле́жный.

hardy ['hɑːdɪ] *adj.* (*bold*) сме́лый (смел, -а́, -о); (*robust*) выно́сливый.

hare [heə(r)] *n.* за́яц (за́йца). **hare-brained** *adj.* опроме́тчивый. **harelip** *n.* за́ячья губа́.

harem ['hɑːriːm, hɑː'riːm] *n.* гаре́м.

haricot (bean) ['hærɪˌkəʊ] *n.* фасо́ль.

hark [hɑːk] *v.i.*: ~ **to, at** слу́шать *impf.*, по~ *pf.*+*a.*; ~ **back to** возвраща́ться *impf.*, верну́ться *pf.* к+*d.*; *int.* чу!

harlot ['hɑːlət] *n.* проститу́тка.

harm [hɑːm] *n.* вред (-а́), зло; *v.t.* вреди́ть *impf.*, по~ *pf.*+*d.* **harmful** *adj.* вре́дный (-ден, -дна́, -дно). **harmless** *adj.* безвре́дный.

harmonic [hɑː'mɒnɪk] *adj.* гармони́ческий. **harmonica** *n.* губна́я гармо́ника. **harmonious** [hɑː'məʊnɪəs] *adj.* гармони́чный; (*amicable*) дру́жный (-жен, -жна́, -жно). **harmonium** *n.* фисгармо́ния. '**harmonize** *v.t.* гармонизи́ровать *impf.* & *pf.*; *v.i.* гармони́ровать *impf.* (**with** с+*i.*). '**harmony** *n.* гармо́ния, созву́чие, согла́сие.

harness ['hɑːnɪs] *n.* у́пряжь, сбру́я; *v.t.* за-, в-, пряга́ть *impf.*, за-, в-, пря́чь (-ягу́, -яжёшь; -я́г, -ягла́) *pf.*; (*fig.*) испо́льзовать *impf.* & *pf.* как исто́чник эне́ргии.

harp [hɑːp] *n.* а́рфа; *v.i.* игра́ть *impf.* на а́рфе; ~ **on** распространя́ться *impf.*, распространи́ться *pf.* о+*p.* **harpist** *n.* арфи́ст, ~ка.

harpoon [hɑː'puːn] *n.* гарпу́н (-а́), острога́.

harpsichord ['hɑːpsɪˌkɔːd] *n.* клавеси́н.

harpy ['hɑːpɪ] *n.* га́рпия; (*fig.*) хи́щник.

harridan ['hærɪd(ə)n] *n.* ве́дьма, карга́.

harrow ['hærəʊ] *n.* борона́ (*a.* -ону; *pl.* -оны, -о́н, -она́м); *v.t.* борони́ть *impf.*, вз~ *pf.*; (*torment*) терза́ть *impf.*

harry ['hærɪ] *v.t.* (*ravage*) опустоша́ть *impf.*, опустоши́ть *pf.*; (*worry*) трево́жить *impf.*, вс~ *pf.*

harsh [hɑːʃ] *adj.* гру́бый (груб, -а́, -о); (*sound*) ре́зкий (-зок, -зка́, -зко); (*cruel*) суро́вый.

hart [hɑːt] *n.* оле́нь *m.*

harvest ['hɑːvɪst] *n.* жа́тва, сбор (плодо́в); (*yield*) урожа́й; (*fig.*) плоды́ *m.pl.*; *v.t.* & *abs.* собира́ть *impf.*, собра́ть (соберу́, -рёшь; собра́л, -а́, -о) *pf.* (урожа́й).

hash [hæʃ] *n.* ру́бленое мя́со; (*medley*) мешани́на; **make a ~ of** напу́тать *pf.* +*a.*, в+*p.*; *v.t.* руби́ть (-блю́, -бишь) *impf.*

hasp [hɑːsp] *n.* застёжка.

hassock ['hæsək] *n.* (*cushion*) поду́шечка; (*tuft of grass*) ко́чка.

haste [heɪst] *n.* поспе́шность, торопли́вость, спе́шка. **hasten** ['heɪs(ə)n] *v.i.* спеши́ть *impf.*, по~ *pf.*; *v.t.* & *i.* торопи́ть(ся) (-плю́(сь), -пишь(ся)) *impf.*, по~ *pf.*; *v.t.* ускоря́ть *impf.*, ускóрить *pf.* **hasty** *adj.* (*hurried*) поспе́шный; (*rash*) опроме́тчивый; (*quick-tempered*) вспы́льчивый.

hat [hæt] *n.* шля́па; **top ~** цили́ндр.

hatch[1] [hætʃ], **-way** *n.* (*naut.*) люк.

hatch[2] [hætʃ] *n.* (*brood*) вы́водок (-дка); *v.t.* выси́живать *impf.*, вы́сидеть (-ижу, -идишь) *pf.*; *v.i.* вылу́пливаться, вылупля́ться *impf.*, вы́лупиться *pf.*

hatchback ['hætʃbæk] *n.* пятидве́рная маши́на.

hatchet ['hætʃɪt] *n.* топо́рик.

hate [heɪt] *n.* не́нависть; *v.t.* ненави́деть (-и́жу, -и́дишь) *impf.* **hateful** *adj.* ненави́стный. **hatred** *n.* не́нависть.

haughty ['hɔːtɪ] *adj.* надме́нный (-нен, -нна), высокоме́рный.

haul [hɔːl] *n.* добы́ча; (*distance*) езда́; *v.t.* тяну́ть (-ну́, -нешь) *impf.*; таска́ть *indet.*, тащи́ть (-щу́, -щишь) *det.*; (*transport*) перевози́ть (-ожу́, -о́зишь) *impf.*, перевезти́ (-езу́, -езёшь; -ёз, -езла́) *pf.*

haunch [hɔːntʃ] *n.* бедро́ (*pl.* бёдра, -дер, -драм), ля́жка.

haunt [hɔːnt] *n.* ча́сто посеща́емое ме́сто; (*of criminals*) прито́н; *v.t.* (*frequent*) ча́сто посеща́ть *impf.*

have [hæv, həv] *v.t.* име́ть *impf.*; **I ~** (*possess*) у меня́ (есть; был, -а́, -о)+*nom.*; **I ~ not** у меня́ нет (*past* не́ было)+*g.*; **I ~ (got) to** я до́лжен (-жна́)+*inf.*; **you had better** вам лу́чше бы+*inf.*; **~ on** (*wear*) быть оде́тым в+*p.*

haven ['heɪv(ə)n] *n.* га́вань; (*refuge*) убе́жище.

haversack ['hævəˌsæk] *n.* ра́нец (-нца).

havoc ['hævək] *n.* (*devastation*) опустоше́ние; (*disorder*) беспоря́док (-дка).

hawk[1] [hɔːk] *n.* (*bird*) я́стреб (*pl.* -ы & -а́).

hawk[2] [hɔːk] *v.t.* (*trade*) торгова́ть *impf.* вразно́с+*i.* **hawker** *n.* разно́счик.

hawser ['hɔːzə(r)] *n.* трос.

hawthorn ['hɔːθɔːn] *n.* боя́рышник.

hay [heɪ] *n.* се́но; **make ~** коси́ть (кошу́, ко́сишь) *impf.*, с~ *pf.* се́но; **~ fever** се́нная лихора́дка. **haycock** *n.* копна́ (*pl.* -пны, -пён, -пна́м). **hayloft** *n.* сенова́л. **haystack** *n.* стог (*loc.* -е & -у́; *pl.* -а́).

hazard ['hæzəd] *n.* риск; *v.t.* рискова́ть *impf.*+*i.* **hazardous** *adj.* риско́ванный (-ан, -анна).

haze [heɪz] *n.* тума́н, ды́мка.

hazel ['heɪz(ə)l] *n.* лещи́на. **hazelnut** *n.* лесно́й оре́х.

hazy ['heɪzɪ] *adj.* (*misty*) тума́нный (-нен, -нна); (*vague*) сму́тный (-тен, -тна́, -тно).

H-bomb ['eɪtʃbɒm] *n.* водоро́дная бо́мба.

he [hiː, hɪ] *pron.* он (его́, ему́, им, о нём).

head [hed] *n.* голова́ (*a.* -ову; *pl.* -овы, -о́в, -ова́м); (*mind*) ум (-а́); (*~ of cattle*) голова́ скота́; (*~ of coin*) лицева́я сторона́ (*a.* -ону) моне́ты; **~s or tails?** орёл и́ли ре́шка?; (*chief*) глава́ (*pl.* -вы) *m.*, нача́льник; *attr.* гла́вный; *v.t.* (*lead*) возглавля́ть *impf.*, возгла́вить *pf.*; (*~ chapter*) озагла́вливать *impf.*, озагла́вить *pf.*; *v.i.*: **~ for** направля́ться *impf.*, напра́виться *pf.* в, на, +*a.*, к+*d.* **headache** *n.* головна́я боль. **headdress** *n.* головно́й убо́р. **heading** *n.* (*title*) заголо́вок (-вка). **headland** *n.* мыс (*loc.* -е & -у́; *pl.* мысы́). **headlight** *n.* фа́ра. **headline** *n.* заголо́вок (-вка). **headlong** *adj.* (*precipitate*) опроме́тчивый; *adv.* стремгла́в. **head'master, -'mistress** *n.* дире́ктор (*pl.* -а́) шко́лы. **headphone** *n.* нау́шник. **head'quarters** *n.* штаб-кварти́ра. **headstone** *n.* надгро́бный ка́мень (-мня; *pl.* -мни, -мне́й) *m.* **headstrong** *adj.* своево́льный. **headway** *n.* движе́ние вперёд. **heady** *adj.* стреми́тельный; (*liquor*) хмельно́й (-лён, -льна́).

heal [hiːl] *v.t.* излечи́вать *impf.*, излечи́ть (-чу́, -чишь) *pf.*; исцеля́ть *impf.*, исцели́ть *pf.*; *v.i.* заживá́ть *impf.*, зажи́ть (-ивёт; за́жил, -а́, -о) *pf.* **healing** *adj.* целе́бный.

health [helθ] *n.* здоро́вье; **~ foods** натура́льная пи́ща; **~ food shop** диетети́ческий магази́н. **healthy** *adj.* здоро́вый; (*beneficial*) поле́зный.

heap [hiːp] *n.* ку́ча, гру́да; *v.t.* нагроможда́ть *impf.*, награмозди́ть *pf.*; (*load*) нагружа́ть *impf.*, нагрузи́ть (-ужу́, -у́зишь) *pf.* (**with** +*i.*).

hear [hɪə(r)] *v.t.* слы́шать (-шу, -шишь) *impf.*, у~ *pf.*; (*listen to*) слу́шать *impf.*, по~ *pf.*; (*learn*) узнава́ть (-наю́, -наёшь) *impf.*, узна́ть *pf.*; **~ out** выслу́шивать *impf.*, вы́слушать *pf.* **hearing** *n.* слух; (*limit*) преде́л слы́шимости; (*leg.*) слуша́ние, разбо́р. **hearsay** *n.* слух.

hearken ['hɑːkən] *v.i.* внима́ть *impf.*, внять (*past only*: внял, -а́, -о) *pf.* (**to** +*d.*).

hearse [hɜːs] *n.* катафа́лк.

heart [hɑːt] *n.* (*organ*; *fig.*) се́рдце (*pl.* -дца́, -де́ц, -дца́м); (*fig.*) душа́ (*a.* -шу; *pl.* -ши); (*courage*) му́жество; (*of tree etc.*) сердцеви́на; (*essence*) суть; *pl.* (*cards*) че́рви (-ве́й) *pl.*; **at ~** в глубине́ души́; **by ~** наизу́сть; **~ attack** серде́чный при́ступ. **heartburn** *n.* изжо́га. **hearten** *v.t.* ободря́ть *impf.*, ободри́ть *pf.* **heartfelt** *adj.* и́скренний (-нен, -нна, -нно & -нне), серде́чный. **heartless**

adj. бессерде́чный. **heart-rending** *adj.* душераздира́ющий. **hearty** *adj.* (*cordial*) серде́чный; (*vigorous*) здоро́вый.
hearth [hɑ:θ] *n.* оча́г (-а́).
heat [hi:t] *n.* жар (*loc.* -е & -у́), жа́ра; (*phys.*) теплота́; (*of feeling*) пыл (*loc.* -у́); (*sport*) забе́г, зае́зд; *v.t.* & *i.* нагрева́ть(ся) *impf.*, нагре́ть(ся) *pf.*; *v.t.* топи́ть (-плю́, -пишь) *impf.* **heater** *n.* нагрева́тель *m.* **heating** *n.* отопле́ние.
heath [hi:θ] *n.* пу́стошь.
heathen ['hi:ð(ə)n] *n.* язы́чник; *adj.* язы́ческий.
heather ['heðə(r)] *n.* ве́реск.
heave [hi:v] *v.t.* (*lift*) поднима́ть *impf.*, подня́ть (подниму́, -мешь; по́дня́л, -а́, -о) *pf.*; (*pull*) тяну́ть (-ну́, -нешь) *impf.*, по~ *pf.*
heaven ['hev(ə)n] *n.* не́бо, рай (*loc.* раю́); *pl.* небеса́ *nt.pl.* **heavenly** *adj.* небе́сный, боже́ственный.
heaviness ['hevɪnɪs] *n.* тя́жесть. **heavy** *adj.* тяжёлый (-л, -ла́); (*strong*) си́льный (си́лён, -льна́, -льно, си́льны́); (*abundant*) оби́льный; (*gloomy*) мра́чный (-чен, -чна́, -чно); (*sea*) бу́рный (-рен, бу́рна́, -рно). **heavyweight** *n.* тяжелове́с.
Hebrew ['hi:bru:] *n.* древнеевре́йский язы́к (-а́); *adj.* (древне)евре́йский.
heckle ['hek(ə)l] *v.t.* препира́ться *impf.* с+*i.*
hectare ['hekteə(r), -tɑ:(r)] *n.* гекта́р.
hectic ['hektɪk] *adj.* лихора́дочный.
hedge [hedʒ] *n.* (*fence*) жива́я и́згородь; (*barrier*) прегра́да; *v.t.* огора́живать *impf.*, огороди́ть (-ожу́, -о́ди́шь) *pf.*; *v.i.* верте́ться (-рчу́сь, -ртишься) *impf.* **hedgerow** *n.* шпале́ра. **hedge-sparrow** *n.* лесна́я завиру́шка.
hedgehog ['hedʒhɒg] *n.* ёж (-а́).
heed [hi:d] *n.* внима́ние; *v.t.* обраща́ть *impf.*, обрати́ть (-ащу́, -ати́шь) *pf.* внима́ние на+*a.* **heedful** *adj.* внима́тельный. **heedless** *adj.* небре́жный.
heel [hi:l] *n.* (*of foot*) пята́ (*pl.* -ты, -т, -та́м); (*of foot*, *sock*) пя́тка; (*of shoe*) каблу́к (-а́).
hefty ['heftɪ] *adj.* дю́жий (дюж, -а́, -о).
hegemony [hɪ'dʒemənɪ, -'gemənɪ] *n.* гегемо́ния.
heifer ['hefə(r)] *n.* тёлка.
height [haɪt] *n.* высота́ (*pl.* -ты), вышина́ (*no pl.*); (*elevation*) возвы́шенность. **heighten** *v.t.* повыша́ть *impf.*, повы́сить *pf.*; (*strengthen*) уси́ливать *impf.*, уси́лить *pf.*
heinous ['heɪnəs, 'hi:nəs] *adj.* гну́сный (-сен, -сна́, -сно).
heir [eə(r)] *n.* насле́дник. **heiress** *n.* насле́дница. **heirloom** ['eəlu:m] *n.* фами́льная вещь (*pl.* -щи, -ще́й).
helicopter ['helɪˌkɒptə(r)] *n.* вертолёт.
heliograph ['hi:lɪəˌgrɑ:f] *n.* гелио́граф. **heliotrope** ['hi:lɪəˌtrəʊp, 'hel-] *n.* гелиотро́п.
helium ['hi:lɪəm] *n.* ге́лий.
helix ['hi:lɪks] *n.* спира́ль.
hell [hel] *n.* ад (*loc.* -у́). **hellish** *adj.* а́дский.
hello, hallo [hə'ləʊ] *int.* приве́т!; (*telephone*) алло́!
helm [helm] *n.* руль (-ля́) *m.*, корми́ло (правле́ния). **helmsman** *n.* рулево́й *sb.*; (*fig.*) ко́рмчий *sb.*
helmet ['helmɪt] *n.* шлем.
help [help] *n.* по́мощь; (*person*) помо́щник, -ица; *v.t.* помога́ть *impf.*, помо́чь (-огу́, -о́жешь; -о́г, -огла́) *pf.*+*d.*; (*with negative*) не мочь (могу́, мо́жешь; мог, -ла́) *impf.* не+*inf.*; ~ **o.s.** брать (беру́, -рёшь; брал, -а́, -о) *impf.*, взять (возьму́, -мёшь; взял, -а́, -о) *pf.* себе́. **helpful** *adj.* поле́зный. **helping** *n.* (*of food*) по́рция. **helpless** *adj.* беспо́мощный.
Helsinki ['helsɪŋkɪ, hel'sɪŋkɪ] *n.* Хе́льсинки *m.indecl.*
helter-skelter [ˌheltə'skeltə(r)] *adv.* как попа́ло.
hem [hem] *n.* рубе́ц (-бца́), кайма́ (*g.pl.* каём); *v.t.* подруба́ть *impf.*, подруби́ть (-блю́, -бишь) *pf.*; ~ **about, in** окружа́ть *impf.*, окружи́ть *pf.*
hemisphere ['hemɪˌsfɪə(r)] *n.* полуша́рие.
hemlock ['hemlɒk] *n.* болиголо́в.
hemp [hemp] *n.* (*plant*) конопля́; (*fibre*) пенька́. **hempen** *adj.* конопля́ный; пенько́вый.
hen [hen] *n.* (*female bird*) са́мка; (*domestic fowl*) ку́рица (*pl.* ку́ры, кур). **henbane** *n.* белена́. **hen-coop** *n.* куря́тник. **henpecked** *adj.*: **be** ~ быть у жены́ под башмако́м, под каблуко́м.
hence [hens] *adv.* (*from here*) отсю́да; (*from this time*) с э́тих пор; (*as a result*) сле́довательно. **hence'forth, hence'forward** *adv.* отны́не.
henchman ['hentʃmən] *n.* приве́рженец (-нца).
henna ['henə] *n.* хна.
her [hɜ:(r), hə(r)] *poss. pron.* её; свой (-оя́, -оё; -ои́).
herald ['her(ə)ld] *n.* геро́льд, предве́стник; *v.t.* возвеща́ть *impf.*, возвести́ть *pf.*
herb [hɜ:b] *n.* трава́ (*pl.* -вы). **herbaceous** [hɜ:'beɪʃəs] *adj.* травяни́стый. **herbal** *adj.* травяно́й. **herbivorous** [ˌhɜ:'bɪvərəs] *adj.* травоя́дный.
herd [hɜ:d] *n.* ста́до (*pl.* -да́); (*of people*) толпа́ (*pl.* -пы); *v.i.* ходи́ть (-ит) *impf.* ста́дом; (*people*) толпи́ться *impf.*, с~ *pf.*; *v.t.* собира́ть *impf.*, собра́ть (соберу́, -рёшь; собра́л, -а́, -о) *pf.* в ста́до. **herdsman** *n.* пасту́х (-а́).
here [hɪə(r)] *adv.* (*position*) здесь, тут; (*direction*) сюда́; ~ **is ...** вот (+*nom.*); ~ **and there** там и сям. **herea'bout(s)** *adv.* побли́зости. **here'after** *adv.* в бу́дущем. **here'by** *adv.* э́тим; таки́м о́бразом. **hereu'pon** *adv.* (*in consequence*) всле́дствие э́того; (*after*) по́сле э́того. **here'with** *adv.* при сём, при э́том, че́рез э́то.
hereditary [hɪ'redɪtərɪ] *adj.* насле́дственный.
heredity [hɪ'redɪtɪ] *n.* насле́дственность.
heresy ['herəsɪ] *n.* е́ресь. **heretic** *n.* ерети́к (-а́). **he'retical** *adj.* ерети́ческий.
heritable ['herɪtəb(ə)l] *adj.* насле́дуемый.

heritage ['herɪtɪdʒ] *n.* наслéдство, наслéдие.
hermaphrodite [hɜː'mæfrə,daɪt] *n.* гермафродúт.
hermetic [hɜː'metɪk] *adj.* герметúческий.
hermit ['hɜːmɪt] *n.* отшéльник, пустынник. **hermitage** *n.* пýстынь; приют (отшéльника, пустынника).
hernia ['hɜːnɪə] *n.* грыжа.
hero ['hɪərəʊ] *n.* герóй. **heroic** [hɪ'rəʊɪk] *adj.* героúческий. **heroine** ['herəʊɪn] *n.* героúня. **heroism** ['herəʊ,ɪz(ə)m] *n.* героúзм.
heron ['herən] *n.* цáпля (*g.pl.* -пель).
herpes ['hɜːpiːz] *n.* лишáй (-ая́).
herring ['herɪŋ] *n.* сельдь (*pl.* -ди, -дéй), селёдка. **herring-bone** *n.* ёлочка; (*attr.*) ёлочкой, в ёлочку.
hers [hɜːz] *poss. pron.* её; свой (-оя́, -оё; -оú).
herself [hə'self] *pron.* (*emph.*) (онá) самá (-мóй, *a.* -мý); (*refl.*) себя́ (себé, собóй); -ся (*suffixed to v.t.*).
hertz [hɜːts] *n.* герц (*g.pl.* -ц).
hesitant ['hezɪt(ə)nt] *adj.* нерешúтельный. **hesitate** *v.i.* колебáться (-блюсь, -блешься) *impf.*, по~ *pf.*; (*in speech*) запинáться *impf.*, запнýться *pf.* **hesi'tation** *n.* колебáние, нерешúтельность.
hessian ['hesɪən] *n.* мешковúна.
heterogeneous [,hetərəʊ'dʒiːnɪəs] *adj.* разнорóдный. **heterosexual** *n.* гетеросексуалúст, ~ка; *adj.* гетеросексуáльный.
hew [hjuː] *v.t.* рубúть (-блю́, -бишь) *impf.*
hexa- [heksə] *in comb.* шести..., гéкса... . **hexagon** ['heksəgən] *n.* шестиугóльник. **hexameter** [hek'sæmɪtə(r)] *n.* гекзáметр.
hey [heɪ] *int.* эй!
heyday ['heɪdeɪ] *n.* расцвéт.
hi [haɪ] *int.* эй!; привéт!
hiatus [haɪ'eɪtəs] *n.* пробéл; (*ling.*) зия́ние.
hibernate ['haɪbə,neɪt] *v.i.* находúться (-ожýсь, -óдишься) *impf.* в зúмней спя́чке; зимовáть *impf.*, пере~, про~ *pf.* **hiber'nation** *n.* зúмняя спя́чка, зимóвка.
hiccough, hiccup ['hɪkʌp] *v.i.* икáть *impf.*, икнýть *pf.*; *n.*: *pl.* икóта.
hide[1] [haɪd] *n.* (*animal's skin*) шкýра, кóжа.
hide[2] [haɪd] *v.t.* & *i.* (*conceal*) пря́тать(ся) (-я́чу(сь), -я́чешь(ся)) *impf.*, с~ *pf.*; скрывáть(ся) *impf.*, скрыть(ся) (скрóю(сь), -óешь(ся)) *pf.*
hideous ['hɪdɪəs] *adj.* отвратúтельный, безобрáзный.
hiding ['haɪdɪŋ] *n.* (*flogging*) пóрка.
hierarchy ['haɪə,rɑːkɪ] *n.* иерáрхия.
hieroglyph ['haɪərəglɪf] *n.* иерóглиф. **hiero'glyphic** *adj.* иероглифúческий.
higgledy-piggledy [,hɪgəldɪ'pɪgəldɪ] *adv.* как придётся.
high [haɪ] *adj.* высóкий (-óк, -окá, -óкó); (*elevated*) возвышенный; (*higher*) высший; (*intense*) сúльный (сúлён, -льнá, -льно, сúльны́); **~er education** высшее образовáние; **~ fidelity** высóкая тóчность воспроизведéния; **~ jump** прыжóк (-жкá) в высотý. **high-class** *adj.* высококáчественный. **high-handed** *adj.* повелúтельный. **highland(s)** *n.* гóрная странá. **highly** *adv.* в высшей стéпени. **highly-strung** *adj.* чувствúтельный, нéрвный (-вен, нéрвнá, -вно). **high-minded** *adj.* благорóдный. **highness** *n.* возвышенность; (*title*) высóчество. **high-pitched** *adj.* высóкий (-óк, -окá, -óкó). **highway** *n.* большáя дорóга, шоссé *nt.indecl.* **highwayman** *n.* разбóйник (с большóй дорóги)
hijack ['haɪdʒæk] *v.t.* похищáть *impf.*, похитúть (-úщу, -úтишь) *pf.* **hijacker** *n.* похитúтель *m.*
hike [haɪk] *n.* похóд.
hilarious [hɪ'leərɪəs] *adj.* весёлый (вéсел, -á, -о, вéселы́). **hilarity** [hɪ'lærɪtɪ] *n.* весéлье.
hill [hɪl] *n.* холм (-á). **hillock** *n.* хóлмик. **hilly** *adj.* холмúстый.
hilt [hɪlt] *n.* рукоя́тка.
Himalayas [,hɪmə'leɪəz] *n.* Гималáи (-ев) *pl.*
himself [hɪm'self] *pron.* (*emph.*) (он) сам (-огó, -омý, -úм, -óм); (*refl.*) себя́ (себé, собóй); -ся (*suffixed to v.t.*).
hind[1] [haɪnd] *n.* (*deer*) сáмка (благорóдного оленя́.
hind[2] [haɪnd] *adj.* (*rear*) зáдний. **hindmost** *adj.* сáмый зáдний.
hinder ['hɪndə(r)] *v.t.* мешáть *impf.*, по~ *pf.*+*d.* **hindrance** *n.* помéха, препя́тствие.
Hindu ['hɪnduː, -'duː] *n.* индýс; *adj.* индýсский.
hinge [hɪndʒ] *n.* шарнúр, пéтля (*g.pl.* -тель); *v.t.* прикрепля́ть *impf.*, прикрепúть *pf.* на пéтлях; *v.i.* вращáться *impf.* на пéтлях; ~ **on** (*fig.*) завúсеть (-сит) *impf.* от+*g.*
hint [hɪnt] *n.* намёк; *v.i.* намекáть *impf.*, намекнýть *pf.* (**at** на+*a.*)
hinterland ['hɪntə,lænd] *n.* глубинá страны́.
hip[1] [hɪp] *n.* (*anat.*) бедрó (*pl.* бёдра, -дер, -драм).
hip[2] [hɪp] *n.* (*fruit*) я́года шипóвника.
hippopotamus [,hɪpə'pɒtəməs] *n.* гиппопотáм.
hire ['haɪə(r)] *n.* наём (нáйма), прокáт; *v.t.* нанимáть *impf.*, наня́ть (наймý, -мёшь; нáнял, -á, -о) *pf.*; брать (берý, -рёшь; брал, -á, -о) *impf.*, взять (возьмý, -мёшь; взял, -á, -о) *pf.* напрокáт; **~ out** отдавáть (-даю́, -даёшь) *impf.*, отдáть (-áм, -áшь, -áст, -адúм; óтдал, -á, -о) *pf.* внаймы́, напрокáт.
hireling ['haɪəlɪŋ] *n.* наёмник.
hire-purchase [,haɪə'pɜːtʃɪs] *n.* покýпка в рассрóчку.
hirsute ['hɜːsjuːt] *adj.* волосáтый.
his [hɪz] *poss. pron.* егó; свой (-оя́, -оё; -оú).
hiss [hɪs] *n.* шипéние, свист; *v.i.* шипéть (-плю́, -пúшь) *impf.*; свистéть (-ищý, -истúшь) *impf.*; *v.t.* освúстывать *impf.*, освистáть (-ищý, -úщешь) *pf.*
historian [hɪ'stɔːrɪən] *n.* истóрик. **historic(al)** [hɪ'stɒrɪk(ə)l] *adj.* историчéский. **history** ['hɪstərɪ] *n.* истóрия.
histrionic [,hɪstrɪ'ɒnɪk] *adj.* театрáльный.

hit [hɪt] *n.* (*blow*) уда́р; (*on target*) попада́ние (в цель); (*success*) успе́х; *v.t.* (*strike*) ударя́ть *impf.*, уда́рить *pf.*; (*target*) попада́ть *impf.*, попа́сть (-аду́, -адёшь; -а́л) *pf.* (в цель); ~ **(up)on** находи́ть (-ожу́, -о́дишь) *impf.*, найти́ (найду́, -дёшь; нашёл, -шла́) *pf.*

hitch [hɪtʃ] *n.* (*jerk*) толчо́к (-чка́); (*knot*) у́зел (узла́); (*stoppage*) заде́ржка; *v.t.* (*move*) подта́лкивать *impf.*, подтолкну́ть *pf.*; (*fasten*) зацепля́ть *impf.*, зацепи́ть (-плю́, -пишь) *pf.*; привя́зывать *impf.*, привяза́ть (-яжу́, -я́жешь) *pf.*; ~ **up** подтя́гивать *impf.*, подтяну́ть (-ну́, -нешь) *pf.* **hitch-hike** *v.i.* голосова́ть *impf.* **hitchhiker** *n.* автосто́повец (-вца).

hither ['hɪðə(r)] *adv.* сюда́. **hither'to** *adv.* до сих пор.

HIV *abbr.* (*of* ***human immunodeficiency virus***) ВИЧ, (***ви́рус иммунодефици́та челове́ка***). **HIV-positive** *adj.* инфици́рованный ВИЧ.

hive [haɪv] *n.* у́лей (у́лья).

hoard [hɔːd] *n.* запа́с; *v.t.* накопля́ть *impf.*, накопи́ть (-плю́, -пишь) *pf.*

hoarding ['hɔːdɪŋ] *n.* рекла́мный щит (-а́).

hoar-frost [hɔː(r)] *n.* и́ней.

hoarse [hɔːs] *adj.* хри́плый (-л, -ла́, -ло).

hoary ['hɔːrɪ] *adj.* седо́й (сед, -а́, -о).

hoax [həʊks] *n.* мистифика́ция; *v.t.* мистифици́ровать *impf.* & *pf.*

hobble ['hɒb(ə)l] *n.* (*for horse*) (ко́нские) пу́ты (-т) *pl.*; *v.i.* прихра́мывать *impf.*; *v.t.* (*horse*) трено́жить *impf.*, с~ *pf.*

hobby ['hɒbɪ] *n.* конёк (-нька́), хо́бби *nt.indecl.*

hobnail ['hɒbneɪl] *n.* сапо́жный гвоздь (-дя́; *pl.* -ди, -де́й) *m.*

hob-nob ['hɒbnɒb] *v.i.* пить (пью, пьёшь) *impf.* вме́сте; ~ **with** якша́ться *impf.* с+*i.*

hock [hɒk] *n.* (*wine*) рейнве́йн (-а(у)).

hockey ['hɒkɪ] *n.* травяно́й хокке́й; **ice** ~ хокке́й (с ша́йбой); ~ **stick** клю́шка.

hod [hɒd] *n.* (*for bricks*) лото́к (-тка́); (*for coal*) ведёрко (*pl.* -рки, -рок, -ркам).

hoe [həʊ] *n.* моты́га; *v.t.* моты́жить *impf.*

hog [hɒg] *n.* бо́ров (*pl.* -ы, -о́в), свинья́ (*pl.* -ньи, -не́й, -ньям).

hoist [hɔɪst] *n.* подъёмник; *v.t.* поднима́ть *impf.*, подня́ть (-ниму́, -ни́мешь; по́днял, -а́, -о) *pf.*

hold[1] [həʊld] *n.* (*naut.*) трюм.

hold[2] [həʊld] *n.* (*grasp*) хва́тка; (*influence*) влия́ние (**on** на+*a.*); *v.t.* (*grasp*) держа́ть (-жу́, -жишь) *impf.*; (*contain*) вмеща́ть *impf.*, вмести́ть *pf.*; (*possess*) владе́ть *impf.*+*i.*; (*conduct*) проводи́ть (-ожу́, -о́дишь) *impf.*, провести́ (-еду́, -едёшь; -ёл, -ела́) *pf.*; (*consider*) счита́ть *impf.*, счесть (сочту́, -тёшь; счёл, сочла́) *pf.* (+*a.* & *i.*, за+*a.*); *v.i.* держа́ться (-жу́сь, -жишься) *impf.*; (*continue*) продолжа́ться *impf.*, продо́лжиться *pf.*; ~ **back** сде́рживать(ся) *impf.*, сдержа́ть(ся) (-жу́(сь), -жишь(ся)) *pf.*; ~ **forth** разглаго́льствовать *impf.*; ~ **out** (*stretch out*) протя́гивать *impf.*, протяну́ть (-ну́, -нешь) *pf.*; (*resist*) не сдава́ться (сдаю́сь, сдаёшься) *impf.*; ~ **over** (*postpone*) откла́дывать *impf.*, отложи́ть (-жу́, -жишь) *pf.*; ~ **up** (*support*) подде́рживать *impf.*, поддержа́ть (-жу́, -жишь) *pf.*; (*display*) выставля́ть *impf.*, вы́ставить *pf.*; (*impede*) заде́рживать *impf.*, задержа́ть (-жу́, -жишь) *pf.* **holdall** *n.* портпле́д. **hold-up** *n.* (*robbery*) налёт; (*delay*) заде́ржка.

hole [həʊl] *n.* дыра́ (*pl.* -ры), я́ма, отве́рстие; (*animal's*) нора́ (*pl.* -ры); **full of ~s** дыря́вый; **pick ~s in** придира́ться *impf.*, придра́ться (придеру́сь, -рёшься; придра́лся, -ала́сь, -а́ло́сь) *pf.* к+*d.*; *v.t.* (*make a ~ in*) продыря́вливать *impf.*, продыря́вить *pf.*

holiday ['hɒlɪˌdeɪ, -dɪ] *n.* (*festival*) пра́здник; (*from work*) о́тпуск; *pl.* кани́кулы (-л) *pl.*; **on** ~ в о́тпуске, -ку́.

holiness ['həʊlɪnɪs] *n.* свя́тость; (**H~**, *title*) святе́йшество.

Holland ['hɒlənd] *n.* Голла́ндия.

hollow ['hɒləʊ] *n.* впа́дина; (*valley*) лощи́на; (*in tree*) дупло́ (*pl.* -пла, -пел, -плам); *adj.* пусто́й (пуст, -а́, -о, пу́сты́), по́лый; (*sunken*) впа́лый; (*sound*) глухо́й (глух, -а́, -о); *v.t.* (~ *out*) выда́лбливать *impf.*, вы́долбить *pf.*

holly ['hɒlɪ] *n.* остроли́ст.

holm [həʊm], **-oak** *n.* ка́менный дуб (*loc.* -е &-у́; *pl.* -ы́).

holocaust ['hɒləˌkɔːst] *n.* (*sacrifice*) всесожже́ние; (*destruction*) уничтоже́ние (в огне́).

holster ['həʊlstə(r)] *n.* кобура́.

holy ['həʊlɪ] *adj.* свято́й (свят, -а́, -о), свяще́нный (-е́н, -е́нна); **H~ Week** Страстна́я неде́ля.

homage ['hɒmɪdʒ] *n.* почте́ние, уваже́ние; **do, pay, ~ to** отдава́ть (-даю́, -даёшь) *impf.*, отда́ть (-а́м, -а́шь, -а́ст, -ади́м; о́тдал, -а́, -о) *pf.* до́лжное+*d.*

home [həʊm] *n.* дом (-а(у); *pl.* -а́); (*native land*) ро́дина; **at ~** до́ма; **feel at ~** чу́вствовать *impf.* себя́ как до́ма; *adj.* дома́шний, родно́й; ~ **economics** домово́дство; **H~ Affairs** вну́тренние дела́ *nt.pl.*; *adv.* (*direction*) домо́й; (*position*) до́ма; (*as aimed*) в цель. **homeland** *n.* ро́дина. **homeless** *adj.* бездо́мный. **home-made** *adj.* дома́шний, самоде́льный. **homesick** *adj.*: **to be ~** тосковать *impf.* по ро́дине. **homewards** *adv.* домо́й, восвоя́си.

homely ['həʊmlɪ] *adj.* просто́й (прост, -а́, -о, про́сты́).

homoeopath ['həʊmɪəʊˌpæθ, 'hɒmɪ-] *n.* гомеопа́т. **homoeo'pathic** *adj.* гомеопати́ческий. **homoeopathy** [ˌhəʊmɪ'ɒpəθɪ, ˌhɒmɪ-] *n.* гомеопа́тия.

homicide ['hɒmɪˌsaɪd] *n.* (*person*) уби́йца *c.g.*; (*action*) уби́йство.

homily ['hɒmɪlɪ] *n.* про́поведь, поуче́ние.

homogeneous [ˌhəʊməʊ'dʒiːnɪəs, ˌhɒməʊ-] *adj.* однoрóдный.

homonym ['hɒmənɪm] *n.* омóним.

homosexual [ˌhəʊməʊ'seksjʊəl, ˌhɒm-] *n.* гомосексуали́ст; *adj.* гомосексуáльный.

hone [həʊn] *n.* точи́льный кáмень (-мня; *pl.* -мни, -мнéй) *m.*; *v.t.* точи́ть (-чý, -чишь) *impf.*, на~ *pf.*

honest ['ɒnɪst] *n.* (*fair*) чéстный (-тен, -тнá, -тно); (*righteous*) правди́вый; (*sincere*) и́скренний (-нен, -нна, -нне & -нно). **honesty** *n.* чéстность; правди́вость; и́скренность.

honey ['hʌnɪ] *n.* мёд (-а(у), *loc.* -ý & -е; *pl.* -ы́). **honeycomb** *n.* медóвые сóты (-тов) *pl.*; *attr.* сóтовый, сотови́дный. **honeymoon** *n.* медóвый мéсяц; *v.i.* проводи́ть (-ожý, -óдишь) *impf.*, провести́ (-едý, -едёшь; -ёл, -елá) *pf.* медóвый мéсяц. **honeysuckle** *n.* жи́молость.

honk [hɒŋk] *v.i.* гоготáть (-очý, -óчешь) *impf.*; (*siren etc.*) гудéть (-ди́т) *impf.*

honorarium [ˌɒnə'reərɪəm] *n.* гонорáр.

honorary ['ɒnərərɪ] *adj.* почётный.

honour ['ɒnə(r)] *n.* честь, почёт; *pl.* пóчести *f.pl.*; **(up)on my** ~ чéстное слóво; *v.t.* (*respect*) почитáть *impf.*; (*confer*) удостáивать *impf.*, удостóить *pf.* (**with** +*g.*). **honourable** *adj.* чéстный (-тен, -тнá, -тно); (*respected*) почтéнный (-нен, -нна).

hood [hʊd] *n.* капюшóн.

hoodlum ['huːdləm] *n.* громи́ла *m.*

hoodwink ['hʊdwɪŋk] *v.t.* втирáть *impf.*, втерéть (вотрý, -рёшь; втёр) *pf.* очки́+*d.*

hoof [huːf] *n.* копы́то.

hook [hʊk] *n.* крюк (-á, *loc.* -é & -ý), крючóк (-чкá); (*trap*) ловýшка; (*cutting instrument*) серп (-á); *v.t.* зацеплять *impf.*, зацепи́ть (-плю́, -пишь) *pf.*; (*catch*) лови́ть (-влю́, -вишь) *impf.*, поймáть *pf.*

hookah ['hʊkə] *n.* кальян.

hooligan ['huːlɪgən] *n.* хулигáн.

hoop [huːp] *n.* óбруч (*pl.* -и, -éй).

hoot [huːt] *v.i.* кричáть (-чý, -чи́шь) *impf.*, кри́кнуть *pf.*; (*owl*) ýхать *impf.*, ýхнуть *pf.*; (*horn*) гудéть (-ди́т) *impf.*

hoover ['huːvə(r)] *n.* (*propr.*) пылесóс; *v.t.* пылесóсить (-сю, -сишь) *impf.*, про~ *pf.*

hop¹ [hɒp] *n.* (*plant*; *collect. hops*) хмель (-ля(-лю)) *m.*

hop² [hɒp] *n.* (*jump*) прыжóк (-жкá); *v.i.* пры́гать *impf.*, пры́гнуть *pf.* (на однóй ногé).

hope [həʊp] *n.* надéжда; *v.i.* надéяться (-éюсь, -éешься) *impf.*, по~ *pf.* (**for** на+*a.*) **hopeful** *adj.* (*hoping*) надéющийся; (*promising*) многообещáющий. **hopeless** *adj.* безнадёжный.

hopper ['hɒpə(r)] *n.* бýнкер (*pl.* -á & -ы); (*rail.*) хóппер.

horde [hɔːd] *n.* (*hist.*, *fig.*) ордá (*pl.* -ды).

horizon [hə'raɪz(ə)n] *n.* горизóнт; (*fig.*) кругозóр. **horizontal** [ˌhɒrɪ'zɒnt(ə)l] *n.* горизонтáль; *adj.* горизонтáльный.

hormone ['hɔːməʊn] *n.* гормóн.

horn [hɔːn] *n.* рог (*pl.* -á); (*mus.*) рожóк (-жкá); (*motor* ~) гудóк (-дкá); *attr.* роговóй. **hornbeam** *n.* граб. **horned** *adj.* рогáтый.

hornet ['hɔːnɪt] *n.* шéршень (-шня) *m.*

horny ['hɔːnɪ] *adj.* роговóй; (*calloused*) мозóлистый.

horoscope ['hɒrəˌskəʊp] *n.* гороскóп; **cast a** ~ составля́ть *impf.*, состáвить *pf.* гороскóп.

horrible ['hɒrɪb(ə)l] *adj.* ужáсный, стрáшный (-шен, -шнá, -шно, стрáшны́). **horrid** *adj.* ужáсный, проти́вный. **horrify** *v.t.* ужасáть *impf.*, ужаснýть *pf.* **horror** *n.* ýжас, отвращéние.

hors-d'oeuvre [ɔː'dɜːvr, -'dɜːv] *n.* закýска (*usu. in pl.*).

horse [hɔːs] *n.* лóшадь (*pl.* -ди, -дéй, *i.* -дьми́), конь (-ня́; *pl.* -ни, -нéй) *m.*; (*collect.*, *cavalry*) кóнница; *attr.* лошади́ный, кóнский. **horse-chestnut** *n.* кóнский каштáн. **horseflesh** *n.* кони́на. **horse-fly** *n.* слепéнь (-пня́) *m.* **horsehair** *n.* кóнский вóлос. **horseman, -woman** *n.* всáдник, -ица. **horseplay** *n.* возня́. **horsepower** *n.* лошади́ная си́ла. **horse-radish** *n.* хрен (-а(у)). **horseshoe** *n.* подкóва. **horsewhip** *n.* хлыст (-á); *v.t.* хлестáть (-ещý, -éщешь) *impf.*, хлестнýть *pf.*

horticulture ['hɔːtɪˌkʌltʃə(r)] *n.* садовóдство.

hose [həʊz] *n.* (*stockings*) чулки́ (*g.* -лóк) *pl.*; (~-*pipe*) шланг, рукáв (-á; *pl.* -á).

hosier ['həʊzɪə(r), 'həʊʒə(r)] *n.* торгóвец (-вца) трикотáжными издéлиями. **hosiery** *n.* чулóчные издéлия *nt.pl.*, трикотáж.

hospitable ['hɒspɪtəb(ə)l, hɒ'spɪt-] *adj.* гостеприи́мный.

hospital ['hɒspɪt(ə)l] *n.* больни́ца; (*military* ~) гóспиталь (*pl.* -ли, -лéй) *m.*

hospitality [ˌhɒspɪ'tælɪtɪ] *n.* гостеприи́мство.

host¹ [həʊst] *n.* (*multitude*) мнóжество; (*army*) вóйско (*pl.* -кá).

host² [həʊst] *n.* (*landlord etc.*) хозя́ин (*pl.* -я́ева, -я́ев).

host³ [həʊst] *n.* (*eccl.*) облáтка.

hostage ['hɒstɪdʒ] *n.* залóжник, -ица.

hostel ['hɒst(ə)l] *n.* (*students'*) общежи́тие; (*tourists'*) турбáза.

hostelry ['hɒstəlrɪ] *n.* постоя́лый двор (-á).

hostess ['həʊstɪs] *n.* хозя́йка; (*air* ~) бортпроводни́ца.

hostile ['hɒstaɪl] *adj.* враждéбный. **hostility** [hɒ'stɪlɪtɪ] *n.* враждéбность; *pl.* воéнные дéйствия *nt.pl.*

hot [hɒt] *adj.* горя́чий (-ч, -чá), жáркий (-рок, -ркá, -рко); (*pungent*) óстрый (остр & остёр, острá, óстрó); (*fresh*) свéжий (свеж, -á, -ó, свéжи́); ~ **air** бахвáльство. **hotbed** *n.* парни́к (-á); (*fig.*) рассáдник. **hot-blooded** *adj.* пы́лкий (-лок, -лкá, -лко).

hotel [həʊ'tel] *n.* гости́ница, отéль *m.*

hotfoot [hɒt'fʊt] *adv.* поспéшно. **hotheaded** *adj.* вспы́льчивый. **hothouse** *n.* тепли́ца. **hotplate** *n.* пли́тка. **hot-water:** ~ **bottle** грéлка.

hound [haʊnd] *n.* го́нчая *sb.*; *v.t.* трави́ть (-влю́, -вишь) *impf.*, за~ *pf.*; ~ **on** подстрека́ть *impf.*, подстрекну́ть *pf.*

hour [aʊə(r)] *n.* (*period*, *specific time*) час (-а́ *with 2,3,4*, *loc.* -у́; *pl.* -ы́); (*time in general*) вре́мя *nt.* **hourly** *adj.* ежеча́сный.

house [haʊs] *n.* дом (-а(у); *pl.* -а́); (*parl.*) пала́та; (*theatre*) теа́тр; (*audience*) пу́блика; (*performance*) сеа́нс; (*dynasty*) дом (*pl.* -а́), дина́стия; *attr.* дома́шний; *v.t.* помеща́ть *impf.*, помести́ть *pf.*; (*provide houses for*) обеспе́чивать *impf.*, обеспе́чить *pf.* жильём. **housebreaker** *n.* взло́мщик. **household** *n.* (*people*) дома́шние *sb.*; (*establishment*) дома́шнее хозя́йство. **house-keeper** *n.* эконо́мка. **housemaid** *n.* го́рничная *sb.* **house-warming** *n.* новосе́лье. **housewife** *n.* хозя́йка. **housework** *n.* дома́шняя рабо́та. **housing** *n.* (*accommodation*) жильё; (*provision of* ~) жили́щное строи́тельство; (*casing*) кожу́х (-а́); ~ **estate** жило́й масси́в.

hovel ['hɒv(ə)l] *n.* лачу́га.

hover ['hɒvə(r)] *v.i.* (*bird*) пари́ть *impf.*; (*helicopter*) висе́ть (-си́т) *impf.*; (*hesitate*) колеба́ться (-блюсь, -блешься) *impf.* **hovercraft** *n.* су́дно (*pl.* -да́, -до́в) на возду́шной поду́шке, СВП.

how [haʊ] *adv.* как, каки́м о́бразом; ~ **do you do?** здра́вствуйте!; ~ **many,** ~ **much** ско́лько (+*g.*). **how'ever** *adv.* как бы ни (+*past*); *conj.* одна́ко, тем не ме́нее; ~ **much** ско́лько бы ни (+*g.* & *past*).

howitzer ['haʊɪtsə(r)] *n.* га́убица.

howl [haʊl] *n.* вой, рёв; *v.i.* выть (во́ю, во́ешь) *impf.*; реве́ть (-ву́, -вёшь) *impf.* **howler** ['haʊlə(r)] *n.* (*mistake*) грубе́йшая оши́бка.

h.p. *abbr.* (*of* **horsepower**) л.с., лошади́ная си́ла.

HQ *abbr.* (*of* **headquarters**) штаб, ста́вка.

hub [hʌb] *n.* (*of wheel*) ступи́ца; (*fig.*) центр (внима́ния); ~ **of the universe** пуп (-а́) земли́.

hubbub ['hʌbʌb] *n.* шум (-а(у)), гам (-а(у)).

huddle ['hʌd(ə)l] *n.* (*heap*) ку́ча; (*confusion*) сумато́ха; *v.t.* (*heap together*) сва́ливать *impf.*, свали́ть (-лю́, -лишь) *pf.* в ку́чу; *v.i.* ~ **together** съёживаться *impf.*, съёжиться *pf.*

hue [hju:] *n.* (*tint*) отте́нок (-нка).

huff [hʌf] *n.* припа́док (-дка) раздраже́ния; *v.t.* & *i.* обижа́ть(ся) *impf.*, оби́деть(ся) (-и́жу(сь), -и́дишь(ся)) *pf.*

hug [hʌg] *n.* объя́тие; (*wrestling*) хва́тка; *v.t.* (*embrace*) обнима́ть *impf.*, обня́ть (обниму́, -мешь; о́бнял, -а́, -о) *pf.*; (*keep close to*) держа́ться (-жу́сь, -жишься) *impf.*+*g.*

huge [hju:dʒ] *adj.* огро́мный.

hulk [hʌlk] *n.* ко́рпус (*pl.* -а́) (корабля́). **hulking** *adj.* (*bulky*) грома́дный; (*clumsy*) неуклю́жий.

hull¹ [hʌl] *n.* (*of pea etc.*) стручо́к (-чка́); (*of grain*) шелуха́; *v.t.* лущи́ть *impf.*, об~ *pf.*

hull² [hʌl] *n.* (*of ship*) ко́рпус (*pl.* -а́); (*of aeroplane*) фюзеля́ж.

hum [hʌm] *n.* жужжа́ние, гуде́ние; *v.i.* жужжа́ть (-жу́, -жи́шь) *impf.*; гуде́ть (гужу́, гуди́шь) *impf.*; *v.t.* напева́ть *impf.*; *int.* гм!

human ['hju:mən] *adj.* челове́ческий, людско́й; *n.* челове́к. **humane** [hju:'meɪn] *adj.* челове́чный, гума́нный (-нен, -нна). **humanism** *n.* гумани́зм. **humanist** *n.* гумани́ст. **humanity** [hju:'mænɪtɪ] *n.* (*human race*) челове́чество; (*humaneness*) гума́нность; **the Humanities** гуманита́рные нау́ки *f.pl.*

humble ['hʌmb(ə)l] *adj.* смире́нный (-е́н, -е́нна), скро́мный (-мен, -мна́, -мно); *v.t.* унижа́ть *impf.*, уни́зить *pf.*

humdrum ['hʌmdrʌm] *adj.* (*banal*) бана́льный; (*dull*) ску́чный (-чен, -чна́, -чно).

humid ['hju:mɪd] *adj.* вла́жный (-жен, -жна́, -жно). **hu'midity** *n.* вла́жность.

humiliate [hju:'mɪlɪˌeɪt] *v.t.* унижа́ть *impf.*, уни́зить *pf.* **humili'ation** *n.* униже́ние.

humility [hju:'mɪlɪtɪ] *n.* смире́ние.

humming-bird ['hʌmɪŋ] *n.* коли́бри *c.g.* *indecl.*

hummock ['hʌmək] *n.* (*hillock*) буго́р (-гра́); (*in ice*) (ледяно́й) торо́с.

humorist ['hju:mərɪst] *n.* юмори́ст. **humorous** *adj.* юмористи́ческий. **humour** *n.* ю́мор; (*mood*) настрое́ние; **out of** ~ не в ду́хе; *v.t.* потака́ть *impf.*+*d.*

hump [hʌmp] *n.* горб (-а́, *loc.* -у́); (*of earth*) буго́р (-гра́); *v.t.* го́рбить *impf.*, с~ *pf.* **humpback** *n.* горб (-а́, *loc.* -у́); (*person*) горбу́н (-а́), ~ья. **humpbacked** *adj.* горба́тый.

humus ['hju:məs] *n.* перегно́й.

hunch [hʌntʃ] *n.* (*hump*) горб (-а́), *loc.* -у́); (*thick piece*) ломо́ть (-мтя́) *m.*; (*suspicion*) подозре́ние; *v.t.* го́рбить *impf.*, с~ *pf.* **hunchback** *n.* горб (-а́), *loc.* -у́); (*person*) горбу́н (-а́), ~ья. **hunchbacked** *adj.* горба́тый.

hundred ['hʌndrəd] *adj.* & *n.* сто (*in oblique cases* ста); (*collect.*) со́тня (*g.pl.* -тен); (*age*) сто лет; **two** ~ две́сти (двухсо́т, двумста́м, двумяста́ми, двухста́х); **three** ~ три́ста (трёхсо́т, трёмста́м, тремяста́ми, трёхста́х); **four** ~ четы́реста (-рёхсо́т, -рёмста́м, -рьмяста́ми, -рёхста́х); **five** ~ пятьсо́т (пятисо́т, пятиста́м, пятьюста́ми, пятиста́х). **hundredfold** *adj.* стокра́тный; *adv.* в сто раз. **hundredth** *adj.* & *n.* со́тый; (*fraction*) со́тая (часть (*pl.* -ти, -те́й)).

Hungarian [hʌŋ'geərɪən] *n.* венгр, венге́рка; *adj.* венге́рский. **Hungary** ['hʌŋgərɪ] *n.* Ве́нгрия.

hunger ['hʌŋgə(r)] *n.* го́лод; (*fig.*) жа́жда (**for** +*g.*); ~ **strike** голодо́вка; *v.i.* голода́ть *impf.*; ~ **for** жа́ждать (-ду, -дешь) *impf.*+*g.* **hungry** *adj.* голо́дный (го́лоден, -дна́, -дно, го́лодны́).

hunk [hʌŋk] *n.* ломо́ть (-мтя́) *m.*

hunt [hʌnt] *n.* охо́та; (*fig.*) по́иски *m.pl.* (**for** +*g.*); *v.t.* охо́титься *impf.* на+*a.*, за+*i.*; трави́ть (-влю́, -вишь) *impf.*, за~ *pf.*; ~

down вы́следить *pf.*; ~ **out** отыска́ть (-ыщу́, -ы́щешь) *pf.* **hunter** *n.* охо́тник. **hunting** *n.* охо́та; *attr.* охо́тничий (-чья, -чье). **huntsman** *n.* охо́тник, е́герь (*pl.* -ря́) *m.*

hurdle [ˈhɜːd(ə)l] *n.* (*fence*) плете́нь (-тня́) *m.*; (*sport*) барье́р; (*fig.*) препя́тствие. **hurdler** *n.* барьери́ст. **hurdles, hurdling** *n.* (*sport*) барье́рный бег.

hurl [hɜːl] *v.t.* швыря́ть *impf.*, швырну́ть *pf.*

hurly-burly [ˈhɜːlɪˌbɜːlɪ] *n.* сумато́ха.

hurrah [hʊˈrɑː], **hurray** [hʊˈreɪ] *int.* ура́!

hurricane [ˈhʌrɪkən, -ˌkeɪn] *n.* урага́н.

hurried [ˈhʌrɪd] *adj.* торопли́вый. **hurry** *n.* спе́шка, торопли́вость; **in a** ~ второпя́х; *v.t.* & *i.* торопи́ть(ся) (-плю́(сь), -пишь(ся)) *impf.*, по~ *pf.*; *v.i.* спеши́ть *impf.*, по~ *pf.*

hurt [hɜːt] *n.* вред (-а́), уще́рб, поврежде́ние; *v.i.* боле́ть (-ли́т) *impf.*; *v.t.* поврежда́ть *impf.*, повреди́ть *pf.*; ~ **the feelings of** задева́ть *impf.*, заде́ть (-е́ну, -е́нешь) *pf.*+*a.*

hurtle [ˈhɜːt(ə)l] *v.i.* (*move swiftly*) нести́сь (несу́сь, -сёшься; нёсся, -сла́сь) *impf.*, по~ *pf.*

husband [ˈhʌzbənd] *n.* муж (*pl.* -ья́, -е́й, -ья́м); *v.t.* эконо́мить *impf.*, с~ *pf.*

hush [hʌʃ] *n.* тишина́, молча́ние; *v.t.* успока́ивать *impf.*, успоко́ить *pf.*; *int.* ти́ше!; тсс!

husk [hʌsk] *n.* шелуха́; *v.t.* шелуши́ть *impf.*

husky[1] [ˈhʌskɪ] *adj.* (*voice*) хри́плый (хрипл, -а́, -о).

husky[2] [ˈhʌskɪ] *n.* (*dog*) эскимо́сская ла́йка.

hussar [hʊˈzɑː(r)] *n.* гуса́р (*g.pl.* -р (*as collect.*) & -ров).

hustle [ˈhʌs(ə)l] *n.* толкотня́; *v.t.* & *i.* (*push*) толка́ть(ся) *impf.*, толкну́ть(ся) *pf.*; (*hurry*) торопи́ть(ся) (-плю́(сь), -пишь(ся)) *impf.*, по~ *pf.*

hut [hʌt] *n.* хи́жина, бара́к.

hutch [hʌtʃ] *n.* кле́тка.

hyacinth [ˈhaɪəsɪnθ] *n.* гиаци́нт.

hybrid [ˈhaɪbrɪd] *n.* гибри́д; *adj.* гибри́дный.

hydra [ˈhaɪdrə] *n.* ги́дра.

hydrangea [haɪˈdreɪndʒə] *n.* горте́нзия.

hydrant [ˈhaɪdrənt] *n.* гидра́нт.

hydrate [ˈhaɪdreɪt] *n.* гидра́т.

hydraulic [haɪˈdrɔːlɪk, -ˈdrɒlɪk] *adj.* гидравли́ческий; ~ **engineering** гидроте́хника. **hydraulics** *n.* гидра́влика.

hydro- [ˈhaɪdrəʊ] *in comb.* гидро... . **hydroˈcarbon** *n.* углеводоро́д. **hydroˈchloric acid** *n.* соляна́я кислота́. **hydrodyˈnamics** *n.* гидродина́мика. **hydroeˈlectric** *adj.* гидроэлектри́ческий; ~ **plant** гидроэлектроста́нция, ГЭС *f.indecl.* **hydrofoil** *n.* подво́дное крыло́ (*pl.* -лья, -льев); (*vessel*) су́дно (*pl.* -да́, -до́в), кора́бль (-ля́) *m.*, на подво́дных кры́льях, СПК, КПК.

hydrogen [ˈhaɪdrədʒ(ə)n] *n.* водоро́д; ~ **bomb** водоро́дная бо́мба. **hydrolysis** [haɪˈdrɒlɪsɪs] *n.* гидро́лиз. **hydroˈphobia** *n.* водобоя́знь. **hydroplane** *n.* (*fin*) горизонта́льный руль (-ля́) *m.*; (*motor boat*) гли́ссер; (*seaplane*) гидросамолёт. **hydroxide** [haɪˈdrɒksaɪd] *n.* гидро́окись.

hyena [haɪˈiːnə] *n.* гие́на.

hygiene [ˈhaɪdʒiːn] *n.* гигие́на. **hyˈgienic** *adj.* гигиени́ческий.

hymn [hɪm] *n.* гимн.

hyperbola [haɪˈpɜːbələ] *n.* гипербо́ла. **hyperbolic** [ˌhaɪpəˈbɒlɪk] *adj.* гиперболи́ческий.

hyperbole [haɪˈpɜːbəlɪ] *n.* гипербо́ла. **hyperbolical** [ˌhaɪpəˈbɒlɪk(ə)l] *adj.* гиперболи́ческий.

hypercritical [ˌhaɪpəˈkrɪtɪk(ə)l] *adj.* придирчивый.

hypersensitive [ˌhaɪpəˈsensɪtɪv] *adj.* сверхчувстви́тельный.

hyphen [ˈhaɪf(ə)n] *n.* дефи́с. **hyphen(ate)** *v.t.* писа́ть (пишу́, -шешь) *impf.*, на~ *pf.* че́рез дефи́с.

hypnosis [hɪpˈnəʊsɪs] *n.* гипно́з. **hypnotic** [hɪpˈnɒtɪk] *adj.* гипноти́ческий; (*soporific*) снотво́рный. **ˈhypnotism** *n.* гипноти́зм. **ˈhypnotist** *n.* гипнотизёр. **ˈhypnotize** *v.t.* гипнотизи́ровать *impf.*, за~ *pf.*

hypocrisy [hɪˈpɒkrɪsɪ] *n.* лицеме́рие. **hypocrite** [ˈhɪpəkrɪt] *n.* лицеме́р. **hypoˈcritical** *adj.* лицеме́рный.

hypodermic [ˌhaɪpəˈdɜːmɪk] *adj.* подко́жный.

hypotenuse [haɪˈpɒtəˌnjuːz] *n.* гипотену́за.

hypothesis [haɪˈpɒθɪsɪs] *n.* гипоте́за, предположе́ние. **hypothesize** *v.i.* стро́ить *impf.*, по~ *pf.* гипоте́зу; де́лать *impf.*, с~ *pf.* предположе́ние. **hypoˈthetical** *adj.* гипотети́ческий; предположи́тельный.

hysteria [hɪˈstɪərɪə] *n.* истери́я. **hysterical** [hɪˈsterɪk(ə)l] *adj.* истери́чный, истери́ческий. **hysterics** *n.* исте́рика, истери́ческий припа́док (-дка).

I

I [aɪ] *pron.* я (меня́, мне, мной & мно́ю, обо мне).

iambic [aɪˈæmbɪk] *adj.* ямби́ческий. **iambus** *n.* ямб.

ibid. [ˈɪbɪˌdem] *abbr.* (*of* **ibidem**) там же.

ice [aɪs] *n.* лёд (льда(у), *loc.* льду); (~ *cream*) моро́женое *sb.*; ~ **age** леднико́вый пери́од; ~ **floe** плаву́чая льди́на; ~ **hockey** хокке́й (с ша́йбой); *v.t.* замора́живать *impf.*, заморо́зить *pf.*; (*cul.*) глазирова́ть *impf.* & *pf.*; *v.i.*: ~ **over, up** обледенева́ть *impf.*, обледене́ть *pf.* **ice-axe** *n.* ледору́б. **iceberg** *n.* а́йсберг. **ice-boat** *n.* бу́ер (*pl.* -а́). **ice-breaker** *n.* ледоко́л. **ice-cream** *n.* моро́женое *sb.*; ~ **parlour** кафе́-моро́женое

nt.indecl. **icicle** *n.* сосу́лька. **icing** *n.* (*cul.*) глазу́рь.
icon ['aɪkɒn] *n.* ико́на.
icy ['aɪsɪ] *adj.* ледяно́й; (*also fig.*) холо́дный (хо́лоден, -дна́, -дно, хо́лодны́).
ID *abbr.* (*of* **identification**) удостовере́ние ли́чности.
idea [aɪ'dɪə] *n.* иде́я, мысль; (*conception*) поня́тие; (*intention*) наме́рение.
ideal [aɪ'di:əl] *n.* идеа́л; *adj.* идеа́льный. **idealism** *n.* идеали́зм. **idealist** *n.* идеали́ст. **idealize** *v.t.* идеализи́ровать *impf.* & *pf.*
identical [aɪ'dentɪk(ə)l] *adj.* (*of one thing*) тот же са́мый; (*of different things*) тожде́ственный (-ен, -енна), одина́ковый. **identifi'cation** *n.* отождествле́ние; (*recognition*) опозна́ние; (*of person*) установле́ние ли́чности. **identify** *v.t.* отождествля́ть *impf.*, отождестви́ть *pf.*; (*recognize*) опознава́ть (-наю́, -наёшь) *impf.*, опозна́ть *pf.* **identity** *n.* (*sameness*) тожде́ственность; (*of person*) ли́чность; (*math.*) то́ждество; ~ **card** удостовере́ние ли́чности.
ideogram ['ɪdɪə,græm], **ideograph** ['ɪdɪə,grɑ:f] *n.* идеогра́мма.
ideological [,aɪdɪə'lɒdʒɪk(ə)l] *adj.* идеологи́ческий. **ide'ologist, 'ideologue** *n.* идео́лог. **ide'ology** *n.* идеоло́гия.
idiocy ['ɪdɪəsɪ] *n.* идиоти́зм.
idiom ['ɪdɪəm] *n.* (*expression*) идио́ма; (*language*) язы́к (-а́), го́вор. **idio'matic** *adj.* идиомати́ческий.
idiosyncrasy [,ɪdɪəʊ'sɪŋkrəsɪ] *n.* склад ума́, идиосинкрази́я.
idiot ['ɪdɪət] *n.* идио́т. **idiotic** [ɪdɪ'ɒtɪk] *adj.* идио́тский.
idle ['aɪd(ə)l] *adj.* (*vain*) тще́тный; (*useless*) бесполе́зный; (*unoccupied*) неза́нятый; (*lazy*) лени́вый; (*machine*) холосто́й (хо́лост, -а́, -о); *v.i.* безде́льничать *impf.*; (*engine*) рабо́тать *impf.* вхолосту́ю; *v.t.*: ~ **away** пра́здно проводи́ть (-ожу́, -о́дишь) *impf.*, провести́ (-еду́, -едёшь; -ёл, -ела́) *pf.* **idleness** *n.* тще́тность; бесполе́зность; пра́здность, безде́лье. **idler** *n.* безде́льник, -ица.
idol ['aɪd(ə)l] *n.* и́дол, куми́р. **idolater** [aɪ'dɒlətə(r)], **-tress** *n.* идолопокло́нник, -ица. **idolatrous** [aɪ'dɒlətrəs] *adj.* идолопокло́ннический. **idolatry** *n.* идолопокло́нство; (*fig.*) обожа́ние. **idolize** *v.t.* боготвори́ть *impf.*
idyll ['ɪdɪl] *n.* иди́ллия. **i'dyllic** *adj.* идилли́ческий.
i.e. *abbr.* (*of* **id est**) т.е., то есть.
if [ɪf] *conj.* (*conditions*) е́сли, е́сли бы; (*whether*) ли; **as** ~ как бу́дто; **even** ~ да́же е́сли; ~ **only** е́сли бы то́лько.
igloo ['ɪglu:] *n.* и́глу *nt.indecl.*
igneous ['ɪgnɪəs] *adj.* о́гненный, огнево́й; (*rock*) вулкани́ческий. **ignite** [ɪg'naɪt] *v.t.* зажига́ть *impf.*, заже́чь (-жгу́, -жжёшь; -жёг, -жгла́) *pf.*; *v.i.* загора́ться *impf.*, загоре́ться (-рю́сь, -ри́шься) *pf.* **ignition** [ɪg'nɪʃ(ə)n] *n.* зажига́ние.
ignoble [ɪg'nəʊb(ə)l] *adj.* ни́зкий (-зок, -зка́, -зко).
ignominious [,ɪgnə'mɪnɪəs] *adj.* позо́рный. **'ignominy** *n.* позо́р.
ignoramus [,ɪgnə'reɪməs] *n.* неве́жда *m.* **ignorance** ['ɪgnərəns] *n.* неве́жество, неве́дение. **'ignorant** *adj.* неве́жественный (-ен, -енна); (*uninformed*) несве́дующий (**of** в+*p.*).
ignore [ɪg'nɔ:(r)] *v.t.* не обраща́ть *impf.* внима́ния на+*a.*; игнори́ровать *impf.* & *pf.*
ill [ɪl] *n.* (*evil*) зло; (*harm*) вред (-а́); *pl.* (*misfortunes*) несча́стья (-тий) *pl.*; *adj.* (*sick*) больно́й (-лен, -льна́); (*evil*) дурно́й (ду́рён, -рна́, -рно, ду́рны́), злой (зол, зла); *adv.* пло́хо, ду́рно; (*scarcely*) едва́ ли; **fall** ~ заболева́ть *impf.*, заболе́ть *pf.* **ill-advised** *adj.* неблагоразу́мный. **ill-bred** *adj.* невоспи́танный (-ан, -анна). **ill-disposed** *adj.* недоброжела́тельный (**towards** к+*d.*).
illegal [ɪ'li:g(ə)l] *adj.* незако́нный (-нен, -нна), нелега́льный. **illegality** [,ɪli:'gælɪtɪ] *n.* незако́нность, нелега́льность.
illegible [ɪ'ledʒɪb(ə)l] *adj.* неразбо́рчивый.
illegitimacy [,ɪlɪ'dʒɪtɪməsɪ] *n.* незако́нность; (*of child*) незаконнорождённость. **illegitimate** *adj.* незако́нный (-нен, -нна); незаконнорождённый (-ён, -ённа).
illiberal [ɪ'lɪbər(ə)l] *adj.* непросвещённый; (*bigoted*) нетерпи́мый; (*stingy*) скупо́й (скуп, -а́, -о).
illicit [ɪ'lɪsɪt] *adj.* незако́нный (-нен, -нна), недозво́ленный (-ен, -енна).
illiteracy [ɪ'lɪtərəsɪ] *n.* негра́мотность. **illiterate** *adj.* негра́мотный.
ill-mannered [ɪl'mænəd] *adj.* неве́жливый. **ill-natured** *adj.* зло́бный.
illness ['ɪlnɪs] *n.* боле́знь.
illogical [ɪ'lɒdʒɪk(ə)l] *adj.* нелоги́чный.
ill-tempered [ɪl'tempəd] *adj.* раздражи́тельный. **ill-treat** *v.t.* пло́хо обраща́ться *impf.* с+*i.*
illuminate [ɪ'lu:mɪ,neɪt, ɪ'lju:-] *v.t.* освеща́ть *impf.*, освети́ть (-ещу́, -ети́шь) *pf.*; (*building*) иллюмини́ровать *impf.* & *pf.*; (*manuscript*) украша́ть *impf.*, укра́сить *pf.* **illumi'nation** *n.* освеще́ние; (*also pl.*) иллюмина́ция; украше́ние (ру́кописи).
illusion [ɪ'lu:ʒ(ə)n, ɪ'lju:-] *n.* иллю́зия. **illusory** *adj.* обма́нчивый, иллюзо́рный.
illustrate ['ɪlə,streɪt] *v.t.* иллюстри́ровать *impf.* & *pf.*, про~ *pf.* **illu'stration** *n.* иллюстра́ция. **illustrative** *adj.* иллюстрати́вный.
illustrious [ɪ'lʌstrɪəs] *adj.* знамени́тый.
image ['ɪmɪdʒ] *n.* (*statue etc.*) изображе́ние; (*optical* ~) отраже́ние; (*semblance*) подо́бие; (*literary* ~ *etc.*) о́браз. **imagery** *n.* о́бразность.
imaginable [ɪ'mædʒɪnəb(ə)l] *adj.* вообрази́мый. **imaginary** *adj.* вообража́емый, мни́мый. **imagi'nation** *n.* воображе́ние, фанта́-

зия. **imagine** *v.t.* воображáть *impf.*, вообразúть *pf.*; (*conceive*) представля́ть *impf.*, предстáвить *pf.* себé.

imbecile ['ɪmbɪˌsiːl] *n.* слабоýмный *sb.*; (*fool*) глупéц (-пцá); *adj.* слабоýмный.

imbibe [ɪm'baɪb] *v.t.* (*absorb*) впúтывать *impf.*, впитáть *pf.*

imbroglio [ɪm'brəʊlɪəʊ] *n.* пýтаница.

imbue [ɪm'bjuː] *v.t.* пропúтывать *impf.*, пропитáть *pf.* (**with** +*i.*); внушáть *impf.*, внушúть *pf.*+*d.* (**with** +*a.*).

imitate ['ɪmɪˌteɪt] *v.t.* подражáть *impf.*+*d.* **imi'tation** *n.* подражáние (**of** +*d.*), имитáция; *attr.* (*counterfeit*) поддéльный; (*artificial*) искýсственный (-ен(ен), -енна). **imitative** *adj.* подражáтельный.

immaculate [ɪ'mækjʊlət] *adj.* незапя́тнанный (-ан, -анна); (*irreproachable*) безупрéчный.

immanent ['ɪmənənt] *adj.* присýщий (**in** +*d.*), имманéнтный.

immaterial [ˌɪmə'tɪərɪəl] *adj.* невещéственный (-ен(ен), -енна); (*unimportant*) несущéственный (-ен(ен), -енна).

immature [ˌɪmə'tjʊə(r)] *adj.* незрéлый.

immeasurable [ɪ'meʒərəb(ə)l] *adj.* неизмерúмый.

immediate [ɪ'miːdɪət] *adj.* (*direct*) непосрéдственный (-ен, -енна); (*swift*) немéдленный (-ен, -ена). **immediately** *adv.* тóтчас, немéдленно; непосрéдственно.

immemorial [ˌɪmɪ'mɔːrɪəl] *adj.* незапáмятный.

immense [ɪ'mens] *adj.* необъя́тный, огрóмный.

immerse [ɪ'mɜːs] *v.t.* погружáть *impf.*, погрузúть *pf.* **immersion** *n.* погружéние.

immigrant ['ɪmɪgrənt] *n.* иммигрáнт, ~ка. **immigrate** *v.i.* иммигрúровать *impf.* & *pf.* **immi'gration** *n.* иммигрáция.

imminent ['ɪmɪnənt] *adj.* блúзкий (-зок, -зкá, -зко, блúзкú); (*danger*) грозя́щий.

immobile [ɪ'məʊbaɪl] *adj.* неподвúжный. **immobility** [ˌɪməʊ'bɪlɪtɪ] *n.* неподвúжность.

immoderate [ɪ'mɒdərət] *adj.* неумéренный (-ен, -енна).

immodest [ɪ'mɒdɪst] *adj.* нескрóмный (-мен, -мнá, -мно).

immolate ['ɪməˌleɪt] *v.t.* приносúть (-ошý, -óсишь) *impf.*, принестú (-есý, -есёшь; -ёс, -еслá) *pf.* в жéртву; жéртвовать *impf.*, по~ *pf.*+*i.*

immoral [ɪ'mɒr(ə)l] *adj.* безнрáвственный (-ен(ен), -енна). **immorality** [ˌɪmə'rælɪtɪ] *n.* безнрáвственность.

immortal [ɪ'mɔːt(ə)l] *adj.* бессмéртный. **immortality** [ˌɪmɔː'tælɪtɪ] *n.* бессмéртие. **immortalize** *v.t.* обессмéртить *pf.*

immovable [ɪ'muːvəb(ə)l] *adj.* неподвúжный, недвúжимый; (*steadfast*) непоколебúмый.

immune [ɪ'mjuːn] *adj.* (*to illness*) невосприúмчивый (**to** к+*d.*); (*free from*) свобóдный (**from** от+*g.*). **immunity** *n.* невосприúмчивость (**to** к+*d.*), иммунитéт; освобождéние (**from** от+*g.*); (*diplomatic etc.*) неприкосновéнность.

immure [ɪ'mjʊə(r)] *v.t.* заточáть *impf.*, заточúть *pf.*

immutable [ɪ'mjuːtəb(ə)l] *adj.* неизмéнный (-нен, -нна).

imp [ɪmp] *n.* бесёнок (-нка; *pl.* -ня́та, -ня́т).

impact ['ɪmpækt] *n.* (*striking*) удáр; (*collision*) столкновéние; (*influence*) влия́ние.

impair [ɪm'peə(r)] *v.t.* (*damage*) повреждáть *impf.*, повредúть *pf.*; (*weaken*) ослабля́ть *impf.*, ослáбить *pf.*

impale [ɪm'peɪl] *v.t.* прокáлывать *impf.*, проколóть (-лю́, -лешь) *pf.*; (*as torture etc.*) сажáть *impf.*, посадúть (-ажý, -áдишь) *pf.* нá кол.

impalpable [ɪm'pælpəb(ə)l] *adj.* неосязáемый.

impart [ɪm'pɑːt] *v.t.* делúться (-лю́сь, -лишься) *impf.*, по~ *pf.*+*i.* (**to** с+*i.*).

impartial [ɪm'pɑːʃ(ə)l] *adj.* беспристрáстный.

impassable [ɪm'pɑːsəb(ə)l] *adj.* непроходúмый, непроéзжий.

impasse ['æmpæs, 'ɪm-] *n.* тупúк (-á).

impassioned [ɪm'pæʃ(ə)nd] *adj.* стрáстный (-тен, -тнá, -тно).

impassive [ɪm'pæsɪv] *adj.* бесстрáстный.

impatience [ɪm'peɪʃəns] *n.* нетерпéние. **impatient** *adj.* нетерпелúвый.

impeach [ɪm'piːtʃ] *v.t.* обвиня́ть *impf.*, обвинúть *pf.* (**of, with** в+*p.*).

impeccable [ɪm'pekəb(ə)l] *adj.* безупрéчный.

impecunious [ˌɪmpɪ'kjuːnɪəs] *adj.* безденéжный.

impedance [ɪm'piːd(ə)ns] *n.* пóлное сопротивлéние. **impede** *v.t.* препя́тствовать *impf.*, вос~ *pf.*+*d.*; задéрживать *impf.*, задержáть (-жý, -жишь) *pf.* **impediment** [ɪm'pedɪmənt] *n.* препя́тствие, задéржка; (*in speech*) заикáние.

impel [ɪm'pel] *v.t.* побуждáть *impf.*, побудúть *pf.* (**to** +*inf.*, к+*d.*).

impend [ɪm'pend] *v.i.* нависáть *impf.*, навúснуть *pf.*

impenetrable [ɪm'penɪtrəb(ə)l] *adj.* непроницáемый.

imperative [ɪm'perətɪv] *adj.* (*imperious*) повелúтельный; (*obligatory*) необходúмый; *n.* (*gram.*) повелúтельное наклонéние.

imperceptible [ˌɪmpə'septɪb(ə)l] *adj.* незамéтный.

imperfect [ɪm'pɜːfɪkt] *n.* имперфéкт; *adj.* (*incomplete*) несовершéнный (-нен, -нна), непóлный (-лон, -лнá, -лно); (*faulty*) дефéктный. **imper'fection** *n.* несовершéнство; (*fault*) недостáток (-тка). **imper'fective** *adj.* (*n.*) несовершéнный (вид).

imperial [ɪm'pɪərɪəl] *adj.* (*of empire*) импéрский; (*of emperor*) императóрский. **imperialism** *n.* империалúзм. **imperialist** *n.* империалúст; *attr.* империалистúческий.

imperil [ɪm'perɪl] *v.t.* подвергáть *impf.*, подвéргнуть (-г) *pf.* опáсности.

imperious [ɪm'pɪərɪəs] *adj.* влáстный.

imperishable [ɪm'perɪʃəb(ə)l] *adj.* вéчный; (*food*) непóртящийся.

impersonal [ɪm'pɜːsən(ə)l] *adj.* безли́чный.
impersonate [ɪm'pɜːsəˌneɪt] *v.t.* (*personify*) олицетворя́ть *impf.*, олицетвори́ть *pf.*; (*play part*) исполня́ть *impf.*, испо́лнить *pf.* роль+*g.*; (*pretend to be*) выдава́ть (-даю́, -даёшь) *impf.*, вы́дать (-ам, -ашь, -аст, -адим) *pf.* себя́ за+*a.*
impertinence [ɪm'pɜːtɪnəns] *n.* де́рзость. **impertinent** *adj.* де́рзкий (-зок, -зка́, -зко).
imperturbable [ˌɪmpə'tɜːbəb(ə)l] *adj.* невозмути́мый.
impervious [ɪm'pɜːvɪəs] *adj.* непроница́емый (**to** для+*g.*); (*not responsive*) глухо́й (глух, -á, -o) (**to** к+*d.*).
impetuous [ɪm'petjʊəs] *adj.* стреми́тельный.
impetus ['ɪmpɪtəs] *n.* дви́жущая си́ла; (*fig.*) и́мпульс.
impiety [ɪm'paɪətɪ] *n.* нечести́вость.
impinge [ɪm'pɪndʒ] *v.i.* & *i.* **(up)on** (*strike*) ударя́ться *impf.*, уда́риться *pf.* о+*a.*; (*encroach*) покуша́ться *impf.*, покуси́ться *pf.* на+*a.*
impious ['ɪmpɪəs] *adj.* нечести́вый.
impish ['ɪmpɪʃ] *adj.* прока́зливый.
implacable [ɪm'plækəb(ə)l] *adj.* неумоли́мый.
implant [ɪm'plɑːnt] *v.t.* насажда́ть *impf.*, насади́ть *pf.*
implement¹ ['ɪmplɪmənt] *n.* (*tool*) ору́дие, инструме́нт; *pl.* принадле́жности *f.pl.*
implement² ['ɪmplɪˌment] *v.t.* (*fulfil*) выполня́ть *impf.*, вы́полнить *pf.*
implicate ['ɪmplɪˌkeɪt] *v.t.* впу́тывать *impf.*, впу́тать *pf.* **impli'cation** *n.* вовлече́ние; (*meaning*) смысл.
implicit [ɪm'plɪsɪt] *adj.* подразумева́емый; (*absolute*) безогово́рочный.
implore [ɪm'plɔː(r)] *v.t.* умоля́ть *impf.*
imply [ɪm'plaɪ] *v.t.* подразумева́ть *impf.*
impolite [ˌɪmpə'laɪt] *adj.* неве́жливый.
imponderable [ɪm'pɒndərəb(ə)l] *adj.* невесо́мый.
import ['ɪmpɔːt; ɪm'pɔːt, 'ɪm-] *n.* (*meaning*) значе́ние; (*of goods*) и́мпорт, ввоз; *v.t.* импорти́ровать *impf.* & *pf.*; ввози́ть (-ожу́, -о́зишь) *impf.*, ввезти́ (ввезу́, -зёшь; ввёз, -ла́) *pf.*
importance [ɪm'pɔːt(ə)ns] *n.* ва́жность. **important** *adj.* ва́жный (-жен, -жна́, -жно, -жны́), значи́тельный.
importunate [ɪm'pɔːtjʊnət] *adj.* назо́йливый.
impose [ɪm'pəʊz] *v.t.* (*tax*) облага́ть *impf.*, обложи́ть (-жу́, -жишь) *pf.*+*i.* (**on** +*a.*); (*obligation*) налага́ть *impf.*, наложи́ть (-жу́, -жишь) *pf.* (**on** на+*a.*); (*force* (*o.s.*) *on*) навя́зывать(ся) *impf.*, навяза́ть(ся) (-яжу́(сь), -я́жешь(ся)) *pf.* (**on** +*d.*). **imposing** *adj.* внуши́тельный. **impo'sition** *n.* обложе́ние, наложе́ние.
impossibility [ɪmˌpɒsɪ'bɪlɪtɪ] *n.* невозмо́жность. **im'possible** *adj.* невозмо́жный.
impostor [ɪm'pɒstə(r)] *n.* самозва́нец (-нца). **imposture** *n.* самозва́нство, обма́н.
impotence ['ɪmpət(ə)ns] *n.* бесси́лие; (*med.*) импоте́нция. **impotent** *adj.* бесси́льный; (*med.*) импоте́нтный.
impound [ɪm'paʊnd] *v.t.* (*cattle*) загоня́ть *impf.*, загна́ть (загоню́, -нишь; загна́л, -á, -o) *pf.*; (*confiscate*) конфискова́ть *impf.* & *pf.*
impoverish [ɪm'pɒvərɪʃ] *v.t.* обедня́ть *impf.*, обедни́ть *pf.*
impracticable [ɪm'præktɪkəb(ə)l] *adj.* невыполни́мый.
imprecation [ˌɪmprɪ'keɪʃ(ə)n] *n.* прокля́тие.
impregnable [ɪm'pregnəb(ə)l] *adj.* непристу́пный.
impregnate ['ɪmpregˌneɪt] *v.t.* (*fertilize*) оплодотворя́ть *impf.*, оплодотвори́ть *pf.*; (*saturate*) пропи́тывать *impf.*, пропита́ть *pf.*
impresario [ˌɪmprɪ'sɑːrɪəʊ] *n.* импреса́рио *m.indecl.*, антрепренёр.
impress ['ɪmpres; ɪm'pres] *n.* отпеча́ток (-тка), печа́ть; *v.t.* (*imprint*) отпеча́тывать *impf.*, отпеча́тать *pf.*; (*affect person*) производи́ть (-ожу́, -о́дишь) *impf.*, произвести́ (-еду́, -едёшь; -ёл, -ела́) *pf.* (како́е-либо) впечатле́ние на+*a.* **im'pression** *n.* (*notion etc.*) впечатле́ние; (*printing*) о́ттиск; (*reprint*) (стереоти́пное) изда́ние; перепеча́тка.
impressionism [ɪm'preʃəˌnɪz(ə)m] *n.* импрессиони́зм.
impressive [ɪm'presɪv] *adj.* вырази́тельный; (*producing great effect*) порази́тельный.
imprint ['ɪmprɪnt; ɪm'prɪnt] *n.* отпеча́ток (-тка); *v.t.* отпеча́тывать *impf.*, отпеча́тать *pf.*; (*on memory etc.*) запечатлева́ть *impf.*, запечатле́ть *pf.*
imprison [ɪm'prɪz(ə)n] *v.t.* заключа́ть *impf.*, заключи́ть *pf.* (в тюрьму́). **imprisonment** *n.* тюре́мное заключе́ние.
improbable [ɪm'prɒbəb(ə)l] *adj.* невероя́тный, неправдоподо́бный.
impromptu [ɪm'prɒmptjuː] *n.* экспро́мт; *adj.* импровизи́рованный (-ан, -ан(н)а); *adv.* без подгото́вки, экспро́мтом.
improper [ɪm'prɒpə(r)] *adj.* (*inaccurate*) непра́вильный; (*indecent*) неприли́чный.
improve [ɪm'pruːv] *v.t.* & *i.* улучша́ть(ся) *impf.*, улу́чшить(ся) *pf.* **improvement** *n.* улучше́ние, усоверше́нствование.
improvidence [ɪm'prɒvɪd(ə)ns] *n.* непредусмотри́тельность. **improvident** *adj.* непредусмотри́тельный.
improvisation [ˌɪmprəvaɪ'zeɪʃ(ə)n] *n.* импровиза́ция. **'improvise** *v.t.* импровизи́ровать *impf.*, сымпровизи́ровать *pf.*
imprudence [ɪm'pruːd(ə)ns] *n.* неосторо́жность. **imprudent** *adj.* неосторо́жный.
impudence ['ɪmpjʊd(ə)nt] *n.* на́глость. **impudent** *adj.* на́глый (нагл, -á, -o).
impugn [ɪm'pjuːn] *v.t.* оспа́ривать *impf.*, оспо́рить *pf.*
impulse ['ɪmpʌls] *n.* (*push*) толчо́к (-чка́); (*impetus*) и́мпульс; (*sudden tendency*) поры́в. **im'pulsive** *adj.* импульси́вный.
impunity [ɪm'pjuːnɪtɪ] *n.* безнака́занность;

with ~ безнака́занно.
impure [ɪm'pjʊə(r)] *adj.* нечи́стый (-т, -та́, -то).
impute [ɪm'pju:t] *v.t.* припи́сывать *impf.*, приписа́ть (-ишу́, -и́шешь) *pf.* (**to** +*d.*); (*fault*) вменя́ть *impf.*, вмени́ть *pf.* в+*a.* (**to** +*d.*).
in [ɪn] *prep.* (*place*) в+*p.*, на+*p.*; (*into*) в+*a.*, на+*a.*; (*point in time*) в+*p.*, на+*p.*; ~ **the morning** (*etc.*) у́тром (*i.*); ~ **spring** (*etc.*) весно́й (*i.*); (*at some stage* ~; *throughout*) во вре́мя+*g.*; (*duration*) за+*a.*; (*after interval of*) че́рез+*a.*; (*during course of*) в тече́ние+*g.*; (*circumstance*) в+*p.*, при+*p.*; *adv.* (*place*) внутри́; (*motion*) внутрь; (*at home*) у себя́, до́ма; (~ *fashion*) в мо́де; ~ **here, there** (*place*) здесь, там; (*motion*) сюда́, туда́; *adj.* вну́тренний; (*fashionable*) мо́дный (-ден, -дна́, -дно); *n.*: **the ~s and outs** все зако́улки *m.pl.*; дета́ли *f.pl.*
inability [ˌɪnə'bɪlɪtɪ] *n.* неспосо́бность, невозмо́жность.
inaccessible [ˌɪnæk'sesɪb(ə)l] *adj.* недосту́пный.
inaccurate [ɪn'ækjʊrət] *adj.* нето́чный (-чен, -чна́, -чно).
inaction [ɪn'ækʃ(ə)n] *n.* безде́йствие. **inactive** *adj.* безде́ятельный. **inac'tivity** *n.* безде́ятельность.
inadequate [ɪn'ædɪkwət] *adj.* недоста́точный, неадеква́тный.
inadmissible [ˌɪnəd'mɪsɪb(ə)l] *adj.* недопусти́мый.
inadvertent [ˌɪnəd'vɜ:t(ə)nt] *adj.* (*inattentive*) невнима́тельный; (*unintentional*) ненаме́ренный (-ен, -енна).
inalienable [ɪn'eɪlɪənəb(ə)l] *adj.* неотъе́млемый, неотчужда́емый.
inane [ɪ'neɪn] *adj.* (*empty*) пусто́й (пуст, -а́, -о, пу́сты́); (*silly*) глу́пый (глуп, -а́, -о).
inanimate [ɪn'ænɪmət] *adj.* (*lifeless*) неодушевлённый (-ён, -ённа); (*dull*) безжи́зненный (-ен, -енна).
inapplicable [ɪn'æplɪkəb(ə)l, ˌɪnə'plɪk-] *adj.* неприменимый.
inapposite [ɪn'æpəzɪt] *adj.* неуме́стный.
inappreciable [ˌɪnə'pri:ʃəb(ə)l] *adj.* незаме́тный.
inappropriate [ˌɪnə'prəʊprɪət] *adj.* неуме́стный.
inapt [ɪn'æpt] *adj.* (*unsuitable*) неподходя́щий; (*unskilful*) неиску́сный. **inaptitude** [ɪn'æptɪˌtju:d] *n.* неуме́стность; неспосо́бность.
inarticulate [ˌɪnɑ:'tɪkjʊlət] *adj.* (*not jointed*) нечленоразде́льный; (*indistinct*) невня́тный.
inasmuch [ˌɪnəz'mʌtʃ] *adv.*: ~ **as** так как; ввиду́ того́, что.
inattention [ˌɪnə'tenʃ(ə)n] *n.* невнима́ние. **inattentive** [ˌɪnə'tentɪv] *adj.* невнима́тельный.
inaudible [ɪn'ɔ:dɪb(ə)l] *adj.* неслы́шный.
inaugural [ɪ'nɔ:gjʊr(ə)l] *adj.* (*lecture etc.*) вступи́тельный. **inaugurate** *v.t.* (*admit to office*) торже́ственно вводи́ть (-ожу́, -о́дишь) *impf.*, ввести́ (введу́, -дёшь; ввёл, -а́) *pf.* в до́лжность; (*open*) открыва́ть *impf.*, откры́ть (-ро́ю, -ро́ешь) *pf.*; (*begin*) начина́ть*impf.*, нача́ть (начну́, -нёшь; на́чал, -а́, -о) *pf.* **inaugu'ration** *n.* торже́ственное введе́ние, вступле́ние, в до́лжность; откры́тие.
inauspicious [ˌɪnɔ:'spɪʃəs] *adj.* неблагоприя́тный.
inborn ['ɪnbɔ:n], **inbred** [ɪn'bred, 'ɪn-] *adj.* врождённый (-ён, -ена́), приро́дный.
incalculable [ɪn'kælkjʊləb(ə)l] *adj.* неисчисли́мый.
incandesce [ˌɪnkæn'des] *v.t.* & *i.* накаля́ть(ся) *impf.*, накали́ть(ся) *pf.* добела́. **incandescence** *n.* бе́лое кале́ние. **incandescent** *adj.* накалённый (-ён, -ена́) добела́.
incantation [ˌɪnkæn'teɪʃ(ə)n] *n.* заклина́ние.
incapability [ɪnˌkeɪpə'bɪlɪtɪ] *n.* неспосо́бность. **in'capable** *adj.* неспосо́бный (**of** к+*d.*, на+*a.*).
incapacitate [ˌɪnkə'pæsɪˌteɪt] *v.t.* де́лать *impf.*, с~ *pf.* неспосо́бным.
incapacity [ˌɪnkə'pæsɪtɪ] *n.* неспосо́бность.
incarcerate [ɪn'kɑ:səˌreɪt] *v.t.* заключа́ть *impf.*, заключи́ть *pf.* (в тюрьму́). **incarce'ration** *n.* заключе́ние (в тюрьму́).
incarnate [ɪn'kɑ:nət; 'ɪnkɑ:ˌneɪt, -'kɑ:neɪt] *adj.* воплощённый (-ён, -ена́); *v.t.* воплоща́ть *impf.*, воплоти́ть (-ощу́, -оти́шь) *pf.* **incar'nation** *n.* воплоще́ние.
incautious [ɪn'kɔ:ʃəs] *adj.* неосторо́жный.
incendiary [ɪn'sendɪərɪ] *adj.* зажига́тельный; *n.* поджига́тель *m.*; (*fig.*) подстрека́тель *m.*; (*bomb*) зажига́тельная бо́мба.
incense[1] ['ɪnsens] *n.* фимиа́м, ла́дан.
incense[2] [ɪn'sens] *v.t.* (*enrage*) разъяря́ть *impf.*, разъяри́ть *pf.*
incentive [ɪn'sentɪv] *n.* побужде́ние.
inception [ɪn'sepʃ(ə)n] *n.* нача́ло.
incessant [ɪn'ses(ə)nt] *adj.* непреста́нный (-нен, -нна).
incest ['ɪnsest] *n.* кровосмеше́ние.
inch [ɪntʃ] *n.* дюйм; ~ **by** ~ ма́ло-пома́лу.
incident *n.* слу́чай, инциде́нт. **incidental** [ˌɪnsɪ'dent(ə)l] *adj.* (*casual*) случа́йный; ~ **to** прису́щий+*d.* **inci'dentally** *adv.* случа́йно; (*by the way*) ме́жду про́чим.
incinerate [ɪn'sɪnəˌreɪt] *v.t.* испепеля́ть *impf.*, испепели́ть *pf.* **incine'ration** *n.* испепеле́ние. **incinerator** *n.* мусоросжига́тельная печь (*pl.* -чи, -че́й).
incipient [ɪn'sɪpɪənt] *adj.* начина́ющийся.
incise [ɪn'saɪz] *v.t.* надре́зывать, надреза́ть *impf.*, надре́зать (-е́жу, -е́зешь) *pf.* **incision** [ɪn'sɪʒ(ə)n] *n.* надре́з (**in** на+*a.*). **incisive** [ɪn'saɪsɪv] *adj.* ре́жущий; (*fig.*) о́стрый (остр & остёр, остра́, о́стро́). **incisor** *n.* резе́ц (-зца́).
incite [ɪn'saɪt] *v.t.* побужда́ть *impf.*, побуди́ть *pf.* (**to** к+*d.*, +*inf.*); подстрека́ть *impf.*, подстрекну́ть *pf.* (**to** к+*d.*). **incitement** *n.*

подстрека́тельство.
incivility [ˌɪnsɪ'vɪlɪtɪ] *n.* неве́жливость.
inclement [ɪn'klemənt] *adj.* суро́вый.
inclination [ˌɪnklɪ'neɪʃ(ə)n] *n.* (*slope*) накло́н; (*propensity*) скло́нность (**for, to** к+*d.*).
incline ['ɪnklaɪn; ɪn'klaɪn] *n.* накло́н; *v.t. & i.* склоня́ть(ся) *impf.*, склони́ть(ся) (-ню́(сь), -нишь(ся)) *pf.* **in'clined** *adj.* (*disposed*) скло́нный (-о́нен, -о́нна́, -о́нно) (**to** к+*d.*).
include [ɪn'klu:d] *v.t.* включа́ть *impf.*, включи́ть *pf.* (**in** в+*a.*); заключа́ть *impf.*, заключи́ть *pf.* в себе́. **including** *prep.* включа́я+*a.* **inclusion** *n.* включе́ние. **inclusive** *adj.* включа́ющий (в себе́); *adv.* включи́тельно.
incognito [ˌɪnkɒg'ni:təʊ] *adv.*, *n.* инко́гнито *adv.*, *m.* & *nt.indecl.*
incoherence [ˌɪnkəʊ'hɪərəns] *n.* бессвя́зность. **incoherent** *adj.* бессвя́зный.
incombustible [ˌɪnkəm'bʌstɪb(ə)l] *adj.* несгора́емый.
income ['ɪnkʌm, 'ɪŋkəm] *n.* дохо́д; ~ **tax** подохо́дный нало́г.
incommensurable [ˌɪnkə'menʃərəb(ə)l, -sjərəb(ə)l] *adj.* несоизмери́мый. **incommensurate** *adj.* несоразме́рный.
incommode [ˌɪnkə'məʊd] *v.t.* беспоко́ить *impf.*, о~ *pf.*
incommodious *adj.* неудо́бный.
incomparable [ɪn'kɒmpərəb(ə)l] *adj.* несравни́мый (**to, with** с+*i.*); (*matchless*) несравне́нный (-нен, -нна).
incompatible [ˌɪnkəm'pætɪb(ə)l] *adj.* несовмести́мый.
incompetence [ɪn'kɒmpɪt(ə)ns] *n.* неспосо́бность; (*leg.*) неправомо́чность. **incompetent** *adj.* неспосо́бный; (*leg.*) неправомо́чный.
incomplete [ˌɪnkəm'pli:t] *adj.* непо́лный (-лон, -лна́, -лно), незако́нченный (-ен, -енна).
incomprehensible [ɪnˌkɒmprɪ'hensɪb(ə)l] *adj.* непоня́тный.
inconceivable [ˌɪnkən'si:vəb(ə)l] *adj.* невообрази́мый.
inconclusive [ˌɪnkən'klu:sɪv] *adj.* неубеди́тельный.
incongruity ['ɪnkɒŋ'gru:ɪtɪ] *n.* несоотве́тствие. **in'congruous** *adj.* несоотве́тственный (-ен, -енна) (**with** +*d.*); (*out of place*) неуме́стный.
inconsequent [ɪn'kɒnsɪkwənt] *adj.* непосле́довательный. **inconsequential** [ɪnˌkɒnsɪ'kwenʃ(ə)l, ˌɪnkɒn-] *adj.* незначи́тельный.
inconsiderable [ˌɪnkən'sɪdərəb(ə)l] *adj.* незначи́тельный.
inconsiderate [ˌɪnkən'sɪdərət] *adj.* (*person*) невнима́тельный; (*action*) необду́манный (-ан, -анна).
inconsistency [ˌɪnkən'sɪst(ə)nsɪ] *n.* непосле́довательность; (*incompatibility*) несовмести́мость. **inconsistent** *adj.* непосле́довательный; (*incompatible*) несовмести́мый.
inconsolable [ˌɪnkən'səʊləb(ə)l] *adj.* безуте́шный.
inconsonant [ɪn'kɒnsənənt] *adj.* несозву́чный (**with** +*d.*).
inconspicuous [ˌɪnkən'spɪkjʊəs] *adj.* незаме́тный.
inconstant [ɪn'kɒnst(ə)nt] *adj.* непостоя́нный (-нен, -нна).
incontestable [ˌɪnkən'testəb(ə)l] *adj.* неоспори́мый.
incontinence [ɪn'kɒntɪnəns] *n.* невозде́ржанность; (*med.*) недержа́ние. **incontinent** *adj.* невозде́ржанный (-ан, -анна).
incontrovertible [ˌɪnkɒntrə'vɜ:tɪb(ə)l] *adj.* неопровержи́мый.
inconvenience [ˌɪnkən'vi:nɪəns] *n.* неудо́бство; *v.t.* причиня́ть *impf.*, причини́ть *pf.* неудо́бство+*d.* **inconvenient** *adj.* неудо́бный.
incorporate [ɪn'kɔ:pəˌreɪt] *v.t.* (*include*) включа́ть *impf.*, включи́ть *pf.*; *v.t. & i.* (*unite*) объединя́ть(ся) *impf.*, объедини́ть(ся) *pf.*; соединя́ть(ся) *impf.*, соедини́ть(ся) *pf.*
incorporeal [ˌɪnkɔ:'pɔ:rɪəl] *adj.* бестеле́сный.
incorrect [ˌɪnkə'rekt] *adj.* непра́вильный.
incorrigible [ɪn'kɒrɪdʒɪb(ə)l] *adj.* неисправи́мый.
incorruptible [ˌɪnkə'rʌptɪb(ə)l] *adj.* неподку́пный; (*not decaying*) непо́ртящийся.
increase ['ɪnkri:s; ɪn'kri:s] *n.* рост, увеличе́ние; (*in pay etc.*) приба́вка; *v.t. & i.* увели́чивать(ся) *impf.*, увели́чить(ся) *pf.*; (*intensify*) уси́ливать(ся) *impf.*, уси́лить(ся) *pf.*
incredible [ɪn'kredɪb(ə)l] *adj.* невероя́тный.
incredulous [ɪn'kredjʊləs] *adj.* недове́рчивый.
increment ['ɪnkrɪmənt] *n.* приба́вка; (*profit*) при́быль.
incriminate [ɪn'krɪmɪˌneɪt] *v.t.* обвиня́ть *impf.*, обвини́ть *pf.* (в преступле́нии).
incubate ['ɪŋkjʊbeɪt] *v.t.* (*eggs*) выводи́ть (-ожу́, -о́дишь) *impf.*, вы́вести (-еду, -едешь; -ел) *pf.* (в инкуба́торе); (*bacteria*) выра́щивать *impf.*, вы́растить *pf.* **incubator** *n.* инкуба́тор.
inculcate ['ɪnkʌlˌkeɪt] *v.t.* внедря́ть *impf.*, внедри́ть *pf.*
incumbent [ɪn'kʌmbənt] *adj.*: **it is** ~ **(up)on you** на вас лежи́т обя́занность.
incur [ɪn'kɜ:(r)] *v.t.* навлека́ть *impf.*, навле́чь (-еку́, -ечёшь; -ёк, -екла́) *pf.* на себя́.
incurable [ɪn'kjʊərəb(ə)l] *adj.* неизлечи́мый.
incurious [ɪn'kjʊərɪəs] *adj.* нелюбопы́тный.
incursion [ɪn'kɜ:ʃ(ə)n] *n.* (*invasion*) вторже́ние; (*attack, raid*) набе́г.
indebted [ɪn'detɪd] *pred.* (*owing money*) в долгу́ (**to** у+*g.*); (*owing gratitude*) обя́зан (-а, -о) (**to** +*d.*).
indecency [ɪn'di:s(ə)nsɪ] *n.* неприли́чие, непристо́йность. **indecent** *adj.* неприли́чный, непристо́йный.
indecision [ˌɪndɪ'sɪʒ(ə)n] *n.* нереши́тельность. **indecisive** [ˌɪndɪ'saɪsɪv] *adj.* нереши́тельный.
indeclinable [ˌɪndɪ'klaɪnəb(ə)l] *adj.* несклоня́емый.
indecorous [ɪn'dekərəs] *adj.* неприли́чный.

indecorum [ˌɪndɪ'kɔːrəm] *n.* неприли́чие.

indeed [ɪn'diːd] *adv.* в са́мом де́ле, действи́тельно; (*interrog.*) неуже́ли?

indefatigable [ˌɪndɪ'fætɪgəb(ə)l] *adj.* неутоми́мый.

indefeasible [ˌɪndɪ'fiːzɪb(ə)l] *adj.* неотъе́млемый.

indefensible [ˌɪndɪ'fensɪb(ə)l] *adj.* (*by arms*) неприго́дный для оборо́ны; (*by argument*) не могу́щий быть опра́вданным.

indefinable [ˌɪndɪ'faɪnəb(ə)l] *adj.* неопредели́мый. **indefinite** [ɪn'defɪnɪt] *adj.* неопределённый (-нён, -нна).

indelible [ɪn'delɪb(ə)l] *adj.* неизглади́мый, несмыва́емый; ~ **pencil** хими́ческий каранда́ш (-а́).

indelicacy [ɪn'delɪkəsɪ] *n.* неделика́тность, беста́ктность. **indelicate** *adj.* неделика́тный, беста́ктный.

indemnify [ɪn'demnɪˌfaɪ] *v.t.*: ~ **against** страхова́ть *impf.*, за~ *pf.* от+*g.*; обезопа́сить *pf.* от+*g.*; ~ **for** (*compensate*) компенси́ровать *impf.* & *pf.* **indemnity** *n.* (*against loss*) гара́нтия от убы́тков; (*compensation*) компенса́ция; (*war* ~) контрибу́ция.

indent [ɪn'dent] *v.t.* (*notch*) зазу́бривать *impf.*, зазубри́ть *pf.*; (*print.*) де́лать *impf.*, с~ *pf.* о́тступ; (*order goods*) зака́зывать *impf.*, заказа́ть (-ажу́, -а́жешь) *pf.* (**for** +*a.*) **inden'tation** *n.* (*notch*) зубе́ц (-бца́); (*print*) о́тступ. **indenture** *n.* контра́кт.

independence [ˌɪndɪ'pend(ə)ns] *n.* незави́симость, самостоя́тельность. **independent** *adj.* незави́симый, самостоя́тельный.

indescribable [ˌɪndɪ'skraɪbəb(ə)l] *adj.* неопису́емый.

indestructible [ˌɪndɪ'strʌktɪb(ə)l] *adj.* неразруши́мый.

indeterminate [ˌɪndɪ'tɜːmɪnət] *adj.* неопределённый (-нен, -нна).

index ['ɪndeks] *n.* и́ндекс, указа́тель *m.*, показа́тель *m.*; (*pointer*) стре́лка; (*finger*) указа́тельный па́лец (-льца); *v.t.* (*provide* ~) снабжа́ть *impf.*, снабди́ть *pf.* указа́телем; (*enter in* ~) заноси́ть (-ошу́, -о́сишь) *impf.*, занести́ (-есу́, есёшь; -ёс, -есла́) *pf.* в указа́тель.

India ['ɪndɪə] *n.* И́ндия. **Indian** *n.* (*from India*) инди́ец (-и́йца), индиа́нка; (*from America*) инде́ец (-е́йца), индиа́нка; *adj.* инди́йский; инде́йский; ~ **club** булава́; ~ **corn** кукуру́за; ~ **ink** тушь; ~ **summer** ба́бье ле́то.

indiarubber [ˌɪndɪə'rʌbə(r)] *n.* каучу́к; (*eraser*) рези́нка.

indicate ['ɪndɪˌkeɪt] *v.t.* ука́зывать *impf.*, указа́ть (-ажу́, -а́жешь) *pf.*; пока́зывать *impf.*, показа́ть (-ажу́, -а́жешь) *pf.* **indi'cation** *n.* указа́ние; (*sign*) при́знак. **in'dicative** *adj.* ука́зывающий; (*gram.*) изъяви́тельный; *n.* изъяви́тельное наклоне́ние. **indicator** *n.* указа́тель *m.*

indict [ɪn'daɪt] *v.t.* обвиня́ть *impf.*, обвини́ть *pf.* (**for** в+*p.*).

indifference [ɪn'dɪfrəns] *n.* равноду́шие, безразли́чие; (*unimportance*) незначи́тельность. **indifferent** *adj.* равноду́шный, безразли́чный; (*mediocre*) посре́дственный (-ен, -енна).

indigenous [ɪn'dɪdʒɪnəs] *adj.* тузе́мный, ме́стный.

indigent ['ɪndɪdʒ(ə)nt] *adj.* нужда́ющийся, бе́дный (-ден, -дна́, -дно, бе́дны́).

indigestible [ˌɪndɪ'dʒestɪb(ə)l] *adj.* неудобовари́мый. **indigestion** *n.* несваре́ние желу́дка.

indignant [ɪn'dɪgnənt] *adj.* негоду́ющий; **be** ~ негодова́ть *impf.* (**with** на+*a.*, про́тив+*g.*). **indig'nation** *n.* негодова́ние.

indignity [ɪn'dɪgnɪtɪ] *n.* оскорбле́ние.

indirect [ˌɪndaɪ'rekt] *adj.* непрямо́й (-м, -ма́, -мо); (*lighting*) отражённый; (*econ.*; *gram.*) ко́свенный.

indiscernible [ˌɪndɪ'sɜːnɪb(ə)l] *adj.* неразличи́мый.

indiscreet [ˌɪndɪ'skriːt] *adj.* нескро́мный (-мен, -мна́, -мно), неосторо́жный. **indiscretion** [ˌɪndɪ'skreʃ(ə)n] *n.* нескро́мность, неосторо́жность, неосмотри́тельность.

indiscriminate [ˌɪndɪ'skrɪmɪnət] *adj.* неразбо́рчивый, огу́льный; (*confused*) беспоря́дочный. **indiscriminately** *adv.* беспоря́дочно; без разбо́ру.

indispensible [ˌɪndɪ'spensəb(ə)l] *adj.* необходи́мый, незамени́мый.

indisposed [ˌɪndɪ'spəʊzd] *pred.* (*unwell*) нездоро́в (-а, -о); (*averse*) не скло́нен (скло́нна́, -но). **indispo'sition** *n.* (*ill health*) нездоро́вье; (*ailment*) неду́г; (*disinclination*) нерасположе́ние.

indisputable [ˌɪndɪ'spjuːtəb(ə)l] *adj.* бесспо́рный.

indissoluble [ˌɪndɪ'sɒljʊb(ə)l] *adj.* неразры́вный; (*in liquid*) нераствори́мый.

indistinct [ˌɪndɪ'stɪŋkt] *adj.* нея́сный (-сен, -сна́, -сно); (*sound only*) невня́тный.

indistinguishable [ˌɪndɪ'stɪŋgwɪʃəb(ə)l] *adj.* неразличи́мый.

individual [ˌɪndɪ'vɪdjʊəl] *n.* индиви́дуум, ли́чность; *adj.* индивидуа́льный, ли́чный. **individualism** *n.* индивидуали́зм. **individualist** *n.* индивидуали́ст. **individua'listic** *adj.* индивидуалисти́ческий. **individu'ality** *n.* индивидуа́льность.

indivisible [ˌɪndɪ'vɪzɪb(ə)l] *adj.* недели́мый.

indoctrinate [ɪn'dɒktrɪˌneɪt] *v.t.* внуша́ть *impf.*, внуши́ть *pf.*+*d.* (**with** +*a.*).

indolence ['ɪndələns] *n.* ле́ность. **indolent** *adj.* лени́вый.

indomitable [ɪn'dɒmɪtəb(ə)l] *adj.* неукроти́мый.

Indonesia [ˌɪndəʊ'niːzɪə] *n.* Индоне́зия.

indoor ['ɪndɔː(r)] *adj.* ко́мнатный, (находя́щийся) внутри́ до́ма. **indoors** *adv.* внутри́ до́ма.

indubitable [ɪn'djuːbɪtəb(ə)l] *adj.* несомне́нный (-е́нен, -е́нна).

induce [ɪn'djuːs] *v.t.* (*prevail on*) заставля́ть *impf.*, заста́вить *pf.*; (*bring about*) вызыва́ть *impf.*, вы́звать (вы́зову, -вешь) *pf.* **inducement** *n.* побужде́ние.

induct [ɪn'dʌkt] *v.t.* вводи́ть (-ожу́, -о́дишь) *impf.*, ввести́ (введу́, -дёшь; ввёл, -а́) *pf.* (в до́лжность).

induction [ɪn'dʌkʃ(ə)n] *n.* инду́кция; (*inducting*) введе́ние в до́лжность.

indulge [ɪn'dʌldʒ] *v.t.* потво́рствовать *impf.+d.*; *v.i.* предава́ться (-даю́сь, -даёшься) *impf.*, преда́ться (-а́мся, -а́шься, -а́стся, -ади́мся; -а́лся, -ала́сь) *pf.* (**in** *+d.*). **indulgence** *n.* снисхожде́ние, потво́рство. **indulgent** *adj.* снисходи́тельный.

industrial [ɪn'dʌstrɪəl] *adj.* промы́шленный. **industrialist** *n.* промы́шленник. **industrious** *adj.* трудолюби́вый, приле́жный. **'industry** *n.* промы́шленность, инду́стри́я; (*diligence*) прилежа́ние.

inebriate [ɪ'niːbrɪət; ɪ'niːbrɪ,eɪt] *n.* пья́ница *c.g.*; *adj.* пья́ный (пьян, -а́, -о); *v.t.* опьяня́ть *impf.*, опьяни́ть *pf.*

inedible [ɪn'edɪb(ə)l] *adj.* несъедо́бный.

ineffable [ɪn'efəb(ə)l] *adj.* несказа́нный.

ineffective [,ɪnɪ'fektɪv] *adj.* безрезульта́тный; (*person*) неспосо́бный.

ineffectual [ɪnɪ'fektjʊəl, -ʃʊəl] *adj.* безрезульта́тный.

inefficiency [,ɪnɪ'fɪʃ(ə)nsɪ] *n.* неэффекти́вность; (*of person*) неспосо́бность. **inefficient** *adj.* неэффекти́вный; неспосо́бный.

inelegant [ɪn'elɪgənt] *adj.* неэлега́нтный.

ineligible [ɪn'elɪdʒɪb(ə)l] *adj.* не могу́щий быть и́збранным.

inept [ɪ'nept] *adj.* (*out of place*) неуме́стный; (*silly*) глу́пый (глуп, -а́, -о); (*unskilful*) неуме́лый.

inequality [,ɪnɪ'kwɒlɪtɪ] *n.* нера́венство, неро́вность.

inequitable [ɪn'ekwɪtəb(ə)l] *adj.* несправедли́вый.

ineradicable [,ɪnɪ'rædɪkəb(ə)l] *adj.* неискорени́мый.

inert [ɪ'nɜːt] *adj.* ине́ртный; (*sluggish*) ко́сный. **inertia** [ɪ'nɜːʃə, -ʃɪə] *n.* (*phys.*) ине́рция; (*sluggishness*) ине́ртность.

inescapable [,ɪnɪ'skeɪpəb(ə)l] *adj.* неизбе́жный.

inessential [,ɪnɪ'senʃ(ə)l] *adj.* несуще́ственный (-ен(ен), -енна).

inestimable [ɪn'estɪməb(ə)l] *adj.* неоцени́мый.

inevitable [ɪn'evɪtəb(ə)l] *adj.* неизбе́жный.

inexact [,ɪnɪg'zækt] *adj.* нето́чный (-чен, -чна́, -чно).

inexcusable [,ɪnɪk'skjuːzəb(ə)l] *adj.* непрости́тельный.

inexhaustible [,ɪnɪg'zɔːstɪb(ə)l] *adj.* неистощи́мый.

inexorable [ɪn'eksərəb(ə)l] *adj.* неумоли́мый.

inexpedient [,ɪnɪk'spiːdɪənt] *adj.* нецелесообра́зный.

inexpensive [,ɪnɪk'spensɪv] *adj.* недорого́й (недо́рог, -а́, -о).

inexperience [,ɪnɪk'spɪərɪəns] *n.* нео́пытность. **inexperienced** *adj.* нео́пытный.

inexpert [ɪn'ekspɜːt] *adj.* неиску́сный.

inexplicable [,ɪnɪk'splɪkəb(ə)l, ɪn'eks-] *adj.* необъясни́мый.

inexpressible [,ɪnɪk'spresɪb(ə)l] *adj.* невыразимый. **inexpressive** *adj.* невырази́тельный.

inextinguishable [,ɪnɪk'stɪŋgwɪʃəb(ə)l] *adj.* неугаси́мый.

inextricable [ɪn'ekstrɪkəb(ə)l, ,ɪnɪk'strɪk-] *adj.* (*of state*) безвы́ходный; (*of problem*) запу́танный (-ан, -анна).

infallible [ɪn'fælɪb(ə)l] *adj.* непогреши́мый.

infamous ['ɪnfəməs] *adj.* (*person*) бесcла́вный, гну́сный (-сен, -сна́, -сно); (*action*) позо́рный. **infamy** *n.* позо́р, дурна́я сла́ва.

infancy ['ɪnfənsɪ] *n.* младе́нчество. **infant** *n.* младе́нец (-нца). **infanticide** [ɪn'fæntɪ,saɪd] *n.* (*action*) детоуби́йство; (*person*) детоуби́йца *c.g.* **infantile** *adj.* младе́нческий, инфанти́льный.

infantry ['ɪnfəntrɪ] *n.* пехо́та; *adj.* пехо́тный. **infantryman** *n.* пехоти́нец (-нца).

infatuate [ɪn'fætjʊ,eɪt] *v.t.* вскружи́ть (-ужу́, -у́жи́шь) *pf.* го́лову+*d.* **infatu'ation** *n.* си́льное увлече́ние.

infect [ɪn'fekt] *v.t.* заража́ть *impf.*, зарази́ть *pf.* (**with** *+i.*). **infection** *n.* зара́за, инфе́кция. **infectious** *adj.* зара́зный; (*fig.*) зарази́тельный.

infelicitous [,ɪnfɪ'lɪsɪtəs] *adj.* несча́стный, неуда́чный. **infelicity** *n.* несча́стье.

infer [ɪn'fɜː(r)] *v.t.* заключа́ть *impf.*, заключи́ть *pf.*; подразумева́ть *impf.* **inference** ['ɪnfərəns] *n.* заключе́ние.

inferior [ɪn'fɪərɪə(r)] *adj.* ни́зший; (*in quality*) ху́дший, плохо́й (плох, -а́, -о, пло́хи́); *n.* подчинённый *sb.* **inferi'ority** *n.* бо́лее ни́зкое положе́ние, бо́лее ни́зкое ка́чество; ~ **complex** ко́мплекс неполноце́нности.

infernal [ɪn'fɜːn(ə)l] *adj.* а́дский. **inferno** *n.* (*hell*) ад (*loc.* -у́); (*conflagration*) пожа́рище.

infertile [ɪn'fɜːtaɪl] *adj.* неплодоро́дный.

infested [ɪn'festɪd] *adj.*: **be ~ with** кише́ть (-шу́, -ши́шь) *impf.+i.*

infidel ['ɪnfɪd(ə)l] *n.* неве́рный *sb.*, неве́рующий *sb.*; *adj.* неве́рующий. **infidelity** [,ɪnfɪ'delɪtɪ] *n.* (*disloyalty*) неве́рность; (*disbelief*) неве́рие.

infiltrate ['ɪnfɪl,treɪt] *v.t.* (*fluid*) фильтрова́ть *impf.*, про~ *pf.*; (*of persons*) постепе́нно проника́ть *impf.*, прони́кнуть (-к) *pf.* в+*a.*

infinite ['ɪnfɪnɪt] *adj.* бесконе́чный, безграни́чный. **infini'tesimal** *adj.* бесконе́чно ма́лый. **in'finitive** *n.* инфинити́в. **in'finity** *n.* бесконе́чность, безграни́чность.

infirm [ɪn'fɜːm] *adj.* не́мощный, сла́бый (слаб, -а́, -о). **infirmary** *n.* больни́ца. **infirmity** *n.* не́мощь, сла́бость.

inflame [ɪn'fleɪm] *v.t. & i.* воспламеня́ть(ся) *impf.*, воспламени́ть(ся) *pf.*; (*excite*) возбуждáть(ся) *impf.*, возбудúть(ся) *pf.*; (*med.*) воспаля́ть(ся) *impf.*, воспалúть(ся) *pf.* **inflammable** [ɪn'flæməb(ə)l] *adj.* огнеопáсный. **infla'mmation** *n.* воспламенéние; (*med.*) воспалéние. **in'flammatory** *adj.* подстрекáтельский; (*med.*) воспалúтельный.

inflate [ɪn'fleɪt] *v.t.* надувáть *impf.*, надýть (-ýю, -ýешь) *pf.*; (*econ.*) проводúть (-ожý, -óдишь) *impf.*, провестú (-едý, -едёшь; -ёл, -елá) *pf.* инфля́цию+*g.* **inflated** *adj.* (*bombastic*) напы́щенный (-ен, -енна). **inflation** *n.* надувáние; (*econ.*) инфля́ция.

inflect [ɪn'flekt] *v.t.* вгибáть *impf.*, вогнýть *pf.*; (*gram.*) изменя́ть *impf.*, изменúть (-ню́, -нишь) *pf.* (окончáние+*g.*). **inflection, -xion** *n.* вгибáние; (*gram.*) флéксия.

inflexible [ɪn'fleksɪb(ə)l] *adj.* негúбкий (-бок, -бкá, -бко); (*fig.*) непреклóнный (-нен, -нна).

inflict [ɪn'flɪkt] *v.t.* (*blow*) наносúть (-ошý, -óсишь) *impf.*, нанестú (-есý, -есёшь; -ёс, -еслá) *pf.* (**(up)on** +*d.*); (*suffering*) причиня́ть *impf.*, причинúть *pf.* (**(up)on** +*d.*); (*penalty*) налагáть *impf.*, наложúть (-жý, -жишь) *pf.* (**(up)on** на+*a.*); ~ **o.s. (up)on** навя́зываться *impf.*, навязáться (-яжýсь, -я́жешься) *pf.*+*d.*

inflow ['ɪnfləʊ] *n.* втекáние, притóк.

influence ['ɪnflʊəns] *n.* влия́ние; *v.t.* влия́ть *impf.*, по~ *pf.* на+*a.* **influential** [ˌɪnflʊ'enʃ(ə)l] *adj.* влия́тельный.

influenza [ˌɪnflʊ'enzə] *n.* грипп.

influx ['ɪnflʌks] *n.* (*of stream*) впадéние; (*of persons*) наплы́в.

inform [ɪn'fɔːm] *v.t.* сообщáть *impf.*, сообщúть *pf.*+*d.* (**of, about** +*a.*, о+*p.*); *v.i.* доносúть (-ошý, -óсишь) *impf.*, донестú (-есý, -есёшь; -ёс, -еслá) *pf.* (**against** на+*a.*).

informal [ɪn'fɔːm(ə)l] *adj.* неофициáльный, неформáльный.

informant [ɪn'fɔːmənt] *n.* осведомúтель *m.* **infor'mation** *n.* информáция, свéдения *nt.pl.*; ~ **science** информáтика. **informer** *n.* донóсчик.

infraction [ɪn'frækʃ(ə)n] *n.* нарушéние.

infra-red [ˌɪnfrə'red] *adj.* инфракрáсный.

infrequent [ɪn'friːkwənt] *adj.* рéдкий (-док, -дкá, -дко).

infringe [ɪn'frɪndʒ] *v.t.* (*violate*) нарушáть *impf.*, нарýшить *pf.*; *v.i.*: ~ **(up)on** посягáть *impf.*, посягнýть *pf.* на+*a.* **infringement** *n.* нарушéние; посягáтельство.

infuriate [ɪn'fjʊərɪˌeɪt] *v.t.* разъяря́ть *impf.*, разъярúть *pf.*

infuse [ɪn'fjuːz] *v.t.* вливáть *impf.*, влить (волью́, -ьёшь; влил, -á, -о) *pf.*; (*fig.*) внушáть *impf.*, внушúть *pf.* (**into** +*d.*); (*steep*) настáивать *impf.*, настоя́ть (-ою́, -оúшь) *pf.* **infusion** *n.* вливáние; внушéние; настóй.

ingenious [ɪn'dʒiːnɪəs] *adj.* изобретáтельный. **inge'nuity** *n.* изобретáтельность.

ingenuous [ɪn'dʒenjʊəs] *adj.* откровéнный (-нен, -нна), бесхúтростный.

inglorious [ɪn'glɔːrɪəs] *adj.* бесслáвный.

ingot ['ɪŋgɒt, -gət] *n.* слúток (-тка).

ingrained [ɪn'greɪnd] *adj.* закоренéлый.

ingratiate [ɪn'greɪʃɪˌeɪt] *v.t.* ~ **o.s.** вкрáдываться *impf.*, вкрáсться (-адýсь, -адёшься; -áлся) *pf.* в мúлость (**with** +*d.*).

ingratitude [ɪn'grætɪˌtjuːd] *n.* неблагодáрность.

ingredient [ɪn'griːdɪənt] *n.* составнáя часть (*pl.* -ти, -тéй).

inhabit [ɪn'hæbɪt] *v.t.* жить (живý, -вёшь; жил, -á, -о) *impf.* в, на, +*p.*; обитáть *impf.* в, на, +*p.* **inhabitant** *n.* жúтель *m.*, ~ница; обитáтель *m.*, ~ница.

inhalation [ˌɪnhə'leɪʃ(ə)n] *n.* вдыхáние. **inhale** [ɪn'heɪl] *v.t.* вдыхáть *impf.*, вдохнýть *pf.*

inherent [ɪn'hɪərənt, ɪn'herənt] *adj.* присýщий (**in** +*d.*).

inherit [ɪn'herɪt] *v.t.* наслéдовать *impf.* & *pf.*, у~ *pf.* **inheritance** *n.* наслéдство. **inheritor** *n.* наслéдник. **inheritress, -trix** *n.* наслéдница.

inhibit [ɪn'hɪbɪt] *v.t.* (*forbid*) запрещáть *impf.*, запретúть (-ещý, -етúшь) *pf.* (+*d.* & *inf.*); (*hinder*) препя́тствовать *impf.*, вос~ *pf.*+*d.* **inhi'bition** *n.* запрещéние; сдéрживание; (*psych.*) торможéние.

inhospitable [ˌɪnhɒ'spɪtəb(ə)l, ɪn'hɒsp-] *adj.* негостеприúмный.

inhuman [ɪn'hjuːmən] *adj.* (*brutal*) бесчеловéчный; (*not human*) нечеловéческий.

inimical [ɪ'nɪmɪk(ə)l] *adj.* враждéбный; (*harmful*) врéдный (-ден, -днá, -дно).

inimitable [ɪ'nɪmɪtəb(ə)l] *adj.* неподражáемый.

iniquitous [ɪ'nɪkwɪtəs] *adj.* несправедлúвый. **iniquity** *n.* несправедлúвость.

initial [ɪ'nɪʃ(ə)l] *adj.* (перво)начáльный; *n.* начáльная бýква; *pl.* инициáлы *m.pl.*; *v.t.* стáвить *impf.*, по~ *pf.* инициáлы на+*a.* **initially** *adv.* в начáле.

initiate [ɪ'nɪʃɪˌeɪt] *v.t.* (*begin*) начинáть *impf.*, начáть (начнý, -нёшь; нáчал, -á, -о) *pf.*; (*admit*) посвящáть *impf.*, посвятúть (-ящý, -ятúшь) *pf.* (**into** в+*a.*).

initiative [ɪ'nɪʃətɪv, ɪ'nɪʃɪətɪv] *n.* почúн, инициатúва.

inject [ɪn'dʒekt] *v.t.* впры́скивать *impf.*, впры́снуть *pf.* **injection** *n.* впры́скивание, инъéкция.

injudicious [ˌɪndʒuː'dɪʃəs] *adj.* неблагоразýмный.

injunction [ɪn'dʒʌŋkʃ(ə)n] *n.* предписáние; (*leg.*) судéбное постановлéние, судéбный запрéт.

injure ['ɪndʒə(r)] *v.t.* вредúть *impf.*, по~ *pf.*+*d.*; повреждáть *impf.*, повредúть *pf.*; (*physically*) рáнить *impf.* & *pf.* **injurious** [ɪn'dʒʊərɪəs] *adj.* врéдный (-ден, -днá, -дно); (*insulting*) оскорбúтельный. **injury** *n.* вред (-á); (*physical*) рáна.

injustice [ɪn'dʒʌstɪs] *n.* несправедлúвость.

ink [ɪŋk] *n.* чернúла (-л) *pl.*; (*printer's* ~) типогрáфская крáска.

inkling ['ɪŋklɪŋ] *n.* (*hint*) намёк (**of** на+*a.*); (*suspicion*) подозре́ние.
ink-well ['ɪŋkwel] *n.* черни́льница.
inland ['ɪnlənd, 'ɪnlænd] *adj.* вну́тренний; *adv.* (*motion*) внутрь страны́; (*place*) внутри́ страны́.
inlay [ɪn'leɪ] *n.* инкруста́ция; *v.t.* инкрусти́ровать *impf.* & *pf.*
inlet ['ɪnlet, -lɪt] *n.* (*of sea*) у́зкий зали́в; впуск.
inmate ['ɪnmeɪt] *n.* жиле́ц (-льца́), жили́ца; (*of prison*) заключённый *sb.*; (*of hospital*) больно́й *sb.*
inmost ['ɪnməʊst, -məst] *adj.* са́мый вну́тренний; (*fig.*) глубоча́йший, сокрове́нный (-е́н, -е́нна).
inn [ɪn] *n.* гости́ница.
innate [ɪ'neɪt, 'ɪ-] *adj.* врождённый (-ён, -ена́).
inner ['ɪnə(r)] *adj.* вну́тренний.
innkeeper ['ɪnˌki:pə(r)] *n.* хозя́ин (*pl.* -я́ева, -я́ев) гости́ницы.
innocence ['ɪnəs(ə)ns] *n.* неви́нность, невино́вность. **innocent** *adj.* неви́нный (-нен, -нна), невино́вный (**of** в+*p.*).
innocuous [ɪ'nɒkjʊəs] *adj.* безвре́дный.
innovate ['ɪnəˌveɪt] *v.i.* вводи́ть (-ожу́, -о́дишь) *impf.*, ввести́ (введу́, -дёшь; ввёл, -а́) *pf.* но́вшества. **inno'vation** *n.* нововведе́ние, но́вшество. **innovative** *adj.* нова́торский. **innovator** *n.* нова́тор.
innuendo [ˌɪnjʊ'endəʊ] *n.* намёк, инсинуа́ция.
innumerable [ɪ'nju:mərəb(ə)l] *adj.* бесчи́сленный (-ен, -енна).
inoculate [ɪ'nɒkjʊˌleɪt] *v.t.* прививáть *impf.*, приви́ть (-вью́, -вьёшь; приви́л, -á, -о) *pf.*+*d.* (**against** +*a.*). **inocu'lation** *n.* приви́вка (**against** от, про́тив+*g.*).
inoffensive [ˌɪnə'fensɪv] *adj.* безоби́дный.
inoperative [ɪn'ɒpərətɪv] *adj.* неде́йствующий.
inopportune [ɪn'ɒpəˌtju:n] *adj.* несвоевре́менный (-нен, -нна).
inordinate [ɪn'ɔ:dɪnət] *adj.* чрезме́рный.
inorganic [ˌɪnɔ:'gænɪk] *adj.* неоргани́ческий.
in-patient ['ɪnˌpeɪʃ(ə)nt] *n.* стациона́рный больно́й *sb.*
input ['ɪnpʊt] *n.* (*action*) ввод, вход; (*power supplied*) вводи́мая мо́щность; (*elec. signal*) входно́й сигна́л; (*econ.*) затра́ты *f.pl.*; (*data*) входны́е да́нные *sb.*; (*device*) устро́йство вво́да.
inquest ['ɪnkwest, 'ɪŋ-] *n.* суде́бное сле́дствие, дозна́ние.
inquire [ɪn'kwaɪə(r), ɪŋ-] *v.t.* спра́шивать *impf.*, спроси́ть (-ошу́, -о́сишь) *pf.*; *v.i.* справля́ться *impf.*, спра́виться *pf.* (**about** о+*p.*); рассле́довать *impf.* & *pf.* (**into** +*a.*) **inquiry** *n.* вопро́с, спра́вка; (*investigation*) рассле́дование; ~ **office** спра́вочное бюро́ *nt.indecl.*
inquisition [ˌɪnkwɪ'zɪʃ(ə)n, ˌɪŋ-] *n.* рассле́дование; **the I~** инквизи́ция. **in'quisitive** *adj.* пытли́вый, любозна́тельный. **in'quisitor** *n.* сле́дователь *m.*; (*hist.*) инквизи́тор.
inroad ['ɪnrəʊd] *n.* набе́г; (*fig.*) посяга́тельство (**on, into** на+*a.*).
insane [ɪn'seɪn] *adj.* душевнобольно́й, безу́мный. **insanity** [ɪn'sænɪtɪ] *n.* безу́мие.
insatiable [ɪn'seɪʃəb(ə)l] *adj.* ненасы́тный.
inscribe [ɪn'skraɪb] *v.t.* надпи́сывать *impf.*, надписа́ть (-ишу́, -и́шешь) *pf.*; впи́сывать *impf.*, вписа́ть (-ишу́, -и́шешь) *pf.*; (*dedicate*) посвяща́ть *impf.*, посвяти́ть (-ящу́, -яти́шь) *pf.* **inscription** [ɪn'skrɪpʃ(ə)n] *n.* на́дпись; посвяще́ние.
inscrutable [ɪn'skru:təb(ə)l] *adj.* непостижи́мый, непроница́емый.
insect ['ɪnsekt] *n.* насеко́мое *sb.* **in'secticide** *n.* инсектици́д. **insec'tivorous** *adj.* насекомоя́дный.
insecure [ˌɪnsɪ'kjʊə(r)] *adj.* (*unsafe*) небезопа́сный; (*not firm*) непро́чный (-чен, -чна́, -чно).
insensate [ɪn'senseɪt] *adj.* бесчу́вственный (-ен, -енна); (*stupid*) глу́пый (глуп, -á, -о).
insensibility [ɪnˌsensɪ'bɪlɪtɪ] *n.* бесчу́вствие. **in'sensible** *adj.* (*inappreciable*) незаме́тный; (*unconscious*) потеря́вший созна́ние; (*insensitive*) нечувстви́тельный.
insensitive [ɪn'sensɪtɪv] *adj.* нечувстви́тельный.
inseparable [ɪn'sepərəb(ə)l] *adj.* неотдели́мый, неразлу́чный.
insert [ɪn'sɜ:t] *v.t.* вставля́ть *impf.*, вста́вить *pf.*; вкла́дывать *impf.*, вложи́ть (-жу́, -о́жишь) *pf.*; (*into newspaper etc.*) помеща́ть *impf.*, помести́ть *pf.* (**in** в+*p.*). **insertion** *n.* (*inserting*) вставле́ние, вкла́дывание; (*thing inserted*) вста́вка; (*in newspaper*) объявле́ние.
inset ['ɪnset] *n.* (*in book*) вкла́дка, вкле́йка; (*in dress*) вста́вка.
inshore [ɪn'ʃɔ:(r), 'ɪn-] *adj.* прибре́жный; *adv.* бли́зко к бе́регу.
inside [ɪn'saɪd] *n.* вну́тренняя сторона́ (*a.* -ону; *pl.* -оны, -о́н, -она́м), вну́тренность; **turn ~ out** вывёртывать *impf.*, вы́вернуть *pf.* наизна́нку; *adj.* вну́тренний; ~ **left, right** (*sport*) ле́вый, пра́вый, полусре́дний *sb.*; *adv.* (*place*) внутри́; (*motion*) внутрь; *prep.* (*place*) внутри́+*g.*, в+*p.*; (*motion*) внутрь+*g.*, в+*a.*
insidious [ɪn'sɪdɪəs] *adj.* кова́рный.
insight ['ɪnsaɪt] *n.* проница́тельность.
insignia [ɪn'sɪgnɪə] *n.* зна́ки *m.pl.* отли́чия, разли́чия.
insignificant [ˌɪnsɪg'nɪfɪkənt] *adj.* незначи́тельный.
insincere [ˌɪnsɪn'sɪə(r)] *adj.* нei̇́скренний (-нен, -нна).
insinuate [ɪn'sɪnjʊˌeɪt] *v.t.* постепе́нно вводи́ть (-ожу́, -о́дишь) *impf.*, ввести́ (введу́, -дёшь; ввёл, -а́) *pf.* (**into** в+*a.*); (*hint*) намека́ть *impf.*, намекну́ть *pf.* на+*a.*; ~ **o.s.** вкра́дываться *impf.*, вкра́сться (-аду́сь, -адёшься; -а́лся) *pf.* (**into** в+*a.*). **insinu'ation** *n.* инсинуа́ция.

insipid [ɪn'sɪpɪd] *adj.* (*tasteless*) безвку́сный; (*dull*) ску́чный (-чен, -чна́, -чно).
insist [ɪn'sɪst] *v.t.* & *i.* утвержда́ть *impf.*; наста́ивать *impf.*, настоя́ть (-ою́, -ои́шь) *pf.* (**on** на+*p.*). **insistent** *adj.* насто́йчивый.
insolence ['ɪnsələns] *n.* на́глость. **insolent** *adj.* на́глый (нагл, -а́, -о).
insoluble [ɪn'sɒljʊb(ə)l] *adj.* (*problem*) неразреши́мый; (*in liquid*) нераствори́мый.
insolvent [ɪn'sɒlv(ə)nt] *adj.* несостоя́тельный.
insomnia [ɪn'sɒmnɪə] *n.* бессо́нница.
insomuch [ˌɪnsəʊ'mʌtʃ] *adv.*: ~ **that** насто́лько..., что; ~ **as** ввиду́ того́, что; так как.
inspect [ɪn'spekt] *v.t.* осма́тривать *impf.*, осмотре́ть (-рю́, -ришь) *pf.*; инспекти́ровать *impf.*, про~ *pf.* **inspection** *n.* осмо́тр, инспе́кция. **inspector** *n.* инспе́ктор (*pl.* -а́), контролёр, ревизо́р.
inspiration [ˌɪnspɪ'reɪʃ(ə)n] *n.* вдохнове́ние; (*breathing in*) вдыха́ние. **inspire** [ɪn'spaɪə(r)] *v.t.* вдохновля́ть *impf.*, вдохнови́ть *pf.*; внуша́ть *impf.*, внуши́ть *pf.*+*d.* (**with** +*a.*); (*breathe in*) вдыха́ть *impf.*, вдохну́ть *pf.*
instability [ˌɪnstə'bɪlɪtɪ] *n.* неусто́йчивость.
install [ɪn'stɔːl] *v.t.* (*person in office*) вводи́ть (-ожу́, -о́дишь) *impf.*, ввести́ (введу́, -дёшь; ввёл, -а́) *pf.* в до́лжность; (*apparatus*) устана́вливать *impf.*, установи́ть (-влю́, -вишь) *pf.* **installation** [ˌɪnstə'leɪʃ(ə)n] *n.* введе́ние в до́лжность; устано́вка; *pl.* сооруже́ния *nt.pl.*
instalment [ɪn'stɔːlmənt] *n.* (*payment*) очередно́й взнос; (*serial publication*) отде́льный вы́пуск; часть (*pl.* -ти, -те́й); **by** ~**s** в рассро́чку, по частя́м.
instance ['ɪnst(ə)ns] *n.* приме́р, слу́чай; (*leg.*) инста́нция; **at the** ~ **of** по тре́бованию+*g.*; **for** ~ наприме́р.
instant ['ɪnst(ə)nt] *n.* мгнове́ние, моме́нт; *adj.* (*immediate*) неме́дленный (-ен, -енна); (*urgent*) настоя́тельный; (*of current month*) теку́щего ме́сяца; (*of coffee etc.*) раствори́мый. **instan'taneous** *adj.* мгнове́нный (-нен, -нна). **instantly** *adv.* неме́дленно, то́тчас.
instead [ɪn'sted] *adv.* вме́сто (**of** +*g.*), взаме́н (**of** +*g.*); ~ **of going** вме́сто того́, что́бый пойти́.
instep ['ɪnstep] *n.* подъём.
instigate ['ɪnstɪˌgeɪt] *v.t.* подстрека́ть *impf.*, подстрекну́ть *pf.* (**to** к+*d.*) **insti'gation** *n.* подстрека́тельство. **instigator** *n.* подстрека́тель *m.*, ~ница.
instil [ɪn'stɪl] *v.t.* (*liquid*) влива́ть *impf.*, влить (волью́, -ьёшь; влил, -а́, -о) *pf.* по ка́пле; (*ideas etc.*) внуша́ть *impf.*, внуши́ть *pf.* (**into** +*d.*).
instinct ['ɪnstɪŋkt] *n.* инсти́нкт. **in'stinctive** *adj.* инстинкти́вный.
institute ['ɪnstɪˌtjuːt] *n.* институ́т, (нау́чное) учрежде́ние; *v.t.* устана́вливать *impf.*, установи́ть (-влю́, -вишь) *pf.*; учрежда́ть *impf.*, учреди́ть *pf.*; (*initiate*) начина́ть *impf.*, нача́ть (начну́, -нёшь; на́чал, -а́, -о) *pf.* **insti'tution** *n.* установле́ние, учрежде́ние.
instruct [ɪn'strʌkt] *v.t.* (*teach*) обуча́ть *impf.*, обучи́ть (-чу́, -чишь) *pf.* (**in** +*d.*); (*inform*) сообща́ть *impf.*, сообщи́ть *pf.*+*d.*; (*command*) прика́зывать *impf.*, приказа́ть (-ажу́, -а́жешь) *pf.*+*d.* **instruction** *n.* инстру́кция; (*teaching*) обуче́ние. **instructive** *adj.* поучи́тельный. **instructor** *n.* инстру́ктор.
instrument ['ɪnstrəmənt] *n.* ору́дие, инструме́нт; (*leg.*) докуме́нт, акт. **instru'mental** *adj.* служа́щий ору́дием; (*mus.*) инструмента́льный; (*gram.*) твори́тельный; **be** ~ **in** спосо́бствовать *impf.*, по~ *pf.*+*d.*; *n.* (*gram.*) твори́тельный паде́ж (-а́). **instrumen'tation** *n.* (*mus.*) инструменто́вка.
insubordinate [ˌɪnsə'bɔːdɪnət] *adj.* неподчиня́ющийся.
insufferable [ɪn'sʌfərəb(ə)l] *adj.* невыноси́мый.
insular ['ɪnsjʊlə(r)] *adj.* (*of island*) островно́й; (*narrow-minded*) ограни́ченный (-ен, -енна).
insulate ['ɪnsjʊˌleɪt] *v.t.* изоли́ровать *impf.* & *pf.*; **insulating tape** изоляцио́нная ле́нта. **insu'lation** *n.* изоля́ция. **insulator** *n.* изоля́тор.
insulin ['ɪnsjʊlɪn] *n.* инсули́н.
insult ['ɪnsʌlt; ɪn'sʌlt] *n.* оскорбле́ние; *v.t.* оскорбля́ть *impf.*, оскорби́ть *pf.* **in'sulting** *adj.* оскорби́тельный.
insurance [ɪn'ʃʊərəns] *n.* страхова́ние; *attr.* страхово́й. **insure** *v.t.* страхова́ть *impf.*, за~ *pf.* (**against** от+*g.*).
insurgent [ɪn'sɜːdʒ(ə)nt] *n.* повста́нец (-нца); *adj.* восста́вший.
insurmountable [ˌɪnsə'maʊntəb(ə)l] *adj.* непреодоли́мый.
insurrection [ˌɪnsə'rekʃ(ə)n] *n.* восста́ние, мяте́ж (-а́).
intact [ɪn'tækt] *adj.* (*untouched*) нетро́нутый; (*entire*) це́лый (цел, -а́, -о).
intake ['ɪnteɪk] *n.* (*action*) впуск, вход; (*mechanism*) впускно́е, приёмное, устро́йство; (*of water*) водозабо́р; (*airway in mine*) вентиляцио́нная вы́работка; (*of persons*) набо́р, о́бщее число́; (*quantity*) потребле́ние.
intangible [ɪn'tændʒɪb(ə)l] *adj.* неосяза́емый.
integral ['ɪntɪgr(ə)l] *adj.* неотъе́млемый; (*whole*) це́льный (-лен, -льна́, -льно); (*math.*) интегра́льный; *n.* интегра́л. **integrate** *v.t.* (*combine*) объединя́ть *impf.*, объедини́ть *pf.*; (*math.*) интегри́ровать *impf.* & *pf.* **inte'gration** *n.* объедине́ние, интегра́ция.
integrity [ɪn'tegrɪtɪ] *n.* (*wholeness*) це́лостность; (*honesty*) че́стность.
intellect ['ɪntɪˌlekt] *n.* интелле́кт, ум (-а́). **inte'llectual** *n.* интеллиге́нт; *adj.* у́мственный; интеллектуа́льный.
intelligence [ɪn'telɪdʒ(ə)ns] *n.* (*intellect*) ум (-а́); (*cleverness*) смышлёность; (*information*) све́дения *nt.pl.*; (~ *service*) разве́дка, разве-

дывательная слу́жба. **intelligent** *adj.* у́мный (умён, умна́, у́мно́).

intelligentsia [ˌɪntelɪˈdʒentsɪə] *n.* интеллиге́нция.

intelligible [ɪnˈtelɪdʒɪb(ə)l] *adj.* поня́тный.

intemperate [ɪnˈtempərət] *adj.* невозде́ржанный.

intend [ɪnˈtend] *v.t.* намерева́ться *impf.+inf.*; быть наме́ренным (-ен)+*inf.*; собира́ться *impf.*, собра́ться (соберу́сь, -рёшься; собра́лся, -ала́сь, -а́ло́сь) *pf.*; (*design*) предназнача́ть *impf.*, предназна́чить *pf.* (**for** для+*g.*, на+*a.*); (*mean*) име́ть *impf.* в виду́.

intense [ɪnˈtens] *adj.* си́льный (си́лён, -льна́, -льно, -си́льны́), напряжённый (-ён, -ённа). **intensify** *v.t. & i.* уси́ливать(ся) *impf.*, уси́лить(ся) *pf.* **intensity** *n.* интенси́вность, напряжённость, си́ла. **intensive** *adj.* интенси́вный.

intent [ɪnˈtent] *n.* наме́рение, цель; *adj.* (*resolved*) стремя́щийся (**on** к+*d.*); (*occupied*) погружённый (-ён, -ена́) (**on** в+*a.*); (*earnest*) внима́тельный. **intention** *n.* наме́рение, цель. **intentional** *adj.* наме́ренный (-ен, -енна), умы́шленный (-ен, -енна).

inter [ɪnˈtɜː(r)] *v.t.* (*bury*) хорони́ть *impf.*, по~ *pf.*

inter- [ˈɪntə(r)] *in comb.* (*mutually*) взаимо...; (*between*) меж..., между...; (*in vv.*) пере... .

interact [ˌɪntərˈækt] *v.i.* взаимоде́йствовать *impf.* **interaction** *n.* взаимоде́йствие. **interactive** *adj.* интеракти́вный, диало́говый.

inter alia [ˌɪntər ˈeɪlɪə, ˈælɪə] *adv.* ме́жду про́чим.

interbreed [ˌɪntəˈbriːd] *v.t. & i.* скре́щивать(ся) *impf.*, скрести́ть(ся) *pf.*

intercede [ˌɪntəˈsiːd] *v.i.* хода́тайствовать *impf.*, по~ *pf.* (**for** за+*a.*; **with** пе́ред+*i.*).

intercept [ˌɪntəˈsept] *v.t.* перехва́тывать *impf.*, перехвати́ть (-ачу́, -а́тишь) *pf.*; (*cut off*) прерыва́ть *impf.*, прерва́ть (-ву́, -вёшь; прерва́л, -а́, -о) *pf.* **interception** *n.* перехва́т.

intercession [ˌɪntəˈseʃ(ə)n] *n.* хода́тайство. **intercessor** *n.* хода́тай.

interchange [ˈɪntəˌtʃeɪndʒ] *n.* (*exchange*) обме́н (**of** +*i.*); (*alternation*) чередова́ние; (*road junction*) тра́нспортная развя́зка; *v.t.* обме́ниваться *impf.*, обменя́ться *pf.+i.*; чередова́ть *impf.* **interchangeable** *adj.* взаимозаменя́емый.

inter-city [ˌɪntəˈsɪtɪ] *adj.* междугоро́дный, межгородско́й.

intercom [ˈɪntəˌkɒm] *n.* вну́тренняя телефо́нная связь; селе́ктор.

interconnection [ˌɪntəkəˈnekʃ(ə)n] *n.* взаимосвя́зь.

intercontinental [ˌɪntəˌkɒntɪˈnent(ə)l] *adj.* межконтинента́льный.

intercourse [ˈɪntəˌkɔːs] *n.* (*social*) обще́ние; (*trade etc.*) сноше́ния *nt.pl.*; (*sexual*) половы́е сноше́ния *nt.pl.*

interdepartmental [ˌɪntəˌdiːpɑːtˈment(ə)l] *adj.* меж(ду)ве́домственный.

interdependent [ˌɪntədɪˈpendənt] *adj.* взаимозави́симый.

interdict [ˈɪntədɪkt] *n.* запреще́ние; *v.t.* запреща́ть *impf.*, запрети́ть (-ещу́, -ети́шь) *pf.* (*person +d.*).

interdisciplinary [ˌɪntəˌdɪsɪˈplɪnərɪ] *adj.* межотраслево́й.

interest [ˈɪntrəst, -trɪst] *n.* интере́с (**in** к+*d.*); (*profit*) вы́года; (*econ.*) проце́нты *m.pl.*; *v.t.* интересова́ть *impf.*; (~ *person in*) заинтересо́вывать *impf.*, заинтересова́ть *pf.* (**in** +*i.*); **be ~ed in** интересова́ться *impf.+i.* **interesting** *adj.* интере́сный.

interethnic [ˌɪntəˈeθnɪk] *adj.* межнациона́льный.

interface [ˈɪntəˌfeɪs] *n.* (*comput.*) интерфе́йс.

interfere [ˌɪntəˈfɪə(r)] *v.i.* меша́ть *impf.*, по~ *pf.* (**with** +*d.*); вме́шиваться *impf.*, вмеша́ться *pf.* (**in** в+*a.*). **interference** *n.* вмеша́тельство; (*radio*) поме́хи *f.pl.*

intergovernmental [ˌɪntəgʌvənˈment(ə)l] *adj.* межправи́тельственный.

interim [ˈɪntərɪm] *n.* промежу́ток (-тка) (вре́мени); **in the ~** тем вре́менем; *adj.* промежу́точный; (*temporary*) вре́менный.

interior [ɪnˈtɪərɪə(r)] *n.* вну́тренность; (*pol.*) вну́тренние дела́ *nt.pl.*; *adj.* вну́тренний.

interjection [ˌɪntəˈdʒekʃ(ə)n] *n.* восклица́ние; (*gram.*) междоме́тие.

interlace [ˌɪntəˈleɪs] *v.t. & i.* переплета́ть(ся) *impf.*, переплести́(сь) (-ету́(сь), -етёшь(ся); -ёл(ся), -ела́(сь)) *pf.*

interlinear [ˌɪntəˈlɪnɪə(r)] *adj.* междустро́чный.

interlock [ˌɪntəˈlɒk] *v.t. & i.* сцепля́ть(ся) *impf.*, сцепи́ть(ся) (-плю́(сь), -пишь(ся)) *pf.*

interlocutor [ˌɪntəˈlɒkjʊtə(r)] *n.* собесе́дник, -ица.

interlope [ˌɪntəˈləʊp] *v.i.* вме́шиваться *impf.*, вмеша́ться *pf.* в чужи́е дела́.

interlude [ˈɪntəˌluːd, -ˌljuːd] *n.* промежу́точный эпизо́д; (*theatr.*) антра́кт.

intermediary [ˌɪntəˈmiːdɪərɪ] *n.* посре́дник; *adj.* посре́днический; (*intermediate*) промежу́точный.

intermediate [ˌɪntəˈmiːdɪət] *adj.* промежу́точный.

interment [ɪnˈtɜːmənt] *n.* погребе́ние.

interminable [ɪnˈtɜːmɪnəb(ə)l] *adj.* бесконе́чный.

intermission [ˌɪntəˈmɪʃ(ə)n] *n.* переры́в, па́уза.

intermittent [ˌɪntəˈmɪt(ə)nt] *adj.* преры́вистый.

intermix [ˌɪntəˈmɪks] *v.t. & i.* переме́шивать(ся) *impf.*, перемеша́ть(ся) *pf.*

intern [ɪnˈtɜːn] *v.t.* интерни́ровать *impf.* & *pf.*

internal [ɪnˈtɜːn(ə)l] *adj.* вну́тренний; **~ combustion engine** дви́гатель *m.* вну́треннего сгора́ния.

international [ˌɪntəˈnæʃən(ə)l] *n.* (*contest*) междунаро́дное состяза́ние; *adj.* междунаро́дный, интернациона́льный. **internationalism** *n.* интернационали́зм.

internecine [ˌɪntəˈniːsaɪn] *adj.* междоусо́бный.

internee [ˌɪntɜːˈniː] *n.* интерни́рованный *sb.* **in'ternment** *n.* интерни́рование.

interplanetary [ˌɪntəˈplænɪtərɪ] *adj.* межплане́тный.

interplay [ˈɪntəˌpleɪ] *n.* взаимоде́йствие.

interpolate [ɪnˈtɜːpəˌleɪt] *v.t.* (*insert*) вставля́ть *impf.*, вста́вить *pf.*; (*math.*) интерполи́ровать *impf.* & *pf.* **interpo'lation** *n.* вста́вка; (*math.*) интерполя́ция.

interpose [ˌɪntəˈpəʊz] *v.t.* (*insert*) вставля́ть *impf.*, вста́вить *pf.*; *v.i.* (*intervene*) вме́шиваться *impf.*, вмеша́ться *pf.*

interpret [ɪnˈtɜːprɪt] *v.t.* толкова́ть *impf.*; (*speech etc.*) у́стно переводи́ть *impf.*, перевести́ (-еду́, -едёшь; -ёл, -ела́) *pf.* **interpre'tation** *n.* толкова́ние. **interpreter** *n.* толкова́тель *m.*; перево́дчик, -ица.

interregnum [ˌɪntəˈregnəm] *n.* междуца́рствие; (*interval*) переры́в.

interrogate [ɪnˈterəˌgeɪt] *v.t.* допра́шивать *impf.*, допроси́ть (-ошу́, -о́сишь) *pf.* **interro'gation** *n.* допро́с; (*question*) вопро́с. **inte'rrogative** *adj.* вопроси́тельный.

interrupt [ˌɪntəˈrʌpt] *v.t.* прерыва́ть *impf.*, прерва́ть (-ву́, -вёшь; -ва́л, -вала́, -ва́ло) *pf.* **interruption** *n.* переры́в.

intersect [ˌɪntəˈsekt] *v.t.* & *i.* пересека́ть(ся) *impf.*, пересе́чь(ся) (-еку́(сь), -ечёшь(ся); -е́к(ся), -екла́(сь)) *pf.* **intersection** *n.* пересече́ние.

intersperse [ˌɪntəˈspɜːs] *v.t.* (*scatter*) рассыпа́ть *impf.*, рассы́пать (-плю, -плешь) *pf.* (**between, among** ме́жду+*i.*, среди́+*g.*); (*diversify*) разнообра́зить *impf.*

intertwine [ˌɪntəˈtwaɪn] *v.t.* & *i.* переплета́ть(ся) *impf.*, переплести́(сь) (-ету́(сь), -етёшь(ся); -ёл(ся), -ела́(сь)) *pf.*

interval [ˈɪntəv(ə)l] *n.* промежу́ток (-тка); (*also mus.*) интерва́л; (*school*) переме́на.

intervene [ˌɪntəˈviːn] *v.i.* (*occur*) происходи́ть (-ит) *impf.*, произойти́ (-ойдёт; -ошёл, -ошла́) *pf.*; ~ **in** вме́шиваться *impf.*, вмеша́ться *pf.* в+*a.* **intervention** [ˌɪntəˈvenʃ(ə)n] *n.* вмеша́тельство; (*pol.*) интерве́нция.

interview [ˈɪntəˌvjuː] *n.* делово́е свида́ние, встре́ча; (*press* ~) интервью́ *nt.indecl.*; *v.t.* интервьюи́ровать *impf.* & *pf.*, про~ *pf.* **interviewer** *n.* интервьюе́р.

interweave [ˌɪntəˈwiːv] *v.t.* вотка́ть (-ку́, -кёшь; -ка́л, -ка́ла́, -ка́ло) *pf.*

intestate [ɪnˈtestət] *adj.* уме́рший без завеща́ния.

intestinal [ˌɪnteˈstaɪn(ə)l] *adj.* кише́чный. **intestine** [ɪnˈtestɪn] *n.* кишка́ (*g.pl.* -шо́к); *pl.* кише́чник.

intimacy [ˈɪntɪməsɪ] *n.* инти́мность, бли́зость. **intimate**[1] [ˈɪntɪmət] *adj.* инти́мный, бли́зкий (-зок, -зка́, -зко, бли́зки́).

intimate[2] [ˈɪntɪˌmeɪt] *v.t.* (*state*) сообща́ть *impf.*, сообщи́ть *pf.*; (*hint*) намека́ть *impf.*, намекну́ть *pf.* на+*a.* **inti'mation** *n.* сообще́ние; намёк.

intimidate [ɪnˈtɪmɪˌdeɪt] *v.t.* запу́гивать *impf.*, запуга́ть *pf.*

into [ˈɪntʊ, ˈɪntə] *prep.* в, во+*a.*, на+*a.*

intolerable [ɪnˈtɒlərəb(ə)l] *adj.* невыноси́мый. **intolerance** *n.* нетерпи́мость. **intolerant** *adj.* нетерпи́мый.

intonation [ˌɪntəˈneɪʃ(ə)n] *n.* интона́ция. **intone** [ɪnˈtəʊn] *v.t.* интони́ровать *impf.*

intoxicant [ɪnˈtɒksɪˌkənt] *adj.* (*n.*) опьяня́ющий (напи́ток (-тка)). **intoxicate** *v.t.* опьяня́ть *impf.*, опьяни́ть *pf.* **intoxi'cation** *n.* опьяне́ние; **in a state of** ~ в нетре́звом состоя́нии.

intra- [ˈɪntrə] *pref.* внутри... .

intractable [ɪnˈtræktəb(ə)l] *adj.* неподатливый.

intransigent [ɪnˈtrænsɪdʒ(ə)nt, -zɪdʒ(ə)nt] *adj.* непримири́мый.

intransitive [ɪnˈtrænsɪtɪv, ɪnˈtrɑːn-, -zɪtɪv] *adj.* неперехо́дный.

intrepid [ɪnˈtrepɪd] *adj.* неустраши́мый.

intricacy [ˈɪntrɪkəsɪ] *n.* запу́танность, сло́жность. **intricate** *adj.* запу́танный (-ан, -анна), сло́жный (-жен, -жна́, -жно).

intrigue [ɪnˈtriːg, ˈɪn-] *n.* интри́га; *v.i.* интригова́ть *impf.*; *v.t.* интригова́ть *impf.*, за~ *pf.* **intriguer** *n.* интрига́н, ~ка.

intrinsic [ɪnˈtrɪnzɪk] *adj.* прису́щий, суще́ственный (-ен, -енна).

introduce [ˌɪntrəˈdjuːs] *v.t.* вводи́ть (-ожу́, -о́дишь) *impf.*, ввести́ (введу́, -дёшь; ввёл, -а́) *pf.*; вноси́ть (-ошу́, -о́сишь) *impf.*, внести́ (внесу́, -сёшь; внёс, -ла́) *pf.*; (*person*) представля́ть *impf.*, предста́вить *pf.* **introduction** *n.* введе́ние, внесе́ние; представле́ние; (*to book*) предисло́вие. **introductory** *adj.* вво́дный, вступи́тельный.

introspection [ˌɪntrəˈspekʃ(ə)n] *n.* самонаблюде́ние.

intrude [ɪnˈtruːd] *v.i.* вторга́ться *impf.*, вто́ргнуться (-г(нул)ся, -глась) *pf.* (**into** в+*a.*); *v.t.* & *i.* навя́зывать(ся) *impf.*, навяза́ть(ся) (-яжу́(сь), -я́жешь(ся)) *pf.* (**upon** +*d.*). **intrusion** *n.* вторже́ние.

intuition [ˌɪntjuːˈɪʃ(ə)n] *n.* интуи́ция. **in'tuitive** *adj.* интуити́вный.

inundate [ˈɪnənˌdeɪt] *v.t.* наводня́ть *impf.*, наводни́ть *pf.* **inun'dation** *n.* наводне́ние.

inure [ɪˈnjʊə(r)] *v.t.* приуча́ть *impf.*, приучи́ть (-чу́, -чишь) *pf.* (**to** к+*d.*, +*inf.*).

invade [ɪnˈveɪd] *v.t.* вторга́ться *impf.*, вто́ргнуться (-г(нул)ся, -глась) *pf.* в+*a.* **invader** *n.* захва́тчик.

invalid[1] [ˈɪnvəˌliːd, -lɪd] *n.* (*disabled person*) инвали́д, больно́й *sb.*; *adj.* (*disabled*) нетрудоспосо́бный.

invalid[2] [ɪnˈvælɪd] *adj.* (*not valid*) недействи́тельный. **invalidate** *v.t.* де́лать *impf.*, с~ *pf.* недействи́тельным.

invaluable [ɪnˈvæljʊəb(ə)l] *adj.* неоцени́мый.

invariable [ɪnˈveərɪəb(ə)l] *adj.* неизме́нный (-нен, -нна); (*math.*) постоя́нный (-нен, -нна).

invasion [ɪn'veɪʒ(ə)n] *n.* вторже́ние (в+*a.*); (*encroachment*) посяга́тельство (на+*a.*).
invective [ɪn'vektɪv] *n.* (*verbal attack*) обличи́тельная речь; (*abuse*) руга́тельства *nt.pl.*
inveigh [ɪn'veɪ] *v.i.* поноси́ть (-ошу́, -о́сишь) *impf.* (**against** +*a.*).
inveigle [ɪn'veɪg(ə)l, -'vi:g(ə)l] *v.t.* завлека́ть *impf.*, завле́чь (-еку́, -ечёшь; -ёк, -екла́) *pf.*
invent [ɪn'vent] *v.t.* изобрета́ть *impf.*, изобрести́ (-ету́, -етёшь; -ёл, -ела́) *pf.*; выду́мывать *impf.*, вы́думать *pf.* **invention** *n.* изобрете́ние; вы́думка. **inventive** *adj.* изобрета́тельный. **inventor** *n.* изобрета́тель *m.*
inventory ['ɪnvəntərɪ] *n.* инвента́рь (-ря́) *m.*, о́пись (иму́щества); *v.t.* инвентаризова́ть *impf.* & *pf.*
inverse ['ɪnvɜ:s, -'vɜ:s] *adj.* обра́тный. **inversion** *n.* перестано́вка.
invertebrate [ɪn'vɜ:tɪbrət, -ˌbreɪt] *adj.* беспозвоно́чный; *n.* беспозвоно́чное *sb.*
invest [ɪn'vest] *v.t.* (*clothe*, *endue*) облека́ть *impf.*, обле́чь (-еку́, -ечёшь; -ёк, -екла́) *pf.* (**in** в+*a.*; **with** +*i.*); (*lay siege to*) осажда́ть *impf.*, осади́ть *pf.*; *v.t.* & *i.* (*econ.*) вкла́дывать *impf.*, вложи́ть (-жу́, -о́жишь) *pf.* (де́ньги) (**in** в+*a.*); инвести́ровать *impf.* & *pf.*
investigate [ɪn'vestɪˌgeɪt] *v.t.* иссле́довать *impf.* & *pf.*; (*leg.*) рассле́довать *impf.* & *pf.* **investi'gation** *n.* иссле́дование; рассле́дование. **investigator** *n.* иссле́дователь *m.*; (*leg.*) сле́дователь *m.*
investiture [ɪn'vestɪˌtjʊə(r)] *n.* введе́ние в до́лжность.
investment [ɪn'vestmənt] *n.* (*econ.*) вложе́ние, вклад, инвести́ция; (*mil.*) оса́да. **investor** *n.* вкла́дчик.
inveterate [ɪn'vetərət] *adj.* закорене́лый, застаре́лый.
invigorate [ɪn'vɪgəˌreɪt] *v.t.* укрепля́ть *impf.*, укрепи́ть *pf.*; (*animate*) оживля́ть *impf.*, оживи́ть *pf.*
invincible [ɪnˌvɪnsɪb(ə)l] *adj.* непобеди́мый.
inviolable [ɪn'vaɪələb(ə)l] *adj.* неприкоснове́нный (-нен, -нна), неруши́мый. **inviolate** *adj.* ненару́шенный.
invisible [ɪn'vɪzɪb(ə)l] *adj.* неви́димый; ~ **ink** симпати́ческие черни́ла (-л) *pl.*
invitation [ˌɪnvɪ'teɪʃ(ə)n] *n.* приглаше́ние. **invite** [ɪn'vaɪt] *v.t.* приглаша́ть *impf.*, пригласи́ть *pf.*; (*request*) проси́ть (-ошу́, -о́сишь) *impf.*, по~ *pf.*; (*attract*) привлека́ть *impf.*, привле́чь (-еку́, -ечёшь; -ёк, -екла́) *pf.* **in'viting** *adj.* привлека́тельный.
invocation [ˌɪnvə'keɪʃ(ə)n] *n.* призы́в.
invoice ['ɪnvɔɪs] *n.* факту́ра, накладна́я *sb.*
invoke [ɪn'vəʊk] *v.t.* призыва́ть *impf.*, призва́ть (-зову́, -зовёшь; призва́л, -а́, -о); взыва́ть *impf.*, воззва́ть (-зову́, -зовёшь) *pf.*
involuntary [ɪn'vɒləntərɪ] *adj.* нево́льный; непроизво́льный.
involve [ɪn'vɒlv] *v.t.* (*entail*) вовлека́ть *impf.*, вовле́чь (-еку́, -ечёшь; -ёк, -екла́) *pf.*; (*include*) включа́ть *impf.*, включи́ть *pf.* в себе́. **involved** *adj.* (*complex*) сло́жный (-жен, -жна́, -жно).
invulnerable [ɪn'vʌlnərəb(ə)l] *adj.* неуязви́мый.
inward ['ɪnwəd] *adj.* вну́тренний. **inwardly** *adv.* внутри́, вну́тренне. **inwards** *adv.* внутрь.
iodine ['aɪəˌdi:n, -ɪn] *n.* йод; *attr.* йо́дный.
ion ['aɪən] *n.* ио́н. **ionic** [aɪ'ɒnɪk] *adj.* ио́нный.
iota [aɪ'əʊtə] *n.* йо́та; **not an** ~ ни на йо́ту.
IOU [ˌaɪəʊ'ju:] *n.* долгова́я распи́ска.
IQ *abbr.* (*of* ***intelligence quotient***) коэффицие́нт у́мственного разви́тия.
Iran [ɪ'rɑ:n] *n.* Ира́н.
Iraq [ɪ'rɑ:k] *n.* Ира́к.
irascible [ɪ'ræsɪb(ə)l] *adj.* раздражи́тельный.
irate [aɪ'reɪt] *adj.* гне́вный (-вен, -вна́, -вно). **ire** *n.* гнев.
Ireland ['aɪələnd] *n.* Ирла́ндия.
iridescent [ˌɪrɪ'des(ə)nt] *adj.* ра́дужный.
iris ['aɪərɪs] *n.* (*anat.*) ра́дужная оболо́чка; (*bot.*) каса́тик.
Irish ['aɪərɪʃ] *adj.* ирла́ндский. **Irishman** *n.* ирла́ндец (-дца). **Irishwoman** *n.* ирла́ндка.
irk [ɜ:k] *v.t.* надоеда́ть *impf.*, надое́сть (-е́м, -е́шь, -е́ст, -еди́м; -е́л) *pf.*+*d.* **irksome** *adj.* ску́чный (-чен, -чна́, -чно).
iron ['aɪən] *n.* желе́зо; (*for clothes*) утю́г (-а́); *pl.* (*fetters*) кандалы́ (-ло́в) *pl.*; *adj.* желе́зный; *v.t.* (*clothes*) утю́жить *impf.*, вы́~, от~ *pf.*; гла́дить *impf.*, вы́~ *pf.*
ironic(al) [aɪ'rɒnɪkəl] *adj.* ирони́ческий. **irony** ['aɪrənɪ] *n.* иро́ния.
irradiate [ɪ'reɪdɪˌeɪt] *v.t.* (*light up*) освеща́ть *impf.*, освети́ть (-ещу́, -ети́шь) *pf.*; (*subject to radiation*) облуча́ть *impf.*, облучи́ть *pf.* **irradi'ation** *n.* освеще́ние; облуче́ние.
irrational [ɪ'ræʃən(ə)l] *adj.* неразу́мный; (*math.*) иррациона́льный.
irreconcilable [ɪ'rekənˌsaɪləb(ə)l] *adj.* (*persons*) непримири́мый; (*ideas*) несовмести́мый.
irrecoverable [ˌɪrɪ'kʌvərəb(ə)l] *adj.* невозвра́тный.
irredeemable [ˌɪrɪ'di:məb(ə)l] *adj.* (*econ.*) не подлежа́щий вы́купу; (*hopeless*) безнадёжный.
irrefutable [ɪ'refjʊtəb(ə)l, ˌɪrɪ'fju:-] *adj.* неопровержи́мый.
irregular [ɪ'regjʊlə(r)] *adj.* нерегуля́рный; (*gram.*) непра́вильный; (*not even*) неро́вный (-вен, -вна́, -вно); (*disorderly*) беспоря́дочный.
irrelevant [ɪ'relɪv(ə)nt] *adj.* неуме́стный.
irreligious [ˌɪrɪ'lɪdʒəs] *adj.* неве́рующий.
irremediable [ˌɪrɪ'mi:dɪəb(ə)l] *adj.* непоправи́мый, неизлечи́мый.
irremovable [ˌɪrɪ'mu:vəb(ə)l] *adj.* неустрани́мый; (*from office*) несменя́емый.
irreparable [ɪ'repərəb(ə)l] *adj.* непоправи́мый.
irreplaceable [ˌɪrɪ'pleɪsəb(ə)l] *adj.* незамени́мый.

irrepressible [ˌɪrɪ'presɪb(ə)l] *adj.* неудержи́мый.

irreproachable [ˌɪrɪ'prəʊtʃəb(ə)l] *adj.* безупре́чный.

irresistible [ˌɪrɪ'zɪstɪb(ə)l] *adj.* неотрази́мый.

irresolute [ɪ'rezəˌluːt, -ˌljuːt] *adj.* нереши́тельный.

irrespective [ˌɪrɪ'spektɪv] *adj.*: ~ **of** безотноси́тельнно к+*d.*, незави́симо от+*g.*

irresponsible [ˌɪrɪ'spɒnsɪb(ə)l] *adj.* (*of conduct etc.*) безотве́тственный (-ен, -енна); (*not responsible*) неотве́тственный (-ен, -енна); (*leg.*) невменя́емый.

irretrievable [ˌɪrɪ'triːvəb(ə)l] *adj.* непоправи́мый, невозвра́тный.

irreverent [ɪ'revərənt] *adj.* непочти́тельный.

irreversible [ˌɪrɪ'vɜːsɪb(ə)l] *adj.* необрати́мый.

irrevocable [ɪ'revəkəb(ə)l] *adj.* неотменя́емый.

irrigate ['ɪrɪˌgeɪt] *v.t.* ороша́ть *impf.*, ороси́ть *pf.* **irri'gation** *n.* ороше́ние, ирригáция.

irritable ['ɪrɪtəb(ə)l] *adj.* раздражи́тельный. **irritate** *v.t.* раздража́ть *impf.*, раздражи́ть *pf.* **irri'tation** *n.* раздраже́ние.

Islam ['ɪzlɑːm, -læm, -'lɑːm] *n.* исла́м. **Islamic** *adj.* мусульма́нский, исламистский.

island ['aɪlənd], **isle** [aɪl] *n.* о́стров (*pl.* -а́); *adj.* островно́й. **islander** *n.* островитя́нин (*pl.* -я́не, -я́н), -я́нка. **islet** *n.* острово́к (-вка́).

iso- ['aɪsəʊ] *in comb.* изо..., равно... . **isobar** *n.* изоба́ра. **isosceles** [aɪ'sɒsɪˌliːz] *adj.* равнобе́дренный. **isotherm** *n.* изоте́рма. **isotope** ['aɪsəˌtəʊp] *n.* изото́п.

isolate ['aɪsəˌleɪt] *v.t.* изоли́ровать *impf.* & *pf.*; обособля́ть *impf.*, обосо́бить *pf.*; (*chem.*) выделя́ть *impf.*, вы́делить *pf.* **iso'lation** *n.* изоля́ция; ~ **hospital** инфекцио́нная больни́ца; ~ **ward** изоля́тор.

Israel ['ɪzreɪl] *n.* Изра́иль *m.* **Is'raeli** *n.* израильтя́нин (*pl.* -я́не, -я́н), -я́нка; *adj.* изра́ильский.

issue ['ɪʃuː, 'ɪsjuː] *n.* (*outlet*) вы́ход; (*outflow*) вытека́ние; (*progeny*) пото́мство; (*outcome*) исхо́д, результа́т; (*question*) (спо́рный) вопро́с; (*of book etc.*) вы́пуск, изда́ние; *v.i.* выходи́ть (-ожу́, -о́дишь) *impf.*, вы́йти (вы́йду, -дешь; вы́шел, -шла) *pf.*; (*flow*) вытека́ть *impf.*, вы́течь (-еку, -ечешь; -ек) *pf.*; *v.t.* выпуска́ть *impf.*, вы́пустить *pf.*; выдава́ть (-даю́, -даёшь) *impf.*, вы́дать (-ам, -ашь, -аст, -адим) *pf.*

isthmus ['ɪsməs, 'ɪsθ-] *n.* перешéек (-е́йка).

it [ɪt] *pron.* он, оно́ (его́, ему́, им, о нём), она́ (её, ей, ей & е́ю, о ней); *demonstrative* э́то.

Italian [ɪ'tæljən] *n.* италья́нец (-нца), -нка; *adj.* италья́нский.

italic [ɪ'tælɪk] *adj.* (**I~**) итали́йский; (*print.*) курси́вный; *n.* курси́в. **italicize** [ɪ'tælɪˌsaɪz] *v.t.* выделя́ть *impf.*, вы́делить *pf.* курси́вом.

Italy ['ɪtəlɪ] *n.* Ита́лия.

itch [ɪtʃ] *n.* зуд, чесо́тка; *v.i.* зуде́ть (-ди́т) *impf.*; чеса́ться (че́шется) *impf.*

item ['aɪtəm] *n.* (*on list*) предме́т; (*in account*) пункт; (*on agenda*) вопро́с; (*in programme*) но́мер (*pl.* -а́); *adv.* та́кже, то́же.

iterate ['ɪtəˌreɪt] *v.t.* повторя́ть *impf.*, повтори́ть *pf.*

itinerant [aɪ'tɪnərənt, ɪ-] *adj.* стра́нствующий. **itinerary** *n.* (*route*) маршру́т; (*guidebook*) путеводи́тель *m.*

its [ɪts] *poss. pron.* его́, её; свой (-оя́, -оё; -ой).

itself [ɪt'self] *pron.* (*emph.*) (он(о́) сам(о́) (-ого́, -ому́, -и́м, -о́м), (она́) сама́ (-мо́й, -му́); (*refl.*) себя́ (себе́, собо́й); -ся (*suffixed to v.t.*)

ITV (*abbr. of* ***Independent Television***) незави́симое (комме́рческое) телеви́дение.

ivory ['aɪvərɪ] *n.* слоно́вая кость.

ivy ['aɪvɪ] *n.* плющ (-а́).

J

jab [dʒæb] *n.* уко́л, толчо́к (-чка́); *v.t.* ты́кать (ты́чу, -чешь) *impf.*, ткнуть *pf.* (+*i.* в+*a.*; +*a.* в+*a.*).

jabber ['dʒæbə(r)] *n.* болтовня́; *v.t.* & *i.* болта́ть *impf.*

jack [dʒæk] *n.* (*cards*) вале́т; (*lifting machine*) домкра́т; *v.t.* (~ *up*) поднима́ть *impf.*, подня́ть (-ниму́, -ни́мешь; по́днял, -а́, -о) *pf.* домкра́том.

jackal ['dʒæk(ə)l] *n.* шака́л.

jackass ['dʒækæs] *n.* осёл (осла́).

jackdaw ['dʒækdɔː] *n.* га́лка.

jacket ['dʒækɪt] *n.* ку́ртка; (*woman's*) жаке́тка; (*tech.*) кожу́х (-а́); (*on boiler*) руба́шка; (*on book*) (супер)обло́жка.

jack-knife ['dʒæknaɪf] *n.* большо́й складно́й нож (-а́).

jaded *adj.* изнурённый (-ён, -ённа).

jade [dʒeɪd] *n.* нефри́т.

jagged ['dʒægɪd] *adj.* зубча́тый, зазу́бренный (-ен, -енна).

jaguar ['dʒægjʊə(r)] *n.* ягуа́р.

jail [dʒeɪl] *n.* тюрьма́ (*pl.* -рьмы, -рем, -рьмам); *v.t.* заключа́ть *impf.*, заключи́ть *pf.* в тюрьму́. **jailer** *n.* тюре́мщик.

jam¹ [dʒæm] *n.* (*crush*) да́вка; (*of machine*) заеда́ние, перебо́й; (*in traffic*) про́бка; *v.t.* (*squeeze*) сжима́ть *impf.*, сжать (сожму́, -мёшь) *pf.*; (*thrust*) впи́хивать *impf.*, впихну́ть *pf.* (**into** в+*a.*); (*block*) загроможда́ть *impf.*, загромозди́ть *pf.*; (*radio*) заглуша́ть *impf.*, заглуши́ть *pf.*; *v.i.* (*machine*) заеда́ть *impf.*, зае́сть (-е́ст; -е́ло) *pf. impers.*+*a.*

jam² [dʒæm] *n.* (*conserve*) варе́нье, джем.
jamb [dʒæm] *n.* кося́к (-а́).
jangle ['dʒæŋg(ə)l] *n.* ре́зкий звук; *v.i.* издава́ть (-даю́, -даёшь) *impf.*, изда́ть (-а́м, -а́шь, -а́ст, -ади́м; изда́л, -а́, -о) *pf.* ре́зкие зву́ки.
janitor ['dʒænɪtə(r)] *n.* (*door-keeper*) приврáтник, -ица; (*caretaker*) дво́рник.
January ['dʒænjʊərɪ] *n.* янва́рь (-ря́) *m.*; *attr.* янва́рский.
Japan [dʒə'pæn] *n.* Япо́ния. **Japanese** [ˌdʒæpə'ni:z] *n.* япо́нец (-нца), -нка; *adj.* япо́нский.
jar¹ [dʒɑ:(r)] *n.* (*container*) ба́нка.
jar² [dʒɑ:(r)] *v.i.* (*sound*) скрипе́ть (-пи́т) *impf.*; (*irritate*) раздража́ть *impf.*, раздражи́ть *pf.* (**upon** +*a.*).
jargon ['dʒɑ:gən] *n.* жарго́н.
jasmin(e) ['dʒæsmɪn, 'dʒæz-] *n.* жасми́н.
jasper ['dʒæspə(r)] *n.* я́шма; *attr.* я́шмовый.
jaundice ['dʒɔ:ndɪs] *n.* желту́ха; (*fig.*) за́висть. **jaundiced** *adj.* желту́шный, больно́й (-лен, -льна́) желту́хой; (*fig.*) зави́стливый.
jaunt [dʒɔ:nt] *n.* прогу́лка, прое́здка. **jaunty** *adj.* бо́дрый (бодр, -а́, -о, бо́дры́).
javelin ['dʒævəlɪn, -vlɪn] *n.* копьё (*pl.* -пья, -пий, -пьям).
jaw [dʒɔ:] *n.* че́люсть; *pl.* пасть, рот (рта, *loc.* во рту́); *pl.* (*of valley etc.*) у́зкий вход; *pl.* (*of vice*) гу́бка.
jay [dʒeɪ] *n.* (*bird*) со́йка; (*fig.*) болту́н (-а́), ~ья.
jazz [dʒæz] *n.* джаз; *adj.* джа́зовый.
jealous ['dʒeləs] *adj.* ревни́вый, зави́стливый; **be ~ of** (*person*) ревнова́ть *impf.*; (*thing*) зави́довать *impf.*, по~ *pf.*+*d.*; (*rights*) ревни́во оберега́ть *impf.*, оберéчь (-егу́, -ежёшь; -ёг, -егла́) *pf.* **jealousy** *n.* ре́вность, за́висть.
jeans [dʒi:nz] *n.* джи́нсы *pl.*
jeep [dʒi:p] *n.* джип.
jeer [dʒɪə(r)] *n.* насме́шка; *v.t.* & *i.* насмеха́ться *impf.* (**at** над+*i.*).
jejune [dʒɪ'dʒu:n] *adj.* (*scanty*) ску́дный (-ден, -дна́, -дно); (*to mind*) неинтере́сный.
jelly ['dʒelɪ] *n.* (*sweet*) желе́ *nt.indecl.*; (*meat, fish*) сту́день (-дня) *m.* **jellyfish** *n.* меду́за.
jemmy ['dʒemɪ] *n.* фо́мка, лом (*pl.* -ы, -ов).
jeopardize ['dʒepəˌdaɪz] *v.t.* подверга́ть *impf.*, подве́ргнуть (-г) *pf.* опа́сности. **jeopardy** *n.* опа́сность.
jerk [dʒɜ:k] *n.* толчо́к (-чка́); (*of muscle*) вздра́гивание; *v.t.* дёргать *impf.*+*i.*; *v.i.* (*twitch*) дёргаться *impf.*, дёрнуться *pf.* **jerky** *adj.* тря́ский (-сок, -ска), отры́вистый.
jersey ['dʒɜ:zɪ] *n.* (*garment*) фуфа́йка; (*fabric*) дже́рси *nt.indecl.*
jest [dʒest] *n.* шу́тка, насме́шка; *v.i.* шути́ть (шучу́, шу́тишь) *impf.*, по~ *pf.* **jester** *n.* шутни́к (-а́), -и́ца; (*hist.*) шут (-а́).
Jesuit ['dʒezjʊɪt] *n.* иезуи́т. **Jesu'itical** *adj.* иезуи́тский.
jet¹ [dʒet] *n.* (*stream*) струя́ (*pl.* -у́и); (*nozzle*) форсу́нка, сопло́ (*pl.* со́пла, со́п(е)л); **~ engine** реакти́вный дви́гатель *m.*; **~ plane** реакти́вный самолёт.
jet² [dʒet] *n.* (*min.*) гага́т; *adj.* гага́товый. **jet-black** *adj.* чёрный (-рен, -рна́, -рно) как смоль.
jetsam ['dʒetsəm] *n.* това́ры *m.pl.*, сбро́шенные с корабля́.
jettison ['dʒetɪs(ə)n, -z(ə)n] *v.t.* выбра́сывать *impf.*, вы́бросить *pf.* за́ борт.
jetty ['dʒetɪ] *n.* (*mole*) мол (*loc.* -у́); (*landing pier*) при́стань (*pl.* -ни, -не́й).
Jew [dʒu:] *n.* евре́й. **Jewess** *n.* евре́йка. **Jewish** *adj.* евре́йский. **Jewry** *n.* евре́йство.
jewel ['dʒu:əl] *n.* драгоце́нность, драгоце́нный ка́мень (-мня; *pl.* -мни, -мне́й) *m.* **jeweller** *n.* ювели́р. **jewellery, jewelry** *n.* драгоце́нности *f.pl.*, ювели́рные изде́лия *nt.pl.*
jib [dʒɪb] *n.* (*naut.*) кли́вер (*pl.* -а́ & -ы); (*of crane*) стрела́ (*pl.* -лы) (кра́на).
jigsaw ['dʒɪgsɔ:] *n.*: **~ puzzle** карти́нка-зага́дка.
jingle ['dʒɪŋg(ə)l] *n.* звя́канье; *v.t.* & *i.* звя́кать *impf.*, звя́кнуть *pf.* (+*i.*).
jingo ['dʒɪŋgəʊ] *n.* ура́-патрио́т. **jingoism** *n.* ура́-патриоти́зм. **jingo'istic** *adj.* ура́-патриоти́ческий.
job [dʒɒb] *n.* (*work*) рабо́та; (*task*) зада́ние; (*position*) ме́сто (*pl.* -а́). **jobless** *adj.* безрабо́тный.
jockey ['dʒɒkɪ] *n.* жоке́й.
jocose [dʒə'kəʊs] *adj.* игри́вый.
jocular ['dʒɒkjʊlə(r)] *adj.* шутли́вый.
jocund ['dʒɒkənd] *adj.* весёлый (ве́сел, -а́, -о, ве́селы́).
jog [dʒɒg] *n.* (*push*) толчо́к (-чка́); (*movement*) ме́дленная ходьба́, езда́; *v.t.* толка́ть *impf.*, толкну́ть *pf.*; (*nudge*) подта́лкивать *impf.*, подтолкну́ть *pf.* **jogger** *n.* люби́тель *m.*, ~ница оздорови́тельного бе́га, джо́ггер. **jogging** *n.* оздорови́тельный бег. **jogtrot** *n.* рысца́.
join [dʒɔɪn] *v.t.* & *i.* соединя́ть(ся) *impf.*, соедини́ть(ся) *pf.*; *v.t.* присоединя́ться *impf.*, присоедини́ться *pf.* к+*d.*; (*become member of*) вступа́ть *impf.*, вступи́ть (-плю́, -пишь) *pf.* в+*a.*; *v.i.*: **~ up** вступа́ть *impf.*, вступи́ть (-плю́, -пишь) *pf.* в а́рмию.
joiner ['dʒɔɪnə(r)] *n.* столя́р (-а́). **joinery** *n.* (*goods*) столя́рные изде́лия *nt.pl.*; (*work*) столя́рная рабо́та.
joint [dʒɔɪnt] *n.* соедине́ние, ме́сто (*pl.* -а́) соедине́ния; (*anat.*) суста́в; (*tech.*) стык, шов (шва), шарни́р; *adj.* соединённый, о́бщий; совме́стный; **~ venture** совме́стное предприя́тие; **~ stock** акционе́рный капита́л; (*attr.*) акционе́рный; *v.t.* (*join*) сочленя́ть *impf.*, сочлени́ть *pf.*; (*divide*) расчленя́ть *impf.*, расчлени́ть *pf.*
joist [dʒɔɪst] *n.* перекла́дина.
joke [dʒəʊk] *n.* шу́тка, остро́та, анекдо́т; *v.i.* шути́ть (щучу́, шу́тишь) *impf.*, по~ *pf.* **joker** *n.* шутни́к (-а́), -и́ца.

jollity ['dʒɒlɪtɪ] *n.* весе́лье. **jolly** *adj.* весёлый (ве́сел, -а́, -о, ве́селы́); *adv.* о́чень.

jolt [dʒəʊlt, dʒɒlt] *n.* тря́ска; *v.t.* трясти́ (-су́, -сёшь; -с, -сла́) *impf.*

jostle ['dʒɒs(ə)l] *n.* толкотня́; *v.t.* & *i.* толка́ть(ся) *impf.*, толкну́ть(ся) *pf.*

jot [dʒɒt] *n.* йо́та; **not a** ~ ни на йо́ту; *v.t.* (~ *down*) бы́стро, кра́тко, запи́сывать *impf.*, записа́ть (-ишу́, -и́шешь) *pf.*

joule [dʒu:l] *n.* джо́уль *m.*

journal ['dʒɜ:n(ə)l] *n.* журна́л, дневни́к (-а́); (*tech.*) ца́пфа, ше́йка. **journa'lese** *n.* газе́тный язы́к (-а́). **journalism** *n.* журнали́стика. **journalist** *n.* журнали́ст.

journey ['dʒɜ:nɪ] *n.* путеше́ствие, пое́здка; (*specific* ~ *of vehicle*) рейс; *v.i.* путеше́ствовать *impf.*

jovial ['dʒəʊvɪəl] *adj.* (*merry*) весёлый (ве́сел, -а́, -о, ве́селы́); (*sociable*) общи́тельный.

jowl [dʒaʊl] *n.* (*jaw*) че́люсть; (*cheek*) щека́ (*a.* щёку; *pl.* щёки, щёк, -а́м).

joy [dʒɔɪ] *n.* ра́дость. **joyful, joyous** *adj.* ра́достный. **joyless** *adj.* безра́достный. **joyrider** *n.* автово́р-лиха́ч (-а́). **joystick** *n.* джо́йстик.

JP *abbr.* (*of* ***Justice of the Peace***) мирово́й судья́.

jubilant ['dʒu:bɪlənt] *adj.* лику́ющий. **jubilate** *v.i.* ликова́ть *impf.*

jubilee ['dʒu:bɪ,li:] *n.* юбиле́й.

Judaic [dʒu:'deɪɪk] *adj.* иуде́йский.

judge [dʒʌdʒ] *n.* судья́ (*pl.* -дьи, -де́й, -дьям) *m.*; (*connoisseur*) цени́тель *m.*; *v.t.* & *i.* суди́ть (сужу́, су́дишь) *impf.*; *v.t.* (*appraise*) оце́нивать *impf.*, оцени́ть (-ню́, -нишь) *pf.* **judgement** *n.* (*sentence*) пригово́р; (*decision*) реше́ние; (*opinion*) мне́ние; (*estimate*) оце́нка.

judicature ['dʒu:dɪkətʃə(r), -'dɪkətʃə(r)] *n.* отправле́ние правосу́дия; (*judiciary*) суде́йская корпора́ция. **judicial** [dʒu:'dɪʃ(ə)l] *adj.* (*of law*) суде́бный; (*of judge*) суде́йский; (*impartial*) беспристра́стный. **ju'dicious** *adj.* здравомы́слящий.

judo ['dʒu:dəʊ] *n.* дзюдо́ *nt.indecl.*

jug [dʒʌg] *n.* кувши́н; *v.t.* туши́ть (-шу́, -шишь) *impf.*, с~ *pf.*

juggle ['dʒʌg(ə)l] *v.i.* жонгли́ровать *impf.* **juggler** *n.* жонглёр.

jugular ['dʒʌgjʊlə(r)] *adj.* ше́йный; ~ **vein** яре́мная ве́на.

juice [dʒu:s] *n.* сок (-а(у), *loc.* -е & -у́); (*fig.*) су́щность. **juicer** *n.* соковыжима́лка. **juicy** *adj.* со́чный (-чен, -чна́, -чно).

July [dʒu:'laɪ] *n.* ию́ль *m.*; *attr.* ию́льский.

jumble ['dʒʌmb(ə)l] *n.* (*disorder*) беспоря́док (-дка); (*articles*) барахло́; *v.t.* перепу́тывать *impf.*, перепу́тать *pf.*

jump [dʒʌmp] *n.* прыжо́к (-жка́), скачо́к (-чка́); (*in price etc.*) ре́зкое повыше́ние; *v.i.* пры́гать *impf.*, пры́гнуть *pf.*; скака́ть (-ачу́, -а́чешь) *impf.*; (*from shock*) вздра́гивать *impf.*, вздро́гнуть *pf.*; (*of price etc.*) подска́кивать *impf.*, подскочи́ть (-ит) *pf.*; *v.t.* (~ *over*) перепры́гивать *impf.*, перепры́гнуть *pf.*; ~ **at** (*accept eagerly*) ухва́тываться *impf.*, ухвати́ться (-ачу́сь, -а́тишься) *pf.* за+*a.*; ~ **the rails** сходи́ть (-ит) *impf.*, сойти́ (сойдёт; сошёл, -шла́) *pf.* с ре́льсов.

jumper ['dʒʌmpə(r)] *n.* (*garment*) дже́мпер.

jumpy ['dʒʌmpɪ] *adj.* не́рвный (-вен, не́рвна́, -вно).

junction ['dʒʌŋkʃ(ə)n] *n.* (*joining*) соедине́ние; (*rail.*) железнодоро́жный у́зел (узла́); (*roads*) перекрёсток (-тка).

juncture ['dʒʌŋktʃə(r)] *n.* (*joining*) соедине́ние; (*state of affairs*) положе́ние дел; **at this** ~ в э́тот моме́нт.

June [dʒu:n] *n.* ию́нь *m.*; *attr.* ию́нский.

jungle ['dʒʌŋg(ə)l] *n.* джу́нгли (-лей) *pl.*

junior ['dʒu:nɪə(r)] *adj.* мла́дший.

juniper ['dʒu:nɪpə(r)] *n.* можжеве́льник.

junk[1] [dʒʌŋk] *n.* (*rubbish*) барахло́.

junk[2] [dʒʌŋk] *n.* (*ship*) джо́нка.

junta ['dʒʌntə] *n.* ху́нта.

Jupiter ['dʒu:pɪtə(r)] *n.* Юпи́тер.

jurisdiction [,dʒʊərɪs'dɪkʃ(ə)n] *n.* (*administration of law*) отправле́ние правосу́дия; (*legal authority*) юрисди́кция.

jurisprudence [,dʒʊərɪs'pru:d(ə)ns] *n.* юриспруде́нция.

jurist ['dʒʊərɪst] *n.* юри́ст.

juror ['dʒʊərə(r)] *n.* прися́жный *sb.*; (*in competition*) член жюри́. **jury** *n.* прися́жные *sb.*; жюри́ *nt.indecl.*

just [dʒʌst] *adj.* (*fair*) справедли́вый; (*deserved*) заслу́женный, до́лжный; *adv.* (*exactly*) то́чно, и́менно; (*barely*) едва́; (*at this, that, moment*) то́лько что; ~ **in case** на вся́кий слу́чай.

justice ['dʒʌstɪs] *n.* правосу́дие; (*fairness*) справедли́вость; (*judge*) судья́ (*pl.* -дьи, -де́й, -дьям); (*proceedings*) суд (-а́); **bring to** ~ отдава́ть (-даю́, -даёшь) *impf.*, отда́ть (-а́м, -а́шь, -а́ст, -ади́м; о́тдал, -а́, -о) *pf.* под суд; **do** ~ **to** отдава́ть (-даю́, -даёшь) *pf.* отда́ть (-а́м, -а́шь, -а́ст, -ади́м; о́тдал, -а́, -о) до́лжное+*d.*

justify ['dʒʌstɪ,faɪ] *v.t.* опра́вдывать *impf.*, оправда́ть *pf.* **justifi'cation** *n.* оправда́ние.

jut [dʒʌt] *v.i.* (~ *out*, *forth*) выдава́ться (-даётся) *impf.*, вы́даться (-астся, -адутся) *pf.*; выступа́ть *impf.*

jute [dʒu:t] *n.* джут.

juvenile ['dʒu:və,naɪl] *n.* ю́ноша *m.*, подро́сток (-тка); *adj.* ю́ный (юн, -а́, -о), ю́ношеский.

juxtapose [,dʒʌkstə'pəʊz] *v.t.* помеща́ть *impf.*, помести́ть *pf.* ря́дом; сопоставля́ть *impf.*, сопоста́вить *pf.* (**with** с+*i.*).

K

K *abbr.* (*of* **kilobyte**) килобайт.
k *abbr.* (*of* **kilometre(s)**) км, киломе́тр.
kale, kail [keɪl] *n.* кормова́я капу́ста.
kaleidoscope [kə'laɪdə,skəʊp] *n.* калейдоско́п.
kangaroo [,kæŋgə'ru:] *n.* кенгуру́ *m.indecl.*
Kazakhstan [,kɑ:zɑ:k'stæn, -'stɑ:n] *n.* Казахста́н.
kebab [kɪ'bæb] *n.* кеба́б, шашлы́к (-á); ~ **house** кеба́бная *sb.*
keel [ki:l] *n.* киль *m.*; *v.t.* & *i.*: ~ **over** опроки́дывать(ся) *impf.*, опроки́нуть(ся) *pf.*
keen [ki:n] *adj.* (*sharp*) о́стрый (остр & остёр, остра́, о́стро́); (*strong*) си́льный (си́лён, -льна́, -льно, си́льны́); (*penetrating*) проница́тельный; (*ardent*) стра́стный (-тен, -тна́, -тно).
keep[1] [ki:p] *n.* (*of castle*) гла́вная ба́шня (*g.pl.* -шен); (*maintenance*) содержа́ние; (*food*) пи́ща.
keep[2] [ki:p] *v.t.* (*observe*) соблюда́ть *impf.*, соблюсти́ (-юду́, -юдёшь; -ю́л, -юла́) *pf.* (*the law*); сде́рживать *impf.*, сдержа́ть (-жу́, -жишь) *pf.* (*one's word*); (*celebrate*) пра́здновать *impf.*, от~ *pf.*; (*possess, maintain*) держа́ть (-жу́, -жишь) *impf.*; храни́ть *impf.*; (*family*) содержа́ть (-жу́, -жишь) *impf.*; (*diary*) вести́ (веду́, -дёшь; вёл, -á) *impf.*; (*detain*) заде́рживать *impf.*, задержа́ть (-жу́, -жишь) *pf.*; (*retain, reserve*) сохраня́ть *impf.*, сохрани́ть *pf.*; *v.i.* (*remain*) остава́ться (-таю́сь, -таёшься) *impf.*, оста́ться (-а́нусь, -а́нешься) *pf.*; (*of food*) не по́ртиться *impf.*; ~ **away** держа́ть(ся) (-жу́(сь), -жишь(ся)) *impf.* в отдале́нии; ~ **back** (*hold back*) уде́рживать *impf.*, удержа́ть (-жу́, -жишь) *pf.*; (*conceal*) скрыва́ть *impf.*, скрыть (-ро́ю, -ро́ешь) *pf.*; ~ **down** подавля́ть *impf.*, подави́ть (-влю́, -вишь) *pf.*; ~ **from** уде́рживаться *impf.*, удержа́ться (-жу́сь, -жишься) *pf.* от+*g.*; ~ **on** продолжа́ть *impf.*, продо́лжить *pf.* (+*inf.*).
keepsake ['ki:pseɪk] *n.* пода́рок (-рка) на па́мять.
keg [keg] *n.* бочо́нок (-нка).
ken [ken] *n.* (*knowledge*) преде́л позна́ний; (*sight*) кругозо́р.
kennel ['ken(ə)l] *n.* конура́.
kerb [kɜ:b] *n.* край (*loc.* -аю́; *pl.* -ая́, -аёв) тротуа́ра. **kerbstone** *n.* бордю́рный ка́мень (-мня; *pl.* -мни, -мне́й) *m.*
kerchief ['kɜ:tʃi:f, -tʃɪf] *n.* (головно́й) плато́к (-тка́).
kernel ['kɜ:n(ə)l] *n.* (*nut*) ядро́ (*pl.* я́дра, я́дер, я́драм); (*grain*) зерно́ (*pl.* зёрна, -рен, -рнам); (*fig.*) суть.
kerosene ['kerə,si:n] *n.* кероси́н (-а(у)).
kestrel ['kestr(ə)l] *n.* пустельга́.
kettle ['ket(ə)l] *n.* ча́йник. **kettledrum** *n.* лита́вра.
key [ki:] *n.* ключ (-á); (*piano, typewriter*) кла́виш(а); (*mus.*) тона́льность; *attr.* веду́щий, ключево́й; *v.t.* (*type*) печа́тать *impf.*, на~ *pf.* **keyboard** *n.* клавиату́ра. **keyhole** *n.* замо́чная сква́жина. **keynote** *n.* (*mus.*) то́ника; (*fig.*) тон. **keystone** *n.* (*archit.*) замко́вый ка́мень (-мня; *pl.* -мни, -мне́й) *m.*; (*fig.*) основно́й при́нцип.
kg. *abbr.* (*of* **kilogram(me)(s)**) кг, (килогра́мм).
KGB *abbr.* (*of Russ.*) КГБ, (*Комите́т госуда́рственной безопа́сности*); ~ **agent** кагебе́шник, гeби́ст.
khaki ['kɑ:kɪ] *n.* & *adj.* ха́ки *nt.indecl.*, *adj.indecl.*
khan [kɑ:n, kæn] *n.* хан. **khanate** *n.* ха́нство.
kick [kɪk] *n.* уда́р ного́й, пино́к (-нка́); (*recoil of gun*) отда́ча; *v.t.* ударя́ть *impf.*, уда́рить *pf.* ного́й; пина́ть *impf.*, пнуть *pf.*; (*score goal*) забива́ть *impf.*, заби́ть (-бью́, -бьёшь) *pf.* (гол, мяч); *v.i.* (*of horse etc.*) ляга́ться *impf.*; ~ **out** вышвы́ривать *impf.*, вы́швырнуть *pf.*
kid[1] [kɪd] *n.* (*goat*) козлёнок (-лёнка; *pl.* -ля́та, -ля́т); (*leather*) ла́йка; (*child*) малы́ш (-á).
kid[2] [kɪd] *v.t.* (*deceive*) обма́нывать *impf.*, обману́ть (-ну́, -нешь) *pf.*; (*tease*) поддра́знивать *impf.*, поддразни́ть (-ню́, -нишь) *pf.*
kidnap ['kɪdnæp] *v.t.* похища́ть *impf.*, похи́тить (-и́щу, -и́тишь) *pf.*
kidney ['kɪdnɪ] *n.* по́чка; *attr.* по́чечный; ~ **bean** фасо́ль.
Kiev ['ki:ef] *n.* Ки́ев.
kill [kɪl] *v.t.* убива́ть *impf.*, уби́ть (убью́, -ьёшь) *pf.*; (*cattle*) ре́зать (ре́жу, -жешь) *impf.*, за~ *pf.*; ~ **off** ликвиди́ровать *impf.* & *pf.* **killer** *n.* уби́йца *c.g.* **killing** *n.* уби́йство; *adj.* (*murderous, fig.*) уби́йственный (-ен, -енна); (*amusing, coll.*) умори́тельный.
kiln [kɪln] *n.* о́бжиговая печь (*pl.* -чи, -че́й).
kilo- ['ki:ləʊ] *in comb.* кило... . **kilobyte** *n.* килоба́йт. **kilocycle, kilohertz** *n.* килоге́рц (*g.pl.* -ц). **kilogram(me)** *n.* килогра́мм. **kilometre** *n.* киломе́тр. **kiloton(ne)** *n.* килото́нна. **kilowatt** *n.* килова́тт (*g.pl.* -т).
kimono [kɪ'məʊnəʊ] *n.* кимоно́ *nt.indecl.*
kin [kɪn] *n.* (*family*) семья́ (*pl.* -мьи, -ме́й, -мьям); (*collect., relatives*) родня́.
kind[1] [kaɪnd] *n.* сорт (*pl.* -á), род (*pl.* -ы, -о́в); **a ~ of** что́-то вро́де+*g.*; **this ~ of** тако́й; **what ~ of** что (э́то, он, *etc.*) за+*nom.*; ~ **of** (*adv.*) как бу́дто, ка́к-то; **pay in ~** плати́ть (-ачу́, -а́тишь) *impf.*, за~ *pf.* нату́рой; **return in ~** отпла́чивать *impf.*, отплати́ть (-ачу́,

-а́тишь) *pf.* то́й же моне́той+*d*.

kind² [kaɪnd] *adj.* до́брый (добр, -а́, -о, до́бры́), любе́зный.

kindergarten ['kɪndəˌgɑːt(ə)n] *n.* де́тский сад (*loc.* -у́; *pl.* -ы́).

kindle ['kɪnd(ə)l] *v.t.* зажига́ть *impf.*, заже́чь (-жгу́, -жжёшь; -жёг, -жгла́) *pf.*; *v.i.* загора́ться *impf.*, загоре́ться (-рю́сь, -ри́шься) *pf.* **kindling** *n.* расто́пка.

kindly ['kaɪndlɪ] *adj.* до́брый (добр, -а́, -о, до́бры́); *adv.* любе́зно; (*with imper.*), (*request*) бу́дьте добры́, +*imper.* **kindness** *n.* доброта́, любе́зность.

kindred ['kɪndrɪd] *n.* (*relationship*) кро́вное родство́; (*relatives*) ро́дственники *m.pl.*; *adj.* ро́дственный (-ен, -енна); (*similar*) схо́дный (-ден, -дна́, -дно).

kinetic [kɪ'netɪk, kaɪ-] *adj.* кинети́ческий.

king [kɪŋ] *n.* коро́ль (-ля́) *m.* (*also chess, cards, fig.*); (*fig.*) царь (-ря́) *m.*; (*draughts*) да́мка **kingdom** *n.* короле́вство; (*fig.*) ца́рство. **kingfisher** *n.* зимоpо́док (-дка). **kingpin** *n.* шкво́рень (-рня) *m.*

kink [kɪŋk] *n.* пе́тля (*g.pl.* -тель), изги́б.

kinsfolk ['kɪnzfəʊk] *n.* кро́вные ро́дственники *m.pl.* **kinship** *n.* родство́; (*similarity*) схо́дство. **kinsman, -woman** *n.* ро́дственник, -ица.

kiosk ['kiːɒsk] *n.* кио́ск; (*telephone*) бу́дка.

kip [kɪp] *v.i.* дры́хнуть (дры́х(нул), -хла) *impf.*

kipper ['kɪpə(r)] *n.* копчёная селёдка.

Kirghizia [kɜː'giːzɪə] *n.* Кирги́зия.

kiss [kɪs] *n.* поцелу́й; *v.t.* целова́ть(ся) *impf.*, по~ *pf.*

kit [kɪt] *n.* (*soldier's*) ли́чное обмундирова́ние; (*clothing*) снаряже́ние; (*tools*) компле́кт. **kitbag** *n.* вещево́й мешо́к (-шка́).

kitchen ['kɪtʃɪn, -tʃ(ə)n] *n.* ку́хня (*g.pl.* -хонь); *attr.* кухо́нный; ~ **garden** огоро́д. **kitchen-maid** *n.* судомо́йка.

kite [kaɪt] *n.* (*bird*) ко́ршун; (*toy*) бума́жный змей.

kith [kɪθ] *n.*: ~ **and kin** знако́мые *sb.* и родня́.

kitten ['kɪt(ə)n] *n.* котёнок (-тёнка; *pl.* -тя́та, -тят); *v.i.* коти́ться *impf.*, о~ *pf.*

kleptomania [ˌkleptəʊ'meɪnɪə] *n.* клептома́ния. **kleptomaniac** *n.* клептома́н.

km. *abbr.* (*of* **kilometre(s)**) км, киломе́тр.

knack [næk] *n.* сноро́вка, трюк.

knacker ['nækə(r)] *n.* живодёр.

knapsack ['næpsæk] *n.* рюкза́к (-а́), ра́нец (-нца).

knave [neɪv] *n.* (*rogue*) плут (-а́); (*cards*) вале́т. **knavery** *n.* плутовство́. **knavish** *adj.* плутовско́й.

knead [niːd] *v.t.* меси́ть (мешу́, ме́сишь) *impf.*, с~ *pf.*

knee [niː] *n.* коле́но (*pl.* (*anat.*) -ни, -ней; (*tech.*) -нья, -ньев). **kneecap** *n.* (*bone*) коле́нная ча́шка; (*protective covering*) наколе́нник. **knee-joint** *n.* коле́нный суста́в.

kneel [niːl] *v.i.* стоя́ть (-ою́, -ои́шь) *impf.* на коле́нях; (~ *down*) станови́ться (-влю́сь, -ви́шься) *impf.*, стать (-а́ну, -нешь) *pf.* на коле́ни.

knell [nel] *n.* похоро́нний звон.

knickers ['nɪkəz] *n.* панталo͏́ны (-н) *pl.*

knick-knack ['nɪknæk] *n.* безделу́шка.

knife [naɪf] *n.* нож (-а́); *v.t.* коло́ть (-лю́, -лешь) *impf.*, за~ *pf.* ножо́м.

knight [naɪt] *n.* ры́царь *m.*; (*holder of order*) кавале́р (о́рдена); (*chess*) конь (-ня́; *pl.* -ни, -не́й) *m.* **knighthood** *n.* ры́царство. **knightly** *adj.* ры́царский.

knit [nɪt] *v.t.* (*garment*) вяза́ть (вяжу́, -жешь) *impf.*, с~ *pf.*; (*unite*) свя́зывать *impf.*, связа́ть (-яжу́, -жешь) *pf.*; *v.t.* & *i.* (*unite*) соединя́ть(ся) *impf.*, соедини́ть(ся) *pf.*; *v.i.* (*bones*) сраста́ться *impf.*, срасти́сь (-тётся; сро́сся, сросла́сь) *pf.*; ~ **one's brows** хму́рить *impf.*, на~ *pf.* бро́ви. **knitting** *n.* (*action*) вяза́ние; (*object*) вяза́нье. **knitting-needle** *n.* спи́ца. **knitwear** *n.* трикота́ж.

knob [nɒb] *n.* ши́шка, кно́пка; (*door handle*) (кру́глая) ру́чка (две́ри). **knobb(l)y** *adj.* шишкова́тый.

knock [nɒk] *n.* (*noise*) стук; (*blow*) уда́р; *v.t.* & *i.* (*strike*) ударя́ть *impf.*, уда́рить *pf.*; (*strike door etc.*) стуча́ть (-чу́, -чи́шь) *impf.*, по~ *pf.* (**at** в+*a.*); ~ **about** (*treat roughly*) колоти́ть (-очу́, -о́тишь) *impf.*, по~ *pf.*; (*wander*) шата́ться *impf.*; ~ **down** (*person*) сбива́ть *impf.*, сбить (собью́, -ьёшь) *pf.* с ног; (*building*) сноси́ть (-ошу́, -о́сишь) *impf.*, снести́ (снесу́, -сёшь; снёс, -ла́) *pf.*; (*at auction*) продава́ть (-даю́, -даёшь) *impf.*, прода́ть (-а́м, -а́шь, -а́ст, -ади́м; про́дал, -а́, -о) *pf.* с молотка́; ~ **in** вбива́ть *impf.*, вбить (вобью́, -ьёшь) *pf.* (в+*a.*); ~ **off** сбива́ть *impf.*, сбить (собью́, -ьёшь) *pf.*; (*leave work*) прекраща́ть *impf.*, прекрати́ть (-ащу́, -ати́шь) *pf.* (рабо́ту); ~ **out** выбива́ть *impf.*, вы́бить (-бью, -бьешь) *pf.*; (*sport*) нокаути́ровать *impf.* & *pf.* **knocker** *n.* (*door-*~) дверно́й молото́к (-тка́). **knock-out** *n.* нока́ут.

knoll [nəʊl] *n.* бугo͏́р (-гра́).

knot [nɒt] *n.* у́зел (узла́) (*also fig., naut.*); (*hard lump*) наро́ст; (*in wood*) сучо́к (-чка́); (*group*) ку́чка; *v.t.* завя́зывать *impf.*, завяза́ть (-яжу́, -жешь) *pf.* узло́м. **knotty** *adj.* узлова́тый; (*fig.*) запу́танный (-ан, -анна).

knout [naʊt, nuːt] *n.* кнут (-а́).

know [nəʊ] *v.t.* знать *impf.*; (~ *how to*) уме́ть *impf.*, с~ *pf.*+*inf.*; (*be acquainted*) быть знако́мым с+*i.*; (*recognize*) узнава́ть (-аю́, -аёшь) *impf.*, узна́ть *pf.* **know -all** *n.* всезна́йка *c.g.* **know-how** *n.* уме́ние. **knowing** *adj.* (*cunning*) хи́трый (-тёр, -тра́, хи́тро́). **knowingly** *adv.* созна́тельно. **knowledge** ['nɒlɪdʒ] *n.* зна́ние, позна́ния (-ний) *pl.*; (*familiarity*) знако́мство (**of** с+*i.*); (*sum of what is known*) нау́ка; **to my** ~ наско́лько мне изве́стно.

knuckle ['nʌk(ə)l] *n.* суста́в па́льца; (*cul.*)

но́жка; *v.i.*: ~ **down to** реши́тельно бра́ться (беру́сь, -рёшься; бра́лся, -ла́сь) *impf.*, взя́ться (возьму́сь, -мёшься; взя́лся, -ла́сь) *pf.* за+*a.*; ~ **under** подчиня́ться *impf.*, подчини́ться *pf.* (**to** +*d.*).

Korea [kəˈriːə] *n.* Коре́я.

kosher [ˈkəʊʃə(r), ˈkɒʃ-] *adj.* коше́рный.

ko(w)tow [kaʊˈtaʊ] *n.* ни́зкий покло́н; *v.i.* ни́зко кла́няться *impf.*, поклони́ться (-ню́сь, -нишься) *pf.*; (*fig.*) раболе́пствовать *impf.* (**to** пе́ред+*i.*).

Kremlin [ˈkremlɪn] *n.* Кремль (-ля́) *m.* **Kremlinologist** [ˌkremlɪnˈɒlədʒɪst] *n.* кремлино́лог. **Kremlinology** *n.* кремлиноло́гия.

kudos [ˈkjuːdɒs] *n.* сла́ва.

kung fu [kʊŋ ˈfuː, kʌŋ] *n.* кун-фу́ *nt. indecl.*

kW *abbr.* (*of* **kilowatt(s)**) кВт, килова́тт.

L

l. *abbr.* (*of* **litre(s)**) л, литр.

label [ˈleɪb(ə)l] *n.* этике́тка; (*also fig.*) ярлы́к (-а́); *v.t.* прикле́ивать *impf.*, прикле́ить *pf.* ярлы́к к+*d.*

labial [ˈleɪbɪəl] *adj.* (*n.*) губно́й (звук).

laboratory [ləˈbɒrətərɪ] *n.* лаборато́рия; ~ **assistant, technician** лабора́нт, ~ка.

laborious [ləˈbɔːrɪəs] *adj.* (*arduous*) тру́дный (-ден, -дна́, -дно, тру́дны́); (*of style*) вы́мученный (-ен).

labour [ˈleɪbə(r)] *n.* труд (-а́), рабо́та; (*workers*) рабо́чие *sb.*; (*task*) зада́ча; (*childbirth*) ро́ды (-дов) *pl.*; *attr.* трудово́й, рабо́чий; ~ **exchange** би́ржа труда́; ~ **force** рабо́чая си́ла; ~ **pains** родовы́е схва́тки *f.pl.*; **L~ Party** лейбори́стская па́ртия; *v.i.* труди́ться *impf.*; рабо́тать *impf.*; *v.t.* (*elaborate*) подро́бно разраба́тывать *impf.*, разрабо́тать *pf.* **laboured** *adj.* затруднённый (-ён, -ённа); (*style*) вы́мученный (-ен). **labourer** *n.* чернорабо́чий *sb.* **labour-intensive** *adj.* трудоёмкий. **labourite** *n.* лейбори́ст. **labour-saving** *adj.* трудосберега́ющий.

laburnum [ləˈbɜːnəm] *n.* золото́й дождь (-дя́) *m.*

labyrinth [ˈlæbərɪnθ] *n.* лабири́нт.

lace [leɪs] *n.* (*fabric*) кру́жево; (*cord*) шнур (-а́), шнуро́к (-рка́); *v.t.* (~ *up*) шнурова́ть *impf.*, за~ *pf.*

lacerate [ˈlæsəˌreɪt] *v.t.* рвать (рву, рвёшь; рвал, -а́, -о) *impf.*; (*fig.*) раздира́ть *impf.* **laceˈration** *n.*(*wound*) рва́ная ра́на.

lachrymose [ˈlækrɪˌməʊs] *adj.* слезли́вый.

lack [læk] *n.* недоста́ток (-тка) (**of** +*g.*, в+*p.*), отсу́тствие; *v.t.* испы́тывать *impf.*, испыта́ть *pf.* недоста́ток в+*p.*; недостава́ть (-таёт) *impf.*, недоста́ть (-а́нет) *pf. impers.* +*d.* (*person*), +*g.* (*object*).

lackadaisical [ˌlækəˈdeɪzɪk(ə)l] *adj.* (*languid*) то́мный (-мен, -мна́, -мно); (*affected*) жема́нный (-нен, -нна).

lackey [ˈlækɪ] *n.* лаке́й.

lack-lustre [ˈlækˌlʌstə(r)] *adj.* ту́склый (-л, -ла́, -ло).

laconic [ləˈkɒnɪk] *adj.* лакони́чный, -ческий.

lacquer [ˈlækə(r)] *n.* лак; *v.t.* лакирова́ть *impf.*, от~ *pf.*

lactic [ˈlæktɪk] *adj.* моло́чный.

lacuna [ləˈkjuːnə] *n.* пробе́л.

lad [læd] *n.* па́рень (-рня; *pl.* -рни, -рне́й) *m.*

ladder [ˈlædə(r)] *n.* ле́стница; (*naut.*) трап.

laden [ˈleɪd(ə)n] *adj.* нагружённый (-ён, -ена́); (*fig.*) обременённый (-ён, -ена́).

ladle [ˈleɪd(ə)l] *n.* (*spoon*) поло́вник; (*for metal*) ковш (-а́); *v.t.* че́рпать *impf.*, черпну́ть *pf.*

lady [ˈleɪdɪ] *n.* да́ма, ле́ди *f.indecl.* **ladybird** *n.* бо́жья коро́вка.

lag¹ [læg] *v.i.*: ~ **behind** отстава́ть (-таю́, -таёшь) *impf.*, отста́ть (-а́ну, -а́нешь) *pf.* (от+*g.*).

lag² [læg] *n.* (*convict*) ка́торжник.

lag³ [læg] *v.t.* (*insulate*) покрыва́ть *impf.*, покры́ть (-ро́ю, -ро́ешь) *pf.* изоля́цией. **lagging** *n.* теплова́я изоля́ция.

lagoon [ləˈguːn] *n.* лагу́на.

lair [leə(r)] *n.* ло́говище, берло́га.

laity [ˈleɪɪtɪ] *n.* (*in religion*) миря́не (-н) *pl.*; (*in profession*) профа́ны (-нов) *pl.*

lake [leɪk] *n.* о́зеро (*pl.* озёра); *attr.* озёрный.

lamb [læm] *n.* ягнёнок (-нка; *pl.* ягня́та, -я́т); (*eccl.*) а́гнец (-нца); *v.i.* ягни́ться *impf.*, о~ *pf.*

lame [leɪm] *adj.* хромо́й (хром, -а́, -о); (*fig.*) неубеди́тельный; **be** ~ хрома́ть *impf.*; **go** ~ хроме́ть *impf.*, о~ *pf.*; *v.t.* кале́чить *impf.*, о~ *pf.* **lameness** *n.* хромота́.

lament [ləˈment] *n.* плач; *v.t.* опла́кивать *impf.*, опла́кать (-а́чу, -а́чешь) *pf.* **lamentable** [ˈlæməntəb(ə)l] *adj.* приско́рбный.

lamina [ˈlæmɪnə] *n.* то́нкая пласти́нка, то́нкий слой (*pl.* -ои́). **laminated** *adj.* листово́й, пласти́нчатый.

lamp [læmp] *n.* ла́мпа, фона́рь (-ря́) *m.* **lamp-post** *n.* фона́рный столб (-а́). **lampshade** *n.* абажу́р.

lampoon [læmˈpuːn] *n.* пасквиль *m.*

lamprey [ˈlæmprɪ] *n.* мино́га.

lance [lɑːns] *n.* пи́ка, копьё (*pl.* -пья, -пий, -пьям); (*fish-spear*) острога́; *v.t.* пронза́ть *impf.*, пронзи́ть *pf.* пи́кой, копьём; (*med.*) вскрыва́ть *impf.*, вскрыть (-ро́ю, -ро́ешь) *pf.* (ланце́том). **lance-corporal** *n.* ефре́йтор. **lancer** *n.* ула́н (*pl.* -нов & -н (*collect.*)).

lancet *n.* ланце́т.

land [lænd] *n.* земля́ (*a.* -млю; *pl.* -мли, -ме́ль, -млям); (*dry* ~) су́ша; (*country*) страна́ (*pl.*

-ы); (*soil*) пóчва; *pl.* (*estates*) помéстья (-тий) *pl.*; *v.t.* (*unload*) выгружáть *impf.*, вы́грузить *pf.*; *v.t.* & *i.* (*persons*) высáживать(ся) *impf.*, вы́садить(ся) *pf.*; (*aeron.*) приземля́ть(ся) *impf.*, приземли́ть(ся) *pf.*

landfall *n.* подхóд к бéрегу. **landing** *n.* вы́садка; (*aeron.*) посáдка; (*mil.*) десáнт; (*on stairs*) лéстничная площáдка; ~ **card** *n.* посáдочный талóн. **landing-stage** *n.* при́стань (*pl.* -ни, -нéй). **landlady** *n.* домовладéлиц, хозя́йка. **landlord** *n.* землевладéлец (-льца); (*of house*) домовладéлец (-льца); (*of inn*) хозя́ин (*pl.* -я́ева, -я́ев). **landmark** *n.* (*boundary stone*; *fig.*) вéха; (*conspicuous object*) ориенти́р. **landowner** *n.* землевладéлец (-льца). **landscape** *n.* ландшáфт; (*also picture*) пейзáж. **landscape-painter** *n.* пейзажи́ст. **landslide, landslip** *n.* óползень (-зня) *m.*

landau [ˈlændɔː] *n.* ландó *nt.indecl.*

lane [leɪn] *n.* у́зкая дорóга; (*street*) переу́лок (-лка); (*passage*) прохóд; (*on road*) ряд (-á *with 2, 3, 4, loc.* -у́; *pl.* -ы́); (*in race*) дорóжка; (*for ships*) морскóй путь (-ти́, -тём) *m.*; (*for aircraft*) трáсса полёта.

language [ˈlæŋgwɪdʒ] *n.* язы́к (-á); (*style, form of speech*) речь.

languid [ˈlæŋgwɪd] *adj.* тóмный (-мен, -мнá, -мно).

languish [ˈlæŋgwɪʃ] *v.i.* (*pine*) томи́ться *impf.*

languor [ˈlæŋgə(r)] *n.* томлéние, тóмность; (*fatigue*) устáлость. **languorous** *adj.* тóмный (-мен, -мнá, -мно); устáлый.

lank [læŋk] *adj.* (*person*) худощáвый; (*hair*) глáдкий (-док, -дкá, -дко). **lanky** *adj.* долговя́зый.

lantern [ˈlænt(ə)n] *n.* фонáрь (-ря́) *m.*

lap¹ [læp] *n.* (*of person*) колéни (-ней) *pl.*; (*racing*) круг (*pl.* -и́).

lap² [læp] *v.t.* (*drink*) лакáть *impf.*, вы́~ *pf.*; *v.i.* (*water*) плескáться (-éщется) *impf.*

lapel [ləˈpel] *n.* отворóт, лáцкан.

lapidary [ˈlæpɪdərɪ] *n.* грани́льщик; *adj.* грани́льный; (*fig.*) сжáтый.

lapse [læps] *n.* (*mistake*) оши́бка; (*of pen*) опи́ска; (*of memory*) провáл пáмяти; (*decline*) падéние; (*expiry*) истечéние; (*of time*) течéние, ход врéмени; *v.i.* впадáть *impf.*, впасть (-аду́, -адёшь; -ал) *pf.* (**into** в+*a.*); (*expire*) истекáть *impf.*, истéчь (-ечёт; -ёк, -еклá) *pf.*

laptop (computer) [ˈlæptɒp] *n.* наколéнный, портати́вный компью́тер.

lapwing [ˈlæpwɪŋ] *n.* чи́бис.

larceny [ˈlɑːsənɪ] *n.* воровствó.

larch [lɑːtʃ] *n.* ли́ственница.

lard [lɑːd] *n.* свинóе сáло; *v.t.* (*cul.*) шпиговáть *impf.*, на~ *pf.*; (*fig.*) уснащáть *impf.*, уснасти́ть *pf.* (**with** +*i.*).

larder [ˈlɑːdə(r)] *n.* кладовáя *sb.*

large [lɑːdʒ] *adj.* большóй, кру́пный (-пен, -пнá, -пно, кру́пны́); (*wide, broad*) ширóкий (-óк, -окá, -óкó); *n.*: **at** ~ (*free*) на свобóде; (*in detail*) подрóбно; (*as a whole*) целикóм. **largely** *adj.* (*to a great extent*) в значи́тельной стéпени.

largess(e) [lɑːˈʒes] *n.* щéдрость.

lark¹ [lɑːk] *n.* (*bird*) жáворонок (-нка).

lark² [lɑːk] *n.* шу́тка, прокáза; *v.i.* (~ *about*) резви́ться *impf.*

larva [ˈlɑːvə] *n.* личи́нка. **larval** *adj.* личи́ночный.

laryngeal [ləˈrɪndʒɪəl] *adj.* гортáнный. **laryngitis** [ˌlærɪnˈdʒaɪtɪs] *n.* ларинги́т. **larynx** [ˈlærɪŋks] *n.* гортáнь.

lascivious [ləˈsɪvɪəs] *adj.* похотли́вый.

laser [ˈleɪzə(r)] *n.* лáзер; *adj.* лáзерный.

lash [læʃ] *n.* плеть (*pl.* -ти, -тéй), бич (-á); (*blow*) удáр плéтью, бичóм; (*eyelash*) ресни́ца; *v.t.* (*beat*) хлестáть (хлещу́, -щешь) *impf.*, хлестну́ть *pf.*; (*with words*) бичевáть (-чу́ю, -чу́ешь) *impf.*; (*fasten*) привя́зывать *impf.*, привязáть (-яжу́, -я́жешь) *pf.* (**to** к+*d.*); ~ **together** свя́зывать *impf.*, связáть (-яжу́, -я́жешь) *pf.*

lass [læs] *n.* дéвушка, дéвочка.

lassitude [ˈlæsɪˌtjuːd] *n.* устáлость.

lasso [læˈsuː, ˈlæsəʊ] *n.* лассó *nt.indecl.*; *v.t.* лови́ть (-влю́, -вишь) *impf.*, поймáть *pf.* лассó.

last¹ [lɑːst] *n.* (*cobbler's*) колóдка.

last² [lɑːst] *adj.* (*final*) послéдний; (*most recent*) прóшлый; (*extreme*) крáйний; **the year before** ~ позапрóшлый год; ~ **but one** предпослéдний; ~ **but two** трéтий (-тья, -тье) с концá; ~ **night** вчерá вéчером, нóчью; *n.* (~*-mentioned*) послéдний *sb.*; (*end*) конéц (-нцá); **at** ~ наконéц, в концé концóв; *adv.* (*after all others*) пóсле всех; (*on last occasion*) в послéдний раз; (*in last place*) в концé.

last³ [lɑːst] *v.i.* (*go on*) продолжáться *impf.*, продóлжиться *pf.*; дли́ться *impf.*, про~ *pf.*; (*food, health*) сохраня́ться *impf.*, сохрани́ться *pf.*; (*suffice*) хватáть *impf.*, хвати́ть (-ит) *pf.* **lasting** *adj.* (*enduring*) дли́тельный; (*permanent*) постоя́нный (-нен, -нна); (*durable*) прóчный (-чен, -чнá, -чно, прóчны́).

lastly [ˈlɑːstlɪ] *adj.* в концé, в заключéние, наконéц.

latch [lætʃ] *n.* щекóлда.

late [leɪt] *adj.* пóздний; (*recent*) недáвний; (*dead*) покóйный; (*former*) бы́вший; **be** ~ **for** опáздывать *impf.*, опоздáть *pf.* на+*a.*; *adv.* пóздно; *n.*: **of** ~ недáвно, за послéднее врéмя.

latent [ˈleɪt(ə)nt] *adj.* скры́тый.

lateral [ˈlætər(ə)l] *adj.* боковóй. **laterally** *adv.* (*from side*) сбóку; (*towards side*) вбок.

latex [ˈleɪteks] *n.* млéчный сок (-а(у), *loc.* -е & -у́); (*synthetic*) лáтекс.

lath [lɑːθ] *n.* рéйка, дрáнка (*also collect.*).

lathe [leɪð] *n.* токáрный станóк (-нкá).

lather [ˈlɑːðə(r), ˈlæðə(r)] *n.* (мы́льная) пéна; (*of horse*) мы́ло; *v.t.* & *i.* мы́лить(ся) *impf.*, на∼ *pf.*; (*of horse*) взмыливаться *impf.*, взмылиться *pf.*

Latin ['lætɪn] *adj.* латинский; (*Romance*) романский; *n.* латинский язык (-á); (*when qualified*) латынь. **Latin-American** *adj.* латиноамериканский.

latitude ['lætɪˌtjuːd] *n.* свобода; (*geog.*) широта.

latrine [lə'triːn] *n.* уборная *sb.*; (*esp. in camp*) отхожее место (*pl.* -тá).

latter ['lætə(r)] *adj.* последний. **latter-day** *adj.* современный. **latterly** *adv.* (*towards end*) к концу; (*of late*) недавно.

lattice ['lætɪs] *n.* решётка. **latticed** *adj.* решётчатый.

Latvia ['lætvɪə] *n.* Латвия.

laud [lɔːd] *n.* хвала; *v.t.* хвалить (-лю, -лишь) *impf.*, по∼ *pf.* **laudable** *adj.* похвальный. **laudatory** *adj.* хвалебный.

laugh [lɑːf] *n.* смех (а(у)), хохот; *v.i.* смеяться (-еюсь, -еёшься) *impf.* (**at** над+*i.*); ∼ **it off** отшучиваться *impf.*, отшутиться (-учусь, -утишься) *pf.* **laughable** *adj.* смешной (-шóн, -шнá). **laughing-stock** *n.* посмешище. **laughter** *n.* смех (-а(у)), хохот.

launch[1] [lɔːntʃ] *v.t.* бросать *impf.*, бросить *pf.*; (*ship*) спускать *impf.*, спустить (-ущу, -устишь) *pf.* на воду; (*rocket*) запускать *impf.*, запустить (-ущу, -устишь) *pf.*; (*undertake*) предпринимать *impf.*, предпринять (-ниму, -нимешь; предпринял, -á, -о) *pf.*; *n.* спуск на воду; запуск. **launcher** *n.* (*for rocket*) пусковая установка. **launching pad** *n.* пусковая площадка.

launch[2] [lɔːntʃ] *n.* (*naut.*) баркас; (*motor-*∼) моторный катер (*pl.* -á).

launder ['lɔːndə(r)] *v.t.* стирать *impf.*, вы∼ *pf.* **laund(e)'rette** *n.* прачечная *sb.* самообслуживания. **laundress** *n.* прачка. **laundry** *n.* (*place*) прачечная *sb.*; (*articles*) бельё.

laurel ['lɒr(ə)l] *n.* лавр(овое дерево); (*ornamental plant, Japanese* ∼) золотое дерево (*pl.* -евья, -евьев); *pl.* лавры *m.pl.*, почести *f.pl.*

lava ['lɑːvə] *n.* лава.

lavatory ['lævətərɪ] *n.* уборная *sb.*

lavender ['lævɪndə(r)] *n.* лаванда.

lavish ['lævɪʃ] *adj.* щедрый (щедр, -á, -о); (*abundant*) обильный; *v.t.* расточать *impf.* (**upon** +*d.*).

law [lɔː] *n.* закон, право; (*jurisprudence*) юриспруденция; (*rule*) правило; ∼ **and order** правопорядок (-дка). **law-court** *n.* суд (-á). **lawful** *adj.* законный (-нен, -нна). **lawgiver** *n.* законодатель. **lawless** *adj.* беззаконный (-нен, -нна).

lawn[1] [lɔːn] *n.* (*fabric*) батист.

lawn[2] [lɔːn] *n.* (*grass*) газон. **lawn-mower** *n.* газонокосилка.

lawsuit ['lɔːsuːt, -sjuːt] *n.* процесс.

lawyer ['lɔɪə(r), 'lɔːjə(r)] *n.* адвокат, юрист.

lax [læks] *adj.* (*loose*) слабый (слаб, -á, -о); (*careless*) небрежный; (*not strict*) нестрогий. **laxity** *n.* слабость; небрежность; (*moral* ∼) распущенность.

laxative ['læksətɪv] *adj.* слабительный; *n.* слабительный *sb.*

lay[1] [leɪ] *adj.* (*non-clerical*) светский; (*non-professional*) непрофессиональный.

lay[2] [leɪ] *n.* (*position*) положение; *v.t.* (*place*) класть (кладу, -дёшь; клал) *impf.*, положить (-жу, -жишь) *pf.*; (*impose*) налагать *impf.*, наложить (-жу, -жишь) *pf.*; (*present*) излагать *impf.*, изложить (-жу, -жишь) *pf.*; (*trap etc.*) устраивать *impf.*, устроить *pf.*; (*crops, dust*) прибивать *impf.*, прибить (-бью, -бьёшь) *pf.*; (*calm*) успокаивать *impf.*, успокоить *pf.*; (*ghost*) изгонять *impf.*, изгнать (изгоню, -нишь; изгнал, -á, -о) *pf.*; (*meal*) накрывать *impf.*, накрыть (-рóю, -рóешь) *pf.* стол к+*d.*; (*eggs*) класть (-адёт; -ал) *impf.*, положить (-ит) *pf.*; *v.abs.* (*lay eggs*) нестись (несётся; нёсся, неслась) *impf.*, с∼ *pf.*; ∼ **bare, open** раскрывать *impf.*, раскрыть (-рóю, -рóешь) *pf.*; ∼ **a bet, wager** держать (-жу, -жишь) *impf.* пари (**on** на+*a.*); ∼ **claim to** иметь *impf.* претензию на+*a.*; ∼ **hands on** (*seize*) завладевать *impf.*, завладеть *pf.*+*i.*; ∼ **siege to** осаждать *impf.*, осадить *pf.*; ∼ **table** накрывать *impf.*, накрыть (-рóю, -óешь) *pf.* стол (**for** (*meal*) к+*d.*); ∼ **waste** опустошать *impf.*, опустошить *pf.*; ∼ **aside** (*put aside*) откладывать *impf.*, отложить (-жу, -жишь) *pf.*; (*save*) приберегать *impf.*, приберечь (-егу, -ежёшь; -ёг, -еглá) *pf.*; ∼ **down** (*relinquish*) отказываться *impf.*, отказаться (-ажусь, -áжешься) *pf.* от+*g.*; (*formulate*) составлять *impf.*, составить *pf.*; (*rule etc.*) устанавливать *impf.*, установить (-влю, -вишь) *pf.*; (*ship etc.*) закладывать *impf.*, заложить (-жу, -жишь) *pf.*; ∼ **down one's arms** складывать, слагать *impf.*, сложить (-жу, -жишь) *pf.* оружие; ∼ **down one's life** положить (-жу, -жишь) *pf.* жизнь (**for** за+*a.*); ∼ **in** (*stock of*), запасать *impf.*, запасти (-су, -сёшь; -с, -слá) *pf.*+*a.*, +*g.*; ∼ **off** (*workmen*) временно увольнять *impf.*, уволить *pf.*; ∼ **out** (*spread*) выкладывать *impf.*, выложить *pf.*; (*arrange*) разбивать *impf.*, разбить (разобью, -ьёшь) *pf.*; (*expend*) тратить *impf.*, ис∼, по∼ *pf.*; ∼ **up** запасать *impf.*, запасти (-су, -сёшь; -с, -слá) *pf.*+*a.*, +*g.*; **be laid up** быть прикованным к постели, к дому. **layabout** *n.* бездельник.

layer ['leɪə(r)] *n.* слой (*pl.* -óй), пласт (-á, *loc.* -у); (*hort.*) отводок (-дка); (*hen*) несушка.

layman ['leɪmən] *n.* мирянин (*pl.* -яне, -ян); (*non-expert*) неспециалист.

laze [leɪz] *v.i.* бездельничать *impf.* **laziness** *n.* лень. **lazy** *adj.* ленивый. **lazy-bones** *n.* лентяй, ∼ка.

lb. [paʊnd(z)] *abbr.* (*of* **libra**) фунт.

lead[1] [liːd] *n.* (*example*) пример; (*leadership*) руководство; (*position*) первое место;

(*theatr.*) гла́вная роль (*pl.* -ли, -ле́й); (*cards*) пе́рвый ход; (*elec.*) про́вод (*pl.* -а́); (*dog's*) поводо́к (-дка́); *v.t.* води́ть (вожу́, во́дишь) *indet.*, вести́ (веду́, -дёшь; вёл, -а́) *det.*; (*guide*) руководи́ть *impf.+i.*; (*army*) кома́ндовать *impf.*, с~ *pf.+i.*; (*induce*) заставля́ть *impf.*, заста́вить *pf.*; *v.t. & i.* (*cards*) ходи́ть (хожу́, хо́дишь) *impf.* (с+*g.*); *v.i.* (*sport*) занима́ть *impf.*, заня́ть (займу́, -мёшь; за́нял, -а́, -о) *pf.* пе́рвое ме́сто; ~ **astray** сбива́ть *impf.*, сбить (собью́, -ьёшь) *pf.* с пути́; ~ **away** уводи́ть (-ожу́, -о́дишь) *impf.*, увести́ (-еду́, -едёшь; увёл, -а́) *pf.*; ~ **on** увлека́ть *impf.*, увле́чь (-еку́, -ечёшь; -ёк, -екла́) *pf.*; ~ **to** (*result in*) приводи́ть (-ит) *impf.*, привести́ (-едёт; -ёл, -ела́) *pf.* к+*d.*

lead² [led] *n.* (*metal*) свине́ц (-нца́); (*naut.*) лот; (*print.*) шпон (-а́). **leaden** *adj.* свинцо́вый.

leader ['li:də(r)] *n.* руководи́тель *m.*, ~ница, ли́дер, вождь (-дя́) *m.*; (*mus.*) концертме́йстер; (*editorial*) передова́я статья́. **leadership** *n.* руково́дство; **under the ~ of** во главе́ с+*i.*

lead-free ['ledfri:] *adj.* неэтили́рованный.

leading ['li:dɪŋ] *adj.* веду́щий, выдаю́щийся; ~ **article** передова́я статья́.

leaf [li:f] *n.* лист (-а́; *pl.* (*plant*) -ья, -ьев & (*paper*) -ы́, -о́в); (*of door*) ство́рка; (*of table*) опускна́я доска́ (*a.* -ску; *pl.* -ски, -со́к, -ска́м); *v.i.*: ~ **through** перели́стывать *impf.*, перелиста́ть *pf.* **leaflet** *n.* листо́вка. **leaf-mould** *n.* листово́й перегно́й. **leafy** *adj.* покры́тый ли́стьями.

league [li:g] *n.* ли́га, сою́з; (*sport*) класс.

leak [li:k] *n.* течь, уте́чка; **spring a ~** дава́ть (даёт) *impf.*, дать (даст; дал, -а́, да́ло́, -и) *pf.* течь; *v.i.* (*escape*) течь (-чёт; тёк, -ла́) *impf.*; (*allow water to ~*) пропуска́ть *impf.* во́ду; ~ **out** проса́чиваться *impf.*, просочи́ться *pf.*

lean¹ [li:n] *adj.* (*thin*) худо́й (худ, -а́, -о); (*meat*) по́стный (-тен, -тна́, -тно); (*meagre*) ску́дный (-ден, -дна́, -дно).

lean² [li:n] *v.t. & i.* прислоня́ть(ся) *impf.*, прислони́ть(ся) (-ню́(сь), -о́нишь(ся)) *pf.* (**against** к+*d.*); *v.i.* (~ *on*, *rely on*) опира́ться *impf.*, опере́ться (обопру́сь, -рёшься; опёрся, опёрла́сь) *pf.* (**on** на+*a.*); (*be inclined*) быть скло́нным (-о́нен, -о́нна́, -о́нно) (**to(wards)** к+*d.*); ~ **back** отки́дываться *impf.*, отки́нуться *pf.*; ~ **out of** высо́вываться *impf.*, вы́сунуться *pf.* в+*a.* **leaning** *n.* скло́нность.

leap [li:p] *n.* прыжо́к (-жка́), скачо́к (-чка́); *v.i.* пры́гать *impf.*, пры́гнуть *pf.*; скака́ть (-ачу́, -а́чешь) *impf.*; *v.t.* (~ *over*) перепры́гивать *impf.*, перепры́гнуть *pf.*; ~ **year** високо́сный год (*loc.* -у́; *pl.* -ы & -а́, -о́в). **leap-frog** *n.* чехарда́.

learn [lɜ:n] *v.t.* учи́ться (учу́сь, у́чишься) *impf.*, об~ *pf.+d.*; (*find out*) узнава́ть (-наю́, -наёшь) *impf.*, узна́ть *pf.* **learned** ['lɜ:nɪd] *adj.* учёный. **learner** *n.* уча́щийся *sb.*, учени́к (-а́). **learning** *n.* (*studies*) уче́ние; (*erudition*) учёность.

lease [li:s] *n.* аре́нда; *v.t.* (*of owner*) сдава́ть (сдаю́, сдаёшь) *impf.*, сдать (-ам, -ашь, -аст, -ади́м; сдал, -а́, -о) *pf.* в аре́нду; (*of tenant*) брать (беру́, -рёшь; брал, -а́, -о) *impf.*, взять (возьму́, -мёшь; взял, -а́, -о) *pf.* в аре́нду. **leaseholder** *n.* аренда́тор.

leash [li:ʃ] *n.* сво́ра, при́вязь.

least [li:st] *adj.* наиме́ньший, мале́йший; *adv.* ме́нее всего́; **at ~** по кра́йней ме́ре; **not in the ~** ничу́ть.

leather ['leðə(r)] *n.* ко́жа; *attr.* ко́жаный.

leave¹ [li:v] *n.* (*permission*) разреше́ние; (~ *of absence*) о́тпуск (*loc.* -е & -у́); **on ~** в о́тпуске, -ку́; **take (one's) ~** проща́ться *impf.*, прости́ться *pf.* (**of** с+*i.*).

leave² [li:v] *v.t. & i.* оставля́ть *impf.*, оста́вить *pf.*; (*abandon*) покида́ть *impf.*, поки́нуть *pf.*; (*go away*) уходи́ть (-ожу́, -о́дишь) *impf.*, уйти́ (уйду́, -дёшь; ушёл, ушла́) *pf.* (**from** от+*g.*); уезжа́ть *impf.*, уе́хать (уе́ду, -дешь) *pf.* (**from** от+*g.*); (*entrust*) предоставля́ть *impf.*, предоста́вить *pf.* (**to** +*d.*); ~ **out** пропуска́ть *impf.*, пропусти́ть (-ущу́, -у́стишь) *pf.*

leaven ['lev(ə)n] *n.* (*yeast*) дро́жжи (-же́й) *pl.*; заква́ска; *v.t.* ста́вить *impf.*, по~ *pf.* на дрожжа́х; заква́шивать *impf.*, заква́сить *pf.*

leavings ['li:vɪŋz] *n.* оста́тки *m.pl.*; (*food*) объе́дки (-ков) *pl.*

lecherous ['letʃərəs] *adj.* распу́тный.

lectern ['lektɜ:n, -t(ə)n] *n.* анало́й.

lecture ['lektʃə(r)] *n.* (*discourse*) ле́кция; (*reproof*) нота́ция; *v.i.* (*deliver ~(s)*) чита́ть *impf.*, про~ *pf.* ле́кцию (-ии) (**on** по+*d.*); *v.t.* (*admonish*) чита́ть *impf.*, про~ *pf.* нота́цию+*d.*; ~ **room** аудито́рия. **lecturer** *n.* ле́ктор; (*univ.*) преподава́тель *m.*, ~ница.

ledge [ledʒ] *n.* вы́ступ; (*under water*) риф.

ledger ['ledʒə(r)] *n.* гла́вная кни́га, гроссбу́х.

lee [li:] *n.* защи́та; ~ **side** подве́тренная сторона́ (*a.* -ону); ~ **shore** подве́тренный бе́рег (*loc.* -у́).

leech [li:tʃ] *n.* (*worm*) пия́вка; (*person*) вымога́тель *m.*

leek [li:k] *n.* лук-поре́й.

leer [lɪə(r)] *v.i.* смотре́ть (-рю́, -ришь) *impf.*, по~ *pf.* и́скоса (**at** на+*a.*).

lees [li:z] *n.* оса́док (-дка), подо́нки (-ков) *pl.*

leeward ['li:wəd, *naut.* 'lu:əd] *n.* подве́тренная сторона́ (*a.* -ону); *adj.* подве́тренный.

leeway ['li:weɪ] *n.* (*naut.*) дрейф.

left [left] *n.* ле́вая сторона́ (*a.* -ону); (**L~**; *pol.*) ле́вые *sb.*; *adj.* ле́вый; *adv.* нале́во, сле́ва (**of** от+*g.*). **left-hander** *n.* левша́ *c.g.*

left-luggage office [left] *n.* ка́мера хране́ния.

leftovers ['left,əʊvəz] *n.* оста́тки *m.pl.*; (*food*) объе́дки (-ков) *pl.*

leg [leg] *n.* нога́ (*a.* -гу; *pl.* -ги, -г, -га́м);

(*furniture etc.*) нóжка; (*support*) подстáвка; (*stage of journey etc.*) этáп; **pull s.o.'s ~** морóчить *impf.* гóлову+*d.*
legacy ['legəsɪ] *n.* наслéдство.
legal ['li:g(ə)l] *adj.* (*of the law*) правовóй; (*lawful*) закóнный; **~ adviser** юрискóнсульт. **legality** [lɪ'gælɪtɪ, li:'g-] *n.* закóнность. **legalize** *v.t.* узакóнивать *impf.*, узакóнить *pf.*
legate [lɪ'geɪt] *n.* легáт.
legatee [ˌlegə'ti:] *n.* наслéдник.
legation [lɪ'geɪʃ(ə)n] *n.* (дипломатúческая) мúссия.
legend ['ledʒ(ə)nd] *n.* легéнда. **legendary** *adj.* легендáрный.
leggings ['legɪŋz] *n.* гамáши *f.pl.*
legible ['ledʒɪb(ə)l] *adj.* разбóрчивый.
legion ['li:dʒ(ə)n] *n.* легиóн; (*great number*) мнóжество. **legionary** *n.* легионéр.
legislate ['ledʒɪsˌleɪt] *v.i.* издавáть (-даю, -даёшь) *impf.*, издáть (-áм, -áшь, -áст, -адúм; издáл, -á, -о) *pf.* закóны. **legis'lation** *n.* законодáтельство. **legislative** *adj.* законодáтельный. **legislator** *n.* законодáтель *m.*
legitimacy [lɪ'dʒɪtɪməsɪ] *n.* закóнность; (*of child*) законнорождённость. **legitimate** *adj.* закóнный; (*child*) законнорождённый. **legitimize** *v.t.* узакóнивать *impf.*, узакóнить *pf.*
leguminous [lɪ'gju:mɪnəs] *adj.* бобóвый, стручкóвый.
leisure ['leʒə(r)] *n.* досýг; **at ~** на досýге. **leisurely** *adj.* нетороплúвый; *adv.* не спешá.
leitmotiv ['laɪtməʊˌti:f] *n.* лейтмотúв.
lemon ['lemən] *n.* лимóн; *attr.* лимóнный. **lemo'nade** *n.* лимонáд.
lend [lend] *v.t.* давáть (даю, даёшь) *impf.*, дать (дам, дашь, даст, дадúм; дал, -á, дáлó, -и) *pf.* взаймы́ (**to** +*d.*); одáлживать *impf.*, одолжúть *pf.* (**to** +*d.*).
length [leŋθ, leŋkθ] *n.* длинá, расстоя́ние; (*duration*) продолжúтельность; (*of cloth*) отрéз; **at ~** (*at last*) наконéц; (*in detail*) подрóбно. **lengthen** *v.t.* & *i.* удлиня́ть(ся) *impf.*, удлинúть(ся) *pf.* **lengthways, -wise** *adv.* в длинý, вдоль. **lengthy** *adj.* длúнный (-нен, -ннá, длúннó).
lenience ['li:nɪəns], **-cy** *n.* снисходúтельность. **lenient** *adj.* снисходúтельный.
Leningrad ['lenɪnˌgræd] *n.* Ленингрáд.
lens [lenz] *n.* лúнза; (*anat.*) хрустáлик глáза.
Lent [lent] *n.* велúкий пост (-á, *loc.* -ý). **Lenten** *adj.* великопóстный; (*food*) пóстный (-тен, -тнá, -тно).
lentil ['lentɪl] *n.* чечевúца.
Leo ['li:əʊ] *n.* Лев (Льва).
leonine ['li:əˌnaɪn] *adj.* львúный.
leopard ['lepəd] *n.* леопáрд.
leotard ['li:əˌtɑ:d] *n.* трикó *nt. indecl.*, леотáрд.
leper ['lepə(r)] *n.* прокажённый *sb.* **leprosy** *n.* прокáза.
lesbian ['lezbɪən] *n.* лесбия́нка; *adj.* лесбúйский.
lesion ['li:ʒ(ə)n] *n.* повреждéние; (*med.*) поражéние.
less [les] *adj.* мéньший; *adv.* мéньше, мéнее; *prep.* без+*g.*, за вы́четом+*g.*
lessee [le'si:] *n.* арендáтор.
lessen ['les(ə)n] *v.t.* & *i.* уменьшáть(ся) *impf.*, умéньшúть(ся) *pf.*
lesser ['lesə(r)] *adj.* мéньший.
lesson ['les(ə)n] *n.* урóк.
lest [lest] *conj.* (*in order that not*) чтóбы не; (*that*) как бы не.
let [let] *n.* (*lease*) сдáча в наём; *v.t.* (*allow*) позволя́ть *impf.*, позвóлить *pf.*+*d.*; разрешáть *impf.*, разрешúть *pf.*+*d.*; (*allow to escape*) пускáть *impf.*, пустúть (пущý, пýстишь) *pf.*; (*rent out*) сдавáть (сдаю, -аёшь) *impf.*, сдать (-áм, -ашь, -аст, -адúм; сдал, -á, -о) *pf.* внаём (**to** +*d.*); *v.aux.* (*imperative*) (*1st person*) давáй(те); (*3rd person*) пусть; (*assumption*) допýстим; **~ alone** оставля́ть *impf.*, остáвить *pf.* в покóе; (*in imperative*) не говоря́ ужé о+*p.*; **~ down** (*lower*) опускáть *impf.*, опустúть (-ущý, -ýстишь) *pf.*; (*fail*) подводúть (-ожý, -óдишь) *impf.*, подвестú (-едý, -едёшь; -ёл, -елá) *pf.*; (*disappoint*) разочарóвывать *impf.*, разочаровáть *pf.*; **~ go** выпускáть *impf.*, вы́пустить *pf.*; **~'s go** пойдёмте!; пошлú!; поéхали!; **~ in(to)** (*admit*) впускáть *impf.*, впустúть (-ущý, -ýстишь) *pf.* в+*a.*; (*into secret*) посвящáть *impf.*, посвятúть (-ящý, -ятúшь) *pf.* в+*a.*; **~ know** давáть (даю, даёшь) *impf.*, дать (дам, дашь, даст, дадúм; дал, -á, дáлó, -и) *pf.* знать+*d.*; **~ off** (*gun*) вы́стрелить *pf.* из+*g.*; (*not punish*) отпускáть *impf.*, отпустúть (-ущý, -ýстишь) *pf.* без наказáния; **~ out** (*release, loosen*) выпускáть *impf.*, вы́пустить *pf.*
lethal ['li:θ(ə)l] *adj.* смертонóсный.
lethargic [lɪ'θɑ:dʒɪk] *adj.* летаргúческий; (*inert*) вя́лый. **lethargy** ['leθədʒɪ] *n.* летаргúя; вя́лость.
letter ['letə(r)] *n.* (*symbol*) бýква; (*print*) лúтера; (*missive*) письмó (*pl.* -сьма, -сем, -сьмам); *pl.* (*literature*) литератýра; *pl.* (*erudition*) учёность; **to the ~** буквáльно. **letter-box** *n.* почтóвый я́щик.
lettuce ['letɪs] *n.* салáт.
leukaemia [lu:'ki:mɪə] *n.* лейкемúя.
level ['lev(ə)l] *n.* ýровень (-вня) *m.*; (*spirit-~*) ватерпáс; (*surveyor's*) нивелúр; (*flat country*) равнúна; *adj.* горизонтáльный, рóвный (-вен, -внá, -вно); **~ crossing** (железнодорóжный) переéзд; *v.t.* (*make ~*) вырáвнивать *impf.*, вы́ровнять *pf.*; (*make equal*) урáвнивать *impf.*, уравня́ть *pf.*; (*raze*) ровня́ть *impf.*, с~ *pf.* с землёй; (*gun*) наводúть (-ожý, -óдишь) *impf.*, навестú (-едý, -едёшь; -ёл, -елá) *pf.* (**at** в, на, +*a.*); (*criticism*) направля́ть *impf.*, напрáвить *pf.* (**at** прóтив+*g.*); (*surveying*) нивелúровать

impf. & *pf.* **level-headed** *adj.* уравнове́шенный (-ен, -ена).

lever ['li:və(r)] *n.* рыча́г (-а́). **leverage** *n.* де́йствие рычага́; (*influence*) влия́ние.

leveret ['levərɪt] *n.* зайчо́нок (-чо́нка; *pl.* -ча́та, -ча́т).

levity ['levɪtɪ] *n.* легкомы́слие.

levy ['levɪ] *n.* (*tax*) сбор; (*mil.*) набо́р; *v.t.* (*tax*) взима́ть *impf.* (**from** с+*g.*); (*mil.*) набира́ть *impf.*, набра́ть (наберу́, -рёшь; набра́л, -а́, -о) *pf.*

lewd [lju:d] *adj.* (*lascivious*) похотли́вый; (*indecent*) непристо́йный.

lexicographer [ˌleksɪ'kɒgrəfə(r)] *n.* лексико́граф. **lexicography** *n.* лексикогра́фия.

lexicon ['leksɪkən] *n.* слова́рь (-ря́) *m.*

liability [ˌlaɪə'bɪlɪtɪ] *n.* (*responsibility*) отве́тственность (**for** за+*a.*); (*obligation*) обяза́тельство; *pl.* (*debts*) долги́ *m.pl.*; (*susceptibility*) подве́рженность (**to** +*d.*). **'liable** *adj.* отве́тственный (-ен, -енна) (**for** за+*a.*); обя́занный (-ан); подве́рженный (-ен) (**to** +*d.*).

liaison [lɪ'eɪzɒn] *n.* любо́вная связь; (*mil.*) связь (взаимоде́йствия); ~ **officer** офице́р свя́зи.

liar ['laɪə(r)] *n.* лгун (-а́), ~ья.

libel ['laɪb(ə)l] *n.* клевета́; *v.t.* клевета́ть (-ещу́, -е́щешь) *impf.*, на~ *pf.* на+*a.* **libellous** ['laɪbələs] *adj.* клеветни́ческий.

liberal ['lɪbər(ə)l] *n.* либера́л; *adj.* либера́льный; (*generous*) ще́дрый (щедр, -а́, -о); (*abundant*) оби́льный.

liberate ['lɪbəˌreɪt] *v.t.* освобожда́ть *impf.*, освободи́ть *pf.* **libe'ration** *n.* освобожде́ние; *attr.* освободи́тельный. **liberator** *n.* освободи́тель *m.*

libertine ['lɪbəˌti:n, -tɪn, -ˌtaɪn] *n.* (*profligate*) распу́тник; (*free-thinker*) вольноду́мец (-мца).

liberty ['lɪbətɪ] *n.* свобо́да, во́льность; **at** ~ на свобо́де.

libidinous [lɪ'bɪdɪnəs] *adj.* похотли́вый.

Libra ['li:brə, 'lɪb-, 'laɪb-] *n.* Весы́ (-со́в) *pl.*

librarian [laɪ'breərɪən] *n.* библиоте́карь *m.* **'library** *n.* библиоте́ка.

libretto [lɪ'bretəʊ] *n.* либре́тто *nt.indecl.*

licence[1] ['laɪs(ə)ns] *n.* (*permission, permit*) разреше́ние, пра́во (*pl.* -ва́), лице́нзия; (*liberty*) (изли́шняя) во́льность. **license, -ce**[2] *v.t.* (*allow*) разреша́ть *impf.*, разреши́ть *pf.*+*d.*; дава́ть (даю́, даёшь) *impf.*, дать (дам, дашь, даст, дади́м; дал, -а́, -о) *pf.* пра́во+*d.*

licentious [laɪ'senʃəs] *adj.* похотли́вый, распу́щенный.

lichen ['laɪkən, 'lɪtʃ(ə)n] *n.* (*bot.*) лиша́йник; (*med.*) лиша́й (-ая́).

lick [lɪk] *n.* лиза́ние; **go at full** ~ нести́сь (несу́сь, -сёшься; нёсся, несла́сь) *det.*, по~ *pf.*; *v.t.* лиза́ть (лижу́, -жешь) *impf.*, лизну́ть *pf.*; (~ *all over*) обли́зывать *impf.*, облиза́ть (-ижу́, -и́жешь) *pf.*; (*thrash*) колоти́ть (-очу́, -о́тишь) *impf.*, по~ *pf.*; (*defeat*) побежда́ть *impf.*, победи́ть (-и́шь). **lickspittle** *n.* подхали́м.

lid [lɪd] *n.* (*cover*) кры́шка; (*eyelid*) ве́ко (*pl.* -ки, -к).

lie[1] [laɪ] *n.* (*untruth*) ложь (лжи, *i.* ло́жью); (*deceit*) обма́н; *v.i.* лгать (лгу, лжёшь; лгал, -а́, -о) *impf.*, со~ *pf.*

lie[2] [laɪ] *n.* (*position*) положе́ние; ~ **of the land** (*fig.*) положе́ние веще́й; *v.i.* лежа́ть (-жу́, -жи́шь) *impf.*; (*be situated*) находи́ться (-ожу́сь, -о́дишься) *impf.*; ~ **down** ложи́ться *impf.*, лечь (ля́гу, ля́жешь; лёг, -ла́) *pf.*; ~ **in wait for** подстерега́ть *impf.*, подстере́чь (-егу́, -ежёшь; -ёг, -егла́) *pf.*+*a.*

lieu [lju:] *n.*: **in** ~ **of** вме́сто+*g.*

lieutenant [lef'tenənt] *n.* лейтена́нт. **lieutenant-colonel** *n.* подполко́вник. **lieutenant-general** *n.* генера́л-лейтена́нт.

life [laɪf] *n.* жизнь; (*way of* ~) о́браз жи́зни; (*energy*) жи́вость; (*biography*) жизнеописа́ние; (*of inanimate object*) срок рабо́ты, слу́жбы; **for** ~ на всю жизнь; **from** ~ с нату́ры. **lifebelt** *n.* спаса́тельный по́яс (*pl.* -а́). **lifeboat** *n.* спаса́тельная шлю́пка. **lifebuoy** *n.* спаса́тельный буй (*pl.* буи́). **lifeguard** *n.* (*bodyguard*) ли́чная охра́на. **Life-Guards** *n.* лейб-гва́рдия. **life-jacket** *n.* спаса́тельный жиле́т. **lifeless** *adj.* безжи́зненный (-ен, -енна). **lifelike** *adj.* сло́вно живо́й (жив, -а́, -о). **lifelong** *adj.* пожи́зненный (-ен, -енна). **life-size(d)** *adj.* в натура́льную величину́. **lifetime** *n.* продолжи́тельность жи́зни.

lift [lɪft] *n.* подня́тие; (*machine*) лифт, подъёмная маши́на, подъёмник; (*force*) подъёмная си́ла; **give a** ~ подвози́ть (-ожу́, -о́зишь) *impf.*, подвезти́ (-езу́, -езёшь; -ёз, -езла́) *pf.*; *v.t.* & *i.* поднима́ть(ся) *impf.*, подня́ть(ся) (-ниму́(сь), -ни́мешь(ся); по́днял/подня́лся́, -ла́(сь), -ло/ло́сь) *pf.*; *v.t.* (*steal*) красть (краду́, -дёшь; крал) *impf.*, у~ *pf.*

ligament ['lɪgəmənt] *n.* свя́зка.

ligature ['lɪgətʃə(r)] *n.* лигату́ра; (*mus.*) ли́га.

light[1] [laɪt] *n.* свет, освеще́ние; (*source of* ~) ого́нь (огня́) *m.*, ла́мпа, фона́рь (-ря́) *m.*; *pl.* (*traffic* ~) светофо́р; **bring to** ~ выводи́ть (-ожу́, -о́дишь) *impf.*, вы́вести (-еду, -едешь; -ел) *pf.* на чи́стую во́ду; **come to** ~ обнару́живаться *impf.*, обнару́житься *pf.*; **shed** ~ **on** пролива́ть *impf.*, проли́ть (-лью́, -льёшь; про́ли́л, -а́, -о) *pf.* свет на+*a.*; ~ **meter** (*phot.*) экспоно́метр; *adj.* (*bright*) све́тлый (-тел, -тла́, -тло); (*pale*) бле́дный (-ден, -дна́, -дно, бле́дны́); **it is** ~ **in the room** в ко́мнате светло́; *v.t.* & *i.* (*ignite*) зажига́ть(ся) *impf.*, заже́чь(ся) (-жгу́(сь), -жжёшь(ся); -жёг(ся), -жгла́(сь)) *pf.*; *v.t.* (*give* ~ *to*) освеща́ть *impf.*, освети́ть (-ещу́, -ети́шь) *pf.*; ~ **up** (*begin to smoke*) закури́ть (-рю́, -ришь) *pf.*

light[2] [laɪt] *adj.* (*not heavy*) лёгкий (-гок, -гка́, -гко́, лёгки́); (*unimportant*) незначи́тельный; (*nimble*) бы́стрый (быстр, -а́, -о, бы́стры́); (*cheerful*) весёлый (ве́сел, -а́, -о, ве́селы́); ~ **industry** лёгкая промы́шленность; ~ **infantry** лёгкая пехо́та.

light³ [laɪt] *v.i.*: ~ **upon** неожи́данно ната́лкиваться *impf.*, натолкну́ться *pf.* на+*a.*

lighten¹ ['laɪt(ə)n] *v.t.* & *i.* (*make lighter*) облегча́ть(ся) *impf.*, облегчи́ть(ся) *pf.*; *v.t.* (*mitigate*) смягча́ть *impf.*, смягчи́ть *pf.*

lighten² ['laɪt(ə)n] *v.t.* (*illuminate*) освеща́ть *impf.*, освети́ть (-ещу́, -ети́шь) *pf.*; *v.i.* (*grow bright*) светле́ть *impf.*, по~ *pf.*; (*flash*) сверка́ть *impf.*, сверкну́ть *pf.*; **it is ~ing** сверка́ет мо́лния.

lighter¹ ['laɪtə(r)] *n.* (*cigarette ~ etc.*) зажига́лка.

lighter² ['laɪtə(r)] *n.* (*boat*) ли́хтер.

light-fingered [laɪt'fɪŋgəd] *adj.* на́ руку нечи́стый (-т, -та́, -то). **light-headed** *adj.* (*frivolous*) легкомы́сленный (-ен, -енна); (*delirious*) *pred.* в бреду́. **light-hearted** *adj.* беззабо́тный.

lighthouse ['laɪthaʊs] *n.* мая́к (-а́).

lighting ['laɪtɪŋ] *n.* освеще́ние; (*lights*) освети́тельные устано́вки *f.pl.*

light-minded [laɪt'maɪndɪd] *adj.* легкомы́сленный (-ен, -енна).

lightning ['laɪtnɪŋ] *n.* мо́лния; **ball** ~ шарова́я мо́лния; **summer** ~ зарни́ца. **lightning-conductor** *n.* молниеотво́д.

lights [laɪts] *n.* (*cul.*) лёгкое *sb.*

lightship ['laɪtʃɪp] *n.* плаву́чий мая́к (-а́).

lightweight ['laɪtweɪt] *n.* (*sport*) легкове́с; *adj.* легкове́сный.

light-year ['laɪtjɪə(r)] *n.* светово́й год (*pl.* го́ды, лет, года́м).

like¹ [laɪk] *adj.* (*similar*) похо́жий (на+*a.*), подо́бный; **what is he ~?** что он за челове́к?; *n.*: **and the ~** и тому́ подо́бное, и т.п.

like² [laɪk] *v.t.* нра́виться *impf.*, по~ *pf. impers.+d.*; люби́ть (-блю́, -бишь) *impf.*; (*wish for*) хоте́ть (хочу́, -чешь, хоти́м) *impf.*; **I should ~** я хоте́л бы; **I would ~** мне хо́чется; **as you ~** как вам удо́бно. **likeable** *adj.* симпати́чный.

likelihood *n.* вероя́тность. **likely** *adj.* (*probable*) вероя́тный; (*suitable*) подходя́щий.

liken ['laɪkən] *v.t.* уподобля́ть *impf.*, уподо́бить *pf.* (**to** +*d.*).

likeness ['laɪknɪs] *n.* (*resemblance*) схо́дство; (*semblance*) вид; (*portrait*) портре́т.

likewise ['laɪkwaɪz] *adv.* (*similarly*) подо́бно; (*also*) то́же, та́кже.

liking ['laɪkɪŋ] *n.* вкус (**for** к+*d.*).

lilac ['laɪlək] *n.* сире́нь; *adj.* сире́невый.

lily ['lɪlɪ] *n.* ли́лия; ~ **of the valley** ла́ндыш.

limb [lɪm] *n.* член те́ла; (*of tree*) сук (-а́, *loc.* -у́; *pl.* -и́, -о́в & су́чья, -ьев).

limber ['lɪmbə(r)] *adj.* (*flexible*) ги́бкий (-бок, -бка́, -бко); (*nimble*) прово́рный; *v.i.*: ~ **up** размина́ться *impf.*, размя́ться (разомну́сь, -нёшься) *pf.*

limbo ['lɪmbəʊ] *n.* преддве́рие а́да; (*fig.*) забро́шенность, забве́ние; состоя́ние неопределённости.

lime¹ [laɪm] *n.* (*min.*) и́звесть. **limekiln** *n.* печь (*loc.* пе́чи́; *pl.* -чи, -че́й) для о́бжига известняка́. **limelight** *n.*: **in the ~** (*fig.*) в це́нтре внима́ния. **limestone** *n.* известня́к (-а́).

lime² [laɪm] *n.* (*fruit*) лайм.

lime³ [laɪm] *n.* (~*-tree*) ли́па.

limit ['lɪmɪt] *n.* грани́ца, преде́л; *v.t.* ограни́чивать *impf.*, ограни́чить *pf.* **limi'tation** *n.* ограниче́ние; (*leg.*) искова́я да́вность. **limitless** *adj.* безграни́чный.

limousine ['lɪmʊˌziːn, ˌlɪmʊ'ziːn, 'lɪməˌziːn] *n.* лимузи́н.

limp¹ [lɪmp] *n.* (*lameness*) хромота́; *v.i.* хрома́ть *impf.*

limp² [lɪmp] *adj.* (*not stiff*) мя́гкий (-гок, -гка́, -гко); (*fig.*) вя́лый.

limpet ['lɪmpɪt] *n.* морско́е блю́дечко (*pl.* -чки, -чек, -чкам).

limpid ['lɪmpɪd] *adj.* прозра́чный.

linchpin ['lɪntʃpɪn] *n.* чека́.

linden ['lɪnd(ə)n] *n.* ли́па.

line¹ [laɪn] *n.* ли́ния, черта́; (*cord*) верёвка; (*fishing ~*) ле́са́ (*pl.* лёсы); (*wrinkle*) морщи́на; (*limit*) грани́ца; (*row*) ряд (-а́ *with* 2, 3, 4, *loc.* -у́; *pl.* -ы́); (*of words*) строка́ (*pl.* -ки, -к, -ка́м); (*of verse*) стих (-а́); *v.t.* (*paper*) линова́ть *impf.*, раз~ *pf.*; *v.t.* & *i.* (~ *up*) выстра́ивать(ся) *impf.*, вы́строить(ся) *pf.* в ряд.

line² [laɪn] *v.t.* (*clothes*) класть (кладу́, -дёшь; клал) *impf.*, положи́ть (-жу́, -жишь) *pf.* на подкла́дку.

lineage ['lɪnɪɪdʒ] *n.* происхожде́ние (по прямо́й ли́нии).

linear ['lɪnɪə(r)] *adj.* лине́йный.

lined¹ [laɪnd] *adj.* (*paper*) лино́ванный; (*face*) морщи́нистый.

lined² [laɪnd] *adj.* (*garment*) на подкла́дке, с подкла́дкой.

linen ['lɪnɪn] *n.* полотно́ (*pl.* -тна, -тен, -тнам); *collect.* бельё; *adj.* льяно́й, полотня́ный.

liner ['laɪnə(r)] *n.* ла́йнер.

linesman ['laɪnzmən] *n.* (*sport*) боково́й судья́ (*pl.* -дьи, -де́й, -дьям) *m.*

linger ['lɪŋgə(r)] *v.i.* ме́длить *impf.*; заде́рживаться *impf.*, задержа́ться (-жу́сь, -жишься) *pf.*

lingerie ['læʒərɪ] *n.* да́мское бельё.

lingering ['lɪŋgərɪŋ] *adj.* (*illness*) затяжно́й.

lingo ['lɪŋgəʊ] *n.* (*special language*) жарго́н.

linguist ['lɪŋgwɪst] *n.* лингви́ст, языкове́д. **lingu'istic** *adj.* лингвисти́ческий. **lingu'istics** *n.* лингви́стика, языкозна́ние.

liniment ['lɪnɪmənt] *n.* жи́дкая мазь.

lining ['laɪnɪŋ] *n.* (*clothing etc.*) подкла́дка; (*tech.*) облицо́вка.

link [lɪŋk] *n.* звено́ (*pl.* -нья, -ньев), связь; *v.t.* соединя́ть *impf.*, соедини́ть *pf.*; свя́зывать *impf.*, связа́ть (свяжу́, -жешь) *pf.*

linnet ['lɪnɪt] *n.* конопля́нка.

lino(leum) ['laɪnəʊ; lɪ'nəʊlɪəm] *n.* линóлеум.
linseed ['lɪnsiːd] *n.* льнянóе сéмя (*g.pl.* -мя́н) *nt.*; ~ **cake** льняны́е жмыхи́ (-хóв) *pl.*; ~ **oil** льнянóе мáсло.
lint [lɪnt] *n.* кóрпия.
lintel ['lɪnt(ə)l] *n.* перемы́чка.
lion ['laɪən] *n.* лев (льва); ~ **cub** львёнок (-нка; *pl.* львя́та, -т). **lioness** *n.* льви́ца.
lip [lɪp] *n.* губá (*pl.* -бы, -б, -бáм); (*of vessel*) край (*loc.* краю́; *pl.* -ая́); (*fig.*) дéрзость. **lipstick** *n.* губнáя помáда.
liquefaction [ˌlɪkwɪ'fækʃ(ə)n] *n.* сжижéние. **liquefy** ['lɪkwɪˌfaɪ] *v.t.* & *i.* превращáть(ся) *impf.*, преврати́ть(ся) (-ащу́, -ати́т(ся)) *pf.* в жи́дкое состоя́ние.
liqueur [lɪ'kjʊə(r)] *n.* ликёр (-а(у)).
liquid ['lɪkwɪd] *n.* жи́дкость; *adj.* жи́дкий (-док, -дкá, -дко); (*transparent*) прозрáчный; (*ling.*) плáвный; (*econ.*) ликви́дный.
liquidate ['lɪkwɪˌdeɪt] *v.t.* ликвиди́ровать *impf.* & *pf.* **liqui'dation** *n.* ликвидáция; **go into** ~ ликвиди́роваться *impf.* & *pf.*
liquidity [lɪ'kwɪdɪtɪ] *n.* жи́дкое состоя́ние.
liquidizer ['lɪkwɪˌdaɪzə(r)] *n.* (*cul.*) ми́ксер.
liquor ['lɪkə(r)] *n.* (спиртнóй) напи́ток (-тка).
liquorice ['lɪkərɪs, -rɪʃ] *n.* (*plant*) лакри́чник, солóдка; (*root*) лакри́ца, солодкóвый кóрень (-рня) *m.*
lissom ['lɪsəm] *adj.* (*lithe*) ги́бкий (-бок, -бкá, -бко); (*agile*) провóрный.
list¹ [lɪst] *n.* (*roll*) спи́сок (-ска), пéречень (-чня) *m.*; *v.t.* составля́ть *impf.*, состáвить *pf.* спи́сок+*g.*; перечисля́ть *impf.*, перечи́слить *pf.*
list² [lɪst] *n.* (*naut.*) крен; *v.i.* накреня́ться *impf.*, крени́ться *impf.*, на~ *pf.*
listen ['lɪs(ə)n] *v.i.* слу́шать *impf.*, по~ *pf.* (**to** +*a.*); (*heed*) прислу́шиваться *impf.*, прислу́шаться *pf.* (**to** к+*d.*); ~ **in** (*telephone*) подслу́шивать *impf.*, подслу́шать *pf.* (**to** +*a.*); (*radio*) слу́шать *impf.* рáдио.
listless ['lɪstlɪs] *adj.* (*languid*) тóмный (-мен, -мнá, -мно); (*indifferent*) безразли́чный.
litany ['lɪtənɪ] *n.* литáния.
literacy ['lɪtərəsɪ] *n.* грáмотность.
literal ['lɪtər(ə)l] *adj.* (*in letters*) бу́квенный; (*sense etc.*) буквáльный.
literary ['lɪtərərɪ] *adj.* литерату́рный.
literate ['lɪtərət] *adj.* грáмотный.
literature ['lɪtərətʃə(r), 'lɪtrə-] *n.* литерату́ра.
lithe [laɪð] *adj.* ги́бкий (-бок, -бкá, -бко).
lithograph ['lɪθəˌgrɑːf, 'laɪθə-] *n.* литогрáфия; *v.t.* литографи́ровать *impf.* & *pf.* **lithographer** [lɪ'θɒgrəfə(r)] *n.* литóграф. **lithographic** [ˌlɪθə'græfɪk] *adj.* литографи́ческий. **lithography** [lɪ'θɒgrəfɪ] *n.* литогрáфия.
Lithuania [ˌlɪθjuː'eɪnɪə, ˌlɪθuː-] *n.* Литвá.
litigant ['lɪtɪgənt] *n.* сторонá (*a.* -ону; *pl.* -оны, -óн, -онáм); *adj.* тя́жущийся. **litigate** *v.i.* суди́ться (сужу́сь, су́дишься) *impf.* **liti'gation** *n.* тя́жба. **litigious** [lɪ'tɪdʒəs] *adj.* сутя́жнический.
litmus ['lɪtməs] *n.* лáкмус; ~ **paper** лáкмусовая бумáга.
litre ['liːtə(r)] *n.* литр.
litter ['lɪtə(r)] *n.* (*vehicle, stretcher*) носи́лки (-лок) *pl.*; (*bedding*) подсти́лка; (*disorder*) беспоря́док (-дка); (*rubbish*) сор (-а(у)); (*brood*) помёт; *v.t.* (*make untidy*) сори́ть *impf.*, на~ *pf.* (**with** +*i.*); (*scatter*) разбрáсывать *impf.*, разбросáть *pf.*
little ['lɪt(ə)l] *n.* немнóгое; ~ **by** ~ мáло-помáлу; **a** ~ немнóго+*g.*; **not a** ~ немáло+*g.*; *adj.* мáленький, небольшóй; (*in height*) небольшóго рóста; (*in distance, time*) корóткий (кóрóток, короткá, кóрóткó); (*unimportant*) незначи́тельный; *adv.* мáло, немнóго; (*not at all*) совсéм не.
littoral ['lɪtər(ə)l] *n.* побережье; *adj.* прибрéжный.
liturgical [lɪ'tɜːdʒɪk(ə)l] *adj.* литурги́ческий. **'liturgy** *n.* литурги́я.
live¹ [laɪv] *adj.* живóй (жив, -á, -о); (*coals*) горя́щий; (*mil.*) боевóй; (*elec.*) под напряжéнием; (*active*) дéятельный; (*real*) жи́зненный (-ен, -енна); ~ **broadcast** прямáя передáча.
live² [lɪv] *v.i.* жить (живу́, -вёшь; жил, -á, -о) *impf.*; существовáть *impf.*; ~ **down** заглáживать *impf.*, заглáдить *pf.*; ~ **on** (*feed on*) питáться *impf.*+*i.*; ~ **through** переживáть *impf.*, пережи́ть (-иву́, -ивёшь; пéрежи́л, -á, -о) *pf.*; ~ **until, to see** доживáть *impf.*, дожи́ть (-иву́, -ивёшь; дóжил, -á, -о) *pf.* до+*g.*; ~ **up to** жить (живу́, -вёшь; жил, -á, -о) *impf.* соглáсно+*d.*
livelihood ['laɪvlɪˌhʊd] *n.* срéдства *nt.pl.* к существовáнию.
lively ['laɪvlɪ] *adj.* живóй (жив, -á, -о), весёлый (вéсел, -á, -о, вéселы́).
liven (up) ['laɪv(ə)n] *v.t.* & *i.* оживля́ть(ся) *impf.*, оживи́ть(ся) *pf.*
liver ['lɪvə(r)] *n.* пéчень; (*cul.*) печёнка.
livery ['lɪvərɪ] *n.* ливрéя.
livestock ['laɪvstɒk] *n.* скот (-á), живóй инвентáрь (-ря́) *m.*
livid ['lɪvɪd] *adj.* (*colour*) синевáто-сéрый; *pred.* (*angry*) зол (зла).
living ['lɪvɪŋ] *n.* срéдства *nt.pl.* к существовáнию; (*eccl.*) бенефи́ция; **earn a** ~ зарабáтывать *impf.*, заработáть *pf.* на жизнь; *adj.* живóй (жив, -á, -о), живу́щий; (*of likeness*) тóчный; ~ **image** кóпия. **living-room** *n.* гости́ная *sb.*
lizard ['lɪzəd] *n.* я́щерица.
lo [ləʊ] *int.* вот!; се!
loach [ləʊtʃ] *n.* голéц (-льцá).
load [ləʊd] *n.* груз; (*also fig.*) брéмя *nt.*; (*tech.*) нагру́зка; *pl.* (*lots*) ку́ча; *v.t.* нагружáть *impf.*, грузи́ть (-ужу́, -у́жишь) *impf.*, на~ *pf.*; (*fig.*) обременя́ть *impf.*, обремени́ть *pf.*; (*gun, camera*) заряжáть *impf.*, заряди́ть (-яжу́, -я́ди́шь) *pf.*
loadstar *see* **lodestar. loadstone** *see* **lodestone**
loaf¹ [ləʊf] *n.* бухáнка; батóн.

loaf² [ləʊf] *v.i.* безде́льничать *impf.*; шата́ться *impf.* **loafer** *n.* безде́льник.
loam [ləʊm] *n.* сугли́нок (-нка).
loan [ləʊn] *n.* заём (за́йма); *v.t.* дава́ть (даю́, даёшь) *impf.*, дать (дам, дашь, даст, дади́м; дал, -а́, да́ло́, -и) *pf.* взаймы́.
loath [ləʊθ] *pred.*: **be ~ to** не хоте́ть (хочу́, -чешь; хоти́м) *impf.*+*inf.*
loathe [ləʊð] *v.t.* пита́ть *impf.* отвраще́ние к+*d.* **loathing** *n.* отвраще́ние. **loathsome** *adj.* отврати́тельный.
lob [lɒb] *n.* (*sport*) свеча́ (*pl.* -чи, -че́й).
lobby ['lɒbɪ] *n.* прихо́жая *sb.*, вестибю́ль *m.*; (*parl.*) кулуа́ры *pl.*
lobe [ləʊb] *n.* до́ля (*pl.* -ли, -ле́й); (*of ear*) мо́чка.
lobster ['lɒbstə(r)] *n.* ома́р. **lobster-pot** *n.* ве́рша для ома́ров.
local ['ləʊk(ə)l] *adj.* ме́стный; (*train*) при́городный.
locality [ləʊ'kælɪtɪ] *n.* (*site*) местоположе́ние; (*district*) ме́стность.
localize ['ləʊkə,laɪz] *v.t.* (*restrict*) локализова́ть *impf.* & *pf.*
locate [ləʊ'keɪt] *v.t.* (*place*) помеща́ть *impf.*, помести́ть *pf.*; (*discover*) обнару́живать *impf.*, обнару́жить *pf.*; **be ~d** находи́ться (-ится) *impf.*
location [ləʊ'keɪʃ(ə)n] *n.* (*position*) местонахожде́ние; определе́ние ме́ста; **on ~** (*cin.*) на нату́ре.
locative ['lɒkətɪv] *adj.* (*n.*) ме́стный (паде́ж (-а́)).
loch [lɒk, lɒx] *n.* (*lake*) о́зеро (*pl.* озёра); (*sea ~*) (у́зкий) зали́в.
lock¹ [lɒk] *n.* (*of hair*) ло́кон; *pl.* во́лосы (воло́с, -а́м) *pl.*
lock² [lɒk] *n.* замо́к (-мка́), запо́р; (*tech.*) сто́пор; (*canal*) шлюз; *v.t.* запира́ть *impf.*, запере́ть (-пру́, -прёшь; за́пер, -ла́, -ло) *pf.*; *v.i.* запира́ться *impf.*, запере́ться (-прётся; за́перся́, -рла́сь, за́перло́сь) *pf.* **locker** ['lɒkə(r)] *n.* шка́фчик.
locket ['lɒkɪt] *n.* медальо́н.
lockjaw ['lɒkdʒɔː] *n.* столбня́к (-а́).
lock-keeper ['lɒkkiːpə(r)] *n.* нача́льник шлю́за.
lockout ['lɒkaʊt] *n.* лока́ут. **locksmith** *n.* сле́сарь (*pl.* -ри & -ря́) *m.* **lock-up** *n.* (*cell*) араста́нтская *sb.*
locomotion [,ləʊkə'məʊʃ(ə)n] *n.* передвиже́ние. **locomotive** *adj.* дви́жущий(ся); *n.* (*rail.*) локомоти́в.
locust ['ləʊkəst] *n.* саранча́ (*also collect.*; *fig.*).
locution [lək'juːʃ(ə)n] *n.* оборо́т ре́чи.
lode [ləʊd] *n.* ру́дная жи́ла. **lodestar, load-** *n.* Поля́рная звезда́; (*fig.*) путево́дная звезда́ (*pl.* звёзды). **lodestone, load-** *n.* магни́тный железня́к (-а́); (*magnet*) магни́т.
lodge [lɒdʒ] *n.* (*hunting*) (охо́тничий) до́мик; (*porter's*) швейца́рская *sb.*, сторо́жка; (*Masonic*) ло́жа; *v.t.* (*accommodate*) помеща́ть *impf.*, помести́ть *pf.*; (*deposit*) дава́ть (даю́, даёшь) *impf.*, дать (дам, дашь, даст, дади́м; дал, -а́, да́ло́, -и) *pf.* на хране́ние (**with** +*d.*); (*complaint*) подава́ть (-даю́, -даёшь) *impf.*, пода́ть (-а́м, -а́шь, -а́ст, -ади́м; по́дал, -а́, -о) *pf.*; *v.i.* (*reside*) жить (живу́, -вёшь; жил, -а́, -о) *impf.* (**with** у+*g.*); (*stick*) заса́живать *impf.*, засе́сть (-ся́дет; -се́л) *pf.* **lodger** *n.* жиле́ц (-льца́), жили́ца. **lodging** *n.* (*also pl.*) кварти́ра, (снима́емая) ко́мната.
loft [lɒft] *n.* (*attic*) черда́к (-а́); (*for hay*) сенова́л; (*for pigeons*) голубя́тня (*g.pl.* -тен); (*gallery*) галере́я.
lofty ['lɒftɪ] *adj.* о́чень высо́кий (-о́к, -ока́, -о́ко́); (*elevated*) возвы́шенный.
log [lɒg] *n.* бревно́ (*pl.* брёвна, -вен, -внам); (*for fire*) поле́но (*pl.* -нья, -ньев); (*naut.*) лаг.
logarithm ['lɒgə,rɪð(ə)m] *n.* логари́фм. **loga'rithmic** *adj.* логарифми́ческий.
log-book ['lɒgbʊk] *n.* (*naut.*) ва́хтенный журна́л; (*aeron.*) бортово́й журна́л; (*registration book*) формуля́р.
loggerhead ['lɒgə,hed] *n.*: **be at ~s** ссо́риться *impf.*, по~ *pf.* (**with** с+*i.*).
logic ['lɒdʒɪk] *n.* ло́гика. **logical** *adj.* (*of logic*) логи́ческий; (*consistent*) логи́чный. **logician** [lə'dʒɪʃ(ə)n] *n.* ло́гик.
logistics [lə'dʒɪstɪks] *n.* материа́льно-техни́ческое обеспе́чение.
loin [lɔɪn] *n.* (*pl.*) поясни́ца; (*cul.*) филе́йная часть.
loiter ['lɔɪtə(r)] *v.i.* слоня́ться *impf.*
London ['lʌnd(ə)n] *n.* Ло́ндон. **Londoner** *n.* ло́ндонец, -ка.
lone [ləʊn], **lonely** *adj.* одино́кий, уединённый (-ён, -ённа). **loneliness** *n.* одино́чество, уединённость.
long¹ [lɒŋ] *v.i.* стра́стно жела́ть *impf.*, по~ *pf.* (**for** +*g.*); тоскова́ть *impf.* (**for** по+*d.*)
long² [lɒŋ] *adj.* (*space*) дли́нный (-нен, -нна́, дли́нно́); (*time*) до́лгий (-лог, -лга́, -лго); (*protracted*) дли́тельный; (*in measurements*) длино́й в+*a.*; **in the ~ run** в коне́чном счёте; *adv.* до́лго; **~ after** спустя́ мно́го вре́мени; **~ ago** (уже́) давно́; **as ~ as** пока́; **~ before** задо́лго до+*g.* **longboat** *n.* барка́с. **longevity** [lɒn'dʒevɪtɪ] *n.* долгове́чность.
longing ['lɒŋɪŋ] *n.* стра́стное жела́ние (**for** +*g.*); тоска́ (**for** по+*d*).
longitude ['lɒŋgɪ,tjuːd, 'lɒndʒ-] *n.* долгота́ (*pl.* -ты).
long-lived [lɒŋ'lɪvd] *adj.* долгове́чный. **long-sighted** *adj.* дальнозо́ркий (-рок, -рка); (*fig.*) дальнови́дный. **long-suffering** *adj.* долготерпели́вый; многострада́льный. **long-term** *adj.* долгосро́чный. **longways** *adv.* в длину́. **long-winded** *adj.* многоре́чивый.
look [lʊk] *n.* (*glance*) взгляд; (*appearance*) вид; (*expression*) выраже́ние; *v.i.* смотре́ть (-рю́, -ришь) *impf.*, по~ *pf.* (**at** на, в, +*a.*); гляде́ть (-яжу́, -яди́шь) *impf.*, по~ *pf.* (**at** на+*a.*); (*appear*) вы́глядеть (-яжу, -ядишь)

impf.+i.; (*face*) выходи́ть (-ит) *impf.* (**towards, onto** на+*a.*); ~ **about** осма́триваться *impf.*, осмотре́ться (-рю́сь, -ришься) *pf.*; ~ **after** (*attend to*) присма́тривать *impf.*, присмотре́ть (-рю́, -ришь) *pf.* за+*i.*; ~ **down on** презира́ть *impf.*; ~ **for** иска́ть (ищу́, и́щешь) *impf.+a.*, +*g.*; ~ **forward to** предвкуша́ть *impf.*, предвкуси́ть (-ушу́, -у́шишь) *pf.*; ~ **in on** загля́дывать *impf.*, загляну́ть (-ну́, -нешь) *pf.* к+*d.*; ~ **into** (*investigate*) разбира́ться *impf.*, разобра́ться (разберу́сь, -рёшься; -а́лся, -ала́сь, -а́ло́сь) *pf.* в+*p.*; ~ **like** быть похо́жим на+*a.*; **it ~s like rain** похо́же на (то, что бу́дет) дождь; ~ **on** (*regard*) счита́ть *impf.*, счесть (сочту́, -тёшь; счёл, сочла́) *pf.* (**as** +*i.*, за+*i.*); ~ **out** выгля́дывать *impf.*, вы́глянуть *pf.* (в окно́); быть настороже́; *imper.* осторо́жно!; береги́(те)сь!; ~ **over, through** просма́тривать *impf.*, просмотре́ть (-рю́, -ришь) *pf.* ~ **up** (*raise eyes*) поднима́ть *impf.*, подня́ть (подниму́, -мешь; по́днял, -а́, -о) *pf.* глаза́; (*in dictionary etc.*) иска́ть (ищу́, и́щешь) *impf.*; (*improve*) улучша́ться *impf.*, улу́чшиться *pf.*; ~ **up to** уважа́ть *impf.* **looker-on** *n.* зри́тель *m.*, ~ница. **looking-glass** *n.* зе́ркало (*pl.* -ла́).

loom¹ [lu:m] *n.* тка́цкий стано́к (-нка́).

loom² [lu:m] *v.i.* нея́сно вырисо́вываться *impf.*, вы́рисоваться; (*fig.*) гото́виться *impf.*

loop [lu:p] *n.* пе́тля (*g.pl.* -тель); *v.i.* образо́вывать *impf.*, образова́ть *pf.* пе́тлю; ~ **the** ~ (*aeron.*) де́лать *impf.*, с~ *pf.* мёртвую пе́тлю.

loophole ['lu:phəʊl] *n.* бойни́ца; (*fig.*) лазе́йка.

loose [lu:s] *adj.* (*free*) свобо́дный; (*not fixed*) неприкреплённый; (*inexact*) нето́чный (-чен, -чна́, -чно); (*not compact*) ры́хлый (рыхл, -а́, -о); (*lax*) распу́щенный (-ен, -енна); **be at a ~ end** безде́льничать *impf.*; *v.t.* (*free*) освобожда́ть *impf.*, освободи́ть *pf.*; (*untie*) отвя́зывать *impf.*, отвяза́ть (-яжу́, -я́жешь) *pf.* **loosen** *v.t.* & *i.* ослабля́ть(ся) *impf.*, осла́бить(ся) *pf.*

loot [lu:t] *n.* добы́ча; *v.t.* гра́бить *impf.*, о~ *pf.*

lop [lɒp] *v.t.* (*tree*) подреза́ть *impf.*, подре́зать (-е́жу, -е́жешь) *pf.*; (~ *off*) отруба́ть *impf.*, отруби́ть (-блю́, -бишь) *pf.*

lope [ləʊp] *v.i.* бе́гать *indet.*, бежа́ть (бегу́, бежи́шь) *det.* вприпры́жку.

lopsided [lɒp'saɪdɪd] *adj.* кривобо́кий.

loquacious [lɒ'kweɪʃəs] *adj.* болтли́вый. **loquacity** [lɒ'kwæsɪtɪ] *n.* болтли́вость.

lord [lɔ:d] *n.* (*master*) господи́н (*pl.* -да́, -д, -да́м), влады́ка *m.*; (**the L~**; *eccl.*) Госпо́дь (-ода, *voc.* -оди); (*peer*; *title*) лорд; *v.t.*: ~ **it over** помыка́ть *impf.+i.* **lordly** *adj.* (*haughty*) высокоме́рный. **lordship** *n.* власть (**over** над+*i.*); (*title*) све́тлость.

lore [lɔ:(r)] *n.* зна́ния *nt.pl.*

lorgnette [lɔ:'njet] *n.* лорне́т.

lorry ['lɒrɪ] *n.* грузови́к (-а́).

lose [lu:z] *v.t.* теря́ть *impf.*, по~ *pf.*; (*forfeit*) лиша́ться *impf.*, лиши́ться *pf.+g.*; (*game etc.*) прои́грывать *impf.*, проигра́ть *pf.*; *v.i.* (*suffer loss*) терпе́ть (-плю́, -пишь) *impf.*, по~ *pf.* уще́рб (**by** от+*g.*); (*clock*) отстава́ть (-таёт) *impf.*, отста́ть (-а́нет) *pf.* **loss** [lɒs] *n.* поте́ря, уще́рб; (*in game*) про́игрыш; **at a ~** (*puzzled*) в затрудне́нии.

lot [lɒt] *n.* жре́бий; (*destiny*) у́часть; (*of goods*) па́ртия; **a ~, ~s** мно́го, ма́сса; **the** ~ всё (всего́), все (всех) *pl.*

lotion ['ləʊʃ(ə)n] *n.* примо́чка.

lottery ['lɒtərɪ] *n.* лотере́я.

lotto ['lɒtəʊ] *n.* лото́ *nt.indecl.*

lotus ['ləʊtəs] *n.* ло́тос.

loud [laʊd] *adj.* (*sound*) гро́мкий (-мок, -мка́, -мко); (*noisy*) шу́мный (-мен, -мна́, -мно); (*colour*) крича́щий; **out ~** вслух. **loudspeaker** *n.* громкоговори́тель *m.*; дина́мик.

lounge [laʊndʒ] *n.* фойе́ *nt.indecl.*; (*sitting room*) гости́ная *sb.*; *v.i.* сиде́ть (сижу́, сиди́шь) *impf.* разваля́сь; (*idle*) безде́льничать *impf.* **lounger** *n.* шезло́нг.

lour ['laʊə(r)], **lower²** ['laʊə(r)] *v.i.* (*person, sky*) хму́риться *impf.*, на~ *pf.*

louse [laʊs] *n.* вошь (вши, *i.* во́шью). **lousy** ['laʊzɪ] *adj.* вши́вый; (*coll.*) парши́вый.

lout [laʊt] *n.* у́валень (-льня) *m.*, грубия́н. **loutish** *adj.* неотёсанный (-ан, -анна).

lovable ['lʌvəb(ə)l] *adj.* ми́лый (мил, -а́, -о, ми́лы́). **love** *n.* любо́вь (-бви́, *i.* -бо́вью) (**of, for** к+*d.*); (*sweetheart*) возлю́бленный *sb.*; **in ~ with** влюблённый (-ён, -ённа) в+*a.*; *v.t.* люби́ть (-блю́, -бишь) *impf.* **lovely** *adj.* краси́вый; (*delightful*) преле́стный. **lover** *n.* любо́вник, -ица.

low¹ [ləʊ] *n.* (*of cow*) мыча́ние; *v.i.* мыча́ть (-чу́, -чи́шь) *impf.*

low² [ləʊ] *adj.* ни́зкий (-зок, -зка́, -зко), невысо́кий (-о́к, -ока́, -о́ко́); (*quiet*) ти́хий (тих, -а́, -о); (*coarse*) гру́бый (груб, -а́, -о); (*weak*) сла́бый (слаб, -а́, -о).

low-alcohol [ˌləʊ'ælkəˌhɒl] *adj.* слабоалкого́льный. **low-calorie** *adj.* малокалори́йный.

lower¹ ['ləʊə(r)] *v.t.* опуска́ть *impf.*, опусти́ть (-ущу́, -у́стишь) *pf.*; снижа́ть *impf.*, сни́зить *pf.*

lower² *see* **lour**

lower³ ['ləʊə(r)] *adj.* ни́зший, ни́жний.

low-fat ['ləʊfæt] *adj.* маложи́рный.

lowland ['ləʊlənd] *n.* ни́зменность.

lowly ['ləʊlɪ] *adj.* скро́мный (-мен, -мна́, -мно).

low-paid ['ləʊpeɪd] *adj.* малоопла́чиваемый.

loyal ['lɔɪəl] *adj.* ве́рный (-рен, -рна́, -рно, ве́рны́), лоя́льный. **loyalty** *n.* ве́рность, лоя́льность.

lozenge ['lɒzɪndʒ] *n.* (*shape*) ромб; (*tablet*) лепёшка.

LP *abbr.* (*of* **long-playing record**) долгоигра́ющая пласти́нка.

L-plate ['elpleɪt] *n.* щито́к с на́дписью

«учёбная» (*на машине*).

Ltd. *abbr.* (*of* ***limited liability company***) с ограниченной ответственностью.

lubricant ['lu:brɪkənt] *n.* смазка, смазочный материал. **lubricate** *v.t.* смазывать *impf.*, смазать (-ажу, -ажешь) *pf.* **lubri'cation** *n.* смазка.

lucerne [lu:'sɜ:n] *n.* люцерна.

lucid ['lu:sɪd] *adj.* ясный (ясен, ясна, ясно, ясны).

luck [lʌk] *n.* (*chance*) случай; (*good* ~) счастье, удача; (*bad* ~) неудача. **luckily** *adv.* к счастью. **luckless** *adj.* несчастный. **lucky** *adj.* счастливый (счастлив); (*successful*) удачный.

lucrative ['lu:krətɪv] *adj.* прибыльный.

lucre ['lu:kə(r)] *n.* прибыль.

ludicrous ['lu:dɪkrəs] *adj.* смехотворный.

lug [lʌg] *v.t.* (*drag*) таскать *indet.*, тащить (-щу, -щишь) *det.*

luggage ['lʌgɪdʒ] *n.* багаж (-а).

lugubrious [lu:'gu:brɪəs, lʊ-] *adj.* печальный.

lukewarm [lu:k'wɔ:m, 'lu:k-] *adj.* тепловатый; (*fig.*) равнодушный.

lull [lʌl] *n.* (*in storm*) затишье; (*interval*) перерыв; *v.t.* (*to sleep*) убаюкивать *impf.*, убаюкать *pf.*; (*suspicions*) усыплять *impf.*, усыпить *pf.*; *v.i.* затихать *impf.*, затихнуть (-х) *pf.*

lullaby ['lʌlə,baɪ] *n.* колыбельная песня (*g.pl.* -сен).

lumbago [lʌm'beɪgəʊ] *n.* люмбаго *nt.indecl.*

lumbar ['lʌmbə(r)] *adj.* поясничный.

lumber[1] ['lʌmbə(r)] *v.i.* (*move*) двигаться (-аюсь, -аешься & движусь, -жешься) *impf.*, двинуться *pf.* тяжело, шумно, неуклюже.

lumber[2] ['lʌmbə(r)] *n.* (*domestic*) рухлядь; (*timber*) лесоматериалы *m.pl.*; *v.t.* загромождать *impf.*, загромоздить *pf.* **lumberjack** *n.* лесоруб. **lumber-room** *n.* чулан.

luminary ['lu:mɪnərɪ] *n.* светило.

luminous ['lu:mɪnəs, 'lju:-] *adj.* светящийся.

lump [lʌmp] *n.* ком (*pl.* -ья, -ьев), кусок (-ска); (*swelling*) опухоль; (*lot*) куча; *v.t.*: ~ **together** смешивать *impf.*, смешать *pf.* (в кучу).

lunacy ['lu:nəsɪ] *n.* безумие.

lunar ['lu:nə(r), 'lju:-] *adj.* лунный.

lunatic ['lu:nətɪk] *adj.* (*n.*) сумасшедший (*sb.*); безумный (*sb.*).

lunch [lʌntʃ] *n.* обед, второй завтрак; *v.i.* обедать *impf.*, по~ *pf.* **lunch-hour, lunch-time** *n.* обеденный перерыв. **luncheon** ['lʌntʃ(ə)n] *n.* официальный обед, завтрак; ~ **voucher** талон на обед.

lung [lʌŋ] *n.* лёгкое *sb.*

lunge [lʌndʒ, lju:-] *n.* (*sport*) выпад; толчок (-чка); *v.i.* (*fencing*) делать *impf.*, с~ *pf.* выпад; наносить (-ошу, -осишь) *impf.*, нанести (-есу, -есёшь; -ёс, -есла) *pf.* удар (с плеча) (**at** +*d.*).

lupin(e) ['lu:pɪn] *n.* люпин.

lupine ['lu:paɪn] *adj.* волчий (-чья, -чье).

lupus ['lu:pəs] *n.* волчанка.

lurch[1] [lɜ:tʃ] *n.*: **leave in the** ~ покидать *impf.*, покинуть *pf.* в беде.

lurch[2] [lɜ:tʃ] *v.i.* (*stagger*) ходить (хожу, ходишь) *indet.*, идти (иду, идёшь; шёл, шла) *det.* шатаясь.

lure [ljʊə(r), lʊə(r)] *n.* приманка; *v.t.* приманивать *impf.*, приманить (-ню, -нишь) *pf.*

lurid ['ljʊərɪd, 'lʊə-] *adj.* мрачный (-чен, -чна, -чно); (*sensational*) сенсационный.

lurk [lɜ:k] *v.i.* прятаться (-ячусь, -ячешься) *impf.*, с~ *pf.*; (*fig.*) таиться *impf.*

luscious ['lʌʃəs] *adj.* приторный.

lush [lʌʃ] *adj.* сочный (-чен, -чна, -чно).

lust [lʌst] *n.* похоть, вожделение (**of, for** к+*d.*); *v.i.* страстно желать *impf.*, по~ *pf.* (**for** +*g.*). **lustful** *adj.* похотливый.

lustre ['lʌstə(r)] *n.* (*gloss*) глянец (-нца); (*splendour*) блеск; (*chandelier*) люстра. **lustrous** *adj.* глянцевитый, блестящий.

lusty ['lʌstɪ] *adj.* (*healthy*) здоровый; (*lively*) живой (жив, -а, -о).

lute[1] [lu:t, lju:t] *n.* (*mus.*) лютня (*g.pl.* -тен).

lute[2] [lu:t, lju:t] *n.* (*clay etc.*) замазка.

Luxemburg ['lʌksəm,bɜ:g] *n.* Люксембург.

luxuriant [lʌg'zjʊərɪənt, lʌk'sj-, lʌg'ʒʊə-] *adj.* пышный (-шен, -шна, -шно).

luxuriate [lʌg'zjʊərɪ,eɪt, lʌk'sj-, lʌg'ʒʊə-] *v.i.* наслаждаться *impf.*, насладиться *pf.* (**in** +*i.*).

luxurious [lʌg'zjʊərɪəs, lʌk'sj-, lʌg'ʒʊə-] *adj.* роскошный. **luxury** ['lʌkʃərɪ] *n.* роскошь.

lye [laɪ] *n.* щёлок (-а(у)).

lymph [lɪmf] *n.* лимфа. **lym'phatic** *adj.* лимфатический.

lynch [lɪntʃ] *v.t.* линчевать (-чую, -чуешь) *impf.* & *pf.*; ~ **law** суд (-а) Линча.

lynx [lɪŋks] *n.* рысь.

lyre ['laɪə(r)] *n.* лира.

lyric ['lɪrɪk] *n.* лирика; *pl.* слова *nt.pl.* песни. **lyrical** *adj.* лирический. **lyricism** ['lɪrɪ,sɪz(ə)m] *n.* лиризм.

M

m. *abbr.* (*of* **metre(s)**) м, метр; (*of* **mile(s)**) миля; (*of* **million(s)**) млн., миллион.

MA *abbr.* (*of* ***Master of Arts***) магистр гуманитарных наук.

macabre [mə'kɑ:br] *adj.* жуткий (-ток, -тка, -тко).

macadam [mə'kædəm] *n.* щебень (-бня) *m.* **macadamize** *v.t.* мостить *impf.*, вы~, за~ *pf.* щебнем.

macaroni [,mækə'rəʊnɪ] *n.* макароны (-н) *pl.*

macaroon [,mækə'ru:n] *n.* миндальное печенье.

macaw [mə'kɔː] *n.* макáо *m.indecl.*

mace [meɪs] *n.* (*weapon*) булавá; (*staff of office*) жезл. **mace-bearer** *n.* жезлонóсец (-сца).

machete [mə'tʃetɪ, mə'ʃetɪ] *n.* мачéте *nt.indecl.*

machination [ˌmækɪ'neɪʃ(ə)n, ˌmæʃ-] *n.* махинáция, интрúга, кóзни (-ней) *pl.*

machine [mə'ʃiːn] *n.* машúна, станóк (-нкá); (*state* ~) аппарáт; *attr.* машúнный; ~ **tool** станóк (-нкá); *v.t.* обрабáтывать *impf.*, обрабóтать *pf.* на станкé; (*sew*) шить (шью, шьёшь) *impf.*, с~ *pf.* (на машúне). **machine-gun** *n.* пулемёт. **machinery** *n.* (*machines*) машúны *f.pl.*; (*mechanism*) механúзм; (*of state*) аппарáт. **machinist** *n.* машинúст; (*sewing*) швéйник, -ица, швеś.

mackerel ['mækr(ə)l] *n.* скýмбрия, макрéль; ~ **sky** нéбо барáшками.

mackintosh ['mækɪnˌtɒʃ] *n.* (*material*) прорезúненная матéрия; (*coat*) непромокáемое пальтó *nt.indecl.*

macrocosm ['mækrəʊˌkɒz(ə)m] *n.* макрокóсм, вселéнная *sb.*

mad [mæd] *adj.* сумасшéдший, помéшанный (-ан, -анна); (*animal*) бéшеный; (*fig.*) безýмный. **madcap** *n.* сорванéц (-нцá). **madden** *v.t.* сводúть (-ожý, -óдишь) *impf.*, свестú (сведý, -дёшь; свёл, -á) *pf.* с умá; (*irritate*) выводúть (-ожý, -óдишь) *impf.*, вы́вести (-еду, -едешь; -ел) *pf.* из себś. **made-to-measure** *adj.* сдéланный (как) на закáз. **madhouse** *n.* сумасшéдший дом (-а(у)); *pl.* -á). **madly** *adv.* безýмно. **madman** *n.* сумасшéдший *sb.*, безýмец (-мца). **madness** *n.* сумасшéствие, безýмие. **madwoman** *n.* сумасшéдшая *sb.*, безýмная *sb.*

made *see* **make**

madder ['mædə(r)] *n.* (*plant*) марéна; (*dye*) крапп.

Madrid [mə'drɪd] *n.* Мадрúд.

madrigal ['mædrɪg(ə)l] *n.* мадригáл.

maestro ['maɪstrəʊ] *n.* маэ́стро *m.indecl.*

mafia ['mæfɪə, 'mɑː-] *n.* мáфия.

magazine [ˌmægə'ziːn] *n.* журнáл; (*mil.*) склад боеприпáсов, вещевóй склад; (*of gun*) магазúн.

maggot ['mægət] *n.* личúнка. **maggoty** *adj.* червúвый.

magic ['mædʒɪk] *n.* мáгия, волшебствó, колдовствó; *adj.* волшéбный, магúческий. **magician** [mə'dʒɪʃ(ə)n] *n.* волшéбник, колдýн (-á); (*conjurer*) фóкусник.

magisterial [ˌmædʒɪ'stɪərɪəl] *adj.* авторитéтный.

magistracy ['mædʒɪstrəsɪ] *n.* магистратýра. **magistrate** ['mædʒɪstrət] *n.* полицéйский судьś (*pl.* -дьи, -дéй, -дьям) *m.*

magma ['mægmə] *n.* мáгма.

magnanimous [mæg'nænɪməs] *adj.* великодýшный.

magnate ['mægneɪt, -nɪt] *n.* магнáт.

magnesia [mæg'niːʒə, -ʃə, -zjə] *n.* óкись мáгния. **magnesium** *n.* мáгний.

magnet ['mægnɪt] *n.* магнúт. **mag'netic** *adj.* магнúтный; (*attractive*) притягáтельный; ~ **tape** магнитолéнта. **magnetism** *n.* магнетúзм; притягáтельность. **magnetize** *v.t.* намагнúчивать *impf.*, намагнúтить *pf.*

magneto [mæg'niːtəʊ] *n.* магнéто *nt.indecl.*

magnification [ˌmægnɪfɪ'keɪʃ(ə)n] *n.* увеличéние.

magnificence [mæg'nɪfɪs(ə)ns] *n.* великолéпие, пы́шность. **magnificent** *adj.* великолéпный, пы́шный (-шен, -шнá, -шно).

magnify ['mægnɪˌfaɪ] *v.t.* увелúчивать *impf.*, увелúчить *pf.*; (*exaggerate*) преувелúчивать *impf.*, преувелúчить *pf.*

magnitude ['mægnɪˌtjuːd] *n.* величинá.

magnolia [mæg'nəʊlɪə] *n.* магнóлия.

magpie ['mægpaɪ] *n.* сорóка.

maharajah [ˌmɑːhə'rɑːdʒə] *n.* магарáджа *m.* **maharanee** [ˌmɑːhə'rɑːnɪ] *n.* магарáни *f.indecl.*

mahogany [mə'hɒgənɪ] *n.* крáсное дéрево.

maid [meɪd] *n.* служáнка, гóрничная *sb.*; ~ **of honour** фрéйлина. **maiden** *adj.* незамýжняя, дéвичий; (*first*) пéрвый; ~ **name** дéвичья фамúлия.

mail[1] [meɪl] *n.* (*letters etc.*) пóчта; (*train*) почтóвый пóезд (*pl.* -á); ~ **order** почтóвый закáз, закáз по пóчте; *v.t.* посылáть *impf.*, послáть (пошлю́, -лёшь) *pf.* по пóчте.

mail[2] [meɪl] *n.* (*armour*) кольчýга; бронś; ~**ed fist** воéнная, физúческая, сúла.

mail-order ['meɪlˌɔːdə(r)] *adj.* торгýющий по почтóвым закáзам; ~ **firm** торгóво-посы́лочная фúрма.

maim [meɪm] *v.t.* калéчить *impf.*, ис~ *pf.*; увéчить *impf.*

main [meɪn] *n.* (*sea*) откры́тое мóре; (*gas* ~; *pl.*) магистрáль; **in the** ~ в основнóм; **with might and** ~ не щадś сил; *adj.* основнóй, глáвный; (*road*) магистрáльный; **by** ~ **force** изо всéх сил; **the** ~ **chance** путь (-тú, -тём) *m.* к нажúве; ~ **line** (*rail.*) магистрáль. **mainland** *n.* матерúк (-á); *attr.* материкóвый. **mainly** *adv.* в основнóм; глáвным óбразом; (*for most part*) бóльшей чáстью. **mainmast** *n.* грот-мáчта. **mainsail** *n.* грот. **mainspring** *n.* ходовáя пружúна. **mainstay** *n.* грóта-штаг; (*fig.*) глáвная опóра.

maintain [meɪn'teɪn] *v.t.* (*continue*) продолжáть *impf.*, продóлжить *pf.*; (*support*) поддéрживать *impf.*, поддержáть (-жý, -жишь) *pf.*; (*family*) содержáть (-жý, -жишь) *impf.*; (*machine*) обслýживать *impf.*, обслужúть (-жý, -жишь) *pf.*; (*assert*) утверждáть *impf.* '**maintenance** *n.* поддéржка; содержáние; обслýживание, ухóд.

maize [meɪz] *n.* кукурýза.

majestic [mə'dʒestɪk] *adj.* велúчественный (-ен, -енна). **majesty** ['mædʒɪstɪ] *n.* велúчественность; (*title*) велúчество.

major[1] ['meɪdʒə(r)] *n.* (*mil.*) майóр.

major[2] ['meɪdʒə(r)] *adj.* (*greater*) бóльший; (*more important*) бóлее вáжный; (*main*) глáвный; (*mus.*) мажóрный; (*senior*) стáр-

ший; *n.* совершеннолéтний *sb.*; (*mus.*) мажóр.
major-general ['meɪdʒə(r)-'dʒenər(ə)l] *n.* генерáл-майóр.
majority [mə'dʒɒrɪtɪ] *n.* (*greater number*) большинствó; (*full age*) совершеннолéтие.
make [meɪk] *n.* мáрка, тип, сорт (*pl.* -á); *v.t.* дéлать *impf.*, с~ *pf.*; (*create*) создавáть (-даю, -даёшь) *impf.*, создáть (-áм, -áшь, -áст, -адим; сóздáл, -á, о) *pf.*; (*produce*) производить (-ожý, -óдишь) *impf.*, произвести (-едý, -едёшь; -ёл, -елá) *pf.*; (*compose*) составлять *impf.*, состáвить *pf.*; (*prepare*) готóвить *impf.*, при~ *pf.*; (*amount to*) равняться *impf.*+*d.*; (*become*) становиться (-влюсь, -вишься) *impf.*, стать (стáну, -нешь) *pf.*+*i.*; (*earn*) зарабáтывать *impf.*, заработать *pf.*; (*compel*) заставлять *impf.*, застáвить *pf.*; **made in the USA** изготóвлено в США; **be made of** состоять (-ою, -оишь) *impf.* из+*g.*;~ **as if, though** дéлать *impf.*, с~ *pf.* вид, что; ~ **a bed** стелить (стелю, -лешь) *impf.*, по~ *pf.* постéль; ~ **believe** притворяться *impf.*, притвориться *pf.*; ~ **do with** довóльствоваться *impf.*, у~ *pf.*+*i.*; ~ **fun of** высмéивать *impf.*, высмеять (-ею, -еешь) *pf.*; ~ **o.s. at home** быть как дóма; ~ **o.s. scarce** исчезáть *impf.*, исчéзнуть (-з) *pf.*; ~ **sure of** удостоверяться *impf.*, удостовéриться *pf.* в+*p.*; ~ **way for** уступáть *impf.*, уступить (-плю, -пишь) *pf.* дорóгу+*d.*; ~ **away with** покóнчить *pf.* с+*i.*; ~ **off** удирáть *impf.*, удрáть (удерý, -рёшь; удрáл, -á, -о) *pf.*; ~ **out** (*document*) составлять *impf.*, состáвить *pf.*; (*cheque*) выписывать *impf.*, выписать (-ишу, -ишешь) *pf.*; (*understand*) разбирáть *impf.*, разобрáть (разберý, -рёшь; разобрáл, -á, -о) *pf.*; ~ **over** передавáть (-даю, -даёшь) *impf.*, передáть (-áм, -áшь, -áст, -адим; пéредал, -á, о) *pf.*; ~ **up** (*compound*) составлять *impf.*, состáвить *pf.*; (*theatr.*) гримировáть(ся) *impf.*, на(за)~ *pf.*; ~ **it up** мириться *impf.*, по~ *pf.* (**with** с+*i.*); ~ **up for** возмещáть *impf.*, возместить *pf.*; ~ **up one's mind** решáться *impf.*, решиться *pf.*; ~ **up to** заискивать *impf.* пéред+*i.* **make-believe** *n.* притвóрство; *adj.* притвóрный. **makeshift** *adj.* врéменный. **make-up** *n.* (*theatr.*) грим; (*cosmetics*) космéтика; (*composition*) состáв. **makeweight** *n.* довéсок (-ска).
malachite ['mælə,kaɪt] *n.* малахит.
maladjusted [,mælə'dʒʌstɪd] *adj.* плóхо приспосóбленный (-ен).
maladministration [,mæləd,mɪnɪ'streɪʃ(ə)n] *n.* плохóе управлéние.
maladroit [,mælə'drɔɪt, 'mæl-] *adj.* нелóвкий (-óвок, -óвкá, -óвко); (*tactless*) бестáктный.
malady ['mælədɪ] *n.* болéзнь.
malaria [mə'leərɪə] *n.* малярия.
malcontent ['mælkən,tent] *n.* недовóльный *sb.*
male [meɪl] *n.* (*animal*) самéц (-мцá); (*person*) мужчина *m.*; *adj.* мужскóй.
malevolence [mə'levələns] *n.* недоброжелáтельность. **malevolent** *adj.* недоброжелáтельный.
malformation [,mælfɔː'meɪʃ(ə)n] *n.* непрáвильное образовáние.
malice ['mælɪs] *n.* злóба; (*leg.*) злой ýмысел (-сла); **with ~ aforethought** со злым ýмыслом. **malicious** [mə'lɪʃəs] *adj.* злóбный.
malign [mə'laɪn] *adj.* пáгубный; *v.t.* клеветáть (-ещý, -éщешь) *impf.*, на~ *pf.* на+*a.* **malignant** [mə'lɪgnənt] *adj.* (*harmful*) зловрéдный; (*malicious*) злóбный; (*med.*) злокáчественный.
malinger [mə'lɪŋgə(r)] *v.i.* притворяться *impf.*, притвориться *pf.* больным. **malingerer** *n.* симулянт.
mallard ['mælɑːd] *n.* кряква.
malleable ['mælɪəb(ə)l] *adj.* кóвкий (-вок, -вкá, -вко); (*fig.*) подáтливый.
mallet ['mælɪt] *n.* (деревянный) молотóк (-ткá).
malnutrition [,mælnjuː'trɪʃ(ə)n] *n.* недоедáние.
malpractice [mæl'præktɪs] *n.* (*wrongdoing*) противозакóнное дéйствие; (*negligence*) престýпная небрéжность.
malt [mɔːlt, mɒlt] *n.* сóлод; *v.t.* солодить *impf.*, на~ *pf.*
maltreat [mæl'triːt] *v.t.* плóхо обращáться *impf.* с+*i.*
mamba *n.* мáмба.
mambo ['mæmbə] *n.* мáмбо *nt.indecl.*
mamma [mə'mɑː] *n.* мáма.
mammal ['mæm(ə)l] *n.* млекопитáющее *sb.* **ma'mmalian** *adj.* млекопитáющий.
mammary ['mæmərɪ] *adj.* груднóй.
mammon ['mæmən] *n.* мамóна, богáтство.
mammoth ['mæməθ] *n.* мáмонт; *adj.* громáдный.
man [mæn] *n.* (*human, person*) человéк (*pl.* люди, -дéй, -дьям, -дьми); (*human race*) человéчество; (*male*) мужчина *m.*; (*husband*) муж (*pl.* -ья, -éй, -ьям); (*servant*) слугá *m.*; (*labourer*) рабóчий *sb.*; *pl.* (*soldiers*) солдáты *m.pl.*, рядовые *sb.*; *pl.* (*sailors*) матрóсы *m.pl.*; (*draughts*) шáшка; ~ **in the street** заурядный человéк; *v.t.* (*furnish with men*) укомплектóвывать *impf.*, укомплектовáть *pf.* личным состáвом; стáвить *impf.*, по~ *pf.* людéй к+*d.*; (*act thus*) становиться (-влюсь, -вишься) *impf.*, стать (стáну, -нешь) *pf.* к+*d.*
manacle ['mænək(ə)l] *n.* нарýчник; *v.t.* надевáть *impf.*, надéть (-éну, -éнешь) *pf.* нарýчники на+*a.*
manage ['mænɪdʒ] *v.t.* (*control*) управлять *impf.*+*i.*; завéдовать *impf.*+*i.*; (*cope*) справляться *impf.*, спрáвиться *pf.* с+*i.* **management** *n.* управлéние (**of** +*i.*), завéдование (**of** +*i.*); (*the* ~) администрáция, дирéкция. **manager** *n.* управляющий *sb.* (**of** +*i.*), завéдующий *sb.* (**of** +*i.*), администрáтор, дирéктор (*pl.* -á); (*good, bad* ~) хозяин; (*in*

entertainment) импреса́рио *m.indecl.*; (*sport*) ме́неджер. **managerial** [ˌmænɪˈdʒɪərɪəl] *adj.* администрати́вный, дире́кторский.

mandarin [ˈmændərɪn] *n.* мандари́н.

mandate [ˈmændeɪt] *n.* манда́т. **mandated** *adj.* подманда́тный. **mandatory** *adj.* обяза́тельный.

mandible [ˈmændɪb(ə)l] *n.* ни́жняя че́люсть; (*of insect*) жва́ло.

mandolin(e) [ˌmændəˈlɪn] *n.* мандоли́на.

mane [meɪn] *n.* гри́ва.

manful [ˈmænfʊl] *adj.* му́жественный (-ен, -енна).

manganese [ˈmæŋgəˌniːz] *n.* ма́рганец (-нца).

manger [ˈmeɪndʒə(r)] *n.* я́сли (-лей) *pl.*; **dog in the ~** соба́ка на се́не.

mangle¹ [ˈmæŋg(ə)l] *n.* (*for clothes*) като́к (-тка́); *v.t.* ката́ть *impf.*, вы́~ *pf.*

mangle² [ˈmæŋg(ə)l] *v.t.* (*mutilate*) кале́чить *impf.*, ис~ *pf.*; (*words*) кове́ркать *impf.*, ис~ *pf.*

mango [ˈmæŋgəʊ] *n.* ма́нго *nt.indecl.*

mangrove [ˈmæŋgrəʊv] *n.* ма́нгровое де́рево (*pl.* -е́вья, -е́вьев).

manhandle [ˈmænˌhænd(ə)l] *v.t.* передвига́ть *impf.*, передви́нуть *pf.* вручну́ю; (*treat roughly*) гру́бо обраща́ться *impf.* с+*i.* **manhole** *n.* смотрово́й коло́дец (-дца). **manhood** *n.* возмужа́лость; (*courage*) му́жественность. **man-hour** *n.* челове́ко-час (*pl.* -ы́).

mania [ˈmeɪnɪə] *n.* ма́ния. **maniac** [ˈmeɪnɪˌæk] *n.* манья́к, -я́чка. **maniacal** *adj.* маниака́льный.

manicure [ˈmænɪˌkjʊə(r)] *n.* маникю́р; *v.t.* де́лать *impf.*, с~ *pf.* маникю́р+*d.* **manicurist** *n.* маникю́рша.

manifest [ˈmænɪˌfest] *adj.* очеви́дный; *v.t.* де́лать *impf.*, с~ *pf.* очеви́дным; (*display*) проявля́ть *impf.*, прояви́ть (-влю́, -вишь) *pf.*; *n.* манифе́ст. **manifeˈstation** *n.* проявле́ние. **maniˈfesto** *n.* манифе́ст.

manifold [ˈmænɪˌfəʊld] *adj.* разнообра́зный; *n.* (*tech.*) колле́ктор, трубопрово́д.

manikin [ˈmænɪkɪn] *n.* (*little man*) челове́чек (-чка); (*lay figure*) манеке́н.

Manil(l)a [məˈnɪlə] *n.* (*hemp*) мани́льская пенька́; (*paper*), мани́льская бума́га.

manipulate [məˈnɪpjʊˌleɪt] *v.t.* манипули́ровать *impf.*+*i.* **manipuˈlation** *n.* манипуля́ция.

manly [ˈmænlɪ] *adj.* му́жественный (-ен, -енна).

mankind [mænˈkaɪnd] *n.* челове́чество.

manna [ˈmænə] *n.* ма́нна (небе́сная).

mannequin [ˈmænɪkɪn] *n.* манеке́нщица.

manner [ˈmænə(r)] *n.* спо́соб, о́браз, мане́ра; *pl.* нра́вы *m.pl.*; *pl.* (*good* ~) (хоро́шие) мане́ры *f.pl.* **mannered** *adj.* вы́чурный, мане́рный. **mannerism** *n.* мане́ра; мане́рность.

mannish [ˈmænɪʃ] *adj.* (*masculine*) мужепо до́бный; (*characteristic of man*) сво́йственный (-ен, -енна) мужчи́не.

manoeuvrable [məˈnuːvrəb(ə)l] *adj.* легко́ управля́емый. **manoeuvre** *n.* манёвр; *v.i.* маневри́ровать *impf.*, с~ *pf.*; проводи́ть (-ожу́, -о́дишь) *impf.*, провести́ (-еду́, -едёшь; -ёл, -ела́) *pf.* манёвры.

man-of-war [ˈmænəfˌwɔː(r)] *n.* вое́нный кора́бль (-ля́) *m.*

manor [ˈmænə(r)] *n.* (*estate*) поме́стье (*g.pl.* -тий); (*house*) поме́щичий дом (-а(у); *pl.* -а́). **manorial** [məˈnɔːrɪəl] *adj.* манориа́льный.

manpower [ˈmænˌpaʊə(r)] *n.* людски́е ресу́рсы *m.pl.*

mansard (roof) [ˈmænsɑːd] *n.* манса́рдная кры́ша.

manservant [ˈmænˌsɜːv(ə)nt] *n.* слуга́ *m.*

mansion [ˈmænʃ(ə)n] *n.* большо́й дом (*pl.* -а́); *pl.* многокварти́рный дом.

manslaughter [ˈmænˌslɔːtə(r)] *n.* человекоуби́йство; (*leg.*) непредумы́шленное уби́йство.

mantelpiece [ˈmænt(ə)lˌpiːs] *n.* ками́нная доска́ (*a.* -ску; *pl.* -ски, -со́к, -ска́м). **mantelshelf** *n.* ками́нная по́лка.

mantis [ˈmæntɪs] *n.* богомо́л.

mantle [ˈmænt(ə)l] *n.* (*cloak*) наки́дка; (*gas* ~) газокали́льная се́тка; (*earth's*) ма́нтия.

manual [ˈmænjʊəl] *adj.* ручно́й; **~ labour** физи́ческий, ручно́й, труд (-а́); *n.* спра́вочник, руково́дство, уче́бник; (*of organ*) мануа́л. **manually** *adv.* вручну́ю.

manufacture [ˌmænjʊˈfæktʃə(r)] *n.* произво́дство, изготовле́ние; *v.t.* производи́ть (-ожу́, -о́дишь) *impf.*, произвести́ (-еду́, -едёшь; -ёл, -ела́) *pf.*; изготовля́ть *impf.*, изгото́вить *pf.*; (*fabricate*) фабрикова́ть *impf.*, с~ *pf.* **manufacturer** *n.* фабрика́нт, промы́шленник, производи́тель *m.*

manure [məˈnjʊə(r)] *n.* наво́з; *v.t.* унаво́живать *impf.*, унаво́зить *pf.*

manuscript [ˈmænjʊskrɪpt] *n.* ру́копись; *adj.* рукопи́сный.

many [ˈmenɪ] *adj.* & *n.* мно́го+*g.*, мно́гие *pl.*; **how ~** ско́лько+*g.*

Maoism [ˈmaʊɪz(ə)m] *n.* маои́зм. **Maoist** *n.* маои́ст; *adj.* маои́стский.

map [mæp] *n.* ка́рта; *v.t.* черти́ть (-рчу́, -ртишь) *impf.*, на~ *pf.* план+*g.*; **~ out** составля́ть *impf.*, соста́вить *pf.* план+*g.*

maple [ˈmeɪp(ə)l] *n.* клён; *attr.* клено́вый.

mar [mɑː(r)] *v.t.* по́ртить *impf.*, ис~ *pf.*

marathon [ˈmærəθ(ə)n] *n.* марафо́н.

marauder [məˈrɔːdə(r)] *n.* мародёр. **marauding** *adj.* мародёрский.

marble [ˈmɑːb(ə)l] *n.* мра́мор; (*toy*) ша́рик; *pl.* (*game*) игра́ в ша́рики; *attr.* мра́морный. **marbled** *adj.* мра́морный.

March¹ [mɑːtʃ] *n.* март; *attr.* ма́ртовский.

march² [mɑːtʃ] *v.i.* марширова́ть *impf.*, про~ *pf.*; *n.* марш; ход; **~ past** прохожде́ние торже́ственным ма́ршем.

mare [meə(r)] *n.* кобы́ла.

margarine [ˌmɑːdʒəˈriːn] *n.* маргари́н (-а(у)).

margin [ˈmɑːdʒɪn] *n.* край (*loc.* краю́; *pl.*

-ая́), каймá (*g.pl.* каём); (*on page*) пóле (*pl.* -ля́); ~ **of error** предéлы *m.pl.* погрéшности; **profit** ~ при́быль; **safety** ~ запáс прóчности.

marigold ['mærɪ,gəʊld] *n.* (*Tagetes*) бáрхатцы (-цев); *pl.*; (*Calendula*) ноготки́ (-кóв) *pl.*

marijuana [,mærɪ'hwɑ:nə] *n.* марихуáна.

marinade [,mærɪ'neɪd, 'mæ-] *n.* маринáд; *v.t.* маринова́ть *impf.*, за~ *pf.*

marine [mə'ri:n] *adj.* (*maritime*) морскóй; (*naval*) воéнно-морскóй; *n.* (*fleet*) морскóй флот; (*soldier*) солдáт морскóй пехóты; *pl.* морскáя пехóта. **mariner** ['mærɪnə(r)] *n.* моря́к (-á), матрóс.

marionette [,mærɪə'net] *n.* марионéтка.

marital ['mærɪt(ə)l] *adj.* супру́жеский, брáчный.

maritime ['mærɪ,taɪm] *adj.* морскóй; (*near sea*) примóрский.

marjoram ['mɑ:dʒərəm] *n.* (*Majorana*) майорáн; (*Origanum*) души́ца.

mark[1] [mɑ:k] *n.* (*coin*) мáрка.

mark[2] [mɑ:k] *n.* (*target*, *aim*) цель; (*sign*) знак; (*school*) отмéтка; (*numerical*) балл; (*trace*) след (*pl.* -ы́); (*level*) у́ровень (-вня) *m.*; **hit the** ~ попадáть *impf.*, попáсть (-аду́, -адёшь; -áл) *pf.* в тóчку; **make one's** ~ отличáться *impf.*, отличи́ться *pf.*; **on your** ~**s** на старт!; *v.t.* отмечáть *impf.*, отмéтить *pf.*; стáвить *impf.*, по~ *pf.* знак, (*goods*) расцéнку, на+*a.*, (*school*) отмéтку, балл, за+*a.*; (*leave trace(s)*) оставля́ть *impf.*, остáвить *pf.* след(ы́) на+*p.*; (*football*) закрывáть *impf.*, закры́ть (-рóю, -рóешь) *pf.*; ~ **my words** попóмни(те) мои́ словá!; ~ **time** топтáться (-пчу́сь, -пчешься) *impf.* на мéсте; ~ **off** отделя́ть *impf.*, отдели́ть (-лю́, -лишь) *pf.*; ~ **out** размечáть *impf.*, размéтить *pf.* **marker** *n.* знак, указáтель *m.*; (*in book*) заклáдка; ~ **(pen)** фломáстер.

market ['mɑ:kɪt] *n.* ры́нок (-нка), базáр; (*demand*) спрос; (*trade*) торгóвля; (*conditions*) конъюнкту́ра; **black** ~ чёрный ры́нок (-нка); **buyer's, seller's,** ~ конъюнкту́ра ры́нка, вы́годная для покупáтеля, для продавцá; **Common M**~ Óбщий ры́нок (-нка); **find a** ~ находи́ть (-ожу́, -óдишь) *impf.*, найти́ (найду́, -дёшь; нашёл, -шлá) *pf.* сбыт; ~ **garden** огорóд; ~ **price** ры́ночная ценá (*a.* -ну; *pl.* -ы); *v.t.* продавáть (-даю́, -даёшь) *impf.*, продáть (-áм, -áшь, -áст, -ади́м; прóдал, -á, -о) *pf.* **marketable** *adj.* хóдкий (-док, -дкá, -дко); (*econ.*) товáрный. **market-day** *n.* базáрный день (дня) *m.* **marketing** *n.* мáркетинг. **market-place** *n.* базáрная плóщадь (*pl.* -ди, -дéй).

marksman ['mɑ:ksmən] *n.* мéткий стрелóк (-лкá). **marksmanship** *n.* мéткая стрельбá.

marmalade ['mɑ:mə,leɪd] *n.* апельси́новый джем.

marmoset ['mɑ:mə,zet] *n.* игру́нка.

marmot ['mɑ:mət] *n.* сурóк (-ркá).

maroon[1] [mə'ru:n] *adj.* (*n.*) (*colour*) тёмно-бордóвый (цвет).

maroon[2] [mə'ru:n] *v.t.* (*put ashore*) высáживать *impf.*, вы́садить *pf.* (на необитáемом óстрове); (*cut off*) отрезáть *impf.*, отрéзать (-éжет) *pf.*

marquee [mɑ:'ki:] *n.* шатёр (-трá).

marquis ['mɑ:kwɪs] *n.* марки́з.

marriage ['mærɪdʒ] *n.* брак; (*wedding*) свáдьба; *attr.* брáчный. **marriageable** *adj.* взрóслый; ~ **age** брáчный вóзраст. **married** *adj.* (*man*) женáтый; (*woman*) заму́жняя, зáмужем; (*of* ~ *persons*) супру́жеский.

marrow ['mærəʊ] *n.* кóстный мозг (*loc.* -у́); (*essence*) су́щность; (*vegetable*) кабачóк (-чкá). **marrowbone** *n.* мозговáя кость (*pl.* -ти, -тéй).

marry ['mærɪ] *v.t.* (*of man*) жени́ться (-ню́сь, -нишься) *impf.* & *pf.* на+*p.*; (*of woman*) выходи́ть (-ожу́, -óдишь) *impf.*, вы́йти (вы́йду, -дешь; вы́шла) *pf.* зáмуж за+*a.*; (*give in marriage*) (*man*) жени́ть (-ню́, -нишь) *impf.* & *pf.*, по~ *pf.* (**to** на+*p.*); (*woman*) выдавáть (-даю́, -даёшь) *impf.*, вы́дать (-ам, -ашь, -аст, -адим) *pf.* зáмуж (**to** за+*a.*).

Mars [mɑ:z] *n.* Марс.

Marseilles [mɑ:'seɪ] *n.* Марсéль *m.*

marsh [mɑ:ʃ] *n.* болóто. **marsh-gas** *n.* болóтный газ. **marshy** *adj.* болóтистый.

marshal ['mɑ:ʃ(ə)l] *n.* мáршал; *v.t.* выстрáивать *impf.*, вы́строить *pf.*; приводи́ть (-ожу́, -óдишь) *impf.*, привести́ (-еду́, -едёшь; -ёл, -елá) *pf.* в поря́док; ~**ling yard** сортирóвочная стáнция.

marsupial [mɑ:'su:pɪəl] *adj.* су́мчатый; *n.* су́мчатое живóтное *sb.*

marten ['mɑ:tɪn] *n.* куни́ца.

martial ['mɑ:ʃ(ə)l] *adj.* воéнный; (*warlike*) вóинский; ~ **law** воéнное положéние.

Martian ['mɑ:ʃ(ə)n] *n.* марсиáнин (*pl.* -áне, -áн); *adj.* марсиáнский.

martin ['mɑ:tɪn] *n.* стриж (-á); (*house-*~) городскáя лáсточка.

martinet [,mɑ:tɪ'net] *n.* сторóнник стрóгой дисципли́ны.

martyr ['mɑ:tə(r)] *n.* му́ченик, -ца; *v.t.* му́чить *impf.*, за~ *pf.* **martyrdom** *n.* му́ченичество.

marvel ['mɑ:v(ə)l] *n.* чу́до (*pl.* -десá), ди́во; *v.i.* изумля́ться *impf.*, изуми́ться *pf.*; удивля́ться *impf.*, удиви́ться *pf.* **marvellous** *adj.* чудéсный, изуми́тельный, удиви́тельный.

Marxian ['mɑ:ksɪən], **Marxist** *n.* маркси́ст; *adj.* маркси́стский. **Marxism** *n.* маркси́зм.

marzipan ['mɑ:zɪ,pæn, -'pæn] *n.* марципáн; *adj.* марципáнный.

mascara [mæ'skɑ:rə] *n.* крáска для ресни́ц.

mascot ['mæskɒt] *n.* талисмáн.

masculine ['mæskjʊlɪn, 'mɑ:s-] *adj.* мужскóй; (*gram.*) мужскóго рóда; (*of woman*) мужеподóбный; *n.* (*gram.*) мужскóй род.

mash [mæʃ] *n.* (*of malt*) су́сло; (*of bran*) пóйло; (*mashed potatoes*) картóфельное пюрé; *nt.indecl.*; *v.t.* разминáть *impf.*, размя́ть (разомну́, -нёшь) *pf.*

mask [mɑ:sk] *n.* ма́ска; (*gas-*~) противога́з; *v.t.* маскирова́ть *impf.*, за~ *pf.*; ~**ed ball** бал-маскара́д.

masochism ['mæsə,kɪz(ə)m] *m.* мазохи́зм. **masochist** *n.* мазохи́ст. **maso'chistic** *adj.* мазохи́стский.

mason ['meɪs(ə)n] *n.* ка́менщик; (**M**~) масо́н. **Masonic** [mə'sɒnɪk] *adj.* масо́нский. **masonry** ['meɪsənrɪ] *n.* ка́менная кла́дка; (**M**~) масо́нство.

masque [mɑ:sk] *n.* ма́ска. **masquer** *n.* уча́стник, -ица, ба́ла-маскара́да. **masquerade** [,mɑ:skə'reɪd, ,mæs-] *n.* маскара́д; *v.i.*: ~ **as** притворя́ться *impf.*, притвори́ться *pf.*+*i.*; выдава́ть (-даю́, -даёшь) *impf.*, вы́дать (-ам, -ашь, -аст, -адим) *pf.* себя́ за+*a.*

mass¹ [mæs] *n.* (*eccl.*) обе́дня (*g.pl.* -ден), ме́сса.

mass² [mæs] *n.* ма́сса; (*majority*) большинство́; *pl.* (*the* ~) наро́дные ма́ссы *f.pl.*; *attr.* ма́ссовый; ~ **media** сре́дства *nt.pl.* ма́ссовой информа́ции; ~ **meeting** ми́тинг; ~ **production** ма́ссовое произво́дство; *v.t.* масси́ровать *impf.* & *pf.*

massacre ['mæsəkə(r)] *n.* резня́; *v.t.* ре́зать (ре́жу, -жешь) *impf.*, за~ *pf.*

massage ['mæsɑ:ʒ, -sɑ:dʒ] *n.* масса́ж; *v.t.* масси́ровать *impf.* & *pf.* **masseur** [mæ'sɜ:(r)], **-euse** [mæ'sɜ:z] *n.* массажи́ст, ~ка.

massif ['mæsi:f, mæ'si:f] *n.* го́рный масси́в.

massive ['mæsɪv] *adj.* масси́вный.

mass-produced [,mæsprə'dju:s] *adj.* ма́ссового произво́дства.

mast [mɑ:st] *n.* ма́чта.

master ['mɑ:stə(r)] *n.* (*owner*) хозя́ин (*pl.* -я́ева, -я́ев), владе́лец (-льца); (*of household, college*) глава́ (*pl.* -вы) *m.* (семьи́, колле́джа); (*of ship*) капита́н; (*teacher*) учи́тель (*pl.* -ля́) *m.*; (**M**~, *univ.*) маги́стр; (*workman; artist*) ма́стер (*pl.* -а́); (*of film*) контро́льная ко́пия; (*of record*) пе́рвый оригина́л; **be** ~ **of** владе́ть *impf.*+*i.*; **M**~ **of Arts** маги́стр гуманита́рных наук; *v.t.* (*overcome*) преодолева́ть *impf.*, преодоле́ть *pf.*; справля́ться *impf.*, спра́виться *pf.* с+*i.*; (*subjugate*) подчиня́ть *impf.*, подчини́ть *pf.* себе́; (*acquire knowledge of*) овладева́ть *impf.*, овладе́ть *pf.*+*i.* **masterful** *adj.* вла́стный. **master-key** *n.* отмы́чка. **masterly** *adj.* мастерско́й. **masterpiece** *n.* шеде́вр. **master-switch** *n.* гла́вный выключа́тель *m.* **mastery** *n.* (*dominion*) госпо́дство; (*skill*) мастерство́; (*knowledge*) соверше́нное владе́ние (**of** +*i.*).

mast-head ['mɑ:sthed] *n.* топ ма́чты.

masticate ['mæstɪ,keɪt] *v.t.* жева́ть (жую́, жуёшь) *impf.*

mastif ['mæstɪf, 'mɑ:s-] *n.* ма́сти́фф.

mastodon ['mæstə,dɒn] *n.* мастодо́нт.

mat [mæt] *n.* ко́врик, полови́к (-а́); (*of rushes, straw*) цино́вка; (*under dish etc.*) подста́вка.

match¹ [mætʃ] *n.* спи́чка. **matchbox** *n.* спи́чечная коро́бка.

match² [mætʃ] *n.* (*equal*) ро́вня *c.g.*; (*contest*) матч, состяза́ние; (*marriage*) брак; **a** ~ **for** па́ра+*d.*; **meet one's** ~ встреча́ть *impf.*, встре́тить *pf.* ра́вного себе́, досто́йного, проти́вника; *v.t.* (*correspond*) соотве́тствовать *impf.*+*d.*; (*of colour*) гармони́ровать *impf.* с+*i.*; (*select*) подбира́ть *impf.*, подобра́ть (подберу́, -рёшь; подобра́л, -а́, -о) *pf.* **matchboard** *n.* шпунтова́я доска́ (*a.* -ску; *pl.* -ски, -со́к, -ска́м). **matchless** *adj.* несравне́нный (-нен, -нна). **matchmaker** *n.* сват, сва́ха.

mate¹ [meɪt] *n.* (*chess*) мат; *v.t.* объявля́ть *impf.*, объяви́ть (-влю́, -вишь) *pf.* мат+*d.*

mate² [meɪt] *n.* (*one of pair*) саме́ц (-мца́), са́мка; (*fellow worker*) напа́рник, това́рищ; (*assistant*) помо́щник; (*naut.*) помо́щник капита́на; *v.i.* (*of animals*) спа́риваться *impf.*, спа́риться *pf.*

material [mə'tɪərɪəl] *adj.* материа́льный; (*essential*) суще́ственный (-ен, -енна); *n.* материа́л; (*cloth*) мате́рия; *pl.* (*necessary articles*) принадле́жности *f.pl.* **materialism** *n.* материали́зм; материалисти́чность. **materialist** *n.* материали́ст. **materia'listic** *adj.* материалисти́чный, -ческий. **materiali'zation** *n.* материализа́ция. **materialize** *v.t.* & *i.* материализова́ть(ся) *impf.* & *pf.*; осуществля́ть(ся) *impf.*, осуществи́ть(ся) *pf.*

maternal [mə'tɜ:n(ə)l] *adj.* матери́нский; (*kinship*) по ма́тери; ~ **grandfather** де́душка с матери́нской стороны́. **maternity** *n.* матери́нство; ~ **benefit** посо́бие роже́нице; ~ **dress** пла́тье (*g.pl.* -в) для бере́менных; ~ **home, hospital** роди́льный дом (-а(у); *pl.* -а́); ~ **leave** декре́тный о́тпуск (*loc.* -е & -у́); ~ **ward** роди́льная пала́та.

mathematical [,mæθɪ'mætɪk(ə)l] *adj.* математи́ческий. **mathematician** [,mæθɪmə'tɪʃ(ə)n] *n.* матема́тик. **mathematics** *n.* матема́тика.

maths *abbr.* = **mathematics**

matinée ['mætɪ,neɪ] *n.* дневно́й спекта́кль *m.*; ~ **coat** распашо́нка.

matins ['mætɪnz] *n.* у́треня.

matriarchal [,meɪtrɪ'ɑ:k(ə)l] *adj.* матриарха́льный. **'matriarchy** *n.* матриарха́т. **matricidal** ['meɪtrɪ,saɪd(ə)l] *adj.* матереуби́йственный. **matricide** *n.* (*action*) матереуби́йство; (*person*) матереуби́йца *c.g.*

matriculate [mə'trɪkjʊ,leɪt] *v.t.* принима́ть *impf.*, приня́ть (приму́, -мешь; при́нял, -а́, -о) *pf.* в вуз; *v.i.* быть при́нятым в вуз. **matricu'lation** *n.* зачисле́ние в вуз; (*examination*) вступи́тельный экза́мен в вуз.

matrimonial [,mætrɪ'məʊnɪəl] *adj.* супру́жеский. **'matrimony** *n.* брак, супру́жество.

matrix ['meɪtrɪks] *n.* (*womb*) ма́тка; (*rock*) ма́точная поро́да; (*mould*) ма́трица.

matron ['meɪtrən] *n.* заму́жняя же́нщина; (*hospital*) сестра́-хозя́йка; (*school*) заве́дующая *sb.* хозя́йством.

matt [mæt] *adj.* ма́товый.

matted ['mætɪd] *adj.* спу́танный (-ан).

matter ['mætə(r)] *n.* (*substance*) вещество́; (*philos.*, *med.*) мате́рия; (*content*) содержа́ние; (*affair*) де́ло (*pl.* -ла́); (*question*) вопро́с; **a ~ of form** форма́льность; **a ~ of life and death** вопро́с жи́зни и сме́рти; **a ~ of opinion** спо́рное де́ло; **a ~ of taste** де́ло вку́са; **an easy ~** просто́е де́ло; **as a ~ of fact** факти́чески; со́бственно говоря́; **for that ~** что каса́ется э́того; в э́том отноше́нии; **money ~s** де́нежные дела́ *nt.pl.*; **no laughing ~** не шу́точное де́ло; **what's the ~?** в чём де́ло?; что случи́лось?; **what's the ~ with him?** что с ним?; *v.i.* име́ть *impf.* значе́ние; (*med.*) гнои́ться *impf.*; **it doesn't ~** э́то не име́ет значе́ния; **it ~s a lot to me** для меня́ э́то о́чень ва́жно; **what does it ~?** како́е э́то име́ет значе́ние? **matter-of-fact** *adj.* прозаи́чный.

matting ['mætɪŋ] *n.* (*rushes*) цино́вка; (*bast*) рого́жа.

mattock ['mætək] *n.* моты́га.

mattress ['mætrɪs] *n.* матра́с, тюфя́к (-а́).

mature [mə'tjʊə(r)] *adj.* зре́лый (зрел, -а́, -о); (*well considered*) хорошо́ обду́манный (-ан, -анна); *v.i.* зреть *impf.*, со~ *pf.*; *v.t.* доводи́ть (-ожу́, -о́дишь) *impf.*, довести́ (-еду́, -едёшь, -ёл, -ела́) *pf.* до зре́лости; (*plan*) обду́мывать *impf.*, обду́мать *pf.* **maturity** *n.* зре́лость.

maul [mɔ:l] *v.t.* терза́ть *impf.*; кале́чить *impf.*, ис~ *pf.*; (*criticize*) раскритикова́ть *pf.*

mausoleum [ˌmɔ:sə'li:əm] *n.* мавзоле́й.

mauve [məʊv] *adj.* (*n.*) розова́то-лило́вый (цвет).

maxim ['mæksɪm] *n.* сенте́нция.

maximum ['mæksɪməm] *n.* ма́ксимум; *adj.* максима́льный.

May[1] [meɪ] *n.* (*month*) май; **~ Day** Пе́рвое *sb.* ма́я; *attr.* ма́йский.

may[2] [meɪ] *v.aux.* (*possibility*, *permission*) мочь (могу́, мо́жешь; мог, -ла́) *impf.*, с~ *pf.*; (*possibility*) возмо́жно, что+*indicative*; (*wish*) пусть+*indicative*.

maybe ['meɪbi:] *adv.* мо́жет быть.

May-bug ['meɪbʌg] *n.* ма́йский жук (-а́).

mayfly *n.* подёнка.

mayonnaise [ˌmeɪə'neɪz] *n.* майоне́з.

mayor [meə(r)] *n.* мэр. **mayoress** *n.* жена́ (*pl.* жёны) мэ́ра; же́нщина-мэр.

maze [meɪz] *n.* лабири́нт; (*fig.*) пу́таница.

mazurka [mə'zɜ:kə] *n.* мазу́рка.

MC *abbr.* (*of* ***Master of Ceremonies***) конферансье́.

MD *abbr.* (*of* ***Doctor of Medicine***) до́ктор медици́ны; (*of* ***Managing Director***) дире́ктор-распоряди́тель.

mead [mi:d] *n.* мёд (-а(у), *loc.* -у́; *pl.* -ы́).

meadow ['medəʊ] *n.* луг (*loc.* -у́; *pl.* -а́).

meagre ['mi:gə(r)] *adj.* ску́дный (-ден, -дна́, -дно).

meal[1] [mi:l] *n.* еда́.

meal[2] [mi:l] *n.* (*ground grain*) мука́ кру́пного помо́ла.

mealtime ['mi:ltaɪm] *n.*: **at ~s** во вре́мя еды́.

mealy ['mi:lɪ] *adj.* рассы́пчатый. **mealy-mouthed** *adj.* сладкоречи́вый.

mean[1] [mi:n] *adj.* (*average*) сре́дний; *n.* (*middle point*) середи́на, сре́днее *sb.*; *pl.* (*method*) сре́дство, спо́соб; *pl.* (*resources*) сре́дства *nt.pl.*, состоя́ние; **by all ~s** коне́чно, пожа́луйста; **by ~s of** при по́мощи+*g.*, посре́дством+*g.*; **by no ~s** совсе́м не; **~s test** прове́рка нужда́емости.

mean[2] [mi:n] *adj.* (*ignoble*) по́длый (подл, -а́, -о), ни́зкий (-зок, -зка́, -зко); (*miserly*) скупо́й (скуп, -а́, -о); (*poor*) убо́гий.

mean[3] [mi:n] *v.t.* (*have in mind*) име́ть *impf.* в виду́; (*intend*) намерева́ться *impf.*+*inf.*; (*signify*) зна́чить *impf.*

meander [mɪ'ændə(r)] *v.i.* (*stream*) извива́ться *impf.*; (*person*) броди́ть (-ожу́, -о́дишь) *impf.* без це́ли. **meandering** *adj.* изви́листый.

meaning ['mi:nɪŋ] *n.* значе́ние, смысл; *adj.* значи́тельный. **meaningful** *adj.* (много)-значи́тельный. **meaningless** *adj.* бессмы́сленный (-ен, -енна).

meantime ['mi:ntaɪm], **meanwhile** *adv.* тем вре́менем, ме́жду тем.

measles ['mi:z(ə)lz] *n.* корь. **measly** *adj.* ничто́жный.

measurable ['meʒərəb(ə)l] *adj.* измери́мый. **measure** *n.* ме́ра; (*size*) ме́рка; (*degree*) сте́пень (*pl.* -ни, -не́й); (*limit*) преде́л; **made to ~** сши́тый по ме́рке; сде́ланный (-ан) на зака́з; *v.t.* измеря́ть *impf.*, изме́рить *pf.*; ме́рить *impf.*, с~ *pf.*; (*for clothes*) снима́ть *impf.*, снять (сниму́, -мешь; снял, -а́, -о) *pf.* ме́рку с+*g.*; (*estimate*) оце́нивать *impf.*, оцени́ть (-ню́, -нишь) *pf.*; *v.i.* (*be of specified size*) име́ть *impf.*+*a.*; **the room ~s 30 feet in length** ко́мната име́ет три́дцать фу́тов в длину́; **~ off** отмеря́ть *impf.*, отме́рить *pf.*; **~ out** (*deal out*) распределя́ть *impf.*, распредели́ть *pf.*; **~ up to** соотве́тствовать *impf.*+*d.* **measured** *adj.* (*rhythmical*) ме́рный. **measurement** *n.* (*action*) измере́ние; *pl.* (*dimensions*) разме́ры *m.pl.*

meat [mi:t] *n.* мя́со. **meaty** *adj.* мясно́й, мяси́стый.

mechanic [mɪ'kænɪk] *n.* меха́ник. **mechanical** *adj.* механи́ческий; (*automatic*) машина́льный; **~ engineer** инжене́р-меха́ник; **~ engineering** машинострое́ние. **mechanics** *n.* меха́ника. **mechanism** ['mekəˌnɪz(ə)m] *n.* механи́зм. **mecha'nistic** *adj.* механисти́ческий. **mechani'zation** *n.* механиза́ция. **'mechanize** *v.t.* механизи́ровать *impf.* & *pf.*

medal ['med(ə)l] *n.* меда́ль. **medallion** [mɪ'dæljən] *n.* медальо́н. **medallist** *n.* (*recipient*) медали́ст.

meddle ['med(ə)l] *v.i.* вме́шиваться *impf.*, вмеша́ться *pf.* (**in, with** в+*a.*).

media ['mi:dɪə] *pl. of* **medium**

mediaeval [ˌmedɪ'i:v(ə)l] *adj.* средневеко́вый.

mediate ['mi:dɪˌeɪt] *v.i.* посре́дничать *impf.*

medi'ation *n.* посре́дничество. **mediator** *n.* посре́дник.

medical ['medɪk(ə)l] *adj.* медици́нский; ~ **jurisprudence** суде́бная медици́на; ~ **man** врач (-а́); ~ **student** ме́дик, -и́чка. **medicated** *adj.* (*impregnated*) пропи́танный (-ан) лека́рством. **medicinal** [mɪ'dɪsɪn(ə)l] *adj.* (*of medicine*) лека́рственный; (*healing*) целе́бный. **medicine** ['medsɪn, -dɪsɪn] *n.* медици́на; (*substance*) лека́рство. **medicine-man** *n.* зна́харь (-ря́) *m.*, шама́н.

mediocre [ˌmiːdɪ'əʊkə(r)] *adj.* посре́дственный (-ен, -енна), зауря́дный. **mediocrity** [ˌmiːdɪ'ɒkrɪtɪ] *n.* посре́дственность.

meditate ['medɪˌteɪt] *v.i.* размышля́ть *impf.* **medi'tation** *n.* размышле́ние. **meditative** *adj.* заду́мчивый.

Mediterranean [ˌmedɪtə'reɪnɪən] *adj.* средиземномо́рский; *n.* Средизе́мное мо́ре.

medium ['miːdɪəm] *n.* (*middle*) середи́на; (*means*) сре́дство; (*environment*; *phys.*) среда́ (*pl.* -ды); (*person*) ме́диум; *pl.* (*mass media*) сре́дства *nt.pl.* ма́ссовой информа́ции; *adj.* сре́дний.

medley ['medlɪ] *n.* смесь, вся́кая вся́чина.

meek [miːk] *adj.* кро́ткий (-ток, -тка́, -тко), смире́нный (-е́н, -е́нна). **meekness** *n.* кро́тость, смире́нность.

meet [miːt] *v.t.* & *i.* встреча́ть(ся) *impf.*, встре́тить(ся) *pf.*; *v.t.* (*make acquaintance*) знако́миться *impf.*, по~ *pf.* с+*i.*; *v.i.* (*assemble*) собира́ться *impf.*, собра́ться (соберётся; собра́лся, -ала́сь, -а́ло́сь) *pf.* **meeting** *n.* встре́ча; собра́ние, заседа́ние, ми́тинг.

mega- ['megə] *in comb.* мега... . **megacycle, megahertz** *n.* мегаге́рц (*g.pl.* -ц). **megalith** ['megəlɪθ] *n.* мегали́т. **mega'lithic** *adj.* мегалити́ческий. **megaphone** *n.* мегафо́н. **megaton(ne)** *n.* мегато́нна. **megavolt** *n.* мегаво́льт (*g.pl.* -т). **megawatt** *n.* мегава́тт (*g.pl.* -т). **megohm** ['megəʊm] *n.* мего́м (*g.pl.* -м).

megalomania [ˌmegələ'meɪnɪə] *n.* мегалома́ния.

melancholia [ˌmelən'kəʊlɪə] *n.* меланхо́лия. **melancholic** [ˌmelən'kɒlɪk] *adj.* меланхоли́ческий. **melancholy** ['melənkəlɪ] *n.* грусть, тоска́; *adj.* уны́лый, гру́стный (-тен, -тна́, -тно).

melée ['meleɪ] *n.* сва́лка.

mellow ['meləʊ] *adj.* (*ripe*) спе́лый (спел, -а́, -о); (*juicy*) со́чный (-чен, -чна́, -чно); (*soft*) мя́гкий (-гок, -гка́, -гко); (*intoxicated*) подвы́пивший; *v.i.* спеть *impf.*; смягча́ться *impf.*, смягчи́ться *pf.*

melodic [mɪ'lɒdɪk] *adj.* мелоди́ческий. **melodious** [mɪ'ləʊdɪəs] *adj.* мелоди́чный. **melody** ['melədɪ] *n.* мело́дия, напе́в.

melodrama ['meləˌdrɑːmə] *n.* мелодра́ма. **melodramatic** [ˌmelədrə'mætɪk] *adj.* мелодрамати́ческий.

melon ['melən] *n.* ды́ня; (*water-*~) арбу́з.

melt [melt] *v.t.* & *i.* раста́пливать(ся) *impf.*, растопи́ть(ся) (-плю́, -пит(ся)) *pf.*; (*smelt*) пла́вить(ся) *impf.*, рас~ *pf.*; (*dissolve*) растворя́ть(ся) *impf.*, раствори́ть(ся) *pf.*; *v.i.* (*thaw*) та́ять (та́ет) *impf.*, рас~ *pf.*; ~**ing point** то́чка плавле́ния.

member ['membə(r)] *n.* член. **membership** *n.* чле́нство; (*number of* ~) коли́чество чле́нов; *attr.* чле́нский.

membrane ['membreɪn] *n.* перепо́нка. **membran(e)ous** *adj.* перепо́нчатый.

memento [mɪ'mentəʊ] *n.* сувени́р. **memoir** ['memwɑː(r)] *n.* кра́ткая биогра́фия; *pl.* мемуа́ры (-ров) *pl.*; воспомина́ния *nt.pl.* **memorable** ['memərəb(ə)l] *adj.* достопа́мятный. **memorandum** [ˌmemə'rændəm] *n.* па́мятная запи́ска; (*diplomatic* ~) мемора́ндум. **memorial** [mɪ'mɔːrɪəl] *adj.* па́мятный, мемориа́льный; *n.* па́мятник. **memorize** ['meməˌraɪz] *v.t.* зау́чивать *impf.*, заучи́ть (-чу́, -чишь) *pf.* наизу́сть. **memory** ['memərɪ] *n.* па́мять; (*recollection*) воспомина́ние; (*comput.*) запомина́ющее устро́йство.

menace ['menɪs] *n.* угро́за; *v.t.* угрожа́ть *impf.*+*d.* **menacing** *adj.* угрожа́ющий.

menagerie [mɪ'nædʒərɪ] *n.* звери́нец (-нца)

mend [mend] *v.t.* чини́ть (-ню́, -нишь) *impf.*, по~ *pf.*; (*clothes*) што́пать *impf.*, за~ *pf.*; (*road*) ремонти́ровать *impf.*, от~ *pf.*; ~ **one's ways** исправля́ться *impf.*, испра́виться *pf.*

mendacious [men'deɪʃəs] *adj.* лжи́вый. **mendacity** [men'dæsɪtɪ] *n.* лжи́вость.

mendicancy ['mendɪkənsɪ] *n.* ни́щенство. **mendicant** *adj.* ни́щий, ни́щенствующий; *n.* ни́щий *sb.*

menial ['miːnɪəl] *adj.* лаке́йский, ни́зкий (-зок, -зка́, -зко).

meningitis [ˌmenɪn'dʒaɪtɪs] *n.* менинги́т.

menopause ['menəˌpɔːz] *n.* кли́макс.

menstrual ['menstrʊəl] *adj.* менструа́льный. **menstru'ation** *n.* менструа́ция.

mental ['ment(ə)l] *adj.* у́мственный, психи́ческий; ~ **arithmetic** счёт в уме́; ~ **deficiency** у́мственная отста́лость; ~ **home, hospital, institution** психиатри́ческая больни́ца. **men'tality** *n.* ум (-а́); (*character*) склад ума́. **mentally** *adv.* у́мственно, мы́сленно.

menthol ['menθɒl] *n.* менто́л.

mention ['menʃ(ə)n] *v.t.* упомина́ть *impf.*, упомяну́ть (-ну́, -нешь) *pf.*; **not to** ~ не говоря́ уже́ о+*p.*; *n.* упомина́ние.

mentor ['mentɔː(r)] *n.* ме́нтор.

menu ['menjuː] *n.* меню́ *nt.indecl.*

mercantile ['mɜːkənˌtaɪl] *adj.* торго́вый; ~ **marine** торго́вый флот.

mercenary ['mɜːsɪnərɪ] *adj.* коры́стный; (*hired*) наёмный; *n.* наёмник.

merchandise ['mɜːtʃənˌdaɪz] *n.* това́ры *m.pl.* **merchant** *n.* купе́ц (-пца́); торго́вец (-вца); *attr.* торго́вый; ~ **navy** торго́вый флот; ~ **ship** торго́вое су́дно (*pl.* -да́, -до́в).

merciful ['mɜːsɪˌfʊl] *adj.* милосе́рдный. **mercifully** *adv.* к сча́стью. **merciless** *adj.* беспоща́дный.

mercurial [mɜː'kjʊərɪəl] *adj.* (*person*) живо́й (жив, -а́, -о); (*of mercury*) рту́тный. **'mercury** *n.* (*metal*) ртуть; (**M~**, *planet*) Мерку́рий.

mercy ['mɜːsɪ] *n.* милосе́рдие; поща́да; **at the ~ of** во вла́сти+*g.*

mere [mɪə(r)] *adj.* просто́й, чи́стый, су́щий; **a ~ child** су́щий ребёнок, всего́ лишь ребёнок. **merely** *adv.* то́лько, про́сто.

meretricious [ˌmerɪ'trɪʃəs] *adj.* показно́й, мишу́рный.

merge [mɜːdʒ] *v.t.* & *i.* слива́ть(ся) *impf.*, слить(ся) (солью́(сь), -ьёшь(ся); сли́л(ся), -ила́(сь), -и́ло/-и́ло́сь) *pf.* **merger** *n.* объедине́ние.

meridian [mə'rɪdɪən] *n.* меридиа́н.

meringue [mə'ræŋ] *n.* мере́нга.

merit ['merɪt] *n.* заслу́га, досто́инство; *v.t.* заслу́живать *impf.*, заслужи́ть (-жу́, -жишь) *pf.*+*g.* **meri'torious** *adj.* похва́льный.

mermaid ['mɜːmeɪd] *n.* руса́лка.

merrily ['merɪlɪ] *adv.* ве́село. **merriment** *n.* весе́лье. **merry** *adj.* весёлый (ве́сел, -а́, -о, ве́селы́). **merry-go-round** *n.* карусе́ль. **merry-making** *n.* весе́лье.

mesh [meʃ] *n.* пе́тля (*g.pl.* -тель); *pl.* (*network*) се́ти (-те́й) *pl.*; *pl.* (*fig.*) западня́; *v.i.* сцепля́ться *impf.*, сцепи́ться (-ится) *pf.*

mesmeric [mez'merɪk] *adj.* гипноти́ческий. **'mesmerize** *v.t.* гипнотизи́ровать *impf.*, за~ *pf.*

mess [mes] *n.* (*disorder*) беспоря́док (-дка); (*trouble*) беда́; (*eating-place*) столо́вая *sb.*; *v.i.* столова́ться *impf.* (**with** вме́сте с+*i.*); **~ about** ло́дырничать *impf.*; **~ up** по́ртить *impf.*, ис~ *pf.*

message ['mesɪdʒ] *n.* сообще́ние; (*errand*) поруче́ние. **messenger** *n.* посы́льный *sb.*, курье́р.

Messiah [mɪ'saɪə] *n.* мессия́ *m.* **Messianic** [ˌmesɪ'ænɪk] *adj.* мессиа́нский.

Messrs ['mesəz] *abbr.* (*of* ***Messieurs***) господа́ (*g.* -д) *m.pl.*

messy ['mesɪ] *adj.* (*untidy*) беспоря́дочный; (*dirty*) гря́зный (-зен, -зна́, -зно).

metabolism [mɪ'tæbəˌlɪz(ə)m] *n.* метаболи́зм, обме́н веще́ств.

metal ['met(ə)l] *n.* мета́лл; (*road-~*) щебень (-бня) *m.*; (*rail.*) балла́ст; *pl.* (*rails*) ре́льсы *m.pl.*; *adj.* металли́ческий; *v.t.* (*road*) шосси́ровать *impf.* & *pf.*; **~ detector** металлоиска́тель *m.*; **~led road** шоссе́ *nt.indecl.* **metallic** [mɪ'tælɪk] *adj.* металли́ческий. **metallurgical** [ˌmetə'lɜːdʒɪk(ə)l] *adj.* металлурги́ческий. **metallurgy** [mɪ'tælədʒɪ, 'metəˌlɜːdʒɪ] *n.* металлу́ргия.

metamorphose [ˌmetə'mɔːfəʊz] *v.t.* подверга́ть *impf.*, подве́ргнуть (-г) *pf.* метаморфо́зе. **meta'mor'phosis** *n.* метаморфо́за; (*biol.*) метаморфо́з.

metaphor ['metəˌfɔː(r)] *n.* мета́фора. **meta'phorical** *adj.* метафори́ческий.

metaphysical [ˌmetə'fɪzɪk(ə)l] *adj.* метафизи́ческий. **metaphy'sician** *n.* метафи́зик. **metaphysics** *n.* метафи́зика.

meteor ['miːtɪə(r)] *n.* метео́р. **meteoric** [ˌmiːtɪ'ɒrɪk] *adj.* метеори́ческий, метео́рный. **meteorite** *n.* метеори́т. **meteoro'logical** *adj.* метеорологи́ческий. **meteo'rologist** *n.* метеоро́лог. **meteo'rology** *n.* метеороло́гия.

meter ['miːtə(r)] *n.* счётчик; *v.t.* измеря́ть *impf.*, изме́рить *pf.* при по́мощи счётчика.

methane ['meθeɪn, 'miːθeɪn] *n.* мета́н.

method ['meθəd] *n.* ме́тод, спо́соб; (*system*) систе́ма. **methodical** [mɪ'θɒdɪk(ə)l] *adj.* системати́ческий, методи́чный.

Methodism ['meθəˌdɪz(ə)m] *n.* методи́зм. **Methodist** *n.* методи́ст; *adj.* методи́стский.

methyl ['meθɪl, 'miːθaɪl] *n.* мети́л; **~ alcohol** мети́ловый спирт. **methylated** ['meθɪˌleɪtɪd] *adj.*: **~ spirit(s)** денатура́т.

meticulous [mə'tɪkjʊləs] *adj.* тща́тельный.

metre ['miːtə(r)] *n.* ме́тр. **metric(al)** ['metrɪk(ə)l] *adj.* метри́ческий.

metronome ['metrəˌnəʊm] *n.* метроно́м.

metropolis [mɪ'trɒpəlɪs] *n.* (*capital*) столи́ца. **metropolitan** [ˌmetrə'pɒlɪt(ə)n] *adj.* столи́чный; *n.* (*eccl.*) митрополи́т.

mettle ['met(ə)l] *n.* темпера́мент; (*ardour*) пыл (-а(у)). **mettlesome** *adj.* горя́чий (-ч, -ча́).

mew *see* **miaow**

Mexico ['meksɪˌkəʊ] *n.* Ме́ксика.

mezzanine ['metsəˌniːn, 'mez-] *n.* антресо́ли *f.pl.*

mezzo-soprano ['metsəʊ] *n.* ме́ццо-сопра́но (*voice*) *nt.* & (*person*) *f.indecl.*

mg. *abbr.* (*of* **milligram(me)(s)**) мг, миллигра́м.

miaow [mɪ'aʊ] *int.* мя́у; *n.* мя́уканье; *v.i.* мя́укать *impf.*, мя́укнуть *pf.*

mica ['maɪkə] *n.* слюда́.

Michaelmas ['mɪkəlməs] *n.* Миха́йлов день (дня) *m.*

micro- ['maɪkrəʊ] *in comb.* микро… . **microbe** *n.* микро́б. **microcircuit** *n.* микросхе́ма. **microcomponent** *n.* микроэлеме́нт. **microcomputer** *n.* микрокомпью́тер. **microcosm** *n.* микроко́см. **microelectronics** *n.* микроэлектро́ника. **microfiche** *n.* микрофи́ша. **microfilm** *n.* микрофи́льм. **micron** ['maɪkrɒn] *n.* микро́н (*g.pl.* -н). **micro-organism** *n.* микроорганизм. **microphone** *n.* микрофо́н. **microscope** *n.* микроско́п. **micro'scopic** *adj.* микроскопи́ческий. **microsecond** *n.* микросеку́нда. **microwave** *adj.* микроволно́вый; *n.* микроволна́ (*pl.* -о́лны, *d.* -о́лна́м); **~ oven** печь сверхвысо́кой частоты́.

mid [mɪd] *adj.* сре́дний, середи́нный. **midday** *n.* по́лдень (полу́дня & по́лдня) *m.*; *attr.* полу́денный. **middle** *n.* середи́на; *adj.*

сре́дний; **M~ Ages** сре́дние века́ *m.pl.*; **~ man** посре́дник. **middle-aged** *adj.* сре́дних лет. **middle-sized** *adj.* сре́днего разме́ра. **middleweight** *n.* сре́дний вес.

midge [mɪdʒ] *n.* мо́шка.

midget ['mɪdʒɪt] *n.* ка́рлик, -ица; *adj.* миниатю́рный.

Midlands ['mɪdləndz] *n.* центра́льные гра́фства *nt.pl.* А́нглии. **midnight** *n.* по́лночь (полу́ночи & по́лночи); *attr.* полу́но́чный. **midriff** *n.* диафра́гма. **midshipman** *n.* кора́бельный гардемари́н. **midst** *n.* середи́на. **mid'summer** *n.* середи́на ле́та. **midway** *adv.* на полпути́, на полдоро́ге. **mid-week** *n.* середи́на неде́ли. **mid'winter** *n.* середи́на зимы́.

midwife ['mɪdwaɪf] *n.* акуше́рка. **midwifery** ['mɪd,wɪfərɪ] *n.* акуше́рство.

might [maɪt] *n.* мощь, могу́щество; си́ла; **with all one's ~, with ~ and main** не щадя́ сил. **mighty** *adj.* могу́щественный (-ен, -енна), мо́щный (-щен, -щна́, -щно).

migraine ['mi:greɪn, 'maɪ-] *n.* мигре́нь.

migrant ['maɪgrənt] *adj.* кочу́ющий; (*bird*) перелётный; *n.* (*person*) переселе́нец (-нца); (*bird*) перелётная пти́ца. **mi'grate** *v.i.* мигри́ровать *impf.* & *pf.*; переселя́ться *impf.*, пересели́ться *pf.* **mi'gration** *n.* мигра́ция. **mi'gratory** *adj.* кочу́ющий; (*bird*) перелётный.

mike [maɪk] *n.* микрофо́н.

milch [mɪltʃ] *adj.* моло́чный. **milch-cow** *n.* до́йная коро́ва.

mild [maɪld] *adj.* (*soft*) мя́гкий (-гок, -гка́, -гко); (*light*) лёгкий (-гок, -гка́, -гко́, лёгки́); (*not sharp*) нео́стрый (не остр & -остёр, остра́, о́стро́); (*not strong*) некре́пкий (-пок, -пка́, -пко); **~ steel** мя́гкая сталь.

mildew ['mɪldju:] *n.* (*fungi*) мильдью́ *nt.indecl.*; (*on paper etc.*) пле́сень.

mile [maɪl] *n.* ми́ля. **mileage** *n.* расстоя́ние в ми́лях; (*distance travelled*) коли́чество про́йденных миль; (*expenses*) де́ньги (-нег, -ньга́м) *pl.* на прое́зд. **milestone** *n.* ми́льный ка́мень (-мня; *pl.* -мни, -мне́й) *m.*; (*fig.*) ве́ха.

militancy ['mɪlɪt(ə)nsɪ] *n.* вои́нственность. **militant** *adj.* вои́нствующий; (*combative*) боево́й; *n.* бое́ц (бойца́); активи́ст. **military** *adj.* вое́нный; **~ band** духово́й орке́стр; *n.* вое́нные *sb.* **militate** *v.i.*: **~ against** говори́ть *impf.* про́тив+*g.* **militia** [mɪ'lɪʃə] *n.* ополче́ние; (*in Russia*) мили́ция. **militiaman** *n.* ополче́нец (-нца); (*in Russia*) милиционе́р.

milk [mɪlk] *n.* молоко́; (*of plants*) мле́чный сок; *attr.* моло́чный; *v.t.* дои́ть *impf.*, по~ *pf.* **milkmaid** *n.* доя́рка. **milkman** *n.* продаве́ц (-вца́) молока́. **milksop** *n.* тря́пка. **milk-tooth** *n.* моло́чный зуб (*pl.* -ы, -о́в). **milky** *adj.* моло́чный; **M~ Way** Мле́чный Путь (-ти́, -тём) *m.*

mill [mɪl] *n.* ме́льница; (*factory*) фа́брика, заво́д; (*rolling-~*) прока́тный стан; *v.t.* (*grain etc.*) моло́ть (мелю́, -лешь) *impf.*, с~ *pf.*; (*cloth*) валя́ть *impf.*, с~ *pf.*; (*metal*) фрезерова́ть *impf.*, от~ *pf.*; (*coin*) гурти́ть *impf.*; **~ed edge** (*of coin*) гурт; *v.i.* кружи́ть (-ужу́, -у́жи́шь) *impf.*

millennium [mɪ'lenɪəm] *n.* тысячеле́тие.

millepede *see* **millipede**

miller ['mɪlə(r)] *n.* ме́льник.

millet ['mɪlɪt] *n.* (*plant*) про́со; (*grain*) пшено́.

mill-hand ['mɪlhænd] *n.* фабри́чный рабо́чий *sb.*

milli- ['mɪlɪ] *in comb.* милли... . **millibar** *n.* миллиба́р. **milligram(me)** *n.* миллигра́мм. **millilitre** *n.* миллили́тр. **millimetre** *n.* миллиме́тр.

milliner ['mɪlɪnə(r)] *n.* моди́стка; шля́пница. **millinery** *n.* да́мские шля́пы *f.pl.*

million ['mɪljən] *n.* миллио́н. **millio'naire** *n.* миллионе́р. **millionth** *adj.* миллио́нный.

millipede ['mɪlɪ,pi:d] *n.* многоно́жка.

mill-pond ['mɪlpɔnd] *n.* ме́льничный пруд (-а́, *loc.* -у́). **mill-race** *n.* ме́льничный лото́к (-тка́). **millstone** *n.* жёрнов (*pl.* -а́); (*fig.*) бре́мя *nt.* **mill-wheel** *n.* ме́льничное колесо́ (*pl.* -ёса).

milt [mɪlt] *n.* моло́ки (-к) *pl.*

mime [maɪm] *n.* мим; *v.t.* изобража́ть *impf.*, изобрази́ть *pf.* мими́чески; *v.i.* исполня́ть *impf.*, испо́лнить *pf.* роль в пантоми́ме. **mimic** ['mɪmɪk] *adj.* мими́ческий, подража́тельный; *n.* мими́ст; *v.t.* имити́ровать *impf.*, сымити́ровать *pf.*; (*ape*) обезья́нничать *impf.*, с~ *pf.* с+*g.* **mimicry** *n.* имита́ция.

mimosa [mɪ'məʊzə] *n.* мимо́за; (*acacia*) ака́ция.

min. *abbr.* (*of* **minute(s)**) мин., мину́та.

minaret [,mɪnə'ret] *n.* минаре́т.

mince [mɪns] *n.* (*meat*) ру́бленое мя́со, фарш; *v.t.* руби́ть (-блю́, -бишь) *impf.*; (*in machine*) пропуска́ть *impf.*, пропусти́ть (-ущу́, -у́стишь) *pf.* че́рез мясору́бку; *v.i.* (*speak*) говори́ть *impf.* жема́нно; (*walk*) семени́ть *impf.*; **not to ~ matters** говори́ть *impf.* пря́мо, без обиняко́в. **mincemeat** *n.* начи́нка из изю́ма, миндаля́ и т.п. **mincer** *n.* мясору́бка.

mind [maɪnd] *n.* ум (-а́), ра́зум; (*memory*) па́мять; (*opinion*) мне́ние; **absence of ~** забы́вчивость, рассе́янность; **bear in ~** име́ть *impf.* в виду́; по́мнить *impf.*; **be in one's right ~** быть в здра́вом уме́; **be out of one's ~** быть не в своём уме́; **change one's ~** переду́мывать *impf.*, переду́мать *pf.*; **make up one's ~** реша́ться *impf.*, реши́ться *pf.*; **presence of ~** прису́тствие ду́ха; *v.t.* (*give heed to*) обраща́ть *impf.*, обрати́ть (-ащу́, -ати́шь) *pf.* внима́ние на+*a.*; (*look after*) присма́тривать *impf.*, присмотре́ть (-рю́, -ришь) *pf.* за+*i.*; **I don't ~** я не возража́ю; я ничего́ не име́ю про́тив; **don't ~ me** не обраща́й(те) внима́ния на меня́!; **~ you don't forget** смотри́ не забу́дь!; **~ your own**

business не вме́шивайтесь в чужи́е дела́!; **never** ~ не беспоко́йтесь!; ничего́! **minded** *adj.* (*disposed*) располо́женный (-ен). **mindful** *adj.* по́мнящий, внима́тельный (**of** к+*d.*).

mine[1] [maɪn] *poss.pron.* мой (моя́, моё; мои́); свой (-оя́, -оё; -ои́).

mine[2] [maɪn] *n.* ша́хта, рудни́к (-а́); (*fig.*) исто́чник; (*mil.*) ми́на; *v.t.* (*obtain from* ~) добыва́ть *impf.*, добы́ть (добу́ду, -дешь; до́бы́л, -а́, -о) *pf.*; (*mil.*) мини́ровать *impf.* & *pf.* **minefield** *n.* ми́нное по́ле (*pl.* -ля́). **minelayer** *n.* ми́нный загради́тель *m.* **miner** *n.* шахтёр, горня́к (-а́). **minesweeper** *n.* ми́нный тра́льщик.

mineral ['mɪnər(ə)l] *n.* минера́л; *adj.* минера́льный; ~ **water** минера́льная вода́ (*a.* -ду). **mine'ralogist** *n.* минерало́г. **mine'ralogy** *n.* минерало́гия.

mingle ['mɪŋg(ə)l] *v.t.* & *i.* сме́шивать(ся) *impf.*, смеша́ть(ся) *pf.*

miniature ['mɪnɪtʃə(r)] *n.* миниатю́ра; *adj.* миниатю́рный. **miniaturist** *n.* миниатюри́ст.

minibus ['mɪnɪˌbʌs] *n.* микроавто́бус.

minim ['mɪnɪm] *n.* (*mus.*) полови́нная но́та. **minimal** *adj.* минима́льный. **minimize** ['mɪnɪˌmaɪz] *v.t.* (*reduce*) доводи́ть (-ожу́, -о́дишь) *impf.*, довести́ (-еду́, -едёшь; -ёл, -ела́) *pf.* до ми́нимума; (*underestimate*) преуменьша́ть *impf.*, преуме́ньшить *pf.* **minimum** *n.* ми́нимум; *adj.* минима́льный.

mining ['maɪnɪŋ] *n.* го́рное де́ло.

miniskirt ['mɪnɪˌskɜːt] *n.* ми́ни-ю́бка.

minister ['mɪnɪstə(r)] *n.* (*pol.*) мини́стр; (*diplomat*) посла́нник; (*eccl.*) свяще́нник. **ministerial** [ˌmɪnɪ'stɪərɪəl] *adj.* министе́рский. **mini'stration** *n.* по́мощь. **ministry** *n.* (*pol.*) министе́рство; (*eccl.*) духове́нство.

mink [mɪŋk] *n.* но́рка; *attr.* но́рковый.

minnow ['mɪnəʊ] *n.* голья́н.

minor ['maɪnə(r)] *adj.* (*lesser*) ме́ньший; (*less important*) второстепе́нный (-нен, -нна); (*mus.*) мино́рный; *n.* (*person under age*) несовершенноле́тний *n.*; (*mus.*) мино́р. **minority** [maɪ'nɒrɪtɪ] *n.* (*small number*) меньшинство́ (*pl.* -ва); (*age*) несовершенноле́тие; **national** ~ нацменьшинство́ (*pl.* -ва).

minstrel ['mɪnstr(ə)l] *n.* менестре́ль *m.*

mint[1] [mɪnt] *n.* (*plant*) мя́та; (*peppermint*) пе́речная мя́та; *attr.* мя́тный.

mint[2] [mɪnt] *n.* (*econ.*) моне́тный двор (-а́); **in** ~ **condition** блестя́щий, но́вый (нов, -а́, -о); (*book etc.*) непотрёпанный (-ан); *v.t.* чека́нить *impf.*, от~, вы́~ *pf.*

minuet [ˌmɪnjʊ'et] *n.* менуэ́т.

minus ['maɪnəs] *prep.* ми́нус+*a.*; без+*g.*; *n.* ми́нус; *adj.* (*math.*, *elec.*) отрица́тельный.

minuscule ['mɪnəˌskjuːl] *adj.* минуску́льный; (о́чень) ма́ленький; *n.* минуску́л.

minute[1] ['mɪnɪt] *n.* мину́та; *pl.* протоко́л; *v.t.* заноси́ть (-ошу́, -о́сишь) *impf.*, занести́ (-есу́, -есёшь; -ёс, -есла́) *pf.* в протоко́л.

minute[2] [maɪ'njuːt] *adj.* ме́лкий (-лок, -лка́, -лко), мельча́йший. **minutiae** [maɪ'njuːʃɪˌiː, mɪ-] *n.* ме́лочи (-че́й) *f.pl.*

minx [mɪŋks] *n.* коке́тка.

miracle ['mɪrək(ə)l] *n.* чу́до (*pl.* -деса́). **miraculous** [mɪ'rækjʊləs] *adj.* чуде́сный.

mirage ['mɪrɑːʒ] *n.* мира́ж.

mire ['maɪə(r)] *n.* (*mud*) грязь (*loc.* -зи́); (*swamp*) боло́то. **miry** *adj.* гря́зный (-зен, -зна́, -зно).

mirror ['mɪrə(r)] *n.* зе́ркало (*pl.* -ла́); (*fig.*) отображе́ние; ~ **image** зерка́льное изображе́ние; *v.t.* отража́ть *impf.*, отрази́ть *pf.*

mirth [mɜːθ] *n.* весе́лье.

misadventure [ˌmɪsəd'ventʃə(r)] *n.* несча́стный слу́чай.

misanthrope ['mɪzənˌθrəʊp, 'mɪs-] *n.* мизантро́п. **misanthropic** [ˌmɪzən'θrɒpɪk, 'mɪs-] *adj.* мизантропи́ческий. **mi'santhropy** *n.* мизантро́пия.

misapplication [mɪsˌæplɪ'keɪʃ(ə)n] *n.* непра́вильное испо́льзование. **misapply** [ˌmɪsə'plaɪ] *v.t.* непра́вильно испо́льзовать *impf.* & *pf.* **misapprehend** *v.t.* непра́вильно понима́ть *impf.*, поня́ть (пойму́, -мёшь; по́нял, -а́, -о) *pf.* **misapprehension** *n.* непра́вильное понима́ние. **misappropriate** *v.t.* незако́нно присва́ивать *impf.*, присво́ить *pf.* **misappropri'ation** *n.* незако́нное присвое́ние. **misbehave** *v.i.* ду́рно вести́ (веду́, -дёшь; вёл, -а́) *impf.* себя́.

miscalculate [ˌmɪs'kælkjʊˌleɪt] *v.t.* непра́вильно рассчи́тывать *impf.*, рассчита́ть *pf.*; (*fig.*, *abs.*) просчи́тываться *impf.*, просчита́ться *pf.* **miscarriage** *n.* (*mistake*) оши́бка; (*med.*) вы́кидыш, або́рт; ~ **of justice** суде́бная оши́бка. **miscarry** *v.i.* терпе́ть (-плю́, -пишь) *impf.*, по~ *pf.* неуда́чу; (*med.*) име́ть *impf.* вы́кидыш. **miscast** *v.t.* непра́вильно распределя́ть *impf.*, распредели́ть *pf.* роль+*d.*

miscellaneous [ˌmɪsə'leɪnɪəs] *adj.* ра́зный, разнообра́зный. **mi'scellany** *n.* (*mixture*) смесь; (*book*) сбо́рник.

mischance [mɪs'tʃɑːns] *n.* несча́стный слу́чай. **mischief** ['mɪstʃɪf] *n.* (*harm*) вред (-а́); (*naughtiness*) озорство́; (*pranks*) прока́зы *f.pl.* **mischievous** *adj.* озорно́й. **misconception** *n.* непра́вильное представле́ние. **misconduct** *n.* дурно́е поведе́ние; (*adultery*) супру́жеская неве́рность; *v.t.*: ~ **o.s.** ду́рно вести́ (веду́, -дёшь; вёл, -а́) *impf.* себя́. **misconstruction** *n.* непра́вильное истолкова́ние. **misconstrue** *v.t.* непра́вильно истолко́вывать *impf.*, истолкова́ть *pf.* **miscount** *n.* оши́бка при подсчёте; непра́вильный подсчёт; *v.t.* ошиба́ться *impf.*, ошиби́ться (-бу́сь, -бёшься; -бся) *pf.* при подсчёте+*g.*

misdeal *v.i.* ошиба́ться *impf.*, ошиби́ться (-бу́сь, -бёшься; -бся) *pf.* при сда́че карт. **misdeed** *n.* злодея́ние. **misdirect** *v.t.* непра́вильно направля́ть *impf.*, напра́вить *pf.*;

(*letter*) непра́вильно адресова́ть *impf.* & *pf.* **misdirection** *n.* непра́вильное указа́ние, руково́дство.

miser ['maɪzə(r)] *n.* скупе́ц (-пца́), скря́га *c.g.* **miserable** ['mɪzərəb(ə)l] *adj.* (*unhappy*) несча́стный; (*wretched*) жа́лкий (-лок, -лка́, -лко), убо́гий. **miserly** ['maɪzəlɪ] *adj.* скупо́й (скуп, -а́, -о). **misery** ['mɪzərɪ] *n.* страда́ние, несча́стье.

misfire [mɪs'faɪə(r)] *v.i.* дава́ть (даёт) *impf.*, дать (даст; дал, -а́, да́ло́, -и) *pf.* осе́чку; *n.* осе́чка. **'misfit** *n.* (*garment*) пло́хо сидя́щее пла́тье (*g.pl.* -в); (*person*) неуда́чник. **misfortune** *n.* несча́стье, беда́. **misgiving** *n.* опасе́ние. **misgovern** *v.t.* пло́хо управля́ть *impf.+i.* **misgovernment** *n.* плохо́е управле́ние. **misguided** *adj.* введённый (-ён, -ена́) в заблужде́ние.

mishap ['mɪshæp] *n.* неуда́ча, несча́стье. **misinform** *v.t.* дезинформи́ровать *impf.* & *pf.* **misinformation** *n.* дезинформа́ция. **misinterpret** *v.t.* неве́рно понима́ть *impf.*, поня́ть (пойму́, -мёшь; по́нял, -а́, -о) *pf.* **misjudge** *v.t.* неве́рно оце́нивать *impf.*, оцени́ть (-ню́, -нишь) *pf.* **misjudgement** *n.* неве́рная оце́нка. **mislay** *v.t.* класть (-аду́, -адёшь; -ал) *impf.*, положи́ть (-жу́, -жишь) *pf.* не на ме́сто; затеря́ть *pf.* **mislead** *v.t.* вводи́ть (-ожу́, -о́дишь) *impf.*, ввести́ (введу́, -дёшь; ввёл, -а́) *pf.* в заблужде́ние. **mismanage** *v.t.* пло́хо управля́ть *impf.+i.* **mismanagement** *n.* плохо́е управле́ние. **misnomer** [mɪs'nəʊmə(r)] *n.* непра́вильное назва́ние.

misogynist [mɪ'sɒdʒɪnɪst] *n.* женоненави́стник. **misogeny** *n.* женоненави́стничество.

misplace [mɪs'pleɪs] *v.t.* класть (-аду́, -дёшь; -ал) *impf.*, положи́ть (-жу́, -жишь) *pf.* не на ме́сто; **~d confidence** незаслу́женное дове́рие. **'misprint** *n.* опеча́тка; *v.t.* непра́вильно печа́тать *impf.*, на~ *pf.* **mispronounce** *v.t.* непра́вильно произноси́ть (-ошу́, -о́сишь) *impf.*, произнести́ (-есу́, -есёшь; -ёс, -сла́) *pf.* **mispronunciation** *n.* непра́вильное произноше́ние. **misquotation** *n.* непра́вильная цита́та; непра́вильное цити́рование. **misquote** *v.t.* непра́вильно цити́ровать *impf.*, про~ *pf.* **misread** *v.t.* непра́вильно чита́ть *impf.*, про~ *pf.* **misrepresent** *v.t.* искажа́ть *impf.*, искази́ть *pf.* **misrepresentation** *n.* искаже́ние.

Miss[1] [mɪs] *n.* (*title*) мисс.

miss[2] [mɪs] *n.* про́мах, неуда́ча; *v.i.* прома́хиваться *impf.*, промахну́ться *pf.*; *v.t.* (*let slip*) упуска́ть *impf.*, упусти́ть (-ущу́, -у́стишь) *pf.*; (*train*) опа́здывать *impf.*, опозда́ть *pf.* на+*a.*; **~ out** пропуска́ть *impf.*, пропусти́ть (-ущу́, -у́стишь) *pf.*; **~ the point** не понима́ть *impf.*, поня́ть (пойму́, -мёшь; по́нял, -а́, -о) *pf.* су́ти.

misshapen [mɪs'ʃeɪpən] *adj.* уро́дливый.

missile ['mɪsaɪl] *n.* снаря́д, раке́та.

missing ['mɪsɪŋ] *adj.* отсу́тствующий, недостаю́щий; (*person*) пропа́вший бе́з ве́сти.

mission ['mɪʃ(ə)n] *n.* ми́ссия; командиро́вка. **missionary** *n.* миссионе́р; *adj.* миссионе́рский. **missive** ['mɪsɪv] *n.* письмо́ (*pl.* -сьма, -сем, -сьмам); посла́ние.

misspell [mɪs'spel] *v.t.* непра́вильно писа́ть (пишу́, -шешь) *impf.*, на~ *pf.* **misspelling** *n.* непра́вильное написа́ние. **misspent** *adj.* растра́ченный (-ен) (впусту́ю). **misstatement** *n.* непра́вильное заявле́ние.

mist [mɪst] *n.* тума́н, мгла.

mistake [mɪ'steɪk] *v.t.* непра́вильно понима́ть *impf.*, поня́ть (пойму́, -мёшь; по́нял, -а́, -о) *pf.*; **~ for** принима́ть *impf.*, приня́ть (приму́, -мешь; при́нял, -а́, -о) *pf.* за+*a.*; *n.* оши́бка; **make a ~** ошиба́ться *impf.*, ошиби́ться (-бу́сь, -бёшься; -бся) *pf.* **mistaken** *adj.* оши́бочный; **be ~** ошиба́ться *impf.*, ошиби́ться (-бу́сь, -бёшься; -бся) *pf.*

mistletoe ['mɪs(ə)l,təʊ] *n.* оме́ла.

mistranslate [,mɪstrænz'leɪt, ,mɪstrɑ:-, -s'leɪt] *v.t.* непра́вильно переводи́ть (-ожу́, -о́дишь) *impf.*, перевести́ (-еду́, -едёшь; -ёл, -ела́) *pf.* **mistranslation** *n.* непра́вильный перево́д.

mistress ['mɪstrɪs] *n.* хозя́йка; (*teacher*) учи́тельница; (*lover*) любо́вница.

mistrust [mɪs'trʌst] *v.t.* не доверя́ть *impf.+d.*; *n.* недове́рие. **mistrustful** *adj.* недове́рчивый.

misty ['mɪstɪ] *adj.* тума́нный.

misunderstand [,mɪsʌndə'stænd] *v.t.* непра́вильно понима́ть *impf.*, поня́ть (пойму́, -мёшь; по́нял, -а́, -о) *pf.* **misunderstanding** *n.* непра́вильное понима́ние, недоразуме́ние; (*disagreement*) размо́лвка.

misuse [mɪs'ju:z; mɪs'ju:s] *v.t.* непра́вильно употребля́ть *impf.*, употреби́ть *pf.*; (*ill-treat*) ду́рно обраща́ться *impf.* с+*i.*; *n.* непра́вильное употребле́ние.

mite [maɪt] *n.* (*cheese-~*) (сы́рный) клещ (-а́); (*child*) ма́ленький ребёнок (-нка; *pl.* де́ти, -те́й, -тям, -тьми́), кро́шка.

mitigate ['mɪtɪ,geɪt] *v.t.* смягча́ть *impf.*, смягчи́ть *pf.* **miti'gation** *n.* смягче́ние.

mitre ['maɪtə(r)] *n.* ми́тра.

mitten ['mɪt(ə)n] *n.* рукави́ца, мите́нка; *pl.* (*boxing-gloves*) боксёрские перча́тки *f.pl.*

mix [mɪks] *v.t.* меша́ть *impf.*, с~ *pf.*; *v.i.* сме́шиваться *impf.*, смеша́ться *pf.*; (*person*) обща́ться *impf.*; **~ up** (*confuse*) пу́тать *impf.*, с~ *pf.*; **get ~ed up in** впу́тываться *impf.*, впу́таться *pf.* в+*a.*; *n.* смесь; (*food ~*) (пищево́й) полуфабрика́т. **mixer** *n.* смеси́тель *m.* **mixture** ['mɪkstʃə(r)] *n.* смесь; (*medicine*) миксту́ра.

ml. *abbr.* (*of* **millilitre(s)**) мл, миллили́тр; (*of* **mile(s)**) ми́ля.

mm. *abbr.* (*of* **millimetre(s)**) мм, миллиме́тр.

mnemonic [nɪ'mɒnɪk] *adj.* мнемони́ческий; *n.* мнемони́ческий приём; *pl.* мнемо́ника.

mo [məʊ] *n.* мину́тка; **half a ~** (одну́) мину́тку!

moan [məʊn] *n.* стон; *v.i.* стона́ть (-ну́, -нешь) *impf.*, про~ *pf.*
moat [məʊt] *n.* (крепостно́й) ров (рва, *loc.* во рву́). **moated** *adj.* обнесённый (-ён, -ена́) рвом.
mob [mɒb] *n.* (*populace*) чернь; (*crowd*) толпа́ (*pl.* -пы); (*gang*) ша́йка; *v.t.* (*attack*) напада́ть *impf.*, напа́сть (-адёт; -а́л) *pf.* толпо́й на+*a.*; (*crowd around*) толпи́ться *impf.* вокру́г+*g.* **mobster** *n.* га́нгстер.
mobile ['məʊbaɪl] *adj.* подвижно́й, передвижно́й. **mobility** [mə'bɪlɪtɪ] *n.* подви́жность. **mobilization** [ˌməʊbɪlaɪ'zeɪʃ(ə)n] *n.* мобилиза́ция. **'mobilize** *v.t.* & *i.* мобилизова́ть(ся) *impf.* & *pf.*
moccasin ['mɒkəsɪn] *n.* мокаси́н (*g.pl.* -н).
mocha ['mɒkə] *n.* мо́кко *m.* & *nt.indecl.*
mock [mɒk] *v.t.* & *i.* издева́ться *impf.* над+*i.*; осме́ивать *impf.*, осмея́ть (-ею́, -еёшь) *pf.*; *adj.* (*sham*) подде́льный; (*pretended*) мни́мый; ~ **turtle soup** суп из теля́чей головы́. **mockery** *n.* (*derision*) издева́тельство, насме́шка; (*travesty*) паро́дия (**of** на+*a.*; +*g.*). **mockingbird** *n.* пересме́шник. **mock-up** *n.* маке́т, моде́ль.
mode [məʊd] *n.* (*manner*) о́браз; (*method*) спо́соб.
model ['mɒd(ə)l] *n.* (*representation*) моде́ль, маке́т; (*pattern*) образе́ц (-зца́); (*artist's*) нату́рщик, -ица; (*mannequin*) манеке́нщик, -ица; *adj.* образцо́вый, приме́рный; *v.t.* лепи́ть (-плю́, -пишь) *impf.*, вы́~, с~ *pf.*; (*document*) оформля́ть *impf.*, офо́рмить *pf.*; *v.i.* (*act as* ~) быть нату́рщиком, -ицей; быть манеке́нщиком, -ицей; ~ **after, on** создава́ть (-даю́, -даёшь) *impf.*, созда́ть (-а́м, -а́шь, -а́ст, -ади́м; со́зда́л, -а́, -о) *pf.* по образцу́+*g.*; ~ **o.s. on** брать (беру́, -рёшь; брал, -а́, -о) *impf.*, взять (возьму́, -мёшь; взял, -а́, -о) *pf.*+*a.* за образе́ц, приме́р.
modem ['məʊdem] *n.* мо́дем.
moderate ['mɒdərət; 'mɒdəˌreɪt] *adj.* (*var. senses*; *pol.*) уме́ренный (-ен, -енна); (*person, conduct*) сде́ржанный (-ан, -анна); (*quantity*) небольшо́й; *v.t.* умеря́ть *impf.*, уме́рить *pf.*; *v.i.* стиха́ть *impf.*, сти́хнуть (-х) *pf.* **mode'ration** *n.* уме́ренность; **in** ~ уме́ренно.
modern ['mɒd(ə)n] *adj.* совреме́нный (-нен, -нна), но́вый (нов, -а́, -о). **modernism** *n.* модерни́зм. **moder'nistic** *adj.* модерни́стский. **modernity** [mɒ'dɜːnɪtɪ] *n.* совреме́нность. **moderni'zation** *n.* модерниза́ция. **modernize** *v.t.* модернизи́ровать *impf.* & *pf.*
modest ['mɒdɪst] *adj.* скро́мный (-мен, -мна́, -мно). **modesty** *n.* скро́мность.
modification [ˌmɒdɪfɪ'keɪʃ(ə)n] *n.* видоизмене́ние, модифика́ция. **modify** ['mɒdɪˌfaɪ] *v.t.* (*soften*) смягча́ть *impf.*, смягчи́ть *pf.*; (*partially change*) модифици́ровать *impf.* & *pf.*
modish ['məʊdɪʃ] *adj.* мо́дный (-ден, -дна́, -дно).
modular ['mɒdjʊlə(r)] *adj.* мо́дульный; бло́чный. **modulate** *v.t.* модули́ровать *impf.* **modu'lation** *n.* модуля́ция. **module** *n.* (*measure*) едини́ца измере́ния; (*unit*) мо́дульный. автоно́мный, отсе́к; **lunar** ~ лу́нная ка́псула. **modulus** *n.* мо́дуль *m.*
mohair ['məʊheə(r)] *n.* мохе́р.
Mohammedan [mə'hæməd(ə)n] *adj.* мусульма́нский; *n.* мусульма́нин (*pl.* -а́не, -а́н), -а́нка. **Mohammedanism** *n.* исла́м.
moiré ['mwɑːreɪ] *adj.* муа́ровый.
moist [mɔɪst] *adj.* сыро́й (сыр, -а́, -о), вла́жный (-жен, -жна́, -жно). **moisten** ['mɔɪs(ə)n] *v.t.* & *i.* увлажня́ть(ся) *impf.*, увлажни́ть(ся) *pf.* **moisture** *n.* вла́га.
molar ['məʊlə(r)] *n.* (*tooth*) коренно́й зуб (*pl.* -ы, -о́в); *adj.* коренно́й.
molasses [mə'læsɪz] *n.* чёрная па́тока.
Moldavia [mɒl'deɪvɪə] *n.* Молда́вия.
mole[1] [məʊl] *n.* (*on skin*) ро́динка.
mole[2] [məʊl] *n.* (*animal*) крот (-а́). **molehill** *n.* кротови́на. **moleskin** *n.* крото́вый мех; (*fabric*) молески́н; *pl.* молески́новые брю́ки (-к) *pl.*
mole[3] [məʊl] *n.* (*pier*) мол (*loc.* -у́).
molecular [mə'lekjʊlə(r)] *adj.* молекуля́рный. **molecule** ['mɒlɪˌkjuːl] *n.* моле́кула.
molest [mə'lest] *v.t.* пристава́ть (-таю́, -таёшь) *impf.*, приста́ть (-а́ну, -а́нешь) *pf.* к+*d.* **molestation** [ˌmɒle'steɪʃ(ə)n, ˌməʊl-] *n.* пристава́ние.
mollify ['mɒlɪˌfaɪ] *v.t.* смягча́ть *impf.*, смягчи́ть *pf.*
mollusc ['mɒləsk] *n.* моллю́ск.
mollycoddle ['mɒlɪˌkɒd(ə)l] *n.* не́женка *c.g.*; *v.t.* не́жить *impf.*
molten ['məʊlt(ə)n] *adj.* распла́вленный (-ен).
moment ['məʊmənt] *n.* моме́нт, миг, мгнове́ние; (*phys.*) моме́нт; (*importance*) значе́ние; **a ~ ago** то́лько что; **at a ~'s notice** по пе́рвому тре́бованию; **at the last** ~ в после́днюю мину́ту; **just a** ~ сейча́с!; погоди́! **momen'tarily** *adv.* на мгнове́ние. **momentary** *adj.* преходя́щий, кратковре́менный (-нен, -нна). **momentous** [mə'mentəs] *adj.* ва́жный (-жен, -жна́, -жно, ва́жны́). **mo'mentum** *n.* количество движе́ния; (*impetus*) дви́жущая си́ла; **gather** ~ набира́ть *impf.*, набра́ть (наберу́, -рёшь; набра́л, -а́, -о) *pf.* ско́рость.
monarch ['mɒnək] *n.* мона́рх, ~иня. **monarchical** [mə'nɑːkɪk(ə)l] *adj.* монархи́ческий. **monarchism** *n.* монархи́зм. **monarchist** *n.* монархи́ст. **monarchy** *n.* мона́рхия.
monastery ['mɒnəstərɪ, -strɪ] *n.* (мужско́й) монасты́рь (-ря́) *m.* **monastic** [mə'næstɪk] *adj.* (*of monastery*) монасты́рский; (*of monks*) мона́шеский. **mo'nasticism** *n.* мона́шество.
Monday ['mʌndeɪ, -dɪ] *n.* понеде́льник.
monetarist ['mʌnɪtəˌrɪst] *n.* монетари́ст; *adj.* монетари́стский. **monetary** *adj.* де́нежный. **money** ['mʌnɪ] *n.* де́ньги (-нег, -ньга́м) *pl.*; ~ **box** копи́лка; ~ **market** де́нежный ры́нок

(-нка); ~ **order** (де́нежный) почто́вый перево́д. **money-changer** *n.* меня́ла *m.* **moneyed** *adj.* бога́тый. **money-grubbing** *adj.* стяжа́тельский. **moneylender** *n.* ростовщи́к (-а́), -и́ца.

Mongol ['mɒŋg(ə)l] *n.* монго́л, ~ка; *adj.* монго́льский. **Mongolia** [mɒŋ'gəʊlɪə] *n.* Монго́лия.

mongoose ['mɒŋgu:s] *n.* мангу́ста.

mongrel ['mʌŋgr(ə)l, 'mɒŋ-] *adj.* нечистокро́вный, сме́шанный; *n.* дворня́жка; (*also fig.*) ублю́док (-дка).

monitor ['mɒnɪt(ə)r] *n.* (*school*) ста́роста *m.* (кла́сса); (*lizard*) вара́н; (*naut.*; *TV*) монито́р; (*of broadcasts etc.*) слуха́ч (-а́); (*of radioactivity*) дозиме́тр; *v.t.* проверя́ть *impf.*, прове́рить *pf.*; контроли́ровать *impf.*, про~ *pf.*; *v.i.* вести́ (веду́, -дёшь; вёл, -а́) *impf.* радиоперехва́т. **monitoring** *n.* радиоперехва́т; монито́ринг; ~ **station** ста́нция радиоперехва́та; **environmental** ~ монито́ринг за окружа́ющей средо́й.

monk [mʌŋk] *n.* мона́х.

monkey ['mʌŋkɪ] *n.* обезья́на; *v.i.*: ~ **(about) with** неуме́ло обраща́ться *impf.* c+*i.*; ~ **business** прока́за; ~ **tricks** ша́лости *f.pl.*; ~ **wrench** разводно́й га́ечный ключ (-а́). **monkey-jacket** *n.* коро́ткая (матро́сская) ку́ртка. **monkey-nut** *n.* земляно́й оре́х. **monkey-puzzle** *n.* араука́рия.

mono- ['mɒnəʊ] *in comb.* одно..., моно..., едино... . **monochrome** ['mɒnə,krəʊm] *adj.* одноцве́тный; *n.* однокра́сочное изображе́ние. **monocle** ['mɒnək(ə)l] *n.* моно́кль *m.* **monogamous** [mə'nɒgəməs] *adj.* единобра́чный. **mo'nogamy** *n.* единобра́чие. **'monogram** *n.* моногра́мма. **'monolith** *n.* моноли́т. **mono'lithic** *adj.* моноли́тный. **'monologue** *n.* моноло́г. **mono'mania** *n.* монома́ния. **mono'maniac** *n.* монома́н. **'monoplane** *n.* монопла́н. **mo'nopolist** *n.* монополи́ст. **mo'nopolize** *v.t.* монополизи́ровать *impf.* & *pf.* **mo'nopoly** *n.* монопо́лия. **'monorail** *n.* моноре́льсовая доро́га. **monosy'llabic** *adj.* односло́жный. **'monosyllable** *n.* односло́жное сло́во (*pl.* -ва́). **'monotheism** *n.* единобо́жие, монотеи́зм. **monothe'istic** *adj.* монотеисти́ческий. **'monotone** *n.* моното́нность; **in a** ~ моното́нно. **mo'notonous** *adj.* моното́нный, однообра́зный. **mo'notony** *n.* моното́нность, однообра́зие. **mo'noxide** *n.* одно́окись.

monsoon [mɒn'su:n] *n.* (*wind*) муссо́н; (*rainy season*) дождли́вый сезо́н.

monster ['mɒnstə(r)] *n.* чудо́вище, уро́д; *adj.* грома́дный. **monstrosity** [mɒn'strɒsɪtɪ] *n.* уро́дство, чудо́вищность; чудо́вище. **monstrous** *adj.* чудо́вищный; (*huge*) грома́дный; (*atrocious*) безобра́зный.

montage [mɒn'tɑ:ʒ] *n.* (*cin.*) монта́ж; (*of photographs*) фотомонта́ж.

Mont Blanc [mɒn'blɒŋk] *n.* Монбла́н.

month [mʌnθ] *n.* ме́сяц. **monthly** *adj.* ежеме́сячный, ме́сячный; *n.* ежеме́сячник; *adv.* ежеме́сячно.

monument ['mɒnjʊmənt] *n.* па́мятник. **monu'mental** *adj.* монумента́льный; (*stupendous*) изуми́тельный, колосса́льный.

moo [mu:] *v.i.* мыча́ть (-чу́, -чи́шь); *n.* мыча́ние.

mood[1] [mu:d] *n.* (*gram.*) наклоне́ние.

mood[2] [mu:d] *n.* настрое́ние. **moody** *adj.* уны́лый, в дурно́м настрое́нии.

moon [mu:n] *n.* (*of earth*) луна́; (*of other planets*) спу́тник; *v.i.* бесце́льно слоня́ться *impf.* **moonlight** *n.* лу́нный свет; *v.i.* халту́рить *impf.* **moonshine** *n.* фанта́зия; (*liquor*) самого́н. **moonstone** *n.* лу́нный ка́мень (-мня) *m.* **moonstruck** *adj.* поме́шанный (-ан).

Moor[1] [mʊə(r), mɔ:(r)] *n.* мавр. **Moorish** *adj.* маврита́нский.

moor[2] [mʊə(r), mɔ:(r)] *n.* ме́стность, поро́сшая ве́реском. **moorcock** *n.* саме́ц (-мца́) шотла́ндской куропа́тки. **moorhen** *n.* (*water-hen*) водяна́я ку́рочка. **moorland** *n.* ве́ресковая пу́стошь.

moor[3] [mʊə(r), mɔ:(r)] *v.t.* & *i.* швартова́ть(ся) *impf.*, при~ *pf.* **mooring** *n.*: *pl.* швартóвы *m.pl.*; (*place*) прича́л.

moose [mu:s] *n.* америка́нский лось (*pl.* -си, -се́й) *m.*

moot [mu:t] *adj.* спо́рный.

mop [mɒp] *n.* шва́бра; (*of hair*) копна́ воло́с; *v.t.* протира́ть *impf.*, протере́ть (-тру́, -трёшь; -тёр) *pf.* (шва́брой); ~ **one's brow** вытира́ть *impf.*, вы́тереть (-тру, -трешь; -тер) *pf.* лоб; ~ **up** вытира́ть *impf.*, вы́тереть (-тру, -трешь; -тер) *pf.*; (*mil.*) очища́ть *impf.*, очи́стить *pf.* (от проти́вника).

mope [məʊp] *v.i.* хандри́ть *impf.*

moped ['məʊped] *n.* мопе́д.

moraine [mə'reɪn] *n.* море́на.

moral ['mɒr(ə)l] *adj.* мора́льный, нра́вственный (-ен, -енна); *n.* мора́ль; *pl.* нра́вы *m.pl.*, нра́вственность. **morale** [mə'rɑ:l] *n.* мора́льное состоя́ние; (*of troops*) боево́й дух. **moralist** *n.* морали́ст, ~ка. **mora'listic** *adj.* моралисти́ческий. **morality** [mə'rælɪtɪ] *n.* нра́вственность, мора́ль. **moralize** *v.i.* морализи́ровать *impf.*

morass [mə'ræs] *n.* боло́то, тряси́на.

moratorium [,mɒrə'tɔ:rɪəm] *n.* морато́рий.

morbid ['mɔ:bɪd] *adj.* боле́зненный (-ен, -енна), нездоро́вый; (*med.*) патологи́ческий.

mordant ['mɔ:d(ə)nt] *adj.* е́дкий (е́док, едка́, е́дко).

more [mɔ:(r)] *adj.* (*larger*) бо́льший; (*greater quantity*) бо́льше+g.; (*additional*) ещё; *adv.* бо́льше; (*in addition*) ещё; (*forming comp.*) бо́лее; **and what is** ~ и вдоба́вок; и бо́льше того́; ~ **fool you** тем ху́же для тебя́; ~ **or less** бо́лее и́ли ме́нее; **once** ~ ещё раз; **what** ~ **do you want?** что ещё ты хо́чешь?; **without** ~ **ado** без дальне́йших церемо́ний.

mo'reover *adv.* сверх того́; кро́ме того́.
mores ['mɔːreɪz, -riːz] *n.* нра́вы *m.pl.*
morganatic [ˌmɔːgə'nætɪk] *adj.* морганати́ческий.
morgue [mɔːg] *n.* морг; (*journ.*) спра́вочный отде́л.
moribund ['mɒrɪˌbʌnd] *adj.* умира́ющий.
morning ['mɔːnɪŋ] *n.* у́тро; **in the ~s** по утра́м; **since ~** с утра́; **towards ~** к утру́; **until ~** до утра́; **at seven o'clock in the ~** в семь часо́в утра́; *attr.* у́тренний; **~ coat** визи́тка.
morocco [mə'rɒkəʊ] *n.* сафья́н; *attr.* сафья́новый.
moron ['mɔːrɒn] *n.* у́мственно отста́лый *sb.* **moronic** [mə'rɒnɪk] *adj.* отста́лый.
morose [mə'rəʊs] *adj.* угрю́мый.
morpheme ['mɔːfiːm] *n.* морфе́ма.
morphine ['mɔːfiːn] *n.* мо́рфий.
morphology [mɔː'fɒlədʒɪ] *n.* морфоло́гия.
Morse (code) [mɔːs] *n.* а́збука Мо́рзе.
morsel ['mɔːs(ə)l] *n.* кусо́чек (-чка).
mortal ['mɔːt(ə)l] *adj.* сме́ртный, смерте́льный; *n.* сме́ртный *sb.* **mortality** [mɔː'tælɪtɪ] *n.* смерте́льность; (*death-rate*) сме́ртность.
mortar ['mɔːtə(r)] *n.* (*vessel*) сту́па, сту́пка; (*cannon*) миномёт, морти́ра; (*cement*) (известко́вый) раство́р. **mortarboard** *n.* академи́ческая ша́почка.
mortgage ['mɔːgɪdʒ] *n.* ипоте́ка; (*deed*) закладна́я *sb.*; *v.t.* закла́дывать *impf.*, заложи́ть (-жу́, -жишь) *pf.*
mortification [ˌmɔːtɪfɪ'keɪʃ(ə)n] *n.* (*humiliation*) униже́ние; (*of the flesh*) умерщвле́ние. **mortify** ['mɔːtɪˌfaɪ] *v.t.* унижа́ть *impf.*, уни́зить *pf.*; умерщвля́ть *impf.*, умертви́ть (-рщвлю́, -ртви́шь) *pf.*
mortise ['mɔːtɪs] *n.* гнездо́ (*pl.* -ёзда), паз (*loc.* -у́; *pl.* -ы́); **~ lock** врезно́й замо́к (-мка́).
mortuary ['mɔːtjʊərɪ] *adj.* похоро́нний; *n.* морг, поко́йницкая *sb.*
mosaic [məʊ'zeɪɪk] *n.* моза́ика; *adj.* моза́ичный.
Moscow ['mɒskəʊ] *n.* Москва́; *attr.* моско́вский.
Moslem ['mɒzləm] *n.* мусульма́нин (*pl.* -а́не, -а́н), -а́нка; *adj.* мусульма́нский.
mosque [mɒsk] *n.* мече́ть.
mosquito [mɒs'kiːtəʊ] *n.* моски́т. **mosquito-net** *n.* моски́тная се́тка.
moss [mɒs] *n.* мох (м(о́)ха, *loc.* м(о́)хе & мху; *pl.* мхи). **moss-grown** *adj.* поро́сший мхом. **mossy** *adj.* мши́стый.
most [məʊst] *adj.* наибо́льший; *n.* наибо́льшее коли́чество; *adj.* & *n.* (*majority*) большинство́+*g.*; бо́льшая часть+*g.*; *adv.* бо́лше всего́, наибо́лее; (*forming superlative*) са́мый. **mostly** *adv.* гла́вным о́бразом.
MOT *abbr.* (*of* ***Ministry of Transport***) Министе́рство тра́нспорта; **~ (test)** листо́к (-тка́) техосмо́тра.
mote [məʊt] *n.* пыли́нка.
motel [məʊ'tel] *n.* моте́ль *m.*
moth [mɒθ] *n.* моль, ночна́я ба́бочка. **mothball** *n.* нафтали́новый ша́рик. **moth-eaten** *adj.* изъе́денный мо́лью.
mother ['mʌðə(r)] *n.* мать (-тери, *i.* -терью; *pl.* -тери, -тере́й); *v.t.* относи́ться (-ошу́сь, -о́сишься) *impf.* по-матери́нски к+*d.*; **~ country** метропо́лия; **~ tongue** родно́й язы́к (-а́). **motherhood** *n.* матери́нство. **mother-in-law** *n.* (*wife's* ~) тёща; (*husband's* ~) свекро́вь. **motherland** *n.* ро́дина. **motherless** *adj.* лишённый (-ён, -ена́) ма́тери. **motherly** *adj.* матери́нский. **mother-of-pearl** *n.* перламу́тр; *adj.* перламу́тровый.
motif [məʊ'tiːf] *n.* основна́я те́ма.
motion ['məʊʃ(ə)n] *n.* движе́ние, ход; (*gesture*) жест; (*proposal*) предложе́ние; (*of bowels*) испражне́ние; **in ~** в движе́нии, на ходу́; *v.t.* пока́зывать *impf.*, показа́ть (-ажу́, -а́жешь) *pf.*+*d.* же́стом, что́бы... . **motionless** *adj.* неподви́жный. **motivate** ['məʊtɪˌveɪt] *v.t.* побужда́ть *impf.*, побуди́ть *pf.* **moti'vation** *n.* побужде́ние. **motive** *n.* по́вод, моти́в; *adj.* дви́жущий, дви́гательный.
motley ['mɒtlɪ] *adj.* (*in colour*) разноцве́тный; (*varied*) пёстрый (-р, -а́, пёстро́); *n.* вся́кая вся́чина; (*costume*) шутовско́й костю́м.
motor ['məʊtə(r)] *n.* дви́гатель *m.*, мото́р; *adj.* дви́гательный, мото́рный; (*of* ~ *vehicles*) автомоби́льный; **~ boat** мото́рная ло́дка; **~ car** (легково́й) автомоби́ль *m.*; **~ cycle** мотоци́кл; **~ oil** *n.* авто́л; **~ racing** автомоби́льные го́нки *f.pl.*; **~ scooter** моторо́ллер; **~ show** *n.* автосало́н; **~ vehicle** автомоби́ль *m.* **motoring** *n.* автомобили́зм. **motorist** *n.* автомобили́ст, ~ка. **motorize** *v.t.* моторизова́ть *impf.* & *pf.* **motorway** *n.* автостра́да.
mottled ['mɒtəld] *adj.* испещрённый (-ён, -ена́), кра́пчатый.
motto ['mɒtəʊ] *n.* деви́з.
mould¹ [məʊld] *n.* (*earth*) взрыхлённая земля́ (*a.* -лю).
mould² [məʊld] *n.* (*shape*) фо́рма, фо́рмочка; *v.t.* формова́ть *impf.*, с~ *pf.*; лепи́ть (-плю́, -пишь) *impf.*, вы́~, с~ *pf.* **moulding** *n.* (*action*) формо́вка; (*decoration*) лепно́е украше́ние; (*in wood*) баге́т.
mould³ [məʊld] *n.* (*fungi*) пле́сень. **mouldy** *adj.* заплесневе́лый.
moulder ['məʊldə(r)] *v.i.* разлага́ться *impf.*, разложи́ться (-ится) *pf.*
moult [məʊlt] *v.i.* линя́ть *impf.*, вы́~ *pf.*; *n.* ли́нька.
mound [maʊnd] *n.* холм (-а́); (*heap*) на́сыпь.
Mount¹ [maʊnt] *n.* (*in names*) гора́ (*a.* -ру).
mount² [maʊnt] *v.t.* (*ascend*) поднима́ться *impf.*, подня́ться (-ниму́сь, -ни́мешься; -ня́лся́, -няла́сь) *pf.* на+*a.*; (~ *a horse etc.*) сади́ться *impf.*, сесть (ся́ду, -дешь; сел) *pf.* на+*a.*; (*picture*) накле́ивать *impf.*, накле́ить *pf.* на карто́н; (*gem*) вставля́ть *impf.*, вста́вить *pf.* в опра́ву; (*gun*) устана́вливать

impf., установи́ть (-влю́, -вишь) *pf.* на лафе́т; ~ **up** (*accumulate*) нака́пливаться *impf.*, накопи́ться (-ится) *pf.*; ~ **guard** стоя́ть (-ою́, -ои́шь) *impf.* на часа́х; *n.* (*for picture*) карто́н, подло́жка; (*for gem*) опра́ва; (*horse*) верхова́я ло́шадь (*pl.* -ди, -де́й; *i.* -дьми́).

mountain ['maʊntɪn] *n.* гора́ (*a.* -ру; *pl.* -ры, -р, -ра́м); *attr.* го́рный; ~ **ash** рябина. **mountai'neer** *n.* альпини́ст. **mountai'neering** *n.* альпини́зм. **mountainous** *adj.* гори́стый; (*huge*) грома́дный.

mountebank ['maʊntɪˌbæŋk] *n.* (*clown*) шут (-а́); (*charlatan*) шарлата́н.

mourn [mɔ:n] *v.t.* опла́кивать *impf.*, опла́кать (-а́чу, -а́чешь) *pf.*; *v.i.* скорбе́ть (-блю́, -би́шь) *impf.* (**over** о+*p.*). **mournful** *adj.* печа́льный, ско́рбный. **mourning** *n.* (*sorrow*) печа́ль; (*dress*) тра́ур.

mouse [maʊs] *n.* мышь (*pl.* -ши, -ше́й); *v.i.* лови́ть (-влю́, -вишь) *impf.*, пойма́ть *pf.* мыше́й. **mouser** *n.* мышело́в. **mousetrap** *n.* мышело́вка.

mousse [mu:s] *n.* мусс.

moustache [mə'stɑ:ʃ] *n.* усы́ (усо́в) *pl.*

mousy ['maʊsɪ] *adj.* мыши́ный; (*timid*) ро́бкий (-бок, -бка́, -бко).

mouth [maʊθ] *n.* рот (рта, *loc.* во рту́); (*poet.*) уста́ (-т) *pl.*; (*entrance*) вход; (*of river*) у́стье (*g.pl.* -в); (*of gun, volcano*) жерло́ (*pl.* -ла); ~ **to feed** едо́к (-а́); **by word of** ~ у́стно; *v.t.* говори́ть *impf.*, сказа́ть (-ажу́, -а́жешь) *pf.* напы́щенно. **mouthful** *n.* по́лный рот (рта); (*small amount*) кусо́к (-ска́), глото́к (-тка́). **mouth-organ** *n.* губна́я гармо́ника. **mouthpiece** *n.* мундшту́к (-а́); (*person*) ру́пор.

movable ['mu:vəb(ə)l] *adj.* подвижно́й; (*property*) дви́жимый.

move [mu:v] *n.* (*in game*) ход (-а(у); *pl.* ходы́); (*change of location*) переме́на ме́ста; (*step*) шаг (*loc.* -у́; *pl.* -и́); *v.t.* & *i.* дви́гать(ся) (-аю(сь), -аешь(ся) & дви́жу(сь), -жешь(ся)) *impf.*, дви́нуться *pf.*; *v.t.* (*affect*) тро́гать *impf.*, тро́нуть *pf.*; (*propose*) вноси́ть (-ошу́, -о́сишь) *impf.*, внести́ (внесу́, -сёшь; внёс, -ла́) *pf.*; *v.i.* (*events*) развива́ться *impf.*, разви́ться (разовьётся; разви́лся, -ила́сь, -и́ло́сь) *pf.*; (~ *house*) переезжа́ть *impf.*, перее́хать (-е́ду, -е́дешь) *pf.*; ~ **away** (*v.i.*) уезжа́ть *impf.*, уе́хать (уе́ду, -дешь) *pf.*; ~ **in** въезжа́ть *impf.*, въе́хать (-е́ду, -е́дешь) *pf.*; ~ **on** идти́ (иду́, идёшь; шёл, шла) *impf.*, пойти́ (пойду́, -дёшь; пошёл, -шла́) *pf.* да́льше; ~ **on!** проходи́те (да́льше)!; ~ **out** съезжа́ть *impf.*, съе́хать (-е́ду, -е́дешь) *pf.* (**of** с+*g.*). **movement** *n.* движе́ние; (*mus.*) часть (*pl.* -ти, -те́й). **moving** *n.* дви́жущийся; (*touching*) тро́гательный; ~ **staircase** эскала́тор.

mow [məʊ] *v.t.* (*also* ~ *down*) коси́ть (кошу́, ко́сишь) *impf.*, с~ *pf.* **mower** *n.* (*person*) косе́ц (-сца́); (*machine*) коси́лка.

MP *abbr.* (*of* ***Member of Parliament***) чле́н парла́мента.

mpg *abbr.* (*of* ***miles per gallon***) ми́ли на галло́н бензи́на.

mph *abbr.* (*of* ***miles per hour***) (*сто́лько-то*) миль в час.

Mr *abbr.* (*of* **mister**) г-н, господи́н, *pl.* -а́; ми́стер.

Mrs ['mɪsɪz] *abbr.* (*of* **mistress**) г-жа, госпожа́; ми́ссис *f.indecl.*

MS *abbr.* (*of* **manuscript**) ру́копись; (*of* ***multiple sclerosis***) рассе́янный *or* мно́жественный склеро́з.

Ms [mɪz, məz] миз, г-жа, госпожа́.

M.Sc. *abbr.* (*of* ***Master of Science***) маги́стр (есте́ственных) нау́к.

Mt. *abbr.* (*of* **Mount, mountain**) г, гора́.

much [mʌtʃ] *adj.* & *n.* мно́го+*g.*; мно́гое *sb.*; *adv.* о́чень (*with comp.adj.*) гора́здо.

muck [mʌk] *n.* (*dung*) наво́з; (*dirt*) грязь (*loc.* -зи́); *v.t.* (*dirty*) па́чкать *impf.*, за~, ис~ *pf.*; ~ **out** чи́стить *impf.*, вы́~ *pf.*; ~ **up** изга́живать *impf.*, изга́дить *pf.*

mucous ['mju:kəs] *adj.* сли́зистый. **mucus** ['mju:kəs] *n.* слизь.

mud [mʌd] *n.* грязь (*loc.* -зи́). **mudguard** *n.* крыло́ (*pl.* -лья, -льев). **mudslinger** ['mʌdslɪŋə(r)] *n.* клеветни́к (-а́).

muddle ['mʌd(ə)l] *v.t.* пу́тать *impf.*, с~ *pf.*; *v.i.*: ~ **along** де́йствовать *impf.* наобу́м; ~ **through** ко́е-как доводи́ть (-ожу́, -о́дишь) *impf.*, довести́ (-еду́, -едёшь; -ёл, -ела́) *pf.* де́ло до конца́; *n.* неразбери́ха, пу́таница. **muddle -headed** *adj.* бестолко́вый.

muddy ['mʌdɪ] *adj.* гря́зный (-зен, -зна́, -зно); (*of liquid*) му́тный (-тен, -тна́, -тно); (*of light*) ту́склый (-л, -ла́, -ло); *v.t.* обры́згивать *impf.*, обры́згать *pf.* гря́зью; (*water*) мути́ть (мучу́, му́ти́шь) *impf.*, вз~, за~ *pf.*

muezzin [mu:'ezɪn] *n.* муэдзи́н.

muff [mʌf] *n.* му́фта.

muffle ['mʌf(ə)l] *v.t.* заку́тывать *impf.*, заку́тать *pf.*; (*sound*) глуши́ть *impf.*, за~ *pf.*; ~**d oars** обмо́танные вёсла (*g.* -сел) *nt.pl.* **muffler** *n.* кашне́ *nt.indecl.*, шарф.

mufti ['mʌftɪ] *n.*: **in** ~ в шта́тском.

mug [mʌg] *n.* (*vessel*) кру́жка; (*face*) мо́рда; *v.t.* напада́ть, напа́сть (-аду́, -адёшь; -а́л) на+*a.* **mugger** *n.* у́личный граби́тель *m.* **mugging** *n.* у́личное ограбле́ние.

muggy ['mʌgɪ] *adj.* сыро́й (сыр, -а́, -о) и тёплый (-пел, -пла́).

mulatto [mju:'lætəʊ] *n.* мула́т, ~ка.

mulberry ['mʌlbərɪ] *n.* (*tree*) шелкови́ца, ту́товое де́рево (*pl.* -е́вья, -е́вьев); (*fruit*) ту́товая я́года.

mulch [mʌltʃ, mʌlʃ] *n.* му́льча; *v.t.* мульчи́ровать *impf.* & *pf.* **mulching** *n.* мульчи́рование.

mule [mju:l] *n.* мул. **mule'teer** *n.* пого́нщик му́лов. **mulish** *adj.* упря́мый как осёл.

mull [mʌl] *v.t.* подогрева́ть *impf.*, подогре́ть *pf.* с пря́ностями; ~**ed wine** глинтве́йн.

mullah ['mʌlə] *n.* мулла́ *m.*

mullet ['mʌlɪt] *n.* (*grey* ~) кефа́ль; (*red* ~) барабу́лька.

mullion ['mʌljən] *n.* сре́дник.

multi- ['mʌltɪ] *in comb.* много... . **multicoloured** *adj.* многокра́сочный. **multifarious** [ˌmʌltɪ'feərɪəs] *adj.* разнообра́зный. **multilateral** *adj.* многосторо́нний. **multimillionaire** *n.* мультимиллионе́р. **multi-purpose** *adj.* универса́льный, многоцелево́й. **multiracial** *adj.* многора́совый. **multistorey** *adj.* многоэта́жный. **multivitamins** *n.* поливитами́ны (-ов) *pl.*

multiple ['mʌltɪp(ə)l] *adj.* составно́й, сло́жный (-жен, -жна́, -жно); (*varied*) разнообра́зный; (*numerous*) многочи́сленный; (*math.*) кра́тный; ~ **sclerosis** рассе́янный склеро́з; ~ **shop** магази́н с филиа́лами; *n.* кра́тное число́ (*pl.* -сла, -сел, -слам); **least common** ~ о́бщее наиме́ньшее кра́тное *sb.* **multiplication** [ˌmʌltɪplɪ'keɪʃ(ə)n] *n.* размноже́ние; (*math.*) умноже́ние. **multi'plicity** *n.* многочи́сленность, многообра́зие. **multiply** ['mʌltɪˌplaɪ] *v.t.* & *i.* размножа́ть(ся) *impf.*, размно́жить(ся) *pf.*; *v.t.* (*math.*) умножа́ть *impf.*, умно́жить *pf.*

multitude ['mʌltɪˌtjuːd] *n.* мно́жество; (*crowd*) толпа́ (*pl.* -пы).

mum[1] [mʌm] *adj.*: ~**'s the word!** (об э́том) ни гугу́!; **keep** ~ молча́ть (-чу́, -чи́шь) *impf.*

mum[2] [mʌm] *n.* (*mother*) ма́ма.

mumble ['mʌmb(ə)l] *v.t.* & *i.* мя́млить *impf.*, про~ *pf.*

mummify ['mʌmɪˌfaɪ] *v.t.* мумифици́ровать *impf.* & *pf.* **mummy**[1] *n.* му́мия.

mummy[2] ['mʌmɪ] *n.* (*mother*) ма́ма, ма́мочка.

mumps [mʌmps] *n.* сви́нка.

munch [mʌntʃ] *v.t.* жева́ть (жую́, жуёшь) *impf.*

mundane [mʌn'deɪn] *adj.* земно́й.

Munich ['mjuːnɪk] *n.* Мю́нхен.

municipal [mjuː'nɪsɪp(ə)l] *adj.* муниципа́льный, городско́й. **municipality** [mjuːˌnɪsɪ'pælɪtɪ] *n.* муниципалите́т.

munificence [mjuː'nɪfɪs(ə)ns] *n.* ще́дрость. **munificent** *adj.* ще́дрый (щедр, -а́, -о).

munitions [mjuː'nɪʃ(ə)ns] *n.* вое́нное иму́щество.

mural ['mjʊər(ə)l] *adj.* стенно́й; *n.* стенна́я ро́спись.

murder ['mɜːdə(r)] *n.* уби́йство; *v.t.* убива́ть *impf.*, уби́ть (убью́, -ьёшь) *pf.*; (*language*) кове́ркать *impf.*, ис~ *pf.* **murderer, murderess** *n.* уби́йца *c.g.* **murderous** *adj.* уби́йственный (-ен, -енна), смертоно́сный.

murky ['mɜːkɪ] *adj.* тёмный (-мен, -мна́), мра́чный (-чен, -чна́, -чно).

murmur ['mɜːmə(r)] *n.* (*of water*) журча́ние; (*of voices*) шёпот; (*of discontent*) ро́пот; **without a** ~ безро́потно; *v.i.* журча́ть (-чи́т) *impf.*; ропта́ть (ропщу́, -щешь) *impf.* (**at** на+*a.*); *v.t.* шепта́ть (шепчу́, -чешь) *impf.*, шепну́ть *pf.*

muscle ['mʌs(ə)l] *n.* мы́шца, му́скул. **muscular** *adj.* мы́шечный, му́скульный; (*person*) му́скулистый.

Muscovite ['mʌskəˌvaɪt] *n.* москви́ч (-а́), ~ка.

muse[1] [mjuːz] *v.i.* размышля́ть *impf.*

muse[2] [mjuːz] *n.* му́за.

museum [mjuː'zɪəm] *n.* музе́й.

mushroom ['mʌʃrʊm, -ruːm] *n.* гриб (-а́); (*cultivated*) шампиньо́н; ~ **cloud** грибови́дное о́блако (*pl.* -ка́, -ко́в).

music ['mjuːzɪk] *n.* му́зыка; (*sheet* ~) но́ты *f.pl.*; **play without** ~ игра́ть *impf.*, сыгра́ть *pf.* без нот; ~ **stand** пюпи́тр. **musical** *adj.* музыка́льный; ~ **comedy** музыка́льная коме́дия; *n.* музыка́льная (кино)коме́дия. **musician** [mjuː'zɪʃ(ə)n] *n.* музыка́нт; (*composer*) компози́тор. **music-hall** *n.* мю́зик-хо́лл. **musi'cologist** *n.* музыкове́д. **musi'cology** *n.* музыкове́дение. **music-paper** *n.* но́тная бума́га.

musk [mʌsk] *n.* му́скус; ~ **deer** кабарга́ (*g.pl.* -ро́г); ~ **melon** ды́ня.

musket ['mʌskɪt] *n.* мушке́т. **muske'teer** *n.* мушкетёр.

muskrat ['mʌskræt] *n.* онда́тра.

musky ['mʌskɪ] *adj.* му́скусный.

muslin ['mʌzlɪn] *n.* мусли́н, кисея́; *adj.* мусли́новый, кисе́йный.

mussel ['mʌs(ə)l] *n.* съедо́бная ми́дия.

must[1] [mʌst] *n.* муст; (*new wine*) молодо́е вино́.

must[2] [mʌst] *v.aux.* (*obligation*) до́лжен (-жна́) *pred.*+*inf.*; на́до *impers.*+*d.* & *inf.*; (*necessity*) ну́жно *impers.*+*d.* & *inf.*; ~ **not** (*prohibition*) нельзя́ *impers.*+*d.* & *inf.*; *n.* необходи́мость.

mustard ['mʌstəd] *n.* горчи́ца; ~ **gas** горчи́чный газ; ~ **plaster** горчи́чник; ~ **pot** горчи́чница.

musty ['mʌstɪ] *adj.* за́тхлый.

mutant ['mjuːt(ə)nt] *adj.* мута́нтный; *n.* мута́нт. **mu'tation** *n.* мута́ция.

mute [mjuːt] *adj.* (*dumb*) немо́й (нем, -а́. -о); (*silent*) безмо́лвный; *n.* немо́й *sb.*; (*mus.*) сурди́нка. **muted** *adj.* приглушённый (-ён, -ена́); **with** ~ **strings** под сурди́нку.

mutilate ['mjuːtɪˌleɪt] *v.t.* уве́чить *impf.*, из~ *pf.*; кале́чить *impf.*, ис~ *pf.* **muti'lation** *n.* уве́чье.

mutineer [ˌmjuːtɪ'nɪə(r)] *n.* мяте́жник. **'mutinous** *adj.* мяте́жный. **'mutiny** *n.* мяте́ж (-а́); *v.i.* бунтова́ть *impf.*, взбунтова́ться *pf.*

mutism ['mjuːtɪz(ə)m] *n.* немота́.

mutter ['mʌtə(r)] *v.i.* бормота́ть (-очу́, -о́чешь) *impf.*; ворча́ть (-чу́, -чи́шь) *impf.*; *n.* бормота́ние, ворча́ние.

mutton ['mʌt(ə)n] *n.* бара́нина.

mutual ['mjuːtʃʊəl, -tjʊəl] *adj.* взаи́мный, взаимо...; (*common*) о́бщий; ~ **benefit** ка́сса взаимопо́мощи; ~ **friend** о́бщий друг (*pl.* друзья́, -зе́й).

muzzle ['mʌz(ə)l] *n.* (*animal's*) мо́рда; (*on animal*) намо́рдник; (*of gun*) ду́ло; *v.t.* надева́ть *impf.*, наде́ть (-е́ну, -е́нешь) *pf.* намо́рдник на+*a.*; (*impose silence*) заставля́ть

impf., заста́вить *pf.* молча́ть.
muzzy ['mʌzɪ] *adj.* тума́нный (-нен, -нна).
MW *abbr.* (*of* **megawatt(s)**) МВт, мегава́тт.
my [maɪ] *poss.pron.* мой (моя́, моё; мои́); свой (своя́, своё; свои́).
myopia [maɪ'əʊpɪə] *n.* близору́кость. **myopic** [maɪ'ɒpɪk] *adj.* близору́кий.
myriad ['mɪrɪəd] *n.* мириа́ды (-д) *pl.*; *adj.* бесчи́сленный (-ен, -енна).
myrrh [mɜː(r)] *n.* ми́рра.
myrtle ['mɜːt(ə)l] *n.* мирт; *attr.* ми́ртовый.
myself [maɪ'self] *pron.* (*emph.*) (я) сам (-ого́, -ому́, -и́м, -о́м), сама́ (-мо́й, *a.* -му́); (*refl.*) себя́ (себе́, собо́й); -ся (*suffixed to v.t.*).
mysterious [mɪ'stɪərɪəs] *adj.* таи́нственный (-ен, -енна). **mystery** ['mɪstərɪ] *n.* та́йна; (*relig. rite*; *play*) мисте́рия.
mystic(al) ['mɪstɪk(ə)l] *adj.* мисти́ческий; *n.* ми́стик. **mysticism** *n.* мистици́зм. **mystifi'cation** *n.* мистифика́ция. **mystify** ['mɪstɪˌfaɪ] *v.t.* озада́чивать *impf.*, озада́чить *pf.*
myth [mɪθ] *n.* миф. **mythical** *adj.* мифи́ческий. **mytho'logical** *adj.* мифологи́ческий. **my'thologist** *n.* мифо́лог. **my'thology** *n.* мифоло́гия.

N

nacre ['neɪkə(r)] *n.* перламу́тр. **nacr(e)ous** *adj.* перламу́тровый.
nadir ['neɪdɪə(r), 'næd-] *n.* нади́р; (*lowest point*) са́мый ни́зкий у́ровень (-вня) *m.*
nag¹ [næg] *n.* (*horse*) ло́шадь (*pl.* -ди, -де́й, *i.* -дьми́).
nag² [næg] *v.i.*: ~ **at** пили́ть (-лю́, -лишь) *impf.+a.*; (*of pain*) ныть (но́ет) *impf.*
naiad ['naɪæd] *n.* ная́да.
nail [neɪl] *n.* (*finger-*, *toe-~*) но́готь (-гтя; *pl.* -гти, -гте́й) *m.*; (*claw*) ко́готь (-гтя; *pl.* -гти, -гте́й) *m.*; (*metal spike*) гвоздь (-дя́; *pl.* -ди, -де́й) *m.*; ~ **varnish** лак для ногте́й; *v.t.* прибива́ть *impf.*, приби́ть (-бью́, -бьёшь) *pf.* (гвоздя́ми). **nail-brush** *n.* щёточка для ногте́й. **nail-file** *n.* пи́лка для ногте́й. **nail-scissors** *n.* но́жницы (-ц) *pl.* для ногте́й.
naive [nɑː'iːv, naɪ'iːv] *adj.* наи́вный. **naivety** *n.* наи́вность.
naked ['neɪkɪd] *adj.* го́лый (гол, -а́, -о), наго́й (наг, -а́, -о); обнажённый (-ён, -ена́); ~ **eye** невооружённый глаз; ~ **light** незащищённый свет; ~ **sword** обнажённый меч (-а́); ~ **truth** чи́стая пра́вда. **nakedness** *n.* нагота́.
name [neɪm] *n.* назва́ние; (*forename*) и́мя *nt.*; (*surname*) фами́лия; (*reputation*) репута́ция; **what is his ~?** как его́ зову́т?; **in the ~ of** во и́мя+*g.*; *v.t.* называ́ть *impf.*, назва́ть (назову́, -вёшь; назва́л, -а́, -о) *pf.*; (*appoint*) назнача́ть *impf.*, назна́чить *pf.* **name-day** *n.* имени́ны (-н) *pl.* **nameless** *adj.* безымя́нный. **namely** *adv.* (а) и́менно; то есть. **name-part** *n.* загла́вная роль. **name-plate** *n.* доще́чка с фами́лией. **namesake** *n.* тёзка *c.g.*
nanny ['nænɪ] *n.* ня́ня. **nanny-goat** *n.* коза́ (*pl.* -зы).
nap¹ [næp] *n.* (*sleep*) коро́ткий сон (сна); *v.i.* вздремну́ть *pf.*
nap² [næp] *n.* (*on cloth*) ворс.
napalm ['neɪpɑːm] *n.* напа́лм.
nape [neɪp] *n.* загри́вок (-вка)
napkin ['næpkɪn] *n.* салфе́тка.
Naples ['neɪp(ə)lz] *n.* Неа́поль (*m.*).
narcissus [nɑː'sɪsəs] *n.* нарци́сс.
narcosis [nɑː'kəʊsɪs] *n.* нарко́з. **narcotic** [nɑː'kɒtɪk] *adj.* наркоти́ческий; *n.* нарко́тик.
nark [nɑːk] *n.* (*spy*) лега́вый *sb.*, стука́ч (-а́); *v.t.* (*irritate*) раздража́ть *impf.*, раздражи́ть *pf.*
narrate [nə'reɪt] *v.t.* расска́зывать *impf.*, рассказа́ть (-ажу́, -а́жешь) *pf.*; повествова́ть *impf.* о+*p.* **narration** *n.* повествова́ние. **narrative** ['nærətɪv] *n.* расска́з, по́весть (*pl.* -ти, -те́й); *adj.* повествова́тельный. **narrator** *n.* расска́зчик, повествова́тель *m.*
narrow ['nærəʊ] *adj.* у́зкий (у́зок, узка́, у́зко; у́зки́), те́сный (-сен, -сна́, -сно); (*restricted*) ограни́ченный (-ен, -енна); *n.*: *pl.* у́зкая часть; (*strait*) у́зкий проли́в; *v.t. & i.* су́живать(ся) *impf.*, су́зить(ся) *pf.* **narrow-gauge** *adj.* узкоколе́йный. **narrowly** *adv.* (*hardly*) чуть, е́ле-е́ле; **he ~ escaped drowning** он чуть не утону́л. **narrow-minded** *adj.* ограни́ченный (-ен, -енна). **narrowness** *n.* у́зость, ограни́ченность.
narwhal ['nɑːw(ə)l] *n.* нарва́л.
NASA ['næsə] *abbr.* (*of* ***National Aeronautics and Space Administration***) НАСА.
nasal ['neɪz(ə)l] *adj.* носово́й; (*voice*) гнуса́вый.
nascent ['næs(ə)nt, 'neɪs-] *adj.* рожда́ющийся.
nasturtium [nə'stɜːʃəm] *n.* насту́рция.
nasty ['nɑːstɪ] *adj.* га́дкий (-док, -дка́, -дко), проти́вный; (*dirty*) гря́зный (-зен, -зна́, -зно); (*person*) зло́бный.
nation ['neɪʃ(ə)n] *n.* на́ция; (*people*) наро́д; (*country*) страна́ (*pl.* -ны). **national** ['næʃən(ə)l] *adj.* национа́льный, наро́дный; (*of the state*) госуда́рственный; *n.* по́дданный *sb.* **nationalism** *n.* национали́зм. **nationalist** *n.* национали́ст, ~ка. **nationa'listic** *adj.* националисти́ческий. **natio'nality** *n.* национа́льность; (*citizenship*) гражда́нство, по́дданство. **nationali'zation** *n.* национализа́ция. **nationalize** *v.t.* национализи́ровать *impf.* & *pf.*
native ['neɪtɪv] *n.* (~ *of*) уроже́нец (-нца), -нка (+*g.*); тузе́мец (-мца), -мка; *adj.* (*natural*) приро́дный; (*of one's birth*) родно́й; (*indig-

enous) тузéмный; (*local*) мéстный; ~ **land** рóдина; ~ **language** роднóй язы́к; ~ **speaker** носи́тель *m.* языкá.

nativity [nəˈtɪvɪtɪ] *n.* Рождествó (Христóво).

NATO [ˈneɪtəʊ] *abbr.* (*of* ***North Atlantic Treaty Organization***) НАТО; ~ **member** нáтовец; *adj.* нáтовский.

natter [ˈnætə(r)] *v.i.* болтáть *impf.*; *n.* болтовня́.

natural [ˈnætʃər(ə)l] *adj.* естéственный (-ен, -енна), прирóдный; ~ **death** естéственная смерть; ~ **resources** прирóдные богáтства *nt.pl.*; ~ **selection** естéственный отбóр; *n.* (*person*) саморóдок (-дка); (*mus.*) бекáр. **naturalism** *n.* натурали́зм. **naturalist** *n.* натурали́ст. **natura'listic** *adj.* натуралисти́ческий. **naturali'zation** *n.* (*of alien*) натурализáция; (*of plant, animal*) акклиматизáция. **naturalize** *v.t.* натурализи́ровать *impf.* & *pf.*; акклиматизи́ровать *impf.* & *pf.* **naturally** *adv.* естéственно, по прирóде; (*of course*) конéчно, как и слéдовало ожидáть. **nature** [ˈneɪtʃə(r)] *n.* прирóда; (*character*) харáктер; **by** ~ по прирóде; **in the** ~ **of** врóде+*g.*; **second** ~ вторáя натýра; **state of** ~ первобы́тное состоя́ние; ~ **reserve** заповéдник. **naturopath** [ˌneɪtʃərəˈpæθ] *n.* натуропáт. **naturopathy** [ˌneɪtʃəˈrɒpəθɪ] *n.* натуропáтия.

naughtiness [ˈnɔːtɪnɪs] *n.* (*disobedience*) непослушáние; (*mischief*) шáлости *f.pl.* **naughty** *adj.* непослýшный; шаловли́вый.

nausea [ˈnɔːzɪə, -sɪə] *n.* тошнотá; (*loathing*) отвращéние. **nauseate** *v.t.* тошни́ть *impf. impers.* от+*g.*; быть проти́вным+*d.*; **the idea ~s me** меня́ тошни́т от э́той мы́сли; э́та мысль мне проти́вна. **nauseous** *adj.* тошнотвóрный; (*loathsome*) отврати́тельный.

nautical [ˈnɔːtɪk(ə)l] *n.* морскóй.

naval [ˈneɪv(ə)l] *adj.* (воéнно-)морскóй, флóтский.

nave [neɪv] *n.* неф.

navel [ˈneɪv(ə)l] *n.* пупóк (-пкá).

navigable [ˈnævɪgəb(ə)l] *adj.* судохóдный. **navigate** *v.t.* (*ship*) вести́ (ведý, -дёшь; вёл, -á) *impf.*; (*sea*) плáвать *impf.* **navi'gation** *n.* навигáция. **navigator** *n.* штýрман.

navvy [ˈnævɪ] *n.* землекóп.

navy [ˈneɪvɪ] *n.* воéнно-морскóй флот (*pl.* -óты, -óтов); ~ **blue** тёмно-си́ний.

Nazi [ˈnɑːtsɪ, ˈnɑːzɪ] *n.* наци́ст, ~ка; *adj.* наци́стский. **Nazism** *n.* наци́зм.

NB *abbr.* (*of* ***nota bene***) нотабéне.

near [nɪə(r)] *adv.* бли́зко, недалекó; **far and** ~ повсю́ду; ~ **at hand** под рукóй; ~ **by** ря́дом; *prep.* вóзле+*g.*, óколо+*g.*, у+*g.*; *adj.* бли́зкий; ~ **miss** бли́зкий прóмах; *v.t.* & *i.*, приближáться *impf.*, прибли́зиться *pf.* к+*d.*; подходи́ть (-ожý, -óдишь) *impf.*, подойти́ (-ойдý, -ойдёшь; -ошёл, -ошлá) *pf.* к+*d.*

nearly [ˈnɪəlɪ] *adv.* почти́, приблизи́тельно.

near-sighted [nɪəˈsaɪtɪd] *adj.* близорýкий.

neat [niːt] *adj.* (*tidy*) опря́тный, аккурáтный; (*clear*) чёткий (-ток, -ткá, -тко); (*undiluted*) неразбáвленный (-ен, -енá).

nebula [ˈnebjʊlə] *n.* тумáнность. **nebular** *adj.* небуля́рный. **nebulous** *adj.* нея́сный (-сен, -снá, -сно), тумáнный (-нен, -нна).

necessarily [ˈnesəsərɪlɪ, -ˈserɪlɪ] *adv.* неизбéжно. **'necessary** *adj.* нýжный (-жен, -жнá, -жно, -жны́), необходи́мый; (*inevitable*) неизбéжный; *n.* необходи́мое *sb.* **ne'cessitate** *v.t.* дéлать *impf.*, с~ *pf.* необходи́мым; (*involve*) влечь (-ечёт, -екýт; влёк, -лá) *impf.* за собóй. **ne'cessity** *n.* необходи́мость; неизбéжность; (*object*) предмéт пéрвой необходи́мости; (*poverty*) нуждá.

neck [nek] *n.* шéя; (*of garment*) вы́рез; (*of bottle*) гóрлышко (*pl.* -шки, -шек, -шкам); (*isthmus*) перешéек (-éйка); **get it in the** ~ получи́ть *pf.* по шée; **risk one's** ~ рисковáть *impf.* головóй; **up to one's** ~ по гóрло, пó ýши; ~ **and** ~ головá в гóлову; ~ **or nothing** ли́бо пан, ли́бо пропáл. **neckband** *n.* вóрот. **neckerchief** *n.* шéйный платóк (-ткá). **necklace** [ˈnekləs, -lɪs] *n.* ожерéлье (*g.pl.* -лий). **necklet** *n.* ожерéлье (*g.pl.* -лий); (*fur*) горжéтка. **neckline** *n.* вы́рез. **necktie** *n.* гáлстук.

necromancer [ˈnekrəʊˌmænsə(r)] *n.* колдýн (-á). **necromancy** *n.* чёрная мáгия, колдовствó.

nectar [ˈnektə(r)] *n.* нектáр.

née [neɪ] *adj.* урождённая.

need [niːd] *n.* нуждá, нáдобность, потрéбность; *v.t.* нуждáться *impf.* в+*p.*; **I** (*etc.*) ~ мне (*d.*) нýжен+*nom.*; **I** ~ **five roubles** мне нýжно пять рублéй.

needle [ˈniːd(ə)l] *n.* иглá (*pl.* -лы), игóлка; (*knitting*) спи́ца; (*pointer*) стрéлка; *pl.* (*pine-*~) хвóя; *v.t.* раздражáть *impf.*, раздражи́ть *pf.*

needless [ˈniːdlɪs] *adj.* ненýжный, изли́шний; ~ **to say** не прихóдится и говори́ть. **needy** *adj.* нуждáющийся, бéдствующий.

negation [nɪˈgeɪʃ(ə)n] *n.* отрицáние. **negative** [ˈnegətɪv] *adj.* отрицáтельный; негати́вный; ~ **quantity** отрицáтельная величинá; ~ **result** негати́вный результáт; *n.* отрицáние; (*gram.*) отрицáтельное слóво (*pl.* -вá); (*phot.*) негати́в; **in the** ~ отрицáтельно; отрицáтельный.

neglect [nɪˈglekt] *v.t.* пренебрегáть *impf.*, пренебрéчь (-егý, -ежёшь; -ёг, -еглá) *pf.*+*i.*; не забóтиться *impf.* о+*p.*; (*abandon*) забрáсывать *impf.*, забрóсить *pf.*; (*not fulfil*) не выполня́ть *impf.*+*g.*; *n.* пренебрежéние; (*condition*) забрóшенность. **neglectful** *adj.* небрéжный, невнимáтельный (**of** к+*d.*). **negligence** [ˈneglɪdʒ(ə)ns] *n.* небрéжность, неради́вость. **negligent** *adj.* небрéжный, неради́вый. **negligible** *adj.* незначи́тельный.

negotiate [nɪˈgəʊʃɪˌeɪt] *v.i.* вести́ (ведý, -дёшь; вёл, -á) *impf.* переговóры; *v.t.* (*arrange*) заключáть *impf.*, заключи́ть *pf.*; (*overcome*) преодолевáть *impf.*, преодолéть *pf.*

negoti'ation *n.* (*discussion*) перегово́ры *m.pl.*
Negress ['ni:grɪs] *n.* негритя́нка. **Negro** *n.* негр; *adj.* негритя́нский.
neigh [neɪ] *n.* ржа́ние; *v.i.* ржать (ржу, ржёшь) *impf.*
neighbour ['neɪbə(r)] *n.* сосе́д (*pl.* -и, -ей), ~ка. **neighbourhood** *n.* (*vicinity*) сосе́дство; (*area*) ме́стность; **in the ~ of** о́коло+*g.* **neighbouring** *adj.* сосе́дний. **neighbourly** *adj.* добрососе́дский.
neither ['naɪðə(r), 'ni:ð-] *adv.* та́кже не, то́же не; *pron.* ни тот, ни друго́й; **~ ... nor** ни... ни.
nemesis ['nemɪsɪs] *n.* возме́здие.
neocolonialism [ˌni:əʊkə'ləʊnɪəˌlɪz(ə)m] *n.* неоколониали́зм.
neolithic [ˌni:ə'lɪθɪk] *adj.* неолити́ческий.
neologism [ni:'ɒlədʒˌɪz(ə)m] *n.* неологи́зм.
neon ['ni:ɒn] *n.* нео́н; *attr.* нео́новый.
nephew ['nevju:, 'nef-] *n.* племя́нник.
nepotism ['nepəˌtɪz(ə)m] *n.* кумовство́.
Neptune ['neptju:n] *n.* Непту́н.
nerve [nɜ:v] *n.* нерв; (*assurance*) самооблада́ние; (*impudence*) на́глость; *pl.* (*nervousness*) нерво́зность; **get on the ~s of** де́йствовать *impf.*, по~ *pf.*+*d.* на не́рвы. **nerveless** *adj.* бесси́льный. **nervous** *adj.* не́рвный (не́рвен, не́рвна́, не́рвно); **~ breakdown** не́рвное расстро́йство. **nervy** *adj.* нерво́зный.
nest [nest] *n.* гнездо́ (*pl.* -ёзда); **~ egg** сбереже́ния *nt.pl.*; *v.i.* гнезди́ться *impf.*; вить (вью, вьёшь; вил, -а́, -о) *impf.*, свить (совью́, -ьёшь; свил, -а́, -о) *pf.* (себе́) гнездо́. **nestle** ['nes(ə)l] *v.i.* льнуть *impf.*, при~ *pf.* **nestling** ['neslɪŋ, 'nest-] *n.* птене́ц (-нца́).
net[1] [net] *n.* сеть (*loc.* сети́; *pl.* -ти, -те́й), се́тка; *v.t.* (*catch*) лови́ть (-влю́, -вишь) *impf.*, пойма́ть *pf.* сетя́ми; (*cover*) закрыва́ть *impf.*, закры́ть (-ро́ю, -ро́ешь) *pf.* се́ткой.
net[2] [net], **nett** *adj.* не́тто; *indecl.* чи́стый (чист, -а́, -о, чи́сты́); **~ price** цена́ не́тто; **~ profit** чи́стая при́быль; **~ weight** чи́стый вес, вес не́тто; *v.t.* получа́ть *impf.*, получи́ть (-чу́, -чишь) *pf.* ... чи́стого дохо́да.
Netherlands ['neðələndz] *n.* Нидерла́нды (-ов) *pl.*
nettle ['net(ə)l] *n.* крапи́ва; *v.t.* (*fig.*) раздража́ть *impf.*, раздражи́ть *pf.* **nettle-rash** *n.* крапи́вница.
network ['netwɜ:k] *n.* сеть (*loc.* сети́; *pl.* -ти, -те́й).
neuralgia [njʊə'rældʒə] *n.* невралги́я. **neurasthenia** [ˌnjʊərəs'θi:nɪə] *n.* неврастени́я. **neuritis** *n.* неври́т. **neurologist** *n.* невро́лог. **neurology** *n.* невроло́гия. **neurosis** *n.* невро́з. **neurotic** *adj.* невроти́ческий; *n.* невро́тик, нервнобольно́й *sb.*
neuter ['nju:tə(r)] *adj.* сре́дний, сре́днего ро́да; *n.* (*gender*) сре́дний род; (*word*) сло́во (*pl.* -ва́) сре́днего ро́да; (*animal*) кастри́рованное живо́тное *sb.*; *v.t.* кастри́ровать *impf.* & *pf.* **neutral** *adj.* нейтра́льный; (*indifferent*) безуча́стный; *n.* (*state*) нейтра́льное госуда́рство; (*person*) граждани́н (*pl.* -ане, -ан), -анка, нейтра́льного госуда́рства; (*gear*) нейтра́льное положе́ние рычага́ коро́бки переда́ч; **in ~** не включённый (-ён, -ена́). **neutrality** [nju:'trælɪtɪ] *n.* нейтралите́т; безуча́стность. **neutrali'zation** *n.* нейтрализа́ция. **neutralize** *v.t.* нейтрализова́ть *impf.* & *pf.* **neutron** *n.* нейтро́н.
Neva ['ni:və] *n.* Нева́.
never ['nevə(r)] *adv.* никогда́; **~!** не мо́жет быть!; **~ again** никогда́ бо́льше, бо́льше не; **~ fear!** будь(те) уве́рен(ы)!; **~ mind** ничего́!; всё равно́!; **~ once** ни ра́зу. **never-never** *n.*: **on the ~** в рассро́чку. **neverthe'less** *conj.*, *adv.* тем не ме́нее.
new [nju:] *adj.* но́вый (нов, -а́, -о); (*fresh*) све́жий (свеж, -а́, -о́, све́жи́); (*young*) молодо́й (мо́лод, -а́, -о); **N~ Year** Но́вый год; **N~ York** Нью-Йо́рк; **N~ Zealand** Но́вая Зела́ндия. **new-born** *adj.* новорождённый. **newcomer** *n.* прише́лец (-льца). **newfangled** *adj.* новомо́дный. **newly** *adv.* (*recently*) неда́вно; (*in new manner*) за́ново, вновь.
newel ['nju:əl] *n.* коло́нка винтово́й ле́стницы.
news [nju:z] *n.* но́вость, -ти *pl.*, изве́стие, -ия *pl.*; **~ agency** аге́нтство печа́ти. **newsagent** *n.* газе́тчик. **newsflash** [nju:z] *n.* сро́чное сообще́ние. **newsletter** *n.* информацио́нный бюллете́нь *m.* **newspaper** *n.* газе́та. **newsprint** *n.* газе́тная бума́га. **newsreel** *n.* кинохро́ника. **news-vendor** *n.* газе́тчик, продаве́ц (-вца́) газе́т.
newt [nju:t] *n.* трито́н.
next [nekst] *adj.* сле́дующий, бу́дущий; *adv.* в сле́дующий раз; пото́м, зате́м; **~ door** по сосе́дству; (*house*) в сосе́днем до́ме; (*flat*) в сосе́дней кварти́ре; **~ door to** (*fig.*) почти́; **~ of kin** ближа́йший ро́дственник; **~ to** ря́дом с+*i.*, о́коло+*g.*; (*fig.*) почти́. **next-door** *adj.* сосе́дний.
nexus ['neksəs] *n.* связь.
NHS *abbr.* (*of* ***National Health Service***) Национа́льная слу́жба здравоохране́ния.
nib [nɪb] *n.* перо́ (*pl.* пе́рья, -ьев).
nibble ['nɪb(ə)l] *v.t.* & *i.* грызть (-зу́, -зёшь; -з) *impf.*; обгрыза́ть *impf.*, обгры́зть (-зу́, -зёшь; -з) *pf.*; (*grass*) щипа́ть (-плет) *impf.*; (*fish*) клева́ть (клюёт) *impf.*
Nice ['ni:s] *n.* Ни́цца.
nice [naɪs] *adj.* (*precise*) то́чный (-чен, -чна́, -чно); (*subtle*) то́нкий (-нок, -нка́, -нко, то́нки́); (*pleasant*) прия́тный (*also iron.*); хоро́ший (-ш, -ша́); (*person*) ми́лый (мил, -а́, -о, ми́лы́), любе́зный. **nicety** ['naɪsɪtɪ] *n.* то́чность; то́нкость; **to a ~** то́чно, вполне́.
niche [nɪtʃ, ni:ʃ] *n.* ни́ша; (*fig.*) своё, надлежа́щее, ме́сто.

nick [nɪk] *n.* зару́бка, засе́чка; **in the ~ of time** в са́мый после́дний моме́нт; как раз во́время; *v.t.* де́лать *impf.*, с~ *pf.* зару́бку, засе́чку, на+*a.*
nickel ['nɪk(ə)l] *n.* ни́кель *m.*; *attr.* ни́келевый. **nickel-plate** *v.t.* никели́ровать *impf.* & *pf.*
nickname ['nɪkneɪm] *n.* про́звище, прозва́ние; *v.t.* прозыва́ть *impf.*, прозва́ть (прозову́, -вёшь; прозва́л, -а́, -о) *pf.*
nicotine ['nɪkəˌtiːn] *n.* никоти́н.
niece [niːs] *n.* племя́нница.
niggardly ['nɪgədlɪ] *adj.* (*miserly*) скупо́й (скуп, -а́, -о); (*scanty*) ску́дный (-ден, -дна́, -дно).
niggling ['nɪglɪŋ] *adj.* ме́лочный.
night [naɪt] *n.* ночь (*loc.* -чи́; *pl.* -чи, -че́й); (*evening*) ве́чер (*pl.* -а́); **at ~** но́чью; **first ~** премье́ра; **last ~** вчера́ ве́чером; **~ and day** непреста́нно; *attr.* ночно́й. **nightcap** *n.* ночно́й колпа́к (-а́); (*drink*) стака́нчик спиртно́го на́ ночь. **nightclub** *n.* ночно́й клуб. **nightdress** *n.* ночна́я руба́шка. **nightfall** *n.* наступле́ние но́чи. **nightgown** *n.* ночна́я руба́шка. **nightingale** *n.* солове́й (-вья́). **nightjar** *n.* козодо́й. **night-light** *n.* ночни́к (-а́). **nightly** *adj.* ночно́й; (*every night*) ежено́щный; *adv.* ежено́щно. **nightmare** *n.* кошма́р. **nightmarish** *adj.* кошма́рный.
nihilism ['naɪɪˌlɪz(ə)m, 'naɪhɪˌlɪz(ə)m] *n.* нигили́зм. **nihilist** *n.* нигили́ст. **nihi'listic** *adj.* нигилисти́ческий.
nil [nɪl] *n.* ноль (-ля́) *m.*
nimble ['nɪmb(ə)l] *adj.* прово́рный; (*mind*) ги́бкий (-бок, -бка́, -бко).
nimbus ['nɪmbəs] *n.* нимб; (*cloud*) дождево́е о́блако (*pl.* -ка́, -ко́в).
nine [naɪn] *adj.* & *n.* де́вять (-ти́, -тью́) (*collect.*; *9 pairs*) де́вятеро (-ры́х); (*cards*; *number 9*) девя́тка; (*time*) де́вять (часо́в); (*age*) де́вять лет. **ninepins** *n.* ке́гли (-лей) *pl.* **nine'teen** *adj.* & *n.* девятна́дцать (-ти, -тью); (*age*) девятна́дцать лет. **nine'teenth** *adj.* & *n.* девятна́дцатый; (*fraction*) девятна́дцатая (часть (*pl.* -ти, -те́й)); (*date*) девятна́дцатое (число́). **ninetieth** *adj.* & *n.* девяно́стый; (*fraction*) девяно́стая (часть (*pl.* -ти, -те́й)). **ninety** *adj.* & *n.* девяно́сто (-та); (*age*) девяно́сто лет; *pl.* (*decade*) девяно́стые го́ды (-до́в) *m.pl.* **ninth** *adj.* & *n.* девя́тый; (*fraction*) девя́тая (часть (*pl.* -ти, -те́й)); (*date*) девя́тое (число́); (*mus.*) но́на.
nip¹ [nɪp] *v.t.* (*pinch*) щипа́ть (-плю́, -плешь) *impf.*, щипну́ть *pf.*; (*bite*) куса́ть *impf.*, укуси́ть (-ушу́, -у́сишь) *pf.*; **~ along** слета́ть *pf.*; **~ in the bud** пресека́ть *impf.*, пресе́чь (-еку́, -ечёшь; -ёк, -екла́) *pf.* в ко́рне; *n.* щипо́к (-пка́); уку́с; **there's a ~ in the air** во́здух па́хнет моро́зцем. **nipper** *n.* (*boy*) мальчуга́н.
nip² [nɪp] *n.* (*drink*) глото́к (-тка́), рю́мочка.
nipple ['nɪp(ə)l] *n.* сосо́к (-ска́); (*tech.*) ни́ппель (*pl.* -ли & -ля́) *m.*
nirvana [nɜː'vɑːnə, nɪə-] *n.* нирва́на.
nit [nɪt] *n.* гни́да.
nitrate ['naɪtreɪt] *n.* нитра́т. **nitre** *n.* сели́тра. **nitric** *adj.* азо́тный. **nitrogen** *n.* азо́т. **nitrogenous** [ˌnaɪ'trɒdʒɪnəs] *adj.* азо́тный. **nitroglycerine** *n.* нитроглицери́н. **nitrous** *adj.* азо́тистый; **~ oxide** за́кись азо́та.
nitwit ['nɪtwɪt] *n.* простофи́ля *c.g.*
No. *abbr.* (*of* **number**) №.
no [nəʊ] *adj.* (*not any*) никако́й, не оди́н; (*not a*) (совсе́м) не; *adv.* нет; (ниско́лько) не+*compar.*; *n.* отрица́ние, отка́з; (*in vote*) го́лос (*pl.* -а́) „про́тив"; **~ doubt** коне́чно, несомне́нно; **~ fear** коне́чно, нет!; **~ longer** уже́ не, бо́льше не; **~ wonder** не удиви́тельно.
no one ['nəʊ wʌn] *pron.* никто́.
Noah's ark ['nəʊə, nɔː] *n.* Но́ев ковче́г.
nobility [nəʊ'bɪlɪtɪ] *n.* (*class*) дворя́нство; (*quality*) благоро́дство. **noble** ['nəʊb(ə)l] *adj.* дворя́нский, зна́тный; благоро́дный. **nobleman** *n.* дворяни́н (*pl.* -я́не, -я́н).
nobody ['nəʊbədɪ] *pron.* никто́; *n.* ничто́жество.
nocturnal [nɒk'tɜːn(ə)l] *adj.* ночно́й. **'nocturne** *n.* ноктю́рн.
nod [nɒd] *v.i.* кива́ть *impf.*, кивну́ть *pf.* голово́й; (*drowsily*) клева́ть (клюю́, клюёшь) *impf.* но́сом; **~ding acquaintance** пове́рхностное знако́мство; *n.* киво́к (-вка́).
nodule ['nɒdjuːl] *n.* узело́к (-лка́).
noggin ['nɒgɪn] *n.* кру́жечка.
noise [nɔɪz] *n.* шум (-а(у)); (*radio*) поме́хи *f.pl.* **noiseless** *adj.* бесшу́мный. **noisy** *adj.* шу́мный (-мен, -мна́, -мно).
nomad ['nəʊmæd] *n.* коче́вник. **no'madic** *adj.* кочево́й, кочу́ющий.
nomenclature [nəʊ'menklətʃə(r), 'nəʊmənˌkleɪtʃə(r)] *n.* номенклату́ра. **nominal** ['nɒmɪn(ə)l] *adj.* номина́льный; (*gram.*) имённо́й. **nominate** *v.t.* (*propose*) выдвига́ть *impf.*, вы́двинуть *pf.*; (*appoint*) назнача́ть *impf.*, назна́чить *pf.* **nomi'nation** *n.* выдвиже́ние; назначе́ние. **nominative** *adj.* (*n.*) имени́тельный (паде́ж (-а́)). **nomi'nee** *n.* кандида́т.
non- [nɒn] *pref.* не..., без... . **non-acceptance** *n.* непринятие.
nonage ['nəʊnɪdʒ, 'nɒn-] *n.* несовершенноле́тие.
nonagenarian [ˌnəʊnədʒɪ'neərɪən, ˌnɒn-] *n.* девяностоле́тний стари́к (-а́), -няя стару́ха.
non-aggression [ˌnɒnə'greʃ(ə)n] *n.* ненападе́ние; **~ pact** пакт о ненападе́нии. **non-alcoholic** *adj.* безалкого́льный. **non-alignment** *n.* неприсоедине́ние. **non-appearance** *n.* (*leg.*) нея́вка (в суд). **non-arrival** *n.* неприбы́тие.
nonchalance ['nɒnʃələns] *n.* (*indifference*) безразли́чие; (*carelessness*) беспе́чность. **nonchalant** *n.* безразли́чный; беспе́чный.
non-combatant [nɒn'kɒmbət(ə)nt] *adj.* не-

строево́й. **non-commissioned** *adj.*; ~ **officer** у́нтер-офице́р. **non-committal** *adj.* уклóнчивый. **non-conductor** *n.* непроводни́к (-á).

non-conformist [ˌnɒnkənˈfɔːmɪst] *n.* диссиде́нт; *adj.* диссиде́нтский.

nondescript [ˈnɒndɪskrɪpt] *adj.* неопределённый (-нен, -нна), неопределённого ви́да.

none [nʌn] *pron.* (*no one*) никто́; (*nothing*) ничто́; (*not one*) не оди́н; *adv.* совсе́м не; ничу́ть не; ~ **the less** тем не ме́нее.

nonentity [nɒˈnentɪtɪ] *n.* ничто́жество.

non-essential [ˌnɒnɪˈsenʃ(ə)l] *adj.* несуще́ственный (-ен(ен), -енна). **non-existence** *n.* небытие́ (*i.* -ие́м, *p.* -ии́). **non-existent** *adj.* несуществу́ющий. **non-ferrous** *adj.* цветно́й. **non-interference, -intervention** *n.* невмеша́тельство. **non-party** *adj.* беспарти́йный. **non-payment** *n.* неплатёж (-á).

nonplus [nɒnˈplʌs] *v.t.* ста́вить *impf.*, по~ *pf.* в тупи́к.

non-proliferation [ˌnɒnprəˌlɪfəˈreɪʃ(ə)n] *n.* нераспростране́ние (я́дерного ору́жия). **non-productive** *adj.* непроизводи́тельный. **non-resident** *adj.* не прожива́ющий по ме́сту слу́жбы. **non-renewable** *adj.* невозобновля́емый. **non-resistance** *n.* непротивле́ние.

nonsense [ˈnɒns(ə)ns] *n.* вздор, ерунда́, чепуха́. **nonsensical** [nɒnˈsensɪk(ə)l] *adj.* бессмы́сленный (-ен, -енна).

non sequitur [nɒn ˈsekwɪtə(r)] *n.* нелоги́чное заключе́ние.

non-skid [nɒnˈskɪd], **-slip** *adj.* нескользя́щий. **non-smoker** *n.* (*person*) некуря́щий *sb.*; (*compartment*) ваго́н, купе́ *nt.indecl.*, для некуря́щих. **non-stick** *adj.* противоприга́рный. **non-stop** *adj.* безостано́вочный; (*flight*) беспоса́дочный; *adv.* без остано́вок; без поса́док. **non-violence** *n.* ненаси́лие. **non-violent** *adj.* ненаси́льственный.

noodles [ˈnuːd(ə)lz] *n.* лапша́.

nook [nʊk] *n.* укро́мный уголо́к (-лка́); **every** ~ **and cranny** все углы́ и закоу́лки *m.pl.*

noon [nuːn] *n.* по́лдень (-лу́дня & -лдня́) *m.*; *attr.* полу́денный.

no one *see* **no**

noose [nuːs] *n.* пе́тля (*g.pl.* -тель); *v.t.* пойма́ть *pf.* арка́ном.

nor [nɔː(r), nə(r)] *conj.* и не; та́кже не, то́же не; **neither ...** ~ ни... ни.

norm [nɔːm] *n.* но́рма. **normal** *adj.* норма́льный. **normality** [nɔːˈmælɪtɪ] *n.* норма́льность. **normalize** *v.t.* нормализова́ть *impf.* & *pf.*

north [nɔːθ] *n.* се́вер; (*naut.*) норд; *adj.* се́верный; (*naut.*) но́рдовый; *adv.* к се́веру, на се́вер; **N~ Star** Поля́рная звезда́; ~ **wind** норд. **north-east** *n.* се́веро-восто́к; (*naut.*) норд-о́ст. **northeaster** *n.* норд-о́ст. **north-easterly, -eastern** *adj.* се́веро-восто́чный; (*naut.*) норд-о́стовый. **northerly** [ˈnɔːðəlɪ] *adj.* се́верный; (*naut.*) но́рдовый. **northern** *adj.* се́верный; ~ **lights** се́верное сия́ние. **northerner** *n.* северя́нин (*pl.* -я́не, -я́н); жи́тель *m.*, ~ница, се́вера. **northernmost** *adj.* са́мый се́верный. **northward(s)** *adv.* к се́веру, на се́вер. **north-west** *n.* се́веро-за́пад; (*naut.*) норд-ве́ст. **northwester** *n.* норд-ве́ст. **north-westerly, -western** *adj.* се́веро-за́падный; (*naut.*) норд-ве́стовый.

Norway [ˈnɔːweɪ] *n.* Норве́гия. **Norwegian** [nɔːˈwiːdʒ(ə)n] *adj.* норве́жский; *n.* норве́жец (-жца), -жка.

nose [nəʊz] *n.* нос (*loc.* -у́; *pl.* -ы́); (*sense*) чутьё; (*of ship etc.*) носова́я часть (*pl.* -ти, -те́й); (*of rocket*) голо́вка; *v.t.* ню́хать *impf.*, по~ *pf.*; ~ **out** разню́хивать *impf.*, разню́хать *pf.*; *v.i.* (*of ship etc.*) осторо́жно продвига́ться *impf.*, продви́нуться *pf.* вперёд. **nosebag** *n.* то́рба. **nosebleed** *n.* кровотече́ние и́з носу. **nosedive** *n.* пике́ *nt.indecl.*; *v.i.* пики́ровать *impf.* & *pf.*

nostalgia [nɒˈstældʒɪə, -dʒə] *n.* тоска́ (по ро́дине, по пре́жнему). **nostalgic** *adj.* вызыва́ющий тоску́.

nostril [ˈnɒstrɪl] *n.* ноздря́ (*pl.* -ри, -ре́й).

not [nɒt] *adv.* не; нет; ни; ~ **at all** ниско́лько, ничу́ть; (*reply to thanks*) не сто́ит (благода́рности); ~ **half** (~ *at all*) совсе́м не; (*very much*) ужа́сно; ~ **once** ни ра́зу; ~ **that** не то, что́бы; ~ **too** дово́льно+*neg.*; ~ **to say** что́бы не сказа́ть; ~ **to speak of** не говоря́ уже́ о+*p.*

notable [ˈnəʊtəb(ə)l] *adj.* заме́тный, замеча́тельный. **notably** *adv.* осо́бенно, заме́тно.

notary (public) [ˈnəʊtərɪ] *n.* нота́риус.

notation [nəʊˈteɪʃ(ə)n] *n.* нота́ция; (*mus.*) но́тное письмо́.

notch [nɒtʃ] *n.* зару́бка; *v.t.* заруба́ть *impf.*, заруби́ть (-блю́, -бишь) *pf.*

note [nəʊt] *n.* (*record*) заме́тка, запи́ска; (*annotation*) примеча́ние; (*letter*) запи́ска; (*banknote*) банкно́т; (*mus.*; *dipl.*) но́та; (*tone*) тон; (*attention*) внима́ние; ~ **of hand** ве́ксель (*pl.* -ля́) *m.*; **man of** ~ выдаю́щийся челове́к; **strike the right (a false)** ~ брать (беру́, -рёшь; брал, -а́, -о) *impf.*, взять (возьму́, -мёшь; взял, -а́, -о) *pf.* (не)ве́рный тон; **take** ~ **of** обраща́ть *impf.*, обрати́ть (-ащу́, -ати́шь) *pf.* внима́ние на+*a.*; *v.t.* отмеча́ть *impf.*, отме́тить *pf.*; ~ **down** запи́сывать *impf.*, записа́ть (-ишу́, -и́шешь) *pf.* **notebook** *n.* записна́я кни́жка, блокно́т. **notecase** *n.* бума́жник. **noted** *adj.* знамени́тый; изве́стный (**for** +*i.*). **notepaper** *n.* почто́вая бума́га. **noteworthy** *adj.* досто́йный (-о́ин, -о́йна) внима́ния.

nothing [ˈnʌθɪŋ] *n.* ничто́, ничего́; ~ **but** ничего́ кро́ме+*g.*, то́лько; ~ **of the kind** ничего́ подо́бного; **come to** ~ конча́ться *impf.*, ко́нчиться *pf.* ниче́м; **for** ~ (*free*) да́ром; (*in vain*) зря, напра́сно; **have** ~ **to do with** не име́ть *impf.* никако́го отноше́ния к+*d.*; **there is (was)** ~ **for it (but to)** ничего́ друго́го не остаётся (остава́лось) (как); придётся (пришло́сь) *+inf.*; **to say ~ of** не говоря́ уже́ о*+p.*

notice ['nəʊtɪs] *n.* (*sign*) объявле́ние; (*intimation*) извеще́ние; (*warning*) предупрежде́ние; (*attention*) внима́ние; (*review*) (печа́тный) о́тзыв; **at a moment's ~** неме́дленно; **give (in) one's ~** подава́ть (-даю́, -даёшь) *impf.*, пода́ть (-а́м, -а́шь, -а́ст, -ади́м; по́дал, -а́, -о) *pf.* заявле́ние об ухо́де с рабо́ты; **give s.o. ~** предупрежда́ть *impf.*, предупреди́ть *pf.* об увольне́нии; **take no ~ of** не обраща́ть *impf.* внима́ния на*+a.*; *v.t.* замеча́ть *impf.*, заме́тить *pf.*; (*take ~ of*) обраща́ть *impf.*, обрати́ть (-ащу́, -ати́шь) *pf.* внима́ние на*+a.* **noticeable** *adj.* заме́тный. **notice-board** *n.* доска́ (*a.* -ску; *pl.* -ски, -со́к, -ска́м) для объявле́ний. **notifiable** ['nəʊtɪˌfaɪəb(ə)l] *adj.* подлежа́щий регистра́ции. **notification** [ˌnəʊtɪfɪ'keɪʃ(ə)n] *n.* извеще́ние, уведомле́ние; (*of death etc.*) регистра́ция. **notify** ['nəʊtɪˌfaɪ] *v.t.* извеща́ть *impf.*, извести́ть *pf.* (**of** о*+p.*); уведомля́ть *impf.*, уве́домить *pf.* (**of** о*+p.*).

notion ['nəʊʃ(ə)n] *n.* поня́тие, представле́ние.

notoriety [ˌnəʊtə'raɪətɪ] *n.* дурна́я сла́ва. **notorious** [nəʊ'tɔːrɪəs] *adj.* пресловý́тый.

notwithstanding [ˌnɒtwɪθ'stændɪŋ, -wɪð'stændɪŋ] *prep.* несмотря́ на*+a.*; *adv.* те́м не ме́нее.

nougat ['nuːgɑː] *n.* нуга́.

nought [nɔːt] *n.* (*nothing*) ничто́; (*figure 0*) нуль (-ля́) *m.*, ноль (-ля́) *m.*; **~s and crosses** кре́стики и но́лики *m.pl.*

noun [naʊn] *n.* (и́мя *nt.*) существи́тельное *sb.*

nourish ['nʌrɪʃ] *v.t.* пита́ть *impf.*, на~ *pf.* **nourishing** *adj.* пита́тельный. **nourishment** *n.* пита́ние.

nova ['nəʊvə] *n.* но́вая звезда́ (*pl.* -ёзды).

novel ['nɒv(ə)l] *adj.* но́вый (нов, -а́, -о); (*unusual*) необыкнове́нный (-нен, -нна); *n.* рома́н. **novelist** *n.* романи́ст. **novelty** *n.* (*newness*) новизна́; (*new thing*) нови́нка.

November [nə'vembə(r)] *n.* ноя́брь (-ря́) *m.*; *attr.* ноя́брьский.

novice ['nɒvɪs] *n.* (*eccl.*) по́слушник, -ица; (*beginner*) новичо́к (-чка́).

now [naʊ] *adv.* тепе́рь, сейча́с; (*immediately*) то́тчас же; (*next*) тогда́; *conj.*: **~ (that)** раз, когда́; **(every) ~ and again, then** вре́мя от вре́мени; **~ ... ~...** то... то...; **by ~** уже́; **from ~ on** в дальне́йшем, впредь. **nowadays** *adv.* в на́ше вре́мя.

nowhere ['nəʊweə(r)] *adv.* (*place*) нигде́; (*direction*) никуда́; *pron.*: **I have ~ to go** мне не́куда пойти́.

noxious ['nɒkʃəs] *adj.* вре́дный (-ден, -дна́, -дно).

nozzle ['nɒz(ə)l] *n.* сопло́ (*pl.* -пла, -п(е)л), форсу́нка, па́трубок (-бка).

nuance ['njuːɑ̃s] *n.* нюа́нс.

nuclear ['njuːklɪə(r)] *adj.* я́дерный. **nucleus** *n.* ядро́ (*pl.* я́дра, я́дер, я́драм).

nude [njuːd] *adj.* обнажённый (-ён, -ена́), наго́й (наг, -а́, -о); *n.* обнажённая фигу́ра.

nudge [nʌdʒ] *v.t.* подта́лкивать *impf.*, подтолкну́ть *pf.* ло́ктем; *n.* лёгкий толчо́к (-чка́).

nudity ['njuːdɪtɪ] *n.* нагота́.

nugget ['nʌgɪt] *n.* (*gold*) саморо́док (-дка).

nuisance ['njuːs(ə)ns] *n.* доса́да, неприя́тность; (*person*) раздража́ющий, надое́дливый, челове́к.

null [nʌl] *adj.*: **~ and void** недействи́тельный. **nullify** ['nʌlɪˌfaɪ] *v.t.* аннули́ровать *impf.* & *pf.* **nullity** *n.* недействи́тельность.

numb [nʌm] *adj.* онеме́лый, оцепене́лый; *v.t.* вызыва́ть *impf.*, вы́звать (-зовет) *pf.* онеме́ние в*+p.*, у*+g.*

number ['nʌmbə(r)] *n.* (*total*) коли́чество; (*total*; *symbol*; *math.*; *gram.*) число́ (*pl.* -сла, -сел, -слам); (*item*) но́мер (*pl.* -а́); *v.t.* (*count*) счита́ть *impf.*, со~, счесть (сочту́, -тёшь; счёл, сочла́) *pf.*; (*assign ~ to*) нумерова́ть *impf.*, за~, про~ *pf.*; (*contain*) начи́тывать *impf.*; **~ among** причисля́ть *impf.*, причи́слить *pf.* к*+d.*; **his days are ~ed** его́ дни сочтены́. **numberless** *adj.* бесчи́сленный (-ен, -енна). **number-plate** *n.* номерна́я доще́чка.

numeral ['njuːmər(ə)l] *adj.* числово́й, цифрово́й; *n.* ци́фра; (*gram.*) (и́мя *nt.*) числи́тельное *sb.* **numerator** *n.* числи́тель *m.* **nu'merical** *adj.* числово́й, цифрово́й. **numerous** *adj.* многочи́сленный (-ен, -енна); (*many*) мно́го*+g.pl.*

numismatic [ˌnjuːmɪz'mætɪk] *adj.* нумизмати́ческий. **numismatics** *n.* нумизма́тика. **numismatist** [ˌnjuː'mɪzmətɪst] *n.* нумизма́т.

numskull ['nʌmskʌl] *n.* тупи́ца *c.g.*, о́лух.

nun [nʌn] *n.* мона́хиня. **nunnery** ['nʌnərɪ] *n.* (же́нский) монасты́рь (-ря́) *m.*

nuptial ['nʌpʃ(ə)l] *adj.* бра́чный, сва́дебный; *n.*: *pl.* сва́дьба (*g.pl.* -деб).

nurse [nɜːs] *n.* (*child's*) ня́ня; (*medical*) медсестра́ (*pl.* -ёстры, -естёр, -ёстрам), сиде́лка; *v.t.* (*suckle*) корми́ть (-млю́, -мишь) *impf.*, на~, по~ *pf.*; (*tend sick*) уха́живать *impf.* за*+i.*; (*treat illness*) лечи́ть (-чу́, -чишь) *impf.*; **nursing home** ча́стная лече́бница, ча́стный санато́рий. **nursery** *n.* (*room*) де́тская *sb.*; (*day ~*) я́сли (-лей) *pl.*; (*for plants*) пито́мник; **~ rhyme** де́тские стишки́ *m.pl.*; **~ school** де́тский сад (*loc.* -у́; *pl.* -ы́). **nurs(e)ling** *n.* пито́мец (-мца), -мица.

nut [nʌt] *n.* оре́х; (*for bolt etc.*) га́йка; (*sl.*, *head*) башка́; (*sl.*, *person*) псих. **nutcrackers** *n.* щипцы́ (-цо́в) *pl.* для оре́хов. **nuthatch** *n.* по́поползень (-зня) *m.* **nutshell** *n.* оре́ховая скорлупа́ (*pl.* -пы); **in a ~** в двух слова́х. **nut-tree** *n.* оре́шник.

nutmeg ['nʌtmeg] *n.* муска́тный оре́х.

nutria ['njuːtrɪə] *n.* ну́трия.

nutriment ['njuːtrɪmənt] *n.* пита́тельная еда́. **nutrition** [njuː'trɪʃ(ə)n] *n.* пита́ние. **nutritionist** *n.* дието́лог. **nu'tritious** *adj.* пита́тельный.

nylon ['naɪlɒn] *n.* нейло́н; *pl.* нейло́новые чулки́ (-ло́к) *pl.*; *attr.* нейло́новый.
nymph [nɪmf] *n.* ни́мфа. **nympho'maniac** *n.* нимфома́нка.

O [əʊ] *int.* о!; ах!; ох!
oaf [əʊf] *n.* неуклю́жий, неотёсанный, челове́к. **oafish** *adj.* неуклю́жий.
oak [əʊk] *n.* (*tree*) дуб (*loc.* -е & -у́; *pl.* -ы́); (*wood*) древеси́на ду́ба; *attr.* дубо́вый.
OAP *abbr.* (*of* **old-age pensioner**) пенсионе́р, ~ка (по ста́рости).
oar [ɔ:(r)] *n.* весло́ (*pl.* вёсла, -сел, -слам). **oarsman** *n.* гребе́ц (-бца́).
oasis [əʊ'eɪsɪs] *n.* оа́зис.
oast-house [əʊst] *n.* хмелесуши́лка.
oat [əʊt] *n.*: *pl.* овёс (овса́) *collect.* **oatcake** *n.* овся́ная лепёшка. **oatmeal** *n.* овся́нка.
oath [əʊθ] *n.* кля́тва, прися́га; (*expletive*) руга́тельство; **on, under,** ~ под прися́гой.
obduracy ['ɒbdjʊrəsɪ] *n.* упря́мство. **obdurate** *adj.* упря́мый.
obedience [əʊ'bi:dɪəns] *n.* послуша́ние. **obedient** *adj.* послу́шный.
obelisk ['ɒbəlɪsk] *n.* обели́ск; (*print.*; *obelus*) кре́стик.
obese [əʊ'bi:s] *n.* ту́чный (-чен, -чна́, -чно). **obesity** *n.* ту́чность.
obey [əʊ'beɪ] *v.t.* слу́шаться *impf.*, по~ *pf.*+*g.*; повинова́ться *impf.* (*also pf. in past*)+*d.*
obituary [ə'bɪtjʊərɪ] *n.* некроло́г; *adj.* некрологи́ческий.
object ['ɒbdʒɪkt; əb'dʒekt] *n.* (*thing*) предме́т; (*aim*) цель; (*gram.*) дополне́ние; *v.i.* возража́ть *impf.*, возрази́ть *pf.* (**to** про́тив+*g.*); протестова́ть *impf.* (**to** про́тив+*g.*); **I don't** ~ я не про́тив. **objection** [əb'dʒekʃ(ə)n] *n.* возраже́ние; **I have no** ~ я не возража́ю. **ob'jectionable** *adj.* неприя́тный. **ob'jective** *adj.* объекти́вный; (*gram.*) объе́ктный; *n.* (*mil.*) объе́кт; (*aim*) цель; (*lens*) объекти́в; (*gram.*) объе́ктный паде́ж (-а́). **objec'tivity** *n.* объекти́вность. **object-lesson** *n.* (*fig.*) нагля́дный приме́р. **ob'jector** *n.* возража́ющий *sb.*
obligation [ˌɒblɪ'geɪʃ(ə)n] *n.* обяза́тельство; **I am under an** ~ я обя́зан(а). **obligatory** [ə'blɪgətərɪ] *adj.* обяза́тельный. **oblige** [ə'blaɪdʒ] *v.t.* обя́зывать *impf.*, обяза́ть (-яжу́, -я́жешь) *pf.*; заставля́ть *impf.*, заста́вить *pf.*; **be ~d to** (*grateful*) быть благода́рным+*d.* **obliging** *adj.* услу́жливый, любе́зный.
oblique [ə'bli:k] *adj.* косо́й (кос, -а́, -о); (*indirect*) непрямо́й (-м, -ма́, -мо); (*gram.*) ко́свенный.
obliterate [ə'blɪtəˌreɪt] *v.t.* (*efface*) стира́ть *impf.*, стере́ть (сотру́, -рёшь; стёр) *pf.*; (*destroy*) уничтожа́ть *impf.*, уничто́жить *pf.* **oblite'ration** *n.* стира́ние; уничтоже́ние.
oblivion [ə'blɪvɪən] *n.* забве́ние. **oblivious** *adj.* (*forgetful*) забы́вчивый; **to be ~ of** не замеча́ть *impf.*+*g.*
oblong ['ɒblɒŋ] *adj.* продолгова́тый.
obnoxious [əb'nɒkʃəs] *adj.* проти́вный.
oboe ['əʊbəʊ] *n.* гобо́й.
obscene [əb'si:n] *adj.* непристо́йный. **obscenity** [əb'senɪtɪ] *n.* непристо́йность.
obscure [əb'skjʊə(r)] *adj.* (*dark*) тёмный (-мен, -мна́); *unclear*) нея́сный (-сен, -сна́, -сно); (*little known*) малоизве́стный; *v.t.* затемня́ть *impf.*, затемни́ть *pf.*; де́лать *impf.*, с~ *pf.* нея́сным. **obscurity** *n.* нея́сность, неизве́стность.
obsequious [əb'si:kwɪəs] *adj.* подобостра́стный.
observance [əb'zɜ:v(ə)ns] *n.* соблюде́ние; (*rite*) обря́д. **observant** *adj.* наблюда́тельный. **observation** [ˌɒbzə'veɪʃ(ə)n] *n.* наблюде́ние; (*remark*) замеча́ние. **observatory** *n.* обсервато́рия. **observe** *v.t.* (*law etc.*) соблюда́ть *impf.*, соблюсти́ (-юду́, -юдёшь; -ю́л, -юла́) *pf.*; (*watch*) наблюда́ть *impf.*; (*remark*) замеча́ть *impf.*, заме́тить *pf.* **observer** *n.* наблюда́тель *m.*
obsess [əb'ses] *v.t.* пресле́довать *impf.*; му́чить *impf.* **obsession** *n.* одержи́мость; (*idea*) навя́зчивая иде́я. **obsessive** *adj.* навя́зчивый.
obsolescence [ˌɒbsə'les(ə)ns] *n.* устарева́ние. **obsolescent** *adj.* устарева́ющий. **obsolete** ['ɒbsəˌli:t] *adj.* устаре́лый, вы́шедший из употребле́ния.
obstacle ['ɒbstək(ə)l] *n.* препя́тствие, поме́ха. **obstacle-race** *n.* бег с препя́тствиями.
obstetric(al) [əb'stetrɪk(əl)] *adj.* акуше́рский. **obstetrician** [ˌɒbstə'trɪʃ(ə)n] *n.* акуше́р. **obstetrics** *n.* акуше́рство.
obstinacy ['ɒbstɪnəsɪ] *n.* упря́мство. **obstinate** *adj.* упря́мый.
obstreperous [əb'strepərəs] *adj.* бу́йный (бу́ен, буйна́, -но).
obstruct [əb'strʌkt] *v.t.* пре-, за-, гражда́ть *impf.*, пре-, за-, гради́ть *pf.*; (*prevent, impede*) препя́тствовать *impf.*, вос~ *pf.*+*d.*; меша́ть *impf.*, по~ *pf.*+*d.* **obstruction** *n.* пре-, за-, гражде́ние; (*obstacle*) препя́тствие. **obstructive** *adj.* пре-, за-, гражда́ющий; препя́тствующий, меша́ющий.
obtain [əb'teɪn] *v.t.* получа́ть *impf.*, получи́ть (-чу́, -чишь) *pf.*; достава́ть (-таю́, -таёшь) *impf.*, доста́ть (-а́ну, -а́нешь) *pf.*
obtrude [əb'tru:d] *v.t.* навя́зывать *impf.*, навяза́ть (-яжу́, -я́жешь) *pf.* ((**up**)**on** +*d.*). **obtrusive** *adj.* навя́зчивый.
obtuse [əb'tju:s] *adj.* тупо́й (туп, -а́, -о, ту́пы́).

obverse ['ɒbvɜːs] *n.* (*of coin etc.*) лицевáя сторонá (*a.* -ону; *pl.* -óны, -óн, -онáм).
obviate ['ɒbvɪˌeɪt] *v.t.* (*remove*) устранять *impf.*, устранить *pf.*; (*get round*) обходить (-ожý, -óдишь) *impf.*, обойти (обойдý, -дёшь; обошёл, -шлá) *pf.*
obvious ['ɒbvɪəs] *adj.* очевидный, явный.
occasion [ə'keɪʒ(ə)n] *n.* (*juncture*) слýчай; (*cause*) пóвод; (*occurrence*) событие; *v.t.* причинять *impf.*, причинить *pf.* **occasional** *adj.* случáйный, рéдкий (-док, -дкá, -дко). **occasionally** *adv.* иногдá, врéмя от врéмени.
Occident ['ɒksɪd(ə)nt] *n.* Зáпад. **Occidental** [ˌɒksɪ'dent(ə)l] *adj.* зáпадный.
occlude [ə'kluːd] *v.t.* преграждáть *impf.*, преградить *pf.* **occlusion** [ə'kluːʒ(ə)n] *n.* преграждéние.
occult [ɒ'kʌlt, 'ɒkʌlt] *adj.* тáйный, оккýльтный.
occupancy ['ɒkjʊpənsɪ] *n.* занятие; (*possession*) владéние (**of** +*i.*). **occupant** ['ɒkjʊpənt] *n.* (*of land*) владéлец (-льца), -лица; (*of house etc.*) житель *m.*, ~ница. **occu'pation** *n.* занятие; (*military* ~) оккупáция; (*profession*) профéссия. **occu'pational** *adj.* профессионáльный; ~ **disease** профессионáльное заболевáние; ~ **therapy** трудотерапия. **occupy** ['ɒkjʊˌpaɪ] *v.t.* занимáть *impf.*, занять (займý, -мёшь; зáнял, -á, -о) *pf.*; (*mil.*) оккупировать *impf.* & *pf.*
occur [ə'kɜː(r)] *v.i.* (*happen*) случáться *impf.*, случиться *pf.*; (*be met with*) встречáться *impf.*; ~ **to** приходить (-ит) *impf.*, прийти (придёт; пришёл, -шлá) *pf.* в гóлову+*d.* **occurrence** [ə'kʌrəns] *n.* слýчай, происшéствие.
ocean ['əʊʃ(ə)n] *n.* океáн; (*fig.*) мáсса, мóре; *attr.* океáнский. **ocean-going** *adj.* океáнский. **oceanic** [ˌəʊʃɪ'ænɪk, ˌəʊsɪ-] *adj.* океáнский, океанический.
ocelot ['ɒsɪˌlɒt] *n.* оцелóт.
ochre ['əʊkə(r)] *n.* óхра.
o'clock [ə'klɒk] *adv.*: **at six** ~ в шесть часóв.
octagon ['ɒktəgən] *n.* восьмиугóльник. **octagonal** [ˌɒk'tægən(ə)l] *adj.* восьмиугóльный.
octane ['ɒkteɪn] *n.* октáн; ~ **number** октáновое числó.
octave ['ɒktɪv] *n.* (*mus.*) октáва.
octet [ɒk'tet] *n.* октéт.
October [ɒk'təʊbə(r)] *n.* октябрь (-ря) *m.*; *attr.* октябрьский.
octogenarian [ˌɒktəʊdʒɪ'neərɪən] *n.* восьмидесятилéтний старик (-á), -няя старýха.
octopus ['ɒktəpəs] *n.* осьминóг, спрут.
ocular ['ɒkjʊlə(r)] *adj.* глазнóй, окулярный. **oculist** *n.* окулист.
odd [ɒd] *adj.* (*number*) нечётный; (*not paired*) непáрный; (*casual*) случáйный; (*strange*) стрáнный (-нен, -ннá, -нно); **five hundred** ~ пятьсóт с лишним; ~ **job** случáйная рабóта; ~ **man out** (трéтий) лишний *sb.* **oddity** *n.* стрáнность; (*person*) чудáк (-á), -áчка. **oddly** *adv.* стрáнно; ~ **enough** как э́то ни стрáнно. **oddment** *n.* остáток (-тка); *pl.* разрóзненные предмéты *m.pl.* **odds** *n.* (*advantage*) перевéс; (*variance*) разноглáсие; (*chance*) шáнсы *m.pl.*; **be at ~ with** (*person*) не лáдить с+*i.*; (*things*) не соответствовать *impf.*+*d.*; **long (short)** ~ нерáвные (почти рáвные) шáнсы *m.pl.*; **the ~ are that** вероятнее всегó, что; ~ **and ends** обрывки *m.pl.*
ode [əʊd] *n.* óда.
odious ['əʊdɪəs] *adj.* ненавистный, отвратительный. **odium** *n.* нéнависть, отвращéние.
odour ['əʊdə(r)] *n.* зáпах; **be in good (bad) ~ with** быть в (не)милости у+*g.* **odourless** *adj.* без зáпаха.
odyssey ['ɒdɪsɪ] *n.* одиссéя.
oedema [ɪ'diːmə] *n.* отёк.
oesophagus [iː'sɒfəgəs] *n.* пищевóд.
of [ɒv, əv] *prep. expressing* **1.** *origin*: из+*g.*: **he comes ~ a working-class family** он из рабóчей семьи; **2.** *cause*: от+*g.*: **he died ~ hunger** он ýмер от гóлода; **3.** *authorship*: *g.*: **the works ~ Pushkin** сочинéния Пýшкина; **4.** *material*: из+*g.*: **made ~ wood** сдéланный из дéрева; *adjective*: **a heart ~ stone** кáменное сéрдце; **5.** *identity*: *apposition*: **the city ~ Moscow** гóрод Москвá; *adjective*: **the University ~ Moscow** Москóвский университéт; **6.** *concern, reference*: о+*p.*: **he talked ~ the past** он говорил о прóшлом; **7.** *quality*: *g.*: **a man ~ strong character** человéк сильного харáктера; *adjective*: **a man ~ importance** вáжный человéк; **8.** *partition*: *g.* (*often in* -ý(-ю)): **a glass ~ milk, tea** стакáн молокá, чáю; из+*g.*: **one ~ them** один из них; **9.** *belonging*: *g.*: **the capital ~ England** столица Англии; *poss. adj.*: **the house ~ his father** отцóвский дом; **10.** *following other parts of speech*: *see individual entries, e.g.* **be afraid** бояться (**of** +*g.*); **dispose** ~ избавляться от+*g.*
off [ɒf] *adv.*: *in phrasal vv., see v., e.g.* **clear** ~ убирáться; *prep.* (*from surface of*) с+*g.*; (*away from*) от+*g.*; *adj.* (*far*) дáльний; (*right hand*) прáвый; (*free*) свобóдный; ~ **and on** врéмя от врéмени; **on the ~ chance** на всякий слýчай; ~ **colour** нездорóвый; ~ **the cuff** без подготóвки; ~ **the point** не относящийся к дéлу.
offal ['ɒf(ə)l] *n.* (*food*) требухá, потрохá (-хóв) *pl.*; (*carrion*) пáдаль.
offence [ə'fens] *n.* (*attack*) нападéние; (*insult*) обида; (*against law*) простýпок (-пка), преступлéние; **take** ~ обижáться *impf.*, обидеться (-ижусь, -идишься) *pf.* (**at** на+*a.*). **offend** *v.t.* оскорблять *impf.*, оскорбить *pf.*; обижáть *impf.*, обидеть (-ижу, -идишь) *pf.*; ~ **against** нарушáть *impf.*, нарýшить *pf.* **offender** *n.* правонарушитель *m.*, ~ница; престýпник, -ица. **offensive** *adj.* (*attacking*) наступáтельный; (*insulting*) оскорбитель-

ный, оби́дный; (*repulsive*) проти́вный; *n.* нападе́ние.

offer ['ɒfə(r)] *v.t.* предлага́ть *impf.*, предложи́ть (-жу́, -жишь) *pf.*; *n.* предложе́ние; **on ~** в прода́же.

offhand [ɒf'hænd, 'ɒfhænd] *adj.* бесцеремо́нный (-нен, -нна), небре́жный; *adv.* (*without preparation*) без подгото́вки, экспро́мтом.

office ['ɒfɪs] *n.* (*position*) до́лжность; (*place, room etc.*) бюро́ *nt.indecl.*, конто́ра, канцеля́рия; (*eccl.*) (церко́вная) слу́жба; **~ equipment** оргте́хника. **officer** *n.* должностно́е лицо́ (*pl.* -ца); (*mil.*) офице́р. **official** [ə'fɪʃ(ə)l] *adj.* служе́бный, должностно́й; (*authorized*) официа́льный; *n.* должностно́е лицо́ (*pl.* -ца). **o'fficiate** *v.i.* (*eccl.*) соверша́ть *impf.*, соверши́ть *pf.* богослуже́ние. **o'fficious** *adj.* (*intrusive*) навя́зчивый.

offing ['ɒfɪŋ] *n.*: **in the ~** в недалёком бу́дущем.

offprint ['ɒfprɪnt] *n.* отде́льный о́ттиск. **offscourings** *n.* отбро́сы (-сов) *pl.*, подо́нки (-ков) *pl.* **offset** *n.* (*compensation*) возмеще́ние; (*offshoot*) о́тпрыск; (*in pipe*) отво́д; **~ process** (*print*) офсе́тный спо́соб; *v.t.* возмеща́ть *impf.*, возмести́ть *pf.* **offshoot** *n.* о́тпрыск. **off'side** *adv.* вне игры́. **offspring** *n.* пото́мок (-мка); (*collect.*) пото́мки *m.pl.*

off-white [ɒf'waɪt] *adj.* не совсе́м бе́лый (бел, -а́, бе́ло́).

often ['ɒf(ə)n, 'ɒft(ə)n] *adv.* ча́сто.

ogle ['əʊg(ə)l] *v.t. & i.* стро́ить *impf.* гла́зки+*d.*

ogre ['əʊgə(r)] *n.* велика́н-людое́д. **ogress** *n.* велика́нша-людое́дка.

oh [əʊ] *int.* о!; ах!; ох!

ohm [əʊm] *n.* ом (*g.pl.* ом).

oho [əʊ'həʊ] *int.* ого́!

oil [ɔɪl] *n.* ма́сло (*pl.* -сла́, -сел, -сла́м); (*petroleum*) нефть; (*lubricant*) жи́дкая сма́зка; *pl.* (*paint*) ма́сло, ма́сляные кра́ски *f.pl.*; *v.t.* сма́зывать *impf.*, сма́зать (сма́жу, -жешь) *pf.*; **~ rig** бурова́я устано́вка; **~ well** нефтяна́я сква́жина. **oilcake** *n.* жмых (-а́). **oilcan** *n.* маслёнка. **oilcloth** *n.* клеёнка. **oilfield** *n.* месторожде́ние не́фти. **oil-paint** *n.* ма́сляная кра́ска. **oil-painting** *n.* карти́на, напи́санная ма́сляными кра́сками. **oilskin** *n.* то́нкая клеёнка; *pl.* дождево́е пла́тье. **oil-tanker** *n.* та́нкер. **oily** *adj.* масляни́стый; (*unctuous*) еле́йный.

ointment ['ɔɪntmənt] *n.* мазь.

OK [əʊ'keɪ] *adv.* хорошо́; *int.* ла́дно!; *v.t.* одобря́ть *impf.*, одо́брить *pf.*

okapi [əʊ'kɑːpɪ] *n.* ока́пи *c.g.indecl.*

old [əʊld] *adj.* ста́рый (стар, -а́, ста́ро́); (*ancient*; *of long standing*) стари́нный; (*former*) бы́вший; **how ~ are you?** ско́лько тебе́, вам, (*d.*) лет?; **she is three years ~** ей (*d.*) три го́да; **the ~** старики́ *m.pl.*; **~ age** ста́рость; **O~ Believer** старообря́дец (-дца); **~ chap, fellow** *etc.* старина́; **the ~ country** ро́дина, оте́чество; **~ maid** ста́рая де́ва; **~ man** (*also father, husband*) стари́к (а́); **~ woman** стару́ха; (*coll.*) стару́шка. **old-age** *adj.*: **~ pension** пе́нсия по ста́рости. **old-fashioned** *adj.* старомо́дный. **old-time** *adj.* стари́нный, пре́жних времён. **old-world** *adj.* стари́нный.

olfactory [ɒl'fæktərɪ] *adj.* обоня́тельный.

oligarch ['ɒlɪ,gɑːk] *n.* олига́рх. **oli'garchic(al)** *adj.* олигархи́ческий. **oligarchy** *n.* олига́рхия.

olive ['ɒlɪv] *n.* (*fruit*) масли́на, оли́вка; (*colour*) оли́вковый цвет; *adj.* оли́вковый; **~ branch** оли́вковая ветвь (*pl.* -ви, -ве́й); **~ oil** оли́вковое ма́сло; **~ tree** масли́на, оли́вковое де́рево (*pl.* дере́вья, -ьев).

Olympic [ə'lɪmpɪk] *adj.* олимпи́йский; **~ games** Олимпи́йские и́гры *f.pl.*

omelet(te) ['ɒmlɪt] *n.* омле́т.

omen ['əʊmən, -men] *n.* предзнаменова́ние. **ominous** ['ɒmɪnəs] *adj.* злове́щий.

omission [ə'mɪʃ(ə)n] *n.* про́пуск; (*neglect*) упуще́ние. **omit** [ə'mɪt] *v.t.* (*leave out*) пропуска́ть *impf.*, пропусти́ть (-ущу́, -у́стишь) *pf.*; (*neglect*) упуска́ть *impf.*, упусти́ть (-ущу́, -у́стишь) *pf.*

omnipotence [ɒm'nɪpət(ə)ns] *n.* всемогу́щество. **omnipotent** *adj.* всемогу́щий. **omni'present** *adj.* вездесу́щий. **omniscient** [ɒm'nɪsɪənt, -ʃɪənt] *adj.* всеве́дующий. **omnivorous** [ɒm'nɪvərəs] *adj.* всея́дный; (*fig.*) всепоглоща́ющий.

on [ɒn] *prep.* (*position*) на+*p.*; **~ the right of** (*relative position*) с пра́вой стороны́ от+*g.*; (*direction*) на+*a.*; (*time*) в+*a.*; **~ the next day** на сле́дующий день; **~ Mondays** (*repeated action*) по понеде́льникам (*d.pl.*); **~ (the morning of) the first of June** (у́тром) пе́рвого ию́ня (*g.*); **~ arrival** по прибы́тии; (*concerning*) по+*p.*, о+*p.*, на+*a.*; *adv.* да́льше, вперёд; *in phrasal vv.*, *see vv.*, *e.g.* **move ~** идти́ да́льше; **and so ~** и так да́лее, и т.д.; **further ~** да́льше; **later ~** по́зже.

once [wʌns] *adv.* (оди́н) раз; (*on past occasion*) одна́жды; **all at ~** неожи́данно; **at ~** сра́зу, неме́дленно; (*if, when*) **~** как то́лько; **~ again, more** ещё раз; **~ and for all** раз навсегда́; **~ or twice** не́сколько раз; **~ upon a time there lived ...** жил-бы́л... .

oncoming ['ɒn,kʌmɪŋ] *adj.* приближа́ющийся; **~ traffic** встре́чное движе́ние.

one [wʌn] *adj.* оди́н (одна́, -но́); (*only, single*) еди́нственный; (*unified*) еди́ный; *n.* оди́н; (*unit*) едини́ца; *pron.*: *not usu. translated*; *v. translated in 2nd pers. sg. or by impers. construction*: **~ never knows** никогда́ не зна́ешь; **where can ~ buy this book?** где мо́жно купи́ть э́ту кни́гу?; **chapter ~** пе́рвая глава́; **I for ~** что каса́ется меня́; я со свое́й стороны́; **~ after another** оди́н за други́м; **~ and all** все до одного́; все как оди́н; **~ and only** еди́нственный; **~ and the same** оди́н и тот же; **~ another** друг дру́га (*d.* -гу, *etc.*); ~ **fine day** в оди́н прекра́сный день; ~ **o'clock** час. **one-armed** *adj.* одноpу́кий. **one-eyed** *adj.* одногла́зый. **one-handed** *adj.* одноpу́кий. **one-legged** *adj.* одноно́гий.

onerous ['ɒnərəs, 'əʊn-] *adj.* тя́гостный.

oneself [wʌn'self] *pron.* себя́ (себе́, собо́й); -ся (*suffixed to v.t.*).

one-sided ['wʌnsaɪdɪd] *adj.* односторо́нний. **one-time** ['wʌntaɪm] *adj.* бы́вший. **one-way** ['wʌnweɪ] *adj.* односторо́нний; ~ **street** у́лица односторо́ннего движе́ния.

onion ['ʌnjən] *n.* (*plant*; *pl. collect.*) лук; (*single* ~) лу́ковица.

onlooker ['ɒn,lʊkə(r)] *n.* наблюда́тель *m.*, ~ница.

only ['əʊnlɪ] *adj.* еди́нственный; *adv.* то́лько; **if** ~ е́сли бы то́лько; ~ **just** то́лько что; *conj.* но.

onomatopoeia [,ɒnə,mætə'pi:ə] *n.* звукоподража́ние. **onomatopoeic** *adj.* звукоподража́тельный.

onset ['ɒnset], **onslaught** ['ɒnslɔ:t] *n.* на́тиск, ата́ка.

onus ['əʊnəs] *n.* (*burden*) бре́мя *nt.*; (*responsibility*) отве́тственность.

onward ['ɒnwəd] *adj.* дви́жущийся вперёд. **onwards** *adv.* вперёд.

onyx ['ɒnɪks] *n.* о́никс; *attr.* о́никсовый.

ooze [u:z] *n.* ил, ти́на; *v.t.* & *i.* сочи́ться *impf.* **oozy** *adj.* и́листый, ти́нистый.

opacity [ə'pæsɪtɪ] *n.* непрозра́чность.

opal ['əʊp(ə)l] *n.* опа́л; ~ **glass** моло́чное стекло́. **opalescence** [,əʊpə'les(ə)ns] *n.* опалесце́нция. **opa'lescent** *adj.* опалесци́рующий. **opaline** ['əʊpə,laɪn] *adj.* опа́ловый.

opaque [əʊ'peɪk] *adj.* непрозра́чный.

open ['əʊpən] *adj.* откры́тый; (*frank*) открове́нный (-нен, -нна); (*accessible*) досту́пный; (*boat*) беспа́лубный; **in the** ~ **air** на откры́том во́здухе; *v.t.* & *i.* открыва́ть(ся) *impf.*, откры́ть(ся) (-ро́ю(сь), -ро́ешь(ся)) *pf.*; (~ *wide*) раскрыва́ть (ся) *impf.*, раскры́ть(ся) (-ро́ю(сь), -ро́ешь(ся)) *pf.*; *v.i.* (*begin*) начина́ться *impf.*, нача́ться (-чнётся; нача́лся́, -ла́сь) *pf.* **opencast** *adj.*: ~ **mining** откры́тые го́рные рабо́ты *f.pl.* **open-handed** *adj.* ще́дрый (щедр, -а́, -о). **opening** *n.* откры́тие; (*aperture*) отве́рстие; (*beginning*) нача́ло; *adj.* вступи́тельный, нача́льный, пе́рвый. **open-minded** *adj.* непредупреждённый (-ён, -ённа). **open-mouthed** *adj.* с рази́нутым ртом. **open-work** *n.* ажу́рный; ажу́рная рабо́та.

opera ['ɒpərə] *n.* о́пера; *attr.* о́перный. **opera-glasses** *n.* бино́кль *m.* **opera-hat** *n.* складно́й цили́ндр. **opera-house** *n.* о́пера, о́перный теа́тр.

operate ['ɒpə,reɪt] *v.i.* де́йствовать *impf.* (**upon** на+*a.*); де́лать *impf.*, с~ *pf.* опера́цию; (*med.*) опери́ровать *impf.* & *pf.* (**on** +*a.*); *v.t.* управля́ть *impf.*+*i.*

operatic [,ɒpə'rætɪk] *adj.* о́перный.

operating-theatre ['ɒpə,reɪtɪŋ] *n.* операцио́нная *sb.* **ope'ration** *n.* де́йствие; (*med.*; *mil.*) опера́ция. **ope'rational** *adj.* операти́вный. **operative** ['ɒpərətɪv] *adj.* де́йствующий, операти́вный; *n.* рабо́чий *sb.* **operator** *n.* опера́тор; (*telephone* ~) телефони́ст, ~ка.

operetta [,ɒpə'retə] *n.* опере́тта.

ophthalmia [ɒf'θælmɪə] *n.* офтальми́я. **ophthalmic** *adj.* глазно́й.

opiate ['əʊpɪət] *n.* опиа́т.

opine [əʊ'paɪn] *v.t.* полага́ть *impf.* **opinion** [ə'pɪnjən] *n.* мне́ние; (*expert's* ~) заключе́ние (специали́ста); ~ **poll** опро́с обще́ственного мне́ния. **opinionated** *adj.* упо́рствующий в свои́х взгля́дах.

opium ['əʊpɪəm] *n.* о́пий, о́пиум; ~ **poppy** снотво́рный мак.

opponent [ə'pəʊnənt] *n.* проти́вник.

opportune ['ɒpə,tju:n] *adj.* своевре́менный (-нен, -нна). **oppor'tunism** *n.* оппортуни́зм. **oppor'tunist** *n.* оппортуни́ст. **oppor'tunity** *n.* слу́чай, возмо́жность.

oppose [ə'pəʊz] *v.t.* (*contrast*) противопоставля́ть *impf.*, противопоста́вить *pf.* (**to** +*d.*); (*resist*) проти́виться *impf.*, вос~ *pf.*+*d.*; (*speak etc. against*) выступа́ть *impf.*, вы́ступить *pf.* про́тив+*g.* **opposed** *adj.* (*contrasted*) противопоста́вленный (-ен); (*of person*) про́тив (**to** +*g.*); **as** ~ **to** в противополо́жность+*d.* **opposite** ['ɒpəzɪt] *adj.* противополо́жный, обра́тный; *n.* противополо́жность; **just the** ~ как раз наоборо́т; *adv.* напро́тив; *prep.* (на)про́тив+*g.* **oppo'sition** *n.* (*contrast*) противопоставле́ние; (*resistance*) сопротивле́ние; (*pol.*) оппози́ция.

oppress [ə'pres] *v.t.* притесня́ть *impf.*, притесни́ть *pf.*; угнета́ть *impf.* **oppression** *n.* притесне́ние, угнете́ние. **oppressive** *adj.* гнету́щий, угнета́тельский; (*weather*) ду́шный (-шен, -шна́, -шно). **oppressor** *n.* угнета́тель *m.*, ~ница.

opprobrious [ə'prəʊbrɪəs] *adj.* оскорби́тельный. **opprobrium** *n.* позо́р.

opt [ɒpt] *v.i.* выбира́ть *impf.*, вы́брать (вы́беру, -решь) *pf.* (**for** +*a.*); ~ **out** не принима́ть *impf.* уча́стия (**of** в+*p.*). **optative (mood)** [ɒp'teɪtɪv, 'ɒptətɪv] *n.* оптати́в.

optic ['ɒptɪk] *adj.* глазно́й, зри́тельный. **optical** *adj.* опти́ческий. **optician** [ɒp'tɪʃ(ə)n] *n.* о́птик. **optics** *n.* о́птика.

optimism ['ɒptɪ,mɪz(ə)m] *n.* оптими́зм. **optimist** *n.* оптими́ст. **opti'mistic** *adj.* оптимисти́чный, -ческий. **optimum** *adj.* оптима́льный.

option ['ɒpʃ(ə)n] *n.* вы́бор; **without the** ~ **(of a fine)** без пра́ва заме́ны штра́фом. **optional** *adj.* необяза́тельный, факультати́вный.

opulence ['ɒpjʊləns] *n.* бога́тство. **opulent** *adj.* бога́тый.

opus ['əʊpəs, 'ɒp-] *n.* о́пус.

or [ɔ:(r), ə(r)] *conj.* и́ли; ~ **else** ина́че; ~ **so** приблизи́тельно.

oracle ['ɒrək(ə)l] *n.* ора́кул. **oracular** [ə'rækjʊlə(r)] *adj.* ора́кульский; (*mysterious*) зага́дочный.

oral ['ɔːr(ə)l] *adj.* у́стный; *n.* у́стный экза́мен.

orange ['ɒrɪndʒ] *n.* (*fruit*) апельси́н; (*colour*) ора́нжевый цвет; *attr.* апельси́нный, апельси́новый; *adj.* ора́нжевый; ~ **blossom** помера́нцевый цвет; (*decoration*) флёрдора́нж; ~ **peel** апельси́новая ко́рка.

orang-(o)utan(g) [ɔːˌræŋuː'tæn] *n.* орангута́нг.

oration [ɔː'reɪʃ(ə)n, ə-] *n.* речь. **orator** ['ɒrətə(r)] *n.* ора́тор. **oratorical** [ˌɒrə'tɒrɪk(ə)l] *adj.* ора́торский.

oratorio [ˌɒrə'tɔːrɪəʊ] *n.* орато́рия.

oratory¹ ['ɒrətərɪ] *n.* (*chapel*) часо́вня (*g.pl.* -вен).

oratory² ['ɒrətərɪ] *n.* (*speech*) ора́торское иску́сство, красноре́чие.

orb [ɔːb] *n.* шар (-á *with 2,3,4*; *pl.* -ы́); (*part of regalia*) держа́ва.

orbit ['ɔːbɪt] *n.* орби́та; (*eye-socket*) глазна́я впа́дина; **in** ~ на орби́те; *v.t.* враща́ться *impf.* по орби́те вокру́г+*g.* **orbital** *adj.* орбита́льный.

orchard ['ɔːtʃəd] *n.* фрукто́вый сад (*loc.* -у́; *pl.* -ы́).

orchestra ['ɔːkɪstrə] *n.* орке́стр. **orchestral** [ɔː'kestr(ə)l] *adj.* оркестро́вый. **orchestrate** *v.t.* оркестрова́ть *impf.* & *pf.* **orche'stration** *n.* оркестро́вка.

orchid ['ɔːkɪd] *n.* орхиде́я.

ordain [ɔː'deɪn] *v.t.* предпи́сывать *impf.*, предписа́ть (-ишу́, -и́шешь) *pf.*; (*eccl.*) посвяща́ть *impf.*, посвяти́ть (-ящу́, -яти́шь) *pf.* (в духо́вный сан) (*v.abs.*); в+*nom.-a.pl.* (*of rank*)).

ordeal [ɔː'diːl] *n.* испыта́ние.

order ['ɔːdə(r)] *n.* поря́док (-дка); (*system*) строй; (*command*) прика́з; (*for goods*) зака́з; (*document*) о́рдер (*pl.* -á); (*archit.*) о́рдер; (*biol.*) отря́д; (*of monks, knights*) о́рден; (*insignia*) о́рден (*pl.* -á); *pl.* (*holy* ~) духо́вный сан; **by** ~ по прика́зу; **in** ~ **to** для того́ что́бы; **made to** ~ сде́ланный (-ан) на зака́з; *v.t.* (*command*) прика́зывать *impf.*, приказа́ть (-ажу́, -а́жешь) *pf.*+*d.*; веле́ть (-лю́, -ли́шь) *impf.* & *pf.*+*d.*; (*goods etc.*) зака́зывать *impf.*, заказа́ть (-ажу́, -а́жешь) *pf.* **orderly** *adj.* аккура́тный, опря́тный; ~ **officer** дежу́рный офице́р; *n.* (*med.*) санита́р; (*mil.*) ордина́рец (-рца).

ordinal ['ɔːdɪn(ə)l] *adj.* поря́дковый; *n.* поря́дковое числи́тельное *sb.*

ordinance ['ɔːdɪnəns] *n.* декре́т.

ordinary ['ɔːdɪnərɪ] *adj.* обыкнове́нный (-нен, -нна), обы́чный; (*mediocre*) зауря́дный.

ordination [ˌɔːdɪ'neɪʃ(ə)n] *n.* посвяще́ние.

ordnance ['ɔːdnəns] *n.* артилле́рия; *attr.* артиллери́йский.

ore [ɔː(r)] *n.* руда́ (*pl.* -ды).

organ ['ɔːgən] *n.* о́рган; (*mus.*) орга́н. **organ-grinder** *n.* шарма́нщик.

organic [ɔː'gænɪk] *adj.* органи́ческий; ~ **whole** еди́ное це́лое *sb.* '**organism** *n.* органи́зм.

organist ['ɔːgənɪst] *n.* органи́ст.

organization [ˌɔːgənaɪ'zeɪʃ(ə)n] *n.* организа́ция. '**organize** *v.t.* организо́вывать *impf.* (*pres. not used*), организова́ть *impf.* (*in pres.*) & *pf.*; устра́ивать *impf.*, устро́ить *pf.* '**organizer** *n.* организа́тор.

orgasm ['ɔːgæz(ə)m] *n.* орга́зм.

orgy ['ɔːdʒɪ] *n.* о́ргия.

oriel ['ɔːrɪəl] *n.* э́ркер; (~ *window*) окно́ (*pl.* о́кна, о́кон, о́кнам) э́ркера.

Orient¹ ['ɔːrɪənt] *n.* Восто́к. **oriental** [ˌɔːrɪ'ent(ə)l, ˌɒr-] *adj.* восто́чный.

orient² ['ɔːrɪənt], **orientate** *v.t.* ориенти́ровать *impf.* & *pf.* (**o.s.** -ся). **orien'tation** *n.* ориента́ция, ориентиро́вка.

orifice ['ɒrɪfɪs] *n.* отве́рстие.

origin ['ɒrɪdʒɪn] *n.* происхожде́ние, нача́ло. **original** [ə'rɪdʒɪn(ə)l] *adj.* оригина́льный; (*initial*) первонача́льный; (*genuine*) по́длинный (-нен, -нна); *n.* оригина́л, по́длинник. **originality** [əˌrɪdʒɪ'nælɪtɪ] *n.* оригина́льность; по́длинность. **o'riginate** *v.t.* порожда́ть *impf.*, породи́ть *pf.*; *v.i.* происходи́ть (-ожу́, -о́дишь) *impf.*, произойти́ (-ойду́, -ойдёшь; -ошёл, -ошла́) *pf.* (**from, in** от+*g.*); брать (беру́, -рёшь; брал, -á, -о) *impf.*, взять (возьму́, -мёшь; взял, -á, -о) *pf.* нача́ло (**from, in** в+*p.*, от+*g.*). **o'riginator** *n.* а́втор, инициа́тор.

oriole ['ɔːrɪəʊl] *n.* и́волга.

ornament ['ɔːnəmənt; 'ɔːnəˌment] *n.* украше́ние, орна́мент; *v.t.* украша́ть *impf.*, укра́сить *pf.* **orna'mental** *adj.* орнамента́льный, декорати́вный.

ornate [ɔː'neɪt] *adj.* разукра́шенный (-ен); (*liter. style*) витиева́тый.

ornithological [ˌɔːnɪθə'lɒdʒɪk(ə)l] *adj.* орнитологи́ческий. **ornithologist** [ˌɔːnɪ'θɒlədʒɪst] *n.* орнито́лог. **orni'thology** *n.* орнитоло́гия.

orphan ['ɔːf(ə)n] *n.* сирота́ (*pl.* -ты) *c.g.*; *v.t.* де́лать *impf.*, с~ *pf.* сирото́й; **be** ~**ed** сироте́ть *impf.*, о~ *pf.* **orphanage** *n.* прию́т, сиро́тский дом (*pl.* -á). **orphaned** *adj.* осироте́лый.

orthodox ['ɔːθəˌdɒks] *adj.* ортодокса́льный; (*eccl.*, **O**~) правосла́вный. **orthodoxy** *n.* ортодо́ксия; (**O**~) правосла́вие.

orthographic(al) [ˌɔːθə'græfɪk((ə)l)] *adj.* орфографи́ческий. **orthography** [ɔː'θɒgrəfɪ] *n.* орфогра́фия, правописа́ние.

orthopaedic [ˌɔːθə'piːdɪk] *adj.* ортопеди́ческий. **orthopaedics** *n.* ортопе́дия.

oscillate ['ɒsɪˌleɪt] *v.i.* вибри́ровать *impf.*; (*also of person*) колеба́ться (-блюсь, -блешься) *impf.*, по~ *pf.* **osci'llation** *n.* вибра́ция, осцилля́ция; колеба́ние. **oscilloscope** [ə'sɪləˌskəʊp] *n.* осциллоско́п.

osier ['əʊzɪə(r)] *n.* (*tree*) и́ва; (*shoot*) лоза́ (*pl.* -зы); *pl.* ивня́к (-á) (*collect*).

osmosis [ɒz'məʊsɪs] *n.* о́смос.

osprey ['ɒsprɪ, -prɪ] *n.* (*bird*) скопа́; (*plume*) эгре́т.

osseous ['ɒsɪəs] *adj.* ко́стный; (*bony*) кости́стый. **ossified** *adj.* окостене́лый.
ostensible [ɒ'stensɪb(ə)l] *adj.* мни́мый. **ostensibly** *adv.* я́кобы.
ostentation [,ɒsten'teɪʃ(ə)n] *n.* показно́е проявле́ние, выставле́ние напока́з. **ostentatious** *adj.* показно́й.
osteopath ['ɒstɪə,pæθ] *n.* остеопа́т. **osteopathy** [,ɒstɪ'ɒpəθɪ] *n.* остеопа́тия.
ostler ['ɒslə(r)] *n.* ко́нюх.
ostracism ['ɒstrə,sɪz(ə)m] *n.* острaки́зм. **ostracize** ['ɒstrə,saɪz] *v.t.* подверга́ть *impf.*, подве́ргнуть (-г) *pf.* острaки́зму.
ostrich ['ɒstrɪtʃ] *n.* стра́ус.
other ['ʌðə(r)] *adj.* друго́й, ино́й; тот; *pl.* други́е *sb.*; **any ~ business** теку́щие дела́ *nt.pl.*, ра́зное *sb.*; **every ~** ка́ждый второ́й; **every ~ day** че́рез день; **in ~ words** ины́ми слова́ми; **on the ~ hand** с друго́й стороны́; **on the ~ side** на той стороне́, по ту сто́рону; **one after the ~** оди́н за други́м; **one or the ~** тот и́ли ино́й; **the ~ day** на дня́х, неда́вно; **the ~ way round** наоборо́т; **the ~s** остальны́е. **otherwise** *adv.* & *conj.* ина́че, а то.
otter ['ɒtə(r)] *n.* вы́дра.
ouch [aʊtʃ] *int.* ай!
ought [ɔːt] *v.aux.* до́лжен (-жна́) (бы) +*inf.*; сле́довало (бы) *impers.+d. & inf.*; (*probability*) веро́ятно, по всей веро́ятности+*finite v.*; **~ not** не сле́довало (бы) *impers.+d. & inf.*; нельзя́+*d. &inf.*
ounce [aʊns] *n.* у́нция.
our ['aʊə(r)], **ours** *poss.pron.* наш (-а, -е; -и); свой (-оя́, -оё; -ои́). **our'selves** *pron.* (*emph.*) (мы) са́ми (-и́х, -и́м, -и́ми); (*refl.*) себя́ (себе́, собо́й); -ся (*suffixed to v.t.*).
oust [aʊst] *v.t.* вытесня́ть *impf.*, вы́теснить *pf.*
out [aʊt] *adv.* **1.** нару́жу, вон; **~ with you!** вон отсю́да!; (*to the end*) до конца́; *in phrasal vv. often rendered by pref.* вы- (вы́- *in pf.*), *e.g.* **pull ~** вытáскивать *impf.*, вы́тащить *pf.*; **2.: to be ~** *in various senses*: **he is ~** (*not at home*) его́ нет до́ма; (*not in office etc.*) он вы́шел; **the workers are ~** (*on strike*) рабо́чие басту́ют; **the secret is ~** та́йна раскры́та; **the truth will ~** пра́вды не скрыть; **to be ~** *rendered by pf. v. in past* (*English pres., past*) *or fut.* (*English fut.*).: (*be at an end*) ко́нчиться *pf.*; (*be ~ of fashion*) вы́йти (вы́йду, -дешь; вы́шел, -шла) *pf.* из мо́ды; (*of book, be published*) вы́йти (вы́йдет; вы́шел, -шла) *pf.* из печа́ти; (*of candle etc.*) потýхнуть (-х) *pf.*; (*of flower*) распусти́ться (-ится) *pf.*; (*of person, be unconscious*) потеря́ть *pf.* созна́ние; (*of rash*) вы́ступить *pf.*; **3.: ~ of** из+*g.*, вне+*g.*; **~ of doors** на откры́том во́здухе; **~ of gear** вы́ключенный (-ен); **~ of order** неиспра́вный; **~ of work** безрабо́тный.
out-and-out ['aʊtənd'aʊt] *adj.* отъя́вленный, соверше́нный.
outbalance [aʊt'bæləns] *v.t.* переве́шивать *impf.*, переве́сить *pf.* **outbid** *v.t.* предлага́ть *impf.*, предложи́ть (-жу́, -жишь) *pf.* бо́лее высо́кую це́ну, чем+*nom.* **'outboard** *adj.*: **~ motor** подвесно́й дви́гатель *m.* **'outbreak** *n.* (*of anger, disease*) вспы́шка; (*of war*) нача́ло. **'outbuilding** *n.* надво́рная постро́йка. **'outburst** *n.* взрыв, вспы́шка. **'outcast** *n.* отве́рженец (-нца); *adj.* отве́рженный. **outclass** *v.t.* оставля́ть *impf.*, оста́вить *pf.* далеко́ позади́. **'outcome** *n.* результа́т, исхо́д. **'outcrop** *n.* обнажённая поро́да. **'outcry** *n.* (шу́мные) проте́сты *m.pl.* **outdistance** *v.t.* обгоня́ть *impf.*, обогна́ть (обгоню́, -нишь; обогна́л, -а́, -о) *pf.* **outdo** *v.t.* превосходи́ть (-ожу́, -о́дишь) *impf.*, превзойти́ (-ойду́, -ойдёшь; -ошёл, -ошла́) *pf.*
outdoor ['aʊtdɔː(r)] *adj.*, **out'doors** *adv.* на откры́том во́здухе, на у́лице.
outer ['aʊtə(r)] *adj.* (*external*) вне́шний, нару́жный; (*far from centre*) отдалённый (от це́нтра). **outermost** *adj.* са́мый да́льний, кра́йний.
outfit ['aʊtfɪt] *n.* снаряже́ние; (*set of things*) набо́р; (*clothes*) оде́жда. **outfitter** *n.* торго́вец (-вца) оде́ждой. **outgoings** *n.* изде́ржки *f.pl.* **out'grow** *v.t.* перераста́ть *impf.*, перерасти́ (-расту́, -растёшь; -ро́с, -росла́) *pf.*; (*clothes*) выраста́ть *impf.*, вы́расти (-ту, -тешь; вы́рос) *pf.* из+*g.*; (*habit*) избавля́ться *impf.*, изба́виться *pf.* с во́зрастом от+*g.* **outhouse** *n.* надво́рная постро́йка.
outing ['aʊtɪŋ] *n.* прогу́лка, экску́рсия.
outlandish [aʊt'lændɪʃ] *adj.* стра́нный (-нен, -нна́, -нно). **outlast** *v.t.* продолжа́ться *impf.*, продо́лжиться *pf.* до́льше, чем+*nom.* **'outlaw** *n.* лицо́ (*pl.* -ца) вне зако́на; банди́т; *v.t.* объявля́ть *impf.*, объяви́ть (-влю́, -вишь) *pf.* вне зако́на. **'outlay** *n.* изде́ржки *f.pl.*, расхо́ды *m.pl.* **'outlet** *n.* вы́пуск; (*fig.*) вы́ход; (*for goods*) торго́вая то́чка. **'outline** *n.* очерта́ние, ко́нтур; (*sketch, draft*) о́черк; *v.t.* оче́рчивать *impf.*, очерти́ть (-рчу́, -ртишь) *pf.* **outlive** *v.t.* пережи́ть (-иву́, -ивёшь; пе́режил, -а́, -о) *pf.* **'outlook** *n.* вид, перспекти́вы *f.pl.* **'outlying** *adj.* отдалённый (-ён, -ённа). **outmoded** *adj.* старомо́дный. **outnumber** *v.t.* чи́сленно превосходи́ть (-ожу́, -о́дишь) *impf.*, превзойти́ (-ойду́, -дёшь; -ошёл, -ошла́) *pf.* **'out-of-date** *adj.* устаре́лый, старомо́дный. **'out-of-the-way** *adj.* отдалённый (-ён, -ённа), тру́дно находи́мый. **'out-patient** *n.* амбулато́рный больно́й *sb.* **'outpost** *n.* аванпо́ст. **'output** *n.* вы́пуск, проду́кция.
outrage ['aʊtreɪdʒ] *n.* (*violation of rights*) наси́льственное наруше́ние чужи́х прав; (*gross offence*) надруга́тельство (**upon** над+*i.*); *v.t.* оскорбля́ть *impf.*, оскорби́ть *pf.*; надруга́ться *pf.* над+*i.*; (*infringe*) наруша́ть *impf.*, нару́шить *pf.* **out'rageous** *adj.* (*immoderate*) возмути́тельный; (*offensive*) оскорби́тельный.

outrigger ['aʊt,rɪgə(r)] *n.* (*boat*) аутри́гер. **outright** *adv.* (*entirely*) вполне́; (*once for all*) раз навсегда́; (*openly*) откры́то; *adj.* прямо́й (прям, -а́, -о, пря́мы́). **outset** *n.* нача́ло; **at the** ~ внача́ле; **from the** ~ с са́мого нача́ла. **out'shine** *v.t.* затмева́ть *impf.*, затми́ть *pf.*

outside [aʊt'saɪd, 'aʊtsaɪd] *n.* (*external side*) нару́жная сторона́ (*a.* -ону; *pl.* -оны, -о́н, -она́м); (*exterior*, *appearance*) нару́жность, вне́шность; **at the** ~ са́мое бо́льшее, в кра́йнем слу́чае; **from the** ~ извне́; **on the** ~ снару́жи; *adj.* нару́жный, вне́шний; (*sport*) кра́йний; *adv.* (*on the* ~) снару́жи; (*to the* ~) нару́жу; (*out of doors*) на откры́том во́здухе, на у́лице; *prep.* вне+*g.*; за+*i.*, за преде́лами+*g.*; (*other than*) кро́ме+*g.* **outsider** *n.* посторо́нний *sb.*; (*sport*) аутса́йдер.

outsize ['aʊtsaɪz] *adj.* бо́льше стандáртного разме́ра. **outskirts** *n.* окра́ина. **out'spoken** *adj.* открове́нный (-нен, -нна), прямо́й (прям, -а́, -о, пря́мы́). **out'spread** *adj.* распростёртый. **out'standing** *adj.* (*person*) выдаю́щийся; (*debt*) неупла́ченный. **out'stay** *v.t.* пересиживать *impf.*, пересиде́ть (-ижу́, -иди́шь) *pf.*; ~ **one's welcome** заси́живаться *impf.*, засиде́ться (-ижу́сь, -ди́шься) *pf.* **out'stretched** *adj.*: **with** ~ **arms** с распростёртыми обья́тиями. **out'strip** *v.t.* обгоня́ть *impf.*, обогна́ть (обгоню́, -нишь; обогна́л, -а́, -о) *pf.* **out'vote** *v.t.* побежда́ть *impf.*, победи́ть (-ди́шь) *pf.* большинство́м голосо́в.

outward ['aʊtwəd] *adj.* (*external*) вне́шний, нару́жный; ~ **bound** уходя́щий в пла́вание. **outwardly** *adv.* вне́шне, на вид. **outwards** *adv.* нару́жу.

outweigh [aʊt'weɪ] *v.t.* переве́шивать *impf.*, переве́сить *pf.* **outwit** [aʊt'wɪt] *v.t.* перехитри́ть *pf.*

oval ['əʊv(ə)l] *adj.* ова́льный; *n.* ова́л.

ovary ['əʊvərɪ] *n.* яи́чник.

ovation [əʊ'veɪʃ(ə)n] *n.* ова́ция.

oven ['ʌv(ə)n] *n.* печь (*loc.* -чи́; *pl.* -чи, -че́й); духо́вка. **ovenproof** *adj.* жаропро́чный.

over ['əʊvə(r)] *adv.* & *prep. with vv*: *see vv.*, *e.g.* **jump** ~ перепры́гивать *impf.*; **think** ~ обду́мывать *impf.*; *adv.* (*in excess*) сли́шком; (*in addition*) вдоба́вок; (*again*) сно́ва; *prep.* (*above*) над+*i.*; (*through*; *covering*) по+*d.*; (*concerning*) о+*p.*; (*across*) че́рез+*a.*; (*on the other side of*) по ту сто́рону+*g.*; (*more than*) свы́ше+*g.*; бо́лее+*g.*; (*with age*) за+*a.*; **all** ~ (*finished*) всё ко́нчено; (*everywhere*) повсю́ду; **all** ~ **the country** по всей стране́; ~ **again** ещё раз; ~ **against** напро́тив+*g.*; (*in contrast to*) по сравне́нию с+*i.*; ~ **and above** сверх+*g.*; не говоря́ уже́ о+*p.*; ~ **the radio** по ра́дио; ~ **there** вон там; ~ **the way** че́рез доро́гу.

overact [,əʊvər'ækt] *v.t.* & *i.* переи́грывать *impf.*, переигра́ть *pf.* **overall** *n.* хала́т; *pl.* комбинезо́н, спецоде́жда; *adj.* о́бщий. **overawe** *v.t.* внуша́ть *impf.*, внуши́ть *pf.* благогове́йный страх+*d.* **overbalance** *v.i.* теря́ть *impf.*, по~ *pf.* равнове́сие. **overbearing** *adj.* вла́стный, повели́тельный. **'overboard** *adv.* (*motion*) за́ борт; (*position*) за бо́ртом. **'overcast** *adj.* (*sky*) покры́тый облака́ми. **'overcoat** *n.* пальто́ *nt.indecl.* **overcome** *v.t.* преодолева́ть *impf.*, преодоле́ть *pf.*; *adj.* охва́ченный (-ен). **overcrowded** *adj.* перепо́лненный (-ен), перенаселённый (-ён, -ена́). **overcrowding** *n.* перенаселённость. **overdo** *v.t.* (*cook*) пережа́ривать *impf.*, пережа́рить *pf.*; ~ **it, things** (*work too hard*) переутомля́ться *impf.*, переутоми́ться *pf.*; (*go too far*) переба́рщивать *impf.*, переборщи́ть *pf.*

overdose ['əʊvə,dəʊs] *n.* чрезме́рная до́за; передозиро́вка. **overdraft** *n.* превыше́ние креди́та; (*amount*) долг ба́нку. **over'draw** *v.i.* превыша́ть *impf.*, превы́сить *pf.* креди́т (в ба́нке). **overdrive** *n.* ускоря́ющая переда́ча. **over'due** *adj.* просро́ченный (-ен); **be** ~ (*late*) запа́здывать *impf.*, запозда́ть *pf.* **over'estimate** *v.t.* переоце́нивать *impf.*, переоцени́ть (-ню́, -нишь) *pf.*; *n.* переоце́нка. **over'flow** *v.i.* перелива́ться *impf.*, перели́ться (-льётся; -ли́лся, -лила́сь, -ли́ло́сь) *pf.*; (*river etc.*) разлива́ться *impf.*, разли́ться (разольётся; разли́лся, -ила́сь, -и́ло́сь) *pf.*; *n.* разли́в; (*outlet*) переливна́я труба́ (*pl.* -бы). **over'grown** *adj.* заро́сший. **overhang** *v.t.* & *i.* выступа́ть *impf.* над+*i.*; (*also fig.*) нависа́ть *impf.*, нави́снуть (-с) *pf.* над+*i.*; *n.* свес, вы́ступ.

overhaul [,əʊvə'hɔːl] *v.t.* разбира́ть *impf.*, разобра́ть (разберу́, -рёшь; разобра́л, -а́, -о) *pf.*; (*repair*) капита́льно ремонти́ровать *impf.* & *pf.*; (*overtake*) догоня́ть *impf.*, догна́ть (догоню́, -нишь; догна́л, -а́, -о) *pf.* **'overhead** *adv.* наверху́, над голово́й; *adj.* возду́шный, подвесно́й; (*expenses*) накладно́й; *n.*: *pl.* накладны́е расхо́ды *m.pl.*; ~ **projector** графопрое́ктор. **overhear** *v.t.* нечая́нно слы́шать (-шу, -шишь) *impf.*, у~ *pf.*; (*eavesdrop*) подслу́шивать *impf.*, подслу́шать *pf.* **overjoyed** *adj.* в восто́рге (**at** от+*g.*), о́чень дово́льный (**at** +*i.*). **'overland** *adj.* сухопу́тный; *adv.* по су́ше. **overlap** *v.t.* & *i.* (*completely*) перекрыва́ть *impf.*, перекры́ть (-ро́ю, -ро́ешь) *pf.* (друг дру́га); *v.t.* (*in part*) части́чно покрыва́ть *impf.*, покры́ть (-ро́ю, -ро́ешь) *pf.*; *v.i.* части́чно совпада́ть *impf.*, совпа́сть (-аду́, -адёшь; -а́л) *pf.*

overleaf *adv.* на обра́тной стороне́ (листа́, страни́цы). **overlook** *v.t.* (*look down on*) смотре́ть (-рю́, -ришь) *impf.* све́рху на+*a.*; (*of window*) выходи́ть (-ит) *impf.* на, в, +*a.*; (*not notice*) не замеча́ть *impf.*, заме́тить *pf.*+*g.*; (~ *offence etc.*) проща́ть *impf.*, прости́ть *pf.* **'overlord** *n.* сюзере́н, влады́ка *m.* **overmaster** *v.t.* подчиня́ть *impf.*, подчини́ть *pf.* себе́; (*fig.*) всеце́ло овладева́ть *impf.*, овладе́ть *pf.*+*i.* **overnight** *adv.* накану́не ве́чером; (*all night*) с ве́чера, всю ночь; (*suddenly*) неожи́данно, ско́ро; **stay** ~ ночева́ть (-чу́ю, -чу́ешь) *impf.*, пере~ *pf.*; *adj.* ночно́й. **'overpass** *n.* путепрово́д. **overpay** *v.t.* перепла́чивать *impf.*, переплати́ть (-ачу́, -а́тишь) *pf.*

over-populated [ˌəʊvəˈpɒpjʊˌleɪtɪd] *adj.* перенаселённый (-ён, -ена́). **over-popuˈlation** *n.* перенаселённость. **overpower** *v.t.* переси́ливать *impf.*, переси́лить *pf.*; (*heat etc.*) одолева́ть *impf.*, одоле́ть *pf.* **over-production** *n.* перепроизво́дство. **overrate** *v.t.* переоце́нивать *impf.*, переоцени́ть (-ню́, -нишь) *pf.* **overreach** *v.t.* перехитри́ть *pf.*; ~ **o.s.** зарыва́ться *impf.*, зарва́ться (-ву́сь, -вёшься; -ва́лся, -вала́сь, -ва́ло́сь) *pf.* **override** *v.t.* (*fig.*) отверга́ть *impf*, отве́ргнуть (-г(нул), -гла) *pf.* **overrule** *v.t.* аннули́ровать *impf.* & *pf.* **overrun** *v.t.* (*flood*) наводня́ть *impf.*, наводни́ть *pf.*; (*ravage*) опустоша́ть *impf.*, опустоши́ть *pf.*

oversea(s) [ˌəʊvəˈsiːz; ˈəʊvəˌsiːz] *adv.* за мо́рем, че́рез мо́ре; *adj.* замо́рский. **oversee** [ˌəʊvəˈsiː] *v.t.* надзира́ть *impf.* за+*i.* **'overseer** *n.* надзира́тель *m.*, ~ница. **overshadow** *v.t.* затмева́ть *impf.*, затми́ть *pf.* **'oversight** *n.* (*supervision*) надзо́р; (*mistake*) недосмо́тр, опло́шность. **oversleep** *v.i.* просыпа́ть *impf.*, проспа́ть (-плю́, -пи́шь; -па́л, -пала́, -па́ло) *pf.* **overstate** *v.t.* преувели́чивать *impf.*, преувели́чить *pf.* **overstatement** *n.* преувеличе́ние. **overstep** *v.t.* переступа́ть *impf.*, переступи́ть (-плю́, -пишь) *pf.*+*a.*, че́рез+*a.*

overt [əʊˈvɜːt, ˈəʊvɜːt] *adj.* я́вный, откры́тый.

overtake [ˌəʊvəˈteɪk] *v.t.* догоня́ть *impf.*, догна́ть (догоню́, -нишь; догна́л, -а́, -о) *pf.*; (*of misfortune etc.*) постига́ть *impf.*, пости́чь & пости́гнуть (-и́гну, -и́гнешь; -иг) *pf.* **overthrow** *v.t.* (*upset*) опроки́дывать *impf.*, опроки́нуть *pf.*; (*from power*) сверга́ть *impf.*, све́ргнуть (-г(нул), -гла) *pf.*; *n.* сверже́ние. **'overtime** *n.* (*time*) сверхуро́чные часы́ *m.pl.*; (*payment*) сверхуро́чное *sb.*; *adv.* сверхуро́чно.

overtone [ˈəʊvəˌtəʊn] *n.* (*mus.*) оберто́н; (*fig.*) скры́тый намёк.

overture [ˈəʊvəˌtjʊə(r)] *n.* предложе́ние, инициати́ва; (*mus.*) увертю́ра.

overturn [ˌəʊvəˈtɜːn] *v.t.* & *i.* опроки́дывать(ся) *impf.*, опроки́нуть(ся) *pf.*; *v.t.* сверга́ть *impf.*, све́ргнуть (-г) *pf.* **overweening** *adj.* высокоме́рный, самонаде́янный (-ян, -янна). **overwhelm** *v.t.* подавля́ть *impf.*, подави́ть (-влю́, -вишь) *pf.*; (*of emotions*) овладева́ть *impf.*, овладе́ть *pf.*+*i.* **overwhelming** *adj.* подавля́ющий. **overwork** *v.t.* & *i.* переутомля́ть(ся) *impf.*, переутоми́ть(ся) *pf.*

owe [əʊ] *v.t.* (~ *money*) быть до́лжным (-жен, -жна́) +*a.* & *d.*; (*be indebted*) быть обя́занным (-ан) +*i.* & *d.*; **he, she, ~s me three roubles** он до́лжен, она́ должна́, мне три рубля́; **she ~s him her life** она́ обя́зана ему́ жи́знью. **owing** *adj.*: **be** ~ причита́ться *impf.* (**to** +*d.*); ~ **to** из-за+*g.*, по причи́не+*g.*, всле́дствие+*g.*

owl [aʊl] *n.* сова́ (*pl.* -вы). **owlet** *n.* совёнок (-нка; *pl.* совя́та, -т).

own [əʊn] *adj.* свой (-оя́, -оё; -ои́); свой (со́бственный); (*relative*) родно́й; **on one's** ~ самостоя́тельно; *v.t.* (*possess*) владе́ть *impf.*+*i.*; (*admit*) признава́ть (признаю́, -наёшь) *impf.*, призна́ть *pf.*; ~ **up** признава́ться (-наю́сь, -наёшься) *impf.*, призна́ться *pf.* **owner** *n.* владе́лец (-льца), со́бственник. **ownership** *n.* владе́ние (**of** +*i.*), со́бственность.

ox [ɒks] *n.* вол (-а́).

oxidation [ˌɒksɪˈdeɪʃ(ə)n] *n.* окисле́ние. **oxide** [ˈɒksaɪd] *n.* о́кись, о́кисел (-сла). **oxidize** [ˈɒksɪˌdaɪz] *v.t.* & *i.* окисля́ть(ся) *impf.*, окисли́ть(ся) *pf.* **oxyacetylene** *adj.* кислоро́дно-ацетиле́новый. **oxygen** *n.* кислоро́д; *attr.* кислоро́дный.

oyster [ˈɔɪstə(r)] *n.* у́стрица.

oz. *abbr.* (*of* **ounce(s)**) у́нция.

ozone [ˈəʊzəʊn] *n.* озо́н; ~ **layer** озо́нный слой. **ozone-friendly** *adj.* озонобезвре́дный.

P

p. *abbr.* (*of* **penny**) пе́нни *nt. indecl.*, пенс; (*of* **page**) стр, страни́ца.

PA *abbr.* (*of* ***personal assistant***) ли́чный секрета́рь.

p.a. [pər ˈænəm] *abbr.* (*of* ***per annum***) в год.

pace [peɪs] *n.* шаг (-а́ *with* 2, 3, 4, *loc.* -у́; *pl.* -и́); (*fig.*) темп; **keep ~ with** идти́ (иду́, идёшь; шёл, шла) *impf.* в но́гу с+*i.*; **set the** ~ задава́ть (-даю́, -даёшь) *impf.*, зада́ть (-а́м, -а́шь, -а́ст, -ади́м; за́дал, -а́, -о) *pf.* темп; *v.i.* шага́ть *impf.*, шагну́ть *pf.*; *v.t.* ~ **out** измеря́ть *impf.*, изме́рить *pf.* шага́ми. **pacemaker** *n.* (*sport*) ли́дер, задаю́щий темп; (*med.*) кардиостимуля́тор.

pachyderm [ˈpækɪˌdɜːm] *n.* толстоко́жее (живо́тное) *sb.*

pacific [pəˈsɪfɪk] *adj.* ми́рный; **P~** тихоокеа́нский; *n.* Ти́хий океа́н. **pacification** [ˌpæsɪfɪˈkeɪʃ(ə)n] *n.* усмире́ние, умиротворе́ние. **'pacifism** *n.* пацифи́зм. **'pacifist** *n.* пацифи́ст. **'pacify** *v.t.* усмиря́ть *impf.*, усмири́ть *pf.*; умиротворя́ть *impf.*, умиротвори́ть *pf.*

pack [pæk] *n.* ýзел (узлá), вьюк (*pl.* -юкú); (*soldier's*) рáнец (-нца); (*hounds*) свóра; (*wolves, birds*) стáя; (*cards*) колóда; ~ **ice** пак, пáковый лёд (льда, *loc.* льду); ~ **of lies** сплошнáя ложь (лжи, *i.* лóжью); *v.t.* паковáть *impf.*, у~ *pf.*; уклáдывать *impf.*, уложúть (-жý, -жишь) *pf.*; (*cram*) набивáть *impf.*, набúть (-бью́, -бьёшь) *pf.* **package** *n.* пакéт, свёрток (-тка); (*packaging*) упакóвка. **packaging** *n.* упакóвка. **packet** *n.* пакéт; пáчка; (*money*) куш. **packhorse** *n.* вью́чная лóшадь (*pl.* -ди, -дéй, *i.* -дьмú). **packing-case** *n.* я́щик. **packing-needle** *n.* упакóвочная иглá (*pl.* -лы).

pact [pækt] *n.* договóр, пакт.

pad¹ [pæd] *v.i.* (*walk*) идтú (идý, идёшь; шёл, шла) *impf.*, пойтú (пойдý, -дёшь; пошёл, -шлá) *pf.* неслы́шным шáгом.

pad² [pæd] *n.* (*cushion*) подýшка, подýшечка; (*guard*) щитóк (-ткá); (*of paper*) блокнóт; (*paw*) лáпа; *v.t.* набивáть *impf.*, набúть (-бью́, -бьёшь) *pf.*; подбивáть *impf.*, подбúть (подобью́, -ьёшь) *pf.* **padding** *n.* набúвка.

paddle¹ ['pæd(ə)l] *n.* (*oar*) (байдáрочное) вёсло (*pl.* вёсла, -сел, -слам); (*of* ~ *wheel*) лóпасть (*pl.* -ти, -тéй); *v.i.* (*row*) грестú (гребý, -бёшь; грёб, -лá) *impf.* байдáрочным веслóм.

paddle² ['pæd(ə)l] *v.i.* (*wade*) ходúть (хожý, хóдишь) *indet.*, идтú (идý, идёшь; шёл, шла) *det.*, пойтú (пойдý, -дёшь; пошёл, -шлá) *pf.* босикóм по водé; **paddling pool** лягушáтник.

paddle-boat ['pæd(ə)l,bəʊt] *n.* колёсный парохóд. **paddle-wheel** *n.* гребнóе колесó (*pl.* -ёса).

paddock ['pædək] *n.* небольшóй луг (*loc.* -ý; *pl.* -á).

padlock ['pædlɒk] *n.* висячий замóк (-мкá); *v.t.* запирáть *impf.*, заперéть (запрý, -рёшь; зáпер, -лá, -ло) *pf.* на висячий замóк.

paediatric [,pi:dɪ'ætrɪk] *adj.* педиатрúческий. **paediatrician** [,pi:dɪə'trɪʃ(ə)n] *n.* педиáтор. **paediatrics** *n.* педиатрúя.

paella [paɪ'elə] *n.* (*cul.*) паэ́лья.

pagan ['peɪgən] *n.* язы́чник, -ица; *adj.* язы́ческий. **paganism** *n.* язы́чество.

page¹ [peɪdʒ] *n.* (~*-boy*) паж (-á), мáльчик-слугá *m.*; *v.t.* (*summon*) вызывáть *impf.*, вы́звать (вы́зову, -вешь) *pf.*

page² [peɪdʒ] *n.* (*of book*) странúца.

pageant ['pædʒ(ə)nt] *n.* пы́шная процéссия; великолéпное зрéлище. **pageantry** *n.* великолéпие.

paginate ['pædʒɪ,neɪt] *v.t.* нумеровáть *impf.*, про~ *pf.* странúцы+*g.*

pagoda [pə'gəʊdə] *n.* пáгода.

paid [peɪd], **paid-up** *adj.* оплáченный (-ен); *see* **pay**

pail [peɪl] *n.* ведрó (*pl.* вёдра, -дер, -драм).

pain [peɪn] *n.* бóль; *pl.* (*efforts*) усúлия *nt.pl.*; **on** ~ **of death** под стрáхом смéрти; **take** ~ **over** прилагáть *impf.*, приложúть (-жý, -жишь) *pf.* усúлия к+*d.*; *v.t.* причинять *impf.*, причинúть *pf.* боль+*d.*; (*fig.*) огорчáть *impf.*, огорчúть *pf.* **painful** *adj.* болéзненный (-ен, -енна); **be** ~ (*part of body*) болéть (-лúт) *impf.* **painkiller** *n.* болеутоляющее срéдство. **painless** *adj.* безболéзненный (-ен, -енна). **painstaking** *adj.* старáтельный, усéрдный.

paint [peɪnt] *n.* крáска; *v.t.* крáсить *impf.*, по~ *pf.*; (*portray*) писáть (пишý, -шешь) *impf.*, на~ *pf.* крáсками. **paintbrush** *n.* кисть (*pl.* -ти, -тéй). **painter¹** *n.* (*artist*) худóжник, -ица; (*decorator*) маляр (-á).

painter² ['peɪntə(r)] *n.* (*rope*) фáлинь *m.*

painting ['peɪntɪŋ] *n.* (*art*) жúвопись; (*picture*) картúна.

pair [peə(r)] *n.* пáра; *not translated with nn. denoting a single object, e.g.* **a** ~ **of scissors** нóжницы (-ц) *pl.*; **one** ~ **of scissors** однú нóжницы; *v.t.* & *i.* располагáть(ся) *impf.*, расположúть(ся) (-жý, -жит(ся)) *pf.* пáрами; ~ **off** уходúть (-ожý, -óдишь) *impf.*, уйтú (уйдý, -дёшь; ушёл, ушлá) *pf.* пáрами.

Pakistan [,pɑ:kɪ'stɑ:n, ,pækɪ-] *n.* Пакистáн.

pal [pæl] *n.* товáрищ, приятель *m.*; ~ **up with** дружúть (-жý, -ýжишь) *impf.*, подружúться (-ужýсь, -ýжишься) *pf.* с+*i.*

palace ['pælɪs] *n.* дворéц (-рцá); *attr.* дворцóвый.

palaeographer [,pælɪ'ɒgrəfə(r)] *n.* палеóграф. **palaeography** *n.* палеогрáфия. **palaeolithic** [,pælɪəʊ'lɪθɪk] *adj.* палеолитúческий. **palaeon'tologist** *n.* палеонтóлог. **palaeon'tology** *n.* палеонтолóгия. **palaeozoic** [,pælɪəʊ'zəʊɪk] *adj.* палеозóйский.

palatable ['pælətəb(ə)l] *adj.* вкýсный (-сен, -снá, -сно); (*fig.*) приятный. **palatal** *adj.* нёбный; (*ling. also*) палатáльный; *n.* палатáльный (звук) *sb.* **palatalize** *v.t.* палатализовáть *impf.* & *pf.* **palate** *n.* нёбо; (*taste*) вкус.

palatial [pə'leɪʃ(ə)l] *adj.* дворцóвый; (*splendid*) великолéпный.

pale¹ [peɪl] *n.* (*stake*) кол (-á, *loc.* -ý; *pl.* -ья); (*boundary*) границa; (*fig.*) предéлы *m.pl.*

pale² [peɪl] *adj.* блéдный (-ден, -днá, -дно, блéдны́); *v.i.* бледнéть *impf.*, по~ *pf.* **paleface** *n.* бледнолúцый *sb.*

palette ['pælɪt] *n.* палúтра. **palette-knife** *n.* мастихúн, штáпель *m.*

paling(s) ['peɪlɪŋ] *n.* частокóл.

palisade [,pælɪ'seɪd] *n.* частокóл, палисáд.

pall¹ [pɔ:l] *n.* покрóв. **pallbearer** *n.* несýщий *sb.* гроб.

pall² [pɔ:l] *v.i.*: ~ **on** надоедáть *impf.*, надоéсть (-éм, -éшь, -éст, -едúм; -éл) *pf.*+*d.*

palliasse ['pælɪ,æs] *n.* солóменный тюфяк (-á).

palliative ['pælɪətɪv] *adj.* смягчáющий, паллиатúвный; *n.* смягчáющее срéдство, паллиатúв.

pallid ['pælɪd] *adj.* блéдный (-ден, -днá, -дно,

бле́дны́). **pallor** *n.* бле́дность.

palm¹ [pɑːm] *n.* (*tree*) па́льма; (*branch*) па́льмовая ветвь (*pl.* -ви, -ве́й); (*willow-branch as substitute*) ве́точка ве́рбы; ~ **oil** па́льмовое ма́сло; **P~ Sunday** Ве́рбное воскресе́нье.

palm² [pɑːm] *n.* (*of hand*) ладо́нь; *v.t.* (*conceal*) пря́тать (-я́чу, -я́чешь) *impf.*, с~ *pf.* в руке́; ~ **off** всу́чивать *impf.*, всучи́ть (-учу́, -у́чи́шь) *pf.* (**on** +*d.*). **palmist** *n.* хирома́нт, ~ка. **palmistry** *n.* хирома́нтия.

palmy ['pɑːmɪ] *adj.* (*flourishing*) цвету́щий.

palpable ['pælpəb(ə)l] *adj.* осяза́емый.

palpitate ['pælpɪˌteɪt] *v.i.* (*throb*) (си́льно) би́ться (бьётся) *impf.*; (*tremble*) трепета́ть (-ещу́, -е́щешь) *impf.* **palpitations** *n.* (си́льное) сердцеби́ение, пульса́ция.

palsy ['pɔːlzɪ, 'pɒl-] *n.* парали́ч (-а́).

paltry ['pɔːltrɪ, 'pɒl-] *adj.* ничто́жный.

pampas ['pæmpəs] *n.* пампа́сы (-сов) *pl.* **pampas-grass** *n.* пампа́сная трава́.

pamper ['pæmpə(r)] *v.t.* балова́ть *impf.*, из~ *pf.*

pamphlet ['pæmflɪt] *n.* брошю́ра.

pan¹ [pæn] *n.* (*saucepan*) кастрю́ля; (*frying-~*) сковорода́ (*pl.* ско́вороды, -о́д, -ода́м); (*bowl*; *of scales*) ча́шка; *v.t.*: ~ **off, out** промыва́ть *impf.*, промы́ть (-мо́ю, -мо́ешь) *pf.*

pan² [pæn] *v.i.* (*cin.*) панорами́ровать *impf.* & *pf.*

panama (hat) ['pænəˌmɑː] *n.* пана́ма.

panacea [ˌpænə'siːə] *n.* панаце́я.

pan-American [ˌpænə'merɪkən] *adj.* панамерика́нский.

pancake ['pænkeɪk] *n.* блин (-а́); *v.i.* (*aeron.*) парашюти́ровать *impf.*, с~ *pf.*

panchromatic [ˌpænkrəʊ'mætɪk] *adj.* панхромати́ческий.

pancreas ['pæŋkrɪəs] *n.* поджелу́дочная железа́ (*pl.* -езы, -ёз, -еза́м).

panda ['pændə] *n.* па́нда; **giant** ~ бамбу́ковый медве́дь *m.*

pandemonium [ˌpændɪ'məʊnɪəm] *n.* гвалт.

pander ['pændə(r)] *n.* сво́дник; *v.i.*: ~ **to** потво́рствовать *impf.*+*d.*

pane [peɪn] *n.* око́нное стекло́ (*pl.* стёкла, -кол, -клам).

panel ['pæn(ə)l] *n.* пане́ль, филёнка; (*control-~*) щит (-а́) управле́ния; (*list of jurors*) спи́сок (-ска) прися́жных; (*jury*) прися́жные *sb.*; (*team in discussion*, *quiz*) уча́стники *m.pl.* (диску́ссии, виктори́ны); (*team of experts*) гру́ппа специали́стов; *v.t.* обшива́ть *impf.*, обши́ть (обошью́, -ьёшь) *pf.* пане́лями. **panelling** *n.* пане́льная обши́вка.

pang [pæŋ] *n.* о́страя боль; *pl.* му́ки (-к) *pl.*

panic ['pænɪk] *n.* па́ника; *v.i.* впада́ть *impf.*, впасть (-аду́, -адёшь; -ал) *pf.* в па́нику. **panicky** *adj.* пани́ческий.

panicle ['pænɪk(ə)l] *n.* метёлка.

panic-monger ['pænɪkˌmʌŋgə] *n.* паникёр. **panic-stricken** *adj.* охва́ченный (-ен) пани́кой; *adj.* пани́ческий.

pannier ['pænɪə(r)] *n.* корзи́нка.

panorama [ˌpænə'rɑːmə] *n.* панора́ма. **panoramic** [ˌpænə'ræmɪk] *adj.* панора́мный.

pansy ['pænzɪ] *n.* аню́тины гла́зки (-зок) *pl.*

pant [pænt] *v.i.* задыха́ться *impf.*, задохну́ться (-о́х(ну́л)ся, -о́х(ну́)лась) *pf.*; пыхте́ть (-хчу́, -хти́шь) *impf.*

pantheism ['pænθɪˌɪz(ə)m] *n.* пантеи́зм. **pantheist** *n.* пантеи́ст. **panthe'istic** *adj.* пантеисти́ческий.

panther ['pænθə(r)] *n.* панте́ра, барс.

panties ['pæntɪz] *n.* тру́сики (-ков) *pl.*

pantomime ['pæntəˌmaɪm] *n.* рожде́ственское представле́ние для дете́й; (*dumb show*) пантоми́ма.

pantry ['pæntrɪ] *n.* кладова́я *sb.*; (*butler's*) буфе́тная *sb.*

pants [pænts] *n.* (*trousers*) брю́ки (-к) *pl.*; (*underpants*) кальсо́ны (-н) *pl.*, трусы́ (-со́в) *pl.*

papacy ['peɪpəsɪ] *n.* па́пство. **papal** *adj.* па́пский.

paper ['peɪpə(r)] *n.* бума́га; *pl.* докуме́нты *m.pl.*; (*newspaper*) газе́та; (*wallpaper*) обо́и (-о́ев) *pl.*; (*dissertation*) докла́д; *adj.* бума́жный; *v.t.* окле́ивать *impf.*, окле́ить *pf.* обо́ями. **paperback** *n.* кни́га в бума́жной обло́жке. **paperclip** *n.* скре́пка. **paperhanger** *n.* обо́йщик. **paper-knife** *n.* разрезно́й нож (-а́). **paper-mill** *n.* бума́жная фа́брика. **paperweight** *n.* пресс-папье́ *nt.indecl.* **papery** *adj.* бума́жный.

papier maché [ˌpæpjeɪ 'mæʃeɪ] *n.* папье́-маше́ *nt.indecl.*

paprika ['pæprɪkə, pə'priːkə] *n.* кра́сный пе́рец (-рца(у)).

papyrus [pə'paɪərəs] *n.* папи́рус.

par [pɑː(r)] *n.* (*equality*) ра́венство; (*normal condition*) норма́льное состоя́ние; ~ **of exchange** парите́т; **above, below,** ~ вы́ше, ни́же, номина́льной цены́; **on a ~ with** наравне́ с+*i.*

parable ['pærəb(ə)l] *n.* при́тча.

parabola [pə'ræbələ] *n.* пара́бола. **parabolic** [ˌpærə'bɒlɪk] *adj.* параболи́ческий.

parachute ['pærəˌʃuːt] *n.* парашю́т; *v.t.* сбра́сывать *impf.*, сбро́сить *pf.* с парашю́том; *v.i.* спуска́ться *impf.*, спусти́ться (-ущу́сь, -у́стишься) *pf.* с парашю́том. **parachutist** *n.* парашюти́ст.

parade [pə'reɪd] *n.* пара́д; (*display*) выставле́ние напока́з; *v.t.* & *i.* стро́ить(ся) *impf.*, по~ *pf.*; *v.t.* (*show off*) выставля́ть *impf.*, вы́ставить *pf.* напока́з. **parade-ground** *n.* плац.

paradigm ['pærəˌdaɪm] *n.* паради́гма.

paradise ['pærəˌdaɪs] *n.* рай (*loc.* раю́).

paradox ['pærəˌdɒks] *n.* парадо́кс. **para'doxical** *adj.* парадокса́льный.

paraffin ['pærəfɪn] *n.* парафи́н; (~ *oil*) кероси́н; **liquid** ~ парафи́новое ма́сло; *attr.* парафи́новый; ~ **wax** твёрдый парафи́н.

paragon ['pærəgən] *n.* образе́ц (-зца́).
paragraph ['pærə,grɑːf] *n.* абза́ц; (*news item*) (газе́тная) заме́тка.
parakeet ['pærə,kiːt] *n.* длиннохво́стый попуга́й.
parallax ['pærə,læks] *n.* паралла́кс.
parallel ['pærə,lel] *adj.* паралле́льный; ~ **bars** паралле́льные бру́сья *m.pl.*; *n.* паралле́ль. **para'llelogram** *n.* параллелогра́мм.
paralyse ['pærə,laɪz] *v.t.* парализова́ть *impf.* & *pf.* **paralysis** [pə'rælɪsɪs] *n.* парали́ч (-а́). **paralytic** [,pærə'lɪtɪk] *n.* парали́тик; *adj.* парали́чный.
parameter [pə'ræmɪtə(r)] *n.* пара́метр.
paramilitary [,pærə'mɪlɪtərɪ] *adj.* полувое́нный.
paramount ['pærə,maʊnt] *adj.* (*supreme*) верхо́вный; (*pre-eminent*) первостепе́нный (-нен, -нна).
paranoia [,pærə'nɔɪə] *n.* парано́йя.
parapet ['pærəpɪt] *n.* парапе́т; (*mil.*) бру́ствер.
paraphernalia [,pærəfə'neɪlɪə] *n.* (*personal belongings*) ли́чное иму́щество; (*accessories*) принадле́жности *f.pl.*
paraphrase ['pærə,freɪz] *n.* переска́з, парафра́за; *v.t.* переска́зывать *impf.*, пересказа́ть (-ажу́, -а́жешь) *pf.*; парафрази́ровать *impf.* & *pf.*
paraplegia [,pærə'pliːdʒə] *n.* параплеги́я.
parapsychology [,pærəsaɪ'kɒlədʒɪ] *n.* парапсихоло́гия.
parasite ['pærə,saɪt] *n.* парази́т; (*person*) туне́ядец (-дца). **parasitic(al)** [,pærə'sɪtɪk(ə)l] *adj.* паразити́ческий, парази́тный.
parasol ['pærə,sɒl] *n.* зо́нтик.
paratrooper ['pærə,truːpə(r)] *n.* парашюти́ст-деса́нтник, авиадеса́нтник. **paratroops** *n.* парашю́тно-деса́нтные войска́ *nt.pl.*
paratyphoid [,pærə'taɪfɔɪd] *n.* парати́ф.
parboil ['pɑːbɔɪl] *v.t.* слегка́ отва́ривать *impf.*, отвари́ть (-рю́, -ришь) *pf.*
parcel ['pɑːs(ə)l] *n.* паке́т, посы́лка; (*of land*) уча́сток (-тка); ~ **post** почто́во-посы́лочная слу́жба; *v.t.*: ~ **out** дели́ть (-лю́, -лишь) *impf.*, раз~ *pf.*; ~ **up** завёртывать *impf.*, заверну́ть *pf.* в паке́т.
parch [pɑːtʃ] *v.t.* иссуша́ть *impf.*, иссуши́ть (-ит) *pf.*; **become** ~**ed** пересыха́ть *impf.*, пересо́хнуть (-х) *pf.*
parchment ['pɑːtʃmənt] *n.* перга́мент; *attr.* перга́мен(т)ный.
pardon ['pɑːd(ə)n] *n.* проще́ние; извине́ние; (*leg.*) поми́лование; *v.t.* проща́ть *impf.*, прости́ть *pf.*; (*leg.*) поми́ловать *pf.* **pardonable** *adj.* прости́тельный.
pare [peə(r)] *v.t.* обреза́ть *impf.*, обре́зать (-е́жу, -е́жешь) *pf.*; (*fruit*) чи́стить *impf.*, о~ *pf.*; ~ **away, down** (*fig.*) сокраща́ть *impf.*, сократи́ть (-ащу́, -ати́шь) *pf.*
parent ['peərənt] *n.* роди́тель *m.*, ~ница; (*forefather*) пре́док (-дка); (*origin*) причи́на. **parentage** *n.* происхожде́ние. **parental** [pə'rent(ə)l] *adj.* роди́тельский.
parenthesis [pə'renθəsɪs] *n.* (*word, clause*) вво́дное сло́во (*pl.* -ва́), предложе́ние; *pl.* (*brackets*) ско́бки *f.pl.*; **in** ~ в ско́бках.
pariah [pə'raɪə, 'pærɪə] *n.* па́рия *c.g.*
parings ['peərɪŋz] *n.* обре́зки *f.pl.*
Paris ['pærɪs] *n.* Пари́ж.
parish ['pærɪʃ] *n.* (*area*) прихо́д; (*inhabitants*) прихожа́не *pl.*; *attr.* прихо́дский. **parishioner** [pə'rɪʃənə(r)] *n.* прихожа́нин (*pl.* -а́не, -а́н), -а́нка.
parity ['pærɪtɪ] *n.* ра́венство; (*econ.*) парите́т.
park [pɑːk] *n.* парк; (*national* ~) запове́дник; (*for cars etc.*) стоя́нка; *v.t.* & *abs.* ста́вить *impf.*, по~ *pf.* (маши́ну); паркова́ть *impf.*, за~ *pf.* (маши́ну). **parking** *n.* стоя́нка. **parking-meter** *n.* парко́вочный автома́т.
parley ['pɑːlɪ] *n.* перегово́ры (-ров) *pl.*; *v.i.* вести́ (веду́, -дёшь; вёл, -а́) *impf.* перегово́ры.
parliament ['pɑːləmənt] *n.* парла́мент. **parliamen'tarian** *n.* знато́к (-а́) парла́ментской пра́ктики. **parlia'mentary** *adj.* парла́ментский.
parlour ['pɑːlə(r)] *n.* гости́ная *sb.*; приёмная *sb.* **parlourmaid** *n.* го́рничная *sb.*
parochial [pə'rəʊkɪəl] *adj.* прихо́дский; (*fig.*) ограни́ченный (-ен, -енна). **parochialism** *n.* ограни́ченность, у́зкость.
parody ['pærədɪ] *n.* паро́дия; *v.t.* пароди́ровать *impf.* & *pf.*
parole [pə'rəʊl] *n.* че́стное сло́во; освобожде́ние под че́стное сло́во; (*password*) паро́ль *m.*; **on** ~ освобождённый (-ён, -ена́) под че́стное сло́во.
paroxysm ['pærək,sɪz(ə)m] *n.* пароксі́зм, припа́док (-дка).
parquet ['pɑːkɪ, -keɪ] *n.* парке́т; *attr.* парке́тный; *v.t.* устила́ть *impf.*, устла́ть (устелю́, -лешь) *pf.* парке́том.
parricidal [,pærɪ'saɪdəl] *adj.* отцеуби́йственный (-ен, -енна). **'parricide** *n.* (*action*) отцеуби́йство; (*person*) отцеуби́йца *c.g.*
parrot ['pærət] *n.* попуга́й; *v.t.* повторя́ть *impf.*, повтори́ть *pf.* как попуга́й.
parry ['pærɪ] *v.t.* пари́ровать *impf.* & *pf.*, от~ *pf.*
parse [pɑːz] *v.t.* де́лать *impf.*, с~ *pf.* разбо́р+*g.*
parsimonious [,pɑːsɪ'məʊnɪəs] *adj.* бережли́вый; (*mean*) скупо́й (скуп, -а́, -о). **parsimony** ['pɑːsɪmənɪ] *n.* бережли́вость; ску́пость.
parsley ['pɑːslɪ] *n.* петру́шка.
parsnip ['pɑːsnɪp] *n.* пастерна́к.
parson ['pɑːs(ə)n] *n.* прихо́дский свяще́нник. **parsonage** *n.* дом (*pl.* -а́) прихо́дского свяще́нника.
part [pɑːt] *n.* часть (*pl.* -ти, -те́й), до́ля (*pl.* -ли, -ле́й); (*taking* ~) уча́стие; (*in play*) роль (*pl.* -ли, -ле́й); (*mus.*) па́ртия; (*in dispute*) сторона́ (*a.* -ону; *pl.* -оны, -о́н, -она́м); **for the most** ~ бо́льшей ча́стью; **in**

~ ча́стью; **for my** ~ что каса́ется меня́; **take ~ in** уча́ствовать *impf.* в+*p.*; ~ **and parcel** неотъе́млемая часть; *v.t.* & *i.* (*divide*) разделя́ть(ся) *impf.*, раздели́ть(ся) (-лю́(сь), -лишь(ся)) *pf.*; *v.i.* (*leave*) расстава́ться (-таю́сь, -таёшься) *impf.*, расста́ться (-а́нусь, -а́нешься) *pf.* (**from, with** с+*i.*); ~ **one's hair** де́лать *impf.*, с~ *pf.* себе́ пробо́р.

partake [pɑːˈteɪk] *v.i.* принима́ть *impf.*, приня́ть (приму́, -мешь; при́нял, -а́, -о) *pf.* уча́стие (**in, of** в+*p.*); (*eat*) есть (ем, ешь, ест, еди́м; ел *impf.*, съ~ *pf.* (**of** +*a.*).

partial [ˈpɑːʃ(ə)l] *adj.* (*incomplete*) части́чный, непо́лный (-лон, -лна́, -лно); (*biased*) пристра́стный; ~ **to** неравноду́шный к+*d.* **partiality** [ˌpɑːʃɪˈælɪtɪ] *n.* пристра́стие (**for** к+*d.*). **partially** *adv.* части́чно.

participant [pɑːˈtɪsɪpənt] *n.* уча́стник, -ица (**in** +*g.*). **participate** *v.i.* уча́ствовать *impf.* (**in** в+*p.*). **partici'pation** *n.* уча́стие (**in** в+*p.*).

participial [ˌpɑːtɪˈsɪpɪ(ə)l] *adj.* прича́стный. **'participle** *n.* прича́стие.

particle [ˈpɑːtɪk(ə)l] *n.* части́ца.

particoloured [ˈpɑːtɪˌkʌləd] *adj.* разноцве́тный.

particular [pəˈtɪkjʊlə(r)] *adj.* осо́бый, осо́бенный; (*careful*) тща́тельный; *n.* подро́бность; *pl.* подро́бный отчёт; **in** ~ в ча́стности.

parting [ˈpɑːtɪŋ] *n.* (*leave-taking*) проща́ние; (*of hair*) пробо́р.

partisan [ˈpɑːtɪˌzæn] *n.* (*adherent*) сторо́нник; (*mil.*) партиза́н (*g.pl.* -н); *attr.* узкопарти́йный; партиза́нский.

partition [pɑːˈtɪʃ(ə)n] *n.* разделе́ние, расчлене́ние; (*wall*) перегоро́дка, перебо́рка; *v.t.* разделя́ть *impf.*, раздели́ть (-лю́, -лишь) *pf.*; ~ **off** отделя́ть *impf.*, отдели́ть (-лю́, -лишь) *pf.* перегоро́дкой.

partitive [ˈpɑːtɪtɪv] *adj.* раздели́тельный; ~ **genitive** роди́тельный раздели́тельный *sb.*

partly [ˈpɑːtlɪ] *adv.* ча́стью, отча́сти.

partner [ˈpɑːtnə(r)] *n.* (со)уча́стник; (*in business*) компаньо́н; (*in dance, game*) партнёр, ~ша. **partnership** *n.* (со)уча́стие, сотру́дничество; (*business*) това́рищество.

partridge [ˈpɑːtrɪdʒ] *n.* куропа́тка.

part-time [pɑːtˈtaɪm] *adj.* (за́нятый (-т, -та́, -то)) непо́лный рабо́чий день.

party [ˈpɑːtɪ] *n.* (*pol.*) па́ртия; (*group*) гру́ппа; (*social gathering*) вечери́нка; (*leg.*) сторона́ (*a.* -ону; *pl.* -оны, -о́н, -она́м); (*accomplice*) (со)уча́стник; **be a ~ to** принима́ть *impf.*, приня́ть (приму́, -мешь; при́нял, -а́. -о) *pf.* уча́стие в+*p.*; *attr.* парти́йный; ~ **line** (*pol.*) ли́ния па́ртии; (*telephone*) о́бщий телефо́нный про́вод (*pl.* -а́). **party-wall** *n.* о́бщая стена́ (*a.* -ну; *pl.* -ны, -н, -на́м).

pasha [ˈpɑːʃə] *n.* паша́ *m.*

pass [pɑːs] *v.t.* & *i.* (*go past*; ~ *test*; *of time*) проходи́ть (-ожу́, -о́дишь) *impf.*, пройти́ (пройду́, -дёшь; прошёл, -шла́) *pf.* (**by** ми́мо+*g.*); (*travel past*) проезжа́ть *impf.*, прое́хать (-е́ду, -е́дешь) *pf.* (**by** ми́мо+*g.*); (*go across*; *change*) переходи́ть (-ожу́, -о́дишь) *impf.*, перейти́ (-ейду́, -ейдёшь; -ешёл, -ешла́) *pf.* (+*a.*, че́рез+*a.*; **to** в+*a.*, к+*d.*); (~ *examination*) сдава́ть (сдаю́, -аёшь) *impf.*, сдать (-ам, -ашь, -аст, -ади́м; сдал, -а́, -о) *pf.* (экза́мен); *v.i.* (*happen*) происходи́ть (-ит) *impf.*, произойти́ (-ойдёт; -ошёл, -ошла́) *pf.*; (*cards*) пасова́ть *impf.*, с~ *pf.*; *v.t.* (*sport*) пасова́ть *impf.*, пасну́ть *pf.*; (*overtake*) обгоня́ть *impf.*, обогна́ть (обгоню́, -нишь; обогна́л, -а́, -о) *pf.*; (*time*) проводи́ть (-ожу́, -о́дишь) *impf.*, провести́ (-еду́, -едёшь; -ёл, -ела́) *pf.*; (*hand on*) передава́ть (-даю́, -даёшь) *impf.*, переда́ть (-а́м, -а́шь, -а́ст, -ади́м; пе́редал, -а́, -о) *pf.*; (*law, resolution*) принима́ть *impf.*, приня́ть (приму́, -мешь; при́нял, -а́, -о) *pf.*; (*sentence*) выноси́ть (-ошу́, -о́сишь) *impf.*, вы́нести (-су, -сешь; -с) *pf.* (**upon** +*d.*); ~ **as, for** слыть (слыву́, -вёшь; слыл, -а́, -о) *impf.*, про~ *pf.*+*i.*, за+*a.*; ~ **away** (*die*) сконча́ться *pf.*; ~ **by** (*omit*) пропуска́ть *impf.*, пропусти́ть (-ущу́, -у́стишь) *pf.*; ~ **off** (постепе́нно; хорошо́) проходи́ть (-ит) *impf.*, пройти́ (-йдёт; прошёл, -шла́) *pf.*; ~ **out** (*coll.*) отключа́ться *impf.*, отключи́ться *pf.*; ~ **over** (*in silence*) обходи́ть (-ожу́, -о́дишь) *impf.*, обойти́ (обойду́, -дёшь; обошёл, -шла́) *pf.* молча́нием; ~ **through** (*experience*) пережива́ть *impf.*, пережи́ть (-иву́, -ивёшь; пе́режи́л, -а́, -о) *pf.*; *n.* (*permit*) про́пуск (*pl.* -а́); (*free* ~) беспла́тный биле́т; (*cards*; *sport*) пас; (*fencing*) вы́пад; (*juggling*) фо́кус; (*hypnotism*) пасс; (*mountain* ~) перева́л; **bring to** ~ соверша́ть *impf.*, соверши́ть *pf.*; **come to** ~ случа́ться *impf.*, случи́ться *pf.*; **make a ~ at** пристава́ть (-таю́, -таёшь) *impf.*, приста́ть (-а́ну, -а́нешь) *pf.* к+*d.*; ~ **degree** дипло́м без отли́чия.

passable [ˈpɑːsəb(ə)l] *adj.* проходи́мый, прое́зжий; (*fairly good*) неплохо́й (-х, -ха́, -хо).

passage [ˈpæsɪdʒ] *n.* прохо́д, прое́зд; (*of time*) ход; (*sea trip*) рейс; (*in house*) коридо́р; (*in book*) отры́вок (-вка); (*musical*) пасса́ж.

passenger [ˈpæsɪndʒə(r)] *n.* пассажи́р.

passer-by [ˌpɑːsəˈbaɪ] *n.* прохо́жий *sb.*

passing [ˈpɑːsɪŋ] *adj.* (*transient*) мимолётный, преходя́щий; (*cursory*) бе́глый; *n.*: **in** ~ мимохо́дом.

passion [ˈpæʃ(ə)n] *n.* страсть (*pl.* -ти, -те́й) (**for** к+*d.*); (*attraction*) увлече́ние; (*anger*) вспы́шка гне́ва; **P~** (*of Christ*; *mus.*) стра́сти (-те́й) *f.pl.* (Христо́вы). **passionate** *adj.* стра́стный (-тен, -тна́, -тно), пы́лкий. **passion-flower** *n.* страстноцве́т.

passive [ˈpæsɪv] *adj.* пасси́вный; (*gram.*) страда́тельный; *n.* страда́тельный зало́г. **pa'ssivity** *n.* пасси́вность.

passkey [ˈpɑːskiː] *n.* отмы́чка.

passmark [ˈpɑːsmɑːk] *n.* посре́дственная оце́нка.

Passover [ˈpɑːsˌəʊvə(r)] *n.* евре́йская па́сха.

passport ['pɑːspɔːt] *n.* пáспорт (*pl.* -á).
password ['pɑːswɜːd] *n.* парóль *m.*
past [pɑːst] *adj.* прóшлый; (*gram.*) прошéдший; *n.* прóшлое *sb.*; (*gram.*) прошéдшее врéмя *nt.*; *prep.* ми́мо+*g.*; (*beyond*) за+*i.*; *adv.* ми́мо.
paste [peɪst] *n.* (*of flour*) тéсто; (*similar mixture*) пáста; (*adhesive*) клéйстер; (*of imitation gem*) страз; *v.t.* наклéивать *impf.*, наклéить *pf.*; ~ **up** расклéивать *impf.*, расклéить *pf.* **pasteboard** *n.* картóн.
pastel ['pæst(ə)l] *n.* (*crayon*) пастéль; (*drawing*) рисýнок (-нка) пастéлью; *attr.* пастéльный.
pastern ['pæst(ə)n] *n.* бáбка.
pasteurization [ˌpɑːstjəraɪ'zeɪʃ(ə)n, ˌpæst-] *n.* пастеризáция. **'pasteurize** *v.t.* пастеризовáть *impf.* & *pf.*
pastiche [pæ'stiːʃ] *n.* смесь.
pastille ['pæstɪl] *n.* лепёшка.
pastime ['pɑːstaɪm] *n.* развлечéние; (*game*) игрá (*pl.* -ры).
pastor ['pɑːstə(r)] *n.* пáстор. **pastoral** *adj.* (*bucolic*) пасторáльный; (*of pastor*) пáсторский; *n.* пасторáль.
pastry ['peɪstrɪ] *n.* печéнье, пирóжное *sb.*
pasturage ['pɑːstʃərɪdʒ] *n.* пастьбá. **pasture** ['pɑːstjə(r)] *n.* (*land*) пáстбище; (*herbage*) поднóжный корм (*loc.* -е & -ý); *v.t.* пасти́ (-сý, -сёшь; -с, -слá) *impf.*
pasty[1] ['pæstɪ] *n.* пирожóк (-жкá).
pasty[2] ['pæstɪ] *adj.* тестообрáзный; (~-*faced*) блéдный (-ден, -днá, -дно, блéдны́).
pat [pæt] *n.* шлепóк (-пкá); (*of butter etc.*) кусóк (-скá); *v.t.* хлопáть *impf.*, по~ *pf.*; *adj.* умéстный; *adv.* кстáти, своеврéменно.
patch [pætʃ] *n.* заплáта; (*over eye*) повя́зка (на глазý); (*on face*) мýшка; (*spot*) пятнó (*pl.* -тна, -тен, -тнам); (*piece of land*) учáсток (-тка) земли́; ~ **pocket** накладнóй кармáн; *v.t.* стáвить *impf.*, по~ *pf.* заплáту, -ы, на+*a.*; ~ **up** (*fig.*) улáживать *impf.*, улáдить *pf.* **patchwork** *n.* лоскýтная рабóта; *attr.* лоскýтный. **patchy** *adj.* пёстрый (пёстр, -á, пёстрó); (*uneven*) неровный (-вен, -внá, -вно).
pâté ['pæteɪ] *n.* паштéт.
patella [pə'telə] *n.* колéнная чáшка.
patent ['peɪt(ə)nt, 'pæt-] *adj.* патентóванный (-ан); (*obvious*) я́вный; ~ **leather** лакирóванная кóжа; *n.* патéнт; *v.t.* патентовáть *impf.*, за~ *pf.* **paten'tee** *n.* владéлец (-льца) патéнта.
paternal [pə'tɜːn(ə)l] *adj.* отцóвский; (*fatherly*) отéческий; ~ **uncle** дя́дя *m.* со стороны́ отцá. **paternity** *n.* отцóвство.
path [pɑːθ] *n.* тропи́нка, тропá (*pl.* -пы, -п, трóпáм); (*way*) путь (-ти́, -тём) *m.*
pathetic [pə'θetɪk] *adj.* жáлостный, трóгательный.
pathless ['pɑːθlɪs] *adj.* бездорóжный.
pathological [ˌpæθə'lɒdʒɪk(ə)l] *adj.* патологи́ческий. **pathologist** [pə'θɒlədʒɪst] *n.* патóлог. **pa'thology** *n.* патолóгия.
pathos ['peɪθɒs] *n.* пáфос.
pathway ['pɑːθweɪ] *n.* тропи́нка, тропá (*pl.* -пы, -п, трóпáм).
patience ['peɪʃ(ə)ns] *n.* терпéние; (*persistence*) упóрство; (*cards*) пасья́нс. **patient** *adj.* терпели́вый; (*persistent*) упóрный; *n.* больнóй *sb.*, пациéнт, ~ка.
patina ['pætɪnə] *n.* пати́на.
patio ['pætɪəʊ] *n.* (*court*) внýтренний дво́рик; (*terrace*) террáса.
patriarch ['peɪtrɪˌɑːk] *n.* патриáрх. **patri'archal** *adj.* патриархáльный; (*relig.*) патриáрший.
patrician [pə'trɪʃ(ə)n] *n.* аристокрáт, ~ка; (*hist.*) патри́ций; *adj.* аристократи́ческий; (*hist.*) патрициáнский.
patricidal *etc. see* **parricide**
patrimonial [ˌpætrɪ'məʊnɪəl] *adj.* наслéдственный. **patrimony** ['pætrɪmənɪ] *n.* наслéдство.
patriot ['peɪtrɪət, 'pæt-] *n.* патриóт, ~ка. **patriotic** [ˌpeɪtrɪ'ɒtɪk, ˌpæt-] *adj.* патриоти́ческий. **patriotism** *n.* патриоти́зм.
patrol [pə'trəʊl] *n.* патрýль (-ля́) *m.*; (*action*) патрули́рование; *v.t.* & *i.* патрули́ровать *impf.*
patron ['peɪtrən] *n.* покрови́тель *m.*; (*of shop*) клиéнт, ~ка; ~ **saint** застýпник, -ица. **patronage** *n.* покрови́тельство. **patroness** *n.* покрови́тельница. **patronize** *v.t.* покрови́тельствовать *impf.*+*d.*; (*shop*) быть клиéнтом, клиéнткой, +*g.*; (*treat condescendingly*) снисходи́тельно относи́ться (-ошýсь, -óсишься) *impf.*, к+*d.*
patronymic [ˌpætrə'nɪmɪk] *n.* родовóе и́мя *nt.*; (*Russian name*) óтчество.
patter[1] ['pætə(r)] *v.i.* (*sound*) постýкивать *impf.*; *n.* постýкивание, лёгкий тóпот.
patter[2] ['pætə(r)] *n.* (*speech*) скороговóрка.
pattern ['pæt(ə)n] *n.* (*paragon*) образéц (-зцá); (*model*) модéль; (*sewing*) вы́кройка; (*design*) узóр.
patty ['pætɪ] *n.* пирожóк (-жкá).
paunch [pɔːntʃ] *n.* брюшкó (*pl.* -ки́, -кóв), пýзо.
pauper ['pɔːpə(r)] *n.* бедня́к (-á), ни́щий *sb.*
pause [pɔːz] *n.* пáуза, переры́в; *v.i.* дéлать *impf.*, с~ *pf.* пáузу; останáвливаться *impf.*, останови́ться (-влю́сь, -ви́шься) *pf.*
pave [peɪv] *v.t.* мости́ть *impf.*, вы́~, за~ *pf.*; ~ **the way** подготовля́ть *impf.*, подготóвить *pf.* пóчву (**for** для+*g.*). **pavement** *n.* тротуáр, панéль.
pavilion [pə'vɪljən] *n.* (*building*) павильóн; (*tent*) палáтка, шатёр (-трá).
paw [pɔː] *n.* лáпа; *v.t.* трóгать *impf.* лáпой; (*horse*) бить (бьёт) *impf.* копы́том.
pawl [pɔːl] *n.* защёлка; (*naut.*) пал.
pawn[1] [pɔːn] *n.* (*chess*) пéшка.
pawn[2] [pɔːn] *n.*: **in** ~ в заклáде; *v.t.* заклáдывать *impf.*, заложи́ть (-жý, -жишь) *pf.*; отдавáть (-даю́, -даёшь) *impf.*, отдáть (-áм, -áшь, -áст, -ади́м; óтдал, -á, -о) *pf.* в залóг.

pawnbroker *n.* ростовщи́к (-а́), -и́ца. **pawnshop** *n.* ломба́рд.

pay [peɪ] *v.t.* плати́ть (-ачу́, -а́тишь) *impf.*, за~, у~ *pf.* (**for** за+*a.*); (*bill etc.*) опла́чивать *impf.*, оплати́ть (-ачу́, -а́тишь) *pf.*; *v.i.* (*be profitable*) окупа́ться *impf.*, окупи́ться (-ится) *pf.*; *n.* (*payment*) упла́та; (*wages*) жа́лованье, зарпла́та. **payable** *adj.* подлежа́щий упла́те. **pa'yee** *n.* получа́тель *m.*, ~ница; (*of cheque etc.*) предъяви́тель *m.*, ~ница. **payload** *n.* поле́зная нагру́зка. **payment** *n.* упла́та, платёж (-а́); ~ **by instalments** платёж (-а́) в рассро́чку; ~ **in kind** пла́та нату́рой. **pay-packet** *n.* полу́чка. **payroll** *n.* платёжная ве́домость.

PC *abbr.* (*of* **Police Constable**) полице́йский, консте́бль; (*of* **personal computer**) ПК, персона́льный компью́тер.

PE *abbr.* (*of* **physical education**) физкульту́ра.

pea [piː] *n.* (*also pl.*, *collect.*) горо́х (-а(у)).

peace [piːs] *n.* мир; (*treaty*) ми́рный догово́р; (*public order*; *tranquillity*) споко́йствие; (*quiet*) поко́й; *attr.* ми́рный; **at** ~ **with** в ми́ре с+*i.*; **in** ~ в поко́е; **make** ~ заключа́ть *impf.*, заключи́ть *pf.* мир; **make one's** ~ мири́ться *impf.*, по~ *pf.* (**with** с+*i.*); ~ **and quiet** мир и тишина́. **peaceable, peaceful** *adj.* ми́рный. **peace-loving** *adj.* миролюби́вый. **peace-offering** *n.* искупи́тельная же́ртва. **peacetime** *n.* ми́рное вре́мя *nt.*

peach [piːtʃ] *n.* пе́рсик; (~-*tree*) пе́рсиковое де́рево (*pl.* дере́вья, -ьев).

peacock ['piːkɒk] *n.* павли́н; ~ **butterfly** дневно́й павли́нный глаз. **peafowl** *n.* павли́н. **peahen** *n.* па́ва.

peak [piːk] *n.* (*of cap*) козырёк (-рька́); (*summit*; *highest point*) верши́на; ~ **hour** часы́ *m.pl.* пик. **peak-load** *n.* максима́льная, пи́ковая, нагру́зка.

peaky ['piːkɪ] *adj.* (*worn out*) измождённый (-ён, -ена́).

peal [piːl] *n.* (*sound*) звон колоколо́в, трезво́н; (*set of bells*) набо́р колоколо́в; (*of thunder*) раска́т; (*of laughter*) взрыв; *v.i.* (*bells*) трезво́нить *impf.*; (*thunder*) греме́ть (-ми́т) *impf.*, по~ *pf.*; ~ **the bells** звони́ть *impf.*, по~ *pf.* в колокола́.

peanut ['piːnʌt] *n.* земляно́й оре́х, ара́хис.

pear [peə(r)] *n.* гру́ша; (~-*tree*) гру́шевое де́рево (*pl.* дере́вья, -ьев). **pear-shaped** *adj.* грушеви́дный.

pearl [pɜːl] *n.* же́мчуг (-а(у); *pl.* -а́); (*single* ~, *also fig.*) жемчу́жина; ~ **barley** перло́вая крупа́; ~ **button** перламу́тровая пу́говица. **pearl-oyster** *n.* жемчу́жница. **pearly** *adj.* жемчу́жный.

peasant ['pez(ə)nt] *n.* крестья́нин (*pl.* -я́не, -я́н), -я́нка; *attr.* крестья́нский; ~ **woman** крестья́нка. **peasantry** *n.* крестья́нство.

peat [piːt] *n.* торф (-а(у)). **peatbog** *n.* торфяни́к (-а́). **peaty** *adj.* торфяно́й.

pebble ['peb(ə)l] *n.* га́лька. **pebbly** *adj.* покры́тый га́лкой.

peccadillo [ˌpekə'dɪləʊ] *n.* грешо́к (-шка́).

peck [pek] *v.t.* & *i.* клева́ть (клюю́, клюёшь) *impf.*, клю́нуть *pf.*; *n.* клево́к (-вка́).

pectoral ['pektər(ə)l] *adj.* грудно́й; (*worn on chest*) нагру́дный.

peculiar [pɪ'kjuːlɪə(r)] *adj.* (*distinctive*) своеобра́зный; (*special*) осо́бенный; (*strange*) стра́нный (-нен, -нна́, -нно); ~ **to** сво́йственный (-ен(ен), -енна) +*d.* **peculiarity** [pɪˌkjuːlɪ'ærɪtɪ] *n.* осо́бенность; стра́нность.

pecuniary [pɪ'kjuːnɪərɪ] *adj.* де́нежный.

pedagogical [ˌpedə'gɒgɪk((ə)l), -'gɒdʒɪk((ə)l)] *adj.* педагоги́ческий. **pedagogics** *n.* педаго́гика. **'pedagogue** *n.* учи́тель (*pl.* -ля́) *m.*, педаго́г.

pedal ['ped(ə)l] *n.* педа́ль; *v.i.* нажима́ть *impf.*, нажа́ть (-жму́, -жмёшь) *pf.* педа́ль; (*ride bicycle*) е́хать (е́ду, е́дешь) *impf.*, по~ *pf.* на велосипе́де.

pedant ['ped(ə)nt] *n.* педа́нт. **pedantic** [pɪ'dæntɪk] *adj.* педанти́чный. **pedantry** *n.* педанти́чность.

peddle ['ped(ə)l] *v.t.* торгова́ть *impf.* вразно́с+*i.*

pedestal ['pedɪst(ə)l] *n.* пьедеста́л, подно́жие; (*of table*) ту́мба.

pedestrian [pɪ'destrɪən] *adj.* пе́ший, пешехо́дный; (*prosaic*) прозаи́ческий; *n.* пешехо́д; ~ **crossing** перехо́д. **pedestrianization** [pɪˌdestrɪəˌnaɪ'zeɪʃ(ə)n] *n.* созда́ние пешехо́дных зон. **pe'destrianize** *v.t.* запреща́ть *impf.*, запрети́ть (-ещу́, -ети́шь) *pf.* автомоби́льное движе́ние.

pedicure ['pedɪˌkjʊə(r)] *n.* педикю́р.

pedigree ['pedɪˌgriː] *n.* (*genealogy*) родосло́вная *sb.*; (*descent*) происхожде́ние; *adj.* поро́дистый, племенно́й.

pediment ['pedɪmənt] *n.* фронто́н.

pedlar ['pedlə(r)] *n.* разно́счик.

pedometer [pɪ'dɒmɪtə(r)] *n.* шагоме́р.

peek [piːk] *v.i.* (~ *in*) загля́дывать *impf.*, загляну́ть (-ну́, -нешь) *pf.*; (~ *out*) выгля́дывать *impf.*, вы́глянуть *pf.*

peel [piːl] *n.* ко́рка, ко́жица; *v.t.* очища́ть *impf.*, очи́стить *pf.*; *v.i.*: ~ **off** (*detach o.s.*) сходи́ть (-ит) *impf.*, сойти́ (сойдёт; сошёл, -шла́) *pf.* **peelings** *n.* очи́стки (-ков) *pl.*, шелуха́.

peep [piːp] *v.i.* (~ *in*) загля́дывать *impf.*, загляну́ть (-ну́, -нешь) *pf.*; (~ *out*) выгля́дывать *impf.*, вы́глянуть *pf.*; *n.* (*glance*) бы́стрый взгляд; ~ **of day** рассве́т. **peephole** *n.* глазо́к (-зка́).

peer[1] [pɪə(r)] *v.i.* всма́триваться *impf.*, всмотре́ться (-рю́сь, -ришься) *pf.* (**at** в+*a.*).

peer[2] [pɪə(r)] *n.* (*noble*) пэр, лорд; (*equal*) ра́вный *sb.*, ро́вня́ *c.g.* **peerage** *n.* (*class*) сосло́вие пэ́ров; (*rank*) зва́ние пэ́ра. **peeress** *n.* (*peer's wife*) супру́га пэ́ра; ле́ди *f.indecl.* **peerless** *adj.* несравне́нный (-е́нен, -е́нна), бесподо́бный.

peeved [piːvd] *adj.* раздражённый (-ён, -ена́).

peevish *adj.* раздражи́тельный, брюзгли́вый.
peewit ['pi:wɪt] *n.* чи́бис.
peg [peg] *n.* ко́лышек (-шка), деревя́нный гвоздь (-дя́; *pl.* -ди, -де́й) *m.*; (*for hat etc.*) ве́шалка; (*on violin etc.*) коло́к (-лка́); **off the ~** гото́вый; **take down a ~** оса́живать *impf.*, осади́ть (-ажу́, -а́дишь) *pf.*; *v.t.* прикрепля́ть *impf.*, прикрепи́ть *pf.* ко́лышком, -ками; (*price etc.*) иску́сственно подде́рживать *impf.*, поддержа́ть (-жу́, -жишь) *pf.*; *v.i.*: **~ away** приле́жно рабо́тать *impf.* (**at** над+*i.*); **~ out** (*die*) помира́ть *impf.*, помере́ть (-мру́, -мрёшь; по́мер, -ла́, -ло) *pf.*
pejorative [pɪ'dʒɒrətɪv, 'pi:dʒə-] *adj.* уничижи́тельный.
peke [pi:k], **Pekin(g)ese** [,pi:kɪ'ni:z] *n.* кита́йский мопс.
pelican ['pelɪkən] *n.* пелика́н.
pellagra [pɪ'lægrə, -'leɪgrə] *n.* пелла́гра.
pellet ['pelɪt] *n.* ка́тышек (-шка); (*shot*) дроби́на.
pellicle ['pelɪk(ə)l] *n.* ко́жица, плёнка.
pell-mell [pel'mel] *adv.* (*in disorder*) беспоря́дочно; (*headlong*) очертя́, сломя́, го́лову.
pellucid [pɪ'lu:sɪd, -'lju:sɪd] *adj.* (*transparent*) прозра́чный; (*clear*) я́сный (я́сен, ясна́, я́сно, я́сны́).
pelmet ['pelmɪt] *n.* ламбреке́н.
pelt[1] [pelt] *n.* (*animal skin*) шку́ра, ко́жа.
pelt[2] [pelt] *v.t.* забра́сывать *impf.*, заброса́ть *pf.*; *v.i.* (*rain*) бараба́нить (-ит) *impf.*; *n.*: **(at) full ~** со всех ног.
pelvic ['pelvɪk] *adj.* та́зовый. **pelvis** *n.* таз (*loc.* -е & -у́; *pl.* -ы́).
pen[1] [pen] *n.* (*for writing*) перо́ (*pl.* -рья, -рьев); **~ and ink** пи́сьменные принадле́жности *f.pl.*; **slip of the ~** опи́ска.
pen[2] [pen] *n.* (*enclosure*) заго́н; *v.t.* загоня́ть *impf.*, загна́ть (загоню́, -нишь; загна́л, -а́, -о) *pf.*
pen[3] [pen] *n.* (*female swan*) са́мка ле́бедя.
penal ['pi:n(ə)l] *adj.* уголо́вный; (*punishable*) наказу́емый; **~ battalion** штрафно́й батальо́н; **~ code** уголо́вный ко́декс; **~ servitude** ка́торжные рабо́ты *f.pl.* **penalize** *v.t.* нака́зывать *impf.*, наказа́ть (-ажу́, -а́жешь) *pf.*; (*sport*) штрафова́ть *impf.*, о~ *pf.* **penalty** ['penəltɪ] *n.* наказа́ние, взыска́ние; (*sport*) штраф; **~ area** штрафна́я площа́дка; **~ kick** штрафно́й уда́р. **penance** ['penəns] *n.* епитимья́ (*g.pl.* -ми́й).
penchant ['pɑ̃ʃɑ̃] *n.* скло́нность (**for** к+*d.*).
pencil ['pensɪl] *n.* каранда́ш (-а́); *v.t.* (*write*) писа́ть (пишу́, -шешь) *impf.*, на~ *pf.* карандашо́м; (*draw*) рисова́ть *impf.*, на~ *pf.* карандашо́м. **pencil-case** *n.* пена́л. **pencil-sharpener** *n.*точи́лка.
pendant ['pend(ə)nt] *n.* подве́ска, куло́н; *adj.* вися́чий.
pending ['pendɪŋ] *adj.* (*awaiting decision*) ожида́ющий реше́ния; **patent ~** пате́нт заявлен; *prep.* (*during*) во вре́мя+*g.*; (*until*) в ожида́нии+*g.*, до+*g.*
pendulous ['pendjʊləs] *adj.* вися́чий, отви́слый.
pendulum ['pendjʊləm] *n.* ма́ятник.
penetrate ['penɪ,treɪt] *v.t.* прони́зывать *impf.*, прониза́ть (-ижу́, -и́жешь) *pf.*; *v.i.* проника́ть *impf.*, прони́кнуть (-к) *pf.* (**into** в+*a.*; **through** че́рез+*a.*). **penetrating** *adj.* проница́тельный; (*sound*) пронзи́тельный. **pene'tration** *n.* проникнове́ние; (*insight*) проница́тельность.
pen-friend ['penfrend] *n.* знако́мый *sb.* по пи́сьмам.
penguin ['peŋgwɪn] *n.* пингви́н.
penicillin [,penɪ'sɪlɪn] *n.* пеницилли́н.
peninsula [pɪ'nɪnsjʊlə] *n.* полуо́стров (*pl.* -а́). **peninsular** *adj.* полуостровно́й.
penis ['pi:nɪs] *n.* муско́й полово́й член.
penitence ['penɪt(ə)ns] *n.* раска́яние, покая́ние. **penitent** *adj.* раска́ивающийся; *n.* ка́ющийся гре́шник. **peni'tential** *adj.* покая́нный.
penknife ['pennaɪf] *n.* перочи́нный нож (-а́).
pen-name ['pennaɪm] *n.* псевдони́м.
pennant ['penənt] *n.* вы́мпел.
penniless ['penɪlɪs] *adj.* безде́нежный; *pred.* без гроша́; (*poor*) бе́дный (-ден, -дна́, -дно, бе́дны́).
penny ['penɪ] *n.* пе́нни *nt.indecl.*, пенс.
pension ['penʃ(ə)n] *n.* пе́нсия; *v.t.*: **~ off** увольня́ть *impf.*, уво́лить *pf.* на пе́нсию. **pensionable** *adj.* даю́щий, име́ющий, пра́во на пе́нсию; (*age*) пенсио́нный. **pensioner** *n.* пенсионе́р, ~ка.
pensive ['pensɪv] *adj.* заду́мчивый.
penta- ['pentə] *in comb.* пяти..., пента... . **pentacle** *n.* маги́ческая фигу́ра. **pentagon** *n.* пятиуго́льник; **the P~** Пентаго́н. **pentagonal** [pen'tægən(ə)l] *adj.* пятиуго́льный. **pentagram** *n.* пентагра́мма. **pentahedron** [,pentə'hi:drən] *n.* пятигра́нник. **pentameter** [pen'tæmɪtə(r)] *n.* пента́метр. **pentathlon** [pen'tæθlən] *n.* пятибо́рье. **pentatonic** [,pentə'tɒnɪk] *adj.* пентато́нный.
Pentecost ['pentɪ,kɒst] *n.* Пятидеся́тница.
penthouse ['penthaʊs] *n.* особня́к (-а́) на кры́ше многоэта́жного до́ма.
pent-up [pent'ʌp] *adj.* (*anger etc.*) сде́рживаемый.
penultimate [pɪ'nʌltɪmət] *adj.* (*n.*) предпосле́дний (слог).
penumbra [pɪ'nʌmbrə] *n.* полуте́нь (*loc.* -ени́; *pl.* -е́ни, -ене́й).
penurious [pɪ'njʊərɪəs] *adj.* бе́дный (-ден, -дна́, -дно, бе́дны́); (*stingy*) скупо́й (скуп, -а́, -о). **penury** ['penjʊrɪ] *n.* нужда́.
peony ['pi:ənɪ] *n.* пио́н.
people ['pi:p(ə)l] *n.* наро́д; (*as pl., persons*) лю́ди (-де́й, -дям, -дьми́) *pl.*; (*relatives*) родны́е *sb.*; (*occupy*) населя́ть *impf.*, насели́ть *pf.*; (*populate*) заселя́ть *impf.*, засели́ть *pf.*
pepper ['pepə(r)] *n.* пе́рец (-рца(у)); *v.t.* пе́рчить *impf.*, на~, по~ *pf.*; (*pelt*) забра́сывать

impf., забросáть *pf.* **peppercorn** *n.* перчúнка. **pepper-pot** *n.* пéречница.

peppermint ['pepəmɪnt] *n.* пéречная мя́та; (*sweet*) мя́тная конфéта.

peppery ['pepərɪ] *adj.* напéрченный; (*fig.*) вспы́льчивый.

per [pɜ:(r)] *prep.* (*by means of*) *expressed by instrumental case* по+*d.*; (*person*) чéрез+*a.*; (*for each*) (*person*) на+*a.*; (*time*) в+*a.*; (*quantity*) за+*a.*; **as ~** соглáсно+*d.*; **~ annum** ежегóдно, в год; **~ capita, ~ head** на человéка; **~ diem** в день; **~ hour** в час; **~ se** сам (-á, -ó) по себé, по существý.

perceive [pə'si:v] *v.t.* воспринимáть *impf.*, восприня́ть (-имý, -и́мешь; воспри́нял, -á, -о) *pf.*

per cent [pə 'sent] *adv.* & *n.* процéнт, на сóтню. **percentage** *n.* процéнтное содержáние, процéнт.

perceptible [pə'septɪb(ə)l] *adj.* воспринимáемый, замéтный. **perception** *n.* восприя́тие, понимáние. **perceptive** *adj.* воспринимáющий, восприи́мчивый.

perch[1] [pɜ:tʃ] *n.* (*fish*) óкунь (*pl.* -ни, -нéй) *m.*

perch[2] [pɜ:tʃ] *n.* (*roost*) насéст, жёрдочка; (*fig.*) высóкое, прóчное, положéние; *v.i.* сади́ться *impf.*, сесть (ся́ду, -дешь; сел) *pf.*; *v.t.* сажáть *impf.*, посади́ть (-ажý, -áдишь) *pf.* (на насéст); высокó помещáть *impf.*, помести́ть *pf.* **perched** *adj.* высокó сидя́щий, располóженный (-ен).

perchance [pə'tʃɑ:ns] *adv.* быть мóжет.

percussion [pə'kʌʃ(ə)n] *n.* удáр, столкновéние; (*mus. instruments*) удáрные инструмéнты *m.pl.*; **~ cap** удáрный кáпсюль *m.* **percussive** [pə'kʌsɪv] *adj.* удáрный.

perdition [pə'dɪʃ(ə)n] *n.* ги́бель.

peregrine (falcon) ['perɪgrɪn] *n.* сóкол, сапсáн.

peremptory [pə'remptərɪ, 'perɪm-] *adj.* повели́тельный.

perennial [pə'renɪəl] *adj.* вéчный; (*plant*) многолéтний; *n.* многолéтнее растéние.

perestroika [ˌpere'strɔɪkə] *n.* перестрóйка.

perfect ['pɜ:fekt] *adj.* совершéнный (-нен, -нна); (*exact*) тóчный (-чен, -чнá, -чно); (*gram.*) перфéктный; (*mus.*) чи́стый; *n.* перфéкт; *v.t.* совершéнствовать *impf.*, у~ *pf.* **per'fection** *n.* совершéнство. **per'fective** *adj.* (*n.*) совершéнный (вид).

perfidious [ˌpɜ:'fɪdɪəs] *adj.* верολóмный, предáтельский. **'perfidy** *n.* верολóмство, предáтельство.

perforate ['pɜ:fəˌreɪt] *v.t.* перфори́ровать *impf.* & *pf.* **perfo'ration** *n.* перфорáция; (*hole*) отвéрстие.

perforce [pə'fɔ:s] *adv.* по необходи́мости, вóлей-невóлей.

perform [pə'fɔ:m] *v.t.* (*carry out*) исполня́ть *impf.*, испóлнить *pf.*; совершáть *impf.*, соверши́ть *pf.*; (*play*; *music*) игрáть *impf.*, сыгрáть *pf.*; *v.i.* выступáть *impf.*, вы́ступить *pf.* **performance** *n.* исполнéние; (*of play etc.*) представлéние, спектáкль *m.*; (*of engine etc.*) эксплуатациóнные кáчества *nt.pl.* **performer** *n.* исполни́тель *m.* **performing** *adj.* (*animal*) дрессирóванный.

perfume ['pɜ:fju:m] *n.* (*sweet smell*) аромáт; (*smell*) зáпах; (*scent*) духи́ (-хóв) *pl.*; *v.t.* души́ть (-шý, -шишь) *impf.*, на~ *pf.* **per'fumery** *n.* парфюмéрия.

perfunctory [pə'fʌŋktərɪ] *adj.* повéрхностный.

pergola ['pɜ:gələ] *n.* пéргола.

perhaps [pə'hæps] *adv.* мóжет быть.

peril ['perɪl] *n.* опáсность, риск. **perilous** *adj.* опáсный, рискóванный (-ан, -анна).

perimeter [pə'rɪmɪtə(r)] *n.* (*geom.*) пери́метр; (*boundary*) внéшняя грани́ца.

period ['pɪərɪəd] *n.* períод; (*term*) срок (-а(у)); (*epoch*) эпóха; (*full stop*) тóчка; *adj.* относя́щийся к определённому периóду. **periodic** [ˌpɪərɪ'ɒdɪk] *adj.* периоди́ческий; **~ table** периоди́ческая систéма элемéнтов Менделéева. **peri'odical** *adj.* периоди́ческий; *n.* периоди́ческое издáние, журнáл. **perio'dicity** *n.* периоди́чность.

peripheral [pə'rɪfər(ə)l] *adj.* перифери́йный; *n.* (*comput.*) перифери́йное устрóйство. **periphery** *n.* (*outline*) кóнтур; перифери́я.

periscope ['perɪˌskəʊp] *n.* перискóп.

perish ['perɪʃ] *v.i.* погибáть *impf.*, поги́бнуть (-б) *pf.*; (*die*) умирáть *impf.*, умерéть (умрý, -рёшь; ýмер, -лá, -ло) *pf.*; (*spoil*) пóртиться *impf.*, ис~ *pf.* **perishable** *adj.* скоропóртящийся; *n.*: *pl.* скоропóртящие товáры *m.pl.*

peritoneum [ˌperɪtə'ni:əm] *adj.* брюши́на. **peritonitis** *n.* воспалéние брюши́ны.

periwinkle[1] ['perɪˌwɪŋk(ə)l] *n.* (*plant*) барви́нок (-нка).

periwinkle[2] ['perɪˌwɪŋk(ə)l] *n.* (*winkle*) литори́на.

perjure ['pɜ:dʒə(r)] *v.*: **~ o.s.** нарушáть *impf.*, нарýшить *pf.* кля́тву. **perjurer** *n.* лжесвидéтель *m.*, ~ница. **perjury** *n.* лóжное показáние под прися́гой, лжесвидéтельство.

perk[1] *see* **perquisite**

perk[2] [pɜ:k] *v.i.*: **~ up** оживля́ться *impf.*, оживи́ться *pf.*; приободря́ться *impf.*, приободри́ться *pf.* **perky** *adj.* бóйкий (бóек, бойкá, -ко); (*pert*) дéрзкий (-зок, -зкá, -зко).

permafrost ['pɜ:məˌfrɒst] *n.* вéчная мерзлотá.

permanence ['pɜ:mənəns] *n.* постоя́нство. **permanency** *n.* постоя́нство; (*permanent employment*) постоя́нная рабóта. **permanent** *adj.* постоя́нный; **~ wave** перманéнт.

permeable ['pɜ:mɪəb(ə)l] *adj.* проницáемый. **permeate** *v.t.* (*penetrate*) проникáть *impf.*, прони́кнуть (-к) *pf.* в+*a.*; (*saturate*) пропи́тывать *impf.*, пропитáть *pf.*; *v.i.* распространя́ться *impf.*, распространи́ться *pf.* **perme'ation** *n.* проникáние.

permissible [pə'mɪsɪb(ə)l] *adj.* допусти́мый, позволи́тельный. **permission** [pə'mɪʃ(ə)n] *n.* разрешéние, позволéние. **permissive**

adj. разреша́ющий, позволя́ющий; (*liberal*) либера́льный. **permissiveness** *n.* (сексуа́льная) вседозво́ленность. **permit** [pə'mɪt; 'pɜːmɪt] *v.t.* разреша́ть *impf.*, разреши́ть *pf.+d.*; позволя́ть *impf.*, позво́лить *pf.+d.*; *v.i.*: ~ **of** допуска́ть *impf.*, допусти́ть (-ущу́, -у́стишь) *pf.+a.*; *n.* про́пуск (*pl.* -á); (*permission*) разреше́ние.

permutation [ˌpɜːmjʊ'teɪʃ(ə)n] *n.* перестано́вка.

pernicious [pə'nɪʃəs] *adj.* па́губный.

peroration [ˌperə'reɪʃ(ə)n] *n.* заключи́тельная часть (*pl.* -ти, -те́й) (ре́чи).

peroxide [pə'rɒksaɪd] *n.* пе́рекись; (*hydrogen* ~) пе́рекись водоро́да; ~ **blonde** хими́ческая блонди́нка.

perpendicular [ˌpɜːpən'dɪkjʊlə(r)] *adj.* перпендикуля́рный; (*cliff etc.*) отве́сный; *n.* перпендикуля́р.

perpetrate ['pɜːpɪˌtreɪt] *v.t.* соверша́ть *impf.*, соверши́ть *pf.* **perpe'tration** *n.* соверше́ние.

perpetual [pə'petjʊəl] *adj.* ве́чный, бесконе́чный; (*for life*) пожи́зненный; (*without limit*) бессро́чный. **perpetuate** *v.t.* увекове́чивать *impf.*, увекове́чить *pf.* **perpetu'ation** *n.* увекове́чение. **perpe'tuity** *n.* ве́чность, бесконе́чность; **in** ~ навсегда́, наве́чно.

perplex [pə'pleks] *v.t.* приводи́ть (-ожу́, -о́дишь) *impf.*, привести́ (-еду́, -едёшь; -ёл, -ела́) в недоуме́ние; озада́чивать *impf.*, озада́чить *pf.* **perplexity** *n.* недоуме́ние, озада́ченность.

perquisite ['pɜːkwɪzɪt], **perk**[1] *n.* случа́йный, дополни́тельный, дохо́д.

persecute ['pɜːsɪˌkjuːt] *v.t.* пресле́довать *impf.*; (*pester*) надоеда́ть *impf.*, надое́сть (-е́м, -е́шь, -е́ст, -еди́м; -е́л) *pf.+d.* (**with** *+i.*). **persecution** *n.* пресле́дование.

perseverance [ˌpɜːsɪ'vɪərəns] *n.* насто́йчивость, сто́йкость. **persevere** *v.i.* сто́йко, насто́йчиво, продолжа́ть *impf.* (**in, at** *etc.* *+a., inf.*).

Persian ['pɜːʃ(ə)n] *n.* перс, ~ия́нка; (*cat*) перси́дская ко́шка; *adj.* перси́дский; **P~ lamb** кара́куль *m.*

persist [pə'sɪst] *v.i.* упо́рствовать *impf.* (**in** в+*p.*); насто́йчиво продолжа́ть *impf.* (**in** *+a., inf.*); (*continue to exist*) продолжа́ть *impf.* существова́ть. **persistence** *n.* упо́рство, насто́йчивость. **persistent** *adj.* упо́рный, насто́йчивый.

person ['pɜːs(ə)n] *n.* челове́к (*pl.* лю́ди, -де́й, -дям, -дьми́), осо́ба; (*appearance*) вне́шность; (*in play*; *gram.*) лицо́ (*pl.* -ца); **in** ~ ли́чно. **personable** *adj.* привлека́тельный. **personage** *n.* осо́ба, (ва́жная) персо́на, выда́ющаяся ли́чность. **personal** *adj.* ли́чный, персона́льный; ~ **property** дви́жимое иму́щество; ~ **remarks** ли́чности *f.pl.*; ~ **stereo** плéер. **personality** [ˌpɜːsə'nælɪtɪ] *n.* ли́чность. **personally** *adv.* ли́чно; **I** ~ что каса́ется меня́. **personalty** *n.* дви́жимое иму́щество. **personification** [pəˌsɒnɪfɪ'keɪʃ(ə)n] *n.* олицетворе́ние. **personify** [pə'sɒnɪˌfaɪ] *v.t.* олицетворя́ть *impf.*, олицетвори́ть *pf.*

personnel [ˌpɜːsə'nel] *n.* ка́дры (-ров) *pl.*, персона́л; (*mil.*) ли́чный соста́в; ~ **carrier** транспортёр; ~ **department** отде́л ка́дров; ~ **manager** нача́льник отде́ла ка́дров.

perspective [pə'spektɪv] *n.* перспекти́ва; *adj.* перспекти́вный.

perspicacious [ˌpɜːspɪ'keɪʃəs] *adj.* проница́тельный. **perspicacity** [ˌpɜːspɪ'kæsɪtɪ] *n.* проница́тельность.

perspiration [ˌpɜːspɪ'reɪʃ(ə)n] *n.* пот (*loc.* -у́; *pl.* -ы́), испа́рина; (*action*) поте́ние. **perspire** [pə'spaɪə(r)] *v.i.* поте́ть *impf.*, вс~ *pf.*

persuade [pə'sweɪd] *v.t.* убежда́ть *impf.*, убеди́ть (-и́шь) *pf.* (**of** в+*p.*); угова́ривать *impf.*, уговори́ть *pf.* **persuasion** *n.* убежде́ние; (*religious belief*) религио́зные убежде́ния *nt.pl.*; (*joc.*) род, сорт. **persuasive** *adj.* убеди́тельный.

pert [pɜːt] *adj.* де́рзкий (-зок, -зка́, -зко).

pertain [pə'teɪn] *v.i.*: ~ **to** (*belong*) принадлежа́ть *impf.+d.*; (*relate*) име́ть *impf.* отноше́ние к+*d.*

pertinence ['pɜːtɪnəns] *n.* уме́стность. **pertinent** *adj.* уме́стный.

perturb [pə'tɜːb] *v.t.* (*disturb*) трево́жить *impf.*, вс~ *pf.*; (*agitate*) волнова́ть *impf.*, вз~ *pf.* **perturbation** [ˌpɜːtə'beɪʃ(ə)n] *n.* трево́га, волне́ние.

perusal [pə'ruːzəl] *n.* внима́тельное чте́ние. **peruse** *v.t.* (*read*) внима́тельно чита́ть *impf.*, про~ *pf.*; (*fig.*) рассма́тривать *impf.*, рассмотре́ть (-рю́, -ришь) *pf.*

pervade [pə'veɪd] *v.t.* (*permeate*) проника́ть *impf.*, прони́кнуть (-к) *pf.* в+*a.*; (*spread*) распространя́ться *impf.*, распространи́ться *pf.* по+*d.*

perverse [pə'vɜːs] *adj.* (*persistent*) упря́мый; (*wayward*) капри́зный; (*perverted*) извращённый (-ён, -ённа). **perversion** *n.* извраще́ние. **perversity** *n.* упря́мство; извращённость. **pervert** [pə'vɜːt; 'pɜːvɜːt] *v.t.* извраща́ть *impf.*, изврати́ть (-ащу́, -ати́шь) *pf.*; *n.* извращённый челове́к.

pessimism ['pesɪˌmɪz(ə)m] *n.* пессими́зм. **pessimist** *n.* пессими́ст. **pessi'mistic** *adj.* пессимисти́ческий.

pest [pest] *n.* вреди́тель *m.*; (*fig.*) я́зва. **pester** *v.t.* надоеда́ть *impf.*, надое́сть (-е́м, -е́шь, -е́ст, -еди́м; -е́л) *pf.+d.*; (*importune*) пристава́ть (-таю́, -таёшь) *impf.*, приста́ть (-а́ну, -а́нешь) *pf.* к+*d.* **pesticide** *n.* пестици́д. **pestilence** *n.* чума́. **pestilent(ial)** ['pestɪlənt, ˌpestɪ'lenʃ(ə)l] *adj.* (*deadly*) смертоно́сный; (*injurious*) вре́дный (-ден, -дна́, -дно); (*of pestilence*) чумно́й; (*coll.*) несно́сный, надое́дливый.

pestle ['pes(ə)l] *n.* пест (-а́), пе́стик.

pet [pet] *n.* (*animal*) люби́мое, дома́шнее, живо́тное *sb.*; (*favourite*) люби́мец (-мца), -мица; ба́ловень (-вня) *m.*; *adj.* (*animal*) ко́мнатный, дома́шний; (*favourite*) любимый; ~ **name** ласка́тельное и́мя *nt.*; ~ **shop** зоомагази́н; *v.t.* ласка́ть *impf.*; балова́ть *impf.*, из~ *pf.*

petal ['pet(ə)l] *n.* лепесто́к (-тка́).

peter ['pi:tə(r)] *v.i.*: ~ **out** истоща́ться *impf.*, истощи́ться *pf.*; (*stream*) иссяка́ть *impf.*, исся́кнуть (-к) *pf.*

petition [pɪ'tɪʃ(ə)n] *n.* хода́тайство, проше́ние; (*formal written* ~) пети́ция; (*leg.*) заявле́ние; *v.t.* подава́ть (-даю́, -даёшь) *impf.*, пода́ть (-а́м, -а́шь, -а́ст, -ади́м; по́дал, -а́, -о) *pf.* проше́ние, хода́тайство, +*d.*; обраща́ться *impf.*, обрати́ться (-ащу́сь, -ати́шься) *pf.* с пети́цией в+*a.* **petitioner** *n.* проси́тель *m.*

petrel ['petr(ə)l] *n.* буреве́стник, качу́рка.

petrified ['petrɪ,faɪd] *adj.* окамене́лый; **be** ~ (*fig.*) оцепене́ть *pf.* (**with** от+*g.*). **'petrify** *v.t.* превраща́ть *impf.*, преврати́ть (-ащу́, -ати́шь) *pf.* в ка́мень; *v.i.* камене́ть *impf.*, о~ *pf.*

petrochemical [,petrəʊ'kemɪk(ə)l] *adj.* нефтехими́ческий. **petrochemistry** [,petrəʊ'kemɪstrɪ] *n.* нефтехи́мия. **petrodollar** *n.* нефтедо́ллар. **petrol** ['petr(ə)l] *n.* бензи́н; *attr.* бензи́новый; ~ **gauge** бензоме́р; ~ **pipe** бензопрово́д; ~ **pump** (*in engine*) бензонасо́с; (*at* ~ *station*) бензоколо́нка; ~ **station** бензозапра́вочная ста́нция; ~ **tank** бензоба́к; ~ **tanker** бензово́з. **pe'troleum** *n.* нефть.

petticoat ['petɪ,kəʊt] *n.* ни́жняя ю́бка.

pettifogger ['petɪ,fɒgə(r)] *n.* крючкотво́р. **pettifoggery** *n.* крючкотво́рство. **pettifogging** *adj.* кляу́зный.

petty ['petɪ] *adj.* ме́лкий (-лок, -лка́, -лко); ~ **bourgeois** мелкобуржуа́зный; ~ **cash** ме́лкие су́ммы *m.pl.*; ~ **officer** старшина́ (*pl.* -ны) *m.*

petulance ['petjʊləns] *n.* нетерпели́вость, раздражи́тельность. **petulant** *adj.* нетерпели́вый, приди́рчивый.

pew [pju:] *n.* церко́вная скамья́ (*pl.* ска́мьи́, -ме́й).

pewit *see* **peewit**

pewter ['pju:tə(r)] *n.* сплав о́лова со свинцо́м; (*dishes*) оловя́нная посу́да.

phalanx ['fælæŋks] *n.* фала́нга.

phallic ['fælɪk] *adj.* фалли́ческий. **phallus** *n.* фа́ллос.

phantom ['fæntəm] *n.* фанто́м, при́зрак.

Pharaoh ['feərəʊ] *n.* фарао́н.

Pharisaic(al) [,færɪ'seɪɪk(ə)l] *adj.* фарисе́йский. **'Pharisee** *n.* фарисе́й.

pharmaceutical [,fɑ:mə'sju:tɪk(ə)l] *adj.* фармацевти́ческий. **'pharmacist** *n.* фармаце́вт. **pharma'cology** *n.* фармаколо́гия. **pharmacopoeia** [,fɑ:məkə'pi:ə] *n.* фармакопе́я. **'pharmacy** *n.* фарма́ция; (*dispensary*) апте́ка.

phase [feɪz] *n.* фа́за, ста́дия.

Ph.D. *abbr.* (*of* ***Doctor of Philosophy***) сте́пень кандида́та нау́к.

pheasant ['fez(ə)nt] *n.* фаза́н.

phenomenal [fɪ'nɒmɪn(ə)l] *adj.* феномена́льный. **phenomenon** *n.* явле́ние; (*also person, event*) фено́мен.

phial ['faɪəl] *n.* скля́нка, пузырёк (-рька́).

philander [fɪ'lændə(r)] *v.i.* волочи́ться (-чу́сь, -чишься) *impf.* (**with** за+*i.*). **philanderer** *n.* волоки́та *m.*

philanthrope ['fɪlən,θrəʊp], **-pist** [fɪ'lænθrəpɪst] *n.* филантро́п. **philanthropic** *adj.* филантропи́ческий. **phi'lanthropy** *n.* филантро́пия.

philatelic [,fɪlə'telɪk] *adj.* филателисти́ческий. **philatelist** [,fɪ'lætəlɪst] *n.* филатели́ст. **phi'lately** *n.* филатели́я.

philharmonic [,fɪlhɑ:'mɒnɪk] *adj.* (*in titles*) филармони́ческий.

Philistine ['fɪlɪ,staɪn] *n.* (*fig.*) фили́стер, меща́нин (*pl.* -а́не, -а́н), -а́нка; *adj.* фили́стерский, меща́нский. **philistinism** ['fɪlɪstɪ,nɪz(ə)m] *n.* фили́стерство, меща́нство.

philological [,fɪlə'lɒdʒɪk(ə)l] *adj.* филологи́ческий. **philologist** [fɪ'lɒlədʒɪst] *n.* фило́лог. **phi'lology** *n.* филоло́гия.

philosopher [fɪ'lɒsəfə(r)] *n.* фило́соф. **philosophic(al)** [,fɪlə'sɒfɪk(ə)l] *adj.* филосо́фский. **philosophize** *v.i.* филосо́фствовать *impf.* **philosophy** *n.* филосо́фия.

philtre ['fɪltə(r)] *n.* приворо́тное зе́лье (*g.pl.* -лий).

phlegm [flem] *n.* мокрота́; (*quality*) флегма. **phlegmatic** [fleg'mætɪk] *adj.* флегмати́ческий.

phobia ['fəʊbɪə] *n.* фоби́я, страх.

phoenix ['fi:nɪks] *n.* фе́никс.

phone [fəʊn] *n.* телефо́н; *v.t.* & *i.* звони́ть *impf.*, по~ *pf.*+*d.* (по телефо́ну).

phoneme ['fəʊni:m] *n.* фоне́ма. **pho'nemic** *adj.* фонемати́ческий. **phonetic** [fə'netɪk] *adj.* фонети́ческий. **phonetician** [,fəʊnɪ'tɪʃ(ə)n] *n.* фонети́ст. **pho'netics** *n.* фоне́тика.

phone-in ['fəʊnɪn] *n.* радиобесе́да.

phonograph ['fəʊnə,grɑ:f] *n.* фоно́граф. **phono'logical** *adj.* фонологи́ческий. **pho'nology** *n.* фоноло́гия.

phosphate ['fɒsfeɪt] *n.* фосфа́т. **phosphorescence** [,fɒsfə'res(ə)ns] *n.* фосфоресце́нсия. **phospho'rescent** *adj.* светя́щийся, фосфоресци́рующий. **phosphorous** *adj.* фо́сфористый. **phosphorus** *n.* фо́сфор.

photo ['fəʊtəʊ] *n.* сни́мок (-мка); *v.t.* снима́ть *impf.*, снять (сниму́, -мешь; снял, -а́, -о) *pf.*; ~ **finish** фотофи́ниш. **photocopier** *n.* фотокопирова́лный аппара́т. **photocopy** *n.* фотоко́пия; *v.t.* ксерокопи́ровать *impf.* & *pf.* **photoelectric** *adj.* фотоэлектри́ческий; ~ **cell** фотоэлеме́нт. **photogenic** [,fəʊtəʊ'dʒenɪk, -'dʒi:nɪk] *adj.* фотогени́чный. **photograph** *n.* фотогра́фия, сни́мок (-мка); *v.t.* фотографи́ровать *impf.*, с~ *pf.*; снима́ть *impf.*, снять (сниму́, -мешь; снял, -а́, о) *pf.* **photographer** [fə'tɒgrəfə(r)] *n.* фото́граф. **photographic** *adj.* фотографи́ческий. **pho-**

tography [fəˈtɒgrəfɪ] *n.* фотогра́фия. **photogravure** *n.* фотогравю́ра. **photolithography** *n.* фотолитогра́фия. **photometer** [fəʊˈtɒmɪtə(r)] *n.* фото́метр. **photosynthesis** *n.* фотоси́нтез.

phrase [freɪz] *n.* фра́за; (*diction*) стиль *m.*; (*expression*) оборо́т (ре́чи); *v.t.* выража́ть *impf.*, вы́разить *pf.* слова́ми. **phraseoˈlogical** *adj.* фразеологи́ческий. **phraseˈology** *n.* фразеоло́гия.

phrenology [frɪˈnɒlədʒɪ] *n.* френоло́гия.

physical [ˈfɪzɪk(ə)l] *adj.* физи́ческий; ~ **culture** физкульту́ра; ~ **examination** медици́нский осмо́тр; ~ **exercises** заря́дка. **physician** [fɪˈzɪʃ(ə)n] *n.* врач (-а́). **physicist** *n.* фи́зик. **physics** *n.* фи́зика.

physiognomy [ˌfɪzɪˈɒnəmɪ] *n.* физионо́мия.

physiological [ˌfɪzɪəˈlɒdʒɪk(ə)l] *n.* физиологи́ческий. **physiologist** [ˌfɪzɪˈɒlədʒɪst] *n.* физио́лог. **physiˈology** *n.* физиоло́гия. **physiotherapist** [ˌfɪzɪəʊˈθerəpɪst] *n.* физиотерапе́вт. **physioˈtherapy** *n.* физиотерапи́я.

physique [fɪˈziːk] *n.* телосложе́ние.

pianist [ˈpɪənɪst] *n.* пиани́ст, ~ка. **piano** [pɪˈænəʊ] *n.* фортепья́но *nt.indecl.*; (*grand*) роя́ль *m.*; (*upright*) пиани́но *nt.indecl.* **pianoforte** *n.* фортепья́но *nt.indecl.*

piccolo [ˈpɪkəˌləʊ] *n.* пи́кколо *nt.indecl.*

pick[1] [pɪk] *v.t.* (*ground*) разрыхля́ть *impf.*, разрыхли́ть *pf.*; (*bone*) обгла́дывать *impf.*, обглода́ть (-ожу́, -о́жешь) *pf.*; (*flower*) срыва́ть *impf.*, сорва́ть (-ву́, -вёшь; сорва́л, -а́, -о) *pf.*; (*gather*) собира́ть *impf.*, собра́ть (соберу́, -рёшь; собра́л, -а́, -о) *pf.*; (*select*) выбира́ть *impf.*, вы́брать (вы́беру, -решь) *pf.*; ~ **s.o.'s brains** присва́ивать *impf.*, присво́ить *pf.* (чужи́е) мы́сли; ~ **a lock** открыва́ть *impf.*, откры́ть (-ро́ю, -ро́ешь) *pf.* замо́к отмы́чкой; ~ **one's nose, teeth** ковыря́ть *impf.*, ковырну́ть *pf.* в носу́, в зуба́х; ~ **a quarrel** иска́ть (ищу́, и́щешь) *impf.* ссо́ры (**with** с+*i.*); ~ **to pieces** (*fig.*) раскритикова́ть *pf.*; ~ **s.o.'s pocket** залеза́ть *impf.*, зале́зть (-зу, -зешь; -з) *pf.* в карма́н+*d.*; ~ **one's way** выбира́ть *impf.*, вы́брать (вы́беру, -решь) *pf.* доро́гу; ~ **off** (*pluck off*) обрыва́ть *impf.*, оборва́ть (-ву́, -вёшь; оборва́л, -а́, -о) *pf.*; (*shoot*) перестре́ливать *impf.*, перестреля́ть *pf.* (одного́ за други́м); ~ **on** (*nag*) пили́ть (-лю́, -лишь) *impf.*; ~ **out** отбира́ть *impf.*, отобра́ть (отберу́, -рёшь; отобра́л, -а́, -о) *pf.*; ~ **up** (*lift*) поднима́ть *impf.*, подня́ть (подниму́, -мешь; по́дня́л, -а́, -о) *pf.*; (*gain*) добыва́ть *impf.*, добы́ть (добу́ду, -дешь; до́бы́л, -а́, -о) *pf.*; (*fetch*) заезжа́ть *impf.*, зае́хать (зае́ду, -дешь) *pf.* за+*i.*; (*recover*) поправля́ться *impf.*, попра́виться *pf.*; ~ **o.s. up** поднима́ться *impf.*, подня́ться (подниму́сь, -мешься; подня́лся́, -ла́сь) *pf.*

pick[2] [pɪk] *n.* вы́бор; (*best part*) лу́чшая часть, са́мое лу́чшее; **take your** ~ выбира́й(те)!

pick[3] [pɪk], **pickaxe** *n.* кирка́ (*pl.* ки́рки́, -рок, ки́рка́м).

picket [ˈpɪkɪt] *n.* (*stake*) кол (-а́, *loc.* -у́; *pl.* -ья, -ьев); (*person*) пике́тчик, -ица; (*collect.*) пике́т; *v.t.* пикети́ровать *impf.*

pickle [ˈpɪk(ə)l] *n.* (*brine*) рассо́л; (*vinegar*) марина́д; *pl.* соле́нье, марина́ды *m.pl.*, пи́кули (-лей) *pl.*; (*plight*) напа́сть; *v.t.* соли́ть (солю́, со́ли́шь) *impf.*, по~ *pf.*; маринова́ть *impf.*, за~ *pf.* **pickled** *adj.* солёный (со́лон, -а́, -о); марино́ванный; (*drunk*) пья́ный (пьян, -а́, -о).

pickpocket [ˈpɪkˌpɒkɪt] *n.* карма́нник.

pick-up [ˈpɪkʌp] *n.* (*truck*) пика́п; (*tech.*) звукоснима́тель *m.*

picnic [ˈpɪknɪk] *n.* пикни́к (-а́); *v.i.* уча́ствовать *impf.* в пикнике́.

pictorial [pɪkˈtɔːrɪəl] *adj.* изобрази́тельный; (*illustrated*) иллюстри́рованный. **picture** [ˈpɪktʃə(r)] *n.* карти́на; (~ *of health etc.*) воплоще́ние; (*film*) фильм; **the** ~**s** кино́ *nt.indecl.*; ~ **postcard** худо́жественная откры́тка; ~ **window** целосте́нное окно́ (*pl.* о́кна, о́кон, о́кнам); *v.t.* изобража́ть *impf.*, изобрази́ть *pf.*; (*to o.s.*) представля́ть *impf.*, предста́вить *pf.* себе́. **picture-book** *n.* кни́га с карти́нками. **picture-gallery** *n.* карти́нная галере́я. **pictuˈresque** *adj.* живопи́сный; (*language etc.*) о́бразный.

pie [paɪ] *n.* пиро́г (-а́), пирожо́к (-жка́).

piebald [ˈpaɪbɔːld] *adj.* пе́гий; *n.* (*horse*) пе́гая ло́шадь (*pl.* -ди, -де́й, *i.* -дьми́).

piece [piːs] *n.* кусо́к (-ска́), часть (*pl.* -ти, -те́й); (*one of set*) шту́ка; (*of land*) уча́сток (-тка); (*of paper*) листо́к (-тка́); (*mus., liter.*) произведе́ние; (*picture*) карти́на; (*drama*) пье́са; (*chess*) фигу́ра; (*coin*) моне́та; **take to** ~**s** разбира́ть *impf.*, разобра́ть (разберу́, -рёшь; разобра́л, -а́, -о) *pf.* (на ча́сти); ~ **of advice** сове́т; ~ **of information** све́дение; ~ **of news** но́вость; *v.t.*: ~ **together** собира́ть *impf.*, собра́ть (соберу́, -рёшь; собра́л, -а́, -о) *pf.* из кусо́чков; своди́ть (-ожу́, -о́дишь) *impf.*, свести́ (сведу́, -дёшь; свёл, -а́) *pf.* воедино́. **piecemeal** *adv.* по частя́м. **piece-work** *n.* сде́льщина. **piece-worker** *n.* сде́льщик.

pied [paɪd] *adj.* разноцве́тный.

pier [pɪə(r)] *n.* (*mole*) мол (*loc.* -у́); (*in harbour*) пирс; (*of bridge*) бык (-а́); (*between windows etc.*) просте́нок (-нка).

pierce [pɪəs] *v.t.* пронза́ть *impf.*, пронзи́ть *pf.*; прока́лывать *impf.*, проколо́ть (-лю́, -лешь) *pf.*; (*of cold look etc.*) прони́зывать *impf.*, прониза́ть (-ижу́, -и́жешь) *pf.* **piercing** *adj.* о́стрый (остр & остёр, остра́, о́стро́), пронзи́тельный.

pier-glass [ˈpɪəglɑːs] трюмо́ *nt.indecl.*

piety [ˈpaɪɪtɪ] *n.* на́божность.

piffle [ˈpɪf(ə)l] *n.* чепуха́, вздор. **piffling** *adj.* ничто́жный.

pig [pɪg] *n.* свинья́ (*pl.* -ньи, -не́й, -ньям) (*also of person*); (*of metal*) болва́нка, чу́шка; *v.t.*:

~ **it** жить (живу́, -вёшь; жил, -á, -о) *impf.* по-сви́нски; *v.abs.* пороси́ться *impf.*, о~ *pf.* **pig'headed** *adj.* упря́мый. **pig-iron** *n.* чугу́н (-á) в чу́шках. **piglet** *n.* поросёнок (-сёнка; *pl.* -ся́та, -ся́т). **pigskin** *n.* свина́я ко́жа. **pigsty** *n.* свина́рник. **pigswill** *n.* помо́и (-о́ев) *pl.* **pigtail** *n.* коси́чка.

pigeon ['pɪdʒɪn, -dʒ(ə)n] *n.* го́лубь (*pl.* -би, -бе́й) *m.* **pigeon-hole** (*n.*) отделе́ние для бума́г; (*v.t.*) раскла́дывать *impf.*, разложи́ть (-ожу́, -о́жишь) *pf.* по отделе́ниям, по я́щикам; (*put aside*) откла́дывать *impf.*, отложи́ть (-ожу́, -о́жишь) *pf.* в до́лгий я́щик.

pigment ['pɪgmənt] *n.* пигме́нт. **pigmen'tation** *n.* пигмента́ция.

pigmy *see* **pygmy**

pike¹ [paɪk] *n.* (*weapon*) пи́ка.

pike² [paɪk] *n.* (*fish*) щу́ка.

pilaster [pɪ'læstə(r)] *n.* пиля́стр.

pilchard ['pɪltʃəd] *n.* сарди́н(к)а.

pile¹ [paɪl] *n.* (*heap*) ку́ча, ки́па; (*funeral* ~) погреба́льный костёр (-тра́); (*building*) огро́мное зда́ние; (*elec.*) батаре́я; (*atomic* ~) я́дерный реа́ктор; *v.t.*: ~ **up** скла́дывать *impf.*, сложи́ть (-жу́, -жишь) *pf.* в ку́чу; сва́ливать *impf.*, свали́ть (-лю́, -лишь) *pf.* в ку́чу; (*load*) нагружа́ть *impf.*, нагрузи́ть (-ужу́, -у́зи́шь) *pf.* (**with** +*i.*); *v.i.*: ~ **in(to), on** забира́ться *impf.*, забра́ться (заберу́сь, -рёшься; забра́лся, -ала́сь, -а́ло́сь) *pf.* в+*a.*; ~ **up** накопля́ться, нака́пливаться *impf.*, накопи́ться (-ится) *pf.*

pile² [paɪl] *n.* (*on cloth etc.*) ворс.

pile³ [paɪl] *n.* (*support*) сва́я. **pile-driver** *n.* копёр (-пра́).

piles [paɪlz] *n.* геморро́й.

pilfer ['pɪlfə(r)] *v.t.* ворова́ть *impf.* **pilfering** *n.* ме́лкая кра́жа.

pilgrim ['pɪlgrɪm] *n.* пилигри́м; пало́мник, -ица. **pilgrimage** *n.* пало́мничество.

pill [pɪl] *n.* пилю́ля; **the** ~ противозача́точная пилю́ля.

pillage ['pɪlɪdʒ] *n.* мародёрство; *v.t.* гра́бить *impf.*, о~ *pf.*; *v.abs.* мародёрствовать *impf.*

pillar ['pɪlə(r)] *n.* столб (-á); (*fig.*) столп (-á). **pillar-box** *n.* стоя́чий почто́вый я́щик.

pillion ['pɪljən] *n.* за́днее сиде́нье (мотоци́кла).

pillory ['pɪlərɪ] *n.* позо́рный столб (-á); *v.t.* (*fig.*) пригвожда́ть *impf.*, пригвозди́ть *pf.* к позо́рному столбу́.

pillow ['pɪləʊ] *n.* поду́шка; *v.t.* подпира́ть *impf.*, подпере́ть (подопру́, -рёшь; подпёр) *pf.* **pillowcase** *n.* на́волочка.

pilot ['paɪlət] *n.* (*naut.*) ло́цман; (*aeron.*) пило́т, лётчик; *adj.* о́пытный, про́бный; *v.t.* управля́ть *impf.*+*i.*; (*aeron.*) пилоти́ровать *impf.*

pimento [ˌpɪmɪ'entəʊ, pɪm'jentəʊ] *n.* пе́рец (-рца(у)).

pimp [pɪmp] *n.* сво́дник, -ица; *v.i.* сво́дничать *impf.*

pimpernel ['pɪmpəˌnel] *n.* о́чный цвет.

pimple ['pɪmp(ə)l] *n.* прыщ (-á). **pimpled, pimply** *adj.* прыща́вый, прыщева́тый.

PIN [pɪn] *abbr.* (*of* ***personal identification number***) персона́льный код.

pin [pɪn] *n.* була́вка; (*peg*) па́лец (-льца); *v.t.* прика́лывать *impf.*, приколо́ть (-лю́, -лешь) *pf.*; (*press*) прижима́ть *impf.*, прижа́ть (-жму́, -жмёшь) *pf.* (**against** к+*d.*).

pinafore ['pɪnəˌfɔː(r)] *n.* пере́дник.

pince-nez ['pænsneɪ, pæ̃s'neɪ] *n.* пенсне́ *nt.indecl.*

pincers ['pɪnsəz] *n.* кле́щи́ (-ще́й) *pl.*, пинце́т; (*crab's*) клешни́ *f.pl.*; **pincer movement** захва́т в кле́щи́.

pinch [pɪntʃ] *v.t.* щипа́ть (-плю́, -плешь) *impf.*, (у)щипну́ть *pf.*; прищемля́ть *impf.*, прищеми́ть *pf.*; (*of shoe*) жать (жмёт) *impf.*; (*steal*) стяну́ть (-ну́, -нешь) *pf.*; (*arrest*) сца́пать *pf.*; *v.i.* скупи́ться *impf.*; **where the shoe ~es** в чём загво́здка; *n.* щипо́к (-пка́); (*of salt*) щепо́тка; (*of snuff*) поню́шка (табаку́); **at a** ~ в кра́йнем слу́чае.

pinchbeck ['pɪntʃbek] *n.* томпа́к (-á); *adj.* томпа́ковый.

pincushion ['pɪnˌkʊʃ(ə)n] *n.* поду́шечка для була́вок.

pine¹ [paɪn] *v.i.* томи́ться *impf.*; ~ **for** тоскова́ть *impf.* по+*d.* & *p.*

pine² [paɪn] *n.* (*tree*) сосна́ (*pl.* -сны, -сен, -снам); *attr.* сосно́вый; ~ **cone** сосно́вая ши́шка; ~ **needles** сосно́вая хво́я *collect.*

pineapple ['paɪnˌæp(ə)l] *n.* анана́с.

ping-pong ['pɪŋpɒŋ] *n.* насто́льный те́ннис, пинг-по́нг.

pinion¹ ['pɪnjən] *n.* (*of wing*) оконе́чность пти́чьего крыла́; (*flight feather*) махово́е перо́ (*pl.* -рья, -рьев); *v.t.* подреза́ть *impf.*, подре́зать (-е́жу, -е́жешь) *pf.* кры́лья+*d.*; (*person*) свя́зывать *impf.*, связа́ть (-яжу́, -я́жешь) *pf.* ру́ки+*d.*

pinion² ['pɪnjən] *n.* (*cog-wheel*) шестерня́ (*g.pl.* -рён).

pink [pɪŋk] *n.* (*flower*) гвозди́ка; (*colour*) ро́зовый цвет; **in the** ~ в прекра́сном состоя́нии; *adj.* ро́зовый.

pinnacle ['pɪnək(ə)l] *n.* (*peak*; *fig.*) верши́на; (*turret*) остроконе́чная ба́шенка.

pinpoint ['pɪnpɔːnt] *v.t.* то́чно определя́ть *impf.*, определи́ть *pf.* **pinprick** *n.* (*fig.*) ме́лкая неприя́тность. **pinstripe** *n.* то́нкая поло́ска.

pint [paɪnt] *n.* пи́нта.

pin-up ['pɪnʌp] *n.* карти́нка (красо́тки), прикреплённая на сте́ну.

pioneer [ˌpaɪə'nɪə(r)] *n.* пионе́р, ~ка; (*mil.*) сапёр; *adj.* пионе́рский; сапёрный.

pious ['paɪəs] *adj.* на́божный.

pip¹ [pɪp] *n.* (*on dice etc.*) очко́ (*pl.* -ки́, -ко́в); (*star*) звёздочка.

pip² [pɪp] *n.* (*seed*) зёрнышко (*pl.* -шки, -шек, -шкам).

pip³ [pɪp] *n.* (*sound*) бип.

pipe [paɪp] *n.* труба́ (*pl.* -бы); (*mus.*) ду́дка, свире́ль; *pl.* волы́нка; (*for smoking*) тру́бка; *v.t.* (*play on* ~) игра́ть *impf.*, сыгра́ть *pf.* на ду́дке, на свире́ли; (*convey by* ~) пуска́ть *impf.*, пусти́ть (пущу́, пу́стишь) *pf.* по труба́м, по трубопрово́ду; *v.i.* ~ **down** замолка́ть *impf.*, замо́лкнуть (-к) *pf.* **pipe-clay** *n.* бе́лая тру́бочная гли́на. **pipedream** *n.* пуста́я мечта́ (*g.pl.* -ний). **pipeline** *n.* трубопрово́д; (*oil* ~) нефтепрово́д. **piper** *n.* волы́нщик. **pipette** [pɪ'pet] *n.* пипе́тка. **piping** *n.* (*on dress etc.*) кант; *adj.* (*voice*) пискли́вый; ~ **hot** с пы́лу, с жа́ру.

piquancy ['piːkənsɪ, -kɑːnsɪ] *n.* пика́нтность. **piquant** *adj.* пика́нтный.

piqué ['piːkeɪ] *n.* пике́ *nt.indecl.*

piracy ['paɪrəsɪ] *n.* пира́тство. **pirate** *n.* пира́т; *v.t.* (*book*) самово́льно переиздава́ть (-даю́, -даёшь) *impf.*, переизда́ть (-а́м, -а́шь, -а́ст, -ади́м; -а́л, -ала́, -а́ло) *pf.* **piratical** [ˌpaɪə'rætɪk(ə)l] *adj.* пира́тский.

pirouette [ˌpɪrʊ'et] *n.* пиру́эт; *v.i.* де́лать *impf.*, с~ *pf.* пиру́эт(ы).

piscatorial [ˌpɪskə'tɔːrɪəl] *adj.* рыболо́вный.

Pisces ['paɪsiːz, 'pɪskiːz] *n.* Ры́бы *f.pl.*

pistachio [pɪ'stɑːʃɪəʊ] *n.* фиста́шка; *attr.* фиста́шковый.

pistol ['pɪst(ə)l] *n.* пистоле́т.

piston ['pɪst(ə)n] *n.* по́ршень (-шня) *m.*; (*in cornet etc.*) писто́н; *adj.* поршнево́й. **piston-ring** *n.* поршнево́е кольцо́ (*pl.* -льца, -ле́ц, -льцам). **piston-rod** *n.* шток по́ршня.

pit [pɪt] *n.* я́ма; (*mine*) ша́хта; (*quarry*) карье́р; (*theatr.*) парте́р; (*in workshop*) ремо́нтная я́ма; (*car-racing*) запра́вочно-ремо́нтный пункт; **the bottomless** ~ преиспо́дняя *sb.*; **in the** ~ **of the stomach** под ло́жечкой; *v.t.*: ~ **against** выставля́ть *impf.*, вы́ставить *pf.* про́тив+*g.*

pit-a-pat ['pɪtəˌpæt] *adv.* с ча́стым бие́нием; **go** ~ (*heart*) затрепета́ть (-е́щет) *pf.*

pitch¹ [pɪtʃ] *n.* (*resin*) смола́; *v.t.* смоли́ть *impf.*, вы́~, о~ *pf.* **pitch-black** *adj.* чёрный (-рен, -рна́) как смоль.

pitch² [pɪtʃ] *v.t.* (*camp, tent*) разбива́ть *impf.*, разби́ть (разобью́, -ьёшь) *pf.*; (*ball*) подава́ть (-даю́, -даёшь) *impf.*, пода́ть (-а́м, -а́шь, -а́ст, -ади́м; по́дал, -а́, -о) *pf.*; (*fling*) кида́ть *impf.*, ки́нуть *pf.*; *v.i.* (*fall*) па́дать *impf.*, (у)па́сть (-аду́, -адёшь; -а́л) *pf.*; (*ship*) испы́тывать *impf.*, испыта́ть *pf.* килеву́ю ка́чку; ~ **into** набра́сываться *impf.*, набро́ситься *pf.* на+*a.*; ~**ed battle** генера́льное сраже́ние; *n.* (*of ship*) килева́я ка́чка; (*of ball*) пода́ча; (*football* ~ *etc.*) площа́дка; (*degree*) у́ровень (-вня) *m.*; (*mus.*) высота́ (*pl.* -ты); (*slope*) укло́н.

pitchblende ['pɪtʃblend] *n.* уранини́т.

pitcher¹ ['pɪtʃə(r)] *n.* (*sport*) подаю́щий *sb.* (мяч).

pitcher² ['pɪtʃə(r)] *n.* (*vessel*) кувши́н.

pitchfork ['pɪtʃfɔːk] *n.* ви́лы (-л) *pl.*

pitch-pipe ['pɪtʃpaɪp] *n.* камерто́н-ду́дка.

piteous ['pɪtɪəs] *adj.* жа́лостный, жа́лкий (-лок, -лка́, -лко).

pitfall ['pɪtfɔːl] *n.* западня́.

pith [pɪθ] *n.* сердцеви́на; (*essence*) суть; (*vigour*) си́ла, эне́ргия.

pit-head ['pɪthed] *n.* надша́хтный копёр;

pithy ['pɪθɪ] *adj.* (*fig.*) сжа́тый, содержа́тельный.

pitiable ['pɪtɪəb(ə)l] *adj.* жа́лкий (-лок, -лка́, -лко), несча́стный. **pitiful** *adj.* жа́лостный, жа́лкий (-лок, -лка́, -лко). **pitiless** *adj.* безжа́лостный.

pittance ['pɪt(ə)ns] *n.* ску́дное жа́лованье, жа́лкие гроши́ (-ше́й) *pl.*

pitted ['pɪtɪd] *adj.* (*of face*) изры́тый, рябо́й (ряб, -а́, -о).

pituitary [pɪ'tjuːɪtərɪ] *adj.* сли́зистый; *n.* (*gland*) гипо́физ.

pity ['pɪtɪ] *n.* сожале́ние; **it's a** ~ жа́лко, жаль; **take** ~ **on** сжа́литься *pf.* над+*i.*; **what a** ~ как жа́лко!; *v.t.* жале́ть *impf.*, по~ *pf.*; **I** ~ **you** мне жаль тебя́.

pivot ['pɪvət] *n.* сте́ржень (-жня) *m.*; (*fig.*) центр; *v.i.* враща́ться *impf.* **pivotal** *adj.* (*fig.*) центра́льный.

pizza ['piːtsə] *n.* пи́цца; ~ **parlour** пиццери́я.

placard ['plækɑːd] *n.* афи́ша, плака́т; *v.t.* (*wall*) раскле́ивать *impf.*, раскле́ить *pf.* афи́ши, плака́ты, на+*p.*, по+*d.*

placate [plə'keɪt, 'plæ-, 'pleɪ-] *v.t.* умиротворя́ть *impf.*, умиротвори́ть *pf.*

place [pleɪs] *n.* ме́сто (*pl.* -та́); **change** ~**s with** обме́ниваться *impf.*, обменя́ться *pf.* места́ми с+*i.*; **give** ~ **to** уступа́ть *impf.*, уступи́ть (-плю́, -пишь) *pf.* ме́сто+*d.*; **in** ~ на ме́сте; (*suitable*) уме́стный; **in** ~ **of** вме́сто+*g.*; **in the first, second,** ~ во-пе́рвых, во-вторы́х; **out of** ~ не на ме́сте; (*unsuitable*) неуме́стный; **take** ~ случа́ться *impf.*, случи́ться *pf.*; (*pre-arranged event*) состоя́ться (-ои́тся) *pf.*; **take the** ~ **of** заменя́ть *impf.*, замени́ть (-ню́, -нишь) *pf.*; *v.t.* помеща́ть *impf.*, помести́ть *pf.*; (*stand*) ста́вить *impf.*, по~ *pf.*; (*lay*) класть (кладу́, -дёшь; -ал) *impf.*, положи́ть (-жу́, -жишь) *pf.*; (*determine*) определя́ть *impf.*, определи́ть *pf.* **place-name** *n.* географи́ческое назва́ние.

placenta [plə'sentə] *n.* плаце́нта.

place-setting ['pleɪsˌsetɪŋ] *n.* столо́вый прибо́р.

placid ['plæsɪd] *adj.* споко́йный. **placidity** [plə'sɪdɪtɪ] *n.* споко́йствие.

plagiarism ['pleɪdʒəˌrɪz(ə)m] *n.* плагиа́т. **plagiarist** *n.* плагиа́тор. **plagiarize** *v.t.* заимствовать *impf.* & *pf.*

plague [pleɪg] *n.* чума́, морова́я я́зва; *v.t.* му́чить *impf.*, за~, из~ *pf.*

plaice [pleɪs] *n.* ка́мбала.

plaid [plæd] *n.* плед; (*cloth*) шотла́ндка; *adj.* в шотла́ндскую кле́тку.

plain [pleɪn] *n.* равни́на; *adj.* (*clear*) я́сный

(я́сен, ясна́, я́сно, я́сны́); (*simple*) просто́й (прост, -а́, -о, про́сты́); (*direct*) прямо́й (прям, -а́, -о, пря́мы́); (*ugly*) некраси́вый; ~ **stitch** пряма́я пе́тля. **plain-clothes** *adj.*: ~ **policeman** шпик (-а́). **plain-spoken** *adj.* открове́нный (-нен, -нна).

plaintiff ['pleɪntɪf] *n.* исте́ц (-тца́), исти́ца.

plaintive ['pleɪntɪv] *adj.* жа́лобный.

plait [plæt] *n.* коса́ (*a.* ко́су́; *pl.* -сы); *v.t.* плести́ (плету́, -тёшь; плёл, -а́) *impf.*, с~ *pf.*

plan [plæn] *n.* план; *v.t.* плани́ровать *impf.*, за~, с~ *pf.*; (*intend*) намерева́ться *impf.+inf.*

plane[1] [pleɪn] *n.* (*tree*) плата́н.

plane[2] [pleɪn] *n.* (*tool*) руба́нок (-нка); *v.t.* строга́ть *impf.*, вы́~ *pf.*

plane[3] [pleɪn] *n.* (*surface*) пло́скость; (*level*) у́ровень (-вня) *m.*; (*aeroplane*) самолёт; *v.i.* плани́ровать *impf.*, с~ *pf.*

plane[4] [pleɪn] *adj.* (*level*) пло́ский (-сок, -ска́, -ско), плоскостно́й.

planet ['plænɪt] *n.* плане́та. **plane'tarium** *n.* планета́рий. **planetary** *adj.* плане́тный, планета́рный.

plank [plæŋk] *n.* доска́ (*a.* -ску; *pl.* -ски, -со́к, -ска́м); (*pol.*) пункт парти́йной програ́ммы; ~ **bed** на́ры (-р) *pl.*; *v.t.* выстила́ть *impf.*, вы́стлать (-телю, -телешь) *pf.* доска́ми. **planking** *n.* насти́л; (*collect.*) до́ски (-со́к, -ска́м) *f.pl.*

plankton ['plæŋkt(ə)n] *n.* планкто́н.

plant [plɑːnt] *n.* расте́ние; (*fixtures*) устано́вка; (*factory*) заво́д; *v.t.* сажа́ть *impf.*, посади́ть (-ажу́, -а́дишь) *pf.*; насажда́ть *impf.*, насади́ть (-ажу́, -а́дишь) *pf.*; (*fix firmly*) про́чно ста́вить *impf.*, по~ *pf.*; (*garden etc.*) заса́живать *impf.*, засади́ть (-ажу́, -а́дишь) *pf.* (**with** +*i.*); (*palm off*) всу́чивать *impf.*, всучи́ть (-учу́, -у́чи́шь) *pf.* (**on** +*d.*); ~ **out** выса́живать *impf.*, вы́садить *pf.* в грунт.

plantain ['plæntɪn] *n.* подоро́жник.

plantation [plæn'teɪʃ(ə)n, plɑːn-] *n.* (*of trees*) (лесо)насажде́ние; (*of cotton etc.*) планта́ция. **planter** ['plɑːntə(r)] *n.* планта́тор.

plaque [plæk, plɑːk] *n.* доще́чка, мемориа́льная доска́ (*a.* -ску; *pl.* -ски, -со́к, -ска́м); (*plate*) декорати́вная таре́лка.

plasma ['plæzmə] *n.* пла́зма; протопла́зма.

plaster ['plɑːstə(r)] *n.* пла́стырь *m.*; (*for walls etc.*) штукату́рка; ~ **of Paris** (*n.*) гипс; (*attr.*) ги́псовый; ~ **cast** (*mould*) ги́псовый сле́пок (-пка); (*for leg etc.*) ги́псовая повя́зка; *v.t.* (*wall*) штукату́рить *impf.*, от~, о~ *pf.*; (*daub*) зама́зывать *impf.*, зама́зать (-а́жу, -а́жешь) *pf.* **plasterboard** *n.* суха́я штукату́рка. **plastered** *adj.* (*drunk*) пья́ный (пьян, -а́, -о). **plasterer** *n.* штукату́р.

plastic ['plæstɪk] *n.* пластма́сса; *adj.* пласти́чный, пласти́ческий; (*made of* ~) пластма́ссовый; ~ **arts** пла́стика; ~ **surgery** пласти́ческая хирурги́я.

plate [pleɪt] *n.* пласти́нка; (*for food*) таре́лка, (*collect.*; *silver*, *gold* ~) столо́вое серебро́, зо́лото; (*metal sheet*) лист (-а́); (*print.*) печа́тная фо́рма; (*illustration*) (вкладна́я) иллюстра́ция; (*name* ~ *etc.*) доще́чка; (*phot.*) фотопласти́нка; ~ **armour** броневы́е пли́ты *f.pl.*; ~ **glass** зерка́льное стекло́; *v.t.* плакирова́ть *impf.* & *pf.*

plateau ['plætəʊ] *n.* плато́ *nt.indecl.*, плоского́рье.

plateful ['pleɪtfʊl] *n.* по́лная таре́лка. **platelayer** *n.* путево́й рабо́чий *sb.* **plate-rack** *n.* суши́лка для посу́ды;

platform ['plætfɔːm] *n.* платфо́рма; (*rail.*) перро́н; ~ **ticket** перро́нный биле́т.

platinum ['plætɪnəm] *n.* пла́тина; *attr.* пла́тиновый.

platitude ['plætɪˌtjuːd] *n.* бана́льность, пло́скость. **plati'tudinous** *adj.* бана́льный, пло́ский (-сок, -ска́, -ско).

platoon [plə'tuːn] *n.* взвод.

platypus ['plætɪpəs] *n.* утконо́с.

plaudits ['plɔːdɪtz] *n.* аплодисме́нты (-тов) *pl.*

plausibility [ˌplɔːzɪ'bɪlɪtɪ] *n.* (*probability*) правдоподо́бие; (*speciosity*) благови́дность. **'plausible** *adj.* правдоподо́бный; благови́дный.

play [pleɪ] *v.t.* & *i.* игра́ть *impf.*, сыгра́ть *pf.* (*game*) в+*a.*, (*instrument*) на+*p.*, (*in* ~) в+*p.*, (*for prize*) на+*a.*, (*opponent*) с+*i.*; *v.t.* (~ *part of*; *also fig.*) игра́ть *impf.*, сыгра́ть *pf.* роль+*g.*; (*musical composition*) исполня́ть *impf.*, испо́лнить *pf.*; (*chessman*, *card*) ходи́ть (хожу́, хо́дишь) *impf.+i.*; (*record*) ста́вить *impf.*, по~ *pf.*; (*searchlight*) направля́ть *impf.*, напра́вить *pf.* (**on** на+*a.*); *v.i.* (*frolic*) резви́ться *impf.*; (*fountain*) бить (бьёт) *impf.*; (*light*) перелива́ться *impf.*; ~ **down** преуменьша́ть *impf.*, преуме́ньшить *pf.*; ~ **fair** че́стно поступа́ть *impf.*, поступи́ть (-плю́, -пишь) *pf.*; ~ **false** изменя́ть *impf.*, измени́ть (-ню́, -нишь) *pf.* (+*d.*); ~ **the fool** валя́ть *impf.* дурака́; ~ **into the hands of** игра́ть *impf.*, сыгра́ть *pf.* на́ руку+*d.*; ~ **a joke, trick, on** подшу́чивать *impf.*, подшути́ть (-учу́, -у́тишь) *pf.* над+*i.*; ~ **off** игра́ть *impf.*, сыгра́ть *pf.* реша́ющую па́ртию; ~ **off against** стра́вливать *impf.*, страви́ть (-влю́, -вишь) *pf.* с+*i.*; ~ **safe** де́йствовать *impf.* наверняка́; ~**ed out** измо́танный (-ан); *n.* игра́; (*theatr.*) пье́са. **playbill** *n.* театра́льная афи́ша. **playboy** *n.* прожига́тель *m.* жи́зни. **player** *n.* игро́к (-а́); (*actor*) актёр, актри́са; (*musician*) музыка́нт. **playful** *adj.* игри́вый. **playgoer** *n.* театра́л. **playground** *n.* площа́дка для игр. **playhouse** *n.* теа́тр. **playing-card** *n.* игра́льная ка́рта. **playing-field** *n.* спортплоща́дка. **playmate** *n.* друг (*pl.* друзья́, -зе́й) де́тства. **play-off** *n.* реша́ющая встре́ча. **plaything** *n.* игру́шка. **playwright** *n.* драмату́рг.

PLC, plc *abbr.* (*of* ***public limited company***)

общéственная компáния с ограни́ченной отвéтственностью.

plea [pliː] *n.* (*appeal*) обращéние; (*entreaty*) мольбá; (*statement*) заявлéние; **on a ~ of** под предлóгом+*g.* **plead** *v.i.* умоля́ть *impf.* (**with** +*a.*); *v.t.* ссылáться *impf.*, сослáться (сошлю́сь, -лёшься) *pf.* на+*a.*; **~ (not) guilty** (не) признавáть (-наю́, -наёшь) *impf.*, признáть *pf.* себя́ винóвным.

pleasant ['plez(ə)nt] *adj.* прия́тный. **pleasantry** *n.* шýтка. **please** [pliːz] *v.t.* нрáвиться *impf.*, по~ *pf.*+*d.*; угождáть *impf.*, угоди́ть *pf.*+*d.*, на+*a.*; *v.i.*: **as you ~** как вам угóдно; **if you ~** пожáлуйста, бýдьте добры́; (*iron.*) представьте себé; *imper.* пожáлуйста; бýдьте добры́. **pleased** *adj.* довóльный; *pred.* рад. **pleasing, pleasurable** ['pleʒərəb(ə)l] *adj.* прия́тный. **pleasure** *n.* (*enjoyment*) удовóльствие; (*will, desire*) вóля, желáние.

pleat [pliːt] *n.* склáдка; *pl.* плиссé *nt.indecl.*; *v.t.* дéлать *impf.*, с~ *pf.* склáдки на+*p.*; плиссировáть *impf.* **pleated** *adj.* плиссé *indecl.* (*follows noun*).

plebeian [plɪ'biːən] *adj.* плебéйский; *n.* плебéй.

plebiscite ['plebɪsɪt, -ˌsaɪt] *n.* плебисци́т.

plectrum ['plektrəm] *n.* плектр.

pledge [pledʒ] *n.* (*security*) залóг; (*promise*) зарóк, обещáние; **sign, take, the ~** дать (дам, дашь, даст, дади́м; дал, -á, дáлó, -и) *pf.* зарóк не пить; *v.t.* отдавáть (-даю́, -даёшь) *impf.*, отдáть (-áм, -áшь, -áст, -ади́м; óтдал, -á, -о) *pf.* в залóг; **~ o.s.** брать (берý, -рёшь; брал, -á, -о) *impf.*, взять (возьмý, -мёшь; взял, -á, -о) *pf.* на себя́ обязáтельство; **~ one's word** давáть (даю́, даёшь) *impf.*, дать (дам, дашь, даст, дади́м; дал, -á, дáлó, -и) *pf.* слóво.

plenary ['pliːnərɪ] *adj.* пóлный (-лон, -лнá, пóлнó); (*assembly*) пленáрный. **plenipotentiary** [ˌplenɪpə'tenʃərɪ] *adj.* (*n.*) полномóчный (представи́тель *m.*). **plenteous** ['plentɪəs], **plentiful** *adj.* оби́льный. **plenty** *n.* изоби́лие, избы́ток (-тка).

plethora ['pleθərə] *n.* изоби́лие.

pleurisy ['plʊərɪsɪ] *n.* плеври́т.

pliability [ˌplaɪə'bɪlɪtɪ], **'pliancy** *n.* ги́бкость; (*fig.*) подáтливость. **'pliable, 'pliant** *adj.* ги́бкий (-бок, -бкá, -бко); (*fig.*) подáтливый.

pliers ['plaɪəz] *n.* плоскогýбцы (-цев) *pl.*; клéщи́ (-щéй) *pl.*

plight [plaɪt] *n.* (бéдственное, трýдное) положéние.

Plimsoll line ['plɪms(ə)l] *n.* грузовáя мáрка. **plimsolls** *n.* спорти́вные тáпочки *f.pl.*, кéды (-д(ов)) *m.pl.*

plinth [plɪnθ] *n.* пли́нтус; (*of wall*) цóколь *m.*

plod [plɒd] *v.i.* плести́сь (плетýсь, -тёшься; плёлся, -лáсь) *impf.*; тащи́ться (-щýсь, -щишься) *impf.*; (*work*) упóрно рабóтать *impf.* (**at** над+*i.*). **plodder** ['plɒdə(r)] *n.* работя́га *c.g.*

plot [plɒt] *n.* (*of land*) учáсток (-тка) (земли́); (*of book etc.*) фáбула; (*conspiracy*) зáговор; *v.t.* (*on graph, map, etc.*) наноси́ть (-ошý, -óсишь) *impf.*, нанести́ (-сý, -сёшь; нанёс, -лá) на грáфик, на кáрту; (*a course*) проклáдывать *impf.*, проложи́ть (-ожý, -óжишь) *pf.*; *v. abs.* (*conspire*) составля́ть *impf.*, состáвить *pf.* зáговор. **plotter** *n.* заговóрщик, -ица.

plough [plaʊ] *n.* плуг (*pl.* -и́); **the P~** (*astron.*) Большáя Медвéдица; (*land*) пáшня; *v.t.* пахáть (пашý, -шешь) *impf.*, вс~ *pf.*; *v.t.* & *i.* (*fail in examination*) провáливать(ся) *impf.*, провали́ть(ся) (-лю́(сь), -лишь(ся)) *pf.*; *v.i.*: **~ through** пробивáться *impf.*, проби́ться (-бью́сь, -бьёшься) *pf.* сквозь+*a.*

plover ['plʌvə(r)] *n.* ржáнка.

ploy [plɔɪ] *n.* улóвка.

pluck [plʌk] *n.* (*cul.*) потрохá (-хóв) *pl.*, ли́вер; (*courage*) мýжество; *v.t.* (*chicken*) щипáть (-плю́, -плешь) *impf.*, об~ *pf.*; **~ up (one's) courage** собирáться *impf.*, собрáться (соберýсь, -рёшься; собрáлся, -алáсь, -алóсь) *pf.* с дýхом; *v.i.*: **~ at** дёргать *impf.*, дёрнуть *pf.* **plucky** *adj.* смéлый (смел, -á, -о).

plug [plʌg] *n.* прóбка; (*elec.*) штéпсельная ви́лка; (*elec. socket*) штéпсель (*pl.* -ля́) *m.*; (*sparking -~*) (запáльная) свечá (*pl.* -чи, -чéй); (*tobacco*) прессóванный табáк (-á(ý)); (*advertisement*) реклáма; *v.t.* (*~ up*) затыкáть *impf.*, заткнýть *pf.*; (*advertise*) реклами́ровать *impf.* & *pf.*; **~ in** включáть *impf.*, включи́ть *pf.*; *v.i.*: **~ away at** корпéть (-плю́, -пи́шь) *impf.* над+*i.*

plum [plʌm] *n.* (*fruit*) сли́ва; (*colour*) тёмно-фиолéтовый цвет; **~ cake** кекс.

plumage ['pluːmɪdʒ] *n.* оперéние, пéрья (-ьев) *nt.pl.*

plumb [plʌm] *n.* отвéс; (*naut.*) лот; *adj.* вертикáльный; (*fig.*) я́вный; *adv.* вертикáльно; (*fig.*) тóчно; *v.t.* измеря́ть *impf.*, измéрить *pf.* глубинý+*g.*; (*fig.*) проникáть *impf.*, прони́кнуть (-к) *pf.* в+*a.*

plumber ['plʌmə(r)] *n.* водопровóдчик. **plumbing** *n.* (*work*) водопровóдное дéло; (*system of pipes*) водопровóдная систéма.

plume [pluːm] *n.* (*feather*) перó (*pl.* -рья, -рьев); (*on hat etc.*) султáн, плюмáж; **~ of smoke** дымóк (-мкá); *v.t.*: **~ o.s. on** кичи́ться *impf.*+*i.*

plummet ['plʌmɪt] *n.* (*plumb*) отвéс; (*sounding-line*) лот; (*on fishing-line*) грузи́ло; *v.i.* слетáть *impf.*, слетéть (-ечý, -ети́шь) *pf.*

plump[1] [plʌmp] *adj.* пóлный (-лон, -лнá, пóлнó), пýхлый (пухл, -á, -о).

plump[2] [plʌmp] *v.t.* & *i.* бýхать(ся) *impf.*, бýхнуть(ся) *pf.*; *v.i.*: **~ for** (*vote for*) голосовáть *impf.*, про~ *pf.* тóлько за+*a.*; (*fig.*) выбирáть *impf.*, вы́брать (вы́беру, -решь) *pf.*

plunder ['plʌndə(r)] *v.t.* грáбить *impf.*, о~ *pf.*; *n.* добы́ча.

plunge [plʌndʒ] *v.t.* & *i.* (*immerse*) погружа́ть(ся) *impf.*, погрузи́ть(ся) *pf.* (**into** в+*a.*); *v.i.* (*dive*) ныря́ть *impf.*, нырну́ть *pf.*; (*rush*) броса́ться *impf.*, бро́ситься *pf.* **plunger** *n.* плу́нжер.

pluperfect [plu:'pɜ:fɪkt] *adj.* предпроше́дший; *n.* предпроше́дшее вре́мя *nt.*

plural ['plʊər(ə)l] *n.* мно́жественное число́; *adj.* мно́жественный. **pluralism** *n.* плюрали́зм. **plura'listic** *adj.* плюралисти́ческий.

plus [plʌs] *prep.* плюс+*a.*; *adj.* (*additional*) доба́вочный; (*positive*) положи́тельный; *n.* (знак) плюс.

plush [plʌʃ] *n.* плюш; *adj.* плю́шевый. **plushy** *adj.* шика́рный.

Pluto ['plu:təʊ] *n.* Плуто́н.

plutocracy [plu:'tɒkrəsɪ] *n.* плутокра́тия. **plutocrat** ['plu:tə,kræt] *n.* плутокра́т. **pluto'cratic** *adj.* плутократи́ческий.

plutonium [plu:'təʊnɪəm] *n.* плуто́ний.

ply[1] [plaɪ] *v.i.* курси́ровать *impf.*; *v.t.* (*tool*) рабо́тать *impf.*+*i.*; (*task*) занима́ться *impf.*+*i.*; ~ **with questions** засыпа́ть *impf.*, засы́пать (-плю, -плешь) *pf.* вопро́сами.

ply[2] [plaɪ] *n.* (*layer*) слой (*pl.* слои́); (*strand*) прядь. **plywood** *n.* фане́ра.

PM *abbr.* (*of* ***Prime Minister***) премье́р-мини́стр.

p.m. *abbr.* (*of* ***post meridiem***) пополу́дни.

pneumatic [nju:'mætɪk] *adj.* пневмати́ческий; ~ **drill** отбо́йный молото́к.

pneumonia [nju:'məʊnɪə] *n.* пневмони́я, воспале́ние лёгких.

PO *abbr.* (*of* ***Post Office***) по́чта; (*of* ***postal order***) почто́вый перево́д.

poach[1] [pəʊtʃ] *v.t.* (*cook*) вари́ть (-рю́, -ришь) *impf.*, опуска́я в кипято́к; кипяти́ть *impf.* на ме́дленном огне́; **~ed egg** яйцо́-пашо́т.

poach[2] [pəʊtʃ] *v.i.* (*hunt*) незако́нно охо́титься *impf.*; (*trespass*) вторга́ться *impf.*, вто́ргнуться (-г(нул)ся, -глась) *pf.* в чужи́е владе́ния; *v.t.* охо́титься *impf.* на+*a.* на чужо́й земле́. **poacher** *n.* браконье́р.

pochard ['pəʊtʃəd] *n.* нырo̲к (-рка́).

pocket ['pɒkɪt] *n.* карма́н; (*billiards*) лу́за; (*air-~*) возду́шная я́ма; **in** ~ в вы́игрыше; **in person's** ~ в рука́х у+*g.*; **out of** ~ в убы́тке; *adj.* карма́нный; *v.t.* класть (-аду́, -адёшь; -ал) *impf.*, положи́ть (-жу́, -жишь) *pf.* в карма́н; (*appropriate*) прикарма́нивать *impf.*, прикарма́нить *pf.*; (*billiards*) загоня́ть *impf.*, загна́ть (загоню́, -нишь; загна́л, -а́, -о) *pf.* в лу́зу. **pocketful** *n.* по́лный карма́н.

pock-marked ['pɒkmɑ:kt] *adj.* рябо́й (ряб, -а́, -о).

pod [pɒd] *n.* стручо́к (-чка́), шелуха́; *v.t.* лущи́ть *impf.*, об~ *pf.*

podgy ['pɒdʒɪ] *adj.* то́лстенький; пу́хлый (пухл, -а́, о).

podium ['pəʊdɪəm] *n.* (*conductor's*) пульт.

poem ['pəʊɪm] *n.* стихотворе́ние; (*longer* ~) поэ́ма. **poet** *n.* поэ́т; **P~ Laureate** поэ́т-лауреа́т. **poetaster** [,pəʊɪ'tæstə(r)] *n.* стихоплёт. **poetess** *n.* поэте́сса. **poetic(al)** [pəʊ'etɪk(ə)l] *adj.* поэти́ческий, поэти́чный; (*in verse*) стихотво́рный. **poetry** *n.* поэ́зия, стихи́ *m.pl.*; (*quality*) поэти́чность.

pogrom ['pɒgrəm, -rɒm] *n.* погро́м.

poignancy ['pɔɪnjənsɪ] *n.* острота́. **poignant** *adj.* о́стрый (остр & остёр, остра́, о́стро́).

point[1] [pɔɪnt] *n.* то́чка; (*place*; *in list*; *print.*) пункт; (*in score*) очко́ (*pl.* -ки́, -ко́в); (*in time*) моме́нт; (*in space*) ме́сто (*pl.* -та́); (*essence*) суть; (*sense*) смысл; (*sharp* ~) остриё; (*tip*) ко́нчик; (*promontory*) мыс (*loc.* -е & -у́; *pl.* мы́сы́); (*decimal* ~) запята́я *sb.*; (*power* ~) ште́псель (*pl.* -ля́) *m.*; *pl.* (*rail.*) стре́лка; **be on the ~ of** (*doing*) собира́ться *impf.*, собра́ться (соберу́сь, -рёшься; собра́лся, -ала́сь, -а́ло́сь) *pf.*+*inf.*; **beside, off, the** ~ некста́ти; **in ~ of fact** факти́чески; **that is the** ~ в э́том и де́ло; **the ~ is that** де́ло в том, что; **there is no** ~ (*in doing*) не име́ет смы́сла (+*inf.*); **to the** ~ кста́ти; **~ of view** то́чка зре́ния.

point[2] [pɔɪnt] *v.t.* (*wall*) расшива́ть *impf.*, расши́ть (разошью́, -ьёшь) *pf.* швы+*g.*; (*gun etc.*) наводи́ть (-ожу́, -о́дишь) *impf.*, навести́ (-еду́, -едёшь; -ёл, -ела́) *pf.* (**at** на+*a.*); *v. abs.* (*dog*) де́лать *impf.*, с~ *pf.* сто́йку; *v.i.* (*with finger*) по-, у-, ка́зывать *impf.*, по-, у-, каза́ть (-ажу́, -а́жешь) *pf.* па́льцем (**at, to** на+*a.*); (*draw attention*; ~ *out*) обраща́ть *impf.*, обрати́ть (-ащу́, -ати́шь) *pf.* внима́ние (**to** на+*a.*).

point-blank [pɔɪnt'blæŋk] *adj.* прямо́й (прям, -а́, -о, пря́мы́). **point-duty** *n.* регули́рование движе́ния.

pointed ['pɔɪntɪd] *adj.* (*sharp*) о́стрый (остр & остёр, остра́, о́стро́); (*of arch etc.*) стре́льчатый; (*of remark*) ко́лкий (-лок, -лка́, -лко). **pointer** *n.* указа́тель *m.*; (*of clock etc.*) стре́лка; (*dog*) по́йнтер (*pl.* -ы & -а́). **pointless** *adj.* бессмы́сленный (-ен, -енна).

poise [pɔɪz] *v.t.* уравнове́шивать *impf.*, уравнове́сить *pf.*; **be ~d** (*hover*) висе́ть (-си́т) *impf.* в во́здухе; *n.* уравнове́шенность.

poison ['pɔɪz(ə)n] *n.* яд (-а(у)), отра́ва; ~ **gas** ядови́тый газ; ~ **ivy** ядоно́сный сума́х; *v.t.* отравля́ть *impf.*, отрави́ть (-влю́, -вишь) *pf.* **poisoner** *n.* отрави́тель *m.* **poisonous** *adj.* ядови́тый. **poison-pen** *adj.*: ~ **letter** анони́мка.

poke [pəʊk] *v.t.* ты́кать (ты́чу, -чешь) *impf.*, ткнуть *pf.*; ~ **fun at** подшу́чивать *impf.*, подшути́ть (-учу́, -у́тишь) *pf.* над+*i.*; ~ **one's nose into** сова́ть (сую́, суёшь) *impf.*, су́нуть *pf.* нос в+*a.*; ~ **the fire** меша́ть *impf.*, по~ *pf.* (кочерго́й) у́гли в ками́не; *n.* тычо́к (-чка́). **poker**[1] *n.* (*metal rod*) кочерга́ (*g.pl.* -рёг).

poker[2] ['pəʊkə(r)] *n.* (*cards*) по́кер. **poker-face** *n.* бесстра́стное лицо́.

poky ['pəʊkɪ] *adj.* те́сный (-сен, -сна́, -сно).

Poland ['pəʊlənd] *n.* По́льша.

polar ['pəʊlə(r)] *adj.* поля́рный; (*phys.*) по́люсный; ~ **bear** бе́лый медве́дь *m.* **polarity** [pə'lærɪtɪ] *n.* поля́рность. **polarize** *v.t.* поляризова́ть *impf.* & *pf.*

pole[1] [pəʊl] *n.* (*geog.*; *phys.*) по́люс; ~ **star** Поля́рная звезда́.

pole[2] [pəʊl] *n.* (*rod*) столб (-а́), шест (-а́).

Pole[3] [pəʊl] *n.* поля́к, по́лька.

pole-axe ['pəʊlæks] *n.* секи́ра, берды́ш (-а́).

polecat ['pəʊlkæt] *n.* хорёк (-рька́).

polemic [pə'lemɪk] *adj.* полеми́ческий; *n.* поле́мика.

pole-vaulter ['pəʊl,vɔ:ltə(r), -,vɒltə(r)] *n.* шестови́к. **pole-vaulting** *n.* прыжо́к (-жка́) с шесто́м.

police [pə'li:s] *n.* поли́ция; (*as pl.*) полице́йские *sb.*; ~ **constable** полице́йский *sb.*; ~ **station** полице́йский уча́сток (-тка). **policeman** *n.* полице́йский *sb.*, полисме́н.

policy[1] ['pɒlɪsɪ] *n.* (*course of action*) поли́тика.

policy[2] ['pɒlɪsɪ] *n.* (*document*) по́лис.

polio(myelitis) [,pəʊlɪəʊ,maɪɪ'laɪtɪs] *n.* полиомиели́т.

Polish[1] ['pəʊlɪʃ] *adj.* по́льский.

polish[2] ['pɒlɪʃ] *n.* (*gloss*) гля́нец (-нца); (*process*) полиро́вка; (*substance*) политу́ра; (*fig.*) изы́сканность; *v.t.* полирова́ть *impf.*, на~, от~ *pf.*; ~ **off** расправля́ться *impf.*, распра́виться *pf.* с+*i.* **polished** *adj.* (*refined*) изы́сканный (-ан, -анна).

polite [pə'laɪt] *adj.* ве́жливый. **politeness** *n.* ве́жливость.

politic ['pɒlɪtɪk] *adj.* полити́чный. **political** [pə'lɪtɪk(ə)l] *adj.* полити́ческий; (*of the state*) госуда́рственный; ~ **economy** политэконо́мика; ~ **prisoner** политзаключённый *sb.* **poli'tician** *n.* поли́тик. **politics** *n.* поли́тика.

polka ['pɒlkə, 'pəʊlkə] *n.* по́лька.

poll [pəʊl] *n.* (*voting*) голосова́ние; (*number of votes*) число́ голосо́в; (*opinion* ~) опро́с; *v.t.* (*receive votes*) получа́ть *impf.*, получи́ть (-чу́, -чишь) *pf.*; *v.i.* голосова́ть *impf.*, про~ *pf.*

pollard ['pɒləd] *v.t.* подстрига́ть *impf.*, подстри́чь (-игу́, -ижёшь; -и́г) *pf.*

pollen ['pɒlən] *n.* пыльца́. **pollinate** *v.t.* опыля́ть *impf.*, опыли́ть *pf.*

polling-booth ['pəʊlɪŋ,bu:ð, -,bu:θ] *n.* каби́на для голосова́ния. **polling-station** *n.* избира́тельный уча́сток (-тка).

pollutant [pə'lu:tənt] *n.* загрязни́тель *m.*, поллюта́нт. **pollute** *v.t.* загрязня́ть *impf.*, загрязни́ть *pf.* **pollution** *n.* загрязне́ние.

polo ['pəʊləʊ] *n.* по́ло *nt.indecl.*

polonaise [,pɒlə'neɪz] *n.* полоне́з.

polo-neck ['pəʊləʊ,nek] *n.* (*garment*) водола́зка.

polyandry ['pɒlɪ,ændrɪ] *n.* полиа́ндрия, многому́жие. **polyester** [,pɒlɪ'estə(r)] *n.* полиэфи́р. **polyethylene** [,pɒlɪ'eθɪ,li:n] *n.* полиэтиле́н. **polygamous** [pə'lɪgəməs] *adj.* многобра́чный. **po'lygamy** *n.* многобра́чие. **polyglot** *n.* полигло́т; *adj.* многоязы́чный; (*person*) говоря́щий на мно́гих языка́х. **polygon** *n.* многоуго́льник. **polymer** *n.* полиме́р.

polyp ['pɒlɪp] *n.* поли́п.

polyphonic [,pɒlɪ'fɒnɪk] *adj.* полифони́ческий. **polyphony** [pə'lɪfənɪ] *n.* полифони́я. **polystyrene** [,pɒlɪ'staɪə,ri:n] *n.* полистиро́л. **polysy'llabic** *adj.* многосло́жный. **polysyllable** *n.* многосло́жное сло́во (*pl.* -ва́). **poly'technic** *n.* полите́хникум. **polytheism** *n.* многобо́жие. **polythene** ['pɒlɪ,θi:n] *n.* полиэтиле́н. **polyunsaturated** [,pɒlɪʌn'sætʃə,reɪtɪd] *adj.*: ~ **fats** полиненасы́щенные жиры́. **polyurethane** [,pɒlɪ'jʊərə,θeɪn] *n.* полиурета́н. **polyvalent** [,pɒlɪ'veɪlənt] *adj.* многовале́нтный.

pomade [pə'mɑ:d] *n.* пома́да; *v.t.* пома́дить *impf.*, на~ *pf.*

pomegranate ['pɒmɪ,grænɪt, 'pɒm,grænɪt] *n.* грана́т.

Pomeranian [,pɒmə'reɪnɪən] *n.* шпиц.

pommel ['pʌm(ə)l] *n.* (*hilt*) голо́вка; (*of saddle*) лука́ (*pl.* -ки).

pomp [pɒmp] *n.* пы́шность, великоле́пие. **pom'posity** *n.* напы́щенность. **pompous** *adj.* напы́щенный (-ен, -енна).

pom-pom ['pɒmpɒm] *n.* помпо́н.

poncho ['pɒntʃəʊ] *n.* по́нчо *nt.indecl.*

pond [pɒnd] *n.* пруд (-а́, *loc.* -у́). **pondweed** *n.* рдест.

ponder ['pɒndə(r)] *v.t.* обду́мывать *impf.*, обду́мать *pf.*; *v.i.* размышля́ть *impf.*, размы́слить *pf.* (**over** о+*p.*).

ponderous ['pɒndərəs] *adj.* тяжелове́сный.

poniard ['pɒnjəd] *n.* кинжа́л.

pontiff ['pɒntɪf] *n.* (*pope*) ри́мский Па́па *m.*; (*bishop*) епи́скоп; (*chief priest*) первосвяще́нник.

pontoon[1] [pɒn'tu:n] *n.* понто́н; ~ **bridge** понто́нный мост (мо́ста́, *loc.* -у́; *pl.* -ы́).

pontoon[2] [pɒn'tu:n] *n.* (*cards*) два́дцать одно́.

pony ['pəʊnɪ] *n.* по́ни *m.indecl.*

poodle ['pu:d(ə)l] *n.* пу́дель (*pl.* -ли & -ля́) *m.*

pooh [pu:] *int.* фу! **pooh-pooh** *v.t.* пренебрега́ть *impf.*, пренебре́чь (-егу́, -ежёшь; -ёг, -егла́) *pf.*+*i.*

pool[1] [pu:l] *n.* (*of water*) прудо́к (-дка́), лу́жа; (*swimming* ~) бассе́йн.

pool[2] [pu:l] *n.* (*collective stakes*) совоку́пность ста́вок; (*common fund*) о́бщий фонд; (*common resources*) объединённые запа́сы *m.pl.*; **car** ~ автоба́за; **typing** ~ машинопи́сное бюро́ *nt.indecl.*; *v.t.* объединя́ть *impf.*, объедини́ть *pf.*

poop [pu:p] *n.* полую́т; (*stern*) корма́.

poor [pʊə(r)] *adj.* бе́дный (-ден, -дна́, -дно, бе́дны́); (*bad*) плохо́й (плох, -а́, -о, пло́хи́); (*scanty*) ску́дный (-ден, -дна́, -дно); (*weak*) сла́бый (слаб, -а́, -о) *n.*: **the** ~ беднота́, бедняки́ *m.pl.* **poorhouse** *n.* рабо́тный дом (*pl.* -а́). **poorly** *pred.* нездоро́в (-а, -о).

pop[1] [pɒp] *v.i.* хло́пать *impf.*, хло́пнуть *pf.*;

щёлкать *impf.*, щёлкнуть *pf.*; *v.t.* бы́стро всу́нуть *pf.* (**into** в+*a.*); ~ **in on** забега́ть *impf.*, забежа́ть (-егу́, -ежи́шь) *pf.* к+*d.*; *n.* хлопо́к (-пка́), щёлк; (*drink*) щипу́чий напи́ток (-тка). **popgun** *n.* (*toy*) пуга́ч (-а́).

pop[2] [pɒp] *adj.* популя́рный, поп-; ~ **art** поп-а́рт; ~ **concert** конце́рт поп-му́зыки; ~ **music** поп-му́зыка.

popcorn ['pɒpkɔːn] *n.* возду́шная кукуру́за.

pope [pəʊp] *n.* Па́па ри́мский *m.* **popery** *n.* папи́зм. **popish** *adj.* папи́стский.

poplar ['pɒplə(r)] *n.* то́поль (*pl.* -ля́) *m.*

poppet ['pɒpɪt] *n.* кро́шка.

poppy ['pɒpɪ] *n.* мак; ~ **seed** (*collect.*) мак (-а(у)).

poppycock ['pɒpɪˌkɒk] *n.* чепуха́.

populace ['pɒpjʊləs] *n.* просто́й наро́д. **popular** *adj.* наро́дный; (*liked*) популя́рный. **popu'larity** *n.* популя́рность. **popularize** *v.t.* популяризи́ровать *impf.* & *pf.* **populate** *v.t.* населя́ть *impf.*, насели́ть *pf.* **popu'lation** *n.* населе́ние. **populous** *adj.* (много)лю́дный.

porcelain ['pɔːsəlɪn] *n.* фарфо́р; *attr.* фарфо́ровый.

porch [pɔːtʃ] *n.* подъе́зд, крыльцо́ (*pl.* -льца, -ле́ц, -льца́м).

porcupine ['pɔːkjʊˌpaɪn] *n.* дикобра́з.

pore[1] [pɔː(r)] *n.* по́ра.

pore[2] [pɔː(r)] *v.i.*: ~ **over** погружа́ться *impf.*, погрузи́ться (-ужу́сь, -у́зи́шься) *pf.* в+*a.*

pork [pɔːk] *n.* свини́на; ~ **pie** пиро́г (-а́) со свини́ной. **pork-butcher** *n.* колба́сник.

pornographic [ˌpɔːnəˈgræfɪk] *adj.* порногра-фи́ческий. **pornography** [pɔːˈnɒgrəfɪ] *n.* порногра́фия.

porous ['pɔːrəs] *adj.* по́ристый.

porphyry ['pɔːrfɪrɪ] *n.* порфи́р.

porpoise ['pɔːpəs] *n.* морска́я свинья́ (*pl.* -ньи, -не́й, -ньям).

porridge ['pɒrɪdʒ] *n.* овся́ная ка́ша.

port[1] [pɔːt] *n.* (*harbour*) порт (*loc.* -у́; *pl.* -ы, -о́в); (*town*) порто́вый го́род (*pl.* -а́).

port[2] [pɔːt] *n.* (*naut.*, *aeron.*) ле́вый борт (*loc.* -у́).

port[3] [pɔːt] *n.* (*wine*) портве́йн (-а(у)).

portable ['pɔːtəb(ə)l] *adj.* портати́вный.

portal ['pɔːt(ə)l] *n.* порта́л.

portcullis [pɔːtˈkʌlɪs] *n.* опускна́я решётка.

portend [pɔːˈtend] *v.t.* предвеща́ть *impf.* **portent** ['pɔːtent, -t(ə)nt] *n.* предзнаменова́ние. **por'tentous** *adj.* злове́щий.

porter[1] ['pɔːtə(r)] *n.* (*gate-*, *door-*, *keeper*) швейца́р, приврáтник; ~**'s lodge** швейца́рская *sb.*, до́мик приврáтника.

porter[2] ['pɔːtə(r)] *n.* (*carrier*) носи́льщик.

portfolio [pɔːtˈfəʊlɪəʊ] *n.* портфе́ль *m.*, па́пка.

porthole ['pɔːthəʊl] *n.* иллюмина́тор.

portico ['pɔːtɪˌkəʊ] *n.* по́ртик.

portion ['pɔːʃ(ə)n] *n.* часть (*pl.* -ти, -те́й), до́ля (*pl.* -ли, -ле́й); (*of food*) по́рция; *v.t.*: ~ **out** разделя́ть *impf.*, раздели́ть *pf.*

portly ['pɔːtlɪ] *adj.* доро́дный.

portmanteau [pɔːtˈmæntəʊ] *n.* чемода́н; ~ **word** сло́во-гибри́д.

portrait ['pɔːtrɪt] *n.* портре́т. **portraiture** *n.* портре́тная жи́вопись. **portray** [pɔːˈtreɪ] *v.t.* рисова́ть *impf.*, на~ *pf.*; изобража́ть *impf.*, изобрази́ть *pf.* **portrayal** *n.* рисова́ние, изображе́ние.

Portugal ['pɔːtjʊg(ə)l] *n.* Португа́лия. **Portuguese** [ˌpɔːtjʊˈgiːz, ˌpɔːtʃ-] *n.* португа́лец (-льца), -лка; *adj.* португа́льский.

pose [pəʊz] *n.* по́за; *v.t.* (*question*) ста́вить *impf.*, по~ *pf.*; *v.i.* пози́ровать *impf.*; ~ **as** принима́ть *impf.*, приня́ть (приму́, -мешь; при́нял, -а́, -о) *pf.* по́зу+*g.*

poser ['pəʊzə(r)] *n.* тру́дный вопро́с, тру́дная зада́ча.

poseur [pəʊˈzɜː(r)] *n.* позёр.

posh [pɒʃ] *adj.* шика́рный.

posit ['pɒzɪt] *v.t.* (*assume*) постули́ровать *impf.* & *pf.*

position [pəˈzɪʃ(ə)n] *n.* положе́ние, пози́ция; **in a ~ to** в состоя́нии+*inf.*; *v.t.* ста́вить *impf.*, по~ *pf.* **positional** *adj.* позицио́нный.

positive ['pɒzɪtɪv] *adj.* положи́тельный; (*person*) уве́ренный (-ен, -енна); (*proof*) несомне́нный (-нен, -нна); (*phot.*) позити́вный; *n.* (*phot.*) позити́в. **positivism** *n.* позитиви́зм.

posse ['pɒsɪ] *n.* отря́д (шери́фа).

possess [pəˈzes] *v.t.* облада́ть *impf.*+*i.*; владе́ть *impf.*+*i.*; (*of feeling etc.*) овладева́ть *impf.*, овладе́ть *pf.*+*i.* **possessed** *adj.* одержи́мый. **possession** *n.* владе́ние (**of** +*i.*); *pl.* со́бственность. **possessive** *adj.* со́бственнический; (*gram.*) притяжа́тельный. **possessor** *n.* облада́тель *m.*, ~ница.

possibility [ˌpɒsɪˈbɪlɪtɪ] *n.* возмо́жность. **'possible** *adj.* возмо́жный; **as much as ~** ско́лько возмо́жно; **as soon as ~** как мо́жно скоре́е; *n.* возмо́жное *sb.* **'possibly** *adv.* возмо́жно, мо́жет (быть).

post[1] [pəʊst] *n.* (*pole*) столб (-а́); *v.t.* (~ *up*) выве́шивать *impf.*, вы́весить *pf.*

post[2] [pəʊst] *n.* (*station*) пост (-а́, *loc.* на -у́); (*trading-~*) факто́рия; *v.t.* (*station*) расставля́ть *impf.*, расста́вить *pf.*; (*appoint*) назнача́ть *impf.*, назна́чить *pf.*

post[3] [pəʊst] *n.* (*letters*, ~ *office*, *etc.*) по́чта; **by return of ~** с обра́тной по́чтой; *attr.* почто́вый; ~ **office** по́чта, почто́вое отделе́ние; **General P~ Office** (гла́вный) почта́мт; *v.t.* (*send by ~*) отправля́ть *impf.*, отпра́вить *pf.* по по́чте; (*put in ~-box*) опуска́ть *impf.*, опусти́ть (-ущу́, -у́стишь) в почто́вый я́щик. **postage** *n.* почто́вая опла́та, почто́вые расхо́ды *m.pl.*; ~ **stamp** почто́вая ма́рка. **postal** *adj.* почто́вый; ~ **order** почто́вый перево́д. **postbox** *n.* почто́вый я́щик. **postcard** *n.* откры́тка. **postcode** *n.* почто́вый и́ндекс.

post-date [pəʊstˈdeɪt] *v.t.* дати́ровать *impf.* & *pf.* бо́лее по́здним число́м.

poster ['pəʊstə(r)] *n.* афи́ша, плака́т.

poste restante [ˌpəʊst reˈstɑ̃t] *n.* (*in address*)

до востре́бования.

posterior [pɒ'stɪərɪə(r)] *adj.* (*later*) после́дующий; (*hinder*) за́дний; *n.* зад (*loc.* -у́; *pl.* -ы́).

posterity [pɒ'sterɪtɪ] *n.* (*descendants*) пото́мство; (*later generations*) после́дующие поколе́ния *nt.pl.*

postern ['pɒst(ə)n, 'pəʊ-] *n.* за́дняя дверь (*loc.* -ри́; *pl.* -ри, -ре́й, *i.* -ря́ми & -рьми́).

post-free [pəʊst'fri:] *adj.* без почто́вой опла́ты.

post-graduate [pəʊst'grædjʊət] *n.* аспира́нт; *adj.* аспира́нтский; ~ **course** аспиранту́ра.

posthumous ['pɒstjʊməs] *adj.* посме́ртный.

postman ['pəʊstmən] *n.* почтальо́н. **postmark** *n.* почто́вый ште́мпель (*pl.* -ля́) *m.*; *v.t.* штемпелева́ть (-лю́ю, -лю́ешь) *impf.*, за~ *pf.* **postmaster, mistress** *n.* нача́льник почто́вого отделе́ния.

post-mortem [pəʊst'mɔ:təm] *n.* вскры́тие тру́па.

post-paid [pəʊst'peɪd] *adj.* с опла́ченными почто́выми расхо́дами.

postpone [pəʊst'pəʊn, pə'spəʊn] *v.t.* отсро́чивать *impf.*, отсро́чить *pf.* **postponement** *n.* отсро́чка.

postprandial [pəʊst'prændɪəl] *adj.* послеобе́денный.

postscript ['pəʊstskrɪpt, 'pəʊskrɪpt] *n.* постскри́птум.

postulate ['pɒstjʊlət; 'pɒstjʊˌleɪt] *n.* постула́т; *v.t.* постули́ровать *impf.* & *pf.*

posture ['pɒstʃə(r)] *n.* по́за, положе́ние; *v.i.* рисова́ться *impf.*

post-war [pəʊst'wɔ:(r), 'pəʊst-] *adj.* послевое́нный.

posy ['pəʊzɪ] *n.* буке́тик.

pot [pɒt] *n.* горшо́к (-шка́), котело́к (-лка́); (*as prize*) ку́бок (-бка); ~**s of money** ку́ча де́нег; ~ **roast** тушёное мя́со; *v.t.* (*plant*) сажа́ть *impf.*, посади́ть (-ажу́, -а́дишь) *pf.* в горшо́к; (*billiards*) загоня́ть *impf.*, загна́ть (загоню́, -нишь; загна́л, -а́, -о) *pf.* в лу́зу.

potash ['pɒtæʃ] *n.* пота́ш (-а́). **potassium** [pə'tæsɪəm] *n.* ка́лий.

potato [pə'teɪtəʊ] *n.* (*plant*; *pl. collect.*) карто́фель *m.* (*no pl.*); карто́фелина; карто́шка (*also collect.*; *coll.*); **two** ~**es** две карто́фелины, карто́шки; ~ **peeler** картофелечи́стка.

pot-bellied [pɒt'belɪd] *adj.* пуза́тый. **pot-belly** *n.* пу́зо. **pot-boiler** *n.* халту́ра; (*person*) халту́рщик.

potence ['pəʊt(ə)ns], **-cy** *n.* си́ла, могу́щество; (*of drug etc.*) де́йственность. **potent** *adj.* (*reason etc.*) убеди́тельный; (*drug etc.*) сильноде́йствующий; (*mighty*) могу́щественный (-ен, -енна). **potentate** *n.* власти́ли́н.

potential [pə'tenʃ(ə)l] *adj.* потенциа́льный, возмо́жный; *n.* потенциа́л, возмо́жность. **potenti'ality** *n.* потенциа́льность.

pot-hole ['pɒthəʊl] *n.* пеще́ра; (*in road*) вы́боина. **pot-holer** *n.* пеще́рник.

potion ['pəʊʃ(ə)n] *n.* до́за лека́рства, зе́лье.

pot-pourri [pəʊ'pʊərɪ, -'ri:] *n.* попурри́ *nt.indecl.*

pot-shot ['pɒtʃɒt] *n.* вы́стрел наугáд.

potter[1] ['pɒtə(r)] *v.i.*: ~ **at, in** рабо́тать *impf.* ко́е-как над+*i.*; ~ **about** ло́дырничать *impf.*

potter[2] ['pɒtə(r)] *n.* гонча́р (-а́). **pottery** *n.* (*goods*) гонча́рные изде́лия *nt.pl.*; (*place*) гонча́рная *sb.*

potty[1] ['pɒtɪ] *adj.* (*trivial*) пустяко́вый; (*crazy*) поме́шанный (-ан) (**about** на+*p.*).

potty[2] ['pɒtɪ] *n.* ночно́й горшо́к (-шка́).

pouch [paʊtʃ] *n.* су́мка, мешо́к (-шка́).

pouffe [pu:f] *n.* пуф.

poulterer ['pəʊltərə(r)] *n.* торго́вец (-вца) дома́шней пти́цей.

poultice ['pəʊltɪs] *n.* припа́рка; *v.t.* ста́вить *impf.*, по~ *pf.* припа́рку+*d.*

poultry ['pəʊltrɪ] *n.* дома́шняя пти́ца; ~ **farm** птицефе́рма.

pounce [paʊns] *v.i.*: ~ **(up)on** налета́ть *impf.*, налете́ть (-ечу́, -ети́шь) *pf.* на+*a.*; набра́сываться *impf.*, набро́ситься *pf.* на+*a.*; (*fig.*) ухвати́ться (-ачу́сь, -а́тишься) *pf.* за+*a.*

pound[1] [paʊnd] *n.* (*measure*) фунт; ~ **sterling** фунт сте́рлингов.

pound[2] [paʊnd] *n.* (*enclosure*) заго́н.

pound[3] [paʊnd] *v.t.* (*crush*) толо́чь (-лку́, -лчёшь; -ло́к, -лкла́) *impf.*, ис~, рас~ *pf.*; (*strike*) колоти́ть (-очу́, -о́тишь) *impf.*, по~ *pf.* по+*d.*, в+*a.*; *v.i.* (*heart*) колоти́ться (-ится) *impf.*; ~ **along** тяжело́ ходи́ть (хожу́, хо́дишь) *impf.*; (*run*) тяжело́ бе́гать *impf.*; ~ **away at** (*with guns*) обстре́ливать *impf.*, обстреля́ть *pf.*

pour [pɔ:(r)] *v.t.* лить (лью, льёшь; лил, -а́, -о) *impf.*; ~ **out** налива́ть *impf.*, нали́ть (налью́, -ьёшь; на́ли́л, -а́, -о) *pf.*; *v.i.* ли́ться (льётся; ли́лся, лила́сь, ли́ло́сь) *impf.*; **it is** ~**ing** (*with rain*) дождь льёт как из ведра́. **pouring** *adj.* (*rain*) проливно́й.

pout [paʊt] *v.t.* & *i.* надува́ть(ся) *impf.*, наду́ть(ся) (-у́ю(сь), -у́ешь(ся)) *pf.*

poverty ['pɒvətɪ] *n.* бе́дность, убо́гость. **poverty-stricken** *adj.* убо́гий.

POW *abbr.* (*of* ***prisoner of war***) военнопле́нный *sb.*

powder ['paʊdə(r)] *n.* порошо́к (-шка́); (*cosmetic*) пу́дра; (*gun*-~) по́рох (-а(у)); ~ **blue** се́ро-голубо́й; ~ **compact** пу́дреница; *v.t.* (*sprinkle with* ~) посыпа́ть *impf.*, посы́пать (-плю, -плешь) *pf.* порошко́м; (*nose etc.*) пу́дрить *impf.*, на~ *pf.*; ~**ed milk** моло́чный порошо́к (-шка́). **powder-keg** *n.* порохова́я бо́чка. **powder-puff** *n.* пухо́вка. **powdery** *adj.* порошкообра́зный.

power ['paʊə(r)] *n.* (*vigour*) си́ла; (*might*) могу́щество; (*ability*) спосо́бность; (*control*) власть; (*authorization*) полномо́чие; (*State*) держа́ва; (*math.*) сте́пень (*pl.* -ни, -не́й); *attr.* силово́й, механи́ческий; **party in** ~ па́ртия у вла́сти; ~ **of attorney** дове́ренность; ~ **cut** прекраще́ние пода́чи эне́ргии; ~

point ште́псель (*pl.* -ля́) *m.*; ~ **station** электроста́нция. **powerful** *adj.* си́льный (си́лён, -льна́, -льно, си́льны́); могу́щественный (-ен, -енна). **powerless** *adj.* беси́льный.

pp. *abbr.* (*of* **page(s)**) стр, страни́цы.

practicable ['præktɪkəb(ə)l] *adj.* осуществи́мый; (*theatr.*) настоя́щий. **practical** *adj.* (*of practice*) практи́ческий; (*useful in practice*; *person*) практи́чный; ~ **joke** гру́бая шу́тка. **practically** *adv.* (*in effect*) факти́чески; (*almost*) почти́. **practice** *n.* пра́ктика; (*custom*) обы́чай; (*exercise*) упражне́ние; **in** ~ на де́ле; **put into** ~ осуществля́ть *impf.*, осуществи́ть *pf.*; *attr.* уче́бный. **practise** *v.t.* (*carry out*) применя́ть *impf.*, примени́ть (-ню́, -нишь) *pf.* на пра́ктике; (*also abs. of doctor etc.*) практикова́ть *impf.*; (*engage in*) занима́ться *impf.*, заня́ться (займу́сь, -мёшься; заня́лся́, -ла́сь) *pf.*+*i.*; упражня́ться *impf.* в+*p.*, (*musical instrument* в игре́ на+*p.*). **practised** *adj.* о́пытный. **prac'titioner** *n.* (*doctor*) практику́ющий врач (-а́); (*lawyer*) практику́ющий юри́ст; **general** ~ врач (-а́) о́бщей пра́ктики.

pragmatic [præg'mætɪk] *adj.* прагмати́ческий. **'pragmatism** *n.* прагмати́зм. **'pragmatist** *n.* прагма́тик.

Prague [prɑ:g] *n.* Пра́га.

prairie ['preərɪ] *n.* степь (*loc.* -пи́; *pl.* -пи, -пе́й); (*in N.America*) пре́рия.

praise [preɪz] *v.t.* хвали́ть (-лю́, -лишь) *impf.*, по~ *pf.*; *n.* похвала́. **praiseworthy** *adj.* похва́льный.

pram [prɑ:m] *n.* де́тская коля́ска.

prance [prɑ:ns] *v.i.* (*horse*) станови́ться (-ится) *impf.*, стать (ста́нет) *pf.* на дыбы́; (*fig.*) задава́ться (-даю́сь, -даёшься) *impf.*

prank [præŋk] *n.* вы́ходка, ша́лость.

prate [preɪt] *v.i.* болта́ть *impf.*

prattle ['præt(ə)l] *v.i.* лепета́ть (-ечу́, -е́чешь); *n.* ле́пет.

prawn [prɔ:n] *n.* креве́тка.

pray [preɪ] *v.t.* моли́ть (-лю́, -лишь) *impf.* (**for** о+*p.*); *v.i.* моли́ться (-лю́сь, -лишься) *impf.*, по~ *pf.* (**to** +*d.*; **for** о+*p.*). **prayer** ['preə(r)] *n.* моли́тва. **prayer-book** *n.* моли́твенник.

preach [pri:tʃ] *v.t.* пропове́дывать *impf.*; *v.i.* произноси́ть (-ошу́, -о́сишь) *impf.*, произнести́ (-есу́, -есёшь; -ёс, -есла́) *pf.* про́поведь. **preacher** *n.* пропове́дник.

preamble [pri:'æmb(ə)l, 'pri:-] *n.* преа́мбула.

pre-arrange [,pri:ə'reɪndʒ] *v.t.* зара́нее плани́ровать *impf.*, за~ *pf.* **pre-arrangement** *n.* предвари́тельная договорённость.

precarious [prɪ'keərɪəs] *adj.* ненадёжный; (*insecure*) непро́чный (-чен, -чна́, -чно).

pre-cast ['pri:kɑ:st] *adj.* сбо́рный.

precaution [prɪ'kɔ:ʃ(ə)n] *n.* предосторо́жность; (*action*) ме́ра предосторо́жности.

precede [prɪ'si:d] *v.t.* предше́ствовать *impf.*+*d.* **precedence** ['presɪd(ə)ns] *n.* предше́ствование; (*seniority*) старшинство́. **precedent** *n.* прецеде́нт.

precept ['pri:sept] *n.* наставле́ние.

precinct ['pri:sɪŋkt] *n.* огоро́женное ме́сто; *pl.* окре́стности *f.pl.*; (*boundary*) преде́л.

precious ['preʃəs] *adj.* драгоце́нный (-нен, -нна); (*beloved*) дорого́й (до́рог, -а́, -о); (*refined*) изы́сканный (-ан, -анна); *adv.* о́чень, весьма́.

precipice ['presɪpɪs] *n.* обры́в; (*also fig.*) про́пасть. **precipitate** [prɪ'sɪpɪtət; prɪ'sɪpɪ,teɪt] *n.* оса́док (-дка); *adj.* стреми́тельный; (*person*) опроме́тчивый; *v.t.* (*throw down*) низверга́ть *impf.*, низве́ргнуть (-г) *pf.*; (*hurry*) ускоря́ть *impf.*, уско́рить *pf.*; (*chem.*) осажда́ть *impf.*, осади́ть (-ажу́, -а́дишь) *pf.* **precipi'tation** *n.* низверже́ние; ускоре́ние; осажде́ние; (*hastiness*) стреми́тельность; (*meteor.*) оса́дки *m.pl.* **pre'cipitous** *adj.* обры́вистый.

précis ['preɪsi:] *n.* конспе́кт.

precise [prɪ'saɪs] *adj.* то́чный (-чен, -чна́, -чно). **precisely** *adv.* то́чно; (*in answer*) и́менно, то́чно так. **precision** [prɪ'sɪʒ(ə)n] *n.* то́чность; *adj.* то́чный.

pre-classical [pri:'klæsɪk(ə)l] *adj.* доклесси́ческий.

preclude [prɪ'klu:d] *v.t.* предотвраща́ть *impf.*, предотврати́ть (-ащу́, -ати́шь) *pf.*

precocious [prɪ'kəʊʃəs] *adj.* не по года́м разви́той (ра́звит, -а́, -о); ра́но разви́вшийся. **precocity** [prɪ'kɒsɪtɪ] *n.* ра́ннее разви́тие.

preconceived [,pri:kən'si:vd] *adj.* предвзя́тый. **preconception** *n.* предвзя́тое мне́ние.

pre-condition [,pri:kən'dɪʃ(ə)n] *n.* предпосы́лка.

precursor [pri:'kɜ:sə(r)] *n.* предте́ча *c.g.*, предше́ственник.

predator ['predətə(r)] *n.* хи́щник. **predatory** *adj.* хи́щнический; (*animal*) хи́щный.

predecease [,pri:dɪ'si:s] *v.t.* умира́ть *impf.*, умере́ть (умру́, -рёшь; у́мер, -ла́, -ло) *pf.* ра́ньше+*g.*

predecessor ['pri:dɪ,sesə(r)] *n.* предше́ственник, -ица.

predestination [pri:,destɪ'neɪʃ(ə)n] *n.* преопределе́ние. **pre'destine** *v.t.* предопределя́ть *impf.*, предопредели́ть *pf.*

predetermine [,pri:dɪ'tɜ:mɪn] *v.t.* предреша́ть *impf.*, предреши́ть *pf.*; предопределя́ть *impf.*, предопредели́ть *pf.*

predicament [prɪ'dɪkəmənt] *n.* затрудни́тельное положе́ние.

predicate ['predɪkət; 'predɪ,keɪt] *n.* (*gram.*) сказу́емое *sb.*, предика́т; *v.t.* утвержда́ть *impf.* **predicative** [prɪ'dɪkətɪv] *adj.* предикати́вный.

predict [prɪ'dɪkt] *v.t.* предска́зывать *impf.*, предсказа́ть (-ажу́, -а́жешь) *pf.* **prediction** *n.* предсказа́ние.

predilection [,pri:dɪ'lekʃ(ə)n] *n.* пристра́стие (**for** к+*d.*).

predispose [,pri:dɪ'spəʊz] *v.t.* предрасполага́ть *impf.*, предрасположи́ть (-ожу́, -о́жишь) *pf.* (**to** к+*d.*). **predispo'sition** *n.* предрасположе́ние (**to** к+*d.*).

predominance [prɪ'dɒmɪnəns] *n.* преоблада́ние. **predominant** *adj.* преоблада́ющий. **predominate** *v.i.* преоблада́ть *impf.*

pre-eminence [priː'emɪnəns] *n.* превосхо́дство. **pre-eminent** *adj.* выдающийся.

pre-empt [priː'empt] *v.t.* покупа́ть *impf.*, купи́ть (-плю́, -пишь) *pf.* пре́жде други́х; (*fig.*) завладева́ть *impf.*, завладе́ть *pf.*+*i.* пре́жде други́х. **pre-emption** *n.* поку́пка пре́жде други́х; (*right*) преиму́щественное пра́во на поку́пку. **pre-emptive** *adj.* преиму́щественный; (*mil.*) упрежда́ющий.

preen [priːn] *v.t.* (*of bird*) чи́стить *impf.*, по~ *pf.* клю́вом; ~ **o.s.** (*smarten*) прихора́шиваться *impf.*; (*be proud*) горди́ться *impf.* собо́й.

pre-fab ['priːfæb] *n.* сбо́рный дом (*pl.* -а́). **prefabricated** [priː'fæbrɪˌkeɪtɪd] *adj.* заводско́го изготовле́ния; сбо́рный.

preface ['prefəs] *n.* предисло́вие; *v.t.* де́лать *impf.*, с~ *pf.* преждвари́тельные замеча́ния к+*d.* **prefatory** *adj.* вступи́тельный.

prefect ['priːfekt] *n.* префе́кт; (*school*) ста́роста *m.* **prefecture** *n.* префекту́ра.

prefer [prɪ'fɜː(r)] *v.t.* (*promote*) продвига́ть *impf.*, продви́нуть *pf.* (по слу́жбе); (*like better*) предпочита́ть *impf.*, предпоче́сть (-чту́, -чтёшь; -чёл, -чла́) *pf.*; ~ **a charge against** выдвига́ть *impf.*, вы́двинуть *pf.* обвине́ние про́тив+*g.* **preferable** ['prefərəb(ə)l] *adj.* предпочти́тельный. '**preference** *n.* предпочте́ние; ~ **share** привилегиро́ванная а́кция. **prefe'rential** *adj.* предпочти́тельный; (*econ.*) преференциа́льный. **preferment** *n.* продвиже́ние по слу́жбе.

prefiguration [priːˌfɪgə'reɪʃ(ə)n] *n.* прообраз. **pre'figure** *v.t.* служи́ть (-жу́, -жишь) *impf.* прообразом+*g.*

prefix ['priːfɪks] *n.* приста́вка, пре́фикс.

pregnancy ['pregnənsɪ] *n.* бере́менность. **pregnant** *adj.* (*woman*) бере́менная; чрева́тый (**with** +*i.*), по́лный (-лон, -лна́, -по́лно́) (**with** +*g.*).

prehensile [priː'hensaɪl] *adj.* хвата́тельный.

prehistoric [ˌpriːhɪ'stɒrɪk] *adj.* доистори́ческий. **pre'history** *n.* (*of situation etc.*) предысто́рия.

pre-ignition [ˌpriːɪg'nɪʃ(ə)n] *n.* преждевре́менное зажига́ние.

prejudge [priː'dʒʌdʒ] *v.t.* предреша́ть *impf.*, предреши́ть *pf.*

prejudice ['predʒʊdɪs] *n.* предрассу́док (-дка); (*bias*) предупрежде́ние; (*injury*) уще́рб; **without** ~ **to** без уще́рба для+*g.*; *v.t.* наноси́ть (-ошу́, -о́сишь) *impf.*, нанести́ (-есу́, -есёшь; -ёс, -есла́) *pf.* уще́рб+*d.*; ~ **against** восстана́вливать *impf.*, восстанови́ть (-влю́, -вишь) *pf.* про́тив+*g.*; ~ **in favour of** располага́ть *impf.*, расположи́ть (-жу́, -жишь) *pf.* в по́льзу+*g.*

prelate ['prelət] *n.* прела́т.

prelim ['priːlɪm, prɪ'lɪm] *n.*: *pl.* (*print.*) сбо́рный лист (-а́). **preliminary** [prɪ'lɪmɪnərɪ] *adj.* предвари́тельный; *n.*: *pl.* (*discussion*) предвари́тельные перегово́ры *m.pl.*

prelude ['preljuːd] *n.* вступле́ние; (*mus.*; *fig.*) прелю́дия.

premarital [priː'mærɪt(ə)l] *adj.* добра́чный.

premature ['preməˌtjʊə(r), -'tjʊə(r)] *adj.* преждевре́менный (-нен, -нна).

premeditated [priː'medɪˌteɪtɪd] *adj.* преднаме́ренный (-ен, -енна). **premedi'tation** *n.* преднаме́ренность.

premier ['premɪə(r)] *adj.* пе́рвый; *n.* премье́р-мини́стр. ***première*** ['premɪˌeə(r)] *n.* премье́ра.

premise, premiss ['premɪs] *n.* (*logic*) (пред)-посы́лка. **premises** *n.* помеще́ние.

premium ['priːmɪəm] *n.* пре́мия.

premonition [ˌpremə'nɪʃ(ə)n, ˌpriː-] *n.* предчу́вствие. **premonitory** [prɪ'mɒnɪtərɪ] *adj.* предупрежда́ющий.

prenatal [priː'neɪt(ə)l] *adj.* предродово́й.

preoccupation [priːˌɒkjʊ'peɪʃ(ə)n] *n.* озабо́ченность. **pre'occupied** *adj.* озабо́ченный (-ен, -ена). **pre'occupy** *v.t.* поглоща́ть *impf.*, поглоти́ть (-ощу́, -о́тишь) *pf.* внима́ние+*g.*

preordain [ˌpriːɔː'deɪn] *v.t.* предопределя́ть *impf.*, предопредели́ть *pf.*

prep [prep] *n.* приготовле́ние уро́ков; *adj.*: ~ **school** приготови́тельная шко́ла.

pre-pack(age) [priː'pækɪdʒ] *v.t.* расфасо́вывать *impf.*, расфасова́ть *pf.*

prepaid [priː'peɪd] *adj.* опла́ченный (-ен) вперёд.

preparation [ˌprepə'reɪʃ(ə)n] *n.* приготовле́ние; *pl.* подгото́вка (**for** к+*d.*); (*medicine etc.*) препара́т. **preparatory** [prɪ'pærətərɪ] *adj.* под-, при-, готови́тельный; ~ **to** пре́жде чем. **prepare** [prɪ'peə(r)] *v.t.* & *i.* при-, под-, гота́вливать(ся) *impf.*, при-, под-, гото́вить(ся) *pf.* (**for** к+*d.*). **prepared** *adj.* гото́вый.

preponderance [prɪ'pɒndərəns] *n.* переве́с. **preponderant** *adj.* преоблада́ющий. **preponderate** *v.i.* име́ть *impf.* переве́с.

preposition [ˌprepə'zɪʃ(ə)n] *n.* предло́г. **prepositional** *adj.* предло́жный.

prepossessing *adj.* привлека́тельный.

preposterous [prɪ'pɒstərəs] *adj.* (*absurd*) неле́пый, абсу́рдный.

prepuce ['priːpjuːs] *n.* кра́йняя плоть.

pre-record [ˌpriːrɪ'kɔːd] *v.t.* предвари́тельно запи́сывать *impf.*, записа́ть (-ишу́, -и́шешь) *pf.*

prerequisite [priː'rekwɪzɪt] *n.* предпосы́лка.

prerogative [prɪ'rɒgətɪv] *n.* прерогати́ва.

presage ['presɪdʒ] *n.* предве́стник, предзнаменова́ние; (*foreboding*) предчу́вствие; *v.t.* предвеща́ть *impf.*

presbyter ['prezbɪtə(r)] *n.* пресви́тер. **Presbyterian** [ˌprezbɪ'tɪərɪən] *n.* пресвитериа́нин (*pl.* -а́не, -а́н), -а́нка; *adj.* пресвитериа́нский. **presbytery** *n.* пресвите́рия.

prescience ['presɪəns] *n.* предви́дение. **pre-**

scient *adj.* предвидящий.

prescribe [prɪ'skraɪb] *v.t.* устанавливать *impf.*, установить (-влю, -вишь) *pf.*; (*med.*) прописывать *impf.*, прописать (-ишу, -ишешь) *pf.* (**to, for** (*person*) +*d.*; **for** (*complaint*) против+*g.*). **prescription** [prɪ'skrɪpʃ(ə)n] *n.* установка; (*med.*) рецепт.

presence ['prez(ə)ns] *n.* присутствие; (*appearance*) (внешний) вид; ~ **of mind** присутствие духа. **present** *adj.* присутствующий; (*being dealt with*) данный; (*existing now*) нынешний; (*also gram.*) настоящий; *pred.* налицо; **be** ~ присутствовать *impf.* (**at** на+*p.*); *n.*: **the** ~ настоящее *sb.*; (*gram.*) настоящее время *nt.*; (*gift*) подарок (-рка); **at** ~ в настоящее, данное, время *nt.*; **for the** ~ пока; *v.t.* (*introduce*) представлять *impf.*, представить *pf.* (**to** +*d.*); (*hand in*) подавать (-даю, -даёшь) *impf.*, подать (-ам, -ашь, -аст, -адим; подал, -а, -о) *pf.*; (*a play*) ставить *impf.*, по~ *pf.*; (*a gift*) подносить (-ошу, -осишь) *impf.*, поднести (-есу, -есёшь; -ёс, -есла) *pf.*+*d.* (**with** +*d.*); ~ **arms** брать (беру, -рёшь; брал, -а, -о) *impf.*, взять (возьму, -мёшь; взял, -а, -о) *pf.* оружие на караул; (*command*) на караул!; ~ **o.s.** являться *impf.*, явиться (явлюсь, явишься) *pf.* **pre'sentable** *adj.* приличный. **presen'tation** *n.* представление, подношение. **present-day** *adj.* нынешний, современный (-нен, -нна).

presentiment [prɪ'zentɪmənt, -'sentɪmənt] *n.* предчувствие.

presently ['prezəntlɪ] *adv.* вскоре, сейчас.

preservation [ˌprezə'veɪʃ(ə)n] *n.* сохранение, предохранение; (*state of* ~) сохранность; (*of game etc.*) охрана. **preservative** [prɪ'zɜːvətɪv] *adj.* предохранительный; *n.* предохраняющее средство. **pre'serve** *v.t.* (*keep safe*) сохранять *impf.*, сохранить *pf.*; (*maintain*, ~ *fruit etc.*) хранить *impf.*; (*food*) консервировать *impf.*, за~ *pf.*; (*game*) охранять *impf.*, охранить *pf.*; *n.* (*for game, fish*) охотничий, рыболовный, заповедник; *pl.* консервы (-вов) *pl.*; (*jam*) джем, варенье.

preside [prɪ'zaɪd] *v.i.* председательствовать *impf.* (**at** на+*p.*). **presidency** ['prezɪdənsɪ] *n.* председательство, президентство. **'president** *n.* председатель *m.*, президент. **presi'dential** *adj.* президентский. **presidium** [prɪ'sɪdɪəm, -'zɪdɪəm] *n.* президиум.

press¹ [pres] *n.* (*of people*) толпа; (*of affairs*) спешка; (*machine*) пресс; (*printing-*~) печатный станок (-нка); (*printing firm*) типография; (*publishing house*) издательство; (*the* ~) пресса, печать; (*cupboard*) шкаф (*loc.* -у; *pl.* -ы); ~ **attaché** пресс-атташе *m.indecl.*; ~ **conference** пресс-конференция; ~ **photographer** фотокорреспондент; *v.t.* жать (жму, жмёшь) *impf.*; (~ *down on*) нажимать *impf.*, нажать (-жму, -жмёшь) *pf.*+*a.*, на+*a.*; (*clasp*) прижимать *impf.*, прижать (-жму, -жмёшь) *pf.* (**to** к+*d.*); (*with iron*) гладить *impf.*, вы~ *pf.*; (*oppress*, ~ *on*) тяготить (-ощу, -отишь) *impf.*; (*insist on*) настаивать *impf.*, настоять (-ою, -оишь) *pf.* на+*p.*; ~ **forward** продвигаться *impf.*, продвинуться *pf.* вперёд.

press² [pres] *v.t.* (*hist.*) насильственно вербовать *impf.*, за~, на~ *pf.* во флот; ~ **into service** пользоваться *impf.*+*i.* **press-gang** *n.* отряд вербовщиков.

pressing ['presɪŋ] *adj.* (*urgent*) неотложный; (*persistent*) настоятельный. **press-stud** *n.* кнопка. **pressure** ['preʃə(r)] *n.* давление, нажим; ~ **gauge** манометр. **pressure-cooker** *n.* скороварка. **pressurized** *adj.* (*aircraft cabin etc.*) герметический.

prestige [pre'stiːʒ] *n.* престиж.

pre-stressed [priː'strest] *adj.* предварительно напряжённый (-ён, -ённа).

presumably [prɪ'zjuːməblɪ] *adv.* вероятно, предположительно. **presume** *v.t.* считать *impf.* доказанным; полагать *impf.*; (*venture*) позволять *impf.* себе. **presumption** [prɪ'zʌmpʃ(ə)n] *n.* предположение; (*arrogance*) самонадеянность. **presumptive** *adj.* предполагаемый. **presumptuous** *adj.* самонадеянный (-ян, -янна), нахальный.

presuppose [ˌpriːsə'pəʊz] *v.t.* предполагать *impf.*

pretence [prɪ'tens] *n.* притворство. **pretend** *v.t.* притворяться *impf.*, притвориться *pf.* (**to be** +*i.*); делать *impf.*, с~ *pf.* вид (что); *v.i.*: ~ **to** претендовать *impf.* на+*a.* **pretender** *n.* претендент. **pretension** *n.* претензия. **pretentious** *adj.* претенциозный.

preternatural [ˌpriːtə'nætʃər(ə)l] *adj.* сверхъестественный (-ен, -енна).

pretext ['priːtekst] *n.* предлог.

pretonic [priː'tɒnɪk] *adj.* предударный.

prettiness ['prɪtɪnɪs] *n.* миловидность. **pretty** *adj.* миловидный; (*also iron.*) хорошенький; **a** ~ **penny** кругленькая сумма; *adv.* довольно.

prevail [prɪ'veɪl] *v.i.* (*predominate*) преобладать *impf.*; ~ **(up)on** уговаривать *impf.*, уговорить *pf.* **prevailing** *adj.* преобладающий. **prevalent** ['prevələnt] *adj.* распространённый (-ён, -ённа).

prevaricate [prɪ'værɪˌkeɪt] *v.i.* говорить *impf.* уклончиво.

prevent [prɪ'vent] *v.t.* предупреждать *impf.*, предупредить *pf.*; мешать *impf.*, по~ *pf.*+*d.* **prevention** *n.* предупреждение. **preventive** *adj.* предупредительный; (*med.*) профилактический; ~ **measures** профилактика.

preview ['priːvjuː] *n.* предварительный просмотр.

previous ['priːvɪəs] *adj.* предыдущий; *adv.*: ~ **to** прежде чем. **previously** *adv.* заранее, прежде.

pre-war [priː'wɔː(r), 'priːwɔː(r)] *adj.* довоенный.

prey [preɪ] *n.* (*animal*) добыча; (*victim*) жертва (**to** +*g.*); **bird of** ~ хищная птица;

v.i.: ~ **(up)on** (*emotion etc.*) му́чить *impf.*

price [praɪs] *n.* цена́ (*a.* -ну; *pl.* -ы); **at any ~** любо́й ценой, во что́ бы то ни ста́ло; **at a ~** по дорого́й цене́; **not at any ~** ни за что́; **what ~ ...** каки́е ша́нсы на+*a.*; *v.t.* назнача́ть *impf.*, назна́чить *pf.* це́ну+*g.*; (*fig.*) оце́нивать *impf.*, оцени́ть (-ню́, -нишь) *pf.* **priceless** *adj.* бесце́нный. **price-list** *n.* прейскура́нт.

prick [prɪk] *v.t.* коло́ть (-лю́, -лешь) *impf.*, ука́лывать *impf.*, уколо́ть (-лю́, -лешь) *pf.*; (*conscience*) му́чить *impf.*; ~ **out** (*plants*) пики́ровать *impf.* & *pf.*; ~ **up one's ears** навостри́ть *pf.* у́ши; *n.* уко́л. **prickle** *n.* (*thorn*) колю́чка; (*spine*) игла́ (*pl.* -лы). **prickly** *adj.* колю́чий; ~ **heat** потни́ца.

pride [praɪd] *n.* го́рдость; (*of lions*) прайд; **take a ~ in, ~ o.s. on** горди́ться *impf.*+*i.*

priest [priːst] *n.* свяще́нник; (*non-Christian*) жрец (-а́). **priestess** *n.* жри́ца. **priesthood** *n.* свяще́нство. **priestly** *adj.* свяще́нниче-ский.

prig [prɪg] *n.* самодово́льный педа́нт. **priggish** *adj.* педанти́чный.

prim [prɪm] *adj.* чо́порный.

primacy ['praɪməsɪ] *n.* пе́рвенство. **primarily** ['praɪmərɪlɪ, -'meərɪlɪ] *adv.* первонача́льно; (*above all*) пре́жде всего́. **primary** *adj.* первичный; (*chief*) основно́й; ~ **colour** основно́й цвет (*pl.* -а́); ~ **feather** махово́е перо́ (*pl.* -рья, -рьев); ~ **school** нача́льная шко́ла. **primate** *n.* при́ма́с; (*zool.*) прима́т. **prime** *n.* расцве́т; **in one's ~, in the ~ of life** в расцве́те сил; *adj.* (*chief*) гла́вный; (*excellent*) превосхо́дный; (*primary*) перви́чный; ~ **cost** себесто́имость; ~ **minister** премье́р-мини́стр; ~ **number** просто́е число́ (*pl.* -сла, -сел, -слам); *v.t.* (*engine*) заправля́ть *impf.*, запра́вить *pf.*; (*with information etc.*) зара́нее снабжа́ть *impf.*, снабди́ть *pf.* (**with** +*i.*); (*with paint etc.*) грунтова́ть *impf.*, за~ *pf.* **primer** *n.* буква́рь (-ря́) *m.*; (*textbook*) уче́бник; (*paint etc.*) грунт. **pri'meval** *adj.* первобы́тный. **priming** *n.* (*with paint etc.*) грунто́вка. **primitive** ['prɪmɪtɪv] *adj.* первобы́тный, примити́вный. **primo'geniture** *n.* перворо́дство. **pri'mordial** *adj.* первобы́тный; (*original*) иско́нный.

primrose ['prɪmrəʊz] *n.* первоцве́т; (*colour*) бле́дно-жёлтый цвет.

primula ['prɪmjʊlə] *n.* первоцве́т.

Primus (stove) ['praɪməs] *n.* (*propr.*) при́мус (*pl.* -сы & -а́).

prince [prɪns] *n.* принц; (*in Russia*) князь (*pl.* -зья́, -зе́й). **princely** *adj.* кня́жеский; (*splendid*) великоле́пный. **princess** *n.* принце́сса; (*wife*) княги́ня; (*daughter*) княжна́ (*g.pl.* -жо́н). **princi'pality** *n.* кня́жество.

principal *n.* гла́вный, основно́й; *n.* нача́льник, -ица; (*of school*) дире́ктор (*pl.* -а́); (*econ.*) капита́л. **principally** *adv.* гла́вным о́бразом, преиму́щественно.

principle *n.* при́нцип; **in ~** в при́нципе; **on ~** принципиа́льно. **principled** *adj.* принципиа́льный.

print [prɪnt] *n.* (*mark*) след (*pl.* -ы́); (*also phot.*) отпеча́ток (-тка); (*fabric*) си́тец (-тца(у)); (*print.*) печа́ть; (*picture*) гравю́ра, эста́мп; **in ~** в прода́же; **out of ~** распро́данный (-ан); *v.t.* (*impress*) запечатлева́ть *impf.*, запечатле́ть *pf.*; (*book etc.*) печа́тать *impf.*, на~ *pf.*; (*write*) писа́ть (пишу́, -шешь) *impf.*, на~ *pf.* печа́тными бу́квами; (*fabric*) набива́ть *impf.*, наби́ть (-бью́, -бьёшь) *pf.*; (*phot.*; ~ *out, off*) отпеча́тывать *impf.*, отпеча́тать *pf.*; ~ **out** (*of computer etc.*) распеча́тывать *impf.*, распеча́тать *pf.*; ~ **run** тира́ж. **printed** *adj.* печа́тный; (*fabric*) набивно́й; ~ **circuit** печа́тная схе́ма; ~ **matter** бандеро́ль. **printer** *n.* (*person*) печа́тник, типо́граф; (*of fabric*) набо́йщик; (*device*) при́нтер; **~'s ink** типогра́фская кра́ска. **printing** *n.* печа́тание, печа́ть. **printing-press** *n.* печа́тный стано́к (-нка́). **printout** *n.* распеча́тка, табулягра́мма.

prior ['praɪə(r)] *n.* настоя́тель *m.*; *adj.* (*earlier*) пре́жний, предше́ствующий; (*more important*) бо́лее ва́жный; *adv.*: ~ **to** до+*g.* **prioress** *n.* настоя́тельница. **priority** [praɪ'ɒrɪtɪ] *n.* приорите́т; **in order of ~** в поря́дке очерёдности. **priory** *n.* монасты́рь (-ря́) *m.*

prise [praɪz] *v.t.*: ~ **open** взла́мывать *impf.*, взлома́ть *pf.* с по́мощью рычага́.

prism ['prɪz(ə)m] *n.* при́зма. **pris'matic** *adj.* призмати́ческий.

prison ['prɪz(ə)n] *n.* тюрьма́ (*pl.* -рьмы, -рем, -рьмам); *attr.* тюре́мный; ~ **camp** ла́герь (*pl.* -ря́) *m.* **prison-break** *n.* побе́г из тюрьмы́. **prisoner** *n.* заключённый *sb.*; (~ *of war*) (военно)пле́нный *sb.*; ~ **of State** политзаключённый *sb.*

pristine ['prɪstiːn, 'prɪstaɪn] *adj.* (*ancient*) первонача́льный; (*untouched*) нетро́нутый.

privacy ['prɪvəsɪ, 'praɪ-] *n.* (*seclusion*) уедине́ние; (*private life*) ча́стная жизнь. **private** ['praɪvət, -vɪt] *adj.* (*personal*) ча́стный, ли́чный; (*unofficial*) неофициа́льный; (*confidential*) конфиденциа́льный; **in ~** наедине́; в ча́стной жи́зни; ~ **view** закры́тый просмо́тр; *n.* рядово́й *sb.* **priva'teer** *n.* ка́пер. **privatization** [ˌpraɪvəˌtaɪ'zeɪʃ(ə)n] *n.* приватиза́ция. **'privatize** *v.t.* приватизи́ровать *impf.* & *pf.*

pri'vation [praɪ'veɪʃ(ə)n] *n.* лише́ние.

privet ['prɪvɪt] *n.* бирючи́на.

privilege ['prɪvɪlɪdʒ] *n.* привиле́гия. **privileged** *adj.* привелигиро́ванный.

privy ['prɪvɪ] *adj.* та́йный; ~ **to** прича́стный к+*d.*, посвящённый (-ён, -ённа) в+*a.*; **P~ Council** та́йный сове́т.

prize [praɪz] *n.* (*reward*) пре́мия, приз, награ́да; *adj.* удосто́енный пре́мии, награ́ды; *v.t.* высоко́ цени́ть (-ню́, -нишь) *impf.* **prizefight** *n.* состяза́ние на приз. **prizefighter** *n.* боксёр-профессиона́л. **prizewinner** *n.* призёр, лауреа́т

pro¹ [prəʊ] *n.*: **~s and cons** до́воды *m.pl.* за и про́тив.

pro² [prəʊ] *n.* (*professional*) профессиона́л; (спортсме́н-)профессиона́л.

probability [ˌprɒbəˈbɪlɪtɪ] *n.* вероя́тность, правдоподо́бие; **in all ~** по всей вероя́тности. **'probable** *adj.* вероя́тный, правдоподо́бный. **'probably** *adv.* вероя́тно.

probate [ˈprəʊbeɪt, -bət] *n.* утвержде́ние завеща́ния.

probation [prəˈbeɪʃ(ə)n] *n.* испыта́ние, стажиро́вка; (*leg.*) усло́вный пригово́р. **probationary** *adj.* испыта́тельный. **probationer** *n.* стажёр.

probe [prəʊb] *n.* (*med.*) зонд; (*spacecraft*) иссле́довательская раке́та; (*fig.*) рассле́дование; *v.t.* зонди́ровать *impf.*; (*fig.*) рассле́довать *impf.* & *pf.*

probity [ˈprəʊbɪtɪ, ˈprɒ-] *n.* че́стность.

problem [ˈprɒbləm] *n.* пробле́ма, вопро́с; (*math., chess, etc.*) зада́ча; **~ child** тру́дный ребёнок (-нка; *pl.* де́ти, -те́й, -тям, -тьми́). **proble'matic(al)** *adj.* проблемати́чный, проблемати́ческий.

proboscis [prəʊˈbɒsɪs] *n.* хо́бот; (*of insects*) хобото́к (-тка́).

procedural [prəˈsiːdjərəl, -dʒərəl] *adj.* процеду́рный. **procedure** *n.* процеду́ра. **proceed** [prəˈsiːd, prəʊ-] *v.i.* (*go further*) идти́ (иду́, идёшь; шёл, шла) *impf.*, пойти́ (пойду́, -дёшь; пошёл, -шла́) *pf.* да́льше; (*act*) поступа́ть *impf.*, поступи́ть (-плю́, -пишь) *pf.*; (*abs.*, *~ to say*) продолжа́ть *impf.*, продо́лжить *pf.*; (*of action*) продолжа́ться *impf.*, продо́лжиться *pf.*; **~ against** возбужда́ть *impf.*, возбуди́ть *pf.* де́ло, проце́сс, про́тив+*g.*; **~ from** исходи́ть (-ожу́, -о́дишь) *impf.* из, от+*g.*; **~ in, with** возобновля́ть *impf.*, возобнови́ть *pf.*; продолжа́ть *impf.*, продо́лжить *pf.*; **~ to** приступа́ть *impf.*, приступи́ть (-плю́, -пишь) *pf.* к+*d.* **proceeding** *n.* (*action*) посту́пок (-пка); *pl.* (*legal ~*) судопроизво́дство; *pl.* (*published report*) труды́ *m.pl.*, запи́ски *f.pl.* **'proceeds** [ˈprəʊsiːdz] *n.* вы́ручка.

process [ˈprəʊses] *n.* (*course*) ход; проце́сс; *v.t.* обраба́тывать *impf.*, обрабо́тать *pf.*; **~ed cheese** пла́вленный сыр (-а(у); *pl.* -ы́). **processing** *n.* обрабо́тка. **pro'cession** *n.* проце́ссия, ше́ствие. **processor** *n.* (*comput.*) проце́ссор.

proclaim [prəˈkleɪm] *v.t.* провозглаша́ть *impf.*, провозгласи́ть *pf.*; объявля́ть *impf.*, объяви́ть (-влю́, -вишь) *pf.* **proclamation** [ˌprɒkləˈmeɪʃ(ə)n] *n.* провозглаше́ние; объявле́ние.

proclivity [prəˈklɪvɪtɪ] *n.* накло́нность (**to(wards)** к+*d.*).

procrastinate [prəʊˈkræstɪˌneɪt] *v.i.* ме́длить *impf.* **procrasti'nation** *n.* оття́жка.

procreation [ˌprəʊkrɪˈeɪʃ(ə)n] *n.* деторожде́ние.

proctor [ˈprɒktə(r)] *n.* про́ктор. **proctorial** [prɒkˈtɔːrɪəl] *adj.* про́кторский.

procuration [ˌprɒkjʊˈreɪʃ(ə)n] *n.* (*obtaining*) получе́ние; (*pimping*) сво́дничество. **pro'cure** *v.t.* добыва́ть *impf.*, добы́ть (добу́ду, -дешь; до́был, -а́, до́было) *pf.*; достава́ть (-таю́, -таёшь) *impf.*, доста́ть (-а́ну, -а́нешь) *pf.*; *v.i.* (*pimp*) сво́дничать *impf.* **pro'curer** *n.* сво́дник. **procuress** *n.* сво́дница.

prod [prɒd] *v.t.* ты́кать (ты́чу, -чешь) *impf.*, ткнуть *pf.*; *n.* тычо́к (-чка́).

prodigal [ˈprɒdɪg(ə)l] *adj.* (*wasteful*) расточи́тельный; (*lavish*) ще́дрый (щедр, -а́, -о) (**of** на+*a.*); **~ son** блу́дный сын; *n.* мот. **prodigality** [ˌprɒdɪˈgælɪtɪ] *n.* мотовство́; изоби́лие.

prodigious [prəˈdɪdʒəs] *adj.* (*amazing*) удиви́тельный; (*enormous*) огро́мный. **prodigy** [ˈprɒdɪdʒɪ] *n.* чу́до (*pl.* -деса́); **infant ~** вундерки́нд.

produce [prəˈdjuːs; ˈprɒdjuːs] *v.t.* (*evidence etc.*) представля́ть *impf.*, предста́вить *pf.*; (*ticket etc.*) предъявля́ть *impf.*, предъяви́ть (-влю́, -вишь) *pf.*; (*play etc.*) ста́вить *impf.*, по~ *pf.*; (*manufacture*; *cause*) производи́ть (-ожу́, -о́дишь) *impf.*, произвести́ (-еду́, -едёшь; -ёл, -ела́) *pf.*; *n.* проду́кция; (*collect*) проду́кты *m.pl.* **pro'ducer** *n.* (*econ.*) производи́тель *m.*; (*of play etc.*) постано́вщик, режиссёр; **~ gas** генера́торный газ. **'product** *n.* проду́кт, фабрика́т; (*result*) результа́т; (*math.*) произведе́ние. **pro'duction** *n.* произво́дство; (*yield*) проду́кция; (*artistic ~*) произведе́ние; (*of play etc.*) постано́вка. **pro'ductive** *adj.* производи́тельный, продукти́вный; (*fruitful*) плодоро́дный. **produc'tivity** *n.* производи́тельность.

profanation [ˌprɒfəˈneɪʃ(ə)n] *n.* профана́ция, оскверне́ние. **profane** [prəˈfeɪn] *adj.* све́тский; (*blasphemous*) богоху́льный; *v.t.* оскверня́ть *impf.*, оскверни́ть *pf.* **profanity** [prəˈfænɪtɪ] *n.* богоху́льство.

profess [prəˈfes] *v.t.* (*pretend*) притворя́ться *impf.*, притвори́ться *pf.* (**to be** +*i.*); (*declare*) заявля́ть *impf.*, заяви́ть (-влю́, -вишь) *pf.*; (*affirm faith*) испове́довать *impf.*; (*engage in*) занима́ться *impf.*, заня́ться (займу́сь, -мёшься; заня́лся́, -ла́сь) *pf.*+*i.* **professed** *adj.* откры́тый; (*alleged*) мни́мый. **profession** *n.* (*declaration*) заявле́ние; (*of faith*) испове́дование; (*vocation*) профе́ссия. **professional** *adj.* профессиона́льный; *n.* (спортсме́н-)профессиона́л. **professor** *n.* профе́ссор (*pl.* -а́). **profe'ssorial** *adj.* профе́ссорский.

proffer [ˈprɒfə(r)] *v.t.* предлага́ть *impf.*, предложи́ть (-ожу́, -о́жишь) *pf.*

proficiency [prəˈfɪʃ(ə)nsɪ] *n.* уме́ние. **proficient** *adj.* уме́лый.

profile [ˈprəʊfaɪl] *n.* про́филь *m.*; (*biographical sketch*) кра́ткий биографи́ческий о́черк.

profit [ˈprɒfɪt] *n.* (*advantage*) по́льза, вы́года; (*gain*) при́быль; **at a ~** с при́былью; *v.t.* приноси́ть (-ит) *impf.*, принести́ (-есёт; -ёс, -есла́) *pf.* по́льзу+*d.*; *v.i.* получа́ть *impf.*, получи́ть (-чу́, -чишь) *pf.* при́быль; ~ **by** по́льзоваться *impf.*, вос~ *pf.*+*i.* **profitable** *adj.* вы́годный, при́быльный. **profi'teer** *v.i.* спекули́ровать *impf.*; *n.* спекуля́нт, ~ка. **profi'teering** *n.* спекуля́ция. **profitless** *adj.* бесполе́зный.

profligacy ['prɒflɪgəsɪ] *n.* распу́тство. **profligate** *n.* распу́тник; *adj.* распу́тный.

pro forma [prəʊ 'fɔːmə] *adv.* для профо́рмы.

profound [prə'faʊnd] *adj.* глубо́кий (-о́к, -ока́, -о́ко́). **profundity** *n.* глубина́.

profuse [prə'fjuːs] *adj.* (*lavish*) ще́дрый (щедр, -á. -о) (**in** на+*a.*); (*abundant*) изоби́льный. **profusion** *n.* изоби́лие.

progenitor [prəʊ'dʒenɪtə(r)] *n.* прароди́тель *m.* **progeny** ['prɒdʒɪnɪ] *n.* пото́мок (-мка); (*collect.*) пото́мство.

prognosis [prɒg'nəʊsɪs] *n.* прогно́з. **prognosticate** [prɒg'nɒstɪˌkeɪt] *v.t.* предска́зывать *impf.*, предсказа́ть (-ажу́, -а́жешь) *pf.* **prognosti'cation** *n.* предсказа́ние.

programme ['prəʊgræm] *n.* програ́мма; *adj.* програ́ммный; *v.t.* программи́ровать *impf.*, за~ *pf.* **programmer** *n.* программи́ст.

progress ['prəʊgres; prə'gres] *n.* прогре́сс; (*success*) успе́хи *m.pl.*; **make** ~ де́лать *impf.*, с~ *pf.* успе́хи; *v.i.* продвига́ться *impf.*, продви́нуться *pf.* вперёд. **pro'gression** *n.* продвиже́ние; (*math.*) прогре́ссия. **pro'gressive** *adj.* прогресси́вный.

prohibit [prə'hɪbɪt] *v.t.* запреща́ть *impf.*, запрети́ть (-ещу́, -ети́шь) *pf.* **prohibition** [ˌprəʊhɪ'bɪʃ(ə)n, ˌprəʊɪ'b-] *n.* запреще́ние; (*on alcohol*) сухо́й зако́н. **prohibitive** *adj.* запрети́тельный; (*price*) недосту́пный.

project [prə'dʒekt; 'prɒdʒekt] *v.t.* (*plan*) проекти́ровать *impf.*, с~ *pf.*; (*cast*)броса́ть *impf.*, бро́сить *pf.*; (*a film*) демонстри́ровать *impf.*, про~ *pf.*; *v.i.* (*jut out*) выступа́ть *impf.*; *n.* прое́кт. **pro'jectile** *n.* снаря́д. **pro'jection** *n.* прое́кция; (*protrusion*) вы́ступ. **pro'jectionist** *n.* киномеха́ник. **pro'jector** *n.* (*apparatus*) проекцио́нный аппара́т.

proletarian [ˌprəʊlɪ'teərɪən] *adj.* пролета́рский; *n.* пролета́рий, -рка. **proletariat** *n.* пролетариа́т.

proliferate [prə'lɪfəˌreɪt] *v.i.* размножа́ться *impf.*, размно́житься; (*spread*) распространя́ться *impf.*, распространи́ться *pf.*

prolific [prə'lɪfɪk] *adj.* плодови́тый; (*abounding*) изоби́лующий (**in** +*i.*).

prolix ['prəʊlɪks, prə'lɪks] *adj.* многосло́вный. **prolixity** *n.* многосло́вие.

prologue ['prəʊlɒg] *n.* проло́г.

prolong [prə'lɒŋ] *v.t.* продлева́ть *impf.*, продли́ть *pf.* **prolongation** [ˌprəʊlɒŋ'geɪʃ(ə)n] *n.* продле́ние.

promenade [ˌprɒmə'nɑːd] *n.* ме́сто (*pl.* -та́) для гуля́нья; (*at seaside*) на́бережная *sb.*; ~ **deck** ве́рхняя па́луба; *v.i.* прогу́ливаться *impf.*, прогуля́ться *pf.*

prominence ['prɒmɪnəns] *n.* возвыше́ние, вы́пуклость; (*distinction*) изве́стность. **prominent** *adj.* вы́пуклый; (*conspicuous*) ви́дный; (*distinguished*) выдаю́щийся.

promiscuity [ˌprɒmɪ'skjuːɪtɪ] *n.* разноро́дность; (*sexual* ~) промискуите́т. **promiscuous** [prə'mɪskjʊəs] *adj.* (*varied*) разноро́дный; (*indiscriminate*) беспоря́дочный; (*casual*) случа́йный.

promise ['prɒmɪs] *n.* обеща́ние; *v.t.* обеща́ть *impf.* & *pf.*; ~**ed land** земля́ (*a.* -лю) обето́ванная. **promising** *adj.* многообеща́ющий, перспекти́вный. **promissory** *adj.*: ~ **note** долгово́е обяза́тельство.

promontory ['prɒməntərɪ] *n.* мыс (*loc.* -е & -у́; *pl.* мысы́).

promote [prə'məʊt] *v.t.* (*advance*) продвига́ть *impf.*, продви́нуть *pf.*; (*assist*) спосо́бствовать *impf.* & *pf.*+*d.*; (*product*) соде́йствовать *impf.* & *pf.* прода́же+*g.*; ~ **to** (*mil.*) производи́ть (-ожу́, -о́дишь) *impf.*, произвести́ (-еду́, -едёшь; -ёл, -ела́) *pf.* в+*nom.-a.pl.* **promoter** *n.* (*company* ~) учреди́тель *m.*; (*of sporting event etc.*) антрепренёр. **promotion** *n.* продвиже́ние, повыше́ние; соде́йствие.

prompt [prɒmpt] *adj.* бы́стрый (быстр, -á, -о, бы́стры́), неме́дленный (-ен, -енна); *adv.* ро́вно; *v.t.* (*incite*) побужда́ть *impf.*, побуди́ть *pf.* (**to** к+*d.*; +*inf.*); (*speaker*; *also fig.*) подска́зывать *impf.*, подсказа́ть (-ажу́, -а́жешь) *pf.*+*d.*; (*theatr.*) суфли́ровать *impf.*+*d.*; *n.* подска́зка. **prompt-box** *n.* суфлёрская бу́дка. **prompter** *n.* суфлёр.

promulgate ['prɒməlˌgeɪt] *v.t.* обнаро́довать *pf.*; публикова́ть *impf.*, о~ *pf.*; (*disseminate*) распространя́ть *impf.*, распространи́ть *pf.* **promul'gation** *n.* обнаро́дование, опублико́вание; распростране́ние.

prone [prəʊn] *adj.* (лежа́щий) ничко́м; *pred.*: ~ **to** скло́нен (-о́нна́, -о́нно) к+*d.*

prong [prɒŋ] *n.* зубе́ц (-бца́).

pronominal [prəʊ'nɒmɪn(ə)l] *adj.* местоиме́нный. **pronoun** ['prəʊnaʊn] *n.* местоиме́ние.

pronounce [prə'naʊns] *v.t.* (*declare*) объявля́ть *impf.*, объяви́ть (-влю́, -вишь) *pf.*; (*articulate*) произноси́ть (-ошу́, -о́сишь) *impf.*, произнести́ (-есу́, -есёшь; -ёс, -есла́) *pf.*; *v.i.* (*give opinion*) выска́зываться *impf.*, вы́сказаться (-ажусь, -ажешься) *pf.* **pronounced** *adj.* ре́зко вы́раженный (-ен). **pronouncement** *n.* выска́зывание. **pronunciation** [prəˌnʌnsɪ'eɪʃ(ə)n] *n.* произноше́ние.

proof [pruːf] *n.* доказа́тельство; (*test*) испыта́ние; (*strength of alcohol*) устано́вленный гра́дус; (*print.*) корректу́ра; (*phot.*) про́бный отпеча́ток (-тка); (*of engraving*) про́бный о́ттиск; *adj.* (*impenetrable*) непроница́емый (**against** для+*g.*); (*not yielding*) неподдаю́щийся (**against** +*d.*). **proofreader** *n.* корре́ктор (*pl.* -ы & -а́).

prop[1] [prɒp] *n.* (*support*) подпо́рка, сто́йка; (*fig.*) опо́ра; *v.t.* (~ *up*) подпира́ть *impf.*, подпере́ть (-допру́, -допрёшь; -дпёр) *pf.*;

(*fig.*) поддéрживать *impf.*, поддержáть (-жý, -жишь) *pf.*
prop² [prɒp] *n.* (*theatr.*): *pl.* (*collect.*) реквизи́т, бутафóрия.
propaganda [ˌprɒpəˈgændə] *n.* пропагáнда. **propagandist** *n.* пропаганди́ст.
propagate [ˈprɒpəˌgeɪt] *v.t.* & *i.* размножáть(ся) *impf.*, размнóжить(ся) *pf.*; (*disseminate*) распространя́ть(ся) *impf.*, распространи́ть(ся) *pf.* **propa'gation** *n.* размножéние; распространéние.
propane [ˈprəʊpeɪn] *n.* пропáн.
propel [prəˈpel] *v.t.* приводи́ть (-ожý, -óдишь) *impf.*, привести́ (-едý, -едёшь; -ёл, -елá) *pf.* в движéние; (*fig.*) дви́гать (-аю, -аешь & дви́жу, -жешь *impf.*, дви́нуть *pf.*; **~ling pencil** автокарандáш (-á). **propellant** *n.* (*in firearm*) пóрох; (*in rocket engine*) тóпливо. **propeller** *n.* (*aeron.*) пропéллер; (*aeron.*; *naut.*) винт (-á).
propensity [prəˈpensɪtɪ] *n.* наклóнность (**to** к+*d.*; +*inf.*).
proper [ˈprɒpə(r)] *adj.* (*characteristic*) свóйственный (-ен(ен), -енна) (**to** +*d.*); (*gram.*) сóбственный; (*correct*) прáвильный; (*strictly so called*; *after n.*) в ýзком смы́сле слóва; (*suitable*) надлежáщий, дóлжный; (*decent*) пристóйный; **~ fraction** прáвильная дробь (*pl.* -би, -бéй). **properly** *adv.* (*fittingly*, *duly*) дóлжным óбразом, как слéдует; (*correctly*) сóбственно; (*decently*) прили́чно.
property [ˈprɒpətɪ] *n.* (*possessions*) сóбственность, имýщество; (*attribute*) свóйство; *pl.* (*theatr.*) реквизи́т, бутафóрия; **~ man** реквизи́тор, бутафóр.
prophecy [ˈprɒfɪsɪ] *n.* пророчество. **prophesy** [ˈprɒfɪˌsaɪ] *v.t.* прорóчить *impf.*, на~ *pf.* **prophet** *n.* прорóк. **prophetess** *n.* прорóчица. **prophetic** [prəˈfetɪk] *adj.* прорóческий.
prophylactic [ˌprɒfɪˈlæktɪk] *adj.* профилакти́ческий; *n.* профилакти́ческое срéдство. **prophylaxis** *n.* профилáктика.
propinquity [prəˈpɪŋkwɪtɪ] *n.* (*nearness*) бли́зость; (*kinship*) родствó.
propitiate [prəˈpɪʃɪˌeɪt] *v.t.* умиротворя́ть *impf.*, умиротвори́ть *pf.* **propiti'ation** *n.* умиротворéние.
propitious [prəˈpɪʃəs] *adj.* благоприя́тный.
proponent [prəˈpəʊnənt] *n.* сторóнник, -ица.
proportion [prəˈpɔːʃ(ə)n] *n.* пропóрция; (*correct relation*) пропорционáльность; *pl.* размéры *m.pl.* **proportional** *adj.* пропорционáльный; **~ representation** пропорционáльное представи́тельство. **proportionate** *adj.* соразмéрный (**to** +*d.*; с+*i.*).
proposal [prəˈpəʊz(ə)l] *n.* предложéние. **propose** *v.t.* предлагáть *impf.*, предложи́ть (-жý, -жишь) *pf.*; (*intend*) предполагáть *impf.*; *v.i.* (**~** *marriage*) дéлать *impf.*, с~ *pf.* предложéние (**to** +*d.*). **proposition** [ˌprɒpəˈzɪʃ(ə)n] *n.* (*assertion*) утверждéние; (*math.*) теорéма; (*proposal*) предложéние; (*undertaking*) (*coll.*) дéло.
propound [prəˈpaʊnd] *v.t.* предлагáть *impf.*, предложи́ть (-жý, -жишь) *pf.* на обсуждéние.
proprietary [prəˈpraɪətərɪ] *adj.* (*of owner*) сóбственнический; (*medicine*) патентóванный. **proprietor** *n.* сóбственник, хозя́ин (*pl.* -я́ева, -я́ев). **proprietress** *n.* сóбственница, хозя́йка.
propriety [prəˈpraɪɪtɪ] *n.* пристóйность, прили́чие.
propulsion [prəˈpʌlʃ(ə)n] *n.* движéние вперёд; (*fig.*) дви́жущая си́ла.
prorogue [prəˈrəʊg] *v.t.* назначáть *impf.*, назнáчить *pf.* переры́в в рабóте+*g.*
prosaic [prəˈzeɪɪk, prəʊ-] *adj.* прозаи́ческий, прозаи́чный.
proscenium [prəˈsiːnɪəm, prəʊ-] *n.* авансцéна.
proscribe [prəˈskraɪb] *v.t.* (*put outside the law*) объявля́ть *impf.*, объяви́ть (-влю́, -вишь) *pf.* вне закóна; (*banish*) изгоня́ть *impf.*, изгнáть (изгоню́, -нишь; изгнáл, -á, -о)) *pf.*; (*forbid*) запрещáть *impf.*, запрети́ть (-ещý, -ети́шь) *pf.*
prose [prəʊz] *n.* прóза.
prosecute [ˈprɒsɪˌkjuːt] *v.t.* (*pursue*) вести́ (ведý, -дёшь; вёл, -á) *impf.*; (*leg.*) преслéдовать *impf.* **prose'cution** *n.* ведéние; (*leg.*) судéбное преслéдование; (*prosecuting party*) обвинéние. **prosecutor** *n.* обвини́тель *m.*
proselyte [ˈprɒsɪˌlaɪt] *n.* прозели́т. **proselytize** [ˈprɒsɪlɪˌtaɪz] *v.t.* обращáть *impf.*, обрати́ть (-ащý, -ати́шь) *pf.* в другýю вéру.
prosody [ˈprɒsədɪ] *n.* просóдия.
prospect [ˈprɒspekt; prəˈspekt] *n.* вид, перспекти́ва; *v.t.* & *i.* развéдывать *impf.*, развéдать *pf.* (**for** на+*a.*). **pro'spective** *adj.* бýдущий, предполагáемый. **pro'spector** *n.* развéдчик. **pro'spectus** *n.* проспéкт.
prosper [ˈprɒspə(r)] *v.i.* процветáть *impf.*; преуспевáть *impf.* **prosperity** [prɒˈsperɪtɪ] *n.* процветáние, преуспевáние. **prosperous** *adj.* процветáющий, преуспевáющий; (*wealthy*) зажи́точный.
prostate (gland) [ˈprɒsteɪt] *n.* предстáтельная железá (*pl.* жéлезы, -лёз, -лезáм).
prostitute [ˈprɒstɪˌtjuːt] *n.* проститýтка; *v.t.* проституи́ровать *impf.* & *pf.* **prosti'tution** *n.* проститýция.
prostrate [ˈprɒstreɪt] *adj.* распростёртый, (лежáщий) ничкóм; (*exhausted*) обесси́ленный (-ен); (*with grief*) уби́тый (**with** +*i.*); *v.t.* (*exhaust*) истощáть *impf.*, истощи́ть *pf.*; **~ o.s.** пáдать *impf.*, пасть (падý, -дёшь; пал) *pf.* ниц. **prost'ration** *n.* прострáция.
protagonist [prəʊˈtægənɪst] *n.* глáвный герóй; (*advocate*) сторóнник.
protean [ˈprəʊtɪən, -ˈtiːən] *adj.* (*having many forms*) многообрáзный; (*versatile*) многосторóнний (-нен, -нняя).
protect [prəˈtekt] *v.t.* защищáть *impf.*, защити́ть (-ищý, -ити́шь) *pf.* (**from** от+*g.*; **against**

про́тив+*g.*). **protection** *n.* защи́та, охра́на; (*patronage*) покрови́тельство. **protectionism** *n.* протекциони́зм. **protective** *adj.* защи́тный, покрови́тельственный. **protector** *n.* защи́тник, покрови́тель *m.*; (*regent*) проте́ктор. **protectorate** *n.* протектора́т.

protégé(e) ['prɒtɪ,ʒeɪ, -te,ʒeɪ, 'prəʊ-] *n.* протеже́ *c.g.indecl.*

protein ['prəʊtiːn] *n.* протеи́н, бело́к (-лка́).

protest ['prəʊtest; prə'test] *n.* проте́ст; *v.i.* протестова́ть *impf.* & *pf.*; *v.t.* (*affirm*) заявля́ть *impf.*, заяви́ть (-влю́, -вишь) *pf.+a.*, о+*p.*, что.

Protestant ['prɒtɪst(ə)nt] *n.* протеста́нт, ~ка; *adj.* протеста́нтский. **Protestantism** *n.* протеста́нство.

protestation [,prɒtɪ'steɪʃ(ə)n] *n.* (торже́ственное) заявле́ние (о+*p.*; что); (*protest*) проте́ст.

protocol [,prəʊtə'kɒl] *n.* протоко́л.

proton ['prəʊtɒn] *n.* прото́н.

protoplasm ['prəʊtə,plæz(ə)m] *n.* протопла́зма.

prototype ['prəʊtə,taɪp] *n.* прототи́п.

protozoan [,prəʊtə'zəʊən] *n.* просте́йшее (живо́тное) *sb.*

protract [prə'trækt] *v.t.* тяну́ть (-ну́, -нешь) *impf.*; (*plan*) черти́ть (-рчу́, -ртишь) *impf.*, на~ *pf.* **protracted** *adj.* дли́тельный. **protraction** *n.* промедле́ние; начерта́ние. **protractor** *n.* (*instrument*) транспорти́р; (*muscle*) разгиба́тельная мы́шца.

protrude [prə'truːd] *v.t.* высо́вывать *impf.*, вы́сунуть *pf.*; *v.i.* выдава́ться (-даётся) *impf.*, вы́даться (-астся) *pf.* **protrusion** *n.* вы́ступ.

protuberance [prə'tjuːbərəns] *n.* вы́пуклость, вы́ступ, бугоро́к (-рка́). **protuberant** *adj.* вы́пуклый; ~ **eyes** глаза́ (-з, -за́м) *m.pl.* навы́кате.

proud [praʊd] *adj.* го́рдый (горд, -а́, -о, го́рды́); **be ~ of** горди́ться *impf.+i.*

provable ['pruːvəb(ə)l] *adj.* доказу́емый. **prove** *v.t.* дока́зывать *impf.*, доказа́ть (-ажу́, -а́жешь) *pf.*; удостоверя́ть *impf.*, удостове́рить *pf.*; (*a will*) утвержда́ть *impf.*, утверди́ть *pf.*; *v.i.* ока́зываться *impf.*, оказа́ться (-ажу́сь, -а́жешься) *pf.* (**to be** +*i.*). **proven** *adj.* дока́занный (-ан).

provenance ['prɒvɪnəns] *n.* происхожде́ние.

provender ['prɒvɪndə(r)] *n.* корм (*loc.* -е́ & -у́; *pl.* -а́).

proverb ['prɒvɜːb] *n.* посло́вица. **proverbial** [prə'vɜːbɪəl] *adj.* воше́дший в погово́рку; (*well known*) общеизве́стный; ~ **saying** погово́рка.

provide [prə'vaɪd] *v.t.* (*stipulate*) ста́вить *impf.*, по~ *pf.* усло́вием (**that** что); (*supply person*) снабжа́ть *impf.*, снабди́ть *pf.* (**with** +*i.*); обеспе́чивать *impf.*, обеспе́чить *pf.* (**with** +*i.*); (*supply thing*) предоставля́ть *impf.*, предоста́вить *pf.* (**to, for** +*d.*); дава́ть (даю́, даёшь) *impf.*, дать (дам, дашь, даст, дади́м; дал, -а́, да́ло́, -и) *pf.* (**to, for** +*d.*); *v.i.*: ~ **against** принима́ть *impf.*, приня́ть (приму́, -мешь; при́нял, -а́, -о) *pf.* ме́ры про́тив+*g.*; ~ **for** предусма́тривать *impf.*, предусмотре́ть (-рю́, -ришь) *pf.+a.*; (~ *for family etc.*) содержа́ть (-жу́,- жишь) *impf.+a.* **provided (that)** *conj.* при усло́вии, что; е́сли то́лько. **providence** ['prɒvɪd(ə)ns] *n.* провиде́ние; (*foresight*) предусмотри́тельность. **'provident** *adj.* предусмотри́тельный; (*thrifty*) бережли́вый. **provi'dential** *adj.* (*lucky*) счастли́вый (сча́стли́в). **providing** *see* **provided (that)**

province ['prɒvɪns] *n.* о́бласть (*pl.* -ти, -те́й) (*also fig.*); прови́нция; *pl.* (*the* ~) прови́нция. **provincial** [prə'vɪnʃ(ə)l] *adj.* провинциа́льный; *n.* провинциа́л, ~ка. **pro'vincialism** *n.* провинциа́льность; (*expression*) областно́е выраже́ние.

provision [prə'vɪʒ(ə)n] *n.* снабже́ние, обеспече́ние; *pl.* прови́зия; (*in agreement etc.*) положе́ние; **make ~ against** принима́ть *impf.*, приня́ть (приму́, -мешь; при́нял, -а́, -о) *pf.* ме́ры про́тив+*g.*; **make ~ for** предусма́тривать *impf.*, предусмотре́ть (-рю́, -ришь) *pf.+a.*; *v.t.* снабжа́ть *impf.*, снабди́ть *pf.* прови́зией. **provisional** *adj.* вре́менный. **proviso** [prə'vaɪzəʊ] *n.* усло́вие, огово́рка. **provisory** [prə'vaɪzərɪ] *adj.* усло́вный.

provocation [,prɒvə'keɪʃ(ə)n] *n.* провока́ция. **provocative** [prə'vɒkətɪv] *adj.* провокацио́нный; ~ **of** вызыва́ющий+*a.* **provoke** [prə'vəʊk] *v.t.* провоци́ровать *impf.*, с~ *pf.*; (*call forth, cause*) вызыва́ть *impf.*, вы́звать (вы́зову, -вешь) *pf.*; (*irritate*) раздража́ть *impf.*, раздражи́ть *pf.*

provost ['prɒvəst] *n.* (*univ.*) ре́ктор; (*mayor*) мэр; ~ **marshal** нача́льник вое́нной поли́ции.

prow [praʊ] *n.* нос (*loc.* -у́; *pl.* -ы́).

prowess ['praʊɪs] *n.* (*valour*) до́блесть; (*skill*) уме́ние.

prowl [praʊl] *v.i.* ры́скать (ры́щу, -щешь) *impf.*; *v.t.* броди́ть (-ожу́, -о́дишь) *impf.* по+*d.*

proximity [prɒk'sɪmɪtɪ] *n.* бли́зость.

proxy ['prɒksɪ] *n.* полномо́чие, дове́ренность; (*person*) уполномо́ченный *sb.*, замести́тель *m.*; **by ~** по дове́ренности; **stand ~ for** быть *impf.* замести́телем+*g.*

prude [pruːd] *n.* скро́мник, -ица.

prudence ['pruːd(ə)ns] *n.* благоразу́мие. **prudent** *adj.* благоразу́мный.

prudery ['pruːdərɪ] *n.* притво́рная стыдли́вость. **prudish** *adj.* ни в ме́ру стыдли́вый.

prune[1] [pruːn] *n.* (*plum*) черносли́вина; *pl.* черносли́в (-а(у)) (*collect.*).

prune[2] [pruːn] *v.t.* (*trim*) об-, под-, реза́ть *impf.*, об-, под-, ре́зать (-е́жу, -е́жешь) *pf.*; (*fig.*) сокраща́ть *impf.*, сократи́ть (-ащу́, -ати́шь) *pf.* **pruning-hook** *n.* приви́вочный нож (-а́).

prurience ['prʊərɪəns] *n.* похотли́вость.

prurient *adj.* похотли́вый.
Prussian ['prʌʃ(ə)n] *n.* прусса́к (-а́), -а́чка; *adj.* пру́сский; ~ **blue** берли́нская лазу́рь.
prussic *adj.*: ~ **acid** сини́льная кислота́.
pry [praɪ] *v.i.* сова́ть (сую́, суёшь) *impf.* нос (**into** в+*a.*). **prying** *adj.* пытли́вый, любопы́тный.
PS (*abbr. of* **postscript**) постскри́птум, припи́ска.
psalm [sɑːm] *n.* псало́м (-лма́). **psalter** ['sɔːltə(r), 'sɒl-] *n.* псалты́рь (-ри & -ря́) *f.* & *m.*
pseudo- ['sjuːdəʊ] *in comb.* псевдо... . **pseudonym** *n.* псевдони́м.
psyche ['saɪkɪ] *n.* пси́хика. **psychi'atric** *adj.* психиатри́ческий. **psychiatrist** [saɪ'kaɪətrɪst] *n.* психиа́тр. **psy'chiatry** *n.* психиатри́я. **psychic(al)** *adj.* психи́ческий, душе́вный; *n.* экстрасе́нс. **psycho** ['saɪkəʊ] *n.* псих. **psycho-** *in comb.* психо... . **psycho-analyse** *v.t.* подверга́ть *impf.*, подве́ргнуть (-г) *pf.* психоана́лизу. **psycho-analysis** *n.* психоана́лиз. **psycho-analyst** *n.* специали́ст по психоана́лизу. **psycho-analytic(al)** *adj.* психоаналити́ческий. **psychological** *adj.* психологи́ческий. **psy'chologist** *n.* психо́лог. **psy'chology** *n.* психоло́гия; (*coll.*) пси́хика. **psychopath** ['saɪkə,pæθ] *n.* психопа́т. **psycho'pathic** *adj.* психопати́ческий. **psychopathology** *n.* психопатоло́гия. **psy'chosis** *n.* психо́з. **psychotherapy** *n.* психотерапи́я.
pt. *n.* (*abbr. of* **pint(s)**) пи́нта.
ptarmigan ['tɑːmɪgən] *n.* тундря́нка.
pterodactyl [,terə'dæktɪl] *n.* птерода́ктиль *m.*
PTO *abbr.* (*of* ***please turn over***) см. на об., смотри́ на оборо́те.
pub [pʌb] *n.* пивна́я *sb.*, каба́к (-а́).
puberty ['pjuːbətɪ] *n.* полова́я зре́лость.
public ['pʌblɪk] *adj.* обще́ственный; (*open*) публи́чный, откры́тый; ~ **health** здравоохране́ние; ~ **house** пивна́я *sb.*; ~ **relations officer** слу́жащий *sb.* отде́ла информа́ции; ~ **school** ча́стная сре́дняя шко́ла; ~ **servant** госуда́рственный слу́жащий *sb.*; ~ **spirit** обще́ственный дух; ~ **utility** предприя́тие обще́ственного по́льзования; *n.* пу́блика, обще́ственность; **in** ~ откры́то, публи́чно. **publi'cation** *n.* (*action*) опубликова́ние; (*also book etc.*) изда́ние. **publicist** *n.* публици́ст. **pub'licity** *n.* рекла́ма; ~ **agent** аге́нт по рекла́ме. **publicize** *v.t.* реклами́ровать *impf.* & *pf.* **publicly** *adv.* публи́чно, откры́то. **publish** *v.t.* публикова́ть *impf.*, о~ *pf.*; (*book*) издава́ть (-даю́, -даёшь) *impf.*, изда́ть (-а́м, -а́шь, -а́ст, -ади́м; изда́л, -а́, -о) *pf.* **publisher** *n.* изда́тель *m.* **publishing** *n.* (*business*) изда́тельское де́ло; ~ **house** изда́тельство.
puce [pjuːs] *adj.* (*n.*) краснова́то-кори́чневый (цвет).
puck [pʌk] *n.* (*in ice hockey*) ша́йба.
pucker ['pʌkə(r)] *v.t.* & *i.* мо́рщить(ся) *impf.*, с~ *pf.*; *n.* морщи́на.
pudding ['pʊdɪŋ] *n.* пу́динг, запека́нка.
puddle ['pʌd(ə)l] *n.* лу́жа.
pudgy ['pʌdʒɪ] *adj.* пу́хлый (пухл, -а́, -о).
puerile ['pjʊəraɪl] *adj.* ребя́ческий. **puerility** [pjʊə'rɪlɪtɪ] *n.* ребя́чество.
puff [pʌf] *n.* (*of wind*) поры́в; (*of smoke*) дымо́к (-мка́); (*on dress*) бу́фы (-ф) *pl. only*; ~ **pastry** слоёное те́сто; ~ **sleeves** рукава́ *m.pl.* с бу́фами; *v.i.* пыхте́ть (-хчу́, -хти́шь) *impf.*; ~ **at** (*pipe etc.*) попы́хивать *impf.*+*i.*; *v.t.*: ~ **up, out** (*inflate*) надува́ть *impf.*, наду́ть (-у́ю, -у́ешь) *pf.*
puffin ['pʌfɪn] *n.* ту́пик.
pug [pʌg] *n.* (*dog*) мопс.
pugilism ['pjuːdʒɪ,lɪz(ə)m] *n.* бокс. **pugilist** *n.* боксёр.
pugnacious [pʌg'neɪʃəs] *adj.* драчли́вый. **pugnacity** [pʌg'næsɪtɪ] *n.* драчли́вость.
pug-nosed ['pʌg,nəʊzd] *adj.* курно́сый.
puissant ['pjuːɪs(ə)nt, 'pwiːs-, 'pwɪs-] *adj.* могу́щественный (-ен, -енна).
puke [pjuːk] *v.i.* рвать (рвёт; рва́ло) *impf.*, вы́~ *pf. impers.*+*a.*; *n.* рво́та.
pull [pʊl] *n.* тя́га; (*fig.*) зару́чка; *v.t.* тяну́ть (-ну́, -нешь) *impf.*, по~ *pf.*; таска́ть *indet.*, тащи́ть (-щу́, -щишь) *det.*, по~ *pf.*; (*a muscle*) растя́гивать *impf.*, растяну́ть (-ну́, -нешь) *pf.*; (*a cork*) выта́скивать *impf.*, вы́тащить *pf.*; (*a tooth*) удаля́ть *impf.*, удали́ть *pf.*; *v.t.* & *i.* дёргать *impf.*, дёрнуть *pf.* (**at** (за)+*a.*); ~ **faces** грима́сничать *impf.*; ~ **s.o's leg** моро́чить *impf.* го́лову+*d.*; ~ **(the) strings, wires** нажима́ть *impf.*, нажа́ть (нажму́, -мёшь) *pf.* на та́йные пружи́ны; ~ **the trigger** спуска́ть *impf.*, спусти́ть (-ущу́, -у́стишь) *pf.* куро́к; ~ **apart, to pieces** разрыва́ть *impf.*, разорва́ть (-ву́, -вёшь; -ва́л, -вала́, -ва́ло) *pf.*; (*fig.*) раскритикова́ть *pf.*; ~ **at** (*pipe etc.*) затя́гиваться *impf.*, затяну́ться (-ну́сь, -нешься) *pf.*+*i.*; ~ **down** (*demolish*) сноси́ть (-ошу́, -о́сишь) *impf.*, снести́ (снесу́, -сёшь; снёс, -ла́) *pf.*; ~ **in** (*earn*) зараба́тывать *impf.*, зарабо́тать *pf.*; (*of train*) прибыва́ть *impf.*, прибы́ть (-бу́дет; при́был, -а́, -о) *pf.*; (*of vehicle*) подъезжа́ть *impf.*, подъе́хать (-е́дет) *pf.* к обо́чине доро́ги; ~ **off** (*garment*) стя́гивать *impf.*, стяну́ть (-ну́, -нешь) *pf.*; (*achieve*) успе́шно заверша́ть *impf.*, заверши́ть *pf.*; (*win*) выи́грывать *impf.*, вы́играть *pf.*; ~ **on** (*garment*) натя́гивать *impf.*, натяну́ть (-ну́, -нешь) *pf.*; ~ **out** (*v.t.*) (*remove*) выта́скивать *impf.*, вы́тащить *pf.*; (*v.i.*) (*withdraw*) отка́зываться *impf.*, отказа́ться (-ажу́сь, -а́жешься) *pf.* от уча́стия (**of** в+*p.*); (*of vehicle*) отъезжа́ть *impf.*, отъе́хать (-е́дет) *pf.* от обо́чины (доро́ги); (*of train*) отходи́ть (-ит) *impf.*, отойти́ (-йдёт; отошёл, -шла́) *pf.* (от ста́нции); ~ **through** выжива́ть *impf.*, вы́жить (вы́живу, -вешь) *pf.*; ~ **o.s. together** брать (беру́, -рёшь; брал, -а́, -о) *impf.*, взять (возьму́, -мёшь; взял, -а́, -о)

pf. себя́ в ру́ки; ~ **up** (*v.t.*) подтя́гивать *impf.*, подтяну́ть (-ну́, -нешь) *pf.*; (*v.t.* & *i.*) (*stop*) остана́вливать(ся) *impf.*, останови́ть(ся) (-влю́(сь), -вишь(ся)) *pf.*

pullet ['pʊlɪt] *n.* моло́дка.

pulley ['pʊlɪ] *n.* блок, шкив (*pl.* -ы́).

Pullman ['pʊlmən] *n.* пу́льман(овский ваго́н).

pullover ['pʊl,əʊvə(r)] *n.* пуло́вер.

pulmonary ['pʌlmənərɪ] *adj.* лёгочный.

pulp [pʌlp] *n.* (*of fruit*) мя́коть; (*anat.*) пу́льпа; (*of paper*) бума́жная ма́сса; *v.t.* превраща́ть *impf.*, преврати́ть (-ащу́, -ати́шь) *pf.* в мя́гкую ма́ссу.

pulpit ['pʊlpɪt] *n.* ка́федра.

pulsar ['pʌlsɑ:(r)] *n.* пульса́р. **pul'sate** *v.i.* пульси́ровать *impf.* **pul'sation** *n.* пульса́ция. **pulse**[1] *n.* (*throbbing*) пульс; *v.i.* пульси́ровать *impf.*

pulse[2] [pʌls] *n.* (*food*) бобо́вые *sb.*

pulverize ['pʌlvə,raɪz] *v.t.* размельча́ть *impf.*, размельчи́ть *pf.*; (*fig.*) сокруша́ть *impf.*, сокруши́ть *pf.*

puma ['pju:mə] *n.* пу́ма.

pumice(-stone) ['pʌmɪs] *n.* пе́мза.

pummel ['pʌm(ə)l] *v.t.* колоти́ть (-очу́, -о́тишь) *impf.*, по~ *pf.*; тузи́ть *impf.*, от~ *pf.*

pump[1] [pʌmp] *n.* (*machine*) насо́с; *v.t.* (*use* ~) кача́ть *impf.*; (*person*) выпра́шивать *impf.*, вы́просить *pf.* у+*g.*; ~ **in(to)** вка́чивать *impf.*, вкача́ть *pf.*; ~ **out** выка́чивать *impf.*, вы́качать *pf.*; ~ **up** нака́чивать *impf.*, накача́ть *pf.*

pump[2] [pʌmp] *n.* (*shoe*) ту́фля (*g.pl.* -фель).

pumpkin ['pʌmpkɪn] *n.* ты́ква.

pun [pʌn] *n.* каламбу́р; *v.i.* каламбу́рить *impf.*, с~ *pf.*

punch[1] [pʌntʃ] *n.* (*drink*) пунш.

punch[2] [pʌntʃ] *v.t.* (*with fist*) ударя́ть *impf.*, уда́рить *pf.* кулако́м; (*pierce*) пробива́ть *impf.*, проби́ть (-бью́, -бьёшь) *pf.*; (*a ticket*) компости́ровать *impf.*, про~ *pf.*; *n.* (*blow*) уда́р кулако́м; (*for tickets*) компо́стер; (*for piercing*) пробо́йник; (*for stamping*) пуансо́н. **punch-ball** *n.* пенчингбо́л, гру́ша. **punch-up** *n.* дра́ка.

punctilious *adj.* соблюда́ющий форма́льности, щепети́льный.

punctual ['pʌŋktjʊəl] *adj.* пунктуа́льный. **punctu'ality** *n.* пунктуа́льность.

punctuate *v.t.* ста́вить *impf.*, по~ *pf.* зна́ки препина́ния в+*a.*; прерыва́ть *impf.*, прерва́ть (-ву́, -вёшь; прерва́л, -а́, -о) *pf.* **punctu'ation** *n.* пунктуа́ция; ~ **marks** зна́ки *m.pl.* препина́ния.

puncture ['pʌŋktʃə(r)] *n.* проко́л; *v.t.* прока́лывать *impf.*, проколо́ть (-лю́, -лешь) *pf.*; *v.i.* получа́ть *impf.*, получи́ть (-чу́, -чишь) *pf.* проко́л

pundit ['pʌndɪt] *n.* (*fig.*) знато́к (-а́).

pungency ['pʌndʒ(ə)nsɪ] *n.* е́дкость. **pungent** *adj.* е́дкий (е́док, едка́, е́дко).

punish ['pʌnɪʃ] *v.t.* нака́зывать *impf.*, наказа́ть (-ажу́, -а́жешь) *pf.* **punishable** *adj.* наказу́емый. **punishment** *n.* наказа́ние. **punitive** ['pju:nɪtɪv] *adj.* кара́тельный.

punk [pʌŋk] *n.* панк; *adj.* па́нковый.

punnet ['pʌnɪt] *n.* корзи́нка.

punster ['pʌnstə(r)] *n.* каламбури́ст.

punt [pʌnt] *n.* (*boat*) плоскодо́нка.

punter ['pʌntə(r)] *n.* (*gambler*) игро́к (-а́).

puny ['pju:nɪ] *adj.* хи́лый (хил, -а́, -о), тщеду́шный.

pup [pʌp] *n.* щено́к (-нка́; *pl.* щенки́, -ко́в & щеня́та, -т); *v.i.* щени́ться *impf.*, о~ *pf.*

pupa ['pju:pə] *n.* ку́колка.

pupil ['pju:pɪl, -p(ə)l] *n.* учени́к (-а́), -и́ца; (*of eye*) зрачо́к (-чка́).

puppet ['pʌpɪt] *n.* марионе́тка, ку́кла (*g.pl.* -кол); ~ **regime** марионе́точный режи́м; ~ **theatre** ку́кольный теа́тр.

puppy ['pʌpɪ] *n.* щено́к (-нка́; *pl.* щенки́, -ко́в & щеня́та, -т).

purblind ['pɜ:blaɪnd] *adj.* близору́кий.

purchase ['pɜ:tʃɪs, -tʃəs] *n.* поку́пка; (*leverage*) то́чка опо́ры; *v.t.* покупа́ть *impf.*, купи́ть (-плю́, -пишь) *pf.* **purchaser** *n.* покупа́тель *m.*, ~ница.

pure [pjʊə(r)] *adj.* чи́стый (чист, -а́, -о, чи́сты́); (*of science*) теорети́ческий. **pure-blooded** *adj.* чистокро́вный. **pure-bred** *adj.* поро́дистый.

purée ['pjʊəreɪ] *n.* пюре́ *nt.indecl.*

purely ['pjʊəlɪ] *adv.* чи́сто; (*entirely*) соверше́нно.

purgative ['pɜ:gətɪv] *adj.* слаби́тельный; (*purifying*) очисти́тельный; *n.* слаби́тельное *sb.* **purgatory** *n.* чисти́лище. **purge** [pɜ:dʒ] *v.t.* (*cleanse*) очища́ть *impf.*, очи́стить *of.*; (*of medicine*; *abs.*) сла́бить *impf.*; (*atone for*) искупа́ть *impf.*, искупи́ть (-плю́, -пишь) *pf.*; (~ *party*, *army etc.*) проводи́ть (-ожу́, -о́дишь) *impf.*, провести́ (-еду́, -едёшь; -ёл, -ела́) *pf.* чи́стку в+*a.*; *n.* очище́ние; (*of party*, *army*, *etc.*) чи́стка.

purification [,pjʊərɪfɪ'keɪʃ(ə)n] *n.* очище́ние, очи́стка. **purify** ['pjʊərɪ,faɪ] *v.t.* очища́ть *impf.*, очи́стить *pf.*

purism ['pjʊərɪz(ə)m] *n.* пури́зм. **purist** *n.* пури́ст.

puritan, P., ['pjʊərɪt(ə)n] *n.* пурита́нин (*pl.* -а́не, -а́н), -а́нка. **puritanical** [,pjʊərɪ'tænɪk(ə)l] *adj.* пурита́нский.

purity ['pjʊərɪtɪ] *n.* чистота́.

purlieu ['pɜ:lju:] *n.*: *pl.* окре́стности *f.pl.*

purloin [pə'lɔɪn] *v.t.* похища́ть *impf.*, похи́тить (-и́щу, -и́тишь) *pf.*

purple ['pɜ:p(ə)l] *adj.* (*n.*) пу́рпу́рный, фиоле́товый (цвет).

purport ['pɜ:pɔ:t] *n.* смысл.

purpose ['pɜ:pəs] *n.* цель, намере́ние; **on** ~ наро́чно; **to no** ~ напра́сно. **purposeful** *adj.* целеустремлённый (-ён, -ённа). **purposeless** *adj.* бесце́льный. **purposely** *adv.* наро́чно.

purr [pɜ:(r)] *n.* мурлы́канье; *v.i.* мурлы́кать (-ы́чу, -ы́чешь) *impf.*

purse [pɜːs] *n.* кошелёк (-лька́); *v.t.* поджима́ть *impf.*, поджа́ть (подожму́, -мёшь) *pf.* **purser** *n.* казначе́й.

pursuance [pə'sjuːəns] *n.* выполне́ние. **pursuant** *adv.*: ~ **to** в соотве́тствии с+*i.*; согла́сно+*d.* **pursue** *v.t.* пресле́довать *impf.* **pursuit** *n.* пресле́дование; (*occupation*) заня́тие.

purulent ['pjuːrʊlənt] *adj.* гно́йный.

purvey [pə'veɪ] *v.t.* поставля́ть *impf.*, поста́вить *pf.* **purveyor** *n.* поставщи́к (-а́).

purview ['pɜːvjuː] *n.* кругозо́р.

pus [pʌs] *n.* гной (-о́я(ю), *loc.* -о́е & -ою́).

push [pʊʃ] *v.t.* толка́ть *impf.*, толкну́ть *pf.*; (*goods*) реклами́ровать *impf.* & *pf.*; *v.i.* толка́ться *impf.*; **be ~ed for** име́ть *impf.* ма́ло+*g.*; **he is ~ing fifty** ему́ ско́ро сту́кнет пятьдеся́т; ~ **one's way** проти́скиваться *impf.*, проти́снуться *pf.*; ~ **ahead, on** продвига́ться *impf.*, продви́нуться *pf.*; ~ **around** (*person*) помыка́ть *impf.* +*i.*; ~ **aside** (*also fig.*) отстраня́ть *impf.*, отстрани́ть *pf.*; ~ **away** отта́лкивать *impf.*, оттолкну́ть *pf.*; ~ **into** (*v.t.*) вта́лкивать *impf.*, втолкну́ть *pf.* в+*a.*; (*urge*) толка́ть *impf.*, толкну́ть *pf.* на+*a.*; ~ **off** (*v.i.*) (*in boat*) отта́лкиваться *impf.*, оттолкну́ться *pf.* (от бе́рега); (*go away*) убира́ться *impf.*, убра́ться (уберу́сь, -рёшься; убра́лся, -ала́сь, -а́лось) *pf.*; ~ **through** (*v.t.*) прота́лкивать *impf.*, протолкну́ть *pf.*; (*conclude*) доводи́ть (-ожу́, -о́дишь) *impf.*, довести́ (-еду́, -едёшь; -ёл, -ела́) *pf.* до конца́; *n.* толчо́к (-чка́); (*energy*) эне́ргия. **push-bike** *n.* велосипе́д. **pushchair** *n.* прогу́лочная коля́ска. **pushing** *adj.* (*of person*) напо́ристый.

puss [pʊs], **pussy(-cat)** *n.* ко́шечка, ки́ска.

pustular ['pʌstjuːlə(r)] *adj.* пустулёзный, прыща́вый. **pustule** *n.* пу́стула, прыщ (-а́).

put [pʊt] *v.t.* класть (кладу́, -дёшь; клал) *impf.*, положи́ть (-жу́, -жишь) *pf.*; (*upright*) ста́вить *impf.*, по~ *pf.*; помеща́ть *impf.*, помести́ть *pf.*; (*into specified state*) приводи́ть (-ожу́, -о́дишь) *impf.*, привести́ (-еду́, -едёшь; -ёл, -ела́) *pf.*; (*estimate*) определя́ть *impf.*, определи́ть *pf.* (**at** в+*a.*); (*express*) выража́ть *impf.*, вы́разить *pf.*; (*translate*) переводи́ть (-ожу́, -о́дишь) *impf.*, перевести́ (-еду́, -едёшь; -ёл, -ела́) *pf.* (**into** на+*a.*); (*a question*) задава́ть (-даю́, -даёшь) *impf.*, зада́ть (-а́м, -а́шь, -а́ст, -ади́м; за́дал, -а́, -о) *pf.*; ~ **an end, a stop, to** класть (кладу́, -дёшь; клал) *impf.*, положи́ть (-жу́, -жишь) *pf.* коне́ц+*d.*; ~ **o.s. in another's place** ста́вить *impf.*, по~ *pf.* себя́ на ме́сто+*g.*; ~ **the shot** толка́ть *impf.*, толкну́ть *pf.* ядро́; ~ **to death** казни́ть *impf.* & *pf.*; ~ **to flight** обраща́ть *impf.*, обрати́ть (-ащу́, -ати́шь) *pf.* в бе́гство; ~ **to shame** стыди́ть *impf.*, при~ *pf.*; ~ **about** (*of ship*) лечь (ля́жет, ля́гут; лёг, -ла́) *pf.* на друго́й галс; (*rumour etc.*) распространя́ть *impf.*, распространи́ть *pf.*; ~ **away** (*for future*) откла́дывать *impf.*, отложи́ть (-жу́, -жишь) *pf.*; (*in prison*) сажа́ть *impf.*, посади́ть (-ажу́, -а́дишь) *pf.*; ~ **back** (*in place*) ста́вить *impf.*, по~ *pf.* на ме́сто; ~ **the clock back** передвига́ть *impf.*, передви́нуть *pf.* стре́лки часо́в наза́д; ~ **by,** (*money*) откла́дывать *impf.*, отложи́ть (-жу́, -жишь) *pf.*; ~ **down** (*suppress*) подавля́ть *impf.*, подави́ть (-влю́, -вишь) *pf.*; (*write down*) запи́сывать *impf.*, записа́ть (-ишу́, -и́шешь) *pf.*; (*passengers*) выса́живать *impf.*, вы́садить *pf.*; (*attribute*) припи́сывать *impf.*, приписа́ть (-ишу́, -и́шешь) *pf.* (**to** +*d.*); ~ **forth** (*of plant*) пуска́ть *impf.*, пусти́ть (-ит) *pf.* (побе́ги); ~ **forward** (*proposal*) предлага́ть *impf.*, предложи́ть (-жу́, -жишь) *pf.*; ~ **the clock forward** передвига́ть *impf.*, передви́нуть *pf.* стре́лки часо́в вперёд; ~ **in** (*install*) устана́вливать *impf.*, установи́ть (-влю́, -вишь) *pf.*; (*a claim*) предъявля́ть *impf.*, предъяви́ть (-влю́, -вишь) *pf.*; (*interpose*) вставля́ть *impf.*, вста́вить *pf.*; (*spend time*) проводи́ть (-ожу́, -о́дишь) *impf.*, провести́ (-еду́, -едёшь; -ёл, -ела́) *pf.*; ~ **in an appearance** появля́ться *impf.*, появи́ться (-влю́сь, -вишься) *pf.*; ~ **off** (*postpone*) откла́дывать *impf.*, отложи́ть (-жу́, -жишь) *pf.*; (*evade*) отде́лываться *impf.*, отде́латься *pf.* от+*g.*; (*dissuade*) отгова́ривать *impf.*, отговори́ть *pf.* от+*g.*, +*inf.*; ~ **on** (*clothes*) надева́ть *impf.*, наде́ть (-е́ну, -е́нешь) *pf.*; (*appearance*) принима́ть *impf.*, приня́ть (приму́, -мешь; при́нял, -а́, -о) *pf.*; (*a play*) ста́вить *impf.*, по~ *pf.*; (*turn on*) включа́ть *impf.*, включи́ть *pf.*; (*add to*) прибавля́ть *impf.*, приба́вить *pf.*; ~ **on airs** ва́жничать *impf.*; ~ **on weight** толсте́ть *impf.*, по~ *pf.*; ~ **out** (*dislocate*) вы́вихнуть *pf.*; (*a fire etc.*) туши́ть (-шу́, -шишь) *impf.*, по~ *pf.*; (*annoy*) раздража́ть *impf.*, раздражи́ть *pf.*; ~ **out to sea** (*of ship*) выходи́ть (-ит) *impf.*, вы́йти (вы́йдет; вы́шел, -шла) *pf.* в мо́ре; ~ **through** (*carry out*) выполня́ть *impf.*, вы́полнить *pf.*; (*on telephone*) соединя́ть *impf.*, соедини́ть *pf.* по телефо́ну; ~ **up** (*building*) стро́ить *impf.*, по~ *pf.*; (*price*) повыша́ть *impf.*, повы́сить *pf.*; (*a guest*) дава́ть (даю́, даёшь) *impf.*, дать (дам, дашь, даст, дади́м; дал, -а́, да́ло́, -и) *pf.* прию́т+*g.*; (*as guest*) остана́вливаться *impf.*, останови́ться (-влю́сь, -вишься) *pf.*; ~ **up to** (*instigate*) подстрека́ть *impf.*, подстрекну́ть *pf.* к+*d.*; ~ **up with** терпе́ть (-плю́, -пишь) *impf.*

putative ['pjuːtətɪv] *adj.* предполага́емый.

putrefaction [ˌpjuːtrɪ'fækʃ(ə)n] *n.* гние́ние. **putrefy** ['pjuːtrɪˌfaɪ] *v.i.* гнить (-ию́, -иёшь; гнил, -а́, -о) *impf.*, с~ *pf.* **'putrid** *adj.* гнило́й (гнил, -а́, -о), гни́лостный.

putsch [pʊtʃ] *n.* путч.

puttee ['pʌtɪ] *n.* обмо́тка.

putty ['pʌtɪ] *n.* зама́зка, шпаклёвка; *v.t.* шпаклева́ть (-лю́ю, -лю́ешь) *impf.*, за~ *pf.*

puzzle ['pʌz(ə)l] *n.* (*perplexity*) недоуме́ние;

(*enigma*) зага́дка; (*toy etc.*) головоло́мка; *v.t.* озада́чивать *impf.*, озада́чить *pf.*; ~ **out** разгада́ть *pf.*; *v.i.*: ~ **over** лома́ть *impf.* себе́ го́лову над+*i.*

PVC *abbr.* (*of* **polyvinyl chloride**) ПХВ, поли-хлорвини́л.

pygmy ['pɪgmɪ] *n.* пигме́й; *adj.* ка́рликовый.

pyjamas [pɪ'dʒɑːməz, pə-] *n.* пижа́м.

pylon ['paɪlən, -lɒn] *n.* пило́н, опо́ра.

pyramid ['pɪrəmɪd] *n.* пирами́да. **pyramidal** [pɪ'ræmɪd(ə)l] *adj.* пирамида́льный.

pyre ['paɪə(r)] *n.* погреба́льный костёр (-тра́).

Pyrenees [,pɪrə'niːz] *n.* Пирене́и (-ев) *pl.*

pyromania [,paɪərəʊ'meɪnɪə] *n.* пирома́ния.

pyrotechnic(al) [,paɪərəʊ'teknɪk(ə)l] *adj.* пиротехни́ческий. **pyrotechnics** [,paɪərəʊ'teknɪks] *n.* пироте́хника.

Pyrrhic ['pɪrɪk] *adj.*: ~ **victory** пи́ррова побе́да.

python ['paɪθ(ə)n] *n.* пито́н.

Q

qua [kwɑː] *conj.* в ка́честве+*g.*

quack[1] [kwæk] *n.* (*sound*) кря́канье; *v.i.* кря́кать *impf.*, кря́кнуть *pf.*

quack[2] [kwæk] *n.* зна́харь *m.*, шарлата́н. **quackery** *n.* зна́харство, шарлата́нство.

quad [kwɒd] *n.* (*quadrangle*) четырёхуго́льный двор (-а́); (*quadrat*) шпа́ция; *pl.* (*quadruplets*) че́тверо (-рых) близнецо́в. **quadrangle** *n.* (*figure*) четырёхуго́льник; (*court*) четырёхуго́льный двор (-а́). **quad'rangular** *adj.* четырёхуго́льный. **quadrant** *n.* квадра́нт. **quadrat** ['kwɒdrət] *n.* шпа́ция. **quad'ratic** *adj.* квадра́тный; ~ **equation** квадра́тное уравне́ние. **quadri'lateral** *adj.* четырёхсторо́нний.

quadrille [kwɒ'drɪl] *n.* кадри́ль.

quadruped ['kwɒdrʊ,ped] *n.* четвероно́гое живо́тное *sb.* **quadruple** ['kwɒdrʊp(ə)l] *adj.* четверно́й, учетверённый (-ён, -ена́); *v.t.* & *i.* учетверя́ть(ся) *impf.*, учетвери́ть(ся) *pf.* **quadruplets** *n.* че́тверо (-ры́х) близнецо́в.

quaff [kwɒf, kwɑːf] *v.t.* пить (пью, пьёшь; пил, -а́, -о) *impf.*, вы́~ *pf.* больши́ми глотка́ми.

quag [kwɒg], **quagmire** *n.* тряси́на; (*also fig.*) боло́то.

quail[1] [kweɪl] *n.* (*bird*) пе́репел (*pl.* -а́), -ёлка.

quail[2] [kweɪl] *v.i.* (*flinch*) дро́гнуть *pf.*; тру́сить *impf.*, с~ *pf.* (**before** +*a.*, пе́ред+*i.*).

quaint [kweɪnt] *adj.* причу́дливый, оригина́льный.

quake [kweɪk] *v.i.* трясти́сь (трясу́сь, -сёшься; тря́сся, -сла́сь) *impf.*; дрожа́ть (-жу́, -жи́шь) *impf.* (**for, with** от+*g.*); *n.* землетрясе́ние.

Quaker ['kweɪkə(r)] *n.* ква́кер, ~ка.

qualification [,kwɒlɪfɪ'keɪʃ(ə)n] *n.* (*restriction*) ограниче́ние, огово́рка; (*for post etc.*) квалифика́ция; (*for citizenship etc.*) ценз; (*description*) характери́стика. **qualify** ['kwɒlɪ,faɪ] *v.t.* (*describe*) квалифици́ровать *impf.* & *pf.*; (*restrict*) ограни́чивать *impf.*, ограни́чить *pf.*; *v.t.* & *i.* (*prepare for*) гото́вить(ся) *impf.* (**for** к+*d.*; +*inf.*).

qualitative ['kwɒlɪtətɪv, -,teɪtɪv] *adj.* ка́чественный. **quality** *n.* ка́чество; сорт; (*excellence*) высо́кое ка́чество; (*ability*) спосо́бность.

qualm [kwɑːm, kwɔːm] *n.* (*queasiness*) при́ступ тошноты́; (*doubt, scruple*) колеба́ние, угрызе́ние со́вести.

quandary ['kwɒndərɪ] *n.* затрудни́тельное положе́ние, диле́мма.

quantify ['kwɒntɪ,faɪ] *v.t.* определя́ть *impf.*, определи́ть *pf.* коли́чество+*g.* **quantitative** *adj.* коли́чественный. **quantity** ['kwɒntɪtɪ] *n.* коли́чество; (*math.*) величина́ (*pl.* -ны).

quantum ['kwɒntəm] *n.* (*amount*) коли́чество; (*share*) до́ля (*pl.* -ли, -ле́й); (*phys.*) квант; *attr.* ква́нтовый.

quarantine ['kwɒrən,tiːn] *n.* каранти́н; *v.t.* подверга́ть *impf.*, подве́ргнуть (-г) *pf.* каранти́ну.

quark [kwɑːk] *n.* кварк.

quarrel ['kwɒr(ə)l] *n.* ссо́ра; *v.i.* ссо́риться *impf.*, по~ *pf.* (**with** с+*i.*; **about, for** из-за+*g.*). **quarrelsome** *adj.* вздо́рный.

quarry[1] ['kwɒrɪ] *n.* (*for stone etc.*) каменоло́мня (*g.pl.* -мен), карье́р; *v.t.* добыва́ть *impf.*, добы́ть (добу́ду, -дешь; до́был, -а́, -о) *pf.*

quarry[2] ['kwɒrɪ] *n.* (*object of pursuit*) пресле́дуемый зверь (*pl.* -ри, -ре́й) *m.*

quart ['kwɔːt] *n.* ква́рта. **quarter** *n.* че́тверть (*pl.* -ти, -те́й); (*of year*; *of town*) кварта́л; (*direction*) сторона́ (*a.* -ону; *pl.* -оны, -о́н, -она́м); (*mercy*) поща́да; *pl.* кварти́ры *f.pl.*; **a ~ to one** без че́тверти час; *v.t.* (*divide*) дели́ть (-лю́, -лишь) *impf.*, раз~ *pf.* на четы́ре (ра́вные) ча́сти; (*traitor's body*) четвертова́ть *impf.* & *pf.*; (*lodge*) расквартиро́вывать *impf.*, расквартирова́ть *pf.* **quarterdeck** *n.* шка́нцы (-цев) *pl.* **quarterfinal** *n.* четверть-фина́л(ьная игра́). **quarterly** *adj.* трёхме́сячный, кварта́льный; *n.* журна́л, выходя́щий раз в три ме́сяца; *adv.* раз в кварта́л, раз в три ме́сяца. **quartermaster** *n.* квартирме́йстер. **quar'tet(te)** *n.* кварте́т. **quarto** *n.* (ин-)ква́рто *nt.indecl.*

quartz [kwɔːts] *n.* кварц.

quasar ['kweɪzɑː(r), -sɑː(r)] *n.* кваза́р.

quash [kwɒʃ] *v.t.* (*annul*) аннули́ровать *impf.* & *pf.*; (*crush*) подавля́ть *impf.*, подави́ть (-влю́, -вишь) *pf.*

quasi *adv.* как бу́дто.
quasi- ['kweɪzaɪ, 'kwɑːzɪ] *in comb.* квази... .
quatercentenary [ˌkwætəsen'tiːnərɪ] *n.* четырёхсотле́тие.
quatrain ['kwɒtreɪn] *n.* четверости́шие.
quaver ['kweɪvə(r)] *v.i.* дрожа́ть (-жу́, -жи́шь) *impf.*; *n.* дрожа́ние; (*mus.*) восьма́я *sb.* но́ты.
quay [kiː] *n.* на́бережная *sb.*
queasy ['kwiːzɪ] *adj.* (*stomach*) сла́бый (слаб, -а́, -о); (*person*) испы́тывающий тошноту́.
queen [kwiːn] *n.* короле́ва; (*cards*) да́ма; (*chess*) ферзь (-зя́) *m.*; **~ bee** ма́тка; **~ mother** вдо́вствующая короле́ва; *v.t.* (*chess*) проводи́ть (-ожу́, -о́дишь) *impf.*, провести́ (-еду́, -едёшь; -ёл, -ела́) *pf.* в ферзи́. **queenly** *adj.* ца́рственный (-ен(ен), -енна).
queer [kwɪə(r)] *adj.* стра́нный (-нен, -нна́, -нно); **feel ~** чу́вствовать *impf.* недомога́ние.
quell [kwel] *v.t.* подавля́ть *impf.*, подави́ть (-влю́, -вишь) *pf.*
quench [kwentʃ] *v.t.* (*thirst*) утоля́ть *impf.*, утоли́ть *pf.*; (*fire, desire*) туши́ть (-шу́, -шишь) *impf.*, по~ *pf.*
querulous ['kwerʊləs] *adj.* ворчли́вый.
query ['kwɪərɪ] *n.* вопро́с, сомне́ние; *v.t.* (*express doubt*) выража́ть *impf.* вы́разить *pf.* сомне́ние в+*p.*
quest [kwest] *n.* по́иски *m.pl.*; **in ~ of** в по́исках+*g.* **question** *n.* вопро́с; (*doubt*) сомне́ние; **beyond all ~** вне сомне́ния; **it is (merely) a ~ of** э́то вопро́с+*g.*; де́ло то́лько в том, что́бы+*inf.*; **it is out of the ~** об э́том не мо́жет быть и ре́чи; **the person in ~** челове́к, о кото́ром идёт речь; **the ~ is this** де́ло в э́том; **~ mark** вопроси́тельный знак; *v.t.* (*ask*) спра́шивать *impf.*, спроси́ть (-ошу́, -о́сишь) *pf.*; (*doubt*) сомнева́ться *impf.* в+*p.* **questionable** *adj.* сомни́тельный. **questio'nnaire** *n.* анке́та, вопро́сник.
queue [kjuː] *n.* о́чередь (*pl.* -ди, -де́й); *v.i.* стоя́ть (-ою́, -ои́шь) *impf.* в о́череди.
quibble ['kwɪb(ə)l] *n.* софи́зм, увёртка; *v.i.* уклоня́ться *impf.*, уклони́ться (-ню́сь, -нишься) *pf.* от су́ти вопро́са, от прямо́го отве́та.
quick [kwɪk] *adj.* ско́рый (скор, -а́, -о), бы́стрый (быстр, -а́, -о, бы́стры́); (*nimble*) прово́рный; (*clever*) смышлёный; *n.*: **to the ~** за живо́е, до мя́са; **the ~ and the dead** живы́е и мёртвые *sb.*; *adv.* скоро, бы́стро; *as imper.* скоре́е! **quicken** *v.t.* & *i.* (*accelerate*) ускоря́ть(ся) *impf.*, уско́рить(ся) *pf.*; *v.t.* (*animate*) оживля́ть *impf.*, оживи́ть *pf.* **quicklime** *n.* негашёная и́звесть. **quickness** *n.* быстрота́; прово́рство. **quicksand** *n.* плыву́н (-а́), зыбу́чий песо́к (-ска́). **quickset** *n.* (*hedge*) жива́я и́згородь. **quicksilver** *n.* ртуть. **quick-tempered** *adj.* вспы́льчивый. **quick-witted** *adj.* остроу́мный.
quid [kwɪd] *n.* фунт.
quiescence [kwɪ'es(ə)ns] *n.* неподви́жность, поко́й. **quiescent** *adj.* неподви́жный, в состоя́нии поко́я. **quiet** ['kwaɪət] *n.* (*silence*) тишина́; (*calm*) споко́йствие; *adj.* ти́хий (тих, -а́, -о); споко́йный; *int.* ти́ше!; *v.t.* & *i.* успока́ивать(ся) *impf.*, успоко́ить(ся) *pf.*
quill [kwɪl] *n.* (*feather*) перо́ (*pl.* -рья, -рьев); (*spine*) игла́ (*pl.* -лы).
quilt [kwɪlt] *n.* (стёганое) одея́ло; *v.t.* стега́ть *impf.*, вы́~ *pf.* **quilting** *n.* стёжка.
quince [kwɪns] *n.* айва́.
quincentenary [ˌkwɪnsen'tiːnərɪ] *n.* пятисотле́тие.
quinine ['kwɪniːn, -'niːn] *n.* хини́н.
quinquennial [kwɪn'kwenɪəl] *adj.* пятиле́тний.
quintessence [kwɪn'tes(ə)ns] *n.* квинтэссе́нция.
quintet(te) [kwɪn'tet] *n.* квинте́т. **quintuple** ['kwɪntjʊp(ə)l] *adj.* пятикра́тный. **quins, quin'tuplets** *n.* пять (-ти́, -тью́) близнецо́в.
quip [kwɪp] *n.* острота́.
quire ['kwaɪə(r)] *n.* (*in manuscript*) тетра́дь; (*24 sheets*) ру́сская десть (*pl.* -ти, -те́й).
quirk [kwɜːk] *n.* причу́да.
quisling ['kwɪzlɪŋ] *n.* кви́слинг.
quit [kwɪt] *v.t.* покида́ть *impf.*, поки́нуть *pf.*; (*dwelling*) выезжа́ть *impf.*, вы́ехать (-еду, -едешь) *pf.* из+*g.*
quite [kwaɪt] *adv.* (*wholly*) совсе́м, вполне́; (*somewhat*) дово́льно; **~ a few** дово́льно мно́го.
quits [kwɪts] *pred.*: **we are ~** мы с тобо́й квиты; **I am ~ with him** я расквита́лся (*past*) с ним.
quiver[1] ['kwɪvə(r)] *n.* (*for arrows*) колча́н.
quiver[2] ['kwɪvə(r)] *v.i.* (*tremble*) трепета́ть (-ещу́, -е́щешь) *impf.*; дрожа́ть (-жу́, -жи́шь) *impf.* (ме́лкой дро́жью); *n.* тре́пет, ме́лкая дрожь.
quixotic [kwɪk'sɒtɪk] *adj.* донкихо́тский.
quiz [kwɪz] *n.* виктори́на. **quizzical** *adj.* насме́шливый.
quoit [kɔɪt] *n.* мета́тельное кольцо́ (*pl.* -льца, -ле́ц, -льцам); *pl.* (*game*) мета́ние коле́ц в цель.
quorum ['kwɔːrəm] *n.* кво́рум.
quota ['kwəʊtə] *n.* кво́та.
quotation [kwəʊ'teɪʃ(ə)n] *n.* (*quoting*) цити́рование; (*passage quoted*) цита́та; (*estimate*) сме́та; (*of stocks etc.*) котиро́вка; **~ marks** кавы́чки (-чек) *pl.* **quote** *v.t.* цити́ровать *impf.*, про~ *pf.*; ссыла́ться *impf.*, сосла́ться (сошлю́сь, -лёшься) *pf.* на+*a.*; (*price*) назнача́ть *impf.*, назна́чить *pf.*
quotidian [kwɒ'tɪdɪən] *adj.* (*daily*) ежедне́вный; (*commonplace*) обы́денный.
quotient ['kwəʊʃ(ə)nt] *n.* ча́стное *sb.*

R

rabbet ['ræbɪt] *n.* шпунт (-á).

rabbi ['ræbaɪ] *n.* равви́н. **rabbinical** [rə'bɪnɪk(ə)l] *adj.* равви́нский.

rabbit ['ræbɪt] *n.* кро́лик; ~ **punch** уда́р в заты́лок.

rabble ['ræb(ə)l] *n.* сброд, чернь.

rabid ['ræbɪd, 'reɪ-] *adj.* бе́шеный. **rabies** ['reɪbi:z] *n.* водобоя́знь, бе́шенство.

RAC *abbr.* (*of* ***Royal Automobile Club***) Короле́вский автомоби́льный клуб.

raccoon *see* **racoon**

race[1] [reɪs] *n.* (*ethnic* ~) ра́са; род.

race[2] [reɪs] *n.* (*contest*) (*on foot*) бег; (*of cars etc.*; *fig.*) го́нка, го́нки *f.pl.*; (*of horses*) ска́чки *f.pl.*; ~ **meeting** ска́чки *f.pl.*; **racing driver** автого́нщик; *v.i.* (*compete*) состяза́ться *impf.* в ско́рости; (*rush*) мча́ться (мчусь, мчи́шься) *impf.*; *v.t.* гнать (гоню́, -нишь; гнал, -á, -o) *impf.* **racecard** *n.* програ́мма ска́чек. **racecourse** *n.* ипподро́м. **racehorse** *n.* скакова́я ло́шадь (*pl.* -ди, -де́й, *i.* -дьми́). **racer** *n.* (*person*) го́нщик; (*car*) го́ночный автомоби́ль *m.* **racetrack** *n.* трек; автомотодро́м; (*for horse* ~) скакова́я доро́жка.

racial ['reɪʃ(ə)l] *adj.* ра́совый. **rac(ial)ism** *n.* раси́зм. **rac(ial)ist** *n.* раси́ст, ~ка; *adj.* раси́стский.

rack[1] [ræk] *n.* (*for fodder*) корму́шка; (*for hats etc.*) ве́шалка; (*for plates etc.*) стелла́ж (-á); (*in train etc.*) се́тка для веще́й; (*for torture*) ды́ба; (*cogged bar*) зубча́тая ре́йка; *v.t.* му́чить *impf.*; пыта́ть *impf.*; ~ **one's brains** лома́ть *impf.* себе́ го́лову.

rack[2] [ræk] *n.*: **go to ~ and ruin** разоря́ться *impf.*, разори́ться *pf.*

racket[1] ['rækɪt] *n.* (*bat*) раке́тка.

racket[2] ['rækɪt] *n.* (*uproar*) шум (-а(у)); (*illegal activity*) рэ́кет. **racke'teer** *n.* рэкети́р.

rac(c)oon [rə'ku:n] *n.* ено́т.

racy ['reɪsɪ] *adj.* колори́тный.

radar ['reɪdɑ:(r)] *n.* (*system*) радиолока́ция; (*apparatus*) радиолока́тор, рада́р; *attr.* радиолокацио́нный, рада́рный.

radial ['reɪdɪəl] *adj.* радиа́льный, лучево́й.

radiance ['reɪdɪəns] *n.* сия́ние. **radiant** *adj.* сия́ющий; лучи́стый; *n.* исто́чник (лучи́стого) тепла́, све́та. **radiate** *v.t.* излуча́ть *impf.*; лучи́ться *impf.+i.*; *v.i.* исходи́ть (-ит) *impf.* из одно́й то́чки; (*diverge*) расходи́ться (-ятся) *impf.* луча́ми. **radi'ation** *n.* излуче́ние, радиа́ция; ~ **sickness** лучева́я боле́знь. **radiator** *n.* радиа́тор; (*in central heating*) батаре́я.

radical ['rædɪk(ə)l] *adj.* коренно́й; (*pol.*) радика́льный; (*ling.*) корнево́й; *n.* (*pol., chem.*) радика́л; (*math., ling.*) ко́рень (-рня; *pl.* -рни, -рне́й) *m.* **radically** *adv.* коренны́м о́бразом, соверше́нно.

radicle ['rædɪk(ə)l] *n.* корешо́к (-шка́).

radio ['reɪdɪəʊ] *n.* ра́дио *nt.indecl.*; *adj.* радио...; *v.t.* ради́ровать *impf.* & *pf.*

radio- ['reɪdɪəʊ] *in comb.* радио...; ~ **telescope** радиотелеско́п; ~ **wave** радиоволна́ (*pl.* -о́лны, *d.* -о́лна́м). **radioactive** *adj.* радиоакти́вный. **radioactivity** *n.* радиоакти́вность. **radiocarbon** *n.* радиоакти́вный изото́п углеро́да; ~ **dating** дати́рование радиоуглеро́дным ме́тодом. **radiogram** *n.* (*X-ray picture*) рентгеногра́мма; (*~-telegram*) радиогра́мма; (*radio and gramophone*) радио́ла. **radiographer** [ˌreɪdɪ'ɒgrəfə(r)] *n.* рентгено́лог. **radi'ography** *n.* радиогра́фия; (*spec. X-ray*) рентгеногра́фия. **radioisotope** *n.* радиоизото́п. **radiolocation** *n.* радиолока́ция. **radiologist** [ˌreɪdɪ'ɒlədʒɪst] *n.* радио́лог; (*spec. X-ray*) рентгено́лог. **radi'ology** *n.* радиоло́гия; рентгеноло́гия. **radi'ometer** *n.* радиоме́тр. **radi'oscopy** *n.* рентгеноскопи́я. **radiosonde** *n.* радиозо́нд. **radiotherapy** *n.* радиотерапи́я; (*specifically X-ray*) рентгенотерапи́я.

radish ['rædɪʃ] *n.* реди́ска; реди́с (*no pl.*: *plant*; *collect.*).

radium ['reɪdɪəm] *n.* ра́дий.

radius ['reɪdɪəs] *n.* (*math.*) ра́диус; (*bone*) лучева́я кость.

RAF *abbr.* (*of* ***Royal Air Force***) BBC (*вое́нно-возду́шные си́лы*) Великобрита́нии.

raffia ['ræfɪə] *n.* ра́фия.

raffish ['ræfɪʃ] *adj.* беспу́тный.

raffle ['ræf(ə)l] *n.* лотере́я; *v.t.* разы́грывать *impf.*, разыгра́ть *pf.* в лотере́е.

raft [rɑ:ft] *n.* плот (-á, *loc.* -ý).

rafter ['rɑ:ftə(r)] *n.* (*beam*) стропи́ло.

raftsman ['rɑ:ftsmən] *n.* плотовщи́к (-á).

rag[1] [ræg] *v.t.* (*tease*) дразни́ть (-ню́, -нишь) *impf.*

rag[2] [ræg] *n.* тря́пка, лоску́т (-á; *pl.* -á, -о́в & -ья, -ьев); *pl.* (*clothes*) лохмо́тья (-ьев) *pl.*; ~ **doll** тряпи́чная ку́кла (*g.pl.* -кол). **ragamuffin** *n.* оборва́нец (-нца). **rag-and-bone man** *n.* старьёвщик.

rage [reɪdʒ] *n.* (*anger*) я́рость, гнев; (*desire*) страсть (for, к+*d.*); **all the ~** после́дний крик мо́ды; *v.i.* беси́ться (бешу́сь, бе́сишься) *impf.*; (*storm etc.*) свире́пствовать *impf.*

ragged ['rægɪd] *adj.* (*jagged*) зазу́бренный (-ен); (*of clothes*) изо́дранный (-ан, -анна); (*of person*) в лохмо́тьях.

raglan ['ræglən] *n.* регла́н; ~ **sleeve** рука́в (-á; *pl.* -á) регла́н (*indecl.*).

ragout [ræ'gu:] *n.* рагу́ *nt.indecl.*
ragtime ['rægtaɪm] *n.* ре́гтайм.
ragwort ['rægwɜ:t] *n.* кресто́вник.
raid [reɪd] *n.* набе́г, налёт; (*by police*) обла́ва; *v.t.* де́лать *impf.*, с~ *pf.* налёт на+*a.*
rail [reɪl] *n.* пери́ла (-л) *pl.*; (*rail.*) рельс; (*railway*) желе́зная доро́га; **by ~** по́ездом, по желе́зной доро́ге; *v.t.*: **~ in, off** обноси́ть (-ошу́, -о́сишь) *impf.*, обнести́ (-есу́, -есёшь; -ёс, -есла́) *pf.* пери́лами. **railhead** *n.* коне́чный пункт (желе́зной доро́ги). **railing** *n.* пери́ла (-л) *pl.*, огра́да.
raillery ['reɪlərɪ] *n.* доброду́шное подшу́чивание.
railway ['reɪlweɪ] *n.* желе́зная доро́га; *attr.* железнодоро́жный. **railwayman** *n.* железнодоро́жник.
raiment ['reɪmənt] *n.* одея́ние.
rain [reɪn] *n.* дождь (-дя́) *m.*; **~ forest** тропи́ческий лес; *pl.* (*the* ~) пери́од (тропи́ческих) дожде́й; *v. impers.* **it is (was) ~ing** идёт (шёл) дождь; *v.t.* осыпа́ть *impf.*, осы́пать (-плю, -плешь) *pf.*+*i.* (**upon** +*a.*); *v.i.* осыпа́ться *impf.*, осы́паться (-плется) *pf.* **rainbow** *n.* ра́дуга; **~ trout** ра́дужная форе́ль. **raincoat** *n.* непромока́емое пальто́ *nt.indecl.*, плащ (-а́). **raindrop** *n.* дождева́я ка́пля (*g.pl.* -пель). **rainfall** *n.* (*shower*) ли́вень (-вня) *m.*; (*amount of rain*) коли́чество оса́дков. **rainproof** *adj.* непромока́емый. **rainwater** *n.* дождева́я вода́ (*a.* -ду). **rainy** *adj.* дождли́вый; **~ day** чёрный день (дня) *m.*
raise [reɪz] *v.t.* (*lift*) поднима́ть *impf.*, подня́ть (подниму́, -мешь; по́днял, -а́, -о) *pf.*; (*heighten*) повыша́ть *impf.*, повы́сить *pf.*; (*erect*) воздвига́ть *impf.*, воздви́гнуть (-г) *pf.*; (*provoke*) вызыва́ть *impf.*, вы́звать (вы́зову, -вешь) *pf.*; (*procure*) добыва́ть *impf.*, добы́ть (добу́ду, -дешь; до́был, -а́, -о) *pf.*; (*children*) расти́ть *impf.*
raisin ['reɪz(ə)n] *n.* изю́минка; *pl.* (*collect.*) изю́м (-а(у)).
raja(h) ['rɑ:dʒə] *n.* ра́джа (*g.pl.* -жей) *m.*
rake[1] [reɪk] *n.* (*tool*) гра́бли (-блей & -бель) *pl.*; *v.t.* (~ *together, up*) сгреба́ть *impf.*, сгрести́ (сгребу́, -бёшь; сгрёб, -бла́) *pf.*; (*with shot*) обстре́ливать *impf.*, обстреля́ть *pf.* продо́льным огнём.
rake[2] [reɪk] *n.* (*person*) пове́са *m.* **rakish** *adj.* распу́тный.
rally[1] ['rælɪ] *v.t.* & *i.* спла́чивать(ся) *impf.*, сплоти́ть(ся) *pf.*; *v.i.* (*after illness etc.*) оправля́ться *impf.*, опра́виться *pf.*; *n.* (*meeting*) слёт; ма́ссовый ми́тинг; (*motoring* ~) (авто)ра́лли *nt.indecl.*; (*tennis*) обме́н уда́рами.
rally[2] ['rælɪ] *v.t.* (*ridicule*) подшу́чивать *impf.*, подшути́ть (-учу́, -у́тишь) *pf.* над+*i.*
RAM [ræm] (*comput.*) (*abbr. of* ***random-access memory***) ЗУПВ, (запомина́ющее устро́йство с произво́льной вы́боркой).
Ramadan ['ræmə,dæn] *n.* рамаза́н.
ram [ræm] *n.* (*sheep*) бара́н; (*the Ram, Aries*) Ове́н (Овна́); (*machine*) тара́н; *v.t.* (*beat down*) трамбова́ть *impf.*, у~ *pf.*; (*drive in*) вбива́ть *impf.*, вбить (вобью́, -ьёшь) *pf.*; (*strike with* ~) тара́нить *impf.*, про~ *pf.*
ramble ['ræmb(ə)l] *v.i.* (*walk*) броди́ть (-ожу́, -о́дишь) *impf.*; (*speak*) говори́ть *impf.* несвя́зно; *n.* прогу́лка. **rambler** *n.* (*hiker*) люби́тель *m.* пешехо́дного тури́зма; (*plant*) вью́щаяся ро́за. **rambling** *n.* пешехо́дный тури́зм; *adj.* (*scattered*) разбро́санный; (*incoherent*) бессвя́зный.
ramification [,ræmɪfɪ'keɪʃ(ə)n] *n.* разветвле́ние. **ramify** ['ræmɪ,faɪ] *v.i.* разветвля́ться *impf.*, разветви́ться *pf.*
ramp [ræmp] *n.* скат, укло́н.
rampage ['ræmpeɪdʒ] *v.i.* неистовствовать *impf.*; *n.* неистовство.
rampant ['ræmpənt] *adj.* (*of lion etc.*) стоя́щий на за́дних ла́пах; (*raging*) свире́пствующий.
rampart ['ræmpɑ:t] *n.* вал (*loc.* -у́; *pl.* -ы́).
ramrod ['ræmrɒd] *n.* шо́мпол (*pl.* -а́).
ramshackle ['ræm,ʃæk(ə)l] *adj.* ве́тхий (ветх, -а́, -о).
ranch [rɑ:ntʃ] *n.* ра́нчо *nt.indecl.*
rancid ['rænsɪd] *adj.* прого́рклый.
rancour ['ræŋkə(r)] *n.* зло́ба. **rancorous** *adj.* зло́бный.
random ['rændəm] *n.*: **at ~** науда́чу, науга́д, наобу́м; *adj.* сде́ланный (-ан), вы́бранный (-ан), науга́д; случа́йный.
range [reɪndʒ] *n.* (*of mountains*) цепь (*pl.* -пи, -пе́й); (*grazing ground*) неогоро́женное па́стбище; (*artillery* ~) полиго́н; (*of voice*) диапазо́н; (*scope*) круг (*loc.* -у́; *pl.* -и́), преде́лы *m.pl.*; (*distance*) да́льность; *v.t.* (*arrange in row*) выстра́ивать *impf.*, вы́строить *pf.* в ряд; *v.i.* (*extend*) тяну́ться (-нется) *impf.*; (*occur*) встреча́ться *impf.*, встре́титься *pf.*; (*vary*) колеба́ться (-блется) *impf.*, по~ *pf.*; (*wander*) броди́ть (-ожу́, -о́дишь) *impf.* **rangefinder** *n.* дальноме́р.
rank[1] [ræŋk] *n.* (*row*) ряд (-а́ *with 2,3,4*; *loc.* -у́; *pl.* -ы́); (*taxi* ~) стоя́нка такси́; (*grade*) зва́ние, чин, ранг; *v.t.* (*classify*) классифици́ровать *impf.* & *pf.*; (*consider*) счита́ть *impf.* (**as** +*i.*); *v.i.*: **~ with** быть (*fut.* бу́ду, -дешь; был, -а́, -о; не́ был, -а́, -о) в числе́+*g.*, на у́ровне+*g.*
rank[2] [ræŋk] *adj.* (*luxuriant*) бу́йный (бу́ен, буйна́, -но); (*in smell*) зловóнный (-нен, -нна); (*repulsive*) отврати́тельный; (*clear*) я́вный.
rankle ['ræŋk(ə)l] *v.i.* причиня́ть *impf.*, причини́ть *pf.* боль.
ransack ['rænsæk] *v.t.* (*search*) обша́ривать *impf.*, обша́рить *pf.*; (*plunder*) гра́бить *impf.*, о~ *pf.*
ransom ['rænsəm] *n.* вы́куп; *v.t.* выкупа́ть *impf.*, вы́купить *pf.*
rant [rænt] *v.t.* & *i.* напы́щенно деклами́ровать *impf.*
rap[1] [ræp] *n.* (*blow*) стук, ре́зкий уда́р; *v.t.*

(ре́зко) ударя́ть *impf.*, уда́рить *pf.*; *v.i.* стуча́ть (-чу́, -чи́шь) *impf.*, сту́кнуть *pf.*; ~ **out** (*words*) отчека́нивать *impf.*, отчека́нить *pf.*

rap² [ræp] *n.*: **not a** ~ нисколько; **I don't care a** ~ мне наплева́ть.

rapacious [rə'peɪʃəs] *adj.* неуме́ренно жа́дный (-ден, -дна́, -дно), хи́щнический.

rape¹ [reɪp] *v.t.* наси́ловать *impf.*, из~ *pf.*; *n.* изнаси́лование; (*abduction*) похище́ние.

rape² [reɪp] *n.* (*plant*) рапс. **rape-oil** *n.* ра́псовое ма́сло.

rapid ['ræpɪd] *adj.* бы́стрый (быстр, -а́, -о, бы́стры́); *n.*: *pl.* поро́г, быстрина́ (*pl.* -ны). **rapidity** [rə'pɪdɪtɪ] *n.* быстрота́.

rapier ['reɪpɪə(r)] *n.* рапи́ра.

rapt [ræpt] *adj.* восхищённый (-ён, -ённа); (*absorbed*) поглощённый (-ен, -ена́). **rapture** *n.* восто́рг. **rapturous** *adj.* восто́рженный (-ен, -енна).

rare¹ [reə(r)] *adj.* (*of meat*) недожа́ренный (-ен).

rare² [reə(r)] *adj.* ре́дкий (-док, -дка́, -дко), ре́дкостный. **rarefy** ['reərɪˌfaɪ] *v.t.* разрежа́ть *impf.*, разреди́ть *pf.* **rarity** *n.* ре́дкость.

rascal ['rɑːsk(ə)l] *n.* плут (-а́).

rase *see* **raze**

rash¹ [ræʃ] *n.* сыпь.

rash² [ræʃ] *adj.* опроме́тчивый.

rasher ['ræʃə(r)] *n.* ло́мтик (беко́на, ветчины́).

rasp [rɑːsp] *n.* (*file*) ра́шпиль *m.*; (*sound*) ре́жущий звук.

raspberry ['rɑːzbərɪ] *n.* (*plant*) мали́на (*also collect., fruit*); *attr.* мали́новый.

rasping ['rɑːspɪŋ] *adj.* (*sound*) ре́жущий, скрипу́чий.

Rastafarian [ˌræstə'feərɪən] *n.* растафа́ри; *adj. indecl.* растафа́ри.

rat [ræt] *n.* кры́са; (*turncoat*) перебе́жчик; ~ **race** бе́шеная пого́ня за успе́хом; *v.i.*: ~ **on** предава́ть (-даю́, -даёшь) *impf.*, преда́ть (-а́м, -а́шь, -а́ст, -ади́м; пре́дал, -а́, -о) *pf.+a.* **rat-catcher** *n.* крысоло́в.

ratchet ['rætʃɪt] *n.* храпови́к (-а́); *attr.* храпово́й.

rate [reɪt] *n.* но́рма, ста́вка; (*speed*) ско́рость; *pl.* ме́стные нало́ги *m.pl.*; **at any** ~ во вся́ком слу́чае, по ме́ньшей ме́ре; **at the** ~ **of** по+*d.*, со ско́ростью+*g.*; *v.t.* оце́нивать *impf.*, оцени́ть (-ню́, -нишь) *pf.*; (*consider*) счита́ть *impf.* **rateable** *adj.* подлежа́щий обложе́нию ме́стным нало́гом; ~ **value** облага́емая сто́имость. **ratepayer** *n.* налогоплате́льщик, -ица.

rather ['rɑːðə(r)] *adv.* лу́чше, скоре́е; (*somewhat*) не́сколько, дово́льно; (*as answer*) ещё бы!; **he (she) had (would)** ~ он (она́) предпочёл (-чла́) бы+*inf.*; **or** ~ (или) верне́е (сказа́ть), точне́е (сказа́ть); ~ ... **than** скоре́е... чем.

ratification [ˌrætɪfɪ'keɪʃ(ə)n] *n.* ратифика́ция. **ratify** ['rætɪˌfaɪ] *v.t.* ратифици́ровать *impf.* & *pf.*

rating ['reɪtɪŋ] *n.* оце́нка; (*naut.*) рядово́й *sb.*

ratio ['reɪʃɪəʊ] *n.* пропо́рция.

ration ['ræʃ(ə)n] *n.* паёк (пайка́), рацио́н; *v.t.* норми́ровать *impf.* & *pf.*; **be** ~**ed** выдава́ться (-даётся) *impf.*, вы́даться (-астся, -адутся) *pf.* по ка́рточкам.

rational ['ræʃən(ə)l] *adj.* разу́мный; (*also math.*) рациона́льный. **rationalism** *n.* рационали́зм. **rationalist** *n.* рационали́ст. **rationalize** *v.t.* дава́ть (даю́, даёшь) *impf.*, дать (дам, дашь, даст, дади́м; дал, -а́, да́ло́, -и) *pf.* рационалисти́ческое объясне́ние+*g.*; (*industry etc.*) рационализи́ровать *impf.* & *pf.*

rattan [rə'tæn] *n.* рота́нг.

rattle ['ræt(ə)l] *v.i.* & *t.* (*sound*) греме́ть (-млю́, -ми́шь) *impf.* (+*i.*); бря́цать *impf.* (+*i.*); *v.i.* (*speak*) болта́ть *impf.*; *v.t.* (*fluster*) смуща́ть *impf.*, смути́ть (-ущу́, -ути́шь) *pf.*; ~ **along** (*move*) мча́ться (мчусь, мчи́шься) *impf.* с гро́хотом; ~ **off** (*utter*) отбараба́нить *pf.*; *n.* (*sound*) треск, гро́хот; (*instrument*) трещо́тка; (*toy*) погрему́шка. **rattlesnake** *n.* грему́чая змея́ (*pl.* -еи, -ей). **rattling** *adj.* (*brisk*) бы́стрый; ~ **good** великоле́пный.

rat-trap ['rættræp] *n.* крысоло́вка.

raucous ['rɔːkəs] *adj.* ре́зкий (-зок, -зка́, -зко).

ravage ['rævɪdʒ] *v.t.* опустоша́ть *impf.*, опустоши́ть *pf.*; *n.*: *pl.* разруши́тельное де́йствие.

rave [reɪv] *v.i.* бре́дить *impf.*; (*wind, sea*) реве́ть (-вёт) *impf.*; ~ **about** бре́дить *impf.+i.*; восторга́ться *impf.+i.*

raven ['reɪv(ə)n] *n.* во́рон.

ravenous ['rævənəs] *adj.* прожо́рливый; (*famished*) голо́дный (го́лоден, -дна́, -дно, го́лодны́) как волк; ~ **appetite** во́лчий аппети́т.

ravine [rə'viːn] *n.* уще́лье (*g.pl.* -лий).

ravioli [ˌrævɪ'əʊlɪ] *n.* равио́ли *nt.* & *pl. indecl.*

ravish ['rævɪʃ] *v.t.* (*rape*) наси́ловать *impf.*, из~ *pf.*; (*charm*) восхища́ть *impf.*, восхити́ть (-ищу́, -ити́шь) *pf.* **ravishing** *adj.* восхити́тельный.

raw [rɔː] *adj.* сыро́й (сыр, -а́, -о); (*brick*) необожжённый; (*alcohol*) неразба́вленный; (*style*) неотде́ланный; (*inexperienced*) нео́пытный; (*stripped of skin*) обо́дранный; (*sensitive*) чувстви́тельный; (*edge of cloth*) неподру́бленный; ~ **material(s)** сырьё (*no pl.*); ~ **place** (*abrasion*) цара́пина; ~ **silk** шёлк-сыре́ц (-рца́); ~ **wound** жива́я ра́на; *n.* больно́е ме́сто; **touch on the** ~ задева́ть *impf.*, заде́ть (-е́ну, -е́нешь) *pf.* за живо́е. **rawhide** *n.* недублёная ко́жа.

ray¹ [reɪ] *n.* (*beam*) луч (-а́); (*fig.*) про́блеск.

ray² [reɪ] *n.* (*fish*) скат.

rayon ['reɪɒn] *n.* виско́за.

raze [reɪz] *v.t.*: ~ **to the ground** ровня́ть *impf.*, с~ *pf.* с землёй.

razor ['reɪzə(r)] *n.* бри́тва. **razor-blade** *n.* ле́звие бри́твы.

RC *abbr.* (*of* ***Roman Catholic***) като́лик.

Rd. *abbr.* (*of* **road**) ул., у́лица.

RE *abbr.* (*of* ***Religious Education***) религио́зное обуче́ние.

reach [ri:tʃ] *v.t.* (*extend*) протя́гивать *impf.*, протяну́ть (-ну́, -нешь) *pf.*; (*attain*, *arrive at*) достига́ть *impf.*, дости́чь & дости́гнуть (-и́гну, -и́гнешь; -и́г) *pf.*+*g.*, до+*g.*; доходи́ть (-ожу́, -о́дишь) *impf.*, дойти́ (дойду́, -дёшь; дошёл, -шла́) *pf.* до+*g.*; *v.i.* (*extend*) простира́ться *impf.*; *n.* досяга́емость; (*of river*) плёс.

react [rɪ'ækt] *v.i.* реаги́ровать *impf.*, от~, про~ *pf.* (**to** на+*a.*). **reaction** *n.* реа́кция. **reactionary** *adj.* реакцио́нный; *n.* реакционе́р, ~ка. **reactive** *adj.* реаги́рующий; (*tech.*) реакти́вный. **reactor** *n.* реа́ктор.

read [ri:d] *v.t.* чита́ть *impf.*, про~, проче́сть (-чту́, -чтёшь; -чёл, -чла́) *pf.*; (*piece of music*) разбира́ть *impf.*, разобра́ть (разберу́, -рёшь; разобра́л, -а́, -о) *pf.*; (*of meter etc.*) пока́зывать *impf.*, показа́ть (-а́жет) *pf.*; (~ *a meter etc.*) снима́ть *impf.*, снять (сниму́, -мешь; снял, -а́, -о) *pf.* показа́ния+*g.*; (*univ.*) изуча́ть *impf.*; (*interpret*) толкова́ть *impf.*; *v.i.* чита́ться *impf.* **readable** *adj.* интере́сный, хорошо́ напи́санный (-ан); (*legible*) разбо́рчивый. **reader** *n.* чита́тель *m.*, ~ница; (*publisher's* ~) реценз́ент; (*printer's* ~) корре́ктор (*pl.* -ы & -а́); (*univ.*) ста́рший преподава́тель *m.*; (*book*) хрестома́тия.

readily ['redɪlɪ] *adv.* (*willingly*) охо́тно; (*easily*) легко́. **readiness** *n.* гото́вность.

reading ['ri:dɪŋ] *n.* чте́ние; (*erudition*) начи́танность; (*variant*) вариа́нт; (*interpretation*) толкова́ние. **reading-lamp** *n.* насто́льная ла́мпа. **reading-matter** *n.* литерату́ра. **reading-room** *n.* чита́льня (*g.pl.* -лен), чита́льный зал.

ready ['redɪ] *adj.* гото́вый (**for** к+*d.*, на+*a.*); ~ **money** нали́чные де́ньги (-нег, -ньга́м) *pl.*; ~ **reckoner** арифмети́ческие табли́цы *f.pl.* **ready-made** *adj.* гото́вый.

reagent [ri:'eɪdʒ(ə)nt] *n.* реакти́в.

real [ri:l] *adj.* настоя́щий, действи́тельный, реа́льный; ~ **estate** недви́жимость. **realism** ['ri:ə,lɪz(ə)m] *n.* реали́зм. **realist** *n.* реали́ст. **rea'listic** *adj.* реалисти́чный, -и́ческий. **reality** *n.* действи́тельность; **in** ~ действи́тельно. **realization** [,rɪəlaɪ'zeɪʃ(ə)n] *n.* (*of plan etc.*) осуществле́ние; (*of assets*) реализа́ция; (*understanding*) осозна́ние. **'realize** *v.t.* (*plan etc.*) осуществля́ть *impf.*, осуществи́ть *pf.*; (*assets*) реализова́ть *impf.* & *pf.*; (*apprehend*) осознава́ть (-на́ю, -наёшь) *impf.*, осозна́ть *pf.* **really** ['rɪəlɪ] *adv.* действи́тельно, в са́мом де́ле.

realm [relm] *n.* (*kingdom*) короле́вство; (*sphere*) о́бласть (*pl.* -ти, -те́й).

ream[1] [ri:m] *n.* стопа́ (*pl.* -пы).

ream[2] [ri:m] *v.t.* развёртывать *impf.*, разверну́ть *pf.*

reap [ri:p] *v.t.* жать (жну, жнёшь) *impf.*, сжать (сожну́, -нёшь) *pf.*; (*fig.*) пожина́ть *impf.*, пожа́ть (-жну́, -жнёшь) *pf.* **reaper** *n.* (*person*) жнец (-а́), жни́ца; (*machine*) жа́тка. **reaping-hook** *n.* серп (-а́).

rear[1] [rɪə(r)] *v.t.* (*lift*) поднима́ть *impf.*, подня́ть (-ниму́, -ни́мешь; по́днял, -а́, -о) *pf.*; (*children*) воспи́тывать *impf.*, воспита́ть *pf.*; *v.i.* (*of horse*) станови́ться (-ится) *impf.*, стать (-а́нет) *pf.* на дыбы́.

rear[2] [rɪə(r)] *n.* тыл (*loc.* -у́; *pl.* -ы́); **bring up the** ~ замыка́ть *impf.*, замкну́ть *pf.* ше́ствие; *adj.* за́дний; (*also mil.*) ты́льный; (*mil.*) тылово́й; ~ **admiral** контр-адмира́л. **rearguard** *n.* арьерга́рд; ~ **action** арьерга́рдный бой (*pl.* бои́). **rear-light** *n.* (*of car*) за́дний фона́рь (-ря́) *m.*

rearm [ri:'ɑ:m] *v.t.* & *i.* перевооружа́ть(ся) *impf.*, перевооружи́ть(ся) *pf.* **rearmament** *n.* перевооруже́ние.

rear-view ['rɪəvju:] *adj.*: ~ **mirror** зе́ркало (*pl.* -ла́) за́дней обзо́рности. **rearwards** *adv.* наза́д, в тыл.

reason ['ri:z(ə)n] *n.* (*cause*) причи́на, основа́ние; (*intellect*) ра́зум, рассу́док (-дка); **it stands to** ~ разуме́ется; **not without** ~ не без основа́ния; *v.t.* (*discuss*) обсужда́ть *impf.*, обсуди́ть (-ужу́, -у́дишь) *pf.*; *v.i.* рассужда́ть *impf.*; ~ **with** (*person*) угова́ривать *impf.*+*a.* **reasonable** *adj.* (*sensible*) разу́мный; (*well-founded*) основа́тельный; (*inexpensive*) недорого́й (недоро́г, -а́, -о).

reassurance [,ri:ə'ʃuərəns] *n.* успока́ивание. **reassure** *v.t.* успока́ивать *impf.*, успоко́ить *pf.*

rebate ['ri:beɪt] *n.* ски́дка.

rebel ['reb(ə)l] *n.* повста́нец (-нца), бунтовщи́к (-а́); *adj.* повста́нческий; *v.i.* бунтова́ть *impf.*, взбунтова́ться *pf.* **rebellion** [rɪ'beljən] *n.* восста́ние, бунт. **re'bellious** *adj.* мяте́жный, повста́нческий.

rebirth [ri:'bɜ:θ, 'ri:-] *n.* возрожде́ние.

rebound [rɪ'baʊnd] *v.i.* отска́кивать *impf.*, отскочи́ть (-чу́, -чишь) *pf.*; *n.* рикоше́т, отско́к.

rebuff [rɪ'bʌf] *n.* отпо́р; *v.t.* дава́ть (даю́, даёшь) *impf.*, дать (дам, дашь, даст, дади́м; дал, -а́, да́ло́, -и) *pf.*+*d.* отпо́р.

rebuke [rɪ'bju:k] *v.t.* упрека́ть *impf.*, упрекну́ть *pf.*; *n.* упрёк.

rebut [rɪ'bʌt] *v.t.* (*refute*) опроверга́ть *impf.*, опрове́ргнуть (-г(нул), -гла) *pf.* **rebuttal** *n.* опроверже́ние.

recalcitrant [rɪ'kælsɪtrənt] *adj.* непоко́рный.

recall [rɪ'kɔ:l; 'ri:kɔl] *v.t.* (*summon*) призыва́ть *impf.*, призва́ть (призову́, -вёшь; призва́л, -а́, -о) *pf.* обра́тно; (*an official*) отзыва́ть *impf.*, отозва́ть (отзову́, -вёшь; отозва́л, -а́, -о) *pf.*; (*remember*) вспомина́ть *impf.*, вспо́мнить *pf.*; (*remind*) напомина́ть *impf.*, напо́мнить *pf.*; (~ *to life*) возвраща́ть *impf.*, верну́ть *pf.* к жи́зни; *n.* призы́в верну́ться; о́тзыв.

recant [rɪ'kænt] *v.t.* & *i.* отрека́ться *impf.*,

отре́чься (-еку́сь, -ечёшься; -ёкся, -екла́сь) *pf.* (от+*g.*). **recan'tation** *n.* отрече́ние

recapitulate [ˌriːkəˈpɪtjʊˌleɪt] *v.t.* резюми́ровать *impf.* & *pf.* **recapitu'lation** *n.* резюме́ *nt.indecl.*

recast [riːˈkɑːst] *v.t.* перераба́тывать *impf.*, перерабо́тать *pf.*; переде́лывать *impf.*, переде́лать *pf.*

recede [rɪˈsiːd] *v.i.* отходи́ть (-ожу́, -о́дишь) *impf.*, отойти́ (отойду́, -дёшь; отошёл, -шла́) *pf.*; отступа́ть *impf.*, отступи́ть (-плю́, -пишь) *pf.*

receipt [rɪˈsiːt] *n.* (*receiving*) получе́ние; *pl.* (*amount*) прихо́д; (*written* ~) распи́ска, квита́нция; *v.t.* распи́сываться *impf.*, расписа́ться (-ишу́сь, -и́шешься) *pf.* на+*p.* **receive** *v.t.* (*accept, admit, entertain*) принима́ть *impf.*, приня́ть (приму́, -мешь; при́нял, -а́, -о) *pf.*; (*acquire, be given, be sent*) получа́ть *impf.*, получи́ть (-чу́, -чишь) *pf.*; (*stolen goods*) укрыва́ть *impf.*, укры́ть (-ро́ю, -ро́ешь) *pf.* **receiver** *n.* (*official* ~) управля́ющий *sb.* иму́ществом (банкро́та); (*of stolen goods*) укрыва́тель *m.* кра́деного; (*radio, television*) приёмник; (*telephone*) тру́бка.

recension [rɪˈsenʃ(ə)n] *n.* изво́д.

recent [ˈriːs(ə)nt] *adj.* неда́вний; (*new*) но́вый (нов, -а́, -о). **recently** *adv.* неда́вно.

receptacle [rɪˈseptək(ə)l] *n.* вмести́лище. **reception** *n.* приём; ~ **room** приёмная *sb.* **receptionist** *n.* секрета́рь (-ря́) *m.*, -рша, в приёмной. **receptive** *adj.* восприи́мчивый.

recess [rɪˈses, ˈriːses] *n.* переры́в в рабо́те; (*parl.*) кани́кулы (-л) *pl.*; (*niche*) ни́ша; *pl.* (*of the heart*) тайники́ *m.pl.* **re'cession** *n.* спад.

recidivist [rɪˈsɪdɪvɪst] *n.* рецидиви́ст.

recipe [ˈresɪpɪ] *n.* реце́пт.

recipient [rɪˈsɪpɪənt] *n.* получа́тель *m.*, ~ница.

reciprocal [rɪˈsɪprək(ə)l] *adj.* взаи́мный; (*corresponding*) соотве́тственный; *n.* (*math.*) обра́тная величина́ (*pl.* -ны). **reciprocate** *v.t.* отвеча́ть *impf.* (взаи́мностью) на+*a.* **reciprocating** *adj.* (*motion*) возвра́тно-поступа́тельный; (*engine*) поршнево́й. **reciprocity** [ˌresɪˈprɒsɪtɪ] *n.* взаи́мность.

recital [rɪˈsaɪt(ə)l] *n.* (*account*) изложе́ние, подро́бное перечисле́ние; (*concert*) (со́льный) конце́рт. **recitation** [ˌresɪˈteɪʃ(ə)n] *n.* публи́чное чте́ние. **recitative** [ˌresɪtəˈtiːv] *n.* речитати́в. **recite** *v.t.* деклами́ровать *impf.*, про~ *pf.*; чита́ть *impf.*, про~ *pf.* вслух; (*enumerate*) перечисля́ть *impf.*, перечи́слить *pf.*

reckless [ˈreklɪs] *adj.* (*rash*) опроме́тчивый; (*careless*) неосторо́жный.

reckon [ˈrekən] *v.t.* подсчи́тывать *impf.*, подсчита́ть *pf.*; (*also regard as*) счита́ть *impf.*, счесть (сочту́, -тёшь; счёл, -сочла́) *pf.* (+*i.*, за+*a.*); *v.i.*: ~ **with** счита́ться *impf.* с+*i.* **reckoning** *n.* счёт, расчёт; **day of** ~ час распла́ты.

reclaim [rɪˈkleɪm] *v.t.* (*reform*) исправля́ть *impf.*, испра́вить *pf.*; (*land*) осва́ивать *impf.*, осво́ить *pf.*

recline [rɪˈklaɪn] *v.i.* отки́дываться *impf.*, отки́нуться *pf.*; полулежа́ть (-жу́, -жи́шь) *impf.*

recluse [rɪˈkluːs] *n.* затво́рник, -ица.

recognition [ˌrekəgˈnɪʃ(ə)n] *n.* узнава́ние; (*acknowledgement*) призна́ние. **recognize** [ˈrekəgˌnaɪz] *v.t.* (*know again*) узнава́ть (-наю́, -наёшь) *impf.*, узна́ть *pf.*; (*acknowledge*) признава́ть (-наю́, -наёшь) *impf.*, призна́ть *pf.*

recoil [ˈriːkɔɪl] *v.i.* отпря́дывать *impf.*, отпря́нуть *pf.*; отша́тываться *impf.*, отшатну́ться *pf.* (**from** от+*g.*); (*of gun*) отдава́ть (-даёт) *impf.*, отда́ть (-а́ст, -аду́т; о́тдал, -а́, -о) *pf.*; *n.* отско́к; отда́ча.

recollect [ˌrekəˈlekt] *v.t.* вспомина́ть *impf.*, вспо́мнить *pf.* **recollection** *n.* воспомина́ние.

recommend [ˌrekəˈmend] *v.t.* рекомендова́ть *impf.* & *pf.*; (*for prize etc.*) представля́ть *impf.*, предста́вить *pf.* (**for** к+*d.*). **recommen'dation** *n.* рекоменда́ция; представле́ние.

recompense [ˈrekəmˌpens] *n.* вознагражде́ние; *v.t.* вознагражда́ть *impf.*, вознагради́ть *pf.*

reconcile [ˈrekənˌsaɪl] *v.t.* примиря́ть *impf.*, примири́ть *pf.*; ~ **o.s.** примиря́ться *impf.*, примири́ться *pf.* (**to** с+*i.*). **reconciliation** [ˌrekənˌsɪlɪˈeɪʃ(ə)n] *n.* примире́ние.

recondition [ˌriːkənˈdɪʃ(ə)n] *v.t.* приводи́ть (-ожу́, -о́дишь) *impf.*, привести́ (-еду́, -едёшь; -ёл, -ела́) *pf.* в испра́вное состоя́ние.

reconnaissance [rɪˈkɒnɪs(ə)ns] *n.* разве́дка. **reconnoitre** [ˌrekəˈnɔɪtə(r)] *v.t.* разве́дывать *impf.*, разве́дать *pf.*

reconstruct [ˌriːkənˈstrʌkt] *v.t.* перестра́ивать *impf.*, перестро́ить *pf.*; реконструи́ровать *impf.* & *pf.*; воссоздава́ть (-даю́, -даёшь) *impf.* воссозда́ть (-а́м, -а́шь, -а́ст, -ади́м; -а́л, -ала́, -о) *pf.* **reconstruction** *n.* перестро́йка; реконстру́кция; воссозда́ние.

record [rɪˈkɔːd; ˈrekɔːd] *v.t.* запи́сывать *impf.*, записа́ть (-ишу́, -и́шешь) *pf.*; *n.* за́пись; (*minutes*) протоко́л; (*gramophone* ~) грампласти́нка; (*sport etc.*) реко́рд; *pl.* архи́в; **off the** ~ неофициа́льно; *adj.* реко́рдный. **record-breaker** *n.* рекордсме́н, ~ка. **re'corder** *n.* (*person who records*) регистра́тор; (*judge*) рико́рдер; (*tech.*) регистри́рующий, самопи́шущий, прибо́р; (*flute*) блок-фле́йта. **record-holder** *n.* рекордсме́н, ~ка. **re'cording** *n.* за́пись; (*sound* ~) звукоза́пись. **record-player** *n.* прои́грыватель *m.*

recount[1] [rɪˈkaʊnt] *v.t.* (*narrate*) переска́зывать *impf.*, пересказа́ть (-ажу́, -а́жешь) *pf.*

re-count[2] [riːˈkaʊnt] *v.t.* (*count again*) пересчи́тывать *impf.*, пересчита́ть *pf.*; *n.* пересчёт.

recoup [rɪˈkuːp] *v.t.* возмеща́ть *impf.*, возмести́ть *pf.* (*person* +*d.*; *loss etc.* +*a.*). **recoupment** *n.* возмеще́ние.

recourse [rɪ'kɔ:s] *n.*: **have ~ to** прибега́ть *impf.*, прибе́гнуть (-г(нул), -гла) *pf.* к по́мощи+*g.*

recover [rɪ'kʌvə(r)] *v.t.* (*regain possession*) получа́ть *impf.*, получи́ть (-чу́, -чишь) *pf.* обра́тно; (*debt etc.*) взы́скивать *impf.*, взыска́ть (-ыщу́, -ы́щешь) *pf.* (**from** с+*g.*); *v.i.* (~ *health*) поправля́ться *impf.*, попра́виться *pf.* (**from** по́сле+*g.*). **recovery** *n.* получе́ние обра́тно; выздоровле́ние.

recreate [ˌri:krɪ'eɪt] *v.t.* вновь создава́ть (-даю́, -даёшь) *impf.*, созда́ть (-а́м, -а́шь, -а́ст, -ади́м; со́зда́л, -а́, -о) *pf.*

recreation [ˌrekrɪ'eɪʃ(ə)n] *n.* развлече́ние, о́тдых.

recrimination [rɪˌkrɪmɪ'neɪʃ(ə)n] *n.* взаи́мное обвине́ние.

recruit [rɪ'kru:t] *n.* новобра́нец (-нца); *v.t.* вербова́ть *impf.*, за~ *pf.* **recruitment** *n.* вербо́вка.

rectangle ['rekˌtæŋg(ə)l] *n.* прямоуго́льник. **rec'tangular** *adj.* прямоуго́льный.

rectification [ˌrektɪfɪ'keɪʃ(ə)n] *n.* исправле́ние; (*chem.*) ректифика́ция; (*elec.*) выпрямле́ние. **rectify** ['rektɪˌfaɪ] *v.t.* исправля́ть *impf.*, испра́вить *pf.*; ректифици́ровать *impf.* & *pf.*; выпрямля́ть *impf.*, вы́прямить *pf.*

rectilinear [ˌrektɪ'lɪnɪə(r)] *adj.* прямолине́йный.

rectitude ['rektɪˌtju:d] *n.* че́стность.

recto ['rektəʊ] *n.* нечётная пра́вая страни́ца; (*of folio*) лицева́я сторона́ (*a.* -ону; *pl.* -оны, -о́н, -она́м).

rector ['rektə(r)] *n.* (*priest*) прихо́дский свяще́нник; (*univ. etc.*) ре́ктор. **rectorship** *n.* ре́кторство. **rectory** *n.* дом (*pl.* -а́) прихо́дского свяще́нника.

rectum ['rektəm] *n.* пряма́я кишка́ (*g.pl.* -шо́к).

recumbent [rɪ'kʌmbənt] *adj.* лежа́чий.

recuperate [rɪ'ku:pəˌreɪt] *v.i.* восстана́вливать *impf.*, восстанови́ть (-влю́, -вишь) *pf.* своё здоро́вье. **recupe'ration** *n.* восстановле́ние здоро́вья.

recur [rɪ'kɜ:(r)] *v.i.* повторя́ться *impf.*, повтори́ться *pf.*; **~ring decimal** периоди́ческая дробь (*pl.* -би, -бе́й). **recurrence** [rɪ'kʌrəns] *n.* повторе́ние. **recurrent** *adj.* повторя́ющийся.

recycle [ri:'saɪk(ə)l] *v.t.* рециркули́ровать *impf.* & *pf.*; **~d paper** бума́га из ути́ля. **recycling** *n.* повто́рное испо́льзование, перерабо́тка.

red [red] *adj.* (*in colour*; *fig.*, *pol.*) кра́сный (-сен, -сна́, -сно); (*of hair*) ры́жий (рыж, -а́, -е); *n.* (*colour*) кра́сный цвет; (*fig.*, *pol.*) кра́сный *sb.*; **in the ~** в долгу́; **~ admiral** адмира́л; **~ cabbage** краснокоча́нная капу́ста; **~ deer** благоро́дный оле́нь *m.*; **~ herring** ло́жный след (*pl.* -ы́); **draw a ~ herring across the track** сбива́ть *impf.*, сбить (собью́, -ьёшь) *pf.* с то́лку; **R~ Indian** инде́ец (-е́йца), индиа́нка; **~ lead** свинцо́вый су́рик; **~ light** кра́сный фона́рь (-ря́) *m.*; **see the ~ light** предчу́вствовать *impf.* приближе́ние опа́сности; **~ pepper** стручко́вый пе́рец (-рца); **~ tape** волоки́та. **red-blooded** *adj.* энерги́чный. **redbreast** *n.* мали́новка. **redcurrant** *n.* кра́сная сморо́дина (*also collect.*). **redden** *v.t.* окра́шивать *impf.*, окра́сить *pf.* в кра́сный цвет; *v.i.* красне́ть *impf.*, по~ *pf.* **reddish** *adj.* краснова́тый; (*hair*) рыжева́тый.

redeem [rɪ'di:m] *v.t.* (*buy back*) выкупа́ть *impf.*, вы́купить *pf.*; (*from sin*) искупа́ть *impf.*, искупи́ть (-плю́, -пишь) *pf.* **redeemer** *n.* искупи́тель *m.* **redemption** [rɪ'dempʃ(ə)n] *n.* вы́куп; искупле́ние.

red-handed [ˌred'hændɪd] *adj.* с поли́чным. **red-hot** *adj.* раскалённый (-ён, -ена́) до́красна́.

redolent ['redələnt] *adj.*: **~ of** па́хнущий+*i.*; **be ~ of** па́хнуть (-х(нул), -хла) *impf.*+*i.*

redouble [ri:'dʌb(ə)l] *v.t.* удва́ивать *impf.*, удво́ить *pf.*

redoubt [rɪ'daʊt] *n.* реду́т.

redoubtable [rɪ'daʊtəb(ə)l] *adj.* гро́зный (-зен, -зна́, -зно).

redound [rɪ'daʊnd] *v.i.* спосо́бствовать *impf.*, по~ *pf.* (**to** +*d.*); **~ to s.o.'s credit** де́лать *impf.*, с~ *pf.* честь+*d.*

redress [rɪ'dres] *v.t.* исправля́ть *impf.*, испра́вить *pf.*; **~ the balance** восстана́вливать *impf.*, восстанови́ть (-влю́, -вишь) *pf.* равнове́сие; *n.* возмеще́ние.

redskin *n.* краснoко́жий *sb.*

reduce [rɪ'dju:s] *v.t.* (*decrease*) уменьша́ть *impf.*, уме́ньшить *pf.*; (*lower*) снижа́ть *impf.*, сни́зить *pf.*; (*shorten*) сокраща́ть *impf.*, сократи́ть (-ащу́, -ати́шь) *pf.*; (*bring to*) приводи́ть (-ожу́, -о́дишь) *impf.*, привести́ (-еду́, -едёшь; ёл, -ела́) *pf.* (**to** в+*a.*); *v.i.* худе́ть *impf.*, по~ *pf.* **reduction** [rɪ'dʌkʃ(ə)n] *n.* уменьше́ние, сниже́ние, сокраще́ние; (*amount of* ~) ски́дка.

redundancy [rɪ'dʌnd(ə)nsɪ] *n.* (*excess of workers*) изли́шек (-шка) рабо́чей си́лы; (*dismissal*) увольне́ние (рабо́чих, слу́жащих). **redundant** *adj.* (*excessive*) изли́шний; (*dismissed*) уво́ленный (-ен) (по сокраще́нию шта́тов).

reduplicate [rɪ'dju:plɪˌkeɪt] *v.t.* удва́ивать *impf.*, удво́ить *pf.* **redupli'cation** *n.* удвое́ние.

redwing ['redwɪŋ] *n.* белобро́вик. **redwood** *n.* секво́йя.

reed [ri:d] *n.* (*plant*) тростни́к (-а́), камы́ш (-а́); (*in musical instrument*) язычо́к (-чка́); (*mus.*) язычко́вый инструме́нт; **a broken ~** ненадёжная опо́ра; *attr.* тростнико́вый, камышо́вый; (*mus.*) язычко́вый. **reed-pipe** *n.* свире́ль. **reedy** ['ri:dɪ] *adj.* (*slender*) то́нкий (-нок, -нка́, -нко, то́нки́); (*voice*) пронзи́тельный.

reef [ri:f] *n.* (*of sail*; *ridge*) риф; *v.abs.* брать (беру́, -рёшь; брал, -а́, -о) *impf.*, взять (возьму́, -мёшь; взял, -а́, -о) *pf.* ри́фы.

reefer *n.* (*jacket*) бушла́т; (*cigarette*) сигаре́та с марихуа́ной. **reef-knot** *n.* ри́фовый у́зел (узла́).

reek [ri:k] *n.* вонь, дурно́й за́пах; *v.i.*: ~ **(of)** воня́ть *impf.* (+*i.*).

reel¹ [ri:l] *n.* кату́шка; (*of film*) руло́н; (*straight*) **off the** ~ (*fig.*) сра́зу, без переры́ва; *v.t.* (*on to* ~) нама́тывать *impf.*, намота́ть *pf.* на кату́шку; ~ **off** разма́тывать *impf.*, размота́ть *pf.*; (*story etc.*) отбараба́нить *pf.*

reel² [ri:l] *v.i.* (*be dizzy*) кружи́ться (-ится) *impf.*, за~ *pf.*; (*stagger*) поша́тываться *impf.*, пошатну́ться *pf.*

reel³ [ri:l] *n.* (*dance*) рил.

refectory [rɪ'fektərɪ, 'refɪktərɪ] *n.* (*in monastery*) трапе́зная *sb.*; (*in college*) столо́вая *sb.*; ~ **table** дли́нный у́зкий обе́денный стол (-а́).

refer [rɪ'fɜ:(r)] *v.t.* (*direct*) отсыла́ть *impf.*, отосла́ть (отошлю́, -лёшь) *pf.* (**to** к+*d.*); *v.i.*: ~ **to** (*cite*) ссыла́ться *impf.*, сосла́ться (сошлю́сь, -лёшься) *pf.* на+*a.*; (*mention*) упомина́ть *impf.*, упомяну́ть (-ну́, -нешь) *pf.*+*a.*; ~ **to drawer** обрати́тесь к чекода́телю. **referee** [ˌrefə'ri:] *n.* судья́ (*pl.* -дьи, -де́й, -дьям) *m.*; *v.t.* суди́ть (сужу́, су́дишь) *impf.* **'reference** *n.* (*to book etc.*) ссы́лка; (*mention*) упомина́ние; (*testimonial*) рекоменда́ция; ~ **book** спра́вочник; ~ **library** спра́вочная библиоте́ка (без вы́дачи книг на́ дом). **refe'rendum** *n.* рефере́ндум.

refine [rɪ'faɪn] *v.t.* очища́ть *impf.*, очи́стить *pf.*; рафини́ровать *impf.* & *pf.* **refined** *adj.* (*in style etc.*) утончённый (-ён, -ённа); (*in manners*) культу́рный; ~ **sugar** рафина́д. **refinery** *n.* (*oil* ~) нефтеочисти́тельный заво́д; (*sugar*-~) рафина́дный заво́д.

refit ['ri:fɪt; ri:'fɪt] *n.* переоборудо́вание; *v.t.* переобору́довать *impf.* & *pf.*

reflect [rɪ'flekt] *v.t.* отража́ть *impf.*, отрази́ть *pf.*; *v.i.* (*meditate*) размышля́ть *impf.*, размы́слить *pf.* (**on** о+*p.*). **reflection** *n.* отраже́ние; размышле́ние; **on** ~ поду́мав. **reflector** *n.* рефле́ктор. **reflex** ['ri:fleks] *n.* рефле́кс; *adj.* рефле́кторный; ~ **camera** зерка́льный фотоаппара́т. **reflexive** *adj.* (*gram.*) возвра́тный.

reform [rɪ'fɔ:m] *v.t.* реформи́ровать *impf.* & *pf.*; *v.t.* & *i.* (*of people*) исправля́ть(ся) *impf.*, испра́вить(ся) *pf.*; *n.* рефо́рма, исправле́ние. **reformation** [ˌrefə'meɪʃ(ə)n] *n.* рефо́рма; **the R**~ Реформа́ция. **reformatory** *adj.* исправи́тельный; *n.* исправи́тельное заведе́ние.

refract [rɪ'frækt] *v.t.* преломля́ть *impf.*, преломи́ть (-ит) *pf.* **refraction** *n.* рефра́кция, преломле́ние. **refractive** *adj.* преломля́ющий. **refractory** *adj.* (*person*) упря́мый, непоко́рный; (*substance*) тугопла́вкий.

refrain¹ [rɪ'freɪn] *n.* припе́в.

refrain² [rɪ'freɪn] *v.i.* уде́рживаться *impf.*, удержа́ться (-жу́сь, -жишься) *pf.* (**from** от+*g.*).

refresh [rɪ'freʃ] *v.t.* освежа́ть *impf.*, освежи́ть *pf.*; ~ **o.s.** подкрепля́ться *impf.*, подкрепи́ться *pf.* **refreshment** *n.* (*drink*) освежа́ющий напи́ток (-тка); *pl.* заку́ска; ~ **room** буфе́т.

refrigerate [rɪ'frɪdʒəˌreɪt] *v.t.* охлажда́ть *impf.*, охлади́ть *pf.* **refrige'ration** *n.* охлажде́ние. **refrigerator** *n.* холоди́льник.

refuge ['refju:dʒ] *n.* убе́жище, прибе́жище; **take** ~ находи́ть (-ожу́, -о́дишь) *impf.*, найти́ (найду́, -дёшь; нашёл, -шла́) *pf.* убе́жище. **refu'gee** *n.* бе́женец (-нца), -нка.

refund [rɪ'fʌnd; 'ri:fʌnd] *v.t.* возвраща́ть *impf.*, возврати́ть (-ащу́, -ати́шь) *pf.*; (*expenses*) возмеща́ть *impf.*, возмести́ть *pf.*; *n.* возмеще́ние.

refusal [rɪ'fju:z(ə)l] *n.* отка́з; **first** ~ пра́во пе́рвого вы́бора. **refuse¹** *v.t.* отка́зывать *impf.*, отказа́ть (-ажу́, -а́жешь) *pf.*

refuse² ['refju:s] *n.* отбро́сы (-сов) *pl.*, му́сор.

refusenik [rɪ'fju:znɪk] *n.* отка́зник, -ица.

refutation [ˌrefjʊ'teɪʃ(ə)n] *n.* опроверже́ние. **refute** [rɪ'fju:t] *v.t.* опроверга́ть *impf.*, опрове́ргнуть (-г(нул), -гла) *pf.*

regain [rɪ'geɪn] *v.t.* (*recover*) сно́ва приобрета́ть *impf.*, приобрести́ (-ету́, -етёшь; -ёл, -ела́) *pf.*; (*reach*) сно́ва достига́ть *impf.*, дости́гнуть & дости́чь (-и́гну, -и́гнешь; -и́г) *pf.*

regal ['ri:g(ə)l] *adj.* короле́вский.

regale [rɪ'geɪl] *v.t.* угоща́ть *impf.*, угости́ть *pf.* (**with** +*i.*).

regalia [rɪ'geɪlɪə] *n.* рега́лии *f.pl.*

regard [rɪ'gɑ:d] *v.t.* смотре́ть (-рю́, -ришь) *impf.*, по~ *pf.* на+*a.*; (*take into account*) счита́ться *impf.* с+*i.*; ~ **as** счита́ть *impf.*+*i.*, за+*i.*; **as** ~**s** что каса́ется+*g.*; *n.* (*esteem*) уваже́ние; (*attention*) внима́ние; *pl.* покло́н, приве́т; **with** ~ **to** относи́тельно+*g.*; что каса́ется+*g.* **regarding** *prep.* относи́тельно+*g.*; что каса́ется+*g.* **regardless** *adv.* не обраща́я внима́ния; ~ **of** не счита́ясь с+*i.*

regatta [rɪ'gætə] *n.* рега́та.

regency ['ri:dʒənsɪ] *n.* реге́нтство.

regenerate [rɪ'dʒenəˌreɪt; rɪ'dʒenərət] *v.t.* перерожда́ть *impf.*, перероди́ть *pf.*; *adj.* перерождённый (-ён, -ена́). **regene'ration** *n.* перерожде́ние.

regent ['ri:dʒ(ə)nt] *n.* ре́гент.

reggae ['regeɪ] *n.* (*mus.*) ре́гги *m. indecl.*

regicide ['redʒɪˌsaɪd] *n.* (*action*) цареуби́йство; (*person*) цареуби́йца *c.g.*

régime [reɪ'ʒi:m] *n.* режи́м. **regimen** ['redʒɪˌmen] *n.* (*med.*) режи́м; (*gram.*) управле́ние.

regiment ['redʒɪmənt] *n.* полк (-а́, *loc.* -у́). **regimental** [ˌredʒɪ'ment(ə)l] *adj.* полково́й. **regimen'tation** *n.* регламента́ция.

region ['ri:dʒ(ə)n] *n.* о́бласть (*pl.* -ти, -те́й). **regional** *adj.* областно́й, региона́льный, ме́стный.

register ['redʒɪstə(r)] *n.* рее́стр, кни́га записе́й; (*also mus.*) реги́стр; *v.t.* регистри́ровать *impf.*, за~ *pf.*; (*express*) выража́ть *impf.*, вы́разить *pf.*; (*a letter*) отправля́ть *impf.*, отпра́вить *pf.* заказны́м. **registered** *adj.* (*letter*) заказно́й. **registrar** [ˌredʒɪs'trɑː(r), 'redʒ-] *n.* регистра́тор. **regi'stration** *n.* регистра́ция, за́пись; ~ **mark** номерно́й знак. **registry** *n.* регистрату́ра; (~ *office*) отде́л за́писей а́ктов гражда́нского состоя́ния, загс.

regression [rɪ'greʃ(ə)n] *n.* регре́сс. **regressive** *adj.* регресси́вный.

regret [rɪ'gret] *v.t.* сожале́ть *impf.* о+*p.*; **I ~ to say** к сожале́нию, должéн сказа́ть; *n.* сожале́ние. **regretful** *adj.* по́лный (-лон, -лна́, по́лно́) **regrettable** *adj.* приско́рбный.

regular ['regjʊlə(r)] *adj.* регуля́рный; (*also gram.*) пра́вильный; (*recurring*) очередно́й; (*of officer*) ка́дровый; *n.* (*coll.*) завсегда́тай. **regularity** [ˌregjʊ'lærɪtɪ] *n.* регуля́рность. **regularize** *v.t.* упоря́дочивать *impf.*, упоря́дочить *pf.* **regulate** *v.t.* регули́ровать *impf.*, у~ *pf.* **regu'lation** *n.* регули́рование; *pl.* пра́вила *nt.pl.*, уста́в; *adj.* устано́вленный.

rehabilitate [ˌriːhə'bɪlɪˌteɪt] *v.t.* реабилити́ровать *impf.* & *pf.* **rehabili'tation** *n.* реабилита́ция.

rehash [riː'hæʃ; 'riːhæʃ] *v.t.* переде́лывать *impf.*, переде́лать *pf.*; *n.* переде́лка.

rehearsal [rɪ'hɜːs(ə)l] *n.* репети́ция. **rehearse** *v.t.* репети́ровать *impf.*, от~ *pf.*

reign [reɪn] *n.* ца́рствование; *v.i.* ца́рствовать *impf.*; (*prevail*) цари́ть *impf.*

reimburse [ˌriːɪm'bɜːs] *v.t.* возмеща́ть *impf.*, возмести́ть *pf.* (+*d. of person*). **reimbursement** *n.* возмеще́ние.

rein [reɪn] *n.* по́вод (*loc.* -у́; *pl.* пово́дья, -ьев); *pl.* во́жжи (-же́й) *pl.*

reincarnation [ˌriːɪnkɑː'neɪʃ(ə)n] *n.* перевоплоще́ние.

reindeer ['reɪndɪə(r)] *n.* се́верный оле́нь *m.*; ~ **moss** оле́ний мох (м(о́)ха, *loc.* мху & м(о́)хе).

reinforce [ˌriːɪn'fɔːs] *v.t.* подкрепля́ть *impf.*, подкрепи́ть (-плю́, -пишь) *pf.*; уси́ливать *impf.*, уси́лить *pf.*; **~d concrete** железобето́н. **reinforcement** *n.* (*also pl.*) подкрепле́ние, усиле́ние.

reinstate [ˌriːɪn'steɪt] *v.t.* восстана́вливать *impf.*, восстанови́ть (-влю́, -вишь) *pf.* **reinstatement** *n.* восстановле́ние.

reinsurance [ˌriːɪn'ʃʊərəns] *n.* перестрахо́вка. **reinsure** *v.t.* перестрахо́вывать *impf.*, перестрахова́ть *pf.*

reiterate [riː'ɪtəˌreɪt] *v.t.* повторя́ть *impf.*, повтори́ть *pf.* **reite'ration** *n.* повторе́ние.

reject [rɪ'dʒekt; 'riːdʒekt] *v.t.* отверга́ть *impf.*, отве́ргнуть (-г(нул), -гла) *pf.*; (*as defective*) бракова́ть *impf.*, за~ *pf.*; *n.* брако́ванное изде́лие. **re'jection** *n.* отка́з (**of** от+*g.*); брако́вка.

rejoice [rɪ'dʒɔɪs] *v.t.* ра́довать *impf.*, об~ *pf.*; *v.i.* ра́доваться *impf.*, об~ *pf.* (**in, at** +*d.*). **rejoicing** *n.* ликова́ние.

rejoin [rɪː'dʒɔɪn] *v.t.* (вновь) присоединя́ться *impf.*, присоедини́ться *pf.* к+*d.*

rejoinder [rɪ'dʒɔɪndə(r)] *n.* отве́т.

rejuvenate [rɪ'dʒuːvɪˌneɪt] *v.t.* & *i.* омола́живать(ся) *impf.*, омолоди́ть(ся) *pf.* **rejuve'nation** *n.* омоложе́ние.

relapse [rɪ'læps] *n.* рециди́в; *v.i.* сно́ва впада́ть *impf.*, впасть (-аду́, -адёшь; -ал) *pf.* (**into** в+*a.*); (*into illness*) сно́ва заболева́ть *impf.*, заболе́ть *pf.*

relate [rɪ'leɪt] *v.t.* (*narrate*) расска́зывать *impf.*, рассказа́ть (-ажу́, -а́жешь) *pf.*; (*establish relation*) устана́вливать *impf.*, установи́ть (-влю́, -вишь) *pf.* связь ме́жду+*i.*; *v.i.* относи́ться (-ится) *impf.* (**to** к+*d.*). **related** *adj.* ро́дственный (-ен, -енна). **relation** *n.* (*narration*) повествова́ние; (*connection etc.*) связь, отноше́ние; (*person*) ро́дственник; **in ~ to** относи́тельно+*g.* **relationship** *n.* родство́. **relative** ['relətɪv] *adj.* относи́тельный; *n.* ро́дственник, -ица. **rela'tivity** *n.* относи́тельность; (*phys.*) тео́рия относи́тельности.

relax [rɪ'læks] *v.t.* & *i.* ослабля́ть(ся) *impf.*, осла́бить(ся) *pf.*; смягча́ть(ся) *impf.*, смягчи́ть(ся) *pf.* **rela'xation** *n.* ослабле́ние, смягче́ние; (*rest*) о́тдых.

relay ['riːleɪ] *n.* сме́на; (*sport*) эстафе́та; (*elec.*) реле́ *nt.indecl.*; (*broadcast etc.*) трансля́ция; *v.t.* сменя́ть *impf.*, смени́ть (-ню́, -нишь) *pf.*; (*radio*) трансли́ровать *impf.* & *pf.*

release [rɪ'liːs] *v.t.* (*set free*) освобожда́ть *impf.*, освободи́ть *pf.*; отпуска́ть *impf.*, отпусти́ть (-ущу́, -у́стишь) *pf.*; (*film etc.*) выпуска́ть *impf.*, вы́пустить *pf.*; *n.* освобожде́ние; вы́пуск.

relegate ['relɪˌgeɪt] *v.t.* переводи́ть (-ожу́, -о́дишь) *impf.*, перевести́ (-еду́, -едёшь; -ёл, -ела́) *pf.* (в бо́лее ни́зкий класс, (*sport*) в ни́зшую ли́гу). **rele'gation** *n.* перево́д (в бо́лее ни́зкий класс, в ни́зшую ли́гу).

relent [rɪ'lent] *v.i.* смягча́ться *impf.*, смягчи́ться *pf.* **relentless** *adj.* неумоли́мый, непрекло́нный (-нен, -нна).

relevance ['relɪv(ə)ns] *n.* уме́стность. **relevant** *adj.* относя́щийся к де́лу; уме́стный.

reliable [rɪ'laɪəb(ə)l] *adj.* надёжный. **reliance** *n.* дове́рие. **reliant** *adj.* уве́ренный (-ен, -енна).

relic ['relɪk] *n.* оста́ток (-тка), рели́квия; *pl.* (*of saint*) мо́щи (-ще́й) *pl.*

relief[1] [rɪ'liːf] *n.* (*art, geol.*) релье́ф.

relief[2] [rɪ'liːf] *n.* (*alleviation*) облегче́ние; (*assistance*) по́мощь; (*in duty*) сме́на; (*raising of siege*) сня́тие оса́ды. **relieve** *v.t.* (*alleviate*) облегча́ть *impf.*, облегчи́ть *pf.*; (*help*) ока́зывать *impf.*, оказа́ть (-ажу́, -а́жешь) *pf.* по́мощь+*d.*; (*replace*) сменя́ть *impf.*, смени́ть (-ню́, -нишь) *pf.*; (*raise siege*) снима́ть *impf.*, снять (сниму́, -мешь; снял, -а́, -о) *pf.* оса́ду с+*g.*

religion [rɪ'lɪdʒ(ə)n] *n.* рели́гия. **religious** *adj.* религио́зный.

relinquish [rɪ'lɪŋkwɪʃ] *v.t.* оставля́ть *impf.*, оста́вить *pf.*; (*right etc.*) отка́зываться *impf.*, отказа́ться (-ажу́сь, -а́жешься) *pf.* от+*g.*
reliquary ['relɪkwərɪ] *n.* ра́ка.
relish ['relɪʃ] *n.* (*enjoyment*) смак, наслажде́ние; (*condiment*) припра́ва; *v.t.* смакова́ть *impf.*
reluctance [rɪ'lʌkt(ə)ns] *n.* неохо́та. **reluctant** *adj.* неохо́тный; **be ~ to** не жела́ть *impf.+inf.*
rely [rɪ'laɪ] *v.i.* полага́ться *impf.*, положи́ться (-жу́сь, -жишься) *pf.* (**on** на+*a.*).
remain [rɪ'meɪn] *v.i.* остава́ться (-аю́сь, -аёшься) *impf.*, оста́ться (-а́нусь, -а́нешься) *pf.* **remainder** *n.* оста́ток (-тка); (*books*) кни́жные оста́тки *m.pl.*; *v.t.* распродава́ть (-даю́, -даёшь) *impf.*, распрода́ть (-а́м, -а́шь, -а́ст, -ади́м; распро́дал, -а́, -о) *pf.* по дешёвой цене́. **remains** *n.* оста́тки *m.pl.*; (*human ~*) оста́нки (-ков) *pl.*
remand [rɪ'mɑːnd] *v.t.* отсыла́ть *impf.*, отосла́ть (отошлю́, -лёшь) *pf.* под стра́жу; *n.* отсы́лка под стра́жу; **prisoner on ~** подсле́дственный *sb.*
remark [rɪ'mɑːk] *v.t.* замеча́ть *impf.*, заме́тить *pf.*; *n.* замеча́ние. **remarkable** *adj.* замеча́тельный.
remedial [rɪ'miːdɪəl] *adj.* лече́бный. **remedy** ['remɪdɪ] *n.* сре́дство (**for** от, про́тив+*g.*); *v.t.* исправля́ть *impf.*, испра́вить *pf.*
remember [rɪ'membə(r)] *v.t.* вспомина́ть *impf.*, вспо́мнить *pf.* о+*p.*; по́мниться *impf. impers.+d.*; (*greet*) передава́ть (-даю́, -даёшь) *impf.*, переда́ть (-а́м, -а́шь, -а́ст, -ади́м; пе́редал, -а́, -о) *pf.* приве́т от+*g.* (**to** +*d.*). **remembrance** [rɪ'membrəns] *n.* па́мять; *pl.* приве́т.
remind [rɪ'maɪnd] *v.t.* напомина́ть *impf.*, напо́мнить *pf.+d.* (**of** +*a.*, о+*p.*). **reminder** *n.* напомина́ние.
reminiscence [ˌremɪ'nɪs(ə)ns] *n.* воспомина́ние. **reminiscent** *adj.* напомина́ющий.
remiss [rɪ'mɪs] *pred.* небре́жен (-жна). **remission** *n.* отпуще́ние. **remit** [rɪ'mɪt] *v.t.* пересыла́ть *impf.*, пересла́ть (-ешлю́, -ешлёшь) *pf.* **remittance** *n.* пересы́лка; (*money*) де́нежный перево́д.
remnant ['remnənt] *n.* оста́ток (-тка).
remonstrance [rɪ'mɒnstrəns] *n.* проте́ст. **remonstrate** ['remənˌstreɪt] *v.i.*: **~ with** увещева́ть *impf.+a.*
remorse [rɪ'mɔːs] *n.* угрызе́ния *nt.pl.* со́вести. **remorseful** *adj.* по́лный (-лон, -лна́, по́лно́) раская́ния. **remorseless** *adj.* беспоща́дный.
remote [rɪ'məʊt] *adj.* да́льний, отдалённый (-ён, -ённа); **~ control** дистанцио́нное управле́ние, телеуправле́ние.
removal [rɪ'muːv(ə)l] *n.* смеще́ние, устране́ние; (*change of house*) перее́зд; **~ firm** трансаге́нтство. **remove** *v.t.* смеща́ть *impf.*, смести́ть *pf.*; устраня́ть *impf.*, устрани́ть *pf.*; *v.i.* переезжа́ть *impf.*, перее́хать (-е́ду, -е́дешь) *pf.*; *n.* шаг, сте́пень (*pl.* -ни, -не́й) (отдале́ния). **removed** *adj.* далёкий (-ёк, -ека́, -ёко́); **once ~** двою́родный; **twice ~** трою́родный.
remuneration [rɪˌmjuːnə'reɪʃ(ə)n] *n.* вознагражде́ние. **re'munerative** *adj.* вы́годный.
renaissance [rɪ'neɪs(ə)ns, rə'n-, -sɑ̃s] *n.* возрожде́ние; **the R~** Ренесса́нс.
renal ['riːn(ə)l] *adj.* по́чечный.
renascence [rɪ'næs(ə)ns] *n.* возрожде́ние.
render ['rendə(r)] *v.t.* воздава́ть (-даю́, -даёшь) *impf.*, возда́ть (-а́м, -а́шь, -а́ст, -ади́м; возда́л, -а́, -о) *pf.*; (*help etc.*) ока́зывать *impf.*, оказа́ть (-ажу́, -а́жешь) *pf.*; (*role etc.*) исполня́ть *impf.*, испо́лнить *pf.*; (*transmit*) передава́ть (-даю́, -даёшь) *impf.*, переда́ть (-а́м, -а́шь, -а́ст, -ади́м; пе́редал, -а́, -о) *pf.*; (*fat*) топи́ть (-плю́, -пишь) *impf.*; (*stone*) штукату́рить *impf.*, о~, от~ *pf.* **rendering** *n.* исполне́ние; переда́ча; выта́пливание.
rendezvous ['rɒndɪˌvuː, -deɪˌvuː] *n.* (*meeting*) свида́ние, встре́ча; (*meeting-place*) ме́сто (*pl.* -та́) свида́ния, встре́чи; *v.i.* встреча́ться *impf.*, встре́титься *pf.*; собира́ться *impf.*, собра́ться (-берётся; собра́лся, -ала́сь, -а́ло́сь) *pf.*
renegade ['renɪˌgeɪd] *n.* ренега́т, ~ка.
renew [rɪ'njuː] *v.t.* (воз)обновля́ть *impf.*, (воз)обнови́ть *pf.*; (*of agreement etc.*) продлева́ть *impf.*, продли́ть *pf.* срок де́йствия+*g.* **renewable** *adj.* возобновля́емый; **~ resources** возобновля́емые ресу́рсы. **renewal** *n.* (воз)обновле́ние; продле́ние (сро́ка де́йствия).
rennet ['renɪt] *n.* сычу́жина.
renounce [rɪ'naʊns] *v.t.* отка́зываться *impf.*, отказа́ться (-ажу́сь, -а́жешься) *pf.* от+*g.*; отрека́ться *impf.*, отре́чься (-еку́сь, -ечёшься; -ёкся, -екла́сь) *pf.* от+*g.*
renovate ['renəˌveɪt] *v.t.* ремонти́ровать *impf.*, от~ *pf.* **reno'vation** *n.* ремо́нт.
renown [rɪ'naʊn] *n.* изве́стность, сла́ва. **renowned** *adj.* изве́стный; **be ~ for** сла́виться *impf.+i.*
rent [rent] *n.* (*for premises*) аре́нда; аре́ндная, кварти́рная, пла́та; (*for land*) ре́нта; *v.t.* (*of tenant*) арендова́ть *impf.* & *pf.*; брать (беру́, -рёшь; брал, -а́, -о) *impf.*, взять (возьму́, -мёшь; взял, -а́, -о) *pf.* в аре́нду; (*of owner*) сдава́ть (сдаю́, сдаёшь) *impf.*, сдать (-ам, -ашь, -аст, -ади́м; сдал, -а́, -о) *pf.* в аре́нду.
renunciation [rɪˌnʌnsɪ'eɪʃ(ə)n] *n.* отка́з, отрече́ние (**of** от+*g.*).
rep[1] [rep], **repp** *n.* (*fabric*) репс.
rep[2] [rep] *n.* (*commercial traveller*) коммивояжёр.
repair[1] [rɪ'peə(r)] *v.i.* (*resort*) направля́ться *impf.*, напра́виться *pf.*
repair[2] [rɪ'peə(r)] *v.t.* (*restore*) ремонти́ровать *impf.*, от~ *pf.*; (*clothing etc.*) чини́ть (-ню́, -нишь) *impf.*, по~ *pf.*; (*error etc.*) исправля́ть *impf.*, испра́вить *pf.*; *n.* (*also pl.*) ремо́нт (*only sg.*); почи́нка; (*good condition*)

испра́вность; **out of** ~ в неиспра́вном состоя́нии; *attr.* ремо́нтный; почи́ночный.
reparation [ˌrepəˈreɪʃ(ə)n] *n.* возмеще́ние; *pl.* репара́ции *f.pl.*
repartee [ˌrepɑːˈtiː] *n.* остроу́мный, нахо́дчивый, отве́т.
repatriate [riːˈpætrɪˌeɪt] *v.t.* репатрии́ровать *impf.* & *pf.* **repatriˈation** *n.* репатриа́ция.
repay [riːˈpeɪ] *v.t.* отпла́чивать *impf.*, отплати́ть (-ачу́, -а́тишь) *pf.* (*person* +*d.*); вознагражда́ть *impf.*, вознагради́ть *pf.* (*action* за+*i.*). **repayment** *n.* отпла́та; вознагражде́ние.
repeal [rɪˈpiːl] *v.t.* отменя́ть *impf.*, отмени́ть (-ню́, -нишь) *pf.*; *n.* отме́на.
repeat [rɪˈpiːt] *v.t.* & *i.* повторя́ть(ся) *impf.*, повтори́ть(ся) *pf.*; *n.* повторе́ние. **repeatedly** *adv.* неоднокра́тно.
repel [rɪˈpel] *v.t.* отта́лкивать *impf.*, оттолкну́ть *pf.*; отража́ть *impf.*, отрази́ть *pf.*
repent [rɪˈpənt] *v.i.* раска́иваться *impf.*, раска́яться (-а́юсь, -а́ешься) *pf.* (**of** в+*p.*). **repentance** *n.* раска́яние. **repentant** *adj.* раска́ивающийся.
repercussion [ˌriːpəˈkʌʃ(ə)n] *n.* (*of event*) после́дствие.
repertoire [ˈrepəˌtwɑː(r)] *n.* репертуа́р. **repertory** [ˈrepətərɪ] *n.* (*store*) запа́с; (*repertoire*) репертуа́р; ~ **company** постоя́нная тру́ппа.
repetition [ˌrepɪˈtɪʃ(ə)n] *n.* повторе́ние. **repetitious, repetitive** [rɪˈpetɪtɪv] *adj.* (беспреста́нно) повторя́ющийся.
replace [rɪˈpleɪs] *v.t.* (*put back*) класть (-аду́, -адёшь; -ал) *impf.*, положи́ть (-жу́, -жишь) *pf.* обра́тно (на ме́сто); (*substitute*) заменя́ть *impf.*, замени́ть (-ню́, -нишь) *pf.* (**by** +*i.*); замеща́ть *impf.*, замести́ть *pf.* **replacement** [rɪˈpleɪsmənt] *n.* заме́на, замеще́ние.
replay [ˈriːpleɪ; riːˈpleɪ] *n.* (*of a game*) переигро́вка; **action** ~ повто́р; *v.t.* переигрывать *impf.*, переигра́ть *pf.*
replenish [rɪˈplenɪʃ] *v.t.* пополня́ть *impf.*, попо́лнить *pf.* **replenishment** *n.* пополне́ние.
replete [rɪˈpliːt] *adj.* пресы́щенный (-ен); (*sated*) сы́тый (сыт, -а́, -о).
replica [ˈreplɪkə] *n.* то́чная ко́пия.
reply [rɪˈplaɪ] *v.t.* & *i.* отвеча́ть *impf.*, отве́тить *pf.* (**to** на+*a.*); *n.* отве́т; ~ **paid** с опла́ченным отве́том.
report [rɪˈpɔːt] *v.t.* (*relate*) сообща́ть *impf.*, сообщи́ть *pf.*; (*formally*) докла́дывать *impf.*, доложи́ть (-жу́, -жишь) *pf.*; *v.i.* (*present o.s.*) явля́ться *impf.*, яви́ться (явлю́сь, я́вишься) *pf.*; *n.* сообще́ние; докла́д; (*school*) та́бель *m.* успева́емости; (*sound*) звук взры́ва, вы́стрела. **reporter** *n.* репортёр, корреспонде́нт.
repose [rɪˈpəʊz] *v.i.* (*lie*) лежа́ть (-жу́, -жи́шь) *impf.*; (*rest*) отдыха́ть *impf.*, отдохну́ть *pf.*; *n.* (*rest*) о́тдых; (*peace*) поко́й.
repository [rɪˈpɒzɪtərɪ] *n.* храни́лище.
repp *see* **rep**[1]
reprehensible [ˌreprɪˈhensɪb(ə)l] *adj.* предосуди́тельный.
represent [ˌreprɪˈzent] *v.t.* представля́ть *impf.*; (*portray*) изобража́ть *impf.*, изобрази́ть *pf.* **represenˈtation** *n.* представи́тельство, представле́ние; изображе́ние. **repreˈsentative** *adj.* изобража́ющий (**of** +*a.*); (*typical*) типи́чный; (*pol.*) представи́тельный; *n.* представи́тель *m.*
repress [rɪˈpres] *v.t.* подавля́ть *impf.*, подави́ть (-влю́, -вишь) *pf.*; репресси́ровать *impf.* & *pf.* **repression** *n.* подавле́ние, репре́ссия. **repressive** *adj.* репресси́вный.
reprieve [rɪˈpriːv] *v.t.* отсро́чивать *impf.*, отсро́чить *pf.*+*d.* приведе́ние в исполне́ние (сме́ртного) пригово́ра; *n.* отсро́чка приведе́ния в исполне́ние (сме́ртного) пригово́ра.
reprimand [ˈreprɪˌmɑːnd] *n.* вы́говор; *v.t.* де́лать *impf.*, с~ *pf.* вы́говор+*d.*
reprint [riːˈprɪnt; ˈriːprɪnt] *v.t.* переиздава́ть (-даю́, -даёшь) *impf.*, переизда́ть (-а́м, -а́шь, -а́ст, -адим; -а́л, -ала́, -а́ло) *pf.*; перепеча́тывать *impf.*, перепеча́тать *pf.*; *n.* переизда́ние; перепеча́тка.
reprisal [rɪˈpraɪz(ə)l] *n.* репресса́лия.
reproach [rɪˈprəʊtʃ] *v.t.* упрека́ть *impf.*, упрекну́ть *pf.* (**with** в+*p.*); укоря́ть *impf.*, укори́ть *pf.* (**with** в+*p.*); *n.* упрёк, уко́р. **reproachful** *adj.* укори́зненный.
reproduce [ˌriːprəˈdjuːs] *v.t.* воспроизводи́ть (-ожу́, -о́дишь) *impf.*, воспроизвести́ (-еду́, -едёшь; -ёл, -ела́) *pf.* **reproduction** [ˌriːprəˈdʌkʃ(ə)n] *n.* (*action*) воспроизведе́ние; (*object*) ко́пия, репроду́кция. **reproductive** *adj.* воспроизводи́тельный.
reproof [rɪˈpruːf] *n.* порица́ние. **reprove** [rɪˈpruːv] *v.t.* порица́ть. *impf.*
reptile [ˈreptaɪl] *n.* пресмыка́ющееся *sb.*
republic [rɪˈpʌblɪk] *n.* респу́блика. **republican** *adj.* республика́нский; *n.* республика́нец (-нца), -нка.
repudiate [rɪˈpjuːdɪˌeɪt] *v.t.* отка́зываться *impf.*, отказа́ться (-ажу́сь, -а́жешься) *pf.* от+*g.*; (*reject*) отверга́ть *impf.*, отве́ргнуть (-г(нул), -гла) *pf.* **repudiˈation** *n.* отка́з (**of** от+*g.*).
repugnance [rɪˈpʌgnəns] *n.* отвраще́ние. **repugnant** *adj.* проти́вный.
repulse [rɪˈpʌls] *v.t.* отража́ть *impf.*, отрази́ть *pf.* **repulsion** *n.* отвраще́ние. **repulsive** *adj.* отврати́тельный, проти́вный.
reputable [ˈrepjʊtəb(ə)l] *adj.* по́льзующийся хоро́шей репута́цией. **repuˈtation, repute** [rɪˈpjuːt] *n.* репута́ция, сла́ва. **reˈputed** *adj.* предполага́емый.
request [rɪˈkwest] *n.* про́сьба; **by, on,** ~ по про́сьбе; **in (great)** ~ в (большо́м) спро́се; ~ **stop** остано́вка по тре́бованию; *v.t.* проси́ть (-ошу́, -о́сишь) *impf.*, по~ *pf.*+*a.*, +*g.*, о+*p.* (*person* +*a.*).
requiem [ˈrekwɪˌem] *n.* ре́квием.
require [rɪˈkwaɪə(r)] *v.t.* (*demand*; *need*) тре́-

бовать *impf.*, по~ *pf.+g.*; (*need*) нужда́ться *impf.* в+*p.* **requirement** *n.* тре́бование; (*necessity*) потре́бность. **requisite** ['rekwɪzɪt] *adj.* необходи́мый; *n.* необходи́мое *sb.*, необходи́мая вещь (*pl.* -щи, -ще́й). **requi'sition** *n.* реквизи́ция *v.t.* реквизи́ровать *impf.* & *pf.*

requite [rɪ'kwaɪt] *v.t.* отпла́чивать *impf.*, отплати́ть (-ачу́, -а́тишь) *pf.* (**for** за+*a.*; **with** +*i.*).

rescind [rɪ'sɪnd] *v.t.* отменя́ть *impf.*, отмени́ть (-ню́, -нишь) *pf.*

rescue ['reskjuː] *v.t.* спаса́ть *impf.*, спасти́ (-су́, -сёшь; -с, -сла́) *pf.*; *n.* спасе́ние; *attr.* спаса́тельный. **rescuer** *n.* спаси́тель *m.*

research [rɪ'sɜːtʃ] *n.* иссле́дование (+*g.*); (*occupation*) нау́чно-иссле́довательская рабо́та; *v.i.* занима́ться *impf.*, заня́ться (займу́сь, -мёшься; заня́лся́, -ла́сь) *pf.* иссле́дованиями, нау́чно-иссле́довательской рабо́той; ~ **into** иссле́довать *impf.* & *pf.+a.* **researcher** *n.* иссле́дователь *m.*

resemblance [rɪ'zembləns] *n.* схо́дство. **resemble** *v.t.* походи́ть (-ожу́, -о́дишь) *impf.* на+*a.*

resent [rɪ'zent] *v.t.* (*be indignant*) негодова́ть *impf.* на+*a.*, про́тив+*g.*; (*take offence*) обижа́ться *impf.*, оби́деться (-и́жусь, -и́дишься) *pf.* на+*a.* **resentful** *adj.* оби́дчивый. **resentment** *n.* негодова́ние; оби́да.

reservation [ˌrezə'veɪʃ(ə)n] *n.* (*proviso etc.*) огово́рка; (*booking*) предвари́тельный зака́з; (*tract of land*) резерва́ция. **reserve** [rɪ'zɜːv] *v.t.* (*postpone*) откла́дывать *impf.*, отложи́ть (-жу́, -жишь) *pf.*; (*keep in stock*) резерви́ровать *impf.* & *pf.*; (*book*) зара́нее зака́зывать *impf.*, заказа́ть (-ажу́, -а́жешь) *pf.*; брони́ровать *impf.*, за~ *pf.*; *n.* (*stock*; *mil.*) запа́с, резе́рв; (*sport*) запасно́й игро́к (-а́); (*nature ~ etc.*) запове́дник; (*proviso*) огово́рка; (~ *price*) ни́зшая отплатна́я цена́ (*a.* -ну); (*self-restraint*) сде́ржанность; *attr.* запасно́й, запа́сный, резе́рвный. **re'served** *adj.* (*person*) сде́ржанный (-ан, -анна). **re'servist** *n.* резерви́ст. **reservoir** ['rezəˌvwɑː(r)] *n.* резервуа́р, водохрани́лище; (*of knowledge etc.*) запа́с.

reside [rɪ'zaɪd] *v.i.* прожива́ть *impf.*; (*of right etc.*) принадлежа́ть (-жи́т) *impf.* (**in** +*d.*). **residence** ['rezɪd(ə)ns] *n.* (*residing*) прожива́ние; (*abode*) местожи́тельство; (*official ~ etc.*) резиде́нция. **'resident** *n.* (постоя́нный) жи́тель *m.*, ~ница; *adj.* прожива́ющий; (*population*) постоя́нный; ~ **physician** врач, живу́щий при больни́це. **resi'dential** *adj.* жило́й; ~ **qualification** ценз осе́длости.

residual [rɪ'zɪdjʊəl] *adj.* оста́точный. **residuary** *adj.* (*of estate*) оста́вшийся. **residue** ['rezɪˌdjuː] *n.* оста́ток (-тка); (*of estate*) оста́вшееся насле́дство.

resign [rɪ'zaɪn] *v.t.* отка́зываться *impf.*, отказа́ться (-ажу́сь, -а́жешься) *pf.* от+*g.*; *v.i.* уходи́ть (-ожу́, -о́дишь) *impf.*, уйти́ (уйду́, -дёшь; ушёл, ушла́) *pf.* в отста́вку; (*chess*) сдава́ть (сдаю́, сдаёшь) *impf.*, сдать (-а́м, -а́шь, -а́ст, -ади́м; сдал, -а́, -о) *pf.* па́ртию; ~ **o.s. to** покоря́ться *impf.*, покори́ться *pf.+d.* **resignation** [ˌrezɪg'neɪʃ(ə)n] *n.* отста́вка, заявле́ние об отста́вке; (*being resigned*) поко́рность; (*chess*) сда́ча. **resigned** *adj.* поко́рный.

resilient [rɪ'zɪlɪənt] *adj.* упру́гий; (*person*) неунывáющий.

resin ['rezɪn] *n.* смола́ (*pl.* -лы). **resinous** *adj.* смоли́стый.

resist [rɪ'zɪst] *v.t.* сопротивля́ться *impf.+d.*; поддава́ться (-даю́сь, -даёшься) *impf.+d.* **resistance** *n.* сопротивле́ние; (~ *movement*) движе́ние сопротивле́ния. **resistant** *adj.* про́чный (-чен, -чна́, -чно, про́чны́). **resistor** *n.* рези́стор.

resolute ['rezəˌluːt, -ˌljuːt] *adj.* реши́тельный. **reso'lution** *n.* (*character*) реши́тельность, реши́мость; (*at meeting etc.*) резолю́ция; (*of problem*; *mus.*) разреше́ние. **resolve** [rɪ'zɒlv] *v.t.* реша́ть *impf.*, реши́ть *pf.*; разреша́ть *impf.*, разреши́ть *pf.*; *v.t.* & *i.* (*decide*) реша́ться *impf.*, реши́ться *pf.+inf.*, на+*a.*; (*of meeting etc.*) выноси́ть (-ит) *impf.*, вы́нести (-сет; -с) *pf.* резолю́цию; *n.* реше́ние.

resonance ['rezənəns] *n.* резона́нс. **resonant** *adj.* раздаю́щийся; зву́чный (-чен, -чна́, -чно). **resonate** *v.i.* резони́ровать *impf.*

resort [rɪ'zɔːt] *v.i.*: ~ **to** прибега́ть *impf.*, прибе́гнуть (-г(нул), -гла) *pf.* к+*d.*; (*visit*) (ча́сто) посеща́ть *impf.+a.*; *n.* (*expedient*) сре́дство; (*health ~ etc.*) куро́рт; **in the last ~** в кра́йнем слу́чае; **without ~ to** не прибега́я к+*d.*

resound [rɪ'zaʊnd] *v.i.* (*of sound etc.*) раздава́ться (-даётся) *impf.*, разда́ться (-а́стся, -аду́тся; -а́лся, -ала́сь) *pf.*; (*of place etc.*) оглаша́ться *impf.*, огласи́ться *pf.* (**with** +*i.*).

resource [rɪ'sɔːs, -'zɔːs] *n.* (*usu. pl.*) ресу́рс, сре́дство; (*expedient*) сре́дство, возмо́жность; (*ingenuity*) нахо́дчивость. **resourceful** *adj.* нахо́дчивый.

respect [rɪ'spekt] *n.* (*relation*) отноше́ние; (*esteem*) уваже́ние; **in ~ of, with ~ to** что каса́ется+*g.*, в отноше́нии+*g.*; *v.t.* уважа́ть *impf.*; почита́ть *impf.* **respecta'bility** *n.* почте́нность, респекта́бельность. **respectable** *adj.* почте́нный (-нен, -нна), респекта́бельный. **respectful** *adj.* почти́тельный. **respective** *adj.* соотве́тственный (-ен, -енна). **respectively** *adv.* соотве́тственно.

respiration [ˌrespɪ'reɪʃ(ə)n] *n.* дыха́ние; **artificial ~** иску́сственное дыха́ние. **'respirator** *n.* респира́тор.

respite ['respaɪt, -pɪt] *n.* переды́шка.

resplendent [rɪ'splend(ə)nt] *adj.* блестя́щий; сверка́ющий.

respond [rɪ'spɒnd] *v.i.*: ~ **to** отзыва́ться *impf.*, отозва́ться (отзову́сь, -вёшься; отозва́лся, -ала́сь, -а́ло́сь) *pf.* на+*a.*; реаги́ровать *impf.*, про~, от~ *pf.* на+*a.* **respondent** *n.* отве́тчик, -ица. **response** *n.* отве́т; о́тклик. **responsi'bility** *n.* отве́тственность, обя́занность. **responsible** *adj.* отве́тственный (-ен, -енна) (**to** перед+*i.*; **for** за+*a.*). **responsive** *adj.* отзы́вчивый.

rest¹ [rest] *v.i.* отдыха́ть *impf.*, отдохну́ть *pf.*; поко́иться *impf.* (**upon** на+*p.*); *v.t.* (*place*) класть (-аду́, -адёшь) *impf.*, положи́ть (-жу́, -жишь) *pf.*; (*allow to* ~) дава́ть (даю́, даёшь) *impf.*, дать (дам, дашь, даст, дади́м; дал, -а́, да́ло́, -и) *pf.* о́тдых+*d.*; *n.* (*repose*) о́тдых; (*peace*) поко́й; (*mus.*) па́уза; (*support*) опо́ра, подста́вка.

rest² [rest] *n.* (*the remainder*) оста́ток (-тка), остально́е *sb.*; (*the others*) остальны́е *sb.*, други́е *sb.*; **for the** ~ что каса́ется остально́го, что до остально́го.

restaurant ['restə,rɒnt, -,rɔ̃] *n.* рестора́н.

restful ['restfʊl] *adj.* споко́йный, ти́хий (тих, -а́, -о); (*soothing*) успока́ивающий.

restitution [,restɪ'tju:ʃ(ə)n] *n.* (*restoring*) возвраще́ние; (*reparation*) возмеще́ние убы́тков.

restive ['restɪv] *adj.* (*horse*) норови́стый; (*person*; *restless*) беспоко́йный; (*wilful*) своенра́вный.

restless ['restlɪs] *adj.* беспоко́йный; (*uneasy*) неспоко́йный, трево́жный.

restoration [,restə'reɪʃ(ə)n] *n.* реставра́ция, восстановле́ние. **restore** [rɪ'stɔ:(r)] *v.t.* реставри́ровать *impf.* & *pf.*; восстана́вливать *impf.*, восстанови́ть (-влю́, -вишь) *pf.*

restrain [rɪ'streɪn] *v.t.* сде́рживать *impf.*, сдержа́ть (-жу́, -жишь) *pf.*; уде́рживать *impf.*, удержа́ть (-жу́, -жишь) *pf.* (**from** от+*g.*). **restraint** *n.* (*reserve*) сде́ржанность; (*restriction*) ограниче́ние; (*confinement*) заключе́ние; **without** ~ свобо́дно, без у́держу.

restrict [rɪ'strɪkt] *v.t.* ограни́чивать *impf.*, ограни́чить *pf.* **restriction** *n.* ограниче́ние. **restrictive** *adj.* ограничи́тельный.

result [rɪ'zʌlt] *v.i.* сле́довать *impf.*; происходи́ть (-ит) *impf.*, произойти́ (-ойдёт; -ошёл, -ошла́) *pf.* в результа́те; ~ **in** конча́ться *impf.*, ко́нчиться *pf.*+*i.*; *n.* результа́т.

resume [rɪ'zju:m] *v.t.* возобновля́ть *impf.*, возобнови́ть *pf.* **résumé** ['rezjʊ,meɪ] *n.* резюме́ *nt.indecl.* **resumption** [rɪ'zʌmpʃ(ə)n] *n.* возобновле́ние.

resurrect [,rezə'rekt] *v.t.* воскреша́ть *impf.*, воскреси́ть *pf.* **resurrection** *n.* (*of the dead*) воскресе́ние; (*to memory etc.*) воскреше́ние.

resuscitate [rɪ'sʌsɪ,teɪt] *v.t.* приводи́ть (-ожу́, -о́дишь) *impf.*, привести́ (-еду́, -едёшь; -ёл, -ела́) *pf.* в созна́ние.

retail ['ri:teɪl] *n.* ро́зничная прода́жа; *attr.* ро́зничный; *adv.* в ро́зницу; *v.t.* продава́ть (-даю́, -даёшь) *impf.*, прода́ть (-а́м, -а́шь, -а́ст, -ади́м; про́дал, -а́, -о) *pf.* в ро́зницу; *v.i.* продава́ться (-даётся) *impf.* в ро́зницу. **retailer** *n.* ро́зничный торго́вец (-вца).

retain [rɪ'teɪn] *v.t.* уде́рживать *impf.*, удержа́ть (-жу́, -жишь) *pf.*; (*preserve*) сохраня́ть *impf.*, сохрани́ть *pf.*

retaliate [rɪ'tælɪ,eɪt] *v.i.* отпла́чивать *impf.*, отплати́ть (-ачу́, -а́тишь) *pf.* тем же (са́мым); (*make reprisals*) применя́ть *impf.*, примени́ть (-ню́, -нишь) *pf.* репресса́лии. **retali'ation** *n.* отпла́та, возме́здие.

retard [rɪ'tɑ:d] *v.t.* замедля́ть *impf.*, заме́длить *pf.* **retarded** *adj.* отста́лый.

retch [retʃ, ri:tʃ] *v.i.* рвать (рвёт; рва́ло) *impf.* *impers.*+*a.*

retention [rɪ'tenʃ(ə)n] *n.* удержа́ние; (*preservation*) сохране́ние. **retentive** *adj.* уде́рживающий; (*memory*) хоро́ший.

reticence ['retɪs(ə)ns] *n.* (*restraint*) сде́ржанность; (*secretiveness*) скры́тность. **reticent** *adj.* сде́ржанный (-ан, -анна); скры́тный.

reticulated [rɪ'tɪkjʊleɪtɪd] *adj.* се́тчатый. **retic-u'lation** *n.* се́тчатый узо́р, се́тчатое строе́ние.

retina ['retɪnə] *n.* сетча́тка.

retinue ['retɪ,nju:] *n.* сви́та.

retire [rɪ'taɪə(r)] *v.i.* (*withdraw*) уединя́ться *impf.*, уедини́ться *pf.*; (*from office etc.*) уходи́ть (-ожу́, -о́дишь) *impf.*, уйти́ (уйду́, -дёшь; ушёл, ушла́) *pf.* в отста́вку. **retired** *adj.* отставно́й, в отста́вке. **retirement** *n.* отста́вка; ~ **age** пенсио́нный во́зраст. **retiring** *adj.* скро́мный (-мен, -мна́, -мно).

retort¹ [rɪ'tɔ:t] *v.t.* отвеча́ть *impf.*, отве́тить *pf.* тем же (**on** на+*a.*); *v.i.* возража́ть *impf.*, возрази́ть *pf.*; *n.* возраже́ние; (*reply*) нахо́дчивый отве́т, остроу́мная ре́плика.

retort² [rɪ'tɔ:t] *n.* (*vessel*) рето́рта.

retouch [ri:'tʌtʃ] *v.t.* ретуши́ровать *impf.* & *pf.*, от~ *pf.*

retrace [rɪ'treɪs] *v.t.*: ~ **one's steps** возвраща́ться *impf.*, возврати́ться (-ащу́сь, -ати́шься) *pf.*

retract [rɪ'trækt] *v.t.* (*draw in*) втя́гивать *impf.*, втяну́ть (-яну́, -я́нешь) *pf.*; (*take back*) брать (беру́, -рёшь; брал, -а́, -о) *impf.*, взять (возьму́, -мёшь; взял, -а́, -о) *pf.* наза́д.

retread [ri:'tred; 'ri:tred] *v.t.* (*tyre*) возобновля́ть *impf.*, возобнови́ть *pf.* проте́ктор+*g.*; *n.* ши́на с возобновлённым проте́ктором.

retreat [rɪ'tri:t] *v.i.* отступа́ть *impf.*, отступи́ть (-плю́, -пишь) *pf.*; *n.* отступле́ние; (*signal*) отбо́й; (*withdrawal*) уедине́ние; (*refuge*) убе́жище.

retrench [rɪ'trentʃ] *v.t.* & *i.* сокраща́ть *impf.*, сократи́ть (-ащу́, -ати́шь) *pf.* (расхо́ды). **retrenchment** *n.* сокраще́ние расхо́дов.

retribution [,retrɪ'bju:ʃ(ə)n] *n.* возме́здие, ка́ра.

retrieval [rɪ'tri:vəl] *n.* (*recovery*) восстановле́ние; (*comput.*) по́иск (информа́ции); (*repair*) исправле́ние; *v.t.* восстана́вливать *impf.*, восстанови́ть (-влю́, -вишь) *pf.*; (*repair*) исправля́ть *impf.*, испра́вить *pf.*

retroactive [,retrəʊ'æktɪv] *adj.* (*leg.*) име́ющий обра́тную си́лу. **'retrograde** *adj.* ретрогра́дный. **retrogress** *v.i.* дви́гаться (-аюсь, -аешься & дви́жусь, -жешься) *impf.* наза́д; регресси́ровать *impf.* **'retrorocket** *n.* ретрораке́та. **'retrospect** *n.* ретроспекти́вный взгляд; **in ~** ретроспекти́вно. **retrospective** *adj.* обращённый (-ён, -ена́) в про́шлое, ретроспекти́вный; (*leg.*) име́ющий обра́тную си́лу.

return [rɪ'tɜːn] *v.t. & i.* (*give back; come back*) возвраща́ть(ся) *impf.*, возврати́ть(ся) (-ащу́(сь), -ати́шь(ся)) *impf.*, верну́ть(ся) *pf.*; *v.t.* (*reply to*) отвеча́ть *impf.*, отве́тить *pf.* на+*a.*; (*elect*) избира́ть *impf.*, избра́ть (изберу́, -рёшь; избра́л, -а́, -о) *pf.*; *n.* возвраще́ние; возвра́т; (*proceeds*) при́быль; **by ~** обра́тной по́чтой; **in ~** взаме́н (**for** +*g.*); **~ match** отве́тный матч; **~ ticket** обра́тный биле́т.

reunion [riː'juːnjən, -nɪən] *n.* встре́ча (друзе́й и т. п.); **family ~** сбор всей семьи́. **reunite** [ˌriːjuː'naɪt] *v.t.* воссоединя́ть *impf.*, воссоедини́ть *pf.*

rev [rev] *n.* оборо́т; *v.t. & i.*: **~ up** ускоря́ть *impf.*, уско́рить *pf.* (дви́гатель *m.*).

revanchism [rɪ'væntʃɪs(ə)m] *n.* реванши́зм. **revanchist** *n.* реванши́ст.

reveal [rɪ'viːl] *v.t.* обнару́живать *impf.*, обнару́жить *pf.*; раскрыва́ть *impf.*, раскры́ть (-ро́ю, -ро́ешь) *pf.*

reveille [rɪ'vælɪ, rɪ'velɪ] *n.* подъём.

revel ['rev(ə)l] *v.i.* пирова́ть *impf.*; **~ in** наслажда́ться *impf.*+*i.*

revelation [ˌrevə'leɪʃ(ə)n] *n.* открове́ние; откры́тие; **R~** (*eccl.*) апокали́псис.

revenge [rɪ'vendʒ] *v.t.*: **~ o.s.** мстить *impf.*, ото~ *pf.* (**for** за+*a.*; **on** +*d.*); *n.* месть, мще́ние. **revengeful** *adj.* мсти́тельный.

revenue ['revəˌnjuː] *n.* дохо́д; *adj.* тамо́женный.

reverberate [rɪ'vɜːbəˌreɪt] *v.i. & i.* отража́ть(ся) *impf.* **reverbe'ration** *n.* отраже́ние; (*fig.*) о́тзвук.

revere [rɪ'vɪə(r)] *v.t.* почита́ть *impf.*, глубоко́ уважа́ть *impf.* **reverence** ['revərəns] *n.* благогове́ние; почте́ние. **'reverend** *adj.*(*in title*) (его́) преподо́бие. **reve'rential** *adj.* благогове́йный.

reverie ['revərɪ] *n.* мечты́ (*g.* -та́ний) *f.pl.*

reversal [rɪ'vɜːsəl] *n.* по́лное измене́ние; (*of decision*) отме́на. **reverse** *adj.* обра́тный; **~ gear** за́дний ход; *v.t.* изменя́ть *impf.*, измени́ть (-ню́, -нишь) *pf.* на обра́тный; (*revoke*) отменя́ть *impf.*, отмени́ть (-ню́, -нишь) *pf.*; *v.i.* дава́ть (даю́, даёшь) *impf.*, да́ть (дам, дашь, даст, дади́м; дал, -а́, да́ло́, -и) *pf.* за́дний ход; *n.* (*the ~*) обра́тное *sb.*, противополо́жное *sb.*; (*~ gear*) за́дний ход; (*~ side*) обра́тная сторона́ (*a.* -ону, *pl.* -оны, -о́н, -она́м); (*misfortune*) неуда́ча; (*defeat*) пораже́ние. **reversible** *adj.* обрати́мый; (*cloth*) двусторо́нний. **reversion** *n.* возвраще́ние, реве́рсия. **revert** *v.i.* возвраща́ться (-ащу́сь, -ати́шься) *impf.* (**to** в+*a.*, к+*d.*); (*leg.*) переходи́ть (-ит) *impf.*, перейти́ (-йдёт; -ешёл, -ешла́) *pf.* к пре́жнему владе́льцу.

review [rɪ'vjuː] *n.* (*leg.*) пересмо́тр; (*mil.*) смотр, пара́д; (*survey*) обзо́р, обозре́ние; (*criticism*) реце́нзия; (*periodical*) журна́л; *v.t.* (*leg.*) пересма́тривать *impf.*, пересмотре́ть (-рю́, -ришь) *pf.*; (*survey*) обозрева́ть *impf.*, обозре́ть (-рю́, -ри́шь) *pf.*; (*of troops etc.*) принима́ть *impf.*, приня́ть (приму́, -мешь; при́нял, -а́, -о) *pf.* пара́д+*g.*; (*book etc.*) рецензи́ровать *impf.*, про~ *pf.* **reviewer** *n.* рецензе́нт.

revise [rɪ'vaɪz] *v.t.* пересма́тривать *impf.*, пересмотре́ть (-рю́, -ришь) *pf.*; исправля́ть *impf.*, испра́вить *pf.*; *n.* втора́я корректу́ра. **revision** [rɪ'vɪʒ(ə)n] *n.* пересмо́тр, исправле́ние.

revival [rɪ'vaɪv(ə)l] *n.* возрожде́ние; (*to life etc.*) оживле́ние. **revive** *v.t.* возрожда́ть *impf.*, возроди́ть *pf.*; оживля́ть *impf.*, оживи́ть *pf.*; *v.i.* ожива́ть *impf.*, ожи́ть (оживу́, -вёшь; о́жил, -а́, -о) *pf.*

revocation [ˌrevə'keɪʃ(ə)n] *n.* отме́на. **revoke** [rɪ'vəʊk] *v.t.* отменя́ть *impf.*, отмени́ть (-ню́, -нишь) *pf.*; *v.i.* (*cards*) объявля́ть *impf.*, объяви́ть (-влю́, -вишь) *pf.* рено́нс.

revolt [rɪ'vəʊlt] *n.* бунт, мяте́ж (-а́); *v.t.* вызыва́ть *impf.*, вы́звать (вы́зову, -вешь) *pf.* отвраще́ние у+*g.*; *v.i.* бунтова́ть *impf.*, взбунтова́ться *pf.* **revolting** *adj.* отврати́тельный.

revolution [ˌrevə'luːʃ(ə)n] *n.* (*motion*) враще́ние; (*single turn*) оборо́т; (*pol. etc.*) револю́ция. **revolutionary** *adj.* революцио́нный; *n.* революционе́р. **revolutionize** *v.t.* революционизи́ровать *impf.* & *pf.* **revolve** [rɪ'vɒlv] *v.t. & i.* враща́ть(ся) *impf.* **revolver** *n.* револьве́р.

revue [rɪ'vjuː] *n.* ревю́ *nt.indecl.*

revulsion [rɪ'vʌlʃ(ə)n] *n.* (*change*) внеза́пное ре́зкое измене́ние; (*dislike*) отвраще́ние.

reward [rɪ'wɔːd] *n.* награ́да, вознагражде́ние; *v.t.* (воз)награжда́ть *impf.*, (воз)награди́ть *pf.*

rewrite [riː'raɪt] *v.t.* (*recast*) переде́лывать *impf.*, переде́лать *pf.*

rhapsodize ['ræpsəˌdaɪz] *v.i.*: **~ over** восторга́ться *impf.*+*i.* **rhapsody** *n.* (*mus.*) рапсо́дия; *pl.* восхище́ние.

rhesus ['riːsəs] *n.* ре́зус; *in comb.* ре́зус-.

rhetoric ['retərɪk] *n.* рито́рика. **rhetorical** [rɪ'tɒrɪk(ə)l] *adj.* ритори́ческий.

rheumatic [ruː'mætɪk] *adj.* ревмати́ческий. **rheumatism** ['ruːməˌtɪz(ə)m] *n.* ревмати́зм. **'rheumatoid** *adj.* ревмато́идный.

Rhine [raɪn] *n.* Рейн.

rhinestone ['raɪnstəʊn] *n.* иску́сственный бриллиа́нт.

rhino ['raɪnəʊ], **rhinoceros** [raɪ'nɒsərəs] *n.* носоро́г.

rhizome ['raɪzəʊm] *n.* ризо́ма, корневи́ще.

rhododendron [ˌrəʊdə'dendrən] *n.* рододе́ндрон.

rhomb [rɒmb] *n.* ромб. **rhombic** *adj.* ромби́ческий. **rhomboid** *n.* ромбо́ид. **rhombus** *n.* ромб.

Rhone [rəʊn] *n.* Ро́на.

rhubarb ['ruːbɑːb] *n.* реве́нь (-ня́) *m.*

rhyme [raɪm] *n.* ри́фма; *pl.* (*verse*) рифмо́ванные стихи́ *m.pl.*; *v.t.* рифмова́ть *impf.*, с~ *pf.*; *v.i.* рифмова́ться *impf.*

rhythm ['rɪð(ə)m] *n.* ритм, ритми́чность. **rhythmic(al)** *adj.* ритми́ческий, -чный.

rib [rɪb] *n.* ребро́ (*pl.* рёбра, -бер, -брам); (*of umbrella*) спи́ца; (*knitting etc.*) ру́бчик; (*of leaf*) жи́лка; (*of ship*) шпанго́ут (*also collect.*).

ribald ['rɪb(ə)ld] *adj.* непристо́йный.

ribbon ['rɪbən] *n.* ле́нта; *pl.* (*reins*) во́жжи (-же́й) *pl.*; *pl.* (*shreds*) кло́чья (-ьев) *m.pl.*; ~ **development** ле́нточная застро́йка.

riboflavin [ˌraɪbəʊ'fleɪvɪn] *n.* рибофлави́н.

ribonucleic [ˌraɪbənjuː'kliːɪk] *adj.* рибонуклеи́новый.

rice [raɪs] *n.* рис; *attr.* ри́совый.

rich [rɪtʃ] *adj.* бога́тый; (*soil*) ту́чный (-чен, -чна́, -чно); (*food*) жи́рный (-рен, -рна́, -рно); (*amusing*) заба́вный. **riches** *n.* бога́тство. **richly** *adv.* (*fully*) вполне́.

rick[1] [rɪk] *n.* стог (*loc.* -е & -у́; *pl.* -а́), скирд(а́) (-а́ & -ы́; *pl.* ски́рды́, -д(о́в), -да́м).

rick[2] [rɪk] *v.t.* растя́гивать *impf.*, растяну́ть (-ну́, -нешь) *pf.*

rickets ['rɪkɪts] *n.* рахи́т. **rickety** *adj.* рахити́чный; (*shaky*) расша́танный.

rickshaw ['rɪkʃɔː] *n.* ри́кша.

ricochet ['rɪkəˌʃeɪ, -ˌʃet] *n.* рикоше́т; *v.i.* рикошети́ровать *impf.* & *pf.*

rid [rɪd] *v.t.* освобожда́ть *impf.*, освободи́ть *pf.* (**of** от+*g.*); **get** ~ **of** избавля́ться *impf.*, изба́виться *pf.* от+*g.* **riddance** *n.*: **good** ~! ска́тертью доро́га!

riddle[1] ['rɪd(ə)l] *n.* (*enigma*) зага́дка.

riddle[2] ['rɪd(ə)l] *n.* (*sieve*) гро́хот; *v.t.* (*sift*) грохоти́ть *impf.*, про~ *pf.*; (*with bullets etc.*) изреше́чивать *impf.*, изрешети́ть *pf.*

ride [raɪd] *v.i.* е́здить *indet.*, е́хать (е́ду, е́дешь) *det.*, по~ *pf.* (*on horseback*, верхо́м); (*lie at anchor*) стоя́ть (-ои́т) *impf.* на я́коре; *v.t.* е́здить *indet.*, е́хать (е́ду, е́дешь) *det.*, по~ *pf.* в, на+*p.*; *n.* пое́здка, езда́. **rider** *n.* вса́дник, -ица; (*clause*) дополне́ние.

ridge [rɪdʒ] *n.* хребе́т (-бта́), гре́бень (-бня) *m.*; (*of roof*) конёк (-нька́). **ridge-pole** *n.* (*of tent*) растя́жка. **ridge-tile** *n.* конько́вая черепи́ца.

ridicule ['rɪdɪˌkjuːl] *n.* насме́шка; *v.t.* осме́ивать *impf.*, осмея́ть (-ею́, -еёшь) *pf.* **ri'diculous** *adj.* неле́пый, смешно́й (-шо́н, -шна́).

riding[1] ['raɪdɪŋ] *n.* (*division of county*) ра́йдинг.

riding[2] ['raɪdɪŋ] *n.* (*horse-*~) (верхова́я) езда́; ~ **habit** амазо́нка. **riding-light** *n.* я́корный ого́нь (огня́) *m.*

Riesling ['riːzlɪŋ, -slɪŋ] *n.* ри́слинг (-а(у)).

rife [raɪf] *pred.* широко́ распространён (-а́), обы́чен (-чна); **be** ~ **with** изоби́ловать *impf.*+*i.*

riff-raff ['rɪfræf] *n.* подо́нки (-ков) *pl.*

rifle ['raɪf(ə)l] *v.t.* (*search*) обы́скивать *impf.*, обыска́ть (-ыщу́, -ы́щешь) *pf.*; (*a gun*) нареза́ть *impf.*, наре́зать (-е́жу, -е́жешь) *pf.*; *n.* винто́вка; *pl.* стрелки́ *m.pl.* **rifle-range** *n.* стре́льбище.

rift [rɪft] *n.* тре́щина; (*dispute*) разры́в.

rig [rɪg] *v.t.* оснаща́ть *impf.*, оснасти́ть *pf.*; ~ **out** наряжа́ть *impf.*, наряди́ть (-яжу́, -я́дишь) *pf.*; ~ **up** стро́ить *impf.*, по~ *pf.* из чего́ попа́ло; *n.* бурова́я устано́вка.

Riga ['riːgə] *n.* Ри́га.

rigging ['rɪgɪŋ] *n.* такела́ж.

right [raɪt] *adj.* (*position*; *justified*; *pol.*) пра́вый (прав, -а́, -о); (*correct*) пра́вильный; (*appropriate*) ну́жный (-жен, -жна́, -жно, -жны́); (*suitable*) подходя́щий; **in one's** ~ **mind** в здра́вом уме́; ~ **angle** прямо́й у́гол (угла́); ~ **side** (*of cloth*) лицева́я сторона́ (*a.* -ону); *v.t.* исправля́ть *impf.*, испра́вить *pf.*; *n.* пра́во (*pl.* -ва́); (~ *side*) пра́вая сторона́ (*a.* -ону); (**R**~; *pol.*) пра́вые *sb.*; **be in the** ~ быть (*fut.* бу́ду, -дешь; был, -а́, -о; не был, -а́, -о) пра́вым; **by** ~ **of** по пра́ву+*g.*; **by** ~**s** по пра́ву, по справедли́вости; **reserve the** ~ оставля́ть *impf.*, оста́вить *pf.* за собо́й пра́во; **set to** ~**s** приводи́ть (-ожу́, -о́дишь) *impf.*, привести́ (-еду́, -едёшь; -ёл, -ела́) *pf.* в поря́док; ~ **of way** пра́во прохо́да, прое́зда; *adv.* (*straight*) пря́мо; (*exactly*) то́чно, как раз; (*to the full*) соверше́нно; (*correctly*) пра́вильно; как сле́дует; (*on the* ~) спра́во (**of** от+*g.*); (*to the* ~) напра́во.

righteous ['raɪtʃəs] *adj.* (*person*) пра́ведный; (*action*) справедли́вый.

rightful ['raɪtfʊl] *adj.* зако́нный.

rigid ['rɪdʒɪd] *adj.* жёсткий (-ток, -тка́, -тко), негну́щийся; (*strict*) стро́гий (-г, -га́, -го). **ri'gidity** *n.* жёсткость; стро́гость.

rigmarole ['rɪgməˌrəʊl] *n.* бессмы́сленная, несвя́зная болтовня́.

rigor mortis [ˌrɪgə 'mɔːtɪs] *n.* тру́пное окочене́ние.

rigorous ['rɪgərəs] *adj.* стро́гий (-г, -га́, -го), суро́вый. **rigour** *n.* стро́гость, суро́вость.

rill [rɪl] *n.* ручеёк (-ейка́).

rim [rɪm] *n.* (*of wheel*) обод (*pl.* обо́дья, -ьев); (*spectacles*) опра́ва. **rimless** *adj.* без опра́вы.

rind [raɪnd] *n.* кожура́, ко́рка.

ring[1] [rɪŋ] *n.* кольцо́ (*pl.* -льца, -ле́ц, -льцам); (*circle*) круг (*loc.* -у́; *pl.* -и́); (*boxing*) ринг; (*circus*) (циркова́я) аре́на; ~ **finger** безымя́нный па́лец (-льца); ~ **road** кольцева́я доро́га; *v.t.* (*encircle*) окружа́ть *impf.*, окружи́ть *pf.* (кольцо́м).

ring[2] [rɪŋ] *v.i.* (*sound*) звене́ть (-ни́т) *impf.*, про~ *pf.*; звони́ть *impf.*, по~ *pf.*; (*of shot etc.*) раздава́ться (-даётся) *impf.*, разда́ться (-а́стся, -аду́тся; а́лся, -ала́сь) *pf.*; (*of place*) оглаша́ться *impf.*, огласи́ться *pf.* (**with** +*i.*); *v.t.* звони́ть *impf.*, по~ *pf.* в+*a.*; ~ **off** дава́ть (даю́, даёшь) *impf.*, дать (дам, дашь, даст, дади́м; дал, -а́, да́ло́, -и) *pf.* отбо́й; ~ **up** звони́ть *impf.*, по~ *pf.*+*d.*; *n.* звон, звоно́к (-нка́).

ring-dove ['rɪŋdʌv] *n.* вя́хирь *m.*

ringleader ['rɪŋ,li:də(r)] *n.* глава́рь (-ря́) *m.*, зачи́нщик.

ringlet ['rɪŋlɪt] *n.* (*of hair*) ло́кон.

ringmaster ['rɪŋ,mɑ:stə(r)] *n.* инспе́ктор (*pl.* -а́ & -ы) мане́жа.

ringworm ['rɪŋwɜ:m] *n.* стригу́щий лиша́й (-ая́).

rink [rɪŋk] *n.* като́к (-тка́).

rinse [rɪns] *v.t.* полоска́ть (-ощу́, -о́щешь) *impf.*, вы́~, про~ *pf.*; *n.* полоска́ние; (*for hair*) кра́ска для воло́с.

riot ['raɪət] *n.* бунт; **run** ~ бу́йствовать *impf.*; переступа́ть *impf.*, переступи́ть (-плю́, -пишь) *pf.* все грани́цы; (*of plants*) бу́йно разраста́ться *impf.*, разрасти́сь (-тётся; разро́сся, -сла́сь) *pf.*; *v.i.* бунтова́ть *impf.*, взбунтова́ться *pf.* **riotous** *adj.* бу́йный (бу́ен, буйна́, -но).

RIP *abbr.* (*of* **rest in peace**) мир пра́ху (*кого*).

rip [rɪp] *v.t.* & *i.* рва́ть(ся) (рву, рвёт(ся); -а́л(ся), -ала́(сь), -а́ло/а́ло́сь) *impf.*; поро́ть(ся) (-рю́, -рет(ся)) *impf.*; *v.t.* (*tear up*) разрыва́ть *impf.*, разорва́ть (-ву́, -вёшь; разорва́л, -а́, -о) *pf.*; *v.i.* (*rush*) мча́ться (мчи́тся) *impf.*; *n.* проре́ха, разре́з. **rip-cord** *n.* вытяжно́й трос.

ripe [raɪp] *adj.* зре́лый (зрел, -а́, -о), спе́лый (спел, -а́, -о). **ripen** *v.t.* де́лать *impf.*, с~ *pf.* зре́лым; *v.i.* созрева́ть *impf.*, созре́ть *pf.* **ripeness** *n.* зре́лость.

ripple ['rɪp(ə)l] *n.* рябь; *v.t.* & *i.* покрыва́ть(ся) *impf.*, покры́ть(ся) (-ро́ет(ся)) *pf.* ря́бью.

rise [raɪz] *v.i.* поднима́ться *impf.*, подня́ться (-нимýсь, -ни́мешься; -ня́лся́, -няла́сь) *pf.*; повыша́ться *impf.*, повы́ситься *pf.*; (*get up*) встава́ть (-таю́, -таёшь) *impf.*, встать (-а́ну, -а́нешь) *pf.*; (*rebel*) восстава́ть (-таю́, -таёшь) *impf.*, восста́ть (-а́ну, -а́нешь) *pf.*; (*sun etc.*) в(о)сходи́ть (-ит) *impf.*, взойти́ (-йдёт; взошёл, -шла́) (*wind*) уси́ливаться *impf.*, уси́литься *pf.*; *n.* подъём, возвыше́ние; (*in pay*) приба́вка; (*of sun etc.*) восхо́д. **riser** *n.* (*of stairs*) по́дступень; **he is an early** ~ он ра́но встаёт. **rising** *n.* (*revolt*) восста́ние.

risk [rɪsk] *n.* риск; *v.t.* рискова́ть *impf.*, рискну́ть *pf.*+*i.* **risky** *adj.* риско́ванный (-ан, -анна).

risqué ['rɪskeɪ, -'keɪ] *adj.* непристо́йный.

rissole ['rɪsəʊl] *n.* котле́та.

rite [raɪt] *n.* обря́д. **ritual** ['rɪtjʊəl] *n.* ритуа́л; *adj.* ритуа́льный, обря́довый.

rival ['raɪv(ə)l] *n.* сопе́рник, -ица; конкуре́нт, ~ка; *adj.* сопе́рничающий; *v.t.* сопе́рничать *impf.* с+*i.*; конкури́ровать *impf.* с+*i.* **rivalry** *n.* сопе́рничество.

river ['rɪvə(r)] *n.* река́ (*a.* ре́ку́; *pl.* ре́ки, рек, ре́ка́м); *adj.* речно́й. **riverside** *n.* прибре́жная полоса́ (*a.* по́лосу́; *pl.* -осы, -о́с, -оса́м); *attr.* прибре́жный.

rivet ['rɪvɪt] *n.* заклёпка; *v.t.* клепа́ть *impf.*; за~, с~, клёпывать *impf.*, за~, с~, клепа́ть *pf.*; (*attention etc.*) прико́вывать *impf.*, прикова́ть (-кую́, -куёшь) *pf.* (**on** к+*d.*).

rivulet ['rɪvjʊlɪt] *n.* ре́чка, ручеёк (-ейка́).

RN *abbr.* (*of* ***Royal Navy***) англи́йский ВМФ (*вое́нно-морско́й флот*).

roach [rəʊtʃ] *n.* (*fish*) плотва́.

road [rəʊd] *n.* доро́га, путь (-ти́, -тём) *m.*; (*highway*) шоссе́ *nt.indecl.*; (*central part; carriageway*) мостова́я *sb.*; (*street*) у́лица; (*naut.*; *usu.pl.*) рейд; ~ **sense** чу́вство доро́ги; ~ **sign** доро́жный знак. **roadblock** *n.* загражде́ние на доро́ге. **road-hog** *n.* лиха́ч (-а́). **road-house** *n.* придоро́жный буфе́т, придоро́жная гости́ница. **road-map** *n.* а́тлас автомоби́льных доро́г. **roadman** *n.* доро́жный рабо́чий *sb.* **roadside** *n.* обо́чина; *attr.* придоро́жный. **roadstead** *n.* рейд. **roadway** *n.* мостова́я *sb.*

roam [rəʊm] *v.t.* & *i.* броди́ть (-ожу́, -о́дишь) *impf.* (по+*d.*); скита́ться *impf.* (по+*d.*).

roan [rəʊn] *adj.* ча́лый.

roar [rɔ:(r)] *n.* (*animal's*) рёв; (*other noise*) гро́хот, шум; *v.i.* реве́ть (-ву́, -вёшь) *impf.*; грохота́ть (-очу́, -о́чешь) *impf.*, про~ *pf.*

roast [rəʊst] *v.t.* & *i.* жа́рить(ся) *impf.*, за~, из~ *pf.*; *adj.* жа́реный; ~ **beef** ро́стбиф; *n.* жарко́е *sb.*, жа́реное *sb.*

rob [rɒb] *v.t.* гра́бить *impf.*, о~ *pf.*; красть (-аду́, -адёшь; -ал) *impf.*, у~ *pf.* у+*g.* (**of** +*a.*); (*deprive*) лиша́ть *impf.*, лиши́ть *pf.* (**of** +*g.*). **robber** *n.* граби́тель *m.* **robbery** *n.* грабёж (-а́).

robe [rəʊb] *n.* (*also pl.*) ма́нтия.

robin ['rɒbɪn] *n.* мали́новка.

robot ['rəʊbɒt] *n.* ро́бот. **ro'botics** *n.* робо(то)те́хника.

robust [rəʊ'bʌst] *adj.* здоро́вый (-в, -ва́), кре́пкий (-пок, -пка́, -пко).

rock[1] [rɒk] *n.* (*geol.*) (го́рная) поро́да; (*cliff etc.*) скала́ (*pl.* -лы); (*large stone*) большо́й ка́мень (-мня; -мни, -мне́й) *m.*; **on the** ~**s** на мели́; (*drink*) со льдом.

rock[2] [rɒk] *v.t.* & *i.* кача́ть(ся) *impf.*, качну́ть(ся) *pf.*; (*sway*) колеба́ть(ся) (-блю(сь), -блешь(ся)) *impf.*, по~ *pf.*; ~ **to sleep** укачивать *impf.*, укача́ть *pf.*; ~ **and roll** рок-н-ро́лл.

rock-bottom [,rɒk'bɒtəm] *adj.* са́мый ни́зкий. **rock-crystal** *n.* го́рный хруста́ль (-ля́) *m.* **'rockery** *n.* сад (*loc.* -у́; *pl.* -ы́) камне́й.

rocket ['rɒkɪt] *n.* раке́та. **rocketry** *n.* ракéтная те́хника.

rocking-chair ['rɒkɪŋ-,tʃeə(r)] *n.* (кре́сло-)кача́лка. **rocking-horse** *n.* конь-кача́лка.

rock-salt ['rɒksɔ:lt] *n.* ка́менная соль. **rocky** *adj.* скали́стый; (*unsteady*) неусто́йчивый.

rococo [rə'kəʊkəʊ] *n.* рококо́ *nt.indecl.*; в

сти́ле рококо́.

rod [rɒd] *n.* прут (-á; *pl.* -ья, -ьев); (*for caning*) ро́зга; (*tech.*) сте́ржень (-жня) *m.*; (*fishing*-~) у́дочка.

rodent ['rəʊd(ə)nt] *n.* грызу́н (-á).

rodeo ['rəʊdɪəʊ, rə'deɪəʊ] *n.* родéо *nt.indecl.*

roe[1] [rəʊ] *n.* (*hard*) икрá; (*soft*) моло́ки (-о́к) *pl.*

roe[2] **(-deer)** [rəʊ] *n.* косу́ля. **roebuck** *n.* саме́ц (-мцá) косу́ли.

rogue [rəʊg] *n.* плут (-á). **roguish** *adj.* плутовско́й; (*mischievous*) прокáзливый.

role [rəʊl] *n.* роль (*pl.* -ли, -ле́й).

roll[1] [rəʊl] *n.* (*cylinder*) руло́н; (*document*) свито́к (-тка); (*register*) спи́сок (-ска), рее́стр; (*bread* ~) бу́лочка.

roll[2] [rəʊl] *v.t.* & *i.* катáть(ся) *indet.*, кати́ть(ся) (качу́(сь), ка́тишь(ся)) *det.*, по~ *pf.*; (~ *up*) свёртывать(ся) *impf.*, сверну́ть(ся) *pf.*; *v.t.* (*road*) укáтывать *impf.*, укатáть *pf.*; (*metal*) прокáтывать *impf.*, прокатáть *pf.*; (*dough*) раскáтывать *impf.*, раскатáть *pf.*; *v.i.* (*sound*) греме́ть (-мит) *impf.*; *n.* катáние; (*of thunder*) раскáт.

roll-call ['rəʊlkɔ:l] *n.* перекли́чка.

roller ['rəʊlə(r)] *n.* вáлик; (*wave*) вал (*loc.* -у́; *pl.* -ы́); *pl.* (*for hair*) бигуди́ *nt.indecl.*; ~ **bearing** ро́ликовый подши́пник; ~ **towel** полоте́нце на ро́лике. **roller-skate** *v.i.* катáться *impf.* на ро́ликах; **roller-skating rink** роликодро́м. **roller-skates** *n.* ро́лики *m.pl.*, коньки́ *m.pl.* на ро́ликах.

rollicking ['rɒlɪkɪŋ] *adj.* разухáбистый.

rolling ['rəʊlɪŋ] *adj.* (*of land*) холми́стый. **rolling-mill** *n.* прокáтный стан. **rolling-pin** *n.* скáлка. **rolling-stock** *n.* подвижно́й состáв.

ROM [rɒm] (*comput.*) *abbr.* (*of* ***read only memory***) ПЗУ, (постоя́нное запоминáющее устро́йство).

Roman ['rəʊmən] *n.* ри́млянин (*pl.* -яне, -ян), -янка; *adj.* ри́мский; ~ **alphabet** лати́нский алфави́т; ~ **Catholic** (*n.*) като́лик, -и́чка; (*adj.*) ри́мско-католи́ческий; ~ **type** прямо́й, све́тлый шрифт.

romance [rəʊ'mæns] *n.* (*tale*; *love affair*) ромáн; (*quality*) ромáнтика; (*mus.*) ромáнс; **R~ languages** ромáнские языки́ *m.pl.*

Romanesque [ˌrəʊmə'nesk] *adj.* ромáнский.

Romania [rəʊ'meɪnɪə] *n.* Румы́ния. **Romanian** *n.* румы́н (*g.pl.* -н), ~ка; *adj.* румы́нский.

romantic [rəʊ'mæntɪk] *adj.* романти́чный, -ческий. **romanticism** *n.* романти́зм.

Rome [rəʊm] *n.* Рим.

romp [rɒmp] *v.i.* вози́ться (вожу́сь, во́зишься) *impf.*; ~ **home** с лёгкостью вы́играть *pf.*

rondo ['rɒndəʊ] *n.* (*mus.*) ро́ндо *nt.indecl.*

rood [ru:d] *n.* распя́тие. **rood-loft** *n.* хо́ры (-р & -ров) *pl.* в це́ркви. **rood-screen** *n.* перегоро́дка в це́ркви.

roof [ru:f] *n.* кры́ша, кро́вля (*g.pl.* -вель); ~ **of the mouth** нёбо; *v.t.* крыть (кро́ю, -о́ешь) *impf.*, покрывáть *impf.*, покры́ть (-ро́ю, -ро́ешь) *pf.*

rook[1] [rʊk] *n.* (*chess*) ладья́.

rook[2] [rʊk] *n.* (*bird*) грач (-á). **rookery** *n.* грачо́вник.

room [ru:m, rʊm] *n.* (*in house*) ко́мната; *pl.* помеще́ние; (*space*) ме́сто; (*opportunity*) возмо́жность. **roomy** *adj.* просто́рный.

roost [ru:st] *n.* насе́ст.

root[1] [ru:t] *n.* (*var. senses*) ко́рень (-рня; *pl.* -рни, -рне́й) *m.*; (*mus.*) основно́й тон (акко́рда); (*plant*) корнепло́д; ~ **and branch** коренны́м о́бразом; *v.i.* пускáть *impf.*, пусти́ть (-ит) *pf.* ко́рни; ~ **to the spot** пригвождáть *impf.*, пригвозди́ть *pf.* к ме́сту.

root[2] [ru:t] *v.i.* (*rummage*) ры́ться (ро́юсь, ро́ешься) *impf.*

rootstock ['ru:tstɒk] *n.* корневи́ще.

rope [rəʊp] *n.* верёвка, канáт, трос; *v.t.* привя́зывать *impf.*, привязáть (-яжу́, -я́жешь) *pf.*; ~ **in, off** о(т)горáживать *impf.*, о(т)городи́ть (-ожу́, -о́ди́шь) *pf.* канáтом. **rope-dancer** *n.* канатохо́дец (-дца). **rope-ladder** *n.* верёвочная ле́стница.

rosary ['rəʊzərɪ] *n.* (*eccl.*) чётки (-ток) *pl.*

rose [rəʊz] *n.* ро́за; (*nozzle*) се́тка; *pl.* (*complexion*) румя́нец (-нца). **rosebud** *n.* буто́н ро́зы. **rose-coloured** *adj.* ро́зовый.

rosemary ['rəʊzmərɪ] *n.* розмари́н.

rosette [rəʊ'zet] *n.* розе́тка. **rose-water** *n.* ро́зовая водá (*a.* -ду). **rose-window** *n.* розе́тка. **'rosewood** *n.* ро́зовое де́рево.

rosin ['rɒzɪn] *n.* канифо́ль; *v.t.* натирáть *impf.*, натере́ть (-тру́, -трёшь; -тёр) *pf.* канифо́лью.

roster ['rɒstə(r), 'rəʊstə(r)] *n.* расписáние (наря́дов, дежу́рств).

rostrum ['rɒstrəm] *n.* трибу́на, кáфедра.

rosy ['rəʊzɪ] *adj.* ро́зовый; (*complexion*) румя́ный.

rot [rɒt] *n.* гниль; (*nonsense*) вздор; *v.i.* гнить (-ию́, -иёшь; гнил, -á, -о) *impf.*, с~ *pf.*; *v.t.* гнои́ть *impf.*, с~ *pf.*

rota ['rəʊtə] *n.* расписáние дежу́рств. **rotary** *adj.* вращáтельный, ротацио́нный. **ro'tate** *v.t.* & *i.* вращáть(ся) *impf.* **ro'tation** *n.* вращéние; **in** ~ по о́череди.

rote [rəʊt] *n.*: **by** ~ наизу́сть.

rotten ['rɒt(ə)n] *adj.* гнило́й (гнил, -á, -о). **rotter** *n.* дрянь.

rotund [rəʊ'tʌnd] *adj.* (*round*) кру́глый (-л, -лá, -ло, кру́глы́); (*plump*) по́лный (-лон, -лнá, по́лно́). **rotunda** *n.* рото́нда. **rotundity** *n.* округлённость, полнотá.

rouble ['ru:b(ə)l] *n.* рубль (-ля́) *m.*

rouge [ru:ʒ] *n.* румя́на (-н) *pl.*; *v.t.* & *i.* румя́нить(ся) *impf.*, на~ *pf.*

rough [rʌf] *adj.* (*uneven*) неро́вный (-вен, -внá, -вно); (*coarse*) гру́бый (груб, -á, -о); (*sea*) бу́рный (-рен, бу́рнá, -но); (*approximate*) приблизи́тельный; ~ **copy** чернови́к (-á); *n.* (~ *ground*) неро́вное по́ле; (*person*) хулигáн. **roughage** *n.* гру́бая пи́ща. **rough-**

and-ready *adj.* грубый но эффективный. **roughcast** *n.* галечная штукатурка. **roughly** *adv.* грубо; ~ **speaking** примерно.

roulette [ruːˈlet] *n.* рулетка.

round [raʊnd] *adj.* круглый (-л, -ла́, -ло, круглы́); (*plump*) полный (-лон, -лна́, по́лно́); ~ **dance** круговой танец; **in** ~ **figures** приблизительно; *n.* (~ *object*) круг (*loc.* -у́; *pl.* -и́); (*circuit*; *also pl.*) обход; (*sport*) тур, раунд; (*series*) ряд (*pl.* -ы́); (*ammunition*) патрон, снаряд; (*of applause*) взрыв; *adv.* вокруг; (*in a circle*) по кругу; **all** ~ кругом; **all the year** ~ круглый год; *prep.* вокруг+*g.*; кругом+*g.*; по+*d.*; ~ **the corner** (*motion*) за угол, (*position*) за углом; *v.t.* & *i.* округлять(ся) *impf.*, округлить(ся) *pf.*; *v.t.* (*pass* ~) огибать *impf.*, обогнуть *pf.*; ~ **off** (*complete*) завершать *impf.*, завершить *pf.*; ~ **up** сгонять *impf.*, согнать (сгоню́, -нишь; согнал, -а́, -о) *pf.* **roundabout** *n.* (*merry-go-round*) карусель; (*road junction*) кольцевая транспортная развязка; *adj.* окольный; **in a** ~ **way** окольным путём. **round-shouldered** *adj.* сутулый. **round-up** *n.* загон; (*police*) облава.

rouse [raʊz] *v.t.* будить (бужу́, бу́дишь) *impf.*, раз~ *pf.*; (*to action etc.*) побуждать *impf.*, побудить (-ужу́, -у́дишь) *pf.* (**to** к+*d.*). **rousing** *adj.* возбуждающий.

rout [raʊt] *n.* (*defeat*) разгром; (*flight*) беспорядочное бегство; *v.t.* обращать *impf.*, обратить (-ащу́, -ати́шь) *pf.* в бегство.

route [ruːt] *n.* маршрут, путь (-ти́, -тём) *m.*; ~ **march** походное движение; *v.t.* отправлять *impf.*, отправить *pf.* (по определённому маршруту).

routine [ruːˈtiːn] *n.* заведённый порядок (-дка), режим; (*pejor.*) рутина; *adj.* установленный; очередной.

rove [rəʊv] *v.i.* скитаться *impf.*; (*of thoughts etc.*) блуждать *impf.* **rover** *n.* скиталец (-льца).

row[1] [rəʊ] *n.* (*line*) ряд (-а́ *with 2,3,4*, *loc.* -у́; *pl.* -ы́).

row[2] [rəʊ] *v.i.* (*in boat*) грести (гребу́, -бёшь; грёб, -ла́) *impf.*; *v.t.* (*convey*) перевозить (-ожу́, -о́зишь) *impf.*, перевезти (-езу́, -езёшь; ёз, -езла́) *pf.* на лодке.

row[3] [raʊ] *n.* (*dispute*) ссора; (*brawl*) скандал; *v.i.* ссориться *impf.*, по~ *pf.*; скандалить *impf.*, на~ *pf.*

rowan [ˈrəʊən, ˈraʊ-] *n.* рябина.

rowdy [ˈraʊdɪ] *adj.* буйный (буен, буйна́, -но); *n.* буян.

rowlock [ˈrɒlək, ˈrʌlək] *n.* уключина.

royal [ˈrɔɪəl] *adj.* королевский, царский; (*majestic*) великолепный. **royalist** [ˈrɔɪəlɪst] *n.* роялист; *adj.* роялистский. **royalty** *n.* член, члены *pl.*, королевской семьи; (*author's fee*) авторский гонорар; (*patentee's fee*) отчисление владельцу патента.

RSVP *abbr.* (*of* ***répondez, s'il vous plaît***) будьте любезны ответить.

rub [rʌb] *v.t.* & *i.* тереть(ся) (тру(сь), трёшь(ся); тёр(ся)) *impf.*; *v.t.* (*polish*; *chafe*) натирать *impf.*, натереть (-тру́, -трёшь; -тёр) *pf.*; (~ *dry*) вытирать *impf.*, вытереть (-тру, -трешь; -тер) *pf.*; ~ **in, on** втирать *impf.*, втереть (вотру́, -рёшь; втёр) *pf.*; ~ **out** стирать *impf.*, стереть (сотру́, -рёшь; стёр) *pf.*; ~ **it in** растравлять *impf.*, растравить (-влю́, -вишь) *pf.* рану; ~ **one's hands** потирать *impf.* руки (**with** (*joy etc.*), от+*g.*); ~ **up the wrong way** гладить *impf.* против шерсти.

rubber[1] [ˈrʌbə(r)] *n.* (*cured*) резина; (*not cured*) каучук; (*eraser*, *also* ~ *band*) резинка, ластик; *attr.* резиновый.

rubber[2] [ˈrʌbə(r)] *n.* (*cards*) роббер.

rubberize [ˈrʌbəˌraɪz] *v.t.* прорезинивать *impf.*, прорезинить *pf.*

rubber-stamp [ˈrʌbəˌstæmp] *v.t.* (*fig.*) штамповать *impf.*

rubbish [ˈrʌbɪʃ] *n.* мусор, хлам; (*nonsense*) чепуха, вздор. **rubbishy** *adj.* дрянной (-нен, -нна́, -нно).

rubble [ˈrʌb(ə)l] *n.* бут.

rubella [ruːˈbelə] *n.* краснуха.

rubicund [ˈruːbɪˌkʌnd] *n.* румяный.

rubric [ˈruːbrɪk] *n.* рубрика.

ruby [ˈruːbɪ] *n.* рубин; *adj.* рубиновый.

ruche [ruːʃ] *n.* рюш.

ruck [rʌk] *v.t.* (~ *up*) мять (мну, мнёшь) *impf.*, из~ (изомну́, -нёшь), с~ (сомну́, -нёшь) *pf.*

rucksack [ˈrʌksæk, ˈrʊk-] *n.* рюкзак (-а́).

rudder [ˈrʌdə(r)] *n.* руль (-ля́) *m.*

ruddy [ˈrʌdɪ] *adj.* красный (-сен, -сна́, -сно); (*face*) невежливый; (*sl.*, *damnable*) проклятый.

rude [ruːd] *adj.* грубый (груб, -а́, -о); (*impolite also*) невежливый; ~ **awakening** глубокое разочарование; ~ **health** крепкое здоровье; ~ **shock** внезапный удар.

rudimentary [ˌruːdɪˈmentərɪ] *adj.* зачаточный, рудиментарный. **ˈrudiments** *n.* (*elements*) начатки (-ков) *pl.*; (*beginning*) зачатки *m.pl.*

rue[1] [ruː] *n.* (*plant*) рута.

rue[2] [ruː] *v.t.* сожалеть *impf.* о+*p.* **rueful** *adj.* печальный, унылый.

ruff[1] [rʌf] *n.* (*frill*) брыжи (-жей) *pl.*; (*of feathers, hair*) кольцо (*pl.* -льца, -лец, -льцам) (перьев, шерсти) вокруг шеи.

ruff[2] [rʌf] *v.t.* (*cards*) покрывать *impf.*, покрыть (-ро́ю, -ро́ешь) *pf.* козырем; *n.* покрытие козырем; козырь (*pl.* -ри, -ре́й) *m.*

ruffian [ˈrʌfɪən] *n.* головорез, хулиган. **ruffianly** *adj.* хулиганский.

ruffle [ˈrʌf(ə)l] *v.t.* (*hair*) ерошить *impf.*, взъ~ *pf.*; (*water*) рябить *impf.*; (*person*) раздражать *impf.*, раздражить *pf.*

rug [rʌg] *n.* (*mat*) коврик, ковёр (-вра́); (*wrap*) плед.

rugby (football) [ˈrʌgbɪ] *n.* регби *nt.indecl.*

rugged [ˈrʌgɪd] *adj.* (*uneven*) неровный (-вен, -вна́, -вно); (*rocky*) скалистый; (*rough*) грубый (груб, -á, -о).

ruin ['ru:ɪn] *n.* (*downfall*) гибель; (*destruction*) разорéние; *pl.* развáлины *f.pl.*, руины *f.pl.*; *v.t.* губить (-блю, -бишь) *impf.*, по~ *pf.*; разорять *impf.*, разорить *pf.* **ruinous** *adj.* губительный, разорительный; (*state*) разрýшенный (-ен).

rule [ru:l] *n.* прáвило; (*carpenter's*, *print*) линéйка; **as a ~** как прáвило, обычно; *v.t. & i.* прáвить *impf.* (+*i.*); (*make lines*) линовáть *impf.*, раз~ *pf.*; (*give decision*) постановлять *impf.*, постановить (-влю, -вишь) *pf.*; **~ out** исключáть *impf.*, исключить *pf.* **ruler** *n.* (*person*) правитель *m.*, ~ница; (*object*) линéйка. **ruling** *n.* (*of court etc.*) постановлéние.

rum[1] [rʌm] *n.* ром.

rum[2] [rʌm] *adj.* стрáнный (-нен, -ннá, -нно), чуднóй (-дён, -днá).

Rumanian *see* **Romanian**

rumba ['rʌmbə] *n.* рýмба.

rumble ['rʌmb(ə)l] *v.i.* громыхáть *impf.*; грохотáть (-óчет) *impf.*; *n.* громыхáние, грóхот.

ruminant ['ru:mɪnənt] *n.* жвáчное (живóтное) *sb.*; *adj.* жвáчный; (*contemplative*) задýмчивый. **ruminate** *v.i.* жевáть (жуёт) *impf.* жвáчку; (*fig.*) размышлять *impf.* (**over, on** о+*p.*). **rumi'nation** *n.* размышлéние.

rummage ['rʌmɪdʒ] *v.i.* рыться (рóюсь, рóешься) *impf.*

rumour ['ru:mə(r)] *n.* слух; *v.t.*: **it is ~ed that** хóдят слýхи (*pl.*), что.

rump [rʌmp] *n.* огýзок (-зка); **~ steak** ромштéкс.

rumple ['rʌmp(ə)l] *v.t.* мять (мну, мнёшь) *impf.*, из~ (изомнý, -нёшь), с~ (сомнý, -нёшь) *pf.*; (*hair*) ерóшить *impf.*, взъ~ *pf.*

run [rʌn] *v.i.* бéгать *indet.*, бежáть (бегý, бежишь) *det.*, по~ *pf.*; (*roll along*) катáться *indet.*, катиться (качýсь, кáтишься) *det.*, по~ *pf.*; (*work, of machines*) рабóтать *impf.*; (*ply, of bus etc.*) ходить (-ит) *indet.*, идти (идёт; шёл, шла) *det.*; (*compete in race*) учáствовать *impf.* (в бéге); (*seek election*) выставлять *impf.*, выставить *pf.* свою кандитатýру; (*be valid*) быть действительным; (*of play etc.*) идти (идёт; шёл, шла) *impf.*; (*spread rapidly*) быстро распространяться *impf.*, распространиться *pf.*; (*of ink, dye*) расплывáться *impf.*, расплыться (-ывётся; -ылся, -ылáсь) *pf.*; (*flow*) течь (течёт; тёк, -лá) *impf.*; (*of document*) гласить *impf.*; *v.t.* (*manage*; *operate a machine*) управлять *impf.*+*i.*; (*a business etc.*) вести (ведý, -дёшь; вёл, -á) *impf.*; **~ dry, low** иссякáть *impf.*, иссякнуть (-к) *pf.*; **~ errands** быть на посылках (**for** у+*g.*); **~ risks** рисковáть *impf.*; **~ to earth** (*fig.*) отыскáть (отыщý, -щешь) *pf.*; **~ across, into** (*meet*) встречáться *impf.*, встрéтиться *pf.* с+*i.*; **~ after** (*fig.*) ухáживать *impf.* за+*i.*; **~ away** (*flee*) убегáть *impf.*, убежáть (-егý, -ежишь) *pf.*; **~ down** (*knock down*) задавить (-влю, -вишь) *pf.*; (*disparage*) умалять *impf.*, умалить *pf.*; **be ~ down** (*of person*) переутомиться *pf.* (*in past tense*); **~ in** (*engine*) обкáтывать *impf.*, обкатáть *pf.*; **~ into** *see* **~ across; ~ out** кончáться *impf.*, кóнчиться *pf.*; **~ out of** истощáть *impf.*, истощить *pf.* свой запáс+*g.*; **~ over** (*glance over*) бéгло просмáтривать *impf.*, просмотрéть (-рю, -ришь) *pf.*; (*injure*) задавить (-влю, -вишь) *pf.*; **~ through** (*pierce*) прокáлывать *impf.*, проколóть (-лю, -лешь) *pf.*; (*money*) промáтывать *impf.*, промотáть *pf.*; (*glance over*) *see* **~ over; ~ to** (*reach*) достигáть *impf.*, достигнуть & достичь (-игну, -игнешь; -иг) *pf.*+*g.*; (*of money*) хватáть *impf.*, хватить (-ит) *pf. impers.*+*g.* на+*a.*; **the money won't ~ to a car** этих дéнег не хвáтит на машину; **~ up against** натáлкиваться *impf.*, натолкнýться *pf.* на+*a.*; бег; (*also distance covered*) пробéг; (*direction*) направлéние; (*course, motion*) ход, течéние; (*regular route*) маршрýт; (*mus.*) рулáда; (*bombing ~*) захóд на цель; **at a ~** бегóм; **~ on** большóй спрос на+*a.*; **common ~ of men** обыкновéнные люди (-дéй, -дям, -дьми) *pl.*; **in the long ~** в концé концóв. **run-down** *adj.* (*decayed*) захудáлый.

rung [rʌŋ] *n.* ступéнь, ступéнька.

runner ['rʌnə(r)] *n.* (*also tech.*) бегýн (-á); (*messenger*) посыльный *sb.*; (*of sledge*) пóлоз (*pl.* полóзья, -ьев); (*cloth*) дорóжка; (*stem*) стéлющийся побéг; **~ bean** фасóль. **runner-up** *n.* учáстник состязáния, занявший вторóе мéсто. **running** *n.* бег; (*of machine*) ход, рабóта; **be in the ~** имéть *impf.* шáнсы на выигрыш; **make the ~** задавáть (-даю, -даёшь) *impf.*, задáть (-áм, -áшь, -áсть, -адим; зáдал, -á, -о) *pf.* темп; *adj.* бегýщий; (*of ~*) беговóй; (*after pl.n., in succession*) подряд; **~ account** текýщий счёт; **~ commentary** (рáдио)репортáж; **~ title** колонтитул; **~ water** протóчная водá (*a.* -ду). **running-board** *n.* поднóжка. **runway** *n.* (*aeron.*) взлётно-посáдочная полосá (*a.* пóлосу; *pl.* -осы, -óс, -осáм).

rupee [ru:'pi:] *n.* рýпия.

rupture ['rʌptʃə(r)] *n.* разрыв; (*hernia*) грыжа.

rural ['rʊər(ə)l] *adj.* сéльский, деревéнский.

ruse [ru:z] *n.* хитрость, улóвка.

rush[1] [rʌʃ] *n.* (*plant*) (*also collect.*) камыш (-á), тростник (-á); (*bot.*) ситник.

rush[2] [rʌʃ] *v.t.* быстро проводить (-ожý, -óдишь) *impf.*, провести (-едý, -едёшь; -ёл, -елá) *pf.*; торопить (-плю, -пишь) *impf.*, по~ *pf.*; *v.i.* бросáться *impf.*, брóситься *pf.*; мчáться (мчусь, мчишься) *impf.*; *n.* стремительное движéние, порыв; (*influx*) наплыв; (*of blood etc.*) прилив; (*hurry*) спéшка; **~ job** аврáл. **rush-hour** *n.* часы *m.pl.* пик.

rusk [rʌsk] *n.* сухáрь (-ря) *m.*

russet ['rʌsɪt] *adj.* красновáто-коричневый.

Russia ['rʌʃə] *n.* Россия; **Holy ~** Святая Русь. **Russian** *n.* русский *sb.*; россиянин (*pl.* -яне, -ян), -янка; *adj.* русский; российский; **~ salad** винегрет.

rust [rʌst] *n.* ржавчина; *v.i.* ржаветь *impf.*, за~ *pf.*

rustic ['rʌstɪk] *adj.* деревенский; (*unpolished, uncouth*) неотёсанный (-ан, -анна); *n.* деревенский, сельский, житель *m.*, ~ница. **rusticate** *v.t.* (*univ.*) временно исключать *impf.*, исключить *pf.* из университета; жить (живу, -вёшь; жил, -а, -о) *impf.* в деревне.

rustle ['rʌs(ə)l] *n.* шелест, шорох, шуршание; *v.i.* шелестеть (-тишь) *impf.*; *v.t.* & *i.* шуршать (-шу, -шишь) *impf.* (+*i.*); *v.t.* (~ *cattle*) красть (-аду, -адёшь; -ал) *impf.*, у~ *pf.*

rust-proof ['rʌstpru:f] *adj.* нержавеющий. **rusty** *adj.* ржавый.

rut [rʌt] *n.* (*groove*) колея.

ruthless ['ru:θlɪs] *adj.* безжалостный.

rye [raɪ] *n.* рожь (ржи); *attr.* ржаной.

S

Sabbath ['sæbəθ] *n.* (*Jewish*) суббота; (*Christian*) воскресенье; (*witches'*) шабаш. **sabbatical** [sə'bætɪk(ə)l] *adj.*: **~ year** годичный отпуск.

sable ['seɪb(ə)l] *n.* (*animal*; *fur*) соболь (*pl.* (*animal*) -ли, -лей & (*fur*) -ля) *m.*; (*fur*) соболий мех (*loc.* -е & -у; *pl.* -а); *attr.* соболиный, соболий.

sabotage ['sæbə,tɑ:ʒ] *n.* саботаж, диверсия; *v.t.* саботировать *impf.* & *pf.* **sabo'teur** *n.* саботажник, диверсант.

sabre ['seɪbə(r)] *n.* сабля (*g.pl.* -бель), шашка. **sabre-rattling** *n.* бряцание оружием.

sac [sæk] *n.* мешочек (-чка).

saccharin ['sækərɪn] *n.* сахарин.

saccharine ['sækə,ri:n] *adj.* сахаристый.

sacerdotal [,sækə'dəʊt(ə)l] *adj.* священнический.

sachet ['sæʃeɪ] *n.* подушечка.

sack[1] [sæk] *v.t.* (*plunder*) разграбить *pf.*

sack[2] [sæk] *n.* куль (-ля) *m.*, мешок (-шка); **the ~** (*dismissal*) увольнение; *v.t.* увольнять *impf.*, уволить *pf.* **sacking** *n.* (*hessian*) мешковина.

sacrament ['sækrəmənt] *n.* таинство; (*Eucharist*) причастие. **sacred** ['seɪkrɪd] *adj.* священный (-ен, -енна), святой (свят, -а, -о). **sacrifice** ['sækrɪ,faɪs] *n.* жертва; *v.t.* жертвовать *impf.*, по~ *pf.*+*i.* **sacrificial** [,sækrɪ'fɪʃ(ə)l] *adj.* жертвенный. **sacrilege** ['sækrɪlɪdʒ] *n.* святотатство. **sacri'legious** *adj.* святотатственный. **sacristy** *n.* ризница. **sacrosanct** *adj.* священный (-ен, -енна).

sad [sæd] *adj.* печальный, грустный (-тен, -тна, -тно). **sadden** *v.t.* печалить *impf.*, о~ *pf.*

saddle ['sæd(ə)l] *n.* седло (*pl.* сёдла, -дел, -длам); *v.t.* седлать *impf.*, о~ *pf.*; (*burden*) обременять *impf.*, обременить *pf.* (**with** +*i.*). **saddler** *n.* седельник, шорник.

sadism ['seɪdɪz(ə)m] *n.* садизм. **sadist** *n.* садист. **sadistic** [sə'dɪstɪk] *adj.* садистский.

sadness ['sædnɪs] *n.* печаль, грусть.

s.a.e. *abbr.* (*of* ***stamped addressed envelope***) конверт с маркой и обратным адресом.

safari [sə'fɑ:rɪ] *n.* сафари *nt. indecl.*; **on ~** на охоте; **~ park** «сафари» зоопарк.

safe [seɪf] *n.* сейф, несгораемый шкаф (*loc.* -у; *pl.* -ы); *adj.* (*uninjured*) невредимый; (*out of danger*) в безопасности; (*secure*) безопасный; (*reliable*) надёжный; **~ and sound** цел (-а, -о) и невредим. **safeguard** *n.* предохранительная мера; *v.t.* предохранять *impf.*, предохранить *pf.* **safety** *n.* безопасность; **~ lamp** рудничная лампа; **~ pin** английская булавка; **~ razor** безопасная бритва. **safety-belt** *n.* предохранительный ремень (-мня) *m.* **safety-catch** *n.* предохранитель *m.* **safety-valve** *n.* предохранительный клапан; (*fig.*) отдушина.

saffron ['sæfrən] *n.* шафран; *adj.* шафранный, шафрановый.

sag [sæg] *v.i.* провисать *impf.*, провиснуть (-с) *pf.*; прогибаться *impf.*, прогнуться *pf.*; *n.* провес, прогиб.

saga ['sɑ:gə] *n.* сага.

sagacious [sə'geɪʃ(ə)s] *adj.* проницательный. **sagacity** [sə'gæsɪtɪ] *n.* проницательность.

sage[1] [seɪdʒ] *n.* (*herb*) шалфей.

sage[2] [seɪdʒ] *n.* (*person*) мудрец (-а); *adj.* мудрый (мудр, -а, -о).

sage-green [seɪdʒ'gri:n] *adj.* серовато-зелёный.

Sagittarius [,sædʒɪ'teərɪəs] *n.* Стрелец (-льца).

sago ['seɪgəʊ] *n.* саго *nt.indecl.*; (*palm*) саговая пальма.

Sahara [sə'hɑ:rə] *n.* Сахара.

sail [seɪl] *n.* парус (*pl.* -а); (*collect.*) паруса *m.pl.*; (*of windmill*) крыло (*pl.* -лья, -льев); *v.t.* (*a ship*) управлять *impf.*+*i.*; *v.i.* плавать *indet.*, плыть (плыву, -вёшь; плыл, -а, -о) *det.*; (*depart*) отплывать *impf.*, отплыть (-ыву, -ывёшь; -ыл, -ыла, -ыло) *pf.* **sailboard** *n.* доска под парусом. **sailboarder** *n.* виндсёрфингист. **sailboarding** *n.* виндсёрфинг. **sailcloth** *n.* парусина. **sailing** *n.* (*sport*) парусный спорт. **sailing-ship** *n.* парусное судно (*pl.* -да, -дов). **sailor** *n.* матрос, моряк (-а).

saint [seɪnt, sənt] *n.* святой *sb.* **saintly** *adj.* святой (свят, -а, -о), безгрешный.

St Petersburg [sənt' pi:təz,bɜ:g] *n.* Санкт-Петербург.

sake [seɪk] *n.*: **for the ~ of** ради+*g.*, для+*g.*

salacious [sə'leɪʃəs] *adj.* непристо́йный; (*lustful*) похотли́вый.

salad ['sæləd] *n.* сала́т, винегре́т; ~ **days** зелёная ю́ность; ~ **oil** расти́тельное, оли́вковое, ма́сло. **salad-dressing** *n.* припра́ва к сала́ту.

salamander ['sælə,mændə(r)] *n.* салама́ндра.

salami [sə'lɑːmɪ] *n.* саля́ми *f.indecl*

salaried ['sælərɪd] *adj.* получа́ющий жа́лованье. **salary** *n.* жа́лованье.

sale [seɪl] *n.* прода́жа; (*also amount sold*) сбыт (*no pl.*); (*at reduced price*) распрода́жа по сни́женным це́нам; **be for** ~ продава́ться (-даётся) *impf.* **saleable** *adj.* хо́дкий (-док, -дка́, -дко). **saleroom** *n.* аукцио́нный зал. **salesman** *n.* продаве́ц (-вца́). **saleswoman** *n.* продавщи́ца.

salient ['seɪlɪənt] *adj.* (*projecting*) выдаю́щийся, выступа́ющий; (*conspicuous*) заме́тный, я́ркий; *n.* вы́ступ.

saline ['seɪlaɪn] *n.* соляно́й.

saliva [sə'laɪvə] *n.* слюна́. **salivary** *adj.* слю́нный. **salivate** ['sælɪ,veɪt] *v.i.* выделя́ть *impf.*, вы́делить *pf.* слюну́. **sali'vation** *n.* слюноте́че́ние.

sallow ['sæləʊ] *adj.* желтова́тый.

sally ['sælɪ] *n.* вы́лазка; (*witticism*) острота́; *v.i.*: ~ **forth, out** отправля́ться *impf.*, отпра́виться *pf.*; ~ **out** (*mil.*) де́лать *impf.*, с~ *pf.* вы́лазку.

salmon ['sæmən] *n.* ло́со́сь *m.*, сёмга; (*cul.*) лососи́на, сёмга.

salon ['sælɒn, -lɔ̃] *n.* сало́н. **saloon** [sə'luːn] *n.* (*hall*) зал; (*on ship*) сало́н; (*rail.*) сало́н-ваго́н; (*bar*) бар; ~ **deck** па́луба пе́рвого кла́сса.

salt [sɔːlt, sɒlt] *n.* соль; ~ **lake** соляно́е о́зеро (*pl.* -ёра); ~ **mine** соляны́е ко́пи (-пей) *pl.*; ~ **water** морска́я вода́ (*a.* -ду); *adj.* солёный (со́лон, -а́, -о); (*preserved in salt also*) засо́ленный (-ен); *v.t.* соли́ть (солю́, со́ли́шь) *impf.*, по~ *pf.*; заса́ливать *impf.*, засоли́ть (-олю́, -о́ли́шь) *pf.*; ~ **away** припря́тывать *impf.*, припря́тать (-я́чу, -я́чешь) *pf.* **salt-cellar** *n.* соло́нка. **salt-marsh** *n.* солонча́к (-а́). **saltpetre** [,sɒlt'piːtə(r), ,sɔːlt-] *n.* сели́тра. **salt-water** *adj.* морско́й. **salty** *adj.* (*also fig.*) солёный (со́лон, -а́, -о).

salubrious [sə'luːbrɪəs, sə'ljuː-] *adj.* здоро́вый.

salutary ['sæljʊtərɪ] *adj.* благотво́рный. **salu'tation** *n.* приве́тствие. **salute** [sə'luːt, -'ljuːt] *n.* приве́тствие; (*mil.*) салю́т; *v.t.* приве́тствовать *impf.* (*in past also pf.*); салютова́ть *impf.* & *pf.*, от~ *pf.+d.*

salvage ['sælvɪdʒ] *n.* спасе́ние; (*property*) спасённое иму́щество; (*ship*) спасённое су́дно (*pl.* -да́, -до́в); (*cargo*) спасённый груз; (*waste material*) ути́ль; *v.t.* спаса́ть *impf.*, спасти́ (-су́, -сёшь; -с, -сла́, -сло) *pf.*

salvation [sæl'veɪʃ(ə)n] *n.* спасе́ние; **S~ Army** А́рмия спасе́ния.

salve [sælv, sɑːv] *n.* мазь, бальза́м; *v.t.*: ~ **one's conscience** успока́ивать *impf.*, успоко́ить *pf.* со́весть.

salver ['sælvə(r)] *n.* подно́с.

salvo ['sælvəʊ] *n.* залп.

sal volatile [,sæl vɒ'lætɪlɪ] *n.* ню́хательная соль.

same [seɪm] *adj.* (*monotonous*) однообра́зный; **the** ~ тот же са́мый; тако́й же, одина́ковый; **just the** ~ то́чно тако́й же; **much the** ~ почти́ тако́й же; *pron.*: **the** ~ одно́ и то́ же, то же са́мое; *adv.*: **the** ~ таки́м же о́бразом, так же; **all the** ~ всё-таки, тем не ме́нее. **sameness** *n.* однообра́зие.

samovar ['sæmə,vɑː(r)] *n.* самова́р.

sample ['sɑːmp(ə)l] *n.* образе́ц (-зца́), про́ба; *v.t.* про́бовать *impf.*, по~ *pf.* **sampler** *n.* обра́зчик вы́шивки.

sanatorium [,sænə'tɔːrɪəm] *n.* санато́рий.

sanctify ['sæŋktɪ,faɪ] *v.t.* освяща́ть *impf.*, освяти́ть (-ящу́, -яти́шь) *pf.* **sanctimonious** [,sæŋktɪ'məʊnɪəs] *adj.* ха́нжеский. **sanction** *n.* са́нкция; *v.t.* санкциони́ровать *impf.* & *pf.* **sanctity** ['sæŋktɪtɪ] *n.* (*holiness*) свя́тость; (*sacredness*) свяще́нность. **sanctuary** ['sæŋktjʊərɪ] *n.* святи́лище, алта́рь (-ря́) *m.*; (*refuge*) убе́жище; (*for animals etc.*) запове́дник. **sanctum** *n.* свята́я *sb.* святы́х; (*joc.*) рабо́чий кабине́т.

sand [sænd] *n.* песо́к (-ска́(у́)); (*grain of* ~, *usu. pl.*) песчи́нка; (*shoal*, *sg. or pl.*) о́тмель; *pl.* (*beach*) пляж; *pl.* (*expanse of* ~) пески́ *m.pl.*; *attr.* песо́чный, песча́ный.

sandal[1] ['sænd(ə)l] *n.* санда́лия.

sandal[2] ['sænd(ə)l], **-wood** *n.* санда́ловое де́рево.

sandbag ['sændbæg] *n.* мешо́к (-шка́) с песко́м; (*as ballast*) балла́стный мешо́к (-шка́); *v.t.* защища́ть *impf.*, защити́ть (-ищу́, -ити́шь) *pf.* мешка́ми с песко́м. **sandbank** *n.* о́тмель. **sand-bar** *n.* песча́ный бар. **sand-blast** *v.t.* обдува́ть *impf.*, обду́ть (-у́ю, -у́ешь) *pf.* песо́чной струёй. **sand-dune** *n.* дю́на. **sand-glass** *n.* песо́чные часы́ (-со́в) *pl.* **sandpaper** *n.* шку́рка; *v.t.* шлифова́ть *impf.*, от~ *pf.* шку́ркой. **sandpiper** *n.* перево́зчик. **sand-pit** *n.* (*children's*) песо́чница. **sandstone** *n.* песча́ник. **sandstorm** *n.* песча́ная бу́ря.

sandwich ['sænwɪdʒ, -wɪtʃ] *n.* са́ндвич, бутербро́д; (*cake*) торт с просло́йкой; ~ **bar** бутербро́дная *sb.*; *v.t.*: ~ **between** вставля́ть *impf.*, вста́вить *pf.* ме́жду+*i.* **sandwich-board** *n.* рекла́мные щиты́ *m.pl.* **sandwich-man** *n.* челове́к-рекла́ма.

sandy ['sændɪ] *adj.* песча́ный, песо́чный; (*hair*) рыжева́тый.

sane [seɪn] *adj.* норма́льный; (*of views*) разу́мный.

sang-froid [sɑ̃'frwɑː] *n.* самооблада́ние.

sanguinary ['sæŋgwɪnərɪ] *adj.* крова́вый. **sanguine** *adj.* сангвини́ческий, оптимисти́ческий.

sanitary ['sænɪtərɪ] *adj.* санита́рный; гигиени́ческий; ~ **towel** гигиени́ческая поду́шка.

sani'tation *n.* санитария; (*disposal of sewage*) водопровод и канализация. **sanity** *n.* нормальная психика; (*good sense*) здравый ум (-а).

Santa Claus ['sæntə ˌklɔːz] *n.* Санта Клаус; (*Russian equivalent*) дед-мороз.

sap[1] [sæp] *n.* (*juice*) сок (*loc.* -е & -у); *v.t.* (*exhaust*) истощать *impf.*, истощить *pf.* (*cf.* **sap[2]**).

sap[2] [sæp] *n.* (*mil.*) сапа; *v.t.* (*undermine*) подрывать *impf.*, подорвать (-ву, -вёшь; -вал, -вала, -вало) *pf.* (*cf.* **sap[1]**).

sapling ['sæplɪŋ] *n.* молодое деревце (*pl.* -вца, -вец, -вцам).

sapper ['sæpə(r)] *n.* сапёр.

sapphire ['sæfaɪə(r)] *n.* сапфир; *adj.* (*colour*) синий (синь, -ня, -не).

Saracen ['særəs(ə)n] *n.* сарацин (*g.pl.* -н).

sarcasm ['sɑːˌkæz(ə)m] *n.* сарказм. **sar'castic** *adj.* саркастический.

sarcoma [sɑː'kəʊmə] *n.* саркома.

sarcophagus [sɑː'kɒfəgəs] *n.* саркофаг.

sardine ['sɑːdaɪn] *n.* сардина.

sardonic [sɑː'dɒnɪk] *adj.* сардонический.

sari ['sɑriː] *n.* сари *nt.indecl.*

sartorial [sɑː'tɔːrɪəl] *adj.* портняжный.

SAS *abbr.* (*of* **Special Air Service**) спецслужба ВВС.

sash[1] [sæʃ] *n.* (*scarf*) пояс (*pl.* -а), кушак (-а).

sash[2] [sæʃ] *n.* (*frame*) скользящая рама. **sash-window** *n.* подъёмное окно (*pl.* окна, окон, окнам).

Satan ['seɪt(ə)n] *n.* сатана *m.* **satanic** [sə'tænɪk] *adj.* сатанинский; (*devilish*) дьявольский.

satchel ['sætʃ(ə)l] *n.* ранец (-нца), сумка.

sate [seɪt] *v.t.* насыщать *impf.*, насытить (-ыщу, -ытишь) *pf.*

sateen [sæ'tiːn] *n.* сатин.

satellite ['sætəˌlaɪt] *n.* спутник, сателлит (*also fig.*); ~ **television** космическое телевидение.

satiate ['seɪʃɪˌeɪt] *v.t.* насыщать *impf.*, насытить (-ыщу, -ытишь) *pf.*; **be ~d** пресыщаться *impf.*, пресытиться (-ыщусь, -ытишься) *pf.* **sati'ation** *n.* насыщение. **satiety** [sə'taɪɪtɪ] *n.* пресыщение, сытость.

satin ['sætɪn] *n.* атлас; *adj.* атласный; ~ **stitch** гладь. **sati'net(te)** *n.* сатинет. **satiny** *adj.* атласный, шелковистый.

satire ['sætaɪə(r)] *n.* сатира. **satirical** [sə'tɪrɪk(ə)l] *adj.* сатирический. **satirist** ['sætərɪst] *n.* сатирик. **satirize** *v.t.* высмеивать *impf.*, высмеять (-ею, -еешь) *pf.*

satisfaction [ˌsætɪs'fækʃ(ə)n] *n.* удовлетворение. **satisfactory** *adj.* удовлетворительный. **satisfy** ['sætɪsˌfaɪ] *v.t.* удовлетворять *impf.*, удовлетворить *pf.*; (*hunger, curiosity*) утолять *impf.*, утолить *pf.*

saturate ['sætʃəˌreɪt, -tjʊˌreɪt] *v.t.* пропитывать *impf.*, пропитать *pf.*; насыщать *impf.*, насытить (-ыщу, -ыщешь) *pf.* **satu'ration** *n.* насыщение, насыщенность.

Saturday ['sætəˌdeɪ, -dɪ] *n.* суббота.

Saturn ['sæt(ə)n] *n.* Сатурн. **saturnine** ['sætəˌnaɪn] *adj.* мрачный (-чен, -чна, -чно), угрюмый.

satyr ['sætə(r)] *n.* сатир.

sauce [sɔːs] *n.* соус; (*insolence*) наглость; **apple** ~ яблочное пюре *nt.indecl.* **sauce-boat** *n.* соусник. **saucepan** *n.* кастрюля. **saucer** *n.* блюдце (*g.pl.* -дец). **saucy** *adj.* наглый (нагл, -а, -о).

Saudi Arabia ['saʊdɪ] Саудовская Аравия.

sauna ['sɔːnə] *n.* финская баня, сауна.

saunter ['sɔːntə(r)] *v.i.* прогуливаться *impf.*; *n.* прогулка.

sausage ['sɒsɪdʒ] *n.* колбаса (*pl.* -сы), сосиска; ~ **meat** колбасный фарш; ~ **roll** пирожок (-жка) с колбасным фаршем.

savage ['sævɪdʒ] *adj.* дикий (дик, -а, -о); (*cruel*) жестокий (-ок, -ока, -око); *n.* дикарь (-ря) *m.*; *v.t.* свирепо нападать *impf.*, напасть (-аду, -адёшь; -ал) *pf.* на+*a.* **savagery** *n.* дикость; жестокость.

savanna(h) [sə'vænə] *n.* саванна.

savant ['sæv(ə)nt, sæ'vɑ̃] *n.* учёный *sb.*

save [seɪv] *v.t.* (*rescue*) спасать *impf.*, спасти (-су, -сёшь; -с, -сла, -сло) *pf.*; (*put aside*) откладывать *impf.*, отложить (-жу, -жишь) *pf.*; (*spare*) беречь (-егу, -ежёшь; -ёг, -егла) *impf.*; *v.i.*: ~ **up** копить (-плю, -пишь) *impf.*, на~ *pf.* деньги. **savings** *n.* сбережения *nt.pl.*; ~ **bank** сберегательная касса. **saviour** *n.* спаситель *m.*

savour ['seɪvə(r)] *n.* вкус; *v.t.* смаковать *impf.*; наслаждаться *impf.*, насладиться *pf.*+*i.*

savoury ['seɪvərɪ] *adj.* (*sharp*) острый (остр & остёр, остра, остро); (*salty*) солёный (солон, -а, -о); (*spicy*) пряный.

savoy [sə'vɔɪ] *n.* савойская капуста.

saw [sɔː] *n.* пила (*pl.* -лы); *v.t.* пилить (-лю, -лишь) *impf.*; ~ **up** распиливать *impf.*, распилить (-лю, -лишь) *pf.* **sawdust** *n.* опилки (-лок) *pl.* **saw-edged** *adj.* пилообразный. **sawfish** *n.* пила-рыба. **sawmill** *n.* лесопильный завод, лесопилка. **sawyer** *n.* пильщик.

saxophone ['sæksəˌfəʊn] *n.* саксофон.

say [seɪ] *v.t.* говорить *impf.*, сказать (-ажу, -ажешь) *pf.*; **to ~ nothing of** не говоря уже о+*p.*; **that is to ~** то есть; (*let us*) ~ скажем; **it is said (that)** говорят (что); *n.* слово; (*opinion*) мнение; (*influence*) влияние; **have one's ~** высказаться (-ажусь, -ажешься) *pf.* **saying** *n.* поговорка.

scab [skæb] *n.* (*on wound*) струп (*pl.* -ья, -ьев), корка; (*mange*) парша; (*strike-breaker*) штрейкбрехер.

scabbard ['skæbəd] *n.* ножны (*g.* -жен) *pl.*

scabies ['skeɪbiːz] *n.* чесотка.

scabious ['skeɪbɪəs] *n.* скабиоза.

scabrous ['skeɪbrəs] *adj.* скабрёзный.

scaffold ['skæfəʊld, -f(ə)ld] *n.* эшафот. **scaffolding** *n.* леса (-сов) *pl.*, подмости (-тей) *pl.*

scald [skɔːld, skɒld] *v.t.* обва́ривать *impf.*, обвари́ть (-рю́, -ришь) *pf.*; *n.* ожо́г.
scale[1] [skeɪl] *n.* (*of fish*) чешу́йка; *pl.* чешуя́ (*collect.*); (*on boiler etc.*) на́кипь; *v.t.* чисти́ть *impf.*, о~ *pf.*; соска́бливать *impf.*, соскобли́ть (-облю́, -обли́шь) *pf.* чешую с+*g.*; *v.i.* шелуши́ться *impf.*
scale[2] [skeɪl] *n.* (~-*pan*) ча́ша весо́в; *pl.* весы́ (-со́в) *pl.*
scale[3] [skeɪl] *n.* (*relative dimensions*) масшта́б; (*set of marks*) шкала́ (*pl.* -лы); (*mus.*) га́мма; (*math.*; ~ *of notation*) систе́ма счисле́ния; *v.t.* (*climb*) взбира́ться *impf.*, взобра́ться (взберу́сь, -рёшься; взобра́лся, -ала́сь, -а́ло́сь) *pf.* (по ле́стнице) на+*a.*; ~ **down** понижа́ть *impf.*, пони́зить *pf.*; ~ **up** повыша́ть *impf.*, повы́сить *pf.*
scallop ['skæləp, 'skɒl-] *n.* (*mollusc*) гребешо́к (-шка́); *pl.* (*decoration*) фесто́ны *m.pl.*; ~ **shell** ра́ковина гребешка́; *v.t.* (*cook*) запека́ть *impf.*, запе́чь (-еку́, -ечёшь; -ёк, -екла́) *pf.* в ра́ковине; (*decorate*) украша́ть *impf.*, укра́сить *pf.* фесто́нами.
scalp [skælp] *n.* ко́жа че́репа; (*as trophy*) скальп; *v.t.* скальпи́ровать *impf.* & *pf.*
scalpel ['skælp(ə)l] *n.* ска́льпель *m.*
scaly ['skeɪlɪ] *adj.* чешу́йчатый; (*of boiler etc.*) покры́тый на́кипью.
scamp [skæmp] *n.* плути́шка *m.*
scamper ['skæmpə(r)] *v.i.* бы́стро бе́гать *impf.*; (*playfully*) резви́ться *impf.*
scampi ['skæmpɪ] *n.* креве́тки *f.pl.*
scan [skæn] *v.t.* & *i.* (*verse*) сканди́ровать(ся) *impf.*; *v.t.* (*intently*) внима́тельно рассма́тривать *impf.*; (*quickly*) бе́гло просма́тривать *impf.*, просмотре́ть (-рю́, -ришь) *pf.*
scandal ['skænd(ə)l] *n.* сканда́л; (*gossip*) спле́тни (-тен) *pl.* **scandalize** *v.t.* шоки́ровать *impf.* & *pf.* **scandalmonger** *n.* спле́тник, -ица. **scandalous** *adj.* сканда́льный.
Scandinavia [ˌskændɪ'neɪvɪə] *n.* Скандина́вия. **Scandinavian** *adj.* скандина́вский.
scanner *n.* (*comput.*, *med.*) ска́нер.
scansion ['skænʃ(ə)n] *n.* сканди́рование.
scanty ['skæntɪ] *adj.* ску́дный (-ден, -дна, -дно); (*insufficient*) недоста́точный.
scapegoat ['skeɪpgəʊt] *n.* козёл (-зла́) отпуще́ния.
scapula ['skæpjʊlə] *n.* лопа́тка.
scar [skɑː(r)] *n.* рубе́ц (-бца́), шрам. **scarred** *adj.* обезобра́женный (-ен) рубца́ми, шра́мами.
scarab ['skærəb] *n.* скарабе́й.
scarce [skeəs] *adj.* дефици́тный, недоста́точный; (*rare*) ре́дкий (-док, -дка́, -дко); **make o.s.** ~ улизну́ть *pf.* **scarcely** *adv.* (*only just*) едва́; (*surely not*) едва́ ли. **scarcity** *n.* недоста́ток (-тка), дефици́т.
scare [skeə(r)] *v.t.* пуга́ть *impf.*, ис~, на~ *pf.*; ~ **away, off** отпу́гивать *impf.*, отпугну́ть *pf.*; *n.* па́ника. **scarecrow** *n.* пу́гало, чу́чело. **scaremonger** *n.* паникёр.
scarf [skɑːf] *n.* шарф.
scarlet ['skɑːlɪt] *adj.* (*n.*) а́лый (цвет); ~ **fever** скарлати́на.
scathing ['skeɪðɪŋ] *adj.* е́дкий (е́док, едка́, е́дко), уничтожа́ющий.
scatter ['skætə(r)] *v.t.* & *i.* рассыпа́ть(ся) *impf.*, рассы́пать(ся) (-плю, -плет(ся)) *pf.*; (*disperse*) рассе́ивать(ся) *impf.*, рассе́ять(ся) (-е́ю, -е́ет(ся)) *pf.*; *v.t.* (*disperse, drive away*) разгоня́ть *impf.*, разогна́ть (разгоню́, -нишь; разогна́л, -а́, -о) *pf.*; *v.i.* (*run*) разбега́ться *impf.*, разбежа́ться (-ежи́тся, -егу́тся) *pf.* **scatterbrained** *adj.* легкомы́сленный (-ен, -енна). **scattered** *adj.* разбро́санный (-ан); (*sporadic*) отде́льный.
scavenger ['skævɪndʒə(r)] *n.* (*person*) му́сорщик; (*animal*) живо́тное *sb.*, пита́ющееся па́далью.
scenario [sɪ'nɑːrɪəʊ, -'neərɪəʊ] *n.* сцена́рий. **scenarist** *n.* сценари́ст. **scene** [siːn] *n.* сце́на; (*part of play also*) явле́ние; (*place of action*) ме́сто де́йствия; (*scenery*) декора́ция; **behind the ~s** за кули́сами; **make a ~** устра́ивать *impf.*, устро́ить *pf.* сце́ну. **scene-painter** *n.* худо́жник-декора́тор. **scenery** *n.* (*theatr.*) декора́ция; (*landscape*) пейза́ж. **scene-shifter** *n.* рабо́чий *sb.* сце́ны. **scenic** *adj.* сцени́ческий.
scent [sent] *n.* (*smell*) арома́т; (*perfume*) духи́ (-хо́в) *pl.*; (*trail*) след (-а(у); *pl.* -ы́); *v.t.* (*discern*) чу́ять (чу́ю, чу́ешь) *impf.*; (*apply perfume*) души́ть (-шу́, -шишь) *impf.*, на~ *pf.*; (*make fragrant*) наполня́ть *impf.*, напо́лнить *pf.* арома́том.
sceptic ['skeptɪk] *n.* ске́птик. **sceptical** *adj.* скепти́ческий. **scepticism** *n.* скептици́зм.
sceptre ['septə(r)] *n.* ски́петр.
schedule ['ʃedjuːl] *n.* (*timetable*) расписа́ние; (*inventory*) о́пись; *v.t.* составля́ть *impf.*, соста́вить *pf.* расписа́ние, о́пись, +*g.*
schematic [skɪ'mætɪk, skiː-] *adj.* схемати́ческий. **scheme** [skiːm] *n.* (*plan*) прое́кт; (*intention*) за́мысел (-сла); (*intrigue*) махина́ция; *v.i.* стро́ить *impf.*, та́йные пла́ны. **'schemer** *n.* интрига́н. **'scheming** *adj.* интригу́ющий.
scherzo ['skeəˌtsəʊ] *n.* ске́рцо *nt.indecl.*
schism ['sɪz(ə)m, 'skɪ-] *n.* раско́л. **schis'matic** *adj.* раско́льнический; *n.* раско́льник.
schizophrenia [ˌskɪtsə'friːnɪə] *n.* шизофрени́я. **schizophrenic** [ˌskɪtsə'frenɪk, -'friːnɪk] *adj.* шизофрени́ческий; *n.* шизофре́ник.
scholar ['skɒlə(r)] *n.* учёный *sb.*: (~*ship holder*) стипендиа́т, ~ка. **scholarly** *adj.* учёный, нау́чный. **scholarship** *n.* учёность, нау́ка; (*payment*) стипе́ндия.
school [skuːl] *n.* шко́ла; (*specialist* ~) учи́лище; (*univ.*) факульте́т; *attr.* шко́льный; *v.t.* (*curb*) обу́здывать *impf.*, обузда́ть *pf.*; (*accustom*) приуча́ть *impf.*, приучи́ть (-чу́, -чишь) *pf.* (**to** к+*d.*, +*inf.*). **school-book** *n.* уче́бник. **schoolboy** *n.* шко́льник, учени́к

(-á). **schoolgirl** *n.* шкóльница, учени́ца. **schooling** *n.* обучéние. **school-leaver** *n.* выпускни́к (-á), -и́ца. **schoolmaster** *n.* шкóльный учи́тель (*pl.* -ля́) *m.* **schoolmistress** *n.* шкóльная учи́тельница.

schooner ['sku:nə(r)] *n.* шхýна.

sciatic [saɪ'ætɪk] *adj.* седáлищный. **sciatica** *n.* и́шиас.

science ['saɪəns] *n.* наýка; (*natural* ~) естéственные наýки *f.pl.*; ~ **fiction** наýчная фантáстика. **scien'tific** *adj.* наýчный; ~ **calculator** компью́тер-калькуля́тор. **scientist** *n.* учёный *sb.*; (*natural* ~) естéственник, -ица.

scintillate ['sɪntɪ,leɪt] *v.i.* и́скри́ться *impf.* **scintillating** *adj.* блистáтельный.

scion ['saɪən] *n.* óтпрыск.

scissors ['sɪzəz] *n.* нóжницы (-ц) *pl.*

sclerosis [sklɪə'rəʊsɪs] *n.* склерóз.

scoff[1] [skɒf] *v.i.* (*mock*) издевáться *impf.* (**at** над+*i.*).

scoff[2] [skɒf] *v.t.* (*eat*) жрать (жру, жрёшь; жрал, -á, -о) *impf.*, со~ *pf.*

scold [skəʊld] *v.t.* брани́ть *impf.*, вы́~ *pf.* **scolding** *n.* нагоня́й.

scollop *see* **scallop**

sconce [skɒns] *n.* (*bracket*) бра *nt.indecl.*; (*candlestick*) подсвéчник.

scone [skɒn, skəʊn] *n.* сдóбная лепёшка.

scoop [sku:p] *n.* черпáк (-á), ковш (-á); *v.t.* (~ *out*, *up*) вычéрпывать *impf.*, вы́черпать *pf.*

scooter ['sku:tə(r)] *n.* (*child's*) самокáт, рóллер; (*motor* ~) моторóллер.

scope [skəʊp] *n.* предéлы *m.pl.*, простóр, размáх.

scorch [skɔ:tʃ] *v.t.* пали́ть *impf.*, с~ *pf.*; подпáливать *impf.*, подпали́ть *pf.*; ~**ed earth policy** тáктика вы́жженной земли́; *n.* **scorching** *adj.* паля́щий, знóйный.

score [skɔ:(r)] *n.* (*notch*) зарýбка; (*account*; *number of points etc.*) счёт; (*mus.*) партитýра; (*twenty*) два деся́тка; *pl.* (*great numbers*) деся́тки *m.pl.*, мнóжество; *v.t.* (*notch*) дéлать *impf.*, с~ *pf.* зарýбки на+*p.*; (*points etc.*) получáть *impf.*, получи́ть (-чý, -чишь) *pf.*; (*mus.*) оркестровáть *impf.* & *pf.*; *v.i.* (*keep* ~) вести́ (ведý, -дёшь; вёл, -á) *impf.*, с~ *pf.* счёт.

scorn [skɔ:n] *n.* презрéние; *v.t.* презирáть *impf.* презрéть (-рю́, -ри́шь) *pf.* **scornful** *adj.* презри́тельный.

Scorpio ['skɔ:pɪəʊ] *n.* Скорпиóн.

scorpion ['skɔ:pɪən] *n.* скорпиóн.

Scot [skɒt] *n.* шотлáндец (-дца), -дка. **Scotch** *adj.* шотлáндский; *n.* (*whisky*) шотлáндское ви́ски; *nt.indecl.*; **the** ~ шотлáндцы *m.pl.*

scot-free ['skɒtfri:] *adv.* безнакáзанно.

Scotland ['skɒtlənd] *n.* Шотлáндия. **Scots, Scottish** *adj.* шотлáндский; *see* **Scotch**

scoundrel ['skaʊndr(ə)l] *n.* негодя́й, подлéц (-á).

scour[1] ['skaʊə(r)] *v.t.* (*cleanse*) отчищáть *impf.*, отчи́стить *pf.* **scourer** *n.* металли́ческая мочáлка.

scour[2] ['skaʊə(r)] *v.t.* & *i.* (*rove*) ры́скать (ры́щу, -щешь) *impf.* (по+*d.*).

scourge [skɜ:dʒ] *n.* бич (-á); *v.t.* бичевáть (-чýю, -чýешь) *impf.*

scout [skaʊt] *n.* развéдчик; (**S**~) бойскáут; *v.i.*: ~ **about** ры́скать (ры́щу, -щешь) *impf.* (**for** в пóисках+*g.*).

scowl [skaʊl] *v.i.* хмýриться *impf.*, на~ *pf.* *n.* хмýрый вид, взгляд.

scrabble ['skræb(ə)l] *v.i.*: ~ **about** ры́ться (рóюсь, рóешься) *impf.*

scramble ['skræmb(ə)l] *v.i.* карáбкаться *impf.*, вс~ *pf.*; (*struggle*) дрáться (дерýсь, -рёшься; дрáлся, -алáсь, -áлóсь) *impf.* (**for** за+*a.*); *v.t.* (*mix together*) перемéшивать *impf.*, перемешáть *pf.*; ~**d eggs** яи́чница-болтýнья.

scrap[1] [skræp] *n.* (*fragment etc.*) клочóк (-чка), обрéзок (-зка), кусóчек (-чка); *pl.* остáтки *m.pl.*; *pl.* (*of food*) объéдки (-ков) *pl.*; ~ **metal** металли́ческий лом, скрап; *v.t.* превращáть *impf.*, преврати́ть (-ащý, -ати́шь) *pf.* в лом; пускáть *impf.*, пусти́ть (пущý, пýстишь) *pf.* на слом.

scrap[2] [skræp] *n.* (*fight*) дрáка; *v.i.* дрáться (дерýсь, -рёшься; дрáлся, -алáсь, -áлóсь) *impf.*

scrape [skreɪp] *v.t.* скрести́ (скребý, -бёшь; скрёб, -лá) *impf.*; скобли́ть (-облю́, -óбли́шь) *impf.*; ~ **off** отскребáть *impf.*, отскрести́ (-ребý, -ребёшь; -рёб, -реблá) *pf.*; ~ **through** (*examination*) с трудóм выдéрживать *impf.*, вы́держать (-жу, -жишь) *pf.*; ~ **together** наскребáть *impf.*, наскрести́ (-ребý, -ребёшь; -рёб, -реблá) *pf.*

scratch [skrætʃ] *v.t.* царáпать *impf.*, о~ *pf.*; *v.t.* & *abs.* чесáть(ся) (чешý(сь), -шешь(ся)) *impf.*, по~ *pf.*; *v.abs.* царáпаться *impf.*; *v.t.* (*erase*, ~ **off, through** *etc.*) вычёркивать *impf.*, вы́черкнуть *pf.*; *n.* царáпина; *adj.* случáйный.

scrawl [skrɔ:l] *n.* карáкули *f.pl.*; *v.t.* писáть (пишý, -шешь) *impf.*, на~ *pf.* карáкулями.

scrawny ['skrɔ:nɪ] *adj.* тóщий (тощ, -á, -е), сухопáрый.

scream [skri:m] *n.* крик, визг; *v.i.* кричáть (-чý, -чи́шь) *impf.*, кри́кнуть *pf.*; *v.t.* выкри́кивать *impf.*, вы́крикнуть *pf.*

screech [skri:tʃ] *n.* визг; *v.i.* визжáть (-жý, -жи́шь) *impf.*

screen [skri:n] *n.* ши́рма; (*cin.*, *television*, *radio*, *etc.*) экрáн; (*sieve*) грóхот; *v.t.* (*shelter*) защищáть *impf.*, защити́ть (-ищý, -ити́шь) *pf.*; заслоня́ть *impf.*, заслони́ть *pf.*; (*show film etc.*) демонстри́ровать *impf.* & *pf.*; (*sieve*) просéивать *impf.*, просéять (-éю, -éешь) *pf.*; ~ **off** отгорáживать *impf.*, отгороди́ть (-ожý, -óди́шь) *pf.* ши́рмой. **screen-play** *n.* сценáрий.

screw [skru:] *n.* (*male* ~; *propeller*) винт (-á); (*female* ~) гáйка; (~-*bolt*) болт (-á); *v.t.* (~ *on*) приви́нчивать *impf.*, привинти́ть *pf.*; (~

up) зави́нчивать *impf.*, завинти́ть *pf.*; ~ **up one's eyes** щу́риться *impf.*, со~ *pf.* **screw-driver** *n.* отвёртка.

scribble ['skrɪb(ə)l] *v.t.* небре́жно, бы́стро, писа́ть (пишу́, -шешь) *impf.*, на~ *pf.*; *n.* кара́кули *f.pl.* **scribbler** *n.* писа́ка *c.g.*

scribe [skraɪb] *n.* писе́ц (-сца́); (*bibl.*) кни́жник.

scrimmage ['skrɪmɪdʒ] *n.* сва́лка.

script [skrɪpt] *n.* по́черк, шрифт; (*of film etc.*) сцена́рий.

Scripture ['skrɪptʃə(r)] *n.* свяще́нное писа́ние.

scriptwriter ['skrɪpt,raɪtə(r)] *n.* сценари́ст.

scrofula ['skrɒfjʊlə] *n.* золоту́ха.

scroll [skrəʊl] *n.* сви́ток (-тка); (*design*) завито́к (-тка́). **scrollwork** *n.* орна́мент в ви́де завитко́в.

scrounge [skraʊndʒ] *v.t.* (*steal*) ти́брить *impf.*, с~ *pf.*; (*cadge*) выкля́нчивать *impf.*, вы́клянчить *pf.*; *v.i.* попроша́йничать *impf.*

scrub[1] [skrʌb] *n.* (*brushwood*) кустáрник; (*area*) поро́сшая куста́рником ме́стность.

scrub[2] [skrʌb] *v.t.* мыть (мо́ю, мо́ешь) *impf.*, вы́~ *pf.* щёткой; *n.* чи́стка. **scrubbing-brush** *n.* жёсткая щётка.

scruff [skrʌf] *n.* загри́вок (-вка); **take by the ~ of the neck** брать (беру́, -рёшь; брал, -а́, -о) *impf.*, взять (возьму́, -мёшь; взял, -а́, -о) *pf.* за ши́ворот.

scruffy ['skrʌfɪ] *adj.* (*of clothes*) потрёпанный (-ан, -анна); (*of person*) неря́шливый.

scrum(mage) ['skrʌmɪdʒ] *n.* схва́тка вокру́г мяча́.

scruple ['skru:p(ə)l] *n.* (*also pl.*) колеба́ние, угрызе́ния *nt.pl.* со́вести; *v.i.* колеба́ться (-блюсь, -блешься) *impf.* **scrupulous** *adj.* скрупулёзный, щепетли́вый.

scrutineer [,skru:tɪ'nɪə(r)] *n.* прове́рщик, -ица. **'scrutinize** *v.t.* рассма́тривать *impf.* **'scrutiny** *n.* рассмотре́ние, прове́рка.

scud [skʌd] *v.i.* нести́сь (несётся; нёсся, несла́сь) *impf.*, по~ *pf.*; скользи́ть *impf.*

scuffed [skʌfd] *adj.* потёртый, поцара́панный.

scuffle ['skʌf(ə)l] *n.* сва́лка; *v.i.* дра́ться (деру́сь, -рёшься; дра́лся, -ала́сь, -а́ло́сь) *impf.*

scull [skʌl] *n.* весло́ (*pl.* вёсла, -сел, -слам); (*stern oar*) кормово́е весло́; *v.i.* грести́ (гребу́, -бёшь; грёб, -ла́) *impf.* (па́рными вёслами); гала́нить *impf.*

scullery ['skʌlərɪ] *n.* судомо́йня (*g.pl.* -о́ен).

sculptor ['skʌlptə(r)] *n.* ску́льптор. **sculptural** ['skʌlptʃərəl] *adj.* скульпту́рный. **sculpture** ['skʌlptʃə(r)] *n.* скульпту́ра.

scum [skʌm] *n.* пе́на, на́кипь; (*fig.*, *people*) подо́нки (-ков) *pl.*

scupper[1] ['skʌpə(r)] *n.* шпига́т.

scupper[2] ['skʌpə(r)] *v.t.* (*ship*) потопля́ть *impf.*, потопи́ть (-плю́, -пишь) *pf.*

scurf [skɜ:f] *n.* пе́рхоть.

scurrility [skʌ'rɪlɪtɪ] *n.* непристо́йность, гру́бость. **'scurrilous** *adj.* непристо́йный, гру́бый (груб, -а́, -о́).

scurry ['skʌrɪ] *v.i.* поспе́шно, суетли́во, бе́гать *indet.*, бежа́ть (бегу́, -бежи́шь) *det.*

scurvy ['skɜ:vɪ] *n.* цинга́; *adj.* по́длый (подл, -а́, -о).

scuttle[1] ['skʌt(ə)l] *n.* (*coal-box*) ведёрка (*pl.* -рки, -рок, -ркам) для у́гля́.

scuttle[2] ['skʌt(ə)l] *v.t.* (*ship*) затопля́ть *impf.*, затопи́ть (-плю́, -пишь) *pf.*

scuttle[3] ['skʌt(ə)l] *v.i.* (*run away*) удира́ть *impf.*, удра́ть (удеру́, -рёшь; удра́л, -а́, -о) *pf.*

scythe [saɪð] *n.* коса́ (*a.* ко́су́; *pl.* -сы).

sea [si:] *n.* мо́ре (*pl.* -ря́); **at ~** в (откры́том) мо́ре; **by ~** мо́рем; *attr.* морско́й; **~ anchor** плаву́чий я́корь (*pl.* -ря́) *m.*; **~ anemone** акти́ния; **~ breeze** ве́тер (-тра) с мо́ря; **~ dog** (*person*) морско́й волк (*pl.* -и, -о́в); **~ front** на́бережная *sb.*; **~ horse** морско́й конёк (-нька́); **~ lane** морско́й путь (-ти́, -тём) *m.*; **~ level** у́ровень (-вня) *m.* мо́ря; **~ lion** морско́й лев (льва); **~ urchin** морско́й ёж (-а́); **~ wall** да́мба. **seaboard** *n.* побере́жье. **seacoast** *n.* побере́жье. **seafaring** *n.* морепла́вание. **seagoing** *adj.* да́льнего пла́вания. **seagull** *n.* ча́йка.

seal[1] [si:l] *n.* (*on document etc.*) печа́ть; *v.t.* скрепля́ть *impf.*, скрепи́ть *pf.* печа́тью; запеча́тывать *impf.*, запеча́тать *pf.*

seal[2] [si:l] *n.* (*animal*) тюле́нь *m.*; (*fur-~*) ко́тик.

sealing-wax ['si:lɪŋ,wæks] *n.* сургу́ч (-а́).

sealskin ['si:lskɪn] *n.* ко́тиковый мех (*loc.* -е & -у́); *attr.* ко́тиковый.

seam [si:m] *n.* шов (шва), рубе́ц (-бца́); (*stratum*) пласт (-а́, *loc.* -у́); *v.t.* сшива́ть *impf.*, сшить (сошью́, -ьёшь) *pf.* шва́ми.

seaman ['si:mən] *n.* моря́к (-а́); (*also rank*) матро́с.

seamstress ['semstrɪs] *n.* швея́.

seamy ['si:mɪ] *adj.* со шва́ми нару́жу; **the ~ side** (*also fig.*) изна́нка.

seance ['seɪɑ̃s] *n.* спирити́ческий сеа́нс.

seaplane ['si:pleɪn] *n.* гидросамолёт. **seaport** *n.* порто́вый го́род (*pl.* -а́).

sear [sɪə(r)] *v.t.* прижига́ть *impf.*, приже́чь (-жгу́, -жжёшь, -жгу́т; -жёг, -жгла́) *pf.*

search [sɜ:tʃ] *v.t.* обы́скивать *impf.*, обыска́ть (-ыщу́, -ы́щешь) *pf.*; *v.i.* иска́ть (ищу́, и́щешь) *impf.* (**for** *+a.*); производи́ть (-ожу́, -о́дишь) *impf.*, произвести́ (-еду́, -едёшь; -ёл, -ела́) *pf.* о́быск; *n.* по́иски *m.pl.*; о́быск; **~ warrant** о́рдер (*pl.* -а́) на о́быск. **searching** *adj.* (*thorough*) тща́тельный; (*look*) испыту́ющий. **searchlight** *n.* проже́ктор (*pl.* -ы & -а́). **search-party** *n.* по́исковая гру́ппа.

seascape ['si:skeɪp] *n.* мари́на. **seashore** *n.* побере́жье. **seasickness** *n.* морска́я боле́знь. **seaside** *n.* бе́рег (*loc.* -у́) мо́ря; (*resort*) морско́й куро́рт.

season ['si:z(ə)n] *n.* сезо́н; (*period in general*) пери́од; (*one of four*) вре́мя *nt.* го́да; **in ~** по сезо́ну; **~ ticket** сезо́нный биле́т; *v.t.*

(*mature*) выдéрживать *impf.*, вы́держать (-жу, -жишь) *pf.*; (*flavour*) приправля́ть *impf.*, припрáвить *pf.* **seasonable** *adj.* по сезóну; (*timely*) своеврéменный (-нен, -нна). **seasonal** *adj.* сезóнный. **seasoning** *n.* приправа.

seat [siːt] *n.* мéсто (*pl.* -тá), сидéнье; (*chair*) стул (*pl.* -ья, -ьев); (*bench*) скамéйка; (*buttocks*) седáлище; (*of trousers*) зад (*loc.* -ý; *pl.* -ы́); (*country* ~) усáдьба; (*ticket*) билéт; *v.t.* сажáть *impf.*, посади́ть (-ажý, -áдишь) *pf.*; (*of room etc.*) вмещáть *impf.*, вмести́ть *pf.*; **be ~ed** сади́ться *impf.*, сесть (ся́ду, -дешь; сел) *pf.* **seat-belt** *n.* привязнóй ремéнь(-мня́) *m.*

seaweed ['siːwiːd] *n.* морскáя вóдоросль.

sebaceous [sɪ'beɪʃəs] *adj.* сáльный.

sec [sek] *n.*: **half a ~!** минýтку!; оди́н момéнт.

sec. *abbr.* (*of* **second(s)**) сек., секýнда.

secateurs [ˌsekə'tɜːz] *n.* секáтор.

secede [sɪ'siːd] *v.i.* откáлываться *impf.*, отколóться (-лю́сь, -лешься) *pf.* **secession** [sɪ'seʃ(ə)n] *n.* откóл.

secluded [sɪ'kluːdɪd] *adj.* укрóмный. **seclusion** *n.* укрóмность; (*place*) укрóмное мéсто.

second[1] ['sekənd] *adj.* вторóй; **be ~ to** (*inferior*) уступáть *impf.*, уступи́ть (-плю́, -пишь) *pf.*+*d.*; **~ ballot** перебаллотирóвка; **~ sight** яснови́дение; **on ~ thoughts** взвéсив всё ещё раз; **have ~ thoughts** передýмывать *impf.*, передýмать *pf.* (**about** +*a.*); **~ wind** вторóе дыхáние; *n.* вторóй *sb.*; (*date*) вторóе (числó) *sb.*; (*mus.*; *time*; *angle*) секýнда; (*coll.*, *moment*) момéнт; (*in duel*) секундáнт; *pl.* товáр вторóго сóрта; *pl.* (~ *helping*) вторáя пóрция; **~ in command** замести́тель *m.* команди́ра; **~ hand** (*of clock etc.*) секýндная стрéлка; *v.t.* (*support*) поддéрживать *impf.*, поддержáть (-жý, -жишь) *pf.*

second[2] [sɪ'kɒnd] *v.t.* (*transfer*) откомандирóвывать *impf.* откомандировáть *pf.*

secondary ['sekəndərɪ] *adj.* втори́чный, второстепéнный (-нен, -нна); (*education*) срéдний. **second-best** *adj.* второсóртный. **second-class** *adj.* второклáссный, второсóртный. **second-hand** *adj.* подéржанный (-ан, -анна); (*of information*) из вторы́х рук. **secondly** *adv.* во-вторы́х. **second-rate** *adj.* второразря́дный.

secrecy ['siːkrɪsɪ] *n.* секрéтность. **secret** *n.* тáйна, секрéт; *adj.* тáйный, секрéтный; (*hidden*) потайнóй.

secretarial [ˌsekrɪ'teərɪəl] *adj.* секретáрский. **secretariat** *n.* секретариáт. **'secretary** *n.* секретáрь (-ря́) *m.*, -рша; (*minister*) мини́стр.

secrete [sɪ'kriːt] *v.t.* (*conceal*) прятать (-я́чу, -я́чешь) *impf.*, с~ *pf.*; (*med.*) выделя́ть *impf.*, вы́делить *pf.* **secretion** *n.* укрывáние; (*med.*) секрéция, выделéние.

secretive ['siːkrɪtɪv] *adj.* скры́тный.

sect [sekt] *n.* сéкта. **sectarian** [sek'teərɪən] *adj.* сектáнтский; *n.* сектáнт.

section ['sekʃ(ə)n] *n.* сéкция, отрéзок (-зка); (*of book*) раздéл; (*of solid*) сечéние, прóфиль, разрéз. **sectional** *adj.* секциóнный. **sector** *n.* сéктор (*pl.* -ы & -á), учáсток (-тка).

secular ['sekjʊlə(r)] *adj.* свéтский, мирскóй; **~ clergy** бéлое духовéнство. **seculari'zation** *n.* секуляризáция. **secularize** *v.t.* секуляризовáть *impf.* & *pf.*

secure [sɪ'kjʊə(r)] *adj.* безопáсный, надёжный; *v.t.* (*fasten*) закрепля́ть *impf.*, закрепи́ть *pf.*; (*guarantee*) обеспéчивать *impf.*, обеспéчить *pf.*; (*obtain*) доставáть (-таю́, -таёшь) *impf.*, достáть (-áну, -áнешь) *pf.* **security** *n.* безопáсность; (*guarantee*) залóг; *pl.* цéнные бумáги *f.pl.*; **S~ Council** Совéт Безопáсности; **~ guard** охрáнник; **~ risk** неблагонадёжный человéк (*pl.* лю́ди, -дéй, -дям, -дьми́); **social ~** социáльное обеспечéние.

sedan(-chair) [sɪ'dæn] *n.* портшéз.

sedate [sɪ'deɪt] *adj.* степéнный (-нен, -нна).

sedation [sɪ'deɪʃ(ə)n] *n.* успокоéние. **sedative** ['sedətɪv] *adj.* успокáивающий; *n.* успокáивающее срéдство.

sedentary ['sedəntərɪ] *adj.* сидя́чий.

sedge [sedʒ] *n.* осóка.

sediment ['sedɪmənt] *n.* осáдок (-дка), отстóй. **sedi'mentary** *adj.* осáдочный.

sedition [sɪ'dɪʃ(ə)n] *n.* подстрекáтельство к мятежý. **seditious** *adj.* подстрекáтельский, мятéжный.

seduce [sɪ'djuːs] *v.t.* соблазня́ть *impf.*, соблазни́ть *pf.*; совращáть *impf.*, соврати́ть (-ащý, -ати́шь) *pf.* **seducer** *n.* соблазни́тель. **seductive** [sɪ'dʌktɪv] *adj.* соблазни́тельный, обольсти́тельный. **seductress** *n.* соблазни́тельница.

sedulous ['sedjʊləs] *adj.* прилéжный.

see[1] [siː] *n.* епáрхия; **Holy S~** пáпский престóл.

see[2] [siː] *v.t.* & *i.* ви́деть (ви́жу, ви́дишь) *impf.*, у~ *pf.*; *v.t.* (*watch, look*) смотрéть (-рю́, -ришь) *impf.*, по~ *pf.*; (*find out*) узнавáть (-наю́, -наёшь) *impf.*, узнáть *pf.*; (*understand*) понимáть *impf.*, поня́ть (поймý, -мёшь; пóнял, -á, -о) *pf.*; (*meet*) ви́деться (ви́жусь, ви́дишься) *impf.*, у~ *pf.* с+*i.*; (*imagine*) представля́ть *impf.*, предстáвить *pf.* себé; (*escort*) провожáть *impf.*, проводи́ть *pf.*; **~ about** (*attend to*) забóтиться *impf.*, по~ *pf.* о+*p.*; **~ over** осмáтривать *impf.*, осмотрéть (-рю́, -ришь) *pf.*; **~ through** (*fig.*) ви́деть (ви́жу, ви́дишь) *impf.*, насквóзь+*a.*

seed [siːd] *n.* сéмя (*g.pl.* -мя́н) *nt.*; (*grain*) зернó. **seed-bed** *n.* парни́к (-á). **seed-cake** *n.* бýлочка с тми́ном. **seed-corn** *n.* посевнóе зернó. **seedling** *n.* сéянец (-нца); *pl.* рассáда. **seed-pearl(s)** *n.* мéлкий жéмчуг. **seedy** *adj.* (*shabby*) потрёпанный (-ан, -анна); (*ill*) нездорóвый.

seeing (that) ['siːɪŋ] *conj.* ввидý тогó, что.

seek [siːk] *v.t.* искáть (ищý, -щешь) *impf.*+*a.* & *g.*

seem [siːm] *v.i.* казáться (кажýсь, -жешься) *impf.*, по~ *pf.* (+*i.*) (*often used parenthetically in impers. forms*). **seeming** *adj.* мни́мый. **seemingly** *adv.* по-ви́димому, на вид.
seemly ['siːmlɪ] *adj.* прили́чный.
seep [siːp] *v.i.* просáчиваться *impf.*, просочи́ться *pf.* **seepage** *n.* просáчивание, течь.
seer ['siːə(r), sɪə(r)] *n.* прови́дец (-дца).
see-saw ['siːsɔː] *n.* (*game*) качáние на доскé; (*board*) дéтские качéли (-лей) *pl.*; *v.i.* качáться *impf.* (на доскé).
seethe [siːð] *v.i.* кипéть (-плю, -пи́шь) *impf.*, вс~ *pf.*
segment ['segmənt] *n.* отрéзок (-зка); (*of orange etc.*) дóлька; (*geom.*) сегмéнт.
segregate ['segrɪgət] *v.t.* отделя́ть *impf.*, отдели́ть *pf.* **segre'gation** *n.* отделéние, сегрегáция.
Seine [seɪn] *n.* Сéна.
seismic ['saɪzmɪk] *adj.* сейсми́ческий. **seismograph** *n.* сейсмóграф. **seis'mology** *n.* сейсмолóгия.
seize [siːz] *v.t.* хватáть *impf.*, схвати́ть (-ачý, -áтишь) *pf.*; *v.i.*: ~ **up** заедáть *impf.*, заéсть (-éст; -éло) *pf. impers.*+*a.*; ~ **upon** ухвáтываться *impf.*, ухвати́ться (-ачýсь, -áтишься) *pf.* за+*a.* **seizure** *n.* захвáт; заедáние; (*stroke*) удáр.
seldom ['seldəm] *adv.* рéдко.
select [sɪ'lekt] *adj.* и́збранный; *v.t.* отбирáть *impf.*, отобрáть (отберý, -рёшь; отобрáл, -á, -о) *pf.* выбирáть *impf.*, вы́брать (вы́беру, -решь) *pf.* **selection** *n.* вы́бор; (*biol.*) отбóр. **selective** *adj.* селекти́вный.
self [self] *n.* сóбственная ли́чность; (*one's interests*) свои́ ли́чные интерéсы *m.pl.*
self- [self] *in comb.* само... . **self-absorbed** *adj.* эгоцентри́чный. **self-assured** *adj.* самоувéренный (-ен, -енна). **self-centred** *adj.* эгоцентри́чный. **self-confidence** *n.* самоувéренность. **self-confident** *adj.* самоувéренный (-ен, -енна). **self-conscious** *adj.* застéнчивый. **self-contained** *adj.* отдéльный. **self-control** *n.* самообладáние. **self-defence** *n.* самооборóна, самозащи́та. **self-denial** *n.* самоотречéние. **self-determination** *n.* самоопределéние. **self-effacing** *adj.* скрóмный (-мен, -мнá, -мно). **self-esteem** *n.* самоуважéние. **self-evident** *adj.* очеви́дный. **self-government** *n.* самоуправлéние. **self-help** *n.* самопóмощь. **self-importance** *n.* самомнéние. **self-interest** *n.* своекоры́стие.
selfish ['selfɪʃ] *adj.* эгоисти́чный, себялюби́вый. **selfless** *adj.* самоотвéрженный (-ен, -енна).
self-made ['selfmeɪd] *adj.* (*man*) вы́бившийся из низóв. **self-portrait** *n.* автопортрéт. **self-possessed** *adj.* хладнокрóвный. **self-preservation** *n.* самосохранéние. **self-propelled** *adj.* самохóдный. **self-reliant** *adj.* надéющийся тóлько на себя́. **self-respect** *n.* чýвство сóбственного достóинства. **self-righteous** *adj.* увéренный (-ен, -енна) в своéй правотé, фарисéйский. **self-sacrifice** *n.* самопожéртвование. **self-satisfied** *adj.* самодовóльный. **self-service** *n.* самообслýживание (*attr.*, *in g. after n.*). **self-starter** *n.* самопýск. **self-styled** *adj.* самозвáнный. **self-sufficient** *adj.* самостоя́тельный. **self-willed** *adj.* самовóльный.
sell [sel] *v.t. & i.* продавáть(ся) (-даю́, -даёт(ся)) *impf.*, продáть(ся) (-áм, -áшь, -áст(ся), -ади́м; -ал/-áлся, -алá(сь), -ало/-алóсь) *pf.*; *v.t.* (*deal in*) торговáть *impf.*+*i.*; ~ **off, out** распродавáть (-даю́, -даёшь) *impf.*, распродáть (-áм, -áшь, -áст, -ади́м; -ал, -алá, -ало) *pf.* **seller** *n.* торгóвец (-вца) (**of** +*i.*), продавéц (-вцá). **selling** *n.* продáжа.
Sellotape ['seləˌteɪp] *n.* (*propr.*) скотч.
selvage ['selvɪdz] *n.* крóмка.
semantic [sɪ'mæntɪk] *adj.* семанти́ческий. **semantics** *n.* семáнтика.
semaphore ['seməˌfɔː(r)] *n.* семафóр.
semblance ['sembləns] *n.* внéшний вид.
semen ['siːmən] *n.* сéмя *nt.*
semi- ['semɪ] *in comb.* полу... . **semibreve** ['semɪˌbriːv] *n.* цéлая нóта. **semicircle** *n.* полукрýг. **semicircular** *adj.* полукрýглый. **semicolon** *n.* тóчка с запятóй. **semiconductor** *n.* полупроводни́к (-á). **semi-conscious** *adj.* полубессознáтельный. **semi-detached** *adj.*: ~ **house** дом, разделённый óбщей стенóй. **semifinal** *n.* полуфинáл. **semifinalist** *n.* полуфинали́ст. **semi-official** *adj.* полуофициáльный; официóзный. **semi-precious** *adj.*: ~ **stone** самоцвéт.
seminar ['semɪˌnɑː(r)] *n.* семинáр. **seminary** ['semɪnərɪ] *n.* (духóвная) семинáрия.
semiquaver ['semɪˌkweɪvə(r)] *n.* шестнáдцатая нóта.
Semite ['siːmaɪt, 'sem-] *n.* семи́т, ~ка. **Semitic** [sɪ'mɪtɪk] *adj.* семити́ческий.
semitone ['semɪˌtəʊn] *n.* полутóн. **semivowel** ['semɪˌvaʊəl] *n.* полуглáсный *sb.*
semolina [ˌsemə'liːnə] *n.* мáнная крупá.
sempstress *see* **seamstress**
senate ['senɪt] *n.* сенáт; (*univ.*) (учёный) совéт. **senator** ['senətə(r)] *n.* сенáтор. **senatorial** [ˌsenə'tɔːrɪəl] *adj.* сенáторский.
send [send] *v.t.* посылáть *impf.*, послáть (пошлю́, -лёшь) *pf.*; ~ **down** (*univ.*) исключáть *impf.*, исключи́ть *pf.* из унирвситéта; ~ **off** отправля́ть *impf.*, ортпрáвить *pf.*; ~ **up** (*ridicule*) высмéивать *impf.*, вы́смеять (-ею, -еешь) *pf.* **sender** *n.* отправи́тель *m.* **send-off** *n.* прóводы (-дов) *pl.*
senile ['siːnaɪl] *adj.* стáрческий, дря́хлый (-л, -лá, -ло). **senility** [sɪ'nɪlɪtɪ] *n.* стáрость, дря́хлость.
senior ['siːnɪə(r)] *adj.* (*n.*) стáрший (*sb.*); ~ **citizen** стари́к (á), старýха; ~ **partner** главá (*pl.* -вы) фи́рмы. **seni'ority** *n.* старшинствó.
senna ['senə] *n.* александри́йский лист (-á).
sensation [sen'seɪʃ(ə)n] *n.* сенсáция; (*feeling*) ощущéние, чýвство. **sensational** *adj.* сенса-

ционный (-нен, -нна).

sense [sens] *n.* чу́вство, ощуще́ние; (*good* ~) здра́вый смысл; (*meaning*) смысл; **in one's ~s** в своём уме́; *v.t.* ощуща́ть *impf.*, ощути́ть (-ущу́, -ути́шь) *pf.*; чу́вствовать *impf.* **senseless** *adj.* бессмы́сленный (-ен, -енна).

sensibility [ˌsensɪˈbɪlɪtɪ] *n.* чувстви́тельность.

sensible [ˈsensɪb(ə)l] *adj.* благоразу́мный.

sensitive [ˈsensɪtɪv] *adj.* чувстви́тельный; (*touchy*) оби́дчивый. **sensiˈtivity** *n.* чувстви́тельность.

sensory [ˈsensərɪ] *adj.* чувстви́тельный.

sensual [ˈsensjʊəl, ˈsenʃʊəl], **sensuous** *adj.* чу́вственный (-ен, -енна).

sentence [ˈsent(ə)ns] *n.* фра́за; (*gram.*) предложе́ние; (*leg.*) пригово́р; *v.t.* осужда́ть *impf.*, осуди́ть (-ужу́, -у́дишь) *pf.* (**to** к+*d.*); пригова́ривать *impf.*, приговори́ть *pf.* (**to** к+*d.*).

sententious [senˈtenʃəs] *adj.* сентенцио́зный.

sentiment [ˈsentɪmənt] *n.* (*feeling*) чу́вство; (*opinion*) мне́ние. **sentimental** [ˌsentɪˈment(ə)l] *adj.* сентимента́льный. **sentimenˈtality** *n.* сентимента́льность.

sentinel [ˈsentɪn(ə)l], **sentry** *n.* часово́й *sb.*

sepal [ˈsep(ə)l, ˈsiː-] *n.* чашели́стник.

separable [ˈsepərəb(ə)l] *adj.* отдели́мый. **separate** [ˈsepərət; ˈsepəˌreɪt] *adj.* отде́льный; (*independent*) самостоя́тельный; *v.t.* & *i.* отделя́ть(ся) *impf.*, отдели́ть(ся) (-лю́(сь), -лишь(ся)) *pf.* **sepaˈration** *n.* отделе́ние. **separatism** *n.* сепарати́зм. **separatist** *n.* сепарати́ст. **separator** *n.* сепара́тор.

sepia [ˈsiːpɪə] *n.* се́пия.

sepoy [ˈsiːpɔɪ] *n.* сипа́й.

sepsis [ˈsepsɪs] *n.* се́псис.

September [sepˈtembə(r)] *n.* сентя́брь (-ря́) *m.*; *attr.* сентя́брьский.

septet [sepˈtet] *n.* септе́т.

septic [ˈseptɪk] *adj.* септи́ческий; ~ **tank** се́птик.

septuple [ˈseptjʊp(ə)l] *adj.* семикра́тный.

sepulchral [sɪˈpʌlkr(ə)l] *adj.* моги́льный, гробово́й. **sepulchre** [ˈsepəlkə(r)] *n.* моги́ла.

sequel [ˈsiːkw(ə)l] *n.* (*result*) после́дствие; (*continuation*) продолже́ние. **sequence** *n.* после́довательность; (*cin.*) эпизо́д; ~ **of events** ход собы́тий.

sequester [sɪˈkwestə(r)] *v.t.* (*isolate*) уединя́ть *impf.*, уедини́ть *pf.*; (*confiscate*) секвестрова́ть *impf.* & *pf.* **sequestered** *adj.* уединённый. **sequestration** [ˌsiːkwɪˈstreɪʃ(ə)n] *n.* секве́стр.

sequin [ˈsiːkwɪn] *n.* блёстка.

sequoia [sɪˈkwɔɪə] *n.* секво́йя.

seraph [ˈserəf] *n.* серафи́м.

Serb(ian) [ˈsɜːbɪən] *adj.* се́рбский; *n.* серб, ~ка. **Serbo-Croat(ian)** [ˌsɜːbəʊkrəʊˈeɪʃ(ə)n] *adj.* сербскохорва́тский.

serenade [ˌserəˈneɪd] *n.* серена́да; *v.t.* исполня́ть *impf.*, испо́лнить *pf.* серена́ду+*d.*

serene [sɪˈriːn, səˈriːn] *adj.* (*calm*) споко́йный; (*clear*) я́сный (я́сен, -ясна́, я́сно, я́сны́). **serenity** [sɪˈrenɪtɪ, səˈr-] *n.* споко́йствие; я́сность.

serf [sɜːf] *n.* крепостно́й *sb.* **serfdom** *n.* крепостно́е пра́во; крепостни́чество.

serge [sɜːdʒ] *n.* са́ржа.

sergeant [ˈsɑːdʒ(ə)nt] *n.* сержа́нт. **sergeant-major** *n.* старшина́ (*pl.* -ны) *m.*

serial [ˈsɪərɪəl] *adj.* сери́йный; (*of story etc.*) выходя́щий отде́льными вы́пусками; *n.* (*story*) рома́н в не́скольких частя́х; (*film*) сери́йный фильм; (*periodical*) периоди́ческое изда́ние. **serialize** *v.t.* издава́ть (-даю́, -даёшь) *impf.*, изда́ть (-а́м, -а́шь, -а́ст, -ади́м; изда́л, -а́, -о) *pf.* вы́пусками, се́риями. **series** *n.* ряд (-а́ *with 2,3,4*, *loc.* -у́; *pl.* -ы́), се́рия.

serious [ˈsɪərɪəs] *adj.* серьёзный. **seriousness** *n.* серьёзность.

sermon [ˈsɜːmən] *n.* про́поведь.

serpent [ˈsɜːpənt] *n.* змея́ (*pl.* -е́и). **serpentine** *adj.* (*coiling*) изви́листый.

serrated [seˈreɪtɪd] *adj.* зазу́бренный, зубча́тый.

serried [ˈserɪd] *adj.* со́мкнутый.

serum [ˈsɪərəm] *n.* сы́воротка.

servant [ˈsɜːv(ə)nt] *n.* слуга́ (*pl.* -ги) *m.*, служа́нка. **serve** *v.t.* служи́ть (-жу́, -жишь) *impf.*, по~ *pf.*+*d.* (**as, for** +*i.*); (*attend to*) обслу́живать *impf.*, обслужи́ть (-жу́, -жишь) *pf.*; (*food, ball*) подава́ть (-даю́, -даёшь) *impf.*, пода́ть (-а́м, -а́шь, -а́ст, -ади́м; по́дал, -а́, -о) *pf.*; (*period*) отбыва́ть *impf.*, отбы́ть (-бу́ду, -бу́дешь; о́тбы́л, -а́, -о) *pf.*; (*writ etc.*) вруча́ть *impf.*, вручи́ть *pf.* (**on** +*d.*); *v.i.* (*be suitable*) годи́ться (**for** на+*a.*, для+*g.*); (*sport*) подава́ть (-даю́, -даёшь) *impf.*, пода́ть (-а́м, -а́шь, -а́ст, -ади́м; по́дал, -а́, -о) *pf.* мяч; **it ~s him right** подело́м ему́ (*d.*). **service** [ˈsɜːvɪs] *n.* слу́жба; (*attendance*) обслу́живание; (*set of dishes etc.*) серви́з; (*sport*) пода́ча; (*transport*) сообще́ние; **at your ~** к ва́шим услу́гам; *v.t.* обслу́живать *impf.*, обслужи́ть (-жу́, -жишь) *pf.* **serviceable** *n.* (*useful*) поле́зный; (*durable*) про́чный (-чен, -чна́, -чно, про́чны́). **serviceman** *n.* военнослу́жащий *sb.* **serviˈette** *n.* салфе́тка. **servile** [ˈsɜːvaɪl] *adj.* ра́бский; (*cringing*) раболе́пный. **servility** [ˌsɜːˈvɪlɪtɪ] *n.* раболе́пие. **serving** *n.* по́рция.

sesame [ˈsesəmɪ] *n.* кунжу́т; **open ~!** сеза́м, откро́йся!

session [ˈseʃ(ə)n] *n.* заседа́ние, се́ссия.

set[1] [set] *v.t.* (*put*; ~ *trap*) ста́вить *impf.*, по~ *pf.*; (*establish*; ~ *clock*) устана́вливать *impf.*, установи́ть (-влю́, -вишь) *pf.*; (*table*) накрыва́ть *impf.*, накры́ть (-ро́ю, -ро́ешь) *pf.*; (*plant*) сажа́ть *impf.*, посади́ть (-ажу́, -а́дишь) *pf.*; (*bone*) вправля́ть *impf.*, впра́вить *pf.*; (*hair*) укла́дывать *impf.*, уложи́ть (-жу́, -жишь) *pf.*; (*jewel*) оправля́ть *impf.*, опра́вить *pf.*; (*print.*, ~ *up*) набира́ть *impf.*, набра́ть (наберу́, -рёшь; набра́л, -а́, -о) *pf.*; (*bring into state*) приводи́ть (-ожу́, -о́дишь) *impf.*, привести́ (-еду́, -едёшь; -ёл, -ела́) *pf.* (**in, to** в+*a.*); (*example*) подава́ть (-даю́, -даёшь) *impf.*, пода́ть (-а́м, -а́шь, -а́ст, -ади́м; по́дал, -а́, -о) *pf.*; (*task*) задава́ть (-аю́, -аёшь) *impf.*, зада́ть (-а́м, -а́шь, -а́ст, -ади́м; за́дал, -а́, -о) *pf.*; *v.i.* (*solidify*) тверде́ть *impf.*, за~ *pf.*; застыва́ть *impf.*, засты́(ну)ть (-ы́нет; -ы́л) *pf.*; (*fruit*) завя́зываться *impf.*, завяза́ться (-я́жется) *pf.*; (*sun etc.*) заходи́ть (-ит) *impf.*, зайти́ (зайдёт; зашёл, -шла́) *pf.*; сади́ться *impf.*, сесть (ся́дет; сел) *pf.*; ~ **eyes on** уви́деть (-и́жу, -и́дишь) *pf.*; ~ **free** освобожда́ть *impf.*, освободи́ть *pf.*; ~ **one's heart on** стра́стно жела́ть *impf.*+*g.*; ~ **to music** положи́ть (-жу́, -жишь) *pf.* на му́зыку; ~ **sail** пуска́ться *impf.*, пусти́ться (пущу́сь, пу́стишься) *pf.* в пла́вание; ~ **about** (*begin*) начина́ть *impf.*, нача́ть (начну́, -нёшь; на́чал, -а́, -о) *pf.*; (*attack*) напада́ть *impf.*, напа́сть (-аду́, -адёшь; -а́л) *pf.* на+*a.*; ~ **back** (*impede*) препя́тствовать *impf.*, вос~ *pf.*+*d.*; ~ **down** (*passenger*) выса́живать *impf.*, вы́садить *pf.*; (*in writing*) запи́сывать *impf.*, записа́ть (-ишу́, -и́шешь) *pf.*; (*attribute*) припи́сывать *impf.*, приписа́ть (-ишу́, -и́шешь) *pf.* (**to** +*d.*); ~ **forth** (*expound*) излага́ть *impf.*, изложи́ть (-жу́, -жишь) *pf.*; (*on journey*) *see* ~ **off;** ~ **in** наступа́ть *impf.*, наступи́ть (-ит) *pf.*; ~ **off** (*on journey*) отправля́ться *impf.*, отпра́виться *pf.*; (*enhance*) оттеня́ть *impf.*, оттени́ть *pf.*; ~ **out** (*state*) излага́ть *impf.*, изложи́ть (-жу́, -жишь) *pf.*; (*on journey*) *see* ~ **off;** ~ **up** (*business*) осно́вывать *impf.*, основа́ть (-ную́, -нуёшь) *pf.*; (*person*) обеспе́чивать *impf.*, обеспе́чить *pf.* (**with** +*i.*).

set² [set] *n.* набо́р, компле́кт, прибо́р; (*of dishes etc.*) серви́з; (*of people*) круг (*loc.* -у́; *pl.* -и́); (*radio*) приёмник; (*television*) телеви́зор; (*tennis*) сет; (*theatr.*) декора́ция; (*cin.*) съёмочная площа́дка.

set³ [set] *adj.* (*established*) устано́вленный (-ен); (*fixed, of smile etc.*) засты́вший; (*of intention*) обду́манный (-ан); ~ **phrase** усто́йчивое словосочета́ние; ~ **square** уго́льник.

set-back ['setbæk] *n.* неуда́ча.

settee [se'ti:] *n.* дива́н.

setter ['setə(r)] *n.* (*dog*) се́ттер; (*person*) устано́вщик.

setting ['setɪŋ] *n.* (*frame*) опра́ва; (*theatr.*) декора́ция, постано́вка; (*mus.*) му́зыка на слова́; (*of sun etc.*) захо́д, зака́т.

settle ['set(ə)l] *v.t.* (*decide*) реша́ть *impf.*, реши́ть *pf.*; (*arrange*) ула́живать *impf.*, ула́дить *pf.*; (*a bill etc.*) опла́чивать *impf.*, оплати́ть (-ачу́, -а́тишь) *pf.*; (*colonize*) заселя́ть *impf.*, засели́ть *pf.*; *v.i.* сели́ться *impf.*, по~ *pf.*; (*subside*) оседа́ть *impf.*, осе́сть (ося́дет; осе́л) *pf.*; ~ **down** уса́живаться *impf.*, усе́сться (уся́дусь, -дешься; усе́лся) *pf.* **settlement** *n.* поселе́ние; (*of dispute*) разреше́ние; (*payment*) упла́та; (*subsidence*) оса́дка, оседа́ние; **marriage** ~ бра́чный контра́кт. **settler** *n.* поселе́нец (-нца).

seven ['sev(ə)n] *adj.* & *n.* семь (-ми́, -мью́); (*collect.*; *7 pairs*) се́меро (-ры́х); (*cards*; *number 7*) семёрка; (*time*) семь (часо́в); (*age*) семь лет. **seventeen** *adj.* & *n.* семна́дцать; (*age*) семна́дцать лет. **seven'teenth** *adj.* & *n.* семна́дцатый; (*fraction*) семна́дцатая (часть (*pl.* -ти, -те́й)); (*date*) семна́дцатое (число́). **seventh** *adj.* & *n.* седьмо́й; (*fraction*) седьма́я (часть(*pl.* -ти, -те́й)); (*date*) седьмо́е (число́). **seventieth** *adj.* & *n.* семидеся́тый; (*fraction*) семидеся́тая (часть (*pl.* -ти, -те́й)). **seventy** *adj.* & *n.* се́мьдесят (-ми́десяти, -мью́десятью); (*age*) се́мьдесят лет; *pl.* (*decade*) семидеся́тые го́ды *m.pl.*

sever ['sevə(r)] *v.t.* (*cut off*) отреза́ть *impf.*, отре́зать (-е́жу, -е́жешь) *pf.*; (*relations*) разрыва́ть *impf.*, разорва́ть (-ву́, -вёшь; -ва́л, -вала́, -ва́ло) *pf.*; (*friendship*) порыва́ть *impf.*, порва́ть (-ву́, -вёшь; порва́л, -а́, -о) *pf.*

several ['sevr(ə)l] *pron.* (*adj.*) не́сколько (+*g.*).

severance ['sevərəns] *n.* разры́в; ~ **pay** выходно́е посо́бие.

severe [sɪ'vɪə(r)] *adj.* стро́гий (строг, -а́, -о), суро́вый; (*illness etc.*) тяжёлый (-л, -ла́). **severity** [sɪ'verɪtɪ] *n.* стро́гость, суро́вость.

sew [səʊ] *v.t.* шить (шью, шьёшь) *impf.*, с~ (сошью́, -ьёшь) *pf.*; ~ **on** пришива́ть *impf.*, приши́ть (-шью́, -шьёшь) *pf.*; ~ **up** зашива́ть *impf.*, заши́ть (-шью́, -шьёшь) *pf.*

sewage ['su:ɪdʒ, 'sju:-] *n.* сто́чные во́ды *f.pl.*, нечисто́ты (-т) *pl.*; ~ **farm** поля́ *nt.pl.* ороше́ния. **sewer** *n.* сто́чная, канализацио́нная, труба́ (*pl.* -бы). **sewerage** *n.* канализа́ция.

sewing ['səʊɪŋ] *n.* шитьё. **sewing-machine** *n.* шве́йная маши́на.

sex [seks] *n.* (*gender*) пол; секс; ~ **appeal** сексапи́льность; **extramarital** ~ секс вне бра́ка; *adj.* сексуа́льный.

sexcentenary [ˌseksen'ti:nərɪ] *n.* шестисотле́тие.

sexism ['seksɪz(ə)m] *n.* дискримина́ция же́нщин. **sexist** *n.* женофо́б; *adj.* женоненави́стнический.

sextant ['sekst(ə)nt] *n.* секста́нт.

sextet [sek'stet] *n.* сексте́т.

sexton ['sekst(ə)n] *n.* понома́рь (-ря́) *m.*, моги́льщик.

sextuple ['seksˌtju:p(ə)l] *adj.* шестикра́тный.

sexual ['seksjʊəl, -ʃʊəl] *adj.* полово́й, сексуа́льный. **sexuality** [ˌseksjʊ'ælɪtɪ, -ʃʊ'ælɪtɪ] *n.* сексуа́льность. **sexy** *adj.* (*alluring*) соблазни́тельный; (*erotic*) эроти́ческий.

sh [ʃ] *int.* ти́ше!; тсс!

shabby ['ʃæbɪ] *adj.* поно́шенный (-ен), потрёпанный (-ан, -анна); (*mean*) по́длый (подл, -а́, -о).

shack [ʃæk] *n.* лачу́га, хи́жина.

shackle ['ʃæk(ə)l] *n.*: *pl.* кандалы́ (-ло́в) *pl.*; (*also fig.*) око́вы (-в) *pl.*; *v.t.* зако́вывать *impf.*, закова́ть (-кую́, -куёшь) *pf.*

shade [ʃeɪd] *n.* тень (*loc.* -ни́; *pl.* -ни, -не́й), полумра́к; (*of colour, meaning*) отте́нок (-нка); (*lamp-*∼) абажу́р; **a** ∼ чуть-чу́ть; *v.t.* затеня́ть *impf.*, затени́ть *pf.*; заслоня́ть *impf.* заслони́ть (-оню́, -о́ни́шь) *pf.*; (*drawing*) тушева́ть (-шу́ю, -шу́ешь) *impf.*, за∼ *pf.*; *v.i.* незаме́тно переходи́ть (-ит) *impf.* (**into** в+*a.*). **shadow** ['ʃædəʊ] *n.* тень (*loc.* -ни́; *pl.* -ни, -не́й); *v.t.* (*follow*) та́йно следи́ть *impf.* за+*i.* **shadowy** *adj.* тёмный (-мен, -мна́), нея́сный (-сен, -сна́, -сно). **shady** *adj.* тени́стый; (*suspicious*) подозри́тельный.

shaft [ʃɑ:ft] *n.* (*of spear*) дре́вко (*pl.* -ки, -ков); (*arrow*; *fig.*) стрела́ (*pl.* -лы); (*of light*) луч (-а́); (*of cart*) огло́бля (*g.pl.* -бель); (*axle*) вал (*loc.* -у́; *pl.* -ы́); (*mine* ∼) ствол (-а́) (ша́хты).

shaggy *adj.* лохма́тый, косма́тый.

shah [ʃɑ:] *n.* шах.

shake [ʃeɪk] *v.t.* & *i.* трясти́(сь) (-су́(сь), -сёшь(ся); -с(ся), -сла́(сь)) *impf.*; *v.i.* (*tremble*) дрожа́ть (-жу́, -жи́шь) *impf.*; *v.t.* (*impair*) колеба́ть (-блю, -блешь) *impf.*, по∼ *pf.*; ∼ **hands** пожима́ть *impf.*, пожа́ть (-жму́, -жмёшь) *pf.* ру́ку+*d.*; ∼ **one's head** покача́ть *pf.* голово́й; ∼ **off** стря́хивать *impf.*, стряхну́ть *pf.*; (*fig.*) избавля́ться *impf.*, изба́виться *pf.* от+*g.*; ∼ **up** (*fig.*) встря́хивать *impf.*, встряхну́ть *pf.*

shako ['ʃeɪkəʊ] *n.* ки́вер (*pl.* -а́).

shaky ['ʃeɪkɪ] *adj.* ша́ткий (-ток, -тка), непро́чный (-чен, -чна́, -чно).

shale [ʃeɪl] *n.* сла́нец (-нца).

shallot [ʃə'lɒt] *n.* лук-шало́т.

shallow ['ʃæləʊ] *adj.* ме́лкий (-лок, -лка́, -лко); (*superficial*) пове́рхностный; *n.* мелково́дье, мель (*loc.* -ли́).

sham [ʃæm] *v.t.* & *i.* притворя́ться *impf.*, притвори́ться *pf.*+*i.*; *n.* притво́рство; (*person*) притво́рщик, -ица; *adj.* притво́рный; (*fake*) подде́льный.

shaman ['ʃæmən] *n.* шама́н.

shamble ['ʃæmb(ə)l] *v.i.* волочи́ть (-чу́, -чишь) *impf.* но́ги.

shambles ['ʃæmb(ə)lz] *n.* бо́йня; (*muddle*) хао́с.

shame [ʃeɪm] *n.* стыд, позо́р; *v.t.* стыди́ть *impf.*, при∼ *pf.* **shamefaced** *adj.* стыдли́вый. **shameful** *adj.* позо́рный. **shameless** *adj.* бессты́дный.

shampoo [ʃæm'pu:] *v.t.* мыть (мо́ю, мо́ешь) *impf.*, по∼ *pf.*; *n.* шампу́нь *m.*

shamrock ['ʃæmrɒk] *n.* трили́стник.

shandy ['ʃændɪ] *n.* смесь (просто́го) пи́ва с лимона́дом, с имби́рным.

shank [ʃæŋk] *n.* (*leg*) нога́ (*a.* -гу; *pl.* -ги, -г, -га́м), го́лень; (*shaft*) сте́ржень (-жня) *m.*

shanty[1] ['ʃæntɪ] *n.* (*hut*) хиба́рка, лачу́га; ∼ **town** бидонви́ль, трущо́ба.

shanty[2] ['ʃæntɪ] *n.* (*song*) матро́сская пе́сня (*g.pl.* -сен).

shape [ʃeɪp] *n.* фо́рма, вид, о́браз; *v.t.* придава́ть (-даю́, -даёшь) *impf.*, прида́ть (-а́м, -а́шь, -а́ст, -ади́м; при́дал, -а́, -о) *pf.* фо́рму+*d.*; *v.i.* принима́ть *impf.*, приня́ть (-и́мет; при́нял, -а́, -о) *pf.* фо́рму. **shapeless** *adj.* бесфо́рменный (-ен, -енна). **shapely** *adj.* стро́йный (-о́ен, -ойна́, -о́йно).

share [ʃeə(r)] *n.* до́ля (*pl.* -ли, -ле́й), часть (*pl.* -ти, -те́й); (*participation*) уча́стие; (*econ.*) а́кция, пай (*pl.* паи́, паёв); *v.t.* дели́ть (-лю́, -лишь) *impf.*, по∼ *pf.*; разделя́ть *impf.*, раздели́ть (-лю́, -лишь) *pf.* **shareholder** *n.* акционе́р, ∼ка; па́йщик, -ица.

shark [ʃɑ:k] *n.* аку́ла.

sharp [ʃɑ:p] *adj.* о́стрый (остр & остёр, остра́, остро́); (*steep*) круто́й (крут, -а́, -о); (*sudden*; *harsh*) ре́зкий (-зок, -зка́, -зко); (*fine*) то́нкий (-нок, -нка́, -нко, то́нки́); *n.* (*mus.*) дие́з; *adv.* (*with time*) ро́вно; (*of angle*) кру́то. **sharpen** ['ʃɑ:pən] *v.t.* точи́ть (-чу́, -чишь) *impf.*, на∼ *pf.*; обостря́ть *impf.*, обостри́ть *pf.*

shatter ['ʃætə(r)] *v.t.* & *i.* разбива́ть(ся) *impf.*, разби́ть(ся) (разобью́, -ьёт(ся)) *pf.* вдре́безги; *v.t.* (*hopes etc.*) разруша́ть *impf.*, разру́шить *pf.*

shave [ʃeɪv] *v.t.* & *i.* бри́ть(ся) (бре́ю(сь), -е́ешь(ся)) *impf.*, по∼ *pf.*; *v.t.* (*plane*) строга́ть *impf.*, вы́∼ *pf.*; *n.* бритьё; **close** ∼ едва́ избе́гнутая опа́сность. **shaver** *n.* электри́ческая бри́тва.

shawl [ʃɔ:l] *n.* шаль.

she [ʃi:] *pron.* она́ (её, ей, ей & е́ю, о ней).

sheaf [ʃi:f] *n.* сноп (-а́); (*of papers etc.*) свя́зка.

shear [ʃɪə(r)] *v.t.* стричь (-игу́, -ижёшь; -иг) *impf.*, о∼ *pf.* **shearer** *n.* стрига́льщик. **shears** *n.* но́жницы (-ц) *pl.*

sheath [ʃi:θ] *n.* (*for sword etc.*) но́жны (*g.* -жен) *pl.*; (*anat.*) оболо́чка; (*for cable etc.*) обши́вка. **sheathe** [ʃi:ð] *v.t.* вкла́дывать *impf.*, вложи́ть (-жу́, -жишь) *pf.* в но́жны; обшива́ть *impf.*, обши́ть (обошью́, -ьёшь) *pf.* **sheathing** *n.* обши́вка.

sheave [ʃi:v] *n.* шкив (*pl.* -ы́).

shed[1] [ʃed] *n.* сара́й.

shed[2] [ʃed] *v.t.* (*tears, blood, light*) пролива́ть *impf.*, проли́ть (-лью́, -льёшь; про́ли́л, -а́, -о) *pf.*; (*skin, clothes*) сбра́сывать *impf.*, сбро́сить *pf.*

sheen [ʃi:n] *n.* блеск.

sheep [ʃi:p] *n.* овца́ (*pl.* о́вцы, ове́ц, о́вцам). **sheepdog** *n.* овча́рка. **sheepfold** *n.* овча́рня (*g.pl.* -рен). **sheepish** *adj.* (*bashful*) засте́нчивый; (*abashed*) сконфу́женный (-ен). **sheepskin** *n.* овчи́на.

sheer [ʃɪə(r)] *adj.* абсолю́тный, су́щий; (*textile*) прозра́чный; (*rock etc.*) отве́сный.

sheet[1] [ʃi:t] *n.* (*on bed*) простыня́ (*pl.* про́стыни, -ы́нь, -ыня́м); (*of glass, paper, etc.*) лист (-а́); (*wide expanse*) пелена́ (*g.pl.*

-ён); *attr.* (*metal, glass etc.*) листово́й; ~ **lightning** зарни́ца.

sheet[2] [ʃiːt] *n.* (*naut.*) шкот; ~ **anchor** запасно́й станово́й я́корь (*pl.* -ря́) *m.*; (*fig.*) я́корь (*pl.* -ря́) *m.* спасе́ния.

sheikh [ʃeɪk] *n.* шейх.

shelf [ʃelf] *n.* по́лка; (*of cliff etc.*) усту́п. **shelf-life** *n.* срок хране́ния. **shelf-mark** *n.* шифр.

shell [ʃel] *n.* (*of mollusc etc.*) ра́ковина; (*of tortoise*) щит (-а́); (*of egg, nut*) скорлупа́ (*pl.* -пы); (*of building etc.*) о́стов; (*explosive* ~) снаря́д; *v.t.* очища́ть *impf.*, очи́стить *pf.*; лущи́ть *impf.*, об~ *pf.*; (*bombard*) обстре́ливать *impf.*, обстреля́ть *pf.*; ~ **out** (*abs.*) раскоше́ливаться *impf.*, раскоше́литься *pf.*

shellac [ʃəˈlæk] *n.* шелла́к.

shellfish [ˈʃeltfɪʃ] *n.* (*mollusc*) моллю́ск; (*crustacean*) ракообра́зное *sb.*

shelter [ˈʃeltə(r)] *n.* прию́т, убе́жище, укры́тие; *v.t.* дава́ть (даю́, даёшь) *impf.*, дать (дам, дашь, даст, дади́м; дал, -а́, да́ло́, -и) *pf.* прию́т+*d.*; служи́ть (-жу́, -жишь) *impf.*, по~ *pf.* убе́жищем, укры́тием+*d.*; *v.t.* & *i.* укрыва́ть(ся) *impf.*, укры́ть(ся) (-ро́ю(сь), -ро́ешь(ся)) *pf.*

shelve[1] [ʃelv] *v.t.* (*defer*) откла́дывать *impf.*, отложи́ть *pf.* (в до́лгий я́щик).

shelve[2] [ʃelv] *v.i.* (*of land*) отло́го спуска́ться *impf.* **shelving**[1] *adj.* отло́гий.

shelving[2] [ˈʃelvɪŋ] *n.* (*shelves*) стелла́ж (-а́).

shepherd [ˈʃepəd] *n.* пасту́х (-а́); (*fig.*) па́стырь *m.*; *v.t.* проводи́ть (-ожу́, -о́дишь) *impf.*, провести́ (-еду́, -едёшь; -ёл, -ела́) *pf.* **shepherdess** *n.* пасту́шка.

sherbet [ˈʃɜːbət] *n.* шербе́т.

sheriff [ˈʃerɪf] *n.* шери́ф.

sherry [ˈʃerɪ] *n.* хе́рес.

shield [ʃiːld] *n.* щит (-а́); *v.t.* прикрыва́ть *impf.*, прикры́ть (-ро́ю, -ро́ешь) *pf.*; заслоня́ть *impf.*, заслони́ть *pf.*

shift [ʃɪft] *v.t.* & *i.* (*change position*) перемеща́ть(ся) *impf.*, перемести́ть(ся) *pf.*; (*change form*) меня́ть(ся) *impf.*; *v.t.* (*move*; ~ *responsibility etc.*) перекла́дывать *impf.*, переложи́ть (-жу́, -жишь) *pf.*; *n.* перемеще́ние; (*of workers*) сме́на. **shiftless** *adj.* неуме́лый. **shifty** *adj.* ненадёжный, нече́стный.

shilly-shally [ˈʃɪlɪˌʃælɪ] *n.* нереши́тельность; *v.i.* колеба́ться (-блюсь, -блешься) *impf.*, по~ *pf.*

shimmer [ˈʃɪmə(r)] *v.i.* мерца́ть *impf.*; *n.* мерца́ние.

shin [ʃɪn] *n.* го́лень; *v.i.*: ~ **up** ла́зить *impf.* по+*d.* **shin-bone** *n.* большеберцо́вая кость (*pl.* -ти, -те́й).

shindy [ˈʃɪndɪ] *n.* шум, сва́лка.

shine [ʃaɪn] *v.i.* свети́ть(ся) (-ит(ся)) *impf.*; блесте́ть (-ещу́, -е́щешь & -ести́шь) *impf.*; (*of sun etc.*) сия́ть *impf.*; *v.t.* полирова́ть *impf.*, от~ *pf.*; *n.* свет, сия́ние, блеск; (*polish*) гля́нец (-нца).

shingle[1] [ˈʃɪŋg(ə)l] *n.* (*for roof*) (кро́вельная) дра́нка.

shingle[2] [ˈʃɪŋg(ə)l] *n.* (*pebbles*) га́лька.

shingles [ˈʃɪŋg(ə)lz] *n.* опоя́сывающий лиша́й (-ая́).

shin-guard [ˈʃɪngɑːd], **-pad** *n.* щито́к (-тка́).

shining [ˈʃaɪnɪŋ], **shiny** *adj.* блестя́щий.

ship [ʃɪp] *n.* кора́бль (-ля́) *m.*; су́дно (*pl.* -да́, -до́в); *v.t.* (*transport*) перевози́ть (-ожу́, -о́зишь) *impf.*, перевезти́ (-езу́, -езёшь; -ёз, -езла́) *pf.* (по воде́); (*dispatch*) отправля́ть *impf.*, отпра́вить *pf.* (по воде́). **shipbuilding** *n.* судостро́ительство. **shipment** *n.* (*loading*) погру́зка; (*consignment*) груз. **shipping** *n.* суда́ (-до́в) *pl.* **shipshape** *adv.* в по́лном поря́дке. **shipwreck** *n.* кораблекруше́ние. **shipwright** *n.* (*shipbuilder*) судострои́тель *m.*; (*carpenter*) корабе́льный пло́тник. **shipyard** *n.* верфь.

shire [ˈʃaɪə(r)] *n.* гра́фство.

shirk [ʃɜːk] *v.t.* увиливать *impf.*, увильну́ть *pf.* от+*g.*

shirt [ʃɜːt] *n.* руба́шка. **shirtsleeves** *n.*: **in** ~ без пиджака́.

shiver [ˈʃɪvə(r)] *v.i.* (*tremble*) дрожа́ть (-жу́, -жи́шь) *impf.*; *n.* дрожь.

shoal[1] [ʃəʊl] *n.* (*bank*) мель (*loc.* -ли́).

shoal[2] [ʃəʊl] *n.* (*of fish*) ста́я, кося́к (-а́).

shock[1] [ʃɒk] *n.* (*impact etc.*) уда́р, толчо́к (-чка́); (*med.*) шок; *attr.* (*troops, brigade, wave*) уда́рный; ~ **absorber** амортиза́тор; ~ **tactics** та́ктика сокруши́тельных уда́ров; ~ **therapy** шокотерапи́я; *v.t.* шоки́ровать *impf.*

shock[2] [ʃɒk] *n.* (*of sheaves*) копна́ (*pl.* -пны, -пён,-пна́м).

shock[3] [ʃɒk] *n.* (*of hair*) копна́ воло́с.

shocking [ˈʃɒkɪŋ] *adj.* возмути́тельный, ужа́сный. **shock-worker** *n.* уда́рник.

shod [ʃɒd] *adj.* обу́тый.

shoddy [ˈʃɒdɪ] *adj.* дрянно́й (-нен, -нна́, -нно).

shoe [ʃuː] *n.* ту́фля (*g.pl.* -фель); (*horse-*~) подко́ва; (*tech.*) башма́к (-а́); *v.t.* подко́вывать *impf.*, подкова́ть (-кую́, -куёшь) *pf.* **shoeblack** *n.* чисти́льщик сапо́г. **shoehorn** *n.* рожо́к (-жка́). **shoe-lace** *n.* шнуро́к (-рка́) для боти́нок. **shoemaker** *n.* сапо́жник. **shoe-string** *n.*: **on a** ~ с небольши́ми сре́дствами.

shoo [ʃuː] *int.* кш!; *v.t.* прогоня́ть *impf.*, прогна́ть (прогоню́, -нишь; прогна́л, -а́, -о) *pf.*

shoot [ʃuːt] *v.t.* & *i.* (*discharge*) стреля́ть *impf.* (*a gun* из+*g.*; **at** в+*a.*, по+*d.*); (*arrow*) пуска́ть *impf.*, пусти́ть (пущу́, пу́стишь) *pf.*; (*kill*) застре́ливать *impf.*, застрели́ть (-лю́, -лишь) *pf.*; (*execute*) расстре́ливать *impf.*, расстреля́ть *pf.*; (*hunt*) охо́титься *impf.* на+*a.*; (*football*) бить (бью, бьёшь) *impf.* (по воро́там); (*cin.*) снима́ть *impf.*, снять (сниму́, -мешь; снял, -а́, -о) *pf.* (фильм); *v.i.* (*go swiftly*) проноси́ться (-ошу́сь, -о́сишься) *impf.*, пронести́сь (-есу́сь, -есёшься; -ёсся, -есла́сь) *pf.*; (*of plant*) пуска́ть *impf.*, пусти́ть (-ит) *pf.* ростки́; ~ **down** (*aircraft*) сбива́ть *impf.*, сбить (собью́, -бьёшь *pf.*; *n.* (*branch*) росто́к (-тка́), побе́г; (*hunt*) охо́та. **shooting** *n.* стрельба́; (*hunting*) охо́та. **shooting-box** *n.* охо́тничий до́мик. **shooting-gallery** *n.* тир. **shooting-range** *n.* стре́льбище.

shop [ʃɒp] *n.* (*for sales*) магази́н, ла́вка; (*for repairs, manufacture*) мастерска́я *sb.*, цех (*loc.* -е & -у́; *pl.* -и & -а́); **talk** ~ говори́ть *impf.*, на узкопрофессиона́льные те́мы, о дела́х; ~ **assistant** продаве́ц (-вца́), -вщи́ца; ~ **steward** цехово́й ста́роста *m.*; *v.i.* де́лать *impf.*, с~ *pf.* поку́пки (*f.pl.*); *v.t.* (*imprison*) сажа́ть *impf.*, посади́ть (-ажу́, -а́дишь) *pf.* в тюрьму́; (*inform against*) доноси́ть (-ошу́, -о́сишь) *impf.*, донести́ (-су́, -сёшь; донёс, -ла́) *pf.* на+*a.* **shop-floor** *n.* (*fig.*) рабо́чие *sb.pl.* **shopkeeper** *n.* ла́вочник. **shoplifter** *n.* магази́нщик. **shopper** *n.* покупа́тель *m.*, ~ница. **shopping** *n.* поку́пки *f.pl.*; **go, do one's** ~ де́лать *impf.*, с~ *pf.* поку́пки. **shopwalker** *n.* дежу́рный администра́тор магази́на. **shop-window** *n.* витри́на.

shore¹ [ʃɔː(r)] *n.* бе́рег (*loc.* -у́; *pl.* -а́); ~ **leave** о́тпуск на бе́рег.

shore² [ʃɔː(r)] *v.t.*: ~ **up** подпира́ть *impf.*, подпере́ть (подопру́, -рёшь; подпёр) *pf.*

shorn [ʃɔːn] *adj.* остри́женный (-ен).

short [ʃɔːt] *adj.* коро́ткий (ко́ро́ток, -тка́, ко́ро́тко́); (*concise*) кра́ткий (-ток, -тка́, -тко); (*not tall*) ни́зкий (-зок, -зка́, -зко, ни́зки́); (*of person*) ни́зкого ро́ста; (*deficient*) недоста́точный; **be** ~ **of** (*have too little*) испы́тывать *impf.*, испыта́ть *pf.* недоста́ток в+*p.*; (*not amount to*) быть (*fut.* бу́ду, -дешь; был, -а́, -о; не́ был, -а́, -о) ме́ньше+*g.*; (*uncivil*) гру́бый (груб, -а́, -о); (*crumbling*) рассы́пчатый; **in** ~ одни́м сло́вом; ~ **(circuit)** коро́ткое замыка́ние; ~ **cut** коро́ткий путь (-ти́, -тём) *m.*; ~ **list** оконча́тельный спи́сок (-ска); ~ **measure** недоме́р; **at** ~ **notice** неме́дленно; ~ **sight** близору́кость; ~ **story** расска́з, нове́лла; **in** ~ **supply** дефици́тный; ~ **wave** коротково́лно́вый; ~ **weight** недове́с; *n.* (*film*) короткометра́жный фильм; (*drink*) спиртно́е *sb.*; *pl.* шо́рты (-т) *pl.* **shortage** *n.* недоста́ток (-тка); дефици́т. **shortbread** *n.* песо́чное пече́нье. **short-change** *v.t.* недодава́ть (-даю́, -даёшь) *impf.*, недода́ть (-а́м, -а́шь, -а́ст, -ади́м; недо́дал, -а́, -о) *pf.* сда́чу+*d.* **short(-circuit)** *v.t.* замыка́ть *impf.*, замкну́ть *pf.* на́коротко. **shortcoming** *n.* недоста́ток (-тка). **shorten** *v.t. & i.* укора́чивать(ся) *impf.*, укороти́ть(ся) *pf.*; сокраща́ть(ся) *impf.*, сократи́ть(ся) (-ащу́, -ати́т(ся)) *pf.*; ~ **sail** убавля́ть *impf.*, уба́вить *pf.* парусо́в. **shortfall** *n.* дефици́т. **shorthand** *n.* стеногра́фия. **shorthorn** *n.* шортго́рнская поро́да скота́. **short-list** *v.t.* включа́ть *impf.*, включи́ть *pf.* в оконча́тельный спи́сок. **short-lived** *adj.* недолгове́чный, мимолётный. **shortly** *adv.*: ~ **after** вско́ре (по́сле+*g.*); ~ **before** незадо́лго (до+*g.*). **short-range** *adj.* краткосро́чный. **short-sighted** *adj.* близору́кий; (*fig.*) недальнови́дный. **short-tempered** *adj.* вспы́льчивый. **short-term** *adj.* краткосро́чный. **short-winded** *adj.* страда́ющий оды́шкой.

shot¹ [ʃɒt] *n.* (*discharge of gun*) вы́стрел; (*for cannon; sport*) ядро́ (*pl.* я́дра, я́дер, я́драм); (*pellet*) дроби́нка; (*as pl., collect.*) дробь; (*person*) стрело́к (-лка́); (*attempt*) попы́тка; (*injection*) уко́л; (*phot.*) сни́мок (-мка); (*cin.*) съёмка; **like a** ~ о́чень охо́тно, неме́дленно; **a** ~ **in the arm** (*fig.*) сти́мул.

shot² [ʃɒt] *adj.* (*of material*) перели́вчатый.

shotgun ['ʃɒtgʌn] *n.* дробови́к (-а́).

shoulder ['ʃəʊldə(r)] *n.* плечо́ (*pl.* -чи, -ч, -ча́м); (*cul.*) лопа́тка; (*of road*) обо́чина; **straight from the** ~ сплеча́; ~ **to** ~ плечо́м к плечу́; *v.t.* взва́ливать *impf.*, взвали́ть (-лю́, -лишь) *pf.* на пле́чи. **shoulder-blade** *n.* лопа́тка. **shoulder-strap** *n.* брете́лька; (*on uniform*) пого́н (*g.pl.* -н).

shout [ʃaʊt] *n.* крик; *v.i.* крича́ть (-чу́, -чи́шь) *impf.*, кри́кнуть *pf.*; ~ **down** перекри́кивать *impf.*, перекрича́ть (-чу́, -чи́шь) *pf.*

shove [ʃʌv] *n.* толчо́к (-чка́); *v.t. & i.* толка́ть(ся) *impf.*, толкну́ть *pf.*; ~ **off** (*coll.*) убира́ться *impf.*, убра́ться (уберу́сь, -рёшься; убра́лся, -ала́сь, -а́ло́сь) *pf.*

shovel ['ʃʌv(ə)l] *n.* сово́к (-вка́), лопа́та; *v.t.* копа́ть *impf.*, вы́~ *pf.*; (~ *up*) сгреба́ть *impf.*, сгрести́ (сгребу́, -бёшь; сгрёб, -ла́) *pf.*

show [ʃəʊ] *v.t.* пока́зывать *impf.*, показа́ть (-ажу́, -а́жешь) *pf.*; (*exhibit*) выставля́ть *impf.*, вы́ставить *pf.*; (*film etc.*) демонстри́ровать *impf.*, про~ *pf.*; *v.i.* быть ви́дным (-ден, -дна́, -дно, ви́дны́), заме́тным; ~ **off** (*v.i.*) рисова́ться *impf.*; *n.* (*exhibition*) вы́ставка; (*theatr.*) спекта́кль *m.*; (*spectacle; pageant*) зре́лище; (*business*) де́ло (*pl.* -ла́); (*appearance*) ви́димость; ~ **of hands** голосова́ние подня́тием руки́. **showboat** *n.* плаву́чий теа́тр. **showcase** *n.* витри́на.

shower ['ʃaʊə(r)] *n.* (*rain*) до́ждик; (*hail; fig.*) град; (~*-bath*) душ; *v.t.* осыпа́ть *impf.*, осы́пать (-плю, -плешь) *pf.*+*i.* (**on** +*a.*); *v.i.* принима́ть *impf.*, приня́ть (приму́, -мешь; при́нял, -а́, -о) *pf.* душ. **showery** *adj.* дождли́вый.

showgirl ['ʃəʊgɜːl] *n.* стати́стка. **showjumping** *n.* соревнова́ние по ска́чкам. **showman** *n.* балага́нщик. **showroom** *n.* сало́н.

showy ['ʃəʊɪ] *adj.* я́ркий (я́рок, ярка́, я́рко); (*gaudy*) бро́ский (-сок, -ска́, -ско).

shrapnel ['ʃræpn(ə)l] *n.* шрапне́ль.

shred [ʃred] *n.* клочо́к (-чка́), лоскуто́к (-тка́); **not a** ~ ни ка́пли; **tear to** ~**s** (*fig.*) по́лностью опроверга́ть *impf.*, опрове́ргнуть (-г(нул), -гла) *pf.*; *v.t.* ре́зать (ре́жу, -жешь) *impf.*, на клочки́; рвать (рву, рвёшь; рвал, -а́, -о) *impf.* в клочки́.

shrew [ʃruː] *n.* (*woman*) сварли́вая, строптйвая, же́нщина; (*animal*) землеро́йка.
shrewd [ʃruːd] *adj.* проница́тельный.
shrewish ['ʃruːɪʃ] *adj.* сварли́вый.
shriek [ʃriːk] *n.* пронзи́тельный крик, визг; *v.i.* визжа́ть (-жу́, -жи́шь) *impf.*; крича́ть (-чу́, -чи́шь) *impf.*, кри́кнуть *pf.*
shrill [ʃrɪl] *adj.* пронзи́тельный, ре́зкий (-зок, -зка́, -зко).
shrimp [ʃrɪmp] *n.* креве́тка.
shrine [ʃraɪn] *n.* (*casket*) ра́ка; (*tomb*) гробни́ца; (*sacred place*) святы́ня.
shrink [ʃrɪŋk] *v.i.* сади́ться *impf.*, сесть (ся́дет; сел) *pf.*; *v.t.* вызыва́ть *impf.*, вы́звать (-зовет) *pf.* уса́дку у+*g.*; ~ **from** уклоня́ться *impf.* от+*g.*; избега́ть *impf.*+*g.* **shrinkage** *n.* уса́дка. **shrink-proof** *adj.* безуса́дочный.
shrivel ['ʃrɪv(ə)l] *v.t.* & *i.* съёживать(ся) *impf.*, съёжить(ся) *pf.*
shroud [ʃraʊd] *n.* са́ван; *pl.* (*naut.*) ва́нты *f.pl.*; *v.t.* (*fig.*) оку́тывать *impf.*, оку́тать *pf.* (**in** +*i.*).
Shrovetide ['ʃrəʊvtaɪd] *n.* Ма́сленица.
shrub [ʃrʌb] *n.* куст (-а́), кустáрник. **shrubbery** *n.* куста́рник.
shrug [ʃrʌg] *v.t.* & *i.* пожима́ть *impf.*, пожа́ть (-жму́, -жмёшь) *pf.* (плеча́ми).
shudder ['ʃʌdə(r)] *n.* содрога́ние; *v.i.* содрога́ться *impf.*, содрогну́ться *pf.*
shuffle ['ʃʌf(ə)l] *v.t.* & *i.* (*one's feet*) ша́ркать *impf.* (нога́ми); *v.t.* (*cards*) тасова́ть *impf.*, с~ *pf.*; (*intermingle, confuse*) переме́шивать *impf.*, перемеша́ть *pf.*; ~ **off** (*blame etc.*) сва́ливать *impf.*, свали́ть (-лю́, -лишь) *pf.* (**on to** на+*a.*); *n.* ша́рканье; тасо́вка.
shun [ʃʌn] *v.t.* избега́ть *impf.*+*g.*
shunt [ʃʌnt] *v.i.* (*rail.*) маневри́ровать *impf.*, с~ *pf.*; *v.t.* (*rail.*) переводи́ть (-ожу́, -о́дишь) *impf.*, перевести́ (-еду́, -едёшь; -ёл, -ела́) *pf.* на запа́сный путь.
shut [ʃʌt] *v.t.* & *i.* закрыва́ть(ся) *impf.*, закры́ть(ся) (-ро́ю, -ро́ет(ся)) *pf.*; ~ **in** запира́ть *impf.*, запере́ть (запру́, -рёшь; за́пер, -ла́, -ло) *pf.*; ~ **up** (*v.i.*) замолча́ть (-чу́, -чи́шь) *pf.*; (*imper.*) заткни́сь!
shutter ['ʃʌtə(r)] *n.* ста́вень (-вня) *m.*, ста́вня (*g.pl.* -вен); (*phot.*) затво́р; *v.t.* закрыва́ть *impf.*, закры́ть (-ро́ю, -ро́ешь) *pf.* ста́внями.
shuttle ['ʃʌt(ə)l] *n.* челно́к (-а́). **shuttlecock** *n.* вола́н.
shy[1] [ʃaɪ] *adj.* засте́нчивый, ро́бкий (-бок, -бка́, -бко).
shy[2] [ʃaɪ] *v.i.* (*in alarm*) пуга́ться *impf.*, ис~ *pf.* (**at** +*g.*).
shy[3] [ʃaɪ] *v.t.* (*throw*) броса́ть *impf.*, бро́сить *pf.*; *n.* бросо́к (-ска́).
Siamese [ˌsaɪə'miːz] *adj.* сиа́мский; ~ **twins** сиа́мские близнецы́ *m.pl.*
Siberia [saɪ'bɪərɪə] *n.* Сиби́рь. **Siberian** *adj.* сиби́рский; *n.* сибиря́к (-а́), -я́чка.
sibilant ['sɪbɪlənt] *adj.* (*n.*) свистя́щий (звук) (*sb.*).
sic [sɪk] *adv.* так!
sick [sɪk] *adj.* больно́й (-лен, -льна́); **be, feel,** ~ тошни́ть *impf.* *impers.*+*a.*; то́шно *impers.*+*d.*; **be** ~ **for** (*pine*) тоскова́ть *impf.* по+*d.*; **be** ~ **of** надоеда́ть *impf.*, надое́сть (-е́м, -е́шь, -е́ст, -еди́м; -е́л) *pf.*+*nom.* (*object*) & *d.* (*subject*); **I'm** ~ **of her** она́ мне надое́ла. **sickbed** *n.* посте́ль больно́го. **sick-benefit** *n.* посо́бие по боле́зни. **sicken** *v.t.* вызыва́ть *impf.*, вы́звать (-зовет) *pf.* тошноту́, (*disgust*) отвраще́ние, у+*g.*; *v.i.* заболева́ть *impf.*, заболе́ть *pf.* **sickening** *adj.* отврати́тельный.
sickle ['sɪk(ə)l] *n.* серп (-а́).
sick-leave ['sɪkliːv] *n.* о́тпуск по боле́зни. **sickly** *adj.* (*ailing*) боле́зненный (-ен, -енна), хи́лый (хил, -а́, -о); (*nauseating*) тошнотво́рный. **sickness** *n.* боле́знь; (*vomiting*) тошнота́; ~ **benefit** посо́бие по боле́зни.
side [saɪd] *n.* сторона́ (*a.* -ону; *pl.* -оны, -о́н, -она́м), бок (*loc.* -у́; *pl.* -а́); ~ **by** ~ бок о́ бок; ря́дом (**with** с+*i.*); **on the** ~ на стороне́, дополни́тельно; *v.i.*: ~ **with** встава́ть (-таю́, -таёшь) *impf.*, встать (-а́ну, -а́нешь) *pf.* на сто́рону+*g.* **sideboard** *n.* серва́нт, буфе́т; *pl.* ба́ки (-к) *pl.* **side-car** *n.* коля́ска (мотоци́кла). **side-effect** *n.* (*of medicine etc.*) побо́чное де́йствие. **sidelight** *n.* боково́й фона́рь (-ря́) *m.* **sideline** *n.* (*work*) побо́чная рабо́та. **sidelong** *adj.* (*glance*) косо́й.
sidereal [saɪ'dɪərɪəl] *adj.* звёздный.
side-saddle ['saɪdˌsæd(ə)l] *n.* да́мское седло́ (*pl.* сёдла, -дел, -длам). **side-slip** *n.* боково́е скольже́ние; (*aeron.*) скольже́ние на крыло́. **sidestep** *v.t.* (*fig.*) уклоня́ться *impf.*, уклони́ться (-ню́сь, -нишься) *pf.* от+*g.* **side-stroke** *n.* пла́вание на боку́. **sidetrack** *v.t.* (*distract*) отвлека́ть *impf.*, отвле́чь (-еку́, -ечёшь; -ёк, -екла́) *pf.*; (*postpone*) откла́дывать *impf.*, отложи́ть (-жу́, -жишь) *pf.* рассмотре́ние+*g.* **side-view** *n.* про́филь *m.*, вид сбо́ку.
sideways ['saɪdweɪz] *adv.* бо́ком; (*from side*) сбо́ку.
siding ['saɪdɪŋ] *n.* запа́сный путь (-ти́, -тём) *m.*
sidle ['saɪd(ə)l] *v.i.* ходи́ть (хожу́, хо́дишь) *impf.* бо́ком.
siege [siːdʒ] *n.* оса́да; **lay** ~ **to** осажда́ть *impf.*, осади́ть *pf.*; **raise the** ~ **of** снима́ть *impf.*, снять (сниму́, -мешь; снял, -а́, -о) *pf.* оса́ду с+*g.*
sienna [sɪ'enə] *n.* сие́на; **burnt** ~ жжёная сие́на.
siesta [sɪ'estə] *n.* сие́ста.
sieve [sɪv] *n.* решето́ (*pl.* -ёта), си́то; *v.t.* просе́ивать *impf.*, просе́ять (-е́ю, -е́ешь) *pf.*
sift [sɪft] *v.t.* просе́ивать *impf.*, просе́ять (-е́ю, -е́ешь) *pf.*; (*evidence etc.*) тща́тельно рассма́тривать *impf.*, рассмотре́ть (-рю́, -ришь) *pf.* **sifter** *n.* си́то.
sigh [saɪ] *v.i.* вздыха́ть *impf.*, вздохну́ть *pf.*; *n.* вздох.
sight [saɪt] *n.* (*faculty*) зре́ние; (*view*; *range*)

вид; (*spectacle*) зре́лище; *pl.* достопримеча́тельности *f.pl.*; (*on gun*) прице́л; **at, on** ~ при ви́де (**of** +*g.*); **at first** ~ с пе́рвого взгля́да; **in** ~ **of** в виду́+*g.*; **long** ~ дальнозо́ркость; **short** ~ близору́кость; **catch** ~ **of** увидеть (-и́жу, -и́дишь) *pf.*; **know by** ~ знать *impf.* в лицо́; **lose** ~ **of** теря́ть *impf.*, по~ *pf.* и́з виду; (*fig.*) упуска́ть *impf.*, упусти́ть (-ущу́, -у́стишь) *pf.* и́з виду. **sightless** *adj.* слепо́й (слеп, -á, -о). **sight-reading** *n.* чте́ние нот с листа́.

sign [saɪn] *n.* знак; (*indication*) при́знак; (~*board*) вы́веска; *v.t.* & *abs.* подпи́сывать(ся) *impf.*, подписа́ть(ся) (-ишу́(сь), -и́шешь(ся)) *pf.*; *v.i.* (*give* ~) подава́ть (-даю́, -даёшь) *impf.*, пода́ть (-а́м, -а́шь, -а́ст, -ади́м; по́дал, -á, -о) *pf.* знак.

signal[1] ['sɪgn(ə)l] *adj.* выдающийся, замеча́тельный.

signal[2] ['sɪgn(ə)l] *n.* сигна́л; *pl.* (*mil.*) связь; *v.t.* & *i.* сигнализи́ровать *impf.* & *pf.*, про~ *pf.* **signal-box** *n.* сигна́льная бу́дка. **signalman** *n.* сигна́льщик.

signatory ['sɪgnətərɪ] *n.* подписа́вший *sb.*; (*of treaty*) сторона́ (*a.* -ону; *pl.* -оны, -о́н, -она́м), подписа́вшая догово́р.

signature ['sɪgnətʃə(r)] *n.* по́дпись; (*print.*) сигнату́ра; (*mus.*) ключ (-á); ~ **tune** музыка́льная ша́пка.

signboard ['saɪnbɔːd] *n.* вы́веска.

signet ['sɪgnɪt] *n.* печа́тка. **signet-ring** *n.* кольцо́ (*pl.* -льца, -ле́ц, -льцам) с печа́ткой.

significance [sɪg'nɪfɪkəns] *n.* значе́ние. **significant** *adj.* значи́тельный. **signify** ['sɪgnɪˌfaɪ] *v.t.* означа́ть *impf.*; (*express*) выража́ть *impf.*, вы́разить *pf.*; *v.i.* быть (*fut.* бу́ду, -дешь; был, -á, -о; не́ был, -á, -о)) *impf.* ва́жным.

signpost ['saɪnpəʊst] *n.* указа́тельный столб (-á).

Sikh [siːk, sɪk] *n.* сикх; *adj.* си́кхский.

silage ['saɪlɪdʒ] *n.* си́лос.

silence ['saɪləns] *n.* молча́ние, тишина́; *v.t.* заста́вить *pf.* замолча́ть. **silencer** *n.* глуши́тель *m.* **silent** *adj.* (*not speaking*) безмо́лвный; (*taciturn*) молчали́вый; (*of film*) немо́й; (*without noise*) ти́хий (тих, -á, -о), бесшу́мный; **be** ~ молча́ть (-чу́, -чи́шь) *impf.*

silhouette [ˌsɪluː'et] *n.* силуэ́т; *v.t.*: **be** ~**d** вырисо́вываться *impf.*, вы́рисоваться *pf.* (**against** на фо́не+*g.*).

silica ['sɪlɪkə] *n.* кремнезём. **silicate** *n.* силика́т. **silicon** *n.* кре́мний; *adj.* кре́мниевый ~ **chip** кре́мниевый криста́лл. **silicone** *n.* силико́н. **sili'cosis** *n.* силико́з.

silk [sɪlk] *n.* шёлк (-а(у), *loc.* -е & -у́; *pl.* -á); **take** ~ станови́ться (-влю́сь, -вишься) *impf.*, стать (-а́ну, -а́нешь) *pf.* короле́вским адвока́том; *attr.* шёлковый; ~ **hat** цили́ндр. **silkworm** *n.* шелкови́чный червь (-вя́; *pl.* -ви, -ве́й) *m.* **silky** *adj.* шелкови́стый.

sill [sɪl] *n.* подоко́нник.

silly ['sɪlɪ] *adj.* глу́пый (глуп, -á, -о).

silo ['saɪləʊ] *n.* си́лос; *v.t.* силосова́ть *impf.* & *pf.*, за~ *pf.*

silt [sɪlt] *n.* ил (-а(у)); *v.i.*: ~ **up** засоря́ться *impf.*, засори́ться *pf.* и́лом.

silver ['sɪlvə(r)] *n.* серебро́; (*cutlery*) столо́вое серебро́; *adj.* (*of* ~) сере́бряный; (*silvery*) серебри́стый; (*hair*) седо́й (сед, -á, -о); ~ **foil** сере́бряная фо́льга; ~ **fox** черно-бу́рая лиса́; ~ **paper** (*tin foil*) стани́оль *m.*; ~ **plate** столо́вое серебро́; *v.t.* серебри́ть *impf.*, вы́~, по~ *pf.*; (*mirror*) покрыва́ть *impf.*, покры́ть (-ро́ю, -ро́ешь) *pf.* амальга́мой рту́ти. **silversmith** *n.* сере́бряных дел ма́стер (*pl.* -á). **silverware** *n.* столо́вое серебро́. **silvery** *adj.* серебри́стый; (*hair*) седо́й (сед, -á, -о).

silviculture ['sɪlvɪˌkʌltʃə(r)] *n.* лесово́дство.

simian ['sɪmɪən] *adj.* обезья́ний.

similar ['sɪmɪlə(r)] *adj.* подо́бный (**to** +*d.*), схо́дный (-ден, -дна́, -дно) (**to** с+*i.*; **in** по+*d.*). **similarity** [ˌsɪmɪ'lærɪtɪ] *n.* схо́дство; (*math.*) подо́бие. **similarly** *adv.* подо́бным о́бразом.

simile ['sɪmɪlɪ] *n.* сравне́ние.

simmer ['sɪmə(r)] *v.t.* кипяти́ть *impf.* на ме́дленном огне́; *v.i.* кипе́ть (-пи́т) *impf.* на ме́дленном огне́; ~ **down** успока́иваться *impf.*, успоко́иться *pf.*

simper ['sɪmpə(r)] *v.i.* жема́нно улыба́ться *impf.*, улыбну́ться *pf.*; *n.* жема́нная улы́бка.

simple ['sɪmp(ə)l] *adj.* просто́й (прост, -á, -о, про́сты́). **simple-hearted** *adj.* простоду́шный. **simple-minded** *adj.* тупова́тый. **simpleton** *n.* проста́к (-á). **sim'plicity** *n.* простота́. **simplify** ['sɪmplɪˌfaɪ] *v.t.* упроща́ть *impf.*, упрости́ть *pf.* **simply** *adv.* про́сто.

simulate ['sɪmjʊˌleɪt] *v.t.* притворя́ться *impf.*, притвори́ться *pf.*+*i.*; (*conditions etc.*) модели́ровать *impf.* & *pf.* **simulated** *adj.* (*pearls etc.*) иску́сственный.

simultaneous [ˌsɪməl'teɪnɪəs] *adj.* одновре́ме́нный (-нен, -нна).

sin [sɪn] *n.* грех (-á); *v.i.* греши́ть *impf.*, со~ *pf.*; ~ **against** наруша́ть *impf.*, наруши́ть *pf.*

since [sɪns] *adv.* с тех пор; (*ago*) (тому́) наза́д; *prep.* с+*g.*; *conj.* с тех пор как; (*reason*) так как.

sincere [sɪn'sɪə(r)] *adj.* и́скренний (-нен, -нна, -нно & -нне). **sincerely** *adv.* искренне; **yours** ~ и́скренне Ваш. **sincerity** [sɪn'serɪtɪ] *n.* и́скренность.

sine [saɪn] *n.* си́нус.

sinecure ['saɪnɪˌkjʊə(r), 'sɪn-] *n.* синеку́ра.

sine die [ˌsaɪnɪ 'daɪiː, ˌsɪneɪ 'diːeɪ] *adv.* на неопределённый срок.

sine qua non [ˌsɪneɪ kwɑː 'nəʊn] *n.* обяза́тельное усло́вие.

sinew ['sɪnjuː] *n.* сухожи́лие. **sinewy** *adj.* жи́листый.

sinful ['sɪnfʊl] *adj.* гре́шный (-шен, -шна́, -шно, гре́шны́). **sinfully** *adv.* грешно́.

sing [sɪŋ] *v.t.* & *i.* петь (пою́, поёшь) *impf.*, про~, с~ *pf.*

singe [sɪndʒ] *v.t.* пали́ть *impf.*, о~ *pf.*; *n.* ожо́г.

singer ['sɪŋə(r)] *n.* певе́ц (-вца́), -ви́ца.

single ['sɪŋg(ə)l] *adj.* оди́н (одна́); (*unmarried*) холосто́й, незаму́жняя; (*solitary*) одино́кий; (*bed*) односпа́льный; ~ **combat** единобо́рство; ~ **father** оте́ц-одино́чка; ~ **mother** мать-одино́чка; **in** ~ **file** гусько́м; ~ **room** ко́мната на одного́; *n.* (*ticket*) биле́т в оди́н коне́ц; *pl.* (*tennis etc.*) одино́чная игра́ *v.t.*: ~ **out** выделя́ть *impf.*, вы́делить *pf.* **single-handed** *adj.* без посторо́нней по́мощи. **single-minded** *adj.* целеустремлённый (-ён, -ённа). **single-seater** *n.* одноме́стный автомоби́ль *m.*

singlet ['sɪŋglɪt] *n.* ма́йка.

singsong ['sɪŋsɒŋ] *adj.* моното́нный.

singular ['sɪŋgjʊlə(r)] *n.* еди́нственное число́; *adj.* еди́нственный; (*unusual*) необыча́йный; (*strange*) стра́нный (-нен, -нна́, -нно). **singularity** [ˌsɪŋgjʊ'lærɪtɪ] *n.* (*peculiarity*) своеобра́зие.

sinister ['sɪnɪstə(r)] *adj.* (*ominous*) злове́щий; (*evil*) злой (зол, зла).

sink [sɪŋk] *v.i.* опуска́ться *impf.*, опусти́ться (-ущу́сь, -у́стишься) *pf.*; (*subside*) оседа́ть *impf.*, осе́сть (ося́дет; осе́л) *pf.*; (*of ship*) тону́ть *impf.*, по~ *pf.*; (*of sick person*) умира́ть *impf.*; *v.t.* (*ship*) топи́ть (-плю́, -пишь) *impf.*, по~ *pf.*; (*well*) рыть (ро́ю, ро́ешь) *impf.*, вы́~ *pf.*; (*shaft*) проходи́ть (-ожу́, -о́дишь) *impf.*, пройти́ (пройду́, -дёшь; прошёл, -шла́) *pf.*; *n.* (*also fig.*) клоа́ка; (*basin*) ра́ковина. **sinker** *n.* грузи́ло.

sinner ['sɪnə(r)] *n.* гре́шник, -ица.

Sino- ['saɪnəʊ] *in comb.* кита́йско-. **sinologist** [saɪ'nɒlədʒɪst, sɪ-] *n.* китаеве́д, сино́лог. **si'nology** *n.* китаеве́дение, синоло́гия.

sinuous ['sɪnjʊəs] *adj.* изви́листый.

sinus ['saɪnəs] *n.* (ло́бная) па́зуха. **sinu'sitis** *n.* синуси́т.

sip [sɪp] *v.t.* пить (пью, пьёшь; пил, -а́, -о) *impf.*, ма́ленькими глотка́ми; *n.* ма́ленький глото́к (-тка́).

siphon ['saɪf(ə)n] *n.* сифо́н.

sir [sɜː(r)] *n.* сэр.

sire ['saɪə(r)] *n.* (*as vocative*) сир; (*stallion etc.*) производи́тель *m.*; *v.t.* быть (*fut.* бу́ду, -дешь; был, -а́, -о; не был, -а́, -о) *impf.* производи́телем+*g.*

siren ['saɪərən] *n.* сире́на.

sirloin ['sɜːlɔɪn] *n.* филе́ *nt.indecl.*

sister ['sɪstə(r)] *n.* сестра́ (*pl.* сёстры, -тёр, -трам). **sisterhood** *n.* (*relig.*) сестри́нская общи́на. **sister-in-law** *n.* (*husband's sister*) золо́вка; (*wife's sister*) своя́ченица. (*brother's wife*) неве́стка.

sit [sɪt] *v.i.* (*be sitting*) сиде́ть (сижу́, сиди́шь) *impf.*; (~ *down*) сади́ться *impf.*, сесть (ся́ду, -дешь; сел) *pf.*; (*parl.*, *leg.*) заседа́ть *impf.*; (*pose*) пози́ровать *impf.* (**for** для+*g.*); *v.t.* уса́живать *impf.*, усади́ть (-ажу́, -а́дишь) *pf.*; (*examination*) сдава́ть (сдаю́, -аёшь) *impf.*; ~ **back** отки́дываться *impf.*, откину́ться *pf.*; ~ **down** сади́ться *impf.*, сесть (ся́ду, -дешь; сел) *pf.*; ~ **on** (*committee etc.*) быть (*fut.* бу́ду, -дешь; был, а́, -о) *impf.* чле́ном+*g.*; ~ **up** приподнима́ться *impf.*, приподня́ться (-ниму́сь, -ни́мешься; -ня́лся, -няла́сь) *pf.*; (*stay out of bed*) не ложи́ться *impf.* спать. **sit-down** *adj.*: ~ **strike** италья́нская забасто́вка.

site [saɪt] *n.* ме́сто (*pl.* -та́), местоположе́ние; **building** ~ строи́тельная площа́дка.

sitter ['sɪtə(r)] *n.* пози́рующий *sb.*; (*model*) нату́рщик, -ица. **sitting** *n.* (*parl. etc.*) заседа́ние; (*for portrait*) сеа́нс; (*for meal*) сме́на; *adj.* сидя́чий, сидя́щий. **sitting-room** *n.* гости́ная *sb.*

situated ['sɪtjʊˌeɪtɪd] *adj.*: **be** ~ находи́ться (-ожу́сь, -о́дишься) *impf.* **situ'ation** *n.* местоположе́ние; (*circumstances*) положе́ние; (*work etc.*) ме́сто (*pl.* -та́).

six [sɪks] *adj.* & *n.* шесть (-ти́, -тью́); (*collect.*; *6 pairs*) ше́стеро (-рых); (*cards*; *number 6*) шестёрка; (*time*) шесть (часо́в); (*age*) шесть лет. **sixteen** *adj.* & *n.* шестна́дцать (-ти, -тью); (*age*) шестна́дцать лет. **sixteenth** *adj.* & *n.* шестна́дцатый; (*fraction*) шестна́дцатая (часть (*pl.* -ти, -те́й)); (*date*) шестна́дцатое (число́). **sixth** *adj.* & *n.* шесто́й; (*fraction*) шеста́я (часть (*pl.* -ти, -те́й)); (*date*) шесто́е (число́); (*mus.*) се́кста. **sixtieth** *adj.* & *n.* шестидеся́тый; (*fraction*) шестидеся́тая (часть (*pl.* -ти, -те́й)). **sixty** *adj.* & *n.* шестьдеся́т (-ти́десяти, -тью́десятью); (*age*) шестьдеся́т лет; *pl.* (*decade*) шестидеся́тые го́ды (-до́в) *m.pl.*

size[1] [saɪz] *n.* (*dimensions*; *of garment etc.*) разме́р; (*magnitude*) величина́; (*capacity*) объём; (*format*) форма́т; *v.t.*: ~ **up** оце́нивать *impf.*, оцени́ть (-ню́, -нишь) *pf.* **sizeable** *adj.* поря́дочных разме́ров.

size[2] [saɪz] *n.* (*solution*) шли́хта; *v.t.* шлихтова́ть *impf.*

sizzle ['sɪz(ə)l] *v.i.* шипе́ть (-пи́т) *impf.*

skate[1] [skeɪt] *n.* (*fish*) скат.

skate[2] [skeɪt] *n.* (*ice-*~) конёк (-нька́); (*roller-*~) конёк (-нька́) на ро́ликах; *v.i.* ката́ться *impf.* на конька́х. **skateboard** *n.* ро́ликовая доска́. **skating-rink** *n.* като́к (-тка́).

skein [skeɪn] *n.* мото́к (-тка́).

skeleton ['skelɪt(ə)n] *n.* скеле́т, о́стов; ~ **key** отмы́чка.

sketch [sketʃ] *n.* набро́сок (-ска), зарисо́вка; (*theatr.*) скетч; *v.t.* & *i.* де́лать *impf.*, с~ *pf.* набро́сок, -ски (+*g.*). **sketch-book** *n.* альбо́м для зарисо́вок. **sketch-map** *n.* кроки́ *nt.indecl.* **sketchy** *adj.* отры́вочный; (*superficial*) пове́рхностный.

skew [skjuː] *adj.* косо́й; *n.* укло́н; **on the** ~ ко́со; *v.t.* перека́шивать *impf.*, перекоси́ть *pf.*; *v.i.* уклоня́ться *impf.*, уклони́ться (-ню́сь, -ни́шься) *pf.*

skewbald ['skjuːbɔːld] *adj.* пе́гий.

skewer ['skju:ə(r)] *n.* вéртел (*pl.* -á); *v.t.* насáживать *impf.*, насадúть (-ажý, -áдишь) *pf.* на вéртел.

ski [ski:] *n.* лы́жа; *v.i.* ходúть (хожý, хóдишь) *impf.* на лы́жах.

skid [skɪd] *n.* занóс; *v.i.* заносúть (-ошý, -óсишь) *impf.*, занестú (-сёт; -слó) *pf. impers.+a.*

skier ['ski:ə(r)] *n.* лы́жник.

skiff [skɪf] *n.* я́лик, скиф.

skiing ['ski:ɪŋ] *n.* лы́жный спорт. **ski-jump** *n.* трамплúн.

skilful ['skɪlfʊl] *adj.* искýсный, умéлый. **skill** *n.* мастерствó, искýсство, умéние. **skilled** *adj.* искýсный; (*worker*) квалифицúрованный.

skim [skɪm] *v.t.* снимáть *impf.*, снять (снимý, -мешь; снял, -á, -о) *pf.* (*cream*) слúвки *pl.*; (*skin on milk*) пéнки *pl.*; (*scum*) нáкипь, с+*g.*; *v.i.* скользúть *impf.* (**over, along** по+*d.*); ~ **through** бéгло просмáтривать *impf.*, просмотрéть (-рю́, -ришь) *pf.*; *adj.*: ~**(med) milk** снятóе молокó.

skimp [skɪmp] *v.t.* & *i.* скупúться *impf.* (на+*a.*). **skimpy** *adj.* скýдный (-ден, -днá, -дно).

skin [skɪn] *n.* кóжа; (*hide*) шкýра; (*of fruit etc.*) кожурá; (*on milk*) пéнка; *v.t.* сдирáть *impf.*, содрáть (сдерý, -рёшь; содрáл, -á, -о) *pf.* кóжу, шкýру, с+*g.*; снимáть *impf.*, снять (снимý, -мешь; снял, -á, -о) *pf.* кожурý с+*g.* **skin-deep** *adj.* повéрхностный. **skin-diver** *n.* аквалангúст. **skinflint** *n.* скря́га *c.g.* **skinny** *adj.* тóщий (тощ, -á, -е).

skint [skɪnt] *adj.* без грошá в кармáне.

skin-tight [skɪn'taɪt] *adj.* в обтя́жку.

skip [skɪp] *v.i.* скакáть (-ачý, -áчешь) *impf.*; (*with rope*) пры́гать *impf.* чéрез скакáлку; *v.t.* (*omit*) пропускáть *impf.*, пропустúть (-ущý, -ýстишь) *pf.*; ~**ping rope** скакáлка.

skipper ['skɪpə(r)] *n.* (*naut.*) шкúпер (*pl.* -ы & -á); (*naut., other senses*) капитáн.

skirmish ['skɜ:mɪʃ] *n.* схвáтка, сты́чка; *v.i.* сражáться *impf.*

skirt [skɜ:t] *n.* ю́бка; *v.t.* обходúть (-ожý, -óдишь) *impf.*, обойтú (обойдý, -дёшь; обошёл, -шлá) *pf.* сторонóй. **skirting-board** *n.* плúнтус.

ski-run ['skirʌn] *n.* лыжня́.

skit [skɪt] *n.* скетч.

skittish ['skɪtɪʃ] *adj.* (*horse*) норовúстый; (*person*) игрúвый.

skittle ['skɪt(ə)l] *n.* кéгля; *pl.* кéгли *f.pl.*

skulk [skʌlk] *v.i.* (*hide*) скрывáться *impf.*; (*creep*) крáсться (крадýсь, -дёшься; крáлся) *impf.*

skull [skʌl] *n.* чéреп (*pl.* -á). **skullcap** *n.* ермóлка.

skunk [skʌŋk] *n.* скунс, воню́чка.

sky [skaɪ] *n.* нéбо (*pl.* -бесá). **sky-blue** *adj.* лазýрный. **skydiving** *n.* парашю́тный спорт. **skyjack** *v.t.* похищáть *impf.*, похúтить (-úщу, -úтишь) *pf.* **skylark** *n.* жáворонок (-нка). **skylight** *n.* oкнó (*pl.* óкна, óкон, óкнам) в кры́ше. **skyline** *n.* горизóнт. **skyscraper** *n.* небоскрёб. **skyway** *n.* авиатрáсса.

slab [slæb] *n.* плитá (*pl.* -ты); (*of cake etc.*) кусóк (-скá).

slack[1] [slæk] *n.* (*coal-dust*) ýгольная пыль.

slack[2] [slæk] *adj.* (*loose*) слáбый (слаб, -á, -о); (*sluggish*) вя́лый; (*inactive*) неактúвный; (*negligent*) небрéжный; (*of rope*) ненатя́нутый; *n.* (*of rope*) слабúна; *pl.* повседнéвные брю́ки (-к) *pl.* **slacken** *v.t.* ослабля́ть *impf.*, ослáбить *pf.*; *v.t.* & *i.* (*slow down*) замедля́ть(ся) *impf.*, замéдлить(ся) *pf.*; *v.i.* ослабевáть *impf.*, ослабéть *pf.* **slacker** *n.* бездéльник, лóдырь *m.*

slag [slæg] *n.* шлак.

slake [sleɪk] *v.t.* (*thirst*) утоля́ть *impf.*, утолúть *pf.*; (*lime*) гасúть (гашý, гáсишь) *impf.*, по~ *pf.*

slalom ['slɑ:ləm] *n.* слáлом.

slam [slæm] *v.t.* & *i.* (*door*) захлóпывать(ся) *impf.*, захлóпнуть(ся) *pf.*; *n.* (*cards*) шлем.

slander ['slɑ:ndə(r)] *n.* клеветá; *v.t.* клеветáть (-ещý, -éщешь) *impf.*, на~ *pf.* на+*a.* **slanderous** *adj.* клеветнúческий.

slang [slæŋ] *n.* сленг, жаргóн; *v.t.* бранúть *impf.*, вы́~ *pf.* **slangy** *adj.* жаргóнный, вульгáрный.

slant [slɑ:nt] *v.t.* & *i.* наклоня́ть(ся) *impf.*, наклонúть(ся) (-ню́, -нит(ся)) *pf.*; *n.* уклóн. **slanting** *adj.* покáтый, косóй (кос, -á, -о).

slap [slæp] *v.t.* хлопáть *impf.*, хлóпнуть *pf.+a.*, *i.*, по+*d.*; шлёпать *impf.*, шлёпнуть *pf.*; *n.* шлепóк (-пкá); *adv.* пря́мо. **slapdash** *adj.* поспéшный, небрéжный. **slapstick** *n.* балагáн.

slash [slæʃ] *v.t.* рубúть (-блю́, -бишь) *impf.*; (*prices etc.*) рéзко снижáть *impf.*, снúзить *pf.*; *n.* разрéз, прóрез.

slat [slæt] *n.* плáнка, филёнка.

slate[1] [sleɪt] *n.* слáнец (-нца); (*for roofing*) шúфер (*no pl.*), шúферная плúтка; (*for writing*) грúфельная доскá (*a.* -ску; *pl.* -ски, -сóк, -скáм); *v.t.* (*roof*) крыть (крóю, -óешь) *impf.*, по~ *pf.* шúферными плúтками.

slate[2] [sleɪt] *v.t.* (*criticize*) раскритиковáть *pf.*

slate-pencil [ˌsleɪt'pensɪl] *n.* грúфель *m.*

slattern ['slæt(ə)n] *n.* неря́ха. **slatternly** *adj.* неря́шливый.

slaughter ['slɔ:tə(r)] *n.* (*of animals*) убóй; (*massacre*) резня́; *v.t.* рéзать (рéжу, -жешь) *impf.*, за~ *pf.*; (*people*) убивáть *impf.*, убúть (убью́, -ьёшь) *pf.* **slaughterhouse** *n.* бóйня (*g.pl.* бóен).

Slav [slɑ:v] *n.* славянúн (*pl.* -я́не, -я́н), -я́нка; *adj.* славя́нский.

slave [sleɪv] *n.* раб (-á), рабы́ня (*g.pl.* -нь); *v.i.* рабóтать *impf.* как раб.

slaver [slævə(r)] *v.i.* пускáть *impf.*, пустúть (пущý, пýстишь) *pf.* слю́ни; *n.* слю́ни (-ней) *pl.*

slavery ['sleɪvərɪ] *n.* рáбство. **slave-trade** *n.* работоргóвля.

Slavic ['slɑːvɪk] *adj.* славя́нский.
slavish ['sleɪvɪʃ] *adj.* ра́бский.
Slavonic [slə'vɒnɪk] *adj.* славя́нский.
slay [sleɪ] *v.t.* убива́ть *impf.*, уби́ть (убью́, -ьёшь) *pf.*
sleazy ['sliːzɪ] *adj.* (*person*) неря́шливый.
sledge [sledʒ] *n.* са́ни (-не́й) *pl.*
sledge-hammer ['sledʒˌhæmə(r)] *n.* кува́лда.
sleek [sliːk] *adj.* гла́дкий (-док, -дка́, -дко).
sleep [sliːp] *n.* сон (сна); **go to ~** засыпа́ть *impf.*, засну́ть *pf.*; *v.i.* спать (сплю, спишь; спал, -а́, -о) *impf.*; (*spend the night*) ночева́ть (-чу́ю, -чу́ешь) *impf.*, пере~ *pf.* **sleeper** *n.* спя́щий *sb.*; (*rail.*, *beam*) шпа́ла; (*sleeping-car*) спа́льный ваго́н. **sleeping** *adj.* спя́щий, спа́льный; **~ partner** пасси́вный партнёр; **~ sickness** со́нная боле́знь. **sleeping-bag** *n.* спа́льный мешо́к (-шка́). **sleeping-car(riage)** *n.* спа́льный ваго́н. **sleeping-pill** *n.* снотво́рная табле́тка. **sleepless** *adj.* бессо́нный (-нен, -нна). **sleepwalker** *n.* луна́тик. **sleepy** *adj.* со́нный (-нен, -нна).
sleet [sliːt] *n.* мо́крый снег (-а(у), *loc.* -у́).
sleeve [sliːv] *n.* рука́в (-а́; *pl.* -а́); (*tech.*) му́фта; (*of record*) конве́рт.
sleigh [sleɪ] *n.* са́ни (-не́й) *pl.* **sleigh-bell** бубе́нчик.
sleight-of-hand [slaɪt] *n.* ло́вкость рук.
slender ['slendə(r)] *adj.* (*slim*) то́нкий (-нок, -нка́, -нко, то́нки́); (*meagre*) ску́дный (-ден, -дна́, -дно); (*of hope etc.*) сла́бый (слаб, -а́, -о).
sleuth [sluːθ] *n.* сы́щик.
slew [sluː] *v.t.* & *i.* бы́стро повора́чивать(ся) *impf.*, поверну́ть(ся) *pf.*
slice [slaɪs] *n.* ло́мтик, ломо́ть (-мтя́) *m.*; (*share*) часть (*pl.* -ти, -те́й); *v.t.* (*~ up*) нареза́ть *impf.*, наре́зать (-е́жу, -е́жешь) *pf.*
slick [slɪk] *adj.* (*dextrous*) ло́вкий (-вок, -вка́, -вко, ло́вки́); (*crafty*) хи́трый (-тёр, -тра́, хи́тро́); (*sleek*) гла́дкий (-док, -дка́, -дко); *n.* нефтяна́я плёнка.
slide [slaɪd] *v.i.* скользи́ть *impf.*; (*on ice*) кати́ться (качу́сь, ка́тишься) *impf.*, по~ *pf.* по льду; *v.t.* (*drawer etc.*) задвига́ть *impf.*, задви́нуть *pf.* (**into** в+*a.*; *n.* (*on ice*) ледяна́я гора́ (*a.* -ру; *pl.* -ры, -р, -ра́м), ледяна́я доро́жка; (*children's ~*) де́тская го́рка; (*chute*) жёлоб (*pl.* -а́); (*microscope ~*) предме́тное стекло́ (*pl.* стёкла, -кол, -клам); (*phot.*) диапозити́в, слайд. **slide-rule** *n.* логарифми́ческая линейка. **slide-valve** *n.* золотни́к (а́). **sliding** *adj.* скользя́щий; (*door*) задвижно́й; **~ seat** слайд.
slight[1] [slaɪt] *adj.* (*slender*) то́нкий (-нок, -нка́, -нко, то́нки́); (*inconsiderable*) незначи́тельный; (*light*) лёгкий (-гок, -гка́, -гко́, лёгки́); **not the ~est** ни мале́йшего, -шей (*g.*); **not in the ~est** ничу́ть.
slight[2] [slaɪt] *v.t.* пренебрега́ть *impf.*, пренебре́чь (-егу́, -ежёшь; -ёг, -егла́) *pf.*+*i.*; *n.* пренебреже́ние, неуваже́ние.
slightly ['slaɪtlɪ] *adv.* слегка́, немно́го.
slim [slɪm] *adj.* то́нкий (-нок, -нка́, -нко, то́нки́); (*chance etc.*) сла́бый (слаб, -а́, -о); *v.i.* худе́ть *impf.*, по~ *pf.*
slime [slaɪm] *n.* слизь. **slimy** *adj.* слизи́стый; (*person*) еле́йный.
sling [slɪŋ] *v.t.* (*throw*) броса́ть *impf.*, бро́сить *pf.*; швыря́ть *impf.*, швырну́ть *pf.*; (*suspend*) подве́шивать *impf.*, подве́сить *pf.*; *n.* (*for throwing*) праща́; (*bandage*) пе́ревязь; (*rope*) строп.
slink [slɪŋk] *v.i.* кра́сться (-аду́сь, -адёшься; -а́лся) *impf.* **slinky** *adj.* (*garment*) отлега́ющий.
slip [slɪp] *n.* (*slipping*) скольже́ние; (*mistake*) оши́бка; (*garment*) комбина́ция; (*pillow-case*) на́волочка; (*building ~*) ста́пель (*pl.* -ля́ & -ли); (*landing*) э́ллинг; (*of paper etc.*) поло́ска; (*print.*) гра́нка; (*cutting*) черено́к (-нка́); (*glaze*) поливна́я глазу́рь; **~ of the pen** опи́ска; **~ of the tongue** обмо́лвка; **give the ~** ускользну́ть *pf.* от+*g.*; *v.i.* скользи́ть *impf.*, скользну́ть *pf.*; поскользну́ться *pf.*; (*from hands etc.*) выска́льзывать *impf.*, вы́скользнуть *pf.*; *v.t.* (*let go*) спуска́ть *impf.*, спусти́ть (-ущу́, -у́стишь) *pf.*; (*insert*) сова́ть (сую́, суёшь) *impf.*, су́нуть *pf.*; **~ off** (*depart*, *v.i.*) ускольза́ть *impf.*, ускользну́ть *pf.*; (*clothes*, *v.t.*) сброса́ть *impf.*, сбро́сить *pf.*; **~ on** (*clothes*) наки́дывать *impf.*, наки́нуть *pf.*; **~ up** (*make mistake*) ошиба́ться *impf.*, ошиби́ться (-бу́сь, -бёшься; -бся) *pf.* **slipper** *n.* (дома́шняя) ту́фля (*g.pl.* -фель); та́почка (*coll.*). **slippery** *adj.* ско́льзкий (-зок, -зка́, -зко); (*fig.*, *shifty*) увёртливый. **slipshod** *adj.* неря́шливый, небре́жный. **slipway** *n.* (*for building*) ста́пель (*pl.* -ля́ & -ли); (*for landing*) э́ллинг.
slit [slɪt] *v.t.* разреза́ть *impf.*, разре́зать (-е́жу, -е́жешь) *pf.*; *n.* щель (*pl.* -ли, -ле́й), разре́з.
slither ['slɪðə(r)] *v.i.* скользи́ть *impf.*
sliver ['slɪvə(r), 'slaɪvə(r)] *n.* ще́пка.
slob [slɒb] *n.* неря́ха *c.g.*
slobber ['slɒbə(r)] *v.i.* пуска́ть *impf.*, пусти́ть (пущу́, пу́стишь) *pf.* слю́ни; *n.* слю́ни (-ней) *pl.*
sloe [sləʊ] *n.* тёрн.
slog [slɒg] *v.t.* (*hit*) си́льно ударя́ть *impf.*, уда́рить *pf.*; (*work*) упо́рно рабо́тать *impf.*
slogan ['sləʊgən] *n.* ло́зунг.
sloop [sluːp] *n.* шлюп.
slop [slɒp] *n.*: *pl.* (*water*) помо́и (-о́ев) *pl.*; (*food*) жи́дкая пи́ща; *v.t.* & *i.* выплёскивать(ся) *impf.*, вы́плескать(ся) (-ещу, -ещет(ся)) *pf.* **slop-basin** *n.* полоска́тельница.
slope [sləʊp] *n.* накло́н, склон; *v.i.* име́ть *impf.* накло́н. **sloping** *adj.* накло́нный (-нен, -нна), пока́тый.
slop-pail ['slɒppeɪl] *n.* помо́йное ведро́ (*pl.* вёдра, -дер, -драм). **sloppy** *adj.* (*ground*) мо́крый (мокр, -а́, -о); (*food*) жи́дкий (-док, -дка́, -дко); (*work*) неря́шливый; (*sentimen-*

tal) сентимента́льный.

slot [slɒt] *n.* щель (*pl.* -ли, -ле́й), паз (*loc.* -у́; *pl.* -ы́).

sloth [sləʊθ] *n.* лень; (*zool.*) лени́вец (-вца). **slothful** *adj.* лени́вый.

slot-machine [ˈslɒtməˌʃiːn] *n.* автома́т.

slouch [slaʊtʃ] *v.i.* (*stoop*) суту́литься *impf.*

slough [slʌf] *v.t.* сбра́сывать *impf.*, сбро́сить *pf.*

sloven [ˈslʌv(ə)n] *n.* неря́ха *c.g.* **slovenly** *adj.* неря́шливый.

slow [sləʊ] *adj.* ме́дленный (-ен(ен), -енна); (*tardy*) медли́тельный; (*stupid*) тупо́й (туп, -а́, -о, ту́пы́); (*business*) вя́лый; **be** ~ (*clock*) отстава́ть (-таёт) *impf.*, отста́ть (-а́нет) *pf.*; *adv.* ме́дленно; *v.t.* & *i.* (~ *down*, *up*) замедля́ть(ся) *impf.*, заме́длить(ся) *pf.* **slowcoach** *n.* копу́н (-а́), ~ья.

slow-worm [ˈsləʊwɜːm] *n.* верете́ница, медя́ница.

sludge [slʌdʒ] *n.* (*mud*) грязь (*loc.* -зи́); (*sediment*) отсто́й.

slug [slʌg] *n.* (*zool.*) слизня́к (-а́); (*piece of metal*) кусо́к (-ска́) мета́лла.

sluggard [ˈslʌgəd] *n.* лентя́й. **sluggish** *adj.* (*inert*) ине́ртный; (*torpid*) вя́лый.

sluice [sluːs] *n.* шлюз; *v.t.* залива́ть *impf.*, зали́ть (-лью́, -льёшь; за́ли́л, -а́, -о́) *pf.*; *v.i.* ли́ться (льётся; ли́лся, лила́сь, ли́ло́сь) *impf.*

slum [slʌm] *n.* трущо́ба.

slumber [ˈslʌmbə(r)] *n.* сон (сна); *v.i.* спать (сплю, спишь; спал, -а́, -о) *impf.*

slump [slʌmp] *n.* ре́зкое паде́ние (цен, спро́са, интере́са); *v.i.* ре́зко па́дать *impf.*, (у)па́сть (-адёт; -а́л) *pf.*; (*of person*) тяжело́ опуска́ться *impf.*, опусти́ться (-ущу́сь, -у́стишься) *pf.*

slur [slɜː(r)] *v.t.* (*speak indistinctly*) невня́тно произноси́ть (-ошу́, -о́сишь) *impf.*, произнести́ (-есу́, -есёшь; -ёс, -есла́) *pf.*; ~ **over** обходи́ть (-ожу́, -о́дишь) *impf.*, обойти́ (обойду́, -дёшь; обошёл, -шла́) *pf.* молча́нием; *n.* (*stigma*) пятно́ (*pl.* -тна, -тен, -тнам); (*mus.*) ли́га.

slush [slʌʃ] *n.* сля́коть. **slushy** *adj.* сля́котный; (*fig.*) сентимента́льный.

slut [slʌt] *n.* (*sloven*) неря́ха; (*trollop*) потаску́ха. **sluttish** *adj.* неря́шливый; распу́щенный.

sly [slaɪ] *adj.* хи́трый (-тёр, -тра́, хи́тро́), лука́вый; **on the** ~ тайко́м.

smack[1] [smæk] *n.* (*flavour*) при́вкус; *v.i.*: ~ **of** па́хнуть *impf.*+*i.*

smack[2] [smæk] *n.* (*slap*) шлепо́к (-пка́); *v.t.* шлёпать *impf.*, шлёпнуть *pf.*

smack[3] [smæk] *n.* (*boat*) смэк.

small [smɔːl] *adj.* ма́ленький, небольшо́й, ма́лый (мал, -а́); (*of agent*, *particles*; *petty*) ме́лкий (-лок, -лка́, -лко); (*unimportant*) незначи́тельный; ~ **capitals** капите́ль; ~ **change** ме́лочь; ~ **fry** ме́лкая со́шка; ~ **talk** све́тская бесе́да; *n.*: ~ **of the back** поясни́ца; *pl.* ме́лочь. **small-minded** *adj.* ме́лкий (-лок, -лка́, -лко). **small-scale** *adj.* мелкомасшта́бный.

smart[1] [smɑːt] *v.i.* са́дни́ть *impf. impers.*

smart[2] [smɑːt] *adj.* (*brisk*) бы́стрый (быстр, -а́, -о, бы́стры́); (*cunning*) ло́вкий (-вок, -вка́, -вко, ло́вки́); (*sharp*) смека́листый (*coll.*); (*in appearance*) элега́нтный.

smash [smæʃ] *v.t.* & *i.* разбива́ть(ся) *impf.*, разби́ть(ся) (разобью́, -ьёт(ся)) *pf.*; *v.i.* (*collide*) ста́лкиваться *impf.*, столкну́ться *pf.* (**into** c+*i.*); *n.* (*disaster*) катастро́фа; (*collision*) столкнове́ние; (*blow*) тяжёлый уда́р.

smattering [ˈsmætərɪŋ] *n.* пове́рхностное зна́ние.

smear [smɪə(r)] *v.t.* сма́зывать *impf.*, сма́зать (-а́жу, -а́жешь) *pf.*; (*dirty*) па́чкать *impf.*, за~, ис~ *pf.*; (*discredit*) поро́чить *impf.*, о~ *pf.*; *n.* (*slander*) клевета́; (*med.*) мазо́к (-зка́).

smell [smel] *n.* (*sense*) обоня́ние; (*odour*) за́пах; *v.t.* чу́вствовать *impf.* за́пах+*g.*; ню́хать *impf.*, по~ *pf.*; *v.i.*: ~ **of** па́хнуть (па́х(нул), па́хла) *impf.*+*i.*; ~ **out** (*also fig.*) разню́хивать *impf.*, разню́хать *pf.*; ~**ing salts** ню́хательная соль. **smelly** *adj.* воню́чий.

smelt [smelt] *v.t.* (*ore*) пла́вить *impf.*; (*metal*) выплавля́ть *impf.*, вы́плавить *pf.*

smile [smaɪl] *v.i.* улыба́ться *impf.*, улыбну́ться *pf.*; *n.* улы́бка.

smirk [smɜːk] *v.i.* ухмыля́ться *impf.*, ухмыльну́ться *pf.*; *n.* ухмы́лка.

smith [smɪθ] *n.* кузне́ц (-а́).

smithereens [ˌsmɪðəˈriːnz] *n.*: **(in)to** ~ вдре́безги.

smithy [ˈsmɪðɪ] *n.* ку́зница.

smock [smɒk] *n.* блу́за.

smog [smɒg] *n.* тума́н с ды́мом.

smoke [sməʊk] *n.* дым (-а(у), *loc.* -у́); (*cigarette etc.*) ку́рево; ~ **bomb** дымова́я бо́мба; *v.i.* дыми́ть *impf.*, на~ *pf.*; (*of lamp*) копти́ть *impf.*, на~ *pf.*; *v.t.* & *i.* (*cigarette etc.*) кури́ть (-рю́, -ришь) *impf.*, по~ *pf.*; *v.t.* (*cure*; *colour*) копти́ть *impf.*, за~ *pf.*; ~ **out** выку́ривать *impf.*, вы́курить *pf.* **smokeless** *adj.* безды́мный. **smoker** *n.* кури́льщик, -ица, куря́щий *sb.* **smokescreen** *n.* дымова́я заве́са. **smoking** *n.*: ~ **compartment** купе́ *nt.indecl.* для куря́щих. **smoking-room** *n.* кури́тельная *sb.* **smoky** *adj.* ды́мный; (*room*) проку́ренный; (*colour*) ды́мчатый.

smooth [smuːð] *adj.* (*surface etc.*) гла́дкий (-док, -дка́, -дко); (*movement etc.*) пла́вный; (*flattering*) льсти́вый; *v.t.* пригла́живать *impf.*, пригла́дить *pf.*; ~ **over** сгла́живать *impf.*, сгла́дить *pf.*

smother [ˈsmʌðə(r)] *v.t.* (*stifle*, *also fig.*) души́ть (-шу́, -шишь) *impf.*, за~ *pf.*; (*cover*) покрыва́ть *impf.*, покры́ть (-ро́ю, -ро́ешь) *pf.*

smoulder [ˈsməʊldə(r)] *v.i.* тлеть *impf.*

smudge [smʌdʒ] *v.t.* па́чкать *impf.*, за~, ис~ *pf.*

smug [smʌg] *adj.* самодово́льный.

smuggle ['smʌg(ə)l] *v.t.* провози́ть (-ожу́, -о́зишь) *impf.*, провезти́ (-езу́, -езёшь; -ёз, -езла́) *pf.* контраба́ндой; (*convey secretly*) та́йно проноси́ть (-ошу́, -о́сишь) *impf.*, пронести́ (-есу́, -есёшь; -ёс, -есла́) *pf.* **smuggler** *n.* контрабанди́ст.

smut [smʌt] *n.* части́ца са́жи, ко́поти; (*indecency*) непристо́йность. **smutty** *adj.* гря́зный (-зен, -зна́, -зно); непристо́йный.

snack [snæk] *n.* заку́ска; ~ **bar** заку́сочная *sb.*, буфе́т.

snaffle ['snæf(ə)l] *n.* тре́нзель (*pl.* -ли & -ля́) *m.*; *v.t.* (*steal*) стащи́ть (-щу́, -щишь) *pf.*

snag [snæg] *n.* (*branch*) сучо́к (-чка́); (*in river*) коря́га; (*fig.*) загво́здка; *v.t.* зацепля́ть *impf.*, зацепи́ть (-плю́, -пишь) *pf.*

snail [sneɪl] *n.* ули́тка; **at a ~'s pace** черепа́хой.

snake [sneɪk] *n.* змея́ (*pl.* -е́и). **snake-charmer** *n.* заклина́тель *m.*, ~ница, змей. **snakeskin** *n.* змеи́ная ко́жа. **snaky** *adj.* змеи́ный; (*winding*) изви́листый.

snap [snæp] *v.i.* (*of dog etc.*) огрыза́ться *impf.*, огрызну́ться *pf.* (**at** на+*a.*); *v.t.* & *i.* говори́ть *impf.* серди́то, раздражённо; (*break*) обрыва́ть(ся) *impf.*, оборва́ть(ся) (-ву́, -вёт(ся); -ва́л(ся), -вала́(сь), -ва́ло/-вало́сь) *pf.*; *v.t.* (*make sound*) щёлкать *impf.*, щёлкнуть *pf.*+*i.*; ~ **up** (*buy*) расхва́тывать *impf.*, расхвата́ть *pf.*; *n.* (*sound*) щёлк; **cold** ~ ре́зкое внеза́пное похолода́ние; *adj.* скоропали́тельный; (*parl.*) внеочередно́й. **snapdragon** *n.* льви́ный зев. **snap-fastener** *n.* кно́пка. **snapshot** *n.* момента́льный сни́мок (-мка).

snare [sneə(r)] *n.* лову́шка; *v.t.* лови́ть (-влю́, -вишь) *impf.*, пойма́ть *pf.* в лову́шку.

snarl [snɑːl] *v.i.* рыча́ть (-чи́т) *impf.*; (*person*) ворча́ть (-чу́, -чи́шь) *impf.*; *n.* рыча́ние; ворча́ние.

snatch [snætʃ] *v.t.* хвата́ть *impf.*, (с)хвати́ть (-ачу́, -а́тишь) *pf.*; (*opportunity etc.*) ухвати́ться (-ачу́сь, -а́тишься) *pf.* за+*a.*; *v.i.*: ~ **at** хвата́ться *impf.*, (с)хвати́ться (-ачу́сь, -а́тишься) *pf.* за+*a.*; *n.* попы́тка схвати́ть; (*fragment*) обры́вок (-вка); **in, by, ~es** уры́вками.

sneak [sniːk] *v.i.* (*slink*) кра́сться (-аду́сь, -адёшься; -а́лся) *impf.*; (*tell tales*) я́бедничать *impf.*, на~ *pf.* (*coll.*); *v.t.* (*steal*) стащи́ть (-щу́, -щишь) *pf.*; *n.* я́бедник, -ица (*coll.*). **sneaking** *adj.* (*hidden*) та́йный; (*of feeling etc.*) неосо́знанный. **sneak-thief** *n.* вори́шка *m.*

sneer [snɪə(r)] *v.i.* (*smile*) насме́шливо улыба́ться *impf.*; (*speak*) насме́шливо говори́ть *impf.*; *n.* насме́шливая улы́бка.

sneeze [sniːz] *v.i.* чиха́ть *impf.*, чихну́ть *pf.*; *n.* чиха́нье.

snick [snɪk] *n.* зару́бка.

snide [snaɪd] *adj.* (*sneering*) насме́шливый.

sniff [snɪf] *v.i.* шмы́гать *impf.*, шмыгну́ть *pf.* но́сом; *v.t.* ню́хать *impf.*, по~ *pf.*

snigger ['snɪgə(r)] *v.i.* хихи́кать *impf.*, хихи́кнуть *pf.*; *n.* хихи́канье.

snip [snɪp] *v.t.* ре́зать (ре́жу, -жешь) *impf.* (но́жницами); ~ **off** среза́ть *impf.*, сре́зать (-е́жу, -е́жешь) *pf.*; *n.* (*purchase*) вы́годная поку́пка.

snipe [snaɪp] *n.* (*bird*) бека́с; *v.i.* стреля́ть *impf.* из укры́тия (**at** в+*a.*). **sniper** *n.* сна́йпер.

snippet ['snɪpɪt] *n.* отре́зок (-зка); *pl.* (*of knowledge etc.*) обры́вки *m.pl.*

snivel ['snɪv(ə)l] *v.i.* (*run at nose*) распуска́ть *impf.*, распусти́ть (-ущу́, -у́стишь) *pf.* со́пли; (*whimper*) хны́кать (хны́чу, -чешь & хны́каю, -аешь) *impf.*

snob [snɒb] *n.* сноб. **snobbery** *n.* снобы́зм. **snobbish** *adj.* снобы́стский.

snook [snuːk] *n.*: **cock a ~ at** показа́ть (-ажу́, -а́жешь) *pf.* дли́нный нос+*d.*

snoop [snuːp] *v.i.* сова́ть (сую́, суёшь) *impf.* нос в чужи́е дела́; ~ **about** шпио́нить *impf.*

snooty ['snuːtɪ] *adj.* чва́нный (-нен, -нна).

snooze [snuːz] *v.i.* вздремну́ть *pf.*; *n.* коро́ткий сон (сна).

snore [snɔː(r)] *v.i.* храпе́ть (-плю́, -пи́шь) *impf.*; *n.* храп.

snorkel ['snɔːk(ə)l] *n.* шно́ркель *m.*; (*diver's*) тру́бка (аквала́нга).

snort [snɔːt] *v.i.* фы́ркать *impf.*, фы́ркнуть *pf.*; *n.* фы́рканье.

snot [snɒt] *n.* со́пли (-ле́й) *pl.*

snout [snaʊt] *n.* ры́ло, мо́рда.

snow [snəʊ] *n.* снег (-а(у), *loc.* -у́; *pl.* -а́); ~ **boot** бот (*g.pl.* -т & -тов); *v.i.*: **it is ~ing** идёт (*past* шёл) снег; **~ed up, in** занесённый (-ён, -ена́) сне́гом. **snowball** *n.* снежо́к (-жка́). **snow-blindness** *n.* сне́жная слепота́. **snowbound** *adj.* заснежённый (-ён, -ена́). **snowdrift** *n.* сугро́б. **snowdrop** *n.* подсне́жник. **snowflake** *n.* снежи́нка. **snowman** *n.* сне́жная ба́ба. **snowplough** *n.* снегоочисти́тель *m.* **snowshoes** *n.* снегосту́пы (-пов) *pl.* **snowstorm** *n.* мете́ль, вьюга. **snow-white** *adj.* белосне́жный. **snowy** *adj.* сне́жный; (*snow-white*) белосне́жный.

snub[1] [snʌb] *v.t.* относи́ться (-ошу́сь, -о́сишься) *impf.*, отнести́сь (-есу́сь, -есёшься; -ёсся, -есла́сь) *pf.* пренебрежи́тельно к+*d.*; (*humiliate*) унижа́ть *impf.*, уни́зить *pf.*

snub[2] [snʌb] *adj.* вздёрнутый. **snub-nosed** *adj.* курно́сый.

snuff[1] [snʌf] *n.* (*tobacco*) ню́хательный таба́к (-а́(у́)); **take ~** ню́хать *impf.*, по~ *pf.* таба́к.

snuff[2] [snʌf] *n.* (*on candle*) нага́р на свече́; *v.t.* снима́ть *impf.*, снять (сниму́, -мешь; снял, -а́, -о) *pf.* нага́р с+*g.*; ~ **out** (*candle*) туши́ть (-шу́, -шишь) *impf.*, по~ *pf.*; (*hopes etc.*) разруша́ть *impf.*, разру́шить *pf.*

snuffbox ['snʌfbɒks] *n.* табаке́рка.

snuffle ['snʌf(ə)l] *v.i.* (*noisily*) сопе́ть (-плю́, -пи́шь) *impf.*

snug [snʌg] *adj.* ую́тный, удо́бный.

snuggle ['snʌg(ə)l] *v.i.*: ~ **up to** прижима́ться

impf., прижа́ться (-жму́сь, -жмёшься) *pf.* к+*d.*

so [səʊ] *adv.* так; (*in this way*) так, таки́м о́бразом; (*thus, at beginning of sentence*) ита́к; (*also*) та́кже, то́же; *conj.* (*therefore*) поэ́тому; **and ~ on** и так да́лее; **if ~** в тако́м слу́чае; **or ~** и́ли о́коло э́того; **~ ... as** так(о́й)... как; **~ as to** с тем что́бы; **~ be it** быть по сему́; **~ far** до сих пор; **(in) ~ far as** насто́лько, поско́льку; **~ long!** пока́!; **~ long as** поско́льку; **~ much** насто́лько; **~ much ~** до тако́й сте́пени; **~ much the better** тем лу́чше; **~ that** что́бы; **~... that** так... что; **~ to say, speak** так сказа́ть; **~ what?** ну и что?

soak [səʊk] *v.t.* & *i.* пропи́тывать(ся) *impf.*, пропита́ть(ся) *pf.* (**in** +*i.*); *v.t.* мочи́ть (-чу́, -чишь) *impf.*, на~ *pf.*; (*drench*) прома́чивать *impf.*, промочи́ть (-чу́, -чишь) *pf.*; **~ up** впи́тывать *impf.*, впита́ть *pf.*; *v.i.*: **~ through** проса́чиваться *impf.*, просочи́ться *pf.*; **get ~ed** промока́ть *impf.*, промо́кнуть (-к) *pf.*; *n.* (*drinker*) пья́ница *c.g.*

so-and-so ['səʊənd,səʊ] *n.* тако́й-то.

soap [səʊp] *n.* мы́ло (*pl.* -ла́); *attr.* мы́льный; *v.t.* мы́лить *impf.*, на~ *pf.*; **~ boiler** мылова́р; **~ bubble** мы́льный пузы́рь (-ря́) *m.*; **~ dish** мы́льница; **~ flakes** мы́льные хло́пья (-ьев) *pl.*; **~ powder** стира́льный порошо́к (-шка́); **~ works** мылова́ренный заво́д. **soapbox** *n.* (*stand*) импровизи́рованная трибу́на. **soapy** *adj.* мы́льный.

soar [sɔː(r)] *v.i.* пари́ть *impf.*; (*aeron.*) плани́ровать *impf.*, с~ *pf.*; (*building etc.*) вы́ситься *impf.*; (*prices*) подска́кивать *impf.*, подскочи́ть *pf.*

sob [sɒb] *v.i.* рыда́ть *impf.*; *n.* рыда́ние.

sober ['səʊbə(r)] *adj.* тре́звый (трезв, -а́, -о); *v.t.* & *i.*: **~ up** (*also fig.*) отрезвля́ться *impf.*, отрезви́ться *pf.*; *v.i.*: **~ up** трезве́ть *impf.*, о~ *pf.* **sobriety** [sə'braɪɪtɪ] *n.* тре́звость.

sobriquet ['səʊbrɪ,keɪ] *n.* про́звище.

so-called ['sɒkɔɪld] *adj.* так называ́емый.

soccer ['sɒkə(r)] *n.* футбо́л.

sociable ['səʊʃəb(ə)l] *adj.* общи́тельный; (*meeting etc.*) дру́жеский. **social** *adj.* обще́ственный, социа́льный; **S~ Democrat** социа́л-демокра́т; **~ sciences** обще́ственные нау́ки *f.pl.*; **~ security** социа́льное обеспе́чение; *n.* вечери́нка. **socialism** *n.* социали́зм. **socialist** *n.* социали́ст; *adj.* социалисти́ческий. **socialize** *v.t.* социализи́ровать *impf.* & *pf.* **society** [sə'saɪətɪ] *n.* о́бщество; (*beau monde*) свет; *attr.* све́тский. **sociolin'guistics** *n.* социолингви́стика. **socio'logical** *adj.* социологи́ческий. **soci'ologist** *n.* социо́лог. **soci'ology** *n.* социоло́гия.

sock[1] [sɒk] *n.* носо́к (-ска́).

sock[2] [sɒk] *v.t.* тузи́ть *impf.*, от~ *pf.*

socket ['sɒkɪt] *n.* впа́дина; (*elec.*) ште́псель (*pl.* -ля́) *m.*; (*for bulb*) патро́н; (*tech.*) гнездо́ (*pl.* -ёзда), растру́б.

sod [sɒd] *n.* (*turf*) дёрн; (*piece of turf*) дерни́на.

soda ['səʊdə] *n.* со́да; **~ water** со́довая вода́ (*a.* -ду).

sodden ['sɒd(ə)n] *adj.* промо́кший, пропи́танный (-ан) вла́гой.

sodium ['səʊdɪəm] *n.* на́трий.

sodomite ['sɒdə,maɪt] *n.* педера́ст. **sodomy** *n.* педера́стия.

sofa ['səʊfə] *n.* дива́н.

soft [sɒft] *adj.* мя́гкий (-гок, -гка́, -гко); (*sound*) ти́хий (тих, -а́, -о); (*colour*) нея́ркий (-рок, -рка́, -рко); (*malleable*) ко́вкий (-вок, -вка́, -вко); (*tender*) не́жный (-жен, -жна́, -жно; не́жны́); **~ drink** безалкого́льный напи́ток (-тка); **~ fruit** я́года; **~ goods** тексти́ль *m.*; **~ toy** мягконабивна́я игру́шка. **soft-boiled** *adj.*: **~ egg** яйцо́ всмя́тку. **soften** ['sɒf(ə)n] *v.t.* & *i.* смягча́ть(ся) *impf.*, смягчи́ть(ся) *pf.* **soft-headed** *adj.* придуркова́тый. **soft-hearted** *adj.* мягкосерде́чный. **softness** *n.* мя́гкость. **soft-pedal** *v.t.* преуменьша́ть *impf.*, преуменьши́ть *pf.* (значе́ние+*g.*). **software** *n.* програ́ммное обеспе́чение. **softwood** *n.* хво́йная древеси́на.

soggy ['sɒgɪ] *adj.* пропи́танный (-ан) водо́й; (*ground*) боло́тистый.

soil[1] [sɔɪl] *n.* по́чва; **~ science** почвове́дение.

soil[2] [sɔɪl] *v.t.* па́чкать *impf.*, за~, ис~ *pf.*

sojourn ['sɒdʒ(ə)n, -dʒɜːn, 'sʌ-] *n.* вре́менное пребыва́ние; *v.i.* вре́менно жить (живу́, -вёшь; жил, -а́, -о) *impf.*

solace ['sɒləs] *n.* утеше́ние; *v.t.* утеша́ть *impf.*, уте́шить *pf.*

solar ['səʊlə(r)] *adj.* со́лнечный.

solarium [sə'leərɪəm] *n.* соля́рий.

solder ['səʊldə(r), 'sɒ-] *n.* припо́й; *v.t.* пая́ть *impf.*; спа́ивать *impf.*, спая́ть *pf.* **soldering-iron** *n.* пая́льник.

soldier ['səʊldʒə(r)] *n.* солда́т (*g.pl.* -т), вое́нный *sb.*; (*toy ~*) солда́тик; **~ of fortune** кондотье́р. **soldierly** *adj.* во́инский.

sole[1] [səʊl] *n.* (*of foot, shoe*) подо́шва; (*of foot*) ступня́; (*of shoe*) подмётка; *v.t.* ста́вить *impf.*, по~ *pf.* подмётку к+*d.*, на+*a.*

sole[2] [səʊl] *n.* (*fish*) морско́й язы́к (-а́).

sole[3] [səʊl] *adj.* еди́нственный; (*exclusive*) исключи́тельный.

solecism ['sɒlɪ,sɪz(ə)m] *n.* солеци́зм.

solemn ['sɒləm] *adj.* торже́ственный (-ен, -енна). **solemnity** [sə'lemnɪtɪ] *n.* торже́ственность; (*celebration*) торжество́.

solicit [sə'lɪsɪt] *v.t.* про́сить (-ошу́, -о́сишь) *impf.*, по~ *pf.*+*a.*, *g.*, о+*p.*; выпра́шивать *impf.*; (*of prostitute*) пристава́ть (-таю́, -таёшь) *impf.*, приста́ть (-а́ну, -а́нешь) *pf.* к+*d.* (*v.abs.* к мужчи́нам). **solicitor** *n.* соли́ситор; юриско́нсульт. **solicitous** *adj.* забо́тливый. **solicitude** *n.* забо́тливость

solid ['sɒlɪd] *adj.* (*not liquid*) твёрдый (твёрд, -а́, -о); (*not hollow; continuous*) сплошно́й; (*of time*) без переры́ва; (*firm*) про́чный

(-чен, -чна́, -чно, про́чны́), пло́тный (-тен, -тна́, -тно, пло́тны́); (*pure*) чи́стый (чист, -а́, -о, чи́сты́); (*of reason etc.*) убеди́тельный; *n.* твёрдое те́ло (*pl.* -ла́); *pl.* твёрдая пи́ща. **solidarity** [ˌsɒlɪ'dærɪtɪ] *n.* солида́рность. **solidify** [sə'lɪdɪˌfaɪ] *v.t. & i.* де́лать(ся) *impf.*, с~ *pf.* твёрдым; *v.i.* затвердева́ть *impf.*, затверде́ть *pf.* **solidity** [sə'lɪdɪtɪ] *n.* твёрдость; про́чность. **solid-state** *adj.*: ~ **physics** фи́зика твёрдого те́ла.

solidus ['sɒlɪdəs] *n.* дели́тельная черта́.

soliloquy [sə'lɪləkwɪ] *n.* моноло́г.

solipsism ['sɒlɪpˌsɪz(ə)m] *n.* солипси́зм.

solitaire ['sɒlɪˌteə(r)] *n.* (*gem*) солите́р.

solitary ['sɒlɪtərɪ] *adj.* одино́кий, уединённый (-ён, -ённа); ~ **confinement** одино́чное заключе́ние. **solitude** *n.* одино́чество.

solo ['səʊləʊ] *n.* со́ло *nt.indecl.*; (*aeron.*) самостоя́тельный полёт; *adj.* со́льный; *adv.* со́ло. **soloist** *n.* соли́ст, ~ка.

solstice ['sɒlstɪs] *n.* солнцестоя́ние.

soluble ['sɒljʊb(ə)l] *adj.* раствори́мый. **solution** [sə'luːʃ(ə)n, -'ljuːʃ(ə)n] *n.* раство́р; (*action*) растворе́ние; (*of puzzle etc.*) реше́ние, разреше́ние. **solve** *v.t.* реша́ть *impf.*, реши́ть *pf.* **solvency** *n.* платёжеспосо́бность. **solvent** *adj.* растворя́ющий; (*financially*) платёжеспосо́бный; *n.* раствори́тель *m.*

sombre ['sɒmbə(r)] *adj.* мра́чный (-чен, -чна́, -чно).

sombrero [sɒm'breərəʊ] *n.* сомбре́ро *nt.indecl.*

some [sʌm] *adj. & pron.* (*any*) како́й-нибудь; (*a certain*) како́й-то; (*a certain amount or number of*) не́который, *or often expressed by noun in* (*partitive*) *g.*; (*several*) не́сколько+*g.*; (*approximately*) о́коло+*g.*; *often expressed by inversion of noun and numeral*; (~ *people, things*) не́которые *pl.*; ~ **day** когда́-нибудь; ~ **more** ещё; ~ **other day** друго́й раз; ~ ... **others** одни́... други́е; **to** ~ **extent** до изве́стной сте́пени. **somebody, someone** *n. & pron.* (*def.*) кто́-то; (*indef.*) кто́-нибудь; (*important pers.*) ва́жная персо́на. **somehow** *adv.* ка́к-то; ка́к-нибудь; (*for some reason*) почему́-то; ~ **or other** так или ина́че.

somersault ['sʌməˌsɒlt] *n.* прыжо́к (-жка́) кувырко́м; *v.i.* кувырка́ться *impf.*, кувыр(к)ну́ться *pf.*

something ['sʌmθɪŋ] *n. & pron.* (*def.*) что́-то; (*indef.*) что́-нибудь; ~ **like** (*approximately*) приблизи́тельно; (*a thing like*) что́-то вро́де+*g.* **sometime** *adv.* не́когда; *adj.* бы́вший. **sometimes** *adv.* иногда́. **somewhat** *adv.* не́сколько, дово́льно. **somewhere** *adv.* (*position*) (*def.*) где́-то; (*indef.*) где́-нибудь; (*motion*) куда́-то; куда́-нибудь.

somnolent ['sɒmnələnt] *adj.* со́нный.

son [sʌn] *n.* сын (*pl.* -овья́, -ове́й).

sonar ['səʊnə(r)] *n.* гидролока́тор.

sonata [sə'nɑːtə] *n.* сона́та.

sonde [sɒnd] *n.* зонд.

song [sɒŋ] *n.* пе́сня (*g.pl.* -сен); (*singing*) пе́ние; ~ **thrush** пе́вчий дрозд (-а́). **songbird** *n.* пе́вчая пти́ца.

sonic ['sɒnɪk] *adj.* звуково́й, акусти́ческий.

son-in-law ['sʌnɪnˌlɔː] *n.* зять (*pl.* -я́, -ёв) *m.*

sonnet ['sɒnɪt] *n.* соне́т.

sonny ['sʌnɪ] *n.* сыно́к.

sonorous ['sɒnərəs, sə'nɔːrəs] *adj.* зву́чный (-чен, -чна́, -чно).

soon [suːn] *adv.* ско́ро, вско́ре; (*early*) ра́но; **as** ~ **as** как то́лько; **as** ~ **as possible** как мо́жно скоре́е; **no** ~**er said than done** ска́зано — сде́лано; ~**er or later** ра́но и́ли по́здно; **the** ~**er the better** чем ра́ньше, тем лу́чше.

soot [sʊt] *n.* са́жа, ко́поть.

soothe [suːð] *v.t.* успока́ивать *impf.*, успоко́ить *pf.*; (*pain*) облегча́ть *impf.*, облегчи́ть *pf.*

soothsayer ['suːθˌseɪə(r)] *n.* предсказа́тель *m.*, ~ница.

sooty ['sʊtɪ] *adj.* запа́чканный (-ан) са́жей, закопте́лый.

sophism ['sɒfɪz(ə)m] *n.* софи́зм.

sophisticated [sə'fɪstɪˌkeɪtɪd] *adj.* (*person*) искушённый; (*tastes*) изощрённый (-ён, -ённа); (*equipment*) усоверше́нствованный.

soporific [ˌsɒpə'rɪfɪk] *adj.* снотво́рный; *n.* снотво́рное *sb.*

soprano [sə'prɑːnəʊ] *n.* сопра́но (*voice*) *nt.* & (*person*) *f.indecl.*, ди́скант.

sorbet ['sɔːbeɪ, -bɪt] *n.* щербе́т.

sorcerer ['sɔːsərə(r)] *n.* колду́н (-а́). **sorceress** *n.* колду́нья (*g.pl.* -ний). **sorcery** *n.* колдовство́.

sordid ['sɔːdɪd] *adj.* (*dirty*) гря́зный (-зен, -зна́, -зно); (*wretched*) убо́гий; (*base*) по́длый (подл, -а́, -о).

sore [sɔː(r)] *n.* боля́чка, я́зва; *adj.* больно́й (-лен, -льна́); **my throat is** ~ у меня́ боли́т го́рло.

sorrel[1] ['sɒr(ə)l] *n.* (*herb*) щаве́ль (-ля́) *m.*

sorrel[2] ['sɒr(ə)l] *adj.* (*of horse*) гнедо́й; *n.* гнеда́я ло́шадь (*pl.* -ди, -де́й, *i.* -дьми́).

sorrow ['sɒrəʊ] *n.* печа́ль, го́ре, скорбь. **sorrowful** *adj.* печа́льный, ско́рбный. **sorry** *adj.* жа́лкий (-лок, -лка́, -лко); *pred.*: **be** ~ жале́ть *impf.* (**about** о+*p.*); жаль *impers.*+*d.* (**for** +*g.*); ~! извини́(те)!

sort [sɔːt] *n.* род (*pl.* -ы́), вид, сорт (*pl.* -а́); *v.t.* сорти́ровать *impf.*; разбира́ть *impf.*, разобра́ть (разберу́, -рёшь; разобра́л, -а́, -о) *pf.* **sorter** *n.* сортиро́вщик, -ица.

sortie ['sɔːtɪ] *n.* вы́лазка.

SOS *n.* (радио)сигна́л бе́дствия.

so-so ['səʊsəʊ] *adj.* так себе́.

sot [sɒt] *n.* пья́ница *c.g.*

sotto voce [ˌsɒtəʊ 'vəʊtʃɪ] *adv.* вполго́лоса.

soubriquet *see* **sobriquet**

soufflé ['suːfleɪ] *n.* суфле́ *nt.indecl.*

soul [səʊl] *n.* душа́ (*a.* -шу; *pl.* -ши); ~ **music** со́ул.

sound[1] [saʊnd] *adj.* (*healthy*) здоро́вый; (*strong*; *of sleep*) кре́пкий (-пок, -пка́, -пко);

(*firm*) про́чный (-чен, -чна́, -чно, про́чны́); *adv.* кре́пко.

sound² [saʊnd] *n.* (*noise*) звук, шум; *attr.* звуково́й; ~ **barrier** звуково́й барье́р; ~ **effects** звуково́е сопровожде́ние; ~ **wave** звукова́я волна́ (*pl.* -ны, -н, во́лна́м); *v.i.* звуча́ть (-чи́т) *impf.*, про~ *pf.*

sound³ [saʊnd] *v.t.* (*test depth*) измеря́ть *impf.*, изме́рить *pf.* глубину́+*g.*; (*med.*, *fig.*) зонди́ровать *impf.*, по~ *pf.*; *n.* зонд.

sound⁴ [saʊnd] *n.* (*strait*) проли́в.

soundproof ['saʊndpru:f] *adj.* звуконепроница́емый. **soundtrack** *n.* звукова́я доро́жка; звуково́е сопровожде́ние.

soup [su:p] *n.* суп (-а(у), *loc.* -е & -у́; *pl.* -ы́); *v.t.*: ~ **up** повыша́ть *impf.*, повы́сить *pf.* мо́щность+*g.* **soup-kitchen** *n.* беспла́тная столо́вая *sb.*

sour ['saʊə(r)] *adj.* ки́слый (-сел, -сла́, -сло); (*of milk etc.*) проки́сший; ~ **cream** смета́на; *v.i.* прокиса́ть *impf.*, проки́снуть (-с) *pf.*; *v.t.* & *i.* озлобля́ть(ся) *impf.*, озло́бить(ся) *pf.*

source [sɔ:s] *n.* исто́чник; (*of river*) исто́ки *m.pl.*

south [saʊθ] *n.* юг; (*naut.*) зюйд; *adj.* ю́жный; (*naut.*) зю́йдовый; *adv.* к ю́гу, на юг; ~ **wind** зюйд. **south-east** *n.* ю́го-восто́к; (*naut.*) зюйд-о́ст. **southeaster** *n.* зюйд-о́ст. **south-easterly, -eastern** *adj.* ю́го-восто́чный; (*naut.*) зюйд-о́стовый. **southerly** ['sʌðəlɪ] *adj.* ю́жный; (*naut.*) зю́йдовый. **southern** ['sʌð(ə)n] *adj.* ю́жный. **southerner** *n.* южа́нин (*pl.* -а́не, -а́н), -а́нка; жи́тель *m.*, ~ница, ю́га. **southernmost** *adj.* са́мый ю́жный. **southpaw** *n.* левша́ *c.g.* **southward(s)** *adv.* к ю́гу, на юг. **south-'west** *n.* ю́го-за́пад; (*naut.*) зюйд-ве́ст. **south'wester** *n.* зюйд-ве́ст. **south-'westerly, -'western** *adj.* ю́го-за́падный; (*naut.*) зюйд-ве́стовый.

souvenir [ˌsu:və'nɪə(r)] *n.* сувени́р.

sou'wester [saʊ'westə(r)] *n.* (*hat*) зюйдве́стка.

sovereign ['sɒvrɪn] *adj.* сувере́нный; *n.* сувере́н, мона́рх; (*coin*) соверéн. **sovereignty** *n.* суверенитéт.

soviet ['səʊvɪət, 'sɒ-] *n.* сове́т; **Supreme S~** Верхо́вный Сове́т; **S~ Union** Сове́тский Сою́з; *adj.* (**S~**) сове́тский.

sow¹ [saʊ] *n.* свинья́ (*pl.* -ньи, -не́й, -ньям), свинома́тка.

sow² [səʊ] *v.t.* (*seed*) се́ять (се́ю, се́ешь) *impf.*, по~ *pf.*; (*field*) засе́ивать *impf.*, засе́ять (-е́ю, -е́ешь) *pf.*; ~**ing machine** се́ялка. **sower** *n.* се́ятель *m.*

soy [sɔɪ] *n.* со́евый со́ус. **soya** ['sɔɪə] *n.* со́я; ~ **bean** со́евый боб (-а́).

sozzled ['sɒz(ə)ld] *pred.* в до́ску пьян (-а́, -о).

spa [spɑ:] *n.* во́ды *f.pl.*, куро́рт.

space [speɪs] *n.* простра́нство; (*distance*) протяже́ние; (*interval*) промежу́ток (-тка); (*place*) ме́сто; (*outer* ~) ко́смос; *attr.* косми́ческий; ~ **station** косми́ческая ста́нция; *v.t.* расставля́ть *impf.*, расста́вить *pf.* с промежу́тками. **space-bar** *n.* кла́виша для интерва́лов. **spacecraft** *n.* косми́ческий кора́бль (-ля́) *m.* **spaceman** *n.* космона́вт, астрона́вт. **spaceship** *n.* косми́ческий кора́бль (-ля́) *m.* **spacesuit** *n.* скафа́ндр (космона́вта). **spacious** ['speɪʃəs] *adj.* просто́рный, помести́тельный.

spade¹ [speɪd] *n.* (*tool*) лопа́та, за́ступ.

spade² [speɪd] *n.* (*cards*) пи́ка.

spaghetti [spə'getɪ] *n.* спаге́тти *nt.indecl.*

Spain [speɪn] *n.* Испа́ния.

span [spæn] *n.* (*of bridge*) пролёт; (*aeron.*) разма́х; (*as measure*) пядь (*pl.* пя́ди, пя́де́й); *v.t.* (*of bridge*) соединя́ть *impf.*, соедини́ть *pf.* сто́роны+*g.*, (*river*) берега́+*g.*

spangle ['spæŋg(ə)l] *n.* блёстка.

Spaniard ['spænjəd] *n.* испа́нец (-нца), -нка.

spaniel ['spænj(ə)l] *n.* спание́ль *m.*

Spanish ['spænɪʃ] *adj.* испа́нский.

spank [spæŋk] *v.t.* шлёпать *impf.*, шлёпнуть *pf.*; *n.* шлепо́к (-пка́).

spanner ['spænə(r)] *n.* га́ечный ключ (-а́).

spar¹ [spɑ:(r)] *n.* (*naut.*) ранго́утное де́рево (*pl.* -е́вья, -е́вьев); (*aeron.*) лонжеро́н.

spar² [spɑ:(r)] *v.i.* бокси́ровать *impf.*; (*fig.*) препира́ться *impf.*

spare [speə(r)] *adj.* (*in reserve*) запасно́й, запа́сный; (*extra, to* ~) ли́шний; (*of seat, time*) свобо́дный; (*thin*) худоща́вый; ~ **parts** запасны́е ча́сти (-те́й) *f.pl.*; ~ **room** ко́мната для госте́й; *n.*: *pl.* запча́сти (-те́й) *pl.*; *v.t.* (*grudge*) жале́ть *impf.*, по~ *pf.*+*a.*, *g.*; **he ~d no pains** он не жале́л трудо́в; (*do without*) обходи́ться (-ожу́сь, -о́дишься) *impf.*, обойти́сь (обойду́сь, -дёшься; обошёлся, -шла́сь) *pf.* без+*g.*; (*time*) уделя́ть *impf.*, удели́ть *pf.*; (*person, feelings, etc.*) щади́ть *impf.*, по~ *pf.*

spare-rib [speə'rɪb] *n.* (свино́е) рёбрышко (*pl.* -шки, -шек, -шкам).

spark [spɑ:k] *n.* и́скра; *v.i.* искри́ть *impf.*; ~**ing plug** запа́льная свеча́ (*pl.* -чи, -че́й).

sparkle ['spɑ:k(ə)l] *v.i.* и́скри́ться *impf.*; сверка́ть *impf.*

sparrow ['spærəʊ] *n.* воробе́й (-бья́). **sparrowhawk** *n.* перепеля́тник.

sparse [spɑ:s] *adj.* ре́дкий (-док, -дка́, -дко); (*population*) разбро́санный (-ан).

spasm ['spæz(ə)m] *n.* спазм, су́дорога. **spasmodic** [spæz'mɒdɪk] *adj.* спазмоди́ческий, су́дорожный.

spastic ['spæstɪk] *adj.* спасти́ческий.

spate [speɪt] *n.* разли́в; (*fig.*) пото́к.

spatial ['speɪʃ(ə)l] *adj.* простра́нственный.

spatter ['spætə(r)] *v.t.* (*liquid*) бры́згать (-зжу, -зжешь) *impf.*+*i.*; (*person etc.*) забры́згивать *impf.*, забры́згать *pf.* (**with** +*i.*); *n.* бры́зги (-г) *pl.*

spatula ['spætjʊlə] *n.* шпа́тель *m.*

spawn [spɔ:n] *v.t.* & *abs.* мета́ть (ме́чет) *impf.* (икру́); *v.t.* (*fig.*) порожда́ть *impf.*, породи́ть *pf.*; *n.* икра́; (*mushroom* ~) грибни́ца; (*offspring*) отро́дье.

speak [spi:k] *v.t.* & *i.* говори́ть *impf.*, сказа́ть (-ажу́, -а́жешь) *pf.*; *v.i.* (*make speech*) выступа́ть *impf.*, вы́ступить *pf.* (с ре́чью); выска́зываться *impf.*, вы́сказаться (-ажусь, -ажешься) *pf.* (**for** за+*a.*; **against** про́тив+*g.*). **speaker** *n.* ора́тор; (*at conference etc.*) докла́дчик; (**S~**, *parl.*) спи́кер; (*loud-~*) громкоговори́тель *m.* **speaking** *n.*: **not be on ~ terms** не разгова́ривать *impf.* (**with** с+*i.*). **speaking-trumpet** *n.* ру́пор. **speaking-tube** *n.* перегово́рная тру́бка.

spear ['spɪə(r)] *n.* копьё (*pl.* -пья, -пий, -пьям); *v.t.* пронза́ть *impf.*, пронзи́ть *pf.* копьём. **spearhead** *n.* передово́й отря́д.

special ['speʃ(ə)l] *adj.* осо́бый, специа́льный; (*extra*) э́кстренный. **specialist** *n.* специали́ст. **speciality** [ˌspeʃɪ'ælɪtɪ] *n.* специа́льность. **speciali'zation** *n.* специализа́ция. **specialize** *v.t.* & *i.* специализи́ровать(ся) *impf.* & *pf.* **specially** *adv.* осо́бенно.

species ['spi:ʃɪz, -ʃi:z, 'spi:s-] *n.* вид.

specific [spɪ'sɪfɪk] *adj.* специфи́ческий; (*biol.*) видово́й; (*phys.*) уде́льный. **specification(s)** [ˌspesɪfɪ'keɪʃ(ə)n] *n.* специфика́ция. **'specify** ['spesɪˌfaɪ] *v.t.* (*mention*) специа́льно упомина́ть *impf.*, упомяну́ть (-ну́, -нешь)+*a.*, о+*p.*; (*include in specifications*) специфици́ровать *impf.* & *pf.*

specimen ['spesɪmən] *n.* образе́ц (-зца́), экземпля́р; **~ page** про́бная страни́ца.

specious ['spi:ʃəs] *adj.* благови́дный, правдоподо́бный.

speck [spek] *n.* кра́пинка, пя́тнышко (*pl.* -шки, -шек, -шкам). **speckled** *adj.* кра́пчатый.

spectacle ['spektək(ə)l] *n.* зре́лище; *pl.* очки́ (-ко́в) *pl.*

spectacular [spek'tækjʊlə(r)] *adj.* эффе́ктный.

spectator [spek'teɪtə(r)] *n.* зри́тель *m.*, ~ница.

spectral ['spektr(ə)l] *adj.* (*ghostlike*) при́зрачный; (*phys.*) спектра́льный. **spectre** *n.* при́зрак.

spectroscope ['spektrəˌskəʊp] *n.* спектроско́п. **spectro'scopic** *adj.* спектроскопи́ческий.

spectrum ['spektrəm] *n.* спектр.

speculate ['spekjʊˌleɪt] *v.i.* (*meditate*) размышля́ть *impf.*, размы́слить *pf.* (**on** о+*p.*); (*in shares etc.*) спекули́ровать *impf.* **specu'lation** *n.* тео́рия, предположе́ние; спекуля́ция. **speculative** *adj.* гипотети́ческий; спекуляти́вный. **speculator** *n.* спекуля́нт, ~ка.

speech [spi:tʃ] *n.* (*faculty*) речь; (*address*) речь (*pl.* -чи, -че́й), выступле́ние; (*language*) язы́к (-а́); **~ day** акт; **~ therapy** логопе́дия. **speechify** ['spi:tʃɪˌfaɪ] *v.i.* ора́торствовать *impf.* **speechless** *adj.* немо́й (нем, -а́, -о); (*with emotion*) онеме́вший.

speed [spi:d] *n.* ско́рость, быстрота́; (*phot.*) светочувстви́тельность; **at full ~** по́лным хо́дом; **~ limit** дозво́ленная ско́рость; *v.i.* спеши́ть *impf.*, по~ *pf.*; *v.t.*: **~ up** ускоря́ть *impf.*, уско́рить *pf.* **speedboat** *n.* быстрохо́дный ка́тер (*pl.* -а́). **spee'dometer** *n.* спидо́метр. **speedway** *n.* доро́жка для мотоцикле́тных го́нок. **speedy** *adj.* бы́стрый (быстр, -а́, -о, бы́стры́), ско́рый (скор, -а́, -о).

speleologist [ˌspi:lɪ'ɒlədʒɪst, ˌspe-] *n.* спелео́лог. **speleology** *n.* спелеоло́гия.

spell¹ [spel] *n.* (*incantation*) заклина́ние.

spell² [spel] *v.t.* (*write*) писа́ть (пишу́, -шешь) *impf.*, на~ *pf.* по бу́квам; (*say*) произноси́ть (-ошу́, -о́сишь) *impf.*, произнести́ (-есу́, -есёшь; -ёс, -есла́) *pf.* по бу́квам; **how do you ~ that word?** как пи́шется э́то сло́во?

spell³ [spel] *n.* (*period*) промежу́ток (-тка) вре́мени.

spellbound ['spelbaʊnd] *adj.* зачаро́ванный (-ан, -ан(н)а).

spelling ['spelɪŋ] *n.* правописа́ние.

spend [spend] *v.t.* (*money*; *effort*) тра́тить *impf.*, ис~, по~ *pf.*; (*time*) проводи́ть (-ожу́, -о́дишь) *impf.*, провести́ (-еду́, -едёшь; -ёл, -ела́) *pf.* **spendthrift** *n.* расточи́тель *m.*, ~ница; мот, ~о́вка.

sperm¹ [spɜ:m] *n.* спе́рма.

sperm² (whale) [spɜ:m] *n.* кашало́т.

spermaceti [ˌspɜ:mə'setɪ] *n.* спермаце́т.

spermatic [spɜ:'mætɪk] *adj.* семенно́й.

spermatozoon [ˌspɜ:mətəʊ'zəʊɒn] *n.* сперматозо́ид.

sphere [sfɪə(r)] *n.* (*var. senses*) сфе́ра; (*ball*) шар (-а́ *with 2,3,4*; *pl.* -ы́). **spherical** ['sferɪk(ə)l] *adj.* сфери́ческий, шарообра́зный. **spheroid** *n.* сферо́ид.

sphincter ['sfɪŋktə(r)] *n.* сфи́нктер.

sphinx [sfɪŋks] *n.* сфинкс.

spice [spaɪs] *n.* спе́ция, пря́ность; *v.t.* приправля́ть *impf.*, припра́вить *pf.* спе́циями.

spick [ˌspɪk] *adj.*: **~ and span** чи́стый (чист, -а́, -о, чи́сты́), опря́тный; (*of person*) оде́тый с иго́лочки.

spicy ['spaɪsɪ] *adj.* пря́ный; (*fig.*) пика́нтный.

spider ['spaɪdə(r)] *n.* пау́к (-а́). **spidery** *adj.* то́нкий (-нок, -нка́, -нко, то́нки́).

spike¹ [spaɪk] *n.* (*bot.*) ко́лос (*pl.* коло́сья, -ьев).

spike² [spaɪk] *n.* (*point*) остриё; (*nail*) гвоздь (-дя́ *pl.* -ди, -де́й) *m.*; (*on shoes*) шип (-а́); (*for papers*) на́колка; *v.t.* снабжа́ть *impf.*, снабди́ть *pf.* шипа́ми; (*gun*) заклёпывать *impf.*, заклепа́ть *pf.*; (*drink*) добавля́ть *impf.*, доба́вить *pf.* спиртно́е в+*a.*

spill [spɪl] *v.t.* & *i.* пролива́ть(ся) *impf.*, проли́ть(ся) (-лью́, -льёт(ся); про́ли́л/проли́лся, -а́(сь), -о/проли́ло́сь) *pf.*; рассыпа́ть(ся) *impf.*, рассы́пать(ся) (-плю, -плет(ся)) *pf.*; *n.* проли́тие, рассы́пка; (*fall*) паде́ние.

spin [spɪn] *v.t.* (*thread etc.*) прясть (пряду́, -дёшь; -ял, -я́ла́, -я́ло) *impf.*, с~ *pf.*; (*top*) запуска́ть *impf.*, запусти́ть (-ущу́, -у́стишь) *pf.*; (*coin*) подбра́сывать *impf.*, подбро́сить *pf.*; *v.t.* & *i.* (*turn*) крути́ть(ся) (-учу́(сь), -у́тишь(ся)) *impf.*; кружи́ть(ся) (-ужу́(сь),

-у́жи́шь(ся)) *impf.*; ~ **out** (*prolong*) затя́гивать *impf.*, затяну́ть (-ну́, -нешь) *pf.*; *n.* круже́ние; (*aeron.*) што́пор; (*excursion*) пое́здка; **go for a** ~ прока́тываться *impf.*, прокати́ться (-ачу́сь, -а́тишься) *pf.*

spinach ['spɪnɪdʒ, -ɪtʃ] *n.* шпина́т.

spinal ['spaɪn(ə)l] *adj.* спинно́й; ~ **column** спинно́й хребе́т (-бта́); ~ **cord** спинно́й мозг.

spindle ['spɪnd(ə)l] *n.* веретено́ (*pl.* -ёна); (*axis*, *pin*) ось (*pl.* о́си, осе́й) *m.*, шпи́ндель *m.* **spindly** *adj.* дли́нный (-нен, -нна́, длинно́) и то́нкий (-нок, -нка́, -нко, то́нки́).

spine [spaɪn] *n.* (*backbone*) позвоно́чник, хребе́т (-бта́); (*bot.*) шип (-а́); (*zool.*) игла́ (*pl.* -лы); (*of book*) корешо́к (-шка́). **spineless** *adj.* (*fig.*) мягкоте́лый, бесхара́ктерный.

spinet [spɪ'net, 'spɪnɪt] *n.* спине́т.

spinnaker ['spɪnəkə(r)] *n.* спи́накер.

spinner ['spɪnə(r)] *n.* пряди́льщик, -ица; (*fishing*) блесна́.

spinney ['spɪnɪ] *n.* ро́щица.

spinning ['spɪnɪŋ] *n.* пряде́ние. **spinning-machine** *n.* пряди́льная маши́на. **spinning-top** *n.* волчо́к (-чка́). **spinning-wheel** *n.* пря́лка.

spinster ['spɪnstə(r)] *n.* незаму́жняя же́нщина.

spiny ['spaɪnɪ] *adj.* колю́чий.

spiral ['spaɪər(ə)l] *adj.* спира́льный, винтово́й; *n.* спира́ль.

spire ['spaɪə(r)] *n.* шпиль *m.*

spirit ['spɪrɪt] *n.* дух, душа́; *pl.* (*mood*) настрое́ние; (*liquid*) спирт (*loc.* -е & -у́; *pl.* -ы́); *pl.* (*drinks*) спиртно́е *sb.*; *v.t.*: ~ **away** та́йно уноси́ть (-ошу́, -о́сишь) *impf.*, унести́ (унесу́, -сёшь; унёс, -ла́) *pf.* **spirited** *adj.* энерги́чный, пы́лкий (-лок, -лка́, -лко). **spirit-lamp** *n.* спирто́вка. **spiritless** *adj.* безжи́зненный (-ен, -енна). **spirit-level** *n.* ватерпа́с. **spiritual** *adj.* духо́вный. **spiritualism** *n.* спирити́зм. **spiritualist** *n.* спири́т. **spirituous** *adj.* спиртно́й.

spit[1] [spɪt] *n.* (*skewer*) ве́ртел (*pl.* -а́); (*of land*) стре́лка, коса́ (*a.* ко́су́; *pl.* -сы); *v.t.* наса́живать *impf.*, насади́ть (-ажу́, -а́дишь) *pf.* на ве́ртел; (*fig.*) пронза́ть *impf.*, пронзи́ть *pf.*

spit[2] [spɪt] *v.i.* плева́ть (плюю́, -юёшь) *impf.*, плю́нуть *pf.*; (*of rain*) мороси́ть *impf.*; (*of fire etc.*) шипе́ть (-пи́т) *impf.*; *v.t.*: ~ **out** выплёвывать *impf.*, вы́плюнуть *pf.*; ~**ing image** то́чная ко́пия; *n.* слюна́, плево́к (-вка́).

spite [spaɪt] *n.* зло́ба, злость; **in** ~ **of** несмотря́ на+*a.* **spiteful** *adj.* зло́бный.

spittle ['spɪt(ə)l] *n.* слюна́, плево́к (-вка́).

spittoon [spɪ'tu:n] *n.* плева́тельница.

spitz [spɪts] *n.* шпиц.

splash [splæʃ] *v.t.* (*person*) забры́згивать *impf.*, забры́згать *pf.* (**with** +*i.*); (~ *liquid*) бры́згать (-зжу, -зжешь) *impf.*+*i.*; *v.i.* плеска́ть(ся) (-ещу́(сь), -е́щешь(ся)) *impf.*, плесну́ть *pf.*; (*move*) шлёпать *impf.*, шлёпнуть *pf.* (**through** по+*d.*); ~ **money about** сори́ть *impf.* деньга́ми; *n.* бры́зги (-г) *pl.*, плеск. **splashdown** *n.* приводне́ние.

splatter ['splætə(r)] *v.i.* плеска́ться (-е́щется) *impf.*

spleen [spli:n] *n.* селезёнка; (*spite*) зло́ба.

splendid ['splendɪd] *adj.* великоле́пный. **splendour** ['splendə(r)] *n.* блеск, великоле́пие.

splenetic [splɪ'netɪk] *adj.* жёлчный.

splice [splaɪs] *v.t.* (*ropes*) сра́щивать *impf.*, срасти́ть *pf.* концы́+*g.*; (*film*, *tape*) скле́ивать *impf.*, скле́ить *pf.* концы́+*g.*; *n.* (*naut.*) спле́сень (-сня) *m.*; (*film*, *tape*) скле́йка, ме́сто скле́йки.

splint [splɪnt] *n.* лубо́к (-бка́), ши́на; *v.t.* накла́дывать *impf.*, наложи́ть (-жу́, -жишь) *pf.* ши́ну на+*a.*; класть (-аду́, -адёшь; -ал) *impf.*, положи́ть (-жу́, -жишь) *pf.* в лубо́к.

splinter ['splɪntə(r)] *n.* оско́лок (-лка), ще́пка; (*in skin*) зано́за; ~ **group** отколо́вшаяся гру́ппа; *v.t.* & *i.* расщепля́ть(ся) *impf.*, расщепи́ть(ся) *pf.*

split [splɪt] *n.* расще́лина, расще́п; (*schism*) раско́л; *pl.* шпага́т; *v.t.* & *i.* расщепля́ть(ся) *impf.*, расщепи́ть(ся) *pf.*; раска́лывать(ся) *impf.*, расколо́ть(ся) (-лю́, -лет(ся)) *pf.*; (*divide*) дели́ть(ся) (-лю́, -лит(ся)) *impf.*, раз~ *pf.* (на ча́сти); *v.i.*: ~ **on** доноси́ть (-ошу́, -о́сишь) *impf.*, донести́ (-есу́, -есёшь; -ёс, -есла́) *pf.* на+*a.*; ~ **hairs** спо́рить *impf.* о мелоча́х; ~ **one's sides** надрыва́ться *impf.* от хо́хота; ~ **pea(s)** лущёный горо́х (-а(у)); ~ **personality** раздвое́ние ли́чности; ~ **pin** шплинт (шпли́нта́); ~ **second** мгнове́ние о́ка. **split-level** *adj.* на ра́зных у́ровнях.

splotch [splɒtʃ] *n.* неро́вное пятно́ (*pl.* -тна, -тен, -тнам), мазо́к (-зка́).

splutter ['splʌtə(r)] *v.i.* бры́згать (-зжу, -зжешь) *impf.* слюно́й; *v.t.* (*utter*) говори́ть *impf.* невня́тно.

spoil [spɔɪl] *n.* (*pl. or collect.*) добы́ча; (*of war*) трофе́и *m.pl.*; *v.t.* & *i.* (*damage*; *decay*) по́ртить(ся) *impf.*, ис~ *pf.*; *v.t.* (*indulge*) балова́ть *impf.*, из~ *pf.*; **be** ~**ing for a fight** рва́ться (рвусь, рвёшься; рва́лся, -ала́сь, -а́ло́сь) *impf.* в дра́ку.

spoke [spəʊk] *n.* спи́ца.

spoken ['spəʊkən] *adj.* (*language*) у́стный. **spokesman, -woman** *n.* представи́тель *m.*, ~ница.

sponge [spʌndʒ] *n.* гу́бка; ~ **cake** бискви́т; ~ **rubber** гу́бчатая рези́на; *v.t.* (*wash*) мыть (мо́ю, мо́ешь) *impf.*, вы́~, по~ *pf.* гу́бкой; (*obtain*) выпра́шивать *impf.*, вы́просить *pf.*; *v.i.*: ~ **on** жить (живу́, -вёшь; жил, -а́, -о) *impf.* на счёт+*g.* **sponger** *n.* прижива́льщик, парази́т. **spongy** *adj.* гу́бчатый.

sponsor ['spɒnsə(r)] *n.* поручи́тель *m.*, ~ница; *v.t.* руча́ться *impf.*, поручи́ться (-чу́сь, -чишься) *pf.* за+*a.*; (*finance*) финансúровать *impf.* & *pf.*

spontaneity [ˌspɒntəˈniːɪtɪ, -ˈneɪɪtɪ] *n.* непосрéдственность, самопроизвóльность. **spontaneous** [spɒnˈteɪnɪəs] *adj.* непосрéдственный (-ен, -енна), самопроизвóльный.

spoof [spuːf] *n.* (*hoax*) мистификáция; (*parody*) парóдия.

spook [spuːk] *n.* привидéние.

spool [spuːl] *n.* шпýлька, катýшка.

spoon [spuːn] *n.* лóжка; *v.t.* чéрпать *impf.*, черпнýть *pf.* лóжкой. **spoon-bait** *n.* блеснá. **spoonbill** *n.* колпúца. **spoonful** *n.* пóлная лóжка.

sporadic [spəˈrædɪk] *adj.* спорадúческий.

spore [spɔː(r)] *n.* спóра.

sport [spɔːt] *n.* спорт; *pl.* спортúвные соревновáния *nt.pl.*; (*fun*) забáва, потéха; (*person*) слáвный мáлый *sb.*; **~s car** спортúвный автомобúль *m.*; **~s coat** спортúвная кýртка; *v.t.* щеголя́ть *impf.*, щегольнýть *pf.*+*i.* **sportsman** *n.* спортсмéн. **sportsmanlike** *adj.* спортсмéнский.

spot [spɒt] *n.* (*place*) мéсто (*pl.* -тá); (*mark*) пятнó (*pl.* -тна, -тен, -тнам) (*also fig.*), крáпинка; (*pimple*) пры́щик; (*on dice etc.*) очкó (*pl.* -кú, -кóв); **on the ~** на мéсте; (*without delay*) немéдленно; **~ check** вы́борочная провéрка; *v.t.* (*mark*; *fig.*) пятнáть *impf.*, за~ *pf.*; (*recognize*) узнавáть (-аю́, -наёшь) *impf.*, узнáть *pf.*; (*notice*) замечáть *impf.*, замéтить *pf.*; *v.i.*: **it's ~ing with rain** накрáпывает дождь. **spotless** *adj.* чúстый (чист, -á, -о, чúсты́); (*fig.*) безупрéчный. **spotlight** *n.* прожéктор (*pl.* -ы & -á); *v.t.* освещáть *impf.*, осветúть (-ещý, -етúшь) *pf.* прожéктором. **spotty** *adj.* прыщевáтый.

spouse [spaʊz, spaʊs] *n.* супрýг, ~а.

spout [spaʊt] *v.i.* бить (бьёт) *impf.* струёй; хлы́нуть *pf.*; *v.t.* выпускáть *impf.*, вы́пустить *pf.* струю́+*g.*; (*verses etc.*) декламúровать *impf.*, про~ *pf.*; *n.* (*tube*) нóсик; (*jet*) струя́ (*pl.* -ýи).

sprain [spreɪn] *v.t.* растя́гивать *impf.*, растянýть (-нý, -нешь) *pf.*; *n.* растяжéние.

sprat [spræt] *n.* кúлька, шпрóта.

sprawl [sprɔːl] *v.i.* (*of person*) развáливаться *impf.*, развалúться (-лю́сь, -лишься) *pf.*; (*of town*) раскúдываться *impf.*, раскúнуться *pf.*

spray¹ [spreɪ] *n.* (*of flowers etc.*) вéт(оч)ка.

spray² [spreɪ] *n.* (*liquid*) бры́зги (-г) *pl.*; (*water*) водянáя пыль; (*atomizer*) распылúтель *m.*; *v.t.* опры́скивать *impf.*, опры́скать *pf.* (**with** +*i.*); (*cause to scatter*) распыля́ть *impf.*, распылúть *pf.* **spray-gun** *n.* краскопýльт.

spread [spred] *v.t.* & *i.* (~ *out*) расстилáть(ся) *impf.*, разостлáть(ся) (расстелю́, -лет(ся)) *pf.*; (*unfurl*, *unroll*) развёртывать(ся) *impf.*, развернýть(ся) *pf.*; (*rumour*, *disease*, *etc.*) распространя́ть(ся) *impf.*, распространúть(ся) *pf.*; *v.i.* (*extend*) простирáться *impf.*, простерéться (-трётся; -тёрся) *pf.*; *v.t.* (*bread etc.* +*a.*; *butter etc.* +*i.*) намáзывать, мáзать (мáжу, -жешь) *impf.*, на~ *pf.*; *n.* распространéние; (*span*) размáх; (*feast*) пир; (*paste*) пáста; (*double page*) разворóт.

spree [spriː] *n.* (*drinking*) кутёж (-á); **go on the ~** кутúть (кучý, кýтишь) *impf.*, кутнýть *pf.*

sprig [sprɪg] *n.* вéточка.

sprightly [ˈspraɪtlɪ] *adj.* бóдрый (бодр, -á, -о, бóдры́).

spring [sprɪŋ] *v.i.* (*jump*) пры́гать *impf.*, пры́гнуть *pf.*; *v.t.* (*disclose unexpectedly*) неожúданно сообщáть *impf.*, сообщúть *pf.* (**on** +*d.*); **~ a leak** давáть (даёт) *impf.*, дать (даст, дадýт; дал, -á, дáлó, -и) *pf.* течь; **~ a surprise on** дéлать *impf.*, с~ *pf.* сюрпрúз+*d.*; **~ from** (*originate*) происходúть (-ожý, -óдишь) *impf.*, произойтú (-ойдý, -ойдёшь; -ошёл, -ошлá) *pf.* из+*g.*; **~ up** (*jump up*) вскáкивать *impf.*, вскочúть (-чý, -чишь) *pf.*; (*arise*) возникáть *impf.*, возникнуть (-к) *pf.*; *n.* (*jump*) прыжóк (-жкá); (*season*) веснá (*pl.* вёсны, -сен, -снам); *attr.* весéнний; (*source*) истóчник, ключ (-á), роднúк (-á); (*elasticity*) упрýгость; (*coil*) пружúна; (*on vehicle*) рессóра; (*fig.*, *motive*) мотúв; **~ balance** пружúнные весы́ (-сóв) *pl.*; **~ mattress** пружúнный матрáс; **~ tide** сизигúйный прилúв; **~ water** ключевáя водá (*a.* -ду). **springboard** *n.* трамплúн. **springbok** *n.* прыгýн (-á). **spring-clean** *n.* генерáльная убóрка; *v.t.* производúть (-ожý, -óдишь) *impf.*, произвестú (-едý, -едёшь; -ёл, -елá) *pf.* генерáльную убóрку+*g.* **springy** *adj.* упрýгий.

sprinkle [ˈsprɪŋk(ə)l] *v.t.* (*with liquid*) опры́скивать *impf.*, опры́скать *pf.* (**with** +*i.*); (*with solid*) посыпáть *impf.*, посы́пать (-плю, -плешь) *pf.* (**with** +*i.*). **sprinkler** *n.* (*for watering*) опры́скиватель *m.*; (*fire-extinguisher*) спрúнклер.

sprint [sprɪnt] *v.i.* бежáть (бегý, бежúшь) *impf.* на корóткую дистáнцию; *n.* спринт. **sprinter** *n.* спрúнтер.

sprocket [ˈsprɒkɪt] *n.* зубéц (-бцá). **sprocket-wheel** *n.* звёздочка, цепнóе колесó (*pl.* -ёса).

sprout [spraʊt] *v.i.* пускáть *impf.*, пустúть (-ит) *pf.* росткú; *n.* ростóк (-ткá), побéг; *pl.* брюссéльская капýста.

spruce¹ [spruːs] *adj.* наря́дный, элегáнтный; *v.t.*: **~ o.s. up** принаряжáться *impf.*, принарядúться (-яжýсь, -я́дишься) *pf.*

spruce² [spruːs] *n.* ель.

spry [spraɪ] *adj.* живóй (жив, -á, -о), бóдрый (бодр, -á, -о, бóдры́).

spud [spʌd] *n.* (*tool*) моты́га; (*potato*) картóшка (*also collect.*).

spume [spjuːm] *n.* пéна.

spur [spɜː(r)] *n.* (*rider's*) шпóра; (*fig.*) стúмул; (*of mountain*) отрóг; **on the ~ of the moment** экспрóмтом; *v.t.*: **~ on** толкáть *impf.*, толкнýть *pf.* (**to** на+*a.*).

spurious ['spjʊərɪəs] *adj.* подде́льный, подло́жный.
spurn [spɜ:n] *v.t.* отверга́ть *impf.*, отве́ргнуть (-г(нул), -гла) *pf.*
spurt [spɜ:t] *n.* (*jet*) струя́ (*pl.* -у́и); (*effort*) рыво́к (-вка́); *v.i.* бить (бьёт) *impf.* струёй; де́лать *impf.*, с~ *pf.* рыво́к.
sputter ['spʌtə(r)] *v.t.* (*utter*) невня́тно говори́ть *impf.*, *v.i.* шипе́ть (-пи́т) *impf.*
sputum ['spju:təm] *n.* слюна́.
spy [spaɪ] *n.* шпио́н; *v.i.* шпио́нить *impf.* (**on** за+*i.*). **spyglass** *n.* подзо́рная труба́ (*pl.* -бы). **spyhole** *n.* глазо́к (-зка́).
Sq. *abbr.* (*of* **square**) пл., пло́щадь.
squabble ['skwɒb(ə)l] *n.* перебра́нка; *v.i.* вздо́рить *impf.*, по~ *pf.*
squad [skwɒd] *n.* кома́нда, гру́ппа.
squadron ['skwɒdrən] *n.* (*mil.*) эскадро́н; (*naut.*) эска́дра; (*aeron.*) эскадри́лья; **S~ Leader** ма́йор авиа́ции.
squalid ['skwɒlɪd] *adj.* гря́зный (-зен, -зна́, -зно), убо́гий.
squall [skwɔ:l] *n.* шквал; *v.i.* визжа́ть (-жу́, -жи́шь) *impf.* **squally** *adj.* шквали́стый.
squalor ['skwɒlə(r)] *n.* грязь (*loc.* -зи́), убо́гость.
squander ['skwɒndə(r)] *v.t.* растра́чивать *impf.*, растра́тить *pf.*; (*fortune*) прома́тывать *impf.*, промота́ть *pf.*
square [skweə(r)] *n.* (*math.*) квадра́т; (*in town*) пло́щадь (*pl.* -ди, -де́й), сквер; (*on paper, material*) кле́тка; (*chess*) по́ле; (*mil.*) каре́ *nt.indecl.*; (*instrument*) науго́льник; **set ~** уго́льник; *adj.* квадра́тный; (*meal*) пло́тный (-тен, -тна́, -тно, пло́тны́); **~ root** квадра́тный ко́рень (-рня) *m.*; **~ sail** прямо́й па́рус (*pl.* -а́); *v.t.* де́лать *impf.*, с~ *pf.* квадра́тным; (*math.*) возводи́ть (-ожу́, -о́дишь) *impf.*, возвести́ (-еду́, -едёшь; -ёл, -ела́) *pf.* в квадра́т; (*bribe*) подкупа́ть *impf.*, подкупи́ть (-плю́, -пишь) *pf.*; **~ accounts with** распла́чиваться *impf.*, расплати́ться (-ачу́сь, -а́тишься) *pf.* с+*i.*
squash [skwɒʃ] *n.* (*crowd*) толку́чка; (*drink*) (фрукто́вый) сок (-а(у), *loc.* -е & -у́); *v.t.* разда́вливать *impf.*, раздави́ть (-влю́, -вишь) *pf.*; (*silence*) заставля́ть *impf.*, заста́вить *pf.* замолча́ть; (*suppress*) подавля́ть *impf.*, пода́вить (-влю́, -вишь) *pf.*; *v.i.* вти́скиваться *impf.*, вти́снуться *pf.*
squat [skwɒt] *adj.* корена́стый, призе́мистый; *v.i.* сиде́ть (сижу́, сиди́шь) *impf.* на ко́рточках; **~ down** сади́ться *impf.*, сесть (ся́ду, -дешь; сел) *pf.* на ко́рточки.
squatter ['skwɒtə(r)] *n.* лицо́, самово́льно поселя́ющееся в чужо́м до́ме.
squaw [skwɔ:] *n.* индиа́нка (в Се́верной Аме́рике).
squawk [skwɔ:k] *n.* пронзи́тельный крик; (*of bird*) клёкот; *v.i.* пронзи́тельно крича́ть (-чу́, -чи́шь) *impf.*, кри́кнуть *pf.*; (*of bird*) клекота́ть (-о́чет) *impf.*
squeak [skwi:k] *n.* писк, скрип; *v.i.* пища́ть (-щу́, -щи́шь) *impf.*, пи́скнуть *pf.*; скрипе́ть (-плю́, -пи́шь) *impf.*, скри́пнуть *pf.* **squeaky** *adj.* пискли́вый, скрипу́чий.
squeal [skwi:l] *n.* визг; *v.i.* визжа́ть (-жу́, -жи́шь) *impf.*, ви́згнуть *pf.*
squeamish ['skwi:mɪʃ] *adj.* брезгли́вый, привере́дливый.
squeeze [skwi:z] *n.* (*crush*) да́вка; (*pressure*) сжа́тие; (*hand*) пожа́тие; *v.t.* дави́ть (давлю́, да́вишь) *impf.*; сжима́ть *impf.*, сжать (сожму́, -мёшь) *pf.*; пожима́ть *impf.*, пожа́ть (пожму́, -мёшь) *pf.*; **~ in** впи́хивать(ся) *impf.*, впихну́ть(ся) *pf.*; вти́скивать(ся) *impf.*, вти́снуть(ся) *pf.*; **~ out** выжима́ть *impf.*, вы́жать (вы́жму, -мешь) *pf.*; **~ through** проти́скивать(ся) *impf.*, проти́снуть(ся) *pf.*
squelch [skweltʃ] *n.* хлю́панье; *v.i.* хлю́пать *impf.*, хлю́пнуть *pf.*
squib [skwɪb] *n.* (*firework*) пета́рда.
squid [skwɪd] *n.* кальма́р.
squiggle ['skwɪg(ə)l] *n.* (*flourish*) загогу́лина; (*scribble*) кара́кули *f.pl.*
squint [skwɪnt] *n.* косогла́зие; *adj.* косо́й (кос, -а́, -о), косогла́зый; *v.i.* коси́ть *impf.*; смотре́ть (-рю́, -ришь) *impf.*, по- *pf.* и́скоса.
squire ['skwaɪə(r)] *n.* сквайр, поме́щик.
squirm [skwɜ:m] *v.i.* (*wriggle*) извива́ться *impf.*, изви́ться (изовью́сь, -вьёшься; изви́лся, извила́сь) *pf.*; (*fidget*) ёрзать *impf.*
squirrel ['skwɪr(ə)l] *n.* бе́лка.
squirt [skwɜ:t] *n.* струя́ (*pl.* -у́и); *v.i.* бить (бьёт) *impf.* струёй; *v.t.* пуска́ть *impf.*, пусти́ть (пущу́, пу́стишь) *pf.* струю́ (*substance* +*g.*; **at** на+*a.*).
St. *abbr.* (*of* **street**) ул., у́лица; (*of* **saint**) св., Свято́й, -а́я.
stab [stæb] *n.* уда́р (ножо́м *etc.*); (*pain*) внеза́пная о́страя боль; *v.i.* наноси́ть (-ошу́, -о́сишь) *impf.*, нанести́ (-есу́, -есёшь; -ёс, -есла́) *pf.* уда́р (ножо́м *etc.*) (**at** +*d.*); *v.t.* коло́ть (-лю́, -лешь) *impf.*, кольну́ть *pf.*
stability [stə'bɪlɪtɪ] *n.* усто́йчивость, про́чность, стаби́льность, постоя́нство. **stabilization** [ˌsteɪbɪˌlaɪ'zeɪʃ(ə)n] *n.* стабилиза́ция. **stabilize** ['steɪbɪˌlaɪz] *v.t.* стабилизи́ровать *impf.* & *pf.* **stabilizer** *n.* стабилиза́тор.
stable ['steɪb(ə)l] *adj.* (*steady*; *of prices, family life etc.*) усто́йчивый; (*lasting, durable*) про́чный (-чен, -чна́, -чно, про́чны́); (*unwavering*) стаби́льный; (*psych.*) уравнове́шенный (-ен, -енна); *n.* коню́шня; *v.t.* ста́вить *impf.*, по~ *pf.* в коню́шню.
staccato [stə'kɑ:təʊ] *n.* (*mus.*) стакка́то *nt.indecl.*; *adv.* (*mus.*) стакка́то.
stack [stæk] *n.* (*hay*) скирд(а́) (-а́ & -ы́; *pl.* ски́рды́, -д(о́в), -да́м), стог (*loc.* -е & -у́; *pl.* -а́); (*heap*) ку́ча, ки́па; (*building materials etc.*) шта́бель (*pl.* -ля́) *m.*; (*chimney*) (дымова́я) труба́ (*pl.* -бы); (*~-room*) (книго)храни́лище; *pl.* ма́сса, мно́жество; *v.t.* скла́дывать *impf.*, сложи́ть (-жу́, -жишь) *pf.* в ку́чу; укла́дывать *impf.*, уложи́ть (-жу́,

-жишь) *pf.* штабеля́ми.

stadium ['steɪdɪəm] *n.* стадио́н.

staff [stɑːf] *n.* (*personnel*) штат, шта́ты (-тов) *pl.*, персона́л, ка́дры (-ров) *pl.*; (*mil.*) штаб (*pl.* -бы́); (*stick*) посо́х, жезл (-а́); (*mus.*) но́тные лине́йки *f.pl.*; *adj.* шта́тный; (*mil.*) штабно́й.

stag [stæg] *n.* саме́ц-оле́нь (самца́-оле́ня) *m.*; ~ **beetle** рога́ч (-а́).

stage [steɪdʒ] *n.* (*theatr.*) сце́на, подмо́стки (-ков) *pl.*, эстра́да; (*platform*) платфо́рма; (*period*) ста́дия, фа́за, эта́п; *v.t.* (*theatr.*) ста́вить *impf.*, по~ *pf.*; (*dramatize*, *feign*) инсцени́ровать *impf.* & *pf.*; (*organize*) организова́ть *impf.* & *pf.*; ~ **whisper** театра́льный шёпот. **stage-manager** *n.* режиссёр.

stagger ['stægə(r)] *n.* поша́тывание, шата́ние; *v.i.* шата́ться *impf.*, шатну́ться *pf.*; кача́ться *impf.*, качну́ться *pf.*; *v.t.* (*surprise*) поража́ть *impf.*, порази́ть *pf.*; потряса́ть *impf.*, потрясти́ (-су́, -сёшь; потря́с, -ла́) *pf.*; (*hours of work etc.*) распределя́ть *impf.*, распредели́ть *pf.* **be staggered** *v.i.* поража́ться *impf.*, порази́ться *pf.* **staggering** *adj.* потряса́ющий, порази́тельный.

stagnancy ['stægnənsɪ], **stagnation** [stæg'neɪʃ(ə)n] *n.* засто́й, ко́сность, ине́ртность. **'stagnant** *adj.* (*water*) стоя́чий; (*fig.*) засто́йный, ко́сный, ине́ртный. **stag'nate** *v.i.* заста́иваться *impf.*, застоя́ться (-ою́сь, -ои́шься) *pf.*; косне́ть *impf.*, за~ *pf.*

stag-party ['stæg,pɑːtɪ] *n.* вечери́нка без же́нщин.

staid [steɪd] *adj.* степе́нный (-нен, -нна), тре́звый (трезв, -а́, -о), соли́дный.

stain [steɪn] *n.* пятно́ (*pl.* -тна, -тен, -тнам); (*dye*) кра́ска; *v.t.* па́чкать *impf.*, за~, ис~ *pf.*; пятна́ть *impf.*, за~ *pf.*; (*dye*) окра́шивать *impf.*, окра́сить *pf.*; ~**ed glass** цветно́е стекло́. **stainless** *adj.* незапя́танный, безупре́чный; ~ **steel** нержаве́ющая сталь.

stair [steə(r)] *n.* ступе́нь, ступе́нька. **staircase, stairs** *n.* ле́стница. **stairwell** *n.* ле́стничная кле́тка. **flight of stairs** *n.* ле́стничный марш.

stake [steɪk] *n.* (*stick*) кол (-а́, *loc.* -у́; *pl.* -ья, -ьев), столб (-а́); (*landmark*) ве́ха; (*bet*) ста́вка, закла́д; **be at** ~ быть поста́вленным на ка́рту; *v.t.* (*mark out*) огора́живать *impf.*, огороди́ть (-ожу́, -о́ди́шь) *pf.* ко́льями; отмеча́ть *impf.*, отме́тить *pf.* ве́хами; (*risk*) ста́вить *impf.*, по~ *pf.* на ка́рту; рискова́ть *impf.*+*i.*

stalactite ['stæləkˌtaɪt, stə'læk-] *n.* сталакти́т.

stalagmite ['stæləgˌmaɪt] *n.* сталагми́т.

stale [steɪl] *adj.* несве́жий (несве́ж, -а́, -е); (*hard, dry*) чёрствый (чёрств, -а́, -о), сухо́й (сух, -а́, -о); (*musty, damp*) за́тхлый; (*hackneyed*) изби́тый; **become, grow** ~ черстве́ть *impf.*, за~, по~ *pf.*

stalemate ['steɪlmeɪt] *n.* пат; (*fig.*) тупи́к (-а́).

stalk [stɔːk] *n.* сте́бель (-ля; *g.pl.* -бле́й) *m.*; *v.t.* высле́живать *impf.*; *v.t* & *i.* (*stride*) ше́ствовать *impf.* (по+*d.*)

stall [stɔːl] *n.* сто́йло; (*booth*) ларёк (-рька́), кио́ск, пала́тка; (*theatr.*) кре́сло (*g.pl.* -сел) в парте́ре; *pl.* (*theatr.*) парте́р; *v.t.* & *i.* остана́вливать(ся) *impf.*, останови́ть(ся) (-влю́(сь), -вишь(ся)) *pf.*; *v.i.* теря́ть *impf.*, по~ *pf.* ско́рость; (*play for time*) оття́гивать *impf.*, оттяну́ть (-ну́, -нешь) *pf.* вре́мя.

stallion ['stæljən] *n.* жеребе́ц (-бца́).

stalwart ['stɔːlwət] *adj.* сто́йкий (-о́ек, -ойка́, -о́йко); *n.* сто́йкий приве́рженец (-нца), -кая приве́рженка.

stamen ['steɪmən] *n.* тычи́нка.

stamina ['stæmɪnə] *n.* выно́сливость.

stammer ['stæmə(r)] *v.i.* заика́ться *impf.*; *n.* заика́ние. **stammerer** *n.* заи́ка *c.g.*

stamp [stæmp] *n.* печа́ть, штамп, ште́мпель (*pl.* -ля́) *m.*; (*hallmark*) клеймо́ (*pl.* -ма); (*postage*) (почто́вая) ма́рка; (*feet*) то́панье; *v.t.* ста́вить *impf.*, по~ *pf.* печа́ть на+*a.*; штампова́ть *impf.*, штемпелева́ть (-лю́ю, -лю́ешь) *impf.*, за~ *pf.*; клейми́ть *impf.*, за~ *pf.*; (*trample*) топта́ть (-пчу́, -пчешь) *impf.*, по~ *pf.*; *v.i.* то́пать *impf.*, то́пнуть *pf.* (нога́ми); ~ **out** подавля́ть *impf.*, подави́ть (-влю́, -вишь) *pf.*; ликвиди́ровать *impf.* & *pf.* **stamp-duty** *n.* ге́рбовый сбор.

stampede [stæm'piːd] *n.* пани́ческое бе́гство; *v.t.* & *i.* обраща́ть(ся) *impf.* в пани́ческое бе́гство.

stanch [stɑːntʃ, stɔːntʃ] *v.t.* остана́вливать *impf.*, останови́ть (-влю́, -вишь) *pf.*

stanchion ['stɑːnʃ(ə)n] *n.* подпо́рка, сто́йка.

stand [stænd] *n.* (*hat, coat*) ве́шалка; (*music*) пюпи́тр; (*umbrella, support*) подста́вка; (*counter*) сто́йка; (*booth*) ларёк (-рька́), кио́ск; (*taxi, bicycle*) стоя́нка; (*tribune*) ка́федра, трибу́на; (*at stadium*) трибу́на; (*position*) пози́ция, ме́сто (*pl.* -та́), положе́ние; (*resistance*) сопротивле́ние; *v.i.* стоя́ть (-ою́, -ои́шь) *impf.*; (*remain in force*) остава́ться (-аю́сь, -аёшься) *impf.*, оста́ться (-а́нусь, -а́нешься) в си́ле; **the matter** ~**s thus** де́ло обстои́т так; **it** ~**s to reason** разуме́ется; *v.t.* (*put*) ста́вить *impf.*, по~ *pf.*; (*endure*) выде́рживать *impf.*, вы́держать (-жу, -жишь) *pf.*; выноси́ть (-ошу́, -о́сишь) *impf.*, вы́нести (-су, -сешь; -с) *pf.*; терпе́ть (-плю́, -пишь) *impf.*, по~ *pf.*; (*treat to*) угоща́ть *impf.*, угости́ть *pf.* (*s.o.* +*a.*; *sth.* +*i.*). ~ **back** отходи́ть (-ожу́, -о́дишь) *impf.*, отойти́ (-йду́, -йдёшь; отошёл, отошла́) *pf.* (**from** от+*g.*); (*not go forward*) держа́ться (-жу́сь, -жишься) *impf.* позади́; ~ **by** (*v.i.*) (*not interfere*) не вме́шиваться *impf.*, вмеша́ться *pf.*; (*prepare*) пригота́вливаться *impf.*, пригото́виться *pf.*; (*v.t.*) (*support*) подде́рживать *impf.*, поддержа́ть (-жу́, -жишь) *pf.*; (*fulfil*) выполня́ть *impf.*, вы́полнить *pf.*; ~ **for** (*signify*) означа́ть *impf.*; (*tolerate*): **I shall not** ~ **for it** я не потерплю́; ~ **in** (*for*) замеща́ть *impf.*, замести́ть *pf.*; ~ **out** выдава́ться (выдаётся) *impf.*, выдаться (-астся, -адутся) *pf.*; выделя́ться *impf.*, вы́делиться *pf.*; ~ **up** встава́ть (встаю́, встаёшь) *impf.*, встать (-а́ну, -а́нешь) *pf.*; ~ **up for** (*defend*) отста́ивать *impf.*, отстоя́ть (-ою́, -ои́шь) *pf.*; защища́ть *impf.*, защити́ть (-ищу́, -ити́шь) *pf.*; ~ **up to** (*endure*) выде́рживать *impf.*, вы́держать (-жу, -жишь) *pf.*; (*not give in to*) не пасова́ть *impf.*, с~ *pf.* пе́ред+*i.*

standard ['stændəd] *n.* (*flag*) зна́мя (*pl.* -мёна) *nt.*, штанда́рт; (*norm*) станда́рт, норм; ~ **of living** жи́зненный у́ровень (-вня) *m.*; **of high** ~ высо́кого ка́чества; ~ **lamp** торше́р; *adj.* норма́льный, станда́ртный, нормати́вный; (*generally accepted*) общепри́нятый; (*exemplary*) образцо́вый. **standard-bearer** *n.* знамено́сец (-сца). **standardi'zation** *n.* нормализа́ция, стандартиза́ция. **standardize** *v.t.* стандартизи́ровать *impf.* & *pf.*; нормализова́ть *impf.* & *pf.*

stand-by ['stændbaɪ] *n.* (*store*) запа́с; (*reliable person*) надёжный челове́к (*pl.* лю́ди, -де́й, -дям, -дьми́); (*support*) опо́ра. **stand-in** *n.* замести́тель *m.*, ~ница.

standing ['stændɪŋ] *n.* положе́ние, ранг, репута́ция; **to be in good ~ (with s.o.)** быть на хоро́шем счету́ (у кого́-л.); *adj.* (*upright*) стоя́чий; (*permanent*) постоя́нный; ~ **army** постоя́нная а́рмия; ~ **committee** постоя́нный комите́т.

standoffish [stænd'ɒfɪʃ] *adj.* высо́комерный.

stand-pipe ['stændpaɪp] *n.* стоя́к (-а́).

standpoint ['stændpɔɪnt] *n.* то́чка зре́ния.

standstill ['stændstɪl] *n.* остано́вка, засто́й, па́уза; **be at a** ~ стоя́ть (-ою́, -ои́шь) *impf.* на мёртвой то́чке; **bring (come) to a** ~ остана́вливать(ся) *impf.*, останови́ть(ся) (-влю́(сь), -вишь(ся)) *pf.*

stanza ['stænzə] *n.* стро́фа (*pl.* -фы, -ф, -фа́м), станс.

staple[1] ['steɪp(ə)l] *n.* (*fastening*) скоба́ (*pl.* -бы, -б, -ба́м).

staple[2] ['steɪp(ə)l] *n.* (*principal product*) гла́вный проду́кт, основно́й това́р; (*principal element*) гла́вный элеме́нт; *adj.* основно́й, гла́вный.

star [stɑː(r)] *n.* звезда́ (*pl.* звёзды); (*asterisk*) звёздочка; *adj.* звёздный; (*chief*) гла́вный; (*celebrated*) знамени́тый; *v.i.* игра́ть *impf.*, сыгра́ть *pf.* гла́вную роль. **starfish** *n.* морска́я звезда́ (*pl.* звёзды). **star-gazer** *n.* астроло́г, звездочёт.

starboard ['stɑːbəd] *n.* пра́вый борт (*loc.* -у́).

starch [stɑːtʃ] *n.* крахма́л; *v.t.* крахма́лить *impf.*, на~ *pf.* **starched** *adj.* крахма́льный, накрахма́ленный. **starchy** *adj.* крахмали́стый; (*prim*) чо́порный.

stare [steə(r)] *n.* при́стальный взгляд; *v.i.* при́стально смотре́ть (-трю́, -тришь) (**at** на+*a.*); ~ **(one) in the face** (*be obvious*) броса́ться *impf.*, бро́ситься *pf.* (+*d.*) в глаза́.

stark [stɑːk] *adj.* (*bare*) го́лый (гол, -а́, -о); (*desolate*) пусты́нный (-нен, -нна); (*sharp*) ре́зкий (-зок, -зка́, -зко); *adv.* соверше́нно.

starling ['stɑːlɪŋ] *n.* скворе́ц (-рца́).

starry ['stɑːrɪ] *adj.* звёздный. **starry-eyed** *adj.* мечта́тельный.

start [stɑːt] *n.* нача́ло; (*setting out*) отправле́ние; (*sport*) старт; (*advantage*) преиму́щество; (*shudder*) рыво́к (-вка́); *v.i.* начина́ться *impf.*, нача́ться (начнётся; начался́, -ла́сь) *pf.*; (*engine*) заводи́ться (-о́дится) *impf.*, завести́сь (-едётся; -ёлся, -ела́сь) *pf.*; (*set out*) отправля́ться *impf.*, отпра́виться *pf.*; (*shudder*) вздра́гивать *impf.*, вздро́гнуть *pf.*; (*sport*) ста́ртовать *impf.* & *pf.*; *v.t.* начина́ть *impf.*, нача́ть (-чну́, -чнёшь; на́чал, -а́, -о) *pf.* (*gerund*, *inf.*, +*inf.*; *by*, +*gerund* с того́, что...; **with** +*i.*, с+*g.*; **from the beginning** с нача́ла); (*set in motion*) пуска́ть *impf.*, пусти́ть (пущу́, пу́стишь) *pf.*; запуска́ть *impf.*, запусти́ть (-ущу́, -у́стишь) *pf.* **starter** *n.* (*tech.*) пуска́тель *m.*, ста́ртёр; (*sport*) ста́ртёр. **starter, starting** *adj.* пусково́й. **starting-point** *n.* отправно́й пункт.

startle ['stɑːt(ə)l] *v.t.* испуга́ть *pf.*; поража́ть *impf.*, порази́ть *pf.* **startled** *adj.* испу́ганный (-ан), потрясённый (-ён, -ена́). **startling** *adj.* порази́тельный, потряса́ющий.

starvation [stɑː'veɪʃ(ə)n] *n.* го́лод, голода́ние. **starve** *v.i.* страда́ть *impf.*, по~ *pf.* от го́лода; (*to death*) умира́ть *impf.*, умере́ть (умру́, -рёшь; у́мер, -ла́, -ло) с го́лоду; *v.t.* мори́ть *impf.*, по~, у~ *pf.* го́лодом. **'starving** *adj.* голода́ющий; (*hungry*) голо́дный (го́лоден, -дна́, -дно, го́лодны́).

state [steɪt] *n.* (*condition*) состоя́ние, положе́ние; (*pomp*) великоле́пие, по́мпа; (*nation*, *government*) госуда́рство, штат; **lie in** ~ поко́иться *impf.* в откры́том гробу́; *adj.* (*ceremonial*) торже́ственный (-ен, -енна); (*apartments*) пара́дный; (*of State*) госуда́рственный; *v.t.* (*announce*) заявля́ть *impf.*, заяви́ть (-влю́, -вишь) *pf.*; (*expound*) излага́ть *impf.*, изложи́ть (-жу́, -жишь) *pf.*; (*maintain*) утвержда́ть *impf.* **stated** *adj.* (*appointed*) назна́ченный. **stateless** *adj.* не име́ющий гражда́нства. **stately** *adj.* вели́чественный (-ен, -енна), велича́вый. **statement** *n.* (*announcement*) заявле́ние; (*exposition*) изложе́ние; (*assertion*) утвержде́ние. **state-of-the-art** *adj.* совреме́нный, нове́йший. **statesman** *n.* госуда́рственный де́ятель *m.*

static ['stætɪk] *adj.* стати́чный, неподви́жный. **statics** *n.* ста́тика.

station ['steɪʃ(ə)n] *n.* (*rail.*) вокза́л, ста́нция; (*position*) ме́сто (*pl.* -та́); (*social*) обще́ственное положе́ние; (*naval etc.*) ба́за; (*meteorological*, *hydro-electric power*, *radio etc.*) ста́нция; (*post*) пост (-а́, *loc.* -у́); *v.t.* ста́вить *impf.*, по~ *pf.*; помеща́ть *impf.*, помести́ть *pf.*; (*mil.*) размеща́ть *impf.*, размести́ть *pf.* **station-master** *n.* нача́льник вокза́ла, ста́нции.

stationary ['steɪʃənərɪ] *adj.* неподви́жный;

(*tech.*) стационáрный; (*constant*) постоя́нный (-нен, -нна), устóйчивый.

stationer ['steɪʃənə(r)] *n.* продавéц (-вцá), -вщи́ца канцеля́рского магази́на; **~'s (shop)** канцеля́рский магази́н. **stationery** *n.* канцеля́рские товáры *m.pl.*; (*writing-paper*) почтóвая бумáга.

statistic [stə'tɪstɪk] *n.* статисти́ческое дáнное, ци́фра. **statistical** *adj.* статисти́ческий. **statistician** [ˌstætɪ'stɪʃ(ə)n] *n.* стати́стик. **statistics** *n.* стати́стика.

statue ['stætjuː, 'stætʃuː] *n.* стáтуя. **statu'esque** *adj.* величáвый. **statu'ette** *n.* статуэ́тка.

stature ['stætʃə(r)] *n.* рост, стан; (*merit*) достóинство, кáчество.

status ['steɪtəs] *n.* стáтус; (*social*) общéственное положéние; (*state*) состоя́ние. **status quo** *n.* стáтус-квó *m.indecl.*

statute ['stætjuːt] *n.* статýт; законодáтельный акт; *pl.* устáв. **statute-book** *n.* свод закóнов. **statutory** ['statjʊtərɪ] *adj.* устнóвленный (-ен) закóном.

staunch [stɔːntʃ] *v.t. see* **stanch**; *adj.* (*loyal*) вéрный (-рен, -рнá, -рно); (*steadfast*) стóйкий (-óек, -ойкá, -óйко), твёрдый (твёрд, -á, -о); прóчный (-чен, -чнá, -чно, прóчны́).

stave [steɪv] *n.* (*of cask*) клёпка; *v.t.* пробивáть *impf.*, проби́ть (-бью́, -бьёшь) *pf.*; разбивáть *impf.*, разби́ть (разобью́, -бьёшь) *pf.*; **~ off** предотвращáть *impf.*, предотврати́ть (-ащý, -ати́шь) *pf.*

stay[1] [steɪ] *n.* (*time spent*) пребывáние; (*suspension*) приостановлéние; (*postponement*) отсрóчка; *v.i.* (*remain*) оставáться (-аю́сь, -аёшься) *impf.*, остáться (-áнусь, -áнешься) *pf.* (**to dinner** обéдать); (*put up*) останáвливаться *impf.*, останови́ться (-влю́сь, -ви́шься) *pf.* (**at** (*place*) в+*p.*; **at** (*friends' etc.*) у+*g.*); гости́ть *impf.* (**with** у+*g.*); (*live*) жить (живý, живёшь; жил, -á, -о); **~ a moment!** подождите минýтку!; **~ away** отсýтствовать *impf.*; **~ behind** оставáться (-аю́сь, -аёшься) *impf.*, остáться (-áнусь, -áнешься) *pf.*; *v.t.* (*check*) задéрживать *impf.*, задержáть (-жý, -жишь) *pf.*; (*hunger, thirst*) утоля́ть *impf.*, утоли́ть *pf.*; (*suspend*) приостанáвливать *impf.*, приостанови́ть (-влю́, -вишь) *pf.*; (*postpone*) отсрóчивать *impf.*, отсрóчить *pf.*; **~ the course** поддéрживаться *impf.*, поддержáться (-жýсь, -жишься) до концá. **stay-at-home** *n.* домосéд, ~ка. **staying-power** *n.* вынóсливость.

stay[2] [steɪ] *n.* (*naut.* штаг; (*support*) поддéржка; *v.t.* (*support*) поддéрживать *impf.*, поддержáть (-жý, -жишь) *pf.* **stays** *n.* корсéт.

stead [sted] *n.*: **to stand s.o. in good ~** окáзываться *impf.*, оказáться (-ажýсь, -áжешься) *pf.* полéзным комý-л.

steadfast ['stedfɑːst, 'stedfəst] *adj.* (*firm, steady*) прóчный (-чен, -чнá, -чно, прóчны́), устóйчивый; (*unshakeable*) стóйкий (-óек, -ойкá, -óйко), непоколеби́мый.

steady ['stedɪ] *adj.* (*firm*) прóчный (-чен, -чнá, -чно, прóчны́), устóйчивый, твёрдый (твёрд, -á, -о); (*continuous*) непреры́вный; (*prices*) устóйчивый; (*wind, temperature*) рóвный (-вен, -внá, -вно); (*speed*) постоя́нный (-нен, -нна); (*unshakeable*) непоколеби́мый; (*staid*) степéнный (-нен, -нна); **~ hand** твёрдая рукá (*a.* -ку; *pl.* -ки, -к, -кáм); *v.t.* (*boat*) приводи́ть (-ожý, -óдишь) *impf.*, привести́ (-едý, -едёшь; -ёл, -елá) *pf.* в равновéсие.

steak [steɪk] *n.* (*before cooking*) тóлстый кусóк (-скá) мя́са (*meat*), говя́дины (*beef*), ры́бы (*fish*), для жарéнья; (*dish*) тóлстый кусóк (-скá) мя́са (*meat*), жáреной ры́бы (*fish*); (*beefsteak*) бифштéкс.

steal [stiːl] *v.t.* ворóвать *impf.*, с~ *pf.*; красть (крадý, -дёшь; крал) *impf.*, у~ *pf.* (*also a kiss*); **~ a glance** украдкой взгля́дывать *impf.*, взгляну́ть (-нý, -нешь) *pf.* (**at** на+*a.*); *v.i.* крáсться (крадýсь, -дёшься; -áлся) *impf.*; подкрáдываться *impf.*, подкрáсться (-адýсь, -адёшься; -áлся) *pf.* **stealing** *n.* воровствó. **stealth** [stelθ] *n.* хи́трость, улóвка; **by ~** укрáдкой, тайкóм. **stealthy** *adj.* воровáтый, тáйный, скры́тый.

steam [stiːm] *n.* пар (*loc.* -ý; *pl.* -ы́); **at full ~** на всех парáх; **get up ~** разводи́ть (-ожý, -óдишь) *impf.*, развести́ (-едý, -едёшь; -ёл, -елá) *pf.* пары́; (*fig.*) собирáться *impf.*, собрáться (-берётся; -брáлся, -бралáсь, -брáлóсь) с си́лами; **let off ~** (*fig.*) давáть (даю́, даёшь) *impf.*, дать (дам, дашь, даст, дади́м; дал, -á, дáлó, -и) *pf.* вы́ход свои́м чýвствам; **under one's own ~** сам (-á, -ó, -и); свои́м хóдом; *adj.* паровóй, паро... *in comb.*; *v.t.* пáрить *impf.*; *v.i.* пáриться *impf.*, по~ *pf.*; (*vessel*) ходи́ть (хóдит) *indet.*, идти́ (идёт; шёл, шла) *det.* на парáх; **~ up** (*mist over*) запотевáть *impf.*, запотéть *pf.*; потéть *impf.*, за~, от~ *pf.*; **~ engine** паровáя маши́на. **steamer** ['stiːmə(r)] *n.* пароxóд. **steaming** *adj.* дымя́щийся. **steam-roller** *n.* паровóй катóк (-ткá). **steamship** *n.* пароxóд.

steed [stiːd] *n.* конь (-ня́, *pl.* -ни, -нéй) *m.*

steel [stiːl] *n.* сталь; *adj.* стальнóй; *v.t.* (*make resolute*) ожесточáть *impf.*, ожесточи́ть *pf.*; **to ~ one's (own) heart** ожесточáться *impf.*, ожесточи́ться *pf.*; **~ foundry** сталелитéйный завóд. **steel-making** *adj.* сталеплави́льный. **steel-rolling** *adj.* сталепрокáтный. **steelworks** *n.* сталеплави́льный завóд. **steely** *adj.* стальнóй; (*cold*) холóдный (хóлоден, -днá, -дно, хóлодны́); (*stern*) сурóвый. **steelyard** *n.* безмéн.

steep[1] [stiːp] *v.t.* (*immerse*) погружáть *impf.*, погрузи́ть *pf.* (**in** в+*a.*); (*saturate*) пропи́тывать *impf.*, пропитáть *pf.* (**in** +*i.*); **be ~ed in** (*also fig.*) погружáться *impf.*, погрузи́ться *pf.* (**in** в+*a.*).

steep[2] [stiːp] *adj.* крутóй (крут, -á, -о); (*excessive*) чрезмéрный; (*improbable*) невероя́тный. **steepness** *n.* крутизнá.

steeple ['sti:p(ə)l] *n.* шпиль *m.* **steeplechase** *n.* ска́чки *f.pl.* с препя́тствиями. **steeplejack** *n.* верхола́з.

steer[1] [stɪə(r)] *n.* молодо́й вол (-а́), бычо́к (-чка́).

steer[2] [stɪə(r)] *v.t.* (*control, navigate*) управля́ть *impf.*, пра́вить *impf.+i.*; (*guide*) руководи́ть *impf.+i.*; *v.abs.* пра́вить *impf.* рулём; рули́ть *impf.* (*coll.*); ~ **clear of** избега́ть *impf.*, избежа́ть (-егу́, -ежи́шь) *pf.+g.* **steering-column** *n.* рулева́я коло́нка. **steering-wheel** *n.* руль (-ля́) *m.*, бара́нка (*coll.*); (*naut.*) штурва́л.

stellar ['stelə(r)] *adj.* звёздный. **stellate** *adj.* звездообра́зный.

stem[1] [stem] *n.* сте́бель (-бля; *pl.* -бли, -бле́й) *m.*; (*trunk*) ствол (-а́); (*wine-glass*) но́жка; (*ling.*) осно́ва; (*naut.*) нос (*loc.* -у́; *pl.* -ы́); **from ~ to stern** от но́са до кормы́; *v.i.*: ~ **from** происходи́ть (-ожу́, -о́дишь) *impf.*, произойти́ (-ойдёт; -ошёл, -ошла́) *pf.* от+*g.*

stem[2] [stem] *v.t.* (*dam*) запру́живать *impf.*, запруди́ть (-ужу́, -у́дишь) *pf.*; (*stop*) остана́вливать *impf.*, останови́ть *pf.*

stench [stentʃ] *n.* злово́ние, смрад.

stencil ['stensɪl] *n.* трафаре́т; (*tech.*) шабло́н; *v.t.* наноси́ть (-ошу́, -о́сишь) *impf.*, нанести́ (-есу́, -есёшь; -ёс, -есла́) *pf.* узо́р по трафаре́ту. **stencilled** *adj.* трафаре́тный.

stentorian [ˌsten'tɔ:rɪən] *adj.* громогла́сный.

step [step] *n.* (*pace, action*) шаг (-а́ *with 2,3,4*, *loc.* -у́; *pl.* -и́); (*gait*) похо́дка; (*dance*) па *nt.indecl.*; (*of stairs, ladder*) ступе́нь (*g.pl.* -е́ней); (*measure*) ме́ра; ~ **by** ~ шаг за ша́гом; **in** ~ в но́гу; **out of** ~ не в но́гу; **watch one's** ~ де́йствовать *impf.* осторо́жно; **take ~s** принима́ть *impf.*, приня́ть (приму́, -мешь; при́нял, -а́, -о) *pf.* ме́ры *v.i.* шага́ть *impf.*, шагну́ть *pf.*; ступа́ть *impf.*, ступи́ть (-плю́, -пишь) *pf.*; ~ **aside** сторони́ться (-ню́сь, -нишься) *impf.*, по~ *pf.*; ~ **back** отступа́ть *impf.*, отступи́ть (-плю́, -пишь) *pf.*; ~ **down** (*resign*) уходи́ть (-ожу́, -о́дишь) *impf.*, уйти́ (уйду́, -дёшь; ушёл, ушла́) *pf.* в отста́вку; ~ **forward** выступа́ть *impf.*, вы́ступить *pf.*; ~ **in** (*intervene*) вме́шиваться *impf.*, вмеша́ться *pf.*; ~ **on** наступа́ть *impf.*, наступи́ть (-плю́, -пишь) *pf.* на+*a.* (**s.o.'s foot** кому́-л. на́ ногу); ~ **over** переша́гивать *impf.*, перешагну́ть *pf.+a.*, че́рез+*a.*; ~ **up** (*increase, promote*) повыша́ть *impf.*, повы́сить *pf.*; (*strengthen*) уси́ливать *impf.*, уси́лить *pf.* **step-ladder** *n.* стремя́нка. **stepped** *adj.* ступе́нчатый. **stepping-stone** *n.* ка́мень (-мня; *pl.* -мни, -мне́й) *m.* для перехо́да че́рез ре́чку *etc.*; (*fig.*) сре́дство к достиже́нию це́ли. **steps** *n.* ле́стница.

stepbrother ['stepˌbrʌðə(r)] *n.* сво́дный брат (*pl.* -ья, -ьев). **stepdaughter** *n.* па́дчерица. **stepfather** *n.* о́тчим. **stepmother** *n.* ма́чеха. **stepsister** *n.* сво́дная сестра́ (*pl.* сёстры, сестёр, сёстрам). **stepson** *n.* па́сынок (-нка).

steppe [step] *n.* степь (*loc.* -пи́; *pl.* -пи, -пе́й); *adj.* степно́й.

stereo ['sterɪəʊ, 'stɪə-] *n.* (*record-player*) стереофони́ческий прои́грыватель *m.*; *adj.* (*recorded in* ~) сте́рео. **stereophonic** *adj.* стереофони́ческий. **stereoscope** *n.* стереоско́п. **stereoscopic** *adj.* стереоскопи́ческий. **stereotype** *n.* стереоти́п; (*tech.*) шабло́н. **stereotyped** *adj.* (*also banal*) стереоти́пный, шабло́нный.

sterile ['steraɪl] *adj.* (*barren, germ-free*) стери́льный. **sterility** [stə'rɪlɪtɪ] *n.* стери́льность. **sterilization** [ˌsterɪlaɪ'zeɪʃ(ə)n] *n.* стерилиза́ция. **sterilize** *v.t.* стерилизова́ть *impf.* & *pf.* **sterilizer** *n.* стерилиза́тор.

sterling ['stɜ:lɪŋ] *n.* сте́рлинг; **pound** ~ фунт сте́рлингов; *adj.* сте́рлинговый; (*irreproachable*) безупре́чный; (*reliable*) надёжный.

stern[1] [stɜ:n] *n.* корма́.

stern[2] [stɜ:n] *adj.* суро́вый, стро́гий (-г, -га́, -го).

sternum ['stɜ:nəm] *n.* груди́на.

stethoscope ['steθəˌskəʊp] *n.* стетоско́п.

stevedore ['sti:vəˌdɔ:(r)] *n.* стивидо́р, гру́зчик.

stew [stju:] *n.* (*cul.*) мя́со тушёное вме́сте с овоща́ми; **be in a** ~ (*coll.*) волнова́ться *impf.*; *v.t.* & *i.* туши́ть(ся) (-шу́(сь), -шишь(ся)) *impf.*, с~ *pf.*; томи́ть(ся) *impf.*; **to ~ in one's own juice** расхлёбывать *impf.* ка́шу, кото́рую сам завари́л. **stewed** *adj.* тушёный; ~ **fruit** компо́т. **stewpan, stewpot** *n.* кастрю́ля, соте́йник.

steward ['stju:əd] *n.* стю́ард, бортпроводни́к (-а́); (*master of ceremonies*) распоряди́тель *m.* **stewardess** *n.* стюарде́сса, бортпроводни́ца.

stick[1] [stɪk] *n.* па́лка; (*of chalk etc.*) па́лочка; (*hockey, walking*) клю́шка; **~s** (*collect.*) хво́рост (-а(у)).

stick[2] [stɪk] *v.t.* (*spear*) зака́лывать *impf.*, заколо́ть (-лю́, -лешь) *pf.*; (*make adhere*) прикле́ивать *impf.*, прикле́ить *pf.* (**to** к+*d.*); прилепля́ть *impf.*, прилепи́ть (-плю́, -пишь) *pf.* (**to** к+*d.*); (*coll.*) (*put*) ста́вить *impf.*, по~ *pf.*; (*lay*) класть (кладу́, -дёшь; клал) *impf.*, положи́ть (-жу́, -жишь) *pf.*; *v.i.* (*adhere*) ли́пнуть (лип) *impf.* (**to** к+*d.*); прилипа́ть *impf.*, прили́пнуть (-нет; прили́п) *pf.* (**to** к+*d.*); прикле́иваться *impf.*, прикле́иться *pf.* (**to** к+*d.*); ~ **in** (*thrust in*) втыка́ть *impf.*, воткну́ть *pf.*; вка́лывать *impf.*, вколо́ть (-лю́, -лешь) *pf.*; **the arrow stuck into the ground** стрела́ воткну́лась в зе́млю; (*into opening*) всо́вывать *impf.*, всу́нуть *pf.*; ~ **on** (*glue on*) накле́ивать *impf.*, накле́ить *pf.*; ~ **out** (*thrust out*) высо́вывать *impf.*, вы́сунуть *pf.* (**from** из+*g.*); (*project*) торча́ть (-чу́, -чи́шь) *impf.*; ~ **to** (*keep to*) приде́рживаться *impf.*, придержа́ться (-жу́сь, -жишься) *pf.+g.*; (*remain at*) не отвлека́ться *impf.* от+*g.*; ~ **together** держа́ться (-жимся) *impf.* вме́сте; ~ **up for** защища́ть *impf.*, защити́ть (-ищу́, -мти́шь) *pf.*; **be, get, stuck** застрева́ть *impf.*, застря́ть (-я́ну, -я́нешь) *pf.* **sticker** *n.* (*label*) этике́тка, ярлы́к (-а́). **sticking-plaster** *n.* ли́пкий пла́стырь *m.*

stickleback ['stɪk(ə)l,bæk] *n.* ко́люшка.

stickler ['stɪklə(r)] *n.* (я́рый) сторо́нник, -ица; приве́рженец (-нца), -нка (**for** +*g.*).

sticky ['stɪkɪ] *adj.* ли́пкий (-пок, -пка́, -пко), клё́йкий; **he will come to a ~ end** он пло́хо ко́нчит.

stiff [stɪf] *adj.* жё́сткий (-ток, -тка́, -тко), неги́бкий (-бок, -бка́, -бко); (*with cold*) окочене́лый; (*prim*) чо́порный; (*difficult*) тру́дный (-ден, -дна́, -дно, тру́дны́); (*breeze*) си́льный (си́лён, -льна́, -льно, си́льны́); **be ~** (*ache*) боле́ть (-ли́т) *impf.* **stiffen** *v.t.* де́лать *impf.*, с~ *pf.* жё́стким; *v.i.* станови́ться (-влю́сь, -вишься) *impf.*, стать (-а́ну, -а́нешь) *pf.* жё́стким. **stiffness** *n.* жё́сткость; (*primness*) чо́порность.

stifle ['staɪf(ə)l] *v.t.* души́ть (-шу́, -шишь) *impf.*, за~ *pf.*; (*suppress*) подавля́ть *impf.*, подави́ть (-влю́, -вишь) *pf.*; (*sound*) заглуша́ть *impf.*, заглуши́ть *pf.*; *v.i.* задыха́ться *impf.*, задохну́ться (-о́х(ну́л)ся, -о́х(ну́)лась) *pf.* **stifling** *adj.* уду́шливый, ду́шный (-шен, -шна́, -шно).

stigma ['stɪgmə] *n.* клеймо́ (*pl.* -ма) позо́ра. **stigmatize** *v.t.* клейми́ть *impf.*, за~ *pf.*

stile [staɪl] *n.* ступе́ньки *f.pl.* для перехо́да че́рез забо́р, перела́з (*coll.*).

stiletto [stɪ'letəʊ] *n.* стиле́т; **~ heels** гво́здики *m.pl.*, шпи́льки *f.pl.*

still[1] [stɪl] *adv.* (всё) ещё, до сих по́р, по-пре́жнему; **~ better** ещё лу́чше; (*nevertheless*) всё же, тем не ме́нее, одна́ко; (*motionless*) неподви́жно; (*quietly*) споко́йно; **stand ~** не дви́гаться (-аюсь, -аешься & дви́жусь, -жешься) *impf.*, дви́нуться *pf.*; **time stood ~** вре́мя останови́лось; **sit ~** сиде́ть (сижу́, сиди́шь) *impf.* сми́рно.

still[2] [stɪl] *n.* (*quiet*) тишина́; (*film*) кадр; *adj.* ти́хий (тих, -а́, -о), споко́йный; (*immobile*) неподви́жный; (*not fizzy*) не шипу́чий; *v.t.* успока́ивать *impf.*, успоко́ить *pf.*

still[3] [stɪl] *n.* перего́нный куб (*pl.* -ы́).

still-born ['stɪlbɔːn] *adj.* мертворождё́нный.

still life ['stɪllaɪf] *n.* натюрмо́рт.

stillness ['stɪlnɪs] *n.* тишина́, споко́йствие; (*immobility*) неподви́жность.

stilt [stɪlt] *n.* ходу́ля; (*tech.*) сто́йка, сва́я. **stilted** *adj.* ходу́льный.

stimulant ['stɪmjʊlənt] *n.* возбужда́ющее сре́дство. **stimulate** *v.t.* возбужда́ть *impf.*, возбуди́ть *pf.*; стимули́ровать *impf.* & *pf.* **stimulating** *adj.* возбуди́тельный. **stimu'lation** *n.* возбужде́ние. **stimulus** *n.* стиму́л, возбуди́тель *m.*, побуди́тельная причи́на.

sting [stɪŋ] *n.* жа́ло (*also fig.*); уку́с (*also wound*); *v.t.* жа́лить *impf.*, у~ *pf.*; укуси́ть (-ушу́, -у́сишь) *pf.*; *v.i.* (*burn*) жечь (жжёт, жгут; жёг, жгла) *impf.* **stinging** *adj.* (*caustic*) язви́тельный; **~ nettle** жгу́чая крапи́ва. **sting-ray** *n.* скат дазиа́тис.

stinginess ['stɪndʒɪnɪs] *n.* ску́пость, ска́редность. **stingy** *adj.* скупо́й (скуп, -а́, -о), ска́редный.

stink [stɪŋk] *n.* злово́ние, вонь, смрад; *v.i.* воня́ть *impf.* (**of** +*i.*); смерде́ть (-ржу́, -рди́шь) *impf.* (**of** +*i.*). **stinking** *adj.* воню́чий, злово́нный (-нен, -нна), смра́дный.

stint [stɪnt] *n.* но́рма; *v.t.* скупи́ться *impf.*, по~ *pf.* на+*a.*

stipend ['staɪpend] *n.* (*salary*) жа́лование; (*grant*) стипе́ндия. **stipendiary** [staɪ'pendjərɪ, stɪ-] *adj.* получа́ющий жа́лование.

stipple ['stɪp(ə)l] *n.* рабо́та, гравирова́ние пункти́ром; *v.t.* & *i.* рисова́ть *impf.*, на~ *pf.*, гравирова́ть *impf.*, вы́~ *pf.*, пункти́ром.

stipulate ['stɪpjʊ,leɪt] *v.i.* ста́вить *impf.*, по~ *pf.* усло́вием (**that** что); *v.t.* обусло́вливать *impf.*, обусло́вить *pf.*+*i.*; (*demand*) тре́бовать *impf.*+*g.* **stipu'lation** *n.* усло́вие.

stir [stɜː(r)] *n.* шевеле́ние, движе́ние; (*uproar*) сумато́ха; **cause a ~** вызыва́ть *impf.*, вы́звать (вы́зову, -вешь) *pf.* волне́ние; *v.t.* (*move*) шевели́ть (шевелю́, -е́ли́шь) *impf.*, шевельну́ть *pf.*+*i.*; дви́гать *impf.*, дви́нуть *pf.*+*i.*; (*mix*) меша́ть *impf.*, по~ *pf.*; разме́шивать *impf.*, размеша́ть *pf.*; (*excite*) волнова́ть *impf.*, вз~ *pf.*; *v.i.* (*move*) шевели́ться (шевелю́сь, -е́ли́шься) *impf.*, шевельну́ться *pf.*; дви́гаться *impf.*, дви́нуться *pf.*; (*be excited*) волнова́ться **~ up** возбужда́ть *impf.*, возбуди́ть *pf.* **stirring** *adj.* волну́ющий.

stirrup ['stɪrəp] *n.* стре́мя (-мени; *pl.* -мена́, -мя́н, -мена́м) *nt.*

stitch [stɪtʃ] *n.* стежо́к (-жка́); (*knitting*) пе́тля (*g.pl.* -тель); (*med.*) шов (шва); (*pain*) ко́лотье (*coll.*); *v.t.* (*embroider, make line of ~es*) строчи́ть (-очу́, -о́чи́шь) *impf.*, про~ *pf.*; (*join by sewing, make, suture*) сшива́ть *impf.*, сшить (сошью́, сошьёшь) *pf.*; (*med.*) накла́дывать *impf.*, наложи́ть (-жу́, -жишь) *pf.* швы на+*a.*; **~ up** зашива́ть *impf.*, заши́ть (-шью́, -шьёшь) *pf.* **stitching** *n.* (*sewing*) шитьё; (*stitches*) стро́чка.

stoat [stəʊt] *n.* горноста́й.

stock [stɒk] *n.* (*store*) запа́с; (*equipment*) инвента́рь (-ря́) *m.*; (*live~*) скот (-а́); (*cul.*) бульо́н; (*family*) семья́ (*pl.* -мьи, -ме́й, -мьям); (*origin, clan*) род (*loc.* -у́; *pl.* -ы́); (*fin.*) а́кции *f.pl.*; *pl.* (*fin.*) фо́нды *m.pl.*; (*punishment*) коло́дки *f.pl.*; **in ~** в нали́чии; **out of ~** распро́дан; **take ~ of** обду́мывать *impf.*, обду́мать *pf.*; *adj.* стандáртный; (*banal*) изби́тый; *v.t.* име́ть в нали́чии; **~ up** запаса́ть *impf.*, запасти́ (-су́, -сёшь; запа́с, -сла́) *pf.* **stock-breeder** *n.* скотово́д. **stock-breeding** *n.* скотово́дство. **stockbroker** *n.* биржево́й ма́клер. **stock-exchange** *n.* фо́ндовая би́ржа.

Stockholm ['stɒkhəʊm] *n.* Стокго́льм.

stock-in-trade ['stɒkɪn,treɪd] *n.* (торго́вый) инвента́рь (-ря́) *m.* **stockpile** *n.* запа́с; *v.t.*

нака́пливать *impf.*, накопи́ть (-плю́, -пишь) *pf.* **stock-still** *adj.* неподви́жный. **stock-taking** *n.* переучёт това́ра, прове́рка инвентаря́. **stockyard** *n.* скотоприго́нный двор (-а́).

stockade [stɒ'keɪd] *n.* частоко́л.

stocking ['stɒkɪŋ] *n.* чуло́к (-лка́; *g.pl.* чуло́к).

stocky ['stɒkɪ] *adj.* приземи́стый, корена́стый.

stodgy ['stɒdʒɪ] *adj.* (*food*) тяжёлый (-л, -ла́); (*boring*) ску́чный (-чен, -чна́, -чно).

stoic ['stəʊɪk] *n.* сто́ик. **stoic(al)** *adj.* стоический. **stoicism** ['stəʊɪˌsɪz(ə)m] *n.* стоици́зм.

stoke [stəʊk] *v.t.* топи́ть (-плю́, -пишь) *impf.* **stokehold, stokehole** *n.* кочега́рка.

stoker ['stəʊkə(r)] *n.* кочега́р, истопни́к (-а́).

stole [stəʊl] *n.* паланти́н.

stolid ['stɒlɪd] *adj.* флегмати́чный.

stomach ['stʌmək] *n.* желу́док (-дка), (*also surface of body*) живо́т (-а́); *adj.* желу́дочный; *v.t.* терпе́ть (-плю́, -пишь) *impf.*, по~ *pf.* **stomach-ache** *n.* боль в животе́.

stone [stəʊn] *n.* (*material, piece of it*) ка́мень (-мня; *pl.* -мни, -мне́й) *m.*; (*fruit*) ко́сточка; *adj.* ка́менный; *v.t.* побива́ть *impf.*, поби́ть (-бью́, -бьёшь) *pf.* камня́ми; (*fruit*) вынима́ть *impf.*, вы́нуть *pf.* ко́сточки из+*g.*; ~ **to death** заби́ть (-бью́, -бьёшь) *pf.* камня́ми на́смерть. **Stone Age** *n.* ка́менный век (*loc.* -у́). **stone-cold** *adj.* соверше́нно холо́дный (хо́лоден, -дна́, -дно, хо́лодны́). **stone-deaf** *adj.* соверше́нно глухо́й (глух, -а́, -о). **stone-mason** *n.* ка́менщик. **stonewall** *v.i.* устра́ивать *impf.*, устро́ить *pf.* обстру́кцию; меша́ть *impf.*, по~ *pf.* диску́ссии. **stonily** *adv.* с ка́менным выраже́нием, хо́лодно. **stony** *adj.* камени́стый; (*fig.*) ка́менный, холо́дный (хо́лоден, -дна́, -дно, хо́лодны́). **stony-broke** *pred.*: **I am** ~ у меня́ нет ни гроша́.

stool [stu:l] *n.* табуре́т, табуре́тка.

stoop [stu:p] *n.* суту́лость; *v.t.* & *i.* суту́лить(ся) *impf.*, с~ *pf.*; (*bend* (*down*)) наклоня́ть(ся) *impf.*, наклони́ть(ся) (-ню́(сь), -нишь(ся)) *pf.*; ~ **to** (*abase o.s.*) унижа́ться *impf.*, уни́зиться *pf.* до+*g.*; (*condescend*) снисходи́ть (-ожу́, -о́дишь) *impf.*, снизойти́ (-ойду́, -ойдёшь; -ошёл, -ошла́) *pf.* до+*g.* **stooped, stooping** *adj.* суту́лый.

stop [stɒp] *n.* остано́вка; (*discontinuance*) прекраще́ние; (*organ*) реги́стр; (*full* ~) то́чка; **request** ~ остано́вка по тре́бованию; *v.t.* остана́вливать *impf.*, останови́ть (-влю́, -вишь) *pf.*; (*discontinue*) прекраща́ть *impf.*, прекрати́ть (-ащу́, -ати́шь) *pf.*; (*restrain*) уде́рживать *impf.*, удержа́ть (-жу́, -жишь) *pf.* (**from** от+*g.*); *v.i.* остана́вливаться *impf.*, останови́ться (-влю́сь, -вишься) *pf.*; (*discontinue*) прекраща́ться *impf.*, прекрати́ться (-и́тся) *pf.*; (*cease*) перестава́ть (-таю́, -таёшь) *impf.*, переста́ть (-а́ну, -а́нешь) *pf.* (+*inf.*); ~ **up** *v.t.* затыка́ть *impf.*, заткну́ть *pf.*; ~ **at nothing** ни перед че́м не остана́вливаться *impf.*, останови́ться (-влю́сь, -вишься) *pf.* **stopcock** *n.* запо́рный кран. **stopgap** *n.* заты́чка. **stop-light** *n.* стоп-сигна́л. **stoppage** *n.* остано́вка; (*strike*) забасто́вка. **stopper** *n.* про́бка; (*tech.*) сто́пор. **stop-press** *n.* э́кстренное сообще́ние в газе́те. **stop-watch** *n.* секундоме́р.

storage ['stɔ:rɪdʒ] *n.* хране́ние. **store** *n.* запа́с; (*storehouse*) склад; (*shop*) магази́н; **set** ~ **by** цени́ть (-ню́, -нишь) *impf.*; **what is in** ~ **for me?** что ждёт меня́ впереди́?; *v.t.* запаса́ть *impf.*, запасти́ (-су́, -сёшь; запа́с, -сла́) *pf.*; (*put into storage*) сдава́ть (сдаю́, сдаёшь) *impf.*, сдать (сдам, сдашь, сдаст, сдади́м; сдал, -а́, -о) *pf.* на хране́ние. **storehouse** *n.* склад, амба́р, храни́лище. **storeroom** кладова́я. *sb.*

storey ['stɔ:rɪ] *n.* эта́ж (-а́).

stork [stɔ:k] *n.* а́ист.

storm [stɔ:m] *n.* бу́ря, гроза́ (*pl.* -зы); (*naut.*) шторм; (*mil.*) штурм, при́ступ; (*outburst*) взрыв; *v.t.* (*mil.*) штурмова́ть *impf.*; брать (беру́, берёшь) *impf.*, взять (возьму́, -мёшь; взял, -а́, -о) *pf.* при́ступом; *v.i.* бушева́ть (-шу́ю, -шу́ешь) *impf.* **stormcloud** *n.* ту́ча. **stormy** *adj.* бу́рный (-рен, бу́рна́, -рно), бу́йный (бу́ен, буйна́, -но).

story ['stɔ:rɪ] *n.* расска́з, по́весть; (*anecdote*) анекдо́т; (*plot*) фа́була, сюже́т; (*history, event*) исто́рия. **story-teller** *n.* расска́зчик.

stout [staʊt] *adj.* (*solid*) пло́тный (-тен, -тна́, -тно, пло́тны́); (*portly*) доро́дный; *n.* кре́пкий по́ртер. **stout-hearted** *adj.* отва́жный. **stoutly** *adv.* (*stubbornly*) упо́рно; (*energetically*) энерги́чно; (*strongly*) кре́пко. **stoutness** *n.* (*strength*) про́чность; (*portliness*) доро́дство; (*courage*) отва́га; (*firmness*) сто́йкость.

stove [stəʊv] *n.* (*with fire inside*) печь (*loc.* -чи́; *pl.* -чи, -че́й); (*cooker*) плита́ (*pl.* -ты).

stow [stəʊ] *v.t.* укла́дывать *impf.*, уложи́ть (-жу́, -жишь) *pf.*; ~ **away** (*travel free*) е́хать (е́ду, е́дешь) *impf.*, по~ *pf.* за́йцем, без биле́та. **stowaway** *n.* за́яц (за́йца), безбиле́тный пассажи́р.

straddle ['stræd(ə)l] *v.i.* широко́ расставля́ть *impf.*, расста́вить *pf.* но́ги; *v.t.* (*sit astride*) сиде́ть (сижу́, сиди́шь) *impf.* верхо́м на+*p.*; (*stand astride*) стоя́ть (-ою́, -ои́шь) *impf.*, расста́вив но́ги над+*i.*

straggle ['stræg(ə)l] *v.i.* (*drop behind*) отстава́ть (-стаю́, -стаёшь) *impf.*, отста́ть (-а́ну, -а́нешь) *pf.* **straggler** *n.* отста́вший *sb.* **straggling** *adj.* (*scattered*) разбро́санный; (*untidy*) беспоря́дочный.

straight [streɪt] *adj.* (*unbent*) прямо́й (-м, -ма́, -мо, пря́мы́); (*honest*) че́стный (-тен, -тна́, -тно); (*undiluted*) неразба́вленный; *pred.* (*properly arranged*) в поря́дке; *adv.* пря́мо; ~ **away** сра́зу. **straighten** *v.t.* & *i.* выпрямля́ть(ся) *impf.*, вы́прямить(ся) *pf.*; *v.t.* (*smooth out*) расправля́ть *impf.*, распра́вить *pf.* **straightforward** *adj.* прямо́й (-м, -ма́, -мо, пря́мы́); (*simple*) просто́й (-т, -та́, -то); (*honest*) че́стный (-тен, -тна́, -тно). **straightness** *n.* прямизна́.

strain[1] [streɪn] *n.* (*pull, tension*) натяже́ние; (*also sprain*) растяже́ние; (*phys., tech.*) напряже́ние; (*tendency*) скло́нность; (*sound*) напе́в, звук; **in the same ~** в том же ду́хе; *v.t.* (*stretch*) натя́гивать *impf.*, натяну́ть (-ну́, -нешь) *pf.*; (*also sprain*) растя́гивать *impf.*, растяну́ть (-ну́, -нешь) *pf.*; (*phys., tech.*) напряга́ть *impf.*, напря́чь (-ягу́, -яжёшь; -яг, -ягла́) *pf.*; (*filter*) проце́живать *impf.*, процеди́ть (-ежу́, -е́дишь) *pf.*; *v.i.* (*also exert o.s.*) напряга́ться *impf.*, напря́чься (-ягу́сь, -яжёшься; -я́гся, -ягла́сь) *pf.* **strained** *adj.* натя́нутый (*also fig.*); растя́нутый (*also sprained*). **strainer** *n.* (*tea ~*) си́течко; (*filter*) фильтр; (*sieve*) си́то.

strain[2] [streɪn] *n.* (*breed*) поро́да; (*hereditary trait*) насле́дственная черта́.

strait(s) [streɪt] *n.* (*geog.*) проли́в. **straiten** *v.t.* ограни́чивать *impf.*, ограни́чить *pf.* **straitened** *adj.*: **in ~ circumstances** в стеснённых обстоя́тельствах. **strait-jacket** *n.* смири́тельная руба́шка. **strait-laced** *adj.* пурита́нский. **straits** *n.* (*difficulties*) затрудни́тельное положе́ние.

strand[1] [strænd] *n.* (*hair, rope*) прядь; (*rope, cable*) стре́нга; (*thread, also fig.*) нить.

strand[2] [strænd] *n.* (*of sea etc.*) бе́рег (*loc.* -у́; *pl.* -а́); *v.t.* сажа́ть *impf.*, посади́ть (-ажу́, -а́дишь) *pf.* на мель. **stranded** *adj.* (*fig.*) без средств.

strange [streɪndʒ] *adj.* стра́нный (-нен, -нна́, -нно); (*unfamiliar*) незнако́мый; (*alien*) чужо́й. **strangely** *adv.* стра́нно. **strangeness** *n.* стра́нность. **stranger** *n.* незнако́мец (-мца), -о́мка; неизве́стный *sb.*; чужо́й *sb.*

strangle [ˈstræŋg(ə)l] *v.t.* души́ть (-шу́, -шишь) *impf.*, за~ *pf.* **stranglehold** *n.* мёртвая хва́тка. **strangulate** *v.t.* сжима́ть *impf.*, сжать (сожму́, -мёшь) *pf.* **strangu'lation** *n.* (*strangling*) удуше́ние; (*strangulating*) зажима́ние.

strap [stræp] *n.* реме́нь (-мня́) *m.*; *v.t.* (*tie up*) стя́гивать *impf.*, стяну́ть (-ну́, -нешь) *pf.* ремнём. **strapping** *adj.* ро́слый.

stratagem [ˈstrætədʒəm] *n.* стратаге́ма, хи́трость. **strategic** [strəˈtiːdʒɪk] *adj.* стратеги́ческий. **strategist** *n.* страте́г. **strategy** *n.* страте́гия.

stratification [ˌstrætɪfɪˈkeɪʃ(ə)n] *n.* расслое́ние. **stratified** [ˈstrætɪˌfaɪd] *adj.* слои́стый. **ˈstratosphere** *n.* стратосфе́ра. **stratum** [ˈstrɑːtəm, ˈstreɪ-] *n.* слой (*pl.* -ои́), пласт (-а́, *loc.* -у́).

straw [strɔː] *n.* соло́ма; (*drinking*) соло́минка; **the last ~** после́дняя ка́пля; *adj.* соло́менный.

strawberry [ˈstrɔːbərɪ] *n.* клубни́ка; (*wild ~*) земляни́ка *collect.*; *adj.* клубни́чный; земляни́чный.

stray [streɪ] *v.i.* сбива́ться *impf.*, сби́ться (собью́сь, -ьёшься) *pf.*; (*roam*) блужда́ть *impf.*; (*digress*) отклоня́ться *impf.*, отклони́ться (-ню́сь, -нишься) *pf.*; *adj.* (*lost*) заблуди́вшийся; (*homeless*) бездо́мный; *n.* (*waif*) беспризо́рный *sb.*; (*from flock*) отби́вшееся от ста́да живо́тное *sb.*; **~ bullet** шальна́я пу́ля.

streak [striːk] *n.* полоса́ (*a.* по́лосу́; *pl.* -осы, -о́с, -оса́м) (**of luck** везе́ния); (*tendency*) жи́лка; (*lightening*) вспы́шка; *v.t.* испещря́ть *impf.*, испещри́ть *pf.*; *v.i.* (*rush*) проноси́ться (-ошу́сь, -о́сишься) *impf.*, пронести́сь (-есу́сь, -есёшься; -ёсся, -есла́сь) *pf.* **streaked** *adj.* с полоса́ми, с прожи́лками (**with** +*g.*). **streaky** *adj.* полоса́тый; (*meat*) с просло́йками жи́ра.

stream [striːm] *n.* (*brook, tears*) руче́й (-чья́); (*brook, flood, tears, people etc.*) пото́к; (*jet*) струя́ (*pl.* -у́и); (*current*) тече́ние; **up/down ~** вверх/вниз по тече́нию; **with/against the ~** по тече́нию, про́тив тече́ния; *v.i.* течь (течёт, теку́т; тёк, текла́) *impf.*; струи́ться (-и́тся) *impf.*; (*rush*) проноси́ться (-ошу́сь, -о́сишься) *impf.*, пронести́сь (-есу́сь, -есёшься; -ёсся, -есла́сь) *pf.*; (*blow*) развева́ться (-а́ется) *impf.* **streamer** *n.* вы́мпел. **stream-lined** *adj.* обтека́емый; (*fig.*) хорошо́ нала́женный.

street [striːt] *n.* у́лица; *adj.* у́личный; **~ lamp** у́личный фона́рь (-ря́) *m.*

strength [streŋθ, streŋkθ] *n.* си́ла, кре́пость; (*numbers*) чи́сленность; **in full ~** в по́лном соста́ве; **on the ~ of** в си́лу+*g.* **strengthen** *v.t.* уси́ливать *impf.*, уси́лить *pf.*; укрепля́ть *impf.*, укрепи́ть *pf.* **strengthening** *n.* усиле́ние, укрепле́ние.

strenuous [ˈstrenjʊəs] *adj.* тре́бующий уси́лий, энерги́чный.

stress [stres] *n.* (*pressure, fig.*) давле́ние; (*tech.*) напряже́ние; (*emphasis*) ударе́ние; *v.t.* де́лать *impf.*, с~ *pf.* ударе́ние на+*a.*; подчёркивать *impf.* подчеркну́ть *pf.*

stretch [stretʃ] *n.* (*expanse*) протяже́ние, простра́нство; **at a ~** (*in succession*) подря́д; *v.t.* & *i.* (*widen, spread out*) растя́гивать(ся) *impf.*, растяну́ть(ся) (-ну́(сь), -нешь(ся)) *pf.*; (*in length, ~ out limbs*) вытя́гивать(ся) *impf.*, вы́тянуть(ся) *pf.*; (*tauten, e.g. bow*) натя́гивать(ся) *impf.*, натяну́ть(ся) (-ну́(сь), -нешь(ся)) *pf.*; (*extend, e.g. rope, ~ forth limbs*) протя́гивать(ся) *impf.*, протяну́ть(ся) (-ну́(сь), -нешь(ся)) *pf.*; *v.i.* (*material, land*) тяну́ться (-нется) *impf.*; *v.t.* (*exaggerate*) преувели́чивать *impf.*, преувели́чить *pf.*; **~ a point** допуска́ть *impf.*, допусти́ть (-ущу́, -у́стишь) *pf.* натя́жку; **~ o.s.** потя́гиваться *impf.*, потяну́ться (-ну́сь, -нешься) *pf.*; **~ one's legs** (*coll.*) размина́ть *impf.*, размя́ть (разомну́, -нёшь) *pf.* но́ги. **stretcher** *n.* носи́лки (-лок) *pl.*

strew [struː] *v.t.* разбра́сывать *impf.*, разброса́ть *pf.*; **~ with** посыпа́ть *impf.*, посы́пать

(-плю, -плешь) *pf.+i.*; усыпа́ть *impf.*, усы́пать (-плю, -плешь) *pf.+i.*

stricken ['strɪkən] *adj.* поражённый (-ён, -ена́), охва́ченный (-ен).

strict [strɪkt] *adj.* стро́гий (-г, -га́, -го); (*precise*) то́чный (-чен, -чна́, -чно). **strictly** *adv.* стро́го, то́чно. **strictness** *n.* стро́гость, то́чность. **stricture(s)** *n.* (стро́гая) кри́тика, осужде́ние.

stride [straɪd] *n.* (большо́й) шаг (-а́ *with 2,3,4*, *loc.* -у́; *pl.* -и́); *pl.* (*fig.*) успе́хи *m.pl.*; **to get into one's ~** принима́ться *impf.*, приня́ться (приму́сь, -мешься; -ня́лся́, -няла́сь) *pf.* за де́ло; **to take sth. in one's ~** преодолева́ть *impf.*, преодоле́ть *pf.* что-л. без уси́лий; *v.i.* шага́ть *impf.* (больши́ми шага́ми).

stridency ['straɪd(ə)nsɪ] *n.* ре́зкость. **strident** *adj.* ре́зкий (-зок, -зка́, -зко).

strife [straɪf] *n.* (*conflict*) борьба́; (*discord*) раздо́р.

strike [straɪk] *n.* (*refusal to work*) забасто́вка, ста́чка; (*discovery*) откры́тие; (*blow*) уда́р; *adj.* забасто́вочный; *v.i.* (*be on ~*) бастова́ть *impf.*; (*go on ~*) забастова́ть *pf.*; объявля́ть *impf.*, объяви́ть (-влю́, -вишь) *pf.* забасто́вку; (*clock*) бить (бьёт) *impf.*, про~ *pf.*; *v.t.* (*hit*) ударя́ть *impf.*, уда́рить *pf.*; (*mil.*, *surprise*) поража́ть *impf.*, порази́ть *pf.*; (*discover*) открыва́ть *impf.*, откры́ть (-ро́ю, -ро́ешь) *pf.*; (*match*) зажига́ть *impf.*, заже́чь (-жгу́, -жжёшь, -жгу́т; -жёг, -жгла́) *pf.*; (*clock*) бить (бьёт) *impf.*, про~ *pf.*; (*occur to*) приходи́ть (-ит) *impf.*, прийти́ (придёт; пришёл, -шла́) *pf.* в го́лову+*d.*; **~ off** вычёркивать *impf.*, вы́черкнуть *pf.*; **~ up** начина́ть *impf.*, нача́ть (-чну́, -чнёшь; на́чал, -а́, -о) *pf.*; **~ upon** напада́ть *impf.*, напа́сть (-аду́, -адёшь; -а́л) *pf.* на+*a.* **strikebreaker** *n.* штрейкбре́хер. **striker** *n.* забасто́вщик, -ица. **striking** *adj.* порази́тельный; **~ distance** досяга́емость.

string [strɪŋ] *n.* бечёвка, верёвка, завя́зка; (*mus.*) стру́на (*pl.* -ны́); (*series*) верени́ца, ряд (-а́ *with 2,3,4*, *loc.* -у́; *pl.* -ы́); (*beads*) ни́тка; *pl.* (*instruments*) стру́нные инструме́нты *m.pl.*; **second ~** запасно́й ресу́рс; **pull ~s** нажима́ть *impf.*, нажа́ть (нажму́, -мёшь) *pf.* на та́йные пружи́ны; **without ~s attached** без каки́х-либо усло́вий; *adj.* стру́нный; *v.t.* (*tie up*) завя́зывать *impf.*, завяза́ть (-яжу́, -я́жешь) *pf.*; (*thread*) низа́ть (нижу́, -жешь) *impf.*, на~ *pf.*; (*beans*) чи́стить *impf.*, о~ *pf.*; **~ along** (*coll.*) (*deceive*) обма́нывать *impf.*, обману́ть (-ну́, -нешь) *pf.*; **~ out** (*prolong*) растя́гивать *impf.*, растяну́ть (-ну́, -нешь) *pf.*; **strung up** (*tense*) напряжённый; **~ bag** аво́ська; **~ vest** се́тка. **stringed** *adj.* стру́нный. **stringy** *adj.* (*fibrous*) волокни́стый; (*meat*) жи́листый.

stringency ['strɪndʒ(ə)nsɪ] *n.* стро́гость. **stringent** *adj.* стро́гий (-г, -га́, -го).

strip¹ [strɪp] *n.* полоса́ (*a.* по́лосу́; *pl.* -осы, -о́с, -оса́м), поло́ска, ле́нта; **~ cartoon** расска́з в рису́нках; **~ light** ла́мпа дневно́го све́та.

strip² [strɪp] *v.t.* (*undress*) раздева́ть *impf.*, разде́ть (-е́ну, -е́нешь) *pf.*; (*deprive*) лиша́ть *impf.*, лиши́ть *pf.* (**of** +*g.*); (*lay bare*) обнажа́ть *impf.*, обнажи́ть *pf.*; **~ off** (*tear off*) сдира́ть *impf.*, содра́ть (сдеру́, -рёшь; -а́л, -ала́, -а́ло); *v.i.* раздева́ться *impf.*, разде́ться (-е́нусь, -е́нешься) *pf.* **strip-tease** *n.* стрипти́з.

stripe [straɪp] *n.* полоса́ (*a.* по́лосу́; *pl.* -осы, -о́с, -оса́м). **striped** *adj.* полоса́тый.

stripling ['strɪplɪŋ] *n.* подро́сток (-тка), ю́ноша *m.*

strive [straɪv] *v.i.* (*endeavour*) стара́ться *impf.*, по~ *pf.*; стреми́ться *impf.* (**for** к+*d.*); (*struggle*) боро́ться (-рю́сь, -решься) *impf.* (**for** за+*a.*; **against** про́тив+*g.*).

stroke [strəʊk] *n.* (*blow*, *med.*) уда́р; (*of oar*) взмах; (*oarsman*) загребно́й *sb.*; (*drawing*) штрих (-а́); (*clock*) бой (*pl.* бои́); (*piston*) ход (*pl.* -ы, -о́в); (*swimming*) стиль *m.*; *v.t.* гла́дить *impf.*, по~ *pf.*

stroll [strəʊl] *n.* прогу́лка; *v.i.* прогу́ливаться *impf.*, прогуля́ться *pf.*

strong [strɒŋ] *adj.* (*also able*; *gram.*) си́льный (си́лён, -льна́, -льно, си́льны́); (*also drinks*) кре́пкий (-пок, -пка́, -пко); (*healthy*) здоро́вый; (*opinion etc.*) твёрдый (-д, -да́, -до). **stronghold** *n.* кре́пость; (*fig.*) опло́т. **strong-minded, strong-willed** *adj.* реши́тельный. **strong-room** ко́мната-сейф.

strop [strɒp] *n.* реме́нь (-мня́) *m.* (для пра́вки бритв); *v.t.* пра́вить *impf.* бри́тву.

structural ['strʌktʃər(ə)l] *adj.* структу́рный; (*building*) конструкти́вный, строи́тельный. **structure** *n.* (*composition*, *arrangement*) структу́ра; (*system*) строй, устро́йство; (*building*) сооруже́ние.

struggle ['strʌg(ə)l] *n.* борьба́; *v.i.* боро́ться (-рю́сь, -решься) *impf.* (**for** за+*a.*; **against** про́тив+*g.*); (*writhe*, **~** *with* (*fig.*)) би́ться (бьюсь, бьёшься) (**with** над+*i.*).

strum [strʌm] *v.i.* бренча́ть (-чу́, -чи́шь) *impf.* (**on** на+*p.*).

strut¹ [strʌt] *n.* (*vertical*) подпо́ра, сто́йка; (*horizontal*) распо́рка; (*angle brace*) подко́с.

strut² [strʌt] *v.i.* ходи́ть (хожу́, хо́дишь) *indet.*, идти́ (иду́, идёшь; шёл, шла) *det.* го́голем.

stub [stʌb] *n.* (*stump*) пень (пня) *m.*; (*pencil*) огры́зок (-зка); (*cigarette*) оку́рок (-рка); (*counterfoil*) корешо́к (-шка́); *v.t.*: **~ one's toe** ударя́ться *impf.*, уда́риться *pf.* ного́й (**on** на+*a.*); **~ out (cigarette)** гаси́ть (гашу́, га́сишь) *impf.*, по~ *pf.* (сигаре́ту).

stubble ['stʌb(ə)l] *n.* стерня́, жнивьё; (*hair*) щети́на.

stubborn ['stʌbən] *adj.* упря́мый, упо́рный. **stubbornness** *n.* упря́мство, упо́рство.

stucco ['stʌkəʊ] *n.* штукату́рка; *adj.* штукату́рный.

stuck-up [stʌ'kʌp] *adj.* (*coll.*) наду́тый.

stud¹ [stʌd] *n.* (*press-button*) кно́пка; (*collar, cuff*) за́понка; (*large-headed nail*) гвоздь (-дя́; *pl.* -ди, -де́й) *m.* с большо́й шля́пкой; *v.t.* (*set with* ~*s*) обива́ть *impf.*, оби́ть (обью́, -ьёшь) *pf.* гвоздя́ми; (*bestrew*) усе́ивать *impf.*, усе́ять (-е́ю, -е́ешь) *pf.* (**with** +*i.*).

stud² [stʌd] *n.* (*horses*) ко́нный заво́д. **stud-horse** *n.* племенно́й жеребе́ц (-бца́).

student ['stju:d(ə)nt] *n.* студе́нт, ~ка.

studied ['stʌdɪd] *adj.* обду́манный (-ан, -анна).

studio ['stju:dɪəʊ] *n.* (*artist's, broadcasting, cinema*) сту́дия; (*artist's*) ателье́ *nt.indecl.*, мастерска́я *sb.*

studious ['stju:dɪəs] *adj.* (*diligent*) приле́жный; (*liking study*) лю́бящий нау́ку.

study ['stʌdɪ] *n.* изуче́ние, иссле́дование; *pl.* заня́тия *nt.pl.*; (*essay*) о́черк; (*art*) эски́з, этю́д; (*mus.*) этю́д; (*room*) кабине́т; *v.t.* изуча́ть *impf.*, изучи́ть (-чу́, -чишь) *pf.*; учи́ться (учу́сь, у́чишься) *impf.*, об~ *pf.*+*d.*; занима́ться *impf.*, заня́ться (займу́сь, -мёшься; заня́лся́, -яла́сь) *pf.*+*i.*; (*research*) иссле́довать *impf.* & *pf.*; (*scrutinize*) рассма́тривать *impf.*, рассмотре́ть (-рю́, -ришь) *pf.*; *v.i.* учи́ться (учу́сь, у́чишься) *impf.*, об~ *pf.*

stuff [stʌf] *n.* (*material*) материа́л; (*substance*) вещество́; ((*woollen*) *fabric*) (шерстяна́я) мате́рия; ~ **and nonsense** вздор; *v.t.* набива́ть *impf.*, наби́ть (набью́, -ьёшь) *pf.*; (*cul.*) начиня́ть *impf.*, начини́ть *pf.*; (*cram into*) запи́хивать *impf.*, запиха́ть *pf.* (**into** в+*a.*); (*thrust, shove into*) сова́ть (сую́, суёшь) *impf.*, су́нуть *pf.* (**into** в+*a.*); *v.i.* (*overeat*) объеда́ться *impf.*, объе́сться (-е́мся, -е́шься, -е́стся, -еди́мся; -е́лся) *pf.* **stuffiness** *n.* духота́, спёртость. **stuffing** *n.* наби́вка; (*cul.*) начи́нка. **stuffy** *adj.* спёртый, ду́шный (-шен, -шна́, -шно).

stumble ['stʌmb(ə)l] *v.i.* (*also fig.*) спотыка́ться *impf.*, споткну́ться *pf.* (**over** о+*a.*); ~ **upon** натыка́ться *impf.*, наткну́ться *pf.* на+*a.* **stumbling-block** *n.* ка́мень (-мня; *pl.* -мни, -мне́й) *m.* преткнове́ния.

stump [stʌmp] *n.* (*tree*) пень (пня) *m.*; (*pencil*) огры́зок (-зка); (*limb*) обру́бок (-бка), культя́; *v.t.* (*perplex*) ста́вить *impf.*, по~ *pf.* в тупи́к; *v.i.* (*coll.*) ковыля́ть *impf.*

stun [stʌn] *v.t.* (*also fig.*) оглуша́ть *impf.*, оглуши́ть *pf.*; (*also fig.*) ошеломля́ть *impf.*, ошеломи́ть *pf.* **stunning** *adj.* (*also fig.*) ошеломи́тельный; (*fig.*) сногсшиба́тельный (*coll.*)

stunt¹ [stʌnt] *n.* трюк; ~ **man** каскадёр, трюка́ч (-а́).

stunt² [stʌnt] *v.t.* заде́рживать *impf.*, задержа́ть (-жу́, -жишь) *pf.* рост+*g.* **stunted** *adj.* ча́хлый, низкоро́слый.

stupefaction [ˌstju:pɪ'fækʃ(ə)n] *n.* ошеломле́ние. **stupefy** ['stju:pɪˌfaɪ] *v.t.* ошеломля́ть *impf.*, ошеломи́ть *pf.* **stu'pendous** *adj.* изуми́тельный; (*huge*) грома́дный. **'stupid** *adj.* (*foolish*) глу́пый (глуп, -па́, -по), дура́цкий (*coll.*); (*dull-witted*) тупо́й (туп, -а́, -о, ту́пы́). **stu'pidity** *n.* глу́пость, ту́пость. **'stupor** *n.* оцепене́ние; (*med.*) сту́пор.

sturdy ['stɜ:dɪ] *adj.* (*robust*) кре́пкий (-пок, -пка́, -пко), здоро́вый (-в, -ва́); (*solid, firm*) твёрдый (-д, -да́, -до).

sturgeon ['stɜ:dʒ(ə)n] *n.* осётр (-а́); (*dish*) осетри́на.

stutter ['stʌtə(r)] *n.* заика́ние; *v.i.* заика́ться *impf.* **stutterer** *n.* заи́ка *c.g.*

sty¹ [staɪ] *n.* (*pig*~) свина́рник.

sty² [staɪ] *n.* (*on eye*) ячме́нь (-ня́) *m.*

style [staɪl] *n.* стиль *m.*; (*manner*) мане́ра; (*taste*) вкус; (*fashion*) мо́да; (*sort*) род (*pl.* -ы́); **in (grand)** ~ с ши́ком; *v.t.* конструи́ровать *impf.* & *pf.* по мо́де. **stylish** *adj.* мо́дный (-ден, -дна́, -дно), шика́рный. **stylist** *n.* стили́ст. **sty'listic** *adj.* стилисти́ческий. **sty'listics** *n.* стили́стика. **stylize** *v.t.* стилизова́ть *impf.* & *pf.*

stylus ['staɪləs] *n.* (грамофо́нная) иго́лка.

suave [swɑ:v] *adj.* обходи́тельный. **suavity** *n.* обходи́тельность.

subaltern ['sʌbəlt(ə)n] *n.* (*mil.*) мла́дший офице́р. **subcommittee** *n.* подкоми́ссия, подкомите́т. **subconscious** *adj.* подсозна́тельный; *n.* подсозна́ние. **subcutaneous** [ˌsʌbkju:'teɪnɪəs] *adj.* подко́жный. **subdivide** *v.t.* подразделя́ть *impf.*, подраздели́ть *pf.* **subdivision** *n.* подразделе́ние. **subdue** *v.t.* покоря́ть *impf.*, покори́ть *pf.* **subdued** *adj.* (*suppressed, dispirited*) пода́вленный; (*soft*) мя́гкий (-гок, -гка́, -гко); (*indistinct*) приглушённый. **sub-editor** *n.* помо́щник, -ица реда́ктора. **sub-heading** *n.* подзаголо́вок (-вка). **subhuman** *adj.* не дости́гший челове́ческого у́ровня.

subject ['sʌbdʒɪkt] *n.* (*theme*) те́ма, сюже́т; (*discipline, theme*) предме́т; (*question*) вопро́с; (*logic, philos., bearer of certain characteristic*) субъе́кт; (*thing on to which action is directed*) объе́кт; (*gram.*) подлежа́щее *sb.*; (*national*) по́дданный *sb.*; *adj.* (*subordinate*) подчинённый (-ён, -ена́) (**to** +*d.*); (*dependent*) подвла́стный (**to** +*d.*); ~ **to** (*susceptible to*) подве́рженный+*d.*; (*on condition that*) при усло́вии, что...; е́сли; ~ **to his agreeing** при усло́вии, что он согласи́тся; е́сли он согласи́тся; **be** ~ **to** (*change etc.*) подлежа́ть (-жи́т) *impf.*+*d.*; *v.t.*: ~ **to** подчиня́ть *impf.*, подчини́ть *pf.*+*d.*; подверга́ть *impf.*, подве́ргнуть (подве́рг, -ла) *pf.*+*d.* **subjection** [səb'dʒekʃ(ə)n] *n.* подчине́ние. **sub'jective** *adj.* субъекти́вный. **subjectivity** [ˌsʌbdʒek'tɪvɪtɪ] *n.* субъекти́вность. **subject-matter** *n.* (*book, lecture*) содержа́ние, те́ма; (*discussion*) предме́т.

sub judice [sʌb 'dʒu:dɪsɪ, sʊb 'ju:dɪˌkeɪ] *adj.* на рассмотре́нии суда́.

subjugate ['sʌbdʒʊˌgeɪt] *v.t.* покоря́ть *impf.*, покори́ть *pf.* **subju'gation** *n.* покоре́ние.

subjunctive (mood) [səb'dʒʌŋktɪv] *n.* сослага́тельное наклоне́ние.

sublet ['sʌblet] *v.t.* передава́ть (-даю́, -даёшь)

impf., передáть (-áм, -áшь, -áст, -адúм; пéредал, -á, -o) *pf.* в субарéнду.

sublimate ['sʌblɪˌmeɪt] *v.t.* (*chem.*, *psych.*) сублимúровать; (*fig.*) возвышáть *impf.*, возвы́сить *pf.* **subli'mation** *n.* (*chem.*, *psych.*) сублимáция; (*fig.*) возвышéние. **sublime** [sə'blaɪm] *adj.* возвы́шенный.

subliminal [səb'lɪmɪn(ə)l] *adj.* подсознáтельный. **sub-machine-gun** *n.* пистолéт-пулемёт, автомáт. **submarine** *adj.* подвóдный; *n.* подвóдная лóдка. **submerge** *v.t.* погружáть *impf.*, погрузúть *pf.*; затоплять *impf.*, затопúть (-плю́, -пишь) *pf.* **submission** *n.* подчинéние; (*for inspection*) представлéние. **submissive** *adj.* покóрный. **submit** *v.i.* подчиня́ться *impf.*, подчинúться *pf.* (**to** +*d.*); покоря́ться *impf.*, покорúться *pf.* (**to** +*d.*); *v.t.* представля́ть *impf.*, представить *pf.* (на рассмотрéние). **subordinate** [sə'bɔːdɪnət; sə'bɔːdɪˌneɪt] *n.* подчинённый *sb.*; *adj.* подчинённый (-ён, -енá); (*secondary*) второстепéнный; (*gram.*) придáточный; *v.t.* подчиня́ть *impf.*, подчинúть *pf.* **subordi'nation** *n.* подчинéние. **suborn** [sə'bɔːn] *v.t.* подкупáть *impf.*, подкупúть (-плю́, -пишь) *pf.* **subpoena** [səb'piːnə, sə'piːnə] *n.* вы́зов, повéстка в суд; *v.t.* вызывáть *impf.*, вы́звать (-зову, -зовешь) *pf.* в суд. **subscribe** *v.i.* подпúсываться *impf.*, подписáться (-ишу́сь, -úшешься) *pf.* (**to** на+*a.*); ~ **to** (*opinion*) присоединя́ться *impf.*, присоединúться *pf.* к+*d.* **subscriber** *n.* (*to newspaper etc.*) подпúсчик -ица; абонéнт, ~ка. **subscription** *n.* (*to newspaper etc.*) подпúска, абонемéнт; (*fee*) взнос. **subsection** *n.* подраздéл. **subsequent** ['sʌbsɪkwənt] *adj.* послéдующий. **subsequently** *adv.* впослéдствии. **subservience** [səb'sɜːvɪəns] *n.* раболéпие, раболéпство. **subservient** *adj.* раболéпный. **subside** [səb'saɪd] *v.i.* (*water*) убывáть *impf.*, убы́ть (убу́ду, -дешь; у́был, -á, -o) *pf.*; (*calm down*, *abate*) уклáдываться *impf.*, улéчься (уля́жется, уля́гутся; улёгся, улеглáсь) *pf.*; (*soil*) оседáть *impf.*, осéсть (ося́дет; осéл) *pf.*; (*collapse*) обвáливаться *impf.*, обвалúться (-ится) *pf.* **subsidence** [səb'saɪd(ə)ns, 'sʌbsɪd(ə)ns] *n.* (*abatement*) спад; (*soil*) оседáние. **subsidiary** [səb'sɪdɪərɪ] *adj.* вспомогáтельный; (*secondary*) второстепéнный. **subsidize** ['sʌbsɪˌdaɪz] *v.t.* субсидúровать *impf.* & *pf.* **subsidy** *n.* субсúдия, дотáция. **subsist** [səb'sɪst] *v.i.* (*exist*) существовáть *impf.*; (*live*) жить (живу́, -вёшь; жил, -á, -o) *impf.* (**on** +*i.*). **subsistence** *n.* существовáние; (*livelihood*) пропитáние. **subsoil** *n.* подпóчва. **subsonic** *adj.* дозвуковóй. **substance** ['sʌbst(ə)ns] *n.* веществó; (*essence*) су́щность, суть; (*content*) содержáние. **substantial** [səb'stænʃ(ə)l] *adj.* (*durable*) прóчный (-чен, -чнá, -чно, прóчны́); (*considerable*) значúтельный; (*food*) плóтный (-тен, -тнá, -тно, плóтны́); (*real*) реáльный; (*material*) вещéственный. **sub'stantially** *adv.* (*basically*) в основнóм; (*considerably*) в значúтельной стéпени. **sub'stantiate** *v.t.* приводúть (-ожу́, -óдишь) *impf.*, привестú (-еду́, -едёшь; -ёл, -елá) *pf.* достáточные основáния+*g.* **sub'stantive** *n.* (úмя *nt.*) существúтельное. **'substitute** *n.* (*person*) заместúтель *m.*, ~ница; (*thing*) замéна; (*tech.*) заменúтель *m.*; *v.t.* заменя́ть *impf.*, заменúть (-ню́, -нишь) *pf.*+*i.* (**for** +*a.*); **I ~ water for milk** заменя́ю молокó водóй. **substi'tution** *n.* замéна, замещéние. **substructure** *n.* фундáмент. **subsume** [səb'sjuːm] *v.t.* относúть (-ошу́, -óсишь) *impf.*, отнестú (-су́, -сёшь; -ёс, -еслá) *pf.* к какóй-л. категóрии. **subtenant** *n.* субарендáтор. **subterfuge** ['sʌbtəˌfjuːdʒ] *n.* увёртка, отговóрка, улóвка. **subterranean** [ˌsʌbtə'reɪnɪən] *adj.* подзéмный. **subtitle** *n.* подзаголóвок (-вка); (*cin.*) субтúтр.

subtle ['sʌt(ə)l] *adj.* (*fine*, *delicate*) тóнкий (-нок, -нкá, -нко); (*mysterious*) таúнственный (-ен, -енна); (*ingenious*) иску́сный; (*cunning*) хúтрый (-тёр, -трá, хúтрó). **subtlety** *n.* (*fineness*, *delicacy*) тóнкость; (*mystery*) тáинственность; (*ingenuity*) иску́сность; (*cunning*) хúтрость.

subtract [səb'trækt] *v.t.* вычитáть *impf.*, вы́честь (-чту, -чтешь; -чел, -чла) *pf.* **subtraction** *n.* вычитáние. **suburb** ['sʌbɜːb] *n.* прúгород. **suburban** [sə'bɜːbən] *adj.* прúгородный. **sub'version** *n.* (*overthrow*) свержéние; (*subversive activities*) подрывнáя дéятельность. **sub'versive** *adj.* подрывнóй. **sub'vert** *v.t.* свергáть *impf.*, свéргнуть (-г(нул), -гла) *pf.* **subway** *n.* тоннéль *m.*; (*pedestrian* ~) подзéмный перехóд.

succeed [sək'siːd] *v.i.* удавáться (удаётся) *impf.*, удáться (удáстся, удаду́тся; удáлся, -лáсь) *pf.*; **the plan will ~** план удáстся; **he ~ed in buying the book** ему́ удалóсь купúть кнúгу; (*be successful*) преуспевáть *impf.*, преуспéть *pf.* (**in** в+*p.*); (*follow*) сменя́ть *impf.*, сменúть (-ню́, -нишь) *pf.*; (*be heir*) наслéдовать *impf.* & *pf.* (**to** +*d.*). **succeeding** *adj.* послéдующий. **success** [sək'ses] *n.* успéх, удáча. **successful** *adj.* успéшный, удáчный. **succession** *n.* преéмственность; (*sequence*) последовáтельность; (*series*) (непреры́вная) цепь (*loc.* -пú; *pl.* -пи, -пéй); (*to throne*) престолонаслéдие; **right of ~** прáво наслéдования; **in ~** подря́д, одúн за другúм. **successive** *adj.* (*consecutive*) последовáтельный. **successor** *n.* наслéдник, -ица; преéмник, -ица.

succinct [sək'sɪŋkt] *adj.* сжáтый.

succour ['sʌkə(r)] *n.* пóмощь; *v.t.* приходúть (-ожу́, -óдишь) *impf.*, прийтú (приду́, -дёшь; пришёл, -шлá) *pf.* на пóмощь+*g.*

succulent ['sʌkjʊlənt] *adj.* сóчный (-чен, -чнá, -чно).

succumb [sə'kʌm] *v.i.* уступáть *impf.*, уступúть (-плю́, -пишь) *pf.* (**to** +*d.*); поддавáться (-даю́сь, -даёшься) *impf.*, поддáться (-áмся,

-áшься, -áстся, -адúмся; -áлся, -алáсь) *pf.* (**to** +*d.*).

such [sʌtʃ] *adj.* такóй, подóбный; ~ **people** такúе лю́ди; **in ~ cases** в такúх, в подóбных, слу́чаях; **in ~ a way** такúм óбразом, так; ~ **as** (*for example*) так напримéр; (*of ~ a kind as*) такóй как; ~ **beauty as yours** такáя красотá как вáша; (*that which*) тот (та, то, те), котóрый; **I shall read ~ books as I like** я бу́ду читáть те кнúги, котóрые мне нрáвятся; ~ **as to** такóй, чтóбы; **his illness was not ~ as to cause anxiety** егó болéзнь былá не такóй (серьёзной), чтóбы вы́звать беспокóйство; *pron.* такóв (-á, -ó, -ы́); тот (та, то, те), такóй; ~ **was his character** такóв был егó харáктер; ~ **as are of my opinion** те, кто соглáсен со мной; **as ~** сам по себе, как таковóй, по существу́; ~ **is not the case** э́то не так. **such-and-such** *adj.* такóй-то. **suchlike** *adj.* подóбный, такóй; *pron.* (*inanimate*) тому́ подóбное; (*people*) такие лю́ди (-дéй, -дям, -дьмú) *pl.*

suck [sʌk] *v.t.* сосáть (сосу́, сосёшь) *impf.*; ~ **in** всáсывать *impf.*, всосáть (-су́, -сёшь) *pf.*; (*engulf*) засáсывать *impf.*, засосáть (-су́, -сёшь) *pf.*; ~ **out** высáсывать *impf.*, вы́сосать (-су, -сешь) *pf.*; ~ **up to** (*coll.*) подлúзываться *impf.*, подлизáться (-ижу́сь, -úжешься) *pf.* к+*d.* **sucker** *n.* (*biol.*, *rubber device*) присóска; (*bot.*) корневóй óтпрыск. **suckle** *v.t.* кормúть (-млю́, -мишь) *impf.*, на~ *pf.* гру́дью. **suckling** *n.* груднóй ребёнок (-нка) (*pl.* дéти, -тéй), сосу́н (-á). **suction** *n.* сосáние, всáсывание.

sudden ['sʌd(ə)n] *adj.* внезáпный, неожúданный (-ан, -анна); ~ **death** скоропостúжная смерть. **suddenly** *adv.* внезáпно, вдруг, неожúданно. **suddenness** *n.* внезáпность, неожúданность.

suds [sʌdz] *n.* мы́льная пéна.

sue [su:, sju:] *v.t.* преслéдовать *impf.* судéбным поря́дком; возбуждáть *impf.*, возбудúть *pf.* дéло прóтив+*g.* (**for** о+*p.*); ~ **s.o. for damages** предъявля́ть *impf.*, предъявúть (-влю́, -вишь) *pf.* (к) кому́-л. иск о возмещéнии ущéрба.

suede [sweɪd] *n.* зáмша; *adj.* зáмшевый.

suet ['su:ɪt, 'sju:ɪt] *n.* пóчечное сáло.

suffer ['sʌfə(r)] *v.t.* страдáть *impf.*, по~ *pf.* +*i.*, от+*g.*; (*experience*) испы́тывать *impf.*, испытáть *pf.*; (*loss*, *defeat*) терпéть (-плю́, -пишь) *impf.*, по~ *pf.*; (*allow*) позволя́ть *impf.*, позвóлить *pf.* +*d.*; дозволя́ть *impf.*, дозвóлить *pf.* +*d.*; (*tolerate*) терпéть (-плю́, -пишь) *impf.*; *v.i.* страдáть *impf.*, по~ *pf.* (**from** +*i.*, от+*g.*). **sufferance** *n.* (*tacit consent*) молчалúвое соглáсие; **he is here on ~** егó здесь тéрпят. **suffering** *n.* страдáние.

suffice [sə'faɪs] *v.i.* &*t.* быть достáточным (для+*g.*); хватáть (-áет) *impf.*, хватúть (-ит) *pf. impers.* +*g.* (+*d.*); **five pounds will ~ me** мне хвáтит пятú фу́нтов. **sufficiency** [sə'fɪʃənsɪ] *n.* (*adequacy*) достáточность; (*prosperity*) достáток (-тка). **sufficient** *adj.* достáточный.

suffix ['sʌfɪks] *n.* су́ффикс.

suffocate ['sʌfə,keɪt] *v.t.* удушáть *impf.*, удушúть (-шу́, -шишь) *pf.*; *v.i.* задыхáться *impf.*, задохну́ться (-óх(ну́л)ся, -óх(ну́)лась) *pf.* **suffocating** *adj.* ду́шный (-шен, -шнá, -шно), уду́шливый. **suffo'cation** *n.* удушéние; (*difficulty in breathing*) уду́шье.

suffrage ['sʌfrɪdʒ] *n.* (*right*) избирáтельное прáво.

suffuse [sə'fju:z] *v.t.* (*light*, *tears*) заливáть *impf.*, залúть (-лью́, -льёшь; зáлúл, -á, зáлúло) *pf.* (**with** +*i.*); (*colour*) покрывáть *impf.*, покры́ть (-рóю, -рóешь) *pf.* (**with** +*i.*). **suffusion** *n.* покры́тие; (*colour*) крáска; (*flush*) румя́нец (-нца).

sugar ['ʃʊgə(r)] *n.* сáхар (-а(у)); *adj.* сáхарный; *v.t.* подслáщивать *impf.*, подсластúть *pf.*; ~ **basin** сáхарница; ~ **beet** сáхарная свёкла; ~ **cane** сáхарный трóстник; ~ **refinery** (сахаро)рафинáдный завóд. **sugary** *adj.* сáхарный; (*sweet*) слáдкий (-док, -дкá, -дко); (*saccharine*) сахарúстый; (*sickly sweet*) прúторный, слащáвый.

suggest [sə'dʒest] *v.t.* (*propose*) предлагáть *impf.*, предложúть (-жу́, -жишь) *pf.*; (*advise*) совéтовать *impf.*, по~ *pf.*; (*call up*) внушáть *impf.*, внушúть *pf.*; ~ **itself to** приходúть (-ит) *impf.*, прийтú (придёт; пришёл, -шлá) *pf.* кому́-л. в гóлову; **a solution ~ itself to me** мне пришлó в гóлову решéние. **suggestible** *adj.* поддáющийся внушéнию. **suggesti'bility** *n.* внушáемость. **suggestion** *n.* (*proposal*) предложéние; (*psych.*) внушéние. **suggestive** *adj.* вызывáющий мы́сли (**of** о+*p.*); (*slightly indecent*) соблазнúтельный.

suicidal [,su:ɪ'saɪd(ə)l, ,sju:-] *adj.* самоубúйственный; (*fig.*) губúтельный. **'suicide** *n.* самоубúйство; (*person*) самоубúйца *c.g.*; (*fig.*) крах по сóбственной винé; **commit ~** совершáть *impf.*, совершúть *pf.* самоубúйство; покóнчить *pf.* с собóй (*coll.*).

suit [su:t, sju:t] *n.* (*clothing*) костю́м; (*leg.*) иск; (*request*) прóсьба; (*cards*) масть; **follow ~** (*cards*) ходúть (хожу́, хóдишь) *impf.* в масть; (*fig.*) слéдовать *impf.*, по~ *pf.* примéру; **in one's birthday ~** в чём мать родилá; *v.t.* (*be convenient for*) устрáивать *impf.*, устрóить *pf.*; (*accommodate*) приспосáбливать *impf.*, приспосóбить *pf.*; (*be ~able for*, *match*) подходúть (-ожу́, -óдишь) *impf.*, подойтú (-йду́, -йдёшь; подошёл, -шлá) *pf.* (+*d.*); (*look attractive on*) идтú (идёт; шёл, шла) *impf.*+*d.*; ~ **o.s.** выбирáть *impf.*, вы́брать (-беру, -берешь) *pf.* по вку́су. **suita'bility** *n.* пригóдность. **suitable** *adj.* (*fitting*) подходя́щий; (*convenient*) удóбный. **suitably** *adv.* соответ́ственно. **suitcase** *n.* чемодáн.

suite [swi:t] *n.* (*retinue*) свúта; (*furniture*) гарнитýр; (*rooms*) апартáменты *m.pl.*; (*mus.*) сюи́та.

suitor ['su:tə(r), 'sju:-] *n.* (*admirer*) поклóнник; (*plaintiff*) истéц (истцá); (*petitioner*) проси́тель *m.*, -ница.

sulk [sʌlk] *v.i.* дýться *impf.* **sulkiness** *n.* сквéрное настроéние. **sulky** *adj.* надýтый, хмýрый (-р, -рá, -ро).

sullen ['sʌlən] *adj.* угрю́мый, хмýрый (-р, -рá, -ро). **sullenness** *n.* угрю́мость.

sully ['sʌlı] *v.t.* пятнáть *impf.*, за~ *pf.*

sulphur *n.* сéра. **sul'phuric** *adj.* сéрный; ~ **acid** сéрная кислотá.

sultan ['sʌlt(ə)n] *n.* (*sovereign*) султáн.

sultana [sʌl'tɑ:nə] *n.* (*raisin*) изю́мина без семя́н; *pl.* кишми́ш (-ишá) (*collect.*).

sultriness ['sʌltrınıs] *n.* зной, духотá. **sultry** *adj.* знóйный; дýшный (-шен, -шнá, -шно); (*passionate*) стрáстный.

sum [sʌm] *n.* сýмма; (*arithmetical problem*) арифмети́ческая задáча; *pl.* арифмéтика; *v.t.* (*add up*) склáдывать *impf.*, сложи́ть (-жý, -жишь) *pf.*; ~ **up** (*summarize*) сумми́ровать *impf.* & *pf.*; резюми́ровать *impf.* & *pf.*; (*appraise*) оцéнивать *impf.*, оцени́ть (-ню́, -нишь) *pf.* **summing-up** *n.* (*leg.*) заключи́тельная речь (*pl.* -чи, -чéй) судьи́.

summarize ['sʌmə,raız] *v.t.* сумми́ровать *impf.* & *pf.*; резюми́ровать *impf.* & *pf.* **summary** *n.* резюмé *nt.indecl.*, конспéкт, свóдка; *adj.* суммáрный, скóрый (-р, -рá, -ро).

summer ['sʌmə(r)] *n.* лéто (*pl.* -тá); **Indian** ~ бáбье лéто (*pl.* -тá); *attr.* лéтний; *v.i.* проводи́ть (-ожý, -óдишь) *impf.*, провести́ (-едý, -едёшь; провёл, -á) *pf.* лéто (*pl.* -тá). **summer-house** *n.* бесéдка. **summery** *adj.* лéтний.

summit ['sʌmıt] *n.* верши́на, верх (-а(у), *loc.* -ý; *pl.* -и́ & -á); (*fig.*) зени́т, предéл; ~ **meeting** совещáние на вы́сшем ýровне.

summon ['sʌmən] *v.t.* вызывáть *impf.*, вы́звать (-зову, -зовешь) *pf.*; (*call*) призывáть *impf.*, призвáть (-зовý, -зовёшь; призвáл, -á, -о) *pf.*; ~ **up one's courage** собирáться *impf.*, собрáться (-берýсь, -берёшься; -брáлся, -бралáсь, -брáлóсь) *pf.* с дýхом. **summons** *n.* вы́зов; (*leg.*) повéстка в суд; *v.t.* вызывáть *impf.*, вы́звать (-зову, -зовешь) *pf.* в суд.

sumptuous ['sʌmptjʊəs] *adj.* роскóшный.

sun [sʌn] *n.* сóлнце; **in the** ~ на сóлнце. **sunbathe** *v.i.* грéться *impf.* на сóлнце, загорáть *impf.* **sunbeam** *n.* сóлнечный луч (-á). **sunburn** *n.* загáр; (*inflammation*) сóлнечный ожóг. **sunburnt** *adj.* загорéлый; **become** ~ загорáть *impf.*, загорéть (-рю́, -ри́шь) *pf.*

Sunday ['sʌndeı, -dı] *n.* воскресéнье; *adj.* воскрéсный.

sundial ['sʌndaıəl] *n.* сóлнечные часы́ *m.pl.*

sundry ['sʌndrı] *adj.* рáзный; **all and** ~ все вмéсте и кáждый в отдéльности.

sunflower ['sʌn,flaʊə(r)] *n.* подсóлнечник; ~ **seeds** сéмечки *nt.pl.* **sun-glasses** *n.* защи́тные очки́ (-кóв) *pl.* от сóлнца.

sunken ['sʌŋkən] *adj.* (*hollow*) впáлый; (*submerged*) погружённый; (*ship*) затóпленный; (*below certain level*) ни́же (какóго-л. ýровня).

sunlight ['sʌnlaıt] *n.* сóлнечный свет. **sunny** *adj.* сóлнечный. **sunrise** *n.* восхóд сóлнца. **sunset** *n.* захóд сóлнца, закáт. **sunshade** *n.* (*parasol*) зóнтик; (*awning*) навéс. **sunshine** *n.* сóлнечный свет. **sunstroke** *n.* сóлнечный удáр. **suntan** *n.* загáр. **sun-tanned** *adj.* загорéлый.

superannuated [,su:pər'ænjʊ,eıtıd, ,sju:-] *adj.* (*pensioner*) вы́шедший на пéнсию; (*obsolete*) устарéлый. **superb** [su:'pɜ:b, sju:-] *adj.* великолéпный, превосхóдный. **supercilious** [,su:pə'sılıəs, ,sju:-] *adj.* надмéнный (-нен, -нна), презри́тельный. **superficial** [,su:pə'fıʃ(ə)l, ,sju:-] *adj.* повéрхностный; (*outward*) внéшний. **superfici'ality** *n.* повéрхностность. **superfluity** [,su:pə'flu:ıtı, ,sju:-] *n.* (*surplus*) изли́шек (-шка); (*abundance*) оби́лие. **superfluous** [su:'pɜ:flʊəs, sju:-] *adj.* ли́шний, ненýжный; (*abundant*) оби́льный. **superhuman** *adj.* сверхчеловéческий. **superimpose** *v.t.* наклáдывать *impf.*, наложи́ть (-жý, -жишь) *pf.* **superintend** *v.t.* завéдовать *impf.*+*i.*; (*supervise*) надзирáть *impf.* за+*i.* **superintendent** *n.* завéдующий *sb.* (**of** +*i.*), надзирáтель *m.*, ~ница (**of** за+*i.*); (*police*) стáрший полицéйский офицéр. **superior** [su:'pıərıə(r), sju:-, sʊ-] *n.* начáльник, -ица; стáрший *sb.*; (*relig.*) настоя́тель *m.*, ~ница; *adj.* (*better*) лýчший, превосходя́щий; (*higher*) вы́сший, стáрший; (*of better quality*) вы́сшего кáчества; (*haughty*) высокомéрный. **superi'ority** *n.* превосхóдство. **superlative** [su:'pɜ:lətıv, sju:-] *adj.* превосхóдный; *n.* (*gram.*) превосхóдная стéпень. **superman** *n.* сверхчеловéк. **supermarket** *n.* универсáм. **supernatural** *adj.* сверхъестéственный (-ен, -енна). **supernumerary** *adj.* сверхштáтный. **superpower** *n.* однá из наибóлее мóщных вели́ких держáв. **supersede** [,su:pə'si:d, ,sju:-] *v.t.* заменя́ть *impf.*, замени́ть (-ню́, -нишь) *pf.* **supersonic** *adj.* сверхзвуковóй. **superstition** [,su:pə'stıʃ(ə)n, ,sju:-] *n.* суевéрие. **superstitious** *adj.* суевéрный. **superstructure** *n.* надстрóйка. **supervene** [,su:pə'vi:n, ,sju:-] *v.i.* слéдовать *impf.*, по~ *pf.* **supervise** ['su:pə,vaız, 'sju:-] *v.t.* наблюдáть *impf.* за+*i.*, надзирáть *impf.* за+*i.* **super'vision** *n.* надзóр, наблюдéние. **supervisor** *n.* надзирáтель *m.*, ~ница; надсмóтрщик, -ица; (*of studies*) наýчный руководи́тель *m.*

supine ['su:paın, 'sju:-] *adj.* (*lying on back*) лежáщий нáвзничь; (*indolent*) лени́вый.

supper ['sʌpə(r)] *n.* ýжин; **have** ~ ýжинать *impf.*, по~ *pf.*; **the Last S**~ Тáйная вéчеря.

supplant [sə'plɑ:nt] *v.t.* вытесня́ть *impf.*, вы́теснить *pf.*

supple ['sʌp(ə)l] *adj.* ги́бкий (-бок, -бкá, -бко).

suppleness *n.* ги́бкость.
supplement ['sʌplɪmənt] *n.* (*to book*) дополне́ние; (*to periodical*) приложе́ние; *v.t.* дополня́ть *impf.*, допо́лнить *pf.* **supplementary** [ˌsʌplɪ'mentərɪ] *adj.* дополни́тельный.
suppliant ['sʌplɪənt] *n.* проси́тель *m.*, ~ница.
supplier [sə'plaɪə(r)] *n.* поставщи́к (-а́) (*animate & inanimate*). **supply** *n.* снабже́ние, поста́вка; (*stock*) запа́с; (*econ.*) предложе́ние; *pl.* припа́сы (-ов) *pl.*, (*provisions*) продово́льствие; ~ **and demand** спрос и предложе́ние; ~ **line** путь (-ти́, -тём) *m.* подво́за; *v.t.* снабжа́ть *impf.*, снабди́ть *pf.* (**with** +*i.*); поставля́ть *impf.*, поста́вить *pf.*
support [sə'pɔːt] *n.* подде́ржка, опо́ра; *v.t.* подде́рживать *impf.*, поддержа́ть (-жу́, -жишь) *pf.*; (*family*) содержа́ть (-жу́, -жишь) *impf.* **supporter** [sə'pɔːtə(r)] *n.* сторо́нник, -ица. **supporting** *adj.* (*tech.*) опо́рный; ~ **actor** исполни́тель *m.*, ~ница второстепе́нной ро́ли.
suppose [sə'pəʊz] *v.t.* (*think*) полага́ть *impf.*; (*presuppose*) предполага́ть *impf.*, предположи́ть (-жу́, -жишь) *pf.*; (*assume*) допуска́ть *impf.*, допусти́ть (-ущу́, -у́стишь) *pf.* **supposed** *adj.* (*pretended*) мни́мый. **supposition** [ˌsʌpə'zɪʃ(ə)n] *n.* предположе́ние. **suppo'sitious** *adj.* предположи́тельный.
suppress [sə'pres] *v.t.* (*uprising, feelings*) подавля́ть *impf.*, подави́ть (-влю́, -вишь) *pf.*; (*laughter, tears*) сде́рживать *impf.*, сдержа́ть (-жу́, -жишь) *pf.*; (*forbid*) запреща́ть *impf.*, запрети́ть (-ещу́, -ети́шь) *pf.* **suppression** *n.* подавле́ние; (*prohibition*) запреще́ние.
supremacy [suː'preməsɪ, sjuː-] *n.* госпо́дство, главе́нство. **supreme** [suː'priːm, sjuː-] *adj.* верхо́вный, вы́сший; (*greatest*) велича́йший; **S~ Soviet (of the USSR)** Верхо́вный Сове́т (СССР); **S~ Court** Верхо́вный суд (-а́).
surcharge ['sɜːtʃɑːdʒ] *n.* припла́та, допла́та.
sure [ʃʊə(r), ʃɔː(r)] *adj.* (*convinced*) уве́ренный (-ен, -ена) (**of** в+*p.*; **that** что); (*unerring*) уве́ренный (-ен, -енна); (*certain, reliable*) ве́рный (-рен, -рна́, -рно, ве́рны́); (*steady*) твёрдый (твёрд, -а́, -о); ~ **enough** действи́тельно, на са́мом де́ле; **he is ~ to come** он обяза́тельно придёт; **make ~ of** (*convince o.s.*) убежда́ться *impf.*, убеди́ться (-ди́шься) *pf.* в+*p.*; (*secure*) обеспе́чивать *impf.*, обеспе́чить *pf.*; **make ~ that** (*check up*) проверя́ть *impf.*, прове́рить *pf.* что; **for ~, surely** *adv.* наверняка́, наве́рное. **surety** *n.* пору́ка; поручи́тель *m.*, ~ница; **stand ~ for** руча́ться *impf.*, поручи́ться (-чу́сь, -чишься) *pf.* за+*a.*
surf [sɜːf] *n.* прибо́й; *v.i.* занима́ться *impf.*, заня́ться (займу́сь, -мёшься; заня́лся́, -ла́сь) *pf.* се́рфингом.
surface ['sɜːfɪs] *n.* пове́рхность; (*exterior*) вне́шность; **on the ~** (*fig.*) вне́шне; **under the ~** (*fig.*) по существу́; *adj.* пове́рхностный; (*exterior*) вне́шний; (*ground*) наземный; *v.i.* всплыва́ть *impf.*, всплыть (-ыву́, -ывёшь; всплыл, -а́, -о) *pf.*
surfeit ['sɜːfɪt] *n.* (*excess*) изли́шество; (*surplus*) изли́шек (-шка); **be ~ed** пресыща́ться *impf.*, пресы́титься (-ы́щусь, -ы́тишься) *pf.* (**with** +*i.*).
surge [sɜːdʒ] *n.* прили́в, (больша́я) волна́ (*pl.* -ы, во́лна́м); *v.i.* (*be agitated, choppy*) волнова́ться *impf.*, вз~ *pf.*; (*rise, heave*) вздыма́ться *impf.*; (*rush, gush*) хлы́нуть *pf.*; ~ **forward** ри́нуться *pf.* вперёд.
surgeon ['sɜːdʒ(ə)n] *n.* хиру́рг; (*mil.*) вое́нный врач (-а́). **surgery** *n.* (*treatment*) хирурги́я; (*place*) кабине́т, приёмная *sb.*, (врача́); (~ *hours*) приёмные часы́ *m.pl.* (врача́). **surgical** *adj.* хирурги́ческий.
surly ['sɜːlɪ] *adj.* (*morose*) угрю́мый; (*rude*) гру́бый (груб, -а́, -о).
surmise [sə'maɪz] *n.* предположе́ние, дога́дка; *v.t. & i.* предполага́ть *impf.*, предположи́ть (-жу́, -жишь) *pf.*; *v.i.* дога́дываться *impf.*, догада́ться *pf.*
surmount [sə'maʊnt] *v.t.* преодолева́ть *impf.*, преодоле́ть *pf.*
surname ['sɜːneɪm] *n.* фами́лия.
surpass [sə'pɑːs] *v.t.* превосходи́ть (-ожу́, -о́дишь) *impf.*, превзойти́ (-ойду́, -ойдёшь; -ошёл, -ошла́) *pf.*
surplus ['sɜːpləs] *n.* изли́шек (-шка), избы́ток (-тка); *adj.* изли́шний (-шен, -шня), избы́точный.
surprise [sə'praɪz] *n.* удивле́ние, неожи́данность, сюрпри́з; **by ~** врасплóх; **to my ~** к моему́ удивле́нию; ~ **attack** внеза́пное нападе́ние; *v.t.* удивля́ть *impf.*, удиви́ть *pf.*; (*come upon suddenly*) застава́ть (-таю́, -таёшь) *impf.*, заста́ть (-а́ну, -а́нешь) *pf.* врасплóх; **be ~d** (*at*) удивля́ться *impf.*, удиви́ться *pf.* (+*d.*). **surprising** *adj.* удиви́тельный, неожи́данный (-ан, -анна).
surreal [sə'rɪəl] *adj.* сюрреалисти́ческий. **surrealism** *n.* сюрреали́зм. **surrealist** *n.* сюрреали́ст; *adj.* сюрреалисти́ческий.
surrender [sə'rendə(r)] *n.* сда́ча; (*renunciation*) отка́з; *v.t.* сдава́ть (сдаю́, сдаёшь) *impf.*, сдать (сдам, сдашь, сдаст, сдади́м; сдал, -а́, -о) *pf.*; (*renounce*) отка́зываться *impf.*, отказа́ться (-ажу́сь, -а́жешься) *pf.* от+*g.*; *v.i.* сдава́ться (сдаю́сь, сдаёшься) *impf.*, сда́ться (сда́мся, сда́шься, сда́стся, сдади́мся; сда́лся, -ла́сь) *pf.*; ~ **o.s. to** предава́ться (-даю́сь, -даёшься) *impf.*, преда́ться (-да́мся, -да́шься, -да́стся, -дади́мся; -да́лся, -ла́сь) *pf.*+*d.*
surreptitious [ˌsʌrəp'tɪʃəs] *adj.* та́йный, сде́ланный тайко́м. **surreptitiously** *adv.* та́йно, тайко́м, исподтишка́ (*coll.*).
surrogate ['sʌrəgət] *n.* (*person*) замести́тель *m.*, ~ница; (*thing*) замени́тель *m.*, суррога́т.
surround [sə'raʊnd] *n.* (*frame*) обрамле́ние; (*edge, selvage*) кро́мка; *v.t.* окружа́ть *impf.*, окружи́ть *pf.* (**with** +*i.*); обступа́ть *impf.*,

обступи́ть (-пит) *pf.*; ~ **with** (*enclose*) обноси́ть (-ошу́, -о́сишь) *impf.*, обнести́ (-есу́, -есёшь; -ёс, -есла́) *pf.+i.* **surrounding** *adj.* окружа́ющий, окре́стный. **surroundings** *n.* (*environs*) окре́стности *f.pl.*; (*milieu*) среда́, окруже́ние; (*locality*) ме́стность.

surveillance [sɜː'veɪləns] *n.* надзо́р, наблюде́ние.

survey ['sɜːveɪ] *n.* обозре́ние, осмо́тр, обзо́р; (*investigation*) обсле́дование; (*geol.*) изыска́ние; (*topog.*) межева́ние; *v.t.* обозрева́ть *impf.*, обозре́ть (-рю́, -ри́шь) *pf.*; осма́тривать *impf.*, осмотре́ть (-рю́, -ришь) *pf.*; (*investigate*) обсле́довать *impf. & pf.*; (*topography*) межева́ть (-жу́ю, -жу́ешь) *impf.* **surveyor** [sə'veɪə(r)] *n.* землеме́р.

survival [sə'vaɪv(ə)l] *n.* (*surviving*) выжива́ние; (*relic*) пережи́ток (-тка). **survive** *v.t.* пережива́ть *impf.*, пережи́ть (-иву́, -ивёшь) *pf.*; *v.i.* выжива́ть *impf.*, вы́жить (-иву, -ивешь) *pf.*; остава́ться (-аю́сь, -аёшься) *impf.*, оста́ться (-а́нусь, -а́нешься) *pf.* в живы́х. **survivor** *n.* оста́вшийся *sb.* в живы́х.

susceptibility [səˌseptɪ'bɪlɪtɪ] *n.* восприи́мчивость; (*sensitivity*) чувстви́тельность. **su'sceptible** *adj.* восприи́мчивый (**to** к+*d.*); (*sensitive*) чувстви́тельный (**to** к+*d.*); (*impressionable*) впечатли́тельный.

suspect ['sʌspekt; sə'spekt] *n.* подозрева́емый *sb.*; *adj.* подозри́тельный; *v.t.* подозрева́ть *impf.* (**of** в+*p.*); (*mistrust*) не доверя́ть *impf.+d.*; (*foresee*) предчу́вствовать *impf.*; (*have reason to believe*) полага́ть *impf.* (**that** что).

suspend [sə'spend] *v.t.* (*hang up*) подве́шивать *impf.*, подве́сить *pf.*; (*call a halt to*) приостана́вливать *impf.*, приостанови́ть (-влю́, -вишь) *pf.*; (*repeal temporarily*) вре́менно отменя́ть *impf.*, отмени́ть (-ню́, -нишь) *pf.*; (*dismiss temporarily*) вре́менно отстраня́ть *impf.*, отстрани́ть *pf.*; **~ed sentence** усло́вный пригово́р. **suspender** *n.* (*stocking*) подвя́зка. **suspense** *n.* (*uncertainty*) неизве́стность, неопределённость; (*anxiety*) беспоко́йство; **keep in ~** держа́ть (-жу́, -жишь) *impf.* в напряжённом ожида́нии. **suspension** *n.* (*halt*) приостано́вка; (*temporary repeal*) вре́менная отме́на; (*temporary dismissal*) вре́менное отстране́ние; (*hanging up*) подве́шивание; (*tech.*) подве́с; **~ bridge** вися́чий мост (мо́ста́, *loc.* -у́; *pl.* -ы́).

suspicion [sə'spɪʃ(ə)n] *n.* подозре́ние; **on ~** по подозре́нию (**of** в+*loc.*); (*trace*) отте́нок (-нка). **suspicious** *adj.* подозри́тельный.

sustain [sə'steɪn] *v.t.* (*support*) подде́рживать *impf.*, поддержа́ть (-жу́, -жишь) *pf.*; (*stand up to*) выде́рживать *impf.*, вы́держать (-жу, -жишь) *pf.*; (*suffer*) потерпе́ть (-плю́, -пишь) *pf.* **sustained** *adj.* (*uninterrupted*) непреры́вный. **sustenance** ['sʌstɪnəns] *n.* пи́ща, пита́ние.

swab [swɒb] *n.* шва́бра; (*med.*) тампо́н; (*smear, specimen*) мазо́к (-зка́); *v.t.* мыть (мо́ю, мо́ешь) *impf.*, вы́~, по~ *pf.* шва́брой; **~ the decks** (*naut.*) дра́ить (-а́ю, -а́ишь) *impf.*, на~ *pf.* па́лубы.

swaddle ['swɒd(ə)l] *v.t.* пелена́ть *impf.*, за~, с~ *pf.* **swaddling-clothes** *n.* пелёнки (*g.* -нок) *pl.*

swagger ['swægə(r)] *v.i.* (*walk with ~*) расха́живать *impf.* с ва́жным ви́дом; (*put on airs*) ва́жничать *impf.*

swallow[1] ['swɒləʊ] *n.* глото́к (-тка́); *v.t.* глота́ть *impf.*, глотну́ть *pf.*; прогла́тывать *impf.*, проглоти́ть (-очу́, -о́тишь) *pf.*; **~ up** поглоща́ть *impf.*, поглоти́ть (-ощу́, -о́тишь) *pf.*

swallow[2] ['swɒləʊ] *n.* (*bird*) ла́сточка.

swamp [swɒmp] *n.* боло́та, топь *v.t.* залива́ть *impf.*, зали́ть (-лью́, -льёшь; за́ли́л, -а́, -о) *pf.*; **~ with** (*letters etc.*) засыпа́ть *impf.*, засы́пать (-плю, -плешь) *pf.+i.* **swampy** *adj.* боло́тистый, то́пкий (-пок, -пка́, -пко).

swan [swɒn] *n.* ле́бедь (*pl.* -ди, -де́й) *m.*

swank [swæŋk] *v.i.* хва́статься *impf.*, по~ *pf.* (**about** *+i.*); (*coll.*) бахва́литься *impf.* (**about** *+i.*).

swansong ['swɒnsɒŋ] *n.* лебеди́ная песнь.

swap [swɒp] *n.* обме́н; *v.t.* меня́ть *impf.*, об~, по~ *pf.*; обме́нивать *impf.*, обменя́ть *pf.*; обме́ниваться *impf.*, обменя́ться *pf.+i.*

swarm [swɔːm] *n.* рой (ро́я, *loc.* рою́; *pl.* рои́, роёв), (*crowd*) толпа́ (*pl.* -пы); *v.i.* рои́ться (-и́тся) *impf.*; толпи́ться (-и́тся) *impf.*; кише́ть (-ши́т) *impf.* (**with** *+i.*).

swarthy ['swɔːðɪ] *adj.* сму́глый (-л, -ла́, -ло).

swastika ['swɒstɪkə] *n.* сва́стика.

swat [swɒt] *v.t.* прихло́пнуть *pf.*; убива́ть *impf.*, уби́ть (убью́, -ьёшь) *pf.*

swathe [sweɪð] *n.* (*bandage*) бинт (-а́); (*puttee*) обмо́тка; *v.t.* (*bandage*) бинтова́ть *impf.*, за~ *pf.*; (*wrap up*) заку́тывать *impf.*, заку́тать *pf.*

sway [sweɪ] *n.* колеба́ние, кача́ние; (*influence*) влия́ние; (*power*) власть *v.t. & i.* колеба́ть(ся) (-блю(сь), -блешь(ся)) *impf.*, по~ *pf.*; кача́ть(ся) *impf.*, качну́ть(ся) *pf.*; *v.t.* (*influence*) име́ть *impf.* влия́ние на+*a.*

swear [sweə(r)] *v.i.* (*vow*) кля́сться (кляну́сь, -нёшься; кля́лся, -ла́сь) *impf.*, по~ *pf.*; (*curse*) руга́ться *impf.*, ругну́ться *pf.*; *v.t.*: **~ in** приводи́ть (-ожу́, -о́дишь) *impf.* привести́ (-еду́, -едёшь; -ёл, -ела́) *pf.* к прися́ге. **swear-word** *n.* руга́тельство, бра́нное сло́во (*pl.* -ва́).

sweat [swet] *n.* пот (*loc.* -у́; *pl.* -ы́); (*perspiration*) испа́рина; *v.i.* поте́ть *impf.*, вс~ *pf.* **sweater** *n.* сви́тер. **sweatshirt** *n.* футбо́лка. **sweaty** *adj.* по́тный (-тен, -тна́, -тно).

Swede [swiːd] *n.* швед, ~дка.

swede [swiːd] *n.* брю́ква.

Sweden ['swiːdən] *n.* Шве́ция. **Swedish** *adj.* шве́дский.

sweep [swiːp] *n.* вымета́ние; (*span*) рахма́х;

(*scope*) охва́т; (*chimney-~*) трубочи́ст; *v.t.* мести́ (мету́, -тёшь; мёл, -á) *impf.*; подмета́ть *impf.*, подмести́ (-ету́, -етёшь; подмёл, -ела́) *pf.*; (*mil.*) обстре́ливать *impf.*, обстреля́ть *pf.*; (*naut.*) (*drag*) тра́лить *impf.*, про~ *pf.*; *v.i.* (*go majestically*) ходи́ть (хожу́, хо́дишь) *indet.*, идти́ (иду́, идёшь; шёл, шла) *det.*, пойти́ (пойду́, -дёшь; пошёл, -шла́) *pf.* велича́во; (*move swiftly*) мча́ться (мчусь, мчи́шься) *impf.*; ~ **away** смета́ть *impf.*, смести́ (смету́, -тёшь; смёл, -á) *pf.* **sweeping** *n.* подмета́ние; (*naut.*) трале́ние; *adj.* широ́кий (-к, -ка́, -о́ко́); (*wholesale*) огу́льный. **sweepstake** *n.* тотализа́тор.

sweet [swi:t] *n.* (*sweetmeat*) конфе́та; (*dessert*) сла́дкое *sb.*; *adj.* сла́дкий (-док, -дка́, -дко); (*fragrant*) души́стый; (*dear*) ми́лый (мил, -á, -о, ми́лы́). **sweetbread** *n.* (*cul.*) сла́дкое мя́со. **sweeten** *v.t.* подсла́щивать *impf.*, подсласти́ть *pf.* **sweetheart** *n.* возлю́бленный, -нная. *sb.* **sweetness** *n.* сла́дость. **sweet'pea** *n.* души́стый горо́шек (-шка(у)) (*collect.*).

swell [swel] *v.i.* (*up*) опуха́ть *impf.*, опу́хнуть (-х) *pf.*; пу́хнуть (-х) *impf.*, вс~, о~ *pf.*; распуха́ть *impf.*, распу́хнуть (-х) *pf.*; (*a sail*) надува́ться *impf.*, наду́ться (-у́ется) *pf.*; (*a bud*) набуха́ть *impf.*, набу́хнуть (-нет; -х) *pf.*; (*increase*) увели́чиваться *impf.*, увели́читься *pf.*; (*sound*) нараста́ть *impf.*, нарасти́ (-тёт; наро́с, -ла́) *pf.*; *v.t.* (*a sail*) надува́ть *impf.*, наду́ть (-у́ю, -у́ешь) *pf.*; (*increase*) увели́чивать *impf.*, увели́чить *pf.*; *n.* вы́пуклость; (*naut.*) мёртвая зыбь (*pl.* -би, -бе́й). **swelling** *n.* о́пухоль; (*bud*) набуха́ние; (*increase*) увеличе́ние.

swelter ['sweltə(r)] *v.i.* томи́ться *impf.*, ис~ *pf.* от жары́. **sweltering** *adj.* зно́йный.

swerve [swɜ:v] *v.i.* отклоня́ться *impf.*, отклони́ться (-ню́сь, -нишься) *pf.*; (*sudden*) ре́зко свора́чивать *impf.*, свороти́ть (-очу́, -о́тишь) *pf.*, сверну́ть *pf.*, в сто́рону.

swift [swɪft] *n.* стриж (-á); *adj.* бы́стрый (быстр, -á, -о, бы́стры́). **swiftness** *n.* быстрота́.

swig [swɪg] *n.* глото́к (-тка́); *v.t.* потя́гивать *impf.* (*coll.*).

swill [swɪl] *n.* по́йло; *v.t.* (*rinse*) полоска́ть (-ощу́, -о́щешь) *impf.*, вы́~ *pf.*; (*sluice*) облива́ть *impf.*, обли́ть (оболью́, -льёшь; о́бли́л, облила́, о́бли́ло) *pf.*

swim [swɪm] *v.i.* пла́вать *indet.*, плыть (плыву́, -вёшь; плыл, -á, -о) *det.*; (*head*) кружи́ться (кру́жи́тся) *impf.*; *v.t.* (*across*) переплыва́ть *impf.*, переплы́ть (-ыву́, -вёшь; переплы́л, -á, -о) *pf.+a.*, че́рез+*a.*; *n.*: **in the** ~ в ку́рсе де́ла. **swimmer** *n.* плове́ц (-вца́), пловчи́ха. **swimming** *n.* пла́вание. **swimming-pool** *n.* бассе́йн для пла́вания.

swindle ['swɪnd(ə)l] *v.t.* обма́нывать *impf.*, обману́ть (-ну́, -нешь) *pf.*; (*coll.*) надува́ть *impf.*, наду́ть (-у́ю, -у́ешь) *pf.*; *n.* обма́н; надува́тельство (*coll.*) **swindler** *n.* плут (-á), ~о́вка; моше́нник, -ица.

swine [swaɪn] *n.* свинья́ (*pl.* -ньи, -не́й). **swineherd** *n.* свинопа́с.

swing [swɪŋ] *v.i.* кача́ться *impf.*, качну́ться *pf.*; колеба́ться (-блюсь, -блешься) *impf.*, по~ *pf.*; раска́чиваться *impf.*, раскача́ться *pf.*; *v.t.* кача́ть *impf.*, качну́ть *pf.+a.*, *i.*; (*arms*) разма́хивать *impf.+i.*; раска́чивать *impf.*, раскача́ть *pf.*; *n.* кача́ние; (*stroke*) мах (-а(у)); (*seat*) каче́ли (-лей) *pl.*; **in full** ~ в по́лном разга́ре. **swing-bridge** *n.* разводно́й мост (мо́ста́, *loc.* -у́; *pl.* -ы́). **swing-door** *n.* дверь (*loc.* -ри́; *pl.* -ри, -ре́й, *i.* -рьми́ & -ря́ми) открыва́ющаяся в любу́ю сто́рону.

swingeing ['swɪndʒɪŋ] *adj.* (*huge*) грома́дный; (*forcible*) си́льный (си́лён, -льна́, -льно, си́льны́).

swinish ['swaɪnɪʃ] *adj.* сви́нский (*coll.*). **swinishness** *n.* сви́нство. (*coll.*).

swipe [swaɪp] *n.* уда́р сплеча́; *v.t.* ударя́ть *impf.*, уда́рить *pf.* сплеча́.

swirl [swɜ:l] *v.i.* кружи́ться (-ужу́сь, -у́жи́шься) *impf.*, верте́ться (-рчу́сь, -ртишься) *impf.*; *v.t.* кружи́ть (-ужу́, -у́жи́шь) *impf.*; *n.* круже́ние; (*whirlpool*) водоворо́т; (*whirlwind*) вихрь *m.*

swish [swɪʃ] *v.i.* (*cut the air*) рассека́ть *impf.*, рассе́чь (-секу́, -сечёшь; -се́к, -ла́) *pf.* во́здух со сви́стом; *v.t.* (*brandish*) разма́хивать *impf.+i.*; *v.t.* & *i.* (*rustle*) шелесте́ть (-ти́шь) *impf.* (+*i.*); шурша́ть (-шу́, -ши́шь) *impf.* (+*i.*); *n.* (*of whip*) свист; (*of scythe*) взмах со сви́стом; (*rustle*) ше́лест, шурша́ние.

Swiss [swɪs] *n.* швейца́рец (-рца), -ца́рка; *adj.* швейца́рский; ~ **roll** руле́т (с варе́ньем).

switch [swɪtʃ] *n.* (*elec.*) выключа́тель *m.*, переключа́тель *m.*; (*rail.*) стре́лка; (*change*) измене́ние; (*twig*) прут (пру́та́; *pl.* -тья, -тьев); (*whip*) хлыст (-á); *v.t.* (*whip*) ударя́ть *impf.*, уда́рить *pf.* пру́то́м, хлысто́м; (*elec.*; *fig.*; *also* ~ *over*) переключа́ть *impf.*, переключи́ть *pf.*; (*wave*) маха́ть (машу́, ма́шешь) *impf.*, махну́ть *pf.+i.*; (*change direction*) (*of conversation etc.*) направля́ть *impf.*, напра́вить *pf.* (разгово́р) в другу́ю сто́рону; (*rail.*) переводи́ть (-ожу́, -о́дишь) *impf.*, перевести́ (-еду́, -едёшь; перевёл, -á) *pf.* (**train** по́езд (*pl.* -á)) на друго́й путь; ~ **off** выключа́ть *impf.*, вы́ключить *pf.*; ~ **on** включа́ть *impf.*, включи́ть *pf.* **switchback** *n.* америка́нские го́ры *f.pl.* **switchboard** *n.* коммута́тор, распредели́тельный щит (-á).

Switzerland ['swɪtsər,lænd] *n.* Швейца́рия.

swivel ['swɪv(ə)l] *v.t.* & *i.* враща́ть(ся) *impf.*; *n.* вертлю́г; ~ **chair** враща́ющийся стул (*pl.* -ья, -ьев).

swollen ['swəʊlən] *adj.* взду́тый. **swollen-headed** *adj.* чванли́вый.

swoon [swu:n] *n.* о́бморок; *v.i.* па́дать *impf.*, упа́сть (упаду́, -дёшь; упа́л) *pf.* в о́бморок.

swoop [swu:p] *v.i.*: ~ **down** налета́ть *impf.*,

налете́ть (-ечу́, -ети́шь) *pf.* (**on** на+*a.*); *n.* налёт; **at one fell ~** одни́м уда́ром, одни́м ма́хом.

sword [sɔːd] *n.* меч (-а́), шпа́га. **sword-fish** *n.* меч-ры́ба. **swordsman** *n.* (иску́сно) владе́ющий *sb.* холо́дным ору́жием; (*fencer*) фехтова́льщик.

sworn [swɔːn] *adj.* (*on oath*) под прися́гой; (*enemy*) закля́тый; (*friend*) закады́чный; (*brother*) назва́ный.

sybaritic [ˌsɪbəˈrɪtɪk] *adj.* сибари́тский.

sycamore [ˈsɪkəˌmɔː(r)] *n.* я́вор.

sycophancy [ˈsɪkəˌfænsɪ] *n.* лесть. **sycophant** *n.* льсте́ц (-а́). **syco'phantic** *adj.* льсти́вый.

Sydney [ˈsɪdnɪ] *n.* Сидне́й.

syllabic [sɪˈlæbɪk] *adj.* слогово́й; (*liter.*) силлаби́ческий. **syllable** [ˈsɪləb(ə)l] *n.* слог (*pl.* -и, -о́в).

syllabus [ˈsɪləbəs] *n.* програ́мма.

symbiosis [ˌsɪmbaɪˈəʊsɪs, ˌsɪmbɪ-] *n.* симбио́з.

symbol [ˈsɪmb(ə)l] *n.* си́мвол, знак. **symbolic(al)** [ˌsɪmˈbɒlɪk(ə)l] *adj.* символи́ческий. **symbolism** *n.* символи́зм. **symbolist** *n.* символи́ст. **symbolize** *v.t.* символизи́ровать *impf.*

symmetrical [ˌsɪˈmetrɪk(ə)l] *adj.* симметри́ческий. **symmetry** [ˈsɪmɪtrɪ] *n.* симметри́я.

sympathetic [ˌsɪmpəˈθetɪk] *adj.* сочу́вственный (-ен, -енна); (*well-disposed*) благожела́тельный; (*physiol.*) симпати́ческий; (*likeable*) симпати́чный. **sympathize** [ˈsɪmpəˌθaɪz] *v.i.* сочу́вствовать *impf.* (**with** +*d.*). **'sympathizer** *n.* (*supporter*) сторо́нник, -ица. **'sympathy** *n.* сочу́вствие; (*condolence*) соболе́знование; (*favour*, *liking*) симпа́тия.

symphonic [sɪmˈfɒnɪk] *adj.* симфони́ческий. **symphony** [ˈsɪmfənɪ] *n.* симфо́ния.

symposium [sɪmˈpəʊzɪəm] *n.* симпо́зиум, совеща́ние.

symptom [ˈsɪmptəm] *n.* симпто́м, при́знак. **sympto'matic** *adj.* симтомати́ческий.

synagogue [ˈsɪnəˌgɒg] *n.* синаго́га.

synchronism [ˈsɪŋkrəˌnɪz(ə)m] *n.* синхрони́зм. **synchroni'zation** *n.* синхрониза́ция. **synchronize** *v.t.* синхронизи́ровать *impf.* & *pf.*; (*cin.*) совмеща́ть *impf.*, совмести́ть *pf.* (**with** с+*i.*).

syncopate [ˈsɪŋkəˌpeɪt] *v.t.* (*mus.*) синкопи́ровать *impf.* & *pf.* **synco'pation** *n.* синко́па.

syndicate [ˈsɪndɪkət; ˈsɪndɪˌkeɪt] *n.* синдика́т; *v.t.* синдици́ровать *impf.* & *pf.*

syndrome [ˈsɪndrəʊm] *n.* синдро́м.

synod [ˈsɪnəd] *n.* сино́д, собо́р. **synodal** *adj.* синода́льный.

synonym [ˈsɪnənɪm] *n.* celsinoни́м. **synonymous** [sɪˈnɒnɪməs] *adj.* синоними́ческий.

synopsis [sɪˈnɒpsɪs] *n.* конспе́кт. **synoptic(al)** *adj.* синопти́ческий.

syntactic(al) [sɪnˈtæktɪkəl] *adj.* синтакси́ческий. **'syntax** *n.* си́нтаксис.

synthesis [ˈsɪnθɪsɪs] *n.* си́нтез. **synthesize** *v.t.* синтези́ровать *impf.* & *pf.* **synthesizer** *n.* синтеза́тор. **synthetic(al)** [sɪnˈθetɪk(əl)] *adj.* синтети́ческий. **synthetics** *n.* синте́тика.

syphilis [ˈsɪfɪlɪs] *n.* си́филис.

Syria [ˈsɪrɪə] *n.* Си́рия. **Syrian** *n.* сири́ец (-и́йца), сири́йка; *adj.* сири́йский.

syringe [sɪˈrɪndʒ, ˈsɪr-] *n.* шприц, спринцо́вка; *v.t.* спринцева́ть *impf.*

syrup [ˈsɪrəp] *n.* сиро́п, па́тока. **syrupy** *adj.* подо́бный сиро́пу.

system [ˈsɪstəm] *n.* систе́ма; (*order*) строй; (*network*) сеть (*loc.* се́ти́; *pl.* -ти, -те́й); (*organism*) органи́зм. **syste'matic** *adj.* системати́ческий. **systematize** *v.t.* систематизи́ровать *impf.* & *pf.* **sy'stemic** *adj.* относя́щийся к всему́ органи́зму.

T

T [tiː] *n.*: **to a T** точь-в-то́чь (*coll.*), как раз.

tab [tæb] *n.* (*loop*) пе́телька; (*on uniform*) петли́ца; (*of boot*) ушко́ (*pl.* -ки́, -ко́в); **keep ~s on** следи́ть *impf.* за+*i.*

tabby [ˈtæbɪ] *n.* полоса́тая ко́шка.

tabernacle [ˈtæbəˌnæk(ə)l] *n.* (*Jewish hist.*) ски́ния; (*receptacle*) дарохрани́тельница.

table [ˈteɪb(ə)l] *n.* (*furniture*, *food*) стол (-а́); (*company*) о́бщество за столо́м; (*list*) табли́ца; (*slab*) доска́ (*a.* -ску; *pl.* -ски, -со́к, -ска́м), плита́ (*pl.* -ты); **bedside ~** ту́мбочка; **~ of contents** оглавле́ние; **~ tennis** насто́льный те́ннис; *v.t.* (*for discussion*) предлага́ть *impf.*, предложи́ть (-жу́, -жишь) *pf.* на обсужде́ние.

tableau [ˈtæbləʊ] *n.* жива́я карти́на; (*dramatic situation*) драмати́ческая ситуа́ция.

tablecloth [ˈteɪb(ə)lˌklɒθ] *n.* ска́терть. **tableland** *n.* плоского́рье.

tablespoon *n.* столо́вая ло́жка.

tablet [ˈtæblɪt] *n.* (*medicine*) табле́тка; (*memorial ~*) мемориа́льная доска́; (*a.* -ску; *pl.* -ски, -со́к, -ска́м); (*name plate*) доще́чка; (*notebook*) блокно́т; (*of soap*) кусо́к (-ска́).

tabloid [ˈtæblɔɪd] *n.* малоформа́тная газе́та; (*pej.*) бульва́рная газе́та.

taboo [təˈbuː] *n.* табу́ *nt.indecl.*, запреще́ние; *adj.* (*prohibited*) запрещённый (-ён, -ена́); (*consecrated*) свяще́нный (-е́н, -е́нна); *v.t.* налага́ть *impf.*, наложи́ть (-жу́, -жишь) *pf.* табу́ на+*a.*

tabular [ˈtæbjʊlə(r)] *adj.* табли́чный; (*flat*) пло́ский (-сок, -ска́, -ско); (*geol.*) слои́стый, пласти́нчатый. **tabulate** *v.t.* располага́ть *impf.*, расположи́ть (-жу́, -жишь) *pf.* в ви́де табли́ц. **tabulator** *n.* (*on typewriter*) табуля́тор; (*person*) состави́тель *m.* табли́ц.

tacit [ˈtæsɪt] *adj.* (*silent*; *implied*) молчали́вый;

(*implied*) подразумева́емый. **taciturn** ['tæsɪ,tɜ:n] *adj.* молчали́вый, неразгово́рчивый. **taci'turnity** *n.* молчали́вость, неразгово́рчивость.

tack [tæk] *n.* (*nail*) гво́здик; (*stitch*) намётка; (*naut.*) галс; (*fig.*) курс; *v.t.* (*fasten*) прикрепля́ть *impf.*, прикрепи́ть *pf.* гво́здиками; (*stitch*) смётывать *impf.*, смета́ть *pf.* на живу́ю ни́тку; (*fig.*) добавля́ть *impf.*, доба́вить *pf.* ((**on**)**to** +*d.*); *v.i.* (*naut.*; *fig.*) лави́ровать *impf.*

tackle ['tæk(ə)l] *n.* (*requisites*) снасть (*collect.*), принадле́жности *f.pl.*; (*equipment*) обору́дование; (*naut.*) такела́ж; (*block and* ~) та́ли (-лей) *pl.*; (*tech.*, ~-*block*) полиспа́ст; (*sport*) блокиро́вка; *v.t.* (*try to overcome*) пыта́ться *impf.*, по~ *pf.* преодоле́ть; (*get down to*) бра́ться (беру́сь, -рёшься) *impf.*, взя́ться (возьму́сь, -мёшься; взя́лся, -ла́сь) *pf.* за+*a.*; (*work on*) занима́ться *impf.*, заня́ться (займу́сь, -мёшься; заня́лся, -ла́сь) *pf.*+*i.*; (*sport*) (*intercept*) перехва́тывать *impf.* перехвати́ть (-ачу́, -а́тишь) *pf.*; блоки́ровать *impf.* & *pf.*; (*secure ball from*) отнима́ть *impf.*, отня́ть (отниму́, -мёшь; о́тнял, -а́, -о) *pf.* мяч у+*g.*

tacky ['tækɪ] *adj.* ли́пкий (-пок, -пка́, -пко), кле́йкий.

tact [tækt] *n.* такт(и́чность). **tactful** *adj.* такти́чный.

tactical ['tæktɪk(ə)l] *adj.* такти́ческий; (*artful*) ло́вкий (-вок, -вка́, -вко, ло́вки́). **tactician** [tæk'tɪʃ(ə)n] *n.* та́ктик. **tactics** *n.* та́ктика.

tactile ['tæktaɪl] *adj.* осяза́тельный; (*tangible*) осяза́емый.

tactless ['tæktlɪs] *adj.* беста́ктный.

tadpole ['tædpəʊl] *n.* голова́стик.

Tadzhikistan [,tædʒɪkɪ'stɑ:n] *n.* Таджикиста́н.

taffeta ['tæfɪtə] *n.* тафта́; *attr.* тафтяно́й.

tag [tæg] *n.* (*label*) ярлы́к (-а́), этике́тка, би́рка; (*of lace*) наконе́чник; (*of boot*) ушко́ (*pl.* -ки́, -ко́в); (*quotation*) избитая цита́та; *v.t.* (*label*) прикрепля́ть *impf.*, прикрепи́ть *pf.* ярлы́к на+*a.*; *v.i.*: ~ **along** (*follow*) сле́довать *impf.*, по~ *pf.* по пята́м (**after** за+*i.*); **may I ~ along?** мо́жно с ва́ми?

tail [teɪl] *n.* (*of animal*, *aircraft*, *kite*, *procession*, *etc.*) хвост; (*of shirt*) ни́жний коне́ц (-нца́); (*of hair*; *of letter*; (*mus.*) *of note*) хво́стик; (*of coat*) фа́лда; (*of coin*) обра́тная сторона́ (*a.* -ону) моне́ты; **heads or ~s?** орёл и́ли ре́шка?; *pl.* (*coat*) фрак; *v.t.* (*shadow*) высле́живать *impf.*; *v.i.*: ~ **away, off** постепе́нно уменьша́ться *impf.*; (*disappear*) исчеза́ть *impf.*; (*grow silent*, *abate*) затиха́ть *impf.* **tailboard** *n.* (*of cart*) откидна́я доска́ (*a.* -ску; *pl.* -ски, -со́к, -ска́м); (*of lorry*) откидно́й борт (*loc.* -у́; *pl.* -а́). **tailcoat** *n.* фрак. **tail-lamp, -light** *n.* за́дний фона́рь (-ря́) *m.*

tailor ['teɪlə(r)] *n.* портно́й *sb.*; *v.t.* шить (шью, шьёшь) *impf.*, сшить (сошью́, сошьёшь) *pf.*; *v.i.* портня́жничать *impf.* (*coll.*). **tailoring** *n.* портня́жное де́ло. **tailor-made** *adj.* сши́тый, изгото́вленный на зака́з; (*fig.*) приспосо́бленный.

tailpiece ['teɪlpi:s] *n.* (*typography*) концо́вка; (*appendage*) за́дний коне́ц (-нца́).

tailspin ['teɪlspɪn] *n.* што́пор. **tailwind** *n.* попу́тный ве́тер (-тра).

taint [teɪnt] *n.* пятно́ (*pl.* -тна, -тен, -тнам), поро́к; (*trace*) налёт; (*infection*) зара́за; *v.t.* & *i.* (*spoil*) по́ртить(ся) *impf.*, ис~ *pf.*; (*infect*) заража́ть(ся) *impf.*, зарази́ть(ся) *pf.* **tainted** *adj.* испо́рченный (-ен).

Taiwan ['taɪ'wɑ:n] *n.* Тайва́нь *m.*

take [teɪk] *v.t.* (*var. senses*) брать (беру́, -рёшь; брал, -а́, -о) *impf.*, взять (возьму́, -мёшь; взял, -а́, -о) *pf.*; (*also seize*, *capture*) захва́тывать *impf.*, захвати́ть (-ачу́, -а́тишь) *pf.*; (*receive*, *accept*; ~ *breakfast*; ~ *medicine*; ~ *steps*) принима́ть *impf.*, приня́ть (приму́, -мешь; при́нял, -а́, -о) *pf.*; (*convey*, *escort*) провожа́ть *impf.*, проводи́ть (-ожу́, -о́дишь) *pf.*; (*public transport*) е́здить *indet.*, е́хать (е́ду, е́дешь) *det.*, по~ *pf.*+*i.*, на+*p.*; (*photograph*) снима́ть *impf.*, снять (сниму́, -мешь; снял, -а́, -о) *pf.*; (*occupy*; ~ *time*) занима́ть *impf.*, заня́ть (займу́, -мёшь; за́нял, -а́, -о) *pf.*; (*impers.*) **how long does it ~?** ско́лько вре́мени ну́жно?; (*size in clothing*) носи́ть (ношу́, но́сишь) *impf.*; (*exam*) сдава́ть (сдаю́, сдаёшь) *impf.*; ~ **courage, heart** мужа́ться *impf.*; ~ **cover** пря́таться (-я́чусь, -я́чешься) *impf.*, с~ *pf.*; ~ **to heart** принима́ть *impf.*, приня́ть (приму́, -мешь; при́нял, -а́, -о) *pf.* бли́зко к се́рдцу; ~ **a liking to** полюби́ться (-блю́сь, -бишься) *pf. impers.*+*d.* (*coll.*); ~ **a turning** swora... сворáчивать *impf.*, сверну́ть *pf.* на у́лицу (*street*), доро́гу (*road*); *v.i.* (*be successful*) име́ть *impf.* успе́х (*of injection*) привива́ться *impf.*, приви́ться (-вьётся; -ви́лся, -вила́сь) *pf.*; ~ **after** походи́ть (-ожу́, -о́дишь) *impf.* на+*a.*; ~ **away** (*remove*) убира́ть *impf.*, убра́ть (уберу́, -рёшь; убра́л, -а́, -о) *pf.*; (*subtract*) вычита́ть *impf.*, вы́честь (-чту, -чтешь; -чел, -чла) *pf.*; ~ **back** брать (беру́, берёшь; брал, -а́, -о) *impf.*, взять (возьму, -мёшь; взял, -а́ -о) *pf.* обра́тно, наза́д; ~ **down** (*in writing*) запи́сывать *impf.*, записа́ть (-ишу́, -и́шешь) *pf.*; ~ **s.o., sth. for, to be** принима́ть *impf.*, приня́ть (приму́, -мешь; при́нял, -а́, -о) *pf.* за+*a.*; счита́ть *impf.*, счесть (сочту́, -тёшь; счёл, сочла́) *pf.*+*i.*, за+*i.*; ~ **from** отнима́ть *impf.*, отня́ть (отниму́, -мешь; о́тнял, -а́, -о) *pf.* у, от+*g.*; ~ **in** (*clothing*) ушива́ть *impf.*, уши́ть (ушью́, -ьёшь) *pf.*; (*understand*) понима́ть *impf.*, поня́ть (пойму́, -мёшь; по́нял, -а́, -о) *pf.*; (*deceive*) обма́нывать *impf.*, обману́ть (-ну́, -нешь) *pf.*; ~ **off** (*clothing*) снима́ть *impf.*, снять (сниму́, -мешь; снял, -а́,-о) *pf.*; (*mimic*) передра́знивать *impf.*, передразни́ть (-ню́, -нишь) *pf.*; (*aeroplane*) взлета́ть *impf.*, взлете́ть (-е́чу, -ети́шь) *pf.*; ~ **on** (*undertake*) брать (беру́, -рёшь; брал, -á, -o) *impf.*, взять (возьму́, -мёшь; взял, -á, -o) *pf.* на себя́; (*at game*) сража́ться *impf.*, срази́ться *pf.* c+*i.* (**at** в+*a.*); ~ **out** вынима́ть *impf.*, вы́нуть *pf.*; (*dog*) выводи́ть (-ожу́, -о́дишь) *impf.*, вы́вести (-еду, -едешь; -ел) *pf.* (**for a walk** на прогу́лку); (*person*) води́ть (вожу́, во́дишь) *indet.*, вести́ (веду́, -дёшь; вёл, -á) *det.*, по~ *pf.*; (*to theatre, restaurant etc.*) приглаша́ть *impf.*, пригласи́ть *pf.* (**to** в+*a.*); **we took them out every night** мы приглаша́ли их куда́-нибудь ка́ждый ве́чер; ~ **over** принима́ть *impf.*, приня́ть (приму́, -мешь; при́нял, -á, -o) *pf.*; (*seize*) завладева́ть *impf.*, завладе́ть *pf.*+*i.*; ~ **to** (*thing*) пристрасти́ться *pf.* к+*d.*; (*person*) привя́зываться *impf.*, привяза́ться (-яжу́сь, -я́жешься) *pf.* к+*d.*; ~ **up** (*enter upon*) бра́ться (беру́сь, -рёшься) *impf.*, взя́ться (возьму́сь, -мёшься; взя́лся, -ла́сь) *pf.* за+*a.*; (*challenge*) принима́ть *impf.*, приня́ть (приму́, -мешь; при́нял, -á, -o) *pf.*; (*time*) занима́ть *impf.*, заня́ть (займу́, -мёшь; за́нял, -á, -o) *pf.*; *n.* (*fishing*) уло́в; (*hunting*) добы́ча; (*cin.*) дубль *m.*, кинока́др. **take-away** *n.* магази́н, где продаю́т на вы́нос. **take-off** *n.* (*imitation*) подража́ние, карикату́ра; (*aeron.*) взлёт.

takings ['teɪkɪŋz] *n.* сбор, барыши́ *m.pl.*

talc(um) ['tælkəm], ~ **powder** *n.* тальк.

tale [teɪl] *n.* расска́з, ска́зка; (*gossip*) сплéтня (*g.pl.* -тен); (*coll., lie*) вы́думка.

talent ['tælənt] *n.* тала́нт. **talented** *adj.* тала́нтливый.

talisman ['tælɪzmən] *n.* талисма́н.

talk [tɔ:k] *v.i.* разгова́ривать *impf.* (**to, with** c+*i.*); (*gossip*) спле́тничать *impf.*, на~ *pf.*; *v.i.* & *i.* говори́ть *impf.*, по~ *pf.*; ~ **down to** говори́ть *impf.* свысока́ c+*i.*; ~ **into** угова́ривать *impf.*, уговори́ть *pf.*+*inf.*; ~ **over** (*discuss*) обсужда́ть *impf.*, обсуди́ть (-ужу́, -у́дишь) *pf.*; ~ **round** (*persuade*) переубежда́ть *impf.*, переубеди́ть *pf.*; (*discuss, reaching no conclusion*) говори́ть *impf.*, по~ *pf.* o+*p.* простра́нно, не каса́ясь существа́ де́ла; ~ **to** (*reprimand*) выгова́ривать *impf.*+*d.*; *n.* (*conversation*) разгово́р, бесе́да; (*chatter, gossip*) болтовня́ (*coll.*); (*lecture*) бесе́да; *pl.* перегово́ры (-ров) *pl.* **talkative** *adj.* болтли́вый, разгово́рчивый. **talker** *n.* говоря́щий *sb.*; (*chatterer*) болту́н (-á) (*coll.*); (*orator*) ора́тор. **talking-to** *n.* (*coll.*) вы́говор.

tall [tɔ:l] *adj.* высо́кий (-о́к, -ока́, -о́ко́); (*in measurements*) высото́й, ро́стом в+*a.* **tallboy** *n.* высо́кий комо́д.

Tallin(n) ['tælɪn] *n.* Та́ллин.

tallow ['tæləʊ] *n.* са́ло. **tallowy** *adj.* са́льный.

tally ['tælɪ] *n.* (*score*) счёт (-a(y)); (*label*) би́рка, ярлы́к (-á); (*duplicate*) ко́пия, дублика́т; *v.i.* соотве́тствовать (**with** +*d.*); *v.t.* подсчи́тывать *impf.*, подсчита́ть *pf.*

tally-ho [ˌtælɪ'həʊ] *int.* ату́!

talon ['tælən] *n.* ко́готь (-гтя; *pl.* -гти, -гте́й) *m.*

tambourine [ˌtæmbə'ri:n] *n.* бу́бен (-бна), тамбури́н.

tame [teɪm] *adj.* ручно́й, приручённый (-ён, -ена́); (*submissive*) поко́рный; (*insipid*) ску́чный (-чен, -чна́, -чно); *v.t.* прируча́ть *impf.*, приручи́ть *pf.*; (*also curb*) укроща́ть *impf.*, укроти́ть (-ощу́, -оти́шь) *pf.* **tameable** *adj.* укроти́мый. **tamer** *n.* укроти́тель *m.*; (*trainer*) дрессиро́вщик; (*fig.*) усмири́тель *m.*

tamp [tæmp] *v.t.* (*road etc.*) трамбова́ть *impf.*, у~ *pf.*; (*pack full*) набива́ть *impf.*, наби́ть (-бью, -бьёшь) *pf.*

tamper ['tæmpə(r)] *v.i.*: ~ **with** (*meddle*) вме́шиваться *impf.*, вмеша́ться *pf.* в+*a.*; (*touch*) тро́гать *impf.*, тро́нуть *pf.*; (*forge*) подде́лывать *impf.*, подде́лать *pf.*

tampon ['tæmpɒn] *n.* тампо́н.

tan [tæn] *n.* (*sun~*) зага́р; (*bark*) толчёная дубова́я кора́; *adj.* желтова́то-кори́чневый; *v.t.* (*of sun*) обжига́ть *impf.*, обже́чь (обожжёт; обжёг, обожгла́) *pf.*; (*hide*) луби́ть *impf.*, вы́~ *pf.*; (*beat*) (*coll.*) дуба́сить *impf.*, от~ *pf.*; *v.i.* загора́ть *impf.*, загоре́ть (-рю́, -ри́шь) *pf.*

tandem ['tændəm] *n.* (*bicycle*) та́ндем; (*horses*) упря́жка цу́гом; **in** ~ (*horses*) цу́гом; (*single file*) гусько́м.

tang [tæŋ] *n.* (*taste*) ре́зкий при́вкус; (*smell*) о́стрый за́пах.

tangent ['tændʒ(ə)nt] *n.* (*math.*) каса́тельная *sb.*; (*trig.*) та́нгенс; **go off at a** ~ (*in conversation etc.*) отклоня́ться *impf.*, отклони́ться (-ню́сь, -нишься) *pf.* от те́мы. **tangential** [tæn'dʒenʃ(ə)l] *adj.* (*diverging*) отклоня́ющийся.

tangerine ['tændʒəˌri:n] *n.* мандари́н.

tangible ['tændʒɪb(ə)l] *adj.* осяза́емый.

tangle ['tæŋg(ə)l] *v.t.* & *i.* запу́тывать(ся) *impf.*, запу́таться *pf.*; *n.* пу́таница.

tango ['tæŋgəʊ] *n.* та́нго *nt.indecl.*

tangy ['tæŋɪ] *adj.* о́стрый (остр & остёр, остра́, о́стро́); ре́зкий (-зок, -зка́, -зко).

tank [tæŋk] *n.* цисте́рна, бак; (*reservoir*) водоём; (*mil.*) танк; *attr.* та́нковый; ~ **engine** танк-парово́з.

tankard ['tæŋkəd] *n.* кру́жка.

tanker ['tæŋkə(r)] *n.* (*sea*) та́нкер; (*road*) автоцисте́рна.

tanner ['tænə(r)] *n.* дуби́льщик. **tannery** *n.* коже́венный заво́д. **tannin** *n.* тани́н. **tanning** *n.* дубле́ние.

tantalize ['tæntəˌlaɪz] *v.t.* дразни́ть (-ню́, -нишь) *impf.* ло́жными наде́ждами; му́чить *impf.*, за~, из~ *pf.*

tantamount ['tæntəˌmaʊnt] *pred.* равноси́лен (-льна, -льно, -льны) (**to** +*d.*).

tantrum ['tæntrəm] *n.* вспы́шка гне́ва, при́ступ раздраже́ния.

tap[1] [tæp] *n.* (*water etc.*) кран; **on** ~ распи́вочно; *v.t.* (*open*) открыва́ть *impf.*, открыть (-ро́ю, -ро́ешь) *pf.*; (*pour out*) налива́ть *impf.*, нали́ть (-лью́, -льёшь; на́лил, -а́, -о) *pf.*; (*med.*) выка́чивать *impf.*, вы́качать *pf.*; (*draw sap from*) подса́чивать *impf.*, подсочи́ть *pf.*; (*telephone conversation*) подслу́шивать *impf.*; ~ **telegraph wires** перехва́тывать *impf.*, перехва́тить (-ачу́, -а́тишь) *pf.* телегра́фное сообще́ние; (*make use of*) испо́льзовать *impf.* & *pf.*

tap² [tæp] *n.* (*knock*) лёгкий стук; *v.t.* стуча́ть (-чу́, -чи́шь) *impf.*, по~ *pf.* в+*a.*, по+*d.* **tap-dance** *v.i.* отбива́ть *impf.*, отби́ть (отобью́, -ьёшь) *pf.* чечётку; *n.* чечётка. **tap-dancer** *n.* чечёточник, -ица.

tape [teɪp] *n.* (*cotton strip*) тесьма́; (*adhesive, magnetic, measuring, etc.*) ле́нта; (*sport*) ле́нточка; ~ **recorder** магнитофо́н; ~ **recording** за́пись; *v.t.* (*seal*) закле́ивать *impf.*, закле́ить *pf.*; (*record*) запи́сывать *impf.*, записа́ть (-ишу́, -и́шешь) *pf.* (на магни́тную ле́нту). **tape-measure** *n.* руле́тка.

taper ['teɪpə(r)] *n.* (*slender candle*) то́нкая све́чка; (*wick*) вощённый фити́ль (-ля́); *m.*; *v.t.* & *i.* су́живать(ся) *impf.*, су́зить(ся) *pf.* к концу́. **tapering** *adj.* су́живающийся к одному́ концу́.

tapestry ['tæpɪstrɪ] *n.* гобеле́н.

tapeworm ['teɪpwɜːm] *n.* ле́нточный глист (-а́).

tapioca [ˌtæpɪ'əʊkə] *n.* тапио́ка.

tapir ['teɪpə(r), -pɪə(r)] *n.* тапи́р.

tar [tɑː(r)] *n.* дёготь (-гтя(-гтю)) *m.*; (*pitch*) смола́; (*tarmac*) гудро́н; *v.t.* ма́зать (ма́жу, -жешь) *impf.*, вы́~, на~, по~ *pf.* дёгтем; смоли́ть *impf.*, вы́~, о~ *pf.*; гудрони́ровать *impf.* & *pf.*

tarantula [tə'ræntjʊlə] *n.* тара́нтул.

tardiness ['tɑːdɪnɪs] *n.* (*slowness*) медли́тельность; (*lateness*) опозда́ние. **tardy** *adj.* (*slow*) медли́тельный; (*late*) по́здний, запозда́лый.

tare¹ [teə(r)] *n.* (*vetch*) ви́ка; *pl.* (*bibl.*) пле́велы *m.pl.*

tare² [teə(r)] *n.* (*comm.*) та́ра; (*allowance*) ски́дка на та́ру.

target ['tɑːgɪt] *n.* мише́нь, цель.

tariff ['tærɪf] *n.* тари́ф; (*price-list*) прейску́рант; *v.t.* тарифици́ровать *impf.* & *pf.*

tarmac ['tɑːmæk] *n.* (*material*) гудро́н; (*road*) гудрони́рованное шоссе́ *nt.indecl.*; (*runway*) бетони́рованная площа́дка; *v.t.* гудрони́ровать *impf.* & *pf.*

tarn [tɑːn] *n.* го́рное озерко́ (*pl.* -ки́, -ко́в).

tarnish ['tɑːnɪʃ] *v.t.* де́лать *impf.*, с~ *pf.* ту́склым; (*discredit*) поро́чить *impf.*, о~ *pf.*; *v.i.* тускне́ть *impf.*, по~ *pf.*; *n.* (*dullness*) ту́склость; (*blemish*) пятно́ (*pl.* -тна, -тен, -тнам). **tarnished** *adj.* ту́склый (-л, -ла́, -ло).

tarpaulin [tɑː'pɔːlɪn] *n.* брезе́нт.

tarragon ['tærəgən] *n.* эстраго́н.

tarry ['tɑːrɪ] *v.i.* ме́длить *impf.*

tart¹ [tɑːt] *adj.* (*taste*) ки́слый (-сел, -сла́, -сло), те́рпкий (-пок, -пка́, -пко); (*biting*) ко́лкий (-лок, -лка́, -лко). **tartness** *n.* кислота́.

tart² [tɑːt] *n.* (*pie*) сла́дкий пиро́г (-а́).

tart³ [tɑːt] *n.* (*prostitute*) шлю́ха.

tartan ['tɑːt(ə)n] *n.* шотла́ндка.

tartar ['tɑːtə(r)] *n.* ви́нный ка́мень (-мня) *m.*

Tartar ['tɑːtə(r)] *n.* тата́рин (*pl.* -ры, -р), -рка; **to catch a** ~ встреча́ть *impf.*, встре́тить *pf.* проти́вника не по си́лам.

task [tɑːsk] *n.* зада́ча, зада́ние; **take to** ~ де́лать *impf.*, с~ *pf.* вы́говор+*d.*; отчи́тывать *impf.*, отчита́ть *pf.* (*coll.*); ~ **force** операти́вная гру́ппа.

taskmaster ['tɑːskˌmɑːstə(r)] *n.* эксплуата́тор.

TASS [tæs] *abbr.* (*of* ***Telegraph Agency of the Soviet Union***) ТАСС, (Телегра́фное аге́нство Сове́тского Сою́за).

tassel ['tæs(ə)l] *n.* ки́сточка, кисть (*pl.* -ти, -те́й).

taste [teɪst] *n.* (*also fig.*) вкус; (*liking*) скло́нность (**for** к+*d.*); (*sample*) про́ба; (*small piece*) ма́ленький кусо́к (-ска́); (*sip*) ма́ленький глото́к (-тка́); ~ **bud** вкусова́я лу́ковица; *v.t.* чу́вствовать *impf.*, по~ *pf.* вкус+*g.*; (*sample*) про́бовать *impf.*, по~ *pf.*; (*fig.*) вкуша́ть *impf.*, вкуси́ть (-ушу́, -у́сишь) *pf.*; (*wine etc.*) дегусти́ровать *impf.* & *pf.*; *v.i.* име́ть *impf.* вкус, при́вкус (**of** +*g.*). **tasteful** *adj.* (сде́ланный) со вку́сом. **tasteless** *adj.* безвку́сный. **tasting** *n.* дегуста́ция. **tasty** *adj.* вку́сный (-сен, -сна́, -сно).

tatter ['tætə(r)] *n.* (*shred*) лоску́т (-а́); *pl.* лохмо́тья (-ьев) *pl.* **tattered** *adj.* обо́рванный; в лохмо́тьях.

tattle ['tæt(ə)l] *n.* (*chatter*) болтовня́; (*gossip*) сплéтни (-тен) *pl.*; *v.i.* (*chatter*) болта́ть *impf.*; (*gossip*) спле́тничать *impf.*, на~ *pf.*

tattoo¹ [tə'tuː, tæ-] *n.* (*mil.*) (*in evening*) сигна́л вече́рней зари́; (*ceremonial*) торже́ственная заря́; **to beat the** ~ бить (бью, бьёшь) *impf.*, по~ *pf.* зо́рю; *v.i.* бараба́нить *impf.* па́льцами.

tattoo² [tə'tuː, tæ-] *n.* (*design*) татуиро́вка; *v.t.* татуи́ровать *impf.* & *pf.*

taunt [tɔːnt] *n.* насме́шка, ко́лкость; *v.t.* насмеха́ться *impf.* над+*i.* **taunting** *adj.* насме́шливый.

Taurus ['tɔːrəs] *n.* Теле́ц (-льца́).

taut [tɔːt] *adj.* ту́го натя́нутый; туго́й (туг, -а́, -о); (*nerves*) взви́нченный. **tauten** *v.t.* & *i.* ту́го натя́гивать(ся) *impf.*, натяну́ть(ся) (-ну́(сь), -нешь(ся)) *pf.* **tautness** *n.* натяже́ние.

tautological [ˌtɔːtə'lɒdʒɪk(ə)l] *adj.* тавтологи́ческий. **tau'tology** *n.* тавтоло́гия.

tavern ['tæv(ə)n] *n.* таве́рна.

tawdriness ['tɔːdrɪnɪs] *n.* мишура́. **tawdry** *adj.* мишу́рный; (*showy*) показно́й.

tawny ['tɔːnɪ] *adj.* рыжева́то-кори́чневый; ~ **owl** нея́сыть.

tax [tæks] *n.* нало́г; (*strain*) напряже́ние; **direct (indirect) ~es** прямы́е (ко́свенные) нало́ги; ~ **collector** сбо́рщик нало́гов; ~

dodger неплате́льщик; *v.t.* облага́ть *impf.*, обложи́ть (-жу́, -жишь) *pf.* нало́гом; (*strain*) напряга́ть *impf.*, напря́чь (-ягу́, -яжёшь; напря́г, -ла́) *pf.*; (*tire*) утомля́ть *impf.*, утоми́ть *pf.*; (*patience*) испы́тывать *impf.*, испыта́ть *pf.*; (*charge*) обвиня́ть *impf.*, обвини́ть *pf.* (**with** в+*p.*). **taxable** *adj.* подлежа́щий обложе́нию нало́гом. **ta'xation** *n.* обложе́ние нало́гом. **tax-free** *adj.* освобождённый (-ён, -ена́) от нало́га. **taxpayer** *n.* налогоплате́льщик.

taxi ['tæksɪ] *n.* такси́ *nt.indecl.*; ~ **rank** стоя́нка такси́; *v.i.* (*aeron.*) рули́ть *impf.*

taxidermist ['tæksɪˌdɜːmɪst] *n.* наби́вщик чу́чел. **taxidermy** *n.* наби́вка чу́чел.

taxi-driver ['tæksɪˌdraɪvə(r)] *n.* води́тель *m.* такси́. **taximeter** *n.* таксо́метр.

Tbilisi [təbɪ'liːsɪ] *n.* Тбили́си *m.indecl.*

tea [tiː] *n.* чай (ча́я(ю); *pl.* чаи́); *attr.* ча́йный; ~ **bag** мешо́чек с зава́ркой ча́я; ~ **caddy** ча́йница; ~ **cloth,** ~ **towel** полоте́нце для посу́ды; ~ **cosy** стёганый чехо́льчик (для ча́йника); ~ **strainer** ча́йное си́течко.

teach [tiːtʃ] *v.t.* учи́ть (учу́, у́чишь) *impf.*, на~ *pf.* (*person* +*a.*; *subject* +*d.*, *inf.*); обуча́ть *impf.*, обучи́ть (-чу́, -чишь) *pf.* (*person* +*a.*; *subject* +*d.*, *inf.*); преподава́ть (-даю́, -даёшь) *impf.* (*subject* +*a.*); (*coll.*) проу́чивать *impf.*, проучи́ть (-чу́, -чишь) *pf.* **teacher** *n.* учи́тель (*pl.* -ля́ & (*fig.*) -ли) *m.*, ~ница; преподава́тель *m.*, ~ница. **teacher-training** *adj.*: ~ **college** педогоги́ческий институ́т. **teaching** *n.* (*instruction*) обуче́ние; (*doctrine*) уче́ние.

teacup ['tiːkʌp] *n.* ча́йная ча́шка.

teak [tiːk] *n.* тик; *attr.* ти́ковый.

tea-leaf ['tiːliːf] *n.* ча́йный лист (-а́; *pl.* -ья, -ьев).

team [tiːm] *n.* (*sport*) кома́нда; (*of people*) брига́да, гру́ппа; (*of horses etc.*) упря́жка; *v.i.* (~ *up*) объединя́ться *impf.*, объедини́ться *pf.* (в кома́нду *etc.*); *v.t.* запряга́ть *impf.*, запря́чь (-ягу́, -я́жешь; -я́г, -ягла́) *pf.* в упря́жку. **team-mate** *n.* (*sport*) игро́к (-а́) той же кома́нды; (*at work*) това́рищ по рабо́те, член той же брига́ды. **teamwork** *n.* брига́дная, совме́стная рабо́та; (*co-operation*) взаимоде́йствие, сотрудни́чество.

tea-pot ['tiːpɒt] *n.* ча́йник.

tear[1] [teə(r)] *n.* (*rent*) проре́ха; (*hole*) дыра́ (*pl.* -ры); (*cut*) разре́з; *v.t.* рвать (рву, рвёшь; рвал, -а́, -о) *impf.*; (*also* ~ *to pieces*) разрыва́ть *impf.*, разорва́ть (-ву́, -вёшь; -вал, -вала́, -ва́ло) *pf.*; *v.i.* рва́ться (рвётся; рва́лся, -ала́сь, -а́ло́сь) *impf.*; разрыва́ться *impf.*, разорва́ться (-вётся; -ва́лся, -вала́сь, -а́ло́сь) *pf.*; (*rush*) мча́ться (мчусь, мчи́шься) *impf.*; ~ **down, off** срыва́ть *impf.*, сорва́ть (-ву́, -вёшь; сорва́л, -а́, -о) *pf.*; ~ **away, off** отрыва́ть *impf.*, оторва́ть (-ву́, -вёшь; оторва́л, -а́, -о) *pf.*; ~ **out** вырыва́ть *impf.*, вы́рвать (-ву, -вешь) *pf.*; ~ **up** изрыва́ть *impf.*, изорва́ть (-ву́, -вёшь; -ва́л, -вала́, -ва́ло) *pf.*

tear[2] [tɪə(r)] *n.* (~-*drop*) слеза́ (*pl.* -ёзы, -ёз, -еза́м). **tearful** *adj.* слезли́вый; (*sad*) печа́льный. **tear-gas** *n.* слезоточи́вый газ (-а(у)).

tease [tiːz] *v.t.* дразни́ть (-ню́, -нишь) *impf.*; (*wool*) чеса́ть (чешу́, -шешь) *impf.*; (*cloth*) ворсова́ть *impf.*, на~ *pf.* **teaser** *n.* (*puzzle*) головоло́мка.

teasel ['tiːz(ə)l], **teazle** *n.* (*plant*) ворся́нка; (*device*) ворши́льная ши́шка.

teaspoon ['tiːspuːn] *n.* ча́йная ло́жка.

teat [tiːt] *n.* сосо́к (-ска́).

technical ['teknɪk(ə)l] *adj.* техни́ческий; (*specialist*) специа́льный; (*formal*) форма́льный; ~ **college** техни́ческое учи́лище. **techni'cality** *n.* техни́ческая сторона́ (*a.* -ону; *pl.* -оны, -о́н, -она́м); форма́льность. **technician** [tek'nɪʃ(ə)n] *n.* те́хник. **tech'nique** *n.* те́хника; (*method*) ме́тод. **tech'nology** *n.* техноло́гия, те́хника. **techno'logical** *adj.* технологи́ческий. **tech'nologist** *n.* техно́лог.

teddy-bear ['tedɪ] *n.* медвежо́нок (-жо́нка; *pl.* -жа́та, -жа́т).

tedious ['tiːdɪəs] *adj.* ску́чный (-чен, -чна́, -чно), утоми́тельный. **tedium** *n.* ску́ка, утоми́тельность.

teem[1] [tiːm] *v.i.* (*abound in*, *be abundant*) кише́ть (-ши́т) *impf.* (**with** +*i.*); (*abound in*) изоби́ловать *impf.* (**with** +*i.*).

teem[2] [tiːm] *v.i.*: **it is** ~**ing (with rain)** дождь льёт как из ведра́.

teenage ['tiːnˌeɪdʒ] *adj.* ю́ношеский. **teenager** *n.* подро́сток (-тка).

teeter ['tiːtə(r)] *v.i.* кача́ться *impf.*, качну́ться *pf.*; поша́тываться *impf.*

teethe [tiːð] *v.i.*: **the child is teething** у ребёнка подре́зываются зу́бы. **teething** *n.* подре́зывание зубо́в; ~ **troubles** (*fig.*) нача́льные пробле́мы. **teething-ring** *n.* де́тское зубно́е кольцо́.

teetotal [tiː'təʊt(ə)l] *adj.* тре́звый (-в, -ва́, -во). **teetotalism** *n.* тре́звенность. **teetotaller** *n.* тре́звенник.

tele- ['telɪ] *in comb.* теле... . **telecommunication(s)** *n.* да́льняя связь. **telegram** *n.* телегра́мма. **telegraph** *n.* телегра́ф; *attr.* телегра́фный; *v.t.* телеграфи́ровать *impf.* & *pf.*; ~ **pole** телегра́фный столб (-а́). **telepathic** *adj.* телепати́ческий. **telepathy** [tɪ'lepəθɪ] *n.* телепа́тия. **telephone** *n.* телефо́н; *attr.* телефо́нный; *v.t.* (*message*) телефони́ровать *impf.* & *pf.* +*a.*, о+*p.*; (*person*) звони́ть *impf.*, по~ *pf.* (по телефо́ну) +*d.*; ~ **box** телефо́нная бу́дка; ~ **directory** телефо́нная кни́га; ~ **exchange** телефо́нная ста́нция; ~ **number** но́мер (*pl.* -а́) телефо́на. **telephonist** [tɪ'lefənɪst] *n.* телефони́ст, ~ка. **telephoto lens** *n.* телеобъекти́в. **teleprinter** *n.* телета́йп. **telescope** *n.* телеско́п; *v.t.* & *i.* телескопи́чески складывать(ся) *impf.*, сложи́ть(ся) (сложу́, сло́жишь) *pf.* **telescopic** *adj.* телескопи́ческий. **televise** *v.t.* пока́зывать *impf.*, показа́ть (покажу́, пока́жешь) *pf.* по телеви́дению; передава́ть (-даю́, -даёшь) *impf.*, переда́ть (-а́м, -а́шь, -а́ст, -ади́м; пе́редал, -а́, -о) *pf.* по телеви́дению. **television** *n.* телеви́дение; (*set*) телеви́зор; *attr.* телевизио́нный. **telex** *n.* те́лекс.

tell [tel] *v.t.* (*relate*) расска́зывать *impf.*, рассказа́ть (-ажу́, -а́жешь) *pf.* (*thing told* +*a.*; *person told* +*d.*); (*utter*, *inform*) говори́ть *impf.*, сказа́ть (скажу́, -жешь) *pf.* (*thing uttered* +*a.*; *thing informed about* о+*p.*; *person informed* +*d.*); (*order*) веле́ть (-лю́, -ли́шь) *impf.* & *pf.*+*d.*; ~ **one thing from another** отлича́ть *impf.*, отличи́ть *pf.*+*a.* от+*g.*; *v.i.* (*have an effect*) ска́зываться *impf.*, сказа́ться (скажу́сь, -жешься) *pf.* (**on** на+*p.*); **all told** итого́; ~ **fortunes** гада́ть *impf.*, по~ *pf.*; ~ **off** (*select*) отбира́ть *impf.*, отобра́ть (отберу́, -рёшь; отобра́л, -а́, -о) *pf.*; (*rebuke*) отде́лывать *impf.*, отде́лать *pf.*; ~ **on**, ~ **tales about** ябе́дничать *impf.*, на~ *pf.* на+*a.* **teller** *n.* (*of story*) расска́зчик, -ица; (*of votes*) счётчик голосо́в; (*in bank*) касси́р, ~ша. **telling** *adj.* (*effective*) эффе́ктный; (*significant*) многозначи́тельный. **telling-'off** *n.* вы́говор. **telltale** *n.* доно́счик, спле́тник; *adj.* преда́тельский.

temerity [tɪ'merɪtɪ] *n.* (*rashness*) безрассу́дство; (*audacity*) дёрзость.

temper ['tempə(r)] *n.* (*metal*) зака́л; (*character*) нрав, хара́ктер; (*mood*) настрое́ние; (*anger*) гнев; **lose one's** ~ выходи́ть (-ожу́, -о́дишь) *impf.*, вы́йти (вы́йду, -дешь; вы́шел, -шла) *pf.* из себя́; *v.t.* (*metal*) отпуска́ть *impf.*, отпусти́ть (-ущу́, -у́стишь) *pf.*; (*moderate*) смягча́ть *impf.*, смягчи́ть *pf.*

temperament ['temprəmənt] *n.* темпера́мент; (*mus.*) темпера́ция. **temperamental** [ˌtemprə'ment(ə)l] *adj.* темпера́ментный.

temperance ['tempərəns] *n.* (*moderation*) уме́ренность; (*sobriety*) тре́звенность.

temperate ['tempərət] *adj.* уме́ренный (-ен, -енна).

temperature ['temprɪtʃə(r)] *n.* температу́ра; (*high* ~) повы́шенная температу́ра; **take s.o.'s** ~ измеря́ть *impf.*, изме́рить *pf.* температу́ру+*d.*

tempest ['tempɪst] *n.* бу́ря. **tempestuous** [tem'pestjʊəs] *adj.* бу́рный (-рен, бу́рна́, -рно), бу́йный (бу́ен, буйна́, -но).

template ['templɪt, -pleɪt] *n.* шабло́н.

temple[1] ['temp(ə)l] *n.* (*religion*) храм.

temple[2] ['temp(ə)l] *n.* (*anat.*) висо́к (-ска́).

tempo ['tempəʊ] *n.* темп.

temporal ['tempər(ə)l] *adj.* (*secular*) мирско́й, све́тский; (*of time*) временно́й.

temporary ['tempərərɪ] *adj.* вре́менный.

temporize ['tempəˌraɪz] *v.i.* приспоса́бливаться *impf.*, приспосо́биться *pf.* ко вре́мени и обстоя́тельствам; (*hesitate*) ме́длить *impf.*

tempt [tempt] *v.t.* искуша́ть *impf.*, искуси́ть *pf.*; соблазня́ть *impf.*, соблазни́ть *pf.*; ~ **fate** испы́тывать *impf.*, испыта́ть *pf.* судьбу́. **temp'tation** *n.* искуше́ние, собла́зн. **tempter, -tress** *n.* искуси́тель *m.*, ~ница. **tempting** *adj.* зама́нчивый, соблазни́тельный.

ten [ten] *adj.* & *n.* де́сять (-ти́, -тью́); (*collect.*; *10 pairs*) де́сятеро (-ры́х); (*cards*; *number 10*) деся́тка; (*time*) де́сять часо́в; (*age*) де́сять лет; (*set of 10*; *10 years*, *decade*) деся́ток (-тка); **in** ~**s** деся́тками. **tenth** *adj.* & *n.* деся́тый; (*fraction*) деся́тая (часть (*pl.* -ти, -те́й)); (*date*) деся́тое (число́); (*mus.*) де́цима.

tenable ['tenəb(ə)l] *adj.* (*strong*) про́чный (-чен, -чна́, -чно, про́чны́); (*logical*) логи́чный; (*of office*) могу́щий быть за́нятым.

tenacious [tɪ'neɪʃəs] *adj.* це́пкий (-пок, -пка́, -пко); (*stubborn*) упо́рный. **tenacity** [tɪ'næsɪtɪ] *n.* це́пкость; упо́рство.

tenancy ['tenənsɪ] *n.* (*renting of property*) наём помеще́ния; (*period*) срок (-а(у)) аре́нды. **tenant** *n.* нанима́тель *m.*, ~ница; аренда́тор.

tend[1] [tend] *v.i.* (*be apt*) име́ть скло́нность (**to** к+*d.*, +*inf.*); (*move*) направля́ться *impf.*, напра́виться *pf.*

tend[2] [tend] *v.t.* (*look after*) (*person*) уха́живать *impf.* за+*i.*; (*machine*) обслу́живать *impf.*, обслужи́ть (-жу́, -жишь) *pf.*

tendency ['tendənsɪ] *n.* тенде́нция, скло́нность. **tendentious** [ten'denʃəs] *adj.* тенденцио́зный.

tender[1] ['tendə(r)] *v.t.* (*offer*) предлага́ть *impf.*, предложи́ть (-жу́, -жишь) *pf.*; (*money*) предоставля́ть *impf.*, предоста́вить *pf.*; *v.i.* (*make* ~ *for*) подава́ть (-даю́, -даёшь) *impf.*, пода́ть (-а́м, -а́шь, -а́ст, -ади́м; по́дал, -а́, -о) *pf.* зая́вку (на торга́х); *n.* предложе́ние; **legal** ~ зако́нное платёжное сре́дство.

tender[2] ['tendə(r)] *n.* (*rail.*) те́ндер; (*naut.*) посы́льное су́дно (*pl.* -да́, -до́в).

tender[3] ['tendə(r)] *adj.* (*delicate*, *affectionate*) не́жный (-жен, -жна́, -жно, не́жны́); (*soft*) мя́гкий (-гок, -гка́, -гко); (*sensitive*) чувстви́тельный. **tenderness** *n.* не́жность; (*softness*) мя́гкость.

tendon ['tend(ə)n] *n.* сухожи́лие.

tendril ['tendrɪl] *n.* у́сик.

tenement ['tenɪmənt] *n.* (убо́гий) многокварти́рный дом (-а(у); *pl.* -а́).

tenet ['tenɪt, 'ti:net] *n.* до́гмат, при́нцип.

tennis ['tenɪs] *n.* те́ннис; *attr.* те́ннисный; ~ **player** тенниси́ст, ~ка.

tenon ['tenən] *n.* шип (-а́).

tenor ['tenə(r)] *n.* (*structure*) укла́д; (*direction*) направле́ние; (*purport*) о́бщее содержа́ние; (*mus.*) те́нор.

tense[1] [tens] *n.* вре́мя *nt.*

tense[2] [tens] *v.t.* напряга́ть *impf.*, напря́чь (-ягу́, -яжёшь; напря́г, -ла́) *pf.*; *adj.* (*tight*) натя́нутый; (*strained*) напряжённый (-ён, -ённа); (*excited*) возбуждённый (-ён, -ена́); (*nervous*) не́рвный (не́рвен, не́рвна́, не́рвно). **tenseness** *n.* натя́нутость, напряжённость. **tensile** *adj.* растяжи́мый. **tension** *n.* напряже́ние (*also fig.*; *elec.*); натяже́ние.

tent [tent] *n.* пала́тка; ~ **peg** ко́лышек (-шка) для пала́тки; ~ **pole** пала́точная сто́йка.

tentacle ['tentək(ə)l] *n.* щу́пальце (*g.pl.* -лец & -льцев).

tentative ['tentətɪv] *adj.* (*experimental*) про́бный; (*preliminary*) предвари́тельный.

tenterhooks ['tentə,hʊks] *n.*: **be on** ~ сиде́ть (сижу́, сиди́шь) *impf.* как на иго́лках.

tenth *see* **ten**

tenuous ['tenjʊəs] *adj.* (*slender*, *subtle*) то́нкий (-нок, -нка́, -нко, то́нки́); (*flimsy*) непро́чный (-чен, -чна́, -чно); (*insignificant*) незначи́тельный; (*rarefied*) разрежённый.

tenure ['tenjə(r)] *n.* (*possession*) владе́ние; (*office*) пребыва́ние в до́лжности; (*period*) срок (-а(у)) (*of possession*) владе́ния, (*of office*) пребыва́ния в до́лжности.

tepid ['tepɪd] *adj.* теплова́тый.

tercentenary [,tɜːsen'tiːnərɪ, -'tenərɪ, tɜː'sentɪnərɪ], **-ennial** [,tɜːsen'tenɪəl] *n.* трёхсотле́тие; *adj.* трёхсотле́тний.

term [tɜːm] *n.* (*period*) срок (-а(у)); (*univ.*) семе́стр; (*school*) че́тверть (*pl.* -ти, -те́й); (*math.*) член; (*leg.*) се́ссия; (*technical word*, *expression*) те́рмин; (*expression*) выраже́ние; (*med.*) норма́льный пери́од бере́менности; *pl.* (*conditions*) усло́вия *nt.pl.* (**of payment** опла́ты); (*relations*) отноше́ния *nt.pl.*; **on good** ~**s** в хоро́ших отноше́ниях; (*language*) язы́к (-а́), выраже́ния *nt.pl.*; **come to** ~**s with** (*resign o.s. to*) покоря́ться *impf.*, покори́ться *pf.* к+*d.*; (*come to an agreement with*) приходи́ть (-ожу́, -о́дишь) *impf.*, прийти́ (приду́, -дёшь; пришёл, -шла́) *pf.* к соглаше́нию с+*i.*; *v.t.* называ́ть *impf.*, назва́ть (назову́, -вёшь; назва́л, -а́, -о) *pf.*; **I do not** ~ **impatience a shortcoming** я не называ́ю нетерпе́ние недоста́тком.

termagant ['tɜːməgənt] *n.* сварли́вая же́нщина; мегера (*coll.*).

terminable ['tɜːmɪnəb(ə)l] *adj.* ограни́ченный сро́ком, сро́чный (-чен, -чна́, -чно).

terminal ['tɜːmɪn(ə)l] *adj.* коне́чный, заключи́тельный; (*univ.*) семестро́вый; (*school*) четвертно́й; (*leg.*) сессио́нный; *n.* (*elec.*) зажи́м; (*computer*) термина́л; (*terminus*) (*rail.*) коне́чная ста́нция; (*bus etc.*) коне́чная остано́вка; (*aeron.*) (*airport buildings*) зда́ния *nt.pl.* аэропо́рта; **air** ~ аэровокза́л.

terminate ['tɜːmɪ,neɪt] *v.t.* & *i.* конча́ть(ся) *impf.*, ко́нчить(ся) *pf.* (**in** +*i.*). **termi'nation** *n.* коне́ц (-нца́), оконча́ние.

terminology [,tɜːmɪ'nɒlədʒɪ] *n.* терминоло́гия. **termino'logical** *adj.* терминологи́ческий.

terminus ['tɜːmɪnəs] *n.* (*rail.*) коне́чная ста́нция; (*bus etc.*) коне́чная остано́вка.

termite ['tɜːmaɪt] *n.* терми́т.

tern [tɜːn] *n.* кра́чка.

terra [,terə] *n.*: ~ ***firma*** су́ша; ~ ***incognita*** неизве́стная страна́.

terrace ['terəs, -rɪs] *n.* терра́са; (*row of houses*) ряд (-а́ *with 2, 3, 4, loc.* -у; *pl.* -ы́) домо́в; *v.t.* террásíровать *impf.* & *pf.*

terracotta [,terə'kɒtə] *n.* террако́та; *adj.* террако́товый.

terrain [te'reɪn, tə-] *n.* ме́стность.

terrapin ['terəpɪn] *n.* (*turtle*) водяна́я черепа́ха.

terrestrial [tə'restrɪəl, tɪ-] *adj.* земно́й; (*ground*) назе́мный.

terrible ['terɪb(ə)l] *adj.* (*frightening*, *dreadful*, *very bad*) ужа́сный; (*excessive*) стра́шный (-шен, -шна́, -шно, стра́шны́) (*coll.*). **terribly** *adv.* ужа́сно, стра́шно.

terrier ['terɪə(r)] *n.* терье́р.

terrific [tə'rɪfɪk] *adj.* (*huge*) огро́мный; (*marvellous*) потряса́ющий. **terrify** ['terɪ,faɪ] *v.t.* ужаса́ть *impf.*, ужасну́ть *pf.*

territorial [,terɪ'tɔːrɪəl] *adj.* территориа́льный. **territory** ['terɪtərɪ, -trɪ] *n.* террито́рия, (*fig.*) о́бласть, сфе́ра.

terror ['terə(r)] *n.* у́жас, страх; (*person*, *thing causing* ~) терро́р. **terrorism** *n.* террори́зм. **terrorist** *n.* террори́ст, ~ка. **terrorize** *v.t.* терроризи́ровать *impf. pf.*

terse [tɜːs] *adj.* сжа́тый, кра́ткий (-ток, -тка́, -тко). **terseness** *n.* сжа́тость, кра́ткость.

tertiary ['tɜːʃərɪ] *adj.* трети́чный; (*education*) вы́сший.

tesselated ['tesə,leɪtɪd] *adj.* моза́ичный.

test [test] *n.* испыта́ние, про́ба; (*exam*) экза́мен; контро́льная *sb.* (*coll.*); (*standard*) крите́рий; (*analysis*) ана́лиз; (*chem.*, *reagent*) реакти́в; ~ **ban** запреще́ние испыта́ний я́дерного ору́жия; ~ **case** де́ло (*pl.* -ла́) име́ющее принципиа́льное значе́ние для разреше́ния аналоги́чных дел; ~ **flight** испыта́тельный полёт; ~ **paper** (*exam*) экзаменацио́нный биле́т; ~ **pilot** лётчик-испыта́тель *m.*; *v.t.* (*try out*) испы́тывать *impf.*, испыта́ть *pf.*; (*check up on*) проверя́ть *impf.*, прове́рить *pf.*; (*give exam to*) экзаменова́ть *impf.*, про~ *pf.*

testament ['testəmənt] *n.* завеща́ние; **Old, New T**~ Ве́тхий, Но́вый заве́т. **testamentary** [,testə'mentərɪ] *adj.* завеща́тельный. **testator** [te'steɪtə(r)] *n.* завеща́тель *m.*, ~ница.

testicle ['testɪk(ə)l] *n.* яи́чко (*pl.* -чки, -чек).

testify ['testɪ,faɪ] *v.i.* свиде́тельствовать *impf.* (**to** в по́льзу+*g.*; **against** про́тив+*g.*); *v.t.* (*declare*) заявля́ть *impf.*, заяви́ть (-влю́, -вишь) *pf.*; (*be evidence of*) свиде́тельствовать о+*p.*

testimonial [,testɪ'məʊnɪəl] *n.* рекоменда́ция, характери́стика. **testimony** ['testɪmənɪ] *n.* показа́ние, -ния *pl.*, свиде́тельство; (*declaration*) заявле́ние.

test-tube ['testtjuːb] *n.* проби́рка.

testy ['testɪ] *adj.* раздражи́тельный.

tetanus ['tetənəs] *n.* столбня́к (-á).
tetchy ['tetʃɪ] *adj.* раздражи́тельный.
tête-à-tête [ˌteɪtɑː'teɪt] *n.* & *adv.* тет-а-те́т.
tether ['teðə(r)] *n.* при́вязь; **be at, come to the end of one's ~** дойти́ (дойду́, -дёшь; дошёл, -шла́) *pf.* до то́чки; *v.t.* привя́зывать *impf.*, привяза́ть (-яжу́, -я́жешь) *pf.*
Teutonic [tjuː'tɒnɪk] *adj.* тевто́нский.
text [tekst] *n.* текст. **textbook** *n.* уче́бник.
textile ['tekstaɪl] *adj.* тексти́льный; *n.* ткань; *pl.* тексти́ль *m.* (*collect*).
textual ['tekstjʊəl] *adj.* текстово́й.
texture ['tekstʃə(r)] *n.* (*consistency*) консисте́нция; (*structure*) строе́ние.
thalidomide [θə'lɪdəˌmaɪd] *n.* талидоми́д.
Thames [temz] *n.* Те́мза.
than [ðən, ðæn] *conj.* (*comparison*) чем; **other ~** (*except*) кро́ме+*g.*; **none other ~** не кто ино́й, как; **nothing else ~** не что ино́е, как.
thank [θæŋk] *v.t.* благодари́ть *impf.*, по~ *pf.* (**for** за+*a.*); **~ God** сла́ва Бо́гу; **~ you** спаси́бо; благодарю́ вас; *n.pl.* благода́рность; спаси́бо; **many ~s** большо́е спаси́бо; **~s to** (*good result*) благодаря́+*d.*; (*bad result*) из-за+*g.* **thankful** *adj.* благода́рный. **thankless** *adj.* неблагода́рный. **thank-offering** *n.* благода́рственная же́ртва. **thanksgiving** *n.* (*service of*) благода́рственный моле́бен (-бна); благодаре́ние.
that [ðæt] *demonstrative adj. & pron.* тот (та, то; *pl.* те); э́тот (э́та, э́то; *pl.* э́ти); **~ which** тот (та, то; те) кото́рый; *relative pron.* кото́рый; *conj.* что; (*purpose*) что́бы; *adv.* так, до тако́й сте́пени.
thatch [θætʃ] *n.* (*straw*) соло́менная, (*reed*) тростнико́вая кры́ша; *v.t.* крыть (кро́ю, кро́ешь) *impf.*, по~ *pf.* соло́мой (*straw*), тростнико́м (*reed*).
thaw [θɔː] *v.t.* раста́пливать *impf.*, растопи́ть (-плю́, -пишь) *pf.*; *v.i.* та́ять (та́ет) *impf.*, рас~ *pf.*; (*fig.*) смягча́ться *impf.*, смягчи́ться *pf.*; *n.* о́ттепель; (*fig.*) смягче́ние.
the [ðɪ, ðə, ðiː] *def. article, not usu. translated*; *adv.* тем; **the ... the ...** чем..., тем; **~ more ~ better** чем бо́льше, тем лу́чше.
theatre ['θɪətə(r)] *n.* теа́тр; (*lecture etc.*) аудито́рия; (*operating*) операцио́нная *sb.* **theatre-goer** *n.* театра́л. **theatrical** [θɪ'ætrɪk(ə)l] *adj.* театра́льный.
theft [θeft] *n.* воровство́, кра́жа.
their [ðeə(r)], **theirs** *poss. pron.* их; свой (-оя́, -оё; -ои́).
theism ['θiːɪz(ə)m] *n.* теи́зм. **theist** *n.* теи́ст. **the'istic(al)** *adj.* теисти́ческий.
thematic [θɪ'mætɪk] *adj.* темати́ческий. **theme** [θiːm] *n.* те́ма, предме́т.
themselves [ðəm'selvz] *pron.* (*emph.*) (они́) са́ми (-и́х, -и́м, -и́ми); (*refl.*) себя́ (себе́, собо́й); -ся (*suffixed to v.t.*).
then [ðen] *adv.* (*at that time*) тогда́, в то вре́мя; (*after that*) пото́м, зате́м; **now and ~** вре́мя от вре́мени; *conj.* в тако́м слу́чае, тогда́; *n.* то вре́мя *nt.*; *adj.* тогда́шний.
thence [ðens] *adv.* отту́да; (*from that*) из э́того. **thence'forth, -'forward** *adv.* с того́/э́того вре́мени.
theodolite [θɪ'ɒdəˌlaɪt] *n.* теодоли́т.
theologian [θɪə'ləʊdʒɪən, -dʒ(ə)n] *n.* тео́лог. **theo'logical** *adj.* теологи́ческий. **theology** [θɪ'ɒlədʒɪ] *n.* теоло́гия.
theorem ['θɪərəm] *n.* теоре́ма. **theo'retical** *adj.* теорети́ческий. **theorist** *n.* теоре́тик. **theorize** *v.i.* теоретизи́ровать *impf.* **theory** *n.* тео́рия.
theosophy [θɪ'ɒsəfɪ] *n.* теосо́фия.
therapeutic(al) [ˌθerə'pjuːtɪk(əl)] *adj.* терапевти́ческий. **therapeutics** *n.* терапе́втика. **'therapist** *n.* терапе́вт. **'therapy** *n.* терапи́я.
there [ðeə(r)] *adv.* (*place*) там; (*direction*) туда́; *int.* вот!; ну!; **~ is, are** есть, име́ется (-е́ются); **~ you are** (*on giving sth.*) пожа́луйста. **thereabouts** *adv.* (*near*) поблизо́сти; (*approximately*) приблизи́тельно. **there'after** *adv.* по́сле э́того. **thereby** *adv.* таки́м о́бразом. **therefore** *adv.* поэ́тому, следова́тельно. **there'in** *adv.* в э́том; (*in that respect*) в э́том отноше́нии. **thereu'pon** *adv.* зате́м.
thermal ['θɜːm(ə)l] *adj.* теплово́й, терми́ческий; **~ springs** горя́чие исто́чники *m.pl.*; **~ unit** едини́ца теплоты́.
thermo- ['θɜːməʊ] *in comb.* термо..., тепло... . **thermodynamics** *n.* термодина́мика. **thermometer** [θə'mɒmɪtə(r)] *n.* термо́метр, гра́дусник. **thermonuclear** *adj.* термоя́дерный. **thermos** ['θɜːməs] *n.* те́рмос. **thermostat** *n.* термоста́т.
thesis ['θiːsɪs] *n.* (*proposition*) те́зис; (*dissertation*) диссерта́ция.
they [ðeɪ] *pron.* они́ (их, им, и́ми, о них).
thick [θɪk] *adj.* то́лстый (-т, -та́, -то, то́лсты́), (*in measurements*) толщино́й в+*a.*; (*line*) жи́рный (-рен, -рна́, -рно); (*dense*) пло́тный (-тен, -тна́, -тно, пло́тны́); густо́й (-т, -та́, -то, гу́сты́); (*turbid*) му́тный (-тен, -тна́, -тно, му́тны́); (*stupid*) тупо́й (туп, -а́, -о, ту́пы́); *n.* гу́ща; (*of fight*) разга́р; **through ~ and thin** не коле́блясь; несмотря́ ни на каки́е препя́тствия. **thicken** *v.t. & i.* утолща́ть(ся) *impf.*, утолсти́ть(ся) *pf.*; (*make, become denser*) сгуща́ть(ся) *impf.*, сгусти́ть(ся) *pf.*; *v.i.* (*become more intricate*) усложня́ться *impf.*, усложни́ться *pf.* **thicket** *n.* ча́ща. **thick-headed** *adj.* тупоголо́вый (*coll.*). **thickness** *n.* (*also dimension*) толщина́; (*density*) пло́тность, густота́; (*layer*) слой (*pl.* слои́). **thick'set** *adj.* корена́стый. **thick-skinned** *adj.* толстоко́жий.
thief [θiːf] *n.* вор (*pl.* -ы, -о́в), ~о́вка. **thieve** *v.i.* ворова́ть *impf.*; *v.t.* красть (-аду́, -адёшь; крал) *impf.*, у~ *pf.* **thievery** *n.* воровство́. **thievish** *adj.* ворова́тый.
thigh [θaɪ] *n.* бедро́ (*pl.* бёдра, -дер, -драм). **thigh-bone** *n.* бе́дренная кость (*pl.* -ти, -те́й).
thimble ['θɪmb(ə)l] *n.* напёрсток (-тка).
thin [θɪn] *adj.* (*slender*; *not thick*) то́нкий

(-нок, -нка́, -нко, то́нки́); (*lean*) худо́й (худ, -а́, -о, ху́ды́); (*too liquid*) жи́дкий (-док, -дка́, -дко); (*sparse*) ре́дкий (-док, -дка́, -дко); (*weak*) сла́бый (-б, -ба́, -бо); *v.t.* & *i.* де́лать(ся) *impf.*, с~ *pf.* то́нким, жи́дким; *v.i.*: ~ **down** худе́ть *impf.*, по~ *pf.*; ~ **out** реде́ть *impf.*, по~ *pf.*; *v.t.*: ~ **out** проре́живать *impf.*, прореди́ть *pf.*

thing [θɪŋ] *n.* вещь (*pl.* -щи, -ще́й); (*object*) предме́т; (*matter*) де́ло (*pl.* -ла́); **poor** ~ (*person*) бедня́жка *c.g.* (*coll.*); *pl.* (*belongings*) пожи́тки (-ков) *pl.* (*coll.*); (*clothes*) оде́жда; (*implements*) у́тварь (*collect.*); (*affairs*) дела́ *nt.pl.* **thingamy** ['θɪŋəmɪ] *n.* (*person*) как бишь его́?; (*thing*) штука.

think [θɪŋk] *v.t.* & *i.* ду́мать *impf.*, по~ *pf.* (**about, of** о+*p.*, над+*i.*); (*consider*) счита́ть *impf.*, счесть (сочту́, -тёшь; счёл, сочла́) *pf.* (**to be** +*i.*, за+*a.*; **that** что); *v.i.* (*think, reason*) мы́слить *impf.*; (*intend*) намерева́ться *impf.* (*of doing* +*inf.*); ~ **out** проду́мывать *impf.*, проду́мать *pf.*; ~ **over** обду́мывать *impf.*, обду́мать *pf.*; ~ **up, of** приду́мывать *impf.*, приду́мать *pf.* **thinker** *n.* мысли́тель *m.* **thinking** *adj.* мы́слящий; *n.* (*reflection*) размышле́ние; **to my way of** ~ по моему́ мне́нию.

thinly ['θɪnlɪ] *adv.* то́нко. **thinness** *n.* то́нкость; (*leanness*) худоба́. **thin-skinned** *adj.* (*fig.*) оби́дчивый.

third [θɜːd] *adj.* & *n.* тре́тий (-тья, -тье); (*fraction*) треть (*pl.* -ти, -те́й); (*date*) тре́тье (число́); (*mus.*) те́рция; ~ **party** тре́тья сторона́ (*a.* -ону; *pl.* -оны, -он, -она́м); **T~ World** стра́ны *f.pl.* тре́тьего ми́ра. **third-rate** *adj.* третьестепе́нный.

thirst [θɜːst] *n.* жа́жда (**for** +*g.* (*fig.*)); *v.i.* (*fig.*) жа́ждать (-ду, -дешь) *impf.* (**for** +*g.*). **thirsty** *adj.*: **be** ~ хоте́ть (хочу́, -чешь; хоти́м) *impf.* пить.

thirteen [θɜː'tiːn, 'θɜː-] *adj.* & *n.* трина́дцать (-ти, -тью); (*age*) трина́дцать лет. **thirteenth** *adj.* & *n.* трина́дцатый; (*fraction*) трина́дцатая (часть (*pl.* -ти, -те́й)); (*date*) трина́дцатое (число́).

thirtieth ['θɜːtɪɪθ] *adj.* & *n.* тридца́тый; (*fraction*) тридца́тая (часть (*pl.* -ти, -те́й)); (*date*) тридца́тое (число́). **thirty** *adj.* & *n.* три́дцать (-ти́, -тью́); (*age*) три́дцать лет; *pl.* (*decade*) тридца́тые го́ды (-до́в) *m.pl.*

this [ðɪs] *demonstrative adj.* & *pron.* э́тот (э́та, э́то; *pl.* э́ти); ~ **way** сюда́; **like** ~ вот так.

thistle ['θɪs(ə)l] *n.* чертополо́х.

thither ['ðɪðə(r)] *adv.* туда́.

thong [θɒŋ] *n.* реме́нь (-мня́) *m.*

thorax ['θɔːræks] *n.* грудна́я кле́тка.

thorn [θɔːn] *n.* шип (-а́), колю́чка (*coll.*). **thorny** *adj.* колю́чий; (*fig.*) терни́стый; (*ticklish*) щекотли́вый.

thorough ['θʌrə] *adj.* основа́тельный, тща́тельный; (*complete*) по́лный (-лон, -лна́, по́лно́), соверше́нный (-нен, -нна). **thoroughbred** *adj.* чистокро́вный, поро́дистый. **thoroughfare** *n.* прое́зд; (*walking*) прохо́д. **thoroughgoing** *adj.* радика́льный. **thoroughly** *adv.* (*completely*) вполне́, соверше́нно. **thoroughness** *n.* основа́тельность, тща́тельность.

though [ðəʊ] *conj.* хотя́; несмотря́ на то, что; **as** ~ как бу́дто; *adv.* одна́ко, всё-таки.

thought [θɔːt] *n.* мысль; (*heed*) внима́ние; (*meditation*) размышле́ние; (*intention*) наме́рение; *pl.* (*opinion*) мне́ние. **thoughtful** *adj.* заду́мчивый; (*considerate*) внима́тельный, забо́тливый. **thoughtless** *adj.* необду́манный (-ан, -анна); (*inconsiderate*) невнима́тельный.

thousand ['θaʊz(ə)nd] *adj.* & *n.* ты́сяча (*i.* -чей & чью). **thousandth** *adj.* & *n.* ты́сячный; (*fraction*) ты́сячная (часть (*pl.* -ти, -те́й).

thraldom ['θrɔːldəm], **thrall** *n.* (*state*) ра́бство; **in** ~ обращённый (-ён, -ена́) в ра́бство.

thrash [θræʃ] *v.t.* бить (бью, бьёшь) *impf.*, по~ *pf.*; ~ **out** (*discuss*) тща́тельно обсужда́ть *impf.*, обсуди́ть (-ужу́, -у́дишь) *pf.*; *v.i.*: ~ **about** мета́ться (мечу́сь, -чешься) *impf.* **thrashing** *n.* (*beating*) взбу́чка (*coll.*).

thread [θred] *n.* ни́тка, нить (*also fig.*); (*of screw etc.*) наре́зка, резьба́; *v.t.* (*needle*) продева́ть *impf.*, проде́ть (-е́ну, -е́нешь) *pf.* нитку́ в+*a.*; (*beads etc.*) нани́зывать *impf.*, наниза́ть (-ижу́, -и́жешь) *pf.*; ~ **one's way** пробира́ться *impf.*, пробра́ться (-беру́сь, -берёшься; -бра́лся, -брала́сь, -бра́ло́сь) *pf.* (**through** че́рез+*a.*). **threadbare** *adj.* (*clothes etc.*) потёртый, изно́шенный; (*hackneyed*) изби́тый.

threat [θret] *n.* угро́за. **threaten** *v.t.* угрожа́ть *impf.*, грози́ть *impf.*, при~ *pf.* (*person* +*d.*; **with** +*i.*; *to do* +*inf.*).

three [θriː] *adj.* & *n.* три (трёх, -ём, -емя́, -ёх); (*collect.*; *3 pairs*) тро́е (-ои́х); (*cards*, *number 3*) тро́йка; (*time*) три часа́; (*age*) три го́да; ~ **times** три́жды; ~ **times four** три́жды четы́ре. **three-dimensional** *adj.* трёхме́рный. **threefold** *adj.* тройно́й; *adv.* втройне́. **three-ply** *adj.* (*wood*) трёхсло́йный; (*rope*) тройно́й. **three-quarters** *n.* три че́тверти. **threesome** *n.* тро́йка.

thresh [θreʃ] *v.t.* молоти́ть (-очу́, -о́тишь) *impf.* **threshing** *n.* молотьба́. **threshing-floor** *n.* ток (*loc.* -у́; *pl.* -а́). **threshing-machine** *n.* молоти́лка.

threshold ['θreʃəʊld, -həʊld] *n.* поро́г.

thrice [θraɪs] *adv.* три́жды.

thrift [θrɪft] *n.* бережли́вость. **thriftless** *adj.* расточи́тельный. **thrifty** *adj.* бережли́вый.

thrill [θrɪl] *n.* (*trepidation*, *excitement*) тре́пет, волне́ние; (*sth.* ~*ing*) что-л. захва́тывающее; *v.t.* & *i.* си́льно волнова́ть(ся) *impf.*, вз~ *pf.* **thriller** *n.* приключе́нческий, детекти́вный (*novel*) рома́н, (*film*) фильм. **thrilling** *adj.* волну́ющий, захва́тывающий.

thrive [θraɪv] *v.i.* процвета́ть *impf.*; (*grow*)

разраста́ться *impf.*, разрасти́сь (-тётся; разро́сся, -сла́сь) *pf.*

throat [θrəʊt] *n.* го́рло. **throaty** *adj.* горта́нный; (*hoarse*) хри́плый (-л, -ла́, -ло).

throb [θrɒb] *v.i.* (*heart*) си́льно би́ться (бьётся) *impf.*; пульси́ровать *impf.*; **his head ~bed** кровь стуча́ла у него́ в виска́х; *n.* бие́ние; пульса́ция.

throe [θrəʊ] *n.* о́страя боль; *pl.* му́ки *f.pl.*; (*of birth*) родовы́е му́ки *f.pl.*; (*of death*) аго́ния.

thrombosis [θrɒm'bəʊsɪs] *n.* тромбо́з.

throne [θrəʊn] *n.* трон, престо́л; **come to the ~** вступа́ть *impf.*, вступи́ть (-плю, -пишь) *pf.* на престо́л.

throng [θrɒŋ] *n.* толпа́ (*pl.* -пы); *v.i.* толпи́ться *impf.*; *v.t.* заполня́ть *impf.*, запо́лнить *pf.* толпо́й.

throttle ['θrɒt(ə)l] *n.* (*gullet*) гло́тка; (*tech.*) дро́ссель *m.*; *v.t.* (*strangle*) души́ть (-шу́, -шишь) *impf.*, за~ *pf.*; (*tech.*) дроссели́ровать *impf.* & *pf.*; **~ down** сбавля́ть *impf.*, сба́вить *pf.* ско́рость+*g.*

through [θru:] *prep.* (*across*, *via*, *~ opening*) че́рез+*a.*; (*esp. ~ thick of*) сквозь+*a.*; (*air*, *streets etc.*) по+*d.*; (*agency*) посре́дством+*g.*; (*reason*) из-за+*g.*; *adv.* насквозь; (*from beginning to end*) с нача́ла до конца́; **be ~ with** (*sth.*) ока́нчивать *impf.*, око́нчить *pf.*; (*s.o.*) порыва́ть *impf.*, порва́ть (-ву́, -вёшь; порва́л, -а́, -о) *pf.* с+*i.*; **put ~** (*on telephone*) соединя́ть *impf.*, соедини́ть *pf.*; **~ and ~** до конца́, соверше́нно; *adj.* сквозно́й. **through'out** *adv.* повсю́ду, во всех отноше́ниях; *prep.* по всему́ (всей, всему́; *pl.* всем)+*d.*; (*from beginning to end*) с нача́ла до конца́+*g.*

throw [θrəʊ] *n.* бросо́к (-ска́), броса́ние; *v.t.* броса́ть *impf.*, бро́сить *pf.*; кида́ть *impf.*, ки́нуть *pf.*; (*rider*) сбра́сывать *impf.*, сбро́сить *pf.*; (*pottery*) формова́ть *impf.*, с~ *pf.*; (*party*) устра́ивать *impf.*, устро́ить *pf.*; **~ o.s. at** набра́сываться *impf.*, набро́ситься *pf.* на+*a.*; **~ o.s. into** броса́ться *impf.*, бро́ситься *pf.* в+*a.*; **~ about** разбра́сывать *impf.*, разброса́ть *pf.*; **~ money about** сори́ть *impf.* деньга́ми; **~ aside, away** отбра́сывать *impf.*, отбро́сить *pf.*; **~ away, out** выбра́сывать *impf.*, вы́бросить *pf.*; **~ back** отбра́сывать *impf.*, отбро́сить *pf.* наза́д; **~ down** сбра́сывать *impf.*, сбро́сить *pf.*; **~ in** (*add*) добавля́ть *impf.*, доба́вить *pf.*; (*sport*) вбра́сывать *impf.*, вбро́сить *pf.*; **~ off** сбра́сывать *impf.*, сбро́сить *pf.*; **~ open** распа́хивать *impf.*, распахну́ть *pf.*; **~ out** (*see also ~ away*) (*expel*) выгоня́ть *impf.*, вы́гнать (вы́гоню, -нишь) *pf.*; (*reject*) отверга́ть *impf.*, отве́ргнуть *pf.*; **~ over, ~ up** (*abandon*, *renounce*) броса́ть *impf.*, бро́сить *pf.* **throw-back** *n.* регре́сс, возвра́т к про́шлому, атави́зм. **throw-in** *n.* вбра́сывание мяча́.

thrush¹ [θrʌʃ] *n.* (*bird*) дрозд (-а́).

thrush² [θrʌʃ] *n.* (*disease*) моло́чница.

thrust [θrʌst] *n.* (*shove*) толчо́к (-чка́); (*lunge*) вы́пад; (*blow*, *stroke*, *mil.*) уда́р; (*tech.*, *of rocket*) тя́га; *v.t.* (*shove*) толка́ть *impf.*, толкну́ть *pf.*; (*~ into*, *out of*; *give quickly*, *carelessly*) сова́ть (сую́, суёшь) *impf.*, су́нуть *pf.*; **~ one's way** пробива́ть *impf.*, проби́ть (-бью, -бьёшь) *pf.* себе́ доро́гу; **~ aside** отта́лкивать *impf.*, оттолкну́ть *pf.*; **~ out** высо́вывать *impf.*, вы́сунуть *pf.*

thud [θʌd] *n.* глухо́й звук, стук; *v.i.* (*fall with ~*) па́дать *impf.*, (у)па́сть ((у)паду́, -дёшь; (у)па́л) *pf.* с глухи́м сту́ком; шлёпаться *impf.*, шлёпнуться *pf.* (*coll.*).

thug [θʌg] *n.* головоре́з (*coll.*).

thumb [θʌm] *n.* большо́й па́лец (-льца); **under the ~ of** под башмако́м у+*g.*; *v.t.*: **~ through** перели́стывать *impf.*, перелиста́ть *pf.*; **~ a lift** голосова́ть *impf.*, про~ *pf.* (*coll.*). **thumbscrew** *n.* тиски́ (-ко́в) *pl.* для больши́х па́льцев.

thump [θʌmp] *n.* (*heavy blow*) тяжёлый уда́р; (*thud*) глухо́й звук, стук; *v.t.* наноси́ть (-ошу́, -о́сишь) *impf.*, нанести́ (-есу́, -есёшь; -ёс, -есла́) *pf.* уда́р+*d.*; колоти́ть (-очу́, -о́тишь) *impf.*, по~ *pf.* в+*a.*, по+*d.*; *v.i.* (*strike with ~*) би́ться (бьюсь, бьёшься) *impf.* с глухи́м шу́мом.

thunder ['θʌndə(r)] *n.* гром (*pl.* -ы, -о́в); (*fig.*) гро́хот; *v.i.* греме́ть (-млю́, -ми́шь) *impf.*; грохота́ть (-очу́, -о́чешь) *impf.*; (*fulminate* (*fig.*)) мета́ть (мечу́, -чешь) *impf.* гро́мы и мо́лнии; **it is ~ing** гром греми́т. **thunderbolt** *n.* уда́р мо́лнии; (*fig.*) гром среди́ я́сного не́ба. **thunderclap** *n.* уда́р гро́ма. **thundercloud** *n.* грозова́я ту́ча. **thunderous** *adj.* громово́й. **thunderstorm** *n.* гроза́ (*pl.* -зы). **thunderstruck** *adj.* (*fig.*) как гро́мом поражённый (-ён, -ена́). **thundery** *adj.* грозово́й.

Thursday ['θɜ:zdeɪ, -dɪ] *n.* четве́рг (-а́).

thus [ðʌs] *adv.* (*in this way*) так, таки́м о́бразом; (*accordingly*) ита́к; **~ far** до сих пор.

thwack [θwæk] *n.* си́льный уда́р; *v.t.* бить (бью, бьёшь) *impf.*, по~ *pf.*

thwart [θwɔ:t] *v.t.* меша́ть *impf.*, по~ *pf.*+*d.*; (*plans*) расстра́ивать *impf.*, расстро́ить *pf.*

thyme [taɪm] *n.* тимья́н.

thyroid ['θaɪrɔɪd] *n.* (*~ gland*) щитови́дная железа́.

tiara [tɪ'ɑ:rə] *n.* тиа́ра.

Tibet [tɪ'bet] *n.* Тибе́т.

tibia ['tɪbɪə] *n.* больша́я берцо́вая кость (*pl.* -ти, -те́й).

tic [tɪk] *n.* тик.

tick¹ [tɪk] *n.* (*noise*) ти́канье; (*moment*) моме́нт, мину́точка; (*mark*) пти́чка; *v.i.* ти́кать *impf.*, ти́кнуть *pf.*; *v.t.* отмеча́ть *impf.*, отме́тить *pf.* пти́чкой; **~ off** (*scold*) отде́лывать *impf.*, отде́лать *pf.* (*coll.*).

tick² [tɪk] *n.* (*mite*) клещ (-а́).

tick³ [tɪk] *n.* (*coll.*) креди́т; **on ~** в креди́т.

ticket ['tɪkɪt] *n.* билéт; (*label*) ярлы́к (-á); (*season* ~) кáрточка; (*cloakroom* ~) номерóк (-ркá); (*receipt*) квитáнция; ~ **collector** контролёр; ~ **office** (билéтная) кáсса; ~ **punch** компóстер; *v.t.* прикрепля́ть *impf.*, прикрепи́ть *pf.* ярлы́к к+*d.*

tickle ['tɪk(ə)l] *n.* щекóтка; *v.t.* щекотáть (-очý, -óчешь) *impf.*, по~ *pf.*; (*amuse*) весели́ть *impf.*, по~, раз~ *pf.*; *v.i.* щекотáть (-óчет) *impf.*, по~ *pf. impers.*; **my throat** ~**s** у меня́ щекóчет в гóрле. **ticklish** *adj.* щекотли́вый (*also fig.*); **to be** ~ боя́ться (боюсь, бои́шься) *impf.* щекóтки.

tidal ['taɪd(ə)l] *adj.* прили́во-отли́вный; ~ **wave** прили́вная волнá (*pl.* -ны, -н, вóлнáм).

tiddlywinks ['tɪdlɪwɪŋks] *n.* (игрá в) блóшки (-шек) *pl.*

tide [taɪd] *n.* прили́в и отли́в; **high** ~ прили́в; **low** ~ отли́в; (*current*, *tendency*) течéние; **the** ~ **turns** (*fig.*) собы́тия принимáют другóй оборóт; *v.t.*: ~ **over** помогáть *impf.*, помóчь (-огý, -óжешь; -óг, -оглá) *pf.* +*d. of person* спрáвиться (*difficulty* с+*i.*); **will this money** ~ **you over?** вы протя́нете с э́тими деньгáми? **tidemark** *n.* отмéтка ýровня пóлной воды́.

tidiness ['taɪdɪnɪs] *n.* опря́тность, аккурáтность. **tidy** *adj.* опря́тный, аккурáтный; (*considerable*) поря́дочный; *v.t.* убирáть *impf.*, убрáть (уберý, -рёшь; убрáл, -á, -о) *pf.*; приводи́ть (-ожý, -óдишь) *impf.*, привести́ (-едý, -едёшь; -ёл, -елá) *pf.* в поря́док.

tie [taɪ] *n.* (*garment*) гáлстук; (*string*, *lace*) завя́зка; (*link*, *bond*; *tech.*) связь; (*equal points etc.*) рáвный счёт; **end in a** ~ закáнчиваться *impf.*, закóнчиться *pf.* вничью́; (*match*) матч; (*mus.*) ли́га; (*burden*) обýза; *pl.* (*bonds*) ýзы (уз) *pl.*; *v.t.* свя́зывать *impf.*, связáть (свяжý, -жешь) *pf.* (*also fig.*); (~ *up*) завя́зывать *impf.*, завязáть (-яжý, -я́жешь) *pf.*; (*restrict*) ограни́чивать *impf.*, ограни́чить *pf.*; ~ **down** (*fasten*) привя́зывать *impf.*, привязáть (-яжý, -я́жешь) *pf.*; ~ **up** (*tether*) привя́зывать *impf.*, привязáть (-яжý, -я́жешь) *pf.*; (*parcel*) перевя́зывать *impf.*, перевязáть (-яжý, -я́жешь) *pf.*; *v.i.* (*be* ~*d*) завя́зываться *impf.*, завязáться (-я́жется) *pf.*; (*sport*) равня́ть *impf.*, с~ *pf.* счёт; сыгрáть *pf.* вничью́; ~ **in, up, with** совпадáть *impf.*, совпáсть *pf.* с+*i.* **tie-pin** *n.* булáвка для гáлстука.

tier [tɪə(r)] *n.* ряд (-á *with 2*, *3*, *4*, *loc.* -ý; *pl.* -ы́), я́рус.

tiff [tɪf] *n.* размóлвка; *v.i.* ссóриться *impf.*, по~ *pf.* (**with** с+*i.*).

tiger ['taɪgə(r)] *n.* тигр. **tigress** *n.* тигри́ца.

tight [taɪt] *adj.* (*compact*) плóтный (-тен, -тнá, -тно, плóтны́); (*cramped*) тéсный (-сен, -снá, -сно), ýзкий (-зок, -зкá, -зко); (*impenetrable*) непроницáемый; (*strict*) стрóгий (-г, -á, -о); (*tense*, *taut*) тугóй (туг, -á, -о), натя́нутый; ~ **corner** (*fig.*) трýдное положéние. **tighten** *v.t.* & *i.* натя́гиваться *impf.*, натянýться *pf.*; (*clench*, *contract*) сжимáть(ся) *impf.*, сжáться (сожмý(сь), -мёшь(ся)) *pf.*; ~ **one's belt** потýже затя́гивать *impf.*, затянýть *pf.* пóяс (*also fig.*); ~ **up** (*discipline etc.*) подтя́гивать *impf.*, подтянýть *pf.* (*coll.*). **tight-fisted** *adj.* скупóй (-п, -пá, -по). **tightly** *adv.* (*strongly*) прóчно; (*closely*, *cramped*) тéсно. **tightness** *n.* теснотá; напряжённость. **tightrope** *n.* тýго натя́нутый канáт. **tights** *n.* колгóтки (-ток) *pl.*

tilde ['tɪldə] *n.* ти́льда.

tile [taɪl] *n.* (*roof*) черепи́ца (*also collect.*); (*decorative*) кáфель *m.* (*also collect.*); *v.t.* крыть (крóю, крóешь) *impf.*, по~ *pf.* черепи́цей, кáфелем. **tiled** *adj.* (*roof*) черепи́чный; (*floor*) кáфельный.

till¹ [tɪl] *prep.* до+*g.*; **not** ~ тóлько (**Friday** в пя́тницу; **the next day** на слéдующий день); *conj.* покá не; **not** ~ тóлько когдá.

till² [tɪl] *n.* кáсса.

till³ [tɪl] *v.t.* воздéлывать *impf.*, воздéлать *pf.* **tillage** *n.* обрабóтка земли́.

tiller¹ ['tɪlə(r)] *n.* землёдéлец (-льца).

tiller² ['tɪlə(r)] *n.* (*naut.*) рýмпель *m.*

tilt [tɪlt] *n.* наклóн; (*naut.*, *aeron.*) крен; **on the** ~ в наклóнном положéнии; **at full** ~ изо всех сил; пóлным хóдом; *v.t.* & *i.* наклоня́ть(ся) *impf.*, наклони́ть(ся) (-ню́(сь), -нишь(ся)) *pf.*; (*heel* (*over*)) крени́ть(ся) *impf.*, на~ *pf.*

timber ['tɪmbə(r)] *n.* лесоматериáл, лес (-а(у)) (*collect.*); (*beam*) бáлка; (*naut.*) ти́мберс. **timbered** *adj.* общи́тый дéревом; деревя́нный. **timbering** *n.* (*work*) плóтничная рабóта.

timbre ['tæmbə(r), 'tæbrə] *n.* тембр.

time [taɪm] *n.* врéмя *nt.*; (*occasion*) раз (*pl.* -зы́, -з); (*term*) срок (-а(у)); (*period*) периóд, эпóха; (*mus.*) темп, такт; (*sport*) тайм; *pl.* (*period*) временá *pl.*; (*in comparison*) раз; **five** ~**s as big** в пять раз бóльше; (*multiplication*) **four** ~**s four** четы́режды четы́ре; **five** ~**s four** пя́тью четы́ре; ~ **and** ~ **again,** ~ **after** ~ не раз, ты́сячу раз; **at a** ~ рáзом, одновремéнно; **at the** ~ в э́то врéмя; **at** ~**s** по временáм; **at the same** ~ в то же врéмя; **before my** ~ до меня́; **for a long** ~ дóлго; (*up to now*) давнó; **for the** ~ **being** покá; **from** ~ **to** ~ врéмя от врéмени; **in** ~ (*early enough*) вó-время; (*with* ~) со врéменем; **in good** ~ заблаговрéменно; **in** ~ **with** в такт+*d.*; **in no** ~ моментáльно; **on** ~ вó-время; **one at a** ~ по одномý; **be in** ~ успевáть *impf.*, успéть *pf.* (**for** к+*d.*, на+*a.*); **I do not have** ~ **for him** (*fig.*) я не хочý трáтить врéмя на негó; **have** ~ **to** (*manage*) успевáть *impf.*, успéть *pf.* +*inf.*; **have a good** ~ хорошó проводи́ть (-ожý, -óдишь) *impf.*, провести́ (-едý, -едёшь; -ёл, -елá) *pf.* врéмя; **it is** ~ порá (**to** +*inf.*); **what is the** ~? котóрый час?; **kill** ~ убивáть *impf.*, уби́ть (убью́, -ьёшь) *pf.* врéмя; **work**

full (part) ~ рабо́тать *impf.* по́лный (непо́лный) рабо́чий день; ~ **bomb** бо́мба заме́дленного де́йствия; ~ **off** о́тпуск; ~ **signal** сигна́л вре́мени; ~ **signature** та́ктовый разме́р; *v.t.* (*choose* ~) выбира́ть *impf.*, вы́брать (-беру, -берешь) *pf.* вре́мя+*g.*; (*arrange* ~) назнача́ть *impf.*, назна́чить *pf.* вре́мя+*g.*; (*ascertain* ~) засека́ть *impf.*, засе́чь (-еку́, -ечёшь; засе́к, -ла́, -ло) *pf.* вре́мя; хронометри́ровать *impf.* & *pf.* **time-consuming** *adj.* отнима́ющий мно́го вре́мени. **time-honoured** *adj.* освящённый века́ми. **timekeeper** *n.* (*person*) та́бельщик; (*sport*) хронометри́ст. **time-lag** отстава́ние во вре́мени; (*tech.*) запа́здывание. **timeless** *adj.* ве́чный. **time-limit** преде́льный срок (-а(у)). **timely** *adj.* своевре́менный. **timepiece** *n.* часы́ (-со́в) *pl.*; хроно́метр. **timetable** *n.* расписа́ние; (*of work*) гра́фик.

timid ['tɪmɪd] *adj.* ро́бкий (-бок, -бка́, -бко), засте́нчивый. **ti'midity** *n.* ро́бкость, засте́нчивость. **timorous** ['tɪmərəs] *adj.* боязли́вый.

tin [tɪn] *n.* (*metal*) о́лово; ~ **plate** бе́лая жесть; *attr.* оловя́нный, жестяно́й; (*container*) (консе́рвная) ба́нка, жестя́нка; (*cake-*~) фо́рма; (*baking* ~) про́тивень (-вня) *m.*; ~ **foil** оловья́нная фо́льга; *v.t.* (*coat with* ~) луди́ть (лужу́, лу́дишь) *impf.*, по~ *pf.*; (*pack in* ~) консерви́ровать *impf.* & *pf.*; ~**ned food** консе́рвы (-вов) *pl.*

tincture ['tɪŋktjə(r), -tʃə(r)] *n.* (*colour*, *fig.*) отте́нок (-нка); (*taste*; *fig.*) при́вкус; (*fig.*) налёт; *v.t.* (*colour*; *fig.*) слегка́ окра́шивать *impf.*, окра́сить *pf.*; (*flavour*) придава́ть (-даю́, -даёшь) *impf.*, прида́ть (-а́м, -а́шь, -а́ст, -ади́м; при́дал, -а́, -о) *pf.* вкус+*d.*

tinder ['tɪndə(r)] *n.* трут. **tinder-box** *n.* тру́тница.

tinge [tɪndʒ] *n.* (*colour*; *fig.*) отте́нок (-нка); (*taste*; *fig.*) при́вкус; (*fig.*) налёт; *v.t.* (*also fig.*) слегка́ окра́шивать *impf.*, окра́сить *pf.*

tingle ['tɪŋg(ə)l] *n.* пока́лывание; (*from cold*) пощи́пывание; *v.i.* (*sting*) коло́ть (ко́лет) *impf. impers.*; **my fingers** ~ у меня́ ко́лет па́льцы; **his nose ~d with the cold** моро́з пощи́пывал ему́ нос; (*burn*) горе́ть (гори́т) *impf.*; (*jingle*) звене́ть (-ни́т) *impf.* в уша́х (*person* у+*g.*).

tinker ['tɪŋkə(r)] *n.* ме́дник, луди́льщик; *v.i.* (*work as a* ~) рабо́тать *impf.* луди́льщиком; ~ **with** вози́ться (вожу́сь, во́зишься) *impf.* с+*i.*

tinkle ['tɪŋk(ə)l] *n.* звон, звя́канье; *v.i.*(*t.*) звене́ть (-ню́, -ни́шь) *impf.* (+*i.*); звя́кать *impf.*, звя́кнуть *pf.* +*i.*; (*on instrument*) бренча́ть (-чу́, -чи́шь) *impf.* (**on** на+*p.*).

tinny ['tɪnɪ] *adj.* (*thin*) то́нкий (-нок, -нка́, -нко, то́нки́); (*piano etc.*) издаю́щий металли́ческий звук; (*sound*) металли́ческий. **tin-opener** *n.* консе́рвный нож (-а́).

tinsel ['tɪns(ə)l] *n.* мишура́ (*also fig.*); *attr.* мишу́рный.

tinsmith ['tɪnsmɪθ] *n.* жестя́нщик.

tint [tɪnt] *n.* отте́нок (-нка); (*faint* ~) бле́дный тон (*pl.* -а́); *v.t.* слегка́ окра́шивать *impf.*, окра́сить *pf.* **tinted** *adj.* окра́шенный; ~ **glasses** тёмные очки́ (-ко́в) *pl.*

tiny ['taɪnɪ] *adj.* о́чень ма́ленький; кро́шечный (*coll.*).

tip¹ [tɪp] *n.* (*end*) ко́нчик; (*of stick*, *spear etc.*) наконе́чник; *v.t.* приставля́ть *impf.*, приста́вить *pf.* наконе́чник к+*d.*; **be on the ~ of s.o.'s tongue** верте́ться (ве́ртится) *impf.* на языке́ у+*g.*

tip² [tɪp] *n.* (*money*) чаевы́е (-ы́х) *pl.*; (*advice*) сове́т, намёк; (*private information*) све́дения *nt.pl.*, полу́ченные ча́стным о́бразом; (*dump*) сва́лка; (*slight push*) лёгкий толчо́к (-чка́); *v.t.* & *i.* наклоня́ть(ся) *impf.*, наклони́ть(ся) (-ню́(сь), -нишь(ся)) *pf.*; *v.t.* (*hit lightly*) слегка́ ударя́ть *impf.*, уда́рить *pf.*; (*give* ~) дава́ть (даю́, даёшь) *impf.*, дать (дам, дашь, даст, дади́м; дал, -ла́, да́ло́, -и) *pf.* (*person* +*d.*; *money* деньги на чай, *information* ча́стную информа́цию); ~ **out** выва́ливать *impf.*, вы́валить *pf.*;~ **over, up** (*v.t.* & *i.*) опроки́дывать(ся) *impf.*, опроки́нуть(ся) *pf.*; ~ **up, back** (*seat*) отки́дывать *impf.*, отки́нуть *pf.*; ~ **the scales** (*fig.*) реша́ть *impf.*, реши́ть *pf.* исхо́д де́ла.

tipple ['tɪp(ə)l] *n.* (алкого́льный) напи́ток (-тка); *v.i.* выпива́ть *impf.*; *v.t.* & *i.* попива́ть *impf.* (*coll.*). **tippler** *n.* пья́ница *c.g.*

tipster ['tɪpstə(r)] *n.* жучо́к (-чка́).

tipsy ['tɪpsɪ] *adj.* подвы́пивший.

tiptoe ['tɪptəʊ] *n.*: **on** ~ на цы́почках.

tip-top ['tɪptɒp] *adj.* первокла́ссный, превосхо́дный.

tip-up ['tɪpʌp] *adj.*: ~ **lorry** самосва́л.

tirade [taɪ'reɪd, tɪ-] *n.* тира́да.

tire¹ ['taɪə(r)] *n.* (*metal*) колёсный банда́ж (-а́).

tire² ['taɪə(r)] *v.t.* (*weary*) утомля́ть *impf.*, утоми́ть *pf.*; (*bore*) надоеда́ть *impf.*, надое́сть (-е́м, -е́шь, -е́ст, -еди́м; -е́л) *pf.* +*d.*; *v.i.* утомля́ться *impf.*, утоми́ться *pf.*; устава́ть (устаю́, -аёшь) *impf.*, уста́ть (-а́ну, -а́нешь) *pf.* **tired** *adj.* уста́лый, утомлённый; **be ~ of, I am ~ of him** он мне надое́л; **I am ~ of playing** мне надое́ло игра́ть; ~ **out** измý-ченный. **tiredness** *n.* уста́лость. **tireless** *adj.* неутоми́мый. **tiresome** *adj.* утоми́тельный, надое́дливый. **tiring** *adj.* утоми́тельный.

tiro ['taɪə,rəʊ] *n.* нович́ок (-чка́).

tissue ['tɪʃuː, 'tɪsjuː] *n.* ткань; (*handkerchief*) бума́жная салфе́тка. **tissue-paper** *n.* папиро́сная бума́га.

tit¹ [tɪt] *n.* (*bird*) сини́ца.

tit² [tɪt] *n.*: ~ **for tat** зуб за́ зуб.

titanic [taɪ'tænɪk, tɪ-] *adj.* (*huge*) титани́ческий.

titbit ['tɪtbɪt] *n.* ла́комый кусо́к (-ска́); (*news*) пика́нтная но́вость.

tithe [taɪð] *n.* деся́тая часть (*pl.* -ти, -те́й); (*hist.*) десяти́на.

titillate ['tɪtɪˌleɪt] *v.t.* щекота́ть (-очу́, -о́чешь) *impf.*, по~ *pf.*; прия́тно возбужда́ть *impf.*, возбуди́ть *pf.*

titivate ['tɪtɪˌveɪt] *v.t.* & *i.* (*coll.*) прихора́шивать(ся) *impf.* (*coll.*).

title ['taɪt(ə)l] *n.* (*of book etc.*) назва́ние; (*heading*) загла́вие; (*rank*) ти́тул, зва́ние; (*cin.*) титр; (*sport*) зва́ние чемпио́на; ~ **role** загла́вная роль (*pl.* -ли, -ле́й). **titled** *adj.* титуло́ванный. **title-deed** *n.* докуме́нт, да́ющий пра́во со́бственности. **title-holder** *n.* чемпио́н. **title-page** *n.* ти́тульный лист (*pl.* -ы́).

titter ['tɪtə(r)] *n.* хихи́канье; *v.i.* хихи́кать *impf.*, хихи́кнуть *pf.*

tittle ['tɪt(ə)l] *n.* чу́точка, ка́пелька. **tittle-tattle** *n.* болтовня́ (*coll.*).

titular ['tɪtjʊlə(r)] *adj.* номина́льный; титуло́ванный.

to [tə, *before a vowel* tʊ, *emph.* tuː] *prep.* (*town, a country, theatre, school, etc.*) в+*a.*; (*the sea, the moon, the ground, post-office, meeting, concert, north, etc.*) на+*a.*; (*the doctor*; *towards, up* ~; ~ *one's surprise etc.*) к+*d.*; (*with accompaniment of*) под+*a.*; (*in toast*) за+*a.*; (*time*): **ten minutes ~ three** без десяти́ три; (*compared with*) в сравне́нии с+*i.*; **it is ten ~ one that** де́вять из десяти́ за то, что; ~ **the left (right)** нале́во (напра́во); (*in order to*) что́бы+*inf.*; *adv.*: **shut the door ~** закро́йте дверь; **come ~** приходи́ть (-ожу́, -о́дишь) *impf.*, прийти́ (-йду́, -йдёшь; пришёл, -шла́) *pf.* в созна́ние; **bring ~** приводи́ть (-ожу́, -о́дишь) *impf.*, привести́ (-еду́, -едёшь; -ёл, -ела́) *pf.* в созна́ние; ~ **and fro** взад и вперёд.

toad [təʊd] *n.* жа́ба. **toadstool** *n.* пога́нка.

toady ['təʊdɪ] *n.* подхали́м; *v.t.* льсти́ть *impf.*, по~ *pf.* +*d.*; *v.t.* & *i.* низкопокло́нничать *impf.* (**to** пе́ред+*i.*).

toast [təʊst] *n.* (*bread*) поджа́ренный хлеб; (*drink*) тост; ~ **rack** подста́вка для поджа́ренного хлеба; *v.t.* (*bread*) поджа́ривать *impf.*, поджа́рить *pf.*; (*drink*) пить (пью, пьёшь; пил, -а́, -о) *impf.*, вы́~ *pf.* за здоро́вье+*g.* **toaster** *n.* то́стер.

toastmaster ['təʊst,mɑːstə(r)] *n.* тамада́ *m.*

tobacco [tə'bækəʊ] *n.* таба́к; *attr.* таба́чный; ~ **pouch** кисе́т. **tobacconist** *n.* торго́вец (-вца) таба́чными изде́лиями; **~'s (shop)** таба́чный магази́н.

toboggan [tə'bɒgən] *n.* сала́зки (-зок) *pl.*; *v.i.* ката́ться *impf.* на сала́зках.

today [tə'deɪ] *adv.* сего́дня; (*nowadays*) в на́ши дни; *n.* сего́дняшний день (дня) *m.*; **~'s newspaper** сего́дняшняя газе́та; **the writers of ~** совреме́нные писа́тели *m.pl.*

toddle ['tɒd(ə)l] *v.i.* ковыля́ть *impf.* (*coll.*); (*learn to walk*) учи́ться (учу́сь, у́чишься) *impf.* ходи́ть; (*stroll*) прогу́ливаться *impf.* **toddler** *n.* ребёнок (-нка; *pl.* де́ти, -те́й), начина́ющий ходи́ть; малы́ш (-а́) (*coll.*).

toddy ['tɒdɪ] *n.* горя́чий пунш.

to-do [tə'duː] *n.* сумато́ха, суета́.

toe [təʊ] *n.* па́лец (-льца) но́ги; (*of sock etc.*) носо́к (-ска́); **from top to ~** с головы́ до пят; *v.t.* (*touch with ~*) каса́ться *impf.*, косну́ться *pf.* носко́м+*g.*; ~ **the line** (*fig.*) подчиня́ться *impf.*, подчини́ться *pf.* тре́бованиям. **toecap** *n.* носо́к (-ска́).

toffee ['tɒfɪ] *n.* (*substance*) ири́с; (*a* ~) ири́ска (*coll.*).

toga ['təʊgə] *n.* то́га.

together [tə'geðə(r)] *adv.* вме́сте, сообща́; (*simultaneously*) одновре́ме́нно; ~ **with** вме́сте с+*i.*; **all ~** все вме́сте; **get ~** собира́ть(ся) *impf.*, собра́ть(ся) (-беру́, -берёшь; -брал(ся), -брала́(сь), -бра́ло, -бра́ло́сь) *pf.*; **join ~** объединя́ть(ся) *impf.*, объедини́ть(ся) *pf.* (**with** с+*i.*

toggle ['tɒg(ə)l] *n.* (*button*) продолгова́тая (деревя́нная) пу́говица.

toil [tɔɪl] *n.* тяжёлый труд; *v.i.* труди́ться (-ужу́сь, -у́дишься) *impf.*; (*drag o.s. along*) тащи́ться (тащу́сь, -щишься) *impf.* **toiler** *n.* тру́женик, -ица.

toilet ['tɔɪlɪt] *n.* туале́т; ~ **paper** туале́тная бума́га; ~ **water** туале́тная вода́ (*a.* во́ду). **toiletries** ['tɔɪlɪtrɪz] *n.pl.* туале́тные принадле́жности *f.pl.*

token ['təʊkən] *n.* (*sign*) знак; (*keepsake*) пода́рок (-рка) на па́мять; (*coupon, counter*) тало́н, жето́н; **as a ~ of** в знак+*g.*; *attr.* символи́ческий; ~ **resistance** ви́димость сопротивле́ния; **by the same ~** (*similarly*) к тому́ же; (*moreover*) кро́ме того́.

Tokyo ['təʊkjəʊ, -kɪ,əʊ] *n.* То́кио *m.indecl.*

tolerable ['tɒlərəb(ə)l] *adj.* (*bearable*) терпи́мый; (*satisfactory*) удовлетвори́тельный, сно́сный (*coll.*). **tolerance** *n.* терпи́мость; (*tech.*) до́пуск; (*med.*) толера́нтность. **tolerant** *adj.* терпи́мый; (*med.*) толера́нтный. **tolerate** *v.t.* терпе́ть (-плю́, -пишь) *impf.*, по~ *pf.*; (*allow*) допуска́ть *impf.*, допусти́ть (-ущу́, -у́стишь) *pf.*; (*med.*) быть толера́нтным. **tole'ration** *n.* терпи́мость.

toll[1] [təʊl] *v.t.* (ме́дленно и ме́рно) ударя́ть *impf.*, уда́рить *pf.* в ко́локол; *v.i.* звони́ть *impf.*, по~ *pf.* (ме́дленно и ме́рно).

toll[2] [təʊl] *n.* (*duty*) по́шлина; **take its ~** наноси́ть (-о́сит) *impf.*, нанести́ (-сёт; нанёс, -есла́) *pf.* тяжёлый уро́н. **toll-bridge** *n.* пла́тный мост (мо́ста́, *loc.* -у́; *pl.* -ы́). **toll-gate** *n.* заста́ва, где взима́ется сбор.

tom(-cat) [tɒm] *n.* кот (-а́).

tomahawk ['tɒmə,hɔːk] *n.* томага́вк; *v.t.* бить (бью, бьёшь) *impf.*, по~ *pf.* томага́вком.

tomato [tə'mɑːtəʊ] *n.* помидо́р; *attr.* тома́тный.

tomb [tuːm] *n.* моги́ла. **tombstone** *n.* моги́льная плита́ (*pl.* -ты).

tomboy ['tɒmbɔː] *n.* сорване́ц (-нца́).

tome [təʊm] *n.* больша́я (тяжёлая) кни́га.

tomfoolery [tɒm'fuːlərɪ] *n.* дура́чества *nt.pl.*

tommy-gun ['tɒmɪ,gʌn] *n.* автома́т.

tomorrow [tə'mɒrəʊ] *adv.* за́втра; *n.* за́втрашний день (дня) *m.*; ~ **morning** за́втра у́тром; **the day after ~** послеза́втра; **see you ~** (*coll.*) до за́втра.

tom-tit ['tɒmtɪt] *n.* сини́ца.

tom-tom ['tɒmtɒm] *n.* тамта́м.

ton [tʌn] *n.* то́нна.

tonal ['təʊn(ə)l] *adj.* тона́льный. **tonality** [tə'nælɪtɪ] *n.* тона́льность. **tone** *n.* тон (*pl.* -ы (*mus. & fig.*), -а́ (*colour*)); (*atmosphere, mood*) атмосфе́ра, настрое́ние; (*med.*) то́нус; **~ control** регуля́ция те́мбра; *v.t.* придава́ть (-даю́, -даёшь) *impf.*, прида́ть (-а́м, а́шь, -а́ст, -ади́м; при́дал, -а́, -о) *pf.* жела́тельный тон+*d.*; *v.i.* (*harmonize*) гармони́ровать *impf.* (**with** с+*i.*); **~ down** смягча́ть(ся) *impf.*, смягчи́ть(ся) *pf.*; **~ up** уси́ливать *impf.*, уси́лить *pf.*; (*med.*) тонизи́ровать *impf. & pf.* **tone-arm** *n.* звукоснима́тель *m.* **tone-deaf** *adj.* с сла́бым музыка́льным слу́хом.

tongs [tɒŋz] *n.* щипцы́ (-цо́в) *pl.*

tongue [tʌŋ] *n.* (*var. senses*) язы́к (-а́); (*of shoe*) язычо́к (-чка́); **give ~** (*of dog*) подава́ть (-аю́, -аёшь) *impf.*, подда́ть (-а́м, -а́шь, -а́ст, -ади́м; по́ддал, -а́, -о) *pf.* го́лос; (*of person*) гро́мко говори́ть *impf.*; **hold one's ~** держа́ть (-жу́, -жишь) *impf.* язы́к за зуба́ми; **lose one's ~** прогла́тывать *impf.*, проглоти́ть (-очу́, -о́тишь) *pf.* язы́к; **put out one's ~** пока́зывать *impf.*, показа́ть (-ажу́, -а́жешь) *pf.* язы́к. **tongue-in-cheek** *adj.* с насме́шкой, ирони́чески. **tongue-tied** *adj.* косноязы́чный. **tongue-twister** *n.* скорогово́рка.

tonic ['tɒnɪk] *n.* (*med.*) тонизи́рующее сре́дство; (*mus.*) то́ника; *adj.* (*med.*) тонизи́рующий; (*mus.*) тони́ческий.

tonight [tə'naɪt] *adv.* сего́дня ве́чером; *n.* сего́дняшний ве́чер.

tonnage ['tʌnɪdʒ] *n.* тонна́ж, грузовмести́мость; (*charge*) кора́бельный сбор.

tonsil ['tɒns(ə)l, -sɪl] *n.* минда́лина. **tonsi'llitis** *n.* анги́на.

tonsure ['tɒnsjə(r), 'tɒnʃə(r)] *n.* тонзу́ра; *v.t.* выбрива́ть *impf.*, вы́брить (-рею, -реешь) *pf.* тонзу́ру+*d.*

too [tuː] *adv.* сли́шком; (*also*) та́кже, то́же; (*very*) о́чень; (*indeed*) действи́тельно; (*moreover*) к тому́ же; **none ~** не сли́шком.

tool [tuːl] *n.* инструме́нт; (*machine-~*) стано́к (-нка́); (*implement*; *fig.*) ору́дие. **tool-box** *n.* я́щик с инструме́нтами.

toot [tuːt] *n.* гудо́к (-дка́); *v.i.* гуде́ть (-ди́т) *impf.*; (*give a hoot*) дава́ть (даю́, даёшь) *impf.*, дать (дам, дашь, даст, дади́м; дал, -а́, да́ло́, -и) *pf.* гудо́к *v.t.* (*blow*) труби́ть *impf.* в+*a.*

tooth [tuːθ] *n.* зуб (*pl.* -ы, -о́в); (*tech.*) зубе́ц (-бца́); *attr.* зубно́й; **false teeth** вставны́е зу́бы (-бо́в) *pl.*; **first ~** моло́чный зуб (*pl.* -ы, -о́в); **loose ~** шата́ющийся зуб (*pl.* -ы, -о́в); **second ~** постоя́нный зуб (*pl.* -ы, -о́в); **~ and nail** (*fiercely*) не на жизнь, а на смерть; (*energetically*) энерги́чно; **in the teeth of** (*in defiance of*) напереко́р+*d.*; (*directly against*) пря́мо про́тив+*g.*; **have one's teeth attended to** лечи́ть (-чу́, -чишь) зу́бы (-бо́в) *pl.*; **he has cut a ~** у него́ проре́зался зуб. **toothache** *n.* зубна́я боль. **toothbrush** *n.* зубна́я щётка. **tooth-comb** *n.* ча́стый гре́бень (-бня) *m.* **toothed** *adj.* зубча́тый. **toothless** *adj.* беззу́бый. **toothpaste** *n.* зубна́я па́ста. **toothpick** *n.* зубочи́стка. **toothy** *adj.* зуба́стый (*coll.*).

top¹ [tɒp] *n.* (*toy*) волчо́к (-чка́).

top² [tɒp] *n.* (*of object*; *fig.*) верх (-а(у), *loc.* -у́; *pl.* -и́); (*of hill etc.*) верши́на; (*of tree*) верху́шка; (*of head*) маку́шка; (*of milk*) сли́вки (-вок) *pl.*; (*lid*) кры́шка; (*upper part*) ве́рхняя часть (*pl.* -ти, -те́й); **~ copy** оригина́л; **~ drawer** (*fig.*) вы́сшее о́бщество; **~ hat** цили́ндр; **(at) ~ level** на вы́сшем у́ровне; (*of high rank*) высокопоста́вленный; **on ~ of** (*position*) на+*p.*, сверх+*g.*; (*on to*) на+*a.*; **on ~ of everything** сверх всего́; **from ~ to bottom** све́рху до́низу; **at the ~ of one's voice** во всё го́рло; **at ~ speed** во весь опо́р; *adj.* ве́рхний, вы́сший, са́мый высо́кий; (*foremost*) пе́рвый; *v.t.* (*cover*) покрыва́ть *impf.*, покры́ть (-ро́ю, -ро́ешь) *pf.*; (*reach ~ of*) поднима́ться *impf.*, подня́ться (-нимусь, -ни́мешься; -ня́лся́, -няла́сь) *pf.* на верши́ну+*g.*; (*excel*) превосходи́ть (-ожу́, -о́дишь) *impf.*, превзойти́ (-ойду́, -ойдёшь; -ошёл, -ошла́) *pf.*; (*cut ~ off*) обреза́ть *impf.*, обре́зать (-е́жу, -е́жешь) *pf.* верху́шку+*g.*; **~ off** заверша́ть *impf.*, заверши́ть *pf.*; **~ up** (*with liquid*) долива́ть *impf.*, доли́ть (-лью́, -льёшь; до́ли́л, -а́, -о) *pf.*; (*with grain etc.*) досыпа́ть *impf.*, досы́пать (-плю, -плешь) *pf.*

topaz ['təʊpæz] *n.* топа́з.

topcoat ['tɒpkəʊt] *n.* пальто́ *nt.indecl.*

top-heavy [tɒp'hevɪ] *adj.* переве́шивающий в свое́й ве́рхней ча́сти. **top-secret** *adj.* соверше́нно секре́тный.

topiary ['təʊpɪərɪ] *n.* иску́сство фигу́рной стри́жки кусто́в.

topic ['tɒpɪk] *n.* те́ма, предме́т. **topical** *adj.* актуа́льный; **~ question** злободне́вный вопро́с. **topi'cality** *n.* актуа́льность.

topknot ['tɒpnɒt] *n.* (*tuft, crest*) хохо́л (-хла́); (*knot*) пучо́к (-чка́) лент (*of ribbons*), воло́с (*of hair*).

topmost ['tɒpməʊst] *adj.* са́мый ве́рхний; са́мый ва́жный.

topographer [tə'pɒgrəfə(r)] *n.* топо́граф. **topographic(al)** [ˌtɒpə'græfɪk(ə)l] *adj.* топографи́ческий. **topography** *n.* топогра́фия.

topology [tə'pɒlədʒɪ] *n.* тополо́гия. **toponymy** [tə'pɒnɪmɪ] *n.* топони́мия.

topple ['tɒp(ə)l] *v.t. & i.* опроки́дывать(ся) *impf.*, опроки́нуть(ся) *pf.*; *v.i.* вали́ться (-лю́сь, -лишься) *impf.*, по~, с~ *pf.*

topsail ['tɒpseɪl, -s(ə)l] *n.* ма́рсель *m.*

topsoil ['tɒpsɔːl] *n.* ве́рхний слой по́чвы.

topsy-turvy [ˌtɒpsɪ'tɜːvɪ] *adj.* повёрнутый

вверх дном; (*disorderly*) беспоря́дочный; *adv.* вверх дном, ши́ворот-навы́ворот.

torch [tɔːtʃ] *n.* фа́кел; (*electric* ~) электри́ческий фона́рик; (*fig.*) све́точ. **torch-bearer** *n.* фа́кельщик, -ица. **torchlight** *n.* свет фа́кела, фона́рика.

toreador ['tɒrɪəˌdɔː(r)] *n.* тореадо́р.

torment ['tɔːment] *n.* муче́ние, му́ка; *v.t.* му́чить *impf.*, за~, из~ *pf.* **tor'mentor** *n.* мучи́тель *m.*

tornado [tɔː'neɪdəʊ] *n.* торна́до; (*fig.*) урага́н.

torpedo [tɔː'piːdəʊ] *n.* торпе́да; *v.t.* торпеди́ровать *impf.* & *pf.*; (*fig.*) прова́ливать *impf.*, провали́ть (-лю́, -лишь) *pf.* **torpedo-boat** *n.* торпе́дный ка́тер (*pl.* -а́).

torpid ['tɔːpɪd] *adj.* (*numb*) онеме́лый; (*sluggish*) вя́лый. **torpor** *n.* онеме́лость; апа́тия.

torque [tɔːk] *n.* (*phys.*, *mechanics*) враща́ющий моме́нт.

torrent ['tɒrənt] *n.* стреми́тельный пото́к; (*fig.*) пото́к; *pl.* ли́вень (-вня) *m.* **torrential** [tə'renʃ(ə)l] *adj.* теку́щий бы́стрым пото́ком; (*of rain*) проливно́й; (*fig.*) оби́льный.

torrid ['tɒrɪd] *adj.* зно́йный.

torsion ['tɔːʃ(ə)n] *n.* скру́ченность; (*tech.*) круче́ние.

torso ['tɔːsəʊ] *n.* ту́ловище; (*of statue*) торс.

tort [tɔːt] *n.* гражда́нское правонаруше́ние.

tortoise ['tɔːtəs] *n.* черепа́ха. **tortoise-shell** *n.* па́нцирь *m.* черепа́хи; (*material*) черепа́ха; *attr.* черепа́ховый; (*cat*) пёстрый.

tortuous ['tɔːtjʊəs] *adj.* изви́листый; (*evasive*) уклóнчивый.

torture ['tɔːtʃə(r)] *n.* пы́тка; *v.t.* пыта́ть *impf.*; (*torment*) му́чить *impf.*, за~, из~ *pf.*; (*distort*) искажа́ть *impf.*, искази́ть *pf.* **torturer** *n.* мучи́тель *m.*, пала́ч (-а́).

toss [tɒs] *n.* бросо́к (-ска́), броса́ние; ~ **of coin** подбра́сывание моне́ты, жеребьёвка (*fig.*); **win (lose) the** ~ (не) выпада́ть *impf.*, вы́пасть (-адет; -ал) *pf.* жре́бий *impers.* (**I won the** ~ мне вы́пал жре́бий); *v.t.* броса́ть *impf.*, бро́сить *pf.*; (*coin*) подбра́сывать *impf.*, подбро́сить *pf.*; (*rider*) сбра́сывать *impf.*, сбро́сить *pf.*; (*of bull etc.*) поднима́ть *impf.*, подня́ть (-ниму́, -ни́мешь; по́дня́л, -а́, -о) *pf.* на рога́; (*head*) вски́дывать *impf.*, вски́нуть *pf.*; (*salad*) переме́шивать *impf.*, перемеша́ть *pf.*; ~ **a pancake** перевора́чивать *impf.*, переверну́ть *pf.* блин, подбро́сив его́; *v.i.* (*of ship*) кача́ться *impf.*, качну́ться *pf.*; (*in bed*) мета́ться (мечу́сь, -чешься) *impf.*; ~ **aside, away** отбра́сывать *impf.*, отбро́сить *pf.*; ~ **off** (*work*) де́лать *impf.*, с~ *pf.* на́спех; (*drink*) пить (пью, пьёшь) *impf.*, вы́~ *pf.* за́лпом; ~ **up** броса́ть *impf.*, бро́сить *pf.* жре́бий. **toss-up** *n.* жеребьёвка; (*doubtful matter*): **it is a** ~ э́то ещё вопро́с.

tot[1] [tɒt] *n.* (*coll.*) (*child*) малы́ш (-а́) (*coll.*); (*glass*) ма́ленькая рю́мка; (*dram*) ма́ленький глото́к (-тка́).

tot[2] [tɒt]: ~ **up** (*coll.*) (*v.t.*) скла́дывать *impf.*, сложи́ть (-жу́, -жишь) *pf.*; (*v.i.*) равня́ться *impf.* (**to** +*d.*).

total ['təʊt(ə)l] *n.* ито́г, су́мма; *adj.* о́бщий; (*complete*) по́лный (-лон, -лна́, по́лно́); **in** ~ в це́лом, вме́сте; ~ **recall** фотографи́ческая па́мять; ~ **war** тота́льная война́; **sum** ~ о́бщая су́мма; *v.t.* подсчи́тывать *impf.*, подсчита́ть *pf.*; *v.i.* равня́ться *impf.*+*d.* **totalitarian** [təʊˌtælɪ'teərɪən] *adj.* тоталита́рный. **totality** [təʊ'tælɪtɪ] *n.* вся су́мма целико́м; **the** ~ **of** весь (вся, всё; все); **in** ~ в це́лом, вме́сте. **totali'zator** *n.* тотализа́тор. **totalize** *v.t.* соединя́ть *impf.*, соедини́ть *pf.* воеди́но. **totally** *adv.* соверше́нно.

totem ['təʊtəm] *n.* тоте́м. **totem-pole** *n.* тоте́мный столб (-а́).

totter ['tɒtə(r)] *v.i.* (*walk unsteadily*) ходи́ть (хожу́, хо́дишь) *indet.*, идти́ (иду́, идёшь; шёл, шла) *det.*, пойти́ (пойду́, -дёшь; пошёл, -шла́) *pf.* неве́рными шага́ми; (*reel*) шата́ться *impf.*; (*toddle*) ковыля́ть *impf.*; (*perish*) ги́бнуть (-б) *impf.*, по~ *pf.*

toucan ['tuːkən] *n.* тука́н.

touch [tʌtʃ] *n.* прикоснове́ние; (*sense*) осяза́ние; (*stroke of brush etc.*) штрих (-а́); (*mus. or art style*) туше́; (*of piano etc.*) уда́р; (*shade*) отте́нок (-нка); (*taste*) при́вкус; (*small amount*) чу́точка; (*of illness*) лёгкий при́ступ; (*sport*) пло́щадь (*pl.* -ди, -де́й) за боковы́ми ли́ниями; (*personal* ~) ли́чный подхо́д; **get in** ~ **with** свя́зываться *impf.*, связа́ться (-яжу́сь, -я́жешься) *pf.* с+*i.*; **keep in (lose)** ~ **with** подде́рживать *impf.*, поддержа́ть (-жу́, -жишь) *pf.* (теря́ть *impf.*, по~ *pf.*) связь, конта́кт с+*i.*; **put the finishing** ~**es to** отде́лывать *impf.*, отде́лать *pf.*; **common** ~ чу́вство ло́ктя; **to the** ~ на о́щупь; *v.t.* (*lightly*) прикаса́ться *impf.*, прикосну́ться *pf.* к+*d.*; каса́ться *impf.*, косну́ться *pf.*+*g.*; (*also disturb*; *affect*) тро́гать *impf.*, тро́нуть *pf.*; (*momentarily reach*) подска́кивать *impf.*, подскочи́ть (-чит) *pf.* до+*g.* (*coll.*); (*be comparable with*) идти́ (иду́, идёшь; шёл, -шла) *impf.* в сравне́нии с+*i.*; *v.i.* (*be contiguous*; *come into contact*) соприкаса́ться *impf.*, соприкосну́ться *pf.*; ~ **down** приземля́ться *impf.*, приземи́ться *pf.*; ~ **off** (*provoke*) вызыва́ть *impf.*, вы́звать (вы́зову, -вешь) *pf.*; ~ **(up)on** (*fig.*) каса́ться *impf.*, косну́ться *pf.*+*g.*; ~ **up** поправля́ть *impf.*, попра́вить *pf.*; ~ **wood!** не сгла́зить бы! **touchdown** *n.* поса́дка. **touched** *adj.* тро́нутый. **touchiness** *n.* оби́дчивость. **touching** *adj.* тро́гательный. **touch-line** *n.* бокова́я ли́ния. **touchstone** *n.* пробирный ка́мень (-мня; *pl.* -мни, -мне́й) *m.* **touch-type** *v.i.* печа́тать *impf.*, напеча́тать *pf.* вслепу́ю. **touch-typing** *n.* слепо́й ме́тод маши́нописи. **touchy** *adj.* оби́дчивый.

tough [tʌf] *adj.* жёсткий (-ток, -тка́, -тко); (*durable*) про́чный (-чен, -чна́, -чно, про́чны́); (*strong*) кре́пкий (-пок, -пка́, -пко);

(*difficult*) тру́дный (-ден, -дна́, -дно, тру́дны́); (*hardy*) выно́сливый; *n.* хулига́н, банди́т. **toughen** *v.t.* & *i.* де́лать(ся) *impf.*, с~ *pf.* жёстким. **toughness** *n.* жёсткость; (*durability*) про́чность.

toupee ['tu:peɪ] *n.* небольшо́й пари́к (-а́).

tour [tʊə(r)] *n.* (*journey*) путеше́ствие, пое́здка; (*excursion*) экску́рсия; (*of artistes*) турне́ *nt.indecl.*; (*of duty*) объе́зд; ~ **de force** проявле́ние си́лы (*strength*), ло́вкости (*skill*); *v.i.* (*t.*) соверша́ть *impf.*, соверши́ть *pf.* путеше́ствие, турне́, объе́зд (по+*d.*). **tourism** *n.* тури́зм. **tourist** *n.* тури́ст, -ка; ~ **class** второ́й класс.

tournament ['tʊənəmənt] *n.* турни́р. **tourney** *v.i.* уча́ствовать *impf.* в турни́ре.

tourniquet ['tʊənɪˌkeɪ] *n.* турнике́т.

tousle ['taʊz(ə)l] *v.t.* взъеро́шивать *impf.*, взъеро́шить *pf.* (*coll.*).

tout [taʊt] *n.* навя́зчивый торго́вец (-вца); (*of horses*) челове́к (*pl.* лю́ди, -де́й, -дям, -дьми) добыва́ющий и прода́ющий све́дения о лошадя́х пе́ред ска́чками; *v.t.* навя́зывать *impf.*, навяза́ть (-яжу́, -я́жешь) *pf.* (*thing* +*a.*; *person* +*d.*).

tow¹ [təʊ] *v.t.* букси́ровать *impf.*; *n.* букси-ро́вка; **on** ~ на букси́ре.

tow² [təʊ] *n.* (*textile*) па́кля.

towards [tə'wɔ:dz, twɔ:dz, tɔ:dz] *prep.* (*in direction of*) (по направле́нию) к+*d.*; (*fig.*) к+*d.*; (*for*) для+*g.*

towel ['taʊəl] *n.* полоте́нце. **towelling** *n.* махро́вая ткань. **towel-rail** *n.* ве́шалка для полоте́нец.

tower ['taʊə(r)] *n.* ба́шня; (*tech.*) вы́шка; (*fig.*): ~ **of strength** надёжная опо́ра; *v.i.* вы́ситься *impf.*, возвыша́ться *impf.* (**above** над+*i.*). **towering** *adj.* (*high*) высо́кий (-о́к, -ока́, -о́ко́); (*rising up*) возвыша́ющийся; (*furious*) нейстовый.

town [taʊn] *n.* го́род (*pl.* -а́); *attr.* городско́й; ~ **clerk** секрета́рь *m.* городско́й корпора́ции; ~ **council** городско́й сове́т, муниципалите́т; ~ **councillor** член городско́го сове́та; ~ **crier** глаша́тай; ~ **hall** ра́туша, мэ́рия; ~ **planning** градострои́тельство. **townsman, -swoman** *n.* горожа́нин (*pl.* -а́не, -а́н), -а́нка.

tow-path ['təʊpɒ:θ] *n.* бечевни́к (-а́). **tow-rope** *n.* букси́р, бечева́ *no pl.*

toxic ['tɒksɪk] *adj.* ядови́тый, токси́ческий. **toxin** *n.* яд (-а(у)); (*med.*) токси́н.

toy [tɔɪ] *n.* игру́шка; ~ **dog** ма́ленькая ко́мнатная соба́чка; ~ **soldier** оловя́нный солда́тик; *v.i.*: ~ **with** (*sth. in hands*) верте́ть (верчу́, -ртишь) *impf.* в рука́х; (*trifle with*) игра́ть *impf.* (с)+*i.*

trace¹ [treɪs] *n.* (*track, mark*) след (*pl.* -ы́); (*small amount*) небольшо́е коли́чество; ~ **element** микроэлеме́нт; *v.t.* (*track* (*down*), *trace* (*through*)) просле́живать *impf.*, проследи́ть *pf.*; (*make copy*) кальки́ровать *impf.*, с~ *pf.*; ~ **back** (*v.i.*) восходи́ть (-ожу́, -о́дишь) *impf.* (**to** к+*d.*); ~ **out** (*plan*) набра́сывать *impf.*, наброса́ть *pf.*; (*map, diagram*) черти́ть (черчу́, -ртишь) *impf.*, на~ *pf.*

trace² [treɪs] *n.* (*of harness*) постро́мка.

tracery ['treɪsərɪ] *n.* узо́р. **tracing** *n.* (*copy*) чертёж (-а́) на ка́льке. **tracing-paper** *n.* ка́лька.

trachea [trə'ki:ə, 'treɪkɪə] *n.* трахе́я.

track [træk] *n.* (*path*) доро́жка, тропи́нка; (*mark*) след (*pl.* -ы́); (*rail.*) путь (-ти́, -тём) *m.*, колея́; (*sport*) трек, доро́жка; (*on tape*) (звукова́я) доро́жка; (*on record*) за́пись; ~ **events** соревнова́ния *nt.pl.* по бегу́; ~ **suit** трениро́вочный костю́м; **off the** ~ на ло́жном пути́; (*fig.*) отклони́вшийся от те́мы; **off the beaten** ~ в глуши́; **be on the** ~ **of** пресле́довать *impf.*; **go off the** ~ (*fig.*) отклоня́ться *impf.*, отклони́ться (-ню́сь, -нишься) *pf.* от те́мы; **keep** ~ **of** следи́ть *impf.* за+*i.*; **lose** ~ **of** теря́ть *impf.*, по~ *pf.* след+*g.*; *v.t.* просле́живать *impf.*, проследи́ть *pf.*; ~ **down** высле́живать *impf.*, вы́следить *pf.*

tract¹ [trækt] *n.* (*expanse*) простра́нство; (*anat.*) тракт.

tract² [trækt] *n.* (*treatise*) тракта́т; (*pamphlet*) брошю́ра.

tractability [ˌtræktə'bɪlɪtɪ] *n.* (*of person*) сгово́рчивость; (*of material*) ко́вкость. **'tractable** *adj.* (*person*) сгово́рчивый; (*material*) ко́вкий (-вок, -вка́, -вко). **'traction** *n.* тя́га; (*therapy*) тра́кция. **traction-engine** *n.* тра́ктор-тяга́ч (-а́). **'tractor** *n.* тра́ктор; ~ **driver** трактори́ст.

trade [treɪd] *n.* торго́вля; (*occupation*) профе́ссия, ремесло́ (*pl.* -ёсла, -ёсел, -ёслам); (*collect.*) торго́вцы *m.pl.*; ~ **mark** фабри́чная ма́рка; (*fig.*) отличи́тельный знак; ~ **name** (*of firm*) назва́ние фи́рмы; ~ **secret** секре́т фи́рмы; ~ **union** профсою́з; ~ **wind** пасса́т; *v.i.* торгова́ть *impf.* (**in** +*i.*); *v.t.* (*swap like things*) обме́ниваться *impf.*, обменя́ться *pf.*+*i.*; (~ *for sth. different*) обме́нивать *impf.*, обменя́ть *pf.* (**for** на+*a.*); ~ **in** сдава́ть (сдаю́, сдаёшь) *impf.*, сдать (сдам, сдашь, сдаст, сдади́м; сдал, -а́, -о) *pf.* в счёт поку́пки но́вого; ~ **on** (*exploit*) испо́льзовать *impf.* & *pf.* **trader, tradesman** *n.* торго́вец (-вца). **trade-unionist** *n.* член профсою́за. **trading** *n.* торго́вля, комме́рция; *attr.* торго́вый; ~ **station** факто́рия.

tradition [trə'dɪʃ(ə)n] *n.* тради́ция; (*legend*) преда́ние. **traditional** *adj.* традицио́нный (-нен, -нна). **traditionalism** *n.* приве́рженность к тради́циям. **traditionally** *adv.* по тради́ции.

traduce [trə'dju:s] *v.t.* клевета́ть (-ещу́, -е́щешь) *impf.*, на~ *pf.* на+*a.* **traducer** *n.* клеветни́к (-а́), -и́ца.

traffic ['træfɪk] *n.* движе́ние; (*trade*) торго́вля; (*transportation*) тра́нспорт; ~ **island** острово́к (-вка́) безопа́сности; ~ **jam** про́бка; *v.i.*

торговáть *impf.* (**in** +*i.*). **trafficator** *n.* указáтель *m.* поворóта. **trafficker** *n.* торгóвец (-вца) (**in** +*i.*). **traffic-lights** *n.* светофóр.

tragedian [trəˈdʒiːdɪən] *n.* трáгик. **tragedy** [ˈtrædʒɪdɪ] *n.* трагéдия. **tragic** [ˈtrædʒɪk] *adj.* трагúческий. **tragicomedy** [ˌtrædʒɪˈkɒmɪdɪ] *n.* трагикомéдия.

trail [treɪl] *n.* (*trace, track*) след (*pl.* -ы́); (*path*) тропúнка; (*course, road*) путь (-тú, -тём) *m.*; *v.t.* (*track*) выслéживать *impf.*, вы́следить *pf.*; *v.t.* & *i.* (*drag*) таскáть(ся) *indet.*, тащúть(ся) (-щу́(сь), -щишь(ся)) *det.*; волочúть(ся) (-чу́(сь), -чишь(ся)) *impf.* **trailer** *n.* (*on vehicle*) прицéп; (*plant*) стéлющееся растéние; (*cin.*) (кино)рóлик.

train [treɪn] *n.* пóезд (*pl.* -á); (*of dress*) шлейф; (*retinue*) свúта; (*mil.*) обóз; (*convoy*) каравáн; (*series*) цепь (*loc.* -пú; *pl.* -пи, -пéй); *v.t.* (*instruct*) обучáть *impf.*, обучúть (-чу́, -чишь) *pf.* (**in** +*d.*); (*prepare*) готóвить *impf.* (**for** к+*d.*); (*sport*) тренировáть *impf.*, на~ *pf.*; (*animals*) дрессировáть *impf.*, вы́~ *pf.*; (*break in*) объезжáть *impf.*, объéздить *pf.*; (*aim, point*) направлять *impf.*, напрáвить *pf.*; (*plant*) направлять *impf.*, напрáвить *pf.* рост+*g.*; *v.i.* приготáвливаться *impf.*, приготóвиться *pf.* (**for** к+*d.*); (*sport*) тренировáться *impf.*, на~ *pf.* **traiˈnee** *n.* стажёр, практикáнт. **trainer** *n.* инстру́ктор; (*sport*) трéнер; (*of animals*) дрессирóвщик; *pl.* (*shoes*) адидáски (-сок), кроссóвки (-вок) *pl.* **training** *n.* обучéние; (*sport*) тренирóвка; (*of animals*) дрессирóвка; ~ **apparatus** тренажёр. **training-college** *n.* (*teachers'*) педагогúческий институ́т, пединститу́т. **training-school** *n.* специáльное учúлище.

traipse [treɪps] *v.i.* таскáться *indet.*, тащúться (-щу́сь, -щишся) *det.*

trait [treɪ, treɪt] *n.* (характéрная) чертá; штрих (-á).

traitor [ˈtreɪtə(r)] *n.* предáтель *m.*, измéнник. **traitorous** *adj.* предáтельский. **traitress** *n.* предáтельница, измéнница.

trajectory [trəˈdʒektərɪ, ˈtrædʒɪk-] *n.* траектóрия.

tram [træm] *n.* трамвáй; ~ **driver** вагоновожáтый *sb.* **tramline** *n.* трамвáйная лúния.

trammel [ˈtræm(ə)l] *n.* (*net*) нéвод (*pl.* -á), трал; (*fig.*) помéха, препятствие; *v.t.* (*fig.*) препятствовать *impf.*, вос~ *pf.*+*d.*

tramp [træmp] *n.* (*vagrant*) бродяга *m.*; (*tread*) тóпот; (*journey on foot*) путешéствие пешкóм; *v.i.* (*of vagrant*) бродяжничать *impf.*; (*go with heavy tread*) тóпать *impf.*; (*go on foot*) ходúть (хожу́, хóдишь) *indet.*, идтú (иду́, идёшь; шёл, шла) *det.*, пойтú (пойду́, -дёшь; пошёл, -шлá) *pf.* пешкóм. **trample** *v.t.* топтáть (топчу́, -чешь) *impf.*, по~, ис~ *pf.*; ~ **down** вытáптывать *impf.*, вы́топтать (-пчу, -пчешь) *pf.*; ~ **on** (*fig.*) попирáть *impf.*, попрáть (-ру́, -рёшь) *pf.*

trampoline [ˈtræmpəˌliːn] *n.* бату́т, бату́д. **trampolining** *n.* бату́тный спорт. **trampolinist** *n.* батутúст, ~ка.

trance [trɑːns] *n.* транс; (*rapture*) состояние экстáза.

tranquil [ˈtræŋkwɪl] *adj.* спокóйный. **tranˈquillity** *n.* спокóйствие. **tranquillize** *v.t.* успокáивать *impf.*, успокóить *pf.* **tranquillizer** *n.* транквилизáтор.

transact [trænˈzækt, trɑːn-, -ˈsækt] *v.t.* (*business*) вестú (веду́, -дёшь; вёл, -á) *impf.*; (*a deal*) заключáть *impf.*, заключúть *pf.* **transaction** *n.* дéло (*pl.* -лá), сдéлка; *pl.* (*publications*) труды́ *m.pl.*; (*minutes*) протокóлы *m.pl.*

transatlantic [ˌtrænzətˈlæntɪk, ˌtrɑːn-, -sətˈlæntɪk] *adj.* трансатлантúческий.

Transcaucasia [ˌtrænskɔːˈkeɪzjə] *n.* Закавкáзье.

transceiver [trænˈsiːvə(r), trɑːn-] *n.* приёмо-передáтчик.

transcend [trænˈsend, trɑːn-] *v.t.* преступáть *impf.*, преступúть (-плю́, -пишь) *pf.* предéлы+*g.*; (*excel*) превосходúть (-ожу́, -óдишь) *impf.*, превзойтú (-ойду́, -ойдёшь; -ошёл, -ошлá) *pf.* **transcendency** *n.* превосхóдство. **transcendent** *adj.* превосхóдный. **transcenˈdental** *adj.* (*philos.*) трансцендентáльный.

transcontinental [trænzˌkɒntɪˈnent(ə)l, trɑːnz, træns-, trɑːns-] *adj.* трансконтинентáльный.

transcribe [trænˈskraɪb, trɑːn-] *v.t.* (*copy out*) перепúсывать *impf.*, переписáть (-ишу́, -úшешь) *pf.*; (*shorthand*) расшифрóвывать *impf.*, расшифровáть *pf.*; (*mus.*) аранжúровать *impf.*; (*phon.*) транскрибúровать *impf.* & *pf.* **transcript** [ˈtrænskrɪpt, ˈtrɑːn-] *n.* кóпия; (*shorthand*) расшифрóвка. **tranˈscription** *n.* (*copying out*) перепúсывание; (*copy*) кóпия; (*mus.*) аранжирóвка; (*phon.*) транскрúпция.

transducer [trænsˈdjuːsə(r)] *n.* преобразовáтель *m.*, дáтчик.

transept [ˈtrænsept, ˈtrɑːn-] *n.* трансéпт.

transfer [ˈtrænsfɜː(r), ˈtrɑːns-] *n.* (*of objects*) перенóс, перемещéние; (*of money; of people*) перевóд; (*leg.*) передáча; (*design*) переводнáя картúнка; *v.t.* (*objects*) переносúть (-ошу́, -óсишь) *impf.*, перенестú (-есу́, -есёшь; -ёс, -еслá) *pf.*; перемещáть *impf.*, переместúть *pf.*; (*money; people; design*) переводúть (-ожу́, -óдишь) *impf.*, перевестú (-еду́, -едёшь; -ёл, -елá) *pf.*; (*leg.*) передавáть (-даю́, -даёшь) *impf.*, передáть (-áм, -áшь, -áст, -адúм; пéредал, -á, -о) *pf.*; *v.i.* (*to different job*) переходúть (-ожу́, -óдишь) *impf.*, перейтú (-ейду́, -ейдёшь; -ешёл, -ешлá) *pf.*; (*change trains etc.*) пересáживаться *impf.*, пересéсть (-сяду, -сядешь; -сéл) *pf.* **transˈferable** *adj.* допускáющий передáчу; (*replaceable*) заменяемый, заменúмый. **transference** *n.* передáча.

transfiguration [trænsˌfɪgjʊˈreɪʃ(ə)n, trɑː-] *n.* преобразовáние; (*spiritual*) преображéние.

trans'figure *v.t.* преобразóвывать *impf.*, преобразовáть *pf.*; (*in spirit*) преображáть *impf.*, преобразúть *pf.*

transfix [træns'fɪks, trɑ:-] *v.t.* (*pierce*) пронзáть *impf.*, пронзúть *pf.*; (*fig.*) пригвождáть *impf.*, пригвоздúть *pf.* к мéсту.

transform [træns'fɔ:m, trɑ:-] *v.t.* & *i.* (*also elec.*) преобразóвывать(ся) *impf.*, преобразовáть(ся) *pf.*; ~ **into** *v.t.* (*i.*) превращáть(ся) *impf.*, превратúть(ся) (-ащý(сь), -атúшь(ся)) *pf.* в+*a.* **transfor'mation** *n.* преобразовáние; превращéние. **transformer** *n.* (*elec.*) трансформáтор.

transfuse [træns'fju:z, trɑ:-] *v.t.* (*med.*) переливáть *impf.*, перелúть (-лью, -льёшь; -лúл, -лилá) *pf.*; (*steep*) пропúтывать *impf.*, пропитáть *pf.* (**in** +*i.*); (*convey*) передавáть (-даю, -даёшь) *impf.*, передáть (-áм, -áшь, -áст, -адúм; пéредал, -á, -о) *pf.* **transfusion** *n.* переливáние (крóви).

transgress [trænz'gres, trɑ:-, -s'gres] *v.t.* переступáть *impf.*, переступúть (-плю, -пишь) *pf.*; нарушáть *impf.*, нарýшить *pf.* **transgression** *n.* простýпок (-пка), нарушéние; (*sin*) грех (-á). **transgressor** *n.* правонарушúтель *m.*; (*sinner*) грéшник, -ица.

transience ['trænzɪəns, 'trɑ:-, -sɪəns] *n.* быстротéчность, мимолётность. **transient** *adj.* преходя́щий; (*fleeting*) мимолётный.

transistor [træn'zɪstə(r), trɑ:-, -'sɪstə(r)] *n.* транзúстор; ~ **radio** транзúсторный приёмник. **transistorized** *adj.* на транзúсторах.

transit ['trænzɪt, 'trɑ:-, -sɪt] *n.* транзúт, прохождéние; (*astron.*) прохождéние планéты; **in** ~ в, по путú; ~ **camp** лáгерь (*pl.* -ря́, -рéй) *m.* перемещённых лиц; ~ **visa** транзúтная вúза. **tran'sition** *n.* перехóд. **tran'sitional** *adj.* перехóдный; (*interim*) промежýточный. **transitive** *adj.* перехóдный. **transitory** *adj.* мимолётный; (*temporary*) врéменный.

translate [træn'sleɪt, trɑ:-, -'zleɪt] *v.t.* переводúть (-ожý, -óдишь) *impf.*, перевестú (-едý, -едёшь; -ёл, -елá) *pf.*; (*explain*) объясня́ть *impf.*, объяснúть *pf.* **translation** *n.* перевóд. **translator** *n.* перевóдчик, -ица.

transliterate [trænz'lɪtəˌreɪt, trɑ:-, -s'lɪtəˌreɪt] *v.t.* транслитерúровать *impf.* & *pf.* **translite'ration** *n.* транслитерáция.

translucency [trænz'lu:s(ə)nsɪ, trɑ:-, -'lju:s(ə)nsɪ, -s'l-] *n.* полупрозрáчность. **translucent** *adj.* просвéчивающий, полупрозрáчный.

transmigration [ˌtrænzmaɪ'greɪʃ(ə)n, ˌtrɑ:-, -smaɪ'greɪʃ(ə)n] *n.* переселéние.

transmission [trænz'mɪʃ(ə)n, trɑ:-, -s'mɪʃ(ə)n] *n.* передáча; (*tech.*) трансмúссия; *attr.* передáточный. **transmit** *v.t.* передавáть (-даю, -даёшь) *impf.*, передáть (-áм, -áшь, -áст, -адúм; пéредал, -á, -о) *pf.* **transmitter** *n.* (радио)передáтчик.

transmutation [trænzˌmju:t'eɪʃ(ə)n, trɑ:-, -sˌmju:t'eɪʃ(ə)n] *n.* превращéние. **trans'mute** *v.t.* превращáть *impf.*, превратúть (-ащý, -атúшь) *pf.*

transparency [træns'pærənsɪ, trɑ:-, -'peərənsɪ] *n.* прозрáчность; (*picture*) транспарáнт; (*phot.*) диапозитúв. **transparent** *adj.* прозрáчный; (*obvious*) очевúдный; (*frank*) откровéнный (-нен, -нна).

transpire [træn'spaɪə(r), trɑ:-] *v.t.* & *i.* испаря́ть(ся) *impf.*, испарúть(ся) *pf.*; *v.i.* (*fig.*) обнарýживаться *impf.*, обнарýжиться *pf.*; (*occur*) случáться *impf.*, случúться *pf.*

transplant [træns'plɑ:nt, trɑ:-; 'trænsplɑ:nt, 'trɑ:-] *v.t.* пересáживать *impf.*, пересадúть (-ажý, -áдишь) *pf.*; (*med.*) дéлать *impf.*, с~ *pf.* пересáдку+*g.*; *n.* (*med.*) пересáдка.

transport ['trænspɔ:t, 'trɑ:-; træns'pɔ:t, trɑ:-] *n.* (*var. senses*) трáнспорт; (*conveyance*) перевóзка; (*of rage etc.*) порыв; *attr.* трáнспортный; *v.t.* перевозúть (-ожý, -óзишь) *impf.*, перевезтú (-езý, -езёшь; -ёз, -езлá) *pf.*; (*exile*) ссылáть *impf.*, сослáть (сошлю, -лёшь) *pf.* **transpor'tation** *n.* трáнспорт, перевóзка; (*exile*) ссылка.

transpose [træns'pəʊz, trɑ:-, -z'pəʊz] *v.t.* перемещáть *impf.*, переместúть *pf.*; (*words*) переставля́ть *impf.*, перестáвить *pf.*; (*mus.*) транспонúровать *impf.* & *pf.* **transpo'sition** *n.* перемещéние, перестанóвка; (*mus.*) транспонирóвка.

transsexual [trænz'seksjʊəl] *n.* транссексуалúст; *adj.* транссексуáльный.

trans-ship [træn'ʃɪp, trɑ:-, trænz-] *v.t.* перегружáть *impf.*, перегрузúть (-ужý, -ýзúшь) *pf.*

transverse ['trænzvɜ:s, 'trɑ:-, -'vɜ:s, -ns-] *adj.* поперéчный.

transvestism [trænz'vestɪz(ə)m, trɑ:-, -s'vestɪz(ə)m] *n.* трансвестúзм *m.* **transvestite** *n.* трансвестúт.

trap [træp] *n.* ловýшка (*also fig.*), западня́, капкáн; (*tech.*) сифóн; (*cart*) рессóрная двукóлка; *v.t.* (*catch*) ловúть (-влю, -вишь) *impf.*, поймáть *pf.* (в ловýшку); (*fig.*) заманивать *impf.*, заманúть (-ню, -нишь) *pf.* в ловýшку. **trapdoor** *n.* люк.

trapeze [trə'pi:z] *n.* трапéция. **trapezium** *n.* трапéция.

trapper ['træpə(r)] *n.* охóтник, стáвящий капкáны.

trappings ['træpɪŋz] *n.* сбрýя (*collect.*); (*fig.*) (*exterior attributes*) внéшние атрибýты *m.pl.*; (*adornments*) украшéния *nt.pl.*

trash [træʃ] *n.* дрянь (*coll.*) **trashy** *adj. adj.* дряннóй (-нен, -ннá, -нно).

trauma ['trɔ:mə, 'traʊ-] *n.* трáвма. **traumatic** [trɔ:'mætɪk, traʊ-] *adj.* травматúческий.

travel ['træv(ə)l] *n.* путешéствие; (*tech.*) передвижéние; ~ **bureau** бюрó *nt.indecl.* путешéствий; ~ **sickness** *n.* болéзнь движéния; *v.i.* путешéствовать *impf.*; (*tech.*) передвигáться *impf.*, передвúнуться *pf.*; *v.t.* объезжáть *impf.*, объéхать (-éду, -éдешь) *pf.* **traveller** *n.* путешéственник, -ица; (*salesman*) коммивояжёр; **~'s cheque** дорóжный чек. **travelling** *n.* путешéствие; *attr.* дорóжный; (*itinerant*) передвижнóй.

travelogue ['trævəˌlɒg] *n.* (*film*) фильм о путеше́ствиях; (*lecture*) ле́кция о путеше́ствии с диапозити́вами. **travel-sick** *adj.*: **be ~** ука́чивать *impf.*, укача́ть *pf. impers.*+*a.*; **I am ~ in cars** меня́ в маши́не ука́чивает.

traverse ['trævəs, trə'vɜːs] *v.t.* пересека́ть *impf.*, пересе́чь (-еку́, -ечёшь; -е́к, -екла́) *pf.*

travesty ['trævɪstɪ] *n.* паро́дия; *v.t.* пароди́ровать *impf.* & *pf.*

trawl [trɔːl] *n.* трал; *v.t.* тра́лить *impf.*; *v.i.* лови́ть (-влю́, -вишь) *impf.* ры́бу тра́ловой се́тью. **trawler** *n.* тра́улер. **trawling** *n.* трале́ние.

tray [treɪ] *n.* подно́с.

treacherous ['tretʃərəs] *adj.* преда́тельский; (*unreliable*) ненадёжный. **treachery** *n.* преда́тельство.

treacle ['triːk(ə)l] *n.* па́тока. **treacly** *adj.* па́точный.

tread [tred] *n.* по́ступь, похо́дка; (*stair*) ступе́нька; (*of tyre*) проте́ктор; *v.i.* ступа́ть *impf.*, ступи́ть (-плю́, -пишь) *pf.*; шага́ть *impf.*, шагну́ть *pf.*; *v.t.* топта́ть (-пчу́, -пчешь) *impf.*; дави́ть (-влю́, -вишь) *impf.* **treadle** *n.* (*of bicycle*) педа́ль; (*of sewing machine*) подно́жка.

treason ['triːz(ə)n] *n.* изме́на; **high ~** госуда́рственная изме́на. **treasonable** *adj.* изме́ннический.

treasure ['treʒə(r)] *n.* сокро́вище, клад; **~ trove** на́йденный клад; *v.t.* (*preserve*) храни́ть *impf.*; (*value*) дорожи́ть *impf.*+*i.*; высо́ко́ цени́ть (-ню́, -нишь) *impf.* **treasurer** *n.* казначе́й. **treasury** *n.* (*also fig.*) сокро́вищница; (**T~**) казна́ *no pl.*; **the T~** госуда́рственное казначе́йство.

treat [triːt] *n.* (*pleasure*) удово́льствие; (*entertainment*) угоще́ние; *v.t.* (*have as guest*) угоща́ть *impf.*, угости́ть *pf.* (**to** +*i.*); (*med.*) лечи́ть (-чу́, -чишь) *impf.* (**for** от+*g.*; **with** +*i.*); (*behave towards*) обраща́ться *impf.* с+*i.*; (*process*) обраба́тывать *impf.*, обрабо́тать *pf.* (**with** +*i.*); (*discuss*) трактова́ть *impf.* о+*p.*; (*regard*) относи́ться (-ошу́сь, -о́сишься) *impf.*, отнести́сь (-есу́сь, -есёшься; -ёсся, -есла́сь) *pf.* к+*d.* (**as** как к+*d.*). **treatise** ['triːtɪs, -ɪz] *n.* тракта́т. **treatment** *n.* (*behaviour*) обраще́ние; (*med.*) лече́ние; (*processing*) обрабо́тка; (*discussion*) тракто́вка. **treaty** *n.* догово́р.

treble ['treb(ə)l] *adj.* тройно́й; (*trebled*) утро́енный (-ен); (*mus.*) дисканто́вый; *adv.* втро́е, втройне́; *n.* тройно́е коли́чество; (*mus.*) ди́ска́нт; *v.t.* & *i.* утра́ивать(ся) *impf.*, утро́ить(ся) *pf.*

tree [triː] *n.* де́рево (*pl.* дере́вья, -ьев). **treeless** *adj.* безле́сный.

trefoil ['trefɔɪl, 'triː-] *n.* трили́стник.

trek [trek] *n.* (*migration*) переселе́ние; (*journey*) путеше́ствие; *v.i.* (*migrate*) переселя́ться *impf.*, пересели́ться *pf.*; (*journey*) путеше́ствовать *impf.*

trellis ['trelɪs] *n.* шпале́ра; (*for creepers*) решётка.

tremble ['tremb(ə)l] *v.i.* трепета́ть (-ещу́, -е́щешь) *impf.* (**at** при+*p.*); дрожа́ть (-жу́, -жи́шь) *impf.* (**with** от+*g.*); трясти́сь (-су́сь, -сёшься; -ся, -сла́сь) *impf.* (**with** от+*g.*). **trembling** *n.* тре́пет, дрожь; **in fear and ~** трепеща́.

tremendous [trɪ'mendəs] *adj.* (*enormous*) огро́мный; (*excellent, remarkable*) потряса́ющий.

tremor ['tremə(r)] *n.* дрожь, тре́пет; (*earthquake*) толчо́к (-чка́). **tremulous** ['tremjʊləs] *adj.* дрожа́щий; (*uneven*) неро́вный (-вен, -вна́, -вно); (*shy*) ро́бкий (-бок, -бка́, -бко).

trench [trentʃ] *n.* кана́ва, ров (рва, *loc.* во рву́); (*mil.*) око́п; **~ coat** тёплая полушине́ль; *v.t.* рыть (ро́ю, ро́ешь) *impf.*, вы́~ *pf.* кана́вы, рвы, око́пы в+*p.*; (*dig over*) перека́пывать *impf.*, перекопа́ть *pf.*

trenchant ['trentʃ(ə)nt] *adj.* о́стрый (остр & остёр, остра́, о́стро́), ре́зкий (-зок, -зка́, -зко). **trenchancy** *n.* острота́, ре́зкость.

trend [trend] *n.* направле́ние, тенде́нция. **trendy** *adj.* мо́дный (-ден, -дна́, -дно).

trepidation [ˌtrepɪ'deɪʃ(ə)n] *n.* (*trembling*) тре́пет; (*alarm*) трево́га.

trespass ['trespəs] *n.* (*on property*) наруше́ние грани́ц; (*misdemeanour*) просту́пок (-пка); *v.i.* наруша́ть *impf.*, нару́шить *pf.* пра́во владе́ния; **~ on** (*property*) наруша́ть *impf.*, нару́шить *pf.* грани́цу+*g.*; (*selfishly exploit*) злоупотребля́ть *impf.*, злоупотреби́ть *pf.*+*i.* **trespasser** *n.* наруши́тель *m.*, ~ница грани́ц.

tress [tres] *n.* ло́кон, коса́ (*a.* ко́су́; *pl.* -сы).

trestle ['tres(ə)l] *n.* ко́злы (-зел, -злам) *pl.*

trial ['traɪəl] *n.* (*test*) испыта́ние (*also ordeal*), про́ба; (*leg.*) проце́сс, суд (-а́); (*sport*) попы́тка; **on ~** (*probation*) на испыта́нии; (*of objects*) взя́тый на про́бу; (*leg.*) под судо́м; **~ period** испыта́тельный срок (-а(у)); **~ run** про́бный пробе́г; (*of ship*) про́бное пла́вание; (*of plane*) испыта́тельный полёт; **~ and error** ме́тод подбо́ра.

triangle ['traɪˌæŋg(ə)l] *n.* треуго́льник. **tri'angular** *adj.* треуго́льный; (*three-edged*) трёхгра́нный.

tribal ['traɪb(ə)l] *adj.* племенно́й, родово́й. **tribe** *n.* пле́мя *nt.*, род (-а(у), *loc.* -у́; *pl.* -ы́). **tribesman** *n.* член пле́мени, ро́да.

tribulation [ˌtrɪbjʊ'leɪʃ(ə)n] *n.* го́ре, несча́стье.

tribunal [traɪ'bjuːn(ə)l, trɪ-] *n.* трибуна́л; (*court*; *fig.*) ка́федра.

tribune¹ ['trɪbjuːn] *n.* (*leader*) трибу́н.

tribune² ['trɪbjuːn] *n.* (*platform*) трибу́на; (*throne*) ка́федра.

tributary ['trɪbjʊtərɪ] *n.* (*geog.*) прито́к; (*hist.*) да́нник. **tribute** *n.* дань (*also fig.*); **pay ~** (*fig.*) отдава́ть (-даю́, -даёшь) *impf.*, отда́ть (-а́м, -а́шь, -а́ст, -ади́м; о́тдал, -а́, -о) *pf.* дань (уваже́ния) (**to** +*d.*).

trice [traɪs] *n.*: **in a ~** мгнове́нно.

trick [trɪk] *n.* (*ruse*) хи́трость; (*deception*) обма́н; (*conjuring ~*) фо́кус; (*feat, stunt*) трюк; (*joke*) шу́тка; (*of trade etc.*) приём; (*habit*) привы́чка; (*cards*) взя́тка; **play a ~ on** игра́ть *impf.*, сыгра́ть *pf.* шу́тку с+*i.*; *v.t.* обма́нывать *impf.*, обману́ть (-ну́, -нешь) *pf.* **trickery** *n.* обма́н, надува́тельство (*coll.*).

trickle ['trɪk(ə)l] *v.i.* ка́пать *impf.*; сочи́ться *impf.*; *n.* стру́йка.

trickster ['trɪkstə(r)] *n.* обма́нщик, -ица. **tricky** *adj.* (*complicated*) сло́жный (-жен, -жна́, -жно); (*crafty*) хи́трый (-тёр, -тра́, хи́тро́).

tricot ['trɪkəʊ, 'tri:-] *n.* трико́ *nt.indecl.*

tricycle ['traɪsɪk(ə)l] *n.* трёхколёсный велосипе́д.

trident ['traɪd(ə)nt] *n.* трезу́бец (-бца).

triennial [traɪ'enɪəl] *adj.* трёхле́тний.

trifle ['traɪf(ə)l] *n.* пустя́к (-а́), ме́лочь (*pl.* -чи, -че́й); (*dish*) бискви́т со сби́тыми сли́вками; **a ~** (*adv.*) немно́го+*g.*; *v.i.* шути́ть (шучу́, шу́тишь) *impf.*, по~ *pf.* (**with** с+*i.*); относи́ться (-ошу́сь, -о́сишься) *impf.*, отнести́сь (-есу́сь, -есёшься; -ёсся, -есла́сь) *pf.* несерьёзно (**with** к+*d.*). **trifling** *adj.* пустяко́вый.

trigger ['trɪgə(r)] *n.* (*of gun*) куро́к (-рка́), спусково́й крючо́к (-чка́); (*releasing catch*) защёлка; *v.t.*: **~ off** вызыва́ть *impf.*, вы́звать (вы́зову, -вешь) *pf.*

trigonometry [ˌtrɪgə'nɒmɪtrɪ] *n.* тригономе́трия.

trilby (hat) ['trɪlbɪ] *n.* мя́гкая фе́тровая шля́па.

trilogy ['trɪlədʒɪ] *n.* трило́гия.

trim [trɪm] *n.* поря́док (-дка), гото́вность; **in fighting ~** в боево́й гото́вности; **in good ~** (*sport*) в хоро́шей фо́рме; (*haircut*) подстри́жка; (*clipping, pruning*) подре́зка; *adj.* (*neat*) аккура́тный, опря́тный; (*smart*) наря́дный; *v.t.* (*cut, clip, cut off*) подреза́ть *impf.*, подре́зать (-е́жу, -е́жешь) *pf.*; (*hair*) подстрига́ть *impf.*, подстри́чь (-игу́, -ижёшь; -и́г) *pf.*; (*square*) обтёсывать *impf.*, обтеса́ть (-ешу, -е́шешь) *pf.*; (*a dress etc.*) отде́лывать *impf.*, отде́лать *pf.*; (*a dish*) украша́ть *impf.*, укра́сить *pf.* **trimming** *n.* (*on dress*) отде́лка; (*to food*) гарни́р, припра́ва.

trimaran ['traɪməˌræn] *n.* тримара́н.

Trinity ['trɪnɪtɪ] *n.* тро́ица; **~ Sunday** Тро́ицын день (дня) *m.*

trinket ['trɪŋkɪt] *n.* безделу́шка, брело́к.

trio ['tri:əʊ] *n.* три́о *nt.indecl.*; (*of people*) тро́йка.

trip [trɪp] *n.* пое́здка, путеше́ствие, экску́рсия; (*business ~*) командиро́вка; (*stumbling*) спотыка́ние; (*sport*) подно́жка; (*light step*) лёгкая похо́дка; (*mistake*) оши́бка; (*tech.*) расцепля́ющее устро́йство; *v.i.* (*run lightly*) бе́гать *indet.*, бежа́ть (бегу́, бежи́шь) *det.*, по~ *pf.* вприпры́жку; (*stumble*) спотыка́ться *impf.*, споткну́ться *pf.* (**over** о+*a.*); (*make a mistake*) ошиба́ться *impf.*, ошиби́ться (-бу́сь, -бёшься; -бся) *pf.*; *v.t.* подставля́ть *impf.*, подста́вить *pf.* но́жку+*d.* (*also fig.*); (*confuse*) запу́тывать *impf.*, запу́тать *pf.*

tripartite [traɪ'pɑ:taɪt] *adj.* трёхсторо́нний.

tripe [traɪp] *n.* (*dish*) рубе́ц (-бца́).

triple ['trɪp(ə)l] *adj.* тройно́й; (*tripled*) утро́енный (-ен); *v.t.* & *i.* утра́ивать(ся) *impf.*, утро́ить(ся) *pf.* **triplet** *n.* (*mus.*) трио́ль; (*one of ~s*) близне́ц (-а́) (из тро́йни); *pl.* тро́йня. **triplicate** ['trɪplɪkət] *n.*: **in ~** в трёх экземпля́рах.

tripod ['traɪpɒd] *n.* трено́жник.

triptych ['trɪptɪk] *n.* три́птих.

trite [traɪt] *adj.* бана́льный, изби́тый.

triumph ['traɪəmf, -ʌmf] *n.* триу́мф (*also event*), торжество́, побе́да; *v.i.* торжествова́ть *impf.*, вос~ *pf.* (**over** над+*i.*). **triumphal** [traɪ'ʌmf(ə)l] *adj.* триумфа́льный. **tri'umphant** *adj.* (*exultant*) торжеству́ющий, лику́ющий; (*victorious*) победоно́сный.

trivia ['trɪvɪə] *n.* ме́лочи (-че́й) *pl.* **trivial** *adj.* незначи́тельный. **triviality** [ˌtrɪvɪ'ælɪtɪ] *n.* тривиа́льность, бана́льность. **trivialize** *v.t.* упроща́ть *impf.*, упрости́ть *pf.*

troglodyte ['trɒgləˌdaɪt] *n.* троглоди́т.

troika ['trɔɪkə] *n.* тро́йка.

Trojan ['trəʊdʒ(ə)n] *adj.* троя́нский; *n.* **work like a ~** рабо́тать *impf.* как вол.

troll [trəʊl] *n.* (*myth.*) тролль *m.*

trolley ['trɒlɪ] *n.* теле́жка, ваго́нетка; (*table on wheels*) сто́лик на колёсиках. **trolleybus** *n.* тролле́йбус.

trollop ['trɒləp] *n.* (*sloven*) неря́ха; (*prostitute*) потаску́ха.

trombone [trɒm'bəʊn] *n.* тромбо́н.

troop [tru:p] *n.* гру́ппа, отря́д; *pl.* (*mil.*) войска́ *nt.pl.*, солда́ты *m.pl.*; *v.i.* (*move in a crowd*) дви́гаться (-ается & дви́жется) *impf.* толпо́й. **trooper** *n.* кавалери́ст. **trooping the colour(s)** *n.* торже́ственный вы́нос зна́мени (знамён). **troop-ship** *n.* войсково́й тра́нспорт.

trophy ['trəʊfɪ] *n.* трофе́й; (*prize*) приз (*pl.* -ы́).

tropic ['trɒpɪk] *n.* тро́пик; **T~ of Cancer** тро́пик Ра́ка; **T~ of Capricorn** тро́пик Козеро́га. **tropical** *adj.* тропи́ческий.

trot [trɒt] *n.* рысь (*loc.* -си́); *v.i.* рыси́ть *impf.*; (*rider*) е́здить *indet.*, е́хать (е́ду, е́дешь) *det.*, по~ *pf.* ры́сью; (*horse*) ходи́ть (-дит) *indet.*, идти́ (идёт; шёл, шла) *det.*, пойти́ (пойду́, -дёшь; пошёл, -шла́) *pf.* ры́сью; **~ out** (*present for inspection*) представля́ть *impf.*, предста́вить *pf.* на рассмотре́ние; (*show off*) щеголя́ть *impf.*, щегольну́ть *pf.*+*i.* **trotter** *n.* (*horse*) рыса́к (-а́); *pl.* (*dish*) но́жки *f.pl.*

troubadour ['tru:bəˌdɔ:(r)] *n.* трубаду́р.

trouble ['trʌb(ə)l] *n.* (*worry*) беспоко́йство, трево́га; (*misfortune*) беда́ (*pl.* -ды), го́ре; (*unpleasantness*) неприя́тности *f.pl.*; (*effort,* *pains*) хло́поты (-о́т) *pl.*, труд; (*care*) забо́та; (*disrepair*) пробле́ма, неприя́тности *f.pl.* (**with** c+*i.*), неиспра́вность (**with** в+*p.*); (*illness*) боле́знь; **heart ~** больно́е се́рдце; **ask for ~** напра́шиваться *impf.*, напроси́ться (-ошу́сь, -о́сишься) *pf.* на неприя́тности; **be in ~** име́ть *impf.* неприя́тности; **cause ~ to** доставля́ть *impf.*, доста́вить *pf.* хло́поты+*d.*; **get into ~** попа́сть (-аду́, -адёшь; -а́л) *pf.* в беду́; **make ~ for** причиня́ть *impf.*, причини́ть *pf.* неприя́тности+*d.*; **take ~** стара́ться *impf.*, по~ *pf.*; **take the ~** труди́ться (-ужу́сь, -у́дишься) *impf.*, по~ *pf.* (**to** +*inf.*); **the ~ is (that)** беда́ в том, что; *v.t.* (*make anxious*, *disturb*, *give pain*) беспоко́ить *impf.*; **may I ~ you for ...?** мо́жно попроси́ть у вас +*a.*?; **may I ~ you to ...?** мо́жно попроси́ть вас+*inf.*?; *v.i.* (*worry*) беспоко́иться *impf.*; (*take the ~*) труди́ться (тружу́сь, тру́дишься) *impf.* **troubled** *adj.* беспоко́йный. **troublemaker** *n.* наруши́тель *m.*, ~ница споко́йствия. **troubleshooter** *n.* авари́йный монтёр. **troublesome** *adj.* (*restless*, *fidgety*) беспоко́йный; (*capricious*) капри́зный; (*difficult*) тру́дный (-ден, -дна́, -дно, тру́дны).

trough [trɒf] *n.* (*for food*) корму́шка, коры́то; (*gutter*) жёлоб (*pl.* -а́); (*of wave*) подо́шва; (*meteor.*) ложби́на ни́зкого давле́ния.

trounce [traʊns] *v.t.* (*beat*) бить (бью, бьёшь) *impf.*, по~ *pf.*; (*punish*) суро́во нака́зывать *impf.*, наказа́ть (-ажу́, -а́жешь) *pf.*; (*scold*) суро́во брани́ть *impf.*, вы́~ *pf.* (*coll.*).

troupe [tru:p] *n.* тру́ппа.

trouser-leg ['traʊzə(r)] *n.* штани́на (*coll.*). **trousers** *n.* брю́ки (-к) *pl.*, штаны́ (-но́в) *pl.* **trouser-suit** *n.* брю́чный костю́м.

trousseau ['tru:səʊ] *n.* прида́ное *sb.*

trout [traʊt] *n.* форе́ль.

trowel ['traʊəl] *n.* (*for plastering etc.*) лопа́тка; (*garden ~*) садо́вый сово́к (-вка́).

truancy ['tru:ənsɪ] *n.* прогу́л. **truant** *n.* прогу́льщик, -ица; **play ~** прогу́ливать *impf.*, прогуля́ть *pf.*; *adj.* пра́здный.

truce [tru:s] *n.* переми́рие; (*respite*) переды́шка.

truck[1] [trʌk] *n.*: **have no ~ with** избега́ть *impf.*, избежа́ть (-егу́, -ежи́шь) *pf.* +*g.*

truck[2] [trʌk] *n.* (*lorry*) грузови́к (-а́); (*rail.*) ваго́н-платфо́рма.

truckle ['trʌk(ə)l] *v.i.* раболе́пствовать *impf.* (**to** пе́ред+*i.*).

truculence ['trʌkjʊləns] *n.* свире́пость. **truculent** *adj.* свире́пый.

trudge [trʌdʒ] *n.* утоми́тельная прогу́лка; *v.i.* уста́ло тащи́ться (-щу́сь, -щишься) *impf.*

true [tru:] *adj.* (*faithful*, *correct*) ве́рный (-рен, -рна́, -рно, ве́рны́); (*correct*) пра́вильный; (*genuine*) по́длинный (-нен, -нна); (*exact*) то́чный (-чен, -чна́, -чно); **come ~** сбыва́ться *impf.*, сбы́ться (сбу́дется; сбы́лся, -ла́сь) *pf.* **true-to-life** *adj.* реалисти́ческий.

truffle ['trʌf(ə)l] *n.* трю́фель (*pl.* -ли, -ле́й) *m.*

truism ['tru:ɪz(ə)m] *n.* трюи́зм. **truly** *adv.* (*sincerely*) и́скренне; (*faithfully*) ве́рно; (*really*, *indeed*) действи́тельно, пои́стине; (*accurately*) то́чно; **yours ~** пре́данный Вам.

trump [trʌmp] *n.* ко́зырь (*pl.* -ри, -ре́й) *m.* (*also fig.*); *v.i.* козыря́ть *impf.*, козырну́ть *pf.* (*coll.*); *v.t.* бить (бью, бьёшь) *impf.*, по~ *pf.* ко́зырем; **~ up** выду́мывать *impf.*, вы́думать *pf.*; фабрикова́ть *impf.*, с~ *pf.*

trumpery *n.* мишура́; (*rubbish*) дрянь (*coll.*).

trumpet ['trʌmpɪt] *n.* труба́ (*pl.* -бы); *v.i.* труби́ть *impf.* (**on** в+*a.*); (*elephant*) реве́ть (-ву́, -вёшь) *impf.*; *v.t.* (*proclaim*) возвеща́ть *impf.*, возвести́ть *pf.* **trumpeter** *n.* труба́ч (-а́).

truncate [trʌŋ'keɪt, 'trʌŋ-] *v.t.* усека́ть *impf.*, усе́чь (-еку́, -ечёшь; усе́к, -ла́) *pf.*; (*cut top off*) среза́ть *impf.*, сре́зать (-е́жу, -е́жешь) *pf.* верху́шку+*g.*; (*abbreviate*) сокраща́ть *impf.*, сократи́ть (-ащу́, -ати́шь) *pf.*

truncheon ['trʌntʃ(ə)n] *n.* (*police*) дуби́нка; (*staff*, *baton*) жезл (-а́).

trundle ['trʌnd(ə)l] *v.t.* & *i.* ката́ть(ся) *indet.*, кати́ть(ся) (качу́(сь), ка́тишь(ся)) *det.*, по~ *pf.*

trunk [trʌŋk] *n.* (*stem*) ствол (-а́); (*anat.*) ту́ловище; (*elephant's*) хо́бот; (*box*) сунду́к (-а́); *pl.* (*swimming*) пла́вки (-вок) *pl.*; (*boxing etc.*) трусы́ (-со́в) *pl.*; **~ call** вы́зов по междугоро́дному телефо́ну; **~ line** магистра́льная ли́ния; **~ road** магистра́льная доро́га.

truss [trʌs] *n.* (*girder*) ба́лка, фе́рма; (*med.*) грыжево́й банда́ж (-а́); (*sheath*, *bunch*) свя́зка; *v.t.* (*tie* (*up*), *bird*) свя́зывать *impf.*, связа́ть (-яжу́, -я́жешь) *pf.*; (*reinforce*) укрепля́ть *impf.*, укрепи́ть *pf.*

trust [trʌst] *n.* дове́рие, ве́ра; (*body of ~ees*) опе́ка; (*property held in ~*) довери́тельная со́бственность; (*econ.*) трест; (*credit*) креди́т; (*responsibility*) отве́тственность; **breach of ~** злоупотребле́ние дове́рием; **on ~** (*credit*) в креди́т; **take on ~** принима́ть *impf.*, приня́ть (приму́, -мешь; при́нял, -а́, -о) *pf.* на ве́ру; *v.t.* доверя́ть *impf.*, дове́рить *pf.*+*d.* (**with** +*a.*; **to** +*inf.*); ве́рить *impf.*, по~ *pf.*+*d.*, в+*a.*; (*entrust*) (*object*) поруча́ть *impf.*, поручи́ть (-чу́, -чишь) *pf.* (**to** +*d.*); (*a secret etc.*) вверя́ть *impf.*, вве́рить *pf.* (**to** +*d.*); *v.i.* (*hope*) наде́яться *impf.*, по~ *pf.* **trus'tee** *n.* попечи́тель *m.*, ~ница, опеку́н, ~ша. **trustful, trusting** *adj.* дове́рчивый. **trustiness** *n.* ве́рность; (*reliability*) надёжность. **trustworthy, trusty** *adj.* надёжный, ве́рный (-рен, -рно, ве́рны́).

truth [tru:θ] *n.* и́стина, пра́вда; **tell the ~** говори́ть *impf.*, сказа́ть (скажу́, -жешь) *pf.* пра́вду; **to tell you the ~** по пра́вде говоря́. **truthful** *adj.* правди́вый.

try [traɪ] *n.* (*attempt*) попы́тка; (*test*, *trial*) испыта́ние, про́ба; *v.t.* (*taste*; *examine effectiveness of*) про́бовать *impf.*, по~ *pf.*; (*test*) испы́тывать *impf.*, испыта́ть *pf.*; (*leg.*)

суди́ть (сужу́, су́дишь) *impf.* (**for** за+*a.*); *v.i.* (*endeavour*) стара́ться *impf.*, по~ *pf.*; (*make an attempt*) пыта́ться *impf.*, по- *pf.*; ~ **on** (*clothes*) примеря́ть *impf.*, приме́рить *pf.* **trying** *adj.* тяжёлый (-л, -ла́); (*tiresome*) доку́чливый (*coll.*).

tsar [zɑ:(r)] *n.* царь (-ря́) *m.* **tsarina** [zɑ:'ri:nə] *n.* цари́ца.

T-shirt ['ti:ʃɜ:t] *n.* те́нниска (*coll.*). **T-square** *n.* рейсши́на.

tub [tʌb] *n.* ка́дка, лоха́нь.

tuba ['tju:bə] *n.* ту́ба.

tubby ['tʌbɪ] *adj.* то́лстенький.

tube [tju:b] *n.* тру́бка, труба́ (*pl.* -бы); (*toothpaste etc.*) тю́бик; (*underground*) метро́ *nt.indecl.*; **cathode-ray** ~ элекроннолучева́я тру́бка; **inner** ~ ка́мера.

tuber ['tju:bə(r)] *n.* клу́бень (-бня) *m.* **tubercular** [tjʊ'bɜ:kjʊlə(r)] *adj.* туберкулёзный. **tubercu'losis** *n.* туберкулёз.

tubing ['tju:bɪŋ] *n.* тру́бы *m.pl.* **tubular** *adj.* тру́бчатый.

tuck [tʌk] *n.* (*in garment*) скла́дка; *v.t.* (*make ~s in*) де́лать *impf.*, с~ *pf.* скла́дки на+*loc.*; (*thrust into*, ~ *away*) засо́вывать *impf.*, засу́нуть *pf.*; (*hide away*) пря́тать (-я́чу, -я́чешь) *impf.*, с~ *pf.*; ~ **in** (*shirt etc.*) заправля́ть *impf.*, запра́вить *pf.*; ~ **in, up** (*blanket, skirt*) подтыка́ть *impf.*, подоткну́ть *pf.*; ~ **up** (*sleeves*) засу́чивать *impf.*, засучи́ть (-чу́, -чишь) *pf.*; (*in bed*) укрыва́ть *impf.*, укры́ть (-ро́ю, -ро́ешь) *pf.*; (*hair etc. out of the way*) подбира́ть *impf.*, подобра́ть (подберу́, -рёшь; подобра́л, а́, -о) *pf.*

Tuesday ['tju:zdeɪ, -dɪ] *n.* вто́рник.

tuft [tʌft] *n.* пучо́к (-чка́). **tufted** *adj.* с хохолко́м.

tug [tʌg] *v.t.* (*sharply*) дёргать *impf.*, дёрнуть *pf.*; (*pull*) тяну́ть (-ну́, -нешь) *impf.*, по~ *pf.*; (*tow*) букси́ровать *impf.*; *n.* рыво́к (-вка́); (*tugboat*) букси́рное судно́ (*pl.* -да́, -до́в); ~ **of war** перетя́гивание на кана́те.

tuition [tju:'ɪʃ(ə)n] *n.* обуче́ние (**in** +*d.*).

tulip ['tju:lɪp] *n.* тюльпа́н.

tulle [tju:l] *n.* тюль *m.*

tumble ['tʌmb(ə)l] *v.i.* (*fall*) па́дать *impf.*, (у)па́сть ((у)паду́, -дёшь; (у)па́л) *pf.*; (*go head over heels*) кувырка́ться *impf.*, кувыркну́ться *pf.*; (*rush headlong*) броса́ться *impf.*, бро́ситься *pf.*; *v.t.* (*disarrange*) приводи́ть (-ожу́, -о́дишь) *impf.*, привести́ (-еду́, -едёшь; -ёл, -ела́) *pf.* в беспоря́док; *n.* паде́ние; кувырка́нье. **tumbledown** *adj.* полуразру́шенный (-ен), развали́вшийся. **tumbler** *n.* (*acrobat*) акроба́т; (*glass*) стака́н.

tumour ['tju:mə(r)] *n.* о́пухоль.

tumult ['tju:mʌlt] *n.* (*uproar*) сумато́ха, шум (-а(у)); (*agitation*) волне́ние. **tumultuous** [tjʊ'mʌltjʊəs] *adj.* шу́мный (-мен, -мна́, -мно).

tumulus ['tju:mjʊləs] *n.* курга́н, моги́льный холм (-а́).

tuna ['tju:nə] *n.* туне́ц (-нца́).

tundra ['tʌndrə] *n.* ту́ндра.

tune [tju:n] *n.* мело́дия, моти́в; **in** ~ в тон, (*of instrument*) настро́енный (-ен); **out of tune** не в тон, фальши́вый, (*of instrument*) расстро́енный (-ен); **be in** ~ **with** (*fig.*) гармони́ровать *impf.* с+*i.*; **be out of** ~ **with** (*fig.*) (*thing*) идти́ (иду́, идёшь; шёл, шла) *impf.* вразре́з с+*i.*; (*person*) быть не в ладу́ с+*i.*; **call the** ~ распоряжа́ться *impf.*; **change one's** ~ (пере)меня́ть *impf.*, перемени́ть (-ню́, -нишь) *pf.* тон; *v.t.* (*instrument*; *radio*) настра́ивать *impf.*, настро́ить *pf.*; (*engine etc.*) регули́ровать *impf.*, от~ *pf.*; (*fig.*) приспособля́ть *impf.*, приспосо́бить *pf.*; ~ **in** настра́ивать *impf.*, настро́ить (*radio*) ра́дио (**to** на+*a.*); *v.i.*: ~ **up** настра́ивать *impf.*, настро́ить *pf.* инструме́нт(ы). **tuneful** *adj.* мелоди́чный, гармони́чный. **tuneless** *adj.* немелоди́чный. **tuner** *n.* настро́йщик.

tungsten ['tʌŋst(ə)n] *n.* вольфра́м.

tunic ['tju:nɪk] *n.* туни́ка; (*of uniform*) ки́тель (*pl.* -ля́ & -ли) *m.*

tuning ['tju:nɪŋ] *n.* настро́йка; (*of engine*) регулиро́вка. **tuning-fork** *n.* камерто́н.

tunnel ['tʌn(ə)l] *n.* тунне́ль *m.*; *v.i.* прокла́дывать *impf.*, проложи́ть (-жу́, -жишь) *pf.* тунне́ль *m.*

tunny ['tʌnɪ] *n.* туне́ц (-нца́).

turban ['tɜ:bən] *n.* тюрба́н, чалма́.

turbid ['tɜ:bɪd] *adj.* му́тный (-тен, -тна́, -тно); (*fig.*) тума́нный (-нен, -нна).

turbine ['tɜ:baɪn] *n.* турби́на. **turbo-jet** *adj.* (*n.*) турбореакти́вный (самолёт). **turboprop** *adj.* (*n.*) турбовинтово́й (самолёт).

turbot ['tɜ:bət] *n.* тюрбо́ *nt.indecl.*

turbulence ['tɜ:bjʊləns] *n.* бу́йность, бу́рность; (*tech.*) турбуле́нтность. **turbulent** *adj.* бу́йный (бу́ен, буйна́, -но), бу́рный (-рен, бу́рна́, -но); (*tech.*) турбуле́нтный.

tureen [tjʊə'ri:n, tə-] *n.* су́пник, су́пница.

turf [tɜ:f] *n.* дёрн; **the** ~ (*track*) бегова́я доро́жка; (*races*) ска́чки *f.pl.*; *v.t.* дернова́ть *impf.*

turgid ['tɜ:dʒɪd] *adj.* (*swollen*) опу́хший; (*pompous*) напы́щенный (-ен, -енна).

Turk [tɜ:k] *n.* ту́рок (-рка), турча́нка. **Turkey** *n.* Ту́рция.

turkey ['tɜ:kɪ] *n.* индю́к (-а́), -ю́шка; (*dish*) инде́йка.

Turkic ['tɜ:kɪk] *adj.* тю́ркский. **Turkish** *adj.* туре́цкий; ~ **bath** туре́цкие ба́ни *f.pl.*; ~ **delight** раха́т-луку́м.

Turkmenistan [tɜ:kmenɪ'stɑ:n] *n.* Туркмениста́н. **Turkoman** *n.* туркме́н, ~ка; *adj.* туркме́нский.

turmoil ['tɜ:mɔɪl] *n.* (*disorder*) беспоря́док (-дка); (*uproar*) сумато́ха, шум (-а(у)).

turn [tɜ:n] *n.* (*change of direction*) поворо́т; (*revolution*) оборо́т; (*service*) услу́га; (*change*) измене́ние; (*one's ~ to do sth.*) о́чередь; (*character*) склад хара́ктера; (*circus, variety*) но́мер (*pl.* -а́); ~ **of phrase** оборо́т ре́чи; **at every** ~ на ка́ждом шагу́; **by, in turn(s)** по о́череди; **to a** ~ как раз в ме́ру; **take a bad**

~ принимáть *impf.*, принять (примý, -мешь; прúнял, -á, -о) *pf.* дурнóй оборóт; **take a ~ for the worse** изменяться *impf.*, измениться (-нюсь, -нишься) *pf.* к хýдшему; *v.t.* (*handle, key, car around etc.*) поворáчивать *impf.*, повернýть *pf.*; (*revolve, rotate*) вращáть *impf.*, (*spin, twirl*) вертéть (-рчý, -ртишь) *impf.* +*a.* & *i.*; (*page on its face*) перевёртывать *impf.*, перевернýть *pf.*; (*direct*) направлять *impf.*, напрáвить *pf.*; (*cause to become*) дéлать *impf.*, с~ *pf.* +*i.*; (*on lathe*) точить (-чý, -чишь) *impf.*; **~ s.o.'s head** кружить (кружý, крýжишь) *impf.*, вс~ *pf.* гóлову+*d.*; **~ one's stomach: that ~ my stomach** меня от этого тошнит; *v.i.* (*change direction*) поворáчивать *impf.*, повернýть *pf.*; завёртывать *impf.*, завернýть *pf.*; (*rotate*) вращáться *impf.*; (*~ round*) поворáчиваться *impf.*, повернýться *pf.*; (*become*) становиться (-влюсь, -вишься) *impf.*, стать (стáну, -нешь) *pf.* +*i.*; **~ against** ополчáться *impf.*, ополчиться *pf.* на+*a.*, прóтив+*g.*; **~ around** *see* **~ round; ~ away** (*v.t.* & *i.*) отворáчивать(ся) *impf.*, отвернýть(ся) *pf.*; **~ back** (*v.i.*) поворáчивать *impf.*, повернýть *pf.* назáд; (*v.t.*) (*bend back*) отгибáть *impf.*, отогнýть *pf.*; **~ down** (*refuse*) отклонять *impf.*, отклонить (-ню, -нишь) *pf.*; (*collar*) отгибáть *impf.*, отогнýть *pf.*; (*make quieter*) дéлать *impf.*, с~ *pf.* тúше; **~ grey** (*v.i.*) седéть *impf.*, по~ *pf.*; **~ in** (*v.t.*) (*hand back*) возвращáть *impf.*, вернýть *pf.*; (*so as to face inwards*) поворáчивать *impf.*, повернýть *pf.* внутрь; **~ inside out** выворáчивать *impf.*, вывернуть *pf.* наизнáнку; **~ into** (*change into*) (*v.t.* & *i.*) превращáть(ся) *impf.*, превратить(ся) (-ащý(сь), -атишь(ся)) *pf.* в+*a.*; (*street*) сворáчивать *impf.*, свернýть *pf.* на+*a.*; **~ off** (*light, radio etc.*) выключáть *impf.*, выключить *pf.*; (*tap*) закрывáть *impf.*, закрыть (-рóю, -рóешь) *pf.*; (*branch off*) сворáчивать *impf.*, свернýть *pf.*; **~ on** (*light, radio etc.*) включáть *impf.*, включить *pf.*; (*tap*) открывáть *impf.*, открыть (-рóю, -рóешь) *pf.*; (*attack*) нападáть *impf.*, напáсть (-адý, -адёшь; -ал) *pf.*; **~ out** (*light etc.*) *see* **~ off**; (*prove to be*) окáзываться *impf.*, оказáться (-ажýсь, -áжешься) *pf.* (**to be** +*i.*); (*drive out*) выгонять *impf.*, выгнать (выгоню, -нишь) *pf.*; (*pockets*) вывёртывать *impf.*, вывернуть *pf.*; (*be present*) приходить (-ожý, -óдишь) *impf.*, прийти (придý, -дёшь; пришёл, -шлá) *pf.*; (*product*) выпускáть *impf.*, выпустить *pf.*; **~ over** (*egg, page, on its face, roll over*) (*v.t.* & *i.*) перевёртывать(ся) *impf.*, перевернýть(ся) *pf.*; (*hand over*) передавáть (-даю, -даёшь) *impf.*, передáть (-áм, -áшь, -áст, -адим; пéредал, -á, -о) *pf.*; (*think about*) обдýмывать *impf.*, обдýмать *pf.*; (*overturn*) (*v.t.* & *i.*) опрокидывать(ся) *impf.*, опрокинуть(ся) *pf.*; (*switch over*) переключáть *impf.*, переключить *pf.* (**to** на+*a.*); **~ pale** бледнéть *impf.*, по~ *pf.*; **~ red** краснéть *impf.*, по~ *pf.*; **~ round** (*v.i.*) (*rotate*; *~ one's back*; *~ to face sth.*) повёртываться *impf.*, повернýться *pf.*; (*~ to face*) оборáчиваться *impf.*, обернýться *pf.*; (*v.t.*) повёртывать *impf.*, повернýть *pf.*; **~ sour** скисáть *impf.*, скиснуть (скис) *pf.*; **~ to** обращáться *impf.*, обратиться (-ащýсь, -атишься) *pf.* к+*d.* (**for** за+*i.*); **~ up** (*appear*) появляться *impf.*, появиться (-влюсь, -вишься) *pf.*; (*be found*) находиться (-ожýсь, -óдишься) *impf.*, найтись (-йдýсь, -йдёшься; нашёлся, -шлáсь) *pf.*; (*shorten garment*) подшивáть *impf.*, подшить (-шью, -шьёшь) *pf.*; (*crop up*) подвёртываться *impf.*, подвернýться *pf.*; (*bend up*; *stick up*) (*v.t.* & *i.*) загибáть(ся) *impf.*, загнýть(ся) *pf.*; (*make louder*) дéлать *impf.*, с~ *pf.* грóмче; **~ up one's nose** воротить (-очý, -óтишь) *impf.* нос (**at** от+*g.*) (*coll.*); **~ upside down** переворáчивать *impf.*, перевернýть *pf.* вверх дном. **turn-out** *n.* количество приходящих. **turn-up** *n.* (*on trousers etc.*) отворóт, обшлáг (-á; *pl.* -á).

turncoat ['tɜːnkəʊt] *n.* ренегáт, перебéжчик.

turner ['tɜːnə(r)] *n.* тóкарь (*pl.* -ри & -ря) *m.*

turning ['tɜːnɪŋ] *n.* (*road*) поворóт. **turning-point** *n.* поворóтный пункт.

turnip ['tɜːnɪp] *n.* рéпа.

turnover ['tɜːnˌəʊvə(r)] *n.* (*turning over*) опрокидывание; (*econ.*) оборóт; (*fluctuation of manpower*) текýчесть рабóчей силы; (*pie*) полукрýглый пирóг (-á) с начинкой.

turnpike ['tɜːnpaɪk] *n.* (*toll gate*) застáва (где взимáется подорóжный сбор).

turnstile ['tɜːnstaɪl] *n.* турникéт.

turntable ['tɜːnteɪbl] *n.* (*rail.*) поворóтный круг (*loc.* -е & -ý; *pl.* -и); (*of record player*) проигрыватель *m.*, вертýшка.

turpentine ['tɜːpənˌtaɪn] *n.* скипидáр.

turpitude ['tɜːpɪˌtjuːd] *n.* низость, порóчность.

turquoise ['tɜːkwɔɪz, -kwɑːz] *n.* (*material, stone*) бирюзá; *adj.* бирюзóвый.

turret ['tʌrɪt] *n.* бáшенка; (*gun ~*) орудийная бáшня.

turtle ['tɜːt(ə)l] *n.* (морскáя) черепáха.

turtle-dove ['tɜːt(ə)l] *n.* гóрлица.

tusk [tʌsk] *n.* бивень (-вня) *m.*, клык (-á).

tussle ['tʌs(ə)l] *n.* дрáка; *v.i.* дрáться (дерýсь, -рёшься; дрáлся, -лáсь, дрáлóсь) *impf.* (**for** за+*a.*).

tut [tʌt] *int.* ах ты!

tutelage ['tjuːtɪlɪdʒ] *n.* (*guardianship*) опекýнство; (*instruction*) обучéние. **tutelar(y)** *adj.* опекýнский. **tutor** *n.* (*private teacher*) чáстный домáшний учитель (*pl.* -ля) *m.*, ~ница; (*coach*) репетитор; (*univ.*) руководитель *m.*, ~ница; (*primer*) учéбник; (*mus. primer*) шкóла игры; *v.t.* (*instruct*) обучáть *impf.*, обучить (-чý, -чишь) *pf.* (**in** +*d.*); (*give lessons to*) давáть (даю, даёшь) *impf.*, дать (дам, дашь, даст, дадим; дал, -á, дáлó, -и) *pf.* урóки+*d.*; (*guide*) руководить *impf.*+*i.*

tutorial [tjuː'tɔːrɪəl] *n.* консульта́ция, встре́ча с руководи́телем.

tutu ['tuːtuː] *n.* (*ballet*) па́чка.

TV *abbr.* (*of* **television**) ТВ, телеви́дение; (*set*) телеви́зор; ~ **addict** телема́н, ~ка; **closed-circuit** ~ за́мкнутое телеви́дение.

twaddle ['twɒd(ə)l] *n.* пуста́я болтовня́, чепуха́.

twang [twæŋ] *n.* (*string*) ре́зкий звук (натя́нутой струны́); (*voice*) гнуса́вость; *v.i.* (*string*) звуча́ть (-чу́, -чи́шь) *impf.*, про~ *pf.*; (*voice*) гнуса́вить; *v.t.* (*pluck*) перебира́ть *impf.*

tweak [twiːk] *n.* щипо́к (-пка́); *v.t.* щипа́ть (-плю́, -плешь) *impf.*, (у)щипну́ть *pf.*

tweed [twiːd] *n.* твид.

tweet [twiːt] *n.* ще́бет; *v.i.* щебета́ть (-ечу́, -е́чешь) *impf.*

tweezers ['twiːzəz] *n.* пинце́т.

twelfth [twelfθ] *adj.* & *n.* двена́дцатый; (*fraction*) двена́дцатая (часть (*pl.* -ти, -те́й)); (*date*) двена́дцатое (число́); **T~ Night** кану́н Креще́ния. **twelve** *adj.* & *n.* двена́дцать (-ти, -тью); (*time*) двена́дцать (часо́в); (*age*) двена́дцать лет.

twentieth ['twentɪɪθ] *adj.* & *n.* двадца́тый; (*fraction*) двадца́тая (часть (*pl.* -ти, -те́й)); (*date*) двадца́тое (число́). **twenty** *adj.* & *n.* два́дцать (-ти́, -тью́); (*age*) два́дцать лет; *pl.* (*decade*) двадца́тые го́ды (-до́в) *m.pl.*

twice [twaɪs] *adv.* (*2 times*, *on 2 occasions*) два́жды; ~ **as** вдво́е, в два ра́за+*comp.*

twiddle ['twɪd(ə)l] *v.t.* (*turn*, *twirl*) верте́ть (-рчу́, -ртишь) *impf.* +*a.*, *i.*; (*toy with*) игра́ть *impf.* +*i.*; ~ **one's thumbs** (*fig.*) безде́льничать *impf.*

twig [twɪg] *n.* ве́точка, прут (пру́та́; *pl.* -тья, -тьев).

twilight ['twaɪlaɪt] *n.* су́мерки (-рек) *pl.*; (*decline*) упа́док (-дка). **twilit** *adj.* су́меречный.

twill [twɪl] *n.* твил, са́ржа.

twin [twɪn] *n.* близне́ц (-а́); *pl.* (*Gemini*) Близнецы́ *m.pl.*; ~ **beds** па́ра односпа́льных крова́тей; ~ **brother** брат (*pl.* -ья, -ьев)-близне́ц (-а́); ~ **town** го́род (*pl.* -а́)-побрати́м; *v.t.* (*unite*) соединя́ть *impf.*, соедини́ть *pf.*

twine [twaɪn] *n.* бечёвка, шпага́т; *v.t.* (*twist*, *weave*) вить (вью, вьёшь; вил, -а́, -о) *impf.*, с~ *pf.*; *v.t.* & *i.* (~ *round*) обвива́ть(ся) *impf.*, обви́ть(ся) (обовью́(сь), -ьёшь(ся); обви́л(ся), -ла́(сь), -ло(сь)) *pf.*

twin-engined [ˌtwɪn'endʒɪnd] *adj.* двухмото́рный.

twinge [twɪndʒ] *n.* при́ступ (бо́ли), о́страя боль; (*of conscience*) угрызе́ние.

twinkle ['twɪŋk(ə)l] *n.* мерца́ние; (*of eyes*) огонёк (-нька); *v.i.* мерца́ть *impf.*, сверка́ть *impf.* **twinkling** *n.* мерца́ние; **in the ~ of an eye** в мгнове́ние о́ка.

twirl [twɜːl] *n.* враще́ние, круче́ние; (*flourish*) ро́счерк; *v.t.* & *i.* (*twist*, *turn*) верте́ть(ся) (-рчу́(сь), -ртишь(ся)) *impf.*; (*whirl*, *spin*) кружи́ть(ся) (-жу́(сь), кру́жи́шь(ся)) *impf.*

twist [twɪst] *n.* (*bend*) изги́б, поворо́т; (~*ing*) круче́ние; (*distortion*) искаже́ние; (*sprain*) вы́вих; (*dance*) твист; (*characteristic*) характе́рная осо́бенность; (*in story*) поворо́т фа́булы; *v.t.* скру́чивать *impf.*, крути́ть (-учу́, -у́тишь) *impf.*, с~ *pf.*; (*wind together*) вить (вью, вьёшь; вил, а́, -о) *impf.*, с~ *pf.*; (*distort*) искажа́ть *impf.*, искази́ть *pf.*; (*sprain*) выви́хивать *impf.*, вы́вихнуть *pf.*; *v.i.* (*bend*, *curve*) изгиба́ться *impf.*, изогну́ться *pf.*; (*climb*, *meander*, *twine*) ви́ться (вьётся) *impf.* **twisted** *adj.* (*bent*, *distorted*) искривлённый (-ён, -ена́) (*also fig.*). **twister** *n.* обма́нщик, -ица.

twit [twɪt] *n.* глупе́ц (-пца́).

twitch [twɪtʃ] *n.* (~*ing*, *jerk*) подёргивание; (*spasm*) су́дорога; *v.t.* & *i.* дёргать(ся) *impf.*, дёрнуть(ся) *pf.* (**at** за+*a.*).

twitter ['twɪtə(r)] *n.* ще́бет; *v.i.* щебета́ть (-ечу́, -е́чешь) *impf.*, чири́кать *impf.*

two [tuː] *adj.* & *n.* два, две (*f.*) (двух, -ум, -умя́, -ух); (*collect.*; *2 pairs*) дво́е (-ои́х); (*cards*, *number 2*) дво́йка; (*time*) два (часа́); (*age*) два го́да; ~ **times** два́жды; ~ **times four** два́жды четы́ре; **in ~** (*in half*) на́двое, попола́м. **two-dimensional** *adj.* двухме́рный. **two-edged** *adj.* обоюдоо́стрый (*also fig.*); (*ambiguous*) двусмы́сленный (-ен, -енна). **twofold** *adj.* двойно́й; *adv.* вдвойне́. **two-ply** *adj.* (*wood*) двухсло́йный; (*rope*) двойно́й. **two-seater** *n.* двухме́стный (автомоби́ль). **twosome** *n.* па́ра, дво́йка. **two-stroke** *adj.* двухта́ктный. **two-way** *adj.* двусторо́нний.

tycoon [taɪ'kuːn] *n.* магна́т.

tympanum ['tɪmpənəm] *n.* (*anat.*) бараба́нная перепо́нка.

type [taɪp] *n.* (*var. senses*) тип; (*model*) типи́чный образе́ц (-зца́); (*sort*, *kind*) род (*pl.* -ды́); (*letter*) ли́тера; (*collect.*) шрифт (*pl.* -ы́); **true to ~** типи́чный; *v.t.* писа́ть (пишу́, -шешь) *impf.*, на~ *pf.* на маши́нке. **typescript** *n.* маши́нопись. **typewriter** *n.* пи́шущая маши́нка. **typewritten** *adj.* машинопи́сный.

typhoid fever ['taɪfɔɪd] *n.* брюшно́й тиф.

typhoon [taɪ'fuːn] *n.* тайфу́н.

typhus ['taɪfəs] *n.* сыпно́й тиф.

typical ['tɪpɪk(ə)l] *adj.* типи́чный. **typify** ['tɪpɪˌfaɪ] *v.t.* служи́ть (-жу́, -жишь) *impf.*, по~ *pf.* типи́чным приме́ром+*g.*; (*personify*) олицетворя́ть *impf.*, олицетвори́ть *pf.*

typist ['taɪpɪst] *n.* машини́стка.

typographical [ˌtaɪpə'græfɪk(ə)l] *adj.* типогра́фский, книгопеча́тный. **ty'pography** *n.* книгопеча́тание; (*style*) оформле́ние.

tyrannical [tɪ'rænɪk(ə)l] *adj.* тирани́ческий, деспоти́чный. **tyrannize** ['tɪrəˌnaɪz] *v.i.* (*t.*) тира́нствовать *impf.* (над+*i.*). **tyrant** ['taɪərənt] *n.* тира́н, де́спот.

tyre ['taɪə(r)] *n.* ши́на. **tyre-gauge** *n.* мано́метр для шин.

U

U-boat ['ju:bəʊt] *n.* неме́цкая подво́дная ло́дка. **ubiquitous** [ju:'bɪkwɪtəs] *adj.* вездесу́щий. **ubiquity** *n.* вездесу́щность.
udder ['ʌdə(r)] *n.* вы́мя *nt.*
UFO *abbr.* (*of* ***unidentified flying object***) НЛО, неопо́знанный лета́ющий объе́кт.
ugh [əx, ʌg, ʌx] *int.* тьфу!
ugliness ['ʌglɪnɪs] *n.* уро́дство. **ugly** *adj.* некраси́вый, уро́дливый, безобра́зный; (*unpleasant*) неприя́тный; (*repulsive*) проти́вный; ~ **duckling** (*fig.*) га́дкий утёнок (-нка; *pl.* утя́та, -т).
неопо́знанный лета́ющий объе́кт.
UK *abbr.* (*of* ***United Kingdom***) Соединённое Короле́вство (Великобрита́нии и Се́верной Ирла́ндии); *adj.* (велико)брита́нский.
Ukraine [ju:'kreɪn] *n.* Украи́на. **Ukrainian** *n.* украи́нец (-нца), -нка; *adj.* украи́нский.
ukulele [ˌju:kə'leɪlɪ] *n.* гава́йская гита́ра.
ulcer ['ʌlsə(r)] *n.* я́зва. **ulcerate** *v.t.* & *i.* изъязвля́ть(ся) *impf.*, изъязви́ть(ся) *pf.* **ulcered, ulcerous** *adj.* изъязвлённый.
ulna ['ʌlnə] *n.* локтева́я кость (*pl.* -ти, -те́й).
ulterior [ʌl'tɪərɪə(r)] *adj.* скры́тый.
ultimate ['ʌltɪmət] *adj.* (*final*) после́дний, оконча́тельный; (*fundamental*) основно́й. **ultimately** *adv.* в коне́чном счёте, в конце́ концо́в. **ultimatum** [ˌʌltɪ'meɪtəm] *n.* ультима́тум.
ultra- ['ʌltrə] *in comb.* ультра..., сверх(ъ)... .
ultramarine [ˌʌltrəmə'ri:n] *n.* ультрамари́н; *adj.* ультрамари́новый. **ultra-violet** [ˌʌltrə'vaɪələt] *adj.* ультрафиоле́товый.
umbilical [ʌm'bɪlɪk(ə)l, ˌʌmbɪ'laɪk(ə)l] *adj.* пупо́чный; ~ **cord** пупови́на.
umbra ['ʌmbrə] *n.* по́лная тень (*loc.* -ни́; *pl.* -ни, -не́й). **umbrage** *n.* оби́да; **take** ~ обижа́ться *impf.*, оби́деться (оби́жусь, -и́дишься) *pf.* (**at** на+*a.*).
umbrella [ʌm'brelə] *n.* зо́нтик, зонт (-а́); ~ **stand** подста́вка для зо́нтов.
umpire ['ʌmpaɪə(r)] *n.* судья́ (*pl.* -дьи, -де́й, -дьям) *m.*; *v.t.* & *i.* суди́ть (сужу́, су́дишь) *impf.*
UN *abbr.* (*of* ***United Nations*** (***Organization***)): **the** ~ ООН *f. indecl.*, Организа́ция Объединённых На́ций; *adj.* (*coll.*) оо́новский.
unabashed [ˌʌnə'bæʃt] *adj.* нерастеря́вшийся; без вся́кого смуще́ния. **unabated** *adj.* неосла́бленный, неосла́бный. **unable** *adj.*: **be** ~ **to** не мочь (могу́, мо́жешь; мог, -ла́) *impf.*, с~ *pf.*; быть не в состоя́нии; (*not know how to*) не уме́ть *impf.*, с~ *pf.* **unabridged** *adj.* несокращённый, без сокраще́ний. **unaccompanied** *adj.* несопровожда́емый; (*mus.*) без аккомпанеме́нта. **unaccountable** *adj.* (*inexplicable*) необъясни́мый. **unaccustomed** *adj.* (*not accustomed*) неприв́ыкший (**to** к+*d.*); (*unusual*) неприв́ычный. **unadulterated** *adj.* настоя́щий, нефальсифици́рованный; чисте́йший. **unaffected** *adj.* и́скренний (-нен, -нна, -нне & -нно); (*not affected*) незатро́нутый. **unaided** *adj.* без по́мощи, самостоя́тельный. **unalloyed** *adj.* беспри́месный, чи́стый (чист, -а́, -о, чи́сты́). **unalterable** *adj.* неизменя́емый, неизме́нный (-нен, -нна). **unambiguous** *adj.* недвусмы́сленный (-ен, -енна).
unanimity [ˌju:nə'nɪmɪtɪ] *n.* единоду́шие. **unanimous** [ju:'nænɪməs] *adj.* единоду́шный.
unanswerable *adj.* (*irrefutable*) неопровержи́мый. **unapproachable** *adj.* непристу́пный; (*unmatched*) несравни́мый. **unarmed** *adj.* безору́жный, невооружённый. **unashamed** *adj.* бессо́вестный, на́глый (нагл, -а́, -о). **unasked** *adj.* доброво́льный, непро́шеный (*coll.*). **unassailable** *adj.* непристу́пный; (*irrefutable*) неопровержи́мый. **unassuming** *adj.* скро́мный (-мен, -мна́, -мно), непритяза́тельный. **unattainable** *adj.* недосяга́емый. **unattended** *adj.* (*unaccompanied*) несопровожда́емый. **unattractive** *adj.* непривлека́тельный. **unauthorized** *adj.* неразрешённый; (*person*) неправомо́чный. **unavailable** *adj.* не име́ющийся в нали́чии, недосту́пный; **be** ~ в нали́чии нет+*g.* **unavailing** *adj.* бесполе́зный, тще́тный. **unavoidable** *adj.* неизбе́жный, немину́емый. **unaware** *pred.*: **be** ~ **of** не сознава́ть (-аю́, -аёшь) *impf.*+*a.*; не знать *impf.* о+*p.* **unawares** *adv.* врасплóх, неожи́данно; (*unintentionally*) нечаянно. **unbalance** *v.t.* (*psych.*) лиша́ть *impf.*, лиши́ть *pf.* душе́вного равнове́сия. **unbalanced** *adj.* (*psych.*) неуравнове́шенный (-ен, -енна). **unbearable** *adj.* невыноси́мый. **unbeatable** *adj.* (*unsurpassable*) не могу́щий быть превзойдённым; (*invincible*) непобеди́мый. **unbeaten** *adj.* (*unsurpassed*) непревзойдённый (-ен, -енна). **unbecoming** *adj.* (*inappropriate*) неподходя́щий; (*unseemly*) неприли́чный; **be** ~ быть не к лицу́ (**to** +*d.*). **unbelief** *n.* неве́рие. **unbelievable** *adj.* невероя́тный. **unbeliever** *n.* неве́рующий *sb.* **unbend** *v.t.* & *i.* (*straighten*) выпрямля́ть(ся) *impf.*, вы́прямить(ся) *pf.*; разгиба́ть(ся) *impf.*, разогну́ть(ся) *pf.*; *v.i.* (*become affable*) станови́ться (-влю́сь, -вишься) *impf.*, стать (-а́ну, -а́нешь) *pf.* приве́тливым. **unbending** *adj.* непрекло́нный (-нен, -нна). **unbias(s)ed** *adj.* беспристра́стный. **unblemished** *adj.* незапя́тнанный. **unblushing** *adj.* беззасте́нчивый. **unbolt** *v.t.*

отпира́ть *impf.*, отпере́ть (отопру́, -рёшь; о́тпер, -ла́, -ло) *pf.* **unborn** *adj.* ещё не рождённый (-ён, -ена́). **unbosom** *v.t.*: ~ **o.s.** открыва́ть *impf.*, откры́ть (-ро́ю, -ро́ешь) *pf.* ду́шу. **unbound** *adj.* (*free*) свобо́дный; (*book*) непереплетённый. **unbounded** *adj.* (*not limited*) неограни́ченный (-ен, -енна); (*joy*) безме́рный; (*infinite*) безграни́чный. **unbreakable** *adj.* небью́щийся. **unbridled** *adj.* разну́зданный (-ан, -анна). **unbroken** *adj.* (*intact*) неразби́тый, це́лый; (*continuous*) непреры́вный; (*unsurpassed*) непоби́тый; (*horse*) необъе́женный. **unbuckle** *v.t.* расстёгивать *impf.*, расстегну́ть *pf.* **unburden** *v.t.*: ~ **o.s.** отводи́ть (-ожу́, -о́дишь) *impf.*, отвести́ (-еду́, -едёшь; -ёл, -ела́) *pf.* ду́шу. **unbutton** *v.t.* расстёгивать *impf.*, расстегну́ть *pf.*

uncalled-for [ʌn'kɔ:ldfɔ:(r)] *adj.* неуме́стный. **uncanny** *adj.* жу́ткий (-ток, -тка́, -тко), сверхъесте́ственный (-ен, -енна). **uncared-for** *adj.* забро́шенный. **unceasing** *adj.* непреры́вный, безостано́вочный. **unceremonious** *adj.* бесцеремо́нный (-нен, -нна). **uncertain** *adj.* (*not certainly known*) то́чно неизве́стный, нея́сный (-сен, -сна́, -сно); (*indecisive*, *hesitating*) неуве́ренный (-ен, -ена); (*lacking belief*, *confidence*) неуве́ренный (-ен, -на); (*indeterminate*) неопределённый (-нен, -нна); (*changeable*) изме́нчивый; **be** ~ (*not know for certain*) то́чно не знать *impf.*; **in no** ~ **terms** в недвусмы́сленных выраже́ниях. **uncertainty** *n.* неизве́стность; неуве́ренность; неопределённость; изме́нчивость. **unchain** *v.t.* спуска́ть *impf.* спусти́ть (-ущу́, -у́стишь) *pf.* с це́пи. **unchallenged** *adj.* не вызыва́ющий возраже́ний. **unchangeable** *adj.* неизмени́мый, неизменя́емый. **unchanged** *adj.* неизмени́вшийся. **unchanging** *adj.* неизменя́ющийся. **uncharacteristic** *adj.* нетипи́чный, нехаракте́рный. **uncharitable** *adj.* немилосе́рдный, жесто́кий (-о́к, -о́ка́, -о́ко). **uncharted** *adj.* (*fig.*) неиссле́дованный. **unchecked** *adj.* (*unrestrained*) необу́зданный (-ан, -анна). **uncivil** *adj.* неве́жливый. **uncivilized** *adj.* нецивилизо́ванный. **unclaimed** *adj.* невостре́бованный. **unclassified** *adj.* неклассифици́рованный; (*not secret*) несекре́тный.

uncle ['ʌŋk(ə)l] *n.* дя́дя (*pl.* -ди, -дей & -дья́, -дьёв) *m.*

unclean [ʌn'kli:n] *adj.* (*not clean*; *bibl. of food*) нечи́стый (-т, -та́, -то). **unclear** *adj.* нея́сный (-сен, -сна́, -сно), непоня́тный. **uncoil** *v.t.* & *i.* разма́тывать(ся) *impf.*, размота́ть(ся) *pf.* **uncomfortable** *adj.* неудо́бный; (*awkward*) нело́вкий (-вок, -вка́, -вко). **uncommon** *adj.* (*unusual*, *remarkable*) необыкнове́нный (-нен, -нна), замеча́тельный; (*rare*) ре́дкий (-док, -дка́, -дко). **uncommunicative** *adj.* необщи́тельный, молчали́вый. **uncomplaining** *adj.* безро́потный. **uncompleted** *adj.* неоко́нченный, незако́нченный. **uncomplimentary** *adj.* неле́стный. **uncompromising** *adj.* не иду́щий на компроми́ссы; (*inflexible*) непрекло́нный (-нен, -нна). **unconcealed** *adj.* нескрыва́емый. **unconcern** *n.* (*freedom from anxiety*) беззабо́тность; (*indifference*) равноду́шие. **unconcerned** *adj.* беззабо́тный; равноду́шный. **unconditional** *adj.* безогово́рочный, безусло́вный. **unconfirmed** *adj.* неподтверждённый. **unconnected** *adj.* ~ **with** не свя́занный (-ан) с+*i.* **unconquerable** *adj.* непобеди́мый. **unconscionable** *adj.* бессо́вестный; (*excessive*) неуме́ренный (-ен, -енна). **unconscious** *adj.* (*also unintentional*) бессозна́тельный; *pred.* без созна́ния; (*unintentional*) нево́льный; **be** ~ **of** не сознава́ть (-аю, -аёшь) *impf.*+*g.*; *n.* подсозна́тельное *sb.* **unconsciousness** *n.* бессозна́тельное состоя́ние; бессозна́тельность. **unconstitutional** *adj.* неконституцио́нный (-нен, -нна). **unconstrained** *adj.* непринуждённый (-ён, -ённа). **uncontrollable** *adj.* неудержи́мый, неукроти́мый. **uncontrolled** *adj.* (*unbridled*) необу́зданный (-ан, -анна). **unconventional** *adj.* чу́ждый (-д, -да́, -до) усло́вности; необы́чный. **unconvincing** *adj.* неубеди́тельный. **uncooked** *adj.* сыро́й (-р, -ра́, -ро). **uncooperative** *adj.* неотзы́вчивый, безуча́стный. **uncork** *v.t.* отку́поривать *impf.*, отку́порить *pf.* **uncouple** *v.t.* расцепля́ть *impf.*, расцепи́ть (-плю́, -пишь) *pf.* **uncouth** [ʌn'ku:θ] *adj.* гру́бый (-б, -ба́, -бо). **uncover** *v.t.* (*remove cover from*) снима́ть *impf.*, снять (сниму́, -мешь; снял, -а́, -о) *pf.* кры́шку с+*g.*; (*reveal*) открыва́ть *impf.*, откры́ть (-ро́ю, -ро́ешь) *pf.*; (*disclose*) обнару́живать *impf.*, обнару́жить *pf.* **uncovered** *adj.* незакры́тый, откры́тый. **uncritical** *adj.* некрити́чный.

unction ['ʌŋkʃ(ə)n] *n.* (*ceremony*) пома́зание; (*process*) втира́ние ма́зи; (*ointment*) мазь; (*balm*) еле́й; (*piety*) на́божность; (*affectedness*) еле́йность; **extreme** ~ собо́рование. **unctuous** *adj.* еле́йный.

uncultivated [ʌn'kʌltɪ,veɪtɪd] *adj.* (*land*) невозде́ланный; (*talent*) неразвито́й (нера́звит, -а́, -о); (*uncultured*) некульту́рный. **uncultured** *adj.* некульту́рный. **uncurl** *v.t.* & *i.* развива́ть(ся) *impf.*, разви́ть(ся) (разовью́, -ьёт(ся); разви́л(ся), -ла́(сь), разви́ло́(сь)) *pf.* **uncut** *adj.* (*unabridged*) несокращённый, без сокраще́ний.

undamaged [ʌn'dæmɪdʒd] *adj.* неповреждённый, неиспо́рченный. **undaunted** *adj.* бесстра́шный. **undeceive** *v.t.* выводи́ть (-ожу́, -о́дишь) *impf.*, вы́вести (-еду, -едешь; -ел) *pf.* из заблужде́ния. **undecided** *adj.* (*not settled*) нерешённый; (*irresolute*) нереши́тельный. **undemanding** *adj.* нетребова́тельный. **undemocratic** *adj.* недемократи́ческий, антидемократи́ческий. **undemonstrative** *adj.* сде́ржанный (-ан, -анна).

undeniable *adj.* неоспори́мый, несомнéнный (-нен, -нна).

under ['ʌndə(r)] *prep.* (*position*) под+*i.*; (*direction*) под+*a.*; (*fig.*) под+*i.*; (*less than*) мéньше+*g.*, ни́же+*g.*; (*according to*) по+*d.*; (*in view of*, *in the reign*, *time of*) при+*p.*; ~ **repair** в ремóнте; ~ **way** на ходу́; **from** ~ из-под+*g.*; *adv.* (*position*) внизу́, ни́же; (*direction*) вниз; (*less*) мéньше; *adj.* ни́жний; (*subordinate*) ни́зший. **under-age** *adj.* несовершеннолéтний.

undercarriage ['ʌndə,kærɪdʒ] *n.* шасси́ *nt.indecl.* **underclothes, underclothing** *n.* ни́жнее бельё. **undercoat** *n.* (*of paint*) грунтóвка. **undercover** *adj.* тáйный, секрéтный. **undercurrent** *n.* подвóдное течéние; (*fig.*) скры́тая тендéнция. **undercut** *v.t.* (*cut away*) подрезáть *impf.*, подрéзать (-éжу, -éжешь) *pf.*; (*price*) назначáть *impf.*, назнáчить *pf.* бóлее ни́зкую цéну чем+*nom.* **underdeveloped** *adj.* недорáзвитый, слаборáзвитый; (*phot.*) недопроя́вленный. **underdog** *n.* неудáчник.

underdone [,ʌndə'dʌn, 'ʌn-] *adj.* недожáренный (-ен). **underemployment** *n.* непóлная зáнятость. **underestimate** *v.t.* недооцéнивать *impf.*, недооцени́ть (-ню́, -нишь) *pf.*; *n.* недооцéнка. **underexpose** *v.t.* недодéрживать *impf.*, недодержáть (-жу́, -жишь) *pf.* **underfed** *adj.* недокóрмленный. **underfelt** *n.* грунт ковра́. **underfloor** *adj.* находя́щийся под полóм. **underfoot** *adv.* под ногáми. **undergarment** *n.* предмéт ни́жнего белья́.

undergo [,ʌndə'gəʊ] *v.t.* подвергáться *impf.*, подвéргнуться (-гся) *pf.*+*d.*; (*endure*) переноси́ть (-ошу́, -óсишь) *impf.*, перенести́ (-есу́, -есёшь; -ёс, -еслá) *pf.* **undergraduate** *n.* студéнт, ~ка. **underground** *n.* (*rail.*) метрó *nt.indecl.*; (*fig.*) подпóлье; *adj.* подзéмный; (*fig.*) подпóльный; *adv.* под землёй; (*fig.*) подпóльно; **go** ~ уходи́ть (-ожу́, -óдишь) *impf.*, уйти́ (уйду́, -дёшь; ушёл, ушлá) *pf.* в подпóлье. **undergrowth** *n.* подлéсок (-ска). **underhand** *adj.* закули́сный, тáйный. **underlie** *v.t.* (*fig.*) лежáть (-жит) *impf.* в оснóве+*g.* **underline** *v.t.* подчёркивать *impf.*, подчеркну́ть *pf.*

underling *n.* подчинённый *sb.*

undermanned [,ʌndə'mænd] *adj.* испы́тывающий недостáток в рабóчей си́ле. **undermentioned** *adj.* нижеупомя́нутый. **undermine** *v.t.* дéлать *impf.*, с~ *pf.* подкóп под+*i.*; (*wash away*) подмывáть *impf.*, подмы́ть (-мóю, -мóешь) *pf.*; (*authority*) подрывáть *impf.*, подорвáть (-ву́, -вёшь; подорвáл, -á, -о) *pf.*; (*health*) разрушáть *impf.*, разру́шить *pf.*

underneath [,ʌndə'ni:θ] *adv.* (*position*) внизу́; (*direction*) вниз; *prep.* (*position*) под+*i.*; (*direction*) под+*a.*; *n.* ни́жняя часть (*pl.* -ти, -тéй); *adj.* ни́жний.

undernourished *adj.* недокóрмленный; **be** ~ недоедáть *impf.* **undernourishment** *n.* недоедáние.

underpaid [,ʌndə'peɪd] *adj.* низкооплáчиваемый. **underpants** *n.* кальсóны (-н) *pl.*, трусы́ (-сóв) *pl.* **underpass** *n.* проéзд под полотнóм дорóги, тоннéль *m.* **underpin** *v.t.* подводи́ть (-ожу́, -óдишь) *impf.*, подвести́ (-еду́, -едёшь; -ёл, -елá) *pf.* фундáмент под+*a.* **underpopulated** *adj.* малонаселённый (-ён, -ённа). **underprivileged** *adj.* пóльзующийся мéньшими правáми; (*poor*) бéдный (-ден, -днá, -дно, бéдны́). **underrate** *v.t.* недооцéнивать *impf.*, недооцени́ть *pf.* **under-secretary** *n.* замести́тель *m.* мини́стра.

undersell [,ʌndə'sel] *v.t.* продавáть (-даю́, -даёшь) *impf.*, продáть (-áм, -áшь, -áсть, -ади́м; прóдал, -á, -о) *pf.* дешéвле+*g.* **underside** *n.* ни́жняя повéрхность. **undersigned** *adj.* (*n.*) нижеподписáвшийся (*sb.*). **undersized** *adj.* маломéрный, нестандáртный; (*dwarfish*) кáрликовый. **underskirt** *n.* ни́жняя ю́бка. **understaffed** *adj.* неукомплектóванный.

understand [,ʌndə'stænd] *v.t.* понимáть *impf.*, поня́ть (пойму́, -мёшь; пóнял, -á, -о) *pf.*; (*have heard say*) слы́шать *impf.* **understandable** *adj.* поня́тный. **understanding** *n.* понимáние; (*intellect*) рáзум; (*mutual* ~) взаимопонимáние; (*agreement*) соглашéние; (*harmony*) соглáсие; *adj.* (*sympathetic*) чу́ткий (-ток, -ткá, -тко), отзы́вчивый.

understate [,ʌndə'steɪt] *v.t.* преуменьшáть *impf.*, преумéньшить *pf.* **understatement** *n.* преуменьшéние.

understudy ['ʌndə,stʌdɪ] *n.* дублёр; *v.t.* дубли́ровать *impf.* роль+*g.*

undertake [,ʌndə'teɪk] *v.t.* (*engage in*, *enter upon*) предпринимáть *impf.*, предприня́ть (-иму́, -и́мешь; предпри́нял, -á, -о) *pf.*; (*responsibility*) брать (беру́, берёшь) *impf.*, взять (возьму́, -мёшь; взял, á, -о) *pf.* на себя́; (+*inf.*) обя́зываться *impf.*, обязáться (-яжу́сь, -я́жешься) *pf.*; (*guarantee*) ручáться *impf.*, поручи́ться (-чу́сь, -чишься) *pf.* (**that** что). **'undertaker** *n.* гробовщи́к (-á). **undertaking** *n.* предприя́тие; (*obligation*) обязáтельство.

undertone ['ʌndə,təʊn] *n.* (*half-tint*) полутóн (*pl.* -ы & -á); (*nuance*) оттéнок (-нка); **speak in** ~**s** говори́ть *impf.* вполгóлоса. **undertow** *n.* глуби́нное течéние, противоположное повéрхностному; подвóдное течéние. **underwater** *adj.* подвóдный. **underwear** *n.* ни́жнее бельё. **underworld** *n.* (*myth.*) преиспóдняя *sb.*; (*criminals*) престу́пный мир (*pl.* -ы́). **underwrite** *v.t.* (*sign*) подпи́сывать *impf.*, подписáть (подпишу́, -шешь) *pf.*; (*accept liability for*) принимáть *impf.*, приня́ть (приму́, -мешь; при́нял, -á, -о) *pf.* на страх; (*guarantee*) гаранти́ровать *impf.* & *pf.* **underwriter** *n.* подпи́счик; страхóвщик; (*company*) страховáя компáния.

undeserved [ˌʌndɪˈzɜːvd] *adj.* незаслу́женный (-ен, -енна). **undeserving** *adj.* незаслу́живающий; ~ **of** не заслу́живающий+*g*. **undesirable** *adj.* нежела́тельный; *n.* нежела́тельное лицо́ (*pl.* -ца). **undeveloped** *adj.* нера́звитый; (*land*) незастро́енный. **undignified** *adj.* недосто́йный (-о́ин, -о́йна). **undiluted** *adj.* неразба́вленный. **undisciplined** *adj.* недисциплини́рованный (-ан, -анна). **undiscovered** *adj.* неоткры́тый; (*unknown*) неизве́стный. **undiscriminating** *adj.* непроница́тельный, неразбо́рчивый. **undisguised** *adj.* откры́тый, я́вный. **undismayed** *adj.* необескура́женный. **undisputed** *adj.* бесспо́рный. **undistinguished** *adj.* невыдаю́щийся. **undisturbed** *adj.* (*untouched*) нетро́нутый; (*peaceful*) споко́йный; (*in order*) в поря́дке. **undivided** *adj.* (*unanimous*) единоду́шный; **give ~ attention** посвяща́ть *impf.*, посвяти́ть (-ящу́, -яти́шь) *pf.* все си́лы (**to** +*d.*). **undo** *v.t.* (*open*) открыва́ть *impf.*, откры́ть (-ро́ю, -ро́ешь) *pf.*; (*untie*) развя́зывать *impf.*, развяза́ть (-яжу́, -я́жешь) *pf.*; (*unbutton*, *unhook*, *unbuckle*) расстёгивать *impf.*, расстегну́ть *pf.*; (*destroy*, *cancel*) уничтожа́ть *impf.*, уничто́жить *pf.*; (*be the ~ing of*) губи́ть (гублю́, -бишь) *impf.*, по~ *pf.* **undoing** *n.* (*ruin*, *downfall*) ги́бель; (*destruction*) уничтоже́ние. **undoubted** *adj.* несомне́нный (-нен, -нна). **undoubtedly** *adv.* несомне́нно. **undress** *v.t.* & *i.* раздева́ть(ся) *impf.*, разде́ть(ся) (-е́ну(сь), -е́нешь(ся)) *pf.* **undrinkable** *adj.* него́дный (-ден, -дна́, -дно) для питья́. **undue** *adj.* чрезме́рный. **unduly** *adv.* чрезме́рно.

undulate [ˈʌndjʊˌleɪt] *v.i.* быть волни́стым, холми́стым. **undulating** *adj.* волни́стый. **unduˈlation** *n.* волни́стость; (*motion*) волнообра́зное движе́ние; (*of surface*) неро́вность пове́рхности.

undying [ʌnˈdaɪɪŋ] *adj.* (*eternal*) ве́чный.

unearned [ʌnˈɜːnd] *adj.* незарабо́танный; (*undeserved*) незаслу́женный (-ен, -енна); ~ **income** нетрудово́й дохо́д. **unearth** *v.t.* (*dig up*) выка́пывать *impf.*, вы́копать *pf.* из земли́; (*fox etc.*) выгоня́ть *impf.*, вы́гнать (вы́гоню, -нишь) *pf.* из но́ры; (*fig.*) раска́пывать *impf.*, раскопа́ть *pf.* **unearthly** *adj.* неземно́й, сверхъесте́ственный (-ен, -енна); (*inconvenient*) кра́йне неудо́бный. **uneasiness** *n.* (*anxiety*) беспоко́йство, трево́га; (*awkwardness*) нело́вкость. **uneasy** *adj.* беспоко́йный, трево́жный; нело́вкий (-вок, нело́вка́, -вко). **uneatable** *adj.* несъедо́бный. **uneconomic** *adj.* нерента́бельный, неэкономи́чный. **uneconomical** *adj.* (*car etc.*) неэкономи́чный; (*person*) неэконо́мный. **uneducated** *adj.* необразо́ванный (-ан, -анна). **unemployed** *adj.* безрабо́тный; (*unoccupied*) неза́нятый (-т, -та́, -то); (*unused*) неиспо́льзованный. **unemployment** *n.* безрабо́тица; ~ **benefit** посо́бие по безрабо́тице. **unending** *adj.* бесконе́чный, несконча́емый. **unenlightened** *adj.* непросвещённый (-ён, -ённа); (*uninformed*) неосведомлённый. **unenterprising** *adj.* непредприи́мчивый, безынициати́вный. **unenviable** *adj.* незави́дный. **unequal** *adj.* нера́вный; (*of ~ value*) неравноце́нный (-нен, -нна); (*unjust*) несправедли́вый; (*inadequate*) неадеква́тный; ~ **to** неподходя́щий для+*g*. **unequalled** *adj.* бесподо́бный, непревзойдённый (-ён, -ённа). **unequivocal** *adj.* недвусмы́сленный (-ен, -енна). **unerring** *adj.* безоши́бочный.

uneven [ʌnˈiːv(ə)n] *adj.* неро́вный (-вен, -вна́, -вно). **uneventful** *adj.* не бога́тый собы́тиями, ти́хий (тих, -а́, -о). **unexceptionable** *adj.* безукори́зненный (-ен, -енна). **unexceptional** *adj.* обы́чный. **unexpected** *adj.* неожи́данный (-ан, -анна); (*sudden*) внеза́пный. **unexplainable** *adj.* необъясни́мый. **unexplored** *adj.* неиссле́дованный. **unexpurgated** *adj.* без купю́р, неподве́ргшийся цензу́ре.

unfailing [ʌnˈfeɪlɪŋ] *adj.* неизме́нный (-нен, -нна); (*faithful*) ве́рный (-рен, -рна́, -рно); (*reliable*) надёжный; (*inexhaustible*) неисчерпа́емый.

unfair *adj.* несправедли́вый; (*dishonest*) нече́стный (-тен, -тна́, -тно). **unfaithful** *adj.* неве́рный (-рен, -рна́, -рно, неве́рны́); (*treacherous*) вероло́мный. **unfamiliar** *adj.* незнако́мый; (*unknown*) неве́домый. **unfashionable** *adj.* немо́дный (-ден, -дна́, -дно). **unfasten** *v.t.* (*detach*, *untie*) открепля́ть *impf.*, открепи́ть *pf.*; (*detach*, *unbutton*) отстёгивать *impf.*, отстегну́ть *pf.*; (*undo*, *unbutton*, *unhook*) расстёгивать *impf.*, расстегну́ть *pf.* **unfathomable** *adj.* (*immeasurable*) неизмери́мый, бездо́нный; (*incomprehensible*) непостижи́мый. **unfavourable** *adj.* неблагоприя́тный; (*not approving*) неблагосклóнный (-нен, -нна). **unfeeling** *adj.* бесчу́вственный (-ен, -енна). **unfeigned** *adj.* и́стинный (-нен, -нна), неподде́льный. **unfinished** *adj.* незако́нченный; (*crude*) необрабо́танный (-ан, -анна). **unfit** *adj.* него́дный (-ден, -дна́, -дно), неприго́дный, неподходя́щий; (*unhealthy*) нездоро́вый. **unfix** *v.t.* открепля́ть *impf.*, открепи́ть *pf.* **unflagging** *adj.* неослабева́ющий. **unfledged** *adj.* неопери́вшийся (*also fig.*). **unfold** *v.t.* & *i.* развёртывать(ся) *impf.*, разверну́ть(ся) *pf.*; (*open up*) раскрыва́ть(ся) *impf.*, раскры́ть(ся) (-ро́ю(сь), -ро́ешь(ся)) *pf.* **unforeseen** *adj.* непредви́денный. **unforgettable** *adj.* незабыва́емый. **unforgivable** *adj.* непрости́тельный. **unforgiving** *adj.* непроща́ющий. **unfortunate** *adj.* несчастли́вый, несча́стный; (*regrettable*) неуда́чный; *n.* несчастли́вец (-вца), неуда́чник, -ица. **unfortunately** *adv.* к несча́стью, к сожале́нию. **unfounded** *adj.* необосно́ванный (-ан, -анна). **unfreeze** *v.t.* & *i.* размора́живать(ся) *impf.*, разморо́зить(ся) *pf.* **un-**

friendly *adj.* недружелю́бный, неприве́тливый. **unfrock** *v.t.* лиша́ть *impf.*, лиши́ть *pf.* духо́вного са́на. **unfruitful** *adj.* беспло́дный. **unfulfilled** *adj.* (*promise etc.*) невы́полненный; (*hopes etc.*) неосуществлённый. **unfurl** *v.t. & i.* развёртывать(ся) *impf.*, развернýть(ся) *pf.* **unfurnished** *adj.* немеблиро́ванный.

ungainly [ʌn'geɪnlɪ] *adj.* нескла́дный, неуклю́жий. **ungentlemanly** *adj.* неблагоро́дный, неве́жливый. **ungodliness** *n.* безбо́жие. **ungodly** *adj.* (*also outrageous*) безбо́жный. **ungovernable** *adj.* необу́зданный (-ан, -анна), неукроти́мый. **ungracious** *adj.* нелюбе́зный. **ungrammatical** *adj.* граммати́чески непра́вильный. **ungrateful** *adj.* неблагода́рный. **unguarded** *adj.* (*incautious*) неосторо́жный.

unguent ['ʌŋgwənt] *n.* мазь.

unhappiness [ʌn'hæpɪnɪs] *n.* несча́стье. **unhappy** *adj.* несча́стливый, несча́стный. **unharmed** *adj.* невреди́мый. **unhealthy** *adj.* (*in var. senses*) нездоро́вый, боле́зненный (-ен, -енна); (*harmful*) вре́дный (-ден, -дна́, -дно). **unheard-of** *adj.* неслы́ханный (-ан, -анна). **unheeded** *adj.* незаме́ченный. **unheeding** *adj.* невнима́тельный. **unhelpful** *adj.* бесполе́зный. **unhesitating** *adj.* реши́тельный. **unhesitatingly** *adv.* без колеба́ния. **unhinge** *v.t.* снима́ть *impf.*, снять (сниму́, -мешь; снял, -а́, -о) *pf.* с пе́тли; (*fig.*) расстра́ивать *impf.*, расстро́ить *pf.* **unholy** *adj.* (*impious*) нечести́вый; (*awful*) ужа́сный. **unhook** *v.t.* снима́ть *impf.*, снять (сниму́, -мешь; снял, -а́, -о) *pf.* с крючка́; (*undo hooks*) расстёгивать *impf.*, расстегну́ть *pf.*; (*uncouple*) расцепля́ть *impf.*, расцепи́ть (-плю́, -пишь) *pf.* **unhoped-for** *adj.* неожи́данный (-ан, -анна). **unhorse** *v.t.* сбра́сывать *impf.*, сбро́сить *pf.* с ло́шади. **unhurt** *adj.* невреди́мый.

unicorn ['ju:nɪˌkɔ:n] *n.* единоро́г.

unification [ˌju:nɪfɪ'keɪʃ(ə)n] *n.* объедине́ние, унифика́ция (*also standardization*).

uniform ['ju:nɪˌfɔ:m] *n.* фо́рма, фо́рменная оде́жда; *adj.* единообра́зный; (*homogeneous*) одноро́дный; (*of* ~) фо́рменный. **uni'formity** *n.* единообра́зие; одноро́дность.

unify ['ju:nɪˌfaɪ] *v.t.* объединя́ть *impf.*, объедини́ть *pf.*; унифици́ровать *impf.* & *pf.* (*also standardize*).

unilateral [ju:nɪ'lætər(ə)l] *adj.* односторо́нний.

unimaginable [ˌʌnɪ'mædʒɪnəb(ə)l] *adj.* невообрази́мый. **unimaginative** *adj.* лишённый (-ён, -ена́) воображе́ния, прозаи́чный. **unimpeachable** *adj.* безупре́чный. **unimportant** *adj.* нева́жный. **uninformed** *adj.* (*ignorant*) несве́дущий (**about** в+*p.*); (*ill-informed*) неосведомлённый. **uninhabitable** *adj.* неприго́дный для жилья́. **uninhabited** *adj.* необита́емый. **uninitiated** *adj.* непосвящённый. **uninspired** *adj.* бана́льный. **unintelligible** *adj.* неразбо́рчивый. **unintentional** *adj.* неумы́шленный (-ен, -енна). **unintentionally** *adv.* неумы́шленно. **uninterested** *adj.* незаинтересо́ванный. **uninteresting** *adj.* неинтере́сный. **uninterrupted** *adj.* непреры́вный. **uninviting** *adj.* непривлека́тельный.

union ['ju:njən, -nɪən] *n.* (*alliance*) сою́з; (*joining together, alliance*) объедине́ние; (*combination*) соедине́ние; (*marriage*) бра́чный сою́з; (*harmony*) согла́сие; (*trade* ~) профсою́з. **unionist** *n.* член профсою́за; (*pol.*) унциони́ст.

unique [jʊ'ni:k, ju:'ni:k] *adj.* еди́нственный (в своём ро́де), уника́льный.

unison ['ju:nɪs(ə)n] *n.* (*mus.*) унисо́н; (*fig.*) согла́сие; **in** ~ (*mus.*) в унисо́н; (*fig.*) в согла́сии.

unit ['ju:nɪt] *n.* едини́ца; (*mil.*) часть (*pl.* -ти, -те́й).

unite [jʊ'naɪt, ju:-] *v.t. & i.* соединя́ть(ся) *impf.*, соедини́ть(ся) *pf.*; объединя́ть(ся) *impf.*, объедини́ть(ся) *pf.* **united** *adj.* соединённый, объединённый; **U~ Kingdom** Соединённое Короле́вство; **U~ Nations** Организа́ция Объединённых На́ций; **U~ States** Соединённые Шта́ты *m.pl.* Аме́рики. **unity** ['ju:nɪtɪ] *n.* еди́нство; (*cohesion*) сплочённость; (*math.*) едини́ца.

universal [ju:nɪ'vɜ:s(ə)l] *adj.* (*general*) всео́бщий; (*world-wide*) всеми́рный; (*many-sided*) универса́льный. **'universe** *n.* вселе́нная *sb.*; (*world*) мир (*pl.* -ы́); (*cosmos*) ко́смос.

university [ˌju:nɪ'vɜ:sɪtɪ] *n.* университе́т; *attr.* университе́тский.

unjust [ʌn'dʒʌst] *adj.* несправедли́вый. **unjustifiable** *adj.* не име́ющий оправда́ния. **unjustified** *adj.* неопра́вданный.

unkempt [ʌn'kempt] *adj.* нечёсаный (-ан); (*untidy*) неопря́тный. **unkind** *adj.* недо́брый, злой (зол, зла, зло). **unknown** *adj.* неизве́стный.

unlace [ʌn'leɪs] *v.t.* расшнуро́вывать *impf.*, расшнурова́ть *pf.* **unlawful** *adj.* незако́нный (-нен, -нна). **unleaded** *adj.* неэтили́рованный. **unlearn** *v.t.* разу́чиваться *impf.*, разучи́ться (-чу́сь, -чишься) *pf.* (**how to** +*inf.*); *v.t.* забыва́ть *impf.*, забы́ть (забу́ду, -дешь) *pf.* **unleash** *v.t.* (*dog*) спуска́ть *impf.*, спусти́ть (-ущу́, -у́стишь) *pf.* с при́вязи; (*also fig.*) развя́зывать *impf.*, развяза́ть (-яжу́, -я́жешь) *pf.* **unleavened** *adj.* бездрожжево́й, пре́сный (-сен, -сна́, -сно).

unless [ʌn'les, ən'les] *conj.* е́сли... не.

unlike [ʌn'laɪk] *adj.* непохо́жий (на+*a.*); (*in contradistinction to*) в отли́чие от+*g.* **unlikely** *adj.* маловероя́тный, неправдоподо́бный; **it is ~ that** вряд ли, едва́ ли. **unlimited** *adj.* (*unrestricted*) неограни́ченный (-ен, -енна); (*boundless*) безграни́чный. **unlined** *adj.* (*clothing*) без подкла́дки. **unload** *v.t.* (*remove load from*) разгружа́ть *impf.*, разгрузи́ть (-ужу́, -у́зишь) *pf.*; (*remove load from, *remove from*) выгружа́ть *impf.*, вы́грузить *pf.*; (*gun*) разряжа́ть *impf.*, разряди́ть *pf.* **unlock** *v.t.* отпира́ть *impf.*, отпере́ть (отопру́, -рёшь; о́тпер, -ла́, -ло) *pf.*; открыва́ть *impf.*, откры́ть (-ро́ю, -ро́ешь) *pf.* **unlucky** *adj.* несчастли́вый; (*unsuccessful*, *unfortunate*) неуда́чный.

unmake [ʌn'meɪk] *v.t.* (*destroy*) уничтожа́ть *impf.*, уничто́жить *pf.*; (*annul*) аннули́ровать *impf.* & *pf.*; (*depose*) понижа́ть *impf.*, пони́зить *pf.* **unmanageable** *adj.* тру́дно поддаю́щийся контро́лю; (*of child*) тру́дный (-ден, -дна́, -дно, тру́дны́). **unmanly** *adj.* недосто́йный (-о́ин, -о́йна) мужчи́ны. **unmarketable** *adj.* него́дный (-ден, -дна, -дно) для прода́жи. **unmarried** *adj.* холосто́й (хо́лост, -а́, -о); (*of man*) нежена́тый; (*of woman*) незаму́жняя. **unmask** *v.t.* (*fig.*) разоблача́ть *impf.*, разоблачи́ть *pf.* **unmentionable** *adj.* незатра́гиваемый, необсужда́емый. **unmerciful** *adj.* безжа́лостный. **unmerited** *adj.* незаслу́женный (-ен, -енна). **unmethodical** *adj.* несистемати́ческий, неметоди́чный. **unmindful** *adj.* невнима́тельный (**of** к+*d.*). **unmistakable** *adj.* несомне́нный (-нен, -нна), я́сный (я́сен, ясна́, я́сно, я́сны́). **unmitigated** *adj.* несмягчённый; (*absolute*) абсолю́тный; (*thorough*) отъя́вленный. **unmoved** *adj.* (*indifferent*) равноду́шный; (*adamant*) непрекло́нный (-нен, -нна).

unnatural [ʌn'nætʃər(ə)l] *adj.* неесте́ственный (-ен, -енна), противоесте́ственный (-ен, -енна). **unnecessary** *adj.* нену́жный, изли́шний (-шен, -шня). **unnerve** *v.t.* лиша́ть *impf.*, лиши́ть *pf.* реши́мости, му́жества. **unnoticed** *adj.* незаме́ченный.

unobjectionable [ˌʌnəb'dʒekʃənəb(ə)l] *adj.* прие́млемый. **unobservant** *adj.* невнима́тельный, ненаблюда́тельный. **unobserved** *adj.* незаме́ченный. **unobtainable** *adj.* тако́й, кото́рого нельзя́ доста́ть; недосту́пный. **unobtrusive** *adj.* ненавя́зчивый. **unoccupied** *adj.* неза́нятый (-т, -та́, -то), свобо́дный; (*uninhabited*) необита́емый. **unofficial** *adj.* неофициа́льный. **unopposed** *adj.* не встре́тивший сопротивле́ния. **unorthodox** *adj.* неортодокса́льный.

unpack [ʌn'pæk] *v.t.* распако́вывать *impf.*, распакова́ть *pf.* **unpaid** *adj.* (*not receiving pay*) не получа́ющий пла́ты; (*work*) беспла́тный. **unpalatable** *adj.* невку́сный; (*unpleasant*) неприя́тный. **unpardonable** *adj.* непрости́тельный. **unpin** *v.t.* отка́лывать *impf.*, отколо́ть (-лю́, -лешь) *pf.* **unpleasant** *adj.* неприя́тный. **unpleasantness** *n.* непривлека́тельность; (*also occurrence*) неприя́тность; (*quarrel*) ссо́ра. **unpopular** *adj.* непопуля́рный. **unprecedented** *adj.* беспрецеде́нтный, бесприме́рный. **unpredictable** *adj.* не могу́щий быть предска́занный. **unprejudiced** *adj.* беспристра́стный. **unpremeditated** *adj.* непреднаме́ренный (-ен, -енна). **unprepared** *adj.* неподгото́вленный, негото́вый. **unprepossessing** *adj.* непривлека́тельный. **unpretentious** *adj.* просто́й (прост, -а́, -о, про́сты́), без прете́нзий. **unprincipled** *adj.* беспринци́пный; (*immoral*) безнра́вственный (-ен(ен), -енна). **unprintable** *adj.* нецензу́рный. **unproductive** *adj.* непродукти́вный. **unprofitable** *adj.* невы́годный. **unpromising** *adj.* не обеща́ющий ничего́ хоро́шего. **unpronounceable** *adj.* непроизноси́мый. **unpropitious** *adj.* неблагоприя́тный. **unprotected** *adj.* (*defenceless*) беззащи́тный; (*area*) откры́тый. **unproven** *adj.* недока́занный. **unprovoked** *adj.* ниче́м не вы́званный, непровоци́рованный. **unpublished** *adj.* неопублико́ванный, неи́зданный. **unpunctual** *adj.* непункту́альный. **unpunished** *adj.* безнака́занный (-ан, -анна).

unqualified [ʌn'kwɒlɪˌfaɪd] *adj.* неквалифици́рованный (-ан, -анна); (*unconditional*) безогово́рочный. **unquenchable** *adj.* неутоли́мый; (*fig.*) неугаси́мый. **unquestionable** *adj.* несомне́нный (-нен, -нна), неоспори́мый. **unquestionably** *adv.* несомне́нно. **unquestioned** *adj.* не вызыва́ющий сомне́ния.

unravel [ʌn'ræv(ə)l] *v.t.* & *i.* распу́тывать(ся) *impf.*, распу́тать(ся) *pf.*; *v.t.* (*solve*) разга́дывать *impf.*, разгада́ть *pf.* **unread** [ʌn'red] *adj.* (*book etc.*) непрочи́танный. **unreadable** *adj.* (*illegible*) неразбо́рчивый; (*boring*) ску́чный (-чен, -чна́, -чно). **unready** *adj.* негото́вый; (*slow-witted*) несообрази́тельный. **unreal** *adj.* ненастоя́щий. **unrealistic** *adj.* нереа́льный. **unreasonable** *adj.* (*unwise*) неблагоразу́мный; (*excessive*) непоме́рный; (*expensive*) непоме́рно дорого́й (до́рог, -а́, -о); (*of price*) непоме́рно высо́кий (-о́к, -ока́, -о́ко́); (*unfounded*; *of demand*) необосно́ванный (-ан, -анна). **unreasoned** *adj.* непроду́манный. **unreasoning** *adj.* немы́слящий. **unreceptive** *adj.* невосприи́мчивый. **unrecognizable** *adj.* неузнава́емый. **unrecognized** *adj.* непри́знанный. **unrefined** *adj.* неочи́щенный; (*manners etc.*) гру́бый (груб, -а́, -о). **unrelenting** *adj.* (*ruthless*) безжа́лостный; (*unremitting*) неосла́бный; (*not abating*) неуменьша́ющийся. **unreliable** *adj.* ненадёжный. **unremitting** *adj.* неосла́бный; (*incessant*) беспреста́нный (-нен, -нна). **unremunerative** *adj.* невы́годный. **unrepeatable** *adj.* (*unique*) неповтори́мый; (*indecent*) неприли́чный. **unrepentant** *adj.* нераска́явшийся. **unrepresentative** *adj.* нехаракте́рный. **unrequited** *adj.*: ~ **love** любо́вь без взаи́мости. **unreserved** *adj.* (*full*) по́лный (-лон, -лна́, по́лно́); (*open*) открове́нный (-нен, -нна); (*unconditional*) безогово́рочный; ~ **seats** незаброни́рованные места́ *nt.pl.* **unresisting** *adj.* несопротивля́ющийся. **unrest** *n.* беспоко́йство; (*pol.*) беспоря́дки *m.pl.*, волне́ния *nt.pl.* **unrestrained** *adj.* несде́ржанный (-ан, анна). **unrestricted** *adj.* неограни́ченный (-ен, -енна). **unripe** *adj.* незре́лый, неспе́лый. **unrivalled** *adj.* бесподо́бный. **unroll** *v.t.* & *i.* развёртывать(ся) *impf.*, разверну́ть(ся) *pf.* **unruffled** *adj.* (*smooth*) гла́дкий (-док, -дка́, -дко); (*calm*) споко́йный. **unruly** [ʌn'ru:lɪ] *adj.* (*wild*) бу́йный (бу́ен, буйна́, -но), (*disobedient*) непослу́шный.

unsafe [ʌn'seɪf] *adj.* опа́сный; (*insecure*) ненадёжный. **unsaid** [ʌn'sed] *adj.*: **leave ~** молча́ть (-чу́, -чи́шь) *impf.* о+*p.* **unsaleable** *adj.* нехо́дкий. **unsalted** *adj.* несолёный (несо́лон, -а́, -о). **unsatisfactory** *adj.* неудовлетвори́тельный. **unsatisfied** *adj.* неудовлетворённый (-ён, -ена́ & -ённа). **unsatisfying** *adj.* неудовлетворя́ющий; (*food*) несы́тный (-тен, -тна́, -тно). **unsavoury** *adj.* невку́сный; (*distasteful*) проти́вный. **unscathed** *adj.* невреди́мый; (*fig.*) жив и невреди́м. **unscheduled** *adj.* внеочередно́й. **unscientific** *adj.* ненау́чный. **unscrew** *v.t.* & *i.* отви́нчивать(ся) *impf.*, отвинти́ть(ся) *pf.* **unscrupulous** *adj.* неразбо́рчивый в сре́дствах, беспринци́пный, бессо́вестный. **unseasonable** *adj.* не по сезо́ну; (*inopportune*) несвоевре́менный (-нен, -нна). **unseasoned** *adj.* (*food*) неприпра́вленный; (*wood*) невы́держанный; (*unaccustomed*) непривы́кший. **unseat** *v.t.* (*of horse*) сбра́сывать *impf.*, сбро́сить *pf.* с седла́; (*parl.*) лиша́ть *impf.*, лиши́ть *pf.* парла́ментского манда́та. **unseemly** *adj.* неподоба́ющий, непристо́йный. **unseen** *adj.* неви́данный; **~ translation** перево́д с листа́. **unselfish** *adj.* бескоры́стный, неэгоисти́чный. **unserviceable** *adj.* неприго́дный. **unsettle** *v.t.* наруша́ть *impf.*, наруши́ть *pf.* распоря́док+*g.*, выбива́ть *impf.*, вы́бить (-бью, -бьешь) *pf.* из колеи́; (*upset*) расстра́ивать *impf.*, расстро́ить *pf.* **unsettled** *adj.*: **the weather is ~** пого́да не установи́лась. **unshakeable** *adj.* непоколеби́мый. **unshaven** *adj.* небри́тый. **unsheathe** *v.t.* вынима́ть *impf.*, вы́нуть *pf.* из но́жен. **unship** *v.t.* (*cargo*) выгружа́ть *impf.*, вы́грузить *pf.*; (*passenger*) выса́живать *impf.*, вы́садить *pf.* на бе́рег. **unsightly** *adj.* непригля́дный, уро́дливый. **unskilful** *adj.* неуме́лый. **unskilled** *adj.* неквалифици́рованный (-ан, -анна). **unsociable** *adj.* необщи́тельный. **unsold** *adj.* непро́данный. **unsolicited** *adj.* непро́шеный. **unsolved** *adj.* нерешённый. **unsophisticated** *adj.* просто́й (прост, -а́, -о, про́сты́), безыску́сственный (-ен, -енна). **unsound** *adj.* (*unhealthy*, *unwholesome*) нездоро́вый; (*rotten*, *also fig.*) гнило́й (гнил, -а́, -о); (*unreliable*) ненадёжный; (*unfounded*) необосно́ванный (-ан, -анна); (*faulty*) дефе́ктный; **of ~ mind** душевнобольно́й. **unsparing** *adj.* (*lavish*) ще́дрый (щедр, -а́, -о); (*merciless*) беспоща́дный. **unspeakable** *adj.* (*inexpressible*) невырази́мый; (*very bad*) отврати́тельный. **unspecified** *adj.* то́чно не устано́вленный (-ен), неопределённый (-нен, -нна). **unspoilt** *adj.* неиспо́рченный. **unspoken** *adj.* невы́сказанный. **unsporting, unsportsmanlike** *adj.* неспорти́вный, недосто́йный (-о́ин, -о́йна) спортсме́на. **unstable** *adj.* неусто́йчивый; (*emotionally*) неуравнове́шенный (-ен, -енна). **unsteady** *adj.* неусто́йчивый. **unsuccessful** *adj.* неуда́чный, безуспе́шный. **unsuitable** *adj.* неподходя́щий, неподоба́ющий. **unsuited** *adj.* (*incompatible*) несовмести́мый. **unsullied** *adj.* незапя́тнанный. **unsupported** *adj.* неподде́ржанный. **unsure** *adj.* (*not convinced*) неуве́ренный (-ен, -ена) (**of o.s.** в себе́); (*hesitating*) неуве́ренный (-ен, -енна). **unsurpassed** *adj.* непревзойдённый (-ён, -ённа). **unsuspected** *adj.* не вызыва́ющий подозре́ний; (*unforeseen*) непредви́денный. **unsuspecting** *adj.* неподозрева́ющий. **unsweetened** *adj.* неподсла́щенный. **unswerving** *adj.* непоколеби́мый. **unsymmetrical** *adj.* несимметри́ческий. **unsympathetic** *adj.* несочу́вствующий; (*unattractive*) несимпати́чный. **unsystematic** *adj.* несистемати́чный.

untainted *adj.* неиспо́рченный. **untalented** *adj.* нетала́нтливый. **untameable** *adj.* не подда́ющийся прируче́нию; (*indomitable*) неукроти́мый. **untapped** *adj.*: **~ resources** неиспо́льзованные ресу́рсы *m.pl.* **untarnished** *adj.* непотускне́вший; (*fig.*) незапя́тнанный. **untenable** *adj.* несостоя́тельный. **unthinkable** *adj.* (*inconceivable*) невообрази́мый; (*unlikely*) невероя́тный; (*out of the question*) исключённый (-ён, -ена́). **unthinking** *adj.* легкомы́сленный (-ен, -енна). **unthread** *v.t.* вынима́ть *impf.*, вы́нуть *pf.* ни́тку из+*g.* **untidiness** *n.* неопря́тность; (*disorder*) беспоря́док (дка). **untidy** *adj.* неопря́тный; (*in disorder*) в беспоря́дке. **untie** *v.t.* развя́зывать *impf.*, развяза́ть (-яжу́, -я́жешь) *pf.*; (*set free*) освобожда́ть *impf.*, освободи́ть *pf.*

until [ən'tɪl, ʌn-] *prep.* до+*g.*; **not ~** не ра́ньше+*g.*; **~ then** до тех пор; *conj.* пока́, пока́... не; **not ~** то́лько когда́.

untimely [ʌn'taɪmlɪ] *adj.* (*premature*) безвре́менный; (*inopportune*) несвоевре́менный (-нен, -нна); (*inappropriate*) неуме́стный. **untiring** *adj.* неутоми́мый. **untold** *adj.* (*innumerable*) бессчётный, несме́тный; (*inexpressible*) невырази́мый. **untouched** *adj.* (*also pure*) нетро́нутый; (*indifferent*) равноду́шный. **untoward** [ˌʌntə'wɔ:d, ʌn'təʊəd] *adj.* (*unfavourable*) неблагоприя́тный; (*refractory*) непоко́рный. **untrained** *adj.* необу́ченный. **untranslatable** *adj.* непереводи́мый. **untried** *adj.* неиспы́танный. **untroubled** *adj.* споко́йный. **untrue** *adj.* (*incorrect*, *disloyal*) неве́рный (-рен, -рна́, -рно, неве́рны́); (*incorrect*) непра́вильный; (*false*) ло́жный. **untrustworthy** *adj.* ненадёжный. **untruth** *n.* непра́вда, ложь. **untruthful** *adj.* лжи́вый.

unusable [ʌn'ju:zəb(ə)l] *adj.* неприго́дный. **unused** *adj.* (*not employed*) неиспо́льзованный; (*not accustomed*) непривы́кший (**to** к+*d.*). **unusual** *adj.* необыкнове́нный (-нен, -нна), необы́чный. **unusually** *adv.* необыкнове́нно. **unutterable** *adj.* невырази́мый.

unvarnished [ʌn'vɑ:nɪʃt] *adj.* (*fig.*) неприкра́шенный. **unvarying** *adj.* неизменя́ющийся. **unveil** *v.t.* снима́ть *impf.*, снять (сниму́, -мешь; снял, -а́, -о) *pf.* покрыва́ло с+*g.*; (*statue*) торже́ственно открыва́ть *impf.*, откры́ть (-ро́ю, -ро́ешь) *pf.*; (*disclose*) открыва́ть *impf.*, откры́ть (-ро́ю, -ро́ешь) *pf.* **unversed** *adj.* несве́дущий (**in** в+*p.*); (*inexperienced*) нео́пытный (**in** в+*p.*).

unwanted [ʌn'wɒntɪd] *adj.* нежела́нный. **unwarranted** *adj.* (*unjustified*) неопра́вданный. **unwary** *adj.* неосторо́жный. **unwavering** *adj.* непоколеби́мый. **unwelcome** *adj.* нежела́нный, нежела́тельный; (*unpleasant*) неприя́тный. **unwell** *adj.* нездоро́вый. **unwholesome** *adj.* нездоро́вый, вре́дный (-ден, -дна́, -дно). **unwieldy** *adj.* громо́здкий, неуклю́жий. **unwilling** *adj.* нерасполо́женный. **unwillingly** *adv.* неохо́тно, про́тив жела́ния. **unwillingness** *n.* нерасположе́ние, неохо́та. **unwind** *v.t.* & *i.* разма́тывать(ся) *impf.*, размота́ть(ся) *pf.*; (*rest*) отдыха́ть *impf.*, отдохну́ть *pf.* **unwise** *adj.* не(благо)разу́мный. **unwitting** *adj.* householder нево́льный, нача́янный. **unwittingly** *adv.* нево́льно, нечаянно. **unwonted** [ʌn'wəʊntɪd] *adj.* непривы́чный, необы́чный. **unworkable** *adj.* непримени́мый. **unworldly** *adj.* не от ми́ра сего́; (*spiritual*) духо́вный. **unworthy** *adj.* недосто́йный (-о́ин, -о́йна). **unwrap** *v.t.* развёртывать *impf.*, разверну́ть *pf.* **unwritten** *adj.*: ~ **law** непи́саный зако́н.

unyielding [ʌn'ji:ldɪŋ] *adj.* упо́рный, непода́тливый.

unzip [ʌn'zɪp] *v.t.* расстёгивать *impf.*, расстегну́ть *pf.* (мо́лнию+*g.*).

up [ʌp] *adv.* (*motion*) наве́рх, вверх; (*position*) наверху́, вверху́; ~ **and down** вверх и вниз (*back and forth*) взад и вперёд; ~ **to** (*towards*) к+*d.*; (*time*) вплоть до+*g.*; ~ **to now** до сих пор; **be** ~ **against** име́ть *impf.* де́ло с+*i.*; **it is** ~ **to you**+*inf.*, э́то вам+*inf.*, вы должны́+*inf.*; **not** ~ **to much** нева́жный (-жен, -жна́, -жно); **what's** ~? что случи́лось?; в чём де́ло?; **your time is** ~ ва́ше вре́мя истекло́; ~ **and about** на нога́х; **he isn't** ~ **yet** он ещё не встал; **he isn't** ~ **to this job** он не годи́тся для э́той рабо́ты; *prep.* вверх по+*d.*; (*along*) (вдоль) по+*d.*; *v.t.* & *i.* поднима́ть(ся) *impf.*, подня́ть(ся) (-ниму́(сь), -ни́мешь(ся); по́днял/подня́лся́, -ла́(сь), -ло/-ло́сь) *pf.*; (*leap* ~) вска́кивать *impf.*, вскочи́ть (-чу́, -чишь) *pf.*; *n.*: ~**s and downs** (*fig.*) превра́тности *f.pl.* судьбы́. **up-and-coming** *adj.* напо́ристый, многообеща́ющий.

upbraid [ʌp'breɪd] *v.t.* брани́ть *impf.*, вы́~ *pf.* (**for** за+*a.*).

upbringing ['ʌp,brɪŋɪŋ] *n.* воспита́ние.

update [ʌp'deɪt] *v.t.* модернизи́ровать *impf.* & *pf.*; (*book*) дополня́ть *impf.*, допо́лнить *pf.*

upgrade ['ʌpgreɪd] *v.t.* повыша́ть *impf.*, повы́сить *pf.* (по слу́жбе).

upheaval [ʌp'hi:v(ə)l] *n.* сдвиг; (*revolution*) переворо́т; (*geol.*) смеще́ние пласто́в.

uphill ['ʌphɪl] *adj.* иду́щий в го́ру; (*fig.*) тяжёлый (-л, -ла́); *adv.* в го́ру.

uphold [ʌp'həʊld] *v.t.* подде́рживать *impf.*, поддержа́ть (-жу́, -жишь) *pf.*; ~ **a view** приде́рживаться *impf.* взгля́да. **upholder** *n.* сторо́нник.

upholster [ʌp'həʊlstə(r)] *v.t.* обива́ть *impf.*, оби́ть (обобью́, -ьёшь) *pf.* (**with, in** +*i.*). **upholsterer** *n.* обо́йщик. **upholstery** *n.* оби́вка.

upkeep ['ʌpki:p] *n.* (*maintenance*, *support*) содержа́ние; (*repair*(*s*)) ремо́нт; (*cost of* ~) сто́имость содержа́ния.

upland ['ʌplənd] *n.* гори́стая часть (*pl.* -ти, -те́й) страны́, наго́рная страна́ (*pl.* -ны); *adj.* наго́рный; (*inland*) лежа́щий внутри́ страны́.

uplift [ʌp'lɪft; 'ʌplɪft] *v.t.* поднима́ть *impf.*, подня́ть (-ниму́, -ни́мешь; по́днял, -а́, -о) *pf.*; *n.* подъём.

upon [ə'pɒn] *prep.* (*position*) на+*p.*, (*motion*) на+*a.*; *see* **on**

upper ['ʌpə(r)] *adj.* ве́рхний; (*socially*, *in rank*) вы́сший; **gain the** ~ **hand** оде́рживать *impf.*, одержа́ть (-жу́, -жишь) *pf.* верх (**over** над+*i.*); ~ **crust** верху́шка о́бщества; **the U~ House** ве́рхняя пала́та; *n.* передо́к (-дка́). **uppermost** *adj.* са́мый ве́рхний, вы́сший; **be** ~ **in person's mind** бо́льше всего́ занима́ть *impf.*, заня́ть (займу́, -мёшь; за́нял, -а́, -о) *pf.* мы́сли кого́-л.

uppish ['ʌpɪʃ] *adj.* спеси́вый, высокоме́рный.

upright ['ʌpraɪt] *n.* подпо́рка, сто́йка; *adj.* вертика́льный; (*straight*) прямо́й (-м, -ма́, -мо, пря́мы́); (*honest*) че́стный (-тен, -тна́, -тно); ~ **piano** пиани́но *nt.indecl.*; *adv.* вертика́льно, пря́мо, стоймя́.

uprising ['ʌp,raɪzɪŋ] *n.* восста́ние, бунт.

uproar ['ʌprɔ:(r)] *n.* шум (-а(у)), гам. **up'roarious** *adj.* шу́мный (-мен, -мна́, -мно), бу́йный (бу́ен, буйна́, -но).

uproot [ʌp'ru:t] *v.t.* вырыва́ть *impf.*, вы́рвать (-ву, -вешь) *pf.* с ко́рнем; (*eradicate*) искореня́ть *impf.*, искорени́ть *pf.*

upset ['ʌpset] *n.* (*disorder*, *confusion*, *discomposure*) расстро́йство; *v.t.* (*disorder*, *discompose*, *spoil* (*plans etc.*)) расстра́ивать *impf.*, расстро́ить *pf.*; *v.t.* & *i.* (*overturn*) опроки́дывать(ся) *impf.*, опроки́нуть(ся) *pf.*; *adj.* (*miserable*) расстро́енный (-ен); ~ **stomach** расстро́йство желу́дка.

upshot ['ʌpʃɒt] *n.* развя́зка, результа́т.

upside-down [,ʌpsaɪd 'daʊn] *adj.* перевёрнутый вверх дном; *adv.* вверх дном; (*in disorder*) в беспоря́дке.

upstairs [ʌp'steəz] *adv.* (*position*) наверху́; (*motion*) наве́рх; *n.* ве́рхний эта́ж (-а́); *adj.* находя́щийся в ве́рхнем этаже́.

upstart ['ʌpstɑːt] *n.* вы́скочка *c.g.*

upstream ['ʌpstriːm] *adv.* про́тив тече́ния; (*situation*) вверх по тече́нию.

upsurge ['ʌpsɜːdʒ] *n.* подъём, волна́ (*pl.* -ны, -н, во́лна́м).

uptake ['ʌpteɪk] *n.*: **be quick on the ~** бы́стро соobража́ть *impf.*, сообрази́ть *pf.*

up-to-date [ˌʌptə'deɪt] *adj.* совреме́нный (-нен, -нна); (*fashionable*) мо́дный (-ден, -дна́, -дно).

upturned ['ʌptɜːnd] *adj.* (*face etc.*) по́днятый (по́днят, -а́, -о) кве́рху; (*inverted*) перевёрнутый.

upward ['ʌpwəd] *adj.* напра́вленный (-ен) вверх, дви́жущийся вверх. **upwards** *adv.* вверх; **~ of** свы́ше+*g.* **upwind** *adv.* про́тив ве́тра.

Urals ['jʊər(ə)lz] *n.* Ура́л.

uranium [jʊ'reɪnɪəm] *n.* ура́н; *attr.* ура́новый.

urban ['ɜːbən] *adj.* городско́й.

urbane [ɜː'beɪn] *adj.* ве́жливый, с изы́сканными мане́рами. **urbanity** [ɜː'bænɪtɪ] *n.* ве́жливость.

urchin ['ɜːtʃɪn] *n.* мальчи́шка *m.*

urge [ɜːdʒ] *n.* (*incitement*) побужде́ние, толчо́к (-чка́); (*desire*) жела́ние; *v.t.* (*impel*, **~** *on*) подгоня́ть *impf.*, подогна́ть (подгоню́, -нишь; подогна́л, -а́, -о) *pf.*; (*induce*, *prompt*) побужда́ть *impf.*, побуди́ть *pf.*; (*advocate*) насто́йчиво убежда́ть *impf.*; (*give as reason*) обраща́ть *impf.*, обрати́ть (-ащу́, -ати́шь) *pf.* внима́ние на+*a.* **urgency** *n.* (*also insistence*) настоя́тельность; (*immediate importance*) безотлага́тельность; **a matter of great ~** сро́чное де́ло (*pl.* -ла́). **urgent** *adj.* сро́чный (-чен, -чна́, -чно); (*also insistent*) настоя́тельный; (*absolutely essential*) кра́йне необходи́мый. **urgently** *adv.* сро́чно.

uric ['jʊərɪk] *adj.* мочево́й. **urinal** [jʊə'raɪn(ə)l, 'jʊərɪn(ə)l] *n.* писсуа́р. **urinate** *v.i.* мочи́ться (-чу́сь, -чишься) *impf.*, по~ *pf.* **uri'nation** *n.* мочеиспуска́ние. **urine** ['jʊərɪn] *n.* моча́.

urn [ɜːn] *n.* у́рна.

US(A) *abbr.* (*of* ***United States of America***) США *pl.*, *indecl.*, Соединённые Шта́ты Аме́рики; *adj.* америка́нский.

usable ['juːzəb(ə)l] *adj.* го́дный (-ден, -дна́, -дно) к употребле́нию. **usage** ['juːsɪdʒ] *n.* употребле́ние; (*custom*) обы́чай; (*treatment*) обраще́ние. **use** *n.* (*also benefit*) по́льза; (*application*) употребле́ние, примене́ние, испо́льзование; **it is of no ~** бесполе́зно; **make ~ of** испо́льзовать *impf.* & *pf.*; по́льзоваться *impf.+i.*; *v.t.* употребля́ть *impf.*, употреби́ть *pf.*; по́льзоваться *impf.+i.*; применя́ть *impf.*, примени́ть (-ню́, -нишь) *pf.*; (*treat*) обраща́ться *impf.* с+*i.*; **I ~d to see him often** я ча́сто его́ встреча́л; **be, get, ~d to** привыка́ть *impf.*, привы́кнуть (-к) *pf.* (**to** к+*d.*) **~ up** расхо́довать *impf.*, из~ *pf.* **used** *adj.* (*second-hand*) подéржанный, ста́рый (стар, -а́, ста́ро́). **useful** *adj.* поле́зный; **come in ~, prove ~** пригоди́ться *pf.* (**to** +*d.*). **useless** *adj.* бесполе́зный, ни куда́ не го́дный (-ден, -дна́, -дно). **user** *n.* потреби́тель *m.* **user-friendly** *adj.* удо́бный в употребле́нии.

usher ['ʌʃə(r)] *n.* (*door-keeper*) швейца́р; (*theatr.*) билетёр; *v.t.* (*lead in*) вводи́ть (ввожу́, -о́дишь) *impf.*, ввести́ (-еду́, -едёшь; -ёл, -ела́) *pf.*; (*proclaim*, **~** *in*) возвеща́ть *impf.*, возвести́ть *pf.* **usherette** *n.* билетёрша.

USSR *abbr.* (*of* ***Union of Soviet Socialist Republics***) СССР, Сою́з Сове́тских Социалисти́ческих Респу́блик.

usual ['juːʒʊəl] *adj.* обыкнове́нный (-нен, -нна), обы́чный; **as ~** как обы́чно. **usually** *adv.* обыкнове́нно, обы́чно.

usurer ['juːʒərə(r)] *n.* ростовщи́к (-а́). **usurious** [jʊ'ʒʊərɪəs] *adj.* ростовщи́ческий.

usurp [jʊ'zɜːp] *v.t.* узурпи́ровать *impf.* & *pf.*; незако́нно захва́тывать *impf.*, захвати́ть (-ачу́, -а́тишь) *pf.* **usurper** *n.* узурпа́тор, захва́тчик.

usury ['juːʒərɪ] *n.* ростовщи́чество.

utensil [juː'tens(ə)l] *n.* инструме́нт, ору́дие; *pl.* у́тварь; принадле́жности *f.pl.*; (*kitchen* **~***s*) посу́да.

uterine ['juːtəˌraɪn, -rɪn] *adj.* ма́точный; (*of one mother*) единоутро́бный. **uterus** *n.* ма́тка.

utilitarian [ˌjʊtɪlɪ'teərɪən] *adj.* утилита́рный; *n.* утилитари́ст. **utilitarianism** *n.* утилитари́зм. **utility** [juː'tɪlɪtɪ] *n.* поле́зность; (*profitableness*) вы́годность; *adj.* утилита́рный; (*practical*) практи́чный. **utilize** ['juːtɪˌlaɪz] *v.t.* испо́льзоваться *impf.* & *pf.*; утилизи́ровать *impf.* & *pf.*

utmost ['ʌtməʊst] *adj.* (*extreme*) кра́йний, преде́льный; (*furthest*) са́мый отдалённый (-ён, -ённа); **this is of the ~ importance to me** э́то для меня́ кра́йне ва́жно; *n.*: **do one's ~** де́лать *impf.*, с~ *pf.* всё возмо́жное.

Utopia [juː'təʊpɪə] *n.* уто́пия. **utopian** *adj.* утопи́ческий; *n.* утопи́ст.

utter ['ʌtə(r)] *attr.* по́лный, соверше́нный, абсолю́тный; (*out-and-out*) отъя́вленный (*coll.*); *v.t.* произноси́ть (-ошу́, -о́сишь) *impf.*, произнести́ (-есу́, -есёшь; -ёс, -есла́) *pf.*; (*let out*) издава́ть (-даю́, -даёшь) *impf.*, изда́ть (-а́м, -а́шь, -а́ст, -ади́м; изда́л, -а́, -о) *pf.* **utterance** *n.* (*uttering*) произнесе́ние; (*pronouncement*) выска́зывание; (*diction*) ди́кция; (*pronunciation*) произноше́ние; **gift of ~** дар сло́ва; **give ~ to** выража́ть *impf.*, вы́разить *pf.* слова́ми. **utterly** *adv.* кра́йне, соверше́нно.

U-turn ['juːtɜːn] *n.* разворо́т; (*fig.*) поворо́т на 180°.

uvula ['juːvjʊlə] *n.* язычо́к (-чка́).

Uzbek ['ʌzbek, 'ʊz-] *n.* узбе́к, -е́чка; *adj.* узбе́кский. **Uzbekistan** [ˌʌzbekɪ'stɑːn, ˌʊz-] *n.* Узбекиста́н.

V

v. *abbr.* (*of* **volt(s)**) В, вольт; (*of* **versus**) про́тив+*g.*; **England ~ France** А́нглия про́тив Фра́нции.

vacancy ['veɪkənsɪ] *n.* (*for job*) вака́нсия, свобо́дное ме́сто (*pl.* -та́); (*at hotel*) свобо́дный но́мер (*pl.* -а́); (*emptiness*) пустота́; (*apathy*) безуча́стность; (*absent-mindedness*) рассе́янность. **vacant** *adj.* (*post*) вака́нтный; (*post*; *not engaged*, *free*) свобо́дный; (*empty*) пусто́й (пуст, -а́, -о, пу́сты́); (*look*) рассе́янный (-ян, -янна); **'~ possession'** «помеще́ние гото́во для въе́зда». **vacantly** *adv.* рассе́янно. **vacate** [və'keɪt, veɪ-] *v.t.* освобожда́ть *impf.*, освободи́ть *pf.*; покида́ть *impf.*, поки́нуть *pf.* **va'cation** *n.* (*school*, *univ.*) кани́кулы (-л) *pl.*; (*leave*) о́тпуск; (*vacating*) оставле́ние, освобожде́ние.

vaccinate ['væksɪˌneɪt] *v.t.* привива́ть *impf.*, приви́ть (-вью́, -вьёшь; приви́л, -а́, -о) *pf.+d.* (**against** *+a.*). **vacci'nation** *n.* приви́вка (**against** от, про́тив+*g.*). **vaccine** ['væksiːn] *n.* вакци́на.

vacillate ['væsɪˌleɪt] *v.i.* колеба́ться (-блюсь, -блешься) *impf.* **vaci'llation** *n.* колеба́ние; (*inconstancy*) непостоя́нство.

vacuity [və'kjuːɪtɪ] *n.* пустота́. **vacuous** ['vækjʊəs] *adj.* пусто́й (пуст, -а́, -о, пу́сты́); (*foolish*) бессмы́сленный (-ен, -енна). **vacuum** *n.* ва́куум; (*fig.*) пустота́; **~ cleaner** пылесо́с; **~ flask** те́рмос. **vacuum-clean** *v.t.* чи́стить *impf.*, вы́~, по~ *pf.* пылесо́сом.

vade-mecum [ˌvɑːdɪ'meɪkəm, ˌveɪdɪ'miːkəm] *n.* путеводи́тель *m.*

vagabond ['vægəˌbɒnd] *n.* бродя́га *m.*; *attr.* бродя́чий. **vagabondage** *n.* бродя́жничество. **vagabondize** *v.i.* скита́ться *impf.*, бродя́жничать *impf.*

vagary ['veɪgərɪ] *n.* капри́з, причу́да.

vagina [və'dʒaɪnə] *n.* влага́лище. **vaginal** *adj.* влага́лищный.

vagrancy ['veɪgrənsɪ] *n.* бродя́жничество. **vagrant** *adj.* бродя́чий; *n.* бродя́га *m.*

vague [veɪg] *adj.* (*indeterminate*, *uncertain*) неопределённый (-нен, -нна); (*unclear*) нея́сный (-сен, -сна́, -сно); (*dim*) сму́тный (-тен, -тна́, -тно); (*absent-minded*) рассе́янный (-ян, -янна). **vagueness** *n.* неопределённость, нея́сность; (*absent-mindedness*) рассе́янность.

vain [veɪn] *adj.* (*futile*) тще́тный, напра́сный; (*empty*) пусто́й (пуст, -а́, -о, пу́сты́); (*conceited*) самовлюблённый, тщесла́вный; **in ~** напра́сно, тще́тно, зря. **vain'glorious** *adj.* тщесла́вный, хвастли́вый. **vain'glory** *n.* тщесла́вие, хвастли́вость.

valance ['væləns] *n.* подзо́р, обо́рка, за́навеска.

vale [veɪl] *n.* дол, доли́на.

valediction [ˌvælɪ'dɪkʃ(ə)n] *n.* проща́ние. **valedictory** *adj.* проща́льный.

valency ['veɪlənsɪ] *n.* вале́нтность.

valentine ['vælənˌtaɪn] *n.* (*sweetheart*) возлю́бленный, -нная; (*card*) любо́вное посла́ние.

valerian [və'lɪərɪən] *n.* валериа́на; (*med.*) валериа́новые ка́пли (-пель) *pl.*

valet ['vælɪt, -leɪ] *n.* камерди́нер, слуга́ (*pl.* -ги) *m.*

valiant ['væljənt] *adj.* хра́брый (храбр, -а́, -о), до́блестный.

valid ['vælɪd] *adj.* действи́тельный, име́ющий си́лу; (*weighty*) ве́ский. **validate** *v.t.* (*ratify*) утвержда́ть *impf.*, утверди́ть *pf.*; (*declare valid*) объявля́ть *impf.*, объяви́ть (-влю́, -вишь) *pf.* действи́тельным. **validity** [və'lɪdɪtɪ] *n.* действи́тельность; (*weightiness*) ве́скость.

valise [və'liːz] *n.* саквоя́ж, чемода́н.

valley ['vælɪ] *n.* доли́на.

valorous ['vælərəs] *adj.* до́блестный. **valour** *n.* до́блесть.

valuable ['væljʊəb(ə)l] *adj.* це́нный (-нен, -нна); (*costly*) дорого́й (до́рог, -а́, -о); *pl.* це́нные ве́щи (-ще́й) *pl.*, драгоце́нности *f.pl.* **valu'ation** *n.* оце́нка. **value** *n.* це́нность; (*cost*, *worth*) цена́ (*pl.* -ны); (*worth*, *econ.*) сто́имость; (*significance*) значе́ние; (*math.*) величина́; (*mus.*) дли́тельность; *pl.* це́нности *f.pl.*; **~ judgement** субъекти́вная оце́нка; *v.t.* (*estimate*) оце́нивать *impf.*, оцени́ть (-ню́, -нишь) *pf.*; (*hold dear*) цени́ть (-ню́, -нишь) *impf.*, дорожи́ть *impf.+i.* **value-added: ~ tax** нало́г на доба́вленную сто́имость. **valueless** *adj.* бесполе́зный, ничего́ не сто́ящий. **valuer** *n.* оце́нщик.

valve [vælv] *n.* (*tech.*, *med.*, *mus.*) кла́пан; (*tech.*) ве́нтиль *m.*; (*bot.*) ство́рка; (*radio*) электро́нная ла́мпа.

vamp[1] [væmp] *n.* (*of shoe*) передо́к (-дка́); (*patched-up article*) что-л. почи́ненное на ско́рую ру́ку; (*mus.*) импровизи́рованный аккомпанеме́нт; *v.t.* (*repair*) чини́ть (-ню́, -нишь) *impf.*, по~ *pf.*; (*mus.*) импровизи́ровать *impf.*, сымпровизи́ровать *pf.* аккомпанеме́нт к+*d.*

vamp[2] [væmp] *n.* (*flirt*) соблазни́тельница.

vampire ['væmpaɪə(r)] *n.* (*also fig.*; *also ~ bat*) вампи́р.

van[1] [væn] *n.* (*road vehicle*, *caravan*) фурго́н; (*rail.*) бага́жный (*luggage*), това́рный (*goods*), служе́бный (*guard's*), ваго́н.

van[2] [væn] *n.* (*vanguard*) авинга́рд.

vandal ['vænd(ə)l] *n.*ванда́л, хулига́н. **vandalism** *n.* вандали́зм, варва́рство. **vandalize** *v.t.* разруша́ть *impf.*, разру́шить *pf.*

vane [veɪn] *n.* (*weathercock*) флю́гер (*pl.* -а́);

(*of windmill*) крыло́ (*pl.* -лья, -льев); (*of propeller*) ло́пасть (*pl.* -ти, -те́й); (*of turbine*) лопа́тка.
vanguard ['vængɑːd] *n.* авангáрд.
vanilla [və'nɪlə] *n.* вани́ль; *attr.* вани́льный.
vanish ['vænɪʃ] *v.i.* исчеза́ть *impf.*, исче́знуть (-е́з) *pf.*; пропада́ть *impf.*, пропа́сть (-аду́, -адёшь; -а́л) *pf.*; **~ing point** то́чка схо́да.
vanity ['vænɪtɪ] *n.* (*futility*) тщета́, суета́; (*vainglory*) тщесла́вие; **~ bag** су́мочка, несессе́р.
vanquish ['væŋkwɪʃ] *v.t.* (*enemy*) побежда́ть *impf.*, победи́ть (-еди́шь, -еди́т) *pf.*; (*fig.*) преодолева́ть *impf.*, преодоле́ть *pf.*
vantage ['vɑːntɪdʒ] *n.* преиму́щество; **~ point** вы́годная пози́ция; (*for observation*) пункт наблюде́ния.
vapid ['væpɪd] *adj.* безвку́сный; (*also fig.*) пре́сный (-сен, -сна́, -сно); (*fig.*) ску́чный (-чен, -чна́, -чно).
vaporize ['veɪpəˌraɪz] *v.t.* & *i.* испаря́ть(ся) *impf.*, испари́ть(ся) *pf.* **vaporizer** *n.* испари́тель *m.* **vaporous** *adj.* парообра́зный; (*vague*) тума́нный (-нен, -нна). **vapour** *n.* (*steam etc.*) пар (*loc.* -у́; *pl.* -ы́); (*mist, haze*) тума́н.
variable ['veərɪəb(ə)l] *adj.* изме́нчивый, непостоя́нный (-нен, -нна); (*weather*) неусто́йчивый, (*also math.*) переме́нный; *n.* (*math.*) переме́нная (величина́). **variance** *n.* (*disagreement*) разногла́сие; (*change*) измене́ние; (*disparity*) несоотве́тствие; **be at ~ with** расходи́ться (-ожу́сь, -о́дишься) *impf.*, разойти́сь (-ойду́сь, -ойдёшься; -ошёлся, -ошла́сь) *pf.* во мне́ниях с+*i.* **variant** *n.* вариа́нт; *adj.* ра́зный. **vari'ation** *n.* (*varying*) измене́ние, переме́на; (*variant*) вариа́нт; (*variety*) разнови́дность; (*mus., math.*) вариа́ция.
varicose ['værɪˌkəʊs] *adj.*: **~ veins** расшире́ние вен.
variegate ['veərɪˌgeɪt, -rɪəˌgeɪt] *v.t.* де́лать *impf.*, с~ *pf.* пёстрым; (*diversify*) разнообра́зить *impf.* **variegated** *adj.* разноцве́тный, пёстрый (-р, -ра́, пёстро́); (*diverse*) разнообра́зный. **variety** [və'raɪətɪ] *n.* разнообра́зие; (*sort*) разнови́дность; (*multitude*) мно́жество; **~ show** варьете́ *nt.indecl.*, эстра́дный конце́рт. **various** *adj.* (*of several kinds*) разли́чный; (*different, several*) ра́зный; (*diverse*) разнообра́зный.
varnish ['vɑːnɪʃ] *n.* лак; (*fig.*) лоск; *v.t.* лакирова́ть *impf.*, от~ *pf.* (*also fig.*). **varnishing** *n.* лакиро́вка.
vary ['veərɪ] *v.t.* разнообра́зить *impf.*, меня́ть *impf.*; *v.i.* (*change*) меня́ться *impf.*, изменя́ться *impf.*, измени́ться (-ню́сь, -нишься) *pf.*; (*differ*) ра́зниться *impf.*; (*disagree*) не соглаша́ться *impf.*
vase [vɑːz] *n.* ва́за.
vaseline ['væsɪˌliːn] *n.* вазели́н.
vassal ['væs(ə)l] *n.* васса́л.
vast [vɑːst] *adj.* грома́дный, обши́рный. **vastly** *adv.* значи́тельно. **vastness** *n.* грома́дность, обши́рность.
VAT *abbr.* (*of* ***value added tax***) нало́г на доба́вленную/приращённую сто́имость.
vat [væt] *n.* чан (*pl.* -ы́), бак.
Vatican ['vætɪkən] *n.* Ватика́н.
vaudeville ['vɔːdəvɪl, 'vəʊ-] *n.* водеви́ль *m.*; (*variety*) варьете́ *nt.indecl.*
vault[1] [vɔːlt, vɒlt] *n.* (*leap*) прыжо́к (-жка́); *v.t.* перепры́гивать *impf.*, перепры́гнуть *pf.*; *v.i.* пры́гать *impf.*, пры́гнуть *pf.* **vaulting-horse** *n.* гимнасти́ческий конь (-ня́; *pl.* -ни, -не́й) *m.*
vault[2] [vɔːlt, vɒlt] *n.* (*arch, covering*) свод; (*cellar*) по́греб, подва́л; (*burial ~*) склеп; *v.t.* возводи́ть (-ожу́, -о́дишь) *impf.*, возвести́ (-еду́, -едёшь; -ёл, -ела́) *pf.* свод над+*i.* **vaulted** *adj.* сво́дчатый.
VCR *abbr.* (*of* **video cassette recorder**) видеомагнитофо́н.
VD *abbr.* (*of* ***venereal disease***) венери́ческая боле́знь.
VDU *abbr.* (*of* ***visual display unit***) диспле́й.
veal [viːl] *n.* теля́тина; *attr.* теля́чий.
vector ['vektə(r)] *n.* (*math.*) ве́ктор; (*carrier of disease*) перено́счик инфе́кции.
veer [vɪə(r)] *v.i.* (*change direction*) изменя́ть *impf.*, измени́ть (-ню́, -нишь) *pf.* направле́ние; (*turn*) повора́чивать *impf.*, повороти́ть (-очу́, -о́тишь) *pf.*; **~ away from** отша́тываться *impf.*, отшатну́ться *pf.* от+*g.*
vegetable ['vedʒɪtəb(ə)l, 'vedʒtəb(ə)l] *n.* о́вощ; *adj.* расти́тельный; (*of vegetables*) овощно́й. **vegetarian** [ˌvedʒɪ'teərɪən] *n.* вегетариа́нец, -нка; *attr.* вегетариа́нский. **vege'tarianism** *n.* вегетариа́нство. **vegetate** *v.i.* расти́ (-ту́, -тёшь; рос, -ла́) *impf.*; (*fig.*) прозяба́ть *impf.* **vege'tation** *n.* расти́тельность; (*fig.*) прозяба́ние. **vegetative** *adj.* расти́тельный; (*biol.*) вегетати́вный; (*fig.*) прозяба́ющий.
vehemence ['viːəməns] *n.* (*force*) си́ла; (*passion*) стра́стность. **vehement** *adj.* (*forceful*) си́льный (си́лён, -льна́, -льно, си́льны́); (*passionate*) стра́стный (-тен, -тна́, -тно).
vehicle ['viːɪk(ə)l, 'vɪək(ə)l] *n.* сре́дство передвиже́ния/перево́зки; (*motor ~*) автомоби́ль *m.*; (*medium*) сре́дство; (*chem.*) носи́тель *m.* **vehicular** [vɪ'hɪkjʊlə(r)] *adj.* (*conveying*) перево́зочный; (*of motor transport*) автомоби́льный; **~ transport** автогужево́й тра́нспорт.
veil [veɪl] *n.* вуа́ль, покрыва́ло; (*fig.*) заве́са, покро́в; (*pretext*) предло́г; *v.t.* покрыва́ть *impf.*, покры́ть (-ро́ю, -ро́ешь) *pf.* вуа́лью, покрыва́лом; (*fig.*) скрыва́ть *impf.*, скрыть (-ро́ю, -ро́ешь) *pf.*
vein [veɪn] *n.* ве́на; (*of leaf; streak*) жи́лка; **in the same ~** в том же ду́хе. **veined** *adj.* испещрённый (-ён, -ена́) жи́лками.
veld [velt] *n.* вельд.
vellum ['veləm] *n.* (*parchment*) то́нкий перга́мент; (*paper*) веле́невая бума́га.
velocity [vɪ'lɒsɪtɪ] *n.* ско́рость.

velour(s) [və'lʊə(r)] *n.* велю́р; (*attr.*) велю́ровый.

velvet ['velvɪt] *n.* барха́т; *adj.* барха́тный. **velveteen** *n.* вельве́т. **velvety** *adj.* бархати́стый.

venal ['viːn(ə)l] *adj.* прода́жный, подку́пный. **venality** [ˌviː'nælɪtɪ] *n.* прода́жность.

vend [vend] *v.t.* продава́ть (-даю́, -даёшь) *impf.*, прода́ть (-а́м, -а́шь, а́ст, -ади́м; про́дал, -а́, -о) *pf.* **vending-machine** *n.* торго́вый автома́т. **vendor** ['vendə(r), -dɔː(r)] *n.* продаве́ц (-вца́), -вщи́ца.

vendetta [ven'detə] *n.* венде́тта, кро́вная месть.

veneer [vɪ'nɪə(r)] *n.* фанеро́вка; (*fig.*) лоск; *v.t.* фанерова́ть *impf.*

venerable ['venərəb(ə)l] *adj.* почте́нный (-нен, -нна); (**V~**) преподо́бный. **venerate** *v.t.* благогове́ть *impf.* пе́ред+*i.* **vene'ration** *n.* благогове́ние, почита́ние. **venerator** *n.* почита́тель *m.*

venereal [vɪ'nɪərɪəl] *adj.* венери́ческий.

venetian blind [vɪ'niːʃ(ə)n] *n.* жалюзи́ *nt.indecl.*

vengeance ['vendʒ(ə)ns] *n.* месть, мще́ние; **take ~** мстить *impf.*, ото~ *pf.* (**on** +*d.*; **for** за+*a.*); **with a ~** в по́лном смы́сле сло́ва; (*with might and main*) вовсю́. **vengeful** *adj.* мсти́тельный.

venial ['viːnɪəl] *adj.* прости́тельный.

Venice ['venɪs] *n.* Вене́ция.

venison ['venɪs(ə)n, -z(ə)n] *n.* оле́нина.

venom ['venəm] *n.* яд (-а(у)). **venomous** *adj.* ядови́тый.

vent¹ [vent] *n.* (*opening*) вы́ход (*also fig.*), отве́рстие; (*air-hole*) отду́шина; *v.t.* (*feelings*) дава́ть (даю́, даёшь) *impf.*, дать (дам, дашь, даст, дади́м; дал, -а́, да́ло́, -и) *pf.* вы́ход+*d.*; излива́ть *impf.*, изли́ть (-лью́, -льёшь; изли́л, -а́, -о) *pf.* (**on** на+*a.*); (*smoke etc.*) выпуска́ть *impf.*, вы́пустить *pf.*; (*opinion*) выска́зывать *impf.*, вы́сказать (-ажу, -ажешь) *pf.*

vent² [vent] *n.* (*slit*) разре́з.

ventilate ['ventɪˌleɪt] *v.t.* прове́тривать *impf.*, прове́трить *pf.*; (*fig.*) обсужда́ть *impf.*, обсуди́ть (-ужу́, -у́дишь) *pf.* **venti'lation** *n.* вентиля́ция, прове́тривание. **ventilator** *n.* вентиля́тор.

ventral ['ventr(ə)l] *adj.* брюшно́й.

ventricle ['ventrɪk(ə)l] *n.* желу́дочек (-чка).

ventriloquism [ven'trɪləˌkwɪz(ə)m], **ventriloquy** *n.* чревовеща́ние. **ventriloquist** *n.* чревовеща́тель *m.* **ventriloquize** *v.i.* чревовеща́ть *impf.*

venture ['ventʃə(r)] *n.* риско́ванное предприя́тие; (*speculation*) спекуля́ция; **at a ~** науда́чу; *v.i.* (*hazard, dare*) отва́живаться *impf.*, отва́житься *pf.*; *v.t.* (*risk*) рискова́ть *impf.*+*i.*; ста́вить *impf.*, по~ *pf.* на ка́рту; **~ an opinion, guess** осме́ливаться *impf.*, осме́литься *pf.* вы́сказать мне́ние, дога́дку. **venturesome** *adj.* (*person*) сме́лый (смел, -а́, -о); (*enterprise*) риско́ванный (-ан, -анна).

venue ['venjuː] *n.* ме́сто (*pl.* -та́) сбо́ра.

veracious [və'reɪʃəs] *adj.* правди́вый. **veracity** [və'ræsɪtɪ] *n.* правди́вость.

veranda(h) [və'rændə] *n.* вера́нда.

verb [vɜːb] *n.* глаго́л. **verbal** *adj.* (*oral*) у́стный; (*relating to words*) слове́сный; (*gram.*) отглаго́льный. **verbalize** *v.t.* выража́ть *impf.*, вы́разить *pf.* слова́ми; *v.i.* быть многосло́вным. **verbatim** [vɜː'beɪtɪm] *adj.* дословный; *adv.* досло́вно. **verbiage** *n.* многосло́вие, пустосло́вие. **verbose** [vɜː'bəʊs] *adj.* многосло́вный. **verbosity** [vɜː'bɒsɪtɪ] *n.* многосло́вие.

verdant ['vɜːd(ə)nt] *adj.* зелёный (зе́лен, -а́, -о).

verdict ['vɜːdɪkt] *n.* верди́кт, реше́ние; (*opinion*) мне́ние.

verdigris ['vɜːdɪgrɪs, -ˌgriːs] *n.* я́рь-медя́нка.

verdure ['vɜːdjə(r)] *n.* зе́лень.

verge¹ [vɜːdʒ] *n.* (*also fig.*) край (*loc.* -а́е & -аю́; *pl.* -ая́); (*of road*) обо́чина; (*fig.*) грань; (*eccl.*) жезл; **on the ~ of** на гра́ни+*g.*; **he was on the ~ of telling all** он чуть не рассказа́л всё.

verge² [vɜːdʒ] *v.i.* клони́ться (-ню́сь, -нишься) *impf.* (**towards** к+*d.*); **~ on** грани́чить *impf.* с+*i.*

verger ['vɜːdʒə(r)] *n.* церко́вный служи́тель *m.*; (*bearer of staff*) жезлоно́сец (-сца).

verification [ˌverɪfɪ'keɪʃ(ə)n] *n.* прове́рка; (*confirmation*) подтвержде́ние. **verify** ['verɪˌfaɪ] *v.t.* проверя́ть *impf.*, прове́рить *pf.*; (*confirm*) подтвержда́ть *impf.*, подтверди́ть *pf.* **verisimilitude** [ˌverɪsɪ'mɪlɪˌtjuːd] *n.* правдоподо́бие. **'veritable** *adj.* настоя́щий. **'verity** *n.* и́стина.

vermicelli [ˌvɜːmɪ'selɪ, -'tʃelɪ] *n.* вермише́ль.

vermilion [və'mɪljən] *adj.* я́рко-кра́сный (-сен, -сна́, -сно); *n.* ки́новарь.

vermin ['vɜːmɪn] *n.* вреди́тели *m.pl.*, паразиты *m.pl.*; (*fig.*) подо́нки (-ков) *pl.* **verminous** *adj.* киша́щий парази́тами; (*fig.*) отврати́тельный.

vermouth ['vɜːməθ, və'muːθ] *n.* ве́рмут.

vernacular [və'nækjʊlə(r)] *adj.* (*native, of language*) родно́й; (*local, of dialect*) ме́стный; (*national, folk*) наро́дный; (*colloquial*) разгово́рный; *n.* родно́й язы́к (-а́); ме́стный диале́кт; (*homely language*) разгово́рный язы́к (-а́).

vernal ['vɜːn(ə)l] *adj.* весе́нний.

verruca [və'ruːkə] *n.* борода́вка.

Versailles [veə'saɪ] *n.* Верса́ль.

versatile ['vɜːsəˌtaɪl] *adj.* многосторо́нний; (*flexible, of mind*) ги́бкий (-бок, -бка́, -бко). **versa'tility** *n.* многосторо́нность; ги́бкость.

verse [vɜːs] *n.* (*also bibl.*) стих (-а́); (*stanza*) строфа́ (*pl.* -фы); (*poetry*) стихи́ *m.pl.*, поэ́зия. **versed** *adj.* о́пытный, све́дущий (**in** в+*p.*). **versify** ['vɜːsɪˌfaɪ] *v.i.* писа́ть (пишу́, -шешь) *impf.*, на~ *pf.* стихи́; *v.t.* перелага́ть *impf.*, переложи́ть (-жу́, -жишь) *pf.* в стихи́.

version ['vɜːʃ(ə)n] *n.* (*variant*) вариа́нт; (*interpretation*) ве́рсия; (*text*) текст.

versus ['vɜ:səs] *prep.* про́тив+*g.*
vertebra ['vɜ:tɪbrə] *n.* позвоно́к (-нка́); *pl.* позвоно́чник. **vertebral** *adj.* позвоно́чный. **vertebrate** *n.* позвоно́чное живо́тное *sb.*
vertex ['vɜ:teks] *n.* верши́на; (*anat.*) маку́шка. **vertical** *adj.* вертика́льный; *n.* вертика́ль.
vertiginous [və'tɪdʒɪnəs] *adj.* (*dizzy*) головокружи́тельный; (*rotating*) крутя́щийся. **vertigo** ['vɜ:tɪ,gəʊ] *n.* головокруже́ние.
verve [vɜ:v] *n.* подъём, энтузиа́зм.
very ['verɪ] *adj.* (*that ~ same*) тот са́мый; (*this ~ same*) э́тот са́мый; **at that ~ moment** в тот са́мый моме́нт; (*precisely*) как раз; **you are the ~ person I was looking for** как раз вас я иска́л; **the ~** (*even the*) да́же, оди́н; **the ~ thought frightens me** одна́, да́же, мысль об э́том меня́ пуга́ет; (*the extreme*) са́мый; **at the ~ end** в са́мом конце́; *adv.* о́чень; **~ much** о́чень; **~ much**+*comp.* гора́здо+*comp.*; **~**+*superl.*, *superl.*; **~ first** са́мый пе́рвый; **~ well** (*agreement*) хорошо́, ла́дно; **not ~** не о́чень, дово́льно+*neg.*
vesicle ['vesɪk(ə)l] *n.* пузырёк (-рька́).
vespers ['vespəz] *n.* вече́рня.
vessel ['ves(ə)l] *n.* сосу́д; (*ship*) кора́бль (-бля́) *m.*, су́дно (*pl.* суда́, -до́в).
vest¹ [vest] *n.* ма́йка; (*waistcoat*) жиле́т.
vest² [vest] *v.t.* (*with power*) облека́ть *impf.*, обле́чь (-еку́, -ечёшь; -ёк, -екла́) *pf.* (**with** +*i.*); (*rights*) наделя́ть *impf.*, надели́ть *pf.*+*i.* (**in** +*a.*). **vested** *adj.*: **~ interest** ли́чная заинтересо́ванность; **~ interests** (*property rights*) иму́щественные права́ *nt.pl.*; (*entrepreneurs*) кру́пные предпринима́тели *m.pl.*; **~ rights** безусло́вные права́ *nt.pl.*
vestal (virgin) ['vest(ə)l] *n.* веста́лка.
vestibule ['vestɪ,bju:l] *n.* вестибю́ль *m.*, пере́дняя *sb.*
vestige ['vestɪdʒ] *n.* (*trace*) след (*pl.* -ы́); (*sign*) при́знак.
vestments ['vestmənts] *n.* одея́ние, оде́жда; (*eccl.*) облаче́ние. **vestry** *n.* ри́зница.
Vesuvius [vɪ'su:vɪəs]: **Mt ~** Везу́вий.
vet [vet] *n.* ветерина́р; *v.t.* (*fig.*) проверя́ть *impf.*, прове́рить *pf.*
vetch [vetʃ] *n.* ви́ка *collect.*
veteran ['vetərən] *n.* ветера́н; *adj.* ста́рый (стар, -а́, ста́ро́).
veterinary ['vetə,rɪnərɪ] *adj.* ветерина́рный; *n.* ветерина́р.
veto ['vi:təʊ] *n.* ве́то *nt.indecl.*, запреще́ние; *v.t.* налага́ть *impf.*, наложи́ть (-жу́, -жишь) *pf.* ве́то на+*a.*; запреща́ть *impf.*, запрети́ть (-ещу́, -ети́шь) *pf.*
vex [veks] *v.t.* досажда́ть *impf.*, досади́ть *pf.*+*d.* **ve'xation** *n.* доса́да. **vexed** *adj.* (*annoyed*) раздоса́дованный (-ан); (*question*) спо́рный. **ve'xatious, vexing** *adj.* доса́дный.
via ['vaɪə] *prep.* че́рез+*a.*
viable ['vaɪəb(ə)l] *adj.* жизнеспосо́бный; (*practicable*) осуществи́мый.
viaduct ['vaɪə,dʌkt] *n.* виаду́к.
vial ['vaɪəl] *n.* пузырёк (-рька́).
vibrant ['vaɪbrənt] *adj.* (*vibrating*) вибри́рующий; (*resonating*) резони́рующий; (*trembling*) дрожа́щий (**with** от+*g.*). **vibraphone** *n.* вибрафо́н. **vi'brate** *v.i.* вибри́ровать *impf.*, дрожа́ть (-жу́, -жи́шь) *impf.*; (*to sound*) звуча́ть (-чу́, -чи́шь) *impf.*, про~ *pf.*; *v.t.* (*make ~*) вызыва́ть *impf.*, вы́звать (вы́зову, -вешь) *pf.* вибра́цию в+*p.* **vi'bration** *n.* вибра́ция, дрожа́ние. **vibrato** [vɪ'brɑ:təʊ] *n.* вибра́то *nt.indecl.*
vicar ['vɪkə(r)] *n.* прихо́дский свяще́нник. **vicarage** *n.* дом (*pl.* -а́) свяще́нника.
vicarious [vɪ'keərɪəs] *adj.* (*deputizing for another*) замеща́ющий друго́го; (*indirect*) ко́свенный.
vice¹ [vaɪs] *n.* (*evil*) поро́к, зло; (*shortcoming*) недоста́ток (-тка).
vice² [vaɪs] *n.* (*tech.*) тиски́ (-ко́в) *pl.*
vice- [vaɪs] *in comb.* вице-, замести́тель *m.*; **~ admiral** вице-адмира́л. **vice-chairman** *n.* замести́тель *m.* председа́теля. **vice-chancellor** *n.* (*univ.*) проре́ктор. **vice-president** *n.* вице-президе́нт. **viceroy** *n.* вице-коро́ль (-ля́) *m.*
vice versa [,vaɪsɪ 'vɜ:sə] *adv.* наоборо́т.
vicinity [vɪ'sɪnɪtɪ] *n.* окре́стности *f.pl.*, сосе́дство, бли́зость; **in the ~** побли́зости (**of** от+*g.*).
vicious ['vɪʃəs] *adj.* поро́чный; (*spiteful*) зло́бный; (*cruel, brutal*) жесто́кий (-о́к, -о́ка́, -о́ко); **~ circle** поро́чный круг (*loc.* -е & -у́; *pl.* -и́). **viciousness** *n.* поро́чность; зло́бность.
vicissitude [vɪ'sɪsɪ,tju:d, vaɪ-] *n.* превра́тность.
victim ['vɪktɪm] *n.* же́ртва. **victimi'zation** *n.* пресле́дование. **victimize** *v.t.* (*harass*) му́чить *impf.*, за~, из~ *pf.*; (*persecute*) пресле́довать *impf.*
victor ['vɪktə(r)] *n.* победи́тель *m.*
Victorian [vɪk'tɔ:rɪən] *adj.* викториа́нский; (*fig.*) старомо́дный.
victorious [vɪk'tɔ:rɪəs] *adj.* (*army*) победоно́сный; (*procession etc.*) побе́дный. **victory** ['vɪktərɪ] *n.* побе́да.
victual ['vɪt(ə)l] *v.t.* снабжа́ть *impf.*, снабди́ть *pf.* прови́зией. **victualler** ['vɪtlə(r)] *n.* поставщи́к продово́льствия. **victuals** *n.* пи́ща, прови́зия *collect.*
vide ['vɪdeɪ, 'vi:-, 'vaɪdɪ] *imper.* смотри́.
video (recorder) *n.* видеомагнитофо́н; **~ cassette** видеокассе́та; **~ recording** видеоза́пись; *v.t.* запи́сывать *impf.*, записа́ть (-ишу́, -и́шешь) *pf.* (на ви́део). **videotape** *n.* видеоле́нта; видеоза́пись.
vie [vaɪ] *v.i.* сопе́рничать *impf.* (**with** с+*i.*; **for** в+*p.*).
Vienna [vɪ'enə] *n.* Ве́на.
Vietnam [,vjet'næm] *n.* Вьетна́м.
view [vju:] *n.* (*prospect, picture*) вид; (*opinion*) взгляд, мне́ние; (*viewing*) просмо́тр; (*inspection*) осмо́тр; **in ~ of** ввиду́+*g.*; **on ~** вы́ставленный (-ен) для обозре́ния; **with a ~ to** с це́лью+*g.*, +*inf.*; *v.t.* (*pictures etc.*)

рассма́тривать *impf.*; (*inspect*) осма́тривать *impf.*, осмотре́ть (-рю́, -ришь) *pf.*; (*mentally*) смотре́ть (-рю́, -ришь) *impf.* на+*a.*; *v.i.* смотре́ть (-рю́, -ришь) *impf.*, по~ *pf.* телеви́зор. **viewer** *n.* зри́тель *m.*, ~ница; (*for slides*) прое́ктор. **viewfinder** *n.* видоиска́тель *m.* **viewpoint** *n.* то́чка зре́ния.

vigil [ˈvɪdʒɪl] *n.* бо́дрствование; **keep** ~ бо́дрствовать *impf.*, дежу́рить *impf.* **vigilance** *n.* бди́тельность. **vigilant** *adj.* бди́тельный. **vigilante** [ˌvɪdʒɪˈlæntɪ] *n.* дружи́нник.

vignette [viːˈnjet] *n.* винье́тка.

vigorous [ˈvɪgərəs] *adj.* си́льный (силён, -льна́, -льно, си́льны́), энерги́чный. **vigour** *n.* си́ла, эне́ргия.

vile [vaɪl] *adj.* (*base*) по́длый (подл, -а́, -о), ни́зкий (-зок, -зка́, -зко); (*disgusting*) отврати́тельный. **vileness** *n.* по́длость; отврати́тельность. **vilify** [ˈvɪlɪˌfaɪ] *v.t.* черни́ть *impf.*, о~ *pf.*

villa [ˈvɪlə] *n.* ви́лла.

village [ˈvɪlɪdʒ] *n.* дере́вня, село́; *attr.* дереве́нский, се́льский. **villager** *n.* дереве́нский, се́льский жи́тель *m.*

villain [ˈvɪlən] *n.* злоде́й. **villainous** *adj.* злоде́йский; (*foul*) ме́рзкий (-зок, -зка́, -зко). **villainy** *n.* злоде́йство.

Vilnius [ˈvɪlnɪəs] *n.* Ви́льнюс.

vim [vɪm] *n.* эне́ргия.

vinaigrette [ˌvɪnɪˈgret] *n.* (*dressing*) припра́ва из у́ксуса и оли́вкового ма́сла.

vindicate [ˈvɪndɪˌkeɪt] *v.t.* (*justify*) опра́вдывать *impf.*, оправда́ть *pf.*; (*stand up for*) отста́ивать *impf.*, отстоя́ть (-ою́, -ои́шь) *pf.* **vindiˈcation** *n.* (*justification*) оправда́ние; (*defence*) защи́та.

vindictive [vɪnˈdɪktɪv] *adj.* мсти́тельный.

vine [vaɪn] *n.* виногра́дная лоза́ (*pl.* -зы).

vinegar [ˈvɪnɪgə(r)] *n.* у́ксус; *attr.* у́ксусный. **vinegary** *adj.* ки́слый (-сел, -сла́, -сло).

vineyard [ˈvɪnjɑːd, -jəd] *n.* виногра́дник.

vintage [ˈvɪntɪdʒ] *n.* сбор, урожа́й, виногра́да; (*wine*) вино́ из сбо́ра определённого го́да; *attr.* (*wine*) ма́рочный; (*car*) ста́рый (стар, -а́, ста́ро́).

viola [ˈvaɪəʊlə] *n.* (*mus.*) альт.

violate [ˈvaɪəˌleɪt] *v.t.* (*treaty, privacy*) наруша́ть *impf.*, нару́шить *pf.*; (*grave*) оскверня́ть *impf.*, оскверни́ть *pf.*; (*rape*) наси́ловать *impf.*, из~ *pf.* **vioˈlation** *n.* наруше́ние; оскверне́ние; наси́лие. **violator** *n.* нару́шитель *m.*

violence [ˈvaɪələns] *n.* (*physical coercion, force*) наси́лие; (*strength, force*) си́ла. **violent** *adj.* (*person*) свире́пый, жесто́кий (-о́к, -о́ка́, -ко); (*storm etc.*) си́льный (си́лён, -льна́, -льно, си́льны́); (*quarrel*) бу́рный (бу́рен, бу́рна́, -но), свире́пый; (*pain*) си́льный (си́лён, -льна́, -льно, си́льны́); (*epoch*) бу́рный (бу́рен, бу́рна́, -но), жесто́кий (-о́к, -о́ка́, -ко); (*death*) наси́льственный. **violently** *adv.* си́льно, о́чень.

violet [ˈvaɪələt] *n.* (*bot.*) фиа́лка; (*colour*) фиоле́товый цвет; *adj.* фиоле́товый.

violin [ˌvaɪəˈlɪn] *n.* скри́пка. **violinist** *n.* скрипа́ч (-а́), ~ка.

VIP *abbr.* (*of* ***very important person***) высокопоста́вленное лицо́ (*pl.* -ца), высо́кий гость.

viper [ˈvaɪpə(r)] *n.* гадю́ка; (*fig.*) змея́ (*pl.* -е́и). **viperous** *adj.* ядови́тый.

virago [vɪˈrɑːgəʊ, -ˈreɪgəʊ] *n.* меѓера.

viral [ˈvaɪər(ə)l] *adj.* ви́русный.

virgin [ˈvɜːdʒɪn] *n.* де́вственник, -ица; **V~ Mary** Де́ва Мари́я; *adj.* (*also fig.*) де́вственный (-ен, -енна); ~ **lands, soil** целина́. **virginal** *adj.* де́вственный (-ен, -енна); (*innocent*) неви́нный (-нен, -нна). **virˈginity** *n.* де́вственность. **Virgo** [ˈvɜːgəʊ] *n.* Де́ва.

virile [ˈvɪraɪl] *adj.* (*mature*) возмужа́лый; (*manly*) му́жественный (-ен, -енна). **virility** [vɪˈrɪlɪtɪ] *n.* возмужа́лость; му́жество.

virtual [ˈvɜːtjʊəl] *adj.* факти́ческий. **virtually** *adv.* факти́чески. **virtue** [ˈvɜːtjuː, -tʃuː] *n.* (*excellence*) доброде́тель; (*merit*) досто́инство; **by ~ of** посре́дством+*g.*, благодаря́+*d.* **virtuˈosity** *n.* виртуо́зность. **virtuoso** [ˌvɜːtjʊˈəʊsəʊ, -zəʊ] *n.* виртуо́з. **virtuous** *adj.* доброде́тельный; (*chaste*) целому́дренный (-ен, -енна).

virulence [ˈvɪrʊləns, ˈvɪrjʊ-] *n.* (*toxicity*) ядови́тость; (*power*) си́ла; (*med.*) вирул́ентность; (*fig.*) зло́ба. **virulent** *adj.* (*poisonous*) ядови́тый; (*of disease*) опа́сный; (*fig.*) зло́бный.

virus [ˈvaɪərəs] *n.* ви́рус.

visa [ˈviːzə] *n.* ви́за; *v.t.* визи́ровать *impf.* & *pf.*, за~ *pf.*

visage [ˈvɪzɪdʒ] *n.* лицо́ (*pl.* -ца); (*aspect*) вид.

vis-à-vis [ˌviːzɑːˈviː] *adv.* визави́, напро́тив; *n.* визави́ *nt.indecl.*; *prep.* (*with regard to*) в отноше́нии+*g.*; (*opposite*) напро́тив+*g.*

viscera [ˈvɪsərə] *n.* вну́тренности *f.pl.*

viscose [ˈvɪskəʊz, -kəʊs] *n.* виско́за.

viscosity [vɪˈskɒsɪtɪ] *n.* вя́зкость.

viscount [ˈvaɪkaʊnt] *n.* вико́нт. **viscountess** *n.* виконте́сса.

viscous [ˈvɪskəs] *adj.* вя́зкий (-зок, -зка́, -зко).

visibility [ˌvɪzɪˈbɪlɪtɪ] *n.* ви́димость. **ˈvisible** *adj.* ви́димый. **ˈvisibly** *adv.* я́вно, заме́тно.

vision [ˈvɪʒ(ə)n] *n.* (*sense*) зре́ние; (*apparition*) виде́ние; (*insight*) проница́тельность; (*foresight*) предви́дение; (*on television screen*) изображе́ние. **visionary** *adj.* (*spectral; illusory*) при́зрачный; (*imaginary, fantastic*) вообража́емый, фантасти́ческий; (*impracticable*) неосуществи́мый; (*given to having visions*) скло́нный (-о́нен, -о́нна́, -о́нно) к галлюцина́циям; *n.* (*dreamer*) мечта́тель *m.*, ~ница, фантазёр; (*one who has visions*) визионе́р.

visit [ˈvɪzɪt] *n.* посеще́ние, визи́т; (*trip*) пое́здка; *v.t.* навеща́ть *impf.*, навести́ть *pf.*; посеща́ть *impf.*, посети́ть (-ещу́, -ети́шь) *pf.*; (*call on*) заходи́ть (-ожу́, -о́дишь) *impf.*, зайти́ (-йду́, -йдёшь; зашёл, -шла́) *pf.* к+*d.*; ходи́ть (хожу́, хо́дишь) *indet.*, идти́ (иду́, идёшь; шёл, шла) *det.*, пойти́ (пойду́, -дёшь;

пошёл, -шла́) *pf.* в го́сти к+*d.*; **be ~ing** быть в гостя́х у+*g.* **visi'tation** *n.* (*official visit*) официа́льное посеще́ние; (*eccl.*) бо́жье наказа́ние. **visiting-card** *n.* визи́тная ка́рточка. **visitor** *n.* гость (*pl.* -ти, -те́й) *m.*, посети́тель *m.*

visor ['vaɪzə(r)] *n.* (*of cap*) козырёк (-рька́); (*in car*) солнцезащи́тный щито́к (-тка́); (*of helmet*) забра́ло.

vista ['vɪstə] *n.* перспекти́ва, вид.

visual ['vɪzjʊəl, 'vɪʒj-] *adj.* (*of vision*) зри́тельный; (*graphic*) нагля́дный; **~ aids** нагля́дные посо́бия *nt.pl.* **visualize** *v.t.* представля́ть *impf.*, предста́вить *pf.* себе́.

vital ['vaɪt(ə)l] *adj.* (*also fig.*) жи́зненный (-ен, -енна); (*fig.*) суще́ственный (-ен, -енна); (*lively*) живо́й (жив, -а́, -о); **~ statistics** стати́стика есте́ственного движе́ния населе́ния. **vitality** [vaɪ'tælɪtɪ] *n.* жизнеспосо́бность; (*liveliness*) жи́вость. **vitalize** *v.t.* оживля́ть *impf.*, оживи́ть *pf.* **vitals** *n.* жи́зненно ва́жные о́рганы *m.pl.*

vitamin ['vɪtəmɪn, 'vaɪt-] *n.* витами́н.

vitiate ['vɪʃɪˌeɪt] *v.t.* по́ртить *impf.*, ис~ *pf.*; (*invalidate*) де́лать *impf.*, с~ *pf.* недействи́тельным; лиша́ть *impf.*, лиши́ть *pf.* си́лы. **viti'ation** *n.* по́рча; (*leg.*) лише́ние си́лы; призна́ние недействи́тельным.

viticulture ['vɪtɪˌkʌltʃə(r)] *n.* виногра́дарство.

vitreous ['vɪtrɪəs] *adj.* стеклови́дный; (*of glass*) стекля́нный. **vitrify** ['vɪtrɪˌfaɪ] *v.t.* & *i.* превраща́ть(ся) *impf.*, преврати́ть(ся) (-ащу́(сь), -ати́шь(ся)) *pf.* в стекло́, в стеклови́дное вещество́.

vitriol ['vɪtrɪəl] *n.* купоро́с; (*fig.*) язви́тельность. **vitriolic** [ˌvɪtrɪ'ɒlɪk] *adj.* купоро́сный; (*fig.*) язви́тельный.

vituperate [vɪ'tju:pəˌreɪt, vaɪ-] *v.t.* брани́ть *impf.*, вы́~ *pf.* **vitupe'ration** *n.* брань.

vivacious [vɪ'veɪʃəs] *adj.* живо́й (жив, -а́, -о), оживлённый (-ён, -ена́). **vivacity** [vɪ'væsɪtɪ] *n.* жи́вость, оживлённость.

viva voce [ˌvaɪvə 'vəʊtʃɪ, 'vəʊsɪ] *adj.* у́стный; *n.* у́стный экза́мен.

vivid ['vɪvɪd] *adj.* (*bright*) я́ркий (я́рок, ярка́, я́рко); (*lively*) живо́й (жив, -а́, -о); (*imagination*) пы́лкий (пы́лок, -лка́, -лко). **vividness** *n.* я́ркость; жи́вость; пы́лкость.

vivify ['vɪvɪˌfaɪ] *v.t.* оживля́ть *impf.*, оживи́ть *pf.*

vivisection [ˌvɪvɪ'sekʃ(ə)n] *n.* вивисе́кция.

vixen ['vɪks(ə)n] *n.* лиси́ца-са́мка; (*fig.*) мегера.

viz. [vɪz] *adv.* то есть, а и́менно.

vizier [vɪ'zɪə(r), 'vɪzɪə(r)] *n.* визи́рь *m.*

V-neck [vi:'nek, 'vi:-] *n.* вы́рез в ви́де бу́квы V.

vocabulary [və'kæbjʊlərɪ] *n.* слова́рь (-ря́) *m.*; (*range of language*) запа́с слов; (*of a language*) слова́рный соста́в.

vocal ['vəʊk(ə)l] *adj.* голосово́й; (*mus.*) вока́льный; (*noisy*) шу́мный (шу́мен, -мна́, -мно); **~ chord** голосова́я свя́зка. **vocalic** [və'kælɪk] *adj.* гла́сный. **vocalist** *n.* певе́ц (-вца́), -ви́ца.

vocation [və'keɪʃ(ə)n] *n.* призва́ние; (*profession*) профе́ссия. **vocational** *adj.* профессиона́льный. **vocative** ['vɒkətɪv] *adj.* (*n.*) зва́тельный (паде́ж(-а́)).

vociferate [və'sɪfəˌreɪt] *v.t.* крича́ть (-чу́, -чи́шь) *impf.*, кри́кнуть *pf.* **vociferous** *adj.* (*clamorous*) крикли́вый; (*noisy*) шу́мный (шу́мен, -мна́, -мно).

vodka ['vɒdkə] *n.* во́дка.

vogue [vəʊg] *n.* мо́да; (*popularity*) популя́рность; **in ~** в мо́де.

voice [vɔɪs] *n.* го́лос; (*gram.*) зало́г; *v.t.* (*express*) выража́ть *impf.*, вы́разить *pf.* **voiced** *adj.* (*phon.*) зво́нкий (-нок, -нка́, -нко). **voiceless** *adj.* (*phon.*) глухо́й (глух, -а́, -о).

void [vɔɪd] *n.* пустота́; *adj.* пусто́й (пуст, -а́, -о, пу́сты́); (*invalid*) недействи́тельный; **~ of** лишённый (-ён, -ена́) +*g.*; *v.t.* (*render invalid*) де́лать *impf.*, с~ *pf.* недействи́тельным; (*excrete*) опорожня́ть *impf.*, опоро́жнить *pf.*

volatile ['vɒləˌtaɪl] *adj.* (*chem.*) лету́чий; (*inconstant*) непостоя́нный (-нен, -нна); (*elusive*) неулови́мый. **vola'tility** *n.* лету́честь; непостоя́нство.

vol-au-vent ['vɒləʊˌvɑ̃] *n.* слоёный пирожо́к (-жка́).

volcanic [vɒl'kænɪk] *adj.* вулкани́ческий (*also fig.*). **volcano** [vɒl'keɪnəʊ] *n.* вулка́н.

vole [vəʊl] *n.* (*zool.*) полёвка.

Volga ['vɒlgə] *n.* Во́лга.

volition [və'lɪʃ(ə)n] *n.* во́ля; **of one's own ~** по свое́й во́ле.

volley ['vɒlɪ] *n.* (*missiles*) залп; (*fig.*; *of arrows etc.*) град; (*sport*) уда́р с лёта; *v.t.* (*sport*) ударя́ть *impf.*, уда́рить *pf.* с лёта. **volleyball** *n.* волейбо́л.

volt [vəʊlt] *n.* вольт. **voltage** *n.* вольта́ж, напряже́ние.

volte-face [vɒlt'fɑ:s] *n.* (*fig.*) ре́зкая переме́на.

volubility [ˌvɒljʊ'bɪlɪtɪ] *n.* говорли́вость. **'voluble** *adj.* говорли́вый.

volume ['vɒlju:m] *n.* (*book*) том (*pl.* -а́); (*capacity, bulk*; *also fig.*) объём; (*loudness*) гро́мкость; (*mus., strength*) си́ла. **voluminous** [və'lju:mɪnəs, və'lu:-] *adj.* (*bulky*) объёмистый, обши́рный; (*of writer*) плодови́тый; (*of many volumes*) многото́мный.

voluntary ['vɒləntərɪ] *adj.* доброво́льный; (*deliberate*) умы́шленный (-ен, -енна); *n.* (*mus.*) со́ло *nt.indecl.* на орга́не. **volun'teer** *n.* доброво́лец (-льца); *v.t.* предлага́ть *impf.*, предложи́ть (-жу́, -жишь) *pf.*; *v.i.* (*offer*) вызыва́ться *impf.*, вы́зваться (вы́зовусь, -вешься) *pf.* (*inf.*, +*inf.*; **for** в+*a.*); (*mil.*) идти́ (иду́, идёшь; шёл, шла) *impf.*, пойти́ (пойду́, -дёшь; пошёл, -шла́) *pf.* доброво́льцем.

voluptuary [və'lʌptjʊərɪ] *n.* сластолю́бец (-бца). **voluptuous** *adj.* сластолюби́вый, чу́вственный (-ен, енна). **voluptuousness** *n.* сластолю́бие.

vomit ['vɒmɪt] *n.* рво́та; *v.t.* рвать (рвёт)

impf., вы́рвать (-вет) *pf. impers.+i.*; **he was ~ing blood** его́ рва́ло кро́вью; (*fig.*) изверга́ть *impf.*, изве́ргнуть *pf.*

voracious [vəˈreɪʃəs] *adj.* прожо́рливый; (*fig.*) ненасы́тный. **voracity** [vəˈræsɪtɪ] *n.* прожо́рливость; ненасы́тность.

vortex [ˈvɔːteks] *n.* (*whirlpool*; *also fig.*) водоворо́т; (*whirlwind*; *also fig.*) вихрь *m.*

votary [ˈvəʊtərɪ] *n.* почита́тель *m.*, ~ница; сторо́нник, -ица.

vote [vəʊt] *n.* (*poll*) голосова́ние; (*individual ~*) го́лос (*pl.* -а́); **the ~** (*suffrage*) пра́во го́лоса; (*resolution*) во́тум *no pl.*; **~ of no confidence** во́тум недове́рия (**in** +*d.*); **~ of thanks** выраже́ние благода́рности; *v.i.* голосова́ть *impf.*, про~ *pf.* (**for** за+*a.*; **against** про́тив+*g.*); *v.t.* (*grant by ~*) ассигнова́ть *impf.* & *pf.*; (*deem*) признава́ть *impf.*, призна́ть *pf.*; **the film was ~d a failure** фильм был при́знан неуда́чным; **~ in** избира́ть *impf.*, избра́ть (изберу́, -рёшь; избра́л, -а́, -о) *pf.* голосова́нием. **voter** *n.* избира́тель *m.* **voting-paper** *n.* избира́тельный бюллете́нь *m.*

votive *adj.* испо́лненный по обе́ту; **~ offering** приноше́ние по обе́ту.

vouch [vaʊtʃ] *v.i.*; **~ for** руча́ться *impf.*, поручи́ться *pf.* за+*a.* **voucher** *n.* (*receipt*) распи́ска; (*coupon*) тало́н. **vouchˈsafe** *v.t.* удоста́ивать *impf.*, удосто́ить+*i.* (*person to whom granted* +*a.*).

vow [vaʊ] *n.* кля́тва, обе́т; *v.t.* кля́сться (кляну́сь, -нёшься; кля́лся, -ла́сь) *impf.*, по~ *pf.* в+*p.*

vowel [ˈvaʊəl] *n.* гла́сный *sb.*

voyage [ˈvɔɪɪdʒ] *n.* путеше́ствие; *v.i.* путеше́ствовать *impf.*

V-sign [ˈviːsaɪn] *n.* (*victory*) знак побе́ды

vulgar [ˈvʌlgə(r)] *adj.* вульга́рный, гру́бый (груб, -а́, -о), по́шлый (пошл, -а́, -о); (*of the common people*) простонаро́дный. **vulgarism** *n.* вульга́рное выраже́ние. **vulgarity** [vʌlˈgærɪtɪ] *n.* вульга́рность, по́шлость. **vulgariˈzation** *n.* вульгариза́ция. **vulgarize** *v.t.* вульгаризи́ровать *impf.* & *pf.*

vulnerable [ˈvʌlnərəb(ə)l] *adj.* уязви́мый.

vulture [ˈvʌltʃə(r)] *n.* гриф; (*fig.*) хи́щник.

vulva [ˈvʌlvə] *n.* ву́льва.

wad [wɒd] *n.* кусо́к (-ска́) ва́ты; (*in gun*) пыж (-а́); **~ of money** па́чка бума́жных де́нег; *v.t.* (*stuff with wadding*) набива́ть *impf.*, наби́ть (набью́, -ьёшь) *pf.* ва́той. **wadding** ва́та; (*padding, packing*) наби́вка.

waddle [ˈwɒd(ə)l] *v.i.* ходи́ть (хожу́, хо́дишь) *indet.*, идти́ (иду́, идёшь; шёл, шла) *det.*, пойти́ (пойду́, -дёшь; пошёл, -шла́) *pf.* вперева́лку (*coll.*).

wade [weɪd] *v.t.* & *i.* (*river*) переходи́ть (-ожу́, -о́дишь) *impf.*, перейти́ (-йду́, -йдёшь; перешёл, -шла́) *pf.* вброд; *v.i.*: **~ through** (*mud etc.*) пробира́ться *impf.*, пробра́ться (проберу́сь, -рёшься; пробра́лся, -ала́сь, -а́ло́сь) *pf.* по+*d.*; (*sth. boring etc.*) одолева́ть *impf.*, одоле́ть *pf.* **wader** *n.* (*bird*) боло́тная пти́ца; (*boot*) боло́тный сапо́г (-а́; *g.pl.* -г).

wafer [ˈweɪfə(r)] *n.* ва́фля (*g.pl.* -фель); (*eccl.*; *paper seal*) обла́тка.

waffle[1] [ˈwɒf(ə)l] *n.* (*dish*) ва́фля (*g.pl.* -фель).

waffle[2] [ˈwɒf(ə)l] *n.* (*blather*) трёп; *v.i.* трепа́ться (-плю́сь, -плешься) *impf.*

waft [wɒft, wɑːft] *v.t.* & *i.* нести́(сь) (несу́(сь), -сёшь(ся); нёс(ся), несла́(сь)) *impf.*, по~ *pf.*

wag[1] [wæg] *n.* (*wave*) взмах; (*of tail*) виля́ние; *v.t.* (*tail*) виля́ть *impf.*, вильну́ть *pf.*+*i.*; (*finger*) грози́ть *impf.*, по~ *pf.*+*i.*; *v.i.* кача́ться *impf.*, качну́ться *pf.*

wag[2] [wæg] *n.* (*joker*) шутни́к (-а́).

wage[1] [weɪdʒ] *v.t.*: **~ war** вести́ (веду́, -дёшь; вёл, -а́) *impf.*, про~ *pf.* войну́.

wage[2] [weɪdʒ] *n.* за́работная пла́та; **~ freeze** замора́живание за́работной пла́ты; **living ~** прожи́точный ми́нимум. **wage-earner** *n.* рабо́чий *sb.*; (*bread-winner*) корми́лец (-льца).

wager [ˈweɪdʒə(r)] *n.* пари́ *nt.indecl.*; (*stake*) ста́вка; *v.i.* (*t.*) держа́ть (-жу́, -жишь) *impf.* пари́ (на+*a.*) (**that** что).

wages *n. see* **wage**[2]

waggish [ˈwægɪʃ] *n.* шаловли́вый.

wag(g)on [ˈwægən] *n.* (*carriage*) пово́зка; (*cart*) теле́га; (*rail.*) ваго́н-платфо́рма; (*van*) фурго́н; (*trolley*) ваго́не́тка. **wag(g)oner** *n.* во́зчик.

wagtail [ˈwægteɪl] *n.* трясогу́зка.

waif [weɪf] *n.* беспризо́рник.

wail [weɪl] *n.* вопль *m.*; *v.i.* вопи́ть *impf.* (*coll.*), выть (во́ю, во́ешь) *impf.* (*coll.*).

wainscot [ˈweɪnskət] *n.* пане́ль; *v.t.* обшива́ть *impf.*, обши́ть (обошью́, -ьёшь) *pf.* пане́лью.

waist [weɪst] *n.* та́лия; (*level of ~*) по́яс (*pl.* -а́). **waistband** *n.* по́яс (*pl.* -а́). **waistcoat** *n.* жиле́т. **waist-deep** *n.* (*adv.*) по по́яс. **waistline** *n.* та́лия.

wait [weɪt] *n.* ожида́ние; **lie in ~** быть в заса́де; **lie in ~ (for)** поджида́ть *impf.*; *v.i.*(*t.*) (*also ~ for*) ждать (жду, ждёшь; ждал, -а́, -о) *impf.* (+*g.*); *v.i.* (*be a ~er, ~ress*) быть официа́нтом, -ткой; **~ on** обслу́живать *impf.*, обслужи́ть (-жу́, -жишь) *pf.* **waiter** *n.* официа́нт. **waiting** *n.* ожида́ние. **waiting-list** *n.* спи́сок (-ска) кандида́тов. **waiting-room** *n.* приёмная *sb.*; (*rail.*) зал ожида́ния. **waitress** *n.* официа́нтка.

waive [weɪv] *v.t.* отка́зываться *impf.*, отказа́ться (-ажу́сь, -а́жешься) *pf.* от+*g.*

wake[1] [weɪk] *n.* (*at funeral*) поми́нки (-нок) *pl.*
wake[2] [weɪk] *n.* (*naut.*) кильва́тер; **in the ~ of** в кильва́тере+*d.*, по пята́м за+*i.*
wake[3] [weɪk] *v.t.* (*also ~ up*) буди́ть (бужу́, бу́дишь) *impf.*, раз~ *pf.*; *v.i.* (*also ~ up*) просыпа́ться *impf.*, просну́ться *pf.*; *v.t. & i.* (*also fig.*) пробужда́ть(ся) *impf.*, пробуди́ть(ся) (-ужу́(сь), -у́дишь(ся)) *pf.* **wakeful** *adj.* (*sleepless*) бессо́нный; (*vigilant*) бди́тельный. **wakefulness** *n.* бди́тельность. **waken** *see* **wake**[3]
Wales [weɪlz] *n.* Уэ́льс.
walk [wɔːk] *n.* (*walking*) ходьба́; (*gait*) похо́дка; (*stroll*) прогу́лка пешко́м; (*path, avenue*) тропа́ (*pl.* -пы, -п, тро́па́м), алле́я; **ten minutes' ~ from here** де́сять мину́т ходьбы́ отсю́да; **go for a ~** идти́ (иду́, идёшь; шёл, шла) *impf.*, пойти́ (пойду́, -дёшь; пошёл, -шла́) *pf.* гуля́ть; **from all ~s of life** всех слоёв о́бщества; *v.i.* ходи́ть (хожу́, хо́дишь) *indet.*, идти́ (иду́, идёшь; шёл, шла) *det.*, пойти́ (пойду́, -дёшь; пошёл, -шла́) *pf.*; гуля́ть *impf.*, по~ *pf.*; **~ away, off** уходи́ть (ухожу́, -о́дишь) *impf.*, уйти́ (уйду́, -дёшь; ушёл, ушла́) *pf.*; **~ in** входи́ть (вхожу́, -о́дишь) *impf.*, войти́ (войду́, -дёшь; вошёл, -шла́) *pf.*; **~ out** выходи́ть (-ожу́, -о́дишь) *impf.*, вы́йти (-йду, -йдешь; вы́шел, -шла) *pf.*; *v.t.* (*traverse*) обходи́ть (-ожу́, -о́дишь) *impf.*, обойти́ (-йду́, -йдёшь; обошёл, -шла́) *pf.*; (*take for ~*) выводи́ть (-ожу́, -о́дишь) *impf.*, вы́вести (-еду, -едешь; -ел) *pf.* гуля́ть. **walker** *n.* ходо́к (-а́). **walkie-talkie** [ˌwɔːkɪˈtɔːkɪ] *n.* (перено́сная) ра́ция. **walking** *n.* ходьба́; *adj.* гуля́ющий; (*med.*; *encyclopaedia*) ходя́чий. **walking-stick** *n.* трость (*pl.* -ти, -те́й).
Walkman [ˈwɔːkmən] *n.* (*propr.*) во́кмен, пле́ер.
walk-on: ~ part роль (*pl.* -ли, -ле́й) без слов. **walk-out** *n.* (*strike*) забасто́вка; (*exit*) демонстрати́вный ухо́д. **walk-over** *n.* лёгкая побе́да.
wall [wɔːl] *n.* стена́ (*a.* -ну; *pl.* -ны, -н, -на́м); (*of object*) сте́нка; *attr.* стенно́й *v.t.* обноси́ть (-ошу́, -о́сишь) *impf.*, обнести́ (-есу́, -есёшь; -ёс, -есла́) *pf.* стено́й; **~ up** (*door, window*) заде́лывать *impf.*, заде́лать *pf.*; (*brick up*) замуро́вывать *impf.*, замурова́ть *pf.*
wallet [ˈwɒlɪt] *n.* бума́жник.
wallflower [ˈwɔːlˌflaʊə(r)] *n.* желтофио́ль.
wallop [ˈwɒləp] *n.* си́льный уда́р; *v.t.* си́льно ударя́ть *impf.*, уда́рить *pf.*; бить (бью, бьёшь) *impf.*, по~ *pf.*
wallow [ˈwɒləʊ] *v.i.* валя́ться *impf.*, бара́хтаться; **~ in** (*give o.s. up to*) предава́ться (-даю́сь, -даёшься) *impf.*, преда́ться (-а́мся, -а́шься, -а́стся, -ади́мся; преда́лся, -ла́сь) *pf.*+*d.*
wallpaper [ˈwɔːlˌpeɪpə(r)] *n.* обо́и (обо́ев) *pl.*
walnut [ˈwɔːlnʌt] *n.* гре́цкий оре́х; (*wood, tree*) оре́ховое де́рево (*pl.* (*tree*) -е́вья, -е́вьев), оре́х.
walrus [ˈwɔːlrəs, ˈwɒl-] *n.* морж (-а́).
waltz [wɔːls, wɔːlts, wɒ-] *n.* вальс; *v.i.* вальси́ровать *impf.*
wan [wɒn] *adj.* (*pale*) бле́дный (-ден, -дна́, -дно, бле́дны́); (*faint*) ту́склый (-л, -ла́, -ло).
wand [wɒnd] *n.* (*of conductor, magician*) па́лочка; (*of official*) жезл (-а́).
wander [ˈwɒndə(r)] *v.i.* броди́ть (брожу́, -о́дишь) *impf.*; (*also of thoughts etc.*) блужда́ть *impf.*; **~ from the point** отклоня́ться *impf.*, отклони́ться (-ню́сь, -нишься) *pf.* от те́мы. **wanderer** *n.* стра́нник, скита́лец (-льца). **wandering** *adj.* бродя́чий; блужда́ющий; (*winding*) изви́листый.
wane [weɪn] *n.* убыва́ние; *v.i.* убыва́ть *impf.*, убы́ть (убу́дет; у́был, -а́, -о) *pf.*; (*diminish*) уменьша́ться *impf.*, уме́ньши́ться *pf.*; (*weaken*) ослабева́ть *impf.*, ослабе́ть *pf.*
wangle [ˈwæŋg(ə)l] *v.t.* ухитя́ться *impf.*, ухитри́ться *pf.* получи́ть.
want [wɒnt] *n.* (*lack*) недоста́ток (-тка); (*need*) нужда́; (*requirement*) потре́бность; (*desire*) жела́ние; *v.t.* хоте́ть (хочу́, -чешь, хоти́м) *impf.*, за~ *pf.*+*g.* & *a.*; (*need*) нужда́ться *impf.* в+*p.*; **I ~ you to come at six** я хочу́, что́бы ты пришёл в шесть. **wanting** *adj.* (*absent*) отсу́тствующий; **be ~** недостава́ть (-таёт) *impf.* (*impers.*+*g.*); **experience is ~** недостаёт о́пыта.
wanton [ˈwɒnt(ə)n] *adj.* (*licentious*) распу́тный; (*senseless*) бессмы́сленный (-ен, -енна); (*luxuriant*) бу́йный (бу́ен, буйна́, -но).
war [wɔː(r)] *n.* война́ (*pl.* -ны); (*attr.*) вое́нный (*in ~ crime, ~ correspondent, ~ debts, ~ loan etc.*); **at ~** в состоя́нии войны́; **~ cry** боево́й клич; **~ dance** вои́нственный та́нец (-нца); **~ memorial** па́мятник па́вшим в войне́; *v.i.* воева́ть (вою́ю, -ю́ешь) *impf.*
warble [ˈwɔːb(ə)l] *n.* трель; *v.i.* издава́ть (-даю́, -даёшь) *impf.*, изда́ть (-а́м, -а́шь, -а́ст, -ади́м; изда́л, -а́, -о) *pf.* тре́ли.
ward[1] [wɔːd] *n.* (*hospital*) пала́та; (*child etc.*) подопе́чный *sb.*; (*district*) администрати́вный райо́н го́рода; избира́тельный о́круг (*pl.* -а́).
ward[2] [wɔːd] *v.t.*: **~ off** отража́ть *impf.*, отрази́ть *pf.*
warden [ˈwɔːd(ə)n] *n.* (*prison*) нача́льник; (*college*) ре́ктор.
warder [ˈwɔːdə(r)] *n.* тюре́мщик.
wardrobe [ˈwɔːdrəʊb] *n.* гардеро́б.
warehouse [ˈweəhaʊs] *n.* склад, пакга́уз. **wares** [weəz] *n.* изде́лия *nt.pl.*, това́ры *m.pl.*
warfare [ˈwɔːfeə(r)] *n.* война́. **war-game** *n.* вое́нная игра́. **warhead** *n.* боева́я голо́вка. **warhorse** *n.* боево́й конь (-ня́; *pl.* -ни, -не́й) *m.*
warily [ˈweərɪlɪ] *adv.* осторо́жно. **wariness** *n.* осторо́жность.
warlike [ˈwɔːlaɪk] *adj.* вои́нственный (-ен, -енна).
warm [wɔːm] *n.* тепло́; *adj.* (*also fig.*) тёплый (тёпел, -пла́, -пло́, -плы); *v.t. & i.* гре́ть(ся) *impf.*; согрева́ть(ся) *impf.*, согре́ть(ся) *pf.*;

~ **up** (*food etc.*) подогрева́ть(ся) *impf.*, подогре́ть(ся) *pf.*; (*liven up*) оживля́ть(ся) *impf.*, оживи́ть(ся) *pf.*; (*sport*) размина́ться *impf.*, размя́ться (разомну́сь, -нёшься) *pf.*; (*mus.*) разы́грываться *impf.*, разыгра́ться *pf.* **warmth** *n.* тепло́; (*cordiality*) серде́чность.

warmonger ['wɔːmʌŋgə(r)] *n.* поджига́тель *m.* войны́.

warn [wɔːn] *v.t.* предупрежда́ть *impf.*, предупреди́ть *pf.* (**about** о+*p.*). **warning** *n.* предупрежде́ние.

warp [wɔːp] *n.* (*of cloth*) осно́ва; (*of wood*) коро́бление *v.t.* & *i.* (*wood*) коро́бить(ся) *impf.*, по~, с~ *pf.*; *v.t.* (*pervert, distort*) извраща́ть *impf.*, изврати́ть (-ащу́, -ати́шь) *pf.*

warpaint ['wɔːpeɪnt] *n.* раскра́ска те́ла пе́ред похо́дом. **warpath** *n.* (*fig.*): **be on the** ~ быть в во́инственном настрое́нии.

warrant ['wɒrənt] *n.* (*for arrest etc.*) о́рдер (*pl.* -а́); (*justification*) оправда́ние; (*proof*) доказа́тельство; *v.t.* (*justify*) опра́вдывать *impf.*, оправда́ть *pf.*; (*guarantee*) гаранти́ровать *impf.* & *pf.*; руча́ться *impf.*, поручи́ться (-чу́сь, -чишься) *pf.* за+*a.* **warranty** *n.* (*basis*) основа́ние; (*guarantee*) гара́нтия.

warren ['wɒrən] *n.* кро́личий садо́к (-дка́).

warrior ['wɒrɪə(r)] *n.* во́ин, бое́ц (бойца́).

Warsaw ['wɔːsɔː] *n.* Варша́ва.

warship ['wɔːʃɪp] *n.* вое́нный кора́бль (-ля́) *m.*

wart [wɔːt] *n.* борода́вка. **wart-hog** *n.* борода́вочник.

wartime ['wɔːtaɪm] *n.*: **in** ~ во вре́мя войны́.

warty ['wɔːtɪ] *adj.* борода́вчатый.

wary ['weərɪ] *adj.* осторо́жный.

wash [wɒʃ] *n.* мытьё; (*thin layer*) то́нкий слой (*pl.* -о́и); (*lotion*) примо́чка; (*surf*) прибо́й; (*backwash*) попу́тная струя́ (*pl.* -у́и); **at the** ~ в сти́рке; **have a** ~ мы́ться (мо́юсь, мо́ешься) *impf.*, по~ *pf.*; *v.t.* & *i.* мы́ть(ся) (мо́ю(сь), мо́ешь(ся)) *impf.*, вы́~ *pf.*; *v.t.* (*clothes*) стира́ть *impf.*, вы́~ *pf.*; (*of sea*) омыва́ть *impf.*; *v.i.* (*clothes*) стира́ться *impf.*; ~ **ashore: the body was ~ed ashore** труп приби́ло к бе́регу (*impers.*); ~ **away, off, out** смыва́ть(ся) *impf.*, смы́ть(ся) (смо́ю, -о́ешь, -о́ет(ся)) *pf.*; (*carry away*) сноси́ть (-ошу́, -о́сишь) *impf.*, снести́ (-есу́, -есёшь; -ёс, -есла́) *pf.*; ~ **out** (*rinse*) спола́скивать *impf.*, сполосну́ть *pf.*; ~ **up** (*dishes*) мыть (мо́ю, мо́ешь) *impf.*, вы́~, по~ *pf.* (посу́ду); ~ **one's hands (of it)** умыва́ть *impf.*, умы́ть (умо́ю, -о́ешь) *pf.* ру́ки. **wash-basin** *n.* умыва́льник. **washed-out** *adj.* (*exhausted*) утомлённый. **washer** *n.* (*tech.*) ша́йба. **washerwoman** *n.* пра́чка. **washing** *n.* (*of clothes*) сти́рка; (*clothes*) бельё. **washing-machine** *n.* стира́льная маши́на. **washing-powder** *n.* стира́льный порошо́к (-шка́).

Washington ['wɒʃɪŋt(ə)n] *n.* Вашингто́н.

washing-up [ˌwɒʃɪŋ-'ʌp] *n.* (*action*) мытьё посу́ды; (*dishes*) гря́зная посу́да. **wash-house** *n.* пра́чечная. **wash-out** *n.* (*fiasco*) прова́л. **washroom** *n.* умыва́льная *sb.* **washtub** *n.* лоха́нь для сти́рки.

wasp [wɒsp] *n.* оса́ (*pl.* о́сы); **~'s nest** оси́ное гнездо́ (*pl.* -ёзда). **waspish** *adj.* (*irritable*) раздражи́тельный; (*caustic*) язви́тельный.

wastage ['weɪstɪdʒ] *n.* уте́чка. **waste** *n.* (*desert*) пусты́ня; (*wastage*) уте́чка; (*refuse*) отбро́сы *m.pl.*; (*of time, money etc.*) (бесполе́зная) тра́та; **go to** ~ пропада́ть *impf.*, пропа́сть (-аду́, -адёшь; -а́л) *pf.* да́ром; ~ **pipe** сто́чная труба́ (*pl.* -бы); *adj.* (*desert*) пусты́нный (-нен, -нна); (*superfluous*) нену́жный; (*uncultivated*) невозде́ланный; **lay** ~ опустоша́ть *impf.*, опустоши́ть *pf.*; ~ **paper** нену́жные бума́ги *f.pl.*; (*for recycling*) макулату́ра; ~ **products** отхо́ды (-дов) *pl.*; *v.t.* тра́тить *impf.*, по~, ис~ *pf.*; (*time*) теря́ть *impf.*, по~ *pf.*; *v.t.* & *i.* (*weaken*) истоща́ть(ся) *impf.*, истощи́ть(ся) *pf.*; *v.i.*; ~ **away** ча́хнуть (-х) *impf.*, за~ *pf.* **wasteful** *adj.* расточи́тельный. **wasteland** *n.* пусты́рь (-ря́) *m.* **waste-paper:** ~ **basket** корзи́на для (нену́жных) бума́г. **wastrel** *n.* (*idler*) безде́льник.

watch [wɒtʃ] *n.* (*timepiece*) часы́ (-со́в) *pl.*; (*duty*) дежу́рство; (*naut.*) ва́хта; **keep** ~ **over** наблюда́ть *impf.* за+*i.*; *v.t.* наблюда́ть *impf.*; следи́ть *impf.* за+*i.*; (*guard*, ~ **over**) охраня́ть *impf.*, охрани́ть *pf.*; (*look after*) смотре́ть (-рю́, -ришь) *impf.*, по~ *pf.* за+*i.*; ~ **television, a film** смотре́ть (-рю́, -ришь) *impf.*, по~ *pf.* телеви́зор, фильм; ~ **out!** осторо́жно! **watch-chain** цепо́чка для часо́в. **watchdog** сторожево́й пёс (пса). **watchful** *adj.* бди́тельный. **watchmaker** часовщи́к (-а́). **watchman** *n.* (ночно́й) сто́рож (*pl.* -а́, -е́й). **watch-spring** часова́я пружи́на. **watch-tower** сторожева́я ба́шня (*g.pl.* -шен). **watchword** *n.* ло́зунг.

water ['wɔːtə(r)] *n.* вода́ (*a.* -ду; *pl.* -ды, -д, во́да́м); *attr.* водяно́й, во́дный; ~ **bird** водяна́я пти́ца; ~ **bottle** графи́н для воды́; ~ **bus** речно́й трамва́й; ~ **jump** во́дное препя́тствие; ~ **lily** водяна́я ли́лия; ~ **main** водопрово́дная магистра́ль; ~ **melon** арбу́з; ~ **polo** во́дное по́ло *nt.indecl.*; *v.t.* (*flowers etc.*) полива́ть *impf.*, поли́ть (-лью́, -льёшь; по́ли́л, -а́, -о) *pf.*; (*animals*) пои́ть (пою́, пои́шь) *impf.*, на~ *pf.*; (*irrigate*) ороша́ть *impf.*, ороси́ть *pf.*; *v.i.* (*eyes*) слези́ться *impf.*; (*mouth*): **my mouth ~s** у меня́ слю́нки теку́т; ~ **down** разбавля́ть *impf.*, разба́вить *pf.* **water-butt** *n.* бо́чка для дождево́й воды́. **water-closet** убо́рная *sb.* **water-colour** *n.* акваре́ль. **watercourse** *n.* (*brook*) руче́й (-чья́); (*bed*) ру́сло (*g.pl.* -л); (*channel*) кана́л. **watercress** *n.* кресс водяно́й. **waterfall** *n.* водопа́д. **waterfront** *n.* часть (*pl.* -ти, -те́й) го́рода примыка́ющая к бе́регу. **water-heater** *n.* кипяти́льник. **water-hole** *n.* (*in desert*) ключ (-а́). **watering-can** *n.* ле́йка. **water-level** *n.* у́ровень (-ня) *m.* воды́. **water-**

line *n.* ватерли́ния. **waterlogged** *adj.* заболо́ченный (-ен); пропи́танный (-ан) водо́й. **watermark** *n.* (*in paper*) водяно́й знак. **water-mill** *n.* водяна́я ме́льница. **water-pipe** *n.* водопрово́дная труба́ (*pl.* -бы). **water-power** *n.* гидроэне́ргия. **waterproof** *adj.* непромока́емый; *n.* непромока́емый плащ (-а́). **water-rat** *n.* водяна́я кры́са. **watershed** *n.* водоразде́л. **waterside** *n.* бе́рег (*loc.* -у́; *pl.* -а́). **water-ski** (*n.*) во́дная лы́жа. **water-supply** *n.* водоснабже́ние. **watertight** *adj.* водонепроница́емый; (*hermetic*) гермети́ческий. **water-tower** *n.* водона́порная ба́шня (*g.pl.* -шен). **waterway** *n.* во́дный путь (-ти́, -тём) *m.* **water-weed** *n.* во́доросль. **water-wheel** *n.* водяно́е колесо́ (-ёса). **waterworks** *n.* водопрово́дные сооруже́ния *nt.pl.* **watery** *adj.* водяни́стый; (*pale*) бле́дный (-ден, -дна́, -дно, бле́дны́).

watt [wɒt] *n.* ватт.

wattle ['wɒt(ə)l] *n.* (*fencing*) плете́нь (-тня́) *m.*; *attr.* плетёный.

wave [weɪv] *v.t.* (*hand etc.*) маха́ть (машу́, -шешь) *impf.*, махну́ть *pf.+i.*; (*hair*) завива́ть *impf.*, зави́ть (-вью́, -вьёшь; зави́л, -а́, -о) *pf.*; *v.i.* (*flutter*) развева́ться *impf.*; (*rock, swing*) кача́ться *impf.*, качну́ться *pf.*; ~ **aside** (*spurn*) отверга́ть *impf.*, отве́ргнуть (-г) *pf.*; ~ **down** дава́ть (даю́, даёшь) *impf.*, дать (дам, дашь, даст, дади́м; дал, -а́, да́ло́, -ли)) *pf.* знак остано́вки+*d.*; *n.* (*in var. senses*) волна́ (*pl.* -ны, -н, во́лна́м); (*of hand*) взмах; (*in hair*) зави́вка. **wavelength** *n.* длина́ волны́. **waver** *v.i.* (*also fig.*) колеба́ться (-блюсь, -блешься) *impf.*; (*flicker, flutter*) колыха́ться (-ы́шется)*impf.*, колыхну́ться *pf.* **wavy** *adj.* волни́стый.

wax [wæks] *n.* воск; (*in ear*) се́ра; *attr.* восково́й; *v.t.* вощи́ть *impf.*, на~ *pf.* **waxen, waxy** *adj.* восково́й; (*like wax*) похо́жий на воск. **waxwork** *n.* восковая фигу́ра; *pl.* галере́я восковы́х фигу́р.

way [weɪ] *n.* (*road, path, route*; *fig.*) доро́га, путь (-ти́, -тём) *m.*; (*manner*) о́браз; (*method*) спо́соб; (*condition*) состоя́ние; (*respect*) отноше́ние; (*habit*) привы́чка; **by the** ~ (*fig.*) кста́ти, ме́жду про́чим; **on the** ~ по доро́ге, по пути́; **this** ~ (*direction*) сюда́; (*in this* ~) таки́м о́бразом; **the other** ~ **round** наоборо́т; **under** ~ на ходу́; **be in the** ~ меша́ть *impf.*; **get out of the** ~ уходи́ть (-ожу́, -о́дишь) *impf.*, уйти́ (уйду́, -дёшь; ушёл, ушла́) *pf.* с доро́ги; **give** ~ (*yield*) поддава́ться (поддаю́сь, -аёшься) *impf.*, подда́ться (-а́мся, -а́шься, -а́стся, -ади́мся; подда́лся, -ла́сь) *pf.* (**to** +*d.*); (*collapse*) обру́шиваться *impf.*, обру́шиться *pf.*; **go out of one's** ~ **to** стара́ться *impf.*, по~ *pf.* изо всех сил+*inf.*; **have it one's own** ~ де́йствовать *impf.* по-сво́ему; **make** ~ уступа́ть *impf.*, уступи́ть (-плю́, -пишь) *pf.* доро́гу (**for** +*d.*). **wayfarer** *n.* пу́тник. **way'lay** *v.t.* (*lie in wait for*) подстерега́ть *impf.*, подстере́чь (-егу́, -ежёшь; подстерёг, -ла́) *pf.*; (*stop*) перехва́тывать *impf.*, перехвати́ть (-ачу́, -а́тишь) *pf.* по пути́. **wayside** *n.* обо́чина; *adj.* придоро́жный.

wayward ['weɪwəd] *adj.* своенра́вый, капри́зный. **waywardness** *n.* своенра́вие, капри́зность.

WC *abbr.* (*of* **water-closet**) убо́рная *sb.*

we [wi:, wɪ] *pron.* мы (нас, нам, на́ми, нас).

weak [wi:k] *adj.* (*in var. senses*) сла́бый (слаб, -а́, -о); (*indecisive*) нереши́тельный; (*unconvincing*) неубеди́тельный. **weaken** *v.t.* ослабля́ть *impf.*, осла́бить *pf.*; *v.i.* слабе́ть *impf.*, о~ *pf.* **weakling** *n.* сла́бый челове́к (*pl.* лю́ди, -де́й, -дям, -дьми́). **weakness** *n.* сла́бость; **have a** ~ **for** име́ть *impf.* сла́бость к+*d.*

weal [wi:l] *n.* (*mark*) рубе́ц (-бца́).

wealth [welθ] *n.* бога́тство; (*abundance*) изоби́лие. **wealthy** *adj.* бога́тый, состоя́тельный.

wean [wi:n] *v.t.* отнима́ть *impf.*, отня́ть (отниму́, -мешь) *pf.* от груди́; (*fig.*) отуча́ть *impf.*, отучи́ть (-чу́, -чишь) *pf.* (**of, from** от+*g.*).

weapon ['wepən] *n.* ору́жие. **weaponless** *adj.* безору́жный. **weaponry** *n.* вооруже́ние, ору́жие.

wear [weə(r)] *n.* (*wearing*) но́ска; (*clothing*) оде́жда; (~ *and tear*) изна́шивание; *v.t.* носи́ть (ношу́, но́сишь) *impf.*; быть в+*p.*; *v.i.* носи́ться (но́сится) *impf.*; ~ **off** (*cease to have effect*) перестава́ть (-таю́, -таёшь) *impf.*, переста́ть (-а́ну, -а́нешь) *pf.* де́йствовать; ~ **out** (*clothes*) изна́шивать(ся) *impf.*, износи́ть(ся) (-ошу́(сь), -о́сишь(ся)) *pf.*; (*exhaust, become exhausted*) истоща́ть(ся) *impf.*, истощи́ть(ся) *pf.*

weariness ['wɪərɪnɪs] *n.* (*tiredness*) уста́лость, утомле́ние; (*tedium*) утоми́тельность. **wearing** ['weərɪŋ], **wearisome** *adj.* утоми́тельный. **weary** *adj.* уста́лый, утомлённый (-ён, -ена́); *v.t.* & *i.* утомля́ть(ся) *impf.*, утоми́ть(ся) *pf.*

weasel ['wi:z(ə)l] *n.* ла́ска (*g.pl.* -сок).

weather ['weðə(r)] *n.* пого́да; ~ **forecast** прогно́з пого́ды; ~ **station** метеорологи́ческая ста́нция; *v.t.* (*storm etc.*) выде́рживать *impf.*, вы́держать (-жу, -жишь) *pf.*; (*expose to atmosphere*) подверга́ть *impf.*, подве́ргнуть (-г) *pf.* атмосфе́рным влия́ниям. **weather-beaten** *adj.* повреждённый (-ён, -ена́) бу́рями; (*of face*) обве́тренный (-ен); (*of person*) закалённый(-ён, -ена́). **weather-chart** *n.* синопти́ческая ка́рта. **weather-cock, weathervane** *n.* флю́гер (*pl.* -а́). **weatherman** *n.* метеоро́лог.

weave[1] [wi:v] *v.t.* & *i.* (*fabric*) ткать (тку, ткёшь; ткал, -а́, -о) *impf.*, со~ *pf.*; *v.t.* (*fig.*; *also wreath etc.*) плести́ (плету́, -тёшь; плёл, -а́) *impf.*, с~ *pf.*; *n.* узо́р тка́ни. **weaver** *n.* ткач, -и́ха. **weaving** *n.* (*the art of* ~) тка́чество; (*the* ~) тканьё.

weave² [wiːv] *v.i.* (*sway*) пока́чиваться *impf.*
web [web] *n.* (*cobweb*, *gossamer*; *fig.*) паути́на; (*membrane*) перепо́нка; (*tissue*) ткань; (*fig.*) сплете́ние. **webbed** *adj.* перепо́нчатый. **webbing** *n.* тка́ная ле́нта, тесьма́.
wed [wed] *v.t.* (*of man*) жени́ться (-ню́сь, -нишься) *impf.* & *pf.* на+*p.*; (*of woman*) выходи́ть (-ожу́, -о́дишь) *impf.*, вы́йти (вы́йду, -дешь; вы́шла) *pf.* за́муж за+*a.*; (*unite*) сочета́ть *impf.* & *pf.*; *v.i.* жени́ться (-ню́сь, -нишься) *pf.* (*coll.*); вступа́ть *impf.*, вступи́ть (-плю́, -пишь) *pf.* в брак. **wedded** *adj.* супру́жеский; ~ **to** (*fig.*) пре́данный (-ан) +*d.* **wedding** *n.* сва́дьба, бракосочета́ние; ~ **cake** сва́дебный торт; ~ **day** день (дня) *m.* сва́дьбы; ~ **dress** подвене́чное пла́тье (*g.pl.* -в); ~ **ring** обруча́льное кольцо́ (*pl.* -льца, -ле́ц, -льцам).
wedge [wedʒ] *n.* клин (*pl.* -ья, -ьев); *v.t.* (~ *open*) закли́нивать *impf.*, заклини́ть *pf.*; *v.t.* & *i.*: ~ **in(to)** вкли́нивать(ся) *impf.*, вкли́нить(ся) *pf.* (в+*a.*).
wedlock ['wedlɒk] *n.* брак, супру́жество; **born out of** ~ рождённый (-ён, -ена́) вне бра́ка, внебра́чный.
Wednesday ['wenzdeɪ, -dɪ] *n.* среда́ (*a.* -ду; *pl.* -ды, -д, -да́м).
weed [wiːd] *n.* сорня́к (-а́); *v.t.* поло́ть (полю́, -лешь) *impf.*, вы́~ *pf.*; ~ **out** удаля́ть *impf.*, удали́ть *pf.* **weed-killer** *n.* гербици́д. **weedy** *adj.* заро́сший сорняка́ми; (*person*) то́щий (тощ, -а́, -е).
week [wiːk] *n.* неде́ля. **weekday** *n.* бу́дний день (дня) *m.* **weekend** *n.* суббо́та и воскресе́нье, уик-э́нд. **weekly** *adj.* еженеде́льный; (*wage*) неде́льный; *adv.* раз в неде́лю; еженеде́льно; *n.* еженеде́льник.
weep [wiːp] *v.i.* пла́кать (пла́чу, -чешь) *impf.*; ~ **over** опла́кивать *impf.*, опла́кать *pf.* **weeping** *n.* плач; *adj.*: ~ **willow** плаку́чая и́ва. **weepy** *adj.* слезли́вый.
weevil ['wiːvɪl] *n.* долгоно́сик.
weft [weft] *n.* уто́к (утка́).
weigh [weɪ] *v.t.* (*also fig.*) взве́шивать *impf.*, взве́сить *pf.*; (*consider*) обду́мывать *impf.*, обду́мать *pf.*; *v.t.* & *i.* (*so much*) ве́сить *impf.*; ~ **down** отягоща́ть *impf.*, отяготи́ть (-ощу́, -оти́шь) *pf.*; ~ **on** тяготи́ть (-ощу́, -оти́шь) *impf.*; ~ **out** отве́шивать *impf.*, отве́сить *pf.*; ~ **up** (*appraise*) оце́нивать *impf.*, оцени́ть (-ню́, -нишь) *pf.* **weight** *n.* (*also authority*) вес (*pl.* -а́); (*load*, *also fig.*) тя́жесть; (*sport*) ги́ря, шта́нга; (*influence*) влия́ние; **lose** ~ худе́ть *impf.*, по~ *pf.*; **put on** ~ толсте́ть *impf.*, по~ *pf.*; прибавля́ть *impf.*, приба́вить *pf.* в ве́се; *v.t.* (*make heavier*) утяжеля́ть *impf.*, утяжели́ть *pf.* **weightless** *adj.* невесо́мый. **weightlessness** *n.* невесо́мость. **weightlifter** *n.* гиреви́к (-а́), штанги́ст. **weightlifting** *n.* подня́тие тя́жестей. **weighty** *adj.* (*also fig.*) ве́ский; (*heavy*) тяжёлый (-л, -ла́); (*important*) ва́жный (-жен, -жна́, -жно, -жны́).
weir [wɪə(r)] *n.* плоти́на, запру́да.
weird [wɪəd] *adj.* (*strange*) стра́нный (-нен, -нна́, -нно).
welcome ['welkəm] *n.* (*greeting*) приве́тствие; (*reception*) приём; *adj.* жела́нный (-ан); (*pleasant*) прия́тный; **you are** ~ (*don't mention it*) не сто́ит благода́рности, пожа́луйста; **you are** ~ **to use my bicycle** мой велосипе́д к ва́шим услу́гам; **you are** ~ **to stay the night** вы мо́жете переночева́ть у меня́/нас; *v.t.* приве́тствовать *impf.* (& *pf.* *in past tense*); *int.* добро́ пожа́ловать!
weld [weld] *n.* сварно́й шов (шва); *v.t.* & *i.* сва́ривать(ся) *impf.*, свари́ть(ся) *pf.*; (*fig.*) спла́чивать *impf.*, сплоти́ть *pf.* **welder** *n.* сва́рщик. **welding** *n.* сва́рка.
welfare ['welfeə(r)] *n.* благосостоя́ние, благополу́чие; **W~ State** госуда́рство всео́бщего благосостоя́ния; ~ **work** рабо́та по социа́льному обеспе́чению.
well¹ [wel] *n.* коло́дец (-дца); (*for stairs*) ле́стничная кле́тка.
well² [wel] *v.i.*: ~ **forth, up** бить (бьёт) *impf.* ключо́м; хлы́нуть *pf.*
well³ [wel] *adj.* (*healthy*) здоро́вый; **feel** ~ чу́вствовать *impf.*, по~ *pf.* себя́ хорошо́, здоро́вым; **get** ~ поправля́ться *impf.*, попра́виться *pf.*; **look** ~ хорошо́ вы́глядеть (-яжу, -ядишь) *impf.*; **all is** ~ всё в поря́дке; *int.* ну(!); *adv.* хорошо́; (*very much*) о́чень; **as** ~ то́же; **as** ~ **as** (*in addition to*) кро́ме+*g.*; **it may** ~ **be true** вполне́ возмо́жно, что э́то так; **very** ~! хорошо́!; ~ **done!** молоде́ц!; ~ **done** (*cooked*) (хорошо́) прожа́ренный (-ен). **well-advised** *adj.* благоразу́мный. **well-balanced** *adj.* уравнове́шенный (-ен, -енна). **well-behaved** *adj.* благонра́вный. **well-being** *n.* благополу́чие. **well-bred** *adj.* благовоспи́танный (-ан, -анна). **well-built** *adj.* кре́пкий (-пок, -пка́, -пко). **well-defined** *adj.* чёткий (-ток, -тка́, -тко). **well-disposed** *adj.* благоскло́нный (-нен, -нна), благожела́тельный. **well-fed** *adj.* отко́рмленный (-ен). **well-groomed** *adj.* (*person*) хо́леный. **well-grounded** *adj.* обосно́ванный (-ан, -анна); (*versed*) све́дущий (**in** в+*p.*). **well-informed** *adj.* (хорошо́) осведомлённый (-ён, -ена́) (**about** в+*p.*). **well-known** *adj.* изве́стный.
wellington (boot) ['welɪŋt(ə)n] *n.* рези́новый сапо́г (-а́; *g.pl.* -г).
well-mannered [ˌwel'mænəd] *adj.* воспи́танный (-ан). **well-meaning** *adj.* име́ющий хоро́шие наме́рения. **wellnigh** ['welnaɪ] *adv.* почти́. **well-paid** *adj.* хорошо́ опла́чиваемый. **well-preserved** *adj.* хорошо́ сохрани́вшийся. **well-proportioned** *adj.* пропорциона́льный. **well-read** *adj.* начи́танный (-ан, -анна). **well-spoken** *adj.* уме́ющий изы́сканно говори́ть. **well-timed** *adj.* своевре́менный (-нен, -нна). **well-wisher** *n.* доброжела́тель *m.* **well-worn** *adj.* (*fig.*) изби́тый.
welsh¹ [welʃ] *v.t.*: ~ **on** (*swindle*) надува́ть

impf., наду́ть (-у́ю, -у́ешь) *pf.* (*coll.*); (*fail to keep*) не сде́рживать *impf.*, сде́ржать (-жу́, -жишь) *pf.*+*g.*

Welsh² [welʃ] *adj.* валли́йский, уэ́льский. **Welshman** *n.* валли́ец. **Welshwoman** *n.* валли́йка.

welt [welt] *n.* (*of shoe*) рант (*loc.* -у́); (*weal*) рубе́ц (-бца́).

welter ['weltə(r)] *n.* (*confusion*) сумбу́р, пу́таница; *v.i.* валя́ться *impf.*

wench [wentʃ] *n.* де́вка.

wend [wend] *v.t.*: ~ **one's way** держа́ть (-жу́, -жишь) *impf.* путь.

wer(e)wolf ['wɪəwʊlf, 'weə-] *n.* о́боротень (-тня) *m.*

west [west] *n.* за́пад; (*naut.*) вест; *adj.* за́падный; *adv.* на за́пад, к за́паду. **westerly** *adj.* за́падный; *n.* за́падный ве́тер (-тра). **western** *adj.* за́падный; *n.* (*film*) ве́стерн. **westernize** *v.t.* европеизи́ровать *impf.* & *pf.* **westward(s)** *adv.* на за́пад, к за́паду.

wet [wet] *adj.* мо́крый (-р, -ра́, -ро); (*paint*) непросо́хший; (*rainy*) дождли́вый; **'W~ Paint'** «осторо́жно, окра́шено»; ~ **through** промо́кший до ни́тки; ~ **suit** водонепроница́емый костю́м; *n.* (*dampness*) вла́жность; (*rain*) дождь (-дя́) *m.*; *v.t.* мочи́ть (-чу́, -чишь) *impf.*, на~ *pf.* **wetness** *n.* вла́жность. **wet-nurse** *n.* корми́лица.

whack [wæk] *n.* (*blow*) си́льный уда́р; *v.t.* колоти́ть (-очу́, -о́тишь) *impf.*, по~ *pf.*

whale [weɪl] *n.* кит (-а́).

wharf [wɔːf] *n.* при́стань (*pl.* -ни, -не́й).

what [wɒt] *pron.* (*interrog.*, *int.*) что (чего́, чему́, чем, чём); (*how much*) ско́лько; (*rel.*) (то,) что (чего́, чему́, чем, чём); ~ **(...) for** заче́м; ~ **if** а что е́сли; ~ **is your name** как вас зову́т?; *adj.* (*interrog.*, *int.*) како́й; ~ **kind of** како́й. **whatever** *pron.* что бы ни+*past* (~ **you think** что бы вы ни ду́мали); всё, что (**take** ~ **you want** возьми́те всё, что хоти́те); *adj.* како́й бы ни+*past* (~ **books he read(s)** каки́е бы ни кни́ги он ни прочита́л); (*at all*): **there is no chance** ~ нет никако́й возмо́жности; **is there any chance** ~? есть ли хоть кака́я-нибу́дь возмо́жность?

wheat [wiːt] *n.* пшени́ца. **wheaten** *adj.* пшени́чный.

wheedle ['wiːd(ə)l] *v.t.* (*coax into doing*) угова́ривать *impf.*, уговори́ть *pf.* с по́мощью ле́сти; ~ **out of** выма́нивать *impf.*, вы́манить *pf.* у+*g.* **wheedling** *adj.* вкра́дчивый, льсти́вый.

wheel [wiːl] *n.* колесо́ (*pl.* -ёса); (*steering* ~, *helm*) руль (-ля́) *m.*, штурва́л; (*potter's*) гонча́рный круг; *v.t.* (*push*) ката́ть *indet.*, кати́ть (качу́, ка́тишь) *det.*, по~ *pf.*; *v.t.* & *i.* (*turn*) повёртывать(ся) *impf.*, поверну́ть(ся) *pf.*; *v.i.* (*circle*) кружи́ться (-ужу́сь, -у́жишься) *impf.* **wheelbarrow** *n.* та́чка. **wheelchair** *n.* инвали́дное кре́сло (*g.pl.* -сел) (на колёсах). **wheelwright** *n.* коле́сник.

wheeze [wiːz] *n.* сопе́ние, хрип; *v.i.* сопе́ть (-плю́, -пи́шь) *impf.*, хрипе́ть (-плю́, -пи́шь) *impf.* **wheezy** *adj.* хри́плый (-л, -ла́, -ло).

whelk [welk] *n.* (*mollusc*) брюхоно́гий моллю́ск.

when [wen] *adv.* когда́; *conj.* когда́, в то вре́мя как; (*whereas*) тогда́ как; (*although*) хотя́. **whence** *adv.* отку́да. **whenever** *adv.* когда́ же; *conj.* (*every time*) вся́кий раз когда́; (*at any time*) в любо́е вре́мя, когда́; (*no matter when*) когда́ бы ни+*past*; **we shall have dinner** ~ **you arrive** во ско́лько бы вы ни прие́хали, мы пообе́даем.

where [weə(r)] *adv.* & *conj.* (*place*) где; (*whither*) куда́; **from** ~ отку́да. **whereabouts** [ˌweərə'baʊts; 'weərəˌbaʊts] *adv.* где; *n.* местонахожде́ние. **where'as** *conj.* тогда́ как; хотя́; (*official*) поско́льку. **where'by** *adv.* & *conj.* посре́дством чего́. **wher'ever** *adv.* & *conj.* (*place*) где бы ни+*past*; (*whither*) куда́ бы ни+*past*; ~ **he goes** куда́ бы он ни пошёл. **wherewithal** ['weəwɪˌðɔːl] *n.* сре́дства *nt.pl.*

whet [wet] *v.t.* точи́ть (-чу́, -чишь) *impf.*, на~ *pf.*; (*stimulate*) возбужда́ть *impf.*, возбуди́ть *pf.* **whetstone** *n.* точи́льный ка́мень (-мня; *pl.* -мни, -мне́й) *m.*

whether ['weðə(r)] *conj.* ли; **I don't know** ~ **he will come** я не зна́ю, придёт ли он; ~ **he comes or not** придёт (ли) он и́ли нет.

whey [weɪ] *n.* сы́воротка.

which [wɪtʃ] *adj.* (*interrog.*, *rel.*) како́й; *pron.* (*interrog.*) како́й; (*person*) кто; (*rel.*) кото́рый; (*rel. to whole statement*) что; ~ **is** ~? (*persons*) кто из них кто?; (*things*) что-что? **which'ever** *adj.* & *pron.* како́й бы ни+*past* (~ **book you choose** каку́ю бы кни́гу ты ни вы́брал); любо́й (**take** ~ **book you want** возьми́те любу́ю кни́гу).

whiff [wɪf] *n.* (*wind*) дунове́ние; (*smoke*) дымо́к (-мка́); (*odour*) за́пах.

while [waɪl] *n.* вре́мя *nt.*; промежу́ток (-тка) вре́мени; **a little** ~ недо́лго; **a long** ~ до́лго; **for a long** ~ (*up to now*) давно́; **for a** ~ на вре́мя; **in a little** ~ ско́ро; **once in a** ~ вре́мя от вре́мени; **it is worth** ~ сто́ит э́то сде́лать; *v.t.*: ~ **away** проводи́ть (-ожу́, -о́дишь) *impf.*, провести́ (-еду́, -едёшь; -ёл, -ела́) *pf.*; *conj.* пока́; в то вре́мя как; (*although*) хотя; несмотря́ на то, что; (*contrast*) а; **we went to the cinema** ~ **they went to the theatre** мы ходи́ли в кино́, а они́ в теа́тр. **whilst** *see* **while**

whim [wɪm] *n.* при́хоть, причу́да, капри́з.

whimper ['wɪmpə(r)] *n.* хны́канье; *v.i.* хны́кать (хны́чу, -чешь & хны́каю, -аешь) *impf.*

whimsical ['wɪmzɪk(ə)l] *adj.* капри́зный; (*odd*) причу́дливый. **whimsy** *n.* капри́з, при́хоть, причу́да.

whine [waɪn] *n.* (*wail*) вой; (*whimper*) хны́канье; *v.i.* скули́ть *impf.*; (*wail*) выть (во́ю, во́ешь); (*whimper*) хны́кать *impf.*

whinny ['wɪnɪ] *n.* ти́хое ржа́ние; *v.i.* ти́хо

ржать (ржу, ржёшь) *impf.*

whip [wɪp] *n.* кнут (-á), хлыст (-á); ~ **hand** контрóль (-ля) *m.*; *v.t.* (*lash*) хлестáть (-ещý, -éщешь) *impf.*, хлестнýть *pf.*; (*urge on*) подгонять *impf.*, подогнáть (подгоню́, -нишь; подогнáл, -á, -о) *pf.*; (*cream*) сбивáть *impf.*, сбить (собью́, -ьёшь) *pf.*; ~ **off** скидывать *impf.*, скинуть *pf.*; ~ **out** выхвáтывать *impf.*, вы́хватить *pf.*; ~ **round** бы́стро повёртываться *impf.*, повернýться *pf.*; ~ **up** (*stir up*) разжигáть *impf.*, разжéчь (разожгý, -ожжёшь; разжёг, разожглá) *pf.* **whipper-snapper** *n.* ничтóжество. **whipping** *n.* побóи (-óев) *pl.* **whip-round** *n.* сбор дéнег.

whirl [wɜːl] *n.* кружéние; (*of dust etc.*) вихрь (-ря) *m.*; (*turmoil*) суматóха, смятéние; *v.t. & i.* кружи́ть(ся) (кружý(сь), крýжишь(ся)) *impf.*, за~ *pf.* **whirlpool** *n.* водоворóт. **whirlwind** *n.* вихрь (-ря) *m.*

whirr [wɜː(r)] *n.* жужжáние; *v.i.* жужжáть (жужжý, -жи́шь) *impf.*

whisk [wɪsk] *n.* (*of twigs etc.*) вéничек (-чка); (*utensil*) мутóвка; (*movement*) помáхивание; *v.t.* (*cream etc.*) сбивáть *impf.*, сбить (собью́, -ьёшь) *pf.*; (*wag, wave*) махáть (машý, -шешь) *impf.*, махнýть *pf.+i.*; ~ **away, off** (*brush off*) смáхивать *impf.*, смахнýть *pf.*; (*take away*) бы́стро уноси́ть (-ошý, -óсишь) *impf.*, унести́ (-есý, -есёшь; -ёс, -еслá) *pf.*; *v.i.* (*scamper away*) юркнýть *pf.*

whisker [ˈwɪskə(r)] *n.* (*human*) вóлос (*pl.* -осы, -óс, -осáм) на лицé; (*animal*) ус (*pl.* -ы́); *pl.* (*human*) бакенбáрды *f.pl.*

whisky [ˈwɪskɪ] *n.* ви́ски *nt.indecl.*

whisper [ˈwɪspə(r)] *n.* шёпот; (*rustle*) шéлест; *v.t. & i.* шептáть (шепчý, -чешь) *impf.*, шепнýть *pf.*; (*rustle*) шелестéть (-ти́шь) *impf.*

whist [wɪst] *n.* вист.

whistle [ˈwɪs(ə)l] *n.* (*sound*) свист; (*instrument*) свистóк (-ткá); *v.i.* свистéть (-ищý, -исти́шь) *impf.*, сви́стнуть *pf.* (*also to dog etc.*); *v.t.* насви́стывать *impf.* **whistler** *n.* свистýн (-á) (*coll.*).

whit [wɪt] *n.*: **not a** ~ ничýть, нискóлько.

white [waɪt] *adj.* бéлый (бел, -á, бéлó); (*hair*) седóй (сед, -á, -о); (*pale*) блéдный (-ден, -днá, -дно, блéдны́); (*transparent*) прозрáчный; (*with milk*) с молокóм; **paint** ~ крáсить *impf.*, по~ *pf.* в бéлый свет; **W~ House** Бéлый дом; ~ **lie** неви́нная ложь (лжи, *i.* лóжью); **W~ Russian** (*n.*) белорýс, ~ка; (*adj.*) белорýсский; *n.* (*colour*) бéлый цвет; (*egg, eye*) белóк (-лкá); (~ *man*) бéлый *sb.* **white-collar** *adj.* контóрский; ~ **worker** слýжащий *sb.* **white-hot** *adj.* раскалённый добелá. **whiten** *v.t.* бели́ть (белю́, бéлишь) *impf.*, на~, по~, вы́~ *pf.*; (*blanch, bleach*) отбéливать *impf.*, отбели́ть *pf.*; *v.i.* белéть *impf.*, по~ *pf.* **whiteness** *n.* белизнá. **whitewash** *n.* раствóр для побéлки; *v.t.* бели́ть (белю́, бéлишь) *impf.*, по~ *pf.*; (*fig.*) обелять *impf.*, обели́ть *pf.*

whither [ˈwɪðə(r)] *adv. & conj.* кудá.

Whitsun [ˈwɪts(ə)n] *n.* недéля пóсле Трóицы.

whittle [ˈwɪt(ə)l] *v.t.* строгáть *impf.*, вы́~ *pf.* ножóм; ~ **down** (*decrease*) уменьшáть *impf.*, умéньши́ть *pf.*

whiz(z) [wɪz] *n.* свист; *v.i.* свистéть (-ищý, -исти́шь) *impf.*

who [huː] *pron.* (*interrog.*) кто (когó, комý, кем, ком); (*rel.*) котóрый.

whoa [wəʊ] *int.* тпру!

whoever [huːˈevə(r)] *pron.* кто бы ни+*past*; (*he who*) тот, кто.

whole [həʊl] *adj.* (*entire*) весь (вся, всё; все), цéлый; (*intact, of number*) цéлый; *n.* (*thing complete*) цéлое *sb.*; (*all there is*) весь (вся, всё; все) *sb.*; (*sum*) сýмма; **as a** ~ в цéлом; **on the** ~ в óбщем. **wholefood** *n.* натурáльные продýкты *m.pl.*; *adj.* натурáльный. **whole-hearted** *adj.*: ~ **support** горячая поддéржка. **whole-heartedly** *adv.* от всей душѝ, от всегó сéрдца. **wholemeal** *n.* непросéянная мукá. **wholesale** *adj.* оптóвый; (*fig.*) мáссовый; *n.* оптóвая торгóвля; *adv.* óптом. **wholesaler** *n.* оптóвый торгóвец (-вца). **wholesome** *adj.* здорóвый, благотвóрный. **wholly** *adv.* пóлностью, целикóм.

whom [huːm] *pron.* (*interrog.*) когó *etc.* (*see* **who**); (*rel.*) котóрого *etc.*

whoop [huːp, wuːp] *n.* крик, ги́канье (*coll.*); *v.i.* кричáть (-чý, -чи́шь) *impf.*, кри́кнуть *pf.*; ги́кать *impf.*, ги́кнуть *pf.* (*coll.*); ~**ing cough** коклю́ш.

whore [hɔː(r)] *n.* проститýтка.

whorl [wɔːl, wɜːl] *n.* (*bot.*) мутóвка; (*on shell*) завитóк (-ткá); (*of spiral*) витóк (-ткá).

whose [huːz] *pron.* (*interrog., rel.*) чей (чья, чьё; чьи); (*rel.*) котóрого.

why [waɪ] *adv.* почемý; *n.* причи́на; *int.* (*surprise*) да ведь!; (*impatience*) ну!

wick [wɪk] *n.* (*of lamp etc.*) фити́ль (-ля́) *m.*

wicked [ˈwɪkɪd] *adj.* злой (зол, зла); (*immoral*) безнрáвственный (-нен, -нна). **wickedness** *n.* злóбность.

wicker [ˈwɪkə(r)] *n.* прýтья *m.pl.* для плетéния; *attr.* плетёный.

wicket [ˈwɪkɪt] *n.* кали́тка; (*cricket*) ворóтца.

wide [waɪd] *adj.* ширóкий (-к, -кá, ширóкó); (*extensive*) обши́рный; (*in measurements*) в+*a.* ширинóй; ~ **awake** бóдрствующий; (*wary*) бди́тельный; ~ **open** широкó откры́тый; (*defenceless*) незащищённый; *adv.* (*off target*) ми́мо цéли. **widely** *adv.* широкó. **widen** *v.t. & i.* расширять(ся) *impf.*, расши́рить(ся) *pf.* **widespread** *adj.* широкó распространённый (-ён, -енá).

widow [ˈwɪdəʊ] *n.* вдовá (*pl.* -вы). **widowed** *adj.* овдовéвший. **widower** *n.* вдовéц (-вцá). **widowhood** *n.* вдовствó.

width [wɪtθ, wɪdθ] *n.* ширинá; (*fig.*) ширинá; (*of cloth*) полóтнище.

wield [wiːld] *v.t.* держáть (-жý, -жишь) *impf.* в рукáх; владéть+*i.*

wife [waɪf] *n.* женá (*pl.* жёны).

wig [wɪg] *n.* пари́к (-á).

wiggle ['wɪg(ə)l] *v.t. & i.* (*move*) шевели́ть(ся) *impf.*, по~, шевельну́ть(ся) *pf.*
wigwam ['wɪgwæm] *n.* вигва́м.
wild [waɪld] *adj.* ди́кий (дик, -á, -о); (*flower*) полево́й; (*uncultivated*) невозде́ланный; (*tempestuous*) бу́йный (бу́ен, буйна́, -но); (*furious*) неи́стовый; (*ill-considered*) необду́манный (-ан, -анна); **be ~ about** быть без ума́ от+*g.*; *n.*: *pl.* пусты́ня, де́бри (-рей) *pl.* **wildcat** *adj.* (*reckless*) риско́ванный; (*unofficial*) неофициа́льный. **wilderness** ['wɪldənɪs] *n.* ди́кая ме́стность; (*desert*) пусты́ня. **wildfire** *n.*: **spread like ~** распространя́ться *impf.*, распространи́ться *pf.* со сверхъесте́ственный быстрото́й. **wild-goose: ~ chase** сумасбро́дная зате́я. **wildlife** *n.* жива́я приро́да. **wildness** *n.* ди́кость.
wile [waɪl] *n.* хи́трость, уло́вка.
wilful ['wɪlfʊl] *adj.* (*obstinate*) упря́мый; (*deliberate*) преднаме́ренный (-ен, -енна), умы́шленный (-ен, -енна). **wilfulness** *n.* упря́мство; преднаме́ренность.
will [wɪl] *n.* во́ля; (*~-power*) си́ла во́ли; (*desire*) во́ля, жела́ние; (*at death*) завеща́ние; **against one's ~** про́тив во́ли; **at ~** по жела́нию; **of one's own free ~** доброво́льно; **with a ~** с энтузиа́змом; **good ~** до́брая во́ля; **make one's ~** писа́ть (пишу́, -шешь) *impf.*, на~ *pf.* завеща́ние; *v.t.* (*want, desire*) хоте́ть (хочу́, -чешь, хоти́м) *impf.*, за~ *pf.+g.*, *a.*; жела́ть *impf.*, по~ *pf.+g.*; (*order*) веле́ть (-лю́, -ли́шь) *impf.* & *pf.*; (*compel by one's ~*) заставля́ть *impf.*, заста́вить *pf.*; (*bequeath*) завеща́ть *impf.* & *pf.* **willing** *adj.* гото́вый, согла́сный; (*assiduous*) стара́тельный. **willingly** *adv.* охо́тно. **willingness** *n.* гото́вность.
will-o'-the-wisp [ˌwɪləðə'wɪsp] *n.* блужда́ющий огонёк (-нька́).
willow ['wɪləʊ] *n.* и́ва.
willy-nilly [ˌwɪlɪ'nɪlɪ] *adv.* во́лей-нево́лей.
wilt [wɪlt] *v.i.* вя́нуть (вял) *impf.*, за~ *pf.*; поника́ть *impf.*, пони́кнуть *pf.*; (*weaken*) слабе́ть *impf.*, о~ *pf.*
wily ['waɪlɪ] *adj.* хи́трый (-тёр, -тра́, хи́тро́), кова́рный.
wimp [wɪmp] *n.* хлю́пик, сопля́к (-ка́). **wimpish** *adj.* бесхара́ктерный.
win [wɪn] *n.* вы́игрыш, побе́да; *v.t. & i.* выи́грывать *impf.*, вы́играть *pf.*; *v.t.* (*obtain*) добива́ться *impf.*, доби́ться (-бью́сь, -бьёшься) *pf.+g.*; **~ over** (*convince*) убежда́ть *impf.*, убеди́ть (-ди́шь) *pf.*; (*gain favour of*) располага́ть *impf.*, расположи́ть (-жу́, -жишь) *pf.* к себе; **~ through** (*overcome*) преодолева́ть *impf.*, преодоле́ть *pf.*
wince [wɪns] *n.* содрога́ние, вздра́гивание; *v.i.* вздра́гивать *impf.*, вздро́гнуть *pf.*
winch [wɪntʃ] *n.* (*windlass*) лебёдка.
wind¹ [wɪnd] *n.* (*air*) ве́тер (-тра); (*breath*) дыха́ние; (*flatulence*) ве́тры *m.pl.*; **~ instrument** духово́й инструме́нт; **get ~ of** проню́хивать *impf.*, проню́хать *pf.*; *v.t.* (*make gasp*) заставля́ть *impf.*, заста́вить *pf.* задохну́ться.
wind² [waɪnd] *v.i.* (*meander*) ви́ться (вью́сь, вьёшься; ви́лся, -ла́сь) *impf.*; извива́ться *impf.*; *v.t. & i.* (*coil*) нама́тывать(ся) *impf.*, намота́ть(ся) *pf.*; *v.t.* (*watch*) заводи́ть (-ожу́, -о́дишь) *impf.*, завести́ (-еду́, -едёшь; -ёл, -ела́) *pf.*; (*wrap*) уку́тывать *impf.*, уку́тать *pf.*; **~ down** (*v.t. & i.*) разма́тывать(ся) *impf.*, размота́ть(ся) *pf.*; **~ up** (*v.t.*) (*reel*) сма́тывать *impf.*, смота́ть *pf.*; (*watch*) *see* **wind²**; (*v.t. & i.*) (*end*) конча́ть(ся) *impf.*, ко́нчить(ся) *pf.* **winding** *adj.* (*twisted*) вито́й, спира́льный; (*meandering*) изви́листый.
windfall ['wɪndfɔːl] *n.* плод (-á), сби́тый ве́тром; (*fig.*) неожи́данное сча́стье. **windmill** *n.* ветряна́я ме́льница.
window ['wɪndəʊ] *n.* окно́ (*pl.* о́кна, о́кон, о́кнам); (*of shop*) витри́на. **window-box** *n.* нару́жный я́щик для расте́ний. **window-dressing** *n.* украше́ние витри́н. **window-frame** *n.* око́нная ра́ма. **window-ledge** *n.* подоко́нник. **window-pane** *n.* око́нное стекло́ (*pl.* стёкла, -кол, -клам). **window-shopping** *n.* рассма́тривание витри́н. **window-sill** *n.* подоко́нник.
windpipe ['wɪndpaɪp] *n.* дыха́тельное го́рло, трахе́я. **windscreen** *n.* пере́днее/ветрово́е стекло́ (*pl.* стёкла, -кол, -клам); **~ wiper** стеклоочисти́тель *m.*, дво́рник (*coll.*). **windsurfer** *n.* виндсёрфинги́ст. **windsurfing** *n.* виндсёрфинг. **wind-swept** *adj.* откры́тый ветра́м. **windward** *n.* наве́тренная сторона́ (*a.* -ону); *adj.* наве́тренный. **windy** *adj.* ве́треный; (*verbose*) многосло́вный.
wine [waɪn] *n.* вино́ (*pl.* -на); **~ bottle** ви́нная буты́лка; **~ cellar** ви́нный по́греб (*pl.* -á); **~ list** ка́рта вин; **~ merchant** торго́вец (-вца) вино́м; *v.i.* пить (пью, пьёшь; пил, -á, -о) *impf.*, вы́~ *pf.* вино́; *v.t.* угоща́ть *impf.*, угости́ть *pf.* вино́м. **wineglass** *n.* рю́мка. **wine-grower** *n.* виногра́дарь *m.* **wine-growing** *n.* виногра́дарство. **winery** *n.* ви́нный заво́д. **wine-tasting** *n.* дегуста́ция вин.
wing [wɪŋ] *n.* (*also pol.*) крыло́ (*pl.* -лья, -льев); (*archit.*) фли́гель (*pl.* -ля́, -ле́й) *m.*; (*sport*) фланг; *pl.* (*theatr.*) кули́сы *f.pl.*; *v.i.* лета́ть *indet.*, лете́ть (лечу́, лети́шь) *det.* по~ *pf.*; *v.t.* (*provide with wings*) снабжа́ть *impf.*, снабди́ть *pf.* кры́льями; (*quicken*) ускоря́ть *impf.*, уско́рить *pf.*; (*inspire*) окрыля́ть *impf.*, окрыли́ть *pf.* **winged** *adj.* крыла́тый. **wing-nut** *n.* крыла́тая га́йка. **wing-span** *n.* разма́х кры́льев.
wink [wɪŋk] *n.* (*blink*) морга́ние; (*as sign*) подми́гивание; **in a ~** момента́льно; *v.i.* морга́ть *impf.*, моргну́ть *pf.*; мига́ть *impf.*, мигну́ть *pf.* (**at** +*d.*); подми́гивать *impf.*, подми́гнуть *pf.* (**at** +*d.*); (*fig.*) смотре́ть (-рю́, -ришь) *impf.*, по~ *pf.* сквозь па́льцы на+*a.*
winkle ['wɪŋk(ə)l] *n.* берегова́я ули́тка; *v.t.*:

~ **out** выковы́ривать *impf.*, вы́ковырять *pf.*
winner ['wɪnə(r)] *n.* победи́тель *m.*, ~ница. **winning** *adj.* выи́грывающий, побежда́ющий; (*of shot etc.*) реша́ющий; (*charming*) обая́тельный; *n.*: *pl.* вы́игрыш. **winning-post** *n.* фи́нишный столб (-а́).
winnow ['wɪnəʊ] *v.t.* (*grain*) ве́ять (ве́ю, ве́ешь) *impf.*; (*sift*) просе́ивать *impf.*, просе́ять (-е́ю, -е́ешь) *pf.*
winsome ['wɪnsəm] *adj.* привлека́тельный, обая́тельный.
winter ['wɪntə(r)] *n.* зима́; *attr.* зи́мний; *v.i.* проводи́ть (-ожу́, -о́дишь) *impf.*, провести́ (-еду́, -едёшь; -ёл, -ела́) *pf.* зиму́; зимова́ть *impf.*, пере~ *pf.* **wintry** *adj.* зи́мний; (*cold*) холо́дный (хо́лоден, -дна́, -дно, хо́лодны́).
wipe [waɪp] *v.t.* (*also* ~ *out inside of*) вытира́ть *impf.*, вы́тереть (вы́тру, -решь; вы́тер, -ла) *pf.*; ~ **away, off** стира́ть *impf.*, стере́ть (сотру́, -рёшь; стёр, -ла) *pf.*; ~ **out** (*exterminate*) уничтожа́ть *impf.*, уничто́жить *pf.*; (*disgrace etc.*) смыва́ть *impf.*, смыть (смо́ю, -о́ешь) *pf.*
wire ['waɪə(r)] *n.* про́волока; (*carrying current*) про́вод (*pl.* -а́); (*telegram*) телегра́мма; *attr.* про́волочный; ~ **netting** про́волочная сеть; *v.t.* (*elec.*) де́лать *impf.*, с~ *pf.* электри́ческую прово́дку в+*a.*; (*telegraph*) телеграфи́ровать *impf.* & *pf.* **wireless** *n.* ра́дио *nt.indecl.*; ~ **set** радиоприёмник. **wiring** *n.* элекропрово́дка. **wiry** *adj.* жи́листый.
wisdom ['wɪzdəm] *n.* му́дрость; ~ **tooth** зуб (*pl.* -ы, -о́в) му́дрости. **wise** [waɪz] *adj.* му́дрый (-р, -ра́, -ро); (*prudent*) благоразу́мный.
wish [wɪʃ] *n.* жела́ние; **with best ~es** всего́ хоро́шего, с наилу́чшими пожела́ниями; *v.t.* хоте́ть (хочу́, -чешь, хоти́м) *impf.*, за~ *pf.* (**I ~ I could see him** мне хоте́лось бы его́ ви́деть; **I ~ to go** я хочу́ пойти́; **I ~ you to come early** я хочу́, что́бы вы ра́но пришли́; **I ~ the day were over** хорошо́ бы день уже́ ко́нчился); жела́ть *impf.*+*g.* (**I ~ you luck** жела́ю вам уда́чи); (*congratulate on*) поздравля́ть *impf.*, поздра́вить *pf.* (**I ~ you a happy birthday** поздравля́ю тебя́ с днём рожде́ния); *v.i.*: ~ **for** жела́ть *impf.*+*g.*; хоте́ть (хочу́, -чешь, хоти́м) *impf.*, за~ *pf.*+*g.* & *a.* **wishbone** *n.* ду́жка. **wishful** *adj.* жела́ющий; ~ **thinking** самообольще́ние; приня́тие жела́емого за действи́тельное.
wishy-washy ['wɪʃɪˌwɒʃɪ] *adj.* (*too liquid*) жи́дкий (-док, -дка́, -лко); (*fig.*) сла́бый (слаб, -а́, -о), бесцве́тный.
wisp [wɪsp] *n.* (*of straw*) пучо́к (-чка́); (*hair*) клочо́к (-чка́); (*smoke*) стру́йка.
wistful ['wɪstfʊl] *adj.* (*pensive*) заду́мчивый; (*melancholy*) тоскли́вый.
wit[1] [wɪt] *n.* (*mind*) ум (-а́); (*wittiness*) остроу́мие; (*person*) остря́к (-а́); **be at one's ~'s end** не знать *impf.* что де́лать.
wit[2] [wɪt] *v.i.*: **to** ~ то́ есть, а и́менно.
witch [wɪtʃ] *n.* ве́дьма, колду́нья (*g.pl.* -ний). **witchcraft** *n.* колдовство́. **witch-doctor** *n.* зна́харь *m.* **witch-hunt** *n.* охо́та за ведьм.
with [wɪð] *prep.* (*in company of, together* ~) (вме́сте) с+*i.*; (*as a result of*) от+*g.*; (*at house of, in keeping of*) у+*g.*; (*by means of*) +*i.*; (*in spite of*) несмотря́ на+*a.*; (*including*) включа́я+*a.*; ~ **each/one another** друг с дру́гом.
withdraw [wɪð'drɔː] *v.t.* (*retract*) брать (беру́, -рёшь; брал, -а́, -о) *impf.*, взять (возьму́, -мёшь; взял, -а́, -о) *pf.* наза́д; (*curtain, hand*) отдёргивать *impf.*, отдёрнуть *pf.*; (*cancel*) снима́ть *impf.*, снять (сниму́, -мешь; снял, -а́, -о) *pf.*; (*mil.*) отводи́ть (-ожу́, -о́дишь) *impf.*, отвести́ (-еду́, -едёшь; -ёл, -ела́) *pf.*; (*money from circulation*) изыма́ть *impf.*, изъя́ть (изыму́, -ы́мешь) из обраще́ния; (*diplomatic representative*) отзыва́ть *impf.*, отозва́ть (отзову́, -вёшь; отозва́л, -а́, -о) *pf.*; (*from bank*) брать (беру́, -рёшь; брал, -а́, -о) *impf.*, взять (возьму́, -мёшь; взял, -а́, -о) *pf.*; *v.i.* удаля́ться *impf.*, удали́ться *pf.*; (*mil.*) отходи́ть (-ожу́, -о́дишь) *impf.*, отойти́ (-йду́, -йдёшь; отошёл, -шла́) *pf.* **withdrawal** *n.* (*retraction*) взя́тие наза́д; (*cancellation*) сня́тие; (*mil.*) отхо́д; (*money from circulation*) изъя́тие; (*departure*) ухо́д; ~ **symptoms** абстине́нтный синдро́м. **withdrawn** *adj.* за́мкнутый.
wither ['wɪðə(r)] *v.i.* вя́нуть (вял) *impf.*, за~ *pf.*; высыха́ть *impf.*, вы́сохнуть (-х) *pf.*; *v.t.* иссуша́ть *impf.*, иссуши́ть (-шу́, -шишь) *pf.* **withering** *adj.* (*fig.*) испепеля́ющий.
withers ['wɪðəz] *n.* хо́лка.
withhold [wɪð'həʊld] *v.t.* (*refuse to grant*) не дава́ть (даю́, даёшь) *impf.*, дать (дам, дашь, даст, дади́м; дал, -а́, да́ло́, -и) *pf.*+*g.*; (*hide*) скрыва́ть *impf.*, скрыть (скро́ю, -о́ешь) *pf.*; (*restrain*) уде́рживать *impf.*, удержа́ть (-жу́, -жишь) *pf.*
within [wɪ'ðɪn] *prep.* (*inside*) внутри́+*g.*, в+*p.*; (~ *the limits of*) в преде́лах+*g.*; (*time*) в тече́ние+*g.*; *adv.* внутри́; (*at home*) до́ма.
without [wɪ'ðaʊt] *prep.* без+*g.*; (*outside*) вне+*g.*, за+*i.*; ~ **saying good-bye** не проща́ясь; **do** ~ обходи́ться (-ожу́сь, -о́дишься) *impf.*, обойти́сь (-йду́сь, -йдёшься; обошёлся, -ошла́сь) *pf.* без+*g.*
withstand [wɪð'stænd] *v.t.* противостоя́ть (-ою́, -ои́шь) *impf.*+*d.*; выде́рживать *impf.*, вы́держать (-жу, -жишь) *pf.*
witless ['wɪtlɪs] *adj.* глу́пый (-п, -па́, -по).
witness ['wɪtnɪs] *n.* (*person*) свиде́тель *m.*; (*eye-~*) очеви́дец (-дца); (*to signature etc.*) завери́тель *m.*; (*evidence*) свиде́тельство; **bear ~ to** свиде́тельствовать *impf.*, за~ *pf.*; *v.t.* быть свиде́телем+*g.*; (*document etc.*) заверя́ть *impf.*, заве́рить *pf.* **witness-box** *n.* ме́сто (*pl.* -а́) для свиде́телей.
witticism ['wɪtɪˌsɪz(ə)m] *n.* остро́та. **wittiness** *n.* остроу́мие. **witty** *adj.* остроу́мный.
wizard ['wɪzəd] *n.* волше́бник, колду́н (-а́). **wizardry** *n.* колдовство́.

wizened ['wɪz(ə)nd] *adj.* (*wrinkled*) морщи́нистый.

wobble ['wɒb(ə)l] *v.t.* & *i.* шата́ть(ся) *impf.*, шатну́ть(ся) *pf.*; кача́ть(ся) *impf.*, качну́ть(ся) *pf.*; *v.i.* (*voice*) дрожа́ть (-жу́, -жи́шь) *impf.* **wobbly** *adj.* ша́ткий.

woe [wəʊ] *n.* го́ре; ~ **is me!** го́ре мне! **woebegone** ['wəʊbɪ,gɒn] *adj.* удручённый, мра́чный (-чен, -чна́, -чно). **woeful** *adj.* ско́рбный, го́рестный.

wolf [wʊlf] *n.* волк (*pl.* -и, -о́в); ~ **cub** волчо́нок (-нка; *pl.* волча́та, -т) *v.t.* пожира́ть *impf.*, пожра́ть (-ру́, -рёшь; пожра́л, -а́, -о) *pf.* (*coll.*) **wolfhound** *n.* волкода́в.

woman ['wʊmən] *n.* же́нщина. **womanhood** *n.* (*maturity*) же́нская зре́лость. **womanish** *adj.* женоподо́бный. **womanly** *adj.* же́нственный (-ен, -енна).

womb [wu:m] *n.* ма́тка; (*fig.*) чре́во.

womenfolk ['wɪmɪn,fəʊk] *n.* же́нщины *f.pl.*; (*of one's family*) же́нская полови́на семьи́. **Women's Liberation** *n.* эмансипа́ция же́нщин; ~ **movement** движе́ние за эмансипа́цию же́нщин.

wonder ['wʌndə(r)] *n.* чу́до (*pl.* -деса́, -де́с); (*amazement*) изумле́ние; **(it's) no** ~ неудиви́тельно; *v.t.* интересова́ться *impf.* (**I** ~ **who will come** интере́сно, кто придёт); *v.i.*: **I shouldn't** ~ **if** неудиви́тельно бу́дет, е́сли; **I** ~ **if you could help me** не могли́ бы вы мне помо́чь?; ~ **at** удивля́ться *impf.*, удиви́ться *pf.*+*d.* **wonderful, wondrous** *adj.* замеча́тельный, удиви́тельный, чуде́сный.

wont [wəʊnt] *n.*: **as is his** ~ по своему́ обыкнове́нию; *pred.*: **be** ~ **to** име́ть привы́чку+*inf.* **wonted** *adj.* привы́чный.

woo [wu:] *v.t.* уха́живать *impf.* за+*i.*; (*fig.*) добива́ться+*g.*

wood [wʊd] *n.* (*forest*) лес (-а(у), *loc.* -у́; *pl.* -а́); (*material*) де́рево; (*firewood*) дрова́ (-в, -ва́м) *pl.*; ~ **pulp** древе́сная ма́сса. **woodbine** *n.* жи́молость. **woodcock** *n.* вальдшне́п. **woodcut** *n.* гравю́ра на де́реве. **wooded** *adj.* леси́стый. **wooden** *adj.* (*also fig.*) деревя́нный. **woodland** *n.* леси́стая ме́стность; *attr.* лесно́й. **woodlouse** *n.* мокри́ца. **woodman** *n.* лесни́к (-а́). **woodpecker** *n.* дя́тел (-тла). **woodpigeon** *n.* лесно́й го́лубь (*pl.* -би, -бе́й) *m.* **woodshed** *n.* сара́й для дров. **woodwind** *n.* деревя́нные духовы́е инструме́нты *m.pl.* **woodwork** *n.* столя́рная рабо́та; (*wooden articles*) деревя́нные изде́лия *nt.pl.*; (*wooden parts of sth.*) деревя́нные ча́сти (-те́й) *pl.* (строе́ния). **woodworm** *n.* (жук-)древото́чец (-чца). **woody** *adj.* (*plant etc.*) деревяни́стый; (*wooded*) леси́стый.

wool [wʊl] *n.* шерсть (*pl.* -ти, -те́й). **woollen** *adj.* шерстяно́й. **woolly** *adj.* (*covered with* ~) покры́тый ше́рстью; (*fleecy*) шерсти́стый; (*indistinct*) нея́сный (-сен, -сна́, -сно); ~ **mind, thinking** пу́таница в голове́; *n.* (*coll.*) сви́тер.

word [wɜ:d] *n.* (*unit of language*; *utterance*; *promise*) сло́во (*pl.* -ва́); (*remark*) замеча́ние; (*news*) изве́стие; **have a** ~ **with** поговори́ть *pf.* с+*i.*; **by** ~ **of mouth** на слова́х, у́стно; **in a** ~ одни́м сло́вом; **in other** ~**s** други́ми слова́ми; ~ **for** ~ сло́во в сло́во; *v.t.* выража́ть *impf.*, вы́разить *pf.* слова́ми; формули́ровать *impf.*, с~ *pf.* **wordiness** *n.* многосло́вие. **wording** *n.* формулиро́вка, реда́кция. **wordy** *adj.* многосло́вный.

work [wɜ:k] *n.* рабо́та; (*labour*; *toil*; *scholarly* ~) труд (-а́); (*occupation*) заня́тие; (*studies*) заня́тия *nt.pl.*; (*of art*) произведе́ние; (*book*) сочине́ние; *pl.* (*factory*) заво́д; (*mechanism*) механи́зм; **at** ~ (*doing*~) за рабо́той; (*at place of* ~) на рабо́те; **out of** ~ безрабо́тный; *v.i.* (*also function*) рабо́тать *impf.* (**at, on** над+*i.*); (*study*) занима́ться *impf.*, заня́ться (займу́сь, -мёшься; за́нялся́, -ла́сь, -ло́сь) *pf.*; (*also toil*, *labour*) труди́ться (-ужу́сь, -у́дишься) *impf.*; (*function*) де́йствовать *impf.*; ~ **to rule** рабо́тать *impf.*, выполня́я сли́шком пунктуа́льно все пра́вила, с це́лью уме́ньшить производи́тельность; *v.t.* (*operate*) управля́ть *impf.*+*i.*; обраща́ться *impf.* с+*i.*; (*wonders*) твори́ть *impf.*, со~ *pf.*; (*soil*) обраба́тывать *impf.*, обрабо́тать *pf.*; (*mine*) разраба́тывать *impf.*, разрабо́тать *pf.*; (*compel to* ~) заставля́ть *impf.*, заста́вить *pf.* рабо́тать; ~ **in** вставля́ть *impf.*, вста́вить *pf.*; ~ **out** (*solve*) реша́ть *impf.*, реши́ть *pf.*; (*plans etc.*) разраба́тывать *impf.*, разрабо́тать *pf.*; (*exhaust*) истоща́ть *impf.*, истощи́ть *pf.*; **everything** ~**ed out well** всё ко́нчилось хорошо́; ~ **out at** (*amount to*) составля́ть *impf.*, соста́вить *pf.*; ~ **up** (*perfect*) обраба́тывать *impf.*, обрабо́тать *pf.*; (*excite*) возбужда́ть *impf.*, возбуди́ть *pf.*; (*appetite*) нагу́ливать *impf.*, нагуля́ть *pf.* **workable** *adj.* осуществи́мый, реа́льный. **workaday** *adj.* бу́дничный. **workaholic** [,wɜ:kə'hɒlɪk] *n.* работома́н. **workbench** верста́к (-а́). **worker** *n.* рабо́чий *sb.*; рабо́тник, -ица. **workforce** рабо́чая си́ла. **working** *adj.*: ~ **class** рабо́чий класс; ~ **conditions** усло́вия *nt.pl.* труда́; ~ **day** рабо́чий день (дня) *m.*; ~ **hours** рабо́чее вре́мя; *nt.*; ~ **party** коми́ссия. **workload** нагру́зка. **workman** *n.* рабо́чий *sb.*, рабо́тник. **workmanlike** *adj.* иску́сный. **workmanship** *n.* иску́сство, мастерство́. **workroom** рабо́чая ко́мната. **workshop** *n.* мастерска́я *sb.* **work-shy** лени́вый.

world [wɜ:ld] *n.* мир (*pl.* -ы́), свет; *attr.* мирово́й; ~ **war** мирова́я война́ (*pl.* -ны). **world-famous** *adj.* всеми́рно изве́стный. **worldly** *adj.* (*earthly*) земно́й; (*temporal*) мирско́й; (*experienced*) о́пытный. **world-view** *n.* мировоззре́ние. **world-weary** *adj.* уста́вший от жи́зни. **worldwide** *adj.* распространённый (-ён, -ена́) по всему́ ми́ру; всеми́рный.

worm [wɜ:m] *n.* червь (-вя́; *pl.* -ви, -ве́й) *m.*; (*also tech.*) червя́к (-а́); (*intestinal*) глист

(-á); *v.t.*: ~ **o.s. into** вкрáдываться *impf.*, вкрáсться (-адýсь, -адёшься; -áлся) *pf.* в+*a.*; ~ **out** вывéдывать *impf.*, вы́ведать *pf.* (**of** у+*g.*); ~ **one's way** пробирáться *impf.*, пробрáться (-берýсь, -берёшься; -брáлся, -бралáсь, -брáлóсь) *pf.* **worm-eaten** *adj.* истóченный (-ен) червя́ми. **wormwood** *n.* полы́нь.

worry ['wʌrɪ] *n.* (*anxiety*) беспокóйство, тревóга; (*care*) забóта; *v.t.* беспокóить *impf.*, о~ *pf.*; тревóжить *impf.*, вс~ *pf.*; (*of dog*) терзáть *impf.*; *v.i.* беспокóиться *impf.*, о~ *pf.* (**about** о+*p.*); мýчиться *impf.*, за~, из~ *pf.* (**about** из-за+*g.*).

worse [wɜːs] *adj.* хýдший; *adv.* хýже; *n.*: **from bad to** ~ всё хýже и хýже. **worsen** *v.t.* & *i.* ухудшáть(ся) *impf.*, ухудши́ть(ся) *pf.*

worship ['wɜːʃɪp] *n.* поклонéние (**of** +*d.*); (*relig.*) богослужéние; *v.t.* поклоня́ться *impf.*+*d.*; (*adore*) обожáть *impf.* **worshipper** *n.* поклóнник, -ица.

worst [wɜːst] *adj.* наихýдший, сáмый плохóй; *adv.* хýже всегó; *n.* сáмое плохóе; *v.t.* побеждáть *impf.*, победи́ть (-и́шь) *pf.*

worsted ['wʊstɪd] *n.* шерстянáя/камвóльная пря́жа.

worth [wɜːθ] *n.* (*value*) ценá (*a.* -ну; *pl.* -ны); (*fig.*) цéнность; (*merit*) достóинство; **give me a pound's** ~ **of apples** дáйте мне я́блок на фунт; *adj.*: **be** ~ (*of value equivalent to*) стóить *impf.* (**what is it** ~**?** скóлько э́то стóит?); (*deserve*) стóить *impf.*+*g.* (**is this film** ~ **seeing?** стóит посмотрéть э́тот фильм?); **for all one is** ~ изо всéх сил. **worthless** *adj.* ничегó не стóящий; (*useless*) бесполéзный. **worthwhile** *adj.* стóящий. **worthy** ['wɜːðɪ] *adj.* достóйный (-óин, -óйна).

would-be ['wʊdbɪ] *adj.*: ~ **actor** человéк (*pl.* лю́ди, -дéй, -дьям, -дьми́) мечтáющий стать актёром.

wound [wuːnd] *n.* рáна, ранéние; (*fig.*) оби́да; *v.t.* рáнить *impf.* & *pf.*; (*fig.*) обижáть *impf.*, оби́деть (-и́жу, -и́дишь) *pf.* **wounded** *adj.* рáненый.

WPC *abbr.* (*of* **woman police constable**) жéнщина-полицéйский.

wraith [reɪθ] *n.* видéние.

wrangle ['ræŋg(ə)l] *n.* пререкáние, спор; *v.i.* пререкáться *impf.*; спóрить *impf.*, по~ *pf.*

wrap [ræp] *n.* (*shawl*) шаль; (*stole*) паланти́н; *v.t.* (*also* ~ *up*) завёртывать *impf.*, завернýть *pf.*; ~ **up** (*v.t.* & *i.*) (*in wraps*) закýтывать(ся) *impf.*, закýтать(ся) *pf.*; (*v.t.*) (*conclude*) завершáть *impf.*, заверши́ть *pf.*; ~**ped up in** (*fig.*) поглощённый (-ён, -енá) +*i.* **wrapper** *n.* обёртка. **wrapping** *n.* обёртка; ~ **paper** обёрточная бумáга.

wrath [rɒθ, rɔːθ] *n.* гнев, я́рость. **wrathful** ['rɒθfʊl] *adj.* гнéвный (-вен, -вná, -вно).

wreak [riːk] *v.t.*: ~ **havoc** производи́ть (-ожý, -óдишь) *impf.*, произвести́ (-едý, -едёшь; -ёл, -елá) *pf.* ужáсные разрушéния; ~ **vengeance** мсти́ть *impf.*, ото~ *pf.* (**on** +*d.*).

wreath [riːθ] *n.* венóк (-нкá); (*of smoke*) кольцó (*pl.* -льца, -лéц, -льцам). **wreathe** [riːð] *v.t.* (*form into wreath*) сплетáть *impf.*, сплести́ (-етý, -етёшь; -ёл, -елá) *pf.*; (*encircle*) обвивáть *impf.*, обви́ть (обовью́, -ьёшь; обви́л, -лá, -ло) *pf.* (**with** +*i.*); *v.i.* (*wind round*) обвивáться *impf.*, обви́ться (обовью́сь, -ьёшься; обви́лся, -лáсь) *pf.*; (*of smoke*) клуби́ться *impf.*

wreck [rek] *n.* (*destruction*) крушéние, авáрия; (*wrecked ship*) óстов разби́того сýдна; (*vehicle, person, building etc.*) развáлина; *v.t.* (*cause destruction of*) вызывáть *impf.*, вы́звать (вы́зову, -вешь) крушéние+*g.*; (*ship*) топи́ть (топлю́, -пишь) *impf.*, по~ *pf.*; (*destroy, also hopes etc.*) разрушáть *impf.*, разрýшить *pf.*; **be** ~**ed** терпéть (-плю́, -пишь) *impf.*, по~ *pf.* крушéние; (*of plans etc.*) рýхнуть *pf.* **wreckage** *n.* облóмки *m.pl.* крушéния.

wren [ren] *n.* крапи́вник.

wrench [rentʃ] *n.* (*jerk*) дёрганье; (*sprain*) растяжéние; (*tech.*) гáечный ключ (-á); (*fig.*) боль; *v.t.* (*snatch, pull out*) вырывáть *impf.*, вы́рвать (-ву, -вешь) *pf.* (**from** у+*g.*); (*sprain*) растя́гивать *impf.*, растянýть (-нý, -нешь) *pf.*; ~ **open** взлáмывать *impf.*, взломáть *pf.*

wrest [rest] *v.t.* (*wrench*) вырывáть *impf.*, вы́рвать (-ву, -вешь) *pf.* (**from** у+*g.*); (*agreement etc.*) исторгáть *impf.*, истóргнуть (-г) *pf.* (**from** у+*g.*); (*distort*) искажáть *impf.*, искази́ть *pf.*

wrestle ['res(ə)l] *v.i.* борóться (-рю́сь, -решься) *impf.* **wrestler** *n.* борéц (-рцá). **wrestling** *n.* борьбá.

wretch [retʃ] *n.* несчáстный *sb.*; (*scoundrel*) негодя́й. **wretched** *adj.* жáлкий (-лок, -лкá, -лко); (*unpleasant*) сквéрный (-рен, -рнá, -рно).

wriggle ['rɪg(ə)l] *v.i.* извивáться *impf.*, изви́ться (изовью́сь, -ьёшься; изви́лся, -лáсь) *pf.*; (*fidget*) ёрзать *impf.*; *v.t.* виля́ть *impf.*, вильнýть *pf.*+*i.*; ~ **out of** увиливать *impf.*, увильнýть от+*g.*

wring [rɪŋ] *v.t.* (*also* ~ *out*) выжимáть *impf.*, вы́жать (вы́жму, -мешь) *pf.*; (*extort*) исторгáть *impf.*, истóргнуть (-г) *pf.* (**from** у+*g.*); (*hand*) крéпко пожимáть *impf.*, пожáть (пожмý, -мёшь) *pf.* (**of** +*d.*); (*neck*) свёртывать *impf.*, свернýть *pf.* (**of** +*d.*); ~ **one's hands** ломáть *impf.*, с~ *pf.* рýки. **wringer** *n.* маши́на для отжимáния белья́.

wrinkle ['rɪŋk(ə)l] *n.* морщи́на; *v.t.* & *i.* мóрщить(ся) *impf.*, с~ *pf.*

wrist [rɪst] *n.* запя́стье. **wrist-watch** *n.* нарýчные часы́ (-сóв) *pl.*

writ [rɪt] *n.* повéстка, предписáние.

write [raɪt] *v.t.* & *i.* (*also fig.*) писáть (пишý, -шешь) *impf.*, на~ *pf.*; ~ **down** запи́сывать *impf.*, записáть (запишý, -шешь) *pf.*; ~ **off** (*cancel*) аннули́ровать *impf.* & *pf.*; (*dispatch letter*) отсылáть *impf.*, отослáть (отошлю́,

-шлёшь) *pf.*; ~ **out** выпи́сывать *impf.*, вы́писать (-ишу, -ишешь) *pf.* (**in full** по́лностью); ~ **up** (*account of*) подро́бно опи́сывать *impf.*, описа́ть (-ишу́, -и́шешь) *pf.*; (*notes*) переписывать *impf.*, переписа́ть (-ишу́, -и́шешь) *pf.* **write-off** *n.*: **the car was a** ~ маши́на была́ соверше́нно испо́рчена. **writer** *n.* писа́тель *m.*, ~ница. **write-up** *n.* (*report*) отчёт.

writhe [raɪð] *v.i.* (*from pain*) ко́рчиться *impf.*, с~ *pf.*; (*fig.*) му́читься *impf.*, за~, из~ *pf.*

writing ['raɪtɪŋ] *n.* (*handwriting*) по́черк; (*work*) произведе́ние; **in** ~ в пи́сьменной фо́рме; **the** ~ **on the wall** злове́щее предзнаменова́ние. **writing-case** *n.* несессе́р для пи́сьменных принадле́жностей. **writing-desk** *n.* пи́сьменный стол (-а́). **writing-paper** *n.* почто́вая бума́га.

wrong [rɒŋ] *adj.* (*incorrect*) непра́вильный, неве́рный (-рен, -рна́, -рно, неве́рны́), оши́бочный; не тот (**I have bought the** ~ **book** я купи́л не ту кни́гу; **you've got the** ~ **number** (*telephone*) вы не туда́ попа́ли); (*mistaken*) непра́вый (-в, -ва́, -во) (**you are** ~ ты непра́в); (*unjust*) несправедли́вый; (*sinful*) дурно́й (дурён, -рна́, -рно, ду́рны́); (*defective*) неиспра́вный; (*side of cloth*) ле́вый; ~ **side out** наизна́нку; ~ **way round** наоборо́т; *n.* зло; (*injustice*) несправедли́вость; **be in the** ~ быть непра́вым; **do** ~ греши́ть *impf.*, со~ *pf.*; *adv.* непра́вильно, неве́рно; **go** ~ не получа́ться *impf.*, получи́ться (-ится) *pf.*; *v.t.* (*harm*) вреди́ть *impf.*, по~ *pf.*+*d.*; обижа́ть *impf.*, оби́деть *pf.*; (*be unjust to*) быть несправедли́вым к+*d.* **wrongdoer** ['rɒŋ,du:ə(r)] *n.* престу́пник, гре́шник, -ица. **wrongful** *adj.* несправедли́вый, непра́вильный. **wrongly** *adv.* непра́вильно, неве́рно.

wrought [rɔ:t] *adj.*: ~ **iron** сва́рочное желе́зо.

wry [raɪ] *adj.* криво́й (-в, -ва́, -во), переко́шенный; ~ **face** грима́са.

xenophobia [,zenə'fəʊbɪə] *n.* ксенофо́бия.

Xerox ['zɪərɒks, 'ze-] *v.t.* размножа́ть *impf.* размно́жить *pf.* на ксе́роксе. **Xerox copy** *n.* ксероко́пия.

X-ray ['eksreɪ] *n.* (*picture*) рентге́н(овский сни́мок (-мка)); *pl.* (*radiation*) рентге́новы лучи́ *m.pl.*; *v.t.* (*photograph*) де́лать *impf.*, с~ *pf.* рентге́н+*g.*; (*examine*) иссле́довать *impf.* & *pf.* рентге́новыми луча́ми.

xylophone ['zaɪlə,fəʊn] *n.* ксилофо́н.

Y

yacht [jɒt] *n.* я́хта. **yacht-club** *n.* яхт-клу́б. **yachting** *n.* па́русный спорт. **yachtsman** *n.* яхтсме́н.

yak [jæk] *n.* як.

Yale lock [jeɪl] *n.* (*propr.*) америка́нский замо́к (-мка́).

Yalta ['jæltə] *n.* Я́лта.

yam [jæm] *n.* ям.

yank [jæŋk] *n.* рыво́к (-вка́); *v.t.* рвану́ть *pf.*

yap [jæp] *n.* тя́вканье; *v.i.* тя́вкать *impf.*, тя́вкнуть *pf.*

yard[1] [jɑ:d] *n.* (*piece of ground*) двор (-а́).

yard[2] [jɑ:d] *n.* (*measure*) ярд; (*naut.*) рей. **yardstick** *n.* (*fig.*) мери́ло.

yarn [jɑ:n] *n.* пря́жа; (*story*) расска́з.

yashmak ['jæʃmæk] *n.* чадра́.

yawl [jɔ:l] *n.* ял.

yawn [jɔ:n] *n.* зево́к (-вка́); *v.i.* (*person*) зева́ть *impf.*, зевну́ть *pf.*; (*chasm etc.*) зия́ть *impf.*

year [jɪə(r), jɜ:(r)] *n.* год (*loc.* -у́; *pl.* -ы & -а́, -о́в & лет, -а́м); **from** ~ **to** ~ год о́т году; ~ **in,** ~ **out** из го́да в год. **yearbook** *n.* ежего́дник. **yearly** *adj.* ежего́дный, годово́й; *adv.* ежего́дно, раз в год.

yearn [jɜ:n] *v.i.* тоскова́ть *impf.* (**for** по+*d.* & *p.*). **yearning** *n.* тоска́ (**for** по+*d.* & *p.*).

yeast [ji:st] *n.* дро́жжи (-же́й) *pl.*

yell [jel] *n.* крик; *v.i.* крича́ть (-чу́, -чи́шь) *impf.*, кри́кнуть *pf.*; *v.t.* выкри́кивать *impf.*, вы́крикнуть *pf.*

yellow ['jeləʊ] *adj.* жёлтый (-т, -та́, жёлто́); (*cowardly*) трусли́вый; *n.* жёлтый цвет; *v.i.* желте́ть *impf.*, по~ *pf.* **yellowish** *adj.* желтова́тый.

yelp [jelp] *n.* визг; *v.i.* визжа́ть (-жу́, -жи́шь) *impf.*, ви́згнуть *pf.*

yen [jen] *n.* (*currency*) ие́на.

yes [jes] *adv.* да; *n.* утвержде́ние, согла́сие; (*in vote*) го́лос (*pl.* -а́) «за». **yes-man** *n.* подпева́ла *c.g.* (*coll.*).

yesterday ['jestə,deɪ] *adv.* вчера́; *n.* вчера́шний день (дня) *m.*; ~ **morning** вчера́ у́тром; **the day before** ~ позавчера́; ~**'s newspaper** вчера́шняя газе́та.

yet [jet] *adv.* (*still*) ещё; (*so far*) до сих пор; (*with comp.*) да́же, ещё; (*in questions*) уже́; (*nevertheless*) тем не ме́нее; **as** ~ пока́, до сих пор; **not** ~ ещё не; *conj.* одна́ко, но.

yeti ['jetɪ] *n.* йе́ти *m.indecl.*

yew [ju:] *n.* тис.

Yiddish ['jɪdɪʃ] *n.* и́диш.

yield [ji:ld] *n.* (*harvest*) урожа́й; (*econ.*) дохо́д; *v.t.* (*fruit, revenue, etc.*) приноси́ть (-ошу́, -о́сишь) *impf.*, принести́ (-есу́, -есёшь; -ёс, -есла́) *pf.*; дава́ть (даю́, даёшь) *impf.*, дать (дам, дашь, даст, дади́м; дал, -а́, да́ло́, -и) *pf.*; (*give up*) сдава́ть (сдаю́, сдаёшь) *impf.*, сдать (-ам, -ашь, -асть, -ади́м; сдал, -а́, -о) *pf.*; *v.i.* (*give in*) (*to enemy etc.*) уступа́ть *impf.*, уступи́ть (-плю́, -пишь) *pf.* (**to** +*d.*); (*to temptation etc.*) поддава́ться (-даю́сь, -даёшься) *impf.*, подда́ться (-а́мся, -а́шься, -а́стся, -ади́мся; -а́лся, -ала́сь) *pf.* (**to** +*d.*).

yodel ['jəʊd(ə)l] *n.* йодль *m.*; *v.i.* петь (пою́, поёшь) *impf.*, про~, с~ *pf.* йо́длем.

yoga ['jəʊgə] *n.* йо́га. **yogi** ['jəʊgɪ] *n.* йог.

yog(h)urt ['jɒgət] *n.* йогу́рт.

yoke [jəʊk] *n.* (*also fig.*) ярмо́ (*pl.* -ма); (*fig.*) и́го; (*for buckets.*) коромы́сло (*g.pl.* -сел); (*of dress*) коке́тка; ~ **of oxen** па́ра запряжённых воло́в; *v.t.* впряга́ть *impf.*, впрячь (-ягу́, -яжёшь; -яг, -ягла́) *pf.* в ярмо́.

yokel ['jəʊk(ə)l] *n.* деревéнщина *c.g.*

yolk [jəʊk] *n.* желто́к (-тка́).

yonder ['jɒndə(r)] *adv.* вон там; *adj.* вон тот (та, то; *pl.* те).

yore [jɔ:(r)] *n.*: **in days of** ~ во вре́мя о́но.

you [ju:] *pron.* (*familiar sg.*) ты (тебя́, тебе́, тобо́й, тебе́); (*familiar pl., polite sg. & pl.*) вы (вас, вам, ва́ми, вас); (*one*) *not usu. translated*; *v. translated in 2nd pers. sg. or by impers. construction*: ~ **never know** никогда́ не зна́ешь.

young [jʌŋ] *adj.* молодо́й (мо́лод, -а́, -о), ю́ный (юн, -а́, -о); (*new*) но́вый (нов, -а́, -о); (*inexperienced*) нео́птный; **the** ~ молодёжь; *n.* (*collect.*) молодня́к (-а́), детёныши *m.pl.* **youngish** *adj.* моложа́вый. **youngster** *n.* ма́льчик, ю́ноша *m.*

your(s) [jɔ:(r), jʊə(r)] *poss. pron.* (*familiar sg.*; *also in letter*) твой (-оя́, -оё; -ои́); (*familiar pl., polite sg. & pl.*; *also in letter*) ваш; свой (-оя́, -оё; -ои́). **yourself** *pron.* (*emph.*) (*familiar sg.*) (ты) сам (-ого́, -ому́, -и́м, -о́м) (*m.*), сама́ (-мо́й, *a.* -му́) (*f.*); (*familiar pl., polite sg. & pl.*) (вы) са́ми (-и́х, -и́м, -и́ми); (*refl.*) себя́ (себе́, собо́й); -ся (*suffixed to v.t.*); **by** ~ (*independently*) самостоя́тельно, сам (-а́; -и); (*alone*) оди́н (одна́; одни́).

youth [ju:θ] *n.* (*age*) мо́лодость, ю́ность; (*young man*) ю́ноша *m.*; (*collect., as pl.*) молодёжь; *attr.* молодёжный; ~ **club** молодёжный клуб; ~ **hostel** молодёжная турба́за. **youthful** *adj.* ю́ношеский.

yo-yo ['jəʊjəʊ] *n.* йо-йо́.

Yugoslavia [ju:gə'slɑ:vɪə] *n.* Югосла́вия. **Yugoslav(ian)** *adj.* югосла́вский; *n.* югосла́в, ~ка.

Z

zany ['zeɪnɪ] *adj.* смешно́й (-шо́н, -шна́).

zeal [zi:l] *n.* рве́ние, усе́рдие. **zealot** ['zelət] *n.* фана́тик. **zealous** ['zeləs] *adj.* ре́вностный, усе́рдный.

zebra ['zebrə, 'zi:-] *n.* зе́бра.

zenith ['zenɪθ, 'zi:-] *n.* зени́т.

zephyr ['zefə(r)] *n.* зефи́р.

zero ['zɪərəʊ] *n.* нуль (-ля́) *m.*, ноль (-ля́) *m.*; ~ **option** (*pol.*) нулево́й вариа́нт.

zest [zest] *n.* (*piquancy*) пика́нтность; (*ardour*) жар, энтузиа́зм; ~ **for life** жизнелю́бие.

zigzag ['zɪgzæg] *n.* зигза́г; *adj.* зигзагообра́зный; *v.i.* де́лать *impf.*, с~ *pf.* зигза́ги.

zinc [zɪŋk] *n.* цинк; *attr.* ци́нковый.

Zionism ['zaɪə,nɪz(ə)m] *n.* сиони́зм. **Zionist** *n.* сиони́ст.

zip [zɪp] *n.* (~ *fastener*) (застёжка-)мо́лния; *v.t. & i.*: ~ **up** застёгивать(ся) *impf.*, застегну́ть(ся) *pf.* на мо́лнию.

zither ['zɪðə(r)] *n.* ци́тра.

zodiac ['zəʊdɪ,æk] *n.* зодиа́к; **sign of the** ~ знак зодиа́ка. **zodiacal** [zə'daɪək(ə)l] *adj.* зодиака́льный.

zonal ['zəʊnəl] *adj.* зона́льный. **zone** *n.* зо́на; (*geog.*) по́яс (*pl.* -а́).

zoo [zu:] *n.* зоопа́рк. **zoological** [,zəʊə'lɒdʒɪk(ə)l] *adj.* зоологи́ческий; ~ **garden(s)** зоопа́рк, зоологи́ческий сад (*loc.* -у́; *pl.* -ы́). **zo'ologist** *n.* зо́олог. **zo'ology** *n.* зооло́гия.

zoom [zu:m] *v.i.* (*aeron.*) де́лать *impf.*, с~ *pf.* го́рку; *n.* го́рка; ~ **lens** объекти́в с переме́нным фо́кусным расстоя́нием.

Zulu ['zu:lu:] *adj.* зулу́сский; *n.* зулу́с, ~ка.

Zurich ['zjʊərɪk] *n.* Цю́рих.